Bill James presents. . .

STATS™ Major League Handbook 1999

STATS, Inc. • Bill James

Published by STATS Publishing
A Division of Sports Team Analysis & Tracking Systems, Inc.

This book is dedicated to my parents for being my biggest fans
when I was a promising, young Little Leaguer. . .
and to my wife and kids (Kathryn, Jessica and Evan) for the
ever-present love and support that continually makes me feel like
a Big Leaguer.
— Marty Gilbert

Cover by Michael Parapetti

Photo by Tony Inzerillo of The Sporting Views

First Edition: November, 1998

Printed in the United States of America

ISBN 1-884064-56-6

Table of Contents

Acknowledgments

Here at the home offices in Skokie, Illinois, they are simply known as "The Fall Three." The STATS *Major League Handbook*, *Minor League Handbook* and *Player Profiles* form the three legs of the triathlon we run each and every October, a triathlon that we are proud to say we've never failed to complete. We are also proud to say that we have built a reputation for finishing first. Here's to a team that boasts strength, stamina, and plenty of flat-out speed.

Over the past 10 years, John Dewan, STATS President and CEO, has taken his love of baseball and the numbers that drive the game and turned that passion into some of the best-selling baseball books in the country. He continues to cultivate an environment of growth and development, and receives plenty of support in that effort from COO Marty Gilbert. Both John and Marty are ably assisted by Jennifer Manicki.

Numbers are the backbone of "The Fall Three," so we're not kidding when we say these books would be quick reads without the work of Jeff Chernow and John Sasman in the Operations Department. Jeff has the daunting task of being our "official" keeper of baseball statistics, while John makes sure we have a live person with a computer in every single press box for every single major league game.

Of course, those numbers have to be tossed together and output in a meaningful way. That's where Allan Spear of the Systems Department comes in mighty handy. Allan handles the programming duties for all three books, and he does so with syntactical grace.

Once the machines stop churning, the Publications Department turns the numbers into books. Led by Vice President of Publications, Don Zminda, the team of Jim Callis, Kevin Fullam, Jim Henzler, Mat Olkin and yours truly take care of the writing, stat-checking and formatting of both *Handbooks* and *Player Profiles*. Chuck Miller deftly coordinates our publications software, while Michael Parapetti produces our eye-catching covers.

Certainly not least are the myriad other individuals who work to keep STATS on the cutting edge of the sports statistics, sports information and fantasy products industries. The STATS management team includes: Doug Abel, Vice President of Operations; Art Ashley, Vice President of Systems; Steve Byrd, Vice President of Fantasy Products; Jim Capuano, Vice President of Interactive Products; Sue Dewan, Vice President of Special Projects; Alan Leib, Vice President of Finance, Legal, Human Resources & Administration; Mary Owen, Vice President of Information Services; and the aforementioned Don Zminda. Thanks also to our other indispensable "triathletes": Andrew Bernstein, Grant Blair, Derek Boyle, Mike Canter, Dave Carlson, Ethan Cooperson, Steve Drago, Marc Elman, Scott Enslen, Drew Faust, Dan Ford, Mike Hammer, Mike Janosi, Sherlinda Johnson, Antoinette Kelly, Greg Kirkorsky, Stefan Kretschmann, Ken Li, Tracy Lickton, Barton Lilje, Walter Lis, Betty Moy, Jim Musso, Steve Olincy, Jim Osborne, Oscar Palacios, Doug Palm, Dean Peterson, Dave Pinto, Pat Quinn, Corey Roberts, Eric Robin, Mike Sarkis, Carol Savier, Jeff Schinski, Leena Sheth, Scott Spencer, Nick Stamm, Bill Stephens, Devin Tuffy, Taasha Veits and Susan Zamechek.

Finally, we saved our biggest debts of gratitude for last. First, thanks to Bill James for blazing the course that we continue to run every fall. And, thanks to you, our loyal readers, for your vigorous and unwavering support at the finish line.

— *Tony Nistler, Assistant Editor*

Introduction

Where were you when they hit No. 62? Were you at home, cheering at your television set? Were you in a restaurant or bar, hugging friends and high-fiving complete strangers? Were you in a car, trying to keep from running off the road while at the same time hoping you didn't loose the signal? Were you vacationing in a foreign country (as was the case with editor Don Zminda), hoping your VCR back home wasn't recording "Melrose Place" instead of Big Mac or Sammy? Were you at a ballpark? Were you at one of *the* ballparks? The locations may have been very different, but the emotions were universal. . . and we'll remember both for a long, long time.

From David Wells' "beanie-baby" perfecto to the Yankees' season-long pursuit of the best record of all time to Barry Bonds' exclusive entry into the 400-400 club to Alex Rodriguez' 40-40 campaign to the end of "The Streak" to the beginning, middle and end of "The Chase," many are already calling 1998 the greatest season in the history of the game. You could throw around terms like "unbelievable," or "awe-inspiring," or "amazing," but you'd fall short every time. *Seventy?* How do you go about describing that number? Words would be about as effective as a fastball in Mark McGwire's wheelhouse.

For those of us here at STATS, Inc. it was an honor to help record so much history in succession. And it was just plain fun. But for us, we had yet *another* reason to celebrate baseball last season. The summer of 1998 also marked the successful launch of two voluminous labors of love: the STATS *All-Time Major League Handbook* and *All-Time Baseball Sourcebook*. We like to think of them as *our* 61st and 62nd home runs, albeit without the same fanfare, and we hope you have the opportunity to thumb through them sometime soon. They are truly the ultimate companions to the *Major League Handbook*. In fact, we even added a section of figures we introduced in the *All-Time Major League Handbook*, namely Component ERA (ERC) and Runs Created per 27 Outs (RC/27), to this edition you are now holding.

As always, thank you for your support of our baseball annuals, and thanks to Bill James for his evolutionary—and revolutionary—measures of the game. Most importantly, thanks to Mark and Sammy. Thanks to your heroics, the summer of '98 will forever be the "Summer of the Sluggers," and 61 will no longer stand as the most daunting number in all of sports.

— *Tony Nistler, Assistant Editor*

What's Official and What's Not

The statistics in this book are technically unofficial. The official Major League Baseball averages are not released until December, but we can't wait that long. If you compare these stats with the official ones, you'll find no major differences. That said, we do not agree with the unofficial stats released by Major League Baseball at the end of the season in the following two instances—both involving intentional walks:

- Mark Grace vs. Rob Stanifer, ChN@Fla (7/19/98), 12th inning
- Jim Edmonds vs. Rocky Coppinger, Ana@Bal (9/13/98), 2nd inning

In both cases, we have counted these walks as intentional and confirmed this with the individual teams involved. As always, we take extraordinary efforts to ensure accuracy.

1

Career Stats

The career data section of this book includes the records of all players who saw major league action in 1998.

You probably know what most of the abbreviations stand for, but just in case:

Age is seasonal age based on July 1, 1999.

For Batters, **B** = bats; **T** = throws; **DH** = designated hitter; **PH** = pinch hitter; **G** = games; **AB** = at-bats; **H** = hits; **2B** = doubles; **3B** = triples; **HR** = home runs; **Hm** = home runs at home; **Rd** = home runs on the road; **TB** = total bases; **R** = runs; **RBI** = runs batted in; **TBB** = total bases on balls; **IBB** = intentional bases on balls; **SO** = strikeouts; **HBP** = times hit by pitches; **SH** = sacrifice hits; **SF** = sacrifice flies; **SB** = stolen bases; **CS** = times caught stealing; **SB%** = stolen base percentage; **GDP** = times grounded into double plays; **Avg** = batting average; **OBP** = on-base percentage; **SLG** = slugging percentage.

For Pitchers, **SP** = starting pitcher; **RP** = relief pitcher; **G** = games pitched; **GS** = games started; **CG** = complete games; **GF** = games finished; **IP** = innings pitched; **BFP** = batters facing pitcher; **H** = hits allowed; **R** = runs allowed; **ER** = earned runs allowed; **HR** = home runs allowed; **SH** = sacrifice hits allowed; **SF** = sacrifice flies allowed; **HB** = hit batsmen; **TBB** = total bases on balls; **IBB** = intentional bases on balls; **SO** = strikeouts; **WP** = wild pitches; **Bk** = balks; **W** = wins; **L** = losses; **Pct.** = winning percentage; **ShO** = shutouts; **Sv** = saves; **Op** = save opportunities; **Hld** = holds; **ERA** = earned run average.

An asterisk (*) by a player's minor league stats indicates that these are his 1998 minor league numbers only; previous minor league experience is not included. Figures in **boldface** indicate the player led the league in that category.

For players who played for more than one major league team in a season, stats for each team are shown just above the bottom-line career totals.

Some Class-A and Rookie Leagues are denoted with a "+" or "-" (like A+) to indicate the caliber of competition within the classification.

Jeff Abbott

Bats: R **Throws:** L **Pos:** CF-38; RF-27; LF-20; PH/PR-14; DH-2 **Ht:** 6'2" **Wt:** 190 **Born:** 8/17/72 **Age:** 26

Year Team	Lg	G	AB	H	2B	3B	HR	(Hm	Rd)	TB	R	RBI	TBB	IBB	SO	HBP	SH	SF	SB	CS	SB%	GDP	Avg	OBP	SLG
1994 White Sox	R	4	15	7	1	0	1	—	—	11	4	3	4	0	0	0	0	0	2	1	.67	1	.467	.579	.733
Hickory	A	63	224	88	16	6	6	—	—	134	47	48	38	1	33	1	1	1	2	1	.67	4	.393	.481	.598
1995 Pr William	A+	70	264	92	16	6	4	—	—	120	41	47	26	0	25	2	1	5	7	1	.88	8	.348	.404	.455
Birmingham	AA	55	197	63	11	1	3	—	—	85	25	28	19	2	20	2	3	2	1	3	.25	3	.320	.382	.431
1996 Nashville	AAA	113	440	143	27	1	14	—	—	214	64	60	32	1	50	2	1	0	12	4	.75	12	.325	.373	.486
1997 Nashville	AAA	118	465	152	35	3	11	—	—	226	88	63	41	0	52	5	2	3	12	7	.63	12	.327	.385	.486
1997 Chicago	AL	19	38	10	1	0	1	(0	1)	14	8	2	0	0	6	0	0	0	0	0	.00	3	.263	.263	.368
1998 Chicago	AL	89	244	68	14	1	12	(5	7)	120	33	41	9	1	28	0	2	5	3	3	.50	2	.279	.298	.492
2 ML YEARS		108	282	78	15	1	13	(5	8)	134	41	43	9	1	34	0	2	5	3	3	.50	5	.277	.294	.475

Jim Abbott

Pitches: Left **Bats:** Left **Pos:** SP-5 **Ht:** 6'3" **Wt:** 210 **Born:** 9/19/67 **Age:** 31

Year Team	Lg	G	GS	CG	GF	IP	BFP	H	R	ER	HR	SH	SF	HB	TBB	IBB	SO	WP	Bk	W	L	Pct.	ShO	Sv-Op	Hld	ERA
1998 Hickory *	A	1	1	0	0	4	15	3	1	1	0	0	0	0	2	0	2	0	0	0	0	.000	0	0--	—	2.25
Winston-Sal *	A+	4	4	0	0	21.2	87	17	13	13	2	0	0	0	7	0	13	4	0	2	1	.667	0	0--	—	5.40
Birmingham *	AA	8	8	0	0	41.2	198	53	33	25	2	0	2	1	21	0	35	5	0	2	3	.400	0	0--	—	5.40
Calgary *	AAA	5	5	1	0	31	126	31	9	9	1	1	0	1	9	0	20	2	0	2	0	1.000	0	0--	—	2.61
1989 California	AL	29	29	4	0	181.1	788	190	95	79	13	11	5	4	74	3	115	8	2	12	12	.500	2	0-0	0	3.92
1990 California	AL	33	33	4	0	211.2	925	246	116	106	16	9	6	5	72	6	105	4	3	10	14	.417	1	0-0	0	4.51
1991 California	AL	34	34	5	0	243	1002	222	85	78	14	7	7	5	73	6	158	1	4	18	11	.621	1	0-0	0	2.89
1992 California	AL	29	29	7	0	211	874	208	73	65	12	8	4	4	68	3	130	2	0	7	15	.318	0	0-0	0	2.77
1993 New York	AL	32	32	4	0	214	906	221	115	104	22	12	4	3	73	4	95	9	0	11	14	.440	1	0-0	0	4.37
1994 New York	AL	24	24	2	0	160.1	692	167	88	81	24	9	5	2	64	1	90	8	1	9	8	.529	0	0-0	0	4.55
1995 ChA-Cal	AL	30	30	4	0	197	842	209	93	81	14	8	4	2	64	1	86	1	0	11	8	.579	1	0-0	0	3.70
1996 California	AL	27	23	1	2	142	654	171	128	118	23	4	10	4	78	3	58	13	1	2	18	.100	0	0-0	0	7.48
1998 Chicago	AL	5	5	0	0	31.2	134	35	16	16	2	0	1	1	12	0	14	0	0	5	0	1.000	0	0-0	0	4.55
1995 Chicago	AL	17	17	3	0	112.1	474	116	50	42	10	5	1	1	35	1	45	0	0	6	4	.600	0	0-0	0	3.36
California	AL	13	13	1	0	84.2	368	93	43	39	4	3	3	1	29	0	41	1	0	5	4	.556	1	0-0	0	4.15
9 ML YEARS		243	239	31	2	1592	6817	1669	809	728	140	68	46	30	578	27	851	46	11	85	100	.459	6	0-0	0	4.12

Kurt Abbott

Bats: R **Throws:** R **Pos:** SS-35; PH/PR-22; LF-9; 2B-7; RF-6; DH-4; 3B-4 **Ht:** 6'0" **Wt:** 190 **Born:** 6/2/69 **Age:** 30

Year Team	Lg	G	AB	H	2B	3B	HR	(Hm	Rd)	TB	R	RBI	TBB	IBB	SO	HBP	SH	SF	SB	CS	SB%	GDP	Avg	OBP	SLG
1998 Edmonton *	AAA	7	25	10	2	0	2	—	—	18	5	4	6	0	8	0	0	0	0	1	.00	1	.400	.516	.720
1993 Oakland	AL	20	61	15	1	0	3	(0	3)	25	11	9	3	0	20	0	3	0	2	0	1.00	3	.246	.281	.410
1994 Florida	NL	101	345	86	17	3	9	(4	5)	136	41	33	16	1	98	5	3	2	3	0	1.00	5	.249	.291	.394
1995 Florida	NL	120	420	107	18	7	17	(12	5)	190	60	60	36	4	110	5	2	5	4	3	.57	6	.255	.318	.452
1996 Florida	NL	109	320	81	18	7	8	(6	2)	137	37	33	22	1	99	3	4	0	3	3	.50	7	.253	.307	.428
1997 Florida	NL	94	252	69	18	2	6	(1	5)	109	35	30	14	3	68	1	6	0	3	1	.75	5	.274	.315	.433
1998 Oak-Col		77	194	51	13	1	5	(3	2)	81	26	24	12	0	53	2	1	3	2	1	.67	5	.263	.308	.418
1998 Oakland	AL	35	123	33	7	1	2	(1	1)	48	17	9	10	0	34	1	1	1	2	1	.67	3	.268	.326	.390
Colorado	NL	42	71	18	6	0	3	(2	1)	33	9	15	2	0	19	1	0	2	0	0	.00	2	.254	.276	.465
6 ML YEARS		521	1592	409	85	20	48	(26	22)	678	210	189	103	9	448	16	19	10	17	8	.68	31	.257	.307	.426

Paul Abbott

Pitches: Right **Bats:** Right **Pos:** SP-4 **Ht:** 6'3" **Wt:** 194 **Born:** 9/15/67 **Age:** 31

Year Team	Lg	G	GS	CG	GF	IP	BFP	H	R	ER	HR	SH	SF	HB	TBB	IBB	SO	WP	Bk	W	L	Pct.	ShO	Sv-Op	Hld	ERA
1998 Mariners *	R	1	0	0	0	3	12	1	0	0	0	0	0	0	6	0	6	0	0	0	0	.000	0	0--	—	0.00
Tacoma *	AAA	3	3	0	0	15	56	9	2	2	2	0	0	0	5	0	20	0	0	1	0	1.000	0	0--	—	1.20
1990 Minnesota	AL	7	7	0	0	34.2	162	37	24	23	0	1	1	1	28	0	25	1	0	0	5	.000	0	0-0	0	5.97
1991 Minnesota	AL	15	3	0	1	47.1	210	38	27	25	5	7	3	0	36	1	43	5	0	3	1	.750	0	0-0	0	4.75
1992 Minnesota	AL	6	0	0	5	11	50	12	4	4	1	0	1	1	5	0	13	1	0	0	0	.000	0	0-0	0	3.27
1993 Cleveland	AL	5	5	0	0	18.1	84	19	15	13	5	0	0	0	11	1	7	1	0	0	1	.000	0	0-0	0	6.38
1998 Seattle	AL	4	4	0	0	24.2	105	24	11	11	2	0	1	0	10	0	22	3	0	3	1	.750	0	0-0	0	4.01
5 ML YEARS		37	19	0	6	136	611	130	81	76	13	8	6	2	90	2	110	11	0	6	8	.429	0	0-0	0	5.03

Bob Abreu

Bats: Left **Throws:** Right **Pos:** RF-146; PH/PR-11 **Ht:** 6'0" **Wt:** 185 **Born:** 3/11/74 **Age:** 25

Year Team	Lg	G	AB	H	2B	3B	HR	(Hm	Rd)	TB	R	RBI	TBB	IBB	SO	HBP	SH	SF	SB	CS	SB%	GDP	Avg	OBP	SLG
1996 Houston	NL	15	22	5	1	0	0	(0	0)	6	1	1	2	0	3	0	0	0	0	0	.00	1	.227	.292	.273
1997 Houston	NL	59	188	47	10	2	3	(3	0)	70	22	26	21	0	48	1	0	0	7	2	.78	0	.250	.329	.372
1998 Philadelphia	NL	151	497	155	29	6	17	(10	7)	247	68	74	84	14	133	0	4	4	19	10	.66	6	.312	.409	.497
3 ML YEARS		225	707	207	40	8	20	(13	7)	323	91	101	107	14	184	1	4	4	26	12	.68	7	.293	.385	.457

Juan Acevedo

Pitches: Right **Bats:** Right **Pos:** RP-41; SP-9   **Ht:** 6'2" **Wt:** 195 **Born:** 5/5/70 **Age:** 29

Year Team	Lg	G	GS	CG	GF	IP	BFP	H	R	ER	HR	SH	SF	HB	TBB	IBB	SO	WP	Bk	W	L	Pct.	ShO	Sv-Op	Hld	ERA
1998 Memphis *	AAA	2	2	0	0	8.2	31	5	0	0	0	0	0	0	1	0	6	0	0	0	0	.000	0	0--	—	0.00
1995 Colorado	NL	17	11	0	0	65.2	291	82	53	47	15	4	2	6	20	2	40	2	1	4	6	.400	0	0-0	1	6.44
1997 New York	NL	25	2	0	4	47.2	215	52	24	19	6	2	5	4	22	2	33	0	1	3	1	.750	0	0-4	3	3.59
1998 St. Louis	NL	50	9	0	29	98.1	394	83	30	28	7	8	1	4	29	2	56	3	0	8	3	.727	0	15-16	3	2.56
3 ML YEARS		92	22	0	33	211.2	900	217	107	94	28	14	8	14	71	6	129	5	2	15	10	.600	0	15-20	7	4.00

Terry Adams

Pitches: Right **Bats:** Right **Pos:** RP-63   **Ht:** 6'3" **Wt:** 205 **Born:** 3/6/73 **Age:** 26

Year Team	Lg	G	GS	CG	GF	IP	BFP	H	R	ER	HR	SH	SF	HB	TBB	IBB	SO	WP	Bk	W	L	Pct.	ShO	Sv-Op	Hld	ERA
1998 Iowa *	AAA	3	0	0	0	4	16	1	1	0	0	0	0	0	3	0	5	1	0	0	0	.000	0	0--	—	0.00
1995 Chicago	NL	18	0	0	7	18	86	22	15	13	0	0	0	0	10	1	15	1	0	1	1	.500	0	1-1	0	6.50
1996 Chicago	NL	69	0	0	22	101	423	84	36	33	6	7	3	1	49	6	78	5	1	3	6	.333	0	4-8	11	2.94
1997 Chicago	NL	74	0	0	39	74	341	91	43	38	3	1	2	1	40	6	64	6	0	2	9	.182	0	18-22	11	4.62
1998 Chicago	NL	63	0	0	15	72.2	330	72	39	35	7	3	3	1	41	3	73	4	3	7	7	.500	0	1-7	13	4.33
4 ML YEARS		224	0	0	83	265.2	1180	269	133	119	16	11	8	3	140	16	230	16	4	13	23	.361	0	24-38	35	4.03

Joel Adamson

Pitches: Left **Bats:** Left **Pos:** SP-5   **Ht:** 6'4" **Wt:** 185 **Born:** 7/2/71 **Age:** 27

Year Team	Lg	G	GS	CG	GF	IP	BFP	H	R	ER	HR	SH	SF	HB	TBB	IBB	SO	WP	Bk	W	L	Pct.	ShO	Sv-Op	Hld	ERA
1996 Florida	NL	9	0	0	1	11	56	18	9	9	1	2	1	1	7	0	7	0	0	0	0	.000	0	0-0	0	7.36
1997 Milwaukee	AL	30	6	0	3	76.1	324	78	36	30	13	4	2	5	19	0	56	0	1	5	3	.625	0	0-0	1	3.54
1998 Arizona	NL	5	5	0	0	23	104	25	21	21	5	1	1	3	11	0	14	0	0	0	3	.000	0	0-0	0	8.22
3 ML YEARS		44	11	0	4	110.1	484	121	66	60	19	7	4	9	37	0	77	0	1	5	6	.455	0	0-0	1	4.89

Benny Agbayani

Bats: Right **Throws:** Right **Pos:** RF-6; PH/PR-3; CF-2; LF-1   **Ht:** 6'0" **Wt:** 225 **Born:** 12/28/71 **Age:** 27

Year Team	Lg	G	AB	H	2B	3B	HR	(Hm Rd)	TB	R	RBI	TBB	IBB	SO	HBP	SH	SF	SB	CS	SB%	GDP	Avg	OBP	SLG
1993 Pittsfield	A-	51	167	42	6	3	2	— —	60	26	22	20	0	43	0	0	0	7	2	.78	4	.251	.332	.359
1994 St. Lucie	A+	119	411	115	13	5	5	— —	153	72	63	58	2	67	10	1	5	8	6	.57	9	.280	.378	.372
1995 St. Lucie	A+	44	155	48	9	3	2	— —	69	24	29	26	1	27	5	1	4	3	3	.73	4	.310	.416	.445
Binghamton	AA	88	295	81	11	2	1	— —	99	38	26	39	0	51	5	1	1	12	3	.80	6	.275	.368	.336
1996 Binghamton	AA	21	53	9	1	0	2	— —	16	7	8	11	0	13	1	1	1	1	0	1.00	2	.170	.318	.302
Norfolk	AAA	99	331	92	13	9	7	— —	144	43	56	30	3	57	3	3	5	14	5	.74	5	.278	.339	.435
1997 Norfolk	AAA	127	468	145	24	2	11	— —	206	90	51	67	0	106	6	0	3	29	14	.67	13	.310	.401	.440
1998 Norfolk	AAA	90	322	91	20	5	11	— —	154	43	53	50	2	58	3	0	3	16	6	.73	9	.283	.381	.478
1998 New York	NL	11	15	2	0	0	0	(0 0)	2	1	0	1	0	5	0	0	0	0	2	.00	1	.133	.188	.133

Rick Aguilera

Pitches: Right **Bats:** Right **Pos:** RP-68   **Ht:** 6'5" **Wt:** 208 **Born:** 12/31/61 **Age:** 37

Year Team	Lg	G	GS	CG	GF	IP	BFP	H	R	ER	HR	SH	SF	HB	TBB	IBB	SO	WP	Bk	W	L	Pct.	ShO	Sv-Op	Hld	ERA
1985 New York	NL	21	19	2	1	122.1	507	118	49	44	8	7	4	2	37	2	74	5	2	10	7	.588	0	0-0	0	3.24
1986 New York	NL	28	20	2	2	141.2	605	145	70	61	15	6	5	7	36	1	104	5	3	10	7	.588	0	0-1	0	3.88
1987 New York	NL	18	17	1	0	115	494	124	53	46	12	7	2	3	33	2	77	9	0	11	3	.786	0	0-0	1	3.60
1988 New York	NL	11	3	0	2	24.2	111	29	20	19	2	2	0	1	10	2	16	1	1	0	4	.000	0	0-0	1	6.93
1989 NYN-Min		47	11	3	19	145	594	130	51	45	8	7	1	3	38	4	137	4	3	9	11	.450	0	7-11	1	2.79
1990 Minnesota	AL	56	0	0	54	65.1	268	55	27	20	5	0	0	4	19	6	61	3	0	5	3	.625	0	32-39	0	2.76
1991 Minnesota	AL	63	0	0	60	69	275	44	20	18	3	1	3	1	30	6	61	3	0	4	5	.444	0	42-51	0	2.35
1992 Minnesota	AL	64	0	0	61	66.2	273	60	28	21	7	1	2	1	17	4	52	5	0	2	6	.250	0	41-48	0	2.84
1993 Minnesota	AL	65	0	0	61	72.1	287	60	25	25	9	2	1	1	14	3	59	1	0	4	3	.571	0	34-40	0	3.11
1994 Minnesota	AL	44	0	0	40	44.2	201	57	23	18	7	4	1	0	10	3	46	2	0	1	4	.200	0	23-29	0	3.63
1995 Min-Bos	AL	52	0	0	51	55.1	223	46	16	16	6	1	4	1	13	1	52	0	0	3	3	.500	0	32-36	0	2.60
1996 Minnesota	AL	19	19	2	0	111.1	484	124	69	67	20	1	3	3	27	1	83	6	0	8	6	.571	0	0-0	0	5.42
1997 Minnesota	AL	61	0	0	57	68.1	285	65	29	29	9	5	3	2	22	3	68	3	0	5	4	.556	0	26-33	0	3.82
1998 Minnesota	AL	68	0	0	64	74.1	307	75	35	35	8	3	2	1	15	1	57	1	0	4	9	.308	0	38-49	0	4.24
1989 New York	NL	36	0	0	19	69.1	284	59	19	18	3	5	1	2	21	3	80	3	3	6	6	.500	0	7-11	1	2.34
Minnesota	AL	11	11	3	0	75.2	310	71	32	27	5	2	0	1	17	1	57	1	0	3	5	.375	0	0-0	0	3.21
1995 Minnesota	AL	22	0	0	21	25	99	20	7	7	2	0	2	1	6	1	29	0	0	1	1	.500	0	12-15	0	2.52
Boston	AL	30	0	0	30	30.1	124	26	9	9	4	1	2	0	7	0	23	0	0	2	2	.500	0	20-21	0	2.67
14 ML YEARS		617	89	10	472	1176	4914	1132	515	464	119	47	31	30	321	39	947	48	9	76	75	.503	0	275-337	3	3.55

Scott Aldred

Pitches: Left **Bats:** Left **Pos:** RP-48 **Ht:** 6'4" **Wt:** 228 **Born:** 6/12/68 **Age:** 31

Year Team	Lg	G	GS	CG	GF	IP	BFP	H	R	ER	HR	SH	SF	HB	TBB	IBB	SO	WP	Bk	W	L	Pct.	ShO	Sv-Op	Hld	ERA
1998 Durham *	AAA	7	7	0	0	35.1	161	44	26	21	3	0	2	4	14	0	19	4	0	2	4	.333	0	0--	—	5.35
1990 Detroit	AL	4	3	0	0	14.1	63	13	6	6	0	2	1	1	10	1	7	0	0	1	2	.333	0	0-0	0	3.77
1991 Detroit	AL	11	11	1	0	57.1	253	58	37	33	9	3	2	0	30	2	35	3	1	2	4	.333	0	0-0	0	5.18
1992 Detroit	AL	16	13	0	0	65	304	80	51	49	12	4	3	3	33	4	34	1	0	3	8	.273	0	0-0	0	6.78
1993 Col-Mon	NL	8	0	0	2	12	65	19	14	12	2	2	0	1	10	1	9	2	0	1	0	1.000	0	0-1	0	9.00
1996 Det-Min	AL	36	25	0	0	165.1	748	194	125	114	29	7	7	6	68	4	111	10	1	6	9	.400	0	0-0	0	6.21
1997 Minnesota	AL	17	15	0	0	77.1	350	102	66	66	20	2	1	3	28	2	33	7	0	2	10	.167	0	0-0	0	7.68
1998 Tampa Bay	AL	48	0	0	8	31.1	135	33	13	13	1	3	0	2	12	3	21	2	0	0	0	.000	0	0-0	8	3.73
1993 Colorado	NL	5	0	0	1	6.2	40	10	10	8	1	2	0	1	9	1	5	1	0	0	0	.000	0	0-0	0	10.80
Montreal	NL	3	0	0	1	5.1	25	9	4	4	1	0	0	0	1	0	4	1	0	1	0	1.000	0	0-1	0	6.75
1996 Detroit	AL	11	8	0	0	43.1	217	60	52	45	9	3	2	3	26	3	36	6	1	0	4	.000	0	0-0	0	9.35
Minnesota	AL	25	17	0	0	122	531	134	73	69	20	4	5	3	42	1	75	4	0	6	5	.545	0	0-0	1	5.09
7 ML YEARS		140	67	1	10	422.2	1918	499	312	293	73	23	14	16	191	17	250	25	2	15	33	.313	0	0-1	9	6.24

Manny Alexander

Bats: R **Throws:** R **Pos:** SS-50; PH/PR-32; 2B-27; 3B-19; DH-2; LF-1 **Ht:** 5'10" **Wt:** 175 **Born:** 3/20/71 **Age:** 28

Year Team	Lg	G	AB	H	2B	3B	HR	(Hm	Rd)	TB	R	RBI	TBB	IBB	SO	HBP	SH	SF	SB	CS	SB%	GDP	Avg	OBP	SLG
1992 Baltimore	AL	4	5	1	0	0	0	(0	0)	1	1	0	0	0	3	0	0	0	0	0	.00	0	.200	.200	.200
1993 Baltimore	AL	3	0	0	0	0	0	(0	0)	0	1	0	0	0	0	0	0	0	0	0	.00	0	.000	.000	.000
1995 Baltimore	AL	94	242	57	9	1	3	(2	1)	77	35	23	20	0	30	2	4	0	11	4	.73	2	.236	.299	.318
1996 Baltimore	AL	54	68	7	0	0	0	(0	0)	7	6	4	3	0	27	0	2	0	3	3	.50	2	.103	.141	.103
1997 NYN-ChN	NL	87	248	66	12	4	3	(0	3)	95	37	22	17	3	54	3	3	1	13	1	.93	6	.266	.320	.383
1998 Chicago	NL	108	264	60	10	1	5	(1	4)	87	34	25	18	1	66	1	5	1	4	1	.80	6	.227	.278	.330
1997 New York	NL	54	149	37	9	3	2	(0	2)	58	26	15	9	1	38	1	1	1	11	0	1.00	3	.248	.294	.389
Chicago	NL	33	99	29	3	1	1	(0	1)	37	11	7	8	2	16	2	2	0	2	1	.67	3	.293	.358	.374
6 ML YEARS		350	827	191	31	6	11	(3	8)	267	114	74	58	4	180	6	14	2	31	9	.78	16	.231	.286	.323

Antonio Alfonseca

Pitches: Right **Bats:** Right **Pos:** RP-58 **Ht:** 6'5" **Wt:** 235 **Born:** 4/16/72 **Age:** 27

Year Team	Lg	G	GS	CG	GF	IP	BFP	H	R	ER	HR	SH	SF	HB	TBB	IBB	SO	WP	Bk	W	L	Pct.	ShO	Sv-Op	Hld	ERA
1991 Expos	R	11	10	0	0	51	225	46	33	22	2	1	4	3	25	0	38	1	0	3	3	.500	0	0--	—	3.88
1992 Expos	R	12	10	1	0	66	282	55	31	27	0	2	6	3	35	0	62	8	2	3	4	.429	1	0--	—	3.68
1993 Jamestown	A-	15	4	0	3	33.2	151	31	26	23	3	0	2	3	22	1	29	4	1	2	2	.500	0	1--	—	6.15
1994 Kane County	A	32	9	0	7	86.1	361	78	41	39	5	2	3	2	21	1	74	14	0	6	5	.545	0	0--	—	4.07
1995 Portland	AA	19	17	1	0	96.1	405	81	43	39	6	3	3	4	42	1	75	5	4	9	3	.750	0	0--	—	3.64
1996 Charlotte	AAA	14	13	0	1	71.2	321	86	47	44	6	1	4	3	22	0	51	2	0	4	4	.500	0	1--	—	5.53
1997 Charlotte	AAA	46	0	0	20	58.1	246	58	34	28	8	2	2	2	20	3	45	3	2	7	2	.778	0	7--	—	4.32
1997 Florida	NL	17	0	0	2	25.2	123	36	16	14	3	1	0	1	10	3	19	1	0	1	3	.250	0	0-2	0	4.91
1998 Florida	NL	58	0	0	27	70.2	316	75	36	32	10	7	6	3	33	9	46	1	0	4	6	.400	0	8-14	9	4.08
2 ML YEARS		75	0	0	29	96.1	439	111	52	46	13	8	6	4	43	12	65	2	0	5	9	.357	0	8-16	9	4.30

Edgardo Alfonzo

Bats: Right **Throws:** Right **Pos:** 3B-144; PH/PR-2; SS-1 **Ht:** 5'11" **Wt:** 187 **Born:** 11/8/73 **Age:** 25

Year Team	Lg	G	AB	H	2B	3B	HR	(Hm	Rd)	TB	R	RBI	TBB	IBB	SO	HBP	SH	SF	SB	CS	SB%	GDP	Avg	OBP	SLG
1995 New York	NL	101	335	93	13	5	4	(0	4)	128	26	41	12	1	37	1	4	4	1	1	.50	7	.278	.301	.382
1996 New York	NL	123	368	96	15	2	4	(2	2)	127	36	40	25	2	56	0	9	5	2	1	1.00	8	.261	.304	.345
1997 New York	NL	151	518	163	27	2	10	(4	6)	224	84	72	63	0	56	5	8	5	11	6	.65	4	.315	.391	.432
1998 New York	NL	144	557	155	28	2	17	(8	9)	238	94	78	65	1	77	3	2	3	8	3	.73	11	.278	.355	.427
4 ML YEARS		519	1778	507	83	11	35	(14	21)	717	240	231	165	4	226	9	23	17	22	10	.69	30	.285	.346	.403

Luis Alicea

Bats: B **Throws:** R **Pos:** 2B-45; PH/PR-32; 3B-26; DH-18; LF-2 **Ht:** 5'9" **Wt:** 176 **Born:** 7/29/65 **Age:** 33

Year Team	Lg	G	AB	H	2B	3B	HR	(Hm	Rd)	TB	R	RBI	TBB	IBB	SO	HBP	SH	SF	SB	CS	SB%	GDP	Avg	OBP	SLG
1988 St. Louis	NL	93	297	63	10	4	1	(1	0)	84	20	24	25	4	32	2	4	2	1	1	.50	12	.212	.276	.283
1991 St. Louis	NL	56	68	13	3	0	0	(0	0)	16	5	0	8	0	19	0	0	0	1	1	.00	0	.191	.276	.235
1992 St. Louis	NL	85	265	65	9	11	2	(2	0)	102	26	32	27	1	40	4	2	4	2	5	.29	5	.245	.320	.385
1993 St. Louis	NL	115	362	101	19	3	3	(2	1)	135	50	46	47	2	54	4	1	7	11	1	.92	9	.279	.362	.373
1994 St. Louis	NL	88	205	57	12	5	5	(3	2)	94	32	29	30	4	38	3	1	3	4	5	.44	1	.278	.373	.459
1995 Boston	AL	132	419	113	20	3	6	(0	6)	157	64	44	63	0	61	7	13	6	13	10	.57	10	.270	.367	.375
1996 St. Louis	NL	129	380	98	26	3	5	(4	1)	145	54	42	52	10	78	5	4	6	11	3	.79	4	.258	.350	.382
1997 Anaheim	AL	128	388	98	16	7	5	(2	3)	143	59	37	69	3	65	8	4	2	22	8	.73	4	.253	.375	.369
1998 Texas	AL	101	259	71	15	3	6	(1	5)	110	51	33	37	0	40	5	4	3	4	3	.57	1	.274	.372	.425
9 ML YEARS		927	2643	679	130	39	33	(15	18)	986	361	287	358	24	427	38	33	36	68	37	.65	46	.257	.350	.373

Jermaine Allensworth

Bats: R **Throws:** R **Pos:** CF-94; RF-27; PH/PR-21; LF-5   **Ht:** 6'0" **Wt:** 190 **Born:** 1/11/72 **Age:** 27

Year Team	Lg	G	AB	H	2B	3B	HR	Hm	Rd	TB	R	RBI	TBB	IBB	SO	HBP	SH	SF	SB	CS	SB%	GDP	Avg	OBP	SLG
1996 Pittsburgh	NL	61	229	60	9	3	4	(4	0)	87	32	31	23	0	50	4	2	2	11	6	.65	2	.262	.337	.380
1997 Pittsburgh	NL	108	369	94	18	2	3	(1	2)	125	55	43	44	1	79	7	9	6	14	7	.67	5	.255	.340	.339
1998 Pit-KC-NYN		133	360	98	20	3	5	(2	3)	139	54	31	28	0	76	12	8	1	15	6	.71	1	.272	.344	.386
1998 Pittsburgh	NL	69	233	72	13	3	3	(2	1)	100	30	24	17	0	43	7	3	1	8	4	.67	1	.309	.372	.429
Kansas City	AL	30	73	15	5	0	0	(0	0)	20	15	3	9	0	17	4	5	0	7	0	1.00	0	.205	.326	.274
New York	AL	34	54	11	2	0	2	(0	2)	19	9	4	2	0	16	1	0	0	0	2	.00	0	.204	.246	.352
3 ML YEARS		302	958	252	47	8	12	(7	5)	351	141	105	95	1	205	23	19	9	40	19	.68	8	.263	.341	.366

Carlos Almanzar

Pitches: Right **Bats:** Right **Pos:** RP-25   **Ht:** 6'2" **Wt:** 200 **Born:** 11/6/73 **Age:** 25

Year Team	Lg	G	GS	CG	GF	IP	BFP	H	R	ER	HR	SH	SF	HB	TBB	IBB	SO	WP	Bk	W	L	Pct.	ShO	Sv-Op	Hld	ERA
1994 Medicine Ha	R+	14	14	0	0	84.2	351	82	38	27	2	7	1	1	19	0	77	3	2	7	4	.636	0	0- -	—	2.87
1995 Knoxville	AA	35	19	0	7	126.1	546	144	77	56	10	3	6	3	32	1	93	4	1	3	12	.200	0	2- -	—	3.99
1996 Knoxville	AA	54	0	0	29	94.2	418	106	58	51	13	1	2	3	33	6	105	3	0	7	8	.467	0	9- -	—	4.85
1997 Knoxville	AA	21	0	0	19	25.2	109	30	14	14	2	2	2	0	5	1	25	0	0	1	1	.500	0	8- -	—	4.91
Syracuse	AAA	32	0	0	17	51	189	30	9	8	2	2	1	2	8	0	47	2	0	5	1	.833	0	3- -	—	1.41
1998 Syracuse	AAA	30	0	0	19	50.2	211	44	21	13	7	1	1	4	13	2	53	2	0	3	6	.333	0	10- -	—	2.31
1997 Toronto	AL	4	0	0	2	3.1	12	1	1	1	1	0	0	0	1	0	4	0	0	0	1	.000	0	0-0	0	2.70
1998 Toronto	AL	25	0	0	8	28.2	129	34	18	17	4	1	0	1	8	2	20	0	0	2	2	.500	0	0-3	1	5.34
2 ML YEARS		29	0	0	10	32	141	35	19	18	5	1	0	1	9	2	24	0	0	2	3	.400	0	0-3	1	5.06

Roberto Alomar

Bats: Both **Throws:** Right **Pos:** 2B-144; PH/PR-4; DH-3   **Ht:** 6'0" **Wt:** 185 **Born:** 2/5/68 **Age:** 31

Year Team	Lg	G	AB	H	2B	3B	HR	Hm	Rd	TB	R	RBI	TBB	IBB	SO	HBP	SH	SF	SB	CS	SB%	GDP	Avg	OBP	SLG
1988 San Diego	NL	143	545	145	24	6	9	(5	4)	208	84	41	47	5	83	3	16	0	24	6	.80	15	.266	.328	.382
1989 San Diego	NL	158	623	184	27	1	7	(3	4)	234	82	56	53	4	76	1	17	8	42	17	.71	10	.295	.347	.376
1990 San Diego	NL	147	586	168	27	5	6	(4	2)	223	80	60	48	1	72	2	5	5	24	7	.77	16	.287	.340	.381
1991 Toronto	AL	161	637	188	41	11	9	(6	3)	278	88	69	57	3	86	4	16	5	53	11	.83	5	.295	.354	.436
1992 Toronto	AL	152	571	177	27	8	8	(5	3)	244	105	76	87	5	52	5	4	5	49	9	.84	8	.310	.405	.427
1993 Toronto	AL	153	589	192	35	6	17	(8	9)	290	109	93	80	5	67	5	4	5	55	15	.79	13	.326	.408	.492
1994 Toronto	AL	107	392	120	25	4	8	(4	4)	177	78	38	51	2	41	2	7	3	19	8	.70	14	.306	.386	.452
1995 Toronto	AL	130	517	155	24	7	13	(7	6)	232	71	66	47	3	45	0	6	7	30	3	.91	16	.300	.354	.449
1996 Baltimore	AL	153	588	193	43	4	22	(14	8)	310	132	94	90	10	65	1	8	12	17	6	.74	14	.328	.411	.527
1997 Baltimore	AL	112	412	137	23	2	14	(10	4)	206	64	60	40	2	43	1	7	7	9	3	.75	10	.333	.390	.500
1998 Baltimore	AL	147	588	166	36	1	14	(7	7)	246	86	56	59	3	70	2	3	5	18	5	.78	11	.282	.347	.418
11 ML YEARS		1563	6048	1825	332	55	127	(73	54)	2648	979	709	659	43	700	28	95	59	340	90	.79	132	.302	.370	.438

Sandy Alomar

Bats: Right **Throws:** Right **Pos:** C-111; PH/PR-4; DH-3   **Ht:** 6'5" **Wt:** 215 **Born:** 6/18/66 **Age:** 33

Year Team	Lg	G	AB	H	2B	3B	HR	Hm	Rd	TB	R	RBI	TBB	IBB	SO	HBP	SH	SF	SB	CS	SB%	GDP	Avg	OBP	SLG
1988 San Diego	NL	1	1	0	0	0	0	(0	0)	0	0	0	0	0	1	0	0	0	0	0	.00	0	.000	.000	.000
1989 San Diego	NL	7	19	4	1	0	1	(1	0)	8	1	6	3	1	3	0	0	0	0	0	.00	1	.211	.318	.421
1990 Cleveland	AL	132	445	129	26	2	9	(5	4)	186	60	66	25	2	46	2	5	6	4	1	.80	10	.290	.326	.418
1991 Cleveland	AL	51	184	40	9	0	0	(0	0)	49	10	7	8	1	24	4	2	1	0	4	.00	4	.217	.264	.266
1992 Cleveland	AL	89	299	75	16	0	2	(1	1)	97	22	26	13	3	32	5	3	0	3	3	.50	7	.251	.293	.324
1993 Cleveland	AL	64	215	58	7	1	6	(3	3)	85	24	32	11	0	28	6	1	4	3	1	.75	3	.270	.318	.395
1994 Cleveland	AL	80	292	84	15	1	14	(4	10)	143	44	43	25	2	31	2	0	1	8	4	.67	7	.288	.347	.490
1995 Cleveland	AL	66	203	61	6	0	10	(4	6)	97	32	35	7	0	26	3	4	1	3	1	.75	3	.300	.332	.478
1996 Cleveland	AL	127	418	110	23	0	11	(3	8)	166	53	50	19	0	42	3	2	2	1	0	1.00	20	.263	.299	.397
1997 Cleveland	AL	125	451	146	37	0	21	(9	12)	246	63	83	19	2	48	3	6	1	0	2	.00	16	.324	.354	.545
1998 Cleveland	AL	117	409	96	26	2	6	(3	3)	144	45	44	18	0	45	3	5	3	0	3	.00	15	.235	.270	.352
11 ML YEARS		859	2936	803	166	6	80	(33	47)	1221	354	392	148	11	326	31	28	19	22	19	.54	91	.274	.313	.416

Moises Alou

Bats: R **Throws:** R **Pos:** LF-152; CF-6; PH/PR-6; DH-1   **Ht:** 6'3" **Wt:** 195 **Born:** 7/3/66 **Age:** 32

Year Team	Lg	G	AB	H	2B	3B	HR	Hm	Rd	TB	R	RBI	TBB	IBB	SO	HBP	SH	SF	SB	CS	SB%	GDP	Avg	OBP	SLG
1990 Pit-Mon	NL	16	20	4	0	1	0	(0	0)	6	4	0	0	0	3	0	1	0	0	0	.00	1	.200	.200	.300
1992 Montreal	NL	115	341	96	28	2	9	(6	3)	155	53	56	25	0	46	1	5	5	16	2	.89	5	.282	.328	.455
1993 Montreal	NL	136	482	138	29	6	18	(10	8)	233	70	85	38	9	53	5	3	7	17	6	.74	9	.286	.340	.483
1994 Montreal	NL	107	422	143	31	5	22	(13	9)	250	81	78	42	10	63	2	0	5	7	6	.54	7	.339	.397	.592
1995 Montreal	NL	93	344	94	22	0	14	(4	10)	158	48	58	29	6	56	9	0	4	4	3	.57	9	.273	.342	.459
1996 Montreal	NL	143	540	152	28	2	21	(14	7)	247	87	96	49	7	83	2	0	7	9	4	.69	15	.281	.339	.457
1997 Florida	NL	150	538	157	29	5	23	(12	11)	265	88	115	70	9	85	4	0	7	9	5	.64	13	.292	.373	.493
1998 Houston	NL	159	584	182	34	5	38	(19	19)	340	104	124	84	11	87	5	0	6	11	3	.79	14	.312	.399	.582
1990 Pittsburgh	NL	2	5	1	0	0	0	(0	0)	1	0	0	0	0	0	0	0	0	0	0	.00	1	.200	.200	.200
Montreal	NL	14	15	3	0	0	0	(0	0)	5	4	0	0	0	1	0	0	0	0	0	.00	0	.200	.200	.333

	BATTING																	BASERUNNING				PERCENTAGES		
Year Team	Lg	G	AB	H	2B	3B	HR	(Hm Rd)	TB	R	RBI	TBB	IBB	SO	HBP	SH	SF	SB	CS	SB%	GDP	Avg	OBP	SLG
8 ML YEARS		919	3271	966	201	26	145	(74 71)	1654	535	612	337	52	476	28	9	41	73	29	.72	73	.295	.362	.506

Gabe Alvarez

Bats: Right **Throws:** Right **Pos:** 3B-55; DH-2; PH/PR-1   **Ht:** 6'1" **Wt:** 205 **Born:** 3/6/74 **Age:** 25

		BATTING																BASERUNNING				PERCENTAGES		
Year Team	Lg	G	AB	H	2B	3B	HR	(Hm Rd)	TB	R	RBI	TBB	IBB	SO	HBP	SH	SF	SB	CS	SB%	GDP	Avg	OBP	SLG
1995 Rancho Cuca	A+	59	212	73	17	2	6	— —	112	41	36	29	0	30	5	0	2	1	0	1.00	3	.344	.431	.528
Memphis	AA	2	9	5	1	0	0	— —	6	0	4	1	0	1	0	0	0	0	0	.00	0	.556	.600	.667
1996 Memphis	AA	104	368	91	23	1	8	— —	140	58	40	64	1	87	0	0	3	2	3	.40	10	.247	.361	.380
1997 Mobile	AA	114	427	128	28	2	14	— —	202	71	78	51	2	64	5	0	6	1	1	.50	21	.300	.376	.473
1998 Toledo	AAA	67	249	68	15	1	20	— —	145	37	58	30	0	60	1	0	3	3	1	.75	7	.273	.350	.582
1998 Detroit	AL	58	199	46	11	0	5	(3 2)	72	16	29	18	1	65	2	0	2	1	3	.25	2	.231	.299	.362

Wilson Alvarez

Pitches: Left **Bats:** Left **Pos:** SP-25   **Ht:** 6'1" **Wt:** 235 **Born:** 3/24/70 **Age:** 29

		HOW MUCH HE PITCHED						WHAT HE GAVE UP											THE RESULTS							
Year Team	Lg	G	GS	CG	GF	IP	BFP	H	R	ER	HR	SH	SF	HB	TBB	IBB	SO	WP	Bk	W	L	Pct.	ShO	Sv-Op	Hld	ERA
1998 Devil Rays *	R	1	1	0	0	3	11	2	0	0	0	0	0	0	1	0	4	0	0	0	0	.000	0	0- —	—	0.00
St. Pete *	A+	1	1	0	0	1.2	12	5	5	5	1	0	0	0	2	0	2	0	0	0	0	.000	0	0- —	—	27.00
Durham *	AAA	1	1	0	0	4.2	19	4	2	2	0	0	0	0	2	0	6	0	0	0	0	.000	0	0- —	—	3.86
1989 Texas	AL	1	1	0	0	0	5	3	3	3	2	0	0	0	2	0	0	0	0	0	1	.000	0	0-0	0	0.00
1991 Chicago	AL	10	9	2	0	56.1	237	47	26	22	9	3	1	0	29	0	32	2	0	3	2	.600	1	0-0	0	3.51
1992 Chicago	AL	34	9	0	4	100.1	455	103	64	58	12	3	4	4	65	2	66	2	0	5	3	.625	0	1-1	3	5.20
1993 Chicago	AL	31	31	1	0	207.2	877	168	78	68	14	13	6	7	122	8	155	2	1	15	8	.652	1	0-0	0	2.95
1994 Chicago	AL	24	24	2	0	161.2	682	147	72	62	16	6	3	0	62	1	108	3	0	12	8	.600	1	0-0	0	3.45
1995 Chicago	AL	29	29	3	0	175	769	171	96	84	21	6	5	2	93	4	118	1	2	8	11	.421	0	0-0	0	4.32
1996 Chicago	AL	35	35	0	0	217.1	946	216	106	102	21	5	2	4	97	3	181	2	0	15	10	.600	0	0-0	0	4.22
1997 ChA-SF		33	33	2	0	212	896	180	97	82	18	10	6	4	91	4	179	5	1	13	11	.542	1	0-0	0	3.48
1998 Tampa Bay	AL	25	25	0	0	142.2	624	130	78	75	18	1	2	9	68	0	107	4	0	6	14	.300	0	0-0	0	4.73
1997 Chicago	AL	22	22	2	0	145.2	613	126	61	49	9	6	5	3	55	1	110	4	0	9	8	.529	1	0-0	0	3.03
San Francisco	NL	11	11	0	0	66.1	283	54	36	33	9	4	1	1	36	3	69	1	1	4	3	.571	0	0-0	0	4.48
9 ML YEARS		222	196	10	4	1273	5491	1165	620	556	131	47	29	30	629	22	946	21	4	77	68	.531	4	1-1	3	3.93

Rich Amaral

B: R **T:** R **Pos:** LF-43; PH/PR-18; 2B-11; RF-9; 1B-7; DH-5; CF-4; 3B-1   **Ht:** 6'0" **Wt:** 175 **Born:** 4/1/62 **Age:** 37

		BATTING																BASERUNNING				PERCENTAGES		
Year Team	Lg	G	AB	H	2B	3B	HR	(Hm Rd)	TB	R	RBI	TBB	IBB	SO	HBP	SH	SF	SB	CS	SB%	GDP	Avg	OBP	SLG
1991 Seattle	AL	14	16	1	0	0	0	(0 0)	1	2	0	1	0	5	1	0	0	0	0	.00	1	.063	.167	.063
1992 Seattle	AL	35	100	24	3	0	1	(0 1)	30	9	7	5	0	16	1	4	0	4	2	.67	4	.240	.276	.300
1993 Seattle	AL	110	373	108	24	1	1	(0 1)	137	53	44	33	0	54	3	7	5	19	11	.63	5	.290	.348	.367
1994 Seattle	AL	77	228	60	10	2	4	(2 2)	86	37	18	24	1	28	1	7	2	5	1	.83	3	.263	.333	.377
1995 Seattle	AL	90	238	67	14	2	2	(1 1)	91	45	19	21	0	33	1	1	0	21	2	.91	3	.282	.342	.382
1996 Seattle	AL	118	312	91	11	3	1	(1 0)	111	69	29	47	0	55	5	4	1	25	6	.81	6	.292	.392	.356
1997 Seattle	AL	89	190	54	5	0	1	(0 1)	62	34	21	10	0	34	3	5	2	12	8	.60	7	.284	.327	.326
1998 Seattle	AL	73	134	37	6	0	1	(1 0)	46	25	4	13	0	24	1	0	1	11	1	.92	1	.276	.342	.343
8 ML YEARS		606	1591	442	73	8	11	(5 6)	564	274	142	154	1	249	15	28	11	97	31	.76	30	.278	.345	.354

Ruben Amaro

Bats: B **Throws:** R **Pos:** PH/PR-58; LF-43; RF-6; CF-3   **Ht:** 5'10" **Wt:** 191 **Born:** 2/12/65 **Age:** 34

		BATTING																BASERUNNING				PERCENTAGES		
Year Team	Lg	G	AB	H	2B	3B	HR	(Hm Rd)	TB	R	RBI	TBB	IBB	SO	HBP	SH	SF	SB	CS	SB%	GDP	Avg	OBP	SLG
1991 California	AL	10	23	5	1	0	0	(0 0)	6	0	2	3	1	3	0	0	0	0	0	.00	1	.217	.308	.261
1992 Philadelphia	NL	126	374	82	15	6	7	(5 2)	130	43	34	37	1	54	9	4	2	11	5	.69	11	.219	.303	.348
1993 Philadelphia	NL	25	48	16	2	2	1	(0 1)	25	7	6	6	0	5	0	3	1	0	0	.00	1	.333	.400	.521
1994 Cleveland	AL	26	23	5	1	0	2	(0 2)	12	5	5	2	0	3	0	0	0	2	1	.67	0	.217	.280	.522
1995 Cleveland	AL	28	60	12	3	0	1	(1 0)	18	5	7	4	0	6	2	2	0	1	3	.25	1	.200	.273	.300
1996 Philadelphia	NL	61	117	37	10	0	2	(1 1)	53	14	15	9	0	18	3	1	0	0	0	.00	3	.316	.380	.453
1997 Philadelphia	NL	117	175	41	6	1	2	(1 1)	55	18	21	21	0	24	2	0	2	1	1	.50	4	.234	.320	.314
1998 Philadelphia	NL	92	107	20	5	0	1	(1 0)	28	7	10	6	0	15	0	1	3	0	0	.00	1	.187	.224	.262
8 ML YEARS		485	927	218	43	9	16	(9 7)	327	99	100	88	2	128	16	11	8	15	10	.60	22	.235	.310	.353

Brady Anderson

Bats: Left **Throws:** Left **Pos:** CF-130; PH/PR-7; DH-1   **Ht:** 6'1" **Wt:** 202 **Born:** 1/18/64 **Age:** 35

		BATTING																BASERUNNING				PERCENTAGES		
Year Team	Lg	G	AB	H	2B	3B	HR	(Hm Rd)	TB	R	RBI	TBB	IBB	SO	HBP	SH	SF	SB	CS	SB%	GDP	Avg	OBP	SLG
1988 Bos-Bal	AL	94	325	69	13	4	1	(1 0)	93	31	21	23	0	75	4	11	1	10	6	.63	4	.212	.272	.286
1989 Baltimore	AL	94	266	55	12	2	4	(2 2)	83	44	16	43	6	45	3	5	0	16	4	.80	4	.207	.324	.312
1990 Baltimore	AL	89	234	54	5	2	3	(1 2)	72	24	24	31	2	46	5	4	5	15	2	.88	4	.231	.327	.308
1991 Baltimore	AL	113	256	59	12	3	2	(1 1)	83	40	27	38	0	44	5	11	3	12	5	.71	7	.230	.338	.324
1992 Baltimore	AL	159	623	169	28	10	21	(15 6)	280	100	80	98	14	98	9	10	9	53	16	.77	2	.271	.373	.449
1993 Baltimore	AL	142	560	147	36	8	13	(2 11)	238	87	66	82	4	99	10	6	6	24	12	.67	4	.263	.363	.425
1994 Baltimore	AL	111	453	119	25	5	12	(7 5)	190	78	48	57	3	75	10	3	2	31	1	.97	7	.263	.356	.419

Year Team	Lg	G	AB	H	2B	3B	HR	(Hm	Rd)	TB	R	RBI	TBB	IBB	SO	HBP	SH	SF	SB	CS	SB%	GDP	Avg	OBP	SLG
1995 Baltimore	AL	143	554	145	33	10	16	(10	6)	246	108	64	87	4	111	10	4	2	26	7	.79	3	.262	.371	.444
1996 Baltimore	AL	149	579	172	37	5	50	(19	31)	369	117	110	76	1	106	22	6	4	21	8	.72	11	.297	.396	.637
1997 Baltimore	AL	151	590	170	39	7	18	(8	10)	277	97	73	84	6	105	19	2	1	18	12	.60	1	.288	.393	.469
1998 Baltimore	AL	133	479	113	28	3	18	(7	11)	201	84	51	75	1	78	15	4	1	21	7	.75	7	.236	.356	.420
1988 Boston	AL	41	148	34	5	3	0	(0	0)	45	14	12	15	0	35	4	4	1	4	2	.67	2	.230	.315	.304
Baltimore	AL	53	177	35	8	1	1	(1	0)	48	17	9	8	0	40	0	7	0	6	4	.60	1	.198	.232	.271
11 ML YEARS		1378	4919	1272	268	59	158	(73	85)	2132	810	580	694	41	882	112	66	34	247	80	.76	47	.259	.361	.433

Brian Anderson

Pitches: Left **Bats:** Both **Pos:** SP-32   **Ht:** 6'1" **Wt:** 190 **Born:** 4/26/72 **Age:** 27

		HOW MUCH HE PITCHED						WHAT HE GAVE UP											THE RESULTS						
Year Team	Lg	G	GS	CG	GF	IP	BFP	H	R	ER	HR	SH	SF	HB	TBB	IBB	SO	WP	Bk	W	L	Pct.	ShO	Sv-Op	Hld	ERA
1993 California	AL	4	1	0	3	11.1	45	11	5	5	1	0	0	0	2	0	4	0	0	0	0	.000	0	0-0	0	3.97
1994 California	AL	18	18	0	0	101.2	441	120	63	59	13	3	6	5	27	0	47	5	5	7	5	.583	0	0-0	0	5.22
1995 California	AL	18	17	1	0	99.2	433	110	66	65	24	5	5	3	30	2	45	1	3	6	8	.429	0	0-0	0	5.87
1996 Cleveland	AL	10	9	0	0	51.1	215	58	29	28	9	2	3	0	14	1	21	2	0	3	1	.750	0	0-0	1	4.91
1997 Cleveland	AL	8	8	0	0	48	199	55	28	25	7	0	5	0	11	0	22	1	0	4	2	.667	0	0-0	0	4.69
1998 Arizona	NL	32	32	2	0	208	845	221	109	100	39	8	3	4	24	2	95	3	6	12	13	.480	1	0-0	0	4.33
6 ML YEARS		90	85	3	3	520	2178	575	300	282	93	18	22	12	108	5	234	12	14	32	29	.525	1	0-0	1	4.88

Garret Anderson

Bats: Left **Throws:** Left **Pos:** RF-122; LF-39; PH/PR-3   **Ht:** 6'3" **Wt:** 215 **Born:** 6/30/72 **Age:** 27

		BATTING																	BASERUNNING				PERCENTAGES		
Year Team	Lg	G	AB	H	2B	3B	HR	(Hm	Rd)	TB	R	RBI	TBB	IBB	SO	HBP	SH	SF	SB	CS	SB%	GDP	Avg	OBP	SLG
1994 California	AL	5	13	5	0	0	0	(0	0)	5	0	1	0	0	2	0	0	0	0	0	.00	0	.385	.385	.385
1995 California	AL	106	374	120	19	1	16	(7	9)	189	50	69	19	4	65	1	2	4	6	2	.75	8	.321	.352	.505
1996 California	AL	150	607	173	33	2	12	(7	5)	246	79	72	27	5	84	0	5	3	7	9	.44	22	.285	.314	.405
1997 Anaheim	AL	154	624	189	36	3	8	(5	3)	255	76	92	30	6	70	2	1	4	10	4	.71	20	.303	.334	.409
1998 Anaheim	AL	156	622	183	41	7	15	(4	11)	283	62	79	29	8	80	1	3	3	8	3	.73	13	.294	.325	.455
5 ML YEARS		571	2240	670	129	13	51	(23	28)	978	267	313	105	23	301	4	11	15	31	18	.63	63	.299	.330	.437

Marlon Anderson

Bats: Left **Throws:** Right **Pos:** 2B-9; PH/PR-8   **Ht:** 5'11" **Wt:** 190 **Born:** 1/6/74 **Age:** 25

		BATTING																	BASERUNNING				PERCENTAGES		
Year Team	Lg	G	AB	H	2B	3B	HR	(Hm	Rd)	TB	R	RBI	TBB	IBB	SO	HBP	SH	SF	SB	CS	SB%	GDP	Avg	OBP	SLG
1995 Batavia	A-	74	312	92	13	4	3	—	—	122	52	40	15	2	20	4	2	4	22	8	.73	2	.295	.331	.391
1996 Clearwater	A+	60	257	70	10	3	2	—	—	92	37	22	14	1	18	2	4	0	26	1	.96	4	.272	.315	.358
Reading	AA	75	314	86	14	3	3	—	—	115	38	28	26	2	44	1	3	1	17	9	.65	5	.274	.330	.366
1997 Reading	AA	137	553	147	18	6	10	—	—	207	88	62	42	1	77	10	9	1	27	15	.64	8	.266	.328	.374
1998 Scranton-WB	AAA	136	575	176	32	14	16	—	—	284	104	86	28	1	77	5	5	5	24	12	.67	11	.306	.343	.494
1998 Philadelphia	NL	17	43	14	3	0	1	(1	0)	20	4	4	1	0	6	0	0	1	2	0	1.00	0	.326	.333	.465

Matt Anderson

Pitches: Right **Bats:** Right **Pos:** RP-42   **Ht:** 6'4" **Wt:** 200 **Born:** 8/17/76 **Age:** 22

		HOW MUCH HE PITCHED						WHAT HE GAVE UP											THE RESULTS						
Year Team	Lg	G	GS	CG	GF	IP	BFP	H	R	ER	HR	SH	SF	HB	TBB	IBB	SO	WP	Bk	W	L	Pct.	ShO	Sv-Op	Hld	ERA
1998 Lakeland	A+	17	0	0	13	26	108	18	4	2	0	2	1	0	8	0	34	2	0	1	0	1.000	0	3--	—	0.69
Jacksonville	AA	13	0	0	12	15	56	7	1	1	1	2	0	0	5	0	11	1	0	1	0	1.000	0	10--	—	0.60
1998 Detroit	AL	42	0	0	10	44	194	38	16	16	3	6	3	2	31	4	44	2	0	5	1	.833	0	0-4	6	3.27

Shane Andrews

Bats: Right **Throws:** Right **Pos:** 3B-147; PH/PR-4   **Ht:** 6'1" **Wt:** 215 **Born:** 8/28/71 **Age:** 27

		BATTING																	BASERUNNING				PERCENTAGES		
Year Team	Lg	G	AB	H	2B	3B	HR	(Hm	Rd)	TB	R	RBI	TBB	IBB	SO	HBP	SH	SF	SB	CS	SB%	GDP	Avg	OBP	SLG
1995 Montreal	NL	84	220	47	10	1	8	(2	6)	83	27	31	17	2	68	1	1	2	1	1	.50	4	.214	.271	.377
1996 Montreal	NL	127	375	85	15	2	19	(8	11)	161	43	64	35	8	119	2	0	2	3	1	.75	2	.227	.295	.429
1997 Montreal	NL	18	64	13	3	0	4	(2	2)	28	10	9	3	0	20	0	0	0	0	0	.00	0	.203	.232	.438
1998 Montreal	NL	150	492	117	30	1	25	(12	13)	224	48	69	58	3	137	0	2	7	1	6	.14	10	.238	.314	.455
4 ML YEARS		379	1151	262	58	4	56	(24	32)	496	128	173	113	13	344	3	3	13	5	8	.38	16	.228	.295	.431

Luis Andujar

Pitches: Right **Bats:** Right **Pos:** RP-5   **Ht:** 6'2" **Wt:** 215 **Born:** 11/22/72 **Age:** 26

		HOW MUCH HE PITCHED						WHAT HE GAVE UP											THE RESULTS						
Year Team	Lg	G	GS	CG	GF	IP	BFP	H	R	ER	HR	SH	SF	HB	TBB	IBB	SO	WP	Bk	W	L	Pct.	ShO	Sv-Op	Hld	ERA
1998 Syracuse *	AAA	20	0	0	14	34	130	23	9	8	5	2	0	4	6	0	24	2	1	3	2	.600	0	8--	—	2.12
Calgary *	AAA	13	9	0	0	50.1	226	62	38	35	8	0	1	5	15	1	46	0	0	3	3	.500	0	0-0	—	6.26
1995 Chicago	AL	5	5	0	0	30.1	128	26	12	11	4	0	1	0	14	2	9	0	0	2	1	.667	0	0-0	0	3.26
1996 ChA-Tor	AL	8	7	0	0	37.1	170	46	30	29	8	1	4	1	16	0	11	1	0	1	3	.250	0	0-0	0	6.99
1997 Toronto	AL	17	8	0	5	50	244	76	45	36	9	3	4	0	21	1	28	2	0	0	0	.000	0	0-0	0	6.48

Year Team	Lg	G	GS	CG	GF	IP	BFP	H	R	ER	HR	SH	SF	HB	TBB	IBB	SO	WP	Bk	W	L	Pct.	ShO	Sv-Op	Hld	ERA
1998 Toronto	AL	5	0	0	3	5.2	30	12	6	6	0	0	0	0	2	0	1	1	0	0	0	.000	0	0-0	0	9.53
1996 Chicago	AL	5	5	0	0	23	113	32	22	21	4	1	2	0	15	0	6	0	0	0	2	.000	0	0-0	0	8.22
Toronto	AL	3	2	0	0	14.1	57	14	8	8	4	0	2	1	1	0	5	1	0	1	1	.500	0	0-0	0	5.02
4 ML YEARS		35	20	0	8	123.1	572	160	93	82	21	4	8	2	53	3	49	4	0	3	10	.231	0	0-0	2	5.98

Kevin Appier

Pitches: Right **Bats:** Right **Pos:** SP-3   **Ht:** 6'2" **Wt:** 200 **Born:** 12/6/67 **Age:** 31

Year Team	Lg	G	GS	CG	GF	IP	BFP	H	R	ER	HR	SH	SF	HB	TBB	IBB	SO	WP	Bk	W	L	Pct.	ShO	Sv-Op	Hld	ERA
1998 Royals *	R	1	1	0	0	3.1	16	3	3	1	0	0	1	0	1	0	2	0	0	0	1	.000	0	0- -	—	2.70
Lansing *	A	1	1	0	0	4	17	4	1	1	0	0	2	0	0	0	5	0	0	0	0	.000	0	0- -	—	2.25
Wichita *	AA	1	1	0	0	6	25	8	4	4	1	0	0	0	2	0	1	0	0	0	1	.000	0	0- -	—	6.00
Omaha *	AAA	6	6	0	0	32	148	41	25	25	7	0	0	0	12	1	22	1	0	3	2	.600	0	0- -	—	7.03
1989 Kansas City	AL	6	5	0	0	21.2	106	34	22	22	3	0	3	0	12	1	10	0	0	1	4	.200	0	0-0	0	9.14
1990 Kansas City	AL	32	24	3	1	185.2	784	179	67	57	13	5	9	6	54	2	127	6	1	12	8	.600	3	0-0	0	2.76
1991 Kansas City	AL	34	31	6	1	207.2	881	205	97	79	13	8	6	2	61	3	158	7	1	13	10	.565	3	0-0	1	3.42
1992 Kansas City	AL	30	30	3	0	208.1	852	167	59	57	10	8	3	2	68	5	150	4	0	15	8	.652	0	0-0	0	2.46
1993 Kansas City	AL	34	34	5	0	238.2	953	183	74	68	8	3	5	1	81	3	186	5	0	18	8	.692	1	0-0	0	**2.56**
1994 Kansas City	AL	23	23	1	0	155	653	137	68	66	11	9	7	4	63	7	145	11	1	7	6	.538	0	0-0	0	3.83
1995 Kansas City	AL	31	31	4	0	201.1	832	163	90	87	17	4	3	8	80	1	185	5	0	15	10	.600	1	0-0	0	3.89
1996 Kansas City	AL	32	32	5	0	211.1	874	192	87	85	17	7	4	5	75	2	207	10	1	14	11	.560	1	0-0	0	3.62
1997 Kansas City	AL	34	34	4	0	235.2	972	215	96	89	24	4	4	7	74	2	196	14	1	9	13	.409	0	0-0	0	3.40
1998 Kansas City	AL	3	3	0	0	15	69	21	13	13	3	0	1	1	5	1	9	1	0	1	2	.333	0	0-0	0	7.80
10 ML YEARS		259	247	31	2	1680.1	6976	1496	673	623	116	47	45	33	573	27	1373	63	5	105	80	.568	10	0-0	1	3.34

Alex Arias

Bats: R **Throws:** R **Pos:** SS-38; PH/PR-17; 3B-5; 2B-1   **Ht:** 6'3" **Wt:** 185 **Born:** 11/20/67 **Age:** 31

Year Team	Lg	G	AB	H	2B	3B	HR	(Hm	Rd)	TB	R	RBI	TBB	IBB	SO	HBP	SH	SF	SB	CS	SB%	GDP	Avg	OBP	SLG
1992 Chicago	NL	32	99	29	6	0	0	(0	0)	35	14	7	11	0	13	2	1	0	0	0	.00	4	.293	.375	.354
1993 Florida	NL	96	249	67	5	1	2	(1	1)	80	27	20	27	0	18	3	1	3	1	1	.50	5	.269	.344	.321
1994 Florida	NL	59	113	27	5	0	0	(0	0)	32	4	15	9	0	19	1	1	1	1	0	1.00	5	.239	.298	.283
1995 Florida	NL	94	216	58	9	2	3	(2	1)	80	22	26	22	1	20	2	3	3	1	0	1.00	8	.269	.337	.370
1996 Florida	NL	100	224	62	11	2	3	(1	2)	86	27	26	17	1	28	3	1	1	2	0	1.00	2	.277	.335	.384
1997 Florida	NL	74	93	23	2	0	1	(0	1)	28	13	11	12	0	12	3	4	0	1	0	1.00	6	.247	.352	.301
1998 Philadelphia	NL	56	133	39	8	0	1	(1	0)	50	17	16	13	3	18	1	1	1	2	1	1.00	1	.293	.358	.376
7 ML YEARS		511	1127	305	46	5	10	(5	5)	391	124	121	111	5	128	15	12	9	6	3	.67	31	.271	.342	.347

George Arias

Bats: Right **Throws:** Right **Pos:** 3B-14; PH/PR-6; 1B-1   **Ht:** 5'11" **Wt:** 190 **Born:** 3/12/72 **Age:** 27

Year Team	Lg	G	AB	H	2B	3B	HR	(Hm	Rd)	TB	R	RBI	TBB	IBB	SO	HBP	SH	SF	SB	CS	SB%	GDP	Avg	OBP	SLG
1998 Las Vegas *	AAA	114	435	134	33	4	36	—	—	283	73	119	37	2	108	5	0	5	0	1	.00	9	.308	.365	.651
1996 California	AL	84	252	60	8	1	6	(5	1)	88	19	28	16	2	50	0	6	0	2	0	1.00	6	.238	.284	.349
1997 Ana-SD	AL	14	28	7	1	0	0	(0	0)	8	3	3	0	0	1	0	0	0	0	0	.00	2	.250	.250	.286
1998 San Diego	NL	20	36	7	1	1	1	(1	0)	13	4	4	3	0	16	2	0	0	0	0	.00	0	.194	.293	.361
1997 Anaheim	AL	3	6	2	0	0	0	(0	0)	2	1	1	0	0	0	0	0	0	0	0	.00	0	.333	.333	.333
San Diego	NL	11	22	5	1	0	0	(0	0)	6	2	2	0	0	1	0	0	0	0	0	.00	2	.227	.227	.273
3 ML YEARS		118	316	74	10	2	7	(6	1)	109	26	35	19	2	67	2	6	0	2	0	1.00	8	.234	.282	.345

Rolando Arrojo

Pitches: Right **Bats:** Right **Pos:** SP-32   **Ht:** 6'4" **Wt:** 215 **Born:** 7/18/68 **Age:** 30

Year Team	Lg	G	GS	CG	GF	IP	BFP	H	R	ER	HR	SH	SF	HB	TBB	IBB	SO	WP	Bk	W	L	Pct.	ShO	Sv-Op	Hld	ERA
1997 St. Pete	A+	16	16	4	0	89.1	349	73	40	34	6	1	3	10	13	0	73	5	1	5	6	.455	1	0- -	—	3.43
1998 Tampa Bay	AL	32	32	2	0	202	853	195	84	80	21	5	3	19	65	2	152	3	1	14	12	.538	2	0-0	0	3.56

Andy Ashby

Pitches: Right **Bats:** Right **Pos:** SP-33   **Ht:** 6'5" **Wt:** 190 **Born:** 7/11/67 **Age:** 31

Year Team	Lg	G	GS	CG	GF	IP	BFP	H	R	ER	HR	SH	SF	HB	TBB	IBB	SO	WP	Bk	W	L	Pct.	ShO	Sv-Op	Hld	ERA
1991 Philadelphia	NL	8	8	0	0	42	186	41	28	28	5	1	3	3	19	0	26	6	0	1	5	.167	0	0-0	0	6.00
1992 Philadelphia	NL	10	8	0	0	37	171	42	31	31	6	2	2	1	21	0	24	2	0	1	3	.250	0	0-0	0	7.54
1993 Col-SD	NL	32	21	0	3	123	577	168	100	93	19	6	7	4	56	5	77	6	3	3	10	.231	0	1-1	0	6.80
1994 San Diego	NL	24	24	4	0	164.1	682	145	75	62	16	11	3	3	43	12	121	5	0	6	11	.353	0	0-0	0	3.40
1995 San Diego	NL	31	**31**	2	0	192.2	800	180	79	63	17	10	4	11	62	3	150	7	0	12	10	.545	2	0-0	0	2.94
1996 San Diego	NL	24	24	1	0	150.2	612	147	60	54	17	6	2	3	34	1	85	3	0	9	5	.643	0	0-0	0	3.23
1997 San Diego	NL	30	30	2	0	200.2	851	207	108	92	17	13	6	5	49	2	144	9	0	9	11	.450	0	0-0	0	4.13
1998 San Diego	NL	33	33	5	0	226.2	939	223	90	84	23	8	5	7	58	8	151	7	0	17	9	.654	1	0-0	0	3.34
1993 Colorado	NL	20	9	0	3	54	277	89	54	51	5	3	3	3	32	4	33	2	3	0	4	.000	0	1-1	0	8.50
San Diego	NL	12	12	0	0	69	300	79	46	42	14	3	4	1	24	1	44	4	0	3	6	.333	0	0-0	0	5.48
8 ML YEARS		192	179	14	3	1137	4818	1153	571	507	120	57	32	37	342	31	778	39	3	58	64	.475	3	1-1	0	4.01

Billy Ashley

Bats: Right **Throws:** Right **Pos:** PH/PR-7; DH-5; 1B-2; LF-2 **Ht:** 6'7" **Wt:** 235 **Born:** 7/11/70 **Age:** 28

Year Team	Lg	G	AB	H	2B	3B	HR	(Hm	Rd)	TB	R	RBI	TBB	IBB	SO	HBP	SH	SF	SB	CS	SB%	GDP	Avg	OBP	SLG
1998 Pawtucket *	AAA	63	218	59	12	0	14	—	—	113	40	51	35	0	72	1	0	2	1	0	1.00	5	.271	.371	.518
1992 Los Angeles	NL	29	95	21	5	0	2	(2	0)	32	6	6	5	0	34	0	0	0	0	0	.00	2	.221	.260	.337
1993 Los Angeles	NL	14	37	9	0	0	0	(0	0)	9	0	0	2	0	11	0	0	0	0	0	.00	0	.243	.282	.243
1994 Los Angeles	NL	2	6	2	1	0	0	(0	0)	3	0	0	0	0	2	0	0	0	0	0	.00	0	.333	.333	.500
1995 Los Angeles	NL	81	215	51	5	0	8	(6	2)	80	17	27	25	4	88	2	0	2	0	0	.00	8	.237	.320	.372
1996 Los Angeles	NL	71	110	22	2	1	9	(5	4)	53	18	25	21	1	44	1	0	1	0	0	.00	3	.200	.331	.482
1997 Los Angeles	NL	71	131	32	7	0	6	(4	2)	57	12	19	8	0	46	1	0	0	0	0	.00	0	.244	.293	.435
1998 Boston	AL	13	24	7	3	0	3	(1	2)	19	3	7	2	0	11	0	0	0	0	0	.00	0	.292	.346	.792
7 ML YEARS		281	618	144	23	1	28	(18	10)	253	56	84	63	5	236	4	0	3	0	0	.00	15	.233	.307	.409

Paul Assenmacher

Pitches: Left **Bats:** Left **Pos:** RP-69 **Ht:** 6'3" **Wt:** 210 **Born:** 12/10/60 **Age:** 38

Year Team	Lg	G	GS	CG	GF	IP	BFP	H	R	ER	HR	SH	SF	HB	TBB	IBB	SO	WP	Bk	W	L	Pct.	ShO	Sv-Op	Hld	ERA
1986 Atlanta	NL	61	0	0	27	68.1	287	61	23	19	5	7	1	0	26	4	56	2	3	7	3	.700	0	7--	—	2.50
1987 Atlanta	NL	52	0	0	10	54.2	251	58	41	31	8	2	1	1	24	4	39	0	0	1	1	.500	0	2-6	10	5.10
1988 Atlanta	NL	64	0	0	32	79.1	329	72	28	27	4	8	1	1	32	11	71	7	0	8	7	.533	0	5-11	8	3.06
1989 Atl-ChN	NL	63	0	0	17	76.2	331	74	37	34	3	9	3	1	28	8	79	3	1	3	4	.429	0	0-3	13	3.99
1990 Chicago	NL	74	1	0	21	103	426	90	33	32	10	10	3	1	36	8	95	2	0	7	2	.778	0	10-20	10	2.80
1991 Chicago	NL	75	0	0	31	102.2	427	85	41	37	10	8	4	3	31	6	117	4	0	7	8	.467	0	15-24	14	3.24
1992 Chicago	NL	70	0	0	23	68	298	72	32	31	6	1	2	3	26	5	67	4	0	4	4	.500	0	8-13	20	4.10
1993 ChN-NYA	NL	72	0	0	21	56	237	54	21	21	5	4	0	1	22	6	45	0	0	4	3	.571	0	0-5	17	3.38
1994 Chicago	AL	44	0	0	11	33	134	26	13	13	2	1	3	1	13	2	29	1	0	1	2	.333	0	1-3	14	3.55
1995 Cleveland	AL	47	0	0	12	38.1	160	32	13	12	3	1	2	3	12	3	40	1	0	6	2	.750	0	0-1	9	2.82
1996 Cleveland	AL	63	0	0	25	46.2	201	46	18	16	1	4	2	4	14	5	44	2	0	4	2	.667	0	1-3	13	3.09
1997 Cleveland	AL	75	0	0	20	49	205	43	17	16	3	4	1	2	15	6	53	4	0	5	0	1.000	0	4-5	20	2.94
1998 Cleveland	AL	69	0	0	17	47	213	54	22	17	5	2	2	1	19	6	43	0	0	2	5	.286	0	3-8	25	3.26
1989 Atlanta	NL	49	0	0	14	57.2	247	55	26	23	2	7	2	1	16	7	64	3	1	1	-3	.250	0	0-2	7	3.59
Chicago	NL	14	0	0	3	19	84	19	11	11	1	2	1	0	12	1	15	0	0	2	1	.667	0	0-1	6	5.21
1993 Chicago	NL	46	0	0	15	38.2	166	44	15	15	5	0	0	1	13	3	34	0	0	2	1	.667	0	0-4	12	3.49
New York	AL	26	0	0	6	17.1	71	10	6	6	0	4	0	1	9	3	11	0	0	2	2	.500	0	0-1	5	3.12
13 ML YEARS		829	1	0	267	822.2	3499	767	339	306	67	58	26	21	298	73	778	30	4	59	43	.578	0	56--	—	3.35

Pedro Astacio

Pitches: Right **Bats:** Right **Pos:** SP-34; RP-1 **Ht:** 6'2" **Wt:** 210 **Born:** 11/28/69 **Age:** 29

Year Team	Lg	G	GS	CG	GF	IP	BFP	H	R	ER	HR	SH	SF	HB	TBB	IBB	SO	WP	Bk	W	L	Pct.	ShO	Sv-Op	Hld	ERA
1992 Los Angeles	NL	11	11	4	0	82	341	80	23	18	1	3	2	2	20	4	43	1	0	5	5	.500	4	0-0	0	1.98
1993 Los Angeles	NL	31	31	3	0	186.1	777	165	80	74	14	7	8	5	68	5	122	8	9	14	9	.609	2	0-0	0	3.57
1994 Los Angeles	NL	23	23	3	0	149	625	142	77	71	18	6	5	4	47	4	108	4	0	6	8	.429	1	0-0	0	4.29
1995 Los Angeles	NL	48	11	1	7	104	436	103	53	49	12	5	3	4	29	5	80	5	0	7	8	.467	1	0-1	2	4.24
1996 Los Angeles	NL	35	32	0	0	211.2	885	207	86	81	18	11	5	9	67	9	130	6	2	9	8	.529	0	0-0	0	3.44
1997 LA-Col	NL	33	31	2	2	202.1	862	200	99	93	24	9	7	9	61	0	166	6	3	12	10	.545	1	0-0	0	4.14
1998 Colorado	NL	35	34	0	0	209.1	938	245	160	145	39	12	3	17	74	0	170	2	0	13	14	.481	0	0-0	0	6.23
1997 Los Angeles	NL	26	24	2	2	153.2	654	151	75	70	15	9	5	4	47	0	115	4	3	7	9	.438	1	0-0	0	4.10
Colorado	NL	7	7	0	0	48.2	208	49	23	23	9	0	2	5	14	0	51	2	0	5	1	.833	0	0-0	0	4.25
7 ML YEARS		216	173	13	9	1144.2	4864	1142	577	531	126	53	33	50	366	27	819	32	14	66	62	.516	9	0-1	2	4.18

Rich Aurilia

Bats: Right **Throws:** Right **Pos:** SS-120; PH/PR-2 **Ht:** 6'1" **Wt:** 182 **Born:** 9/2/71 **Age:** 27

Year Team	Lg	G	AB	H	2B	3B	HR	(Hm	Rd)	TB	R	RBI	TBB	IBB	SO	HBP	SH	SF	SB	CS	SB%	GDP	Avg	OBP	SLG
1995 San Francisco	NL	9	19	9	3	0	2	(0	2)	18	4	4	1	0	2	0	1	1	1	0	1.00	1	.474	.476	.947
1996 San Francisco	NL	105	318	76	7	1	9	(1	2)	94	27	26	25	2	52	1	6	2	4	1	.80	1	.239	.295	.296
1997 San Francisco	NL	46	102	28	8	0	5	(1	4)	51	16	19	8	0	15	0	1	2	1	1	.50	3	.275	.321	.500
1998 San Francisco	NL	122	413	110	27	2	9	(5	4)	168	54	49	31	3	62	2	5	3	3	3	.50	3	.266	.319	.407
4 ML YEARS		282	852	223	45	3	19	(7	12)	331	101	98	65	5	131	3	13	8	9	5	.64	8	.262	.314	.388

Brad Ausmus

Bats: Right **Throws:** Right **Pos:** C-124; PH/PR-5 **Ht:** 5'11" **Wt:** 195 **Born:** 4/14/69 **Age:** 30

Year Team	Lg	G	AB	H	2B	3B	HR	(Hm	Rd)	TB	R	RBI	TBB	IBB	SO	HBP	SH	SF	SB	CS	SB%	GDP	Avg	OBP	SLG
1993 San Diego	NL	49	160	41	8	1	5	(4	1)	66	18	12	6	0	28	0	0	0	2	0	1.00	5	.256	.283	.413
1994 San Diego	NL	101	327	82	12	1	7	(6	1)	117	45	24	30	12	63	1	6	2	5	1	.83	8	.251	.314	.358
1995 San Diego	NL	103	328	96	16	4	5	(2	3)	135	44	34	31	3	56	2	4	4	16	5	.76	6	.293	.353	.412
1996 SD-Det		125	375	83	16	0	5	(2	3)	114	46	35	39	4	72	5	6	2	4	8	.33	7	.221	.302	.304
1997 Houston	NL	130	425	113	25	1	4	(1	3)	152	45	44	38	4	78	3	6	6	14	6	.70	8	.266	.326	.358
1998 Houston	NL	128	412	111	10	4	6	(2	4)	147	62	45	53	11	60	3	3	1	10	3	.77	18	.269	.356	.357
1996 San Diego	NL	50	149	27	4	0	1	(0	1)	34	16	13	13	0	27	3	1	0	1	4	.20	1	.181	.261	.228
Detroit	AL	75	226	56	12	0	4	(2	2)	80	30	22	26	1	45	2	5	2	3	4	.43	4	.248	.328	.354

Year Team	Lg		BATTING																		BASERUNNING				PERCENTAGES		
		G	AB	H	2B	3B	HR	(Hm	Rd)	TB	R	RBI	TBB	IBB	SO	HBP	SH	SF	SB	CS	SB%	GDP	Avg	OBP	SLG
6 ML YEARS		636	2027	526	87	11	32	(17	15)	731	260	194	197	31	357	14	25	15	51	23	.69	50	.259	.327	.361

Steve Avery

Pitches: Left **Bats:** Left **Pos:** SP-23; RP-11 **Ht:** 6'4" **Wt:** 205 **Born:** 4/14/70 **Age:** 29

Year Team	Lg	HOW MUCH HE PITCHED						WHAT HE GAVE UP											THE RESULTS						ERA
		G	GS	CG	GF	IP	BFP	H	R	ER	HR	SH	SF	HB	TBB	IBB	SO	WP	Bk	W	L	Pct.	ShO	Sv-Op	Hld	
1998 Pawtucket *	AAA	3	3	0	0	11.1	53	9	9	7	2	3	2	1	9	0	6	0	0	0	2	.000	0	0- -	—	5.56
1990 Atlanta	NL	21	20	1	1	99	466	121	79	62	7	14	4	2	45	2	75	5	1	3	11	.214	1	0-0	0	5.64
1991 Atlanta	NL	35	35	3	0	210.1	868	189	89	79	21	8	4	3	65	0	137	4	1	18	8	.692	1	0-0	0	3.38
1992 Atlanta	NL	35	35	2	0	233.2	969	216	95	83	14	12	8	0	71	3	129	7	3	11	11	.500	2	0-0	0	3.20
1993 Atlanta	NL	35	35	3	0	223.1	891	216	81	73	14	12	8	0	43	5	125	3	1	18	6	.750	1	0-0	0	2.94
1994 Atlanta	NL	24	24	1	0	151.2	628	127	71	68	15	4	6	4	55	4	122	5	2	8	3	.727	0	0-0	0	4.04
1995 Atlanta	NL	29	29	3	0	173.1	724	165	92	90	22	6	4	6	52	4	141	3	0	7	13	.350	1	0-0	0	4.67
1996 Atlanta	NL	24	23	1	0	131	567	146	70	65	10	7	3	4	40	8	86	5	0	7	10	.412	0	0-0	0	4.47
1997 Boston	AL	22	18	0	1	96.2	453	127	76	69	15	1	4	2	49	0	51	4	0	6	7	.462	0	0-0	1	6.42
1998 Boston	AL	34	23	0	4	123.2	546	128	74	69	14	3	0	4	64	0	57	7	0	10	7	.588	0	0-1	1	5.02
9 ML YEARS		259	242	14	6	1442.2	6112	1435	727	664	132	67	41	25	484	26	923	43	8	88	76	.537	6	0-1	2	4.10

Bobby Ayala

Pitches: Right **Bats:** Right **Pos:** RP-62 **Ht:** 6'3" **Wt:** 210 **Born:** 7/8/69 **Age:** 29

Year Team	Lg	HOW MUCH HE PITCHED						WHAT HE GAVE UP											THE RESULTS						ERA
		G	GS	CG	GF	IP	BFP	H	R	ER	HR	SH	SF	HB	TBB	IBB	SO	WP	Bk	W	L	Pct.	ShO	Sv-Op	Hld	
1992 Cincinnati	NL	5	5	0	0	29	127	33	15	14	1	2	0	1	13	2	23	0	0	2	1	.667	0	0-0	0	4.34
1993 Cincinnati	NL	43	9	0	8	98	450	106	72	61	16	9	2	7	45	4	65	5	0	7	10	.412	0	3-5	6	5.60
1994 Seattle	AL	46	0	0	40	56.2	236	42	25	18	2	1	2	0	26	0	76	2	0	4	3	.571	0	18-24	0	2.86
1995 Seattle	AL	63	0	0	50	71	320	73	42	35	9	2	3	6	30	4	77	3	0	6	5	.545	0	19-27	2	4.44
1996 Seattle	AL	50	0	0	26	67.1	285	65	45	44	10	2	2	2	25	3	61	2	0	6	3	.667	0	3-6	7	5.88
1997 Seattle	AL	71	0	0	33	96.2	403	91	45	41	14	3	6	3	41	3	92	6	0	10	5	.667	0	8-12	15	3.82
1998 Seattle	AL	62	0	0	36	75.1	351	100	66	61	7	8	6	1	26	4	68	4	0	1	10	.091	0	8-17	5	7.29
7 ML YEARS		340	14	0	193	494	2172	510	310	274	61	27	21	20	206	20	462	22	0	36	37	.493	0	59-91	35	4.99

Manny Aybar

Pitches: Right **Bats:** Right **Pos:** SP-14; RP-6 **Ht:** 6'1" **Wt:** 165 **Born:** 10/5/74 **Age:** 24

Year Team	Lg	HOW MUCH HE PITCHED						WHAT HE GAVE UP											THE RESULTS						ERA
		G	GS	CG	GF	IP	BFP	H	R	ER	HR	SH	SF	HB	TBB	IBB	SO	WP	Bk	W	L	Pct.	ShO	Sv-Op	Hld	
1994 Cardinals	R	13	13	1	0	72.1	295	69	25	17	0	4	9	4	9	0	79	4	3	6	1	.857	0	0- -	—	2.12
1995 Savannah	A	18	18	2	0	112.2	461	82	46	38	8	7	4	2	36	0	99	8	1	3	8	.273	1	0- -	—	3.04
St. Pete	A+	9	9	0	0	48.1	202	42	27	18	4	0	1	1	16	0	43	7	1	2	5	.286	0	0- -	—	3.35
1996 Arkansas	AA	20	20	0	0	121	507	120	53	41	10	6	3	0	34	0	83	3	3	8	6	.571	0	0- -	—	3.05
Louisville	AAA	5	5	0	0	30.2	123	26	12	11	1	0	1	0	7	0	25	3	2	2	2	.500	0	0- -	—	3.23
1997 Louisville	AAA	22	22	3	0	137	579	131	60	53	10	2	2	4	45	2	114	7	3	5	8	.385	2	0- -	—	3.48
1998 Fresno	AAA	1	1	0	0	6.2	28	5	0	0	0	1	0	0	3	0	4	0	0	0	0	.000	0	0- -	—	0.00
Memphis	AAA	13	13	0	0	83	324	62	34	24	7	3	2	3	17	0	63	1	4	10	0	1.000	0	0- -	—	2.60
1997 St. Louis	NL	12	12	0	0	68	295	66	33	32	8	7	4	4	29	0	41	1	0	1	2	.333	0	0-0	0	4.24
1998 St. Louis	NL	20	14	0	1	81.1	369	90	58	54	6	4	1	2	42	1	57	2	0	6	6	.500	0	0-0	0	5.98
2 ML YEARS		32	26	0	1	149.1	664	156	91	86	14	11	5	6	71	1	98	3	1	8	10	.444	0	0-0	0	5.18

Carlos Baerga

Bats: Both **Throws:** Right **Pos:** 2B-144; PH/PR-7 **Ht:** 5'11" **Wt:** 215 **Born:** 11/4/68 **Age:** 30

Year Team	Lg	BATTING																		BASERUNNING				PERCENTAGES		
		G	AB	H	2B	3B	HR	(Hm	Rd)	TB	R	RBI	TBB	IBB	SO	HBP	SH	SF	SB	CS	SB%	GDP	Avg	OBP	SLG
1990 Cleveland	AL	108	312	81	17	2	7	(3	4)	123	46	47	16	2	57	4	1	5	0	2	.00	4	.260	.300	.394
1991 Cleveland	AL	158	593	171	28	2	11	(2	9)	236	80	69	48	5	74	6	4	3	3	2	.60	12	.288	.346	.398
1992 Cleveland	AL	161	657	205	32	1	20	(9	11)	299	92	105	35	10	76	13	2	9	10	2	.83	15	.312	.354	.455
1993 Cleveland	AL	154	624	200	28	6	21	(8	13)	303	105	114	34	7	68	6	3	13	15	4	.79	17	.321	.355	.486
1994 Cleveland	AL	103	442	139	32	2	19	(8	11)	232	81	80	10	1	45	6	3	8	8	2	.80	10	.314	.333	.525
1995 Cleveland	AL	135	557	175	28	2	15	(7	8)	252	87	90	35	6	31	3	0	5	11	2	.85	15	.314	.355	.452
1996 Cle-NYN		126	507	129	28	0	12	(5	7)	193	59	66	21	0	27	9	2	5	1	1	.50	23	.254	.293	.381
1997 New York	NL	133	467	131	25	1	9	(4	5)	185	53	52	20	1	54	3	3	5	2	6	.25	13	.281	.311	.396
1998 New York	NL	147	511	136	27	1	7	(3	4)	186	46	53	24	6	55	6	3	7	0	1	.00	21	.266	.303	.364
1996 Cleveland	AL	100	424	113	25	0	10	(5	5)	168	54	55	16	0	25	7	2	4	1	1	.50	15	.267	.302	.396
New York	NL	26	83	16	3	0	2	(0	2)	25	5	11	5	0	2	2	0	1	0	0	.00	8	.193	.253	.301
9 ML YEARS		1225	4670	1367	245	17	121	(49	72)	2009	649	676	243	38	487	56	21	60	50	22	.69	130	.293	.331	.430

11

Jeff Bagwell

Bats: Right **Throws:** Right **Pos:** 1B-147; PH/PR-1 **Ht:** 6'0" **Wt:** 195 **Born:** 5/27/68 **Age:** 31

Year Team	Lg	G	AB	H	2B	3B	HR	(Hm	Rd)	TB	R	RBI	TBB	IBB	SO	HBP	SH	SF	SB	CS	SB%	GDP	Avg	OBP	SLG
1991 Houston	NL	156	554	163	26	4	15	(6	9)	242	79	82	75	5	116	13	1	7	7	4	.64	12	.294	.387	.437
1992 Houston	NL	162	586	160	34	6	18	(8	10)	260	87	96	84	13	97	12	2	13	10	6	.63	17	.273	.368	.444
1993 Houston	NL	142	535	171	37	4	20	(9	11)	276	76	88	62	6	73	3	0	9	13	4	.76	20	.320	.388	.516
1994 Houston	NL	110	400	147	32	2	39	(23	16)	300	104	116	65	14	65	4	0	10	15	4	.79	12	.368	.451	.750
1995 Houston	NL	114	448	130	29	0	21	(10	11)	222	88	87	79	12	102	6	0	6	12	5	.71	9	.290	.399	.496
1996 Houston	NL	162	568	179	48	2	31	(16	15)	324	111	120	135	20	114	10	0	6	21	7	.75	15	.315	.451	.570
1997 Houston	NL	162	566	162	40	2	43	(22	21)	335	109	135	127	27	122	16	0	8	31	10	.76	10	.286	.425	.592
1998 Houston	NL	147	540	164	33	1	34	(20	14)	301	124	111	109	8	90	7	0	5	19	7	.73	14	.304	.424	.557
8 ML YEARS		1155	4197	1276	279	21	221	(114	107)	2260	778	835	736	105	779	71	3	64	128	47	.73	109	.304	.411	.538

Scott Bailes

Pitches: Left **Bats:** Left **Pos:** RP-46 **Ht:** 6'2" **Wt:** 171 **Born:** 12/18/62 **Age:** 36

		HOW MUCH HE PITCHED						WHAT HE GAVE UP										THE RESULTS					
Year Team	Lg	G	GS	CG	GF	IP	BFP	H	R	ER	HR	SH	SF	HB	TBB	IBB	SO	WP	Bk	W	L	Pct.	ShO	Sv-Op Hld	ERA
1998 Tulsa *	AA	2	0	0	2	1.2	9	4	2	2	0	0	0	0	0	0	4	0	0	0	1	.000	0	1- -	10.80
Oklahoma *	AAA	1	0	0	0	1.1	6	2	0	0	0	0	0	0	0	0	2	0	0	0	0	--	0	0- -	0.00
1986 Cleveland	AL	62	10	0	22	112.2	500	123	70	62	12	7	4	1	43	5	60	4	2	10	10	.500	0	7-13 8	4.95
1987 Cleveland	AL	39	17	0	15	120.1	551	145	75	62	21	4	6	4	47	1	65	3	0	7	8	.467	0	6-8 1	4.64
1988 Cleveland	AL	37	21	5	7	145	617	149	89	79	22	5	4	2	46	0	53	2	3	9	14	.391	2	0-2 4	4.90
1989 Cleveland	AL	34	11	0	9	113.2	473	116	57	54	7	5	5	3	29	4	47	3	0	5	9	.357	0	0-1 2	4.28
1990 California	AL	27	0	0	6	35.1	173	46	30	25	8	1	5	1	20	0	16	0	0	2	0	1.000	0	0-0 4	6.37
1991 California	AL	42	0	0	14	51.2	219	41	26	24	5	3	2	4	22	5	41	2	0	1	2	.333	0	0-1 8	4.18
1992 California	AL	32	0	0	10	38.2	200	59	34	32	7	1	2	1	28	4	25	2	1	3	1	.750	0	0-0 4	7.45
1997 Texas	AL	24	0	0	7	22	91	18	9	7	2	2	1	0	10	2	14	0	0	1	0	1.000	0	0-0 5	2.86
1998 Texas	AL	46	0	0	13	40.1	187	61	33	29	5	0	2	0	11	0	30	3	0	1	0	1.000	0	0-0 5	6.47
9 ML YEARS		343	59	5	103	679.2	3011	758	423	374	89	28	31	16	256	21	351	19	6	39	44	.470	2	13-25 36	4.95

Cory Bailey

Pitches: Right **Bats:** Right **Pos:** RP-5 **Ht:** 6'1" **Wt:** 202 **Born:** 1/24/71 **Age:** 28

		HOW MUCH HE PITCHED						WHAT HE GAVE UP										THE RESULTS					
Year Team	Lg	G	GS	CG	GF	IP	BFP	H	R	ER	HR	SH	SF	HB	TBB	IBB	SO	WP	Bk	W	L	Pct.	ShO	Sv-Op Hld	ERA
1998 Fresno *	AAA	57	0	0	25	94.2	375	79	31	26	4	1	2	3	18	4	76	4	2	7	2	.778	0	10- -	2.47
1993 Boston	AL	11	0	0	5	15.2	66	12	7	6	0	1	1	0	12	3	11	2	1	0	1	.000	0	0-0 0	3.45
1994 Boston	AL	5	0	0	2	4.1	24	10	6	6	2	0	0	0	3	1	4	0	0	0	0	.000	0	0-1 0	12.46
1995 St. Louis	NL	3	0	0	0	3.2	15	2	3	3	0	0	0	0	2	1	5	1	0	0	0	.000	0	0-0 0	7.36
1996 St. Louis	NL	51	0	0	12	57	251	57	21	19	1	2	1	1	30	3	38	3	0	5	2	.714	0	0-1 10	3.00
1997 San Francisco	NL	7	0	0	4	9.2	45	15	9	9	1	0	1	0	4	0	5	0	0	0	0	.000	0	0-0 0	8.38
1998 San Francisco	NL	5	0	0	1	3.1	13	2	1	1	1	0	0	0	1	0	2	0	0	0	0	.000	0	0-0 0	2.70
6 ML YEARS		82	0	0	24	93.2	414	98	47	44	5	3	3	1	52	8	65	6	1	5	5	.500	0	0-2 10	4.23

Harold Baines

Bats: Left **Throws:** Left **Pos:** DH-80; PH/PR-28 **Ht:** 6'2" **Wt:** 195 **Born:** 3/15/59 **Age:** 40

Year Team	Lg	G	AB	H	2B	3B	HR	(Hm	Rd)	TB	R	RBI	TBB	IBB	SO	HBP	SH	SF	SB	CS	SB%	GDP	Avg	OBP	SLG
1980 Chicago	AL	141	491	125	23	6	13	(3	10)	199	55	49	19	7	65	1	2	5	2	4	.33	15	.255	.281	.405
1981 Chicago	AL	82	280	80	11	7	10	(3	7)	135	42	41	12	4	41	2	0	2	6	2	.75	6	.286	.318	.482
1982 Chicago	AL	161	608	165	29	8	25	(11	14)	285	89	105	49	10	95	0	2	9	10	3	.77	12	.271	.321	.469
1983 Chicago	AL	156	596	167	33	2	20	(12	8)	264	76	99	49	13	85	1	3	6	7	5	.58	15	.280	.333	.443
1984 Chicago	AL	147	569	173	28	10	29	(16	13)	308	72	94	54	9	75	0	1	5	1	2	.33	12	.304	.361	.541
1985 Chicago	AL	160	640	198	29	3	22	(13	9)	299	86	113	42	8	89	1	0	10	1	1	.50	23	.309	.348	.467
1986 Chicago	AL	145	570	169	29	2	21	(8	13)	265	72	88	38	9	89	2	0	8	2	1	.67	14	.296	.338	.465
1987 Chicago	AL	132	505	148	26	4	20	(12	8)	242	59	93	46	2	82	1	0	7	0	0	.00	14	.293	.352	.479
1988 Chicago	AL	158	599	166	39	1	13	(5	8)	246	55	81	67	14	109	1	0	7	0	0	.00	21	.277	.347	.411
1989 ChA-Tex	AL	146	505	156	29	1	16	(5	11)	235	73	72	73	13	79	1	0	3	0	0	.00	15	.309	.395	.465
1990 Tex-Oak	AL	135	415	118	15	1	16	(9	7)	183	52	65	67	10	80	0	0	3	0	0	.00	17	.284	.378	.441
1991 Oakland	AL	141	488	144	25	1	20	(11	9)	231	76	90	72	22	67	1	0	5	0	1	.00	12	.295	.383	.473
1992 Oakland	AL	140	478	121	18	0	16	(10	6)	187	58	76	59	6	61	0	0	3	1	3	.25	11	.253	.331	.391
1993 Baltimore	AL	118	416	130	22	0	20	(12	8)	212	64	78	57	9	52	0	0	4	0	0	.00	14	.313	.390	.510
1994 Baltimore	AL	94	326	96	12	1	16	(11	5)	158	44	54	30	6	49	1	0	0	0	0	.00	9	.294	.356	.485
1995 Baltimore	AL	127	385	115	19	1	24	(7	17)	208	60	63	70	13	45	0	0	4	0	2	.00	17	.299	.403	.540
1996 Chicago	AL	143	495	154	29	0	22	(13	9)	249	80	95	73	7	62	1	0	3	3	1	.75	20	.311	.399	.503
1997 ChA-Bal	AL	137	452	136	23	0	16	(6	10)	207	55	67	55	11	62	0	0	0	0	1	.00	12	.301	.375	.458
1998 Baltimore	AL	104	293	88	17	0	9	(5	4)	132	40	57	32	4	40	1	0	2	0	0	.00	17	.300	.369	.451
1989 Chicago	AL	96	333	107	20	1	13	(4	9)	168	55	56	60	13	52	1	0	1	0	0	.00	11	.321	.423	.505
Texas		50	172	49	9	0	3	(1	2)	67	18	16	13	0	27	0	0	2	0	0	.00	4	.285	.333	.390
1990 Texas	AL	103	321	93	10	1	13	(6	7)	144	41	44	47	9	63	0	0	3	0	0	.00	13	.290	.377	.449
Oakland		32	94	25	5	0	3	(3	0)	39	11	21	20	1	17	0	0	0	0	0	.00	4	.266	.381	.415
1997 Chicago	AL	93	318	97	18	0	12	(5	7)	151	40	52	41	10	47	0	0	0	0	1	.00	9	.305	.382	.475
Baltimore		44	134	39	5	0	4	(1	3)	56	15	15	14	1	15	0	0	0	0	0	.00	3	.291	.356	.418
19 ML YEARS		2567	9111	2649	456	48	348	(168	180)	4245	1208	1480	964	177	1327	14	9	94	33	32	.51	274	.291	.356	.466

Paul Bako

Bats: Left **Throws:** Right **Pos:** C-94; PH/PR-5 **Ht:** 6'2" **Wt:** 205 **Born:** 6/20/72 **Age:** 27

Year Team	Lg	G	AB	H	2B	3B	HR	(Hm	Rd)	TB	R	RBI	TBB	IBB	SO	HBP	SH	SF	SB	CS	SB%	GDP	Avg	OBP	SLG
1993 Billings	R+	57	194	61	11	0	4	—	—	84	34	30	22	0	37	1	1	3	5	1	.83	5	.314	.382	.433
1994 Winston-Sal	A+	90	289	59	9	1	3	—	—	79	29	26	35	0	81	4	8	0	2	2	.50	6	.204	.299	.273
1995 Winston-Sal	A+	82	249	71	11	2	7	—	—	107	29	27	42	6	66	1	6	1	3	1	.75	6	.285	.389	.430
1996 Chattanooga	AA	110	360	106	27	0	8	—	—	157	53	48	48	5	93	5	2	4	1	0	1.00	5	.294	.381	.436
1997 Indianapolis	AAA	104	321	78	14	1	8	—	—	118	34	43	34	3	81	2	1	4	0	5	.00	7	.243	.316	.368
1998 Toledo	AAA	13	48	14	3	1	1	—	—	22	5	6	1	0	13	0	0	1	0	0	.00	1	.292	.300	.458
1998 Detroit	AL	96	305	83	12	1	3	(2	1)	106	23	30	23	4	82	0	1	4	1	1	.50	3	.272	.319	.348

James Baldwin

Pitches: Right **Bats:** Right **Pos:** SP-24; RP-13 **Ht:** 6'3" **Wt:** 210 **Born:** 7/15/71 **Age:** 27

Year Team	Lg	G	GS	CG	GF	IP	BFP	H	R	ER	HR	SH	SF	HB	TBB	IBB	SO	WP	Bk	W	L	Pct.	ShO	Sv-Op	Hld	ERA
1995 Chicago	AL	6	4	0	0	14.2	81	32	22	21	6	0	0	1	9	1	10	1	0	0	1	.000	0	0-0	0	12.89
1996 Chicago	AL	28	28	0	0	169	719	168	88	83	24	2	2	4	57	3	127	12	1	11	6	.647	0	0-0	0	4.42
1997 Chicago	AL	32	32	1	0	200	879	205	128	117	19	3	6	5	83	3	140	14	3	12	15	.444	0	0-0	0	5.27
1998 Chicago	AL	37	24	1	3	159	712	176	103	94	18	3	5	10	60	2	108	5	1	13	6	.684	0	0-1	0	5.32
4 ML YEARS		103	88	2	3	542.2	2391	581	341	315	67	8	13	19	209	9	385	32	5	36	28	.563	0	0-1	0	5.22

Jeff Ball

Bats: Right **Throws:** Right **Pos:** 1B-1; PH/PR-1 **Ht:** 5'10" **Wt:** 185 **Born:** 4/17/69 **Age:** 30

Year Team	Lg	G	AB	H	2B	3B	HR	(Hm	Rd)	TB	R	RBI	TBB	IBB	SO	HBP	SH	SF	SB	CS	SB%	GDP	Avg	OBP	SLG
1990 Auburn	A-	70	263	76	18	1	5	—	—	111	40	38	22	1	35	4	3	5	20	5	.80	4	.289	.347	.422
1991 Osceola	A+	118	392	96	15	3	5	—	—	132	53	51	49	4	74	10	3	4	20	8	.71	9	.245	.341	.337
1992 Jackson	AA	93	278	53	14	1	5	—	—	84	27	24	20	1	58	10	2	1	5	3	.63	9	.191	.269	.302
1993 Quad City	A	112	389	114	28	2	14	—	—	188	68	76	58	3	63	7	1	5	40	19	.68	11	.293	.390	.483
1994 Jackson	AA	111	358	113	30	3	13	—	—	188	65	57	34	3	74	5	5	3	9	8	.53	9	.316	.380	.525
1995 Tucson	AAA	110	362	106	25	2	4	—	—	147	58	56	25	3	66	7	4	5	11	5	.69	13	.293	.346	.406
1996 Tucson	AAA	116	429	139	31	2	19	—	—	231	64	73	34	1	83	1	0	1	10	8	.56	12	.324	.374	.538
1997 Phoenix	AAA	126	470	151	38	3	18	—	—	249	90	103	58	5	84	5	1	7	10	4	.71	12	.321	.396	.530
1998 Fresno	AAA	124	456	135	29	0	21	—	—	227	81	80	55	6	86	8	0	5	5	2	.71	18	.296	.381	.498
1998 San Francisco	NL	2	4	1	0	0	0	(0	0)	0	0	0	0	0	0	0	0	0	0	0	.00	0	.250	.250	.250

Brian Banks

Bats: B **Throws:** R **Pos:** PH/PR-19; C-5; 1B-2; 3B-1; LF-1 **Ht:** 6'3" **Wt:** 200 **Born:** 9/28/70 **Age:** 28

Year Team	Lg	G	AB	H	2B	3B	HR	(Hm	Rd)	TB	R	RBI	TBB	IBB	SO	HBP	SH	SF	SB	CS	SB%	GDP	Avg	OBP	SLG
1993 Helena	R+	12	18	7	1	1	2	—	—	28	8	8	11	0	8	0	0	1	1	2	.33	2	.396	.500	.583
Beloit	A	38	147	36	5	1	4	—	—	55	21	19	7	0	34	1	0	0	1	2	.33	1	.245	.284	.374
1994 Stockton	A+	67	246	58	9	1	4	—	—	81	29	28	38	2	46	2	3	2	3	8	.27	8	.236	.340	.329
Beloit	A	65	237	71	13	1	9	—	—	113	41	47	29	5	40	2	1	4	11	1	.92	3	.300	.375	.477
1995 El Paso	AA	128	441	136	39	10	12	—	—	231	81	78	81	6	113	3	3	8	9	9	.50	10	.308	.413	.524
1996 New Orleans	AAA	137	487	132	29	7	16	—	—	223	71	64	66	3	105	2	2	7	17	8	.68	6	.271	.356	.458
1997 Tucson	AAA	98	378	112	26	3	10	—	—	174	53	63	35	2	83	1	2	5	7	3	.70	6	.296	.353	.460
1998 Louisville	AAA	85	299	87	18	1	21	—	—	170	58	66	52	3	72	2	0	2	14	3	.82	5	.291	.397	.569
1996 Milwaukee	AL	4	7	4	2	0	1	(0	1)	9	2	2	1	0	2	0	0	0	0	0	.00	0	.571	.625	1.286
1997 Milwaukee	AL	28	68	14	1	0	1	(0	1)	18	9	8	6	0	17	0	0	1	0	1	.00	1	.206	.267	.265
1998 Milwaukee	NL	24	24	7	2	0	1	(0	1)	12	3	5	4	0	7	0	0	0	0	0	.00	0	.292	.393	.500
3 ML YEARS		56	99	25	5	0	3		(0 | 3)	39	14	15	11	0	26	0	0	1	0	1	.00	1	.253	.324	.394

Willie Banks

Pitches: Right **Bats:** Right **Pos:** RP-42 **Ht:** 6'1" **Wt:** 200 **Born:** 2/27/69 **Age:** 30

Year Team	Lg	G	GS	CG	GF	IP	BFP	H	R	ER	HR	SH	SF	HB	TBB	IBB	SO	WP	Bk	W	L	Pct.	ShO	Sv-Op	Hld	ERA
1991 Minnesota	AL	5	3	0	2	17.1	85	21	15	11	1	0	0	0	12	0	16	3	0	1	1	.500	0	0-0	0	5.71
1992 Minnesota	AL	16	12	0	2	71	324	80	46	45	6	2	5	2	37	0	37	5	1	4	4	.500	0	0-0	0	5.70
1993 Minnesota	AL	31	30	0	1	171.1	754	186	91	77	17	4	4	3	78	2	138	9	5	11	12	.478	0	0-0	0	4.04
1994 Chicago	NL	23	23	1	0	138.1	598	139	88	83	16	5	2	2	56	3	91	8	1	8	12	.400	1	0-0	0	5.40
1995 ChN-LA-Fla	NL	25	15	0	2	90.2	430	106	71	57	14	6	3	2	58	7	62	9	1	2	6	.250	0	0-1	1	5.66
1997 New York	AL	5	1	0	1	14	57	9	3	3	0	1	0	0	6	0	8	0	0	3	0	1.000	0	0-1	0	1.93
1998 NYA-Ari		42	0	0	13	58	265	54	37	31	6	6	1	2	37	4	40	5	1	2	3	.400	0	1-2	5	4.81
1995 Chicago	NL	10	0	0	2	11.2	73	27	23	20	5	1	0	0	12	4	9	3	0	0	1	.000	0	0-1	1	15.43
Los Angeles	NL	6	6	0	0	29	138	36	21	13	2	1	1	1	16	2	23	4	1	0	2	.000	0	0-0	0	4.03
Florida	NL	9	9	0	0	50	219	43	27	24	7	4	1	1	30	1	30	2	0	2	3	.400	0	0-0	0	4.32
1998 New York	AL	9	0	0	5	14.1	77	20	16	16	4	2	0	1	12	2	8	1	0	1	1	.500	0	0-0	0	10.05
Arizona	NL	33	0	0	8	43.2	188	34	21	15	2	4	1	1	25	2	32	4	1	1	2	.333	0	1-2	5	3.09
7 ML YEARS		147	84	1	21	560.2	2513	595	351	307	60	25	15	12	284	16	392	39	9	31	38	.449	1	1-4	6	4.93

Travis Baptist

Pitches: Left   **Bats:** Left   **Pos:** RP-13   **Ht:** 6'0"   **Wt:** 195   **Born:** 12/30/71   **Age:** 27

Year Team	Lg	G	GS	CG	GF	IP	BFP	H	R	ER	HR	SH	SF	HB	TBB	IBB	SO	WP	Bk	W	L	Pct.	ShO	Sv-Op	Hld	ERA
1991 Medicine Ha	R+	14	14	1	0	85.1	379	100	52	39	5	2	2	1	21	0	48	4	1	4	4	.500	1	0--	—	4.11
1992 Myrtle Bch	A	19	19	2	0	118	455	81	24	19	2	6	2	4	22	0	97	5	4	11	4	.846	1	0--	—	1.45
1993 Knoxville	AA	7	7	0	0	33	139	37	17	15	2	2	3	2	7	0	24	3	0	1	3	.250	0	0--	—	4.09
1994 Syracuse	AAA	24	22	1	0	122.2	539	145	80	62	20	3	4	0	33	2	42	6	2	8	8	.500	0	0--	—	4.55
1995 Syracuse	AAA	15	13	0	0	79	356	83	56	38	12	2	3	2	32	2	52	4	1	3	4	.429	0	0--	—	4.33
1996 Syracuse	AAA	30	21	2	1	141	633	187	91	85	15	5	10	2	48	2	77	7	2	7	6	.538	0	0--	—	5.43
1997 New Britain	AA	36	3	0	7	60.2	247	49	27	23	6	8	1	2	26	2	50	4	0	5	6	.455	0	0--	—	3.41
Salt Lake	AAA	7	6	1	0	47.2	194	47	16	11	3	0	1	9	0	28	2	1	4	1	.800	1	0--	—	2.08
1998 Salt Lake	AAA	21	21	1	0	135.2	559	128	53	47	12	3	0	4	41	1	98	7	1	8	5	.615	0	0--	—	3.12
1998 Minnesota	AL	13	0	0	4	27	123	34	18	17	5	0	6	0	11	1	11	0	0	0	1	.000	0	0-0	0	5.67

Brian Barber

Pitches: Right   **Bats:** Right   **Pos:** SP-8   **Ht:** 6'1"   **Wt:** 175   **Born:** 3/4/73   **Age:** 26

Year Team	Lg	G	GS	CG	GF	IP	BFP	H	R	ER	HR	SH	SF	HB	TBB	IBB	SO	WP	Bk	W	L	Pct.	ShO	Sv-Op	Hld	ERA
1991 Johnson Cty	R+	14	14	0	0	73.1	325	62	48	44	5	1	1	5	38	0	84	4	6	4	6	.400	0	0--	—	5.40
1992 Springfield	A	8	8	0	0	50.2	215	39	21	21	7	2	0	1	24	0	56	2	1	3	4	.429	0	0--	—	3.73
St. Pete	A+	19	19	1	0	113.1	473	99	51	41	7	1	2	5	46	0	102	4	0	5	5	.500	0	0--	—	3.26
1993 Arkansas	AA	24	24	1	0	143.1	625	154	70	64	19	7	4	4	56	2	126	10	2	9	8	.529	0	0--	—	4.02
Louisville	AAA	1	1	0	0	5.2	25	4	3	3	0	1	0	0	4	0	5	0	1	0	1	.000	0	0--	—	4.76
1994 Arkansas	AA	6	6	0	0	36	152	31	15	13	4	1	0	0	16	2	54	2	0	1	3	.250	0	0--	—	3.25
Louisville	AAA	19	18	0	1	85.1	376	79	58	51	7	4	3	5	46	1	95	7	0	4	7	.364	0	1--	—	5.38
1995 Louisville	AAA	20	19	0	0	107.1	465	105	67	56	14	2	6	4	40	1	94	1	0	6	5	.545	0	0--	—	4.70
1996 Louisville	AAA	11	11	1	0	49.2	222	49	37	31	12	0	1	3	26	1	33	2	0	0	6	.000	0	0--	—	5.62
1997 Pr William	A+	2	2	0	0	11	44	10	5	5	3	0	0	0	5	0	13	0	0	1	1	.500	0	0--	—	4.09
Arkansas	AA	3	3	0	0	16.1	80	28	19	19	2	0	2	3	5	0	15	0	1	0	1	.000	0	0--	—	10.47
Louisville	AAA	18	18	0	0	92.2	431	111	80	71	20	2	4	3	44	1	74	5	0	4	8	.333	0	0--	—	6.90
1998 Omaha	AAA	22	22	2	0	136.2	568	114	63	57	24	4	3	3	53	0	100	0	1	8	4	.667	1	0--	—	3.75
1995 St. Louis	NL	9	4	0	2	29.1	130	31	17	17	4	0	3	0	16	0	27	3	0	2	1	.667	0	0-0	0	5.22
1996 St. Louis	NL	1	1	0	0	3	20	4	5	5	0	0	2	1	6	0	1	0	0	0	0	.000	0	0-0	0	15.00
1998 Kansas City	AL	8	8	0	0	42	180	45	28	28	5	0	3	1	13	1	24	4	0	2	4	.333	0	0-0	0	6.00
3 ML YEARS		18	13	0	2	74.1	330	80	50	50	9	0	8	2	35	1	52	7	0	4	5	.444	0	0-0	0	6.05

Brian Barkley

Pitches: Left   **Bats:** Left   **Pos:** RP-6   **Ht:** 6'2"   **Wt:** 180   **Born:** 12/8/75   **Age:** 23

Year Team	Lg	G	GS	CG	GF	IP	BFP	H	R	ER	HR	SH	SF	HB	TBB	IBB	SO	WP	Bk	W	L	Pct.	ShO	Sv-Op	Hld	ERA
1994 Red Sox	R	4	3	0	0	18.2	71	11	7	2	1	1	0	0	4	0	14	2	1	1	0	1.000	0	0--	—	0.96
1995 Sarasota	A+	24	24	2	0	146.2	611	147	66	53	5	2	3	5	37	3	70	4	1	8	10	.444	2	0--	—	3.25
1996 Trenton	AA	22	21	0	0	119.2	535	126	79	76	17	6	5	5	56	4	89	7	2	8	8	.500	0	0--	—	5.72
1997 Trenton	AA	29	29	4	0	178.2	797	208	113	98	18	3	6	3	79	0	121	3	2	12	9	.571	0	0--	—	4.94
1998 Pawtucket	AAA	23	23	1	0	139.1	609	161	81	76	22	3	10	7	50	4	88	5	2	7	9	.438	0	0--	—	4.91
1998 Boston	AL	6	0	0	0	11	59	16	13	12	2	0	2	1	9	1	2	1	0	0	0	.000	0	0-0	0	9.82

Michael Barrett

Bats: Right   **Throws:** Right   **Pos:** C-3; 3B-3; PH/PR-2   **Ht:** 6'3"   **Wt:** 185   **Born:** 10/22/76   **Age:** 22

Year Team	Lg	G	AB	H	2B	3B	HR	(Hm	Rd)	TB	R	RBI	TBB	IBB	SO	HBP	SH	SF	SB	CS	SB%	GDP	Avg	OBP	SLG
1995 Expos	R	50	183	57	13	4	0	—	—	78	22	19	15	1	19	0	0	1	7	6	.54	1	.311	.362	.426
Vermont	A-	3	10	1	0	0	0	—	—	1	0	1	1	0	1	0	0	1	0	0	.00	0	.100	.167	.100
1996 Delmarva	A	129	474	113	29	4	4	—	—	162	57	62	18	0	42	9	2	5	5	11	.31	9	.238	.277	.342
1997 Wst Plm Bch	A+	119	423	120	30	0	8	—	—	174	52	61	36	1	49	5	2	10	7	4	.64	11	.284	.340	.411
1998 Harrisburg	AA	120	453	145	32	2	19	—	—	238	78	87	27	5	43	2	2	4	7	6	.54	16	.320	.358	.525
1998 Montreal	NL	8	23	7	2	0	1	(0	1)	12	3	2	3	0	6	1	0	0	0	0	.00	0	.304	.407	.522

Manuel Barrios

Pitches: Right   **Bats:** Right   **Pos:** RP-3   **Ht:** 6'0"   **Wt:** 185   **Born:** 9/21/74   **Age:** 24

Year Team	Lg	G	GS	CG	GF	IP	BFP	H	R	ER	HR	SH	SF	HB	TBB	IBB	SO	WP	Bk	W	L	Pct.	ShO	Sv-Op	Hld	ERA
1994 Quad City	A	43	0	0	11	65	295	73	44	43	4	5	2	7	23	4	63	8	2	0	6	.000	0	4--	—	5.95
1995 Quad City	A	50	0	0	48	52	219	44	16	13	1	2	1	4	17	1	55	1	0	1	5	.167	0	23--	—	2.25
1996 Jackson	AA	60	0	0	53	68.1	298	60	29	18	4	4	2	3	29	5	69	3	0	6	4	.600	0	23--	—	2.37
1997 New Orleans	AAA	57	0	0	17	82.2	350	70	32	30	5	10	4	1	34	9	77	2	0	4	8	.333	0	0--	—	3.27
1998 Albuquerque	AAA	20	2	0	7	36	170	47	25	24	7	1	1	2	15	0	33	4	0	1	3	.250	0	0--	—	6.00
Charlotte	AAA	18	1	0	6	24.1	98	19	10	10	3	0	0	1	5	0	22	0	0	0	0	.000	0	0--	—	3.70
1997 Houston	NL	2	0	0	1	3	18	6	4	4	0	0	0	0	3	0	3	0	0	0	0	.000	0	0--	—	12.00
1998 Fla-LA	NL	3	0	0	1	3.2	17	4	1	1	1	0	0	0	4	0	1	0	0	0	0	.000	0	0-0	1	2.45
1998 Florida	NL	2	0	0	0	2.2	13	4	1	1	1	0	0	0	2	0	1	0	0	0	0	.000	0	0-0	0	3.38
Los Angeles	NL	1	0	0	1	1	4	0	0	0	0	0	0	0	2	0	0	0	0	0	0	.000	0	0-0	0	0.00
2 ML YEARS		5	0	0	1	6.2	35	10	5	5	1	0	0	0	7	0	4	0	0	0	0	.000	0	0-0	1	6.75

Jeff Barry

Bats: Both **Throws:** Right **Pos:** CF-8; PH/PR-6; RF-5; LF-1 **Ht:** 6'0" **Wt:** 200 **Born:** 9/22/68 **Age:** 30

Year Team	Lg	G	AB	H	2B	3B	HR	(Hm	Rd)	TB	R	RBI	TBB	IBB	SO	HBP	SH	SF	SB	CS	SB%	GDP	Avg	OBP	SLG
1990 Jamestown	A-	51	197	62	6	1	4	—	—	82	30	23	17	2	25	0	2	0	25	5	.83	1	.315	.369	.416
1991 Wst Plm Bch	A+	116	437	92	16	3	4	—	—	126	47	31	34	4	67	4	2	2	20	14	.59	7	.211	.273	.288
1992 St. Lucie	A+	3	9	3	2	0	0	—	—	5	0	1	0	0	0	0	0	0	0	0	.00	0	.333	.333	.556
Mets	R	8	23	4	1	0	0	—	—	5	5	2	6	1	2	0	0	0	2	0	1.00	1	.174	.345	.217
1993 St. Lucie	A+	114	420	108	17	5	4	—	—	147	68	50	49	4	37	5	2	6	17	14	.55	7	.257	.338	.350
1994 Binghamton	AA	110	388	118	24	3	9	—	—	175	48	69	35	4	62	6	1	8	10	11	.48	10	.304	.364	.451
1995 Norfolk	AAA	12	41	9	2	0	0	—	—	11	3	6	3	0	6	1	0	2	0	0	.00	2	.220	.277	.268
Binghamton	AA	80	290	78	17	6	11	—	—	140	49	53	31	6	90	9	0	9	4	1	.80	4	.269	.348	.483
1996 Las Vegas	AAA	4	12	1	0	0	0	—	—	1	0	3	0	0	0	0	0	0	0	0	.00	0	.083	.267	.083
Memphis	AA	91	226	55	7	0	3	—	—	71	29	25	29	5	48	1	1	6	3	7	.30	6	.243	.324	.314
1997 New Haven	AA	40	146	32	4	0	5	—	—	51	21	12	4	0	34	3	1	1	3	2	.60	3	.219	.253	.349
Colo Sprngs	AAA	81	273	82	13	3	13	—	—	140	46	70	30	2	45	4	0	2	5	0	1.00	5	.300	.375	.513
1998 Colo Sprngs	AAA	100	349	91	19	6	8	—	—	146	55	55	46	3	52	7	0	2	5	1	.83	6	.261	.356	.418
1995 New York	NL	15	15	2	1	0	0	(0	0)	3	2	0	1	0	8	0	0	0	0	0	.00	0	.133	.188	.200
1998 Colorado	NL	15	34	6	1	0	0	(0	0)	7	4	2	2	0	11	0	0	1	0	0	.00	0	.176	.216	.206
2 ML YEARS		30	49	8	2	0	0	(0	0)	10	6	2	3	0	19	0	0	1	0	0	.00	0	.163	.208	.204

Kimera Bartee

Bats: B **Throws:** R **Pos:** PH/PR-30; CF-18; LF-11; DH-10; RF-1 **Ht:** 6'0" **Wt:** 185 **Born:** 7/21/72 **Age:** 26

Year Team	Lg	G	AB	H	2B	3B	HR	(Hm	Rd)	TB	R	RBI	TBB	IBB	SO	HBP	SH	SF	SB	CS	SB%	GDP	Avg	OBP	SLG
1998 Toledo *	AAA	51	215	53	10	0	2	—	—	69	24	13	16	1	42	2	0		6	3	.67	2	.247	.305	.321
1996 Detroit	AL	110	217	55	6	1	1	(0	1)	66	32	14	17	0	77	0	13	0	20	10	.67	1	.253	.308	.304
1997 Detroit	AL	12	5	1	0	0	0	(0	0)	1	4	0	2	0	2	1	0	0	3	1	.75	0	.200	.500	.200
1998 Detroit	AL	57	98	19	5	1	3	(3	0)	35	20	15	6	0	35	0	0	1	9	5	.64	1	.194	.238	.357
3 ML YEARS		179	320	75	11	2	4	(3	1)	102	56	29	25	0	114	1	13	1	32	16	.67	2	.234	.291	.319

Jason Bates

Bats: B **Throws:** R **Pos:** PH/PR-39; 2B-17; 3B-3; SS-3 **Ht:** 5'10" **Wt:** 192 **Born:** 1/5/71 **Age:** 28

Year Team	Lg	G	AB	H	2B	3B	HR	(Hm	Rd)	TB	R	RBI	TBB	IBB	SO	HBP	SH	SF	SB	CS	SB%	GDP	Avg	OBP	SLG
1998 Colo Sprngs *	AAA	49	182	59	9	1	5	—	—	85	37	20	17	0	31	1	1	1	1	2	.33	4	.324	.383	.467
1995 Colorado	NL	116	322	86	17	4	8	(4	4)	135	42	46	42	3	70	2	2	0	3	6	.33	4	.267	.355	.419
1996 Colorado	NL	88	160	33	8	1	1	(1	0)	46	19	9	23	1	34	2	1	1	2	1	.67	7	.206	.312	.288
1997 Colorado	NL	62	121	29	10	0	3	(1	2)	48	17	11	15	1	27	3	0	0	0	1	.00	3	.240	.338	.397
1998 Colorado	NL	53	74	14	3	0	0	(0	0)	17	10	3	8	1	21	0	0	0	0	0	.00	0	.189	.268	.230
4 ML YEARS		319	677	162	38	5	12	(6	6)	246	88	69	88	6	152	7	3	1	5	8	.38	18	.239	.332	.363

Miguel Batista

Pitches: Right **Bats:** Right **Pos:** RP-43; SP-13 **Ht:** 6'0" **Wt:** 190 **Born:** 2/19/71 **Age:** 28

Year Team	Lg	G	GS	CG	GF	IP	BFP	H	R	ER	HR	SH	SF	HB	TBB	IBB	SO	WP	Bk	W	L	Pct.	ShO	Sv-Op	Hld	ERA
1992 Pittsburgh	NL	1	0	0	1	2	13	4	2	2	1	0	0	0	3	0	1	0	0	0	0	.000	0	0-0	0	9.00
1996 Florida	NL	9	0	0	4	11.1	49	9	8	7	0	3	0	0	7	2	6	1	0	0	0	.000	0	0-0	0	5.56
1997 Chicago	NL	11	6	0	2	36.1	168	36	24	23	4	4	4	1	24	2	27	2	0	0	5	.000	0	0-0	0	5.70
1998 Montreal	NL	56	13	0	12	135	598	141	66	57	12	7	5	6	65	7	92	6	1	3	5	.375	0	0-0	3	3.80
4 ML YEARS		77	19	0	19	184.2	828	190	100	89	17	14	9	7	99	11	126	9	1	3	10	.231	0	0-0	3	4.34

Tony Batista

Bats: R **Throws:** R **Pos:** 2B-41; SS-34; PH/PR-31; 3B-15 **Ht:** 6'0" **Wt:** 195 **Born:** 12/9/73 **Age:** 25

Year Team	Lg	G	AB	H	2B	3B	HR	(Hm	Rd)	TB	R	RBI	TBB	IBB	SO	HBP	SH	SF	SB	CS	SB%	GDP	Avg	OBP	SLG
1996 Oakland	AL	74	238	71	10	2	6	(1	5)	103	38	25	19	0	49	1	0	2	7	3	.70	2	.298	.350	.433
1997 Oakland	AL	68	188	38	10	1	4	(0	4)	62	22	18	14	0	31	2	3	0	2	2	.50	8	.202	.265	.330
1998 Arizona	NL	106	293	80	16	1	18	(0	9)	152	46	41	18	0	52	3	0	4	1	1	.50	7	.273	.318	.519
3 ML YEARS		248	719	189	36	4	28	(10	18)	317	106	84	51	0	132	6	3	6	10	6	.63	17	.263	.315	.441

Justin Baughman

Bats: R **Throws:** R **Pos:** 2B-59; PH/PR-4; SS-3; DH-1 **Ht:** 5'11" **Wt:** 180 **Born:** 8/1/74 **Age:** 24

Year Team	Lg	G	AB	H	2B	3B	HR	(Hm	Rd)	TB	R	RBI	TBB	IBB	SO	HBP	SH	SF	SB	CS	SB%	GDP	Avg	OBP	SLG
1995 Boise	A-	58	215	50	4	3	1	—	—	63	26	20	18	0	38	2	4	1	19	4	.83	2	.233	.297	.293
1996 Cedar Rapds	A	127	464	115	17	8	5	—	—	163	78	48	45	2	78	6	15	1	50	17	.75	13	.248	.322	.351
1997 Lk Elsinore	A+	134	478	131	14	3	2	—	—	157	71	48	40	3	79	13	11	5	68	15	.82	9	.274	.343	.328
1998 Vancouver	AAA	54	222	66	10	4	0	—	—	84	35	15	13	0	28	4	5	2	26	8	.76	7	.297	.344	.378
1998 Anaheim	AL	63	196	50	9	1	1	(0	1)	64	24	20	10	0	36	1	5	3	10	4	.71	4	.255	.277	.327

Danny Bautista

Bats: R **Throws:** R **Pos:** LF-53; PH/PR-34; RF-4; DH-1; CF-1   **Ht:** 5'11"   **Wt:** 170   **Born:** 5/24/72   **Age:** 27

Year Team	Lg	G	AB	H	2B	3B	HR	(Hm	Rd)	TB	R	RBI	TBB	IBB	SO	HBP	SH	SF	SB	CS	SB%	GDP	Avg	OBP	SLG
1998 Greenville *	AA	2	6	2	0	0	1	—	—	5	1	2	1	1	1	0	0	0	0	0	.00	0	.333	.429	.833
1993 Detroit	AL	17	61	19	3	0	1	(0	1)	25	6	9	1	0	10	0	0	1	3	1	.75	1	.311	.317	.410
1994 Detroit	AL	31	99	23	4	1	4	(1	3)	41	12	15	3	0	18	0	0	0	1	2	.33	3	.232	.255	.414
1995 Detroit	AL	89	271	55	9	0	7	(3	4)	85	28	27	12	0	68	0	6	0	4	1	.80	6	.203	.237	.314
1996 Det-Atl		42	84	19	2	0	2	(1	1)	27	13	9	11	0	20	1	0	0	1	2	.33	4	.226	.323	.321
1997 Atlanta	NL	64	103	25	3	2	3	(1	2)	41	14	9	5	1	24	1	2	1	2	0	1.00	3	.243	.282	.398
1998 Atlanta	NL	82	144	36	11	0	3	(2	1)	56	17	17	7	0	21	0	3	2	1	0	1.00	0	.250	.281	.389
1996 Detroit	AL	25	64	16	2	0	2	(1	1)	24	12	8	9	0	15	0	0	0	1	2	.33	1	.250	.342	.375
Atlanta	NL	17	20	3	0	0	0	(0	0)	3	1	1	2	0	5	1	0	0	0	0	.00	3	.150	.261	.150
6 ML YEARS		325	762	177	32	3	20	(8	12)	275	90	86	39	1	161	2	11	4	12	6	.67	21	.232	.270	.361

Trey Beamon

Bats: L **Throws:** R **Pos:** PH/PR-18; DH-11; LF-2; RF-2   **Ht:** 6'0"   **Wt:** 192   **Born:** 2/11/74   **Age:** 25

Year Team	Lg	G	AB	H	2B	3B	HR	(Hm	Rd)	TB	R	RBI	TBB	IBB	SO	HBP	SH	SF	SB	CS	SB%	GDP	Avg	OBP	SLG
1998 Lakeland *	A+	2	6	3	0	0	0	—	—	3	2	0	3	0	0	0	0	0	0	0	.00	0	.500	.667	.500
Toledo *	AAA	56	207	49	6	0	3	—	—	64	31	18	28	0	38	2	0	3	16	2	.89	2	.237	.329	.309
1996 Pittsburgh	NL	24	51	11	2	0	0	(0	0)	13	7	6	4	0	6	0	1	0	1	1	.50	0	.216	.273	.255
1997 San Diego	NL	43	65	18	3	0	0	(0	0)	21	5	7	2	0	17	1	0	0	1	2	.33	1	.277	.309	.323
1998 Detroit	AL	28	42	11	4	0	0	(0	0)	15	4	2	5	0	13	0	1	0	1	0	1.00	3	.262	.340	.357
3 ML YEARS		95	158	40	9	0	0	(0	0)	49	16	15	11	0	36	1	2	0	3	3	.50	4	.253	.306	.310

Rod Beck

Pitches: Right   **Bats:** Right   **Pos:** RP-81   **Ht:** 6'1"   **Wt:** 235   **Born:** 8/3/68   **Age:** 30

Year Team	Lg	G	GS	CG	GF	IP	BFP	H	R	ER	HR	SH	SF	HB	TBB	IBB	SO	WP	Bk	W	L	Pct.	ShO	Sv-Op	Hld	ERA
1991 San Francisco	NL	31	0	0	10	52.1	214	53	22	22	4	4	2	1	13	2	38	0	0	1	1	.500	0	1-1	1	3.78
1992 San Francisco	NL	65	0	0	42	92	352	62	20	18	4	6	2	2	15	2	87	5	2	3	3	.500	0	17-23	4	1.76
1993 San Francisco	NL	76	0	0	71	79.1	309	57	20	19	11	6	3	3	13	4	86	4	0	3	1	.750	0	48-52	0	2.16
1994 San Francisco	NL	48	0	0	47	48.2	207	49	17	15	10	3	3	0	13	2	39	0	0	2	4	.333	0	28-28	0	2.77
1995 San Francisco	NL	60	0	0	52	58.2	255	60	31	29	7	4	3	2	21	3	42	1	0	5	6	.455	0	33-43	0	4.45
1996 San Francisco	NL	63	0	0	58	62	248	56	23	23	9	0	2	1	10	2	48	1	0	0	9	.000	0	35-42	0	3.34
1997 San Francisco	NL	73	0	0	66	70	281	67	31	27	7	1	0	2	8	2	53	1	0	7	4	.636	0	37-45	1	3.47
1998 Chicago	NL	81	0	0	70	80.1	349	86	33	27	11	2	5	2	20	4	81	2	0	3	4	.429	0	51-58	1	3.02
8 ML YEARS		497	0	0	416	543.1	2215	490	197	180	63	26	20	13	113	21	474	15	2	24	32	.429	0	250-292	7	2.98

Rich Becker

Bats: L **Throws:** L **Pos:** RF-56; PH/PR-50; CF-27; LF-22; DH-2   **Ht:** 5'10"   **Wt:** 193   **Born:** 2/1/72   **Age:** 27

Year Team	Lg	G	AB	H	2B	3B	HR	(Hm	Rd)	TB	R	RBI	TBB	IBB	SO	HBP	SH	SF	SB	CS	SB%	GDP	Avg	OBP	SLG
1993 Minnesota	AL	3	7	2	2	0	0	(0	0)	4	3	0	5	0	4	0	0	0	1	1	.50	0	.286	.583	.571
1994 Minnesota	AL	28	98	26	3	0	1	(1	0)	32	12	8	13	0	25	0	1	0	6	1	.86	2	.265	.351	.327
1995 Minnesota	AL	106	392	93	15	1	2	(1	1)	116	45	33	34	0	95	4	6	2	8	9	.47	9	.237	.303	.296
1996 Minnesota	AL	148	525	153	31	4	12	(8	4)	228	92	71	68	1	118	2	5	4	19	5	.79	14	.291	.372	.434
1997 Minnesota	AL	132	443	117	22	3	10	(4	6)	175	61	45	62	1	130	1	2	2	17	5	.77	4	.264	.354	.395
1998 NYN-Bal		128	213	42	5	2	6	(4	2)	69	37	21	43	2	76	2	2	0	5	1	.83	7	.197	.337	.324
1998 New York	NL	49	100	19	4	2	3	(3	0)	36	15	10	21	2	42	0	0	0	3	1	.75	1	.190	.331	.360
Baltimore	AL	79	113	23	1	0	3	(1	2)	33	22	11	22	0	34	2	2	0	2	0	1.00	6	.204	.343	.292
6 ML YEARS		545	1678	433	78	10	31	(18	13)	624	250	178	225	4	448	9	16	8	56	22	.72	36	.258	.347	.372

Matt Beech

Pitches: Left   **Bats:** Left   **Pos:** SP-21   **Ht:** 6'2"   **Wt:** 194   **Born:** 1/20/72   **Age:** 27

Year Team	Lg	G	GS	CG	GF	IP	BFP	H	R	ER	HR	SH	SF	HB	TBB	IBB	SO	WP	Bk	W	L	Pct.	ShO	Sv-Op	Hld	ERA
1996 Philadelphia	NL	8	8	0	0	41.1	182	49	32	32	8	2	6	3	11	0	33	0	0	1	4	.200	0	0-0	0	6.97
1997 Philadelphia	NL	24	24	0	0	136.2	602	147	81	77	25	7	6	5	57	9	120	6	2	4	9	.308	0	0-0	0	5.07
1998 Philadelphia	NL	21	21	0	0	117	531	126	78	67	19	4	2	4	63	2	113	8	0	3	9	.250	0	0-0	0	5.15
3 ML YEARS		53	53	0	0	295	1315	322	191	176	52	13	14	12	131	11	266	14	2	8	22	.267	0	0-0	0	5.37

Tim Belcher

Pitches: Right   **Bats:** Right   **Pos:** SP-34   **Ht:** 6'3"   **Wt:** 225   **Born:** 10/19/61   **Age:** 37

Year Team	Lg	G	GS	CG	GF	IP	BFP	H	R	ER	HR	SH	SF	HB	TBB	IBB	SO	WP	Bk	W	L	Pct.	ShO	Sv-Op	Hld	ERA
1987 Los Angeles	NL	6	5	0	1	34	135	30	11	9	2	2	1	0	7	0	23	0	1	4	2	.667	0	0-0	0	2.38
1988 Los Angeles	NL	36	27	4	5	179.2	719	143	65	58	8	6	1	2	51	7	152	4	0	12	6	.667	1	4-5	0	2.91
1989 Los Angeles	NL	39	30	10	6	230	937	182	81	72	20	6	6	7	80	5	200	7	2	15	12	.556	8	1-1	1	2.82
1990 Los Angeles	NL	24	24	5	0	153	627	136	76	68	17	5	6	6	48	0	102	6	1	9	9	.500	2	0-0	0	4.00
1991 Los Angeles	NL	33	33	2	0	209.1	880	189	76	61	10	11	3	2	75	3	156	7	0	10	9	.526	1	0-0	0	2.62

Year Team	Lg	G	GS	CG	GF	IP	BFP	H	R	ER	HR	SH	SF	HB	TBB	IBB	SO	WP	Bk	W	L	Pct.	ShO	Sv-Op	Hld	ERA
		HOW MUCH HE PITCHED						**WHAT HE GAVE UP**												**THE RESULTS**						
1992 Cincinnati	NL	35	34	2	1	227.2	949	201	104	99	17	12	11	3	80	2	149	3	1	15	14	.517	1	0-0	0	3.91
1993 Cin-ChA		34	33	5	0	208.2	886	198	108	103	19	8	4	8	74	4	135	6	0	12	11	.522	3	0-0	0	4.44
1994 Detroit	AL	25	25	3	0	162	750	192	124	106	21	3	3	4	78	10	76	6	1	7	15	.318	0	0-0	0	5.89
1995 Seattle	AL	28	28	1	0	179.1	802	188	101	90	19	4	5	5	88	5	96	6	0	10	12	.455	0	0-0	0	4.52
1996 Kansas City	AL	35	35	4	0	238.2	1021	262	116	104	28	6	10	6	68	4	113	7	0	15	11	.577	1	0-0	0	3.92
1997 Kansas City	AL	32	32	3	0	213.1	927	242	128	119	31	7	4	5	70	2	113	7	1	13	12	.520	1	0-0	0	5.02
1998 Kansas City	AL	34	34	2	0	234	1003	247	127	111	37	5	9	7	73	0	130	6	1	14	14	.500	0	0-0	0	4.27
1993 Cincinnati	NL	22	22	4	0	137	590	134	72	68	16	3	7		47	4	101	6	0	9	6	.600	2	0-0	0	4.47
Chicago	AL	12	11	1	0	71.2	296	64	36	35	8	2	1		27	0	34	0	0	3	5	.375	1	0-0	0	4.40
12 ML YEARS		361	340	41	13	2269.2	9636	2210	1118	1000	229	75	63	51	792	42	1445	65	8	136	127	.517	18	5-6	1	3.97

Stan Belinda

Pitches: Right **Bats:** Right **Pos:** RP-40   **Ht:** 6'3" **Wt:** 215 **Born:** 8/6/66 **Age:** 32

Year Team	Lg	G	GS	CG	GF	IP	BFP	H	R	ER	HR	SH	SF	HB	TBB	IBB	SO	WP	Bk	W	L	Pct.	ShO	Sv-Op	Hld	ERA
		HOW MUCH HE PITCHED						**WHAT HE GAVE UP**												**THE RESULTS**						
1989 Pittsburgh	NL	8	0	0	2	10.1	46	13	8	7	0	0	0	0	2	0	10	1	0	0	1	.000	0	0-0	2	6.10
1990 Pittsburgh	NL	55	0	0	17	58.1	245	48	23	23	4	2	2	1	29	3	55	1	0	3	4	.429	0	8-13	9	3.55
1991 Pittsburgh	NL	60	0	0	37	78.1	318	50	30	30	10	4	3	4	35	4	71	2	0	7	5	.583	0	16-20	6	3.45
1992 Pittsburgh	NL	59	0	0	42	71.1	299	58	26	25	8	4	6	0	29	5	57	1	0	6	4	.600	0	18-24	0	3.15
1993 Pit-KC		63	0	0	44	69.2	287	65	31	30	6	3	2	2	17	4	55	2	0	4	2	.667	0	19-23	8	3.88
1994 Kansas City	AL	37	0	0	10	49	220	47	36	28	6	0	3	5	24	3	37	1	0	2	2	.500	0	1-2	5	5.14
1995 Boston	AL	63	0	0	30	69.2	285	51	25	24	5	0	4	4	28	3	57	2	0	8	1	.889	0	10-14	17	3.10
1996 Boston	AL	31	0	0	10	28.2	139	31	22	21	3	1	0	4	20	1	18	2	0	2	1	.667	0	2-4	7	6.59
1997 Cincinnati	NL	84	0	0	18	99.1	420	84	42	41	11	6	5	9	33	6	114	5	0	1	5	.167	0	1-5	28	3.71
1998 Cincinnati	NL	40	0	0	24	61.1	254	46	23	22	7	7	1	1	28	6	57	3	0	4	8	.333	0	1-2	4	3.23
1993 Pittsburgh	NL	40	0	0	37	42.1	171	35	18	18	4	1	2	1	11	4	30	0	0	3	1	.750	0	19-22	0	3.61
Kansas City	AL	23	0	0	7	27.1	116	30	13	12	2	2	0	1	6	0	25	2	0	1	1	.500	0	0-1	8	4.28
10 ML YEARS		500	0	0	234	596	2513	493	266	251	60	27	26	30	245	35	531	20	0	37	33	.529	0	76-107	86	3.79

David Bell

Bats: R **Throws:** R **Pos:** 2B-116; 3B-15; 1B-6; PH/PR-4; SS-1; LF-1   **Ht:** 5'10" **Wt:** 175 **Born:** 9/14/72 **Age:** 26

Year Team	Lg	G	AB	H	2B	3B	HR	Hm	Rd	TB	R	RBI	TBB	IBB	SO	HBP	SH	SF	SB	CS	SB%	GDP	Avg	OBP	SLG
		BATTING																	**BASERUNNING**				**PERCENTAGES**		
1995 Cle-StL		41	146	36	7	2	2	(1	1)	53	13	19	4	0	25	2	0	1	1	2	.33	0	.247	.275	.363
1996 St. Louis	NL	62	145	31	6	0	1	(1	0)	40	12	9	10	2	22	1	0	1	1	1	.50	3	.214	.268	.276
1997 St. Louis	NL	66	142	30	7	1	1	(1	0)	44	9	12	10	2	28	0	2	1	1	0	1.00	2	.211	.261	.310
1998 StL-Cle-Sea		132	429	117	30	2	10	(2	8)	181	48	49	27	4	65	2	1	5		4	.00	11	.273	.315	.422
1995 Cleveland	AL	2	2	0	0	0	0	(0	0)	0	0	0	0	0	0	0	0	0	0	0	.00	0	.000	.000	.000
St. Louis	NL	39	144	36	7	2	2	(1	1)	53	13	19	4	0	25	2	0	1	1	2	.33	0	.250	.278	.368
1998 St. Louis	NL	4	9	2	1	0	0	(0	0)	3	0	0	0	0	3	0	0	0	0	0	.00	0	.222	.222	.333
Cleveland	AL	107	340	89	21	2	10	(2	8)	144	37	41	22	4	54	2	1	5	0	4	.00	8	.262	.306	.424
Seattle	AL	21	80	26	8	0	0	(0	0)	34	11	8	5	0	8	0	0	0	0	0	.00	3	.325	.365	.425
4 ML YEARS		301	862	214	50	6	14	(5	9)	318	82	89	51	8	140	5	3	8	3	7	.30	16	.248	.292	.369

Derek Bell

Bats: Right **Throws:** Right **Pos:** RF-154; PH/PR-3   **Ht:** 6'2" **Wt:** 215 **Born:** 12/11/68 **Age:** 30

Year Team	Lg	G	AB	H	2B	3B	HR	Hm	Rd	TB	R	RBI	TBB	IBB	SO	HBP	SH	SF	SB	CS	SB%	GDP	Avg	OBP	SLG
		BATTING																	**BASERUNNING**				**PERCENTAGES**		
1991 Toronto	AL	18	28	4	0	0	0	(0	0)	4	5	1	6	0	5	1	0	0	3	2	.60	0	.143	.314	.143
1992 Toronto	AL	61	161	39	6	3	2	(2	0)	57	23	15	15	1	34	5	2	1	7	2	.78	6	.242	.324	.354
1993 San Diego	NL	150	542	142	19	1	21	(12	9)	226	73	72	23	5	122	12	0	8	26	5	.84	7	.262	.303	.417
1994 San Diego	NL	108	434	135	20	0	14	(8	6)	197	54	54	29	5	88	1	0	2	24	8	.75	14	.311	.354	.454
1995 Houston	NL	112	452	151	21	2	8	(3	5)	200	63	86	33	2	71	8	0	6	27	9	.75	10	.334	.385	.442
1996 Houston	NL	158	627	165	40	3	17	(8	9)	262	84	113	40	8	123	8	0	9	29	3	.91	18	.263	.311	.418
1997 Houston	NL	129	493	136	29	3	15	(7	8)	216	67	71	40	3	94	12	0	2	15	7	.68	16	.276	.344	.438
1998 Houston	NL	156	630	198	41	2	22	(12	10)	309	111	108	51	0	126	4	0	10	13	3	.81	14	.314	.364	.490
8 ML YEARS		892	3367	970	176	14	99	(52	47)	1471	480	520	237	24	663	51	2	38	144	39	.79	85	.288	.341	.437

Jay Bell

Bats: Right **Throws:** Right **Pos:** SS-138; 2B-15; PH/PR-4   **Ht:** 6'0" **Wt:** 182 **Born:** 12/11/65 **Age:** 33

Year Team	Lg	G	AB	H	2B	3B	HR	Hm	Rd	TB	R	RBI	TBB	IBB	SO	HBP	SH	SF	SB	CS	SB%	GDP	Avg	OBP	SLG
		BATTING																	**BASERUNNING**				**PERCENTAGES**		
1986 Cleveland	AL	5	14	5	2	0	1	(0	1)	10	3	4	2	0	3	0	0	0	0	0	.00	0	.357	.438	.714
1987 Cleveland	AL	38	125	27	9	1	2	(1	1)	44	14	13	8	0	31	1	3	0	2	0	1.00	1	.216	.269	.352
1988 Cleveland	AL	73	211	46	5	1	2	(2	0)	59	23	21	21	0	53	1	1	2	4	2	.67	3	.218	.289	.280
1989 Pittsburgh	NL	78	271	70	13	3	2	(1	1)	95	33	27	19	0	47	1	10	2	5	3	.63	9	.258	.307	.351
1990 Pittsburgh	NL	159	583	148	28	7	7	(1	6)	211	93	52	65	0	109	3	**39**	6	10	6	.63	14	.254	.329	.362
1991 Pittsburgh	NL	157	608	164	32	8	16	(7	9)	260	96	67	52	1	99	4	**30**	3	10	6	.63	15	.270	.330	.428
1992 Pittsburgh	NL	159	632	167	36	9	9	(5	4)	242	87	55	55	0	103	4	19	2	7	5	.58	12	.264	.326	.383
1993 Pittsburgh	NL	154	604	187	32	9	9	(3	6)	264	102	51	77	6	122	6	13	1	16	10	.62	16	.310	.392	.437
1994 Pittsburgh	NL	110	424	117	35	4	9	(3	6)	187	68	45	49	1	82	3	8	3	2	0	1.00	15	.276	.353	.441
1995 Pittsburgh	NL	138	530	139	28	4	13	(8	5)	214	79	55	55	1	110	4	3	1	2	5	.29	13	.262	.336	.404
1996 Pittsburgh	NL	151	527	132	29	3	13	(7	6)	206	65	71	54	5	108	5	6	6	6	4	.60	10	.250	.323	.391
1997 Kansas City	AL	153	573	167	28	3	21	(10	11)	264	89	92	71	2	101	4	3	6	10	6	.63	13	.291	.368	.461

Year Team	Lg	G	AB	H	2B	3B	HR	(Hm	Rd)	TB	R	RBI	TBB	IBB	SO	HBP	SH	SF	SB	CS	SB%	GDP	Avg	OBP	SLG
1998 Arizona	NL	155	549	138	29	5	20	(11	9)	237	79	67	81	3	129	7	5	3	3	5	.38	14	.251	.353	.432
13 ML YEARS		1530	5651	1507	306	54	124	(59	65)	2293	831	620	609	19	1097	43	140	38	77	52	.60	134	.267	.340	.406

Albert Belle

Bats: Right **Throws:** Right **Pos:** LF-159; DH-4   **Ht:** 6'2" **Wt:** 210 **Born:** 8/25/66 **Age:** 32

Year Team	Lg	G	AB	H	2B	3B	HR	(Hm	Rd)	TB	R	RBI	TBB	IBB	SO	HBP	SH	SF	SB	CS	SB%	GDP	Avg	OBP	SLG
1989 Cleveland	AL	62	218	49	8	4	7	(3	4)	86	22	37	12	0	55	2	0	2	2	2	.50	4	.225	.269	.394
1990 Cleveland	AL	9	23	4	0	0	1	(1	0)	7	1	3	1	0	6	0	1	0	0	0	.00	1	.174	.208	.304
1991 Cleveland	AL	123	461	130	31	2	28	(8	20)	249	60	95	25	2	99	5	0	5	3	1	.75	24	.282	.323	.540
1992 Cleveland	AL	153	585	152	23	1	34	(15	19)	279	81	112	52	5	128	4	1	8	8	2	.80	18	.260	.320	.477
1993 Cleveland	AL	159	594	172	36	3	38	(20	18)	328	93	129	76	13	96	8	1	14	23	12	.66	18	.290	.370	.552
1994 Cleveland	AL	106	412	147	35	2	36	(21	15)	294	90	101	58	9	71	4	1	4	9	6	.60	5	.357	.438	.714
1995 Cleveland	AL	143	546	173	52	1	50	(25	25)	377	121	126	73	5	80	6	1	4	5	2	.71	24	.317	.401	.690
1996 Cleveland	AL	158	602	187	38	3	48	(22	26)	375	124	148	99	15	87	7	0	7	11	0	1.00	20	.311	.410	.623
1997 Chicago	AL	161	634	174	45	1	30	(14	16)	311	90	116	53	6	105	6	0	6	4	4	.50	26	.274	.332	.491
1998 Chicago	AL	163	609	200	48	2	49	(29	20)	399	113	152	81	10	84	1	0	15	6	4	.60	17	.328	.399	.655
10 ML YEARS		1237	4684	1388	316	19	321	(158	163)	2705	795	1019	530	65	811	44	4	67	71	33	.68	157	.296	.368	.577

Mark Bellhorn

Bats: B **Throws:** R **Pos:** 3B-5; PH/PR-5; DH-2; SS-2; 2B-1   **Ht:** 6'1" **Wt:** 190 **Born:** 8/23/74 **Age:** 24

Year Team	Lg	G	AB	H	2B	3B	HR	(Hm	Rd)	TB	R	RBI	TBB	IBB	SO	HBP	SH	SF	SB	CS	SB%	GDP	Avg	OBP	SLG
1995 Modesto	A+	56	229	59	12	0	6	—	—	89	35	31	27	0	52	4	2	0	5	2	.71	9	.258	.346	.389
1996 Huntsville	AA	131	468	117	24	5	10	—	—	181	84	71	73	7	124	4	7	4	19	2	.90	7	.250	.353	.387
1997 Edmonton	AAA	70	241	79	18	3	11	—	—	136	54	46	64	2	59	2	3	0	6	6	.50	4	.328	.472	.564
1998 Edmonton	AAA	87	309	77	20	4	10	—	—	135	57	44	62	0	90	6	0	1	6	2	.75	8	.249	.384	.437
1997 Oakland	AL	68	224	51	9	1	6	(3	3)	80	33	19	32	0	70	0	5	0	7	1	.88	1	.228	.324	.357
1998 Oakland	AL	11	12	1	0	0	0	(0	0)	2	1	1	3	0	4	1	0	0	2	0	1.00	0	.083	.313	.167
2 ML YEARS		79	236	52	10	1	6	(3	3)	82	34	20	35	0	74	1	5	0	9	1	.90	1	.220	.324	.347

Rafael Belliard

Bats: Right **Throws:** Right **Pos:** SS-7   **Ht:** 5'6" **Wt:** 160 **Born:** 10/24/61 **Age:** 37

Year Team	Lg	G	AB	H	2B	3B	HR	(Hm	Rd)	TB	R	RBI	TBB	IBB	SO	HBP	SH	SF	SB	CS	SB%	GDP	Avg	OBP	SLG
1998 Richmond *	AAA	13	43	6	0	0	1	—	—	9	6	2	0	0	6	0	1	0	0	0	.00	2	.140	.140	.209
1982 Pittsburgh	NL	9	2	1	0	0	0	(0	0)	1	3	0	0	0	0	0	0	0	1	0	1.00	0	.500	.500	.500
1983 Pittsburgh	NL	4	1	0	0	0	0	(0	0)	0	1	0	0	0	1	0	0	0	0	0	.00	0	.000	.000	.000
1984 Pittsburgh	NL	20	22	5	0	0	0	(0	0)	5	3	0	0	0	1	0	0	0	4	1	.80	0	.227	.227	.227
1985 Pittsburgh	NL	17	20	4	0	0	0	(0	0)	4	1	1	0	0	5	0	0	0	0	0	.00	0	.200	.200	.200
1986 Pittsburgh	NL	117	309	72	5	2	0	(0	0)	81	33	31	26	6	54	3	11	1	12	2	.86	8	.233	.298	.262
1987 Pittsburgh	NL	81	203	42	4	3	1	(0	1)	55	26	15	20	6	25	3	2	1	5	1	.83	4	.207	.286	.271
1988 Pittsburgh	NL	122	286	61	4	0	0	(0	0)	69	28	11	26	3	47	4	5	0	7	1	.88	10	.213	.288	.241
1989 Pittsburgh	NL	67	154	33	4	0	0	(0	0)	37	10	8	8	2	22	0	3	0	5	2	.71	1	.214	.253	.240
1990 Pittsburgh	NL	47	54	11	3	0	0	(0	0)	14	10	6	5	0	13	1	1	0	1	2	.33	2	.204	.283	.259
1991 Atlanta	NL	149	353	88	9	2	0	(0	0)	101	36	27	22	2	63	2	7	1	3	1	.75	4	.249	.296	.286
1992 Atlanta	NL	144	285	60	6	1	0	(0	0)	68	20	14	14	4	43	3	13	0	0	1	.00	6	.211	.255	.239
1993 Atlanta	NL	91	79	18	5	0	0	(0	0)	23	6	6	4	0	13	3	3	0	0	0	.00	4	.228	.291	.291
1994 Atlanta	NL	46	120	29	7	1	0	(0	0)	38	9	9	2	1	29	2	2	1	0	2	.00	4	.242	.264	.317
1995 Atlanta	NL	75	180	40	2	1	0	(0	0)	44	12	7	6	2	28	2	4	0	2	2	.50	4	.222	.255	.244
1996 Atlanta	NL	87	142	24	7	0	0	(0	0)	31	9	3	2	0	22	0	3	1	3	1	.75	6	.169	.179	.218
1997 Atlanta	NL	72	71	15	3	0	1	(0	1)	21	9	3	1	0	17	0	4	1	0	1	.00	1	.211	.219	.296
1998 Atlanta	NL	7	20	5	0	0	0	(0	0)	5	1	1	0	0	1	0	0	0	0	0	.00	2	.250	.250	.250
17 ML YEARS		1155	2301	508	55	14	2	(0	2)	597	217	142	136	26	384	23	58	6	43	17	.72	53	.221	.270	.259

Ron Belliard

Bats: Right **Throws:** Right **Pos:** PH/PR-7; 2B-1   **Ht:** 5'8" **Wt:** 180 **Born:** 4/7/75 **Age:** 24

Year Team	Lg	G	AB	H	2B	3B	HR	(Hm	Rd)	TB	R	RBI	TBB	IBB	SO	HBP	SH	SF	SB	CS	SB%	GDP	Avg	OBP	SLG
1994 Brewers	R	39	143	42	7	3	0	—	—	55	32	27	14	1	25	3	2	1	7	0	1.00	3	.294	.366	.385
1995 Beloit	A	130	461	137	28	5	13	—	—	214	76	76	36	2	67	7	2	1	16	12	.57	10	.297	.356	.464
1996 El Paso	AA	109	416	116	20	8	3	—	—	161	73	57	60	1	51	4	4	3	26	10	.72	11	.279	.373	.387
1997 Tucson	AAA	118	443	125	35	4	4	—	—	180	80	55	61	1	69	11	3	5	10	7	.59	13	.282	.379	.406
1998 Louisville	AAA	133	507	163	36	7	14	—	—	255	114	73	69	2	77	8	1	4	33	12	.73	17	.321	.408	.503
1998 Milwaukee	NL	8	5	1	0	0	0	(0	0)	1	1	0	0	0	0	0	0	0	0	0	.00	0	.200	.200	.200

Carlos Beltran

Bats: Both **Throws:** Right **Pos:** CF-14   **Ht:** 6'0" **Wt:** 175 **Born:** 4/24/77 **Age:** 22

Year Team	Lg	G	AB	H	2B	3B	HR	(Hm	Rd)	TB	R	RBI	TBB	IBB	SO	HBP	SH	SF	SB	CS	SB%	GDP	Avg	OBP	SLG
1995 Royals	R	52	180	50	9	0	0	—	—	59	29	23	13	0	30	3	1	3	5	3	.63	1	.278	.332	.328
1996 Lansing	A	11	42	6	2	0	0	—	—	8	3	0	1	0	11	0	0	0	1	0	1.00	0	.143	.163	.190

Year Team	Lg	G	AB	H	2B	3B	HR	(Hm	Rd)	TB	R	RBI	TBB	IBB	SO	HBP	SH	SF	SB	CS	SB%	GDP	Avg	OBP	SLG
								BATTING											**BASERUNNING**				**PERCENTAGES**		
Spokane	A-	59	215	58	8	3	7	—	—	93	29	29	31	0	65	0	3	2	10	2	.83	4	.270	.359	.433
1997 Wilmington	A+	120	419	96	15	4	11	—	—	152	57	46	46	3	96	4	3	1	17	7	.71	10	.229	.311	.363
1998 Wilmington	A+	52	192	53	14	0	5	—	—	82	32	32	25	0	39	2	0	1	11	7	.61	2	.276	.364	.427
Wichita	AA	47	182	64	13	3	14	—	—	125	50	44	23	3	30	1	2	0	7	1	.88	4	.352	.427	.687
1998 Kansas City	AL	14	58	16	5	3	0	(0	0)	27	12	7	3	0	12	1	0	1	3	0	1.00	2	.276	.317	.466

Rigo Beltran

Pitches: Left **Bats:** Left **Pos:** RP-7　　　　**Ht:** 5'11" **Wt:** 185 **Born:** 11/13/69 **Age:** 29

Year Team	Lg	G	GS	CG	GF	IP	BFP	H	R	ER	HR	SH	SF	HB	TBB	IBB	SO	WP	Bk	W	L	Pct.	ShO	Sv-Op	Hld	ERA
			HOW MUCH HE PITCHED							**WHAT HE GAVE UP**											**THE RESULTS**				
1991 Hamilton	A-	21	4	0	4	48	206	41	17	14	4	4	2	2	19	0	69	3	12	5	2	.714	0	0- --	—	2.63
1992 Savannah	A	13	13	2	0	83	316	38	20	20	4	1	0	4	40	0	106	8	6	6	1	.857	1	0- --	—	2.17
St. Pete	A+	2	2	0	0	8	30	6	0	0	1	0	0	0	2	0	3	0	0	0	0	.000	0	0- --	—	0.00
1993 Arkansas	AA	18	16	0	1	88.2	376	74	39	32	8	5	0	6	38	1	82	11	4	5	5	.500	0	0- --	—	3.25
1994 Arkansas	AA	4	4	1	0	28	95	12	3	2	2	1	0	0	3	0	21	0	0	4	0	1.000	1	0- --	—	0.64
Louisville	AAA	23	23	1	0	138.1	624	147	82	78	15	7	7	5	68	2	87	18	5	11	11	.500	0	0- --	—	5.07
1995 Louisville	AAA	24	24	0	0	129.2	575	156	81	75	12	2	8	5	34	0	92	4	2	8	9	.471	0	0- --	—	5.21
1996 Louisville	AAA	38	16	3	5	130.1	548	132	67	63	17	2	4	5	24	1	132	8	1	8	6	.571	1	0- --	—	4.35
1997 Louisville	AAA	9	8	1	0	54.1	227	45	17	14	7	0	1	1	21	0	46	0	0	5	2	.714	0	0- --	—	2.32
1998 Norfolk	AAA	36	11	0	7	94.1	418	104	51	45	16	2	2	1	40	1	98	5	1	6	5	.545	0	1- --	—	4.29
1997 St. Louis	NL	35	4	0	16	54.1	224	47	25	21	3	6	3	0	17	0	50	1	0	1	2	.333	0	1-1	2	3.48
1998 New York	NL	7	0	0	0	8	33	6	3	3	1	0	1	0	4	0	5	0	0	0	0	.000	0	0-0	0	3.38
2 ML YEARS		42	4	0	16	62.1	257	53	28	24	4	6	4	0	21	0	55	1	0	1	2	.333	0	1-1	2	3.47

Adrian Beltre

Bats: Right **Throws:** Right **Pos:** 3B-74; PH/PR-5; SS-2　　**Ht:** 5'11" **Wt:** 165 **Born:** 4/7/78 **Age:** 21

Year Team	Lg	G	AB	H	2B	3B	HR	(Hm	Rd)	TB	R	RBI	TBB	IBB	SO	HBP	SH	SF	SB	CS	SB%	GDP	Avg	OBP	SLG
								BATTING											**BASERUNNING**				**PERCENTAGES**		
1996 Savannah	A	68	244	75	14	3	16	—	—	143	48	59	35	2	46	7	0	2	4	3	.57	7	.307	.406	.586
San Berndno	A+	63	238	62	13	1	10	—	—	107	40	40	19	0	44	5	1	5	3	4	.43	3	.261	.322	.450
1997 Vero Beach	A+	123	435	138	24	2	26	—	—	244	95	104	67	12	66	6	0	11	25	9	.74	9	.317	.407	.561
1998 San Antonio	AA	64	246	79	21	2	13	—	—	143	49	56	39	2	37	2	0	5	20	4	.83	5	.321	.411	.581
1998 Los Angeles	NL	77	195	42	9	0	7	(5	2)	72	18	22	14	0	37	3	2	0	3	1	.75	4	.215	.278	.369

Marvin Benard

Bats: L **Throws:** L **Pos:** RF-64; PH/PR-45; LF-12; CF-9; DH-2　　**Ht:** 5'9" **Wt:** 183 **Born:** 1/20/70 **Age:** 29

Year Team	Lg	G	AB	H	2B	3B	HR	(Hm	Rd)	TB	R	RBI	TBB	IBB	SO	HBP	SH	SF	SB	CS	SB%	GDP	Avg	OBP	SLG
								BATTING											**BASERUNNING**				**PERCENTAGES**		
1995 San Francisco	NL	13	34	13	2	0	1	(0	1)	18	5	4	1	0	7	0	0	0	1	0	1.00	1	.382	.400	.529
1996 San Francisco	NL	135	488	121	14	4	5	(2	3)	161	89	27	59	2	84	4	6	1	25	11	.69	8	.248	.333	.330
1997 San Francisco	NL	84	114	26	4	0	1	(0	1)	33	13	13	13	0	29	2	0	1	3	1	.75	2	.228	.315	.289
1998 San Francisco	NL	121	286	92	21	1	3	(2	1)	124	41	36	34	1	39	2	4	1	11	4	.73	3	.322	.396	.434
4 ML YEARS		353	922	252	44	5	10	(4	6)	336	148	80	107	3	159	8	10	3	40	16	.71	14	.273	.353	.364

Alan Benes

Pitches: Right **Bats:** Right **Pos:** SP　　　　**Ht:** 6'5" **Wt:** 215 **Born:** 1/21/72 **Age:** 27

Year Team	Lg	G	GS	CG	GF	IP	BFP	H	R	ER	HR	SH	SF	HB	TBB	IBB	SO	WP	Bk	W	L	Pct.	ShO	Sv-Op	Hld	ERA
			HOW MUCH HE PITCHED							**WHAT HE GAVE UP**											**THE RESULTS**				
1995 St. Louis	NL	3	3	0	0	16	76	24	15	15	2	1	0	1	4	0	20	3	0	1	2	.333	0	0-0	0	8.44
1996 St. Louis	NL	34	32	3	1	191	840	192	120	104	27	15	9	7	87	3	131	5	1	13	10	.565	1	0-0	0	4.90
1997 St. Louis	NL	23	23	2	0	161.2	666	128	60	52	13	5	4	4	68	3	160	9	2	9	9	.500	0	0-0	0	2.89
3 ML YEARS		60	58	5	1	368.2	1582	344	195	171	42	21	13	12	159	6	311	17	3	23	21	.523	1	0-0	0	4.17

Andy Benes

Pitches: Right **Bats:** Right **Pos:** SP-34　　　　**Ht:** 6'6" **Wt:** 245 **Born:** 8/20/67 **Age:** 31

Year Team	Lg	G	GS	CG	GF	IP	BFP	H	R	ER	HR	SH	SF	HB	TBB	IBB	SO	WP	Bk	W	L	Pct.	ShO	Sv-Op	Hld	ERA
			HOW MUCH HE PITCHED							**WHAT HE GAVE UP**											**THE RESULTS**				
1989 San Diego	NL	10	10	0	0	66.2	280	51	28	26	7	6	2	1	31	0	66	0	3	6	3	.667	0	0-0	0	3.51
1990 San Diego	NL	32	31	2	1	192.1	811	177	87	77	18	5	4	1	69	5	140	2	5	10	11	.476	0	0-0	0	3.60
1991 San Diego	NL	33	33	4	0	223	908	194	76	75	23	5	4	4	59	7	167	3	4	15	11	.577	1	0-0	0	3.03
1992 San Diego	NL	34	34	2	0	231.1	961	**230**	90	86	14	19	6	5	61	6	169	1	1	13	14	.481	2	0-0	0	3.35
1993 San Diego	NL	34	34	4	0	230.2	968	200	111	97	23	10	6	4	86	7	179	14	2	15	15	.500	2	0-0	0	3.78
1994 San Diego	NL	25	25	2	0	172.1	717	155	82	74	20	11	1	1	51	2	**189**	4	0	6	14	.300	2	0-0	0	3.86
1995 SD-Sea		31	31	1	0	181.2	809	193	100	96	18	4	8	6	78	5	171	5	0	11	9	.550	1	0-0	0	4.76
1996 St. Louis	NL	36	34	3	1	230.1	963	215	107	98	28	2	6	6	77	7	160	6	0	18	10	.643	1	1-1	0	3.83
1997 St. Louis	NL	26	26	0	0	177	727	149	64	61	9	6	7	5	61	4	175	7	0	10	7	.588	0	0-0	0	3.10
1998 Arizona	NL	34	34	1	0	231.1	979	221	104	102	25	11	8	6	74	6	164	9	1	14	13	.519	0	0-0	0	3.97
1995 San Diego	NL	19	19	1	0	118.2	518	121	65	55	10	3	4	4	45	3	126	3	0	4	7	.364	1	0-0	0	4.17
Seattle	AL	12	12	0	0	63	291	72	42	41	8	1	4	2	33	2	45	2	0	7	2	.778	0	0-0	0	5.86
10 ML YEARS		295	292	19	2	1936.2	8123	1785	863	792	185	79	54	39	647	46	1580	51	16	118	107	.524	9	1-1	0	3.68

19

Armando Benitez

Pitches: Right **Bats:** Right **Pos:** RP-71   **Ht:** 6'4" **Wt:** 225 **Born:** 11/3/72 **Age:** 26

Year Team	Lg	G	GS	CG	GF	IP	BFP	H	R	ER	HR	SH	SF	HB	TBB	IBB	SO	WP	Bk	W	L	Pct.	ShO	Sv-Op	Hld	ERA
1994 Baltimore	AL	3	0	0	1	10	42	8	1	1	0	0	0	1	4	0	14	0	0	0	0	.000	0	0-0	0	0.90
1995 Baltimore	AL	44	0	0	18	47.2	221	37	33	30	8	2	3	5	37	2	56	3	1	1	5	.167	0	2-5	6	5.66
1996 Baltimore	AL	18	0	0	8	14.1	56	7	6	6	2	0	1	0	6	0	20	1	0	1	0	1.000	0	4-5	1	3.77
1997 Baltimore	AL	71	0	0	26	73.1	307	49	22	20	7	2	4	1	43	5	106	1	0	4	5	.444	0	9-10	20	2.45
1998 Baltimore	AL	71	0	0	54	68.1	289	48	29	29	10	3	2	4	39	2	87	0	0	5	6	.455	0	22-26	3	3.82
5 ML YEARS		207	0	0	107	213.2	915	149	91	86	27	7	10	11	129	9	283	5	1	11	16	.407	0	37-46	30	3.62

Yamil Benitez

Bats: R **Throws:** R **Pos:** LF-49; PH/PR-35; RF-13; DH-2   **Ht:** 6'2" **Wt:** 195 **Born:** 5/10/72 **Age:** 27

Year Team	Lg	G	AB	H	2B	3B	HR	(Hm	Rd)	TB	R	RBI	TBB	IBB	SO	HBP	SH	SF	SB	CS	SB%	GDP	Avg	OBP	SLG
1995 Montreal	NL	14	39	15	2	1	2	(1	1)	25	8	7	1	0	7	0	0	0	0	2	.00	1	.385	.400	.641
1996 Montreal	NL	11	12	2	0	0	0	(0	0)	2	0	2	0	0	4	0	0	0	0	0	.00	0	.167	.167	.167
1997 Kansas City	NL	53	191	51	7	1	8	(5	3)	84	22	21	10	0	49	1	2	0	2	2	.50	2	.267	.307	.440
1998 Arizona	NL	91	206	41	7	1	9	(4	5)	77	17	30	14	1	46	4	0	1	2	2	.50	6	.199	.262	.374
4 ML YEARS		169	448	109	16	3	19	(10	9)	188	47	60	25	1	106	5	2	1	4	6	.40	9	.243	.290	.420

Mike Benjamin

Bats: R **Throws:** R **Pos:** 2B-87; SS-20; 3B-11; PH/PR-11; 1B-10; DH-2   **Ht:** 6'0" **Wt:** 169 **Born:** 11/22/65 **Age:** 33

Year Team	Lg	G	AB	H	2B	3B	HR	(Hm	Rd)	TB	R	RBI	TBB	IBB	SO	HBP	SH	SF	SB	CS	SB%	GDP	Avg	OBP	SLG
1989 San Francisco	NL	14	6	1	0	0	0	(0	0)	1	6	0	0	0	1	0	0	0	0	0	.00	0	.167	.167	.167
1990 San Francisco	NL	22	56	12	3	1	2	(2	0)	23	7	3	3	1	10	0	4	0	1	0	1.00	0	.214	.254	.411
1991 San Francisco	NL	54	106	13	3	0	2	(0	2)	22	12	8	7	2	26	2	3	2	3	0	1.00	1	.123	.188	.208
1992 San Francisco	NL	40	75	13	2	1	1	(0	1)	20	4	3	4	1	15	0	3	0	1	0	1.00	1	.173	.215	.267
1993 San Francisco	NL	63	146	29	7	0	4	(3	1)	48	22	16	9	2	23	4	6	0	0	0	.00	3	.199	.264	.329
1994 San Francisco	NL	38	62	16	5	1	1	(1	0)	26	9	9	5	1	16	3	5	0	5	0	1.00	1	.258	.343	.419
1995 San Francisco	NL	68	186	41	6	0	3	(1	2)	56	19	12	8	3	51	1	7	0	11	1	.92	3	.220	.256	.301
1996 Philadelphia	NL	35	103	23	5	1	4	(0	4)	42	13	13	12	5	21	2	1	0	3	1	.75	2	.223	.316	.408
1997 Boston	AL	49	116	27	9	1	0	(0	0)	38	12	7	4	0	27	1	1	1	2	3	.40	2	.233	.262	.328
1998 Boston	AL	124	349	95	23	0	4	(2	2)	130	46	39	15	1	73	6	13	2	3	0	1.00	11	.272	.312	.373
10 ML YEARS		507	1205	270	63	5	21	(9	12)	406	150	110	67	16	263	19	39	5	29	5	.85	26	.224	.275	.337

Gary Bennett

Bats: Right **Throws:** Right **Pos:** C-9   **Ht:** 6'0" **Wt:** 190 **Born:** 4/17/72 **Age:** 27

Year Team	Lg	G	AB	H	2B	3B	HR	(Hm	Rd)	TB	R	RBI	TBB	IBB	SO	HBP	SH	SF	SB	CS	SB%	GDP	Avg	OBP	SLG
1990 Martinsvlle	R+	16	52	14	2	1	0	—	—	18	3	10	4	0	15	0	0	1	0	1	.00	0	.269	.316	.346
1991 Martinsvlle	R+	41	136	32	7	0	1	—	—	42	15	16	17	0	26	5	1	1	0	1	.00	5	.235	.340	.309
1992 Batavia	A-	47	146	30	2	0	0	—	—	32	22	12	15	0	27	2	3	0	2	1	.67	2	.205	.288	.219
1993 Spartanburg	A	42	126	32	4	1	0	—	—	38	18	15	12	0	22	1	2	1	0	2	.00	2	.254	.321	.302
Clearwater	A+	17	55	18	0	0	1	—	—	21	5	6	3	0	10	1	2	0	0	1	.00	1	.327	.373	.382
1994 Clearwater	A+	19	55	13	3	0	0	—	—	16	6	10	8	0	6	0	1	0	0	0	.00	1	.236	.328	.291
Reading	AA	63	208	48	9	0	3	—	—	66	13	22	14	0	26	0	3	3	0	1	.00	6	.231	.276	.317
1995 Reading	AA	86	271	64	11	0	4	—	—	87	27	40	22	1	36	3	3	2	0	0	.00	12	.236	.299	.321
Scranton-WB	AAA	7	20	3	0	0	0	—	—	3	1	1	2	1	2	0	1	0	0	0	.00	0	.150	.227	.150
1996 Scranton-WB	AAA	91	286	71	15	1	8	—	—	112	37	37	24	2	43	3	3	3	1	0	1.00	10	.248	.310	.392
1997 Pawtucket	AAA	71	224	48	7	1	4	—	—	69	16	22	18	0	39	2	1	1	1	1	.50	10	.214	.278	.308
1998 Scranton-WB	AAA	86	282	72	18	0	10	—	—	120	33	40	25	0	41	2	2	4	0	0	.00	6	.255	.316	.426
1995 Philadelphia	NL	1	1	0	0	0	0	(0	0)	0	0	0	0	0	1	0	0	0	0	0	.00	0	.000	.000	.000
1996 Philadelphia	NL	6	16	4	0	0	0	(0	0)	4	0	1	2	1	6	0	0	0	0	0	.00	0	.250	.333	.250
1998 Philadelphia	NL	9	31	9	0	0	0	(0	0)	9	4	3	5	0	5	0	0	1	0	0	.00	1	.290	.378	.290
3 ML YEARS		16	48	13	0	0	0	(0	0)	13	4	4	7	1	12	0	0	1	0	0	.00	1	.271	.357	.271

Joel Bennett

Pitches: Right **Bats:** Right **Pos:** RP-2   **Ht:** 6'1" **Wt:** 160 **Born:** 1/31/70 **Age:** 29

Year Team	Lg	G	GS	CG	GF	IP	BFP	H	R	ER	HR	SH	SF	HB	TBB	IBB	SO	WP	Bk	W	L	Pct.	ShO	Sv-Op	Hld	ERA
1991 Red Sox	R	2	2	0	0	10	38	6	2	2	0	0	1	1	4	0	8	2	1	0	0	.000	0	0--	—	1.80
Elmira	A-	13	12	1	0	81	325	60	29	22	3	3	1	6	30	0	75	7	0	5	3	.625	1	0--	—	2.44
1992 Winter Havn	A+	26	26	4	0	161.2	690	161	86	76	7	7	5	7	55	0	154	7	3	7	11	.389	1	0--	—	4.23
1993 Lynchburg	A+	29	29	3	0	181	754	151	93	77	17	7	9	4	67	6	221	18	0	7	12	.368	1	0--	—	3.83
1994 New Britain	AA	23	23	1	0	130.2	560	119	65	59	9	2	2	4	56	0	130	10	0	11	7	.611	1	0--	—	4.06
Pawtucket	AAA	4	4	0	0	21	91	19	16	16	8	0	0	1	12	0	24	1	0	1	3	.250	0	0--	—	6.86
1995 Pawtucket	AAA	20	13	0	2	77	357	91	57	50	6	0	4	3	45	3	50	6	0	4	4	.333	0	0--	—	5.84
1996 Trenton	AA	3	0	0	1	4.1	18	3	4	4	2	0	0	0	2	0	8	0	0	1	0	1.000	0	0--	—	8.31
Newburgh	IND	9	9	2	0	57	211	18	8	5	2	0	1	2	16	0	82	3	0	6	0	1.000	1	0--	—	0.79
Bowie	AA	10	8	1	0	54.2	211	36	21	20	5	0	0	1	17	0	48	0	0	5	3	.400	0	0--	—	3.29
1997 Bowie	AA	44	10	0	12	113.1	461	89	45	40	12	6	3	4	40	6	146	2	1	6	8	.429	0	4--	—	3.18
1998 Rochester	AAA	18	15	1	0	101.1	425	99	46	41	9	2	3	2	37	1	99	3	0	10	0	1.000	0	0--	—	3.64

20

		HOW MUCH HE PITCHED			WHAT HE GAVE UP											THE RESULTS					
Year Team	Lg	G GS CG GF	IP	BFP	H	R	ER	HR SH SF HB	TBB IBB	SO	WP	Bk	W	L	Pct.	ShO	Sv-Op	Hld	ERA
Scranton-WB	AAA	8 7 0 0	47.2	215	51	29	28	6 0 1 1	25 1	35	0	0	1	2	.333	0	0- -	—	5.29
1998 Baltimore	AL	2 0 0 2	2	11	2	1	1	0 0 0 0	3 0	0	0	0	0	0	.000	0	0-0	0	4.50

Shayne Bennett

Pitches: Right **Bats:** Right **Pos:** RP-62   **Ht:** 6'5" **Wt:** 215 **Born:** 4/10/72 **Age:** 27

		HOW MUCH HE PITCHED			WHAT HE GAVE UP											THE RESULTS					
Year Team	Lg	G GS CG GF	IP	BFP	H	R	ER	HR SH SF HB	TBB IBB	SO	WP	Bk	W	L	Pct.	ShO	Sv-Op	Hld	ERA
1993 Red Sox	R	2 1 0 1	7	25	2	1	1	1 0 0 0	1 0	4	1	0	0	0	.000	0	1- -	—	1.29
Ft. Laud	A+	23 0 0 18	31.1	128	26	8	6	1 4 1 0	11 1	23	2	2	1	2	.333	0	6- -	—	1.72
1994 Sarasota	A+	15 8 0 4	48.1	216	46	31	24	1 2 1 3	27 0	28	1	1	1	6	.143	0	3- -	—	4.47
1995 Sarasota	A+	52 0 0 43	59.2	255	50	23	17	3 4 2 4	21 4	69	5	1	5	.286	0	24- -	—	2.56
Trenton	AA	10 0 0 6	10.2	48	16	6	6	0 3 1 0	3 0	6	1	0	0	1	.000	0	3- -	—	5.06
1996 Harrisburg	AA	53 0 0 27	92.2	393	83	32	26	6 3 3 5	35 2	89	2	2	8	8	.500	0	12- -	—	2.53
1997 Harrisburg	AA	23 1 0 7	47	210	47	28	23	6 3 1 4	20 0	38	1	0	4	2	.667	0	2- -	—	4.40
Ottawa	AAA	25 0 0 21	34.1	142	23	8	6	0 2 1 2	21 1	29	2	0	1	2	.333	0	14- -	—	1.57
1997 Montreal	NL	16 0 0 3	22.2	98	21	9	8	2 1 3 0	9 3	18	0	0	1	0	.000	0	0-0	0	3.18
1998 Montreal	NL	62 0 0 11	91.2	417	97	61	56	8 9 6 6	45 3	59	3	1	5	5	.500	0	1-2	0	5.50
2 ML YEARS		78 0 0 14	114.1	515	118	70	64	10 10 9 6	54 6	67	3	1	5	6	.455	0	1-2	0	5.04

Jason Bere

Pitches: Right **Bats:** Right **Pos:** SP-22; RP-5   **Ht:** 6'3" **Wt:** 215 **Born:** 5/26/71 **Age:** 28

		HOW MUCH HE PITCHED			WHAT HE GAVE UP											THE RESULTS					
Year Team	Lg	G GS CG GF	IP	BFP	H	R	ER	HR SH SF HB	TBB IBB	SO	WP	Bk	W	L	Pct.	ShO	Sv-Op	Hld	ERA
1993 Chicago	AL	24 24 1 0	142.2	610	109	60	55	12 4 2 5	81 0	129	8	0	12	5	.706	0	0-0	0	3.47
1994 Chicago	AL	24 24 0 0	141.2	608	119	65	60	17 4 4 1	80 0	127	2	0	12	2	.857	0	0-0	0	3.81
1995 Chicago	AL	27 27 1 0	137.2	668	151	120	110	21 4 7 6	106 6	110	8	0	8	15	.348	0	0-0	0	7.19
1996 Chicago	AL	5 5 0 0	16.2	93	26	19	19	3 1 1 0	18 1	19	2	0	0	1	.000	0	0-0	0	10.26
1997 Chicago	AL	6 6 0 0	28.2	123	20	15	15	4 1 1 3	17 0	21	1	0	4	2	.667	0	0-0	0	4.71
1998 ChA-Cin		27 22 0 2	127.1	588	137	91	80	17 4 7 3	78 0	84	8	0	6	9	.400	0	0-0	0	5.65
1998 Chicago	AL	18 15 0 0	83.2	404	98	71	60	14 4 5 2	58 0	53	7	0	3	7	.300	0	0-0	0	6.45
Cincinnati	NL	9 7 0 2	43.2	184	39	20	20	3 0 2 1	20 0	31	1	0	3	2	.600	0	0-0	0	4.12
6 ML YEARS		113 108 2 2	594.2	2690	562	370	339	74 18 22 18	380 7	490	29	0	42	34	.553	0	0-0	0	5.13

Dave Berg

Bats: R **Throws:** R **Pos:** 2B-27; 3B-25; PH/PR-20; SS-17   **Ht:** 5'11" **Wt:** 185 **Born:** 9/3/70 **Age:** 28

		BATTING															BASERUNNING				PERCENTAGES		
Year Team	Lg	G	AB	H	2B	3B	HR	(Hm Rd)	TB	R	RBI	TBB	IBB	SO	HBP	SH	SF	SB	CS	SB%	GDP	Avg	OBP	SLG
1993 Elmira	A-	75	281	74	13	1	4	— —	101	37	28	35	1	37	8	4	3	6	4	.60	8	.263	.358	.359
1994 Kane County	A	121	437	117	27	8	9	— —	187	80	53	54	0	80	8	15	6	8	6	.57	10	.268	.354	.428
1995 Brevard Cty	A+	114	382	114	18	1	3	— —	143	71	39	68	1	61	8	7	9	4	4	.69	5	.298	.407	.374
1996 Portland	AA	109	414	125	28	5	6	— —	190	64	73	42	1	60	5	8	6	17	7	.71	10	.302	.368	.459
1997 Charlotte	AAA	117	424	125	26	6	9	— —	190	76	47	55	1	71	3	10	3	16	7	.70	13	.295	.377	.448
1998 Florida	NL	81	182	57	11	0	2	(1 1)	74	18	21	26	1	46	0	4	3	3	0	1.00	1	.313	.393	.407

Sean Bergman

Pitches: Right **Bats:** Right **Pos:** SP-27; RP-4   **Ht:** 6'4" **Wt:** 225 **Born:** 4/11/70 **Age:** 29

		HOW MUCH HE PITCHED			WHAT HE GAVE UP											THE RESULTS					
Year Team	Lg	G GS CG GF	IP	BFP	H	R	ER	HR SH SF HB	TBB IBB	SO	WP	Bk	W	L	Pct.	ShO	Sv-Op	Hld	ERA
1993 Detroit	AL	9 6 1 0	39.2	189	47	29	25	6 3 2 1	23 3	19	3	1	1	4	.200	0	0-0	0	5.67
1994 Detroit	AL	3 3 0 0	17.2	82	22	11	11	2 0 1 1	7 0	12	1	0	2	1	.667	0	0-0	0	5.60
1995 Detroit	AL	28 28 1 0	135.1	630	169	95	77	19 5 3 4	67 8	86	13	0	7	10	.412	1	0-0	0	5.12
1996 San Diego	NL	41 14 0 11	113.1	482	119	63	55	14 8 4 2	33 3	85	7	2	6	8	.429	0	0-0	1	4.37
1997 San Diego	NL	44 9 0 13	99	451	126	72	67	11 7 4 3	38 4	74	6	0	2	4	.333	0	0-2	1	6.09
1998 Houston	NL	31 27 1 1	172	733	183	81	71	20 3 1 5	42 3	100	8	1	12	9	.571	0	0-0	0	3.72
6 ML YEARS		156 87 3 26	577	2567	666	351	306	72 26 15 16	210 21	376	38	4	30	36	.455	1	0-2	2	4.77

Geronimo Berroa

Bats: R **Throws:** R **Pos:** DH-42; PH/PR-18; LF-16; RF-2   **Ht:** 6'0" **Wt:** 210 **Born:** 3/18/65 **Age:** 34

		BATTING															BASERUNNING				PERCENTAGES		
Year Team	Lg	G	AB	H	2B	3B	HR	(Hm Rd)	TB	R	RBI	TBB	IBB	SO	HBP	SH	SF	SB	CS	SB%	GDP	Avg	OBP	SLG
1989 Atlanta	NL	81	136	36	4	0	2	(1 1)	46	7	9	7	1	32	0	0	0	0	1	.00	2	.265	.301	.338
1990 Atlanta	NL	7	4	0	0	0	0	(0 0)	0	0	0	1	1	1	0	0	0	0	0	.00	0	.000	.200	.000
1992 Cincinnati	NL	13	15	4	1	0	0	(0 0)	5	2	0	2	0	1	1	0	0	0	1	.00	1	.267	.389	.333
1993 Florida	NL	14	34	4	1	0	0	(0 0)	5	3	0	2	0	7	0	0	0	0	0	.00	2	.118	.167	.147
1994 Oakland	AL	96	340	104	18	2	13	(4 9)	165	55	65	41	0	62	3	0	7	7	2	.78	5	.306	.379	.485
1995 Oakland	AL	141	546	152	22	3	22	(10 12)	246	87	88	63	2	98	1	0	6	7	4	.64	12	.278	.351	.451
1996 Oakland	AL	153	586	170	32	1	36	(21 15)	312	101	106	47	0	122	4	0	6	3	0	.00	16	.290	.344	.532
1997 Oak-Bal	AL	156	561	159	25	0	26	(11 15)	262	88	90	76	4	120	4	0	7	4	4	.50	18	.283	.369	.467
1998 Cle-Det	AL	72	190	43	7	2	1	(1 0)	57	23	13	24	1	44	2	0	0	1	1	.50	5	.225	.318	.298
1997 Oakland	AL	73	261	81	12	0	16	(6 10)	141	40	42	36	2	58	1	0	1	3	2	.60	12	.310	.395	.540
Baltimore	AL	83	300	78	13	0	10	(5 5)	121	48	48	40	2	62	3	0	6	1	2	.33	6	.260	.347	.403
1998 Cleveland	AL	20	65	13	3	1	0	(0 0)	18	6	3	7	0	17	0	0	0	1	0	1.00	2	.200	.278	.277

Year Team	Lg	G	AB	H	2B	3B	HR	(Hm	Rd)	TB	R	RBI	TBB	IBB	SO	HBP	SH	SF	SB	CS	SB%	GDP	Avg	OBP	SLG
Detroit	AL	52	126	30	4	1	1	(1	0)	39	17	10	17	1	27	2	0	0	0	1	.00	3	.238	.338	.310
9 ML YEARS		733	2413	672	110	8	100	(48	52)	1098	366	371	263	9	487	15	0	26	19	16	.54	61	.278	.350	.455

Sean Berry

Bats: Right **Throws:** Right **Pos:** 3B-87; PH/PR-21; DH-1   **Ht:** 5'11" **Wt:** 200 **Born:** 3/22/66 **Age:** 33

Year Team	Lg	G	AB	H	2B	3B	HR	(Hm	Rd)	TB	R	RBI	TBB	IBB	SO	HBP	SH	SF	SB	CS	SB%	GDP	Avg	OBP	SLG
1990 Kansas City	AL	8	23	5	1	1	0	(0	0)	8	2	4	2	0	5	0	0	0	0	0	.00	0	.217	.280	.348
1991 Kansas City	AL	31	60	8	3	0	0	(0	0)	11	5	1	5	0	23	1	0	0	0	0	.00	1	.133	.212	.183
1992 Montreal	NL	24	57	19	1	0	1	(0	1)	23	5	4	1	0	11	0	0	0	2	1	.67	1	.333	.345	.404
1993 Montreal	NL	122	299	78	15	2	14	(5	9)	139	50	49	41	6	70	2	3	6	12	2	.86	4	.261	.348	.465
1994 Montreal	NL	103	320	89	19	2	11	(4	7)	145	43	41	32	7	50	3	2	2	14	0	1.00	4	.278	.347	.453
1995 Montreal	NL	103	314	100	22	1	14	(5	9)	166	38	55	25	1	53	2	2	5	3	8	.27	5	.318	.367	.529
1996 Houston	NL	132	431	121	38	1	17	(4	13)	212	55	95	23	1	58	9	2	4	12	6	.67	11	.281	.328	.492
1997 Houston	NL	96	301	77	24	1	8	(4	4)	127	37	43	25	1	53	5	1	6	1	5	.17	8	.256	.318	.422
1998 Houston	NL	102	299	94	17	1	13	(7	6)	152	48	52	31	3	50	7	1	4	3	1	.75	8	.314	.387	.508
9 ML YEARS		721	2104	591	140	9	78	(29	49)	983	283	344	185	19	373	29	11	27	47	23	.67	45	.281	.343	.467

Brian Bevil

Pitches: Right **Bats:** Right **Pos:** RP-39   **Ht:** 6'4" **Wt:** 225 **Born:** 9/5/71 **Age:** 27

Year Team	Lg	G	GS	CG	GF	IP	BFP	H	R	ER	HR	SH	SF	HB	TBB	IBB	SO	WP	Bk	W	L	Pct.	ShO	Sv-Op	Hld	ERA
1991 Royals	R	13	12	2	1	65.1	262	56	20	14	0	1	0	2	19	0	70	3	3	5	3	.625	0	0- --	—	1.93
1992 Appleton	A	26	26	4	0	156	646	129	67	59	17	5	4	5	63	0	168	9	0	9	7	.563	2	0- --	—	3.40
1993 Wilmington	A+	12	12	2	0	74.1	286	46	21	19	2	2	2	4	23	0	61	4	0	7	1	.875	0	0- --	—	2.30
Memphis	AA	6	6	0	0	33	146	36	17	16	4	2	2	0	14	0	26	3	0	3	3	.500	0	0- --	—	4.36
1994 Memphis	AA	17	17	0	0	100	408	75	42	39	6	3	5	3	40	0	78	12	0	5	4	.556	0	0- --	—	3.51
1995 Omaha	AAA	6	6	0	0	22	119	40	31	23	7	1	0	3	14	1	10	2	0	1	3	.250	0	0- --	—	9.41
Wichita	AA	15	15	0	0	74	334	85	51	48	7	0	3	3	35	0	57	7	0	5	7	.417	0	0- --	—	5.84
1996 Wichita	AA	13	13	2	0	75.2	301	56	22	17	4	1	3	2	26	0	74	6	0	9	2	.818	0	0- --	—	2.02
Omaha	AAA	12	12	0	0	67.2	289	62	36	31	10	0	0	5	19	0	73	6	0	7	5	.583	0	0- --	—	4.12
1997 Wichita	AA	4	2	0	2	8	38	11	8	5	0	0	1	1	4	0	10	1	0	0	0	.000	0	0- --	—	5.63
Omaha	AAA	26	3	0	12	39	171	34	22	19	8	1	2	2	22	0	47	0	0	2	1	.667	0	1- --	—	4.38
1998 Royals	R	3	3	0	0	4	19	4	2	1	0	0	0	0	2	0	7	1	0	0	0	.000	0	0- --	—	2.25
Omaha	AAA	10	0	0	2	13	55	10	2	2	1	0	0	1	4	1	19	2	0	1	0	1.000	0	1- --	—	1.38
1996 Kansas City	AL	3	1	0	1	11	44	9	7	7	2	0	1	0	5	0	7	0	0	1	0	1.000	0	0-0	1	5.73
1997 Kansas City	AL	18	0	0	11	16.1	72	16	13	12	1	0	2	1	9	2	13	2	0	1	2	.333	0	1-5	1	6.61
1998 Kansas City	AL	39	0	0	10	40	194	47	29	28	4	1	2	3	22	1	47	6	0	3	1	.750	0	0-2	5	6.30
3 ML YEARS		60	1	0	22	67.1	310	72	49	47	7	1	5	4	36	3	67	8	0	5	3	.625	0	1-7	7	6.28

Dante Bichette

Bats: R **Throws:** R **Pos:** LF-134; RF-29; PH/PR-4; DH-1   **Ht:** 6'3" **Wt:** 228 **Born:** 11/18/63 **Age:** 35

Year Team	Lg	G	AB	H	2B	3B	HR	(Hm	Rd)	TB	R	RBI	TBB	IBB	SO	HBP	SH	SF	SB	CS	SB%	GDP	Avg	OBP	SLG
1988 California	AL	21	46	12	2	0	0	(0	0)	14	1	8	0	0	7	0	0	4	0	0	.00	0	.261	.240	.304
1989 California	AL	48	138	29	7	0	3	(2	1)	45	13	15	6	0	24	0	0	2	3	0	1.00	3	.210	.240	.326
1990 California	AL	109	349	89	15	1	15	(8	7)	151	40	53	16	1	79	3	1	2	5	2	.71	9	.255	.292	.433
1991 Milwaukee	AL	134	445	106	18	3	15	(6	9)	175	53	59	22	4	107	1	1	6	14	8	.64	9	.238	.272	.393
1992 Milwaukee	AL	112	387	111	27	2	5	(3	2)	157	37	41	16	3	74	3	2	3	18	7	.72	13	.287	.318	.406
1993 Colorado	NL	141	538	167	43	5	21	(11	10)	283	93	89	28	2	99	7	0	8	14	8	.64	7	.310	.348	.526
1994 Colorado	NL	116	484	147	33	2	27	(15	12)	265	74	95	19	3	70	4	0	2	21	8	.72	17	.304	.334	.548
1995 Colorado	NL	139	579	197	38	2	40	(31	9)	359	102	128	22	5	96	4	0	7	13	9	.59	16	.340	.364	.620
1996 Colorado	NL	159	633	198	39	3	31	(22	9)	336	114	141	45	4	105	6	0	10	31	12	.72	18	.313	.359	.531
1997 Colorado	NL	151	561	173	31	2	26	(20	6)	286	81	118	30	1	90	3	0	7	6	5	.55	13	.308	.343	.510
1998 Colorado	NL	161	662	219	48	2	22	(17	5)	337	97	122	28	2	76	1	0	4	14	4	.78	22	.331	.357	.509
11 ML YEARS		1291	4822	1448	301	22	205	(135	70)	2408	705	869	232	25	827	32	4	55	139	63	.69	127	.300	.333	.499

Steve Bieser

Bats: Left **Throws:** Right **Pos:** PH/PR-12; LF-1   **Ht:** 5'10" **Wt:** 170 **Born:** 8/4/67 **Age:** 31

Year Team	Lg	G	AB	H	2B	3B	HR	(Hm	Rd)	TB	R	RBI	TBB	IBB	SO	HBP	SH	SF	SB	CS	SB%	GDP	Avg	OBP	SLG
1989 Batavia	A-	25	75	18	3	1	1	—	—	26	13	13	12	0	20	2	2	2	1	.67	1	.240	.352	.347
1990 Batavia	A-	54	160	37	11	1	0	—	—	50	36	12	26	1	27	1	2	2	13	2	.87	3	.231	.339	.313
1991 Spartanburg	A	60	168	41	6	0	0	—	—	47	25	13	31	0	35	3	4	3	17	4	.81	4	.244	.366	.280
1992 Clearwater	A+	73	203	58	6	5	0	—	—	74	33	10	39	3	28	9	8	0	8	8	.50	2	.286	.422	.365
Reading	AA	33	139	38	5	4	0	—	—	51	20	8	6	0	25	4	4	0	8	3	.73	3	.273	.322	.367
1993 Reading	AA	53	170	53	6	3	1	—	—	68	21	19	15	1	24	2	1	0	9	5	.64	2	.312	.374	.400
Scranton-WB	AAA	26	83	21	4	0	0	—	—	25	3	4	2	0	14	1	1	0	3	0	1.00	6	.253	.279	.301
1994 Scranton-WB	AAA	93	228	61	13	1	0	—	—	76	42	15	17	1	40	5	4	2	12	8	.60	2	.268	.329	.333
1995 Scranton-WB	AAA	95	245	66	12	6	1	—	—	93	37	33	22	1	56	10	6	2	14	5	.74	5	.269	.351	.380
1996 Ottawa	AAA	123	382	123	24	4	1	—	—	158	63	32	35	4	55	6	23	6	27	7	.79	6	.322	.386	.414
1997 Norfolk	AAA	41	122	20	5	0	0	—	—	25	6	4	9	0	20	5	2	0	4	3	.57	1	.164	.250	.205
1998 Nashville	AAA	82	206	53	11	4	1	—	—	75	30	24	33	1	30	10	4	6	13	2	.87	4	.257	.376	.364
1997 New York	NL	47	69	17	3	0	0	(0	0)	20	16	4	7	1	20	4	0	1	2	3	.40	0	.246	.346	.290

Year Team	Lg	G	AB	H	2B	3B	HR	(Hm	Rd)	TB	R	RBI	TBB	IBB	SO	HBP	SH	SF	SB	CS	SB%	GDP	Avg	OBP	SLG
1998 Pittsburgh	NL	13	11	3	1	0	0	(0	0)	4	2	1	2	0	2	0	0	0	0	0	.00	1	.273	.385	.364
2 ML YEARS		60	80	20	4	0	0	(0	0)	24	18	5	9	1	22	4	0	1	2	3	.40	1	.250	.351	.300

Craig Biggio

Bats: Right **Throws:** Right **Pos:** 2B-159; DH-1; PH/PR-1   **Ht:** 5'11" **Wt:** 180 **Born:** 12/14/65 **Age:** 33

Year Team	Lg	G	AB	H	2B	3B	HR	(Hm	Rd)	TB	R	RBI	TBB	IBB	SO	HBP	SH	SF	SB	CS	SB%	GDP	Avg	OBP	SLG
1988 Houston	NL	50	123	26	6	1	3	(1	2)	43	14	5	7	2	29	0	1	0	6	1	.86	1	.211	.254	.350
1989 Houston	NL	134	443	114	21	2	13	(6	7)	178	64	60	49	8	64	6	6	5	21	3	.88	7	.257	.336	.402
1990 Houston	NL	150	555	153	24	2	4	(2	2)	193	53	42	53	1	79	3	9	1	25	11	.69	11	.276	.342	.348
1991 Houston	NL	149	546	161	23	4	4	(0	4)	204	79	46	53	3	71	2	5	3	19	6	.76	2	.295	.358	.374
1992 Houston	NL	162	613	170	32	3	6	(3	3)	226	96	39	94	9	95	7	5	2	38	15	.72	5	.277	.378	.369
1993 Houston	NL	155	610	175	41	5	21	(8	13)	289	98	64	77	7	93	10	4	5	15	17	.47	10	.287	.373	.474
1994 Houston	NL	114	437	139	44	5	6	(4	2)	211	88	56	62	1	58	8	2	2	39	4	.91	5	.318	.411	.483
1995 Houston	NL	141	553	167	30	2	22	(6	16)	267	123	77	80	1	85	22	11	7	33	8	.80	6	.302	.406	.483
1996 Houston	NL	162	605	174	24	4	15	(7	8)	251	113	75	75	0	72	27	8	8	25	7	.78	10	.288	.386	.415
1997 Houston	NL	162	619	191	37	8	22	(7	15)	310	146	81	84	6	107	34	0	7	47	10	.82	0	.309	.415	.501
1998 Houston	NL	160	646	210	51	2	20	(10	10)	325	123	88	64	6	113	23	1	4	50	8	.86	10	.325	.403	.503
11 ML YEARS		1539	5750	1680	333	38	136	(54	82)	2497	997	633	698	44	866	142	52	44	318	90	.78	67	.292	.380	.434

Willie Blair

Pitches: Right **Bats:** Right **Pos:** SP-25; RP-9   **Ht:** 6'1" **Wt:** 185 **Born:** 12/18/65 **Age:** 33

Year Team	Lg	G	GS	CG	GF	IP	BFP	H	R	ER	HR	SH	SF	HB	TBB	IBB	SO	WP	Bk	W	L	Pct.	ShO	Sv-Op	Hld	ERA
1990 Toronto	AL	27	6	0	8	68.2	297	66	33	31	4	0	4	1	28	4	43	3	0	3	5	.375	0	0-0	1	4.06
1991 Cleveland	AL	11	5	0	1	36	168	58	27	27	7	1	2	1	10	0	13	1	0	2	3	.400	0	0-1	0	6.75
1992 Houston	NL	29	8	0	1	78.2	331	74	47	35	5	4	3	2	25	2	48	2	0	5	7	.417	0	0-0	1	4.00
1993 Colorado	NL	46	18	1	5	146	664	184	90	77	20	10	8	3	42	4	84	6	1	6	10	.375	0	0-0	3	4.75
1994 Colorado	NL	47	1	0	13	77.2	365	98	57	50	9	3	1	4	39	3	68	4	0	0	5	.000	0	3-6	2	5.79
1995 San Diego	NL	40	12	0	11	114	485	112	60	55	11	8	2	2	45	3	83	4	0	7	5	.583	0	0-0	3	4.34
1996 San Diego	NL	60	0	0	17	88	377	80	52	45	13	4	3	7	29	5	67	2	0	2	6	.250	0	1-5	3	4.60
1997 Detroit	AL	29	27	2	0	175	739	186	85	81	18	3	6	3	46	2	90	6	1	16	8	.667	0	0-0	0	4.17
1998 Ari-NYN	AL	34	25	0	2	175.1	750	188	101	97	31	14	4	4	61	2	92	6	0	5	16	.238	0	0-0	0	4.98
1998 Arizona	NL	23	23	0	0	146.2	634	165	91	87	27	11	3	3	51	2	71	5	0	4	15	.211	0	0-0	0	5.34
New York	NL	11	2	0	2	28.2	116	23	10	10	4	3	1	1	10	0	21	1	0	1	1	.500	0	0-0	0	3.14
9 ML YEARS		323	102	3	58	959.1	4176	1046	552	498	118	47	33	27	325	25	588	34	2	46	65	.414	0	4-12	13	4.67

Jeff Blauser

Bats: Right **Throws:** Right **Pos:** SS-106; PH/PR-14   **Ht:** 6'1" **Wt:** 180 **Born:** 11/8/65 **Age:** 33

Year Team	Lg	G	AB	H	2B	3B	HR	(Hm	Rd)	TB	R	RBI	TBB	IBB	SO	HBP	SH	SF	SB	CS	SB%	GDP	Avg	OBP	SLG
1987 Atlanta	NL	51	165	40	6	3	2	(1	1)	58	11	15	18	1	34	3	1	0	7	3	.70	4	.242	.328	.352
1988 Atlanta	NL	18	67	16	3	1	2	(2	0)	27	7	7	2	0	11	1	3	1	0	1	.00	1	.239	.268	.403
1989 Atlanta	NL	142	456	123	24	2	12	(5	7)	187	63	46	38	2	101	1	8	4	5	2	.71	7	.270	.325	.410
1990 Atlanta	NL	115	386	104	24	3	8	(3	5)	158	46	39	35	1	70	3	3	0	3	5	.38	4	.269	.338	.409
1991 Atlanta	NL	129	352	91	14	3	11	(7	4)	144	49	54	54	4	59	2	4	3	5	6	.45	4	.259	.358	.409
1992 Atlanta	NL	123	343	90	19	3	14	(5	9)	157	61	46	46	2	82	4	7	3	5	5	.50	2	.262	.354	.458
1993 Atlanta	NL	161	597	182	29	2	15	(4	11)	260	110	73	85	0	109	16	5	7	16	6	.73	13	.305	.401	.436
1994 Atlanta	NL	96	380	98	21	4	6	(3	3)	145	56	45	38	0	64	5	5	6	1	3	.25	11	.258	.329	.382
1995 Atlanta	NL	115	431	91	16	2	12	(7	5)	147	60	31	57	2	107	12	2	2	8	5	.62	6	.211	.319	.341
1996 Atlanta	NL	83	265	65	14	1	10	(4	6)	111	48	35	40	3	54	6	0	1	6	0	1.00	7	.245	.356	.419
1997 Atlanta	NL	151	519	160	31	4	17	(9	8)	250	90	70	70	6	101	20	5	9	5	1	.83	13	.308	.405	.482
1998 Chicago	NL	119	361	79	11	3	4	(0	4)	108	49	26	60	1	93	3	3	3	2	2	.50	5	.219	.340	.299
12 ML YEARS		1303	4322	1139	212	31	113	(50	63)	1752	650	487	543	22	885	83	46	39	63	39	.62	77	.264	.354	.405

Ron Blazier

Pitches: Right **Bats:** Right **Pos:** RP   **Ht:** 6'5" **Wt:** 249 **Born:** 7/30/71 **Age:** 27

Year Team	Lg	G	GS	CG	GF	IP	BFP	H	R	ER	HR	SH	SF	HB	TBB	IBB	SO	WP	Bk	W	L	Pct.	ShO	Sv-Op	Hld	ERA
1996 Philadelphia	NL	27	0	0	9	38.1	173	49	26	25	6	3	2	0	10	3	25	3	0	3	1	.750	0	0-0	0	5.87
1997 Philadelphia	NL	36	0	0	7	53.2	240	62	31	30	8	1	4	0	21	3	42	2	0	1	1	.500	0	0-0	0	5.03
2 ML YEARS		63	0	0	16	92	413	111	61	55	14	4	6	0	31	6	67	5	0	4	2	.667	0	0-0	0	5.38

Mike Blowers

Bats: R **Throws:** R **Pos:** 3B-120; PH/PR-15; 1B-8; DH-2   **Ht:** 6'2" **Wt:** 210 **Born:** 4/24/65 **Age:** 34

Year Team	Lg	G	AB	H	2B	3B	HR	(Hm	Rd)	TB	R	RBI	TBB	IBB	SO	HBP	SH	SF	SB	CS	SB%	GDP	Avg	OBP	SLG
1989 New York	AL	13	38	10	0	0	0	(0	0)	10	2	3	3	0	13	0	0	0	0	0	.00	1	.263	.317	.263
1990 New York	AL	48	144	27	4	0	5	(1	4)	46	16	21	12	1	50	0	1	0	1	0	1.00	3	.188	.255	.319
1991 New York	AL	15	35	7	0	0	1	(0	1)	10	3	1	4	0	3	0	1	0	0	0	.00	1	.200	.282	.286
1992 Seattle	AL	31	73	14	3	0	1	(0	1)	20	7	2	6	0	20	0	1	0	0	0	.00	3	.192	.253	.274
1993 Seattle	AL	127	379	106	23	3	15	(8	7)	180	55	57	44	3	98	2	3	1	1	5	.17	12	.280	.357	.475

Year Team	Lg	G	AB	H	2B	3B	HR	(Hm	Rd)	TB	R	RBI	TBB	IBB	SO	HBP	SH	SF	SB	CS	SB%	GDP	Avg	OBP	SLG
1994 Seattle	AL	85	270	78	13	0	9	(3	6)	118	37	49	25	2	60	1	1	3	2	2	.50	12	.289	.348	.437
1995 Seattle	AL	134	439	113	24	1	23	(17	6)	208	59	96	53	0	128	0	3	3	2	1	.67	18	.257	.335	.474
1996 Los Angeles	NL	92	317	84	19	2	6	(4	2)	125	31	38	37	2	77	1	0	3	0	0	.00	11	.265	.341	.394
1997 Seattle	AL	68	150	44	5	0	5	(5	0)	64	22	20	21	1	33	0	4	2	0	0	.00	4	.293	.376	.427
1998 Oakland	AL	129	409	97	24	2	11	(2	9)	158	56	71	39	1	116	1	2	4	1	0	1.00	13	.237	.302	.386
10 ML YEARS		742	2254	580	115	8	76	(40	36)	939	288	358	244	10	598	6	15	16	7	8	.47	78	.257	.329	.417

Doug Bochtler

Pitches: Right **Bats:** Right **Pos:** RP-51   **Ht:** 6'3" **Wt:** 200 **Born:** 7/5/70 **Age:** 28

Year Team	Lg	G	GS	CG	GF	IP	BFP	H	R	ER	HR	SH	SF	HB	TBB	IBB	SO	WP	Bk	W	L	Pct.	ShO	Sv-Op	Hld	ERA
1995 San Diego	NL	34	0	0	11	45.1	181	38	18	18	5	2	1	0	19	0	45	1	0	4	4	.500	0	1-4	8	3.57
1996 San Diego	NL	63	0	0	17	65.2	278	45	25	22	6	5	2	1	39	8	68	8	2	2	4	.333	0	3-7	20	3.02
1997 San Diego	NL	54	0	0	13	60.1	281	51	35	32	3	4	3	1	50	4	46	5	0	3	6	.333	0	2-3	9	4.77
1998 Detroit	AL	51	0	0	11	67.1	312	73	48	46	17	2	3	3	42	6	45	6	0	0	2	.000	0	0-2	2	6.15
4 ML YEARS		202	0	0	52	238.2	1052	207	126	118	31	13	9	5	150	18	204	20	2	9	16	.360	0	6-16	39	4.45

Brian Boehringer

Pitches: Right **Bats:** Both **Pos:** RP-55; SP-1   **Ht:** 6'2" **Wt:** 190 **Born:** 1/8/70 **Age:** 29

Year Team	Lg	G	GS	CG	GF	IP	BFP	H	R	ER	HR	SH	SF	HB	TBB	IBB	SO	WP	Bk	W	L	Pct.	ShO	Sv-Op	Hld	ERA
1995 New York	AL	7	3	0	1	17.2	99	24	27	27	5	0	1	2	22	1	10	3	0	0	3	.000	0	0-1	0	13.75
1996 New York	AL	15	3	0	1	46.1	205	46	28	28	6	3	3	1	21	2	37	1	0	2	4	.333	0	0-1	4	5.44
1997 New York	AL	34	0	0	11	48	210	39	16	14	4	3	2	0	32	6	53	2	0	3	2	.600	0	0-3	5	2.63
1998 San Diego	NL	56	1	0	18	76.1	347	75	38	37	10	5	1	4	45	4	67	1	0	5	2	.714	0	0-1	7	4.36
4 ML YEARS		112	7	0	30	188.1	861	184	109	106	25	11	7	6	120	13	167	7	0	10	11	.476	0	0-6	16	5.07

Tim Bogar

Bats: R **Throws:** R **Pos:** SS-55; 2B-11; 3B-11; PH/PR-10; DH-1   **Ht:** 6'2" **Wt:** 198 **Born:** 10/28/66 **Age:** 32

Year Team	Lg	G	AB	H	2B	3B	HR	(Hm	Rd)	TB	R	RBI	TBB	IBB	SO	HBP	SH	SF	SB	CS	SB%	GDP	Avg	OBP	SLG
1993 New York	NL	78	205	50	13	0	3	(1	2)	72	19	25	14	2	29	3	1	1	0	1	.00	2	.244	.300	.351
1994 New York	NL	50	52	8	0	0	2	(0	2)	14	5	5	4	1	11	0	2	1	1	0	1.00	1	.154	.211	.269
1995 New York	NL	78	145	42	7	0	1	(0	1)	52	17	21	9	0	25	0	2	1	1	0	1.00	2	.290	.329	.359
1996 New York	NL	91	89	19	4	0	0	(0	0)	23	17	6	8	0	20	2	3	2	1	3	.25	0	.213	.287	.258
1997 Houston	NL	97	241	60	14	4	4	(3	1)	94	30	30	24	1	42	3	3	4	4	1	.80	4	.249	.320	.390
1998 Houston	NL	79	156	24	4	1	1	(0	1)	33	12	8	9	2	36	2	1	1	2	1	.67	5	.154	.208	.212
6 ML YEARS		473	888	203	42	5	11	(4	7)	288	100	95	68	6	163	10	12	10	9	6	.60	14	.229	.288	.324

Wade Boggs

Bats: Left **Throws:** Right **Pos:** 3B-78; DH-33; PH/PR-15   **Ht:** 6'2" **Wt:** 197 **Born:** 6/15/58 **Age:** 41

Year Team	Lg	G	AB	H	2B	3B	HR	(Hm	Rd)	TB	R	RBI	TBB	IBB	SO	HBP	SH	SF	SB	CS	SB%	GDP	Avg	OBP	SLG
1982 Boston	AL	104	338	118	14	1	5	(4	1)	149	51	44	35	4	21	0	4	4	1	0	1.00	9	.349	.406	.441
1983 Boston	AL	153	582	210	44	7	5	(2	3)	283	100	74	92	2	36	1	3	7	3	3	.50	15	.361	.444	.486
1984 Boston	AL	158	625	203	31	4	6	(5	1)	260	109	55	89	6	44	0	8	4	3	2	.60	13	.325	.407	.416
1985 Boston	AL	161	653	240	42	3	8	(6	2)	312	107	78	96	5	61	4	3	2	2	1	.67	20	.368	.450	.478
1986 Boston	AL	149	580	207	47	2	8	(3	5)	282	107	71	105	14	44	0	4	4	0	4	.00	11	.357	.453	.486
1987 Boston	AL	147	551	200	40	6	24	(10	14)	324	108	89	105	19	48	2	1	8	1	3	.25	13	.363	.461	.588
1988 Boston	AL	155	584	214	45	6	5	(4	1)	286	128	58	125	18	34	3	0	7	2	3	.40	23	.366	.476	.490
1989 Boston	AL	156	621	205	51	7	3	(2	1)	279	113	54	107	19	51	7	0	7	2	6	.25	19	.330	.430	.449
1990 Boston	AL	155	619	187	44	5	6	(3	3)	259	89	63	87	19	68	1	0	6	0	0	.00	14	.302	.386	.418
1991 Boston	AL	144	546	181	42	2	8	(6	2)	251	93	51	89	25	32	0	0	6	1	2	.33	16	.332	.421	.460
1992 Boston	AL	143	514	133	22	4	7	(4	3)	184	62	50	74	19	31	4	0	6	1	3	.25	10	.259	.353	.358
1993 New York	AL	143	560	169	26	1	2	(1	1)	203	83	59	74	4	49	0	1	9	0	1	.00	10	.302	.378	.363
1994 New York	AL	97	366	125	19	1	11	(6	5)	179	61	55	61	3	29	1	2	4	2	1	.67	10	.342	.433	.489
1995 New York	AL	126	460	149	22	4	5	(4	1)	194	76	63	74	5	50	0	0	5	1	1	.50	13	.324	.412	.422
1996 New York	AL	132	501	156	29	2	2	(2	0)	195	80	41	67	7	32	0	1	5	1	2	.33	10	.311	.389	.389
1997 New York	AL	104	353	103	23	1	4	(0	4)	140	55	28	48	3	38	0	2	4	0	1	.00	10	.292	.373	.397
1998 Tampa Bay	AL	123	435	122	23	4	7	(7	0)	174	51	52	46	6	54	0	0	3	3	2	.60	13	.280	.348	.400
17 ML YEARS		2350	8888	2922	564	60	116	(69	47)	3954	1473	985	1374	178	722	23	29	92	23	35	.40	222	.329	.416	.445

Brian Bohanon

Pitches: Left **Bats:** Left **Pos:** RP-21; SP-18   **Ht:** 6'3" **Wt:** 219 **Born:** 8/1/68 **Age:** 30

Year Team	Lg	G	GS	CG	GF	IP	BFP	H	R	ER	HR	SH	SF	HB	TBB	IBB	SO	WP	Bk	W	L	Pct.	ShO	Sv-Op	Hld	ERA
1990 Texas	AL	11	6	0	1	34	158	40	30	25	6	0	3	2	18	0	15	1	0	0	3	.000	0	0-0	0	6.62
1991 Texas	AL	11	11	1	0	61.1	273	66	35	33	4	2	5	2	23	0	34	3	1	4	3	.571	0	0-0	0	4.84
1992 Texas	AL	18	7	0	3	45.2	220	57	38	32	7	0	2	1	25	0	29	2	0	1	1	.500	0	0-0	0	6.31
1993 Texas	AL	36	8	0	4	92.2	418	107	54	49	8	2	5	4	43	5	45	10	0	4	4	.500	0	0-1	1	4.76
1994 Texas	AL	11	5	0	0	37.1	169	51	31	30	7	1	0	1	8	1	26	0	0	2	2	.500	0	0-0	0	7.23
1995 Detroit	AL	52	10	0	7	105.2	474	121	68	65	10	0	5	4	41	5	63	3	0	1	1	.500	0	1-1	10	5.54

Year Team	Lg	G	GS	CG	GF	IP	BFP	H	R	ER	HR	SH	SF	HB	TBB	IBB	SO	WP	Bk	W	L	Pct.	ShO	Sv-Op	Hld	ERA
1996 Toronto	AL	20	0	0	6	22	112	27	19	19	4	0	2	2	19	4	17	2	0	0	1	.000	0	1-1	2	7.77
1997 New York	NL	19	14	0	0	94.1	412	95	49	40	9	6	0	4	34	2	66	3	1	6	4	.600	0	0-0	0	3.82
1998 NYN-LA	NL	39	18	2	4	151.2	626	121	56	45	13	7	2	11	57	2	111	3	0	7	11	.389	0	0-1	1	2.67
1998 New York	NL	25	4	0	4	54.1	230	47	21	19	4	2	0	6	21	2	39	1	0	2	4	.333	0	0-1	1	3.15
Los Angeles	NL	14	14	2	0	97.1	396	74	35	26	9	5	2	5	36	0	72	2	0	5	7	.417	0	0-0	0	2.40
9 ML YEARS		217	79	3	26	644.2	2862	685	380	338	68	18	24	31	271	17	406	32	2	25	30	.455	0	2-4	14	4.72

Frank Bolick

Bats: B **Throws:** R **Pos:** DH-9; PH/PR-9; 3B-7; 1B-1; RF-1   **Ht:** 5'10" **Wt:** 200 **Born:** 6/28/66 **Age:** 33

Year Team	Lg	G	AB	H	2B	3B	HR	(Hm	Rd)	TB	R	RBI	TBB	IBB	SO	HBP	SH	SF	SB	CS	SB%	GDP	Avg	OBP	SLG
1987 Helena	R+	52	156	39	8	1	10	—	—	79	41	28	41	1	44	3	1	0	4	0	1.00	3	.250	.415	.506
1988 Beloit	A	55	180	41	14	1	2	—	—	63	28	16	43	0	49	1	1	0	3	3	.50	3	.228	.379	.350
Brewers	R	23	80	30	9	3	1	—	—	48	20	20	22	0	8	0	0	3	1	0	1.00	0	.375	.495	.600
Helena	R+	40	131	39	10	1	10	—	—	81	35	28	32	2	31	1	1	2	5	1	.83	2	.298	.434	.618
1989 Beloit	A	88	299	90	23	0	9	—	—	140	44	41	47	5	52	6	0	2	9	6	.60	3	.301	.404	.468
1990 Stockton	A+	50	164	51	9	1	8	—	—	86	39	36	38	1	33	2	0	5	5	3	.63	0	.311	.435	.524
San Berndno	A+	78	277	92	24	4	10	—	—	154	61	66	53	6	53	2	0	8	3	6	.33	2	.332	.432	.556
1991 Jacksnville	AA	136	468	119	19	0	16	—	—	186	69	73	84	3	115	5	2	7	5	4	.56	7	.254	.369	.397
1992 Jacksnville	AA	63	224	60	9	0	13	—	—	108	32	42	42	1	38	1	0	4	1	4	.20	3	.268	.380	.482
Calgary	AAA	78	274	79	18	6	14	—	—	151	35	54	39	2	52	1	1	4	4	4	.50	4	.288	.374	.551
1993 Ottawa	AAA	2	8	1	0	0	0	—	—	1	0	0	0	0	0	0	0	0	0	0	.00	0	.125	.125	.125
1994 Buffalo	AAA	35	95	25	6	0	2	—	—	37	18	8	27	3	29	2	1	2	0	1	.00	0	.263	.429	.389
New Haven	AA	85	301	76	13	0	21	—	—	152	53	63	41	3	57	3	1	2	2	2	.50	10	.252	.346	.505
1995 Colo Sprngs	AAA	23	68	16	3	1	2	—	—	27	8	7	8	0	14	0	0	0	0	0	.00	0	.235	.316	.397
Lubbock	IND	59	214	76	17	1	7	—	—	116	42	56	46	7	33	1	0	5	1	1	.50	5	.355	.462	.542
Buffalo	AAA	20	65	16	6	0	3	—	—	31	11	10	3	0	13	1	0	0	0	1	.00	3	.246	.290	.477
1996 Lubbock	IND	33	125	45	15	1	6	—	—	82	22	35	19	2	14	0	0	2	0	1	.00	0	.376	.452	.656
1997 Midland	AA	28	97	32	5	1	8	—	—	63	26	27	26	0	18	1	0	0	0	0	.00	1	.330	.476	.649
Vancouver	AAA	102	362	110	27	4	16	—	—	193	61	66	46	4	70	1	1	2	4	1	.80	12	.304	.382	.533
1998 Vancouver	AAA	75	269	71	10	2	13	—	—	124	40	29	28	1	47	2	0	0	0	0	.00	9	.264	.336	.461
1993 Montreal	NL	95	213	45	13	0	4	(2	2)	70	25	24	23	2	37	4	0	2	1	0	1.00	4	.211	.298	.329
1998 Anaheim	AL	21	45	7	2	0	1	(0	1)	12	3	2	11	0	8	0	0	0	0	0	.00	1	.156	.321	.267
2 ML YEARS		116	258	52	15	0	5	(2	3)	82	28	26	34	2	45	4	0	2	1	0	1.00	4	.202	.302	.318

Barry Bonds

Bats: Left **Throws:** Left **Pos:** LF-155; PH/PR-2   **Ht:** 6'2" **Wt:** 206 **Born:** 7/24/64 **Age:** 34

Year Team	Lg	G	AB	H	2B	3B	HR	(Hm	Rd)	TB	R	RBI	TBB	IBB	SO	HBP	SH	SF	SB	CS	SB%	GDP	Avg	OBP	SLG
1986 Pittsburgh	NL	113	413	92	26	3	16	(9	7)	172	72	48	65	2	102	2	2	2	36	7	.84	4	.223	.330	.416
1987 Pittsburgh	NL	150	551	144	34	9	25	(12	13)	271	99	59	54	3	88	3	0	3	32	10	.76	4	.261	.329	.492
1988 Pittsburgh	NL	144	538	152	30	5	24	(14	10)	264	97	58	72	14	82	2	0	3	17	11	.61	3	.283	.368	.491
1989 Pittsburgh	NL	159	580	144	34	6	19	(7	12)	247	96	58	93	22	93	1	1	4	32	10	.76	9	.248	.351	.426
1990 Pittsburgh	NL	151	519	156	32	3	33	(14	19)	293	104	114	93	15	83	3	0	6	52	13	.80	8	.301	.406	**.565**
1991 Pittsburgh	NL	153	510	149	28	5	25	(12	13)	262	95	116	107	25	73	4	0	13	43	13	.77	8	.292	**.410**	.514
1992 Pittsburgh	NL	140	473	147	36	5	34	(15	19)	295	109	103	127	32	69	5	0	7	39	8	.83	9	.311	**.456**	**.624**
1993 San Francisco	NL	159	539	181	38	4	46	(21	25)	365	129	123	126	43	79	2	0	7	29	12	.71	11	.336	**.458**	**.677**
1994 San Francisco	NL	112	391	122	18	1	37	(15	22)	253	89	81	74	18	43	6	0	3	29	9	.76	3	.312	.426	.647
1995 San Francisco	NL	144	506	149	30	7	33	(16	17)	292	109	104	120	22	83	5	0	4	31	10	.76	12	.294	**.431**	.577
1996 San Francisco	NL	158	517	159	27	3	42	(23	19)	318	122	129	151	30	76	1	0	6	40	7	.85	11	.308	.461	.615
1997 San Francisco	NL	159	532	155	26	5	40	(24	16)	311	123	101	**145**	34	87	8	0	5	37	8	.82	13	.291	.446	.585
1998 San Francisco	NL	156	552	167	44	7	37	(21	16)	336	120	122	130	29	92	8	1	6	28	12	.70	15	.303	.438	.609
13 ML YEARS		1898	6621	1917	403	63	411	(203	208)	3679	1364	1216	1357	289	1050	50	4	68	445	130	.77	110	.290	.411	.556

Ricky Bones

Pitches: Right **Bats:** Right **Pos:** RP-32   **Ht:** 6'0" **Wt:** 190 **Born:** 4/7/69 **Age:** 30

Year Team	Lg	G	GS	CG	GF	IP	BFP	H	R	ER	HR	SH	SF	HB	TBB	IBB	SO	WP	Bk	W	L	Pct.	ShO	Sv-Op	Hld	ERA
1998 Salt Lake *	AAA	8	8	0	0	47.1	200	41	20	18	5	1	3	3	19	1	41	1	0	5	1	.833	0	0- —	—	3.42
Omaha *	AAA	3	3	0	0	14.2	70	19	16	14	5	0	0	0	10	1	8	1	0	1	2	.333	0	0- —	—	8.59
1991 San Diego	NL	11	11	0	0	54	234	57	33	29	3	0	4	0	18	0	31	4	0	4	6	.400	0	0-0	0	4.83
1992 Milwaukee	AL	31	28	0	0	163.1	705	169	90	83	27	2	5	9	48	0	65	3	2	9	10	.474	0	0-0	0	4.57
1993 Milwaukee	AL	32	31	3	1	203.2	883	222	122	110	28	5	7	8	63	3	63	6	1	11	11	.500	0	0-0	0	4.86
1994 Milwaukee	AL	24	24	4	0	170.2	708	166	76	65	17	4	5	3	45	1	57	8	0	10	9	.526	1	0-0	0	3.43
1995 Milwaukee	AL	32	31	3	0	200.1	877	218	100	103	26	3	11	4	83	2	77	5	2	10	12	.455	0	0-0	0	4.63
1996 Mil-NYA	AL	36	24	0	2	152	699	184	115	105	30	5	5	10	68	2	63	2	0	7	14	.333	0	0-0	3	6.22
1997 Cin-KC	NL	30	13	1	2	96	450	133	81	72	12	3	8	7	36	4	44	1	0	4	8	.333	0	0-1	2	6.75
1998 Kansas City	AL	32	0	0	12	53.1	231	49	18	18	4	5	0	1	24	5	38	2	0	2	2	.500	0	1-2	3	3.04
1996 Milwaukee	AL	32	23	0	2	145	658	170	104	94	28	4	4	9	62	2	59	2	0	7	14	.333	0	0-0	3	5.83
New York	AL	4	1	0	0	7	41	14	11	11	2	1	1	1	6	0	4	0	0	0	0	.000	0	0-0	0	14.14
1997 Cincinnati	NL	9	2	0	2	17.2	98	31	22	20	2	1	2	2	11	2	11	0	0	0	1	.000	0	0-0	0	10.19
Kansas City	AL	21	11	1	2	78.1	352	102	59	52	10	2	6	5	25	2	36	1	0	4	7	.364	0	0-1	2	5.97
8 ML YEARS		228	162	11	19	1093.1	4787	1198	643	585	147	27	45	42	385	17	438	31	5	57	72	.442	1	1-3	8	4.82

Bobby Bonilla

Bats: Both   **Throws:** Right   **Pos:** 3B-85; LF-12; PH/PR-5   **Ht:** 6'3"   **Wt:** 240   **Born:** 2/23/63   **Age:** 36

Year Team	Lg	G	AB	H	2B	3B	HR	(Hm Rd)	TB	R	RBI	TBB	IBB	SO	HBP	SH	SF	SB	CS	SB%	GDP	Avg	OBP	SLG
1986 ChA-Pit		138	426	109	16	4	3	(2 1)	142	55	43	62	3	88	2	5	1	8	5	.62	9	.256	.352	.333
1987 Pittsburgh	NL	141	466	140	33	3	15	(7 8)	224	58	77	39	4	64	2	0	8	3	5	.38	8	.300	.351	.481
1988 Pittsburgh	NL	159	584	160	32	7	24	(9 15)	278	87	100	85	19	82	4	0	8	3	5	.38	4	.274	.366	.476
1989 Pittsburgh	NL	163	616	173	37	10	24	(13 11)	302	96	86	76	20	93	1	0	5	8	8	.50	10	.281	.358	.490
1990 Pittsburgh	NL	160	625	175	39	7	32	(13 19)	324	112	120	45	9	103	1	0	15	4	3	.57	11	.280	.322	.518
1991 Pittsburgh	NL	157	577	174	44	6	18	(9 9)	284	102	100	90	8	67	2	0	11	2	4	.33	14	.302	.391	.492
1992 New York	NL	128	438	109	23	0	19	(5 14)	189	62	70	66	10	73	1	0	1	4	3	.57	11	.249	.348	.432
1993 New York	NL	139	502	133	21	3	34	(18 16)	262	81	87	72	11	96	0	0	8	3	3	.50	12	.265	.352	.522
1994 New York	NL	108	403	117	24	1	20	(8 12)	203	60	67	55	9	101	0	0	2	1	3	.25	10	.290	.374	.504
1995 NYN-Bal		141	554	182	37	8	28	(14 14)	319	96	99	54	10	79	2	0	4	0	5	.00	22	.329	.388	.576
1996 Baltimore	AL	159	595	171	27	5	28	(9 19)	292	107	116	75	5	85	5	0	17	1	3	.25	13	.287	.363	.491
1997 Florida	NL	153	562	167	39	3	17	(8 9)	263	77	96	73	8	94	5	0	8	6	6	.50	18	.297	.378	.468
1998 Fla-LA	NL	100	333	83	11	1	11	(8 3)	129	39	45	41	4	59	0	0	6	1	2	.33	16	.249	.326	.387
1986 Chicago	AL	75	234	63	10	2	2	(2 0)	83	27	26	33	2	49	1	2	1	4	1	.80	4	.269	.361	.355
Pittsburgh	NL	63	192	46	6	2	1	(0 1)	59	28	17	29	1	39	1	3	0	4	4	.50	5	.240	.342	.307
1995 New York	NL	80	317	103	25	4	18	(7 11)	190	49	53	31	10	48	1	0	2	0	3	.00	11	.325	.385	.599
Baltimore	AL	61	237	79	12	4	10	(7 3)	129	47	46	23	0	31	1	0	2	0	2	.00	11	.333	.392	.544
1998 Florida	NL	28	97	27	5	0	4	(3 1)	44	11	15	12	1	22	0	0	1	0	1	.00	6	.278	.355	.454
Los Angeles	NL	72	236	56	6	1	7	(5 2)	85	28	30	29	3	37	0	0	5	1	1	.50	10	.237	.315	.360
13 ML YEARS		1846	6681	1893	383	58	273	(123 150)	3211	1032	1106	833	122	1084	25	5	94	44	55	.44	158	.283	.360	.481

Aaron Boone

Bats: R   **Throws:** R   **Pos:** 3B-52; PH/PR-7; 2B-1; SS-1   **Ht:** 6'2"   **Wt:** 200   **Born:** 3/9/73   **Age:** 26

Year Team	Lg	G	AB	H	2B	3B	HR	(Hm Rd)	TB	R	RBI	TBB	IBB	SO	HBP	SH	SF	SB	CS	SB%	GDP	Avg	OBP	SLG
1994 Billings	R+	67	256	70	15	5	7	— —	116	48	55	36	3	35	3	0	6	6	3	.67	7	.273	.362	.453
1995 Chattanooga	AA	23	66	15	3	0	0	— —	18	6	3	5	0	12	0	1	2	2	0	1.00	5	.227	.274	.273
Winston-Sal	A+	108	395	103	19	1	14	— —	166	61	50	43	7	77	9	4	2	11	7	.61	4	.261	.345	.420
1996 Chattanooga	AA	136	548	158	44	7	17	— —	267	86	95	38	4	77	5	1	4	21	10	.68	5	.288	.338	.487
1997 Indianapolis	AAA	131	476	138	30	4	22	— —	242	79	75	40	3	81	1	3	3	12	4	.75	11	.290	.344	.508
1998 Indianapolis	AAA	87	332	80	18	1	7	— —	121	56	38	31	2	71	8	0	6	17	5	.77	6	.241	.316	.364
1997 Cincinnati	NL	16	49	12	1	0	0	(0 0)	13	5	5	2	0	5	0	1	0	1	0	1.00	1	.245	.275	.265
1998 Cincinnati	NL	58	181	51	13	2	2	(2 0)	74	24	28	15	1	36	5	3	2	6	1	.86	3	.282	.350	.409
2 ML YEARS		74	230	63	14	2	2	(2 0)	87	29	33	17	1	41	5	4	2	7	1	.88	4	.274	.335	.378

Bret Boone

Bats: Right   **Throws:** Right   **Pos:** 2B-156; PH/PR-2   **Ht:** 5'10"   **Wt:** 180   **Born:** 4/6/69   **Age:** 30

Year Team	Lg	G	AB	H	2B	3B	HR	(Hm Rd)	TB	R	RBI	TBB	IBB	SO	HBP	SH	SF	SB	CS	SB%	GDP	Avg	OBP	SLG
1992 Seattle	AL	33	129	25	4	0	4	(2 2)	41	15	15	4	0	34	1	1	0	1	1	.50	4	.194	.224	.318
1993 Seattle	AL	76	271	68	12	2	12	(7 5)	120	31	38	17	1	52	4	6	4	2	3	.40	6	.251	.301	.443
1994 Cincinnati	NL	108	381	122	25	2	12	(5 7)	187	59	68	24	1	74	8	5	6	3	4	.43	10	.320	.368	.491
1995 Cincinnati	NL	138	513	137	34	2	15	(6 9)	220	63	68	41	0	84	6	5	5	5	1	.83	14	.267	.326	.429
1996 Cincinnati	NL	142	520	121	21	3	12	(5 7)	184	56	69	31	0	100	3	5	9	3	2	.60	9	.233	.275	.354
1997 Cincinnati	NL	139	443	99	25	1	7	(4 3)	147	40	46	45	4	101	4	4	5	5	5	.50	11	.223	.298	.332
1998 Cincinnati	NL	157	583	155	38	1	24	(13 11)	267	76	95	48	3	104	4	9	4	6	4	.60	23	.266	.324	.458
7 ML YEARS		793	2840	727	159	11	86	(44 42)	1166	340	399	210	9	549	30	35	33	25	20	.56	77	.256	.311	.411

Josh Booty

Bats: Right   **Throws:** Right   **Pos:** 3B-7   **Ht:** 6'3"   **Wt:** 220   **Born:** 4/29/75   **Age:** 24

Year Team	Lg	G	AB	H	2B	3B	HR	(Hm Rd)	TB	R	RBI	TBB	IBB	SO	HBP	SH	SF	SB	CS	SB%	GDP	Avg	OBP	SLG
1994 Marlins	R	10	36	8	0	0	1	— —	11	5	2	5	0	8	0	1	0	1	0	1.00	2	.222	.317	.306
Elmira	A-	4	16	4	1	0	0	— —	5	1	1	0	0	4	0	0	0	0	0	.00	1	.250	.250	.313
1995 Kane County	A	31	109	11	2	0	1	— —	16	6	6	11	0	45	0	0	1	1	0	1.00	1	.101	.182	.147
Elmira	A-	74	287	63	18	1	6	— —	101	33	37	19	0	85	5	0	2	4	4	.50	12	.220	.278	.352
1996 Kane County	A	128	475	98	25	1	21	— —	188	62	87	46	0	195	1	1	6	2	3	.40	11	.206	.275	.396
1997 Portland	AA	122	448	94	19	2	20	— —	177	42	69	27	1	166	1	0	4	2	2	.50	12	.210	.254	.395
1998 Charlotte	AAA	38	127	18	3	0	3	— —	30	9	11	7	2	44	0	0	2	0	1	.00	5	.142	.184	.236
Portland	AA	71	247	50	8	3	10	— —	94	28	39	20	0	74	1	1	4	1	1	.50	10	.202	.261	.381
1996 Florida	NL	2	2	1	0	0	0	(0 0)	1	1	0	0	0	0	0	0	0	0	0	.00	0	.500	.500	.500
1997 Florida	NL	4	5	3	0	0	0	(0 0)	3	2	1	1	0	1	0	0	0	0	0	.00	1	.600	.667	.600
1998 Florida	NL	7	19	3	1	0	0	(0 0)	4	0	3	3	0	8	0	0	0	0	0	.00	1	.158	.273	.211
3 ML YEARS		13	26	7	1	0	0	(0 0)	8	3	4	4	0	9	0	0	0	0	0	.00	1	.269	.367	.308

Pat Borders

Bats: Right **Throws:** Right **Pos:** C-53; PH/PR-3; 3B-1   **Ht:** 6'2" **Wt:** 200 **Born:** 5/14/63 **Age:** 36

Year Team	Lg	G	AB	H	2B	3B	HR	(Hm	Rd)	TB	R	RBI	TBB	IBB	SO	HBP	SH	SF	SB	CS	SB%	GDP	Avg	OBP	SLG
1988 Toronto	AL	56	154	42	6	3	5	(2	3)	69	15	21	3	0	24	0	2	1	0	0	.00	5	.273	.285	.448
1989 Toronto	AL	94	241	62	11	1	3	(1	2)	84	22	29	11	2	45	1	1	1	2	1	.67	7	.257	.290	.349
1990 Toronto	AL	125	346	99	24	2	15	(10	5)	172	36	49	18	2	57	0	1	3	0	1	.00	17	.286	.319	.497
1991 Toronto	AL	105	291	71	17	0	5	(2	3)	103	22	36	11	1	45	1	6	3	0	0	.00	8	.244	.271	.354
1992 Toronto	AL	138	480	116	26	2	13	(7	6)	185	47	53	33	3	75	2	1	5	1	1	.50	11	.242	.290	.385
1993 Toronto	AL	138	488	124	30	0	9	(6	3)	181	38	55	20	2	66	2	7	3	2	2	.50	18	.254	.285	.371
1994 Toronto	AL	85	295	73	13	1	3	(3	0)	97	24	26	15	0	50	0	1	1	1	1	.50	7	.247	.284	.329
1995 KC-Hou		63	178	37	8	1	4	(1	3)	59	15	13	9	2	29	0	0	0	0	0	.00	3	.208	.246	.331
1996 StL-Cal-ChA		76	220	61	7	0	5	(3	2)	83	15	18	9	0	43	0	5	0	0	2	.00	4	.277	.306	.377
1997 Cleveland	AL	55	159	47	7	1	4	(0	4)	68	17	15	9	0	27	2	0	0	0	2	.00	5	.296	.341	.428
1998 Cleveland	AL	54	160	38	6	0	0	(0	0)	44	12	6	10	0	40	2	2	1	0	2	.00	3	.238	.289	.275
1995 Kansas City	AL	52	143	33	8	1	4	(1	3)	55	14	13	7	1	22	0	0	0	0	0	.00	1	.231	.267	.385
Houston	NL	11	35	4	0	0	0	(0	0)	4	1	0	2	1	7	0	0	0	0	0	.00	2	.114	.162	.114
1996 St. Louis	NL	26	69	22	3	0	0	(0	0)	25	3	4	1	0	14	0	1	0	0	1	.00	1	.319	.329	.362
California	AL	19	57	13	3	0	2	(2	0)	22	6	8	3	0	11	0	1	0	0	1	.00	1	.228	.267	.386
Chicago	AL	31	94	26	1	0	3	(1	2)	36	6	6	5	0	18	0	3	0	0	0	.00	2	.277	.313	.383
11 ML YEARS		989	3012	770	155	11	66	(35	31)	1145	263	321	148	12	501	10	26	18	6	12	.33	88	.256	.291	.380

Mike Bordick

Bats: Right **Throws:** Right **Pos:** SS-150; PH/PR-1   **Ht:** 5'11" **Wt:** 175 **Born:** 7/21/65 **Age:** 33

Year Team	Lg	G	AB	H	2B	3B	HR	(Hm	Rd)	TB	R	RBI	TBB	IBB	SO	HBP	SH	SF	SB	CS	SB%	GDP	Avg	OBP	SLG
1990 Oakland	AL	25	14	1	0	0	0	(0	0)	1	0	0	1	0	4	0	0	0	0	0	.00	0	.071	.133	.071
1991 Oakland	AL	90	235	56	5	1	0	(0	0)	63	21	21	14	0	37	3	12	1	3	4	.43	3	.238	.289	.268
1992 Oakland	AL	154	504	151	19	4	3	(3	0)	187	62	48	40	2	59	9	14	5	12	6	.67	10	.300	.358	.371
1993 Oakland	AL	159	546	136	21	2	3	(2	1)	170	60	48	60	2	58	11	10	6	10	10	.50	9	.249	.332	.311
1994 Oakland	AL	114	391	99	18	4	2	(1	1)	131	38	37	38	1	44	3	3	5	7	2	.78	9	.253	.320	.335
1995 Oakland	AL	126	428	113	13	0	8	(2	6)	150	46	44	35	2	48	5	7	3	11	3	.79	8	.264	.325	.350
1996 Oakland	AL	155	525	126	18	4	5	(2	3)	167	46	54	52	0	59	1	4	5	5	6	.45	8	.240	.307	.318
1997 Baltimore	AL	153	509	120	19	1	7	(5	2)	162	55	46	33	1	66	2	12	4	0	2	.00	23	.236	.283	.318
1998 Baltimore	AL	151	465	121	29	1	13	(10	3)	191	59	51	39	0	65	10	15	4	6	7	.46	13	.260	.328	.411
9 ML YEARS		1127	3617	923	142	17	41	(25	16)	1222	387	349	312	8	440	44	77	33	54	40	.57	83	.255	.319	.338

Toby Borland

Pitches: Right **Bats:** Right **Pos:** RP-6   **Ht:** 6'6" **Wt:** 193 **Born:** 5/29/69 **Age:** 30

Year Team	Lg	G	GS	CG	GF	IP	BFP	H	R	ER	HR	SH	SF	HB	TBB	IBB	SO	WP	Bk	W	L	Pct.	ShO	Sv-Op	Hld	ERA
1998 Reading *	AA	8	0	0	8	9.1	51	18	12	10	4	1	0	0	5	0	13	1	0	1	3	.250	0	3- -	—	9.64
Scranton-WB *	AAA	13	0	0	8	12.2	52	14	8	8	1	0	1	1	3	0	15	1	0	0	2	.000	0	5- -	—	5.68
Charlotte *	AAA	19	0	0	6	36.2	158	33	12	11	3	0	1	1	21	1	26	4	1	3	0	1.000	0	1- -	—	2.70
1994 Philadelphia	NL	24	0	0	7	34.1	144	31	10	9	1	1	0	4	14	3	26	4	0	1	0	1.000	0	1-1	0	2.36
1995 Philadelphia	NL	50	0	0	18	74	339	81	37	31	3	3	2	5	37	7	59	12	0	1	3	.250	0	6-9	11	3.77
1996 Philadelphia	NL	69	0	0	11	90.2	399	83	51	41	9	4	1	3	43	3	76	10	0	7	3	.700	0	0-2	10	4.07
1997 NYN-Bos		16	0	0	5	16.2	89	17	14	14	2	0	0	3	21	0	8	3	0	0	1	.000	0	1-2	1	7.56
1998 Philadelphia	NL	6	0	0	3	9	39	8	5	5	1	1	0	0	5	0	9	2	0	0	0	.000	0	0-0	1	5.00
1997 New York	NL	13	0	0	5	13.1	65	11	9	9	1	0	0	1	14	0	7	3	0	0	1	.000	0	1-2	1	6.08
Boston	AL	3	0	0	0	3.1	24	6	5	5	1	0	0	2	7	0	1	0	0	0	0	.000	0	0-0	0	13.50
5 ML YEARS		165	0	0	44	224.2	1010	220	117	100	16	9	3	15	120	13	178	31	0	9	7	.563	0	8-14	22	4.01

Joe Borowski

Pitches: Right **Bats:** Right **Pos:** RP-8   **Ht:** 6'2" **Wt:** 225 **Born:** 5/4/71 **Age:** 28

Year Team	Lg	G	GS	CG	GF	IP	BFP	H	R	ER	HR	SH	SF	HB	TBB	IBB	SO	WP	Bk	W	L	Pct.	ShO	Sv-Op	Hld	ERA
1998 Columbus *	AAA	45	0	0	10	73.2	320	66	25	24	6	3	4	2	39	1	67	3	0	3	3	.500	0	4- -	—	2.93
1995 Baltimore	AL	6	0	0	3	7.1	30	5	1	1	0	0	0	0	4	0	3	0	0	0	0	.000	0	0-0	0	1.23
1996 Atlanta	NL	22	0	0	8	26	121	33	15	14	4	5	0	1	13	4	15	1	0	4	4	.333	0	0-0	1	4.85
1997 Atl-NYA		21	0	0	9	26	123	29	13	12	2	1	0	0	20	5	8	0	0	2	3	.400	0	0-0	2	4.15
1998 New York	AL	8	0	0	6	9.2	42	11	7	7	0	0	0	0	4	0	7	0	0	1	0	1.000	0	0-0	0	6.52
1997 Atlanta	NL	20	0	0	8	24	111	27	11	10	2	1	0	0	16	4	6	0	0	2	2	.500	0	0-0	2	3.75
New York	AL	1	0	0	1	2	12	2	2	2	0	0	0	0	4	1	2	0	0	0	1	.000	0	0-0	0	9.00
4 ML YEARS		57	0	0	26	69	316	78	36	34	6	6	0	1	41	9	33	1	0	5	7	.417	0	0-0	3	4.43

Shawn Boskie

Pitches: Right **Bats:** Right **Pos:** SP-5   **Ht:** 6'3" **Wt:** 210 **Born:** 3/28/67 **Age:** 32

Year Team	Lg	G	GS	CG	GF	IP	BFP	H	R	ER	HR	SH	SF	HB	TBB	IBB	SO	WP	Bk	W	L	Pct.	ShO	Sv-Op	Hld	ERA
1998 Ottawa *	AAA	13	13	0	0	87	375	100	48	44	7	0	2	5	21	1	51	5	0	5	7	.417	0	0- -	—	4.55
1990 Chicago	NL	15	15	1	0	97.2	415	99	42	40	8	8	2	1	31	3	49	3	2	5	6	.455	0	0-0	0	3.69
1991 Chicago	NL	28	20	0	2	129	582	150	78	75	14	8	6	5	52	4	62	1	1	4	9	.308	0	0-0	0	5.23
1992 Chicago	NL	23	18	0	2	91.2	393	96	55	51	14	9	6	4	36	3	39	5	1	5	11	.313	0	0-0	0	5.01

	HOW MUCH HE PITCHED						WHAT HE GAVE UP												THE RESULTS						
Year Team	Lg	G	GS	CG	GF	IP	BFP	H	R	ER	HR	SH	SF	HB	TBB	IBB	SO	WP	Bk	W	L	Pct.	ShO	Sv-Op	Hld	ERA
1993 Chicago	NL	39	2	0	10	65.2	277	63	30	25	7	4	1	7	21	2	39	5	0	5	3	.625	0	0-3	6	3.43
1994 ChN-Phi-Sea		22	15	1	1	90.2	394	92	58	51	15	2	3	3	30	3	61	7	0	4	7	.364	0	0-1	0	5.06
1995 California	AL	20	20	1	0	111.2	494	127	73	70	16	4	6	7	25	0	51	4	0	7	7	.500	0	0-0	0	5.64
1996 California	AL	37	28	1	1	189.1	860	226	126	112	**40**	6	4	**13**	67	7	133	10	0	12	11	.522	0	0-0	1	5.32
1997 Baltimore	AL	28	9	0	8	77	349	95	57	55	14	2	7	2	26	1	50	1	0	6	6	.500	0	1-1	1	6.43
1998 Montreal	NL	5	5	0	0	17.2	90	34	21	18	5	1	1	2	4	1	10	0	0	1	3	.250	0	0-0	0	9.17
1994 Chicago	NL	2	0	0	0	3.2	14	3	0	0	0	0	0	0	0	0	2	1	0	0	0	.000	0	0-0	0	0.00
Philadelphia		18	14	1	1	84.1	367	85	56	49	14	2	3	3	29	2	59	6	0	4	6	.400	0	0-1	0	5.23
Seattle	AL	2	1	0	0	2.2	13	4	2	2	1	0	0	0	1	1	0	0	0	0	1	.000	0	0-0	0	6.75
9 ML YEARS		217	132	4	24	870.1	3854	982	540	497	133	44	36	44	292	24	494	36	4	49	63	.438	0	1-5	8	5.14

Ricky Bottalico

Pitches: Right **Bats:** Left **Pos:** RP-39 **Ht:** 6'1" **Wt:** 217 **Born:** 8/26/69 **Age:** 29

	HOW MUCH HE PITCHED						WHAT HE GAVE UP												THE RESULTS						
Year Team	Lg	G	GS	CG	GF	IP	BFP	H	R	ER	HR	SH	SF	HB	TBB	IBB	SO	WP	Bk	W	L	Pct.	ShO	Sv-Op	Hld	ERA
1998 Scranton-WB *	AAA	10	5	0	3	12.1	54	8	4	4	1	1	1	1	9	0	4	1	0	1	0	1.000	0	1--		2.92
1994 Philadelphia	NL	3	0	0	3	3	13	3	0	0	0	0	0	0	1	0	3	0	0	0	0	.000	0	0-0	0	0.00
1995 Philadelphia	NL	62	0	0	20	87.2	350	50	25	24	7	3	1	4	42	3	87	1	0	5	3	.625	0	1-5	**20**	2.46
1996 Philadelphia	NL	61	0	0	56	67.2	269	47	24	24	6	4	2	2	23	2	74	3	0	4	5	.444	0	34-38	0	3.19
1997 Philadelphia	NL	69	0	0	61	74	324	68	31	30	7	1	2	2	42	4	89	3	0	2	5	.286	0	34-41	0	3.65
1998 Philadelphia	NL	39	0	0	28	43.1	206	54	31	31	7	1	2	1	25	5	27	2	0	1	5	.167	0	6-7	3	6.44
5 ML YEARS		234	0	0	168	275.2	1162	222	111	109	27	9	7	9	133	14	280	9	0	12	18	.400	0	75-91	23	3.56

Kent Bottenfield

Pitches: Right **Bats:** Right **Pos:** RP-27; SP-17 **Ht:** 6'3" **Wt:** 240 **Born:** 11/14/68 **Age:** 30

	HOW MUCH HE PITCHED						WHAT HE GAVE UP												THE RESULTS						
Year Team	Lg	G	GS	CG	GF	IP	BFP	H	R	ER	HR	SH	SF	HB	TBB	IBB	SO	WP	Bk	W	L	Pct.	ShO	Sv-Op	Hld	ERA
1992 Montreal	NL	10	4	0	2	32.1	135	26	9	8	1	1	2	1	11	1	14	0	0	1	2	.333	0	1-1	1	2.23
1993 Mon-Col	NL	37	25	1	2	159.2	710	179	102	90	24	**21**	4	6	71	3	63	4	1	5	10	.333	0	0-0	0	5.07
1994 Col-SF	NL	16	1	0	3	26.1	121	33	18	18	2	1	0	2	10	0	15	2	0	3	1	.750	0	1-1	0	6.15
1996 Chicago	NL	48	0	0	10	61.2	258	59	25	18	3	5	0	3	19	4	33	2	0	3	5	.375	0	1-3	4	2.63
1997 Chicago	NL	64	0	0	20	84	361	82	39	36	13	4	4	2	35	7	74	2	0	2	3	.400	0	2-4	8	3.86
1998 St. Louis	NL	44	17	0	11	133.2	578	128	72	66	13	11	3	4	57	3	98	3	2	4	6	.400	0	4-5	6	4.44
1993 Montreal	NL	23	11	0	2	83	373	93	49	38	11	11	1	5	33	2	33	4	1	2	5	.286	0	0-0	0	4.12
Colorado	NL	14	14	1	0	76.2	337	86	53	52	13	10	3	1	38	1	30	0	0	3	5	.375	0	0-0	0	6.10
1994 Colorado	NL	15	1	0	3	24.2	112	28	16	16	1	1	0	2	10	0	15	2	0	3	1	.750	0	1-1	0	5.84
San Francisco	NL	1	0	0	0	1.2	9	5	2	2	1	0	0	0	0	0	0	0	0	0	0	.000	0	0-0	0	10.80
6 ML YEARS		219	47	1	48	497.2	2163	507	265	236	56	43	13	18	203	18	297	13	3	18	27	.400	0	9-14	19	4.27

Rafael Bournigal

Bats: R **Throws:** R **Pos:** 2B-48; SS-38; PH/PR-7; DH-1 **Ht:** 5'11" **Wt:** 176 **Born:** 5/12/66 **Age:** 33

	BATTING																	BASERUNNING				PERCENTAGES		
Year Team	Lg	G	AB	H	2B	3B	HR	(Hm	Rd)	TB	R	RBI	TBB	IBB	SO	HBP	SH	SF	SB	CS	SB%	GDP	Avg	OBP	SLG
1992 Los Angeles	NL	10	20	3	1	0	0	(0	0)	4	1	0	1	0	2	1	0	0	0	0	.00	0	.150	.227	.200
1993 Los Angeles	NL	8	18	9	1	0	0	(0	0)	10	0	3	0	0	2	0	0	0	0	0	.00	0	.500	.500	.556
1994 Los Angeles	NL	40	116	26	3	1	0	(0	0)	31	2	11	9	1	5	2	5	0	0	0	.00	4	.224	.291	.267
1996 Oakland	AL	88	252	61	14	2	0	(0	0)	79	33	18	16	0	19	1	8	0	4	3	.57	6	.242	.290	.313
1997 Oakland	AL	79	222	62	9	0	1	(0	1)	74	29	20	16	1	19	4	7	0	2	1	.67	11	.279	.339	.333
1998 Oakland	AL	85	209	47	11	0	1	(1	0)	61	23	19	10	1	11	2	6	2	6	1	.86	6	.225	.265	.292
6 ML YEARS		310	837	208	39	3	2	(1	1)	259	88	71	52	3	58	10	26	2	12	5	.71	27	.249	.300	.309

Chad Bradford

Pitches: Right **Bats:** Right **Pos:** RP-29 **Ht:** 6'5" **Wt:** 205 **Born:** 9/14/74 **Age:** 24

	HOW MUCH HE PITCHED						WHAT HE GAVE UP												THE RESULTS						
Year Team	Lg	G	GS	CG	GF	IP	BFP	H	R	ER	HR	SH	SF	HB	TBB	IBB	SO	WP	Bk	W	L	Pct.	ShO	Sv-Op	Hld	ERA
1996 Hickory	A	28	0	0	27	30	121	21	7	3	1	2	1	3	7	1	27	0	0	0	2	.000	0	18--	—	0.90
1997 Winston-Sal	A+	46	0	0	41	54.2	247	51	30	24	2	4	0	5	25	5	43	2	0	3	7	.300	0	15--	—	3.95
1998 Birmingham	AA	10	0	0	7	17.1	72	13	6	5	2	0	0	0	8	0	14	2	0	1	1	.500	0	1--	—	2.60
Calgary	AAA	29	0	0	10	51	205	50	12	11	3	0	1	1	11	2	27	2	2	4	1	.800	0	0--	—	1.94
1998 Chicago	AL	29	0	0	8	30.2	125	27	16	11	0	0	0	0	7	0	11	1	1	2	1	.667	0	1-3	9	3.23

Ryan Bradley

Pitches: Right **Bats:** Right **Pos:** RP-4; SP-1 **Ht:** 6'4" **Wt:** 226 **Born:** 10/26/75 **Age:** 23

	HOW MUCH HE PITCHED						WHAT HE GAVE UP												THE RESULTS						
Year Team	Lg	G	GS	CG	GF	IP	BFP	H	R	ER	HR	SH	SF	HB	TBB	IBB	SO	WP	Bk	W	L	Pct.	ShO	Sv-Op	Hld	ERA
1997 Oneonta	A-	14	0	0	9	26.2	103	22	5	4	1	0	0	0	5	1	22	0	1	3	1	.750	0	1--	—	1.35
1998 Tampa	A+	32	11	1	18	94.2	383	59	29	25	5	1	1	6	30	4	112	16	2	7	4	.636	1	7--	—	2.38
Norwich	AA	3	3	0	0	25	89	8	4	4	1	0	0	0	8	0	25	0	0	2	0	1.000	1	0--	—	1.44
Columbus	AAA	3	3	0	0	16	72	15	13	11	0	0	0	0	13	0	12	1	0	0	1	.000	0	0--	—	6.19
1998 New York	AL	5	1	0	1	12.2	59	12	9	8	2	0	1	1	9	0	13	0	0	2	1	.667	0	0-0	0	5.68

Darren Bragg

Bats: L **Throws:** R **Pos:** RF-112; CF-12; PH/PR-11; LF-7; DH-4   **Ht:** 5'9" **Wt:** 180 **Born:** 9/7/69 **Age:** 29

Year Team	Lg	G	AB	H	2B	3B	HR	(Hm	Rd)	TB	R	RBI	TBB	IBB	SO	HBP	SH	SF	SB	CS	SB%	GDP	Avg	OBP	SLG
1994 Seattle	AL	8	19	3	1	0	0	(0	0)	4	4	2	2	1	5	0	0	0	0	0	.00	0	.158	.238	.211
1995 Seattle	AL	52	145	34	5	1	3	(1	2)	50	20	12	18	1	37	4	1	2	9	0	1.00	2	.234	.331	.345
1996 Sea-Bos	AL	127	417	109	26	2	10	(7	3)	169	74	47	69	6	74	4	2	7	14	9	.61	5	.261	.366	.405
1997 Boston	AL	153	513	132	35	2	9	(3	6)	198	65	57	61	5	102	3	5	4	10	6	.63	16	.257	.337	.386
1998 Boston	AL	129	409	114	29	3	8	(3	5)	173	51	57	42	0	99	6	4	4	5	3	.63	16	.279	.351	.423
1996 Seattle	AL	69	195	53	12	1	7	(4	3)	88	36	25	33	4	35	2	1	4	8	5	.62	2	.272	.376	.451
Boston	AL	58	222	56	14	1	3	(3	0)	81	38	22	36	2	39	2	1	3	6	4	.60	3	.252	.357	.365
5 ML YEARS		469	1503	392	96	8	30	(14	16)	594	214	175	192	13	317	17	12	17	38	18	.68	39	.261	.348	.395

Jeff Branson

Bats: L **Throws:** R **Pos:** 2B-31; PH/PR-22; 3B-20; 1B-3; SS-2   **Ht:** 6'0" **Wt:** 180 **Born:** 1/26/67 **Age:** 32

Year Team	Lg	G	AB	H	2B	3B	HR	(Hm	Rd)	TB	R	RBI	TBB	IBB	SO	HBP	SH	SF	SB	CS	SB%	GDP	Avg	OBP	SLG
1998 Buffalo *	AAA	12	46	12	4	1	0	—	—	18	5	2	5	1	9	0	0	0	0	0	.00	0	.261	.333	.391
1992 Cincinnati	NL	72	115	34	7	1	0	(0	0)	43	12	15	5	2	16	0	2	1	0	1	.00	4	.296	.322	.374
1993 Cincinnati	NL	125	381	92	15	1	3	(2	1)	118	40	22	19	2	73	0	8	4	4	1	.80	4	.241	.275	.310
1994 Cincinnati	NL	58	109	31	4	1	6	(1	5)	55	18	16	5	2	16	0	2	0	0	0	.00	4	.284	.316	.505
1995 Cincinnati	NL	122	331	86	18	2	12	(9	3)	144	43	45	44	14	69	2	1	6	2	1	.67	9	.260	.345	.435
1996 Cincinnati	NL	129	311	76	16	4	9	(5	4)	127	34	37	31	4	67	1	7	3	2	0	1.00	8	.244	.312	.408
1997 Cin-Cle		94	170	34	7	1	3	(3	0)	52	14	12	14	1	40	1	1	2	1	2	.33	4	.200	.262	.306
1998 Cleveland	AL	63	100	20	4	1	1	(1	0)	29	6	9	3	0	21	0	1	0	0	0	.00	1	.200	.221	.290
1997 Cincinnati	NL	65	98	15	3	1	1	(1	0)	23	9	5	7	1	23	0	1	0	1	0	1.00	3	.153	.210	.235
Cleveland	AL	29	72	19	4	0	2	(2	0)	29	5	7	7	0	17	1	0	2	0	2	.00	1	.264	.329	.403
7 ML YEARS		663	1517	373	71	11	34	(21	13)	568	167	156	121	25	302	4	22	17	9	5	.64	35	.246	.300	.374

Jeff Brantley

Pitches: Right **Bats:** Right **Pos:** RP-48   **Ht:** 5'10" **Wt:** 190 **Born:** 9/5/63 **Age:** 35

		HOW MUCH HE PITCHED						WHAT HE GAVE UP											THE RESULTS					
Year Team	Lg	G	GS	CG	GF	IP	BFP	H	R	ER	HR	SH	SF	HB	TBB	IBB	SO	WP	Bk	W	L	Pct.	ShO	Sv-Op	Hld	ERA
1998 Arkansas *	AA	2	0	0	0	1.2	6	0	0	0	0	1	0	1	0	3	0	0	0	0	.000	0	0- -	—	0.00
1988 San Francisco	NL	9	1	0	2	20.2	88	22	13	13	2	1	0	1	6	1	11	0	1	0	1	.000	0	1-1	0	5.66
1989 San Francisco	NL	59	1	0	15	97.1	422	101	50	44	10	7	3	2	37	8	69	3	2	7	1	.875	0	0-1	11	4.07
1990 San Francisco	NL	55	0	0	32	86.2	361	77	18	15	3	2	2	3	33	6	61	0	3	5	3	.625	0	19-24	8	1.56
1991 San Francisco	NL	67	0	0	39	95.1	411	78	27	26	8	4	4	5	52	10	81	6	0	5	2	.714	0	15-19	12	2.45
1992 San Francisco	NL	56	4	0	32	91.2	381	67	32	30	8	7	3	3	45	5	86	3	1	7	7	.500	0	7-9	3	2.95
1993 San Francisco	NL	53	12	0	9	113.2	496	112	60	54	19	5	5	7	46	2	76	3	4	5	6	.455	0	0-3	10	4.28
1994 Cincinnati	NL	50	0	0	35	65.1	262	46	20	18	6	5	1	0	28	5	63	1	0	6	6	.500	0	15-21	1	2.48
1995 Cincinnati	NL	56	0	0	49	70.1	283	53	22	22	11	2	3	1	20	3	62	2	2	3	2	.600	0	28-32	3	2.82
1996 Cincinnati	NL	66	0	0	61	71	288	54	21	19	7	4	5	0	28	6	76	2	0	1	2	.333	0	44-49	0	2.41
1997 Cincinnati	NL	13	0	0	9	11.2	53	9	5	5	2	0	0	2	7	1	16	2	0	1	1	.500	0	1-3	0	3.86
1998 St. Louis	NL	48	0	0	33	50.2	209	40	26	25	12	5	3	1	18	3	48	1	0	0	5	.000	0	14-22	3	4.44
11 ML YEARS		532	18	0	316	774.1	3254	659	294	271	88	42	29	25	320	50	649	23	13	40	36	.526	0	144-184	48	3.15

Russ Branyan

Bats: Left **Throws:** Right **Pos:** 3B-1   **Ht:** 6'3" **Wt:** 195 **Born:** 12/19/75 **Age:** 23

Year Team	Lg	G	AB	H	2B	3B	HR	(Hm	Rd)	TB	R	RBI	TBB	IBB	SO	HBP	SH	SF	SB	CS	SB%	GDP	Avg	OBP	SLG
1994 Burlington	R+	55	171	36	10	0	5	—	—	61	21	13	25	2	64	4	0	1	4	2	.67	3	.211	.323	.357
1995 Columbus	A	76	277	71	8	6	19	—	—	148	46	55	27	2	120	3	0	3	1	1	.50	6	.256	.326	.534
1996 Columbus	A	130	482	129	20	4	40	—	—	277	102	106	62	5	166	5	0	3	7	4	.64	4	.268	.355	.575
1997 Kinston	A+	83	297	86	26	2	27	—	—	197	59	75	52	4	94	5	0	5	3	1	.75	9	.290	.398	.663
Akron	AA	41	137	32	4	0	12	—	—	72	26	30	28	1	56	2	0	1	0	0	.00	1	.234	.369	.526
1998 Akron	AA	43	163	48	11	3	16	—	—	113	35	46	35	4	58	0	0	1	1	1	.50	2	.294	.417	.693
1998 Cleveland	AL	1	4	0	0	0	0	(0	0)	0	0	0	0	0	2	0	0	0	0	0	.00	0	.000	.000	.000

Brent Brede

Bats: L **Throws:** L **Pos:** PH/PR-41; RF-39; LF-26; 1B-12; DH-1   **Ht:** 6'4" **Wt:** 208 **Born:** 9/13/71 **Age:** 27

Year Team	Lg	G	AB	H	2B	3B	HR	(Hm	Rd)	TB	R	RBI	TBB	IBB	SO	HBP	SH	SF	SB	CS	SB%	GDP	Avg	OBP	SLG
1998 Tucson *	AAA	29	96	30	8	1	2	—	—	46	16	16	21	0	20	0	0	1	2	1	.67	3	.313	.432	.479
1996 Minnesota	AL	10	20	6	0	1	0	(0	0)	8	2	1	2	1	5	0	0	0	0	0	.00	1	.300	.333	.400
1997 Minnesota	AL	61	190	52	11	1	3	(2	1)	74	25	21	21	0	38	1	1	1	7	2	.78	1	.274	.347	.389
1998 Arizona	NL	98	212	48	9	3	2	(1	1)	69	23	17	24	2	43	2	0	0	1	0	1.00	6	.226	.311	.325
3 ML YEARS		169	422	106	20	5	5	(3	2)	151	50	40	46	2	86	3	1	1	8	2	.80	8	.251	.328	.358

Billy Brewer

Pitches: Left **Bats:** Left **Pos:** RP-2   **Ht:** 6'1" **Wt:** 175 **Born:** 4/15/68 **Age:** 31

Year Team	Lg	G	GS	CG	GF	IP	BFP	H	R	ER	HR	SH	SF	HB	TBB	IBB	SO	WP	Bk	W	L	Pct.	ShO	Sv-Op	Hld	ERA
1993 Kansas City	AL	46	0	0	14	39	157	31	16	15	6	1	1	0	20	4	28	2	1	2	2	.500	0	0-2	5	3.46
1994 Kansas City	AL	50	0	0	17	38.2	157	28	11	11	4	2	2	2	16	1	25	3	0	4	1	.800	0	3-7	12	2.56
1995 Kansas City	AL	48	0	0	13	45.1	209	54	28	28	9	1	0	2	20	1	31	5	1	2	4	.333	0	0-4	7	5.56
1996 New York	AL	4	0	0	1	5.2	32	7	6	6	0	0	0	0	8	0	8	0	0	1	0	1.000	0	0-0	0	9.53
1997 Oak-Phi		28	0	0	5	24	105	19	11	11	3	0	3	0	13	0	17	1	0	1	2	.333	0	0-2	5	4.13
1998 Philadelphia	NL	2	0	0	0	0.1	6	3	4	4	0	0	0	0	2	0	0	0	0	0	1	.000	0	0-0	0	108.00
1997 Oakland	AL	3	0	0	1	2	12	4	3	3	1	0	1	0	2	0	1	0	0	0	0	.000	0	0-0	0	13.50
Philadelphia	NL	25	0	0	4	22	93	15	8	8	2	0	2	0	11	0	16	1	0	1	2	.333	0	0-2	5	3.27
6 ML YEARS		178	0	0	50	153	666	142	76	75	22	4	6	4	79	6	109	11	2	10	10	.500	0	3-15	29	4.41

Doug Brocail

Pitches: Right **Bats:** Left **Pos:** RP-60   **Ht:** 6'5" **Wt:** 235 **Born:** 5/16/67 **Age:** 32

Year Team	Lg	G	GS	CG	GF	IP	BFP	H	R	ER	HR	SH	SF	HB	TBB	IBB	SO	WP	Bk	W	L	Pct.	ShO	Sv-Op	Hld	ERA
1992 San Diego	NL	3	3	0	0	14	64	17	10	10	2	2	0	0	5	0	15	0	0	0	0	.000	0	0-0	0	6.43
1993 San Diego	NL	24	24	0	0	128.1	571	143	75	65	16	10	8	4	42	4	70	4	1	4	13	.235	0	0-0	0	4.56
1994 San Diego	NL	12	0	0	4	17	78	21	13	11	1	1	1	2	5	3	11	1	1	0	0	.000	0	0-1	0	5.82
1995 Houston	NL	36	7	0	12	77.1	339	87	40	36	10	1	1	4	22	2	39	1	1	6	4	.600	0	1-1	0	4.19
1996 Houston	NL	23	4	0	4	53	231	58	31	27	7	3	2	2	23	1	34	0	0	1	5	.167	0	0-0	1	4.58
1997 Detroit	AL	61	4	0	20	78	332	74	31	28	10	1	3	3	36	4	60	6	0	3	4	.429	0	2-9	16	3.23
1998 Detroit	AL	60	0	0	24	62.2	247	47	23	19	2	2	3	1	18	3	55	6	0	5	2	.714	0	0-1	11	2.73
7 ML YEARS		219	42	0	64	430.1	1862	447	223	196	48	20	18	16	151	17	284	18	3	19	28	.404	0	3-12	28	4.10

Chris Brock

Pitches: Right **Bats:** Right **Pos:** RP-13   **Ht:** 6'0" **Wt:** 180 **Born:** 2/5/70 **Age:** 29

Year Team	Lg	G	GS	CG	GF	IP	BFP	H	R	ER	HR	SH	SF	HB	TBB	IBB	SO	WP	Bk	W	L	Pct.	ShO	Sv-Op	Hld	ERA
1992 Idaho Falls	R+	15	15	1	0	78	333	61	27	20	3	3	2	3	48	0	72	12	8	6	4	.600	0	0--	—	2.31
1993 Macon	A	14	14	1	0	80	333	61	31	24	3	1	0	2	33	0	92	8	1	7	5	.583	0	0--	—	2.70
Durham	A+	12	12	1	0	79	335	63	28	22	7	1	2	5	35	0	67	6	0	5	2	.714	0	0--	—	2.51
1994 Greenville	AA	25	23	2	0	137.1	576	128	68	57	9	4	4	5	47	0	94	8	3	7	6	.538	2	0--	—	3.74
1995 Richmond	AAA	22	9	0	5	60	270	68	37	36	2	3	3	1	27	2	43	1	2	4	16	.200	0	0--	—	5.40
1996 Richmond	AAA	26	25	3	0	150.1	652	137	95	78	20	3	8	6	61	0	112	9	0	10	11	.476	0	0--	—	4.67
1997 Richmond	AAA	20	19	0	0	118.2	497	97	50	44	9	8	4	1	51	0	83	8	1	10	6	.625	0	0--	—	3.34
1998 Fresno	AAA	17	17	2	0	115	483	111	47	42	11	5	2	11	33	2	112	8	1	11	3	.786	0	0--	—	3.29
1997 Atlanta	NL	7	6	0	1	30.2	144	34	23	19	2	3	4	0	19	2	16	2	1	0	0	.000	0	0-0	0	5.58
1998 San Francisco	NL	13	0	0	4	27.2	120	31	13	12	3	2	0	0	7	1	19	0	0	0	0	.000	0	0-0	0	3.90
2 ML YEARS		20	6	0	5	58.1	264	65	36	31	5	5	4	0	26	3	35	2	1	0	0	.000	0	0-0	0	4.78

Rico Brogna

Bats: Left **Throws:** Left **Pos:** 1B-151; PH/PR-3   **Ht:** 6'2" **Wt:** 200 **Born:** 4/18/70 **Age:** 29

Year Team	Lg	G	AB	H	2B	3B	HR	(Hm	Rd)	TB	R	RBI	TBB	IBB	SO	HBP	SH	SF	SB	CS	SB%	GDP	Avg	OBP	SLG
1992 Detroit	AL	9	26	5	1	0	1	(1	0)	9	3	3	3	0	5	0	0	0	0	0	.00	0	.192	.276	.346
1994 New York	NL	39	131	46	11	2	7	(2	5)	82	16	20	6	0	29	0	1	0	1	0	1.00	1	.351	.380	.626
1995 New York	NL	134	495	143	27	2	22	(13	9)	240	72	76	39	7	111	2	2	2	0	0	.00	10	.289	.342	.485
1996 New York	NL	55	188	48	10	1	7	(5	2)	81	18	30	19	1	50	0	0	4	0	0	.00	4	.255	.318	.431
1997 Philadelphia	NL	148	543	137	36	1	20	(9	11)	235	68	81	33	4	116	0	0	4	12	3	.80	12	.252	.293	.433
1998 Philadelphia	NL	153	565	150	36	3	20	(11	9)	252	77	104	49	8	125	0	0	10	7	7	.50	12	.265	.319	.446
6 ML YEARS		538	1948	529	121	9	77	(41	36)	899	254	314	149	20	436	2	3	20	20	10	.67	40	.272	.321	.461

Scott Brosius

Bats: R **Throws:** R **Pos:** 3B-150; 1B-3; PH/PR-2; RF-1   **Ht:** 6'1" **Wt:** 202 **Born:** 8/15/66 **Age:** 32

Year Team	Lg	G	AB	H	2B	3B	HR	(Hm	Rd)	TB	R	RBI	TBB	IBB	SO	HBP	SH	SF	SB	CS	SB%	GDP	Avg	OBP	SLG
1991 Oakland	AL	36	68	16	5	0	2	(1	1)	27	9	4	3	0	11	0	1	0	3	1	.75	2	.235	.268	.397
1992 Oakland	AL	38	87	19	2	0	4	(1	3)	33	13	13	3	1	13	2	0	1	3	0	1.00	6	.218	.258	.379
1993 Oakland	AL	70	213	53	10	1	6	(3	3)	83	26	25	14	0	37	1	3	2	6	0	1.00	6	.249	.296	.390
1994 Oakland	AL	96	324	77	14	1	14	(9	5)	135	31	49	24	0	57	2	4	6	2	6	.25	7	.238	.289	.417
1995 Oakland	AL	123	389	102	19	2	17	(12	5)	176	69	46	41	0	67	8	1	4	4	2	.67	5	.262	.342	.452
1996 Oakland	AL	114	428	130	25	0	22	(15	7)	221	73	71	59	4	85	7	1	5	7	2	.78	11	.304	.393	.516
1997 Oakland	AL	129	479	97	20	1	11	(7	4)	152	59	41	34	1	102	4	5	4	9	4	.69	9	.203	.259	.317
1998 New York	AL	152	530	159	34	0	19	(8	11)	250	86	98	52	1	97	10	8	3	11	8	.58	4	.300	.371	.472
8 ML YEARS		758	2518	653	129	5	95	(56	39)	1077	366	347	230	7	469	34	23	25	45	23	.66	44	.259	.327	.428

Scott Brow

Pitches: Right **Bats:** Right **Pos:** RP-17 **Ht:** 6'3" **Wt:** 200 **Born:** 3/17/69 **Age:** 30

Year Team	Lg	G	GS	CG	GF	IP	BFP	H	R	ER	HR	SH	SF	HB	TBB	IBB	SO	WP	Bk	W	L	Pct.	ShO	Sv-Op	Hld	ERA
1998 Columbus *	AAA	30	3	0	8	59.1	273	74	42	36	8	2	3	1	26	0	35	3	0	3	2	.600	0	0- --		5.46
1993 Toronto	AL	6	3	0	1	18	83	19	15	12	2	1	2	1	10	1	7	0	0	1	1	.500	0	0-0	0	6.00
1994 Toronto	AL	18	0	0	9	29	141	34	27	19	4	1	2	1	19	2	15	6	0	0	3	.000	0	2-2	0	5.90
1996 Toronto	AL	18	1	0	9	38.2	180	45	25	24	5	1	1	0	25	1	23	2	1	1	0	1.000	0	0-1	0	5.59
1998 Arizona	NL	17	0	0	5	21.1	98	22	17	17	2	2	1	0	14	2	13	0	0	1	0	1.000	0	0-0	1	7.17
4 ML YEARS		59	4	0	24	107	502	120	84	72	13	5	6	2	68	6	58	8	1	3	4	.429	0	2-3	1	6.06

Adrian Brown

Bats: B **Throws:** R **Pos:** CF-34; LF-3; PH/PR-3; RF-1 **Ht:** 6'0" **Wt:** 182 **Born:** 2/7/74 **Age:** 25

Year Team	Lg	G	AB	H	2B	3B	HR	(Hm	Rd)	TB	R	RBI	TBB	IBB	SO	HBP	SH	SF	SB	CS	SB%	GDP	Avg	OBP	SLG
1992 Pirates	R	39	121	31	2	2	0	—	—	37	11	12	0	0	12	2	0	0	8	4	.67	3	.256	.268	.306
1993 Lethbridge	R+	69	282	75	12	9	3	—	—	114	47	27	17	1	34	5	3	0	22	7	.76	8	.266	.319	.404
1994 Augusta	A	79	308	80	17	1	1	—	—	102	41	18	14	0	38	0	6	0	19	12	.61	2	.260	.292	.331
1995 Augusta	A	76	287	86	15	4	4	—	—	121	64	31	33	0	23	1	3	2	25	14	.64	2	.300	.372	.422
Lynchburg	A+	54	215	52	5	2	1	—	—	64	30	14	12	0	20	1	4	1	11	6	.65	3	.242	.284	.298
1996 Lynchburg	A+	52	215	69	9	3	4	—	—	96	39	25	14	1	24	2	1	0	18	9	.67	1	.321	.368	.447
Carolina	AA	84	341	101	11	3	3	—	—	127	48	25	25	3	40	1	5	1	27	11	.71	4	.296	.345	.372
1997 Carolina	AA	37	145	44	4	4	2	—	—	62	29	15	18	1	12	2	3	0	9	5	.64	1	.303	.388	.428
Calgary	AAA	62	248	79	10	1	1	—	—	94	53	19	27	1	38	0	2	2	20	4	.83	9	.319	.383	.379
1998 Nashville	AAA	85	311	90	12	5	3	—	—	121	58	27	28	1	38	0	6	2	25	7	.78	7	.289	.346	.389
1997 Pittsburgh	NL	48	147	28	6	0	1	(0	1)	37	17	10	13	0	18	4	2	1	8	4	.67	3	.190	.273	.252
1998 Pittsburgh	NL	41	152	43	4	1	0	(0	0)	49	20	5	9	0	18	0	4	0	4	1	1.00	3	.283	.323	.322
2 ML YEARS		89	299	71	10	1	1	(0	1)	86	37	15	22	0	36	4	6	1	12	4	.75	6	.237	.298	.288

Brant Brown

Bats: L **Throws:** L **Pos:** CF-69; LF-48; PH/PR-28; 1B-7 **Ht:** 6'3" **Wt:** 205 **Born:** 6/22/71 **Age:** 28

Year Team	Lg	G	AB	H	2B	3B	HR	(Hm	Rd)	TB	R	RBI	TBB	IBB	SO	HBP	SH	SF	SB	CS	SB%	GDP	Avg	OBP	SLG
1998 Iowa *	AAA	3	11	4	0	0	0	—	—	4	1	0	0	0	6	0	0	0	0	0	.00	0	.364	.364	.364
1996 Chicago	NL	29	69	21	1	0	5	(3	2)	37	11	9	2	1	17	1	0	1	3	3	.50	1	.304	.329	.536
1997 Chicago	NL	46	137	32	7	1	5	(3	2)	56	15	15	7	0	28	1	0	2	2	1	.67	2	.234	.286	.409
1998 Chicago	NL	124	347	101	17	7	14	(10	4)	174	56	48	30	2	95	1	1	1	4	5	.44	1	.291	.348	.501
3 ML YEARS		199	553	154	25	8	24	(16	8)	267	82	72	39	3	140	5	2	2	9	9	.50	4	.278	.331	.483

Dermal Brown

Bats: Left **Throws:** Right **Pos:** PH/PR-5; DH-3; RF-2 **Ht:** 5'11" **Wt:** 210 **Born:** 3/27/78 **Age:** 21

Year Team	Lg	G	AB	H	2B	3B	HR	(Hm	Rd)	TB	R	RBI	TBB	IBB	SO	HBP	SH	SF	SB	CS	SB%	GDP	Avg	OBP	SLG
1996 Royals	R	7	20	1	1	0	0	—	—	2	1	1	0	0	6	1	0	0	0	2	.00	0	.050	.095	.100
1997 Spokane	A-	73	298	97	20	6	13	—	—	168	67	73	38	5	65	2	0	1	17	4	.81	5	.326	.404	.564
1998 Wilmington	A+	128	442	114	30	2	10	—	—	178	64	58	53	5	115	7	1	0	26	10	.72	12	.258	.347	.403
1998 Kansas City	AL	5	3	0	0	0	0	(0	0)	0	2	0	0	0	1	0	0	0	0	0	.00	0	.000	.000	.000

Emil Brown

Bats: Right **Throws:** Right **Pos:** LF-9; PH/PR-3; CF-1; RF-1 **Ht:** 6'2" **Wt:** 195 **Born:** 12/29/74 **Age:** 24

Year Team	Lg	G	AB	H	2B	3B	HR	(Hm	Rd)	TB	R	RBI	TBB	IBB	SO	HBP	SH	SF	SB	CS	SB%	GDP	Avg	OBP	SLG
1994 Athletics	R	32	86	19	1	1	3	—	—	31	13	12	13	0	12	4	0	0	5	1	.83	2	.221	.350	.360
1995 W Michigan	A	124	459	115	17	3	3	—	—	147	63	67	52	0	77	11	0	6	35	19	.65	17	.251	.337	.320
1996 Athletics	R	4	15	4	3	0	0	—	—	7	5	2	3	0	2	1	0	0	1	1	.50	0	.267	.421	.467
Modesto	A+	57	211	64	10	1	10	—	—	106	50	47	32	1	51	6	0	2	13	5	.72	5	.303	.406	.502
1998 Carolina	AA	123	466	154	31	2	14	—	—	231	89	67	50	2	71	11	0	9	24	7	.77	12	.330	.401	.496
1997 Pittsburgh	NL	66	95	17	2	1	2	(1	1)	27	16	6	10	1	32	7	0	0	5	1	.83	1	.179	.304	.284
1998 Pittsburgh	NL	13	39	10	1	0	0	(0	0)	11	2	3	1	0	11	1	0	0	0	0	.00	0	.256	.293	.282
2 ML YEARS		79	134	27	3	1	2	(1	1)	38	18	9	11	1	43	8	0	0	5	1	.83	1	.201	.301	.284

Kevin Brown

Pitches: Right **Bats:** Right **Pos:** SP-35; RP-1 **Ht:** 6'4" **Wt:** 200 **Born:** 3/14/65 **Age:** 34

Year Team	Lg	G	GS	CG	GF	IP	BFP	H	R	ER	HR	SH	SF	HB	TBB	IBB	SO	WP	Bk	W	L	Pct.	ShO	Sv-Op	Hld	ERA
1986 Texas	AL	5	1	0	0	5	19	6	2	2	0	0	0	0	4	0	1	0	0	1	0	1.000	0	0-0	0	3.60
1988 Texas	AL	4	4	1	0	23.1	110	33	15	11	2	1	0	1	8	0	12	1	0	1	1	.500	0	0-0	0	4.24
1989 Texas	AL	28	28	7	0	191	798	167	81	71	10	3	6	4	70	2	104	7	2	12	9	.571	0	0-0	0	3.35
1990 Texas	AL	26	26	6	0	180	757	175	84	72	13	2	7	3	60	3	88	3	2	12	10	.545	2	0-0	0	3.60
1991 Texas	AL	33	33	0	0	210.2	934	233	116	103	17	6	4	13	90	5	96	12	3	9	12	.429	0	0-0	0	4.40
1992 Texas	AL	35	35	11	0	265.2	1108	262	117	98	11	7	8	10	76	2	173	8	2	21	11	.656	1	0-0	0	3.32
1993 Texas	AL	34	34	12	0	233	1001	228	105	93	14	5	3	15	74	5	142	1	1	15	12	.556	3	0-0	0	3.59

Year Team	Lg	G	GS	CG	GF	IP	BFP	H	R	ER	HR	SH	SF	HB	TBB	IBB	SO	WP	Bk	W	L	Pct.	ShO	Sv-Op	Hld	ERA
1994 Texas	AL	26	25	3	1	170	760	218	109	91	18	2	7	6	50	3	123	7	0	7	9	.438	0	0-0	0	4.82
1995 Baltimore	AL	26	26	3	0	172.1	706	155	73	69	10	5	2	9	48	1	117	3	0	10	9	.526	1	0-0	0	3.60
1996 Florida	NL	32	32	5	0	233	906	187	60	49	8	4	4	16	33	2	159	6	1	17	11	.607	3	0-0	0	1.89
1997 Florida	NL	33	33	6	0	237.1	976	214	77	71	10	5	1	14	66	7	205	7	1	16	8	.667	2	0-0	0	2.69
1998 San Diego	NL	36	35	7	0	257	1032	225	77	68	8	13	3	10	49	4	257	10	0	18	7	.720	3	0-0	1	2.38
12 ML YEARS		314	312	61	1	2178.1	9107	2103	916	798	121	53	45	101	624	34	1480	78	12	139	99	.584	15	0-0	1	3.30

Kevin L. Brown

Bats: Right **Throws:** Right **Pos:** C-52; PH/PR-1   **Ht:** 6'2" **Wt:** 200 **Born:** 4/21/73 **Age:** 26

						BATTING												BASERUNNING				PERCENTAGES		
Year Team	Lg	G	AB	H	2B	3B	HR	(Hm	Rd)	TB	R	RBI	TBB	IBB	SO	HBP	SH	SF	SB	CS	SB%	GDP	Avg	OBP	SLG
1994 Hudson Vall	A-	68	232	57	19	1	6	—	—	96	33	32	23	0	86	4	0	6	0	1	.00	4	.246	.317	.414
1995 Charlotte	A+	107	355	94	25	1	11	—	—	154	48	57	50	0	96	9	1	4	2	3	.40	9	.265	.366	.434
Okla City	AAA	3	10	4	1	0	0	—	—	5	1	0	2	0	4	0	0	0	0	0	.00	0	.400	.500	.500
1996 Tulsa	AA	128	460	121	27	1	26	—	—	228	77	86	73	0	150	11	0	6	0	3	.00	5	.263	.373	.496
1997 Okla City	AAA	116	403	97	18	2	19	—	—	176	56	50	38	1	111	5	1	2	2	2	.50	11	.241	.313	.437
1998 Syracuse	AAA	2	8	5	2	0	0	—	—	7	2	0	0	0	2	0	0	0	0	0	.00	0	.625	.625	.875
1996 Texas	AL	3	4	0	0	0	0	(0	0)	0	1	1	2	0	2	1	0	1	0	0	.00	0	.000	.375	.000
1997 Texas	AL	4	5	2	0	0	1	(0	1)	5	1	1	0	0	0	0	0	0	0	0	.00	0	.400	.400	1.000
1998 Toronto	AL	52	110	29	7	1	2	(1	1)	44	17	15	9	0	31	2	3	4	0	0	.00	1	.264	.320	.400
3 ML YEARS		59	119	31	7	1	3	(1	2)	49	19	17	11	0	33	3	3	5	0	0	.00	1	.261	.326	.412

Mark Brownson

Pitches: Right **Bats:** Left **Pos:** SP-2   **Ht:** 6'2" **Wt:** 185 **Born:** 6/17/75 **Age:** 24

		HOW MUCH HE PITCHED						WHAT HE GAVE UP												THE RESULTS					
Year Team	Lg	G	GS	CG	GF	IP	BFP	H	R	ER	HR	SH	SF	HB	TBB	IBB	SO	WP	Bk	W	L	Pct.	ShO	Sv-Op	Hld	ERA
1994 Rockies	R	19	4	0	6	54.1	224	48	18	10	2	2	2	3	6	0	72	2	2	4	1	.800	0	3--	—	1.66
1995 Asheville	A	23	12	0	4	98.2	422	106	52	44	12	2	2	4	29	0	94	4	2	6	7	.462	0	1--	—	4.01
New Haven	AA	1	1	0	0	6	24	4	2	1	1	0	0	1	1	0	4	0	0	0	0	.000	0	0--	—	1.50
Salem	A+	9	1	0	5	15.2	71	16	8	7	0	0	0	1	10	4	9	4	0	2	1	.667	0	1--	—	4.02
1996 New Haven	AA	37	19	1	10	144	619	141	73	56	10	6	3	6	43	5	155	7	2	8	13	.381	0	3--	—	3.50
1997 New Haven	AA	29	29	2	0	184.2	779	172	101	86	24	8	5	14	55	1	170	5	2	10	9	.526	0	0--	—	4.19
1998 Colo Sprngs	AAA	21	21	3	0	124.2	542	131	85	74	22	5	8	14	37	0	82	2	3	6	8	.429	0	0--	—	5.34
1998 Colorado	NL	2	2	1	0	13.1	57	16	7	7	2	0	0	1	2	0	8	0	0	1	0	1.000	1	0-0	0	4.73

Will Brunson

Pitches: Left **Bats:** Left **Pos:** RP-10   **Ht:** 6'6" **Wt:** 185 **Born:** 3/20/70 **Age:** 29

		HOW MUCH HE PITCHED						WHAT HE GAVE UP												THE RESULTS					
Year Team	Lg	G	GS	CG	GF	IP	BFP	H	R	ER	HR	SH	SF	HB	TBB	IBB	SO	WP	Bk	W	L	Pct.	ShO	Sv-Op	Hld	ERA
1992 Princeton	R+	13	13	0	0	72.2	313	68	34	29	6	4	2	3	28	0	48	2	0	5	5	.500	0	0--	—	3.59
1993 Chston-WV	A	37	15	0	4	123.2	545	119	68	54	10	4	4	11	50	1	103	7	2	5	6	.455	0	0--	—	3.93
1994 Winston-Sal	A+	30	22	3	3	165	711	161	83	73	22	5	7	12	58	2	129	6	4	12	7	.632	0	0--	—	3.98
1995 San Berndno	AA	13	13	0	0	83.1	334	68	24	19	4	3	5	5	21	0	70	3	0	10	0	1.000	0	0--	—	2.05
San Antonio	AA	14	14	0	0	80	356	105	46	44	4	3	1	4	22	0	44	5	1	4	5	.444	0	0--	—	4.95
1996 San Antonio	AA	11	5	0	1	42	166	32	13	10	2	2	0	1	15	0	38	2	1	3	1	.750	0	0--	—	2.14
Albuquerque	AAA	9	9	1	0	54.1	239	53	29	27	7	2	1	2	23	1	47	2	0	3	4	.429	0	0--	—	4.47
1997 Albuquerque	AAA	27	0	0	9	26.1	125	39	19	19	3	1	1	1	10	1	25	0	0	1	1	.500	0	0--	—	6.49
San Antonio	AA	17	11	2	4	72.2	299	68	30	28	8	3	1	6	13	0	71	2	0	5	5	.500	1	0--	—	3.47
1998 Albuquerque	AAA	34	15	1	5	120	520	135	69	62	11	5	3	4	40	1	100	3	1	5	8	.385	0	2--	—	4.65
1998 LA-Det		10	0	0	2	5.1	22	5	3	3	0	0	0	0	3	0	2	1	0	0	1	.000	0	0-0	2	5.06
1998 Los Angeles	NL	2	0	0	1	2.1	11	3	3	3	0	0	0	0	2	0	1	0	0	0	1	.000	0	0-0	1	11.57
Detroit	AL	8	0	0	1	3	11	2	0	0	0	0	0	0	1	0	1	1	0	0	0	.000	0	0-0	1	0.00

Jim Bruske

Pitches: Right **Bats:** Right **Pos:** RP-41; SP-1   **Ht:** 6'1" **Wt:** 185 **Born:** 10/7/64 **Age:** 34

		HOW MUCH HE PITCHED						WHAT HE GAVE UP												THE RESULTS					
Year Team	Lg	G	GS	CG	GF	IP	BFP	H	R	ER	HR	SH	SF	HB	TBB	IBB	SO	WP	Bk	W	L	Pct.	ShO	Sv-Op	Hld	ERA
1998 Las Vegas *	AAA	5	0	0	4	6	25	8	4	4	1	0	0	0	1	0	2	0	0	0	1	.000	0	1--	—	6.00
Columbus *	AAA	4	0	0	3	7.2	31	7	1	1	0	0	0	0	2	0	9	0	0	0	0	.000	0	1--	—	1.17
1995 Los Angeles	NL	9	0	0	3	10	45	12	7	5	0	0	0	1	4	0	5	1	0	0	0	.000	0	1-1	0	4.50
1996 Los Angeles	NL	11	0	0	5	12.2	58	17	8	8	2	0	0	1	3	1	12	1	0	0	0	.000	0	0-0	0	5.68
1997 San Diego	NL	28	0	0	6	44.2	193	37	22	18	4	2	3	1	25	1	32	4	0	4	1	.800	0	0-1	5	3.63
1998 LA-SD-NYA		42	1	0	11	60	265	66	25	23	5	0	0	3	24	3	38	3	0	4	0	1.000	0	1-2	4	3.45
1998 Los Angeles	NL	35	0	0	10	44	195	47	18	17	2	0	0	3	19	1	31	3	0	3	0	1.000	0	1-2	2	3.48
San Diego	NL	4	0	0	1	7	34	10	4	3	1	0	0	0	4	2	4	0	0	0	0	.000	0	0-0	1	3.86
New York	AL	3	1	0	0	9	36	9	3	3	2	0	0	0	1	0	3	0	0	1	0	1.000	0	0-0	1	3.00
4 ML YEARS		90	1	0	25	127.1	561	132	62	54	11	2	3	6	56	5	87	9	0	8	1	.889	0	2-4	9	3.82

Mike Buddie

Pitches: Right **Bats:** Right **Pos:** RP-22; SP-2   **Ht:** 6'3" **Wt:** 210 **Born:** 12/12/70 **Age:** 28

Year Team	Lg	G	GS	CG	GF	IP	BFP	H	R	ER	HR	SH	SF	HB	TBB	IBB	SO	WP	Bk	W	L	Pct.	ShO	Sv-Op	Hld	ERA
1992 Oneonta	A-	13	13	1	0	67.1	301	69	36	29	3	0	1	3	34	0	87	7	5	1	4	.200	0	0- --	—	3.88
1993 Greensboro	A	27	26	0	0	155.1	686	138	104	84	19	2	4	8	89	0	143	22	2	13	10	.565	0	0- --	—	4.87
1994 Tampa	A+	25	24	2	0	150.1	643	143	75	67	7	5	8	5	66	2	113	9	4	12	5	.706	0	0- --	—	4.01
1995 Norwich	AA	29	27	2	1	149.2	689	155	102	80	4	6	8	15	81	2	106	13	1	10	12	.455	0	1- --	—	4.81
1996 Norwich	AA	29	26	4	0	159.2	708	176	101	79	10	8	5	8	71	5	103	16	0	7	12	.368	0	0- --	—	4.45
1997 Norwich	AA	1	0	0	0	1	3	0	0	0	0	0	0	0	0	0	3	0	0	0	0	.000	0	0- --	—	0.00
Columbus	AAA	53	0	0	13	75	319	85	24	22	4	4	3	2	25	0	67	5	0	6	6	.500	0	2- --	—	2.64
1998 Columbus	AAA	26	0	0	12	42.2	170	35	15	13	0	1	1	0	15	0	30	2	0	5	0	1.000	0	4- --	—	2.74
1998 New York	AL	24	2	0	8	41.2	180	46	29	26	5	1	1	3	13	1	20	2	1	4	1	.800	0	0-0	0	5.62

Damon Buford

Bats: R **Throws:** R **Pos:** CF-67; PH/PR-29; DH-15; 2B-1; 3B-1   **Ht:** 5'10" **Wt:** 170 **Born:** 6/12/70 **Age:** 29

Year Team	Lg	G	AB	H	2B	3B	HR	(Hm	Rd)	TB	R	RBI	TBB	IBB	SO	HBP	SH	SF	SB	CS	SB%	GDP	Avg	OBP	SLG
1993 Baltimore	AL	53	79	18	5	0	2	(0	2)	29	18	9	9	0	19	1	1	0	2	2	.50	1	.228	.315	.367
1994 Baltimore	AL	4	2	1	0	0	0	(0	0)	1	2	0	0	0	1	0	0	0	0	0	.00	0	.500	.500	.500
1995 Bal-NYN		68	168	34	5	0	4	(2	2)	51	30	14	25	0	35	5	3	3	10	8	.56	3	.202	.318	.304
1996 Texas	AL	90	145	41	9	0	6	(3	3)	68	30	20	15	0	34	0	1	1	8	5	.62	3	.283	.348	.469
1997 Texas	AL	122	366	82	18	0	8	(4	4)	124	49	39	30	0	83	3	3	2	18	7	.72	5	.224	.287	.339
1998 Boston	AL	86	216	61	14	4	10	(4	6)	113	37	42	22	1	43	1	0	2	5	5	.50	2	.282	.349	.523
1995 Baltimore	AL	24	32	2	0	0	0	(0	0)	2	6	2	6	0	7	0	3	1	3	1	.75	0	.063	.205	.063
New York	NL	44	136	32	5	0	4	(2	2)	49	24	12	19	0	28	5	0	2	7	7	.50	3	.235	.346	.360
6 ML YEARS		423	976	237	51	4	30	(13	17)	386	166	124	101	1	215	10	8	8	43	27	.61	20	.243	.318	.395

Jay Buhner

Bats: Right **Throws:** Right **Pos:** RF-70; DH-1; PH/PR-1   **Ht:** 6'3" **Wt:** 215 **Born:** 8/13/64 **Age:** 34

Year Team	Lg	G	AB	H	2B	3B	HR	(Hm	Rd)	TB	R	RBI	TBB	IBB	SO	HBP	SH	SF	SB	CS	SB%	GDP	Avg	OBP	SLG
1998 Tacoma *	AAA	2	4	2	0	0	0	—	—	4	2	2	2	0	2	0	0	1	0	0	.00	0	.500	.571	1.000
1987 New York	AL	7	22	5	2	0	0	(0	0)	7	0	1	1	0	6	0	0	0	0	0	.00	0	.227	.261	.318
1988 NYA-Sea	AL	85	261	56	13	1	13	(8	5)	110	36	38	28	1	93	6	1	3	1	1	.50	5	.215	.302	.421
1989 Seattle	AL	58	204	56	15	1	9	(7	2)	100	27	33	19	0	55	2	0	1	1	4	.20	0	.275	.341	.490
1990 Seattle	AL	51	163	45	12	0	7	(2	5)	78	16	33	17	1	50	4	0	1	2	2	.50	6	.276	.357	.479
1991 Seattle	AL	137	406	99	14	4	27	(14	13)	202	64	77	53	5	117	6	2	4	0	1	.00	10	.244	.337	.498
1992 Seattle	AL	152	543	132	16	3	25	(9	16)	229	69	79	71	2	146	6	1	8	0	6	.00	12	.243	.333	.422
1993 Seattle	AL	158	563	153	28	3	27	(13	14)	268	91	98	100	11	144	4	2	8	2	5	.29	12	.272	.379	.476
1994 Seattle	AL	101	358	100	23	4	21	(8	13)	194	74	68	66	3	63	5	2	5	0	1	.00	15	.279	.394	.542
1995 Seattle	AL	126	470	123	23	0	40	(21	19)	266	86	121	60	7	120	1	2	6	0	1	.00	11	.262	.343	.566
1996 Seattle	AL	150	564	153	29	0	44	(21	23)	314	107	138	84	5	159	9	0	10	0	0	.00	11	.271	.369	.557
1997 Seattle	AL	157	540	131	18	2	40	(13	27)	273	104	109	119	3	175	5	0	1	0	0	.00	23	.243	.383	.506
1998 Seattle	AL	72	244	59	7	1	15	(8	7)	113	33	45	38	0	71	1	1	2	0	0	.00	2	.242	.344	.463
1988 New York	AL	25	69	13	0	0	3	(1	2)	22	8	13	3	0	25	3	0	1	0	0	.00	1	.188	.250	.319
Seattle	AL	60	192	43	13	1	10	(7	3)	88	28	25	25	1	68	3	1	2	1	1	.50	4	.224	.320	.458
12 ML YEARS		1254	4338	1112	200	19	268	(124	144)	2154	707	840	656	38	1199	47	11	49	6	22	.21	104	.256	.357	.497

Jim Bullinger

Pitches: Right **Bats:** Right **Pos:** SP-1; RP-1   **Ht:** 6'2" **Wt:** 180 **Born:** 8/21/65 **Age:** 33

Year Team	Lg	G	GS	CG	GF	IP	BFP	H	R	ER	HR	SH	SF	HB	TBB	IBB	SO	WP	Bk	W	L	Pct.	ShO	Sv-Op	Hld	ERA
1998 Tacoma *	AAA	20	16	0	2	101.2	459	106	64	57	13	1	1	8	58	1	73	4	0	8	7	.533	0	0- --	—	5.05
1992 Chicago	NL	39	9	1	15	85	380	72	49	44	9	9	4	4	54	6	36	4	0	2	8	.200	0	7-7	4	4.66
1993 Chicago	NL	15	0	0	6	16.2	75	18	9	8	1	0	1	0	9	0	10	0	0	1	0	1.000	0	1-1	3	4.32
1994 Chicago	NL	33	10	1	10	100	412	87	43	40	6	3	3	1	34	2	72	4	1	6	2	.750	0	2-2	1	3.60
1995 Chicago	NL	24	24	1	0	150	665	152	80	69	14	12	5	9	65	7	93	5	1	12	8	.600	1	0-0	0	4.14
1996 Chicago	NL	37	20	1	6	129.1	598	144	101	94	15	8	5	8	68	5	90	7	0	6	10	.375	1	1-1	0	6.54
1997 Montreal	NL	36	25	2	4	155.1	697	165	106	96	17	8	6	12	74	5	87	7	0	7	12	.368	2	0-1	0	5.56
1998 Seattle	AL	2	1	0	0	5.2	33	13	10	10	3	0	1	0	2	0	4	0	0	0	1	.000	0	0-0	0	15.88
7 ML YEARS		186	89	6	41	642	2860	651	398	361	65	40	25	34	306	25	392	27	2	34	41	.453	4	11-12	8	5.06

Kirk Bullinger

Pitches: Right **Bats:** Right **Pos:** RP-8   **Ht:** 6'2" **Wt:** 170 **Born:** 10/28/69 **Age:** 29

Year Team	Lg	G	GS	CG	GF	IP	BFP	H	R	ER	HR	SH	SF	HB	TBB	IBB	SO	WP	Bk	W	L	Pct.	ShO	Sv-Op	Hld	ERA
1992 Hamilton	A-	35	0	0	7	48.2	191	24	7	6	0	1	2	2	8	4	61	3	1	2	2	.500	0	2- --	—	1.11
1993 Springfield	A	50	0	0	46	51.1	208	26	19	13	5	3	2	2	21	4	72	6	0	1	3	.250	0	33- --	—	2.28
1994 St. Pete	A+	39	0	0	18	53.2	220	37	16	7	0	4	0	1	20	5	50	4	3	2	0	1.000	0	6- --	—	1.17
1995 Harrisburg	AA	56	0	0	39	67	282	61	22	18	4	4	1	0	25	5	42	2	1	5	3	.625	0	7- --	—	2.42
1996 Ottawa	AAA	10	0	0	4	15.1	62	10	6	6	3	0	0	0	9	1	9	1	0	2	1	.667	0	0- --	—	3.52
Harrisburg	AA	47	0	0	40	45.2	193	46	16	10	5	3	1	1	18	3	29	3	0	3	4	.429	0	22- --	—	1.97
1997 Wst Plm Bch	A+	2	0	0	0	3.2	15	3	0	0	0	0	0	0	0	1	7	1	0	2	0	1.000	0	0- --	—	0.00

Year Team	Lg	HOW MUCH HE PITCHED					WHAT HE GAVE UP									SO	WP	Bk	THE RESULTS		Pct	ShO	Sv-Op	Hld	ERA
		G	GS	CG	GF	IP	BFP	H	R	ER	HR	SH	SF	HB	TBB	IBB				W	L					
Harrisburg	AA	21	0	0	12	27	106	22	9	8	4	1	0	1	6	0	21	0	0	3	0	1.000	0	6--	—	2.67
Ottawa	AAA	22	0	0	14	31.2	119	17	7	6	0	2	1	0	10	0	15	1	0	3	4	.429	0	5--	—	1.71
1998 Expos	R	2	2	0	0	4	14	2	0	0	0	0	0	0	0	0	7	0	0	0	0	.000	0	0--	—	0.00
Jupiter	A+	8	0	0	1	10	42	9	7	6	1	0	0	1	2	0	12	2	0	0	0	.000	0	0--	—	5.40
Ottawa	AAA	13	0	0	4	17	72	16	2	2	0	1	0	0	6	1	7	0	0	0	0	.000	0	3--	—	1.06
1998 Montreal	NL	8	0	0	1	7	35	14	8	7	1	0	0	0	0	0	2	0	1	1	0	1.000	0	0-1	0	9.00

Dave Burba

Pitches: Right **Bats:** Right **Pos:** SP-31; RP-1 **Ht:** 6'4" **Wt:** 240 **Born:** 7/7/66 **Age:** 32

Year Team	Lg	HOW MUCH HE PITCHED						WHAT HE GAVE UP									SO	WP	Bk	THE RESULTS		Pct	ShO	Sv-Op	Hld	ERA
		G	GS	CG	GF	IP	BFP	H	R	ER	HR	SH	SF	HB	TBB	IBB				W	L					
1990 Seattle	AL	6	0	0	2	8	35	8	6	4	2	0	1	0	2	0	4	0	0	0	0	.000	0	0-0	0	4.50
1991 Seattle	AL	22	2	0	11	36.2	153	34	16	15	6	0	0	0	14	3	16	1	0	2	2	.500	0	1-1	0	3.68
1992 San Francisco	NL	23	11	0	4	70.2	318	80	43	39	4	2	4	2	31	2	47	1	1	2	7	.222	0	0-0	0	4.97
1993 San Francisco	NL	54	5	0	9	95.1	408	95	49	45	14	6	3	3	37	5	88	4	0	10	3	.769	0	0-0	10	4.25
1994 San Francisco	NL	57	0	0	13	74	322	59	39	36	5	3	1	6	45	3	84	3	0	3	6	.333	0	0-3	11	4.38
1995 SF-Cin	NL	52	9	1	7	106.2	451	90	50	47	9	4	1	0	51	3	96	5	0	10	4	.714	1	0-1	5	3.97
1996 Cincinnati	NL	34	33	0	0	195	849	179	96	83	18	5	12	2	97	9	148	9	1	11	13	.458	0	0-0	0	3.83
1997 Cincinnati	NL	30	27	2	1	160	706	157	88	84	22	6	3	9	73	10	131	6	0	11	10	.524	0	0-0	0	4.73
1998 Cleveland	AL	32	31	0	0	203.2	870	210	100	93	30	3	10	7	69	4	132	6	0	15	10	.600	0	0-0	0	4.11
1995 Cincinnati	NL	37	0	0	7	43.1	191	38	26	24	5	3	1	0	25	2	46	2	0	4	2	.667	0	0-1	5	4.98
Cincinnati	NL	15	9	1	0	63.1	260	52	24	23	4	1	0	0	26	1	50	3	0	6	2	.750	1	0-0	0	3.27
9 ML YEARS		310	118	3	47	950	4112	912	487	446	108	31	34	30	419	39	746	35	2	64	55	.538	1	1-5	26	4.23

John Burkett

Pitches: Right **Bats:** Right **Pos:** SP-32 **Ht:** 6'3" **Wt:** 215 **Born:** 11/28/64 **Age:** 34

Year Team	Lg	HOW MUCH HE PITCHED						WHAT HE GAVE UP									SO	WP	Bk	THE RESULTS		Pct	ShO	Sv-Op	Hld	ERA
		G	GS	CG	GF	IP	BFP	H	R	ER	HR	SH	SF	HB	TBB	IBB				W	L					
1987 San Francisco	NL	3	0	0	1	6	28	7	4	3	2	1	0	1	3	0	5	0	0	0	0	.000	0	0-0	0	4.50
1990 San Francisco	NL	33	32	2	1	204	857	201	92	86	18	6	5	4	61	7	118	3	3	14	7	.667	0	1-1	0	3.79
1991 San Francisco	NL	36	34	3	0	206.2	890	223	103	96	19	8	6	8	60	2	131	5	0	12	11	.522	1	0-0	1	4.18
1992 San Francisco	NL	32	32	3	0	189.2	799	194	96	81	13	11	4	4	45	6	107	0	0	13	9	.591	1	0-0	0	3.84
1993 San Francisco	NL	34	34	2	0	231.2	942	224	100	94	18	8	4	11	40	4	145	1	2	22	7	.759	1	0-0	0	3.65
1994 San Francisco	NL	25	25	0	0	159.1	676	176	72	64	14	12	5	7	36	7	85	2	0	6	8	.429	0	0-0	0	3.62
1995 Florida	NL	30	30	4	0	188.1	810	208	95	90	22	10	0	6	57	5	126	2	1	14	14	.500	0	0-0	0	4.30
1996 Fla-Tex		34	34	2	0	222.2	934	229	117	105	19	12	6	5	58	4	155	0	0	11	12	.478	1	0-0	0	4.24
1997 Texas	AL	30	30	2	0	189.1	828	240	106	96	20	4	7	4	30	1	139	1	0	9	12	.429	0	0-0	0	4.56
1998 Texas	AL	32	32	0	0	195	854	230	131	123	19	7	5	8	46	1	131	3	0	9	13	.409	0	0-0	0	5.68
1996 Florida	NL	24	24	1	0	154	645	154	84	74	15	11	4	3	42	2	108	0	0	6	10	.375	1	0-0	0	4.32
Texas	AL	10	10	1	0	68.2	289	75	33	31	4	1	2	2	16	2	47	0	0	5	2	.714	1	0-0	0	4.06
10 ML YEARS		289	283	18	2	1792.2	7618	1932	916	838	164	79	44	60	436	37	1142	17	6	110	93	.542	4	1-1	1	4.21

Ellis Burks

Bats: R **Throws:** R **Pos:** CF-114; LF-45; RF-10; PH/PR-4 **Ht:** 6'2" **Wt:** 209 **Born:** 9/11/64 **Age:** 34

Year Team	Lg	BATTING									R	RBI	TBB	IBB	SO	HBP	SH	SF	BASERUNNING				PERCENTAGES		
		G	AB	H	2B	3B	HR	(Hm	Rd)	TB									SB	CS	SB%	GDP	Avg	OBP	SLG
1987 Boston	AL	133	558	152	30	2	20	(11	9)	246	94	59	41	0	98	2	4	1	27	6	.82	1	.272	.324	.441
1988 Boston	AL	144	540	159	37	5	18	(8	10)	260	93	92	62	1	89	3	4	6	25	9	.74	8	.294	.367	.481
1989 Boston	AL	97	399	121	19	6	12	(6	6)	188	73	61	36	2	52	5	2	4	21	5	.81	8	.303	.365	.471
1990 Boston	AL	152	588	174	33	8	21	(10	11)	286	89	89	48	4	82	1	2	2	9	11	.45	18	.296	.349	.486
1991 Boston	AL	130	474	119	33	3	14	(8	6)	200	56	56	39	2	81	6	2	3	6	11	.35	7	.251	.314	.422
1992 Boston	AL	66	235	60	8	3	8	(4	4)	98	35	30	25	2	48	1	0	2	5	2	.71	5	.255	.327	.417
1993 Chicago	AL	146	499	137	24	4	17	(7	10)	220	75	74	60	2	97	4	3	8	6	9	.40	11	.275	.352	.441
1994 Colorado	NL	42	149	48	8	3	13	(7	6)	101	33	24	16	3	39	0	0	0	3	1	.75	3	.322	.388	.678
1995 Colorado	NL	103	278	74	10	6	14	(8	6)	138	41	49	39	0	72	2	1	1	7	3	.70	7	.266	.359	.496
1996 Colorado	NL	156	613	211	45	8	40	(23	17)	392	142	128	61	2	114	6	3	2	32	6	.84	19	.344	.408	.639
1997 Colorado	NL	119	424	123	19	2	32	(17	15)	242	91	82	47	0	75	3	1	2	7	2	.78	17	.290	.363	.571
1998 Col-SF	NL	142	504	147	28	6	21	(10	11)	250	76	76	58	1	111	5	6	9	11	8	.58	12	.292	.365	.496
1998 Colorado	NL	100	357	102	22	5	16	(8	8)	182	54	54	39	0	80	2	2	5	8	1	.30	10	.286	.355	.510
San Francisco	NL	42	147	45	6	1	5	(2	3)	68	22	22	19	1	31	3	4	4	3	1	.89	2	.306	.387	.463
12 ML YEARS		1430	5261	1525	294	56	230	(119	111)	2621	898	820	532	19	958	38	28	40	159	73	.69	116	.290	.357	.498

Jeromy Burnitz

Bats: Left **Throws:** Right **Pos:** RF-161; PH/PR-3; CF-1 **Ht:** 6'0" **Wt:** 205 **Born:** 4/15/69 **Age:** 30

Year Team	Lg	BATTING									R	RBI	TBB	IBB	SO	HBP	SH	SF	BASERUNNING				PERCENTAGES		
		G	AB	H	2B	3B	HR	(Hm	Rd)	TB									SB	CS	SB%	GDP	Avg	OBP	SLG
1993 New York	NL	86	263	64	10	6	13	(6	7)	125	49	38	38	4	66	1	2	2	3	6	.33	2	.243	.339	.475
1994 New York	NL	45	143	34	4	0	3	(2	1)	47	26	15	23	0	45	1	1	0	1	1	.50	2	.238	.347	.329
1995 Cleveland	AL	9	7	4	1	0	0	(0	0)	5	4	0	0	0	0	0	0	0	0	0	.00	0	.571	.571	.714
1996 Cle-Mil	AL	94	200	53	14	0	9	(5	4)	94	38	40	33	2	47	4	0	2	4	1	.80	4	.265	.377	.470
1997 Milwaukee	AL	153	494	139	37	8	27	(18	9)	273	85	85	75	8	111	5	3	0	20	13	.61	8	.281	.382	.553
1998 Milwaukee	NL	161	609	160	28	1	38	(17	21)	304	92	125	70	7	158	4	1	7	7	4	.64	9	.263	.339	.499
1996 Cleveland	AL	71	128	36	10	0	7	(4	3)	67	30	26	25	1	31	2	0	0	2	1	.67	2	.281	.406	.523
Milwaukee	AL	23	72	17	4	0	2	(1	1)	27	8	14	8	1	16	2	0	2	2	0	1.00	1	.236	.321	.375

				BATTING														BASERUNNING				PERCENTAGES		
Year Team	Lg	G	AB	H	2B	3B	HR	(Hm | Rd)	TB	R	RBI	TBB	IBB	SO	HBP	SH	SF	SB	CS	SB%	GDP	Avg	OBP	SLG
6 ML YEARS		548	1716	454	94	15	90	(48 | 42)	848	294	303	239	21	427	15	7	11	35	25	.58	25	.265	.357	.494

Mike Busby

Pitches: Right **Bats:** Right **Pos:** RP-24; SP-2   **Ht:** 6'4" **Wt:** 210 **Born:** 12/27/72 **Age:** 26

		HOW MUCH HE PITCHED						WHAT HE GAVE UP											THE RESULTS						
Year Team	Lg	G	GS	CG	GF	IP	BFP	H	R	ER	HR	SH	SF	HB	TBB	IBB	SO	WP	Bk	W	L	Pct.	ShO	Sv-Op	Hld	ERA
1991 Cardinals	R	11	11	0	0	59	267	67	35	23	1	0	2	2	29	0	71	3	1	4	3	.571	0	0--	—	3.51
1992 Savannah	A	28	28	1	0	149.2	665	145	96	61	11	1	7	17	67	0	84	16	1	4	13	.235	0	0--	—	3.67
1993 Savannah	A	23	21	1	0	143.2	579	116	49	39	8	6	4	10	31	0	125	5	2	12	2	.857	1	0--	—	2.44
1994 St. Pete	A+	26	26	1	0	151.2	663	166	82	75	11	8	5	14	49	1	89	5	2	6	13	.316	0	0--	—	4.45
1995 Arkansas	AA	20	20	1	0	134	565	125	63	49	8	3	3	6	35	1	95	5	0	7	6	.538	0	0--	—	3.29
Louisville	AAA	6	6	1	0	38.1	154	28	18	14	2	2	2	3	11	0	26	2	0	2	2	.500	0	0--	—	3.29
1996 Louisville	AAA	14	14	0	0	72	343	89	57	51	11	3	1	6	44	1	53	7	2	2	5	.286	0	0--	—	6.38
1997 Louisville	AAA	15	14	1	0	93.2	395	95	49	48	12	0	1	7	30	1	65	8	0	4	8	.333	1	0--	—	4.61
1998 Memphis	AAA	7	2	0	2	8	29	5	3	3	1	0	1	0	2	0	5	1	0	0	0	.000	0	0--	—	3.38
1996 St. Louis	NL	1	1	0	0	4	28	9	13	8	4	1	0	1	4	0	4	0	0	0	1	.000	0	0-0	0	18.00
1997 St. Louis	NL	3	3	0	0	14.1	67	24	14	14	2	1	1	0	4	0	6	0	0	0	2	.000	0	0-0	0	8.79
1998 St. Louis	NL	26	2	0	7	46	202	45	23	23	3	3	2	5	15	0	33	3	0	5	2	.714	0	0-2	5	4.50
3 ML YEARS		30	6	0	7	64.1	297	78	50	45	9	5	3	6	23	0	43	3	0	5	5	.500	0	0-2	5	6.30

Homer Bush

Bats: R **Throws:** R **Pos:** 2B-24; PH/PR-21; DH-13; 3B-3; SS-2   **Ht:** 5'10" **Wt:** 175 **Born:** 11/12/72 **Age:** 26

					BATTING														BASERUNNING				PERCENTAGES		
Year Team	Lg	G	AB	H	2B	3B	HR	(Hm	Rd)	TB	R	RBI	TBB	IBB	SO	HBP	SH	SF	SB	CS	SB%	GDP	Avg	OBP	SLG
1991 Padres	R	32	127	41	3	2	0	—	—	48	16	16	4	1	33	1	0	0	11	7	.61	2	.323	.348	.378
1992 Chston-SC	A	108	367	86	10	5	0	—	—	106	37	18	13	0	85	3	0	2	14	11	.56	3	.234	.265	.289
1993 Waterloo	A	130	472	152	16	3	5	—	—	192	63	51	19	0	87	1	1	1	39	14	.74	10	.322	.349	.407
1994 Rancho Cuca	A+	39	161	54	10	3	0	—	—	70	37	16	9	0	29	4	1	1	9	2	.82	2	.335	.383	.435
Wichita	AA	59	245	73	11	4	3	—	—	101	35	14	10	0	39	3	1	0	20	7	.74	6	.298	.333	.412
1995 Memphis	AA	108	432	121	12	5	5	—	—	158	53	37	15	0	83	2	4	0	34	12	.74	6	.280	.307	.366
1996 Las Vegas	AAA	32	116	42	11	1	2	—	—	61	24	3	3	1	33	2	5	0	3	5	.38	2	.362	.388	.526
1997 Las Vegas	AAA	38	155	43	10	1	3	—	—	64	25	14	7	0	40	2	1	4	5	1	.83	1	.277	.310	.413
Columbus	AAA	74	275	68	10	3	2	—	—	90	36	26	25	0	56	1	7	4	12	7	.63	6	.247	.308	.327
1997 New York	AL	10	11	4	0	0	0	(0	0)	4	2	3	0	0	0	0	0	0	0	0	.00	0	.364	.364	.364
1998 New York	AL	45	71	27	3	0	1	(1	0)	33	17	5	5	0	19	0	2	0	6	3	.67	1	.380	.421	.465
2 ML YEARS		55	82	31	3	0	1	(1	0)	37	19	8	5	0	19	0	2	0	6	3	.67	1	.378	.414	.451

Adam Butler

Pitches: Left **Bats:** Left **Pos:** RP-8   **Ht:** 6'2" **Wt:** 225 **Born:** 8/17/73 **Age:** 25

			HOW MUCH HE PITCHED					WHAT HE GAVE UP											THE RESULTS						
Year Team	Lg	G	GS	CG	GF	IP	BFP	H	R	ER	HR	SH	SF	HB	TBB	IBB	SO	WP	Bk	W	L	Pct.	ShO	Sv-Op	Hld	ERA
1995 Eugene	A-	23	0	0	18	25.1	109	15	9	7	0	1	0	3	12	5	50	1	0	4	1	.800	0	8--	—	2.49
1996 Macon	A	12	0	0	12	14.2	53	5	3	2	1	0	0	1	3	0	23	1	0	0	1	.000	0	8--	—	1.23
Durham	A+	9	0	0	9	11	41	2	0	0	0	0	0	1	7	0	14	0	0	0	0	.000	0	5--	—	0.00
Greenville	AA	38	0	0	31	35.1	161	36	22	20	6	5	3	2	16	3	31	3	0	1	4	.200	0	17--	—	5.09
1997 Greenville	AA	46	0	0	38	49	203	40	16	14	3	3	2	4	15	2	56	1	0	5	1	.833	0	22--	—	2.57
1998 Richmond	AAA	48	4	0	34	100	427	96	41	40	9	6	6	6	28	1	92	3	1	3	7	.300	0	14--	—	3.60
1998 Atlanta	NL	8	0	0	1	5	28	5	7	6	1	2	1	1	6	1	7	1	0	0	1	.000	0	0-0	1	10.80

Rich Butler

Bats: Left **Throws:** Right **Pos:** LF-39; RF-22; PH/PR-13   **Ht:** 6'1" **Wt:** 205 **Born:** 5/1/73 **Age:** 26

					BATTING														BASERUNNING				PERCENTAGES		
Year Team	Lg	G	AB	H	2B	3B	HR	(Hm	Rd)	TB	R	RBI	TBB	IBB	SO	HBP	SH	SF	SB	CS	SB%	GDP	Avg	OBP	SLG
1991 Blue Jays	R	59	213	56	6	7	0	—	—	76	30	13	17	1	45	0	4	0	10	6	.63	0	.263	.317	.357
1992 Myrtle Bch	A	130	441	100	14	1	2	—	—	122	43	43	37	1	90	7	6	0	11	15	.42	6	.227	.297	.277
1993 Dunedin	A+	110	444	136	19	8	11	—	—	204	68	65	48	10	64	3	1	4	11	13	.46	4	.306	.375	.459
Knoxville	AA	6	21	2	0	1	0	—	—	4	3	0	3	0	5	0	0	0	0	0	.00	0	.095	.208	.190
1994 Knoxville	AA	53	192	56	7	4	3	—	—	80	29	22	19	1	31	2	1	1	7	4	.64	1	.292	.360	.417
Syracuse	AAA	94	302	73	6	2	3	—	—	92	34	27	22	0	66	0	2	1	8	8	.50	6	.242	.292	.305
1995 Syracuse	AAA	69	199	32	4	2	2	—	—	46	20	14	9	0	45	0	1	1	2	3	.40	5	.161	.196	.231
Knoxville	AA	58	217	58	12	3	4	—	—	88	27	33	25	1	41	2	1	0	11	3	.79	5	.267	.348	.406
1996 Dunedin	A+	10	28	2	0	0	0	—	—	2	1	1	5	0	9	0	0	0	4	1	.80	1	.071	.212	.071
1997 Syracuse	AAA	137	537	161	30	9	24	—	—	281	93	87	60	2	107	4	3	3	20	7	.74	11	.300	.373	.523
1998 Durham	AAA	38	145	43	8	0	8	—	—	75	28	35	22	3	24	2	0	3	6	2	.75	1	.297	.390	.517
1997 Toronto	AL	7	14	4	1	0	0	(0	0)	5	3	2	2	0	3	0	0	0	0	1	.00	0	.286	.375	.357
1998 Tampa Bay	AL	72	217	49	3	3	7	(6	1)	79	25	20	15	0	37	2	0	3	4	2	.67	4	.226	.278	.364
2 ML YEARS		79	231	53	4	3	7	(6	1)	84	28	22	17	0	40	2	0	3	4	3	.57	4	.229	.285	.364

Paul Byrd

Pitches: Right **Bats:** Right **Pos:** SP-8; RP-1   **Ht:** 6'1" **Wt:** 185 **Born:** 12/3/70 **Age:** 28

Year Team	Lg	G	GS	CG	GF	IP	BFP	H	R	ER	HR	SH	SF	HB	TBB	IBB	SO	WP	Bk	W	L	Pct.	ShO	Sv-Op	Hld	ERA
1998 Richmond *	AAA	17	17	2	0	102.1	424	92	44	42	9	2	2	2	36	2	84	3	1	5	5	.500	0	0- -	-	3.69
1995 New York	NL	17	0	0	6	22	91	18	6	5	1	0	2	1	7	1	26	1	2	2	0	1.000	0	0-0	3	2.05
1996 New York	NL	38	0	0	14	46.2	204	48	22	22	7	1	1	0	21	4	31	3	0	1	2	.333	0	0-2	3	4.24
1997 Atlanta	NL	31	4	0	9	53	236	47	34	31	6	2	2	4	28	4	37	3	1	4	4	.500	0	0-0	1	5.26
1998 Atl-Phi	NL	9	8	2	0	57	233	45	19	17	6	2	1	0	18	1	39	2	0	5	2	.714	1	0-0	0	2.68
1998 Atlanta	NL	1	0	0	0	2	11	4	3	3	0	0	0	0	1	0	1	0	0	0	0	.000	0	0-0	0	13.50
Philadelphia	NL	8	8	2	0	55	222	41	16	14	6	2	1	0	17	1	38	2	0	5	2	.714	1	0-0	0	2.29
4 ML YEARS		95	12	2	29	178.2	764	158	81	75	20	5	6	5	74	10	133	9	3	12	8	.600	1	0-2	7	3.78

Tim Byrdak

Pitches: Left **Bats:** Left **Pos:** RP-3   **Ht:** 5'11" **Wt:** 160 **Born:** 10/31/73 **Age:** 25

Year Team	Lg	G	GS	CG	GF	IP	BFP	H	R	ER	HR	SH	SF	HB	TBB	IBB	SO	WP	Bk	W	L	Pct.	ShO	Sv-Op	Hld	ERA
1994 Eugene	A-	15	15	0	0	73.1	302	60	33	25	6	2	2	4	20	0	77	1	1	4	5	.444	0	0- -	-	3.07
1995 Wilmington	A+	27	26	0	0	166.1	657	118	46	40	7	3	3	10	45	2	127	1	0	11	5	.688	0	0- -	-	2.16
1996 Wichita	AA	15	15	0	0	84.2	388	112	73	65	15	5	1	0	44	0	47	8	0	5	7	.417	0	0- -	-	6.91
1997 Wilmington	A+	22	2	0	15	41	169	34	17	16	3	5	1	2	12	4	47	4	0	4	3	.571	0	3- -	-	3.51
1998 Wichita	AA	34	0	0	10	52	242	58	29	24	3	4	4	2	28	1	37	2	3	3	5	.375	0	2- -	-	4.15
Omaha	AAA	26	0	0	8	36.2	161	31	13	10	3	4	0	2	20	0	32	2	0	2	1	.667	0	1- -	-	2.45
1998 Kansas City	AL	3	0	0	0	1.2	9	5	1	1	1	0	0	0	0	0	0	1	0	0	0	.000	0	0-0	0	5.40

Jolbert Cabrera

Bats: Right **Throws:** Right **Pos:** SS-1   **Ht:** 6'0" **Wt:** 177 **Born:** 12/8/72 **Age:** 26

Year Team	Lg	G	AB	H	2B	3B	HR	(Hm	Rd)	TB	R	RBI	TBB	IBB	SO	HBP	SH	SF	SB	CS	SB%	GDP	Avg	OBP	SLG
1991 Sumter	A	101	324	66	4	0	1	—	—	73	33	20	19	0	62	4	4	2	10	11	.48	5	.204	.255	.225
1992 Albany	A	118	377	86	9	2	0	—	—	99	44	23	34	0	77	1	6	0	22	11	.67	8	.228	.294	.263
1993 Burlington	A	128	507	129	24	2	0	—	—	157	62	38	39	0	93	7	11	4	31	11	.74	13	.254	.314	.310
1994 Wst Plm Bch	A+	83	266	54	4	0	0	—	—	58	32	13	14	0	48	8	4	0	7	10	.41	4	.203	.264	.218
San Berndno	A+	30	109	27	5	1	0	—	—	34	14	11	14	0	24	0	4	2	2	2	.50	1	.248	.328	.312
Harrisburg	AA	3	2	0	0	0	0	—	—	0	0	0	0	0	1	0	0	0	0	0	.00	0	.000	.000	.000
1995 Wst Plm Bch	A+	103	357	102	23	2	1	—	—	132	62	25	38	0	61	8	6	4	19	12	.61	3	.286	.364	.370
Harrisburg	AA	9	35	10	2	0	0	—	—	12	4	1	1	0	3	0	2	0	3	1	.75	1	.286	.306	.343
1996 Harrisburg	AA	107	354	85	18	2	3	—	—	116	40	29	23	3	63	1	5	4	10	5	.67	9	.240	.285	.328
1997 Harrisburg	AA	48	171	43	9	0	2	—	—	58	28	11	28	0	28	1	3	0	5	4	.56	4	.251	.360	.339
Ottawa	AAA	68	191	54	10	4	0	—	—	72	28	12	11	0	31	0	4	1	15	5	.75	5	.283	.320	.377
1998 Buffalo	AAA	129	494	157	24	1	10	—	—	213	94	45	68	0	71	13	8	2	25	15	.63	10	.318	.412	.431
1998 Cleveland	AL	1	2	0	0	0	0	(0	0)	0	0	0	0	0	1	0	0	0	0	0	.00	0	.000	.000	.000

Jose Cabrera

Pitches: Right **Bats:** Right **Pos:** RP-3   **Ht:** 6'0" **Wt:** 160 **Born:** 3/24/72 **Age:** 27

Year Team	Lg	G	GS	CG	GF	IP	BFP	H	R	ER	HR	SH	SF	HB	TBB	IBB	SO	WP	Bk	W	L	Pct.	ShO	Sv-Op	Hld	ERA
1992 Burlington	R+	13	13	1	0	92.1	367	74	27	18	6	2	4	2	18	0	79	3	1	8	3	.727	0	0- -	-	1.75
1993 Columbus	A	26	26	1	0	155.1	624	122	54	46	8	2	4	1	53	2	105	8	4	11	6	.647	0	0- -	-	2.67
1994 Kinston	A+	24	24	0	0	133.2	575	134	84	66	15	6	3	5	43	0	110	5	5	4	13	.235	0	0- -	-	4.44
1995 Canton-Akrn	AA	24	11	1	4	85	350	83	32	31	7	1	6	1	21	1	61	0	2	5	3	.625	1	0- -	-	3.28
1996 Bakersfield	A+	7	7	0	0	41.1	183	40	25	18	7	2	2	1	21	0	52	5	0	2	2	.500	0	0- -	-	3.92
Kinston	A+	4	3	0	0	17.2	68	7	2	2	0	1	1	1	8	0	19	3	0	1	1	.500	0	0- -	-	1.02
Canton-Akrn	AA	15	9	1	4	62.1	278	78	45	39	10	2	3	1	17	2	40	4	0	4	3	.571	0	0- -	-	5.63
1997 Buffalo	AAA	5	0	0	2	15	57	8	2	2	2	0	0	1	7	1	11	1	0	3	0	1.000	0	0- -	-	1.20
New Orleans	AAA	31	0	0	5	46	181	31	13	13	2	1	0	2	13	3	48	0	0	2	2	.500	0	0- -	-	2.54
1998 New Orleans	AAA	5	0	0	2	5	19	2	3	3	2	0	0	1	1	0	6	1	1	0	0	.000	0	1- -	-	5.40
1997 Houston	NL	12	0	0	6	15.1	57	6	2	2	1	0	3	0	6	0	18	0	0	0	0	.000	0	0-1	2	1.17
1998 Houston	NL	3	0	0	1	4.1	19	7	4	4	0	0	0	0	1	1	1	0	0	0	0	.000	0	0-0	0	8.31
2 ML YEARS		15	0	0	7	19.2	76	13	6	6	1	0	3	0	7	1	19	0	0	0	0	.000	0	0-1	2	2.75

Orlando Cabrera

Bats: Right **Throws:** Right **Pos:** SS-52; 2B-28; PH/PR-5   **Ht:** 5'9" **Wt:** 165 **Born:** 11/2/74 **Age:** 24

Year Team	Lg	G	AB	H	2B	3B	HR	(Hm	Rd)	TB	R	RBI	TBB	IBB	SO	HBP	SH	SF	SB	CS	SB%	GDP	Avg	OBP	SLG
1993 Expos	R	11	0	0	0	0	0	—	—	0	0	0	0	0	0	0	0	0	0	0	.00	0	.000	.000	.000
1994 Expos	R	22	73	23	4	1	0	—	—	29	13	11	5	0	8	0	1	0	5	0	1.00	2	.315	.359	.397
1995 Wst Plm Bch	A+	3	5	1	0	0	0	—	—	1	0	0	0	0	0	0	0	0	1	0	1.00	0	.200	.200	.200
Vermont	A-	65	248	70	12	5	3	—	—	101	37	33	16	0	28	1	2	4	15	8	.65	3	.282	.323	.407
1996 Delmarva	A	134	512	129	28	4	14	—	—	207	86	65	54	4	63	5	5	4	51	18	.74	4	.252	.327	.404
1997 Wst Plm Bch	A+	69	279	77	19	2	5	—	—	115	56	26	27	0	33	0	1	0	32	12	.73	1	.276	.340	.412
Harrisburg	AA	35	133	41	13	2	5	—	—	73	34	20	15	0	18	0	1	0	7	2	.78	1	.308	.378	.549
Ottawa	AAA	31	122	32	5	2	2	—	—	47	17	14	7	0	16	2	1	3	8	1	.89	0	.262	.306	.385
1998 Ottawa	AAA	66	272	63	9	4	0	—	—	80	31	26	28	0	27	0	2	5	19	9	.68	8	.232	.298	.294

Year Team	Lg	BATTING G	AB	H	2B	3B	HR	(Hm	Rd)	TB	R	RBI	TBB	IBB	SO	HBP	SH	SF	BASERUNNING SB	CS	SB%	GDP	PERCENTAGES Avg	OBP	SLG
1997 Montreal	NL	16	18	4	0	0	0	(0	0)	4	4	2	1	0	3	0	1	0	1	2	.33	1	.222	.263	.222
1998 Montreal	NL	79	261	73	16	5	3	(2	1)	108	44	22	18	1	27	0	5	1	6	2	.75	6	.280	.325	.414
2 ML YEARS		95	279	77	16	5	3	(2	1)	112	48	24	19	1	30	0	6	1	7	4	.64	7	.276	.321	.401

Greg Cadaret

Pitches: Left **Bats:** Left **Pos:** RP-50 **Ht:** 6'3" **Wt:** 230 **Born:** 2/27/62 **Age:** 37

Year Team	Lg	HOW MUCH HE PITCHED G	GS	CG	GF	IP	BFP	WHAT HE GAVE UP H	R	ER	HR	SH	SF	HB	TBB	IBB	SO	WP	Bk	THE RESULTS W	L	Pct.	ShO	Sv-Op	Hld	ERA
1998 Vancouver *	AAA	9	0	0	3	10	36	4	2	0	0	1	0	0	3	0	12	1	0	2	1	.667	0	1--	--	0.00
1987 Oakland	AL	29	0	0	7	39.2	176	37	22	20	6	2	2	1	24	1	30	1	0	6	2	.750	0	0-1	3	4.54
1988 Oakland	AL	58	0	0	16	71.2	311	60	26	23	2	5	3	1	36	1	64	5	3	5	2	.714	0	3-4	17	2.89
1989 Oak-NYA	AL	46	13	3	7	120	531	130	62	54	7	3	5	2	57	4	80	6	2	5	5	.500	0	0-2	6	4.05
1990 New York	AL	54	6	0	9	121.1	525	120	62	56	8	9	4	1	64	5	80	14	0	4	4	.556	0	3-4	8	4.15
1991 New York	AL	68	5	0	17	121.2	517	110	52	49	8	6	3	2	59	6	105	3	1	8	6	.571	0	3-7	11	3.62
1992 New York	AL	46	11	1	9	103.2	471	104	53	49	12	3	3	2	74	7	73	5	1	4	8	.333	1	1-3	7	4.25
1993 Cin-KC		47	0	0	18	48	220	54	24	23	3	4	0	2	30	5	25	2	0	3	2	.600	0	1-1	5	4.31
1994 Tor-Det	AL	38	0	0	17	40	191	41	24	21	4	0	0	0	33	5	29	9	0	1	1	.500	0	2-2	4	4.73
1997 Anaheim	AL	15	0	0	6	13.2	61	11	5	5	1	1	0	2	8	2	11	3	0	0	0	.000	0	0-0	1	3.29
1998 Ana-Tex	AL	50	0	0	14	44.2	203	49	21	21	7	2	1	3	18	0	42	8	0	1	2	.333	0	1-2	7	4.23
1989 Oakland	AL	26	0	0	6	27.2	119	21	9	7	0	0	2	0	19	3	14	0	0	0	0	.000	0	0-1	5	2.28
New York	AL	20	13	3	1	92.1	412	109	53	47	7	3	3	2	38	1	66	6	2	5	5	.500	1	0-1	1	4.58
1993 Cincinnati	NL	34	0	0	15	32.2	158	40	19	18	3	3	0	1	23	5	23	2	0	2	1	.667	0	1-1	4	4.96
Kansas City	AL	13	0	0	3	15.1	62	14	5	5	0	1	0	1	7	0	2	0	0	1	1	.500	0	0-0	1	2.93
1994 Toronto	AL	21	0	0	8	20	100	24	15	13	4	0	0	0	17	2	15	6	0	0	1	.000	0	0-0	4	5.85
Detroit	AL	17	0	0	9	20	91	17	9	8	0	0	0	0	16	3	14	3	0	1	0	1.000	0	2-2	0	3.60
1998 Anaheim	AL	39	0	0	11	37	167	38	17	17	6	1	0	3	15	0	37	5	0	1	2	.333	0	1-2	7	4.14
Texas	AL	11	0	0	3	7.2	36	11	4	4	1	1	1	0	3	0	5	3	0	0	0	.000	0	0-0	0	4.70
10 ML YEARS		451	35	4	120	724.1	3206	716	351	321	58	35	21	16	403	36	539	56	7	38	32	.543	2	14-26	69	3.99

Miguel Cairo

Bats: Right **Throws:** Right **Pos:** 2B-148; PH/PR-6; DH-1 **Ht:** 6'1" **Wt:** 160 **Born:** 5/4/74 **Age:** 25

Year Team	Lg	BATTING G	AB	H	2B	3B	HR	(Hm	Rd)	TB	R	RBI	TBB	IBB	SO	HBP	SH	SF	BASERUNNING SB	CS	SB%	GDP	PERCENTAGES Avg	OBP	SLG
1992 Dodgers	R	21	76	23	5	2	0	—	—	32	10	9	2	0	6	2	2	1	1	0	1.00	1	.303	.333	.421
Vero Beach	A+	36	125	28	0	0	0	—	—	28	7	7	11	0	12	0	3	1	5	3	.63	3	.224	.285	.224
1993 Vero Beach	A+	89	343	108	10	1	1	—	—	123	49	23	26	0	22	7	10	0	23	16	.59	2	.315	.375	.359
1994 Bakersfield	A+	133	533	155	23	4	2	—	—	192	76	48	34	3	37	6	15	4	44	23	.66	9	.291	.338	.360
1995 San Antonio	AA	107	435	121	20	1	1	—	—	146	53	41	26	0	32	5	4	4	33	16	.67	6	.278	.323	.336
1996 Syracuse	AAA	120	465	129	14	4	3	—	—	160	71	48	26	1	44	8	5	5	27	9	.75	5	.277	.323	.344
1997 Iowa	AAA	135	569	159	35	4	5	—	—	217	82	46	24	0	54	6	6	3	40	15	.73	9	.279	.314	.381
1996 Toronto	AL	9	27	6	2	0	0	(0	0)	8	5	1	2	0	9	1	0	0	0	0	.00	1	.222	.300	.296
1997 Chicago	NL	16	29	7	1	0	0	(0	0)	8	7	1	2	0	3	1	0	0	0	0	.00	0	.241	.313	.276
1998 Tampa Bay	AL	150	515	138	26	5	5	(3	2)	189	49	46	24	0	44	6	11	2	19	8	.70	9	.268	.307	.367
3 ML YEARS		175	571	151	29	5	5	(3	2)	205	61	48	28	0	56	8	11	2	19	8	.70	10	.264	.307	.359

Mike Cameron

Bats: Right **Throws:** Right **Pos:** CF-136; PH/PR-9; RF-2 **Ht:** 6'2" **Wt:** 190 **Born:** 1/8/73 **Age:** 26

Year Team	Lg	BATTING G	AB	H	2B	3B	HR	(Hm	Rd)	TB	R	RBI	TBB	IBB	SO	HBP	SH	SF	BASERUNNING SB	CS	SB%	GDP	PERCENTAGES Avg	OBP	SLG
1995 Chicago	AL	28	38	7	2	0	1	(0	1)	12	4	2	3	0	15	0	3	0	0	0	.00	0	.184	.244	.316
1996 Chicago	AL	11	11	1	0	0	0	(0	0)	1	1	0	1	0	3	0	0	0	0	1	.00	0	.091	.167	.091
1997 Chicago	AL	116	379	98	18	3	14	(10	4)	164	63	55	55	1	105	5	2	5	23	2	.92	8	.259	.356	.433
1998 Chicago	AL	141	396	83	16	5	8	(5	3)	133	53	43	37	0	101	6	1	3	27	11	.71	6	.210	.285	.336
4 ML YEARS		296	824	189	36	8	23	(15	8)	310	121	100	96	1	224	11	6	8	50	14	.78	14	.229	.315	.376

Ken Caminiti

Bats: Both **Throws:** Right **Pos:** 3B-126; PH/PR-5 **Ht:** 6'0" **Wt:** 200 **Born:** 4/21/63 **Age:** 36

Year Team	Lg	BATTING G	AB	H	2B	3B	HR	(Hm	Rd)	TB	R	RBI	TBB	IBB	SO	HBP	SH	SF	BASERUNNING SB	CS	SB%	GDP	PERCENTAGES Avg	OBP	SLG
1987 Houston	NL	63	203	50	7	1	3	(2	1)	68	10	23	12	1	44	0	2	1	0	0	.00	6	.246	.287	.335
1988 Houston	NL	30	83	15	2	0	1	(0	1)	20	5	7	5	0	18	0	0	1	0	0	.00	3	.181	.225	.241
1989 Houston	NL	161	585	149	31	3	10	(3	7)	216	71	72	51	9	93	3	3	4	4	1	.80	8	.255	.316	.369
1990 Houston	NL	153	541	131	20	2	4	(2	2)	167	52	51	48	7	97	0	3	4	9	4	.69	15	.242	.302	.309
1991 Houston	NL	152	574	145	30	3	13	(9	4)	220	65	80	46	7	85	5	3	4	4	5	.44	15	.253	.312	.383
1992 Houston	NL	135	506	149	31	2	13	(7	6)	223	68	62	44	13	68	1	2	4	10	4	.71	14	.294	.350	.441
1993 Houston	NL	143	543	142	31	0	13	(5	8)	212	75	75	49	10	88	0	1	3	8	5	.62	15	.262	.321	.390
1994 Houston	NL	111	406	115	28	2	18	(6	12)	201	63	75	43	13	71	2	0	3	4	3	.57	8	.283	.352	.495
1995 San Diego	NL	143	526	159	33	0	26	(16	10)	270	74	94	69	8	94	1	0	6	12	5	.71	11	.302	.380	.513
1996 San Diego	NL	146	546	178	37	2	40	(20	20)	339	109	130	78	16	99	4	0	10	11	5	.69	15	.326	.408	.621
1997 San Diego	NL	137	486	141	28	0	26	(15	11)	247	92	90	80	9	118	3	0	7	11	2	.85	12	.290	.389	.508
1998 San Diego	NL	131	452	114	29	0	29	(14	15)	230	87	82	71	4	108	4	0	8	6	2	.75	6	.252	.353	.509
12 ML YEARS		1505	5451	1488	307	15	196	(99	97)	2413	771	841	596	97	983	23	14	55	79	36	.69	131	.273	.344	.443

Tom Candiotti

Pitches: Right **Bats:** Right **Pos:** SP-33 **Ht:** 6'2" **Wt:** 221 **Born:** 8/31/57 **Age:** 41

Year Team	Lg	G	GS	CG	GF	IP	BFP	H	R	ER	HR	SH	SF	HB	TBB	IBB	SO	WP	Bk	W	L	Pct.	ShO	Sv-Op	Hld	ERA
1983 Milwaukee	AL	10	8	2	1	55.2	233	62	21	20	4	0	2	2	16	0	21	0	0	4	4	.500	1	0- -	—	3.23
1984 Milwaukee	AL	8	6	0	0	32.1	147	38	21	19	5	0	0	0	10	0	23	1	0	2	2	.500	0	0- -	—	5.29
1986 Cleveland	AL	36	34	17	1	252.1	1078	234	112	100	18	3	9	8	106	0	167	12	4	16	12	.571	3	0- -	—	3.57
1987 Cleveland	AL	32	32	7	0	201.2	888	193	132	107	28	8	10	4	93	2	111	13	2	7	18	.280	2	0-0	0	4.78
1988 Cleveland	AL	31	31	11	0	216.2	903	225	86	79	15	12	5	6	53	3	137	5	7	14	8	.636	1	0-0	0	3.28
1989 Cleveland	AL	31	31	4	0	206	847	188	80	71	10	6	4	4	55	5	124	4	8	13	10	.565	0	0-0	0	3.10
1990 Cleveland	AL	31	29	3	1	202	856	207	92	82	23	4	3	6	55	1	128	9	3	15	11	.577	1	0-0	0	3.65
1991 Cle-Tor	AL	34	34	6	0	238	981	202	82	70	12	4	11	6	73	1	167	11	0	13	13	.500	2	0-0	0	2.65
1992 Los Angeles	NL	32	30	6	1	203.2	839	177	78	68	13	20	6	3	63	5	152	9	2	11	15	.423	2	0-0	0	3.00
1993 Los Angeles	NL	33	32	2	0	213.2	898	192	86	74	12	15	9	6	71	1	155	6	0	8	10	.444	0	0-0	0	3.12
1994 Los Angeles	NL	23	22	5	0	153	652	149	77	70	9	9	8	5	54	2	102	9	0	7	7	.500	0	0-0	0	4.12
1995 Los Angeles	NL	30	30	1	0	190.1	812	187	93	74	18	7	5	9	58	2	141	7	0	7	14	.333	1	0-0	0	3.50
1996 Los Angeles	NL	28	27	1	0	152.1	657	172	91	76	18	8	5	3	43	3	79	3	1	9	11	.450	0	0-0	0	4.49
1997 Los Angeles	NL	41	18	0	6	135	573	128	60	54	21	3	2	11	40	4	89	4	0	10	7	.588	0	0-0	2	3.60
1998 Oakland	AL	33	33	3	0	201	878	222	140	108	30	7	8	9	63	2	98	14	0	11	16	.407	0	0-0	0	4.84
1991 Cleveland	AL	15	15	3	0	108.1	442	88	35	27	6	1	7	2	28	0	86	6	0	7	6	.538	0	0-0	0	2.24
Toronto	AL	19	19	3	0	129.2	539	114	47	43	6	3	4	4	45	1	81	5	0	6	7	.462	2	0-0	0	2.98
15 ML YEARS		433	397	68	10	2653.2	11242	2576	1235	1072	236	106	87	82	853	31	1694	107	27	147	158	.482	11	0- -	—	3.64

John Cangelosi

Bats: B **Throws:** L **Pos:** PH/PR-72; CF-33; LF-9; RF-8; DH-1 **Ht:** 5'8" **Wt:** 160 **Born:** 3/10/63 **Age:** 36

Year Team	Lg	G	AB	H	2B	3B	HR	(Hm	Rd)	TB	R	RBI	TBB	IBB	SO	HBP	SH	SF	SB	CS	SB%	GDP	Avg	OBP	SLG
1985 Chicago	AL	5	2	0	0	0	0	(0	0)	0	2	0	0	0	1	1	1	0	0	0	.00	0	.000	.333	.000
1986 Chicago	AL	137	438	103	16	3	2	(1	1)	131	65	32	71	0	61	7	6	3	50	17	.75	5	.235	.349	.299
1987 Pittsburgh	NL	104	182	50	8	3	4	(2	2)	76	44	18	46	1	33	3	1	1	21	6	.78	3	.275	.427	.418
1988 Pittsburgh	NL	75	118	30	4	1	0	(0	0)	36	18	8	17	0	16	1	3	0	9	4	.69	0	.254	.353	.305
1989 Pittsburgh	NL	112	160	35	4	2	0	(0	0)	43	18	9	35	2	20	3	1	2	11	8	.58	1	.219	.365	.269
1990 Pittsburgh	NL	58	76	15	2	0	0	(0	0)	17	13	1	11	0	12	1	2	0	7	2	.78	2	.197	.307	.224
1992 Texas	AL	73	85	16	2	0	1	(0	1)	21	12	6	18	0	16	0	3	0	6	5	.55	0	.188	.330	.247
1994 New York	NL	62	111	28	4	0	0	(0	0)	32	14	4	19	1	20	2	3	0	5	1	.83	1	.252	.371	.288
1995 Houston	NL	90	201	64	5	2	2	(2	0)	79	46	18	48	2	42	4	2	1	21	5	.81	3	.318	.457	.393
1996 Houston	NL	108	262	69	11	4	1	(1	0)	91	49	16	44	0	41	5	1	1	17	9	.65	4	.263	.378	.347
1997 Florida	NL	103	192	47	8	0	1	(1	0)	58	28	12	19	1	33	3	1	1	5	1	.83	3	.245	.321	.302
1998 Florida	NL	104	171	43	8	0	1	(0	1)	54	19	10	30	0	23	1	5	1	2	3	.40	5	.251	.365	.316
12 ML YEARS		1031	1998	500	72	15	12	(7	5)	638	328	134	358	7	318	31	29	10	154	61	.72	27	.250	.371	.319

Jose Canseco

Bats: Right **Throws:** Right **Pos:** DH-78; LF-50; RF-26 **Ht:** 6'4" **Wt:** 240 **Born:** 7/2/64 **Age:** 34

Year Team	Lg	G	AB	H	2B	3B	HR	(Hm	Rd)	TB	R	RBI	TBB	IBB	SO	HBP	SH	SF	SB	CS	SB%	GDP	Avg	OBP	SLG
1985 Oakland	AL	29	96	29	3	0	5	(4	1)	47	16	13	4	0	31	0	0	0	1	1	.50	1	.302	.330	.490
1986 Oakland	AL	157	600	144	29	1	33	(14	19)	274	85	117	65	1	175	8	0	9	15	7	.68	12	.240	.318	.457
1987 Oakland	AL	159	630	162	35	3	31	(16	15)	296	81	113	50	2	157	2	0	9	15	3	.83	16	.257	.310	.470
1988 Oakland	AL	158	610	187	34	4	42	(16	26)	347	120	124	78	10	128	10	1	6	40	16	.71	15	.307	.391	.569
1989 Oakland	AL	65	227	61	9	1	17	(8	9)	123	40	57	23	4	69	2	0	6	6	3	.67	4	.269	.333	.542
1990 Oakland	AL	131	481	132	14	2	37	(18	19)	261	83	101	72	8	158	5	0	5	19	10	.66	9	.274	.371	.543
1991 Oakland	AL	154	572	152	32	1	44	(16	28)	318	115	122	78	8	152	9	0	6	26	6	.81	16	.266	.359	.556
1992 Oak-Tex	AL	119	439	107	15	0	26	(15	11)	200	74	87	63	2	128	6	0	4	6	7	.46	16	.244	.344	.456
1993 Texas	AL	60	231	59	14	1	10	(6	4)	105	30	46	16	2	62	3	0	3	6	6	.50	6	.255	.308	.455
1994 Texas	AL	111	429	121	19	2	31	(17	14)	237	88	90	69	8	114	5	0	2	15	8	.65	20	.282	.386	.552
1995 Boston	AL	102	396	121	25	1	24	(10	14)	220	64	81	42	4	93	7	0	5	4	0	1.00	9	.306	.378	.556
1996 Boston	AL	96	360	104	22	1	28	(17	11)	212	68	82	63	3	82	6	0	3	3	1	.75	7	.289	.400	.589
1997 Oakland	AL	108	388	91	19	0	23	(10	13)	179	56	74	51	1	122	3	0	4	8	2	.80	15	.235	.325	.461
1998 Toronto	AL	151	583	138	26	0	46	(25	21)	302	98	107	65	5	159	6	0	4	29	17	.63	7	.237	.318	.518
1992 Oakland	AL	97	366	90	11	0	22	(12	10)	167	66	72	48	1	104	3	0	4	5	7	.42	15	.246	.335	.456
Texas	AL	22	73	17	4	0	4	(3	1)	33	8	15	15	1	24	3	0	0	1	0	1.00	1	.233	.385	.452
14 ML YEARS		1600	6042	1608	296	13	397	(192	205)	3121	1018	1214	739	58	1630	72	1	66	193	87	.69	153	.266	.350	.517

Dan Carlson

Pitches: Right **Bats:** Right **Pos:** RP-10 **Ht:** 6'1" **Wt:** 185 **Born:** 1/26/70 **Age:** 29

Year Team	Lg	G	GS	CG	GF	IP	BFP	H	R	ER	HR	SH	SF	HB	TBB	IBB	SO	WP	Bk	W	L	Pct.	ShO	Sv-Op	Hld	ERA
1990 Everett	A-	17	11	0	3	62.1	279	60	42	37	5	1	4	1	39	1	77	9	5	2	6	.250	0	0- -	—	5.34
1991 Clinton	A	27	27	5	0	181.1	740	149	69	62	11	3	3	2	76	0	164	18	5	16	7	.696	3	0- -	—	3.08
1992 Shreveport	AA	27	27	4	0	186	765	166	85	66	15	5	3	1	60	3	157	4	0	15	9	.625	1	0- -	—	3.19
1993 Phoenix	AAA	13	12	0	0	70	320	79	54	51	12	2	1	5	32	1	48	4	0	5	6	.455	0	0- -	—	6.56
Shreveport	AA	15	15	2	0	100.1	397	86	30	25	9	4	4	0	26	3	81	5	0	7	4	.636	1	0- -	—	2.24
1994 Phoenix	AAA	31	22	0	2	151.1	665	173	80	78	21	3	9	1	55	1	117	10	0	13	6	.684	0	0- -	—	4.64
1995 Phoenix	AAA	23	22	2	1	132.2	582	138	67	63	11	7	7	3	66	0	93	6	1	9	5	.643	0	1- -	—	4.27
1996 Phoenix	AAA	33	15	2	3	146.2	604	135	61	56	18	5	5	2	46	0	123	3	0	13	6	.684	0	1- -	—	3.44
1997 Bakersfield	A+	2	2	0	0	6	22	3	0	0	0	0	0	0	1	0	7	0	0	0	0	.000	0	0- -	—	0.00

Year Team	Lg	G	GS	CG	GF	IP	BFP	H	R	ER	HR	SH	SF	HB	TBB	IBB	SO	WP	Bk	W	L	Pct.	ShO	Sv-Op	Hld	ERA
Phoenix	AAA	29	14	0	7	109	451	102	53	47	12	3	3	2	36	1	108	6	1	13	3	.813	0	3--	—	3.88
1998 Durham	AAA	19	11	0	3	68	316	87	52	48	8	1	1	3	28	0	59	4	1	3	5	.375	0	0--	—	6.35
1996 San Francisco	NL	5	0	0	3	10	46	13	6	3	2	0	2	0	2	0	4	0	0	1	0	1.000	0	0-0	0	2.70
1997 San Francisco	NL	6	0	0	2	15.1	72	20	14	13	5	0	1	0	8	1	14	0	0	0	0	.000	0	0-0	0	7.63
1998 Tampa Bay	AL	10	0	0	1	17.2	86	25	15	15	3	2	1	3	8	0	16	0	0	0	0	.000	0	0-0	0	7.64
3 ML YEARS		21	0	0	6	43	204	58	35	31	10	2	4	3	18	1	34	0	0	1	0	1.000	0	0-0	0	6.49

Chris Carpenter

Pitches: Right **Bats:** Right **Pos:** SP-24; RP-9 **Ht:** 6'6" **Wt:** 215 **Born:** 4/27/75 **Age:** 24

Year Team	Lg	G	GS	CG	GF	IP	BFP	H	R	ER	HR	SH	SF	HB	TBB	IBB	SO	WP	Bk	W	L	Pct.	ShO	Sv-Op	Hld	ERA
1994 Medicine Ha	R+	15	15	0	0	84.2	366	76	40	26	3	2	3	8	39	0	80	9	2	6	3	.667	0	0--	—	2.76
1995 Dunedin	A+	15	15	0	0	99.1	420	83	29	24	3	2	0	4	50	0	56	9	3	3	5	.375	0	0--	—	2.17
Knoxville	AA	12	12	0	0	64.1	287	71	47	37	3	1	4	1	31	1	53	9	0	3	7	.300	0	0--	—	5.18
1996 Knoxville	AA	28	28	1	0	171.1	755	161	94	75	13	9	3	8	91	4	150	8	2	7	9	.438	0	0--	—	3.94
1997 Syracuse	AAA	19	19	3	0	120	499	113	64	60	16	2	1	3	53	0	97	8	0	4	9	.308	2	0--	—	4.50
1997 Toronto	AL	14	13	1	1	81.1	374	108	55	46	7	1	2	2	37	0	55	7	1	3	7	.300	1	0-0	0	5.09
1998 Toronto	AL	33	24	1	4	175	742	177	97	85	18	4	5	5	61	1	136	5	0	12	7	.632	1	0-0	0	4.37
2 ML YEARS		47	37	2	5	256.1	1116	285	152	131	25	5	7	7	98	1	191	12	1	15	14	.517	2	0-0	0	4.60

Hector Carrasco

Pitches: Right **Bats:** Right **Pos:** RP-63 **Ht:** 6'2" **Wt:** 175 **Born:** 10/22/69 **Age:** 29

Year Team	Lg	G	GS	CG	GF	IP	BFP	H	R	ER	HR	SH	SF	HB	TBB	IBB	SO	WP	Bk	W	L	Pct.	ShO	Sv-Op	Hld	ERA
1994 Cincinnati	NL	45	0	0	29	56.1	237	42	17	14	3	5	0	2	30	1	41	3	1	5	6	.455	0	6-8	3	2.24
1995 Cincinnati	NL	64	0	0	28	87.1	391	86	45	40	1	2	6	2	46	5	64	15	0	2	7	.222	0	5-9	11	4.12
1996 Cincinnati	NL	56	0	0	10	74.1	325	58	37	31	6	4	4	1	45	5	59	8	1	4	3	.571	0	0-2	15	3.75
1997 Cin-KC		66	0	0	22	86	388	80	46	42	7	4	3	8	41	5	76	11	2	2	8	.200	0	0-2	8	4.40
1998 Minnesota	AL	63	0	0	20	61.2	287	75	30	30	4	0	8	1	31	1	46	8	0	4	2	.667	0	1-2	10	4.38
1997 Cincinnati	NL	38	0	0	11	51.1	237	51	25	21	3	3	1	4	25	2	46	3	2	1	2	.333	0	0-0	5	3.68
Kansas City	AL	28	0	0	11	34.2	151	29	21	21	4	1	2	4	16	3	30	8	0	1	6	.143	0	0-2	3	5.45
5 ML YEARS		294	0	0	109	365.2	1628	341	175	157	21	15	21	14	193	17	286	45	4	17	26	.395	0	12-23	47	3.86

Joe Carter

Bats: R **Throws:** R **Pos:** RF-61; DH-32; PH/PR-31; 1B-17; LF-7 **Ht:** 6'3" **Wt:** 230 **Born:** 3/7/60 **Age:** 39

Year Team	Lg	G	AB	H	2B	3B	HR	(Hm	Rd)	TB	R	RBI	TBB	IBB	SO	HBP	SH	SF	SB	CS	SB%	GDP	Avg	OBP	SLG
1983 Chicago	NL	23	51	9	1	1	0	(0	0)	12	6	1	0	0	21	0	1	0	1	0	1.00	1	.176	.176	.235
1984 Cleveland	AL	66	244	67	6	1	13	(9	4)	114	32	41	11	0	48	1	0	1	2	4	.33	2	.275	.307	.467
1985 Cleveland	AL	143	489	128	27	0	15	(5	10)	200	64	59	25	2	74	2	3	4	24	6	.80	9	.262	.298	.409
1986 Cleveland	AL	162	663	200	36	9	29	(14	15)	341	108	121	32	3	95	5	1	8	29	7	.81	6	.302	.335	.514
1987 Cleveland	AL	149	588	155	27	2	32	(9	23)	282	83	106	27	6	105	9	1	4	31	6	.84	8	.264	.304	.480
1988 Cleveland	AL	157	621	168	36	6	27	(16	11)	297	85	98	35	6	82	7	1	6	27	5	.84	6	.271	.314	.478
1989 Cleveland	AL	162	651	158	32	4	35	(16	19)	303	84	105	39	8	112	8	2	5	13	5	.72	6	.243	.292	.465
1990 San Diego	NL	162	634	147	27	1	24	(12	12)	248	79	115	48	19	93	7	0	8	22	6	.79	12	.232	.290	.391
1991 Toronto	AL	162	638	174	42	3	33	(23	10)	321	89	108	49	12	112	10	1	9	20	9	.69	6	.273	.330	.503
1992 Toronto	AL	158	622	164	30	7	34	(21	13)	310	97	119	36	4	109	11	1	13	12	5	.71	14	.264	.309	.498
1993 Toronto	AL	155	603	153	33	5	33	(21	12)	295	92	121	47	5	113	9	0	10	8	3	.73	10	.254	.312	.489
1994 Toronto	AL	111	435	118	25	2	27	(18	9)	228	70	103	33	6	64	2	0	13	11	0	1.00	6	.271	.317	.524
1995 Toronto	AL	139	558	141	23	0	25	(13	12)	239	70	76	37	5	87	3	0	5	12	1	.92	11	.253	.300	.428
1996 Toronto	AL	157	625	158	35	7	30	(14	16)	297	84	107	44	2	106	7	0	9	7	6	.54	12	.253	.306	.475
1997 Toronto	AL	157	612	143	30	4	21	(11	10)	244	76	102	40	5	105	7	0	9	8	2	.80	12	.234	.284	.399
1998 Bal-SF		126	388	101	22	1	18	(11	7)	179	51	63	24	4	61	2	0	4	4	1	.80	9	.260	.304	.461
1998 Baltimore	AL	85	283	70	15	1	11	(6	5)	120	36	34	18	4	48	2	0	0	3	1	.75	7	.247	.297	.424
San Francisco	NL	41	105	31	7	0	7	(5	2)	59	15	29	6	0	13	0	0	4	1	0	1.00	2	.295	.322	.562
16 ML YEARS		2189	8422	2184	432	53	396	(213	183)	3910	1170	1445	527	86	1387	90	10	105	231	66	.78	132	.259	.306	.464

Mike Caruso

Bats: Left **Throws:** Right **Pos:** SS-131; PH/PR-4 **Ht:** 6'1" **Wt:** 172 **Born:** 5/27/77 **Age:** 22

Year Team	Lg	G	AB	H	2B	3B	HR	(Hm	Rd)	TB	R	RBI	TBB	IBB	SO	HBP	SH	SF	SB	CS	SB%	GDP	Avg	OBP	SLG
1996 Bellingham	A-	73	312	91	13	1	2	—	—	112	48	24	16	2	23	2	3	6	24	10	.71	2	.292	.324	.359
1997 San Jose	A+	108	441	147	24	11	2	—	—	199	76	50	38	3	19	6	4	3	11	16	.41	3	.333	.391	.451
Winston-Sal	A+	28	119	27	3	2	0	—	—	34	12	14	4	0	8	2	0	0	3	0	1.00	0	.227	.264	.286
1998 Chicago	AL	133	523	160	17	6	5	(3	2)	204	81	55	14	0	38	7	8	3	22	6	.79	8	.306	.331	.390

Raul Casanova

Bats: Both **Throws:** Right **Pos:** C-14; PH/PR-2 **Ht:** 6'0" **Wt:** 195 **Born:** 8/23/72 **Age:** 26

Year Team	Lg	G	AB	H	2B	3B	HR	(Hm	Rd)	TB	R	RBI	TBB	IBB	SO	HBP	SH	SF	SB	CS	SB%	GDP	Avg	OBP	SLG
1998 Toledo *	AAA	50	171	44	8	0	7	—	—	73	17	26	22	1	28	3	0	1	0	1	.00	6	.257	.350	.427
1996 Detroit	AL	25	85	16	1	0	4	(1	3)	29	6	9	6	0	18	0	0	0	0	0	.00	6	.188	.242	.341

Year Team	Lg	G	AB	H	2B	3B	HR	(Hm	Rd)	TB	R	RBI	TBB	IBB	SO	HBP	SH	SF	SB	CS	SB%	GDP	Avg	OBP	SLG
1997 Detroit	AL	101	304	74	10	1	5	(5	0)	101	27	24	26	1	48	3	0	1	1	1	.50	10	.243	.308	.332
1998 Detroit	AL	16	42	6	2	0	1	(1	0)	11	4	3	5	0	10	1	0	0	0	0	.00	0	.143	.250	.262
3 ML YEARS		142	431	96	13	1	10	(7	3)	141	37	36	37	1	76	4	0	1	1	1	.50	16	.223	.290	.327

Sean Casey

Bats: Left **Throws:** Right **Pos:** 1B-86; PH/PR-15 **Ht:** 6'4" **Wt:** 215 **Born:** 7/2/74 **Age:** 24

Year Team	Lg	G	AB	H	2B	3B	HR	(Hm	Rd)	TB	R	RBI	TBB	IBB	SO	HBP	SH	SF	SB	CS	SB%	GDP	Avg	OBP	SLG
1995 Watertown	A-	55	207	68	18	0	2	—	—	92	26	37	18	4	21	1	0	3	3	0	1.00	6	.329	.380	.444
1996 Kinston	A+	92	344	114	31	3	12	—	—	187	62	57	36	3	47	6	0	2	1	1	.50	5	.331	.402	.544
1997 Akron	AA	62	241	93	19	1	10	—	—	144	38	66	23	2	34	5	0	1	0	1	.00	5	.386	.448	.598
Buffalo	AAA	20	72	26	7	0	5	—	—	48	12	18	9	0	11	1	0	0	0	0	.00	0	.361	.439	.667
1998 Indianaplis	AAA	27	95	31	8	1	1	—	—	44	14	13	14	1	10	1	0	0	0	0	.00	0	.326	.418	.463
1997 Cleveland	AL	6	10	2	0	0	0	(0	0)	2	1	1	1	0	2	1	0	0	0	0	.00	0	.200	.333	.200
1998 Cincinnati	NL	96	302	82	21	1	7	(3	4)	126	44	52	43	3	45	3	0	3	1	1	.50	11	.272	.365	.417
2 ML YEARS		102	312	84	21	1	7	(3	4)	128	45	53	44	3	47	4	0	3	1	1	.50	11	.269	.364	.410

Larry Casian

Pitches: Left **Bats:** Right **Pos:** RP-4 **Ht:** 6'0" **Wt:** 175 **Born:** 10/28/65 **Age:** 33

		HOW MUCH HE PITCHED						WHAT HE GAVE UP										THE RESULTS						
Year Team	Lg	G	GS	CG	GF	IP	BFP	H	R	ER	HR	SH	SF	HB	TBB	IBB	SO	WP	Bk	W	L	Pct.	ShO	Sv-Op	Hld	ERA
1998 Calgary *	AAA	43	0	0	12	52	216	53	22	21	5	2	1	1	16	2	44	3	0	4	1	.800	0	4- -	—	3.63
1990 Minnesota	AL	5	3	0	1	22.1	90	26	9	8	2	0	1	0	4	0	11	0	0	2	1	.667	0	0-0	0	3.22
1991 Minnesota	AL	15	0	0	4	18.1	87	28	16	15	4	0	0	1	7	2	6	2	0	0	0	.000	0	0-0	2	7.36
1992 Minnesota	AL	6	0	0	1	6.2	28	7	2	2	0	0	0	0	1	0	2	0	0	1	0	1.000	0	0-0	1	2.70
1993 Minnesota	AL	54	0	0	8	56.2	241	59	23	19	1	3	3	1	14	2	31	2	0	5	3	.625	0	1-3	15	3.02
1994 Min-Cle	AL	40	0	0	10	49	231	73	43	40	1	7	2	2	16	3	20	1	0	1	5	.167	0	1-1	6	7.35
1995 Chicago	NL	42	0	0	5	23.1	107	23	6	5	1	1	2	0	15	6	11	2	0	1	0	1.000	0	0-3	5	1.93
1996 Chicago	NL	35	0	0	4	24	90	14	5	5	2	2	1	1	11	3	15	1	0	1	1	.500	0	0-1	5	1.88
1997 ChN-KC		44	0	0	7	36.1	164	48	24	23	8	1	3	1	8	2	23	1	0	3	0	.000	0	0-2	5	5.70
1998 Chicago	AL	4	0	0	3	4	23	8	5	5	0	0	0	2	1	0	0	0	0	0	0	.000	0	0-0	0	11.25
1994 Minnesota	AL	33	0	0	8	40.2	188	57	34	32	1	6	2	2	12	2	18	0	0	1	3	.250	0	1-1	5	7.08
Cleveland	AL	7	0	0	2	8.1	43	16	9	8	1	1	0	0	4	1	2	1	0	0	2	.000	0	0-0	1	8.64
1997 Chicago	NL	12	0	0	1	9.2	49	16	9	8	3	0	2	1	2	1	7	0	0	0	1	.000	0	0-0	1	7.45
Kansas City	AL	32	0	0	6	26.2	115	32	15	15	5	1	1	0	6	1	16	1	0	3	2	.000	0	0-2	5	5.06
9 ML YEARS		245	3	0	43	240.2	1061	286	133	122	30	14	12	8	77	18	125	9	0	11	13	.458	0	2-10	38	4.56

Vinny Castilla

Bats: Right **Throws:** Right **Pos:** 3B-162; SS-1 **Ht:** 6'1" **Wt:** 204 **Born:** 7/4/67 **Age:** 31

Year Team	Lg	G	AB	H	2B	3B	HR	(Hm	Rd)	TB	R	RBI	TBB	IBB	SO	HBP	SH	SF	SB	CS	SB%	GDP	Avg	OBP	SLG
1991 Atlanta	NL	12	5	1	0	0	0	(0	0)	1	1	0	0	0	2	0	1	0	0	0	.00	0	.200	.200	.200
1992 Atlanta	NL	9	16	4	1	0	0	(0	0)	5	1	1	1	1	4	1	0	0	0	0	.00	0	.250	.333	.313
1993 Colorado	NL	105	337	86	9	7	9	(5	4)	136	36	30	13	4	45	2	0	5	2	5	.29	10	.255	.283	.404
1994 Colorado	NL	52	130	43	11	1	3	(1	2)	65	16	18	7	1	23	0	1	3	2	1	.67	3	.331	.357	.500
1995 Colorado	NL	139	527	163	34	2	32	(23	9)	297	82	90	30	2	87	4	4	6	2	8	.20	15	.309	.347	.564
1996 Colorado	NL	160	629	191	34	0	40	(27	13)	345	97	113	35	7	88	5	0	4	7	2	.78	20	.304	.343	.548
1997 Colorado	NL	159	612	186	25	2	40	(21	19)	335	94	113	44	9	108	8	0	4	2	4	.33	17	.304	.356	.547
1998 Colorado	NL	162	645	206	28	4	46	(26	20)	380	108	144	40	7	89	6	0	6	5	9	.36	24	.319	.362	.589
8 ML YEARS		798	2901	880	142	16	170	(103	67)	1564	435	509	170	31	446	26	6	28	20	29	.41	89	.303	.344	.539

Alberto Castillo

Bats: Right **Throws:** Right **Pos:** C-35; PH/PR-4; DH-1 **Ht:** 6'0" **Wt:** 185 **Born:** 2/10/70 **Age:** 29

Year Team	Lg	G	AB	H	2B	3B	HR	(Hm	Rd)	TB	R	RBI	TBB	IBB	SO	HBP	SH	SF	SB	CS	SB%	GDP	Avg	OBP	SLG
1998 Norfolk *	AAA	21	49	9	2	0	1	—	—	14	4	6	11	2	12	0	0	0	0	0	.00	0	.184	.333	.286
1995 New York	NL	13	29	3	0	0	0	(0	0)	3	2	0	3	0	9	1	0	0	1	0	1.00	0	.103	.212	.103
1996 New York	NL	6	11	4	0	0	0	(0	0)	4	1	0	0	0	4	0	0	0	0	0	.00	0	.364	.364	.364
1997 New York	NL	35	59	12	1	0	0	(0	0)	13	3	7	9	0	16	0	2	1	0	1	.00	3	.203	.304	.220
1998 New York	NL	38	83	17	4	0	2	(0	2)	27	13	7	9	0	17	1	6	0	0	2	.00	1	.205	.290	.325
4 ML YEARS		92	182	36	5	0	2	(0	2)	47	19	14	21	0	46	2	8	1	1	3	.25	4	.198	.286	.258

Carlos Castillo

Pitches: Right **Bats:** Right **Pos:** RP-52; SP-2 **Ht:** 6'2" **Wt:** 250 **Born:** 4/21/75 **Age:** 24

		HOW MUCH HE PITCHED						WHAT HE GAVE UP										THE RESULTS						
Year Team	Lg	G	GS	CG	GF	IP	BFP	H	R	ER	HR	SH	SF	HB	TBB	IBB	SO	WP	Bk	W	L	Pct.	ShO	Sv-Op	Hld	ERA
1994 White Sox	R	12	12	0	0	59	239	53	20	17	4	2	2	2	10	0	57	3	4	4	3	.571	0	0- -	—	2.59
Hickory	A	3	1	0	2	12	42	3	0	0	0	0	0	1	2	0	17	0	0	2	0	1.000	0	0- -	—	0.00
1995 Hickory	A	14	12	2	2	79.2	343	85	42	33	11	1	3	3	18	0	67	3	6	5	6	.455	0	1- -	—	3.73
1996 South Bend	A	20	19	5	1	133.1	557	131	74	60	12	3	9	5	29	0	128	9	6	9	9	.500	0	0- -	—	4.05
Pr William	A+	6	6	4	0	43.1	180	45	22	19	0	3	5	2	4	1	30	1	1	2	4	.333	0	0- -	—	3.95
1997 Nashville	AAA	4	0	0	4	6	24	4	1	1	0	0	0	0	0	0	4	0	0	0	0	.000	0	3- -	—	1.50

Year Team	Lg	G	GS	CG	GF	IP	BFP	H	R	ER	HR	SH	SF	HB	TBB	IBB	SO	WP	Bk	W	L	Pct.	ShO	Sv-Op	Hld	ERA
1998 Calgary	AAA	2	2	0	0	8	40	12	8	8	4	0	0	0	4	0	4	0	0	1	1	.500	0	0- --	—	9.00
1997 Chicago	AL	37	2	0	14	66.1	295	68	35	33	9	0	4	1	33	3	43	3	0	2	1	.667	0	1-1	3	4.48
1998 Chicago	AL	54	2	0	11	100.1	431	94	61	57	17	2	7	5	35	4	64	4	3	6	4	.600	0	0-2	3	5.11
2 ML YEARS		91	4	0	25	166.2	726	162	96	90	26	2	11	6	68	4	107	7	3	8	5	.615	0	1-3	6	4.86

Frank Castillo

Pitches: Right **Bats:** Right **Pos:** SP-19; RP-8   **Ht:** 6'1" **Wt:** 200 **Born:** 4/1/69 **Age:** 30

Year Team	Lg	G	GS	CG	GF	IP	BFP	H	R	ER	HR	SH	SF	HB	TBB	IBB	SO	WP	Bk	W	L	Pct.	ShO	Sv-Op	Hld	ERA
1998 Lakeland *	A+	1	1	0	0	5	18	2	0	0	0	1	0	1	0	0	4	0	0	1	0	1.000	0	0- --	—	0.00
1991 Chicago	NL	18	18	4	0	111.2	467	107	56	54	5	6	3	0	33	2	73	5	1	6	7	.462	0	0-0	0	4.35
1992 Chicago	NL	33	33	0	0	205.1	856	179	91	79	19	11	5	6	63	6	135	11	0	10	11	.476	0	0-0	0	3.46
1993 Chicago	NL	29	25	2	0	141.1	614	162	83	76	20	10	3	9	39	4	84	5	3	5	8	.385	0	0-0	0	4.84
1994 Chicago	NL	4	4	1	0	23	96	25	13	11	3	1	0	0	5	0	19	0	0	2	1	.667	0	0-0	0	4.30
1995 Chicago	NL	29	29	2	0	188	795	179	75	67	22	11	3	6	52	4	135	3	1	11	10	.524	2	0-0	0	3.21
1996 Chicago	NL	33	33	1	0	182.1	789	209	112	107	28	4	5	8	46	4	139	2	1	7	16	.304	1	0-0	0	5.28
1997 ChN-Col	AL	34	33	0	0	184.1	830	220	121	111	25	17	2	6	69	4	126	3	0	12	12	.500	0	0-0	0	5.42
1998 Detroit	AL	27	19	0	4	116	531	150	91	88	17	2	6	5	44	0	81	0	0	3	9	.250	0	1-1	0	6.83
1997 Chicago	NL	20	19	0	0	98	446	113	64	59	9	11	0	4	44	1	67	1	0	6	9	.400	0	0-0	0	5.42
Colorado	NL	14	14	0	0	86.1	384	107	57	52	16	6	2	4	25	3	59	2	0	6	3	.667	0	0-0	0	5.42
8 ML YEARS		207	194	10	4	1152	4978	1231	642	593	139	62	27	42	351	24	792	29	6	56	74	.431	3	1-1	0	4.63

Luis Castillo

Bats: Right **Throws:** Right **Pos:** 2B-44; PH/PR-1   **Ht:** 5'11" **Wt:** 175 **Born:** 9/12/75 **Age:** 23

Year Team	Lg	G	AB	H	2B	3B	HR	(Hm	Rd)	TB	R	RBI	TBB	IBB	SO	HBP	SH	SF	SB	CS	SB%	GDP	Avg	OBP	SLG
1998 Charlotte *	AAA	100	381	109	11	2	0	—	—	124	74	15	75	1	68	0	4	1	41	15	.73	6	.286	.403	.325
1996 Florida	NL	41	164	43	2	1	1	(0	1)	50	26	8	14	0	46	0	2	0	17	4	.81	0	.262	.320	.305
1997 Florida	NL	75	263	63	8	0	0	(0	0)	71	27	8	27	0	53	0	1	0	16	10	.62	6	.240	.310	.270
1998 Florida	NL	44	153	31	3	2	1	(0	1)	41	21	10	22	0	33	1	1	0	3	0	1.00	1	.203	.307	.268
3 ML YEARS		160	580	137	13	3	2	(0	2)	162	74	26	63	0	132	1	4	0	36	14	.72	7	.236	.312	.279

Tony Castillo

Pitches: Left **Bats:** Left **Pos:** RP-25   **Ht:** 5'10" **Wt:** 190 **Born:** 3/1/63 **Age:** 36

Year Team	Lg	G	GS	CG	GF	IP	BFP	H	R	ER	HR	SH	SF	HB	TBB	IBB	SO	WP	Bk	W	L	Pct.	ShO	Sv-Op	Hld	ERA
1988 Toronto	AL	14	0	0	6	15	54	10	5	5	2	0	2	0	2	0	14	0	0	1	0	1.000	0	0-0	1	3.00
1989 Tor-Atl		29	0	0	9	27	127	31	19	17	0	3	4	1	14	6	15	3	0	1	2	.333	0	1-1	6	5.67
1990 Atlanta	NL	52	3	0	7	76.2	337	93	41	36	5	4	4	1	20	3	64	2	2	5	1	.833	0	1-2	3	4.23
1991 Atl-NYN	NL	17	3	0	6	32.1	148	40	16	12	4	2	1	0	11	1	18	0	0	2	1	.667	0	0-0	1	3.34
1993 Toronto	AL	51	0	0	10	50.2	211	44	19	19	4	5	2	0	22	5	28	1	0	3	2	.600	0	0-1	13	3.38
1994 Toronto	AL	41	0	0	8	68	291	66	22	19	7	3	3	3	28	1	43	0	0	5	2	.714	0	1-4	13	2.51
1995 Toronto	AL	55	0	0	31	72.2	298	64	27	26	7	3	4	3	24	1	38	0	0	1	5	.167	0	13-21	5	3.22
1996 Tor-ChA	AL	55	0	0	13	95	398	95	45	38	10	3	5	3	24	2	57	3	0	5	4	.556	0	2-6	9	3.60
1997 Chicago	AL	64	0	0	20	62.1	283	74	48	34	6	9	0	1	23	7	42	0	0	4	4	.500	0	4-9	15	4.91
1998 Chicago	AL	25	0	0	4	27	129	38	25	24	7	0	0	2	11	0	14	0	0	1	2	.333	0	0-0	1	8.00
1989 Toronto	AL	17	0	0	8	17.2	86	23	14	12	0	2	4	1	10	5	10	3	0	1	1	.500	0	1-1	2	6.11
Atlanta	NL	12	0	0	1	9.1	41	8	5	5	0	1	0	0	4	1	5	0	0	0	1	.000	0	0-0	4	4.82
1991 Atlanta	NL	7	0	0	5	8.2	44	13	9	7	3	1	0	0	5	0	8	0	0	1	1	.500	0	0-0	0	7.27
New York	NL	10	3	0	1	23.2	104	27	7	5	1	1	1	0	6	1	10	0	0	1	0	1.000	0	0-0	1	1.90
1996 Toronto	AL	40	0	0	7	72.1	304	72	38	34	9	3	2	2	20	1	48	2	0	2	3	.400	0	1-2	6	4.23
Chicago	AL	15	0	0	6	22.2	94	23	7	4	1	0	3	1	4	1	9	1	0	3	1	.750	0	1-4	3	1.59
10 ML YEARS		403	6	0	114	526.2	2276	555	267	230	52	32	26	14	179	26	333	9	2	28	23	.549	0	22-44	67	3.93

Juan Castro

Bats: R **Throws:** R **Pos:** SS-47; 2B-38; 3B-12; PH/PR-11   **Ht:** 5'10" **Wt:** 187 **Born:** 6/20/72 **Age:** 27

Year Team	Lg	G	AB	H	2B	3B	HR	(Hm	Rd)	TB	R	RBI	TBB	IBB	SO	HBP	SH	SF	SB	CS	SB%	GDP	Avg	OBP	SLG
1995 Los Angeles	NL	11	4	1	0	0	0	(0	0)	1	0	0	1	0	1	0	0	0	0	0	.00	0	.250	.400	.250
1996 Los Angeles	NL	70	132	26	5	3	0	(0	0)	37	16	5	10	0	27	0	4	0	1	0	1.00	3	.197	.254	.280
1997 Los Angeles	NL	40	75	11	3	1	0	(0	0)	16	3	4	7	1	20	0	2	0	0	0	.00	2	.147	.220	.213
1998 Los Angeles	NL	89	220	43	7	0	2	(0	2)	56	25	14	15	0	37	0	9	2	0	0	.00	5	.195	.245	.255
4 ML YEARS		210	431	81	15	4	2	(0	2)	110	44	23	33	1	85	0	15	2	1	0	1.00	10	.188	.245	.255

Frank Catalanotto

Bats: L **Throws:** R **Pos:** PH/PR-38; 2B-31; DH-22; 1B-18; 3B-3   **Ht:** 6'0" **Wt:** 190 **Born:** 4/27/74 **Age:** 25

Year Team	Lg	G	AB	H	2B	3B	HR	(Hm	Rd)	TB	R	RBI	TBB	IBB	SO	HBP	SH	SF	SB	CS	SB%	GDP	Avg	OBP	SLG
1992 Bristol	R+	21	50	10	2	0	0	—	—	12	6	4	8	0	8	0	0	0	0	1	.00	0	.200	.310	.240
1993 Bristol	R+	55	199	61	9	5	3	—	—	89	37	22	15	1	19	3	3	0	3	6	.33	3	.307	.364	.447
1994 Fayetteville	A	119	458	149	24	8	3	—	—	198	72	56	37	1	54	3	5	1	4	5	.44	4	.325	.379	.432
1995 Jacksnville	AA	134	491	111	19	5	8	—	—	164	66	48	49	4	56	9	6	4	13	8	.62	9	.226	.306	.334

Year Team	Lg	G	AB	H	2B	3B	HR	(Hm	Rd)	TB	R	RBI	TBB	IBB	SO	HBP	SH	SF	SB	CS	SB%	GDP	Avg	OBP	SLG
												BATTING							BASERUNNING				PERCENTAGES		
1996 Jacksnville	AA	132	497	148	34	6	17	—	—	245	105	67	74	8	69	11	3	3	15	14	.52	8	.298	.398	.493
1997 Toledo	AAA	134	500	150	32	3	16	—	—	236	75	68	47	6	80	10	1	6	12	11	.52	9	.300	.368	.472
1998 Toledo	AAA	28	105	35	6	3	4	—	—	59	20	28	14	0	21	7	1	2	0	0	.00	2	.333	.438	.562
1997 Detroit	AL	13	26	8	2	0	0	(0	0)	10	2	3	3	0	7	0	0	0	0	0	.00	0	.308	.379	.385
1998 Detroit	AL	89	213	60	13	2	6	(3	3)	95	23	25	12	1	39	4	0	5	3	2	.60	4	.282	.325	.446
2 ML YEARS		102	239	68	15	2	6	(3	3)	105	25	28	15	1	46	4	0	5	3	2	.60	4	.285	.331	.439

Mike Cather

Pitches: Right **Bats:** Right **Pos:** RP-36   **Ht:** 6'2" **Wt:** 195 **Born:** 12/17/70 **Age:** 28

Year Team	Lg	G	GS	CG	GF	IP	BFP	H	R	ER	HR	SH	SF	HB	TBB	IBB	SO	WP	Bk	W	L	Pct.	ShO	Sv-Op	Hld	ERA
		HOW MUCH HE PITCHED						WHAT HE GAVE UP												THE RESULTS						
1993 Rangers	R	25	0	0	17	30.2	124	20	7	6	0	0	0	3	9	0	30	2	1	1	1	.500	0	4- -	—	1.76
1994 Charlotte	A+	44	0	0	37	60.1	270	56	33	26	2	3	2	3	40	3	53	1	0	8	6	.571	0	6- -	—	3.88
1995 Tulsa	AA	18	0	0	12	21.2	90	20	11	8	0	4	1	1	7	5	15	0	0	0	2	.000	0	1- -	—	3.32
Winnipeg	IND	27	0	0	24	31	123	18	6	5	1	2	0	0	12	3	35	2	0	4	2	.667	0	8- -	—	1.45
1996 Greenville	AA	53	0	0	18	87.2	384	89	42	36	2	6	2	8	29	5	61	2	1	3	4	.429	0	5- -	—	3.70
1997 Greenville	AA	22	0	0	2	37.1	153	37	18	18	2	1	2	6	7	1	29	0	0	5	2	.714	0	1- -	—	4.34
Richmond	AAA	13	0	0	10	26	102	17	6	5	1	2	0	1	9	1	22	0	0	0	0	.000	0	3- -	—	1.73
1998 Richmond	AAA	11	0	0	2	15.1	72	22	12	10	1	2	0	0	6	0	10	2	0	1	1	.000	0	0- -	—	5.87
1997 Atlanta	NL	35	0	0	10	37.2	155	23	12	10	1	2	0	2	19	4	29	0	0	2	4	.333	0	0-3	4	2.39
1998 Atlanta	NL	36	0	0	11	41.1	173	39	21	18	7	4	2	2	12	1	33	0	0	2	2	.500	0	0-3	1	3.92
2 ML YEARS		71	0	0	21	79	328	62	33	28	8	6	2	4	31	5	62	0	0	4	6	.400	0	0-6	5	3.19

Domingo Cedeno

Bats: B **Throws:** R **Pos:** SS-35; PH/PR-27; DH-15; 2B-7   **Ht:** 6'0" **Wt:** 170 **Born:** 11/4/68 **Age:** 30

Year Team	Lg	G	AB	H	2B	3B	HR	(Hm	Rd)	TB	R	RBI	TBB	IBB	SO	HBP	SH	SF	SB	CS	SB%	GDP	Avg	OBP	SLG
												BATTING							BASERUNNING				PERCENTAGES		
1993 Toronto	AL	15	46	8	0	0	0	(0	0)	8	5	7	1	0	10	0	2	1	1	0	1.00	2	.174	.188	.174
1994 Toronto	AL	47	97	19	2	3	0	(0	0)	27	14	10	10	0	31	0	3	4	1	2	.33	1	.196	.261	.278
1995 Toronto	AL	51	161	38	6	1	4	(1	3)	58	18	14	10	0	35	2	1	0	1	0	1.00	3	.236	.289	.360
1996 Tor-ChA	AL	89	301	82	12	2	2	(0	2)	104	46	20	15	0	64	2	8	3	6	3	.67	7	.272	.308	.346
1997 Texas	AL	113	365	103	19	6	4	(2	2)	146	49	36	27	0	77	2	2	1	3	3	.50	5	.282	.334	.400
1998 Texas	AL	61	141	37	9	1	2	(1	1)	54	19	21	10	0	32	0	1	1	2	1	.67	4	.262	.309	.383
1996 Toronto	AL	77	282	79	10	2	2	(0	2)	99	44	17	15	0	60	2	7	1	5	3	.63	6	.280	.320	.351
Chicago	AL	12	19	3	2	0	0	(0	0)	5	2	3	0	0	4	0	1	2	1	0	1.00	1	.158	.143	.263
6 ML YEARS		376	1111	287	48	13	12	(4	8)	397	151	108	73	0	249	6	17	10	13	10	.57	22	.258	.305	.357

Roger Cedeno

Bats: B **Throws:** R **Pos:** LF-45; PH/PR-40; CF-29; RF-10   **Ht:** 6'1" **Wt:** 205 **Born:** 8/16/74 **Age:** 24

Year Team	Lg	G	AB	H	2B	3B	HR	(Hm	Rd)	TB	R	RBI	TBB	IBB	SO	HBP	SH	SF	SB	CS	SB%	GDP	Avg	OBP	SLG
												BATTING							BASERUNNING				PERCENTAGES		
1998 Vero Beach *	A+	6	21	9	0	1	1	—	—	14	5	6	5	0	5	0	0	0	1	0	1.00	2	.429	.538	.667
1995 Los Angeles	NL	40	42	10	2	0	0	(0	0)	12	4	3	3	0	10	0	0	1	1	0	1.00	1	.238	.283	.286
1996 Los Angeles	NL	86	211	52	11	1	2	(0	2)	71	26	18	24	0	47	1	2	0	5	1	.83	0	.246	.326	.336
1997 Los Angeles	NL	80	194	53	10	2	3	(3	0)	76	31	17	25	2	44	3	3	2	9	1	.90	1	.273	.362	.392
1998 Los Angeles	NL	105	240	58	11	1	2	(2	0)	77	33	17	27	2	57	0	3	1	8	2	.80	1	.242	.317	.321
4 ML YEARS		311	687	173	34	4	7	(5	2)	236	94	55	79	4	158	4	8	4	23	4	.85	3	.252	.331	.344

Norm Charlton

Pitches: Left **Bats:** Both **Pos:** RP-49   **Ht:** 6'3" **Wt:** 205 **Born:** 1/6/63 **Age:** 36

Year Team	Lg	G	GS	CG	GF	IP	BFP	H	R	ER	HR	SH	SF	HB	TBB	IBB	SO	WP	Bk	W	L	Pct.	ShO	Sv-Op	Hld	ERA
		HOW MUCH HE PITCHED						WHAT HE GAVE UP												THE RESULTS						
1998 Richmond *	AAA	2	0	0	1	2	8	2	0	0	0	0	0	0	0	0	1	0	0	0	0	.000	0	0- -	—	0.00
1988 Cincinnati	NL	10	10	0	0	61.1	259	60	27	27	6	1	2	2	20	2	39	3	2	4	5	.444	0	0-0	0	3.96
1989 Cincinnati	NL	69	0	0	27	95.1	393	67	38	31	5	9	2	2	40	7	98	2	4	8	3	.727	0	0-1	8	2.93
1990 Cincinnati	NL	56	16	1	13	154.1	650	131	53	47	10	7	2	4	70	4	117	9	1	12	9	.571	1	2-3	9	2.74
1991 Cincinnati	NL	39	11	0	10	108.1	438	92	37	35	6	7	1	6	34	4	77	11	0	3	5	.375	0	1-4	3	2.91
1992 Cincinnati	NL	64	0	0	46	81.1	341	79	39	27	7	7	3	3	26	4	90	8	0	4	2	.667	0	26-34	7	2.99
1993 Seattle	AL	34	0	0	29	34.2	141	22	12	9	4	0	1	0	17	0	48	6	0	1	3	.250	0	18-21	1	2.34
1995 Phi-Sea		55	0	0	27	69.2	284	46	31	26	4	4	2	4	31	3	70	6	1	4	6	.400	0	14-16	12	3.36
1996 Seattle	AL	70	0	0	50	75.2	323	68	37	34	7	3	2	1	38	1	73	9	0	4	7	.364	0	20-27	8	4.04
1997 Seattle	AL	71	0	0	38	69.1	343	89	59	56	7	7	0	4	42	2	55	7	1	3	8	.273	0	14-25	9	7.27
1998 Bal-Atl		49	0	0	19	48	231	53	29	29	5	2	2	1	33	0	47	7	0	2	1	.667	0	1-2	5	5.44
1995 Philadelphia	NL	25	0	0	5	22	102	23	19	18	2	1	1	3	15	3	12	1	0	2	5	.286	0	0-1	9	7.36
Seattle		30	0	0	22	47.2	182	23	12	8	2	3	1	1	16	0	58	5	1	2	1	.667	0	14-15	3	1.51
1998 Baltimore	AL	36	0	0	11	35	178	46	27	27	5	1	1	0	25	0	41	5	0	2	1	.667	0	0-1	3	6.94
Atlanta	NL	13	0	0	8	13	53	7	2	2	0	1	1	1	8	0	6	2	0	0	0	.000	0	1-1	2	1.38
10 ML YEARS		517	37	1	259	798	3403	707	362	321	61	47	17	27	356	27	714	68	9	45	49	.479	1	96-133	62	3.62

Eric Chavez

Bats: Left **Throws:** Right **Pos:** 3B-13; PH/PR-5 **Ht:** 6'1" **Wt:** 195 **Born:** 12/7/77 **Age:** 21

Year Team	Lg	G	AB	H	2B	3B	HR	(Hm	Rd)	TB	R	RBI	TBB	IBB	SO	HBP	SH	SF	SB	CS	SB%	GDP	Avg	OBP	SLG
1997 Visalia	A+	134	520	141	30	3	18	—	—	231	67	100	37	1	91	2	3	2	13	7	.65	20	.271	.321	.444
1998 Huntsville	AA	88	335	110	27	1	22	—	—	205	66	86	42	4	61	1	3	3	12	4	.75	6	.328	.402	.612
Edmonton	AAA	47	194	63	18	0	11	--	—	114	38	40	12	0	32	1	0	2	2	3	.40	4	.325	.364	.588
1998 Oakland	AL	16	45	14	4	1	0	(0	0)	20	6	6	3	1	5	0	0	0	1	1	.50	1	.311	.354	.444

Raul Chavez

Bats: Right **Throws:** Right **Pos:** C-1 **Ht:** 5'11" **Wt:** 175 **Born:** 3/18/73 **Age:** 26

Year Team	Lg	G	AB	H	2B	3B	HR	(Hm	Rd)	TB	R	RBI	TBB	IBB	SO	HBP	SH	SF	SB	CS	SB%	GDP	Avg	OBP	SLG
1990 Astros	R	48	155	50	8	1	0	—	—	60	23	23	7	0	12	2	2	1	5	3	.63	7	.323	.358	.387
1991 Burlington	A	114	420	108	17	0	3	—	—	134	54	41	25	1	64	10	3	4	1	4	.20	13	.257	.312	.319
1992 Asheville	A	95	348	99	22	1	2	—	—	129	37	40	16	1	39	4	1	4	1	0	1.00	11	.284	.320	.371
1993 Osceola	A+	58	197	45	5	1	0	—	—	52	13	16	8	0	19	1	1	1	1	1	.50	12	.228	.261	.264
1994 Jackson	AA	89	251	55	7	0	1	—	—	65	17	22	17	3	41	2	2	1	1	0	1.00	5	.219	.273	.259
1995 Jackson	AA	58	188	54	8	0	4	—	—	74	16	25	8	1	17	3	4	2	0	4	.00	7	.287	.323	.394
Tucson	AAA	32	103	27	5	0	0	—	—	32	14	10	8	0	13	2	1	1	0	1	.00	7	.262	.325	.311
1996 Ottawa	AAA	60	198	49	10	0	2	—	—	65	15	24	11	0	31	1	4	0	0	2	.00	7	.247	.290	.328
1997 Ottawa	AAA	92	310	76	17	0	4	—	—	105	31	46	18	1	42	4	3	3	1	3	.25	9	.245	.293	.339
1998 Ottawa	AAA	11	31	7	0	0	0	—	—	7	2	1	5	0	5	0	1	0	0	0	.00	1	.226	.333	.226
Tacoma	AAA	76	233	52	6	0	4	—	—	70	27	34	22	1	41	4	2	6	1	2	.33	7	.223	.294	.300
1996 Montreal	NL	4	5	1	0	0	0	(0	0)	1	1	0	1	0	1	0	0	0	1	0	1.00	0	.200	.333	.200
1997 Montreal	NL	13	26	7	0	0	0	(0	0)	7	0	2	0	0	5	0	0	0	1	0	1.00	0	.269	.259	.269
1998 Seattle	AL	1	1	0	0	0	0	(0	0)	0	0	0	0	0	0	0	0	0	0	0	.00	1	.000	.000	.000
3 ML YEARS		18	32	8	0	0	0	(0	0)	8	1	2	1	0	6	0	0	0	2	0	1.00	1	.250	.265	.250

Robinson Checo

Pitches: Right **Bats:** Right **Pos:** SP-2 **Ht:** 6'1" **Wt:** 185 **Born:** 9/9/71 **Age:** 27

Year Team	Lg	G	GS	CG	GF	IP	BFP	H	R	ER	HR	SH	SF	HB	TBB	IBB	SO	WP	Bk	W	L	Pct.	ShO	Sv-Op	Hld	ERA
1997 Sarasota	A+	11	11	0	0	56	250	54	37	33	9	3	5	1	27	0	63	4	5	1	4	.200	0	0--	—	5.30
Trenton	AA	1	1	0	0	7.2	29	6	3	2	0	0	1	0	1	0	9	0	0	1	0	1.000	0	0--	—	2.35
Pawtucket	AAA	9	9	2	0	55.1	220	41	22	21	8	1	0	0	16	0	56	3	0	4	2	.667	1	0--	—	3.42
1998 Red Sox	R	3	3	0	0	9	37	9	5	3	1	0	0	1	0	0	13	0	0	1	0	1.000	0	0--	—	3.00
Sarasota	A+	1	1	0	0	2	10	3	2	2	0	0	0	0	1	0	4	0	0	0	1	.000	0	0--	—	9.00
Pawtucket	AAA	11	10	0	0	53.1	233	48	30	27	9	0	2	5	26	1	46	4	0	6	2	.750	0	0--	—	4.56
1997 Boston	AL	5	2	0	1	13.1	54	12	5	5	0	0	0	0	3	0	14	0	0	1	1	.500	0	0-0	1	3.38
1998 Boston	AL	2	2	0	0	7.2	34	11	8	8	3	0	0	0	5	0	5	1	0	0	2	.000	0	0-0	—	9.39
2 ML YEARS		7	4	0	1	21	88	23	13	13	3	0	0	0	8	0	19	1	0	1	3	.250	0	0-0	1	5.57

Bruce Chen

Pitches: Left **Bats:** Both **Pos:** SP-4 **Ht:** 6'1" **Wt:** 150 **Born:** 6/19/77 **Age:** 22

Year Team	Lg	G	GS	CG	GF	IP	BFP	H	R	ER	HR	SH	SF	HB	TBB	IBB	SO	WP	Bk	W	L	Pct.	ShO	Sv-Op	Hld	ERA
1994 Braves	R	9	7	0	2	42.2	180	42	21	18	2	0	3	2	3	0	26	3	0	1	4	.200	0	1--	—	3.80
1995 Danville	R+	14	13	1	0	70.1	310	78	42	31	3	1	4	3	19	1	56	4	1	4	4	.500	0	0--	—	3.97
1996 Eugene	A-	11	8	0	0	35.2	151	23	13	9	1	1	0	3	14	0	55	2	1	4	1	.800	0	0--	—	2.27
1997 Macon	A	28	28	1	0	146.1	602	120	67	57	19	4	5	7	44	0	182	5	1	12	7	.632	1	0--	—	3.51
1998 Greenville	AA	24	23	1	0	139.1	572	106	57	51	14	2	8	5	48	0	164	6	0	13	7	.650	0	0--	—	3.29
Richmond	AAA	4	4	0	0	24	104	17	5	5	1	1	0	1	19	1	29	1	0	2	1	.667	0	0--	—	1.88
1998 Atlanta	NL	4	4	0	0	20.1	91	23	9	9	3	1	0	1	9	1	17	0	0	2	0	1.000	0	0-0	0	3.98

Jin Ho Cho

Pitches: Right **Bats:** Right **Pos:** SP-4 **Ht:** 6'3" **Wt:** 207 **Born:** 8/16/75 **Age:** 23

Year Team	Lg	G	GS	CG	GF	IP	BFP	H	R	ER	HR	SH	SF	HB	TBB	IBB	SO	WP	Bk	W	L	Pct.	ShO	Sv-Op	Hld	ERA
1998 Sarasota	A+	5	5	0	0	32	132	33	14	11	1	0	4	0	5	0	30	2	0	3	1	.750	0	0--	—	3.09
Trenton	AA	13	13	1	0	74	299	59	21	18	4	3	4	3	19	2	62	0	0	5	2	.714	1	0--	—	2.19
1998 Boston	AL	4	4	0	0	18.2	87	28	17	17	4	0	1	1	3	0	15	1	0	0	3	.000	0	0-0	0	8.20

Bobby Chouinard

Pitches: Right **Bats:** Right **Pos:** RP-25; SP-2 **Ht:** 6'1" **Wt:** 188 **Born:** 5/1/72 **Age:** 27

Year Team	Lg	G	GS	CG	GF	IP	BFP	H	R	ER	HR	SH	SF	HB	TBB	IBB	SO	WP	Bk	W	L	Pct.	ShO	Sv-Op	Hld	ERA
1990 Bluefield	R+	10	10	2	0	56	237	61	34	23	10	1	2	1	14	0	30	2	2	2	5	.286	1	0--	—	3.70
1991 Kane County	A	6	6	1	0	33	147	45	24	17	3	0	3	2	5	0	17	3	1	2	4	.333	0	0--	—	4.64
Bluefield	R+	6	6	0	0	33.2	150	44	19	13	1	0	0	2	11	0	31	1	2	5	1	.833	0	0--	—	3.48
1992 Kane County	A	26	24	9	0	181.2	735	151	60	42	4	9	7	6	38	3	112	13	5	10	14	.417	2	0--	—	2.08
1993 Modesto	A+	24	24	1	0	145.2	623	154	75	69	15	3	8	4	56	1	82	4	1	8	10	.444	0	0--	—	4.26

Year Team	Lg	G	GS	CG	GF	IP	BFP	H	R	ER	HR	SH	SF	HB	TBB	IBB	SO	WP	Bk	W	L	Pct.	ShO	Sv-Op	Hld	ERA
1994 Modesto	A+	29	20	0	5	145.2	599	147	53	42	5	8	2	8	32	1	74	5	1	12	5	.706	0	3--	—	2.59
1995 Huntsville	AA	29	29	1	0	166.2	694	155	81	67	10	9	1	4	50	5	106	4	0	14	8	.636	1	0--	—	3.62
1996 Edmonton	AAA	15	15	0	0	84.1	344	70	32	26	7	1	2	1	24	2	45	1	0	10	2	.833	0	0--	—	2.77
1997 Edmonton	AAA	25	21	1	1	100	446	129	80	67	19	1	1	0	26	0	58	6	0	6	6	.500	0	0--	—	6.03
1998 Louisville	AAA	7	7	0	0	42	192	52	31	23	5	1	1	0	15	0	33	1	1	2	1	.667	0	0--	—	4.93
Tucson	AAA	4	0	0	3	6.1	25	6	3	3	1	0	0	0	0	0	6	1	0	0	0	.000	0	1--	—	4.26
1996 Oakland	AL	13	11	0	0	59	278	75	41	40	10	3	3	3	32	3	32	0	0	4	2	.667	0	0-0	0	6.10
1998 Mil-Ari	NL	27	2	0	9	41.1	181	46	24	19	5	4	2	0	11	2	27	5	0	0	2	.000	0	0-1	6	4.14
1998 Milwaukee	NL	1	0	0	0	3	12	5	1	1	0	0	0	0	0	0	1	0	0	0	0	.000	0	0-0	0	3.00
Arizona	NL	26	2	0	9	38.1	169	41	23	18	5	4	1	0	11	2	26	5	0	0	2	.000	0	0-1	6	4.23
2 ML YEARS		40	13	0	9	100.1	459	121	65	59	15	7	5	3	43	5	59	5	0	4	4	.500	0	0-1	6	5.29

Ryan Christenson

Bats: R **Throws:** R **Pos:** CF-113; PH/PR-6; RF-4; LF-1   **Ht:** 5'11" **Wt:** 175 **Born:** 3/28/74 **Age:** 25

Year Team	Lg	G	AB	H	2B	3B	HR	(Hm	Rd)	TB	R	RBI	TBB	IBB	SO	HBP	SH	SF	SB	CS	SB%	GDP	Avg	OBP	SLG
1995 Sou. Oregon	A-	49	158	30	4	1	1	—	—	39	14	16	22	0	33	0	1	2	5	5	.50	3	.190	.286	.247
1996 Sou. Oregon	A-	36	136	39	11	0	5	—	—	65	31	21	19	1	21	1	1	1	8	6	.57	3	.287	.376	.478
W Michigan	A	33	122	38	2	2	2	—	—	50	21	18	13	0	22	4	1	3	4	4	.33	2	.311	.387	.410
1997 Visalia	A+	83	308	90	18	8	13	—	—	163	69	54	70	1	72	2	3	1	20	11	.65	4	.292	.425	.529
Huntsville	AA	29	120	44	9	3	2	—	—	65	39	18	24	0	23	0	0	1	5	4	.56	3	.367	.469	.542
Edmonton	AAA	16	49	14	2	2	2	—	—	26	12	5	11	0	11	2	0	0	2	0	1.00	1	.286	.435	.531
1998 Edmonton	AAA	22	88	23	6	1	1	—	—	34	17	7	15	0	24	0	0	1	4	1	.80	1	.261	.365	.386
1998 Oakland	AL	117	370	95	22	2	5	(2	3)	136	56	40	36	0	106	1	10	4	5	6	.45	1	.257	.321	.368

Jason Christiansen

Pitches: Left **Bats:** Right **Pos:** RP-60   **Ht:** 6'5" **Wt:** 246 **Born:** 9/21/69 **Age:** 29

Year Team	Lg	G	GS	CG	GF	IP	BFP	H	R	ER	HR	SH	SF	HB	TBB	IBB	SO	WP	Bk	W	L	Pct.	ShO	Sv-Op	Hld	ERA
1995 Pittsburgh	NL	63	0	0	13	56.1	255	49	26	25	6	5	3	3	34	9	53	4	1	3	3	.250	0	0-4	12	4.15
1996 Pittsburgh	NL	33	0	0	9	44.1	205	56	34	33	7	2	3	1	19	2	38	4	1	3	3	.500	0	0-2	5	6.70
1997 Pittsburgh	NL	39	0	0	9	33.2	154	37	11	11	2	0	0	2	17	3	37	4	0	3	0	1.000	0	0-2	8	2.94
1998 Pittsburgh	NL	60	0	0	19	64.2	269	51	22	18	2	5	1	0	27	7	71	3	0	3	3	.500	0	6-10	15	2.51
4 ML YEARS		195	0	0	50	199	883	193	95	88	16	13	7	6	97	21	199	15	2	10	9	.526	0	6-18	37	3.98

Archi Cianfrocco

Bats: R **Throws:** R **Pos:** 1B-19; 3B-13; PH/PR-13; 2B-3; RF-3   **Ht:** 6'5" **Wt:** 215 **Born:** 10/6/66 **Age:** 32

Year Team	Lg	G	AB	H	2B	3B	HR	(Hm	Rd)	TB	R	RBI	TBB	IBB	SO	HBP	SH	SF	SB	CS	SB%	GDP	Avg	OBP	SLG
1998 Las Vegas *	AAA	38	127	36	8	1	6	—	—	64	15	16	11	0	35	1	0	0	3	1	.75	2	.283	.345	.504
1992 Montreal	NL	86	232	56	5	2	6	(3	3)	83	25	30	11	0	66	1	1	2	3	0	1.00	2	.241	.276	.358
1993 Mon-SD	NL	96	296	72	11	2	12	(6	6)	123	30	48	17	1	69	3	2	5	2	0	1.00	9	.243	.287	.416
1994 San Diego	NL	59	146	32	8	0	4	(3	1)	52	9	13	3	0	39	4	1	2	2	0	1.00	2	.219	.252	.356
1995 San Diego	NL	51	118	31	7	0	5	(1	4)	53	22	31	11	1	28	2	0	1	0	2	.00	3	.263	.333	.449
1996 San Diego	NL	79	192	54	13	3	2	(0	2)	79	21	32	8	0	56	2	0	1	1	0	1.00	4	.281	.315	.411
1997 San Diego	NL	89	220	54	12	0	4	(3	1)	78	25	26	25	1	80	3	1	2	7	1	.88	11	.245	.328	.355
1998 San Diego	NL	40	72	9	3	0	1	(1	0)	15	4	5	5	0	22	1	2	0	1	0	1.00	1	.125	.192	.208
1993 Montreal	NL	12	17	4	1	0	1	(0	1)	8	3	1	0	0	5	0	0	0	0	0	.00	0	.235	.235	.471
San Diego	NL	84	279	68	10	2	11	(6	5)	115	27	47	17	1	64	3	2	5	2	0	1.00	9	.244	.289	.412
7 ML YEARS		500	1276	308	59	7	34	(17	17)	483	136	185	80	3	360	16	7	13	16	3	.84	34	.241	.292	.379

Jeff Cirillo

Bats: Right **Throws:** Right **Pos:** 3B-149; 1B-6; PH/PR-2   **Ht:** 6'2" **Wt:** 193 **Born:** 9/23/69 **Age:** 29

Year Team	Lg	G	AB	H	2B	3B	HR	(Hm	Rd)	TB	R	RBI	TBB	IBB	SO	HBP	SH	SF	SB	CS	SB%	GDP	Avg	OBP	SLG
1994 Milwaukee	AL	39	126	30	9	0	3	(1	2)	48	17	12	11	0	16	2	0	0	0	1	.00	4	.238	.309	.381
1995 Milwaukee	AL	125	328	91	19	4	9	(6	3)	145	57	39	47	0	42	4	1	4	7	2	.78	8	.277	.371	.442
1996 Milwaukee	AL	158	566	184	46	5	15	(6	9)	285	101	83	58	0	69	7	6	6	4	9	.31	14	.325	.391	.504
1997 Milwaukee	AL	154	580	167	46	2	10	(6	4)	247	74	82	60	0	74	14	4	3	4	3	.57	13	.288	.367	.426
1998 Milwaukee	NL	156	604	194	31	1	14	(6	8)	269	97	68	79	3	88	4	5	3	10	4	.71	26	.321	.402	.445
5 ML YEARS		632	2204	666	151	12	51	(25	26)	994	346	284	255	3	289	31	16	15	25	19	.57	65	.302	.380	.451

Dave Clark

Bats: L **Throws:** R **Pos:** PH/PR-72; RF-13; LF-9; DH-4   **Ht:** 6'2" **Wt:** 209 **Born:** 9/3/62 **Age:** 36

Year Team	Lg	G	AB	H	2B	3B	HR	(Hm	Rd)	TB	R	RBI	TBB	IBB	SO	HBP	SH	SF	SB	CS	SB%	GDP	Avg	OBP	SLG
1986 Cleveland	AL	18	58	16	1	0	3	(1	2)	26	10	9	7	0	11	0	2	1	1	0	1.00	1	.276	.348	.448
1987 Cleveland	AL	29	87	18	5	0	3	(1	2)	32	11	12	2	0	24	0	0	1	1	0	1.00	4	.207	.225	.368
1988 Cleveland	AL	63	156	41	4	1	3	(2	1)	56	11	18	17	2	28	0	0	1	0	2	.00	8	.263	.333	.379
1989 Cleveland	AL	102	253	60	12	0	8	(4	4)	96	21	29	30	5	63	0	1	1	0	2	.00	7	.237	.317	.379
1990 Chicago	NL	84	171	47	4	2	5	(3	2)	70	22	20	8	1	40	0	0	2	7	1	.88	4	.275	.304	.409
1991 Kansas City	AL	11	10	2	0	0	0	(0	0)	2	1	1	1	0	1	0	0	0	0	0	.00	0	.200	.273	.200

Year Team	Lg	G	AB	H	2B	3B	HR	(Hm	Rd)	TB	R	RBI	TBB	IBB	SO	HBP	SH	SF	SB	CS	SB%	GDP	Avg	OBP	SLG
1992 Pittsburgh	NL	23	33	7	0	0	2	(2	0)	13	3	7	6	0	8	0	0	1	0	0	.00	0	.212	.325	.394
1993 Pittsburgh	NL	110	277	75	11	2	11	(8	3)	123	43	46	38	5	58	1	0	2	1	0	1.00	10	.271	.358	.444
1994 Pittsburgh	NL	86	223	66	11	1	10	(7	3)	109	37	46	22	0	48	0	1	3	2	2	.50	5	.296	.355	.489
1995 Pittsburgh	NL	77	196	55	6	0	4	(2	2)	73	30	24	24	1	38	1	0	2	3	3	.50	9	.281	.359	.372
1996 Pit-LA	NL	107	226	61	12	2	8	(6	2)	101	28	36	34	3	53	0	0	1	2	1	.67	6	.270	.364	.447
1997 Chicago	NL	102	143	43	8	0	5	(1	4)	66	19	32	19	3	34	2	0	2	1	0	1.00	2	.301	.386	.462
1998 Houston	NL	93	131	27	7	0	0	(0	0)	34	12	4	14	1	45	1	0	0	1	1	.50	2	.206	.288	.260
1996 Pittsburgh	NL	92	211	58	12	2	8	(6	2)	98	28	35	31	3	51	0	0	0	2	1	.67	6	.275	.366	.464
Los Angeles	NL	15	15	3	0	0	0	(0	0)	3	0	1	3	0	2	0	0	0	0	0	.00	0	.200	.333	.200
13 ML YEARS		905	1964	518	81	8	62	(37	25)	801	248	284	222	21	451	5	4	16	19	12	.61	58	.264	.338	.408

Mark Clark

Pitches: Right **Bats:** Right **Pos:** SP-33   **Ht:** 6'5" **Wt:** 235 **Born:** 5/12/68 **Age:** 31

		HOW MUCH HE PITCHED						WHAT HE GAVE UP												THE RESULTS						
Year Team	Lg	G	GS	CG	GF	IP	BFP	H	R	ER	HR	SH	SF	HB	TBB	IBB	SO	WP	Bk	W	L	Pct.	ShO	Sv-Op	Hld	ERA
1991 St. Louis	NL	7	2	0	1	22.1	93	17	10	10	3	0	3	0	11	0	13	2	0	1	1	.500	0	0-0	1	4.03
1992 St. Louis	NL	20	20	1	0	113.1	488	117	59	56	12	7	4	0	36	2	44	4	0	3	10	.231	1	0-0	0	4.45
1993 Cleveland	AL	26	15	1	1	109.1	454	119	55	52	18	1	1	1	25	1	57	1	0	7	5	.583	0	0-0	2	4.28
1994 Cleveland	AL	20	20	4	0	127.1	540	133	61	54	14	2	7	4	40	0	60	9	1	11	3	.786	1	0-0	0	3.82
1995 Cleveland	AL	22	21	2	0	124.2	552	143	77	73	13	3	6	4	42	0	68	8	0	9	7	.563	0	0-0	0	5.27
1996 New York	NL	32	32	2	0	212.1	883	217	98	81	20	8	4	3	48	8	142	6	2	14	11	.560	0	0-0	0	3.43
1997 NYN-ChN	NL	32	31	3	0	205	866	213	96	87	24	9	4	4	59	3	123	4	1	14	8	.636	0	0-0	0	3.82
1998 Chicago	NL	33	33	2	0	213.2	918	236	116	115	23	12	6	4	48	4	161	5	2	9	14	.391	0	0-0	0	4.84
1997 New York	NL	23	22	1	0	142	608	158	74	67	18	9	2	3	47	2	72	4	0	8	7	.533	0	0-0	0	4.25
Chicago	NL	9	9	2	0	63	258	55	22	20	6	0	2	1	12	1	51	0	1	6	1	.857	0	0-0	0	2.86
8 ML YEARS		192	174	15	2	1128	4794	1195	572	528	127	42	35	20	309	18	668	39	6	68	59	.535	3	0-0	3	4.21

Tony Clark

Bats: Both **Throws:** Right **Pos:** 1B-142; DH-15   **Ht:** 6'7" **Wt:** 245 **Born:** 6/15/72 **Age:** 27

Year Team	Lg	G	AB	H	2B	3B	HR	(Hm	Rd)	TB	R	RBI	TBB	IBB	SO	HBP	SH	SF	SB	CS	SB%	GDP	Avg	OBP	SLG
1995 Detroit	AL	27	101	24	5	1	3	(0	3)	40	10	11	8	0	30	0	0	0	0	0	.00	2	.238	.294	.396
1996 Detroit	AL	100	376	94	14	0	27	(17	10)	189	56	72	29	1	127	0	0	6	0	1	.00	7	.250	.299	.503
1997 Detroit	AL	159	580	160	28	3	32	(18	14)	290	105	117	93	13	144	3	0	5	1	3	.25	11	.276	.376	.500
1998 Detroit	AL	157	602	175	37	0	34	(18	16)	314	84	103	63	5	128	3	0	5	3	3	.50	11	.291	.358	.522
4 ML YEARS		443	1659	453	84	4	96	(53	43)	833	255	303	193	19	429	6	0	16	4	7	.36	36	.273	.348	.502

Will Clark

Bats: Left **Throws:** Left **Pos:** 1B-134; DH-15; PH/PR-1   **Ht:** 6'1" **Wt:** 200 **Born:** 3/13/64 **Age:** 35

Year Team	Lg	G	AB	H	2B	3B	HR	(Hm	Rd)	TB	R	RBI	TBB	IBB	SO	HBP	SH	SF	SB	CS	SB%	GDP	Avg	OBP	SLG
1986 San Francisco	NL	111	408	117	27	2	11	(7	4)	181	66	41	34	10	76	3	9	4	4	7	.36	3	.287	.343	.444
1987 San Francisco	NL	150	529	163	29	5	35	(22	13)	307	89	91	49	11	98	5	3	2	5	17	.23	2	.308	.371	.580
1988 San Francisco	NL	162	575	162	31	6	29	(14	15)	292	102	**109**	100	27	129	4	0	10	9	1	.90	9	.282	.386	.508
1989 San Francisco	NL	159	588	196	38	9	23	(14	9)	321	**104**	111	74	14	103	5	0	8	8	3	.73	6	.333	.407	.546
1990 San Francisco	NL	154	600	177	25	5	19	(8	11)	269	91	95	62	9	97	3	0	13	8	2	.80	7	.295	.357	.448
1991 San Francisco	NL	148	565	170	32	7	29	(17	12)	**303**	84	116	51	12	91	2	0	4	4	2	.67	5	.301	.359	**.536**
1992 San Francisco	NL	144	513	154	40	1	16	(11	5)	244	69	73	73	23	82	4	0	11	12	7	.63	5	.300	.384	.476
1993 San Francisco	NL	132	491	139	27	2	14	(9	5)	212	82	73	63	6	68	6	1	6	2	2	.50	10	.283	.367	.432
1994 Texas	AL	110	389	128	24	2	13	(9	4)	195	73	80	71	11	59	3	0	6	5	1	.83	5	.329	.431	.501
1995 Texas	AL	123	454	137	27	3	16	(10	6)	218	85	92	68	6	50	4	0	11	0	1	.00	1	.302	.389	.480
1996 Texas	AL	117	436	124	25	1	13	(9	4)	190	69	72	64	5	67	5	0	7	2	1	.67	10	.284	.377	.436
1997 Texas	AL	110	393	128	29	1	12	(6	6)	195	69	51	49	11	62	3	0	5	0	0	.00	4	.326	.400	.496
1998 Texas	AL	149	554	169	41	1	23	(11	12)	281	98	102	72	5	97	3	0	7	1	0	1.00	15	.305	.384	.507
13 ML YEARS		1769	6495	1964	395	45	253	(138	115)	3208	1068	1106	830	150	1079	50	13	94	60	44	.58	88	.302	.381	.494

Royce Clayton

Bats: Right **Throws:** Right **Pos:** SS-142; PH/PR-3   **Ht:** 6'0" **Wt:** 183 **Born:** 1/2/70 **Age:** 29

Year Team	Lg	G	AB	H	2B	3B	HR	(Hm	Rd)	TB	R	RBI	TBB	IBB	SO	HBP	SH	SF	SB	CS	SB%	GDP	Avg	OBP	SLG
1991 San Francisco	NL	9	26	3	1	0	0	(0	0)	4	0	2	1	0	6	0	0	0	0	0	.00	1	.115	.148	.154
1992 San Francisco	NL	98	321	72	7	4	4	(3	1)	99	31	24	26	3	63	0	3	2	8	4	.67	11	.224	.281	.308
1993 San Francisco	NL	153	549	155	21	5	6	(5	1)	204	54	70	38	2	91	5	8	7	11	10	.52	16	.282	.331	.372
1994 San Francisco	NL	108	385	91	14	6	3	(1	2)	126	38	30	30	2	74	3	3	2	23	3	.88	7	.236	.295	.327
1995 San Francisco	NL	138	509	124	29	3	5	(2	3)	174	56	58	38	1	109	4	3	4	24	9	.73	7	.244	.298	.342
1996 St. Louis	NL	129	491	136	20	4	6	(6	0)	182	64	35	33	4	89	1	2	4	33	15	.69	13	.277	.321	.371
1997 St. Louis	NL	154	576	153	39	5	9	(5	4)	229	75	61	33	4	109	3	2	5	30	10	.75	19	.266	.306	.398
1998 StL-Tex	NL	142	541	136	31	2	9	(2	7)	198	89	53	53	1	83	3	6	5	24	11	.69	16	.251	.319	.366
1998 St. Louis	NL	90	355	83	19	1	4	(1	3)	116	59	29	40	1	51	2	3	2	19	6	.76	10	.234	.313	.327
Texas	AL	52	186	53	12	1	5	(1	4)	82	30	24	13	0	32	1	3	3	5	5	.50	6	.285	.330	.441
8 ML YEARS		931	3398	870	162	29	42	(24	18)	1216	407	333	252	17	624	18	28	28	153	62	.71	90	.256	.308	.358

Roger Clemens

Pitches: Right Bats: Right Pos: SP-33 Ht: 6'4" Wt: 230 Born: 8/4/62 Age: 36

Year Team	Lg	G	GS	CG	GF	IP	BFP	H	R	ER	HR	SH	SF	HB	TBB	IBB	SO	WP	Bk	W	L	Pct.	ShO	Sv-Op	Hld	ERA
1984 Boston	AL	21	20	5	0	133.1	575	146	67	64	13	2	3	2	29	3	126	4	0	9	4	.692	1	0-0	0	4.32
1985 Boston	AL	15	15	3	0	98.1	407	83	38	36	5	1	2	3	37	0	74	1	3	7	5	.583	1	0-0	0	3.29
1986 Boston	AL	33	33	10	0	254	997	179	77	70	21	4	6	4	67	0	238	11	3	24	4	.857	1	0-0	0	2.48
1987 Boston	AL	36	36	18	0	281.2	1157	248	100	93	19	6	4	9	83	4	256	4	3	20	9	.690	7	0-0	0	2.97
1988 Boston	AL	35	35	14	0	264	1063	217	93	86	17	6	3	6	62	4	291	4	7	18	12	.600	8	0-0	0	2.93
1989 Boston	AL	35	35	8	0	253.1	1044	215	101	88	20	9	5	8	93	5	230	7	0	17	11	.607	3	0-0	0	3.13
1990 Boston	AL	31	31	7	0	228.1	920	193	59	49	7	7	5	7	54	3	209	8	0	21	6	.778	4	0-0	0	1.93
1991 Boston	AL	35	35	13	0	271.1	1077	219	93	79	15	6	8	5	65	12	241	6	0	18	10	.643	4	0-0	0	2.62
1992 Boston	AL	32	32	11	0	246.2	989	203	80	66	11	5	5	9	62	5	208	3	0	18	11	.621	5	0-0	0	2.41
1993 Boston	AL	29	29	2	0	191.2	808	175	99	95	17	5	7	11	67	4	160	3	1	11	14	.440	1	0-0	0	4.46
1994 Boston	AL	24	24	3	0	170.2	692	124	62	54	15	2	5	4	71	1	168	4	0	9	7	.563	1	0-0	0	2.85
1995 Boston	AL	23	23	0	0	140	623	141	70	65	15	2	3	14	60	0	132	9	0	10	5	.667	0	0-0	0	4.18
1996 Boston	AL	34	34	6	0	242.2	1032	216	106	98	19	4	7	4	106	2	257	8	1	10	13	.435	2	0-0	0	3.63
1997 Toronto	AL	34	34	9	0	264	1044	204	65	60	9	5	2	12	68	1	292	4	0	21	7	.750	3	0-0	0	2.05
1998 Toronto	AL	33	33	5	0	234.2	961	169	78	69	11	8	2	7	88	0	271	6	0	20	6	.769	3	0-0	0	2.65
15 ML YEARS		450	449	114	0	3274.2	13389	2732	1188	1072	214	72	67	105	1012	44	3153	82	18	233	124	.653	44	0-0	0	2.95

Matt Clement

Pitches: Right Bats: Right Pos: SP-2; RP-2 Ht: 6'3" Wt: 190 Born: 8/12/74 Age: 24

Year Team	Lg	G	GS	CG	GF	IP	BFP	H	R	ER	HR	SH	SF	HB	TBB	IBB	SO	WP	Bk	W	L	Pct.	ShO	Sv-Op	Hld	ERA
1994 Spokane	A-	2	2	0	0	7.1	39	8	7	5	0	0	0	1	11	0	4	1	1	1	1	.500	0	0--	—	6.14
Padres	R	13	13	0	0	67	286	65	38	33	0	1	0	6	17	0	76	10	0	8	5	.615	0	0--	—	4.43
1995 Rancho Cuca	A+	12	12	0	0	57.1	267	61	37	27	1	2	4	5	49	0	33	12	0	3	4	.429	0	0--	—	4.24
Idaho Falls	R+	14	14	0	0	81	349	61	53	39	3	6	3	13	42	0	65	19	2	6	3	.667	0	0--	—	4.33
1996 Clinton	A	16	16	1	0	96.1	410	66	31	30	3	1	3	9	52	0	109	15	0	8	3	.727	1	0--	—	2.80
Rancho Cuca	A+	11	11	0	0	56.1	261	61	40	35	8	5	3	9	26	0	75	5	1	4	5	.444	0	0--	—	5.59
1997 Rancho Cuca	A+	14	14	2	0	101	410	74	30	18	3	2	1	9	31	1	109	6	0	6	3	.667	1	0--	—	1.60
Mobile	AA	13	13	1	0	88	382	83	37	25	4	4	1	12	32	0	92	12	0	6	5	.545	1	0--	—	2.56
1998 Las Vegas	AAA	27	27	1	0	171.2	763	157	94	76	12	4	4	30	85	2	160	18	2	10	9	.526	0	0--	—	3.98
1998 San Diego	NL	4	2	0	0	13.2	62	15	8	7	0	2	0	0	7	1	13	2	0	2	0	1.000	0	0-0	0	4.61

Edgard Clemente

Bats: Right Throws: Right Pos: RF-6; PH/PR-5; CF-1 Ht: 5'11" Wt: 188 Born: 12/15/75 Age: 23

Year Team	Lg	G	AB	H	2B	3B	HR	(Hm	Rd)	TB	R	RBI	TBB	IBB	SO	HBP	SH	SF	SB	CS	SB%	GDP	Avg	OBP	SLG
1993 Rockies	R	39	147	36	4	2	2	—	—	50	20	20	16	0	35	0	2	2	7	5	.58	2	.245	.315	.340
1994 Asheville	A	119	447	106	22	3	11	—	—	167	50	39	23	0	120	3	3	2	9	9	.50	14	.237	.278	.374
1995 Salem	A+	131	497	149	25	6	13	—	—	225	74	69	40	4	102	4	3	7	7	10	.41	17	.300	.352	.453
1996 New Haven	AA	132	486	141	29	4	19	—	—	235	72	62	53	5	114	4	0	6	6	2	.75	7	.290	.365	.484
1997 Colo Sprngs	AAA	120	438	123	24	10	17	—	—	218	70	73	34	2	119	6	1	2	6	3	.67	8	.281	.340	.498
1998 Colo Sprngs	AAA	135	493	124	21	7	22	—	—	225	79	82	40	0	117	4	1	5	5	5	.50	6	.252	.310	.456
1998 Colorado	NL	11	17	6	0	1	0	(0	0)	8	2	2	2	0	8	0	0	0	0	0	.00	0	.353	.421	.471

Brad Clontz

Pitches: Right Bats: Right Pos: RP-20 Ht: 6'1" Wt: 180 Born: 4/25/71 Age: 28

Year Team	Lg	G	GS	CG	GF	IP	BFP	H	R	ER	HR	SH	SF	HB	TBB	IBB	SO	WP	Bk	W	L	Pct.	ShO	Sv-Op	Hld	ERA
1998 Albuquerque *	AAA	6	0	0	2	7	38	11	10	6	2	0	0	0	5	0	12	3	0	1	2	.333	0	0--	—	7.71
Norfolk *	AAA	28	0	0	7	42	185	43	26	16	4	0	1	1	16	3	49	2	0	2	4	.333	0	0--	—	3.43
1995 Atlanta	NL	59	0	0	14	69	295	71	29	28	5	3	2	4	22	4	55	0	0	8	1	.889	0	4-6	6	3.65
1996 Atlanta	NL	81	0	0	11	80.2	350	78	53	51	11	5	4	2	33	8	49	0	1	6	3	.667	0	1-6	17	5.69
1997 Atlanta	NL	51	0	0	16	48	203	52	24	20	3	0	2	1	18	3	42	1	0	5	1	.833	0	1-2	0	3.75
1998 LA-NYN	NL	20	0	0	6	23.2	101	19	16	16	4	0	0	2	12	4	16	0	0	2	0	1.000	0	0-1	3	6.08
1998 Los Angeles	NL	18	0	0	6	20.2	87	15	13	13	3	0	0	2	10	4	14	0	0	2	0	1.000	0	0-1	3	5.66
New York	NL	2	0	0	0	3	14	4	3	3	1	0	0	0	2	0	2	0	0	0	0	.000	0	0-0	0	9.00
4 ML YEARS		211	0	0	47	221.1	949	220	122	115	23	8	8	9	85	19	162	1	1	21	5	.808	0	6-15	26	4.68

Ken Cloude

Pitches: Right Bats: Right Pos: SP-30 Ht: 6'1" Wt: 180 Born: 1/9/75 Age: 24

Year Team	Lg	G	GS	CG	GF	IP	BFP	H	R	ER	HR	SH	SF	HB	TBB	IBB	SO	WP	Bk	W	L	Pct.	ShO	Sv-Op	Hld	ERA
1994 Mariners	R	12	7	0	2	52.1	209	36	22	12	1	2	2	6	19	0	61	9	0	3	4	.429	0	0--	—	2.06
1995 Wisconsin	A	25	25	4	0	161	677	137	64	58	8	1	7	8	63	4	140	10	1	9	8	.529	0	0--	—	3.24
1996 Lancaster	A+	28	28	1	0	168.1	727	167	94	79	15	4	6	8	60	0	161	6	1	15	4	.789	0	0--	—	4.22
1997 Memphis	AA	22	22	3	0	132.2	567	131	62	57	15	1	2	11	48	2	124	7	0	11	7	.611	2	0--	—	3.87
1998 Tacoma	AAA	1	1	0	0	4	16	4	3	3	1	0	0	0	1	0	4	0	0	1	0	1.000	0	0--	—	6.75
1997 Seattle	AL	10	9	0	0	51	219	41	32	29	8	1	1	3	26	0	46	2	0	4	2	.667	0	0-0	0	5.12
1998 Seattle	AL	30	30	0	0	155.1	722	187	116	110	29	4	4	3	80	4	114	2	1	8	10	.444	0	0-0	0	6.37
2 ML YEARS		40	39	0	0	206.1	941	228	148	139	37	5	5	6	106	4	160	4	1	12	12	.500	0	0-0	0	6.06

Danny Clyburn

Bats: Right **Throws:** Right **Pos:** LF-5; RF-5; PH/PR-3; DH-1   **Ht:** 6'4" **Wt:** 220 **Born:** 4/6/74 **Age:** 25

Year Team	Lg	G	AB	H	2B	3B	HR	(Hm	Rd)	TB	R	RBI	TBB	IBB	SO	HBP	SH	SF	SB	CS	SB%	GDP	Avg	OBP	SLG
1992 Pirates	R	39	149	51	9	0	4	—	—	72	26	25	5	0	20	1	0	2	7	3	.70	4	.342	.363	.483
1993 Augusta	A	127	457	121	21	4	9	—	—	177	55	66	37	1	97	5	0	0	5	5	.50	7	.265	.327	.387
1994 Salem	A+	118	461	126	19	0	22	—	—	211	57	90	20	2	96	0	0	5	4	5	.44	7	.273	.300	.458
1995 Winston-Sal	A+	59	227	59	10	2	11	—	—	106	27	41	13	1	59	4	0	2	2	4	.33	5	.260	.309	.467
Frederick	A+	15	45	9	4	0	0	—	—	13	4	4	4	0	18	2	0	0	1	1	.50	0	.200	.294	.289
High Desert	A+	45	160	45	3	1	12	—	—	86	20	37	17	1	41	4	0	3	2	1	.67	3	.281	.359	.538
1996 Bowie	AA	95	365	92	14	5	18	—	—	170	51	55	17	1	88	4	0	4	4	3	.57	5	.252	.290	.466
1997 Rochester	AAA	137	520	156	33	5	20	—	—	259	91	76	53	3	107	8	0	2	14	4	.78	7	.300	.372	.498
1998 Rochester	AAA	84	322	92	21	1	14	—	—	157	58	54	34	0	72	4	0	3	11	5	.69	9	.286	.358	.488
1997 Baltimore	AL	2	3	0	0	0	0	(0	0)	0	0	0	0	0	2	0	0	0	0	0	.00	0	.000	.000	.000
1998 Baltimore	AL	11	25	7	0	0	1	(0	1)	10	6	3	1	0	10	0	0	0	0	0	.00	0	.280	.308	.400
2 ML YEARS		13	28	7	0	0	1	(0	1)	10	6	3	1	0	12	0	0	0	0	0	.00	0	.250	.276	.357

Greg Colbrunn

Bats: R **Throws:** R **Pos:** PH/PR-52; 1B-36; RF-6; DH-3; C-1   **Ht:** 6'0" **Wt:** 205 **Born:** 7/26/69 **Age:** 29

Year Team	Lg	G	AB	H	2B	3B	HR	(Hm	Rd)	TB	R	RBI	TBB	IBB	SO	HBP	SH	SF	SB	CS	SB%	GDP	Avg	OBP	SLG
1992 Montreal	NL	52	168	45	8	0	2	(1	1)	59	12	18	6	1	34	2	0	4	3	2	.60	1	.268	.294	.351
1993 Montreal	NL	70	153	39	9	0	4	(2	2)	60	15	23	6	1	33	1	1	3	4	2	.67	1	.255	.282	.392
1994 Florida	NL	47	155	47	10	0	6	(3	3)	75	17	31	9	0	27	2	0	2	1	1	.50	3	.303	.345	.484
1995 Florida	NL	138	528	146	22	1	23	(12	11)	239	70	89	22	4	69	6	0	4	11	3	.79	15	.277	.311	.453
1996 Florida	NL	141	511	146	26	2	16	(7	9)	224	60	69	25	1	76	14	0	5	4	5	.44	22	.286	.333	.438
1997 Min-Atl	NL	98	271	76	17	0	7	(3	4)	114	27	35	10	1	49	2	1	2	1	2	.33	8	.280	.309	.421
1998 Col-Atl	NL	90	166	51	11	2	3	(1	2)	75	18	23	10	0	34	4	0	0	4	3	.57	1	.307	.361	.452
1997 Minnesota	AL	70	217	61	14	0	5	(2	3)	90	24	26	8	1	38	1	0	2	1	2	.33	7	.281	.307	.415
Atlanta	NL	28	54	15	3	0	2	(1	1)	24	3	9	2	0	11	1	1	0	0	0	.00	1	.278	.316	.444
1998 Colorado	NL	62	122	38	8	2	2	(1	1)	56	12	13	8	0	23	1	0	0	3	3	.50	1	.311	.359	.459
Atlanta	NL	28	44	13	3	0	1	(0	1)	19	6	10	2	0	11	3	0	0	1	0	1.00	0	.295	.367	.432
7 ML YEARS		636	1952	550	103	5	61	(29	32)	846	219	288	88	8	322	31	2	20	28	18	.61	51	.282	.320	.433

Lou Collier

Bats: Right **Throws:** Right **Pos:** SS-107; PH/PR-4   **Ht:** 5'10" **Wt:** 183 **Born:** 8/21/73 **Age:** 25

Year Team	Lg	G	AB	H	2B	3B	HR	(Hm	Rd)	TB	R	RBI	TBB	IBB	SO	HBP	SH	SF	SB	CS	SB%	GDP	Avg	OBP	SLG
1993 Welland	A-	50	201	61	6	2	1	—	—	74	35	19	12	0	31	5	1	1	8	7	.53	2	.303	.356	.368
1994 Augusta	A	85	318	89	17	4	7	—	—	135	48	40	25	0	53	8	3	3	32	10	.76	4	.280	.345	.425
Salem	A+	43	158	42	4	1	6	—	—	66	25	16	15	0	29	6	2	2	5	8	.38	4	.266	.348	.418
1995 Lynchburg	A+	114	399	110	19	3	4	—	—	147	68	38	51	4	60	7	3	3	31	11	.74	13	.276	.365	.368
1996 Carolina	AA	119	443	124	20	3	3	—	—	159	76	49	48	4	73	7	2	6	29	9	.76	11	.280	.355	.359
1997 Calgary	AAA	112	397	131	31	5	1	—	—	175	65	48	37	2	47	6	8	3	17	7	.63	13	.330	.393	.441
1998 Lynchburg	A+	5	18	3	2	0	0	—	—	5	4	0	2	0	0	1	0	0	2	0	1.00	0	.167	.286	.278
1997 Pittsburgh	NL	18	37	5	0	0	0	(0	0)	5	3	3	1	0	11	0	0	0	1	0	1.00	1	.135	.158	.135
1998 Pittsburgh	NL	110	334	82	13	6	2	(1	1)	113	30	34	31	6	70	6	3	5	2	2	.50	8	.246	.316	.338
2 ML YEARS		128	371	87	13	6	2	(1	1)	118	33	37	32	6	81	6	3	5	3	2	.60	9	.235	.302	.318

Bartolo Colon

Pitches: Right **Bats:** Right **Pos:** SP-31   **Ht:** 6'0" **Wt:** 185 **Born:** 5/24/75 **Age:** 24

Year Team	Lg	G	GS	CG	GF	IP	BFP	H	R	ER	HR	SH	SF	HB	TBB	IBB	SO	WP	Bk	W	L	Pct.	ShO	Sv-Op	Hld	ERA
1994 Burlington	R+	12	12	0	0	66	291	46	32	23	3	2	1	4	44	0	84	6	2	7	4	.636	0	0- --	—	3.14
1995 Kinston	A+	21	21	0	0	128.2	493	91	31	28	8	1	2	0	39	0	152	4	3	13	3	.813	0	0- --	—	1.96
1996 Canton-Akrn	AA	13	12	0	0	62	253	44	17	12	2	0	1	2	25	0	56	3	1	2	2	.500	0	0- --	—	1.74
Buffalo	AAA	8	0	0	1	15	69	16	10	10	2	1	1	0	8	0	19	2	0	0	0	.000	0	0- --	—	6.00
1997 Buffalo	AAA	10	10	0	0	56.2	230	45	15	14	4	2	1	0	23	0	54	1	1	7	1	.875	1	0- --	—	2.22
1997 Cleveland	AL	19	17	1	0	94	427	107	66	59	12	4	1	3	45	1	66	5	0	4	7	.364	0	0-0	0	5.65
1998 Cleveland	AL	31	31	6	0	204	883	205	91	84	15	10	2	3	79	5	158	4	0	14	9	.609	2	0-0	0	3.71
2 ML YEARS		50	48	7	0	298	1310	312	157	143	27	14	3	6	124	6	224	9	0	18	16	.529	2	0-0	0	4.32

David Cone

Pitches: Right **Bats:** Left **Pos:** SP-31   **Ht:** 6'1" **Wt:** 190 **Born:** 1/2/63 **Age:** 36

Year Team	Lg	G	GS	CG	GF	IP	BFP	H	R	ER	HR	SH	SF	HB	TBB	IBB	SO	WP	Bk	W	L	Pct.	ShO	Sv-Op	Hld	ERA
1986 Kansas City	AL	11	0	0	5	22.2	108	29	14	14	2	0	0	1	13	1	21	3	0	0	0	.000	0	0- --	—	5.56
1987 New York	NL	21	13	1	3	99.1	420	87	46	41	11	4	3	5	44	1	68	2	4	5	6	.455	0	1-1	2	3.71
1988 New York	NL	35	28	8	0	231.1	936	178	67	57	10	11	5	4	80	7	213	10	10	20	3	.870	4	0-0	1	2.22
1989 New York	NL	34	33	7	0	219.2	910	183	92	86	20	6	4	4	74	6	190	14	4	14	8	.636	2	0-0	0	3.52
1990 New York	NL	31	30	6	1	211.2	860	177	84	76	21	4	6	1	65	1	233	10	4	14	10	.583	2	0-0	0	3.23
1991 New York	NL	34	34	5	0	232.2	966	204	95	85	13	13	7	5	73	2	241	17	1	14	14	.500	2	0-0	0	3.29
1992 NYN-Tor		35	34	7	0	249.2	1055	201	91	78	15	6	9	12	111	7	261	12	1	17	10	.630	5	0-0	0	2.81
1993 Kansas City	AL	34	34	6	0	254	1060	205	102	94	20	7	9	10	114	2	191	14	2	11	14	.440	1	0-0	0	3.33

47

		HOW MUCH HE PITCHED						WHAT HE GAVE UP												THE RESULTS						
Year Team	Lg	G	GS	CG	GF	IP	BFP	H	R	ER	HR	SH	SF	HB	TBB	IBB	SO	WP	Bk	W	L	Pct.	ShO	Sv-Op	Hld	ERA
1994 Kansas City	AL	23	23	4	0	171.2	690	130	60	56	15	1	5	7	54	0	132	5	1	16	5	.762	2	0-0	0	2.94
1995 Tor-NYA	AL	30	30	6	0	**229.1**	954	195	95	91	24	2	3	6	88	2	191	11	1	18	8	.692	2	0-0	0	3.57
1996 New York	AL	11	11	1	0	72	295	50	25	23	3	1	5	2	34	0	71	4	1	7	2	.778	0	0-0	0	2.88
1997 New York	AL	29	29	1	0	195	805	155	67	61	17	3	2	4	86	2	222	**14**	2	12	6	.667	0	0-0	0	2.82
1998 New York	AL	31	31	3	0	207.2	866	186	89	82	20	4	4	15	59	1	209	6	0	**20**	7	.741	0	0-0	0	3.55
1992 New York	NL	27	27	7	0	196.2	831	162	75	63	12	6	6	9	82	5	214	9	1	13	7	.650	5	0-0	0	2.88
Toronto	AL	8	7	0	0	53	224	39	16	15	3	0	3	3	29	2	47	3	0	4	3	.571	0	0-0	0	2.55
1995 Toronto	AL	17	17	5	0	130.1	537	113	53	49	12	2	2	5	41	2	102	6	1	9	6	.600	2	0-0	0	3.38
New York	AL	13	13	1	0	99	417	82	42	42	12	0	1	1	47	0	89	5	0	9	2	.818	0	0-0	0	3.82
13 ML YEARS		359	330	55	9	2396.2	9925	1980	927	844	191	62	62	76	895	32	2243	122	31	168	93	.644	21	1--	—	3.17

Jeff Conine

Bats: R **Throws:** R **Pos:** LF-50; RF-31; 1B-12; PH/PR-4; DH-3   **Ht:** 6'1" **Wt:** 220 **Born:** 6/27/66 **Age:** 33

		BATTING																	BASERUNNING				PERCENTAGES		
Year Team	Lg	G	AB	H	2B	3B	HR	(Hm	Rd)	TB	R	RBI	TBB	IBB	SO	HBP	SH	SF	SB	CS	SB%	GDP	Avg	OBP	SLG
1998 Omaha *	AAA	2	9	0	0	0	0	(—	—)	0	0	0	0	0	3	0	0	0	0	0	.00	0	.000	.000	.000
1990 Kansas City	AL	9	20	5	2	0	0	(0	0)	7	3	2	2	0	5	0	0	0	0	0	.00	1	.250	.318	.350
1992 Kansas City	AL	28	91	23	5	2	0	(0	0)	32	10	9	8	1	23	0	0	0	0	0	.00	1	.253	.313	.352
1993 Florida	NL	**162**	595	174	24	3	12	(5	7)	240	75	79	52	2	135	5	0	0	2	2	.50	14	.292	.351	.403
1994 Florida	NL	115	451	144	27	6	18	(8	10)	237	60	82	40	4	92	1	0	4	1	2	.33	8	.319	.373	.525
1995 Florida	NL	133	483	146	26	2	25	(13	12)	251	72	105	66	5	94	1	0	12	2	0	1.00	13	.302	.379	.520
1996 Florida	NL	157	597	175	32	2	26	(15	11)	289	84	95	62	1	121	4	0	7	1	4	.20	17	.293	.360	.484
1997 Florida	NL	151	405	98	13	1	17	(7	10)	164	46	61	57	3	89	2	0	2	2	0	1.00	11	.242	.337	.405
1998 Kansas City	AL	93	309	79	26	0	8	(4	4)	129	30	43	26	1	68	2	0	6	3	0	1.00	8	.256	.312	.417
8 ML YEARS		848	2951	844	155	16	106	(52	54)	1349	380	476	313	17	627	15	0	37	11	8	.58	73	.286	.353	.457

Steve Connelly

Pitches: Right **Bats:** Right **Pos:** RP-3   **Ht:** 6'4" **Wt:** 210 **Born:** 4/27/74 **Age:** 25

		HOW MUCH HE PITCHED						WHAT HE GAVE UP												THE RESULTS						
Year Team	Lg	G	GS	CG	GF	IP	BFP	H	R	ER	HR	SH	SF	HB	TBB	IBB	SO	WP	Bk	W	L	Pct.	ShO	Sv-Op	Hld	ERA
1995 Sou. Oregon	A-	17	0	0	10	28.1	133	29	17	12	1	3	2	4	14	4	19	6	0	2	4	.333	0	2--	—	3.81
1996 Modesto	A+	52	0	0	42	64.2	283	58	33	27	5	1	1	5	32	1	65	5	2	4	7	.364	0	14--	—	3.76
1997 Huntsville	AA	43	0	0	22	69.2	297	74	33	29	3	2	1	4	20	2	49	5	0	3	3	.500	0	7--	—	3.75
1998 Edmonton	AAA	55	0	0	27	76	310	64	34	32	7	1	2	6	24	2	62	5	0	6	0	1.000	0	13--	—	3.79
1998 Oakland	AL	3	0	0	1	4.2	28	10	1	1	0	0	0	1	4	0	1	0	0	0	0	.000	0	0-0	0	1.93

Dennis Cook

Pitches: Left **Bats:** Left **Pos:** RP-73   **Ht:** 6'3" **Wt:** 190 **Born:** 10/4/62 **Age:** 36

		HOW MUCH HE PITCHED						WHAT HE GAVE UP												THE RESULTS						
Year Team	Lg	G	GS	CG	GF	IP	BFP	H	R	ER	HR	SH	SF	HB	TBB	IBB	SO	WP	Bk	W	L	Pct.	ShO	Sv-Op	Hld	ERA
1988 San Francisco	NL	4	4	1	0	22	86	9	8	7	1	0	3	0	11	1	13	1	0	2	1	.667	1	0-0	0	2.86
1989 SF-Phi	NL	23	18	2	1	121	499	110	59	50	18	5	2	2	38	6	67	4	2	7	8	.467	1	0-0	0	3.72
1990 Phi-LA	NL	47	16	2	4	156	663	156	74	68	20	7	7	2	56	9	64	6	3	9	4	.692	1	1-2	4	3.92
1991 Los Angeles	NL	20	1	0	5	17.2	69	12	3	1	0	1	2	0	7	1	8	0	0	1	0	1.000	0	0-1	0	0.51
1992 Cleveland	AL	32	25	1	1	158	669	156	79	67	29	3	3	2	50	2	96	4	5	5	7	.417	0	0-0	0	3.82
1993 Cleveland	AL	25	6	0	2	54	233	62	36	34	9	3	2	2	16	1	34	0	1	5	5	.500	0	0-2	2	5.67
1994 Chicago	AL	38	0	0	8	33	143	29	17	13	4	3	0	1	14	3	26	0	1	3	1	.750	0	0-1	3	3.55
1995 Cle-Tex	AL	46	1	0	10	57.2	255	63	32	29	9	4	5	2	26	3	53	1	0	0	1	.000	0	2-2	6	4.53
1996 Texas	AL	60	0	0	9	70.1	298	53	34	32	2	3	5	7	35	7	64	0	0	5	2	.714	0	0-2	11	4.09
1997 Florida	NL	59	0	0	12	62.1	272	64	28	27	1	1	2	1	28	4	63	0	0	1	3	.333	0	0-2	13	3.90
1998 New York	NL	73	0	0	18	68	286	60	21	18	5	3	3	3	27	4	79	1	1	8	4	.667	0	1-5	21	2.38
1989 San Francisco	NL	2	2	1	0	15	58	13	3	3	1	0	0	0	5	0	9	1	0	1	0	1.000	0	0-0	0	1.80
Philadelphia	NL	21	16	1	1	106	441	97	56	47	17	5	2	2	33	6	58	3	2	6	8	.429	1	0-0	0	3.99
1990 Philadelphia	NL	42	13	2	4	141.2	594	132	61	56	13	5	5	2	54	9	58	6	3	8	3	.727	1	1-2	3	3.56
Los Angeles	NL	5	3	0	0	14.1	69	23	13	12	7	2	2	0	2	0	6	0	0	1	1	.500	0	0-0	0	7.53
1995 Cleveland	AL	11	0	0	1	12.2	62	16	9	9	3	1	0	1	10	2	13	0	0	0	0	.000	0	0-0	0	6.39
Texas	AL	35	1	0	9	45	193	47	23	20	6	3	5	1	16	1	40	1	0	0	2	.000	0	2-2	5	4.00
11 ML YEARS		427	71	6	70	820	3473	773	391	346	101	33	33	22	308	41	567	17	13	46	36	.561	3	4-17	62	3.80

Steve Cooke

Pitches: Left **Bats:** Right **Pos:** SP-1   **Ht:** 6'6" **Wt:** 240 **Born:** 1/14/70 **Age:** 29

		HOW MUCH HE PITCHED						WHAT HE GAVE UP												THE RESULTS						
Year Team	Lg	G	GS	CG	GF	IP	BFP	H	R	ER	HR	SH	SF	HB	TBB	IBB	SO	WP	Bk	W	L	Pct.	ShO	Sv-Op	Hld	ERA
1998 Indianapols *	AAA	2	2	0	0	1.2	13	3	7	7	0	0	0	0	5	0	0	0	0	0	1	.000	0	0--	—	37.80
1992 Pittsburgh	NL	11	0	0	8	23	91	22	9	9	2	0	0	0	4	1	10	0	0	2	0	1.000	0	1-1	1	3.52
1993 Pittsburgh	NL	32	32	3	0	210.2	882	207	101	91	22	13	6	3	59	4	132	3	3	10	10	.500	1	0-0	0	3.89
1994 Pittsburgh	NL	25	23	2	1	134.1	590	157	79	75	21	9	3	5	46	7	74	3	0	4	11	.267	0	0-0	0	5.02
1996 Pittsburgh	NL	3	0	0	1	8.1	41	11	7	7	1	0	0	1	5	0	7	1	0	0	0	.000	0	0-0	0	7.56
1997 Pittsburgh	NL	32	32	1	0	167.1	756	184	95	80	15	**18**	5	9	77	**11**	109	8	1	9	15	.375	0	0-0	0	4.30
1998 Cincinnati	NL	1	1	0	0	6	23	4	1	1	0	0	1	0	3	0	3	0	0	1	0	1.000	0	0-0	0	1.50
6 ML YEARS		104	88	5	10	549.2	2383	585	292	263	61	40	15	18	191	23	335	15	4	26	36	.419	1	1-1	1	4.31

Ron Coomer

Bats: R **Throws:** R **Pos:** 3B-76; 1B-54; DH-13; PH/PR-10; RF-3   **Ht:** 5'11" **Wt:** 206 **Born:** 11/18/66 **Age:** 32

Year Team	Lg	G	AB	H	2B	3B	HR	(Hm	Rd)	TB	R	RBI	TBB	IBB	SO	HBP	SH	SF	SB	CS	SB%	GDP	Avg	OBP	SLG
1995 Minnesota	AL	37	101	26	3	1	5	(2	3)	46	15	19	9	0	11	1	0	0	0	1	.00	9	.257	.324	.455
1996 Minnesota	AL	95	233	69	12	1	12	(5	7)	119	34	41	17	1	24	0	0	3	3	0	1.00	10	.296	.340	.511
1997 Minnesota	AL	140	523	156	30	2	13	(4	9)	229	63	85	22	5	91	0	0	5	4	3	.57	11	.298	.324	.438
1998 Minnesota	AL	137	529	146	22	1	15	(6	9)	215	54	72	18	1	72	0	0	8	2	2	.50	22	.276	.295	.406
4 ML YEARS		409	1386	397	67	5	45	(17	28)	609	166	217	66	7	198	1	0	16	9	6	.60	52	.286	.316	.439

Rocky Coppinger

Pitches: Right **Bats:** Right **Pos:** RP-5; SP-1   **Ht:** 6'5" **Wt:** 245 **Born:** 3/19/74 **Age:** 25

Year Team	Lg	G	GS	CG	GF	IP	BFP	H	R	ER	HR	SH	SF	HB	TBB	IBB	SO	WP	Bk	W	L	Pct.	ShO	Sv-Op	Hld	ERA
1998 Bowie *	AA	7	6	0	0	31	128	26	16	15	4	2	1	1	11	1	30	0	0	2	2	.500	0	0--	—	4.35
Rochester *	AAA	14	13	1	1	87.1	379	80	38	34	11	2	3	3	43	1	64	0	0	8	3	.727	0	0--	—	3.50
1996 Baltimore	AL	23	22	0	1	125	548	126	76	72	25	2	5	2	60	1	104	4	0	10	6	.625	0	0-0	0	5.18
1997 Baltimore	AL	5	4	0	1	20	95	21	14	14	2	0	1	1	16	1	22	1	0	1	1	.500	0	0-0	0	6.30
1998 Baltimore	AL	6	1	0	3	15.2	72	16	9	9	3	0	0	0	7	1	13	0	0	0	0	.000	0	0-0	0	5.17
3 ML YEARS		34	27	0	5	160.2	715	163	99	95	30	2	6	3	83	3	139	5	0	11	7	.611	0	0-0	0	5.32

Alex Cora

Bats: Left **Throws:** Right **Pos:** SS-21; PH/PR-5; 2B-4   **Ht:** 6'0" **Wt:** 180 **Born:** 10/18/75 **Age:** 23

Year Team	Lg	G	AB	H	2B	3B	HR	(Hm	Rd)	TB	R	RBI	TBB	IBB	SO	HBP	SH	SF	SB	CS	SB%	GDP	Avg	OBP	SLG
1996 Vero Beach	A+	61	214	55	5	4	0	—	—	68	26	26	12	0	36	3	4	0	5	5	.50	1	.257	.306	.318
1997 San Antonio	AA	127	448	105	20	4	3	—	—	142	52	48	25	4	60	3	7	1	12	9	.57	17	.234	.279	.317
1998 Albuquerque	AAA	81	299	79	16	6	5	—	—	122	42	45	15	1	38	3	6	3	10	7	.59	1	.264	.303	.408
1998 Los Angeles	NL	29	33	4	0	1	0	(0	0)	6	1	0	2	0	8	1	2	0	0	0	.00	0	.121	.194	.182

Joey Cora

Bats: Both **Throws:** Right **Pos:** 2B-151; PH/PR-8   **Ht:** 5'8" **Wt:** 162 **Born:** 5/14/65 **Age:** 34

Year Team	Lg	G	AB	H	2B	3B	HR	(Hm	Rd)	TB	R	RBI	TBB	IBB	SO	HBP	SH	SF	SB	CS	SB%	GDP	Avg	OBP	SLG
1987 San Diego	NL	77	241	57	7	2	0	(0	0)	68	23	13	28	1	26	1	5	1	15	11	.58	4	.237	.317	.282
1989 San Diego	NL	12	19	6	1	0	0	(0	0)	7	5	1	1	0	0	0	0	0	1	0	1.00	0	.316	.350	.368
1990 San Diego	NL	51	100	27	3	0	0	(0	0)	30	12	2	6	1	9	0	0	0	8	3	.73	1	.270	.311	.300
1991 Chicago	AL	100	228	55	2	3	0	(0	0)	63	37	18	20	0	21	5	8	3	11	6	.65	1	.241	.313	.276
1992 Chicago	AL	68	122	30	7	1	0	(0	0)	39	27	9	22	1	13	4	2	3	10	3	.77	2	.246	.371	.320
1993 Chicago	AL	153	579	155	15	13	2	(0	2)	202	95	51	67	0	63	0	19	4	20	8	.71	14	.268	.351	.349
1994 Chicago	AL	90	312	86	13	4	2	(2	0)	113	55	30	38	0	32	2	11	5	8	4	.67	8	.276	.353	.362
1995 Seattle	AL	120	427	127	19	2	3	(1	2)	159	64	39	37	0	31	6	13	4	18	7	.72	8	.297	.359	.372
1996 Seattle	AL	144	530	154	37	6	6	(2	4)	221	90	45	35	1	32	7	6	5	5	5	.50	9	.291	.340	.417
1997 Seattle	AL	149	574	172	40	4	11	(4	7)	253	105	54	53	2	49	5	8	9	7	.46	6	.300	.359	.441
1998 Sea-Cle	AL	155	602	166	27	6	6	(2	4)	223	111	32	73	0	59	5	12	3	15	6	.71	5	.276	.357	.370
1998 Seattle	AL	131	519	147	23	6	6	(2	4)	200	95	26	62	0	50	4	10	3	13	5	.72	2	.283	.362	.385
Cleveland	AL	24	83	19	4	0	0	(0	0)	23	16	6	11	0	9	1	2	0	2	1	.67	3	.229	.326	.277
11 ML YEARS		1119	3734	1035	171	41	30	(11	19)	1378	624	294	380	6	335	44	84	37	117	60	.66	58	.277	.348	.369

Wil Cordero

Bats: R **Throws:** R **Pos:** 1B-83; RF-8; LF-4; PH/PR-4   **Ht:** 6'2" **Wt:** 195 **Born:** 10/3/71 **Age:** 27

Year Team	Lg	G	AB	H	2B	3B	HR	(Hm	Rd)	TB	R	RBI	TBB	IBB	SO	HBP	SH	SF	SB	CS	SB%	GDP	Avg	OBP	SLG
1998 Birmingham *	AA	11	35	10	2	0	2	—	—	18	6	11	7	0	3	0	0	0	0	0	.00	1	.286	.405	.514
1992 Montreal	NL	45	126	38	4	1	2	(1	1)	50	17	8	9	0	31	1	1	0	0	0	.00	3	.302	.353	.397
1993 Montreal	NL	138	475	118	32	2	10	(8	2)	184	56	58	34	8	60	7	4	1	12	3	.80	12	.248	.308	.387
1994 Montreal	NL	110	415	122	30	3	15	(5	10)	203	65	63	41	3	62	6	2	3	16	3	.84	8	.294	.363	.489
1995 Montreal	NL	131	514	147	35	2	10	(2	8)	216	64	49	36	4	88	9	1	4	9	5	.64	11	.286	.341	.420
1996 Boston	AL	59	198	57	14	0	3	(2	1)	80	29	37	11	4	31	2	1	1	2	1	.67	8	.288	.330	.404
1997 Boston	AL	140	570	160	26	3	18	(11	7)	246	82	72	31	7	122	4	0	4	1	3	.25	11	.281	.320	.432
1998 Chicago	AL	96	341	91	18	2	13	(6	8)	152	58	49	22	0	66	3	1	4	2	1	.67	7	.267	.314	.446
7 ML YEARS		719	2639	733	159	13	71	(34	37)	1131	371	336	184	26	460	32	10	17	42	16	.72	60	.278	.330	.429

Francisco Cordova

Pitches: Right **Bats:** Right **Pos:** SP-33   **Ht:** 5'11" **Wt:** 183 **Born:** 4/26/72 **Age:** 27

Year Team	Lg	G	GS	CG	GF	IP	BFP	H	R	ER	HR	SH	SF	HB	TBB	IBB	SO	WP	Bk	W	L	Pct.	ShO	Sv-Op	Hld	ERA
1996 Pittsburgh	NL	59	6	0	41	99	414	103	49	45	11	1	0	2	20	6	95	2	1	4	7	.364	0	12-18	3	4.09
1997 Pittsburgh	NL	29	29	2	0	178.2	744	175	80	72	14	3	7	9	49	4	121	4	0	11	8	.579	2	0-0	0	3.63
1998 Pittsburgh	NL	33	33	3	0	220.1	921	204	91	81	22	9	6	3	69	5	157	1	1	13	14	.481	2	0-0	0	3.31
3 ML YEARS		121	68	5	41	498	2079	482	220	198	47	13	13	14	138	15	373	7	2	28	29	.491	4	12-18	3	3.58

Marty Cordova

Bats: Right **Throws:** Right **Pos:** LF-115; DH-4; PH/PR-1　　　　　**Ht:** 6'0" **Wt:** 206 **Born:** 7/10/69 **Age:** 29

		BATTING																BASERUNNING				PERCENTAGES		
Year Team	Lg	G	AB	H	2B	3B	HR	(Hm	Rd)	TB	R	RBI	TBB	IBB	SO	HBP	SH	SF	SB	CS	SB%	GDP	Avg	OBP	SLG
1995 Minnesota	AL	137	512	142	27	4	24	(16	8)	249	81	84	52	1	111	10	0	5	20	7	.74	10	.277	.352	.486
1996 Minnesota	AL	145	569	176	46	1	16	(10	6)	272	97	111	53	4	96	8	0	9	11	5	.69	18	.309	.371	.478
1997 Minnesota	AL	103	378	93	18	4	15	(4	11)	164	44	51	30	2	92	3	0	2	5	3	.63	13	.246	.305	.434
1998 Minnesota	AL	119	438	111	20	2	10	(6	4)	165	52	69	50	3	103	5	0	6	3	6	.33	14	.253	.333	.377
4 ML YEARS		504	1897	522	111	11	65	(36	29)	850	274	315	185	10	402	26	0	22	39	21	.65	55	.275	.344	.448

Bryan Corey

Pitches: Right **Bats:** Right **Pos:** RP-3　　　　　**Ht:** 6'0" **Wt:** 170 **Born:** 10/21/73 **Age:** 25

		HOW MUCH HE PITCHED						WHAT HE GAVE UP												THE RESULTS					
Year Team	Lg	G	GS	CG	GF	IP	BFP	H	R	ER	HR	SH	SF	HB	TBB	IBB	SO	WP	Bk	W	L	Pct.	ShO	Sv-Op	Hld	ERA
1995 Jamestown	A-	29	0	0	28	28	116	21	14	12	2	0	1	1	12	1	41	4	0	2	2	.500	0	10- -	—	3.86
1996 Fayetteville	A	60	0	0	53	82	315	50	19	11	2	4	6	2	17	3	101	6	2	6	4	.600	0	34- -	—	1.21
1997 Jacksonville	AA	52	0	0	36	68	298	74	42	36	8	5	3	1	21	3	37	4	0	3	8	.273	0	9- -	—	4.76
1998 Tucson	AAA	39	10	0	14	87.2	401	116	61	53	14	1	2	6	24	0	50	2	2	4	6	.400	0	2- -	—	5.44
1998 Arizona	NL	3	0	0	2	4	20	6	4	4	1	1	0	1	2	0	1	0	0	0	0	.000	0	0-0	0	9.00

Jim Corsi

Pitches: Right **Bats:** Right **Pos:** RP-59　　　　　**Ht:** 6'1" **Wt:** 220 **Born:** 9/9/61 **Age:** 37

		HOW MUCH HE PITCHED						WHAT HE GAVE UP												THE RESULTS					
Year Team	Lg	G	GS	CG	GF	IP	BFP	H	R	ER	HR	SH	SF	HB	TBB	IBB	SO	WP	Bk	W	L	Pct.	ShO	Sv-Op	Hld	ERA
1998 Pawtucket *	AAA	1	1	0	0	2	8	3	0	0	0	0	0	0	0	0	1	0	0	0	0	.000	0	0- -	—	0.00
1988 Oakland	AL	11	1	0	7	21.1	89	20	10	9	1	3	3	0	6	1	10	1	1	0	1	1.000	0	0-0	0	3.80
1989 Oakland	AL	22	0	0	14	38.1	149	26	8	8	2	2	2	1	10	0	21	0	0	1	2	.333	0	0-0	2	1.88
1991 Houston	NL	47	0	0	15	77.2	322	76	37	32	6	3	2	0	23	5	53	1	1	0	5	.000	0	0-3	4	3.71
1992 Oakland	AL	32	0	0	16	44	185	44	12	7	2	4	2	0	18	2	19	0	0	4	2	.667	0	0-4	1	1.43
1993 Florida	NL	15	0	0	6	20.1	97	28	15	15	1	3	1	0	10	3	7	0	0	0	2	.000	0	0-0	1	6.64
1995 Oakland	AL	38	0	0	7	45	187	31	14	11	2	5	1	2	26	1	26	0	0	2	4	.333	0	2-4	13	2.20
1996 Oakland	AL	56	0	0	19	73.2	312	71	33	33	6	9	2	3	34	4	43	1	0	6	0	1.000	0	3-6	10	4.03
1997 Boston	AL	52	0	0	14	57.2	251	56	26	22	1	3	4	3	21	7	40	2	0	5	3	.625	0	2-9	11	3.43
1998 Boston	AL	59	0	0	9	66	274	58	23	19	6	2	1	1	23	2	49	3	0	3	2	.600	0	0-3	18	2.59
9 ML YEARS		332	1	0	107	444	1866	410	178	156	27	34	17	11	171	25	268	8	2	21	21	.500	0	7-25	63	3.16

Craig Counsell

Bats: Left **Throws:** Right **Pos:** 2B-104; PH/PR-5　　　　　**Ht:** 6'0" **Wt:** 170 **Born:** 8/21/70 **Age:** 28

		BATTING																	BASERUNNING				PERCENTAGES		
Year Team	Lg	G	AB	H	2B	3B	HR	(Hm	Rd)	TB	R	RBI	TBB	IBB	SO	HBP	SH	SF	SB	CS	SB%	GDP	Avg	OBP	SLG
1995 Colorado	NL	3	1	0	0	0	0	(0	0)	0	0	0	1	0	0	0	0	0	0	0	.00	0	.000	.500	.000
1997 Col-Fla	NL	52	164	49	9	2	1	(1	0)	65	20	16	18	2	17	3	3	1	1	1	.50	5	.299	.376	.396
1998 Florida	NL	107	335	84	19	5	4	(2	2)	125	43	40	51	7	47	4	8	1	3	0	1.00	5	.251	.355	.373
1997 Colorado	NL	1	0	0	0	0	0	(0	0)	0	0	0	0	0	0	0	0	0	0	0	.00	0	.000	.000	.000
Florida	NL	51	164	49	9	2	1	(1	0)	65	20	16	18	2	17	3	3	1	1	1	.50	5	.299	.376	.396
3 ML YEARS		162	500	133	28	7	5	(3	2)	190	63	56	70	9	64	7	11	2	4	1	.80	10	.266	.363	.380

Tim Crabtree

Pitches: Right **Bats:** Right **Pos:** RP-64　　　　　**Ht:** 6'4" **Wt:** 205 **Born:** 10/13/69 **Age:** 29

		HOW MUCH HE PITCHED						WHAT HE GAVE UP												THE RESULTS					
Year Team	Lg	G	GS	CG	GF	IP	BFP	H	R	ER	HR	SH	SF	HB	TBB	IBB	SO	WP	Bk	W	L	Pct.	ShO	Sv-Op	Hld	ERA
1995 Toronto	AL	31	0	0	19	32	141	30	16	11	1	0	1	2	13	0	21	2	0	0	2	.000	0	0-2	1	3.09
1996 Toronto	AL	53	0	0	21	67.1	284	59	26	19	4	2	2	3	22	4	57	3	0	5	3	.625	0	1-5	17	2.54
1997 Toronto	AL	37	0	0	16	40.2	199	65	32	32	7	4	2	2	17	3	26	4	0	3	3	.500	0	2-5	8	7.08
1998 Texas	AL	64	0	0	14	85.1	371	86	40	34	3	1	6	3	35	2	60	6	0	6	1	.857	0	0-1	10	3.59
4 ML YEARS		185	0	0	70	225.1	995	240	114	96	15	7	11	10	87	9	164	15	0	14	9	.609	0	3-13	36	3.83

Rickey Cradle

Bats: Right **Throws:** Right **Pos:** PH/PR-3; CF-2; LF-1; RF-1　　　　　**Ht:** 6'2" **Wt:** 180 **Born:** 6/20/73 **Age:** 26

		BATTING																	BASERUNNING				PERCENTAGES		
Year Team	Lg	G	AB	H	2B	3B	HR	(Hm	Rd)	TB	R	RBI	TBB	IBB	SO	HBP	SH	SF	SB	CS	SB%	GDP	Avg	OBP	SLG
1991 Blue Jays	R	44	132	28	4	3	1	—	—	41	16	6	24	1	37	3	1	1	4	5	.44	4	.212	.344	.311
1992 Medicine Hat	R+	65	217	49	8	0	9	—	—	84	38	36	42	0	69	6	1	2	16	2	.89	5	.226	.363	.387
1993 Hagerstown	A	129	441	112	26	4	13	—	—	185	72	62	68	2	125	11	1	4	19	14	.58	5	.254	.365	.420
1994 Dunedin	A+	114	344	88	14	3	10	—	—	138	65	39	59	0	87	9	0	1	20	10	.67	5	.256	.378	.401
1995 Knoxville	AA	41	117	21	5	1	4	—	—	40	17	13	17	0	29	3	1	1	3	3	.50	3	.179	.297	.342
Dunedin	A+	50	178	49	10	3	7	—	—	86	33	27	28	0	42	1	0	4	6	2	.75	2	.275	.376	.483
1996 Knoxville	AA	92	333	94	23	2	12	—	—	157	59	47	55	1	65	10	7	7	15	11	.58	2	.282	.393	.471
Syracuse	AAA	40	130	26	5	3	8	—	—	61	22	22	14	1	39	1	0	2	1	0	1.00	2	.200	.279	.469
1997 Syracuse	AAA	11	25	3	0	0	1	—	—	6	4	3	2	0	9	2	0	0	0	1	.00	0	.120	.241	.240
Knoxville	AA	84	257	55	16	1	10	—	—	103	50	34	41	0	67	7	2	1	5	6	.45	5	.214	.337	.401
1998 Tacoma	AAA	82	297	86	25	1	12	—	—	149	53	53	26	1	76	4	0	0	9	5	.64	4	.290	.349	.502

						BATTING			(Hm	Rd)										BASERUNNING				PERCENTAGES		
Year Team	Lg	G	AB	H	2B	3B	HR	(Hm	Rd)	TB	R	RBI	TBB	IBB	SO	HBP	SH	SF	SB	CS	SB%	GDP	Avg	OBP	SLG
1998 Seattle	AL	5	7	1	0	0	0	(0	0)	1	0	2	1	0	5	0	0	0	1	0	1.00	0	.143	.250	.143

Felipe Crespo

Bats: B **Throws:** R **Pos:** RF-25; PH/PR-22; LF-19; 2B-8; DH-2; 3B-2; 1B-1   **Ht:** 5'11"   **Wt:** 200   **Born:** 3/5/73   **Age:** 26

						BATTING			(Hm	Rd)										BASERUNNING				PERCENTAGES		
Year Team	Lg	G	AB	H	2B	3B	HR	(Hm	Rd)	TB	R	RBI	TBB	IBB	SO	HBP	SH	SF	SB	CS	SB%	GDP	Avg	OBP	SLG
1996 Toronto	AL	22	49	9	4	0	0	(0	0)	13	6	4	12	0	13	3	0	0	1	0	1.00	0	.184	.375	.265
1997 Toronto	AL	12	28	8	0	1	1	(0	1)	13	3	5	2	0	4	0	1	0	0	0	.00	1	.286	.333	.464
1998 Toronto	AL	66	130	34	8	1	1	(0	1)	47	11	15	15	1	27	2	4	2	4	3	.57	1	.262	.342	.362
3 ML YEARS		100	207	51	12	2	2	(0	2)	73	20	24	29	1	44	5	5	2	5	3	.63	2	.246	.350	.353

Tripp Cromer

Bats: Right **Throws:** Right **Pos:** PH/PR-6   **Ht:** 6'2"   **Wt:** 166   **Born:** 11/21/67   **Age:** 31

						BATTING			(Hm	Rd)										BASERUNNING				PERCENTAGES		
Year Team	Lg	G	AB	H	2B	3B	HR	(Hm	Rd)	TB	R	RBI	TBB	IBB	SO	HBP	SH	SF	SB	CS	SB%	GDP	Avg	OBP	SLG
1998 Albuquerque * AAA		12	30	10	1	0	2	—	—	17	3	5	1	0	5	0	0	1	0	1	.00	0	.333	.344	.567
San Berndno * A+		4	15	6	1	0	2	—	—	13	3	6	0	0	2	0	0	0	0	0	.00	0	.400	.400	.867
1993 St. Louis	NL	10	23	2	0	0	0	(0	0)	2	1	0	1	0	6	0	0	0	0	0	.00	0	.087	.125	.087
1994 St. Louis	NL	2	0	0	0	0	0	(0	0)	0	1	0	0	0	0	0	0	0	0	0	.00	0	.000	.000	.000
1995 St. Louis	NL	105	345	78	19	0	5	(2	3)	112	36	18	14	2	66	4	1	5	0	0	.00	14	.226	.261	.325
1997 Los Angeles	NL	28	86	25	3	0	4	(2	2)	40	8	20	6	3	16	0	2	1	0	1	.00	2	.291	.333	.465
1998 Los Angeles	NL	6	6	1	0	0	1	(0	1)	4	1	1	0	0	2	0	0	0	0	0	.00	0	.167	.167	.667
5 ML YEARS		151	460	106	22	0	10	(4	6)	158	47	39	21	5	90	4	3	6	0	1	.00	16	.230	.267	.343

Rich Croushore

Pitches: Right **Bats:** Right **Pos:** RP-41   **Ht:** 6'4"   **Wt:** 210   **Born:** 8/7/70   **Age:** 28

		HOW MUCH HE PITCHED						WHAT HE GAVE UP										THE RESULTS					
Year Team	Lg	G	GS	CG	GF	IP	BFP	H	R	ER	HR	SH	SF	HB	TBB	IBB	SO	WP	Bk	W	L	Pct.	ShO	Sv-Op	Hld	ERA
1993 Glens Falls	A-	31	0	0	11	41.1	184	38	16	14	1	4	1	2	22	4	36	6	0	4	1	.800	0	1- —	—	3.05
1994 Madison	A	62	0	0	14	94.1	410	90	49	43	5	4	2	5	46	2	103	10	4	6	6	.500	0	0- —	—	4.10
1995 St. Pete	A+	12	11	0	0	59	251	44	25	23	2	3	1	4	32	0	57	5	0	6	4	.600	0	0- —	—	3.51
1996 Arkansas	AA	34	17	2	11	108	486	113	75	59	18	4	1	2	51	1	85	7	0	5	10	.333	0	3- —	—	4.92
1997 Arkansas	AA	17	16	1	1	92.2	421	111	52	43	7	1	5	4	37	0	67	8	2	7	5	.583	0	0- —	—	4.18
Louisville	AAA	14	6	0	3	43.2	173	37	14	12	3	0	0	0	13	0	41	4	0	1	2	.333	0	1- —	—	2.47
1998 Memphis	AAA	23	0	0	9	28.2	115	21	16	15	3	1	0	1	9	0	40	2	0	0	3	.000	0	2- —	—	4.71
1998 St. Louis	NL	41	0	0	15	54.1	243	44	31	30	6	2	1	4	29	2	47	6	0	0	3	.000	0	8-11	6	4.97

Dean Crow

Pitches: Right **Bats:** Left **Pos:** RP-32   **Ht:** 6'4"   **Wt:** 215   **Born:** 8/21/72   **Age:** 26

		HOW MUCH HE PITCHED						WHAT HE GAVE UP										THE RESULTS					
Year Team	Lg	G	GS	CG	GF	IP	BFP	H	R	ER	HR	SH	SF	HB	TBB	IBB	SO	WP	Bk	W	L	Pct.	ShO	Sv-Op	Hld	ERA
1993 Bellingham	A-	25	0	0	12	47.2	190	31	14	10	1	1	2	0	21	1	38	0	0	5	3	.625	0	4- —	—	1.89
1994 Appleton	A	16	0	0	8	15.1	80	25	15	12	4	2	3	1	7	4	11	1	0	2	4	.333	0	2- —	—	7.04
1995 Riverside	A+	51	0	0	47	61.2	249	54	21	18	1	3	2	3	13	0	46	2	0	3	4	.429	0	22- —	—	2.63
1996 Port City	AA	60	0	0	49	68	285	64	35	23	4	5	1	1	20	0	43	6	0	2	3	.400	0	26- —	—	3.04
1997 Tacoma	AAA	33	0	0	23	43.1	200	56	25	23	3	2	3	1	19	1	36	3	0	4	2	.667	0	7- —	—	4.78
Toledo	AAA	18	0	0	10	18.1	90	26	16	16	1	2	1	2	10	1	10	0	0	3	0	1.000	0	2- —	—	7.85
1998 Toledo	AAA	24	0	0	21	24.1	97	21	8	4	1	1	1	1	3	0	12	0	0	2	0	1.000	0	10- —	—	1.48
1998 Detroit	AL	32	0	0	15	45.2	197	55	22	20	6	2	1	2	16	6	18	0	0	2	2	.500	0	0-0	0	3.94

Deivi Cruz

Bats: Right **Throws:** Right **Pos:** SS-135   **Ht:** 6'0"   **Wt:** 184   **Born:** 6/11/75   **Age:** 24

						BATTING			(Hm	Rd)										BASERUNNING				PERCENTAGES		
Year Team	Lg	G	AB	H	2B	3B	HR	(Hm	Rd)	TB	R	RBI	TBB	IBB	SO	HBP	SH	SF	SB	CS	SB%	GDP	Avg	OBP	SLG
1993 Giants	R	28	82	28	3	0	0	—	—	31	8	15	4	0	5	0	3	1	3	0	1.00	3	.341	.368	.378
1994 Giants	R	18	53	16	8	0	0	—	—	24	10	5	5	0	3	1	1	1	0	1	.00	1	.302	.367	.453
1995 Burlington	A	16	58	8	1	0	1	—	—	12	2	9	4	0	7	0	1	0	1	1	.50	1	.138	.194	.207
Bellingham	A-	62	223	66	17	0	3	—	—	92	32	28	19	3	21	0	1	2	6	3	.67	5	.296	.348	.413
1996 Burlington	A	127	517	152	27	2	9	—	—	210	72	64	35	3	49	4	4	3	12	5	.71	20	.294	.342	.406
1998 Lakeland	A+	2	9	0	0	0	0	—	—	0	0	1	0	0	1	0	0	0	0	0	.00	0	.000	.000	.000
Toledo	AAA	2	9	1	1	0	0	—	—	2	1	2	2	0	3	0	0	0	0	0	.00	0	.111	.273	.222
1997 Detroit	AL	147	436	105	26	0	2	(0	2)	137	35	40	14	0	55	0	14	3	3	6	.33	9	.241	.263	.314
1998 Detroit	AL	135	454	118	22	3	5	(5	0)	161	52	45	13	0	55	3	5	2	3	4	.43	11	.260	.284	.355
2 ML YEARS		282	890	223	48	3	7	(5	2)	298	87	85	27	0	110	3	19	5	6	10	.38	20	.251	.274	.335

Jacob Cruz

Bats: Left **Throws:** Left **Pos:** PH/PR-4   **Ht:** 6'0" **Wt:** 179 **Born:** 1/28/73 **Age:** 26

Year Team	Lg	G	AB	H	2B	3B	HR	Hm	Rd	TB	R	RBI	TBB	IBB	SO	HBP	SH	SF	SB	CS	SB%	GDP	Avg	OBP	SLG
1994 San Jose	A+	31	118	29	7	0	0	—	—	36	14	12	9	0	22	2	2	2	0	2	.00	6	.246	.305	.305
1995 Shreveport	AA	127	458	136	33	1	13	—	—	210	88	77	57	6	72	8	4	2	9	8	.53	15	.297	.383	.459
1996 Phoenix	AAA	121	435	124	26	4	7	—	—	179	60	75	62	5	77	10	2	11	5	9	.36	16	.285	.378	.411
1997 Phoenix	AAA	127	493	178	45	3	12	—	—	265	97	95	64	9	64	3	0	5	18	3	.86	11	.361	.434	.538
1998 Fresno	AAA	89	342	102	17	3	18	—	—	179	60	62	46	2	57	8	2	1	12	5	.71	9	.298	.393	.523
Buffalo	AAA	43	169	56	8	2	13	—	—	107	32	36	13	0	26	1	0	1	3	2	.40	3	.331	.380	.633
1996 San Francisco	NL	33	77	18	3	0	3	(3	0)	30	10	10	12	0	24	2	1	0	0	1	.00	2	.234	.352	.390
1997 San Francisco	NL	16	25	4	1	0	0	(0	0)	5	3	3	3	0	4	0	0	1	0	0	.00	3	.160	.241	.200
1998 SF-Cle		4	4	0	0	0	0	(0	0)	0	0	0	0	0	3	0	0	0	0	0	.00	0	.000	.000	.000
1998 San Francisco	NL	3	3	0	0	0	0	(0	0)	0	0	0	0	0	2	0	0	0	0	0	.00	0	.000	.000	.000
Cleveland	AL	1	1	0	0	0	0	(0	0)	0	0	0	0	0	1	0	0	0	0	0	.00	0	.000	.000	.000
3 ML YEARS		53	106	22	4	0	3	(3	0)	35	13	13	15	0	31	2	1	1	0	1	.00	5	.208	.315	.330

Jose Cruz Jr.

Bats: Both **Throws:** Right **Pos:** CF-103; LF-6; PH/PR-3   **Ht:** 6'0" **Wt:** 200 **Born:** 4/19/74 **Age:** 25

Year Team	Lg	G	AB	H	2B	3B	HR	Hm	Rd	TB	R	RBI	TBB	IBB	SO	HBP	SH	SF	SB	CS	SB%	GDP	Avg	OBP	SLG
1995 Everett	A-	3	11	5	0	0	0	—	—	5	6	2	3	0	3	0	0	0	1	0	1.00	0	.455	.571	.455
Riverside	A+	35	144	37	7	1	7	—	—	67	34	29	24	1	50	0	0	2	3	1	.75	1	.257	.359	.465
1996 Lancaster	A+	53	203	66	17	1	6	—	—	103	38	43	39	1	33	0	0	6	7	1	.88	4	.325	.423	.507
Port City	AA	47	181	51	10	2	3	—	—	74	39	31	27	4	38	0	0	1	5	0	1.00	8	.282	.373	.409
Tacoma	AAA	22	76	18	1	2	6	—	—	41	15	15	18	1	12	0	0	1	1	1	.50	2	.237	.383	.539
1997 Tacoma	AAA	50	190	51	16	2	6	—	—	89	33	30	34	1	44	1	1	0	3	0	1.00	4	.268	.382	.468
1998 Syracuse	AAA	40	141	42	14	1	7	—	—	79	29	23	32	0	32	0	0	1	8	4	.67	2	.298	.425	.560
1997 Sea-Tor	AL	104	395	98	19	1	26	(11	15)	197	59	68	41	2	117	0	1	5	7	2	.78	5	.248	.315	.499
1998 Toronto	AL	105	352	89	14	3	11	(4	7)	142	55	42	57	3	99	0	0	4	11	4	.73	6	.253	.354	.403
1997 Seattle	AL	49	183	49	12	1	12	(7	5)	99	28	34	13	0	45	0	1	1	1	0	1.00	3	.268	.315	.541
Toronto	AL	55	212	49	7	0	14	(4	10)	98	31	34	28	2	72	0	0	4	6	2	.75	2	.231	.316	.462
2 ML YEARS		209	747	187	33	4	37	(15	22)	339	114	110	98	5	216	0	1	9	18	6	.75	5	.250	.334	.454

Midre Cummings

Bats: Left **Throws:** Right **Pos:** PH/PR-36; DH-31; RF-17   **Ht:** 6'0" **Wt:** 190 **Born:** 10/14/71 **Age:** 27

Year Team	Lg	G	AB	H	2B	3B	HR	Hm	Rd	TB	R	RBI	TBB	IBB	SO	HBP	SH	SF	SB	CS	SB%	GDP	Avg	OBP	SLG
1993 Pittsburgh	NL	13	36	4	1	0	0	(0	0)	5	5	3	4	0	9	0	0	1	0	0	.00	1	.111	.195	.139
1994 Pittsburgh	NL	24	86	21	4	0	1	(1	0)	28	11	12	4	0	18	1	0	1	0	0	.00	0	.244	.283	.326
1995 Pittsburgh	NL	59	152	37	7	1	2	(1	1)	52	13	15	13	3	30	0	0	0	1	0	1.00	1	.243	.303	.342
1996 Pittsburgh	NL	24	85	19	3	1	3	(2	1)	33	11	7	0	0	16	0	1	1	0	0	.00	0	.224	.221	.388
1997 Pit-Phi	NL	115	314	83	22	6	4	(3	1)	129	35	31	31	0	56	1	2	2	2	3	.40	3	.264	.330	.411
1998 Boston	AL	67	120	34	8	0	5	(4	1)	57	20	15	17	0	19	2	1	0	3	3	.50	2	.283	.381	.475
1997 Pittsburgh	NL	52	106	20	6	2	3	(2	1)	39	11	8	8	0	26	1	1	0	0	0	.00	0	.189	.252	.368
Philadelphia	NL	63	208	63	16	4	1	(1	0)	90	24	23	23	0	30	0	1	2	2	3	.40	2	.303	.369	.433
6 ML YEARS		302	793	198	45	8	15	(11	4)	304	95	83	69	3	148	4	4	5	6	6	.50	7	.250	.311	.383

Will Cunnane

Pitches: Right **Bats:** Right **Pos:** RP-3   **Ht:** 6'2" **Wt:** 175 **Born:** 4/24/74 **Age:** 25

Year Team	Lg	G	GS	CG	GF	IP	BFP	H	R	ER	HR	SH	SF	HB	TBB	IBB	SO	WP	Bk	W	L	Pct.	ShO	Sv-Op	Hld	ERA
1993 Marlins	R	16	9	0	4	66.2	290	75	32	20	1	3	0	0	8	0	64	2	1	3	3	.500	0	2-	—	2.70
1994 Kane County	A	32	16	5	6	138.2	540	110	27	22	2	4	1	6	23	4	106	5	1	11	3	.786	4	1-	—	1.43
1995 Portland	AA	21	21	1	0	117.2	497	120	48	48	10	3	0	5	34	1	83	2	0	9	2	.818	1	0-	—	3.67
1996 Portland	AA	25	25	4	0	151.2	631	156	73	63	15	5	2	1	30	6	101	4	0	10	12	.455	0	0-	—	3.74
1998 Las Vegas	AAA	33	0	0		36	171	45	26	21	1	2	2	3	19	4	30	2	0	1	2	.333	0	4-	—	5.25
1997 San Diego	NL	54	8	0	16	91.1	430	114	69	59	11	1	5		49	3	79	3	0	6	3	.667	0	0-2	4	5.81
1998 San Diego	NL	3	0	0	1	3	14	4	2	2	1	0	0	0	1	1	1	3	0	0	0	.000	0	0-0	—	6.00
2 ML YEARS		57	8	0	17	94.1	444	118	71	61	12	1	5		50	4	80	3	0	6	3	.667	0	0-2	4	5.82

Chad Curtis

Bats: R **Throws:** R **Pos:** LF-100; CF-45; PH/PR-12; RF-9; DH-2   **Ht:** 5'10" **Wt:** 185 **Born:** 11/6/68 **Age:** 30

Year Team	Lg	G	AB	H	2B	3B	HR	Hm	Rd	TB	R	RBI	TBB	IBB	SO	HBP	SH	SF	SB	CS	SB%	GDP	Avg	OBP	SLG
1992 California	AL	139	441	114	16	2	10	(5	5)	164	59	46	51	2	71	6	5	7	43	18	.70	10	.259	.341	.372
1993 California	AL	152	583	166	25	3	6	(3	3)	215	94	59	70	2	89	4	7	7	48	24	.67	16	.285	.361	.369
1994 California	AL	114	453	116	23	4	11	(8	3)	180	67	50	37	0	69	5	7	4	25	11	.69	10	.256	.317	.397
1995 Detroit	AL	144	586	157	29	3	21	(11	10)	255	96	67	70	3	93	7	2	4	27	15	.64	12	.268	.349	.435
1996 Det-LA		147	504	127	25	1	12	(3	9)	190	85	46	70	0	88	1	6	6	18	11	.62	15	.252	.341	.377
1997 Cle-NYA	AL	115	349	99	22	1	15	(4	11)	168	59	56	43	1	59	5	2	9	12	6	.67	7	.284	.362	.481
1998 New York	AL	151	456	111	21	1	10	(6	4)	164	79	56	75	3	80	7	1	6	21	5	.81	11	.243	.355	.360
1996 Detroit	AL	104	400	105	20	1	10	(2	8)	157	65	37	53	0	73	1	6	6	16	10	.62	14	.263	.346	.393
Los Angeles	NL	43	104	22	5	0	2	(1	1)	33	20	9	17	0	15	0	0	0	2	1	.67	1	.212	.322	.317

Year Team	Lg	G	AB	H	2B	3B	HR	(Hm	Rd)	TB	R	RBI	TBB	IBB	SO	HBP	SH	SF	SB	CS	SB%	GDP	Avg	OBP	SLG
1997 Cleveland	AL	22	29	6	1	0	3	(1	2)	16	8	5	7	0	10	0	0	0	0	0	.00	1	.207	.361	.552
New York	AL	93	320	93	21	1	12	(3	9)	152	51	50	36	1	49	5	2	9	12	6	.67	6	.291	.362	.475
7 ML YEARS		962	3372	890	161	15	85	(40	45)	1336	539	379	416	11	549	35	28	43	194	90	.68	81	.264	.347	.396

Milt Cuyler

Bats: Both **Throws:** Right **Pos:** PH/PR-4; DH-3; CF-3 **Ht:** 5'10" **Wt:** 185 **Born:** 10/7/68 **Age:** 30

Year Team	Lg	G	AB	H	2B	3B	HR	(Hm	Rd)	TB	R	RBI	TBB	IBB	SO	HBP	SH	SF	SB	CS	SB%	GDP	Avg	OBP	SLG
1998 Nashua *	IND	73	249	77	18	6	6	—	—	125	62	33	39	1	42	6	7	1	21	8	.72	4	.309	.414	.502
Oklahoma *	AAA	2	6	0	0	0	0	—	—	0	0	0	2	0	4	0	0	0	0	1	.00	0	.000	.250	.000
1990 Detroit	AL	19	51	13	3	1	0	(0	0)	18	8	8	5	0	10	0	2	1	1	2	.33	1	.255	.316	.353
1991 Detroit	AL	154	475	122	15	7	3	(1	2)	160	77	33	52	0	92	5	12	2	41	10	.80	4	.257	.335	.337
1992 Detroit	AL	89	291	70	11	1	3	(1	2)	92	39	28	10	0	62	4	8	0	8	5	.62	4	.241	.275	.316
1993 Detroit	AL	82	249	53	11	7	0	(0	0)	78	46	19	19	0	53	3	4	1	13	2	.87	2	.213	.276	.313
1994 Detroit	AL	48	116	28	3	1	1	(1	0)	36	20	11	13	0	21	1	2	2	5	3	.63	3	.241	.318	.310
1995 Detroit	AL	41	88	18	1	4	0	(0	0)	27	15	5	8	0	16	0	2	0	2	1	.67	0	.205	.271	.307
1996 Boston	AL	50	110	22	1	2	2	(0	2)	33	19	12	13	0	19	3	7	1	7	3	.70	1	.200	.299	.300
1998 Texas	AL	7	6	3	2	0	1	(0	1)	8	3	3	1	0	0	0	0	0	0	0	.00	0	.500	.571	1.333
8 ML YEARS		490	1386	329	47	23	10	(3	7)	452	227	119	121	0	273	16	37	7	77	26	.75	15	.237	.305	.326

Omar Daal

Pitches: Left **Bats:** Left **Pos:** SP-23; RP-10 **Ht:** 6'3" **Wt:** 185 **Born:** 3/1/72 **Age:** 27

Year Team	Lg	G	GS	CG	GF	IP	BFP	H	R	ER	HR	SH	SF	HB	TBB	IBB	SO	WP	Bk	W	L	Pct.	ShO	Sv-Op	Hld	ERA
1998 Tucson *	AAA	1	1	0	0	3	13	3	2	1	0	0	0	0	1	0	4	0	0	0	0	.000	0	0- —	—	3.00
1993 Los Angeles	NL	47	0	0	12	35.1	155	36	20	20	5	2	2	0	21	3	19	1	2	2	3	.400	0	0-1	7	5.09
1994 Los Angeles	NL	24	0	0	5	13.2	55	12	5	5	1	1	0	0	5	0	9	1	1	0	0	.000	0	0-0	3	3.29
1995 Los Angeles	NL	28	0	0	9	20	100	29	16	16	1	1	1	1	15	4	11	0	1	4	0	1.000	0	0-1	4	7.20
1996 Montreal	NL	64	6	0	9	87.1	366	74	40	39	10	2	2	1	37	3	82	1	1	4	5	.444	0	0-4	9	4.02
1997 Mon-Tor		42	3	0	6	57.1	270	82	48	45	7	7	1	2	21	3	44	2	0	2	3	.400	0	1-3	5	7.06
1998 Arizona	NL	33	23	3	4	162.2	664	146	60	52	12	9	6	3	51	3	132	0	1	8	12	.400	1	0-0	1	2.88
1997 Montreal	NL	33	0	0	6	30.1	150	48	35	33	4	5	1	2	15	3	16	1	0	1	2	.333	0	1-3	3	9.79
Toronto	AL	9	3	0	0	27	120	34	13	12	3	2	0	0	6	0	28	1	0	1	1	.500	0	0-0	0	4.00
6 ML YEARS		238	32	3	36	376.1	1610	379	189	177	36	22	12	7	150	16	297	5	6	20	23	.465	1	1-9	27	4.23

Mark Dalesandro

Bats: R **Throws:** R **Pos:** C-18; 3B-8; PH/PR-7; 1B-2; RF-1 **Ht:** 6'0" **Wt:** 185 **Born:** 5/14/68 **Age:** 31

Year Team	Lg	G	AB	H	2B	3B	HR	(Hm	Rd)	TB	R	RBI	TBB	IBB	SO	HBP	SH	SF	SB	CS	SB%	GDP	Avg	OBP	SLG
1998 Syracuse	AAA	45	164	44	9	1	10	—	—	85	25	30	12	1	20	5	0	1	1	0	1.00	3	.268	.335	.518
1994 California	AL	19	25	5	1	0	1	(1	0)	9	5	2	2	0	4	0	0	0	0	0	.00	0	.200	.259	.360
1995 California	AL	11	10	1	1	0	0	(0	0)	2	1	0	0	0	2	0	0	0	0	0	.00	0	.100	.100	.200
1998 Toronto	AL	32	67	20	5	0	2	(1	1)	31	8	14	1	0	6	0	0	1	0	0	.00	3	.299	.304	.463
3 ML YEARS		62	102	26	7	0	3	(2	1)	42	14	16	3	0	12	0	0	1	0	0	.00	5	.255	.274	.412

Jeff D'Amico

Pitches: Right **Bats:** Right **Pos:** SP **Ht:** 6'7" **Wt:** 250 **Born:** 12/27/75 **Age:** 23

Year Team	Lg	G	GS	CG	GF	IP	BFP	H	R	ER	HR	SH	SF	HB	TBB	IBB	SO	WP	Bk	W	L	Pct.	ShO	Sv-Op	Hld	ERA
1996 Milwaukee	AL	17	17	0	0	86	367	88	53	52	21	3	3	0	31	0	53	1	1	6	6	.500	0	0-0	0	5.44
1997 Milwaukee	AL	23	23	1	0	135.2	585	139	81	71	25	4	4	8	43	2	94	3	1	9	7	.563	1	0-0	0	4.71
2 ML YEARS		40	40	1	0	221.2	952	227	134	123	46	7	7	8	74	2	147	4	2	15	13	.536	1	0-0	0	4.99

Johnny Damon

Bats: L **Throws:** L **Pos:** CF-130; RF-24; LF-14; PH/PR-6 **Ht:** 6'2" **Wt:** 190 **Born:** 11/5/73 **Age:** 25

Year Team	Lg	G	AB	H	2B	3B	HR	(Hm	Rd)	TB	R	RBI	TBB	IBB	SO	HBP	SH	SF	SB	CS	SB%	GDP	Avg	OBP	SLG
1995 Kansas City	AL	47	188	53	11	5	3	(1	2)	83	32	23	12	0	22	1	2	3	7	0	1.00	2	.282	.324	.441
1996 Kansas City	AL	145	517	140	22	5	6	(3	3)	190	61	50	31	3	64	3	10	5	25	5	.83	4	.271	.313	.368
1997 Kansas City	AL	146	472	130	12	8	8	(3	5)	182	70	48	42	2	70	3	6	1	16	10	.62	4	.275	.338	.386
1998 Kansas City	AL	161	642	178	30	10	18	(11	7)	282	104	66	58	4	84	4	3	3	26	12	.68	4	.277	.339	.439
4 ML YEARS		499	1819	501	75	28	35	(18	17)	737	267	187	143	9	240	11	21	12	74	27	.73	13	.275	.330	.405

Vic Darensbourg

Pitches: Left **Bats:** Left **Pos:** RP-59   **Ht:** 5'10" **Wt:** 165 **Born:** 11/13/70 **Age:** 28

Year Team	Lg	G	GS	CG	GF	IP	BFP	H	R	ER	HR	SH	SF	HB	TBB	IBB	SO	WP	Bk	W	L	Pct.	ShO	Sv-Op	Hld	ERA
1992 Marlins	R	8	4	0	2	42	161	28	5	3	1	0	0	3	11	2	37	0	0	2	1	.667	0	2--	--	0.64
1993 Kane County	A	46	0	0	31	71.1	300	58	17	17	3	3	3	4	28	3	89	2	0	9	1	.900	0	16--	--	2.14
High Desert	A+	1	0	0	0	1	4	1	0	0	0	0	0	0	0	1	0	0	0	0	0	.000	0	0--	--	0.00
1994 Portland	AA	34	21	1	9	149	631	146	76	63	18	7	4	6	60	3	103	4	2	10	7	.588	1	4--	--	3.81
1996 Brevard Cty	A+	2	0	0	1	3	10	1	0	0	0	0	0	0	1	0	5	0	0	0	0	.000	0	0--	--	0.00
Charlotte	AAA	47	0	0	25	63.1	280	61	30	26	7	3	2	2	32	3	66	3	1	1	5	.167	0	7--	--	3.69
1997 Charlotte	AAA	27	0	0	6	24.2	110	22	12	12	4	2	0	2	15	3	21	1	0	4	2	.667	0	2--	--	4.38
1998 Florida	NL	59	0	0	10	71	287	52	29	29	5	3	3	0	30	6	74	4	0	0	7	.000	0	1-2	13	3.68

Danny Darwin

Pitches: Right **Bats:** Right **Pos:** SP-25; RP-8   **Ht:** 6'3" **Wt:** 202 **Born:** 10/25/55 **Age:** 43

Year Team	Lg	G	GS	CG	GF	IP	BFP	H	R	ER	HR	SH	SF	HB	TBB	IBB	SO	WP	Bk	W	L	Pct.	ShO	Sv-Op	Hld	ERA
1978 Texas	AL	3	1	0	2	8.2	36	11	4	4	0	0	1	0	1	0	8	0	0	1	0	1.000	0	0--	--	4.15
1979 Texas	AL	20	6	1	4	78	313	50	36	35	5	3	6	5	30	2	58	0	1	4	4	.500	0	0--	--	4.04
1980 Texas	AL	53	2	0	35	109.2	468	98	37	32	4	5	7	2	50	7	104	3	0	13	4	.765	0	8--	--	2.63
1981 Texas	AL	22	22	6	0	146	601	115	67	59	12	8	3	6	57	5	98	1	0	9	9	.500	2	0-0	0	3.64
1982 Texas	AL	56	1	0	41	89	394	95	38	34	6	10	5	2	37	8	61	2	1	10	8	.556	0	7--	--	3.44
1983 Texas	AL	28	26	9	0	183	780	175	86	71	9	7	7	3	62	3	92	2	0	8	13	.381	2	0-0	0	3.49
1984 Texas	AL	35	32	5	2	223.2	955	249	110	98	19	3	3	4	54	2	123	3	0	8	12	.400	1	0-0	0	3.94
1985 Milwaukee	AL	39	29	11	8	217.2	919	212	112	92	**34**	7	9	4	65	4	125	6	0	8	18	.308	1	2-2	0	3.80
1986 Mil-Hou		39	22	6	6	184.2	759	170	81	65	16	6	9	3	44	1	120	7	1	11	10	.524	1	0-1	0	3.17
1987 Houston	NL	33	30	3	0	195.2	833	184	87	78	17	8	3	5	69	12	134	3	1	9	10	.474	1	0-0	1	3.59
1988 Houston	NL	44	20	3	9	192	804	189	86	82	20	10	9	7	48	9	129	1	2	8	13	.381	0	3-3	3	3.84
1989 Houston	NL	68	0	0	26	122	482	92	34	32	8	8	5	2	33	9	104	2	3	11	4	.733	0	7-11	8	2.36
1990 Houston	NL	48	17	3	14	162.2	646	136	42	40	11	4	2	4	31	4	109	0	1	11	4	.733	0	2-4	0	**2.21**
1991 Boston	AL	12	12	0	0	68	292	71	39	39	15	1	2	4	15	1	42	2	0	3	6	.333	0	0-0	0	5.16
1992 Boston	AL	51	15	2	21	161.1	688	159	76	71	11	7	5	5	53	9	124	5	0	9	9	.500	0	3-6	1	3.96
1993 Boston	AL	34	34	2	0	229.1	919	196	93	83	31	6	9	3	49	8	130	5	1	15	11	.577	1	0-0	0	3.26
1994 Boston	AL	13	13	0	0	75.2	350	101	54	53	13	1	5	1	24	6	54	0	0	7	5	.583	0	0-0	0	6.30
1995 Tor-Tex	AL	20	15	1	0	99	448	131	87	82	25	3	5	4	31	3	58	2	0	3	10	.231	0	0-0	0	7.45
1996 Pit-Hou	NL	34	25	0	1	164.2	677	160	79	69	16	8	7	12	27	3	96	3	3	10	11	.476	0	0-2	1	3.77
1997 ChA-SF		31	24	1	0	157.1	692	181	86	76	26	7	6	2	45	1	92	1	2	5	11	.313	0	0-0	0	4.35
1998 San Francisco	NL	33	25	0	2	148.2	660	176	97	91	23	12	3	3	49	4	81	4	0	8	10	.444	0	0-0	0	5.51
1986 Milwaukee	AL	27	14	5	4	130.1	537	120	62	51	13	5	6	3	35	1	80	5	0	6	8	.429	1	0-1	0	3.52
Houston	NL	12	8	1	2	54.1	222	50	19	14	3	1	3	0	9	0	40	2	1	5	2	.714	0	0-0	0	2.32
1995 Toronto	AL	13	11	1	0	65	303	91	60	55	13	3	5	3	24	2	36	1	0	1	8	.111	0	0-0	0	7.62
Texas	AL	7	4	0	0	34	145	40	27	27	12	0	0	1	7	1	22	1	0	2	2	.500	0	0-0	0	7.15
1996 Pittsburgh	NL	19	19	0	0	122.1	493	117	48	41	9	5	4	6	16	0	69	3	3	7	9	.438	0	0-0	0	3.02
Houston	NL	15	6	0	1	42.1	184	43	31	28	7	3	3	6	11	3	27	0	0	3	2	.600	0	0-2	1	5.95
1997 Chicago	AL	21	17	1	0	113.1	496	130	60	52	21	4	5	1	31	1	62	1	2	4	8	.333	0	0-0	0	4.13
San Francisco	NL	10	7	0	0	44	196	51	26	24	5	3	1	1	14	0	30	0	0	1	3	.250	0	0-0	0	4.91
21 ML YEARS		716	371	53	171	3016.2	12716	2951	1431	1286	321	124	111	81	874	101	1942	52	17	171	182	.484	9	32--	--	3.84

Brian Daubach

Bats: Left **Throws:** Right **Pos:** PH/PR-6; 1B-4   **Ht:** 6'1" **Wt:** 201 **Born:** 2/11/72 **Age:** 27

Year Team	Lg	G	AB	H	2B	3B	HR	(Hm	Rd)	TB	R	RBI	TBB	IBB	SO	HBP	SH	SF	SB	CS	SB%	GDP	Avg	OBP	SLG
1990 Mets	R	45	152	41	8	4	1	--	--	60	26	19	22	0	41	2	0	3	2	1	.67	2	.270	.363	.395
1991 Kingsport	R+	65	217	52	9	1	7	--	--	84	30	42	33	5	64	6	1	2	1	3	.25	1	.240	.353	.387
1992 Pittsfield	A-	72	260	63	15	2	2	--	--	88	26	40	30	2	61	3	1	4	4	0	1.00	5	.242	.323	.338
1993 Capital Cty	A	102	379	106	19	3	7	--	--	152	50	72	52	5	84	5	1	7	6	1	.86	14	.280	.368	.401
1994 St. Lucie	A+	129	450	123	30	2	6	--	--	175	52	74	58	5	120	5	3	4	14	9	.61	3	.273	.360	.389
1995 Binghamton	AA	135	469	115	25	2	10	--	--	174	61	72	51	5	104	7	1	7	6	2	.75	5	.245	.324	.371
Norfolk	AAA	2	7	0	0	0	0	--	--	0	0	0	2	1	0	0	0	0	0	0	.00	0	.000	.222	.000
1996 Norfolk	AAA	17	54	11	2	0	0	--	--	13	7	6	6	0	14	0	0	1	1	1	.50	1	.204	.279	.241
Binghamton	AA	122	436	129	24	1	22	--	--	221	80	76	74	9	103	7	0	4	7	9	.44	8	.296	.403	.510
1997 Charlotte	AAA	136	461	128	40	2	21	--	--	235	66	93	65	4	126	6	1	10	1	8	.11	7	.278	.367	.510
1998 Charlotte	AAA	140	497	157	45	4	35	--	--	315	102	124	80	9	114	15	0	7	9	3	.75	15	.316	.421	.634
1998 Florida	NL	10	15	3	1	0	0	(0	0)	4	0	3	1	0	5	1	0	0	0	0	.00	0	.200	.294	.267

Ben Davis

Bats: Both **Throws:** Right **Pos:** C-1   **Ht:** 6'4" **Wt:** 205 **Born:** 3/10/77 **Age:** 22

Year Team	Lg	G	AB	H	2B	3B	HR	(Hm	Rd)	TB	R	RBI	TBB	IBB	SO	HBP	SH	SF	SB	CS	SB%	GDP	Avg	OBP	SLG
1995 Idaho Falls	R+	52	197	55	8	3	5	--	--	84	36	46	17	1	36	1	3	1	0	0	.00	3	.279	.338	.426
1996 Rancho Cuca	A+	98	353	71	10	1	6	--	--	101	35	41	31	0	89	0	4	2	1	1	.50	8	.201	.264	.286
1997 Rancho Cuca	A+	122	474	132	30	1	17	--	--	215	67	76	28	2	107	2	2	3	3	1	.75	11	.278	.320	.454
1998 Mobile	AA	116	433	124	29	2	14	--	--	199	65	75	42	3	60	6	1	7	4	2	.67	11	.286	.352	.460
1998 San Diego	NL	1	1	0	0	0	0	(0	0)	0	0	0	0	0	0	0	0	0	0	0	.00	0	.000	.000	.000

Chili Davis

Bats: Both **Throws:** Right **Pos:** DH-34; PH/PR-9   **Ht:** 6'3" **Wt:** 220 **Born:** 1/17/60 **Age:** 39

Year Team	Lg	G	AB	H	2B	3B	HR	(Hm	Rd)	TB	R	RBI	TBB	IBB	SO	HBP	SH	SF	SB	CS	SB%	GDP	Avg	OBP	SLG
1998 Norwich *	AA	11	37	9	3	0	1	—	—	15	2	5	9	3	7	1	0	0	0	0	.00	4	.243	.404	.405
Columbus *	AAA	6	22	8	1	0	0	—	—	9	4	3	4	0	3	1	0	0	0	0	.00	0	.364	.481	.409
1981 San Francisco	NL	8	15	2	0	0	0	(0	0)	2	1	0	1	0	2	0	0	0	2	0	1.00	1	.133	.188	.133
1982 San Francisco	NL	154	641	167	27	6	19	(6	13)	263	86	76	45	2	115	2	7	6	24	13	.65	13	.261	.308	.410
1983 San Francisco	NL	137	486	113	21	2	11	(7	4)	171	54	59	55	6	108	0	3	9	10	12	.45	9	.233	.305	.352
1984 San Francisco	NL	137	499	157	21	6	21	(7	14)	253	87	81	42	6	74	1	2	2	12	8	.60	13	.315	.368	.507
1985 San Francisco	NL	136	481	130	25	2	13	(7	6)	198	53	56	62	12	74	0	1	7	15	7	.68	16	.270	.349	.412
1986 San Francisco	NL	153	526	146	28	3	13	(7	6)	219	71	70	84	23	96	1	2	5	16	13	.55	11	.278	.375	.416
1987 San Francisco	NL	149	500	125	22	1	24	(9	15)	221	80	76	72	15	109	2	0	4	16	9	.64	8	.250	.344	.442
1988 California	AL	158	600	161	29	3	21	(11	10)	259	81	93	56	14	118	0	1	10	9	10	.47	13	.268	.326	.432
1989 California	AL	154	560	152	24	1	22	(6	16)	244	81	90	61	12	109	0	3	6	3	0	1.00	21	.271	.340	.436
1990 California	AL	113	412	109	17	1	12	(10	2)	164	58	58	61	4	89	0	0	3	1	2	.33	14	.265	.357	.398
1991 Minnesota	AL	153	534	148	34	1	29	(14	15)	271	84	93	95	13	117	1	0	4	5	6	.45	17	.277	.385	.507
1992 Minnesota	AL	138	444	128	27	2	12	(6	6)	195	63	66	73	11	76	3	0	9	4	5	.44	11	.288	.386	.439
1993 California	AL	153	573	139	32	0	27	(13	14)	252	74	112	71	12	135	1	0	0	4	1	.80	18	.243	.327	.440
1994 California	AL	108	392	122	18	1	26	(14	12)	220	72	84	69	11	84	1	0	6	3	2	.60	12	.311	.410	.561
1995 California	AL	119	424	135	23	0	20	(11	9)	218	81	86	89	12	79	0	0	9	3	3	.50	12	.318	.429	.514
1996 California	AL	145	530	155	24	0	28	(15	13)	263	73	95	86	11	99	0	1	6	5	2	.71	18	.292	.387	.496
1997 Kansas City	AL	140	477	133	20	0	30	(21	9)	243	71	90	85	16	96	1	0	4	6	3	.67	15	.279	.386	.509
1998 New York	AL	35	103	30	7	0	3	(1	2)	46	11	9	14	1	18	0	0	1	0	0	.00	6	.291	.373	.447
18 ML YEARS		2290	8197	2252	399	29	331	(165	166)	3702	1181	1294	1121	181	1598	13	20	91	138	97	.59	220	.275	.359	.452

Eric Davis

Bats: R **Throws:** R **Pos:** RF-64; DH-54; PH/PR-17; CF-11   **Ht:** 6'3" **Wt:** 200 **Born:** 5/29/62 **Age:** 37

Year Team	Lg	G	AB	H	2B	3B	HR	(Hm	Rd)	TB	R	RBI	TBB	IBB	SO	HBP	SH	SF	SB	CS	SB%	GDP	Avg	OBP	SLG
1984 Cincinnati	NL	57	174	39	10	1	10	(3	7)	81	33	30	24	0	48	1	0	1	10	2	.83	1	.224	.320	.466
1985 Cincinnati	NL	56	122	30	3	3	8	(1	7)	63	26	18	7	0	39	0	2	0	16	3	.84	1	.246	.287	.516
1986 Cincinnati	NL	132	415	115	15	3	27	(12	15)	217	97	71	68	5	100	1	0	3	80	11	.88	6	.277	.378	.523
1987 Cincinnati	NL	129	474	139	23	4	37	(17	20)	281	120	100	84	8	134	1	0	3	50	6	.89	6	.293	.399	.593
1988 Cincinnati	NL	135	472	129	18	3	26	(14	12)	231	81	93	65	10	124	3	0	3	35	3	.92	11	.273	.363	.489
1989 Cincinnati	NL	131	462	130	14	2	34	(15	19)	250	74	101	68	12	116	1	0	11	21	7	.75	16	.281	.367	.541
1990 Cincinnati	NL	127	453	118	26	2	24	(13	11)	220	84	86	60	6	100	2	0	3	21	3	.88	7	.260	.347	.486
1991 Cincinnati	NL	89	285	67	10	0	11	(5	6)	110	39	33	48	5	92	5	0	2	14	2	.88	4	.235	.353	.386
1992 Los Angeles	NL	76	267	61	8	1	5	(1	4)	86	21	32	36	2	71	3	0	2	19	1	.95	9	.228	.325	.322
1993 LA-Det		131	451	107	18	1	20	(10	10)	187	71	68	55	7	106	1	0	4	35	7	.83	12	.237	.319	.415
1994 Detroit	AL	37	120	22	4	0	3	(3	0)	35	19	13	18	0	45	0	0	0	5	0	1.00	4	.183	.290	.292
1996 Cincinnati	NL	129	415	119	20	0	26	(8	18)	217	81	83	70	3	121	6	1	4	23	9	.72	8	.287	.394	.523
1997 Baltimore	AL	42	158	48	11	0	8	(7	1)	83	29	25	14	0	47	1	0	3	6	0	1.00	2	.304	.358	.525
1998 Baltimore	AL	131	452	148	29	1	28	(16	12)	263	81	89	44	0	108	5	0	7	7	6	.54	13	.327	.388	.582
1993 Los Angeles	NL	108	376	88	17	0	14	(7	7)	147	57	53	41	6	88	1	0	4	33	5	.87	8	.234	.308	.391
Detroit	AL	23	75	19	1	1	6	(3	3)	40	14	15	14	1	18	0	0	0	2	2	.50	4	.253	.371	.533
14 ML YEARS		1402	4720	1272	209	21	267	(125	142)	2324	856	842	661	58	1251	30	3	46	342	60	.85	100	.269	.360	.492

Russ Davis

Bats: Right **Throws:** Right **Pos:** 3B-137; PH/PR-5; LF-3   **Ht:** 6'0" **Wt:** 195 **Born:** 9/13/69 **Age:** 29

Year Team	Lg	G	AB	H	2B	3B	HR	(Hm	Rd)	TB	R	RBI	TBB	IBB	SO	HBP	SH	SF	SB	CS	SB%	GDP	Avg	OBP	SLG
1994 New York	AL	4	14	2	0	0	0	(0	0)	2	0	1	0	0	4	0	0	0	0	0	.00	1	.143	.143	.143
1995 New York	AL	40	98	27	5	2	2	(2	0)	42	14	12	10	0	26	1	0	0	0	0	.00	0	.276	.349	.429
1996 Seattle	AL	51	167	39	9	0	5	(3	2)	63	24	18	17	1	50	2	4	0	2	0	1.00	1	.234	.312	.377
1997 Seattle	AL	119	420	114	29	1	20	(11	9)	205	57	63	27	2	100	2	3	2	6	2	.75	11	.271	.317	.488
1998 Seattle	AL	141	502	130	30	1	20	(7	13)	222	68	82	34	1	134	3	2	9	4	3	.57	10	.259	.305	.442
5 ML YEARS		355	1201	312	73	4	47	(23	24)	534	163	176	88	4	314	8	9	11	12	5	.71	23	.260	.312	.445

Rick DeHart

Pitches: Left **Bats:** Left **Pos:** RP-26   **Ht:** 6'1" **Wt:** 190 **Born:** 3/21/70 **Age:** 29

Year Team	Lg	G	GS	CG	GF	IP	BFP	H	R	ER	HR	SH	SF	HB	TBB	IBB	SO	WP	Bk	W	L	Pct.	ShO	Sv-Op	Hld	ERA
1992 Albany	A	38	10	1	15	117	476	91	42	32	11	5	5	4	40	1	133	5	6	9	6	.600	1	3- -	—	2.46
1993 San Berndno	A+	9	9	0	0	53.1	237	56	28	18	4	3	1	0	25	0	44	0	0	4	3	.571	0	0- -	—	3.04
Harrisburg	AA	12	7	0	1	34	163	45	31	29	5	1	2	2	19	0	18	2	0	2	4	.333	0	0- -	—	7.68
Wst Plm Bch	A+	7	7	1	0	42	175	42	14	14	0	1	1	1	17	0	33	2	0	1	3	.250	1	0- -	—	3.00
1994 Wst Plm Bch	A+	30	20	3	5	136.1	566	132	61	51	12	7	2	3	34	0	88	7	1	9	7	.563	2	0- -	—	3.37
1995 Harrisburg	AA	35	12	0	4	93	417	94	62	50	13	4	6	5	39	3	64	4	4	6	7	.462	0	0- -	—	4.84
1996 Harrisburg	AA	30	2	0	14	43.2	196	46	19	13	4	1	2	3	19	0	30	1	0	1	2	.333	0	1- -	—	2.68
1997 Ottawa	AAA	43	0	0	14	63	264	60	33	28	6	2	1	4	22	0	57	1	0	0	4	.000	0	2- -	—	4.00
1998 Ottawa	AAA	38	0	0	18	53	220	46	19	19	5	1	0	2	17	2	48	1	0	7	1	.875	0	4- -	—	3.23
1997 Montreal	NL	23	0	0	7	29.1	130	33	21	18	7	1	2	0	14	4	29	2	0	2	1	.667	0	0-1	1	5.52
1998 Montreal	NL	26	0	0	6	28	134	34	22	15	3	3	1	0	13	1	14	1	1	0	0	.000	0	1-2	4	4.82
2 ML YEARS		49	0	0	13	57.1	264	67	43	33	10	4	3	0	27	5	43	3	1	2	1	.667	0	1-3	5	5.18

Mike DeJean

Pitches: Right **Bats:** Right **Pos:** RP-58; SP-1 **Ht:** 6'2" **Wt:** 208 **Born:** 9/28/70 **Age:** 28

		HOW MUCH HE PITCHED						WHAT HE GAVE UP												THE RESULTS						
Year Team	Lg	G	GS	CG	GF	IP	BFP	H	R	ER	HR	SH	SF	HB	TBB	IBB	SO	WP	Bk	W	L	Pct.	ShO	Sv-Op	Hld	ERA
1992 Oneonta	A-	20	0	0	19	20.2	78	12	3	1	1	0	0	0	3	0	20	0	0	0	0	.000	0	16--	—	0.44
1993 Greensboro	A	20	0	0	18	18	87	22	12	10	1	1	1	0	8	2	16	1	0	2	3	.400	0	9--	—	5.00
1994 Tampa	A+	34	0	0	33	34	156	39	15	9	1	1	2	2	13	0	22	0	0	0	2	.000	0	16--	—	2.38
Albany-Colo	AA	16	0	0	10	24.2	110	22	14	12	1	4	1	2	15	3	13	6	0	0	4	.000	0	4--	—	4.38
1995 Norwich	AA	59	0	0	40	78.1	323	58	29	26	5	2	3	5	34	2	57	4	1	5	5	.500	0	20--	—	2.99
1996 New Haven	AA	16	0	0	15	22.1	90	20	9	8	2	0	1	0	8	0	12	2	0	0	0	.000	0	11--	—	3.22
Colo Sprngs	AAA	30	0	0	17	40.1	186	52	24	23	3	0	0	2	21	3	31	2	0	0	2	.000	0	1--	—	5.13
1997 Colo Sprngs	AAA	10	0	0	10	10	50	17	6	6	0	0	1	0	7	1	9	0	0	0	1	.000	0	4--	—	5.40
New Haven	AA	2	0	0	0	3	14	3	2	2	0	0	0	1	2	0	2	0	0	0	1	.000	0	0--	—	6.00
1997 Colorado	NL	55	0	0	15	67.2	295	74	34	30	4	3	1	3	24	2	38	2	0	5	0	1.000	0	2-4	13	3.99
1998 Colorado	NL	59	1	0	9	74.1	307	78	29	25	4	4	4	1	24	1	27	3	0	3	1	.750	0	2-3	11	3.03
2 ML YEARS		114	1	0	24	142	602	152	63	55	8	7	5	4	48	3	65	5	0	8	1	.889	0	4-7	24	3.49

Carlos Delgado

Bats: Left **Throws:** Right **Pos:** 1B-141; DH-1 **Ht:** 6'3" **Wt:** 225 **Born:** 6/25/72 **Age:** 27

		BATTING																BASERUNNING				PERCENTAGES		
Year Team	Lg	G	AB	H	2B	3B	HR	(Hm Rd)	TB	R	RBI	TBB	IBB	SO	HBP	SH	SF	SB	CS	SB%	GDP	Avg	OBP	SLG
1998 Dunedin *	A+	4	16	5	1	0	2	—	12	4	7	2	0	4	0	0	0	0	0	.00	1	.313	.389	.750
Syracuse *	AAA	2	7	4	2	0	1	—	9	4	6	2	0	0	0	0	0	0	0	.00	0	.571	.667	1.286
1993 Toronto	AL	2	1	0	0	0	0	(0 0)	0	0	0	1	0	0	0	0	0	0	0	.00	0	.000	.500	.000
1994 Toronto	AL	43	130	28	2	0	9	(5 4)	57	17	24	25	4	46	3	0	1	1	1	.50	5	.215	.352	.438
1995 Toronto	AL	37	91	15	3	0	3	(2 1)	27	7	11	6	0	26	0	0	2	0	0	.00	5	.165	.212	.297
1996 Toronto	AL	138	488	132	28	2	25	(12 13)	239	68	92	58	2	139	9	0	8	0	0	.00	13	.270	.353	.490
1997 Toronto	AL	153	519	136	42	3	30	(17 13)	274	79	91	64	9	133	8	0	4	0	3	.00	6	.262	.350	.528
1998 Toronto	AL	142	530	155	43	1	38	(20 18)	314	94	115	73	13	139	11	0	6	3	0	1.00	8	.292	.385	.592
6 ML YEARS		515	1759	466	118	6	105	(56 49)	911	265	333	227	28	483	31	0	21	4	4	.50	33	.265	.355	.518

Wilson Delgado

Bats: Both **Throws:** Right **Pos:** SS-6; PH/PR-6 **Ht:** 5'11" **Wt:** 155 **Born:** 7/15/75 **Age:** 23

		BATTING																BASERUNNING				PERCENTAGES		
Year Team	Lg	G	AB	H	2B	3B	HR	(Hm Rd)	TB	R	RBI	TBB	IBB	SO	HBP	SH	SF	SB	CS	SB%	GDP	Avg	OBP	SLG
1994 Mariners	R	39	149	56	5	4	0	— —	69	30	10	15	0	24	1	0	0	13	5	.72	2	.376	.436	.463
Appleton	A	9	31	6	0	0	0	— —	6	2	0	0	0	8	0	0	0	0	0	.00	0	.194	.194	.194
1995 Port City	AA	13	41	8	4	0	0	— —	12	3	1	6	0	8	0	0	0	0	0	.00	1	.195	.298	.293
Wisconsin	A	19	70	17	3	0	0	— —	20	13	7	3	0	15	0	2	0	3	0	1.00	0	.243	.274	.286
Burlington	A	93	365	113	20	3	5	— —	154	52	37	32	1	57	2	2	1	9	9	.50	7	.310	.368	.422
San Jose	A+	1	2	0	0	0	0	— —	0	1	0	0	0	0	0	0	0	0	0	.00	0	.000	.000	.000
1996 San Jose	A+	121	462	124	19	6	2	— —	161	59	54	48	0	89	2	4	4	8	2	.80	8	.268	.337	.348
Phoenix	AAA	12	43	6	0	1	0	— —	8	1	1	3	1	7	0	0	0	0	1	.00	1	.140	.196	.186
1997 Phoenix	AAA	119	416	120	22	4	9	— —	177	47	59	24	4	70	1	6	4	9	3	.75	9	.288	.326	.425
1998 Fresno	AAA	127	512	142	22	2	12	— —	204	87	63	52	2	92	3	4	4	9	5	.64	5	.277	.345	.398
1996 San Francisco	NL	6	22	8	0	0	0	(0 0)	8	3	2	1	0	5	2	0	0	1	0	1.00	0	.364	.440	.364
1997 San Francisco	NL	8	7	1	1	0	0	(0 0)	2	1	0	0	0	2	0	1	0	0	0	.00	0	.143	.143	.286
1998 San Francisco	NL	10	12	2	1	0	0	(0 0)	3	1	1	1	0	3	0	0	0	0	0	.00	0	.167	.231	.250
3 ML YEARS		24	41	11	2	0	0	(0 0)	13	5	3	2	0	10	2	1	0	1	0	1.00	0	.268	.333	.317

David Dellucci

Bats: L **Throws:** L **Pos:** LF-95; CF-19; PH/PR-16; RF-15 **Ht:** 5'10" **Wt:** 180 **Born:** 10/31/73 **Age:** 25

		BATTING																BASERUNNING				PERCENTAGES		
Year Team	Lg	G	AB	H	2B	3B	HR	(Hm Rd)	TB	R	RBI	TBB	IBB	SO	HBP	SH	SF	SB	CS	SB%	GDP	Avg	OBP	SLG
1995 Bluefield	R+	20	69	23	5	1	2	— —	36	11	12	6	1	7	1	0	1	3	1	.75	1	.333	.390	.522
Frederick	A+	28	96	27	3	0	1	— —	33	16	10	12	1	10	3	0	0	1	2	.33	3	.281	.378	.344
1996 Frederick	A+	59	185	60	11	1	4	— —	85	33	28	38	3	34	0	0	1	5	6	.45	2	.324	.438	.459
Bowie	AA	66	251	73	14	1	2	— —	95	27	33	28	1	56	1	2	1	2	7	.22	4	.291	.363	.378
1997 Bowie	AA	107	385	126	29	3	20	— —	221	71	55	58	1	69	5	0	1	11	4	.73	6	.327	.421	.574
1998 Tucson	AAA	17	72	22	4	3	1	— —	35	17	11	5	0	8	0	0	1	4	0	1.00	0	.306	.346	.486
1997 Baltimore	AL	17	27	6	1	0	1	(0 1)	10	3	3	4	1	7	1	0	0	0	0	.00	2	.222	.344	.370
1998 Arizona	NL	124	416	108	19	12	5	(1 4)	166	43	51	33	2	103	3	0	1	3	5	.38	6	.260	.318	.399
2 ML YEARS		141	443	114	20	12	6	(1 5)	176	46	54	37	3	110	4	0	1	3	5	.38	8	.257	.320	.397

Valerio De Los Santos

Pitches: Left **Bats:** Left **Pos:** RP-13 **Ht:** 6'2" **Wt:** 180 **Born:** 10/6/75 **Age:** 23

		HOW MUCH HE PITCHED						WHAT HE GAVE UP												THE RESULTS						
Year Team	Lg	G	GS	CG	GF	IP	BFP	H	R	ER	HR	SH	SF	HB	TBB	IBB	SO	WP	Bk	W	L	Pct.	ShO	Sv-Op	Hld	ERA
1995 Brewers	R	14	12	0	1	82	341	81	34	20	3	5	4	6	12	2	57	6	2	4	6	.400	0	0--	—	2.20
1996 Beloit	A	33	23	5	10	164.2	715	164	83	65	11	8	5	3	59	4	137	8	3	10	8	.556	1	4--	—	3.55
1997 El Paso	AA	26	16	1	3	114.1	516	146	83	73	6	5	4	4	38	2	61	7	1	6	10	.375	0	2--	—	5.75
1998 El Paso	AA	42	4	0	32	66.2	305	81	34	29	2	5	3	1	25	1	62	5	1	6	2	.750	0	10--	—	3.92
Louisville	AAA	5	0	0	2	5	19	4	2	2	0	0	0	0	0	0	5	0	0	0	0	.000	0	0--	—	3.60
1998 Milwaukee	NL	13	0	0	3	21.2	75	11	7	7	4	0	0	0	2	0	18	1	0	0	0	.000	0	0-0	0	2.91

Rich DeLucia

Pitches: Right **Bats:** Right **Pos:** RP-61   **Ht:** 6'0" **Wt:** 190 **Born:** 10/7/64 **Age:** 34

		HOW MUCH HE PITCHED					WHAT HE GAVE UP											THE RESULTS					
Year Team	Lg	G	GS	CG	GF	IP	BFP	H	R	ER	HR	SH	SF	HB	TBB	IBB	SO	WP	Bk	W	L	Pct.	ShO	Sv-Op	Hld	ERA
1990 Seattle	AL	5	5	1	0	36	144	30	9	8	2	2	0	4	9	0	20	0	0	1	2	.333	0	0-0	0	2.00
1991 Seattle	AL	32	31	0	0	182	779	176	107	103	31	5	14	4	78	4	98	10	0	12	13	.480	0	0-0	0	5.09
1992 Seattle	AL	30	11	0	6	83.2	382	100	55	51	13	2	2	2	35	1	66	1	0	3	6	.333	0	1-3	3	5.49
1993 Seattle	AL	30	1	0	11	42.2	195	46	24	22	5	1	1	1	23	3	48	4	0	3	6	.333	0	0-4	6	4.64
1994 Cincinnati	NL	8	0	0	2	10.2	47	9	6	5	4	0	0	0	5	0	15	1	0	0	0	.000	0	0-0	0	4.22
1995 St. Louis	NL	56	1	0	8	82.1	342	63	38	31	9	5	2	3	36	2	76	5	0	8	7	.533	0	0-1	9	3.39
1996 San Francisco	NL	56	0	0	20	61.2	279	62	44	40	8	4	2	3	31	6	55	7	0	3	6	.333	0	0-2	11	5.84
1997 SF-Ana		36	0	0	13	44	186	35	21	19	5	2	2	1	27	2	44	2	0	6	4	.600	0	3-7	8	3.89
1998 Anaheim	AL	61	0	0	18	71.2	314	56	36	34	10	5	7	3	46	5	73	8	1	2	6	.250	0	3-6	12	4.27
1997 San Francisco	NL	3	0	0	0	1.2	12	6	3	2	0	0	0	0	0	0	2	1	0	0	0	.000	0	0-0	1	10.80
Anaheim	AL	33	0	0	13	42.1	174	29	18	17	5	2	2	1	27	2	42	1	0	6	4	.600	0	3-7	7	3.61
9 ML YEARS		314	49	1	78	614.2	2668	577	340	313	87	26	30	17	290	23	495	38	1	38	50	.432	0	7-23	49	4.58

Ryan Dempster

Pitches: Right **Bats:** Right **Pos:** SP-11; RP-3   **Ht:** 6'2" **Wt:** 195 **Born:** 5/3/77 **Age:** 22

		HOW MUCH HE PITCHED					WHAT HE GAVE UP											THE RESULTS					
Year Team	Lg	G	GS	CG	GF	IP	BFP	H	R	ER	HR	SH	SF	HB	TBB	IBB	SO	WP	Bk	W	L	Pct.	ShO	Sv-Op	Hld	ERA
1995 Rangers	R	8	6	1	0	34.1	154	34	21	9	1	0	1	2	17	0	37	2	1	3	1	.750	0	0- -		2.36
Hudson Vall	A-	1	1	0	0	5.2	24	7	2	2	0	1	0	0	1	0	6	0	0	1	0	1.000	0	0- -		3.18
1996 Chston-SC	A	23	23	2	0	144.1	603	120	71	53	13	6	9	6	58	1	141	17	5	7	11	.389	0	0- -		3.30
Kane County	A	4	4	1	0	26.1	109	18	10	8	0	1	0	1	18	0	16	2	0	2	1	.667	1	0- -		2.73
1997 Brevard Cty	A+	28	26	2	0	165.1	721	190	100	90	19	3	4	13	46	1	131	8	1	10	9	.526	1	0- -		4.90
1998 Portland	AA	7	7	0	0	44.2	180	34	20	16	8	3	0	3	15	0	33	1	0	4	3	.571	0	0- -		3.22
Charlotte	AAA	5	5	1	0	33	137	33	14	12	4	0	2	1	12	1	24	2	0	3	1	.750	0	0- -		3.27
1998 Florida	NL	14	11	0	1	54.2	272	72	47	43	6	5	6	9	38	1	35	5	0	1	5	.167	0	0-1	0	7.08

Mark DeRosa

Bats: Right **Throws:** Right **Pos:** SS-4; PH/PR-3   **Ht:** 6'1" **Wt:** 190 **Born:** 2/2/75 **Age:** 24

		BATTING																BASERUNNING				PERCENTAGES		
Year Team	Lg	G	AB	H	2B	3B	HR	(Hm	Rd)	TB	R	RBI	TBB	IBB	SO	HBP	SH	SF	SB	CS	SB%	GDP	Avg	OBP	SLG
1996 Eugene	A-	70	255	66	13	1	2	—	—	87	43	28	38	1	48	5	0	2	3	4	.43	10	.259	.363	.341
1997 Durham	A+	92	346	93	11	3	8	—	—	134	51	37	25	2	73	10	2	4	6	8	.43	12	.269	.332	.387
1998 Greenville	AA	125	461	123	26	2	8	—	—	177	67	49	60	2	57	5	5	2	7	13	.35	18	.267	.356	.384
1998 Atlanta	NL	5	3	1	0	0	0	(0	0)	1	2	0	0	0	1	0	0	0	0	0	.00	0	.333	.333	.333

Delino DeShields

Bats: Left **Throws:** Right **Pos:** 2B-111; PH/PR-14; 1B-1   **Ht:** 6'1" **Wt:** 175 **Born:** 1/15/69 **Age:** 30

		BATTING																BASERUNNING				PERCENTAGES		
Year Team	Lg	G	AB	H	2B	3B	HR	(Hm	Rd)	TB	R	RBI	TBB	IBB	SO	HBP	SH	SF	SB	CS	SB%	GDP	Avg	OBP	SLG
1998 Arkansas *	AA	4	13	2	0	0	0	—	—	2	1	0	2	0	6	0	0	0	0	1	.00	0	.154	.267	.154
1990 Montreal	NL	129	499	144	28	6	4	(3	1)	196	69	45	66	3	96	4	1	2	42	22	.66	10	.289	.375	.393
1991 Montreal	NL	151	563	134	15	4	10	(3	7)	187	83	51	95	2	151	2	8	5	56	23	.71	6	.238	.347	.332
1992 Montreal	NL	135	530	155	19	8	7	(1	6)	211	82	56	54	4	108	3	9	3	46	15	.75	10	.292	.359	.398
1993 Montreal	NL	123	481	142	17	7	2	(2	0)	179	75	29	72	3	64	3	4	2	43	10	.81	6	.295	.389	.372
1994 Los Angeles	NL	89	320	80	11	3	2	(1	1)	103	51	33	54	0	53	0	1	1	27	7	.79	9	.250	.357	.322
1995 Los Angeles	NL	127	425	109	18	3	8	(2	6)	157	66	37	63	4	83	1	3	1	39	14	.74	6	.256	.353	.369
1996 Los Angeles	NL	154	581	130	12	8	5	(3	2)	173	75	41	53	7	124	1	2	5	48	11	.81	12	.224	.288	.298
1997 St. Louis	NL	150	572	169	26	14	11	(6	5)	256	92	58	55	1	72	3	7	6	55	14	.80	5	.295	.357	.448
1998 St. Louis	NL	117	420	122	21	8	7	(3	4)	180	74	44	56	2	61	0	4	4	26	10	.72	6	.290	.371	.429
9 ML YEARS		1175	4391	1185	167	61	56	(24	32)	1642	667	394	568	26	812	17	39	29	382	126	.75	70	.270	.354	.374

Elmer Dessens

Pitches: Right **Bats:** Right **Pos:** RP-38; SP-5   **Ht:** 6'0" **Wt:** 178 **Born:** 1/13/72 **Age:** 27

		HOW MUCH HE PITCHED					WHAT HE GAVE UP											THE RESULTS					
Year Team	Lg	G	GS	CG	GF	IP	BFP	H	R	ER	HR	SH	SF	HB	TBB	IBB	SO	WP	Bk	W	L	Pct.	ShO	Sv-Op	Hld	ERA
1995 Carolina	AA	27	27	1	0	152	638	170	62	42	10	11	4	3	21	3	68	7	2	15	8	.652	0	0- -		2.49
1996 Calgary	AAA	6	6	0	0	34.1	150	40	14	12	5	2	1	1	15	1	15	2	1	2	2	.500	0	0- -		3.15
Carolina	AA	5	1	0	2	11.2	55	15	8	7	1	0	0	1	4	0	7	0	0	0	1	.000	0	0- -		5.40
1998 Nashville	AAA	5	5	0	0	30	127	32	12	11	2	2	1	1	6	1	13	0	0	3	1	.750	0	0- -		3.30
1996 Pittsburgh	NL	15	3	0	1	25	112	40	23	23	2	3	1	0	4	0	13	0	0	2	2	.000	0	0-0	3	8.28
1997 Pittsburgh	NL	3	0	0	1	3.1	13	2	0	0	0	0	0	0	0	0	2	0	0	0	0	.000	0	0-0	0	0.00
1998 Pittsburgh	NL	43	5	0	8	74.2	332	90	50	47	10	4	3	0	25	2	43	1	0	2	6	.250	0	0-1	6	5.67
3 ML YEARS		61	8	0	10	103	457	132	73	70	12	7	4	1	29	2	58	1	0	2	8	.200	0	0-1	9	6.12

Mike Devereaux

Bats: Right **Throws:** Right **Pos:** PH/PR-5; CF-3; LF-1; RF-1   **Ht:** 6'0" **Wt:** 195 **Born:** 4/10/63 **Age:** 36

Year Team	Lg	G	AB	H	2B	3B	HR	(Hm	Rd)	TB	R	RBI	TBB	IBB	SO	HBP	SH	SF	SB	CS	SB%	GDP	Avg	OBP	SLG
1998 Las Vegas *	AAA	34	120	32	10	1	2	—	—	50	19	12	9	1	13	0	0	0	1	0	1.00	6	.267	.318	.417
1987 Los Angeles	NL	19	54	12	3	0	0	(0	0)	15	7	4	3	0	10	0	1	0	3	1	.75	0	.222	.263	.278
1988 Los Angeles	NL	30	43	5	1	0	0	(0	0)	6	4	2	2	0	10	0	0	0	0	1	.00	0	.116	.156	.140
1989 Baltimore	AL	122	391	104	14	3	8	(4	4)	148	55	46	36	0	60	2	2	3	22	11	.67	7	.266	.329	.379
1990 Baltimore	AL	108	367	88	18	1	12	(6	6)	144	48	49	28	0	48	0	4	4	13	12	.52	10	.240	.291	.392
1991 Baltimore	AL	149	608	158	27	10	19	(10	9)	262	82	59	47	2	115	2	7	4	16	9	.64	13	.260	.313	.431
1992 Baltimore	AL	156	653	180	29	11	24	(14	10)	303	76	107	44	1	94	4	0	9	10	8	.56	14	.276	.321	.464
1993 Baltimore	AL	131	527	132	31	3	14	(8	6)	211	72	75	43	0	99	1	2	4	3	3	.50	13	.250	.306	.400
1994 Baltimore	AL	85	301	61	8	2	9	(5	4)	100	35	33	22	0	72	1	2	4	1	2	.33	6	.203	.256	.332
1995 ChA-Atl		121	388	116	24	1	11	(5	6)	175	55	63	27	3	62	0	0	3	8	6	.57	11	.299	.342	.451
1996 Baltimore	AL	127	323	74	11	2	8	(5	3)	113	49	34	34	0	53	2	2	2	8	2	.80	8	.229	.305	.350
1997 Texas	AL	29	72	15	3	0	0	(0	0)	18	8	7	7	0	10	0	0	1	1	0	1.00	0	.208	.275	.250
1998 Los Angeles	NL	9	13	4	1	0	0	(0	0)	5	0	1	3	0	2	0	0	0	1	0	1.00	2	.308	.438	.385
1995 Chicago	AL	92	333	102	21	1	10	(4	6)	155	48	55	25	3	51	0	0	3	6	6	.50	10	.306	.352	.465
Atlanta	NL	29	55	14	3	0	1	(1	0)	20	7	8	2	0	11	0	0	0	2	0	1.00	1	.255	.281	.364
12 ML YEARS		1086	3740	949	170	33	105	(57	48)	1500	491	480	296	6	635	12	20	34	85	56	.60	84	.254	.308	.401

Alex Diaz

Bats: B **Throws:** R **Pos:** PH/PR-16; CF-15; LF-4; RF-3   **Ht:** 5'11" **Wt:** 180 **Born:** 10/5/68 **Age:** 30

Year Team	Lg	G	AB	H	2B	3B	HR	(Hm	Rd)	TB	R	RBI	TBB	IBB	SO	HBP	SH	SF	SB	CS	SB%	GDP	Avg	OBP	SLG
1998 Fresno *	AAA	11	39	7	0	0	0	—	—	7	2	2	2	0	5	0	1	1	1	3	.25	3	.179	.214	.179
1992 Milwaukee	AL	22	9	1	0	0	0	(0 | 0)	1	5	1	0	0	0	0	0	0	0	3	2	.60	0	.111	.111	.111
1993 Milwaukee	AL	32	69	22	2	0	0	(0	0)	24	9	1	0	0	12	0	3	0	5	3	.63	3	.319	.319	.348
1994 Milwaukee	AL	79	187	47	5	7	1	(0	1)	69	17	17	10	1	19	0	3	3	5	5	.50	5	.251	.285	.369
1995 Seattle	AL	103	270	67	14	0	3	(3	0)	90	44	27	13	2	27	2	5	2	18	8	.69	3	.248	.286	.333
1996 Seattle	AL	38	79	19	2	0	1	(1	0)	24	11	5	2	0	8	2	0	1	6	3	.67	2	.241	.274	.304
1997 Texas	AL	28	90	20	4	0	2	(0	2)	30	8	12	5	0	13	1	0	1	1	1	.50	3	.222	.268	.333
1998 San Francisco	NL	34	62	8	2	0	0	(0	0)	10	5	5	0	0	15	0	0	0	1	1	.50	0	.129	.129	.161
7 ML YEARS		336	766	184	29	7	7	(4	3)	248	99	68	30	3	94	5	11	7	39	23	.63	16	.240	.271	.324

Edwin Diaz

Bats: Right **Throws:** Right **Pos:** 2B-3; PH/PR-1   **Ht:** 5'11" **Wt:** 170 **Born:** 1/15/75 **Age:** 24

Year Team	Lg	G	AB	H	2B	3B	HR	(Hm	Rd)	TB	R	RBI	TBB	IBB	SO	HBP	SH	SF	SB	CS	SB%	GDP	Avg	OBP	SLG
1993 Rangers	R	43	154	47	10	5	1	—	—	70	27	23	19	1	21	4	0	2	12	5	.71	4	.305	.391	.455
1994 Chston-SC	A	122	413	109	22	7	11	—	—	178	52	60	22	0	107	8	9	8	11	14	.44	7	.264	.308	.431
1995 Charlotte	A+	115	450	128	26	5	8	—	—	188	48	56	33	0	94	7	3	2	8	13	.38	10	.284	.341	.418
1996 Tulsa	AA	121	499	132	33	6	16	—	—	225	70	65	25	4	122	9	8	4	8	9	.47	9	.265	.309	.451
1997 Okla City	AAA	20	73	8	3	1	1	—	—	16	6	4	2	0	27	2	1	1	1	1	.50	1	.110	.156	.219
Tulsa	AA	105	440	121	31	1	15	—	—	199	65	46	33	0	102	8	2	2	6	9	.40	6	.275	.335	.452
1998 Tucson	AAA	131	510	134	31	12	2	—	—	195	61	49	27	0	105	4	2	5	9	6	.60	9	.263	.302	.382
1998 Arizona	NL	3	7	0	0	0	0	(0	0)	0	0	0	0	0	2	0	0	0	0	0	.00	0	.000	.000	.000

Einar Diaz

Bats: Right **Throws:** Right **Pos:** C-17; PH/PR-1   **Ht:** 5'10" **Wt:** 165 **Born:** 12/28/72 **Age:** 26

Year Team	Lg	G	AB	H	2B	3B	HR	(Hm	Rd)	TB	R	RBI	TBB	IBB	SO	HBP	SH	SF	SB	CS	SB%	GDP	Avg	OBP	SLG
1992 Burlington	R+	52	178	37	3	0	1	—	—	43	19	14	20	0	9	3	2	2	2	3	.40	4	.208	.296	.242
1993 Burlington	R+	60	231	69	15	3	5	—	—	105	40	33	8	0	7	4	2	4	7	3	.70	5	.299	.328	.455
Columbus	A	1	5	0	0	0	0	—	—	0	0	0	0	0	0	0	0	0	0	0	.00	0	.000	.000	.000
1994 Columbus	A	120	491	137	23	2	16	—	—	212	67	71	17	0	34	21	1	1	4	4	.50	18	.279	.330	.432
1995 Kinston	A+	104	373	98	21	0	6	—	—	137	46	43	12	2	29	8	1	4	3	6	.33	6	.263	.297	.367
1996 Canton-Akrn	AA	104	395	111	26	2	3	—	—	150	47	35	12	0	22	9	1	1	3	2	.60	11	.281	.317	.380
1997 Buffalo	AAA	109	336	86	18	2	3	—	—	117	40	31	18	1	34	5	4	2	2	6	.25	12	.256	.302	.348
1998 Buffalo	AAA	115	415	130	21	3	8	—	—	181	62	63	21	3	33	6	0	2	3	3	.50	8	.313	.354	.436
1996 Cleveland	AL	4	1	0	0	0	0	(0	0)	0	0	0	0	0	0	0	0	0	0	0	.00	0	.000	.000	.000
1997 Cleveland	AL	5	7	1	1	0	0	(0	0)	2	1	1	0	0	2	0	0	0	0	0	.00	0	.143	.143	.286
1998 Cleveland	AL	17	48	11	1	0	2	(1	1)	18	8	9	3	0	2	2	0	3	0	0	.00	2	.229	.286	.375
3 ML YEARS		26	56	12	2	0	2	(1	1)	20	9	10	3	0	4	2	0	3	0	0	.00	2	.214	.266	.357

Jason Dickson

Pitches: Right **Bats:** Left **Pos:** SP-18; RP-9   **Ht:** 6'0" **Wt:** 202 **Born:** 3/30/73 **Age:** 26

			HOW MUCH HE PITCHED					WHAT HE GAVE UP										THE RESULTS					
Year Team	Lg	G	GS	CG	GF	IP	BFP	H	R	ER	HR	SH	SF	HB	TBB	IBB	SO	WP	Bk	W	L	Pct.	ShO	Sv-Op	Hld	ERA
1998 Vancouver *	AAA	4	4	0	0	25.1	100	26	5	5	2	2	0	1	4	0	18	0	1	2	1	.667	0	0--	—	1.78
1996 California	AL	7	7	0	0	43.1	192	52	22	22	6	2	1	1	18	1	20	1	0	1	4	.200	0	0-0	0	4.57
1997 Anaheim	AL	33	32	2	1	203.2	888	236	111	97	32	4	5	7	56	3	115	4	1	13	9	.591	1	0-0	0	4.29
1998 Anaheim	AL	27	18	0	5	122	545	147	89	82	17	4	9	6	41	1	61	6	0	10	10	.500	0	0-0	0	6.05
3 ML YEARS		67	57	2	6	369	1625	435	222	201	55	10	15	14	115	5	196	11	2	24	23	.511	1	0-0	0	4.90

Mike DiFelice

Bats: Right **Throws:** Right **Pos:** C-84   **Ht:** 6'2" **Wt:** 205 **Born:** 5/28/69 **Age:** 30

							BATTING											BASERUNNING				PERCENTAGES		
Year Team	Lg	G	AB	H	2B	3B	HR	(Hm | Rd)	TB	R	RBI	TBB	IBB	SO	HBP	SH	SF	SB	CS	SB%	GDP	Avg	OBP	SLG
1996 St. Louis	NL	4	7	2	1	0	0	(0 | 0)	3	0	2	0	0	1	0	0	0	0	0	.00	0	.286	.286	.429
1997 St. Louis	NL	93	260	62	10	1	4	(1 | 3)	86	16	30	19	0	61	3	6	1	1	1	.50	11	.238	.297	.331
1998 Tampa Bay	AL	84	248	57	12	3	3	(1 | 2)	84	17	23	15	0	56	1	3	2	0	0	.00	12	.230	.274	.339
3 ML YEARS		181	515	121	23	4	7	(2 | 5)	173	33	55	34	0	118	4	9	3	1	1	.50	23	.235	.286	.336

Jerry Dipoto

Pitches: Right **Bats:** Right **Pos:** RP-68   **Ht:** 6'2" **Wt:** 207 **Born:** 5/24/68 **Age:** 31

		HOW MUCH HE PITCHED						WHAT HE GAVE UP										THE RESULTS						
Year Team	Lg	G	GS	CG	GF	IP	BFP	H	R	ER	HR	SH	SF	HB	TBB	IBB	SO	WP	Bk	W	L	Pct.	ShO	Sv-Op	Hld	ERA
1993 Cleveland	AL	46	0	0	26	56.1	247	57	21	15	0	3	2	1	30	7	41	0	0	4	4	.500	0	11-17	6	2.40
1994 Cleveland	AL	7	0	0	1	15.2	79	26	14	14	1	0	4	1	10	0	9	0	0	0	0	.000	0	0-0	1	8.04
1995 New York	NL	58	0	0	26	78.2	330	77	41	33	2	6	3	4	29	8	49	3	1	4	6	.400	0	2-6	8	3.78
1996 New York	NL	57	0	0	21	77.1	364	91	44	36	5	7	4	3	45	8	52	3	3	7	2	.778	0	0-5	3	4.19
1997 Colorado	NL	74	0	0	33	95.2	422	108	56	50	6	3	7	4	33	5	74	4	1	5	3	.625	0	16-21	10	4.70
1998 Colorado	NL	68	0	0	51	71.1	295	61	31	28	8	2	2	3	25	3	49	7	0	3	4	.429	0	19-23	7	3.53
6 ML YEARS		310	0	0	158	395	1737	420	207	176	22	21	22	16	172	31	274	17	5	23	19	.548	0	48-72	35	4.01

Gary DiSarcina

Bats: Right **Throws:** Right **Pos:** SS-157; PH/PR-1   **Ht:** 6'2" **Wt:** 205 **Born:** 11/19/67 **Age:** 31

							BATTING											BASERUNNING				PERCENTAGES		
Year Team	Lg	G	AB	H	2B	3B	HR	(Hm	Rd)	TB	R	RBI	TBB	IBB	SO	HBP	SH	SF	SB	CS	SB%	GDP	Avg	OBP	SLG
1989 California	AL	2	0	0	0	0	0	(0	0)	0	0	0	0	0	0	0	0	0	0	0	.00	0	.000	.000	.000
1990 California	AL	18	57	8	1	1	0	(0	0)	11	8	0	3	0	10	0	1	0	1	0	1.00	3	.140	.183	.193
1991 California	AL	18	57	12	2	0	0	(0	0)	14	5	3	3	0	4	2	2	0	0	0	.00	0	.211	.274	.246
1992 California	AL	157	518	128	19	0	3	(2	1)	156	48	42	20	0	50	7	5	3	9	7	.56	15	.247	.283	.301
1993 California	AL	126	416	99	20	1	3	(2	1)	130	44	45	15	0	38	6	5	3	5	7	.42	13	.238	.273	.313
1994 California	AL	112	389	101	14	2	3	(2	1)	128	53	33	18	0	28	2	10	2	3	7	.30	10	.260	.294	.329
1995 California	AL	99	362	111	28	6	5	(1	4)	166	61	41	20	0	25	2	7	3	7	4	.64	10	.307	.344	.459
1996 California	AL	150	536	137	26	4	5	(2	3)	186	62	48	21	0	36	2	16	1	2	1	.67	16	.256	.286	.347
1997 Anaheim	AL	154	549	135	28	2	4	(2	2)	179	52	47	17	0	29	4	8	5	7	8	.47	18	.246	.271	.326
1998 Anaheim	AL	157	551	158	39	3	3	(0	3)	212	73	56	21	0	51	8	12	3	11	7	.61	11	.287	.321	.385
10 ML YEARS		993	3435	889	177	19	26	(11	15)	1182	406	315	138	0	271	33	66	20	45	41	.52	96	.259	.292	.344

Robert Dodd

Pitches: Left **Bats:** Left **Pos:** RP-4   **Ht:** 6'3" **Wt:** 195 **Born:** 3/14/73 **Age:** 26

		HOW MUCH HE PITCHED						WHAT HE GAVE UP										THE RESULTS						
Year Team	Lg	G	GS	CG	GF	IP	BFP	H	R	ER	HR	SH	SF	HB	TBB	IBB	SO	WP	Bk	W	L	Pct.	ShO	Sv-Op	Hld	ERA
1994 Batavia	A-	14	7	0	2	52	209	42	16	13	0	2	1	2	14	1	44	4	0	2	4	.333	0	1- -	—	2.25
1995 Clearwater	A+	26	26	0	0	151	636	144	64	53	4	3	6	1	58	0	110	3	7	8	7	.533	0	0- -	—	3.16
Reading	AA	1	0	0	0	1.1	5	0	0	0	0	0	0	0	2	0	0	0	0	0	0	.000	0	0- -	—	0.00
1996 Reading	AA	18	5	0	4	43	185	41	21	17	4	4	3	3	24	2	35	0	1	2	3	.400	0	0- -	—	3.56
Scranton-WB	AAA	8	2	0	2	20	101	32	21	18	4	0	0	1	9	0	12	1	0	0	0	.000	0	0- -	—	8.10
1997 Reading	AA	63	0	0	23	80.1	314	61	29	29	8	6	0	0	21	1	94	1	0	9	4	.692	0	8- -	—	3.25
1998 Scranton-WB	AAA	42	0	0	16	41.2	177	37	15	15	4	2	1	1	19	2	41	0	0	4	1	.800	0	6- -	—	3.24
1998 Philadelphia	NL	4	0	0	3	5	25	7	6	4	1	0	2	1	1	0	4	1	1	1	0	1.000	0	0-0	0	7.20

Jim Dougherty

Pitches: Right **Bats:** Right **Pos:** RP-9   **Ht:** 6'0" **Wt:** 210 **Born:** 3/8/68 **Age:** 31

		HOW MUCH HE PITCHED						WHAT HE GAVE UP										THE RESULTS						
Year Team	Lg	G	GS	CG	GF	IP	BFP	H	R	ER	HR	SH	SF	HB	TBB	IBB	SO	WP	Bk	W	L	Pct.	ShO	Sv-Op	Hld	ERA
1998 Edmonton *	AAA	45	0	0	26	57.2	254	57	24	24	7	2	1	2	33	4	45	1	0	2	1	.667	0	6- -	—	3.75
1995 Houston	NL	56	0	0	11	67.2	294	76	37	37	7	3	3	3	25	1	49	1	0	8	4	.667	0	0-2	5	4.92
1996 Houston	NL	12	0	0	2	13	64	14	14	13	2	1	1	0	11	1	6	0	0	0	2	.000	0	0-1	1	9.00
1998 Oakland	AL	9	0	0	4	12	59	17	11	11	2	1	0	1	7	0	3	0	0	0	2	.000	0	0-1	0	8.25
3 ML YEARS		77	0	0	17	92.2	417	107	62	61	11	5	4	5	43	2	58	1	0	8	8	.500	0	0-4	6	5.92

Doug Drabek

Pitches: Right **Bats:** Right **Pos:** SP-21; RP-2   **Ht:** 6'1" **Wt:** 190 **Born:** 7/25/62 **Age:** 36

		HOW MUCH HE PITCHED						WHAT HE GAVE UP										THE RESULTS						
Year Team	Lg	G	GS	CG	GF	IP	BFP	H	R	ER	HR	SH	SF	HB	TBB	IBB	SO	WP	Bk	W	L	Pct.	ShO	Sv-Op	Hld	ERA
1998 Bowie *	AA	1	1	0	0	5	16	0	0	0	0	0	0	0	3	0	0	0	0	0	0	.000	0	0- -	—	0.00
1986 New York	AL	27	21	0	2	131.2	561	126	64	60	13	5	2	3	50	1	76	2	0	7	8	.467	0	0-0	0	4.10
1987 Pittsburgh	NL	29	28	1	0	176.1	721	165	86	76	22	3	4	0	46	2	120	5	1	11	12	.478	1	0-0	0	3.88
1988 Pittsburgh	NL	33	32	3	0	219.1	880	194	83	75	21	7	5	6	50	4	127	4	1	15	7	.682	1	0-0	0	3.08
1989 Pittsburgh	NL	35	34	8	1	244.1	994	215	83	76	21	13	7	3	69	3	123	3	0	14	12	.538	5	0-0	0	2.80
1990 Pittsburgh	NL	33	33	9	0	231.1	918	190	78	71	15	10	3	5	56	2	131	6	0	22	6	.786	3	0-0	0	2.76
1991 Pittsburgh	NL	35	35	5	0	234.2	977	245	92	80	16	12	6	3	62	6	142	5	0	15	14	.517	2	0-0	0	3.07
1992 Pittsburgh	NL	34	34	10	0	256.2	1021	218	84	79	17	8	8	6	54	8	177	11	0	15	11	.577	4	0-0	0	2.77

Year Team	Lg	G	GS	CG	GF	IP	BFP	H	R	ER	HR	SH	SF	HB	TBB	IBB	SO	WP	Bk	W	L	Pct.	ShO	Sv-Op	Hld	ERA
		HOW MUCH HE PITCHED						WHAT HE GAVE UP												THE RESULTS						
1993 Houston	NL	34	34	7	0	237.2	991	242	108	100	18	14	8	3	60	12	157	12	0	9	18	.333	2	0-0	0	3.79
1994 Houston	NL	23	23	6	0	164.2	657	132	58	52	14	5	6	2	45	2	121	2	0	12	6	.667	2	0-0	0	2.84
1995 Houston	NL	31	31	2	0	185	797	205	104	98	18	4	3	8	54	4	143	8	1	10	9	.526	1	0-0	0	4.77
1996 Houston	NL	30	30	1	0	175.1	786	208	102	89	21	12	8	7	60	5	137	9	0	7	9	.438	0	0-0	0	4.57
1997 Chicago	AL	31	31	0	0	169.1	731	170	109	108	30	4	2	4	69	5	85	12	2	12	11	.522	0	0-0	0	5.74
1998 Baltimore	AL	23	21	1	1	108.2	484	138	90	88	20	0	7	5	29	2	55	1	0	6	11	.353	0	0-0	0	7.29
13 ML YEARS		398	387	53	4	2535	10518	2448	1141	1052	246	97	69	53	704	56	1594	80	6	155	134	.536	21	0- --	—	3.73

Darren Dreifort

Pitches: Right **Bats:** Right **Pos:** SP-26; RP-6   **Ht:** 6'2" **Wt:** 211 **Born:** 5/18/72 **Age:** 27

Year Team	Lg	G	GS	CG	GF	IP	BFP	H	R	ER	HR	SH	SF	HB	TBB	IBB	SO	WP	Bk	W	L	Pct.	ShO	Sv-Op	Hld	ERA
		HOW MUCH HE PITCHED						WHAT HE GAVE UP												THE RESULTS						
1994 Los Angeles	NL	27	0	0	15	29	148	45	21	20	0	3	4	0	15	3	22	1	0	0	5	.000	0	6-9	1	6.21
1996 Los Angeles	NL	19	0	0	5	23.2	106	23	13	13	2	3	1	0	12	4	24	2	1	1	4	.200	0	0-2	1	4.94
1997 Los Angeles	NL	48	0	0	15	63	265	45	21	20	3	5	2	1	34	2	63	3	1	5	2	.714	0	4-7	9	2.86
1998 Los Angeles	NL	32	26	1	0	180	752	171	84	80	12	11	6	10	57	2	168	9	0	8	12	.400	1	0-0	0	4.00
4 ML YEARS		126	26	1	35	295.2	1271	284	139	133	17	22	9	15	118	11	277	15	2	14	23	.378	1	10-18	13	4.05

J.D. Drew

Bats: Left **Throws:** Right **Pos:** LF-6; RF-5; PH/PR-4; CF-2   **Ht:** 6'1" **Wt:** 195 **Born:** 11/20/75 **Age:** 23

Year Team	Lg	G	AB	H	2B	3B	HR	(Hm	Rd)	TB	R	RBI	TBB	IBB	SO	HBP	SH	SF	SB	CS	SB%	GDP	Avg	OBP	SLG
		BATTING																	BASERUNNING				PERCENTAGES		
1997 St. Paul	IND	44	170	58	6	1	18	—	—	120	51	50	30	0	40	2	0	1	5	3	.63	1	.341	.443	.706
1998 St. Paul	IND	30	114	44	11	2	9	—	—	86	27	33	21	5	32	6	0	0	8	1	.89	2	.386	.504	.754
Arkansas	AA	19	67	22	3	1	5	—	—	42	18	11	13	1	15	1	0	0	2	1	.67	0	.328	.444	.627
Memphis	AAA	26	79	25	8	1	2	—	—	41	15	13	22	0	18	1	0	0	1	3	.25	1	.316	.471	.519
1998 St. Louis	NL	14	36	15	3	1	5	(4	1)	35	9	13	4	0	10	0	0	0	0	0	.00	4	.417	.463	.972

Rob Ducey

Bats: L **Throws:** R **Pos:** RF-61; LF-23; PH/PR-22; CF-6   **Ht:** 6'2" **Wt:** 180 **Born:** 5/24/65 **Age:** 34

Year Team	Lg	G	AB	H	2B	3B	HR	(Hm	Rd)	TB	R	RBI	TBB	IBB	SO	HBP	SH	SF	SB	CS	SB%	GDP	Avg	OBP	SLG
		BATTING																	BASERUNNING				PERCENTAGES		
1987 Toronto	AL	34	48	9	1	0	1	(1	0)	13	12	6	8	0	10	0	0	1	2	0	1.00	0	.188	.298	.271
1988 Toronto	AL	27	54	17	4	1	0	(0	0)	23	15	6	5	0	7	0	2	2	1	0	1.00	1	.315	.361	.426
1989 Toronto	AL	41	76	16	4	0	0	(0	0)	20	5	7	9	1	25	0	1	0	1	1	.67	2	.211	.294	.263
1990 Toronto	AL	19	53	16	5	0	0	(0	0)	21	7	7	7	0	15	1	0	1	1	1	.50	0	.302	.387	.396
1991 Toronto	AL	39	68	16	2	2	1	(0	1)	25	8	4	6	0	26	0	1	0	2	0	1.00	1	.235	.297	.368
1992 Tor-Cal	AL	54	80	15	4	0	0	(0	0)	19	7	2	5	0	22	0	0	1	2	4	.33	1	.188	.233	.238
1993 Texas	AL	27	85	24	6	3	2	(2	0)	42	15	9	10	2	17	0	0	2	2	3	.40	1	.282	.351	.494
1994 Texas	AL	11	29	5	1	0	0	(0	0)	6	1	1	2	0	1	0	0	0	0	0	.00	1	.172	.226	.207
1997 Seattle	AL	76	143	41	15	2	5	(0	5)	75	25	10	6	0	31	0	0	2	3	3	.50	3	.287	.311	.524
1998 Seattle	AL	97	217	52	18	2	5	(2	3)	89	30	23	23	2	61	9	0	1	4	3	.57	4	.240	.336	.410
1992 Toronto	AL	23	21	1	1	0	0	(0	0)	2	3	0	0	0	10	0	0	0	0	1	.00	0	.048	.048	.095
California	AL	31	59	14	3	0	0	(0	0)	17	4	2	5	0	12	0	0	1	2	3	.40	1	.237	.292	.288
10 ML YEARS		425	853	211	60	10	14	(5	9)	333	125	75	81	5	215	10	6	10	19	15	.56	14	.247	.317	.390

Shawon Dunston

Bats: R **Throws:** R **Pos:** PH/PR-41; 2B-25; SS-23; LF-11; DH-7; CF-7   **Ht:** 6'1" **Wt:** 180 **Born:** 3/21/63 **Age:** 36

Year Team	Lg	G	AB	H	2B	3B	HR	(Hm	Rd)	TB	R	RBI	TBB	IBB	SO	HBP	SH	SF	SB	CS	SB%	GDP	Avg	OBP	SLG
		BATTING																	BASERUNNING				PERCENTAGES		
1985 Chicago	NL	74	250	65	12	4	4	(3	1)	97	40	18	19	3	42	0	1	2	11	3	.79	3	.260	.310	.388
1986 Chicago	NL	150	581	145	37	3	17	(10	7)	239	66	68	21	5	114	3	4	2	13	11	.54	5	.250	.278	.411
1987 Chicago	NL	95	346	85	18	3	5	(3	2)	124	40	22	10	1	68	1	0	2	12	3	.80	6	.246	.267	.358
1988 Chicago	NL	155	575	143	23	6	9	(5	4)	205	69	56	16	8	108	2	4	2	30	9	.77	6	.249	.271	.357
1989 Chicago	NL	138	471	131	20	6	9	(3	6)	190	52	60	30	15	86	1	6	4	19	11	.63	7	.278	.320	.403
1990 Chicago	NL	146	545	143	22	8	17	(7	10)	232	73	66	15	1	87	3	4	6	25	5	.83	9	.262	.283	.426
1991 Chicago	NL	142	492	128	22	7	12	(7	5)	200	59	50	23	5	64	4	4	11	21	6	.78	9	.260	.292	.407
1992 Chicago	NL	18	73	23	3	1	0	(0	0)	28	8	2	3	0	13	0	0	0	2	3	.40	0	.315	.342	.384
1993 Chicago	NL	7	10	4	2	0	0	(0	0)	6	3	2	0	0	0	0	0	0	0	0	.00	0	.400	.400	.600
1994 Chicago	NL	88	331	92	19	0	11	(2	9)	144	38	35	16	3	48	2	5	2	3	8	.27	4	.278	.313	.435
1995 Chicago	NL	127	477	141	30	6	14	(8	6)	225	58	69	10	3	75	6	7	3	10	5	.67	8	.296	.317	.472
1996 San Francisco	NL	82	287	86	12	2	5	(3	2)	117	27	25	13	0	40	1	5	1	8	0	1.00	8	.300	.331	.408
1997 ChN-Pit	NL	132	490	147	22	5	14	(10	4)	221	71	57	8	0	75	3	5	5	32	8	.80	9	.300	.312	.451
1998 Cle-SF	NL	98	207	46	13	3	3	(2	4)	83	36	20	6	0	28	4	1	3	9	4	.69	3	.222	.255	.401
1997 Chicago	NL	114	419	119	18	4	9	(7	2)	172	57	41	8	0	64	3	3	4	29	7	.81	7	.284	.300	.411
Pittsburgh		18	71	28	4	1	5	(3	2)	49	14	16	0	0	11	0	2	1	3	1	.75	2	.394	.389	.690
1998 Cleveland	AL	62	156	37	11	3	3	(1	2)	63	26	12	6	0	18	1	0	3	9	2	.82	2	.237	.265	.404
San Francisco	NL	36	51	9	2	0	3	(1	2)	20	10	8	0	0	10	3	1	0	0	2	.00	1	.176	.222	.392
14 ML YEARS		1452	5135	1379	255	54	123	(63	60)	2111	640	550	190	44	849	30	46	43	195	76	.72	77	.269	.296	.411

Todd Dunwoody

Bats: Left **Throws:** Left **Pos:** CF-111; PH/PR-12 **Ht:** 6'1" **Wt:** 195 **Born:** 4/11/75 **Age:** 24

Year Team	Lg	G	AB	H	2B	3B	HR	(Hm	Rd)	TB	R	RBI	TBB	IBB	SO	HBP	SH	SF	SB	CS	SB%	GDP	Avg	OBP	SLG
1993 Marlins	R	31	109	21	2	2	0	—	—	27	13	7	7	0	28	2	1	1	5	0	1.00	2	.193	.252	.248
1994 Kane County	A	15	45	5	0	0	1	—	—	8	7	1	5	0	17	0	1	0	1	0	1.00	1	.111	.200	.178
Marlins	R	46	169	44	6	6	1	—	—	65	32	25	21	1	28	4	1	1	11	3	.79	1	.260	.354	.385
1995 Kane County	A	132	494	140	20	8	14	—	—	218	89	89	52	7	105	8	2	9	39	11	.78	7	.283	.355	.441
1996 Portland	AA	138	552	153	30	6	24	—	—	267	88	93	45	6	149	7	0	5	24	19	.56	10	.277	.337	.484
1997 Charlotte	AAA	107	401	105	16	7	23	—	—	204	74	62	39	2	129	3	0	1	25	3	.89	8	.262	.331	.509
1998 Charlotte	AAA	28	102	31	6	3	6	—	—	61	20	22	12	0	28	4	0	0	4	2	.67	2	.304	.398	.598
1997 Florida	NL	19	50	13	2	2	2	(0	2)	25	7	7	7	0	21	1	0	0	2	0	1.00	1	.260	.362	.500
1998 Florida	NL	116	434	109	27	7	5	(2	3)	165	53	28	21	0	113	4	3	0	5	1	.83	6	.251	.292	.380
2 ML YEARS		135	484	122	29	9	7	(2	5)	190	60	35	28	0	134	5	3	0	7	1	.88	7	.252	.300	.393

Roberto Duran

Pitches: Left **Bats:** Left **Pos:** RP-18 **Ht:** 6'0" **Wt:** 205 **Born:** 3/6/73 **Age:** 26

Year Team	Lg	G	GS	CG	GF	IP	BFP	H	R	ER	HR	SH	SF	HB	TBB	IBB	SO	WP	Bk	W	L	Pct.	ShO	Sv-Op	Hld	ERA
1992 Dodgers	R	9	8	0	0	38.2	166	22	17	12	1	1	1	2	31	0	57	8	0	4	3	.571	0	0--	—	2.79
Vero Beach	A+	2	1	0	0	5	24	6	5	5	1	0	0	1	4	0	5	1	0	0	0	.000	0	0--	—	9.00
1993 Vero Beach	A+	8	0	0	2	9.2	43	10	4	4	0	0	0	0	8	1	9	0	0	1	1	.500	0	0--	—	3.72
Yakima	A-	20	3	0	6	40	201	37	34	31	3	1	2	6	42	0	50	10	0	2	2	.500	0	0--	—	6.98
1994 Bakersfield	A+	42	4	0	29	65.1	300	61	43	35	5	3	4	5	48	0	86	6	0	6	5	.545	0	10--	—	4.82
1995 Vero Beach	A+	23	22	0	0	101.1	446	82	42	38	8	3	1	1	70	0	114	12	2	7	4	.636	0	0--	—	3.38
1996 Dunedin	A+	8	8	1	0	48.1	188	31	9	6	1	1	1	2	19	0	54	5	0	3	1	.750	1	0--	—	1.12
Knoxville	AA	19	16	0	1	80.2	366	72	52	46	8	1	1	3	61	1	74	13	2	4	6	.400	0	0--	—	5.13
1997 Jacksnville	AA	50	0	0	34	60.2	265	41	19	16	2	2	5	2	39	0	95	11	0	4	2	.667	0	16--	—	2.37
1998 Toledo	AAA	1	0	0	0	0.2	5	1	2	2	0	0	0	0	2	0	1	0	0	0	0	.000	0	0--	—	27.00
Lakeland	A+	8	0	0	2	8.2	46	4	5	4	0	1	1	2	13	1	9	1	0	0	0	.000	0	0--	—	4.15
1997 Detroit	AL	13	0	0	1	10.2	56	7	9	9	0	0	1	3	15	0	11	1	1	0	0	.000	0	0-0	0	7.59
1998 Detroit	AL	18	0	0	5	15.1	74	9	10	10	0	2	0	2	17	0	12	2	0	0	1	.000	0	0-0	0	5.87
2 ML YEARS		31	0	0	6	26	130	16	19	19	0	2	1	5	32	0	23	3	1	0	1	.000	0	0-0	0	6.58

Ray Durham

Bats: Both **Throws:** Right **Pos:** 2B-158; PH/PR-2 **Ht:** 5'8" **Wt:** 170 **Born:** 11/30/71 **Age:** 27

Year Team	Lg	G	AB	H	2B	3B	HR	(Hm	Rd)	TB	R	RBI	TBB	IBB	SO	HBP	SH	SF	SB	CS	SB%	GDP	Avg	OBP	SLG
1995 Chicago	AL	125	471	121	27	6	7	(1	6)	181	68	51	31	2	83	6	5	4	18	5	.78	8	.257	.309	.384
1996 Chicago	AL	156	557	153	33	5	10	(3	7)	226	79	65	58	4	95	10	7	7	30	4	**.88**	6	.275	.350	.406
1997 Chicago	AL	155	634	172	27	5	11	(3	8)	242	106	53	61	0	96	6	2	6	33	16	.67	14	.271	.337	.382
1998 Chicago	AL	158	635	181	35	8	19	(10	9)	289	126	67	73	3	105	6	6	3	36	9	.80	5	.285	.363	.455
4 ML YEARS		594	2297	627	122	24	47	(17	30)	938	379	236	223	9	379	28	20	22	117	34	.77	33	.273	.342	.408

Mike Duvall

Pitches: Left **Bats:** Right **Pos:** RP-3 **Ht:** 6'0" **Wt:** 185 **Born:** 10/11/74 **Age:** 24

Year Team	Lg	G	GS	CG	GF	IP	BFP	H	R	ER	HR	SH	SF	HB	TBB	IBB	SO	WP	Bk	W	L	Pct.	ShO	Sv-Op	Hld	ERA
1995 Marlins	R	16	1	0	10	28.1	120	15	8	7	1	0	0	2	12	1	34	4	2	5	0	1.000	0	1--	—	2.22
1996 Kane County	A	41	0	0	28	48	210	43	20	11	0	2	0	0	21	2	46	3	0	4	1	.800	0	8--	—	2.06
1997 Brevard Cty	A+	11	0	0	11	12.1	45	7	1	1	0	0	0	0	3	1	9	0	0	1	0	1.000	0	6--	—	0.73
Portland	AA	45	0	0	25	68.1	291	63	20	14	4	9	1	2	20	2	49	2	0	4	6	.400	0	18--	—	1.84
1998 St. Pete	A+	2	0	0	2	3.1	16	4	1	1	0	0	0	0	2	0	3	2	0	0	0	.000	0	0--	—	2.70
Durham	AAA	32	9	1	5	72.2	314	74	31	26	3	0	1	2	32	3	55	5	0	5	3	.625	0	0--	—	3.22
1998 Tampa Bay	AL	3	0	0	0	4	17	4	3	3	0	0	0	0	2	0	1	0	0	0	0	.000	0	0-0	0	6.75

Jermaine Dye

Bats: Right **Throws:** Right **Pos:** RF-59; PH/PR-2 **Ht:** 6'4" **Wt:** 220 **Born:** 1/28/74 **Age:** 25

Year Team	Lg	G	AB	H	2B	3B	HR	(Hm	Rd)	TB	R	RBI	TBB	IBB	SO	HBP	SH	SF	SB	CS	SB%	GDP	Avg	OBP	SLG
1998 Omaha *	AAA	41	157	47	6	0	12	—	—	89	29	35	19	0	29	1	1	2	7	0	1.00	8	.299	.374	.567
1996 Atlanta	NL	98	292	82	16	0	12	(4	8)	134	32	37	8	0	67	3	0	3	1	4	.20	11	.281	.304	.459
1997 Kansas City	AL	75	263	62	14	0	7	(3	4)	97	26	22	17	0	51	1	1	1	2	1	.67	6	.236	.284	.369
1998 Kansas City	AL	60	214	50	5	1	5	(3	2)	72	24	23	11	2	46	1	0	4	2	2	.50	8	.234	.270	.336
3 ML YEARS		233	769	194	35	1	24	(10	14)	303	82	82	36	2	164	5	1	8	5	7	.42	25	.252	.287	.394

Radhames Dykhoff

Pitches: Left **Bats:** Left **Pos:** RP-1 **Ht:** 6'0" **Wt:** 160 **Born:** 9/27/74 **Age:** 24

Year Team	Lg	G	GS	CG	GF	IP	BFP	H	R	ER	HR	SH	SF	HB	TBB	IBB	SO	WP	Bk	W	L	Pct.	ShO	Sv-Op	Hld	ERA
1993 Orioles	R	14	3	0	1	45	184	37	22	17	2	3	3	2	11	0	29	3	0	1	2	.333	0	1--	—	3.40
1994 Orioles	R	12	12	1	0	73	307	69	34	27	2	0	5	0	17	0	67	4	1	3	6	.333	0	0--	—	3.33

Year Team	Lg	G	GS	CG	GF	IP	BFP	H	R	ER	HR	SH	SF	HB	TBB	IBB	SO	WP	Bk	W	L	Pct.	ShO	Sv-Op	Hld	ERA
						HOW MUCH HE PITCHED					WHAT HE GAVE UP											THE RESULTS				
1995 High Desert	A+	34	2	0	10	80.2	389	95	68	45	8	7	7	0	44	2	88	0	2	1	5	.167	0	3--	—	5.02
1996 Frederick	A+	33	0	0	15	62	290	77	45	39	7	4	4	1	22	2	75	0	0	2	6	.250	0	3--	—	5.66
1997 Bowie	AA	7	0	0	4	8.2	43	10	9	8	2	0	0	0	7	0	7	0	0	0	0	.000	0	0--	—	8.31
Delmarva	A	1	0	0	1	3	12	3	0	0	0	0	0	0	0	0	3	0	0	0	0	.000	0	1--	—	0.00
Frederick	A+	31	0	0	18	67	282	48	19	18	4	6	1	0	38	3	98	0	1	3	3	.500	0	5--	—	2.42
1998 Bowie	AA	38	8	0	9	93.2	411	83	51	49	10	2	3	4	52	1	98	3	0	3	7	.300	0	1--	—	4.71
1998 Baltimore	AL	1	0	0	1	1	6	2	2	2	0	0	0	0	1	0	1	0	0	0	0	.000	0	0-0	0	18.00

Damion Easley

Bats: R **Throws:** R **Pos:** 2B-140; SS-30; DH-2; PH/PR-1   **Ht:** 5'11" **Wt:** 185 **Born:** 11/11/69 **Age:** 29

Year Team	Lg	G	AB	H	2B	3B	HR	(Hm	Rd)	TB	R	RBI	TBB	IBB	SO	HBP	SH	SF	SB	CS	SB%	GDP	Avg	OBP	SLG
								BATTING												BASERUNNING			PERCENTAGES		
1992 California	AL	47	151	39	5	0	1	(1	0)	47	14	12	8	0	26	3	2	1	9	5	.64	2	.258	.307	.311
1993 California	AL	73	230	72	13	2	2	(0	2)	95	33	22	28	2	35	3	1	2	6	6	.50	5	.313	.392	.413
1994 California	AL	88	316	68	16	1	6	(4	2)	104	41	30	29	0	48	4	4	2	4	5	.44	8	.215	.288	.329
1995 California	AL	114	357	77	14	2	4	(1	3)	107	35	35	32	1	47	6	6	4	5	2	.71	11	.216	.288	.300
1996 Cal-Det	AL	49	112	30	2	0	4	(1	3)	44	14	17	10	0	25	1	5	1	3	1	.75	0	.268	.331	.393
1997 Detroit	AL	151	527	139	37	3	22	(12	10)	248	97	72	68	3	102	16	4	5	28	13	.68	18	.264	.362	.471
1998 Detroit	AL	153	594	161	38	2	27	(19	8)	284	84	100	39	2	112	16	0	2	15	5	.75	8	.271	.332	.478
1996 California	AL	28	45	7	1	0	2	(1	1)	14	4	7	6	0	12	0	3	0	0	0	.00	0	.156	.255	.311
Detroit	AL	21	67	23	1	0	2	(0	2)	30	10	10	4	0	13	1	2	1	3	1	.75	0	.343	.384	.448
7 ML YEARS		675	2287	586	125	10	66	(38	28)	929	318	288	214	8	395	49	22	17	70	37	.65	52	.256	.331	.406

Angel Echevarria

Bats: R **Throws:** R **Pos:** PH/PR-11; 1B-4; LF-3; RF-1   **Ht:** 6'3" **Wt:** 214 **Born:** 5/25/71 **Age:** 28

Year Team	Lg	G	AB	H	2B	3B	HR	(Hm	Rd)	TB	R	RBI	TBB	IBB	SO	HBP	SH	SF	SB	CS	SB%	GDP	Avg	OBP	SLG
								BATTING												BASERUNNING			PERCENTAGES		
1998 Colo Sprngs *	AAA	85	301	98	21	2	15		—	168	50	60	14	0	47	3	0	2	0	1	.00	8	.326	.359	.558
1996 Colorado	NL	26	21	6	0	0	0	(0	0)	6	2	6	2	0	5	1	0	2	0	0	.00	0	.286	.346	.286
1997 Colorado	NL	15	20	5	2	0	0	(0	0)	7	4	0	2	0	5	0	0	0	0	0	.00	0	.250	.318	.350
1998 Colorado	NL	19	29	11	3	0	1	(1	0)	17	7	9	2	0	3	2	0	0	0	0	.00	4	.379	.455	.586
3 ML YEARS		60	70	22	5	0	1	(1	0)	30	13	15	6	0	13	3	0	2	0	0	.00	4	.314	.383	.429

Dennis Eckersley

Pitches: Right **Bats:** Right **Pos:** RP-50   **Ht:** 6'2" **Wt:** 195 **Born:** 10/3/54 **Age:** 44

Year Team	Lg	G	GS	CG	GF	IP	BFP	H	R	ER	HR	SH	SF	HB	TBB	IBB	SO	WP	Bk	W	L	Pct.	ShO	Sv-Op	Hld	ERA
						HOW MUCH HE PITCHED					WHAT HE GAVE UP											THE RESULTS				
1998 Pawtucket *	AAA	2	0	0	2	2	8	2	1	1	1	0	0	0	0	0	2	0	0	0	0	.000	0	0--	—	4.50
1975 Cleveland	AL	34	24	6	5	186.2	794	147	61	54	16	6	7	7	90	8	152	4	2	13	7	.650	2	2-3	0	2.60
1976 Cleveland	AL	36	30	9	3	199.1	821	155	82	76	13	10	4	5	78	2	200	6	1	13	12	.520	3	1-1	0	3.43
1977 Cleveland	AL	33	33	12	0	247.1	1006	214	100	97	31	11	6	7	54	11	191	3	0	14	13	.519	3	0-0	0	3.53
1978 Boston	AL	35	35	16	0	268.1	1121	258	99	89	30	7	8	7	71	8	162	3	0	20	8	.714	2	0-0	0	2.99
1979 Boston	AL	33	33	17	0	246.2	1018	234	89	82	29	10	6	6	59	4	150	1	1	17	10	.630	2	0-0	0	2.99
1980 Boston	AL	30	30	8	0	197.2	818	188	101	94	25	7	8	2	44	7	121	0	0	12	14	.462	0	0-0	0	4.28
1981 Boston	AL	23	23	8	0	154	649	160	82	73	9	6	5	3	35	2	79	0	0	9	8	.529	2	0-0	0	4.27
1982 Boston	AL	33	33	11	0	224.1	926	228	101	93	31	4	4	2	43	3	127	1	0	13	13	.500	3	0-0	0	3.73
1983 Boston	AL	28	28	2	0	176.1	787	223	119	110	27	1	5	6	39	4	77	1	0	9	13	.409	0	0-0	0	5.61
1984 Bos-ChN		33	33	4	0	225	932	223	97	90	21	11	9	5	49	9	114	3	2	14	12	.538	0	0-0	0	3.60
1985 Chicago	NL	25	25	6	0	169.1	664	145	61	58	15	6	2	3	19	4	117	0	3	11	7	.611	2	0-0	0	3.08
1986 Chicago	NL	33	32	1	0	201	862	226	109	102	21	13	10	3	43	3	137	2	5	6	11	.353	0	0-0	0	4.57
1987 Oakland	AL	54	2	0	33	115.2	460	99	41	39	11	3	3	3	17	3	113	1	0	6	8	.429	0	16-20	2	3.03
1988 Oakland	AL	60	0	0	53	72.2	279	52	20	19	5	1	3	1	11	2	70	0	0	4	2	.667	0	45-53	0	2.35
1989 Oakland	AL	51	0	0	46	57.2	206	32	10	10	5	0	4	1	3	0	55	0	0	4	0	1.000	0	33-39	1	1.56
1990 Oakland	AL	63	0	0	61	73.1	262	41	9	5	2	0	1	0	4	1	73	0	0	4	2	.667	0	48-50	0	0.61
1991 Oakland	AL	67	0	0	59	76	299	60	26	25	11	1	0	1	9	3	87	1	0	5	4	.556	0	43-51	0	2.96
1992 Oakland	AL	69	0	0	65	80	309	62	17	17	5	3	0	1	11	6	93	0	0	7	1	.875	0	51-54	0	1.91
1993 Oakland	AL	64	0	0	52	67	276	67	32	31	7	2	2	2	13	4	80	0	0	2	4	.333	0	36-46	0	4.16
1994 Oakland	AL	45	0	0	39	44.1	193	49	26	21	5	1	0	1	13	2	47	0	0	5	4	.556	0	19-25	0	4.26
1995 Oakland	AL	52	0	0	48	50.1	212	53	29	27	5	1	2	1	11	0	40	0	0	4	6	.400	0	29-38	0	4.83
1996 St. Louis	NL	63	0	0	53	60	251	65	26	22	8	1	3	4	6	2	49	0	0	0	6	.000	0	30-34	0	3.30
1997 St. Louis	NL	57	0	0	47	53	218	49	24	23	9	2	1	3	8	0	45	2	0	1	5	.167	0	36-43	0	3.91
1998 Boston	AL	50	0	0	13	39.2	171	46	21	21	6	2	1	2	8	3	22	0	0	4	1	.800	0	1-4	9	4.76
1984 Boston	AL	9	9	2	0	64.2	270	71	38	36	10	3	3	1	13	2	33	2	0	4	4	.500	0	0-0	0	5.01
Chicago	NL	24	24	2	0	160.1	662	152	59	54	11	8	6	4	36	7	81	1	2	10	8	.556	0	0-0	0	3.03
24 ML YEARS		1071	361	100	577	3285.2	13534	3076	1382	1278	347	109	93	75	738	91	2401	28	16	197	171	.535	20	390-461	17	3.50

Jim Edmonds

Bats: Left **Throws:** Left **Pos:** CF-153; PH/PR-1   **Ht:** 6'1" **Wt:** 218 **Born:** 6/27/70 **Age:** 29

Year Team	Lg	G	AB	H	2B	3B	HR	(Hm	Rd)	TB	R	RBI	TBB	IBB	SO	HBP	SH	SF	SB	CS	SB%	GDP	Avg	OBP	SLG
								BATTING												BASERUNNING			PERCENTAGES		
1993 California	AL	18	61	15	4	1	0	(0	0)	21	5	4	2	1	16	0	0	0	0	2	.00	1	.246	.270	.344
1994 California	AL	94	289	79	13	1	5	(3	2)	109	35	37	30	3	72	1	1	1	4	2	.67	3	.273	.343	.377
1995 California	AL	141	558	162	30	4	33	(16	17)	299	120	107	51	4	130	5	1	5	1	4	.20	10	.290	.352	.536
1996 California	AL	114	431	131	28	3	27	(17	10)	246	73	66	46	2	101	4	0	2	4	0	1.00	8	.304	.375	.571

Year Team	Lg	G	AB	H	2B	3B	HR	(Hm	Rd)	TB	R	RBI	TBB	IBB	SO	HBP	SH	SF	SB	CS	SB%	GDP	Avg	OBP	SLG
1997 Anaheim	AL	133	502	146	27	0	26	(14	12)	251	82	80	60	5	80	4	0	5	5	7	.42	8	.291	.368	.500
1998 Anaheim	AL	154	599	184	42	1	25	(9	16)	303	115	91	57	7	114	1	1	1	7	5	.58	16	.307	.368	.506
6 ML YEARS		654	2440	717	144	10	116	(59	57)	1229	430	385	246	22	513	15	3	14	21	20	.51	46	.294	.360	.504

Brian Edmondson

Pitches: Right **Bats:** Right **Pos:** RP-53   **Ht:** 6'2" **Wt:** 175 **Born:** 1/29/73 **Age:** 26

Year Team	Lg	G	GS	CG	GF	IP	BFP	H	R	ER	HR	SH	SF	HB	TBB	IBB	SO	WP	Bk	W	L	Pct.	ShO	Sv-Op	Hld	ERA
1991 Bristol	R+	12	12	1	0	69	289	72	38	35	7	1	2	3	23	1	42	5	2	4	4	.500	0	0--	—	4.57
1992 Fayetteville	A	28	27	3	0	155.1	665	145	69	58	10	5	3	6	67	0	125	6	2	10	6	.625	1	0--	—	3.36
1993 Lakeland	A+	19	19	1	0	114.1	483	115	44	38	6	1	0	3	43	0	64	7	0	8	5	.615	0	0--	—	2.99
London	AA	5	5	1	0	23	109	30	23	16	2	1	0	0	13	0	17	1	0	0	4	.000	0	0--	—	6.26
1994 Trenton	AA	26	26	2	0	162	703	171	89	82	12	2	6	6	61	1	90	11	2	11	9	.550	0	0--	—	4.56
1995 Binghamton	AA	23	22	2	0	134.1	601	150	82	71	17	5	5	6	59	2	69	7	0	7	11	.389	1	0--	—	4.76
1996 Binghamton	AA	39	13	1	9	114.1	502	130	69	54	16	7	7	4	38	5	83	3	1	6	6	.500	0	0--	—	4.25
1997 Binghamton	AA	14	0	0	7	22	85	17	4	3	0	2	0	0	7	0	18	1	0	2	0	1.000	0	3--	—	1.23
Norfolk	AAA	31	4	0	8	68.1	296	62	27	22	5	3	3	4	37	2	65	4	1	4	3	.571	0	1--	—	2.90
1998 Atl-Fla	NL	53	0	0	13	76	334	76	38	33	10	5	3	3	37	5	40	5	0	4	4	.500	0	0-3	5	3.91
1998 Atlanta	NL	10	0	0	3	16.2	73	14	10	8	2	0	0	0	8	1	8	4	0	0	1	.000	0	0-1	0	4.32
Florida	NL	43	0	0	10	59.1	261	62	28	25	8	5	3	3	29	4	32	1	0	4	3	.571	0	0-2	5	3.79

Dave Eiland

Pitches: Right **Bats:** Right **Pos:** SP-1   **Ht:** 6'3" **Wt:** 210 **Born:** 7/5/66 **Age:** 32

Year Team	Lg	G	GS	CG	GF	IP	BFP	H	R	ER	HR	SH	SF	HB	TBB	IBB	SO	WP	Bk	W	L	Pct.	ShO	Sv-Op	Hld	ERA
1998 Durham *	AAA	28	28	2	0	171.2	693	177	70	57	13	0	4	1	27	1	112	2	0	13	5	.722	1	0--	—	2.99
1988 New York	AL	3	3	0	0	12.2	57	15	9	9	4	0	0	2	4	0	7	0	0	0	0	.000	0	0-0	0	6.39
1989 New York	AL	6	6	0	0	34.1	152	44	25	22	5	1	2	2	13	3	11	0	0	1	3	.250	0	0-0	0	5.77
1990 New York	AL	5	5	0	0	30.1	127	31	14	12	2	0	0	0	5	0	16	0	0	2	1	.667	0	0-0	0	3.56
1991 New York	AL	18	13	0	4	72.2	317	87	51	43	10	0	3	3	23	1	18	0	0	2	5	.286	0	0-0	0	5.33
1992 San Diego	NL	7	7	0	0	27	120	33	21	17	1	0	0	0	5	0	10	0	1	0	2	.000	0	0-0	0	5.67
1993 San Diego	NL	10	9	0	0	48.1	217	58	33	28	5	2	2	1	17	1	14	1	0	0	3	.000	0	0-0	0	5.21
1995 New York	AL	4	1	0	1	10	51	16	10	7	1	0	1	1	3	1	6	1	0	1	1	.500	0	0-0	0	6.30
1998 Tampa Bay	AL	1	1	0	0	2.2	17	6	6	6	0	0	0	0	3	0	1	0	0	0	1	.000	0	0-0	0	20.25
8 ML YEARS		54	45	0	5	238	1058	290	169	144	30	3	8	9	73	6	83	2	1	6	16	.273	0	0-0	0	5.45

Jim Eisenreich

Bats: L **Throws:** L **Pos:** PH/PR-58; LF-27; 1B-19; RF-5; DH-2   **Ht:** 5'11" **Wt:** 200 **Born:** 4/18/59 **Age:** 40

Year Team	Lg	G	AB	H	2B	3B	HR	(Hm	Rd)	TB	R	RBI	TBB	IBB	SO	HBP	SH	SF	SB	CS	SB%	GDP	Avg	OBP	SLG
1982 Minnesota	AL	34	99	30	6	0	2	(1	1)	42	10	9	11	0	13	1	0	0	0	0	.00	1	.303	.378	.424
1983 Minnesota	AL	2	7	2	1	0	0	(0	0)	3	1	0	1	0	1	0	0	0	0	0	.00	0	.286	.375	.429
1984 Minnesota	AL	12	32	7	1	0	0	(0	0)	8	1	3	2	1	4	0	0	0	2	0	1.00	1	.219	.250	.250
1987 Kansas City	AL	44	105	25	8	2	4	(3	1)	49	10	21	7	2	13	0	0	3	1	1	.50	2	.238	.278	.467
1988 Kansas City	AL	82	202	44	8	1	1	(0	1)	57	26	19	6	1	31	0	2	4	9	3	.75	2	.218	.236	.282
1989 Kansas City	AL	134	475	139	33	7	9	(4	5)	213	64	59	37	9	44	0	3	4	27	8	.77	5	.293	.341	.448
1990 Kansas City	AL	142	496	139	29	7	5	(2	3)	197	61	51	42	2	51	1	2	4	12	14	.46	7	.280	.335	.397
1991 Kansas City	AL	135	375	113	22	3	2	(2	0)	147	47	47	20	1	35	1	3	6	5	3	.63	10	.301	.333	.392
1992 Kansas City	AL	113	353	95	13	3	2	(1	1)	120	31	28	24	4	36	0	0	3	11	6	.65	6	.269	.313	.340
1993 Philadelphia	NL	153	362	115	17	4	7	(3	4)	161	51	54	26	5	36	1	3	2	5	0	1.00	6	.318	.363	.445
1994 Philadelphia	NL	104	290	87	15	4	4	(3	1)	122	42	43	33	3	31	1	3	2	6	2	.75	4	.300	.371	.421
1995 Philadelphia	NL	129	377	119	22	2	10	(5	5)	175	46	55	38	4	44	1	2	5	10	0	1.00	7	.316	.375	.464
1996 Philadelphia	NL	113	338	122	24	3	3	(1	2)	161	45	41	31	9	32	1	0	3	11	1	.92	7	.361	.413	.476
1997 Florida	NL	120	293	82	19	1	2	(2	0)	109	36	34	30	4	28	1	3	4	0	0	.00	7	.280	.345	.372
1998 Fla-LA	NL	105	191	41	3	2	1	(1	0)	51	21	13	16	2	36	0	1	0	6	0	1.00	3	.215	.275	.267
1998 Florida	NL	30	64	16	1	0	1	(1	0)	20	9	7	4	1	14	0	0	0	2	0	1.00	1	.250	.294	.313
Los Angeles	NL	75	127	25	2	2	0	(0	0)	31	12	6	12	1	22	0	1	0	4	0	1.00	2	.197	.266	.244
15 ML YEARS		1422	3995	1160	221	39	52	(28	24)	1615	492	477	324	47	435	8	22	42	105	38	.73	75	.290	.341	.404

Scott Elarton

Pitches: Right **Bats:** Right **Pos:** RP-26; SP-2   **Ht:** 6'7" **Wt:** 240 **Born:** 2/23/76 **Age:** 23

Year Team	Lg	G	GS	CG	GF	IP	BFP	H	R	ER	HR	SH	SF	HB	TBB	IBB	SO	WP	Bk	W	L	Pct.	ShO	Sv-Op	Hld	ERA
1994 Astros	R	5	5	0	0	28	92	9	0	0	0	0	0	0	5	0	28	1	0	4	0	1.000	0	0--	—	0.00
Quad City	A	9	9	0	0	54.2	220	42	23	20	4	2	2	1	18	0	42	3	1	4	1	.800	0	0--	—	3.29
1995 Quad City	A	26	26	0	0	149.2	668	149	86	74	12	8	4	8	71	2	112	12	0	13	7	.650	0	0--	—	4.45
1996 Kissimmee	A+	27	27	3	0	172.1	715	154	67	56	13	7	6	8	54	0	130	5	0	12	7	.632	1	0--	—	2.92
1997 Jackson	AA	20	20	2	0	133.1	544	103	57	48	6	3	1	2	47	3	141	5	0	7	4	.636	1	0--	—	3.24
New Orleans	AAA	9	9	0	0	54	228	51	36	32	5	3	1	1	17	1	50	4	0	4	4	.500	0	0--	—	5.33
1998 New Orleans	AAA	14	14	2	0	92	383	71	42	41	6	0	3	4	41	3	100	3	0	9	4	.692	1	0--	—	4.01
1998 Houston	NL	28	2	0	7	57	227	40	21	21	5	1	1	4	20	0	56	1	0	2	1	.667	0	2-3	2	3.32

Cal Eldred

Pitches: Right **Bats:** Right **Pos:** SP-23   **Ht:** 6'4" **Wt:** 237 **Born:** 11/24/67 **Age:** 31

Year Team	Lg	G	GS	CG	GF	IP	BFP	H	R	ER	HR	SH	SF	HB	TBB	IBB	SO	WP	Bk	W	L	Pct.	ShO	Sv-Op	Hld	ERA
1991 Milwaukee	AL	3	3	0	0	16	73	20	9	8	2	0	0	0	6	0	10	0	0	2	0	1.000	0	0-0	0	4.50
1992 Milwaukee	AL	14	14	2	0	100.1	394	76	21	20	4	1	0	2	23	0	62	3	0	11	2	.846	1	0-0	0	1.79
1993 Milwaukee	AL	36	36	8	0	258	1087	232	120	115	32	5	12	10	91	5	180	2	0	16	16	.500	1	0-0	0	4.01
1994 Milwaukee	AL	25	25	6	0	179	769	158	96	93	23	5	7	4	84	0	98	2	0	11	11	.500	0	0-0	0	4.68
1995 Milwaukee	AL	4	4	0	0	23.2	104	24	10	9	4	1	0	1	10	0	18	1	1	1	1	.500	0	0-0	0	3.42
1996 Milwaukee	AL	15	15	0	0	84.2	363	82	43	42	8	0	4	4	38	0	50	1	0	4	4	.500	0	0-0	0	4.46
1997 Milwaukee	AL	34	34	1	0	202	885	207	118	112	31	4	6	9	89	0	122	5	0	13	15	.464	1	0-0	0	4.99
1998 Milwaukee	NL	23	23	0	0	133	602	157	82	71	14	5	3	4	61	3	86	6	0	4	8	.333	0	0-0	0	4.80
8 ML YEARS		154	154	17	0	996.2	4277	956	499	470	118	21	32	34	402	8	626	20	1	62	57	.521	3	0-0	0	4.24

Kevin Elster

Bats: Right **Throws:** Right **Pos:** SS-84   **Ht:** 6'2" **Wt:** 205 **Born:** 8/3/64 **Age:** 34

Year Team	Lg	G	AB	H	2B	3B	HR	(Hm	Rd)	TB	R	RBI	TBB	IBB	SO	HBP	SH	SF	SB	CS	SB%	GDP	Avg	OBP	SLG
1986 New York	NL	19	30	5	1	0	0	(0	0)	6	3	0	3	1	8	0	0	0	0	0	.00	0	.167	.242	.200
1987 New York	NL	5	10	4	2	0	0	(0	0)	6	1	1	0	0	1	0	0	0	0	0	.00	1	.400	.400	.600
1988 New York	NL	149	406	87	11	1	9	(6	3)	127	41	37	35	12	47	3	6	0	2	0	1.00	5	.214	.282	.313
1989 New York	NL	151	458	106	25	2	10	(5	5)	165	52	55	34	11	77	2	6	8	4	3	.57	13	.231	.283	.360
1990 New York	NL	92	314	65	20	1	9	(2	7)	114	36	45	30	2	54	1	1	6	2	0	1.00	4	.207	.274	.363
1991 New York	NL	115	348	84	16	2	6	(3	3)	122	33	36	40	6	53	1	1	4	2	3	.40	4	.241	.318	.351
1992 New York	NL	6	18	4	0	0	0	(0	0)	4	0	0	0	0	2	0	0	0	0	0	.00	1	.222	.222	.222
1994 New York	AL	7	20	0	0	0	0	(0	0)	0	0	1	0	0	6	0	1	0	0	0	.00	0	.000	.048	.000
1995 NYA-Phi		36	70	13	5	1	1	(1	0)	23	11	9	8	1	19	1	2	2	0	0	.00	1	.186	.272	.329
1996 Texas	AL	157	515	130	32	2	24	(9	15)	238	79	99	52	1	138	2	16	11	4	1	.80	8	.252	.317	.462
1997 Pittsburgh	NL	39	138	31	6	2	7	(3	4)	62	14	25	21	0	39	1	2	2	0	2	.00	1	.225	.327	.449
1998 Texas	AL	84	297	69	10	1	8	(3	5)	105	33	37	33	0	66	2	2	2	0	2	.00	7	.232	.311	.354
1995 New York	AL	10	17	2	1	0	0	(0	0)	3	1	0	1	0	5	0	0	0	0	0	.00	0	.118	.167	.176
Philadelphia	NL	26	53	11	4	1	1	(1	0)	20	10	9	7	1	14	1	2	2	0	0	.00	1	.208	.302	.377
12 ML YEARS		860	2624	598	128	12	74	(32	42)	972	303	344	257	34	510	13	37	35	14	11	.56	45	.228	.296	.370

Alan Embree

Pitches: Left **Bats:** Left **Pos:** RP-55   **Ht:** 6'2" **Wt:** 190 **Born:** 1/23/70 **Age:** 29

Year Team	Lg	G	GS	CG	GF	IP	BFP	H	R	ER	HR	SH	SF	HB	TBB	IBB	SO	WP	Bk	W	L	Pct.	ShO	Sv-Op	Hld	ERA
1992 Cleveland	AL	4	4	0	0	18	81	19	14	14	2	0	2	1	8	0	12	1	1	0	2	.000	0	0-0	0	7.00
1995 Cleveland	AL	23	0	0	8	24.2	111	23	16	14	2	2	2	0	16	0	23	1	0	3	2	.600	0	1-1	6	5.11
1996 Cleveland	AL	24	0	0	2	31	141	30	26	22	10	1	3	0	21	3	33	3	0	1	1	.500	0	0-0	1	6.39
1997 Atlanta	NL	66	0	0	15	46	190	36	13	13	1	4	1	2	20	2	45	3	1	3	1	.750	0	0-0	16	2.54
1998 Atl-Ari	NL	55	0	0	16	53.2	237	56	32	25	7	4	1	1	23	0	43	3	0	4	2	.667	0	1-3	12	4.19
1998 Atlanta	NL	20	0	0	5	18.2	87	23	14	9	2	1	1	0	10	0	19	0	0	1	0	1.000	0	0-1	6	4.34
Arizona	NL	35	0	0	11	35	150	33	18	16	5	3	0	1	13	0	24	3	0	3	2	.600	0	1-2	6	4.11
5 ML YEARS		172	4	0	41	173.1	760	164	101	88	23	11	9	4	88	5	156	11	2	11	8	.579	0	2-4	35	4.57

Juan Encarnacion

Bats: R **Throws:** R **Pos:** RF-21; CF-13; LF-8; DH-1; PH/PR-1   **Ht:** 6'3" **Wt:** 187 **Born:** 3/8/76 **Age:** 23

Year Team	Lg	G	AB	H	2B	3B	HR	(Hm	Rd)	TB	R	RBI	TBB	IBB	SO	HBP	SH	SF	SB	CS	SB%	GDP	Avg	OBP	SLG
1994 Fayetteville	A	24	83	16	1	1	1	—	—	22	6	4	8	1	36	1	0	0	1	1	.50	2	.193	.272	.265
Bristol	R+	54	197	49	7	1	4	—	—	70	16	31	13	1	54	5	1	1	9	2	.82	2	.249	.310	.355
Lakeland	A+	3	6	2	0	0	0	—	—	2	1	0	0	0	3	1	0	0	0	0	.00	0	.333	.429	.333
1995 Fayetteville	A	124	457	129	31	7	16	—	—	222	62	72	30	0	113	8	1	2	5	6	.45	10	.282	.336	.486
1996 Lakeland	A+	131	499	120	31	2	15	—	—	200	54	58	24	2	104	12	0	3	11	5	.69	10	.240	.290	.401
1997 Jacksnville	AA	131	493	159	31	4	26	—	—	276	91	90	43	6	86	19	0	6	17	3	.85	8	.323	.394	.560
1998 Lakeland	A+	4	16	4	0	1	0	—	—	6	4	4	2	0	4	1	0	0	4	0	1.00	0	.250	.368	.375
Toledo	AAA	92	356	102	17	3	8	—	—	149	55	41	29	1	85	10	0	4	24	4	.86	9	.287	.353	.419
1997 Detroit	AL	11	33	7	1	1	1	(1	0)	13	3	5	3	0	12	2	0	0	3	1	.75	1	.212	.316	.394
1998 Detroit	AL	40	164	54	9	4	7	(4	3)	92	30	21	7	0	31	1	0	3	7	4	.64	2	.329	.354	.561
2 ML YEARS		51	197	61	10	5	8	(5	3)	105	33	26	10	0	43	3	0	3	10	5	.67	3	.310	.347	.533

Todd Erdos

Pitches: Right **Bats:** Right **Pos:** RP-2   **Ht:** 6'1" **Wt:** 205 **Born:** 11/21/73 **Age:** 25

Year Team	Lg	G	GS	CG	GF	IP	BFP	H	R	ER	HR	SH	SF	HB	TBB	IBB	SO	WP	Bk	W	L	Pct.	ShO	Sv-Op	Hld	ERA
1992 Padres	R	12	9	1	2	57.2	233	36	28	17	1	3	1	3	18	0	61	8	3	3	4	.429	0	0- -	—	2.65
Spokane	A-	2	2	0	0	13	53	9	2	1	0	1	0	1	5	0	11	0	0	1	0	1.000	0	0- -	—	0.69
1993 Waterloo	A	11	11	0	0	47.2	235	64	51	44	9	2	3	4	31	2	27	8	1	1	9	.100	0	0- -	—	8.31
Spokane	A-	15	15	0	0	90.1	384	73	39	32	13	4	2	3	53	2	64	1	0	5	6	.455	0	0- -	—	3.19
1995 Rancho Cuca	A+	1	0	0	0	2.2	13	5	4	4	0	0	1	0	0	0	4	0	0	0	0	.000	0	0- -	—	13.50
Clinton	A	5	1	0	1	5	27	4	4	3	0	0	0	0	8	1	1	2	0	0	0	.000	0	0- -	—	5.40
Idaho Falls	R+	32	0	0	20	41.1	185	34	19	16	1	2	5	1	30	2	48	8	0	5	3	.625	0	1- -	—	3.48

Year Team	Lg	G	GS	CG	GF	IP	BFP	H	R	ER	HR	SH	SF	HB	TBB	IBB	SO	WP	Bk	W	L	Pct.	ShO	Sv-Op	Hld	ERA
1996 Rancho Cuca	A+	55	0	0	41	67.1	305	63	33	28	2	7	2	6	37	3	82	6	0	3	3	.500	0	17- -	—	3.74
1997 Mobile	AA	55	0	0	50	59	244	45	22	22	4	2	1	0	22	4	49	2	1	1	4	.200	0	27- -	—	3.36
1998 Columbus	AAA	39	0	0	33	48.2	216	52	27	25	4	1	3	2	20	0	50	2	0	3	2	.600	0	16- -	—	4.62
1997 San Diego	NL	11	0	0	2	13.2	64	17	9	8	1	0	0	2	4	0	13	3	0	2	0	1.000	0	0-0	0	5.27
1998 New York	AL	2	0	0	1	2	11	5	2	2	0	0	0	0	1	1	0	0	0	0	0	.000	0	0-0	0	9.00
2 ML YEARS		13	0	0	3	15.2	75	22	11	10	1	0	0	2	5	1	13	3	0	2	0	1.000	0	0-0	0	5.74

John Ericks

Pitches: Right   Bats: Right   Pos: RP   Ht: 6'7"   Wt: 245   Born: 9/16/67   Age: 31

Year Team	Lg	G	GS	CG	GF	IP	BFP	H	R	ER	HR	SH	SF	HB	TBB	IBB	SO	WP	Bk	W	L	Pct.	ShO	Sv-Op	Hld	ERA
1995 Pittsburgh	NL	19	18	1	0	106	472	108	59	54	7	5	5	2	50	4	80	11	1	3	9	.250	0	0-0	0	4.58
1996 Pittsburgh	NL	28	4	0	13	46.2	213	56	35	30	11	1	1	0	19	2	46	2	0	4	5	.444	0	8-10	1	5.79
1997 Pittsburgh	NL	10	0	0	10	9.1	39	7	3	2	1	0	0	0	4	0	6	0	0	1	0	1.000	0	6-7	0	1.93
3 ML YEARS		57	22	1	23	162	724	171	97	86	19	6	6	2	73	6	132	13	1	8	14	.364	0	14-17	1	4.78

Scott Erickson

Pitches: Right   Bats: Right   Pos: SP-36   Ht: 6'4"   Wt: 230   Born: 2/2/68   Age: 31

Year Team	Lg	G	GS	CG	GF	IP	BFP	H	R	ER	HR	SH	SF	HB	TBB	IBB	SO	WP	Bk	W	L	Pct.	ShO	Sv-Op	Hld	ERA
1990 Minnesota	AL	19	17	1	1	113	485	108	49	36	9	5	2	5	51	4	53	3	0	8	4	.667	0	0-0	0	2.87
1991 Minnesota	AL	32	32	5	0	204	851	189	80	72	13	5	7	6	71	3	108	4	0	20	8	.714	0	0-0	0	3.18
1992 Minnesota	AL	32	32	5	0	212	888	197	86	80	18	9	7	8	83	3	101	6	1	13	12	.520	3	0-0	0	3.40
1993 Minnesota	AL	34	34	1	0	218.2	976	266	138	126	17	10	13	10	71	1	116	5	0	8	19	.296	0	0-0	0	5.19
1994 Minnesota	AL	23	23	2	0	144	654	173	95	87	15	3	4	9	59	0	104	10	0	8	11	.421	1	0-0	0	5.44
1995 Min-Bal	AL	32	31	7	1	196.1	836	213	108	105	18	3	3	5	67	0	106	3	2	13	10	.565	2	0-0	0	4.81
1996 Baltimore	AL	34	34	6	0	222.1	968	262	137	124	21	5	5	11	66	2	100	1	0	13	12	.520	2	0-0	0	5.02
1997 Baltimore	AL	34	33	3	0	221.2	922	218	100	91	16	3	4	5	61	5	131	11	0	16	7	.696	2	0-0	0	3.69
1998 Baltimore	AL	36	36	11	0	251.1	1102	284	125	112	23	7	2	13	69	4	186	4	0	16	13	.552	2	0-0	0	4.01
1995 Minnesota	AL	15	15	0	0	87.2	390	102	61	58	11	2	1	4	32	0	45	1	0	4	6	.400	0	0-0	0	5.95
Baltimore	AL	17	16	7	1	108.2	446	111	47	47	7	1	2	1	35	0	61	2	2	9	4	.692	2	0-0	0	3.89
9 ML YEARS		276	272	41	2	1783.1	7682	1910	918	833	150	50	47	72	598	24	1005	47	3	115	96	.545	13	0-0	0	4.20

Darin Erstad

Bats: L Throws: L   Pos: 1B-70; LF-70; PH/PR-4; CF-3; DH-2   Ht: 6'2"   Wt: 210   Born: 6/4/74   Age: 25

Year Team	Lg	G	AB	H	2B	3B	HR	(Hm	Rd)	TB	R	RBI	TBB	IBB	SO	HBP	SH	SF	SB	CS	SB%	GDP	Avg	OBP	SLG
1996 California	AL	57	208	59	5	1	4	(1	3)	78	34	20	17	1	29	0	1	3	3	3	.50	3	.284	.333	.375
1997 Anaheim	AL	139	539	161	34	4	16	(8	8)	251	99	77	51	4	86	4	5	6	23	8	.74	5	.299	.360	.466
1998 Anaheim	AL	133	537	159	39	3	16	(9	10)	261	84	82	43	7	77	6	1	3	20	6	.77	2	.296	.353	.486
3 ML YEARS		329	1284	379	78	8	39	(18	21)	590	217	179	111	12	192	10	7	12	46	17	.73	10	.295	.353	.460

Kelvim Escobar

Pitches: Right   Bats: Right   Pos: RP-12; SP-10   Ht: 6'1"   Wt: 205   Born: 4/11/76   Age: 23

Year Team	Lg	G	GS	CG	GF	IP	BFP	H	R	ER	HR	SH	SF	HB	TBB	IBB	SO	WP	Bk	W	L	Pct.	ShO	Sv-Op	Hld	ERA
1994 Blue Jays	R	11	10	1	0	65	257	56	23	17	0	0	1	2	18	0	64	5	3	4	4	.500	0	0- -	—	2.35
1995 Medicine Ha	R+	14	14	1	0	69.1	307	66	47	44	6	2	5	6	33	0	75	4	4	3	3	.500	1	0- -	—	5.71
1996 Dunedin	A+	18	18	1	0	110.1	460	101	44	33	5	2	1	3	33	0	113	7	2	9	5	.643	0	0- -	—	2.69
Knoxville	AA	10	10	0	0	54	238	61	36	32	7	0	1	1	24	0	44	6	1	3	4	.429	0	0- -	—	5.33
1997 Dunedin	A+	3	2	0	0	12	55	16	9	5	0	1	1	1	3	0	16	1	0	1	0	1.000	0	0- -	—	3.75
Knoxville	AA	5	5	1	0	24.1	108	20	13	10	1	0	0	2	16	0	31	1	2	2	1	.667	0	0- -	—	3.70
1998 Syracuse	AAA	13	10	0	2	59.2	253	51	26	25	7	1	1	4	24	0	64	3	0	2	2	.500	0	1- -	—	3.77
1997 Toronto	AL	27	0	0	23	31	139	28	12	10	1	2	0	0	19	2	36	0	0	3	2	.600	0	14-17	5	2.90
1998 Toronto	AL	22	10	0	2	79.2	342	72	37	33	5	0	3	0	35	0	72	0	0	7	3	.700	0	0-1	5	3.73
2 ML YEARS		49	10	0	25	110.2	481	100	49	43	6	2	3	0	54	2	108	0	0	10	5	.667	0	14-18	6	3.50

Vaughn Eshelman

Pitches: Left   Bats: Left   Pos: RP/SP   Ht: 6'3"   Wt: 205   Born: 5/22/69   Age: 30

Year Team	Lg	G	GS	CG	GF	IP	BFP	H	R	ER	HR	SH	SF	HB	TBB	IBB	SO	WP	Bk	W	L	Pct.	ShO	Sv-Op	Hld	ERA
1995 Boston	AL	23	14	0	4	81.2	356	86	47	44	3	0	3	1	36	0	41	4	0	6	3	.667	0	0-0	1	4.85
1996 Boston	AL	39	10	0	1	87.2	428	112	79	69	13	3	5	2	58	4	59	4	0	6	3	.667	0	0-0	8	7.08
1997 Boston	AL	21	6	0	6	42.2	198	58	32	30	3	1	2	2	17	5	18	2	0	3	3	.500	0	0-1	0	6.33
3 ML YEARS		83	30	0	11	212	982	256	158	143	19	4	10	5	111	9	118	10	0	15	9	.625	0	0-1	9	6.07

Bobby Estalella

Bats: Right **Throws:** Right **Pos:** C-47   **Ht:** 6'1" **Wt:** 210 **Born:** 8/23/74 **Age:** 24

Year Team	Lg	G	AB	H	2B	3B	HR	(Hm	Rd)	TB	R	RBI	TBB	IBB	SO	HBP	SH	SF	SB	CS	SB%	GDP	Avg	OBP	SLG
1993 Martinsvlle	R+	35	122	36	11	0	3	—	—	56	14	19	14	2	24	2	0	0	0	1	.00	6	.295	.377	.459
Clearwater	A+	11	35	8	0	0	0	—	—	8	4	4	2	0	3	0	0	0	0	0	.00	1	.229	.270	.229
1994 Spartanburg	A	86	299	65	19	1	9	—	—	113	34	41	31	0	85	1	1	4	0	1	.00	5	.217	.290	.378
Clearwater	A+	13	46	12	1	0	2	—	—	19	3	9	3	0	17	0	2	1	0	1	.00	1	.261	.300	.413
1995 Clearwater	A+	117	404	105	24	1	15	—	—	176	61	58	56	2	76	2	3	4	0	3	.00	12	.260	.350	.436
Reading	AA	10	34	8	1	0	2	—	—	15	5	9	4	1	7	1	0	0	0	0	.00	0	.235	.333	.441
1996 Reading	AA	111	365	89	14	2	23	—	—	176	48	67	5	104	5	1	4	2	4	.33	7		.244	.365	.482
Scranton-WB	AAA	11	36	9	3	0	3	—	—	21	7	8	5	0	10	0	0	0	0	0	.00	0	.250	.341	.583
1997 Scranton-WB	AAA	123	433	101	32	0	16	—	—	181	63	65	56	0	109	9	0	2	3	0	1.00	14	.233	.332	.418
1998 Scranton-WB	AAA	76	242	68	14	1	17	—	—	135	49	49	66	0	49	2	0	2	0	0	.00	13	.281	.436	.558
1996 Philadelphia	NL	7	17	6	0	0	2	(0	2)	12	5	4	1	0	6	0	0	0	1	0	1.00	0	.353	.389	.706
1997 Philadelphia	NL	13	29	10	1	0	4	(1	3)	23	9	9	7	0	7	0	0	0	0	0	.00	2	.345	.472	.793
1998 Philadelphia	NL	47	165	31	6	1	8	(3	5)	63	16	20	13	0	49	1	0	3	0	0	.00	4	.188	.247	.382
3 ML YEARS		67	211	47	7	1	14	(4	10)	98	30	33	21	0	62	1	0	3	1	0	1.00	6	.223	.292	.464

Shawn Estes

Pitches: Left **Bats:** Right **Pos:** SP-25   **Ht:** 6'2" **Wt:** 195 **Born:** 2/18/73 **Age:** 26

Year Team	Lg	G	GS	CG	GF	IP	BFP	H	R	ER	HR	SH	SF	HB	TBB	IBB	SO	WP	Bk	W	L	Pct.	ShO	Sv-Op	Hld	ERA
1998 Bakersfield *	A+	1	1	0	0	4.1	17	3	0	0	0	0	0	0	1	0	5	0	0	0	0	.000	0	0--	—	0.00
Fresno *	AAA	1	1	0	0	5	19	3	1	1	0	0	0	0	3	0	6	6	0	1	0	1.000	0	0--	—	1.80
1995 San Francisco	NL	3	3	0	0	17.1	76	16	14	13	2	0	0	1	5	0	14	4	0	0	3	.000	0	0-0	0	6.75
1996 San Francisco	NL	11	11	0	0	70	305	63	30	28	3	5	0	2	36	4	60	4	0	3	5	.375	0	0-0	0	3.60
1997 San Francisco	NL	32	32	3	0	201	849	162	80	71	12	13	2	8	100	2	181	10	2	19	5	.792	2	0-0	0	3.18
1998 San Francisco	NL	25	25	1	0	149.1	661	150	89	84	14	15	4	5	80	6	136	6	1	7	12	.368	1	0-0	0	5.06
4 ML YEARS		71	71	4	0	437.2	1891	391	213	196	31	33	6	16	224	11	391	24	3	29	25	.537	3	0-0	0	4.03

Tony Eusebio

Bats: Right **Throws:** Right **Pos:** C-54; PH/PR-15   **Ht:** 6'2" **Wt:** 210 **Born:** 4/27/67 **Age:** 32

Year Team	Lg	G	AB	H	2B	3B	HR	(Hm	Rd)	TB	R	RBI	TBB	IBB	SO	HBP	SH	SF	SB	CS	SB%	GDP	Avg	OBP	SLG
1991 Houston	NL	10	19	2	1	0	0	(0	0)	3	4	0	6	0	8	0	0	0	0	0	.00	1	.105	.320	.158
1994 Houston	NL	55	159	47	9	1	5	(1	4)	73	18	30	8	0	33	0	2	5	0	1	.00	4	.296	.320	.459
1995 Houston	NL	113	368	110	21	1	6	(5	1)	151	46	58	31	1	59	3	1	5	0	2	.00	12	.299	.354	.410
1996 Houston	NL	58	152	41	7	2	1	(1	0)	55	15	19	18	2	20	0	0	2	1	0	.00	5	.270	.343	.362
1997 Houston	NL	60	164	45	2	0	1	(0	1)	50	12	18	19	1	27	4	0	0	1	0	.00	4	.274	.364	.305
1998 Houston	NL	66	182	46	6	1	1	(1	0)	57	13	36	18	2	31	1	0	2	1	0	1.00	8	.253	.320	.313
6 ML YEARS		362	1044	291	46	5	14	(8	6)	389	108	161	100	6	178	8	3	14	1	5	.17	34	.279	.342	.373

Bart Evans

Pitches: Right **Bats:** Right **Pos:** RP-8   **Ht:** 6'2" **Wt:** 210 **Born:** 12/30/70 **Age:** 28

Year Team	Lg	G	GS	CG	GF	IP	BFP	H	R	ER	HR	SH	SF	HB	TBB	IBB	SO	WP	Bk	W	L	Pct.	ShO	Sv-Op	Hld	ERA
1992 Eugene	A-	13	1	0	4	26	126	17	20	18	1	1	2	4	31	0	39	14	0	1	1	.500	0	0--	—	6.23
1993 Rockford	A	27	16	0	4	99	439	95	52	48	5	1	2	4	60	0	120	10	1	10	4	.714	0	0--	—	4.36
1994 Wilmington	A+	26	26	0	0	145	587	107	53	48	7	1	0	4	61	0	145	10	0	10	3	.769	0	0--	—	2.98
1995 Wichita	AA	7	7	0	0	22.1	123	22	28	26	3	1	0	1	45	0	13	7	1	0	4	.000	0	0--	—	10.48
Wilmington	A+	16	6	0	4	46.2	215	30	21	15	0	0	1	5	44	0	47	7	0	4	1	.800	0	2--	—	2.89
1996 Wichita	AA	9	7	0	0	24.1	146	31	38	32	7	3	2	6	36	0	16	12	0	1	2	.333	0	0--	—	11.84
1997 Wichita	A+	16	2	0	8	20.2	101	22	18	15	1	0	2	3	15	0	22	3	0	1	0	.000	0	0--	—	6.53
Wichita	AA	32	0	0	22	33.1	148	45	20	17	4	2	1	0	8	2	28	1	0	1	2	.333	0	6--	—	4.59
1998 Omaha	AAA	49	0	0	40	57	236	50	18	16	4	2	0	2	22	2	54	3	0	3	1	.750	0	27--	—	2.53
1998 Kansas City	AL	8	0	0	3	9	34	7	3	2	1	0	0	0	0	0	7	0	0	0	0	.000	0	0-0	0	2.00

Tom Evans

Bats: Right **Throws:** Right **Pos:** 3B-7   **Ht:** 6'1" **Wt:** 200 **Born:** 7/9/74 **Age:** 24

Year Team	Lg	G	AB	H	2B	3B	HR	(Hm	Rd)	TB	R	RBI	TBB	IBB	SO	HBP	SH	SF	SB	CS	SB%	GDP	Avg	OBP	SLG
1992 Medicine Ha	R+	52	166	36	3	0	1	—	—	42	17	21	33	0	29	1	1	1	4	3	.57	4	.217	.348	.253
1993 Hagerstown	A	119	389	100	25	1	7	—	—	148	47	54	53	2	61	3	0	4	9	2	.82	7	.257	.347	.380
1994 Hagerstown	A	95	322	88	16	2	13	—	—	147	52	48	51	1	80	1	1	1	2	1	.67	3	.273	.373	.457
1995 Dunedin	A+	130	444	124	29	3	9	—	—	186	63	66	51	0	80	8	3	7	7	2	.78	10	.279	.359	.419
1996 Knoxville	AA	120	394	111	27	1	17	—	—	191	87	65	115	0	113	9	0	2	4	0	1.00	7	.282	.452	.485
1997 Dunedin	A+	15	42	11	2	0	2	—	—	19	8	4	11	0	10	4	0	1	0	0	.00	0	.262	.448	.452
Syracuse	AAA	107	376	99	17	1	15	—	—	163	60	65	53	1	104	9	1	3	1	2	.33	4	.263	.365	.434
1998 Syracuse	AAA	109	400	120	32	1	15	—	—	199	57	55	50	1	74	8	0	1	11	7	.61	13	.300	.388	.498
1997 Toronto	AL	12	38	11	2	0	1	(1	0)	16	7	2	10	0	12	1	0	0	0	0	.00	1	.289	.341	.421
1998 Toronto	AL	7	10	0	0	0	0	(0	0)	0	0	0	1	0	2	0	0	0	0	1	.00	1	.000	.091	.000
2 ML YEARS		19	48	11	2	0	1	(1	0)	16	7	2	3	0	12	1	0	0	0	1	.00	1	.229	.288	.333

Carl Everett

Bats: Both **Throws:** Right **Pos:** CF-121; PH/PR-13; RF-5 **Ht:** 6'0" **Wt:** 190 **Born:** 6/3/71 **Age:** 28

Year Team	Lg	G	AB	H	2B	3B	HR	(Hm	Rd)	TB	R	RBI	TBB	IBB	SO	HBP	SH	SF	SB	CS	SB%	GDP	Avg	OBP	SLG
1993 Florida	NL	11	19	2	0	0	0	(0	0)	2	0	0	1	0	9	0	0	0	1	0	1.00	0	.105	.150	.105
1994 Florida	NL	16	51	11	1	0	2	(2	0)	18	7	6	3	0	15	0	0	0	4	0	1.00	0	.216	.259	.353
1995 New York	NL	79	289	75	13	1	12	(9	3)	126	48	54	39	2	67	2	1	0	2	5	.29	11	.260	.352	.436
1996 New York	NL	101	192	46	8	1	1	(1	0)	59	29	16	21	2	53	4	1	1	6	0	1.00	4	.240	.326	.307
1997 New York	NL	142	443	110	28	3	14	(11	3)	186	58	57	32	3	102	7	3	2	17	9	.65	3	.248	.308	.420
1998 Houston	NL	133	467	138	34	4	15	(5	10)	225	72	76	44	2	102	3	3	2	14	12	.54	11	.296	.359	.482
6 ML YEARS		482	1461	382	84	9	44	(28	16)	616	214	209	140	9	348	16	8	5	44	26	.63	29	.261	.332	.422

Bryan Eversgerd

Pitches: Left **Bats:** Right **Pos:** RP-8 **Ht:** 6'1" **Wt:** 185 **Born:** 2/11/69 **Age:** 30

		HOW MUCH HE PITCHED						WHAT HE GAVE UP										THE RESULTS						
Year Team	Lg	G	GS	CG	GF	IP	BFP	H	R	ER	HR	SH	SF	HB	TBB	IBB	SO	WP	Bk	W	L	Pct.	ShO	Sv-Op	Hld	ERA
1998 Memphis *	AAA	49	0	0	17	56.2	238	51	25	21	9	1	0	1	20	1	50	2	1	2	5	.286	0	0- --		3.34
1994 St. Louis	NL	40	1	0	8	67.2	283	75	36	34	8	5	2	2	20	1	47	3	1	2	3	.400	0	0-1	0	4.52
1995 Montreal	NL	25	0	0	5	21	95	22	13	12	2	1	2	1	9	2	8	1	0	0	0	.000	0	0-0	3	5.14
1997 Texas	AL	3	0	0	1	1.1	12	5	3	3	0	0	0	0	3	0	2	0	0	0	0	.000	0	0-0	0	20.25
1998 St. Louis	NL	8	0	0	2	6	31	9	7	6	1	0	2	1	2	0	4	0	0	0	0	.000	0	0-0	4	9.00
4 ML YEARS		76	1	0	16	96	421	111	59	55	11	6	6	4	34	3	61	4	1	2	5	.286	0	0-1	7	5.16

Scott Eyre

Pitches: Left **Bats:** Left **Pos:** SP-17; RP-16 **Ht:** 6'1" **Wt:** 190 **Born:** 5/30/72 **Age:** 27

		HOW MUCH HE PITCHED						WHAT HE GAVE UP										THE RESULTS						
Year Team	Lg	G	GS	CG	GF	IP	BFP	H	R	ER	HR	SH	SF	HB	TBB	IBB	SO	WP	Bk	W	L	Pct.	ShO	Sv-Op	Hld	ERA
1992 Butte	R+	15	14	2	0	80.2	339	71	30	26	6	1	0	4	39	0	94	6	1	7	3	.700	1	0- --		2.90
1993 Chston-SC	A	26	26	0	0	143.2	597	115	74	55	6	3	6	6	59	1	154	2	1	11	7	.611	0	0- --		3.45
1994 South Bend	A	19	18	2	1	111.2	481	108	56	43	7	2	4	3	37	0	111	8	3	8	4	.667	0	0- --		3.47
1995 White Sox	R	9	9	0	0	27.1	106	16	7	7	0	0	1	1	12	0	40	2	0	0	2	.000	0	0- --		2.30
1996 Birmingham	AA	27	27	0	0	158.1	709	170	90	77	12	3	6	8	79	3	137	12	0	12	7	.632	0	0- --		4.38
1997 Birmingham	AA	22	22	0	0	126.2	538	110	61	54	14	1	1	5	55	2	127	9	1	13	5	.722	0	0- --		3.84
1997 Chicago	AL	11	11	0	0	60.2	267	62	36	34	11	1	2	1	31	1	36	2	0	4	4	.500	0	0-0	0	5.04
1998 Chicago	AL	33	17	0	10	107	491	114	78	64	24	2	3	2	64	0	73	7	0	3	8	.273	0	0-0	0	5.38
2 ML YEARS		44	28	0	10	167.2	758	176	114	98	35	3	5	3	95	1	109	9	0	7	12	.368	0	0-0	0	5.26

Jorge Fabregas

Bats: Left **Throws:** Right **Pos:** C-53; PH/PR-18 **Ht:** 6'3" **Wt:** 215 **Born:** 3/13/70 **Age:** 29

Year Team	Lg	G	AB	H	2B	3B	HR	(Hm	Rd)	TB	R	RBI	TBB	IBB	SO	HBP	SH	SF	SB	CS	SB%	GDP	Avg	OBP	SLG
1998 Tucson *	AAA	6	20	5	1	0	0	—	—	6	2	3	3	0	1	0	0	0	0	0	.00	2	.250	.348	.300
1994 California	AL	43	127	36	3	0	0	(0	0)	39	12	16	7	1	18	0	1	0	2	1	.67	5	.283	.321	.307
1995 California	AL	73	227	56	10	0	1	(1	0)	69	24	22	17	0	28	0	3	1	0	2	.00	9	.247	.298	.304
1996 California	AL	90	254	73	6	0	2	(1	1)	85	18	26	17	3	27	0	3	5	0	1	.00	7	.287	.326	.335
1997 Ana-ChA	AL	121	360	93	11	1	7	(1	6)	127	33	51	14	0	46	1	6	4	1	1	.50	16	.258	.285	.353
1998 Ari-NYN	NL	70	183	36	4	0	2	(0	2)	46	11	20	14	1	32	1	1	2	0	0	.00	4	.197	.255	.251
1997 Anaheim	AL	21	38	3	1	0	0	(0	0)	4	2	3	3	0	3	0	2	0	0	0	.00	2	.079	.146	.105
Chicago	AL	100	322	90	10	1	7	(1	6)	123	31	48	11	0	43	1	4	4	1	1	.50	14	.280	.302	.382
1998 Arizona	NL	50	151	30	4	0	1	(0	1)	37	8	15	13	1	26	1	0	2	0	0	.00	3	.199	.263	.245
New York	NL	20	32	6	0	0	1	(0	1)	9	3	5	1	0	6	0	1	0	0	0	.00	1	.188	.212	.281
5 ML YEARS		397	1151	294	34	1	12	(3	9)	366	98	135	69	5	151	2	14	12	3	5	.38	41	.255	.296	.318

Sal Fasano

Bats: Right **Throws:** Right **Pos:** C-70; 1B-5; 3B-1; PH/PR-1 **Ht:** 6'2" **Wt:** 220 **Born:** 8/10/71 **Age:** 27

Year Team	Lg	G	AB	H	2B	3B	HR	(Hm	Rd)	TB	R	RBI	TBB	IBB	SO	HBP	SH	SF	SB	CS	SB%	GDP	Avg	OBP	SLG
1998 Omaha *	AAA	4	14	3	1	0	1	—	—	7	1	2	1	0	4	0	0	0	0	1	.00	0	.214	.267	.500
1996 Kansas City	AL	51	143	29	2	0	6	(1	5)	49	20	19	14	0	25	2	1	0	1	1	.50	3	.203	.283	.343
1997 Kansas City	AL	13	38	8	2	0	1	(0	1)	13	4	1	1	0	12	0	0	0	0	0	.00	1	.211	.231	.342
1998 Kansas City	AL	74	216	49	10	0	8	(4	4)	83	21	31	10	1	56	16	3	2	1	0	1.00	4	.227	.307	.384
3 ML YEARS		138	397	86	14	0	15	(5	10)	145	45	51	25	1	93	18	4	2	2	1	.67	8	.217	.292	.365

Jeff Fassero

Pitches: Left **Bats:** Left **Pos:** SP-32 **Ht:** 6'1" **Wt:** 195 **Born:** 1/5/63 **Age:** 36

		HOW MUCH HE PITCHED						WHAT HE GAVE UP										THE RESULTS						
Year Team	Lg	G	GS	CG	GF	IP	BFP	H	R	ER	HR	SH	SF	HB	TBB	IBB	SO	WP	Bk	W	L	Pct.	ShO	Sv-Op	Hld	ERA
1991 Montreal	NL	51	0	0	30	55.1	223	39	17	15	1	6	0	1	17	1	42	4	0	2	5	.286	0	8-11	7	2.44
1992 Montreal	NL	70	0	0	22	85.2	368	81	35	27	1	5	2	2	34	6	63	7	1	8	7	.533	0	1-7	12	2.84
1993 Montreal	NL	56	15	1	10	149.2	616	119	50	38	7	7	4	0	54	0	140	5	0	12	5	.706	0	1-3	6	2.29
1994 Montreal	NL	21	21	1	0	138.2	569	119	54	46	13	7	2	1	40	4	119	6	0	8	6	.571	0	0-0	0	2.99
1995 Montreal	NL	30	30	1	0	189	833	207	102	91	15	**19**	7	2	74	3	164	7	1	13	14	.481	0	0-0	0	4.33

		HOW MUCH HE PITCHED						WHAT HE GAVE UP										THE RESULTS					
Year Team	Lg	G	GS	CG	GF	IP	BFP	H	R	ER	HR	SH	SF	HB	TBB	IBB	SO	WP	Bk	W	L	Pct.	ShO	Sv-Op	Hld	ERA
1996 Montreal	NL	34	34	5	0	231.2	967	217	95	85	20	16	5	3	55	3	222	5	2	15	11	.577	1	0-0	0	3.30
1997 Seattle	AL	35	35	2	0	234.1	1010	226	108	94	21	7	10	3	84	6	189	13	2	16	9	.640	1	0-0	0	3.61
1998 Seattle	AL	32	32	7	0	224.2	954	223	115	99	33	8	8	10	66	2	176	12	0	13	12	.520	0	0-0	0	3.97
8 ML YEARS		329	167	17	62	1309	5540	1231	576	495	111	75	38	22	424	25	1115	59	6	87	69	.558	2	10-21	25	3.40

Carlos Febles

Bats: Right **Throws:** Right **Pos:** 2B-11; PH/PR-2   **Ht:** 5'11" **Wt:** 170 **Born:** 5/24/76 **Age:** 23

					BATTING													BASERUNNING				PERCENTAGES		
Year Team	Lg	G	AB	H	2B	3B	HR	(Hm	Rd)	TB	R	RBI	TBB	IBB	SO	HBP	SH	SF	SB	CS	SB%	GDP	Avg	OBP	SLG
1995 Royals	R	54	188	53	13	5	3	—	—	85	40	20	26	0	30	4	1	0	16	8	.67	5	.282	.381	.452
1996 Lansing	A	102	363	107	23	5	5	—	—	155	84	43	66	0	64	11	7	4	30	14	.68	8	.295	.414	.427
1997 Wilmington	A+	122	438	104	27	6	3	—	—	152	78	29	51	2	95	12	3	0	49	11	.82	13	.237	.333	.347
1998 Wichita	AA	126	432	141	28	9	14	—	—	229	110	52	80	1	70	11	5	3	51	16	.76	6	.326	.441	.530
1998 Kansas City	AL	11	25	10	1	2	0	(0	0)	15	5	2	4	0	7	0	0	0	2	1	.67	0	.400	.483	.600

Alex Fernandez

Pitches: Right **Bats:** Right **Pos:** SP   **Ht:** 6'1" **Wt:** 215 **Born:** 8/13/69 **Age:** 29

		HOW MUCH HE PITCHED						WHAT HE GAVE UP												THE RESULTS					
Year Team	Lg	G	GS	CG	GF	IP	BFP	H	R	ER	HR	SH	SF	HB	TBB	IBB	SO	WP	Bk	W	L	Pct.	ShO	Sv-Op	Hld	ERA
1990 Chicago	AL	13	13	3	0	87.2	378	89	40	37	6	5	0	3	34	0	61	1	0	5	5	.500	0	0-0	1	3.80
1991 Chicago	AL	34	32	2	1	191.2	827	186	100	96	16	7	11	2	88	2	145	4	1	9	13	.409	0	0-0	1	4.51
1992 Chicago	AL	29	29	3	0	187.2	804	199	100	89	21	6	4	8	50	3	95	3	0	8	11	.421	2	0-0	0	4.27
1993 Chicago	AL	34	34	3	0	247.1	1004	221	95	86	27	9	3	6	67	5	169	4	0	18	9	.667	1	0-0	0	3.13
1994 Chicago	AL	24	24	4	0	170.1	712	163	83	73	25	4	6	1	50	4	122	3	1	11	7	.611	3	0-0	0	3.86
1995 Chicago	AL	30	30	5	0	203.2	858	200	98	86	19	4	6	0	65	7	159	3	0	12	8	.600	2	0-0	0	3.80
1996 Chicago	AL	35	35	6	0	258	1071	248	110	99	34	5	7	7	72	4	200	5	0	16	10	.615	1	0-0	0	3.45
1997 Florida	NL	32	32	5	0	220.2	904	193	93	88	25	14	5	4	69	2	183	9	0	17	12	.586	1	0-0	0	3.59
8 ML YEARS		231	229	32	1	1567	6558	1499	719	654	173	54	42	31	495	27	1134	36	2	96	75	.561	10	0-0	1	3.76

Tony Fernandez

Bats: B **Throws:** R **Pos:** 2B-82; 3B-54; PH/PR-3; DH-1   **Ht:** 6'2" **Wt:** 175 **Born:** 6/30/62 **Age:** 37

					BATTING													BASERUNNING			PERCENTAGES		
Year Team	Lg	G	AB	H	2B	3B	HR	(Hm | Rd)	TB	R	RBI	TBB	IBB	SO	HBP	SH	SF	SB	CS	SB%	GDP	Avg	OBP	SLG
1983 Toronto	AL	15	34	9	1	1	0	(0 | 0)	12	5	2	2	0	2	1	1	0	0	1	.00	1	.265	.324	.353
1984 Toronto	AL	88	233	63	5	3	3	(1 | 2)	83	29	19	17	0	15	0	2	2	5	7	.42	3	.270	.317	.356
1985 Toronto	AL	161	564	163	31	10	2	(1 | 1)	220	71	51	43	2	41	2	7	2	13	6	.68	12	.289	.340	.390
1986 Toronto	AL	163	687	213	33	9	10	(4 | 6)	294	91	65	27	0	52	4	5	4	25	12	.68	8	.310	.338	.428
1987 Toronto	AL	146	578	186	29	8	5	(1 | 4)	246	90	67	51	3	48	5	4	4	32	12	.73	14	.322	.379	.426
1988 Toronto	AL	154	648	186	41	4	5	(3 | 2)	250	76	70	45	3	65	4	3	4	15	5	.75	9	.287	.335	.386
1989 Toronto	AL	140	573	147	25	9	11	(2 | 9)	223	64	64	29	1	51	3	2	10	22	6	.79	9	.257	.291	.389
1990 Toronto	AL	161	635	175	27	17	4	(2 | 2)	248	84	66	71	4	70	7	2	6	26	13	.67	17	.276	.352	.391
1991 San Diego	NL	145	558	152	27	5	4	(1 | 3)	201	81	38	55	0	74	0	7	1	23	9	.72	12	.272	.337	.360
1992 San Diego	NL	155	622	171	32	4	4	(3 | 1)	223	84	37	56	4	62	4	9	3	20	20	.50	6	.275	.337	.359
1993 NYN-Tor		142	526	147	23	11	5	(1 | 4)	207	65	64	56	3	45	1	8	3	21	10	.68	16	.279	.348	.394
1994 Cincinnati	NL	104	366	102	18	6	8	(3 | 5)	156	50	50	44	8	40	5	4	3	12	7	.63	5	.279	.361	.426
1995 New York	AL	108	384	94	20	2	5	(3 | 2)	133	57	45	42	4	40	4	3	5	6	6	.50	14	.245	.322	.346
1997 Cleveland	AL	120	409	117	21	1	11	(7 | 4)	173	55	44	22	0	47	2	6	3	6	6	.50	11	.286	.323	.423
1998 Toronto	AL	138	486	156	36	2	9	(4 | 5)	223	71	72	45	5	53	11	3	6	8	5	.62	11	.321	.387	.459
1993 New York	NL	48	173	39	5	2	1	(0 | 1)	51	20	14	25	0	19	1	3	2	6	2	.75	3	.225	.323	.295
Toronto	AL	94	353	108	18	9	4	(1 | 3)	156	45	50	31	3	26	0	5	1	15	8	.65	13	.306	.361	.442
15 ML YEARS		1940	7303	2081	369	92	86	(36 | 50)	2892	973	754	605	37	705	53	66	56	239	128	.65	148	.285	.342	.396

Mike Fetters

Pitches: Right **Bats:** Right **Pos:** RP-60   **Ht:** 6'4" **Wt:** 226 **Born:** 12/19/64 **Age:** 34

		HOW MUCH HE PITCHED						WHAT HE GAVE UP												THE RESULTS					
Year Team	Lg	G	GS	CG	GF	IP	BFP	H	R	ER	HR	SH	SF	HB	TBB	IBB	SO	WP	Bk	W	L	Pct.	ShO	Sv-Op	Hld	ERA
1989 California	AL	1	0	0	0	3.1	16	5	4	3	1	0	0	0	1	0	4	2	0	0	0	.000	0	0-0	0	8.10
1990 California	AL	26	2	0	10	67.2	291	77	33	31	9	1	0	2	20	0	35	3	0	1	1	.500	0	1-1	1	4.12
1991 California	AL	19	4	0	8	44.2	206	53	29	24	4	1	0	3	28	2	24	4	0	2	5	.286	0	0-1	0	4.84
1992 Milwaukee	AL	50	0	0	11	62.2	243	38	15	13	3	5	2	7	24	2	43	4	1	5	1	.833	0	2-5	8	1.87
1993 Milwaukee	AL	45	0	0	14	59.1	246	59	29	22	4	5	5	2	22	4	23	0	0	3	3	.500	0	0-0	8	3.34
1994 Milwaukee	AL	42	0	0	31	46	202	41	16	13	0	2	3	1	27	5	31	3	1	1	4	.200	0	17-20	3	2.54
1995 Milwaukee	AL	40	0	0	34	34.2	163	40	16	13	3	2	1	0	20	4	33	5	0	0	3	.000	0	22-27	2	3.38
1996 Milwaukee	AL	61	0	0	55	61.1	268	65	28	23	4	4	4	1	26	4	53	5	0	3	3	.500	0	32-38	1	3.38
1997 Milwaukee	AL	51	0	0	20	70.1	298	62	30	27	4	6	4	1	33	3	62	2	1	1	5	.167	0	6-11	11	3.45
1998 Oak-Ana	AL	60	0	0	28	58.2	264	62	34	28	5	4	2	1	25	2	43	6	0	2	8	.200	0	5-9	11	4.30
1998 Oakland	AL	48	0	0	22	47.1	214	48	26	21	3	4	2	1	21	2	34	3	0	1	6	.143	0	5-8	10	3.99
Anaheim	AL	12	0	0	6	11.1	50	14	8	7	2	0	0	0	4	0	9	3	0	1	2	.333	0	0-1	1	5.56
10 ML YEARS		395	6	0	211	508.2	2197	502	234	197	37	26	21	18	226	26	351	34	3	18	33	.353	0	85-112	45	3.49

Robert Fick

Bats: Left **Throws:** Right **Pos:** C-3; DH-2; 1B-1; PH/PR-1 **Ht:** 6'1" **Wt:** 189 **Born:** 3/15/74 **Age:** 25

Year Team	Lg	G	AB	H	2B	3B	HR	(Hm	Rd)	TB	R	RBI	TBB	IBB	SO	HBP	SH	SF	SB	CS	SB%	GDP	Avg	OBP	SLG
1996 Jamestown	A-	43	133	33	6	0	1	—	—	42	18	14	12	1	25	0	0	2	3	1	.75	4	.248	.306	.316
1997 W Michigan	A	122	463	158	50	3	16	—	—	262	100	90	75	11	74	1	0	7	13	4	.76	10	.341	.429	.566
1998 Jacksnville	AA	130	515	164	47	6	18	—	—	277	101	114	71	6	83	6	0	9	8	4	.67	8	.318	.401	.538
1998 Detroit	AL	7	22	8	1	0	3	(0	3)	18	6	7	2	0	7	0	0	0	1	0	1.00	1	.364	.417	.818

Cecil Fielder

Bats: Right **Throws:** Right **Pos:** 1B-75; DH-41; PH/PR-4 **Ht:** 6'3" **Wt:** 261 **Born:** 9/21/63 **Age:** 35

Year Team	Lg	G	AB	H	2B	3B	HR	(Hm	Rd)	TB	R	RBI	TBB	IBB	SO	HBP	SH	SF	SB	CS	SB%	GDP	Avg	OBP	SLG
1985 Toronto	AL	30	74	23	4	0	4	(2	2)	39	6	16	6	0	16	1	0	1	0	0	.00	2	.311	.358	.527
1986 Toronto	AL	34	83	13	2	0	4	(0	4)	27	7	13	6	0	27	1	0	0	0	0	.00	3	.157	.222	.325
1987 Toronto	AL	82	175	47	7	1	14	(10	4)	98	30	32	20	2	48	1	0	1	0	1	.00	6	.269	.345	.560
1988 Toronto	AL	74	174	40	6	1	9	(6	3)	75	24	23	14	0	53	1	0	1	0	1	.00	6	.230	.289	.431
1990 Detroit	AL	159	573	159	25	1	**51**	(25	26)	**339**	104	**132**	90	11	**182**	5	0	5	0	1	.00	15	.277	.377	**.592**
1991 Detroit	AL	**162**	624	163	25	0	**44**	(27	17)	320	102	133	78	12	151	6	0	4	0	0	.00	17	.261	.347	.513
1992 Detroit	AL	155	594	145	22	0	35	(18	17)	272	80	**124**	73	8	151	2	0	7	0	0	.00	14	.244	.325	.458
1993 Detroit	AL	154	573	153	23	0	30	(20	10)	266	80	117	90	15	125	4	0	5	0	1	.00	22	.267	.368	.464
1994 Detroit	AL	109	425	110	16	2	28	(12	16)	214	67	90	50	4	110	2	0	4	0	1	.00	17	.259	.337	.504
1995 Detroit	AL	136	494	120	18	1	31	(16	15)	233	70	82	75	8	116	5	0	4	0	1	.00	17	.243	.346	.472
1996 Det-NYA	AL	160	591	149	20	0	39	(18	21)	286	85	117	87	12	139	5	0	5	2	0	1.00	18	.252	.350	.484
1997 New York	AL	98	361	94	15	0	13	(6	7)	148	40	61	51	3	87	7	0	6	0	1	.00	14	.260	.358	.410
1998 Ana-Cle	AL	117	416	97	17	1	17	(7	10)	167	49	68	53	1	111	4	0	3	0	1	.00	18	.233	.324	.401
1996 Detroit	AL	107	391	97	12	0	26	(9	17)	187	55	80	63	8	91	3	0	3	2	0	1.00	11	.248	.354	.478
New York	AL	53	200	52	8	0	13	(9	4)	99	30	37	24	4	48	2	0	2	0	0	.00	7	.260	.342	.495
1998 Anaheim	AL	103	381	92	16	1	17	(7	10)	161	48	68	52	1	98	3	0	3	0	1	.00	17	.241	.335	.423
Cleveland	AL	14	35	5	1	0	0	(0	0)	6	1	0	1	0	13	1	0	0	0	0	.00	1	.143	.189	.171
13 ML YEARS		1470	5157	1313	200	7	319	(167	152)	2484	744	1008	693	76	1316	43	0	46	2	6	.25	169	.255	.345	.482

Mike Figga

Bats: Right **Throws:** Right **Pos:** C-1 **Ht:** 6'0" **Wt:** 200 **Born:** 7/31/70 **Age:** 28

Year Team	Lg	G	AB	H	2B	3B	HR	(Hm	Rd)	TB	R	RBI	TBB	IBB	SO	HBP	SH	SF	SB	CS	SB%	GDP	Avg	OBP	SLG
1990 Yankees	R	40	123	35	1	1	2	—	—	44	19	18	17	2	33	1	0	1	4	2	.67	2	.285	.373	.358
1991 Pr William	A+	55	174	34	6	0	3	—	—	49	15	17	19	0	51	0	2	1	2	1	.67	9	.195	.273	.282
1992 Pr William	A+	3	10	2	1	0	0	—	—	3	0	0	2	0	3	0	0	0	1	0	1.00	0	.200	.333	.300
Ft. Laud	A+	80	249	44	13	0	1	—	—	60	12	15	13	1	78	2	3	0	3	1	.75	7	.177	.223	.241
1993 San Berndno	A+	83	308	82	17	1	25	—	—	176	48	71	17	0	84	2	2	3	2	3	.40	7	.266	.306	.571
Albany-Colo	AA	6	22	5	0	0	0	—	—	5	3	2	2	0	9	0	0	0	1	0	1.00	0	.227	.292	.227
1994 Albany-Colo	AA	1	2	1	0	0	0	—	—	2	1	0	0	0	1	0	0	0	0	0	.00	0	.500	.500	1.000
Tampa	A+	111	420	116	17	5	15	—	—	188	48	75	22	1	94	2	1	5	3	0	1.00	12	.276	.312	.448
1995 Norwich	AA	109	399	108	22	4	13	—	—	177	59	61	43	3	90	1	2	6	1	0	1.00	10	.271	.339	.444
Columbus	AAA	8	25	7	1	0	1	—	—	11	2	3	3	0	5	0	1	0	0	0	.00	0	.280	.357	.440
1996 Columbus	AAA	4	11	3	1	0	0	—	—	4	3	0	1	0	3	0	0	0	0	0	.00	0	.273	.333	.364
1997 Columbus	AAA	110	390	95	14	4	12	—	—	153	48	54	18	0	104	2	1	3	3	3	.50	9	.244	.278	.392
1998 Columbus	AAA	123	461	129	30	3	26	—	—	243	57	95	35	4	109	2	0	1	2	2	.50	15	.280	.333	.527
1997 New York	AL	2	4	0	0	0	0	(0	0)	0	0	0	0	0	3	0	0	0	0	0	.00	0	.000	.000	.000
1998 New York	AL	1	4	1	0	0	0	(0	0)	1	1	0	0	0	1	0	0	0	0	0	.00	0	.250	.250	.250
2 ML YEARS		3	8	1	0	0	0			1	1	0	0	0	4	0	0	0	0	0	.00	0	.125	.125	.125

Chuck Finley

Pitches: Left **Bats:** Left **Pos:** SP-34 **Ht:** 6'6" **Wt:** 226 **Born:** 11/26/62 **Age:** 36

Year Team	Lg	G	GS	CG	GF	IP	BFP	H	R	ER	HR	SH	SF	HB	TBB	IBB	SO	WP	Bk	W	L	Pct.	ShO	Sv-Op	Hld	ERA
1986 California	AL	25	0	0	7	46.1	198	40	17	17	2	4	0	1	23	1	37	2	0	3	1	.750	0	0-0	1	3.30
1987 California	AL	35	3	0	17	90.2	405	102	54	47	7	2	2	3	43	3	63	4	3	2	7	.222	0	0-2	0	4.67
1988 California	AL	31	31	2	0	194.1	831	191	95	90	15	7	10	6	82	7	111	5	8	9	15	.375	0	0-0	0	4.17
1989 California	AL	29	29	9	0	199.2	827	171	64	57	13	7	3	2	82	0	156	4	2	16	9	.640	1	0-0	0	2.57
1990 California	AL	32	32	7	0	236	962	210	77	63	17	8	3	1	81	3	177	9	0	18	9	.667	2	0-0	0	2.40
1991 California	AL	34	34	4	0	227.1	955	205	102	96	23	4	3	8	101	1	171	6	3	18	9	.667	2	0-0	0	3.80
1992 California	AL	31	31	4	0	204.1	885	212	99	90	24	10	10	3	98	2	124	6	0	7	12	.368	1	0-0	0	3.96
1993 California	AL	35	35	13	0	251.1	1065	243	108	88	22	11	7	6	82	1	187	8	1	16	14	.533	2	0-0	0	3.15
1994 California	AL	25	**25**	7	0	**183.1**	774	178	95	88	21	**9**	6	3	71	0	148	10	0	10	10	.500	2	0-0	0	4.32
1995 California	AL	32	32	2	0	203	880	192	106	95	20	4	5	7	93	1	195	13	1	15	12	.556	1	0-0	0	4.21
1996 California	AL	35	35	4	0	238	1037	241	124	110	27	7	9	11	94	5	215	**17**	2	15	16	.484	1	0-0	0	4.16
1997 Anaheim	AL	25	25	3	0	164	690	152	79	77	20	3	4	5	65	0	155	10	2	13	6	.684	1	0-0	0	4.23
1998 Anaheim	AL	34	34	1	0	223.1	976	210	97	84	20	3	5	6	109	1	212	8	0	11	9	.550	1	0-0	0	3.39
13 ML YEARS		403	346	56	24	2461.2	10485	2347	1117	1002	231	83	67	63	1024	25	1951	102	22	153	129	.543	14	0-2	1	3.66

Steve Finley

Bats: Left **Throws:** Left **Pos:** CF-157; PH/PR-7   **Ht:** 6'2" **Wt:** 180 **Born:** 3/12/65 **Age:** 34

Year Team	Lg	G	AB	H	2B	3B	HR	(Hm	Rd)	TB	R	RBI	TBB	IBB	SO	HBP	SH	SF	SB	CS	SB%	GDP	Avg	OBP	SLG
1989 Baltimore	AL	81	217	54	5	2	2	(0	2)	69	35	25	15	1	30	1	6	2	17	3	.85	3	.249	.298	.318
1990 Baltimore	AL	142	464	119	16	4	3	(1	2)	152	46	37	32	3	53	2	10	5	22	9	.71	8	.256	.304	.328
1991 Houston	NL	159	596	170	28	10	8	(0	8)	242	84	54	42	5	65	2	10	6	34	18	.65	8	.285	.331	.406
1992 Houston	NL	162	607	177	29	13	5	(5	0)	247	84	55	58	6	63	3	16	2	44	9	.83	10	.292	.355	.407
1993 Houston	NL	142	545	145	15	13	8	(1	7)	210	69	44	28	1	65	3	6	3	19	6	.76	8	.266	.304	.385
1994 Houston	NL	94	373	103	16	5	11	(4	7)	162	64	33	28	0	52	2	13	1	13	7	.65	3	.276	.329	.434
1995 San Diego	NL	139	562	167	23	8	10	(6	4)	236	104	44	59	5	62	3	4	2	36	12	.75	8	.297	.366	.420
1996 San Diego	NL	161	655	195	45	9	30	(15	15)	348	126	95	56	5	87	4	1	5	22	8	.73	20	.298	.354	.531
1997 San Diego	NL	143	560	146	26	5	28	(5	23)	266	101	92	43	2	92	3	2	7	15	3	.83	10	.261	.313	.475
1998 San Diego	NL	159	619	154	40	6	14	(8	6)	248	92	67	45	0	103	3	3	4	12	3	.80	9	.249	.301	.401
10 ML YEARS		1382	5198	1430	243	75	119	(43	76)	2180	805	546	406	28	672	26	71	37	234	78	.75	87	.275	.329	.419

John Flaherty

Bats: Right **Throws:** Right **Pos:** C-91   **Ht:** 6'1" **Wt:** 200 **Born:** 10/21/67 **Age:** 31

Year Team	Lg	G	AB	H	2B	3B	HR	(Hm	Rd)	TB	R	RBI	TBB	IBB	SO	HBP	SH	SF	SB	CS	SB%	GDP	Avg	OBP	SLG
1998 Durham *	AAA	6	23	3	1	0	0	—	—	4	1	2	1	0	5	0	0	1	0	0	.00	1	.130	.160	.174
1992 Boston	AL	35	66	13	2	0	0	(0	0)	15	3	2	3	0	7	0	1	1	0	0	.00	0	.197	.229	.227
1993 Boston	AL	13	25	3	0	0	0	(0	0)	5	3	2	2	0	6	1	1	0	0	0	.00	0	.120	.214	.200
1994 Detroit	AL	34	40	6	1	0	0	(0	0)	7	2	4	1	0	11	0	2	1	0	1	.00	1	.150	.167	.175
1995 Detroit	AL	112	354	86	22	1	11	(6	5)	143	39	40	18	0	47	3	8	2	0	0	.00	8	.243	.284	.404
1996 Det-SD		119	416	118	24	0	13	(8	5)	181	40	64	17	2	61	3	4	4	3	3	.50	13	.284	.314	.435
1997 San Diego	NL	129	439	120	21	1	9	(4	5)	170	38	46	33	7	62	0	2	2	4	4	.50	11	.273	.323	.387
1998 Tampa Bay	AL	91	304	63	11	0	3	(1	2)	83	21	24	22	0	46	1	4	3	0	5	.00	9	.207	.261	.273
1996 Detroit	AL	47	152	38	12	0	4	(2	2)	62	18	23	8	1	25	1	3	1	1	0	1.00	5	.250	.290	.408
San Diego	NL	72	264	80	12	0	9	(6	3)	119	22	41	9	1	36	2	1	3	2	3	.40	8	.303	.327	.451
7 ML YEARS		533	1644	409	83	2	36	(19	17)	604	146	182	96	9	240	8	22	13	7	13	.35	42	.249	.291	.367

Darrin Fletcher

Bats: Left **Throws:** Right **Pos:** C-121; PH/PR-8; DH-1   **Ht:** 6'1" **Wt:** 200 **Born:** 10/3/66 **Age:** 32

Year Team	Lg	G	AB	H	2B	3B	HR	(Hm	Rd)	TB	R	RBI	TBB	IBB	SO	HBP	SH	SF	SB	CS	SB%	GDP	Avg	OBP	SLG
1989 Los Angeles	NL	5	8	4	0	0	1	(1	0)	7	1	2	1	0	0	0	0	0	0	0	.00	0	.500	.556	.875
1990 LA-Phi	NL	11	23	3	1	0	0	(0	0)	4	3	1	1	0	6	0	0	0	0	0	.00	0	.130	.167	.174
1991 Philadelphia	NL	46	136	31	8	0	1	(1	0)	42	5	12	5	0	15	0	1	0	0	1	.00	2	.228	.255	.309
1992 Montreal	NL	83	222	54	10	2	2	(0	2)	74	13	26	14	3	28	2	2	4	0	2	.00	8	.243	.289	.333
1993 Montreal	NL	133	396	101	20	1	9	(5	4)	150	33	60	34	2	40	6	5	4	0	0	.00	7	.255	.320	.379
1994 Montreal	NL	94	285	74	18	1	10	(4	6)	124	28	57	25	4	23	0	0	12	0	0	.00	6	.260	.314	.435
1995 Montreal	NL	110	350	100	21	1	11	(3	8)	156	42	45	32	1	23	4	1	2	0	1	.00	15	.286	.351	.446
1996 Montreal	NL	127	394	105	22	0	12	(7	5)	163	41	57	27	4	42	6	1	3	0	0	.00	13	.266	.321	.414
1997 Montreal	NL	96	310	86	20	1	17	(10	7)	159	39	55	17	3	35	5	0	2	1	1	.50	6	.277	.323	.513
1998 Toronto	AL	124	407	115	23	1	9	(3	6)	167	37	52	25	7	39	6	1	7	0	0	.00	19	.283	.328	.410
1990 Los Angeles	NL	2	1	0	0	0	0	(0	0)	0	0	0	0	0	1	0	0	0	0	0	.00	0	.000	.000	.000
Philadelphia	NL	9	22	3	1	0	0	(0	0)	4	3	1	1	0	5	0	0	0	0	0	.00	0	.136	.174	.182
10 ML YEARS		829	2531	673	143	7	72	(34	38)	1046	242	367	181	24	251	32	11	34	1	5	.17	76	.266	.319	.413

Bryce Florie

Pitches: Right **Bats:** Right **Pos:** RP-26; SP-16   **Ht:** 5'11" **Wt:** 192 **Born:** 5/21/70 **Age:** 29

		HOW MUCH HE PITCHED						WHAT HE GAVE UP										THE RESULTS				
Year Team	Lg	G	GS	CG	GF	IP	BFP	H	R	ER	HR	SH	SF	HB	TBB	IBB	SO	WP	Bk	W	L	Pct.	ShO	Sv-Op	Hld	ERA
1998 Toledo *	AAA	1	1	0	0	4	12	0	0	0	0	0	0	0	3	0	3	0	0	0	0	.000	0	0- -	—	0.00
1994 San Diego	NL	9	0	0	4	9.1	37	8	1	1	0	0	1	0	3	0	8	1	0	0	0	.000	0	0-0	0	0.96
1995 San Diego	NL	47	0	0	10	68.2	290	49	30	23	8	5	1	4	38	3	68	7	2	2	2	.500	0	1-4	9	3.01
1996 SD-Mil		54	0	0	16	68.1	312	65	40	36	4	1	3	6	40	5	63	6	1	2	3	.400	0	0-3	8	4.74
1997 Milwaukee	AL	32	8	0	6	75	332	74	43	36	4	1	4	3	42	2	53	4	1	4	4	.500	0	0-1	0	4.32
1998 Detroit	AL	42	16	0	6	133	580	141	80	71	16	3	2	4	59	6	97	9	0	8	9	.471	0	0-0	4	4.80
1996 San Diego	NL	39	0	0	11	49.1	222	45	24	22	1	0	1	6	27	3	51	3	1	2	2	.500	0	0-1	4	4.01
Milwaukee	AL	15	0	0	5	19	90	20	16	14	3	1	2	0	13	2	12	3	0	0	1	.000	0	0-2	4	6.63
5 ML YEARS		184	24	0	42	354.1	1551	337	194	167	32	10	11	17	182	16	289	27	4	16	18	.471	0	1-8	21	4.24

Cliff Floyd

Bats: L **Throws:** R **Pos:** LF-146; PH/PR-5; DH-3; CF-2   **Ht:** 6'4" **Wt:** 235 **Born:** 12/5/72 **Age:** 26

Year Team	Lg	G	AB	H	2B	3B	HR	(Hm	Rd)	TB	R	RBI	TBB	IBB	SO	HBP	SH	SF	SB	CS	SB%	GDP	Avg	OBP	SLG
1993 Montreal	NL	10	31	7	0	0	1	(0	1)	10	3	2	0	0	9	0	0	0	0	0	.00	0	.226	.226	.323
1994 Montreal	NL	100	334	94	19	4	4	(2	2)	133	43	41	24	0	63	3	2	3	10	3	.77	3	.281	.332	.398
1995 Montreal	NL	29	69	9	1	0	1	(1	0)	13	6	8	7	0	22	1	0	0	3	0	1.00	3	.130	.221	.188
1996 Montreal	NL	117	227	55	15	4	6	(3	3)	96	29	26	30	1	52	5	1	3	7	1	.88	3	.242	.340	.423
1997 Florida	NL	61	137	32	9	1	6	(2	4)	61	23	19	24	0	33	2	1	1	6	2	.75	3	.234	.354	.445
1998 Florida	NL	153	588	166	45	3	22	(10	12)	283	85	90	47	7	112	3	0	3	27	14	.66	10	.282	.337	.481

			BATTING																	BASERUNNING				PERCENTAGES		
Year Team	Lg	G	AB	H	2B	3B	HR	(Hm	Rd)	TB	R	RBI	TBB	IBB	SO	HBP	SH	SF	SB	CS	SB%	GDP	Avg	OBP	SLG
6 ML YEARS		470	1386	363	89	12	40	(18	22)	596	189	186	132	8	291	14	4	10	53	20	.73	20	.262	.330	.430

Joe Fontenot

Pitches: Right **Bats:** Right **Pos:** SP-8　　　　**Ht:** 6'2" **Wt:** 185 **Born:** 3/20/77 **Age:** 22

		HOW MUCH HE PITCHED						WHAT HE GAVE UP										THE RESULTS						
Year Team	Lg	G	GS	CG	GF	IP	BFP	H	R	ER	HR	SH	SF	HB	TBB	IBB	SO	WP	Bk	W	L	Pct.	ShO	Sv-Op	Hld	ERA
1995 Bellingham	A-	6	6	0	0	18.2	77	14	5	4	0	0	0	0	10	0	14	0	2	0	3	.000	0	0- --	--	1.93
1996 San Jose	A+	26	23	0	1	144	642	137	87	71	7	10	6	11	74	0	124	13	1	9	4	.692	0	0- --	--	4.44
1997 Shreveport	AA	26	26	1	0	151.1	688	171	105	93	12	8	1	12	65	0	103	10	0	10	11	.476	0	0- --	--	5.53
1998 Portland	AA	7	7	0	0	38	167	37	16	13	1	2	1	4	13	1	31	3	0	3	1	.750	0	0- --	--	3.08
Charlotte	AAA	1	1	0	0	3	15	4	4	4	1	0	0	0	2	0	0	0	0	0	1	.000	0	0- --	--	12.00
1998 Florida	NL	8	8	0	0	42.2	204	56	34	30	5	3	1	5	20	1	24	6	0	0	7	.000	0	0-0	0	6.33

P.J. Forbes

Bats: Right **Throws:** Right **Pos:** 2B-7; PH/PR-2; 3B-1; SS-1　　　**Ht:** 5'10" **Wt:** 160 **Born:** 9/22/67 **Age:** 31

			BATTING																	BASERUNNING				PERCENTAGES		
Year Team	Lg	G	AB	H	2B	3B	HR	(Hm	Rd)	TB	R	RBI	TBB	IBB	SO	HBP	SH	SF	SB	CS	SB%	GDP	Avg	OBP	SLG
1990 Boise	A-	43	170	42	9	1	0	—	—	53	29	19	23	1	21	0	7	1	11	4	.73	5	.247	.335	.312
1991 Palm Spring	A+	94	349	93	14	2	2	—	—	117	45	26	36	1	44	4	12	0	18	8	.69	7	.266	.342	.335
1992 Quad City	A	105	376	106	16	5	2	—	—	138	53	46	44	1	51	2	24	5	15	6	.71	4	.282	.356	.367
1993 Midland	AA	126	498	159	23	2	15	—	—	231	90	64	26	1	50	4	14	2	6	8	.43	13	.319	.357	.464
Vancouver	AAA	5	16	4	2	0	0	—	—	6	1	3	0	0	3	0	1	0	0	0	.00	1	.250	.250	.375
1994 Angels	R	2	6	0	0	0	0	—	—	0	1	0	0	0	1	0	0	0	0	0	.00	0	.000	.000	.000
Vancouver	AAA	90	318	91	21	2	1	—	—	119	39	40	22	0	42	2	7	5	4	2	.67	6	.286	.331	.374
1995 Vancouver	AAA	109	369	101	22	3	1	—	—	132	47	52	21	0	46	2	7	10	4	6	.40	4	.274	.308	.358
1996 Vancouver	AAA	117	409	112	24	2	0	—	—	140	58	46	42	3	44	5	10	4	4	3	.57	13	.274	.346	.342
1997 Rochester	AAA	116	434	118	22	2	8	—	—	168	67	54	35	0	42	6	8	3	15	4	.79	11	.272	.333	.387
1998 Rochester	AAA	116	460	135	37	3	6	—	—	196	74	52	36	1	54	8	3	8	10	2	.83	15	.293	.349	.426
1998 Baltimore	AL	9	10	1	0	0	0	(0	0)	1	0	2	0	0	0	0	0	0	0	0	.00	0	.100	.100	.100

Ben Ford

Pitches: Right **Bats:** Right **Pos:** RP-8　　　　**Ht:** 6'7" **Wt:** 200 **Born:** 8/15/75 **Age:** 23

		HOW MUCH HE PITCHED						WHAT HE GAVE UP										THE RESULTS						
Year Team	Lg	G	GS	CG	GF	IP	BFP	H	R	ER	HR	SH	SF	HB	TBB	IBB	SO	WP	Bk	W	L	Pct.	ShO	Sv-Op	Hld	ERA
1994 Yankees	R	18	0	0	11	34	143	27	13	9	0	0	0	6	8	0	31	3	0	2	2	.500	0	3- --	--	2.38
1995 Greensboro	A	7	0	0	2	7	31	4	4	4	1	1	0	0	5	1	8	2	0	0	0	.000	0	0- --	--	5.14
Oneonta	A-	29	0	0	10	52	224	39	23	5	1	0	2	5	16	0	50	8	0	5	0	1.000	0	0- --	--	0.87
1996 Greensboro	A	43	0	0	16	82.1	359	75	48	39	3	4	1	11	33	6	84	9	0	2	6	.250	0	2- --	--	4.26
1997 Tampa	A+	32	0	0	30	37.1	155	27	8	8	1	2	0	6	14	1	37	4	0	4	0	1.000	0	18- --	--	1.93
Norwich	AA	28	0	0	14	42.2	183	35	28	20	1	1	2	3	19	1	38	4	0	4	3	.571	0	1- --	--	4.22
1998 Tucson	AAA	48	0	0	36	68.1	313	68	41	33	6	3	3	2	33	5	63	7	1	2	5	.286	0	13- --	--	4.35
1998 Arizona	NL	8	0	0	2	10	49	13	12	11	2	0	0	2	3	0	5	1	0	0	0	.000	0	0-0	0	9.90

Tom Fordham

Pitches: Left **Bats:** Left **Pos:** RP-24; SP-5　　　**Ht:** 6'2" **Wt:** 205 **Born:** 2/20/74 **Age:** 25

		HOW MUCH HE PITCHED						WHAT HE GAVE UP										THE RESULTS						
Year Team	Lg	G	GS	CG	GF	IP	BFP	H	R	ER	HR	SH	SF	HB	TBB	IBB	SO	WP	Bk	W	L	Pct.	ShO	Sv-Op	Hld	ERA
1993 White Sox	R	3	0	0	1	10	41	9	2	2	0	0	0	0	3	0	12	1	0	1	1	.500	0	0- --	--	1.80
Sarasota	A+	2	0	0	1	5	21	3	1	0	0	0	0	0	3	2	5	1	1	0	0	.000	0	0- --	--	0.00
Hickory	A	8	8	1	0	48.2	194	36	21	21	3	1	6	0	21	0	27	3	2	4	3	.571	1	0- --	--	3.88
1994 Hickory	A	17	17	1	0	109	452	101	47	38	10	1	1	3	30	1	121	5	4	10	5	.667	1	0- --	--	3.14
South Bend	A	11	11	0	0	74.2	315	82	46	36	4	4	3	0	14	0	48	4	0	4	4	.500	1	0- --	--	4.34
1995 Pr William	A+	13	13	1	0	84	340	66	20	19	7	2	1	2	35	2	78	1	0	9	0	1.000	1	0- --	--	2.04
Birmingham	AA	14	14	2	0	82.2	348	79	35	31	9	2	2	0	28	2	61	3	0	6	3	.667	1	0- --	--	3.38
1996 Birmingham	AA	6	6	0	0	37.1	147	26	13	11	4	0	2	0	14	1	37	2	0	2	1	.667	0	0- --	--	2.65
Nashville	AAA	22	22	3	0	140.2	589	117	60	54	15	4	2	4	69	1	118	7	1	10	8	.556	2	0- --	--	3.45
1997 Nashville	AAA	21	20	2	0	114	493	113	64	60	14	1	5	1	53	1	90	6	1	4	7	.462	0	0- --	--	4.74
1998 Calgary	AAA	9	9	0	0	56.2	225	38	21	19	6	1	3	0	26	0	39	3	0	4	2	.667	0	0- --	--	3.02
1997 Chicago	AL	7	1	0	1	17.1	78	17	13	12	2	1	2	1	10	2	10	0	0	1	0	1.000	0	0-1	1	6.23
1998 Chicago	AL	29	5	0	5	48	228	51	36	36	7	1	1	1	42	0	23	1	0	1	2	.333	0	0-0	0	6.75
2 ML YEARS		36	6	0	6	65.1	306	68	49	48	9	2	3	2	52	2	33	1	0	1	3	.250	0	0-1	1	6.61

Brook Fordyce

Bats: Right **Throws:** Right **Pos:** C-54; PH/PR-5　　　**Ht:** 6'1" **Wt:** 185 **Born:** 5/7/70 **Age:** 29

			BATTING																	BASERUNNING				PERCENTAGES		
Year Team	Lg	G	AB	H	2B	3B	HR	(Hm	Rd)	TB	R	RBI	TBB	IBB	SO	HBP	SH	SF	SB	CS	SB%	GDP	Avg	OBP	SLG
1998 Indianapols *	AAA	6	24	6	1	0	2	—	—	13	4	3	1	0	2	0	0	0	0	0	.00	1	.250	.280	.542
1995 New York	NL	4	2	1	1	0	0	(0	0)	2	1	0	1	0	0	0	0	0	0	0	.00	0	.500	.667	1.000
1996 Cincinnati	NL	4	7	2	1	0	0	(0	0)	3	0	1	3	0	1	0	0	0	0	0	.00	0	.286	.500	.429
1997 Cincinnati	NL	47	96	20	5	0	1	(1	0)	28	7	8	8	1	15	0	0	1	2	0	1.00	0	.208	.267	.292
1998 Cincinnati	NL	57	146	37	9	0	3	(3	0)	55	8	14	11	3	28	0	1	0	0	1	.00	2	.253	.306	.377
4 ML YEARS		112	251	60	16	0	4	(4	0)	88	16	23	23	4	44	0	1	1	2	1	.67	2	.239	.302	.351

Tony Fossas

Pitches: Left **Bats:** Left **Pos:** RP-41 **Ht:** 6'0" **Wt:** 198 **Born:** 9/23/57 **Age:** 41

Year Team	Lg	G	GS	CG	GF	IP	BFP	H	R	ER	HR	SH	SF	HB	TBB	IBB	SO	WP	Bk	W	L	Pct.	ShO	Sv-Op	Hld	ERA
1998 Iowa *	AAA	10	0	0	5	5	26	10	4	2	0	0	0	0	2	0	2	0	0	0	0	.000	0	0--	--	3.60
Oklahoma *	AAA	4	0	0	3	6.2	27	6	4	4	0	1	0	0	4	1	3	0	0	0	0	.000	0	0--	--	5.40
1988 Texas	AL	5	0	0	1	5.2	28	11	3	3	0	0	0	0	2	0	1	0	0	0	0	.000	0	0-0	0	4.76
1989 Milwaukee	AL	51	0	0	16	61	256	57	27	24	3	7	3	1	22	7	42	1	3	2	2	.500	0	1-3	13	3.54
1990 Milwaukee	AL	32	0	0	9	29.1	146	44	23	21	5	2	1	0	10	2	24	0	0	2	3	.400	0	0-2	8	6.44
1991 Boston	AL	64	0	0	18	57	244	49	27	22	3	5	0	3	28	9	29	2	0	3	2	.600	0	1-2	18	3.47
1992 Boston	AL	60	0	0	17	29.2	129	31	9	8	1	3	0	1	14	3	19	0	0	1	2	.333	0	2-3	14	2.43
1993 Boston	AL	71	0	0	19	40	175	38	28	23	4	0	1	2	15	4	39	1	1	1	1	.500	0	0-2	13	5.18
1994 Boston	AL	44	0	0	14	34	151	35	18	18	6	2	0	1	15	1	31	1	0	2	0	1.000	0	1-1	9	4.76
1995 St. Louis	NL	58	0	0	20	36.2	145	28	6	6	1	2	1	1	10	3	40	1	0	3	0	1.000	0	0-0	19	1.47
1996 St. Louis	NL	65	0	0	11	47	209	43	19	14	7	1	1	0	21	3	36	3	0	1	0	1.000	0	2-7	15	2.68
1997 St. Louis	NL	71	0	0	14	51.2	239	62	32	22	7	3	1	1	26	3	41	0	0	2	7	.222	0	0-1	16	3.83
1998 Sea-ChN-Tex		41	0	0	10	22.2	110	30	15	15	1	2	1	0	16	0	23	1	0	1	3	.250	0	0-1	4	5.96
1998 Seattle	AL	23	0	0	8	11.1	55	19	11	11	1	1	1	0	6	0	10	0	0	0	3	.000	0	0-1	3	8.74
Chicago	NL	8	0	0	1	4	26	8	4	4	0	1	0	0	6	0	6	0	0	0	0	.000	0	0-0	1	9.00
Texas	AL	10	0	0	1	7.1	29	3	0	0	0	0	0	0	4	0	7	1	0	1	0	1.000	0	0-0	0	0.00
11 ML YEARS		562	0	0	149	414.2	1832	428	207	176	38	27	9	10	179	35	324	11	4	17	24	.415	0	7-22	129	3.82

Kevin Foster

Pitches: Right **Bats:** Right **Pos:** RP-3 **Ht:** 6'1" **Wt:** 175 **Born:** 1/13/69 **Age:** 30

Year Team	Lg	G	GS	CG	GF	IP	BFP	H	R	ER	HR	SH	SF	HB	TBB	IBB	SO	WP	Bk	W	L	Pct.	ShO	Sv-Op	Hld	ERA
1998 Daytona *	A+	3	0	0	0	2.2	19	2	7	3	1	0	0	0	7	1	3	0	0	0	0	.000	0	0--	--	10.13
West Tenn *	AA	2	0	0	0	4	17	5	1	1	0	0	0	0	1	0	5	0	0	1	0	1.000	0	0--	--	2.25
Iowa *	AAA	17	11	1	4	67	300	74	52	51	19	1	2	0	38	0	75	5	0	5	6	.455	1	0--	--	6.85
1993 Philadelphia	NL	2	1	0	0	6.2	40	13	11	11	3	0	0	0	7	0	6	2	0	0	1	.000	0	0-0	0	14.85
1994 Chicago	NL	13	13	0	0	81	337	70	31	26	7	1	1	1	35	1	75	1	1	3	4	.429	0	0-0	0	2.89
1995 Chicago	NL	30	28	0	0	167.2	703	149	90	84	32	4	6	6	65	4	146	2	2	12	11	.522	0	0-0	0	4.51
1996 Chicago	NL	17	16	1	0	87	386	98	63	60	16	5	4	2	35	3	53	2	0	7	6	.538	0	0-0	0	6.21
1997 Chicago	NL	26	25	1	0	146.1	637	141	79	75	27	9	7	2	66	4	118	3	0	10	7	.588	0	0-0	0	4.61
1998 Chicago	NL	3	0	0	1	3.1	20	8	6	6	1	0	2	0	2	0	3	0	0	0	0	.000	0	0-0	0	16.20
6 ML YEARS		91	83	2	2	492	2123	479	280	262	86	19	20	11	210	12	401	10	3	32	29	.525	0	0-0	0	4.79

Keith Foulke

Pitches: Right **Bats:** Right **Pos:** RP-54 **Ht:** 6'0" **Wt:** 200 **Born:** 10/19/72 **Age:** 26

Year Team	Lg	G	GS	CG	GF	IP	BFP	H	R	ER	HR	SH	SF	HB	TBB	IBB	SO	WP	Bk	W	L	Pct.	ShO	Sv-Op	Hld	ERA
1994 Everett	A-	4	4	0	0	19.1	79	17	4	2	0	1	0	2	3	0	22	0	0	2	0	1.000	0	0--	--	0.93
1995 San Jose	A+	28	26	2	0	177.1	723	166	85	69	16	10	3	7	32	0	168	6	2	13	6	.684	1	0--	--	3.50
1996 Shreveport	AA	27	27	4	0	182.2	712	149	61	56	16	6	7	3	35	0	129	6	1	12	7	.632	2	0--	--	2.76
1997 Phoenix	AAA	12	12	0	0	76	321	79	38	38	11	2	5	6	15	0	54	1	2	5	4	.556	0	0--	--	4.50
Nashville	AAA	1	1	0	0	4.2	20	8	3	3	1	0	0	0	0	0	4	1	0	0	0	.000	0	0--	--	5.79
1997 SF-ChA		27	8	0	0	73.1	326	88	52	52	13	3	1	4	23	2	54	1	0	4	5	.444	0	3-6	5	6.38
1998 Chicago	AL	54	0	0	18	65.1	267	51	31	30	9	2	2	4	20	3	57	3	1	3	2	.600	0	1-2	13	4.13
1997 San Francisco	NL	11	8	0	0	44.2	209	60	41	41	9	2	0	4	18	1	33	1	0	1	5	.167	0	0-1	0	8.26
Chicago	AL	16	0	0	5	28.2	117	28	11	11	4	1	1	0	5	1	21	0	0	3	0	1.000	0	3-5	5	3.45
2 ML YEARS		81	8	0	23	138.2	593	139	83	82	22	5	3	8	43	5	111	4	1	7	7	.500	0	4-8	18	5.32

Andy Fox

Bats: L **Throws:** R **Pos:** 2B-60; RF-33; 3B-26; PH/PR-15; 1B-12; LF-10; CF-8 **Ht:** 6'4" **Wt:** 205 **Born:** 1/12/71 **Age:** 28

Year Team	Lg	G	AB	H	2B	3B	HR	(Hm	Rd)	TB	R	RBI	TBB	IBB	SO	HBP	SH	SF	SB	CS	SB%	GDP	Avg	OBP	SLG
1996 New York	AL	113	189	37	4	0	3	(1	2)	50	26	13	20	0	28	1	9	0	11	3	.79	2	.196	.276	.265
1997 New York	AL	22	31	7	1	0	0	(0	0)	8	13	1	7	0	9	0	2	0	1	1	.67	1	.226	.368	.258
1998 Arizona	NL	139	502	139	21	6	9	(5	4)	199	67	44	43	0	97	18	0	1	14	7	.67	2	.277	.355	.396
3 ML YEARS		274	722	183	26	6	12	(6	6)	257	106	58	70	0	134	19	11	1	27	11	.71	5	.253	.335	.356

Chad Fox

Pitches: Right **Bats:** Right **Pos:** RP-49 **Ht:** 6'3" **Wt:** 175 **Born:** 9/3/70 **Age:** 28

Year Team	Lg	G	GS	CG	GF	IP	BFP	H	R	ER	HR	SH	SF	HB	TBB	IBB	SO	WP	Bk	W	L	Pct.	ShO	Sv-Op	Hld	ERA
1992 Princeton	R+	15	8	0	4	49.1	238	55	43	26	2	1	1	2	34	1	37	6	2	4	2	.667	0	0--	--	4.74
1993 Chston-WV	A	27	26	0	0	135.2	638	138	100	81	7	6	8	13	97	0	81	15	1	9	12	.429	0	0--	--	5.37
1994 Winston-Sal	A+	25	25	1	0	156.1	674	121	77	67	18	5	5	9	94	0	137	20	1	12	5	.706	0	0--	--	3.86
1995 Chattanooga	AA	20	17	0	1	80	363	76	49	45	2	2	3	2	52	1	56	14	0	4	5	.444	0	0--	--	5.06
1996 Richmond	AAA	18	18	1	0	93.1	415	91	57	49	9	8	6	3	49	1	87	8	1	3	10	.231	0	0--	--	4.73
1997 Richmond	AAA	13	0	0	0	24.1	105	24	10	10	1	2	1	0	14	0	25	4	0	1	0	1.000	0	0--	--	3.70
1998 Beloit	A	2	1	0	0	2	7	1	1	1	0	1	0	0	0	0	3	0	0	0	0	.000	0	0--	--	4.50
1997 Atlanta	NL	30	0	0	8	27.1	120	24	12	10	4	0	0	0	16	0	28	4	0	0	1	.000	0	0-1	7	3.29
1998 Milwaukee	NL	49	0	0	12	57	242	56	27	25	4	4	1	0	20	0	64	5	0	0	1	.200	0	0-2	20	3.95

Year Team	Lg	G	GS	CG	GF	IP	BFP	H	R	ER	HR	SH	SF	HB	TBB	IBB	SO	WP	Bk	W	L	Pct.	ShO	Sv-Op	Hld	ERA
2 ML YEARS		79	0	0	20	84.1	362	80	39	35	8	6	0	1	36	0	92	9	0	1	5	.167	0	0-3	27	3.74

John Franco

Pitches: Left **Bats:** Left **Pos:** RP-61 **Ht:** 5'10" **Wt:** 185 **Born:** 9/17/60 **Age:** 38

				HOW MUCH HE PITCHED				WHAT HE GAVE UP												THE RESULTS						
Year Team	Lg	G	GS	CG	GF	IP	BFP	H	R	ER	HR	SH	SF	HB	TBB	IBB	SO	WP	Bk	W	L	Pct.	ShO	Sv-Op	Hld	ERA
1984 Cincinnati	NL	54	0	0	30	79.1	335	74	28	23	3	4	4	2	36	4	55	2	0	6	2	.750	0	4-8	2	2.61
1985 Cincinnati	NL	67	0	0	33	99	407	83	27	24	5	11	1	1	40	8	61	4	0	12	3	.800	0	12-14	11	2.18
1986 Cincinnati	NL	74	0	0	52	101	429	90	40	33	7	8	3	2	44	12	84	4	2	6	6	.500	0	29-38	2	2.94
1987 Cincinnati	NL	68	0	0	60	82	344	76	26	23	6	5	2	0	27	6	61	1	0	8	5	.615	0	32-41	0	2.52
1988 Cincinnati	NL	70	0	0	61	86	336	60	18	15	3	5	1	0	27	3	46	1	0	6	6	.500	0	**39-42**	1	1.57
1989 Cincinnati	NL	60	0	0	50	80.2	345	77	35	28	3	7	3	0	36	8	60	3	2	4	8	.333	0	32-39	1	3.12
1990 New York	NL	55	0	0	48	67.2	287	66	22	19	4	3	1	0	21	2	56	7	2	5	3	.625	0	**33-39**	0	2.53
1991 New York	NL	52	0	0	48	55.1	247	61	27	18	2	3	0	1	18	4	45	6	0	5	9	.357	0	30-35	0	2.93
1992 New York	NL	31	0	0	30	33	128	24	6	6	1	0	2	0	11	2	20	0	0	6	2	.750	0	15-17	1	1.64
1993 New York	NL	35	0	0	30	36.1	172	46	24	21	6	4	1	1	19	3	29	5	0	4	3	.571	0	10-17	0	5.20
1994 New York	NL	47	0	0	43	50	216	47	20	15	2	2	1	1	19	0	42	1	0	1	4	.200	0	**30-36**	0	2.70
1995 New York	NL	48	0	0	41	51.2	213	48	17	14	4	4	1	0	17	2	41	0	0	5	3	.625	0	29-36	0	2.44
1996 New York	NL	51	0	0	44	54	235	54	15	11	2	6	0	0	21	0	48	2	0	4	3	.571	0	28-36	0	1.83
1997 New York	NL	59	0	0	53	60	244	49	18	17	3	4	5	3	20	2	53	6	0	5	3	.625	0	36-42	0	2.55
1998 New York	NL	61	0	0	53	64.2	289	66	28	26	4	4	5	4	29	7	59	2	0	0	8	.000	0	38-46	0	3.62
15 ML YEARS		832	0	0	677	1000.2	4227	921	351	293	55	71	26	13	385	63	760	44	8	77	68	.531	0	397-486	18	2.64

Matt Franco

Bats: L **Throws:** R **Pos:** PH/PR-71; 3B-13; LF-12; 1B-11; DH-2; RF-1 **Ht:** 6'1" **Wt:** 210 **Born:** 8/19/69 **Age:** 29

					BATTING													BASERUNNING				PERCENTAGES		
Year Team	Lg	G	AB	H	2B	3B	HR	(Hm | Rd)	TB	R	RBI	TBB	IBB	SO	HBP	SH	SF	SB	CS	SB%	GDP	Avg	OBP	SLG
1998 Norfolk *	AAA	5	19	7	1	0	0	—	—	8	2	1	3	0	1	0	0	0	2	0	1.00	1	.368	.455	.421
1995 Chicago	NL	16	17	5	1	0	0	(0 | 0)	6	3	1	0	0	4	0	0	0	0	0	.00	0	.294	.294	.353
1996 New York	NL	14	31	6	1	0	1	(0 | 1)	10	3	2	1	0	5	1	0	1	0	0	.00	1	.194	.235	.323
1997 New York	NL	112	163	45	5	0	5	(3 | 2)	65	21	21	13	4	23	0	0	0	1	0	1.00	6	.276	.330	.399
1998 New York	NL	103	161	44	7	2	1	(1 | 0)	58	20	13	23	6	26	1	0	1	0	1	.00	8	.273	.366	.360
4 ML YEARS		245	372	100	14	2	7	(4 | 3)	139	47	37	37	10	58	2	0	2	1	1	.50	13	.269	.337	.374

Mike Frank

Bats: L **Throws:** L **Pos:** CF-25; RF-2; LF-1; PH/PR-1 **Ht:** 6'2" **Wt:** 190 **Born:** 1/14/75 **Age:** 24

					BATTING													BASERUNNING				PERCENTAGES		
Year Team	Lg	G	AB	H	2B	3B	HR	(Hm | Rd)	TB	R	RBI	TBB	IBB	SO	HBP	SH	SF	SB	CS	SB%	GDP	Avg	OBP	SLG
1997 Billings	R+	69	266	100	22	6	10	—	—	164	62	62	35	5	24	2	0	3	18	8	.69	7	.376	.448	.617
1998 Indianapolis	AAA	22	88	30	4	0	0	—	—	34	8	13	7	0	9	0	0	0	1	0	1.00	1	.341	.389	.386
Chattanooga	AA	58	231	75	12	4	12	—	—	131	43	43	19	1	28	1	0	3	5	2	.71	3	.325	.374	.567
1998 Cincinnati	NL	28	89	20	6	0	0	(0 | 0)	26	14	7	7	0	12	0	1	1	0	0	.00	3	.225	.278	.292

John Frascatore

Pitches: Right **Bats:** Right **Pos:** RP-69 **Ht:** 6'1" **Wt:** 210 **Born:** 2/4/70 **Age:** 29

				HOW MUCH HE PITCHED				WHAT HE GAVE UP												THE RESULTS						
Year Team	Lg	G	GS	CG	GF	IP	BFP	H	R	ER	HR	SH	SF	HB	TBB	IBB	SO	WP	Bk	W	L	Pct.	ShO	Sv-Op	Hld	ERA
1994 St. Louis	NL	1	1	0	0	3.1	16	7	6	6	2	0	0	2	0	2	1	0	0	1	0	1.000	0	0-0	0	16.20
1995 St. Louis	NL	14	4	0	3	32.2	151	39	19	16	3	1	1	2	16	1	21	0	0	1	1	.500	0	0-0	0	4.41
1997 St. Louis	NL	59	0	0	17	80	348	74	25	22	5	5	5	6	33	5	58	4	0	5	2	.714	0	0-4	3	2.48
1998 St. Louis	NL	69	0	0	15	95.2	415	95	48	44	11	4	1	3	36	3	49	2	0	3	4	.429	0	0-2	13	4.14
4 ML YEARS		143	5	0	35	211.2	932	215	98	88	21	10	7	11	87	9	130	7	0	9	8	.529	0	0-6	16	3.74

Lou Frazier

Bats: Both **Throws:** Right **Pos:** PH/PR-4; CF-3; DH-1 **Ht:** 6'2" **Wt:** 175 **Born:** 1/26/65 **Age:** 34

					BATTING													BASERUNNING				PERCENTAGES		
Year Team	Lg	G	AB	H	2B	3B	HR	(Hm | Rd)	TB	R	RBI	TBB	IBB	SO	HBP	SH	SF	SB	CS	SB%	GDP	Avg	OBP	SLG
1998 Calgary *	AAA	101	397	107	26	3	14	—	—	181	81	50	57	1	84	3	2	2	42	8	.84	2	.270	.364	.456
1993 Montreal	NL	112	189	54	7	1	1	(1 | 0)	66	27	16	16	0	24	0	5	1	17	2	.89	3	.286	.340	.349
1994 Montreal	NL	76	140	38	3	1	0	(0 | 0)	43	25	14	18	0	23	1	1	0	20	4	.83	1	.271	.358	.307
1995 Mon-Tex		84	162	33	4	0	0	(0 | 0)	37	25	11	15	0	32	4	3	1	13	1	.93	3	.204	.286	.228
1996 Texas	AL	30	50	13	2	1	0	(0 | 0)	17	5	5	8	0	10	1	1	0	4	2	.67	2	.260	.373	.340
1998 Chicago	AL	7	7	0	0	0	0	(0 | 0)	0	0	0	2	0	6	0	1	0	4	0	1.00	0	.000	.222	.000
1995 Montreal	NL	35	63	12	2	0	0	(0 | 0)	14	6	3	8	0	12	2	0	1	4	0	1.00	1	.190	.297	.222
Texas	AL	49	99	21	2	0	0	(0 | 0)	23	19	8	7	0	20	2	3	0	9	1	.90	2	.212	.278	.232
5 ML YEARS		309	548	138	16	3	1	(1 | 0)	163	82	46	59	0	95	6	11	2	58	9	.87	9	.252	.330	.297

Hanley Frias

Bats: Both **Throws:** Right **Pos:** PH/PR-9; 2B-3; 3B-2; SS-2 **Ht:** 6'0" **Wt:** 165 **Born:** 12/5/73 **Age:** 25

Year Team	Lg	G	AB	H	2B	3B	HR	(Hm	Rd)	TB	R	RBI	TBB	IBB	SO	HBP	SH	SF	SB	CS	SB%	GDP	Avg	OBP	SLG
1992 Rangers	R	58	205	50	9	2	0	—	—	63	37	28	27	0	30	2	2	5	28	6	.82	1	.244	.335	.307
1993 Chston-SC	A	132	473	109	20	4	4	—	—	149	61	37	40	0	108	3	4	4	27	14	.66	8	.230	.292	.315
1994 High Desert	A+	124	452	115	17	6	3	—	—	153	70	59	41	1	74	2	5	3	37	12	.76	9	.254	.317	.338
1995 Charlotte	A+	33	120	40	6	3	0	—	—	52	23	14	15	1	11	1	3	1	8	6	.57	0	.333	.409	.433
Tulsa	AA	93	360	101	18	4	0	—	—	127	44	27	45	0	53	1	8	2	14	12	.54	6	.281	.360	.353
1996 Tulsa	AA	134	505	145	24	12	2	—	—	199	73	41	30	2	73	0	5	3	9	9	.50	1	.287	.325	.394
1997 Okla City	AAA	132	484	128	17	4	5	—	—	168	64	46	56	2	72	1	8	3	35	15	.70	19	.264	.340	.347
1998 Tucson	AAA	63	253	73	10	4	1	—	—	94	32	21	24	0	41	0	2	3	16	7	.70	4	.289	.346	.372
1997 Texas	AL	14	26	5	1	0	0	(0	0)	6	4	1	1	0	4	0	0	0	0	0	.00	1	.192	.222	.231
1998 Arizona	NL	15	23	3	0	1	1	(1	0)	8	4	2	0	0	5	0	0	0	0	0	.00	1	.130	.130	.348
2 ML YEARS		29	49	8	1	1	1	(1	0)	14	8	3	1	0	9	0	0	0	0	0	.00	2	.163	.180	.286

Jeff Frye

Bats: R **Throws:** R **Pos:** 2B **Ht:** 5'9" **Wt:** 165 **Born:** 8/31/66 **Age:** 32

Year Team	Lg	G	AB	H	2B	3B	HR	(Hm	Rd)	TB	R	RBI	TBB	IBB	SO	HBP	SH	SF	SB	CS	SB%	GDP	Avg	OBP	SLG
1992 Texas	AL	67	199	51	9	1	1	(0	1)	65	24	12	16	0	27	3	11	1	1	3	.25	2	.256	.320	.327
1994 Texas	AL	57	205	67	20	3	0	(0	0)	93	37	18	29	0	23	1	5	3	6	1	.86	1	.327	.408	.454
1995 Texas	AL	90	313	87	15	2	4	(2	2)	118	38	29	24	0	45	5	8	4	3	3	.50	7	.278	.335	.377
1996 Boston	AL	105	419	120	27	2	4	(3	1)	163	74	41	54	0	57	5	5	3	18	4	.82	6	.286	.372	.389
1997 Boston	AL	127	404	126	36	2	3	(2	1)	175	56	51	27	1	44	2	2	7	19	8	.70	12	.312	.352	.433
5 ML YEARS		446	1540	451	107	10	12	(7	5)	614	229	151	150	1	196	16	31	18	47	19	.71	28	.293	.358	.399

Travis Fryman

Bats: Right **Throws:** Right **Pos:** 3B-144; SS-3; DH-2 **Ht:** 6'1" **Wt:** 195 **Born:** 3/25/69 **Age:** 30

Year Team	Lg	G	AB	H	2B	3B	HR	(Hm	Rd)	TB	R	RBI	TBB	IBB	SO	HBP	SH	SF	SB	CS	SB%	GDP	Avg	OBP	SLG
1990 Detroit	AL	66	232	69	11	1	9	(5	4)	109	32	27	17	0	51	1	1	0	3	3	.50	3	.297	.348	.470
1991 Detroit	AL	149	557	144	36	3	21	(8	13)	249	65	91	40	0	149	3	6	6	12	5	.71	13	.259	.309	.447
1992 Detroit	AL	161	**659**	175	31	4	20	(9	11)	274	87	96	45	1	144	6	5	6	8	4	.67	13	.266	.316	.416
1993 Detroit	AL	151	607	182	37	5	22	(13	9)	295	98	97	77	1	128	4	1	6	9	4	.69	6	.300	.379	.486
1994 Detroit	AL	114	**464**	122	34	5	18	(10	8)	220	66	85	45	1	**128**	5	1	**13**	2	2	.50	6	.263	.326	.474
1995 Detroit	AL	144	567	156	21	5	15	(9	6)	232	79	81	63	4	100	3	0	7	4	2	.67	18	.275	.347	.409
1996 Detroit	AL	157	616	165	32	3	22	(10	12)	269	90	100	57	2	118	4	1	10	4	3	.57	18	.268	.329	.437
1997 Detroit	AL	154	595	163	27	3	22	(13	9)	262	90	102	46	5	113	5	0	11	16	3	.84	15	.274	.326	.440
1998 Cleveland	AL	146	557	160	33	2	28	(16	12)	281	74	96	44	0	125	3	0	4	10	8	.56	12	.287	.340	.504
9 ML YEARS		1242	4854	1336	262	31	177	(93	84)	2191	681	775	434	14	1056	34	15	63	68	34	.67	106	.275	.335	.451

Brad Fullmer

Bats: Left **Throws:** Right **Pos:** 1B-137; PH/PR-4 **Ht:** 6'1" **Wt:** 205 **Born:** 1/17/75 **Age:** 24

Year Team	Lg	G	AB	H	2B	3B	HR	(Hm	Rd)	TB	R	RBI	TBB	IBB	SO	HBP	SH	SF	SB	CS	SB%	GDP	Avg	OBP	SLG
1995 Albany	A	123	468	151	38	4	8	—	—	221	69	67	36	4	33	17	0	6	10	10	.50	9	.323	.387	.472
1996 Wst Plm Bch	A+	102	380	115	29	1	5	—	—	161	52	63	32	2	43	11	0	8	4	6	.40	9	.303	.367	.424
Harrisburg	AA	24	98	27	4	1	4	—	—	45	11	14	3	0	8	2	0	0	0	0	.00	3	.276	.311	.459
1997 Harrisburg	AA	94	357	111	24	2	19	—	—	196	60	62	30	5	25	7	0	4	6	4	.60	11	.311	.372	.549
Ottawa	AAA	24	91	27	7	0	3	—	—	43	13	17	3	0	10	2	0	5	1	1	.50	3	.297	.317	.473
1997 Montreal	NL	19	40	12	2	0	3	(1	2)	23	4	8	2	1	7	1	0	0	0	0	.00	0	.300	.349	.575
1998 Montreal	NL	140	505	138	44	2	13	(3	10)	225	58	73	39	4	70	2	0	1	6	6	.50	12	.273	.327	.446
2 ML YEARS		159	545	150	46	2	16	(4	12)	248	62	81	41	5	77	3	0	1	6	6	.50	12	.275	.329	.455

Chris Fussell

Pitches: Right **Bats:** Right **Pos:** SP-2; RP-1 **Ht:** 6'2" **Wt:** 200 **Born:** 5/19/76 **Age:** 23

	HOW MUCH HE PITCHED						WHAT HE GAVE UP												THE RESULTS						
Year Team	Lg	G	GS	CG	GF	IP	BFP	H	R	ER	HR	SH	SF	HB	TBB	IBB	SO	WP	Bk	W	L	Pct.	ShO	Sv-Op	Hld	ERA
1994 Orioles	R	14	8	0	2	56.1	245	53	30	26	2	1	4	4	24	0	65	6	1	2	3	.400	0	0- —	—	4.15
1995 Bluefield	R+	12	12	1	0	65.2	265	37	18	16	4	1	1	7	32	0	98	3	1	9	1	.900	1	0- —	—	2.19
1996 Frederick	A+	15	14	1	0	86.1	369	71	36	27	8	1	1	5	44	0	94	5	0	5	2	.714	1	0- —	—	2.81
1997 Bowie	AA	19	18	0	0	82.1	398	102	71	65	12	1	5	10	58	3	71	7	0	1	8	.111	0	0- —	—	7.11
Frederick	A+	9	9	1	0	50	218	42	23	22	5	2	3	3	31	2	54	3	0	3	3	.500	1	0- —	—	3.96
1998 Bowie	AA	18	18	0	0	93	413	87	54	44	13	1	6	4	52	1	84	4	0	3	7	.300	0	0- —	—	4.26
Rochester	AAA	10	10	0	0	58.2	249	50	30	26	4	1	3	5	28	0	51	5	0	5	2	.714	0	0- —	—	3.99
1998 Baltimore	AL	3	2	0	0	9.2	47	11	9	9	1	1	1	0	9	1	8	0	0	0	1	.000	0	0-0	0	8.38

Gary Gaetti

Bats: R **Throws:** R **Pos:** 3B-119; PH/PR-10; 1B-3; P-1; 2B-1; RF-1   **Ht:** 6'0" **Wt:** 200 **Born:** 8/19/58 **Age:** 40

Year Team	Lg	G	AB	H	2B	3B	HR	(Hm	Rd)	TB	R	RBI	TBB	IBB	SO	HBP	SH	SF	SB	CS	SB%	GDP	Avg	OBP	SLG
1981 Minnesota	AL	9	26	5	0	0	2	(1	1)	11	4	3	0	0	6	0	0	0	0	0	.00	1	.192	.192	.423
1982 Minnesota	AL	145	508	117	25	4	25	(15	10)	225	59	84	37	2	107	3	4	13	0	4	.00	16	.230	.280	.443
1983 Minnesota	AL	157	584	143	30	3	21	(7	14)	242	81	78	54	2	121	4	0	8	7	1	.88	18	.245	.309	.414
1984 Minnesota	AL	162	588	154	29	4	5	(2	3)	206	55	65	44	1	81	4	3	5	11	5	.69	9	.262	.315	.350
1985 Minnesota	AL	160	560	138	31	0	20	(10	10)	229	71	63	37	3	89	7	3	1	13	5	.72	15	.246	.301	.409
1986 Minnesota	AL	157	596	171	34	1	34	(16	18)	309	91	108	52	4	108	6	1	6	14	15	.48	18	.287	.347	.518
1987 Minnesota	AL	154	584	150	36	2	31	(18	13)	283	95	109	37	7	92	5	1	3	10	7	.59	25	.257	.303	.485
1988 Minnesota	AL	133	468	141	29	2	28	(9	19)	258	66	88	36	5	85	5	1	6	7	4	.64	10	.301	.353	.551
1989 Minnesota	AL	130	498	125	11	4	19	(10	9)	201	63	75	25	5	87	3	1	9	6	2	.75	12	.251	.286	.404
1990 Minnesota	AL	154	577	132	27	5	16	(7	9)	217	61	85	36	1	101	3	1	8	6	1	.86	22	.229	.274	.376
1991 California	AL	152	586	144	22	1	18	(12	6)	222	58	66	33	4	104	8	2	5	5	5	.50	13	.246	.293	.379
1992 California	AL	130	456	103	13	2	12	(8	4)	156	41	48	21	4	79	6	0	3	3	1	.75	9	.226	.267	.342
1993 Cal-KC	AL	102	331	81	20	1	14	(6	8)	145	40	50	21	0	87	8	2	7	1	3	.25	5	.245	.300	.438
1994 Kansas City	AL	90	327	94	15	3	12	(5	7)	151	53	57	19	3	63	2	1	3	0	2	.00	9	.287	.328	.462
1995 Kansas City	AL	137	514	134	27	0	35	(16	19)	266	76	96	47	6	91	8	3	6	3	3	.50	7	.261	.329	.518
1996 St. Louis	NL	141	522	143	27	4	23	(13	10)	247	71	80	35	6	97	8	4	5	2	2	.50	10	.274	.326	.473
1997 St. Louis	NL	148	502	126	24	1	17	(7	10)	203	63	69	36	3	88	6	4	6	7	3	.70	20	.251	.305	.404
1998 StL-ChN	NL	128	434	122	34	1	19	(5	14)	215	60	70	43	2	62	10	1	4	1	1	.50	12	.281	.356	.495
1993 California	AL	20	50	9	2	0	0	(0	0)	11	3	4	5	0	12	0	0	1	1	0	1.00	3	.180	.250	.220
Kansas City		82	281	72	18	1	14	(6	8)	134	37	46	16	0	75	8	2	6	0	3	.00	2	.256	.309	.477
1998 St. Louis	NL	91	306	81	23	1	11	(1	10)	139	39	43	31	2	39	5	0	3	1	1	.50	10	.265	.339	.454
Chicago	NL	37	128	41	11	0	8	(4	4)	76	21	27	12	1	23	5	1	1	0	0	.00	2	.320	.397	.594
18 ML YEARS		2389	8661	2223	434	38	351	(167	184)	3786	1108	1294	613	57	1548	94	32	98	96	64	.60	231	.257	.310	.437

Eddie Gaillard

Pitches: Right **Bats:** Right **Pos:** RP-6   **Ht:** 6'1" **Wt:** 180 **Born:** 8/13/70 **Age:** 28

Year Team	Lg	G	GS	CG	GF	IP	BFP	H	R	ER	HR	SH	SF	HB	TBB	IBB	SO	WP	Bk	W	L	Pct.	ShO	Sv-Op	Hld	ERA
1993 Niagara Fal	A-	3	3	0	0	14.2	63	15	6	6	0	0	0	0	4	0	12	0	0	1	2	.333	0	0--	—	3.68
Fayettevlle	A	11	11	0	0	61.2	261	64	30	28	8	2	0	4	20	0	41	1	1	5	2	.714	0	0--	—	4.09
1994 Lakeland	A+	30	9	0	8	92	389	82	37	29	3	1	2	10	29	0	51	3	1	6	1	.857	0	2--	—	2.84
1995 Jacksnville	AA	8	0	0	2	8	42	11	5	5	0	2	1	0	5	1	4	0	0	0	1	.000	0	0--	—	5.63
Lakeland	A+	43	0	0	38	55	227	48	13	8	1	1	3	0	18	2	51	2	1	2	4	.333	0	25--	—	1.31
1996 Jacksnville	AA	56	0	0	24	88	389	82	40	33	8	4	3	5	50	7	76	10	0	9	6	.600	0	1--	—	3.38
1997 Toledo	AAA	55	0	0	46	53	235	52	27	25	7	3	1	2	24	2	54	4	1	1	4	.200	0	28--	—	4.25
1998 St. Pete	A+	1	1	0	0	2	7	1	0	0	0	0	0	0	0	0	2	0	0	0	0	.000	0	0--	—	0.00
Devil Rays	R	2	2	0	0	4	13	0	0	0	0	0	0	0	1	0	5	0	0	0	0	.000	0	0--	—	0.00
Durham	AAA	18	0	0	1	20	98	27	18	17	5	0	1	3	11	0	21	3	0	2	0	1.000	0	0--	—	7.65
1997 Detroit	AL	16	0	0	5	20.1	88	16	12	12	2	0	2	0	10	2	12	0	0	1	0	1.000	0	1-2	0	5.31
1998 Tampa Bay	AL	6	0	0	1	7.2	30	4	5	5	3	0	0	0	3	0	5	0	0	0	0	.000	0	0-0	0	5.87
2 ML YEARS		22	0	0	6	28	118	20	17	17	5	0	2	0	13	2	17	0	0	1	0	1.000	0	1-2	0	5.46

Steve Gajkowski

Pitches: Right **Bats:** Right **Pos:** RP-9   **Ht:** 6'2" **Wt:** 185 **Born:** 12/30/69 **Age:** 29

Year Team	Lg	G	GS	CG	GF	IP	BFP	H	R	ER	HR	SH	SF	HB	TBB	IBB	SO	WP	Bk	W	L	Pct.	ShO	Sv-Op	Hld	ERA
1990 Burlington	R+	14	10	1	1	63.2	287	74	34	29	0	0	3	3	23	0	44	0	1	2	6	.250	0	0--	—	4.10
1991 Columbus	A	3	0	0	2	6	24	3	2	2	0	0	0	0	5	0	5	0	0	0	0	.000	0	0--	—	3.00
Watertown	A-	20	4	0	7	48	221	41	36	28	0	1	2	6	32	1	34	7	2	3	3	.500	0	0--	—	5.25
1992 Utica	A-	29	0	0	26	47	184	33	14	7	1	0	2	1	10	1	38	6	0	3	2	.600	0	14--	—	1.34
1993 Sarasota	A+	43	0	0	38	69.2	273	52	21	16	1	3	3	4	17	5	45	5	1	3	3	.500	0	15--	—	2.07
Birmingham	AA	1	0	0	0	2.1	8	0	0	0	0	0	0	0	2	0	0	0	0	0	0	.000	0	0--	—	0.00
1994 Birmingham	AA	58	0	0	32	82.1	355	78	35	28	6	6	3	5	26	1	44	2	0	11	5	.688	0	8--	—	3.06
1995 Nashville	AAA	15	0	0	5	24.2	103	26	15	7	2	0	1	1	8	1	12	1	0	0	1	.000	0	2--	—	2.55
Birmingham	AA	35	0	0	14	51.2	230	64	27	24	4	2	0	2	16	1	29	1	0	4	4	.500	0	2--	—	4.18
1996 Nashville	AAA	49	8	0	17	107.1	472	113	61	47	11	4	5	5	41	5	47	6	0	5	6	.455	0	2--	—	3.94
1997 Tacoma	AAA	44	3	0	10	93	394	100	43	40	11	2	1	5	24	0	48	3	1	5	3	.625	0	2--	—	3.87
1998 Tacoma	AAA	53	0	0	44	73.2	299	60	23	21	3	2	2	2	20	3	61	0	0	3	3	.500	0	24--	—	2.57
1998 Seattle	AL	9	0	0	3	8.2	42	14	8	7	0	0	0	2	4	0	3	0	0	0	0	.000	0	0-0	0	7.27

Andres Galarraga

Bats: Right **Throws:** Right **Pos:** 1B-149; DH-2; PH/PR-2   **Ht:** 6'3" **Wt:** 235 **Born:** 6/18/61 **Age:** 38

Year Team	Lg	G	AB	H	2B	3B	HR	(Hm	Rd)	TB	R	RBI	TBB	IBB	SO	HBP	SH	SF	SB	CS	SB%	GDP	Avg	OBP	SLG
1985 Montreal	NL	24	75	14	1	0	2	(0	2)	21	9	4	3	0	18	1	0	0	1	2	.33	0	.187	.228	.280
1986 Montreal	NL	105	321	87	13	0	10	(4	6)	130	39	42	30	5	79	3	1	1	6	5	.55	8	.271	.338	.405
1987 Montreal	NL	147	551	168	40	3	13	(7	6)	253	72	90	41	13	127	10	0	4	7	10	.41	11	.305	.361	.459
1988 Montreal	NL	157	609	184	42	8	29	(14	15)	329	99	92	39	9	153	10	0	3	13	4	.76	12	.302	.352	.540
1989 Montreal	NL	152	572	147	30	1	23	(13	10)	248	76	85	48	10	158	13	0	3	12	5	.71	12	.257	.327	.434
1990 Montreal	NL	155	579	148	29	0	20	(6	14)	237	65	87	40	8	169	4	0	5	10	1	.91	14	.256	.306	.409
1991 Montreal	NL	107	375	82	13	2	9	(3	6)	126	34	33	23	5	86	2	0	0	5	6	.45	8	.219	.268	.336
1992 St. Louis	NL	95	325	79	14	2	10	(4	6)	127	38	39	11	0	69	8	0	3	5	4	.56	8	.243	.282	.391

Year Team	Lg	G	AB	H	2B	3B	HR	(Hm	Rd)	TB	R	RBI	TBB	IBB	SO	HBP	SH	SF	SB	CS	SB%	GDP	Avg	OBP	SLG
1993 Colorado	NL	120	470	174	35	4	22	(13	9)	283	71	98	24	12	73	6	0	6	2	4	.33	9	.370	.403	.602
1994 Colorado	NL	103	417	133	21	0	31	(16	15)	247	77	85	19	8	93	8	0	5	8	3	.73	10	.319	.356	.592
1995 Colorado	NL	143	554	155	29	3	31	(18	13)	283	89	106	32	6	146	13	0	5	12	2	.86	14	.280	.331	.511
1996 Colorado	NL	159	626	190	39	3	47	(32	15)	376	119	150	40	3	157	17	0	8	18	8	.69	6	.304	.357	.601
1997 Colorado	NL	154	600	191	31	3	41	(21	20)	351	120	140	54	2	141	17	0	3	15	8	.65	16	.318	.389	.585
1998 Atlanta	NL	153	555	169	27	1	44	(16	28)	330	103	121	63	11	146	25	0	5	7	6	.54	8	.305	.397	.595
14 ML YEARS		1774	6629	1921	364	30	332	(167	165)	3341	1011	1172	467	92	1615	137	1	51	121	68	.64	134	.290	.347	.504

Ron Gant

Bats: Right **Throws:** Right **Pos:** LF-104; PH/PR-19   **Ht:** 6'0" **Wt:** 200 **Born:** 3/2/65 **Age:** 34

Year Team	Lg	G	AB	H	2B	3B	HR	(Hm	Rd)	TB	R	RBI	TBB	IBB	SO	HBP	SH	SF	SB	CS	SB%	GDP	Avg	OBP	SLG
1987 Atlanta	NL	21	83	22	4	0	2	(1	1)	32	9	9	1	0	11	0	1	1	4	2	.67	3	.265	.271	.386
1988 Atlanta	NL	146	563	146	28	8	19	(7	12)	247	85	60	46	4	118	3	2	4	19	10	.66	7	.259	.317	.439
1989 Atlanta	NL	75	260	46	8	3	9	(5	4)	87	26	25	20	0	63	1	2	2	9	6	.60	0	.177	.237	.335
1990 Atlanta	NL	152	575	174	34	3	32	(18	14)	310	107	84	50	0	86	1	1	4	33	16	.67	8	.303	.357	.539
1991 Atlanta	NL	154	561	141	35	3	32	(18	14)	278	101	105	71	8	104	5	0	5	34	15	.69	6	.251	.338	.496
1992 Atlanta	NL	153	544	141	22	6	17	(10	7)	226	74	80	45	5	101	7	0	6	32	10	.76	10	.259	.321	.415
1993 Atlanta	NL	157	606	166	27	4	36	(17	19)	309	113	117	67	2	117	2	0	7	26	9	.74	14	.274	.345	.510
1995 Cincinnati	NL	119	410	113	19	4	29	(12	17)	227	79	88	74	5	108	3	1	5	23	8	.74	11	.276	.386	.554
1996 St. Louis	NL	122	419	103	14	2	30	(17	13)	211	74	82	73	5	98	3	1	4	13	4	.76	9	.246	.359	.504
1997 St. Louis	NL	139	502	115	21	4	17	(11	6)	195	68	62	58	3	162	1	0	1	14	6	.70	2	.229	.310	.388
1998 St. Louis	NL	121	383	92	17	1	26	(14	12)	189	60	67	51	2	92	2	0	2	8	0	1.00	6	.240	.331	.493
11 ML YEARS		1359	4906	1259	229	38	249	(130	119)	2311	796	779	556	34	1060	28	8	41	215	86	.71	76	.257	.333	.471

Rich Garces

Pitches: Right **Bats:** Right **Pos:** RP-30   **Ht:** 6'0" **Wt:** 215 **Born:** 5/18/71 **Age:** 28

		HOW MUCH HE PITCHED						WHAT HE GAVE UP												THE RESULTS						
Year Team	Lg	G	GS	CG	GF	IP	BFP	H	R	ER	HR	SH	SF	HB	TBB	IBB	SO	WP	Bk	W	L	Pct.	ShO	Sv-Op	Hld	ERA
1998 Pawtucket *	AAA	7	0	0	7	8.1	33	6	5	5	1	1	0	0	2	1	10	1	0	0	1	.000	0	3- --	—	5.40
Red Sox *	R	7	7	0	0	11	43	11	4	4	0	0	0	0	0	0	8	0	2	0	0	.000	0	0- --	—	3.27
1990 Minnesota	AL	5	0	0	3	5.2	24	4	2	1	0	0	0	0	4	0	1	0	0	0	0	.000	0	2-2	0	1.59
1993 Minnesota	AL	3	0	0	1	4	18	4	2	0	0	0	0	0	2	0	3	0	0	0	0	.000	0	0-0	0	0.00
1995 ChN-Fla	NL	18	0	0	7	24.1	108	25	15	12	1	1	0	0	11	2	22	0	0	0	2	.000	0	0-1	1	4.44
1996 Boston	AL	37	0	0	9	44	205	42	26	24	5	0	5	0	33	5	55	0	0	3	2	.600	0	0-2	4	4.91
1997 Boston	AL	12	0	0	4	13.2	66	14	9	7	2	0	1	1	9	0	12	0	0	0	1	.000	0	0-2	1	4.61
1998 Boston	AL	30	0	0	11	46	201	36	19	17	6	2	1	2	27	3	34	1	1	1	1	.500	0	1-3	6	3.33
1995 Chicago	NL	7	0	0	4	11	46	11	6	4	0	0	0	0	3	0	6	0	0	0	0	.000	0	0-0	0	3.27
Florida	NL	11	0	0	3	13.1	62	14	9	8	1	1	0	0	8	2	16	0	0	0	2	.000	0	0-1	1	5.40
6 ML YEARS		105	0	0	35	137.2	622	125	73	61	14	3	7	3	86	10	127	1	1	4	6	.400	0	3-10	12	3.99

Carlos Garcia

Bats: R **Throws:** R **Pos:** 2B-11; PH/PR-6; SS-5; DH-3   **Ht:** 6'1" **Wt:** 197 **Born:** 10/15/67 **Age:** 31

Year Team	Lg	G	AB	H	2B	3B	HR	(Hm	Rd)	TB	R	RBI	TBB	IBB	SO	HBP	SH	SF	SB	CS	SB%	GDP	Avg	OBP	SLG
1998 Vancouver *	AAA	44	161	41	6	0	3	—	—	56	18	15	8	1	22	2	0	1	2	5	.29	2	.255	.297	.348
1990 Pittsburgh	NL	4	4	2	0	0	0	(0	0)	2	1	0	0	0	2	0	0	0	0	0	.00	0	.500	.500	.500
1991 Pittsburgh	NL	12	24	6	0	2	0	(0	0)	10	2	1	1	0	8	0	0	0	0	0	.00	1	.250	.280	.417
1992 Pittsburgh	NL	22	39	8	1	0	0	(0	0)	9	4	4	0	0	9	0	1	2	0	0	.00	1	.205	.195	.231
1993 Pittsburgh	NL	141	546	147	25	5	12	(7	5)	218	77	47	31	2	67	9	6	5	18	11	.62	9	.269	.316	.399
1994 Pittsburgh	NL	98	412	114	15	2	6	(4	2)	151	49	28	16	2	67	4	1	4	18	9	.67	6	.277	.309	.367
1995 Pittsburgh	NL	104	367	108	24	2	6	(4	2)	154	41	50	25	5	55	2	5	3	8	4	.67	4	.294	.340	.420
1996 Pittsburgh	NL	101	390	111	18	4	6	(3	3)	155	66	44	23	3	58	4	3	2	16	6	.73	3	.285	.329	.397
1997 Toronto	AL	103	350	77	18	2	3	(0	3)	108	29	23	15	0	60	2	10	4	11	3	.79	7	.220	.253	.309
1998 Anaheim	AL	19	35	5	1	0	0	(0	0)	6	4	0	3	0	11	1	1	0	2	0	1.00	0	.143	.231	.171
9 ML YEARS		604	2167	578	102	17	33	(18	15)	813	273	197	114	12	337	22	27	17	73	33	.69	31	.267	.308	.375

Freddy Garcia

Bats: Right **Throws:** Right **Pos:** 3B-47; PH/PR-5; 1B-4   **Ht:** 6'3" **Wt:** 219 **Born:** 8/1/72 **Age:** 26

Year Team	Lg	G	AB	H	2B	3B	HR	(Hm	Rd)	TB	R	RBI	TBB	IBB	SO	HBP	SH	SF	SB	CS	SB%	GDP	Avg	OBP	SLG
1998 Nashville *	AAA	88	326	88	24	4	22	—	—	186	52	55	25	0	89	4	0	3	0	2	.00	12	.270	.327	.571
1995 Pittsburgh	NL	42	57	8	1	1	0	(0	0)	11	5	1	8	0	17	0	1	0	0	1	.00	0	.140	.246	.193
1997 Pittsburgh	NL	20	40	6	1	0	3	(0	3)	16	4	5	2	0	17	0	0	0	0	0	.00	0	.150	.190	.400
1998 Pittsburgh	NL	56	172	44	11	1	9	(2	7)	84	27	26	18	3	45	2	0	1	0	2	.00	3	.256	.332	.488
3 ML YEARS		118	269	58	13	2	12	(2	10)	111	36	32	28	3	79	2	1	1	0	3	.00	3	.216	.293	.413

Guillermo Garcia

Bats: Right **Throws:** Right **Pos:** C-11; PH/PR-2   **Ht:** 6'3" **Wt:** 215 **Born:** 4/4/72 **Age:** 27

								BATTING											BASERUNNING				PERCENTAGES		
Year Team	Lg	G	AB	H	2B	3B	HR	(Hm	Rd)	TB	R	RBI	TBB	IBB	SO	HBP	SH	SF	SB	CS	SB%	GDP	Avg	OBP	SLG
1990 Mets	R	42	136	25	1	2	0	—	—	30	9	6	7	1	34	1	2	1	1	1	.50	2	.184	.228	.221
1991 Kingsport	R+	15	33	8	1	1	0	—	—	11	9	2	4	0	4	0	0	0	0	0	.00	1	.242	.324	.333
Pittsfield	A-	45	157	43	13	2	0	—	—	60	22	24	15	0	38	1	3	3	4	1	.80	5	.274	.335	.382
1992 Pittsfield	A-	73	272	54	11	1	2	—	—	73	36	26	20	0	52	2	0	3	3	4	.43	5	.199	.256	.268
1993 Capital Cty	A	119	429	124	28	2	3	—	—	165	64	72	49	1	60	10	1	3	10	8	.56	11	.289	.373	.385
1994 St. Lucie	A+	55	203	48	9	1	1	—	—	62	22	23	13	1	24	3	2	0	0	2	.00	6	.236	.292	.305
1995 Winston-Sal	A+	78	245	58	10	2	3	—	—	81	26	29	28	0	32	1	2	2	2	2	.50	7	.237	.315	.331
1996 Indianapols	AAA	16	47	12	2	0	0	—	—	14	4	0	2	2	6	0	0	0	0	0	.00	5	.255	.286	.298
Chattanooga	AA	60	203	64	12	0	6	—	—	94	25	36	12	2	32	1	2	1	3	3	.50	3	.315	.355	.463
1997 Chattanooga	AA	20	74	21	1	1	4	—	—	36	11	19	8	0	13	0	0	1	0	0	.00	1	.284	.349	.486
Indianapols	AAA	55	151	36	2	0	10	—	—	68	16	20	9	0	46	1	0	2	0	2	.00	4	.238	.282	.450
1998 Indianapols	AAA	93	334	85	20	0	19	—	—	162	48	60	22	1	81	0	1	0	0	0	.00	2	.254	.301	.485
1998 Cincinnati	NL	12	36	7	2	0	2	(1	1)	15	3	4	2	0	13	0	0	0	0	0	.00	2	.194	.237	.417

Karim Garcia

Bats: Left **Throws:** Left **Pos:** RF-100; PH/PR-15; CF-8   **Ht:** 6'0" **Wt:** 172 **Born:** 10/29/75 **Age:** 23

								BATTING											BASERUNNING				PERCENTAGES		
Year Team	Lg	G	AB	H	2B	3B	HR	(Hm	Rd)	TB	R	RBI	TBB	IBB	SO	HBP	SH	SF	SB	CS	SB%	GDP	Avg	OBP	SLG
1993 Bakersfield	A+	123	460	111	20	9	19	—	—	206	61	54	37	4	109	2	0	2	5	3	.63	5	.241	.299	.448
1994 Vero Beach	A+	121	452	120	28	10	21	—	—	231	72	84	37	8	112	1	0	6	8	3	.73	7	.265	.319	.511
1995 Albuquerque	AAA	124	474	151	26	10	20	—	—	257	88	91	38	5	102	2	2	3	12	6	.67	12	.319	.369	.542
1996 San Antonio	AA	35	129	32	6	1	5	—	—	55	21	22	9	0	38	0	0	0	1	1	.50	1	.248	.297	.426
Albuquerque	AAA	84	327	97	17	10	13	—	—	173	54	58	29	8	67	1	0	3	4	6	.60	9	.297	.353	.529
1997 Albuquerque	AAA	71	262	80	17	6	20	—	—	169	53	66	23	4	70	0	1	0	11	5	.69	4	.305	.361	.645
1998 Tucson	AAA	27	106	33	4	2	10	—	—	71	21	27	15	1	24	0	0	1	5	1	.83	2	.311	.393	.670
1995 Los Angeles	NL	13	20	4	0	0	0	(0	0)	4	1	0	0	0	4	0	0	0	0	0	.00	0	.200	.200	.200
1996 Los Angeles	NL	1	1	0	0	0	0	(0	0)	0	0	0	0	0	1	0	0	0	0	0	.00	0	.000	.000	.000
1997 Los Angeles	NL	15	39	5	0	0	1	(0	1)	8	5	8	6	1	14	0	0	0	0	0	.00	0	.128	.239	.205
1998 Arizona	NL	113	333	74	10	8	9	(4	5)	127	39	43	18	1	78	0	0	3	5	4	.56	6	.222	.260	.381
4 ML YEARS		142	393	83	10	8	10	(4	6)	139	45	51	24	2	97	0	0	4	5	4	.56	6	.211	.254	.354

Ramon Garcia

Pitches: Right **Bats:** Right **Pos:** SP   **Ht:** 6'2" **Wt:** 200 **Born:** 12/9/69 **Age:** 29

				HOW MUCH HE PITCHED						WHAT HE GAVE UP									THE RESULTS						
Year Team	Lg	G	GS	CG	GF	IP	BFP	H	R	ER	HR	SH	SF	HB	TBB	IBB	SO	WP	Bk	W	L	Pct.	ShO	Sv-Op	Hld	ERA
1991 Chicago	AL	16	15	0	0	78.1	332	79	50	47	13	3	2	2	31	2	40	0	2	4	4	.500	0	0-0	0	5.40
1996 Milwaukee	AL	37	2	0	14	75.2	326	84	58	56	17	1	5	6	21	3	40	2	1	4	4	.500	0	4-7	6	6.66
1997 Houston	NL	42	20	1	5	158.2	665	155	71	65	20	10	2	9	52	1	120	3	2	9	8	.529	1	1-1	1	3.69
3 ML YEARS		95	37	1	19	312.2	1323	318	179	168	50	14	9	17	104	6	200	5	5	17	16	.515	1	5-8	7	4.84

Nomar Garciaparra

Bats: Right **Throws:** Right **Pos:** SS-143   **Ht:** 6'0" **Wt:** 175 **Born:** 7/23/73 **Age:** 25

								BATTING											BASERUNNING				PERCENTAGES		
Year Team	Lg	G	AB	H	2B	3B	HR	(Hm	Rd)	TB	R	RBI	TBB	IBB	SO	HBP	SH	SF	SB	CS	SB%	GDP	Avg	OBP	SLG
1996 Boston	AL	24	87	21	2	3	4	(1	3)	41	11	16	4	0	14	0	1	1	5	0	1.00	5	.241	.272	.471
1997 Boston	AL	153	684	209	44	11	30	(11	19)	365	122	98	35	2	92	6	2	7	22	9	.71	9	.306	.342	.534
1998 Boston	AL	143	604	195	37	8	35	(17	18)	353	111	122	33	1	62	8	0	7	12	6	.67	20	.323	.362	.584
3 ML YEARS		320	1375	425	83	22	69	(31	38)	759	244	236	72	3	168	14	3	15	39	15	.72	29	.309	.346	.552

Mark Gardner

Pitches: Right **Bats:** Right **Pos:** SP-33   **Ht:** 6'1" **Wt:** 215 **Born:** 3/1/62 **Age:** 37

				HOW MUCH HE PITCHED						WHAT HE GAVE UP									THE RESULTS						
Year Team	Lg	G	GS	CG	GF	IP	BFP	H	R	ER	HR	SH	SF	HB	TBB	IBB	SO	WP	Bk	W	L	Pct.	ShO	Sv-Op	Hld	ERA
1989 Montreal	NL	7	4	0	1	26.1	117	26	16	15	2	0	0	2	11	1	21	0	0	0	3	.000	0	0-0	0	5.13
1990 Montreal	NL	27	26	3	1	152.2	642	129	62	58	13	4	7	9	61	5	135	2	4	7	9	.438	3	0-0	0	3.42
1991 Montreal	NL	27	27	0	0	168.1	692	139	78	72	17	7	4	8	75	1	107	2	1	9	11	.450	0	0-0	0	3.85
1992 Montreal	NL	33	30	0	1	179.2	778	179	91	87	15	12	7	9	60	2	132	2	0	12	10	.545	0	0-0	0	4.36
1993 Kansas City	AL	17	16	0	0	91.2	387	92	65	63	17	1	7	4	36	0	54	2	0	4	6	.400	0	0-0	0	6.19
1994 Florida	NL	20	14	0	3	92.1	391	97	53	50	14	4	5	1	30	2	57	3	1	4	4	.500	0	0-0	0	4.87
1995 Florida	NL	39	11	1	7	102.1	456	109	60	51	14	7	0	5	43	5	87	3	1	5	5	.500	1	1-1	4	4.49
1996 San Francisco	NL	30	28	0	0	179.1	782	200	105	88	28	6	5	8	57	3	145	2	0	12	7	.632	1	0-0	1	4.42
1997 San Francisco	NL	30	30	2	0	180.1	764	188	92	86	28	10	6	1	57	6	136	3	3	12	9	.571	1	0-0	0	4.29
1998 San Francisco	NL	33	33	4	0	212	886	203	106	102	29	6	7	6	65	5	151	5	1	13	6	.684	2	0-0	0	4.33
10 ML YEARS		263	219	14	13	1385	5895	1362	728	672	177	57	46	49	495	30	1025	24	11	78	70	.527	8	1-1	5	4.37

Brent Gates

Bats: B **Throws:** R **Pos:** 3B-77; 2B-21; PH/PR-17; DH-2; 1B-1; SS-1   **Ht:** 6'1"   **Wt:** 190   **Born:** 3/14/70   **Age:** 29

							BATTING											BASERUNNING				PERCENTAGES		
Year Team	Lg	G	AB	H	2B	3B	HR	(Hm | Rd)	TB	R	RBI	TBB	IBB	SO	HBP	SH	SF	SB	CS	SB%	GDP	Avg	OBP	SLG
1993 Oakland	AL	139	535	155	29	2	7	(4 | 3)	209	64	69	56	4	75	4	6	8	7	3	.70	17	.290	.357	.391
1994 Oakland	AL	64	233	66	11	1	2	(0 | 2)	85	29	24	21	1	32	1	3	6	3	0	1.00	8	.283	.337	.365
1995 Oakland	AL	136	524	133	24	4	5	(3 | 2)	180	60	56	46	2	84	0	4	11	3	3	.50	15	.254	.308	.344
1996 Oakland	AL	64	247	65	19	2	2	(1 | 1)	94	26	30	18	0	35	2	5	2	1	1	.50	9	.263	.316	.381
1997 Seattle	AL	65	151	36	8	0	3	(1 | 2)	53	18	20	14	0	21	0	2	3	0	0	.00	6	.238	.298	.351
1998 Minnesota	AL	107	333	83	15	0	3	(1 | 2)	107	31	42	36	0	46	2	3	3	3	3	.50	6	.249	.324	.321
6 ML YEARS		575	2023	538	106	9	22	(10 | 12)	728	228	241	191	7	293	9	23	33	17	10	.63	61	.266	.327	.360

Jason Giambi

Bats: Left **Throws:** Right **Pos:** 1B-146; DH-7   **Ht:** 6'3"   **Wt:** 235   **Born:** 1/8/71   **Age:** 28

							BATTING											BASERUNNING				PERCENTAGES		
Year Team	Lg	G	AB	H	2B	3B	HR	(Hm	Rd)	TB	R	RBI	TBB	IBB	SO	HBP	SH	SF	SB	CS	SB%	GDP	Avg	OBP	SLG
1995 Oakland	AL	54	176	45	7	0	6	(3	3)	70	27	25	28	0	31	3	1	2	2	1	.67	4	.256	.364	.398
1996 Oakland	AL	140	536	156	40	1	20	(6	14)	258	84	79	51	3	95	5	1	5	0	1	.00	15	.291	.355	.481
1997 Oakland	AL	142	519	152	41	2	20	(14	6)	257	66	81	55	3	89	6	0	8	0	1	.00	11	.293	.362	.495
1998 Oakland	AL	153	562	166	28	0	27	(12	15)	275	92	110	81	7	102	5	0	9	2	2	.50	16	.295	.384	.489
4 ML YEARS		489	1793	519	116	3	73	(35	38)	860	269	295	215	13	317	19	2	24	4	5	.44	46	.289	.367	.480

Jeremy Giambi

Bats: Left **Throws:** Left **Pos:** LF-9; DH-7; PH/PR-2   **Ht:** 6'0"   **Wt:** 185   **Born:** 9/30/74   **Age:** 24

							BATTING											BASERUNNING				PERCENTAGES		
Year Team	Lg	G	AB	H	2B	3B	HR	(Hm	Rd)	TB	R	RBI	TBB	IBB	SO	HBP	SH	SF	SB	CS	SB%	GDP	Avg	OBP	SLG
1996 Spokane	A-	67	231	63	17	0	6	—	—	98	58	39	61	2	32	8	0	0	22	5	.81	5	.273	.440	.424
1997 Lansing	A	31	116	39	11	1	5	—	—	67	33	21	23	2	16	2	0	1	5	1	.83	1	.336	.451	.578
Wichita	AA	74	268	86	15	1	11	—	—	136	50	52	44	3	47	6	0	4	4	4	.50	7	.321	.422	.507
1998 Omaha	AAA	96	325	121	21	2	20	—	—	206	68	66	57	8	64	6	2	4	8	5	.62	4	.372	.469	.634
1998 Kansas City	AL	18	58	13	4	0	2	(0	2)	23	6	8	11	0	9	0	0	1	0	1	.00	3	.224	.343	.397

Derrick Gibson

Bats: Right **Throws:** Right **Pos:** LF-7   **Ht:** 6'2"   **Wt:** 244   **Born:** 2/5/75   **Age:** 24

							BATTING											BASERUNNING				PERCENTAGES		
Year Team	Lg	G	AB	H	2B	3B	HR	(Hm	Rd)	TB	R	RBI	TBB	IBB	SO	HBP	SH	SF	SB	CS	SB%	GDP	Avg	OBP	SLG
1993 Rockies	R	34	119	18	2	2	0	—	—	24	13	10	5	0	55	3	0	1	3	0	1.00	1	.151	.203	.202
1994 Bend	A-	73	284	75	19	5	12	—	—	140	47	57	29	5	102	9	0	1	14	4	.78	4	.264	.350	.493
1995 Asheville	A	135	506	148	16	10	32	—	—	280	91	115	29	5	136	19	1	6	31	13	.70	10	.292	.350	.553
1996 New Haven	AA	122	449	115	21	4	15	—	—	189	58	62	31	1	125	8	1	4	3	12	.20	15	.256	.313	.421
1997 New Haven	AA	119	461	146	24	2	23	—	—	243	91	75	36	7	100	10	0	2	20	13	.61	8	.317	.377	.527
Colo Sprngs	AAA	21	78	33	7	0	3	—	—	49	14	12	5	1	9	0	0	0	2	2	.00	1	.423	.458	.628
1998 Colo Sprngs	AAA	126	497	145	20	3	14	—	—	213	84	81	35	2	110	3	0	2	14	6	.70	17	.292	.341	.429
1998 Colorado	NL	7	21	9	1	0	0	(0	0)	10	4	2	1	0	4	1	0	0	0	0	.00	0	.429	.478	.476

Shawn Gilbert

Bats: Right **Throws:** Right **Pos:** PH/PR-6; 2B-2; 3B-1   **Ht:** 5'9"   **Wt:** 185   **Born:** 3/12/68   **Age:** 31

							BATTING											BASERUNNING				PERCENTAGES		
Year Team	Lg	G	AB	H	2B	3B	HR	(Hm	Rd)	TB	R	RBI	TBB	IBB	SO	HBP	SH	SF	SB	CS	SB%	GDP	Avg	OBP	SLG
1987 Visalia	A+	82	272	61	5	0	5	—	—	81	39	27	34	0	59	7	4	4	6	4	.60	8	.224	.322	.298
1988 Visalia	A+	14	43	16	3	2	0	—	—	23	10	8	10	0	7	1	0	0	1	1	.50	0	.372	.500	.535
Kenosha	A	108	402	112	21	2	3	—	—	146	80	44	63	2	61	2	0	5	49	10	.83	6	.279	.375	.363
1989 Visalia	A+	125	453	113	17	1	2	—	—	138	52	49	54	1	70	3	6	3	42	16	.72	11	.249	.331	.305
1990 Orlando	AA	123	433	110	18	2	4	—	—	144	68	44	61	0	69	5	4	3	31	9	.78	10	.254	.351	.333
1991 Orlando	AA	138	529	135	12	5	3	—	—	166	69	38	53	1	70	11	6	6	43	19	.69	18	.255	.332	.314
1992 Portland	AAA	138	444	109	17	2	3	—	—	139	60	52	36	2	55	4	5	2	31	8	.79	10	.245	.307	.314
1993 Nashville	AAA	104	278	63	17	2	0	—	—	84	28	17	12	0	41	2	2	1	6	2	.75	4	.227	.263	.302
1994 Scranton-WB	AAA	141	547	139	33	4	7	—	—	201	81	52	66	3	86	7	3	3	20	15	.57	9	.254	.340	.367
1995 Scranton-WB	AAA	136	536	141	26	2	2	—	—	177	84	42	64	0	102	6	4	4	16	11	.59	8	.263	.346	.330
1996 Norfolk	AAA	131	493	126	28	1	9	—	—	183	76	50	46	0	97	5	14	4	17	9	.65	5	.256	.323	.371
1997 Norfolk	AAA	78	288	76	13	1	8	—	—	115	53	33	43	1	64	2	3	1	16	4	.80	2	.264	.362	.399
1998 Norfolk	AAA	39	133	36	8	0	2	—	—	50	21	12	16	1	28	2	0	2	7	2	.78	2	.271	.353	.376
Memphis	AAA	62	216	58	15	2	7	—	—	98	37	32	29	1	53	6	0	3	7	4	.64	3	.269	.366	.454
1997 New York	NL	29	22	3	0	0	1	(1	0)	6	3	1	1	0	8	0	0	0	1	0	1.00	0	.136	.174	.273
1998 NYN-StL	NL	7	5	1	0	0	0	(0	0)	1	1	0	0	0	2	0	0	0	1	0	1.00	0	.200	.200	.200
1998 New York	NL	3	3	0	0	0	0	(0	0)	0	1	0	0	0	1	0	0	0	0	0	.00	0	.000	.000	.000
St. Louis	NL	4	2	1	0	0	0	(0	0)	1	0	0	0	0	1	0	0	0	1	0	1.00	0	.500	.500	.500
2 ML YEARS		36	27	4	0	0	1	(1	0)	7	4	1	1	0	10	0	0	0	2	0	1.00	0	.148	.179	.259

Brian Giles

Bats: L **Throws:** L **Pos:** LF-95; PH/PR-8; DH-6; RF-6; CF-3   **Ht:** 5'11" **Wt:** 200 **Born:** 1/20/71 **Age:** 28

Year Team	Lg	G	AB	H	2B	3B	HR	(Hm	Rd)	TB	R	RBI	TBB	IBB	SO	HBP	SH	SF	SB	CS	SB%	GDP	Avg	OBP	SLG
1998 Buffalo *	AAA	13	46	11	2	0	2	(—	—)	19	5	7	6	0	8	0	0	0	0	0	.00	2	.239	.327	.413
1995 Cleveland	AL	6	9	5	0	0	1	(0	1)	8	6	3	0	0	1	0	0	0	0	0	.00	0	.556	.556	.889
1996 Cleveland	AL	51	121	43	14	1	5	(2	3)	74	26	27	19	4	13	0	0	3	3	0	1.00	6	.355	.434	.612
1997 Cleveland	AL	130	377	101	15	3	17	(7	10)	173	62	61	63	2	50	1	3	7	13	3	.81	10	.268	.368	.459
1998 Cleveland	AL	112	350	94	19	0	16	(10	6)	161	56	66	73	8	75	3	1	3	10	5	.67	7	.269	.396	.460
4 ML YEARS		299	857	243	48	4	39	(19	20)	416	150	157	155	14	139	4	4	13	26	8	.76	23	.284	.391	.485

Bernard Gilkey

Bats: R **Throws:** R **Pos:** LF-103; PH/PR-11; RF-4; CF-1   **Ht:** 6'0" **Wt:** 200 **Born:** 9/24/66 **Age:** 32

Year Team	Lg	G	AB	H	2B	3B	HR	(Hm	Rd)	TB	R	RBI	TBB	IBB	SO	HBP	SH	SF	SB	CS	SB%	GDP	Avg	OBP	SLG
1990 St. Louis	NL	18	64	19	5	2	1	(0	1)	31	11	3	8	0	5	0	0	0	6	1	.86	1	.297	.375	.484
1991 St. Louis	NL	81	268	58	7	2	5	(2	3)	84	28	20	39	0	33	1	1	2	14	8	.64	14	.216	.316	.313
1992 St. Louis	NL	131	384	116	19	4	7	(3	4)	164	56	43	39	1	52	1	3	4	18	12	.60	5	.302	.364	.427
1993 St. Louis	NL	137	557	170	40	5	16	(7	9)	268	99	70	56	2	66	4	0	5	15	10	.60	16	.305	.370	.481
1994 St. Louis	NL	105	380	96	22	1	6	(0	6)	138	52	45	39	2	65	10	0	2	15	8	.65	5	.253	.336	.363
1995 St. Louis	NL	121	480	143	33	4	17	(5	12)	235	73	69	42	3	70	5	1	3	12	6	.67	17	.298	.358	.490
1996 New York	NL	153	571	181	44	3	30	(14	16)	321	108	117	73	7	125	4	0	8	17	9	.65	18	.317	.393	.562
1997 New York	NL	145	518	129	31	1	18	(7	11)	216	85	78	70	1	111	6	0	12	7	11	.39	11	.249	.338	.417
1998 NYN-Ari	NL	111	365	85	15	0	5	(2	3)	115	41	33	43	1	80	5	3	3	9	3	.75	11	.233	.320	.315
1998 New York	NL	82	264	60	15	0	4	(1	3)	87	33	28	32	1	66	4	2	3	5	1	.83	6	.227	.317	.330
Arizona	NL	29	101	25	0	0	1	(1	0)	28	8	5	11	0	14	1	1	0	4	2	.67	5	.248	.327	.277
9 ML YEARS		1002	3587	997	216	22	105	(40	65)	1572	553	478	409	17	607	36	8	39	113	68	.62	97	.278	.354	.438

Ed Giovanola

Bats: L **Throws:** R **Pos:** PH/PR-39; 3B-37; 2B-36; SS-2   **Ht:** 5'10" **Wt:** 170 **Born:** 3/4/69 **Age:** 30

Year Team	Lg	G	AB	H	2B	3B	HR	(Hm	Rd)	TB	R	RBI	TBB	IBB	SO	HBP	SH	SF	SB	CS	SB%	GDP	Avg	OBP	SLG
1998 Las Vegas *	AAA	4	15	5	0	0	0	(0	0)	5	4	1	2	0	3	0	0	0	0	1	.00	0	.333	.412	.333
1995 Atlanta	NL	13	14	1	0	0	0	(0	0)	1	2	0	3	0	5	0	0	0	0	0	.00	1	.071	.235	.071
1996 Atlanta	NL	43	82	19	2	0	0	(0	0)	21	10	7	8	0	13	1	2	1	1	0	1.00	3	.232	.304	.256
1997 Atlanta	NL	14	8	2	0	0	0	(0	0)	2	0	0	2	1	1	0	0	0	0	0	.00	2	.250	.400	.250
1998 San Diego	NL	92	139	32	3	3	1	(1	0)	44	19	9	22	0	22	0	5	0	1	2	.33	2	.230	.335	.317
4 ML YEARS		162	243	54	5	3	1	(1	0)	68	31	16	35	1	41	1	7	1	2	2	.50	8	.222	.321	.280

Charles Gipson

Bats: R **Throws:** R **Pos:** PH/PR-17; LF-14; RF-13; CF-11; 3B-4; DH-1   **Ht:** 6'2" **Wt:** 180 **Born:** 12/16/72 **Age:** 26

Year Team	Lg	G	AB	H	2B	3B	HR	(Hm	Rd)	TB	R	RBI	TBB	IBB	SO	HBP	SH	SF	SB	CS	SB%	GDP	Avg	OBP	SLG
1992 Mariners	R	39	124	39	2	0	0	—	—	41	30	14	13	1	19	6	2	1	11	5	.69	0	.315	.403	.331
1993 Appleton	A	109	348	89	13	1	0	—	—	104	63	20	61	0	76	27	9	1	21	15	.58	5	.256	.405	.299
1994 Riverside	A+	128	481	141	12	3	1	—	—	162	102	41	76	4	67	12	7	2	34	15	.69	8	.293	.401	.337
1995 Port City	AA	112	391	87	11	2	0	—	—	102	36	29	30	0	66	8	7	1	10	12	.45	13	.223	.291	.261
1996 Port City	AA	119	407	109	12	3	1	—	—	130	54	30	41	1	62	7	6	0	26	15	.63	9	.268	.345	.319
1997 Tacoma	AAA	11	35	11	2	0	0	—	—	13	5	5	4	0	3	1	0	0	0	1	.00	0	.314	.400	.371
Memphis	AA	88	320	79	9	4	1	—	—	99	56	28	34	2	71	13	2	1	31	6	.84	4	.247	.342	.309
1998 Tacoma	AAA	75	278	67	16	2	0	—	—	87	39	11	27	1	50	6	3	0	14	11	.56	17	.241	.322	.313
1998 Seattle	AL	44	51	12	1	0	0	(0	0)	13	11	2	5	1	9	1	0	0	2	1	.67	1	.235	.316	.255

Joe Girardi

Bats: Right **Throws:** Right **Pos:** C-78   **Ht:** 5'11" **Wt:** 195 **Born:** 10/14/64 **Age:** 34

Year Team	Lg	G	AB	H	2B	3B	HR	(Hm	Rd)	TB	R	RBI	TBB	IBB	SO	HBP	SH	SF	SB	CS	SB%	GDP	Avg	OBP	SLG
1989 Chicago	NL	59	157	39	10	0	1	(0	1)	52	15	14	11	1	26	2	1	1	2	1	.67	4	.248	.304	.331
1990 Chicago	NL	133	419	113	24	2	1	(1	0)	144	36	38	17	11	50	3	4	4	8	3	.73	13	.270	.300	.344
1991 Chicago	NL	21	47	9	2	0	0	(0	0)	11	3	6	6	1	6	0	1	0	0	0	.00	0	.191	.283	.234
1992 Chicago	NL	91	270	73	3	1	1	(1	0)	81	19	12	19	3	38	1	0	1	0	2	.00	7	.270	.320	.300
1993 Colorado	NL	86	310	90	14	5	3	(2	1)	123	35	31	24	0	41	3	12	1	6	6	.50	6	.290	.346	.397
1994 Colorado	NL	93	330	91	9	4	4	(1	3)	120	47	34	21	1	48	2	6	2	3	3	.50	13	.276	.321	.364
1995 Colorado	NL	125	462	121	17	2	8	(6	2)	166	63	55	29	0	76	2	12	1	3	3	.50	15	.262	.308	.359
1996 New York	AL	124	422	124	22	3	2	(1	1)	158	55	45	30	1	55	5	11	3	13	4	.76	11	.294	.346	.374
1997 New York	AL	112	398	105	23	1	1	(1	0)	133	38	50	26	1	53	2	5	2	2	3	.40	10	.264	.311	.334
1998 New York	AL	78	254	70	11	4	3	(1	2)	98	31	31	14	1	38	2	8	1	2	4	.33	10	.276	.317	.386
10 ML YEARS		922	3069	835	135	22	24	(14	10)	1086	342	316	197	24	431	22	60	16	39	29	.57	95	.272	.319	.354

Doug Glanville

Bats: Right **Throws:** Right **Pos:** CF-158; PH/PR-1   **Ht:** 6'2" **Wt:** 175 **Born:** 8/25/70 **Age:** 28

Year Team	Lg	G	AB	H	2B	3B	HR	(Hm	Rd)	TB	R	RBI	TBB	IBB	SO	HBP	SH	SF	SB	CS	SB%	GDP	Avg	OBP	SLG
1996 Chicago	NL	49	83	20	5	1	1	(1	0)	30	10	10	3	0	11	0	2	1	2	0	1.00	0	.241	.264	.361
1997 Chicago	NL	146	474	142	22	5	4	(2	2)	186	79	35	24	0	46	1	9	2	19	11	.63	9	.300	.333	.392
1998 Philadelphia	NL	158	678	189	28	7	8	(3	5)	255	106	49	42	1	89	6	5	4	23	6	.79	7	.279	.325	.376
3 ML YEARS		353	1235	351	55	13	13	(6	7)	471	195	94	69	1	146	7	16	7	44	17	.72	16	.284	.324	.381

Keith Glauber

Pitches: Right **Bats:** Right **Pos:** RP-3   **Ht:** 6'2" **Wt:** 190 **Born:** 1/18/72 **Age:** 27

Year Team	Lg	G	GS	CG	GF	IP	BFP	H	R	ER	HR	SH	SF	HB	TBB	IBB	SO	WP	Bk	W	L	Pct.	ShO	Sv-Op	Hld	ERA
1994 New Jersey	A-	17	10	0	3	68.2	289	67	36	32	3	4	2	2	26	1	51	8	0	4	6	.400	0	0- —	—	4.19
1995 Savannah	A	40	0	0	3	62.2	277	50	29	26	2	4	5	3	36	3	62	9	1	2	1	.667	0	0- —	—	3.73
1996 Peoria	A	54	0	0	36	64	276	54	31	22	2	2	5	1	26	2	80	2	1	3	3	.500	0	14- —	—	3.09
1997 Arkansas	AA	50	0	0	22	59	245	48	22	18	3	2	4	2	25	2	53	5	0	5	7	.417	0	3- —	—	2.75
Louisville	AAA	15	0	0	12	15.2	71	18	14	9	2	1	0	1	4	0	14	0	0	1	3	.250	0	5- —	—	5.17
1998 Burlington	A	7	1	0	1	14	73	13	9	6	1	0	0	2	6	0	13	2	0	0	1	.000	0	0- —	—	3.86
Chattanooga	AA	2	2	0	0	9	35	3	4	4	1	0	0	0	6	0	5	0	0	1	1	.500	0	0- —	—	4.00
Indianapolis	AAA	4	4	0	0	16	78	20	17	16	1	3	2	1	14	0	15	3	0	1	3	.250	0	0- —	—	9.00
1998 Cincinnati	NL	3	0	0	2	7.2	31	6	2	2	0	0	2	0	1	0	4	2	0	0	0	.000	0	0-0	0	2.35

Troy Glaus

Bats: Right **Throws:** Right **Pos:** 3B-48   **Ht:** 6'5" **Wt:** 225 **Born:** 8/3/76 **Age:** 22

Year Team	Lg	G	AB	H	2B	3B	HR	(Hm	Rd)	TB	R	RBI	TBB	IBB	SO	HBP	SH	SF	SB	CS	SB%	GDP	Avg	OBP	SLG
1998 Midland	AA	50	188	58	11	2	19	—	—	130	51	51	39	3	41	2	0	1	4	2	.67	4	.309	.430	.691
Vancouver	AAA	59	219	67	16	0	16	—	—	131	33	42	21	0	55	3	0	0	3	2	.60	1	.306	.374	.598
1998 Anaheim	AL	48	165	36	9	0	1	(0	1)	48	19	23	15	0	51	0	0	2	1	0	1.00	3	.218	.280	.291

Tom Glavine

Pitches: Left **Bats:** Left **Pos:** SP-33   **Ht:** 6'1" **Wt:** 185 **Born:** 3/25/66 **Age:** 33

Year Team	Lg	G	GS	CG	GF	IP	BFP	H	R	ER	HR	SH	SF	HB	TBB	IBB	SO	WP	Bk	W	L	Pct.	ShO	Sv-Op	Hld	ERA
1987 Atlanta	NL	9	9	0	0	50.1	238	55	34	31	5	2	3	3	33	4	20	1	1	2	4	.333	0	0-0	0	5.54
1988 Atlanta	NL	34	34	1	0	195.1	844	201	111	99	12	17	11	8	63	7	84	2	1	7	17	.292	0	0-0	0	4.56
1989 Atlanta	NL	29	29	6	0	186	766	172	88	76	20	11	4	2	40	3	90	2	0	14	8	.636	4	0-0	0	3.68
1990 Atlanta	NL	33	33	1	0	214.1	929	232	111	102	18	21	7	2	78	10	129	8	1	10	12	.455	0	0-0	0	4.28
1991 Atlanta	NL	34	34	9	0	246.2	989	201	83	70	17	7	6	2	69	6	192	10	2	20	11	.645	1	0-0	0	2.55
1992 Atlanta	NL	33	33	7	0	225	919	197	81	69	6	2	6	2	70	7	129	5	0	20	8	.714	5	0-0	0	2.76
1993 Atlanta	NL	36	36	4	0	239.1	1014	236	91	85	16	10	2	2	90	7	120	4	0	22	6	.786	2	0-0	0	3.20
1994 Atlanta	NL	25	25	2	0	165.1	731	173	76	73	10	9	6	1	70	10	140	8	1	13	9	.591	0	0-0	0	3.97
1995 Atlanta	NL	29	29	3	0	198.2	822	182	76	68	9	7	5	5	66	0	127	3	0	16	7	.696	1	0-0	0	3.08
1996 Atlanta	NL	36	36	1	0	235.1	994	222	91	78	14	15	2	0	85	7	181	4	0	15	10	.600	0	0-0	0	2.98
1997 Atlanta	NL	33	33	5	0	240	970	197	86	79	20	11	6	4	79	9	152	3	0	14	7	.667	2	0-0	0	2.96
1998 Atlanta	NL	33	33	4	0	229.1	934	202	67	63	13	6	2	2	74	2	157	3	0	20	6	.769	3	0-0	0	2.47
12 ML YEARS		364	364	43	0	2425.2	10150	2270	995	893	160	118	55	32	817	72	1521	53	7	173	105	.622	18	0-0	0	3.31

Wayne Gomes

Pitches: Right **Bats:** Right **Pos:** RP-71   **Ht:** 6'2" **Wt:** 226 **Born:** 1/15/73 **Age:** 26

Year Team	Lg	G	GS	CG	GF	IP	BFP	H	R	ER	HR	SH	SF	HB	TBB	IBB	SO	WP	Bk	W	L	Pct.	ShO	Sv-Op	Hld	ERA
1993 Batavia	A-	5	0	0	3	7.1	32	1	1	1	0	0	0	0	8	0	11	0	1	1	0	1.000	0	0- —	—	1.23
Clearwater	A+	9	0	0	8	7.2	37	4	1	1	0	0	0	0	9	0	13	2	0	0	0	.000	0	4- —	—	1.17
1994 Clearwater	A+	23	21	1	0	104.1	474	85	63	55	5	2	4	3	82	1	102	27	4	6	8	.429	1	0- —	—	4.74
1995 Reading	AA	22	22	1	0	104.2	462	89	54	46	8	3	1	1	70	0	102	6	6	7	4	.636	1	0- —	—	3.96
1996 Reading	AA	67	0	0	55	64.1	291	53	35	32	7	1	3	1	48	3	79	14	0	4	4	.000	0	24- —	—	4.48
1997 Scranton-WB	AAA	26	0	0	15	38	166	31	11	10	2	1	1	0	24	2	36	2	0	3	1	.750	0	7- —	—	2.37
1997 Philadelphia	NL	37	0	0	13	42.2	191	45	26	25	4	2	0	1	24	0	24	2	0	5	1	.833	0	0-1	5	5.27
1998 Philadelphia	NL	71	0	0	16	93.1	408	94	48	44	9	5	1	3	35	4	86	6	0	9	6	.600	0	1-8	13	4.24
2 ML YEARS		108	0	0	29	136	599	139	74	69	13	7	1	4	59	4	110	8	0	14	7	.667	0	1-9	16	4.57

Chris Gomez

Bats: Right **Throws:** Right **Pos:** SS-143; PH/PR-3   **Ht:** 6'1" **Wt:** 195 **Born:** 6/16/71 **Age:** 28

Year Team	Lg	G	AB	H	2B	3B	HR	(Hm	Rd)	TB	R	RBI	TBB	IBB	SO	HBP	SH	SF	SB	CS	SB%	GDP	Avg	OBP	SLG
1993 Detroit	AL	46	128	32	7	1	0	(0	0)	41	11	11	9	0	17	1	3	0	2	2	.50	2	.250	.304	.320
1994 Detroit	AL	84	296	76	19	2	8	(5	3)	119	32	53	33	0	64	3	1	1	5	3	.63	8	.257	.336	.402
1995 Detroit	AL	123	431	96	20	2	11	(5	6)	153	49	50	41	0	96	3	3	4	4	1	.80	13	.223	.292	.355
1996 Det-SD		137	456	117	21	1	4	(2	2)	152	53	45	57	1	84	7	6	2	3	3	.50	16	.257	.347	.333
1997 San Diego	NL	150	522	132	19	2	5	(2	3)	170	62	54	53	1	114	5	3	3	5	8	.38	16	.253	.326	.326

Year Team	Lg	G	AB	H	2B	3B	HR	(Hm	Rd)	TB	R	RBI	TBB	IBB	SO	HBP	SH	SF	SB	CS	SB%	GDP	Avg	OBP	SLG
1998 San Diego	NL	145	449	120	32	3	4	(3	1)	170	55	39	51	7	87	5	7	3	1	3	.25	11	.267	.346	.379
1996 Detroit	AL	48	128	31	5	0	1	(1	0)	39	21	16	18	0	20	1	3	0	1	1	.50	5	.242	.340	.305
San Diego	NL	89	328	86	16	1	3	(1	2)	113	32	29	39	1	64	6	3	2	2	2	.50	11	.262	.349	.345
6 ML YEARS		685	2282	573	118	9	32	(17	15)	805	262	252	244	9	462	24	25	13	20	20	.50	66	.251	.328	.353

Alex Gonzalez

Bats: Right **Throws:** Right **Pos:** SS-158 **Ht:** 6'0" **Wt:** 190 **Born:** 4/8/73 **Age:** 26

Year Team	Lg	G	AB	H	2B	3B	HR	(Hm	Rd)	TB	R	RBI	TBB	IBB	SO	HBP	SH	SF	SB	CS	SB%	GDP	Avg	OBP	SLG
1994 Toronto	AL	15	53	8	3	1	0	(0	0)	13	7	1	4	0	17	1	1	0	3	0	1.00	2	.151	.224	.245
1995 Toronto	AL	111	367	89	19	4	10	(8	2)	146	51	42	44	1	114	1	9	4	4	4	.50	7	.243	.322	.398
1996 Toronto	AL	147	527	124	30	5	14	(3	11)	206	64	64	45	0	127	5	7	3	16	6	.73	12	.235	.300	.391
1997 Toronto	AL	126	426	102	23	2	12	(4	8)	165	46	35	34	1	94	5	11	2	15	6	.71	9	.239	.302	.387
1998 Toronto	AL	158	568	136	28	1	13	(7	6)	205	70	51	28	1	121	6	13	3	21	6	.78	13	.239	.281	.361
5 ML YEARS		557	1941	459	103	13	49	(22	27)	735	238	193	155	3	473	18	41	12	59	22	.73	43	.236	.297	.379

Alex Gonzalez

Bats: Right **Throws:** Right **Pos:** SS-25; PH/PR-1 **Ht:** 6'0" **Wt:** 170 **Born:** 2/15/77 **Age:** 22

Year Team	Lg	G	AB	H	2B	3B	HR	(Hm	Rd)	TB	R	RBI	TBB	IBB	SO	HBP	SH	SF	SB	CS	SB%	GDP	Avg	OBP	SLG
1995 Brevard Cty	A+	17	59	12	2	1	0	—	—	16	6	8	1	0	14	1	0	0	1	1	.50	2	.203	.230	.271
Marlins	R	53	187	55	7	4	2	—	—	76	30	30	19	0	27	2	1	4	11	2	.85	2	.294	.358	.406
1996 Marlins	R	10	41	16	3	0	0	—	—	19	6	6	2	0	4	0	0	0	1	0	1.00	1	.390	.419	.463
Kane County	A	4	10	2	0	0	0	—	—	2	2	0	2	0	4	1	1	0	0	0	.00	1	.200	.385	.200
Portland	AA	11	34	8	0	1	0	—	—	10	4	1	2	2	10	1	0	0	0	0	.00	2	.235	.297	.294
1997 Portland	AA	133	449	114	16	4	19	—	—	195	69	65	27	5	83	7	3	3	4	7	.36	7	.254	.305	.434
1998 Charlotte	AAA	108	422	117	20	10	10	—	—	187	71	51	28	2	80	6	8	2	4	7	.36	6	.277	.330	.443
1998 Florida	NL	25	86	13	2	0	3	(1	2)	24	11	7	9	0	30	1	2	0	0	0	.00	2	.151	.240	.279

Gabe Gonzalez

Pitches: Left **Bats:** Left **Pos:** RP-3 **Ht:** 6'1" **Wt:** 150 **Born:** 5/24/72 **Age:** 27

Year Team	Lg	HOW MUCH HE PITCHED						WHAT HE GAVE UP											THE RESULTS						
		G	GS	CG	GF	IP	BFP	H	R	ER	HR	SH	SF	HB	TBB	IBB	SO	WP	Bk	W	L	Pct.	ShO	Sv-Op	Hld	ERA
1995 Kane County	A	32	0	0	10	43.1	181	32	18	11	0	2	1	2	14	2	41	1	0	4	4	.500	0	1--	—	2.28
1996 Charlotte	AAA	2	0	0	1	3	15	4	1	1	0	0	0	2	0	3	0	0	0	0	0	.000	0	0--	—	3.00
Brevard Cty	A+	47	0	0	32	76.1	308	56	20	15	2	9	1	3	23	7	62	2	0	2	7	.222	0	9--	—	1.77
1997 Portland	AA	29	0	0	10	42.2	171	43	12	10	1	3	3	0	5	1	28	1	0	3	2	.600	0	3--	—	2.11
Charlotte	AAA	37	1	0	11	42.2	176	38	15	13	3	1	2	1	14	1	24	0	0	2	2	.500	0	3--	—	2.74
1998 Charlotte	AAA	57	4	0	13	87	412	101	67	53	3	8	7	1	53	5	41	2	1	3	9	.250	0	2--	—	5.48
1998 Florida	NL	3	0	0	1	1	5	1	1	1	0	0	0	1	1	0	0	0	0	0	0	.000	0	0-0	0	9.00

Jeremi Gonzalez

Pitches: Right **Bats:** Right **Pos:** SP-20 **Ht:** 6'2" **Wt:** 205 **Born:** 1/8/75 **Age:** 24

Year Team	Lg	HOW MUCH HE PITCHED						WHAT HE GAVE UP											THE RESULTS						
		G	GS	CG	GF	IP	BFP	H	R	ER	HR	SH	SF	HB	TBB	IBB	SO	WP	Bk	W	L	Pct.	ShO	Sv-Op	Hld	ERA
1992 Rockies/Cub	R	14	7	0	1	45	238	65	54	39	0	0	6	10	22	0	39	11	1	0	5	.000	0	0--	—	7.80
1993 Huntington	R+	12	12	1	0	67.2	319	82	59	47	6	1	2	5	38	0	42	5	2	3	9	.250	0	0--	—	6.25
1994 Peoria	A	13	13	1	0	71.1	325	86	53	44	4	2	3	7	32	0	39	5	2	1	7	.125	0	0--	—	5.55
Williamsprt	A-	16	12	1	2	80.2	357	83	46	38	6	3	3	10	29	0	64	4	1	4	6	.400	1	1--	—	4.24
1995 Rockford	A	12	12	1	0	65.1	297	63	43	37	4	1	4	8	28	0	36	8	1	4	4	.500	0	4--	—	5.10
Daytona	A+	19	2	0	7	44.1	178	34	15	6	0	1	2	1	13	1	30	4	2	5	1	.833	0	4--	—	1.22
1996 Orlando	AA	17	14	0	2	97	415	95	39	36	6	1	2	4	28	1	85	2	0	6	3	.667	0	0--	—	3.34
1997 Iowa	AAA	10	10	1	0	62	249	47	27	24	8	1	1	1	21	0	58	2	0	2	2	.500	1	0--	—	3.48
1997 Chicago	NL	23	23	1	0	144	613	126	73	68	16	4	5	2	69	5	93	1	1	11	9	.550	1	0-0	0	4.25
1998 Chicago	NL	20	20	1	0	110	493	124	72	65	13	5	2	3	41	5	70	2	3	7	7	.500	1	0-0	0	5.32
2 ML YEARS		43	43	2	0	254	1106	250	145	133	29	9	7	5	110	10	163	3	4	18	16	.529	2	0-0	0	4.71

Juan Gonzalez

Bats: Right **Throws:** Right **Pos:** RF-116; DH-38; PH/PR-1 **Ht:** 6'3" **Wt:** 220 **Born:** 10/16/69 **Age:** 29

Year Team	Lg	G	AB	H	2B	3B	HR	(Hm	Rd)	TB	R	RBI	TBB	IBB	SO	HBP	SH	SF	SB	CS	SB%	GDP	Avg	OBP	SLG
1989 Texas	AL	24	60	9	3	0	1	(1	0)	15	6	7	6	0	17	0	2	0	0	0	.00	4	.150	.227	.250
1990 Texas	AL	25	90	26	7	1	4	(3	1)	47	11	12	2	0	18	2	0	1	0	1	.00	2	.289	.316	.522
1991 Texas	AL	142	545	144	34	1	27	(7	20)	261	78	102	42	7	118	5	0	3	4	4	.50	10	.264	.321	.479
1992 Texas	AL	155	584	152	24	2	43	(19	24)	309	77	109	35	1	143	5	0	6	0	1	.00	16	.260	.304	.529
1993 Texas	AL	140	536	166	33	1	46	(24	22)	339	105	118	37	7	99	13	0	1	4	1	.80	12	.310	.368	.632
1994 Texas	AL	107	422	116	18	4	19	(6	13)	199	57	85	30	10	66	7	0	4	6	4	.60	18	.275	.330	.472
1995 Texas	AL	90	352	104	20	2	27	(15	12)	209	57	82	17	3	66	0	0	5	0	0	.00	15	.295	.324	.594
1996 Texas	AL	134	541	170	33	2	47	(23	24)	348	89	144	45	12	82	3	0	3	2	0	1.00	12	.314	.368	.643
1997 Texas	AL	133	533	158	24	3	42	(18	24)	314	87	131	33	7	107	3	0	10	0	0	.00	12	.296	.335	.589
1998 Texas	AL	154	606	193	50	2	45	(21	24)	382	110	157	46	9	126	6	0	11	2	1	.67	20	.318	.366	.630
10 ML YEARS		1104	4269	1238	246	18	301	(137	164)	2423	677	947	293	56	842	44	2	46	18	12	.60	119	.290	.339	.568

Lariel Gonzalez

Pitches: Right **Bats:** Right **Pos:** RP-1   **Ht:** 6'4" **Wt:** 228 **Born:** 5/25/76 **Age:** 23

Year Team	Lg	HOW MUCH HE PITCHED						WHAT HE GAVE UP											THE RESULTS					
		G	GS	CG	GF	IP	BFP	H	R	ER	HR	SH	SF	HB	TBB	IBB	SO	WP	Bk	W	L	Pct.	ShO	Sv-Op	Hld	ERA
1995 Portland	A-	15	11	0	2	57.2	258	44	31	26	4	1	1	7	43	0	48	9	5	3	4	.429	0	2- -	—	4.06
1996 Asheville	A	35	0	0	24	45	208	37	21	18	2	0	0	1	37	0	53	4	2	1	1	.500	0	4- -	—	3.60
1997 Salem	A+	44	0	0	25	57	237	42	19	16	3	2	2	3	23	1	79	4	0	5	0	1.000	0	8- -	—	2.53
1998 New Haven	AA	58	0	0	45	58	255	46	30	27	5	3	3	3	40	2	63	11	0	4	4	.000	0	22- -	—	4.19
1998 Colorado	NL	1	0	0	1	1	3	0	0	0	0	0	0	0	0	0	0	0	0	0	0	.000	0	0-0	0	0.00

Luis Gonzalez

Bats: L **Throws:** R **Pos:** LF-132; DH-19; PH/PR-6; CF-3   **Ht:** 6'2" **Wt:** 190 **Born:** 9/3/67 **Age:** 31

Year Team	Lg	BATTING															BASERUNNING				PERCENTAGES		
		G	AB	H	2B	3B	HR	(Hm | Rd)	TB	R	RBI	TBB	IBB	SO	HBP	SH	SF	SB	CS	SB%	GDP	Avg	OBP	SLG
1990 Houston	NL	12	21	4	2	0	0	(0 | 0)	6	1	0	2	1	5	0	0	0	0	0	.00	0	.190	.261	.286
1991 Houston	NL	137	473	120	28	9	13	(4 | 9)	205	51	69	40	4	101	8	1	4	10	7	.59	9	.254	.320	.433
1992 Houston	NL	122	387	94	19	3	10	(4 | 6)	149	40	55	24	3	52	2	1	2	7	7	.50	6	.243	.289	.385
1993 Houston	NL	154	540	162	34	3	15	(8 | 7)	247	82	72	47	7	83	10	3	10	20	9	.69	9	.300	.361	.457
1994 Houston	NL	112	392	107	29	4	8	(3 | 5)	168	57	67	49	6	57	3	0	6	15	13	.54	10	.273	.353	.429
1995 Hou-ChN	NL	133	471	130	29	8	13	(6 | 7)	214	69	69	57	8	63	6	1	6	6	8	.43	16	.276	.357	.454
1996 Chicago	NL	146	483	131	30	4	15	(6 | 9)	214	70	79	61	8	49	4	1	6	9	6	.60	13	.271	.354	.443
1997 Houston	NL	152	550	142	31	2	10	(4 | 6)	207	78	68	71	7	67	5	0	5	10	7	.59	12	.258	.345	.376
1998 Detroit	AL	154	547	146	35	5	23	(15 | 8)	260	84	71	57	7	62	8	0	6	12	7	.63	9	.267	.340	.475
1995 Houston	NL	56	209	54	10	4	6	(1 | 5)	90	35	35	18	3	30	›3	1	3	1	3	.25	8	.258	.322	.431
Chicago	NL	77	262	76	19	4	7	(5 | 2)	124	34	34	39	5	33	3	0	3	5	5	.50	8	.290	.384	.473
9 ML YEARS		1122	3864	1036	237	38	107	(50 | 57)	1670	532	550	408	51	539	46	7	47	89	64	.58	84	.268	.341	.432

Dwight Gooden

Pitches: Right **Bats:** Right **Pos:** SP-23   **Ht:** 6'3" **Wt:** 210 **Born:** 11/16/64 **Age:** 34

Year Team	Lg	HOW MUCH HE PITCHED						WHAT HE GAVE UP											THE RESULTS					
		G	GS	CG	GF	IP	BFP	H	R	ER	HR	SH	SF	HB	TBB	IBB	SO	WP	Bk	W	L	Pct.	ShO	Sv-Op	Hld	ERA
1998 Buffalo *	AAA	4	4	0	0	16	74	23	16	16	5	0	0	0	7	0	18	1	0	1	2	.333	0	0-0	0	9.00
1984 New York	NL	31	31	7	0	218	879	161	72	63	7	3	2	2	73	2	276	3	7	17	9	.654	3	0-0	0	2.60
1985 New York	NL	35	35	16	0	276.2	1065	198	51	47	13	6	2	2	69	4	268	6	2	24	4	.857	8	0-0	0	1.53
1986 New York	NL	33	33	12	0	250	1020	197	92	79	17	10	8	4	80	3	200	4	1	17	6	.739	2	0-0	0	2.84
1987 New York	NL	25	25	7	0	179.2	730	162	68	64	11	5	5	2	53	2	148	1	1	15	7	.682	3	0-0	0	3.21
1988 New York	NL	34	34	10	0	248.1	1024	242	98	88	8	10	6	6	57	4	175	5	5	18	9	.667	3	0-0	0	3.19
1989 New York	NL	19	17	0	1	118.1	497	93	42	38	9	4	3	2	47	2	101	7	3	9	4	.692	0	1-1	1	2.89
1990 New York	NL	34	34	2	0	232.2	983	229	106	99	10	10	7	7	70	3	223	6	3	19	7	.731	1	0-0	0	3.83
1991 New York	NL	27	27	3	0	190	789	185	80	76	12	5	4	3	56	2	150	5	2	13	7	.650	1	0-0	0	3.60
1992 New York	NL	31	31	3	0	206	863	197	93	84	11	10	7	3	70	7	145	3	1	10	13	.435	3	0-0	0	3.67
1993 New York	NL	29	29	7	0	208.2	866	188	89	80	16	11	7	9	61	1	149	5	2	12	15	.444	2	0-0	0	3.45
1994 New York	NL	7	7	0	0	41.1	182	46	32	29	9	3	0	1	15	1	40	2	0	3	4	.429	0	0-0	0	6.31
1996 New York	AL	29	29	1	0	170.2	756	169	101	95	19	1	5	8	88	4	126	9	1	11	7	.611	1	0-0	0	5.01
1997 New York	AL	20	19	0	0	106.1	472	116	61	58	14	0	2	7	53	1	66	8	0	9	5	.643	0	0-0	0	4.91
1998 Cleveland	AL	23	23	0	0	134	580	135	59	56	13	1	4	9	51	0	83	3	0	8	6	.571	0	0-0	0	3.76
14 ML YEARS		377	374	68	1	2580.2	10706	2318	1044	956	169	79	62	66	843	36	2150	67	33	185	103	.642	24	1-1	1	3.33

Curtis Goodwin

Bats: L **Throws:** L **Pos:** CF-74; PH/PR-48; LF-14; RF-7   **Ht:** 5'11" **Wt:** 180 **Born:** 9/30/72 **Age:** 26

Year Team	Lg	BATTING															BASERUNNING				PERCENTAGES		
		G	AB	H	2B	3B	HR	(Hm | Rd)	TB	R	RBI	TBB	IBB	SO	HBP	SH	SF	SB	CS	SB%	GDP	Avg	OBP	SLG
1995 Baltimore	AL	87	289	76	11	3	1	(0 | 1)	96	40	24	15	0	53	2	7	3	22	4	.85	5	.263	.301	.332
1996 Cincinnati	NL	49	136	31	3	0	0	(0 | 0)	34	20	5	19	0	34	0	1	0	15	6	.71	1	.228	.323	.250
1997 Cincinnati	NL	85	265	67	11	0	1	(1 | 0)	81	27	12	24	0	53	1	6	1	22	13	.63	6	.253	.316	.306
1998 Colorado	NL	119	159	39	7	0	1	(1 | 0)	49	27	6	16	0	40	0	10	1	5	1	.83	3	.245	.313	.308
4 ML YEARS		340	849	213	32	3	3	(2 | 1)	260	114	47	74	0	180	3	24	5	64	24	.73	15	.251	.311	.306

Tom Goodwin

Bats: Left **Throws:** Right **Pos:** CF-150; PH/PR-13; DH-1   **Ht:** 6'1" **Wt:** 175 **Born:** 7/27/68 **Age:** 30

Year Team	Lg	BATTING															BASERUNNING				PERCENTAGES		
		G	AB	H	2B	3B	HR	(Hm | Rd)	TB	R	RBI	TBB	IBB	SO	HBP	SH	SF	SB	CS	SB%	GDP	Avg	OBP	SLG
1991 Los Angeles	NL	16	7	1	0	0	0	(0 | 0)	1	3	0	0	0	0	0	0	0	1	1	.50	0	.143	.143	.143
1992 Los Angeles	NL	57	73	17	1	1	0	(0 | 0)	20	15	3	6	0	10	0	0	0	7	3	.70	0	.233	.291	.274
1993 Los Angeles	NL	30	17	5	1	0	0	(0 | 0)	6	6	1	1	0	4	0	0	0	1	2	.33	1	.294	.333	.353
1994 Kansas City	AL	2	2	0	0	0	0	(0 | 0)	0	0	0	0	0	1	0	0	0	0	0	.00	0	.000	.000	.000
1995 Kansas City	AL	133	480	138	16	3	4	(2 | 2)	172	72	28	38	0	72	5	14	4	50	18	.74	7	.288	.346	.358
1996 Kansas City	AL	143	524	148	14	4	1	(0 | 1)	173	80	35	39	0	79	2	21	4	66	22	.75	3	.282	.334	.330
1997 KC-Tex	AL	150	574	149	26	6	2	(0 | 2)	193	90	39	44	1	88	3	11	3	50	16	.76	7	.260	.314	.336
1998 Texas	AL	154	520	151	13	3	2	(2 | 0)	176	102	33	73	0	90	2	10	3	38	20	.66	2	.290	.378	.338
1997 Kansas City	AL	97	367	100	13	4	2	(0 | 2)	127	51	22	19	0	51	2	11	1	34	10	.77	5	.272	.311	.346
Texas	AL	53	207	49	13	2	0	(0 | 0)	66	39	17	25	1	37	1	0	2	16	6	.73	2	.237	.319	.319
8 ML YEARS		685	2197	609	71	17	9	(4 | 5)	741	368	139	201	1	344	12	56	7	213	82	.72	20	.277	.340	.337

Tom Gordon

Pitches: Right **Bats:** Right **Pos:** RP-73   **Ht:** 5'9" **Wt:** 180 **Born:** 11/18/67 **Age:** 31

		HOW MUCH HE PITCHED						WHAT HE GAVE UP										THE RESULTS						
Year Team	Lg	G	GS	CG	GF	IP	BFP	H	R	ER	HR	SH	SF	HB	TBB	IBB	SO	WP	Bk	W	L	Pct.	ShO	Sv-Op	Hld	ERA
1988 Kansas City	AL	5	2	0	0	15.2	67	16	9	9	1	0	0	0	7	0	18	0	0	0	2	.000	0	0-0	2	5.17
1989 Kansas City	AL	49	16	1	16	163	677	122	67	66	10	4	4	1	86	4	153	12	0	17	9	.654	1	1-7	3	3.64
1990 Kansas City	AL	32	32	6	0	195.1	858	192	99	81	17	8	2	3	99	1	175	11	0	12	11	.522	1	0-0	0	3.73
1991 Kansas City	AL	45	14	1	11	158	684	129	76	68	16	5	3	4	87	6	167	5	0	9	14	.391	0	1-4	4	3.87
1992 Kansas City	AL	40	11	0	13	117.2	516	116	67	60	9	2	6	4	55	4	98	5	2	6	10	.375	0	0-2	0	4.59
1993 Kansas City	AL	48	14	2	18	155.2	651	125	65	62	11	6	6	1	77	5	143	17	0	12	6	.667	0	1-6	2	3.58
1994 Kansas City	AL	24	24	0	0	155.1	675	136	79	75	15	3	8	3	87	3	126	12	1	11	7	.611	0	0-0	0	4.35
1995 Kansas City	AL	31	31	2	0	189	843	204	110	93	12	7	11	4	89	4	119	9	0	12	12	.500	0	0-0	0	4.43
1996 Boston	AL	34	34	4	0	215.2	998	249	143	**134**	22	7	5	11	105	5	171	6	1	12	9	.571	1	0-0	0	5.59
1997 Boston	AL	42	25	2	16	182.2	774	155	85	76	10	3	4	3	78	1	159	5	0	6	10	.375	1	11-13	0	3.74
1998 Boston	AL	73	0	0	**69**	79.1	317	55	24	24	2	2	2	0	25	1	78	9	0	7	4	.636	0	**46**-47	0	2.72
11 ML YEARS		423	203	18	143	1627.1	7060	1499	824	748	131	42	57	27	795	34	1407	91	4	104	94	.525	4	60-79	11	4.14

Rick Gorecki

Pitches: Right **Bats:** Right **Pos:** SP-3   **Ht:** 6'3" **Wt:** 167 **Born:** 8/27/73 **Age:** 25

		HOW MUCH HE PITCHED						WHAT HE GAVE UP										THE RESULTS						
Year Team	Lg	G	GS	CG	GF	IP	BFP	H	R	ER	HR	SH	SF	HB	TBB	IBB	SO	WP	Bk	W	L	Pct.	ShO	Sv-Op	Hld	ERA
1991 Great Falls	R+	13	10	0	0	51	219	44	34	25	3	2	0	1	27	0	56	4	5	0	3	.000	0	0- -	—	4.41
1992 Bakersfield	A+	25	24	0	1	129	580	122	68	58	11	0	2	7	90	2	115	17	0	11	7	.611	0	0- -	—	4.05
1993 San Antonio	AA	26	26	1	0	156	653	136	76	58	6	3	5	5	62	2	118	5	1	6	9	.400	0	0- -	—	3.35
1994 Albuquerque	AAA	22	21	0	0	103	481	119	65	58	11	2	3	7	60	1	73	11	0	8	6	.571	0	0- -	—	5.07
1995 Vero Beach	A+	6	5	0	0	27	110	19	6	2	0	1	1	4	9	0	24	1	0	1	2	.333	0	0- -	—	0.67
1997 San Berndno	A+	14	14	0	0	51	215	38	22	22	4	0	2	2	32	0	58	4	0	2	3	.400	0	0- -	—	3.88
San Antonio	AA	7	7	0	0	45.1	174	26	8	7	3	3	1	1	15	0	33	2	0	4	2	.667	0	0- -	—	1.39
1998 Devil Rays	R	2	2	0	0	5	20	3	0	0	0	1	0	0	2	0	5	0	0	0	0	.000	0	0- -	—	0.00
St. Pete	A+	1	1	0	0	4.2	19	4	0	0	0	0	0	0	1	0	7	0	0	0	0	.000	0	0- -	—	0.00
1997 Los Angeles	NL	4	1	0	2	6	32	9	10	10	3	0	0	0	6	1	6	0	0	1	0	1.000	0	0-0	0	15.00
1998 Tampa Bay	AL	3	3	0	0	16.2	70	15	9	9	1	0	2	0	10	0	7	1	0	1	2	.333	0	0-0	0	4.86
2 ML YEARS		7	4	0	2	22.2	102	24	19	19	4	0	2	0	16	1	13	1	0	2	2	.500	0	0-0	0	7.54

Mark Grace

Bats: Left **Throws:** Left **Pos:** 1B-156; PH/PR-3   **Ht:** 6'2" **Wt:** 200 **Born:** 6/28/64 **Age:** 35

		BATTING																	BASERUNNING				PERCENTAGES		
Year Team	Lg	G	AB	H	2B	3B	HR	(Hm	Rd)	TB	R	RBI	TBB	IBB	SO	HBP	SH	SF	SB	CS	SB%	GDP	Avg	OBP	SLG
1988 Chicago	NL	134	486	144	23	4	7	(0	7)	196	65	57	60	5	43	0	0	4	3	3	.50	12	.296	.371	.403
1989 Chicago	NL	142	510	160	28	3	13	(8	5)	233	74	79	80	13	42	0	3	3	14	7	.67	13	.314	.405	.457
1990 Chicago	NL	157	589	182	32	1	9	(4	5)	243	72	82	59	5	54	5	1	8	15	6	.71	10	.309	.372	.413
1991 Chicago	NL	160	**619**	169	28	5	8	(5	3)	231	87	58	70	7	53	3	4	7	3	4	.43	6	.273	.346	.373
1992 Chicago	NL	158	603	185	37	5	9	(5	4)	259	72	79	72	8	36	4	2	8	6	1	.86	14	.307	.380	.430
1993 Chicago	NL	155	594	193	39	4	14	(5	9)	282	86	98	71	14	32	1	1	9	8	4	.67	**25**	.325	.393	.475
1994 Chicago	NL	106	403	120	23	3	6	(5	1)	167	55	44	48	5	41	0	0	3	0	1	.00	10	.298	.370	.414
1995 Chicago	NL	143	552	180	**51**	3	16	(4	12)	285	97	92	65	9	46	2	1	7	6	2	.75	10	.326	.395	.516
1996 Chicago	NL	142	547	181	39	1	9	(4	5)	249	88	75	62	8	41	1	0	6	2	3	.40	18	.331	.396	.455
1997 Chicago	NL	151	555	177	32	5	13	(6	7)	258	87	78	88	3	45	2	1	8	2	4	.33	18	.319	.409	.465
1998 Chicago	NL	158	595	184	39	3	17	(7	10)	280	92	89	93	9	56	3	0	7	4	7	.36	17	.309	.401	.471
11 ML YEARS		1606	6053	1875	371	37	121	(53	68)	2683	875	831	768	86	489	21	13	70	63	42	.60	153	.310	.385	.443

Mike Grace

Pitches: Right **Bats:** Right **Pos:** SP-15; RP-6   **Ht:** 6'4" **Wt:** 219 **Born:** 6/20/70 **Age:** 29

		HOW MUCH HE PITCHED						WHAT HE GAVE UP										THE RESULTS						
Year Team	Lg	G	GS	CG	GF	IP	BFP	H	R	ER	HR	SH	SF	HB	TBB	IBB	SO	WP	Bk	W	L	Pct.	ShO	Sv-Op	Hld	ERA
1998 Scranton-WB *	AAA	11	10	2	0	75	327	92	44	42	8	9	3	5	18	1	39	2	0	3	6	.333	0	0- -	—	5.04
1995 Philadelphia	NL	2	2	0	0	11.1	47	10	4	4	0	1	0	0	4	0	7	0	0	1	1	.500	0	0-0	0	3.18
1996 Philadelphia	NL	12	12	1	0	80	323	72	33	31	9	4	0	1	16	1	49	0	1	7	2	.778	1	0-0	0	3.49
1997 Philadelphia	NL	6	6	0	0	39	151	32	16	15	3	0	1	1	10	1	26	2	0	3	2	.600	1	0-0	0	3.46
1998 Philadelphia	NL	21	15	0	1	90.1	418	116	61	55	10	7	1	8	30	1	46	1	1	4	7	.364	0	0-0	1	5.48
4 ML YEARS		41	35	2	1	220.2	939	230	114	105	22	12	2	10	60	3	128	3	2	15	12	.556	2	0-0	1	4.28

Tony Graffanino

Bats: R **Throws:** R **Pos:** 2B-93; PH/PR-30; SS-2; 3B-1   **Ht:** 6'1" **Wt:** 195 **Born:** 6/6/72 **Age:** 27

		BATTING																	BASERUNNING				PERCENTAGES		
Year Team	Lg	G	AB	H	2B	3B	HR	(Hm	Rd)	TB	R	RBI	TBB	IBB	SO	HBP	SH	SF	SB	CS	SB%	GDP	Avg	OBP	SLG
1996 Atlanta	NL	22	46	8	1	1	0	(0	0)	11	7	2	4	0	13	1	0	1	0	0	.00	0	.174	.250	.239
1997 Atlanta	NL	104	186	48	9	1	8	(5	3)	83	33	20	26	1	46	1	3	5	6	4	.60	3	.258	.344	.446
1998 Atlanta	NL	105	289	61	14	1	5	(3	2)	92	32	22	24	0	68	2	1	1	1	4	.20	7	.211	.275	.318
3 ML YEARS		231	521	117	24	3	13	(8	5)	186	72	44	54	1	127	4	4	7	7	8	.47	10	.225	.299	.357

Danny Graves

Pitches: Right **Bats:** Right **Pos:** RP-62 **Ht:** 5'11" **Wt:** 200 **Born:** 8/7/73 **Age:** 25

Year Team	Lg	HOW MUCH HE PITCHED						WHAT HE GAVE UP													THE RESULTS						
		G	GS	CG	GF	IP	BFP	H	R	ER	HR	SH	SF	HB	TBB	IBB	SO	WP	Bk	W	L	Pct.	ShO	Sv-Op	Hld	ERA
1998 Indianapols *	AAA	13	0	0	2	14	58	15	3	3	0	0	0	0	3	0	11	1	0	1	0	1.000	0	0--	—	1.93
1996 Cleveland	AL	15	0	0	5	29.2	129	29	18	15	2	0	1	0	10	0	22	1	0	2	0	1.000	0	0-1	0	4.55
1997 Cle-Cin	AL	15	0	0	3	26	134	41	22	16	2	3	2	0	20	1	11	1	0	0	0	.000	0	0-0	1	5.54
1998 Cincinnati	NL	62	0	0	35	81.1	340	76	31	30	6	2	5	2	28	4	44	4	0	2	1	.667	0	8-8	6	3.32
1997 Cleveland	AL	5	0	0	2	11.1	56	15	8	6	2	0	1	0	9	0	4	0	0	0	0	.000	0	0-0	1	4.76
Cincinnati	NL	10	0	0	1	14.2	78	26	14	10	0	3	1	0	11	1	7	1	0	0	0	.000	0	0-0	1	6.14
3 ML YEARS		92	0	0	43	137	603	146	71	61	10	5	8	2	58	5	77	6	0	4	1	.800	0	8-9	7	4.01

Craig Grebeck

Bats: R **Throws:** R **Pos:** 2B-91; SS-6; PH/PR-6; 3B-4 **Ht:** 5'7" **Wt:** 148 **Born:** 12/29/64 **Age:** 34

Year Team	Lg	BATTING																	BASERUNNING				PERCENTAGES		
		G	AB	H	2B	3B	HR	(Hm	Rd)	TB	R	RBI	TBB	IBB	SO	HBP	SH	SF	SB	CS	SB%	GDP	Avg	OBP	SLG
1998 Syracuse *	AAA	1	3	1	0	0	0	(—	—)	1	0	0	0	0	0	0	0	0	0	0	.00	0	.333	.333	.333
1990 Chicago	AL	59	119	20	3	1	1	(1	0)	28	7	9	8	0	24	2	3	3	0	0	.00	2	.168	.227	.235
1991 Chicago	AL	107	224	63	16	3	6	(3	3)	103	37	31	38	0	40	1	4	1	1	3	.25	3	.281	.386	.460
1992 Chicago	AL	88	287	77	21	2	3	(2	1)	111	24	35	30	0	34	3	10	3	0	3	.00	5	.268	.341	.387
1993 Chicago	AL	72	190	43	5	0	1	(0	1)	51	25	12	26	0	26	0	7	0	1	2	.33	9	.226	.319	.268
1994 Chicago	AL	35	97	30	5	0	0	(0	0)	35	17	5	12	0	5	1	3	0	0	0	.00	1	.309	.391	.361
1995 Chicago	AL	53	154	40	12	0	1	(0	1)	55	19	18	21	0	23	3	4	0	0	0	.00	6	.260	.360	.357
1996 Florida	NL	50	95	20	1	0	1	(0	1)	24	8	9	4	1	14	1	1	2	0	0	.00	2	.211	.245	.253
1997 Anaheim	AL	63	126	34	9	0	1	(1	0)	46	12	6	18	1	11	0	5	1	0	1	.00	6	.270	.359	.365
1998 Toronto	AL	102	301	77	17	2	2	(2	0)	104	33	27	29	0	42	4	8	2	2	2	.50	8	.256	.327	.346
9 ML YEARS		629	1593	404	89	8	16	(9	7)	557	182	152	186	2	219	15	45	12	4	11	.27	40	.254	.335	.350

Shawn Green

Bats: Left **Throws:** Left **Pos:** RF-127; CF-33; PH/PR-3 **Ht:** 6'4" **Wt:** 195 **Born:** 11/10/72 **Age:** 26

Year Team	Lg	BATTING																	BASERUNNING				PERCENTAGES		
		G	AB	H	2B	3B	HR	(Hm	Rd)	TB	R	RBI	TBB	IBB	SO	HBP	SH	SF	SB	CS	SB%	GDP	Avg	OBP	SLG
1993 Toronto	AL	3	6	0	0	0	0	(0	0)	0	0	0	0	0	1	0	0	0	0	0	.00	0	.000	.000	.000
1994 Toronto	AL	14	33	3	1	0	0	(0	0)	4	1	1	1	0	8	0	0	0	1	0	1.00	1	.091	.118	.121
1995 Toronto	AL	121	379	109	31	4	15	(5	10)	193	52	54	20	3	68	3	0	3	1	2	.33	4	.288	.326	.509
1996 Toronto	AL	132	422	118	32	3	11	(7	4)	189	52	45	33	3	75	8	0	2	5	1	.83	9	.280	.342	.448
1997 Toronto	AL	135	429	123	22	4	16	(10	6)	201	57	53	36	4	99	1	1	4	14	3	.82	4	.287	.340	.469
1998 Toronto	AL	158	630	175	33	4	35	(21	14)	321	106	100	50	2	142	5	1	3	35	12	.74	6	.278	.334	.510
6 ML YEARS		563	1899	528	119	15	77	(43	34)	908	268	253	140	12	393	17	2	12	56	18	.76	24	.278	.331	.478

Tyler Green

Pitches: Right **Bats:** Right **Pos:** SP-27 **Ht:** 6'5" **Wt:** 208 **Born:** 2/18/70 **Age:** 29

Year Team	Lg	HOW MUCH HE PITCHED						WHAT HE GAVE UP													THE RESULTS						
		G	GS	CG	GF	IP	BFP	H	R	ER	HR	SH	SF	HB	TBB	IBB	SO	WP	Bk	W	L	Pct.	ShO	Sv-Op	Hld	ERA
1993 Philadelphia	NL	3	2	0	1	7.1	41	16	9	6	1	0	0	0	5	0	7	2	0	0	0	.000	0	0-0	0	7.36
1995 Philadelphia	NL	26	25	4	0	140.2	623	157	86	83	15	5	6	4	66	3	85	9	2	8	9	.471	2	0-0	0	5.31
1997 Philadelphia	NL	14	14	0	0	76.2	340	72	50	42	8	0	3	1	45	4	58	7	0	4	4	.500	0	0-0	0	4.93
1998 Philadelphia	NL	27	27	0	0	159.1	699	142	97	89	23	5	6	9	85	1	113	8	0	6	12	.333	0	0-0	0	5.03
4 ML YEARS		70	68	4	1	384	1703	387	242	220	47	10	15	14	201	8	263	26	2	18	25	.419	2	0-0	0	5.16

Charlie Greene

Bats: Right **Throws:** Right **Pos:** C-13 **Ht:** 6'2" **Wt:** 190 **Born:** 1/23/71 **Age:** 28

Year Team	Lg	BATTING																	BASERUNNING				PERCENTAGES		
		G	AB	H	2B	3B	HR	(Hm	Rd)	TB	R	RBI	TBB	IBB	SO	HBP	SH	SF	SB	CS	SB%	GDP	Avg	OBP	SLG
1991 Padres	R	49	183	52	15	1	5	(—	—)	84	27	39	16	0	23	3	2	6	6	1	.86	7	.284	.341	.459
1992 Chston-SC	A	98	298	55	9	1	1	(—	—)	69	22	24	11	0	60	5	3	2	1	2	.33	7	.185	.225	.232
1993 Waterloo	A	84	213	38	8	0	2	(—	—)	52	19	20	13	0	33	3	6	3	0	0	.00	5	.178	.233	.244
1994 Binghamton	AA	30	106	18	4	0	0	(—	—)	22	13	2	6	1	18	1	0	1	0	0	.00	3	.170	.219	.208
St. Lucie	A+	69	224	57	4	0	0	(—	—)	61	23	21	9	0	31	4	4	1	0	1	.00	3	.254	.294	.272
1995 Binghamton	AA	100	346	82	13	0	2	(—	—)	101	26	34	15	4	47	5	3	4	2	1	.67	10	.237	.276	.292
Norfolk	AAA	27	88	17	3	0	0	(—	—)	20	6	4	3	0	28	0	1	0	1	1	.00	1	.193	.220	.227
1996 Binghamton	AA	100	336	82	17	0	2	(—	—)	105	35	27	17	0	52	0	2	4	2	0	1.00	8	.244	.277	.313
1997 Norfolk	AAA	76	238	49	7	0	8	(—	—)	80	27	28	9	0	54	2	0	2	1	0	1.00	8	.206	.239	.336
1998 Rochester	AAA	77	250	53	10	0	4	(—	—)	75	23	28	9	0	54	3	5	0	1	1	.50	4	.212	.248	.300
1996 New York	NL	2	5	0	0	0	0	(0	0)	0	0	0	0	0	0	0	0	0	0	0	.00	0	.000	.000	.000
1997 Baltimore	AL	5	2	0	0	0	0	(0	0)	0	0	1	0	0	1	0	0	0	0	0	.00	0	.000	.000	.000
1998 Baltimore	AL	13	21	4	1	0	0	(0	0)	5	1	0	0	0	8	0	1	0	0	0	.00	1	.190	.190	.238
3 ML YEARS		20	24	4	1	0	0	(0	0)	5	1	1	0	0	9	0	1	0	0	0	.00	1	.167	.167	.208

Todd Greene

Bats: R **Throws:** R **Pos:** PH/PR-13; LF-12; DH-4; 1B-3   **Ht:** 5'10" **Wt:** 208 **Born:** 5/8/71 **Age:** 28

						BATTING												BASERUNNING				PERCENTAGES		
Year Team	Lg	G	AB	H	2B	3B	HR	(Hm | Rd)	TB	R	RBI	TBB	IBB	SO	HBP	SH	SF	SB	CS	SB%	GDP	Avg	OBP	SLG
1998 Lk Elsinore *	A+	12	44	10	2	0	1	—	—	15	9	6	4	0	7	0	0	1	1	0	1.00	1	.227	.286	.341
Vancouver *	AAA	30	108	30	12	0	7	—	—	63	16	20	2	0	17	3	0	2	1	0	1.00	1	.278	.360	.583
1996 California	AL	29	79	15	1	0	2	(1 | 1)	22	9	9	4	0	11	1	0	0	2	0	1.00	4	.190	.238	.278
1997 Anaheim	AL	34	124	36	6	0	9	(5 | 4)	69	24	24	7	1	25	0	0	0	2	0	1.00	1	.290	.328	.556
1998 Anaheim	AL	29	71	18	4	0	1	(0 | 1)	25	3	7	2	0	20	0	0	0	0	0	.00	0	.254	.274	.352
3 ML YEARS		92	274	69	11	0	12	(6 | 6)	116	36	40	13	1	56	1	0	0	4	0	1.00	5	.252	.288	.423

Willie Greene

Bats: L **Throws:** R **Pos:** 3B-76; RF-35; PH/PR-26; LF-10; DH-2; SS-2   **Ht:** 5'11" **Wt:** 192 **Born:** 9/23/71 **Age:** 27

						BATTING												BASERUNNING				PERCENTAGES		
Year Team	Lg	G	AB	H	2B	3B	HR	(Hm	Rd)	TB	R	RBI	TBB	IBB	SO	HBP	SH	SF	SB	CS	SB%	GDP	Avg	OBP	SLG
1992 Cincinnati	NL	29	93	25	5	2	2	(2	0)	40	10	13	10	0	23	0	0	1	0	2	.00	1	.269	.337	.430
1993 Cincinnati	NL	15	50	8	1	1	2	(2	0)	17	7	5	2	0	19	0	0	1	0	0	.00	1	.160	.189	.340
1994 Cincinnati	NL	16	37	8	2	0	0	(0	0)	10	5	3	6	1	14	0	0	1	0	0	.00	1	.216	.318	.270
1995 Cincinnati	NL	8	19	2	0	0	0	(0	0)	2	1	0	3	0	7	0	0	0	0	0	.00	1	.105	.227	.105
1996 Cincinnati	NL	115	287	70	5	5	19	(11	8)	142	48	63	36	6	88	0	1	1	0	1	.00	5	.244	.327	.495
1997 Cincinnati	NL	151	495	125	22	1	26	(13	13)	227	62	91	78	5	111	1	1	3	6	0	1.00	10	.253	.354	.459
1998 Cin-Bal		135	396	102	19	1	15	(9	6)	168	65	54	69	2	90	3	0	2	7	3	.70	9	.258	.370	.424
1998 Cincinnati	NL	111	356	96	18	1	14	(8	6)	158	57	49	56	2	80	3	0	2	6	3	.67	7	.270	.372	.444
Baltimore	AL	24	40	6	1	0	1	(1	0)	10	8	5	13	0	10	0	0	0	1	0	1.00	2	.150	.358	.250
7 ML YEARS		469	1377	340	54	10	64	(37	27)	606	198	229	204	14	352	4	2	9	13	6	.68	28	.247	.344	.440

Rusty Greer

Bats: Left **Throws:** Left **Pos:** LF-154; PH/PR-2; CF-2   **Ht:** 6'0" **Wt:** 195 **Born:** 1/21/69 **Age:** 30

						BATTING												BASERUNNING				PERCENTAGES		
Year Team	Lg	G	AB	H	2B	3B	HR	(Hm	Rd)	TB	R	RBI	TBB	IBB	SO	HBP	SH	SF	SB	CS	SB%	GDP	Avg	OBP	SLG
1994 Texas	AL	80	277	87	16	1	10	(3	7)	135	36	46	46	2	46	2	2	4	0	0	.00	3	.314	.410	.487
1995 Texas	AL	131	417	113	21	2	13	(7	6)	177	58	61	55	1	66	1	2	3	3	1	.75	9	.271	.355	.424
1996 Texas	AL	139	542	180	41	6	18	(9	9)	287	96	100	62	4	86	3	0	10	9	0	1.00	9	.332	.397	.530
1997 Texas	AL	157	601	193	42	3	26	(18	8)	319	112	87	83	4	87	3	1	2	9	5	.64	11	.321	.405	.531
1998 Texas	AL	155	598	183	31	5	16	(8	8)	272	107	108	80	1	93	4	0	9	2	4	.33	18	.306	.386	.455
5 ML YEARS		662	2435	756	151	17	83	(45	38)	1190	409	402	326	12	378	13	5	28	23	10	.70	50	.310	.391	.489

Seth Greisinger

Pitches: Right **Bats:** Right **Pos:** SP-21   **Ht:** 6'3" **Wt:** 200 **Born:** 7/29/75 **Age:** 23

		HOW MUCH HE PITCHED						WHAT HE GAVE UP										THE RESULTS					
Year Team	Lg	G	GS	CG	GF	IP	BFP	H	R	ER	HR	SH	SF	HB	TBB	IBB	SO	WP	Bk	W	L	Pct.	ShO	Sv-Op	Hld	ERA
1997 Jacksnville	AA	28	28	1	0	159.1	710	194	103	92	29	3	6	3	53	0	105	12	2	10	6	.625	0	0--	—	5.20
1998 Toledo	AAA	10	10	0	0	58.2	247	50	21	19	5	1	1	5	22	0	37	3	2	3	4	.429	0	0--	—	2.91
1998 Detroit	AL	21	21	0	0	130	562	142	79	74	17	2	5	4	48	2	66	3	0	6	9	.400	0	0-0	0	5.12

Ben Grieve

Bats: Left **Throws:** Right **Pos:** RF-151; DH-3; PH/PR-2   **Ht:** 6'4" **Wt:** 226 **Born:** 5/4/76 **Age:** 23

						BATTING												BASERUNNING				PERCENTAGES		
Year Team	Lg	G	AB	H	2B	3B	HR	(Hm	Rd)	TB	R	RBI	TBB	IBB	SO	HBP	SH	SF	SB	CS	SB%	GDP	Avg	OBP	SLG
1994 Sou. Oregon	A-	72	252	83	13	0	7	—	—	117	44	50	51	7	48	10	0	3	2	2	.50	6	.329	.456	.464
1995 W Michigan	A	102	371	97	16	1	4	—	—	127	53	62	60	6	75	4	0	6	11	3	.79	10	.261	.371	.342
Modesto	A+	28	107	28	5	0	2	—	—	39	17	14	15	1	22	0	0	2	2	0	1.00	3	.262	.347	.364
1996 Modesto	A+	72	281	100	20	1	11	—	—	155	61	51	38	2	52	1	1	3	8	7	.53	5	.356	.430	.552
Huntsville	AA	63	232	55	8	1	8	—	—	89	34	32	35	5	53	2	0	3	1	0	1.00	3	.237	.338	.384
1997 Huntsville	AA	100	372	122	19	2	24	—	—	227	100	108	81	0	75	9	0	4	5	1	.83	8	.328	.455	.610
Edmonton	AAA	27	108	46	11	1	7	—	—	80	27	28	12	0	16	1	1	1	0	0	1.00	4	.426	.484	.741
1997 Oakland	AL	24	93	29	6	0	3	(3	0)	44	12	24	13	1	25	1	1	0	0	0	.00	1	.312	.402	.473
1998 Oakland	AL	155	583	168	41	2	18	(5	13)	267	94	89	85	3	123	9	0	1	2	2	.50	18	.288	.386	.458
2 ML YEARS		179	676	197	47	2	21	(8	13)	311	106	113	98	4	148	10	1	1	2	2	.50	19	.291	.389	.460

Ken Griffey Jr.

Bats: L **Throws:** L **Pos:** CF-158; DH-3; 1B-1; LF-1; RF-1   **Ht:** 6'3" **Wt:** 205 **Born:** 11/21/69 **Age:** 29

						BATTING												BASERUNNING				PERCENTAGES		
Year Team	Lg	G	AB	H	2B	3B	HR	(Hm	Rd)	TB	R	RBI	TBB	IBB	SO	HBP	SH	SF	SB	CS	SB%	GDP	Avg	OBP	SLG
1989 Seattle	AL	127	455	120	23	0	16	(10	6)	191	61	61	44	8	83	2	1	4	16	7	.70	4	.264	.329	.420
1990 Seattle	AL	155	597	179	28	7	22	(8	14)	287	91	80	63	12	81	2	0	4	16	11	.59	12	.300	.366	.481
1991 Seattle	AL	154	548	179	42	1	22	(16	6)	289	76	100	71	21	82	1	4	9	18	6	.75	10	.327	.399	.527
1992 Seattle	AL	142	565	174	39	4	27	(16	11)	302	83	103	44	15	67	5	0	3	10	5	.67	15	.308	.361	.535
1993 Seattle	AL	156	582	180	38	3	45	(21	24)	359	113	109	96	25	91	6	0	7	17	9	.65	14	.309	.408	.617
1994 Seattle	AL	111	433	140	24	4	40	(18	22)	292	94	90	56	19	73	2	0	2	11	3	.79	9	.323	.402	.674
1995 Seattle	AL	72	260	67	7	0	17	(13	4)	125	52	42	52	6	53	0	0	2	4	2	.67	4	.258	.379	.481
1996 Seattle	AL	140	545	165	26	2	49	(26	23)	342	125	140	78	13	104	7	1	7	16	1	.94	7	.303	.392	.628

Year Team	Lg	G	AB	H	2B	3B	HR	(Hm	Rd)	TB	R	RBI	TBB	IBB	SO	HBP	SH	SF	SB	CS	SB%	GDP	Avg	OBP	SLG
1997 Seattle	AL	157	608	185	34	3	56	(27	29)	393	125	147	76	23	121	8	0	12	15	4	.79	12	.304	.382	.646
1998 Seattle	AL	161	633	180	33	3	56	(30	26)	387	120	146	76	11	121	7	0	4	20	5	.80	14	.284	.365	.611
10 ML YEARS		1375	5226	1569	294	27	350	(185	165)	2967	940	1018	656	153	876	40	6	54	143	53	.73	101	.300	.379	.568

Marquis Grissom

Bats: Right **Throws:** Right **Pos:** CF-137; PH/PR-8   **Ht:** 5'11" **Wt:** 190 **Born:** 4/17/67 **Age:** 32

Year Team	Lg	G	AB	H	2B	3B	HR	(Hm	Rd)	TB	R	RBI	TBB	IBB	SO	HBP	SH	SF	SB	CS	SB%	GDP	Avg	OBP	SLG
1989 Montreal	NL	26	74	19	2	0	1	(0	1)	24	16	2	12	0	21	0	1	0	1	0	1.00	1	.257	.360	.324
1990 Montreal	NL	98	288	74	14	2	3	(2	1)	101	42	29	27	2	40	0	4	1	22	2	.92	3	.257	.320	.351
1991 Montreal	NL	148	558	149	23	9	6	(3	3)	208	73	39	34	0	89	1	4	0	76	17	.82	8	.267	.310	.373
1992 Montreal	NL	159	653	180	39	6	14	(8	6)	273	99	66	42	6	81	5	3	4	78	13	.86	12	.276	.322	.418
1993 Montreal	NL	157	630	188	27	2	19	(9	10)	276	104	95	52	6	76	3	0	8	53	10	.84	9	.298	.351	.438
1994 Montreal	NL	110	475	137	25	4	11	(4	7)	203	96	45	41	4	66	1	0	4	36	6	.86	10	.288	.344	.427
1995 Atlanta	NL	139	551	142	23	3	12	(5	7)	207	80	42	47	4	61	3	1	4	29	9	.76	8	.258	.317	.376
1996 Atlanta	NL	158	671	207	32	10	23	(11	12)	328	106	74	41	6	73	3	4	4	28	11	.72	12	.308	.349	.489
1997 Cleveland	AL	144	558	146	27	6	12	(5	7)	221	74	66	43	1	89	6	6	9	22	13	.63	12	.262	.317	.396
1998 Milwaukee	NL	142	542	147	28	1	10	(2	8)	207	57	60	24	2	78	2	2	2	13	8	.62	12	.271	.304	.382
10 ML YEARS		1281	5000	1389	240	43	111	(49	62)	2048	747	518	363	31	674	24	25	36	358	89	.80	87	.278	.327	.410

Buddy Groom

Pitches: Left **Bats:** Left **Pos:** RP-75   **Ht:** 6'2" **Wt:** 208 **Born:** 7/10/65 **Age:** 33

Year Team	Lg	G	GS	CG	GF	IP	BFP	H	R	ER	HR	SH	SF	HB	TBB	IBB	SO	WP	Bk	W	L	Pct.	ShO	Sv-Op	Hld	ERA
1992 Detroit	AL	12	7	0	3	38.2	177	48	28	25	4	3	2	0	22	4	15	0	1	0	5	.000	0	1-2	0	5.82
1993 Detroit	AL	19	3	0	8	36.2	170	48	25	24	4	2	4	2	13	5	15	2	1	0	2	.000	0	0-0	1	6.14
1994 Detroit	AL	40	0	0	10	32	139	31	14	14	4	0	3	2	13	2	27	0	0	0	1	.000	0	1-1	11	3.94
1995 Det-Fla		37	4	0	11	55.2	274	81	47	46	8	2	2	2	32	4	35	3	0	2	5	.286	0	1-3	0	7.44
1996 Oakland	AL	72	1	0	16	77.1	341	85	37	33	8	2	0	3	34	3	57	5	0	5	0	1.000	0	2-4	10	3.84
1997 Oakland	AL	78	0	0	7	64.2	285	75	38	37	9	0	4	0	24	1	45	3	0	2	2	.500	0	3-5	12	5.15
1998 Oakland	AL	75	0	0	13	57.1	251	62	30	27	4	1	3	1	20	1	36	1	0	3	1	.750	0	0-6	16	4.24
1995 Detroit	AL	23	4	0	6	40.2	203	55	35	34	6	2	2	2	26	4	23	3	0	1	3	.250	0	1-3	0	7.52
Florida	NL	14	0	0	5	15	71	26	12	12	2	0	0	0	6	0	12	0	0	1	2	.333	0	0-0	0	7.20
7 ML YEARS		333	15	0	68	362.1	1637	430	219	207	41	10	18	10	158	20	230	14	2	12	16	.429	0	8-21	50	5.14

Mark Grudzielanek

Bats: Right **Throws:** Right **Pos:** SS-156   **Ht:** 6'1" **Wt:** 185 **Born:** 6/30/70 **Age:** 29

Year Team	Lg	G	AB	H	2B	3B	HR	(Hm	Rd)	TB	R	RBI	TBB	IBB	SO	HBP	SH	SF	SB	CS	SB%	GDP	Avg	OBP	SLG
1995 Montreal	NL	78	269	66	12	2	1	(1	0)	85	27	20	14	4	47	7	3	0	8	3	.73	7	.245	.300	.316
1996 Montreal	NL	153	657	201	34	4	6	(5	1)	261	99	49	26	3	83	9	1	3	33	7	.83	10	.306	.340	.397
1997 Montreal	NL	156	649	177	54	3	4	(1	3)	249	76	51	23	0	76	10	3	3	25	9	.74	13	.273	.307	.384
1998 Mon-LA	NL	156	589	160	21	1	10	(5	5)	213	62	62	26	2	73	11	8	7	18	5	.78	18	.272	.311	.362
1998 Montreal	NL	105	396	109	15	1	8	(3	5)	150	51	41	21	1	50	9	5	4	11	5	.275	.323	.379
Los Angeles	NL	51	193	51	6	0	2	(2	0)	63	11	21	5	1	23	2	3	3	7	0	1.00	7	.264	.286	.326
4 ML YEARS		543	2164	604	121	10	21	(12	9)	808	264	182	89	9	279	37	15	13	84	24	.78	48	.279	.317	.373

Mike Grzanich

Pitches: Right **Bats:** Right **Pos:** RP-1   **Ht:** 6'1" **Wt:** 180 **Born:** 8/24/72 **Age:** 26

Year Team	Lg	G	GS	CG	GF	IP	BFP	H	R	ER	HR	SH	SF	HB	TBB	IBB	SO	WP	Bk	W	L	Pct.	ShO	Sv-Op	Hld	ERA
1992 Astros	R	17	3	0	9	33.2	159	38	21	17	0	2	3	6	14	0	29	1	0	2	5	.286	0	3- -	—	4.54
1993 Auburn	A-	16	14	4	1	93.1	409	106	63	50	11	3	3	3	27	0	71	7	1	5	8	.385	1	0- -	—	4.82
1994 Quad City	A	23	22	3	1	142.2	598	145	55	49	5	2	1	11	43	2	101	5	0	11	7	.611	0	0- -	—	3.09
1995 Jackson	AA	50	0	0	23	65.2	276	55	22	20	0	5	3	6	38	5	44	4	0	5	3	.625	0	8- -	—	2.74
1996 Jackson	AA	57	0	0	19	72.1	316	60	47	32	10	4	2	8	43	2	80	6	0	5	4	.556	0	6- -	—	3.98
1997 Jackson	AA	38	13	0	21	101.2	472	114	68	56	10	4	5	8	46	2	73	2	0	7	6	.538	0	12- -	—	4.96
1998 Kissimmee	A+	4	0	0	1	7.1	36	9	7	5	0	2	0	1	5	0	8	1	0	1	1	.500	0	0- -	—	6.14
New Orleans	AAA	34	0	0	16	39.2	165	27	13	10	2	2	3	3	21	0	39	5	0	1	2	.333	0	5- -	—	2.27
1998 Houston	NL	1	0	0	0	1	6	1	2	2	0	0	1	0	2	0	1	0	0	0	0	.000	0	0-0	0	18.00

Eddie Guardado

Pitches: Left **Bats:** Right **Pos:** RP-79   **Ht:** 6'0" **Wt:** 194 **Born:** 10/2/70 **Age:** 28

Year Team	Lg	G	GS	CG	GF	IP	BFP	H	R	ER	HR	SH	SF	HB	TBB	IBB	SO	WP	Bk	W	L	Pct.	ShO	Sv-Op	Hld	ERA
1993 Minnesota	AL	19	16	0	2	94.2	426	123	68	65	13	1	3	1	36	2	46	0	0	3	8	.273	0	0-0	0	6.18
1994 Minnesota	AL	4	4	0	0	17	81	26	16	16	3	1	2	0	4	0	8	0	0	0	2	.000	0	0-0	0	8.47
1995 Minnesota	AL	51	5	0	10	91.1	410	99	54	52	13	6	5	0	45	2	71	5	1	4	9	.308	0	2-5	5	5.12
1996 Minnesota	AL	83	0	0	17	73.2	313	61	45	43	12	6	4	3	33	4	74	3	0	6	5	.545	0	4-7	18	5.25
1997 Minnesota	AL	69	0	0	20	46	201	45	23	20	7	2	1	2	17	2	54	2	0	0	4	.000	0	1-1	13	3.91
1998 Minnesota	AL	79	0	0	12	65.2	286	66	34	33	10	3	6	0	28	6	53	2	0	3	1	.750	0	0-4	16	4.52
6 ML YEARS		305	25	0	61	388.1	1717	420	240	229	58	19	21	6	163	16	306	12	1	16	29	.356	0	7-17	52	5.31

Vladimir Guerrero

Bats: Right **Throws:** Right **Pos:** RF-157; PH/PR-2 **Ht:** 6'2" **Wt:** 200 **Born:** 2/9/76 **Age:** 23

Year Team	Lg	G	AB	H	2B	3B	HR	(Hm	Rd)	TB	R	RBI	TBB	IBB	SO	HBP	SH	SF	SB	CS	SB%	GDP	Avg	OBP	SLG
1996 Montreal	NL	9	27	5	0	0	1	(0	1)	8	2	1	0	0	3	0	0	0	0	0	.00	1	.185	.185	.296
1997 Montreal	NL	90	325	98	22	2	11	(5	6)	157	44	40	19	2	39	7	0	3	3	4	.43	11	.302	.350	.483
1998 Montreal	NL	159	623	202	37	7	38	(19	19)	367	108	109	42	13	95	7	0	5	11	9	.55	15	.324	.371	.589
3 ML YEARS		258	975	305	59	9	50	(24	26)	532	154	150	61	15	137	14	0	8	14	13	.52	27	.313	.359	.546

Wilton Guerrero

Bats: B **Throws:** R **Pos:** 2B-84; PH/PR-20; SS-14; LF-6; CF-1 **Ht:** 5'11" **Wt:** 175 **Born:** 10/24/74 **Age:** 24

Year Team	Lg	G	AB	H	2B	3B	HR	(Hm	Rd)	TB	R	RBI	TBB	IBB	SO	HBP	SH	SF	SB	CS	SB%	GDP	Avg	OBP	SLG
1998 Albuquerque *	AAA	30	121	36	3	2	1	—		46	15	10	9	0	12	1	2	0	11	3	.79	2	.298	.351	.380
1996 Los Angeles	NL	5	2	0	0	0	0	(0	0)	0	1	0	0	0	2	0	0	0	0	0	.00	0	.000	.000	.000
1997 Los Angeles	NL	111	357	104	10	9	4	(2	2)	144	39	32	8	1	52	0	13	2	6	5	.55	7	.291	.305	.403
1998 LA-Mon	NL	116	402	114	14	9	2	(0	2)	152	50	27	14	0	63	1	6	3	8	2	.80	4	.284	.307	.378
1998 Los Angeles	NL	64	180	51	4	3	0	(0	0)	61	21	7	4	0	33	1	3	2	5	2	.71	3	.283	.299	.339
Montreal	NL	52	222	63	10	6	2	(0	2)	91	29	20	10	0	30	0	3	1	3	0	1.00	1	.284	.313	.410
3 ML YEARS		232	761	218	24	18	6	(2	4)	296	90	59	22	1	117	1	19	5	14	7	.67	11	.286	.305	.389

Giomar Guevara

Bats: Both **Throws:** Right **Pos:** 2B-5; SS-5; PH/PR-4; DH-1 **Ht:** 5'8" **Wt:** 150 **Born:** 10/23/72 **Age:** 26

Year Team	Lg	G	AB	H	2B	3B	HR	(Hm	Rd)	TB	R	RBI	TBB	IBB	SO	HBP	SH	SF	SB	CS	SB%	GDP	Avg	OBP	SLG
1993 Bellingham	A-	62	211	48	8	3	1	—		65	31	23	34	2	46	2	4	0	4	7	.36	3	.227	.340	.308
1994 Appleton	A	110	385	116	23	3	8	—		169	57	46	42	1	77	2	5	1	9	16	.36	6	.301	.372	.439
Jacksonville	AA	7	20	4	2	0	1	—		9	2	3	2	0	9	0	1	0	0	0	.00	0	.200	.273	.450
1995 Riverside	A+	83	292	71	12	3	2	—		95	53	34	30	1	71	1	6	6	7	4	.64	4	.243	.310	.325
1996 Port City	AA	119	414	110	18	2	2	—		138	60	41	54	1	102	4	9	4	21	7	.75	12	.266	.353	.333
1997 Tacoma	AAA	54	176	43	5	1	2	—		56	29	13	5	0	39	1	5	0	3	7	.30	2	.244	.269	.318
Memphis	AA	65	228	60	10	4	4	—		90	30	28	20	0	42	0	0	1	5	5	.50	3	.263	.321	.395
1998 Lancaster	A+	19	61	15	4	0	0	—		19	15	3	14	0	20	1	0	0	1	1	.50	1	.246	.395	.311
Orlando	AA	14	45	15	5	1	0	—		22	13	6	8	0	11	0	1	0	0	0	.00	3	.333	.434	.489
1997 Seattle	AL	5	4	0	0	0	0	(0	0)	0	0	0	0	0	2	0	0	0	1	0	1.00	0	.000	.000	.000
1998 Seattle	AL	11	13	3	2	0	0	(0	0)	5	4	0	4	0	4	1	0	0	0	0	.00	1	.231	.444	.385
2 ML YEARS		16	17	3	2	0	0	(0	0)	5	4	0	4	0	6	1	0	0	1	0	1.00	1	.176	.364	.294

Carlos Guillen

Bats: Both **Throws:** Right **Pos:** 2B-10 **Ht:** 6'1" **Wt:** 180 **Born:** 9/30/75 **Age:** 23

Year Team	Lg	G	AB	H	2B	3B	HR	(Hm	Rd)	TB	R	RBI	TBB	IBB	SO	HBP	SH	SF	SB	CS	SB%	GDP	Avg	OBP	SLG
1995 Astros	R	30	105	31	4	2	2	—		45	17	15	9	1	17	1	1	2	17	1	.94	0	.295	.350	.429
1996 Quad City	A	29	112	37	7	1	3	—		55	23	17	16	2	25	0	0	3	13	6	.68	1	.330	.405	.491
1997 Jackson	AA	115	390	99	16	1	10	—		147	47	39	38	1	78	2	4	2	6	5	.55	9	.254	.322	.377
New Orleans	AAA	3	13	4	1	0	0	—		5	3	0	0	0	4	0	0	0	0	0	.00	0	.308	.308	.385
1998 New Orleans	AAA	100	374	109	18	4	12	—		171	67	51	31	1	61	5	6	4	3	4	.43	5	.291	.350	.457
Tacoma	AAA	24	92	21	1	1	1	—		27	8	4	9	0	17	0	1	0	1	2	.33	1	.228	.297	.293
1998 Seattle	AL	10	39	13	1	1	0	(0	0)	16	9	5	5	0	9	0	0	0	2	0	1.00	0	.333	.381	.410

Jose Guillen

Bats: Right **Throws:** Right **Pos:** RF-149; CF-2; PH/PR-2 **Ht:** 5'11" **Wt:** 196 **Born:** 5/17/76 **Age:** 23

Year Team	Lg	G	AB	H	2B	3B	HR	(Hm	Rd)	TB	R	RBI	TBB	IBB	SO	HBP	SH	SF	SB	CS	SB%	GDP	Avg	OBP	SLG
1994 Pirates	R	30	110	29	4	1	4	—		47	17	11	7	0	15	6	0	0	2	1	.67	0	.264	.341	.427
1995 Erie	A-	66	258	81	17	1	12	—		136	41	46	10	0	44	12	0	1	1	5	.17	5	.314	.367	.527
Augusta	A	10	34	8	1	1	2	—		17	6	6	2	0	9	2	0	0	0	0	.00	0	.235	.316	.500
1996 Lynchburg	A+	136	528	170	30	0	21	—		263	78	94	20	1	73	13	1	8	24	13	.65	16	.322	.357	.498
1997 Pittsburgh	NL	143	498	133	20	5	14	(5	9)	205	58	70	17	0	88	8	0	3	1	2	.33	16	.267	.300	.412
1998 Pittsburgh	NL	153	573	153	38	2	14	(10	4)	237	60	84	21	0	100	6	1	4	3	5	.38	7	.267	.298	.414
2 ML YEARS		296	1071	286	58	7	28	(15	13)	442	118	154	38	0	188	14	1	7	4	7	.36	23	.267	.299	.413

Ozzie Guillen

Bats: L **Throws:** R **Pos:** SS-77; PH/PR-23; 2B-2; 3B-2; 1B-1 **Ht:** 5'11" **Wt:** 164 **Born:** 1/20/64 **Age:** 35

Year Team	Lg	G	AB	H	2B	3B	HR	(Hm	Rd)	TB	R	RBI	TBB	IBB	SO	HBP	SH	SF	SB	CS	SB%	GDP	Avg	OBP	SLG
1985 Chicago	AL	150	491	134	21	9	1	(1	0)	176	71	33	12	1	36	1	8	1	7	4	.64	5	.273	.291	.358
1986 Chicago	AL	159	547	137	19	4	2	(1	1)	170	58	47	12	1	52	1	4	5	8	4	.67	14	.250	.265	.311
1987 Chicago	AL	149	560	156	22	7	2	(2	0)	198	64	51	22	2	52	1	13	6	25	8	.76	10	.279	.303	.354
1988 Chicago	AL	156	566	148	16	7	0	(0	0)	178	58	39	25	3	40	2	10	3	25	13	.66	14	.261	.294	.314
1989 Chicago	AL	155	597	151	20	8	1	(0	1)	190	63	54	15	3	48	0	11	3	36	17	.68	8	.253	.270	.318
1990 Chicago	AL	160	516	144	21	4	1	(1	0)	176	61	58	26	8	37	1	15	5	13	17	.43	6	.279	.312	.341

Year Team	Lg	G	AB	H	2B	3B	HR	(Hm	Rd)	TB	R	RBI	TBB	IBB	SO	HBP	SH	SF	SB	CS	SB%	GDP	Avg	OBP	SLG
1991 Chicago	AL	154	524	143	20	3	3	(1	2)	178	52	49	11	1	38	0	13	7	21	15	.58	7	.273	.284	.340
1992 Chicago	AL	12	40	8	4	0	0	(0	0)	12	5	7	1	0	5	0	1	1	1	0	1.00	1	.200	.214	.300
1993 Chicago	AL	134	457	128	23	4	4	(3	1)	171	44	50	10	0	41	0	13	6	5	4	.56	6	.280	.292	.374
1994 Chicago	AL	100	365	105	9	5	1	(0	1)	127	46	39	14	2	35	0	7	4	5	4	.56	5	.288	.311	.348
1995 Chicago	AL	122	415	103	20	3	1	(1	0)	132	50	41	13	1	25	0	4	1	6	7	.46	11	.248	.270	.318
1996 Chicago	AL	150	499	131	24	8	4	(0	4)	183	62	45	10	0	27	0	12	7	6	5	.55	10	.263	.273	.367
1997 Chicago	AL	142	490	120	21	6	4	(1	3)	165	59	52	22	1	24	0	11	4	5	3	.63	7	.245	.275	.337
1998 Bal-Atl		95	280	74	15	1	1	(1	0)	94	37	22	25	0	27	1	5	2	1	5	.17	3	.264	.325	.336
1998 Baltimore	AL	12	16	1	0	0	0	(0	0)	1	2	0	1	0	2	0	1	0	0	1	.00	1	.063	.118	.063
Atlanta	NL	83	264	73	15	1	1	(1	0)	93	35	22	24	0	25	1	4	2	1	4	.20	2	.277	.337	.352
14 ML YEARS		1838	6347	1682	255	69	25	(12	13)	2150	730	587	218	23	487	7	135	57	164	106	.61	107	.265	.288	.339

Eric Gunderson

Pitches: Left **Bats:** Right **Pos:** RP-67; SP-1 **Ht:** 6'0" **Wt:** 190 **Born:** 3/29/66 **Age:** 33

	HOW MUCH HE PITCHED						WHAT HE GAVE UP												THE RESULTS						
Year Team	Lg	G	GS	CG	GF	IP	BFP	H	R	ER	HR	SH	SF	HB	TBB	IBB	SO	WP	Bk	W	L	Pct.	ShO	Sv-Op	Hld	ERA
1990 San Francisco	NL	7	4	0	1	19.2	94	24	14	12	2	1	0	0	11	1	14	0	0	1	2	.333	0	0-0	0	5.49
1991 San Francisco	NL	2	0	0	1	3.1	18	6	4	2	0	0	0	0	1	0	2	0	0	0	0	.000	0	1-1	0	5.40
1992 Seattle	AL	9	0	0	4	9.1	45	12	12	9	1	0	2	1	5	3	2	0	2	2	1	.667	0	0-0	0	8.68
1994 New York	NL	14	0	0	3	9	31	5	0	0	0	0	0	0	4	0	4	0	0	0	0	.000	0	0-0	2	0.00
1995 NYN-Bos		49	0	0	8	36.2	161	38	17	17	2	2	2	3	17	4	28	1	0	3	2	.600	0	0-3	6	4.17
1996 Boston	AL	28	0	0	2	17.1	82	21	17	16	5	0	2	2	8	2	7	3	0	1	0	.000	0	0-0	3	8.31
1997 Texas	AL	60	0	0	11	49.2	209	45	19	18	5	2	3	2	15	3	31	2	1	2	1	.667	0	1-4	12	3.26
1998 Texas	AL	68	1	0	13	67.2	303	88	43	39	13	1	3	1	19	4	41	4	0	3	0	.000	0	0-2	5	5.19
1995 New York	NL	30	0	0	7	24.1	103	25	10	10	2	0	1	1	8	3	19	1	0	1	1	.500	0	0-3	0	3.70
Boston	AL	19	0	0	1	12.1	58	13	7	7	0	2	1	2	9	1	9	0	0	2	1	.667	0	0-0	6	5.11
8 ML YEARS		237	5	0	43	212.2	943	239	126	113	28	6	12	9	80	17	129	10	3	8	10	.444	0	2-10	32	4.78

Mark Guthrie

Pitches: Left **Bats:** Right **Pos:** RP-53 **Ht:** 6'4" **Wt:** 211 **Born:** 9/22/65 **Age:** 33

	HOW MUCH HE PITCHED						WHAT HE GAVE UP												THE RESULTS						
Year Team	Lg	G	GS	CG	GF	IP	BFP	H	R	ER	HR	SH	SF	HB	TBB	IBB	SO	WP	Bk	W	L	Pct.	ShO	Sv-Op	Hld	ERA
1989 Minnesota	AL	13	8	0	2	57.1	254	66	32	29	7	1	5	1	21	1	38	1	0	2	4	.333	0	0-0	0	4.55
1990 Minnesota	AL	24	21	3	0	144.2	603	154	65	61	8	6	0	1	39	3	101	9	0	7	9	.438	1	0-0	0	3.79
1991 Minnesota	AL	41	12	0	13	98	432	116	52	47	11	4	3	1	41	2	72	7	0	7	5	.583	0	2-2	5	4.32
1992 Minnesota	AL	54	0	0	15	75	303	59	27	24	7	4	2	0	23	7	76	2	0	2	3	.400	0	5-7	19	2.88
1993 Minnesota	AL	22	0	0	2	21	94	20	11	11	2	1	2	0	16	2	15	1	3	2	1	.667	0	0-1	8	4.71
1994 Minnesota	AL	50	2	0	13	51.1	234	65	43	35	8	2	6	2	18	2	38	7	0	4	2	.667	0	1-3	12	6.14
1995 Min-LA		60	0	0	14	62	272	66	33	29	6	4	0	2	25	5	67	5	1	5	5	.500	0	0-2	15	4.21
1996 Los Angeles	NL	66	0	0	16	73	302	65	21	18	3	4	4	1	22	2	56	1	0	2	3	.400	0	1-3	12	2.22
1997 Los Angeles	NL	62	0	0	18	69.1	305	71	44	41	12	10	3	0	30	6	42	2	1	1	4	.200	0	1-4	13	5.32
1998 Los Angeles	NL	53	0	0	11	54	241	56	26	21	3	5	0	2	24	1	45	2	0	2	1	.667	0	0-1	8	3.50
1995 Minnesota	AL	36	0	0	7	42.1	181	47	22	21	5	2	0	2	16	3	48	3	1	5	3	.625	0	0-2	10	4.46
Los Angeles	NL	24	0	0	7	19.2	91	19	11	8	1	2	0	0	9	2	19	2	0	0	2	.000	0	0-0	5	3.66
10 ML YEARS		445	43	3	104	705.2	3040	738	354	316	67	41	25	10	259	31	550	37	5	34	37	.479	1	10-23	92	4.03

Ricky Gutierrez

Bats: Right **Throws:** Right **Pos:** SS-141; PH/PR-5 **Ht:** 6'1" **Wt:** 175 **Born:** 5/23/70 **Age:** 29

	BATTING																		BASERUNNING				PERCENTAGES		
Year Team	Lg	G	AB	H	2B	3B	HR	(Hm	Rd)	TB	R	RBI	TBB	IBB	SO	HBP	SH	SF	SB	CS	SB%	GDP	Avg	OBP	SLG
1993 San Diego	NL	133	438	110	10	5	5	(5	0)	145	76	26	50	2	97	5	1	1	4	3	.57	7	.251	.334	.331
1994 San Diego	NL	90	275	66	11	2	1	(1	0)	84	27	28	32	1	54	2	2	3	2	6	.25	8	.240	.321	.305
1995 Houston	NL	52	156	43	6	0	0	(0	0)	49	22	12	10	3	33	1	1	1	5	0	1.00	4	.276	.321	.314
1996 Houston	NL	89	218	62	8	1	1	(1	0)	75	28	15	23	3	42	3	4	1	6	1	.86	4	.284	.359	.344
1997 Houston	NL	102	303	79	14	4	3	(0	3)	110	33	34	21	2	50	3	0	0	5	2	.71	17	.261	.315	.363
1998 Houston	NL	141	491	128	24	3	2	(1	1)	164	55	46	54	5	84	6	3	7	13	7	.65	20	.261	.337	.334
6 ML YEARS		607	1881	488	73	15	12	(8	4)	627	241	161	190	16	360	20	11	13	35	19	.65	60	.259	.332	.333

Juan Guzman

Pitches: Right **Bats:** Right **Pos:** SP-33 **Ht:** 5'11" **Wt:** 195 **Born:** 10/28/66 **Age:** 32

	HOW MUCH HE PITCHED						WHAT HE GAVE UP												THE RESULTS						
Year Team	Lg	G	GS	CG	GF	IP	BFP	H	R	ER	HR	SH	SF	HB	TBB	IBB	SO	WP	Bk	W	L	Pct.	ShO	Sv-Op	Hld	ERA
1991 Toronto	AL	23	23	1	0	138.2	574	98	53	46	6	2	5	4	66	0	123	10	0	10	3	.769	0	0-0	0	2.99
1992 Toronto	AL	28	28	1	0	180.2	733	135	56	53	6	5	3	1	72	2	165	14	2	16	5	.762	0	0-0	0	2.64
1993 Toronto	AL	33	33	2	0	221	963	211	107	98	17	5	9	3	110	2	194	26	1	14	3	.824	1	0-0	0	3.99
1994 Toronto	AL	25	25	2	0	147.1	671	165	93	90	20	1	6	3	76	1	124	13	1	12	11	.522	0	0-0	0	5.68
1995 Toronto	AL	24	24	3	0	135.1	619	151	101	95	13	3	2	3	73	6	94	8	0	4	14	.222	0	0-0	0	6.32
1996 Toronto	AL	27	27	4	0	187.2	756	158	68	61	20	2	2	7	53	3	165	7	0	11	8	.579	1	0-0	0	2.93
1997 Toronto	AL	13	13	0	0	60	261	48	42	33	14	1	2	2	31	0	52	4	0	3	3	.500	0	0-0	0	4.95
1998 Tor-Bal	AL	33	33	2	0	211	918	193	117	102	23	2	5	8	98	2	168	11	0	10	16	.385	0	0-0	0	4.35
1998 Toronto	AL	22	22	2	0	145	632	133	83	71	19	2	3	6	65	1	113	6	0	6	12	.333	0	0-0	0	4.41
Baltimore	AL	11	11	0	0	66	286	60	34	31	4	0	2	2	33	1	55	5	0	4	4	.500	0	0-0	0	4.08
8 ML YEARS		206	206	15	0	1281.2	5495	1159	646	581	119	21	34	31	579	16	1085	93	4	80	66	.548	2	0-0	0	4.08

Tony Gwynn

Bats: Left **Throws:** Left **Pos:** RF-116; PH/PR-9; DH-3 **Ht:** 5'11" **Wt:** 220 **Born:** 5/9/60 **Age:** 39

Year Team	Lg	G	AB	H	2B	3B	HR	(Hm	Rd)	TB	R	RBI	TBB	IBB	SO	HBP	SH	SF	SB	CS	SB%	GDP	Avg	OBP	SLG
1982 San Diego	NL	54	190	55	12	2	1	(0	1)	74	33	17	14	0	16	0	4	1	8	3	.73	5	.289	.337	.389
1983 San Diego	NL	86	304	94	12	2	1	(0	1)	113	34	37	23	5	21	0	4	3	7	4	.64	9	.309	.355	.372
1984 San Diego	NL	158	606	**213**	21	10	5	(3	2)	269	88	71	59	13	23	2	6	2	33	18	.65	15	**.351**	.410	.444
1985 San Diego	NL	154	622	197	29	5	6	(3	3)	254	90	46	45	4	33	2	1	1	14	11	.56	17	.317	.364	.408
1986 San Diego	NL	160	**642**	211	33	7	14	(8	6)	300	**107**	59	52	11	35	3	2	2	37	9	.80	20	.329	.381	.467
1987 San Diego	NL	157	589	218	36	13	7	(5	2)	301	119	54	82	26	35	3	2	4	56	12	.82	13	**.370**	.447	.511
1988 San Diego	NL	133	521	163	22	5	7	(3	4)	216	64	70	51	13	40	0	4	2	26	11	.70	11	**.313**	.373	.415
1989 San Diego	NL	158	604	203	27	7	4	(3	1)	256	82	62	56	16	30	1	11	7	40	16	.71	12	**.336**	.389	.424
1990 San Diego	NL	141	573	177	29	10	4	(2	2)	238	79	72	44	20	23	1	7	4	17	8	.68	13	.309	.357	.415
1991 San Diego	NL	134	530	168	27	11	4	(1	3)	229	69	62	34	8	19	0	0	5	8	8	.50	11	.317	.355	.432
1992 San Diego	NL	128	520	165	27	3	6	(4	2)	216	77	41	46	12	16	0	0	3	3	6	.33	13	.317	.371	.415
1993 San Diego	NL	122	489	175	41	3	7	(4	3)	243	70	59	36	11	19	1	1	4	14	1	.93	18	.358	.398	.497
1994 San Diego	NL	110	419	165	35	1	12	(4	8)	238	79	64	48	16	19	2	1	5	5	0	1.00	20	**.394**	.454	.568
1995 San Diego	NL	135	535	197	33	1	9	(5	4)	259	82	90	35	10	15	1	0	6	17	5	.77	20	**.368**	.404	.484
1996 San Diego	NL	116	451	159	27	2	3	(2	1)	199	67	50	39	12	17	1	1	6	11	4	.73	17	**.353**	.400	.441
1997 San Diego	NL	149	592	220	49	2	17	(8	9)	324	97	119	43	12	28	3	1	**12**	12	5	.71	12	**.372**	.409	.547
1998 San Diego	NL	127	461	148	35	0	16	(5	11)	231	65	69	35	6	18	1	0	8	3	1	.75	14	.321	.364	.501
17 ML YEARS		2222	8648	2928	495	84	123	(60	63)	3960	1302	1042	742	195	407	21	45	78	311	122	.72	240	.339	.389	.458

Jerry Hairston Jr.

Bats: Right **Throws:** Right **Pos:** 2B-4; PH/PR-3 **Ht:** 5'10" **Wt:** 172 **Born:** 5/29/76 **Age:** 23

Year Team	Lg	G	AB	H	2B	3B	HR	(Hm	Rd)	TB	R	RBI	TBB	IBB	SO	HBP	SH	SF	SB	CS	SB%	GDP	Avg	OBP	SLG
1997 Bluefield	R+	59	221	73	13	4	2	—	—	100	44	36	21	0	29	10	4	2	13	9	.59	4	.330	.409	.452
1998 Frederick	A+	80	293	83	22	3	5	—	—	126	56	33	28	3	32	12	1	3	13	7	.65	4	.283	.366	.430
Bowie	AA	55	221	72	12	3	5	—	—	105	42	37	20	0	25	5	2	1	6	4	.60	5	.326	.393	.475
1998 Baltimore	AL	6	7	0	0	0	0	(0	0)	0	2	0	0	0	1	0	0	0	0	0	.00	0	.000	.000	.000

John Halama

Pitches: Left **Bats:** Left **Pos:** SP-6 **Ht:** 6'5" **Wt:** 200 **Born:** 2/22/72 **Age:** 27

Year Team	Lg	G	GS	CG	GF	IP	BFP	H	R	ER	HR	SH	SF	HB	TBB	IBB	SO	WP	Bk	W	L	Pct.	ShO	Sv-Op	Hld	ERA
1994 Auburn	A-	6	3	0	3	28	107	18	5	4	1	2	0	0	5	0	27	1	1	4	1	.800	0	1- -	—	1.29
Quad City	A	9	9	1	0	51.1	222	63	31	26	2	3	0	2	18	1	37	3	0	3	4	.429	1	0- -	—	4.56
1995 Quad City	A	55	0	0	26	62.1	241	48	16	14	7	2	1	3	22	1	56	1	0	1	2	.333	0	2- -	—	2.02
1996 Jackson	AA	27	27	0	0	162.2	691	151	77	58	10	7	7	8	59	0	110	7	0	9	10	.474	0	0- -	—	3.21
1997 New Orleans	AAA	26	24	1	2	171	673	150	57	49	9	4	7	1	32	1	126	2	2	13	3	.813	0	0- -	—	2.58
1998 New Orleans	AAA	17	17	4	0	121	488	118	48	43	11	3	4	3	16	1	86	3	3	12	3	.800	1	0- -	—	3.20
1998 Houston	NL	6	6	0	0	32.1	147	37	21	21	0	3	4	2	13	0	21	2	1	1	1	.500	0	0-0	0	5.85

Darren Hall

Pitches: Right **Bats:** Right **Pos:** RP-11 **Ht:** 6'3" **Wt:** 207 **Born:** 7/14/64 **Age:** 34

Year Team	Lg	G	GS	CG	GF	IP	BFP	H	R	ER	HR	SH	SF	HB	TBB	IBB	SO	WP	Bk	W	L	Pct.	ShO	Sv-Op	Hld	ERA
1998 San Antonio *	AA	2	2	0	0	1.2	7	1	2	2	1	0	0	0	1	0	2	0	0	0	0	.000	0	0- -	—	10.80
San Berndno *	A+	8	2	0	2	9.2	33	4	0	0	0	1	0	0	2	0	8	0	0	1	0	1.000	0	0- -	—	0.00
1994 Toronto	AL	30	0	0	28	31.2	131	26	12	12	3	1	0	1	14	1	28	1	0	2	3	.400	0	17-20	1	3.41
1995 Toronto	AL	17	0	0	11	16.1	77	21	9	8	2	0	0	0	9	0	11	0	0	0	2	.000	0	3-4	2	4.41
1996 Los Angeles	NL	9	0	0	3	12	53	13	9	8	2	0	0	0	5	0	12	0	0	0	2	.000	0	0-1	2	6.00
1997 Los Angeles	NL	63	0	0	20	54.2	233	58	15	14	3	1	1	0	26	7	39	0	0	3	2	.600	0	2-5	15	2.30
1998 Los Angeles	NL	11	0	0	2	11.1	56	17	14	13	2	0	1	1	5	0	8	0	0	0	3	.000	0	0-1	0	10.32
5 ML YEARS		130	0	0	64	126	550	135	59	55	12	2	2	2	59	8	98	1	0	5	12	.294	0	22-31	20	3.93

Roy Halladay

Pitches: Right **Bats:** Right **Pos:** SP-2 **Ht:** 6'6" **Wt:** 205 **Born:** 5/14/77 **Age:** 22

Year Team	Lg	G	GS	CG	GF	IP	BFP	H	R	ER	HR	SH	SF	HB	TBB	IBB	SO	WP	Bk	W	L	Pct.	ShO	Sv-Op	Hld	ERA
1995 Blue Jays	R	10	8	0	1	50.1	203	35	25	19	4	2	0	1	16	0	48	9	2	3	5	.375	0	0- -	—	3.40
1996 Dunedin	A+	27	27	2	0	164.2	688	158	75	50	7	5	1	6	46	0	109	1	4	15	7	.682	2	0- -	—	2.73
1997 Knoxville	AA	7	7	0	0	36.2	165	46	26	22	4	1	0	0	11	0	30	4	0	2	3	.400	0	0- -	—	5.40
Syracuse	AAA	22	22	2	0	125.2	537	132	74	64	13	4	1	1	53	1	64	8	3	7	10	.412	2	0- -	—	4.58
1998 Syracuse	AAA	21	21	1	0	116.1	500	107	52	49	11	2	2	8	53	3	71	9	0	9	5	.643	1	0- -	—	3.79
1998 Toronto	AL	2	2	1	0	14	53	9	4	3	2	0	0	0	2	0	13	0	0	1	0	1.000	0	0-0	0	1.93

Shane Halter

Bats: R **Throws:** R **Pos:** SS-66; PH/PR-10; 3B-8; 2B-6; LF-6; RF-3; P-1; 1B-1 **Ht:** 6'0" **Wt:** 180 **Born:** 11/8/69 **Age:** 29

Year Team	Lg	G	AB	H	2B	3B	HR	(Hm	Rd)	TB	R	RBI	TBB	IBB	SO	HBP	SH	SF	SB	CS	SB%	GDP	Avg	OBP	SLG
1991 Eugene	A-	64	236	55	9	1	1	—	—	69	41	18	49	0	59	3	2	1	12	6	.67	3	.233	.370	.292
1992 Appleton	A	80	313	83	22	3	3	—	—	120	50	33	41	1	54	1	5	3	21	6	.78	4	.265	.349	.383
Baseball Cy	A+	44	117	28	1	0	1	—	—	32	11	14	24	0	31	0	5	4	5	5	.50	2	.239	.359	.274
1993 Wilmington	A+	54	211	63	8	5	5	—	—	96	44	32	27	2	55	2	12	4	5	4	.56	3	.299	.377	.455
Memphis	AA	81	306	79	7	0	4	—	—	98	50	20	30	1	74	2	10	3	4	7	.36	3	.258	.326	.320
1994 Memphis	AA	129	494	111	23	1	6	—	—	154	61	35	39	0	102	3	15	6	10	14	.42	10	.225	.282	.312
1995 Omaha	AAA	124	392	90	19	3	8	—	—	139	42	39	40	0	97	0	19	1	2	3	.40	6	.230	.300	.355
1996 Charlotte	AAA	16	41	12	1	0	0	—	—	13	3	4	2	0	8	0	0	2	0	0	.00	0	.293	.311	.317
Omaha	AAA	93	299	77	24	0	3	—	—	110	43	33	31	0	49	2	8	1	7	2	.78	6	.258	.330	.368
1997 Omaha	AAA	14	49	13	1	1	2	—	—	22	10	9	6	0	10	1	0	2	0	0	.00	1	.265	.345	.449
1998 Omaha	AAA	22	97	30	6	1	1	—	—	41	15	13	6	1	15	0	4	0	4	1	.80	2	.309	.350	.423
1997 Kansas City	AL	74	123	34	5	1	2	(1	1)	47	16	10	10	0	28	2	4	0	4	3	.57	1	.276	.341	.382
1998 Kansas City	AL	86	204	45	12	0	2	(0	2)	63	17	13	12	0	38	1	7	2	2	5	.29	3	.221	.265	.309
2 ML YEARS		160	327	79	17	1	4	(1	3)	110	33	23	22	0	66	3	11	2	6	8	.43	4	.242	.294	.336

Bob Hamelin

Bats: Left **Throws:** Left **Pos:** PH/PR-66; 1B-51; DH-1 **Ht:** 6'0" **Wt:** 235 **Born:** 11/29/67 **Age:** 31

Year Team	Lg	G	AB	H	2B	3B	HR	(Hm	Rd)	TB	R	RBI	TBB	IBB	SO	HBP	SH	SF	SB	CS	SB%	GDP	Avg	OBP	SLG
1993 Kansas City	AL	16	49	11	3	0	2	(1	1)	20	2	5	6	0	15	0	0	0	0	0	.00	2	.224	.309	.408
1994 Kansas City	AL	101	312	88	25	1	24	(13	11)	187	64	65	56	3	62	1	0	5	4	3	.57	4	.282	.388	.599
1995 Kansas City	AL	72	208	35	7	1	7	(3	4)	65	20	25	26	1	56	6	0	1	0	1	.00	6	.168	.278	.313
1996 Kansas City	AL	89	239	61	14	1	9	(2	7)	104	31	40	54	2	58	2	0	4	5	2	.71	7	.255	.391	.435
1997 Detroit	AL	110	318	86	15	0	18	(10	8)	155	47	52	48	3	72	1	0	2	2	1	.67	8	.270	.366	.487
1998 Milwaukee	NL	109	146	32	6	0	7	(5	2)	59	15	22	16	1	30	1	1	3	0	1	.00	7	.219	.295	.404
6 ML YEARS		497	1272	313	70	3	67	(34	33)	590	179	209	206	10	293	11	1	15	11	8	.58	34	.246	.352	.464

Darryl Hamilton

Bats: Left **Throws:** Right **Pos:** CF-144; PH/PR-7 **Ht:** 6'1" **Wt:** 185 **Born:** 12/3/64 **Age:** 34

Year Team	Lg	G	AB	H	2B	3B	HR	(Hm	Rd)	TB	R	RBI	TBB	IBB	SO	HBP	SH	SF	SB	CS	SB%	GDP	Avg	OBP	SLG
1988 Milwaukee	AL	44	103	19	4	0	1	(1	0)	26	14	11	12	0	9	1	0	1	7	3	.70	2	.184	.274	.252
1990 Milwaukee	AL	89	156	46	5	0	1	(1	0)	54	27	18	9	0	12	0	3	0	10	3	.77	2	.295	.333	.346
1991 Milwaukee	AL	122	405	126	15	6	1	(0	1)	156	64	57	33	2	38	0	7	3	16	6	.73	10	.311	.361	.385
1992 Milwaukee	AL	128	470	140	19	7	5	(1	4)	188	67	62	45	0	42	1	4	7	41	14	.75	10	.298	.356	.400
1993 Milwaukee	AL	135	520	161	21	1	9	(5	4)	211	74	48	45	5	62	3	4	1	21	13	.62	9	.310	.367	.406
1994 Milwaukee	AL	36	141	37	10	1	1	(0	1)	52	23	13	15	1	17	0	2	1	3	0	1.00	6	.262	.331	.369
1995 Milwaukee	AL	112	398	108	20	6	5	(3	2)	155	54	44	47	3	35	3	8	3	11	1	.92	9	.271	.350	.389
1996 Texas	AL	148	627	184	29	4	6	(2	4)	239	94	51	54	4	66	2	7	6	15	5	.75	15	.293	.348	.381
1997 San Francisco	NL	125	460	124	23	3	5	(1	4)	168	78	43	61	1	61	0	6	2	15	10	.60	6	.270	.354	.365
1998 SF-Col	NL	148	561	173	28	3	6	(3	3)	225	95	51	82	1	73	3	12	3	13	9	.59	6	.308	.398	.401
1998 San Francisco	NL	97	367	108	19	2	1	(1	0)	134	65	26	59	0	53	2	6	2	9	8	.53	6	.294	.393	.365
Colorado	NL	51	194	65	9	1	5	(2	3)	91	30	25	23	1	20	1	6	1	4	1	.80	0	.335	.406	.469
10 ML YEARS		1087	3841	1118	174	31	40	(17	23)	1474	590	398	403	17	415	13	53	27	152	64	.70	71	.291	.358	.384

Joey Hamilton

Pitches: Right **Bats:** Right **Pos:** SP-34 **Ht:** 6'4" **Wt:** 230 **Born:** 9/9/70 **Age:** 28

Year Team	Lg	G	GS	CG	GF	IP	BFP	H	R	ER	HR	SH	SF	HB	TBB	IBB	SO	WP	Bk	W	L	Pct.	ShO	Sv-Op	Hld	ERA
1994 San Diego	NL	16	16	1	0	108.2	447	98	40	36	7	4	2	6	29	3	61	6	0	9	6	.600	1	0-0	0	2.98
1995 San Diego	NL	31	30	2	1	204.1	850	189	89	70	17	12	4	11	56	5	123	2	0	6	9	.400	2	0-0	0	3.08
1996 San Diego	NL	34	33	3	0	211.2	908	206	100	98	19	6	5	9	83	3	184	14	1	15	9	.625	1	0-0	1	4.17
1997 San Diego	NL	31	29	1	1	192.2	831	199	100	91	22	8	8	12	69	2	124	7	0	12	7	.632	0	0-0	0	4.25
1998 San Diego	NL	34	34	0	0	217.1	958	220	113	103	15	13	6	8	106	10	147	4	0	13	13	.500	0	0-0	0	4.27
5 ML YEARS		146	142	7	2	934.2	3994	912	442	398	80	43	25	46	343	23	639	33	1	55	44	.556	4	0-0	1	3.83

Chris Hammond

Pitches: Left **Bats:** Left **Pos:** SP-3 **Ht:** 6'1" **Wt:** 195 **Born:** 1/21/66 **Age:** 33

Year Team	Lg	G	GS	CG	GF	IP	BFP	H	R	ER	HR	SH	SF	HB	TBB	IBB	SO	WP	Bk	W	L	Pct.	ShO	Sv-Op	Hld	ERA
1998 Charlotte *	AAA	5	5	0	0	28	129	35	15	15	2	3	1	0	14	2	22	0	0	1	3	.250	0	0- –	—	4.82
1990 Cincinnati	NL	3	3	0	0	11.1	56	13	9	8	2	1	0	0	12	1	4	1	3	0	2	.000	0	0-0	0	6.35
1991 Cincinnati	NL	20	18	0	0	99.2	425	92	51	45	4	6	1	2	48	3	50	3	0	7	7	.500	0	0-0	0	4.06
1992 Cincinnati	NL	28	26	0	1	147.1	627	149	75	69	13	5	3	3	55	6	79	6	0	7	10	.412	0	0-0	0	4.21
1993 Florida	NL	32	32	1	0	191	826	207	106	99	18	10	2	1	66	2	108	10	5	11	12	.478	0	0-0	0	4.66
1994 Florida	NL	13	13	1	0	73.1	312	79	30	25	5	5	2	1	23	1	40	3	0	4	4	.500	1	0-0	0	3.07
1995 Florida	NL	25	24	3	0	161	683	157	73	68	17	7	7	9	47	2	126	3	1	9	6	.600	2	0-0	0	3.80
1996 Florida	NL	38	9	0	5	81	368	104	65	59	14	3	4	4	27	3	50	1	0	5	8	.385	0	0-0	5	6.56
1997 Boston	AL	29	8	0	6	65.1	293	81	45	43	5	0	3	2	27	4	48	2	0	3	4	.429	0	1-2	4	5.92
1998 Florida	NL	3	3	0	0	13.2	67	20	11	10	3	2	0	0	8	0	0	0	0	0	2	.000	0	0-0	0	6.59

Year Team	Lg	G	GS	CG	GF	IP	BFP	H	R	ER	HR	SH	SF	HB	TBB	IBB	SO	WP	Bk	W	L	Pct.	ShO	Sv-Op	Hld	ERA
		HOW MUCH HE PITCHED						WHAT HE GAVE UP												THE RESULTS						
9 ML YEARS		191	136	5	12	843.2	3657	902	465	426	81	39	22	23	313	22	513	29	9	46	55	.455	3	1-2	9	4.54

Jeffrey Hammonds

Bats: R **Throws:** R **Pos:** CF-49; RF-29; PH/PR-15; DH-7; LF-7   **Ht:** 6'0" **Wt:** 195 **Born:** 3/5/71 **Age:** 28

		BATTING																BASERUNNING				PERCENTAGES		
Year Team	Lg	G	AB	H	2B	3B	HR	(Hm | Rd)	TB	R	RBI	TBB	IBB	SO	HBP	SH	SF	SB	CS	SB%	GDP	Avg	OBP	SLG
1998 Bowie *	AA	3	6	2	0	0	0	—	—	2	4	0	2	0	2	1	0	0	3	1	.75	0	.333	.556	.333
1993 Baltimore	AL	33	105	32	8	0	3	(2 | 1)	49	10	19	2	1	16	0	1	2	4	0	1.00	3	.305	.312	.467
1994 Baltimore	AL	68	250	74	18	2	8	(6 | 2)	120	45	31	17	1	39	2	0	5	5	0	1.00	3	.296	.339	.480
1995 Baltimore	AL	57	178	43	9	1	4	(2 | 2)	66	18	23	9	0	30	1	1	2	4	2	.67	1	.242	.279	.371
1996 Baltimore	AL	71	248	56	10	1	9	(3 | 6)	95	38	27	23	1	53	4	6	1	3	3	.50	7	.226	.301	.383
1997 Baltimore	AL	118	397	105	19	3	21	(9 | 12)	193	71	55	32	1	73	3	0	2	15	1	.94	6	.264	.323	.486
1998 Bal-Cin		89	257	72	16	2	6	(1 | 5)	110	50	39	39	1	56	3	3	4	8	3	.73	2	.280	.376	.428
1998 Baltimore	AL	63	171	46	12	1	6	(1 | 5)	78	36	28	26	1	38	3	0	3	7	2	.78	2	.269	.369	.456
Cincinnati	NL	26	86	26	4	1	0	(0 | 0)	32	14	11	13	0	18	0	3	1	1	1	.50	0	.302	.390	.372
6 ML YEARS		436	1435	382	80	9	51	(23 | 28)	633	232	194	122	5	267	13	11	16	39	9	.81	24	.266	.326	.441

Mike Hampton

Pitches: Left **Bats:** Right **Pos:** SP-32   **Ht:** 5'10" **Wt:** 180 **Born:** 9/9/72 **Age:** 26

		HOW MUCH HE PITCHED						WHAT HE GAVE UP												THE RESULTS					
Year Team	Lg	G	GS	CG	GF	IP	BFP	H	R	ER	HR	SH	SF	HB	TBB	IBB	SO	WP	Bk	W	L	Pct.	ShO	Sv-Op	Hld	ERA
1993 Seattle	AL	13	3	0	2	17	95	28	20	18	3	1	1	0	17	3	8	1	1	1	3	.250	0	1-1	2	9.53
1994 Houston	NL	44	0	0	7	41.1	181	46	19	17	4	0	0	2	16	1	24	5	1	2	1	.667	0	0-1	10	3.70
1995 Houston	NL	24	24	0	0	150.2	641	141	73	56	13	11	5	4	49	3	115	3	1	9	8	.529	0	0-0	0	3.35
1996 Houston	NL	27	27	2	0	160.1	691	175	79	64	12	10	3	3	49	1	101	7	2	10	10	.500	1	0-0	0	3.59
1997 Houston	NL	34	34	7	0	223	941	217	105	95	16	11	7	2	77	2	139	6	1	15	10	.600	2	0-0	0	3.83
1998 Houston	NL	32	32	1	0	211.2	917	227	92	79	18	7	7	5	81	1	137	4	2	11	7	.611	1	0-0	0	3.36
6 ML YEARS		174	120	10	9	804	3466	834	388	329	66	40	23	16	289	11	524	26	8	48	39	.552	4	1-2	12	3.68

Chris Haney

Pitches: Left **Bats:** Left **Pos:** RP-26; SP-12   **Ht:** 6'3" **Wt:** 210 **Born:** 11/16/68 **Age:** 30

		HOW MUCH HE PITCHED						WHAT HE GAVE UP												THE RESULTS					
Year Team	Lg	G	GS	CG	GF	IP	BFP	H	R	ER	HR	SH	SF	HB	TBB	IBB	SO	WP	Bk	W	L	Pct.	ShO	Sv-Op	Hld	ERA
1998 Royals *	R	1	1	0	0	2.1	11	2	2	0	0	0	0	0	0	0	1	0	0	0	1	.000	0	0- —	—	0.00
1991 Montreal	NL	16	16	0	0	84.2	387	94	49	38	8	6	1	1	43	1	51	9	0	3	7	.300	0	0-0	0	4.04
1992 Mon-KC		16	13	2	0	80	339	75	43	41	11	0	6	4	26	2	54	5	1	4	6	.400	2	0-0	0	4.61
1993 Kansas City	AL	23	23	1	0	124	556	141	87	83	13	3	4	3	53	2	65	6	1	9	9	.500	1	0-0	0	6.02
1994 Kansas City	AL	6	6	0	0	28.1	127	36	25	23	2	3	4	1	11	1	18	2	0	2	2	.500	0	0-0	0	7.31
1995 Kansas City	AL	16	13	1	0	81.1	338	78	35	33	7	1	4	2	33	0	31	2	0	3	4	.429	0	0-0	2	3.65
1996 Kansas City	AL	35	35	4	0	228	988	267	136	119	29	5	8	6	51	0	115	8	0	10	14	.417	1	0-0	0	4.70
1997 Kansas City	AL	8	3	0	1	24.2	110	29	16	12	1	2	1	2	5	2	16	1	0	1	2	.333	0	0-0	1	4.38
1998 KC-ChN		38	12	0	2	102.1	469	128	82	80	20	2	11	5	37	0	55	4	1	6	6	.500	0	0-1	0	7.04
1992 Montreal	NL	9	6	1	2	38	165	40	25	23	6	0	3	4	10	0	27	5	1	2	3	.400	1	0-0	0	5.45
Kansas City	AL	7	7	1	0	42	174	35	18	18	5	0	3	0	16	2	27	0	0	2	3	.400	1	0-0	0	3.86
1998 Kansas City	AL	33	12	0	2	97.1	450	125	78	76	18	2	11	5	36	0	51	4	1	6	6	.500	0	0-1	0	7.03
Chicago	NL	5	0	0	0	5	19	3	4	4	2	0	0	0	1	0	4	0	0	0	0	.000	0	0-0	0	7.20
8 ML YEARS		158	121	8	5	753.1	3314	848	473	429	89	22	39	24	259	8	405	37	3	38	50	.432	4	0-1	3	5.13

Todd Haney

Bats: Right **Throws:** Right **Pos:** PH/PR-3; 2B-1; LF-1   **Ht:** 5'9" **Wt:** 165 **Born:** 7/30/65 **Age:** 33

		BATTING																BASERUNNING				PERCENTAGES		
Year Team	Lg	G	AB	H	2B	3B	HR	(Hm | Rd)	TB	R	RBI	TBB	IBB	SO	HBP	SH	SF	SB	CS	SB%	GDP	Avg	OBP	SLG
1998 St. Lucie *	A+	1	4	1	0	0	0	—	—	1	1	0	0	0	0	0	0	0	0	0	.00	0	.250	.250	.250
Norfolk *	AAA	117	440	152	33	4	3	—	—	202	84	51	55	1	44	5	5	1	11	2	.85	13	.345	.423	.459
1992 Montreal	NL	7	10	3	1	0	0	(0 | 0)	4	0	1	0	0	0	0	0	0	0	0	.00	1	.300	.300	.400
1994 Chicago	NL	17	37	6	0	0	1	(0 | 1)	9	6	2	3	0	3	1	1	1	2	1	.67	0	.162	.238	.243
1995 Chicago	NL	25	73	30	8	0	2	(1 | 1)	44	11	6	7	0	11	0	1	0	0	0	.00	0	.411	.463	.603
1996 Chicago	NL	49	82	11	1	0	0	(0 | 0)	12	11	3	7	0	15	0	2	1	1	0	1.00	1	.134	.200	.146
1998 New York	NL	3	3	0	0	0	0	(0 | 0)	0	0	0	1	0	0	0	0	0	0	0	.00	0	.000	.250	.000
5 ML YEARS		101	205	50	10	0	3	(1 | 2)	69	28	12	18	0	29	1	5	2	3	1	.75	2	.244	.305	.337

Jed Hansen

Bats: Right **Throws:** Right **Pos:** 2B-2; PH/PR-2   **Ht:** 6'1" **Wt:** 195 **Born:** 8/19/72 **Age:** 26

		BATTING																BASERUNNING				PERCENTAGES		
Year Team	Lg	G	AB	H	2B	3B	HR	(Hm | Rd)	TB	R	RBI	TBB	IBB	SO	HBP	SH	SF	SB	CS	SB%	GDP	Avg	OBP	SLG
1994 Eugene	A-	66	235	57	8	2	3	—	—	78	26	17	24	2	56	8	2	1	6	4	.60	1	.243	.332	.332
1995 Springfield	A	122	414	107	27	7	9	—	—	175	86	50	78	0	73	7	6	1	44	10	.81	8	.258	.384	.423
1996 Wichita	AA	99	405	116	27	4	12	—	—	187	60	50	29	0	72	4	4	2	14	8	.64	6	.286	.339	.462
Omaha	AAA	29	99	23	4	0	3	—	—	36	14	9	12	0	22	3	1	1	2	0	1.00	1	.232	.330	.364
1997 Omaha	AAA	114	380	102	20	2	11	—	—	159	43	44	32	0	78	2	5	2	8	1	.89	9	.268	.327	.418
1998 Omaha	AAA	127	417	116	19	7	16	—	—	197	63	56	44	0	125	4	4	7	17	9	.65	7	.278	.347	.472
1997 Kansas City	AL	34	94	29	6	1	1	(1 | 0)	40	11	14	13	0	29	1	2	1	3	2	.60	2	.309	.394	.426

			BATTING																	BASERUNNING				PERCENTAGES		
Year Team	Lg	G	AB	H	2B	3B	HR	(Hm	Rd)	TB	R	RBI	TBB	IBB	SO	HBP	SH	SF		SB	CS	SB%	GDP	Avg	OBP	SLG
1998 Kansas City	AL	4	3	0	0	0	0	(0	0)	0	0	0	0	0	3	0	0	0		0	0	.00	0	.000	.000	.000
2 ML YEARS		38	97	29	6	1	1	(1	0)	40	11	14	13	0	32	1	2	1		3	2	.60	2	.299	.384	.412

Erik Hanson

Pitches: Right **Bats:** Right **Pos:** SP-8; RP-3   **Ht:** 6'6" **Wt:** 215 **Born:** 5/18/65 **Age:** 34

		HOW MUCH HE PITCHED						WHAT HE GAVE UP											THE RESULTS						
Year Team	Lg	G	GS	CG	GF	IP	BFP	H	R	ER	HR	SH	SF	HB	TBB	IBB	SO	WP	Bk	W	L	Pct.	ShO	Sv-Op	Hld	ERA
1998 Dunedin *	A+	1	1	0	0	4	18	4	1	1	0	0	0	0	2	0	5	0	0	0	0	.000	0	0- -	—	2.25
Vancouver *	AAA	14	14	2	0	82	353	82	43	41	7	4	2	3	36	0	60	6	0	5	5	.500	1	0- -	—	4.50
1988 Seattle	AL	6	6	0	0	41.2	168	35	17	15	4	3	0	1	12	1	36	2	2	2	3	.400	0	0-0	0	3.24
1989 Seattle	AL	17	17	1	0	113.1	465	103	44	40	7	4	1	5	32	1	75	3	0	9	5	.643	0	0-0	0	3.18
1990 Seattle	AL	33	33	5	0	236	964	205	88	85	15	5	6	2	68	6	211	10	0	18	9	.667	1	0-0	0	3.24
1991 Seattle	AL	27	27	2	0	174.2	744	182	82	74	16	2	8	2	56	2	143	14	1	8	8	.500	1	0-0	0	3.81
1992 Seattle	AL	31	30	6	0	186.2	809	209	110	100	14	8	9	7	57	1	112	6	0	8	17	.320	1	0-0	0	4.82
1993 Seattle	AL	31	30	7	0	215	898	215	91	83	17	10	4	5	60	6	163	8	0	11	12	.478	1	0-0	0	3.47
1994 Cincinnati	NL	22	21	0	1	122.2	519	137	60	56	10	5	4	3	23	3	101	8	1	5	5	.500	0	0-0	0	4.11
1995 Boston	AL	29	29	1	0	186.2	800	187	94	88	17	6	8	1	59	0	139	5	0	15	5	.750	1	0-0	0	4.24
1996 Toronto	AL	35	35	4	0	214.2	955	243	143	129	26	4	5	2	102	2	156	13	0	13	17	.433	1	0-0	0	5.41
1997 Toronto	AL	3	2	0	1	15	65	15	13	13	3	0	0	0	6	0	18	1	0	0	0	.000	0	0-0	0	7.80
1998 Toronto	AL	11	8	0	3	49	243	73	34	34	10	3	0	1	29	1	21	1	1	0	3	.000	0	0-0	0	6.24
11 ML YEARS		245	238	26	5	1555.1	6630	1604	776	717	139	50	45	29	504	23	1175	71	6	89	84	.514	5	0-0	0	4.15

Jason Hardtke

Bats: B **Throws:** R **Pos:** PH/PR-12; 3B-7; DH-1; RF-1   **Ht:** 5'10" **Wt:** 175 **Born:** 9/15/71 **Age:** 27

			BATTING																	BASERUNNING				PERCENTAGES		
Year Team	Lg	G	AB	H	2B	3B	HR	(Hm	Rd)	TB	R	RBI	TBB	IBB	SO	HBP	SH	SF		SB	CS	SB%	GDP	Avg	OBP	SLG
1990 Burlington	R+	58	215	58	7	0	4	—	—	57	18	16	23	0	19	2	0	0		1	0	.92	1	.268	.377	.401
1991 Columbus	A	139	534	155	26	8	12	—	—	233	104	81	75	5	48	7	6	6		22	4	.85	6	.290	.381	.436
1992 Kinston	A+	6	19	4	0	0	0	—	—	4	3	1	4	0	4	0	0	0		0	0	.00	0	.211	.348	.211
Waterloo	A	110	411	125	27	4	8	—	—	184	75	47	38	3	33	5	1	5		9	7	.56	9	.304	.366	.448
High Desert	A+	10	41	11	1	0	2	—	—	18	9	8	4	0	4	1	0	1		1	1	.50	1	.268	.340	.439
1993 Rancho Cuca	A+	130	523	167	38	7	11	—	—	252	98	85	61	2	54	2	2	6		7	8	.47	12	.319	.389	.482
1994 Wichita	AA	75	255	60	15	1	5	—	—	92	26	29	21	1	44	0	2	4		1	2	.33	4	.235	.289	.361
Rancho Cuca	A+	4	13	4	0	0	0	—	—	4	2	0	3	0	2	0	0	0		0	1	.00	0	.308	.438	.308
1995 Norfolk	AAA	4	7	2	1	0	0	—	—	3	1	0	2	0	0	0	0	0		1	1	.50	0	.286	.444	.429
Binghamton	AA	121	455	130	42	4	4	—	—	192	65	52	66	1	58	4	2	9		6	8	.43	7	.286	.375	.422
1996 Binghamton	AA	35	137	36	11	0	3	—	—	56	23	16	16	1	16	0	1	0		0	1	.00	3	.263	.340	.409
Norfolk	AAA	71	257	77	17	2	9	—	—	125	49	35	29	1	29	0	4	2		4	6	.40	4	.300	.368	.486
1997 Norfolk	AAA	97	388	107	23	3	11	—	—	169	46	45	40	1	54	0	4	1		3	6	.33	9	.276	.343	.436
Binghamton	AA	6	26	10	2	0	1	—	—	15	3	4	2	0	2	0	0	0		0	0	.00	0	.385	.429	.577
1998 Iowa	AAA	91	333	96	20	1	11	—	—	151	67	53	35	1	46	4	1	2		7	7	.50	7	.288	.361	.453
1996 New York	NL	19	57	11	5	0	0	(0	0)	16	3	6	2	0	12	1	0	0		0	0	.00	1	.193	.233	.281
1997 New York	NL	30	56	15	2	0	2	(0	2)	23	9	8	4	1	6	1	0	1		1	1	.50	3	.268	.323	.411
1998 Chicago	NL	18	21	5	0	0	0	(0	0)	5	2	2	2	0	6	0	0	0		0	0	.00	0	.238	.304	.238
3 ML YEARS		67	134	31	7	0	2	(0	2)	44	14	16	8	1	24	2	0	1		1	1	.50	4	.231	.283	.328

Pete Harnisch

Pitches: Right **Bats:** Right **Pos:** SP-32   **Ht:** 6'0" **Wt:** 228 **Born:** 9/23/66 **Age:** 32

		HOW MUCH HE PITCHED						WHAT HE GAVE UP											THE RESULTS						
Year Team	Lg	G	GS	CG	GF	IP	BFP	H	R	ER	HR	SH	SF	HB	TBB	IBB	SO	WP	Bk	W	L	Pct.	ShO	Sv-Op	Hld	ERA
1988 Baltimore	AL	2	2	0	0	13	61	13	8	8	1	2	0	0	9	1	10	1	0	0	2	.000	0	0-0	0	5.54
1989 Baltimore	AL	18	17	2	1	103.1	468	97	55	53	10	4	5	4	64	3	70	5	1	5	9	.357	0	0-0	0	4.62
1990 Baltimore	AL	31	31	3	0	188.2	821	189	96	91	17	6	5	1	86	5	122	2	2	11	11	.500	2	0-0	0	4.34
1991 Houston	NL	33	33	4	0	216.2	900	169	71	65	14	9	7	5	83	3	172	5	2	12	9	.571	2	0-0	0	2.70
1992 Houston	NL	34	34	0	0	206.2	859	182	92	85	18	5	5	5	64	3	164	4	1	9	10	.474	0	0-0	0	3.70
1993 Houston	NL	33	33	5	0	217.2	896	171	84	72	20	9	4	6	79	5	185	3	1	16	9	.640	4	0-0	0	2.98
1994 Houston	NL	17	17	1	0	95	419	100	59	57	13	3	2	3	39	1	62	0	0	8	5	.615	0	0-0	0	5.40
1995 New York	NL	18	18	0	0	110	462	111	55	45	13	4	6	3	24	4	82	0	1	2	8	.200	0	0-0	0	3.68
1996 New York	NL	31	31	2	0	194.2	839	195	103	91	30	13	9	7	61	5	114	7	3	8	12	.400	1	0-0	0	4.21
1997 NYN-Mil		10	8	0	0	39.2	186	48	33	31	6	0	2	1	23	1	22	2	0	1	2	.333	0	0-0	0	7.03
1998 Cincinnati	NL	32	32	2	0	209	854	176	79	73	24	8	5	6	64	4	157	4	1	14	7	.667	1	0-0	0	3.14
1997 New York	NL	6	5	0	0	25.2	121	35	24	23	5	0	2	1	11	1	12	1	0	0	1	.000	0	0-0	0	8.06
Milwaukee	AL	4	3	0	0	14	65	13	9	8	1	0	0	0	12	0	10	1	0	1	1	.500	0	0-0	0	5.14
11 ML YEARS		259	256	19	1	1594.1	6765	1451	735	671	166	63	50	42	596	35	1160	35	12	86	84	.506	8	0-0	0	3.79

Denny Harriger

Pitches: Right **Bats:** Right **Pos:** SP-2; RP-2   **Ht:** 5'11" **Wt:** 185 **Born:** 7/21/69 **Age:** 29

		HOW MUCH HE PITCHED						WHAT HE GAVE UP											THE RESULTS						
Year Team	Lg	G	GS	CG	GF	IP	BFP	H	R	ER	HR	SH	SF	HB	TBB	IBB	SO	WP	Bk	W	L	Pct.	ShO	Sv-Op	Hld	ERA
1987 Kingsport	R+	12	7	0	2	43.2	198	43	31	21	3	4	1	4	22	0	24	1	0	2	5	.286	0	0- -	—	4.33
1988 Kingsport	R+	13	13	2	0	92.1	375	83	35	22	3	1	1	0	24	1	59	2	1	7	2	.778	1	0- -	—	2.14
1989 Pittsfield	A-	3	3	1	0	21	84	20	4	4	0	2	0	1	0	0	17	0	0	2	0	1.000	1	0- -	—	1.71
St. Lucie	A+	11	11	0	0	67.2	284	72	33	24	6	0	0	2	17	0	17	1	0	5	3	.625	0	0- -	—	3.19
1990 St. Lucie	A+	27	7	1	9	71.2	293	73	36	28	0	0	0	1	20	0	47	2	1	5	3	.625	0	2- -	—	3.52

Year Team	Lg	G	GS	CG	GF	IP	BFP	H	R	ER	HR	SH	SF	HB	TBB	IBB	SO	WP	Bk	W	L	Pct.	ShO	Sv-Op	Hld	ERA
1991 Columbia	A	2	2	1	0	11	37	5	0	0	0	1	0	0	2	0	13	0	0	2	0	1.000	1	0- –	—	0.00
St. Lucie	A+	14	11	2	1	71.1	286	67	20	18	2	4	2	1	12	0	37	1	0	6	1	.857	2	0- –	—	2.27
1992 Binghamton	AA	11	0	0	5	21.1	88	22	11	9	2	2	0	1	7	0	8	0	0	2	2	.500	0	0- –	—	3.80
St. Lucie	A+	27	10	0	9	88.1	372	89	30	22	1	6	0	3	14	1	65	5	1	7	3	.700	0	3- –	—	2.24
1993 Binghamton	AA	35	24	4	4	170.2	716	174	69	56	8	6	2	7	40	0	89	9	1	13	10	.565	3	1- –	—	2.95
1994 Las Vegas	AAA	30	25	3	0	157.1	720	216	122	104	16	6	5	4	44	0	87	3	1	6	11	.353	0	0- –	—	5.95
1995 Las Vegas	AAA	29	28	7	0	177	776	187	94	80	12	6	5	4	60	2	97	4	1	9	9	.500	2	0- –	—	4.07
1996 Las Vegas	AAA	26	25	1	0	164.1	711	183	91	77	12	3	8	7	51	1	102	4	1	10	7	.588	0	0- –	—	4.22
1997 Toledo	AAA	27	27	2	0	167	717	159	87	74	19	5	1	5	63	2	109	3	0	11	8	.579	1	0- –	—	3.99
1998 Toledo	AAA	22	22	4	0	142.1	603	151	78	72	15	4	5	2	48	0	87	2	0	5	12	.294	1	0- –	—	4.55
1998 Detroit	AL	4	2	0	2	12	61	17	11	9	1	1	0	0	8	2	3	0	0	0	3	.000	0	0-0	0	6.75

Lenny Harris

B: L **T:** R **Pos:** RF-73; PH/PR-51; LF-34; 3B-10; 2B-2; DH-1; P-1; 1B-1; CF-1 **Ht:** 5'10" **Wt:** 210 **B:** 10/28/64 **Age:** 34

Year Team	Lg	G	AB	H	2B	3B	HR	(Hm	Rd)	TB	R	RBI	TBB	IBB	SO	HBP	SH	SF	SB	CS	SB%	GDP	Avg	OBP	SLG
1988 Cincinnati	NL	16	43	16	1	0	0	(0	0)	17	7	8	5	0	4	0	1	2	4	1	.80	0	.372	.420	.395
1989 Cin-LA	NL	115	335	79	10	1	3	(1	2)	100	36	26	20	0	33	2	1	0	14	9	.61	14	.236	.283	.299
1990 Los Angeles	NL	137	431	131	16	4	2	(0	2)	161	61	29	29	2	31	1	3	1	15	10	.60	8	.304	.348	.374
1991 Los Angeles	NL	145	429	123	16	1	3	(1	2)	150	59	38	37	5	32	5	12	2	12	3	.80	16	.287	.349	.350
1992 Los Angeles	NL	135	347	94	11	0	0	(0	0)	105	28	30	24	2	24	1	6	2	19	7	.73	10	.271	.318	.303
1993 Los Angeles	NL	107	160	38	6	1	2	(0	2)	52	20	11	15	4	15	0	1	0	3	1	.75	4	.238	.303	.325
1994 Cincinnati	NL	66	100	31	3	1	0	(0	0)	36	13	14	5	0	13	0	0	1	7	2	.78	6	.310	.340	.360
1995 Cincinnati	NL	101	197	41	8	3	2	(0	2)	61	32	16	14	0	22	0	3	1	10	1	.91	6	.208	.259	.310
1996 Cincinnati	NL	125	302	86	17	2	5	(2	3)	122	33	32	21	1	31	1	6	3	14	6	.70	3	.285	.330	.404
1997 Cincinnati	NL	120	238	65	13	1	3	(2	1)	89	32	28	18	1	18	2	3	2	4	3	.57	10	.273	.327	.374
1998 Cin-NYN	NL	132	290	75	15	0	6	(2	4)	108	30	27	17	3	21	2	4	4	6	5	.55	13	.259	.300	.372
1989 Cincinnati	NL	61	188	42	4	0	2	(0	2)	52	17	11	9	0	20	1	1	0	10	6	.63	5	.223	.263	.277
Los Angeles	NL	54	147	37	6	1	1	(1	0)	48	19	15	11	0	13	1	0	0	4	3	.57	9	.252	.308	.327
1998 Cincinnati	NL	57	122	36	8	0	0	(0	0)	44	12	10	8	2	9	1	0	2	1	3	.25	8	.295	.338	.361
New York	NL	75	168	39	7	0	6	(2	4)	64	18	17	9	1	12	1	4	2	5	2	.71	5	.232	.272	.381
11 ML YEARS		1199	2872	779	116	14	26	(8	18)	1001	351	259	205	19	242	14	40	18	108	48	.69	84	.271	.321	.349

Pep Harris

Pitches: Right **Bats:** Right **Pos:** RP-49 **Ht:** 6'2" **Wt:** 253 **Born:** 9/23/72 **Age:** 26

Year Team	Lg	G	GS	CG	GF	IP	BFP	H	R	ER	HR	SH	SF	HB	TBB	IBB	SO	WP	Bk	W	L	Pct.	ShO	Sv-Op	Hld	ERA
1998 Lk Elsinore *	A+	4	1	0	0	9.1	38	9	5	0	0	0	0	0	2	0	12	0	0	0	1	.000	0	0- –	—	0.00
Vancouver *	AAA	2	0	0	1	6.1	25	4	2	2	0	0	0	0	3	0	7	1	0	0	1	1.000	0	1- –	—	2.84
1996 California	AL	11	3	0	0	32.1	146	31	16	14	4	0	4	3	17	2	20	4	0	2	0	1.000	0	0-0	2	3.90
1997 Anaheim	AL	61	0	0	17	79.2	346	82	33	32	7	3	4	2	38	6	56	3	0	5	4	.556	0	0-3	10	3.62
1998 Anaheim	AL	49	0	0	13	60	257	55	32	29	7	3	1	0	23	4	34	2	0	3	1	.750	0	0-1	14	4.35
3 ML YEARS		121	3	0	30	172	749	168	81	75	18	6	9	5	78	12	110	9	0	10	5	.667	0	0-4	26	3.92

Reggie Harris

Pitches: Right **Bats:** Right **Pos:** RP-6 **Ht:** 6'1" **Wt:** 217 **Born:** 8/12/68 **Age:** 30

Year Team	Lg	G	GS	CG	GF	IP	BFP	H	R	ER	HR	SH	SF	HB	TBB	IBB	SO	WP	Bk	W	L	Pct.	ShO	Sv-Op	Hld	ERA
1998 New Orleans *	AAA	51	0	0	41	52.2	221	38	27	26	7	2	0	0	28	3	53	2	0	2	3	.400	0	23- –	—	4.44
1990 Oakland	AL	16	1	0	9	41.1	168	25	16	16	5	1	2	2	21	1	31	2	0	0	0	1.000	0	0-0	0	3.48
1991 Oakland	AL	2	0	0	1	3	15	5	4	4	0	0	1	0	3	1	2	2	0	0	0	.000	0	0-0	0	12.00
1996 Boston	AL	4	0	0	1	4.1	24	7	6	6	2	0	0	1	5	0	4	0	0	0	0	.000	0	0-1	0	12.46
1997 Philadelphia	NL	50	0	0	13	54.1	264	55	33	32	1	3	4	5	43	1	45	5	1	1	3	.250	0	0-0	1	5.30
1998 Houston	NL	6	0	0	2	6	26	6	4	4	1	0	1	0	2	0	2	0	0	0	0	.000	0	0-0	1	6.00
5 ML YEARS		78	1	0	26	109	497	98	63	62	9	4	8	8	74	3	84	9	1	2	3	.400	0	0-1	2	5.12

Dean Hartgraves

Pitches: Left **Bats:** Left **Pos:** RP-5 **Ht:** 6'0" **Wt:** 185 **Born:** 8/12/66 **Age:** 32

Year Team	Lg	G	GS	CG	GF	IP	BFP	H	R	ER	HR	SH	SF	HB	TBB	IBB	SO	WP	Bk	W	L	Pct.	ShO	Sv-Op	Hld	ERA
1998 Fresno *	AAA	38	1	0	11	70.1	295	67	35	31	8	2	5	1	19	4	64	1	0	2	3	.400	0	3- –	—	3.97
1995 Houston	NL	40	0	0	11	36.1	150	30	14	13	2	1	1	0	16	2	24	1	0	2	0	1.000	0	0-3	4	3.22
1996 Hou-Atl	NL	39	0	0	9	37.2	167	34	21	20	4	1	2	2	23	3	30	2	0	1	0	1.000	0	0-0	6	4.78
1998 San Francisco	NL	5	0	0	1	5.2	32	10	7	6	1	0	2	0	4	0	4	1	0	0	0	.000	0	0-0	0	9.53
1996 Houston	NL	19	0	0	5	19	89	18	11	11	1	1	1	1	16	3	16	2	0	0	0	.000	0	0-0	4	5.21
Atlanta	NL	20	0	0	4	18.2	78	16	10	9	3	0	1	1	7	0	14	0	0	1	0	1.000	0	0-0	2	4.34
3 ML YEARS		84	0	0	21	79.2	349	74	42	39	7	2	5	2	43	5	58	4	0	3	0	1.000	0	0-3	10	4.41

Shigetoshi Hasegawa

Pitches: Right **Bats:** Right **Pos:** RP-61 **Ht:** 5'11" **Wt:** 170 **Born:** 8/1/68 **Age:** 30

		HOW MUCH HE PITCHED					WHAT HE GAVE UP											THE RESULTS						
Year Team	Lg	G	GS	CG	GF	IP	BFP	H	R	ER	HR	SH	SF	HB	TBB	IBB	SO	WP	Bk	W	L	Pct.	ShO	Sv-Op	Hld	ERA
1997 Anaheim	AL	50	7	0	17	116.2	497	118	60	51	14	5	5	3	46	6	83	2	1	3	7	.300	0	0-1	3	3.93
1998 Anaheim	AL	61	0	0	20	97.1	401	86	37	34	14	4	6	2	32	2	73	5	2	8	3	.727	0	5-7	10	3.14
2 ML YEARS		111	7	0	37	214	898	204	97	85	28	9	11	5	78	8	156	7	3	11	10	.524	0	5-8	13	3.57

Bill Haselman

Bats: Right **Throws:** Right **Pos:** C-36; PH/PR-4; DH-3 **Ht:** 6'3" **Wt:** 223 **Born:** 5/25/66 **Age:** 33

							BATTING												BASERUNNING				PERCENTAGES		
Year Team	Lg	G	AB	H	2B	3B	HR	(Hm	Rd)	TB	R	RBI	TBB	IBB	SO	HBP	SH	SF	SB	CS	SB%	GDP	Avg	OBP	SLG
1990 Texas	AL	7	13	2	0	0	0	(0	0)	2	0	3	1	0	5	0	0	0	0	0	.00	0	.154	.214	.154
1992 Seattle	AL	8	19	5	0	0	0	(0	0)	5	1	0	0	0	7	0	0	0	0	0	.00	1	.263	.263	.263
1993 Seattle	AL	58	137	35	8	0	5	(3	2)	58	21	16	12	0	19	1	2	2	2	1	.67	5	.255	.316	.423
1994 Seattle	AL	38	83	16	7	1	1	(1	0)	28	11	8	3	0	11	1	1	0	1	0	1.00	2	.193	.230	.337
1995 Boston	AL	64	152	37	6	1	5	(3	2)	60	22	23	17	0	30	2	0	3	2	0	.00	6	.243	.322	.395
1996 Boston	AL	77	237	65	13	1	8	(5	3)	104	33	34	19	3	52	1	0	0	4	2	.67	13	.274	.331	.439
1997 Boston	AL	67	212	50	15	0	6	(3	3)	83	22	26	15	2	44	2	1	2	0	2	.00	8	.236	.290	.392
1998 Texas	AL	40	105	33	6	0	6	(4	2)	57	11	17	3	0	17	0	0	2	0	0	.00	2	.314	.327	.543
8 ML YEARS		359	958	243	55	3	31	(19	12)	397	121	127	70	5	185	7	4	9	7	7	.50	35	.254	.307	.414

Chris Hatcher

Bats: Right **Throws:** Right **Pos:** LF-5; PH/PR-3 **Ht:** 6'3" **Wt:** 220 **Born:** 1/7/69 **Age:** 30

							BATTING												BASERUNNING				PERCENTAGES		
Year Team	Lg	G	AB	H	2B	3B	HR	(Hm	Rd)	TB	R	RBI	TBB	IBB	SO	HBP	SH	SF	SB	CS	SB%	GDP	Avg	OBP	SLG
1990 Auburn	A-	72	259	64	10	0	9	—	—	101	37	45	27	3	86	5	0	5	8	2	.80	4	.247	.324	.390
1991 Burlington	A	129	497	117	23	6	13	—	—	191	69	65	46	4	180	9	0	4	10	5	.67	6	.235	.309	.384
1992 Osceola	A+	97	367	103	19	6	17	—	—	185	49	68	20	1	97	5	0	5	11	0	1.00	5	.281	.322	.504
1993 Jackson	AA	101	367	95	15	3	15	—	—	161	45	64	11	0	104	11	0	3	5	8	.38	8	.259	.298	.439
1994 Tucson	AAA	108	349	104	28	4	12	—	—	176	55	73	19	0	90	4	0	6	5	1	.83	6	.298	.336	.504
1995 Jackson	AA	11	39	12	1	0	1	—	—	16	5	3	4	0	6	1	0	1	0	2	.00	1	.308	.378	.410
Tucson	AAA	94	290	83	19	2	14	—	—	148	59	50	42	2	107	4	1	2	7	3	.70	5	.286	.382	.510
1996 Jackson	AA	41	156	48	9	1	13	—	—	98	29	36	9	2	39	4	0	1	2	1	.67	5	.308	.359	.628
Tucson	AAA	95	348	105	21	4	18	—	—	188	53	61	14	1	87	5	0	5	10	8	.56	9	.302	.333	.540
1997 Wichita	AA	11	42	11	0	0	5	—	—	26	7	7	4	0	16	1	0	0	1	0	1.00	4	.262	.340	.619
Omaha	AAA	68	242	56	9	0	11	—	—	93	34	24	17	2	68	6	0	3	0	1	.00	4	.230	.298	.419
1998 Omaha	AAA	126	485	150	21	2	46	—	—	313	84	106	25	3	125	3	0	3	8	6	.57	9	.309	.345	.645
1998 Kansas City	AL	8	15	1	0	0	0	(0	0)	1	0	1	1	0	7	0	0	0	0	0	.00	0	.067	.125	.067

Scott Hatteberg

Bats: Left **Throws:** Right **Pos:** C-108; PH/PR-5 **Ht:** 6'1" **Wt:** 195 **Born:** 12/14/69 **Age:** 29

							BATTING												BASERUNNING				PERCENTAGES		
Year Team	Lg	G	AB	H	2B	3B	HR	(Hm	Rd)	TB	R	RBI	TBB	IBB	SO	HBP	SH	SF	SB	CS	SB%	GDP	Avg	OBP	SLG
1995 Boston	AL	2	2	1	0	0	0	(0	0)	1	1	0	0	0	0	0	0	0	0	0	.00	1	.500	.500	.500
1996 Boston	AL	10	11	2	1	0	0	(0	0)	3	3	0	3	0	2	0	0	0	0	0	.00	2	.182	.357	.273
1997 Boston	AL	114	350	97	23	1	10	(5	5)	152	46	44	40	2	70	2	2	1	0	1	.00	11	.277	.354	.434
1998 Boston	AL	112	359	99	23	1	12	(4	8)	160	46	43	43	3	58	5	0	3	0	0	.00	11	.276	.359	.446
4 ML YEARS		238	722	199	47	2	22	(9	13)	316	96	87	86	5	130	7	2	4	0	1	.00	25	.276	.357	.438

LaTroy Hawkins

Pitches: Right **Bats:** Right **Pos:** SP-33 **Ht:** 6'5" **Wt:** 204 **Born:** 12/21/72 **Age:** 26

			HOW MUCH HE PITCHED					WHAT HE GAVE UP											THE RESULTS						
Year Team	Lg	G	GS	CG	GF	IP	BFP	H	R	ER	HR	SH	SF	HB	TBB	IBB	SO	WP	Bk	W	L	Pct.	ShO	Sv-Op	Hld	ERA
1995 Minnesota	AL	6	6	1	0	27	131	39	29	26	3	0	3	1	12	0	9	1	1	2	3	.400	0	0-0	0	8.67
1996 Minnesota	AL	7	6	0	1	26.1	124	42	24	24	8	1	1	0	9	0	24	1	1	1	1	.500	0	0-0	0	8.20
1997 Minnesota	AL	20	20	0	0	103.1	478	134	71	67	19	2	2	4	47	0	58	6	3	6	12	.333	0	0-0	0	5.84
1998 Minnesota	AL	33	33	0	0	190.1	840	227	126	111	27	4	10	5	61	1	105	10	2	7	14	.333	0	0-0	0	5.25
4 ML YEARS		66	65	1	1	347	1573	442	250	228	57	7	16	10	129	1	196	18	7	16	30	.348	0	0-0	0	5.91

Charlie Hayes

Bats: R **Throws:** R **Pos:** 3B-46; 1B-45; PH/PR-24; DH-2 **Ht:** 6'0" **Wt:** 215 **Born:** 5/29/65 **Age:** 34

							BATTING												BASERUNNING				PERCENTAGES		
Year Team	Lg	G	AB	H	2B	3B	HR	(Hm	Rd)	TB	R	RBI	TBB	IBB	SO	HBP	SH	SF	SB	CS	SB%	GDP	Avg	OBP	SLG
1988 San Francisco	NL	7	11	1	0	0	0	(0	0)	1	0	0	0	0	3	0	0	0	0	0	.00	0	.091	.091	.091
1989 SF-Phi	NL	87	304	78	15	1	8	(3	5)	119	26	43	11	1	50	0	2	3	3	1	.75	6	.257	.280	.391
1990 Philadelphia	NL	152	561	145	20	0	10	(3	7)	195	56	57	28	3	91	2	0	6	4	4	.50	12	.258	.293	.348
1991 Philadelphia	NL	142	460	106	23	1	12	(6	6)	167	34	53	16	3	75	1	2	1	3	3	.50	13	.230	.257	.363
1992 New York	AL	142	509	131	19	2	18	(7	11)	208	52	66	28	0	100	3	3	6	3	5	.38	12	.257	.297	.409
1993 Colorado	NL	157	573	175	45	2	25	(17	8)	299	89	98	43	6	82	5	1	8	11	6	.65	25	.305	.355	.522
1994 Colorado	NL	113	423	122	23	4	10	(4	6)	183	46	50	36	4	71	3	0	1	3	6	.33	11	.288	.348	.433
1995 Philadelphia	NL	141	529	146	30	3	11	(6	5)	215	58	85	50	4	88	4	0	6	5	1	.83	22	.276	.340	.406

Year Team	Lg	G	AB	H	2B	3B	HR	(Hm	Rd)	TB	R	RBI	TBB	IBB	SO	HBP	SH	SF	SB	CS	SB%	GDP	Avg	OBP	SLG
1996 Pit-NYA		148	526	133	24	2	12	(5	7)	197	58	75	37	4	90	0	3	3	6	0	1.00	17	.253	.300	.375
1997 New York	AL	100	353	91	16	0	11	(5	6)	140	39	53	40	2	66	1	0	4	3	2	.60	13	.258	.332	.397
1998 San Francisco	NL	111	329	94	8	0	12	(7	5)	138	39	62	34	0	61	0	1	2	2	1	.67	4	.286	.351	.419
1989 San Francisco	NL	3	5	1	0	0	0	(0	0)	1	0	0	0	0	1	0	0	0	0	0	.00	0	.200	.200	.200
Philadelphia	NL	84	299	77	15	1	8	(3	5)	118	26	43	11	1	49	0	2	3	3	1	.75	6	.258	.281	.395
1996 Pittsburgh	NL	128	459	114	21	2	10	(5	5)	169	51	62	36	4	78	0	2	3	6	0	1.00	16	.248	.301	.368
New York	AL	20	67	19	3	0	2	(0	2)	28	7	13	1	0	12	0	1	0	0	0	.00	1	.284	.294	.418
11 ML YEARS		1300	4578	1222	223	15	129	(63	66)	1862	497	642	323	25	777	19	12	40	43	29	.60	135	.267	.315	.407

Jimmy Haynes

Pitches: Right **Bats:** Right **Pos:** SP-33 **Ht:** 6'3" **Wt:** 180 **Born:** 9/5/72 **Age:** 26

Year Team	Lg	G	GS	CG	GF	IP	BFP	H	R	ER	HR	SH	SF	HB	TBB	IBB	SO	WP	Bk	W	L	Pct.	ShO	Sv-Op	Hld	ERA
1995 Baltimore	AL	4	3	0	0	24	94	11	6	6	2	0	0	1	12	1	22	0	0	2	1	.667	0	0-0	0	2.25
1996 Baltimore	AL	26	11	0	8	89	435	122	84	82	14	4	5	2	58	1	65	5	0	3	6	.333	0	1-1	0	8.29
1997 Oakland	AL	13	13	0	0	73.1	329	74	38	36	7	1	4	2	40	1	65	4	1	3	6	.333	0	0-0	0	4.42
1998 Oakland	AL	33	33	1	0	194.1	875	229	124	110	25	5	9	5	88	4	134	11	0	11	9	.550	1	0-0	0	5.09
4 ML YEARS		76	60	1	8	380.2	1733	436	252	234	48	11	18	9	198	7	286	20	1	19	22	.463	1	1-1	0	5.53

Mike Heathcott

Pitches: Right **Bats:** Right **Pos:** RP-1 **Ht:** 6'3" **Wt:** 180 **Born:** 5/16/69 **Age:** 30

Year Team	Lg	G	GS	CG	GF	IP	BFP	H	R	ER	HR	SH	SF	HB	TBB	IBB	SO	WP	Bk	W	L	Pct.	ShO	Sv-Op	Hld	ERA
1991 Utica	A-	6	6	0	0	33	138	26	19	13	4	1	1	1	14	0	14	1	0	3	1	.750	0	0- --	---	3.55
1992 South Bend	A	15	14	0	1	82	340	67	28	14	3	5	2	0	32	0	49	8	0	9	5	.643	0	0- --	---	1.54
1993 Sarasota	A+	26	26	6	0	179.1	739	174	90	72	5	12	10	4	62	7	83	16	1	11	10	.524	1	0- --	---	3.61
1994 Birmingham	AA	17	17	0	0	98	449	126	71	63	11	1	6	2	44	4	44	9	0	3	7	.300	0	0- --	---	5.79
Pr William	A+	9	8	1	1	43	193	51	28	19	7	1	0	1	23	0	27	6	0	1	2	.333	0	0- --	---	3.98
1995 Pr William	A+	27	14	1	4	88.2	387	96	56	46	8	2	7	2	36	3	68	18	0	4	9	.308	0	3- --	---	4.67
1996 Birmingham	AA	23	23	1	0	147.2	625	138	72	66	9	5	5	4	55	3	108	5	0	11	8	.579	0	0- --	---	4.02
1997 Nashville	AAA	17	0	0	7	27	129	39	25	22	5	1	0	0	12	0	23	6	0	2	3	.400	0	0- --	---	7.33
Birmingham	AA	30	1	0	12	59	247	50	20	12	2	3	0	1	25	0	47	3	0	3	1	.750	0	7- --	---	1.83
1998 Calgary	AAA	39	13	1	10	109	483	113	65	61	12	2	4	5	51	2	77	8	0	9	6	.600	0	1- --	---	5.04
1998 Chicago	AL	1	0	0	0	3	12	2	1	1	0	0	0	0	1	0	3	2	0	0	0	.000	0	0-0	0	3.00

Rick Helling

Pitches: Right **Bats:** Right **Pos:** SP-33 **Ht:** 6'3" **Wt:** 220 **Born:** 12/15/70 **Age:** 28

Year Team	Lg	G	GS	CG	GF	IP	BFP	H	R	ER	HR	SH	SF	HB	TBB	IBB	SO	WP	Bk	W	L	Pct.	ShO	Sv-Op	Hld	ERA
1994 Texas	AL	9	9	1	0	52	228	62	34	34	14	0	0	0	18	0	25	4	1	3	2	.600	1	0-0	0	5.88
1995 Texas	AL	3	3	0	0	12.1	62	17	11	9	2	0	2	2	8	0	5	0	0	0	2	.000	0	0-0	0	6.57
1996 Tex-Fla		11	6	0	2	48	198	37	23	23	9	1	1	0	16	0	42	1	1	3	3	.500	0	0-0	1	4.31
1997 Fla-Tex		41	16	0	3	131	550	108	67	65	17	3	9	6	69	2	99	3	0	5	9	.357	0	0-1	6	4.47
1998 Texas	AL	33	33	4	0	216.1	922	209	109	106	27	6	10	1	78	6	164	10	0	20	7	.741	2	0-0	0	4.41
1996 Texas	AL	6	2	0	2	20.1	92	23	17	17	7	0	1	0	9	0	16	1	0	1	2	.333	0	0-0	1	7.52
Florida	NL	5	4	0	0	27.2	106	14	6	6	2	1	0	0	7	0	26	0	1	2	1	.667	0	0-0	0	1.95
1997 Florida	NL	31	8	0	8	76	324	61	38	37	12	2	7	4	48	2	53	0	1	2	6	.250	0	0-1	6	4.38
Texas	AL	10	8	0	1	55	226	47	29	28	5	1	2	2	21	0	46	3	0	3	3	.500	0	0-0	0	4.58
5 ML YEARS		97	67	5	11	459.2	1960	433	244	237	69	10	22	9	189	8	335	18	2	31	23	.574	3	0-1	7	4.64

Wes Helms

Bats: Right **Throws:** Right **Pos:** 3B-4; PH/PR-4 **Ht:** 6'4" **Wt:** 230 **Born:** 5/12/76 **Age:** 23

Year Team	Lg	G	AB	H	2B	3B	HR	(Hm	Rd)	TB	R	RBI	TBB	IBB	SO	HBP	SH	SF	SB	CS	SB%	GDP	Avg	OBP	SLG
1994 Braves	R	56	184	49	15	1	4	—	—	78	22	29	22	0	36	4	0	1	6	1	.86	3	.266	.355	.424
1995 Macon	A	136	539	149	32	1	11	—	—	216	89	85	50	0	107	10	0	3	2	2	.50	8	.276	.347	.401
1996 Durham	A+	67	258	83	19	2	13	—	—	145	40	54	12	0	51	7	0	1	1	1	.50	7	.322	.367	.562
Greenville	AA	64	231	59	13	2	4	—	—	88	24	22	13	2	48	4	1	0	2	1	.67	6	.255	.306	.381
1997 Richmond	AAA	32	110	21	4	0	3	—	—	34	11	15	10	1	34	5	0	1	1	1	.50	4	.191	.286	.309
Greenville	AA	86	314	93	14	1	11	—	—	142	50	44	33	2	50	6	0	3	3	4	.43	14	.296	.371	.452
1998 Richmond	AAA	125	451	124	27	1	13	—	—	192	56	75	35	2	103	13	0	4	6	2	.75	11	.275	.342	.426
1998 Atlanta	NL	7	13	4	1	0	1	(0	1)	8	2	2	0	0	4	0	0	0	0	0	.00	0	.308	.308	.615

Todd Helton

Bats: Left **Throws:** Left **Pos:** 1B-146; PH/PR-14 **Ht:** 6'2" **Wt:** 202 **Born:** 8/20/73 **Age:** 25

Year Team	Lg	G	AB	H	2B	3B	HR	(Hm	Rd)	TB	R	RBI	TBB	IBB	SO	HBP	SH	SF	SB	CS	SB%	GDP	Avg	OBP	SLG
1995 Asheville	A	54	201	51	11	1	1	—	—	67	24	15	25	1	32	1	0	0	1	1	.50	7	.254	.339	.333
1996 New Haven	AA	93	319	106	24	2	7	—	—	155	46	51	51	5	37	1	3	1	2	5	.29	8	.332	.425	.486
Colo Sprngs	AAA	21	71	25	4	1	2	—	—	37	13	13	11	0	12	0	0	0	0	0	.00	3	.352	.439	.521
1997 Colo Sprngs	AAA	99	392	138	31	2	16	—	—	221	87	88	61	4	68	0	1	6	3	1	.75	10	.352	.434	.564
1997 Colorado	NL	35	93	26	2	1	5	(3	2)	45	13	11	8	0	11	0	0	0	0	1	.00	1	.280	.337	.484

Year Team	Lg	G	AB	H	2B	3B	HR	(Hm	Rd)	TB	R	RBI	TBB	IBB	SO	HBP	SH	SF	SB	CS	SB%	GDP	Avg	OBP	SLG
1998 Colorado	NL	152	530	167	37	1	25	(13	12)	281	78	97	53	5	54	6	1	5	3	3	.50	15	.315	.380	.530
2 ML YEARS		187	623	193	39	2	30	(16	14)	326	91	108	61	5	65	6	1	5	3	4	.43	16	.310	.374	.523

Rickey Henderson

Bats: Right **Throws:** Left **Pos:** LF-142; CF-24; PH/PR-7   **Ht:** 5'10" **Wt:** 190 **Born:** 12/25/58 **Age:** 40

Year Team	Lg	G	AB	H	2B	3B	HR	(Hm	Rd)	TB	R	RBI	TBB	IBB	SO	HBP	SH	SF	SB	CS	SB%	GDP	Avg	OBP	SLG
1979 Oakland	AL	89	351	96	13	3	1	(1	0)	118	49	26	34	0	39	2	8	3	33	11	.75	4	.274	.338	.336
1980 Oakland	AL	158	591	179	22	4	9	(3	6)	236	111	53	117	7	54	5	6	3	100	26	.79	6	.303	.420	.399
1981 Oakland	AL	108	423	135	18	7	6	(5	1)	185	89	35	64	4	68	2	0	4	56	22	.72	7	.319	.408	.437
1982 Oakland	AL	149	536	143	24	4	10	(5	5)	205	119	51	116	1	94	2	0	2	130	42	.76	5	.267	.398	.382
1983 Oakland	AL	145	513	150	25	7	9	(5	4)	216	105	48	103	8	80	4	1	1	108	19	.85	11	.292	.414	.421
1984 Oakland	AL	142	502	147	27	4	16	(7	9)	230	113	58	86	1	81	5	1	3	66	18	.79	7	.293	.399	.458
1985 New York	AL	143	547	172	28	5	24	(8	16)	282	146	72	99	1	65	3	0	5	80	10	.89	8	.314	.419	.516
1986 New York	AL	153	608	160	31	5	28	(13	15)	285	130	74	89	2	81	2	0	2	87	18	.83	12	.263	.358	.469
1987 New York	AL	95	358	104	17	3	17	(10	7)	178	78	37	80	1	52	2	0	0	41	8	.84	10	.291	.423	.497
1988 New York	AL	140	554	169	30	2	6	(2	4)	221	118	50	82	1	54	3	2	6	93	13	.88	6	.305	.394	.399
1989 NYA-Oak	AL	150	541	148	26	3	12	(7	5)	216	113	57	126	5	68	3	0	4	77	14	.85	8	.274	.411	.399
1990 Oakland	AL	136	489	159	33	3	28	(8	20)	282	119	61	97	2	60	4	2	2	65	10	.87	13	.325	.439	.577
1991 Oakland	AL	134	470	126	17	1	18	(8	10)	199	105	57	98	7	73	7	0	3	58	18	.76	7	.268	.400	.423
1992 Oakland	AL	117	396	112	18	3	15	(10	5)	181	77	46	95	5	56	6	0	3	48	11	.81	5	.283	.426	.457
1993 Oak-Tor	AL	134	481	139	22	2	21	(10	11)	228	114	59	120	7	65	4	1	4	53	8	.87	9	.289	.432	.474
1994 Oakland	AL	87	296	77	13	0	6	(4	2)	108	66	20	72	1	45	5	1	2	22	7	.76	0	.260	.411	.365
1995 Oakland	AL	112	407	122	31	1	9	(3	6)	182	67	54	72	2	66	4	1	3	32	10	.76	8	.300	.407	.447
1996 San Diego	NL	148	465	112	17	2	9	(6	3)	160	110	29	125	2	90	10	0	2	37	15	.71	5	.241	.410	.344
1997 SD-Ana		120	403	100	14	0	8	(6	2)	138	84	34	97	2	85	6	1	2	45	8	.85	10	.248	.400	.342
1998 Oakland	AL	152	542	128	16	1	14	(6	8)	188	101	57	118	0	114	5	2	3	66	13	.84	5	.236	.376	.347
1989 New York	AL	65	235	58	13	1	3	(1	2)	82	41	22	56	0	29	1	0	1	25	8	.76	0	.247	.392	.349
Oakland	AL	85	306	90	13	2	9	(6	3)	134	72	35	70	5	39	2	0	3	52	6	.90	8	.294	.425	.438
1993 Oakland	AL	90	318	104	19	1	17	(8	9)	176	77	47	85	6	46	2	0	2	31	6	.84	8	.327	.469	.553
Toronto	AL	44	163	35	3	1	4	(2	2)	52	37	12	35	1	19	2	1	2	22	2	.92	1	.215	.356	.319
1997 San Diego	NL	88	288	79	11	0	6	(5	1)	108	63	27	71	2	62	4	0	2	29	4	.88	7	.274	.422	.375
Anaheim	AL	32	115	21	3	0	2	(1	1)	30	21	7	26	0	23	2	1	0	16	4	.80	3	.183	.343	.261
20 ML YEARS		2612	9473	2678	442	60	266	(127	139)	4038	2014	978	1890	59	1390	84	26	57	1297	301	.81	146	.283	.404	.426

Rodney Henderson

Pitches: Right **Bats:** Right **Pos:** RP-2   **Ht:** 6'4" **Wt:** 193 **Born:** 3/11/71 **Age:** 28

Year Team	Lg	G	GS	CG	GF	IP	BFP	H	R	ER	HR	SH	SF	HB	TBB	IBB	SO	WP	Bk	W	L	Pct.	ShO	Sv-Op	Hld	ERA
1992 Jamestown	A-	1	1	0	0	3	13	2	3	2	0	0	0	0	5	0	2	0	0	0	0	.000	0	0--	—	6.00
1993 Wst Plm Bch	A+	22	22	1	0	143	580	110	50	46	3	4	5	6	44	0	127	8	6	12	7	.632	1	0--	—	2.90
Harrisburg	AA	5	5	0	0	29.2	125	20	10	6	1	0	0	0	15	0	25	2	1	5	0	1.000	0	0--	—	1.82
1994 Harrisburg	AA	2	2	0	0	12	44	5	2	2	1	0	0	0	4	0	16	0	0	2	0	1.000	0	0--	—	1.50
Ottawa	AAA	23	21	0	1	122.2	545	123	67	63	16	2	5	2	67	3	100	1	0	6	9	.400	0	1--	—	4.62
1995 Harrisburg	AA	12	12	0	0	56.1	240	51	28	27	4	0	1	5	18	0	53	1	0	3	6	.333	0	0--	—	4.31
1996 Ottawa	AAA	25	23	3	0	121.1	528	117	75	70	12	1	4	4	52	1	83	2	0	4	11	.267	1	0--	—	5.19
1997 Ottawa	AAA	26	20	2	3	123.2	542	136	72	68	18	4	2	6	49	3	103	6	0	5	9	.357	1	1--	—	4.95
1998 Ottawa	AAA	6	0	0	1	11	66	23	17	11	3	1	0	0	12	0	12	0	0	0	0	.000	0	0--	—	9.00
El Paso	AA	1	0	0	0	1.2	10	4	1	1	0	0	0	0	1	0	0	0	0	0	0	.000	0	0--	—	5.40
Louisville	AAA	22	19	1	1	121.1	493	100	45	40	4	2	1	4	39	0	68	1	0	11	5	.688	0	0--	—	2.97
1994 Montreal	NL	3	2	0	0	6.2	37	9	9	7	1	3	0	0	7	0	3	0	0	0	1	.000	0	0-0	0	9.45
1998 Milwaukee	NL	2	0	0	0	3.2	17	5	4	4	2	0	0	1	0	0	1	0	0	0	0	.000	0	0-0	0	9.82
2 ML YEARS		5	2	0	0	10.1	54	14	13	11	3	3	0	1	7	0	4	0	0	0	1	.000	0	0-0	0	9.58

Bob Henley

Bats: Right **Throws:** Right **Pos:** C-35; PH/PR-7   **Ht:** 6'2" **Wt:** 205 **Born:** 1/30/73 **Age:** 26

Year Team	Lg	G	AB	H	2B	3B	HR	(Hm	Rd)	TB	R	RBI	TBB	IBB	SO	HBP	SH	SF	SB	CS	SB%	GDP	Avg	OBP	SLG
1993 Jamestown	A-	60	206	53	10	4	7	—	—	92	25	29	20	1	60	1	1	1	0	1	.00	5	.257	.325	.447
1994 Burlington	A	98	346	104	20	1	20	—	—	186	72	67	49	1	91	10	1	3	1	2	.33	8	.301	.400	.538
1995 Albany	A	102	335	94	20	1	3	—	—	125	45	46	83	1	57	11	1	2	1	2	.33	11	.281	.436	.373
1996 Harrisburg	AA	103	289	66	12	1	3	—	—	89	33	27	70	1	78	3	9	2	1	2	.33	14	.228	.382	.308
1997 Harrisburg	AA	79	280	85	19	0	12	—	—	140	41	49	32	2	40	5	0	4	5	1	.83	7	.304	.380	.500
1998 Jupiter	A+	13	50	17	3	0	2	—	—	26	10	14	5	1	5	2	0	1	1	1	.50	4	.340	.414	.520
Ottawa	AAA	37	126	31	6	1	4	—	—	51	13	20	12	0	34	1	1	2	1	1	.50	3	.246	.312	.405
1998 Montreal	NL	41	115	35	8	1	3	(1	2)	54	16	18	11	0	26	3	2	1	3	0	1.00	4	.304	.377	.470

Oscar Henriquez

Pitches: Right **Bats:** Right **Pos:** RP-15   **Ht:** 6'6" **Wt:** 220 **Born:** 1/28/74 **Age:** 25

Year Team	Lg	G	GS	CG	GF	IP	BFP	H	R	ER	HR	SH	SF	HB	TBB	IBB	SO	WP	Bk	W	L	Pct.	ShO	Sv-Op	Hld	ERA
1993 Asheville	A	27	26	2	0	150	679	154	95	74	12	6	5	10	70	2	117	7	3	9	10	.474	1	0--	—	4.44
1995 Kissimmee	A+	20	0	0	7	44.2	207	40	29	25	2	2	2	6	30	0	36	3	0	3	4	.429	0	1--	—	5.04
1996 Kissimmee	A+	37	0	0	33	34	162	28	18	15	0	1	1	3	29	2	40	4	0	0	4	.000	0	15--	—	3.97

Year Team	Lg	G	GS	CG	GF	IP	BFP	H	R	ER	HR	SH	SF	HB	TBB	IBB	SO	WP	Bk	W	L	Pct.	ShO	Sv-Op	Hld	ERA
1997 New Orleans	AAA	60	0	0	37	74	313	65	28	23	4	6	3	5	27	3	80	7	1	4	5	.444	0	12--	—	2.80
1998 Charlotte	AAA	26	0	0	19	31.2	134	29	12	9	3	0	1	2	12	0	37	4	0	1	0	1.000	0	11--	—	2.56
1997 Houston	NL	4	0	0	1	4	17	2	2	2	0	1	0	1	3	0	3	0	0	0	1	.000	0	0-0	1	4.50
1998 Florida	NL	15	0	0	4	20	100	26	22	19	4	0	2	1	12	0	19	1	0	0	0	.000	0	0-0	0	8.55
2 ML YEARS		19	0	0	5	24	117	28	24	21	4	1	2	2	15	0	22	1	0	0	1	.000	0	0-0	1	7.88

Butch Henry

Pitches: Left **Bats:** Left **Pos:** SP-2 **Ht:** 6'1" **Wt:** 205 **Born:** 10/7/68 **Age:** 30

Year Team	Lg	G	GS	CG	GF	IP	BFP	H	R	ER	HR	SH	SF	HB	TBB	IBB	SO	WP	Bk	W	L	Pct.	ShO	Sv-Op	Hld	ERA
1998 Sarasota *	A+	1	1	0	0	6.2	23	4	2	1	0	0	0	0	0	0	5	0	0	0	1	.000	0	0--	—	1.35
1992 Houston	NL	28	28	2	0	165.2	710	185	81	74	16	12	7	1	41	7	96	2	2	6	9	.400	1	0-0	0	4.02
1993 Col-Mon	NL	30	16	1	4	103	467	135	76	70	15	6	6	1	28	2	47	1	0	3	9	.250	0	0-0	0	6.12
1994 Montreal	NL	24	15	0	1	107.1	433	97	30	29	10	5	3	2	20	1	70	1	0	8	3	.727	0	1-1	2	2.43
1995 Montreal	NL	21	21	1	0	126.2	524	133	47	40	11	7	3	2	28	3	60	0	1	7	9	.438	1	0-0	0	2.84
1997 Boston	AL	36	5	0	13	84.1	345	89	36	33	6	2	3	0	19	2	51	0	0	7	3	.700	0	6-8	4	3.52
1998 Boston	AL	2	2	0	0	9	38	8	4	4	2	0	0	1	3	0	6	0	0	0	0	.000	0	0-0	0	4.00
1993 Colorado	NL	20	15	1	1	84.2	390	117	66	62	14	6	5	1	24	2	39	1	0	2	8	.200	0	0-0	0	6.59
Montreal	NL	10	1	0	3	18.1	77	18	10	8	1	0	1	0	4	0	8	0	0	1	1	.500	0	0-0	0	3.93
6 ML YEARS		141	87	4	18	596	2517	647	274	250	60	32	22	7	139	15	330	4	3	31	33	.484	2	7-9	6	3.78

Doug Henry

Pitches: Right **Bats:** Right **Pos:** RP-59 **Ht:** 6'4" **Wt:** 205 **Born:** 12/10/63 **Age:** 35

Year Team	Lg	G	GS	CG	GF	IP	BFP	H	R	ER	HR	SH	SF	HB	TBB	IBB	SO	WP	Bk	W	L	Pct.	ShO	Sv-Op	Hld	ERA
1991 Milwaukee	AL	32	0	0	25	36	137	16	4	4	1	2	0	1	14	1	28	0	0	2	1	.667	0	15-16	3	1.00
1992 Milwaukee	AL	68	0	0	56	65	277	64	34	29	6	1	2	0	24	4	52	4	0	1	4	.200	0	29-33	1	4.02
1993 Milwaukee	AL	54	0	0	41	55	260	67	37	34	7	5	4	3	25	8	38	4	0	4	4	.500	0	17-24	0	5.56
1994 Milwaukee	AL	25	0	0	7	31.1	143	32	17	16	7	1	0	1	23	1	20	3	0	2	3	.400	0	0-0	4	4.60
1995 New York	NL	51	0	0	20	67	273	48	23	22	7	3	2	1	25	6	62	6	1	3	6	.333	0	4-7	6	2.96
1996 New York	NL	58	0	0	33	75	343	82	48	39	7	3	3	1	36	6	58	6	1	2	8	.200	0	9-14	8	4.68
1997 San Francisco	NL	75	0	0	25	70.2	317	70	45	37	5	4	3	1	41	6	69	3	0	4	5	.444	0	3-6	21	4.71
1998 Houston	NL	59	0	0	25	71	296	55	25	24	9	3	3	0	35	5	59	7	0	8	2	.800	0	2-5	11	3.04
8 ML YEARS		422	0	0	232	471	2046	434	233	205	49	21	19	7	223	37	386	33	2	26	33	.441	0	79-105	54	3.92

Pat Hentgen

Pitches: Right **Bats:** Right **Pos:** SP-29 **Ht:** 6'2" **Wt:** 200 **Born:** 11/13/68 **Age:** 30

Year Team	Lg	G	GS	CG	GF	IP	BFP	H	R	ER	HR	SH	SF	HB	TBB	IBB	SO	WP	Bk	W	L	Pct.	ShO	Sv-Op	Hld	ERA
1991 Toronto	AL	3	1	0	1	7.1	30	5	2	2	1	1	0	2	3	0	3	1	0	0	0	.000	0	0-0	0	2.45
1992 Toronto	AL	28	2	0	10	50.1	229	49	30	30	7	2	2	0	32	5	39	2	1	5	2	.714	0	0-1	1	5.36
1993 Toronto	AL	34	32	3	0	216.1	926	215	103	93	27	6	5	7	74	0	122	11	1	19	9	.679	0	0-0	0	3.87
1994 Toronto	AL	24	24	6	0	174.2	728	158	74	66	21	6	3	3	59	1	147	5	1	13	8	.619	3	0-0	0	3.40
1995 Toronto	AL	30	30	2	0	200.2	913	236	129	114	24	2	1	5	90	6	135	7	2	10	14	.417	0	0-0	0	5.11
1996 Toronto	AL	35	35	10	0	265.2	1100	238	105	95	20	5	8	5	94	3	177	8	0	20	10	.667	3	0-0	0	3.22
1997 Toronto	AL	35	35	9	0	264	1085	253	116	108	31	9	3	7	71	2	160	6	2	15	10	.600	3	0-0	0	3.68
1998 Toronto	AL	29	29	0	0	177.2	795	208	109	102	28	5	7	5	69	1	94	7	1	12	11	.522	0	0-0	0	5.17
8 ML YEARS		218	188	30	11	1356.2	5806	1362	668	610	159	36	29	34	492	18	877	47	8	94	64	.595	9	0-1	1	4.05

Felix Heredia

Pitches: Left **Bats:** Left **Pos:** RP-69; SP-2 **Ht:** 6'0" **Wt:** 175 **Born:** 6/18/76 **Age:** 23

Year Team	Lg	G	GS	CG	GF	IP	BFP	H	R	ER	HR	SH	SF	HB	TBB	IBB	SO	WP	Bk	W	L	Pct.	ShO	Sv-Op	Hld	ERA
1996 Florida	NL	21	0	0	5	16.2	78	21	8	8	1	0	1	0	10	1	10	2	0	1	1	.500	0	0-0	2	4.32
1997 Florida	NL	56	0	0	10	56.2	259	53	30	27	3	2	2	5	30	1	54	2	0	5	3	.625	0	0-1	7	4.29
1998 Fla-ChN	NL	71	2	0	18	58.2	268	57	39	33	2	1	2	5	38	3	54	6	1	3	3	.500	0	2-5	17	5.06
1998 Florida	NL	41	2	0	12	41	194	38	30	25	1	1	2	5	32	2	38	5	1	0	3	.000	0	2-3	9	5.49
Chicago	NL	30	0	0	6	17.2	74	19	9	8	1	0	0	0	6	1	16	1	0	3	0	1.000	0	0-2	8	4.08
3 ML YEARS		148	2	0	33	132	605	131	77	68	6	3	5	6	78	5	118	10	1	9	7	.563	0	2-6	26	4.64

Gil Heredia

Pitches: Right **Bats:** Right **Pos:** SP-6; RP-2 **Ht:** 6'1" **Wt:** 195 **Born:** 10/26/65 **Age:** 33

Year Team	Lg	G	GS	CG	GF	IP	BFP	H	R	ER	HR	SH	SF	HB	TBB	IBB	SO	WP	Bk	W	L	Pct.	ShO	Sv-Op	Hld	ERA
1998 Edmonton *	AAA	29	19	6	7	144.2	595	154	69	59	13	5	8	2	18	3	99	2	1	10	8	.556	1	1--	—	3.67
1991 San Francisco	NL	7	4	0	1	33	126	27	14	14	4	2	1	0	7	2	13	1	0	2	0	.000	0	0-0	0	3.82
1992 SF-Mon	NL	20	5	0	4	44.2	187	44	23	21	4	2	1	1	20	2	22	1	0	2	3	.400	0	0-1	4	4.23
1993 Montreal	NL	20	9	1	2	57.1	246	66	28	25	4	4	1	2	14	2	40	0	0	4	2	.667	0	2-3	1	3.92
1994 Montreal	NL	39	3	0	8	75.1	325	85	34	29	7	3	4	2	13	2	62	4	1	6	3	.667	0	0-0	5	3.46
1995 Montreal	NL	40	18	0	5	119	509	137	60	57	7	9	4	5	21	1	74	1	0	5	6	.455	0	1-3	1	4.31
1996 Texas	AL	44	0	0	21	73.1	320	91	50	48	12	1	2	1	14	2	43	2	0	2	5	.286	0	1-4	7	5.89
1998 Oakland	AL	8	6	0	2	42.2	175	43	14	13	4	1	0	3	3	0	27	0	0	3	3	.500	0	0-0	0	2.74

		HOW MUCH HE PITCHED						WHAT HE GAVE UP												THE RESULTS				
Year Team	Lg	G	GS	CG	GF	IP	BFP	H	R	ER	HR	SH	SF	HB	TBB	IBB	SO	WP	Bk	W	L	Pct.	ShO	Sv-Op	Hld	ERA
1992 San Francisco	NL	13	4	0	3	30	132	32	20	18	3	0	0	1	16	1	15	1	0	2	3	.400	0	0-0	1	5.40
Montreal	NL	7	1	0	1	14.2	55	12	3	3	1	2	1	0	4	0	7	0	0	0	0	.000	0	0-0	0	1.84
7 ML YEARS		178	45	1	43	445.1	1888	493	223	207	42	22	13	14	92	11	281	9	1	22	24	.478	0	4-10	15	4.18

Dustin Hermanson

Pitches: Right **Bats:** Right **Pos:** SP-30; RP-2   **Ht:** 6'2" **Wt:** 200 **Born:** 12/21/72 **Age:** 26

		HOW MUCH HE PITCHED						WHAT HE GAVE UP												THE RESULTS				
Year Team	Lg	G	GS	CG	GF	IP	BFP	H	R	ER	HR	SH	SF	HB	TBB	IBB	SO	WP	Bk	W	L	Pct.	ShO	Sv-Op	Hld	ERA
1995 San Diego	NL	26	0	0	6	31.2	151	35	26	24	8	3	0	1	22	1	19	3	0	3	1	.750	0	0-0	1	6.82
1996 San Diego	NL	8	0	0	4	13.2	62	18	15	13	3	2	3	0	4	0	11	0	1	1	0	1.000	0	0-0	0	8.56
1997 Montreal	NL	32	28	1	0	158.1	656	134	68	65	15	10	6	1	66	2	136	4	1	8	8	.500	1	0-0	0	3.69
1998 Montreal	NL	32	30	1	0	187	768	163	80	65	21	9	3	3	56	3	154	4	3	14	11	.560	0	0-0	1	3.13
4 ML YEARS		98	58	2	10	390.2	1637	350	189	167	47	24	12	5	148	6	320	11	5	26	20	.565	1	0-0	2	3.85

Carlos Hernandez

Bats: Right **Throws:** Right **Pos:** C-122; PH/PR-13; 1B-1   **Ht:** 5'11" **Wt:** 215 **Born:** 5/24/67 **Age:** 32

		BATTING																	BASERUNNING				PERCENTAGES		
Year Team	Lg	G	AB	H	2B	3B	HR	(Hm	Rd)	TB	R	RBI	TBB	IBB	SO	HBP	SH	SF	SB	CS	SB%	GDP	Avg	OBP	SLG
1990 Los Angeles	NL	10	20	4	1	0	0	(0	0)	5	2	1	0	0	2	0	0	0	0	0	.00	0	.200	.200	.250
1991 Los Angeles	NL	15	14	3	1	0	0	(0	0)	4	1	1	0	0	5	1	0	1	1	0	1.00	0	.214	.250	.286
1992 Los Angeles	NL	69	173	45	4	0	3	(1	2)	58	11	17	11	1	21	4	0	2	0	1	.00	8	.260	.316	.335
1993 Los Angeles	NL	50	99	25	5	0	2	(1	1)	36	6	7	2	0	11	0	1	0	0	0	.00	0	.253	.267	.364
1994 Los Angeles	NL	32	64	14	2	0	2	(0	2)	22	6	6	1	0	14	0	0	0	0	0	.00	0	.219	.231	.344
1995 Los Angeles	NL	45	94	14	1	0	2	(1	1)	21	3	8	7	0	25	1	1	0	0	0	.00	5	.149	.216	.223
1996 Los Angeles	NL	13	14	4	0	0	0	(0	0)	4	1	0	2	0	2	0	0	0	0	0	.00	0	.286	.375	.286
1997 San Diego	NL	50	134	42	7	1	3	(2	1)	60	15	14	3	0	27	0	1	0	0	2	.00	5	.313	.328	.448
1998 San Diego	NL	129	390	102	15	0	9	(7	2)	144	34	52	16	2	54	9	0	2	2	2	.50	19	.262	.305	.369
9 ML YEARS		413	1002	253	36	1	21	(12	9)	354	79	106	42	3	161	15	3	5	3	5	.38	39	.252	.291	.353

Jose Hernandez

B: R **T:** R **Pos:** 3B-72; SS-45; LF-31; CF-31; PH/PR-14; 1B-3; 2B-2; RF-2   **Ht:** 6'1" **Wt:** 185 **Born:** 7/14/69 **Age:** 29

		BATTING																	BASERUNNING				PERCENTAGES		
Year Team	Lg	G	AB	H	2B	3B	HR	(Hm	Rd)	TB	R	RBI	TBB	IBB	SO	HBP	SH	SF	SB	CS	SB%	GDP	Avg	OBP	SLG
1991 Texas	AL	45	98	18	2	1	0	(0	0)	22	8	4	3	0	31	0	6	0	0	1	.00	2	.184	.208	.224
1992 Cleveland	AL	3	4	0	0	0	0	(0	0)	0	0	0	0	0	2	0	0	0	0	0	.00	0	.000	.000	.000
1994 Chicago	NL	56	132	32	2	3	1	(0	1)	43	18	9	8	0	29	1	5	0	2	2	.50	4	.242	.291	.326
1995 Chicago	NL	93	245	60	11	4	13	(6	7)	118	37	40	13	3	69	0	8	2	1	0	1.00	8	.245	.281	.482
1996 Chicago	NL	131	331	80	14	1	10	(4	6)	126	52	41	24	4	97	1	5	2	4	0	1.00	10	.242	.293	.381
1997 Chicago	NL	121	183	50	8	5	7	(4	3)	89	33	26	14	2	42	0	1	1	2	5	.29	5	.273	.323	.486
1998 Chicago	NL	149	488	124	23	7	23	(11	12)	230	76	75	40	3	140	1	2	2	4	6	.40	12	.254	.311	.471
7 ML YEARS		598	1481	364	60	21	54	(25	29)	628	224	195	102	12	410	3	27	7	13	14	.48	41	.246	.294	.424

Livan Hernandez

Pitches: Right **Bats:** Right **Pos:** SP-33   **Ht:** 6'2" **Wt:** 220 **Born:** 2/20/75 **Age:** 24

		HOW MUCH HE PITCHED						WHAT HE GAVE UP												THE RESULTS				
Year Team	Lg	G	GS	CG	GF	IP	BFP	H	R	ER	HR	SH	SF	HB	TBB	IBB	SO	WP	Bk	W	L	Pct.	ShO	Sv-Op	Hld	ERA
1996 Florida	NL	1	0	0	0	3	13	3	0	0	0	0	0	0	2	0	2	0	0	0	0	.000	0	0-0	0	0.00
1997 Florida	NL	17	17	0	0	96.1	405	81	39	34	5	4	7	3	38	1	72	0	0	9	3	.750	0	0-0	0	3.18
1998 Florida	NL	33	33	9	0	234.1	1040	265	133	123	37	8	5	6	104	8	162	4	3	10	12	.455	0	0-0	0	4.72
3 ML YEARS		51	50	9	0	333.2	1458	349	172	157	42	12	12	9	144	9	236	4	3	19	15	.559	0	0-0	0	4.23

Orlando Hernandez

Pitches: Right **Bats:** Right **Pos:** SP-21   **Ht:** 6'3" **Wt:** 210 **Born:** 10/11/69 **Age:** 29

		HOW MUCH HE PITCHED						WHAT HE GAVE UP												THE RESULTS				
Year Team	Lg	G	GS	CG	GF	IP	BFP	H	R	ER	HR	SH	SF	HB	TBB	IBB	SO	WP	Bk	W	L	Pct.	ShO	Sv-Op	Hld	ERA
1998 Tampa	A+	2	2	0	0	9	37	3	2	1	0	0	0	4	3	0	15	1	0	1	1	.500	0	0--	—	1.00
Columbus	AAA	7	7	0	0	42.1	182	41	19	18	2	2	1	5	17	0	59	1	0	6	0	1.000	0	0--	—	3.83
1998 New York	AL	21	21	3	0	141	574	113	53	49	11	3	5	6	52	1	131	5	2	12	4	.750	1	0-0	0	3.13

Roberto Hernandez

Pitches: Right **Bats:** Right **Pos:** RP-67   **Ht:** 6'4" **Wt:** 235 **Born:** 11/11/64 **Age:** 34

		HOW MUCH HE PITCHED						WHAT HE GAVE UP												THE RESULTS				
Year Team	Lg	G	GS	CG	GF	IP	BFP	H	R	ER	HR	SH	SF	HB	TBB	IBB	SO	WP	Bk	W	L	Pct.	ShO	Sv-Op	Hld	ERA
1991 Chicago	AL	9	3	0	1	15	69	18	15	13	1	0	0	0	7	0	6	1	0	1	0	1.000	0	0-0	0	7.80
1992 Chicago	AL	43	0	0	42	71	277	45	15	13	4	0	3	4	20	1	68	2	0	7	3	.700	0	12-16	6	1.65
1993 Chicago	AL	70	0	0	67	78.2	314	66	21	20	6	2	2	0	20	1	71	2	0	3	4	.429	0	38-44	5	2.29
1994 Chicago	AL	45	0	0	43	47.2	206	44	29	26	5	0	1	1	19	1	50	1	0	4	4	.500	0	14-20	0	4.91
1995 Chicago	AL	60	0	0	57	59.2	272	63	30	26	9	4	0	3	28	4	84	1	0	3	7	.300	0	32-42	0	3.92
1996 Chicago	AL	72	0	0	61	84.2	355	65	21	18	2	2	2	0	38	5	85	6	0	6	5	.545	0	38-46	0	1.91

Year Team	Lg	G	GS	CG	GF	IP	BFP	H	R	ER	HR	SH	SF	HB	TBB	IBB	SO	WP	Bk	W	L	Pct.	ShO	Sv-Op	Hld	ERA
						HOW MUCH HE PITCHED				WHAT HE GAVE UP												THE RESULTS				
1997 ChA-SF		74	0	0	50	80.2	340	67	24	22	7	2	1	1	38	5	82	3	0	10	3	.769	0	31-39	9	2.45
1998 Tampa Bay	AL	67	0	0	58	71.1	310	55	33	32	5	4	0	5	41	4	55	1	0	2	6	.250	0	26-35	4	4.04
1997 Chicago	AL	46	0	0	43	48	203	38	15	13	5	1	1	1	24	4	47	2	0	5	1	.833	0	27-31	0	2.44
San Francisco	NL	28	0	0	7	32.2	137	29	9	9	2	1	0	0	14	1	35	1	0	5	2	.714	0	4-8	9	2.48
8 ML YEARS		440	3	0	364	508.2	2143	423	188	170	39	14	9	14	211	21	501	17	0	36	32	.529	0	191-242	15	3.01

Xavier Hernandez

Pitches: Right **Bats:** Right **Pos:** RP-46   **Ht:** 6'2" **Wt:** 195 **Born:** 8/16/65 **Age:** 33

Year Team	Lg	G	GS	CG	GF	IP	BFP	H	R	ER	HR	SH	SF	HB	TBB	IBB	SO	WP	Bk	W	L	Pct.	ShO	Sv-Op	Hld	ERA
1998 Tulsa *	AA	2	2	0	0	3	13	3	1	1	1	0	0	1	0	0	2	1	0	0	0	.000	0	0--	—	3.00
Oklahoma *	AAA	5	0	0	1	6.2	26	5	1	1	0	0	0	1	1	0	9	2	0	0	0	.000	0	0--	—	1.35
1989 Toronto	AL	7	0	0	2	22.2	101	25	15	12	2	0	2	1	8	0	7	1	0	1	0	1.000	0	0-0	1	4.76
1990 Houston	NL	34	1	0	10	62.1	268	60	34	32	8	2	4	4	24	5	24	6	0	2	1	.667	0	0-1	1	4.62
1991 Houston	NL	32	6	0	8	63	285	66	34	33	6	1	1	0	32	7	55	0	0	2	7	.222	0	3-6	5	4.71
1992 Houston	NL	77	0	0	25	111	454	81	31	26	5	3	2	3	42	7	96	5	0	9	1	.900	0	7-10	8	2.11
1993 Houston	NL	72	0	0	29	96.2	389	75	37	28	6	3	3	1	28	3	101	6	0	4	5	.444	0	9-17	22	2.61
1994 New York	AL	31	0	0	14	40	187	48	27	26	7	2	2	2	21	3	37	3	0	4	4	.500	0	6-8	1	5.85
1995 Cincinnati	NL	59	0	0	19	90	391	95	45	46	8	6	2	4	31	1	84	7	0	7	2	.778	0	3-4	6	4.60
1996 Cin-Hou	NL	61	0	0	27	78	340	77	45	40	13	8	3	2	28	5	81	9	0	5	5	.500	0	6-10	7	4.62
1997 Texas	AL	44	0	0	20	49.1	221	51	27	25	7	1	1	2	22	4	36	5	0	0	4	.000	0	0-1	13	4.56
1998 Texas	AL	46	0	0	15	58	243	43	27	23	5	2	2	1	30	1	41	4	0	6	6	.500	0	1-6	9	3.57
1996 Cincinnati	NL	3	0	0	0	3.1	19	8	6	5	2	0	0	0	2	0	3	0	0	0	0	.000	0	0-0	1	13.50
Houston	NL	58	0	0	27	74.2	321	69	39	35	11	8	3	2	26	5	78	9	0	5	5	.500	0	6-10	7	4.22
10 ML YEARS		463	7	0	169	671	2879	621	324	291	67	28	22	20	266	36	562	46	0	40	35	.533	0	35-63	73	3.90

Orel Hershiser

Pitches: Right **Bats:** Right **Pos:** SP-34   **Ht:** 6'3" **Wt:** 195 **Born:** 9/16/58 **Age:** 40

Year Team	Lg	G	GS	CG	GF	IP	BFP	H	R	ER	HR	SH	SF	HB	TBB	IBB	SO	WP	Bk	W	L	Pct.	ShO	Sv-Op	Hld	ERA
1983 Los Angeles	NL	8	0	0	4	8	37	7	6	3	1	1	0	0	6	0	5	1	0	0	0	.000	0	1-1	0	3.38
1984 Los Angeles	NL	45	20	8	10	189.2	771	160	65	56	9	2	3	4	50	8	150	8	1	11	8	.579	4	2-3	0	2.66
1985 Los Angeles	NL	36	34	9	1	239.2	953	179	72	54	8	5	4	6	68	5	157	5	0	19	3	.864	5	0-0	0	2.03
1986 Los Angeles	NL	35	35	8	0	231.1	988	213	112	99	13	14	6	5	86	11	153	12	3	14	14	.500	1	0-0	0	3.85
1987 Los Angeles	NL	37	35	10	2	264.2	1093	247	105	90	17	8	2	9	74	5	190	11	2	16	16	.500	1	1-1	0	3.06
1988 Los Angeles	NL	35	34	15	1	267	1068	208	73	67	18	9	6	4	73	10	178	6	5	23	8	.742	8	1-1	0	2.26
1989 Los Angeles	NL	35	33	8	0	256.2	1047	226	75	66	9	19	6	3	77	14	178	8	4	15	15	.500	4	0-0	0	2.31
1990 Los Angeles	NL	4	4	0	0	25.1	106	26	12	12	1	1	0	1	4	0	16	0	1	1	1	.500	0	0-0	0	4.26
1991 Los Angeles	NL	21	21	0	0	112	473	112	43	43	3	2	1	5	32	6	73	2	4	7	2	.778	0	0-0	0	3.46
1992 Los Angeles	NL	33	33	1	0	210.2	910	209	101	86	15	15	6	8	69	13	130	10	0	10	15	.400	1	0-0	0	3.67
1993 Los Angeles	NL	33	33	5	0	215.2	913	201	106	86	17	12	4	7	72	13	141	7	0	12	14	.462	1	0-0	0	3.59
1994 Los Angeles	NL	21	21	0	0	135.1	575	146	67	57	15	4	3	2	42	6	72	6	2	6	6	.500	0	0-0	0	3.79
1995 Cleveland	AL	26	26	1	0	167.1	683	151	76	72	21	3	4	5	51	1	111	3	0	16	6	.727	1	0-0	0	3.87
1996 Cleveland	AL	33	33	1	0	206	908	238	115	97	21	5	4	12	58	4	125	11	1	15	9	.625	0	0-0	0	4.24
1997 Cleveland	AL	32	32	1	0	195.1	826	199	105	97	26	6	8	11	69	2	107	11	0	14	6	.700	0	0-0	0	4.47
1998 San Francisco	NL	34	34	0	0	202	887	200	105	99	22	12	5	13	85	7	126	12	0	11	10	.524	0	0-0	0	4.41
16 ML YEARS		468	428	68	18	2926.2	12238	2722	1238	1084	216	118	62	95	916	105	1912	113	23	190	133	.588	25	5-6	0	3.33

Richard Hidalgo

Bats: R **Throws:** R **Pos:** CF-57; RF-13; LF-9; PH/PR-6   **Ht:** 6'3" **Wt:** 190 **Born:** 7/2/75 **Age:** 23

Year Team	Lg	G	AB	H	2B	3B	HR	(Hm	Rd)	TB	R	RBI	TBB	IBB	SO	HBP	SH	SF	SB	CS	SB%	GDP	Avg	OBP	SLG
1992 Astros	R	51	184	57	7	3	1	—	—	73	20	27	13	0	27	3	1	3	14	5	.74	1	.310	.360	.397
1993 Asheville	A	111	403	109	23	3	10	—	—	168	49	55	30	0	76	4	2	5	21	13	.62	3	.270	.324	.417
1994 Quad City	A	124	476	139	47	6	12	—	—	234	68	76	23	1	80	7	1	4	12	12	.50	6	.292	.331	.492
1995 Jackson	AA	133	489	130	28	6	14	—	—	212	59	59	32	1	76	2	0	7	8	9	.47	11	.266	.309	.434
1996 Jackson	AA	130	513	151	34	2	14	—	—	231	66	78	29	2	55	1	1	7	11	7	.61	24	.294	.341	.450
1997 New Orleans	AAA	134	526	147	37	5	11	—	—	227	74	78	35	3	57	8	0	7	6	10	.38	16	.279	.330	.432
1998 New Orleans	AAA	10	24	4	2	0	0	—	—	6	0	1	3	0	2	0	0	0	0	0	—	3	.167	.259	.250
1997 Houston	NL	19	62	19	5	0	2	(0	2)	30	8	6	4	0	18	1	0	1	1	0	1.00	1	.306	.358	.484
1998 Houston	NL	74	211	64	15	0	7	(3	4)	100	31	35	17	0	37	2	0	4	3	3	.50	5	.303	.355	.474
2 ML YEARS		93	273	83	20	0	9	(3	6)	130	39	41	21	0	55	3	0	4	4	3	.57	5	.304	.355	.476

Bob Higginson

Bats: L **Throws:** R **Pos:** RF-136; LF-17; DH-2; PH/PR-2   **Ht:** 5'11" **Wt:** 195 **Born:** 8/18/70 **Age:** 28

Year Team	Lg	G	AB	H	2B	3B	HR	(Hm	Rd)	TB	R	RBI	TBB	IBB	SO	HBP	SH	SF	SB	CS	SB%	GDP	Avg	OBP	SLG
1995 Detroit	AL	131	410	92	17	5	14	(10	4)	161	61	43	62	3	107	5	2	7	6	4	.60	5	.224	.329	.393
1996 Detroit	AL	130	440	141	35	0	26	(15	11)	254	75	81	65	7	66	1	3	6	6	3	.67	7	.320	.404	.577
1997 Detroit	AL	146	546	163	30	5	27	(16	11)	284	94	101	70	2	85	3	0	4	12	7	.63	10	.299	.379	.520
1998 Detroit	AL	157	612	174	37	4	25	(10	15)	294	92	85	63	2	101	6	0	4	3	3	.50	16	.284	.355	.480
4 ML YEARS		564	2008	570	119	14	92	(51	41)	993	322	310	260	14	359	15	5	21	27	17	.61	38	.284	.367	.495

Glenallen Hill

Bats: Right **Throws:** Right **Pos:** LF-99; PH/PR-20; RF-6   **Ht:** 6'2" **Wt:** 225 **Born:** 3/22/65 **Age:** 34

							BATTING										BASERUNNING				PERCENTAGES		
Year Team	Lg	G	AB	H	2B	3B	HR	(Hm | Rd)	TB	R	RBI	TBB	IBB	SO	HBP	SH	SF	SB	CS	SB%	GDP	Avg	OBP	SLG
1989 Toronto	AL	19	52	15	0	0	1	(1 | 0)	18	4	7	3	0	12	0	0	0	2	1	.67	0	.288	.327	.346
1990 Toronto	AL	84	260	60	11	3	12	(7 | 5)	113	47	32	18	0	62	0	0	0	8	3	.73	5	.231	.281	.435
1991 Tor-Cle	AL	72	221	57	8	2	8	(3 | 5)	93	29	25	23	0	54	0	1	3	6	4	.60	7	.258	.324	.421
1992 Cleveland	AL	102	369	89	16	1	18	(7 | 11)	161	38	49	20	0	73	4	0	1	9	6	.60	11	.241	.287	.436
1993 Cle-ChN	AL	97	261	69	14	2	15	(5 | 10)	132	33	47	17	1	71	1	1	4	8	3	.73	4	.264	.307	.506
1994 Chicago	NL	89	269	80	12	1	10	(3 | 7)	124	48	38	29	0	57	0	0	1	19	6	.76	5	.297	.365	.461
1995 San Francisco	NL	132	497	131	29	4	24	(13 | 11)	240	71	86	39	4	98	1	0	2	25	5	.83	11	.264	.317	.483
1996 San Francisco	NL	98	379	106	26	0	19	(9 | 10)	189	56	67	33	3	95	6	0	3	6	3	.67	6	.280	.344	.499
1997 San Francisco	NL	128	398	104	28	4	11	(3 | 8)	173	47	64	19	0	87	4	0	7	7	4	.64	8	.261	.297	.435
1998 Sea-ChN	AL	122	390	121	25	2	20	(11 | 9)	210	63	56	28	2	79	3	0	1	1	1	.50	16	.310	.360	.538
1991 Toronto	AL	35	99	25	5	2	3	(2 | 1)	43	14	11	7	0	24	0	0	2	2	2	.50	2	.253	.296	.434
Cleveland	AL	37	122	32	3	0	5	(1 | 4)	50	15	14	16	0	30	0	1	1	4	2	.67	5	.262	.345	.410
1993 Cleveland	AL	66	174	39	7	2	5	(0 | 5)	65	19	25	11	1	50	1	1	4	7	3	.70	3	.224	.268	.374
Chicago	NL	31	87	30	7	0	10	(5 | 5)	67	14	22	6	0	21	0	0	0	1	0	1.00	1	.345	.387	.770
1998 Seattle	AL	74	259	75	20	2	12	(5 | 7)	135	37	33	14	1	45	3	0	1	1	1	.50	13	.290	.332	.521
Chicago	NL	48	131	46	5	0	8	(6 | 2)	75	26	23	14	1	34	0	0	0	0	0	.00	3	.351	.414	.573
10 ML YEARS		943	3096	832	169	19	138	(62 | 76)	1453	436	471	229	10	688	19	2	22	91	36	.72	73	.269	.321	.469

Ken Hill

Pitches: Right **Bats:** Right **Pos:** SP-19   **Ht:** 6'2" **Wt:** 214 **Born:** 12/14/65 **Age:** 33

		HOW MUCH HE PITCHED						WHAT HE GAVE UP											THE RESULTS					
Year Team	Lg	G	GS	CG	GF	IP	BFP	H	R	ER	HR	SH	SF	HB	TBB	IBB	SO	WP	Bk	W	L	Pct.	ShO	Sv-Op	Hld	ERA
1998 Cedar Rapds *	A	2	2	0	0	7.1	28	7	1	1	0	1	0	0	1	0	6	1	0	0	0	.000	0	0--	—	1.23
Lk Elsinore *	A+	1	1	0	0	4	21	5	4	3	0	0	1	0	5	0	2	1	0	0	0	.000	0	0--	—	6.75
1988 St. Louis	NL	4	1	0	0	14	62	16	9	8	0	0	0	0	6	0	6	1	0	0	1	.000	0	0-0	0	5.14
1989 St. Louis	NL	33	33	2	0	196.2	862	186	92	83	9	14	5	5	99	6	112	11	2	7	15	.318	1	0-0	0	3.80
1990 St. Louis	NL	17	14	1	1	78.2	343	79	49	48	7	5	5	1	33	1	58	5	0	5	6	.455	0	0-0	1	5.49
1991 St. Louis	NL	30	30	0	0	181.1	743	147	76	72	15	7	7	6	67	4	121	7	1	11	10	.524	0	0-0	0	3.57
1992 Montreal	NL	33	33	3	0	218	908	187	76	65	13	15	3	9	75	4	150	11	4	16	9	.640	3	0-0	0	2.68
1993 Montreal	NL	28	28	2	0	183.2	780	163	84	66	7	9	7	6	74	7	90	6	2	9	7	.563	0	0-0	0	3.23
1994 Montreal	NL	23	23	2	0	154.2	647	145	61	57	12	6	6	6	44	7	85	3	0	16	5	.762	1	0-0	0	3.32
1995 StL-Cle		30	29	1	0	185	817	202	107	95	21	12	3	1	77	4	98	6	0	10	8	.556	0	0-0	0	4.62
1996 Texas	AL	35	35	7	0	250.2	1061	250	110	101	19	4	7	6	95	3	170	5	4	16	10	.615	3	0-0	0	3.63
1997 Tex-Ana	AL	31	31	1	0	190	833	194	103	96	19	3	7	3	95	3	106	7	0	9	12	.429	0	0-0	0	4.55
1998 Anaheim	AL	19	19	0	0	103	458	123	60	57	6	7	5	3	47	0	57	3	0	9	6	.600	0	0-0	0	4.98
1995 St. Louis	NL	18	18	0	0	110.1	493	125	71	62	16	9	2	0	45	4	50	3	0	6	7	.462	0	0-0	0	5.06
Cleveland	AL	12	11	1	0	74.2	324	77	36	33	5	3	1	1	32	0	48	3	0	4	1	.800	0	0-0	0	3.98
1997 Texas	AL	19	19	0	0	111	499	129	69	64	11	2	6	2	56	3	68	5	0	5	8	.385	0	0-0	0	5.19
Anaheim	AL	12	12	1	0	79	334	65	34	32	8	1	1	1	39	0	38	2	0	4	4	.500	0	0-0	0	3.65
11 ML YEARS		283	276	19	1	1755.2	7514	1692	827	748	128	82	55	40	712	39	1053	65	13	108	89	.548	8	0-0	1	3.83

A.J. Hinch

Bats: Right **Throws:** Right **Pos:** C-118; PH/PR-3   **Ht:** 6'1" **Wt:** 205 **Born:** 5/15/74 **Age:** 25

							BATTING										BASERUNNING				PERCENTAGES		
Year Team	Lg	G	AB	H	2B	3B	HR	(Hm | Rd)	TB	R	RBI	TBB	IBB	SO	HBP	SH	SF	SB	CS	SB%	GDP	Avg	OBP	SLG
1997 Modesto	A+	95	333	103	25	3	20	—	—	194	70	73	42	3	68	11	4	4	8	3	.73	9	.309	.400	.583
Edmonton	AAA	39	125	47	7	4	1	—	—	66	23	24	20	1	13	3	0	0	2	0	1.00	7	.376	.473	.528
1998 Oakland	AL	120	337	78	10	0	9	(4 | 5)	115	34	35	30	0	89	4	13	7	3	0	1.00	6	.231	.296	.341

Sterling Hitchcock

Pitches: Left **Bats:** Left **Pos:** SP-27; RP-12   **Ht:** 6'1" **Wt:** 192 **Born:** 4/29/71 **Age:** 28

		HOW MUCH HE PITCHED						WHAT HE GAVE UP											THE RESULTS					
Year Team	Lg	G	GS	CG	GF	IP	BFP	H	R	ER	HR	SH	SF	HB	TBB	IBB	SO	WP	Bk	W	L	Pct.	ShO	Sv-Op	Hld	ERA
1992 New York	AL	3	3	0	0	13	68	23	12	12	2	0	0	1	6	0	6	0	0	0	2	.000	0	0-0	0	8.31
1993 New York	AL	6	6	0	0	31	135	32	18	16	4	0	2	1	14	1	26	3	0	1	2	.333	0	0-0	0	4.65
1994 New York	AL	23	5	1	4	49.1	218	48	24	23	3	1	7	0	29	1	37	5	0	4	1	.800	0	0-0	0	4.20
1995 New York	AL	27	27	4	0	168.1	719	155	91	88	22	5	9	5	68	1	121	5	2	11	10	.524	1	0-0	0	4.70
1996 Seattle	AL	35	35	0	0	196.2	885	245	131	117	27	3	8	7	73	4	132	4	1	13	9	.591	0	0-0	0	5.35
1997 San Diego	NL	32	28	1	1	161	693	172	102	93	24	7	4	4	55	2	106	6	2	10	11	.476	0	0-0	0	5.20
1998 San Diego	NL	39	27	2	3	176.1	743	169	83	77	29	9	3	9	48	2	158	11	1	9	7	.563	1	1-2	3	3.93
7 ML YEARS		165	131	8	8	795.2	3461	844	461	426	111	25	33	27	293	11	586	34	8	48	42	.533	2	3-4	6	4.82

Denny Hocking

B: B **T:** R **Pos:** 2B-48; SS-28; PH/PR-19; 3B-11; RF-7; DH-2; 1B-2; CF-1   **Ht:** 5'10" **Wt:** 183 **B:** 4/2/70 **Age:** 29

							BATTING										BASERUNNING				PERCENTAGES		
Year Team	Lg	G	AB	H	2B	3B	HR	(Hm | Rd)	TB	R	RBI	TBB	IBB	SO	HBP	SH	SF	SB	CS	SB%	GDP	Avg	OBP	SLG
1993 Minnesota	AL	15	36	5	1	0	0	(0 | 0)	6	7	0	6	0	8	0	0	0	1	0	1.00	1	.139	.262	.167
1994 Minnesota	AL	11	31	10	3	0	0	(0 | 0)	13	3	2	0	0	4	0	0	0	2	0	1.00	1	.323	.323	.419
1995 Minnesota	AL	9	25	5	0	2	0	(0 | 0)	9	4	3	2	1	2	0	1	0	1	0	1.00	1	.200	.259	.360
1996 Minnesota	AL	49	127	25	6	0	1	(0 | 1)	34	16	10	8	0	24	0	1	1	3	3	.50	3	.197	.243	.268

Year Team	Lg	G	AB	H	2B	3B	HR	(Hm	Rd)	TB	R	RBI	TBB	IBB	SO	HBP	SH	SF	SB	CS	SB%	GDP	Avg	OBP	SLG
																	BATTING					**BASERUNNING**			**PERCENTAGES**	
1997 Minnesota	AL	115	253	65	12	4	2	(0	2)	91	28	25	18	0	51	1	5	1	3	5	.38	6	.257	.308	.360
1998 Minnesota	AL	110	198	40	6	1	3	(1	2)	57	32	15	16	1	44	0	3	2	2	1	.67	2	.202	.259	.288
6 ML YEARS		309	670	150	28	7	6	(1	5)	210	90	55	50	2	133	1	10	4	12	9	.57	14	.224	.277	.313

Trevor Hoffman

Pitches: Right **Bats:** Right **Pos:** RP-66   **Ht:** 6'0" **Wt:** 205 **Born:** 10/13/67 **Age:** 31

Year Team	Lg	G	GS	CG	GF	IP	BFP	H	R	ER	HR	SH	SF	HB	TBB	IBB	SO	WP	Bk	W	L	Pct.	ShO	Sv-Op	Hld	ERA
				HOW MUCH HE PITCHED						**WHAT HE GAVE UP**												**THE RESULTS**				
1993 Fla-SD	NL	67	0	0	26	90	391	80	43	39	10	4	5	1	39	13	79	5	0	4	6	.400	0	5-8	15	3.90
1994 San Diego	NL	47	0	0	41	56	225	39	16	16	4	1	2	0	20	6	68	3	0	4	4	.500	0	20-23	1	2.57
1995 San Diego	NL	55	0	0	51	53.1	218	48	25	23	10	0	0	0	14	3	52	1	0	7	4	.636	0	31-38	0	3.88
1996 San Diego	NL	70	0	0	62	88	348	50	23	22	6	2	2	2	31	5	111	2	0	9	5	.643	0	42-49	0	2.25
1997 San Diego	NL	70	0	0	59	81.1	322	59	25	24	9	2	1	0	24	4	111	7	0	6	4	.600	0	37-44	0	2.66
1998 San Diego	NL	66	0	0	61	73	274	41	12	12	2	3	0	1	21	2	86	8	0	4	2	.667	0	53-54	0	1.48
1993 Florida	NL	28	0	0	13	35.2	152	24	13	13	5	2	1	0	19	7	26	3	0	2	2	.500	0	2-3	8	3.28
San Diego	NL	39	0	0	13	54.1	239	56	30	26	5	2	4	1	20	6	53	2	0	2	4	.333	0	3-5	7	4.31
6 ML YEARS		375	0	0	300	441.2	1778	317	144	136	41	12	10	4	149	33	507	26	0	34	25	.576	0	188-216	16	2.77

Chris Hoiles

Bats: R **Throws:** R **Pos:** C-83; PH/PR-10; DH-6; 1B-6   **Ht:** 6'0" **Wt:** 220 **Born:** 3/20/65 **Age:** 34

Year Team	Lg	G	AB	H	2B	3B	HR	(Hm	Rd)	TB	R	RBI	TBB	IBB	SO	HBP	SH	SF	SB	CS	SB%	GDP	Avg	OBP	SLG
															BATTING						**BASERUNNING**			**PERCENTAGES**	
1989 Baltimore	AL	6	9	1	0	0	0	(0	0)	2	0	1	1	0	3	0	0	0	0	0	.00	0	.111	.200	.222
1990 Baltimore	AL	23	63	12	3	0	1	(1	0)	18	7	6	5	1	12	0	0	0	0	0	.00	0	.190	.250	.286
1991 Baltimore	AL	107	341	83	15	0	11	(5	6)	131	36	31	29	1	61	1	0	1	0	2	.00	1	.243	.304	.384
1992 Baltimore	AL	96	310	85	10	1	20	(8	12)	157	49	40	55	2	60	2	1	3	0	0	.00	8	.274	.384	.506
1993 Baltimore	AL	126	419	130	28	0	29	(16	13)	245	80	82	69	4	94	9	3	3	1	1	.50	10	.310	.416	.585
1994 Baltimore	AL	99	332	82	10	0	19	(11	8)	149	45	53	63	2	73	5	1	4	2	0	1.00	6	.247	.371	.449
1995 Baltimore	AL	114	352	88	15	1	19	(9	10)	162	53	58	67	3	80	1	0	3	1	0	1.00	11	.250	.373	.460
1996 Baltimore	AL	127	407	105	13	0	25	(13	12)	193	64	73	57	1	97	9	1	7	1	0	1.00	7	.258	.356	.474
1997 Baltimore	AL	99	320	83	15	0	12	(9	3)	134	45	49	51	3	86	10	0	3	1	0	1.00	7	.259	.375	.419
1998 Baltimore	AL	97	267	70	12	0	15	(5	10)	127	36	56	38	0	50	4	5	4	0	1	.00	5	.262	.358	.476
10 ML YEARS		894	2820	739	122	2	151	(77	74)	1318	415	449	435	17	616	44	11	28	5	7	.42	65	.262	.366	.467

Ray Holbert

Bats: Right **Throws:** Right **Pos:** SS-7; PH/PR-3; 2B-1   **Ht:** 6'0" **Wt:** 175 **Born:** 9/25/70 **Age:** 28

Year Team	Lg	G	AB	H	2B	3B	HR	(Hm	Rd)	TB	R	RBI	TBB	IBB	SO	HBP	SH	SF	SB	CS	SB%	GDP	Avg	OBP	SLG
															BATTING						**BASERUNNING**			**PERCENTAGES**	
1998 Richmond *	AAA	1	1	0	0	0	0	—	—	0	1	0	2	0	1	0	0	0	0	0	.00	0	.000	.667	.000
Ottawa *	AAA	86	266	82	17	4	2	—	—	113	38	25	29	3	66	0	4	0	10	5	.67	2	.308	.376	.425
1994 San Diego	NL	5	5	1	0	0	0	(0	0)	1	1	0	0	0	4	0	0	0	0	0	.00	0	.200	.200	.200
1995 San Diego	NL	63	73	13	2	1	2	(1	1)	23	11	5	8	1	20	2	3	0	4	0	1.00	3	.178	.277	.315
1998 Atl-Mon	NL	10	20	2	0	0	0	(0	0)	2	2	1	2	0	5	0	0	1	0	0	.00	0	.100	.174	.100
1998 Atlanta	NL	8	15	2	0	0	0	(0	0)	2	2	1	2	0	4	0	0	1	0	0	.00	0	.133	.222	.133
Montreal	NL	2	5	0	0	0	0	(0	0)	0	0	0	0	0	1	0	0	0	0	0	.00	0	.000	.000	.000
3 ML YEARS		78	98	16	2	1	2	(1	1)	26	14	6	10	1	29	2	3	1	4	0	1.00	3	.163	.252	.265

David Holdridge

Pitches: Right **Bats:** Right **Pos:** RP-7   **Ht:** 6'3" **Wt:** 190 **Born:** 2/5/69 **Age:** 30

Year Team	Lg	G	GS	CG	GF	IP	BFP	H	R	ER	HR	SH	SF	HB	TBB	IBB	SO	WP	Bk	W	L	Pct.	ShO	Sv-Op	Hld	ERA
				HOW MUCH HE PITCHED						**WHAT HE GAVE UP**												**THE RESULTS**				
1988 Quad City	A	28	28	0	0	153.2	686	151	92	66	4	5	4	13	79	1	110	8	4	6	12	.333	0	0- —	—	3.87
1989 Clearwater	A+	24	24	3	0	132.1	610	147	100	84	11	2	6	8	77	0	77	16	1	7	10	.412	0	0- —	—	5.71
1990 Reading	AA	24	24	1	0	127.2	571	114	74	64	13	3	5	6	79	0	78	8	0	8	12	.400	0	0- —	—	4.51
1991 Reading	AA	7	7	0	0	26.1	135	26	24	16	3	2	3	1	34	0	19	3	0	0	2	.000	0	0- —	—	5.47
Clearwater	A+	15	0	0	4	25	126	34	23	21	2	0	2	1	21	0	23	4	0	0	0	.000	0	1- —	—	7.56
1992 Palm Spring	A+	28	27	3	0	159	726	169	99	75	5	5	3	5	87	4	135	21	0	12	12	.500	2	0- —	—	4.25
1993 Midland	AA	27	27	1	0	151	700	202	117	102	13	4	2	11	55	0	123	13	1	8	10	.444	1	0- —	—	6.08
1994 Vancouver	AAA	4	0	0	1	7	36	12	7	4	1	0	1	1	4	0	4	0	0	0	0	.000	0	0- —	—	5.14
Midland	AA	38	2	0	17	66.1	286	66	33	29	4	1	3	5	23	0	59	2	0	7	4	.636	0	2- —	—	3.93
1995 Lk Elsinore	A+	12	0	0	8	18.1	74	13	3	2	0	1	1	2	5	1	24	3	0	3	0	1.000	0	0- —	—	0.98
Midland	AA	14	0	0	11	25.1	100	20	8	5	1	1	0	1	8	0	23	2	0	1	0	1.000	0	1- —	—	1.78
Vancouver	AAA	11	0	0	6	13.2	68	18	10	7	0	2	0	1	7	1	13	0	0	2	2	.000	0	1- —	—	4.61
1996 Vancouver	AAA	29	0	0	17	35	163	39	19	18	4	0	2	2	23	2	26	3	0	2	1	.667	0	1- —	—	4.63
Lk Elsinore	A+	12	0	0	12	13	53	11	3	3	1	0	0	1	2	0	21	0	0	0	0	.000	0	6- —	—	2.08
1997 Memphis	AA	30	0	0	27	35	149	31	14	13	2	1	1	2	17	1	37	2	0	0	3	.000	0	17- —	—	3.34
Tacoma	AAA	15	0	0	8	24.1	105	21	9	8	0	1	1	3	13	0	24	0	0	1	1	.500	0	1- —	—	2.96
1998 Tacoma	AAA	42	0	0	17	70.2	299	55	28	26	2	6	2	7	34	5	73	3	1	7	5	.583	0	7- —	—	3.31
1998 Seattle	AL	7	0	0	3	6.2	31	6	3	3	0	0	1	0	4	0	6	3	0	0	0	.000	0	0-0	0	4.05

Todd Hollandsworth

Bats: L **Throws:** L **Pos:** LF-48; CF-10; PH/PR-6; RF-1 **Ht:** 6'2" **Wt:** 215 **Born:** 4/20/73 **Age:** 26

Year Team	Lg	G	AB	H	2B	3B	HR	(Hm	Rd)	TB	R	RBI	TBB	IBB	SO	HBP	SH	SF	SB	CS	SB%	GDP	Avg	OBP	SLG
1995 Los Angeles	NL	41	103	24	2	0	5	(3	2)	41	16	13	10	2	29	1	0	1	2	1	.67	1	.233	.304	.398
1996 Los Angeles	NL	149	478	139	26	4	12	(2	10)	209	64	59	41	1	93	2	3	2	21	6	.78	2	.291	.348	.437
1997 Los Angeles	NL	106	296	73	20	2	4	(1	3)	109	39	31	17	2	60	0	2	2	5	5	.50	8	.247	.286	.368
1998 Los Angeles	NL	55	175	47	6	4	3	(1	2)	70	23	20	9	0	42	1	2	0	4	3	.57	2	.269	.308	.400
4 ML YEARS		351	1052	283	54	10	24	(7	17)	429	142	123	77	5	224	4	7	5	32	15	.68	13	.269	.320	.408

Damon Hollins

Bats: Right **Throws:** Left **Pos:** RF-4; LF-3; PH/PR-2 **Ht:** 5'11" **Wt:** 180 **Born:** 6/12/74 **Age:** 25

Year Team	Lg	G	AB	H	2B	3B	HR	(Hm	Rd)	TB	R	RBI	TBB	IBB	SO	HBP	SH	SF	SB	CS	SB%	GDP	Avg	OBP	SLG
1992 Braves	R	49	179	41	12	1	1	—	—	58	35	15	30	0	22	2	2	0	15	2	.88	3	.229	.346	.324
1993 Danville	R+	62	240	77	15	2	7	—	—	117	37	51	19	0	30	1	0	3	10	2	.83	5	.321	.369	.488
1994 Durham	A+	131	485	131	28	0	23	—	—	228	76	88	45	0	115	4	2	3	12	7	.63	9	.270	.335	.470
1995 Greenville	AA	129	466	115	26	2	18	—	—	199	64	77	44	6	120	4	0	6	6	6	.50	7	.247	.313	.427
1996 Richmond	AAA	42	146	29	9	0	0	—	—	38	16	8	16	1	37	0	1	0	2	3	.40	2	.199	.278	.260
1997 Richmond	AAA	134	498	132	31	3	20	—	—	229	73	63	45	4	84	3	6	1	7	2	.78	18	.265	.329	.460
1998 Richmond	AAA	119	436	115	26	3	13	—	—	186	61	48	45	2	85	0	1	4	10	2	.83	16	.264	.330	.427
1998 Atl-LA	NL	8	15	3	0	0	0	(0	0)	3	1	2	0	0	3	0	0	0	0	1	.00	0	.200	.200	.200
1998 Atlanta	NL	3	6	1	0	0	0	(0	0)	1	0	0	0	0	1	0	0	0	0	0	.00	0	.167	.167	.167
Los Angeles	NL	5	9	2	0	0	0	(0	0)	2	1	2	0	0	2	0	0	0	0	1	.00	0	.222	.222	.222

Dave Hollins

Bats: B **Throws:** R **Pos:** 3B-91; 1B-7; PH/PR-3; DH-2 **Ht:** 6'1" **Wt:** 232 **Born:** 5/25/66 **Age:** 33

Year Team	Lg	G	AB	H	2B	3B	HR	(Hm	Rd)	TB	R	RBI	TBB	IBB	SO	HBP	SH	SF	SB	CS	SB%	GDP	Avg	OBP	SLG
1990 Philadelphia	NL	72	114	21	0	0	5	(2	3)	36	14	15	10	3	28	1	0	2	0	0	.00	1	.184	.252	.316
1991 Philadelphia	NL	56	151	45	10	2	6	(3	3)	77	18	21	17	1	26	3	0	1	1	1	.50	2	.298	.378	.510
1992 Philadelphia	NL	156	586	158	28	4	27	(14	13)	275	104	93	76	4	110	19	0	4	9	6	.60	8	.270	.369	.469
1993 Philadelphia	NL	143	543	148	30	4	18	(9	9)	240	104	93	85	5	109	5	0	7	2	3	.40	15	.273	.372	.442
1994 Philadelphia	NL	44	162	36	7	1	4	(1	3)	57	28	26	23	0	32	4	0	3	1	0	1.00	6	.222	.328	.352
1995 Phi-Bos		70	218	49	12	2	7	(5	2)	86	48	26	57	4	45	5	0	4	1	1	.50	4	.225	.391	.394
1996 Min-Sea	AL	149	516	135	29	0	16	(7	9)	212	88	78	84	7	117	13	1	2	6	6	.50	11	.262	.377	.411
1997 Anaheim	AL	149	572	165	29	2	16	(15	1)	246	101	85	62	2	124	8	1	5	16	6	.73	12	.288	.363	.430
1998 Anaheim	AL	101	363	88	16	2	11	(4	7)	141	60	39	44	2	69	7	2	2	11	3	.79	5	.242	.334	.388
1995 Philadelphia	NL	65	205	47	12	2	7	(5	2)	84	46	25	53	4	38	5	0	4	1	1	.50	4	.229	.393	.410
Boston	AL	5	13	2	0	0	0	(0	0)	2	2	1	4	0	7	0	0	0	0	0	.00	0	.154	.353	.154
1996 Minnesota	AL	121	422	102	26	0	13	(6	7)	167	71	53	71	5	102	10	0	0	6	4	.60	9	.242	.364	.396
Seattle	AL	28	94	33	3	0	3	(1	2)	45	17	25	13	2	15	3	1	2	0	2	.00	2	.351	.438	.479
9 ML YEARS		940	3225	845	161	17	110	(60	50)	1370	565	476	458	28	660	65	4	30	47	26	.64	64	.262	.362	.425

Darren Holmes

Pitches: Right **Bats:** Right **Pos:** RP-34 **Ht:** 6'0" **Wt:** 202 **Born:** 4/25/66 **Age:** 33

Year Team	Lg	G	GS	CG	GF	IP	BFP	H	R	ER	HR	SH	SF	HB	TBB	IBB	SO	WP	Bk	W	L	Pct.	ShO	Sv-Op	Hld	ERA
1998 Tampa *	A+	2	1	0	0	2	11	4	2	1	0	0	0	0	0	0	6	0	0	0	1	.000	0	0- -	—	4.50
1990 Los Angeles	NL	14	0	0	1	17.1	77	15	10	10	1	2	0	0	11	3	19	1	0	0	1	.000	0	0-0	0	5.19
1991 Milwaukee	AL	40	0	0	9	76.1	344	90	43	40	6	8	3	1	27	1	59	6	0	1	4	.200	0	3-6	3	4.72
1992 Milwaukee	AL	41	0	0	25	42.1	173	35	12	12	1	4	0	2	11	4	31	0	0	4	4	.500	0	6-8	2	2.55
1993 Colorado	NL	62	0	0	51	66.2	274	56	31	30	6	0	0	2	20	1	60	2	1	3	3	.500	0	25-29	2	4.05
1994 Colorado	NL	29	0	0	14	28.1	142	35	25	20	5	4	1	1	24	4	33	2	0	0	3	.000	0	3-8	3	6.35
1995 Colorado	NL	68	0	0	33	66.2	286	59	26	24	3	5	3	1	28	3	61	7	1	6	1	.857	0	14-18	13	3.24
1996 Colorado	NL	62	0	0	21	77	333	78	41	34	8	2	1	1	28	2	73	2	0	5	4	.556	0	1-8	7	3.97
1997 Colorado	NL	42	6	0	10	89.1	406	113	58	53	12	6	4	0	36	3	70	4	0	9	2	.818	0	3-4	5	5.34
1998 New York	AL	34	0	0	13	51.1	215	53	19	19	4	0	2	0	14	3	31	1	0	0	3	.000	0	2-3	2	3.33
9 ML YEARS		392	6	0	177	515.1	2250	534	265	242	46	30	17	10	199	24	437	25	2	28	25	.528	0	57-84	37	4.23

Mike Holtz

Pitches: Left **Bats:** Left **Pos:** RP-53 **Ht:** 5'9" **Wt:** 175 **Born:** 10/10/72 **Age:** 26

Year Team	Lg	G	GS	CG	GF	IP	BFP	H	R	ER	HR	SH	SF	HB	TBB	IBB	SO	WP	Bk	W	L	Pct.	ShO	Sv-Op	Hld	ERA
1998 Vancouver *	AAA	10	0	0	5	10.1	48	10	4	2	1	0	0	1	6	0	18	0	0	0	0	.000	0	2- -	—	1.74
1996 California	AL	30	0	0	8	29.1	127	21	11	8	1	1	1	3	19	2	31	1	0	3	3	.500	0	0-0	5	2.45
1997 Anaheim	AL	66	0	0	11	43.1	187	38	21	16	7	1	2	2	15	4	40	1	0	3	4	.429	0	2-8	14	3.32
1998 Anaheim	AL	53	0	0	9	30.1	137	38	16	16	0	1	2	1	15	1	29	4	0	2	2	.500	0	1-2	13	4.75
3 ML YEARS		149	0	0	28	103	451	97	48	40	8	3	5	6	49	7	100	6	0	8	9	.471	0	3-10	32	3.50

102

Mark Holzemer

Pitches: Left **Bats:** Left **Pos:** RP-13   **Ht:** 6'0" **Wt:** 165 **Born:** 8/20/69 **Age:** 29

		HOW MUCH HE PITCHED						WHAT HE GAVE UP											THE RESULTS						
Year Team	Lg	G	GS	CG	GF	IP	BFP	H	R	ER	HR	SH	SF	HB	TBB	IBB	SO	WP	Bk	W	L	Pct.	ShO	Sv-Op	Hld	ERA
1998 Edmonton *	AAA	30	0	0	8	39	168	41	15	14	2	3	4	3	11	1	27	2	0	1	1	.500	0	6- -	—	3.23
1993 California	AL	5	4	0	1	23.1	117	34	24	23	2	1	0	3	13	0	10	1	0	0	3	.000	0	0-0	0	8.87
1995 California	AL	12	0	0	5	8.1	45	11	6	5	1	1	0	1	7	1	5	0	0	1	0	1.000	0	0-0	0	5.40
1996 California	AL	25	0	0	3	24.2	119	35	28	24	7	0	1	3	8	1	20	0	0	1	0	1.000	0	0-0	1	8.76
1997 Seattle	AL	14	0	0	2	9	44	9	6	6	0	0	0	0	8	0	7	0	0	0	0	.000	0	1-1	1	6.00
1998 Oakland	AL	13	0	0	4	9.2	44	13	6	6	1	0	1	1	3	0	3	1	0	1	0	1.000	0	0-0	2	5.59
5 ML YEARS		69	4	0	15	75	369	102	70	64	11	2	2	8	39	2	45	2	0	2	4	.333	0	1-1	4	7.68

Tyler Houston

Bats: L **Throws:** R **Pos:** C-63; PH/PR-24; 3B-12; 1B-7   **Ht:** 6'1" **Wt:** 205 **Born:** 1/17/71 **Age:** 28

		BATTING																BASERUNNING				PERCENTAGES		
Year Team	Lg	G	AB	H	2B	3B	HR	(Hm	Rd)	TB	R	RBI	TBB	IBB	SO	HBP	SH	SF	SB	CS	SB%	GDP	Avg	OBP	SLG
1996 Atl-ChN	NL	79	142	45	9	1	3	(1	2)	65	21	27	9	1	27	0	0	0	3	2	.60	5	.317	.358	.458
1997 Chicago	NL	72	196	51	10	0	2	(0	2)	67	15	28	9	1	35	0	0	2	1	0	1.00	4	.260	.290	.342
1998 Chicago	NL	95	255	65	7	1	9	(4	5)	101	26	33	13	1	53	0	1	1	2	2	.50	6	.255	.290	.396
1996 Atlanta	NL	33	27	6	2	1	1	(1	0)	13	3	8	1	0	9	0	0	0	0	0	.00	1	.222	.250	.481
Chicago	NL	46	115	39	7	0	2	(0	2)	52	18	19	8	1	18	0	0	0	3	2	.60	4	.339	.382	.452
3 ML YEARS		246	593	161	26	2	14	(5	9)	233	62	88	31	3	115	0	1	3	6	4	.60	15	.272	.306	.393

David Howard

Bats: B **Throws:** R **Pos:** 2B-19; SS-16; 3B-14; PH/PR-7; CF-2; RF-1   **Ht:** 6'0" **Wt:** 175 **Born:** 2/26/67 **Age:** 32

		BATTING																BASERUNNING				PERCENTAGES		
Year Team	Lg	G	AB	H	2B	3B	HR	(Hm	Rd)	TB	R	RBI	TBB	IBB	SO	HBP	SH	SF	SB	CS	SB%	GDP	Avg	OBP	SLG
1991 Kansas City	AL	94	236	51	7	0	1	(0	1)	61	20	17	16	0	45	1	9	2	3	2	.60	1	.216	.267	.258
1992 Kansas City	AL	74	219	49	6	2	1	(1	0)	62	19	18	15	0	43	0	8	2	3	4	.43	3	.224	.271	.283
1993 Kansas City	AL	15	24	8	0	1	0	(0	0)	10	5	2	2	0	5	0	2	1	1	0	1.00	0	.333	.370	.417
1994 Kansas City	AL	46	83	19	4	0	1	(0	1)	26	9	13	11	0	23	0	3	3	3	2	.60	1	.229	.309	.313
1995 Kansas City	AL	95	255	62	13	4	0	(0	0)	83	23	19	24	1	41	1	6	1	6	1	.86	7	.243	.310	.325
1996 Kansas City	AL	143	420	92	14	5	4	(3	1)	128	51	48	40	0	74	4	17	4	5	6	.45	5	.219	.291	.305
1997 Kansas City	AL	80	162	39	8	1	1	(0	1)	52	24	13	10	1	31	1	3	1	2	2	.50	1	.241	.287	.321
1998 St. Louis	NL	46	102	25	1	1	2	(2	0)	34	15	12	12	2	22	0	2	1	0	0	.00	2	.245	.322	.333
8 ML YEARS		593	1501	345	53	14	10	(6	4)	456	166	142	130	4	284	7	50	15	23	17	.58	21	.230	.292	.304

Thomas Howard

Bats: L **Throws:** R **Pos:** PH/PR-25; CF-13; LF-11; RF-6; DH-1   **Ht:** 6'2" **Wt:** 205 **Born:** 12/11/64 **Age:** 34

		BATTING																BASERUNNING				PERCENTAGES		
Year Team	Lg	G	AB	H	2B	3B	HR	(Hm	Rd)	TB	R	RBI	TBB	IBB	SO	HBP	SH	SF	SB	CS	SB%	GDP	Avg	OBP	SLG
1990 San Diego	NL	20	44	12	2	0	0	(0	0)	14	4	0	0	0	11	0	1	0	0	1	.00	1	.273	.273	.318
1991 San Diego	NL	106	281	70	12	3	4	(4	0)	100	30	22	24	4	57	1	2	1	10	7	.59	4	.249	.309	.356
1992 SD-Cle		122	361	100	15	2	2	(1	1)	125	37	32	17	1	60	0	11	2	15	8	.65	4	.277	.308	.346
1993 Cle-Cin		112	319	81	15	3	7	(5	2)	123	48	36	24	1	63	0	0	5	10	7	.59	9	.254	.302	.386
1994 Cincinnati	NL	83	178	47	11	0	5	(4	1)	73	24	24	10	1	30	0	3	1	4	2	.67	2	.264	.302	.410
1995 Cincinnati	NL	113	281	85	15	2	3	(1	2)	113	42	26	20	0	37	1	1	1	17	8	.68	3	.302	.350	.402
1996 Cincinnati	NL	121	360	98	19	10	6	(1	5)	155	50	42	17	3	51	3	2	4	6	5	.55	5	.272	.307	.431
1997 Houston	NL	107	255	63	16	1	3	(0	3)	90	24	22	26	1	48	3	1	1	2	3	.33	1	.247	.323	.353
1998 Los Angeles	NL	47	76	14	4	0	2	(1	1)	24	9	4	3	0	15	0	0	0	1	0	1.00	2	.184	.215	.316
1992 San Diego	NL	5	3	1	0	0	0	(0	0)	1	1	0	0	0	0	0	1	0	0	0	.00	0	.333	.333	.333
Cleveland	AL	117	358	99	15	2	2	(1	1)	124	36	32	17	1	60	0	10	2	15	8	.65	4	.277	.308	.346
1993 Cleveland	AL	74	178	42	7	0	3	(3	0)	58	26	23	12	0	42	0	0	4	5	1	.83	5	.236	.278	.326
Cincinnati	NL	38	141	39	8	3	4	(2	2)	65	22	13	12	0	21	0	0	1	5	6	.45	4	.277	.331	.461
9 ML YEARS		831	2155	570	109	21	32	(17	15)	817	268	208	141	10	372	8	21	15	64	40	.62	33	.265	.310	.379

Jack Howell

Bats: Left **Throws:** Right **Pos:** PH/PR-13; 1B-10; 3B-2   **Ht:** 6'0" **Wt:** 190 **Born:** 8/18/61 **Age:** 37

		BATTING																BASERUNNING				PERCENTAGES		
Year Team	Lg	G	AB	H	2B	3B	HR	(Hm	Rd)	TB	R	RBI	TBB	IBB	SO	HBP	SH	SF	SB	CS	SB%	GDP	Avg	OBP	SLG
1985 California	AL	43	137	27	4	0	5	(2	3)	46	19	18	16	2	33	0	4	1	1	1	.50	1	.197	.279	.336
1986 California	AL	63	151	41	14	2	4	(1	3)	71	26	21	19	0	28	0	3	2	2	0	1.00	1	.272	.349	.470
1987 California	AL	138	449	110	18	5	23	(15	8)	207	64	64	57	4	118	2	1	2	4	3	.57	7	.245	.331	.461
1988 California	AL	154	500	127	32	2	16	(9	7)	211	59	63	46	8	130	6	4	2	2	6	.25	8	.254	.323	.422
1989 California	AL	144	474	108	19	4	20	(9	11)	195	56	52	52	9	125	3	3	1	0	3	.00	8	.228	.308	.411
1990 California	AL	105	316	72	19	4	8	(3	5)	117	35	33	46	1	61	1	1	2	3	0	1.00	3	.228	.326	.370
1991 Cal-SD		90	241	50	5	1	8	(3	5)	81	35	23	29	1	44	0	1	0	1	1	.50	2	.207	.293	.336
1996 California	AL	66	126	34	4	1	8	(4	4)	64	20	21	10	0	30	0	0	0	0	0	.00	3	.270	.324	.508
1997 Anaheim	AL	77	174	45	7	0	14	(5	9)	94	25	34	13	2	36	0	1	3	1	0	1.00	4	.259	.305	.540
1998 Houston	NL	24	38	11	5	0	1	(1	0)	19	4	7	4	0	12	0	0	0	0	0	.00	1	.289	.357	.500
1991 California	AL	32	81	17	2	0	2	(0	2)	25	11	7	11	0	11	0	0	0	1	1	.50	1	.210	.304	.309
San Diego	NL	58	160	33	3	1	6	(3	3)	56	24	16	18	1	33	0	1	0	0	0	.00	1	.206	.287	.350
10 ML YEARS		904	2606	625	127	16	107	(52	55)	1105	343	336	292	31	617	12	18	13	14	15	.48	38	.240	.318	.424

Bob Howry

Pitches: Right **Bats:** Left **Pos:** RP-44   **Ht:** 6'5" **Wt:** 215 **Born:** 8/4/73 **Age:** 25

Year Team	Lg	G	GS	CG	GF	IP	BFP	H	R	ER	HR	SH	SF	HB	TBB	IBB	SO	WP	Bk	W	L	Pct.	ShO	Sv-Op	Hld	ERA
1994 Everett	A-	5	5	0	0	19	97	29	19	15	3	0	1	1	10	2	16	5	0	0	4	.000	0	0--	—	7.11
Clinton	A	9	8	0	0	49.1	219	61	29	23	1	3	4	3	16	0	22	4	2	1	3	.250	0	0--	—	4.20
1995 San Jose	A+	27	25	1	1	165.1	695	171	79	65	6	12	4	8	54	0	107	7	3	12	10	.545	0	0--	—	3.54
1996 Shreveport	AA	27	27	0	0	156.2	682	163	90	81	17	6	4	9	56	3	57	3	1	10	8	.556	0	0--	—	4.65
1997 Shreveport	AA	48	0	0	39	55	240	58	35	30	6	1	3	0	21	0	43	3	1	6	3	.667	0	22--	—	4.91
Birmingham	AA	12	0	0	11	12.2	54	16	4	4	1	0	0	0	3	0	3	0	0	0	0	.000	0	2--	—	2.84
1998 Calgary	AAA	23	0	0	11	31.2	130	25	12	12	2	2	0	2	10	3	22	4	0	1	2	.333	0	5--	—	3.41
1998 Chicago	AL	44	0	0	15	54.1	217	37	20	19	7	2	3	2	19	2	51	2	0	0	3	.000	0	9-11	19	3.15

Mike Hubbard

Bats: Right **Throws:** Right **Pos:** C-24; PH/PR-8; 2B-1   **Ht:** 6'1" **Wt:** 180 **Born:** 2/16/71 **Age:** 28

Year Team	Lg	G	AB	H	2B	3B	HR	(Hm	Rd)	TB	R	RBI	TBB	IBB	SO	HBP	SH	SF	SB	CS	SB%	GDP	Avg	OBP	SLG
1998 Ottawa *	AAA	20	70	16	5	0	0	—	—	21	9	8	3	0	13	0	0	1	0	0	.00	3	.229	.257	.300
1995 Chicago	NL	15	23	4	0	0	0	(0	0)	4	2	1	2	0	2	0	0	0	0	0	.00	1	.174	.240	.174
1996 Chicago	NL	21	38	4	0	0	1	(1	0)	7	1	4	0	0	15	0	0	1	0	0	.00	1	.105	.103	.184
1997 Chicago	NL	29	64	13	0	0	1	(0	1)	16	4	2	2	1	21	0	0	0	0	0	.00	0	.203	.227	.250
1998 Montreal	NL	32	55	8	1	0	1	(1	0)	12	3	3	0	0	17	1	0	0	0	0	.00	1	.145	.161	.218
4 ML YEARS		97	180	29	1	0	3	(2	1)	39	10	10	4	1	55	1	0	1	0	0	.00	4	.161	.183	.217

Trenidad Hubbard

Bats: R **Throws:** R **Pos:** CF-46; LF-34; PH/PR-30; RF-4; 3B-1   **Ht:** 5'9" **Wt:** 185 **Born:** 5/11/66 **Age:** 33

Year Team	Lg	G	AB	H	2B	3B	HR	(Hm	Rd)	TB	R	RBI	TBB	IBB	SO	HBP	SH	SF	SB	CS	SB%	GDP	Avg	OBP	SLG
1998 Albuquerque *	AAA	11	30	9	0	0	3	—	—	18	6	5	5	0	5	1	0	0	2	1	.67	1	.300	.417	.600
1994 Colorado	NL	18	25	7	1	1	1	(1	0)	13	3	3	3	0	4	0	0	0	0	0	.00	1	.280	.357	.520
1995 Colorado	NL	24	58	18	4	0	3	(2	1)	31	13	9	8	0	6	0	1	0	2	1	.67	2	.310	.394	.534
1996 Col-SF	NL	55	89	19	5	2	2	(2	0)	34	15	14	11	0	27	1	0	0	2	0	1.00	1	.213	.307	.382
1997 Cleveland	AL	7	12	3	1	0	0	(0	0)	4	3	0	1	0	3	0	0	0	2	0	1.00	0	.250	.308	.333
1998 Los Angeles	NL	94	208	62	6	1	7	(2	5)	94	29	18	18	0	46	3	3	3	9	5	.64	5	.298	.358	.452
1996 Colorado	NL	45	60	13	5	1	1	(1	0)	23	12	12	9	0	22	1	0	0	2	0	1.00	1	.217	.329	.383
San Francisco	NL	10	29	6	0	1	1	(1	0)	11	3	2	2	0	5	0	0	0	0	0	.00	2	.207	.258	.379
5 ML YEARS		198	392	109	20	4	13	(7	6)	176	63	44	41	0	86	4	4	3	15	6	.71	11	.278	.350	.449

John Hudek

Pitches: Right **Bats:** Both **Pos:** RP-58   **Ht:** 6'2" **Wt:** 210 **Born:** 8/8/66 **Age:** 32

Year Team	Lg	G	GS	CG	GF	IP	BFP	H	R	ER	HR	SH	SF	HB	TBB	IBB	SO	WP	Bk	W	L	Pct.	ShO	Sv-Op	Hld	ERA
1994 Houston	NL	42	0	0	33	39.1	159	24	14	13	5	0	2	1	18	2	39	0	0	0	2	.000	0	16-18	1	2.97
1995 Houston	NL	19	0	0	16	20	83	19	12	12	3	1	0	0	5	0	29	2	0	2	2	.500	0	7-9	0	5.40
1996 Houston	NL	15	0	0	6	16	65	12	5	5	2	2	0	0	5	2	14	1	1	2	0	1.000	0	2-4	1	2.81
1997 Houston	NL	40	0	0	20	40.2	188	38	27	27	8	1	0	3	33	2	36	4	0	1	3	.250	0	4-8	2	5.98
1998 NYN-Cin	NL	58	0	0	23	64	289	50	27	22	8	5	5	4	47	4	68	1	0	5	6	.455	0	0-1	6	3.09
1998 New York	NL	28	0	0	15	27	123	23	13	12	2	3	2	2	19	3	28	0	0	1	4	.200	0	0-0	0	4.00
Cincinnati	NL	30	0	0	8	37	166	27	14	10	6	2	3	2	28	1	40	1	0	4	2	.667	0	0-1	6	2.43
5 ML YEARS		174	0	0	98	180	784	143	85	79	26	9	7	8	108	10	186	8	1	10	13	.435	0	29-38	10	3.95

Rex Hudler

Bats: R **Throws:** R **Pos:** PH/PR-16; RF-5; LF-3; 1B-1; CF-1   **Ht:** 6'0" **Wt:** 202 **Born:** 9/2/60 **Age:** 38

Year Team	Lg	G	AB	H	2B	3B	HR	(Hm	Rd)	TB	R	RBI	TBB	IBB	SO	HBP	SH	SF	SB	CS	SB%	GDP	Avg	OBP	SLG
1998 Buffalo *	AAA	11	36	7	1	0	0	—	—	8	4	2	4	0	10	2	1	0	0	0	.00	1	.194	.310	.222
1984 New York	AL	9	7	1	1	0	0	(0	0)	2	2	0	1	0	5	1	0	0	0	0	.00	0	.143	.333	.286
1985 New York	AL	20	51	8	0	1	0	(0	0)	10	4	1	1	0	9	0	5	0	0	1	.00	0	.157	.173	.196
1986 Baltimore	AL	14	1	0	0	0	0	(0	0)	0	1	0	0	0	0	0	0	0	1	0	1.00	0	.000	.000	.000
1988 Montreal	NL	77	216	59	14	2	4	(1	3)	89	38	14	10	6	34	0	1	2	29	7	.81	2	.273	.303	.412
1989 Montreal	NL	92	155	38	7	0	6	(3	3)	63	21	13	6	2	23	1	0	0	15	4	.79	2	.245	.278	.406
1990 Mon-StL	NL	93	220	62	11	2	7	(2	5)	98	31	22	12	1	32	2	2	1	18	10	.64	3	.282	.323	.445
1991 St. Louis	NL	101	207	47	10	2	1	(1	0)	64	21	15	10	1	29	0	2	2	12	8	.60	1	.227	.260	.309
1992 St. Louis	NL	61	98	24	4	0	3	(2	1)	37	17	5	2	0	23	1	1	1	2	6	.25	0	.245	.265	.378
1994 California	AL	56	124	37	8	0	8	(4	4)	69	17	20	6	0	28	0	4	1	2	2	.50	7	.298	.326	.556
1995 California	AL	84	223	59	16	0	6	(4	2)	93	30	27	10	1	48	5	2	1	13	0	1.00	1	.265	.310	.417
1996 California	AL	92	302	94	20	3	16	(6	10)	168	60	40	9	0	54	3	2	1	14	5	.74	7	.311	.337	.556
1997 Philadelphia	NL	50	122	27	4	0	5	(5	0)	46	17	10	6	1	28	1	1	0	1	0	1.00	2	.221	.264	.377
1998 Philadelphia	NL	25	41	5	1	0	0	(0	0)	6	2	2	1	0	12	0	0	0	0	0	.00	1	.122	.200	.146
1990 Montreal	NL	4	3	1	0	0	0	(0	0)	1	1	0	0	0	1	0	0	0	0	0	.00	1	.333	.333	.333
St. Louis	NL	89	217	61	11	2	7	(2	5)	97	30	22	12	1	31	2	2	1	18	10	.64	3	.281	.323	.447
13 ML YEARS		774	1767	461	96	10	56	(28	28)	745	261	169	77	12	325	14	20	10	107	43	.71	27	.261	.296	.422

104

Joe Hudson

Pitches: Right **Bats:** Right **Pos:** RP-1 **Ht:** 6'1" **Wt:** 180 **Born:** 9/29/70 **Age:** 28

		HOW MUCH HE PITCHED					WHAT HE GAVE UP										THE RESULTS						
Year Team	Lg	G	GS	CG	GF	IP	BFP	H	R	ER	HR	SH	SF	HB	TBB	IBB	SO	WP	Bk	W	L	Pct.	ShO	Sv-Op	Hld	ERA
1998 Pawtucket *	AAA	46	0	0	26	47.2	222	57	32	24	3	2	2	0	23	3	32	4	0	2	2	.500	0	10--	—	4.53
Louisville *	AAA	9	0	0	1	12.1	57	13	7	7	1	0	1	2	5	1	4	0	0	1	0	1.000	0	0--	—	5.11
1995 Boston	AL	39	0	0	11	46	205	53	21	21	2	3	1	2	23	1	29	6	0	0	1	.000	0	1-4	8	4.11
1996 Boston	AL	36	0	0	16	45	214	57	35	27	4	1	2	0	32	4	19	0	0	3	5	.375	0	1-5	3	5.40
1997 Boston	AL	26	0	0	9	35.2	154	39	16	14	1	1	0	4	14	2	14	1	0	3	1	.750	0	0-0	0	3.53
1998 Milwaukee	NL	1	0	0	0	0.1	7	2	6	6	0	0	0	0	4	1	0	0	0	0	0	.000	0	0-0	0	162.00
4 ML YEARS		102	0	0	36	127	580	151	78	68	7	5	4	6	73	8	62	7	0	6	7	.462	0	2-9	11	4.82

Bobby Hughes

Bats: Right **Throws:** Right **Pos:** C-72; PH/PR-16; RF-3 **Ht:** 6'4" **Wt:** 237 **Born:** 4/10/71 **Age:** 28

		BATTING																BASERUNNING				PERCENTAGES		
Year Team	Lg	G	AB	H	2B	3B	HR	(Hm	Rd)	TB	R	RBI	TBB	IBB	SO	HBP	SH	SF	SB	CS	SB%	GDP	Avg	OBP	SLG
1992 Helena	R+	11	40	7	1	1	0	—	—	10	5	6	4	0	14	2	0	0	0	0	.00	0	.175	.283	.250
1993 Beloit	A	98	321	89	11	3	17	—	—	157	42	56	23	0	77	6	5	0	1	3	.25	2	.277	.337	.489
1994 El Paso	AA	12	36	10	4	1	0	—	—	16	3	12	5	0	7	1	0	2	0	1	.00	1	.278	.364	.444
Stockton	A+	95	322	81	24	3	11	—	—	144	54	53	33	0	83	9	1	2	1	2	.67	8	.252	.336	.447
1995 Stockton	A+	52	179	42	9	2	8	—	—	79	22	31	17	1	41	1	0	3	2	2	.50	10	.235	.300	.441
El Paso	AA	51	173	46	12	0	7	—	—	79	11	27	12	1	30	2	0	4	0	2	.00	4	.266	.317	.457
1996 New Orleans	AAA	37	125	25	5	0	4	—	—	42	11	15	4	0	31	3	0	0	1	1	.50	2	.200	.242	.336
El Paso	AA	67	237	72	18	1	15	—	—	137	43	39	30	1	40	2	0	3	3	3	.50	5	.304	.382	.578
1997 Tucson	AAA	89	290	90	29	2	7	—	—	144	43	51	24	1	46	9	0	4	0	0	.00	9	.310	.376	.497
1998 Milwaukee	NL	85	218	50	7	2	9	(4	5)	88	28	29	16	1	54	1	1	1	1	2	.33	5	.229	.284	.404

Todd Hundley

Bats: Both **Throws:** Right **Pos:** LF-34; PH/PR-17; C-2 **Ht:** 5'11" **Wt:** 199 **Born:** 5/27/69 **Age:** 30

		BATTING																BASERUNNING				PERCENTAGES		
Year Team	Lg	G	AB	H	2B	3B	HR	(Hm	Rd)	TB	R	RBI	TBB	IBB	SO	HBP	SH	SF	SB	CS	SB%	GDP	Avg	OBP	SLG
1998 Mets *	R	1	2	0	0	0	0	—	—	0	0	0	2	0	1	0	0	0	0	0	.00	0	.000	.500	.000
St. Lucie *	A+	12	42	9	2	0	1	—	—	14	4	6	12	1	8	0	0	0	0	1	.00	1	.214	.389	.333
Norfolk *	AAA	10	30	13	1	0	4	—	—	26	9	15	14	1	10	0	0	0	0	0	.00	0	.433	.614	.867
1990 New York	NL	36	67	14	6	0	0	(0	0)	20	8	2	6	0	18	0	1	0	0	0	.00	1	.209	.274	.299
1991 New York	NL	21	60	8	0	1	1	(1	0)	13	5	7	6	0	14	1	1	1	0	0	.00	0	.133	.221	.217
1992 New York	NL	123	358	75	17	0	7	(2	5)	113	32	32	19	4	76	4	7	2	3	0	1.00	8	.209	.256	.316
1993 New York	NL	130	417	95	17	2	11	(5	6)	149	40	53	23	7	62	2	2	4	1	1	.50	10	.228	.269	.357
1994 New York	NL	91	291	69	10	1	16	(8	8)	129	45	42	25	4	73	3	3	1	2	0	1.00	4	.237	.303	.443
1995 New York	NL	90	275	77	11	0	15	(6	9)	133	39	51	42	5	64	5	1	3	1	0	1.00	4	.280	.382	.484
1996 New York	NL	153	540	140	32	1	41	(20	21)	297	85	112	79	15	146	3	0	2	1	3	.25	9	.259	.356	.550
1997 New York	NL	132	417	114	21	2	30	(14	16)	229	78	86	83	16	116	3	0	5	2	3	.40	10	.273	.394	.549
1998 New York	NL	53	124	20	4	0	3	(1	2)	33	8	12	16	0	55	1	0	1	1	1	.50	0	.161	.261	.266
9 ML YEARS		829	2549	612	118	7	124	(57	67)	1116	340	397	299	51	624	22	15	19	11	9	.55	48	.240	.323	.438

Brian Hunter

Bats: R **Throws:** L **Pos:** PH/PR-31; LF-16; RF-12; 1B-10; DH-1 **Ht:** 6'0" **Wt:** 225 **Born:** 3/4/68 **Age:** 31

		BATTING																BASERUNNING				PERCENTAGES		
Year Team	Lg	G	AB	H	2B	3B	HR	(Hm	Rd)	TB	R	RBI	TBB	IBB	SO	HBP	SH	SF	SB	CS	SB%	GDP	Avg	OBP	SLG
1998 Calgary *	AAA	11	31	3	1	0	0	—	—	4	1	6	2	1	9	2	0	2	0	0	.00	1	.097	.189	.129
1991 Atlanta	NL	97	271	68	16	1	12	(7	5)	122	32	50	17	0	48	1	0	2	0	2	.00	6	.251	.296	.450
1992 Atlanta	NL	102	238	57	13	2	14	(9	5)	116	34	41	21	3	50	0	1	8	1	2	.33	1	.239	.292	.487
1993 Atlanta	NL	37	80	11	3	1	0	(0	0)	16	4	8	2	1	15	0	0	3	0	0	.00	1	.138	.153	.200
1994 Pit-Cin	NL	85	256	60	16	1	15	(4	11)	123	34	57	17	2	56	0	0	5	0	0	.00	3	.234	.277	.480
1995 Cincinnati	NL	40	79	17	6	0	1	(0	1)	26	9	9	11	1	21	1	0	2	2	1	.67	1	.215	.312	.329
1996 Seattle	AL	75	198	53	10	0	7	(2	5)	84	21	28	15	2	43	4	1	3	1	0	.00	6	.268	.327	.424
1998 St. Louis	NL	62	112	23	9	1	4	(2	2)	46	11	19	7	0	23	1	3	0	1	1	.50	4	.205	.258	.411
1994 Pittsburgh	NL	76	233	53	15	1	11	(4	7)	103	28	47	15	2	55	0	0	4	0	0	.00	3	.227	.270	.442
Cincinnati	NL	9	23	7	1	0	4	(0	4)	20	6	10	2	0	1	0	0	1	0	0	.00	0	.304	.346	.870
7 ML YEARS		498	1234	289	73	6	53	(24	29)	533	145	206	90	9	256	7	5	23	4	7	.36	24	.234	.285	.432

Brian L. Hunter

Bats: Right **Throws:** Right **Pos:** CF-139; PH/PR-4 **Ht:** 6'3" **Wt:** 180 **Born:** 3/5/71 **Age:** 28

		BATTING																BASERUNNING				PERCENTAGES		
Year Team	Lg	G	AB	H	2B	3B	HR	(Hm	Rd)	TB	R	RBI	TBB	IBB	SO	HBP	SH	SF	SB	CS	SB%	GDP	Avg	OBP	SLG
1994 Houston	NL	6	24	6	1	0	0	(0	0)	7	2	0	1	0	6	0	1	0	2	1	.67	0	.250	.280	.292
1995 Houston	NL	78	321	97	14	5	2	(0	2)	127	52	28	21	0	52	2	2	3	24	7	.77	2	.302	.346	.396
1996 Houston	NL	132	526	145	27	2	5	(1	4)	191	74	35	17	0	92	2	1	7	35	9	.80	6	.276	.297	.363
1997 Detroit	AL	162	658	177	29	7	4	(2	2)	232	112	45	66	1	121	1	8	5	74	18	.80	13	.269	.334	.353
1998 Detroit	AL	142	595	151	29	3	4	(1	3)	198	67	36	36	0	94	2	2	1	42	12	.78	8	.254	.298	.333
5 ML YEARS		520	2124	576	100	17	15	(4	11)	755	307	144	141	1	365	7	14	16	177	47	.79	29	.271	.316	.355

Torii Hunter

Bats: Right **Throws:** Right **Pos:** CF-6; PH/PR-1 **Ht:** 6'2" **Wt:** 201 **Born:** 7/18/75 **Age:** 23

Year Team	Lg	G	AB	H	2B	3B	HR	(Hm	Rd)	TB	R	RBI	TBB	IBB	SO	HBP	SH	SF	SB	CS	SB%	GDP	Avg	OBP	SLG
1993 Twins	R	28	100	19	3	0	0	—	—	22	6	8	4	0	23	9	1	0	4	2	.67	1	.190	.283	.220
1994 Fort Wayne	A	91	335	98	17	1	10	—	—	147	57	50	25	1	80	10	0	2	8	10	.44	5	.293	.358	.439
1995 Fort Myers	A+	113	391	96	15	2	7	—	—	136	64	36	38	1	77	12	5	1	7	4	.64	8	.246	.330	.348
1996 Fort Myers	A+	4	16	3	0	0	0	—	—	3	1	1	2	0	5	0	0	0	1	1	.50	1	.188	.278	.188
Hardware City	AA	99	342	90	20	3	7	—	—	137	49	33	28	1	60	7	9	1	7	7	.50	7	.263	.331	.401
1997 New Britain	AA	127	471	109	22	2	8	—	—	159	57	56	47	1	94	3	6	1	8	8	.50	6	.231	.305	.338
1998 New Britain	AA	82	308	87	24	3	6	—	—	135	42	32	19	1	64	4	4	3	11	9	.55	2	.282	.329	.438
Salt Lake	AAA	26	92	31	7	0	4	—	—	50	15	20	1	0	13	1	2	1	2	2	.50	3	.337	.347	.543
1997 Minnesota	AL	1	0	0	0	0	0	(0	0)	0	0	0	0	0	0	0	0	0	0	0	.00	0	.000	.000	.000
1998 Minnesota	AL	6	17	4	1	0	0	(0	0)	5	0	2	2	0	6	0	0	0	0	1	.00	1	.235	.316	.294
2 ML YEARS		7	17	4	1	0	0	(0	0)	5	0	2	2	0	6	0	0	0	0	1	.00	1	.235	.316	.294

Butch Huskey

Bats: Right **Throws:** Right **Pos:** RF-103; PH/PR-16; DH-1 **Ht:** 6'3" **Wt:** 244 **Born:** 11/10/71 **Age:** 27

Year Team	Lg	G	AB	H	2B	3B	HR	(Hm	Rd)	TB	R	RBI	TBB	IBB	SO	HBP	SH	SF	SB	CS	SB%	GDP	Avg	OBP	SLG
1998 Norfolk *	AAA	2	8	2	0	0	0	—	—	2	0	3	0	0	1	0	0	1	0	0	.00	0	.250	.222	.250
1993 New York	NL	13	41	6	1	0	0	(0	0)	7	2	3	1	1	13	0	0	2	0	0	.00	0	.146	.159	.171
1995 New York	NL	28	90	17	1	0	3	(2	1)	27	8	11	10	0	16	0	1	1	1	0	1.00	3	.189	.267	.300
1996 New York	NL	118	414	115	16	2	15	(9	6)	180	43	60	27	3	77	0	0	4	1	2	.33	10	.278	.319	.435
1997 New York	NL	142	471	135	26	2	24	(7	17)	237	61	81	25	5	84	1	0	8	8	5	.62	21	.287	.319	.503
1998 New York	NL	113	369	93	18	0	13	(4	9)	150	43	59	26	3	66	1	2	4	7	6	.54	13	.252	.300	.407
5 ML YEARS		414	1385	366	62	4	55	(22	33)	601	157	214	89	12	256	2	3	19	17	13	.57	47	.264	.306	.434

Jeff Huson

Bats: L **Throws:** R **Pos:** PH/PR-9; 2B-8; 3B-8; 1B-7; DH-1; SS-1; RF-1 **Ht:** 6'1" **Wt:** 185 **Born:** 8/15/64 **Age:** 34

Year Team	Lg	G	AB	H	2B	3B	HR	(Hm	Rd)	TB	R	RBI	TBB	IBB	SO	HBP	SH	SF	SB	CS	SB%	GDP	Avg	OBP	SLG
1998 Tucson *	AAA	27	82	25	4	1	1	—	—	34	7	12	5	0	14	1	0	0	0	2	.00	0	.305	.352	.415
1988 Montreal	NL	20	42	13	2	0	0	(0	0)	15	7	3	4	2	3	0	0	0	2	1	.67	0	.310	.370	.357
1989 Montreal	NL	32	74	12	5	0	0	(0	0)	17	1	2	6	3	6	0	3	0	3	0	1.00	6	.162	.225	.230
1990 Texas	AL	145	396	95	12	2	0	(0	0)	111	57	28	46	0	54	2	7	3	12	4	.75	8	.240	.320	.280
1991 Texas	AL	119	268	57	8	3	2	(1	1)	77	36	26	39	0	32	0	9	1	8	3	.73	6	.213	.312	.287
1992 Texas	AL	123	318	83	14	3	4	(0	4)	115	49	24	41	2	43	1	8	6	18	6	.75	7	.261	.342	.362
1993 Texas	AL	23	45	6	1	0	0	(0	0)	9	3	2	0	0	10	0	1	0	0	0	.00	0	.133	.133	.200
1995 Baltimore	AL	66	161	40	4	2	1	(0	1)	51	24	19	15	1	20	1	2	1	5	4	.56	4	.248	.315	.317
1996 Baltimore	AL	17	28	9	1	0	0	(0	0)	10	5	2	1	0	3	0	0	1	0	0	.00	0	.321	.333	.357
1997 Milwaukee	AL	84	143	29	3	0	0	(0	0)	32	12	11	5	0	15	2	2	1	3	0	1.00	7	.203	.238	.224
1998 Seattle	AL	31	49	8	1	0	1	(0	1)	12	8	4	5	0	6	0	0	0	1	1	.50	0	.163	.241	.245
10 ML YEARS		660	1524	352	51	11	8	(1	7)	449	202	121	162	8	192	6	32	13	52	19	.73	40	.231	.305	.295

Mark Hutton

Pitches: Right **Bats:** Right **Pos:** RP-8; SP-2 **Ht:** 6'6" **Wt:** 240 **Born:** 2/6/70 **Age:** 29

Year Team	Lg	G	GS	CG	GF	IP	BFP	H	R	ER	HR	SH	SF	HB	TBB	IBB	SO	WP	Bk	W	L	Pct.	ShO	Sv-Op	Hld	ERA
1998 Indianapolis *	AAA	16	16	0	0	83.1	370	91	50	41	7	3	4	5	37	0	47	4	0	4	6	.400	0	0-	—	4.43
1993 New York	AL	7	4	0	2	22	104	24	17	14	2	2	2	1	17	0	12	0	0	1	1	.500	0	0-0	0	5.73
1994 New York	AL	2	0	0	1	3.2	16	4	3	2	0	0	0	0	1	0	1	0	0	0	0	.000	0	0-0	0	4.91
1996 NYA-Fla		25	11	0	5	86.2	374	79	42	40	9	0	3	4	36	1	56	2	0	5	3	.625	0	0-0	1	4.15
1997 Fla-Col	NL	40	1	0	9	60.1	272	72	34	30	10	7	4	6	26	3	39	3	1	3	2	.600	0	0-3	4	4.48
1998 Cincinnati	NL	10	2	0	2	17	87	24	14	14	2	0	0	1	17	0	3	1	0	0	0	.000	0	0-0	0	7.41
1996 New York	AL	12	2	0	5	30.1	140	32	19	17	3	0	2	1	18	1	25	0	0	0	2	.000	0	0-0	1	5.04
Florida	NL	13	9	0	0	56.1	234	47	23	23	6	0	1	3	18	0	31	2	0	5	1	.833	0	0-0	0	3.67
1997 Florida	NL	32	0	0	9	47.2	204	50	24	20	7	5	3	2	19	3	29	3	1	3	1	.750	0	0-2	3	3.78
Colorado	NL	8	1	0	0	12.2	68	22	10	10	3	2	1	4	7	0	10	0	0	0	1	.000	0	0-1	1	7.11
5 ML YEARS		84	18	0	19	189.2	853	203	110	100	23	9	9	12	96	4	111	6	1	9	7	.563	0	0-3	5	4.75

Raul Ibanez

Bats: L **Throws:** R **Pos:** 1B-16; RF-12; PH/PR-9; LF-6; DH-1 **Ht:** 6'2" **Wt:** 200 **Born:** 6/2/72 **Age:** 27

Year Team	Lg	G	AB	H	2B	3B	HR	(Hm	Rd)	TB	R	RBI	TBB	IBB	SO	HBP	SH	SF	SB	CS	SB%	GDP	Avg	OBP	SLG
1992 Mariners	R	33	120	37	8	2	1	—	—	52	25	16	9	1	18	2	0	0	1	2	.33	3	.308	.366	.433
1993 Appleton	A	52	157	43	9	0	5	—	—	67	26	21	24	2	31	1	1	2	0	2	.00	2	.274	.370	.427
Bellingham	A-	43	134	38	5	2	0	—	—	47	16	15	21	1	23	0	0	1	0	3	.00	0	.284	.378	.351
1994 Appleton	A	91	327	102	30	3	7	—	—	159	55	59	32	3	37	2	0	2	10	5	.67	8	.312	.375	.486
1995 Riverside	A+	95	361	120	23	9	20	—	—	221	59	108	41	1	49	2	1	9	4	3	.57	7	.332	.395	.612
1996 Port City	AA	19	76	28	8	1	1	—	—	41	12	13	8	1	7	0	0	1	3	2	.60	1	.368	.424	.539
Tacoma	AAA	111	405	115	20	3	11	—	—	174	59	47	44	2	56	2	0	5	7	7	.50	4	.284	.353	.430
1997 Tacoma	AAA	111	438	133	30	5	15	—	—	218	84	84	32	1	75	1	3	4	7	5	.58	12	.304	.349	.498
1998 Tacoma	AAA	52	190	41	8	1	6	—	—	69	24	25	24	2	47	1	0	3	1	1	.50	3	.216	.301	.363

		BATTING																	BASERUNNING				PERCENTAGES		
Year Team	Lg	G	AB	H	2B	3B	HR	(Hm	Rd)	TB	R	RBI	TBB	IBB	SO	HBP	SH	SF	SB	CS	SB%	GDP	Avg	OBP	SLG
1996 Seattle	AL	4	5	0	0	0	0	(0	0)	0	0	0	0	0	1	1	0	0	0	0	.00	0	.000	.167	.000
1997 Seattle	AL	11	26	4	0	1	1	(1	0)	9	3	4	0	0	6	0	0	0	0	0	.00	0	.154	.154	.346
1998 Seattle	AL	37	98	25	7	1	2	(1	1)	40	12	12	5	0	22	0	0	0	0	0	.00	4	.255	.291	.408
3 ML YEARS		52	129	29	7	2	3	(2	1)	49	15	16	5	0	29	1	0	0	0	0	.00	4	.225	.259	.380

Pete Incaviglia

Bats: Right **Throws:** Right **Pos:** PH/PR-14; DH-4; LF-4   **Ht:** 6'1" **Wt:** 225 **Born:** 4/2/64 **Age:** 35

		BATTING																	BASERUNNING				PERCENTAGES		
Year Team	Lg	G	AB	H	2B	3B	HR	(Hm	Rd)	TB	R	RBI	TBB	IBB	SO	HBP	SH	SF	SB	CS	SB%	GDP	Avg	OBP	SLG
1998 New Orleans *	AAA	76	281	91	10	1	23	—	—	172	57	66	34	0	63	9	0	2	11	3	.79	9	.324	.411	.612
1986 Texas	AL	153	540	135	21	2	30	(17	13)	250	82	88	55	2	185	4	0	7	3	2	.60	9	.250	.320	.463
1987 Texas	AL	139	509	138	26	4	27	(11	16)	253	85	80	48	1	168	1	0	5	9	3	.75	8	.271	.332	.497
1988 Texas	AL	116	418	104	19	3	22	(12	10)	195	59	54	39	3	153	7	0	3	6	4	.60	6	.249	.321	.467
1989 Texas	AL	133	453	107	27	4	21	(13	8)	205	48	81	32	0	136	6	0	4	5	7	.42	12	.236	.293	.453
1990 Texas	AL	153	529	123	27	0	24	(15	9)	222	59	85	45	5	146	9	0	4	3	4	.43	18	.233	.302	.420
1991 Detroit	AL	97	337	72	12	1	11	(6	5)	119	38	38	36	0	92	1	1	2	1	3	.25	6	.214	.290	.353
1992 Houston	NL	113	349	93	22	1	11	(6	5)	150	31	44	25	2	99	3	0	2	2	2	.50	6	.266	.319	.430
1993 Philadelphia	NL	116	368	101	16	3	24	(15	9)	195	60	89	21	1	82	6	0	7	1	1	.50	9	.274	.318	.530
1994 Philadelphia	NL	80	244	56	10	1	13	(6	7)	107	28	32	16	3	71	1	0	2	1	0	1.00	3	.230	.278	.439
1996 Phi-Bal		111	302	73	9	2	18	(6	12)	140	37	50	30	2	89	4	0	1	2	0	1.00	6	.242	.318	.464
1997 Bal-NYA	AL	53	154	38	4	0	5	(2	3)	57	19	12	11	2	46	3	0	1	0	0	.00	1	.247	.308	.370
1998 Det-Hou		20	30	3	1	0	0	(0	0)	4	0	2	2	0	10	0	0	0	0	0	.00	1	.100	.156	.133
1996 Philadelphia	NL	99	269	63	7	2	16	(6	10)	122	33	42	30	2	82	3	0	0	2	0	1.00	6	.234	.318	.454
Baltimore	AL	12	33	10	2	0	2	(0	2)	18	4	8	0	0	7	1	0	1	0	0	.00	0	.303	.314	.545
1997 Baltimore	AL	48	138	34	4	0	5	(2	3)	53	18	12	11	2	43	3	0	1	0	0	.00	1	.246	.314	.384
New York	AL	5	16	4	0	0	0	(0	0)	4	1	0	0	0	3	0	0	0	0	0	.00	0	.250	.250	.250
1998 Detroit	AL	7	14	1	0	0	0	(0	0)	1	0	0	1	0	6	0	0	0	0	0	.00	0	.071	.133	.071
Houston	NL	13	16	2	1	0	0	(0	0)	3	0	2	1	0	4	0	0	0	0	0	.00	1	.125	.176	.188
12 ML YEARS		1284	4233	1043	194	21	206	(109	97)	1897	546	655	360	21	1277	45	1	38	33	26	.56	85	.246	.310	.448

Hideki Irabu

Pitches: Right **Bats:** Right **Pos:** SP-28; RP-1   **Ht:** 6'4" **Wt:** 240 **Born:** 5/5/69 **Age:** 30

		HOW MUCH HE PITCHED					WHAT HE GAVE UP											THE RESULTS					
Year Team	Lg	G	GS	CG	GF	IP	BFP	H	R	ER	HR	SH	SF	HB	TBB	IBB	SO	WP	Bk	W	L	Pct.	ShO	Sv-Op	Hld	ERA
1997 Tampa	A+	2	2	0	0	9	29	4	0	0	0	0	0	0	0	0	12	0	3	1	0	1.000	0	0- —	—	0.00
Norwich	AA	2	2	0	0	10	41	13	5	5	1	0	0	0	0	0	9	0	1	1	1	.500	0	0- —	—	4.50
Columbus	AAA	4	4	1	0	27	101	19	7	5	1	1	1	0	5	0	28	2	3	2	0	1.000	1	0- —	—	1.67
1997 New York	AL	13	9	0	0	53.1	246	69	47	42	15	1	2	1	20	0	56	4	3	5	4	.556	0	0-0	1	7.09
1998 New York	AL	29	28	2	0	173	732	148	79	78	27	6	6	9	76	1	126	6	1	13	9	.591	1	0-0	0	4.06
2 ML YEARS		42	37	2	0	226.1	978	217	126	120	42	7	8	10	96	1	182	10	4	18	13	.581	1	0-0	1	4.77

Jason Isringhausen

Pitches: Right **Bats:** Right **Pos:** SP   **Ht:** 6'3" **Wt:** 210 **Born:** 9/7/72 **Age:** 26

		HOW MUCH HE PITCHED					WHAT HE GAVE UP											THE RESULTS					
Year Team	Lg	G	GS	CG	GF	IP	BFP	H	R	ER	HR	SH	SF	HB	TBB	IBB	SO	WP	Bk	W	L	Pct.	ShO	Sv-Op	Hld	ERA
1995 New York	NL	14	14	1	0	93	385	88	29	29	6	3	3	2	31	2	55	4	1	9	2	.818	1	0-0	0	2.81
1996 New York	NL	27	27	2	0	171.2	766	190	103	91	13	7	9	8	73	5	114	14	0	6	14	.300	1	0-0	0	4.77
1997 New York	NL	6	6	0	0	29.2	145	40	27	25	3	1	2	1	22	0	25	3	0	2	2	.500	0	0-0	0	7.58
3 ML YEARS		47	47	3	0	294.1	1296	318	159	145	22	11	14	11	126	7	194	21	1	17	18	.486	1	0-0	0	4.43

Damian Jackson

Bats: Right **Throws:** Right **Pos:** SS-10; CF-3; PH/PR-1   **Ht:** 5'11" **Wt:** 185 **Born:** 8/16/73 **Age:** 25

		BATTING																	BASERUNNING				PERCENTAGES		
Year Team	Lg	G	AB	H	2B	3B	HR	(Hm	Rd)	TB	R	RBI	TBB	IBB	SO	HBP	SH	SF	SB	CS	SB%	GDP	Avg	OBP	SLG
1992 Burlington	R+	62	226	56	12	1	0	—	—	70	32	23	32	0	31	6	6	3	29	5	.85	1	.248	.352	.310
1993 Columbus	A	108	350	94	19	3	6	—	—	137	70	45	41	0	61	5	5	1	26	7	.79	1	.269	.353	.391
1994 Canton-Akrn	AA	138	531	143	29	5	5	—	—	197	85	46	60	2	121	6	5	5	37	16	.70	8	.269	.346	.371
1995 Canton-Akrn	AA	131	484	120	20	2	3	—	—	153	67	34	65	0	103	9	7	0	40	22	.65	6	.248	.348	.316
1996 Buffalo	AAA	133	452	116	15	1	12	—	—	169	77	49	48	0	78	7	8	6	24	7	.77	7	.257	.333	.374
1997 Buffalo	AAA	73	266	78	12	0	4	—	—	102	51	13	37	2	45	3	3	2	20	8	.71	2	.293	.383	.383
Indianapolis	AAA	19	71	19	6	1	0	—	—	27	12	7	10	0	17	1	0	1	4	1	.80	1	.268	.361	.380
1998 Indianapolis	AAA	131	517	135	36	10	6	—	—	209	102	49	62	0	125	10	3	4	25	10	.71	2	.261	.349	.404
1996 Cleveland	AL	5	10	3	0	0	0	(0	0)	5	2	1	1	0	4	0	0	0	0	0	.00	0	.300	.364	.500
1997 Cle-Cin		20	36	7	2	1	1	(0	1)	14	8	2	4	1	8	1	1	0	2	1	.67	0	.194	.293	.389
1998 Cincinnati	NL	13	38	12	5	0	0	(0	0)	17	4	7	6	0	4	0	0	1	2	0	1.00	0	.316	.400	.447
1997 Cleveland	AL	8	9	1	0	0	0	(0	0)	1	2	0	0	0	1	1	0	0	1	0	1.00	0	.111	.200	.111
Cincinnati	NL	12	27	6	2	1	1	(0	1)	13	6	2	4	1	7	0	1	0	1	1	.50	0	.222	.323	.481
3 ML YEARS		38	84	22	9	1	1	(0	1)	36	14	10	11	1	16	1	1	1	4	1	.80	0	.262	.351	.429

107

Darrin Jackson

Bats: R **Throws:** R **Pos:** LF-55; CF-43; PH/PR-34; RF-5; DH-2 **Ht:** 6'0" **Wt:** 191 **Born:** 8/22/63 **Age:** 35

								BATTING											BASERUNNING				PERCENTAGES		
Year Team	Lg	G	AB	H	2B	3B	HR	(Hm	Rd)	TB	R	RBI	TBB	IBB	SO	HBP	SH	SF	SB	CS	SB%	GDP	Avg	OBP	SLG
1985 Chicago	NL	5	11	1	0	0	0	(0	0)	1	0	0	0	0	3	0	0	0	0	0	.00	0	.091	.091	.091
1987 Chicago	NL	7	5	4	0	0	0	(0	0)	5	2	0	0	0	0	0	0	0	0	0	.00	0	.800	.800	1.000
1988 Chicago	NL	100	188	50	11	3	6	(3	3)	85	29	20	5	1	28	1	2	1	4	1	.80	3	.266	.287	.452
1989 ChN-SD	NL	70	170	37	7	0	4	(1	3)	56	17	20	13	5	34	0	0	2	1	4	.20	2	.218	.270	.329
1990 San Diego	NL	58	113	29	3	0	3	(1	2)	41	10	9	5	1	24	0	1	1	3	0	1.00	1	.257	.286	.363
1991 San Diego	NL	122	359	94	12	1	21	(12	9)	171	51	49	27	2	66	2	3	3	5	3	.63	5	.262	.315	.476
1992 San Diego	NL	155	587	146	23	5	17	(11	6)	230	72	70	26	4	106	4	6	5	14	3	.82	21	.249	.283	.392
1993 Tor-NYN		77	263	55	9	0	6	(4	2)	82	19	26	10	0	75	0	0	4	1	2	.00	9	.209	.237	.312
1994 Chicago	AL	104	369	115	17	3	10	(4	6)	168	43	51	27	3	56	3	2	2	7	1	.88	5	.312	.362	.455
1997 Min-Mil	AL	75	211	55	9	1	5	(4	1)	81	26	36	6	0	31	0	5	2	4	1	.80	5	.261	.279	.384
1998 Milwaukee	AL	114	204	49	13	1	4	(2	2)	76	20	20	9	0	37	1	0	1	1	1	.50	5	.240	.276	.373
1989 Chicago	NL	45	83	19	4	0	1	(0	1)	26	7	8	6	1	17	0	0	0	1	2	.33	1	.229	.281	.313
San Diego		25	87	18	3	0	3	(1	2)	30	10	12	7	4	17	0	0	2	0	2	.00	1	.207	.260	.345
1993 Toronto	AL	46	176	38	8	0	5	(4	1)	61	15	19	8	0	53	0	5	0	0	2	.00	5	.216	.250	.347
New York	NL	31	87	17	1	0	1	(0	1)	21	4	7	2	0	22	0	1	1	0	0	.00	9	.195	.211	.241
1997 Minnesota	AL	49	130	33	2	1	3	(3	0)	46	19	21	4	0	21	0	3	2	2	1	1.00	0	.254	.272	.354
Milwaukee	AL	26	81	22	7	0	2	(1	1)	35	7	15	2	0	10	0	2	0	2	1	.67	3	.272	.289	.432
11 ML YEARS		887	2480	635	105	14	76	(42	34)	996	289	301	128	16	460	11	25	17	39	16	.71	56	.256	.294	.402

Mike Jackson

Pitches: Right **Bats:** Right **Pos:** RP-69 **Ht:** 6'2" **Wt:** 225 **Born:** 12/22/64 **Age:** 34

		HOW MUCH HE PITCHED						WHAT HE GAVE UP												THE RESULTS					
Year Team	Lg	G	GS	CG	GF	IP	BFP	H	R	ER	HR	SH	SF	HB	TBB	IBB	SO	WP	Bk	W	L	Pct.	ShO	Sv-Op	Hld	ERA
1986 Philadelphia	NL	9	0	0	4	13.1	54	12	5	5	2	0	0	2	4	1	3	0	0	0	0	.000	0	0-1	0	3.38
1987 Philadelphia	NL	55	7	0	8	109.1	468	88	55	51	16	3	4	3	56	6	93	6	8	3	10	.231	0	1-2	6	4.20
1988 Seattle	AL	62	0	0	29	99.1	412	74	37	29	10	3	10	2	43	10	76	6	6	6	5	.545	0	4-11	10	2.63
1989 Seattle	AL	65	0	0	27	99.1	431	81	43	35	8	6	2	6	54	6	94	1	2	4	6	.400	0	7-10	9	3.17
1990 Seattle	AL	63	0	0	28	77.1	338	64	42	39	8	8	5	2	44	12	69	9	2	5	7	.417	0	3-12	13	4.54
1991 Seattle	AL	72	0	0	35	88.2	363	64	35	32	5	4	0	6	34	11	74	3	0	7	7	.500	0	14-22	9	3.25
1992 San Francisco	NL	67	0	0	24	82	346	76	35	34	7	5	2	4	33	10	80	1	0	6	6	.500	0	2-3	9	3.73
1993 San Francisco	NL	81	0	0	17	77.1	317	58	28	26	7	4	2	3	24	6	70	2	2	6	6	.500	0	1-6	34	3.03
1994 Seattle	AL	36	0	0	12	42.1	158	23	8	7	4	4	2	1	11	0	51	0	0	3	2	.600	0	4-6	9	1.49
1995 Cincinnati	NL	40	0	0	10	49	200	38	13	13	5	1	1	1	19	1	41	1	1	1	6	.857	0	2-4	9	2.39
1996 Seattle	AL	73	0	0	23	72	302	61	32	29	11	0	1	6	24	3	70	2	0	1	1	.500	0	6-8	15	3.63
1997 Cleveland	AL	71	0	0	38	75	313	59	33	27	3	3	4	3	29	5	74	2	0	5	5	.286	0	15-17	14	3.24
1998 Cleveland	AL	69	0	0	57	64	239	43	11	11	4	1	0	4	13	0	55	1	3	1	1	.500	0	40-45	1	1.55
13 ML YEARS		763	7	0	312	949	3941	741	377	338	90	42	31	45	388	71	850	34	24	50	57	.467	0	99-147	138	3.21

Ryan Jackson

Bats: L **Throws:** L **Pos:** 1B-44; PH/PR-38; RF-23; LF-10; DH-5 **Ht:** 6'3" **Wt:** 185 **Born:** 11/11/71 **Age:** 27

								BATTING											BASERUNNING				PERCENTAGES		
Year Team	Lg	G	AB	H	2B	3B	HR	(Hm	Rd)	TB	R	RBI	TBB	IBB	SO	HBP	SH	SF	SB	CS	SB%	GDP	Avg	OBP	SLG
1994 Elmira	A-	72	276	80	18	1	6	—	—	118	46	41	22	1	40	1	0	6	4	3	.57	2	.290	.338	.428
1995 Kane County	A	132	471	138	39	6	10	—	—	219	78	82	67	7	74	4	0	5	13	8	.62	9	.293	.382	.465
1996 Marlins	R	7	25	9	0	0	0	—	—	9	5	5	1	0	3	1	0	0	2	0	1.00	0	.360	.407	.360
Brevard Cty	A+	6	26	8	2	0	1	—	—	13	4	4	1	0	7	0	0	0	1	0	1.00	0	.308	.333	.500
1997 Portland	AA	134	491	153	28	4	26	—	—	267	87	98	51	2	85	3	1	0	2	5	.29	6	.312	.380	.544
1998 Charlotte	AAA	13	50	19	4	0	2	—	—	29	5	11	4	0	14	0	0	0	2	0	1.00	1	.380	.426	.580
1998 Florida	NL	111	260	65	15	1	5	(3	2)	97	26	31	20	0	73	1	2	1	1	1	.50	3	.250	.305	.373

Jason Jacome

Pitches: Left **Bats:** Left **Pos:** SP-1 **Ht:** 6'1" **Wt:** 185 **Born:** 11/24/70 **Age:** 28

		HOW MUCH HE PITCHED						WHAT HE GAVE UP												THE RESULTS					
Year Team	Lg	G	GS	CG	GF	IP	BFP	H	R	ER	HR	SH	SF	HB	TBB	IBB	SO	WP	Bk	W	L	Pct.	ShO	Sv-Op	Hld	ERA
1998 Buffalo *	AAA	24	24	2	0	154.2	642	161	62	56	13	2	2	3	38	0	109	5	1	14	2	.875	0	0- —	—	3.26
1994 New York	NL	8	8	1	0	54	222	54	17	16	3	3	1	0	17	2	30	2	0	4	3	.571	1	0-0	0	2.67
1995 NYN-KC		20	19	1	0	105	474	134	76	74	18	3	4	2	36	2	50	1	1	4	10	.286	0	0-0	0	6.34
1996 Kansas City	AL	49	2	0	21	47.2	226	67	27	25	5	3	0	2	22	5	32	1	0	0	4	.000	0	1-4	6	4.72
1997 KC-Cle	AL	28	4	0	2	49.1	218	58	33	32	10	0	1	1	20	5	27	2	0	2	0	1.000	0	0-1	1	5.84
1998 Cleveland	AL	1	1	0	0	5	26	10	8	8	2	0	0	3	0	2	0	0	1	0	1.000	0	0-0		14.40
1995 New York	NL	5	5	0	0	21	110	33	24	24	3	1	1		15	0	11	1	0	0	4	.000	0	0-0	0	10.29
Kansas City	AL	15	14	1	0	84	364	101	52	50	15	2	3	1	21	2	39	0	1	4	6	.400	0	0-0	0	5.36
1997 Kansas City	AL	7	0	0	0	6.2	35	13	7	7	2	0	0	1	5	1	3	0	0	0	0	.000	0	0-0	0	9.45
Cleveland	AL	21	4	0	2	42.2	183	45	26	25	8	0	1	0	15	4	24	2	0	2	0	1.000	0	0-1	1	5.27
5 ML YEARS		106	34	2	23	261	1166	323	161	155	38	9	6	5	98	14	141	6	1	10	18	.357	1	1-5	7	5.34

John Jaha

Bats: Right **Throws:** Right **Pos:** 1B-57; PH/PR-9; DH-8   **Ht:** 6'1" **Wt:** 224 **Born:** 5/27/66 **Age:** 33

		BATTING															**BASERUNNING**				**PERCENTAGES**			
Year Team *	Lg	G	AB	H	2B	3B	HR	(Hm | Rd)	TB	R	RBI	TBB	IBB	SO	HBP	SH	SF	SB	CS	SB%	GDP	Avg	OBP	SLG
1998 Beloit *	A	2	4	0	0	0	0	—	—	0	1	0	2	0	2	1	0	0	0	0	.00	0	.000	.429	.000
1992 Milwaukee	AL	47	133	30	3	1	2	(1 | 1)	41	17	10	12	1	30	2	1	4	10	0	1.00	1	.226	.291	.308
1993 Milwaukee	AL	153	515	136	21	0	19	(5 | 14)	214	78	70	51	4	109	8	4	4	13	9	.59	6	.264	.337	.416
1994 Milwaukee	AL	84	291	70	14	0	12	(5 | 7)	120	45	39	32	3	75	10	1	4	3	3	.50	8	.241	.332	.412
1995 Milwaukee	AL	88	316	99	20	2	20	(8 | 12)	183	59	65	36	0	66	4	0	1	2	1	.67	4	.313	.389	.579
1996 Milwaukee	AL	148	543	163	28	1	34	(17 | 17)	295	108	118	85	1	118	5	0	3	1	3	.25	16	.300	.398	.543
1997 Milwaukee	AL	46	162	40	7	0	11	(1 | 10)	80	25	26	25	1	40	3	0	2	1	0	1.00	6	.247	.354	.494
1998 Milwaukee	NL	73	216	45	6	1	7	(2 | 5)	74	29	38	49	3	66	6	0	2	1	3	.25	5	.208	.366	.343
7 ML YEARS		639	2176	583	99	5	105	(39 | 66)	1007	361	366	290	13	504	38	6	20	33	17	.66	50	.268	.361	.463

Mike James

Pitches: Right **Bats:** Right **Pos:** RP-11   **Ht:** 6'3" **Wt:** 180 **Born:** 8/15/67 **Age:** 31

		HOW MUCH HE PITCHED						**WHAT HE GAVE UP**										**THE RESULTS**						
Year Team	Lg	G	GS	CG	GF	IP	BFP	H	R	ER	HR	SH	SF	HB	TBB	IBB	SO	WP	Bk	W	L	Pct.	ShO	Sv-Op Hld	ERA
1995 California	AL	46	0	0	11	55.2	237	49	27	24	6	2	0	3	26	2	36	1	0	3	0	1.000	0	1-2 3	3.88
1996 California	AL	69	0	0	23	81	353	62	27	24	7	6	5	10	42	7	65	5	0	5	5	.500	0	1-6 18	2.67
1997 Anaheim	AL	58	0	0	22	62.2	284	69	32	30	3	6	1	5	28	4	57	1	0	5	5	.500	0	7-13 12	4.31
1998 Anaheim	AL	11	0	0	3	14	55	10	3	3	0	0	0	0	7	0	12	0	0	0	0	.000	0	0-0 2	1.93
4 ML YEARS		184	0	0	59	213.1	929	190	89	81	16	14	6	18	103	13	170	7	0	13	10	.565	0	9-21 35	3.42

Stan Javier

Bats: B **Throws:** R **Pos:** RF-95; CF-29; PH/PR-20; LF-6   **Ht:** 6'0" **Wt:** 195 **Born:** 1/9/64 **Age:** 35

		BATTING															**BASERUNNING**				**PERCENTAGES**			
Year Team	Lg	G	AB	H	2B	3B	HR	(Hm | Rd)	TB	R	RBI	TBB	IBB	SO	HBP	SH	SF	SB	CS	SB%	GDP	Avg	OBP	SLG
1984 New York	AL	7	7	1	0	0	0	(0 | 0)	1	1	0	0	0	1	0	0	0	0	0	.00	0	.143	.143	.143
1986 Oakland	AL	59	114	23	8	0	0	(0 | 0)	31	13	8	16	0	27	1	0	0	8	0	1.00	2	.202	.305	.272
1987 Oakland	AL	81	151	28	3	1	2	(1 | 1)	39	22	9	19	3	33	0	6	0	3	2	.60	2	.185	.276	.258
1988 Oakland	AL	125	397	102	13	3	2	(0 | 2)	127	49	35	32	1	63	2	6	3	20	1	.95	13	.257	.313	.320
1989 Oakland	AL	112	310	77	12	3	1	(1 | 0)	98	42	28	31	1	45	1	4	2	12	2	.86	6	.248	.317	.316
1990 Oak-LA		123	309	92	9	6	3	(1 | 2)	122	60	27	40	2	50	0	6	2	15	7	.68	6	.298	.376	.395
1991 Los Angeles	NL	121	176	36	5	3	1	(0 | 1)	50	21	11	16	0	36	0	3	2	7	1	.88	4	.205	.268	.284
1992 LA-Phi	NL	130	334	83	17	1	1	(1 | 0)	105	42	29	37	2	54	3	3	2	18	3	.86	4	.249	.327	.314
1993 California	NL	92	237	69	10	4	3	(0 | 3)	96	33	28	27	1	33	1	1	3	12	2	.86	7	.291	.362	.405
1994 Oakland	AL	109	419	114	23	0	10	(1 | 9)	167	75	44	49	1	76	2	7	3	24	7	.77	7	.272	.349	.399
1995 Oakland	AL	130	442	123	20	2	8	(3 | 5)	171	81	56	49	3	63	4	5	4	36	5	.88	8	.278	.353	.387
1996 San Francisco	NL	71	274	74	25	0	2	(1 | 1)	105	44	22	25	0	51	2	5	0	14	2	.88	4	.270	.336	.383
1997 San Francisco	NL	142	440	126	16	4	8	(6 | 2)	174	69	50	56	1	70	5	2	7	25	3	.89	5	.286	.368	.395
1998 San Francisco	NL	135	417	121	13	5	4	(1 | 3)	156	63	49	65	4	63	1	4	3	21	5	.81	13	.290	.385	.374
1990 Oakland	AL	19	33	8	0	2	0	(0 | 0)	12	4	3	3	0	6	0	0	0	0	0	.00	0	.242	.306	.364
Los Angeles	NL	104	276	84	9	4	3	(1 | 2)	110	56	24	37	2	44	0	6	2	15	7	.68	6	.304	.384	.399
1992 Los Angeles	NL	56	58	11	3	0	1	(1 | 0)	17	6	5	6	2	11	1	1	0	1	2	.33	0	.190	.277	.293
Philadelphia	NL	74	276	72	14	1	0	(0 | 0)	88	36	24	31	0	43	2	2	2	17	1	.94	4	.261	.338	.319
14 ML YEARS		1437	4027	1069	174	32	45	(16 | 29)	1442	615	396	462	19	665	22	52	31	215	40	.84	81	.265	.342	.358

Gregg Jefferies

Bats: Both **Throws:** Right **Pos:** LF-136; PH/PR-7; 1B-3   **Ht:** 5'10" **Wt:** 185 **Born:** 8/1/67 **Age:** 31

		BATTING															**BASERUNNING**				**PERCENTAGES**			
Year Team	Lg	G	AB	H	2B	3B	HR	(Hm | Rd)	TB	R	RBI	TBB	IBB	SO	HBP	SH	SF	SB	CS	SB%	GDP	Avg	OBP	SLG
1987 New York	NL	6	6	3	1	0	0	(0 | 0)	4	0	2	0	0	0	0	0	0	0	0	.00	0	.500	.500	.667
1988 New York	NL	29	109	35	8	2	6	(3 | 3)	65	19	17	8	0	10	0	0	1	5	1	.83	1	.321	.364	.596
1989 New York	NL	141	508	131	28	2	12	(7 | 5)	199	72	56	39	8	46	5	2	5	21	6	.78	16	.258	.314	.392
1990 New York	NL	153	604	171	40	3	15	(6 | 9)	262	96	68	46	2	40	5	0	4	11	2	.85	12	.283	.337	.434
1991 New York	NL	136	486	132	19	2	9	(5 | 4)	182	59	62	47	2	38	2	1	3	26	5	.84	12	.272	.336	.374
1992 Kansas City	AL	152	604	172	36	3	10	(3 | 7)	244	66	75	43	4	29	1	0	9	19	9	.68	24	.285	.329	.404
1993 St. Louis	NL	142	544	186	24	3	16	(10 | 6)	264	89	83	62	7	32	2	0	4	46	9	.84	15	.342	.408	.485
1994 St. Louis	NL	103	397	129	27	1	12	(7 | 5)	194	52	55	45	12	26	1	0	4	12	5	.71	9	.325	.391	.489
1995 Philadelphia	NL	114	480	147	31	2	11	(4 | 7)	215	69	56	35	5	26	0	0	5	9	5	.64	15	.306	.349	.448
1996 Philadelphia	NL	104	404	118	17	3	7	(4 | 3)	162	59	51	36	6	21	1	0	5	20	6	.77	9	.292	.348	.401
1997 Philadelphia	NL	130	476	122	25	3	11	(4 | 7)	186	68	48	53	7	27	2	0	0	12	6	.67	8	.256	.333	.391
1998 Phi-Ana		144	555	167	28	3	9	(3 | 6)	228	72	58	29	4	32	1	1	6	12	3	.80	19	.301	.333	.411
1998 Philadelphia	NL	125	483	142	22	3	8	(3 | 5)	194	65	48	29	4	27	1	1	6	11	3	.79	17	.294	.331	.402
Anaheim	AL	19	72	25	6	0	1	(0 | 1)	34	7	10	0	0	5	0	0	0	1	0	1.00	2	.347	.347	.472
12 ML YEARS		1354	5173	1513	284	27	118	(57 | 61)	2205	721	631	443	57	327	20	4	47	193	57	.77	140	.292	.348	.426

Reggie Jefferson

Bats: Left **Throws:** Left **Pos:** DH-48; PH/PR-8; 1B-7 **Ht:** 6'4" **Wt:** 215 **Born:** 9/25/68 **Age:** 30

Year Team	Lg	G	AB	H	2B	3B	HR	(Hm Rd)	TB	R	RBI	TBB	IBB	SO	HBP	SH	SF	SB	CS	SB%	GDP	Avg	OBP	SLG
1998 Red Sox *	R	1	4	0	0	0	0	— —	0	0	0	0	0	1	0	0	0	0	0	.00	0	.000	.000	.000
Sarasota *	A+	4	14	5	0	0	0	— —	5	2	2	1	0	3	0	0	0	0	0	.00	1	.357	.400	.357
1991 Cin-Cle	R	31	108	21	3	0	3	(2 1)	33	11	13	4	0	24	0	0	1	0	0	.00	1	.194	.221	.306
1992 Cleveland	AL	24	89	30	6	2	1	(1 0)	43	8	6	1	0	17	1	0	0	0	0	.00	2	.337	.352	.483
1993 Cleveland	AL	113	366	91	11	2	10	(4 6)	136	35	34	28	7	78	5	3	1	1	3	.25	7	.249	.310	.372
1994 Seattle	AL	63	162	53	11	0	8	(4 4)	88	24	32	17	5	32	1	0	1	0	0	.00	6	.327	.392	.543
1995 Boston	AL	46	121	35	8	0	5	(1 4)	58	21	26	9	1	24	1	0	2	0	0	.00	3	.289	.333	.479
1996 Boston	AL	122	386	134	30	4	19	(12 7)	229	67	74	25	5	89	3	0	4	0	0	.00	11	.347	.388	.593
1997 Boston	AL	136	489	156	33	1	13	(6 7)	230	74	67	24	5	93	7	1	3	1	2	.33	17	.319	.358	.470
1998 Boston	AL	62	196	60	16	1	8	(2 6)	102	24	31	21	2	40	1	0	1	0	0	.00	7	.306	.374	.470
1991 Cincinnati	NL	5	7	1	0	0	1	(1 0)	4	1	1	1	0	2	0	0	0	0	0	.00	0	.143	.250	.571
Cleveland	AL	26	101	20	3	0	2	(1 1)	29	10	12	3	0	22	0	0	1	0	0	.00	1	.198	.219	.287
8 ML YEARS		597	1917	580	118	10	67	(32 35)	919	264	283	129	25	397	18	4	13	2	5	.29	54	.303	.350	.479

Geoff Jenkins

Bats: Left **Throws:** Right **Pos:** LF-81; PH/PR-11; RF-1 **Ht:** 6'1" **Wt:** 200 **Born:** 7/21/74 **Age:** 24

Year Team	Lg	G	AB	H	2B	3B	HR	(Hm Rd)	TB	R	RBI	TBB	IBB	SO	HBP	SH	SF	SB	CS	SB%	GDP	Avg	OBP	SLG
1995 Helena	R+	7	28	9	0	1	0	— —	11	2	9	3	0	11	0	0	1	0	2	.00	0	.321	.375	.393
Stockton	A+	13	47	12	2	0	3	— —	23	13	12	10	0	12	0	0	2	2	0	1.00	0	.255	.373	.489
El Paso	AA	22	79	22	4	2	1	— —	33	12	13	8	0	23	0	0	1	3	1	.75	1	.278	.341	.418
1996 El Paso	AA	22	77	22	5	4	1	— —	38	17	11	12	1	21	2	0	1	1	2	.33	2	.286	.391	.494
Stockton	A+	37	138	48	8	4	3	— —	73	27	25	20	1	32	3	1	3	3	3	.50	3	.348	.433	.529
1997 Tucson	AAA	93	347	82	24	3	10	— —	142	44	56	33	1	87	3	0	0	2	2	.00	7	.236	.308	.409
1998 Louisville	AAA	55	215	71	10	4	7	— —	110	38	52	14	3	39	5	0	2	1	1	.50	6	.330	.381	.512
1998 Milwaukee	NL	84	262	60	12	1	9	(4 5)	101	33	28	20	4	61	2	0	1	1	3	.25	7	.229	.288	.385

Marcus Jensen

Bats: Both **Throws:** Right **Pos:** C-1; PH/PR-1 **Ht:** 6'4" **Wt:** 204 **Born:** 12/14/72 **Age:** 26

Year Team	Lg	G	AB	H	2B	3B	HR	(Hm Rd)	TB	R	RBI	TBB	IBB	SO	HBP	SH	SF	SB	CS	SB%	GDP	Avg	OBP	SLG
1998 Louisville *	AAA	74	246	52	13	0	10	— —	95	29	33	33	1	64	1	0	0	0	3	.00	5	.226	.326	.413
1996 San Francisco	NL	9	19	4	1	0	0	(0 0)	5	4	4	8	0	7	0	0	0	0	0	.00	1	.211	.444	.263
1997 SF-Det		38	85	13	2	0	1	(1 0)	18	6	4	8	1	28	0	0	0	0	0	.00	2	.153	.226	.212
1998 Milwaukee	NL	2	2	0	0	0	0	(0 0)	0	0	0	0	0	2	0	0	0	0	0	.00	0	.000	.000	.000
1997 San Francisco	NL	30	74	11	2	0	1	(1 0)	16	5	3	7	1	23	0	0	0	0	0	.00	2	.149	.222	.216
Detroit	AL	8	11	2	0	0	0	(0 0)	2	1	1	1	0	5	0	0	0	0	0	.00	0	.182	.250	.182
3 ML YEARS		49	106	17	3	0	1	(1 0)	23	10	8	16	1	37	0	0	0	0	0	.00	3	.160	.270	.217

Mike Jerzembeck

Pitches: Right **Bats:** Right **Pos:** SP-2; RP-1 **Ht:** 6'1" **Wt:** 185 **Born:** 5/18/72 **Age:** 27

Year Team	Lg	G	GS	CG	GF	IP	BFP	H	R	ER	HR	SH	SF	HB	TBB	IBB	SO	WP	Bk	W	L	Pct.	ShO	Sv-Op	Hld	ERA
1993 Oneonta	A-	14	14	0	0	77.1	327	70	25	23	1	3	1	3	26	0	76	2	2	8	4	.667	0	0--	—	2.68
1994 Tampa	A+	16	16	0	0	68.2	274	59	27	24	6	1	2	2	22	0	45	2	1	4	3	.571	0	0--	—	3.15
1995 Tampa	A+	2	0	0	0	3	17	5	4	3	1	0	0	0	2	0	1	1	0	0	1	.000	0	0--	—	9.00
1996 Columbus	AAA	1	0	0	0	1.2	7	1	1	1	0	0	0	0	1	0	0	0	0	0	0	.000	0	0--	—	5.40
Norwich	AA	14	13	1	0	69.2	303	74	38	35	9	4	2	3	26	0	65	2	4	3	6	.333	1	0--	—	4.52
Tampa	A+	12	12	0	0	73.1	297	67	26	24	4	1	1	0	13	0	60	3	0	4	2	.667	0	0--	—	2.95
1997 Norwich	AA	8	8	0	0	42	164	21	10	8	1	2	0	0	16	0	42	2	1	2	1	.667	0	0--	—	1.71
Columbus	AAA	20	20	2	0	130.1	540	125	55	52	14	4	5	2	37	0	118	4	0	7	5	.583	0	0--	—	3.59
1998 Columbus	AAA	24	24	0	0	140.1	624	158	82	76	20	1	1	3	55	1	107	4	1	4	9	.308	0	0--	—	4.87
1998 New York	AL	3	2	0	1	6.1	31	9	9	9	2	0	1	0	4	0	1	1	1	0	1	.000	0	0-0	0	12.79

Derek Jeter

Bats: Right **Throws:** Right **Pos:** SS-148; PH/PR-1 **Ht:** 6'3" **Wt:** 185 **Born:** 6/26/74 **Age:** 25

Year Team	Lg	G	AB	H	2B	3B	HR	(Hm Rd)	TB	R	RBI	TBB	IBB	SO	HBP	SH	SF	SB	CS	SB%	GDP	Avg	OBP	SLG
1998 Columbus *	AAA	1	5	2	2	0	0	— —	4	2	0	0	0	2	0	0	0	0	0	.00	0	.400	.400	.800
1995 New York	AL	15	48	12	4	1	0	(0 0)	18	5	7	3	0	11	0	0	0	0	0	.00	0	.250	.294	.375
1996 New York	AL	157	582	183	25	6	10	(3 7)	250	104	78	48	1	102	9	6	9	14	7	.67	13	.314	.370	.430
1997 New York	AL	159	654	190	31	7	10	(5 5)	265	116	70	74	0	125	10	8	2	23	12	.66	14	.291	.370	.405
1998 New York	AL	149	626	203	25	8	19	(9 10)	301	127	84	57	1	119	5	3	3	30	6	.83	13	.324	.384	.481
4 ML YEARS		480	1910	588	85	22	39	(17 22)	834	352	239	182	2	357	24	17	14	67	25	.73	40	.308	.373	.437

Jose Jimenez

Pitches: Right **Bats:** Right **Pos:** SP-3; RP-1   **Ht:** 6'3" **Wt:** 170 **Born:** 7/7/73 **Age:** 25

Year Team	Lg	G	GS	CG	GF	IP	BFP	H	R	ER	HR	SH	SF	HB	TBB	IBB	SO	WP	Bk	W	L	Pct.	ShO	Sv-Op	Hld	ERA
1995 Johnson Cty	R+	14	14	1	0	90.1	380	81	48	35	3	3	1	5	25	0	85	7	1	5	7	.417	1	0--	—	3.49
1996 Peoria	A	28	27	3	0	172.1	720	158	75	56	6	5	6	9	53	0	129	8	1	12	9	.571	1	0--	—	2.92
1997 Pr William	A+	24	24	2	0	145.2	609	128	73	50	12	2	2	9	42	2	81	10	2	9	7	.563	0	0--	—	3.09
1998 Arkansas	AA	26	26	1	0	179.2	743	156	71	62	9	6	4	12	68	1	88	13	0	15	6	.714	1	0--	—	3.11
1998 St. Louis	NL	4	3	0	0	21.1	94	22	8	7	0	1	1	0	8	0	12	0	0	3	0	1.000	0	0-0	0	2.95

Doug Johns

Pitches: Left **Bats:** Right **Pos:** RP-21; SP-10   **Ht:** 6'2" **Wt:** 195 **Born:** 12/19/67 **Age:** 31

Year Team	Lg	G	GS	CG	GF	IP	BFP	H	R	ER	HR	SH	SF	HB	TBB	IBB	SO	WP	Bk	W	L	Pct.	ShO	Sv-Op	Hld	ERA
1998 Rochester *	AAA	2	2	0	0	10.2	45	7	3	2	2	0	2	0	6	0	4	0	0	0	1	.000	0	0--	—	1.69
1995 Oakland	AL	11	9	1	1	54.2	229	44	32	28	5	2	1	5	26	1	25	5	1	5	3	.625	1	0-0	0	4.61
1996 Oakland	AL	40	23	1	4	158	710	187	112	105	21	2	3	6	69	5	71	9	0	6	12	.333	0	1-2	0	5.98
1998 Baltimore	AL	31	10	0	5	86.2	382	108	46	44	9	4	6	4	32	2	34	3	0	3	3	.500	0	1-1	2	4.57
3 ML YEARS		82	42	2	10	299.1	1321	339	190	177	35	8	10	15	127	8	130	17	1	14	18	.438	1	2-3	2	5.32

Keith Johns

Bats: Right **Throws:** Right **Pos:** DH-1; 2B-1; PH/PR-1   **Ht:** 6'1" **Wt:** 175 **Born:** 7/19/71 **Age:** 27

Year Team	Lg	G	AB	H	2B	3B	HR	(Hm	Rd)	TB	R	RBI	TBB	IBB	SO	HBP	SH	SF	SB	CS	SB%	GDP	Avg	OBP	SLG
1992 Hamilton	A-	70	275	78	11	1	1	—	—	94	36	23	27	0	42	1	1	3	15	10	.60	5	.284	.346	.342
1993 Springfield	A	132	467	121	24	1	2	—	—	153	74	40	70	0	68	4	9	5	40	20	.67	8	.259	.357	.328
1994 St. Pete	A+	122	464	106	20	1	3	—	—	135	52	47	37	1	49	2	12	4	18	9	.67	7	.228	.286	.291
1995 Arkansas	AA	111	396	111	13	2	2	—	—	134	69	28	55	0	53	2	11	2	14	7	.67	11	.280	.369	.338
Louisville	AAA	5	10	0	0	0	0	—	—	0	0	0	0	0	2	0	0	0	0	0	.00	0	.000	.000	.000
1996 Arkansas	AA	127	447	110	17	1	1	—	—	132	52	40	47	0	61	4	7	1	8	9	.47	17	.246	.323	.295
1997 Tucson	AAA	112	333	88	21	3	5	—	—	130	45	36	43	0	61	2	6	2	4	2	.67	7	.264	.350	.390
Rochester	AAA	1	1	0	0	0	0	—	—	0	0	0	0	0	0	1	0	0	0	0	.00	0	.000	.500	.000
1998 Pawtucket	AAA	96	329	75	12	1	8	—	—	113	31	38	28	0	82	4	1	5	2	6	.25	10	.228	.292	.343
1998 Boston	AL	2	0	0	0	0	0	(0	0)	0	0	0	1	0	0	0	0	0	0	0	.00	0	.000	1.000	.000

Brian Johnson

Bats: Right **Throws:** Right **Pos:** C-95; PH/PR-5; LF-1   **Ht:** 6'2" **Wt:** 210 **Born:** 1/8/68 **Age:** 31

Year Team	Lg	G	AB	H	2B	3B	HR	(Hm	Rd)	TB	R	RBI	TBB	IBB	SO	HBP	SH	SF	SB	CS	SB%	GDP	Avg	OBP	SLG
1998 Fresno *	AAA	5	19	6	1	0	2	—	—	13	4	3	1	0	5	0	0	0	0	0	.00	1	.316	.350	.684
1994 San Diego	NL	36	93	23	4	1	3	(3	0)	38	7	16	5	0	21	0	2	1	0	0	.00	4	.247	.283	.409
1995 San Diego	NL	68	207	52	9	0	3	(1	2)	70	20	29	11	2	39	1	1	4	0	0	.00	4	.251	.287	.338
1996 San Diego	NL	82	243	66	13	1	8	(3	5)	105	18	35	4	2	36	4	2	4	0	0	.00	8	.272	.290	.432
1997 Det-SF	NL	101	318	83	13	3	13	(8	5)	141	32	45	19	8	45	2	5	4	1	1	.50	11	.261	.303	.443
1998 San Francisco	NL	99	308	73	8	1	13	(7	6)	122	34	34	28	4	67	5	4	1	0	2	.00	11	.237	.310	.396
1997 Detroit	AL	45	139	33	6	1	2	(2	0)	47	13	18	5	1	19	0	2	1	1	0	1.00	3	.237	.262	.338
San Francisco	NL	56	179	50	7	2	11	(6	5)	94	19	27	14	7	26	2	3	3	0	1	.00	8	.279	.333	.525
5 ML YEARS		386	1169	297	47	6	40	(22	18)	476	111	159	67	16	208	12	14	14	1	3	.25	36	.254	.298	.407

Charles Johnson

Bats: Right **Throws:** Right **Pos:** C-131; PH/PR-3   **Ht:** 6'2" **Wt:** 215 **Born:** 7/20/71 **Age:** 27

Year Team	Lg	G	AB	H	2B	3B	HR	(Hm	Rd)	TB	R	RBI	TBB	IBB	SO	HBP	SH	SF	SB	CS	SB%	GDP	Avg	OBP	SLG
1994 Florida	NL	4	11	5	1	0	1	(1	0)	9	5	4	1	0	4	0	0	1	0	0	.00	1	.455	.462	.818
1995 Florida	NL	97	315	79	15	1	11	(3	8)	129	40	39	46	2	71	4	4	2	0	2	.00	11	.251	.351	.410
1996 Florida	NL	120	386	84	13	1	13	(9	4)	138	34	37	40	6	91	2	2	4	1	0	1.00	20	.218	.292	.358
1997 Florida	NL	124	416	104	26	1	19	(7	12)	189	43	63	60	6	109	3	3	2	0	2	.00	13	.250	.347	.454
1998 Fla-LA	NL	133	459	100	18	0	19	(14	5)	175	44	58	45	1	129	1	0	1	0	2	.00	12	.218	.289	.381
1998 Florida	NL	31	113	25	5	0	7	(5	2)	51	13	23	16	0	30	0	0	1	0	1	.00	3	.221	.315	.451
Los Angeles	NL	102	346	75	13	0	12	(9	3)	124	31	35	29	1	99	1	0	0	0	1	.00	9	.217	.279	.358
5 ML YEARS		478	1587	372	73	3	63	(34	29)	640	166	201	192	15	404	10	9	10	1	6	.14	57	.234	.319	.403

Jason Johnson

Pitches: Right **Bats:** Right **Pos:** SP-13   **Ht:** 6'6" **Wt:** 220 **Born:** 10/27/73 **Age:** 25

Year Team	Lg	G	GS	CG	GF	IP	BFP	H	R	ER	HR	SH	SF	HB	TBB	IBB	SO	WP	Bk	W	L	Pct.	ShO	Sv-Op	Hld	ERA
1992 Pirates	R	5	0	0	4	7.1	32	6	3	3	0	0	0	0	6	0	3	1	0	2	0	1.000	0	0--	—	3.68
1993 Pirates	R	9	9	0	0	54	217	48	22	14	0	0	1	1	14	0	39	0	1	1	4	.200	0	0--	—	2.33
Welland	A-	6	6	1	0	35	152	33	24	18	0	4	1	2	9	0	19	1	0	1	5	.167	0	0--	—	4.63
1994 Augusta	A	20	19	1	0	102.2	465	119	67	46	5	4	4	7	32	0	69	12	2	2	12	.143	0	0--	—	4.03
1995 Augusta	A	11	11	1	0	53.2	233	57	32	26	2	1	1	4	17	0	42	3	0	3	5	.375	0	0--	—	4.36
Lynchburg	A+	10	10	0	0	55	236	58	37	30	9	0	3	2	20	0	41	2	0	1	4	.200	0	0--	—	4.91

111

Year Team	Lg	G	GS	CG	GF	IP	BFP	H	R	ER	HR	SH	SF	HB	TBB	IBB	SO	WP	Bk	W	L	Pct.	ShO	Sv-Op	Hld	ERA
		HOW MUCH HE PITCHED						WHAT HE GAVE UP												THE RESULTS						
1996 Lynchburg	A+	15	5	0	1	44.1	204	56	37	32	6	5	1	1	12	0	27	0	0	1	4	.200	0	0--	—	6.50
Augusta	A	14	14	1	0	84	359	82	40	29	2	5	3	6	25	0	83	5	2	4	4	.500	1	0--	—	3.11
1997 Lynchburg	A+	17	17	0	0	99.1	411	98	43	41	4	4	2	6	30	1	92	7	0	8	4	.667	0	0--	—	3.71
Carolina	AA	9	9	1	0	57.1	244	56	31	26	6	1	1	1	16	0	63	1	0	3	3	.500	0	0--	—	4.08
1998 Durham	AAA	2	2	0	0	12.1	44	6	4	4	2	0	0	0	0	14	0	1	0	1.000	0	0--	—	2.92
1997 Pittsburgh	NL	3	0	0	0	6	27	10	4	4	2	0	0	0	1	0	3	0	0	0	0	.000	0	0--	—	6.00
1998 Tampa Bay	AL	13	13	0	0	60	274	74	38	38	9	1	1	3	27	0	36	2	0	2	5	.286	0	0-0	0	5.70
2 ML YEARS		16	13	0	0	66	301	84	42	42	11	1	2	3	28	0	39	2	0	2	5	.286	0	0-0	0	5.73

Jonathan Johnson

Pitches: Right **Bats:** Right **Pos:** SP-1 **Ht:** 6'0" **Wt:** 180 **Born:** 7/16/74 **Age:** 24

Year Team	Lg	G	GS	CG	GF	IP	BFP	H	R	ER	HR	SH	SF	HB	TBB	IBB	SO	WP	Bk	W	L	Pct.	ShO	Sv-Op	Hld	ERA
		HOW MUCH HE PITCHED						WHAT HE GAVE UP												THE RESULTS						
1995 Charlotte	A+	8	7	1	1	43.1	178	34	14	13	2	2	0	1	16	0	25	3	3	1	5	.167	0	0--	—	2.70
1996 Okla City	AAA	1	1	1	0	9	29	2	0	0	0	0	0	0	1	0	6	0	0	1	0	1.000	0	0--	—	0.00
Tulsa	AA	26	25	6	1	174.1	728	176	86	69	15	3	5	6	41	1	97	2	3	13	10	.565	0	0--	—	3.56
1997 Okla City	AAA	13	12	1	0	58	276	83	54	47	6	1	3	1	29	3	33	2	1	1	8	.111	0	0--	—	7.29
Tulsa	AA	10	10	4	0	71.2	297	70	35	28	3	1	3	2	15	0	47	4	0	5	4	.556	0	0--	—	3.52
1998 Charlotte	A+	3	3	0	0	11.2	51	16	6	6	2	0	1	2	4	0	11	0	0	0	2	.000	0	0--	—	4.63
Oklahoma	AAA	19	18	1	1	112	474	109	66	61	15	0	4	11	32	0	94	6	2	6	6	.500	0	1--	—	4.90
1998 Texas	AL	1	1	0	0	4.1	22	5	4	4	0	0	1	0	5	0	3	0	0	0	0	.000	0	0-0	0	8.31

Lance Johnson

Bats: Left **Throws:** Left **Pos:** CF-78; PH/PR-9 **Ht:** 5'11" **Wt:** 165 **Born:** 7/6/63 **Age:** 35

Year Team	Lg	G	AB	H	2B	3B	HR	(Hm	Rd)	TB	R	RBI	TBB	IBB	SO	HBP	SH	SF	SB	CS	SB%	GDP	Avg	OBP	SLG
		BATTING																	BASERUNNING				PERCENTAGES		
1987 St. Louis	NL	33	59	13	2	1	0	(0	0)	17	4	7	4	1	6	0	0	0	6	1	.86	2	.220	.270	.288
1988 Chicago	AL	33	124	23	4	1	0	(0	0)	29	11	6	6	0	11	0	2	0	6	2	.75	1	.185	.223	.234
1989 Chicago	AL	50	180	54	8	2	0	(0	0)	66	28	16	17	0	24	0	2	0	16	3	.84	1	.300	.360	.367
1990 Chicago	AL	151	541	154	18	9	1	(0	1)	193	76	51	33	2	45	1	8	4	36	22	.62	12	.285	.325	.357
1991 Chicago	AL	160	588	161	14	13	0	(0	0)	201	72	49	26	2	58	1	6	3	26	11	.70	14	.274	.304	.342
1992 Chicago	AL	157	567	158	15	12	3	(2	1)	206	67	47	34	4	33	1	4	5	41	14	.75	20	.279	.318	.363
1993 Chicago	AL	147	540	168	18	14	0	(0	0)	214	75	47	36	1	33	0	3	0	35	7	.83	16	.311	.354	.396
1994 Chicago	AL	106	412	114	11	14	3	(1	2)	162	56	54	26	5	23	2	0	3	26	6	.81	8	.277	.321	.393
1995 Chicago	AL	142	607	186	18	12	10	(2	8)	258	98	57	32	2	31	1	2	3	40	6	.87	7	.306	.341	.425
1996 New York	NL	160	682	227	31	21	9	(1	8)	327	117	69	33	8	40	1	3	5	50	12	.81	8	.333	.362	.479
1997 NYN-ChN	NL	111	410	126	16	8	5	(4	1)	173	60	39	42	3	31	0	0	2	20	12	.63	8	.307	.370	.422
1998 Chicago	NL	85	304	85	8	4	2	(1	1)	107	51	21	26	1	22	0	1	1	10	6	.63	5	.280	.335	.352
1997 New York	NL	72	265	82	10	6	1	(1	0)	107	43	24	33	2	21	0	0	1	15	10	.60	6	.309	.385	.404
Chicago	NL	39	145	44	6	2	4	(3	1)	66	17	15	9	1	10	0	0	1	5	2	.71	2	.303	.342	.455
12 ML YEARS		1335	5014	1469	163	111	33	(11	22)	1953	715	463	315	29	357	7	31	26	312	102	.75	96	.293	.334	.390

Mark Johnson

Bats: Left **Throws:** Left **Pos:** 1B-5; PH/PR-5; DH-2 **Ht:** 6'4" **Wt:** 230 **Born:** 10/17/67 **Age:** 31

Year Team	Lg	G	AB	H	2B	3B	HR	(Hm	Rd)	TB	R	RBI	TBB	IBB	SO	HBP	SH	SF	SB	CS	SB%	GDP	Avg	OBP	SLG
		BATTING																	BASERUNNING				PERCENTAGES		
1998 Indianapols *	AAA	116	357	107	33	1	22	—	—	208	65	75	68	3	82	0	0	3	2	2	.50	0	.300	.409	.583
1995 Pittsburgh	NL	79	221	46	6	1	13	(7	6)	93	32	28	37	2	66	2	0	1	5	2	.71	2	.208	.326	.421
1996 Pittsburgh	NL	127	343	94	24	0	13	(10	3)	157	55	47	44	3	64	5	0	4	6	4	.60	5	.274	.361	.458
1997 Pittsburgh	NL	78	219	47	10	0	4	(2	2)	69	30	29	43	1	78	2	0	0	1	1	.50	1	.215	.345	.315
1998 Anaheim	AL	10	14	1	0	0	0	(0	0)	1	1	0	0	0	6	0	0	0	0	0	.00	1	.071	.071	.071
4 ML YEARS		294	797	188	40	1	30	(19	11)	320	118	104	124	6	214	9	0	8	12	7	.63	9	.236	.342	.402

Mark L. Johnson

Bats: Left **Throws:** Right **Pos:** C-7 **Ht:** 6'0" **Wt:** 185 **Born:** 9/12/75 **Age:** 23

Year Team	Lg	G	AB	H	2B	3B	HR	(Hm	Rd)	TB	R	RBI	TBB	IBB	SO	HBP	SH	SF	SB	CS	SB%	GDP	Avg	OBP	SLG
		BATTING																	BASERUNNING				PERCENTAGES		
1994 White Sox	R	32	87	21	5	0	0	—	—	26	10	14	14	0	15	3	0	0	1	1	.50	0	.241	.365	.299
1995 Hickory	A	107	319	58	9	0	2	—	—	73	31	17	59	1	52	3	2	2	3	5	.38	4	.182	.313	.229
1996 South Bend	A	67	214	55	14	3	2	—	—	81	29	27	39	2	25	1	4	4	3	3	.50	8	.257	.368	.379
Pr William	A+	18	58	14	3	0	0	—	—	17	9	3	13	0	6	1	0	0	0	0	.00	0	.241	.389	.293
1997 Winston-Sal	A+	120	375	95	27	4	4	—	—	142	59	46	106	2	85	5	0	5	4	2	.67	7	.253	.420	.379
1998 Birmingham	AA	117	382	108	17	3	9	—	—	158	68	59	105	0	72	6	0	1	0	1	.00	5	.283	.443	.414
1998 Chicago	AL	7	23	2	0	2	0	(0	0)	6	2	1	1	0	8	0	0	0	0	0	.00	0	.087	.125	.261

Mike Johnson

Pitches: Right **Bats:** Right **Pos:** SP-2 **Ht:** 6'2" **Wt:** 175 **Born:** 10/3/75 **Age:** 23

Year Team	Lg	G	GS	CG	GF	IP	BFP	H	R	ER	HR	SH	SF	HB	TBB	IBB	SO	WP	Bk	W	L	Pct.	ShO	Sv-Op	Hld	ERA
		HOW MUCH HE PITCHED						WHAT HE GAVE UP												THE RESULTS						
1993 Blue Jays	R	16	1	0	7	44.1	208	59	40	24	4	1	3	2	22	0	31	4	2	0	2	.000	0	1--	—	4.87
1994 Medicine Ha	R+	9	9	0	0	36.1	170	48	31	18	2	2	0	1	22	0	8	8	1	1	3	.250	0	0--	—	4.46
1995 Blue Jays	R	3	3	0	0	15	74	20	15	12	1	0	0	3	8	0	13	7	0	0	2	.000	0	0--	—	7.20

Year Team	Lg	G	GS	CG	GF	IP	BFP	H	R	ER	HR	SH	SF	HB	TBB	IBB	SO	WP	Bk	W	L	Pct.	ShO	Sv-Op	Hld	ERA
Medicine Ha	R+	19	0	0	7	49	217	46	26	21	2	2	2	0	25	1	32	6	0	4	1	.800	0	3--	—	3.86
1996 Hagerstown	A	29	23	5	1	162.2	671	157	74	57	6	5	5	8	39	0	155	12	1	11	8	.579	3	0--	—	3.15
1998 Harrisburg	AA	7	7	0	0	33.2	148	35	27	26	9	1	0	2	10	0	38	4	0	3	2	.600	0	0--	—	6.95
Ottawa	AAA	18	18	1	0	109	473	105	63	52	20	3	4	8	38	0	88	4	1	4	9	.308	0	0--	—	4.29
1997 Bal-Mon		25	16	0	5	89.2	403	106	70	68	20	2	4	1	37	4	57	5	0	2	6	.250	0	2-2	0	6.83
1998 Montreal	NL	2	2	0	0	7.1	40	16	12	12	4	0	1	0	2	0	4	0	0	0	0	.000	0	0-0	0	14.73
1997 Baltimore	AL	14	5	0	5	39.2	183	52	36	35	12	0	2	1	16	2	29	1	0	0	1	.000	0	2-2	0	7.94
Montreal	NL	11	11	0	0	50	220	54	34	33	8	2	2	0	21	2	28	4	0	2	5	.286	0	0-0	0	5.94
2 ML YEARS		27	18	0	5	97	443	122	82	80	24	2	4	2	39	4	61	5	0	2	8	.200	0	2-2	0	7.42

Randy Johnson

Pitches: Left **Bats:** Right **Pos:** SP-34 **Ht:** 6'10" **Wt:** 230 **Born:** 9/10/63 **Age:** 35

Year Team	Lg	G	GS	CG	GF	IP	BFP	H	R	ER	HR	SH	SF	HB	TBB	IBB	SO	WP	Bk	W	L	Pct.	ShO	Sv-Op	Hld	ERA
1988 Montreal	NL	4	4	1	0	26	109	23	8	7	3	0	0	0	7	0	25	3	0	3	0	1.000	0	0-0	0	2.42
1989 Mon-Sea		29	28	2	1	160.2	715	147	100	86	13	10	13	3	96	2	130	7	7	7	13	.350	0	0-0	0	4.82
1990 Seattle	AL	33	33	5	0	219.2	944	174	103	89	26	7	6	5	120	2	194	4	2	14	11	.560	2	0-0	0	3.65
1991 Seattle	AL	33	33	2	0	201.1	889	151	96	89	15	9	8	12	152	0	228	12	2	13	10	.565	1	0-0	0	3.98
1992 Seattle	AL	31	31	6	0	210.1	922	154	104	88	13	3	8	18	144	1	241	13	1	12	14	.462	2	0-0	0	3.77
1993 Seattle	AL	35	34	10	1	255.1	1043	185	97	92	22	8	7	16	99	1	308	8	2	19	8	.704	3	1-1	0	3.24
1994 Seattle	AL	23	23	9	0	172	694	132	65	61	14	3	1	6	72	2	204	5	0	13	6	.684	4	0-0	0	3.19
1995 Seattle	AL	30	30	6	0	214.1	866	159	65	59	12	2	1	6	65	1	294	5	2	18	2	.900	3	0-0	0	2.48
1996 Seattle	AL	14	8	0	2	61.1	256	48	27	25	8	1	0	2	25	1	85	3	1	5	0	1.000	0	1-2	0	3.67
1997 Seattle	AL	30	29	5	0	213	852	147	60	54	20	4	1	10	77	2	291	4	0	20	4	.833	2	0-0	0	2.28
1998 Sea-Hou		34	34	10	0	244.1	1014	203	102	89	23	5	2	14	86	1	329	7	2	19	11	.633	6	0-0	0	3.28
1989 Montreal	NL	7	6	0	1	29.2	143	29	25	22	2	3	4	0	26	1	26	2	2	0	4	.000	0	0-0	0	6.67
Seattle	AL	22	22	2	0	131	572	118	75	64	11	7	9	3	70	1	104	5	5	7	9	.438	0	0-0	0	4.40
1998 Seattle	AL	23	23	6	0	160	685	146	90	77	19	5	1	11	60	0	213	7	2	9	10	.474	2	0-0	0	4.33
Houston	NL	11	11	4	0	84.1	329	57	12	12	4	0	1	3	26	1	116	0	0	10	1	.909	4	0-0	0	1.28
11 ML YEARS		296	287	56	4	1978.1	8302	1523	827	739	169	52	47	92	943	12	2329	71	19	143	79	.644	23	2-3	0	3.36

Russ Johnson

Bats: Right **Throws:** Right **Pos:** 3B-5; PH/PR-3; 2B-1 **Ht:** 5'10" **Wt:** 180 **Born:** 2/22/73 **Age:** 26

Year Team	Lg	G	AB	H	2B	3B	HR	(Hm	Rd)	TB	R	RBI	TBB	IBB	SO	HBP	SH	SF	SB	CS	SB%	GDP	Avg	OBP	SLG
1995 Jackson	AA	132	475	118	16	2	9	—	—	165	65	53	50	1	60	8	2	5	10	5	.67	11	.248	.327	.347
1996 Jackson	AA	132	496	154	24	5	15	—	—	233	86	74	56	1	50	3	5	3	9	4	.69	16	.310	.382	.470
1997 New Orleans	AAA	122	445	123	16	6	4	—	—	163	72	49	66	1	78	1	2	2	7	4	.64	10	.276	.370	.366
1998 New Orleans	AAA	122	453	140	28	2	7	—	—	193	95	52	90	2	64	5	4	6	11	11	.50	10	.309	.424	.426
1997 Houston	NL	21	60	18	1	0	2	(2	0)	25	7	9	6	0	14	0	1	0	1	1	.50	2	.300	.364	.417
1998 Houston	NL	8	13	3	1	0	0	(0	0)	4	2	0	1	0	5	1	0	0	1	0	1.00	1	.231	.333	.308
2 ML YEARS		29	73	21	2	0	2	(2	0)	29	9	9	7	0	19	1	1	0	2	1	.67	3	.288	.358	.397

John Johnstone

Pitches: Right **Bats:** Right **Pos:** RP-70 **Ht:** 6'3" **Wt:** 195 **Born:** 11/25/68 **Age:** 30

Year Team	Lg	G	GS	CG	GF	IP	BFP	H	R	ER	HR	SH	SF	HB	TBB	IBB	SO	WP	Bk	W	L	Pct.	ShO	Sv-Op	Hld	ERA
1993 Florida	NL	7	0	0	3	10.2	54	16	8	7	1	0	0	0	7	0	5	1	0	0	2	.000	0	0-0	0	5.91
1994 Florida	NL	17	0	0	7	21.1	105	23	20	14	4	1	0	1	16	5	23	0	0	1	2	.333	0	0-0	3	5.91
1995 Florida	NL	4	0	0	0	4.2	23	7	2	2	1	0	0	0	2	1	3	0	0	0	0	.000	0	0-0	0	3.86
1996 Houston	NL	9	0	0	6	13	60	17	8	8	2	0	2	0	5	0	5	0	0	1	0	1.000	0	0-0	0	5.54
1997 SF-Oak		18	0	0	3	25	112	22	9	9	1	2	4	4	14	0	19	0	0	0	0	.000	0	0-0	1	3.24
1998 San Francisco	NL	70	0	0	13	88	370	72	32	30	10	4	5	1	38	8	86	4	0	6	5	.545	0	0-1	15	3.07
1997 San Francisco	NL	13	0	0	2	18.2	80	15	7	7	1	2	3	4	7	0	15	0	0	0	0	.000	0	0-0	0	3.38
Oakland	AL	5	0	0	1	6.1	32	7	2	2	0	0	1	0	7	0	4	0	0	0	0	.000	0	0-0	0	2.84
6 ML YEARS		125	0	0	32	162.2	724	157	79	70	19	7	11	6	82	14	141	5	0	8	9	.471	0	0-1	19	3.87

Andruw Jones

Bats: Right **Throws:** Right **Pos:** CF-159; PH/PR-3 **Ht:** 6'1" **Wt:** 185 **Born:** 4/23/77 **Age:** 22

Year Team	Lg	G	AB	H	2B	3B	HR	(Hm	Rd)	TB	R	RBI	TBB	IBB	SO	HBP	SH	SF	SB	CS	SB%	GDP	Avg	OBP	SLG
1996 Atlanta	NL	31	106	23	7	1	5	(3	2)	47	11	13	7	0	29	0	0	0	3	0	1.00	1	.217	.265	.443
1997 Atlanta	NL	153	399	92	18	1	18	(5	13)	166	60	70	56	2	107	4	5	3	20	11	.65	11	.231	.329	.416
1998 Atlanta	NL	159	582	158	33	8	31	(16	15)	300	89	90	40	8	129	4	1	4	27	4	.87	10	.271	.321	.515
3 ML YEARS		343	1087	273	58	10	54	(24	30)	513	160	173	103	10	265	8	6	7	50	15	.77	22	.251	.319	.472

Bobby Jones

Pitches: Right **Bats:** Right **Pos:** SP-30 **Ht:** 6'4" **Wt:** 216 **Born:** 2/10/70 **Age:** 29

Year Team	Lg	HOW MUCH HE PITCHED						WHAT HE GAVE UP												THE RESULTS						
		G	GS	CG	GF	IP	BFP	H	R	ER	HR	SH	SF	HB	TBB	IBB	SO	WP	Bk	W	L	Pct.	ShO	Sv-Op	Hld	ERA
1993 New York	NL	9	9	0	0	61.2	265	61	35	25	6	5	3	2	22	3	35	1	0	2	4	.333	1	0-0	0	3.65
1994 New York	NL	24	24	1	0	160	685	157	75	56	10	11	4	4	56	9	80	1	3	12	7	.632	1	0-0	0	3.15
1995 New York	NL	30	30	3	0	195.2	839	209	107	91	20	11	6	7	53	6	127	2	1	10	10	.500	1	0-0	0	4.19
1996 New York	NL	31	31	3	0	195.2	826	219	102	96	26	12	5	3	46	6	116	2	0	12	8	.600	1	0-0	0	4.42
1997 New York	NL	30	30	2	0	193.1	806	177	88	78	24	6	4	2	63	3	125	3	1	15	9	.625	1	0-0	0	3.63
1998 New York	NL	30	30	0	0	195.1	804	192	94	88	23	4	7	8	53	2	115	2	2	9	9	.500	0	0-0	0	4.05
6 ML YEARS		154	154	9	0	1001.2	4225	1015	501	434	109	49	29	26	293	29	598	11	7	60	47	.561	4	0-0	0	3.90

Bobby Jones

Pitches: Left **Bats:** Right **Pos:** SP-20; RP-15 **Ht:** 6'0" **Wt:** 185 **Born:** 4/11/72 **Age:** 27

Year Team	Lg	HOW MUCH HE PITCHED						WHAT HE GAVE UP												THE RESULTS						
		G	GS	CG	GF	IP	BFP	H	R	ER	HR	SH	SF	HB	TBB	IBB	SO	WP	Bk	W	L	Pct.	ShO	Sv-Op	Hld	ERA
1992 Helena	R+	14	13	1	0	76.1	341	93	51	37	7	4	2	1	23	0	53	6	5	5	4	.556	0	0- -	—	4.36
1993 Beloit	A	25	25	4	0	144.2	661	159	82	66	9	1	6	9	65	1	115	4	4	10	10	.500	0	0- -	—	4.11
1994 Stockton	A+	26	26	2	0	147.2	638	131	90	69	12	4	4	4	64	1	147	5	2	6	12	.333	0	0- -	—	4.21
1995 Colo Sprngs	AAA	11	8	0	0	40.2	204	50	38	33	5	4	1	2	33	1	48	4	1	1	2	.333	0	0- -	—	7.30
New Haven	AA	27	8	0	9	73.1	315	61	27	21	4	3	3	8	36	2	70	7	0	5	2	.714	0	3- -	—	2.58
1996 Colo Sprngs	AAA	57	0	0	17	88.2	410	88	54	49	8	5	2	4	63	4	78	7	2	2	8	.200	0	3- -	—	4.97
1997 Colo Sprngs	AAA	25	21	0	2	133	593	135	89	76	16	1	5	12	71	2	104	2	0	7	11	.389	0	0- -	—	5.14
1997 Colorado	NL	4	4	0	0	19.1	96	30	18	18	2	2	3	0	12	0	5	0	1	1	1	.500	0	0-0	0	8.38
1998 Colorado	NL	35	20	1	1	141.1	630	153	87	82	12	9	6	6	66	0	109	4	1	7	8	.467	0	0-0	1	5.22
2 ML YEARS		39	24	1	1	160.2	726	183	105	100	14	11	9	6	78	0	114	4	1	8	9	.471	0	0-0	1	5.60

Chipper Jones

Bats: Both **Throws:** Right **Pos:** 3B-158; PH/PR-1 **Ht:** 6'3" **Wt:** 200 **Born:** 4/24/72 **Age:** 27

Year Team	Lg	BATTING																	BASERUNNING				PERCENTAGES		
		G	AB	H	2B	3B	HR	(Hm	Rd)	TB	R	RBI	TBB	IBB	SO	HBP	SH	SF	SB	CS	SB%	GDP	Avg	OBP	SLG
1993 Atlanta	NL	8	3	2	1	0	0	(0	0)	3	2	0	1	0	1	0	0	0	0	0	.00	0	.667	.750	1.000
1995 Atlanta	NL	140	524	139	22	3	23	(15	8)	236	87	86	73	1	99	0	1	4	8	4	.67	10	.265	.353	.450
1996 Atlanta	NL	157	598	185	32	5	30	(18	12)	317	114	110	87	0	88	0	1	7	14	1	.93	14	.309	.393	.530
1997 Atlanta	NL	157	597	176	41	3	21	(7	14)	286	100	111	76	8	88	0	0	6	20	5	.80	19	.295	.371	.479
1998 Atlanta	NL	160	601	188	29	5	34	(17	17)	329	123	107	96	1	93	1	1	8	16	6	.73	17	.313	.404	.547
5 ML YEARS		622	2323	690	125	16	108	(57	51)	1171	426	414	333	10	369	1	3	25	58	16	.78	60	.297	.382	.504

Chris Jones

Bats: R **Throws:** R **Pos:** RF-31; PH/PR-28; LF-6; DH-2 **Ht:** 6'2" **Wt:** 205 **Born:** 12/16/65 **Age:** 33

Year Team	Lg	BATTING																	BASERUNNING				PERCENTAGES		
		G	AB	H	2B	3B	HR	(Hm	Rd)	TB	R	RBI	TBB	IBB	SO	HBP	SH	SF	SB	CS	SB%	GDP	Avg	OBP	SLG
1998 Fresno *	AAA	25	60	16	1	3	3	(—	—)	32	11	8	6	0	12	0	1	0	2	1	.67	0	.267	.333	.533
1991 Cincinnati	NL	52	89	26	1	2	3	(0	2)	37	14	6	2	0	31	0	0	0	2	1	.67	2	.292	.304	.416
1992 Houston	NL	54	63	12	2	1	1	(1	0)	19	7	4	7	0	21	0	3	0	0	1	.00	0	.190	.271	.302
1993 Colorado	NL	86	209	57	11	4	6	(2	4)	94	29	31	10	1	48	0	5	1	9	4	.69	6	.273	.305	.450
1994 Colorado	NL	21	40	12	2	1	0	(0	0)	16	6	2	2	1	14	0	0	0	1	0	1.00	1	.300	.333	.400
1995 New York	NL	79	182	51	6	2	8	(4	4)	85	33	31	13	1	45	1	2	3	2	1	.67	2	.280	.327	.467
1996 New York	NL	89	149	36	7	0	4	(2	2)	55	22	18	12	1	42	2	0	0	1	0	1.00	3	.242	.307	.369
1997 San Diego	NL	92	152	37	9	0	7	(4	3)	67	24	25	16	0	45	2	1	1	7	2	.78	4	.243	.322	.441
1998 Ari-SF	NL	63	121	23	3	1	2	(2	0)	34	17	13	11	0	37	0	1	2	2	1	.67	2	.190	.254	.281
1998 Arizona	NL	20	31	6	1	0	0	(0	0)	7	3	3	3	0	9	0	0	0	0	0	.00	2	.194	.265	.226
San Francisco	NL	43	90	17	2	1	2	(2	0)	27	14	10	8	0	28	0	1	2	2	1	.67	0	.189	.250	.300
8 ML YEARS		536	1005	254	41	11	30	(15	15)	407	152	130	73	4	283	5	11	8	26	10	.72	21	.253	.304	.405

Doug Jones

Pitches: Right **Bats:** Right **Pos:** RP-69 **Ht:** 6'2" **Wt:** 224 **Born:** 6/24/57 **Age:** 42

Year Team	Lg	HOW MUCH HE PITCHED						WHAT HE GAVE UP												THE RESULTS						
		G	GS	CG	GF	IP	BFP	H	R	ER	HR	SH	SF	HB	TBB	IBB	SO	WP	Bk	W	L	Pct.	ShO	Sv-Op	Hld	ERA
1982 Milwaukee	AL	4	0	0	2	2.2	14	5	3	3	1	0	0	0	1	0	1	0	0	0	0	.000	0	0-0	0	10.13
1986 Cleveland	AL	11	0	0	5	18	79	18	5	5	0	1	1	0	6	1	12	0	0	1	0	1.000	0	1-3	0	2.50
1987 Cleveland	AL	49	0	0	29	91.1	400	101	45	32	4	5	5	6	24	6	87	0	0	6	5	.545	0	8-12	0	3.15
1988 Cleveland	AL	51	0	0	46	83.1	338	69	26	21	1	3	0	2	16	3	72	2	3	3	4	.429	0	37-43	0	2.27
1989 Cleveland	AL	59	0	0	53	80.2	331	76	25	21	4	8	6	1	13	4	65	1	1	7	10	.412	0	32-41	0	2.34
1990 Cleveland	AL	66	0	0	64	84.1	331	66	26	24	5	2	2	2	22	4	55	2	0	5	5	.500	0	43-51	0	2.56
1991 Cleveland	AL	36	4	0	29	63.1	293	87	42	39	7	2	0	6	21	6	48	1	0	4	8	.333	0	7-12	0	5.54
1992 Houston	NL	80	0	0	70	111.2	440	96	29	23	5	9	0	5	17	5	93	2	1	11	8	.579	0	36-42	0	1.85
1993 Houston	NL	71	0	0	60	85.1	381	102	46	43	7	9	4	5	21	6	66	3	0	4	10	.286	0	26-34	1	4.54
1994 Philadelphia	NL	47	0	0	42	54	226	55	14	13	2	4	0	0	6	0	38	1	0	2	4	.333	0	27-29	0	2.17
1995 Baltimore	AL	52	0	0	47	46.2	211	55	30	26	6	1	0	2	16	2	42	0	0	0	4	.000	0	22-25	0	5.01
1996 ChN-Mil		52	0	0	21	64	282	72	33	30	7	1	2	3	20	6	60	1	0	7	2	.778	0	3-11	2	4.22
1997 Milwaukee	AL	75	0	0	73	80.1	307	62	20	18	4	1	5	3	9	1	82	2	0	6	6	.500	0	36-38	0	2.02
1998 Mil-Cle		69	0	0	42	85.1	372	99	44	43	17	5	6	4	17	4	71	0	1	4	6	.400	0	13-22	5	4.54
1996 Chicago	NL	28	0	0	13	32.1	143	41	20	18	4	1	0	1	7	4	26	0	0	2	2	.500	0	2-7	0	5.01

Year Team	Lg	G	GS	CG	GF	IP	BFP	H	R	ER	HR	SH	SF	HB	TBB	IBB	SO	WP	Bk	W	L	Pct.	ShO	Sv-Op	Hld	ERA
				HOW MUCH HE PITCHED							WHAT HE GAVE UP											THE RESULTS				
Milwaukee	AL	24	0	0	8	31.2	139	31	13	12	3	0	2	2	13	2	34	1	0	5	0	1.000	0	1-4	2	3.41
1998 Milwaukee	NL	46	0	0	34	54	239	65	32	31	15	3	3	4	11	1	43	0	0	3	4	.429	0	12-20	1	5.17
Cleveland	AL	23	0	0	8	31.1	133	34	12	12	2	2	3	0	6	3	28	0	1	1	2	.333	0	1-2	4	3.45
14 ML YEARS		722	4	0	583	951	4005	963	388	341	70	51	33	34	205	46	792	15	6	60	72	.455	0	291-363	9	3.23

Terry Jones

Bats: Both   Throws: Right   Pos: CF-60; PH/PR-2   Ht: 5'10"   Wt: 165   Born: 2/15/71   Age: 28

Year Team	Lg	G	AB	H	2B	3B	HR	(Hm	Rd)	TB	R	RBI	TBB	IBB	SO	HBP	SH	SF	SB	CS	SB%	GDP	Avg	OBP	SLG
					BATTING														BASERUNNING				PERCENTAGES		
1993 Bend	A-	33	138	40	5	4	0	—	—	53	21	18	12	1	19	0	2	0	16	6	.73	0	.290	.347	.384
Central Val	A+	21	73	21	1	0	0	—	—	22	16	7	10	0	15	1	1	0	5	0	1.00		.288	.381	.301
1994 Central Val	A+	129	536	157	20	1	2	—	—	185	94	34	42	1	85	1	10	1	44	12	.79	12	.293	.345	.345
1995 New Haven	AA	124	472	127	12	1	1	—	—	144	78	26	39	0	104	3	3	3	51	19	.73	6	.269	.327	.305
1996 Colo Sprngs	AAA	128	497	143	7	4	0	—	—	158	75	33	37	3	80	1	4	2	26	14	.65	5	.288	.337	.318
1997 Colo Sprngs	AAA	92	363	98	14	4	1	—	—	123	70	25	25	0	49	0	6	2	36	6	.86	3	.270	.315	.339
1998 Ottawa	AAA	81	278	66	3	4	0	—	—	77	36	21	32	1	48	0	8	2	35	6	.85	8	.237	.314	.277
1996 Colorado	NL	12	10	3	0	0	0	(0	0)	3	6	1	0	0	3	0	0	1	0	0	.00	0	.300	.273	.300
1998 Montreal	NL	60	212	46	7	2	1	(1	0)	60	30	15	21	1	46	0	15	0	16	4	.80	2	.217	.288	.283
2 ML YEARS		72	222	49	7	2	1	(1	0)	63	36	16	21	1	49	0	15	1	16	4	.80	2	.221	.287	.284

Todd Jones

Pitches: Right   Bats: Left   Pos: RP-65   Ht: 6'3"   Wt: 230   Born: 4/24/68   Age: 31

Year Team	Lg	G	GS	CG	GF	IP	BFP	H	R	ER	HR	SH	SF	HB	TBB	IBB	SO	WP	Bk	W	L	Pct.	ShO	Sv-Op	Hld	ERA
				HOW MUCH HE PITCHED							WHAT HE GAVE UP											THE RESULTS				
1993 Houston	NL	27	0	0	8	37.1	150	28	14	13	4	2	1	1	15	2	25	1	1	1	2	.333	0	2-3	6	3.13
1994 Houston	NL	48	0	0	20	72.2	288	52	23	22	3	3	1	1	26	4	63	1	0	5	2	.714	0	5-9	8	2.72
1995 Houston	NL	68	0	0	40	99.2	442	89	38	34	8	5	4	6	52	17	96	5	0	6	5	.545	0	15-20	8	3.07
1996 Houston	NL	51	0	0	37	57.1	263	61	30	28	5	2	1	5	32	6	44	3	0	6	3	.667	0	17-23	1	4.40
1997 Detroit	AL	68	0	0	51	70	301	60	29	24	3	1	4	1	35	2	70	7	1	4	4	.556	0	31-36	5	3.09
1998 Detroit	AL	65	0	0	53	63.1	279	58	38	35	7	2	6	2	36	4	57	5	0	1	4	.200	0	28-32	0	4.97
6 ML YEARS		327	0	0	209	400.1	1723	348	172	156	30	15	17	16	196	35	355	22	1	24	20	.545	0	98-123	28	3.51

Brian Jordan

Bats: R   Throws: R   Pos: RF-124; CF-33; PH/PR-8; DH-3; 3B-1   Ht: 6'1"   Wt: 205   Born: 3/29/67   Age: 32

Year Team	Lg	G	AB	H	2B	3B	HR	(Hm	Rd)	TB	R	RBI	TBB	IBB	SO	HBP	SH	SF	SB	CS	SB%	GDP	Avg	OBP	SLG
					BATTING														BASERUNNING				PERCENTAGES		
1992 St. Louis	NL	55	193	40	9	4	5	(3	2)	72	17	22	10	1	48	1	0	0	7	2	.78	6	.207	.250	.373
1993 St. Louis	NL	67	223	69	10	6	10	(4	6)	121	33	44	12	0	35	4	0	3	6	6	.50	6	.309	.351	.543
1994 St. Louis	NL	53	178	46	8	2	5	(4	1)	73	14	15	16	0	40	1	0	2	4	3	.57	6	.258	.320	.410
1995 St. Louis	NL	131	490	145	20	4	22	(14	8)	239	83	81	22	4	79	11	0	2	24	9	.73	5	.296	.339	.488
1996 St. Louis	NL	140	513	159	36	1	17	(3	14)	248	82	104	29	4	84	7	2	9	22	5	.81	6	.310	.349	.483
1997 St. Louis	NL	47	145	34	5	0	0	(0	0)	39	17	10	10	1	21	6	0	0	6	1	.86	4	.234	.311	.269
1998 St. Louis	NL	150	564	178	34	7	25	(9	16)	301	100	91	40	1	66	9	0	4	17	5	.77	18	.316	.368	.534
7 ML YEARS		643	2306	671	122	24	84	(37	47)	1093	346	367	139	11	373	39	2	20	86	31	.74	51	.291	.339	.474

Kevin Jordan

Bats: R   Throws: R   Pos: PH/PR-58; 1B-24; 2B-22; DH-8; 3B-6   Ht: 6'1"   Wt: 207   Born: 10/9/69   Age: 29

Year Team	Lg	G	AB	H	2B	3B	HR	(Hm	Rd)	TB	R	RBI	TBB	IBB	SO	HBP	SH	SF	SB	CS	SB%	GDP	Avg	OBP	SLG
					BATTING														BASERUNNING				PERCENTAGES		
1995 Philadelphia	NL	24	54	10	1	0	2	(1	1)	17	6	6	2	1	9	1	0	0	0	0	.00	0	.185	.228	.315
1996 Philadelphia	NL	43	131	37	10	0	3	(2	1)	56	15	12	5	0	20	1	3	2	2	1	.67	3	.282	.309	.427
1997 Philadelphia	NL	84	177	47	8	0	6	(4	2)	73	19	30	3	0	26	0	0	3	1	0	.00	5	.266	.273	.412
1998 Philadelphia	NL	112	250	69	13	0	2	(1	1)	88	23	27	8	1	30	2	0	1	0	0	.00	5	.276	.303	.352
4 ML YEARS		263	612	163	32	0	13	(8	5)	234	63	75	18	2	85	4	3	6	2	2	.50	13	.266	.289	.382

Ricardo Jordan

Pitches: Left   Bats: Left   Pos: RP-6   Ht: 6'0"   Wt: 190   Born: 6/27/70   Age: 29

Year Team	Lg	G	GS	CG	GF	IP	BFP	H	R	ER	HR	SH	SF	HB	TBB	IBB	SO	WP	Bk	W	L	Pct.	ShO	Sv-Op	Hld	ERA
				HOW MUCH HE PITCHED							WHAT HE GAVE UP											THE RESULTS				
1998 Indianapolis *	AAA	37	6	0	6	69.2	309	70	39	27	8	2	3	2	33	2	52	1	0	2	4	.349	0	0- —		3.49
Columbus *	AAA	5	5	0	0	26	119	28	15	14	4	0	1	1	17	0	22	0	0	2	0	1.000	0	0- —		4.85
1995 Toronto	AL	15	0	0	3	15	76	18	11	11	3	0	2	2	13	1	10	1	0	1	0	1.000	0	1-1	1	6.60
1996 Philadelphia	NL	26	0	0	2	25	103	18	6	5	0	1	1	0	12	0	17	1	0	2	2	.500	0	0-0	4	1.80
1997 New York	NL	22	0	0	4	27	123	31	17	16	1	2	2	2	15	2	19	0	0	1	2	.333	0	0-0	1	5.33
1998 Cincinnati	NL	6	0	0	0	3.1	21	4	9	9	2	0	1	0	7	0	1	0	0	1	0	1.000	0	0-0		24.30
4 ML YEARS		69	0	0	9	70.1	323	71	43	41	6	3	6	4	47	3	47	2	0	5	4	.556	0	1-1	6	5.25

Wally Joyner

Bats: Left **Throws:** Left **Pos:** 1B-127; PH/PR-10   **Ht:** 6'2" **Wt:** 200 **Born:** 6/16/62 **Age:** 37

Year Team	Lg	G	AB	H	2B	3B	HR	(Hm	Rd)	TB	R	RBI	TBB	IBB	SO	HBP	SH	SF	SB	CS	SB%	GDP	Avg	OBP	SLG
1986 California	AL	154	593	172	27	3	22	(11	11)	271	82	100	57	8	58	2	10	12	5	2	.71	11	.290	.348	.457
1987 California	AL	149	564	161	33	1	34	(19	15)	298	100	117	72	12	64	5	2	10	8	2	.80	14	.285	.366	.528
1988 California	AL	158	597	176	31	2	13	(6	7)	250	81	85	55	14	51	5	0	6	8	2	.80	16	.295	.356	.419
1989 California	AL	159	593	167	30	2	16	(8	8)	249	78	79	46	7	58	6	1	8	2	1	.67	15	.282	.335	.420
1990 California	AL	83	310	83	15	0	8	(5	3)	122	35	41	41	4	34	1	1	5	2	1	.67	10	.268	.350	.394
1991 California	AL	143	497	145	34	3	21	(4	11)	269	79	96	52	4	66	1	2	5	2	0	1.00	11	.301	.360	.488
1992 Kansas City	AL	149	572	154	36	2	9	(1	8)	221	66	66	55	4	50	4	0	2	11	5	.69	19	.269	.336	.386
1993 Kansas City	AL	141	497	145	36	3	15	(4	11)	232	83	65	66	13	67	3	2	5	5	9	.36	6	.292	.375	.467
1994 Kansas City	AL	97	363	113	20	3	8	(2	6)	163	52	57	47	3	43	0	2	5	3	2	.60	12	.311	.386	.449
1995 Kansas City	AL	131	465	144	28	0	12	(6	6)	208	69	83	69	10	65	2	5	9	3	2	.60	10	.310	.394	.447
1996 San Diego	NL	121	433	120	29	1	8	(5	3)	175	59	65	69	8	71	3	1	4	5	3	.63	6	.277	.377	.404
1997 San Diego	NL	135	455	149	29	2	13	(6	7)	221	59	83	51	5	51	2	0	10	3	5	.38	14	.327	.390	.486
1998 San Diego	NL	131	439	131	30	1	12	(4	8)	199	58	80	51	8	44	1	0	3	1	2	.33	11	.298	.370	.453
13 ML YEARS		1751	6432	1881	378	23	191	(87	104)	2878	901	1017	731	100	722	35	26	84	59	37	.61	155	.292	.363	.447

Mike Judd

Pitches: Right **Bats:** Right **Pos:** RP-7   **Ht:** 6'1" **Wt:** 217 **Born:** 6/30/75 **Age:** 24

Year Team	Lg	G	GS	CG	GF	IP	BFP	H	R	ER	HR	SH	SF	HB	TBB	IBB	SO	WP	Bk	W	L	Pct.	ShO	Sv-Op	Hld	ERA
1995 Yankees	R	21	0	0	18	32.1	123	18	5	4	0	0	0	4	6	0	30	4	0	1	1	.500	0	8- -	—	1.11
Greensboro	A	1	0	0	1	2.2	11	2	0	0	0	0	0	0	0	0	1	0	0	0	0	.000	0	0- -	—	0.00
1996 Greensboro	A	29	0	0	2	28.1	119	22	14	12	2	2	0	2	8	3	36	2	1	2	2	.500	0	10- -	—	3.81
Savannah	A	15	8	1	7	55.1	220	40	21	15	2	2	0	2	15	0	62	9	0	4	2	.667	0	3- -	—	2.44
1997 Vero Beach	A+	14	14	1	0	86.2	361	67	37	34	4	3	3	1	39	1	104	4	1	6	5	.545	0	0- -	—	3.53
San Antonio	AA	12	12	0	0	79	323	69	27	24	0	0	2	3	33	0	65	8	2	4	2	.667	0	0- -	—	2.73
1998 Albuquerque	AAA	17	17	3	0	94.2	424	98	62	48	17	4	2	6	44	0	77	6	3	5	7	.417	1	0- -	—	4.56
1997 Los Angeles	NL	2	0	0	0	2.2	11	4	0	0	0	0	0	0	0	0	4	0	0	0	0	.000	0	0-0	0	0.00
1998 Los Angeles	NL	7	0	0	3	11.1	63	19	19	19	4	2	0	1	9	1	14	0	0	0	0	.000	0	0-0	0	15.09
2 ML YEARS		8	0	0	3	14	74	23	19	19	4	2	0	1	9	1	18	0	0	0	0	.000	0	0-0	0	12.21

Jeff Juden

Pitches: Right **Bats:** Both **Pos:** SP-30; RP-2   **Ht:** 6'8" **Wt:** 265 **Born:** 1/19/71 **Age:** 28

Year Team	Lg	G	GS	CG	GF	IP	BFP	H	R	ER	HR	SH	SF	HB	TBB	IBB	SO	WP	Bk	W	L	Pct.	ShO	Sv-Op	Hld	ERA
1991 Houston	NL	4	3	0	0	18	81	19	14	12	3	2	3	0	7	1	11	0	1	0	2	.000	0	0-0	0	6.00
1993 Houston	NL	2	0	0	1	5	23	4	3	3	1	0	1	0	4	1	7	0	0	1	1	.000	0	0-0	0	5.40
1994 Philadelphia	NL	6	5	0	0	27.2	121	29	25	19	4	1	2	1	12	0	22	0	2	1	4	.200	0	0-0	0	6.18
1995 Philadelphia	NL	13	10	1	0	62.2	271	53	31	28	6	5	4	5	31	0	47	4	1	2	4	.333	0	0-0	0	4.02
1996 SF-Mon	NL	58	0	0	16	74.1	318	61	35	27	8	3	3	5	34	2	61	5	0	5	0	1.000	0	0-0	3	3.27
1997 Mon-Cle		30	27	3	0	161.1	706	157	86	80	23	7	6	10	72	0	136	8	1	11	6	.647	0	0-0	0	4.46
1998 Mil-Ana		32	30	2	1	178.1	801	182	123	115	27	9	7	12	84	0	148	10	0	8	14	.364	0	0-0	0	5.80
1996 San Francisco	NL	36	0	0	9	41.2	180	39	23	19	7	1	2	1	20	2	35	3	0	4	0	1.000	0	0-0	3	4.10
Montreal	NL	22	0	0	7	32.2	138	22	12	8	1	2	1	4	14	0	26	2	0	1	0	1.000	0	0-0	0	2.20
1997 Montreal	NL	22	22	3	0	130	565	125	64	61	17	5	4	9	57	0	107	7	1	11	5	.688	0	0-0	0	4.22
Cleveland	AL	8	5	0	0	31.1	141	32	21	19	6	2	2	1	15	0	29	1	0	0	1	.000	0	0-0	0	5.46
1998 Milwaukee	NL	24	24	2	0	138.1	629	149	91	85	20	9	7	10	66	0	109	6	0	7	11	.389	0	0-0	0	5.53
Anaheim	AL	8	6	0	1	40	172	33	32	30	7	0	0	2	18	0	39	4	0	1	3	.250	0	0-0	0	6.75
7 ML YEARS		145	75	6	18	527.1	2321	505	316	284	72	27	26	33	244	6	432	27	5	27	31	.466	0	0-0	3	4.85

David Justice

Bats: L **Throws:** L **Pos:** DH-123; LF-19; PH/PR-10; RF-2   **Ht:** 6'3" **Wt:** 200 **Born:** 4/14/66 **Age:** 33

Year Team	Lg	G	AB	H	2B	3B	HR	(Hm	Rd)	TB	R	RBI	TBB	IBB	SO	HBP	SH	SF	SB	CS	SB%	GDP	Avg	OBP	SLG
1989 Atlanta	NL	16	51	12	3	0	1	(1	0)	18	7	3	3	1	9	1	1	0	2	1	.67	1	.235	.291	.353
1990 Atlanta	NL	127	439	124	23	2	28	(19	9)	235	76	78	64	4	92	0	0	1	11	6	.65	2	.282	.373	.535
1991 Atlanta	NL	109	396	109	25	1	21	(11	10)	199	67	87	65	9	81	3	0	5	8	8	.50	4	.275	.377	.503
1992 Atlanta	NL	144	484	124	19	5	21	(10	11)	216	78	72	79	8	85	2	0	6	2	4	.33	1	.256	.359	.446
1993 Atlanta	NL	157	585	158	15	4	40	(18	22)	301	90	120	78	12	90	3	0	4	3	5	.38	9	.270	.357	.515
1994 Atlanta	NL	104	352	110	16	2	19	(9	10)	187	61	59	69	5	45	2	0	1	2	4	.33	8	.313	.427	.531
1995 Atlanta	NL	120	411	104	17	2	24	(15	9)	197	73	78	73	5	68	2	0	5	2	2	.67	5	.253	.365	.479
1996 Atlanta	NL	40	140	45	9	0	6	(5	1)	72	23	25	21	1	22	1	0	2	1	1	.50	5	.321	.409	.514
1997 Cleveland	AL	139	495	163	31	1	33	(17	16)	295	84	101	80	11	79	0	0	7	3	5	.38	12	.329	.418	.596
1998 Cleveland	AL	146	540	151	39	2	21	(7	14)	257	94	88	76	7	98	0	0	9	9	3	.75	9	.280	.363	.476
10 ML YEARS		1102	3893	1100	197	19	214	(112	102)	1977	653	711	608	63	669	14	1	40	45	39	.54	56	.283	.378	.508

Scott Kamieniecki

Pitches: Right **Bats:** Right **Pos:** SP-11; RP-1   **Ht:** 6'0" **Wt:** 200 **Born:** 4/19/64 **Age:** 35

			HOW MUCH HE PITCHED					WHAT HE GAVE UP										THE RESULTS						
Year Team	Lg	G	GS	CG	GF	IP	BFP	H	R	ER	HR	SH	SF	HB	TBB	IBB	SO	WP	Bk	W	L	Pct.	ShO	Sv-Op	Hld	ERA
1998 Bowie *	AA	3	3	0	0	11.1	49	13	6	6	1	0	0	0	2	0	5	1	0	1	0	1.000	0	0--	--	4.76
1991 New York	AL	9	9	0	0	55.1	239	54	24	24	8	2	1	3	22	1	34	1	0	4	4	.500	0	0-0	0	3.90
1992 New York	AL	28	28	4	0	188	804	193	100	91	13	3	5	5	74	9	88	9	1	6	14	.300	0	0-0	0	4.36
1993 New York	AL	30	20	2	4	154.1	659	163	73	70	17	3	5	3	59	7	72	2	0	10	7	.588	0	1-1	0	4.08
1994 New York	AL	22	16	1	2	117.1	509	115	53	49	13	4	3	3	59	5	71	4	0	8	6	.571	0	0-0	1	3.76
1995 New York	AL	17	16	1	1	89.2	391	83	43	40	8	1	0	3	49	1	43	4	0	7	6	.538	0	0-0	0	4.01
1996 New York	AL	7	5	0	0	22.2	120	36	30	28	6	0	0	2	19	1	15	1	0	1	2	.333	0	0-1	0	11.12
1997 Baltimore	AL	30	30	0	0	179.1	764	179	83	80	20	1	6	4	67	2	109	5	0	10	6	.625	0	0-0	0	4.01
1998 Baltimore	AL	12	11	0	1	54.2	249	67	41	41	7	3	2	4	26	0	25	2	0	2	6	.250	0	0-0	0	6.75
8 ML YEARS		155	135	8	8	861.1	3735	890	447	423	92	17	22	27	375	26	457	28	1	48	51	.485	0	1-2	1	4.42

Gabe Kapler

Bats: Right **Throws:** Right **Pos:** RF-6; DH-1; PH/PR-1   **Ht:** 6'2" **Wt:** 190 **Born:** 8/31/75 **Age:** 23

							BATTING												BASERUNNING				PERCENTAGES		
Year Team	Lg	G	AB	H	2B	3B	HR	(Hm	Rd)	TB	R	RBI	TBB	IBB	SO	HBP	SH	SF	SB	CS	SB%	GDP	Avg	OBP	SLG
1995 Jamestown	A-	63	236	68	19	4	4	—	—	107	38	34	23	0	37	2	0	4	1	2	.33	4	.288	.351	.453
1996 Fayetteville	A	138	524	157	45	0	26	—	—	280	81	99	62	6	73	7	3	5	14	4	.78	6	.300	.378	.534
1997 Lakeland	A+	137	519	153	40	6	19	—	—	262	87	87	54	4	68	5	0	10	8	6	.57	8	.295	.361	.505
1998 Jacksnville	AA	139	547	176	47	6	28	—	—	319	113	146	66	5	93	5	0	11	6	4	.60	6	.322	.393	.583
1998 Detroit	AL	7	25	5	0	1	0	(0	0)	7	3	0	1	0	4	0	0	0	2	0	1.00	0	.200	.231	.280

Matt Karchner

Pitches: Right **Bats:** Right **Pos:** RP-61   **Ht:** 6'4" **Wt:** 210 **Born:** 6/28/67 **Age:** 32

				HOW MUCH HE PITCHED					WHAT HE GAVE UP										THE RESULTS						
Year Team	Lg	G	GS	CG	GF	IP	BFP	H	R	ER	HR	SH	SF	HB	TBB	IBB	SO	WP	Bk	W	L	Pct.	ShO	Sv-Op	Hld	ERA
1995 Chicago	AL	31	0	0	10	32	137	33	8	6	2	0	4	1	12	2	24	1	0	4	2	.667	0	0-0	13	1.69
1996 Chicago	AL	50	0	0	13	59.1	278	61	42	38	10	2	4	2	41	8	46	4	0	7	4	.636	0	1-9	13	5.76
1997 Chicago	AL	52	0	0	25	52.2	224	50	18	17	4	3	1	0	26	4	30	6	0	3	1	.750	0	15-16	12	2.91
1998 ChA-ChN		61	0	0	26	64.2	299	63	39	37	8	5	4	7	33	8	52	1	0	5	5	.500	0	11-18	10	5.15
1998 Chicago	AL	32	0	0	23	36.2	167	33	21	21	2	3	4	5	19	6	30	0	0	2	4	.333	0	11-15	1	5.15
Chicago	NL	29	0	0	3	28	132	30	18	16	6	2	0	2	14	2	22	1	0	3	1	.750	0	0-3	9	5.14
4 ML YEARS		194	0	0	74	208.2	938	207	107	98	24	10	13	10	112	22	152	12	0	19	12	.613	0	27-43	48	4.23

Scott Karl

Pitches: Left **Bats:** Left **Pos:** SP-33   **Ht:** 6'2" **Wt:** 206 **Born:** 8/9/71 **Age:** 27

				HOW MUCH HE PITCHED					WHAT HE GAVE UP										THE RESULTS						
Year Team	Lg	G	GS	CG	GF	IP	BFP	H	R	ER	HR	SH	SF	HB	TBB	IBB	SO	WP	Bk	W	L	Pct.	ShO	Sv-Op	Hld	ERA
1995 Milwaukee	AL	25	18	1	3	124	548	141	65	57	10	3	3	3	50	6	59	0	0	6	7	.462	0	0-0	1	4.14
1996 Milwaukee	AL	32	32	3	0	207.1	905	220	124	112	29	2	7	11	72	0	121	5	1	13	9	.591	1	0-0	0	4.86
1997 Milwaukee	AL	32	32	1	0	193.1	839	212	103	96	23	5	2	4	67	1	119	6	0	10	13	.435	0	0-0	0	4.47
1998 Milwaukee	NL	33	33	0	0	192.1	843	219	104	94	21	14	3	4	66	4	102	6	0	10	11	.476	0	0-0	0	4.40
4 ML YEARS		122	115	5	3	717	3135	792	396	359	83	24	15	22	255	11	401	17	1	39	40	.494	1	0-0	1	4.51

Eric Karros

Bats: Right **Throws:** Right **Pos:** 1B-136; DH-2; PH/PR-1   **Ht:** 6'4" **Wt:** 226 **Born:** 11/4/67 **Age:** 31

							BATTING												BASERUNNING				PERCENTAGES		
Year Team	Lg	G	AB	H	2B	3B	HR	(Hm	Rd)	TB	R	RBI	TBB	IBB	SO	HBP	SH	SF	SB	CS	SB%	GDP	Avg	OBP	SLG
1998 San Berndno *	A+	4	15	4	1	0	0			5	3	1	0	0	0	0	0	0	0	0	.00	0	.267	.267	.333
1991 Los Angeles	NL	14	14	1	1	0	0	(0	0)	2	0	1	1	0	6	0	0	0	0	0	.00	0	.071	.133	.143
1992 Los Angeles	NL	149	545	140	30	1	20	(6	14)	232	63	88	37	3	103	2	0	5	2	4	.33	15	.257	.304	.426
1993 Los Angeles	NL	158	619	153	27	2	23	(13	10)	253	74	80	34	1	82	0	0	3	0	0	.00	17	.247	.287	.409
1994 Los Angeles	NL	111	406	108	21	1	14	(5	9)	173	51	46	29	1	53	2	0	11	2	0	1.00	4	.266	.310	.426
1995 Los Angeles	NL	143	551	164	29	3	32	(19	13)	295	83	105	61	4	115	4	0	4	4	4	.50	14	.298	.369	.535
1996 Los Angeles	NL	154	608	158	29	1	34	(16	18)	291	84	111	53	2	121	1	0	8	8	0	1.00	27	.260	.316	.479
1997 Los Angeles	NL	162	628	167	28	0	31	(13	18)	288	86	104	61	2	116	2	0	9	15	7	.68	10	.266	.329	.459
1998 Los Angeles	NL	139	507	150	20	2	23	(9	14)	241	59	87	47	1	93	3	0	7	7	2	.78	7	.296	.355	.475
8 ML YEARS		1030	3878	1041	185	9	177	(81	96)	1775	500	622	323	14	689	16	0	47	38	18	.68	103	.268	.324	.458

Steve Karsay

Pitches: Right **Bats:** Right **Pos:** RP-10; SP-1   **Ht:** 6'3" **Wt:** 209 **Born:** 3/24/72 **Age:** 27

				HOW MUCH HE PITCHED					WHAT HE GAVE UP										THE RESULTS						
Year Team	Lg	G	GS	CG	GF	IP	BFP	H	R	ER	HR	SH	SF	HB	TBB	IBB	SO	WP	Bk	W	L	Pct.	ShO	Sv-Op	Hld	ERA
1998 Buffalo *	AAA	16	14	0	0	79	342	89	39	33	5	0	1	3	15	0	63	2	0	6	4	.600	0	0--	--	3.76
1993 Oakland	AL	8	8	0	0	49	210	49	23	22	4	0	2	2	16	1	33	1	0	3	3	.500	0	0-0	0	4.04
1994 Oakland	AL	4	4	1	0	28	115	26	8	8	1	2	1	1	8	0	15	0	0	1	1	.500	0	0-0	0	2.57
1997 Oakland	AL	24	24	0	0	132.2	609	166	92	85	20	2	5	9	47	3	92	7	0	3	12	.200	0	0-0	0	5.77
1998 Cleveland	AL	11	1	0	4	24.1	111	31	16	16	3	1	2	2	6	1	13	2	0	0	2	.000	0	0-0	2	5.92
4 ML YEARS		47	37	1	4	234	1045	272	139	131	28	5	10	14	77	5	153	10	0	7	18	.280	0	0-0	2	5.04

Greg Keagle

Pitches: Right **Bats:** Right **Pos:** SP-7; RP-2   **Ht:** 6'2" **Wt:** 195 **Born:** 6/28/71 **Age:** 28

Year Team	Lg	G	GS	CG	GF	IP	BFP	H	R	ER	HR	SH	SF	HB	TBB	IBB	SO	WP	Bk	W	L	Pct.	ShO	Sv-Op	Hld	ERA
1998 Toledo *	AAA	15	14	0	1	81.2	365	94	48	42	12	1	2	6	32	0	61	1	2	5	3	.625	0	0- -	—	4.63
1996 Detroit	AL	26	6	0	5	87.2	435	104	76	72	13	2	7	9	68	5	70	2	0	3	6	.333	0	0-0	0	7.39
1997 Detroit	AL	11	10	0	0	45.1	214	58	33	33	9	2	1	5	18	0	33	1	0	3	5	.375	0	0-0	0	6.55
1998 Detroit	AL	9	7	0	0	38.2	180	46	26	24	5	0	0	4	20	0	25	2	0	0	5	.000	0	0-0	0	5.59
3 ML YEARS		46	23	0	5	171.2	829	208	135	129	27	4	8	18	106	5	128	5	0	6	16	.273	0	0-0	0	6.76

Mike Kelly

Bats: R **Throws:** R **Pos:** RF-51; LF-43; PH/PR-26; DH-6   **Ht:** 6'4" **Wt:** 195 **Born:** 6/2/70 **Age:** 29

								BATTING									BASERUNNING				PERCENTAGES		
Year Team	Lg	G	AB	H	2B	3B	HR	(Hm	Rd)	TB	R	RBI	TBB	IBB	SO	HBP	SH	SF	SB	CS	SB%	GDP	Avg	OBP	SLG
1998 Durham *	AAA	4	12	1	0	0	0	—	—	1	2	0	4	0	5	0	0	0	0	0	.00	1	.083	.313	.083
1994 Atlanta	NL	30	77	21	10	1	2	(0	2)	39	14	9	2	0	17	1	0	0	0	1	.00	1	.273	.300	.506
1995 Atlanta	NL	97	137	26	6	1	3	(0	3)	43	26	17	11	0	49	2	2	1	7	3	.70	2	.190	.258	.314
1996 Cincinnati	NL	19	49	9	4	0	1	(0	1)	16	5	7	9	0	11	2	0	0	4	0	1.00	2	.184	.333	.327
1997 Cincinnati	NL	73	140	41	13	2	6	(3	3)	76	27	19	10	0	30	0	0	1	6	1	.86	3	.293	.338	.543
1998 Tampa Bay	AL	106	279	67	11	2	10	(4	6)	112	39	33	22	1	80	0	1	1	13	6	.68	8	.240	.295	.401
5 ML YEARS		325	682	164	44	6	22	(7	15)	286	111	85	54	1	187	5	3	3	30	11	.73	16	.240	.300	.419

Pat Kelly

Bats: R **Throws:** R **Pos:** 2B-41; PH/PR-11; LF-3; SS-2   **Ht:** 6'0" **Wt:** 182 **Born:** 10/14/67 **Age:** 31

								BATTING									BASERUNNING				PERCENTAGES		
Year Team	Lg	G	AB	H	2B	3B	HR	(Hm	Rd)	TB	R	RBI	TBB	IBB	SO	HBP	SH	SF	SB	CS	SB%	GDP	Avg	OBP	SLG
1998 Syracuse *	AAA	80	291	82	22	3	17			161	58	39	39	2	60	6	8	2	18	6	.75	4	.282	.376	.553
1991 New York	AL	96	298	72	12	4	3	(3	0)	101	35	23	15	0	52	5	2	2	12	1	.92	5	.242	.288	.339
1992 New York	AL	106	318	72	22	2	7	(3	4)	119	38	27	25	1	72	10	6	3	8	5	.62	6	.226	.301	.374
1993 New York	AL	127	406	111	24	1	7	(4	3)	158	49	51	24	0	68	5	10	6	14	11	.56	9	.273	.317	.389
1994 New York	AL	93	286	80	21	2	3	(1	2)	114	35	41	19	1	51	1	5	4	6	5	.55	10	.280	.330	.399
1995 New York	AL	89	270	64	12	1	4	(1	3)	90	32	29	23	0	65	5	10	2	8	3	.73	5	.237	.307	.333
1996 New York	AL	13	21	3	0	0	0	(0	0)	3	4	2	2	0	9	0	1	0	1	0	1.00	1	.143	.217	.143
1997 New York	AL	67	120	29	6	1	2	(1	1)	43	25	10	14	1	37	1	2	1	8	1	.89	4	.242	.324	.358
1998 St. Louis	NL	53	153	33	5	0	4	(3	1)	50	18	14	13	0	48	2	1	1	5	1	.83	3	.216	.284	.327
8 ML YEARS		644	1872	464	102	11	30	(16	14)	678	236	197	135	3	402	33	45	20	61	28	.69	43	.248	.307	.362

Roberto Kelly

Bats: R **Throws:** R **Pos:** CF-41; RF-31; LF-14; PH/PR-14; DH-2   **Ht:** 6'2" **Wt:** 198 **Born:** 10/1/64 **Age:** 34

								BATTING									BASERUNNING				PERCENTAGES		
Year Team	Lg	G	AB	H	2B	3B	HR	(Hm | Rd)	TB	R	RBI	TBB	IBB	SO	HBP	SH	SF	SB	CS	SB%	GDP	Avg	OBP	SLG
1987 New York	AL	23	52	14	3	0	1	(0 | 1)	20	12	7	5	0	15	0	1	1	9	3	.75	0	.269	.328	.385
1988 New York	AL	38	77	19	4	1	1	(1 | 0)	28	9	7	3	0	15	0	3	1	5	2	.71	0	.247	.272	.364
1989 New York	AL	137	441	133	18	3	9	(2 | 7)	184	65	48	41	3	89	6	8	0	35	12	.74	9	.302	.369	.417
1990 New York	AL	162	641	183	32	4	15	(5 | 10)	268	85	61	33	0	148	4	4	4	42	17	.71	7	.285	.323	.418
1991 New York	AL	126	486	130	22	2	20	(11 | 9)	216	68	69	45	2	77	5	2	5	32	9	.78	14	.267	.333	.444
1992 New York	AL	152	580	158	31	2	10	(6 | 4)	223	81	66	41	4	96	4	1	6	28	5	.85	19	.272	.322	.384
1993 Cincinnati	NL	78	320	102	17	3	9	(4 | 5)	152	44	35	17	0	43	2	0	3	21	5	.81	10	.319	.354	.475
1994 Cin-Atl	NL	110	434	127	23	3	9	(4 | 5)	183	73	45	35	1	71	3	0	3	19	11	.63	8	.293	.347	.422
1995 Mon-LA	NL	136	504	140	23	2	7	(2 | 5)	188	58	57	22	6	79	6	0	7	19	10	.66	14	.278	.312	.373
1996 Minnesota	AL	98	322	104	17	4	6	(3 | 3)	147	41	47	23	0	53	7	0	5	10	2	.83	17	.323	.375	.457
1997 Min-Sea	AL	105	368	107	26	2	12	(8 | 4)	173	58	59	22	0	67	3	2	3	9	5	.64	6	.291	.333	.470
1998 Texas	AL	75	257	83	7	3	16	(6 | 10)	144	48	46	8	0	46	3	1	1	0	2	.00	4	.323	.349	.560
1994 Cincinnati	NL	47	179	54	8	0	3	(1 | 2)	71	29	21	11	1	35	3	0	1	9	8	.53	3	.302	.351	.397
Atlanta	NL	63	255	73	15	3	6	(3 | 3)	112	44	24	24	0	36	0	0	2	10	3	.77	5	.286	.345	.439
1995 Montreal	NL	24	95	26	4	0	1	(0 | 1)	33	11	9	7	1	14	2	0	0	4	3	.57	4	.274	.337	.347
Los Angeles	NL	112	409	114	19	2	6	(2 | 4)	155	47	48	15	5	65	4	0	7	15	7	.68	10	.279	.306	.379
1997 Minnesota	NL	75	247	71	19	2	5	(5 | 0)	109	39	37	17	0	50	2	1	2	7	4	.64	4	.287	.336	.441
Seattle	AL	30	121	36	7	0	7	(3 | 4)	64	19	22	5	0	17	1	1	1	2	1	.67	2	.298	.328	.529
12 ML YEARS		1240	4482	1300	223	29	115	(52 | 63)	1926	642	547	295	16	799	43	22	39	229	83	.73	108	.290	.337	.430

Jason Kendall

Bats: Right **Throws:** Right **Pos:** C-144; PH/PR-5   **Ht:** 6'0" **Wt:** 190 **Born:** 6/26/74 **Age:** 25

								BATTING									BASERUNNING				PERCENTAGES		
Year Team	Lg	G	AB	H	2B	3B	HR	(Hm | Rd)	TB	R	RBI	TBB	IBB	SO	HBP	SH	SF	SB	CS	SB%	GDP	Avg	OBP	SLG
1996 Pittsburgh	NL	130	414	124	23	5	3	(2 | 1)	166	54	42	35	11	30	15	3	4	5	2	.71	7	.300	.372	.401
1997 Pittsburgh	NL	144	486	143	36	4	8	(5 | 3)	211	71	49	49	2	53	31	1	5	18	6	.75	11	.294	.391	.434
1998 Pittsburgh	NL	149	535	175	36	3	12	(6 | 6)	253	95	75	51	3	51	31	2	8	26	5	.84	6	.327	.411	.473
3 ML YEARS		423	1435	442	95	12	23	(13 | 10)	630	220	166	135	16	134	77	6	17	49	13	.79	24	.308	.393	.439

Jeff Kent

Bats: Right **Throws:** Right **Pos:** 2B-134; PH/PR-2; 1B-1   **Ht:** 6'1" **Wt:** 190 **Born:** 3/7/68 **Age:** 31

Year Team	Lg	G	AB	H	2B	3B	HR	(Hm	Rd)	TB	R	RBI	TBB	IBB	SO	HBP	SH	SF	SB	CS	SB%	GDP	Avg	OBP	SLG
1992 Tor-NYN		102	305	73	21	2	11	(4	7)	131	52	50	27	0	76	7	0	4	2	3	.40	5	.239	.312	.430
1993 New York	NL	140	496	134	24	0	21	(9	12)	221	65	80	30	2	88	8	6	4	4	4	.50	11	.270	.320	.446
1994 New York	NL	107	415	121	24	5	14	(10	4)	197	53	68	23	3	84	10	1	3	1	4	.20	7	.292	.341	.475
1995 New York	NL	125	472	131	22	3	20	(11	9)	219	65	65	29	3	89	8	1	4	3	3	.50	9	.278	.327	.464
1996 NYN-Cle		128	437	124	27	1	12	(4	8)	189	61	55	31	1	78	2	1	6	6	4	.60	8	.284	.330	.432
1997 San Francisco	NL	155	580	145	38	2	29	(13	16)	274	90	121	48	6	133	13	0	10	11	3	.79	14	.250	.316	.472
1998 San Francisco	NL	137	526	156	37	3	31	(17	14)	292	94	128	48	4	110	9	1	10	9	4	.69	16	.297	.359	.555
1992 Toronto	AL	65	192	46	13	1	8	(2	6)	85	36	35	20	0	47	6	0	4	2	1	.67	3	.240	.324	.443
New York	NL	37	113	27	8	1	3	(2	1)	46	16	15	7	0	29	1	0	0	0	2	.00	2	.239	.289	.407
1996 New York	NL	89	335	97	20	1	9	(2	7)	146	45	39	21	1	56	1	1	3	4	3	.57	7	.290	.331	.436
Cleveland	AL	39	102	27	7	0	3	(2	1)	43	16	16	10	0	22	1	0	3	2	1	.67	1	.265	.328	.422
7 ML YEARS		894	3231	884	193	16	138	(68	70)	1523	480	567	236	19	658	57	10	41	36	25	.59	70	.274	.330	.471

Jimmy Key

Pitches: Left **Bats:** Right **Pos:** RP-14; SP-11   **Ht:** 6'1" **Wt:** 190 **Born:** 4/22/61 **Age:** 38

Year Team	Lg	G	GS	CG	GF	IP	BFP	H	R	ER	HR	SH	SF	HB	TBB	IBB	SO	WP	Bk	W	L	Pct.	ShO	Sv-Op	Hld	ERA
1998 Frederick *	A+	1	1	0	0	6	22	4	2	2	0	0	0	2	0	6	0	0	1	0	1.000	0	0--	—	3.00
1984 Toronto	AL	63	0	0	24	62	285	70	37	32	8	6	1	1	32	8	44	3	1	4	5	.444	0	10--	—	4.65
1985 Toronto	AL	35	32	3	0	212.2	856	188	77	71	22	5	5	2	50	1	85	6	1	14	6	.700	0	0--	—	3.00
1986 Toronto	AL	36	35	4	0	232	959	222	98	92	24	10	6	3	74	1	141	0	0	14	11	.560	2	0--	—	3.57
1987 Toronto	AL	36	36	8	0	261	1033	210	93	80	24	11	3	2	66	6	161	8	5	17	8	.680	1	0-0	0	2.76
1988 Toronto	AL	21	21	2	0	131.1	551	127	55	48	13	4	3	5	30	2	65	1	0	12	5	.706	2	0-0	0	3.29
1989 Toronto	AL	33	33	5	0	216	886	226	99	93	18	9	9	3	27	2	118	4	1	13	14	.481	1	0-0	0	3.88
1990 Toronto	AL	27	27	0	0	154.2	636	169	79	73	20	5	6	1	22	2	88	0	1	13	7	.650	0	0-0	0	4.25
1991 Toronto	AL	33	33	2	0	209.1	877	207	84	71	12	10	5	3	44	3	125	1	0	16	12	.571	2	0-0	0	3.05
1992 Toronto	AL	33	33	4	0	216.2	900	205	88	85	24	2	7	4	59	0	117	5	0	13	13	.500	2	0-0	0	3.53
1993 New York	AL	34	34	4	0	236.2	948	219	84	79	26	6	9	1	43	1	173	3	0	18	6	.750	2	0-0	0	3.00
1994 New York	AL	25	25	1	0	168	710	177	68	61	10	4	2	3	52	0	97	8	1	17	4	.810	0	0-0	0	3.27
1995 New York	AL	5	5	0	0	30.1	134	40	20	19	3	3	1	0	6	1	14	1	0	1	2	.333	0	0-0	0	5.64
1996 New York	AL	30	30	0	0	169.1	715	171	93	88	21	7	5	2	58	1	116	2	0	12	11	.522	0	0-0	0	4.68
1997 Baltimore	AL	34	34	1	0	212.1	902	210	90	81	24	5	6	5	82	1	141	4	1	16	10	.615	1	0-0	0	3.43
1998 Baltimore	AL	25	11	0	4	79.1	327	77	39	37	5	1	1	3	23	0	53	1	1	6	3	.667	0	0-1	3	4.20
15 ML YEARS		470	389	34	28	2591.2	10719	2518	1104	1010	254	88	69	38	668	29	1538	50	12	186	117	.614	13	10--	—	3.51

Darryl Kile

Pitches: Right **Bats:** Right **Pos:** SP-35; RP-1   **Ht:** 6'5" **Wt:** 185 **Born:** 12/2/68 **Age:** 30

Year Team	Lg	G	GS	CG	GF	IP	BFP	H	R	ER	HR	SH	SF	HB	TBB	IBB	SO	WP	Bk	W	L	Pct.	ShO	Sv-Op	Hld	ERA
1991 Houston	NL	37	22	0	5	153.2	689	144	81	63	16	9	5	6	84	4	100	5	4	7	11	.389	0	0-1	0	3.69
1992 Houston	NL	22	22	2	0	125.1	554	124	61	55	8	5	6	4	63	4	90	3	4	5	10	.333	0	0-0	0	3.95
1993 Houston	NL	32	26	4	0	171.2	733	152	73	67	12	5	7	15	69	1	141	9	3	15	8	.652	2	0-0	0	3.51
1994 Houston	NL	24	24	0	0	147.2	664	153	84	75	13	14	2	9	82	6	105	10	0	9	6	.600	0	0-0	0	4.57
1995 Houston	NL	25	21	0	1	127	570	114	81	70	5	7	3	12	73	2	113	11	1	4	12	.250	0	0-0	0	4.96
1996 Houston	NL	35	33	4	1	219	975	233	113	102	16	10	9	16	97	8	219	13	3	12	11	.522	0	0-0	0	4.19
1997 Houston	NL	34	34	6	0	255.2	1056	208	87	73	19	17	10	10	94	2	205	7	1	19	7	.731	4	0-0	0	2.57
1998 Colorado	NL	36	35	4	1	230.1	1020	257	141	133	28	15	8	7	96	4	158	12	0	13	17	.433	1	0-0	0	5.20
8 ML YEARS		245	217	20	8	1430.1	6261	1385	721	638	117	82	50	79	658	31	1131	70	16	84	82	.506	7	0-1	0	4.01

Curtis King

Pitches: Right **Bats:** Right **Pos:** RP-36   **Ht:** 6'5" **Wt:** 205 **Born:** 10/25/70 **Age:** 28

Year Team	Lg	G	GS	CG	GF	IP	BFP	H	R	ER	HR	SH	SF	HB	TBB	IBB	SO	WP	Bk	W	L	Pct.	ShO	Sv-Op	Hld	ERA
1994 New Jersey	A-	5	4	0	0	20.2	92	19	7	6	0	0	1	0	11	0	14	2	1	1	0	1.000	0	0--	—	2.61
Savannah	A	8	8	2	0	53	202	37	14	11	4	2	1	4	9	0	40	1	0	4	1	.800	2	0--	—	1.87
1995 St. Pete	A+	28	21	3	1	136	567	117	49	39	3	4	2	11	49	2	65	6	0	7	8	.467	0	0--	—	2.58
1996 Arkansas	AA	5	0	0	3	5	37	15	12	11	1	0	0	0	6	1	5	0	0	0	1	.000	0	1--	—	19.80
St. Pete	A+	48	0	0	46	55.2	232	41	20	17	0	5	2	5	24	4	27	2	0	3	3	.500	0	30--	—	2.75
1997 Arkansas	AA	32	0	0	27	36.1	154	38	19	18	7	2	0	1	10	1	29	1	0	2	3	.400	0	16--	—	4.46
Louisville	AAA	16	0	0	9	22	89	19	5	5	1	5	0	0	6	1	9	0	0	2	1	.667	0	3--	—	2.05
1998 Memphis	AAA	27	0	0	18	25.2	110	31	6	6	1	3	0	2	6	1	23	2	0	0	1	.000	0	12--	—	2.10
1997 St. Louis	NL	30	0	0	8	29.1	136	38	14	9	0	4	3	1	11	0	13	2	0	4	2	.667	0	0-3	10	2.76
1998 St. Louis	NL	36	0	0	11	51	218	50	20	20	5	2	2	3	20	4	28	0	0	2	0	1.000	0	2-8	3	3.53
2 ML YEARS		66	0	0	19	80.1	354	88	34	29	5	6	5	4	31	4	41	2	0	6	2	.750	0	2-11	13	3.25

Jeff King

Bats: R **Throws:** R **Pos:** 1B-112; DH-16; 3B-4; PH/PR-3   **Ht:** 6'1" **Wt:** 190 **Born:** 12/26/64 **Age:** 34

Year Team	Lg	G	AB	H	2B	3B	HR	(Hm	Rd)	TB	R	RBI	TBB	IBB	SO	HBP	SH	SF	SB	CS	SB%	GDP	Avg	OBP	SLG
1989 Pittsburgh	NL	75	215	42	13	3	5	(3	2)	76	31	19	20	1	34	2	2	4	4	2	.67	3	.195	.266	.353
1990 Pittsburgh	NL	127	371	91	17	1	14	(9	5)	152	46	53	21	1	50	1	2	7	3	3	.50	12	.245	.283	.410
1991 Pittsburgh	NL	33	109	26	1	1	4	(3	1)	41	16	18	14	3	15	1	0	1	3	1	.75	3	.239	.328	.376
1992 Pittsburgh	NL	130	480	111	21	2	14	(6	8)	178	56	65	27	3	56	2	8	5	4	6	.40	8	.231	.272	.371
1993 Pittsburgh	NL	158	611	180	35	3	9	(4	5)	248	82	98	59	4	54	4	1	8	8	6	.57	17	.295	.356	.406
1994 Pittsburgh	NL	94	339	89	23	0	5	(2	3)	127	36	42	30	1	38	0	2	7	3	2	.60	7	.263	.316	.375
1995 Pittsburgh	NL	122	445	118	27	2	18	(7	11)	203	61	87	55	5	63	1	0	8	7	4	.64	10	.265	.342	.456
1996 Pittsburgh	NL	155	591	160	36	4	30	(14	16)	294	91	111	70	3	95	2	1	8	15	1	.94	17	.271	.346	.497
1997 Kansas City	AL	155	543	129	30	1	28	(11	17)	245	84	112	89	4	96	2	1	12	16	5	.76	9	.238	.341	.451
1998 Kansas City	AL	131	486	128	17	1	24	(13	11)	219	83	93	42	1	73	2	0	10	10	2	.83	10	.263	.319	.451
10 ML YEARS		1180	4190	1074	220	18	151	(72	79)	1783	586	698	427	26	574	17	17	70	73	32	.70	96	.256	.323	.426

Gene Kingsale

Bats: Both **Throws:** Right **Pos:** PH/PR-7; CF-4; DH-1   **Ht:** 6'3" **Wt:** 190 **Born:** 8/20/76 **Age:** 22

Year Team	Lg	G	AB	H	2B	3B	HR	(Hm	Rd)	TB	R	RBI	TBB	IBB	SO	HBP	SH	SF	SB	CS	SB%	GDP	Avg	OBP	SLG
1994 Orioles	R	50	168	52	2	3	0	—	—	60	26	9	18	0	24	2	1	1	15	8	.65	1	.310	.381	.357
1995 Bluefield	R+	47	171	54	11	2	0	—	—	69	45	16	27	0	31	5	4	2	20	8	.71	0	.316	.420	.404
1996 Frederick	A+	49	166	45	6	4	0	—	—	59	26	9	19	1	32	6	3	2	23	4	.85	1	.271	.363	.355
1997 Orioles	R	6	17	5	0	0	0	—	—	5	2	0	2	0	2	1	0	0	1	0	1.00	0	.294	.400	.294
Bowie	AA	13	46	19	6	0	0	—	—	25	8	4	5	0	4	1	1	0	5	1	.83	2	.413	.481	.543
1998 Rochester	AAA	18	55	12	1	1	0	—	—	15	3	2	4	0	8	1	1	0	3	3	.50	3	.218	.283	.273
Bowie	AA	111	427	112	11	5	1	—	—	136	69	34	48	2	79	12	10	4	29	12	.71	6	.262	.350	.319
1996 Baltimore	AL	3	0	0	0	0	0	(0	0)	0	0	0	0	0	0	0	0	0	0	0	.00	0	.000	.000	.000
1998 Baltimore	AL	11	2	0	0	0	0	(0	0)	0	1	0	0	0	1	0	0	0	0	0	.00	0	.000	.000	.000
2 ML YEARS		14	2	0	0	0	0	(0	0)	0	1	0	0	0	1	0	0	0	0	0	.00	0	.000	.000	.000

Mike Kinkade

Bats: Right **Throws:** Right **Pos:** PH/PR-2; 3B-1   **Ht:** 6'1" **Wt:** 210 **Born:** 5/6/73 **Age:** 26

Year Team	Lg	G	AB	H	2B	3B	HR	(Hm	Rd)	TB	R	RBI	TBB	IBB	SO	HBP	SH	SF	SB	CS	SB%	GDP	Avg	OBP	SLG
1995 Helena	R+	69	266	94	19	1	4	—	—	127	76	39	43	2	38	10	0	6	26	9	.74	6	.353	.452	.477
1996 Beloit	A	135	499	151	33	4	15	—	—	237	105	100	47	7	69	32	3	6	23	12	.66	10	.303	.394	.475
1997 El Paso	AA	125	468	180	35	12	12	—	—	275	112	109	52	0	66	13	1	6	17	4	.81	13	.385	.455	.588
1998 Louisville	AAA	80	291	90	24	6	7	—	—	147	57	46	36	1	52	6	1	7	10	2	.83	7	.309	.394	.505
Norfolk	AAA	30	125	35	5	0	1	—	—	43	12	18	3	0	24	5	1	2	6	1	.86	5	.280	.319	.344
1998 New York	NL	3	2	0	0	0	0	(0	0)	0	2	0	0	0	0	0	0	0	0	0	.00	0	.000	.000	.000

Wayne Kirby

Bats: L **Throws:** R **Pos:** RF-12; PH/PR-12; CF-4; LF-3   **Ht:** 5'10" **Wt:** 190 **Born:** 1/22/64 **Age:** 35

Year Team	Lg	G	AB	H	2B	3B	HR	(Hm	Rd)	TB	R	RBI	TBB	IBB	SO	HBP	SH	SF	SB	CS	SB%	GDP	Avg	OBP	SLG
1998 Memphis *	AAA	58	227	64	15	3	5	—	—	100	36	32	15	1	33	0	2	0	10	2	.83	2	.282	.326	.441
Norfolk *	AAA	42	162	50	8	3	5	—	—	79	32	23	21	1	18	2	1	0	11	5	.69	1	.309	.395	.488
1991 Cleveland	AL	21	43	9	2	0	0	(0	0)	11	4	5	2	0	6	0	1	1	1	2	.33	2	.209	.239	.256
1992 Cleveland	AL	21	18	3	1	0	1	(0	1)	7	9	1	3	0	2	0	0	0	0	3	.00	1	.167	.286	.389
1993 Cleveland	AL	131	458	123	19	5	6	(4	2)	170	71	60	37	2	58	3	7	6	17	5	.77	8	.269	.323	.371
1994 Cleveland	AL	78	191	56	6	0	5	(3	2)	77	33	23	13	0	30	1	2	0	11	4	.73	1	.293	.341	.403
1995 Cleveland	AL	101	188	39	10	2	1	(0	1)	56	29	14	13	0	32	1	1	2	10	3	.77	4	.207	.260	.298
1996 Cle-LA		92	204	55	11	1	1	(0	1)	71	26	12	19	1	19	1	1	1	4	3	.57	4	.270	.333	.348
1997 Los Angeles	NL	46	65	11	2	0	0	(0	0)	13	6	4	10	0	12	0	0	0	0	0	.00	1	.169	.280	.200
1998 New York	NL	26	31	6	0	1	0	(0	0)	8	5	0	1	0	9	0	1	0	1	1	.50	0	.194	.219	.258
1996 Cleveland	AL	27	16	4	1	0	0	(0	0)	5	3	1	2	0	2	0	0	0	1	1	.00	1	.250	.333	.313
Los Angeles	NL	65	188	51	10	1	1	(0	1)	66	23	11	17	1	17	1	1	1	4	2	.67	3	.271	.333	.351
8 ML YEARS		516	1198	302	51	9	14	(7	7)	413	183	119	98	3	168	6	13	10	44	21	.68	21	.252	.309	.345

Danny Klassen

Bats: Right **Throws:** Right **Pos:** 2B-29; PH/PR-1   **Ht:** 6'0" **Wt:** 175 **Born:** 9/22/75 **Age:** 23

Year Team	Lg	G	AB	H	2B	3B	HR	(Hm	Rd)	TB	R	RBI	TBB	IBB	SO	HBP	SH	SF	SB	CS	SB%	GDP	Avg	OBP	SLG
1993 Brewers	R	38	117	26	5	0	2	—	—	37	26	20	24	3	28	8	1	4	14	3	.82	2	.222	.379	.316
Helena	R+	18	45	9	1	0	0	—	—	10	8	3	7	0	11	2	1	0	2	1	.67	2	.200	.333	.222
1994 Beloit	A	133	458	119	20	3	6	—	—	163	61	54	58	0	123	12	17	3	28	14	.67	3	.260	.356	.356
1995 Beloit	A	59	218	60	15	2	2	—	—	85	27	25	16	0	43	4	0	3	12	4	.75	4	.275	.332	.390
1996 Stockton	A+	118	432	116	22	4	2	—	—	152	58	46	34	0	77	10	5	2	14	8	.64	12	.269	.335	.352
1997 El Paso	AA	135	519	172	30	6	14	—	—	256	112	81	48	1	104	10	4	4	16	9	.64	13	.331	.396	.493
1998 Tucson	AAA	73	281	82	25	2	10	—	—	141	47	47	19	1	54	6	0	5	6	2	.75	11	.292	.344	.502
1998 Arizona	NL	29	108	21	2	1	3	(3	0)	34	12	8	9	0	33	1	0	0	1	1	.50	5	.194	.263	.315

Ryan Klesko

Bats: Left **Throws:** Left **Pos:** LF-120; 1B-7; PH/PR-5   **Ht:** 6'3" **Wt:** 220 **Born:** 6/12/71 **Age:** 28

					BATTING														BASERUNNING				PERCENTAGES		
Year Team	Lg	G	AB	H	2B	3B	HR	(Hm Rd)	TB	R	RBI	TBB	IBB	SO	HBP	SH	SF	SB	CS	SB%	GDP	Avg	OBP	SLG
1992 Atlanta	NL	13	14	0	0	0	0	(0 0)	0	0	1	0	0	5	1	0	0	0	0	.00	0	.000	.067	.000
1993 Atlanta	NL	22	17	6	1	0	2	(2 0)	13	3	5	3	1	4	0	0	0	0	0	.00	0	.353	.450	.765
1994 Atlanta	NL	92	245	68	13	3	17	(7 10)	138	42	47	26	3	48	1	0	4	1	0	1.00	8	.278	.344	.563
1995 Atlanta	NL	107	329	102	25	2	23	(15 8)	200	48	70	47	10	72	2	0	3	5	4	.56	8	.310	.396	.608
1996 Atlanta	NL	153	528	149	21	4	34	(20 14)	280	90	93	68	10	129	2	0	4	6	3	.67	10	.282	.364	.530
1997 Atlanta	NL	143	467	122	23	6	24	(10 14)	229	67	84	48	5	130	4	1	2	4	4	.50	12	.261	.334	.490
1998 Atlanta	NL	129	427	117	29	1	18	(8 10)	202	69	70	56	5	66	3	0	4	5	3	.63	9	.274	.359	.473
7 ML YEARS		659	2027	564	112	16	118	(62 56)	1062	319	370	248	34	454	13	1	17	21	14	.60	47	.278	.358	.524

Steve Kline

Pitches: Left **Bats:** Both **Pos:** RP-78   **Ht:** 6'2" **Wt:** 210 **Born:** 8/22/72 **Age:** 26

		HOW MUCH HE PITCHED						WHAT HE GAVE UP										THE RESULTS						
Year Team	Lg	G	GS	CG	GF	IP	BFP	H	R	ER	HR	SH	SF	HB	TBB	IBB	SO	WP	Bk	W	L	Pct.	ShO	Sv-Op	Hld	ERA
1993 Burlington	R+	2	1	0	0	7.1	34	11	4	4	0	1	0	0	2	1	4	0	0	1	1	.500	0	0--	—	4.91
Watertown	A-	13	13	2	0	79	332	77	36	28	3	3	2	4	12	0	45	5	0	5	4	.556	1	0--	—	3.19
1994 Columbus	A	28	28	2	0	185.2	744	175	67	62	14	1	2	7	36	0	174	6	2	18	5	.783	1	0--	—	3.01
1995 Canton-Akrn	AA	14	14	0	0	89.1	377	86	34	24	6	4	1	1	30	3	45	1	1	2	3	.400	0	0--	—	2.42
1996 Canton-Akrn	AA	25	24	0	0	146.2	658	168	98	89	16	10	4	6	55	2	107	5	1	8	12	.400	0	0--	—	5.46
1997 Buffalo	AAA	20	4	0	5	51.1	219	53	26	23	4	3	0	3	13	1	41	5	0	3	3	.500	0	1--	—	4.03
1998 Ottawa	AAA	2	0	0	0	2.2	8	1	0	0	0	0	0	0	1	0	0	0	0	0	0	.000	0	0--	—	0.00
1997 Cle-Mon		46	1	0	7	52.2	248	73	37	35	10	4	2	2	23	4	37	4	1	4	4	.500	0	0-3	5	5.98
1998 Montreal	NL	78	0	0	18	71.2	319	62	25	22	4	1	2	3	41	7	76	5	0	3	6	.333	0	1-2	18	2.76
1997 Cleveland	AL	20	1	0	0	26.1	130	42	19	17	6	1	0	1	13	1	17	3	1	3	1	.750	0	0-2	4	5.81
Montreal	NL	26	0	0	7	26.1	118	31	18	18	4	3	2	1	10	3	20	1	0	1	3	.250	0	0-1	1	6.15
2 ML YEARS		124	1	0	25	124.1	567	135	62	57	14	5	4	5	64	11	113	9	1	7	10	.412	0	1-5	23	4.13

Scott Klingenbeck

Pitches: Right **Bats:** Right **Pos:** SP-4   **Ht:** 6'2" **Wt:** 205 **Born:** 2/3/71 **Age:** 28

		HOW MUCH HE PITCHED						WHAT HE GAVE UP										THE RESULTS						
Year Team	Lg	G	GS	CG	GF	IP	BFP	H	R	ER	HR	SH	SF	HB	TBB	IBB	SO	WP	Bk	W	L	Pct.	ShO	Sv-Op	Hld	ERA
1998 Indianapols *	AAA	10	10	0	0	63	249	57	26	20	7	1	2	0	10	0	50	0	0	6	2	.750	0	0--	—	2.86
Nashville *	AAA	6	6	0	0	29.1	137	45	24	20	3	2	2	2	7	0	15	0	1	2	2	.500	0	0--	—	6.14
1994 Baltimore	AL	1	1	0	0	7	31	6	4	3	1	0	1	1	4	1	5	0	0	1	0	1.000	0	0-0	0	3.86
1995 Bal-Min	AL	24	9	0	4	79.2	373	101	65	63	22	3	1	4	42	0	42	7	0	2	4	.333	0	0-0	0	7.12
1996 Minnesota	AL	10	3	0	2	28.2	137	42	28	25	5	1	1	1	10	0	15	1	0	1	1	.500	0	0-1	0	7.85
1998 Cincinnati	NL	4	4	0	0	22.2	102	26	17	15	6	2	1	1	7	0	13	0	0	1	3	.250	0	0-0	0	5.96
1995 Baltimore	AL	6	5	0	0	31.1	137	32	17	17	6	0	0	1	18	0	15	2	0	2	2	.500	0	0-0	0	4.88
Minnesota	AL	18	4	0	4	48.1	236	69	48	46	16	3	1	4	24	0	27	5	0	0	2	.000	0	0-0	0	8.57
4 ML YEARS		39	17	0	6	138	643	175	114	106	34	6	4	7	63	1	75	8	0	5	8	.385	0	0-1	0	6.91

Chuck Knoblauch

Bats: Right **Throws:** Right **Pos:** 2B-149; DH-1   **Ht:** 5'9" **Wt:** 170 **Born:** 7/7/68 **Age:** 30

					BATTING														BASERUNNING				PERCENTAGES		
Year Team	Lg	G	AB	H	2B	3B	HR	(Hm Rd)	TB	R	RBI	TBB	IBB	SO	HBP	SH	SF	SB	CS	SB%	GDP	Avg	OBP	SLG
1991 Minnesota	AL	151	565	159	24	6	1	(1 0)	198	78	50	59	0	40	4	1	5	25	5	**.83**	8	.281	.351	.350
1992 Minnesota	AL	155	600	178	19	6	2	(0 2)	215	104	56	88	1	60	5	2	12	34	13	.72	8	.297	.384	.358
1993 Minnesota	AL	153	602	167	27	4	2	(2 0)	208	82	41	65	1	44	9	4	5	29	11	.73	11	.277	.354	.346
1994 Minnesota	AL	109	445	139	**45**	3	5	(1 4)	205	85	51	41	2	56	10	0	3	35	6	.85	13	.312	.381	.461
1995 Minnesota	AL	136	538	179	34	8	11	(4 7)	262	107	63	78	3	95	10	0	3	46	18	.72	15	.333	.424	.487
1996 Minnesota	AL	153	578	197	35	**14**	13	(7 6)	299	140	72	98	6	74	19	0	6	45	14	.76	9	.341	.448	.517
1997 Minnesota	AL	156	611	178	26	10	9	(2 7)	251	117	58	84	6	84	17	0	4	62	10	.86	11	.291	.390	.411
1998 New York	AL	150	603	160	25	4	17	(5 12)	244	117	64	76	1	70	**18**	2	7	31	12	.72	13	.265	.361	.405
8 ML YEARS		1163	4542	1357	235	55	60	(22 38)	1882	830	455	589	20	523	92	9	45	307	89	.78	88	.299	.387	.414

Randy Knorr

Bats: Right **Throws:** Right **Pos:** C-15   **Ht:** 6'2" **Wt:** 215 **Born:** 11/12/68 **Age:** 30

					BATTING														BASERUNNING				PERCENTAGES		
Year Team	Lg	G	AB	H	2B	3B	HR	(Hm Rd)	TB	R	RBI	TBB	IBB	SO	HBP	SH	SF	SB	CS	SB%	GDP	Avg	OBP	SLG
1998 Charlotte *	AAA	68	201	66	15	0	7	(— —)	102	30	39	34	0	41	1	0	4	1	2	.33	3	.328	.421	.507
1991 Toronto	AL	3	1	0	0	0	0	(0 0)	0	0	0	1	0	1	0	0	0	0	0	.00	0	.000	.500	.000
1992 Toronto	AL	8	19	5	0	0	1	(0 1)	8	1	2	1	1	5	0	0	0	0	0	.00	0	.263	.300	.421
1993 Toronto	AL	39	101	25	3	2	4	(2 2)	44	11	20	9	0	29	0	2	0	0	0	.00	2	.248	.309	.436
1994 Toronto	AL	40	124	30	2	0	7	(4 3)	53	20	19	10	0	35	1	0	1	0	0	.00	7	.242	.301	.427
1995 Toronto	AL	45	132	28	8	0	3	(2 1)	45	18	16	11	0	28	0	1	0	0	0	.00	5	.212	.273	.341
1996 Houston	NL	37	87	17	5	0	1	(1 0)	25	7	7	5	2	18	1	0	1	0	1	.00	1	.195	.245	.287
1997 Houston	NL	4	8	3	0	0	1	(1 0)	6	1	1	0	0	2	0	0	0	0	0	.00	0	.375	.375	.750
1998 Florida	NL	15	49	10	4	1	2	(0 2)	22	4	11	1	0	10	0	0	1	0	0	.00	0	.204	.216	.449
8 ML YEARS		191	521	118	22	3	19	(10 9)	203	62	76	38	3	128	2	3	3	0	1	.00	15	.226	.280	.390

Paul Konerko

Bats: R **Throws:** R **Pos:** 1B-30; 3B-20; LF-18; PH/PR-11; DH-3   **Ht:** 6'3" **Wt:** 211 **Born:** 3/5/76 **Age:** 23

								BATTING											BASERUNNING				PERCENTAGES		
Year Team	Lg	G	AB	H	2B	3B	HR	(Hm	Rd)	TB	R	RBI	TBB	IBB	SO	HBP	SH	SF	SB	CS	SB%	GDP	Avg	OBP	SLG
1994 Yakima	A-	67	257	74	15	2	6	—	—	111	25	58	36	4	52	6	0	7	1	0	1.00	6	.288	.379	.432
1995 San Berndno	A+	118	448	124	21	1	19	—	—	204	77	77	59	2	88	4	2	6	3	1	.75	12	.277	.362	.455
1996 San Antonio	AA	133	470	141	23	2	29	—	—	255	78	86	72	6	85	8	0	7	1	3	.25	7	.300	.397	.543
Albuquerque	AAA	4	14	6	0	0	1	—	—	9	2	2	1	0	2	0	0	0	0	1	.00	0	.429	.467	.643
1997 Albuquerque	AAA	130	483	156	31	1	37	—	—	300	97	127	64	3	61	8	0	5	2	3	.40	16	.323	.407	.621
1998 Albuquerque	AAA	24	87	33	10	0	6	—	—	61	16	26	11	0	12	0	0	3	0	0	.00	3	.379	.436	.701
Indianapolis	AAA	39	150	49	8	0	8	—	—	81	25	39	19	0	18	2	0	3	1	0	1.00	3	.327	.402	.540
1997 Los Angeles	NL	6	7	1	0	0	0	(0	0)	1	0	0	1	0	2	0	0	0	0	0	.00	1	.143	.250	.143
1998 LA-Cin	NL	75	217	47	4	0	7	(2	5)	72	21	29	16	0	40	3	0	3	0	1	.00	10	.217	.276	.332
1998 Los Angeles	NL	49	144	31	1	0	4	(2	2)	44	14	16	10	0	30	2	0	2	0	0	.00	5	.215	.272	.306
Cincinnati	NL	26	73	16	3	0	3	(0	3)	28	7	13	6	0	10	1	0	1	0	0	.00	5	.219	.284	.384
2 ML YEARS		81	224	48	4	0	7	(2	5)	73	21	29	17	0	42	3	0	3	0	1	.00	11	.214	.275	.326

Corey Koskie

Bats: Left **Throws:** Right **Pos:** 3B-10; PH/PR-2   **Ht:** 6'3" **Wt:** 217 **Born:** 6/28/73 **Age:** 26

								BATTING											BASERUNNING				PERCENTAGES		
Year Team	Lg	G	AB	H	2B	3B	HR	(Hm	Rd)	TB	R	RBI	TBB	IBB	SO	HBP	SH	SF	SB	CS	SB%	GDP	Avg	OBP	SLG
1994 Elizabethtn	R+	34	107	25	2	1	3	—	—	38	16	8	16	0	27	2	0	0	3	0	.00	3	.234	.354	.355
1995 Fort Wayne	A	123	462	143	37	5	16	—	—	238	64	78	38	3	79	9	1	5	2	4	.33	10	.310	.370	.515
1996 Fort Myers	A+	95	338	88	19	4	9	—	—	142	43	55	40	0	76	1	1	3	1	1	.50	4	.260	.338	.420
1997 New Britain	AA	131	437	125	26	6	23	—	—	232	88	79	90	10	106	7	0	2	9	5	.64	13	.286	.414	.531
1998 Salt Lake	AAA	135	505	152	32	5	26	—	—	272	91	105	51	4	104	8	0	10	15	7	.68	17	.301	.368	.539
1998 Minnesota	AL	11	29	4	0	0	1	(1	0)	7	2	2	2	0	10	0	0	0	0	0	.00	0	.138	.194	.241

Mark Kotsay

Bats: L **Throws:** L **Pos:** RF-107; CF-46; PH/PR-13; 1B-3   **Ht:** 6'0" **Wt:** 180 **Born:** 12/2/75 **Age:** 23

								BATTING											BASERUNNING				PERCENTAGES		
Year Team	Lg	G	AB	H	2B	3B	HR	(Hm	Rd)	TB	R	RBI	TBB	IBB	SO	HBP	SH	SF	SB	CS	SB%	GDP	Avg	OBP	SLG
1996 Kane County	A	17	60	17	5	0	2	—	—	28	16	8	16	0	8	1	0	1	3	0	1.00	5	.283	.436	.467
1997 Portland	AA	114	438	134	27	2	20	—	—	225	103	77	75	3	65	0	0	3	17	5	.77	16	.306	.405	.514
1997 Florida	NL	14	52	10	1	1	0	(0	0)	13	5	4	4	0	7	0	1	0	3	0	1.00	1	.192	.250	.250
1998 Florida	NL	154	578	161	25	7	11	(5	6)	233	72	68	34	2	61	1	7	3	10	5	.67	17	.279	.318	.403
2 ML YEARS		168	630	171	26	8	11	(5	6)	246	77	72	38	2	68	1	8	3	13	5	.72	18	.271	.313	.390

Chad Kreuter

Bats: Both **Throws:** Right **Pos:** C-94; PH/PR-5   **Ht:** 6'2" **Wt:** 200 **Born:** 8/26/64 **Age:** 34

								BATTING											BASERUNNING				PERCENTAGES		
Year Team	Lg	G	AB	H	2B	3B	HR	(Hm	Rd)	TB	R	RBI	TBB	IBB	SO	HBP	SH	SF	SB	CS	SB%	GDP	Avg	OBP	SLG
1988 Texas	AL	16	51	14	2	1	1	(0	1)	21	3	5	7	0	13	0	0	0	0	0	.00	1	.275	.362	.412
1989 Texas	AL	87	158	24	3	0	5	(2	3)	42	16	9	27	0	40	0	6	1	0	1	.00	4	.152	.274	.266
1990 Texas	AL	22	22	1	1	0	0	(0	0)	2	2	2	8	0	9	0	1	1	0	0	.00	0	.045	.290	.091
1991 Texas	AL	3	4	0	0	0	0	(0	0)	0	0	0	0	0	1	0	0	0	0	0	.00	0	.000	.000	.000
1992 Detroit	AL	67	190	48	9	0	2	(2	0)	63	22	16	20	1	38	0	3	2	0	1	.00	8	.253	.321	.332
1993 Detroit	AL	119	374	107	23	3	15	(9	6)	181	59	51	49	4	92	3	2	3	2	1	.67	5	.286	.371	.484
1994 Detroit	AL	65	170	38	8	0	1	(1	0)	49	17	19	28	0	36	0	2	4	0	1	.00	3	.224	.327	.288
1995 Seattle	AL	26	75	17	5	0	1	(0	1)	25	12	8	5	0	22	1	0	0	0	0	.00	2	.227	.293	.333
1996 Chicago	AL	46	114	25	8	0	3	(2	1)	42	14	18	13	0	29	2	2	1	0	0	.00	2	.219	.308	.368
1997 ChA-Ana	AL	89	255	59	9	2	5	(3	2)	87	25	21	29	0	66	0	1	0	0	3	.00	8	.231	.310	.341
1998 ChA-Ana	AL	96	252	63	10	1	2	(2	0)	81	27	33	33	1	49	3	5	1	1	0	1.00	8	.250	.343	.321
1997 Chicago	AL	19	37	8	2	1	1	(1	0)	15	6	3	8	0	9	0	0	0	0	1	.00	1	.216	.356	.405
Anaheim	AL	70	218	51	7	1	4	(2	2)	72	19	18	21	0	57	0	1	0	0	2	.00	7	.234	.301	.330
1998 Chicago	AL	93	245	62	9	1	2	(2	0)	79	26	33	32	1	45	3	5	1	1	0	1.00	8	.253	.345	.322
Anaheim	AL	3	7	1	1	0	0	(0	0)	2	1	0	1	0	4	0	0	0	0	0	.00	0	.143	.250	.286
11 ML YEARS		636	1665	396	78	7	35	(21	14)	593	197	182	219	6	395	10	23	13	3	7	.30	38	.238	.328	.356

Rick Krivda

Pitches: Left **Bats:** Right **Pos:** RP-25; SP-2   **Ht:** 6'1" **Wt:** 185 **Born:** 1/19/70 **Age:** 29

		HOW MUCH HE PITCHED						WHAT HE GAVE UP												THE RESULTS					
Year Team	Lg	G	GS	CG	GF	IP	BFP	H	R	ER	HR	SH	SF	HB	TBB	IBB	SO	WP	Bk	W	L	Pct.	ShO	Sv-Op	Hld	ERA
1995 Baltimore	AL	13	13	1	0	75.1	319	76	40	38	9	0	4	4	25	1	53	2	2	2	7	.222	0	0-0	0	4.54
1996 Baltimore	AL	22	11	0	4	81.2	359	89	48	45	14	2	2	1	39	2	54	3	1	3	5	.375	0	0-0	1	4.96
1997 Baltimore	AL	10	10	0	0	50	225	67	36	35	7	1	2	0	18	1	29	0	2	4	2	.667	0	0-0	0	6.30
1998 Cle-Cin	AL	27	2	0	6	51.1	250	65	44	42	9	3	1	3	35	2	29	2	2	2	2	.500	0	0-1	1	7.36
1998 Cleveland	AL	11	1	0	5	25	112	24	10	9	2	0	0	0	16	1	10	1	1	2	0	1.000	0	0-0	0	3.24
Cincinnati	NL	16	1	0	1	26.1	138	41	34	33	7	3	1	3	19	1	19	1	1	0	2	.000	0	0-1	1	11.28
4 ML YEARS		72	36	1	10	258.1	1153	297	168	160	39	6	9	8	117	6	165	7	7	11	16	.407	0	0-1	2	5.57

Marc Kroon

Pitches: Right **Bats:** Right **Pos:** RP-6   **Ht:** 6'2" **Wt:** 195 **Born:** 4/2/73 **Age:** 26

Year Team	Lg	G	GS	CG	GF	IP	BFP	H	R	ER	HR	SH	SF	HB	TBB	IBB	SO	WP	Bk	W	L	Pct.	ShO	Sv-Op	Hld	ERA
1991 Mets	R	12	10	1	2	47.2	208	39	33	24	1	0	1	4	22	0	39	10	5	2	3	.400	0	0--	—	4.53
1992 Kingsport	R+	12	12	0	0	68	307	52	41	31	3	0	3	1	57	0	60	13	2	3	5	.375	0	0--	—	4.10
1993 Capital Cty	A	29	19	0	8	124.1	542	123	65	48	6	1	4	8	70	0	122	10	2	2	11	.154	0	2--	—	3.47
1994 Rancho Cuca	A+	26	26	0	0	143.1	655	143	86	77	14	4	9	11	81	1	153	9	3	11	6	.647	0	0--	—	4.83
1995 Memphis	AA	22	19	0	2	115.1	497	90	49	45	12	2	2	6	61	1	123	16	1	7	5	.583	0	2--	—	3.51
1996 Memphis	AA	44	0	0	43	46.2	208	33	19	15	4	1	4	3	28	1	56	6	1	2	4	.333	0	22--	—	2.89
1997 Las Vegas	AAA	46	0	0	33	41.2	175	34	22	21	5	2	2	3	22	0	53	6	0	1	3	.250	0	15--	—	4.54
1998 Indianapols	AAA	39	0	0	9	46.1	219	39	29	29	6	1	2	5	47	0	36	14	0	3	2	.600	0	1--	—	5.63
1995 San Diego	NL	2	0	0	1	1.2	7	1	2	2	0	0	0	0	2	0	2	0	0	0	1	.000	0	0-0	—	10.80
1997 San Diego	NL	12	0	0	2	11.1	56	14	9	9	2	0	0	1	5	0	12	1	0	0	1	.000	0	0-0	—	7.15
1998 SD-Cin	NL	6	0	0	4	7.2	38	7	8	8	0	0	0	1	9	0	6	2	1	0	0	.000	0	0-0	—	9.39
1998 San Diego	NL	2	0	0	2	2.1	8	0	0	0	0	0	0	0	1	0	2	0	0	0	0	.000	0	0-0	—	0.00
Cincinnati	NL	4	0	0	2	5.1	30	7	8	8	0	0	0	1	8	0	4	2	1	0	0	.000	0	0-0	—	13.50
3 ML YEARS		20	0	0	7	20.2	101	22	19	19	2	0	0	2	16	0	20	3	1	0	2	.000	0	0-0	1	8.27

Jeff Kubenka

Pitches: Left **Bats:** Right **Pos:** RP-6   **Ht:** 6'1" **Wt:** 191 **Born:** 8/24/74 **Age:** 24

Year Team	Lg	G	GS	CG	GF	IP	BFP	H	R	ER	HR	SH	SF	HB	TBB	IBB	SO	WP	Bk	W	L	Pct.	ShO	Sv-Op	Hld	ERA
1996 Yakima	A-	28	0	0	24	32.1	127	20	11	9	2	0	0	0	10	1	61	4	1	5	1	.833	0	14--	—	2.51
1997 San Berndno	A+	34	0	0	32	39	152	24	4	4	1	4	2	1	11	1	62	3	0	5	1	.833	0	19--	—	0.92
Albuquerque	AAA	8	0	0	6	7.1	37	11	9	7	2	0	0	0	2	0	10	3	0	0	2	.000	0	2--	—	8.59
San Antonio	AA	19	0	0	17	25.2	93	10	2	2	1	0	1	0	6	0	38	1	0	3	0	1.000	0	4--	—	0.70
1998 San Antonio	AA	9	0	0	6	9	47	10	11	7	2	0	1	1	7	0	10	3	1	0	0	.000	0	0--	—	7.00
Albuquerque	AAA	28	0	0	22	40.1	163	32	11	11	1	1	3	0	12	2	40	1	0	2	5	.286	0	9--	—	2.45
1998 Los Angeles	NL	6	0	0	2	9.1	40	4	1	1	0	2	1	0	8	0	10	1	0	1	0	1.000	0	0-1	2	0.96

Kerry Lacy

Pitches: Right **Bats:** Right **Pos:** RP   **Ht:** 6'2" **Wt:** 215 **Born:** 8/7/72 **Age:** 26

Year Team	Lg	G	GS	CG	GF	IP	BFP	H	R	ER	HR	SH	SF	HB	TBB	IBB	SO	WP	Bk	W	L	Pct.	ShO	Sv-Op	Hld	ERA
1996 Boston	AL	11	0	0	3	10.2	54	15	5	4	2	0	0	1	8	0	9	0	0	2	0	1.000	0	0-2	1	3.38
1997 Boston	AL	33	0	0	12	45.2	215	60	34	31	7	0	2	0	22	4	18	0	0	1	1	.500	0	3-3	5	6.11
2 ML YEARS		44	0	0	15	56.1	269	75	39	35	9	0	2	1	30	4	27	0	0	3	1	.750	0	3-5	6	5.59

Tim Laker

Bats: Right **Throws:** Right **Pos:** PH/PR-10; 1B-4; C-3; DH-1   **Ht:** 6'3" **Wt:** 200 **Born:** 11/27/69 **Age:** 29

Year Team	Lg	G	AB	H	2B	3B	HR	(Hm	Rd)	TB	R	RBI	TBB	IBB	SO	HBP	SH	SF	SB	CS	SB%	GDP	Avg	OBP	SLG
1998 Durham *	AAA	40	134	32	7	0	11	—	—	72	36	26	28	1	32	1	0	1	1	1	.50	4	.239	.372	.537
Nashville *	AAA	44	152	54	16	1	11	—	—	105	30	34	24	0	26	3	0	1	1	0	1.00	6	.355	.441	.691
1992 Montreal	NL	28	46	10	3	0	0	(0	0)	13	8	4	2	0	14	0	0	0	1	1	.50	1	.217	.250	.283
1993 Montreal	NL	43	86	17	2	1	0	(0	0)	21	3	7	2	0	16	1	3	1	2	0	1.00	2	.198	.222	.244
1995 Montreal	NL	64	141	33	8	1	3	(1	2)	52	17	20	14	4	38	1	1	1	0	1	.00	5	.234	.306	.369
1997 Baltimore	AL	7	14	0	0	0	0	(0	0)	0	0	1	2	0	9	0	0	1	0	0	.00	0	.000	.118	.000
1998 TB-Pit		17	29	10	1	0	1	(0	1)	14	3	2	2	0	4	0	0	1	0	1	.00	1	.345	.375	.483
1998 Tampa Bay	AL	3	5	1	0	0	0	(0	0)	1	1	0	1	0	1	0	0	0	0	1	.00	0	.200	.333	.200
Pittsburgh	NL	14	24	9	1	0	1	(0	1)	13	2	2	1	0	3	0	0	1	0	0	.00	1	.375	.385	.542
5 ML YEARS		159	316	70	14	2	4	(1	3)	100	31	34	22	4	81	2	5	4	3	3	.50	9	.222	.273	.316

Tom Lampkin

Bats: L **Throws:** R **Pos:** C-62; PH/PR-29; LF-4; 1B-2; RF-1   **Ht:** 5'11" **Wt:** 195 **Born:** 3/4/64 **Age:** 35

Year Team	Lg	G	AB	H	2B	3B	HR	(Hm	Rd)	TB	R	RBI	TBB	IBB	SO	HBP	SH	SF	SB	CS	SB%	GDP	Avg	OBP	SLG
1988 Cleveland	AL	4	4	0	0	0	0	(0	0)	0	0	0	1	0	0	0	0	0	0	0	.00	1	.000	.200	.000
1990 San Diego	NL	26	63	14	0	1	1	(1	0)	19	4	4	4	1	9	0	0	0	0	1	.00	2	.222	.269	.302
1991 San Diego	NL	38	58	11	3	1	0	(0	0)	16	4	3	3	0	9	0	0	0	0	0	.00	0	.190	.230	.276
1992 San Diego	NL	9	17	4	0	0	0	(0	0)	4	3	0	6	0	1	1	0	0	2	0	1.00	0	.235	.458	.235
1993 Milwaukee	AL	73	162	32	8	0	4	(1	3)	52	22	25	20	3	26	0	2	4	7	3	.70	2	.198	.280	.321
1995 San Francisco	NL	65	76	21	2	0	1	(1	0)	26	8	9	9	1	8	1	0	0	2	0	1.00	1	.276	.360	.342
1996 San Francisco	NL	66	177	41	8	0	6	(5	1)	67	26	29	20	2	22	5	0	2	1	5	.17	2	.232	.324	.379
1997 St. Louis	NL	108	229	56	8	1	7	(2	5)	87	28	22	28	5	30	4	4	2	2	1	.67	8	.245	.335	.380
1998 St. Louis	NL	93	216	50	12	1	6	(4	2)	82	25	28	24	5	32	7	1	0	3	2	.60	5	.231	.328	.380
9 ML YEARS		482	1002	229	41	4	25	(14	11)	353	120	120	115	17	137	18	7	8	17	12	.59	21	.229	.317	.352

Mark Langston

Pitches: Left   Bats: Right   Pos: SP-16; RP-6   Ht: 6'2"   Wt: 185   Born: 8/20/60   Age: 38

Year Team	Lg	G	GS	CG	GF	IP	BFP	H	R	ER	HR	SH	SF	HB	TBB	IBB	SO	WP	Bk	W	L	Pct.	ShO	Sv-Op	Hld	ERA
1984 Seattle	AL	35	33	5	0	225	965	188	99	85	16	13	7	8	118	5	204	4	2	17	10	.630	2	0--	—	3.40
1985 Seattle	AL	24	24	2	0	126.2	577	122	85	77	22	3	2	2	91	2	72	3	3	7	14	.333	0	0-0	0	5.47
1986 Seattle	AL	37	36	9	1	239.1	1057	234	142	129	30	5	8	4	123	1	245	10	3	12	14	.462	0	0--	—	4.85
1987 Seattle	AL	35	35	14	0	272	1152	242	132	116	30	12	6	5	114	0	262	9	2	19	13	.594	3	0-0	0	3.84
1988 Seattle	AL	35	35	9	0	261.1	1078	222	108	97	32	6	5	3	110	2	235	7	4	15	11	.577	3	0-0	0	3.34
1989 Sea-Mon	AL	34	34	8	0	250	1037	198	87	76	16	9	7	4	112	6	235	6	4	16	14	.533	5	0-0	0	2.74
1990 California	AL	33	33	5	0	223	950	215	120	109	13	6	6	5	104	1	195	8	0	10	17	.370	1	0-0	0	4.40
1991 California	AL	34	34	7	0	246.1	992	190	89	82	30	4	6	2	96	3	183	6	0	19	8	.704	0	0-0	0	3.00
1992 California	AL	32	32	9	0	229	941	206	103	93	14	4	5	6	74	2	174	5	0	13	14	.481	2	0-0	0	3.66
1993 California	AL	35	35	7	0	256.1	1039	220	100	91	22	3	8	1	85	2	196	10	2	16	11	.593	0	0-0	0	3.20
1994 California	AL	18	18	2	0	119.1	517	121	67	62	19	3	8	0	54	1	109	6	0	7	8	.467	1	0-0	0	4.68
1995 California	AL	31	31	2	0	200.1	859	212	109	103	21	11	3	3	64	1	142	5	1	15	7	.682	1	0-0	0	4.63
1996 California	AL	18	18	2	0	123.1	518	116	68	66	18	0	2	2	45	0	83	4	0	6	5	.545	0	0-0	0	4.82
1997 Anaheim	AL	9	9	0	0	47.2	226	61	34	31	8	2	2	0	29	1	30	1	0	2	4	.333	0	0-0	0	5.85
1998 San Diego	NL	22	16	0	0	81.1	380	107	55	53	11	5	4	1	41	1	56	3	1	4	6	.400	0	0-1	2	5.86
1989 Seattle	AL	10	10	2	0	73.1	297	60	30	29	3	0	3	4	19	0	60	1	2	4	5	.444	1	0-0	0	3.56
Montreal	NL	24	24	6	0	176.2	740	138	57	47	13	9	4	0	93	6	175	5	2	12	9	.571	4	0-0	0	2.39
15 ML YEARS		432	423	81	1	2901	12288	2654	1398	1270	302	86	79	46	1260	28	2421	87	22	178	156	.533	18	0--	—	3.94

Frank Lankford

Pitches: Right   Bats: Right   Pos: RP-12   Ht: 6'2"   Wt: 190   Born: 3/26/71   Age: 28

Year Team	Lg	G	GS	CG	GF	IP	BFP	H	R	ER	HR	SH	SF	HB	TBB	IBB	SO	WP	Bk	W	L	Pct.	ShO	Sv-Op	Hld	ERA
1993 Oneonta	A-	16	7	0	1	64.2	276	60	41	24	3	3	2	1	22	0	61	5	0	4	5	.444	0	0--	—	3.34
1994 Greensboro	A	54	0	0	27	82.1	352	79	37	27	3	6	1	1	18	3	74	7	1	7	6	.538	0	7--	—	2.95
1995 Tampa	A+	55	0	0	36	73	305	64	29	21	0	7	0	2	22	6	58	1	0	4	6	.400	0	15--	—	2.59
1996 Norwich	AA	61	0	0	25	88	392	82	42	26	4	9	1	2	40	6	61	3	0	7	8	.467	0	4--	—	2.66
1997 Norwich	AA	11	11	2	0	68.1	277	58	28	22	3	1	1	2	15	1	39	1	1	4	2	.667	0	0--	—	2.90
Columbus	AAA	15	13	1	2	93.2	374	84	33	28	2	3	1	2	22	1	40	1	0	7	4	.636	1	0--	—	2.69
1998 Columbus	AAA	15	15	3	0	94	413	110	60	53	12	3	0	1	32	0	58	3	0	5	9	.357	0	0--	—	5.07
1998 Los Angeles	NL	12	0	0	9	19.2	89	23	13	13	2	0	0	2	7	0	7	1	0	0	2	.000	0	1-1	0	5.95

Ray Lankford

Bats: Left   Throws: Left   Pos: CF-145; PH/PR-16; DH-1   Ht: 5'11"   Wt: 198   Born: 6/5/67   Age: 32

Year Team	Lg	G	AB	H	2B	3B	HR	(Hm	Rd)	TB	R	RBI	TBB	IBB	SO	HBP	SH	SF	SB	CS	SB%	GDP	Avg	OBP	SLG
1990 St. Louis	NL	39	126	36	10	1	3	(2	1)	57	12	12	13	0	27	0	0	0	8	2	.80	1	.286	.353	.452
1991 St. Louis	NL	151	566	142	23	15	9	(4	5)	222	83	69	41	1	114	1	4	3	44	20	.69	4	.251	.301	.392
1992 St. Louis	NL	153	598	175	40	6	20	(13	7)	287	87	86	72	6	147	5	2	5	42	24	.64	5	.293	.371	.480
1993 St. Louis	NL	127	407	97	17	3	7	(6	1)	141	64	45	81	7	111	3	1	3	14	14	.50	5	.238	.366	.346
1994 St. Louis	NL	109	416	111	25	5	19	(8	11)	203	89	57	58	3	113	4	0	4	11	10	.52	0	.267	.359	.488
1995 St. Louis	NL	132	483	134	35	2	25	(16	9)	248	81	63	63	6	110	2	0	5	24	8	.75	10	.277	.360	.513
1996 St. Louis	NL	149	545	150	36	8	21	(8	13)	265	100	86	79	10	133	3	1	7	35	7	.83	12	.275	.366	.486
1997 St. Louis	NL	133	465	137	36	3	31	(10	21)	272	94	98	95	10	125	0	0	5	21	11	.66	9	.295	.411	.585
1998 St. Louis	NL	154	533	156	37	1	31	(20	11)	288	94	105	86	5	151	3	0	4	26	5	.84	4	.293	.391	.540
9 ML YEARS		1147	4139	1138	259	44	166	(87	79)	1983	704	640	588	48	1031	21	8	36	225	101	.69	50	.275	.365	.479

Mike Lansing

Bats: Right   Throws: Right   Pos: 2B-153; PH/PR-2; 3B-1   Ht: 6'0"   Wt: 185   Born: 4/3/68   Age: 31

Year Team	Lg	G	AB	H	2B	3B	HR	(Hm	Rd)	TB	R	RBI	TBB	IBB	SO	HBP	SH	SF	SB	CS	SB%	GDP	Avg	OBP	SLG
1993 Montreal	NL	141	491	141	29	1	3	(1	2)	181	64	45	46	2	56	5	10	3	23	5	.82	16	.287	.352	.369
1994 Montreal	NL	106	394	105	21	2	5	(3	2)	145	44	35	30	3	37	7	2	2	12	8	.60	10	.266	.328	.368
1995 Montreal	NL	127	467	119	30	2	10	(4	6)	183	47	62	28	2	65	3	1	3	27	4	.87	14	.255	.299	.392
1996 Montreal	NL	159	641	183	40	2	11	(3	8)	260	99	53	44	1	85	10	9	1	23	8	.74	19	.285	.341	.406
1997 Montreal	NL	144	572	161	45	2	20	(11	9)	270	86	70	45	2	92	5	6	3	11	5	.69	9	.281	.338	.472
1998 Colorado	NL	153	584	161	39	2	12	(7	5)	240	73	66	39	4	88	5	7	3	10	3	.77	18	.276	.325	.411
6 ML YEARS		830	3149	870	204	11	61	(29	32)	1279	413	331	232	14	423	35	35	15	106	33	.76	86	.276	.331	.406

Andy Larkin

Pitches: Right   Bats: Right   Pos: SP-14; RP-3   Ht: 6'4"   Wt: 190   Born: 6/27/74   Age: 25

Year Team	Lg	G	GS	CG	GF	IP	BFP	H	R	ER	HR	SH	SF	HB	TBB	IBB	SO	WP	Bk	W	L	Pct.	ShO	Sv-Op	Hld	ERA
1992 Marlins	R	14	4	0	2	41.1	187	41	26	24	0	1	1	7	19	0	20	4	0	1	2	.333	0	2--	—	5.23
1993 Elmira	A-	14	14	4	0	88	368	74	43	29	1	1	3	12	23	0	89	9	1	5	7	.417	1	0--	—	2.97
1994 Kane County	A	21	21	3	0	140	577	125	53	44	6	3	3	19	27	1	125	4	0	9	7	.563	1	0--	—	2.83
1995 Portland	AA	9	9	0	0	40	160	29	16	15	5	4	0	6	11	2	23	1	0	1	2	.333	0	0--	—	3.38
1996 Brevard Cty	A+	6	6	0	0	27.2	126	34	20	13	0	0	1	7	7	0	18	3	0	0	4	.000	0	0--	—	4.23
Portland	AA	8	8	0	0	49.1	195	45	18	17	6	2	0	2	10	0	40	3	0	4	1	.800	0	0--	—	3.10
1997 Charlotte	AAA	28	27	3	0	144.1	669	166	109	97	23	3	3	15	76	2	103	4	1	6	11	.353	0	0--	—	6.05

Year Team	Lg	G	GS	CG	GF	IP	BFP	H	R	ER	HR	SH	SF	HB	TBB	IBB	SO	WP	Bk	W	L	Pct.	ShO	Sv-Op	Hld	ERA
1998 Charlotte	AAA	11	10	0	0	53.2	246	55	39	38	8	2	0	4	32	2	41	2	0	4	1	.800	0	0--	—	6.37
1996 Florida	NL	1	1	0	0	5	22	3	1	1	0	0	0	1	4	0	2	0	0	0	0	.000	0	0-0	0	1.80
1998 Florida	NL	17	14	0	0	74.2	373	101	87	80	12	5	2	4	55	3	43	3	0	3	8	.273	0	0-0	0	9.64
2 ML YEARS		18	15	0	0	79.2	395	104	88	81	12	5	2	5	59	3	45	3	0	3	8	.273	0	0-0	0	9.15

Barry Larkin

Bats: Right **Throws:** Right **Pos:** SS-145; PH/PR-3 **Ht:** 6'0" **Wt:** 185 **Born:** 4/28/64 **Age:** 35

Year Team	Lg	G	AB	H	2B	3B	HR	(Hm	Rd)	TB	R	RBI	TBB	IBB	SO	HBP	SH	SF	SB	CS	SB%	GDP	Avg	OBP	SLG
1986 Cincinnati	NL	41	159	45	4	3	3	(3	0)	64	27	19	9	1	21	0	0	1	8	0	1.00	2	.283	.320	.403
1987 Cincinnati	NL	125	439	107	16	2	12	(6	6)	163	64	43	36	3	52	1	5	3	21	6	.78	8	.244	.306	.371
1988 Cincinnati	NL	151	588	174	32	5	12	(9	3)	252	91	56	41	3	24	8	10	5	40	7	.85	7	.296	.347	.429
1989 Cincinnati	NL	97	325	111	14	4	4	(1	3)	145	47	36	20	5	23	2	2	8	10	5	.67	7	.342	.375	.446
1990 Cincinnati	NL	158	614	185	25	6	7	(4	3)	243	85	67	49	3	49	7	7	4	30	5	.86	14	.301	.358	.396
1991 Cincinnati	NL	123	464	140	27	4	20	(16	4)	235	88	69	55	1	64	3	3	2	24	6	.80	7	.302	.378	.506
1992 Cincinnati	NL	140	533	162	32	6	12	(8	4)	242	76	78	63	8	58	4	2	7	15	4	.79	13	.304	.377	.454
1993 Cincinnati	NL	100	384	121	20	3	8	(4	4)	171	57	51	51	6	33	1	1	3	14	1	.93	13	.315	.394	.445
1994 Cincinnati	NL	110	427	119	23	5	9	(3	6)	179	78	52	64	3	58	0	5	5	26	2	.93	6	.279	.369	.419
1995 Cincinnati	NL	131	496	158	29	6	15	(8	7)	244	98	66	61	2	49	3	3	4	51	5	.91	6	.319	.394	.492
1996 Cincinnati	NL	152	517	154	32	4	33	(14	19)	293	117	89	96	3	52	7	0	7	36	10	.78	20	.298	.410	.567
1997 Cincinnati	NL	73	224	71	17	3	4	(0	4)	106	34	20	47	6	24	3	1	1	14	3	.82	3	.317	.440	.473
1998 Cincinnati	NL	145	538	166	34	10	17	(8	9)	271	93	72	79	5	69	2	4	3	26	3	.90	12	.309	.397	.504
13 ML YEARS		1546	5708	1713	305	61	156	(84	72)	2608	955	718	671	49	576	45	43	53	315	57	.85	118	.300	.375	.457

Stephen Larkin

Bats: Left **Throws:** Left **Pos:** 1B-1 **Ht:** 6'0" **Wt:** 190 **Born:** 7/24/73 **Age:** 25

Year Team	Lg	G	AB	H	2B	3B	HR	(Hm	Rd)	TB	R	RBI	TBB	IBB	SO	HBP	SH	SF	SB	CS	SB%	GDP	Avg	OBP	SLG
1994 Hudson Vall	A-	66	237	47	10	1	2	—	—	65	26	22	30	1	47	1	0	3	10	5	.67	3	.198	.288	.274
1995 Chston-SC	A	113	369	94	19	1	5	—	—	130	50	45	54	2	80	1	3	5	18	10	.64	1	.255	.347	.352
Winston-Sal	A+	13	50	11	1	0	0	—	—	12	2	4	3	1	12	0	0	1	2	2	.50	0	.220	.259	.240
1996 Winston-Sal	A+	39	117	21	2	0	3	—	—	32	13	6	14	2	25	0	1	1	6	1	.86	6	.179	.264	.274
Chston-WV	A	58	203	55	7	2	5	—	—	81	30	33	35	1	40	4	1	1	5	4	.56	2	.271	.387	.399
1997 Chston-WV	A	129	464	129	23	10	13	—	—	211	88	79	52	1	83	5	0	5	28	9	.76	6	.278	.354	.455
1998 Chattanooga	AA	80	267	61	22	1	3	—	—	94	33	31	23	0	52	1	1	4	3	4	.43	7	.228	.288	.352
1998 Cincinnati	NL	1	3	1	0	0	0	(0	0)	1	0	0	0	0	0	0	0	0	0	0	.00	0	.333	.333	.333

Chris Latham

Bats: B **Throws:** R **Pos:** CF-15; LF-13; PH/PR-6; RF-5 **Ht:** 6'0" **Wt:** 195 **Born:** 5/26/73 **Age:** 26

Year Team	Lg	G	AB	H	2B	3B	HR	(Hm	Rd)	TB	R	RBI	TBB	IBB	SO	HBP	SH	SF	SB	CS	SB%	GDP	Avg	OBP	SLG
1991 Dodgers	R	43	109	26	2	1	0	—	—	30	17	11	16	0	45	0	0	1	14	4	.78	0	.239	.333	.275
1992 Great Falls	R+	17	37	12	2	0	0	—	—	14	8	3	8	0	8	0	0	0	1	1	.50	0	.324	.444	.378
Dodgers	R	14	48	11	2	0	0	—	—	13	4	2	5	1	17	0	1	1	2	3	.40	0	.229	.296	.271
1993 Yakima	A-	54	192	50	2	6	4	—	—	76	46	17	39	0	53	1	0	0	24	9	.73	2	.260	.388	.396
Bakersfield	A+	6	27	5	1	0	0	—	—	6	1	3	4	0	5	0	0	0	2	2	.50	0	.185	.290	.222
1994 Bakersfield	A+	52	191	41	5	2	2	—	—	56	29	15	28	1	49	2	4	0	28	7	.80	2	.215	.321	.293
Yakima	A-	71	288	98	19	8	5	—	—	148	69	32	55	7	66	2	3	0	33	20	.62	1	.340	.449	.514
1995 Vero Beach	A+	71	259	74	13	4	6	—	—	113	53	39	56	4	54	2	2	3	42	11	.79	2	.286	.413	.436
San Antonio	AA	58	214	64	14	5	9	—	—	115	38	37	33	0	59	2	1	1	11	11	.50	2	.299	.396	.537
Albuquerque	AAA	5	18	3	0	1	0	—	—	5	2	3	1	0	4	0	0	1	1	0	1.00	0	.167	.200	.278
1996 Salt Lake	AAA	115	376	103	16	6	9	—	—	158	59	50	36	1	91	2	4	3	26	9	.74	5	.274	.338	.420
1997 Salt Lake	AAA	118	492	152	22	5	8	—	—	208	78	58	58	0	110	4	4	1	21	19	.53	8	.309	.386	.423
1998 Salt Lake	AAA	97	377	122	21	4	11	—	—	184	81	51	56	4	99	1	4	0	29	5	.85	5	.324	.412	.488
1997 Minnesota	AL	15	22	4	1	0	0	(0	0)	5	4	1	0	0	8	0	0	0	0	0	.00	0	.182	.182	.227
1998 Minnesota	AL	34	94	15	1	0	1	(1	0)	19	14	5	13	0	36	0	1	0	4	2	.67	0	.160	.262	.202
2 ML YEARS		49	116	19	2	0	1	(1	0)	24	18	6	13	0	44	0	1	0	4	2	.67	0	.164	.248	.207

Sean Lawrence

Pitches: Left **Bats:** Left **Pos:** RP-4; SP-3 **Ht:** 6'4" **Wt:** 215 **Born:** 9/2/70 **Age:** 28

Year Team	Lg	G	GS	CG	GF	IP	BFP	H	R	ER	HR	SH	SF	HB	TBB	IBB	SO	WP	Bk	W	L	Pct.	ShO	Sv-Op	Hld	ERA
1992 Welland	A-	15	15	0	0	74	330	75	55	43	10	2	2	2	34	1	71	6	3	3	6	.333	0	0--	—	5.23
1993 Augusta	A	22	22	0	0	121	516	108	59	42	9	7	4	4	50	1	96	6	0	6	8	.429	0	0--	—	3.12
Salem	A+	4	4	0	0	15	77	25	19	17	1	2	1	0	9	0	14	2	0	1	3	.250	0	0--	—	10.20
1994 Salem	A+	12	12	0	0	72	312	76	38	21	8	1	2	3	18	0	66	2	0	4	2	.667	0	0--	—	2.63
1995 Carolina	AA	12	3	0	3	21.1	96	27	13	13	2	0	0	1	8	1	19	0	1	0	2	.000	0	0--	—	5.48
Lynchburg	A+	20	19	0	0	111	465	115	56	52	16	3	3	1	25	0	82	3	0	5	8	.385	0	0--	—	4.22
1996 Carolina	AA	37	9	0	13	82	362	80	40	36	11	2	1	3	36	1	81	0	1	3	5	.375	0	2--	—	3.95
1997 Calgary	AAA	26	26	2	0	143.1	641	154	83	67	17	9	6	3	57	3	116	6	0	8	9	.471	0	0--	—	4.21
1998 Nashville	AAA	26	26	0	0	147	634	153	86	82	20	7	2	6	57	1	126	4	1	12	9	.571	0	0--	—	5.02
1998 Pittsburgh	NL	7	3	0	0	19.2	92	25	16	16	4	0	2	0	10	0	12	1	0	2	1	.667	0	0-0	0	7.32

Matt Lawton

Bats: L **Throws:** R **Pos:** RF-100; CF-47; LF-12; PH/PR-3   **Ht:** 5'10" **Wt:** 186 **Born:** 11/3/71 **Age:** 27

Year Team	Lg	G	AB	H	2B	3B	HR	(Hm	Rd)	TB	R	RBI	TBB	IBB	SO	HBP	SH	SF	SB	CS	SB%	GDP	Avg	OBP	SLG
1995 Minnesota	AL	21	60	19	4	1	1	(1	0)	28	11	12	7	0	11	3	0	0	1	1	.50	1	.317	.414	.467
1996 Minnesota	AL	79	252	65	7	1	6	(1	5)	92	34	42	28	1	28	4	0	2	4	4	.50	6	.258	.339	.365
1997 Minnesota	AL	142	460	114	29	3	14	(8	6)	191	74	60	76	3	81	10	1	1	7	4	.64	7	.248	.366	.415
1998 Minnesota	AL	152	557	155	36	6	21	(11	10)	266	91	77	86	6	64	15	0	4	16	8	.67	10	.278	.387	.478
4 ML YEARS		394	1329	353	76	11	42	(21	21)	577	210	191	197	10	184	32	1	7	28	17	.62	24	.266	.372	.434

Ricky Ledee

Bats: L **Throws:** L **Pos:** LF-36; PH/PR-6; RF-4; CF-3   **Ht:** 6'1" **Wt:** 160 **Born:** 11/22/73 **Age:** 25

Year Team	Lg	G	AB	H	2B	3B	HR	(Hm	Rd)	TB	R	RBI	TBB	IBB	SO	HBP	SH	SF	SB	CS	SB%	GDP	Avg	OBP	SLG
1990 Yankees	R	19	37	4	2	0	0	—	—	6	5	1	6	0	18	0	0	0	2	0	1.00	1	.108	.233	.162
1991 Yankees	R	47	165	44	6	2	0	—	—	54	22	18	22	0	41	0	0	1	3	1	.75	3	.267	.351	.327
1992 Yankees	R	52	179	41	9	2	2	—	—	60	25	23	24	1	47	1	0	1	4	2	.20	2	.229	.322	.335
1993 Oneonta	A-	52	192	49	7	6	8	—	—	92	32	20	25	0	46	2	1	0	7	5	.58	2	.255	.347	.479
1994 Greensboro	A	134	484	121	23	9	22	—	—	228	87	71	91	4	126	4	3	6	10	11	.48	7	.250	.369	.471
1995 Greensboro	A	89	335	90	16	6	14	—	—	160	65	49	51	6	66	2	0	1	10	4	.71	3	.269	.368	.478
1996 Norwich	AA	39	137	50	11	1	8	—	—	87	27	37	16	0	25	1	1	5	2	2	.50	4	.365	.421	.635
Columbus	AAA	96	358	101	22	6	21	—	—	198	79	64	44	2	95	1	0	2	6	3	.67	4	.282	.360	.553
1997 Yankees	R	7	21	7	1	0	0	—	—	8	3	2	2	1	4	1	0	0	0	0	.00	1	.333	.417	.381
Columbus	AAA	43	170	52	12	1	10	—	—	96	38	39	21	0	49	1	0	0	4	0	1.00	5	.306	.385	.565
1998 Columbus	AAA	96	360	102	21	1	19	—	—	182	70	41	54	5	108	4	1	5	7	2	.78	7	.283	.378	.506
1998 New York	AL	42	79	19	5	2	1	(0	1)	31	13	12	7	0	29	0	0	1	3	1	.75	1	.241	.299	.392

Aaron Ledesma

Bats: R **Throws:** R **Pos:** SS-57; 2B-19; PH/PR-17; 3B-7; DH-6; 1B-3   **Ht:** 6'2" **Wt:** 200 **Born:** 6/3/71 **Age:** 28

Year Team	Lg	G	AB	H	2B	3B	HR	(Hm	Rd)	TB	R	RBI	TBB	IBB	SO	HBP	SH	SF	SB	CS	SB%	GDP	Avg	OBP	SLG
1995 New York	NL	21	33	8	0	0	0	(0	0)	8	4	3	6	1	7	0	0	0	0	0	.00	2	.242	.359	.242
1997 Baltimore	AL	43	88	31	5	1	2	(1	1)	44	24	11	13	0	9	1	1	1	1	0	1.00	1	.352	.437	.500
1998 Tampa Bay	AL	95	299	97	16	3	0	(1	0)	119	30	29	9	1	51	1	4	2	9	7	.56	8	.324	.344	.398
3 ML YEARS		159	420	136	21	4	2	(1	1)	171	58	43	28	2	67	2	5	3	10	7	.59	11	.324	.366	.407

Derrek Lee

Bats: Right **Throws:** Right **Pos:** 1B-132; PH/PR-16   **Ht:** 6'5" **Wt:** 205 **Born:** 9/6/75 **Age:** 23

Year Team	Lg	G	AB	H	2B	3B	HR	(Hm	Rd)	TB	R	RBI	TBB	IBB	SO	HBP	SH	SF	SB	CS	SB%	GDP	Avg	OBP	SLG
1993 Padres	R	15	52	17	1	1	2	—	—	26	11	5	6	1	7	0	0	0	4	0	1.00	1	.327	.397	.500
Rancho Cuca	A+	20	73	20	5	1	1	—	—	30	13	10	10	0	20	1	0	0	2	2	.00	0	.274	.369	.411
1994 Rancho Cuca	A+	126	442	118	19	2	8	—	—	165	66	53	42	2	95	7	0	6	18	14	.56	11	.267	.336	.373
1995 Rancho Cuca	A+	128	502	151	25	2	23	—	—	249	82	95	49	2	130	7	0	7	14	7	.67	8	.301	.366	.496
Memphis	AA	2	9	1	0	0	0	—	—	1	0	1	0	0	2	0	0	0	0	0	.00	0	.111	.111	.111
1996 Memphis	AA	134	500	140	39	2	34	—	—	285	98	104	65	3	170	2	0	8	13	6	.68	8	.280	.360	.570
1997 Las Vegas	AAA	125	472	153	29	2	13	—	—	225	86	64	60	4	116	0	0	2	17	3	.85	9	.324	.399	.477
1997 San Diego	NL	22	54	14	3	0	1	(0	1)	20	9	4	9	0	24	0	0	0	0	0	.00	1	.259	.365	.370
1998 Florida	NL	141	454	106	29	1	17	(4	13)	188	62	74	47	1	120	10	0	2	5	2	.71	12	.233	.318	.414
2 ML YEARS		163	508	120	32	1	18	(4	14)	208	71	78	56	1	144	10	0	2	5	2	.71	13	.236	.323	.409

Travis Lee

Bats: Left **Throws:** Left **Pos:** 1B-146   **Ht:** 6'3" **Wt:** 210 **Born:** 5/26/75 **Age:** 24

Year Team	Lg	G	AB	H	2B	3B	HR	(Hm	Rd)	TB	R	RBI	TBB	IBB	SO	HBP	SH	SF	SB	CS	SB%	GDP	Avg	OBP	SLG
1997 High Desert	A+	61	226	82	18	1	18	—	—	156	63	63	47	6	36	3	0	3	5	1	.83	9	.363	.473	.690
Tucson	AAA	59	227	68	16	2	14	—	—	130	42	46	31	2	46	2	0	1	2	0	1.00	10	.300	.387	.573
1998 Arizona	NL	146	562	151	20	2	22	(12	10)	241	71	72	67	5	123	0	0	6	8	1	.89	13	.269	.346	.429

Al Leiter

Pitches: Left **Bats:** Left **Pos:** SP-28   **Ht:** 6'3" **Wt:** 220 **Born:** 10/23/65 **Age:** 33

| | | HOW MUCH HE PITCHED | | | | | | WHAT HE GAVE UP | | | | | | | | | | | | THE RESULTS | | | | | |
Year Team	Lg	G	GS	CG	GF	IP	BFP	H	R	ER	HR	SH	SF	HB	TBB	IBB	SO	WP	Bk	W	L	Pct.	ShO	Sv-Op	Hld	ERA
1987 New York	AL	4	4	0	0	22.2	104	24	16	16	2	1	0	0	15	0	28	4	0	2	2	.500	0	0-0	0	6.35
1988 New York	AL	14	14	0	0	57.1	251	49	27	25	7	1	0	5	33	0	60	1	4	4	4	.500	0	0-0	0	3.92
1989 NYA-Tor	AL	5	5	0	0	33.1	154	32	23	21	2	1	1	2	23	0	26	2	1	1	2	.333	0	0-0	0	5.67
1990 Toronto	AL	4	0	0	0	6.1	22	1	0	0	0	0	0	0	2	0	5	0	0	0	0	.000	0	0-0	0	0.00
1991 Toronto	AL	3	0	0	1	1.2	13	3	5	5	0	1	0	0	5	0	1	0	0	0	0	.000	0	0-0	0	27.00
1992 Toronto	AL	1	0	0	0	1	7	1	1	1	0	0	0	0	2	0	0	0	0	0	0	.000	0	0-0	0	9.00
1993 Toronto	AL	34	12	1	4	105	454	93	52	48	8	3	3	4	56	2	66	2	2	9	6	.600	1	2-3	3	4.11
1994 Toronto	AL	20	20	1	0	111.2	516	125	68	63	6	3	8	2	65	3	100	7	5	6	7	.462	0	0-0	0	5.08
1995 Toronto	AL	28	28	2	0	183	805	162	80	74	15	6	4	6	108	1	153	14	0	11	11	.500	1	0-0	0	3.64

126

Year Team	Lg	G	GS	CG	GF	IP	BFP	H	R	ER	HR	SH	SF	HB	TBB	IBB	SO	WP	Bk	W	L	Pct.	ShO	Sv-Op	Hld	ERA
1996 Florida	NL	33	33	2	0	215.1	896	153	74	70	14	7	3	11	**119**	3	200	5	0	16	12	.571	1	0-0	0	2.93
1997 Florida	NL	27	27	0	0	151.1	668	133	78	73	13	10	3	12	91	4	132	2	0	11	9	.550	0	0-0	0	4.34
1998 New York	NL	28	28	4	0	193	789	151	55	53	8	6	2	11	71	2	174	4	1	17	6	.739	2	0-0	0	2.47
1989 New York	AL	4	4	0	0	26.2	123	23	20	18	1	1	1	2	21	0	22	1	1	1	2	.333	0	0-0	0	6.08
Toronto	AL	1	1	0	0	6.2	31	9	3	3	1	0	0	0	2	0	4	1	0	0	0	.000	0	0-0	0	4.05
12 ML YEARS		201	171	10	7	1081.2	4679	927	479	449	75	39	24	53	590	15	945	41	13	77	59	.566	5	2-3	3	3.74

Mark Leiter

Pitches: Right **Bats:** Right **Pos:** RP-69   **Ht:** 6'3" **Wt:** 220 **Born:** 4/13/63 **Age:** 36

Year Team	Lg	G	GS	CG	GF	IP	BFP	H	R	ER	HR	SH	SF	HB	TBB	IBB	SO	WP	Bk	W	L	Pct.	ShO	Sv-Op	Hld	ERA
1990 New York	AL	8	3	0	2	26.1	119	33	20	20	5	2	1	2	9	0	21	0	0	1	1	.500	0	0-0	0	6.84
1991 Detroit	AL	38	15	1	7	134.2	578	125	66	63	16	5	6	6	50	4	103	2	0	9	7	.563	0	1-2	2	4.21
1992 Detroit	AL	35	14	1	7	112	475	116	57	52	9	2	8	3	43	5	75	3	0	8	5	.615	0	0-0	3	4.18
1993 Detroit	AL	27	13	1	4	106.2	471	111	61	56	17	3	5	3	44	5	70	5	0	6	6	.500	0	0-1	1	4.73
1994 California	AL	40	7	0	15	95.1	425	99	56	50	13	4	4	9	35	6	71	2	0	4	7	.364	0	2-3	3	4.72
1995 San Francisco	NL	30	29	7	0	195.2	817	185	91	83	19	10	6	17	55	4	129	9	3	10	12	.455	1	0-0	0	3.82
1996 SF-Mon	NL	35	34	2	0	205	904	219	128	112	**37**	12	6	**16**	69	8	164	6	4	8	12	.400	0	0-0	0	4.92
1997 Philadelphia	NL	31	31	3	0	182.2	832	216	**132**	115	25	11	8	9	64	4	148	11	2	10	**17**	.370	0	0-0	0	5.67
1998 Philadelphia	NL	69	0	0	50	88.2	378	67	36	35	8	9	4	8	47	5	84	5	0	7	5	.583	0	23-35	1	3.55
1996 San Francisco	NL	23	22	1	0	135.1	602	151	93	78	25	7	3	9	50	7	118	2	3	4	10	.286	0	0-0	0	5.19
Montreal	NL	12	12	1	0	69.2	302	68	35	34	12	5	3	7	19	1	46	4	1	4	2	.667	0	0-0	0	4.39
9 ML YEARS		313	146	15	85	1147	4999	1171	647	586	149	58	48	73	416	41	865	43	9	63	72	.467	1	26-41	10	4.60

Scott Leius

Bats: R **Throws:** R **Pos:** 3B-15; PH/PR-4; SS-2; DH-1   **Ht:** 6'3" **Wt:** 200 **Born:** 9/24/65 **Age:** 33

								BATTING										BASERUNNING				PERCENTAGES		
Year Team	Lg	G	AB	H	2B	3B	HR	(Hm	Rd)	TB	R	RBI	TBB	IBB	SO	HBP	SH	SF	SB	CS	SB%	GDP	Avg	OBP	SLG
1998 Omaha *	AAA	71	258	77	10	0	15	—	—	132	40	46	17	0	30			3	7	3	.70	14	.298	.343	.512
1990 Minnesota	AL	14	25	6	1	0	1	(0	1)	10	4	4	2	0	2	0	1	0	0	0	.00	2	.240	.296	.400
1991 Minnesota	AL	109	199	57	7	2	5	(2	3)	83	35	20	30	1	35	0	5	1	5	5	.50	4	.286	.378	.417
1992 Minnesota	AL	129	409	102	18	2	2	(2	0)	130	50	35	34	0	61	1	5	0	6	5	.55	10	.249	.309	.318
1993 Minnesota	AL	10	18	3	0	0	0	(0	0)	3	4	2	2	0	4	0	0	2	0	0	.00	1	.167	.227	.167
1994 Minnesota	AL	97	350	86	16	1	14	(7	7)	146	57	49	37	0	58	1	1	2	2	4	.33	9	.246	.318	.417
1995 Minnesota	AL	117	372	92	16	5	4	(2	2)	130	51	45	49	3	54	2	0	4	2	1	.67	14	.247	.335	.349
1996 Cleveland	AL	27	43	6	4	0	1	(0	1)	13	3	3	2	0	8	0	1	0	0	0	.00	1	.140	.178	.302
1998 Kansas City	AL	17	46	8	0	0	0	(0	0)	8	2	4	1	0	6	0	0	0	0	0	.00	2	.174	.191	.174
8 ML YEARS		520	1462	360	62	10	27	(13	14)	523	206	162	157	4	228	4	13	9	15	15	.50	43	.246	.319	.358

Mark Lemke

Bats: Both **Throws:** Right **Pos:** 2B-31   **Ht:** 5'9" **Wt:** 167 **Born:** 8/13/65 **Age:** 33

								BATTING										BASERUNNING				PERCENTAGES		
Year Team	Lg	G	AB	H	2B	3B	HR	(Hm	Rd)	TB	R	RBI	TBB	IBB	SO	HBP	SH	SF	SB	CS	SB%	GDP	Avg	OBP	SLG
1988 Atlanta	NL	16	58	13	4	0	0	(0	0)	17	8	2	4	0	5	0	2	0	0	2	.00	1	.224	.274	.293
1989 Atlanta	NL	14	55	10	2	1	2	(1	1)	20	4	10	5	0	7	0	0	0	0	1	.00	1	.182	.250	.364
1990 Atlanta	NL	102	239	54	13	0	0	(0	0)	67	22	21	21	3	22	0	4	2	0	1	.00	6	.226	.286	.280
1991 Atlanta	NL	136	269	63	11	2	2	(2	0)	84	36	23	29	2	27	0	6	4	1	2	.33	9	.234	.305	.312
1992 Atlanta	NL	155	427	97	7	4	6	(4	2)	130	38	26	50	11	39	0	12	4	0	3	.00	9	.227	.307	.304
1993 Atlanta	NL	151	493	124	19	2	7	(3	4)	168	52	49	65	13	50	0	5	6	1	2	.33	21	.252	.335	.341
1994 Atlanta	NL	104	350	103	15	0	3	(2	1)	127	40	31	38	12	37	0	6	0	0	3	.00	11	.294	.363	.363
1995 Atlanta	NL	116	399	101	16	5	5	(3	2)	142	42	38	44	4	40	0	7	3	2	2	.50	17	.253	.325	.356
1996 Atlanta	NL	135	498	127	17	0	5	(3	2)	159	64	37	53	1	48	0	5	6	5	2	.71	9	.255	.323	.319
1997 Atlanta	NL	109	351	86	17	1	2	(2	0)	111	33	26	33	2	51	0	8	5	2	0	1.00	10	.245	.306	.316
1998 Boston	AL	31	91	17	4	0	0	(0	0)	21	10	7	6	0	15	0	1	2	0	1	.00	0	.187	.232	.231
11 ML YEARS		1069	3230	795	125	15	32	(20	12)	1046	349	270	348	48	341	0	56	30	11	19	.37	94	.246	.317	.324

Patrick Lennon

Bats: Right **Throws:** Right **Pos:** RF-2   **Ht:** 6'2" **Wt:** 240 **Born:** 4/27/68 **Age:** 31

								BATTING										BASERUNNING				PERCENTAGES		
Year Team	Lg	G	AB	H	2B	3B	HR	(Hm	Rd)	TB	R	RBI	TBB	IBB	SO	HBP	SH	SF	SB	CS	SB%	GDP	Avg	OBP	SLG
1998 Syracuse *	AAA	126	438	127	22	4	27	—	—	238	87	95	87	3	121	2	0	2	12	4	.75	21	.290	.408	.543
1991 Seattle	AL	9	8	1	1	0	0	(0	0)	2	2	1	3	0	1	0	0	0	0	0	.00	0	.125	.364	.250
1992 Seattle	AL	1	2	0	0	0	0	(0	0)	0	0	0	0	0	0	0	0	0	0	0	.00	0	.000	.000	.000
1996 Kansas City	AL	14	30	7	3	0	0	(0	0)	10	5	1	7	0	10	0	0	0	0	0	.00	0	.233	.378	.333
1997 Oakland	AL	56	116	34	6	1	1	(1	0)	45	14	14	15	0	35	0	0	0	0	1	.00	3	.293	.374	.388
1998 Toronto	AL	2	4	2	2	0	0	(0	0)	4	1	0	0	0	1	0	0	0	0	0	.00	0	.500	.500	1.000
5 ML YEARS		82	160	44	12	1	1	(1	0)	61	22	16	25	0	47	0	0	0	0	1	.00	6	.275	.373	.381

Brian Lesher

Bats: Right **Throws:** Left **Pos:** LF-4; PH/PR-3; 1B-1   **Ht:** 6'5" **Wt:** 216 **Born:** 3/5/71 **Age:** 28

Year Team	Lg	G	AB	H	2B	3B	HR	(Hm	Rd)	TB	R	RBI	TBB	IBB	SO	HBP	SH	SF	SB	CS	SB%	GDP	Avg	OBP	SLG
1998 Edmonton *	AAA	99	360	108	31	1	11	—	—	174	62	60	46	1	96	2	0	2	3	4	.43	11	.300	.380	.483
1996 Oakland	AL	26	82	19	3	0	5	(2	3)	37	11	16	5	0	17	1	1	1	0	0	.00	2	.232	.281	.451
1997 Oakland	AL	46	131	30	4	1	4	(2	2)	48	17	16	9	0	30	0	0	2	4	1	.80	1	.229	.275	.366
1998 Oakland	AL	7	7	1	1	0	0	(0	0)	2	0	1	0	0	3	0	0	0	0	0	.00	0	.143	.143	.286
3 ML YEARS		79	220	50	8	1	9	(4	5)	87	28	33	14	0	50	1	1	3	4	1	.80	6	.227	.273	.395

Curt Leskanic

Pitches: Right **Bats:** Right **Pos:** RP-66   **Ht:** 6'0" **Wt:** 187 **Born:** 4/2/68 **Age:** 31

		HOW MUCH HE PITCHED						WHAT HE GAVE UP											THE RESULTS					
Year Team	Lg	G	GS	CG	GF	IP	BFP	H	R	ER	HR	SH	SF	HB	TBB	IBB	SO	WP	Bk	W	L	Pct.	ShO	Sv-Op	Hld	ERA
1993 Colorado	NL	18	8	0	1	57	260	59	40	34	7	5	4	2	27	1	30	8	2	1	5	.167	0	0-0	0	5.37
1994 Colorado	NL	8	3	0	2	22.1	98	27	14	14	2	2	0	0	10	0	17	2	0	1	1	.500	0	0-0	0	5.64
1995 Colorado	NL	76	0	0	27	98	406	83	38	37	7	3	2	0	33	1	107	6	1	6	3	.667	0	10-16	19	3.40
1996 Colorado	NL	70	0	0	32	73.2	334	82	51	51	12	3	3	2	38	1	76	6	2	7	5	.583	0	6-10	9	6.23
1997 Colorado	NL	55	0	0	23	58.1	248	59	36	36	8	2	4	0	24	0	53	4	0	4	0	1.000	0	2-4	6	5.55
1998 Colorado	NL	66	0	0	20	75.2	332	75	37	37	9	0	0	1	40	2	55	3	1	6	4	.600	0	2-5	12	4.40
6 ML YEARS		293	11	0	105	385	1678	385	216	209	45	15	13	5	172	5	338	29	6	25	18	.581	0	20-35	46	4.89

Al Levine

Pitches: Right **Bats:** Left **Pos:** RP-30   **Ht:** 6'3" **Wt:** 180 **Born:** 5/22/68 **Age:** 31

		HOW MUCH HE PITCHED						WHAT HE GAVE UP											THE RESULTS					
Year Team	Lg	G	GS	CG	GF	IP	BFP	H	R	ER	HR	SH	SF	HB	TBB	IBB	SO	WP	Bk	W	L	Pct.	ShO	Sv-Op	Hld	ERA
1998 Oklahoma *	AAA	12	7	0	4	53.1	223	51	33	28	7	1	1	2	17	0	30	1	0	1	3	.250	0	1- -	—	4.73
1996 Chicago	AL	16	0	0	5	18.1	85	22	14	11	1	0	1	1	7	1	12	0	0	1	0	1.000	0	0-1	0	5.40
1997 Chicago	AL	25	0	0	6	27.1	133	35	22	21	4	1	2	2	16	1	22	2	0	2	2	.500	0	0-1	3	6.91
1998 Texas	AL	30	0	0	11	58	251	68	30	29	6	1	3	0	16	1	19	5	0	0	1	.000	0	0-0	0	4.50
3 ML YEARS		71	0	0	22	103.2	469	125	66	61	11	2	6	3	39	3	53	7	0	2	4	.333	0	0-2	3	5.30

Jesse Levis

Bats: Left **Throws:** Right **Pos:** C-14; PH/PR-9   **Ht:** 5'9" **Wt:** 200 **Born:** 4/14/68 **Age:** 31

Year Team	Lg	G	AB	H	2B	3B	HR	(Hm	Rd)	TB	R	RBI	TBB	IBB	SO	HBP	SH	SF	SB	CS	SB%	GDP	Avg	OBP	SLG
1992 Cleveland	AL	28	43	12	4	0	1	(0	1)	19	2	3	0	0	5	0	0	0	0	0	.00	1	.279	.279	.442
1993 Cleveland	AL	31	63	11	2	0	0	(0	0)	13	7	4	2	0	10	0	1	1	0	0	.00	0	.175	.197	.206
1994 Cleveland	AL	1	1	1	0	0	0	(0	0)	1	0	0	0	0	0	0	0	0	0	0	.00	0	1.000	1.000	1.000
1995 Cleveland	AL	12	18	6	2	0	0	(0	0)	8	1	3	1	0	0	0	0	1	0	0	.00	1	.333	.333	.444
1996 Milwaukee	AL	104	233	55	6	1	1	(0	1)	66	27	21	38	0	15	2	1	0	0	0	.00	7	.236	.348	.283
1997 Milwaukee	AL	99	200	57	7	0	1	(1	0)	67	19	19	24	0	17	1	5	2	1	0	1.00	3	.285	.361	.335
1998 Milwaukee	NL	22	37	13	0	0	0	(0	0)	13	4	4	7	2	6	2	1	1	1	0	1.00	3	.351	.468	.351
7 ML YEARS		297	595	155	21	1	3	(1	2)	187	60	54	72	2	53	5	9	6	2	0	1.00	16	.261	.342	.314

Darren Lewis

Bats: R **Throws:** R **Pos:** CF-109; RF-55; LF-4; PH/PR-4; DH-1   **Ht:** 6'0" **Wt:** 189 **Born:** 8/28/67 **Age:** 31

Year Team	Lg	G	AB	H	2B	3B	HR	(Hm	Rd)	TB	R	RBI	TBB	IBB	SO	HBP	SH	SF	SB	CS	SB%	GDP	Avg	OBP	SLG
1990 Oakland	AL	25	35	8	0	0	0	(0	0)	8	4	1	7	0	4	1	3	0	2	0	1.00	0	.229	.372	.229
1991 San Francisco	NL	72	222	55	5	3	1	(0	1)	69	41	15	36	0	30	2	7	0	13	7	.65	1	.248	.358	.311
1992 San Francisco	NL	100	320	74	8	1	1	(0	1)	87	38	18	29	0	46	1	10	2	28	8	.78	3	.231	.295	.272
1993 San Francisco	NL	136	522	132	17	7	2	(2	0)	169	84	48	30	0	40	7	12	1	46	15	.75	4	.253	.302	.324
1994 San Francisco	NL	114	451	116	15	9	4	(4	0)	161	70	29	53	0	50	4	4	1	30	13	.70	6	.257	.340	.357
1995 SF-Cin	NL	132	472	118	13	3	1	(0	1)	140	66	24	34	0	57	8	12	1	32	18	.64	9	.250	.311	.297
1996 Chicago	AL	141	337	77	12	2	4	(0	4)	105	55	53	45	1	40	3	15	5	21	5	.81	9	.228	.321	.312
1997 ChA-LA		107	154	41	4	1	1	(0	1)	50	22	15	17	0	31	0	7	0	14	6	.70	3	.266	.339	.325
1998 Boston	AL	155	585	157	25	3	8	(5	3)	212	95	63	70	0	94	8	2	5	29	12	.71	12	.268	.352	.362
1995 San Francisco	NL	74	309	78	10	3	1	(1	0)	97	47	16	17	0	37	6	7	1	21	7	.75	6	.252	.303	.314
Cincinnati	NL	58	163	40	3	0	0	(0	0)	43	19	8	17	0	20	2	5	0	11	11	.50	3	.245	.324	.264
1997 Chicago	AL	81	77	18	1	0	0	(0	0)	19	15	5	11	0	14	0	5	0	11	4	.73	2	.234	.330	.247
Los Angeles	NL	26	77	23	3	1	1	(0	1)	31	7	10	6	0	17	0	2	0	3	2	.60	1	.299	.349	.403
9 ML YEARS		982	3098	778	99	29	22	(13	9)	1001	475	266	321	1	392	34	72	15	215	84	.72	49	.251	.327	.323

Mark Lewis

Bats: Right **Throws:** Right **Pos:** 2B-140; PH/PR-3   **Ht:** 6'1" **Wt:** 185 **Born:** 11/30/69 **Age:** 29

Year Team	Lg	G	AB	H	2B	3B	HR	(Hm	Rd)	TB	R	RBI	TBB	IBB	SO	HBP	SH	SF	SB	CS	SB%	GDP	Avg	OBP	SLG
1991 Cleveland	AL	84	314	83	15	1	0	(0	0)	100	29	30	15	0	45	0	2	5	2	2	.50	12	.264	.293	.318
1992 Cleveland	AL	122	413	109	21	0	5	(2	3)	145	44	30	25	1	69	3	1	4	4	5	.44	12	.264	.308	.351
1993 Cleveland	AL	14	52	13	2	0	1	(1	0)	18	6	5	0	0	7	0	1	0	3	0	1.00	1	.250	.250	.346
1994 Cleveland	AL	20	73	15	5	0	1	(1	0)	23	6	8	2	0	13	0	1	0	1	0	1.00	2	.205	.227	.315

Year Team	Lg	G	AB	H	2B	3B	HR	(Hm	Rd)	TB	R	RBI	TBB	IBB	SO	HBP	SH	SF	SB	CS	SB%	GDP	Avg	OBP	SLG
1995 Cincinnati	NL	81	171	58	13	1	3	(1	2)	82	25	30	21	2	33	0	0	2	0	3	.00	1	.339	.407	.480
1996 Detroit	AL	145	545	147	30	3	11	(8	3)	216	69	55	42	0	109	5	4	3	6	1	.86	12	.270	.326	.396
1997 San Francisco	NL	118	341	91	14	6	10	(4	6)	147	50	42	23	2	62	4	1	3	3	2	.60	8	.267	.318	.431
1998 Philadelphia	NL	142	518	129	21	2	9	(4	5)	181	52	54	48	2	111	3	3	8	3	3	.50	17	.249	.312	.349
8 ML YEARS		726	2427	645	121	13	40	(21	19)	912	281	254	176	7	449	15	13	25	22	16	.58	65	.266	.316	.376

Richie Lewis

Pitches: Right **Bats:** Right **Pos:** SP-1; RP-1 **Ht:** 5'10" **Wt:** 175 **Born:** 1/25/66 **Age:** 33

Year Team	Lg	G	GS	CG	GF	IP	BFP	H	R	ER	HR	SH	SF	HB	TBB	IBB	SO	WP	Bk	W	L	Pct.	ShO	Sv-Op	Hld	ERA
1998 Rochester *	AAA	21	21	2	0	124	526	107	77	69	17	1	3	7	42	0	131	10	0	5	7	.417	0	0--	0	5.01
1992 Baltimore	AL	2	2	0	0	6.2	40	13	8	8	1	0	1	0	7	0	4	0	0	1	1	.500	0	0-0	0	10.80
1993 Florida	NL	57	0	0	14	77.1	341	68	37	28	7	8	4	1	43	6	65	9	1	6	3	.667	0	0-2	3	3.26
1994 Florida	NL	45	0	0	9	54	261	62	44	34	7	3	1	1	38	9	45	10	1	1	4	.200	0	0-0	0	5.67
1995 Florida	NL	21	1	0	6	36	152	30	15	15	9	2	0	1	15	5	32	1	2	0	1	.000	0	0-0	0	3.75
1996 Detroit	AL	72	0	0	19	90.1	412	78	45	42	9	5	10	4	65	9	78	14	2	4	6	.400	0	2-6	6	4.18
1997 Oak-Cin		18	0	0	5	24.1	119	28	26	24	10	3	1	1	18	0	16	2	0	2	0	1.000	0	0-0	0	8.88
1998 Baltimore	AL	2	1	0	0	4.2	25	8	8	8	2	0	1	0	5	0	4	1	0	0	0	.000	0	0-0	0	15.43
1997 Oakland	AL	14	0	0	5	18.2	94	24	21	20	7	1	1	1	15	0	12	2	0	2	0	1.000	0	0-0	0	9.64
Cincinnati	NL	4	0	0	0	5.2	25	4	5	4	3	2	0	0	3	0	4	0	0	0	0	.000	0	0-0	0	6.35
7 ML YEARS		217	4	0	53	293.1	1350	287	183	159	45	21	18	8	191	29	244	37	6	14	15	.483	0	2-8	13	4.88

Jim Leyritz

Bats: R **Throws:** R **Pos:** PH/PR-40; DH-39; C-25; 1B-21; 3B-1; LF-1 **Ht:** 6'0" **Wt:** 195 **Born:** 12/27/63 **Age:** 35

Year Team	Lg	G	AB	H	2B	3B	HR	(Hm	Rd)	TB	R	RBI	TBB	IBB	SO	HBP	SH	SF	SB	CS	SB%	GDP	Avg	OBP	SLG
1990 New York	AL	92	303	78	13	1	5	(1	4)	108	28	25	27	1	51	7	1	1	2	3	.40	11	.257	.331	.356
1991 New York	AL	32	77	14	3	0	0	(0	0)	17	8	4	13	0	15	0	1	0	0	1	.00	0	.182	.300	.221
1992 New York	AL	63	144	37	6	0	7	(3	4)	64	17	26	14	1	22	6	0	3	0	1	.00	2	.257	.341	.444
1993 New York	AL	95	259	80	14	0	14	(6	8)	136	43	53	37	3	59	8	0	1	0	0	.00	12	.309	.410	.525
1994 New York	AL	75	249	66	12	0	17	(4	13)	129	47	58	35	1	61	6	0	3	0	0	.00	9	.265	.365	.518
1995 New York	AL	77	264	71	12	0	7	(3	4)	104	37	37	37	2	73	8	0	1	1	1	.50	4	.269	.374	.394
1996 New York	AL	88	265	70	10	0	7	(3	4)	101	23	40	30	3	68	9	2	3	2	0	1.00	11	.264	.355	.381
1997 Ana-Tex	AL	121	379	105	11	0	11	(3	8)	149	58	64	60	2	78	6	4	6	2	1	.67	13	.277	.379	.393
1998 Bos-SD		114	272	75	16	0	12	(7	5)	127	34	42	42	1	74	9	0	5	0	0	.00	6	.276	.384	.467
1997 Anaheim	AL	84	294	81	7	0	11	(3	8)	121	47	50	37	2	56	3	3	5	1	1	.50	11	.276	.357	.412
Texas	AL	37	85	24	4	0	0	(0	0)	28	11	14	23	0	22	3	1	1	1	0	1.00	2	.282	.446	.329
1998 Boston	AL	52	129	37	6	0	8	(6	2)	67	17	24	21	1	34	2	0	4	0	0	.00	4	.287	.385	.519
San Diego	NL	62	143	38	10	0	4	(1	3)	60	17	18	21	0	40	7	0	1	0	0	.00	2	.266	.384	.420
9 ML YEARS		757	2212	596	97	1	80	(30	50)	935	295	349	295	14	501	59	8	23	7	7	.50	68	.269	.367	.423

Jon Lieber

Pitches: Right **Bats:** Left **Pos:** SP-28; RP-1 **Ht:** 6'2" **Wt:** 227 **Born:** 4/2/70 **Age:** 29

Year Team	Lg	G	GS	CG	GF	IP	BFP	H	R	ER	HR	SH	SF	HB	TBB	IBB	SO	WP	Bk	W	L	Pct.	ShO	Sv-Op	Hld	ERA
1994 Pittsburgh	NL	17	17	1	0	108.2	460	116	62	45	12	3	3	1	25	3	71	2	3	6	7	.462	0	0-0	0	3.73
1995 Pittsburgh	NL	21	12	0	3	72.2	327	103	56	51	7	5	6	4	14	0	45	3	0	4	7	.364	0	0-1	3	6.32
1996 Pittsburgh	NL	51	15	0	6	142	600	156	70	63	19	7	3	3	28	2	94	0	0	9	5	.643	0	1-4	9	3.99
1997 Pittsburgh	NL	33	32	1	0	188.1	799	193	102	94	23	6	7	1	51	8	160	3	1	11	14	.440	0	0-0	0	4.49
1998 Pittsburgh	NL	29	28	2	1	171	731	182	93	78	23	7	4	3	40	4	138	0	3	8	14	.364	0	1-1	0	4.11
5 ML YEARS		151	104	4	10	682.2	2917	750	383	331	84	28	22	12	158	17	508	8	7	38	47	.447	0	2-6	12	4.36

Mike Lieberthal

Bats: Right **Throws:** Right **Pos:** C-83; PH/PR-6 **Ht:** 6'0" **Wt:** 186 **Born:** 1/18/72 **Age:** 27

Year Team	Lg	G	AB	H	2B	3B	HR	(Hm	Rd)	TB	R	RBI	TBB	IBB	SO	HBP	SH	SF	SB	CS	SB%	GDP	Avg	OBP	SLG
1994 Philadelphia	NL	24	79	21	3	1	1	(1	0)	29	6	5	3	0	5	1	1	0	0	0	.00	4	.266	.301	.367
1995 Philadelphia	NL	16	47	12	2	0	0	(0	0)	14	1	4	5	0	5	0	2	0	0	0	.00	1	.255	.327	.298
1996 Philadelphia	NL	50	166	42	8	0	7	(4	3)	71	21	23	10	0	30	2	0	4	0	0	.00	4	.253	.297	.428
1997 Philadelphia	NL	134	455	112	27	1	20	(11	9)	201	59	77	44	1	76	4	0	7	3	4	.43	10	.246	.314	.442
1998 Philadelphia	NL	86	313	80	15	3	8	(5	3)	125	39	45	17	1	44	7	0	5	2	1	.67	4	.256	.304	.399
5 ML YEARS		310	1060	267	55	5	36	(21	15)	440	126	154	79	2	160	14	3	16	5	5	.50	23	.252	.308	.415

Kerry Ligtenberg

Pitches: Right **Bats:** Right **Pos:** RP-75 **Ht:** 6'2" **Wt:** 205 **Born:** 5/11/71 **Age:** 28

Year Team	Lg	G	GS	CG	GF	IP	BFP	H	R	ER	HR	SH	SF	HB	TBB	IBB	SO	WP	Bk	W	L	Pct.	ShO	Sv-Op	Hld	ERA
1994 Minneapolis	IND	19	19	2	0	114.1	487	103	47	42	11	5	3	3	44	4	94	6	0	5	5	.500	0	0--	—	3.31
1996 Durham	A+	49	0	0	42	59.2	255	58	20	16	3	3	2	3	16	3	76	4	1	7	4	.636	0	20--	—	2.41
1997 Greenville	AA	31	0	0	27	35.1	140	20	8	8	3	0	1	1	14	1	43	1	0	3	1	.750	0	16--	—	2.04
Richmond	AAA	14	0	0	6	25	94	21	13	12	3	1	2	0	2	0	35	3	0	0	3	.000	0	1--	—	4.32
1997 Atlanta	NL	15	0	0	9	15	61	12	5	5	4	0	0	0	4	2	19	0	0	1	0	1.000	0	1-1	0	3.00

		HOW MUCH HE PITCHED				WHAT HE GAVE UP												THE RESULTS					
Year Team	Lg	G GS CG GF	IP	BFP	H	R	ER	HR	SH	SF	HB	TBB	IBB	SO	WP	Bk	W	L	Pct.	ShO	Sv-Op	Hld	ERA
1998 Atlanta	NL	75 0 0 56	73	290	51	24	22	6	1	0		24	1	79	3	0	3	2	.600	0	30-34	11	2.71
2 ML YEARS		90 0 0 65	88	351	63	29	27	10	1	1	0	28	3	98	3	0	4	2	.667	0	31-35	11	2.76

Jose Lima

Pitches: Right **Bats:** Right **Pos:** SP-33   **Ht:** 6'2" **Wt:** 205 **Born:** 9/30/72 **Age:** 26

		HOW MUCH HE PITCHED				WHAT HE GAVE UP												THE RESULTS					
Year Team	Lg	G GS CG GF	IP	BFP	H	R	ER	HR	SH	SF	HB	TBB	IBB	SO	WP	Bk	W	L	Pct.	ShO	Sv-Op	Hld	ERA
1994 Detroit	AL	3 1 0 1	6.2	34	11	10	10	2	0	0	0	3	1	7	1	0	0	1	.000	0	0-0	0	13.50
1995 Detroit	AL	15 15 0 0	73.2	320	85	52	50	10	2	1	4	18	4	37	5	0	3	9	.250	0	0-0	0	6.11
1996 Detroit	AL	39 4 0 15	72.2	329	87	48	46	13	5	3	5	22	4	59	3	0	5	6	.455	0	3-7	6	5.70
1997 Houston	NL	52 1 0 15	75	321	79	45	44	9	6	3	5	16	2	63	2	0	1	6	.143	0	2-2	3	5.28
1998 Houston	NL	33 33 3 0	233.1	950	229	100	96	34	11	5	7	32	1	169	4	0	16	8	.667	1	0-0	0	3.70
5 ML YEARS		142 54 3 31	461.1	1954	491	255	246	68	24	12	21	91	12	335	15	0	25	30	.455	1	5-9	9	4.80

Felipe Lira

Pitches: Right **Bats:** Right **Pos:** RP-7   **Ht:** 6'1" **Wt:** 205 **Born:** 4/26/72 **Age:** 27

		HOW MUCH HE PITCHED				WHAT HE GAVE UP												THE RESULTS					
Year Team	Lg	G GS CG GF	IP	BFP	H	R	ER	HR	SH	SF	HB	TBB	IBB	SO	WP	Bk	W	L	Pct.	ShO	Sv-Op	Hld	ERA
1998 Tacoma *	AAA	20 20 2 0	129	560	142	69	61	10	6	6	11	42	0	88	2	0	6	8	.429	1	0- -	1	4.26
1995 Detroit	AL	37 22 0 7	146.1	635	151	74	70	17	4	9	8	56	7	89	5	1	9	13	.409	1	1-3	1	4.31
1996 Detroit	AL	32 32 3 0	194.2	850	204	123	113	30	5	11	10	66	2	113	7	0	6	14	.300	2	0-0	0	5.22
1997 Det-Sea	AL	28 18 1 3	110.2	516	132	82	78	18	2	4	6	55	2	73	7	0	5	11	.313	1	0-0	1	6.34
1998 Seattle	AL	7 0 0 3	15.2	75	22	10	8	5	0	1	0	5	0	16	1	0	1	0	1.000	0	0-0	1	4.60
1997 Detroit	AL	20 15 1 1	92	415	101	61	59	15	2	2	2	45	2	64	7	0	5	7	.417	1	0-0	0	5.77
Seattle	AL	8 3 0 2	18.2	101	31	21	19	3	0	2	4	10	0	9	0	0	0	4	.000	0	0-0	1	9.16
4 ML YEARS		104 72 4 13	467.1	2076	509	289	269	70	11	25	24	182	11	291	20	1	21	38	.356	3	1-3	2	5.18

Nelson Liriano

Bats: Both **Throws:** Right **Pos:** PH/PR-8; 2B-3; SS-1   **Ht:** 5'10" **Wt:** 185 **Born:** 6/3/64 **Age:** 35

		BATTING																BASERUNNING				PERCENTAGES		
Year Team	Lg	G	AB	H	2B	3B	HR	(Hm	Rd)	TB	R	RBI	TBB	IBB	SO	HBP	SH	SF	SB	CS	SB%	GDP	Avg	OBP	SLG
1998 Colo Sprngs *	AAA	87	286	90	16	3	7	—	—	133	44	44	39	2	42	3	0	4	8	10	.44	12	.315	.398	.465
1987 Toronto	AL	37	158	38	6	2	2	(1	—)	54	29	10	16	2	22	0	2	0	13	2	.87	3	.241	.310	.342
1988 Toronto	AL	99	276	73	6	2	3	(0	3)	92	36	23	11	0	40	2	5	1	12	5	.71	4	.264	.297	.333
1989 Toronto	AL	132	418	110	26	3	5	(3	2)	157	51	53	43	0	51	2	10	5	16	7	.70	10	.263	.331	.376
1990 Tor-Min	AL	103	355	83	12	9	1	(1	0)	116	46	28	38	0	44	1	4	2	8	7	.53	8	.234	.308	.327
1991 Kansas City	AL	10	22	9	0	0	0	(0	0)	9	5	1	0	0	2	1	0	1	0	1	.00	0	.409	.409	.409
1993 Colorado	NL	48	151	46	6	3	2	(0	2)	64	28	15	18	2	22	0	5	1	6	4	.60	6	.305	.376	.424
1994 Colorado	NL	87	255	65	17	5	3	(2	1)	101	39	31	42	5	44	0	3	3	0	2	.00	4	.255	.357	.396
1995 Pittsburgh	NL	107	259	74	12	1	5	(2	3)	103	29	38	24	3	34	2	1	3	2	2	.50	2	.286	.347	.398
1996 Pittsburgh	NL	112	217	58	14	2	3	(0	3)	85	23	30	14	2	22	0	0	3	2	0	1.00	4	.267	.308	.392
1997 Los Angeles	NL	76	88	20	6	0	1	(0	1)	29	10	11	6	1	12	0	2	1	0	0	.00	1	.227	.274	.330
1998 Colorado	NL	12	17	0	0	0	0	(0	0)	0	0	0	0	0	7	0	0	0	0	0	.00	1	.000	.000	.000
1990 Toronto	AL	50	170	36	7	2	1	(1	0)	50	16	15	16	0	20	1	1	1	3	5	.38	5	.212	.282	.294
Minnesota	AL	53	185	47	5	7	0	(0	0)	66	30	13	22	0	24	0	3	1	5	2	.71	3	.254	.332	.357
11 ML YEARS		823	2216	576	105	27	25	(9	16)	810	296	240	212	15	300	7	33	19	59	30	.66	40	.260	.324	.366

Mark Little

Bats: Right **Throws:** Right **Pos:** RF-4; LF-3   **Ht:** 6'0" **Wt:** 195 **Born:** 7/11/72 **Age:** 26

		BATTING																BASERUNNING				PERCENTAGES		
Year Team	Lg	G	AB	H	2B	3B	HR	(Hm	Rd)	TB	R	RBI	TBB	IBB	SO	HBP	SH	SF	SB	CS	SB%	GDP	Avg	OBP	SLG
1994 Hudson Vall	A-	54	208	61	15	5	3	—	—	95	33	27	22	1	38	1	0	4	14	5	.74	4	.293	.357	.457
1995 Charlotte	A+	115	438	112	31	8	9	—	—	186	75	50	51	1	108	14	2	2	20	14	.59	4	.256	.350	.425
1996 Tulsa	AA	101	409	119	24	2	13	—	—	186	69	50	48	0	88	10	5	3	22	10	.69	5	.291	.377	.455
1997 Okla City	AAA	121	415	109	23	4	15	—	—	185	72	45	39	1	100	8	8	0	21	9	.70	6	.263	.338	.446
1998 Oklahoma	AAA	69	274	81	20	4	8	—	—	133	58	46	16	0	60	10	0	5	9	6	.60	4	.296	.351	.485
Memphis	AAA	19	63	17	3	3	0	—	—	26	9	6	6	1	10	2	0	2	0	3	.00	0	.270	.342	.413
1998 St. Louis	NL	7	12	1	0	0	0	(0	0)	1	0	0	2	0	5	0	1	0	1	0	1.00	0	.083	.214	.083

Scott Livingstone

Bats: L **Throws:** R **Pos:** PH/PR-54; 3B-17; DH-5; 1B-3   **Ht:** 6'0" **Wt:** 190 **Born:** 7/15/65 **Age:** 33

		BATTING																BASERUNNING				PERCENTAGES		
Year Team	Lg	G	AB	H	2B	3B	HR	(Hm	Rd)	TB	R	RBI	TBB	IBB	SO	HBP	SH	SF	SB	CS	SB%	GDP	Avg	OBP	SLG
1991 Detroit	AL	44	127	37	5	0	2	(1	1)	48	19	11	10	0	25	0	1	1	2	1	.67	0	.291	.341	.378
1992 Detroit	AL	117	354	100	21	0	4	(2	2)	133	43	46	21	1	36	0	3	4	1	3	.25	4	.282	.319	.376
1993 Detroit	AL	98	304	89	10	2	2	(1	1)	109	39	39	19	1	32	0	1	6	1	3	.25	4	.293	.328	.359
1994 Det-SD		72	203	54	13	1	2	(1	1)	75	11	11	7	0	26	0	0	1	2	2	.50	5	.266	.289	.369
1995 San Diego	NL	99	196	66	15	0	5	(1	4)	96	26	32	15	1	22	0	0	2	2	1	.67	6	.337	.380	.490
1996 San Diego	NL	102	172	51	4	1	2	(0	2)	63	20	20	9	0	22	0	0	0	0	1	.00	6	.297	.331	.366
1997 SD-StL	NL	65	67	11	2	0	0	(0	0)	13	4	6	3	0	11	0	0	2	1	0	1.00	1	.164	.194	.194
1998 Montreal	NL	76	110	23	6	0	0	(0	0)	29	1	12	5	2	15	0	1	3	1	1	.50	2	.209	.237	.264
1994 Detroit	AL	15	23	5	1	0	0	(0	0)	6	0	1	1	0	4	0	0	0	0	0	.00	0	.217	.250	.261

Year Team	Lg	G	AB	H	2B	3B	HR	(Hm	Rd)	TB	R	RBI	TBB	IBB	SO	HBP	SH	SF	SB	CS	SB%	GDP	Avg	OBP	SLG
San Diego	NL	57	180	49	12	1	2	(1	1)	69	11	10	6	0	22	0	0	1	2	2	.50	5	.272	.294	.383
1997 San Diego	NL	23	26	4	1	0	0	(0	0)	5	1	3	2	0	1	0	0	0	0	0	.00	0	.154	.214	.192
St. Louis	NL	42	41	7	1	0	0	(0	0)	8	3	3	1	0	10	0	0	2	1	0	1.00	1	.171	.182	.195
8 ML YEARS		673	1533	431	76	4	17	(6	11)	566	163	177	89	5	189	0	5	19	10	12	.45	29	.281	.317	.369

Graeme Lloyd

Pitches: Left **Bats:** Left **Pos:** RP-50   **Ht:** 6'7" **Wt:** 234 **Born:** 4/9/67 **Age:** 32

		HOW MUCH HE PITCHED						WHAT HE GAVE UP											THE RESULTS						
Year Team	Lg	G	GS	CG	GF	IP	BFP	H	R	ER	HR	SH	SF	HB	TBB	IBB	SO	WP	Bk	W	L	Pct.	ShO	Sv-Op	Hld	ERA
1993 Milwaukee	AL	55	0	0	12	63.2	269	64	24	20	5	1	2	3	13	3	31	4	0	3	4	.429	0	0-4	6	2.83
1994 Milwaukee	AL	43	0	0	21	47	203	49	28	27	4	1	2	3	15	6	31	2	0	2	3	.400	0	3-6	3	5.17
1995 Milwaukee	AL	33	0	0	14	32	127	28	16	16	4	1	4	0	8	2	13	3	0	0	5	.000	0	4-6	9	4.50
1996 Mil-NYA	AL	65	0	0	15	56.2	252	61	30	27	4	5	3	1	22	4	30	4	0	2	6	.250	0	0-5	17	4.29
1997 New York	AL	46	0	0	17	49	217	55	24	18	6	3	5	1	20	7	26	3	0	1	1	.500	0	1-1	2	3.31
1998 New York	AL	50	0	0	8	37.2	145	26	10	7	3	0	1	2	6	2	20	2	0	3	0	1.000	0	0-2	9	1.67
1996 Milwaukee	AL	52	0	0	15	51	217	49	19	16	3	5	1	1	17	3	24	0	0	2	4	.333	0	0-3	15	2.82
New York	AL	13	0	0	0	5.2	35	12	11	11	1	0	2	0	5	1	6	4	0	0	2	.000	0	0-2	2	17.47
6 ML YEARS		292	0	0	87	286	1213	283	132	115	26	11	17	10	84	24	151	18	0	11	19	.367	0	8-24	46	3.62

Esteban Loaiza

Pitches: Right **Bats:** Right **Pos:** SP-28; RP-7   **Ht:** 6'3" **Wt:** 205 **Born:** 12/31/71 **Age:** 27

		HOW MUCH HE PITCHED						WHAT HE GAVE UP											THE RESULTS						
Year Team	Lg	G	GS	CG	GF	IP	BFP	H	R	ER	HR	SH	SF	HB	TBB	IBB	SO	WP	Bk	W	L	Pct.	ShO	Sv-Op	Hld	ERA
1995 Pittsburgh	NL	32	31	1	0	172.2	762	205	115	99	21	10	9	5	55	3	85	6	1	8	9	.471	0	0-0	0	5.16
1996 Pittsburgh	NL	10	10	1	0	52.2	236	65	32	29	11	3	1	2	19	2	32	0	0	2	3	.400	1	0-0	0	4.96
1997 Pittsburgh	NL	33	32	1	0	196.1	851	214	99	90	17	10	7	12	56	9	122	2	3	11	11	.500	0	0-0	0	4.13
1998 Pit-Tex		35	28	1	3	171	751	199	107	98	28	7	12	5	52	4	108	4	2	9	11	.450	0	0-1	0	5.16
1998 Pittsburgh	NL	21	14	0	3	91.2	394	96	50	46	13	5	7	3	30	1	53	1	2	6	5	.545	0	0-1	0	4.52
Texas	AL	14	14	1	0	79.1	357	103	57	52	15	2	5	2	22	3	55	3	0	3	6	.333	0	0-0	0	5.90
4 ML YEARS		110	101	4	3	592.2	2600	683	353	316	77	30	29	24	182	18	347	12	6	30	34	.469	1	0-1	0	4.80

Keith Lockhart

Bats: L **Throws:** R **Pos:** 2B-98; PH/PR-19; DH-2; 3B-1   **Ht:** 5'10" **Wt:** 170 **Born:** 11/10/64 **Age:** 34

		BATTING																	BASERUNNING				PERCENTAGES		
Year Team	Lg	G	AB	H	2B	3B	HR	(Hm	Rd)	TB	R	RBI	TBB	IBB	SO	HBP	SH	SF	SB	CS	SB%	GDP	Avg	OBP	SLG
1994 San Diego	NL	27	43	9	0	0	2	(2	0)	15	4	6	4	0	10	1	1	1	1	0	1.00	2	.209	.286	.349
1995 Kansas City	AL	94	274	88	19	3	6	(3	3)	131	41	33	14	2	21	4	1	7	8	1	.89	2	.321	.355	.478
1996 Kansas City	AL	138	433	118	33	3	7	(4	3)	178	49	55	30	4	40	2	1	5	11	6	.65	7	.273	.319	.411
1997 Atlanta	NL	96	147	41	5	3	6	(3	3)	70	25	32	14	0	17	1	3	4	0	0	.00	4	.279	.337	.476
1998 Atlanta	NL	109	366	94	21	0	9	(4	5)	142	50	37	29	0	37	1	2	3	2	2	.50	2	.257	.311	.388
5 ML YEARS		464	1263	350	78	9	30	(16	14)	536	169	163	91	6	125	9	8	20	22	9	.71	17	.277	.325	.424

Paul LoDuca

Bats: Right **Throws:** Right **Pos:** C-4; PH/PR-4   **Ht:** 5'10" **Wt:** 185 **Born:** 4/12/72 **Age:** 27

		BATTING																	BASERUNNING				PERCENTAGES		
Year Team	Lg	G	AB	H	2B	3B	HR	(Hm	Rd)	TB	R	RBI	TBB	IBB	SO	HBP	SH	SF	SB	CS	SB%	GDP	Avg	OBP	SLG
1993 Vero Beach	A+	39	134	42	6	0	0	—	—	48	17	13	13	0	22	2	0	1	0	0	.00	2	.313	.380	.358
1994 Bakersfield	A+	123	455	141	32	1	6	—	—	193	65	68	52	2	49	3	0	4	16	9	.64	5	.310	.381	.424
1995 San Antonio	AA	61	199	49	8	0	1	—	—	60	27	8	26	0	25	2	0	0	5	5	.50	12	.246	.339	.302
1996 Vero Beach	A+	124	439	134	22	0	3	—	—	165	54	66	70	2	38	2	0	4	8	2	.80	14	.305	.400	.376
1997 San Antonio	AA	105	385	126	28	2	7	—	—	179	63	69	46	3	27	3	4	5	16	8	.67	17	.327	.399	.465
1998 Albuquerque	AAA	126	451	144	30	3	8	—	—	204	69	58	59	2	40	5	1	7	6	19	7	.73	20	.319	.399	.452
1998 Los Angeles	NL	6	14	4	1	0	0	(0	0)	5	2	1	0	0	1	0	0	0	0	0	.00	0	.286	.286	.357

Carlton Loewer

Pitches: Right **Bats:** Right **Pos:** SP-21   **Ht:** 6'6" **Wt:** 220 **Born:** 9/24/73 **Age:** 25

		HOW MUCH HE PITCHED						WHAT HE GAVE UP											THE RESULTS						
Year Team	Lg	G	GS	CG	GF	IP	BFP	H	R	ER	HR	SH	SF	HB	TBB	IBB	SO	WP	Bk	W	L	Pct.	ShO	Sv-Op	Hld	ERA
1995 Clearwater	A+	20	20	1	0	114.2	502	124	59	42	6	3	5	5	36	0	83	7	3	7	5	.583	0	0- -	—	3.30
Reading	AA	8	8	0	0	50	212	42	17	12	3	1	0	1	31	0	35	4	0	4	1	.800	0	0- -	—	2.16
1996 Reading	AA	27	27	3	0	171	753	191	115	100	24	7	3	8	57	3	119	9	1	7	10	.412	1	0- -	—	5.26
1997 Scranton-WB	AAA	29	29	4	0	184	797	198	120	94	20	8	4	7	50	6	152	3	0	5	13	.278	0	0- -	—	4.60
1998 Scranton-WB	AAA	12	12	5	0	94	385	89	34	30	5	5	2	5	22	0	69	0	0	7	3	.700	2	0-' -	—	2.87
1998 Philadelphia	NL	21	21	1	0	122.2	549	154	86	83	18	5	8	3	39	1	58	4	0	7	8	.467	0	0-0	0	6.09

Kenny Lofton

Bats: Left **Throws:** Left **Pos:** CF-154 **Ht:** 6'0" **Wt:** 180 **Born:** 5/31/67 **Age:** 32

Year Team	Lg	G	AB	H	2B	3B	HR	(Hm	Rd)	TB	R	RBI	TBB	IBB	SO	HBP	SH	SF	SB	CS	SB%	GDP	Avg	OBP	SLG
1991 Houston	NL	20	74	15	1	0	0	(0	0)	16	9	0	5	0	19	0	0	0	2	1	.67	0	.203	.253	.216
1992 Cleveland	AL	148	576	164	15	8	5	(3	2)	210	96	42	68	3	54	2	4	1	66	12	.85	7	.285	.362	.365
1993 Cleveland	AL	148	569	185	28	8	1	(1	0)	232	116	42	81	6	83	1	2	4	70	14	.83	8	.325	.408	.408
1994 Cleveland	AL	112	459	**160**	32	9	12	(10	2)	246	105	57	52	5	56	2	4	6	60	12	.83	5	.349	.412	.536
1995 Cleveland	AL	118	481	149	22	**13**	7	(5	2)	218	93	53	40	6	49	1	4	3	54	15	.78	6	.310	.362	.453
1996 Cleveland	AL	154	**662**	210	35	4	14	(7	7)	295	132	67	61	3	82	0	7	6	75	17	.82	7	.317	.372	.446
1997 Atlanta	NL	122	493	164	20	6	5	(3	2)	211	90	48	64	5	83	2	2	3	27	20	.57	10	.333	.409	.428
1998 Cleveland	AL	154	600	169	31	6	12	(6	6)	248	101	64	87	1	80	2	3	6	54	10	**.84**	7	.282	.371	.413
8 ML YEARS		976	3914	1216	184	54	56	(35	21)	1676	742	373	458	29	506	10	26	29	408	101	.80	50	.311	.382	.428

Rich Loiselle

Pitches: Right **Bats:** Right **Pos:** RP-54 **Ht:** 6'5" **Wt:** 240 **Born:** 1/12/72 **Age:** 27

Year Team	Lg	G	GS	CG	GF	IP	BFP	H	R	ER	HR	SH	SF	HB	TBB	IBB	SO	WP	Bk	W	L	Pct.	ShO	Sv-Op	Hld	ERA
1998 Nashville *	AAA	4	0	0	3	5	18	3	0	0	0	0	0	0	0	0	6	0	0	0	0	.000	0	2- --		0.00
1996 Pittsburgh	NL	5	3	0	0	20.2	90	22	8	7	3	0	0	0	8	1	9	3	0	1	0	1.000	0	0-0	1	3.05
1997 Pittsburgh	NL	72	0	0	58	72.2	312	76	29	25	7	2	2	1	24	3	66	4	0	1	5	.167	0	29-34	5	3.10
1998 Pittsburgh	NL	54	0	0	43	55	258	56	26	21	2	5	1	2	36	9	48	0	0	2	7	.222	0	19-27	1	3.44
3 ML YEARS		131	3	0	101	148.1	660	154	63	53	12	7	3	3	68	13	123	7	0	4	12	.250	0	48-61	7	3.22

George Lombard

Bats: Left **Throws:** Right **Pos:** PH/PR-5; RF-2 **Ht:** 6'0" **Wt:** 208 **Born:** 9/14/75 **Age:** 23

Year Team	Lg	G	AB	H	2B	3B	HR	(Hm	Rd)	TB	R	RBI	TBB	IBB	SO	HBP	SH	SF	SB	CS	SB%	GDP	Avg	OBP	SLG
1994 Braves	R	40	129	18	2	0	0	—	—	20	10	5	18	0	47	3	0	0	10	4	.71	1	.140	.260	.155
1995 Macon	A	49	180	37	6	1	3	—	—	54	32	16	27	3	44	5	1	0	16	4	.80	4	.206	.325	.300
Eugene	A-	68	262	66	5	3	5	—	—	92	38	19	23	0	91	5	2	1	35	13	.73	0	.252	.323	.351
1996 Macon	A	116	444	109	16	8	15	—	—	186	76	51	36	0	122	7	8	2	24	17	.59	4	.245	.311	.419
1997 Durham	A+	131	462	122	25	7	14	—	—	203	65	72	66	9	145	9	2	2	35	7	.83	4	.264	.365	.439
1998 Greenville	AA	122	422	130	25	4	22	—	—	229	84	65	71	10	140	5	5	4	35	5	.88	2	.308	.410	.543
1998 Atlanta	NL	6	6	2	0	0	1	(0	1)	5	2	1	0	0	1	0	0	0	1	0	1.00	0	.333	.333	.833

Braden Looper

Pitches: Right **Bats:** Right **Pos:** RP-4 **Ht:** 6'4" **Wt:** 210 **Born:** 10/28/74 **Age:** 24

Year Team	Lg	G	GS	CG	GF	IP	BFP	H	R	ER	HR	SH	SF	HB	TBB	IBB	SO	WP	Bk	W	L	Pct.	ShO	Sv-Op	Hld	ERA
1997 Pr William	A+	12	12	0	0	64.1	287	71	38	32	6	1	1	3	25	0	58	1	2	3	6	.333	0	0- --		4.48
Arkansas	AA	19	0	0	14	21.1	94	24	14	14	2	1	1	1	7	2	20	1	2	1	4	.200	0	5- --		5.91
1998 Memphis	AAA	40	0	0	32	40.2	177	43	16	14	3	2	1	2	13	1	43	3	0	2	3	.400	0	20- --		3.10
1998 St. Louis	NL	4	0	0	3	3.1	16	5	4	2	1	0	1	0	1	0	4	1	0	0	1	.000	0	0-2	0	5.40

Albie Lopez

Pitches: Right **Bats:** Right **Pos:** RP-54 **Ht:** 6'2" **Wt:** 185 **Born:** 8/18/71 **Age:** 27

Year Team	Lg	G	GS	CG	GF	IP	BFP	H	R	ER	HR	SH	SF	HB	TBB	IBB	SO	WP	Bk	W	L	Pct.	ShO	Sv-Op	Hld	ERA
1998 Durham *	AAA	2	0	0	0	3	13	4	0	0	0	0	0	0	1	0	2	0	0	0	0	.000	0	0- --		0.00
St. Pete *	A+	1	1	0	0	1	5	2	2	2	1	0	0	0	0	0	1	0	0	0	1	.000	0	0- --		18.00
1993 Cleveland	AL	9	9	0	0	49.2	222	49	34	33	7	1	1	1	32	1	25	0	0	3	1	.750	0	0-0	0	5.98
1994 Cleveland	AL	4	4	1	0	17	76	20	11	8	3	0	1	1	6	0	18	3	0	1	2	.333	1	0-0	0	4.24
1995 Cleveland	AL	6	2	0	0	23	92	17	8	8	4	0	1	1	7	1	22	2	0	0	0	.000	0	0-0	0	3.13
1996 Cleveland	AL	13	10	0	0	62	282	80	47	44	14	0	1	2	22	1	45	2	0	5	4	.556	0	0-0	0	6.39
1997 Cleveland	AL	37	6	0	10	76.2	364	101	61	59	11	3	2	4	40	9	63	5	0	3	7	.300	0	0-1	4	6.93
1998 Tampa Bay	AL	54	0	0	12	79.2	335	73	31	23	7	4	3	3	32	4	62	5	0	7	4	.636	0	1-5	4	2.60
6 ML YEARS		123	31	1	22	308	1371	340	192	175	46	8	8	12	139	16	235	17	0	19	18	.514	1	1-6	8	5.11

Javy Lopez

Bats: Right **Throws:** Right **Pos:** C-128; PH/PR-9; DH-1 **Ht:** 6'3" **Wt:** 200 **Born:** 11/5/70 **Age:** 28

Year Team	Lg	G	AB	H	2B	3B	HR	(Hm	Rd)	TB	R	RBI	TBB	IBB	SO	HBP	SH	SF	SB	CS	SB%	GDP	Avg	OBP	SLG
1992 Atlanta	NL	9	16	6	2	0	0	(0	0)	8	3	2	0	0	1	0	0	0	0	0	.00	0	.375	.375	.500
1993 Atlanta	NL	8	16	6	1	1	1	(0	1)	12	1	2	0	0	2	1	0	0	0	0	.00	0	.375	.412	.750
1994 Atlanta	NL	80	277	68	9	0	13	(4	9)	116	27	35	17	0	61	5	2	2	0	2	.00	12	.245	.299	.419
1995 Atlanta	NL	100	333	105	11	4	14	(8	6)	166	37	51	14	0	57	2	0	3	0	1	.00	13	.315	.344	.498
1996 Atlanta	NL	138	489	138	19	1	23	(10	13)	228	56	69	28	5	84	3	1	5	1	6	.14	17	.282	.322	.466
1997 Atlanta	NL	123	414	122	28	1	23	(11	12)	221	52	68	40	10	82	5	1	1	1	1	.50	9	.295	.361	.534
1998 Atlanta	NL	133	489	139	21	1	34	(18	16)	264	73	106	30	1	85	6	1	8	5	3	.63	22	.284	.328	.540
7 ML YEARS		591	2034	584	91	8	108	(51	57)	1015	249	333	129	16	372	22	5	22	7	13	.35	73	.287	.333	.499

Luis Lopez

Bats: B **Throws:** R **Pos:** 2B-50; PH/PR-46; SS-39; 3B-11; LF-8; RF-1   **Ht:** 5'11"   **Wt:** 166   **Born:** 9/4/70   **Age:** 28

							BATTING									BASERUNNING				PERCENTAGES		
Year Team	Lg	G	AB	H	2B	3B	HR	(Hm | Rd)	TB	R	RBI	TBB	IBB	SO	HBP	SH	SF	SB	CS	SB%	GDP	Avg	OBP	SLG
1993 San Diego	NL	17	43	5	1	0	0	(0 | 0)	6	1	1	0	0	8	0	0	1	0	0	.00	0	.116	.114	.140
1994 San Diego	NL	77	235	65	16	1	2	(2 | 0)	89	29	20	15	2	39	3	2	2	3	2	.60	7	.277	.325	.379
1996 San Diego	NL	63	139	25	3	0	2	(1 | 1)	34	10	11	9	1	35	1	1	0	0	0	.00	7	.180	.233	.245
1997 New York	NL	78	178	48	12	1	1	(1 | 0)	65	19	19	12	2	42	4	2	0	2	4	.33	2	.270	.330	.365
1998 New York	NL	117	266	67	13	2	2	(1 | 1)	90	37	22	20	3	60	4	3	2	2	2	.50	10	.252	.312	.338
5 ML YEARS		352	861	210	45	4	7	(5 | 2)	284	96	73	56	8	184	12	8	6	7	8	.47	26	.244	.297	.330

Mendy Lopez

Bats: Right **Throws:** Right **Pos:** SS-72; 3B-2   **Ht:** 6'2"   **Wt:** 190   **Born:** 10/15/74   **Age:** 24

							BATTING									BASERUNNING				PERCENTAGES		
Year Team	Lg	G	AB	H	2B	3B	HR	(Hm | Rd)	TB	R	RBI	TBB	IBB	SO	HBP	SH	SF	SB	CS	SB%	GDP	Avg	OBP	SLG
1994 Royals	R	59	235	85	19	3	5	—	—	125	56	50	22	0	27	3	2	5	19	2	.90	5	.362	.415	.532
1995 Wilmington	A+	130	428	116	29	3	2	—	—	157	42	36	28	0	73	5	7	2	18	10	.64	12	.271	.322	.367
1996 Wichita	AA	93	327	92	20	5	6	—	—	140	47	32	26	1	67	4	2	1	14	4	.78	6	.281	.341	.428
1997 Omaha	AAA	17	52	12	2	0	1	—	—	17	6	6	8	0	21	0	1	0	0	0	.00	0	.231	.333	.327
Wichita	AA	101	357	83	16	3	5	—	—	120	56	42	36	0	70	3	5	5	7	5	.58	8	.232	.304	.336
1998 Omaha	AAA	60	195	35	6	1	3	—	—	52	18	14	18	0	44	1	3	0	2	3	.40	0	.179	.252	.267
1998 Kansas City	AL	74	206	50	10	2	1	(1 | 0)	67	18	15	12	0	40	1	5	1	5	2	.71	6	.243	.286	.325

Mark Loretta

Bats: R **Throws:** R **Pos:** 1B-70; SS-56; PH/PR-23; 3B-22; 2B-13; LF-1   **Ht:** 6'0"   **Wt:** 180   **Born:** 8/14/71   **Age:** 27

							BATTING									BASERUNNING				PERCENTAGES		
Year Team	Lg	G	AB	H	2B	3B	HR	(Hm | Rd)	TB	R	RBI	TBB	IBB	SO	HBP	SH	SF	SB	CS	SB%	GDP	Avg	OBP	SLG
1995 Milwaukee	AL	19	50	13	3	0	1	(0 | 1)	19	13	3	4	0	7	1	1	0	1	1	.50	1	.260	.327	.380
1996 Milwaukee	AL	73	154	43	3	0	1	(0 | 1)	49	20	13	14	0	15	0	2	0	2	1	.67	7	.279	.339	.318
1997 Milwaukee	AL	132	418	120	17	5	5	(2 | 3)	162	56	47	47	2	60	2	5	10	5	5	.50	15	.287	.354	.388
1998 Milwaukee	NL	140	434	137	29	6	1	(3 | 3)	184	55	54	42	1	47	7	4	4	9	6	.60	14	.316	.382	.424
4 ML YEARS		364	1056	313	52	5	13	(5 | 8)	414	144	117	107	3	129	10	12	14	17	13	.57	37	.296	.362	.392

Andrew Lorraine

Pitches: Left **Bats:** Left **Pos:** RP-4   **Ht:** 6'3"   **Wt:** 195   **Born:** 8/11/72   **Age:** 26

		HOW MUCH HE PITCHED					WHAT HE GAVE UP										THE RESULTS					
Year Team	Lg	G	GS	CG	GF	IP	BFP	H	R	ER	HR	SH	SF	HB	TBB	IBB	SO	WP	Bk	W	L	Pct.	ShO	Sv-Op	Hld	ERA
1998 Tacoma *	AAA	52	4	0	10	80.1	359	93	44	43	10	3	3	2	36	2	70	2	0	7	4	.636	0	2--	—	4.82
1994 California	AL	4	3	0	0	18.2	96	30	23	22	7	2	1	0	11	0	10	0	0	0	2	.000	0	0-0	0	10.61
1995 Chicago	AL	5	0	0	2	8	30	3	3	3	0	0	1	0	2	0	5	0	0	0	0	.000	0	0-0	1	3.38
1997 Oakland	AL	12	6	0	1	29.2	146	45	22	21	2	0	3	1	15	0	18	0	0	3	1	.750	0	0-0	0	6.37
1998 Seattle	AL	4	0	0	1	3.2	16	3	1	1	0	0	0	0	4	0	0	1	0	0	0	.000	0	0-0	1	2.45
4 ML YEARS		25	9	0	4	60	288	81	49	47	9	2	4	2	32	0	33	1	0	3	3	.500	0	0-0	2	7.05

Torey Lovullo

Bats: Both **Throws:** Right **Pos:** 2B-5; 3B-1   **Ht:** 6'0"   **Wt:** 185   **Born:** 7/25/65   **Age:** 33

							BATTING									BASERUNNING				PERCENTAGES		
Year Team	Lg	G	AB	H	2B	3B	HR	(Hm | Rd)	TB	R	RBI	TBB	IBB	SO	HBP	SH	SF	SB	CS	SB%	GDP	Avg	OBP	SLG
1998 Buffalo *	AAA	92	328	107	17	4	17	—	—	183	66	65	54	1	32	1	1	9	3	3	.50	9	.326	.413	.558
1988 Detroit	AL	12	21	8	1	1	1	(0 | 1)	14	2	2	1	0	2	0	1	0	0	0	.00	1	.381	.409	.667
1989 Detroit	AL	29	87	10	2	0	1	(0 | 1)	15	8	4	14	0	20	0	1	2	0	0	.00	3	.115	.233	.172
1991 New York	AL	22	51	9	2	0	0	(0 | 0)	11	0	2	5	1	7	0	3	0	0	0	.00	0	.176	.250	.216
1993 California	AL	116	367	92	20	0	6	(4 | 2)	130	42	30	36	1	49	1	3	2	7	6	.54	8	.251	.318	.354
1994 Seattle	AL	36	72	16	5	0	2	(2 | 0)	27	9	7	9	1	13	0	0	1	1	0	1.00	2	.222	.309	.375
1996 Oakland	AL	65	82	18	4	0	3	(0 | 3)	31	15	9	11	0	17	2	3	1	1	2	.33	0	.220	.323	.378
1998 Cleveland	AL	6	19	4	1	0	0	(0 | 0)	5	1	1	1	0	2	0	1	0	0	0	.00	1	.211	.250	.263
7 ML YEARS		286	699	157	35	1	13	(6 | 7)	233	77	55	77	3	110	3	12	5	9	8	.53	15	.225	.302	.333

Derek Lowe

Pitches: Right **Bats:** Right **Pos:** RP-53; SP-10   **Ht:** 6'6"   **Wt:** 170   **Born:** 6/1/73   **Age:** 26

		HOW MUCH HE PITCHED					WHAT HE GAVE UP										THE RESULTS					
Year Team	Lg	G	GS	CG	GF	IP	BFP	H	R	ER	HR	SH	SF	HB	TBB	IBB	SO	WP	Bk	W	L	Pct.	ShO	Sv-Op	Hld	ERA
1991 Mariners	R	12	12	0	0	71	295	58	26	19	2	1	4	2	21	0	60	4	6	5	3	.625	0	0--	—	2.41
1992 Bellingham	A-	14	13	2	0	85.2	349	69	34	23	2	3	1	4	22	0	66	5	4	7	3	.700	1	0--	—	2.42
1993 Riverside	A+	27	26	3	1	154	687	189	104	90	9	2	2	6	60	0	80	12	9	12	9	.571	2	0--	—	5.26
1994 Jacksonville	AA	26	26	2	0	151.1	676	177	92	83	7	6	3	9	50	1	75	11	7	7	10	.412	0	0--	—	4.94
1995 Mariners	R	2	2	0	0	9.2	35	5	1	1	0	0	0	0	2	0	11	0	0	1	0	1.000	0	0--	—	0.93
Port City	AA	10	10	1	0	53.1	244	70	41	36	8	3	2	3	22	1	30	2	0	1	6	.143	0	0--	—	6.08
1996 Port City	AA	10	10	0	0	65	258	56	27	22	7	0	2	1	17	0	33	0	0	5	3	.625	0	0--	—	3.05
Tacoma	AAA	17	16	1	0	105	463	118	64	53	7	4	5	3	37	1	54	1	2	6	9	.400	1	0--	—	4.54
1997 Tacoma	AAA	10	9	1	0	57.1	242	53	26	22	3	1	1	2	20	0	49	1	0	3	4	.429	0	0--	—	3.45
Pawtucket	AAA	6	5	0	1	30.1	121	23	8	8	3	1	0	1	11	0	21	0	0	4	0	1.000	0	0--	—	2.37

			HOW MUCH HE PITCHED						WHAT HE GAVE UP											THE RESULTS						
Year Team	Lg	G	GS	CG	GF	IP	BFP	H	R	ER	HR	SH	SF	HB	TBB	IBB	SO	WP	Bk	W	L	Pct.	ShO	Sv-Op	Hld	ERA
1997 Sea-Bos	AL	20	9	0	1	69	298	74	49	47	11	4	2	4	23	3	52	2	0	2	6	.250	0	0-2	1	6.13
1998 Boston	AL	63	10	0	8	123	527	126	65	55	5	4	5	4	42	5	77	8	0	3	9	.250	0	4-9	12	4.02
1997 Seattle	AL	12	9	0	0	53	234	59	43	41	11	2	1	2	20	2	39	2	0	2	4	.333	0	0-0	0	6.96
Boston	AL	8	0	0	0	16	64	15	6	6	0	2	1	2	3	1	13	0	0	0	2	.000	0	0-2	1	3.38
2 ML YEARS		83	19	0	9	192	825	200	114	102	16	8	7	8	65	8	129	10	0	5	15	.250	0	4-11	13	4.78

Sean Lowe

Pitches: Right **Bats:** Right **Pos:** RP-3; SP-1   **Ht:** 6'2" **Wt:** 205 **Born:** 3/29/71 **Age:** 28

			HOW MUCH HE PITCHED						WHAT HE GAVE UP											THE RESULTS						
Year Team	Lg	G	GS	CG	GF	IP	BFP	H	R	ER	HR	SH	SF	HB	TBB	IBB	SO	WP	Bk	W	L	Pct.	ShO	Sv-Op	Hld	ERA
1992 Hamilton	A-	5	5	0	0	28	109	14	8	5	0	0	0	1	14	0	22	1	1	2	0	1.000	0	0- --	--	1.61
1993 St. Pete	A+	25	25	0	0	132.2	594	152	80	63	6	2	5	6	62	1	87	4	5	6	11	.353	0	0- --	--	4.27
1994 St. Pete	A+	21	21	0	0	114	488	119	51	44	6	3	2	5	37	0	92	3	0	5	6	.455	0	0- --	--	3.47
Arkansas	AA	3	3	0	0	19.1	76	13	3	3	0	2	0	0	8	0	11	0	0	2	1	.667	0	0- --	--	1.40
1995 Arkansas	AA	24	24	0	0	129	578	143	84	70	2	5	4	5	64	0	77	9	0	9	8	.529	0	0- --	--	4.88
1996 Arkansas	AA	6	6	0	0	33	150	32	24	22	2	1	1	2	15	1	25	1	0	2	3	.400	0	0- --	--	6.00
Louisville	AAA	25	18	0	1	115	515	127	72	60	7	4	6	7	51	7	76	6	0	8	9	.471	0	0- --	--	4.70
1997 Louisville	AAA	26	23	1	2	131.2	581	142	74	64	13	3	3	10	53	4	117	5	2	6	10	.375	0	1- --	--	4.37
1998 Memphis	AAA	25	21	0	0	153	637	147	57	54	17	6	1	4	61	1	114	2	0	12	8	.600	0	0- --	--	3.18
1997 St. Louis	NL	6	4	0	1	17.1	89	27	21	18	2	1	2	1	10	0	8	0	0	0	2	.000	0	0-0	0	9.35
1998 St. Louis	NL	4	1	0	2	5.1	31	11	9	9	1	1	0	0	5	0	2	0	0	0	3	.000	0	0-0	0	15.19
2 ML YEARS		10	5	0	3	22.2	120	38	30	27	3	2	2	1	15	0	10	0	0	0	5	.000	0	0-0	0	10.72

Mike Lowell

Bats: Right **Throws:** Right **Pos:** 3B-7; PH/PR-2; DH-1   **Ht:** 6'4" **Wt:** 195 **Born:** 2/24/74 **Age:** 25

			BATTING																BASERUNNING				PERCENTAGES		
Year Team	Lg	G	AB	H	2B	3B	HR	(Hm	Rd)	TB	R	RBI	TBB	IBB	SO	HBP	SH	SF	SB	CS	SB%	GDP	Avg	OBP	SLG
1995 Oneonta	A-	72	281	73	18	0	1	—	—	94	36	27	23	0	34	3	0	6	3	1	.75	5	.260	.316	.335
1996 Greensboro	A	113	433	122	33	0	8	—	—	179	54	46	46	0	43	4	2	2	10	3	.77	7	.282	.355	.413
Tampa	A+	24	78	22	5	0	0	—	—	27	8	11	3	0	13	0	1	1	1	1	.50	2	.282	.298	.346
1997 Norwich	AA	78	285	98	17	0	15	—	—	160	60	47	48	1	30	4	1	3	2	1	.67	11	.344	.439	.561
Columbus	AAA	57	210	58	13	1	15	—	—	118	36	45	23	0	34	3	1	6	2	4	.33	6	.276	.347	.562
1998 Columbus	AAA	126	510	155	34	3	26	—	—	273	79	99	37	2	85	6	0	5	4	0	1.00	10	.304	.355	.535
1998 New York	AL	8	15	4	0	0	0	(0	0)	4	1	0	0	0	1	0	0	0	0	0	.00	0	.267	.267	.267

Terrell Lowery

Bats: Right **Throws:** Right **Pos:** CF-20; PH/PR-9; LF-2   **Ht:** 6'3" **Wt:** 195 **Born:** 10/25/70 **Age:** 28

			BATTING																BASERUNNING				PERCENTAGES		
Year Team	Lg	G	AB	H	2B	3B	HR	(Hm	Rd)	TB	R	RBI	TBB	IBB	SO	HBP	SH	SF	SB	CS	SB%	GDP	Avg	OBP	SLG
1991 Butte	R+	54	214	64	10	7	3	—	—	97	38	33	29	0	44	1	0	2	23	12	.66	2	.299	.382	.453
1993 Charlotte	A+	65	257	77	7	9	3	—	—	111	46	36	46	2	47	2	1	1	14	15	.48	2	.300	.408	.432
Tulsa	AA	66	258	62	5	1	3	—	—	78	29	14	28	1	50	1	1	1	10	12	.45	5	.240	.316	.302
1994 Tulsa	AA	129	496	142	34	8	8	—	—	216	89	54	59	0	113	5	5	5	33	15	.69	7	.286	.365	.435
1995 Rangers	R	10	34	9	3	1	3	—	—	23	10	7	6	0	7	0	0	0	1	0	1.00	1	.265	.375	.676
Charlotte	A+	11	35	9	2	2	0	—	—	15	4	4	6	0	6	1	0	0	1	0	1.00	2	.257	.381	.429
1996 Binghamton	AA	62	211	58	13	4	7	—	—	100	34	32	44	2	44	2	2	3	5	6	.45	4	.275	.400	.474
Norfolk	AAA	62	193	45	7	2	4	—	—	68	25	21	22	0	44	1	3	2	6	3	.67	1	.233	.312	.352
1997 Iowa	AAA	110	386	116	28	3	17	—	—	201	69	71	65	2	97	1	1	1	9	8	.53	8	.301	.401	.521
1998 Iowa	AAA	65	246	73	14	1	12	—	—	125	41	49	27	0	63	2	1	2	5	2	.71	10	.297	.368	.508
1997 Chicago	NL	9	14	4	0	0	0	(0	0)	4	2	0	3	0	3	0	0	0	1	0	1.00	0	.286	.412	.286
1998 Chicago	NL	24	15	3	1	0	0	(0	0)	4	2	1	3	0	7	0	0	0	0	0	.00	0	.200	.333	.267
2 ML YEARS		33	29	7	1	0	0	(0	0)	8	4	1	6	0	10	0	0	0	1	0	1.00	0	.241	.371	.276

Eric Ludwick

Pitches: Right **Bats:** Right **Pos:** RP-7; SP-6   **Ht:** 6'5" **Wt:** 210 **Born:** 12/14/71 **Age:** 27

			HOW MUCH HE PITCHED						WHAT HE GAVE UP											THE RESULTS						
Year Team	Lg	G	GS	CG	GF	IP	BFP	H	R	ER	HR	SH	SF	HB	TBB	IBB	SO	WP	Bk	W	L	Pct.	ShO	Sv-Op	Hld	ERA
1993 Pittsfield	A-	10	10	1	0	51	219	51	27	18	0	3	1	0	18	0	40	4	2	4	4	.500	0	0- --	--	3.18
1994 St. Lucie	A+	27	27	3	0	150.1	671	162	102	76	6	1	12	6	77	1	77	3	5	7	13	.350	0	0- --	--	4.55
1995 Binghamton	AA	23	22	3	0	143.1	590	108	52	47	9	4	6	2	68	1	131	6	0	12	5	.706	2	0- --	--	2.95
Norfolk	AAA	4	3	0	0	20	88	22	15	13	3	0	0	1	7	0	9	1	0	1	1	.500	0	0- --	--	5.85
1996 Louisville	AAA	11	11	0	0	60.1	253	55	24	19	4	2	2	1	24	0	73	2	0	3	4	.429	1	0- --	--	2.83
1997 Louisville	AAA	24	11	1	12	80	325	67	31	26	7	1	1	4	26	0	85	4	0	6	8	.429	0	4- --	--	2.93
Edmonton	AAA	6	3	0	0	19	84	22	7	7	1	1	2	0	4	0	20	2	0	1	1	.500	0	0- --	--	3.32
1998 Charlotte	AAA	8	8	0	0	26.2	118	25	17	11	1	1	0	1	13	0	26	3	0	1	3	.250	0	0- --	--	3.71
1996 St. Louis	NL	6	1	0	2	10	45	11	11	10	4	0	1	1	3	0	12	0	0	0	1	.000	0	0-0	0	9.00
1997 StL-Oak		11	5	0	3	30.2	152	44	31	29	8	2	0	1	22	1	21	0	0	1	5	.167	0	0-0	0	8.51
1998 Florida	NL	13	6	0	0	32.2	159	46	31	27	7	2	2	0	17	1	27	2	0	1	4	.200	0	0-1	0	7.44
1997 St. Louis	NL	5	0	0	3	6.2	36	12	7	7	1	0	0	0	6	0	7	0	0	1	0	.000	0	0-0	0	9.45
Oakland	AL	6	5	0	0	24	116	32	24	22	7	2	0	1	16	1	14	0	0	1	5	.200	0	0-0	0	8.25
3 ML YEARS		30	12	0	5	73.1	356	101	73	66	19	4	3	2	42	2	60	2	0	2	10	.167	0	0-1	0	8.10

Matt Luke

Bats: L **Throws:** L **Pos:** LF-50; PH/PR-35; 1B-18; RF-14   **Ht:** 6'5" **Wt:** 220 **Born:** 2/26/71 **Age:** 28

Year Team	Lg	G	AB	H	2B	3B	HR	(Hm	Rd)	TB	R	RBI	TBB	IBB	SO	HBP	SH	SF	SB	CS	SB%	GDP	Avg	OBP	SLG
1992 Oneonta	A-	69	271	67	11	7	2	—	—	98	30	34	19	3	32	2	0	3	4	1	.80	9	.247	.298	.362
1993 Greensboro	A	135	549	157	37	5	21	—	—	267	83	91	47	4	79	7	0	6	11	3	.79	9	.286	.346	.486
1994 Albany-Colo	AA	63	236	67	11	2	8	—	—	106	34	40	28	0	50	2	3	1	6	4	.60	6	.284	.363	.449
Tampa	A+	57	222	68	11	2	16	—	—	131	52	42	28	2	27	1	0	1	4	1	.80	7	.306	.385	.590
1995 Norwich	AA	93	365	95	17	5	8	—	—	146	48	53	20	2	68	2	3	4	5	4	.56	6	.260	.299	.400
Columbus	AAA	23	77	23	4	1	3	—	—	38	11	12	2	0	12	1	1	0	1	1	.50	3	.299	.325	.494
1996 Tampa	A+	2	7	2	0	0	0	—	—	2	1	1	1	0	1	0	0	0	0	0	.00	0	.286	.375	.286
Columbus	AAA	74	264	74	14	2	19	—	—	149	46	70	17	0	52	6	1	5	1	1	.50	9	.280	.332	.564
1997 Columbus	AAA	87	337	77	19	3	8	—	—	126	42	45	29	1	64	4	0	1	0	3	.00	9	.228	.296	.374
1996 New York	AL	1	0	0	0	0	0	(0	0)	0	1	0	0	0	0	0	0	0	0	0	.00	0	.000	.000	.000
1998 LA-Cle		104	239	56	12	1	12	(7	5)	106	34	34	17	2	60	1	1	1	2	1	.67	4	.234	.287	.444
1998 Los Angeles	NL	102	237	56	12	1	12	(7	5)	106	34	34	17	2	60	1	1	1	2	1	.67	4	.236	.289	.447
Cleveland	AL	2	2	0	0	0	0	(0	0)	0	0	0	0	0	0	0	0	0	0	0	.00	0	.000	.000	.000
2 ML YEARS		105	239	56	12	1	12	(7	5)	106	35	34	17	2	60	1	1	1	2	1	.67	4	.234	.287	.444

John Mabry

Bats: L **Throws:** R **Pos:** LF-46; 3B-38; RF-37; PH/PR-31; 1B-16   **Ht:** 6'4" **Wt:** 195 **Born:** 10/17/70 **Age:** 28

Year Team	Lg	G	AB	H	2B	3B	HR	(Hm	Rd)	TB	R	RBI	TBB	IBB	SO	HBP	SH	SF	SB	CS	SB%	GDP	Avg	OBP	SLG
1994 St. Louis	NL	6	23	7	3	0	0	(0	0)	10	2	3	2	0	4	0	0	0	0	0	.00	0	.304	.360	.435
1995 St. Louis	NL	129	388	119	21	1	5	(2	3)	157	35	41	24	5	45	2	0	4	0	3	.00	6	.307	.347	.405
1996 St. Louis	NL	151	543	161	30	2	13	(3	10)	234	63	74	37	11	84	3	3	5	3	2	.60	21	.297	.342	.431
1997 St. Louis	NL	116	388	110	19	0	5	(5	0)	144	40	36	39	9	77	3	2	2	0	1	.00	11	.284	.352	.371
1998 St. Louis	NL	142	377	94	22	0	9	(4	5)	143	41	46	30	6	76	1	3	2	0	2	.00	6	.249	.305	.379
5 ML YEARS		544	1719	491	95	3	32	(14	18)	688	181	200	132	31	286	9	8	13	3	8	.27	44	.286	.337	.400

Mike Macfarlane

Bats: Right **Throws:** Right **Pos:** C-73; PH/PR-13   **Ht:** 6'1" **Wt:** 205 **Born:** 4/12/64 **Age:** 35

Year Team	Lg	G	AB	H	2B	3B	HR	(Hm	Rd)	TB	R	RBI	TBB	IBB	SO	HBP	SH	SF	SB	CS	SB%	GDP	Avg	OBP	SLG
1987 Kansas City	AL	8	19	4	1	0	0	(0	0)	5	0	3	2	0	2	0	0	0	0	0	.00	1	.211	.286	.263
1988 Kansas City	AL	70	211	56	15	0	4	(2	2)	83	25	26	21	2	37	1	1	2	0	0	.00	5	.265	.332	.393
1989 Kansas City	AL	69	157	35	6	0	2	(0	2)	47	13	19	7	0	27	2	0	1	0	0	.00	8	.223	.263	.299
1990 Kansas City	AL	124	400	102	24	4	6	(1	5)	152	37	58	25	2	69	7	1	6	1	0	1.00	9	.255	.306	.380
1991 Kansas City	AL	84	267	74	18	2	13	(6	7)	135	34	41	17	0	52	6	1	4	1	0	1.00	4	.277	.330	.506
1992 Kansas City	AL	129	402	94	28	3	17	(7	10)	179	51	48	30	2	89	15	1	2	1	5	.17	8	.234	.310	.445
1993 Kansas City	AL	117	388	106	27	0	20	(7	13)	193	55	67	40	2	83	16	1	6	2	5	.29	8	.273	.360	.497
1994 Kansas City	AL	92	314	80	17	3	14	(9	5)	145	53	47	35	1	71	18	0	3	1	0	1.00	9	.255	.359	.462
1995 Boston	AL	115	364	82	18	1	15	(7	8)	147	45	51	38	0	78	14	0	4	2	1	.67	9	.225	.319	.404
1996 Kansas City	AL	112	379	104	24	2	19	(9	10)	189	58	54	31	5	57	7	0	2	3	3	.50	4	.274	.339	.499
1997 Kansas City	AL	82	257	61	14	2	8	(5	3)	103	34	35	24	3	47	6	3	1	0	2	.00	4	.237	.316	.401
1998 KC-Oak	AL	81	218	53	12	0	7	(5	2)	86	29	34	12	0	36	4	1	3	1	0	1.00	3	.243	.291	.394
1998 Kansas City	AL	3	11	1	0	0	0	(0	0)	1	1	0	0	0	2	0	0	0	0	0	.00	0	.091	.091	.091
Oakland	AL	78	207	52	12	0	7	(5	2)	85	28	34	12	0	34	4	1	3	1	0	1.00	3	.251	.301	.411
12 ML YEARS		1083	3376	851	204	17	125	(58	67)	1464	434	483	282	17	648	96	9	34	12	16	.43	72	.252	.324	.434

Robert Machado

Bats: Right **Throws:** Right **Pos:** C-34   **Ht:** 6'1" **Wt:** 205 **Born:** 6/3/73 **Age:** 26

Year Team	Lg	G	AB	H	2B	3B	HR	(Hm	Rd)	TB	R	RBI	TBB	IBB	SO	HBP	SH	SF	SB	CS	SB%	GDP	Avg	OBP	SLG
1991 White Sox	R	38	126	31	4	1	0	—	—	37	11	15	6	0	21	6	0	1	2	1	.67	2	.246	.309	.294
1992 Utica	A-	45	161	44	13	1	2	—	—	65	16	20	5	0	26	0	0	1	1	5	.17	3	.273	.293	.404
1993 South Bend	A	75	281	86	14	3	2	—	—	112	34	33	19	0	59	4	2	4	1	2	.33	6	.306	.354	.399
1994 Pr William	A+	93	312	81	17	1	11	—	—	133	45	47	27	0	68	4	2	1	0	1	.00	10	.260	.326	.426
1995 Nashville	AAA	16	49	7	3	0	1	—	—	13	7	5	7	0	12	0	0	0	0	1	.00	1	.143	.250	.265
Pr William	A+	83	272	69	14	0	6	—	—	101	37	31	40	5	47	7	2	1	0	0	.00	6	.254	.363	.371
1996 Birmingham	AA	87	309	74	16	0	6	—	—	108	35	28	20	1	56	3	10	1	1	4	.20	9	.239	.291	.350
1997 Nashville	AAA	84	308	83	18	0	8	—	—	125	43	30	12	0	61	1	5	2	5	0	1.00	6	.269	.297	.406
1998 Calgary	AAA	66	239	63	19	0	4	—	—	94	31	27	20	0	33	3	5	2	2	2	.50	9	.264	.326	.393
1996 Chicago	AL	4	6	4	1	0	0	(0	0)	5	1	2	0	0	0	0	0	0	0	0	.00	1	.667	.667	.833
1997 Chicago	AL	10	15	3	0	1	0	(0	0)	5	1	2	1	0	6	0	1	0	0	0	.00	0	.200	.250	.333
1998 Chicago	AL	34	111	23	6	0	3	(2	1)	38	14	15	7	0	22	0	3	0	0	0	.00	3	.207	.254	.342
3 ML YEARS		48	132	30	7	1	3	(2	1)	48	16	19	8	0	28	0	4	0	0	0	.00	4	.227	.271	.364

Shane Mack

Bats: R **Throws:** R **Pos:** LF-30; DH-21; PH/PR-18; RF-3   **Ht:** 6'0" **Wt:** 190 **Born:** 12/7/63 **Age:** 35

Year Team	Lg	G	AB	H	2B	3B	HR	(Hm	Rd)	TB	R	RBI	TBB	IBB	SO	HBP	SH	SF	SB	CS	SB%	GDP	Avg	OBP	SLG
1987 San Diego	NL	105	238	57	11	3	4	(2	2)	86	28	25	18	0	47	3	6	2	4	6	.40	11	.239	.299	.361
1988 San Diego	NL	56	119	29	3	0	0	(0	0)	32	13	12	14	0	21	3	3	1	5	1	.83	2	.244	.336	.269

Year Team	Lg	G	AB	H	2B	3B	HR	(Hm	Rd)	TB	R	RBI	TBB	IBB	SO	HBP	SH	SF	SB	CS	SB%	GDP	Avg	OBP	SLG
																			BASERUNNING				PERCENTAGES		
1990 Minnesota	AL	125	313	102	10	4	8	(5	3)	144	50	44	29	1	69	5	6	0	13	4	.76	7	.326	.392	.460
1991 Minnesota	AL	143	442	137	27	8	18	(4	14)	234	79	74	34	1	79	6	2	5	13	9	.59	11	.310	.363	.529
1992 Minnesota	AL	156	600	189	31	6	16	(10	6)	280	101	75	64	1	106	15	11	2	26	14	.65	8	.315	.394	.467
1993 Minnesota	AL	128	503	139	30	4	10	(3	7)	207	66	61	41	1	76	4	3	2	15	5	.75	13	.276	.335	.412
1994 Minnesota	AL	81	303	101	21	2	15	(8	7)	171	55	61	32	1	51	6	1	5	4	1	.80	11	.333	.402	.564
1997 Boston	AL	60	130	41	7	0	3	(2	1)	57	13	17	9	1	24	3	2	2	2	1	.67	3	.315	.368	.438
1998 Oak-KC	AL	69	209	58	15	1	6	(3	3)	93	31	29	15	0	36	6	0	1	8	2	.80	6	.278	.342	.445
1998 Oakland	AL	3	2	0	0	0	0	(0	0)	0	1	0	0	0	0	0	0	0	0	0	.00	0	.000	.000	.000
Kansas City	AL	66	207	58	15	1	6	(3	3)	93	30	29	15	0	36	6	0	1	8	2	.80	6	.280	.345	.449
9 ML YEARS		923	2857	853	155	28	80	(37	43)	1304	436	398	256	6	509	51	34	20	90	43	.68	72	.299	.364	.456

Greg Maddux

Pitches: Right **Bats:** Right **Pos:** SP-34   **Ht:** 6'0" **Wt:** 175 **Born:** 4/14/66 **Age:** 33

Year Team	Lg	G	GS	CG	GF	IP	BFP	H	R	ER	HR	SH	SF	HB	TBB	IBB	SO	WP	Bk	W	L	Pct.	ShO	Sv-Op	Hld	ERA
1986 Chicago	NL	6	5	1	0	31	144	44	20	19	3	1	0	1	11	2	20	2	0	2	4	.333	0	0-0	0	5.52
1987 Chicago	NL	30	27	1	2	155.2	701	181	111	97	17	7	1	4	74	13	101	4	7	6	14	.300	1	0-0	0	5.61
1988 Chicago	NL	34	34	9	0	249	1047	230	97	88	13	11	2	9	81	16	140	3	6	18	8	.692	3	0-0	0	3.18
1989 Chicago	NL	35	35	7	0	238.1	1002	222	90	78	13	18	6	6	82	13	135	5	3	19	12	.613	1	0-0	0	2.95
1990 Chicago	NL	35	35	8	0	237	1011	242	116	91	11	18	5	4	71	10	144	3	3	15	15	.500	2	0-0	0	3.46
1991 Chicago	NL	37	37	7	0	263	1070	232	113	98	18	16	3	6	66	9	198	6	3	15	11	.577	2	0-0	0	3.35
1992 Chicago	NL	35	35	9	0	268	1061	201	68	65	7	15	3	14	70	7	199	5	0	20	11	.645	4	0-0	0	2.18
1993 Atlanta	NL	36	36	8	0	267	1064	228	85	70	14	15	7	6	52	7	197	5	1	20	10	.667	1	0-0	0	2.36
1994 Atlanta	NL	25	25	10	0	202	774	150	44	35	4	6	5	6	31	3	156	3	0	16	6	.727	3	0-0	0	1.56
1995 Atlanta	NL	28	28	10	0	209.2	785	147	39	38	8	9	1	4	23	3	181	1	0	19	2	.905	3	0-0	0	1.63
1996 Atlanta	NL	35	35	5	0	245	978	225	85	74	11	8	5	3	28	11	172	4	0	15	11	.577	1	0-0	0	2.72
1997 Atlanta	NL	33	33	5	0	232.2	893	200	58	57	9	11	7	6	20	6	177	0	0	19	4	.826	2	0-0	0	2.20
1998 Atlanta	NL	34	34	9	0	251	987	201	75	62	13	15	5	7	45	10	204	4	0	18	9	.667	5	0-0	0	2.22
13 ML YEARS		403	399	89	3	2849.1	11517	2503	1001	872	141	150	50	76	654	110	2024	45	24	202	117	.633	28	0-0	0	2.75

Mike Maddux

Pitches: Right **Bats:** Left **Pos:** RP-51   **Ht:** 6'2" **Wt:** 185 **Born:** 8/27/61 **Age:** 37

Year Team	Lg	G	GS	CG	GF	IP	BFP	H	R	ER	HR	SH	SF	HB	TBB	IBB	SO	WP	Bk	W	L	Pct.	ShO	Sv-Op	Hld	ERA
1986 Philadelphia	NL	16	16	0	0	78	351	88	56	47	6	3	3	4	34	4	44	4	2	3	7	.300	0	0-0	0	5.42
1987 Philadelphia	NL	7	2	0	0	17	72	17	5	5	0	0	0	0	5	0	15	1	0	2	0	1.000	0	0-0	0	2.65
1988 Philadelphia	NL	25	11	0	4	88.2	380	91	41	37	6	7	3	5	34	4	59	4	2	4	3	.571	0	0-0	0	3.76
1989 Philadelphia	NL	16	4	2	1	43.2	191	52	29	25	3	3	1	2	14	3	26	3	1	1	3	.250	1	1-1	2	5.15
1990 Los Angeles	NL	11	2	0	3	20.2	88	24	15	15	3	0	1	1	4	0	11	2	0	0	1	.000	0	0-0	0	6.53
1991 San Diego	NL	64	1	0	27	98.2	388	78	30	27	4	5	2	1	27	3	57	5	0	7	2	.778	0	5-7	9	2.46
1992 San Diego	NL	50	1	0	14	79.2	330	71	25	21	2	2	3	0	24	4	60	4	1	2	2	.500	0	5-9	8	2.37
1993 New York	NL	58	0	0	31	75	320	67	34	30	3	7	6	4	27	7	57	4	1	3	8	.273	0	5-11	3	3.60
1994 New York	NL	27	0	0	12	44	186	45	25	25	7	0	2	0	13	4	32	0	0	2	1	.667	0	2-4	1	5.11
1995 Pit-Bos		44	4	0	7	98.2	409	100	49	45	5	1	1	2	18	4	69	6	0	5	1	.833	0	1-1	6	4.10
1996 Boston	AL	23	7	0	2	64.1	295	76	37	32	12	3	2	5	27	2	32	1	0	3	2	.600	0	0-0	2	4.48
1997 Seattle	AL	6	0	0	1	10.2	59	20	12	12	1	0	0	1	8	2	7	1	0	1	0	1.000	0	0-0	0	10.13
1998 Montreal	NL	51	0	0	20	55.2	228	50	24	23	3	3	3	1	15	1	33	3	1	3	4	.429	0	1-2	7	3.72
1995 Pittsburgh	NL	8	0	0	1	9	42	14	9	9	0	0	0	0	3	1	4	1	0	1	0	1.000	0	0-2	2	9.00
Boston	AL	36	4	0	6	89.2	367	86	40	36	5	1	1	2	15	3	65	5	0	4	1	.800	0	1-1	4	3.61
13 ML YEARS		398	48	2	122	774.2	3297	779	382	344	55	34	27	25	250	38	502	40	8	36	34	.514	1	20-35	39	4.00

Dave Magadan

Bats: Left **Throws:** Right **Pos:** 3B-30; 1B-7; PH/PR-6   **Ht:** 6'4" **Wt:** 215 **Born:** 9/30/62 **Age:** 36

Year Team	Lg	G	AB	H	2B	3B	HR	(Hm	Rd)	TB	R	RBI	TBB	IBB	SO	HBP	SH	SF	SB	CS	SB%	GDP	Avg	OBP	SLG
1986 New York	NL	10	18	8	0	0	0	(0	0)	8	3	3	3	0	1	0	0	0	0	0	.00	1	.444	.524	.444
1987 New York	NL	85	192	61	13	1	3	(2	1)	85	21	24	22	2	22	0	0	1	0	0	.00	5	.318	.386	.443
1988 New York	NL	112	314	87	15	0	1	(1	0)	105	39	35	60	4	39	2	1	3	0	1	.00	9	.277	.393	.334
1989 New York	NL	127	374	107	22	3	4	(3	1)	147	47	41	49	6	37	1	1	4	1	0	1.00	9	.286	.367	.393
1990 New York	NL	144	451	148	28	6	6	(2	4)	206	74	72	74	4	55	2	4	10	2	1	.67	11	.328	.417	.457
1991 New York	NL	124	418	108	23	0	4	(2	2)	143	58	51	83	3	50	2	7	7	1	1	.50	5	.258	.378	.342
1992 New York	NL	99	321	91	9	1	3	(2	1)	111	33	28	56	3	44	0	2	2	1	0	1.00	6	.283	.390	.346
1993 Fla-Sea		137	455	124	23	0	5	(3	2)	162	49	50	80	7	63	1	2	6	2	1	.67	12	.273	.378	.356
1994 Florida	NL	74	211	58	7	0	1	(1	0)	68	30	17	39	0	25	1	0	3	0	0	.00	8	.275	.386	.322
1995 Houston	NL	127	348	109	24	0	2	(1	1)	139	44	51	71	9	56	0	1	2	2	1	.67	9	.313	.428	.399
1996 Chicago	NL	78	169	43	10	0	3	(2	1)	62	23	17	29	3	23	0	1	2	0	2	.00	3	.254	.360	.367
1997 Oakland	AL	128	271	82	10	1	4	(2	2)	106	38	30	50	1	40	2	4	1	1	0	1.00	7	.303	.414	.391
1998 Oakland	AL	35	109	35	8	0	1	(0	1)	46	12	13	11	1	12	0	0	1	1	0	1.00	5	.321	.390	.422
1993 Florida	NL	66	227	65	12	0	4	(3	1)	89	22	29	44	4	30	1	0	3	0	1	.00	5	.286	.398	.392
Seattle	AL	71	228	59	11	0	1	(0	1)	73	27	21	36	3	33	0	2	3	2	0	1.00	9	.259	.356	.320
13 ML YEARS		1280	3651	1061	192	12	37	(20	17)	1388	471	432	629	43	467	11	24	40	10	8	.56	83	.291	.393	.380

Wendell Magee

Bats: Right **Throws:** Right **Pos:** LF-19; PH/PR-1 **Ht:** 6'0" **Wt:** 220 **Born:** 8/3/72 **Age:** 26

Year Team	Lg	G	AB	H	2B	3B	HR	(Hm	Rd)	TB	R	RBI	TBB	IBB	SO	HBP	SH	SF	SB	CS	SB%	GDP	Avg	OBP	SLG
1998 Scranton-WB *AAA		126	507	147	30	7	24	—	—	263	86	72	46	3	102	3	0	5	7	7	.50	11	.290	.349	.519
1996 Philadelphia	NL	38	142	29	7	0	2	(2	0)	42	9	14	9	0	33	0	0	0	0	0	.00	2	.204	.252	.296
1997 Philadelphia	NL	38	115	23	4	0	1	(0	1)	30	7	9	9	1	20	0	0	2	1	4	.20	8	.200	.254	.261
1998 Philadelphia	NL	20	75	22	6	1	1	(0	1)	33	9	11	7	0	11	0	0	0	0	0	.00	4	.293	.354	.440
3 ML YEARS		96	332	74	17	1	4	(2	2)	105	25	34	25	1	64	0	0	2	1	4	.20	14	.223	.276	.316

Mike Magnante

Pitches: Left **Bats:** Left **Pos:** RP-48 **Ht:** 6'1" **Wt:** 185 **Born:** 6/17/65 **Age:** 34

Year Team	Lg	G	GS	CG	GF	IP	BFP	H	R	ER	HR	SH	SF	HB	TBB	IBB	SO	WP	Bk	W	L	Pct.	ShO	Sv-Op	Hld	ERA
1991 Kansas City	AL	38	0	0	10	55	236	55	19	15	3	2	1	0	23	3	42	1	0	0	1	.000	0	0-0	2	2.45
1992 Kansas City	AL	44	12	0	11	89.1	403	115	53	49	5	5	7	2	35	5	31	2	0	4	9	.308	0	0-3	4	4.94
1993 Kansas City	AL	7	6	0	0	35.1	145	37	16	16	3	1	1	1	11	1	16	1	0	1	2	.333	0	0-0	0	4.08
1994 Kansas City	AL	36	1	0	10	47	211	55	27	24	5	2	3	0	16	1	21	3	0	2	3	.400	0	0-0	6	4.60
1995 Kansas City	AL	28	0	0	7	44.2	190	45	23	21	6	2	2	2	16	1	28	2	0	1	1	.500	0	0-1	5	4.23
1996 Kansas City	AL	38	0	0	9	54	238	58	38	34	5	0	4	4	24	1	32	3	0	2	2	.500	0	0-1	5	5.67
1997 Houston	NL	40	0	0	14	47.2	191	39	16	12	2	3	2	0	11	2	43	2	2	3	1	.750	0	1-5	3	2.27
1998 Houston	NL	48	0	0	20	51.2	237	56	28	28	2	3	1	4	26	4	39	3	0	4	7	.364	0	2-4	3	4.88
8 ML YEARS		279	19	0	81	424.2	1851	460	220	199	31	18	21	13	162	18	252	17	2	17	26	.395	0	3-14	28	4.22

Ron Mahay

Pitches: Left **Bats:** Left **Pos:** RP-29 **Ht:** 6'2" **Wt:** 189 **Born:** 6/28/71 **Age:** 28

Year Team	Lg	G	GS	CG	GF	IP	BFP	H	R	ER	HR	SH	SF	HB	TBB	IBB	SO	WP	Bk	W	L	Pct.	ShO	Sv-Op	Hld	ERA
1996 Sarasota	A+	31	4	0	13	70.2	295	61	33	30	5	1	4	5	35	0	68	4	1	2	2	.500	0	2- -	—	3.82
Trenton	AA	1	1	0	0	3.2	19	12	13	12	1	0	0	0	6	0	1	0	1	0	1	.000	0	0- -	—	29.45
1997 Trenton	AA	17	4	0	9	40.2	165	29	16	14	0	0	0	1	13	0	47	2	0	3	3	.500	0	5- -	—	3.10
Pawtucket	AAA	2	0	0	0	4.2	18	3	0	0	0	0	0	0	1	0	6	0	0	1	0	1.000	0	0- -	—	0.00
1998 Pawtucket	AAA	23	1	0	8	41	179	37	20	19	8	0	2	0	19	2	41	3	0	3	1	.750	0	3- -	—	4.17
1997 Boston	AL	28	0	0	7	25	105	19	7	7	3	1	0	0	11	0	22	3	0	3	0	1.000	0	0-1	5	2.52
1998 Boston	AL	29	0	0	6	26	120	26	16	10	2	0	4	2	15	1	14	3	0	1	1	.500	0	1-2	7	3.46
2 ML YEARS		57	0	0	13	51	225	45	23	17	5	1	4	2	26	1	36	6	0	4	1	.800	0	1-3	12	3.00

Marty Malloy

Bats: Left **Throws:** Right **Pos:** 2B-10; PH/PR-1 **Ht:** 5'10" **Wt:** 160 **Born:** 7/6/72 **Age:** 26

Year Team	Lg	G	AB	H	2B	3B	HR	(Hm	Rd)	TB	R	RBI	TBB	IBB	SO	HBP	SH	SF	SB	CS	SB%	GDP	Avg	OBP	SLG
1992 Idaho Falls	R+	62	251	79	18	1	2	—	—	105	45	28	11	0	43	2	0	1	8	4	.67	4	.315	.347	.418
1993 Macon	A	109	376	110	19	3	2	—	—	141	55	36	39	3	70	2	3	3	24	8	.75	4	.293	.360	.375
1994 Durham	A+	118	428	113	22	1	6	—	—	155	53	35	52	2	69	2	2	3	18	12	.60	9	.264	.344	.362
1995 Greenville	AA	124	461	128	20	3	10	—	—	184	73	59	39	1	58	0	7	8	11	12	.48	6	.278	.329	.399
1996 Richmond	AAA	18	64	13	2	1	0	—	—	17	7	8	5	1	7	0	2	1	3	0	1.00	1	.203	.257	.266
Greenville	AA	111	429	134	27	2	4	—	—	177	82	36	54	6	50	4	6	2	11	10	.52	11	.312	.393	.413
1997 Richmond	AAA	108	414	118	19	5	2	—	—	153	66	25	41	1	61	1	5	0	17	7	.71	6	.285	.351	.370
1998 Richmond	AAA	124	483	140	25	3	7	—	—	192	75	54	51	2	65	5	5	4	20	7	.74	12	.290	.361	.398
1998 Atlanta	NL	11	28	5	1	0	1	(0	1)	9	3	1	2	0	2	0	0	0	0	0	.00	0	.179	.233	.321

Sean Maloney

Pitches: Right **Bats:** Right **Pos:** RP-11 **Ht:** 6'7" **Wt:** 210 **Born:** 5/25/71 **Age:** 28

Year Team	Lg	G	GS	CG	GF	IP	BFP	H	R	ER	HR	SH	SF	HB	TBB	IBB	SO	WP	Bk	W	L	Pct.	ShO	Sv-Op	Hld	ERA
1993 Helena	R+	17	3	1	10	47.2	209	55	31	23	2	3	2	2	11	1	35	3	0	2	2	.500	0	0- -	—	4.34
1994 Beloit	A	51	0	0	41	59	272	73	42	36	3	2	5	4	10	5	53	6	1	2	6	.250	0	22- -	—	5.49
1995 El Paso	AA	43	0	0	27	64.2	292	69	41	30	4	4	4	3	28	9	54	5	0	7	5	.583	0	15- -	—	4.18
1996 El Paso	AA	51	0	0	49	56.2	230	49	11	9	1	2	1	1	12	1	57	6	1	3	2	.600	0	38- -	—	1.43
1997 Tucson	AAA	15	0	0	10	18.2	82	24	10	10	3	5	0	0	3	3	21	1	0	0	2	.000	0	5- -	—	4.82
1998 Albuquerque	AAA	26	0	0	23	35	150	38	21	18	6	1	0	1	8	1	38	4	0	3	2	.600	0	9- -	—	4.63
1997 Milwaukee	AL	3	0	0	2	7	29	7	4	4	1	0	2	2	2	0	5	2	0	0	0	.000	0	0-0	0	5.14
1998 Los Angeles	NL	11	0	0	2	12.2	57	13	7	7	2	1	0	2	5	0	11	1	0	0	1	.000	0	0-1	1	4.97
2 ML YEARS		14	0	0	4	19.2	86	20	11	11	3	1	2	4	7	0	16	3	0	0	1	.000	0	0-1	1	5.03

Matt Mantei

Pitches: Right **Bats:** Right **Pos:** RP-42 **Ht:** 6'1" **Wt:** 190 **Born:** 7/7/73 **Age:** 25

Year Team	Lg	G	GS	CG	GF	IP	BFP	H	R	ER	HR	SH	SF	HB	TBB	IBB	SO	WP	Bk	W	L	Pct.	ShO	Sv-Op	Hld	ERA
1998 Charlotte *	AAA	16	0	0	8	16.1	76	11	10	10	2	0	2	0	18	1	25	2	0	1	2	.333	0	3- -	—	5.51
1995 Florida	NL	12	0	0	3	13.1	64	12	8	7	1	1	1	0	13	0	15	1	0	0	1	.000	0	0-0	0	4.73
1996 Florida	NL	14	0	0	1	18.1	89	13	13	13	2	1	0	1	21	1	25	2	0	1	0	1.000	0	0-1	0	6.38

Year Team	Lg	HOW MUCH HE PITCHED					WHAT HE GAVE UP											THE RESULTS						
		G	GS	CG	GF	IP	BFP	H	R	ER	HR	SH	SF	HB	TBB	IBB	SO	WP	Bk	W	L	Pct.	ShO	Sv-Op	Hld	ERA
1998 Florida	NL	42	0	0	23	54.2	224	38	19	18	1	3	4	7	23	3	63	0	0	3	4	.429	0	9-12	2	2.96
3 ML YEARS		68	0	0	27	86.1	377	63	40	38	4	5	5	8	57	4	103	3	0	4	5	.444	0	9-13	2	3.96

Jeff Manto

Bats: R **Throws:** R **Pos:** 1B-17; 3B-8; DH-6; PH/PR-6; 2B-1; LF-1 **Ht:** 6'3" **Wt:** 210 **Born:** 8/23/64 **Age:** 34

Year Team	Lg	BATTING																BASERUNNING				PERCENTAGES		
		G	AB	H	2B	3B	HR	(Hm | Rd)	TB	R	RBI	TBB	IBB	SO	HBP	SH	SF	SB	CS	SB%	GDP	Avg	OBP	SLG
1998 Buffalo *	AAA	62	209	65	11	0	23	—	—	145	46	63	58	0	48	1	0	2	4	2	.67	2	.311	.459	.694
1990 Cleveland	AL	30	76	17	5	1	2	(1 | 1)	30	12	14	21	1	18	0	0	0	0	1	.00	0	.224	.392	.395
1991 Cleveland	AL	47	128	27	7	0	2	(0 | 2)	40	15	13	14	0	22	4	1	1	2	0	1.00	3	.211	.306	.313
1993 Philadelphia	NL	8	18	1	0	0	0	(0 | 0)	1	0	0	0	0	3	1	0	0	0	0	.00	0	.056	.105	.056
1995 Baltimore	AL	89	254	65	9	0	17	(12 | 5)	125	31	38	24	0	69	2	0	0	0	3	.00	6	.256	.325	.492
1996 Bos-Sea	AL	43	102	20	6	1	3	(3 | 0)	37	15	10	17	0	24	1	0	0	0	1	.00	5	.196	.317	.363
1997 Cleveland	AL	16	30	8	3	0	2	(2 | 0)	17	3	7	1	0	10	0	0	0	0	0	.00	0	.267	.290	.567
1998 Cle-Det	AL	31	67	16	3	0	3	(1 | 2)	28	14	9	5	0	21	1	0	0	1	1	.50	5	.239	.301	.418
1996 Boston	AL	22	48	10	3	1	2	(2 | 0)	21	8	6	8	0	12	1	0	0	0	0	.00	4	.208	.333	.438
Seattle	AL	21	54	10	3	0	1	(1 | 0)	16	7	4	9	0	12	0	0	0	0	1	.00	1	.185	.302	.296
1998 Cleveland	AL	15	37	8	1	0	2	(1 | 1)	15	8	6	2	0	10	1	0	0	0	0	.00	4	.216	.256	.405
Detroit	AL	16	30	8	2	0	1	(0 | 1)	13	6	3	3	0	11	1	0	0	1	1	.50	1	.267	.353	.433
7 ML YEARS		264	675	154	33	2	29	(19 | 10)	278	90	91	82	1	167	9	1	1	3	6	.33	18	.228	.319	.412

Barry Manuel

Pitches: Right **Bats:** Right **Pos:** RP-13 **Ht:** 5'11" **Wt:** 185 **Born:** 8/12/65 **Age:** 33

Year Team	Lg	HOW MUCH HE PITCHED						WHAT HE GAVE UP												THE RESULTS						
		G	GS	CG	GF	IP	BFP	H	R	ER	HR	SH	SF	HB	TBB	IBB	SO	WP	Bk	W	L	Pct.	ShO	Sv-Op	Hld	ERA
1998 Diamondbcks *	R	1	0	0	0	2	7	1	0	0	0	0	0	0	0	0	2	0	0	0	0	.000	0	0--	—	0.00
Tucson *	AAA	23	0	0	12	41.1	170	28	12	12	2	0	0	2	16	2	40	1	1	3	2	.600	0	0--	1	2.61
1991 Texas	AL	8	0	0	5	16	58	7	2	2	0	0	3	0	6	0	5	2	0	1	0	1.000	0	0-0	0	1.13
1992 Texas	AL	3	0	0	0	5.2	25	6	3	3	2	0	1	1	1	0	9	0	0	1	0	1.000	0	0-0	0	4.76
1996 Montreal	NL	53	0	0	7	86	360	70	34	31	10	6	2	7	26	4	62	4	0	4	1	.800	0	0-0	2	3.24
1997 New York	NL	19	0	0	6	25.2	123	35	18	15	6	1	0	1	13	1	21	0	0	1	1	.500	0	0-0	1	5.26
1998 Arizona	NL	13	0	0	3	15.2	79	17	14	13	5	0	0	1	14	3	12	0	0	1	0	1.000	0	0-0	0	7.47
5 ML YEARS		96	0	0	21	149	645	135	71	64	23	7	5	10	60	8	109	6	0	7	2	.778	0	0-0	3	3.87

Kirt Manwaring

Bats: Right **Throws:** Right **Pos:** C-108; PH/PR-6 **Ht:** 5'11" **Wt:** 198 **Born:** 7/15/65 **Age:** 33

Year Team	Lg	BATTING																BASERUNNING				PERCENTAGES		
		G	AB	H	2B	3B	HR	(Hm | Rd)	TB	R	RBI	TBB	IBB	SO	HBP	SH	SF	SB	CS	SB%	GDP	Avg	OBP	SLG
1987 San Francisco	NL	6	7	1	0	0	0	(0 | 0)	1	0	0	0	0	1	1	0	0	0	0	.00	1	.143	.250	.143
1988 San Francisco	NL	40	116	29	7	0	1	(0 | 1)	39	12	15	2	0	21	3	1	1	0	1	.00	1	.250	.279	.336
1989 San Francisco	NL	85	200	42	4	2	0	(0 | 0)	50	14	18	11	1	28	4	7	1	2	1	.67	5	.210	.264	.250
1990 San Francisco	NL	8	13	2	0	1	0	(0 | 0)	4	0	1	0	0	3	0	0	0	0	0	.00	0	.154	.154	.308
1991 San Francisco	NL	67	178	40	9	0	0	(0 | 0)	49	16	19	9	0	22	3	7	2	1	1	.50	2	.225	.271	.275
1992 San Francisco	NL	109	349	85	10	5	4	(1 | 3)	117	24	26	29	0	42	5	6	0	2	1	.67	12	.244	.311	.335
1993 San Francisco	NL	130	432	119	15	1	5	(3 | 2)	151	48	49	41	13	76	6	5	2	1	3	.25	14	.275	.345	.350
1994 San Francisco	NL	97	316	79	17	1	1	(0 | 1)	101	30	29	25	3	50	3	4	3	1	1	.50	14	.250	.308	.320
1995 San Francisco	NL	118	379	95	15	2	4	(4 | 0)	126	21	36	27	6	72	10	4	4	1	0	1.00	8	.251	.314	.332
1996 SF-Hou	NL	86	227	52	9	0	1	(1 | 0)	64	14	18	19	1	40	5	2	2	1	0	1.00	4	.229	.300	.282
1997 Colorado	NL	104	337	76	6	4	1	(1 | 0)	93	22	27	30	0	78	2	4	2	1	5	.17	10	.226	.291	.276
1998 Colorado	NL	110	291	72	12	3	2	(1 | 1)	96	30	26	38	3	49	3	2	1	1	5	.17	11	.247	.339	.330
1996 San Francisco	NL	49	145	34	6	0	1	(1 | 0)	43	9	14	16	1	24	3	1	2	0	1	.00	2	.234	.319	.297
Houston	NL	37	82	18	3	0	0	(0 | 0)	21	5	4	3	0	16	2	1	0	0	0	.00	2	.220	.264	.256
12 ML YEARS		960	2845	692	104	19	19	(11 | 8)	891	231	264	231	27	482	45	42	18	10	19	.34	78	.243	.308	.313

Eli Marrero

Bats: Right **Throws:** Right **Pos:** C-73; PH/PR-10; 1B-2 **Ht:** 6'1" **Wt:** 180 **Born:** 11/17/73 **Age:** 25

Year Team	Lg	BATTING																BASERUNNING				PERCENTAGES		
		G	AB	H	2B	3B	HR	(Hm | Rd)	TB	R	RBI	TBB	IBB	SO	HBP	SH	SF	SB	CS	SB%	GDP	Avg	OBP	SLG
1993 Johnson Cty	R+	18	61	22	8	0	2	—	—	36	10	14	12	0	9	1	0	1	1	2	.33	0	.361	.467	.590
1994 Savannah	A	116	421	110	16	3	21	—	—	195	71	79	39	3	92	5	2	5	5	4	.56	6	.261	.328	.463
1995 St. Pete	A+	107	383	81	16	1	10	—	—	129	43	55	23	2	55	1	0	7	9	4	.69	10	.211	.254	.337
1996 Arkansas	AA	116	374	101	17	3	19	—	—	181	65	65	34	1	55	6	0	2	9	6	.60	7	.270	.336	.484
1997 Louisville	AAA	112	395	108	21	7	20	—	—	203	60	68	25	2	53	3	1	5	4	4	.50	8	.273	.318	.514
1998 Memphis	AAA	32	130	31	5	0	7	—	—	57	22	21	13	1	23	0	0	1	5	4	.56	3	.238	.306	.438
1997 St. Louis	NL	17	45	11	2	0	2	(0 | 2)	19	4	7	2	1	13	0	1	0	4	0	1.00	1	.244	.271	.422
1998 St. Louis	NL	83	254	62	18	1	4	(2 | 2)	94	28	20	28	5	42	0	1	2	6	2	.75	5	.244	.318	.370
2 ML YEARS		100	299	73	20	1	6	(2 | 4)	113	32	27	30	6	55	0	1	2	10	2	.83	6	.244	.311	.378

Al Martin

Bats: Left **Throws:** Left **Pos:** LF-114; PH/PR-12; DH-2   **Ht:** 6'2" **Wt:** 207 **Born:** 11/24/67 **Age:** 31

Year Team	Lg	G	AB	H	2B	3B	HR	(Hm	Rd)	TB	R	RBI	TBB	IBB	SO	HBP	SH	SF	SB	CS	SB%	GDP	Avg	OBP	SLG
1992 Pittsburgh	NL	12	12	2	0	1	0	(0	0)	4	1	2	0	0	5	0	0	1	0	0	.00	0	.167	.154	.333
1993 Pittsburgh	NL	143	480	135	26	8	18	(15	3)	231	85	64	42	5	122	1	2	3	16	9	.64	5	.281	.338	.481
1994 Pittsburgh	NL	82	276	79	12	4	9	(6	3)	126	48	33	34	3	56	2	0	1	15	6	.71	3	.286	.367	.457
1995 Pittsburgh	NL	124	439	124	25	3	13	(8	5)	194	70	41	44	6	92	2	1	0	20	11	.65	5	.282	.351	.442
1996 Pittsburgh	NL	155	630	189	40	1	18	(8	10)	285	101	72	54	2	116	2	1	7	38	12	.76	9	.300	.354	.452
1997 Pittsburgh	NL	113	423	123	24	7	13	(8	5)	200	64	59	45	7	83	3	1	5	23	7	.77	7	.291	.359	.473
1998 Pittsburgh	NL	125	440	105	15	2	12	(5	7)	160	57	47	32	2	91	5	0	2	20	3	.87	13	.239	.296	.364
7 ML YEARS		754	2700	757	142	26	83	(50	33)	1200	426	318	251	25	565	15	5	19	132	48	.73	42	.280	.343	.444

Norberto Martin

Bats: R **Throws:** R **Pos:** 2B-54; PH/PR-17; DH-10; 3B-5; LF-5; SS-2   **Ht:** 5'10" **Wt:** 182 **Born:** 12/10/66 **Age:** 32

Year Team	Lg	G	AB	H	2B	3B	HR	(Hm	Rd)	TB	R	RBI	TBB	IBB	SO	HBP	SH	SF	SB	CS	SB%	GDP	Avg	OBP	SLG
1993 Chicago	AL	8	14	5	0	0	0	(0	0)	5	3	2	1	0	1	0	0	0	0	0	.00	0	.357	.400	.357
1994 Chicago	AL	45	131	36	7	1	1	(0	1)	48	19	16	9	0	16	0	3	2	4	2	.67	2	.275	.317	.366
1995 Chicago	AL	72	160	43	7	4	2	(1	1)	64	17	17	3	0	25	1	2	3	5	0	1.00	5	.269	.281	.400
1996 Chicago	AL	70	140	49	7	0	1	(0	1)	59	30	14	6	0	17	0	4	1	10	2	.83	4	.350	.374	.421
1997 Chicago	AL	71	213	64	7	1	2	(1	1)	79	24	27	6	0	31	0	0	0	1	4	.20	2	.300	.320	.371
1998 Anaheim	AL	79	195	42	2	0	1	(0	1)	47	20	13	6	0	29	0	3	2	3	1	.75	9	.215	.236	.241
6 ML YEARS		345	853	239	30	6	7	(2	5)	302	113	89	31	0	119	1	12	8	23	9	.72	22	.280	.303	.354

Tom Martin

Pitches: Left **Bats:** Left **Pos:** RP-14   **Ht:** 6'1" **Wt:** 200 **Born:** 5/21/70 **Age:** 29

Year Team	Lg	G	GS	CG	GF	IP	BFP	H	R	ER	HR	SH	SF	HB	TBB	IBB	SO	WP	Bk	W	L	Pct.	ShO	Sv-Op	Hld	ERA
1989 Bluefield	R+	8	8	0	0	39	176	36	28	20	3	1	1	0	25	0	31	2	1	3	3	.500	0	0- -	—	4.62
Erie	A-	7	7	0	0	40.2	190	42	39	30	2	0	2	1	25	0	44	11	2	0	5	.000	0	0- -	—	6.64
1990 Wausau	A	9	9	0	0	40	183	31	25	11	1	3	0	5	27	0	45	4	0	2	3	.400	0	0- -	—	2.48
1991 Kane County	A	38	10	0	19	99	442	92	50	40	4	6	4	3	56	3	106	13	0	4	10	.286	0	6- -	—	3.64
1992 High Desert	A+	11	0	0	8	16.1	85	23	19	17	4	0	0	0	16	0	10	2	0	0	2	.000	0	0- -	—	9.37
Waterloo	A	39	2	0	11	55	248	62	38	26	3	5	1	4	22	4	57	5	0	2	6	.250	0	3- -	—	4.25
1993 Rancho Cuca	A+	47	1	0	16	59.1	290	72	41	37	4	1	7	7	39	2	53	9	0	1	4	.200	0	0- -	—	5.61
1994 Greenville	AA	36	6	0	9	74	324	82	40	38	4	1	4	4	27	3	51	3	0	6	5	.455	0	0- -	—	4.62
1995 Richmond	AAA	7	0	0	2	9	45	10	9	9	4	0	0	0	10	2	3	0	0	0	0	.000	0	0- -	—	9.00
1996 Tucson	AAA	5	0	0	3	6	25	6	0	0	0	0	0	0	2	2	1	0	0	0	0	.000	0	0- -	—	0.00
Jackson	AA	57	0	0	18	75	338	71	35	27	8	5	3	4	42	4	58	4	0	6	2	.750	0	3- -	—	3.24
1998 Buffalo	AAA	41	0	0	8	36	167	46	25	24	4	1	1	3	13	0	35	1	0	3	1	.750	0	0- -	—	6.00
1997 Houston	NL	55	0	0	18	56	236	52	13	13	7	2	6	1	23	2	36	3	0	5	3	.625	0	2-3	7	2.09
1998 Cleveland	AL	14	0	0	1	14.2	85	29	21	21	3	1	1	0	12	0	9	2	0	1	1	.500	0	0-0	3	12.89
2 ML YEARS		69	0	0	19	70.2	321	81	34	34	5	7	2	1	35	2	45	5	0	6	4	.600	0	2-3	10	4.33

Dave Martinez

Bats: L **Throws:** L **Pos:** RF-85; PH/PR-6; CF-2; DH-1; 1B-1   **Ht:** 5'10" **Wt:** 175 **Born:** 9/26/64 **Age:** 34

Year Team	Lg	G	AB	H	2B	3B	HR	(Hm	Rd)	TB	R	RBI	TBB	IBB	SO	HBP	SH	SF	SB	CS	SB%	GDP	Avg	OBP	SLG
1986 Chicago	NL	53	108	15	1	1	1	(1	0)	21	13	7	6	0	22	1	0	1	4	2	.67	1	.139	.190	.194
1987 Chicago	NL	142	459	134	18	8	8	(5	3)	192	70	36	57	4	96	2	1	1	16	8	.67	4	.292	.372	.418
1988 ChN-Mon	NL	138	447	114	13	6	6	(2	4)	157	51	46	38	8	94	2	2	5	23	9	.72	3	.255	.313	.351
1989 Montreal	NL	126	361	99	16	7	3	(1	2)	138	41	27	27	2	57	0	7	1	23	4	.85	1	.274	.324	.382
1990 Montreal	NL	118	391	109	13	5	11	(5	6)	165	60	39	24	2	48	1	3	2	13	11	.54	8	.279	.321	.422
1991 Montreal	NL	124	396	117	18	5	7	(3	4)	166	47	42	20	3	54	1	3	3	16	7	.70	3	.295	.332	.419
1992 Cincinnati	NL	135	393	100	20	5	3	(3	0)	139	47	31	42	4	54	0	6	4	12	8	.60	6	.254	.323	.354
1993 San Francisco	NL	91	241	58	12	1	5	(1	4)	87	28	27	27	3	39	0	0	0	6	3	.67	5	.241	.317	.361
1994 San Francisco	NL	97	235	58	9	3	4	(1	3)	85	23	27	21	1	22	2	2	0	3	4	.43	6	.247	.314	.362
1995 Chicago	AL	119	303	93	16	4	5	(2	3)	132	49	37	32	2	41	1	9	4	8	2	.80	6	.307	.371	.436
1996 Chicago	AL	146	440	140	20	8	10	(3	7)	206	85	53	52	1	52	0	3	3	15	7	.68	4	.318	.393	.468
1997 Chicago	AL	145	504	144	16	6	12	(5	7)	208	78	55	57	6	69	3	5	6	12	6	.67	4	.286	.356	.413
1998 Tampa Bay	AL	90	309	79	11	0	3	(1	2)	99	31	20	35	4	52	2	0	1	8	7	.53	5	.256	.334	.320
1988 Chicago	NL	75	256	65	10	1	4	(2	2)	89	27	34	21	5	46	2	0	4	7	3	.70	2	.254	.311	.348
Montreal	NL	63	191	49	3	5	2	(0	2)	68	24	12	17	3	48	0	2	1	16	6	.73	1	.257	.316	.356
13 ML YEARS		1524	4587	1260	183	59	78	(34	44)	1795	623	447	436	41	700	20	42	29	159	78	.67	56	.275	.338	.391

Dennis Martinez

Pitches: Right **Bats:** Right **Pos:** RP-48; SP-5   **Ht:** 6'1" **Wt:** 180 **Born:** 5/14/55 **Age:** 44

Year Team	Lg	G	GS	CG	GF	IP	BFP	H	R	ER	HR	SH	SF	HB	TBB	IBB	SO	WP	Bk	W	L	Pct.	ShO	Sv-Op	Hld	ERA
1976 Baltimore	AL	4	2	1	1	27.2	106	23	8	8	1	1	0	0	8	0	18	1	0	1	2	.333	0	0- -	—	2.60
1977 Baltimore	AL	42	13	5	19	166.2	709	157	86	76	10	8	8	8	64	5	107	5	0	14	7	.667	0	4- -	—	4.10
1978 Baltimore	AL	40	38	15	0	276.1	1140	257	121	108	20	8	7	3	93	4	142	8	0	16	11	.593	2	0- -	—	3.52
1979 Baltimore	AL	40	**39**	**18**	0	**292.1**	**1206**	279	129	119	28	12	**12**	1	78	1	132	9	2	15	16	.484	3	0- -	—	3.66

		HOW MUCH HE PITCHED					WHAT HE GAVE UP									THE RESULTS						
Year Team	Lg	G	GS	CG	GF	IP	BFP	H	R	ER	HR	SH	SF	HB	TBB	IBB	SO	WP	Bk	W	L	Pct.	ShO	Sv-Op	Hld	ERA
1980 Baltimore	AL	25	12	2	8	99.2	428	103	44	44	12	1	3	2	44	6	42	0	1	6	4	.600	0	1--	—	3.97
1981 Baltimore	AL	25	24	9	0	179	753	173	84	66	10	2	5	2	62	1	88	6	1	14	5	.737	2	0-0	0	3.32
1982 Baltimore	AL	40	39	10	0	252	1093	262	123	118	30	11	7	7	87	2	111	7	1	16	12	.571	2	0-0	0	4.21
1983 Baltimore	AL	32	25	4	3	153	688	209	108	94	21	3	5	2	45	0	71	2	0	7	16	.304	0	0-1	0	5.53
1984 Baltimore	AL	34	20	2	4	141.2	599	145	81	79	26	0	5	5	37	2	77	13	0	6	9	.400	0	0-0	0	5.02
1985 Baltimore	AL	33	31	3	1	180	789	203	110	103	29	0	11	9	63	3	68	4	1	13	11	.542	0	0-0	0	5.15
1986 Bal-Mon		23	15	1	2	104.2	449	114	57	55	11	8	2	3	30	4	65	3	2	3	6	.333	1	0-0	0	4.73
1987 Montreal	NL	22	22	2	0	144.2	599	133	59	53	9	4	3	6	40	2	84	4	2	11	4	.733	1	0-0	0	3.30
1988 Montreal	NL	34	34	9	0	235.1	968	215	94	71	21	2	6	6	55	3	120	5	10	15	13	.536	2	0-0	0	2.72
1989 Montreal	NL	34	33	5	1	232	950	227	88	82	21	8	2	7	49	4	142	5	2	16	7	.696	2	0-0	0	3.18
1990 Montreal	NL	32	32	7	0	226	908	191	80	74	16	11	3	6	49	9	156	1	1	10	11	.476	2	0-0	0	2.95
1991 Montreal	NL	31	31	9	0	222	905	187	70	59	9	7	3	4	62	3	123	3	0	14	11	.560	5	0-0	0	2.39
1992 Montreal	NL	32	32	6	0	226.1	900	172	75	62	12	12	5	9	60	3	147	2	0	16	11	.593	0	0-0	0	2.47
1993 Montreal	NL	35	34	2	1	224.2	945	211	110	96	27	10	4	11	64	7	138	2	4	15	9	.625	0	1-1	0	3.85
1994 Cleveland	AL	24	24	7	0	176.2	730	166	75	69	14	3	5	7	44	2	92	4	3	11	6	.647	3	0-0	0	3.52
1995 Cleveland	AL	28	28	3	0	187	771	174	71	64	17	4	4	12	46	2	99	3	0	12	5	.706	2	0-0	0	3.08
1996 Cleveland	AL	20	20	1	0	112	483	122	63	56	12	2	3	2	37	2	48	0	0	9	6	.600	1	0-0	0	4.50
1997 Seattle	AL	9	9	0	0	49	239	65	46	42	8	1	3	7	29	1	17	0	0	1	5	.167	0	0-0	0	7.71
1998 Atlanta	NL	53	5	1	11	91	396	109	53	45	8	2	3	3	19	5	62	2	0	4	6	.400	1	2-4	12	4.45
1986 Baltimore	AL	4	0	0	1	6.2	33	11	5	5	0	0	1	0	2	0	2	1	0	0	0	.000	0	0-0	0	6.75
Montreal	NL	19	15	1	1	98	416	103	52	50	11	8	1	3	28	4	63	2	2	3	6	.333	1	0-0	0	4.59
23 ML YEARS		692	562	122	51	3999.2	16754	3897	1835	1643	372	120	109	122	1165	71	2149	89	30	245	193	.559	30	8- -	—	3.70

Edgar Martinez

Bats: Right **Throws:** Right **Pos:** DH-147; 1B-4; PH/PR-3 **Ht:** 5'11" **Wt:** 200 **Born:** 1/2/63 **Age:** 36

		BATTING																BASERUNNING				PERCENTAGES		
Year Team	Lg	G	AB	H	2B	3B	HR	(Hm	Rd)	TB	R	RBI	TBB	IBB	SO	HBP	SH	SF	SB	CS	SB%	GDP	Avg	OBP	SLG
1987 Seattle	AL	13	43	16	5	2	0	(0	0)	25	6	5	2	0	5	1	0	0	0	0	.00	0	.372	.413	.581
1988 Seattle	AL	14	32	9	4	0	0	(0	0)	13	0	5	4	0	7	0	1	1	0	0	.00	0	.281	.351	.406
1989 Seattle	AL	65	171	41	5	0	2	(0	2)	52	20	20	17	1	26	3	2	3	2	1	.67	3	.240	.314	.304
1990 Seattle	AL	144	487	147	27	2	11	(3	8)	211	71	49	74	3	62	5	1	3	1	4	.20	13	.302	.397	.433
1991 Seattle	AL	150	544	167	35	1	14	(8	6)	246	98	52	84	9	72	8	2	4	0	3	.00	19	.307	.405	.452
1992 Seattle	AL	135	528	181	46	3	18	(11	7)	287	100	73	54	2	61	4	1	5	14	4	.78	15	.343	.404	.544
1993 Seattle	AL	42	135	32	7	0	4	(1	3)	51	20	13	28	1	19	0	1	1	0	0	.00	4	.237	.366	.378
1994 Seattle	AL	89	326	93	23	1	13	(4	9)	157	47	51	53	3	42	3	2	3	6	2	.75	2	.285	.387	.482
1995 Seattle	AL	145	511	182	52	0	29	(16	13)	321	121	113	116	19	87	8	0	4	3	3	.57	11	.356	.479	.628
1996 Seattle	AL	139	499	163	52	2	26	(14	12)	297	121	103	123	12	84	8	0	4	3	3	.50	15	.327	.464	.595
1997 Seattle	AL	155	542	179	35	1	28	(12	16)	300	104	108	119	11	86	11	0	6	2	4	.33	21	.330	.456	.554
1998 Seattle	AL	154	556	179	46	1	29	(17	12)	314	86	102	106	4	96	3	0	7	1	1	.50	13	.322	.429	.565
12 ML YEARS		1245	4374	1389	337	13	174	(86	88)	2274	794	694	780	65	647	54	10	41	33	25	.57	116	.318	.424	.520

Felix Martinez

Bats: Both **Throws:** Right **Pos:** SS-32; PH/PR-4; 2B-2 **Ht:** 6'0" **Wt:** 180 **Born:** 5/18/74 **Age:** 25

		BATTING																BASERUNNING				PERCENTAGES		
Year Team	Lg	G	AB	H	2B	3B	HR	(Hm	Rd)	TB	R	RBI	TBB	IBB	SO	HBP	SH	SF	SB	CS	SB%	GDP	Avg	OBP	SLG
1993 Royals	R	57	165	42	5	1	0	—	—	49	23	12	17	0	26	3	1	0	22	5	.81	2	.255	.335	.297
1994 Wilmington	A+	117	400	107	16	4	2	—	—	137	65	43	30	0	91	3	12	2	19	8	.70	10	.268	.322	.343
1995 Wichita	AA	127	426	112	15	3	3	—	—	142	53	30	31	0	71	6	4	1	44	20	.69	5	.263	.321	.333
1996 Omaha	AAA	118	395	93	13	3	5	—	—	127	54	35	44	0	79	5	10	0	18	10	.64	11	.235	.320	.322
1997 Omaha	AAA	112	410	104	19	4	2	—	—	137	55	36	29	0	86	7	5	1	21	11	.66	11	.254	.313	.334
1998 Omaha	AAA	51	164	41	8	3	2	—	—	61	27	16	15	0	40	1	5	1	6	2	.75	1	.250	.315	.372
1997 Kansas City	AL	16	31	7	1	1	0	(0	0)	10	3	3	6	0	8	0	1	0	0	0	.00	1	.226	.351	.323
1998 Kansas City	AL	34	85	11	1	1	0	(0	0)	14	7	5	5	0	21	1	4	0	3	1	.75	1	.129	.187	.165
2 ML YEARS		50	116	18	2	2	0	(0	0)	24	10	8	11	0	29	1	5	0	3	1	.75	2	.155	.234	.207

Greg Martinez

Bats: Both **Throws:** Right **Pos:** PH/PR-10; LF-6 **Ht:** 5'10" **Wt:** 168 **Born:** 1/27/72 **Age:** 27

		BATTING																BASERUNNING				PERCENTAGES		
Year Team	Lg	G	AB	H	2B	3B	HR	(Hm	Rd)	TB	R	RBI	TBB	IBB	SO	HBP	SH	SF	SB	CS	SB%	GDP	Avg	OBP	SLG
1993 Brewers	R	5	19	12	0	0	0	—	—	12	6	3	4	0	0	1	0	0	7	1	.88	0	.632	.708	.632
Helena	R+	52	183	53	4	2	0	—	—	61	45	19	30	0	26	6	3	5	30	6	.83	0	.290	.397	.333
1994 Beloit	A	81	224	62	8	1	0	—	—	72	39	20	25	1	32	3	6	1	27	11	.71	4	.277	.356	.321
1995 Stockton	A+	114	410	113	8	2	0	—	—	125	80	43	69	1	64	2	10	1	55	9	.86	7	.276	.382	.305
1996 Stockton	A+	73	286	82	5	1	0	—	—	89	51	26	29	0	34	0	8	2	30	9	.77	3	.287	.350	.311
El Paso	AA	41	166	52	2	2	1	—	—	61	27	21	13	0	19	3	6	1	14	4	.78	4	.313	.372	.367
1997 El Paso	AA	95	381	111	10	10	1	—	—	144	75	29	32	0	55	3	9	2	39	7	.85	5	.291	.349	.378
Tucson	AAA	3	12	5	2	0	0	—	—	7	2	3	0	0	1	0	0	0	0	0	.00	0	.417	.417	.583
1998 Louisville	AAA	115	376	98	4	11	4	—	—	136	65	25	51	0	80	0	10	0	43	7	.86	3	.261	.349	.362
1998 Milwaukee	NL	13	3	0	0	0	0	(0	0)	0	2	0	1	0	2	0	0	0	2	0	1.00	0	.000	.250	.000

Javier Martinez

Pitches: Right **Bats:** Right **Pos:** RP-37 **Ht:** 6'2" **Wt:** 210 **Born:** 2/5/77 **Age:** 22

		HOW MUCH HE PITCHED						WHAT HE GAVE UP										THE RESULTS						
Year Team	Lg	G	GS	CG	GF	IP	BFP	H	R	ER	HR	SH	SF	HB	TBB	IBB	SO	WP	Bk	W	L	Pct.	ShO	Sv-Op	Hld	ERA
1994 Huntington	R+	9	8	0	1	35	147	24	20	15	1	1	2	3	21	0	31	9	2	2	1	.667	0	0--	—	3.86
1995 Rockford	A	18	18	1	0	104.2	455	100	56	46	6	5	4	12	39	0	53	15	2	6	6	.500	0	0--	—	3.96
1996 Cubs	R	3	3	0	0	15	62	11	4	1	0	0	0	1	6	0	15	1	0	2	1	.667	0	0--	—	0.60
Rockford	A	10	10	3	0	59	250	49	26	22	5	2	2	1	30	0	53	9	0	4	3	.571	0	0--	—	3.36
1997 Daytona	A+	9	9	2	0	51.1	238	65	40	33	8	1	3	3	26	0	34	3	2	2	6	.250	0	0--	—	5.79
Rockford	A	17	17	1	0	79	369	85	61	50	7	3	2	3	50	1	70	10	0	1	7	.125	0	0--	—	5.70
1998 Pittsburgh	NL	37	0	0	13	41	199	39	32	22	5	1	3	4	34	1	42	5	0	0	1	.000	0	0-0	2	4.83

Manny Martinez

Bats: R **Throws:** R **Pos:** CF-37; LF-26; PH/PR-12; RF-3; DH-2 **Ht:** 6'2" **Wt:** 169 **Born:** 10/3/70 **Age:** 28

		BATTING																	BASERUNNING				PERCENTAGES		
Year Team	Lg	G	AB	H	2B	3B	HR	(Hm	Rd)	TB	R	RBI	TBB	IBB	SO	HBP	SH	SF	SB	CS	SB%	GDP	Avg	OBP	SLG
1990 Sou. Oregon	A-	66	244	60	5	0	2	—	—	71	35	17	16	0	59	5	1	0	6	4	.60	5	.246	.306	.291
1991 Modesto	A+	125	502	136	32	3	3	—	—	183	73	55	34	2	80	7	7	3	26	19	.58	7	.271	.324	.365
1992 Modesto	A+	121	495	125	23	1	9	—	—	177	70	45	39	3	75	4	12	5	17	13	.57	7	.253	.309	.358
1993 San Berndno	A+	109	459	148	26	3	11	—	—	213	88	52	41	2	60	5	6	4	28	21	.57	10	.322	.381	.464
Tacoma	AAA	20	59	18	2	0	1	—	—	23	9	6	4	0	12	0	1	0	2	3	.40	2	.305	.349	.390
1994 Tacoma	AAA	137	536	137	25	5	9	—	—	199	76	60	28	3	72	10	9	5	18	10	.64	14	.256	.302	.371
1995 Iowa	AAA	122	397	115	17	8	8	—	—	172	63	49	20	0	64	3	7	2	11	8	.58	3	.290	.327	.433
1996 Tacoma	AAA	66	277	87	15	1	4	—	—	116	54	24	23	1	41	2	3	3	14	10	.58	6	.314	.367	.419
Scranton-WB	AAA	17	67	14	1	1	0	—	—	17	8	5	4	0	17	1	0	0	3	0	1.00	1	.209	.264	.254
1997 Calgary	AAA	109	420	139	34	1	16	—	—	223	78	66	33	4	80	0	2	1	17	9	.65	3	.331	.379	.531
1998 Nashville	AAA	22	75	18	5	0	1	—	—	26	12	6	7	0	20	0	0	0	5	3	.63	1	.240	.305	.347
1996 Sea-Phi		22	53	12	2	3	0	(0	0)	20	5	3	4	0	16	1	1	0	4	1	.80	2	.226	.293	.377
1998 Pittsburgh	NL	73	180	45	11	2	4	(5	1)	78	21	24	9	0	44	2	3	2	0	3	.00	3	.250	.290	.433
1996 Seattle	AL	9	17	4	2	1	0	(0	0)	8	3	3	3	0	5	0	0	0	2	0	1.00	1	.235	.350	.471
Philadelphia	NL	13	36	8	0	2	0	(0	0)	12	2	0	1	0	11	1	1	0	2	1	.67	1	.222	.263	.333
2 ML YEARS		95	233	57	13	5	6	(5	1)	98	26	27	13	0	60	3	4	2	4	4	.50	5	.245	.291	.421

Pedro Martinez

Pitches: Right **Bats:** Right **Pos:** SP-33 **Ht:** 5'11" **Wt:** 170 **Born:** 10/25/71 **Age:** 27

		HOW MUCH HE PITCHED						WHAT HE GAVE UP										THE RESULTS						
Year Team	Lg	G	GS	CG	GF	IP	BFP	H	R	ER	HR	SH	SF	HB	TBB	IBB	SO	WP	Bk	W	L	Pct.	ShO	Sv-Op	Hld	ERA
1992 Los Angeles	NL	2	1	0	1	8	31	6	2	2	0	0	0	0	1	0	8	0	0	1	0	.000	0	0-0	0	2.25
1993 Los Angeles	NL	65	2	0	20	107	444	76	34	31	5	0	5	4	57	4	119	3	1	10	5	.667	0	2-3	14	2.61
1994 Montreal	NL	24	23	1	1	144.2	584	115	58	55	11	2	3	11	45	3	142	6	0	11	5	.688	1	1-1	0	3.42
1995 Montreal	NL	30	30	2	0	194.2	784	158	79	76	21	7	3	11	66	1	174	5	2	14	10	.583	2	0-0	0	3.51
1996 Montreal	NL	33	33	4	0	216.2	901	189	100	89	19	9	6	3	70	3	222	6	0	13	10	.565	1	0-0	0	3.70
1997 Montreal	NL	31	31	13	0	241.1	947	158	65	51	16	9	1	9	67	5	305	3	1	17	8	.680	4	0-0	0	1.90
1998 Boston	AL	33	33	3	0	233.2	951	188	82	75	26	4	7	8	67	3	251	9	0	19	7	.731	2	0-0	0	2.89
7 ML YEARS		218	153	23	22	1146	4642	890	420	379	98	31	25	46	373	19	1221	32	4	84	46	.646	10	3-4	14	2.98

Ramon Martinez

Pitches: Right **Bats:** Both **Pos:** SP-15 **Ht:** 6'4" **Wt:** 184 **Born:** 3/22/68 **Age:** 31

		HOW MUCH HE PITCHED						WHAT HE GAVE UP										THE RESULTS						
Year Team	Lg	G	GS	CG	GF	IP	BFP	H	R	ER	HR	SH	SF	HB	TBB	IBB	SO	WP	Bk	W	L	Pct.	ShO	Sv-Op	Hld	ERA
1988 Los Angeles	NL	9	6	0	0	35.2	151	27	17	15	0	4	0	0	22	1	23	1	0	1	3	.250	0	0-0	1	3.79
1989 Los Angeles	NL	15	15	2	0	98.2	410	79	39	35	11	4	0	5	41	1	89	1	0	6	4	.600	2	0-0	0	3.19
1990 Los Angeles	NL	33	33	12	0	234.1	950	191	89	76	22	7	5	4	67	5	223	3	3	20	6	.769	3	0-0	0	2.92
1991 Los Angeles	NL	33	33	6	0	220.1	916	190	89	80	18	4	7	6	69	4	150	6	0	17	13	.567	4	0-0	0	3.27
1992 Los Angeles	NL	25	25	1	0	150.2	662	141	82	67	11	12	1	5	69	4	101	9	0	8	11	.421	1	0-0	0	4.00
1993 Los Angeles	NL	32	32	4	0	211.2	918	202	88	81	15	12	5	4	104	9	127	2	2	10	12	.455	3	0-0	0	3.44
1994 Los Angeles	NL	24	24	4	0	170	718	160	83	75	18	6	8	6	56	2	119	2	0	12	7	.632	3	0-0	0	3.97
1995 Los Angeles	NL	30	30	4	0	206.1	859	176	95	84	19	7	5	5	81	5	138	3	0	17	7	.708	2	0-0	0	3.66
1996 Los Angeles	NL	28	27	2	1	168.2	732	153	76	64	12	7	6	8	86	5	133	2	1	15	6	.714	2	0-0	0	3.42
1997 Los Angeles	NL	22	22	1	0	133.2	590	123	64	54	14	5	4	6	68	1	120	1	0	10	5	.667	0	0-0	0	3.64
1998 Los Angeles	NL	15	15	1	0	101.2	418	76	41	32	8	2	3	3	41	1	91	0	0	7	3	.700	0	0-0	0	2.83
11 ML YEARS		266	262	37	1	1731.2	7324	1518	763	663	148	74	41	53	704	38	1314	32	7	123	77	.615	20	0-0	1	3.45

Ramon E. Martinez

Bats: Right **Throws:** Right **Pos:** 2B-14; PH/PR-6 **Ht:** 6'1" **Wt:** 170 **Born:** 10/10/72 **Age:** 26

		BATTING																	BASERUNNING				PERCENTAGES		
Year Team	Lg	G	AB	H	2B	3B	HR	(Hm	Rd)	TB	R	RBI	TBB	IBB	SO	HBP	SH	SF	SB	CS	SB%	GDP	Avg	OBP	SLG
1993 Royals	R	37	97	23	5	0	0	—	—	28	16	9	8	0	6	2	2	2	3	0	1.00	1	.237	.303	.289
Wilmington	A+	24	75	19	4	0	0	—	—	23	8	6	11	0	9	1	3	1	1	4	.20	2	.253	.352	.307
1994 Rockford	A	6	18	5	0	0	0	—	—	5	3	4	0	2	0	1	0	1	0	1.00	1	.278	.409	.278
Wilmington	A+	90	325	87	13	2	2	—	—	110	40	35	35	0	25	4	20	5	6	3	.67	14	.268	.341	.338
1995 Wichita	AA	103	393	108	20	2	3	—	—	141	58	51	42	1	50	4	18	9	11	8	.58	11	.275	.344	.359
1996 Omaha	AAA	85	320	81	12	3	6	—	—	117	35	41	21	1	34	3	13	0	3	2	.60	6	.253	.305	.366
Wichita	AA	26	93	32	4	1	1	—	—	41	16	8	7	0	8	0	7	0	4	1	.80	4	.344	.390	.441

Year Team	Lg	G	AB	H	2B	3B	HR	(Hm	Rd)	TB	R	RBI	TBB	IBB	SO	HBP	SH	SF	SB	CS	SB%	GDP	Avg	OBP	SLG
1997 Phoenix	AAA	18	57	16	2	0	1	—	—	21	6	7	5	0	9	0	1	1	1	0	1.00	1	.281	.333	.368
Shreveport	AA	105	404	129	32	4	5	—	—	184	72	54	40	1	48	3	4	3	4	5	.44	6	.319	.382	.455
1998 Fresno	AAA	98	364	114	21	2	14	—	—	181	58	60	38	3	42	2	4	7	0	3	.00	11	.313	.375	.497
1998 San Francisco	NL	19	19	6	1	0	0	(0	0)	7	4	0	4	0	2	0	1	0	0	0	.00	0	.316	.435	.368

Sandy Martinez

Bats: Left **Throws:** Right **Pos:** C-33; PH/PR-18 **Ht:** 6'2" **Wt:** 205 **Born:** 10/3/72 **Age:** 26

Year Team	Lg	G	AB	H	2B	3B	HR	(Hm	Rd)	TB	R	RBI	TBB	IBB	SO	HBP	SH	SF	SB	CS	SB%	GDP	Avg	OBP	SLG
1995 Toronto	AL	62	191	46	12	0	2	(1	1)	64	12	25	7	0	45	1	0	1	0	0	.00	1	.241	.270	.335
1996 Toronto	AL	76	229	52	9	3	3	(2	1)	76	17	18	16	0	58	4	1	1	0	0	.00	4	.227	.288	.332
1997 Toronto	AL	3	2	0	0	0	0	(0	0)	0	1	0	1	0	1	0	0	0	0	0	.00	0	.000	.333	.000
1998 Chicago	NL	45	87	23	9	1	0	(0	0)	34	7	7	13	0	21	1	0	1	1	0	1.00	3	.264	.363	.391
4 ML YEARS		186	509	121	30	4	5	(3	2)	174	37	50	37	0	125	6	1	3	1	0	1.00	8	.238	.295	.342

Tino Martinez

Bats: Left **Throws:** Right **Pos:** 1B-142; PH/PR-1 **Ht:** 6'2" **Wt:** 210 **Born:** 12/7/67 **Age:** 31

Year Team	Lg	G	AB	H	2B	3B	HR	(Hm	Rd)	TB	R	RBI	TBB	IBB	SO	HBP	SH	SF	SB	CS	SB%	GDP	Avg	OBP	SLG
1990 Seattle	AL	24	68	15	4	0	0	(0	0)	19	4	5	9	0	9	0	0	1	0	0	.00	0	.221	.308	.279
1991 Seattle	AL	36	112	23	2	0	4	(3	1)	37	11	9	11	0	24	0	0	2	0	0	.00	2	.205	.272	.330
1992 Seattle	AL	136	460	118	19	2	16	(10	6)	189	53	66	42	9	77	2	1	8	2	1	.67	24	.257	.316	.411
1993 Seattle	AL	109	408	108	25	1	17	(9	8)	186	48	60	45	9	56	5	3	3	0	3	.00	7	.265	.343	.456
1994 Seattle	AL	97	329	86	21	0	20	(8	12)	167	42	61	29	2	52	1	4	3	1	2	.33	9	.261	.320	.508
1995 Seattle	AL	141	519	152	35	3	31	(14	17)	286	92	111	62	15	91	4	2	6	0	0	.00	10	.293	.369	.551
1996 New York	AL	155	595	174	28	0	25	(9	16)	277	82	117	68	4	85	2	1	5	2	1	.67	18	.292	.364	.466
1997 New York	AL	158	594	176	31	2	44	(18	26)	343	96	141	75	14	75	3	0	13	3	1	.75	15	.296	.371	.577
1998 New York	AL	142	531	149	33	1	28	(12	16)	268	92	123	61	3	83	6	0	10	2	1	.67	18	.281	.355	.505
9 ML YEARS		998	3616	1001	198	9	185	(83	102)	1772	520	693	402	56	552	23	11	51	10	9	.53	103	.277	.348	.490

John Marzano

Bats: Right **Throws:** Right **Pos:** C-48; PH/PR-3; DH-1 **Ht:** 5'11" **Wt:** 195 **Born:** 2/14/63 **Age:** 36

Year Team	Lg	G	AB	H	2B	3B	HR	(Hm	Rd)	TB	R	RBI	TBB	IBB	SO	HBP	SH	SF	SB	CS	SB%	GDP	Avg	OBP	SLG
1987 Boston	AL	52	168	41	11	0	5	(4	1)	67	20	24	7	0	41	3	2	2	0	1	.00	3	.244	.283	.399
1988 Boston	AL	10	29	4	1	0	0	(0	0)	5	3	1	1	0	3	0	0	0	0	0	.00	1	.138	.167	.172
1989 Boston	AL	7	18	8	3	0	1	(1	0)	14	5	3	0	0	2	0	1	1	0	0	.00	1	.444	.421	.778
1990 Boston	AL	32	83	20	4	0	0	(0	0)	24	8	6	5	0	10	0	2	1	0	1	.00	0	.241	.281	.289
1991 Boston	AL	49	114	30	8	0	0	(0	0)	38	10	5	1	0	16	1	1	2	0	0	.00	5	.263	.271	.333
1992 Boston	AL	19	50	4	2	1	0	(0	0)	8	4	1	2	0	12	1	1	0	0	0	.00	0	.080	.132	.160
1995 Texas	AL	2	6	2	0	0	0	(0	0)	2	1	0	0	0	0	0	0	0	0	0	.00	0	.333	.333	.333
1996 Seattle	AL	41	106	26	6	0	0	(0	0)	32	8	6	7	0	15	4	3	0	0	0	.00	2	.245	.316	.302
1997 Seattle	AL	39	87	25	3	0	1	(1	0)	31	7	10	7	0	15	0	2	0	0	0	.00	2	.287	.340	.356
1998 Seattle	AL	50	133	31	7	1	4	(0	4)	52	13	12	9	1	24	9	2	0	0	0	.00	3	.233	.325	.391
10 ML YEARS		301	794	191	45	2	11	(6	5)	273	79	72	39	1	138	18	14	6	0	2	.00	17	.241	.289	.344

Damon Mashore

Bats: R **Throws:** R **Pos:** RF-28; PH/PR-12; DH-7; CF-7; LF-1 **Ht:** 5'11" **Wt:** 209 **Born:** 10/31/69 **Age:** 29

Year Team	Lg	G	AB	H	2B	3B	HR	(Hm	Rd)	TB	R	RBI	TBB	IBB	SO	HBP	SH	SF	SB	CS	SB%	GDP	Avg	OBP	SLG
1998 Vancouver *	AAA	42	143	39	7	0	2	—	—	52	19	15	18	0	28	1	1	1	1	1	.50	2	.273	.358	.364
1996 Oakland	AL	50	105	28	7	1	3	(1	2)	46	20	12	16	0	31	1	1	1	4	0	1.00	2	.267	.366	.438
1997 Oakland	AL	92	279	69	10	2	3	(1	2)	92	55	18	50	1	82	5	7	1	5	4	.56	5	.247	.370	.330
1998 Anaheim	AL	43	98	23	6	0	2	(0	2)	35	13	11	9	0	22	3	1	0	1	0	1.00	3	.235	.318	.357
3 ML YEARS		185	482	120	23	3	8	(2	6)	173	88	41	75	1	135	9	9	2	10	4	.71	10	.249	.359	.359

Mike Matheny

Bats: Right **Throws:** Right **Pos:** C-107; PH/PR-1 **Ht:** 6'3" **Wt:** 205 **Born:** 9/22/70 **Age:** 28

Year Team	Lg	G	AB	H	2B	3B	HR	(Hm	Rd)	TB	R	RBI	TBB	IBB	SO	HBP	SH	SF	SB	CS	SB%	GDP	Avg	OBP	SLG
1998 Beloit *	A	2	8	2	1	0	0	—	—	3	1	2	1	0	3	0	0	0	0	0	.00	0	.250	.333	.375
1994 Milwaukee	AL	28	53	12	3	0	1	(1	0)	18	3	2	3	0	13	2	1	0	0	1	.00	1	.226	.293	.340
1995 Milwaukee	AL	80	166	41	9	1	0	(0	0)	52	13	21	12	0	28	2	1	0	2	1	.67	3	.247	.306	.313
1996 Milwaukee	AL	106	313	64	15	2	8	(5	3)	107	31	46	14	0	80	3	7	4	3	2	.60	9	.204	.243	.342
1997 Milwaukee	AL	123	320	78	16	1	4	(2	2)	108	29	32	17	0	68	7	9	3	1	0	1.00	9	.244	.294	.338
1998 Milwaukee	NL	108	320	76	13	0	6	(4	2)	107	24	27	11	0	63	7	3	0	1	0	1.00	6	.238	.278	.334
5 ML YEARS		445	1172	271	56	4	19	(12	7)	392	100	128	57	0	252	21	21	7	6	5	.55	28	.231	.278	.334

T.J. Mathews

Pitches: Right   **Bats:** Right   **Pos:** RP-66   **Ht:** 6'2"   **Wt:** 200   **Born:** 1/19/70   **Age:** 29

Year Team	Lg	G	GS	CG	GF	IP	BFP	H	R	ER	HR	SH	SF	HB	TBB	IBB	SO	WP	Bk	W	L	Pct.	ShO	Sv-Op	Hld	ERA
1998 Edmonton *	AAA	1	0	0	0	1.1	5	2	1	1	1	0	0	0	0	0	1	0	0	0	1	.000	0	0--	—	6.75
1995 St. Louis	NL	23	0	0	12	29.2	120	21	7	5	1	4	0	0	11	1	28	2	0	1	1	.500	0	2-2	7	1.52
1996 St. Louis	NL	67	0	0	23	83.2	345	62	32	28	8	5	0	2	32	4	80	1	0	2	6	.250	0	6-11	9	3.01
1997 StL-Oak		64	0	0	26	74.2	329	75	32	25	9	8	1	2	30	4	70	1	0	10	6	.625	0	3-9	12	3.01
1998 Oakland	AL	66	0	0	15	72.2	319	71	44	37	6	2	9	4	29	3	53	1	0	7	4	.636	0	1-4	19	4.58
1997 St. Louis	NL	40	0	0	12	46	197	41	14	11	4	6	0	1	18	3	46	1	0	4	4	.500	0	0-3	8	2.15
Oakland	AL	24	0	0	14	28.2	132	34	18	14	5	2	1	1	12	1	24	0	0	6	2	.750	0	3-6	4	4.40
4 ML YEARS		220	0	0	76	260.2	1113	229	115	95	24	19	10	8	102	12	231	5	0	20	17	.541	0	12-26	47	3.28

Terry Mathews

Pitches: Right   **Bats:** Left   **Pos:** RP-17   **Ht:** 6'2"   **Wt:** 225   **Born:** 10/5/64   **Age:** 34

Year Team	Lg	G	GS	CG	GF	IP	BFP	H	R	ER	HR	SH	SF	HB	TBB	IBB	SO	WP	Bk	W	L	Pct.	ShO	Sv-Op	Hld	ERA
1998 Bowie *	AA	1	1	0	0	3	12	3	2	2	1	0	0	0	1	0	2	0	0	0	0	.000	0	0--	—	6.00
Rochester *	AAA	1	1	0	0	3	15	4	1	1	0	0	0	0	2	0	4	0	0	0	1	.000	0	0--	—	3.00
Edmonton *	AAA	13	8	0	1	43.1	186	47	22	22	9	1	0	3	11	0	33	2	0	2	2	.500	0	1--	—	4.57
1991 Texas	AL	34	2	0	8	57.1	236	54	24	23	5	2	0	1	18	3	51	5	0	4	0	1.000	0	1-3	2	3.61
1992 Texas	AL	40	0	0	11	42.1	199	48	29	28	4	1	3	1	31	3	26	2	1	2	4	.333	0	0-4	6	5.95
1994 Florida	NL	24	2	0	5	43	179	45	16	16	4	1	0	1	9	1	21	1	0	2	1	.667	0	0-1	3	3.35
1995 Florida	NL	57	0	0	14	82.2	332	70	32	31	9	5	1	1	27	4	72	3	0	4	4	.500	0	3-7	11	3.38
1996 Fla-Bal		71	0	0	24	73.2	326	79	40	37	10	3	1	1	34	5	62	0	0	4	6	.400	0	4-6	15	4.52
1997 Baltimore	AL	57	0	0	19	63.1	285	63	35	31	8	9	4	0	36	2	39	3	0	4	4	.500	0	1-2	8	4.41
1998 Baltimore	AL	17	0	0	2	20.1	90	26	15	14	6	5	1	0	8	3	10	0	0	0	1	.000	0	0-1	1	6.20
1996 Florida	NL	57	0	0	19	55	247	59	33	30	7	2	1	1	27	5	49	0	0	2	4	.333	0	4-5	11	4.91
Baltimore	AL	14	0	0	5	18.2	79	20	7	7	3	1	0	0	7	0	13	0	0	2	2	.500	0	0-1	4	3.38
7 ML YEARS		300	4	0	83	382.2	1647	385	191	180	46	26	10	5	163	21	281	14	1	20	20	.500	0	9-24	46	4.23

Jason Maxwell

Bats: Right   **Throws:** Right   **Pos:** PH/PR-6; 2B-1   **Ht:** 6'1"   **Wt:** 185   **Born:** 3/26/72   **Age:** 27

Year Team	Lg	G	AB	H	2B	3B	HR	(Hm	Rd)	TB	R	RBI	TBB	IBB	SO	HBP	SH	SF	SB	CS	SB%	GDP	Avg	OBP	SLG
1993 Huntington	R+	61	179	52	7	2	7	—	—	84	50	38	35	0	39	4	2	1	6	5	.55	0	.291	.416	.469
1994 Daytona	A+	116	368	85	18	2	10	—	—	137	71	32	55	0	96	8	6	2	7	7	.50	6	.231	.342	.372
1995 Daytona	A+	117	388	102	13	3	10	—	—	151	66	58	63	1	68	6	1	8	12	7	.63	6	.263	.368	.389
1996 Orlando	AA	126	433	115	20	1	9	—	—	164	64	45	56	3	77	6	4	3	19	4	.83	5	.266	.355	.379
1997 Orlando	AA	122	409	114	22	6	14	—	—	190	87	58	82	1	72	4	5	9	12	9	.57	6	.279	.397	.465
1998 Iowa	AAA	124	483	144	40	3	15	—	—	235	86	60	52	1	93	8	1	4	8	1	.89	6	.298	.373	.487
1998 Chicago	NL	7	3	1	0	0	1	(1	0)	4	2	2	0	0	2	0	1	0	0	0	.00	0	.333	.333	1.333

Derrick May

Bats: Left   **Throws:** Right   **Pos:** LF-48; PH/PR-40; DH-2   **Ht:** 6'4"   **Wt:** 225   **Born:** 7/14/68   **Age:** 30

Year Team	Lg	G	AB	H	2B	3B	HR	(Hm	Rd)	TB	R	RBI	TBB	IBB	SO	HBP	SH	SF	SB	CS	SB%	GDP	Avg	OBP	SLG
1998 Ottawa *	AAA	21	69	26	6	0	6	—	—	50	16	21	13	0	7	1	0	0	1	0	.00	1	.377	.482	.725
1990 Chicago	NL	17	61	15	3	0	1	(1	0)	21	8	11	2	0	7	0	0	0	1	0	1.00	1	.246	.270	.344
1991 Chicago	NL	15	22	5	2	0	1	(1	0)	10	4	3	2	0	1	0	0	0	0	0	.00	1	.227	.280	.455
1992 Chicago	NL	124	351	96	11	0	8	(3	5)	131	33	45	14	4	40	3	2	1	5	3	.63	10	.274	.306	.373
1993 Chicago	NL	128	465	131	25	2	10	(3	7)	196	62	77	31	6	41	1	0	6	10	3	.77	15	.295	.336	.422
1994 Chicago	NL	100	345	98	19	2	8	(5	3)	145	43	51	30	4	34	0	1	2	3	2	.60	11	.284	.340	.420
1995 Mil-Hou		110	319	90	18	2	9	(4	5)	139	44	50	24	0	42	2	0	3	5	1	.83	5	.282	.333	.436
1996 Houston	NL	109	259	65	12	3	5	(2	3)	98	24	33	30	8	33	2	0	3	2	2	.50	3	.251	.330	.378
1997 Philadelphia	NL	83	149	34	5	1	1	(0	1)	44	8	13	8	3	26	0	1	4	4	1	.80	4	.228	.266	.295
1998 Montreal	NL	85	180	43	8	0	5	(1	4)	66	13	15	11	1	24	0	0	0	0	0	.00	5	.239	.281	.367
1995 Milwaukee	AL	32	113	28	3	1	1	(1	0)	36	15	9	5	0	18	1	0	0	0	1	.00	1	.248	.286	.319
Houston	NL	78	206	62	15	1	8	(3	5)	103	29	41	19	0	24	1	0	3	5	0	1.00	4	.301	.358	.500
9 ML YEARS		771	2151	583	103	10	48	(20	28)	850	239	298	152	26	248	8	3	18	30	12	.71	55	.271	.319	.395

Brent Mayne

Bats: Left   **Throws:** Right   **Pos:** C-88; PH/PR-12   **Ht:** 6'1"   **Wt:** 190   **Born:** 4/19/68   **Age:** 31

Year Team	Lg	G	AB	H	2B	3B	HR	(Hm	Rd)	TB	R	RBI	TBB	IBB	SO	HBP	SH	SF	SB	CS	SB%	GDP	Avg	OBP	SLG
1990 Kansas City	AL	5	13	3	0	0	0	(0	0)	3	2	1	3	0	3	0	0	0	0	1	.00	0	.231	.375	.231
1991 Kansas City	AL	85	231	58	8	0	3	(2	1)	75	22	31	23	4	42	0	2	3	2	4	.33	6	.251	.315	.325
1992 Kansas City	AL	82	213	48	10	0	0	(0	0)	58	16	18	11	0	26	0	2	3	0	4	.00	5	.225	.260	.272
1993 Kansas City	AL	71	205	52	9	1	2	(0	2)	69	22	22	18	7	31	1	3	0	3	2	.60	6	.254	.317	.337
1994 Kansas City	AL	46	144	37	5	1	2	(1	1)	50	19	20	14	1	27	0	0	0	1	0	1.00	3	.257	.323	.347
1995 Kansas City	AL	110	307	77	18	1	1	(1	0)	100	23	27	25	1	41	3	11	0	0	1	.00	16	.251	.313	.326
1996 New York	NL	70	99	26	6	0	1	(0	1)	35	9	6	12	1	22	0	2	0	0	1	.00	5	.263	.342	.354
1997 Oakland	AL	85	256	74	12	0	6	(4	2)	104	29	22	18	1	33	4	2	2	1	0	1.00	6	.289	.343	.406
1998 San Francisco	NL	94	275	75	15	0	3	(0	3)	99	26	32	37	3	47	1	2	2	2	1	.67	8	.273	.359	.360

Year Team	Lg	G	AB	H	2B	3B	HR	(Hm	Rd)	TB	R	RBI	TBB	IBB	SO	HBP	SH	SF	SB	CS	SB%	GDP	Avg	OBP	SLG
																								BATTING		
																							BASERUNNING	PERCENTAGES	
9 ML YEARS		648	1743	450	83	3	18	(8	10)	593	168	179	161	18	272	9	24	11	9	14	.39	54	.258	.322	.340

Greg McCarthy

Pitches: Left **Bats:** Left **Pos:** RP-29   **Ht:** 6'2" **Wt:** 215 **Born:** 10/30/68 **Age:** 30

		HOW MUCH HE PITCHED						WHAT HE GAVE UP									THE RESULTS						
Year Team	Lg	G	GS	CG	GF	IP	BFP	H	R	ER	HR	SH	SF	HB	TBB	IBB	SO	WP	Bk	W	L	Pct.	ShO	Sv-Op	Hld	ERA
1998 Tacoma *	AAA	19	0	0	6	19.1	95	15	14	9	2	1	1	2	22	0	24	4	0	1	2	.333	0	1- -	—	4.19
1996 Seattle	AL	10	0	0	1	9.2	45	8	2	2	0	1	1	4	4	0	7	4	0	0	0	.000	0	0-0	1	1.86
1997 Seattle	AL	37	0	0	4	29.2	130	26	21	18	4	0	0	1	16	0	34	4	0	1	1	.500	0	0-0	8	5.46
1998 Seattle	AL	29	0	0	5	23.1	106	18	13	13	6	2	0	3	17	2	25	1	0	1	2	.333	0	0-1	3	5.01
3 ML YEARS		76	0	0	10	62.2	281	52	36	33	10	3	1	8	37	2	66	5	0	2	3	.400	0	0-1	12	4.74

Dave McCarty

Bats: Right **Throws:** Left **Pos:** RF-5; 1B-2; PH/PR-1   **Ht:** 6'5" **Wt:** 215 **Born:** 11/23/69 **Age:** 29

								BATTING										BASERUNNING				PERCENTAGES		
Year Team	Lg	G	AB	H	2B	3B	HR	(Hm	Rd)	TB	R	RBI	TBB	IBB	SO	HBP	SH	SF	SB	CS	SB%	GDP	Avg	OBP	SLG
1998 Tacoma *	AAA	108	398	126	30	2	15	—		193	73	52	59	3	85	6	1	2	9	6	.60	15	.317	.411	.485
1993 Minnesota	AL	98	350	75	15	2	2	(2	0)	100	36	21	19	0	80	1	1	0	2	6	.25	13	.214	.257	.286
1994 Minnesota	AL	44	131	34	8	2	1	(1	0)	49	21	12	7	1	32	5	0	0	2	1	.67	3	.260	.322	.374
1995 Min-SF		37	75	17	4	1	0	(0	0)	23	11	6	6	0	22	1	0	1	1	1	.50	1	.227	.289	.307
1996 San Francisco	NL	91	175	38	3	0	6	(5	1)	59	16	24	18	0	43	2	0	2	2	1	.67	5	.217	.294	.337
1998 Seattle	AL	8	18	5	0	0	1	(1	0)	8	1	2	5	0	4	0	0	0	1	0	1.00	0	.278	.435	.444
1995 Minnesota	AL	25	55	12	3	1	0	(0	0)	17	10	4	4	0	18	1	0	1	0	1	.00	1	.218	.279	.309
San Francisco	NL	12	20	5	1	0	0	(0	0)	6	1	2	2	0	4	0	0	0	1	0	1.00	0	.250	.318	.300
5 ML YEARS		278	749	169	30	5	10	(9	1)	239	85	65	55	1	181	9	1	3	8	9	.47	22	.226	.286	.319

Scott McClain

Bats: Right **Throws:** Right **Pos:** 1B-5; 3B-3; PH/PR-2   **Ht:** 6'4" **Wt:** 210 **Born:** 5/19/72 **Age:** 27

								BATTING										BASERUNNING				PERCENTAGES		
Year Team	Lg	G	AB	H	2B	3B	HR	(Hm	Rd)	TB	R	RBI	TBB	IBB	SO	HBP	SH	SF	SB	CS	SB%	GDP	Avg	OBP	SLG
1990 Bluefield	R+	40	107	21	2	0	4	—	—	35	20	15	22	0	35	2	0	4	2	3	.40	1	.196	.333	.327
1991 Kane County	A	25	81	18	0	0	0	—	—	18	9	4	17	0	25	0	1	0	1	1	.50	4	.222	.357	.222
Bluefield	R+	41	149	39	5	0	0	—	—	44	16	24	14	0	39	3	0	1	5	3	.63	3	.262	.335	.295
1992 Kane County	A	96	316	84	12	2	3	—	—	109	43	30	48	1	62	6	6	1	7	4	.64	5	.266	.372	.345
1993 Frederick	A+	133	427	111	22	2	9	—	—	164	65	54	70	0	88	6	3	2	10	6	.63	8	.260	.370	.384
1994 Bowie	AA	133	427	103	29	1	11	—	—	167	71	58	72	2	89	1	2	7	6	3	.67	14	.241	.347	.391
1995 Rochester	AAA	61	199	50	9	1	8	—	—	85	32	22	23	0	34	1	1	0	0	1	.00	1	.251	.329	.427
Bowie	AA	70	259	72	14	1	13	—	—	127	41	61	25	1	44	3	0	4	2	1	.67	13	.278	.344	.490
1996 Rochester	AAA	131	463	130	23	4	17	—	—	212	76	69	61	1	109	1	0	7	8	6	.57	6	.281	.361	.458
1997 Norfolk	AAA	127	429	120	29	2	21	—	—	216	71	64	64	5	93	2	1	8	1	3	.25	8	.280	.370	.503
1998 Durham	AAA	126	472	141	35	2	34	—	—	278	91	109	66	5	113	2	1	3	6	2	.75	9	.299	.385	.589
1998 Tampa Bay	AL	9	20	2	0	0	0	(0	0)	2	2	0	2	0	6	1	0	0	0	0	.00	0	.100	.217	.100

Quinton McCracken

Bats: Both **Throws:** Right **Pos:** CF-103; LF-58; PH/PR-7   **Ht:** 5'7" **Wt:** 173 **Born:** 3/16/70 **Age:** 29

								BATTING										BASERUNNING				PERCENTAGES		
Year Team	Lg	G	AB	H	2B	3B	HR	(Hm	Rd)	TB	R	RBI	TBB	IBB	SO	HBP	SH	SF	SB	CS	SB%	GDP	Avg	OBP	SLG
1995 Colorado	NL	3	1	0	0	0	0	(0	0)	0	0	0	0	0	1	0	0	0	0	0	.00	0	.000	.000	.000
1996 Colorado	NL	124	283	82	13	4	3	(2	1)	116	50	40	32	4	62	1	12	1	17	6	.74	5	.290	.363	.410
1997 Colorado	NL	147	325	95	11	1	3	(1	2)	117	69	36	42	0	62	1	6	1	28	11	.72	6	.292	.374	.360
1998 Tampa Bay	AL	155	614	179	38	7	7	(5	2)	252	77	59	41	1	107	3	9	8	19	10	.66	12	.292	.335	.410
4 ML YEARS		429	1223	356	62	14	13	(8	5)	485	196	135	115	5	232	5	27	10	64	27	.70	23	.291	.352	.397

Jeff McCurry

Pitches: Right **Bats:** Right **Pos:** RP-16   **Ht:** 6'6" **Wt:** 220 **Born:** 1/21/70 **Age:** 29

		HOW MUCH HE PITCHED						WHAT HE GAVE UP									THE RESULTS						
Year Team	Lg	G	GS	CG	GF	IP	BFP	H	R	ER	HR	SH	SF	HB	TBB	IBB	SO	WP	Bk	W	L	Pct.	ShO	Sv-Op	Hld	ERA
1998 Nashville *	AAA	40	0	0	35	45.1	193	45	26	25	9	4	0	0	15	6	34	2	0	2	5	.286	0	23- -	—	4.96
1995 Pittsburgh	NL	55	0	0	10	61	282	82	38	34	9	4	0	5	30	4	27	2	0	1	4	.200	0	1-2	5	5.02
1996 Detroit	AL	2	0	0	1	3.1	21	9	9	9	3	0	0	0	2	0	0	0	0	0	0	.000	0	0-0	0	24.30
1997 Colorado	NL	33	0	0	14	40.2	179	43	22	20	7	3	1	0	20	0	19	2	0	1	4	.200	0	0-2	4	4.43
1998 Pittsburgh	NL	16	0	0	8	19.1	87	24	14	14	4	2	1	1	9	0	11	0	0	1	3	.250	0	0-0	0	6.52
4 ML YEARS		106	0	0	33	124.1	569	158	83	77	23	9	2	6	61	4	57	4	0	3	11	.214	0	1-4	9	5.57

144

Allen McDill

Pitches: Left **Bats:** Left **Pos:** RP-7 **Ht:** 6'1" **Wt:** 160 **Born:** 8/23/71 **Age:** 27

Year Team	Lg	G	GS	CG	GF	IP	BFP	H	R	ER	HR	SH	SF	HB	TBB	IBB	SO	WP	Bk	W	L	Pct.	ShO	Sv-Op	Hld	ERA
1992 Kingsport	R+	1	0	0	0	0.1	3	0	0	0	0	0	0	0	0	0	0	0	0	0	0	.000	0	0--	—	0.00
Mets	R	10	9	0	0	53.1	216	36	23	16	3	0	0	4	15	0	60	3	0	3	4	.429	0	0--	—	2.70
1993 Kingsport	R+	9	9	0	0	53.1	224	52	19	13	1	1	2	0	14	0	42	2	2	5	2	.714	0	0--	—	2.19
Pittsfield	A-	5	5	0	0	28.1	132	31	22	17	0	2	2	1	15	0	24	3	0	2	3	.400	0	0--	—	5.40
1994 Capital City	A	19	19	1	0	111.2	461	101	52	44	11	5	2	4	38	2	102	9	0	9	6	.600	0	0--	—	3.55
1995 St. Lucie	A+	7	7	1	0	49.1	190	36	11	9	2	1	0	1	13	0	28	3	0	4	2	.667	1	0--	—	1.64
Binghamton	AA	12	12	1	0	73	324	69	42	37	5	1	4	3	38	2	44	3	1	3	5	.375	0	0--	—	4.56
Wichita	AA	12	1	0	5	21.1	85	16	7	5	2	0	0	1	5	0	20	1	0	1	0	1.000	0	1--	—	2.11
1996 Omaha	AAA	2	0	0	0	0.1	5	3	2	2	0	0	0	0	1	0	1	1	2	0	1	.000	0	0--	—	54.00
Wichita	AA	54	0	0	30	65	288	79	43	40	10	2	4	1	21	3	62	7	0	1	5	.167	0	11--	—	5.54
1997 Omaha	AAA	23	6	0	5	64.1	295	80	42	42	10	2	1	5	26	2	51	2	0	5	2	.714	0	2--	—	5.88
Wichita	AA	16	0	0	7	17.1	72	18	7	6	0	1	0	0	7	1	14	1	0	0	1	.000	0	3--	—	3.12
1998 Omaha	AAA	61	0	0	22	60.1	246	54	22	16	4	3	0	0	24	3	62	0	1	6	4	.600	0	4--	—	2.39
1997 Kansas City	AL	3	0	0	1	4	24	3	6	6	1	1	0	1	8	0	2	0	0	0	0	.000	0	0-0	1	13.50
1998 Kansas City	AL	7	0	0	1	6	29	9	7	7	3	0	0	0	2	0	3	0	0	0	0	.000	0	0-0	1	10.50
2 ML YEARS		10	0	0	2	10	53	12	13	13	4	1	0	1	10	0	5	0	0	0	0	.000	0	0-0	1	11.70

Jason McDonald

Bats: B **Throws:** R **Pos:** CF-33; RF-25; PH/PR-15; LF-11; DH-1 **Ht:** 5'7" **Wt:** 182 **Born:** 3/20/72 **Age:** 27

Year Team	Lg	G	AB	H	2B	3B	HR	(Hm	Rd)	TB	R	RBI	TBB	IBB	SO	HBP	SH	SF	SB	CS	SB%	GDP	Avg	OBP	SLG
1993 Sou. Oregon	A-	35	112	33	5	2	0	—	—	42	26	8	31	2	17	0	2	0	22	4	.85	0	.295	.448	.375
1994 W Michigan	A	116	404	96	11	9	2	—	—	131	67	31	81	1	87	4	9	1	52	23	.69	5	.238	.369	.324
1995 Modesto	A+	133	493	129	25	7	6	—	—	186	109	50	110	0	84	6	8	2	70	20	.78	6	.262	.401	.377
1996 Edmonton	AAA	137	479	114	7	5	8	—	—	155	71	46	63	0	82	15	10	6	33	13	.72	8	.238	.341	.324
1997 Edmonton	AAA	79	276	73	14	6	4	—	—	111	74	30	74	0	58	7	8	1	31	9	.78	4	.264	.430	.402
1998 Huntsville	AA	7	20	6	2	0	2	—	—	14	9	4	8	0	6	0	0	0	4	0	1.00	0	.300	.500	.700
Edmonton	AAA	12	43	10	1	1	2	—	—	19	12	5	15	0	11	0	0	0	7	0	1.00	0	.233	.431	.442
1997 Oakland	AL	78	236	62	11	4	4	(1	3)	93	47	14	36	0	49	1	2	1	13	8	.62	0	.263	.361	.394
1998 Oakland	AL	70	175	44	9	0	1	(1	0)	56	25	16	27	0	33	3	6	1	10	4	.71	2	.251	.359	.320
2 ML YEARS		148	411	106	20	4	5	(2	3)	149	72	30	63	0	82	4	8	2	23	12	.66	2	.258	.360	.363

Jack McDowell

Pitches: Right **Bats:** Right **Pos:** SP-14 **Ht:** 6'5" **Wt:** 188 **Born:** 1/16/66 **Age:** 33

Year Team	Lg	G	GS	CG	GF	IP	BFP	H	R	ER	HR	SH	SF	HB	TBB	IBB	SO	WP	Bk	W	L	Pct.	ShO	Sv-Op	Hld	ERA
1998 Vancouver *	AAA	1	1	0	0	3	14	4	2	2	0	0	0	0	2	0	0	1	0	0	0	.000	0	0--	—	6.00
Lk Elsinore *	A+	1	1	0	0	5	22	7	5	5	1	0	0	0	0	0	4	0	0	0	1	.000	0	0--	—	9.00
Midland **	AA	1	1	0	0	7	28	5	3	3	1	0	0	0	2	0	5	0	0	0	1	.000	0	0--	—	3.86
1987 Chicago	AL	4	4	0	0	28	103	16	6	6	1	0	0	2	6	0	15	0	0	3	0	1.000	0	0-0	0	1.93
1988 Chicago	AL	26	26	1	0	158.2	687	147	85	70	12	6	7	7	68	5	84	11	1	5	10	.333	1	0-0	0	3.97
1990 Chicago	AL	33	33	4	0	205	866	189	93	87	20	1	5	7	77	0	165	7	1	14	9	.609	0	0-0	0	3.82
1991 Chicago	AL	35	35	15	0	253.2	1028	212	97	96	19	8	4	4	82	2	191	10	1	17	10	.630	3	0-0	0	3.41
1992 Chicago	AL	34	34	13	0	260.2	1079	247	95	92	21	8	6	7	75	9	178	6	0	20	10	.667	1	0-0	0	3.18
1993 Chicago	AL	34	34	10	0	256.2	1067	261	104	96	20	8	6	3	69	6	158	8	1	22	10	.688	4	0-0	0	3.37
1994 Chicago	AL	25	25	6	0	181	755	186	82	75	12	4	4	5	42	0	127	4	0	10	9	.526	2	0-0	0	3.73
1995 New York	AL	30	30	8	0	217.2	927	211	106	95	25	8	6	5	78	1	157	9	1	15	10	.600	1	0-0	0	3.93
1996 Cleveland	AL	30	30	5	0	192	846	214	119	109	22	10	5	4	67	2	141	5	0	13	9	.591	1	0-0	0	5.11
1997 Cleveland	AL	8	6	0	0	40.2	181	44	25	23	6	4	2	1	18	1	38	1	0	3	3	.500	0	0-0	0	5.09
1998 Anaheim	AL	14	14	0	0	76	334	96	45	43	11	3	2	1	19	1	45	2	0	5	3	.625	0	0-0	0	5.09
11 ML YEARS		273	271	62	0	1870	7873	1823	857	792	169	60	47	46	601	29	1299	63	5	127	83	.605	13	0-0	0	3.81

Chuck McElroy

Pitches: Left **Bats:** Left **Pos:** RP-78 **Ht:** 6'0" **Wt:** 195 **Born:** 10/1/67 **Age:** 31

Year Team	Lg	G	GS	CG	GF	IP	BFP	H	R	ER	HR	SH	SF	HB	TBB	IBB	SO	WP	Bk	W	L	Pct.	ShO	Sv-Op	Hld	ERA
1989 Philadelphia	NL	11	0	0	4	10.1	46	12	2	2	1	0	0	0	4	1	8	0	0	0	0	.000	0	0-0	0	1.74
1990 Philadelphia	NL	16	0	0	8	14	76	24	13	12	0	1	0	0	10	2	16	0	0	0	1	.000	0	0-0	0	7.71
1991 Chicago	NL	71	0	0	12	101.1	419	73	33	22	7	9	6	0	57	7	92	1	0	6	2	.750	0	3-6	10	1.95
1992 Chicago	NL	72	0	0	30	83.2	369	73	40	33	5	5	5	0	51	10	83	3	0	4	7	.364	0	6-11	3	3.55
1993 Chicago	NL	49	0	0	11	47.1	214	51	30	24	4	5	1	1	25	5	31	3	0	2	2	.500	0	0-0	4	4.56
1994 Cincinnati	NL	52	0	0	13	57.2	230	52	15	15	3	2	0	0	15	2	38	4	0	1	2	.333	0	5-11	10	2.34
1995 Cincinnati	NL	44	0	0	11	40.1	178	46	29	27	5	1	3	1	15	3	27	1	0	3	4	.429	0	0-3	5	6.02
1996 Cin-Cal		52	0	0	12	49	210	45	22	21	4	1	1	2	23	3	45	1	0	7	1	.875	0	0-2	7	3.86
1997 Ana-ChA		61	0	0	16	75	320	73	36	32	5	3	3	2	22	1	62	1	0	1	3	.250	0	1-6	15	3.84
1998 Colorado	NL	78	0	0	27	68.1	281	68	23	22	3	0	3	0	24	0	61	0	0	6	4	.600	0	2-6	19	2.90
1996 Cincinnati	NL	12	0	0	1	12.1	59	13	10	9	2	0	0	0	10	1	13	0	0	2	0	1.000	0	0-0	1	6.57
California	AL	40	0	0	11	36.2	151	32	12	12	2	1	1	2	13	2	32	1	0	5	1	.833	0	0-2	6	2.95
1997 Anaheim	AL	13	0	0	3	15.2	66	17	7	6	2	0	0	0	3	0	18	0	0	0	0	.000	0	0-2	4	3.45
Chicago	AL	48	0	0	13	59.1	254	56	29	26	3	3	3	2	19	1	44	1	0	1	3	.250	0	1-4	11	3.94
10 ML YEARS		506	0	0	144	547	2343	517	243	210	37	26	23	6	246	34	463	14	0	30	26	.536	0	17-45	71	3.46

Joe McEwing

Bats: R **Throws:** R **Pos:** 2B-6; PH/PR-6; LF-1; CF-1; RF-1 **Ht:** 5'10" **Wt:** 170 **Born:** 10/19/72 **Age:** 26

Year Team	Lg	G	AB	H	2B	3B	HR	(Hm	Rd)	TB	R	RBI	TBB	IBB	SO	HBP	SH	SF	SB	CS	SB%	GDP	Avg	OBP	SLG
1992 Cardinals	R	55	211	71	4	2	0	—	—	79	55	13	24	0	18	5	1	1	23	7	.77	1	.336	.415	.374
1993 Savannah	A	138	511	127	35	1	0	—	—	164	94	43	89	0	73	4	15	4	22	9	.71	7	.249	.362	.321
1994 Madison	A	90	346	112	24	2	4	—	—	152	58	47	32	4	53	1	5	3	18	15	.55	5	.324	.380	.439
St. Pete	A+	50	197	49	7	0	1	—	—	59	22	20	19	0	32	1	4	3	8	4	.67	4	.249	.314	.299
1995 St. Pete	A+	75	281	64	13	0	1	—	—	80	33	23	25	3	49	1	6	4	2	3	.40	5	.228	.289	.285
Arkansas	AA	42	121	30	4	0	2	—	—	40	16	12	9	2	13	1	6	0	3	2	.60	4	.248	.305	.331
1996 Arkansas	AA	106	216	45	7	3	2	—	—	64	27	14	13	0	32	0	5	1	2	4	.33	8	.208	.252	.296
1997 Arkansas	AA	103	263	68	6	3	4	—	—	92	33	35	19	4	39	1	3	2	2	4	.33	6	.259	.309	.350
1998 Arkansas	AA	60	223	79	21	4	9	—	—	135	45	46	21	4	18	1	1	2	4	2	.67	2	.354	.409	.605
Memphis	AAA	78	329	110	30	7	6	—	—	172	52	46	21	0	39	3	1	1	11	10	.52	4	.334	.379	.523
1998 St. Louis	NL	10	20	4	1	0	0	(0	0)	5	5	1	1	0	3	1	1	0	0	1	.00	0	.200	.273	.250

Willie McGee

Bats: B **Throws:** R **Pos:** LF-56; PH/PR-45; RF-38; CF-7; DH-3; 1B-1 **Ht:** 6'1" **Wt:** 185 **Born:** 11/2/58 **Age:** 40

Year Team	Lg	G	AB	H	2B	3B	HR	(Hm	Rd)	TB	R	RBI	TBB	IBB	SO	HBP	SH	SF	SB	CS	SB%	GDP	Avg	OBP	SLG
1982 St. Louis	NL	123	422	125	12	8	4	(2	2)	165	43	56	12	2	58	2	2	1	24	12	.67	9	.296	.318	.391
1983 St. Louis	NL	147	601	172	22	8	5	(4	1)	225	75	75	26	2	98	0	1	3	39	8	.83	8	.286	.314	.374
1984 St. Louis	NL	145	571	166	19	11	6	(2	4)	225	82	50	29	2	80	1	0	3	43	10	.81	12	.291	.325	.394
1985 St. Louis	NL	152	612	216	26	18	10	(3	7)	308	114	82	34	2	86	0	1	5	56	16	.78	3	.353	.384	.503
1986 St. Louis	NL	124	497	127	22	7	7	(7	0)	184	65	48	37	7	82	1	0	4	19	16	.54	8	.256	.306	.370
1987 St. Louis	NL	153	620	177	37	11	11	(6	5)	269	76	105	24	5	90	2	1	5	16	4	.80	24	.285	.312	.434
1988 St. Louis	NL	137	562	164	24	6	3	(1	2)	209	73	50	32	5	84	1	2	3	41	6	.87	10	.292	.329	.372
1989 St. Louis	NL	58	199	47	10	2	3	(1	2)	70	23	17	10	0	34	1	0	1	8	6	.57	2	.236	.275	.352
1990 StL-Oak		154	614	199	35	7	3	(1	2)	257	99	77	48	6	104	1	0	1	31	9	.78	13	.324	.373	.419
1991 San Francisco	NL	131	497	155	30	3	4	(2	2)	203	67	43	34	3	74	2	8	2	17	9	.65	11	.312	.357	.408
1992 San Francisco	NL	138	474	141	20	2	1	(0	1)	168	56	36	29	3	88	1	5	1	13	4	.76	7	.297	.339	.354
1993 San Francisco	NL	130	475	143	28	1	4	(0	4)	185	53	46	38	7	67	1	3	2	10	9	.53	12	.301	.353	.389
1994 San Francisco	NL	45	156	44	3	0	5	(2	3)	62	19	23	15	2	24	0	1	4	3	0	1.00	6	.282	.337	.397
1995 Boston	AL	67	200	57	11	3	2	(1	1)	80	32	15	9	0	41	0	5	3	5	2	.71	5	.285	.311	.400
1996 St. Louis	NL	123	309	95	15	2	5	(2	3)	129	52	41	18	2	60	2	1	1	5	2	.71	4	.307	.348	.417
1997 St. Louis	NL	122	300	90	19	4	3	(2	1)	126	29	38	22	2	59	0	0	1	8	2	.80	6	.300	.347	.420
1998 St. Louis	NL	120	269	68	10	1	3	(0	3)	89	27	34	14	5	49	0	0	3	7	2	.78	6	.253	.287	.331
1990 St. Louis	NL	125	501	168	32	5	3	(1	2)	219	76	62	38	6	86	1	0	2	28	9	.76	9	.335	.382	.437
Oakland	AL	29	113	31	3	2	0	(0	0)	38	23	15	10	0	18	0	0	0	3	0	1.00	4	.274	.333	.336
17 ML YEARS		2069	7378	2186	343	94	79	(36	43)	2954	985	836	431	55	1178	15	30	44	345	117	.75	152	.296	.335	.400

Fred McGriff

Bats: Left **Throws:** Left **Pos:** 1B-135; DH-14; PH/PR-3 **Ht:** 6'3" **Wt:** 215 **Born:** 10/31/63 **Age:** 35

Year Team	Lg	G	AB	H	2B	3B	HR	(Hm	Rd)	TB	R	RBI	TBB	IBB	SO	HBP	SH	SF	SB	CS	SB%	GDP	Avg	OBP	SLG
1986 Toronto	AL	3	5	1	0	0	0	(0	0)	1	1	0	0	0	2	0	0	0	0	0	.00	0	.200	.200	.200
1987 Toronto	AL	107	295	73	16	0	20	(7	13)	149	58	43	60	4	104	1	0	0	3	2	.60	3	.247	.376	.505
1988 Toronto	AL	154	536	151	35	4	34	(18	16)	296	100	82	79	3	149	4	0	4	6	1	.86	15	.282	.376	.552
1989 Toronto	AL	161	551	148	27	3	36	(18	18)	289	98	92	119	12	132	4	1	5	7	4	.64	14	.269	.399	.525
1990 Toronto	AL	153	557	167	21	1	35	(14	21)	295	91	88	94	12	108	2	1	4	5	3	.63	7	.300	.400	.530
1991 San Diego	NL	153	528	147	19	1	31	(18	13)	261	84	106	105	26	135	2	0	7	4	1	.80	14	.278	.396	.494
1992 San Diego	NL	152	531	152	30	4	35	(21	14)	295	79	104	96	23	108	1	0	4	8	6	.57	14	.286	.394	.556
1993 SD-Atl	NL	151	557	162	29	2	37	(15	22)	306	111	101	76	6	106	2	0	5	5	3	.63	14	.291	.375	.549
1994 Atlanta	NL	113	424	135	25	1	34	(13	21)	264	81	94	50	8	76	1	0	3	7	3	.70	8	.318	.389	.623
1995 Atlanta	NL	144	528	148	27	1	27	(15	12)	258	85	93	65	6	99	5	0	6	3	6	.33	19	.280	.361	.489
1996 Atlanta	NL	159	617	182	37	1	28	(17	11)	305	81	107	68	12	116	2	0	4	7	3	.70	20	.295	.365	.494
1997 Atlanta	NL	152	564	156	25	1	22	(8	14)	249	77	97	68	4	112	4	0	5	5	0	1.00	22	.277	.356	.441
1998 Tampa Bay	AL	151	564	160	33	0	19	(14	5)	250	73	81	79	9	118	2	0	4	7	2	.78	14	.284	.371	.443
1993 San Diego	NL	83	302	83	11	1	18	(7	11)	150	52	46	42	4	55	1	0	4	4	3	.57	9	.275	.361	.497
Atlanta	NL	68	255	79	18	1	19	(8	11)	156	59	55	34	2	51	1	0	1	1	0	1.00	5	.310	.392	.612
13 ML YEARS		1753	6257	1782	324	19	358	(178	180)	3218	1019	1088	959	125	1365	30	2	51	67	34	.66	164	.285	.380	.514

Ryan McGuire

Bats: L **Throws:** L **Pos:** 1B-78; LF-33; PH/PR-24; RF-8; CF-7 **Ht:** 6'2" **Wt:** 200 **Born:** 11/23/71 **Age:** 27

Year Team	Lg	G	AB	H	2B	3B	HR	(Hm	Rd)	TB	R	RBI	TBB	IBB	SO	HBP	SH	SF	SB	CS	SB%	GDP	Avg	OBP	SLG
1993 Ft. Laud	A+	58	213	69	12	2	4	—	—	97	23	38	27	3	34	2	1	3	2	4	.33	11	.324	.400	.455
1994 Lynchburg	A+	137	489	133	29	0	10	—	—	192	70	73	79	2	77	2	4	7	10	9	.53	19	.272	.371	.393
1995 Trenton	AA	109	414	138	29	1	7	—	—	190	59	59	58	5	51	4	4	4	11	8	.58	10	.333	.414	.459
1996 Ottawa	AAA	134	451	116	21	2	12	—	—	177	62	60	59	4	80	2	1	3	11	4	.73	12	.257	.344	.392
1997 Ottawa	AAA	50	184	55	11	1	3	—	—	77	37	15	36	2	29	0	0	2	5	2	.71	4	.299	.410	.418
1997 Montreal	NL	84	199	51	15	2	3	(2	1)	79	22	17	19	1	34	0	3	1	1	4	.20	3	.256	.320	.397
1998 Montreal	NL	130	210	39	9	0	1	(1	0)	51	17	10	32	0	55	0	1	1	0	0	.00	9	.186	.292	.243
2 ML YEARS		214	409	90	24	2	4	(3	1)	130	39	27	51	1	89	0	4	2	1	4	.20	12	.220	.305	.318

Mark McGwire

Bats: Right **Throws:** Right **Pos:** 1B-151; PH/PR-3   **Ht:** 6'5" **Wt:** 250 **Born:** 10/1/63 **Age:** 35

Year Team	Lg	G	AB	H	2B	3B	HR	(Hm	Rd)	TB	R	RBI	TBB	IBB	SO	HBP	SH	SF	SB	CS	SB%	GDP	Avg	OBP	SLG
1986 Oakland	AL	18	53	10	1	0	3	(1	2)	20	10	9	4	0	18	1	0	0	0	1	.00	0	.189	.259	.377
1987 Oakland	AL	151	557	161	28	4	49	(21	28)	344	97	118	71	8	131	5	0	8	1	1	.50	6	.289	.370	**.618**
1988 Oakland	AL	155	550	143	22	1	32	(12	20)	263	87	99	76	4	117	4	1	4	0	0	.00	15	.260	.352	.478
1989 Oakland	AL	143	490	113	17	0	33	(12	21)	229	74	95	83	5	94	3	0	11	1	1	.50	23	.231	.339	.467
1990 Oakland	AL	156	523	123	16	0	39	(14	25)	256	87	108	**110**	9	116	7	1	9	2	1	.67	13	.235	.370	.489
1991 Oakland	AL	154	483	97	22	0	22	(15	7)	185	62	75	93	3	116	3	1	5	2	1	.67	13	.201	.330	.383
1992 Oakland	AL	139	467	125	22	0	42	(24	18)	273	87	104	90	12	105	5	0	9	0	1	.00	10	.268	.385	**.585**
1993 Oakland	AL	27	84	28	6	0	9	(5	4)	61	16	24	21	5	19	1	0	1	0	1	.00	0	.333	.467	.726
1994 Oakland	AL	47	135	34	3	0	9	(6	3)	64	26	25	37	3	40	0	0	0	0	0	.00	3	.252	.413	.474
1995 Oakland	AL	104	317	87	13	0	39	(15	24)	217	75	90	88	5	77	11	0	6	1	1	.50	9	.274	.441	.685
1996 Oak-StL	AL	130	423	132	21	0	**52**	(24	28)	309	104	113	116	16	112	8	0	1	0	0	.00	14	.312	**.467**	**.730**
1997 Oak-StL		156	540	148	27	0	58	(30	28)	349	86	123	101	16	159	9	0	7	3	0	1.00	9	.274	.393	.646
1998 St. Louis	NL	155	509	152	21	0	**70**	(38	32)	383	130	147	**162**	28	155	6	0	4	0	1	.00	8	.299	**.470**	**.752**
1997 Oakland	AL	105	366	104	24	0	34	(17	17)	230	48	81	58	8	98	4	0	5	1	0	1.00	9	.284	.383	.628
St. Louis	NL	51	174	44	3	0	24	(13	11)	119	38	42	43	8	61	5	0	2	2	0	1.00	0	.253	.411	.684
13 ML YEARS		1535	5131	1353	219	5	457	(217	240)	2953	941	1130	1052	114	1259	63	3	65	11	8	.58	123	.264	.391	.576

Mark McLemore

Bats: Both **Throws:** Right **Pos:** 2B-122; PH/PR-3; DH-2   **Ht:** 5'11" **Wt:** 207 **Born:** 10/4/64 **Age:** 34

Year Team	Lg	G	AB	H	2B	3B	HR	(Hm	Rd)	TB	R	RBI	TBB	IBB	SO	HBP	SH	SF	SB	CS	SB%	GDP	Avg	OBP	SLG
1986 California	AL	5	4	0	0	0	0	(0	0)	0	0	0	1	0	2	0	1	0	0	1	.00	0	.000	.200	.000
1987 California	AL	138	433	102	13	3	3	(3	0)	130	61	41	48	0	72	0	15	3	25	8	.76	7	.236	.310	.300
1988 California	AL	77	233	56	11	2	2	(1	0)	77	38	16	25	0	28	0	5	2	13	7	.65	6	.240	.312	.330
1989 California	AL	32	103	25	3	1	0	(0	0)	30	12	14	7	0	19	1	3	1	6	1	.86	2	.243	.295	.291
1990 Cal-Cle	AL	28	60	9	2	0	0	(0	0)	11	6	2	4	0	15	0	1	0	1	0	1.00	1	.150	.203	.183
1991 Houston	NL	21	61	9	1	0	0	(0	0)	10	6	2	6	0	13	0	0	1	1	0	1.00	1	.148	.221	.164
1992 Baltimore	AL	101	228	56	7	2	0	(0	0)	67	40	27	21	1	26	0	6	1	11	5	.69	6	.246	.308	.294
1993 Baltimore	AL	148	581	165	27	5	4	(2	2)	214	81	72	64	4	92	1	11	6	21	15	.58	21	.284	.353	.368
1994 Baltimore	AL	104	343	88	11	1	3	(2	1)	110	44	29	51	3	50	1	4	1	20	5	.80	7	.257	.354	.321
1995 Texas	AL	129	467	122	20	5	5	(3	2)	167	73	41	59	6	71	3	10	3	21	11	.66	10	.261	.346	.358
1996 Texas	AL	147	517	150	23	4	5	(3	2)	196	84	46	87	5	69	0	2	5	27	10	.73	16	.290	.389	.379
1997 Texas	AL	89	349	91	17	2	1	(0	1)	115	47	25	40	1	54	2	6	2	7	5	.58	5	.261	.338	.330
1998 Texas	AL	126	461	114	15	1	5	(4	1)	146	79	53	89	2	64	2	12	3	12	4	.75	15	.247	.369	.317
1990 California	AL	20	48	7	2	0	0	(0	0)	9	4	2	4	0	9	0	1	0	1	0	1.00	1	.146	.212	.188
Cleveland	AL	8	12	2	0	0	0	(0	0)	2	2	0	0	0	6	0	0	0	0	0	.00	0	.167	.167	.167
13 ML YEARS		1145	3840	987	150	26	28	(18	10)	1273	571	368	502	21	575	10	76	28	164	73	.69	97	.257	.342	.332

Greg McMichael

Pitches: Right **Bats:** Right **Pos:** RP-64   **Ht:** 6'3" **Wt:** 222 **Born:** 12/1/66 **Age:** 32

Year Team	Lg	G	GS	CG	GF	IP	BFP	H	R	ER	HR	SH	SF	HB	TBB	IBB	SO	WP	Bk	W	L	Pct.	ShO	Sv-Op	Hld	ERA
1993 Atlanta	NL	74	0	0	40	91.2	365	68	22	21	3	4	2	0	29	4	89	6	1	2	3	.400	0	19-21	12	2.06
1994 Atlanta	NL	51	0	0	41	58.2	259	66	29	25	1	3	1	0	19	6	47	3	1	4	6	.400	0	21-31	1	3.84
1995 Atlanta	NL	67	0	0	16	80.2	337	64	27	25	8	5	0	0	32	9	74	3	0	7	2	.778	0	2-4	**20**	2.79
1996 Atlanta	NL	73	0	0	14	86.2	366	84	34	31	4	3	3	1	27	7	78	4	1	5	3	.625	0	2-8	18	3.22
1997 New York	NL	73	0	0	23	87.2	355	73	34	29	8	9	4	2	27	6	81	5	0	7	10	.412	0	7-18	19	2.98
1998 NYN-LA	NL	64	0	0	19	68	317	81	39	31	9	6	3	4	35	10	55	6	1	5	4	.556	0	2-7	10	4.10
1998 New York	NL	52	0	0	18	53.2	251	64	31	24	8	3	2	3	29	7	44	5	1	5	3	.625	0	1-4	8	4.02
Los Angeles	NL	12	0	0	1	14.1	66	17	8	7	1	3	1	1	6	3	11	1	0	0	1	.000	0	1-3	2	4.40
6 ML YEARS		402	0	0	153	473.1	1999	436	188	162	33	30	13	7	169	42	424	27	4	30	28	.517	0	53-89	80	3.08

Brian McRae

Bats: Both **Throws:** Right **Pos:** CF-154; PH/PR-10   **Ht:** 6'0" **Wt:** 195 **Born:** 8/27/67 **Age:** 31

Year Team	Lg	G	AB	H	2B	3B	HR	(Hm	Rd)	TB	R	RBI	TBB	IBB	SO	HBP	SH	SF	SB	CS	SB%	GDP	Avg	OBP	SLG
1990 Kansas City	AL	46	168	48	8	3	2	(1	1)	68	21	23	9	0	29	0	3	2	4	3	.57	5	.286	.318	.405
1991 Kansas City	AL	152	629	164	28	9	8	(3	5)	234	86	64	24	1	99	2	3	5	20	11	.65	12	.261	.288	.372
1992 Kansas City	AL	149	533	119	23	5	4	(2	2)	164	63	52	42	1	88	6	7	4	18	5	.78	10	.223	.285	.308
1993 Kansas City	AL	153	627	177	28	9	12	(5	7)	259	78	69	37	1	105	4	14	3	23	14	.62	8	.282	.325	.413
1994 Kansas City	AL	114	436	119	22	6	4	(2	2)	165	71	40	54	3	67	6	6	3	28	8	.78	3	.273	.359	.378
1995 Chicago	NL	137	580	167	38	7	12	(6	6)	255	92	48	47	1	92	7	3	1	27	8	.77	12	.288	.348	.440
1996 Chicago	NL	157	624	172	32	5	17	(9	8)	265	111	66	73	6	84	12	2	5	37	9	.80	11	.276	.360	.425
1997 ChN-NYN	NL	153	562	136	32	7	11	(6	5)	215	86	43	65	2	84	6	4	2	17	10	.63	13	.242	.326	.383
1998 New York	NL	159	552	146	36	5	9	(12	9)	255	79	79	80	3	90	5	3	5	20	11	.65	5	.264	.360	.462
1997 Chicago	NL	108	417	100	27	5	6	(4	3)	155	63	28	52	2	62	4	3	1	14	6	.70	11	.240	.329	.372
New York	NL	45	145	36	5	2	5	(2	3)	60	23	15	13	0	22	2	1	1	3	4	.43	2	.248	.317	.414
9 ML YEARS		1220	4711	1248	247	56	91	(46	45)	1880	687	484	431	18	738	48	45	30	194	79	.71	79	.265	.331	.399

Brian Meadows

Pitches: Right **Bats:** Right **Pos:** SP-31 | **Ht:** 6'4" **Wt:** 200 **Born:** 11/21/75 **Age:** 23

Year Team	Lg	HOW MUCH HE PITCHED						WHAT HE GAVE UP												THE RESULTS						
		G	GS	CG	GF	IP	BFP	H	R	ER	HR	SH	SF	HB	TBB	IBB	SO	WP	Bk	W	L	Pct.	ShO	Sv-Op	Hld	ERA
1994 Marlins	R	8	7	0	0	37	151	34	9	8	1	0	0	1	6	0	33	0	0	3	0	1.000	0	0--	—	1.95
1995 Kane County	A	26	26	1	0	147	646	163	90	69	11	8	4	12	41	0	103	3	2	9	9	.500	1	0--	—	4.22
1996 Brevard Cty	A+	24	23	3	1	146	600	129	73	58	13	3	4	10	25	1	69	4	1	8	7	.533	1	0--	—	3.58
Portland	AA	4	4	1	0	27	108	26	15	13	1	3	1	1	4	0	13	0	0	0	1	.000	0	0--	—	4.33
1997 Portland	AA	29	29	4	0	175.2	763	204	90	90	23	9	2	4	48	4	115	7	1	9	7	.563	0	0--	—	4.61
1998 Florida	NL	31	31	1	0	174.1	772	222	106	101	20	14	4	3	46	3	88	5	1	11	13	.458	0	0-0	0	5.21

Pat Meares

Bats: Right **Throws:** Right **Pos:** SS-149; PH/PR-2 | **Ht:** 6'0" **Wt:** 187 **Born:** 9/6/68 **Age:** 30

Year Team	Lg	BATTING																	BASERUNNING				PERCENTAGES		
		G	AB	H	2B	3B	HR	(Hm	Rd)	TB	R	RBI	TBB	IBB	SO	HBP	SH	SF	SB	CS	SB%	GDP	Avg	OBP	SLG
1993 Minnesota	AL	111	346	87	14	3	0	(0	0)	107	33	33	7	0	52	1	4	3	4	5	.44	11	.251	.266	.309
1994 Minnesota	AL	80	229	61	12	1	2	(0	2)	81	29	24	14	0	50	2	6	3	5	1	.83	3	.266	.310	.354
1995 Minnesota	AL	116	390	105	19	4	12	(3	9)	168	57	49	15	0	68	11	4	5	10	4	.71	17	.269	.311	.431
1996 Minnesota	AL	152	517	138	26	7	8	(3	5)	202	66	67	17	1	90	9	4	7	9	4	.69	19	.267	.298	.391
1997 Minnesota	AL	134	439	121	23	3	10	(5	5)	180	63	60	18	0	86	16	3	7	7	7	.50	9	.276	.323	.410
1998 Minnesota	AL	149	543	141	26	3	9	(2	7)	200	56	70	24	1	86	6	3	5	7	4	.64	12	.260	.296	.368
6 ML YEARS		742	2464	653	120	21	41	(13	28)	938	304	303	95	2	432	45	24	30	42	25	.63	71	.265	.301	.381

Jim Mecir

Pitches: Right **Bats:** Both **Pos:** RP-68 | **Ht:** 6'1" **Wt:** 195 **Born:** 5/16/70 **Age:** 29

Year Team	Lg	HOW MUCH HE PITCHED						WHAT HE GAVE UP												THE RESULTS						
		G	GS	CG	GF	IP	BFP	H	R	ER	HR	SH	SF	HB	TBB	IBB	SO	WP	Bk	W	L	Pct.	ShO	Sv-Op	Hld	ERA
1995 Seattle	AL	2	0	0	1	4.2	21	5	1	0	0	0	0	0	2	0	3	0	0	0	0	.000	0	0-0	0	0.00
1996 New York	AL	26	0	0	10	40.1	185	42	24	23	6	5	4	0	23	4	38	6	0	1	1	.500	0	0-0	0	5.13
1997 New York	AL	25	0	0	11	33.2	142	36	23	22	5	0	1	2	10	1	25	1	0	0	4	.000	0	0-1	1	5.88
1998 Tampa Bay	AL	68	0	0	23	84	343	68	30	29	6	3	2	3	33	5	77	2	0	7	2	.778	0	0-3	14	3.11
4 ML YEARS		121	0	0	45	162.2	691	151	78	74	17	8	7	5	68	10	143	9	0	8	7	.533	0	0-4	15	4.09

Rafael Medina

Pitches: Right **Bats:** Right **Pos:** SP-12 | **Ht:** 6'3" **Wt:** 195 **Born:** 2/15/75 **Age:** 24

Year Team	Lg	HOW MUCH HE PITCHED						WHAT HE GAVE UP												THE RESULTS						
		G	GS	CG	GF	IP	BFP	H	R	ER	HR	SH	SF	HB	TBB	IBB	SO	WP	Bk	W	L	Pct.	ShO	Sv-Op	Hld	ERA
1993 Yankees	R	5	5	0	0	27.1	107	16	6	2	0	1	1	1	12	0	21	1	1	2	0	1.000	0	0--	—	0.66
1994 Oneonta	A-	14	14	1	0	73.1	316	67	54	38	7	2	5	1	35	0	59	7	3	3	7	.300	0	0--	—	4.66
1995 Greensboro	A	19	19	1	0	98.2	418	86	48	44	8	0	5	6	38	0	108	6	3	4	4	.500	0	0--	—	4.01
Tampa	A+	6	6	0	0	30.1	131	29	12	8	0	0	0	1	12	0	25	0	2	2	2	.500	0	0--	—	2.37
1996 Norwich	AA	19	19	1	0	103	446	78	48	35	7	5	1	6	55	2	112	11	4	5	8	.385	0	0--	—	3.06
1997 Rancho Cuca	A+	3	3	0	0	18	68	13	4	4	1	1	0	0	5	0	14	1	0	2	0	1.000	0	0--	—	2.00
Las Vegas	AAA	13	13	0	0	66.2	322	90	60	56	12	1	2	3	39	1	50	8	2	4	5	.444	0	0--	—	7.56
1998 Charlotte	AAA	11	9	3	1	57.2	245	53	27	25	8	0	2	2	26	1	41	4	1	4	2	.667	1	0--	—	3.90
1998 Florida	NL	12	12	0	0	67.1	327	76	50	45	8	5	4	3	52	3	49	5	0	2	6	.250	0	0-0	0	6.01

Mitch Meluskey

Bats: Both **Throws:** Right **Pos:** PH/PR-6; C-3 | **Ht:** 6'0" **Wt:** 185 **Born:** 9/18/73 **Age:** 25

Year Team	Lg	BATTING																	BASERUNNING				PERCENTAGES		
		G	AB	H	2B	3B	HR	(Hm	Rd)	TB	R	RBI	TBB	IBB	SO	HBP	SH	SF	SB	CS	SB%	GDP	Avg	OBP	SLG
1992 Burlington	R+	43	126	29	7	0	3	—	—	45	23	16	29	0	36	0	0	2	3	0	1.00	0	.230	.369	.357
1993 Columbus	A	101	342	84	18	3	3	—	—	117	36	47	35	4	69	4	4	7	1	1	.50	5	.246	.317	.342
1994 Kinston	A+	100	319	77	16	1	3	—	—	104	36	41	49	0	62	2	2	4	3	4	.43	4	.241	.342	.326
1995 Kinston	A+	8	29	7	5	0	0	—	—	12	5	2	2	0	9	0	0	0	0	0	.00	1	.241	.290	.414
Kissimmee	A+	78	261	56	18	0	1	—	—	85	23	31	27	2	33	1	2	4	3	1	.00	12	.215	.287	.326
1996 Kissimmee	A+	74	231	77	19	0	1	—	—	99	29	31	29	5	26	1	1	5	1	1	.50	9	.333	.402	.429
Jackson	AA	38	134	42	11	0	0	—	—	53	18	21	18	0	24	1	1	1	0	0	.00	6	.313	.396	.396
1997 Jackson	AA	73	241	82	18	0	14	—	—	142	49	46	31	4	39	3	0	3	1	3	.25	7	.340	.417	.589
New Orleans	AA	51	172	43	7	0	3	—	—	59	22	21	25	1	38	1	0	1	0	0	.00	4	.250	.347	.343
1998 New Orleans	AAA	121	397	140	41	0	17	—	—	232	76	71	85	10	59	3	0	5	2	0	1.00	15	.353	.465	.584
1998 Houston	NL	8	8	2	1	0	0	(0	0)	3	1	0	1	0	4	0	0	0	0	0	.00	1	.250	.333	.375

Ramiro Mendoza

Pitches: Right **Bats:** Right **Pos:** RP-27; SP-14 | **Ht:** 6'2" **Wt:** 154 **Born:** 6/15/72 **Age:** 27

Year Team	Lg	HOW MUCH HE PITCHED						WHAT HE GAVE UP												THE RESULTS						
		G	GS	CG	GF	IP	BFP	H	R	ER	HR	SH	SF	HB	TBB	IBB	SO	WP	Bk	W	L	Pct.	ShO	Sv-Op	Hld	ERA
1996 New York	AL	12	11	0	0	53	249	80	43	40	5	1	4	1	10	1	34	2	1	4	5	.444	0	0-0	0	6.79
1997 New York	AL	39	15	0	9	133.2	578	157	67	63	15	3	5	5	28	2	82	2	1	8	6	.571	0	2-4	4	4.24
1998 New York	AL	41	14	1	6	130.1	548	131	50	47	9	6	7	9	30	6	56	3	0	10	2	.833	1	1-4	5	3.25
3 ML YEARS		92	40	1	15	317	1375	368	160	150	29	10	13	18	68	9	172	7	2	22	13	.629	1	3-8	9	4.26

Orlando Merced

Bats: L Throws: R Pos: 1B-38; PH/PR-23; RF-14; DH-9; LF-4   Ht: 6'1" Wt: 195 Born: 11/2/66 Age: 32

Year Team	Lg	G	AB	H	2B	3B	HR	(Hm	Rd)	TB	R	RBI	TBB	IBB	SO	HBP	SH	SF	SB	CS	SB%	GDP	Avg	OBP	SLG
1990 Pittsburgh	NL	25	24	5	1	0	0	(0	0)	6	3	0	1	0	9	0	0	0	0	0	.00	1	.208	.240	.250
1991 Pittsburgh	NL	120	411	113	17	2	10	(5	5)	164	83	50	64	4	81	1	1	1	8	4	.67	6	.275	.373	.399
1992 Pittsburgh	NL	134	405	100	28	5	6	(4	2)	156	50	60	52	8	63	2	1	5	5	4	.56	6	.247	.332	.385
1993 Pittsburgh	NL	137	447	140	26	4	8	(3	5)	198	68	70	77	10	64	1	0	2	3	3	.50	9	.313	.414	.443
1994 Pittsburgh	NL	108	386	105	21	3	9	(4	5)	159	48	51	42	5	58	1	0	2	4	1	.80	17	.272	.343	.412
1995 Pittsburgh	NL	132	487	146	29	4	15	(8	7)	228	75	83	52	9	74	1	0	5	7	2	.78	9	.300	.365	.468
1996 Pittsburgh	NL	120	453	130	24	1	17	(9	8)	207	69	80	51	5	74	0	0	3	8	4	.67	9	.287	.357	.457
1997 Toronto	AL	98	368	98	23	2	9	(3	6)	152	45	40	47	1	62	3	0	2	7	3	.70	6	.266	.352	.413
1998 Min-Bos-ChN		84	223	62	12	0	6	(4	2)	92	24	40	20	3	34	1	0	3	1	4	.20	6	.278	.336	.413
1998 Minnesota	AL	63	204	59	12	0	5	(3	2)	86	22	33	17	3	29	1	0	1	1	4	.20	4	.289	.345	.422
Boston	AL	9	9	0	0	0	0	(0	0)	0	0	2	2	0	3	0	0	0	0	0	.00	0	.000	.167	.000
Chicago	NL	12	10	3	0	0	1	(1	0)	6	2	5	1	0	2	0	0	1	0	0	.00	2	.300	.333	.600
9 ML YEARS		958	3204	899	181	21	80	(40	40)	1362	465	474	406	45	519	10	2	23	43	25	.63	69	.281	.361	.425

Jose Mercedes

Pitches: Right Bats: Right Pos: SP-5; RP-2   Ht: 6'1" Wt: 208 Born: 3/5/71 Age: 28

Year Team	Lg	G	GS	CG	GF	IP	BFP	H	R	ER	HR	SH	SF	HB	TBB	IBB	SO	WP	Bk	W	L	Pct.	ShO	Sv-Op	Hld	ERA
1998 El Paso *	AA	1	1	0	0	3.1	18	9	4	4	2	0	1	0	0	0	0	0	0	0	0	.000	0	0- -	—	10.80
1994 Milwaukee	AL	19	0	0	5	31	120	22	9	8	4	0	0	2	16	1	11	0	1	2	0	1.000	0	0-1	3	2.32
1995 Milwaukee	AL	5	0	0	0	7.1	42	12	9	8	1	0	2	0	8	0	6	1	0	0	1	.000	0	0-2	1	9.82
1996 Milwaukee	AL	11	0	0	4	16.2	74	20	18	17	6	0	1	0	5	0	6	2	0	0	2	.000	0	0-1	2	9.18
1997 Milwaukee	AL	29	23	2	1	159	653	146	76	67	24	3	4	5	53	2	80	1	1	7	10	.412	1	0-0	1	3.79
1998 Milwaukee	NL	7	5	0	0	32	146	42	25	24	5	1	2	1	9	1	11	0	0	2	2	.500	0	0-0	0	6.75
5 ML YEARS		71	28	2	10	246	1035	242	137	124	40	4	9	8	91	4	114	4	2	11	15	.423	1	0-4	7	4.54

Kent Mercker

Pitches: Left Bats: Left Pos: SP-29; RP-1   Ht: 6'2" Wt: 195 Born: 2/1/68 Age: 31

Year Team	Lg	G	GS	CG	GF	IP	BFP	H	R	ER	HR	SH	SF	HB	TBB	IBB	SO	WP	Bk	W	L	Pct.	ShO	Sv-Op	Hld	ERA
1989 Atlanta	NL	2	1	0	1	4.1	26	8	6	6	0	0	0	0	6	0	4	0	0	0	0	.000	0	0-0	0	12.46
1990 Atlanta	NL	36	0	0	28	48.1	211	43	22	17	6	1	2	2	24	3	39	2	0	4	7	.364	0	7-10	0	3.17
1991 Atlanta	NL	50	4	0	28	73.1	306	56	23	21	5	2	2	1	35	3	62	4	1	5	3	.625	0	6-8	3	2.58
1992 Atlanta	NL	53	0	0	18	68.1	289	51	27	26	4	4	1	3	35	1	49	6	0	3	2	.600	0	6-9	6	3.42
1993 Atlanta	NL	43	6	0	9	66	283	52	24	21	2	0	0	2	36	3	59	5	1	3	1	.750	0	0-3	4	2.86
1994 Atlanta	NL	20	17	2	0	112.1	461	90	46	43	16	4	3	0	45	3	111	4	1	9	4	.692	1	0-0	0	3.45
1995 Atlanta	NL	29	26	0	1	143	622	140	73	66	16	8	7	3	61	2	102	6	2	7	8	.467	0	0-0	0	4.15
1996 Bal-Cle	AL	24	12	0	2	69.2	329	83	60	54	13	3	6	3	38	2	29	3	1	4	6	.400	0	0-0	0	6.98
1997 Cincinnati	NL	28	25	0	0	144.2	616	135	65	63	16	8	4	2	62	6	75	2	1	8	11	.421	0	0-0	0	3.92
1998 St. Louis	NL	30	29	0	1	161.2	716	199	99	91	11	10	9	3	53	4	72	6	4	11	11	.500	0	0-0	0	5.07
1996 Baltimore	AL	14	12	0	0	58	283	73	56	50	12	3	4	3	35	1	22	3	1	3	6	.333	0	0-0	0	7.76
Cleveland	AL	10	0	0	2	11.2	46	10	4	4	1	0	2	0	3	1	7	0	0	1	0	1.000	0	0-0	2	3.09
10 ML YEARS		315	120	2	88	891.2	3859	857	445	408	89	40	34	19	395	27	602	38	11	54	53	.505	1	19-30	15	4.12

Lou Merloni

Bats: R Throws: R Pos: 2B-32; 3B-5; PH/PR-2; SS-1   Ht: 5'10" Wt: 194 Born: 4/6/71 Age: 28

Year Team	Lg	G	AB	H	2B	3B	HR	(Hm	Rd)	TB	R	RBI	TBB	IBB	SO	HBP	SH	SF	SB	CS	SB%	GDP	Avg	OBP	SLG
1993 Red Sox	R	4	14	5	1	0	0	—	—	6	4	1	1	0	1	1	0	0	1	1	.50	0	.357	.438	.429
Ft. Laud	A+	44	156	38	1	1	2	—	—	47	14	21	13	1	26	1	0	4	1	1	.50	6	.244	.299	.301
1994 Sarasota	A+	113	419	120	16	2	1	—	—	143	59	63	36	4	57	7	7	10	5	2	.71	11	.286	.345	.341
1995 Trenton	AA	93	318	88	16	1	1	—	—	109	42	30	39	3	50	11	11	2	7	7	.50	1	.277	.373	.343
1996 Trenton	AA	28	95	22	6	1	3	—	—	39	11	16	9	1	18	5	1	0	0	2	.00	2	.232	.330	.411
Red Sox	R	1	4	1	0	0	0	—	—	1	1	1	0	0	0	0	0	0	0	0	.00	0	.250	.200	.250
Pawtucket	AAA	38	115	29	6	0	1	—	—	38	19	12	10	0	20	3	4	0	1	0	1.00	1	.252	.328	.330
1997 Trenton	AA	69	255	79	17	4	5	—	—	119	49	37	30	1	43	12	1	4	3	2	.60	2	.310	.402	.467
Pawtucket	AAA	49	165	49	10	0	5	—	—	74	24	24	15	2	20	4	1	1	0	2	.00	4	.297	.368	.448
1998 Pawtucket	AAA	27	88	34	3	1	8	—	—	63	17	22	16	0	13	8	1	0	2	2	.50	2	.386	.518	.716
Red Sox	R	1	1	0	0	0	0	—	—	0	0	0	0	0	0	0	0	0	0	0	.00	0	.000	.000	.000
1998 Boston	AL	39	96	27	6	0	1	(1	0)	36	10	15	7	1	20	2	1	0	1	0	1.00	1	.281	.343	.375

Jose Mesa

Pitches: Right Bats: Right Pos: RP-76   Ht: 6'3" Wt: 225 Born: 5/22/66 Age: 33

Year Team	Lg	G	GS	CG	GF	IP	BFP	H	R	ER	HR	SH	SF	HB	TBB	IBB	SO	WP	Bk	W	L	Pct.	ShO	Sv-Op	Hld	ERA
1987 Baltimore	AL	6	5	0	0	31.1	143	38	23	21	7	0	0	0	15	0	17	4	0	1	3	.250	0	0-0	1	6.03
1990 Baltimore	AL	7	7	0	0	46.2	202	37	20	20	2	2	2	1	27	2	24	1	1	3	2	.600	0	0-0	0	3.86
1991 Baltimore	AL	23	23	2	0	123.2	566	151	86	82	11	5	4	3	62	2	64	3	0	6	11	.353	1	0-0	0	5.97
1992 Bal-Cle	AL	28	23	1	1	160.2	700	169	86	82	14	2	5	4	70	1	62	2	0	7	12	.368	1	0-0	0	4.59
1993 Cleveland	AL	34	33	3	0	208.2	897	232	122	114	21	9	9	7	62	2	118	8	2	10	12	.455	0	0-0	0	4.92

Year Team	Lg	HOW MUCH HE PITCHED						WHAT HE GAVE UP												THE RESULTS						
		G	GS	CG	GF	IP	BFP	H	R	ER	HR	SH	SF	HB	TBB	IBB	SO	WP	Bk	W	L	Pct.	ShO	Sv-Op	Hld	ERA
1994 Cleveland	AL	51	0	0	22	73	315	71	33	31	3	3	4	3	26	7	63	3	0	7	5	.583	0	2-6	8	3.82
1995 Cleveland	AL	62	0	0	57	64	250	49	9	8	3	4	2	0	17	2	58	5	0	3	0	1.000	0	46-48	0	1.13
1996 Cleveland	AL	69	0	0	60	72.1	304	69	32	30	6	2	2	3	28	4	64	4	0	2	7	.222	0	39-44	0	3.73
1997 Cleveland	AL	66	0	0	38	82.1	356	83	28	22	7	2	2	3	28	3	69	1	0	4	4	.500	0	16-21	9	2.40
1998 Cle-SF		76	0	0	36	84.2	383	91	50	43	8	6	2	4	38	5	63	10	0	8	7	.533	0	1-4	13	4.57
1992 Baltimore	AL	13	12	0	1	67.2	300	77	41	39	9	0	3	2	27	1	22	2	0	3	8	.273	0	0-0	0	5.19
Cleveland	AL	15	15	1	0	93	400	92	45	43	5	2	2	2	43	0	40	0	0	4	4	.500	1	0-0	0	4.16
1998 Cleveland	AL	44	0	0	18	54	244	61	36	31	7	2	2	4	20	3	35	2	0	3	4	.429	0	1-3	7	5.17
San Francisco	NL	32	0	0	18	30.2	139	30	14	12	1	4	0	0	18	2	28	8	0	5	3	.625	0	0-1	6	3.52
10 ML YEARS		422	95	6	214	947.1	4116	990	489	453	82	35	32	28	373	28	602	41	3	51	63	.447	2	104-123	31	4.30

Mike Metcalfe

Bats: Right **Throws:** Right **Pos:** PH/PR-4; 2B-1   **Ht:** 5'10" **Wt:** 175 **Born:** 1/2/73 **Age:** 26

Year Team	Lg	BATTING									TB	R	RBI	TBB	IBB	SO	HBP	SH	SF	BASERUNNING				PERCENTAGES		
		G	AB	H	2B	3B	HR	(Hm	Rd)											SB	CS	SB%	GDP	Avg	OBP	SLG
1994 Bakersfield	A+	69	275	78	10	0	0	—	—	88	44	18	28	0	34	1	4	2	41	13	.76	6	.284	.350	.320
1995 San Antonio	AA	10	41	10	1	0	0	—	—	11	10	2	7	0	2	0	1	1	1	2	.33	0	.244	.347	.268
Vero Beach	A+	120	435	131	13	3	3	—	—	159	86	35	60	2	37	3	6	5	60	27	.69	8	.301	.386	.366
1996 Vero Beach	A+	2	5	0	0	0	0	—	—	0	0	0	0	0	0	0	0	0	0	0	.00	0	.000	.000	.000
1997 San Berndno	A+	132	519	147	28	7	3	—	—	198	83	47	55	0	79	4	6	1	67	32	.68	5	.283	.356	.382
1998 San Antonio	AA	57	213	60	5	5	3	—	—	84	35	19	30	1	24	1	3	2	19	15	.56	3	.282	.370	.394
1998 Los Angeles	NL	4	1	0	0	0	0	(0	0)	0	0	0	0	0	1	0	0	0	2	0	1.00	0	.000	.000	.000

Hensley Meulens

Bats: Right **Throws:** Right **Pos:** RF-4; PH/PR-3   **Ht:** 6'3" **Wt:** 210 **Born:** 6/23/67 **Age:** 32

Year Team	Lg	BATTING								TB	R	RBI	TBB	IBB	SO	HBP	SH	SF	BASERUNNING				PERCENTAGES		
		G	AB	H	2B	3B	HR	(Hm	Rd)											SB	CS	SB%	GDP	Avg	OBP	SLG
1998 Tucson *	AAA	76	268	67	16	2	13	—	—	126	45	37	30	0	67	2	0	3	2	1	.67	12	.250	.327	.470
Calgary *	AAA	2	8	3	1	0	2	—	—	10	3	3	0	0	2	0	0	0	0	0	.00	1	.375	.375	1.250
1989 New York	AL	8	28	5	0	0	0	(0	0)	5	2	1	2	0	8	0	0	0	0	1	.00	0	.179	.233	.179
1990 New York	AL	23	83	20	7	0	3	(2	1)	36	12	10	9	0	25	3	0	0	1	0	1.00	3	.241	.337	.434
1991 New York	AL	96	288	64	8	1	6	(4	2)	92	37	29	18	1	97	4	1	2	3	0	1.00	7	.222	.276	.319
1992 New York	AL	2	5	3	0	0	0	(1	0)	6	1	1	1	0	0	0	0	0	0	0	.00	1	.600	.667	1.200
1993 New York	AL	30	53	9	1	1	2	(1	1)	18	8	5	8	0	19	0	0	0	0	1	.00	2	.170	.279	.340
1997 Montreal	NL	16	24	7	1	0	2	(1	1)	14	6	6	4	0	10	0	0	1	0	1	.00	0	.292	.379	.583
1998 Arizona	NL	7	15	1	0	0	0	(0	1)	4	1	1	0	0	6	0	0	0	0	1	.00	0	.067	.067	.267
7 ML YEARS		182	496	109	17	2	15	(9	6)	175	67	53	42	1	165	7	1	3	4	3	.57	15	.220	.288	.353

Dan Miceli

Pitches: Right **Bats:** Right **Pos:** RP-67   **Ht:** 6'0" **Wt:** 216 **Born:** 9/9/70 **Age:** 28

Year Team	Lg	HOW MUCH HE PITCHED						WHAT HE GAVE UP												THE RESULTS						
		G	GS	CG	GF	IP	BFP	H	R	ER	HR	SH	SF	HB	TBB	IBB	SO	WP	Bk	W	L	Pct.	ShO	Sv-Op	Hld	ERA
1993 Pittsburgh	NL	9	0	0	1	5.1	25	6	3	3	0	0	0	0	3	0	4	0	1	0	0	.000	0	0-0	0	5.06
1994 Pittsburgh	NL	28	0	0	9	27.1	121	28	19	18	5	1	2	2	11	2	27	2	0	2	1	.667	0	2-3	4	5.93
1995 Pittsburgh	NL	58	0	0	51	58	264	61	30	30	7	2	4	4	28	5	56	4	0	4	4	.500	0	21-27	2	4.66
1996 Pittsburgh	NL	44	9	0	17	85.2	398	99	65	55	15	3	7	3	45	5	66	9	0	2	10	.167	0	1-1	4	5.78
1997 Detroit	AL	71	0	0	24	82.2	357	77	49	46	13	5	3	1	38	4	79	3	0	3	2	.600	0	3-8	11	5.01
1998 San Diego	NL	67	0	0	18	72.2	302	64	28	26	6	3	2	1	27	4	70	5	1	10	5	.667	0	2-8	20	3.22
6 ML YEARS		277	9	0	120	331.2	1467	335	194	178	46	14	18	11	152	20	302	23	2	21	22	.488	0	29-47	41	4.83

Chris Michalak

Pitches: Left **Bats:** Left **Pos:** RP-5   **Ht:** 6'2" **Wt:** 195 **Born:** 1/4/71 **Age:** 28

Year Team	Lg	HOW MUCH HE PITCHED						WHAT HE GAVE UP												THE RESULTS						
		G	GS	CG	GF	IP	BFP	H	R	ER	HR	SH	SF	HB	TBB	IBB	SO	WP	Bk	W	L	Pct.	ShO	Sv-Op	Hld	ERA
1993 Sou. Oregon	A-	16	15	0	0	79	346	77	41	25	2	2	5	6	36	0	57	4	3	7	3	.700	0	0-—	—	2.85
1994 W Michigan	A	15	10	0	2	67	291	66	32	29	3	4	2	8	28	0	38	2	3	5	3	.625	0	0-—	—	3.90
Modesto	A+	17	10	1	3	77.1	310	67	28	25	13	2	3	3	20	1	46	4	3	5	3	.625	0	2-—	—	2.91
1995 Huntsville	AA	7	0	0	4	5.2	32	10	7	7	1	1	0	1	5	0	4	2	0	1	1	.500	0	1-—	—	11.12
Modesto	A+	44	0	0	16	65.1	266	56	26	19	3	4	3	4	27	1	49	2	1	3	2	.600	0	2-—	—	2.62
1996 Modesto	A+	21	0	0	13	38.2	173	37	21	13	4	0	2	2	17	0	39	0	2	2	2	.500	0	4-—	—	3.03
Huntsville	AA	21	0	0	4	23.1	123	32	29	20	2	1	1	1	26	4	15	4	0	4	0	1.000	0	0-—	—	7.71
1997 High Desert	A+	49	0	0	17	85	362	76	36	25	4	3	0	9	31	1	74	6	1	3	7	.300	0	4-—	—	2.65
1998 Tulsa	AA	10	0	0	3	19.2	73	10	4	4	2	2	0	2	2	0	15	0	2	1	2	.333	0	1-—	—	1.83
Tucson	AAA	29	9	0	6	73.1	326	91	47	41	11	2	5	4	29	3	50	4	3	3	8	.273	0	0-—	—	5.03
1998 Arizona	NL	5	0	0	2	5.1	29	9	7	7	1	0	1	0	4	0	5	0	0	0	0	.000	0	0-0	—	11.81

Doug Mientkiewicz

Bats: Left **Throws:** Right **Pos:** 1B-8; PH/PR-1   **Ht:** 6'2" **Wt:** 193 **Born:** 6/19/74 **Age:** 25

Year Team	Lg	BATTING								TB	R	RBI	TBB	IBB	SO	HBP	SH	SF	BASERUNNING				PERCENTAGES		
		G	AB	H	2B	3B	HR	(Hm	Rd)											SB	CS	SB%	GDP	Avg	OBP	SLG
1995 Fort Myers	A+	38	110	27	6	1	1	—	—	38	9	15	18	1	19	1	2	0	2	2	.50	1	.245	.357	.345
1996 Fort Myers	A+	133	492	143	36	4	5	—	—	202	69	79	66	3	47	3	1	6	12	2	.86	10	.291	.374	.411

Year Team	Lg	G	AB	H	2B	3B	HR	(Hm	Rd)	TB	R	RBI	TBB	IBB	SO	HBP	SH	SF	SB	CS	SB%	GDP	Avg	OBP	SLG
1997 New Britain	AA	132	467	119	28	2	15	—	—	196	87	61	98	2	67	7	5	2	21	8	.72	8	.255	.390	.420
1998 New Britain	AA	139	502	162	45	0	16	—	—	255	96	88	96	7	58	6	0	7	11	4	.73	6	.323	.432	.508
1998 Minnesota	AL	8	25	5	1	0	0	(0	0)	6	1	2	4	0	3	0	0	0	1	1	.50	0	.200	.310	.240

Matt Mieske

Bats: R **Throws:** R **Pos:** LF-50; PH/PR-36; RF-12; CF-3 **Ht:** 6'0" **Wt:** 195 **Born:** 2/13/68 **Age:** 31

Year Team	Lg	G	AB	H	2B	3B	HR	(Hm	Rd)	TB	R	RBI	TBB	IBB	SO	HBP	SH	SF	SB	CS	SB%	GDP	Avg	OBP	SLG
1998 Iowa *	AAA	35	106	27	5	0	7	—	—	53	17	19	10	0	27	3	0	1	0	0	.00	6	.255	.333	.500
1993 Milwaukee	AL	23	58	14	0	0	3	(1	2)	23	9	7	4	0	14	0	1	0	2	2	.00	1	.241	.290	.397
1994 Milwaukee	AL	84	259	67	13	1	10	(7	3)	112	39	38	21	0	62	3	2	1	3	5	.38	6	.259	.320	.432
1995 Milwaukee	AL	117	267	67	13	1	12	(3	9)	118	42	48	27	0	45	4	0	-5	2	4	.33	8	.251	.323	.442
1996 Milwaukee	AL	127	374	104	24	3	14	(9	5)	176	46	64	26	2	76	2	1	6	1	5	.17	9	.278	.324	.471
1997 Milwaukee	AL	84	253	63	15	3	5	(1	4)	99	39	21	19	2	50	0	0	1	1	0	1.00	12	.249	.300	.391
1998 Chicago	NL	77	97	29	7	0	1	(1	0)	39	16	12	11	1	17	1	1	1	0	0	.00	1	.299	.373	.402
6 ML YEARS		512	1308	344	72	8	45	(22	23)	567	191	190	108	5	264	10	5	14	7	16	.30	37	.263	.321	.433

Kevin Millar

Bats: Right **Throws:** Right **Pos:** 3B-2; PH/PR-1 **Ht:** 6'0" **Wt:** 185 **Born:** 9/24/71 **Age:** 27

Year Team	Lg	G	AB	H	2B	3B	HR	(Hm	Rd)	TB	R	RBI	TBB	IBB	SO	HBP	SH	SF	SB	CS	SB%	GDP	Avg	OBP	SLG
1994 Kane County	A	135	477	144	35	2	19	—	—	240	75	93	74	2	88	13	0	6	3	3	.50	12	.302	.405	.503
1995 Brevard Cty	A+	129	459	132	32	2	13	—	—	207	53	68	70	2	66	12	0	10	4	4	.50	8	.288	.388	.451
1996 Portland	AA	130	472	150	32	0	18	—	—	236	69	86	37	4	53	9	0	5	6	5	.55	13	.318	.375	.500
1997 Portland	AA	135	511	175	34	2	32	—	—	309	94	131	66	9	53	10	0	7	2	3	.40	11	.342	.423	.605
1998 Charlotte	AAA	14	46	15	3	0	4	—	—	30	14	15	9	0	7	2	0	1	1	0	1.00	3	.326	.448	.652
1998 Florida	NL	2	2	1	0	0	0	(0	0)	1	1	0	1	0	0	0	0	0	0	0	.00	0	.500	.667	.500

Damian Miller

Bats: R **Throws:** R **Pos:** C-46; PH/PR-12; DH-2; RF-2; 1B-1 **Ht:** 6'2" **Wt:** 190 **Born:** 10/13/69 **Age:** 29

Year Team	Lg	G	AB	H	2B	3B	HR	(Hm	Rd)	TB	R	RBI	TBB	IBB	SO	HBP	SH	SF	SB	CS	SB%	GDP	Avg	OBP	SLG
1990 Elizabethtn	R+	14	45	10	1	0	1	—	—	14	7	6	9	0	3	0	0	0	1	0	1.00	2	.222	.352	.311
1991 Kenosha	A	80	267	62	11	1	3	—	—	84	28	34	24	1	53	2	2	3	3	2	.60	4	.232	.297	.315
1992 Kenosha	A	115	377	110	27	2	5	—	—	156	53	56	53	1	66	7	2	4	6	1	.86	13	.292	.385	.414
1993 Fort Myers	A+	87	325	69	12	1	1	—	—	86	31	26	31	0	44	0	1	0	6	3	.67	5	.212	.281	.265
Nashville	AA	4	13	3	0	0	0	—	—	3	0	0	2	0	4	0	0	0	0	0	.00	0	.231	.333	.231
1994 Nashville	AA	103	328	88	10	0	8	—	—	122	36	35	35	2	51	1	2	5	4	6	.40	11	.268	.336	.372
1995 Salt Lake	AAA	83	295	84	23	1	3	—	—	118	39	41	15	1	39	3	5	2	2	4	.33	4	.285	.324	.400
1996 Salt Lake	AAA	104	385	110	27	1	7	—	—	160	54	55	25	2	58	6	2	4	1	4	.20	13	.286	.336	.416
1997 Salt Lake	AAA	85	314	106	19	3	11	—	—	164	48	82	29	0	62	3	1	3	6	1	.86	7	.338	.395	.522
1998 Tucson	AAA	18	63	22	7	1	0	—	—	31	14	11	9	1	9	2	0	2	0	0	.00	2	.349	.434	.492
1997 Minnesota	AL	25	66	18	1	0	2	(1	1)	25	5	13	2	0	12	0	0	3	0	0	.00	2	.273	.282	.379
1998 Arizona	NL	57	168	48	14	2	3	(2	1)	75	17	14	11	2	43	2	2	0	1	0	1.00	2	.286	.337	.446
2 ML YEARS		82	234	66	15	2	5	(3	2)	100	22	27	13	2	55	2	2	3	1	0	1.00	4	.282	.321	.427

Kurt Miller

Pitches: Right **Bats:** Right **Pos:** RP-3 **Ht:** 6'5" **Wt:** 220 **Born:** 8/24/72 **Age:** 26

Year Team	Lg	G	GS	CG	GF	IP	BFP	H	R	ER	HR	SH	SF	HB	TBB	IBB	SO	WP	Bk	W	L	Pct.	ShO	Sv-Op	Hld	ERA
1998 Iowa *	AAA	28	27	2	0	167.2	711	153	77	71	13	4	5	3	77	0	145	6	0	14	3	.824	0	0--	—	3.81
1994 Florida	NL	4	4	0	0	20	92	26	18	18	3	0	1	2	7	0	11	0	0	1	3	.250	0	0-0	0	8.10
1996 Florida	NL	26	5	0	6	46.1	222	57	41	35	5	4	1	2	33	8	30	1	1	1	3	.250	0	0-2	0	6.80
1997 Florida	NL	7	0	0	1	7.1	41	12	8	8	2	0	0	1	7	0	7	0	0	0	1	.000	0	0-0	0	9.82
1998 Chicago	NL	3	0	0	1	4	15	3	0	0	0	0	0	0	0	0	6	0	0	0	0	.000	0	0-0	0	0.00
4 ML YEARS		40	9	0	8	77.2	370	98	67	61	10	4	2	5	47	8	54	1	1	2	7	.222	0	0-2	0	7.07

Travis Miller

Pitches: Left **Bats:** Right **Pos:** RP-14 **Ht:** 6'3" **Wt:** 209 **Born:** 11/2/72 **Age:** 26

Year Team	Lg	G	GS	CG	GF	IP	BFP	H	R	ER	HR	SH	SF	HB	TBB	IBB	SO	WP	Bk	W	L	Pct.	ShO	Sv-Op	Hld	ERA
1998 Salt Lake *	AAA	34	2	0	15	57.2	262	60	33	31	3	3	2	1	31	1	65	4	0	3	4	.429	0	9--	—	4.84
1996 Minnesota	AL	7	7	0	0	26.1	126	45	29	27	7	1	0	0	9	0	15	0	0	1	2	.333	0	0-0	0	9.23
1997 Minnesota	AL	13	7	0	0	48.1	227	64	49	41	8	1	2	1	23	2	26	5	0	1	5	.167	0	0-0	0	7.63
1998 Minnesota	AL	14	0	0	2	23.1	104	25	10	10	0	0	1	0	11	1	23	2	0	0	2	.000	0	0-0	0	3.86
3 ML YEARS		34	14	0	3	98	457	134	88	78	15	2	3	1	43	3	64	7	0	2	9	.182	0	0-0	0	7.16

Trever Miller

Pitches: Left **Bats:** Right **Pos:** RP-36; SP-1   **Ht:** 6'4" **Wt:** 195 **Born:** 5/29/73 **Age:** 26

Year Team	Lg	G	GS	CG	GF	IP	BFP	H	R	ER	HR	SH	SF	HB	TBB	IBB	SO	WP	Bk	W	L	Pct.	ShO	Sv-Op	Hld	ERA
1991 Bristol	R+	13	13	0	0	54	253	60	44	34	7	3	3	2	29	0	46	9	1	2	7	.222	0	0--	—	5.67
1992 Bristol	R+	12	12	1	0	69.1	311	75	45	38	4	3	3	1	27	0	64	4	1	3	8	.273	0	0--	—	4.93
1993 Fayetteville	A	28	28	2	0	161	699	151	99	75	7	2	8	5	67	0	116	10	0	8	13	.381	0	0--	—	4.19
1994 Trenton	AA	26	26	6	0	174.1	754	198	95	85	9	10	8	3	51	0	73	3	1	7	16	.304	0	0--	—	4.39
1995 Jacksnville	AA	31	16	3	4	122.1	512	122	46	37	5	4	2	5	34	0	77	1	0	8	2	.800	2	0--	—	2.72
1996 Toledo	AAA	27	27	0	0	165.1	722	167	98	90	19	4	1	9	65	1	115	3	2	13	6	.684	0	0--	—	4.90
1997 New Orleans	AAA	29	27	2	0	163.2	694	177	71	60	15	8	4	3	54	1	99	6	0	6	7	.462	0	0--	—	3.30
1996 Detroit	AL	5	4	0	0	16.2	88	28	17	17	3	2	2	2	9	0	8	0	0	0	0	.000	0	0-0	—	9.18
1998 Houston	NL	37	1	0	15	53.1	235	57	21	18	4	0	0	1	20	1	30	1	0	2	0	1.000	0	1-2	1	3.04
2 ML YEARS		42	5	0	15	70	323	85	38	35	7	2	2	3	29	1	38	1	0	2	4	.333	0	1-2	1	4.50

Ralph Milliard

Bats: Right **Throws:** Right **Pos:** 2B-5; PH/PR-4; SS-1   **Ht:** 5'11" **Wt:** 175 **Born:** 12/30/73 **Age:** 25

Year Team	Lg	G	AB	H	2B	3B	HR	(Hm	Rd)	TB	R	RBI	TBB	IBB	SO	HBP	SH	SF	SB	CS	SB%	GDP	Avg	OBP	SLG
1998 Norfolk *	AAA	127	417	108	24	4	15	—	—	185	73	52	79	0	59	8	5	2	17	6	.74	4	.259	.385	.444
1996 Florida	NL	24	62	10	2	0	0	(0	0)	12	7	1	14	1	16	0	0	1	2	0	1.00	1	.161	.312	.194
1997 Florida	NL	8	30	6	1	0	0	(0	0)	6	2	2	3	0	3	2	1	0	1	1	.50	2	.200	.314	.200
1998 New York	NL	10	1	0	0	0	0	(0	0)	0	3	0	0	0	1	0	0	0	0	0	.00	0	.000	.000	.000
3 ML YEARS		42	93	16	2	0	0	(0	0)	18	12	3	17	1	20	2	1	1	3	1	.75	3	.172	.310	.194

Alan Mills

Pitches: Right **Bats:** Both **Pos:** RP-72   **Ht:** 6'1" **Wt:** 195 **Born:** 10/18/66 **Age:** 32

Year Team	Lg	G	GS	CG	GF	IP	BFP	H	R	ER	HR	SH	SF	HB	TBB	IBB	SO	WP	Bk	W	L	Pct.	ShO	Sv-Op	Hld	ERA
1990 New York	AL	36	0	0	18	41.2	200	48	21	19	4	4	1	1	33	6	24	3	0	1	5	.167	0	0-2	3	4.10
1991 New York	AL	6	2	0	3	16.1	72	16	9	8	1	0	1	0	8	0	11	2	0	1	1	.500	0	0-0	0	4.41
1992 Baltimore	AL	35	3	0	12	103.1	428	78	33	30	5	6	5	1	54	10	60	2	0	10	4	.714	0	2-3	2	2.61
1993 Baltimore	AL	45	0	0	18	100.1	421	80	39	36	14	4	6	4	51	5	68	3	0	5	4	.556	0	4-7	4	3.23
1994 Baltimore	AL	47	0	0	16	45.1	199	43	26	26	7	1	1	2	24	2	44	2	0	3	3	.500	0	2-4	14	5.16
1995 Baltimore	AL	21	0	0	1	23	118	30	20	19	4	0	1	2	18	4	16	1	0	3	0	1.000	0	0-1	1	7.43
1996 Baltimore	AL	49	0	0	23	54.2	233	40	26	26	10	3	2	1	35	2	50	6	0	3	2	.600	0	3-8	9	4.28
1997 Baltimore	AL	39	0	0	11	38.2	192	41	23	21	5	4	1	1	33	1	32	2	0	2	3	.400	0	0-0	7	4.89
1998 Baltimore	AL	72	0	0	13	77	327	55	32	32	8	2	1	1	50	8	57	4	0	3	4	.429	0	2-5	19	3.74
9 ML YEARS		350	5	0	115	500.1	2190	431	229	217	58	24	21	13	306	38	362	25	0	31	26	.544	0	13-30	59	3.90

Kevin Millwood

Pitches: Right **Bats:** Right **Pos:** SP-29; RP-2   **Ht:** 6'4" **Wt:** 220 **Born:** 12/24/74 **Age:** 24

Year Team	Lg	G	GS	CG	GF	IP	BFP	H	R	ER	HR	SH	SF	HB	TBB	IBB	SO	WP	Bk	W	L	Pct.	ShO	Sv-Op	Hld	ERA
1993 Braves	R	12	9	0	1	50	219	36	27	17	3	2	1	4	28	0	49	5	1	3	3	.500	0	0--	—	3.06
1994 Macon	A	12	4	0	2	32.2	165	31	31	21	4	2	1	2	32	1	24	4	0	0	5	.000	0	1--	—	5.79
Danville	R+	13	5	0	2	46	211	42	25	19	4	4	1	2	34	2	56	1	0	3	3	.500	0	1--	—	3.72
1995 Macon	A	29	12	0	5	103	458	86	65	53	10	3	4	5	57	0	89	10	0	5	6	.455	0	1--	—	4.63
1996 Durham	A+	33	20	1	3	149.1	638	138	77	71	17	9	6	8	58	0	139	8	3	6	9	.400	0	1--	—	4.28
1997 Greenville	AA	11	11	0	0	61.1	264	59	37	28	8	2	2	0	24	0	61	7	0	3	5	.375	0	0--	—	4.11
Richmond	AAA	9	9	1	0	60.2	232	38	13	13	2	2	0	1	16	0	46	2	0	7	0	1.000	0	0--	—	1.93
1997 Atlanta	NL	12	8	0	2	51.1	227	55	26	23	1	3	5	2	21	1	42	1	0	5	3	.625	0	0-0	0	4.03
1998 Atlanta	NL	31	29	3	1	174.1	748	175	86	79	18	8	3	3	56	3	163	6	1	17	8	.680	1	0-0	1	4.08
2 ML YEARS		43	37	3	3	225.2	975	230	112	102	19	11	8	5	77	4	205	7	1	22	11	.667	1	0-0	1	4.07

Eric Milton

Pitches: Left **Bats:** Left **Pos:** SP-32   **Ht:** 6'3" **Wt:** 200 **Born:** 8/4/75 **Age:** 23

Year Team	Lg	G	GS	CG	GF	IP	BFP	H	R	ER	HR	SH	SF	HB	TBB	IBB	SO	WP	Bk	W	L	Pct.	ShO	Sv-Op	Hld	ERA
1997 Tampa	A+	14	14	1	0	93.1	371	78	35	32	8	2	1	3	14	0	95	4	3	8	3	.727	0	0--	—	3.09
Norwich	AA	14	14	1	0	77.2	322	59	29	27	2	1	4	0	36	0	67	3	4	6	3	.667	0	0--	—	3.13
1998 Minnesota	AL	32	32	1	0	172.1	772	195	113	108	25	2	6	2	70	0	107	1	0	8	14	.364	0	0-0	0	5.64

Ryan Minor

Bats: Right **Throws:** Right **Pos:** 3B-6; 1B-3; DH-1; PH/PR-1   **Ht:** 6'7" **Wt:** 225 **Born:** 1/5/74 **Age:** 25

Year Team	Lg	G	AB	H	2B	3B	HR	(Hm	Rd)	TB	R	RBI	TBB	IBB	SO	HBP	SH	SF	SB	CS	SB%	GDP	Avg	OBP	SLG
1996 Bluefield	R+	25	87	22	6	0	4	—	—	40	14	9	7	0	32	3	0	0	1	0	1.00	0	.253	.330	.460
1997 Delmarva	A	134	488	150	42	1	24	—	—	266	83	97	51	2	102	15	0	4	7	3	.70	8	.307	.387	.545
1998 Bowie	AA	138	521	130	20	3	17	—	—	207	73	71	34	2	152	13	0	13	2	3	.40	13	.250	.311	.397
1998 Baltimore	AL	9	14	6	1	0	0	(0	0)	7	3	1	0	0	3	0	0	0	0	0	.00	0	.429	.429	.500

Doug Mirabelli

Bats: Right **Throws:** Right **Pos:** C-10; PH/PR-1   **Ht:** 6'1" **Wt:** 215 **Born:** 10/18/70 **Age:** 28

Year Team	Lg	G	AB	H	2B	3B	HR	(Hm	Rd)	TB	R	RBI	TBB	IBB	SO	HBP	SH	SF	SB	CS	SB%	GDP	Avg	OBP	SLG
1992 San Jose	A+	53	177	41	11	1	0	—	—	54	30	21	24	0	18	4	2	2	1	3	.25	7	.232	.333	.305
1993 San Jose	A+	113	371	100	19	2	1	—	—	126	58	48	72	1	55	4	2	4	4	0	.00	7	.270	.390	.340
1994 Shreveport	AA	85	255	56	8	0	4	—	—	76	23	24	36	5	48	0	2	0	3	1	.75	6	.220	.316	.298
1995 Phoenix	AAA	23	66	11	0	1	0	—	—	13	3	7	12	1	10	1	0	2	1	0	1.00	5	.167	.296	.197
Shreveport	AA	40	126	38	13	0	0	—	—	51	14	16	20	1	14	0	2	0	1	0	1.00	3	.302	.397	.405
1996 Phoenix	AAA	14	47	14	7	0	0	—	—	21	10	7	4	0	7	1	0	0	0	0	.00	1	.298	.365	.447
Shreveport	AA	115	380	112	23	0	21	—	—	198	60	70	76	0	49	6	1	1	0	1	.00	9	.295	.419	.521
1997 Phoenix	AAA	100	332	88	23	2	8	—	—	139	49	48	58	2	69	7	3	1	1	2	.33	9	.265	.384	.419
1998 Fresno	AAA	85	265	69	12	2	13	—	—	124	45	53	52	6	55	3	3	1	2	0	1.00	9	.260	.386	.468
1996 San Francisco	NL	9	18	4	1	0	0	(0	0)	5	2	1	3	0	4	0	0	0	0	0	.00	0	.222	.333	.278
1997 San Francisco	NL	6	7	1	0	0	0	(0	0)	1	0	0	1	0	3	0	0	0	0	0	.00	0	.143	.250	.143
1998 San Francisco	NL	10	17	4	2	0	1	(1	0)	9	2	4	2	0	6	0	0	0	0	0	.00	0	.235	.316	.529
3 ML YEARS		25	42	9	3	0	1	(1	0)	15	4	5	6	0	13	0	0	0	0	0	.00	0	.214	.313	.357

Keith Mitchell

Bats: R **Throws:** R **Pos:** DH-12; PH/PR-12; RF-6; LF-4   **Ht:** 5'10" **Wt:** 180 **Born:** 8/6/69 **Age:** 29

Year Team	Lg	G	AB	H	2B	3B	HR	(Hm	Rd)	TB	R	RBI	TBB	IBB	SO	HBP	SH	SF	SB	CS	SB%	GDP	Avg	OBP	SLG
1998 Trenton *	AA	12	41	8	2	0	2	—	—	16	4	7	8	0	5	0	0	1	0	0	.00	1	.195	.320	.390
Pawtucket *	AAA	63	211	66	15	0	12	—	—	117	55	45	44	2	37	1	0	4	3	3	.50	5	.313	.427	.555
1991 Atlanta	NL	48	66	21	0	0	0	(1	1)	27	11	5	8	0	12	0	0	0	3	1	.75	1	.318	.392	.409
1994 Seattle	AL	46	128	29	2	0	5	(2	3)	46	21	15	18	0	22	1	1	1	0	0	.00	2	.227	.324	.359
1996 Cincinnati	NL	11	15	4	1	0	1	(1	0)	8	2	3	1	0	3	0	0	0	0	0	.00	0	.267	.313	.533
1998 Boston	AL	23	33	9	2	0	0	(0	0)	11	4	6	7	1	5	0	0	0	1	0	1.00	0	.273	.400	.333
4 ML YEARS		128	242	63	5	0	8	(4	4)	92	38	29	34	1	42	1	1	1	4	1	.80	3	.260	.353	.380

Kevin Mitchell

Bats: R **Throws:** R **Pos:** DH-23; PH/PR-23; LF-10; 1B-2   **Ht:** 5'11" **Wt:** 210 **Born:** 1/13/62 **Age:** 37

Year Team	Lg	G	AB	H	2B	3B	HR	(Hm	Rd)	TB	R	RBI	TBB	IBB	SO	HBP	SH	SF	SB	CS	SB%	GDP	Avg	OBP	SLG
1998 Edmonton *	AAA	6	23	8	2	0	0	—	—	10	4	1	1	0	2	0	0	0	0	1	.00	0	.348	.375	.435
1984 New York	NL	7	14	3	0	0	0	(0	0)	3	0	1	0	0	3	0	0	0	0	1	.00	0	.214	.214	.214
1986 New York	NL	108	328	91	22	2	12	(4	8)	153	51	43	33	0	61	1	1	1	3	3	.50	6	.277	.344	.466
1987 SD-SF	NL	131	464	130	20	2	22	(9	13)	220	68	70	48	4	88	2	0	1	9	6	.60	10	.280	.350	.474
1988 San Francisco	NL	148	505	127	25	7	19	(10	9)	223	60	80	48	7	85	1	5	7	5	5	.50	9	.251	.319	.442
1989 San Francisco	NL	154	543	158	34	6	47	(22	25)	345	100	125	87	32	115	3	0	7	3	4	.43	6	.291	.388	.635
1990 San Francisco	NL	140	524	152	24	2	35	(15	20)	285	90	93	58	9	87	2	0	5	4	7	.36	8	.290	.360	.544
1991 San Francisco	NL	113	371	95	13	1	27	(9	18)	191	52	69	43	8	57	5	0	4	2	3	.40	6	.256	.338	.515
1992 Seattle	AL	99	360	103	24	0	9	(5	4)	154	48	67	35	4	46	3	2	0	4	2	.00	4	.286	.351	.428
1993 Cincinnati	NL	93	323	110	21	3	19	(10	9)	194	56	64	25	4	48	1	0	4	1	0	1.00	14	.341	.385	.601
1994 Cincinnati	NL	95	310	101	18	1	30	(18	12)	211	57	77	59	15	62	3	0	8	2	0	1.00	12	.326	.429	.681
1996 Bos-Cin	NL	64	206	65	15	0	4	(6	2)	104	27	39	37	2	30	1	0	1	0	0	.00	5	.316	.420	.505
1997 Cleveland	AL	20	59	9	1	0	4	(1	3)	22	7	11	9	2	11	1	0	0	1	0	1.00	2	.153	.275	.373
1998 Oakland	AL	51	127	29	7	1	2	(1	1)	44	14	21	9	0	26	0	0	0	0	0	.00	5	.228	.279	.346
1987 San Diego	NL	62	196	48	7	1	7	(2	5)	78	19	26	20	3	38	0	0	5	0	0	.00	5	.245	.313	.398
San Francisco	NL	69	268	82	13	1	15	(7	8)	142	49	44	28	1	50	2	0	0	9	6	.60	5	.306	.376	.530
1996 Boston	AL	27	92	28	4	0	2	(1	1)	38	9	13	11	0	14	1	0	0	0	0	.00	3	.304	.385	.413
Cincinnati	NL	37	114	37	11	0	6	(5	1)	66	18	26	26	2	16	0	0	0	0	0	.00	5	.325	.447	.579
13 ML YEARS		1223	4134	1173	224	25	234	(110	124)	2149	630	760	491	87	719	27	2	42	30	31	.49	89	.284	.360	.520

Dave Mlicki

Pitches: Right **Bats:** Right **Pos:** SP-30   **Ht:** 6'4" **Wt:** 205 **Born:** 6/8/68 **Age:** 31

Year Team	Lg	G	GS	CG	GF	IP	BFP	H	R	ER	HR	SH	SF	HB	TBB	IBB	SO	WP	Bk	W	L	Pct.	ShO	Sv-Op	Hld	ERA
1992 Cleveland	AL	4	4	0	0	21.2	101	23	14	12	3	2	0	1	16	0	16	1	0	0	2	.000	0	0-0	0	4.98
1993 Cleveland	AL	3	3	0	0	13.1	58	11	6	5	2	0	0	2	6	0	7	2	0	0	0	.000	0	0-0	0	3.38
1995 New York	NL	29	25	0	1	160.2	696	160	82	76	23	8	5	4	54	2	123	5	1	9	7	.563	0	0-0	0	4.26
1996 New York	NL	51	2	0	16	90	393	95	46	43	9	8	3	6	33	8	83	7	0	6	7	.462	0	1-3	8	3.30
1997 New York	NL	32	32	1	0	193.2	838	194	89	86	21	3	6	5	76	7	157	5	1	8	12	.400	1	0-0	0	4.00
1998 NYN-LA	NL	30	30	3	0	181.1	789	188	102	92	23	8	7	7	63	5	117	10	0	8	7	.533	1	0-0	0	4.57
1998 New York	NL	10	10	1	0	57	264	68	38	36	8	2	3	5	25	4	39	4	0	1	4	.200	0	0-0	0	5.68
Los Angeles	NL	20	20	2	0	124.1	525	120	64	56	15	6	4	2	38	1	78	6	0	7	3	.700	1	0-0	0	4.05
6 ML YEARS		149	96	4	17	660.2	2875	671	339	304	81	29	21	25	248	22	503	30	2	31	35	.470	2	1-3	8	4.14

Brian Moehler

Pitches: Right Bats: Right Pos: SP-33 Ht: 6'3" Wt: 235 Born: 12/31/71 Age: 27

		HOW MUCH HE PITCHED						WHAT HE GAVE UP											THE RESULTS						
Year Team	Lg	G	GS	CG	GF	IP	BFP	H	R	ER	HR	SH	SF	HB	TBB	IBB	SO	WP	Bk	W	L	Pct.	ShO	Sv-Op	Hld	ERA
1996 Detroit	AL	2	2	0	0	10.1	51	11	10	5	1	1	0	0	8	1	2	1	0	0	1	.000	0	0-0	0	4.35
1997 Detroit	AL	31	31	2	0	175.1	770	198	97	91	22	1	8	5	61	1	97	3	0	11	12	.478	1	0-0	0	4.67
1998 Detroit	AL	33	33	4	0	221.1	912	220	103	96	30	3	3	2	56	1	123	4	0	14	13	.519	3	0-0	0	3.90
3 ML YEARS		66	66	6	0	407	1733	429	210	192	53	5	11	7	125	3	222	8	0	25	26	.490	4	0-0	0	4.25

Mike Mohler

Pitches: Left Bats: Right Pos: RP-57 Ht: 6'2" Wt: 208 Born: 7/26/68 Age: 30

		HOW MUCH HE PITCHED						WHAT HE GAVE UP											THE RESULTS						
Year Team	Lg	G	GS	CG	GF	IP	BFP	H	R	ER	HR	SH	SF	HB	TBB	IBB	SO	WP	Bk	W	L	Pct.	ShO	Sv-Op	Hld	ERA
1993 Oakland	AL	42	9	0	4	64.1	290	57	45	40	10	5	2	2	44	4	42	0	1	1	6	.143	0	0-1	1	5.60
1994 Oakland	AL	1	1	0	0	2.1	14	2	3	2	1	0	0	0	2	0	4	0	0	0	1	.000	0	0-0	0	7.71
1995 Oakland	AL	28	0	0	6	23.2	100	16	8	8	0	1	0	0	18	1	15	1	0	1	1	.500	0	1-2	4	3.04
1996 Oakland	AL	72	0	0	30	81	352	79	36	33	9	6	4	1	41	6	64	9	0	6	3	.667	0	7-13	13	3.67
1997 Oakland	AL	62	10	0	16	101.2	462	116	65	58	11	9	7	7	54	8	66	4	0	1	10	.091	0	1-4	11	5.13
1998 Oakland	AL	57	0	0	16	61	277	70	38	35	6	3	2	4	26	3	42	3	1	3	3	.500	0	0-1	8	5.16
6 ML YEARS		262	20	0	72	334	1495	340	195	176	37	24	15	14	185	22	233	17	2	12	24	.333	0	9-21	37	4.74

Ben Molina

Bats: Right Throws: Right Pos: C-2; PH/PR-1 Ht: 5'11" Wt: 200 Born: 7/20/74 Age: 24

		BATTING															BASERUNNING				PERCENTAGES		
Year Team	Lg	G	AB	H	2B	3B	HR	(Hm | Rd)	TB	R	RBI	TBB	IBB	SO	HBP	SH	SF	SB	CS	SB%	GDP	Avg	OBP	SLG
1993 Angels	R	27	80	21	6	2	0	—	—	31	9	10	10	0	4	1	0	1	0	2	.00	1	.263	.348	.388
1994 Cedar Rapds	A	48	171	48	8	2	3	—	—	65	14	16	8	0	12	3	1	0	1	2	.33	3	.281	.324	.380
1995 Vancouver	AAA	1	2	0	0	0	0	—	—	0	0	0	0	0	1	0	0	0	0	0	.00	0	.000	.000	.000
Cedar Rapds	A	39	133	39	9	0	4	—	—	60	15	17	15	0	11	1	1	1	1	1	.50	4	.293	.367	.451
Lk Elsinore	A+	27	96	37	7	2	2	—	—	54	21	12	8	1	7	4	3	1	0	0	.00	2	.385	.450	.563
1996 Midland	AA	108	365	100	21	2	8	—	—	149	45	54	25	1	25	6	4	5	0	1	.00	16	.274	.327	.408
1997 Lk Elsinore	A+	36	149	42	10	2	4	—	—	68	18	33	7	2	9	0	0	3	0	1	.00	5	.282	.308	.456
Midland	AA	29	106	35	8	0	6	—	—	61	18	30	10	0	7	0	0	2	0	0	.00	7	.330	.381	.575
1998 Midland	AA	41	154	55	8	0	9	—	—	90	28	39	14	2	7	3	0	1	0	1	.00	7	.357	.419	.584
Vancouver	AAA	49	184	54	9	1	1	—	—	68	13	22	5	0	14	0	1	1	1	1	.50	6	.293	.311	.370
1998 Anaheim	AL	2	1	0	0	0	0	(0 | 0)	0	0	0	0	0	0	0	0	0	0	0	.00	0	.000	.000	.000

Izzy Molina

Bats: Right Throws: Right Pos: C-5; PH/PR-2; DH-1 Ht: 6'1" Wt: 224 Born: 6/3/71 Age: 28

		BATTING															BASERUNNING				PERCENTAGES		
Year Team	Lg	G	AB	H	2B	3B	HR	(Hm | Rd)	TB	R	RBI	TBB	IBB	SO	HBP	SH	SF	SB	CS	SB%	GDP	Avg	OBP	SLG
1998 Edmonton *	AAA	86	303	73	15	2	8	—	—	116	29	38	17	0	60	4	1	3	3	0	1.00	16	.241	.287	.383
1996 Oakland	AL	14	25	5	2	0	0	(0 | 0)	7	0	1	1	0	3	0	0	0	0	0	.00	0	.200	.231	.280
1997 Oakland	AL	48	111	22	3	1	3	(1 | 2)	36	6	7	3	0	17	0	1	0	0	0	.00	1	.198	.219	.324
1998 Oakland	AL	6	2	1	0	0	0	(0 | 0)	1	1	0	0	0	0	0	0	0	0	0	.00	0	.500	.500	.500
3 ML YEARS		68	138	28	5	1	3	(1 | 2)	44	7	8	4	0	20	0	1	0	0	0	.00	1	.203	.225	.319

Paul Molitor

Bats: Right Throws: Right Pos: DH-115; 1B-9; PH/PR-2 Ht: 6'0" Wt: 195 Born: 8/22/56 Age: 42

		BATTING															BASERUNNING				PERCENTAGES		
Year Team	Lg	G	AB	H	2B	3B	HR	(Hm | Rd)	TB	R	RBI	TBB	IBB	SO	HBP	SH	SF	SB	CS	SB%	GDP	Avg	OBP	SLG
1998 Salt Lake *	AAA	2	10	5	1	0	0	—	—	6	0	0	0	0	0	0	0	0	0	0	.00	1	.500	.500	.600
1978 Milwaukee	AL	125	521	142	26	4	6	(4 | 2)	194	73	45	19	2	54	4	7	5	30	12	.71	5	.273	.301	.372
1979 Milwaukee	AL	140	584	188	27	16	9	(3 | 6)	274	88	62	48	5	48	2	6	5	33	13	.72	9	.322	.372	.469
1980 Milwaukee	AL	111	450	137	29	2	9	(2 | 7)	197	81	37	48	4	48	3	6	5	34	7	.83	9	.304	.372	.438
1981 Milwaukee	AL	64	251	67	11	0	2	(1 | 1)	84	45	19	25	1	29	3	5	0	10	6	.63	3	.267	.341	.335
1982 Milwaukee	AL	160	666	201	26	8	19	(9 | 10)	300	136	71	69	1	93	1	10	5	41	9	.82	9	.302	.366	.450
1983 Milwaukee	AL	152	608	164	28	6	15	(9 | 6)	249	95	47	59	4	74	2	7	6	41	8	.84	12	.270	.333	.410
1984 Milwaukee	AL	13	46	10	1	0	0	(0 | 0)	11	3	6	2	0	8	0	0	1	1	0	1.00	0	.217	.245	.239
1985 Milwaukee	AL	140	576	171	28	3	10	(6 | 4)	235	93	48	54	6	80	1	7	4	21	7	.75	12	.297	.356	.408
1986 Milwaukee	AL	105	437	123	24	6	9	(5 | 4)	186	62	55	40	0	81	0	2	3	20	5	.80	9	.281	.340	.426
1987 Milwaukee	AL	118	465	164	41	5	16	(7 | 9)	263	114	75	69	2	67	2	5	1	45	10	.82	4	.353	.438	.566
1988 Milwaukee	AL	154	609	190	34	6	13	(9 | 4)	275	115	60	71	8	54	2	5	3	41	10	.80	10	.312	.384	.452
1989 Milwaukee	AL	155	615	194	35	4	11	(6 | 5)	270	84	56	64	4	67	4	4	9	27	11	.71	11	.315	.379	.439
1990 Milwaukee	AL	103	418	119	27	6	12	(6 | 6)	194	64	45	37	4	51	1	0	2	18	3	.86	7	.285	.343	.464
1991 Milwaukee	AL	158	665	216	32	13	17	(7 | 10)	325	133	75	77	16	62	6	0	1	19	8	.70	11	.325	.399	.489
1992 Milwaukee	AL	158	609	195	36	7	12	(4 | 8)	281	89	89	73	12	66	3	4	11	31	6	.84	13	.320	.389	.461
1993 Toronto	AL	160	636	211	37	5	22	(13 | 9)	324	121	111	77	3	71	3	1	8	22	4	.85	13	.332	.402	.509
1994 Toronto	AL	115	454	155	30	4	14	(8 | 6)	235	86	75	55	4	48	1	0	5	20	0	1.00	10	.341	.410	.518
1995 Toronto	AL	130	525	142	31	2	15	(6 | 9)	222	63	60	61	1	57	5	3	4	12	0	1.00	10	.270	.350	.423
1996 Minnesota	AL	161	660	225	41	8	9	(6 | 3)	309	99	113	56	10	72	0	9	8	18	6	.75	21	.341	.390	.468
1997 Minnesota	AL	135	538	164	32	4	10	(5 | 5)	234	63	89	45	4	73	0	2	12	11	4	.73	8	.305	.351	.435
1998 Minnesota	AL	126	502	141	29	5	4	(0 | 4)	192	75	69	45	5	41	1	1	5	9	2	.82	19	.281	.335	.382
21 ML YEARS		2683	10835	3319	605	114	234	(116 | 118)	4854	1782	1307	1094	100	1244	47	75	109	504	131	.79	209	.306	.369	.448

Shane Monahan

Bats: L **Throws:** R **Pos:** LF-61; CF-3; RF-2; PH/PR-1   **Ht:** 6'0" **Wt:** 195 **Born:** 8/12/74 **Age:** 24

Year Team	Lg	G	AB	H	2B	3B	HR	(Hm	Rd)	TB	R	RBI	TBB	IBB	SO	HBP	SH	SF	SB	CS	SB%	GDP	Avg	OBP	SLG
1995 Wisconsin	A	59	233	66	9	6	1	—	—	90	34	32	11	0	40	2	7	3	9	2	.82	4	.283	.317	.386
1996 Lancaster	A+	132	585	164	31	12	14	—	—	261	107	97	30	2	124	4	3	8	19	5	.79	8	.280	.316	.446
1997 Memphis	AA	107	401	121	24	6	12	—	—	193	52	76	30	2	100	2	1	4	14	7	.67	4	.302	.352	.481
Tacoma	AAA	21	85	25	4	0	2	—	—	35	15	12	5	0	21	1	2	0	5	1	.83	1	.294	.341	.412
1998 Tacoma	AAA	69	277	69	8	5	4	—	—	99	32	33	19	3	47	0	4	2	6	4	.60	3	.249	.295	.357
1998 Seattle	AL	62	211	51	8	1	4	(2	2)	73	17	28	8	0	53	0	4	0	1	2	.33	0	.242	.269	.346

Raul Mondesi

Bats: Right **Throws:** Right **Pos:** CF-94; RF-54   **Ht:** 5'11" **Wt:** 215 **Born:** 3/12/71 **Age:** 28

Year Team	Lg	G	AB	H	2B	3B	HR	(Hm	Rd)	TB	R	RBI	TBB	IBB	SO	HBP	SH	SF	SB	CS	SB%	GDP	Avg	OBP	SLG
1993 Los Angeles	NL	42	86	25	3	1	4	(2	2)	42	13	10	4	0	16	0	1	0	4	1	.80	1	.291	.322	.488
1994 Los Angeles	NL	112	434	133	27	8	16	(10	6)	224	63	56	16	5	78	2	0	2	11	8	.58	9	.306	.333	.516
1995 Los Angeles	NL	139	536	153	23	6	26	(13	13)	266	91	88	33	4	96	4	0	7	27	4	.87	7	.285	.328	.496
1996 Los Angeles	NL	157	634	188	40	7	24	(11	13)	314	98	88	32	9	122	5	0	2	14	7	.67	6	.297	.334	.495
1997 Los Angeles	NL	159	616	191	42	5	30	(16	14)	333	95	87	44	7	105	6	1	3	32	15	.68	11	.310	.360	.541
1998 Los Angeles	NL	148	580	162	26	5	30	(13	17)	288	85	90	30	4	112	3	0	4	16	10	.62	8	.279	.316	.497
6 ML YEARS		757	2886	852	161	32	130	(65	65)	1467	445	419	159	29	529	20	2	18	104	45	.70	42	.295	.334	.508

Jeff Montgomery

Pitches: Right **Bats:** Right **Pos:** RP-56   **Ht:** 5'11" **Wt:** 175 **Born:** 1/7/62 **Age:** 37

		HOW MUCH HE PITCHED						WHAT HE GAVE UP										THE RESULTS						
Year Team	Lg	G	GS	CG	GF	IP	BFP	H	R	ER	HR	SH	SF	HB	TBB	IBB	SO	WP	Bk	W	L	Pct.	ShO	Sv-Op	Hld	ERA
1987 Cincinnati	NL	14	1	0	6	19.1	89	25	15	14	2	0	0	0	9	1	13	1	1	2	2	.500	0	0-0	1	6.52
1988 Kansas City	AL	45	0	0	13	62.2	271	54	25	24	6	3	2	2	30	1	47	3	6	7	2	.778	0	1-3	9	3.45
1989 Kansas City	AL	63	0	0	39	92	363	66	16	14	3	1	1	2	25	4	94	6	1	7	3	.700	0	18-24	11	1.37
1990 Kansas City	AL	73	0	0	59	94.1	400	81	36	25	6	5	3	5	34	8	94	3	0	6	5	.545	0	24-34	7	2.39
1991 Kansas City	AL	67	0	0	55	90	376	83	32	29	6	6	2	2	28	2	77	6	0	4	4	.500	0	33-39	3	2.90
1992 Kansas City	AL	65	0	0	62	82.2	333	61	23	20	5	4	2	3	27	2	69	2	0	1	6	.143	0	39-46	0	2.18
1993 Kansas City	AL	69	0	0	63	87.1	347	65	22	22	3	5	1	2	23	4	66	3	0	7	5	.583	0	45-51	0	2.27
1994 Kansas City	AL	42	0	0	38	44.2	193	48	21	20	5	2	1	1	15	1	50	2	0	2	3	.400	0	27-32	0	4.03
1995 Kansas City	AL	54	0	0	46	65.2	275	60	27	25	7	5	5	2	25	4	49	1	1	2	3	.400	0	31-38	0	3.43
1996 Kansas City	AL	48	0	0	41	63.1	261	59	31	30	14	3	1	3	19	3	45	0	1	4	6	.400	0	24-34	0	4.26
1997 Kansas City	AL	55	0	0	37	59.1	245	53	24	23	9	4	2	0	18	5	48	5	0	1	4	.200	0	14-17	3	3.49
1998 Kansas City	AL	56	0	0	54	56	247	58	35	31	8	2	1	2	22	2	54	0	1	2	5	.286	0	36-41	0	4.98
12 ML YEARS		651	1	0	513	817.1	3400	713	307	277	74	37	20	24	275	37	706	32	10	45	48	.484	0	292-359	34	3.05

Ray Montgomery

Bats: Right **Throws:** Right **Pos:** PH/PR-5; LF-1; RF-1   **Ht:** 6'3" **Wt:** 195 **Born:** 8/8/69 **Age:** 29

		BATTING																	BASERUNNING				PERCENTAGES		
Year Team	Lg	G	AB	H	2B	3B	HR	(Hm	Rd)	TB	R	RBI	TBB	IBB	SO	HBP	SH	SF	SB	CS	SB%	GDP	Avg	OBP	SLG
1998 New Orleans * AAA		75	272	79	18	1	9	—	—	126	42	45	26	0	48	3	0	4	4	2	.67	8	.290	.354	.463
1996 Houston	NL	12	14	3	1	0	1	(1	0)	7	4	4	1	0	5	0	0	0	0	0	.00	0	.214	.267	.500
1997 Houston	NL	29	68	16	4	1	0	(0	0)	22	8	4	5	0	18	0	0	3	0	0	.00	2	.235	.276	.324
1998 Houston	NL	6	5	2	0	0	0	(0	0)	2	2	0	0	0	0	0	0	0	0	0	.00	0	.400	.400	.400
3 ML YEARS		47	87	21	5	1	1	(1	0)	31	14	8	6	0	23	0	0	3	0	0	.00	2	.241	.281	.356

Trey Moore

Pitches: Left **Bats:** Left **Pos:** SP-11; RP-2   **Ht:** 6'1" **Wt:** 200 **Born:** 10/2/72 **Age:** 26

		HOW MUCH HE PITCHED						WHAT HE GAVE UP										THE RESULTS						
Year Team	Lg	G	GS	CG	GF	IP	BFP	H	R	ER	HR	SH	SF	HB	TBB	IBB	SO	WP	Bk	W	L	Pct.	ShO	Sv-Op	Hld	ERA
1994 Bellingham	A-	11	10	1	0	61.2	247	48	18	18	4	0	2	2	24	0	73	4	0	5	2	.714	0	0- -	0	2.63
1995 Riverside	A+	24	24	0	0	148.1	605	122	65	51	6	2	5	2	58	1	134	6	1	14	6	.700	0	0- -	0	3.09
1996 Port City	AA	11	11	0	0	53.2	265	73	54	46	6	2	5	0	33	0	42	4	1	1	6	.143	0	0- -	0	7.71
Lancaster	A+	15	15	2	0	94.1	413	106	57	43	10	2	0	7	31	0	77	7	0	7	5	.583	0	0- -	0	4.10
1997 Harrisburg	AA	27	27	2	0	162.2	701	152	91	75	15	6	3	10	66	1	137	4	0	11	6	.647	2	0- -	0	4.15
1998 Ottawa	AAA	3	3	0	0	13	59	18	8	8	1	0	1	0	8	1	8	1	0	1	1	.500	0	0- -	0	5.54
1998 Montreal	NL	13	11	0	1	61	277	78	37	34	5	1	3	1	17	3	35	2	0	2	5	.286	0	0-0	0	5.02

Mickey Morandini

Bats: Left **Throws:** Right **Pos:** 2B-152; PH/PR-6   **Ht:** 5'11" **Wt:** 176 **Born:** 4/22/66 **Age:** 33

		BATTING																	BASERUNNING				PERCENTAGES		
Year Team	Lg	G	AB	H	2B	3B	HR	(Hm	Rd)	TB	R	RBI	TBB	IBB	SO	HBP	SH	SF	SB	CS	SB%	GDP	Avg	OBP	SLG
1990 Philadelphia	NL	25	79	19	4	0	1	(1	0)	26	9	3	6	0	19	0	2	0	3	0	1.00	1	.241	.294	.329
1991 Philadelphia	NL	98	325	81	11	4	1	(1	0)	103	38	20	29	0	45	2	6	2	13	2	.87	7	.249	.313	.317
1992 Philadelphia	NL	127	422	112	8	8	3	(2	1)	145	47	30	25	2	64	0	6	2	8	3	.73	4	.265	.305	.344
1993 Philadelphia	NL	120	425	105	19	9	3	(2	1)	151	57	33	34	2	73	5	4	2	13	2	.87	7	.247	.309	.355
1994 Philadelphia	NL	87	274	80	16	5	2	(1	1)	112	40	26	34	5	33	4	4	0	10	5	.67	4	.292	.378	.409

Year Team	Lg	G	AB	H	2B	3B	HR	(Hm	Rd)	TB	R	RBI	TBB	IBB	SO	HBP	SH	SF	SB	CS	SB%	GDP	Avg	OBP	SLG
1995 Philadelphia	NL	127	494	140	34	7	6	(3	3)	206	65	49	42	3	80	9	4	1	9	6	.60	11	.283	.350	.417
1996 Philadelphia	NL	140	539	135	24	6	3	(2	1)	180	64	32	49	0	87	9	5	4	26	5	.84	15	.250	.321	.334
1997 Philadelphia	NL	150	553	163	40	2	1	(1	0)	210	83	39	62	0	91	8	12	5	16	13	.55	8	.295	.371	.380
1998 Chicago	NL	154	582	172	20	4	8	(4	4)	224	93	53	72	4	84	9	4	2	13	1	.93	14	.296	.380	.385
9 ML YEARS		1028	3693	1007	176	45	28	(17	11)	1357	496	285	353	16	576	46	47	18	111	37	.75	71	.273	.342	.367

Mike Mordecai

Bats: R **Throws:** R **Pos:** SS-30; 2B-21; PH/PR-18; 3B-11; 1B-1   **Ht:** 5'11" **Wt:** 175 **Born:** 12/13/67 **Age:** 31

					BATTING														BASERUNNING				PERCENTAGES		
Year Team	Lg	G	AB	H	2B	3B	HR	(Hm	Rd)	TB	R	RBI	TBB	IBB	SO	HBP	SH	SF	SB	CS	SB%	GDP	Avg	OBP	SLG
1998 Jupiter *	A+	2	8	0	0	0	0	—	—	0	0	0	1	0	3	0	0	0	0	0	.00	1	.000	.111	.000
Ottawa *	AAA	6	22	5	2	0	0	—	—	7	2	1	3	0	3	0	0	0	0	0	.00	1	.227	.320	.318
1994 Atlanta	NL	4	4	1	0	0	1	(1	0)	4	1	3	1	0	0	0	0	0	0	0	.00	0	.250	.400	1.000
1995 Atlanta	NL	69	75	21	6	0	3	(1	2)	36	10	11	9	0	16	0	2	1	0	0	.00	0	.280	.353	.480
1996 Atlanta	NL	66	108	26	5	0	2	(0	2)	37	12	12	9	1	24	0	4	1	1	0	1.00	1	.241	.297	.343
1997 Atlanta	NL	61	81	14	2	1	0	(0	0)	18	8	3	6	0	16	0	1	1	0	1	.00	4	.173	.227	.222
1998 Montreal	NL	73	119	24	4	2	3	(1	2)	41	12	10	9	0	20	0	2	0	1	0	1.00	2	.202	.258	.345
5 ML YEARS		273	387	86	17	3	9	(3	6)	136	43	35	34	1	76	0	9	3	2	1	.67	7	.222	.283	.351

Mike Morgan

Pitches: Right **Bats:** Right **Pos:** SP-22; RP-1   **Ht:** 6'2" **Wt:** 220 **Born:** 10/8/59 **Age:** 39

		HOW MUCH HE PITCHED						WHAT HE GAVE UP											THE RESULTS						
Year Team	Lg	G	GS	CG	GF	IP	BFP	H	R	ER	HR	SH	SF	HB	TBB	IBB	SO	WP	Bk	W	L	Pct.	ShO	Sv-Op	Hld	ERA
1978 Oakland	AL	3	3	1	0	12.1	60	19	12	10	1	1	0	0	8	0	0	0	0	0	3	.000	0	0-0	0	7.30
1979 Oakland	AL	13	13	2	0	77.1	368	102	57	51	7	4	4	3	50	0	17	7	0	2	10	.167	0	0-0	0	5.94
1982 New York	AL	30	23	2	2	150.1	661	167	77	73	15	2	4	2	67	5	71	6	0	7	11	.389	0	0-0	0	4.37
1983 Toronto	AL	16	4	0	2	45.1	198	48	26	26	6	0	1	0	21	0	22	3	0	0	3	.000	0	0-0	0	5.16
1985 Seattle	AL	2	2	0	0	6	33	11	8	8	2	0	0	0	5	0	2	1	0	1	1	.500	0	0-0	0	12.00
1986 Seattle	AL	37	33	9	2	216.1	951	243	122	109	24	7	3	4	86	3	116	8	1	11	17	.393	1	1-1	0	4.53
1987 Seattle	AL	34	31	8	0	207	898	245	117	107	25	8	5	5	53	3	85	11	0	12	17	.414	2	0-0	0	4.65
1988 Baltimore	AL	22	10	2	6	71.1	299	70	45	43	6	1	0	1	23	1	29	5	0	1	6	.143	0	1-1	0	5.43
1989 Los Angeles	NL	40	19	0	7	152.2	604	130	51	43	6	8	6	2	33	8	72	6	0	8	11	.421	0	0-1	1	2.53
1990 Los Angeles	NL	33	33	6	0	211	891	216	100	88	19	11	4	5	60	5	106	4	0	11	15	.423	4	0-0	0	3.75
1991 Los Angeles	NL	34	33	5	1	236.1	949	197	85	73	12	10	4	3	61	10	140	6	0	14	10	.583	1	1-1	0	2.78
1992 Chicago	NL	34	34	6	0	240	966	203	80	68	14	10	5	3	79	10	123	11	0	16	8	.667	1	0-0	0	2.55
1993 Chicago	NL	32	32	1	0	207.2	883	206	100	93	15	11	5	7	74	8	111	8	2	10	15	.400	1	0-0	0	4.03
1994 Chicago	NL	15	15	1	0	80.2	380	111	65	60	12	7	6	4	35	2	57	5	0	2	10	.167	0	0-0	0	6.69
1995 ChN-StL	NL	21	21	1	0	131.1	548	133	56	52	12	12	5	6	34	2	61	6	0	7	7	.500	0	0-0	0	3.56
1996 StL-Cin	NL	23	23	0	0	130.1	567	146	72	67	16	6	7	1	47	0	74	2	0	6	11	.353	0	0-0	0	4.63
1997 Cincinnati	NL	31	30	1	0	162	688	165	91	86	13	9	2	8	49	6	103	7	0	9	12	.429	0	0-0	0	4.78
1998 Min-ChN		23	22	0	0	120.2	524	138	62	56	21	3	3	8	39	2	60	1	0	4	3	.571	0	0-0	0	4.18
1995 Chicago	NL	4	4	0	0	24.2	100	19	8	6	2	2	0	1	9	1	15	0	0	2	1	.667	0	0-0	0	2.19
St. Louis	NL	17	17	1	0	106.2	448	114	48	46	10	10	5	5	25	1	46	6	0	5	6	.455	0	0-0	0	3.88
1996 St. Louis	NL	18	18	0	0	103	452	118	63	60	14	4	6	0	40	0	55	2	0	4	8	.333	0	0-0	0	5.24
Cincinnati	NL	5	5	0	0	27.1	115	28	9	7	2	1	1	1	7	0	19	0	0	2	3	.400	0	0-0	0	2.30
1998 Minnesota	AL	18	17	0	0	98	412	108	41	38	13	0	3	7	24	1	50	1	0	4	2	.667	0	0-0	0	3.49
Chicago	NL	5	5	0	0	22.2	112	30	21	18	8	3	0	1	15	1	10	0	0	0	1	.000	0	0-0	0	7.15
18 ML YEARS		443	381	45	22	2458.2	10468	2550	1226	1113	226	110	64	62	824	65	1249	97	4	121	170	.416	10	3-4	2	4.07

Alvin Morman

Pitches: Left **Bats:** Right **Pos:** RP-40   **Ht:** 6'3" **Wt:** 210 **Born:** 1/6/69 **Age:** 30

		HOW MUCH HE PITCHED						WHAT HE GAVE UP											THE RESULTS						
Year Team	Lg	G	GS	CG	GF	IP	BFP	H	R	ER	HR	SH	SF	HB	TBB	IBB	SO	WP	Bk	W	L	Pct.	ShO	Sv-Op	Hld	ERA
1998 Buffalo *	AAA	2	0	0	0	2	8	3	0	0	0	0	0	0	0	0	4	0	0	0	0	.000	0	0- -	—	0.00
Fresno *	AAA	4	1	0	1	4.1	19	7	2	2	1	0	0	0	0	0	3	1	0	2	0	1.000	0	0- -	—	4.15
1996 Houston	NL	53	0	0	9	42	192	43	24	23	8	2	1	0	24	6	31	3	1	4	1	.800	0	0-2	7	4.93
1997 Cleveland	AL	34	0	0	7	18.1	86	19	13	12	2	0	0	1	14	3	13	1	0	0	0	.000	0	2-2	5	5.89
1998 Cle-SF		40	0	0	8	29	128	33	17	17	5	0	1	0	14	1	23	2	0	0	2	.000	0	0-2	9	5.28
1998 Cleveland	AL	31	0	0	5	22	96	25	13	13	1	0	1	0	11	1	16	2	0	0	1	.000	0	0-1	9	5.32
San Francisco	NL	9	0	0	3	7	32	8	4	4	4	0	0	0	3	0	7	0	0	0	1	.000	0	0-1	0	5.14
3 ML YEARS		127	0	0	24	89.1	406	95	54	52	15	2	2	1	52	10	67	6	1	4	3	.571	0	2-6	21	5.24

Hal Morris

Bats: L **Throws:** L **Pos:** 1B-46; DH-39; LF-39; PH/PR-10   **Ht:** 6'2" **Wt:** 195 **Born:** 4/9/65 **Age:** 34

					BATTING														BASERUNNING				PERCENTAGES		
Year Team	Lg	G	AB	H	2B	3B	HR	(Hm	Rd)	TB	R	RBI	TBB	IBB	SO	HBP	SH	SF	SB	CS	SB%	GDP	Avg	OBP	SLG
1988 New York	AL	15	20	2	0	0	0	(0	0)	2	1	0	0	0	9	0	0	0	0	0	.00	0	.100	.100	.100
1989 New York	AL	15	18	5	0	0	0	(0	0)	5	2	4	1	0	4	0	0	0	0	0	.00	2	.278	.316	.278
1990 Cincinnati	NL	107	309	105	22	3	7	(3	4)	154	50	36	21	4	32	1	3	2	9	3	.75	12	.340	.381	.498
1991 Cincinnati	NL	136	478	152	33	1	14	(9	5)	229	72	59	46	4	61	1	5	7	10	4	.71	4	.318	.374	.479
1992 Cincinnati	NL	115	395	107	21	3	6	(3	3)	152	41	53	45	8	53	2	2	2	6	6	.50	12	.271	.347	.385
1993 Cincinnati	NL	101	379	120	18	0	7	(2	5)	159	48	49	34	4	51	2	0	6	2	2	.50	5	.317	.371	.420
1994 Cincinnati	NL	112	436	146	30	4	10	(5	5)	214	60	78	34	4	62	5	2	6	6	2	.75	16	.335	.385	.491
1995 Cincinnati	NL	101	359	100	25	2	11	(6	5)	162	53	51	29	1	58	1	1	1	1	1	.50	10	.279	.333	.451

Year Team	Lg	G	AB	H	2B	3B	HR	(Hm	Rd)	TB	R	RBI	TBB	IBB	SO	HBP	SH	SF	SB	CS	SB%	GDP	Avg	OBP	SLG
1996 Cincinnati	NL	142	528	165	32	4	16	(7	9)	253	82	80	50	5	76	5	5	6	7	5	.58	12	.313	.374	.479
1997 Cincinnati	NL	96	333	92	20	1	1	(1	0)	117	42	33	23	2	43	3	4	1	3	1	.75	10	.276	.328	.351
1998 Kansas City	AL	127	472	146	27	2	1	(0	1)	180	50	40	32	6	52	1	4	7	1	0	1.00	15	.309	.350	.381
11 ML YEARS		1067	3727	1140	228	20	73	(36	37)	1627	501	483	315	51	501	21	26	38	45	24	.65	98	.306	.360	.437

Matt Morris

Pitches: Right **Bats:** Right **Pos:** SP-17 **Ht:** 6'5" **Wt:** 210 **Born:** 8/9/74 **Age:** 24

Year Team	Lg	G	GS	CG	GF	IP	BFP	H	R	ER	HR	SH	SF	HB	TBB	IBB	SO	WP	Bk	W	L	Pct.	ShO	Sv-Op	Hld	ERA
1995 New Jersey	A-	2	2	0	0	11	45	12	3	2	1	0	0	0	3	0	13	0	3	2	0	1.000	0	0- —	—	1.64
St. Pete	A+	6	6	1	0	34	134	22	16	9	1	2	0	0	11	0	31	0	2	3	2	.600	1	0- —	—	2.38
1996 Arkansas	AA	27	27	4	0	167	711	178	79	72	14	8	4	2	48	1	120	9	0	12	12	.500	4	0- —	—	3.88
Louisville	AAA	1	1	0	0	8	32	8	3	3	0	0	0	0	1	0	9	0	0	0	1	.000	0	0- —	—	3.38
1998 Arkansas	AA	1	0	0	1	4	17	4	0	0	0	0	0	0	0	0	2	0	0	0	0	.000	0	1- —	—	0.00
Memphis	AAA	4	4	0	0	14	60	16	8	7	1	0	0	0	4	0	21	1	0	1	0	1.000	0	0- —	—	4.50
1997 St. Louis	NL	33	33	3	0	217	900	208	88	77	12	11	7	7	69	2	149	5	3	12	9	.571	0	0-0	0	3.19
1998 St. Louis	NL	17	17	2	0	113.2	468	101	37	32	8	6	1	3	42	6	79	3	0	7	5	.583	0	0-0	0	2.53
2 ML YEARS		50	50	5	0	330.2	1368	309	125	109	20	17	8	10	111	8	228	8	3	19	14	.576	0	0-0	0	2.97

James Mouton

Bats: R **Throws:** R **Pos:** PH/PR-32; LF-16; RF-14; CF-4; DH-1 **Ht:** 5'9" **Wt:** 175 **Born:** 12/29/68 **Age:** 30

Year Team	Lg	G	AB	H	2B	3B	HR	(Hm	Rd)	TB	R	RBI	TBB	IBB	SO	HBP	SH	SF	SB	CS	SB%	GDP	Avg	OBP	SLG
1998 Las Vegas *	AAA	50	192	68	17	3	4	—	—	103	38	31	17	0	31	1	0	1	15	1	.94	9	.354	.408	.536
1994 Houston	NL	99	310	76	11	0	2	(1	1)	93	43	16	27	0	69	5	2	1	24	5	.83	6	.245	.315	.300
1995 Houston	NL	104	298	78	18	2	4	(2	2)	112	42	27	25	1	59	4	3	1	25	8	.76	5	.262	.326	.376
1996 Houston	NL	122	300	79	15	1	3	(2	1)	105	40	34	38	2	55	0	2	3	21	9	.70	9	.263	.343	.350
1997 Houston	NL	86	180	38	9	1	3	(1	2)	58	24	23	18	0	30	2	2	2	9	7	.56	3	.211	.287	.322
1998 San Diego	NL	55	63	12	2	1	0	(0	0)	16	8	7	7	1	11	0	0	1	4	3	.57	3	.190	.268	.254
5 ML YEARS		466	1151	283	55	5	12	(6	6)	384	157	107	115	4	224	11	9	8	83	32	.72	26	.246	.318	.334

Lyle Mouton

Bats: R **Throws:** R **Pos:** RF-12; LF-6; PH/PR-4; DH-2 **Ht:** 6'4" **Wt:** 240 **Born:** 5/13/69 **Age:** 30

Year Team	Lg	G	AB	H	2B	3B	HR	(Hm	Rd)	TB	R	RBI	TBB	IBB	SO	HBP	SH	SF	SB	CS	SB%	GDP	Avg	OBP	SLG
1998 Rochester *	AAA	37	137	44	9	2	7	—	—	78	23	32	13	0	31	2	0	0	1	1	.50	8	.321	.388	.569
1995 Chicago	AL	58	179	54	16	0	5	(4	1)	85	23	27	19	0	46	2	0	1	1	0	1.00	1	.302	.373	.475
1996 Chicago	AL	87	214	63	8	1	7	(4	3)	94	25	39	22	4	50	2	0	3	3	0	1.00	3	.294	.361	.439
1997 Chicago	AL	88	242	65	9	0	5	(4	1)	89	26	23	14	1	66	1	0	3	4	4	.50	8	.269	.308	.368
1998 Baltimore	AL	18	39	12	2	0	2	(0	2)	20	5	7	4	0	8	0	0	0	0	0	.00	6	.308	.372	.513
4 ML YEARS		251	674	194	35	1	19	(12	7)	288	79	96	59	5	170	5	0	7	8	4	.67	18	.288	.346	.427

Jamie Moyer

Pitches: Left **Bats:** Left **Pos:** SP-34 **Ht:** 6'0" **Wt:** 170 **Born:** 11/18/62 **Age:** 36

Year Team	Lg	G	GS	CG	GF	IP	BFP	H	R	ER	HR	SH	SF	HB	TBB	IBB	SO	WP	Bk	W	L	Pct.	ShO	Sv-Op	Hld	ERA
1986 Chicago	NL	16	16	1	0	87.1	395	107	52	49	10	3	3	3	42	1	45	3	3	7	4	.636	1	0-0	0	5.05
1987 Chicago	NL	35	33	1	1	201	899	210	127	114	28	14	7	5	97	9	147	11	2	12	15	.444	0	0-0	0	5.10
1988 Chicago	NL	34	30	3	1	202	855	212	84	78	20	14	4	4	55	7	121	4	0	9	15	.375	1	0-2	0	3.48
1989 Texas	AL	15	15	1	0	76	337	84	51	41	10	1	4	2	33	0	44	1	0	4	9	.308	0	0-0	0	4.86
1990 Texas	AL	33	10	1	6	102.1	447	115	59	53	6	7	7	4	39	4	58	1	0	2	6	.250	0	0-0	0	4.66
1991 St. Louis	NL	8	7	0	0	31.1	142	38	21	20	5	4	2	1	16	0	20	2	1	0	5	.000	0	0-0	0	5.74
1993 Baltimore	AL	25	25	3	0	152	630	154	63	58	11	3	1	6	38	2	90	1	1	12	9	.571	1	0-0	0	3.43
1994 Baltimore	AL	23	23	0	0	149	631	158	81	79	23	5	2	2	38	3	87	1	0	5	7	.417	0	0-0	0	4.77
1995 Baltimore	AL	27	18	0	3	115.2	483	117	70	67	18	5	3	3	30	0	65	0	0	8	6	.571	0	0-0	0	5.21
1996 Bos-Sea	AL	34	21	0	1	160.2	703	177	86	71	23	7	6	2	46	5	79	3	1	13	3	.813	0	0-0	0	3.98
1997 Seattle	AL	30	30	2	0	188.2	787	187	82	81	21	6	1	7	43	2	113	3	0	17	5	.773	0	0-0	0	3.86
1998 Seattle	AL	34	34	4	0	234.1	974	234	99	92	23	4	3	10	42	2	158	3	1	15	9	.625	3	0-0	0	3.53
1996 Boston	AL	23	10	0	1	90	405	111	50	45	14	4	3	1	27	2	50	2	1	7	1	.875	0	0-0	0	4.50
Seattle	AL	11	11	0	0	70.2	298	66	36	26	9	3	3	1	19	3	29	1	0	6	2	.750	0	0-0	0	3.31
12 ML YEARS		314	262	16	13	1700.1	7283	1793	875	803	198	67	43	49	519	35	1027	33	9	104	93	.528	6	0-2	2	4.25

Bill Mueller

Bats: Both **Throws:** Right **Pos:** 3B-137; 2B-10; PH/PR-8 **Ht:** 6'0" **Wt:** 170 **Born:** 3/17/71 **Age:** 28

Year Team	Lg	G	AB	H	2B	3B	HR	(Hm	Rd)	TB	R	RBI	TBB	IBB	SO	HBP	SH	SF	SB	CS	SB%	GDP	Avg	OBP	SLG
1996 San Francisco	NL	55	200	66	15	1	0	(0	0)	83	31	19	24	0	26	1	1	2	0	0	.00	1	.330	.401	.415
1997 San Francisco	NL	128	390	114	26	3	7	(5	2)	167	51	44	48	1	71	3	6	6	4	3	.57	10	.292	.369	.428
1998 San Francisco	NL	145	534	157	27	0	9	(1	8)	211	93	59	79	1	83	1	3	5	3	3	.50	12	.294	.383	.395
3 ML YEARS		328	1124	337	68	4	16	(6	10)	461	175	122	151	2	180	5	10	13	7	6	.54	23	.300	.381	.410

Terry Mulholland

Pitches: Left **Bats:** Right **Pos:** RP-64; SP-6   **Ht:** 6'3" **Wt:** 200 **Born:** 3/9/63 **Age:** 36

Year Team	Lg	G	GS	CG	GF	IP	BFP	H	R	ER	HR	SH	SF	HB	TBB	IBB	SO	WP	Bk	W	L	Pct.	ShO	Sv-Op	Hld	ERA
1986 San Francisco	NL	15	10	0	1	54.2	245	51	33	30	3	5	1	1	35	2	27	6	0	1	7	.125	0	0--	—	4.94
1988 San Francisco	NL	9	6	2	1	46	191	50	20	19	3	5	0	1	7	0	18	1	0	2	1	.667	1	0-0	1	3.72
1989 SF-Phi	NL	25	18	2	4	115.1	513	137	66	63	8	7	1	4	36	3	66	3	0	4	7	.364	1	0-0	1	4.92
1990 Philadelphia	NL	33	26	6	2	180.2	746	172	78	67	15	7	12	2	42	7	75	7	2	9	10	.474	1	0-1	0	3.34
1991 Philadelphia	NL	34	34	8	0	232	956	231	100	93	15	11	6	3	49	2	142	3	0	16	13	.552	3	0-0	0	3.61
1992 Philadelphia	NL	32	32	12	0	229	937	227	101	97	14	10	7	3	46	3	125	3	0	13	11	.542	2	0-0	0	3.81
1993 Philadelphia	NL	29	28	7	0	191	786	177	80	69	20	5	4	3	40	2	116	5	0	12	9	.571	2	0-0	0	3.25
1994 New York	AL	24	19	2	4	120.2	542	150	94	87	24	3	4	3	37	1	72	5	0	6	7	.462	0	0-0	0	6.49
1995 San Francisco	NL	29	24	2	2	149	666	190	112	96	25	11	6	4	38	1	65	4	0	5	13	.278	0	0-0	0	5.80
1996 Phi-Sea	NL	33	33	3	0	202.2	871	232	112	105	22	11	8	5	49	4	86	6	0	13	11	.542	0	0-0	0	4.66
1997 ChN-SF	NL	40	27	1	5	186.2	794	190	100	88	24	17	4	11	51	3	99	3	0	6	13	.316	0	0-0	1	4.24
1998 Chicago	NL	70	6	0	14	112	476	100	49	36	7	5	3	4	39	7	72	4	0	6	5	.545	0	3-5	19	2.89
1989 San Francisco	NL	5	1	0	2	11	51	15	5	5	0	0	0	0	4	0	6	0	0	0	0	.000	0	0-0	0	4.09
Philadelphia	NL	20	17	2	2	104.1	462	122	61	58	8	7	1	4	32	3	60	3	0	4	7	.364	1	0-0	0	5.00
1996 Philadelphia	NL	21	21	3	0	133.1	571	157	74	69	17	6	5	3	21	1	52	5	0	8	7	.533	0	0-0	0	4.66
Seattle	AL	12	12	0	0	69.1	300	75	38	36	5	5	3	2	28	3	34	1	0	5	4	.556	0	0-0	0	4.67
1997 Chicago	NL	25	25	1	0	157	668	162	79	71	20	13	3	9	45	2	74	2	0	6	12	.333	0	0-0	0	4.07
San Francisco	NL	15	2	0	5	29.2	126	28	21	17	4	4	1	2	6	1	25	1	0	0	1	.000	0	0-0	1	5.16
12 ML YEARS		373	263	45	33	1819.2	7723	1907	945	850	180	97	56	44	469	35	963	50	2	93	107	.465	10	3- -	—	4.20

Greg Mullins

Pitches: Left **Bats:** Left **Pos:** RP-2   **Ht:** 5'10" **Wt:** 160 **Born:** 12/13/71 **Age:** 27

Year Team	Lg	G	GS	CG	GF	IP	BFP	H	R	ER	HR	SH	SF	HB	TBB	IBB	SO	WP	Bk	W	L	Pct.	ShO	Sv-Op	Hld	ERA
1995 Helena	R+	4	4	0	0	23	98	7	7	7	0	0	0	2	6	0	14	0	2	4	0	1.000	0	0--	—	2.74
Beloit	A	15	4	0	6	36.1	151	26	16	16	2	0	1	5	14	0	48	2	3	3	1	.750	0	2--	—	3.96
1996 El Paso	AA	23	1	0	6	28	130	30	25	22	7	3	0	1	17	2	28	0	1	1	5	.167	0	2--	—	7.07
Stockton	A+	10	0	0	3	11.1	51	13	5	5	0	0	0	1	4	0	12	0	0	0	0	.000	0	0--	—	3.97
1997 Stockton	A+	30	0	0	30	33	131	22	9	8	2	0	0	1	12	0	52	4	0	0	2	.000	0	19--	—	2.18
El Paso	AA	25	0	0	22	23.1	100	19	8	7	2	2	1	1	11	1	21	2	0	1	1	.500	0	13--	—	2.70
1998 Louisville	AAA	61	0	0	39	66	279	57	26	26	5	2	2	2	23	2	86	2	1	1	3	.250	0	18--	—	3.55
1998 Milwaukee	NL	2	0	0	1	1	5	1	0	0	0	0	0	1	0	0	1	0	0	0	0	.000	0	0-0	0	0.00

Bobby Munoz

Pitches: Right **Bats:** Right **Pos:** RP-8; SP-1   **Ht:** 6'7" **Wt:** 237 **Born:** 3/3/68 **Age:** 31

Year Team	Lg	G	GS	CG	GF	IP	BFP	H	R	ER	HR	SH	SF	HB	TBB	IBB	SO	WP	Bk	W	L	Pct.	ShO	Sv-Op	Hld	ERA
1998 Rochester *	AAA	44	0	0	34	59.1	228	40	9	7	5	1	1	5	13	0	46	4	0	3	1	.750	0	19--	—	1.06
1993 New York	AL	38	0	0	12	45.2	208	48	27	27	1	1	3	0	26	5	33	2	0	3	3	.500	0	0-2	6	5.32
1994 Philadelphia	NL	21	14	1	1	104.1	447	101	40	31	8	5	5	1	35	0	59	5	1	7	5	.583	0	1-2	0	2.67
1995 Philadelphia	NL	3	3	0	0	15.2	70	15	13	10	2	0	2	3	9	0	6	0	0	0	2	.000	0	0-0	0	5.74
1996 Philadelphia	NL	6	6	0	0	25.1	123	42	28	22	5	2	1	1	7	1	8	0	0	0	3	.000	0	0-0	0	7.82
1997 Philadelphia	NL	8	7	0	1	33.1	161	47	35	33	4	2	3	2	15	1	20	3	1	1	5	.167	0	0-0	0	8.91
1998 Baltimore	AL	9	1	0	5	12	58	18	13	13	4	1	3	1	6	0	6	0	0	0	0	.000	0	0-0	0	9.75
6 ML YEARS		85	31	1	19	236.1	1067	271	156	136	24	11	17	8	98	7	132	10	3	11	18	.379	0	1-4	6	5.18

Mike Munoz

Pitches: Left **Bats:** Left **Pos:** RP-40   **Ht:** 6'2" **Wt:** 198 **Born:** 7/12/65 **Age:** 33

Year Team	Lg	G	GS	CG	GF	IP	BFP	H	R	ER	HR	SH	SF	HB	TBB	IBB	SO	WP	Bk	W	L	Pct.	ShO	Sv-Op	Hld	ERA
1989 Los Angeles	NL	3	0	0	1	2.2	14	5	5	5	1	0	0	0	2	0	3	0	0	0	0	.000	0	0-0	0	16.88
1990 Los Angeles	NL	8	0	0	3	5.2	24	6	2	2	0	1	0	0	3	0	2	0	0	0	1	.000	0	0-1	2	3.18
1991 Detroit	AL	6	0	0	4	9.1	46	14	10	10	0	0	1	0	5	0	3	1	0	0	0	.000	0	0-0	0	9.64
1992 Detroit	AL	65	0	0	15	48	210	44	16	16	3	4	2	0	25	6	23	2	0	1	2	.333	0	2-3	15	3.00
1993 Det-Col		29	0	0	10	21	101	25	14	11	2	3	2	0	15	4	17	2	0	2	2	.500	0	0-2	2	4.71
1994 Colorado	NL	57	0	0	8	45.2	200	37	22	19	3	2	1	0	31	5	32	2	0	4	2	.667	0	1-2	12	3.74
1995 Colorado	NL	64	0	0	19	43.2	208	54	38	36	9	2	2	1	27	0	37	5	0	2	4	.333	0	2-4	12	7.42
1996 Colorado	NL	54	0	0	7	44.2	203	55	33	33	4	3	1	1	16	2	45	0	0	2	2	.500	0	0-3	13	6.65
1997 Colorado	NL	64	0	0	16	45.2	192	52	25	23	4	0	2	0	13	0	26	3	0	3	3	.500	0	2-2	19	4.53
1998 Colorado	NL	40	0	0	13	41.1	186	53	32	26	2	1	1	1	16	2	24	1	0	2	2	.500	0	3-4	1	5.66
1993 Detroit	AL	8	0	0	3	3	19	4	2	2	1	0	0	0	6	1	1	0	0	0	1	.000	0	0-0	1	6.00
Colorado	NL	21	0	0	7	18	82	21	12	9	1	3	2	0	9	3	16	2	0	2	1	.667	0	0-2	1	4.50
10 ML YEARS		390	0	0	96	307.2	1387	345	197	181	28	16	12	3	153	19	212	16	0	16	18	.471	0	10-21	76	5.29

Mike Mussina

Pitches: Right   **Bats:** Both   **Pos:** SP-29   **Ht:** 6'2"   **Wt:** 185   **Born:** 12/8/68   **Age:** 30

Year Team	Lg	G	GS	CG	GF	IP	BFP	H	R	ER	HR	SH	SF	HB	TBB	IBB	SO	WP	Bk	W	L	Pct.	ShO	Sv-Op	Hld	ERA
1991 Baltimore	AL	12	12	2	0	87.2	349	77	31	28	7	3	2	1	21	0	52	3	1	4	5	.444	0	0-0	0	2.87
1992 Baltimore	AL	32	32	8	0	241	957	212	70	68	16	13	6	2	48	2	130	6	0	18	5	.783	4	0-0	0	2.54
1993 Baltimore	AL	25	25	3	0	167.2	693	163	84	83	20	6	4	3	44	2	117	5	0	14	6	.700	2	0-0	0	4.46
1994 Baltimore	AL	24	24	3	0	176.1	712	163	63	60	19	3	9	1	42	1	99	0	0	16	5	.762	0	0-0	0	3.06
1995 Baltimore	AL	32	32	7	0	221.2	882	187	86	81	24	2	2	1	50	4	158	2	0	19	9	.679	4	0-0	0	3.29
1996 Baltimore	AL	36	36	4	0	243.1	1039	264	137	130	31	4	4	3	69	0	204	3	0	19	11	.633	1	0-0	0	4.81
1997 Baltimore	AL	33	33	4	0	224.2	905	197	87	80	27	3	2	3	54	3	218	5	0	15	8	.652	1	0-0	0	3.20
1998 Baltimore	AL	29	29	4	0	206.1	835	189	85	80	22	6	3	4	41	3	175	10	0	13	10	.565	2	0-0	0	3.49
8 ML YEARS		223	223	35	0	1568.2	6372	1452	643	610	166	40	32	18	369	15	1153	34	1	118	59	.667	14	0-0	0	3.50

Greg Myers

Bats: Left   **Throws:** Right   **Pos:** C-52; PH/PR-24   **Ht:** 6'2"   **Wt:** 208   **Born:** 4/14/66   **Age:** 33

Year Team	Lg	G	AB	H	2B	3B	HR	(Hm	Rd)	TB	R	RBI	TBB	IBB	SO	HBP	SH	SF	SB	CS	SB%	GDP	Avg	OBP	SLG
1998 Rancho Cuca *	A+	3	9	0	0	0	0	—	—	0	1	0	2	0	1	0	0	0	0	0	.00	1	.000	.182	.000
Las Vegas *	AAA	3	9	5	0	0	0	—	—	5	0	1	0	0	0	0	0	0	0	0	.00	0	.556	.556	.556
1987 Toronto	AL	7	9	1	0	0	0	(0	0)	1	1	0	0	0	3	0	0	0	0	0	.00	2	.111	.111	.111
1989 Toronto	AL	17	44	5	2	0	0	(0	0)	7	0	1	2	0	9	0	0	0	0	1	.00	2	.114	.152	.159
1990 Toronto	AL	87	250	59	7	1	5	(3	2)	83	33	22	22	0	33	0	1	4	0	1	.00	12	.236	.293	.332
1991 Toronto	AL	107	309	81	22	0	8	(5	3)	127	25	36	21	4	45	0	0	3	0	0	.00	13	.262	.306	.411
1992 Tor-Cal	AL	30	78	18	7	0	1	(0	1)	28	4	13	5	0	11	0	1	2	0	0	.00	2	.231	.271	.359
1993 California	AL	108	290	74	10	0	7	(4	3)	105	27	40	17	2	47	2	3	3	3	3	.50	8	.255	.298	.362
1994 California	AL	45	126	31	6	0	2	(1	1)	43	10	8	10	3	27	0	5	1	0	2	.00	3	.246	.299	.341
1995 California	AL	85	273	71	12	2	9	(6	3)	114	35	38	17	3	49	1	1	2	0	0	.00	4	.260	.304	.418
1996 Minnesota	AL	97	329	94	22	3	6	(3	3)	140	37	47	19	3	52	0	0	5	0	0	.00	11	.286	.320	.426
1997 Min-Atl		71	174	45	11	1	5	(3	2)	73	24	29	17	2	32	0	0	4	0	0	.00	4	.259	.321	.420
1998 San Diego	NL	69	171	42	10	0	4	(1	3)	64	19	20	17	1	36	0	0	1	0	1	.00	6	.246	.312	.374
1992 Toronto	AL	22	61	14	6	0	1	(0	1)	23	4	13	5	0	5	0	0	2	0	0	.00	2	.230	.279	.377
California	AL	8	17	4	1	0	0	(0	0)	5	0	0	0	0	6	0	1	0	0	0	.00	0	.235	.235	.294
1997 Minnesota	AL	62	165	44	11	1	5	(3	2)	72	24	28	16	2	29	0	0	4	0	0	.00	4	.267	.328	.436
Atlanta	NL	9	9	1	0	0	0	(0	0)	1	0	1	1	0	3	0	0	0	0	0	.00	0	.111	.200	.111
11 ML YEARS		723	2053	521	109	7	47	(26	21)	785	215	254	147	18	344	3	11	23	3	9	.25	67	.254	.301	.382

Mike Myers

Pitches: Left   **Bats:** Left   **Pos:** RP-70   **Ht:** 6'4"   **Wt:** 205   **Born:** 6/26/69   **Age:** 30

Year Team	Lg	G	GS	CG	GF	IP	BFP	H	R	ER	HR	SH	SF	HB	TBB	IBB	SO	WP	Bk	W	L	Pct.	ShO	Sv-Op	Hld	ERA
1995 Fla-Det		13	0	0	5	8.1	42	11	7	7	1	0	1	2	7	0	4	0	0	1	0	1.000	0	0-1	1	7.56
1996 Detroit	AL	83	0	0	25	64.2	298	70	41	36	6	2	1	4	34	8	69	2	0	1	5	.167	0	6-8	17	5.01
1997 Detroit	AL	88	0	0	23	53.2	246	58	36	34	12	4	3	2	25	2	50	0	0	0	4	.000	0	2-5	18	5.70
1998 Milwaukee	NL	70	0	0	14	50	211	44	19	15	5	4	2	6	22	1	40	2	1	2	2	.500	0	1-3	23	2.70
1995 Florida	NL	2	0	0	2	2	9	1	0	0	0	0	0	0	3	0	0	0	0	0	0	.000	0	0-0	0	0.00
Detroit	AL	11	0	0	3	6.1	33	10	7	7	1	0	1	2	4	0	4	0	0	1	0	1.000	0	0-1	1	9.95
4 ML YEARS		254	0	0	67	176.2	797	183	103	92	24	10	7	14	88	11	163	4	1	4	11	.267	0	9-17	59	4.69

Randy Myers

Pitches: Left   **Bats:** Left   **Pos:** RP-62   **Ht:** 6'1"   **Wt:** 225   **Born:** 9/19/62   **Age:** 36

Year Team	Lg	G	GS	CG	GF	IP	BFP	H	R	ER	HR	SH	SF	HB	TBB	IBB	SO	WP	Bk	W	L	Pct.	ShO	Sv-Op	Hld	ERA
1985 New York	NL	1	0	0	1	2	7	0	0	0	0	0	0	1	0	2	0	0	0	0	.000	0	0-0	0	0.00
1986 New York	NL	10	0	0	5	10.2	53	11	5	5	1	0	0	0	9	1	13	0	0	0	0	.000	0	0-0	0	4.22
1987 New York	NL	54	0	0	18	75	314	61	36	33	6	7	6	0	30	5	92	3	0	3	6	.333	0	6-9	7	3.96
1988 New York	NL	55	0	0	44	68	261	45	15	13	5	3	2	2	17	2	69	2	0	7	3	.700	0	26-29	3	1.72
1989 New York	NL	65	0	0	47	84.1	349	62	23	22	4	6	2	0	40	4	88	3	0	7	4	.636	0	24-29	2	2.35
1990 Cincinnati	NL	66	0	0	59	86.2	353	59	24	20	6	4	2	0	38	8	98	2	1	4	6	.400	0	31-37	0	2.08
1991 Cincinnati	NL	58	12	1	18	132	575	116	61	52	8	6	1	1	80	5	108	2	1	6	13	.316	0	6-10	8	3.55
1992 San Diego	NL	66	0	0	57	79.2	348	84	38	38	7	7	5	1	34	3	66	5	0	3	6	.333	0	38-46	0	4.29
1993 Chicago	NL	73	0	0	69	75.1	313	65	26	26	7	1	2	1	26	2	86	3	0	2	4	.333	0	53-59	0	3.11
1994 Chicago	NL	38	0	0	34	40.1	174	40	18	17	3	3	1	0	16	1	32	2	0	1	5	.167	0	21-26	0	3.79
1995 Chicago	NL	57	0	0	47	55.2	240	49	25	24	7	2	3	0	28	1	59	0	0	1	2	.333	0	38-44	0	3.88
1996 Baltimore	AL	62	0	0	58	58.2	262	60	24	23	7	3	3	1	29	4	74	3	0	4	4	.500	0	31-38	0	3.53
1997 Baltimore	AL	61	0	0	57	59.2	241	47	12	10	2	2	0	0	22	2	56	3	0	2	3	.400	0	45-46	2	1.51
1998 Tor-SD		62	0	0	42	56.2	254	59	31	31	6	4	1	2	26	5	41	4	0	4	7	.364	0	28-34	8	4.92
1998 Toronto	AL	41	0	0	37	42.1	190	44	21	21	4	2	1	2	19	4	32	2	0	3	4	.429	0	28-33	0	4.46
San Diego	NL	21	0	0	5	14.1	64	15	10	10	2	2	0	0	7	1	9	2	0	1	3	.250	0	0-1	8	6.28
14 ML YEARS		728	12	1	548	884.2	3744	758	338	314	69	50	33	12	396	43	884	32	2	44	63	.411	0	347-407	32	3.19

Rodney Myers

Pitches: Right **Bats:** Right **Pos:** RP-12   **Ht:** 6'1" **Wt:** 205 **Born:** 6/26/69 **Age:** 3

		HOW MUCH HE PITCHED					WHAT HE GAVE UP											THE RESULTS					
Year Team	Lg	G	GS	CG	GF	IP	BFP	H	R	ER	HR	SH	SF	HB	TBB	IBB	SO	WP	Bk	W	L	Pct.	ShO	Sv-Op	Hld	ERA
1998 Iowa *	AAA	33	13	2	17	101.1	429	84	47	44	10	5	2	5	45	1	86	6	0	7	5	.583	1	11- -	—	3.91
1996 Chicago	NL	45	0	0	8	67.1	298	61	38	35	6	1	5	3	38	3	50	4	1	2	1	.667	0	0-0	1	4.68
1997 Chicago	NL	5	1	0	2	9	44	12	6	6	1	0	0	1	7	1	6	0	0	0	0	.000	0	0-0	0	6.00
1998 Chicago	NL	12	0	0	3	18	82	26	14	14	3	0	0	0	6	0	15	1	0	0	0	.000	0	0-1	0	7.00
3 ML YEARS		62	1	0	13	94.1	424	99	58	55	10	1	5	4	51	4	71	5	1	2	1	.667	0	0-1	1	5.25

Tim Naehring

Bats: Right **Throws:** Right **Pos:** 3B   **Ht:** 6'2" **Wt:** 203 **Born:** 2/1/67 **Age:** 32

		BATTING																	BASERUNNING				PERCENTAGES		
Year Team	Lg	G	AB	H	2B	3B	HR	(Hm	Rd)	TB	R	RBI	TBB	IBB	SO	HBP	SH	SF	SB	CS	SB%	GDP	Avg	OBP	SLG
1990 Boston	AL	24	85	23	6	0	2	(2	0)	35	10	12	8	1	15	0	0	0	0	0	.00	2	.271	.333	.412
1991 Boston	AL	20	55	6	1	0	0	(0	0)	7	1	3	6	0	15	0	4	0	0	0	.00	0	.109	.197	.127
1992 Boston	AL	72	186	43	8	0	3	(0	3)	60	12	14	18	0	31	3	6	1	0	0	.00	1	.231	.308	.323
1993 Boston	AL	39	127	42	10	0	1	(0	1)	55	14	17	10	0	26	0	3	1	1	0	1.00	3	.331	.377	.433
1994 Boston	AL	80	297	82	18	1	7	(4	3)	123	41	42	30	1	56	4	7	1	1	3	.25	11	.276	.349	.414
1995 Boston	AL	126	433	133	27	2	10	(5	5)	194	61	57	77	5	66	4	4	2	0	2	.00	16	.307	.415	.448
1996 Boston	AL	116	430	124	16	0	17	(9	8)	191	77	65	49	4	63	4	2	4	2	1	.67	14	.288	.363	.444
1997 Boston	AL	70	259	74	18	1	9	(4	5)	121	38	40	38	0	40	1	0	1	1	1	.50	10	.286	.375	.467
8 ML YEARS		547	1872	527	104	4	49	(24	25)	786	254	250	236	11	312	16	26	12	5	7	.42	57	.282	.365	.420

Charles Nagy

Pitches: Right **Bats:** Left **Pos:** SP-33   **Ht:** 6'3" **Wt:** 200 **Born:** 5/5/67 **Age:** 32

		HOW MUCH HE PITCHED						WHAT HE GAVE UP												THE RESULTS					
Year Team	Lg	G	GS	CG	GF	IP	BFP	H	R	ER	HR	SH	SF	HB	TBB	IBB	SO	WP	Bk	W	L	Pct.	ShO	Sv-Op	Hld	ERA
1990 Cleveland	AL	9	8	0	1	45.2	208	58	31	30	7	1	1	1	21	1	26	1	1	2	4	.333	0	0-0	0	5.91
1991 Cleveland	AL	33	33	6	0	211.1	914	228	103	97	15	5	9	6	66	7	109	6	2	10	15	.400	1	0-0	0	4.13
1992 Cleveland	AL	33	33	10	0	252	1018	245	91	83	11	6	9	2	57	1	169	7	0	17	10	.630	3	0-0	0	2.96
1993 Cleveland	AL	9	9	1	0	48.2	223	66	38	34	6	2	1	2	13	1	30	2	0	2	6	.250	0	0-0	0	6.29
1994 Cleveland	AL	23	23	3	0	169.1	717	175	76	65	15	2	2	5	48	1	108	5	1	10	8	.556	0	0-0	0	3.45
1995 Cleveland	AL	29	29	2	0	178	771	194	95	90	20	2	5	6	61	0	139	2	0	16	6	.727	1	0-0	0	4.55
1996 Cleveland	AL	32	32	5	0	222	921	217	89	84	21	2	4	3	61	2	167	7	0	17	5	.773	0	0-0	0	3.41
1997 Cleveland	AL	34	34	1	0	227	991	253	115	108	27	6	6	7	77	4	149	5	0	15	11	.577	1	0-0	0	4.28
1998 Cleveland	AL	33	33	2	0	210.1	930	250	139	122	34	8	6	9	66	12	120	3	0	15	10	.600	0	0-0	0	5.22
9 ML YEARS		235	234	30	1	1564.1	6693	1686	777	713	156	33	43	41	470	29	1017	38	4	104	75	.581	6	0-0	0	4.10

Dan Naulty

Pitches: Right **Bats:** Right **Pos:** RP-19   **Ht:** 6'6" **Wt:** 224 **Born:** 1/6/70 **Age:** 29

		HOW MUCH HE PITCHED						WHAT HE GAVE UP												THE RESULTS					
Year Team	Lg	G	GS	CG	GF	IP	BFP	H	R	ER	HR	SH	SF	HB	TBB	IBB	SO	WP	Bk	W	L	Pct.	ShO	Sv-Op	Hld	ERA
1998 Salt Lake *	AAA	5	0	0	2	5.1	24	8	4	4	0	0	0	0	2	0	5	0	0	1	0	1.000	0	0- -	—	6.75
1996 Minnesota	AL	49	0	0	15	57	245	43	26	24	5	2	0	0	35	3	56	2	0	3	2	.600	0	4-9	4	3.79
1997 Minnesota	AL	29	0	0	8	30.2	128	29	20	20	8	0	4	0	10	0	23	3	0	1	1	.500	0	1-3	8	5.87
1998 Minnesota	AL	19	0	0	9	23.2	104	25	16	13	3	0	1	0	10	1	15	0	0	0	2	.000	0	0-1	0	4.94
3 ML YEARS		97	0	0	32	111.1	477	97	62	57	16	2	5	0	55	4	94	5	0	4	5	.444	0	5-13	12	4.61

Jaime Navarro

Pitches: Right **Bats:** Right **Pos:** SP-27; RP-10   **Ht:** 6'4" **Wt:** 230 **Born:** 3/27/68 **Age:** 31

		HOW MUCH HE PITCHED						WHAT HE GAVE UP												THE RESULTS					
Year Team	Lg	G	GS	CG	GF	IP	BFP	H	R	ER	HR	SH	SF	HB	TBB	IBB	SO	WP	Bk	W	L	Pct.	ShO	Sv-Op	Hld	ERA
1989 Milwaukee	AL	19	17	1	1	109.2	470	119	47	38	6	5	2	1	32	3	56	3	0	7	8	.467	0	0-0	0	3.12
1990 Milwaukee	AL	32	22	3	2	149.1	654	176	83	74	11	4	5	4	41	3	75	6	5	8	7	.533	0	1-2	3	4.46
1991 Milwaukee	AL	34	34	10	0	234	1002	237	117	102	18	7	8	6	73	3	114	10	0	15	12	.556	2	0-0	0	3.92
1992 Milwaukee	AL	34	34	5	0	246	1004	224	98	91	14	9	13	6	64	4	100	6	0	17	11	.607	3	0-0	0	3.33
1993 Milwaukee	AL	35	34	5	0	214.1	955	254	135	127	21	6	17	11	73	4	114	11	0	11	12	.478	1	0-0	0	5.33
1994 Milwaukee	AL	29	10	0	7	89.2	411	115	71	66	10	2	4	4	35	4	65	3	0	4	9	.308	0	0-0	0	6.62
1995 Chicago	NL	29	29	1	0	200.1	837	194	79	73	19	2	3	3	56	7	128	1	0	14	6	.700	1	0-0	0	3.28
1996 Chicago	NL	35	35	4	0	236.2	1007	244	116	103	25	10	7	10	72	5	158	10	0	15	12	.556	1	0-0	0	3.92
1997 Chicago	AL	33	33	2	0	209.2	957	267	155	135	22	2	14	3	73	6	142	14	1	9	14	.391	0	0-0	0	5.79
1998 Chicago	AL	37	27	1	4	172.2	802	223	135	122	30	3	7	7	77	1	71	18	0	8	16	.333	0	1-1	0	6.36
10 ML YEARS		317	275	32	14	1862.1	8099	2053	1036	931	176	50	80	55	596	40	1023	82	6	108	107	.502	8	2-3	3	4.50

Denny Neagle

Pitches: Left **Bats:** Left **Pos:** SP-31; RP-1   **Ht:** 6'2" **Wt:** 225 **Born:** 9/13/68 **Age:** 30

		HOW MUCH HE PITCHED						WHAT HE GAVE UP												THE RESULTS					
Year Team	Lg	G	GS	CG	GF	IP	BFP	H	R	ER	HR	SH	SF	HB	TBB	IBB	SO	WP	Bk	W	L	Pct.	ShO	Sv-Op	Hld	ERA
1991 Minnesota	AL	7	3	0	2	20	92	28	9	9	3	0	0	0	7	2	14	1	0	0	1	.000	0	0-0	0	4.05
1992 Pittsburgh	NL	55	6	0	8	86.1	380	81	46	43	9	4	3	2	43	8	77	3	2	4	6	.400	0	2-4	5	4.48
1993 Pittsburgh	NL	50	7	0	13	81.1	360	82	49	48	10	1	1	3	37	3	73	5	0	3	5	.375	0	1-1	6	5.31

			HOW MUCH HE PITCHED			WHAT HE GAVE UP												THE RESULTS					
Year Team	Lg	G GS CG GF	IP	BFP	H	R	ER	HR	SH	SF	HB	TBB	IBB	SO	WP	Bk	W	L	Pct.	ShO	Sv-Op	Hld	ERA
1994 Pittsburgh	NL	24 24 2 0	137	587	135	80	78	18	7	6	3	49	3	122	2	0	9	10	.474	0	0-0	0	5.12
1995 Pittsburgh	NL	31 **31** 5 0	**209.2**	**876**	**221**	91	80	20	13	6	3	45	3	150	6	0	13	8	.619	1	0-0	0	3.43
1996 Pit-Atl	NL	33 33 2 0	221.1	910	226	93	86	26	10	4	3	48	2	149	3	1	16	9	.640	0	0-0	0	3.50
1997 Atlanta	NL	34 34 4 0	233.1	947	204	87	77	18	12	6	6	49	5	172	3	0	**20**	5	.800	4	0-0	0	2.97
1998 Atlanta	NL	32 31 5 0	210.1	861	196	91	83	25	7	3	6	60	3	165	6	1	16	11	.593	2	0-0	0	3.55
1996 Pittsburgh	NL	27 27 1 0	182.2	745	186	67	62	21	9	3	3	34	2	131	2	1	14	6	.700	0	0-0	0	3.05
Atlanta	NL	6 6 1 0	38.2	165	40	26	24	5	1	1	0	14	0	18	1	0	2	3	.400	0	0-0	0	5.59
8 ML YEARS		266 169 18 23	1199.1	5013	1173	546	504	129	54	29	26	338	29	922	29	4	81	55	.596	7	3-5	11	3.78

Mike Neill

Bats: Left **Throws:** Left **Pos:** LF-4; CF-2; PH/PR-1 **Ht:** 6'2" **Wt:** 190 **Born:** 4/27/70 **Age:** 29

								BATTING												BASERUNNING				PERCENTAGES		
Year Team	Lg	G	AB	H	2B	3B	HR	(Hm	Rd)	TB	R	RBI	TBB	IBB	SO	HBP	SH	SF		SB	CS	SB%	GDP		Avg	OBP	SLG
1991 Sou. Oregon	A-	63	240	84	14	0	5	—	—	113	42	42	35	3	54	0	4	1		9	3	.75	1		.350	.431	.471
1992 Reno	A+	130	473	159	26	7	5	—	—	214	101	76	81	2	96	5	6	2		23	11	.68	15		.336	.437	.452
Huntsville	AA	5	16	5	0	0	0	—	—	5	4	2	2	0	7	0	1	1		1	0	1.00	0		.313	.368	.313
1993 Huntsville	AA	54	179	44	8	0	1	—	—	55	30	15	34	0	45	1	0	1		3	4	.43	4		.246	.367	.307
Modesto	A+	17	62	12	3	0	0	—	—	15	4	4	12	0	12	0	1	0		0	1	.00	0		.194	.324	.242
1994 Tacoma	AAA	7	22	5	1	0	0	—	—	6	1	2	3	0	7	0	0	0		0	0	.00	2		.227	.320	.273
Modesto	A+	47	165	48	4	1	2	—	—	60	22	18	26	1	50	1	2	1		1	1	.50	4		.291	.389	.364
1995 Modesto	A+	71	257	71	17	1	6	—	—	108	39	36	34	2	65	2	5	1		4	4	.50	6		.276	.364	.420
Huntsville	AA	33	107	32	6	1	2	—	—	46	11	16	12	1	29	0	0	1		1	0	1.00	1		.299	.367	.430
1996 Edmonton	AAA	6	20	3	1	0	1	—	—	7	4	4	2	0	3	0	1	0		0	0	.00	0		.150	.227	.350
Modesto	A+	114	442	150	20	6	19	—	—	239	101	78	68	4	123	4	2	2		28	7	.80	3		.339	.430	.541
1997 Edmonton	AAA	7	21	4	0	0	0	—	—	4	3	3	7	0	7	0	2	0		1	1	.50	1		.190	.393	.190
Huntsville	AA	122	486	165	30	2	14	—	—	241	129	80	72	0	113	4	3	3		16	7	.70	8		.340	.427	.496
1998 Edmonton	AAA	99	371	112	18	4	10	—	—	168	72	48	65	0	91	2	6	1		6	5	.55	12		.302	.408	.453
Huntsville	AA	12	35	9	5	0	0	—	—	14	1	2	4	1	13	0	1	0		0	0	.00	0		.257	.333	.400
1998 Oakland	AL	6	15	4	1	0	0	(0	0)	5	2	0	2	0	4	0	0	0		0	0	.00	0		.267	.353	.333

Jeff Nelson

Pitches: Right **Bats:** Right **Pos:** RP-45 **Ht:** 6'8" **Wt:** 225 **Born:** 11/17/66 **Age:** 32

			HOW MUCH HE PITCHED			WHAT HE GAVE UP												THE RESULTS					
Year Team	Lg	G GS CG GF	IP	BFP	H	R	ER	HR	SH	SF	HB	TBB	IBB	SO	WP	Bk	W	L	Pct.	ShO	Sv-Op	Hld	ERA
1998 Tampa *	A+	2 1 0 0	2	9	1	1	0	0	0	0	1	1	0	4	0	0	0	0	.000	0	0- -	—	0.00
1992 Seattle	AL	66 0 0 27	81	352	71	34	31	7	9	3	6	44	**12**	46	2	0	1	7	.125	0	6-14	6	3.44
1993 Seattle	AL	71 0 0 13	60	269	57	30	29	5	2	4	8	34	10	61	2	0	5	3	.625	0	1-11	17	4.35
1994 Seattle	AL	28 0 0 7	42.1	185	35	18	13	3	1	1	8	20	4	44	2	0	0	0	.000	0	0-0	2	2.76
1995 Seattle	AL	62 0 0 24	78.2	318	58	21	19	4	5	3	6	27	5	96	1	0	7	3	.700	0	2-4	14	2.17
1996 New York	AL	73 0 0 27	74.1	328	75	38	36	6	3	1	2	36	1	91	4	0	4	4	.500	0	2-4	10	4.36
1997 New York	AL	77 0 0 22	78.2	328	53	32	25	7	7	2	4	37	**12**	81	4	0	3	7	.300	0	2-8	22	2.86
1998 New York	AL	45 0 0 13	40.1	192	44	18	17	1	1	3	8	22	4	35	2	0	5	3	.625	0	3-6	10	3.79
7 ML YEARS		422 0 0 133	455.1	1971	393	191	170	33	28	17	42	220	48	454	17	0	25	27	.481	0	16-47	81	3.36

Robb Nen

Pitches: Right **Bats:** Right **Pos:** RP-78 **Ht:** 6'5" **Wt:** 210 **Born:** 11/28/69 **Age:** 29

			HOW MUCH HE PITCHED			WHAT HE GAVE UP												THE RESULTS					
Year Team	Lg	G GS CG GF	IP	BFP	H	R	ER	HR	SH	SF	HB	TBB	IBB	SO	WP	Bk	W	L	Pct.	ShO	Sv-Op	Hld	ERA
1993 Tex-Fla		24 4 0 5	56	272	63	45	42	6	1	2	0	46	0	39	6	1	2	1	.667	0	0-0	0	6.75
1994 Florida	NL	44 0 0 28	58	228	46	20	19	6	3	1	0	17	2	60	3	2	5	5	.500	0	15-15	1	2.95
1995 Florida	NL	62 0 0 **54**	65.2	279	62	26	24	6	0	1	1	23	3	68	2	0	0	7	.000	0	23-29	0	3.29
1996 Florida	NL	75 0 0 66	83	326	67	21	18	2	5	1	1	21	6	92	4	0	5	1	.833	0	35-42	0	1.95
1997 Florida	NL	73 0 0 65	74	332	72	35	32	7	1	3	0	40	7	81	5	0	9	3	.750	0	35-42	0	3.89
1998 San Francisco	NL	78 0 0 67	88.2	357	59	21	15	4	2	2	1	25	5	110	3	0	7	7	.500	0	40-45	0	1.52
1993 Texas	AL	9 3 0 3	22.2	113	28	17	16	1	0	1	0	26	0	12	2	1	1	1	.500	0	0-0	0	6.35
Florida	NL	15 1 0 2	33.1	159	35	28	26	5	1	1	0	20	0	27	4	0	1	0	1.000	0	0-0	0	7.02
6 ML YEARS		356 4 0 285	425.1	1794	369	168	150	31	12	10	3	172	23	450	23	3	28	24	.538	0	148-173	1	3.17

Phil Nevin

Bats: Right **Throws:** Right **Pos:** C-69; DH-3; PH/PR-3; 1B-2 **Ht:** 6'2" **Wt:** 231 **Born:** 1/19/71 **Age:** 28

								BATTING												BASERUNNING				PERCENTAGES		
Year Team	Lg	G	AB	H	2B	3B	HR	(Hm	Rd)	TB	R	RBI	TBB	IBB	SO	HBP	SH	SF		SB	CS	SB%	GDP		Avg	OBP	SLG
1995 Hou-Det		47	156	28	4	1	2	(2	0)	40	13	13	18	1	40	4	1	0		1	0	1.00	5		.179	.281	.256
1996 Detroit	AL	38	120	35	5	0	8	(3	5)	64	15	19	8	0	39	1	0	1		1	0	1.00	1		.292	.338	.533
1997 Detroit	AL	93	251	59	16	1	9	(4	5)	104	32	35	25	1	68	1	0	1		0	1	.00	5		.235	.306	.414
1998 Anaheim	AL	75	237	54	8	1	8	(3	5)	88	27	27	17	0	67	5	0	2		0	0	.00	5		.228	.291	.371
1995 Houston	NL	18	60	7	1	0	0	(0	0)	8	4	1	7	1	13	1	1	0		1	0	1.00	2		.117	.221	.133
Detroit	AL	29	96	21	3	1	2	(2	0)	32	9	12	11	0	27	3	0	0		0	0	.00	3		.219	.318	.333
4 ML YEARS		253	764	176	33	3	27	(12	15)	296	87	94	68	2	214	11	1	4		2	1	.67	17		.230	.301	.387

Marc Newfield

Bats: Right **Throws:** Right **Pos:** LF-55; PH/PR-40; DH-2 **Ht:** 6'4" **Wt:** 226 **Born:** 10/19/72 **Age:** 26

Year Team	Lg	G	AB	H	2B	3B	HR	(Hm	Rd)	TB	R	RBI	TBB	IBB	SO	HBP	SH	SF	SB	CS	SB%	GDP	Avg	OBP	SLG
1993 Seattle	AL	22	66	15	3	0	1	(1	0)	21	5	7	2	0	8	1	0	1	0	1	.00	2	.227	.257	.318
1994 Seattle	AL	12	38	7	1	0	1	(0	1)	11	3	4	2	0	4	0	0	0	0	0	.00	2	.184	.225	.289
1995 Sea-SD		45	140	33	8	1	4	(1	3)	55	13	21	5	1	24	1	0	0	0	0	.00	5	.236	.267	.393
1996 SD-Mil		133	370	103	26	0	12	(5	7)	165	48	57	27	2	70	6	0	7	1	2	.33	8	.278	.332	.446
1997 Milwaukee	AL	50	157	36	8	0	1	(0	1)	47	14	18	14	0	27	2	0	3	0	0	.00	4	.229	.295	.299
1998 Milwaukee	NL	93	186	44	7	0	3	(2	1)	60	15	25	19	1	29	1	0	3	0	1	.00	7	.237	.306	.323
1995 Seattle	AL	24	85	16	3	0	3	(0	3)	28	7	14	3	1	16	1	0	0	0	0	.00	2	.188	.225	.329
San Diego	NL	21	55	17	5	1	1	(1	0)	27	6	7	2	0	8	0	0	0	0	0	.00	3	.309	.333	.491
1996 San Diego	NL	84	191	48	11	0	5	(1	4)	74	27	26	16	1	44	2	0	3	1	1	.50	7	.251	.311	.387
Milwaukee	AL	49	179	55	15	0	7	(4	3)	91	21	31	11	1	26	4	0	4	0	1	.00	1	.307	.354	.508
6 ML YEARS		355	957	238	53	1	22	(9	13)	359	98	132	69	4	162	11	0	14	1	4	.20	28	.249	.303	.375

Warren Newson

Bats: Left **Throws:** Left **Pos:** LF-6; DH-3; PH/PR-1 **Ht:** 5'7" **Wt:** 202 **Born:** 7/3/64 **Age:** 34

Year Team	Lg	G	AB	H	2B	3B	HR	(Hm	Rd)	TB	R	RBI	TBB	IBB	SO	HBP	SH	SF	SB	CS	SB%	GDP	Avg	OBP	SLG
1998 Oklahoma *	AAA	111	398	122	21	1	21	—	—	208	75	75	66	4	106	0	1	5	7	5	.58	11	.307	.401	.523
1991 Chicago	AL	71	132	39	5	0	4	(1	3)	56	20	25	28	1	34	0	0	0	2	2	.50	4	.295	.419	.424
1992 Chicago	AL	63	136	30	3	0	1	(1	0)	36	19	11	37	2	38	0	0	0	3	0	1.00	4	.221	.387	.265
1993 Chicago	AL	26	40	12	0	0	2	(2	0)	18	9	6	9	1	12	0	0	0	1	0	.00	2	.300	.429	.450
1994 Chicago	AL	63	102	26	5	0	2	(2	0)	37	16	7	14	1	23	0	2	0	1	0	1.00	3	.255	.345	.363
1995 ChA-Sea	AL	84	157	41	2	2	5	(4	1)	62	34	15	39	0	45	1	0	0	2	1	.67	3	.261	.411	.395
1996 Texas	AL	91	235	60	14	1	10	(5	5)	106	34	31	37	1	82	0	0	1	3	0	1.00	3	.255	.355	.451
1997 Texas	AL	81	169	36	10	1	10	(2	8)	78	23	23	31	2	53	0	0	0	3	0	1.00	4	.213	.333	.462
1998 Texas	AL	10	21	4	1	0	0	(0	0)	5	1	2	1	1	5	0	0	0	0	0	.00	1	.190	.227	.238
1995 Chicago	AL	51	85	20	0	2	3	(3	0)	33	19	9	23	0	27	1	0	0	1	1	.50	2	.235	.404	.388
Seattle	AL	33	72	21	2	0	2	(1	1)	29	15	6	16	0	18	0	0	0	1	0	1.00	1	.292	.420	.403
8 ML YEARS		489	992	248	40	4	34	(17	17)	398	156	120	196	9	292	1	2	2	14	3	.82	24	.250	.374	.401

Jose Nieves

Bats: Right **Throws:** Right **Pos:** SS-1; PH/PR-1 **Ht:** 6'1" **Wt:** 180 **Born:** 6/16/75 **Age:** 24

Year Team	Lg	G	AB	H	2B	3B	HR	(Hm	Rd)	TB	R	RBI	TBB	IBB	SO	HBP	SH	SF	SB	CS	SB%	GDP	Avg	OBP	SLG
1995 Williamsprt	A-	69	276	59	13	1	4	—	—	86	46	44	21	1	39	6	0	3	11	10	.52	4	.214	.281	.312
1996 Rockford	A	113	396	96	20	4	5	—	—	139	55	57	33	1	59	5	4	3	17	9	.65	8	.242	.307	.351
1997 Daytona	A+	85	331	91	20	1	4	—	—	125	51	42	17	0	55	4	4	6	16	6	.73	7	.275	.313	.378
1998 West Tenn	AA	82	314	91	27	5	8	—	—	152	42	39	18	0	55	1	2	3	17	10	.63	9	.290	.327	.484
Iowa	AAA	19	75	19	4	0	0	—	—	23	7	4	2	0	11	0	0	2	1	1	.50	2	.253	.273	.307
1998 Chicago	NL	2	1	0	0	0	0	(0	0)	0	0	0	0	0	1	0	1	0	0	0	.00	0	.000	.000	.000

Melvin Nieves

Bats: B **Throws:** R **Pos:** PH/PR-60; RF-22; DH-3; LF-3 **Ht:** 6'2" **Wt:** 220 **Born:** 12/28/71 **Age:** 27

Year Team	Lg	G	AB	H	2B	3B	HR	(Hm	Rd)	TB	R	RBI	TBB	IBB	SO	HBP	SH	SF	SB	CS	SB%	GDP	Avg	OBP	SLG
1998 Indianapolis *	AAA	15	53	15	4	0	2	—	—	25	10	13	9	0	11	0	0	0	0	0	.00	0	.283	.387	.472
1992 Atlanta	NL	12	19	4	1	0	0	(0	0)	5	0	1	2	0	7	0	0	0	0	0	.00	0	.211	.286	.263
1993 San Diego	NL	19	47	9	2	0	2	(2	0)	15	4	3	3	0	21	1	0	0	0	0	.00	0	.191	.255	.319
1994 San Diego	NL	10	19	5	1	0	1	(0	1)	9	2	4	3	0	10	0	0	0	0	0	.00	0	.263	.364	.474
1995 San Diego	NL	98	234	48	6	1	14	(5	9)	98	32	38	19	0	88	5	1	3	2	3	.40	9	.205	.276	.419
1996 Detroit	AL	120	431	106	23	4	24	(10	14)	209	71	60	44	2	158	6	0	3	1	2	.33	10	.246	.322	.485
1997 Detroit	AL	116	359	82	18	4	20	(7	13)	162	46	64	39	6	157	5	0	2	1	7	.13	9	.228	.311	.451
1998 Cincinnati	NL	83	119	30	4	0	2	(1	1)	40	8	17	26	1	42	0	0	2	0	0	.00	3	.252	.381	.336
7 ML YEARS		458	1228	284	53	6	63	(25	38)	538	163	187	136	9	483	17	1	10	4	12	.25	25	.231	.314	.438

Dave Nilsson

Bats: L **Throws:** R **Pos:** 1B-49; LF-37; PH/PR-14; C-7; RF-3 **Ht:** 6'3" **Wt:** 229 **Born:** 12/14/69 **Age:** 29

Year Team	Lg	G	AB	H	2B	3B	HR	(Hm	Rd)	TB	R	RBI	TBB	IBB	SO	HBP	SH	SF	SB	CS	SB%	GDP	Avg	OBP	SLG
1998 Beloit *	A	4	12	5	3	0	1	—	—	11	3	7	2	0	0	0	0	1	0	0	.00	1	.417	.467	.917
El Paso *	AA	5	17	5	3	0	0	—	—	8	4	5	2	0	0	0	0	0	1	0	1.00	0	.294	.368	.471
1992 Milwaukee	AL	51	164	38	8	0	4	(1	3)	58	15	25	17	1	18	0	2	0	2	2	.50	1	.232	.304	.354
1993 Milwaukee	AL	100	296	76	10	2	7	(5	2)	111	35	40	37	5	36	0	4	3	3	6	.33	10	.257	.336	.375
1994 Milwaukee	AL	109	397	109	28	3	12	(4	8)	179	51	69	34	9	61	0	1	8	1	0	1.00	7	.275	.326	.451
1995 Milwaukee	AL	81	263	73	12	1	12	(7	5)	123	41	53	24	4	41	2	0	5	2	0	1.00	9	.278	.337	.468
1996 Milwaukee	AL	123	453	150	33	2	17	(3	14)	238	81	84	57	6	68	3	0	4	2	3	.40	9	.331	.407	.525
1997 Milwaukee	AL	156	554	154	33	0	20	(5	15)	247	71	81	65	8	88	2	1	7	2	3	.40	7	.278	.352	.446
1998 Milwaukee	NL	102	309	83	14	0	12	(6	6)	135	39	56	33	1	48	1	2	2	2	2	.50	12	.269	.339	.437
7 ML YEARS		722	2436	683	138	9	84	(31	53)	1091	333	408	267	34	360	8	10	28	14	16	.47	50	.280	.350	.448

C.J. Nitkowski

Pitches: Left **Bats:** Left **Pos:** RP-43 **Ht:** 6'3" **Wt:** 205 **Born:** 3/9/73 **Age:** 26

Year Team	Lg	G	GS	CG	GF	IP	BFP	H	R	ER	HR	SH	SF	HB	TBB	IBB	SO	WP	Bk	W	L	Pct.	ShO	Sv-Op	Hld	ERA
1998 New Orleans *AAA		5	3	0	1	15	75	22	12	10	1	1	0	2	7	0	18	2	0	0	1	.000	0	1--	—	6.00
1995 Cin-Det		20	18	0	0	71.2	338	94	57	53	11	2	4	5	35	3	31	2	0	2	7	.222	0	0-1	0	6.66
1996 Detroit	AL	11	8	0	0	45.2	234	62	44	41	7	0	2	7	38	1	36	2	0	2	3	.400	0	0-0	0	8.08
1998 Houston	NL	43	0	0	11	59.2	250	49	27	25	4	4	2	6	23	2	44	3	1	3	3	.500	0	3-5	8	3.77
1995 Cincinnati	NL	9	7	0	0	32.1	154	41	25	22	4	2	1	2	15	1	18	1	2	1	3	.250	0	0-1	0	6.12
Detroit	AL	11	11	0	0	39.1	184	53	32	31	7	0	3	3	20	2	13	1	0	1	4	.200	0	0-0	0	7.09
3 ML YEARS		74	26	0	11	177	822	205	128	119	22	6	8	18	96	6	111	7	3	7	13	.350	0	3-6	8	6.05

Otis Nixon

Bats: Both **Throws:** Right **Pos:** CF-108; PH/PR-2 **Ht:** 6'2" **Wt:** 180 **Born:** 1/9/59 **Age:** 40

Year Team	Lg	G	AB	H	2B	3B	HR	(Hm	Rd)	TB	R	RBI	TBB	IBB	SO	HBP	SH	SF	SB	CS	SB%	GDP	Avg	OBP	SLG
1983 New York	AL	13	14	2	0	0	0	(0	0)	2	2	0	1	0	5	0	1	0	2	0	1.00	0	.143	.200	.143
1984 Cleveland	AL	49	91	14	0	0	0	(0	0)	14	16	1	8	0	11	0	3	1	12	6	.67	2	.154	.220	.154
1985 Cleveland	AL	104	162	38	4	0	3	(1	2)	51	34	9	8	0	27	0	4	0	20	11	.65	2	.235	.271	.315
1986 Cleveland	AL	105	95	25	4	1	0	(0	0)	31	33	8	13	0	12	0	2	0	23	6	.79	1	.263	.352	.326
1987 Cleveland	AL	19	17	1	0	0	0	(0	0)	1	2	1	3	0	4	0	0	0	2	3	.40	0	.059	.200	.059
1988 Montreal	NL	90	271	66	8	2	0	(0	0)	78	47	15	28	0	42	0	4	2	46	13	.78	0	.244	.312	.288
1989 Montreal	NL	126	258	56	7	2	0	(0	0)	67	41	21	33	1	36	0	2	0	37	12	.76	4	.217	.306	.260
1990 Montreal	NL	119	231	58	6	2	1	(0	1)	71	46	20	28	0	33	0	3	1	50	13	.79	2	.251	.331	.307
1991 Atlanta	NL	124	401	119	10	1	0	(0	0)	131	81	26	47	3	40	2	7	3	72	21	.77	5	.297	.371	.327
1992 Atlanta	NL	120	456	134	14	2	2	(1	1)	158	79	22	39	0	54	0	5	2	41	18	.69	4	.294	.348	.346
1993 Atlanta	NL	134	461	124	12	3	1	(1	0)	145	77	24	61	2	63	0	5	5	47	13	.78	10	.269	.351	.315
1994 Boston	AL	103	398	109	15	1	0	(0	0)	126	60	25	55	1	65	0	6	2	42	10	.81	0	.274	.360	.317
1995 Texas	AL	139	589	174	21	2	0	(0	0)	199	87	45	58	1	85	0	6	3	50	21	.70	6	.295	.357	.338
1996 Toronto	AL	125	496	142	15	1	1	(1	0)	162	87	29	71	1	68	1	7	0	54	13	.81	9	.286	.377	.327
1997 Tor-LA		145	576	153	18	3	2	(0	2)	183	84	44	65	0	78	0	8	6	59	12	.83	12	.266	.337	.318
1998 Minnesota	AL	110	448	133	6	6	1	(0	1)	154	71	20	44	0	56	2	4	2	37	7	.84	14	.297	.361	.344
1997 Toronto	AL	103	401	105	12	1	1	(0	1)	122	54	26	52	0	54	0	6	5	47	10	.82	10	.262	.343	.304
Los Angeles	NL	42	175	48	6	2	1	(0	1)	61	30	18	13	0	24	0	2	1	12	2	.86	2	.274	.323	.349
16 ML YEARS		1625	4964	1348	140	26	11	(5	6)	1573	847	310	562	9	679	5	66	27	594	179	.77	71	.272	.345	.317

Trot Nixon

Bats: Left **Throws:** Left **Pos:** PH/PR-7; RF-6; DH-4; LF-1 **Ht:** 6'2" **Wt:** 196 **Born:** 4/11/74 **Age:** 25

Year Team	Lg	G	AB	H	2B	3B	HR	(Hm	Rd)	TB	R	RBI	TBB	IBB	SO	HBP	SH	SF	SB	CS	SB%	GDP	Avg	OBP	SLG
1994 Lynchburg	A+	71	264	65	12	6	12	—	—	113	33	43	44	1	53	3	1	3	10	3	.77	5	.246	.357	.428
1995 Sarasota	A+	73	264	80	11	4	5	—	—	114	43	39	45	3	46	1	0	2	7	5	.58	5	.303	.404	.432
Trenton	AA	25	94	15	3	1	2	—	—	26	9	8	7	0	20	0	2	2	2	1	.67	0	.160	.214	.277
1996 Trenton	AA	123	438	110	11	4	11	—	—	162	55	63	50	3	65	3	6	5	7	9	.44	6	.251	.329	.370
1997 Pawtucket	AAA	130	475	116	18	3	20	—	—	200	80	61	63	2	86	1	9	4	11	4	.73	11	.244	.331	.421
1998 Pawtucket	AAA	135	509	158	26	4	23	—	—	261	97	74	76	6	81	5	0	7	26	13	.67	10	.310	.400	.513
1996 Boston	AL	2	4	2	1	0	0	(0	0)	3	2	0	0	0	1	0	0	0	1	0	1.00	0	.500	.500	.750
1998 Boston	AL	13	27	7	1	0	0	(0	0)	8	3	0	1	0	3	0	0	0	0	0	.00	0	.259	.286	.296
2 ML YEARS		15	31	9	2	0	0	(0	0)	11	5	0	1	0	4	0	0	0	1	0	1.00	0	.290	.313	.355

Hideo Nomo

Pitches: Right **Bats:** Right **Pos:** SP-28; RP-1 **Ht:** 6'2" **Wt:** 220 **Born:** 8/31/68 **Age:** 30

Year Team	Lg	G	GS	CG	GF	IP	BFP	H	R	ER	HR	SH	SF	HB	TBB	IBB	SO	WP	Bk	W	L	Pct.	ShO	Sv-Op	Hld	ERA
1995 Los Angeles	NL	28	28	4	0	191.1	780	124	63	54	14	11	4	5	78	2	236	19	5	13	6	.684	3	0-0	0	2.54
1996 Los Angeles	NL	33	33	3	0	228.1	932	180	93	81	23	12	6	2	85	6	234	11	3	16	11	.593	2	0-0	0	3.19
1997 Los Angeles	NL	33	33	1	0	207.1	904	193	104	93	23	7	1	9	92	2	233	10	4	14	12	.538	0	0-0	0	4.25
1998 LA-NYN	NL	29	28	3	0	157.1	687	130	88	86	19	8	5	4	94	2	167	13	4	6	12	.333	0	0-0	0	4.92
1998 Los Angeles	NL	12	12	2	0	67.2	295	57	39	38	8	2	3	1	38	0	73	4	1	2	7	.222	0	0-0	0	5.05
New York	NL	17	16	1	0	89.2	392	73	49	48	11	6	3	1	56	2	94	9	3	4	5	.444	0	0-0	0	4.82
4 ML YEARS		123	122	11	0	784.1	3303	627	348	319	79	38	16	20	349	12	870	53	16	49	41	.544	5	0-0	0	3.66

Greg Norton

Bats: B **Throws:** R **Pos:** 1B-79; PH/PR-22; 3B-11; DH-2; 2B-1 **Ht:** 6'1" **Wt:** 190 **Born:** 7/6/72 **Age:** 26

Year Team	Lg	G	AB	H	2B	3B	HR	(Hm	Rd)	TB	R	RBI	TBB	IBB	SO	HBP	SH	SF	SB	CS	SB%	GDP	Avg	OBP	SLG
1993 White Sox	R	3	9	2	0	0	0	—	—	2	1	2	1	0	1	0	0	0	0	0	.00	0	.222	.300	.222
Hickory	A	71	254	62	12	2	4	—	—	90	36	36	41	1	44	1	1	4	0	2	.00	6	.244	.347	.354
1994 South Bend	A	127	477	137	22	2	6	—	—	181	73	64	62	4	71	2	2	3	5	3	.63	7	.287	.369	.379
1995 Birmingham	AA	133	469	117	23	2	6	—	—	162	65	60	64	7	90	5	3	10	19	12	.61	10	.249	.339	.345
1996 Birmingham	AA	76	287	81	14	3	8	—	—	125	40	44	33	5	55	1	1	5	5	5	.50	5	.282	.357	.436
Nashville	AAA	43	164	47	14	2	7	—	—	86	28	26	17	3	42	0	0	2	3	3	.40	1	.287	.350	.524
1997 Nashville	AAA	114	414	114	27	1	26	—	—	221	82	76	57	2	101	4	1	3	3	5	.38	9	.275	.366	.534
1996 Chicago	AL	11	23	5	0	0	2	(0	2)	11	4	3	4	0	6	0	0	0	0	1	.00	0	.217	.333	.478

Year Team	Lg	G	AB	H	2B	3B	HR	(Hm	Rd)	TB	R	RBI	TBB	IBB	SO	HBP	SH	SF	SB	CS	SB%	GDP	Avg	OBP	SLG
1997 Chicago	AL	18	34	9	2	2	0	(0	0)	15	5	1	2	0	8	0	1	0	0	0	.00	0	.265	.306	.441
1998 Chicago	AL	105	299	71	17	2	9	(6	3)	119	38	36	26	1	77	2	1	2	3	3	.50	11	.237	.301	.398
3 ML YEARS		134	356	85	19	4	11	(6	5)	145	47	40	32	1	91	2	2	2	3	4	.43	11	.239	.304	.407

Abraham Nunez

Bats: Both **Throws:** Right **Pos:** SS-23; PH/PR-3 **Ht:** 5'11" **Wt:** 177 **Born:** 3/16/76 **Age:** 23

Year Team	Lg	G	AB	H	2B	3B	HR	(Hm	Rd)	TB	R	RBI	TBB	IBB	SO	HBP	SH	SF	SB	CS	SB%	GDP	Avg	OBP	SLG
1996 St. Cathari	A-	75	297	83	6	4	3	—	—	106	43	26	31	0	43	4	8	2	37	14	.73	2	.279	.353	.357
1997 Lynchburg	A+	78	304	79	9	4	3	—	—	105	45	32	23	0	47	1	9	1	29	14	.67	5	.260	.313	.345
Carolina	AA	47	198	65	6	1	1	—	—	76	31	14	20	1	28	0	2	3	10	5	.67	2	.328	.385	.384
1998 Lynchburg	A+	5	18	4	1	0	0	—	—	5	2	2	3	0	1	0	0	0	1	0	1.00	1	.222	.333	.278
Nashville	AAA	94	366	91	12	3	3	—	—	118	50	32	39	0	73	5	2	1	16	8	.67	9	.249	.328	.322
1997 Pittsburgh	NL	19	40	9	2	2	0	(0	0)	15	3	6	3	0	10	1	0	1	1	0	1.00	1	.225	.289	.375
1998 Pittsburgh	NL	24	52	10	2	0	1	(0	1)	15	6	2	12	0	14	0	3	0	4	2	.67	1	.192	.344	.288
2 ML YEARS		43	92	19	4	2	1	(0	1)	30	9	8	15	0	24	1	3	1	5	2	.71	2	.207	.321	.326

Vladimir Nunez

Pitches: Right **Bats:** Right **Pos:** RP-4 **Ht:** 6'4" **Wt:** 235 **Born:** 3/15/75 **Age:** 24

Year Team	Lg	G	GS	CG	GF	IP	BFP	H	R	ER	HR	SH	SF	HB	TBB	IBB	SO	WP	Bk	W	L	Pct.	ShO	Sv-Op	Hld	ERA
1996 Visalia	A+	12	10	0	0	53	233	64	45	32	10	1	3	3	17	0	37	3	2	1	6	.143	0	0--	—	5.43
Lethbridge	R+	14	13	0	0	85	342	78	25	21	4	1	1	9	10	0	93	6	0	10	1	1.000	0	0--	—	2.22
1997 High Desert	A+	28	28	1	0	158.1	682	169	102	91	36	1	3	14	40	1	142	10	2	8	5	.615	1	0--	—	5.17
1998 Tucson	AAA	31	13	1	8	95.1	422	103	58	52	12	2	4	7	37	0	78	5	0	4	4	.500	0	2--	—	4.91
1998 Arizona	NL	4	0	0	2	5.1	25	7	6	6	0	0	1	0	2	0	2	0	1	0	0	.000	0	0-0	0	10.13

Jon Nunnally

Bats: L **Throws:** R **Pos:** RF-53; CF-24; PH/PR-13; LF-6 **Ht:** 5'10" **Wt:** 190 **Born:** 11/9/71 **Age:** 27

Year Team	Lg	G	AB	H	2B	3B	HR	(Hm	Rd)	TB	R	RBI	TBB	IBB	SO	HBP	SH	SF	SB	CS	SB%	GDP	Avg	OBP	SLG
1998 Indianapols *	AAA	79	290	73	18	2	11	—	—	128	53	53	47	0	71	2	1	6	7	4	.64	3	.252	.354	.441
1995 Kansas City	AL	119	303	74	15	6	14	(6	8)	143	51	42	51	5	86	2	4	0	6	4	.60	4	.244	.357	.472
1996 Kansas City	AL	35	90	19	5	1	5	(2	3)	41	16	17	13	2	25	0	0	1	0	0	.00	0	.211	.308	.456
1997 KC-Cin		78	230	71	12	4	14	(7	7)	133	46	39	31	0	58	2	1	1	7	3	.70	2	.309	.394	.578
1998 Cincinnati	NL	74	174	36	9	0	7	(2	5)	66	29	20	34	3	38	1	1	3	3	4	.43	4	.207	.335	.379
1997 Kansas City	AL	13	29	7	0	1	1	(1	0)	12	8	4	5	0	7	0	0	0	0	0	.00	0	.241	.353	.414
Cincinnati	NL	65	201	64	12	3	13	(6	7)	121	38	35	26	0	51	2	1	1	7	3	.70	2	.318	.400	.602
4 ML YEARS		306	797	200	41	11	40	(17	23)	383	142	118	129	10	207	5	6	5	16	11	.59	10	.251	.357	.481

Ryan Nye

Pitches: Right **Bats:** Right **Pos:** RP-1 **Ht:** 6'2" **Wt:** 195 **Born:** 6/24/73 **Age:** 26

Year Team	Lg	G	GS	CG	GF	IP	BFP	H	R	ER	HR	SH	SF	HB	TBB	IBB	SO	WP	Bk	W	L	Pct.	ShO	Sv-Op	Hld	ERA
1994 Batavia	A-	13	12	1	0	71.2	301	64	27	21	3	1	0	6	15	0	71	2	1	7	2	.778	0	0--	—	2.64
1995 Clearwater	A+	27	27	5	0	167	681	164	71	63	8	5	5	6	33	1	116	4	3	12	7	.632	1	0--	—	3.40
1996 Reading	AA	14	14	0	0	86.2	365	76	41	37	9	1	3	6	30	1	90	3	1	8	2	.800	0	0--	—	3.84
Scranton-WB	AAA	14	14	0	0	80.2	362	97	52	45	10	0	2	3	30	0	51	1	1	5	2	.714	0	0--	—	5.02
1997 Scranton-WB	AAA	17	17	0	0	109.1	465	117	70	67	20	2	2	2	32	1	85	2	1	4	10	.286	0	0--	—	5.52
1998 Scranton-WB	AAA	23	22	3	0	140	595	139	73	63	8	4	2	7	49	2	118	7	2	9	6	.600	2	0--	—	4.05
1997 Philadelphia	NL	4	2	0	1	12	65	20	11	11	2	1	2	2	9	0	7	0	0	0	2	.000	0	0-0	0	8.25
1998 Philadelphia	NL	1	0	0	1	1	6	3	3	3	1	0	0	1	2	0	3	0	0	0	0	.000	0	0-0	0	27.00
2 ML YEARS		5	2	0	2	13	71	23	14	14	3	1	2	3	11	0	10	0	0	0	2	.000	0	0-0	0	9.69

Charlie O'Brien

Bats: Right **Throws:** Right **Pos:** C-62 **Ht:** 6'2" **Wt:** 205 **Born:** 5/1/61 **Age:** 38

Year Team	Lg	G	AB	H	2B	3B	HR	(Hm	Rd)	TB	R	RBI	TBB	IBB	SO	HBP	SH	SF	SB	CS	SB%	GDP	Avg	OBP	SLG
1998 Midland *	AA	5	17	2	0	0	0	—	—	2	1	2	1		4	0	0	0	1	0	1.00	0	.118	.211	.118
1985 Oakland	AL	16	11	3	1	0	0	(0	0)	4	3	1	3	0	3	0	0	0	0	0	.00	0	.273	.429	.364
1987 Milwaukee	AL	10	35	7	1	0	0	(0	0)	12	2	0	4	0	4	0	1	0	0	1	.00	0	.200	.282	.343
1988 Milwaukee	AL	40	118	26	6	0	2	(2	0)	38	12	9	5	0	16	0	4	0	0	1	.00	3	.220	.252	.322
1989 Milwaukee	AL	62	188	44	10	0	6	(4	2)	72	22	35	21	1	11	9	8	0	0	0	.00	11	.234	.339	.383
1990 Mil-NYN		74	213	38	10	2	0	(0	0)	52	17	20	21	3	34	3	10	2	0	0	.00	5	.178	.259	.244
1991 New York	NL	69	168	31	6	0	4	(1	1)	43	16	14	17	1	25	4	0	2	0	2	.00	5	.185	.272	.256
1992 New York	NL	68	156	33	12	0	2	(1	1)	51	15	13	16	1	18	1	4	0	0	1	.00	5	.212	.289	.327
1993 New York	NL	67	188	48	11	0	4	(1	3)	71	15	23	14	1	14	2	3	1	1	1	.50	4	.255	.312	.378
1994 Atlanta	NL	51	152	37	11	0	8	(6	2)	72	24	28	15	2	24	3	1	1	0	0	.00	5	.243	.322	.474
1995 Atlanta	NL	67	198	45	7	0	9	(4	5)	79	18	23	29	2	40	6	0	0	0	0	.00	3	.227	.343	.399
1996 Toronto	AL	109	324	77	17	0	13	(8	5)	133	33	44	29	1	68	17	3	2	0	0	.00	8	.238	.331	.410
1997 Toronto	AL	69	225	49	15	1	4	(2	2)	78	22	27	22	1	45	11	3	6	0	0	.00	6	.218	.311	.347
1998 ChA-Ana	AL	62	175	45	9	0	4	(0	4)	66	13	18	10	0	33	2	3	0	0	0	.00	6	.257	.300	.377

Year Team	Lg	G	AB	H	2B	3B	HR	(Hm	Rd)	TB	R	RBI	TBB	IBB	SO	HBP	SH	SF	SB	CS	SB%	GDP	Avg	OBP	SLG
1990 Milwaukee	AL	46	145	27	7	2	0	(0	0)	38	11	11	11	1	26	2	8	0	0	0	.00	3	.186	.253	.262
New York	NL	28	68	11	3	0	0	(0	0)	14	6	9	10	2	8	1	2	2	0	0	.00	1	.162	.272	.206
1998 Chicago	AL	57	164	43	9	0	4	(0	4)	64	12	18	9	0	31	2	3	3	0	0	.00	3	.262	.303	.390
Anaheim	AL	5	11	2	0	0	0	(0	0)	2	1	0	1	0	2	0	0	0	0	0	.00	0	.182	.250	.182
13 ML YEARS		764	2151	483	118	4	54	(29	25)	771	212	255	206	13	335	58	40	17	1	10	.09	61	.225	.307	.358

Alex Ochoa

Bats: R **Throws:** R **Pos:** RF-52; PH/PR-25; LF-21; CF-4; DH-3 **Ht:** 6'0" **Wt:** 195 **Born:** 3/29/72 **Age:** 27

Year Team	Lg	G	AB	H	2B	3B	HR	(Hm	Rd)	TB	R	RBI	TBB	IBB	SO	HBP	SH	SF	SB	CS	SB%	GDP	Avg	OBP	SLG
1995 New York	NL	11	37	11	1	0	0	(0	0)	12	7	0	2	0	10	0	0	0	1	0	1.00	1	.297	.333	.324
1996 New York	NL	82	282	83	19	3	4	(1	3)	120	37	33	17	0	30	2	0	3	4	3	.57	2	.294	.336	.426
1997 New York	NL	113	238	58	14	1	3	(1	2)	83	31	22	18	0	32	2	2	2	3	4	.43	7	.244	.300	.349
1998 Minnesota	AL	94	249	64	14	2	2	(1	1)	88	35	25	10	0	35	1	0	0	6	3	.67	7	.257	.288	.353
4 ML YEARS		300	806	216	48	6	9	(3	6)	303	110	80	47	0	107	5	2	5	14	10	.58	17	.268	.311	.376

Jose Offerman

Bats: Both **Throws:** Right **Pos:** 2B-152; DH-6; PH/PR-1 **Ht:** 6'0" **Wt:** 190 **Born:** 11/8/68 **Age:** 30

Year Team	Lg	G	AB	H	2B	3B	HR	(Hm	Rd)	TB	R	RBI	TBB	IBB	SO	HBP	SH	SF	SB	CS	SB%	GDP	Avg	OBP	SLG
1990 Los Angeles	NL	29	58	9	0	0	1	(1	0)	12	7	7	4	1	14	0	1	0	1	0	1.00	1	.155	.210	.207
1991 Los Angeles	NL	52	113	22	2	0	0	(0	0)	24	10	3	25	2	32	1	1	0	3	2	.60	5	.195	.345	.212
1992 Los Angeles	NL	149	534	139	20	8	1	(1	0)	178	67	30	57	4	98	0	5	2	23	16	.59	5	.260	.331	.333
1993 Los Angeles	NL	158	590	159	21	6	1	(1	0)	195	77	62	71	7	75	2	25	4	30	13	.70	12	.269	.346	.331
1994 Los Angeles	NL	72	243	51	8	4	1	(0	1)	70	27	25	38	4	38	0	6	2	2	1	.67	6	.210	.314	.288
1995 Los Angeles	NL	119	429	123	14	6	4	(2	2)	161	69	33	69	0	67	3	10	0	2	7	.22	5	.287	.389	.375
1996 Kansas City	AL	151	561	170	33	8	5	(1	4)	234	85	47	74	3	98	1	7	2	24	10	.71	9	.303	.384	.417
1997 Kansas City	AL	106	424	126	23	6	2	(2	0)	167	59	39	41	3	64	0	6	0	9	10	.47	5	.297	.359	.394
1998 Kansas City	AL	158	607	191	28	13	7	(4	3)	266	102	66	89	1	96	5	2	6	45	12	.79	7	.315	.403	.438
9 ML YEARS		994	3559	990	149	51	22	(12	10)	1307	503	312	468	25	582	12	63	20	139	71	.66	54	.278	.362	.367

Chad Ogea

Pitches: Right **Bats:** Right **Pos:** RP-10; SP-9 **Ht:** 6'2" **Wt:** 220 **Born:** 11/9/70 **Age:** 28

		HOW MUCH HE PITCHED						WHAT HE GAVE UP											THE RESULTS					
Year Team	Lg	G	GS	CG	GF	IP	BFP	H	R	ER	HR	SH	SF	HB	TBB	IBB	SO	WP	Bk	W	L	Pct.	ShO	Sv-Op	Hld	ERA
1998 Buffalo *	AAA	9	9	1	0	42.1	178	42	19	17	2	1	1	4	5	0	34	1	0	2	1	.667	0	0- -	—	3.61
1994 Cleveland	AL	4	1	0	0	16.1	80	21	11	11	2	0	1	0	10	2	11	0	0	0	1	.000	0	0-0	0	6.06
1995 Cleveland	AL	20	14	1	3	106.1	442	95	38	36	11	0	5	1	29	0	57	3	1	8	3	.727	0	0-0	0	3.05
1996 Cleveland	AL	29	21	1	2	146.2	620	151	82	78	22	3	3	5	42	3	101	2	0	10	6	.625	1	0-0	0	4.79
1997 Cleveland	AL	21	21	1	0	126.1	552	139	79	70	13	3	5	5	47	4	80	4	2	8	9	.471	0	0-0	0	4.99
1998 Cleveland	AL	19	9	0	1	69	307	74	44	43	9	1	3	7	25	1	43	0	0	5	4	.556	0	0-1	0	5.61
5 ML YEARS		93	66	3	6	464.2	2001	480	254	238	57	7	16	19	153	10	292	9	3	31	23	.574	1	0-1	0	4.61

Kirt Ojala

Pitches: Left **Bats:** Left **Pos:** RP-28; SP-13 **Ht:** 6'2" **Wt:** 200 **Born:** 12/24/68 **Age:** 30

		HOW MUCH HE PITCHED						WHAT HE GAVE UP											THE RESULTS					
Year Team	Lg	G	GS	CG	GF	IP	BFP	H	R	ER	HR	SH	SF	HB	TBB	IBB	SO	WP	Bk	W	L	Pct.	ShO	Sv-Op	Hld	ERA
1990 Oneonta	A-	14	14	1	0	79	353	75	28	19	2	5	2	4	43	0	87	1	2	7	2	.778	0	0- -	—	2.16
1991 Pr William	A+	25	23	1	0	156.2	636	120	52	44	5	3	4	4	61	1	112	3	1	8	7	.533	0	0- -	—	2.53
1992 Albany-Colo	AA	24	23	2	0	151.2	642	130	71	61	10	3	7	0	80	0	116	10	0	12	8	.600	1	0- -	.	3.62
1993 Albany-Colo	AA	1	1	0	0	6.1	26	5	0	0	0	0	0	0	2	0	6	2	0	1	0	1.000	0	0- -	—	0.00
Columbus	AAA	31	20	0	3	126	575	145	85	77	13	4	5	3	71	2	83	13	1	8	9	.471	0	0- -	—	5.50
1994 Columbus	AAA	25	23	1	0	148	638	157	78	63	12	2	4	2	46	1	81	10	1	11	7	.611	1	0- -	—	3.83
1995 Columbus	AAA	32	20	0	5	145.2	619	138	74	64	15	6	2	3	54	3	107	7	1	8	7	.533	0	1- -	—	3.95
1996 Indianapolis	AAA	22	21	3	0	133.2	569	143	67	56	15	2	6	6	31	0	92	3	0	7	7	.500	0	0- -	—	3.77
1997 Charlotte	AAA	25	24	0	1	149	627	148	74	58	13	4	1	3	55	2	119	4	0	8	7	.533	0	0- -	—	3.50
1997 Florida	NL	7	5	0	1	28.2	130	28	10	10	4	0	1	0	18	0	19	0	0	1	2	.333	0	0-0	0	3.14
1998 Florida	NL	41	13	1	4	125	554	128	71	59	14	10	2	4	59	4	75	6	0	2	7	.222	0	0-0	1	4.25
2 ML YEARS		48	18	1	5	153.2	684	156	81	69	18	10	3	4	77	4	94	6	0	3	9	.250	0	0-0	1	4.04

Troy O'Leary

Bats: Left **Throws:** Left **Pos:** LF-155; PH/PR-2 **Ht:** 6'0" **Wt:** 198 **Born:** 8/4/69 **Age:** 29

Year Team	Lg	G	AB	H	2B	3B	HR	(Hm	Rd)	TB	R	RBI	TBB	IBB	SO	HBP	SH	SF	SB	CS	SB%	GDP	Avg	OBP	SLG
1993 Milwaukee	AL	19	41	12	3	0	0	(0	0)	15	3	3	5	0	9	0	3	0	0	0	.00	1	.293	.370	.366
1994 Milwaukee	AL	27	66	18	1	1	2	(0	2)	27	9	7	5	0	12	1	0	1	1	1	.50	1	.273	.329	.409
1995 Boston	AL	112	399	123	31	6	10	(5	5)	196	60	49	29	4	64	1	3	2	5	3	.63	8	.308	.355	.491
1996 Boston	AL	149	497	129	28	5	15	(10	5)	212	68	81	47	3	80	4	1	3	3	2	.60	13	.260	.327	.427
1997 Boston	AL	146	499	154	32	4	15	(5	10)	239	65	80	39	7	70	2	1	4	0	5	.00	13	.309	.358	.479
1998 Boston	AL	156	611	165	36	8	23	(12	11)	286	95	83	36	2	108	5	0	5	2	2	.50	17	.270	.314	.468
6 ML YEARS		609	2113	601	131	24	65	(32	33)	975	300	303	161	16	343	13	8	15	11	13	.46	52	.284	.337	.461

John Olerud

Bats: Left **Throws:** Left **Pos:** 1B-157; PH/PR-6   **Ht:** 6'5" **Wt:** 220 **Born:** 8/5/68 **Age:** 30

Year Team	Lg	G	AB	H	2B	3B	HR	(Hm	Rd)	TB	R	RBI	TBB	IBB	SO	HBP	SH	SF	SB	CS	SB%	GDP	Avg	OBP	SLG
1989 Toronto	AL	6	8	3	0	0	0	(0	0)	3	2	0	0	0	1	0	0	0	0	0	.00	0	.375	.375	.375
1990 Toronto	AL	111	358	95	15	1	14	(11	3)	154	43	48	57	6	75	1	1	4	0	0	.00	5	.265	.364	.430
1991 Toronto	AL	139	454	116	30	1	17	(7	10)	199	64	68	68	9	84	6	3	10	0	2	.00	12	.256	.353	.438
1992 Toronto	AL	138	458	130	28	0	16	(4	12)	206	68	66	70	11	61	1	1	7	1	0	1.00	15	.284	.375	.450
1993 Toronto	AL	158	551	200	54	2	24	(9	15)	330	109	107	114	33	65	7	0	7	0	2	.00	12	.363	.473	.599
1994 Toronto	AL	108	384	114	29	2	12	(6	6)	183	47	67	61	12	53	3	0	5	1	2	.33	11	.297	.393	.477
1995 Toronto	AL	135	492	143	32	0	8	(1	7)	199	72	54	84	10	54	4	0	1	0	0	.00	17	.291	.398	.404
1996 Toronto	AL	125	398	109	25	0	18	(9	9)	188	59	61	60	6	37	10	0	1	1	0	1.00	10	.274	.382	.472
1997 New York	NL	154	524	154	34	1	22	(13	9)	256	90	102	85	5	67	13	0	8	0	0	.00	19	.294	.400	.489
1998 New York	NL	160	557	197	36	4	22	(13	9)	307	91	93	96	11	73	4	1	7	2	2	.50	15	.354	.447	.551
10 ML YEARS		1234	4184	1261	283	11	153	(73	80)	2025	645	666	695	103	570	49	6	50	5	10	.33	116	.301	.403	.484

Omar Olivares

Pitches: Right **Bats:** Right **Pos:** SP-26; RP-11   **Ht:** 6'1" **Wt:** 205 **Born:** 7/6/67 **Age:** 31

Year Team	Lg	G	GS	CG	GF	IP	BFP	H	R	ER	HR	SH	SF	HB	TBB	IBB	SO	WP	Bk	W	L	Pct.	ShO	Sv-Op	Hld	ERA
1990 St. Louis	NL	9	6	0	0	49.1	201	45	17	16	2	1	0	2	17	0	20	1	1	1	1	.500	0	0-0	1	2.92
1991 St. Louis	NL	28	24	0	2	167.1	688	148	72	69	13	11	2	5	61	1	91	3	1	11	7	.611	0	1-1	0	3.71
1992 St. Louis	NL	32	30	1	1	197	818	189	84	84	20	8	7	4	63	5	124	2	0	9	9	.500	0	0-0	0	3.84
1993 St. Louis	NL	58	9	0	11	118.2	537	134	60	55	10	4	4	9	54	7	63	4	3	5	3	.625	0	1-5	2	4.17
1994 St. Louis	NL	14	12	1	2	73.2	333	84	53	47	10	3	3	4	37	0	26	5	0	3	4	.429	0	1-1	0	5.74
1995 Col-Phi	NL	16	6	0	4	41.2	195	55	34	32	5	2	2	3	23	0	22	4	0	1	4	.200	0	0-0	0	6.91
1996 Detroit	AL	25	25	4	0	160	708	169	90	87	16	3	6	9	75	4	81	4	1	7	11	.389	0	0-0	0	4.89
1997 Det-Sea	AL	32	31	3	0	177.1	794	191	109	98	18	2	7	13	81	4	103	5	0	6	10	.375	2	0-0	0	4.97
1998 Anaheim	AL	37	26	1	6	183	805	189	92	82	19	6	4	5	91	1	112	5	0	9	9	.500	0	0-0	0	4.03
1995 Colorado	NL	11	6	0	1	31.2	151	44	28	26	4	1	2	2	21	0	15	4	0	1	3	.250	0	0-0	0	7.39
Philadelphia	NL	5	0	0	3	10	44	11	6	6	1	1	0	1	2	0	7	0	0	0	1	.000	0	0-0	0	5.40
1997 Detroit	AL	19	19	3	0	115	502	110	68	60	8	2	4	9	53	1	74	5	0	5	6	.455	2	0-0	0	4.70
Seattle	AL	13	12	0	0	62.1	292	81	41	38	10	0	3	4	28	3	29	0	0	1	4	.200	0	0-0	0	5.49
9 ML YEARS		251	169	10	26	1168	5079	1204	611	570	113	40	35	54	502	22	642	33	6	52	58	.473	2	3-7	3	4.39

Darren Oliver

Pitches: Left **Bats:** Right **Pos:** SP-29   **Ht:** 6'2" **Wt:** 210 **Born:** 10/6/70 **Age:** 28

Year Team	Lg	G	GS	CG	GF	IP	BFP	H	R	ER	HR	SH	SF	HB	TBB	IBB	SO	WP	Bk	W	L	Pct.	ShO	Sv-Op	Hld	ERA
1998 Oklahoma *	AAA	1	1	0	0	5	18	2	0	0	0	0	0	1	1	0	1	0	0	0	0	.000	0	0- -	—	0.00
1993 Texas	AL	2	0	0	1	3.1	14	2	1	1	1	0	0	0	1	1	4	0	0	0	0	.000	0	0-0	0	2.70
1994 Texas	AL	43	0	0	10	50	226	40	24	19	4	6	0	6	35	4	50	2	2	4	0	1.000	0	2-3	9	3.42
1995 Texas	AL	17	7	0	0	49	222	47	25	23	3	5	1	1	32	1	39	4	0	4	2	.667	0	0-0	0	4.22
1996 Texas	AL	30	30	1	0	173.2	777	190	97	90	20	2	7	10	76	3	112	5	1	14	6	.700	1	0-0	0	4.66
1997 Texas	AL	32	32	3	0	201.1	887	213	114	94	29	2	5	11	82	3	104	7	0	13	12	.520	1	0-0	0	4.20
1998 Tex-StL		29	29	2	0	160.1	749	204	115	102	18	8	8	10	66	2	87	7	4	10	11	.476	0	0-0	0	5.73
1998 Texas	AL	19	19	2	0	103.1	493	140	84	75	11	3	6	10	43	1	58	6	1	6	7	.462	0	0-0	0	6.53
St. Louis	NL	10	10	0	0	57	256	64	31	27	7	5	2	0	23	1	29	1	3	4	4	.500	0	0-0	0	4.26
6 ML YEARS		153	98	6	12	637.2	2875	696	373	329	75	23	21	38	292	14	396	25	7	45	31	.592	2	2-3	9	4.64

Joe Oliver

Bats: Right **Throws:** Right **Pos:** C-77; PH/PR-4; 1B-2; DH-1   **Ht:** 6'3" **Wt:** 220 **Born:** 7/24/65 **Age:** 33

Year Team	Lg	G	AB	H	2B	3B	HR	(Hm	Rd)	TB	R	RBI	TBB	IBB	SO	HBP	SH	SF	SB	CS	SB%	GDP	Avg	OBP	SLG
1989 Cincinnati	NL	49	151	41	8	0	3	(1	2)	58	13	23	6	1	28	1	1	2	0	0	.00	3	.272	.300	.384
1990 Cincinnati	NL	121	364	84	23	0	8	(3	5)	131	34	52	37	15	75	2	5	1	1	1	.50	6	.231	.304	.360
1991 Cincinnati	NL	94	269	58	11	0	11	(7	4)	102	21	41	18	5	53	0	4	0	0	0	.00	14	.216	.265	.379
1992 Cincinnati	NL	143	485	131	25	1	10	(7	3)	188	42	57	35	19	75	1	6	7	2	3	.40	12	.270	.316	.388
1993 Cincinnati	NL	139	482	115	28	0	14	(7	7)	185	40	75	27	2	91	1	2	9	0	0	.00	13	.239	.276	.384
1994 Cincinnati	NL	6	19	4	0	0	1	(1	0)	7	1	5	2	1	3	0	0	0	0	0	.00	1	.211	.286	.368
1995 Milwaukee	AL	97	337	92	20	0	12	(4	8)	148	43	51	27	1	66	3	2	0	2	4	.33	11	.273	.332	.439
1996 Cincinnati	NL	106	289	70	12	1	11	(6	5)	117	31	46	28	6	54	2	3	3	2	0	1.00	8	.242	.311	.405
1997 Cincinnati	NL	111	349	90	13	0	14	(7	7)	145	28	43	25	1	58	5	2	5	1	3	.25	7	.258	.313	.415
1998 Det-Sea	AL	79	240	54	11	0	6	(3	3)	83	20	32	17	0	48	0	2	4	1	1	.50	8	.225	.272	.346
1998 Detroit	AL	50	155	35	8	0	4	(2	2)	55	8	22	7	0	33	0	0	4	0	0	.00	5	.226	.253	.355
Seattle	AL	29	85	19	3	0	2	(1	1)	28	12	10	10	0	15	0	2	0	1	1	.50	3	.224	.305	.329
10 ML YEARS		945	2985	739	151	2	90	(46	44)	1164	273	425	222	51	551	15	27	31	9	12	.43	83	.248	.300	.390

Gregg Olson

Pitches: Right **Bats:** Right **Pos:** RP-64   **Ht:** 6'4" **Wt:** 210 **Born:** 10/11/66 **Age:** 32

Year Team	Lg	G	GS	CG	GF	IP	BFP	H	R	ER	HR	SH	SF	HB	TBB	IBB	SO	WP	Bk	W	L	Pct.	ShO	Sv-Op	Hld	ERA
1988 Baltimore	AL	10	0	0	4	11	51	10	4	4	1	0	0	0	10	1	9	0	1	1	1	.500	0	0-1	1	3.27
1989 Baltimore	AL	64	0	0	52	85	356	57	17	16	1	4	1	1	46	10	90	9	3	5	2	.714	0	27-33	1	1.69

Year Team	Lg	G	GS	CG	GF	IP	BFP	H	R	ER	HR	SH	SF	HB	TBB	IBB	SO	WP	Bk	W	L	Pct.	ShO	Sv-Op	Hld	ERA
1990 Baltimore	AL	64	0	0	58	74.1	305	57	20	20	3	1	2	3	31	3	74	5	0	6	5	.545	0	37-42	0	2.42
1991 Baltimore	AL	72	0	0	62	73.2	319	74	28	26	1	5	1	1	29	5	72	8	1	4	6	.400	0	31-39	1	3.18
1992 Baltimore	AL	60	0	0	56	61.1	244	46	14	14	3	0	2	0	24	0	58	4	0	1	5	.167	0	36-44	0	2.05
1993 Baltimore	AL	50	0	0	45	45	188	37	9	8	1	2	2	0	18	3	44	5	0	0	2	.000	0	29-35	1	1.60
1994 Atlanta	NL	16	0	0	6	14.2	77	19	15	15	1	2	1	1	13	3	10	0	2	0	2	.000	0	1-1	1	9.20
1995 Cle-KC	AL	23	0	0	12	33	141	28	15	15	4	1	2	0	19	2	21	1	0	3	3	.500	0	3-5	2	4.09
1996 Det-Hou		52	0	0	30	52.1	243	55	30	29	7	1	1	1	35	6	37	6	0	4	0	1.000	0	8-10	1	4.99
1997 Min-KC	AL	45	0	0	18	50	226	58	35	31	3	2	1	1	28	4	34	1	0	4	3	.571	0	1-4	5	5.58
1998 Arizona	NL	64	0	0	49	68.2	281	56	25	23	4	3	1	0	25	1	55	2	0	3	4	.429	0	30-34	0	3.01
1995 Cleveland	AL	3	0	0	2	2.2	14	5	4	4	1	0	0	0	2	0	0	0	0	0	0	.000	0	0-0	0	13.50
Kansas City	AL	20	0	0	10	30.1	127	23	11	11	3	1	2	0	17	2	21	1	0	3	3	.500	0	3-5	2	3.26
1996 Detroit	AL	43	0	0	28	43	196	43	25	24	6	1	0	1	28	4	29	5	0	3	0	1.000	0	8-10	1	5.02
Houston	NL	9	0	0	2	9.1	47	12	5	5	1	0	1	0	7	2	8	1	0	1	0	1.000	0	0-0	0	4.82
1997 Minnesota	AL	11	0	0	5	8.1	55	19	17	17	0	0	0	0	11	1	6	0	0	0	0	.000	0	0-0	1	18.36
Kansas City	AL	34	0	0	13	41.2	171	39	18	14	3	2	1	1	17	3	28	1	0	4	3	.571	0	1-4	4	3.02
11 ML YEARS		520	0	0	392	569	2431	497	212	201	29	21	14	9	278	38	504	41	7	31	33	.484	0	203-248	12	3.18

Paul O'Neill

Bats: Left   **Throws:** Left   **Pos:** RF-150; PH/PR-2; DH-1   **Ht:** 6'4"   **Wt:** 215   **Born:** 2/25/63   **Age:** 36

Year Team	Lg	G	AB	H	2B	3B	HR	(Hm	Rd)	TB	R	RBI	TBB	IBB	SO	HBP	SH	SF	SB	CS	SB%	GDP	Avg	OBP	SLG
1985 Cincinnati	NL	5	12	4	1	0	0	(0	0)	5	1	1	0	0	2	0	0	0	0	0	.00	0	.333	.333	.417
1986 Cincinnati	NL	3	2	0	0	0	0	(0	0)	0	0	0	1	0	1	0	0	0	0	0	.00	0	.000	.333	.000
1987 Cincinnati	NL	84	160	41	14	1	7	(4	3)	78	24	28	18	1	29	0	0	2	2	1	.67	9	.256	.331	.488
1988 Cincinnati	NL	145	485	122	25	3	16	(12	4)	201	58	73	38	5	65	2	3	5	8	6	.57	7	.252	.306	.414
1989 Cincinnati	NL	117	428	118	24	2	15	(11	4)	191	49	74	46	4	64	2	0	4	20	5	.80	7	.276	.346	.446
1990 Cincinnati	NL	145	503	136	28	0	16	(10	6)	212	59	78	53	13	103	2	1	5	13	11	.54	12	.270	.339	.421
1991 Cincinnati	NL	152	532	136	36	0	28	(20	8)	256	71	91	73	14	107	1	0	1	12	7	.63	8	.256	.346	.481
1992 Cincinnati	NL	148	496	122	19	1	14	(6	8)	185	59	66	77	15	85	2	3	6	6	3	.67	10	.246	.346	.373
1993 New York	AL	141	498	155	34	1	20	(8	12)	251	71	75	44	5	69	2	0	3	2	4	.33	13	.311	.367	.504
1994 New York	AL	103	368	132	25	1	21	(10	11)	222	68	83	72	13	56	0	0	3	5	4	.56	16	**.359**	.460	.603
1995 New York	AL	127	460	138	30	4	22	(10	12)	242	82	96	71	8	76	1	0	11	1	2	.33	25	.300	.387	.526
1996 New York	AL	150	546	165	35	1	19	(7	12)	259	89	91	102	6	76	4	0	8	0	1	.00	21	.302	.411	.474
1997 New York	AL	149	553	179	42	0	21	(10	11)	284	89	117	75	8	92	0	0	9	10	7	.59	16	.324	.399	.514
1998 New York	AL	152	602	191	40	2	24	(10	14)	307	95	116	57	2	103	2	0	11	15	1	.94	22	.317	.372	.510
14 ML YEARS		1621	5645	1639	353	16	223	(120	103)	2693	815	989	727	100	928	18	7	66	94	52	.64	160	.290	.369	.477

Mike Oquist

Pitches: Right   **Bats:** Right   **Pos:** SP-29; RP-2   **Ht:** 6'2"   **Wt:** 189   **Born:** 5/30/68   **Age:** 31

Year Team	Lg	G	GS	CG	GF	IP	BFP	H	R	ER	HR	SH	SF	HB	TBB	IBB	SO	WP	Bk	W	L	Pct.	ShO	Sv-Op	Hld	ERA
1993 Baltimore	AL	5	0	0	2	11.2	50	12	5	5	0	0	0	0	4	1	8	0	0	0	0	.000	0	0-0	0	3.86
1994 Baltimore	AL	15	9	0	3	58.1	278	75	41	40	7	3	4	6	30	4	39	3	0	3	3	.500	0	0-0	0	6.17
1995 Baltimore	AL	27	0	0	3	54	255	51	27	25	6	1	4	2	41	3	27	2	0	2	1	.667	0	0-1	0	4.17
1996 San Diego	NL	8	0	0	3	7.2	30	2	2	2	0	0	4	0	4	2	4	1	0	0	0	.000	0	0-0	0	2.35
1997 Oakland	AL	19	17	1	0	107.2	473	111	62	60	15	3	3	6	43	3	72	2	0	4	6	.400	0	0-0	0	5.02
1998 Oakland	AL	31	29	0	2	175	777	210	125	121	27	5	6	5	57	1	112	4	0	7	11	.389	0	0-0	0	6.22
6 ML YEARS		105	55	1	12	414.1	1863	465	262	253	55	12	17	19	179	14	262	12	0	16	21	.432	0	0-1	0	5.50

Luis Ordaz

Bats: R   **Throws:** R   **Pos:** SS-54; 3B-2; PH/PR-2; 2B-1   **Ht:** 5'11"   **Wt:** 170   **Born:** 8/12/75   **Age:** 23

Year Team	Lg	G	AB	H	2B	3B	HR	(Hm	Rd)	TB	R	RBI	TBB	IBB	SO	HBP	SH	SF	SB	CS	SB%	GDP	Avg	OBP	SLG
1993 Princeton	R+	57	217	65	9	7	2	—	—	94	28	39	7	2	32	2	0	5	3	1	.75	2	.300	.320	.433
1994 Chston-WV	A	9	31	7	0	0	0	—	—	7	3	0	1	0	4	1	1	0	1	0	1.00	1	.226	.273	.226
Princeton	R+	60	211	52	12	3	0	—	—	70	33	12	10	1	27	2	5	1	7	5	.58	2	.246	.286	.332
1995 Chston-WV	A	112	359	83	14	7	2	—	—	117	43	42	13	1	47	6	8	4	12	5	.71	10	.231	.267	.326
1996 St. Pete	A+	126	423	115	13	3	3	—	—	143	46	49	30	0	53	1	7	6	10	5	.67	10	.272	.317	.338
1997 Arkansas	AA	115	390	112	20	6	4	—	—	156	44	58	22	1	39	2	7	6	11	10	.52	19	.287	.324	.400
1998 Memphis	AAA	59	214	62	9	2	6	—	—	93	29	35	16	0	20	1	4	1	3	3	.50	6	.290	.341	.435
1997 St. Louis	NL	12	22	6	1	0	0	(0	0)	7	3	1	1	0	2	0	0	0	3	0	1.00	0	.273	.304	.318
1998 St. Louis	NL	57	153	31	5	0	0	(0	0)	36	9	8	12	1	18	0	4	0	2	0	1.00	3	.203	.261	.235
2 ML YEARS		69	175	37	6	0	0	(0	0)	43	12	9	13	1	20	0	4	0	5	0	1.00	3	.211	.266	.246

Magglio Ordonez

Bats: Right   **Throws:** Right   **Pos:** RF-136; CF-22   **Ht:** 5'11"   **Wt:** 170   **Born:** 1/28/74   **Age:** 25

Year Team	Lg	G	AB	H	2B	3B	HR	(Hm	Rd)	TB	R	RBI	TBB	IBB	SO	HBP	SH	SF	SB	CS	SB%	GDP	Avg	OBP	SLG
1992 White Sox	R	38	111	20	10	2	1	—	—	37	17	14	13	0	26	2	0	1	6	4	.60	2	.180	.276	.333
1993 Hickory	A	84	273	59	14	4	3	—	—	90	32	20	26	0	66	0	2	0	5	5	.50	6	.216	.284	.330
1994 Hickory	A	132	490	144	24	5	11	—	—	211	86	69	45	1	57	1	7	3	16	7	.70	11	.294	.353	.431
1995 Pr William	A+	131	487	116	24	2	12	—	—	180	61	65	41	0	71	3	0	4	11	5	.69	16	.238	.299	.370
1996 Birmingham	AA	130	479	126	41	0	18	—	—	221	66	67	39	4	74	9	1	6	9	10	.47	16	.263	.330	.461
1997 Nashville	AAA	135	523	172	29	3	14	—	—	249	65	90	32	5	61	2	2	9	14	10	.58	18	.329	.364	.476

Year Team	Lg	G	AB	H	2B	3B	HR	(Hm	Rd)	TB	R	RBI	TBB	IBB	SO	HBP	SH	SF	SB	CS	SB%	GDP	Avg	OBP	SLG
1997 Chicago	AL	21	69	22	6	0	4	(2	2)	40	12	11	2	0	8	0	1	0	1	2	.33	1	.319	.338	.580
1998 Chicago	AL	145	535	151	25	2	14	(8	6)	222	70	65	28	1	53	9	2	4	9	7	.56	19	.282	.326	.415
2 ML YEARS		166	604	173	31	2	18	(10	8)	262	82	76	30	1	61	9	3	4	10	9	.53	20	.286	.328	.434

Rey Ordonez

Bats: Right **Throws:** Right **Pos:** SS-151; PH/PR-4   **Ht:** 5'9" **Wt:** 159 **Born:** 11/11/72 **Age:** 26

Year Team	Lg	G	AB	H	2B	3B	HR	(Hm	Rd)	TB	R	RBI	TBB	IBB	SO	HBP	SH	SF	SB	CS	SB%	GDP	Avg	OBP	SLG
1996 New York	NL	151	502	129	12	4	1	(0	1)	152	51	30	22	12	53	1	4	1	1	3	.25	12	.257	.289	.303
1997 New York	NL	120	356	77	5	3	1	(1	0)	91	35	33	18	3	36	1	14	2	11	5	.69	10	.216	.255	.256
1998 New York	NL	153	505	124	20	2	1	(0	1)	151	46	42	23	7	60	1	15	4	3	6	.33	11	.246	.278	.299
3 ML YEARS		424	1363	330	37	9	3	(1	2)	394	132	105	63	22	149	3	33	7	15	14	.52	33	.242	.276	.289

Kevin Orie

Bats: Right **Throws:** Right **Pos:** 3B-105; PH/PR-8   **Ht:** 6'4" **Wt:** 215 **Born:** 9/1/72 **Age:** 26

Year Team	Lg	G	AB	H	2B	3B	HR	(Hm	Rd)	TB	R	RBI	TBB	IBB	SO	HBP	SH	SF	SB	CS	SB%	GDP	Avg	OBP	SLG
1993 Peoria	A	65	238	64	17	1	7	—	—	104	28	45	21	1	51	10	2	2	3	5	.38	7	.269	.351	.437
1994 Daytona	A+	6	17	7	3	1	1	—	—	15	4	5	8	1	4	1	0	0	0	1	.00	1	.412	.615	.882
1995 Daytona	A+	119	409	100	17	4	9	—	—	152	54	51	42	2	71	15	0	6	5	4	.56	11	.244	.333	.372
1996 Orlando	AA	82	296	93	25	0	8	—	—	142	42	58	48	3	52	0	0	6	2	0	1.00	7	.314	.403	.480
Iowa	AAA	14	48	10	1	0	2	—	—	17	5	6	6	1	10	0	0	0	0	0	.00	1	.208	.296	.354
1997 Orlando	AA	3	13	5	2	0	2	—	—	13	3	6	2	1	1	0	0	0	0	0	.00	0	.385	.467	1.000
Iowa	AAA	9	32	12	4	0	1	—	—	19	7	8	5	0	5	0	0	0	0	0	.00	0	.375	.459	.594
1998 Iowa	AAA	24	92	34	8	0	9	—	—	69	27	24	12	1	15	2	0	0	1	0	1.00	3	.370	.453	.750
1997 Chicago	NL	114	364	100	23	5	8	(6	2)	157	40	44	39	3	57	5	3	4	2	2	.50	13	.275	.350	.431
1998 ChN-Fla	NL	112	379	83	22	1	8	(2	6)	131	47	38	32	2	59	8	2	4	2	1	.67	8	.219	.291	.346
1998 Chicago	NL	64	204	37	14	0	2	(1	1)	57	24	21	18	0	35	3	1	4	1	1	.50	4	.181	.253	.279
Florida	NL	48	175	46	8	1	6	(1	5)	74	23	17	14	2	24	5	1	0	1	0	1.00	4	.263	.335	.423
2 ML YEARS		226	743	183	45	6	16	(8	8)	288	87	82	71	5	116	13	5	8	4	3	.57	21	.246	.320	.388

Jesse Orosco

Pitches: Left **Bats:** Right **Pos:** RP-69   **Ht:** 6'2" **Wt:** 205 **Born:** 4/21/57 **Age:** 42

Year Team	Lg	G	GS	CG	GF	IP	BFP	H	R	ER	HR	SH	SF	HB	TBB	IBB	SO	WP	Bk	W	L	Pct.	ShO	Sv-Op	Hld	ERA
1979 New York	NL	18	2	0	6	35	154	33	20	19	4	3	0	2	22	0	22	0	0	1	2	.333	0	0-0	0	4.89
1981 New York	NL	8	0	0	4	17.1	69	13	4	3	2	2	0	0	6	2	18	0	1	0	1	.000	0	1-1	0	1.56
1982 New York	NL	54	2	0	22	109.1	451	92	37	33	7	5	4	2	40	2	89	3	2	4	10	.286	0	4-5	5	2.72
1983 New York	NL	62	0	0	42	110	432	76	27	18	3	4	3	1	38	7	84	1	2	13	7	.650	0	17-22	1	1.47
1984 New York	NL	60	0	0	52	87	355	58	29	25	7	3	3	2	46	7	85	1	1	10	6	.625	0	31-38	2	2.59
1985 New York	NL	54	0	0	39	79	331	66	26	24	6	1	1	0	34	7	68	4	0	8	6	.571	0	17-25	1	2.73
1986 New York	NL	58	0	0	40	81	338	64	23	21	6	2	3	3	35	3	62	2	0	8	6	.571	0	21-29	1	2.33
1987 New York	NL	58	0	0	41	77	335	78	41	38	5	5	4	2	31	9	78	2	0	3	9	.250	0	16-22	4	4.44
1988 Los Angeles	NL	55	0	0	21	53	229	41	18	16	4	3	3	2	30	3	43	1	0	3	2	.600	0	9-15	14	2.72
1989 Cleveland	AL	69	0	0	29	78	312	54	20	18	7	8	3	2	26	4	79	0	0	3	4	.429	0	3-7	12	2.08
1990 Cleveland	AL	55	0	0	28	64.2	289	58	35	28	9	5	3	0	38	7	55	1	0	5	4	.556	0	2-3	2	3.90
1991 Cleveland	AL	47	0	0	20	45.2	202	52	20	19	4	1	3	1	15	8	36	1	1	2	0	1.000	0	0-0	3	3.74
1992 Milwaukee	AL	59	0	0	14	39	158	33	15	14	5	0	2	1	13	1	40	2	0	3	1	.750	0	1-2	11	3.23
1993 Milwaukee	AL	57	0	0	27	56.2	233	47	25	22	7	2	2	3	17	3	67	3	1	3	5	.375	0	8-13	11	3.18
1994 Milwaukee	AL	40	0	0	5	39	174	32	26	22	4	0	2	4	26	2	36	0	0	3	1	.750	0	0-4	8	5.08
1995 Baltimore	AL	65	0	0	23	49.2	200	28	19	18	4	2	4	1	27	7	58	2	1	2	4	.333	0	3-6	15	3.26
1996 Baltimore	AL	66	0	0	10	55.2	236	42	22	21	5	2	1	2	28	4	52	2	0	3	1	.750	0	0-3	15	3.40
1997 Baltimore	AL	71	0	0	12	50.1	205	29	13	13	6	1	2	0	30	0	46	1	1	6	3	.667	0	0-4	21	2.32
1998 Baltimore	AL	69	0	0	26	56.2	243	46	20	20	6	4	2	1	28	1	50	3	1	4	1	.800	0	7-9	9	3.18
19 ML YEARS		1025	4	0	461	1184	4946	942	440	390	96	52	45	27	518	76	1068	29	11	84	73	.535	0	140-208	137	2.96

David Ortiz

Bats: Left **Throws:** Left **Pos:** 1B-71; DH-10; PH/PR-6   **Ht:** 6'4" **Wt:** 230 **Born:** 11/18/75 **Age:** 23

Year Team	Lg	G	AB	H	2B	3B	HR	(Hm	Rd)	TB	R	RBI	TBB	IBB	SO	HBP	SH	SF	SB	CS	SB%	GDP	Avg	OBP	SLG
1994 Mariners	R	53	167	41	10	1	2	—	—	59	14	20	14	2	46	2	1	4	1	4	.20	2	.246	.305	.353
1995 Mariners	R	48	184	61	18	4	4	—	—	99	30	37	23	1	52	1	0	3	2	0	1.00	2	.332	.403	.538
1996 Wisconsin	A	130	487	156	34	2	18	—	—	248	89	93	52	8	108	5	2	4	3	4	.43	5	.320	.389	.509
1997 Fort Myers	A+	61	239	79	15	0	13	—	—	133	45	58	22	3	53	1	0	3	2	1	.67	2	.331	.385	.556
New Britain	AA	69	258	83	22	2	14	—	—	151	40	56	21	1	78	4	0	2	2	6	.25	6	.322	.379	.585
Salt Lake	AAA	10	42	9	1	0	4	—	—	22	5	10	2	0	11	0	0	0	0	1	.00	0	.214	.250	.524
1998 Salt Lake	AAA	11	37	9	3	0	2	—	—	18	5	5	3	0	9	0	0	0	0	0	.00	0	.243	.300	.486
1997 Minnesota	AL	15	49	16	3	0	1	(0	1)	22	10	6	2	0	19	0	0	0	0	0	.00	1	.327	.353	.449
1998 Minnesota	AL	86	278	77	20	0	9	(2	7)	124	47	46	39	3	72	5	0	4	1	0	1.00	8	.277	.371	.446
2 ML YEARS		101	327	93	23	0	10	(2	8)	146	57	52	41	3	91	5	0	4	1	0	1.00	9	.284	.369	.446

Hector Ortiz

Bats: Right **Throws:** Right **Pos:** C-3; 1B-1 **Ht:** 6'0" **Wt:** 205 **Born:** 10/14/69 **Age:** 29

Year Team	Lg	G	AB	H	2B	3B	HR	(Hm	Rd)	TB	R	RBI	TBB	IBB	SO	HBP	SH	SF	SB	CS	SB%	GDP	Avg	OBP	SLG
1988 Salem	A-	32	77	11	1	0	0	—	—	12	5	4	5	0	16	1	1	0	0	2	.00	5	.143	.205	.156
1989 Vero Beach	A+	42	85	12	0	1	0	—	—	14	5	4	6	0	15	2	4	0	0	0	.00	1	.141	.215	.165
Salem	A-	44	140	32	3	1	0	—	—	37	13	12	4	0	24	1	2	0	2	1	.67	6	.229	.255	.264
1990 Yakima	A-	52	173	47	3	1	0	—	—	52	16	12	5	0	15	1	1	0	1	1	.50	6	.272	.296	.301
1991 Vero Beach	A+	42	123	28	2	0	0	—	—	30	3	8	5	0	8	3	0	0	0	0	.00	2	.228	.275	.244
1992 Bakersfield	A+	63	206	58	8	1	1	—	—	71	19	31	21	0	16	5	3	2	2	3	.40	8	.282	.359	.345
San Antonio	AA	26	59	12	1	0	0	—	—	13	1	5	11	0	13	1	1	0	0	0	.00	2	.203	.338	.220
1993 San Antonio	AA	49	131	28	5	0	1	—	—	36	6	6	9	2	17	0	3	0	0	2	.00	3	.214	.264	.275
Albuquerque	AAA	18	44	8	1	1	0	—	—	11	0	3	0	0	6	1	2	0	0	0	.00	1	.182	.200	.250
1994 Albuquerque	AAA	34	93	28	1	1	0	—	—	31	7	10	3	0	12	0	0	1	0	0	.00	7	.301	.320	.333
San Antonio	AA	24	75	9	0	0	0	—	—	9	4	4	2	0	7	1	0	2	0	0	.00	4	.120	.150	.120
1995 Orlando	AA	96	299	70	12	0	0	—	—	82	13	18	20	0	39	1	1	4	0	5	.00	10	.234	.281	.274
1996 Orlando	AA	78	216	47	8	0	0	—	—	55	16	15	26	2	23	0	1	3	1	2	.33	12	.218	.298	.255
Iowa	AAA	27	79	19	2	0	0	—	—	21	6	3	3	1	16	0	0	1	0	0	.00	5	.241	.265	.266
1997 Omaha	AAA	21	63	12	3	0	0	—	—	15	7	3	13	0	15	0	0	0	0	0	.00	1	.190	.329	.238
Wichita	AA	59	180	45	3	0	1	—	—	51	20	25	21	0	15	2	4	2	1	2	.33	10	.250	.332	.283
1998 Wichita	AA	4	13	2	0	0	0	—	—	2	1	0	2	0	1	0	0	0	0	1	.00	0	.154	.267	.154
Omaha	AAA	63	191	43	7	0	0	—	—	50	17	12	9	0	26	1	2	0	0	0	.00	10	.225	.264	.262
1998 Kansas City	AL	4	4	0	0	0	0	(0	0)	0	1	0	0	0	0	0	0	0	0	0	.00	0	.000	.000	.000

Russ Ortiz

Pitches: Right **Bats:** Right **Pos:** SP-13; RP-9 **Ht:** 6'1" **Wt:** 190 **Born:** 6/5/74 **Age:** 25

Year Team	Lg	G	GS	CG	GF	IP	BFP	H	R	ER	HR	SH	SF	HB	TBB	IBB	SO	WP	Bk	W	L	Pct.	ShO	Sv-Op	Hld	ERA
1995 Bellingham	A-	25	0	0	20	34.1	131	19	4	2	1	0	1	0	13	0	55	2	1	2	0	1.000	0	11--	—	0.52
San Jose	A+	5	0	0	5	6	24	4	1	1	0	0	1	0	2	0	7	0	0	0	1	.000	0	0--	—	1.50
1996 San Jose	A+	34	0	0	31	36.2	145	16	2	1	0	0	0	0	20	0	63	0	0	0	0	.000	0	23--	—	0.25
Shreveport	AA	26	0	0	20	26.2	123	22	14	12	0	0	0	0	21	3	29	1	0	1	2	.333	0	13--	—	4.05
1997 Shreveport	AA	12	12	0	0	56.2	249	52	28	26	3	4	1	1	37	0	50	2	1	2	3	.400	0	0--	—	4.13
Phoenix	AAA	14	14	0	0	85	376	96	57	52	11	2	3	2	34	0	70	3	1	4	3	.571	0	0--	—	5.51
1998 Fresno	AAA	10	10	0	0	50.2	209	35	10	9	3	5	1	4	22	0	59	1	0	3	1	.750	0	0--	—	1.60
1998 San Francisco	NL	22	13	0	3	88.1	394	90	51	49	11	5	4	4	46	1	75	3	0	4	4	.500	0	0-0	1	4.99

Donovan Osborne

Pitches: Left **Bats:** Left **Pos:** SP-14 **Ht:** 6'2" **Wt:** 195 **Born:** 6/21/69 **Age:** 30

Year Team	Lg	G	GS	CG	GF	IP	BFP	H	R	ER	HR	SH	SF	HB	TBB	IBB	SO	WP	Bk	W	L	Pct.	ShO	Sv-Op	Hld	ERA
1998 Memphis *	AAA	1	1	0	0	4.1	19	5	4	3	2	0	0	0	0	0	6	0	0	0	0	.000	0	0--	—	6.23
Arkansas *	AA	5	5	0	0	19	76	16	9	9	2	0	0	0	3	0	21	0	0	2	0	1.000	0	0--	—	4.26
1992 St. Louis	NL	34	29	0	2	179	754	193	91	75	14	7	4	2	38	2	104	6	0	11	9	.550	0	0-0		3.77
1993 St. Louis	NL	26	26	1	0	155.2	657	153	73	65	18	6	2	7	47	4	83	4	0	10	7	.588	0	0-0	0	3.76
1995 St. Louis	NL	19	19	0	0	113.1	477	112	58	48	17	8	3	2	34	2	82	0	0	4	6	.400	0	0-0	0	3.81
1996 St. Louis	NL	30	30	2	0	198.2	822	191	84	78	22	7	4	1	57	5	134	6	1	13	9	.591	0	0-0	0	3.53
1997 St. Louis	NL	14	14	0	0	80.1	337	84	46	44	10	3	3	1	23	2	51	0	0	3	7	.300	0	0-0	0	4.93
1998 St. Louis	NL	14	14	1	0	83.2	358	84	42	38	11	3	4	1	22	0	60	1	0	5	4	.556	1	0-0	0	4.09
6 ML YEARS		137	132	4	2	810.2	3405	817	397	348	92	34	20	14	221	17	514	18	1	46	42	.523	2	0-0		3.86

Keith Osik

Bats: Right **Throws:** Right **Pos:** C-26; PH/PR-8; 3B-7 **Ht:** 6'0" **Wt:** 198 **Born:** 10/22/68 **Age:** 30

Year Team	Lg	G	AB	H	2B	3B	HR	(Hm	Rd)	TB	R	RBI	TBB	IBB	SO	HBP	SH	SF	SB	CS	SB%	GDP	Avg	OBP	SLG
1996 Pittsburgh	NL	48	140	41	14	1	1	(0	1)	60	18	14	14	1	22	1	1	0	1	0	1.00	3	.293	.361	.429
1997 Pittsburgh	NL	49	105	27	9	1	0	(0	0)	38	10	7	9	1	21	1	2	0	0	1	.00	4	.257	.322	.362
1998 Pittsburgh	NL	39	98	21	4	0	0	(0	0)	25	8	7	13	2	16	2	2	1	1	2	.33	4	.214	.316	.255
3 ML YEARS		136	343	89	27	2	1	(0	1)	123	36	28	36	4	59	4	5	1	2	3	.40	8	.259	.336	.359

Antonio Osuna

Pitches: Right **Bats:** Right **Pos:** RP-54 **Ht:** 5'11" **Wt:** 206 **Born:** 4/12/73 **Age:** 26

Year Team	Lg	G	GS	CG	GF	IP	BFP	H	R	ER	HR	SH	SF	HB	TBB	IBB	SO	WP	Bk	W	L	Pct.	ShO	Sv-Op	Hld	ERA
1995 Los Angeles	NL	39	0	0	8	44.2	186	39	22	22	5	2	1	1	20	2	46	1	0	2	4	.333	0	0-2	11	4.43
1996 Los Angeles	NL	73	0	0	21	84	342	65	33	28	6	7	5	2	32	12	85	3	2	9	6	.600	0	4-9	16	3.00
1997 Los Angeles	NL	48	0	0	18	61.2	245	46	15	15	6	4	1	1	19	2	68	2	0	4	4	.429	0	0-0	10	2.19
1998 Los Angeles	NL	54	0	0	25	64.2	272	50	26	22	8	2	2	2	32	1	72	1	0	7	1	.875	0	6-11	12	3.06
4 ML YEARS		214	0	0	72	255	1045	200	96	87	25	15	9	6	103	16	271	7	2	21	15	.583	0	10-22	49	3.07

Willis Otanez

Bats: Right **Throws:** Right **Pos:** RF-2; PH/PR-1 **Ht:** 6'1" **Wt:** 200 **Born:** 4/19/73 **Age:** 26

Year Team	Lg	G	AB	H	2B	3B	HR	(Hm	Rd)	TB	R	RBI	TBB	IBB	SO	HBP	SH	SF	SB	CS	SB%	GDP	Avg	OBP	SLG
1991 Great Falls	R+	58	222	64	9	2	6	—	—	95	38	39	19	0	34	2	1	4	3	3	.50	7	.288	.344	.428
1992 Vero Beach	A+	117	390	86	18	0	3	—	—	113	27	27	24	0	60	4	5	3	2	4	.33	10	.221	.271	.290
1993 Bakersfield	A+	95	325	85	11	2	10	—	—	130	34	39	29	1	63	2	4	2	1	4	.20	9	.262	.324	.400
1994 Vero Beach	A+	131	476	132	27	1	19	—	—	218	77	72	53	2	98	4	0	7	4	2	.67	10	.277	.350	.458
1995 Vero Beach	A+	92	354	92	24	0	10	—	—	146	39	53	28	3	59	2	0	5	1	1	.50	15	.260	.314	.412
San Antonio	AA	27	100	24	4	1	1	—	—	33	8	7	6	0	25	0	0	3	0	1	.00	3	.240	.278	.330
1996 Bowie	AA	138	506	134	27	2	24	—	—	237	60	75	45	2	97	1	2	5	3	7	.30	17	.265	.323	.468
1997 Orioles	R	8	25	8	2	0	2	—	—	16	5	3	2	0	4	1	0	0	0	0	.00	1	.320	.393	.640
Bowie	AA	19	78	26	9	0	3	—	—	44	13	13	9	0	19	0	0	1	0	0	.00	3	.333	.398	.564
Rochester	AAA	49	168	35	9	0	5	—	—	59	20	25	15	0	35	0	0	3	0	0	.00	8	.208	.269	.351
1998 Rochester	AAA	124	481	137	24	2	27	—	—	246	87	100	41	6	104	6	1	8	1	0	1.00	8	.285	.343	.511
1998 Baltimore	AL	3	5	1	0	0	0	(0	0)	1	0	0	0	0	2	0	0	0	0	0	.00	0	.200	.200	.200

Eric Owens

Bats: R **Throws:** R **Pos:** PH/PR-15; LF-10; CF-5; 2B-4; RF-2 **Ht:** 6'1" **Wt:** 184 **Born:** 2/3/71 **Age:** 28

Year Team	Lg	G	AB	H	2B	3B	HR	(Hm	Rd)	TB	R	RBI	TBB	IBB	SO	HBP	SH	SF	SB	CS	SB%	GDP	Avg	OBP	SLG
1998 Louisville *	AAA	77	254	85	11	4	5	—	—	119	48	40	34	0	30	0	0	4	21	6	.78	7	.335	.408	.469
1995 Cincinnati	NL	2	2	2	0	0	0	(0	0)	2	0	1	0	0	0	0	1	0	0	0	.00	0	1.000	1.000	1.000
1996 Cincinnati	NL	88	205	41	6	0	0	(0	0)	47	26	9	23	1	38	1	1	2	16	2	.89	2	.200	.281	.229
1997 Cincinnati	NL	27	57	15	0	0	0	(0	0)	15	8	3	4	0	11	0	0	0	3	2	.60	2	.263	.311	.263
1998 Milwaukee	NL	34	40	5	2	0	1	(0	1)	10	5	4	2	0	6	0	1	0	0	0	.00	3	.125	.167	.250
4 ML YEARS		151	304	63	8	0	1	(0	1)	74	39	17	29	1	55	1	3	2	19	4	.83	7	.207	.277	.243

Tom Pagnozzi

Bats: Right **Throws:** Right **Pos:** C-44; PH/PR-9 **Ht:** 6'1" **Wt:** 190 **Born:** 7/30/62 **Age:** 36

Year Team	Lg	G	AB	H	2B	3B	HR	(Hm	Rd)	TB	R	RBI	TBB	IBB	SO	HBP	SH	SF	SB	CS	SB%	GDP	Avg	OBP	SLG
1998 Peoria *	A	4	8	1	0	0	0	—	—	1	2	1	6	0	1	0	0	0	0	0	.00	0	.125	.500	.125
1987 St. Louis	NL	27	48	9	1	0	2	(2	0)	16	8	9	4	2	13	0	1	0	1	0	1.00	1	.188	.250	.333
1988 St. Louis	NL	81	195	55	9	0	0	(0	0)	64	17	15	11	1	32	0	2	1	0	0	.00	5	.282	.319	.328
1989 St. Louis	NL	52	80	12	2	0	0	(0	0)	14	3	3	6	2	19	1	0	1	0	0	.00	7	.150	.216	.175
1990 St. Louis	NL	69	220	61	15	0	2	(2	0)	82	20	23	14	1	37	1	0	2	1	1	.50	7	.277	.321	.373
1991 St. Louis	NL	140	459	121	24	5	2	(2	0)	161	38	57	36	6	63	4	6	5	9	13	.41	10	.264	.319	.351
1992 St. Louis	NL	139	485	121	26	3	7	(3	4)	174	33	44	28	9	64	1	6	3	2	5	.29	15	.249	.290	.359
1993 St. Louis	NL	92	330	85	15	1	7	(1	6)	123	31	41	19	6	30	1	0	5	1	0	1.00	7	.258	.296	.373
1994 St. Louis	NL	70	243	66	12	1	7	(2	5)	101	21	40	21	5	39	0	0	3	0	0	.00	3	.272	.327	.416
1995 St. Louis	NL	62	219	47	14	1	2	(1	1)	69	17	15	11	0	31	1	0	1	0	1	.00	9	.215	.254	.315
1996 St. Louis	NL	119	407	110	23	0	13	(9	4)	172	48	55	24	2	78	2	3	4	4	1	.80	9	.270	.311	.423
1997 St. Louis	NL	25	50	11	3	0	1	(1	0)	17	4	8	1	0	7	0	0	0	0	0	.00	2	.220	.235	.340
1998 St. Louis	NL	51	160	35	9	0	1	(0	1)	47	7	10	14	0	37	0	3	1	0	0	.00	4	.219	.280	.294
12 ML YEARS		927	2896	733	153	11	44	(23	21)	1040	247	320	189	34	450	11	21	25	18	21	.46	71	.253	.299	.359

Lance Painter

Pitches: Left **Bats:** Left **Pos:** RP-65 **Ht:** 6'1" **Wt:** 197 **Born:** 7/21/67 **Age:** 31

Year Team	Lg	G	GS	CG	GF	IP	BFP	H	R	ER	HR	SH	SF	HB	TBB	IBB	SO	WP	Bk	W	L	Pct.	ShO	Sv-Op	Hld	ERA
1993 Colorado	NL	10	6	1	2	39	166	52	26	26	5	1	0	0	9	0	16	2	0	2	2	.500	0	0-0	0	6.00
1994 Colorado	NL	15	14	0	1	73.2	336	91	51	50	9	3	5	1	26	2	41	3	1	4	6	.400	0	0-0	0	6.11
1995 Colorado	NL	33	1	0	7	45.1	198	55	23	22	9	0	0	2	10	0	36	4	1	3	0	1.000	0	1-1	4	4.37
1996 Colorado	NL	34	1	0	4	50.2	234	56	37	33	12	3	3	3	25	3	48	1	0	4	2	.667	0	0-1	4	5.86
1997 St. Louis	NL	14	0	0	4	17	69	13	9	9	1	0	0	0	8	2	11	0	0	1	1	.500	0	0-0	3	4.76
1998 St. Louis	NL	65	0	0	9	47.1	207	42	24	21	5	4	2	4	28	3	39	2	0	4	0	1.000	0	1-2	21	3.99
6 ML YEARS		171	22	1	27	273	1210	309	170	161	41	11	10	10	106	10	191	12	2	18	11	.621	0	2-4	32	5.31

Donn Pall

Pitches: Right **Bats:** Right **Pos:** RP-23 **Ht:** 6'1" **Wt:** 180 **Born:** 1/11/62 **Age:** 37

Year Team	Lg	G	GS	CG	GF	IP	BFP	H	R	ER	HR	SH	SF	HB	TBB	IBB	SO	WP	Bk	W	L	Pct.	ShO	Sv-Op	Hld	ERA
1998 Charlotte *	AAA	29	0	0	25	34.2	147	33	17	16	1	2	2	0	10	0	33	1	0	1	2	.333	0	14--	—	4.15
1988 Chicago	AL	17	0	0	6	28.2	130	39	11	11	1	2	1	0	8	1	16	1	0	0	2	.000	0	0-0	4	3.45
1989 Chicago	AL	53	0	0	27	87	370	90	35	32	9	8	2	8	19	3	58	4	1	4	5	.444	0	6-10	5	3.31
1990 Chicago	AL	56	0	0	11	76	306	63	33	28	7	4	0	8	24	8	39	2	0	3	5	.375	0	2-3	13	3.32
1991 Chicago	AL	51	0	0	7	71	282	59	22	19	7	4	0	3	20	3	40	2	0	7	2	.778	0	0-1	12	2.41
1992 Chicago	AL	39	0	0	12	73	323	79	43	40	9	1	3	2	27	8	27	1	2	5	2	.714	0	1-2	2	4.93
1993 ChA-Phi		47	0	0	11	76.1	320	77	32	26	8	1	2	1	14	3	40	3	1	3	3	.500	0	1-2	9	3.07
1994 NYA-ChN		28	0	0	7	39	176	51	20	16	4	0	1	1	10	0	23	2	0	1	2	.333	0	0-0	3	3.69
1996 Florida	NL	12	0	0	2	18.2	80	16	15	12	3	1	1	0	9	1	9	1	0	1	1	.500	0	0-0	1	5.79
1997 Florida	NL	2	0	0	0	2.1	11	3	1	1	1	0	0	0	1	0	1	0	0	0	0	.000	0	0-1	0	3.86
1998 Florida	NL	23	0	0	11	33.1	141	42	19	19	5	3	1	1	7	2	26	0	0	1	0	1.000	0	0-0	2	5.13

Year Team	Lg	G	GS	CG	GF	IP	BFP	H	R	ER	HR	SH	SF	HB	TBB	IBB	SO	WP	Bk	W	L	Pct.	ShO	Sv-Op	Hld	ERA
1993 Chicago	AL	39	0	0	9	58.2	251	62	25	21	5	6	1	2	11	3	29	3	0	2	3	.400	0	1-2	8	3.22
Philadelphia	NL	8	0	0	2	17.2	69	15	7	5	1	1	0	0	3	0	11	0	1	1	0	1.000	0	0-0	1	2.55
1994 New York	AL	26	0	0	7	35	157	43	18	14	3	0	1	1	9	0	21	2	0	1	2	.333	0	0-0	3	3.60
Chicago	NL	2	0	0	0	4	19	8	2	2	1	0	0	0	1	0	2	0	0	0	0	.000	0	0-0	0	4.50
10 ML YEARS		328	0	0	94	505.1	2139	519	231	204	52	30	12	21	139	29	278	18	4	24	23	.511	0	10-19	51	3.63

Orlando Palmeiro

Bats: L **Throws:** L **Pos:** LF-46; PH/PR-27; CF-6; RF-4; DH-3 **Ht:** 5'11" **Wt:** 175 **Born:** 1/19/69 **Age:** 30

Year Team	Lg	G	AB	H	2B	3B	HR	(Hm	Rd)	TB	R	RBI	TBB	IBB	SO	HBP	SH	SF	SB	CS	SB%	GDP	Avg	OBP	SLG
1998 Vancouver *	AAA	43	140	42	13	3	1	—	—	64	21	29	16	0	10	0	8	4	3	1	.75	2	.300	.363	.457
1995 California	AL	15	20	7	0	0	0	(0	0)	7	3	1	1	0	1	0	0	0	0	0	.00	0	.350	.381	.350
1996 California	AL	50	87	25	6	1	0	(0	0)	33	6	6	8	1	13	2	1	0	0	1	.00	1	.287	.361	.379
1997 Anaheim	AL	74	134	29	2	2	0	(0	0)	35	19	8	17	1	11	1	3	1	2	2	.50	4	.216	.307	.261
1998 Anaheim	AL	75	165	53	7	2	0	(0	0)	64	28	21	20	1	11	0	7	0	5	4	.56	2	.321	.395	.388
4 ML YEARS		214	406	114	15	5	0	(0	0)	139	56	36	46	3	36	3	11	1	7	7	.50	7	.281	.357	.342

Rafael Palmeiro

Bats: Left **Throws:** Left **Pos:** 1B-159; DH-3; PH/PR-1 **Ht:** 6'0" **Wt:** 190 **Born:** 9/24/64 **Age:** 34

Year Team	Lg	G	AB	H	2B	3B	HR	(Hm	Rd)	TB	R	RBI	TBB	IBB	SO	HBP	SH	SF	SB	CS	SB%	GDP	Avg	OBP	SLG
1986 Chicago	NL	22	73	18	4	0	3	(1	2)	31	9	12	4	0	6	1	0	0	1	1	.50	4	.247	.295	.425
1987 Chicago	NL	84	221	61	15	1	14	(5	9)	120	32	30	20	1	26	1	0	2	2	2	.50	4	.276	.336	.543
1988 Chicago	NL	152	580	178	41	5	8	(8	0)	253	75	53	38	6	34	3	2	6	12	2	.86	11	.307	.349	.436
1989 Texas	AL	156	559	154	23	4	8	(4	4)	209	76	64	63	3	48	6	2	2	4	3	.57	18	.275	.354	.374
1990 Texas	AL	154	598	191	35	6	14	(9	5)	280	72	89	40	6	59	3	2	8	3	3	.50	24	.319	.361	.468
1991 Texas	AL	159	631	203	49	3	26	(12	14)	336	115	88	68	10	72	6	2	7	4	3	.57	17	.322	.389	.532
1992 Texas	AL	159	608	163	27	4	22	(8	14)	264	84	85	72	8	83	10	5	6	2	3	.40	10	.268	.352	.434
1993 Texas	AL	160	597	176	40	2	37	(22	15)	331	124	105	73	22	85	5	2	9	22	3	.88	8	.295	.371	.554
1994 Baltimore	AL	111	436	139	32	0	23	(11	12)	240	82	76	54	1	63	2	0	6	7	3	.70	11	.319	.392	.550
1995 Baltimore	AL	143	554	172	30	2	39	(21	18)	323	89	104	62	5	65	3	0	5	3	1	.75	12	.310	.380	.583
1996 Baltimore	AL	162	626	181	40	2	39	(21	18)	342	110	142	95	12	96	3	0	8	8	0	1.00	9	.289	.381	.546
1997 Baltimore	AL	158	614	156	24	2	38	(20	18)	298	95	110	67	7	109	5	0	4	5	2	.71	14	.254	.329	.485
1998 Baltimore	AL	162	619	183	36	1	43	(25	18)	350	98	121	79	8	91	7	0	4	11	7	.61	14	.296	.379	.565
13 ML YEARS		1782	6716	1975	396	32	314	(167	147)	3377	1061	1079	735	89	837	55	15	69	84	33	.72	156	.294	.365	.503

Dean Palmer

Bats: Right **Throws:** Right **Pos:** 3B-129; DH-22; PH/PR-1 **Ht:** 6'1" **Wt:** 210 **Born:** 12/27/68 **Age:** 30

Year Team	Lg	G	AB	H	2B	3B	HR	(Hm	Rd)	TB	R	RBI	TBB	IBB	SO	HBP	SH	SF	SB	CS	SB%	GDP	Avg	OBP	SLG
1989 Texas	AL	16	19	2	0	0	0	(0	0)	4	0	1	0	0	12	0	0	1	0	0	.00	0	.105	.100	.211
1991 Texas	AL	81	268	50	9	2	15	(6	9)	108	38	37	32	0	98	3	1	0	0	2	.00	4	.187	.281	.403
1992 Texas	AL	152	541	124	25	0	26	(11	15)	227	74	72	62	2	154	4	2	4	10	4	.71	9	.229	.311	.420
1993 Texas	AL	148	519	127	31	2	33	(12	21)	261	88	96	53	4	154	8	0	5	11	10	.52	5	.245	.321	.503
1994 Texas	AL	93	342	84	14	2	19	(11	8)	159	50	59	26	0	89	2	0	1	3	4	.43	7	.246	.302	.465
1995 Texas	AL	36	119	40	6	0	9	(5	4)	73	30	24	21	1	21	4	0	1	1	1	.50	2	.336	.448	.613
1996 Texas	AL	154	582	163	26	2	38	(19	19)	307	98	107	59	4	145	5	0	6	2	0	1.00	15	.280	.348	.527
1997 Tex-KC	AL	143	542	139	31	1	23	(10	13)	241	70	86	41	2	134	3	1	5	2	2	.50	7	.256	.310	.445
1998 Kansas City	AL	152	572	159	27	2	34	(21	13)	292	84	119	48	3	134	6	0	13	2	2	.80	18	.278	.333	.510
1997 Texas	AL	94	355	87	21	0	14	(6	8)	150	47	55	26	2	84	1	1	3	1	0	1.00	4	.245	.296	.423
Kansas City	AL	49	187	52	10	1	9	(4	5)	91	23	31	15	0	50	2	0	2	1	2	.33	3	.278	.335	.487
9 ML YEARS		975	3504	888	171	11	197	(95	102)	1672	532	601	342	16	941	35	4	36	37	25	.60	67	.253	.323	.477

Jose Paniagua

Pitches: Right **Bats:** Right **Pos:** RP-18 **Ht:** 6'2" **Wt:** 185 **Born:** 8/20/73 **Age:** 25

Year Team	Lg	G	GS	CG	GF	IP	BFP	H	R	ER	HR	SH	SF	HB	TBB	IBB	SO	WP	Bk	W	L	Pct.	ShO	Sv-Op	Hld	ERA
1998 Tacoma *	AAA	44	0	0	18	68.1	292	66	25	24	2	4	4	4	22	1	61	0	0	3	1	.750	0	5- -	—	2.77
1996 Montreal	NL	13	11	0	0	51	223	55	24	20	7	1	1	3	23	0	27	2	2	2	4	.333	0	0-0	0	3.53
1997 Montreal	NL	9	3	0	0	18	100	29	24	24	2	1	1	4	16	1	8	1	0	1	2	.333	0	0-0	0	12.00
1998 Seattle	AL	18	0	0	2	22	83	15	5	5	3	0	0	3	5	0	16	2	0	2	0	1.000	0	1-2	6	2.05
3 ML YEARS		40	14	0	2	91	406	99	53	49	12	2	2	10	44	1	51	5	2	5	6	.455	0	1-2	6	4.85

Craig Paquette

Bats: Right **Throws:** Right **Pos:** 3B-4; 1B-2; PH/PR-2; LF-1 **Ht:** 6'0" **Wt:** 190 **Born:** 3/28/69 **Age:** 30

Year Team	Lg	G	AB	H	2B	3B	HR	(Hm	Rd)	TB	R	RBI	TBB	IBB	SO	HBP	SH	SF	SB	CS	SB%	GDP	Avg	OBP	SLG
1998 Norfolk *	AAA	15	61	17	1	1	3	—	—	29	11	14	1	0	13	0	0	1	2	1	.67	2	.279	.286	.475
1993 Oakland	AL	105	393	86	20	4	12	(8	4)	150	35	46	14	2	108	1	1	4	4	2	.67	7	.219	.245	.382
1994 Oakland	AL	14	49	7	2	0	0			9	0	0	0	0	14	0	1	0	1	0	1.00	0	.143	.143	.184
1995 Oakland	AL	105	283	64	13	1	13	(8	5)	118	42	49	12	0	88	1	3	5	5	2	.71	5	.226	.256	.417
1996 Kansas City	AL	118	429	111	15	1	22	(12	10)	194	61	67	23	2	101	2	3	5	5	3	.63	11	.259	.296	.452

Year Team	Lg	BATTING																		BASERUNNING				PERCENTAGES		
		G	AB	H	2B	3B	HR	(Hm	Rd)	TB	R	RBI	TBB	IBB	SO	HBP	SH	SF		SB	CS	SB%	GDP	Avg	OBP	SLG
1997 Kansas City	AL	77	252	58	15	1	8	(7	1)	99	26	33	10	0	57	2	1	2		2	2	.50	13	.230	.263	.393
1998 New York	NL	7	19	5	2	0	0	(0	0)	7	3	0	0	0	6	0	0	0		1	0	1.00	3	.263	.263	.368
6 ML YEARS		426	1425	331	67	7	55	(35	20)	577	167	195	59	4	374	5	9	13		18	9	.67	39	.232	.263	.405

Mark Parent

Bats: Right **Throws:** Right **Pos:** C-34   **Ht:** 6'5" **Wt:** 245 **Born:** 9/16/61 **Age:** 37

Year Team	Lg	BATTING																		BASERUNNING				PERCENTAGES		
		G	AB	H	2B	3B	HR	(Hm	Rd)	TB	R	RBI	TBB	IBB	SO	HBP	SH	SF		SB	CS	SB%	GDP	Avg	OBP	SLG
1986 San Diego	NL	8	14	2	0	0	0	(0	0)	2	1	0	1	0	3	0	0	0		0	0	.00	1	.143	.200	.143
1987 San Diego	NL	12	25	2	0	0	0	(0	0)	2	0	2	0	0	9	0	0	0		0	0	.00	0	.080	.080	.080
1988 San Diego	NL	41	118	23	3	0	6	(4	2)	44	9	15	6	0	23	0	0	1		0	0	.00	1	.195	.232	.373
1989 San Diego	NL	52	141	27	4	0	7	(6	1)	52	12	21	8	2	34	0	1	4		1	0	1.00	5	.191	.229	.369
1990 San Diego	NL	65	189	42	11	0	3	(1	2)	62	13	16	16	3	29	0	3	0		1	0	1.00	1	.222	.283	.328
1991 Texas	AL	3	1	0	0	0	0	(0	0)	0	0	0	0	0	1	0	0	0		0	0	.00	0	.000	.000	.000
1992 Baltimore	AL	17	34	8	1	0	2	(0	2)	15	4	4	3	0	7	1	2	0		0	0	.00	1	.235	.316	.441
1993 Baltimore	AL	22	54	14	2	0	4	(1	3)	28	7	12	3	0	14	0	3	1		0	0	.00	1	.259	.293	.519
1994 Chicago	AL	44	99	26	4	0	3	(0	3)	39	8	16	13	1	24	1	1	2		0	1	.00	6	.263	.348	.394
1995 Pit-ChN	NL	81	265	62	11	0	18	(7	11)	127	30	38	26	2	69	0	1	0		0	0	.00	6	.234	.302	.479
1996 Det-Bal	AL	56	137	31	7	0	9	(4	5)	65	17	23	5	0	37	0	1	1		0	0	.00	3	.226	.252	.474
1997 Philadelphia	NL	39	113	17	3	0	0	(0	0)	20	4	8	7	0	39	0	0	1		0	0	.00	1	.150	.198	.177
1998 Philadelphia	NL	34	113	25	4	0	1	(0	1)	32	7	13	10	0	30	0	0	3		1	1	.50	1	.221	.278	.283
1995 Pittsburgh	NL	69	233	54	9	0	15	(5	10)	108	25	33	23	2	62	0	1	0		0	0	.00	5	.232	.301	.464
Chicago	NL	12	32	8	2	0	3	(2	1)	19	5	5	3	0	7	0	0	0		0	0	.00	1	.250	.314	.594
1996 Detroit	AL	38	104	25	6	0	7	(4	3)	52	13	17	3	0	27	0	0	0		0	0	.00	2	.240	.259	.500
Baltimore	AL	18	33	6	1	0	2	(0	2)	13	4	6	2	0	10	0	1	0		0	0	.00	1	.182	.229	.394
13 ML YEARS		474	1303	279	50	0	53	(23	30)	488	112	168	98	8	319	2	12	13		3	3	.50	28	.214	.268	.375

Chan Ho Park

Pitches: Right **Bats:** Right **Pos:** SP-34   **Ht:** 6'2" **Wt:** 204 **Born:** 6/30/73 **Age:** 26

Year Team	Lg	HOW MUCH HE PITCHED						WHAT HE GAVE UP												THE RESULTS						
		G	GS	CG	GF	IP	BFP	H	R	ER	HR	SH	SF	HB	TBB	IBB	SO	WP	Bk	W	L	Pct.	ShO	Sv-Op	Hld	ERA
1994 Los Angeles	NL	2	0	0	1	4	23	5	5	5	1	0	0	1	5	0	6	0	0	0	0	.000	0	0-0	0	11.25
1995 Los Angeles	NL	2	1	0	0	4	16	2	2	2	1	0	0	2	2	0	7	0	1	0	0	.000	0	0-0	0	4.50
1996 Los Angeles	NL	48	10	0	7	108.2	477	82	48	44	7	8	1	4	71	3	119	4	3	5	5	.500	0	0-0	4	3.64
1997 Los Angeles	NL	32	29	2	1	192	792	149	80	72	24	9	5	8	70	1	166	4	1	14	8	.636	0	0-0	0	3.38
1998 Los Angeles	NL	34	34	2	0	220.2	946	199	101	91	16	11	10	11	97	1	191	6	2	15	9	.625	0	0-0	0	3.71
5 ML YEARS		118	74	4	9	529.1	2254	437	236	214	49	28	16	24	245	5	489	14	7	34	22	.607	0	0-0	4	3.64

Jim Parque

Pitches: Left **Bats:** Left **Pos:** SP-21   **Ht:** 5'11" **Wt:** 165 **Born:** 2/8/75 **Age:** 24

Year Team	Lg	HOW MUCH HE PITCHED						WHAT HE GAVE UP												THE RESULTS						
		G	GS	CG	GF	IP	BFP	H	R	ER	HR	SH	SF	HB	TBB	IBB	SO	WP	Bk	W	L	Pct.	ShO	Sv-Op	Hld	ERA
1997 Winston-Sal	A+	11	11	0	0	61.2	231	29	19	19	3	0	1	0	23	0	76	2	2	7	2	.778	0	0--	—	2.77
Nashville	AAA	2	2	0	0	10.2	49	9	5	5	0	0	1	0	9	0	5	1	0	1	0	1.000	0	0--	—	4.22
1998 Calgary	AAA	8	8	0	0	48	213	49	26	21	7	0	1	1	25	0	31	1	0	3	2	.400	0	0--	—	3.94
1998 Chicago	AL	21	21	0	0	113	507	135	72	64	14	1	0	6	49	0	77	0	3	7	5	.583	0	0-0	0	5.10

Steve Parris

Pitches: Right **Bats:** Right **Pos:** SP-16; RP-2   **Ht:** 6'0" **Wt:** 195 **Born:** 12/17/67 **Age:** 31

Year Team	Lg	HOW MUCH HE PITCHED						WHAT HE GAVE UP												THE RESULTS						
		G	GS	CG	GF	IP	BFP	H	R	ER	HR	SH	SF	HB	TBB	IBB	SO	WP	Bk	W	L	Pct.	ShO	Sv-Op	Hld	ERA
1998 Indianapols *	AAA	13	13	1	0	84.1	347	74	38	36	8	2	3	1	26	1	102	6	0	6	1	.857	1	0--	—	3.84
1995 Pittsburgh	NL	15	15	1	0	82	360	89	49	49	12	3	2	7	33	1	61	4	0	6	6	.500	1	0-0	0	5.38
1996 Pittsburgh	NL	8	4	0	3	26.1	123	35	22	21	4	1	1	1	11	0	27	2	0	0	3	.000	0	0-0	0	7.18
1998 Cincinnati	NL	18	16	1	0	99	421	89	44	41	9	7	1	4	32	3	77	1	1	6	5	.545	1	0-0	0	3.73
3 ML YEARS		41	35	2	3	207.1	904	213	115	111	25	11	4	12	76	4	165	7	1	12	14	.462	2	0-0	0	4.82

Bronswell Patrick

Pitches: Right **Bats:** Right **Pos:** RP-29; SP-3   **Ht:** 6'1" **Wt:** 205 **Born:** 9/16/70 **Age:** 28

Year Team	Lg	HOW MUCH HE PITCHED						WHAT HE GAVE UP												THE RESULTS						
		G	GS	CG	GF	IP	BFP	H	R	ER	HR	SH	SF	HB	TBB	IBB	SO	WP	Bk	W	L	Pct.	ShO	Sv-Op	Hld	ERA
1988 Athletics	R	14	13	2	0	96.1	390	99	37	32	7	1	2	2	16	1	64	1	2	8	3	.727	0	0--	—	2.99
1989 Madison	A	12	10	0	1	54.1	238	62	29	22	3	2	0	0	14	0	32	3	2	2	5	.286	0	0--	—	3.64
1990 Modesto	A+	14	14	0	0	74.2	340	92	58	43	10	3	1	4	32	0	37	5	1	3	7	.300	0	0--	—	5.18
Madison	A	13	12	3	0	80	337	88	44	32	6	5	4	1	19	0	40	3	0	3	7	.300	0	0--	—	3.60
1991 Modesto	A+	28	26	3	1	169.2	716	158	77	61	9	4	4	1	60	4	95	7	0	12	12	.500	1	0--	—	3.24
1992 Huntsville	AA	29	29	3	0	179.1	758	187	84	75	20	1	3	4	46	0	98	3	0	13	7	.650	0	0--	—	3.76
1993 Tacoma	AAA	35	13	1	12	104.2	496	156	88	82	12	3	12	4	42	3	56	3	0	3	8	.273	0	1--	—	7.05
1994 Huntsville	AA	7	3	0	1	27.2	120	31	11	9	2	1	0	2	10	0	16	1	1	2	0	1.000	0	1--	—	2.93
Tacoma	AAA	30	0	0	9	47.1	208	50	31	25	5	3	1	0	20	2	38	2	0	1	1	.500	0	2--	—	4.75
1995 Tucson	AAA	43	4	0	10	81.2	352	91	42	38	3	2	3	1	21	1	62	4	0	5	1	.833	0	1--	—	4.19
1996 Tucson	AAA	33	15	0	2	118	521	137	59	46	7	1	1	0	33	4	82	1	0	7	3	.700	0	1--	—	3.51

Year Team	Lg	G	GS	CG	GF	IP	BFP	H	R	ER	HR	SH	SF	HB	TBB	IBB	SO	WP	Bk	W	L	Pct.	ShO	Sv-Op	Hld	ERA
1997 New Orleans	AAA	30	12	1	10	100.2	426	108	45	36	10	6	2	0	30	4	88	5	0	6	5	.545	1	0- -	—	3.22
1998 Louisville	AAA	6	6	0	0	37.2	167	43	21	18	6	0	1	1	9	0	28	3	0	3	1	.750	0	0- -	—	4.30
1998 Milwaukee	NL	32	3	0	8	78.2	334	83	43	41	9	4	3	0	29	1	49	2	0	4	1	.800	0	0-0	0	4.69

Bob Patterson

Pitches: Left **Bats:** Right **Pos:** RP-33   **Ht:** 6'1" **Wt:** 195 **Born:** 5/16/59 **Age:** 40

Year Team	Lg	G	GS	CG	GF	IP	BFP	H	R	ER	HR	SH	SF	HB	TBB	IBB	SO	WP	Bk	W	L	Pct.	ShO	Sv-Op	Hld	ERA
1985 San Diego	NL	3	0	0	2	4	26	13	11	11	2	0	0	0	3	0	1	0	1	0	0	.000	0	0- -	—	24.75
1986 Pittsburgh	NL	11	5	0	2	36.1	159	49	20	20	0	1	1	0	5	2	20	0	1	2	3	.400	0	0- -	—	4.95
1987 Pittsburgh	NL	15	7	0	2	43	201	49	34	32	5	6	3	1	22	4	27	1	0	1	4	.200	0	0-0	0	6.70
1989 Pittsburgh	NL	12	3	0	2	26.2	109	23	13	12	3	1	1	0	8	2	20	0	0	4	3	.571	0	1-1	0	4.05
1990 Pittsburgh	NL	55	5	0	19	94.2	386	88	33	31	9	5	3	3	21	7	70	1	2	8	5	.615	0	5-8	8	2.95
1991 Pittsburgh	NL	54	1	0	19	65.2	270	67	32	30	7	2	2	0	15	1	57	0	0	4	3	.571	0	2-3	13	4.11
1992 Pittsburgh	NL	60	0	0	26	64.2	268	59	22	21	7	3	2	0	23	6	43	3	0	6	3	.667	0	9-13	10	2.92
1993 Texas	AL	52	0	0	29	52.2	224	59	28	28	8	1	2	1	11	0	46	0	0	2	4	.333	0	1-2	6	4.78
1994 California	AL	47	0	0	11	42	170	35	21	19	6	0	0	2	15	2	30	1	0	2	3	.400	0	1-1	10	4.07
1995 California	AL	62	0	0	20	53.1	212	48	18	18	6	2	1	1	13	3	41	0	0	5	2	.714	0	0-1	12	3.04
1996 Chicago	NL	79	0	0	27	54.2	230	46	19	19	6	2	4	1	22	7	53	1	1	3	3	.500	0	8-10	15	3.13
1997 Chicago	NL	76	0	0	12	59.1	231	47	23	22	9	5	4	0	10	1	58	1	0	1	6	.143	0	0-3	22	3.34
1998 Chicago	NL	33	0	0	4	20.1	107	36	20	17	2	1	2	0	12	3	17	0	0	1	1	.500	0	1-2	5	7.52
13 ML YEARS		559	21	0	175	617.1	2593	619	294	280	70	29	25	9	180	38	483	8	6	39	40	.494	0	28- -	—	4.08

Danny Patterson

Pitches: Right **Bats:** Right **Pos:** RP-56   **Ht:** 6'0" **Wt:** 185 **Born:** 2/17/71 **Age:** 28

Year Team	Lg	G	GS	CG	GF	IP	BFP	H	R	ER	HR	SH	SF	HB	TBB	IBB	SO	WP	Bk	W	L	Pct.	ShO	Sv-Op	Hld	ERA
1998 Tulsa *	AA	2	1	0	1	4	14	3	2	2	1	0	0	0	4	0	4	0	0	0	0	.000	0	0- -	—	4.50
Oklahoma *	AAA	1	0	0	0	2	11	4	1	1	0	0	0	0	1	0	2	0	0	0	0	.000	0	0- -	—	4.50
1996 Texas	AL	7	0	0	5	8.2	38	10	4	0	0	0	0	0	3	1	5	0	0	0	0	.000	0	0-0	0	0.00
1997 Texas	AL	54	0	0	17	71	296	70	29	27	3	4	3	0	23	4	69	7	1	10	6	.625	0	1-8	9	3.42
1998 Texas	AL	56	0	0	21	60.2	257	64	31	30	11	1	1	2	19	2	33	3	0	2	5	.286	0	2-2	19	4.45
3 ML YEARS		117	0	0	43	140.1	591	144	64	57	14	5	4	2	45	7	107	10	1	12	11	.522	0	3-10	28	3.66

Carl Pavano

Pitches: Right **Bats:** Right **Pos:** SP-23; RP-1   **Ht:** 6'5" **Wt:** 225 **Born:** 1/8/76 **Age:** 23

Year Team	Lg	G	GS	CG	GF	IP	BFP	H	R	ER	HR	SH	SF	HB	TBB	IBB	SO	WP	Bk	W	L	Pct.	ShO	Sv-Op	Hld	ERA
1994 Red Sox	R	9	7	0	0	44	176	31	14	9	1	0	1	1	7	0	47	4	1	4	3	.571	0	0- -	—	1.84
1995 Michigan	A	22	22	1	0	141.1	591	118	63	54	7	6	7	6	52	0	138	9	0	6	6	.500	0	0- -	—	3.44
1996 Trenton	AA	27	26	6	1	185	741	154	66	54	16	5	7	11	47	2	146	7	1	16	5	.762	2	0- -	—	2.63
1997 Pawtucket	AAA	23	23	3	0	161.2	663	148	62	56	13	1	3	6	34	2	147	7	1	11	6	.647	0	0- -	—	3.12
1998 Jupiter	A+	4	4	0	0	15	63	20	11	11	1	0	0	0	3	0	14	0	0	0	0	.000	0	0- -	—	6.60
Ottawa	AAA	3	3	0	0	18.2	75	12	5	5	1	0	0	5	7	0	14	1	0	1	0	1.000	0	0- -	—	2.41
1998 Montreal	NL	24	23	0	0	134.2	580	130	70	63	18	5	6	8	43	1	83	1	0	6	9	.400	0	0-0	0	4.21

Roger Pavlik

Pitches: Right **Bats:** Right **Pos:** RP-5   **Ht:** 6'2" **Wt:** 220 **Born:** 10/4/67 **Age:** 31

Year Team	Lg	G	GS	CG	GF	IP	BFP	H	R	ER	HR	SH	SF	HB	TBB	IBB	SO	WP	Bk	W	L	Pct.	ShO	Sv-Op	Hld	ERA
1992 Texas	AL	13	12	1	0	62	275	66	32	29	3	0	2	3	34	0	45	9	0	4	4	.500	0	0-0	0	4.21
1993 Texas	AL	26	26	2	0	166.1	712	151	67	63	18	6	4	5	80	3	131	6	0	12	6	.667	0	0-0	0	3.41
1994 Texas	AL	11	11	0	0	50.1	245	61	45	43	8	4	4	4	30	1	31	5	1	2	5	.286	0	0-0	0	7.69
1995 Texas	AL	31	31	2	0	191.2	819	174	96	93	19	4	5	4	90	5	149	10	1	10	10	.500	1	0-0	0	4.37
1996 Texas	AL	34	34	7	0	201	877	216	120	116	28	3	4	5	81	5	127	8	0	15	8	.652	0	0-0	0	5.19
1997 Texas	AL	11	11	0	0	57.2	256	59	29	28	7	2	1	1	31	1	35	0	0	3	5	.375	0	0-0	0	4.37
1998 Texas	AL	5	0	0	2	14	63	16	8	6	2	0	1	1	5	1	8	1	0	1	1	.500	0	1-1	0	3.86
7 ML YEARS		131	125	12	2	743	3247	743	397	378	85	19	21	23	351	16	526	39	2	47	39	.547	1	1-1	0	4.58

Jay Payton

Bats: Right **Throws:** Right **Pos:** PH/PR-9; LF-8; RF-1   **Ht:** 5'10" **Wt:** 185 **Born:** 11/22/72 **Age:** 26

Year Team	Lg	G	AB	H	2B	3B	HR	(Hm	Rd)	TB	R	RBI	TBB	IBB	SO	HBP	SH	SF	SB	CS	SB%	GDP	Avg	OBP	SLG
1994 Pittsfield	A-	58	219	80	16	2	3	—	—	109	47	37	23	2	18	9	0	4	10	2	.83	1	.365	.439	.498
Binghamton	AA	8	25	7	1	0	0	—	—	8	3	1	2	0	3	1	0	0	1	1	.50	1	.280	.357	.320
1995 Binghamton	AA	85	357	123	20	3	14	—	—	191	59	54	29	2	32	2	0	2	16	7	.70	11	.345	.395	.535
Norfolk	AAA	50	196	47	11	4	4	—	—	78	33	30	11	0	22	2	4	2	11	3	.79	5	.240	.284	.398
1996 Mets	R	3	13	5	1	0	1	—	—	9	3	2	0	0	1	0	0	0	1	0	1.00	0	.385	.385	.692
Binghamton	AA	4	10	2	0	0	0	—	—	2	0	2	2	1	2	0	0	2	1	0	1.00	0	.200	.286	.200
St. Lucie	A+	9	26	8	2	0	0	—	—	10	4	1	4	1	5	0	0	0	2	1	.67	1	.308	.400	.385
Norfolk	AAA	55	153	47	6	3	6	—	—	77	30	26	11	1	25	3	0	1	10	1	.91	3	.307	.363	.503
1998 St. Lucie	A+	3	7	1	0	0	0	—	—	1	0	0	3	2	1	0	0	0	0	0	.00	0	.143	.400	.143

Year Team	Lg	G	AB	H	2B	3B	HR	(Hm	Rd)	TB	R	RBI	TBB	IBB	SO	HBP	SH	SF	SB	CS	SB%	GDP	Avg	OBP	SLG
Norfolk	AAA	82	322	84	14	4	8	—		130	45	30	26	0	50	1	1	0	12	7	.63	5	.261	.318	.404
1998 New York	NL	15	22	7	1	0	0	(0	0)	8	2	0	1	0	4	0	0	0	0	0	.00	0	.318	.348	.364

Angel Pena

Bats: Right **Throws:** Right **Pos:** C-4; PH/PR-3 **Ht:** 5'10" **Wt:** 228 **Born:** 2/16/75 **Age:** 24

Year Team	Lg	G	AB	H	2B	3B	HR	(Hm	Rd)	TB	R	RBI	TBB	IBB	SO	HBP	SH	SF	SB	CS	SB%	GDP	Avg	OBP	SLG
1995 Great Falls	R+	49	138	40	11	1	4	—		65	24	15	21	2	32	3	0	3	2	1	.67	5	.290	.388	.471
1996 Savannah	A	36	127	26	4	0	0	—		48	13	16	7	1	37	0	1	0	1	1	.50	1	.205	.246	.378
1997 San Berndno	A+	86	322	89	22	4	16	—		167	53	64	32	4	84	2	0	2	3	5	.38	9	.276	.344	.519
1998 San Antonio	AA	126	483	162	32	2	22	—		264	81	105	48	3	80	6	3	2	9	5	.64	7	.335	.401	.547
1998 Los Angeles	NL	6	13	3	0	0	0	(0	0)	3	1	0	0	0	6	0	0	0	0	0	.00	0	.231	.231	.231

Terry Pendleton

Bats: Both **Throws:** Right **Pos:** DH-40; 3B-23; PH/PR-22 **Ht:** 5'9" **Wt:** 195 **Born:** 7/16/60 **Age:** 38

Year Team	Lg	G	AB	H	2B	3B	HR	(Hm	Rd)	TB	R	RBI	TBB	IBB	SO	HBP	SH	SF	SB	CS	SB%	GDP	Avg	OBP	SLG
1998 Omaha *	AAA	7	25	9	4	0	1	—		16	2	6	4	0	3	0	0	0	0	0	.00	0	.360	.448	.640
1984 St. Louis	NL	67	262	85	16	3	1	(0	1)	110	37	33	16	3	32	0	0	5	20	5	.80	7	.324	.357	.420
1985 St. Louis	NL	149	559	134	16	3	5	(3	2)	171	56	69	37	4	75	0	3	3	17	12	.59	18	.240	.285	.306
1986 St. Louis	NL	159	578	138	26	5	1	(0	1)	177	56	59	34	10	59	1	6	7	24	6	.80	12	.239	.279	.306
1987 St. Louis	NL	159	583	167	29	4	12	(5	7)	240	82	96	70	6	74	2	3	9	19	12	.61	18	.286	.360	.412
1988 St. Louis	NL	110	391	99	20	2	6	(3	3)	141	44	53	21	4	51	2	4	3	3	3	.50	9	.253	.293	.361
1989 St. Louis	NL	162	613	162	28	5	13	(8	5)	239	83	74	44	3	81	0	2	2	9	5	.64	16	.264	.313	.390
1990 St. Louis	NL	121	447	103	20	2	6	(6	0)	145	46	58	30	8	58	1	0	6	7	5	.58	12	.230	.277	.324
1991 Atlanta	NL	153	586	**187**	34	8	22	(13	9)	**303**	94	86	43	8	70	1	7	7	10	2	.83	16	**.319**	.363	.517
1992 Atlanta	NL	160	640	**199**	39	1	21	(13	8)	303	98	105	37	8	67	0	5	7	5	2	.71	16	.311	.345	.473
1993 Atlanta	NL	161	633	172	33	1	17	(9	8)	258	81	84	36	5	97	3	3	7	5	1	.83	18	.272	.311	.408
1994 Atlanta	NL	77	309	78	18	3	7	(3	4)	123	25	30	12	3	57	0	3	0	2	0	1.00	8	.252	.280	.398
1995 Florida	NL	133	513	149	32	1	14	(8	6)	225	70	78	38	7	84	2	0	4	1	2	.33	7	.290	.339	.439
1996 Fla-Atl	NL	153	568	135	26	1	11	(6	5)	196	51	75	41	6	111	3	1	5	2	3	.40	18	.238	.290	.345
1997 Cincinnati	NL	50	113	28	9	0	1	(1	0)	40	11	17	12	1	14	0	1	0	2	1	.67	1	.248	.290	.345
1998 Kansas City	AL	79	237	61	10	0	3	(2	1)	80	17	29	15	1	49	0	0	2	1	0	1.00	3	.257	.299	.338
1996 Florida	NL	111	406	102	20	1	7	(4	3)	145	30	58	26	5	75	3	1	5	0	2	.00	10	.251	.298	.357
Atlanta	NL	42	162	33	6	0	4	(2	2)	51	21	17	15	1	36	0	0	0	2	1	.67	8	.204	.271	.315
15 ML YEARS		1893	7032	1897	356	39	140	(80	60)	2751	851	946	486	77	979	15	37	67	127	59	.68	178	.270	.316	.391

Brad Pennington

Pitches: Left **Bats:** Left **Pos:** RP-1 **Ht:** 6'6" **Wt:** 215 **Born:** 4/14/69 **Age:** 30

Year Team	Lg	G	GS	CG	GF	IP	BFP	H	R	ER	HR	SH	SF	HB	TBB	IBB	SO	WP	Bk	W	L	Pct.	ShO	Sv-Op	Hld	ERA
1998 Durham *	AAA	45	6	0	11	100	442	77	55	54	12	0	3	6	65	0	125	8	1	4	4	.500	0	1--	--	4.86
1993 Baltimore	AL	34	0	0	16	33	158	34	25	24	7	2	1	2	25	0	39	3	0	3	2	.600	0	4-7	5	6.55
1994 Baltimore	AL	8	0	0	3	6	35	9	8	8	2	1	0	0	8	0	7	2	0	0	1	.000	0	0-1	1	12.00
1995 Bal-Cin		14	0	0	4	16.1	80	12	15	12	1	0	2	1	22	1	17	4	0	1	0	1.000	0	0-1	0	6.61
1996 Bos-Cal	AL	22	0	0	8	20.1	102	11	15	14	2	0	1	0	31	1	20	2	0	0	2	.000	0	0-1	1	6.20
1998 Tampa Bay	AL	1	0	0	0	0	4	1	1	1	0	0	0	0	3	0	0	0	0	0	0	.000	0	0-0	1	0.00
1995 Baltimore	AL	8	0	0	2	6.2	33	3	7	6	1	0	0	0	11	1	10	1	0	0	1	.000	0	0-1	0	8.10
Cincinnati	NL	6	0	0	2	9.2	47	9	8	6	0	0	2	1	11	0	7	3	0	0	0	.000	0	0-0	0	5.59
1996 Boston	AL	14	0	0	6	13	59	6	5	4	1	0	1	0	15	1	13	1	0	0	2	.000	0	0-0	0	2.77
California	AL	8	0	0	2	7.1	43	5	10	10	1	0	0	0	16	0	7	1	0	0	0	.000	0	0-0	0	12.27
5 ML YEARS		79	0	0	31	75.2	379	67	64	59	12	3	4	3	89	2	83	11	0	3	6	.333	0	4-9	7	7.02

Troy Percival

Pitches: Right **Bats:** Right **Pos:** RP-67 **Ht:** 6'3" **Wt:** 230 **Born:** 8/9/69 **Age:** 29

Year Team	Lg	G	GS	CG	GF	IP	BFP	H	R	ER	HR	SH	SF	HB	TBB	IBB	SO	WP	Bk	W	L	Pct.	ShO	Sv-Op	Hld	ERA
1995 California	AL	62	0	0	16	74	284	37	19	16	6	4	1	1	26	2	94	2	2	3	2	.600	0	3-6	29	1.95
1996 California	AL	62	0	0	52	74	291	38	20	19	8	2	1	4	31	4	100	2	0	0	0	.000	0	36-39	2	2.31
1997 Anaheim	AL	55	0	0	46	52	224	40	20	20	6	1	2	4	22	2	72	5	0	5	5	.500	0	27-31	0	3.46
1998 Anaheim	AL	67	0	0	60	66.2	287	45	31	27	5	3	2	3	37	4	87	3	0	2	7	.222	0	42-48	3	3.65
4 ML YEARS		246	0	0	174	266.2	1086	160	90	82	25	10	6	10	116	12	353	12	2	10	16	.385	0	108-124	31	2.77

Carlos Perez

Pitches: Left **Bats:** Left **Pos:** SP-34 **Ht:** 6'3" **Wt:** 210 **Born:** 1/14/71 **Age:** 28

Year Team	Lg	G	GS	CG	GF	IP	BFP	H	R	ER	HR	SH	SF	HB	TBB	IBB	SO	WP	Bk	W	L	Pct.	ShO	Sv-Op	Hld	ERA
1998 Expos *	R	5	1	0	0	5	20	5	2	0	1	0	0	1	1	0	2	0	0	1	0	1.000	0	0--	--	0.00
1995 Montreal	NL	28	23	2	2	141.1	592	142	61	58	18	6	1	5	28	2	106	8	4	10	8	.556	1	0-0	1	3.69
1997 Montreal	NL	33	32	8	0	206.2	857	206	109	89	21	5	7	4	48	1	110	2	1	12	13	.480	5	0-0	0	3.88
1998 Mon-LA	NL	34	34	7	0	241	1009	244	109	96	21	14	3	3	63	4	128	7	1	11	14	.440	2	0-0	0	3.59
1998 Montreal	NL	23	23	3	0	163.1	690	177	79	68	12	11	3	3	33	3	82	5	1	7	10	.412	0	0-0	0	3.75

Year Team	Lg	G	GS	CG	GF	IP	BFP	H	R	ER	HR	SH	SF	HB	TBB	IBB	SO	WP	Bk	W	L	Pct.	ShO	Sv-Op	Hld	ERA
Los Angeles	NL	11	11	4	0	77.2	319	67	30	28	9	3	0	0	30	1	46	2	0	4	4	.500	2	0-0	0	3.24
3 ML YEARS		95	89	17	2	589	2458	592	279	243	60	25	11	12	139	7	344	17	6	33	35	.485	8	0-0	1	3.71

Eddie Perez

Bats: R **Throws:** R **Pos:** C-45; PH/PR-13; 1B-8; DH-1   **Ht:** 6'1" **Wt:** 185 **Born:** 5/4/68 **Age:** 31

Year Team	Lg	G	AB	H	2B	3B	HR	(Hm	Rd)	TB	R	RBI	TBB	IBB	SO	HBP	SH	SF	SB	CS	SB%	GDP	Avg	OBP	SLG
1995 Atlanta	NL	7	13	4	1	0	1	(0	1)	8	1	4	0	0	2	0	0	0	0	0	.00	0	.308	.308	.615
1996 Atlanta	NL	68	156	40	9	1	4	(2	2)	63	19	17	8	0	19	1	0	0	0	0	.00	6	.256	.293	.404
1997 Atlanta	NL	73	191	41	5	0	6	(4	2)	64	20	18	10	0	35	2	1	2	0	1	.00	8	.215	.259	.335
1998 Atlanta	NL	61	149	50	12	0	6	(3	3)	80	18	32	15	0	28	2	1	0	1	1	.50	3	.336	.404	.537
4 ML YEARS		209	509	135	27	1	17	(9	8)	215	58	71	33	0	84	5	2	4	1	2	.33	17	.265	.314	.422

Eduardo Perez

Bats: R **Throws:** R **Pos:** 1B-51; PH/PR-42; 3B-1; LF-1   **Ht:** 6'4" **Wt:** 215 **Born:** 9/11/69 **Age:** 29

Year Team	Lg	G	AB	H	2B	3B	HR	(Hm	Rd)	TB	R	RBI	TBB	IBB	SO	HBP	SH	SF	SB	CS	SB%	GDP	Avg	OBP	SLG
1993 California	AL	52	180	45	6	2	4	(2	2)	67	16	30	9	0	39	2	0	1	5	4	.56	4	.250	.292	.372
1994 California	AL	38	129	27	7	0	5	(3	2)	49	10	16	12	1	29	0	1	1	3	0	1.00	5	.209	.275	.380
1995 California	AL	29	71	12	4	1	1	(0	1)	21	9	7	12	0	9	2	0	1	0	2	.00	3	.169	.302	.296
1996 Cincinnati	NL	18	36	8	0	0	3	(3	0)	17	8	5	5	1	9	0	0	0	0	0	.00	2	.222	.317	.472
1997 Cincinnati	NL	106	299	75	18	0	16	(7	9)	141	44	52	29	1	76	2	0	2	5	1	.83	6	.253	.321	.475
1998 Cincinnati	NL	84	172	41	4	0	4	(1	3)	57	20	30	21	2	45	2	1	2	0	1	.00	2	.238	.325	.331
6 ML YEARS		327	885	208	39	3	33	(16	17)	352	107	140	88	5	207	8	2	7	13	8	.62	22	.235	.308	.398

Neifi Perez

Bats: Both **Throws:** Right **Pos:** SS-162; PH/PR-2; C-1   **Ht:** 6'0" **Wt:** 177 **Born:** 2/2/75 **Age:** 24

Year Team	Lg	G	AB	H	2B	3B	HR	(Hm	Rd)	TB	R	RBI	TBB	IBB	SO	HBP	SH	SF	SB	CS	SB%	GDP	Avg	OBP	SLG
1996 Colorado	NL	17	45	7	2	0	0	(0	0)	9	4	3	0	0	8	0	1	0	2	2	.50	2	.156	.156	.200
1997 Colorado	NL	83	313	91	13	10	5	(3	2)	139	46	31	21	4	43	1	5	3	4	3	.57	3	.291	.333	.444
1998 Colorado	NL	162	647	177	25	9	9	(6	3)	247	80	59	38	0	70	1	22	4	5	6	.45	8	.274	.313	.382
3 ML YEARS		262	1005	275	40	19	14	(9	5)	395	130	93	59	4	121	2	28	8	11	11	.50	13	.274	.313	.393

Odalis Perez

Pitches: Left **Bats:** Left **Pos:** RP-10   **Ht:** 6'0" **Wt:** 150 **Born:** 6/7/78 **Age:** 21

Year Team	Lg	G	GS	CG	GF	IP	BFP	H	R	ER	HR	SH	SF	HB	TBB	IBB	SO	WP	Bk	W	L	Pct.	ShO	Sv-Op	Hld	ERA
1995 Braves	R	12	12	1	0	65	264	48	22	16	0	3	0	3	18	0	62	7	3	3	5	.375	1	0- --	--	2.22
1996 Eugene	A-	10	6	0	0	23.2	110	26	16	10	2	2	0	0	11	0	38	3	0	2	1	.667	0	0- --	--	3.80
1997 Macon	A	36	0	0	12	87.1	358	67	31	16	4	4	1	5	27	1	100	3	0	4	5	.444	0	5- --	--	1.65
1998 Greenville	AA	23	21	0	0	132	558	127	67	59	15	3	3	2	53	2	143	4	1	6	5	.545	0	0- --	--	4.02
Richmond	AAA	13	0	0	10	24.1	100	26	10	8	4	1	0	0	7	1	22	2	0	1	2	.333	0	3- --	--	2.96
1998 Atlanta	NL	10	0	0	0	10.2	45	10	5	5	1	0	0	0	4	0	5	0	0	0	1	.000	0	0-1	5	4.22

Robert Perez

Bats: Right **Throws:** Right **Pos:** LF-31; PH/PR-31; RF-15   **Ht:** 6'3" **Wt:** 195 **Born:** 6/4/69 **Age:** 30

Year Team	Lg	G	AB	H	2B	3B	HR	(Hm	Rd)	TB	R	RBI	TBB	IBB	SO	HBP	SH	SF	SB	CS	SB%	GDP	Avg	OBP	SLG
1994 Toronto	AL	4	8	1	0	0	0	(0	0)	1	0	0	0	0	1	0	0	0	0	0	.00	1	.125	.125	.125
1995 Toronto	AL	17	48	9	2	0	1	(1	0)	14	2	3	0	0	5	0	0	0	0	0	.00	1	.188	.188	.292
1996 Toronto	AL	86	202	66	10	0	2	(0	2)	82	30	21	8	0	17	1	4	1	3	0	1.00	6	.327	.354	.406
1997 Toronto	AL	37	78	15	4	1	2	(0	2)	27	4	6	0	0	16	0	0	0	0	0	.00	2	.192	.192	.346
1998 Sea-Mon		69	141	31	2	0	3	(3	0)	42	12	14	2	0	28	1	0	1	0	0	.00	5	.220	.234	.298
1998 Seattle	AL	17	35	6	1	0	2	(2	0)	13	3	6	0	0	5	0	0	0	0	0	.00	1	.171	.171	.371
Montreal	NL	52	106	25	1	0	1	(1	0)	29	9	8	2	0	23	1	0	1	0	0	.00	4	.236	.255	.274
5 ML YEARS		213	477	122	18	1	8	(4	4)	166	48	44	10	0	67	2	4	2	3	0	1.00	15	.256	.273	.348

Tomas Perez

Bats: Right **Throws:** Right **Pos:** SS-4; 2B-1; PH/PR-1   **Ht:** 5'11" **Wt:** 177 **Born:** 12/29/73 **Age:** 25

Year Team	Lg	G	AB	H	2B	3B	HR	(Hm	Rd)	TB	R	RBI	TBB	IBB	SO	HBP	SH	SF	SB	CS	SB%	GDP	Avg	OBP	SLG
1998 Syracuse *	AAA	116	404	102	15	4	3	—	—	134	40	37	18	0	67	0	4	0	4	7	.36	10	.252	.284	.332
1995 Toronto	AL	41	98	24	3	1	1	(1	0)	32	12	8	7	0	18	0	1	0	0	1	.00	6	.245	.292	.327
1996 Toronto	AL	91	295	74	13	4	1	(1	0)	98	24	19	25	0	29	1	6	1	1	2	.33	10	.251	.311	.332
1997 Toronto	AL	40	123	24	3	2	0	(0	0)	31	9	9	11	0	28	1	3	0	1	1	.50	2	.195	.267	.252
1998 Toronto	AL	6	9	1	0	0	0	(0	0)	1	1	0	1	0	3	0	1	0	0	0	.00	1	.111	.200	.111
4 ML YEARS		178	525	123	19	7	2	(2	0)	162	46	36	44	0	78	2	10	2	2	4	.33	19	.234	.295	.309

Yorkis Perez

Pitches: Left Bats: Both Pos: RP-57

Ht: 6'0" Wt: 180 Born: 9/30/67 Age: 31

Year Team	Lg	G	GS	CG	GF	IP	BFP	H	R	ER	HR	SH	SF	HB	TBB	IBB	SO	WP	Bk	W	L	Pct.	ShO	Sv-Op	Hld	ERA
1998 Reading *	AA	1	1	0	0	1	3	0	0	0	0	0	0	0	0	0	1	0	0	0	0	.000	0	0- -	—	0.00
Scranton-WB *	AAA	4	1	0	1	4.1	17	2	1	0	0	0	0	1	1	0	3	0	0	0	0	.000	0	0- -	—	0.00
1991 Chicago	NL	3	0	0	0	4.1	16	2	1	1	0	0	2	0	2	0	3	2	0	1	0	1.000	0	0-1	0	2.08
1994 Florida	NL	44	0	0	11	40.2	167	33	18	16	4	2	0	1	14	3	41	4	1	3	0	1.000	0	0-2	15	3.54
1995 Florida	NL	69	0	0	11	46.2	205	35	29	27	6	2	1	2	28	4	47	2	0	2	6	.250	0	1-4	16	5.21
1996 Florida	NL	64	0	0	15	47.2	222	51	28	28	2	2	2	1	31	4	47	2	0	3	4	.429	0	0-2	10	5.29
1997 New York	NL	9	0	0	1	8.2	45	15	8	8	2	0	1	0	4	0	7	1	0	0	1	.000	0	0-1	1	8.31
1998 Philadelphia	NL	57	0	0	7	52	221	40	23	22	3	2	3	0	25	0	42	7	0	0	2	.000	0	0-0	13	3.81
6 ML YEARS		246	0	0	45	200	876	176	107	102	17	8	9	4	104	11	187	18	1	9	13	.409	0	1-10	55	4.59

Matt Perisho

Pitches: Left Bats: Left Pos: SP-2

Ht: 6'0" Wt: 190 Born: 6/8/75 Age: 24

Year Team	Lg	G	GS	CG	GF	IP	BFP	H	R	ER	HR	SH	SF	HB	TBB	IBB	SO	WP	Bk	W	L	Pct.	ShO	Sv-Op	Hld	ERA
1993 Angels	R	11	11	1	0	64	266	58	32	26	1	1	3	2	23	0	65	2	2	7	3	.700	1	0- -	—	3.66
1994 Cedar Rapds	A	27	27	0	0	147.2	689	165	90	71	11	7	7	4	88	0	107	8	3	12	9	.571	0	0- -	—	4.33
1995 Lk Elsinore	A+	24	22	0	0	115.1	541	137	91	81	10	0	8	6	60	0	68	7	0	8	9	.471	0	0- -	—	6.32
1996 Lk Elsinore	A+	21	18	1	1	128.2	565	131	72	60	9	8	7	7	58	0	97	5	4	7	5	.583	1	0- -	—	4.20
Midland	AA	8	8	0	0	53.1	222	48	22	19	4	4	1	2	20	0	50	1	0	3	2	.600	0	0- -	—	3.21
1997 Midland	AA	10	10	3	0	73	299	60	26	24	5	0	1	0	26	1	62	1	2	5	2	.714	1	0- -	—	2.96
Vancouver	AAA	9	9	1	0	52.1	254	68	42	31	3	3	2	3	29	1	47	5	3	4	4	.500	0	0- -	—	5.33
1998 Tulsa	AA	1	1	0	0	3	22	3	2	2	0	0	0	3	3	0	1	0	0	0	0	.000	0	0- -	—	6.00
Oklahoma	AAA	15	15	1	0	90.1	394	91	41	39	6	2	3	6	42	0	60	6	1	8	5	.615	0	0- -	—	3.89
1997 Anaheim	AL	11	8	0	2	45	217	59	34	30	6	2	2	3	28	0	35	5	2	0	2	.000	0	0-0	0	6.00
1998 Texas	AL	2	2	0	0	5	40	15	17	15	2	0	0	2	8	0	2	0	0	0	2	.000	0	0-0	0	27.00
2 ML YEARS		13	10	0	2	50	257	74	51	45	8	2	2	5	36	0	37	5	2	0	4	.000	0	0-0	0	8.10

Robert Person

Pitches: Right Bats: Right Pos: RP-27

Ht: 6'0" Wt: 190 Born: 10/6/69 Age: 29

Year Team	Lg	G	GS	CG	GF	IP	BFP	H	R	ER	HR	SH	SF	HB	TBB	IBB	SO	WP	Bk	W	L	Pct.	ShO	Sv-Op	Hld	ERA
1998 Syracuse *	AAA	20	6	1	12	59	238	38	17	15	9	1	1	1	29	2	55	3	0	3	3	.500	0	6- -	—	2.29
1995 New York	NL	3	1	0	0	12	44	5	1	1	0	0	0	2	0	10	0	0	1	0	1.000	0	0-0	0	0.75
1996 New York	NL	27	13	0	1	89.2	390	86	50	45	16	1	4	2	35	3	76	3	0	4	5	.444	0	0-0	1	4.52
1997 Toronto	AL	23	22	0	0	128.1	566	125	86	80	19	4	6	5	60	2	99	7	0	5	10	.333	0	0-0	0	5.61
1998 Toronto	AL	27	0	0	14	38.1	184	45	31	30	9	2	5	2	22	1	31	0	0	3	1	.750	0	6-8	0	7.04
4 ML YEARS		80	36	0	15	268.1	1184	261	168	156	45	7	15	9	119	6	216	10	0	13	16	.448	0	6-8	1	5.23

Roberto Petagine

Bats: L Throws: L Pos: PH/PR-18; 1B-15; RF-15; LF-1

Ht: 6'1" Wt: 170 Born: 6/2/71 Age: 28

Year Team	Lg	G	AB	H	2B	3B	HR	(Hm	Rd)	TB	R	RBI	TBB	IBB	SO	HBP	SH	SF	SB	CS	SB%	GDP	Avg	OBP	SLG
1998 Indianapols *	AAA	102	363	120	30	1	24	—	—	224	79	109	70	6	71	3	0	7	3	1	.75	14	.331	.436	.617
1994 Houston	NL	8	7	0	0	0	0	(0	0)	0	0	0	1	0	3	0	0	0	0	0	.00	0	.000	.125	.000
1995 San Diego	NL	89	124	29	8	0	3	(2	1)	46	15	17	26	2	41	0	2	0	0	0	.00	4	.234	.367	.371
1996 New York	NL	50	99	23	3	0	4	(2	2)	38	10	17	9	1	27	3	1	1	0	0	.00	2	.232	.313	.384
1997 New York	NL	12	15	1	0	0	0	(0	0)	1	2	2	3	0	6	0	0	0	0	0	.00	0	.067	.222	.067
1998 Cincinnati	NL	34	62	16	2	1	3	(1	2)	29	14	7	16	0	11	0	0	2	1	0	1.00	2	.258	.405	.468
5 ML YEARS		193	307	69	13	1	10	(5	5)	114	41	43	55	3	88	3	3	3	1	2	.33	8	.225	.346	.371

Chris Peters

Pitches: Left Bats: Left Pos: SP-21; RP-18

Ht: 6'1" Wt: 175 Born: 1/28/72 Age: 27

Year Team	Lg	G	GS	CG	GF	IP	BFP	H	R	ER	HR	SH	SF	HB	TBB	IBB	SO	WP	Bk	W	L	Pct.	ShO	Sv-Op	Hld	ERA
1996 Pittsburgh	NL	16	10	0	0	64	283	72	43	40	9	3	3	1	25	0	28	4	0	2	4	.333	0	0-0	2	5.63
1997 Pittsburgh	NL	31	1	0	5	37.1	167	38	23	19	6	5	1	3	21	4	17	4	0	2	2	.500	0	0-1	2	4.58
1998 Pittsburgh	NL	39	21	1	7	148	630	142	63	57	13	4	5	3	55	4	103	4	1	8	10	.444	0	1-1	2	3.47
3 ML YEARS		86	32	1	12	249.1	1080	252	129	116	28	12	9	7	101	8	148	12	1	12	16	.429	0	1-2	6	4.19

Mark Petkovsek

Pitches: Right Bats: Right Pos: RP-38; SP-10

Ht: 6'0" Wt: 185 Born: 11/18/65 Age: 33

Year Team	Lg	G	GS	CG	GF	IP	BFP	H	R	ER	HR	SH	SF	HB	TBB	IBB	SO	WP	Bk	W	L	Pct.	ShO	Sv-Op	Hld	ERA
1991 Texas	AL	4	1	0	1	9.1	53	21	16	15	4	0	1	0	4	0	6	2	0	0	1	.000	0	0-0	0	14.46
1993 Pittsburgh	NL	26	0	0	8	32.1	145	43	25	25	7	4	1	0	9	2	14	4	0	3	0	1.000	0	0-0	0	6.96
1995 St. Louis	NL	26	21	1	0	137.1	569	136	71	61	14	4	9	4	35	3	71	1	1	6	6	.500	1	0-0	0	4.00
1996 St. Louis	NL	48	6	0	7	88.2	377	83	37	35	9	5	1	5	35	2	45	2	1	11	2	.846	0	0-3	10	3.55
1997 St. Louis	NL	55	2	0	19	96	414	109	61	54	14	2	2	6	31	4	51	2	0	4	7	.364	0	2-2	5	5.06

		HOW MUCH HE PITCHED				WHAT HE GAVE UP											THE RESULTS					
Year Team	Lg	G GS CG GF	IP	BFP	H	R	ER	HR SH SF HB	TBB IBB	SO WP Bk	W	L	Pct.	ShO	Sv-Op	Hld	ERA
1998 St. Louis	NL	48 10 0 7	105.2	476	131	63	56	9 9 3 8	36 3	55 1 1	7	4	.636	0	0-5	6	4.77
6 ML YEARS		207 40 1 43	469.1	2034	523	273	246	54 24 12 25	150 14	242 12 3	31	20	.608	1	2-10	21	4.72

Andy Pettitte

Pitches: Left **Bats:** Left **Pos:** SP-32; RP-1 **Ht:** 6'5" **Wt:** 235 **Born:** 6/15/72 **Age:** 27

		HOW MUCH HE PITCHED				WHAT HE GAVE UP											THE RESULTS					
Year Team	Lg	G GS CG GF	IP	BFP	H	R	ER	HR SH SF HB	TBB IBB	SO WP Bk	W	L	Pct.	ShO	Sv-Op	Hld	ERA
1995 New York	AL	31 26 3 1	175	745	183	86	81	15 4 5 1	63 3	114 8 1	12	9	.571	0	0-0	0	4.17
1996 New York	AL	35 34 2 1	221	929	229	105	95	23 7 3 3	72 2	162 6 1	21	8	.724	0	0-0	0	3.87
1997 New York	AL	35 35 4 0	240.1	986	233	86	77	7 6 2 3	65 0	166 7 0	18	7	.720	1	0-0	0	2.88
1998 New York	AL	33 32 5 0	216.1	932	226	110	102	20 6 7 6	87 1	146 5 0	16	11	.593	0	0-0	0	4.24
4 ML YEARS		134 127 14 2	852.2	3592	871	387	355	65 23 17 13	287 6	588 26 2	67	35	.657	1	0-0	0	3.75

J.R. Phillips

Bats: Left **Throws:** Left **Pos:** PH/PR-21; 1B-12; LF-6 **Ht:** 6'1" **Wt:** 185 **Born:** 4/29/70 **Age:** 29

		BATTING															BASERUNNING				PERCENTAGES		
Year Team	Lg	G	AB	H	2B	3B	HR	(Hm	Rd)	TB	R	RBI	TBB	IBB	SO	HBP SH SF	SB	CS	SB%	GDP	Avg	OBP	SLG
1998 New Orleans *	AAA	56	225	68	18	0	21	—	—	149	51	60	21	2	65	1 0 2	1	1	.50	4	.302	.361	.662
1993 San Francisco	NL	11	16	5	1	1	1	(0	1)	11	1	4	0	0	5	0 0 0	0	0	.00	0	.313	.313	.688
1994 San Francisco	NL	15	38	5	0	0	1	(0	1)	8	1	3	1	0	13	0 0 1	1	0	1.00	1	.132	.150	.211
1995 San Francisco	NL	92	231	45	9	0	9	(5	4)	81	27	28	19	2	69	0 2 0	1	1	.50	3	.195	.256	.351
1996 SF-Phi	NL	50	104	17	5	0	7	(4	3)	43	12	15	11	1	51	1 0 0	0	0	.00	1	.163	.250	.413
1997 Houston	NL	13	15	2	0	0	1	(1	0)	5	2	4	0	0	7	0 0 1	0	0	.00	0	.133	.125	.333
1998 Houston	NL	36	58	11	0	0	2	(0	2)	17	4	9	7	1	22	0 0 0	0	0	.00	1	.190	.277	.293
1996 San Francisco	NL	15	25	5	0	0	2	(0	2)	11	3	5	1	0	13	0 0 0	0	0	.00	0	.200	.231	.440
Philadelphia	NL	35	79	12	5	0	5	(4	1)	32	9	10	10	1	38	1 0 0	0	0	.00	1	.152	.256	.405
6 ML YEARS		217	462	85	15	1	21	(10	11)	165	47	63	38	4	167	1 2 2	2	1	.67	6	.184	.247	.357

Tony Phillips

Bats: Both **Throws:** Right **Pos:** LF-54; RF-19; PH/PR-3 **Ht:** 5'10" **Wt:** 175 **Born:** 4/25/59 **Age:** 40

		BATTING															BASERUNNING				PERCENTAGES		
Year Team	Lg	G	AB	H	2B	3B	HR	(Hm	Rd)	TB	R	RBI	TBB	IBB	SO	HBP SH SF	SB	CS	SB%	GDP	Avg	OBP	SLG
1998 Syracuse *	AAA	10	32	8	1	0	1	—	—	12	7	4	15	0	10	0 0 0	2	1	.67	0	.250	.489	.375
1982 Oakland	AL	40	81	17	2	2	0	(0	0)	23	11	8	12	0	26	2 5 0	2	3	.40	0	.210	.326	.284
1983 Oakland	AL	148	412	102	12	3	4	(1	3)	132	54	35	48	1	70	2 11 3	16	5	.76	5	.248	.327	.320
1984 Oakland	AL	154	451	120	24	3	4	(2	2)	162	62	37	42	1	86	0 7 5	10	6	.63	5	.266	.325	.359
1985 Oakland	AL	42	161	45	12	2	4	(2	2)	73	23	17	13	0	34	0 1 1	3	2	.60	1	.280	.331	.453
1986 Oakland	AL	118	441	113	14	5	5	(3	2)	152	76	52	76	0	82	3 9 3	15	10	.60	2	.256	.367	.345
1987 Oakland	AL	111	379	91	20	0	10	(5	5)	141	48	46	57	1	76	0 2 3	7	6	.54	9	.240	.337	.372
1988 Oakland	AL	79	212	43	8	4	2	(2	0)	65	32	17	36	0	50	1 1 1	0	2	.00	6	.203	.320	.307
1989 Oakland	AL	143	451	118	15	6	4	(2	2)	157	48	47	58	2	66	3 5 7	3	8	.27	17	.262	.345	.348
1990 Detroit	AL	152	573	144	23	5	8	(4	4)	201	97	55	99	0	85	4 9 2	19	9	.68	10	.251	.364	.351
1991 Detroit	AL	146	564	160	28	4	17	(9	8)	247	87	72	79	5	95	3 3 6	10	5	.67	8	.284	.371	.438
1992 Detroit	AL	159	606	167	32	3	10	(3	7)	235	114	64	114	2	93	1 5 7	12	10	.55	13	.276	.387	.388
1993 Detroit	AL	151	566	177	27	0	7	(3	4)	225	113	57	132	5	102	4 5 4	16	11	.59	11	.313	.443	.398
1994 Detroit	AL	114	438	123	19	3	19	(12	7)	205	91	61	95	3	105	2 0 3	13	5	.72	8	.281	.409	.468
1995 California	AL	139	525	137	21	1	27	(13	14)	241	119	61	113	6	135	3 1 1	13	10	.57	5	.261	.394	.459
1996 Chicago	AL	153	581	161	29	3	12	(6	6)	232	119	63	125	9	132	4 1 8	13	8	.62	6	.277	.404	.399
1997 ChA-Ana	AL	141	534	147	34	2	8	(5	3)	209	96	57	102	5	118	3 5 4	13	10	.57	11	.275	.392	.391
1998 Tor-NYN	AL	65	236	59	16	0	4	(3	1)	87	34	21	47	1	50	2 1 3	1	1	.50	3	.250	.375	.369
1997 Chicago	AL	36	129	40	6	0	2	(1	1)	52	23	9	29	0	29	1 2 0	4	1	.80	3	.310	.440	.403
Anaheim	AL	105	405	107	28	2	6	(4	2)	157	73	48	73	5	89	2 3 4	9	9	.50	8	.264	.376	.388
1998 Toronto	AL	13	48	17	5	0	1	(0	1)	25	9	7	9	1	6	2 0 1	0	0	.00	2	.354	.467	.521
New York	NL	52	188	42	11	0	3	(3	0)	62	25	14	38	0	44	0 1 2	1	1	.50	1	.223	.351	.330
17 ML YEARS		2055	7211	1924	336	46	145	(75	70)	2787	1224	770	1248	41	1405	37 69 61	166	111	.60	120	.267	.375	.386

Mike Piazza

Bats: Right **Throws:** Right **Pos:** C-140; PH/PR-7; DH-4 **Ht:** 6'3" **Wt:** 200 **Born:** 9/4/68 **Age:** 30

		BATTING															BASERUNNING				PERCENTAGES		
Year Team	Lg	G	AB	H	2B	3B	HR	(Hm	Rd)	TB	R	RBI	TBB	IBB	SO	HBP SH SF	SB	CS	SB%	GDP	Avg	OBP	SLG
1992 Los Angeles	NL	21	69	16	3	0	1	(1	0)	22	5	7	4	0	12	1 0 0	0	0	.00	1	.232	.284	.319
1993 Los Angeles	NL	149	547	174	24	2	35	(21	14)	307	81	112	46	6	86	3 0 6	3	4	.43	10	.318	.370	.561
1994 Los Angeles	NL	107	405	129	18	0	24	(13	11)	219	64	92	33	10	65	1 0 2	1	3	.25	11	.319	.370	.541
1995 Los Angeles	NL	112	434	150	17	0	32	(9	23)	263	82	93	39	10	80	1 0 1	1	0	1.00	10	.346	.400	.606
1996 Los Angeles	NL	148	547	184	16	0	36	(14	22)	308	87	105	81	21	93	1 0 2	0	3	.00	21	.336	.422	.563
1997 Los Angeles	NL	152	556	201	32	1	40	(22	18)	355	104	124	69	11	77	3 0 5	5	1	.83	19	.362	.431	.638
1998 LA-Fla-NYN	NL	151	561	184	38	1	32	(15	17)	320	88	111	58	14	80	2 0 5	1	0	1.00	15	.328	.390	.570
1998 Los Angeles	NL	37	149	42	5	0	9	(5	4)	74	20	30	11	4	27	0 0 0	0	0	.00	3	.282	.329	.497
Florida	NL	5	18	5	0	1	0	(0	0)	7	1	5	0	0	0	0 0 0	0	0	.00	0	.278	.263	.389
New York	NL	109	394	137	33	0	23	(10	13)	239	67	76	47	10	53	2 0 3	1	0	1.00	12	.348	.417	.607
7 ML YEARS		840	3119	1038	148	4	200	(95	105)	1794	511	644	330	72	493	12 0 21	11	11	.50	87	.333	.396	.575

Hipolito Pichardo

Year Team	Lg	G	GS	CG	GF	IP	BFP	H	R	ER	HR	SH	SF	HB	TBB	IBB	SO	WP	Bk	W	L	Pct.	ShO	Sv-Op	Hld	ERA
1998 Lansing *	A	1	0	0	0	1	3	0	0	0	0	0	0	0	0	0	0	0	0	0	0	.000	0	0- --	—	0.00
1992 Kansas City	AL	31	24	1	0	143.2	615	148	71	63	9	4	5	3	49	1	59	3	1	9	6	.600	0	0-0	0	3.95
1993 Kansas City	AL	30	25	2	2	165	720	183	85	74	10	3	8	6	53	2	70	5	3	7	8	.467	0	0-0	1	4.04
1994 Kansas City	AL	45	0	0	19	67.2	303	82	42	37	4	4	2	7	24	5	36	3	0	5	3	.625	0	3-5	6	4.92
1995 Kansas City	AL	44	0	0	16	64	287	66	34	31	4	3	1	4	30	7	43	4	1	8	4	.667	0	1-2	7	4.36
1996 Kansas City	AL	57	0	0	28	68	294	74	41	41	5	3	2	2	26	5	43	4	0	3	5	.375	0	3-5	15	5.43
1997 Kansas City	AL	47	0	0	26	49	215	51	24	23	7	2	0	1	24	8	34	2	1	3	5	.375	0	11-13	4	4.22
1998 Kansas City	AL	27	18	0	2	112.1	503	126	73	64	11	3	3	4	43	2	55	2	0	7	8	.467	0	1-1	2	5.13
7 ML YEARS		281	67	3	93	669.2	2937	730	370	333	50	22	21	27	249	30	340	23	6	42	39	.519	1	19-26	35	4.48

Calvin Pickering

Bats: Left Throws: Left Pos: 1B-5; DH-3; PH/PR-1   Ht: 6'5" Wt: 283 Born: 9/29/76 Age: 22

		BATTING															BASERUNNING				PERCENTAGES		
Year Team	Lg	G	AB	H	2B	3B	HR	(Hm	Rd)	TB	R	RBI	TBB	IBB	SO	HBP	SH	SF	SB	CS	SB%	GDP	Avg	OBP	SLG
1995 Orioles	R	15	60	30	10	0	1	—	—	43	8	22	2	0	6	0	0	1	0	0	.00	3	.500	.508	.717
1996 Bluefield	R+	60	200	65	14	1	18	—	—	135	45	66	28	4	64	2	0	1	8	2	.80	4	.325	.411	.675
1997 Delmarva	A	122	444	138	31	1	25	—	—	246	88	79	53	2	139	9	0	1	6	3	.67	14	.311	.394	.554
1998 Bowie	AA	139	488	151	28	2	31	—	—	276	93	114	98	16	119	11	0	2	4	6	.40	20	.309	.434	.566
1998 Baltimore	AL	9	21	5	0	0	2	(1	1)	11	4	3	3	0	4	0	0	0	1	0	1.00	2	.238	.333	.524

Ricky Pickett

Pitches: Left Bats: Left Pos: RP-2   Ht: 6'1" Wt: 200 Born: 1/19/70 Age: 29

Year Team	Lg	G	GS	CG	GF	IP	BFP	H	R	ER	HR	SH	SF	HB	TBB	IBB	SO	WP	Bk	W	L	Pct.	ShO	Sv-Op	Hld	ERA
1992 Billings	R+	20	4	0	4	53.2	225	35	21	14	2	1	2	5	28	0	41	3	1	1	2	.333	0	2- --	—	2.35
1993 Chston-WV	A	44	1	0	5	43.2	227	42	40	33	1	1	1	5	48	0	65	6	3	1	2	.333	0	0- --	—	6.80
1994 Chston-WV	A	28	0	0	19	27.1	121	14	8	6	1	0	1	2	20	0	48	4	0	1	1	.500	0	13- --	—	1.98
Winston-Sal	A+	21	0	0	17	24	112	16	11	10	0	1	1	2	23	1	33	2	0	2	1	.667	0	4- --	—	3.75
1995 Chattanooga	AA	40	0	0	19	46.2	203	22	20	17	3	2	0	0	44	3	69	1	0	5	4	.444	0	0- --	—	3.28
Shreveport	AA	14	0	0	9	21	82	9	5	4	1	0	1	0	9	0	23	2	1	0	4	.000	0	9- --	—	1.71
1996 Phoenix	AAA	8	0	0	2	8.1	43	12	8	8	1	0	0	1	5	0	7	1	0	0	3	.000	0	3- --	—	8.64
Shreveport	AA	29	0	0	12	48.2	214	35	21	15	4	3	2	3	35	3	51	2	0	4	1	.800	0	2- --	—	2.77
1997 Phoenix	AAA	61	0	0	29	67.2	302	52	27	24	2	4	1	4	49	3	85	4	0	3	3	.500	0	12- --	—	3.19
1998 Fresno	AAA	5	0	0	3	7	42	6	4	3	1	3	0	0	14	1	11	0	0	1	1	.500	0	0- --	—	3.86
Tucson	AAA	5	0	0	1	4.2	29	7	8	8	1	0	0	0	9	0	5	1	0	0	0	.000	0	0- --	—	15.43
Oklahoma	AAA	24	10	2	5	80	349	69	39	33	7	2	1	0	52	0	78	3	0	6	6	.500	2	1- --	—	3.71
1998 Arizona	NL	2	0	0	0	0.2	9	3	6	6	0	0	0	0	4	0	0	0	0	0	0	.000	0	0-0	0	81.00

A.J. Pierzynski

Bats: Left Throws: Right Pos: C-6; PH/PR-1   Ht: 6'3" Wt: 218 Born: 12/30/76 Age: 22

		BATTING															BASERUNNING				PERCENTAGES		
Year Team	Lg	G	AB	H	2B	3B	HR	(Hm	Rd)	TB	R	RBI	TBB	IBB	SO	HBP	SH	SF	SB	CS	SB%	GDP	Avg	OBP	SLG
1994 Twins	R	43	152	44	8	1	1	—	—	57	21	19	12	0	19	0	0	2	0	2	.00	3	.289	.337	.375
1995 Fort Wayne	A	22	84	26	5	1	2	—	—	39	10	14	2	0	10	0	0	1	0	0	.00	1	.310	.322	.464
Elizabethtn	R+	56	205	68	13	1	7	—	—	104	29	45	14	1	23	0	0	1	0	2	.00	4	.332	.373	.507
1996 Fort Wayne	A+	114	431	118	30	3	7	—	—	175	48	70	22	1	53	2	0	6	0	4	.00	10	.274	.308	.406
1997 Fort Myers	A+	118	412	115	23	1	9	—	—	167	49	64	16	1	59	6	1	4	2	1	.67	9	.279	.313	.405
1998 New Britain	AA	59	212	63	11	0	3	—	—	83	30	17	10	4	25	2	2	1	0	2	.00	4	.297	.333	.392
Salt Lake	AAA	59	208	53	7	2	7	—	—	85	29	30	9	2	24	0	2	1	3	1	.75	4	.255	.284	.409
1998 Minnesota	AL	7	10	3	0	0	0	(0	0)	3	1	1	1	0	2	1	0	1	0	0	.00	0	.300	.385	.300

Marc Pisciotta

Pitches: Right Bats: Right Pos: RP-43   Ht: 6'5" Wt: 225 Born: 8/7/70 Age: 28

Year Team	Lg	G	GS	CG	GF	IP	BFP	H	R	ER	HR	SH	SF	HB	TBB	IBB	SO	WP	Bk	W	L	Pct.	ShO	Sv-Op	Hld	ERA
1991 Welland	A-	24	0	0	21	34	143	16	4	1	0	2	1	3	20	1	47	7	1	1	1	.500	0	8- --	—	0.26
1992 Augusta	A	20	12	1	5	79.1	372	91	51	40	4	5	1	10	43	2	54	12	2	4	5	.444	0	1- --	—	4.54
1993 Augusta	A	34	0	0	28	43.2	188	31	18	13	0	5	0	5	17	1	49	5	0	5	2	.714	0	12- --	—	2.68
Salem	A+	20	0	0	18	18.1	88	23	13	6	0	1	1	0	13	0	13	2	0	0	0	.000	0	12- --	—	2.95
1994 Carolina	AA	26	0	0	17	25.2	127	32	21	16	2	6	2	3	15	2	21	1	1	3	4	.429	0	5- --	—	5.61
Salem	A+	31	0	0	30	29.1	134	24	14	5	1	2	1	3	13	1	23	2	0	1	4	.200	0	19- --	—	1.53
1995 Carolina	AA	56	0	0	27	69.1	313	60	37	32	2	7	3	6	45	8	57	4	0	6	4	.600	0	9- --	—	4.15
1996 Calgary	AAA	57	0	0	27	65.2	308	71	38	30	3	1	2	2	46	8	46	7	0	2	7	.222	0	1- --	—	4.11
1997 Iowa	AAA	42	0	0	38	45.2	194	29	12	12	2	4	0	2	23	3	48	6	0	6	2	.750	0	22- --	—	2.36
1998 Iowa	AAA	28	0	0	24	30.2	140	34	24	22	4	3	1	2	16	1	29	4	0	3	5	.375	0	8- --	—	6.46
1997 Chicago	NL	24	0	0	7	28.1	119	20	10	10	1	1	1	1	16	0	21	2	0	3	1	.750	0	0-1	10	3.18
1998 Chicago	NL	43	0	0	12	44	206	44	21	20	4	1	1	2	32	3	31	6	0	1	2	.333	0	0-0	7	4.09
2 ML YEARS		67	0	0	19	72.1	325	64	31	30	5	2	2	3	48	3	52	8	0	4	3	.571	0	0-1	17	3.73

Jim Pittsley

Pitches: Right **Bats:** Right **Pos:** RP-37; SP-2 **Ht:** 6'7" **Wt:** 220 **Born:** 4/3/74 **Age:** 25

		HOW MUCH HE PITCHED					WHAT HE GAVE UP										THE RESULTS					
Year Team	Lg	G	GS	CG	GF	IP	BFP	H	R	ER	HR	SH	SF	HB	TBB	IBB	SO	WP	Bk	W	L	Pct.	ShO	Sv-Op	Hld	ERA
1995 Kansas City	AL	1	1	0	0	3.1	17	7	5	5	3	0	0	0	1	0	0	0	0	0	0	.000	0	0-0		13.50
1997 Kansas City	AL	21	21	0	0	112	501	120	72	68	15	2	6	6	54	1	52	3	0	5	8	.385	0	0-0		5.46
1998 Kansas City	AL	39	2	0	11	68.1	320	88	56	50	13	3	5	2	37	1	44	6	0	1	1	.500	0	0-0	1	6.59
3 ML YEARS		61	24	0	11	183.2	838	215	133	123	31	5	11	8	92	2	96	9	0	6	9	.400	0	0-0	1	6.03

Dan Plesac

Pitches: Left **Bats:** Left **Pos:** RP-78 **Ht:** 6'5" **Wt:** 217 **Born:** 2/4/62 **Age:** 37

		HOW MUCH HE PITCHED					WHAT HE GAVE UP										THE RESULTS					
Year Team	Lg	G	GS	CG	GF	IP	BFP	H	R	ER	HR	SH	SF	HB	TBB	IBB	SO	WP	Bk	W	L	Pct.	ShO	Sv-Op	Hld	ERA
1986 Milwaukee	AL	51	0	0	33	91	377	81	34	30	5	6	5	4	29	1	75	4	0	10	7	.588	0	14-20	5	2.97
1987 Milwaukee	AL	57	0	0	47	79.1	325	63	30	23	8	1	2	3	23	1	89	6	0	5	6	.455	0	23-36	0	2.61
1988 Milwaukee	AL	50	0	0	48	52.1	211	46	14	14	2	2	0	0	12	2	52	4	6	1	2	.333	0	30-35	0	2.41
1989 Milwaukee	AL	52	0	0	51	61.1	242	47	16	16	6	0	4	0	17	1	52	0	0	3	4	.429	0	33-40	0	2.35
1990 Milwaukee	AL	66	0	0	52	69	299	67	36	34	5	2	2	3	31	6	65	2	0	3	7	.300	0	24-34	2	4.43
1991 Milwaukee	AL	45	10	0	25	92.1	402	92	49	44	12	3	7	3	39	1	61	2	1	2	7	.222	0	8-12	1	4.29
1992 Milwaukee	AL	44	4	0	13	79	330	64	28	26	5	8	4	3	35	5	54	3	1	5	4	.556	0	1-3	1	2.96
1993 Chicago	NL	57	0	0	12	62.2	276	74	37	33	10	4	3	0	21	6	47	5	2	2	1	.667	0	0-2	12	4.74
1994 Chicago	NL	54	0	0	14	54.2	235	61	30	28	9	1	1	1	13	0	53	0	0	2	3	.400	0	1-3	14	4.61
1995 Pittsburgh	NL	58	0	0	16	60.1	259	53	25	24	3	4	3	1	27	7	57	1	0	4	4	.500	0	3-5	11	3.58
1996 Pittsburgh	NL	73	0	0	30	70.1	300	67	35	32	4	2	3	0	24	6	76	4	0	6	5	.545	0	11-17	11	4.09
1997 Toronto	AL	73	0	0	18	50.1	215	47	22	20	8	2	1	0	19	4	61	2	0	2	4	.333	0	1-5	27	3.58
1998 Toronto	AL	78	0	0	16	50	203	41	23	21	4	0	3	0	16	1	55	0	0	4	3	.571	0	4-5	27	3.78
13 ML YEARS		758	14	0	375	872.2	3674	803	380	345	81	35	38	15	306	41	797	33	10	49	57	.462	0	153-217	111	3.56

Eric Plunk

Pitches: Right **Bats:** Right **Pos:** RP-63 **Ht:** 6'6" **Wt:** 220 **Born:** 9/3/63 **Age:** 35

		HOW MUCH HE PITCHED					WHAT HE GAVE UP										THE RESULTS					
Year Team	Lg	G	GS	CG	GF	IP	BFP	H	R	ER	HR	SH	SF	HB	TBB	IBB	SO	WP	Bk	W	L	Pct.	ShO	Sv-Op	Hld	ERA
1986 Oakland	AL	26	15	0	2	120.1	537	91	75	71	14	2	3	5	102	2	98	9	6	4	7	.364	0	0--		5.31
1987 Oakland	AL	32	11	0	11	95	432	91	53	50	8	3	5	2	62	3	90	5	2	4	6	.400	0	2-5	1	4.74
1988 Oakland	AL	49	0	0	22	78	331	62	27	26	6	3	2	1	39	4	79	4	7	7	2	.778	0	5-9	5	3.00
1989 Oak-NYA	AL	50	7	0	17	104.1	445	82	43	38	10	3	4	1	64	2	85	10	3	8	6	.571	0	1-3	7	3.28
1990 New York	AL	47	0	0	16	72.2	310	58	27	22	6	7	0	2	43	4	67	4	2	6	3	.667	0	0-1	3	2.72
1991 New York	AL	43	8	0	6	111.2	521	128	69	59	18	6	4	1	62	1	103	6	2	2	5	.286	0	0-0	2	4.76
1992 Cleveland	AL	58	0	0	20	71.2	309	61	31	29	5	3	2	0	38	2	50	5	0	9	6	.600	0	4-8	1	3.64
1993 Cleveland	AL	70	0	0	40	71	306	61	29	22	5	4	2	0	30	4	77	6	0	4	5	.444	0	15-18	16	2.79
1994 Cleveland	AL	41	0	0	18	71	306	61	25	20	3	2	1	2	37	5	73	7	0	7	2	.778	0	3-7	8	2.54
1995 Cleveland	AL	56	0	0	22	64	263	48	19	19	5	2	2	4	27	2	71	3	0	6	2	.750	0	2-5	10	2.67
1996 Cleveland	AL	56	0	0	12	77.2	318	56	21	21	6	1	4	3	34	2	85	4	1	3	2	.600	0	2-3	15	2.43
1997 Cleveland	AL	55	0	0	22	65.2	293	62	37	34	12	1	1	1	36	7	66	6	0	4	5	.444	0	0-2	10	4.66
1998 Cle-Mil		63	0	0	13	72.2	321	77	37	35	9	4	4	5	30	2	74	1	0	4	3	.571	0	1-6	12	4.33
1989 Oakland	AL	23	0	0	12	28.2	113	17	7	7	1	1	0	1	12	0	24	4	0	1	1	.500	0	1-3	5	2.20
New York	AL	27	7	0	5	75.2	332	65	36	31	9	2	4	0	52	2	61	6	3	7	5	.583	0	0-0	2	3.69
1998 Cleveland	AL	37	0	0	6	41	178	44	23	22	6	3	2	2	15	1	38	0	0	3	1	.750	0	0-3	7	4.83
Milwaukee	NL	26	0	0	7	31.2	143	33	14	13	3	1	2	3	15	1	36	1	0	1	2	.333	0	1-3	5	3.69
13 ML YEARS		646	41	0	221	1075.2	4692	938	493	446	107	41	35	27	604	40	1018	70	23	68	54	.557	0	35--		3.73

Placido Polanco

Bats: Right **Throws:** Right **Pos:** SS-28; 2B-14; PH/PR-6 **Ht:** 5'10" **Wt:** 168 **Born:** 10/10/75 **Age:** 23

		BATTING																BASERUNNING				PERCENTAGES		
Year Team	Lg	G	AB	H	2B	3B	HR	(Hm	Rd)	TB	R	RBI	TBB	IBB	SO	HBP	SH	SF	SB	CS	SB%	GDP	Avg	OBP	SLG
1994 Cardinals	R	32	127	27	4	0	1	—	—	34	17	10	7	0	15	1	0	0	2	1	.67	2	.213	.259	.268
1995 Peoria	A	103	361	96	7	4	2	—	—	117	43	41	18	0	30	2	11	2	7	6	.54	8	.266	.303	.324
1996 St. Pete	A+	137	540	157	29	5	0	—	—	196	65	51	24	1	34	5	6	7	4	4	.50	31	.291	.323	.363
1997 Arkansas	AA	129	508	148	16	3	2	—	—	176	71	51	29	1	51	3	6	3	19	5	.79	11	.291	.331	.346
1998 Memphis	AAA	70	246	69	19	1	1	—	—	93	36	21	16	1	15	3	4	1	6	3	.67	8	.280	.331	.378
1998 St. Louis	NL	45	114	29	3	2	1	(1	0)	39	10	11	5	0	9	1	2	0	2	0	1.00	1	.254	.292	.342

Kevin Polcovich

Bats: R **Throws:** R **Pos:** SS-54; 2B-15; PH/PR-14; 3B-8 **Ht:** 5'9" **Wt:** 182 **Born:** 6/28/70 **Age:** 29

		BATTING																BASERUNNING				PERCENTAGES		
Year Team	Lg	G	AB	H	2B	3B	HR	(Hm	Rd)	TB	R	RBI	TBB	IBB	SO	HBP	SH	SF	SB	CS	SB%	GDP	Avg	OBP	SLG
1992 Carolina	AA	13	35	6	0	0	0	—	—	6	1	1	4	0	4	2	0	0	1	1	.00	1	.171	.293	.171
Augusta	A	46	153	40	6	2	0	—	—	50	24	10	18	0	30	8	3	0	7	7	.50	1	.261	.369	.327
1993 Augusta	A	14	48	13	2	0	0	—	—	15	9	4	7	0	8	0	2	1	2	1	.67	1	.271	.357	.313
Carolina	AA	4	11	3	0	0	0	—	—	3	1	1	1	0	1	0	2	0	0	1	.00	1	.273	.333	.273
Salem	A+	94	282	72	10	3	1	—	—	91	44	25	49	0	42	12	6	3	13	6	.68	7	.255	.384	.323
1994 Carolina	AA	125	406	95	14	2	2	—	—	119	46	33	38	4	70	11	10	8	4	9	.69	6	.234	.311	.293
1995 Carolina	AA	64	221	70	8	0	3	—	—	87	27	18	14	1	29	5	3	1	10	5	.67	3	.317	.369	.394
Calgary	AAA	62	213	60	8	1	3	—	—	79	31	27	11	0	32	8	2	3	5	6	.45	7	.282	.336	.371

			BATTING																	BASERUNNING				PERCENTAGES		
Year Team	Lg	G	AB	H	2B	3B	HR	(Hm	Rd)	TB	R	RBI	TBB	IBB	SO	HBP	SH	SF		SB	CS	SB%	GDP	Avg	OBP	SLG
1996 Calgary	AAA	104	336	92	21	3	1	—	—	122	53	46	18	3	49	14	5	2		7	6	.54	9	.274	.335	.363
1997 Carolina	AA	17	50	16	5	0	3	—	—	30	13	7	10	0	4	2	2	0		4	2	.67	1	.320	.452	.600
Calgary	AAA	17	62	19	4	0	1	—	—	26	7	9	1	0	7	1	0	1		0	0	.00	1	.306	.323	.419
1997 Pittsburgh	NL	84	245	67	16	1	4	(0	4)	97	37	21	21	4	45	9	2	2		2	2	.50	11	.273	.350	.396
1998 Pittsburgh	NL	81	212	40	12	0	0	(0	0)	52	18	14	15	2	33	5	3	3		4	3	.57	7	.189	.255	.245
2 ML YEARS		165	457	107	28	1	4	(0	4)	149	55	35	36	6	78	14	5	5		6	5	.55	18	.234	.307	.326

Cliff Politte

Pitches: Right **Bats:** Right **Pos:** SP-8 **Ht:** 5'11" **Wt:** 185 **Born:** 2/27/74 **Age:** 25

		HOW MUCH HE PITCHED						WHAT HE GAVE UP												THE RESULTS						
Year Team	Lg	G	GS	CG	GF	IP	BFP	H	R	ER	HR	SH	SF	HB	TBB	IBB	SO	WP	Bk	W	L	Pct.	ShO	Sv-Op	Hld	ERA
1996 Peoria	A	25	25	0	0	149.2	603	108	50	43	8	3	2	7	47	0	151	5	1	14	6	.700	0	0--	—	2.59
1997 Pr William	A+	19	19	0	0	120.1	475	89	37	30	11	0	3	2	31	0	118	2	2	11	1	.917	0	0--	—	2.24
Arkansas	AA	6	6	0	0	37.2	152	35	15	9	3	6	1	0	9	1	26	0	0	4	1	.800	0	0--	—	2.15
1998 Memphis	AAA	10	10	0	0	50.2	244	71	46	43	10	3	2	0	24	0	42	3	0	1	4	.200	0	0--	—	7.64
Arkansas	AA	10	10	1	0	67	265	56	25	22	6	3	1	1	16	0	61	0	0	5	3	.625	1	0--	—	2.96
1998 St. Louis	NL	8	8	0	0	37	172	45	32	26	3	1	1	1	18	0	22	2	1	2	3	.400	0	0-0	0	6.32

Sidney Ponson

Pitches: Right **Bats:** Right **Pos:** SP-20; RP-11 **Ht:** 6'1" **Wt:** 200 **Born:** 11/2/76 **Age:** 22

		HOW MUCH HE PITCHED						WHAT HE GAVE UP												THE RESULTS						
Year Team	Lg	G	GS	CG	GF	IP	BFP	H	R	ER	HR	SH	SF	HB	TBB	IBB	SO	WP	Bk	W	L	Pct.	ShO	Sv-Op	Hld	ERA
1994 Orioles	R	12	11	1	0	73	300	68	30	24	5	1	3	2	17	0	53	2	4	4	3	.571	0	0--	—	2.96
1995 Bluefield	R+	13	13	0	0	77.2	324	79	44	36	7	1	2	1	16	0	56	4	3	6	3	.667	0	0--	—	4.17
1996 Frederick	A+	18	16	3	2	107	443	98	56	41	6	3	4	5	28	0	110	6	3	7	6	.538	0	0--	—	3.45
1997 Bowie	AA	13	13	1	0	74.2	328	77	51	45	11	4	3	3	32	2	56	1	1	2	7	.222	1	0--	—	5.42
Orioles	R	1	0	0	0	2	6	0	0	0	0	0	0	0	0	0	1	0	1	1	0	1.000	0	0--	—	0.00
1998 Rochester	AAA	1	1	0	0	5	20	4	0	0	0	0	1	0	1	0	3	0	0	1	0	1.000	0	0--	—	0.00
1998 Baltimore	AL	31	20	0	5	135	588	157	82	79	19	3	4	3	42	2	85	4	1	8	9	.471	0	1-2	0	5.27

Jim Poole

Pitches: Left **Bats:** Left **Pos:** RP-38 **Ht:** 6'2" **Wt:** 195 **Born:** 4/28/66 **Age:** 33

		HOW MUCH HE PITCHED						WHAT HE GAVE UP												THE RESULTS						
Year Team	Lg	G	GS	CG	GF	IP	BFP	H	R	ER	HR	SH	SF	HB	TBB	IBB	SO	WP	Bk	W	L	Pct.	ShO	Sv-Op	Hld	ERA
1998 Buffalo *	AAA	13	0	0	4	10.1	40	6	3	1	0	0	0	1	2	0	16	0	0	1	0	1.000	0	0--	—	0.87
1990 Los Angeles	NL	16	0	0	4	10.2	46	7	5	5	1	0	0	0	8	4	6	1	0	0	0	.000	0	0-0	2	4.22
1991 Tex-Bal	AL	29	0	0	5	42	166	29	14	11	3	3	3	0	12	2	38	2	0	3	2	.600	0	1-1	4	2.36
1992 Baltimore	AL	6	0	0	1	3.1	14	3	3	0	0	0	0	0	1	0	3	2	0	0	0	.000	0	0-1	0	0.00
1993 Baltimore	AL	55	0	0	11	50.1	197	30	18	12	2	3	2	0	21	5	29	0	0	2	1	.667	0	2-3	14	2.15
1994 Baltimore	AL	38	0	0	10	20.1	100	32	15	15	4	0	3	0	11	2	18	1	0	1	0	1.000	0	0-2	10	6.64
1995 Cleveland	AL	42	0	0	9	50.1	206	40	22	21	7	1	2	2	17	0	41	2	1	3	3	.500	0	0-0	6	3.75
1996 Cle-SF		67	0	0	13	50.1	218	44	22	16	5	3	1	1	27	7	38	3	0	6	1	.857	0	0-4	10	2.86
1997 San Francisco	NL	63	0	0	11	49.1	242	73	44	39	6	2	4	2	25	4	26	5	0	3	1	.750	0	0-9	9	7.11
1998 SF-Cle		38	0	0	9	39.1	174	47	24	23	5	4	1	1	12	6	27	2	0	1	3	.250	0	0-3	6	5.26
1991 Texas	AL	5	0	0	2	6	31	10	4	3	0	0	1	0	3	0	4	0	0	0	0	.000	0	1-1	2	4.50
Baltimore	AL	24	0	0	3	36	135	19	10	8	3	3	2	0	9	2	34	2	0	3	2	.600	0	0-0	4	2.00
1996 Cleveland	AL	32	0	0	8	26.2	121	29	15	9	3	0	1	0	14	4	19	2	0	4	0	1.000	0	0-1	5	3.04
San Francisco	NL	35	0	0	5	23.2	97	15	7	7	2	3	0	1	13	3	19	1	0	2	1	.667	0	0-3	5	2.66
1998 San Francisco	NL	26	0	0	8	32.1	140	38	20	19	5	4	1	0	9	5	16	2	0	1	3	.250	0	0-2	3	5.29
Cleveland	AL	12	0	0	1	7	34	9	4	4	0	0	0	1	3	1	11	0	0	0	0	.000	0	0-1	3	5.14
9 ML YEARS		354	0	0	73	316	1363	305	167	142	33	18	14	8	134	30	226	16	1	19	11	.633	0	3-14	61	4.04

Mark Portugal

Pitches: Right **Bats:** Right **Pos:** SP-26 **Ht:** 6'0" **Wt:** 190 **Born:** 10/30/62 **Age:** 36

		HOW MUCH HE PITCHED						WHAT HE GAVE UP												THE RESULTS						
Year Team	Lg	G	GS	CG	GF	IP	BFP	H	R	ER	HR	SH	SF	HB	TBB	IBB	SO	WP	Bk	W	L	Pct.	ShO	Sv-Op	Hld	ERA
1985 Minnesota	AL	6	4	0	0	24.1	105	24	16	15	3	0	2	0	14	0	12	1	1	1	3	.250	0	0-0	0	5.55
1986 Minnesota	AL	27	15	3	7	112.2	481	112	56	54	10	5	3	1	50	1	67	5	0	6	10	.375	0	1-2	2	4.31
1987 Minnesota	AL	13	7	0	3	44	204	58	40	38	13	0	1	1	24	1	28	2	0	1	3	.250	0	0-1	0	7.77
1988 Minnesota	AL	26	0	0	9	57.2	242	60	30	29	11	2	3	1	17	1	31	2	2	3	3	.500	0	3-4	0	4.53
1989 Houston	NL	20	15	2	1	108	440	91	34	33	7	8	1	2	37	0	86	3	0	7	1	.875	1	0-0	1	2.75
1990 Houston	NL	32	32	1	0	196.2	831	187	90	79	21	7	6	4	67	4	136	6	0	11	10	.524	0	0-0	0	3.62
1991 Houston	NL	32	27	1	3	168.1	710	163	91	84	19	6	6	2	59	5	120	4	1	10	12	.455	0	1-2	1	4.49
1992 Houston	NL	18	16	1	0	101.1	405	76	32	30	7	5	1	1	41	3	62	1	1	6	3	.667	1	0-0	0	2.66
1993 Houston	NL	33	33	1	0	208	876	194	75	64	10	11	3	4	77	3	131	9	2	18	4	.818	1	0-0	0	2.77
1994 San Francisco	NL	21	21	1	0	137.1	580	135	68	60	17	6	4	6	45	2	87	5	0	10	8	.556	0	0-0	0	3.93
1995 SF-Cin		31	31	1	0	181.2	775	185	91	81	19	9	1	4	56	2	96	7	0	11	10	.524	0	0-0	0	4.01
1996 Cincinnati	NL	27	26	1	0	156	646	146	77	69	20	7	6	2	42	2	93	6	0	8	9	.471	0	0-0	0	3.98
1997 Philadelphia	NL	3	3	0	0	13.2	60	17	8	7	0	1	1	0	5	0	2	0	0	0	2	.000	0	0-0	0	4.61
1998 Philadelphia	NL	26	26	1	0	166.1	704	186	88	82	26	8	2	4	32	2	104	4	0	10	5	.667	0	0-0	0	4.44
1995 San Francisco	NL	17	17	1	0	104	445	106	56	48	10	5	0	2	34	2	63	2	0	5	5	.500	0	0-0	0	4.15
Cincinnati	NL	14	14	0	0	77.2	330	79	35	33	7	4	1	2	22	0	33	5	0	6	5	.545	0	0-0	0	3.82
14 ML YEARS		315	256	15	23	1676	7059	1634	796	725	181	75	40	32	566	26	1055	55	7	102	83	.551	4	5-9	4	3.89

Jorge Posada

Bats: B **Throws:** R **Pos:** C-99; PH/PR-19; DH-6; 1B-1   **Ht:** 6'2" **Wt:** 205 **Born:** 8/17/71 **Age:** 27

								BATTING											BASERUNNING				PERCENTAGES		
Year Team	Lg	G	AB	H	2B	3B	HR	(Hm	Rd)	TB	R	RBI	TBB	IBB	SO	HBP	SH	SF	SB	CS	SB%	GDP	Avg	OBP	SLG
1995 New York	AL	1	1	0	0	0	0	(0	0)	0	0	0	0	0	0	0	0	0	0	0	.00	0	.000	.000	.000
1996 New York	AL	8	14	1	0	0	0	(0	0)	1	0	1	0	6	0	0	0	0	0	0	.00	1	.071	.133	.071
1997 New York	AL	60	188	47	12	0	6	(2	4)	77	29	25	30	2	33	3	1	2	1	2	.33	2	.250	.359	.410
1998 New York	AL	111	358	96	23	0	17	(6	11)	170	56	63	47	7	92	0	0	4	0	1	.00	14	.268	.350	.475
4 ML YEARS		180	560	144	35	0	23	(8	15)	248	86	88	78	9	131	3	1	6	1	3	.25	17	.257	.348	.443

Brian Powell

Pitches: Right **Bats:** Right **Pos:** SP-16; RP-2   **Ht:** 6'2" **Wt:** 205 **Born:** 10/10/73 **Age:** 25

		HOW MUCH HE PITCHED						WHAT HE GAVE UP												THE RESULTS						
Year Team	Lg	G	GS	CG	GF	IP	BFP	H	R	ER	HR	SH	SF	HB	TBB	IBB	SO	WP	Bk	W	L	Pct.	ShO	Sv-Op	Hld	ERA
1995 Jamestown	A-	5	5	0	0	26.1	108	19	12	9	1	0	1	5	8	0	15	3	0	2	1	.667	0	0--	—	3.08
Fayetteville	A	5	5	0	0	28	111	15	5	5	0	1	1	2	11	0	37	2	0	4	0	1.000	0	0--	—	1.61
1996 Lakeland	A+	29	27	5	2	174.1	746	195	106	95	12	9	2	7	47	0	84	1	2	8	13	.381	0	0--	—	4.90
1997 Lakeland	A+	27	27	8	0	183.1	732	153	70	51	9	4	5	6	35	2	122	5	0	13	9	.591	2	0--	—	2.50
1998 Jacksnville	AA	14	14	2	0	93.2	379	84	37	32	5	0	3	4	24	0	51	3	2	10	2	.833	1	0--	—	3.07
Toledo	AAA	1	1	0	0	7	27	5	0	0	0	0	0	0	0	0	7	0	0	0	0	.000	0	0--	—	0.00
1998 Detroit	AL	18	16	0	1	83.2	383	101	67	59	17	1	1	2	36	2	46	3	0	3	8	.273	0	0-0	0	6.35

Dante Powell

Bats: Right **Throws:** Right **Pos:** CF-8; PH/PR-2   **Ht:** 6'2" **Wt:** 180 **Born:** 8/25/73 **Age:** 25

								BATTING											BASERUNNING				PERCENTAGES		
Year Team	Lg	G	AB	H	2B	3B	HR	(Hm	Rd)	TB	R	RBI	TBB	IBB	SO	HBP	SH	SF	SB	CS	SB%	GDP	Avg	OBP	SLG
1994 Everett	A-	41	165	51	15	1	5	—	—	83	31	25	19	1	47	4	0	2	27	1	.96	1	.309	.389	.503
San Jose	A+	1	4	2	0	1	0	—	—	4	0	0	0	0	1	0	0	0	0	0	.00	0	.500	.500	1.000
1995 San Jose	A+	135	505	125	23	8	10	—	—	194	74	70	46	2	131	3	1	4	43	12	.78	8	.248	.312	.384
1996 Shreveport	AA	135	508	142	27	2	21	—	—	236	92	78	72	4	92	3	1	2	43	23	.65	6	.280	.371	.465
Phoenix	AAA	2	8	2	0	1	0	—	—	4	0	0	2	0	3	0	0	0	1	0	1.00	0	.250	.400	.500
1997 Phoenix	AAA	108	452	109	24	4	11	—	—	174	91	42	52	1	105	3	3	0	34	10	.77	9	.241	.323	.385
1998 Fresno	AAA	134	448	103	17	3	14	—	—	168	83	52	71	1	138	14	3	4	41	9	.82	6	.230	.350	.375
1997 San Francisco	NL	27	39	12	1	0	1	(1	0)	16	8	3	4	0	11	0	1	0	1	1	.50	0	.308	.372	.410
1998 San Francisco	NL	8	4	2	0	0	1	(1	0)	5	2	1	3	0	0	0	0	0	0	0	.00	0	.500	.714	1.250
2 ML YEARS		35	43	14	1	0	2	(2	0)	21	10	4	7	0	11	0	1	0	1	1	.50	0	.326	.420	.488

Jay Powell

Pitches: Right **Bats:** Right **Pos:** RP-62   **Ht:** 6'4" **Wt:** 225 **Born:** 1/19/72 **Age:** 27

		HOW MUCH HE PITCHED						WHAT HE GAVE UP												THE RESULTS						
Year Team	Lg	G	GS	CG	GF	IP	BFP	H	R	ER	HR	SH	SF	HB	TBB	IBB	SO	WP	Bk	W	L	Pct.	ShO	Sv-Op	Hld	ERA
1995 Florida	NL	9	0	0	1	8.1	38	7	2	1	0	1	0	2	6	1	4	0	0	0	0	.000	0	0-0	2	1.08
1996 Florida	NL	67	0	0	16	71.1	321	71	41	36	5	2	1	4	36	1	52	3	0	4	3	.571	0	2-5	10	4.54
1997 Florida	NL	74	0	0	23	79.2	337	71	35	29	3	6	4	4	30	3	65	3	0	7	2	.778	0	2-4	24	3.28
1998 Fla-Hou	NL	62	0	0	35	70.1	302	58	28	26	6	3	1	3	37	9	62	1	0	7	7	.500	0	7-11	3	3.33
1998 Florida	NL	33	0	0	26	36.1	165	36	19	17	5	3	1	2	22	6	24	1	0	4	4	.500	0	3-6	0	4.21
Houston	NL	29	0	0	9	34	137	22	9	9	1	0	0	1	15	3	38	0	0	3	3	.500	0	4-5	3	2.38
4 ML YEARS		212	0	0	75	229.2	998	207	106	92	14	12	6	13	109	14	183	7	0	18	12	.600	0	11-20	39	3.61

Jeremy Powell

Pitches: Right **Bats:** Right **Pos:** SP-6; RP-1   **Ht:** 6'6" **Wt:** 225 **Born:** 6/28/76 **Age:** 23

		HOW MUCH HE PITCHED						WHAT HE GAVE UP												THE RESULTS						
Year Team	Lg	G	GS	CG	GF	IP	BFP	H	R	ER	HR	SH	SF	HB	TBB	IBB	SO	WP	Bk	W	L	Pct.	ShO	Sv-Op	Hld	ERA
1994 Expos	R	9	9	1	0	43	171	37	16	14	1	0	1	2	14	0	36	2	2	2	2	.500	0	0--	—	2.93
1995 Albany	A	1	1	0	0	5.2	20	4	1	1	0	0	1	0	1	0	6	1	0	1	0	1.000	0	0--	—	1.59
Vermont	A-	15	15	0	0	87	373	88	48	42	5	2	2	6	34	1	47	6	2	5	5	.500	0	0--	—	4.34
1996 Delmarva	A	27	27	1	0	157.2	665	127	68	53	9	1	6	15	66	0	109	11	4	12	9	.571	0	0--	—	3.03
1997 Wst Plm Bch	A+	26	26	1	0	155	675	162	75	52	3	9	5	12	62	0	121	12	2	9	10	.474	0	0--	—	3.02
1998 Oklahoma	AAA	1	0	0	0	2	13	3	5	3	1	0	0	1	2	0	4	0	0	0	0	.000	0	0--	—	13.50
Harrisburg	AA	22	22	1	0	131.2	546	115	54	44	13	7	2	9	37	0	77	6	1	9	7	.563	0	0--	—	3.01
1998 Montreal	NL	7	6	0	1	25	112	27	25	22	5	2	4	1	11	0	14	0	0	1	5	.167	0	0-0	0	7.92

Todd Pratt

Bats: Right **Throws:** Right **Pos:** PH/PR-24; C-16; 1B-3   **Ht:** 6'3" **Wt:** 220 **Born:** 2/9/67 **Age:** 32

								BATTING											BASERUNNING				PERCENTAGES		
Year Team	Lg	G	AB	H	2B	3B	HR	(Hm	Rd)	TB	R	RBI	TBB	IBB	SO	HBP	SH	SF	SB	CS	SB%	GDP	Avg	OBP	SLG
1998 St. Lucie *	A+	5	20	9	1	0	1	—	—	13	2	3	1	0	5	2	0	0	1	0	1.00	0	.450	.522	.650
Mets *	R	2	4	1	0	0	0	—	—	1	0	4	0	1	0	0	0	0	0	0	.00	0	.250	.625	.250
Norfolk *	AAA	35	118	42	6	0	7	—	—	69	16	30	15	0	19	4	1	1	2	0	1.00	4	.356	.442	.585
1992 Philadelphia	NL	16	46	13	1	0	2	(2	0)	20	6	10	4	0	12	0	0	2	0	0	.00	2	.283	.340	.435
1993 Philadelphia	NL	33	87	25	6	0	5	(4	1)	46	8	13	5	0	19	1	1	1	0	0	.00	2	.287	.330	.529
1994 Philadelphia	NL	28	102	20	6	1	2	(1	1)	34	10	9	12	0	29	0	0	0	0	1	.00	3	.196	.281	.333

BATTING																			BASERUNNING				PERCENTAGES		
Year Team	Lg	G	AB	H	2B	3B	HR	(Hm	Rd)	TB	R	RBI	TBB	IBB	SO	HBP	SH	SF	SB	CS	SB%	GDP	Avg	OBP	SLG
1995 Chicago	NL	25	60	8	2	0	0	(0	0)	10	3	4	6	1	21	0	0	1	0	0	.00	1	.133	.209	.167
1997 New York	NL	39	106	30	6	0	2	(1	1)	42	12	19	13	0	32	2	0	0	0	1	.00	0	.283	.372	.396
1998 New York	NL	41	69	19	9	1	2	(1	1)	36	9	18	2	0	20	0	0	0	0	0	.00	0	.275	.296	.522
6 ML YEARS		182	470	115	30	2	13	(9	4)	188	48	73	42	1	133	3	1	2	0	2	.00	9	.245	.309	.400

Curtis Pride

Bats: L **Throws:** R **Pos:** PH/PR-47; RF-14; LF-8; DH-2   **Ht:** 6'0" **Wt:** 210 **Born:** 12/17/68 **Age:** 30

BATTING																			BASERUNNING				PERCENTAGES		
Year Team	Lg	G	AB	H	2B	3B	HR	(Hm	Rd)	TB	R	RBI	TBB	IBB	SO	HBP	SH	SF	SB	CS	SB%	GDP	Avg	OBP	SLG
1998 Richmond *	AAA	21	78	19	2	1	2	—	—	29	11	6	15	2	17	0	0	0	8	0	1.00	3	.244	.366	.372
1993 Montreal	NL	10	9	4	1	1	1	(0	1)	10	3	5	0	0	3	0	0	0	1	0	1.00	0	.444	.444	1.111
1995 Montreal	NL	48	63	11	1	0	0	(0	0)	12	10	2	5	0	16	0	1	0	3	2	.60	2	.175	.235	.190
1996 Detroit	AL	95	267	80	17	5	10	(5	5)	137	52	31	31	1	63	0	3	0	11	6	.65	2	.300	.372	.513
1997 Det-Bos	AL	81	164	35	4	4	3	(3	0)	56	22	20	24	1	46	1	2	1	6	4	.60	4	.213	.316	.341
1998 Atlanta	NL	70	107	27	6	1	3	(1	2)	44	19	9	9	0	29	3	1	1	4	0	1.00	2	.252	.325	.411
1997 Detroit	AL	79	162	34	4	4	2	(2	0)	52	21	19	24	1	45	1	2	1	6	4	.60	4	.210	.314	.321
Boston	AL	2	2	1	0	0	1	(1	0)	4	1	1	0	0	1	0	0	0	0	0	.00	0	.500	.500	2.000
5 ML YEARS		304	610	157	29	11	17	(9	8)	259	106	67	69	2	157	4	7	2	25	12	.68	10	.257	.336	.425

Eddie Priest

Pitches: Left **Bats:** Right **Pos:** SP-2   **Ht:** 6'1" **Wt:** 200 **Born:** 4/8/74 **Age:** 25

HOW MUCH HE PITCHED							WHAT HE GAVE UP											THE RESULTS						
Year Team	Lg	G	GS	CG	GF	IP	BFP	H	R	ER	HR	SH	SF	HB	TBB	IBB	SO	WP	Bk	W	L	Pct.	ShO	Sv-Op	Hld	ERA
1994 Billings	R+	13	13	2	0	85	333	74	31	24	3	1	0	1	14	0	82	2	1	7	4	.636	0	0- -	—	2.54
1995 Winston-Sal	A+	12	12	1	0	67	275	60	32	27	7	2	2	0	22	0	60	2	0	5	5	.500	1	0- -	—	3.63
1996 Winston-Sal	A+	4	4	0	0	12.1	48	5	2	1	1	0	0	0	6	0	9	1	0	1	0	1.000	0	0- -	—	0.73
1997 Chston-WV	A	14	14	0	0	77	321	79	38	31	6	2	3	2	10	0	70	5	0	5	3	.625	0	0- -	—	3.62
Chattanooga	AA	14	14	1	0	91.2	379	101	39	35	7	2	2	0	17	1	63	3	1	4	6	.400	0	0- -	—	3.44
1998 Chattanooga	AA	4	4	0	0	26	105	15	6	5	1	1	0	0	10	1	29	1	0	1	2	.333	0	0- -	—	1.73
Indianapolis	AAA	6	6	0	0	34	147	36	19	18	6	2	0	1	7	0	21	2	0	4	1	.800	0	0- -	—	4.76
Buffalo	AAA	16	16	0	0	88	390	103	56	48	10	2	1	2	28	1	44	2	0	3	5	.375	0	0- -	—	4.91
1998 Cincinnati	NL	2	2	0	0	6	29	12	8	7	2	0	1	0	1	0	1	0	0	0	1	.000	0	0-0	0	10.50

Ariel Prieto

Pitches: Right **Bats:** Right **Pos:** SP-2   **Ht:** 6'2" **Wt:** 245 **Born:** 10/22/69 **Age:** 29

HOW MUCH HE PITCHED							WHAT HE GAVE UP											THE RESULTS						
Year Team	Lg	G	GS	CG	GF	IP	BFP	H	R	ER	HR	SH	SF	HB	TBB	IBB	SO	WP	Bk	W	L	Pct.	ShO	Sv-Op	Hld	ERA
1998 Edmonton *	AAA	10	10	1	0	52.2	212	47	20	15	3	0	2	0	12	0	50	3	1	5	1	.833	0	0- -	—	2.56
1995 Oakland	AL	14	9	1	1	58	258	57	35	32	4	3	2	5	32	1	37	4	1	2	6	.250	0	0-0	0	4.97
1996 Oakland	AL	21	21	2	0	125.2	547	130	66	58	9	5	5	7	54	2	75	6	2	6	7	.462	0	0-0	0	4.15
1997 Oakland	AL	22	22	0	0	125	588	155	84	70	16	3	4	5	70	3	90	7	1	6	8	.429	0	0-0	0	5.04
1998 Oakland	AL	2	2	0	0	8.1	47	17	11	11	2	0	0	1	5	1	8	0	0	0	1	.000	0	0-0	0	11.88
4 ML YEARS		59	54	3	1	317	1440	359	196	171	31	11	11	18	161	7	210	17	4	14	22	.389	0	0-0	0	4.85

Tom Prince

Bats: Right **Throws:** Right **Pos:** C-32; PH/PR-6   **Ht:** 5'11" **Wt:** 206 **Born:** 8/13/64 **Age:** 34

BATTING																			BASERUNNING				PERCENTAGES		
Year Team	Lg	G	AB	H	2B	3B	HR	(Hm	Rd)	TB	R	RBI	TBB	IBB	SO	HBP	SH	SF	SB	CS	SB%	GDP	Avg	OBP	SLG
1987 Pittsburgh	NL	4	9	2	1	0	1	(0	1)	6	1	2	0	0	2	0	0	0	0	0	.00	0	.222	.222	.667
1988 Pittsburgh	NL	29	74	13	2	0	0	(0	0)	15	3	6	4	0	15	0	2	0	0	0	.00	5	.176	.218	.203
1989 Pittsburgh	NL	21	52	7	4	0	0	(0	0)	11	1	5	6	1	12	0	0	1	1	1	.50	1	.135	.220	.212
1990 Pittsburgh	NL	4	10	1	0	0	0	(0	0)	1	1	1	0	0	2	0	0	0	0	0	.00	0	.100	.182	.100
1991 Pittsburgh	NL	26	34	9	3	0	1	(0	1)	15	4	2	7	0	3	1	0	0	0	0	.00	3	.265	.405	.441
1992 Pittsburgh	NL	27	44	4	2	0	0	(0	0)	6	1	5	6	0	9	0	0	2	1	1	.50	2	.091	.192	.136
1993 Pittsburgh	NL	66	179	35	14	0	2	(2	0)	55	14	24	13	2	38	7	2	3	1	1	.50	5	.196	.272	.307
1994 Los Angeles	NL	3	6	2	0	0	0	(0	0)	2	2	1	1	0	3	0	0	0	0	0	.00	0	.333	.429	.333
1995 Los Angeles	NL	18	40	8	2	1	1	(0	1)	15	3	4	4	0	10	0	0	0	0	0	.00	0	.200	.273	.375
1996 Los Angeles	NL	40	64	19	6	0	1	(0	1)	28	6	11	6	2	15	2	3	2	0	0	.00	0	.297	.365	.438
1997 Los Angeles	NL	47	100	22	5	0	3	(2	1)	36	17	14	5	0	15	3	4	1	0	0	.00	2	.220	.275	.360
1998 Los Angeles	NL	37	81	15	5	1	0	(0	0)	22	7	5	7	1	24	2	2	0	0	0	.00	0	.185	.267	.272
12 ML YEARS		322	693	137	44	2	9	(4	5)	212	60	79	60	6	148	15	13	9	3	4	.43	18	.198	.273	.306

Chris Pritchett

Bats: Left **Throws:** Right **Pos:** 1B-29; PH/PR-8   **Ht:** 6'4" **Wt:** 212 **Born:** 1/31/70 **Age:** 29

BATTING																			BASERUNNING				PERCENTAGES		
Year Team	Lg	G	AB	H	2B	3B	HR	(Hm	Rd)	TB	R	RBI	TBB	IBB	SO	HBP	SH	SF	SB	CS	SB%	GDP	Avg	OBP	SLG
1991 Boise	A-	70	255	68	10	3	9	—	—	111	41	50	47	3	41	0	0	3	1	0	1.00	7	.267	.381	.435
1992 Quad City	A	128	448	130	19	1	13	—	—	190	79	72	71	6	88	5	2	5	9	4	.69	7	.290	.389	.424
1993 Midland	AA	127	464	143	30	6	2	—	—	191	61	66	61	2	72	2	6	7	3	7	.30	17	.308	.386	.412
1994 Midland	AA	127	460	142	25	4	6	—	—	193	86	91	92	9	87	2	3	7	5	3	.63	8	.309	.421	.420
1995 Vancouver	AAA	123	434	120	27	4	8	—	—	179	66	53	56	6	79	5	2	1	2	3	.40	7	.276	.365	.412
1996 Vancouver	AAA	130	485	143	39	1	16	—	—	232	78	73	71	11	96	6	0	6	5	4	.56	7	.295	.387	.478

			BATTING																BASERUNNING				PERCENTAGES		
Year Team	Lg	G	AB	H	2B	3B	HR	(Hm Rd)	TB	R	RBI	TBB	IBB	SO	HBP	SH	SF		SB	CS	SB%	GDP	Avg	OBP	SLG
1997 Vancouver	AAA	109	383	107	30	3	7	(— —)	164	60	47	42	6	72	5	5	2		5	3	.63	9	.279	.356	.428
1998 Vancouver	AAA	104	374	97	21	1	4	(— —)	141	42	41	37	3	72	0	3	5		2	2	.50	14	.259	.322	.377
1996 California	AL	5	13	2	0	0	0	(0 0)	2	1	1	0	0	3	0	0	0		0	0	.00	0	.154	.154	.154
1998 Anaheim	AL	31	80	23	2	1	2	(0 2)	33	12	8	4	0	16	0	0	0		2	0	1.00	3	.288	.321	.413
2 ML YEARS		36	93	25	2	1	2	(0 2)	35	13	9	4	0	19	0	0	0		2	0	1.00	3	.269	.299	.376

Bill Pulsipher

Pitches: Left **Bats:** Left **Pos:** RP-15; SP-11 **Ht:** 6'3" **Wt:** 200 **Born:** 10/9/73 **Age:** 25

		HOW MUCH HE PITCHED						WHAT HE GAVE UP												THE RESULTS						
Year Team	Lg	G	GS	CG	GF	IP	BFP	H	R	ER	HR	SH	SF	HB	TBB	IBB	SO	WP	Bk	W	L	Pct.	ShO	Sv-Op	Hld	ERA
1992 Pittsfield	A-	14	14	0	0	95	413	88	40	30	3	0	1	3	56	0	83	16	1	6	3	.667	0	0--	—	2.84
1993 Capital Cty	A	6	6	1	0	43.1	175	34	17	10	1	2	0	1	12	0	29	1	1	2	3	.400	0	0--	—	2.08
St. Lucie	A+	13	13	3	0	96.1	374	63	27	24	2	3	1	0	39	0	102	3	1	7	3	.700	1	0--	—	2.24
1994 Binghamton	AA	28	28	5	0	201	849	179	90	72	18	7	1	3	89	2	171	9	5	14	9	.609	1	0--	—	3.22
1995 Norfolk	AAA	13	13	4	0	91.2	377	84	36	32	3	5	3	1	33	0	63	2	3	6	4	.600	0	0--	—	3.14
1997 Norfolk	AAA	8	5	0	1	27.2	142	23	29	24	1	3	0	1	38	0	18	5	1	0	5	.000	0	0--	—	7.81
Mets	R	2	2	0	0	5	18	3	1	1	0	0	0	1	0	4	0	0	0	0	0	.000	0	0--	—	1.80
St. Lucie	A+	12	7	0	2	36.2	178	29	27	24	1	2	1	4	35	0	35	14	5	1	4	.200	0	0--	—	5.89
Binghamton	AA	10	0	0	4	12.2	55	11	3	2	0	2	0	0	7	1	12	0	0	0	0	.000	0	0--	—	1.42
1998 Norfolk	AAA	14	14	1	0	86.1	378	91	50	38	12	2	0	2	41	1	58	8	0	7	5	.583	0	0--	—	3.96
1995 New York	NL	17	17	2	0	126.2	530	122	58	56	11	2	1	4	45	0	81	2	1	5	7	.417	0	0-0	0	3.98
1998 NYN-Mil	NL	26	11	0	2	72.1	320	86	41	41	8	4	4	1	31	4	51	2	2	3	4	.429	0	0-1	2	5.10
1998 New York	NL	15	1	0	1	14.1	68	23	11	11	2	1	0	0	5	1	13	0	0	0	0	.000	0	0-1	2	6.91
Milwaukee	NL	11	10	0	1	58	252	63	30	30	6	3	4	1	26	3	38	2	2	3	4	.429	0	0-0	0	4.66
2 ML YEARS		43	28	2	2	199	850	208	99	97	19	6	5	5	76	4	132	4	3	8	11	.421	0	0-1	2	4.39

Paul Quantrill

Pitches: Right **Bats:** Left **Pos:** RP-82 **Ht:** 6'1" **Wt:** 185 **Born:** 11/3/68 **Age:** 30

		HOW MUCH HE PITCHED						WHAT HE GAVE UP												THE RESULTS						
Year Team	Lg	G	GS	CG	GF	IP	BFP	H	R	ER	HR	SH	SF	HB	TBB	IBB	SO	WP	Bk	W	L	Pct.	ShO	Sv-Op	Hld	ERA
1992 Boston	AL	27	0	0	10	49.1	213	55	18	12	1	4	2	1	15	5	24	1	0	2	3	.400	0	1-5	3	2.19
1993 Boston	AL	49	14	1	8	138	594	151	73	60	13	4	2	2	44	14	66	0	1	6	12	.333	1	1-2	3	3.91
1994 Bos-Phi		35	1	0	9	53	236	64	31	29	7	5	3	5	15	4	28	0	2	3	3	.500	0	1-4	3	4.92
1995 Philadelphia	NL	33	29	0	1	179.1	784	212	102	93	20	9	6	6	44	3	103	0	3	11	12	.478	0	0-0	0	4.67
1996 Toronto	AL	38	20	0	7	134.1	609	172	90	81	27	5	7	2	51	3	86	1	1	5	14	.263	0	0-2	1	5.43
1997 Toronto	AL	77	0	0	29	88	373	103	25	19	5	5	3	1	17	3	56	1	0	6	7	.462	0	5-10	16	1.94
1998 Toronto	AL	82	0	0	32	80	345	88	26	23	5	7	4	3	22	6	59	1	0	3	4	.429	0	7-14	27	2.59
1994 Boston	AL	17	0	0	4	23	101	25	10	9	4	2	2	2	5	1	15	0	0	1	1	.500	0	0-2	2	3.52
Philadelphia	NL	18	1	0	5	30	135	39	21	20	3	3	1	3	10	3	13	0	2	2	2	.500	0	1-2	1	6.00
7 ML YEARS		341	64	1	96	722	3154	845	365	317	78	39	27	20	208	38	422	4	7	36	55	.396	1	15-37	53	3.95

Scott Radinsky

Pitches: Left **Bats:** Left **Pos:** RP-62 **Ht:** 6'3" **Wt:** 221 **Born:** 3/3/68 **Age:** 31

		HOW MUCH HE PITCHED						WHAT HE GAVE UP												THE RESULTS						
Year Team	Lg	G	GS	CG	GF	IP	BFP	H	R	ER	HR	SH	SF	HB	TBB	IBB	SO	WP	Bk	W	L	Pct.	ShO	Sv-Op	Hld	ERA
1990 Chicago	AL	62	0	0	18	52.1	237	47	29	28	1	2	2	2	36	1	46	2	1	6	1	.857	0	4-5	10	4.82
1991 Chicago	AL	67	0	0	19	71.1	289	53	18	16	4	4	4	1	23	2	49	0	0	5	5	.500	0	8-15	15	2.02
1992 Chicago	AL	68	0	0	33	59.1	261	54	21	18	3	2	1	2	34	5	48	3	0	3	7	.300	0	15-23	16	2.73
1993 Chicago	AL	73	0	0	24	54.2	250	61	33	26	3	2	0	1	19	3	44	0	4	8	2	.800	0	4-5	12	4.28
1995 Chicago	AL	46	0	0	10	38	171	46	23	23	7	1	4	0	17	4	14	0	0	2	1	.667	0	1-3	8	5.45
1996 Los Angeles	NL	58	0	0	19	52.1	221	52	19	14	2	4	3	0	17	4	48	0	3	5	1	.833	0	1-4	7	2.41
1997 Los Angeles	NL	75	0	0	14	62.1	258	54	22	20	4	3	4	1	21	5	44	0	0	5	1	.833	0	3-5	26	2.89
1998 Los Angeles	NL	62	0	0	30	61.2	264	63	21	18	5	6	2	4	20	1	45	0	3	6	6	.500	0	13-24	8	2.63
8 ML YEARS		511	0	0	167	452	1951	430	186	163	29	24	20	11	187	26	338	5	11	40	24	.625	0	49-84	102	3.25

Brad Radke

Pitches: Right **Bats:** Right **Pos:** SP-32 **Ht:** 6'2" **Wt:** 190 **Born:** 10/27/72 **Age:** 26

		HOW MUCH HE PITCHED						WHAT HE GAVE UP												THE RESULTS						
Year Team	Lg	G	GS	CG	GF	IP	BFP	H	R	ER	HR	SH	SF	HB	TBB	IBB	SO	WP	Bk	W	L	Pct.	ShO	Sv-Op	Hld	ERA
1995 Minnesota	AL	29	28	2	0	181	772	195	112	107	32	2	9	4	47	0	75	4	0	11	14	.440	1	0-0	0	5.32
1996 Minnesota	AL	35	35	3	0	232	973	231	125	115	40	5	6	4	57	2	148	1	0	11	16	.407	0	0-0	0	4.46
1997 Minnesota	AL	35	35	4	0	239.2	989	238	114	103	28	2	9	3	48	1	174	1	1	20	10	.667	3	0-0	0	3.87
1998 Minnesota	AL	32	32	5	0	213.2	904	238	109	102	23	9	3	9	43	1	146	3	1	12	14	.462	1	0-0	0	4.30
4 ML YEARS		131	130	14	0	866.1	3638	902	460	427	123	18	27	20	195	4	543	9	2	54	54	.500	3	0-0	0	4.44

Ryan Radmanovich

Bats: Left **Throws:** Right **Pos:** RF-24; 1B-1; PH/PR-1 **Ht:** 6'2" **Wt:** 185 **Born:** 8/9/71 **Age:** 27

			BATTING																BASERUNNING				PERCENTAGES		
Year Team	Lg	G	AB	H	2B	3B	HR	(Hm Rd)	TB	R	RBI	TBB	IBB	SO	HBP	SH	SF		SB	CS	SB%	GDP	Avg	OBP	SLG
1993 Fort Wayne	A	62	204	59	7	5	8	(— —)	100	36	38	30	2	60	7	2	2		8	2	.80	4	.289	.395	.490
1994 Fort Myers	A+	26	85	16	4	0	2	(— —)	26	11	9	7	0	19	2	0	0		3	1	.75	0	.188	.266	.306
Fort Wayne	A	101	383	105	20	6	19	(— —)	194	64	69	45	3	98	3	1	1		19	14	.58	7	.274	.354	.507

Year Team	Lg	G	AB	H	2B	3B	HR	(Hm	Rd)	TB	R	RBI	TBB	IBB	SO	HBP	SH	SF	SB	CS	SB%	GDP	Avg	OBP	SLG
1995 Fort Myers	A+	12	41	13	2	0	0	—	—	15	3	5	2	0	8	1	0	0	0	0	.00	0	.317	.364	.366
1996 Hardware City	AA	125	453	127	31	2	25	—	—	237	77	86	49	6	122	3	3	2	4	11	.27	12	.280	.353	.523
1997 Salt Lake	AAA	133	485	128	25	4	28	—	—	245	92	78	67	7	138	4	1	5	11	4	.73	4	.264	.355	.505
1998 Tacoma	AAA	110	397	119	33	2	15	—	—	201	73	65	46	3	83	1	5	7	2	4	.33	6	.300	.368	.506
1998 Seattle	AL	25	69	15	4	0	2	(2	0)	25	5	10	4	1	25	0	2	0	1	1	.50	0	.217	.260	.362

Brady Raggio

Pitches: Right **Bats:** Right **Pos:** RP-3; SP-1 **Ht:** 6'4" **Wt:** 210 **Born:** 9/17/72 **Age:** 26

Year Team	Lg	G	GS	CG	GF	IP	BFP	H	R	ER	HR	SH	SF	HB	TBB	IBB	SO	WP	Bk	W	L	Pct.	ShO	Sv-Op	Hld	ERA
1992 Cardinals	R	14	6	3-	4	48.1	207	51	26	19	1	2	2	3	7	1	48	5	0	4	3	.571	0	1- —	—	3.54
1994 New Jersey	A-	4	4	0	0	27	115	28	7	5	0	0	1	0	4	0	20	1	0	3	0	1.000	0	0- —	—	1.67
Madison	A	11	11	1	0	67.1	277	63	31	24	8	3	2	3	14	1	66	3	0	4	3	.571	0	0- —	—	3.21
1995 Peoria	A	8	8	3	0	48.2	181	42	13	10	1	1	1	0	2	0	34	0	0	3	0	1.000	2	0- —	—	1.85
St. Pete	A+	20	3	0	4	47.1	195	43	24	20	2	3	1	1	13	2	35	2	1	2	3	.400	0	0- —	—	3.80
1996 Arkansas	AA	26	24	4	0	162.1	667	160	68	58	17	8	5	3	40	2	123	3	2	9	10	.474	1	0- —	—	3.22
1997 Louisville	AAA	22	22	2	0	138	576	145	68	64	18	5	3	6	32	0	91	3	1	8	11	.421	0	0- —	—	4.17
1998 Memphis	AAA	24	23	2	0	152.1	616	156	57	52	11	3	3	4	31	0	100	4	1	8	9	.471	1	0- —	—	3.07
1997 St. Louis	NL	15	4	0	5	31.1	151	44	24	24	1	1	2	1	16	0	21	3	0	1	2	.333	0	0-0	0	6.89
1998 St. Louis	NL	4	1	0	2	7	43	22	12	12	1	0	1	1	3	0	3	0	0	1	1	.500	0	0-0	0	15.43
2 ML YEARS		19	5	0	7	38.1	194	66	36	36	2	1	3	2	19	0	24	3	0	2	3	.400	0	0-0	0	8.45

Tim Raines

Bats: Both **Throws:** Right **Pos:** DH-56; LF-47; PH/PR-25 **Ht:** 5'8" **Wt:** 186 **Born:** 9/16/59 **Age:** 39

Year Team	Lg	G	AB	H	2B	3B	HR	(Hm	Rd)	TB	R	RBI	TBB	IBB	SO	HBP	SH	SF	SB	CS	SB%	GDP	Avg	OBP	SLG
1979 Montreal	NL	6	0	0	0	0	0	(0	0)	0	3	0	0	0	0	0	0	0	2	0	1.00	0	.000	.000	.000
1980 Montreal	NL	15	20	1	0	0	0	(0	0)	1	5	0	6	0	3	0	1	0	5	0	1.00	0	.050	.269	.050
1981 Montreal	NL	88	313	95	13	7	5	(3	2)	137	61	37	45	5	31	2	0	3	71	11	.87	7	.304	.391	.438
1982 Montreal	NL	156	647	179	32	8	4	(1	3)	239	90	43	75	9	83	2	6	1	78	16	.83	6	.277	.353	.369
1983 Montreal	NL	156	615	183	32	8	11	(5	6)	264	133	71	97	9	70	2	2	4	90	14	.87	12	.298	.393	.429
1984 Montreal	NL	160	622	192	38	9	8	(2	6)	272	106	60	87	7	69	2	3	4	75	10	.88	7	.309	.393	.437
1985 Montreal	NL	150	575	184	30	13	11	(4	7)	273	115	41	81	13	60	3	3	3	70	9	.89	9	.320	.405	.475
1986 Montreal	NL	151	580	194	35	10	9	(4	5)	276	91	62	78	9	60	2	1	3	70	9	.89	6	.334	.413	.476
1987 Montreal	NL	139	530	175	34	8	18	(9	9)	279	123	68	90	26	52	4	0	3	50	5	.91	9	.330	.429	.526
1988 Montreal	NL	109	429	116	19	7	12	(5	7)	185	66	48	53	14	44	2	0	4	33	7	.83	8	.270	.350	.431
1989 Montreal	NL	145	517	148	29	6	9	(6	3)	216	76	60	93	18	48	3	0	5	41	9	.82	8	.286	.395	.418
1990 Montreal	NL	130	457	131	11	5	9	(6	3)	179	65	62	70	8	43	3	0	8	49	16	.75	9	.287	.379	.392
1991 Chicago	AL	155	609	163	20	6	5	(1	4)	210	102	50	83	9	68	5	9	3	51	15	.77	7	.268	.359	.345
1992 Chicago	AL	144	551	162	22	9	7	(4	3)	223	102	54	81	4	48	0	4	8	45	6	.88	5	.294	.380	.405
1993 Chicago	AL	115	415	127	16	4	16	(7	9)	199	75	54	64	4	35	3	2	2	21	7	.75	7	.306	.401	.480
1994 Chicago	AL	101	384	102	15	5	10	(5	5)	157	80	52	61	3	43	1	4	3	13	0	1.00	10	.266	.365	.409
1995 Chicago	AL	133	502	143	25	4	12	(6	6)	212	81	67	70	3	52	1	3	3	13	2	.87	8	.285	.374	.422
1996 New York	AL	59	201	57	10	0	9	(7	2)	94	45	33	34	1	29	1	0	4	10	1	.91	5	.284	.383	.468
1997 New York	AL	74	271	87	20	2	4	(3	1)	123	56	38	41	0	34	0	0	6	8	5	.62	4	.321	.403	.454
1998 New York	AL	109	321	93	13	1	5	(2	3)	123	53	47	55	1	49	3	0	3	8	3	.73	5	.290	.395	.383
20 ML YEARS		2295	8559	2532	414	112	164	(80	84)	3662	1528	947	1264	143	921	41	38	70	803	145	.85	132	.296	.386	.428

Jason Rakers

Pitches: Right **Bats:** Right **Pos:** RP-1 **Ht:** 6'2" **Wt:** 200 **Born:** 6/29/73 **Age:** 26

Year Team	Lg	G	GS	CG	GF	IP	BFP	H	R	ER	HR	SH	SF	HB	TBB	IBB	SO	WP	Bk	W	L	Pct.	ShO	Sv-Op	Hld	ERA
1995 Watertown	A-	14	14	1	0	75	315	72	27	25	3	0	2	0	24	1	73	6	2	4	3	.571	1	0- —	—	3.00
1996 Columbus	A	14	14	1	0	77.1	319	84	37	31	5	1	1	3	17	0	64	8	1	5	4	.556	1	0- —	—	3.61
1997 Kinston	A+	17	17	2	0	102.2	405	93	41	35	10	1	0	1	18	0	105	2	1	8	5	.615	2	0- —	—	3.07
Buffalo	AAA	1	1	0	0	7	26	5	0	0	0	0	1	0	0	0	3	0	0	1	0	1.000	0	0- —	—	0.00
Akron	AA	7	7	1	0	41	168	36	21	20	3	1	2	4	11	0	31	1	0	1	4	.200	1	0- —	—	4.39
1998 Akron	AA	5	5	0	0	31.1	130	35	10	9	2	2	1	0	7	0	27	2	0	3	1	.750	0	0- —	—	2.59
Buffalo	AAA	21	21	1	0	126	542	134	70	64	13	2	6	8	38	0	89	7	1	8	6	.571	0	0- —	—	4.57
1998 Cleveland	AL	1	0	0	1	1	6	0	1	1	0	0	1	0	3	0	0	0	0	0	0	.000	0	0-0	0	9.00

Alex Ramirez

Bats: Right **Throws:** Right **Pos:** LF-2; RF-1 **Ht:** 5'11" **Wt:** 176 **Born:** 10/3/74 **Age:** 24

Year Team	Lg	G	AB	H	2B	3B	HR	(Hm	Rd)	TB	R	RBI	TBB	IBB	SO	HBP	SH	SF	SB	CS	SB%	GDP	Avg	OBP	SLG
1993 Burlington	R+	64	252	68	14	4	13	—	—	129	44	58	13	1	52	4	0	3	12	8	.60	4	.270	.313	.512
Kinston	A+	3	12	2	0	0	0	—	—	2	0	1	0	0	5	0	0	0	0	1	.00	0	.167	.167	.167
1994 Columbus	A	125	458	115	23	3	18	—	—	198	64	57	26	0	100	4	0	4	7	5	.58	11	.251	.295	.432
1995 Bakersfield	A+	98	406	131	25	2	10	—	—	190	56	52	18	1	76	3	0	1	13	9	.59	9	.323	.355	.468
Canton-Akrn	AA	33	133	33	3	4	1	—	—	47	15	11	5	1	24	0	1	1	3	5	.38	5	.248	.273	.353
1996 Canton-Akrn	AA	131	513	169	28	12	14	—	—	263	79	85	16	1	74	3	1	3	18	10	.64	8	.329	.353	.513
1997 Buffalo	AAA	119	416	119	19	8	11	—	—	187	59	44	24	0	95	4	6	3	10	5	.67	9	.286	.329	.450
1998 Buffalo	AAA	121	521	156	21	8	34	—	—	295	94	103	16	4	101	5	0	4	6	4	.60	11	.299	.324	.566
1998 Cleveland	AL	3	8	1	0	0	0	(0	0)	1	1	0	0	0	3	0	0	0	0	0	.00	0	.125	.125	.125

Aramis Ramirez

Bats: Right **Throws:** Right **Pos:** 3B-71; PH/PR-1 **Ht:** 6'1" **Wt:** 190 **Born:** 6/25/78 **Age:** 21

Year Team	Lg	G	AB	H	2B	3B	HR	(Hm	Rd)	TB	R	RBI	TBB	IBB	SO	HBP	SH	SF	SB	CS	SB%	GDP	Avg	OBP	SLG
1996 Erie	A-	61	223	68	14	4	9	—	—	117	37	42	31	1	41	7	0	2	0	0	.00	7	.305	.403	.525
Augusta	A	6	20	4	1	0	1	—	—	8	3	2	1	0	7	2	0	0	0	2	.00	—	.200	.304	.400
1997 Lynchburg	A+	137	482	134	24	2	29	—	—	249	85	114	80	9	103	12	0	5	5	3	.63	12	.278	.390	.517
1998 Nashville	AAA	47	168	46	10	0	5	—	—	71	19	18	24	0	28	4	0	2	0	2	.00	3	.274	.374	.423
1998 Pittsburgh	NL	72	251	59	9	1	6	(3	3)	88	23	24	18	0	72	4	1		0	1	.00	3	.235	.296	.351

Manny Ramirez

Bats: Right **Throws:** Right **Pos:** RF-148; DH-2 **Ht:** 6'0" **Wt:** 205 **Born:** 5/30/72 **Age:** 27

Year Team	Lg	G	AB	H	2B	3B	HR	(Hm	Rd)	TB	R	RBI	TBB	IBB	SO	HBP	SH	SF	SB	CS	SB%	GDP	Avg	OBP	SLG
1993 Cleveland	AL	22	53	9	1	0	2	(0	2)	16	5	5	2	0	8	0	0	0	0	0	.00	3	.170	.200	.302
1994 Cleveland	AL	91	290	78	22	0	17	(9	8)	151	51	60	42	4	72	0	0	4	4	2	.67	4	.269	.357	.521
1995 Cleveland	AL	137	484	149	26	1	31	(12	19)	270	85	107	75	6	112	5	2	5	6	6	.50	13	.308	.402	.558
1996 Cleveland	AL	152	550	170	45	3	33	(19	14)	320	94	112	85	8	104	3	0	9	8	5	.62	18	.309	.399	.582
1997 Cleveland	AL	150	561	184	40	0	26	(14	12)	302	99	88	79	5	115	7	0	4	2	3	.40	19	.328	.415	.538
1998 Cleveland	AL	150	571	168	35	2	45	(25	20)	342	108	145	76	6	121	6	0	10	5	3	.63	18	.294	.377	.599
6 ML YEARS		702	2509	758	169	6	154	(79	75)	1401	442	517	359	29	532	21	2	32	25	19	.57	77	.302	.390	.558

Roberto Ramirez

Pitches: Left **Bats:** Left **Pos:** RP-21 **Ht:** 6'1" **Wt:** 171 **Born:** 8/17/72 **Age:** 26

Year Team	Lg	G	GS	CG	GF	IP	BFP	H	R	ER	HR	SH	SF	HB	TBB	IBB	SO	WP	Bk	W	L	Pct.	ShO	Sv-Op	Hld	ERA
1990 Pirates	R	11	3	0	0	33.2	133	20	4	2	1	0	0	1	18	0	27	1	1	2	1	.667	0	0--	—	0.53
1991 Welland	A-	16	12	0	2	74.1	316	66	43	34	7	2	2	2	35	0	71	3	3	2	6	.250	0	1--	—	4.12
1994 Carolina	AA	6	6	0	0	27.1	129	38	19	16	2	3	0	1	8	0	21	1	0	0	1	.000	0	0--	—	5.27
1998 Las Vegas	AAA	26	1	0	7	29.2	120	23	14	8	2	2	1	0	10	2	33	2	0	1	1	.500	0	2--	—	2.43
1998 San Diego	NL	21	0	0	4	14.2	70	12	13	10	4	1	0	0	12	1	17	3	1	1	0	1.000	0	0-0	6	6.14

Joe Randa

Bats: R **Throws:** R **Pos:** 3B-118; 2B-20; PH/PR-12; DH-1; 1B-1 **Ht:** 5'11" **Wt:** 190 **Born:** 12/18/69 **Age:** 29

Year Team	Lg	G	AB	H	2B	3B	HR	(Hm	Rd)	TB	R	RBI	TBB	IBB	SO	HBP	SH	SF	SB	CS	SB%	GDP	Avg	OBP	SLG
1995 Kansas City	AL	34	70	12	2	0	1	(1	0)	17	6	5	6	0	17	0	0	0	0	1	.00	2	.171	.237	.243
1996 Kansas City	AL	110	337	102	24	1	6	(2	4)	146	36	47	26	4	72	1	2	4	13	4	.76	10	.303	.351	.433
1997 Pittsburgh	NL	126	443	134	27	9	7	(5	2)	200	58	60	41	1	64	6	4	5	4	2	.67	10	.302	.366	.451
1998 Detroit	AL	138	460	117	21	2	9	(3	6)	169	56	50	41	1	70	7	3	3	8	7	.53	9	.254	.323	.367
4 ML YEARS		408	1310	365	74	12	23	(11	12)	532	156	162	114	6	198	14	9	12	25	14	.64	31	.279	.340	.406

Pat Rapp

Pitches: Right **Bats:** Right **Pos:** SP-32 **Ht:** 6'3" **Wt:** 215 **Born:** 7/13/67 **Age:** 31

Year Team	Lg	G	GS	CG	GF	IP	BFP	H	R	ER	HR	SH	SF	HB	TBB	IBB	SO	WP	Bk	W	L	Pct.	ShO	Sv-Op	Hld	ERA
1992 San Francisco	NL	3	2	0	1	10	43	8	8	8	0	2	0	1	6	1	3	0	0	0	2	.000	0	0-0	0	7.20
1993 Florida	NL	16	16	1	0	94	412	101	49	42	7	8	4	2	39	1	57	6	0	4	6	.400	0	0-0	0	4.02
1994 Florida	NL	24	23	2	1	133.1	568	132	67	57	13	8	4	7	69	3	75	5	1	7	8	.467	1	0-0	0	3.85
1995 Florida	NL	28	28	3	0	167.1	716	158	72	64	10	8	0	7	76	2	102	7	0	14	7	.667	2	0-0	0	3.44
1996 Florida	NL	30	29	0	1	162.1	728	184	95	92	12	15	8	3	91	6	86	13	0	8	**16**	.333	0	0-0	0	5.10
1997 Fla-SF	NL	27	25	1	0	141.2	638	158	83	76	16	6	6	5	72	4	92	8	0	5	8	.385	1	0-0	0	4.83
1998 Kansas City	AL	32	32	1	0	188.1	855	208	117	111	24	3	6	10	107	7	132	14	0	12	13	.480	1	0-0	0	5.30
1997 Florida	NL	19	19	1	0	108.2	484	121	59	54	11	4	3	3	51	3	64	5	0	4	6	.400	1	0-0	0	4.47
San Francisco	NL	8	6	0	0	33	154	37	24	22	5	2	3	2	21	1	28	3	0	1	2	.333	0	0-0	0	6.00
7 ML YEARS		160	155	8	3	897	3976	949	491	450	82	50	28	35	460	24	547	53	1	50	60	.455	5	0-0	0	4.52

Fred Rath

Pitches: Right **Bats:** Right **Pos:** RP-2 **Ht:** 6'3" **Wt:** 220 **Born:** 1/5/73 **Age:** 26

Year Team	Lg	G	GS	CG	GF	IP	BFP	H	R	ER	HR	SH	SF	HB	TBB	IBB	SO	WP	Bk	W	L	Pct.	ShO	Sv-Op	Hld	ERA
1995 Elizabethtn	R+	27	0	0	25	33.1	134	20	8	5	2	2	0	1	11	1	50	3	0	1	1	.500	0	12--	—	1.35
1996 Fort Wayne	A	32	0	0	29	41.2	163	26	12	7	1	0	2	0	10	0	63	3	0	1	2	.333	0	14--	—	1.51
Fort Myers	A+	22	0	0	16	29	123	25	10	9	1	1	0	2	10	0	29	3	0	2	5	.286	0	4--	—	2.79
1997 Fort Myers	A+	17	0	0	11	22	87	18	4	4	2	1	0	3	3	1	22	1	0	4	0	1.000	0	2--	—	1.64
New Britain	AA	33	0	0	23	50.1	200	43	17	15	1	1	3	1	13	0	33	3	0	3	3	.500	0	12--	—	2.68
Salt Lake	AAA	10	0	0	9	11	46	11	2	2	1	0	0	0	2	0	11	0	0	0	1	.000	0	3--	—	1.64
1998 Salt Lake	AAA	27	0	0	22	31.2	133	35	16	16	4	1	0	2	8	0	15	3	0	1	2	.333	0	8--	—	4.55
Colo Spngs	AAA	23	0	0	14	28.1	132	37	17	16	2	1	2	2	15	1	20	4	0	5	1	.833	0	4--	—	5.08
1998 Colorado	NL	2	0	0	1	5.1	23	6	1	1	0	1	0	1	2	0	2	0	0	0	0	.000	0	0-0	0	1.69

Gary Rath

Pitches: Left **Bats:** Left **Pos:** RP-3 **Ht:** 6'2" **Wt:** 186 **Born:** 1/10/73 **Age:** 26

Year Team	Lg	G	GS	CG	GF	IP	BFP	H	R	ER	HR	SH	SF	HB	TBB	IBB	SO	WP	Bk	W	L	Pct.	ShO	Sv-Op	Hld	ERA
1994 Vero Beach	A+	13	11	0	0	62.2	261	55	26	19	3	3	3	2	23	0	50	4	0	5	6	.455	0	0- --	—	2.73
1995 San Antonio	AA	18	18	3	0	117	483	96	42	36	6	3	2	4	48	0	81	4	2	13	3	.813	1	0- --	—	2.77
Albuquerque	AAA	8	8	0	0	39	178	46	31	22	4	1	1	2	20	0	23	2	0	3	5	.375	0	0- --	—	5.08
1996 Albuquerque	AAA	30	30	1	0	180.1	784	177	97	84	13	9	4	3	89	8	125	8	0	10	11	.476	1	0- --	—	4.19
1997 Albuquerque	AAA	24	24	0	0	132.1	615	177	107	89	17	7	4	4	49	1	100	7	0	7	11	.389	0	0- --	—	6.05
1998 Albuquerque	AAA	28	24	1	3	157.1	687	184	91	79	17	5	1	4	52	1	119	2	0	9	7	.563	0	1- --	—	4.52
1998 Los Angeles	NL	3	0	0	1	3.1	15	3	4	4	1	1	0	0	2	0	4	0	0	0	0	.000	0	0-0	0	10.80

Jeff Reboulet

Bats: R **Throws:** R **Pos:** 2B-28; SS-28; 3B-23; PH/PR-14 **Ht:** 5'11" **Wt:** 170 **Born:** 4/30/64 **Age:** 35

Year Team	Lg	G	AB	H	2B	3B	HR	(Hm	Rd)	TB	R	RBI	TBB	IBB	SO	HBP	SH	SF	SB	CS	SB%	GDP	Avg	OBP	SLG
1992 Minnesota	AL	73	137	26	7	1	1	(1	0)	38	15	16	23	0	26	1	7	0	3	2	.60	0	.190	.311	.277
1993 Minnesota	AL	109	240	62	8	0	1	(0	1)	73	33	15	35	0	37	2	5	1	5	5	.50	6	.258	.356	.304
1994 Minnesota	AL	74	189	49	11	1	3	(2	1)	71	28	23	18	0	23	1	2	0	0	0	.00	4	.259	.327	.376
1995 Minnesota	AL	87	216	63	11	0	4	(1	3)	86	39	23	27	0	34	1	2	0	1	2	.33	3	.292	.373	.398
1996 Minnesota	AL	107	234	52	9	0	0	(0	0)	61	20	23	25	1	34	1	4	2	4	2	.67	10	.222	.298	.261
1997 Baltimore	AL	99	228	54	9	0	4	(2	2)	75	26	27	23	0	44	1	11	2	3	0	1.00	3	.237	.307	.329
1998 Baltimore	AL	79	126	31	6	0	1	(1	0)	40	20	8	19	0	34	2	7	1	0	1	.00	3	.246	.351	.317
7 ML YEARS		628	1370	337	61	2	14	(7	7)	444	181	135	170	1	232	9	38	6	16	12	.57	31	.246	.332	.324

Mike Redmond

Bats: Right **Throws:** Right **Pos:** C-37 **Ht:** 6'1" **Wt:** 185 **Born:** 5/5/71 **Age:** 28

Year Team	Lg	G	AB	H	2B	3B	HR	(Hm	Rd)	TB	R	RBI	TBB	IBB	SO	HBP	SH	SF	SB	CS	SB%	GDP	Avg	OBP	SLG
1993 Kane County	A	43	100	20	2	0	0	—	—	22	10	10	6	0	17	4	2	0	2	0	1.00	1	.200	.273	.220
1994 Kane County	A	92	306	83	10	0	1	—	—	96	39	24	26	0	31	9	6	2	3	4	.43	10	.271	.344	.314
Brevard Cty	A+	12	42	11	4	0	0	—	—	15	4	2	3	0	4	1	0	0	0	0	.00	1	.262	.326	.357
1995 Portland	AA	105	333	85	11	1	3	—	—	107	37	39	22	2	27	3	4	3	2	2	.50	9	.255	.305	.321
1996 Portland	AA	120	394	113	22	0	4	—	—	147	43	44	26	2	45	5	5	5	3	4	.43	12	.287	.335	.373
1997 Charlotte	AAA	22	61	13	5	1	1	—	—	23	8	2	1	1	10	3	2	0	0	1	.00	1	.213	.262	.377
Marlins	R	16	55	19	3	0	0	—	—	22	7	5	9	0	5	0	0	0	2	0	1.00	1	.345	.463	.400
Brevard Cty	A+	5	17	0	0	0	0	—	—	0	2	0	2	0	2	0	0	0	0	0	.00	2	.000	.105	.000
1998 Portland	AA	8	28	9	4	0	1	—	—	16	7	7	2	0	2	1	0	0	0	0	.00	2	.321	.406	.571
Charlotte	AAA	18	58	14	2	0	2	—	—	22	4	7	0	0	3	1	0	2	0	0	.00	3	.241	.246	.379
1998 Florida	NL	37	118	39	9	0	2	(1	1)	54	10	12	5	2	16	2	4	0	0	0	.00	6	.331	.368	.458

Jeff Reed

Bats: Left **Throws:** Right **Pos:** C-99; PH/PR-36 **Ht:** 6'2" **Wt:** 204 **Born:** 11/12/62 **Age:** 36

Year Team	Lg	G	AB	H	2B	3B	HR	(Hm	Rd)	TB	R	RBI	TBB	IBB	SO	HBP	SH	SF	SB	CS	SB%	GDP	Avg	OBP	SLG
1984 Minnesota	AL	18	21	3	3	0	0	(0	0)	6	3	1	2	0	6	0	1	0	0	0	.00	0	.143	.217	.286
1985 Minnesota	AL	7	10	2	0	0	0	(0	0)	2	2	0	0	0	3	0	0	0	0	0	.00	0	.200	.200	.200
1986 Minnesota	AL	68	165	39	6	1	2	(1	1)	53	13	9	16	0	19	1	3	0	1	0	1.00	2	.236	.308	.321
1987 Montreal	NL	75	207	44	11	0	1	(1	0)	58	15	21	12	1	20	1	4	4	0	1	.00	6	.213	.254	.280
1988 Mon-Cin	NL	92	265	60	9	2	1	(1	0)	76	20	16	28	1	41	0	1	1	1	0	1.00	5	.226	.299	.287
1989 Cincinnati	NL	102	287	64	11	0	3	(1	2)	84	16	23	34	5	46	2	3	4	0	0	.00	7	.223	.306	.293
1990 Cincinnati	NL	72	175	44	8	1	3	(2	1)	63	12	16	24	5	26	0	5	1	0	0	.00	4	.251	.340	.360
1991 Cincinnati	NL	91	270	72	15	2	3	(1	2)	100	20	31	23	3	38	1	1	5	0	1	.00	6	.267	.321	.370
1992 Cincinnati	NL	15	25	4	0	0	0	(0	0)	4	2	2	1	1	4	0	0	0	0	0	.00	1	.160	.192	.160
1993 San Francisco	NL	66	119	31	3	0	6	(5	1)	52	10	12	16	4	22	0	0	1	0	0	.00	2	.261	.346	.437
1994 San Francisco	NL	50	103	18	3	0	1	(0	1)	24	11	7	11	4	21	0	0	0	0	0	.00	3	.175	.254	.233
1995 San Francisco	NL	66	113	30	2	0	0	(0	0)	32	12	9	20	3	17	0	1	0	0	0	.00	1	.265	.376	.283
1996 Colorado	NL	116	341	97	20	1	8	(7	1)	143	34	37	43	8	65	2	6	3	2	2	.50	8	.284	.365	.419
1997 Colorado	NL	90	256	76	10	0	17	(9	8)	137	45	47	35	1	55	2	5	0	2	1	.67	8	.297	.386	.535
1998 Colorado	NL	113	259	75	17	1	9	(6	3)	121	43	39	37	4	57	1	3	3	0	0	.00	6	.290	.377	.467
1988 Montreal	NL	43	123	27	3	2	0	(0	0)	34	10	9	13	1	22	0	1	1	1	0	1.00	3	.220	.292	.276
Cincinnati	NL	49	142	33	6	0	1	(1	0)	42	10	7	15	0	19	0	0	0	0	0	.00	2	.232	.306	.296
15 ML YEARS		1041	2616	659	118	8	54	(34	20)	955	256	270	302	40	440	10	33	22	6	6	.50	62	.252	.329	.365

Rick Reed

Pitches: Right **Bats:** Right **Pos:** SP-31 **Ht:** 6'1" **Wt:** 195 **Born:** 8/16/65 **Age:** 33

Year Team	Lg	G	GS	CG	GF	IP	BFP	H	R	ER	HR	SH	SF	HB	TBB	IBB	SO	WP	Bk	W	L	Pct.	ShO	Sv-Op	Hld	ERA
1988 Pittsburgh	NL	2	2	0	0	12	47	10	4	4	1	2	0	0	2	0	6	0	0	1	0	1.000	0	0-0	0	3.00
1989 Pittsburgh	NL	15	7	0	2	54.2	232	62	35	34	5	2	3	2	11	3	34	0	3	1	4	.200	0	0-0	0	5.60
1990 Pittsburgh	NL	13	8	1	2	53.2	238	62	32	26	6	2	1	1	12	6	27	0	0	2	3	.400	1	1-1	1	4.36
1991 Pittsburgh	NL	1	1	0	0	4.1	21	8	5	5	1	0	0	0	1	0	2	0	0	0	0	.000	0	0-0	0	10.38
1992 Kansas City	AL	19	18	1	0	100.1	419	105	47	41	10	2	5	5	20	3	49	0	0	3	7	.300	0	0-0	0	3.68
1993 KC-Tex	AL	3	0	0	0	7.2	36	12	5	5	1	0	0	2	2	0	5	0	0	1	0	1.000	0	0-0	0	5.87

Year Team	Lg	G	GS	CG	GF	IP	BFP	H	R	ER	HR	SH	SF	HB	TBB	IBB	SO	WP	Bk	W	L	Pct.	ShO	Sv-Op	Hld	ERA
1994 Texas	AL	4	3	0	0	16.2	75	17	13	11	3	0	0	1	7	0	12	0	0	1	1	.500	0	0-0	0	5.94
1995 Cincinnati	NL	4	3	0	1	17	70	18	12	11	5	1	0	0	3	0	10	0	0	0	0	.000	0	0-0	0	5.82
1997 New York	NL	33	31	2	0	208.1	824	186	76	67	19	7	3	5	31	4	113	0	0	13	9	.591	0	0-0	0	2.89
1998 New York	NL	31	31	2	0	212.1	845	208	84	82	30	8	5	6	29	2	153	1	0	16	11	.593	1	0-0	0	3.48
1993 Kansas City	AL	1	0	0	0	3.2	18	6	4	4	0	0	0	1	1	0	3	0	0	0	0	.000	0	0-0	0	9.82
Texas	AL	2	0	0	0	4	18	6	1	1	0	1	0	0	1	0	2	0	0	1	0	1.000	0	0-0	0	2.25
10 ML YEARS		125	104	6	5	687	2807	688	314	286	81	24	17	22	118	18	411	1	3	38	35	.521	3	1-1	1	3.75

Steve Reed

Pitches: Right **Bats:** Right **Pos:** RP-70 **Ht:** 6'2" **Wt:** 212 **Born:** 3/11/66 **Age:** 33

Year Team	Lg	G	GS	CG	GF	IP	BFP	H	R	ER	HR	SH	SF	HB	TBB	IBB	SO	WP	Bk	W	L	Pct.	ShO	Sv-Op	Hld	ERA
1992 San Francisco	NL	18	0	0	2	15.2	63	13	5	4	2	0	0	1	3	0	11	0	0	1	0	1.000	0	0-0	1	2.30
1993 Colorado	NL	64	0	0	14	84.1	347	80	47	42	13	2	3	3	30	5	51	1	0	9	5	.643	0	3-6	9	4.48
1994 Colorado	NL	61	0	0	11	64	297	79	33	28	9	0	7	6	26	3	51	1	0	3	2	.600	0	3-10	14	3.94
1995 Colorado	NL	71	0	0	15	84	327	61	24	20	8	3	1	6	21	3	79	0	2	5	2	.714	0	3-6	11	2.14
1996 Colorado	NL	70	0	0	7	75	307	66	38	33	11	2	4	6	19	0	51	1	0	4	3	.571	0	0-6	22	3.96
1997 Colorado	NL	63	0	0	23	62.1	260	49	28	28	10	3	1	5	27	1	43	0	1	4	6	.400	0	6-13	10	4.04
1998 SF-Cle		70	0	0	19	80.1	322	56	29	28	8	2	0	5	27	5	73	0	0	4	3	.571	0	1-6	21	3.14
1998 San Francisco	NL	50	0	0	14	54.2	213	30	10	9	4	2	0	4	19	5	50	0	0	2	1	.667	0	1-5	13	1.48
Cleveland	AL	20	0	0	5	25.2	109	26	19	19	4	0	0	1	8	0	23	0	0	2	2	.500	0	0-1	8	6.66
7 ML YEARS		417	0	0	91	465.2	1923	404	204	183	61	12	16	27	153	17	359	3	2	30	21	.588	0	16-47	88	3.54

Pokey Reese

Bats: R **Throws:** R **Pos:** 3B-32; SS-18; PH/PR-10; 2B-3 **Ht:** 5'11" **Wt:** 180 **Born:** 6/10/73 **Age:** 26

Year Team	Lg	G	AB	H	2B	3B	HR	(Hm	Rd)	TB	R	RBI	TBB	IBB	SO	HBP	SH	SF	SB	CS	SB%	GDP	Avg	OBP	SLG
1991 Princeton	R+	62	231	55	8	3	3	—	—	78	30	27	23	0	44	0	0	2	10	8	.56	4	.238	.305	.338
1992 Chston-WV	A	106	380	102	19	3	6	—	—	145	50	53	24	0	75	5	4	7	19	8	.70	2	.268	.315	.382
1993 Chattanooga	AA	102	345	73	17	4	3	—	—	107	35	37	23	1	77	1	3	7	8	5	.62	2	.212	.258	.310
1994 Chattanooga	AA	134	484	130	23	4	12	—	—	197	77	49	43	1	75	7	6	1	21	4	.84	6	.269	.336	.407
1995 Indianapols	AAA	89	343	82	21	1	10	—	—	135	51	46	36	0	81	4	1	3	8	5	.62	3	.239	.316	.394
1996 Indianapols	AAA	79	280	65	16	0	1	—	—	84	26	23	21	0	46	5	4	3	5	2	.71	10	.232	.294	.300
1997 Indianapols	AAA	17	72	17	2	0	4	—	—	31	12	11	9	0	12	0	0	0	4	0	1.00	1	.236	.321	.431
1997 Cincinnati	NL	128	397	87	15	0	4	(3	1)	114	48	26	31	2	82	5	4	0	25	7	.78	1	.219	.284	.287
1998 Cincinnati	NL	59	133	34	2	2	1	(0	1)	43	20	16	14	1	28	0	2	2	3	2	.60	3	.256	.322	.323
2 ML YEARS		187	530	121	17	2	5	(3	2)	157	68	42	45	3	110	5	6	2	28	9	.76	4	.228	.294	.296

Bryan Rekar

Pitches: Right **Bats:** Right **Pos:** SP-15; RP-1 **Ht:** 6'3" **Wt:** 210 **Born:** 6/3/72 **Age:** 27

Year Team	Lg	G	GS	CG	GF	IP	BFP	H	R	ER	HR	SH	SF	HB	TBB	IBB	SO	WP	Bk	W	L	Pct.	ShO	Sv-Op	Hld	ERA
1998 St. Pete *	A+	4	4	0	0	13	45	6	2	1	0	0	0	0	2	0	15	1	0	0	0	.000	0	0- —	—	0.69
Durham *	AAA	3	3	0	0	11	44	10	4	4	3	0	0	0	2	0	9	0	0	0	1	.000	0	0- —	—	3.27
1995 Colorado	NL	15	14	1	0	85	375	95	51	47	11	7	4	3	24	2	60	0	3	4	6	.400	0	0-0	1	4.98
1996 Colorado	NL	14	11	0	0	58.1	289	87	61	58	11	3	3	5	26	1	25	4	0	2	4	.333	0	0-0	0	8.95
1997 Colorado	NL	2	2	0	0	9.1	46	11	7	6	3	1	0	0	6	0	4	0	0	1	0	1.000	0	0-0	0	5.79
1998 Tampa Bay	AL	16	15	1	1	86.2	369	95	56	48	16	1	8	2	21	0	55	1	0	2	8	.200	0	0-0	0	4.98
4 ML YEARS		47	42	2	1	239.1	1079	288	175	159	41	12	15	10	77	3	144	8	2	9	18	.333	0	0-1	1	5.98

Desi Relaford

Bats: Both **Throws:** Right **Pos:** SS-137; PH/PR-6 **Ht:** 5'8" **Wt:** 170 **Born:** 9/16/73 **Age:** 25

Year Team	Lg	G	AB	H	2B	3B	HR	(Hm	Rd)	TB	R	RBI	TBB	IBB	SO	HBP	SH	SF	SB	CS	SB%	GDP	Avg	OBP	SLG
1991 Mariners	R	46	163	43	7	3	0	—	—	56	36	18	22	1	24	1	1	5	15	3	.83	0	.264	.346	.344
1992 Peninsula	A+	130	445	96	18	1	3	—	—	125	53	34	39	1	88	1	4	6	27	7	.79	7	.216	.277	.281
1993 Jacksnville	AA	133	472	115	16	4	8	—	—	163	49	47	50	1	103	7	6	4	16	12	.57	4	.244	.323	.345
1994 Jacksnville	AA	37	143	29	7	3	3	—	—	51	24	11	22	0	28	0	2	2	10	1	.91	2	.203	.305	.357
Riverside	A+	99	374	116	27	5	5	—	—	168	95	59	78	6	78	4	3	6	27	6	.82	7	.310	.429	.449
1995 Port City	AA	90	352	101	11	2	7	—	—	137	51	27	41	2	58	2	2	0	25	9	.74	4	.287	.365	.389
Tacoma	AAA	30	113	27	5	1	2	—	—	40	20	7	13	2	24	0	0	2	6	0	1.00	2	.239	.313	.354
1996 Tacoma	AAA	93	317	65	12	0	4	—	—	89	27	32	23	0	58	1	4	3	10	6	.63	7	.205	.259	.281
Scranton-WB	AAA	21	85	20	4	1	1	—	—	29	12	11	8	0	19	1	1	1	7	1	.88	0	.235	.305	.341
1997 Scranton-WB	AAA	131	517	138	34	4	9	—	—	207	82	53	43	0	77	7	4	5	29	8	.78	12	.267	.329	.400
1996 Philadelphia	NL	15	40	7	2	0	0	(0	0)	9	2	1	9	0	9	0	1	0	1	0	1.00	1	.175	.233	.225
1997 Philadelphia	NL	15	38	7	1	2	0	(0	0)	12	3	6	5	0	6	0	1	0	3	0	1.00	0	.184	.279	.316
1998 Philadelphia	NL	142	494	121	25	3	5	(4	1)	167	45	41	33	4	87	3	10	6	9	5	.64	9	.245	.293	.338
3 ML YEARS		172	572	135	28	5	5	(4	1)	188	50	48	41	4	102	3	12	6	13	5	.72	10	.236	.288	.329

Mike Remlinger

Pitches: Left **Bats:** Left **Pos:** SP-28; RP-7   **Ht:** 6'1" **Wt:** 215 **Born:** 3/23/66 **Age:** 33

Year Team	Lg	G	GS	CG	GF	IP	BFP	H	R	ER	HR	SH	SF	HB	TBB	IBB	SO	WP	Bk	W	L	Pct.	ShO	Sv-Op	Hld	ERA
1991 San Francisco	NL	8	6	1	1	35	155	36	17	17	5	1	1	0	20	1	19	2	1	2	1	.667	1	0-0	0	4.37
1994 New York	NL	10	9	0	0	54.2	252	55	30	28	9	2	3	1	35	4	33	3	0	1	5	.167	0	0-0	1	4.61
1995 NYN-Cin	NL	7	0	0	4	6.2	34	9	6	5	1	1	0	0	5	0	7	0	0	0	0	.000	0	0-1	0	6.75
1996 Cincinnati	NL	19	4	0	2	27.1	125	24	17	17	4	3	1	3	19	2	19	2	2	0	0	.000	0	0-0	1	5.60
1997 Cincinnati	NL	69	12	2	10	124	525	100	61	57	11	6	4	7	60	6	145	12	2	8	8	.500	0	2-2	14	4.14
1998 Cincinnati	NL	35	28	1	0	164.1	727	164	96	88	23	12	7	5	87	1	144	11	1	8	15	.348	1	0-0	0	4.82
1995 New York	NL	5	0	0	4	5.2	27	7	5	4	1	0	0	0	2	0	6	0	0	0	1	.000	0	0-1	0	6.35
Cincinnati	NL	2	0	0	0	1	7	2	1	1	0	0	0	0	3	0	1	0	0	0	0	.000	0	0-0	0	9.00
6 ML YEARS		148	59	4	17	412	1818	388	227	212	53	25	16	16	226	14	367	30	6	19	31	.380	2	2-3	16	4.63

Edgar Renteria

Bats: Right **Throws:** Right **Pos:** SS-130; PH/PR-4   **Ht:** 6'1" **Wt:** 180 **Born:** 8/7/75 **Age:** 23

								BATTING											BASERUNNING				PERCENTAGES		
Year Team	Lg	G	AB	H	2B	3B	HR	(Hm	Rd)	TB	R	RBI	TBB	IBB	SO	HBP	SH	SF	SB	CS	SB%	GDP	Avg	OBP	SLG
1996 Florida	NL	106	431	133	18	3	5	(2	3)	172	68	31	33	0	68	2	2	3	16	2	.89	12	.309	.358	.399
1997 Florida	NL	154	617	171	21	3	4	(3	1)	210	90	52	45	1	108	4	19	6	32	15	.68	17	.277	.327	.340
1998 Florida	NL	133	517	146	18	2	3	(2	1)	177	79	31	48	1	78	4	9	2	41	22	.65	13	.282	.347	.342
3 ML YEARS		393	1565	450	57	8	12	(7	5)	559	237	114	126	2	254	10	30	11	89	39	.70	42	.288	.342	.357

Al Reyes

Pitches: Right **Bats:** Right **Pos:** RP-50   **Ht:** 6'1" **Wt:** 206 **Born:** 4/10/71 **Age:** 28

Year Team	Lg	G	GS	CG	GF	IP	BFP	H	R	ER	HR	SH	SF	HB	TBB	IBB	SO	WP	Bk	W	L	Pct.	ShO	Sv-Op	Hld	ERA
1998 Louisville *	AAA	3	2	0	0	4.1	20	5	5	4	1	0	1	0	2	0	5	0	0	1	0	.000	0	0- -	1	8.31
1995 Milwaukee	AL	27	0	0	13	33.1	138	19	9	9	3	1	2	3	18	2	29	0	0	1	1	.500	0	1-1	4	2.43
1996 Milwaukee	AL	5	0	0	2	5.2	27	8	5	5	1	0	0	0	2	0	2	2	0	1	0	1.000	0	0-0	0	7.94
1997 Milwaukee	AL	19	0	0	7	29.2	131	32	19	18	4	2	0	3	9	0	28	1	0	1	2	.333	0	1-1	1	5.46
1998 Milwaukee	NL	50	0	0	13	57	253	55	26	25	9	2	1	2	31	1	58	2	0	5	1	.833	0	0-1	10	3.95
4 ML YEARS		101	0	0	35	125.2	549	114	59	57	17	5	3	8	60	3	117	5	0	8	4	.667	0	2-3	15	4.08

Carlos Reyes

Pitches: Right **Bats:** Both **Pos:** RP-46   **Ht:** 6'1" **Wt:** 190 **Born:** 4/4/69 **Age:** 30

Year Team	Lg	G	GS	CG	GF	IP	BFP	H	R	ER	HR	SH	SF	HB	TBB	IBB	SO	WP	Bk	W	L	Pct.	ShO	Sv-Op	Hld	ERA
1998 Las Vegas *	AAA	1	0	0	0	1.2	6	1	0	0	0	0	0	0	0	0	2	0	0	0	0	.000	0	0- -	0	0.00
1994 Oakland	AL	27	9	0	8	78	344	71	38	36	10	2	3	2	44	1	57	3	0	0	3	.000	0	1-1	0	4.15
1995 Oakland	AL	40	1	0	19	69	306	71	43	39	10	4	0	5	28	4	48	5	0	4	6	.400	0	0-1	4	5.09
1996 Oakland	AL	46	10	0	14	122.1	550	134	71	65	19	2	8	2	61	8	78	2	1	7	10	.412	0	0-0	1	4.78
1997 Oakland	AL	37	6	0	9	77.1	352	101	52	50	13	3	2	2	25	2	43	2	1	3	4	.429	0	0-1	1	5.82
1998 SD-Bos		46	0	0	18	66	267	58	26	26	6	2	2	3	20	2	47	3	1	3	3	.500	0	1-2	3	3.55
1998 San Diego	NL	22	0	0	8	27.2	109	23	11	11	4	2	1	2	6	0	24	0	1	2	2	.500	0	1-2	1	3.58
Boston	AL	24	0	0	10	38.1	158	35	15	15	2	0	1	1	14	2	23	3	0	1	1	.500	0	0-0	2	3.52
5 ML YEARS		196	26	0	68	412.2	1819	435	230	216	58	13	15	14	178	17	273	15	3	17	26	.395	0	2-5	9	4.71

Dennis Reyes

Pitches: Left **Bats:** Right **Pos:** SP-10; RP-9   **Ht:** 6'3" **Wt:** 246 **Born:** 4/19/77 **Age:** 22

Year Team	Lg	G	GS	CG	GF	IP	BFP	H	R	ER	HR	SH	SF	HB	TBB	IBB	SO	WP	Bk	W	L	Pct.	ShO	Sv-Op	Hld	ERA
1994 Vero Beach	A+	9	9	0	0	41.2	199	58	37	31	6	1	1	0	18	0	25	1	1	2	4	.333	0	0- -	—	6.70
Great Falls	R+	14	9	0	2	66.2	294	71	37	28	0	0	0	2	25	0	70	10	1	7	1	.875	0	0- -	—	3.78
1995 Vero Beach	A+	3	2	0	0	10	43	8	2	2	0	1	0	0	6	0	9	0	1	1	0	1.000	0	0- -	—	1.80
1996 San Berndno	A+	29	28	0	0	166	731	166	106	77	11	4	2	6	77	0	176	9	3	11	12	.478	0	0- -	—	4.17
1997 San Antonio	AA	12	12	1	0	80.1	335	79	33	27	6	3	1	1	28	1	66	2	2	8	1	.889	0	0- -	—	3.02
Albuquerque	AAA	10	10	1	0	57.1	271	70	40	36	4	1	1	1	33	0	45	5	0	6	3	.667	0	0- -	—	5.65
1998 Albuquerque	AAA	7	7	1	0	43.2	176	31	13	7	5	0	0	1	18	0	58	1	0	1	4	.200	1	0- -	—	1.44
Indianapolis	AAA	4	4	0	0	24	100	20	10	8	1	0	0	0	14	0	27	5	0	2	0	1.000	0	0- -	—	3.00
1997 Los Angeles	NL	14	5	0	0	47	207	51	21	20	4	5	1	1	18	3	36	2	1	2	3	.400	0	0-0	0	3.83
1998 LA-Cin	NL	19	10	0	4	67.1	300	62	36	34	3	7	2	1	47	5	77	6	1	3	5	.375	0	0-0	0	4.54
1998 Los Angeles	NL	11	3	0	0	28.2	130	27	17	15	1	3	1	0	20	4	33	1	1	0	4	.000	0	0-0	0	4.71
Cincinnati	NL	8	7	0	0	38.2	170	35	19	19	2	4	1	1	27	1	44	5	0	3	1	.750	0	0-0	0	4.42
2 ML YEARS		33	15	0	4	114.1	507	113	57	54	7	12	3	2	65	8	113	8	2	5	8	.385	0	0-0	0	4.25

Shane Reynolds

Pitches: Right **Bats:** Right **Pos:** SP-35   **Ht:** 6'3" **Wt:** 210 **Born:** 3/26/68 **Age:** 31

Year Team	Lg	G	GS	CG	GF	IP	BFP	H	R	ER	HR	SH	SF	HB	TBB	IBB	SO	WP	Bk	W	L	Pct.	ShO	Sv-Op	Hld	ERA
1992 Houston	NL	8	5	0	0	25.1	122	42	22	20	6	1	0	6	6	1	10	1	1	1	3	.250	0	0-0	0	7.11
1993 Houston	NL	5	1	0	0	11	49	11	4	1	2	0	0	0	6	1	10	0	0	0	0	.000	0	0-0	0	0.82

Year Team	Lg	G	GS	CG	GF	IP	BFP	H	R	ER	HR	SH	SF	HB	TBB	IBB	SO	WP	Bk	W	L	Pct.	ShO	Sv-Op	Hld	ERA
1994 Houston	NL	33	14	1	5	124	517	128	46	42	10	4	0	6	21	3	110	3	2	8	5	.615	1	0-0	5	3.05
1995 Houston	NL	30	30	3	0	189.1	792	196	87	73	15	8	0	2	37	6	175	7	1	10	11	.476	2	0-0	0	3.47
1996 Houston	NL	35	35	4	0	239	981	227	103	97	20	11	7	8	44	3	204	5	1	16	10	.615	1	0-0	0	3.65
1997 Houston	NL	30	30	2	0	181	773	189	92	85	19	9	5	3	47	5	152	5	2	9	10	.474	0	0-0	0	4.23
1998 Houston	NL	35	35	3	0	233.1	986	257	99	91	25	5	7	2	53	2	209	5	0	19	8	.704	1	0-0	0	3.51
7 ML YEARS		176	150	13	5	1003	4220	1050	453	409	91	43	20	21	214	21	870	26	7	63	47	.573	5	0-0	5	3.67

Armando Reynoso

Pitches: Right **Bats:** Right **Pos:** SP-11   **Ht:** 6'0" **Wt:** 204 **Born:** 5/1/66 **Age:** 33

Year Team	Lg	G	GS	CG	GF	IP	BFP	H	R	ER	HR	SH	SF	HB	TBB	IBB	SO	WP	Bk	W	L	Pct.	ShO	Sv-Op	Hld	ERA
1998 St. Lucie *	A+	4	4	0	0	12	51	14	6	5	2	0	0	0	1	0	6	1	0	0	1	.000	0	0--	—	3.75
Norfolk *	AAA	2	2	0	0	9.1	45	14	11	11	1	0	1	0	4	1	8	1	0	0	2	.000	0	0--	—	10.61
1991 Atlanta	NL	6	5	0	1	23.1	103	26	18	16	4	3	0	3	10	1	10	2	0	2	1	.667	0	0-0	0	6.17
1992 Atlanta	NL	3	1	0	1	7.2	32	11	4	4	2	1	0	1	2	1	2	0	0	1	0	1.000	0	1-1	0	4.70
1993 Colorado	NL	30	30	4	0	189	830	206	101	84	22	5	8	9	63	7	117	7	6	12	11	.522	0	0-0	0	4.00
1994 Colorado	NL	9	9	1	0	52.1	226	54	30	28	5	2	2	6	22	1	25	2	2	3	4	.429	0	0-0	0	4.82
1995 Colorado	NL	20	18	0	0	93	418	116	61	55	12	8	2	5	36	3	40	2	0	7	7	.500	0	0-0	0	5.32
1996 Colorado	NL	30	30	0	0	168.2	733	195	97	93	27	3	3	9	49	0	88	4	3	8	9	.471	0	0-0	0	4.96
1997 New York	NL	16	16	1	0	91.1	388	95	47	46	7	3	5	6	29	4	47	4	1	6	3	.667	1	0-0	0	4.53
1998 New York	NL	11	11	0	0	68.1	292	64	31	29	4	4	1	5	32	3	40	2	2	7	3	.700	0	0-0	0	3.82
8 ML YEARS		125	120	6	2	693.2	3022	767	389	355	83	29	21	44	243	20	369	23	14	46	38	.548	1	1-1	0	4.61

Arthur Rhodes

Pitches: Left **Bats:** Left **Pos:** RP-45   **Ht:** 6'2" **Wt:** 205 **Born:** 10/24/69 **Age:** 29

Year Team	Lg	G	GS	CG	GF	IP	BFP	H	R	ER	HR	SH	SF	HB	TBB	IBB	SO	WP	Bk	W	L	Pct.	ShO	Sv-Op	Hld	ERA
1998 Rochester *	AAA	1	1	0	0	2	10	3	1	1	0	0	0	0	1	0	1	0	0	0	0	.000	0	0--	—	4.50
1991 Baltimore	AL	8	8	0	0	36	174	47	34	32	4	1	3	0	23	0	23	2	0	0	3	.000	0	0-0	0	8.00
1992 Baltimore	AL	15	15	2	0	94.1	394	87	39	38	6	5	1	1	38	2	77	2	1	7	5	.583	1	0-0	0	3.63
1993 Baltimore	AL	17	17	0	0	85.2	387	91	62	62	16	2	3	1	49	1	49	2	0	5	6	.455	0	0-0	0	6.51
1994 Baltimore	AL	10	10	3	0	52.2	238	51	34	34	8	2	3	2	30	1	47	3	0	3	5	.375	2	0-0	0	5.81
1995 Baltimore	AL	19	9	0	3	75.1	336	68	53	52	13	4	0	6	48	1	77	3	1	2	5	.286	0	0-1	0	6.21
1996 Baltimore	AL	28	2	0	5	53	224	48	28	24	6	1	1	0	23	3	62	0	0	9	1	.900	0	1-1	2	4.08
1997 Baltimore	AL	53	0	0	6	95.1	378	75	32	32	9	0	4	4	26	5	102	2	0	10	3	.769	0	1-2	9	3.02
1998 Baltimore	AL	45	0	0	10	77	321	65	30	30	8	2	5	1	34	2	83	1	1	4	4	.500	0	4-8	10	3.51
8 ML YEARS		195	61	5	24	569.1	2452	532	313	304	70	17	20	9	271	15	520	15	3	40	32	.556	3	6-12	21	4.81

Ricardo Rincon

Pitches: Left **Bats:** Left **Pos:** RP-60   **Ht:** 5'10" **Wt:** 187 **Born:** 4/13/70 **Age:** 29

Year Team	Lg	G	GS	CG	GF	IP	BFP	H	R	ER	HR	SH	SF	HB	TBB	IBB	SO	WP	Bk	W	L	Pct.	ShO	Sv-Op	Hld	ERA
1998 Carolina	AA	2	0	0	2	3	16	5	2	1	1	0			2	0	1	0	0	0	0	.000	0	0--	—	6.00
Nashville	AAA	1	0	0	0	1	3	0	0	0	0	0	0	0	0	0	1	0	0	0	0	.000	0	0--	—	0.00
1997 Pittsburgh	NL	62	0	0	23	60	254	51	26	23	5	5	1	2	24	6	71	2	3	4	8	.333	0	4-6	18	3.45
1998 Pittsburgh	NL	60	0	0	27	65	272	50	31	21	6	1	2	0	29	2	64	2	0	0	2	.000	0	14-17	11	2.91
2 ML YEARS		122	0	0	50	125	526	101	57	44	11	6	3	2	53	8	135	4	3	4	10	.286	0	18-23	29	3.17

Armando Rios

Bats: Left **Throws:** Left **Pos:** PH/PR-8; LF-2; RF-2; CF-1   **Ht:** 5'9" **Wt:** 185 **Born:** 9/13/71 **Age:** 27

Year Team	Lg	G	AB	H	2B	3B	HR	(Hm	Rd)	TB	R	RBI	TBB	IBB	SO	HBP	SH	SF	SB	CS	SB%	GDP	Avg	OBP	SLG
1994 Clinton	A	119	407	120	23	4	8	—	—	175	67	60	59	2	69	4	1	7	16	12	.57	7	.295	.384	.430
1995 San Jose	A+	128	488	143	34	3	8	—	—	207	76	75	74	3	75	1	4	7	51	10	.84	8	.293	.382	.424
1996 Shreveport	AA	92	329	93	22	2	12	—	—	155	62	49	44	3	42	1	3	4	9	9	.50	2	.283	.365	.471
1997 Shreveport	AA	127	461	133	30	6	14	—	—	217	86	79	63	1	85	0	4	6	17	7	.71	11	.289	.370	.471
1998 Fresno	AAA	125	445	134	23	1	26	—	—	237	85	103	55	4	73	3	4	5	17	5	.77	9	.301	.378	.533
1998 San Francisco	NL	12	7	4	0	0	2	(0	2)	10	3	3	3	0	2	0	0	0	0	0	.00	0	.571	.700	1.429

Danny Rios

Pitches: Right **Bats:** Right **Pos:** RP-5   **Ht:** 6'2" **Wt:** 208 **Born:** 11/11/72 **Age:** 26

Year Team	Lg	G	GS	CG	GF	IP	BFP	H	R	ER	HR	SH	SF	HB	TBB	IBB	SO	WP	Bk	W	L	Pct.	ShO	Sv-Op	Hld	ERA
1993 Yankees	R	24	0	0	17	38.1	170	34	18	15	0	2	1	5	16	0	29	9	3	2	1	.667	0	6--	—	3.52
1994 Greensboro	A	37	0	0	34	41.1	164	32	4	4	1	2	0	3	13	1	36	3	0	3	2	.600	0	17--	—	0.87
Tampa	A+	9	0	0	8	10.1	41	6	2	0	0	0	1	1	4	0	11	0	0	0	0	.000	0	2--	—	0.00
1995 Tampa	A+	57	0	0	52	67.1	296	67	24	15	1	5	2	8	20	4	72	2	0	4	4	.500	0	24--	—	2.00
1996 Norwich	AA	38	0	0	29	43	183	34	14	10	0	2	0	3	21	1	38	3	2	3	1	.750	0	17--	—	2.09
Columbus	AAA	24	0	0	6	27.2	111	22	7	6	1	0	2	4	6	0	22	1	0	4	1	.800	0	0--	—	1.95
1997 Columbus	AAA	58	0	0	14	84.2	351	73	37	29	8	3	4	1	31	1	53	5	0	7	4	.636	0	3--	—	3.08
1998 Omaha	AAA	25	18	2	4	123	563	159	90	77	14	2	4	6	41	0	51	6	0	6	7	.462	0	1--	—	5.63
1997 New York	AL	2	0	0	0	2.1	19	9	5	5	3	0	0	1	2	0	1	0	0	0	0	.000	0	0-0	0	19.29

		HOW MUCH HE PITCHED						WHAT HE GAVE UP												THE RESULTS					
Year Team	Lg	G	GS	CG	GF	IP	BFP	H	R	ER	HR	SH	SF	HB	TBB	IBB	SO	WP	Bk	W	L	Pct.	ShO	Sv-Op	Hld	ERA
1998 Kansas City	AL	5	0	0	1	7.1	38	9	9	5	1	0	1	1	6	0	6	1	0	0	1	.000	0	0-0	0	6.14
2 ML YEARS		7	0	0	1	9.2	57	18	14	10	4	0	1	2	8	0	7	1	0	0	1	.000	0	0-0	0	9.31

Billy Ripken

Bats: R **Throws:** R **Pos:** SS-21; 1B-2; 2B-2; 3B-2; DH-1   **Ht:** 6'1" **Wt:** 190 **Born:** 12/16/64 **Age:** 34

							BATTING											BASERUNNING				PERCENTAGES		
Year Team	Lg	G	AB	H	2B	3B	HR	(Hm	Rd)	TB	R	RBI	TBB	IBB	SO	HBP	SH	SF	SB	CS	SB%	GDP	Avg	OBP	SLG
1998 Toledo *	AAA	5	19	6	1	0	0	—	—	7	3	1	2	0	0	0	0	0	0	0	.00	2	.316	.381	.368
1987 Baltimore	AL	58	234	72	9	0	2	(0	2)	87	27	20	21	0	23	0	1	1	4	1	.80	3	.308	.363	.372
1988 Baltimore	AL	150	512	106	18	1	2	(0	2)	132	52	34	33	0	63	5	6	3	8	2	.80	14	.207	.260	.258
1989 Baltimore	AL	115	318	76	11	2	2	(0	2)	97	31	26	22	0	53	0	19	5	1	2	.33	12	.239	.284	.305
1990 Baltimore	AL	129	406	118	28	1	3	(2	1)	157	48	38	28	2	43	4	17	1	5	2	.71	7	.291	.342	.387
1991 Baltimore	AL	104	287	62	11	1	0	(0	0)	75	24	14	15	0	31	0	11	2	0	1	.00	14	.216	.253	.261
1992 Baltimore	AL	111	330	76	15	0	4	(3	1)	103	35	36	18	1	26	3	10	2	2	3	.40	10	.230	.275	.312
1993 Texas	AL	50	132	25	4	0	0	(0	0)	29	12	11	11	0	19	4	5	1	0	2	.00	6	.189	.270	.220
1994 Texas	AL	32	81	25	5	0	0	(0	0)	30	9	6	3	0	11	0	1	0	2	0	1.00	5	.309	.333	.370
1995 Cleveland	AL	8	17	7	0	0	2	(1	1)	13	4	3	0	0	3	0	0	0	0	0	.00	0	.412	.412	.765
1996 Baltimore	AL	57	135	31	8	0	2	(1	1)	45	19	12	9	0	18	1	1	1	0	0	.00	4	.230	.281	.333
1997 Texas	AL	71	203	56	9	1	3	(1	2)	76	18	24	9	0	32	0	1	5	0	1	.00	7	.276	.300	.374
1998 Detroit	AL	27	74	20	3	0	0	(0	0)	23	8	5	5	0	10	1	0	1	3	2	.60	2	.270	.321	.311
12 ML YEARS		912	2729	674	121	6	20	(8	12)	867	287	229	174	3	332	18	72	22	25	16	.61	81	.247	.294	.318

Cal Ripken

Bats: Right **Throws:** Right **Pos:** 3B-161   **Ht:** 6'4" **Wt:** 220 **Born:** 8/24/60 **Age:** 38

							BATTING											BASERUNNING				PERCENTAGES		
Year Team	Lg	G	AB	H	2B	3B	HR	(Hm	Rd)	TB	R	RBI	TBB	IBB	SO	HBP	SH	SF	SB	CS	SB%	GDP	Avg	OBP	SLG
1981 Baltimore	AL	23	39	5	0	0	0	(0	0)	5	1	0	1	0	8	0	0	0	0	0	.00	4	.128	.150	.128
1982 Baltimore	AL	160	598	158	32	5	28	(11	17)	284	90	93	46	3	95	3	2	6	3	3	.50	16	.264	.317	.475
1983 Baltimore	AL	162	663	211	47	2	27	(12	15)	343	121	102	58	0	97	0	0	5	0	4	.00	24	.318	.371	.517
1984 Baltimore	AL	162	641	195	37	7	27	(16	11)	327	103	86	71	1	89	2	0	2	2	1	.67	16	.304	.374	.510
1985 Baltimore	AL	161	642	181	32	5	26	(15	11)	301	116	110	67	1	68	1	0	8	2	3	.40	32	.282	.347	.469
1986 Baltimore	AL	162	627	177	35	1	25	(10	15)	289	98	81	70	5	60	4	0	6	4	2	.67	19	.282	.355	.461
1987 Baltimore	AL	162	624	157	28	3	27	(17	10)	272	97	98	81	0	77	1	0	11	3	5	.38	19	.252	.333	.436
1988 Baltimore	AL	161	575	152	25	1	23	(11	12)	248	87	81	102	7	69	2	0	10	2	2	.50	10	.264	.372	.431
1989 Baltimore	AL	162	646	166	30	0	21	(13	8)	259	80	93	57	5	72	3	0	6	3	2	.60	22	.257	.317	.401
1990 Baltimore	AL	161	600	150	28	4	21	(8	13)	249	78	84	82	18	66	5	1	7	3	1	.75	25	.250	.341	.415
1991 Baltimore	AL	162	650	210	46	5	34	(16	18)	368	99	114	53	15	46	5	0	9	6	1	.86	19	.323	.374	.566
1992 Baltimore	AL	162	637	160	29	1	14	(5	9)	233	73	72	64	14	50	7	0	7	4	3	.57	13	.251	.323	.366
1993 Baltimore	AL	162	641	165	26	3	24	(14	10)	269	87	90	65	19	58	6	0	6	1	4	.20	17	.257	.329	.420
1994 Baltimore	AL	112	444	140	19	3	13	(5	8)	204	71	75	32	3	41	4	0	4	1	0	1.00	17	.315	.364	.459
1995 Baltimore	AL	144	550	144	33	2	17	(10	7)	232	71	88	52	6	59	2	1	8	0	1	.00	15	.262	.324	.422
1996 Baltimore	AL	163	640	178	40	1	26	(10	16)	298	94	102	59	3	78	4	0	4	1	2	.33	28	.278	.341	.466
1997 Baltimore	AL	162	615	166	30	0	17	(10	7)	247	79	84	56	3	73	5	0	10	1	0	1.00	19	.270	.331	.402
1998 Baltimore	AL	161	601	163	27	1	14	(8	6)	234	65	61	51	0	68	4	1	2	0	2	.00	9	.271	.331	.389
18 ML YEARS		2704	10433	2878	544	44	384	(191	193)	4662	1510	1514	1067	103	1174	58	5	111	36	36	.50	311	.276	.343	.447

Bill Risley

Pitches: Right **Bats:** Right **Pos:** RP-44   **Ht:** 6'2" **Wt:** 215 **Born:** 5/29/67 **Age:** 32

				HOW MUCH HE PITCHED						WHAT HE GAVE UP									THE RESULTS					
Year Team	Lg	G	GS	CG	GF	IP	BFP	H	R	ER	HR	SH	SF	HB	TBB	IBB	SO	WP	Bk	W	L	Pct.	ShO	Sv-Op	Hld	ERA
1992 Montreal	NL	1	1	0	0	5	19	4	1	1	0	1	0	0	1	0	2	0	0	1	0	1.000	0	0-0	0	1.80
1993 Montreal	NL	2	0	0	1	3	14	2	3	2	1	1	0	1	2	0	2	0	0	0	0	.000	0	0-0	0	6.00
1994 Seattle	AL	37	0	0	7	52.1	203	31	20	20	7	0	2	0	19	4	61	2	0	9	6	.600	0	0-2	5	3.44
1995 Seattle	AL	45	0	0	5	60.1	249	55	21	21	7	2	3	1	18	1	65	2	0	2	1	.667	0	1-7	13	3.13
1996 Toronto	AL	25	0	0	11	41.2	177	33	20	18	7	1	2	0	25	0	29	1	0	0	1	.000	0	0-2	4	3.89
1997 Toronto	AL	3	0	0	1	4.1	18	3	4	4	2	0	0	0	2	0	2	0	0	0	1	.000	0	0-1	0	8.31
1998 Toronto	AL	44	0	0	18	54.2	245	52	37	32	7	3	3	4	34	4	42	3	1	3	4	.429	0	0-0	3	5.27
7 ML YEARS		157	1	0	43	221.1	925	180	106	98	31	8	10	6	101	9	203	8	1	15	13	.536	0	1-12	25	3.98

Todd Ritchie

Pitches: Right **Bats:** Right **Pos:** RP-15   **Ht:** 6'3" **Wt:** 219 **Born:** 11/7/71 **Age:** 27

				HOW MUCH HE PITCHED						WHAT HE GAVE UP									THE RESULTS					
Year Team	Lg	G	GS	CG	GF	IP	BFP	H	R	ER	HR	SH	SF	HB	TBB	IBB	SO	WP	Bk	W	L	Pct.	ShO	Sv-Op	Hld	ERA
1990 Elizabethtn	R+	11	11	1	0	65	261	45	24	14	5	2	2	6	24	0	49	2	3	5	2	.714	0	0--	—	1.94
1991 Kenosha	A	21	21	0	0	116.2	498	113	53	46	3	4	1	7	50	0	101	10	1	7	6	.538	0	0--	—	3.55
1992 Visalia	A+	28	28	3	0	172.2	763	193	113	97	13	6	6	7	65	2	129	16	1	11	9	.550	1	0--	—	5.06
1993 Nashville	AA	12	10	0	0	46.2	194	46	21	19	2	1	1	0	15	0	41	5	1	3	2	.600	0	0--	—	3.66
1994 Nashville	AA	4	4	0	0	17	74	24	10	8	1	1	0	0	7	0	9	2	0	0	2	.000	0	0--	—	4.24
1995 Hardware City	AA	24	21	0	0	113	515	135	78	72	12	4	5	6	54	0	60	8	0	4	9	.308	0	0--	—	5.73
1996 Hardware City	AA	29	10	0	14	82.2	376	101	55	50	6	3	4	3	30	1	53	4	0	3	7	.300	0	4--	—	5.44
Salt Lake	AAA	16	0	0	4	24.2	113	27	15	15	5	2	1	1	11	0	19	4	0	1	4	.000	0	4--	—	5.47
1998 Salt Lake	AAA	36	0	0	18	60.2	271	55	38	28	5	2	4	4	31	3	62	2	0	1	3	.250	0	4--	—	4.15
1997 Minnesota	AL	42	0	0	19	74.2	331	87	41	38	11	0	1	2	28	0	44	11	0	2	3	.400	0	0-2	3	4.58
1998 Minnesota	AL	15	0	0	7	24	113	30	17	15	1	0	0	0	9	0	21	3	0	0	0	.000	0	0-0	0	5.63

Year Team	Lg	G	GS	CG	GF	IP	BFP	H	R	ER	HR	SH	SF	HB	TBB	IBB	SO	WP	Bk	W	L	Pct.	ShO	Sv-Op	Hld	ERA
		HOW MUCH HE PITCHED						WHAT HE GAVE UP												THE RESULTS						
2 ML YEARS		57	0	0	26	98.2	444	117	58	53	12	0	1	2	37	0	65	14	0	2	3	.400	0	0-2	3	4.83

Kevin Ritz

Pitches: Right **Bats:** Right **Pos:** SP-2 **Ht:** 6'4" **Wt:** 226 **Born:** 6/8/65 **Age:** 34

Year Team	Lg	G	GS	CG	GF	IP	BFP	H	R	ER	HR	SH	SF	HB	TBB	IBB	SO	WP	Bk	W	L	Pct.	ShO	Sv-Op	Hld	ERA
		HOW MUCH HE PITCHED						WHAT HE GAVE UP												THE RESULTS						
1998 New Haven *	AA	3	3	1	0	17	65	17	7	7	3	0	1	1	3	0	14	0	0	1	2	.333	0	0--	—	3.71
Colo Sprngs *	AAA	4	4	0	0	17.1	90	25	23	16	2	2	3	1	9	0	7	0	0	0	2	.000	0	0--	—	8.31
1989 Detroit	AL	12	12	1	0	74	334	75	41	36	2	1	5	1	44	5	56	6	0	4	6	.400	0	0-0	0	4.38
1990 Detroit	AL	4	4	0	0	7.1	52	14	12	9	0	3	0	0	14	2	3	3	0	0	4	.000	0	0-0	0	11.05
1991 Detroit	AL	11	5	0	3	15.1	86	17	22	20	1	1	2	2	22	1	9	0	0	0	3	.000	0	0-1	0	11.74
1992 Detroit	AL	23	11	0	4	80.1	368	88	52	50	4	1	4	3	44	4	57	7	1	2	5	.286	0	0-0	0	5.60
1994 Colorado	NL	15	15	0	0	73.2	335	88	49	46	5	4	2	4	35	4	53	6	1	5	6	.455	0	0-0	0	5.62
1995 Colorado	NL	31	28	0	3	173.1	743	171	91	81	16	8	5	6	65	3	120	6	0	11	11	.500	0	2-2	0	4.21
1996 Colorado	NL	35	35	2	0	213	966	236	**135**	**125**	24	8	4	12	105	3	105	10	1	17	11	.607	0	0-0	0	5.28
1997 Colorado	NL	18	18	1	0	107.1	486	122	72	70	16	4	5	1	46	3	56	7	0	6	8	.429	0	0-0	0	5.87
1998 Colorado	NL	2	2	0	0	9	46	17	11	11	1	0	0	1	2	0	3	1	0	0	2	.000	0	0-0	0	11.00
9 ML YEARS		151	130	4	10	753.1	3416	848	485	448	69	30	27	30	377	25	462	46	3	45	56	.446	0	2-3	0	5.35

Luis Rivera

Bats: R **Throws:** R **Pos:** SS-30; 2B-6; 3B-6; PH/PR-4 **Ht:** 5'10" **Wt:** 175 **Born:** 1/3/64 **Age:** 35

Year Team	Lg	G	AB	H	2B	3B	HR	(Hm	Rd)	TB	R	RBI	TBB	IBB	SO	HBP	SH	SF	SB	CS	SB%	GDP	Avg	OBP	SLG
		BATTING																	BASERUNNING				PERCENTAGES		
1998 New Orleans *	AAA	33	82	19	2	1	1	—	—	26	17	7	9	0	8	0	1	0	2	1	.67	2	.232	.308	.317
1986 Montreal	NL	55	166	34	11	1	0	(0	0)	47	20	13	17	0	33	2	1	1	1	1	.50	1	.205	.285	.283
1987 Montreal	NL	18	32	5	2	0	0	(0	0)	7	0	1	1	0	8	0	0	0	0	0	.00	0	.156	.182	.219
1988 Montreal	NL	123	371	83	17	3	4	(2	2)	118	35	30	24	4	69	1	3	3	3	4	.43	9	.224	.271	.318
1989 Boston	AL	93	323	83	17	1	5	(4	1)	117	35	29	20	1	60	1	4	1	2	3	.40	2	.257	.301	.362
1990 Boston	AL	118	346	78	20	0	7	(4	3)	119	38	45	25	0	58	1	1	2	4	3	.57	10	.225	.279	.344
1991 Boston	AL	129	414	107	22	3	8	(4	4)	159	64	40	35	0	86	3	12	4	4	4	.50	10	.258	.318	.384
1992 Boston	AL	102	288	62	11	1	0	(0	0)	75	17	29	26	0	56	3	5	4	4	3	.57	5	.215	.287	.260
1993 Boston	AL	62	130	27	8	1	1	(1	0)	40	13	7	11	0	36	1	2	1	1	2	.33	2	.208	.273	.308
1994 New York	NL	32	43	12	2	1	3	(2	1)	25	11	5	4	0	14	2	0	0	0	1	.00	1	.279	.367	.581
1997 Houston	NL	7	13	3	0	1	0	(0	0)	5	2	3	1	0	6	0	1	0	0	0	.00	0	.231	.286	.385
1998 Kansas City	AL	42	89	22	4	0	0	(0	0)	26	14	7	7	0	17	0	2	0	1	1	.50	1	.247	.302	.292
11 ML YEARS		781	2215	516	114	12	28	(17	11)	738	249	209	171	5	443	14	42	11	20	22	.48	46	.233	.291	.333

Mariano Rivera

Pitches: Right **Bats:** Right **Pos:** RP-54 **Ht:** 6'2" **Wt:** 168 **Born:** 11/29/69 **Age:** 29

Year Team	Lg	G	GS	CG	GF	IP	BFP	H	R	ER	HR	SH	SF	HB	TBB	IBB	SO	WP	Bk	W	L	Pct.	ShO	Sv-Op	Hld	ERA
		HOW MUCH HE PITCHED						WHAT HE GAVE UP												THE RESULTS						
1995 New York	AL	19	10	0	2	67	301	71	43	41	11	0	2	2	30	0	51	0	1	5	3	.625	0	0-1	0	5.51
1996 New York	AL	61	0	0	14	107.2	425	73	25	25	1	2	1	2	34	3	130	1	0	8	3	.727	0	5-8	27	2.09
1997 New York	AL	66	0	0	56	71.2	301	65	17	15	5	3	4	0	20	6	68	2	0	6	4	.600	0	43-**52**	0	1.88
1998 New York	AL	54	0	0	49	61.1	246	48	13	13	3	2	3	1	17	1	36	0	0	3	0	1.000	0	36-41	0	1.91
4 ML YEARS		200	10	0	121	307.2	1273	257	98	94	20	7	10	5	101	10	285	3	1	22	10	.688	0	84-102	27	2.75

Ruben Rivera

Bats: R **Throws:** R **Pos:** RF-73; PH/PR-27; LF-13; CF-13 **Ht:** 6'3" **Wt:** 200 **Born:** 11/14/73 **Age:** 25

Year Team	Lg	G	AB	H	2B	3B	HR	(Hm	Rd)	TB	R	RBI	TBB	IBB	SO	HBP	SH	SF	SB	CS	SB%	GDP	Avg	OBP	SLG
		BATTING																	BASERUNNING				PERCENTAGES		
1992 Yankees	R	53	194	53	10	3	1	—	—	72	37	20	42	0	49	6	2	0	21	6	.78	2	.273	.417	.371
1993 Oneonta	A-	55	199	55	7	6	13	—	—	113	45	47	32	1	66	5	1	3	11	5	.69	2	.276	.385	.568
1994 Greensboro	A	105	400	115	24	3	28	—	—	229	83	81	47	1	125	8	0	2	36	5	.88	6	.288	.372	.573
Tampa	A+	34	134	35	4	3	5	—	—	60	18	20	8	0	38	1	0	0	12	5	.71	7	.261	.308	.448
1995 Norwich	AA	71	256	75	16	8	9	—	—	134	49	39	37	2	77	11	0	2	16	8	.67	4	.293	.402	.523
Columbus	AAA	48	174	47	8	2	15	—	—	104	37	35	26	0	62	3	0	1	8	4	.67	5	.270	.373	.598
1996 Columbus	AAA	101	362	85	20	4	10	—	—	143	59	46	40	4	96	8	1	1	15	10	.60	4	.235	.324	.395
1997 Rancho Cuca	A+	6	23	4	1	0	1	—	—	8	6	3	3	0	9	0	0	1	1	0	1.00	1	.174	.259	.348
Las Vegas	AAA	12	48	12	5	1	1	—	—	22	6	6	1	0	20	1	0	1	1	0	1.00	0	.250	.280	.458
1998 Las Vegas	AAA	30	104	15	3	0	3	—	—	27	9	11	11	0	42	0	0	2	4	0	1.00	3	.144	.222	.260
1995 New York	AL	5	1	0	0	0	0	(0	0)	0	0	0	0	0	1	0	0	0	0	0	.000	0	.000	.000	.000
1996 New York	AL	46	88	25	6	1	2	(0	2)	39	17	16	13	0	26	2	1	0	6	2	.75	1	.284	.381	.443
1997 San Diego	NL	17	20	5	1	0	0	(0	0)	6	2	1	2	0	9	0	0	0	2	1	.67	0	.250	.318	.300
1998 San Diego	NL	95	172	36	7	2	6	(2	4)	65	31	29	28	0	52	2	1	1	5	1	.83	1	.209	.325	.378
4 ML YEARS		163	281	66	14	3	8	(2	6)	110	50	46	43	0	88	4	2	3	13	4	.76	2	.235	.341	.391

Todd Rizzo

Pitches: Left **Bats:** Right **Pos:** RP-9 **Ht:** 6'2" **Wt:** 220 **Born:** 5/24/71 **Age:** 28

Year Team	Lg	G	GS	CG	GF	IP	BFP	H	R	ER	HR	SH	SF	HB	TBB	IBB	SO	WP	Bk	W	L	Pct.	ShO	Sv-Op	Hld	ERA
		HOW MUCH HE PITCHED						WHAT HE GAVE UP												THE RESULTS						
1992 Yakima	A-	15	0	0	8	26	121	21	13	13	3	0	1	2	24	0	26	6	0	2	0	1.000	0	0--	—	4.50

		HOW MUCH HE PITCHED						WHAT HE GAVE UP												THE RESULTS						
Year Team	Lg	G	GS	CG	GF	IP	BFP	H	R	ER	HR	SH	SF	HB	TBB	IBB	SO	WP	Bk	W	L	Pct.	ShO	Sv-Op	Hld	ERA
Dodgers	R	3	1	0	1	7	31	4	4	3	0	0	0	1	8	0	7	0	0	0	1	.000	0	0--	—	3.86
1995 Pr William	A+	36	0	0	10	68	307	68	30	21	2	2	1	3	39	8	59	13	0	3	5	.375	0	1--	—	2.78
1996 Birmingham	AA	46	0	0	19	68.2	300	61	28	21	0	3	2	1	40	7	48	7	0	4	4	.500	0	10--	—	2.75
1997 Nashville	AAA	54	0	0	23	70.2	318	63	39	28	6	3	1	3	33	3	60	9	0	4	5	.444	0	6--	—	3.57
1998 Calgary	AAA	50	0	0	19	72	358	102	62	54	6	3	3	3	39	3	58	10	1	7	3	.700	0	4--	—	6.75
1998 Chicago	AL	9	0	0	1	6.2	38	12	12	10	0	0	1	0	6	0	3	2	0	0	0	.000	0	0-0	0	13.50

Bip Roberts

B: B **T:** R **Pos:** 2B-31; DH-29; PH/PR-21; CF-12; LF-10; 3B-3; RF-3   **Ht:** 5'7"   **Wt:** 165   **Born:** 10/27/63   **Age:** 35

		BATTING																BASERUNNING				PERCENTAGES		
Year Team	Lg	G	AB	H	2B	3B	HR	(Hm	Rd)	TB	R	RBI	TBB	IBB	SO	HBP	SH	SF	SB	CS	SB%	GDP	Avg	OBP	SLG
1998 Toledo *	AAA	6	19	5	0	0	0	—	—	5	2	0	2	1	4	1	0	0	2	0	1.00	5	.263	.364	.263
1986 San Diego	NL	101	241	61	5	2	1	(0	1)	73	34	12	14	1	29	0	2	1	14	12	.54	2	.253	.293	.303
1988 San Diego	NL	5	9	3	0	0	0	(0	0)	3	1	0	1	0	2	0	0	0	0	2	.00	0	.333	.400	.333
1989 San Diego	NL	117	329	99	15	8	3	(2	1)	139	81	25	49	0	45	1	6	2	21	11	.66	3	.301	.391	.422
1990 San Diego	NL	149	556	172	36	3	9	(4	5)	241	104	44	55	1	65	6	8	4	46	12	.79	8	.309	.375	.433
1991 San Diego	NL	117	424	119	13	3	3	(3	0)	147	66	32	37	0	71	4	4	3	26	11	.70	6	.281	.342	.347
1992 Cincinnati	NL	147	532	172	34	6	4	(3	1)	230	92	45	62	4	54	2	1	4	44	16	.73	7	.323	.393	.432
1993 Cincinnati	NL	83	292	70	13	0	1	(0	1)	86	46	18	38	1	46	3	0	3	26	6	.81	7	.240	.330	.295
1994 San Diego	NL	105	403	129	15	5	2	(1	1)	160	52	31	39	1	57	3	2	2	21	7	.75	7	.320	.383	.397
1995 San Diego	NL	73	296	90	14	0	2	(2	0)	110	40	25	17	1	36	2	1	0	20	2	.91	2	.304	.346	.372
1996 Kansas City	AL	90	339	96	21	2	0	(0	0)	121	39	52	25	8	38	2	0	6	12	9	.57	8	.283	.331	.357
1997 KC-Cle	AL	120	431	130	20	2	4	(1	3)	166	63	44	28	2	67	3	1	5	18	3	.86	5	.302	.345	.385
1998 Det-Oak	AL	95	295	79	17	0	1	(0	1)	99	45	24	31	0	38	4	3	1	16	4	.80	7	.268	.344	.336
1997 Kansas City	AL	97	346	107	17	2	1	(0	1)	131	44	36	21	2	53	1	1	3	15	3	.83	6	.309	.348	.379
Cleveland	AL	23	85	23	3	0	3	(1	2)	35	19	8	7	0	14	2	0	2	3	0	1.00	1	.271	.333	.412
1998 Detroit	AL	34	113	28	6	0	0	(0	0)	34	17	9	16	0	14	2	1	0	6	1	.86	3	.248	.351	.301
Oakland	AL	61	182	51	11	0	1	(0	1)	65	28	15	15	0	24	2	1	1	10	3	.77	4	.280	.340	.357
12 ML YEARS		1202	4147	1220	203	31	30	(16	14)	1575	663	352	396	19	548	30	27	31	264	95	.74	59	.294	.358	.380

Mike Robertson

Bats: Left   **Throws:** Left   **Pos:** PH/PR-10; DH-2   **Ht:** 6'0"   **Wt:** 189   **Born:** 10/9/70   **Age:** 28

		BATTING																BASERUNNING				PERCENTAGES		
Year Team	Lg	G	AB	H	2B	3B	HR	(Hm	Rd)	TB	R	RBI	TBB	IBB	SO	HBP	SH	SF	SB	CS	SB%	GDP	Avg	OBP	SLG
1991 Utica	A-	13	54	9	2	1	0	—	—	13	6	8	5	0	10	0	0	0	2	1	.67	0	.167	.237	.241
South Bend	A	54	210	69	16	2	1	—	—	92	30	26	18	3	24	3	3	3	7	6	.54	5	.329	.385	.438
1992 Sarasota	A+	106	395	99	21	3	10	—	—	156	50	59	50	3	55	7	1	3	5	7	.42	8	.251	.343	.395
Birmingham	AA	27	90	17	8	1	1	—	—	30	6	9	10	1	19	0	1	1	0	1	.00	1	.189	.267	.333
1993 Birmingham	AA	138	511	138	31	3	11	—	—	208	73	73	59	4	97	3	0	8	10	5	.67	10	.270	.344	.407
1994 Birmingham	AA	53	196	62	20	2	3	—	—	95	32	30	31	4	34	2	0	2	6	3	.67	5	.316	.411	.485
Nashville	AAA	67	213	48	8	1	8	—	—	82	21	21	15	4	27	3	0	0	0	3	.00	4	.225	.286	.385
1995 Nashville	AAA	139	499	124	17	4	19	—	—	206	55	52	50	7	72	11	3	2	2	4	.33	8	.248	.329	.413
1996 Nashville	AAA	138	450	116	16	4	21	—	—	203	64	74	38	4	83	5	9	2	1	2	.33	10	.258	.321	.451
1997 Scranton-WB	AAA	121	416	124	17	3	12	—	—	183	61	72	58	4	67	4	1	6	0	2	.00	9	.298	.384	.440
1998 Tucson	AAA	111	411	112	14	3	13	—	—	171	49	70	33	1	56	7	0	3	1	0	1.00	15	.273	.335	.416
1996 Chicago	AL	6	7	1	0	0	0	(0	0)	2	0	0	0	0	0	0	0	0	0	0	.00	0	.143	.143	.286
1997 Philadelphia	NL	22	38	8	2	1	0	(0	0)	12	3	4	0	0	6	0	0	0	1	0	1.00	0	.211	.268	.316
1998 Arizona	NL	11	13	2	0	0	0	(0	0)	2	0	0	0	0	2	0	0	0	0	0	.00	0	.154	.154	.154
3 ML YEARS		39	58	11	3	1	0	(0	0)	16	3	4	0	0	9	3	0	0	1	0	1.00	0	.190	.230	.276

Rich Robertson

Pitches: Left   **Bats:** Left   **Pos:** RP-5   **Ht:** 6'4"   **Wt:** 182   **Born:** 9/15/68   **Age:** 30

		HOW MUCH HE PITCHED						WHAT HE GAVE UP												THE RESULTS						
Year Team	Lg	G	GS	CG	GF	IP	BFP	H	R	ER	HR	SH	SF	HB	TBB	IBB	SO	WP	Bk	W	L	Pct.	ShO	Sv-Op	Hld	ERA
1998 Vancouver *	AAA	27	27	2	0	175	744	171	85	74	14	5	5	8	68	0	123	9	0	11	12	.478	0	0--	—	3.81
1993 Pittsburgh	NL	9	0	0	2	9	44	15	6	6	0	1	0	0	4	0	5	0	0	0	1	.000	0	0-1	0	6.00
1994 Pittsburgh	NL	8	0	0	1	15.2	76	20	12	12	2	1	1	0	10	4	8	0	0	0	0	.000	0	0-0	1	6.89
1995 Minnesota	AL	25	4	1	8	51.2	228	48	28	22	4	5	2	0	31	4	38	0	1	2	0	1.000	0	0-0	1	3.83
1996 Minnesota	AL	36	31	5	1	186.1	853	197	113	106	22	2	4	9	116	2	114	7	0	7	17	.292	3	0-1	1	5.12
1997 Minnesota	AL	31	26	0	2	147	666	169	105	93	19	3	8	6	70	3	69	10	0	8	12	.400	0	0-0	0	5.69
1998 Anaheim	AL	5	0	0	0	5.2	31	11	11	10	3	0	1	0	2	0	3	0	0	0	0	.000	0	0-0	1	15.88
6 ML YEARS		114	61	6	14	415.1	1898	460	275	249	50	12	16	15	233	13	237	17	1	17	30	.362	3	0-2	3	5.40

Kerry Robinson

Bats: Left   **Throws:** Left   **Pos:** LF-2   **Ht:** 6'0"   **Wt:** 175   **Born:** 10/3/73   **Age:** 25

		BATTING																BASERUNNING				PERCENTAGES		
Year Team	Lg	G	AB	H	2B	3B	HR	(Hm	Rd)	TB	R	RBI	TBB	IBB	SO	HBP	SH	SF	SB	CS	SB%	GDP	Avg	OBP	SLG
1995 Johnson Cty	R+	60	250	74	12	8	1	—	—	105	44	26	16	1	30	0	3	2	14	10	.58	3	.296	.336	.420
1996 Peoria	A	123	440	158	17	14	2	—	—	209	98	47	51	5	51	3	4	8	50	26	.66	2	.359	.422	.475
1997 Arkansas	AA	136	523	168	16	3	2	—	—	196	80	62	54	2	64	2	5	2	40	23	.63	7	.321	.386	.375
Louisville	AAA	2	9	1	0	0	0	—	—	1	0	0	0	0	1	0	0	0	0	0	.00	0	.111	.111	.111
1998 Orlando	AA	72	309	83	7	5	2	—	—	106	45	26	27	0	28	0	4	2	28	9	.76	6	.269	.325	.343
Durham	AAA	58	242	73	7	4	1	—	—	91	28	28	23	0	30	0	2	1	18	11	.62	1	.302	.361	.376
1998 Tampa Bay	AL	2	3	0	0	0	0	(0	0)	0	0	0	0	0	0	0	0	0	0	0	.00	0	.000	.000	.000

John Rocker

Pitches: Left **Bats:** Right **Pos:** RP-47 **Ht:** 6'4" **Wt:** 210 **Born:** 10/17/74 **Age:** 24

Year Team	Lg	G	GS	CG	GF	IP	BFP	H	R	ER	HR	SH	SF	HB	TBB	IBB	SO	WP	Bk	W	L	Pct.	ShO	Sv-Op	Hld	ERA
1994 Danville	R+	12	12	1	0	63.2	285	50	36	25	4	3	4	6	38	1	72	13	4	1	5	.167	0	0--	—	3.53
1995 Macon	A	16	16	0	0	86	375	86	50	43	5	1	4		52	0	61	5	1	4	4	.500	0	0--	—	4.50
Eugene	A-	12	12	0	0	59.1	260	45	40	34	4	1	1	2	36	0	74	7	2	1	5	.167	0	0--	—	5.16
1996 Macon	A	20	19	2	1	106.1	453	85	60	46	7	1	4	6	63	1	107	12	3	5	3	.625	2	0--	—	3.89
Durham	A+	9	9	0	0	58.1	245	63	24	22	4	0	0	1	25	0	43	4	0	4	3	.571	0	0--	—	3.39
1997 Durham	A+	11	1	0	3	35.1	157	33	21	17	3	2	1	2	22	0	39	5	1	1	1	.500	0	0--	—	4.33
Greenville	AA	22	18	0	1	113	507	119	69	61	12	3	1	0	61	0	96	17	2	5	6	.455	0	0--	—	4.86
1998 Richmond	AAA	9	0	0	4	19	81	13	4	3	1	1	0	0	10	0	22	1	1	1	1	.500	0	1--	—	1.42
1998 Atlanta	NL	47	0	0	16	38	156	22	10	9	4	3	0	3	22	4	42	6	0	1	3	.250	0	2-4	15	2.13

Alex Rodriguez

Bats: Right **Throws:** Right **Pos:** SS-160; DH-1 **Ht:** 6'3" **Wt:** 195 **Born:** 7/27/75 **Age:** 23

Year Team	Lg	G	AB	H	2B	3B	HR	(Hm	Rd)	TB	R	RBI	TBB	IBB	SO	HBP	SH	SF	SB	CS	SB%	GDP	Avg	OBP	SLG
1994 Seattle	AL	17	54	11	0	0	0	(0	0)	11	4	2	3	0	20	0	1	1	3	0	1.00	0	.204	.241	.204
1995 Seattle	AL	48	142	33	6	2	5	(1	4)	58	15	19	6	0	42	0	1	0	4	2	.67	0	.232	.264	.408
1996 Seattle	AL	146	601	215	54	1	36	(18	18)	379	141	123	59	1	104	4	6	7	15	4	.79	15	.358	.414	.631
1997 Seattle	AL	141	587	176	40	3	23	(16	7)	291	100	84	41	1	99	5	4	1	29	6	.83	14	.300	.350	.496
1998 Seattle	AL	161	686	213	35	5	42	(18	24)	384	123	124	45	0	121	10	3	4	46	13	.78	12	.310	.360	.560
5 ML YEARS		513	2070	648	135	11	106	(53	53)	1123	383	352	154	2	386	19	15	13	97	25	.80	41	.313	.364	.543

Felix Rodriguez

Pitches: Right **Bats:** Right **Pos:** RP-43 **Ht:** 6'1" **Wt:** 180 **Born:** 12/5/72 **Age:** 26

Year Team	Lg	G	GS	CG	GF	IP	BFP	H	R	ER	HR	SH	SF	HB	TBB	IBB	SO	WP	Bk	W	L	Pct.	ShO	Sv-Op	Hld	ERA
1998 Diamondbcks *	R	3	2	0	0	4.1	18	3	4	2	0	0	0	1	2	0	5	0	0	0	0	.000	0	0--	—	4.15
Tucson *	AAA	1	0	0	0	1	6	1	1	1	0	0	0	0	2	0	0	0	0	0	0	.000	0	0--	—	9.00
1995 Los Angeles	NL	11	0	0	5	10.2	45	11	3	3	2	0	0	0	5	0	5	0	0	1	1	.500	0	0-1	0	2.53
1997 Cincinnati	NL	26	1	0	13	46	212	48	23	22	2	0	1	6	28	2	34	4	1	0	0	.000	0	0-0	0	4.30
1998 Arizona	NL	43	0	0	23	44	207	44	31	30	5	4	3	1	29	1	36	5	2	0	2	.000	0	5-8	0	6.14
3 ML YEARS		80	1	0	41	100.2	464	103	57	55	9	4	4	7	62	3	75	9	3	1	3	.250	0	5-9	0	4.92

Frank Rodriguez

Pitches: Right **Bats:** Right **Pos:** SP-11; RP-9 **Ht:** 6'0" **Wt:** 200 **Born:** 12/11/72 **Age:** 26

Year Team	Lg	G	GS	CG	GF	IP	BFP	H	R	ER	HR	SH	SF	HB	TBB	IBB	SO	WP	Bk	W	L	Pct.	ShO	Sv-Op	Hld	ERA
1998 Salt Lake *	AAA	16	16	2	0	96.1	419	97	63	50	7	3	3	5	35	0	79	7	1	5	7	.417	1	0--	—	4.67
1995 Bos-Min	AL	25	18	0	1	105.2	478	114	83	72	11	1	4	5	57	1	59	9	0	5	8	.385	0	0-0	1	6.13
1996 Minnesota	AL	38	33	3	4	206.2	899	218	129	116	27	6	8	5	78	1	110	2	1	13	14	.481	0	2-2	0	5.05
1997 Minnesota	AL	43	15	0	5	142.1	613	147	82	73	12	4	2	4	60	9	65	6	0	3	6	.333	0	0-2	4	4.62
1998 Minnesota	AL	20	11	0	4	70	329	88	58	51	6	1	5	3	30	0	62	6	1	4	6	.400	0	0-0	0	6.56
1995 Boston	AL	9	2	0	1	15.1	75	21	19	18	3	0	0	0	10	1	14	4	0	0	2	.000	0	0-0	1	10.57
Minnesota	AL	16	16	0	0	90.1	403	93	64	54	8	1	4	5	47	0	45	5	0	5	6	.455	0	0-0	0	5.38
4 ML YEARS		126	77	3	14	524.2	2319	567	352	312	56	12	19	17	225	11	296	23	1	25	34	.424	0	2-4	5	5.35

Henry Rodriguez

Bats: Left **Throws:** Left **Pos:** LF-114; PH/PR-11; DH-5 **Ht:** 6'2" **Wt:** 220 **Born:** 11/8/67 **Age:** 31

Year Team	Lg	G	AB	H	2B	3B	HR	(Hm	Rd)	TB	R	RBI	TBB	IBB	SO	HBP	SH	SF	SB	CS	SB%	GDP	Avg	OBP	SLG
1992 Los Angeles	NL	53	146	32	7	0	3	(2	1)	48	11	14	8	0	30	0	1	1	0	0	.00	2	.219	.258	.329
1993 Los Angeles	NL	76	176	39	10	0	8	(5	3)	73	20	23	11	2	39	0	0	1	1	0	1.00	6	.222	.266	.415
1994 Los Angeles	NL	104	306	82	14	2	8	(5	3)	124	33	49	17	2	58	2	1	4	0	0	.00	9	.268	.307	.405
1995 LA-Mon	NL	45	138	33	4	1	2	(1	1)	45	13	15	11	2	28	0	0	1	0	1	.00	5	.239	.293	.326
1996 Montreal	NL	145	532	147	42	1	36	(20	16)	299	81	103	37	7	160	3	0	4	2	0	1.00	6	.276	.325	.562
1997 Montreal	NL	132	476	116	28	3	26	(14	12)	228	55	83	42	5	149	2	0	3	3	3	.50	6	.244	.306	.479
1998 Chicago	NL	128	415	104	21	1	31	(16	15)	220	56	85	54	7	113	0	0	4	1	3	.25	6	.251	.334	.530
1995 Los Angeles	NL	21	80	21	4	1	1	(0	1)	30	6	10	5	2	17	0	0	1	0	1	.00	3	.263	.306	.375
Montreal	NL	24	58	12	0	0	1	(1	0)	15	7	5	6	0	11	0	0	1	0	0	.00	2	.207	.277	.259
7 ML YEARS		683	2189	553	126	8	114	(63	51)	1037	269	372	180	25	577	7	2	18	7	8	.47	39	.253	.309	.474

Ivan Rodriguez

Bats: Right **Throws:** Right **Pos:** C-139; DH-6; PH/PR-1 **Ht:** 5'9" **Wt:** 205 **Born:** 11/30/71 **Age:** 27

Year Team	Lg	G	AB	H	2B	3B	HR	(Hm	Rd)	TB	R	RBI	TBB	IBB	SO	HBP	SH	SF	SB	CS	SB%	GDP	Avg	OBP	SLG
1991 Texas	AL	88	280	74	16	0	3	(3	0)	99	24	27	5	0	42	0	2	1	0	1	.00	10	.264	.276	.354
1992 Texas	AL	123	420	109	16	1	8	(4	4)	151	39	37	24	2	73	1	7	2	0	0	.00	15	.260	.300	.360
1993 Texas	AL	137	473	129	28	4	10	(7	3)	195	56	66	29	3	70	4	5	8	8	7	.53	16	.273	.315	.412
1994 Texas	AL	99	363	108	19	1	16	(7	9)	177	56	57	31	5	42	7	0	4	6	3	.67	10	.298	.360	.488

	BATTING																		BASERUNNING				PERCENTAGES		
Year Team	Lg	G	AB	H	2B	3B	HR	(Hm	Rd)	TB	R	RBI	TBB	IBB	SO	HBP	SH	SF	SB	CS	SB%	GDP	Avg	OBP	SLG
1995 Texas	AL	130	492	149	32	2	12	(5	7)	221	56	67	16	2	48	4	0	5	0	2	.00	11	.303	.327	.449
1996 Texas	AL	153	639	192	47	3	19	(10	9)	302	116	86	38	7	55	4	0	4	5	0	1.00	15	.300	.342	.473
1997 Texas	AL	150	597	187	34	4	20	(12	8)	289	98	77	38	7	89	8	1	4	7	3	.70	18	.313	.360	.484
1998 Texas	AL	145	579	186	40	4	21	(12	9)	297	88	91	32	4	88	3	0	3	9	0	1.00	18	.321	.358	.513
8 ML YEARS		1025	3843	1134	232	19	109	(60	49)	1731	533	508	213	30	507	31	15	31	35	16	.69	113	.295	.335	.450

Nerio Rodriguez

Pitches: Right **Bats:** Right **Pos:** RP-9; SP-4   **Ht:** 6'0" **Wt:** 165 **Born:** 3/22/73 **Age:** 26

	HOW MUCH HE PITCHED						WHAT HE GAVE UP											THE RESULTS						
Year Team	Lg	G	GS	CG	GF	IP	BFP	H	R	ER	HR	SH	SF	HB	TBB	IBB	SO	WP	Bk	W	L	Pct.	ShO	Sv-Op	Hld	ERA
1995 High Desert	A+	7	0	0	3	10	44	8	2	2	0	0	0	0	7	0	10	0	0	0	1	.000	0	0- -	—	1.80
1996 Frederick	A+	24	17	1	7	111.1	462	83	42	28	10	5	0	4	40	0	114	6	1	8	7	.533	0	2- -	—	2.26
Rochester	AAA	2	2	0	0	15	58	10	3	3	0	0	0	0	2	0	6	2	0	1	0	1.000	0	0- -	—	1.80
1997 Rochester	AAA	27	27	1	0	168.1	688	124	82	73	23	6	0	8	62	0	160	4	3	11	10	.524	1	0- -	—	3.90
1998 Rochester	AAA	5	5	0	0	24.2	108	24	16	15	6	1	1	1	10	0	19	0	1	1	4	.200	0	0- -	—	5.47
Bowie	AA	2	2	0	0	4	18	6	2	2	0	0	0	0	0	0	7	0	0	0	1	.000	0	0- -	—	4.50
1996 Baltimore	AL	8	1	0	2	16.2	77	18	11	8	2	0	1	1	7	0	12	0	0	1	0	.000	0	0-0	0	4.32
1997 Baltimore	AL	6	2	0	1	22	98	21	15	12	2	1	4	1	8	0	11	1	0	2	1	.667	0	0-1	0	4.91
1998 Bal-Tor	AL	13	4	0	3	27.1	133	35	26	26	1	0	2	1	17	0	11	1	0	2	3	.400	0	0-0	0	8.56
1998 Baltimore	AL	6	4	0	0	19	89	25	17	17	0	0	2	0	9	0	8	1	0	1	3	.250	0	0-0	0	8.05
Toronto	AL	7	0	0	3	8.1	44	10	9	9	1	0	0	1	8	0	3	0	0	1	0	1.000	0	0-0	0	9.72
3 ML YEARS		27	7	0	6	66	308	74	52	46	5	1	7	3	32	0	34	2	0	4	5	.444	0	0-1	0	6.27

Rich Rodriguez

Pitches: Left **Bats:** Left **Pos:** RP-68   **Ht:** 6'0" **Wt:** 200 **Born:** 3/1/63 **Age:** 36

	HOW MUCH HE PITCHED						WHAT HE GAVE UP											THE RESULTS						
Year Team	Lg	G	GS	CG	GF	IP	BFP	H	R	ER	HR	SH	SF	HB	TBB	IBB	SO	WP	Bk	W	L	Pct.	ShO	Sv-Op	Hld	ERA
1990 San Diego	NL	32	0	0	15	47.2	201	52	17	15	2	2	1	1	16	4	22	1	1	1	1	.500	0	1-1	3	2.83
1991 San Diego	NL	64	1	0	19	80	335	66	31	29	8	7	2	0	44	8	40	4	1	3	1	.750	0	0-2	8	3.26
1992 San Diego	NL	61	1	0	15	91	369	77	28	24	4	2	2	0	29	4	64	1	1	6	3	.667	0	0-1	5	2.37
1993 SD-Fla	NL	70	0	0	21	76	331	73	38	32	10	5	0	2	33	8	43	3	0	2	4	.333	0	3-7	10	3.79
1994 St. Louis	NL	56	0	0	15	60.1	260	62	30	27	6	2	1	1	26	4	43	4	0	3	5	.375	0	0-3	15	4.03
1995 St. Louis	NL	1	0	0	0	1.2	4	0	0	0	0	0	0	0	0	0	0	0	0	0	0	.000	0	0-0	0	0.00
1997 San Francisco	NL	71	0	0	15	65.1	271	65	24	23	7	3	0	1	21	4	32	0	0	4	3	.571	0	1-5	14	3.17
1998 San Francisco	NL	68	0	0	11	65.2	278	69	28	27	7	2	2	0	20	5	44	3	0	4	0	1.000	0	2-6	22	3.70
1993 San Diego	NL	34	0	0	10	30	133	34	15	11	2	2	0	1	9	3	22	1	0	2	3	.400	0	2-5	8	3.30
Florida	NL	36	0	0	11	46	198	39	23	21	8	3	0	1	24	5	21	2	0	0	1	.000	0	1-2	2	4.11
8 ML YEARS		423	2	0	111	487.2	2049	464	196	177	44	23	8	5	189	37	288	16	3	23	17	.575	0	7-25	77	3.27

Kenny Rogers

Pitches: Left **Bats:** Left **Pos:** SP-34   **Ht:** 6'1" **Wt:** 205 **Born:** 11/10/64 **Age:** 34

	HOW MUCH HE PITCHED						WHAT HE GAVE UP											THE RESULTS						
Year Team	Lg	G	GS	CG	GF	IP	BFP	H	R	ER	HR	SH	SF	HB	TBB	IBB	SO	WP	Bk	W	L	Pct.	ShO	Sv-Op	Hld	ERA
1989 Texas	AL	73	0	0	24	73.2	314	60	28	24	2	6	3	4	42	9	63	6	0	3	4	.429	0	2-5	16	2.93
1990 Texas	AL	69	3	0	46	97.2	428	93	40	34	6	7	4	1	42	5	74	5	0	10	6	.625	0	15-23	6	3.13
1991 Texas	AL	63	9	0	20	109.2	511	121	80	66	14	9	5	6	61	7	73	3	1	10	10	.500	0	5-6	11	5.42
1992 Texas	AL	81	0	0	38	78.2	337	80	32	27	7	4	1	0	26	8	70	4	1	3	6	.333	0	6-10	16	3.09
1993 Texas	AL	35	33	5	0	208.1	885	210	108	95	18	7	5	4	71	2	140	6	5	16	10	.615	0	0-0	1	4.10
1994 Texas	AL	24	24	6	0	167.1	714	169	93	83	24	3	6	3	52	1	120	3	1	11	8	.579	2	0-0	0	4.46
1995 Texas	AL	31	31	3	0	208	877	192	87	78	26	3	5	2	76	1	140	8	1	17	7	.708	1	0-0	0	3.38
1996 New York	AL	30	30	2	0	179	786	179	97	93	16	6	3	8	83	2	92	5	0	12	8	.600	1	0-0	0	4.68
1997 New York	AL	31	22	1	4	145	651	161	100	91	18	2	4	7	62	1	78	2	2	6	7	.462	0	0-0	1	5.65
1998 Oakland	AL	34	34	7	0	238.2	970	215	96	84	19	4	5	7	67	0	138	5	2	16	8	.667	1	0-0	0	3.17
10 ML YEARS		471	186	24	132	1506	6473	1480	761	675	150	51	41	42	582	36	988	47	13	104	74	.584	5	28-44	51	4.03

Mel Rojas

Pitches: Right **Bats:** Right **Pos:** RP-50   **Ht:** 5'11" **Wt:** 212 **Born:** 12/10/66 **Age:** 32

	HOW MUCH HE PITCHED						WHAT HE GAVE UP											THE RESULTS						
Year Team	Lg	G	GS	CG	GF	IP	BFP	H	R	ER	HR	SH	SF	HB	TBB	IBB	SO	WP	Bk	W	L	Pct.	ShO	Sv-Op	Hld	ERA
1990 Montreal	NL	23	0	0	5	40	173	34	17	16	5	2	0	2	24	4	26	2	0	3	1	.750	0	1-2	1	3.60
1991 Montreal	NL	37	0	0	13	48	200	42	21	20	4	0	2	1	13	1	37	3	0	3	3	.500	0	6-9	7	3.75
1992 Montreal	NL	68	0	0	26	100.2	399	71	17	16	2	4	2	2	34	8	70	2	0	7	1	.875	0	10-11	13	1.43
1993 Montreal	NL	66	0	0	25	88.1	378	80	39	29	6	8	6	4	30	3	48	5	0	5	8	.385	0	10-19	14	2.95
1994 Montreal	NL	58	0	0	27	84	341	71	35	31	11	2	1	4	21	0	84	0	0	3	2	.600	0	16-18	19	3.32
1995 Montreal	NL	59	0	0	48	67.2	302	69	32	31	2	2	1	7	29	4	61	6	0	1	4	.200	0	30-39	3	4.12
1996 Montreal	NL	74	0	0	64	81	326	56	30	29	5	2	4	2	28	3	92	5	0	7	4	.636	0	36-40	1	3.22
1997 ChN-NYN	NL	77	0	0	50	85.1	370	78	47	44	15	2	2	7	36	2	93	3	0	0	6	.000	0	15-22	7	4.64
1998 New York	NL	50	0	0	19	58	262	68	39	39	9	4	2	3	30	5	41	2	0	5	2	.714	0	2-6	5	6.05
1997 Chicago	NL	54	0	0	38	59	259	54	30	29	11	2	1	5	30	1	61	2	0	0	4	.000	0	13-19	2	4.42
New York	NL	23	0	0	12	26.1	111	24	17	15	4	0	1	2	6	1	32	1	0	0	2	.000	0	2-3	5	5.13
9 ML YEARS		512	0	0	277	653	2751	569	277	255	59	26	20	32	245	30	552	29	0	34	31	.523	0	126-166	72	3.51

194

Scott Rolen

Bats: Right **Throws:** Right **Pos:** 3B-159; PH/PR-1   **Ht:** 6'4" **Wt:** 223 **Born:** 4/4/75 **Age:** 24

Year Team	Lg	G	AB	H	2B	3B	HR	(Hm	Rd)	TB	R	RBI	TBB	IBB	SO	HBP	SH	SF	SB	CS	SB%	GDP	Avg	OBP	SLG
1996 Philadelphia	NL	37	130	33	7	0	4	(2	2)	52	10	18	13	0	27	1	0	2	0	2	.00	4	.254	.322	.400
1997 Philadelphia	NL	156	561	159	35	3	21	(11	10)	263	93	92	76	4	138	13	0	7	16	6	.73	6	.283	.377	.469
1998 Philadelphia	NL	160	601	174	45	4	31	(19	12)	320	120	110	93	6	141	11	0	6	14	7	.67	10	.290	.391	.532
3 ML YEARS		353	1292	366	87	7	56	(32	24)	635	223	220	182	10	306	25	0	15	30	15	.67	20	.283	.378	.491

Mandy Romero

Bats: Both **Throws:** Right **Pos:** C-10; PH/PR-9; DH-3   **Ht:** 6'0" **Wt:** 180 **Born:** 10/29/67 **Age:** 31

Year Team	Lg	G	AB	H	2B	3B	HR	(Hm	Rd)	TB	R	RBI	TBB	IBB	SO	HBP	SH	SF	SB	CS	SB%	GDP	Avg	OBP	SLG
1988 Princeton	R+	30	71	22	6	0	2	—	—	34	7	11	13	0	15	1	0	0	1	0	1.00		.310	.424	.479
1989 Augusta	A	121	388	87	26	3	4	—	—	131	58	55	67	4	74	6	3	6	8	5	.62	10	.224	.343	.338
1990 Salem	A+	124	460	134	31	3	17	—	—	222	62	90	55	3	68	5	2	4	0	2	.00	10	.291	.370	.483
1991 Carolina	AA	98	323	70	12	0	3	—	—	91	28	31	45	4	53	1	2	2	1	2	.33	9	.217	.313	.282
1992 Carolina	AA	80	269	58	16	0	3	—	—	83	28	27	29	0	39	1	1	2	0	3	.00	10	.216	.292	.309
1993 Buffalo	AAA	42	136	31	6	1	2	—	—	45	11	14	6	1	12	0	1	1	1	0	1.00	5	.228	.259	.331
1994 Buffalo	AAA	7	23	3	0	0	0	—	—	3	3	1	2	0	1	0	1	0	0	0	.00	1	.130	.200	.130
1995 Wichita	AA	121	440	133	32	1	21	—	—	230	73	82	69	10	60	5	0	1	1	3	.25	15	.302	.402	.523
1996 Memphis	AA	88	297	80	15	0	10	—	—	125	40	46	41	2	52	1	1	2	3	1	.75	15	.269	.358	.421
1997 Mobile	AA	61	222	71	22	0	13	—	—	132	50	52	38	3	31	2	0	1	0	0	.00	4	.320	.422	.595
Las Vegas	AAA	33	91	28	4	1	3	—	—	43	19	13	11	1	19	1	0	1	0	0	.00	4	.308	.385	.473
1998 Las Vegas	AAA	40	131	38	8	0	8	—	—	70	25	22	20	1	25	1	1	0	0	1	.00	9	.290	.388	.534
Pawtucket	AAA	45	139	46	5	0	8	—	—	75	20	27	24	6	15	0	2	4	0	0	.00	1	.331	.419	.540
1997 San Diego	NL	21	48	10	0	0	2	(1	1)	16	7	4	2	0	18	0	0	0	1	0	1.00	1	.208	.240	.333
1998 SD-Bos		18	22	3	1	0	0	(0	0)	4	3	1	4	0	6	0	0	0	0	0	.00	1	.136	.269	.182
1998 San Diego	NL	6	9	0	0	0	0	(0	0)	0	1	0	1	0	3	0	0	0	0	0	0		.000	.100	.000
Boston	AL	12	13	3	1	0	0	(0	0)	4	2	1	3	0	3	0	0	0	0	0	.00	1	.231	.375	.308
2 ML YEARS		39	70	13	1	0	2	(1	1)	20	10	5	6	0	24	0	0	0	1	0	1.00	2	.186	.250	.286

Rafael Roque

Pitches: Left **Bats:** Left **Pos:** SP-9   **Ht:** 6'4" **Wt:** 186 **Born:** 1/1/72 **Age:** 27

Year Team	Lg	G	GS	CG	GF	IP	BFP	H	R	ER	HR	SH	SF	HB	TBB	IBB	SO	WP	Bk	W	L	Pct.	ShO	Sv-Op	Hld	ERA
1992 Mets	R	20	0	0	18	33.2	149	28	13	8	0	4	0	1	16	2	33	3	1	3	1	.750	0	8--	—	2.14
1993 Kingsport	R+	14	7	0	4	45.1	222	58	44	31	9	3	2	7	26	0	36	8	1	1	3	.250	0	0--	—	6.15
1994 St. Lucie	A+	2	0	0	2	3	15	2	1	0	0	1	1	1	3	1	2	0	0	0	0	.000	0	0--	—	0.00
Capital City	A	15	15	1	0	86.1	353	73	26	23	6	1	3	4	30	1	74	7	1	6	3	.667	0	0--	—	2.40
1995 St. Lucie	A+	24	24	2	0	136.2	582	114	65	54	7	2	4	4	72	1	81	11	4	6	9	.400	1	0--	—	3.56
1996 Binghamton	AA	13	13	0	0	60.2	291	71	57	49	8	2	1	2	39	0	46	4	0	0	4	.000	0	0--	—	7.27
St. Lucie	A+	14	12	1	1	76.1	311	57	22	18	2	5	0	3	39	0	59	8	0	6	4	.600	0	0--	—	2.12
1997 Binghamton	AA	16	0	0	5	26.1	126	35	26	20	7	2	0	1	17	1	23	1	0	1	1	.500	0	0--	—	6.84
St. Lucie	A+	17	13	1	1	77.2	325	81	42	37	8	3	4	1	25	0	54	2	1	2	10	.167	0	0--	—	4.29
1998 El Paso	AA	16	16	1	0	94	432	113	56	46	8	2	2	4	35	2	70	4	0	5	6	.455	0	0--	—	4.40
Louisville	AAA	9	8	0	0	49.2	207	42	21	20	2	2	4	4	19	1	43	1	0	5	2	.714	0	0--	—	3.62
1998 Milwaukee	NL	9	9	0	0	48	206	42	28	26	9	4	0	1	24	0	34	3	1	4	2	.667	0	0-0	0	4.88

Jose Rosado

Pitches: Left **Bats:** Left **Pos:** SP-25; RP-13   **Ht:** 6'0" **Wt:** 185 **Born:** 11/9/74 **Age:** 24

Year Team	Lg	G	GS	CG	GF	IP	BFP	H	R	ER	HR	SH	SF	HB	TBB	IBB	SO	WP	Bk	W	L	Pct.	ShO	Sv-Op	Hld	ERA
1996 Kansas City	AL	16	16	2	0	106.2	441	101	39	38	7	1	4	4	26	1	64	5	1	8	6	.571	1	0-0	0	3.21
1997 Kansas City	AL	33	33	2	0	203.1	881	208	117	106	26	6	11	4	73	3	129	4	2	9	12	.429	0	0-0	0	4.69
1998 Kansas City	AL	38	25	2	1	174.2	757	180	106	91	25	1	3	5	57	2	135	6	1	8	11	.421	1	1-1	2	4.69
3 ML YEARS		87	74	6	1	484.2	2079	489	262	235	58	8	18	13	156	6	328	15	4	25	29	.463	2	1-1	2	4.36

Brian Rose

Pitches: Right **Bats:** Right **Pos:** SP-8   **Ht:** 6'3" **Wt:** 212 **Born:** 2/13/76 **Age:** 23

Year Team	Lg	G	GS	CG	GF	IP	BFP	H	R	ER	HR	SH	SF	HB	TBB	IBB	SO	WP	Bk	W	L	Pct.	ShO	Sv-Op	Hld	ERA
1995 Michigan	A	21	20	2	0	136	561	127	63	52	5	3	1	9	31	0	105	4	0	8	5	.615	0	0--	—	3.44
1996 Trenton	AA	27	27	4	0	163.2	687	157	82	73	21	6	4	13	45	3	115	1	1	12	7	.632	2	0--	—	4.01
1997 Pawtucket	AAA	27	26	3	0	190.2	787	188	74	64	21	1	5	7	46	2	116	5	0	17	5	.773	0	0--	—	3.02
1998 Pawtucket	AAA	6	6	0	0	17.2	84	24	19	15	5	0	0	2	4	0	17	0	0	0	3	.000	0	0--	—	7.64
1997 Boston	AL	1	1	0	0	3	16	5	4	4	0	0	0	0	2	0	3	0	0	0	0	.000	0	0-0	0	12.00
1998 Boston	AL	8	8	0	0	37.2	168	43	32	29	9	0	1	2	14	0	18	0	0	1	4	.200	0	0-0	0	6.93
2 ML YEARS		9	9	0	0	40.2	184	48	36	33	9	0	1	2	16	0	21	0	0	1	4	.200	0	0-0	0	7.30

John Roskos

Bats: Right **Throws:** Right **Pos:** PH/PR-9; 1B-1   **Ht:** 5'11" **Wt:** 195 **Born:** 11/19/74 **Age:** 24

Year Team	Lg	G	AB	H	2B	3B	HR	(Hm	Rd)	TB	R	RBI	TBB	IBB	SO	HBP	SH	SF	SB	CS	SB%	GDP	Avg	OBP	SLG
1993 Marlins	R	11	40	7	1	0	1	—	—	11	6	3	5	0	11	1	0	0	1	1	.50	0	.175	.283	.275
1994 Elmira	A-	39	136	38	7	0	4	—	—	57	11	23	27	0	37	0	0	2	0	1	.00	0	.279	.394	.419
1995 Kane County	A	114	418	124	36	3	12	—	—	202	74	88	42	1	86	6	0	6	2	0	1.00	6	.297	.364	.483
1996 Portland	AA	121	396	109	26	3	9	—	—	168	53	58	67	4	102	5	0	2	3	4	.43	5	.275	.385	.424
1997 Portland	AA	123	451	139	31	1	24	—	—	244	66	84	50	2	81	0	2	6	4	6	.40	17	.308	.373	.541
1998 Charlotte	AAA	115	416	118	23	1	10	—	—	173	54	62	43	0	84	3	0	3	0	4	.00	15	.284	.353	.416
1998 Florida	NL	10	10	1	0	0	0	(0	0)	1	1	0	0	0	5	0	0	0	0	0	.00	0	.100	.100	.100

Rico Rossy

Bats: R **Throws:** R **Pos:** 3B-25; 2B-6; SS-4; PH/PR-3; DH-1   **Ht:** 5'10" **Wt:** 175 **Born:** 2/16/64 **Age:** 35

Year Team	Lg	G	AB	H	2B	3B	HR	(Hm	Rd)	TB	R	RBI	TBB	IBB	SO	HBP	SH	SF	SB	CS	SB%	GDP	Avg	OBP	SLG
1998 Tacoma *	AAA	56	210	60	18	0	8			102	33	36	26	2	36	0	2	0	1	1	.50	7	.286	.364	.486
1991 Atlanta	NL	5	1	0	0	0	0	(0	0)	0	0	0	0	0	1	0	0	0	0	0	.00	0	.000	.000	.000
1992 Kansas City	AL	59	149	32	8	1	1	(0	1)	45	21	12	20	1	20	1	7	1	0	3	.00	6	.215	.310	.302
1993 Kansas City	AL	46	86	19	4	0	2	(2	0)	29	10	12	9	0	11	1	1	0	0	0	.00	0	.221	.302	.337
1998 Seattle	AL	37	81	16	6	0	1	(1	0)	25	12	4	6	0	13	0	0	0	0	0	.00	0	.198	.253	.309
4 ML YEARS		147	317	67	18	1	4	(3	1)	99	43	28	35	1	45	2	10	1	0	3	.00	6	.211	.293	.312

Matt Ruebel

Pitches: Left **Bats:** Left **Pos:** RP-6; SP-1   **Ht:** 6'2" **Wt:** 180 **Born:** 10/16/69 **Age:** 29

		HOW MUCH HE PITCHED						WHAT HE GAVE UP										THE RESULTS						
Year Team	Lg	G	GS	CG	GF	IP	BFP	H	R	ER	HR	SH	SF	HB	TBB	IBB	SO	WP	Bk	W	L	Pct.	ShO	Sv-Op	Hld	ERA
1998 Durham *	AAA	24	23	1	0	129	569	141	73	68	17	0	3	5	45	1	87	2	0	9	6	.600	1	0- —	—	4.74
1996 Pittsburgh	NL	26	7	0	3	58.2	265	64	38	30	7	0	3	6	25	0	22	2	0	1	1	.500	0	1-1	4	4.60
1997 Pittsburgh	NL	44	0	0	9	62.2	296	77	50	44	8	3	5	5	27	3	50	4	0	3	2	.600	0	0-1	8	6.32
1998 Tampa Bay	AL	7	1	0	1	8.2	39	11	7	6	3	0	0	0	4	0	6	0	0	0	2	.000	0	0-0	1	6.23
3 ML YEARS		77	8	0	13	130	600	152	95	80	18	3	8	11	56	3	78	6	0	4	5	.444	0	1-2	13	5.54

Kirk Rueter

Pitches: Left **Bats:** Left **Pos:** SP-33   **Ht:** 6'3" **Wt:** 207 **Born:** 12/1/70 **Age:** 28

		HOW MUCH HE PITCHED						WHAT HE GAVE UP										THE RESULTS						
Year Team	Lg	G	GS	CG	GF	IP	BFP	H	R	ER	HR	SH	SF	HB	TBB	IBB	SO	WP	Bk	W	L	Pct.	ShO	Sv-Op	Hld	ERA
1993 Montreal	NL	14	14	1	0	85.2	341	85	33	26	5	1	0	0	18	1	31	0	0	8	0	1.000	0	0-0	0	2.73
1994 Montreal	NL	20	20	0	0	92.1	397	106	60	53	11	6	6	2	23	1	50	2	0	7	3	.700	0	0-0	0	5.17
1995 Montreal	NL	9	9	0	0	47.1	184	38	17	17	3	4	0	1	9	0	28	0	0	5	3	.625	1	0-0	0	3.23
1996 Mon-SF	NL	20	19	0	0	102	430	109	50	45	12	4	2	1	27	0	46	2	0	6	8	.429	0	0-0	0	3.97
1997 San Francisco	NL	32	32	1	0	190.2	802	194	83	73	17	10	6	1	51	8	115	3	0	13	6	.684	0	0-0	0	3.45
1998 San Francisco	NL	33	33	1	0	187.2	806	193	100	91	27	5	8	7	57	3	102	6	0	16	9	.640	0	0-0	0	4.36
1996 Montreal	NL	16	16	0	0	78.2	338	91	44	40	12	4	1	2	22	0	30	0	0	5	6	.455	0	0-0	0	4.58
San Francisco	NL	4	3	0	0	23.1	92	18	6	5	0	0	1	0	5	0	16	2	0	1	2	.333	0	0-0	0	1.93
6 ML YEARS		128	127	3	0	705.2	2960	725	343	305	75	30	21	13	185	13	372	13	0	55	29	.655	1	0-0	0	3.89

Sean Runyan

Pitches: Left **Bats:** Left **Pos:** RP-88   **Ht:** 6'3" **Wt:** 200 **Born:** 6/21/74 **Age:** 25

		HOW MUCH HE PITCHED						WHAT HE GAVE UP										THE RESULTS						
Year Team	Lg	G	GS	CG	GF	IP	BFP	H	R	ER	HR	SH	SF	HB	TBB	IBB	SO	WP	Bk	W	L	Pct.	ShO	Sv-Op	Hld	ERA
1992 Astros	R	10	10	0	0	45	203	54	19	16	0	1	0	5	16	0	30	8	1	3	3	.500	0	0- —	—	3.20
1993 Astros	R	12	12	0	0	66.1	302	66	35	22	2	1	3	2	24	0	52	4	0	4	3	.571	0	0- —	—	2.98
1994 Auburn	A-	14	14	2	0	95.1	396	90	49	37	5	1	1	2	19	0	66	12	1	7	5	.583	1	0- —	—	3.49
1995 Quad City	A	22	11	0	2	76.1	327	67	37	31	10	1	2	3	29	0	65	4	0	4	6	.400	0	0- —	—	3.66
1996 Quad City	A	29	17	0	3	132.1	551	128	61	57	10	1	5	14	30	0	104	4	1	9	4	.692	0	0- —	—	3.88
1997 Mobile	AA	40	1	0	15	61.2	261	54	25	16	4	2	1	3	28	3	52	1	1	5	2	.714	0	1- —	—	2.34
1998 Detroit	AL	88	0	0	11	50.1	223	47	23	20	7	2	7	2	28	4	39	5	0	1	4	.200	0	1-3	11	3.58

Glendon Rusch

Pitches: Left **Bats:** Left **Pos:** SP-24; RP-5   **Ht:** 6'1" **Wt:** 195 **Born:** 11/7/74 **Age:** 24

		HOW MUCH HE PITCHED						WHAT HE GAVE UP										THE RESULTS						
Year Team	Lg	G	GS	CG	GF	IP	BFP	H	R	ER	HR	SH	SF	HB	TBB	IBB	SO	WP	Bk	W	L	Pct.	ShO	Sv-Op	Hld	ERA
1993 Royals	R	11	10	0	0	62	234	43	14	11	0	3	1	1	11	0	48	2	1	4	2	.667	0	0- —	—	1.60
Rockford	A	2	2	0	0	8	40	10	6	3	0	0	1	0	7	0	8	1	0	0	1	.000	0	0- —	—	3.38
1994 Rockford	A	28	17	1	5	114	485	111	61	59	5	4	5	6	34	2	122	7	1	8	5	.615	1	1- —	—	4.66
1995 Wilmington	A+	26	26	1	0	165.2	629	110	41	32	5	4	3	4	34	3	147	3	1	14	6	.700	1	0- —	—	1.74
1996 Omaha	AAA	28	28	1	0	169.2	723	177	88	75	15	7	8	6	40	3	117	3	0	11	9	.550	0	0- —	—	3.98
1997 Omaha	AAA	1	1	0	0	6	25	7	3	3	3	0	0	1	0	1	2	1	0	0	1	.000	0	0- —	—	4.50
1998 Omaha	AAA	3	3	0	0	14.2	72	20	18	13	4	1	1	1	6	0	14	0	0	1	1	.500	0	0- —	—	7.98
1997 Kansas City	AL	30	27	1	2	170.1	758	206	111	104	28	8	7	7	52	0	116	0	1	6	9	.400	0	0-0	0	5.50
1998 Kansas City	AL	29	24	1	2	154.2	686	191	104	101	22	1	2	4	50	0	94	1	0	6	15	.286	1	1-1	0	5.88

Year Team	Lg	G	GS	CG	GF	IP	BFP	H	R	ER	HR	SH	SF	HB	TBB	IBB	SO	WP	Bk	W	L	Pct.	ShO	Sv-Op	Hld	ERA
2 ML YEARS		59	51	2	2	325	1444	397	215	205	50	9	9	11	102	0	210	1	1	12	24	.333	1	1-1	0	5.68

Ken Ryan

Pitches: Right **Bats:** Right **Pos:** RP-16; SP-1   **Ht:** 6'3" **Wt:** 230 **Born:** 10/24/68 **Age:** 30

Year Team	Lg	G	GS	CG	GF	IP	BFP	H	R	ER	HR	SH	SF	HB	TBB	IBB	SO	WP	Bk	W	L	Pct.	ShO	Sv-Op	Hld	ERA
1998 Clearwater *	A+	4	4	0	0	9	34	5	3	3	0	0	0	1	3	0	10	1	0	0	0	.000	0	0- -	—	3.00
Scranton-WB *	AAA	6	0	0	3	8	34	7	0	0	0	0	0	1	3	0	9	0	0	1	0	1.000	0	1- -	—	0.00
1992 Boston	AL	7	0	0	6	7	30	4	5	5	2	1	1	0	5	0	5	0	0	0	0	.000	0	1-1	0	6.43
1993 Boston	AL	47	0	0	26	50	223	43	23	20	2	4	4	3	29	5	49	3	0	7	2	.778	0	1-4	3	3.60
1994 Boston	AL	42	0	0	26	48	202	46	14	13	1	4	0	1	17	3	32	2	0	2	3	.400	0	13-16	5	2.44
1995 Boston	AL	28	0	0	20	32.2	153	34	20	18	4	1	0	1	24	6	34	1	0	0	4	.000	0	7-10	0	4.96
1996 Philadelphia	NL	62	0	0	26	89	370	71	32	24	4	5	0	1	45	8	70	4	3	5	.375	0	8-13	15	2.43
1997 Philadelphia	NL	22	0	0	10	20.2	108	31	23	22	5	1	2	2	13	1	10	0	0	1	0	1.000	0	0-0	1	9.58
1998 Philadelphia	NL	17	1	0	6	22.2	108	21	12	11	1	2	2	1	20	1	16	4	0	0	0	.000	0	0-0	1	4.37
7 ML YEARS		225	1	0	120	270	1194	250	129	113	19	18	9	9	153	24	216	14	3	13	14	.481	0	30-44	25	3.77

Bret Saberhagen

Pitches: Right **Bats:** Right **Pos:** SP-31   **Ht:** 6'1" **Wt:** 200 **Born:** 4/11/64 **Age:** 35

Year Team	Lg	G	GS	CG	GF	IP	BFP	H	R	ER	HR	SH	SF	HB	TBB	IBB	SO	WP	Bk	W	L	Pct.	ShO	Sv-Op	Hld	ERA
1984 Kansas City	AL	38	18	2	9	157.2	634	138	71	61	13	8	5	2	36	4	73	7	1	10	11	.476	1	1- -	—	3.48
1985 Kansas City	AL	32	32	10	0	235.1	931	211	79	75	19	9	7	1	38	1	158	1	1	20	6	.769	1	0-0	0	2.87
1986 Kansas City	AL	30	25	4	4	156	652	165	77	72	15	3	3	2	29	1	112	1	1	7	12	.368	2	0- -	—	4.15
1987 Kansas City	AL	33	33	15	0	257	1048	246	99	96	27	8	5	6	53	2	163	6	0	18	10	.643	4	0-0	0	3.36
1988 Kansas City	AL	35	35	9	0	260.2	1089	**271**	122	110	18	8	10	4	59	5	171	9	0	14	16	.467	0	0-0	0	3.80
1989 Kansas City	AL	36	35	**12**	0	262.1	1021	209	74	63	13	9	6	2	43	6	193	8	1	**23**	6	.793	4	0-0	0	**2.16**
1990 Kansas City	AL	20	20	5	0	135	561	146	52	49	9	4	4	1	28	1	87	1	0	5	9	.357	0	0-0	0	3.27
1991 Kansas City	AL	28	28	7	0	196.1	789	165	76	67	12	8	3	0	45	5	136	8	1	13	8	.619	2	0-0	0	3.07
1992 New York	NL	17	15	1	0	97.2	397	84	39	38	6	3	3	4	27	1	81	1	2	3	5	.375	1	0-1	0	3.50
1993 New York	NL	19	19	4	0	139.1	556	131	55	51	11	6	6	3	17	4	93	2	2	7	7	.500	1	0-0	0	3.29
1994 New York	NL	24	24	4	0	177.1	696	169	58	54	13	9	5	4	13	0	143	0	0	14	4	.778	1	0-0	0	2.74
1995 NYN-Col	NL	25	25	3	0	153	658	165	78	71	21	7	3	10	33	3	100	3	0	7	6	.538	0	0-0	0	4.18
1997 Boston	AL	6	6	0	0	26	120	30	20	19	5	1	3	2	10	0	14	1	0	0	1	.000	0	0-0	0	6.58
1998 Boston	AL	31	31	0	0	175	725	181	82	77	22	2	3	6	29	1	100	4	0	15	8	.652	0	0-0	0	3.96
1995 New York	NL	16	16	3	0	110	452	105	45	41	13	5	3	5	20	2	71	2	0	5	5	.500	0	0-0	0	3.35
Colorado	NL	9	9	0	0	43	206	60	33	30	8	2	0	5	13	1	29	1	0	2	1	.667	0	0-0	0	6.28
14 ML YEARS		374	346	76	13	2428.2	9877	2311	982	903	204	85	66	56	460	34	1624	52	12	156	109	.589	16	1- -	—	3.35

Donnie Sadler

Bats: R **Throws:** R **Pos:** 2B-50; PH/PR-14; DH-4; SS-4   **Ht:** 5'6" **Wt:** 165 **Born:** 6/17/75 **Age:** 24

Year Team	Lg	G	AB	H	2B	3B	HR	(Hm	Rd)	TB	R	RBI	TBB	IBB	SO	HBP	SH	SF	SB	CS	SB%	GDP	Avg	OBP	SLG
1994 Red Sox	R	53	206	56	8	6	1			79	52	16	23	0	27	3	1	3	32	8	.80	1	.272	.349	.383
1995 Michigan	A	118	438	124	25	8	9	—	—	192	103	59	79	0	85	6	3	3	41	13	.76	5	.283	.397	.438
1996 Trenton	AA	115	454	121	20	8	6	—	—	175	68	46	38	3	75	6	6	3	34	8	.81	6	.267	.329	.385
1997 Pawtucket	AAA	125	481	102	18	2	11	—	—	157	74	36	57	0	121	2	3	6	20	14	.59	11	.212	.295	.326
1998 Pawtucket	AAA	36	131	29	5	1	2	—	—	42	25	10	26	0	23	0	1	1	11	1	.92	1	.221	.348	.321
1998 Boston	AL	58	124	28	4	4	3	(0	3)	49	21	15	6	0	28	3	5	1	4	0	1.00	1	.226	.276	.395

A.J. Sager

Pitches: Right **Bats:** Right **Pos:** RP-28; SP-3   **Ht:** 6'4" **Wt:** 220 **Born:** 3/3/65 **Age:** 34

Year Team	Lg	G	GS	CG	GF	IP	BFP	H	R	ER	HR	SH	SF	HB	TBB	IBB	SO	WP	Bk	W	L	Pct.	ShO	Sv-Op	Hld	ERA
1998 Toledo *	AAA	14	0	0	5	24	107	27	8	8	1	1	1	0	13	1	16	0	0	1	2	.333	0	1- -	—	3.00
1994 San Diego	NL	22	3	0	4	46.2	217	62	34	31	4	6	2	2	16	5	26	0	0	1	4	.200	0	0-0	0	5.98
1995 Colorado	NL	10	0	0	2	14.2	70	19	16	12	1	2	0	0	7	1	10	0	0	0	0	.000	0	0-1	0	7.36
1996 Detroit	AL	22	9	0	1	79	347	91	46	44	10	3	3	2	29	2	52	1	0	4	5	.444	0	0-0	1	5.01
1997 Detroit	AL	38	1	0	8	84	350	81	43	39	10	5	6	1	24	6	53	0	0	3	4	.429	0	3-4	10	4.18
1998 Detroit	AL	31	3	0	7	59.1	274	79	47	43	7	5	2	1	23	4	23	4	0	4	2	.667	0	2-3	1	6.52
5 ML YEARS		123	16	0	22	283.2	1258	332	186	169	32	21	13	6	99	18	164	5	0	12	15	.444	0	5-8	12	5.36

Mike Saipe

Pitches: Right **Bats:** Right **Pos:** SP-2   **Ht:** 6'1" **Wt:** 188 **Born:** 9/10/73 **Age:** 25

Year Team	Lg	G	GS	CG	GF	IP	BFP	H	R	ER	HR	SH	SF	HB	TBB	IBB	SO	WP	Bk	W	L	Pct.	ShO	Sv-Op	Hld	ERA
1994 Bend	A-	16	16	0	0	84.1	363	73	56	39	7	3	4	7	34	0	74	6	2	3	7	.300	0	0- -	—	4.16
1995 Salem	A+	21	9	0	7	85.1	347	68	35	33	7	1	4	2	32	4	90	9	1	4	5	.444	0	3- -	—	3.48
1996 New Haven	AA	32	19	1	5	138	562	114	53	47	12	4	3	4	42	6	126	4	4	10	7	.588	1	3- -	—	3.07
1997 New Haven	AA	19	19	4	0	136.2	562	127	57	47	18	3	1	5	29	2	123	4	1	8	5	.615	2	0- -	—	3.10
Colo Sprngs	AAA	10	10	1	0	60.1	278	74	42	37	10	1	0	4	24	3	40	2	3	4	3	.571	0	0- -	—	5.52
1998 Colo Sprngs	AAA	24	24	2	0	139.2	632	167	96	80	19	3	6	5	51	1	124	4	2	5	11	.313	0	0- -	—	5.16

Year Team	Lg	G	GS	CG	GF	IP	BFP	H	R	ER	HR	SH	SF	HB	TBB	IBB	SO	WP	Bk	W	L	Pct.	ShO	Sv-Op	Hld	ERA
		HOW MUCH HE PITCHED						**WHAT HE GAVE UP**												**THE RESULTS**						
1998 Colorado	NL	2	2	0	0	10	54	22	12	12	5	1	0	2	0	0	2	0	0	0	1	.000	0	0-0	0	10.80

Tim Salmon

Bats: Right **Throws:** Right **Pos:** DH-111; RF-19; PH/PR-6   **Ht:** 6'3" **Wt:** 241 **Born:** 8/24/68 **Age:** 30

Year Team	Lg	G	AB	H	2B	3B	HR	(Hm	Rd)	TB	R	RBI	TBB	IBB	SO	HBP	SH	SF	SB	CS	SB%	GDP	Avg	OBP	SLG
								BATTING											**BASERUNNING**				**PERCENTAGES**		
1992 California	AL	23	79	14	1	0	2	(1	1)	21	8	6	11	1	23	1	0	1	1	1	.50	1	.177	.283	.266
1993 California	AL	142	515	146	35	1	31	(23	8)	276	93	95	82	5	135	5	0	8	5	6	.45	6	.283	.382	.536
1994 California	AL	100	373	107	18	2	23	(12	11)	198	67	70	54	2	102	5	0	3	1	3	.25	3	.287	.382	.531
1995 California	AL	143	537	177	34	3	34	(15	19)	319	111	105	91	2	111	6	0	4	5	5	.50	9	.330	.429	.594
1996 California	AL	156	581	166	27	4	30	(18	12)	291	90	98	93	7	125	4	0	3	4	2	.67	8	.286	.386	.501
1997 Anaheim	AL	157	582	172	28	1	33	(17	16)	301	95	129	95	5	142	7	0	11	9	12	.43	7	.296	.394	.517
1998 Anaheim	AL	136	463	139	28	1	26	(13	13)	247	84	88	90	5	100	3	0	10	0	1	.00	4	.300	.410	.533
7 ML YEARS		857	3130	921	171	12	179	(99	80)	1653	548	591	516	27	738	31	0	40	25	30	.45	38	.294	.395	.528

Benj Sampson

Pitches: Left **Bats:** Right **Pos:** RP-3; SP-2   **Ht:** 6'2" **Wt:** 210 **Born:** 4/27/75 **Age:** 24

Year Team	Lg	G	GS	CG	GF	IP	BFP	H	R	ER	HR	SH	SF	HB	TBB	IBB	SO	WP	Bk	W	L	Pct.	ShO	Sv-Op	Hld	ERA
		HOW MUCH HE PITCHED						**WHAT HE GAVE UP**												**THE RESULTS**						
1993 Elizabethtn	R+	11	6	0	2	42.1	171	33	12	9	1	2	0	1	15	1	34	5	0	4	1	.800	0	1- —	—	1.91
1994 Fort Wayne	A	25	25	0	0	139.2	617	149	72	59	10	7	5	5	60	0	111	5	0	6	9	.400	0	0- —	—	3.80
1995 Fort Myers	A+	28	27	3	1	160	664	148	71	62	11	8	8	4	52	0	95	5	0	11	9	.550	2	0- —	—	3.49
1996 Fort Myers	A+	11	11	2	0	70	282	55	28	27	5	1	2	1	26	0	65	1	0	7	1	.875	0	0- —	—	3.47
Hardware City	AA	16	16	1	0	75.1	353	108	54	48	8	0	2	2	25	0	51	2	1	5	7	.417	0	0- —	—	5.73
1997 New Britain	AA	25	20	0	1	118	498	112	56	55	12	2	5	1	49	1	92	4	2	10	6	.625	0	0- —	—	4.19
1998 Salt Lake	AAA	28	28	0	0	161	726	198	99	92	24	4	6	2	52	0	132	8	4	10	7	.588	0	0- —	—	5.14
1998 Minnesota	AL	5	2	0	1	17.1	67	10	3	3	0	0	2	0	7	0	16	2	0	1	0	1.000	0	0-0	0	1.56

Juan Samuel

Bats: R **Throws:** R **Pos:** PH/PR-28; DH-11; LF-8; 1B-3; 2B-2; RF-2   **Ht:** 5'11" **Wt:** 190 **Born:** 12/9/60 **Age:** 38

Year Team	Lg	G	AB	H	2B	3B	HR	(Hm	Rd)	TB	R	RBI	TBB	IBB	SO	HBP	SH	SF	SB	CS	SB%	GDP	Avg	OBP	SLG
								BATTING											**BASERUNNING**				**PERCENTAGES**		
1983 Philadelphia	NL	18	65	18	1	2	2	(1	1)	29	14	5	4	1	16	1	0	1	3	2	.60	1	.277	.324	.446
1984 Philadelphia	NL	160	701	191	36	19	15	(8	7)	310	105	69	28	2	168	7	0	1	72	15	.83	6	.272	.307	.442
1985 Philadelphia	NL	161	663	175	31	13	19	(8	11)	289	101	74	33	2	141	6	2	5	53	19	.74	8	.264	.303	.436
1986 Philadelphia	NL	145	591	157	36	12	16	(10	6)	265	90	78	26	3	142	8	1	7	42	14	.75	8	.266	.302	.448
1987 Philadelphia	NL	160	655	178	37	15	28	(15	13)	329	113	100	60	5	162	5	0	6	35	15	.70	12	.272	.335	.502
1988 Philadelphia	NL	157	629	153	32	9	12	(7	5)	239	68	67	39	6	151	12	0	5	33	10	.77	8	.243	.298	.380
1989 Phi-NYN	NL	137	532	125	16	2	11	(5	6)	178	69	48	42	2	120	11	2	2	42	12	.78	7	.235	.303	.335
1990 Los Angeles	NL	143	492	119	24	3	13	(6	7)	188	62	52	51	5	126	5	5	5	38	20	.66	8	.242	.316	.382
1991 Los Angeles	NL	153	594	161	22	6	12	(4	8)	231	74	58	49	4	133	3	10	3	23	8	.74	4	.271	.328	.389
1992 LA-KC		76	224	61	8	4	0	(0	0)	77	22	23	14	4	49	2	4	2	8	3	.73	2	.272	.318	.344
1993 Cincinnati	NL	103	261	60	10	4	4	(1	3)	90	31	26	23	3	53	3	0	2	9	7	.56	2	.230	.298	.345
1994 Detroit	AL	59	136	42	9	5	5	(4	1)	76	32	21	10	0	26	0	1	1	5	2	.71	4	.309	.364	.559
1995 Det-KC	AL	91	206	54	10	1	12	(6	6)	102	31	39	29	1	49	2	1	0	6	4	.60	3	.263	.360	.498
1996 Toronto	AL	69	188	48	8	3	8	(4	4)	86	34	26	15	0	65	3	0	1	9	1	.90	2	.255	.319	.457
1997 Toronto	AL	45	95	27	5	4	3	(2	1)	49	13	15	10	1	28	2	1	1	5	3	.63	2	.284	.364	.516
1998 Toronto	AL	43	50	9	2	0	1	(1	0)	14	14	2	7	0	13	1	1	0	13	8	.62	0	.180	.293	.280
1989 Philadelphia	NL	51	199	49	3	1	8	(3	5)	78	32	20	18	1	45	1	0	1	11	3	.79	2	.246	.311	.392
New York		86	333	76	13	1	3	(2	1)	100	37	28	24	1	75	10	2	1	31	9	.78	5	.228	.299	.300
1992 Los Angeles	NL	47	122	32	3	1	0	(0	0)	37	7	15	7	3	22	1	4	2	2	2	.50	0	.262	.303	.303
Kansas City	AL	29	102	29	5	3	0	(0	0)	40	15	8	7	1	27	1	0	0	6	1	.86	2	.284	.336	.392
1995 Detroit	AL	76	171	48	10	1	10	(6	4)	90	28	34	24	0	38	2	1	0	5	4	.56	3	.281	.376	.526
Kansas City	AL	15	34	6	0	0	2	(0	2)	12	3	5	5	1	11	0	0	0	1	0	1.00	0	.176	.282	.353
16 ML YEARS		1720	6081	1578	287	102	161	(82	79)	2552	873	703	440	38	1442	74	27	42	396	143	.73	81	.259	.315	.420

Jesus Sanchez

Pitches: Left **Bats:** Left **Pos:** SP-29; RP-6   **Ht:** 5'10" **Wt:** 153 **Born:** 10/11/74 **Age:** 24

Year Team	Lg	G	GS	CG	GF	IP	BFP	H	R	ER	HR	SH	SF	HB	TBB	IBB	SO	WP	Bk	W	L	Pct.	ShO	Sv-Op	Hld	ERA
		HOW MUCH HE PITCHED						**WHAT HE GAVE UP**												**THE RESULTS**						
1994 Kingsport	R+	13	12	3	0	87.1	346	61	27	19	2	1	1	4	24	0	71	7	1	7	4	.636	0	0- —	—	1.96
1995 Capital City	A	27	27	4	0	169.2	705	154	76	59	9	2	5	7	58	0	177	10	4	9	7	.563	0	0- —	—	3.13
1996 St. Lucie	A+	16	16	2	0	92	344	53	22	20	6	3	1	1	24	0	81	4	2	9	3	.750	1	0- —	—	1.96
1997 Binghamton	AA	26	26	3	0	165.1	693	146	87	79	25	4	6	5	61	2	176	4	3	13	10	.565	0	0- —	—	4.30
1998 Florida	NL	35	29	0	1	173	765	178	98	86	18	12	4	4	91	2	137	8	5	7	9	.438	0	0-1	0	4.47

198

Rey Sanchez

Bats: Right **Throws:** Right **Pos:** SS-76; 2B-36; PH/PR-13   **Ht:** 5'9" **Wt:** 170 **Born:** 10/5/67 **Age:** 31

Year Team	Lg	G	AB	H	2B	3B	HR	(Hm	Rd)	TB	R	RBI	TBB	IBB	SO	HBP	SH	SF	SB	CS	SB%	GDP	Avg	OBP	SLG
1991 Chicago	NL	13	23	6	0	0	0	(0	0)	6	1	2	4	0	3	0	0	0	0	0	.00	0	.261	.370	.261
1992 Chicago	NL	74	255	64	14	3	1	(1	0)	87	24	19	10	1	17	3	5	2	2	1	.67	7	.251	.285	.341
1993 Chicago	NL	105	344	97	11	2	0	(0	0)	112	35	28	15	7	22	3	9	2	1	1	.50	8	.282	.316	.326
1994 Chicago	NL	96	291	83	13	1	0	(0	0)	98	26	24	20	4	29	7	4	1	2	5	.29	9	.285	.345	.337
1995 Chicago	NL	114	428	119	22	2	3	(0	3)	154	57	27	14	2	48	1	8	2	6	4	.60	9	.278	.301	.360
1996 Chicago	NL	95	289	61	9	0	1	(1	0)	73	28	12	22	8	42	3	8	2	7	1	.88	6	.211	.272	.253
1997 ChN-NYA		135	343	94	21	0	2	(1	1)	121	35	27	16	2	47	1	9	1	4	6	.40	8	.274	.307	.353
1998 San Francisco	NL	109	316	90	14	2	2	(0	2)	114	44	30	16	0	47	4	1	2	0	0	.00	11	.285	.325	.361
1997 Chicago	NL	97	205	51	9	0	1	(1	0)	63	14	12	11	2	26	0	4	0	4	2	.67	7	.249	.287	.307
New York	AL	38	138	43	12	0	1	(0	1)	58	21	15	5	0	21	1	5	1	0	4	.00	1	.312	.338	.420
8 ML YEARS		741	2289	614	104	10	9	(3	6)	765	250	169	117	22	255	22	44	12	22	18	.55	58	.268	.309	.334

Reggie Sanders

Bats: Right **Throws:** Right **Pos:** CF-88; RF-57; PH/PR-10   **Ht:** 6'1" **Wt:** 185 **Born:** 12/1/67 **Age:** 31

Year Team	Lg	G	AB	H	2B	3B	HR	(Hm	Rd)	TB	R	RBI	TBB	IBB	SO	HBP	SH	SF	SB	CS	SB%	GDP	Avg	OBP	SLG
1991 Cincinnati	NL	9	40	8	0	0	1	(0	1)	11	6	3	0	0	9	0	0	0	1	1	.50	1	.200	.200	.275
1992 Cincinnati	NL	116	385	104	26	6	12	(6	6)	178	62	36	48	2	98	4	0	1	16	7	.70	6	.270	.356	.462
1993 Cincinnati	NL	138	496	136	16	4	20	(8	12)	220	90	83	51	7	118	5	3	8	27	10	.73	10	.274	.343	.444
1994 Cincinnati	NL	107	400	105	20	8	17	(10	7)	192	66	62	41	1	114	2	1	3	21	9	.70	2	.263	.332	.480
1995 Cincinnati	NL	133	484	148	36	6	28	(9	19)	280	91	99	69	4	122	8	0	6	36	12	.75	9	.306	.397	.579
1996 Cincinnati	NL	81	287	72	17	1	14	(7	7)	133	49	33	44	4	86	2	0	1	24	8	.75	8	.251	.353	.463
1997 Cincinnati	NL	86	312	79	19	2	19	(11	8)	159	52	56	42	3	93	3	1	0	13	7	.65	9	.253	.347	.510
1998 Cincinnati	NL	135	481	129	18	6	14	(7	7)	201	83	59	51	2	137	7	4	2	20	9	.69	10	.268	.346	.418
8 ML YEARS		805	2885	781	152	33	125	(58	67)	1374	499	431	346	23	777	31	9	21	158	63	.71	55	.271	.353	.476

Scott Sanders

Pitches: Right **Bats:** Right **Pos:** RP-24; SP-2   **Ht:** 6'4" **Wt:** 220 **Born:** 3/25/69 **Age:** 30

Year Team	Lg	G	GS	CG	GF	IP	BFP	H	R	ER	HR	SH	SF	HB	TBB	IBB	SO	WP	Bk	W	L	Pct.	ShO	Sv-Op	Hld	ERA
1998 Las Vegas *	AAA	15	3	0	6	36.2	151	34	14	14	2	2	1	2	12	3	43	0	0	1	2	.333	0	3- —	—	3.44
1993 San Diego	NL	9	9	0	0	52.1	231	54	32	24	4	1	2	1	23	1	37	0	1	3	3	.500	0	0-0	—	4.13
1994 San Diego	NL	23	20	0	2	111	485	103	63	59	10	6	5	5	48	4	109	10	1	4	8	.333	0	1-1	1	4.78
1995 San Diego	NL	17	15	1	0	90	383	79	46	43	14	2	2	2	31	4	88	6	1	5	5	.500	0	0-0	1	4.30
1996 San Diego	NL	46	16	0	6	144	594	117	58	54	10	7	7	2	48	5	157	7	0	9	5	.643	0	0-0	3	3.38
1997 Sea-Det	AL	47	20	1	15	139.2	626	152	92	91	30	3	10	4	62	6	120	8	0	6	14	.300	1	2-4	4	5.86
1998 Det-SD		26	2	0	8	40.1	188	57	39	33	6	4	0	0	11	3	32	2	0	3	3	.500	0	0-0	1	7.36
1997 Seattle	AL	33	6	0	15	65.1	309	73	48	47	16	2	5	3	38	5	62	4	0	3	6	.333	0	2-4	4	6.47
Detroit	AL	14	14	1	0	74.1	317	79	44	44	14	1	5	1	24	1	58	4	0	3	8	.273	1	0-0	0	5.33
1998 Detroit	AL	3	2	0	1	9.2	57	24	19	19	1	0	0	0	6	2	6	1	0	0	2	.000	0	0-0	0	17.69
San Diego	NL	23	0	0	7	30.2	131	33	20	14	5	4	0	0	5	1	26	1	0	3	1	.750	0	0-0	1	4.11
6 ML YEARS		168	82	2	31	577.1	2507	562	330	304	74	23	26	14	223	23	543	33	3	30	38	.441	1	3-5	10	4.74

Chance Sanford

Bats: Left **Throws:** Right **Pos:** PH/PR-8; 3B-5; 2B-1; SS-1   **Ht:** 5'10" **Wt:** 175 **Born:** 6/2/72 **Age:** 27

Year Team	Lg	G	AB	H	2B	3B	HR	(Hm	Rd)	TB	R	RBI	TBB	IBB	SO	HBP	SH	SF	SB	CS	SB%	GDP	Avg	OBP	SLG
1992 Welland	A-	59	214	61	11	3	5	—	—	93	36	21	35	4	39	0	0	3	13	4	.76	2	.285	.381	.435
Augusta	A	14	46	5	1	0	0	—	—	6	3	2	3	0	10	1	0	0	0	2	.00	0	.109	.180	.130
1993 Salem	A+	115	428	109	21	5	10	—	—	170	54	37	33	0	80	1	3	2	11	10	.52	0	.255	.308	.397
1994 Salem	A+	127	474	130	32	6	19	—	—	231	81	78	56	0	95	0	4	4	12	6	.67	7	.274	.351	.487
1995 Carolina	AA	16	36	10	3	1	3	—	—	24	6	10	5	1	7	1	0	0	3	1	.75	0	.278	.381	.667
Pirates	R	6	19	4	0	0	1	—	—	7	2	1	2	0	2	0	0	0	0	0	.00	0	.211	.286	.368
Lynchburg	A+	16	66	22	4	0	3	—	—	35	8	14	7	0	13	0	0	1	1	0	1.00	1	.333	.392	.530
1996 Carolina	AA	131	470	115	16	13	4	—	—	169	62	56	72	2	108	0	2	7	11	11	.50	9	.245	.341	.360
1997 Carolina	AA	44	149	39	10	2	9	—	—	80	30	36	20	1	39	2	2	4	3	1	.75	1	.262	.349	.537
Calgary	AAA	89	325	95	27	9	6	—	—	158	58	60	39	0	82	3	1	5	9	7	.56	5	.292	.368	.486
1998 Nashville	AAA	27	81	21	7	1	4	—	—	42	17	21	16	0	12	0	0	0	0	1	.00	1	.259	.381	.519
1998 Pittsburgh	NL	14	28	4	1	1	0	(0	0)	7	3	3	1	0	6	0	0	0	0	0	.00	1	.143	.172	.250

Julio Santana

Pitches: Right **Bats:** Right **Pos:** SP-19; RP-16   **Ht:** 6'0" **Wt:** 185 **Born:** 1/20/73 **Age:** 26

Year Team	Lg	G	GS	CG	GF	IP	BFP	H	R	ER	HR	SH	SF	HB	TBB	IBB	SO	WP	Bk	W	L	Pct.	ShO	Sv-Op	Hld	ERA
1993 Rangers	R	26	0	0	12	39	153	31	9	6	0	0	0	1	7	0	50	1	0	4	1	.800	0	7- —	—	1.38
1994 Chston-SC	A	16	16	0	0	91.1	383	65	36	25	3	0	4	7	44	0	103	7	1	6	7	.462	0	0- —	—	2.46
Tulsa	AA	11	11	2	0	71.1	290	50	26	23	1	1	2	2	41	0	45	2	0	7	2	.778	0	0- —	—	2.90
1995 Okla City	AAA	2	2	0	0	3	25	9	14	13	3	0	0	0	7	0	6	1	1	0	2	.000	0	0- —	—	39.00
Charlotte	A+	5	5	1	0	31.1	136	32	16	13	1	1	1	0	16	0	27	7	2	0	3	.000	0	0- —	—	3.73
Tulsa	AA	15	15	3	0	103	438	91	40	36	8	2	4	0	52	2	71	8	1	6	4	.600	0	0- —	—	3.15

Year Team	Lg	G	GS	CG	GF	IP	BFP	H	R	ER	HR	SH	SF	HB	TBB	IBB	SO	WP	Bk	W	L	Pct.	ShO	Sv-Op	Hld	ERA
									HOW MUCH HE PITCHED			WHAT HE GAVE UP									THE RESULTS				
1996 Okla City	AAA	29	29	4	0	185.2	787	171	102	83	12	5	9	5	66	1	113	12	1	11	12	.478	1	0--	—	4.02
1997 Okla City	AAA	1	1	0	0	3	20	9	6	5	0	0	0	0	2	0	1	0	0	0	0	.000	0	0--	—	15.00
1997 Texas	AL	30	14	0	3	104	496	141	86	78	16	1	5	4	49	2	64	8	1	4	6	.400	0	0-1	1	6.75
1998 Tex-TB	AL	35	19	1	5	145.2	630	151	77	71	18	2	5	5	62	3	61	3	0	5	6	.455	0	0-0	0	4.39
1998 Texas	AL	3	0	0	0	5.1	27	7	5	5	0	0	0	0	4	1	1	0	0	0	0	.000	0	0-0	0	8.44
Tampa Bay	AL	32	19	1	5	140.1	603	144	72	66	18	2	5	5	58	2	60	3	0	5	6	.455	0	0-0	0	4.23
2 ML YEARS		65	33	1	8	249.2	1126	292	163	149	34	3	10	9	111	5	125	11	1	9	12	.429	0	0-1	1	5.37

Marino Santana

Pitches: Right **Bats:** Right **Pos:** RP-7   **Ht:** 6'1" **Wt:** 175 **Born:** 5/10/72 **Age:** 27

Year Team	Lg	G	GS	CG	GF	IP	BFP	H	R	ER	HR	SH	SF	HB	TBB	IBB	SO	WP	Bk	W	L	Pct.	ShO	Sv-Op	Hld	ERA
						HOW MUCH HE PITCHED				WHAT HE GAVE UP												THE RESULTS				
1993 Bellingham	A-	15	0	0	8	21.2	117	27	19	14	3	0	1	0	22	1	24	4	2	0	1	.000	0	0--	—	5.82
1994 Bellingham	A-	15	15	1	0	80	331	68	35	28	3	1	1	3	26	0	88	10	3	6	3	.667	0	0--	—	3.15
1995 Wisconsin	A	15	15	2	0	96.2	368	57	26	19	5	2	2	1	25	0	110	6	0	8	3	.727	1	0--	—	1.77
Riverside	A+	9	9	0	0	48	214	44	47	33	10	3	4	2	25	0	57	2	3	3	5	.375	0	0--	—	6.19
1996 Lancaster	A+	28	28	1	0	157.1	688	164	105	88	26	5	8	8	57	0	167	18	6	8	15	.348	0	0--	—	5.03
1997 Jacksonville	AA	39	0	0	10	74	317	55	28	27	8	1	1	1	43	0	98	13	1	4	1	.800	0	1--	—	3.28
1998 Toledo	AAA	44	0	0	24	68.1	277	44	30	22	10	1	4	1	34	1	94	10	2	6	3	.667	0	7--	—	2.90
1998 Detroit	AL	7	0	0	2	7.1	39	9	3	3	1	1	0	1	8	2	10	3	0	0	0	.000	0	0-0	1	3.68

F.P. Santangelo

Bats: B **Throws:** R **Pos:** LF-72; 2B-35; CF-23; PH/PR-10; 3B-1; RF-1   **Ht:** 5'10" **Wt:** 180 **Born:** 10/24/67 **Age:** 31

Year Team	Lg	G	AB	H	2B	3B	HR	(Hm	Rd)	TB	R	RBI	TBB	IBB	SO	HBP	SH	SF	SB	CS	SB%	GDP	Avg	OBP	SLG
						BATTING													BASERUNNING				PERCENTAGES		
1998 Ottawa *	AAA	2	8	2	0	0	0	—	—	2	1	1	0	0	3	1	0	0	0	0	.00	0	.250	.333	.250
1995 Montreal	NL	35	98	29	5	1	1	(1	0)	39	11	9	12	0	9	2	1	0	1	1	.50	1	.296	.384	.398
1996 Montreal	NL	152	393	109	20	5	7	(5	2)	160	54	56	49	4	61	11	9	5	5	2	.71	6	.277	.369	.407
1997 Montreal	NL	130	350	87	19	5	5	(5	0)	131	56	31	50	1	73	25	12	3	8	5	.62	1	.249	.379	.374
1998 Montreal	NL	122	383	82	18	0	4	(2	2)	112	53	23	44	1	72	23	11	1	7	3	.70	5	.214	.330	.292
4 ML YEARS		439	1224	307	62	11	17	(13	4)	442	174	119	155	6	215	61	33	9	21	11	.66	12	.251	.361	.361

Benito Santiago

Bats: Right **Throws:** Right **Pos:** C-15; PH/PR-4   **Ht:** 6'1" **Wt:** 195 **Born:** 3/9/65 **Age:** 34

Year Team	Lg	G	AB	H	2B	3B	HR	(Hm	Rd)	TB	R	RBI	TBB	IBB	SO	HBP	SH	SF	SB	CS	SB%	GDP	Avg	OBP	SLG
						BATTING													BASERUNNING				PERCENTAGES		
1998 Dunedin *	A+	11	37	6	1	0	1	—	—	10	4	5	3	0	9	0	0	0	3	0	1.00	1	.162	.225	.270
Syracuse *	AAA	5	22	5	2	0	0	—	—	7	0	2	1	0	3	0	0	0	0	0	.00	1	.227	.261	.318
1986 San Diego	NL	17	62	18	2	0	3	(2	1)	29	10	6	2	0	12	0	0	1	0	1	.00	0	.290	.308	.468
1987 San Diego	NL	146	546	164	33	2	18	(11	7)	255	64	79	16	2	112	5	1	4	21	12	.64	12	.300	.324	.467
1988 San Diego	NL	139	492	122	22	2	10	(3	7)	178	49	46	24	2	82	1	5	5	15	7	.68	18	.248	.282	.362
1989 San Diego	NL	129	462	109	16	3	16	(8	8)	179	50	62	26	6	89	1	3	2	11	6	.65	9	.236	.277	.387
1990 San Diego	NL	100	344	93	8	5	11	(5	6)	144	42	53	27	2	55	3	1	7	5	5	.50	4	.270	.323	.419
1991 San Diego	NL	152	580	155	22	3	17	(6	11)	234	60	87	23	5	114	4	0	7	8	10	.44	21	.267	.296	.403
1992 San Diego	NL	106	386	97	21	0	10	(8	2)	148	37	42	21	1	52	0	0	4	2	5	.29	14	.251	.287	.383
1993 Florida	NL	139	469	108	19	6	13	(6	7)	178	49	50	37	2	88	5	0	4	10	7	.59	9	.230	.291	.380
1994 Florida	NL	101	337	92	14	2	11	(4	7)	143	35	41	25	1	57	1	2	4	1	2	.33	11	.273	.322	.424
1995 Cincinnati	NL	81	266	76	20	0	11	(7	4)	129	40	44	24	1	48	4	0	2	2	2	.50	7	.286	.351	.485
1996 Philadelphia	NL	136	481	127	21	2	30	(8	22)	242	71	85	49	7	104	1	0	2	2	0	1.00	8	.264	.332	.503
1997 Toronto	AL	97	341	83	10	0	13	(7	6)	132	31	42	17	1	80	2	1	5	1	0	1.00	1	.243	.279	.387
1998 Toronto	AL	15	29	9	5	0	0	(0	0)	14	3	4	1	0	6	0	0	0	0	0	.00	1	.310	.333	.483
13 ML YEARS		1358	4795	1253	213	25	163	(75	88)	2005	541	641	292	30	899	27	13	47	78	57	.58	124	.261	.305	.418

Jose Santiago

Pitches: Right **Bats:** Right **Pos:** RP-2   **Ht:** 6'3" **Wt:** 215 **Born:** 11/5/74 **Age:** 24

Year Team	Lg	G	GS	CG	GF	IP	BFP	H	R	ER	HR	SH	SF	HB	TBB	IBB	SO	WP	Bk	W	L	Pct.	ShO	Sv-Op	Hld	ERA
						HOW MUCH HE PITCHED				WHAT HE GAVE UP												THE RESULTS				
1994 Royals	R	10	1	0	7	19	84	17	7	5	1	0	0	1	7	0	10	2	1	1	0	1.000	0	2--	—	2.37
1995 Spokane	A-	22	0	0	10	48.2	227	60	26	17	1	1	2	5	20	4	32	3	0	2	4	.333	0	1--	—	3.14
1996 Lansing	A	54	0	0	46	77	331	78	34	22	4	7	1	5	21	3	55	3	1	7	6	.538	0	19--	—	2.57
1997 Wilmington	A+	4	0	0	4	3.2	18	3	3	2	0	1	0	1	1	0	1	0	0	1	1	.500	0	2--	—	4.91
Lansing	A	9	0	0	6	13	57	10	6	3	0	0	1	0	6	1	8	0	0	1	0	1.000	0	1--	—	2.08
Wichita	AA	22	0	0	8	27	120	32	13	12	1	1	2	2	8	1	12	0	0	1	2	.333	0	3--	—	4.00
1998 Wichita	AA	52	0	0	41	72.1	316	79	36	29	9	6	1	1	27	7	31	1	0	3	4	.429	0	22--	—	3.61
Omaha	AAA	4	0	0	2	7.2	40	10	9	6	0	1	0	1	5	2	4	1	0	0	0	.000	0	1--	—	7.04
1997 Kansas City	AL	4	0	0	3	4.2	24	7	2	1	0	0	0	1	2	1	1	0	0	0	0	.000	0	0-0	0	1.93
1998 Kansas City	AL	2	0	0	2	2	9	4	2	2	0	0	0	0	0	0	2	0	0	0	0	.000	0	0-0	0	9.00
2 ML YEARS		6	0	0	5	6.2	33	11	4	3	0	0	0	1	2	1	3	0	0	0	0	.000	0	0-0	0	4.05

Rob Sasser

Bats: Right **Throws:** Right **Pos:** PH/PR-1   **Ht:** 6'3" **Wt:** 205 **Born:** 3/9/75 **Age:** 24

Year Team	Lg	G	AB	H	2B	3B	HR	(Hm	Rd)	TB	R	RBI	TBB	IBB	SO	HBP	SH	SF	SB	CS	SB%	GDP	Avg	OBP	SLG
1993 Braves	R	33	113	27	4	0	0	—	—	31	19	7	6	0	25	4	0	2	2	1	.67	1	.239	.296	.274
1994 Idaho Falls	R+	58	219	50	9	6	2	—	—	77	32	26	19	3	58	1	0	1	13	1	.93	3	.228	.292	.352
1995 Danville	R+	12	47	15	2	1	0	—	—	19	8	7	4	1	7	0	0	1	5	1	.83	1	.319	.365	.404
Eugene	A-	57	216	58	9	1	9	—	—	96	40	32	23	1	51	3	0	2	14	4	.78	2	.269	.344	.444
1996 Macon	A	135	465	122	35	3	8	—	—	187	64	64	65	4	108	5	3	6	38	8	.83	4	.262	.355	.402
1997 Cedar Rapds	A	134	497	135	26	5	17	—	—	222	103	77	69	6	92	8	0	3	37	13	.74	11	.272	.367	.447
1998 Charlotte	A+	4	13	4	2	0	0	—	—	6	1	3	3	0	5	0	0	1	1	0	1.00	1	.308	.438	.462
Tulsa	AA	111	417	117	25	2	8	—	—	170	57	62	60	0	98	3	1	4	18	12	.60	11	.281	.372	.408
1998 Texas	AL	1	1	0	0	0	0	(0	0)	0	0	0	0	0	0	0	0	0	0	0	.00	0	.000	.000	.000

Tony Saunders

Pitches: Left **Bats:** Left **Pos:** SP-31   **Ht:** 6'2" **Wt:** 205 **Born:** 4/29/74 **Age:** 25

Year Team	Lg	G	GS	CG	GF	IP	BFP	H	R	ER	HR	SH	SF	HB	TBB	IBB	SO	WP	Bk	W	L	Pct.	ShO	Sv-Op	Hld	ERA
1992 Marlins	R	24	0	0	16	45.2	180	29	10	6	0	2	3	1	13	2	37	4	0	4	1	.800	0	7--	—	1.18
1993 Kane County	A	23	10	2	1	83.1	344	72	23	21	3	6	0	2	32	3	87	2	1	6	1	.857	0	1--	—	2.27
1994 Brevard Cty	A+	10	10	1	0	60	237	54	24	21	4	2	1	2	9	0	46	2	0	5	5	.500	0	0--	—	3.15
1995 Brevard Cty	A+	13	13	0	0	71	275	60	29	24	6	1	4	7	15	0	54	3	0	6	5	.545	0	0--	—	3.04
1996 Portland	AA	26	26	2	0	167.2	669	121	51	49	10	8	4	0	62	3	156	8	1	13	4	.765	0	0--	—	2.63
1997 Portland	AA	1	1	0	0	2	10	3	2	2	0	0	0	0	1	0	3	0	0	0	0	.000	0	0--	—	9.00
Charlotte	AAA	3	3	0	0	13	50	9	4	4	1	1	0	0	6	0	9	0	0	1	0	1.000	0	0--	—	2.77
1997 Florida	NL	22	21	0	0	111.1	483	99	62	57	12	8	4	2	64	1	102	2	1	4	6	.400	0	0-0	0	4.61
1998 Tampa Bay	AL	31	31	2	0	192.1	855	191	95	88	15	6	10	7	111	1	172	2	1	6	15	.286	0	0-0	0	4.12
2 ML YEARS		53	52	2	0	303.2	1338	290	157	145	27	14	14	9	175	2	274	4	2	10	21	.323	0	0-0	0	4.30

Bob Scanlan

Pitches: Right **Bats:** Right **Pos:** RP-27   **Ht:** 6'7" **Wt:** 215 **Born:** 8/9/66 **Age:** 32

Year Team	Lg	G	GS	CG	GF	IP	BFP	H	R	ER	HR	SH	SF	HB	TBB	IBB	SO	WP	Bk	W	L	Pct.	ShO	Sv-Op	Hld	ERA
1998 New Orleans *	AAA	14	12	1	0	61.1	295	90	50	44	6	3	5	2	24	0	35	2	0	5	4	.556	0	0--	—	6.46
1991 Chicago	NL	40	13	0	16	111	482	114	60	48	5	8	6	3	40	3	44	5	1	7	8	.467	0	1-2	2	3.89
1992 Chicago	NL	69	0	0	41	87.1	360	76	32	28	4	4	2	1	30	6	42	6	4	3	6	.333	0	14-18	7	2.89
1993 Chicago	NL	70	0	0	13	75.1	323	79	41	38	6	2	6	3	28	7	44	0	2	4	5	.444	0	0-3	25	4.54
1994 Milwaukee	AL	30	12	0	9	103	441	117	53	47	11	1	2	4	28	2	65	3	1	2	6	.250	0	2-3	3	4.11
1995 Milwaukee	AL	17	14	0	1	83.1	389	101	66	61	9	0	6	7	44	3	29	3	0	4	7	.364	0	0-0	0	6.59
1996 Det-KC	AL	17	0	0	4	22.1	105	29	19	17	2	1	0	2	12	2	6	1	0	0	1	.000	0	0-1	5	6.85
1998 Houston	NL	27	0	0	9	26.1	118	24	12	9	4	3	3	1	13	0	9	5	0	0	1	.000	0	0-0	3	3.08
1996 Detroit	AL	8	0	0	2	11	57	16	15	13	1	1	0	1	9	1	3	1	0	0	0	.000	0	0-0	0	10.64
Kansas City	AL	9	0	0	2	11.1	48	13	4	4	1	0	0	1	3	1	3	0	0	0	1	.000	0	0-1	5	3.18
7 ML YEARS		270	39	0	93	508.2	2218	540	283	248	41	19	25	21	195	23	239	23	8	20	34	.370	0	17-27	45	4.39

Curt Schilling

Pitches: Right **Bats:** Right **Pos:** SP-35   **Ht:** 6'4" **Wt:** 228 **Born:** 11/14/66 **Age:** 32

Year Team	Lg	G	GS	CG	GF	IP	BFP	H	R	ER	HR	SH	SF	HB	TBB	IBB	SO	WP	Bk	W	L	Pct.	ShO	Sv-Op	Hld	ERA
1988 Baltimore	AL	4	4	0	0	14.2	76	22	19	16	3	0	3	1	10	1	4	2	0	0	3	.000	0	0-0	0	9.82
1989 Baltimore	AL	5	1	0	0	8.2	38	10	6	6	2	0	0	0	3	0	6	1	0	0	1	.000	0	0-0	0	6.23
1990 Baltimore	AL	35	0	0	16	46	191	38	13	13	1	2	4	0	19	0	32	0	0	1	2	.333	0	3-9	5	2.54
1991 Houston	NL	56	0	0	34	75.2	336	79	35	32	2	5	1	0	39	7	71	4	1	3	5	.375	0	8-11	5	3.81
1992 Philadelphia	NL	42	26	10	10	226.1	895	165	67	59	11	7	8	1	59	4	147	4	0	14	11	.560	4	2-3	0	2.35
1993 Philadelphia	NL	34	34	7	0	235.1	982	234	114	105	23	9	7	4	57	6	186	9	3	16	7	.696	2	0-0	0	4.02
1994 Philadelphia	NL	13	13	1	0	82.1	360	87	42	41	10	6	1	3	28	3	58	3	1	2	8	.200	0	0-0	0	4.48
1995 Philadelphia	NL	17	17	1	0	116	473	96	52	46	12	5	2	3	26	2	114	0	1	7	5	.583	0	0-0	0	3.57
1996 Philadelphia	NL	26	26	8	0	183.1	732	149	69	65	16	6	4	3	50	5	182	5	0	9	10	.474	2	0-0	0	3.19
1997 Philadelphia	NL	35	35	7	0	254.1	1009	208	96	84	25	8	6	3	58	3	319	5	1	17	11	.607	2	0-0	0	2.97
1998 Philadelphia	NL	35	35	15	0	268.2	1089	236	101	97	23	14	7	6	61	3	300	12	0	15	14	.517	2	0-0	0	3.25
11 ML YEARS		302	191	49	60	1511.1	6181	1324	614	564	128	62	45	26	410	34	1419	45	7	84	77	.522	12	13-23	10	3.36

Jason Schmidt

Pitches: Right **Bats:** Right **Pos:** SP-33   **Ht:** 6'5" **Wt:** 207 **Born:** 1/29/73 **Age:** 26

Year Team	Lg	G	GS	CG	GF	IP	BFP	H	R	ER	HR	SH	SF	HB	TBB	IBB	SO	WP	Bk	W	L	Pct.	ShO	Sv-Op	Hld	ERA
1995 Atlanta	NL	9	2	0	1	25	119	27	16	16	2	2	4	1	18	3	19	1	0	2	2	.500	0	0-1	0	5.76
1996 Atl-Pit	NL	19	17	1	0	96.1	445	108	67	61	10	4	9	2	53	0	74	8	1	5	6	.455	0	0-0	0	5.70
1997 Pittsburgh	NL	32	32	2	0	187.2	825	193	106	96	16	10	3	9	76	2	136	8	0	10	9	.526	0	0-0	0	4.60
1998 Pittsburgh	NL	33	33	0	0	214.1	916	228	100	97	24	10	3	4	71	3	158	15	1	11	14	.440	0	0-0	0	4.07
1996 Atlanta	NL	13	11	0	0	58.2	274	69	48	44	8	3	6	0	32	0	48	5	1	3	4	.429	0	0-0	0	6.75
Pittsburgh	NL	6	6	1	0	37.2	171	39	19	17	2	1	3	2	21	0	26	3	0	2	2	.500	0	0-0	0	4.06
4 ML YEARS		93	84	3	1	523.1	2305	556	296	270	52	26	19	16	218	8	387	32	2	28	31	.475	0	0-1	0	4.64

Pete Schourek

Pitches: Left   **Bats:** Left   **Pos:** SP-23; RP-2   **Ht:** 6'5"   **Wt:** 205   **Born:** 5/10/69   **Age:** 30

Year Team	Lg	G	GS	CG	GF	IP	BFP	H	R	ER	HR	SH	SF	HB	TBB	IBB	SO	WP	Bk	W	L	Pct.	ShO	Sv-Op	Hld	ERA
1998 Kissimmee *	A+	2	1	0	0	8.1	38	8	1	1	0	2	0	1	4	0	9	0	0	0	0	.000	0	0--	--	1.08
1991 New York	NL	35	8	1	7	86.1	385	82	49	41	7	5	4	2	43	4	67	1	0	4	5	.556	1	2-3	1	4.27
1992 New York	NL	22	21	0	0	136	578	137	60	55	9	4	4	2	44	6	60	4	2	6	8	.429	0	0-0	0	3.64
1993 New York	NL	41	18	0	6	128.1	586	168	90	85	13	3	8	3	45	7	72	1	2	5	12	.294	0	0-1	2	5.96
1994 Cincinnati	NL	22	10	0	3	81.1	354	90	39	37	11	6	2	3	29	4	69	0	0	7	2	.778	0	0-0	0	4.09
1995 Cincinnati	NL	29	29	2	0	190.1	754	158	72	68	17	4	4	8	45	3	160	1	1	18	7	.720	0	0-0	0	3.22
1996 Cincinnati	NL	12	12	0	0	67.1	304	79	48	45	7	3	4	3	24	1	54	3	0	4	5	.444	0	0-0	0	6.01
1997 Cincinnati	NL	18	17	0	0	84.2	371	78	59	51	18	4	1	4	38	0	59	2	0	5	8	.385	0	0-0	0	5.42
1998 Hou-Bos		25	23	0	0	124	537	127	64	61	17	5	7	5	50	1	95	7	0	8	9	.471	0	0-0	1	4.43
1998 Houston	NL	15	15	0	0	80	354	82	43	40	10	5	4	4	36	0	59	5	0	7	6	.538	0	0-0	0	4.50
Boston	AL	10	8	0	0	44	183	45	21	21	7	0	3	1	14	1	36	2	0	1	3	.250	0	0-0	1	4.30
8 ML YEARS		204	138	3	16	898.1	3869	919	481	443	99	34	34	30	318	26	636	19	5	58	55	.513	1	2-4	6	4.44

Rudy Seanez

Pitches: Right   **Bats:** Right   **Pos:** RP-34   **Ht:** 5'10"   **Wt:** 190   **Born:** 10/20/68   **Age:** 30

Year Team	Lg	G	GS	CG	GF	IP	BFP	H	R	ER	HR	SH	SF	HB	TBB	IBB	SO	WP	Bk	W	L	Pct.	ShO	Sv-Op	Hld	ERA
1998 Richmond *	AAA	16	0	0	13	21	85	13	9	3	1	0	0	0	7	1	33	1	0	2	0	1.000	0	7--	--	1.29
1989 Cleveland	AL	5	0	0	2	5	20	1	2	2	0	0	2	0	4	1	7	1	1	0	0	.000	0	0-0	0	3.60
1990 Cleveland	AL	24	0	0	12	27.1	127	22	17	17	2	0	1	1	25	1	24	5	0	2	1	.667	0	0-0	3	5.60
1991 Cleveland	AL	5	0	0	0	5	33	10	12	9	2	0	0	0	7	0	7	2	0	0	0	.000	0	0-1	0	16.20
1993 San Diego	NL	3	0	0	3	3.1	20	8	6	5	1	1	0	0	2	0	1	0	0	0	0	.000	0	0-0	0	13.50
1994 Los Angeles	NL	17	0	0	6	23.2	104	24	7	7	2	4	2	1	9	1	18	3	0	1	1	.500	0	0-1	1	2.66
1995 Los Angeles	NL	37	0	0	12	34.2	159	39	27	26	5	3	0	1	18	3	29	0	0	1	3	.250	0	3-4	6	6.75
1998 Atlanta	NL	34	0	0	8	36	148	25	13	11	2	1	2	1	16	0	50	2	0	4	1	.800	0	2-4	8	2.75
7 ML YEARS		125	0	0	43	135	611	129	84	77	14	9	7	4	81	6	136	13	1	8	6	.571	0	5-10	18	5.13

Kevin Sefcik

Bats: R   **Throws:** R   **Pos:** PH/PR-52; LF-35; RF-20; CF-8; 3B-2; DH-1; 2B-1   **Ht:** 5'10"   **Wt:** 181   **Born:** 2/10/71   **Age:** 28

Year Team	Lg	G	AB	H	2B	3B	HR	(Hm	Rd)	TB	R	RBI	TBB	IBB	SO	HBP	SH	SF	SB	CS	SB%	GDP	Avg	OBP	SLG
1995 Philadelphia	NL	5	4	0	0	0	0	(0	0)	0	1	0	0	0	0	2	0	0	0	0	.00	0	.000	.000	.000
1996 Philadelphia	NL	44	116	33	5	3	0	(0	0)	44	10	9	9	3	16	2	1	2	3	0	1.00	4	.284	.341	.379
1997 Philadelphia	NL	61	119	32	3	0	2	(2	0)	41	11	6	4	0	9	1	7	0	1	2	.33	4	.269	.298	.345
1998 Philadelphia	NL	104	169	53	7	2	3	(2	1)	73	27	20	25	0	32	7	3	1	4	2	.67	3	.314	.421	.432
4 ML YEARS		214	408	118	15	5	5	(4	1)	158	49	35	38	3	59	10	11	3	8	4	.67	11	.289	.362	.387

David Segui

Bats: Both   **Throws:** Left   **Pos:** 1B-134; PH/PR-9; LF-1   **Ht:** 6'1"   **Wt:** 202   **Born:** 7/19/66   **Age:** 32

Year Team	Lg	G	AB	H	2B	3B	HR	(Hm	Rd)	TB	R	RBI	TBB	IBB	SO	HBP	SH	SF	SB	CS	SB%	GDP	Avg	OBP	SLG
1990 Baltimore	AL	40	123	30	7	0	2	(1	1)	43	14	15	11	2	15	1	1	0	0	0	.00	12	.244	.311	.350
1991 Baltimore	AL	86	212	59	7	0	2	(1	1)	72	15	22	12	2	19	0	3	1	1	1	.50	7	.278	.316	.340
1992 Baltimore	AL	115	189	44	9	0	1	(1	0)	56	21	17	20	3	23	0	2	0	1	0	1.00	4	.233	.306	.296
1993 Baltimore	AL	146	450	123	27	0	10	(6	4)	180	54	60	58	4	53	0	3	8	2	1	.67	18	.273	.351	.400
1994 New York	NL	92	336	81	17	1	10	(5	5)	130	46	43	33	6	43	1	1	3	0	0	.00	6	.241	.308	.387
1995 NYN-Mon	NL	130	456	141	25	4	12	(6	6)	210	68	68	40	5	47	3	8	3	2	7	.22	10	.309	.367	.461
1996 Montreal	NL	115	416	119	30	1	11	(6	5)	184	69	58	60	4	54	0	0	1	4	4	.50	9	.286	.375	.442
1997 Montreal	NL	125	459	141	22	3	21	(10	11)	232	75	68	57	12	66	1	0	6	1	0	1.00	9	.307	.380	.505
1998 Seattle	AL	143	522	159	36	1	19	(10	9)	254	79	84	49	4	80	0	0	9	3	1	.75	12	.305	.359	.487
1995 New York	NL	33	73	24	3	1	2	(2	0)	35	9	11	12	1	9	1	4	2	1	3	.25	2	.329	.420	.479
Montreal	NL	97	383	117	22	3	10	(4	6)	175	59	57	28	4	38	2	4	1	1	4	.20	8	.305	.355	.457
9 ML YEARS		992	3163	897	180	10	88	(46	42)	1361	441	435	340	42	400	6	18	31	14	14	.50	86	.284	.351	.430

Fernando Seguignol

Bats: Both   **Throws:** Right   **Pos:** LF-8; 1B-7; RF-1; PH/PR-1   **Ht:** 6'5"   **Wt:** 190   **Born:** 1/19/75   **Age:** 24

Year Team	Lg	G	AB	H	2B	3B	HR	(Hm	Rd)	TB	R	RBI	TBB	IBB	SO	HBP	SH	SF	SB	CS	SB%	GDP	Avg	OBP	SLG
1993 Yankees	R	45	161	35	3	3	2	--	--	50	16	20	9	0	37	5	0	0	2	0	1.00	6	.217	.280	.311
1994 Oneonta	A-	73	266	77	14	9	2	--	--	115	36	32	16	1	61	2	0	0	4	6	.40	6	.289	.335	.432
1995 Albany	A	121	457	95	22	2	12	--	--	157	59	66	28	3	141	6	1	6	12	8	.60	6	.208	.260	.344
1996 Delmarva	A	118	410	98	14	5	8	--	--	146	59	55	48	4	126	6	0	1	12	13	.48	6	.239	.327	.356
1997 Wst Plm Bch	A+	124	456	116	27	5	18	--	--	207	70	83	30	3	129	5	0	14	5	5	.50	1	.254	.299	.454
1998 Harrisburg	AA	80	281	81	13	0	25	--	--	169	54	69	29	4	77	6	0	1	6	1	.86	6	.288	.366	.601
Ottawa	AAA	32	109	28	8	0	6	--	--	54	16	16	12	0	43	1	1	1	0	0	.00	1	.257	.333	.495
1998 Montreal	NL	16	42	11	4	0	2	(2	0)	21	6	3	3	0	15	0	0	1	0	0	.00	1	.262	.304	.500

Aaron Sele

Pitches: Right   Bats: Right   Pos: SP-33   Ht: 6'5"   Wt: 215   Born: 6/25/70   Age: 29

		HOW MUCH HE PITCHED						WHAT HE GAVE UP										THE RESULTS					
Year Team	Lg	G	GS	CG	GF	IP	BFP	H	R	ER	HR	SH	SF	HB	TBB	IBB	SO	WP	Bk	W	L	Pct.	ShO	Sv-Op	Hld	ERA
1993 Boston	AL	18	18	0	0	111.2	484	100	42	34	5	2	5	7	48	2	93	5	0	7	2	.778	0	0-0	0	2.74
1994 Boston	AL	22	22	2	0	143.1	615	140	68	61	13	4	5	9	60	2	105	4	0	8	7	.533	0	0-0	0	3.83
1995 Boston	AL	6	6	0	0	32.1	146	32	14	11	3	1	1	3	14	0	21	3	0	3	1	.750	0	0-0	0	3.06
1996 Boston	AL	29	29	1	0	157.1	722	192	110	93	14	6	7	8	67	2	137	2	0	7	11	.389	0	0-0	0	5.32
1997 Boston	AL	33	33	1	0	177.1	810	196	115	106	25	5	7	15	80	4	122	7	0	13	12	.520	0	0-0	0	5.38
1998 Texas	AL	33	33	3	0	212.2	954	239	116	100	14	5	7	13	84	6	167	4	0	19	11	.633	2	0-0	0	4.23
6 ML YEARS		141	141	7	0	834.2	3731	899	465	405	74	23	32	55	353	16	645	25	0	57	44	.564	2	0-0	0	4.37

Dan Serafini

Pitches: Left   Bats: Both   Pos: RP-19; SP-9   Ht: 6'1"   Wt: 191   Born: 1/25/74   Age: 25

		HOW MUCH HE PITCHED						WHAT HE GAVE UP										THE RESULTS					
Year Team	Lg	G	GS	CG	GF	IP	BFP	H	R	ER	HR	SH	SF	HB	TBB	IBB	SO	WP	Bk	W	L	Pct.	ShO	Sv-Op	Hld	ERA
1992 Twins	R	8	6	0	0	29.2	130	27	16	12	0	1	1	1	15	0	33	3	1	1	0	1.000	0	0- -	—	3.64
1993 Fort Wayne	A	27	27	1	0	140.2	606	117	72	57	5	2	2	6	83	0	147	12	2	10	8	.556	1	0- -	—	3.65
1994 Fort Myers	A+	23	23	2	0	136.2	600	149	84	70	11	7	5	6	57	1	130	7	1	9	9	.500	1	0- -	—	4.61
1995 Hardware City	AA	27	27	1	0	162.2	692	155	74	61	7	3	4	12	72	0	123	3	4	12	9	.571	1	0- -	—	3.38
Salt Lake	AAA	1	0	0	1	4	17	4	3	3	2	0	0	0	1	0	4	0	0	0	0	.000	0	1- -	—	6.75
1996 Salt Lake	AAA	25	23	1	1	130.2	588	164	84	81	20	5	6	2	58	1	109	9	2	7	7	.500	0	0- -	—	5.58
1997 Salt Lake	AAA	28	24	2	1	152	660	166	87	84	18	4	3	8	55	0	118	3	0	9	7	.563	0	0- -	—	4.97
1998 Salt Lake	AAA	9	8	0	1	53.1	233	56	29	22	4	0	0	3	21	0	39	4	0	2	4	.333	0	0- -	—	3.71
1996 Minnesota	AL	1	1	0	0	4.1	23	7	5	5	1	1	1	2	2	0	1	0	0	0	1	.000	0	0-0	0	10.38
1997 Minnesota	AL	6	4	1	0	26.1	111	27	11	10	1	1	0	0	11	0	15	1	0	2	1	.667	0	0-0	0	3.42
1998 Minnesota	AL	28	9	0	3	75	345	95	58	54	10	3	6	1	29	1	46	2	0	7	4	.636	0	0-0	2	6.48
3 ML YEARS		35	14	1	4	105.2	479	129	74	69	12	4	7	2	42	1	62	3	0	9	6	.600	0	0-0	2	5.88

Scott Servais

Bats: Right   Throws: Right   Pos: C-110; PH/PR-16; 1B-1   Ht: 6'2"   Wt: 210   Born: 6/4/67   Age: 32

		BATTING																BASERUNNING				PERCENTAGES		
Year Team	Lg	G	AB	H	2B	3B	HR	(Hm	Rd)	TB	R	RBI	TBB	IBB	SO	HBP	SH	SF	SB	CS	SB%	GDP	Avg	OBP	SLG
1991 Houston	NL	16	37	6	3	0	0	(0	0)	9	0	6	4	0	8	0	1	0	0	0	.00	0	.162	.244	.243
1992 Houston	NL	77	205	49	9	0	0	(0	0)	58	12	15	11	2	25	5	6	0	0	0	.00	7	.239	.294	.283
1993 Houston	NL	85	258	63	11	0	11	(5	6)	107	24	32	22	2	45	5	3	3	0	0	.00	6	.244	.313	.415
1994 Houston	NL	78	251	49	15	1	9	(3	6)	93	27	41	10	0	44	4	7	3	0	0	.00	6	.195	.235	.371
1995 Hou-ChN	NL	80	264	70	22	0	13	(8	5)	131	38	47	32	8	52	3	2	3	2	2	.50	9	.265	.348	.496
1996 Chicago	NL	129	445	118	20	0	11	(6	5)	171	42	63	30	1	75	14	3	7	0	2	.00	18	.265	.327	.384
1997 Chicago	NL	122	385	100	21	0	6	(4	2)	139	36	45	24	7	56	6	7	3	0	1	.00	7	.260	.311	.361
1998 Chicago	NL	113	325	72	15	1	7	(5	2)	110	35	36	26	6	51	5	3	1	1	0	1.00	6	.222	.289	.338
1995 Houston	NL	28	89	20	10	0	1	(1	0)	33	7	12	9	2	15	1	1	0	0	1	.00	4	.225	.300	.371
Chicago	NL	52	175	50	12	0	12	(7	5)	98	31	35	23	6	37	2	1	2	2	1	.67	5	.286	.371	.560
8 ML YEARS		700	2170	527	116	2	57	(31	26)	818	214	285	159	26	356	42	32	20	3	5	.38	65	.243	.304	.377

Scott Service

Pitches: Right   Bats: Right   Pos: RP-73   Ht: 6'6"   Wt: 230   Born: 2/26/67   Age: 32

		HOW MUCH HE PITCHED						WHAT HE GAVE UP										THE RESULTS					
Year Team	Lg	G	GS	CG	GF	IP	BFP	H	R	ER	HR	SH	SF	HB	TBB	IBB	SO	WP	Bk	W	L	Pct.	ShO	Sv-Op	Hld	ERA
1988 Philadelphia	NL	5	0	0	1	5.1	23	7	1	1	0	0	0	1	1	0	6	0	0	0	0	.000	0	0-0	1	1.69
1992 Montreal	NL	5	0	0	0	7	41	15	11	11	1	0	0	0	5	0	11	0	0	0	0	.000	0	0-0	1	14.14
1993 Col-Cin	NL	29	0	0	7	46	197	44	24	22	6	2	4	2	16	4	43	0	0	2	2	.500	0	2-2	3	4.30
1994 Cincinnati	NL	6	0	0	2	7.1	35	8	9	6	2	2	0	0	3	0	5	0	0	1	2	.333	0	0-0	0	7.36
1995 San Francisco	NL	28	0	0	6	31	129	18	11	11	4	3	2	2	20	4	30	3	0	3	1	.750	0	0-0	7	3.19
1996 Cincinnati	NL	34	1	0	5	48	213	51	21	21	7	4	1	6	18	4	46	5	0	1	0	1.000	0	0-0	3	3.94
1997 Cin-KC		16	0	0	3	22.1	95	28	16	16	2	2	1	0	6	0	22	2	0	0	3	.000	0	0-1	3	6.45
1998 Kansas City	AL	73	0	0	26	82.2	353	70	35	32	7	2	5	9	34	4	95	10	1	6	4	.600	0	4-8	18	3.48
1993 Colorado	NL	3	0	0	0	4.2	24	8	5	5	1	0	2	1	1	0	3	0	0	0	0	.000	0	0-0	0	9.64
Cincinnati		26	0	0	7	41.1	173	36	19	17	5	2	2	1	15	4	40	0	0	2	2	.500	0	2-2	3	3.70
1997 Cincinnati	NL	4	0	0	2	5.1	26	11	7	7	1	1	0	0	1	0	3	2	0	0	0	.000	0	0-0	1	11.81
Kansas City	AL	12	0	0	1	17	69	17	9	9	1	1	1	0	5	0	19	0	0	0	3	.000	0	0-1	2	4.76
8 ML YEARS		196	1	0	50	249.2	1086	241	128	120	29	15	13	20	103	16	258	20	1	13	12	.520	0	6-11	35	4.33

Richie Sexson

Bats: R   Throws: R   Pos: 1B-45; PH/PR-4; LF-3; DH-2   Ht: 6'7"   Wt: 206   Born: 12/29/74   Age: 24

		BATTING																BASERUNNING				PERCENTAGES		
Year Team	Lg	G	AB	H	2B	3B	HR	(Hm	Rd)	TB	R	RBI	TBB	IBB	SO	HBP	SH	SF	SB	CS	SB%	GDP	Avg	OBP	SLG
1993 Burlington	R+	40	97	18	3	0	1	—	—	24	11	5	18	2	21	1	2	1	1	1	.50	1	.186	.316	.247
1994 Columbus	A	130	488	133	25	2	14	—	—	204	88	77	37	2	87	14	0	5	7	3	.70	5	.273	.338	.418
1995 Kinston	A+	131	494	151	34	0	22	—	—	251	80	85	43	5	115	10	0	7	4	6	.40	8	.306	.368	.508
1996 Canton-Akrn	AA	133	518	143	38	3	16	—	—	230	85	76	39	5	118	6	0	5	1	0	.67	13	.276	.331	.444
1997 Buffalo	AAA	115	434	113	20	2	31	—	—	230	57	88	27	4	87	4	3	4	5	1	.83	11	.260	.307	.530
1998 Buffalo	AAA	89	344	102	20	1	21	—	—	187	58	74	50	2	68	3	0	5	1	2	.33	11	.297	.386	.544
1997 Cleveland	AL	5	11	3	0	0	0	(0	0)	3	0	0	0	0	4	0	0	0	0	0	.00	2	.273	.273	.273

		BATTING																	BASERUNNING				PERCENTAGES		
Year Team	Lg	G	AB	H	2B	3B	HR	(Hm	Rd)	TB	R	RBI	TBB	IBB	SO	HBP	SH	SF	SB	CS	SB%	GDP	Avg	OBP	SLG
1998 Cleveland	AL	49	174	54	14	1	11	(9	2)	103	28	35	6	0	42	3	0	0	1	1	.50	3	.310	.344	.592
2 ML YEARS		54	185	57	14	1	11	(9	2)	106	29	35	6	0	44	3	0	0	1	1	.50	5	.308	.340	.573

Jon Shave

Bats: R **Throws:** R **Pos:** 3B-15; PH/PR-7; DH-1; 1B-1; SS-1   **Ht:** 6'0" **Wt:** 185 **Born:** 11/4/67 **Age:** 31

		BATTING																	BASERUNNING				PERCENTAGES		
Year Team	Lg	G	AB	H	2B	3B	HR	(Hm	Rd)	TB	R	RBI	TBB	IBB	SO	HBP	SH	SF	SB	CS	SB%	GDP	Avg	OBP	SLG
1990 Butte	R+	64	250	88	9	3	2	—	—	109	41	42	25	0	27	3	2	4	21	7	.75	8	.352	.411	.436
1991 Gastonia	A	55	213	62	11	0	2	—	—	79	29	24	20	0	26	1	3	0	11	9	.55	3	.291	.355	.371
Charlotte	A+	56	189	43	4	1	1	—	—	52	17	20	18	1	30	5	2	4	7	7	.50	3	.228	.306	.275
1992 Tulsa	AA	118	453	130	23	5	2	—	—	169	57	36	37	1	59	4	7	5	6	7	.46	10	.287	.343	.373
1993 Okla City	AAA	100	399	105	17	3	4	—	—	140	58	41	20	0	60	2	9	1	4	3	.57	12	.263	.301	.351
1994 Okla City	AAA	95	332	73	15	2	1	—	—	95	29	31	14	1	61	5	12	5	6	2	.75	6	.220	.258	.286
1995 Okla City	AAA	32	83	17	1	0	0	—	—	18	10	5	7	0	28	1	1	0	1	0	1.00	1	.205	.275	.217
1996 Okla City	AAA	116	414	110	20	2	7	—	—	155	54	41	41	0	97	10	4	4	8	6	.57	7	.266	.343	.374
1997 Salt Lake	AAA	103	395	130	27	3	7	—	—	184	75	60	39	0	62	6	1	8	6	6	.50	3	.329	.391	.466
1998 Salt Lake	AAA	90	317	107	20	1	4	—	—	141	63	41	34	1	46	13	5	1	8	9	.47	7	.338	.422	.445
1993 Texas	AL	17	47	15	2	0	0	(0	0)	17	3	7	0	0	8	0	3	2	1	3	.25	0	.319	.306	.362
1998 Minnesota	AL	19	40	10	3	0	1	(0	1)	16	7	5	3	0	10	0	0	0	1	2	.33	0	.250	.302	.400
2 ML YEARS		36	87	25	5	0	1	(0	1)	33	10	12	3	0	18	0	3	2	2	5	.29	0	.287	.304	.379

Jeff Shaw

Pitches: Right **Bats:** Right **Pos:** RP-73   **Ht:** 6'2" **Wt:** 200 **Born:** 7/7/66 **Age:** 32

		HOW MUCH HE PITCHED					WHAT HE GAVE UP												THE RESULTS						
Year Team	Lg	G	GS	CG	GF	IP	BFP	H	R	ER	HR	SH	SF	HB	TBB	IBB	SO	WP	Bk	W	L	Pct.	ShO	Sv-Op	Hld	ERA
1990 Cleveland	AL	12	9	0	0	48.2	229	73	38	36	11	1	3	0	20	0	25	3	0	3	4	.429	0	0-0	0	6.66
1991 Cleveland	AL	29	1	0	9	72.1	311	72	34	27	6	1	4	4	27	5	31	6	0	0	5	.000	0	1-4	0	3.36
1992 Cleveland	AL	2	1	0	1	7.2	33	7	7	7	2	2	0	0	4	0	3	0	0	0	0	.000	0	0-0	0	8.22
1993 Montreal	NL	55	8	0	13	95.2	404	91	47	44	12	5	2	7	32	2	50	2	0	2	7	.222	0	0-1	4	4.14
1994 Montreal	NL	46	0	0	15	67.1	287	67	32	29	8	2	4	2	15	2	47	5	0	5	2	.714	0	1-2	10	3.88
1995 Mon-ChA		59	0	0	18	72	309	70	42	39	6	7	1	4	27	4	51	0	0	1	6	.143	0	3-5	6	4.88
1996 Cincinnati	NL	78	0	0	24	104.2	434	99	34	29	8	5	5	2	29	11	69	0	0	8	6	.571	0	4-11	22	2.49
1997 Cincinnati	NL	78	0	0	62	94.2	367	79	26	25	7	3	3	1	12	3	74	1	0	4	2	.667	0	42-49	0	2.38
1998 Cin-LA	NL	73	0	0	69	85	339	75	22	20	8	5	2	1	19	5	55	0	0	3	8	.273	0	48-57	0	2.12
1995 Montreal	NL	50	0	0	17	62.1	268	58	35	32	4	6	1	3	26	4	45	0	0	1	6	.143	0	3-5	5	4.62
Chicago	AL	9	0	0	1	9.2	41	12	7	7	2	1	0	1	1	0	6	0	0	0	0	.000	0	0-0	1	6.52
1998 Cincinnati	NL	39	0	0	35	49.2	192	40	11	10	2	4	2	1	12	4	29	0	0	2	4	.333	0	23-28	0	1.81
Los Angeles	NL	34	0	0	34	35.1	147	35	11	10	6	1	0	0	7	1	26	0	0	1	4	.200	0	25-29	0	2.55
9 ML YEARS		432	19	0	211	648	2713	633	282	256	68	31	24	21	185	32	405	17	0	26	41	.388	0	99-129	47	3.56

Andy Sheets

Bats: R **Throws:** R **Pos:** SS-39; 3B-23; 2B-22; PH/PR-19; 1B-2   **Ht:** 6'2" **Wt:** 180 **Born:** 11/19/71 **Age:** 27

		BATTING																	BASERUNNING				PERCENTAGES		
Year Team	Lg	G	AB	H	2B	3B	HR	(Hm	Rd)	TB	R	RBI	TBB	IBB	SO	HBP	SH	SF	SB	CS	SB%	GDP	Avg	OBP	SLG
1996 Seattle	AL	47	110	21	8	0	0	(0	0)	29	18	9	10	0	41	1	2	1	2	0	1.00	2	.191	.262	.264
1997 Seattle	AL	32	89	22	3	0	4	(2	2)	37	18	9	7	0	34	0	5	1	2	0	1.00	1	.247	.299	.416
1998 San Diego	NL	88	194	47	5	3	7	(2	5)	79	31	29	21	3	62	1	2	1	7	2	.78	4	.242	.318	.407
3 ML YEARS		167	393	90	16	3	11	(4	7)	145	67	47	38	3	137	2	9	3	11	2	.85	7	.229	.298	.369

Gary Sheffield

Bats: Right **Throws:** Right **Pos:** RF-126; PH/PR-4   **Ht:** 5'11" **Wt:** 190 **Born:** 11/18/68 **Age:** 30

		BATTING																	BASERUNNING				PERCENTAGES		
Year Team	Lg	G	AB	H	2B	3B	HR	(Hm	Rd)	TB	R	RBI	TBB	IBB	SO	HBP	SH	SF	SB	CS	SB%	GDP	Avg	OBP	SLG
1988 Milwaukee	AL	24	80	19	1	0	4	(1	3)	32	12	12	7	0	7	0	1	1	3	1	.75	5	.238	.295	.400
1989 Milwaukee	AL	95	368	91	18	0	5	(2	3)	124	34	32	27	0	33	4	3	3	10	6	.63	4	.247	.303	.337
1990 Milwaukee	AL	125	487	143	30	1	10	(3	7)	205	67	67	44	1	41	3	4	9	25	10	.71	11	.294	.350	.421
1991 Milwaukee	AL	50	175	34	12	2	2	(2	0)	56	25	22	19	1	15	3	1	5	5	5	.50	3	.194	.277	.320
1992 San Diego	NL	146	557	184	34	3	33	(23	10)	323	87	100	48	5	40	6	0	7	5	6	.45	19	.330	.385	.580
1993 SD-Fla	NL	140	494	145	20	5	20	(10	10)	235	67	73	47	6	64	9	0	7	17	5	.77	11	.294	.361	.476
1994 Florida	NL	87	322	89	16	1	27	(15	12)	188	61	78	51	11	50	6	0	5	12	6	.67	10	.276	.380	.584
1995 Florida	NL	63	213	69	8	0	16	(4	12)	125	46	46	55	8	45	4	0	2	19	4	.83	3	.324	.467	.587
1996 Florida	NL	161	519	163	33	1	42	(19	23)	324	118	120	142	19	66	10	0	6	16	9	.64	16	.314	.465	.624
1997 Florida	NL	135	444	111	22	1	21	(13	8)	198	86	71	121	11	79	15	0	2	11	7	.61	7	.250	.424	.446
1998 Fla-LA	NL	130	437	132	27	2	22	(11	11)	229	73	85	95	12	46	8	0	9	22	7	.76	7	.302	.428	.524
1993 San Diego	NL	68	258	76	12	2	10	(6	4)	122	34	36	18	0	30	3	0	3	5	1	.83	9	.295	.344	.473
Florida	NL	72	236	69	8	3	10	(4	6)	113	33	37	29	6	34	6	0	4	12	4	.75	2	.292	.378	.479
1998 Florida	NL	40	136	37	11	1	6	(6	0)	68	21	28	26	1	16	2	0	2	4	2	.67	3	.272	.392	.500
Los Angeles	NL	90	301	95	16	1	16	(5	11)	161	52	57	69	11	30	6	0	7	18	5	.78	4	.316	.444	.535
11 ML YEARS		1156	4096	1180	221	16	202	(103	99)	2039	676	706	656	74	486	68	9	56	145	66	.69	96	.288	.390	.498

Scott Sheldon

Bats: R **Throws:** R **Pos:** PH/PR-4; 3B-3; SS-2; DH-1; 1B-1   **Ht:** 6'3" **Wt:** 185 **Born:** 11/28/68 **Age:** 30

Year Team	Lg	G	AB	H	2B	3B	HR	(Hm	Rd)	TB	R	RBI	TBB	IBB	SO	HBP	SH	SF	SB	CS	SB%	GDP	Avg	OBP	SLG
1991 Sou. Oregon	A-	65	229	58	10	3	0	—	—	74	34	24	23	0	44	2	3	1	9	5	.64	5	.253	.325	.323
1992 Madison	A	74	279	76	16	0	6	—	—	110	41	24	32	1	78	1	3	4	5	4	.56	2	.272	.345	.394
1993 Madison	A	131	428	91	22	1	8	—	—	139	67	67	49	3	121	8	3	8	8	7	.53	8	.213	.300	.325
1994 Huntsville	AA	91	268	62	10	1	0	—	—	74	31	28	28	1	69	7	7	3	7	1	.88	4	.231	.317	.276
1995 Edmonton	AAA	45	128	33	7	1	4	—	—	54	21	12	15	0	15	2	4	1	4	2	.67	0	.258	.342	.422
Huntsville	AA	66	235	51	10	2	4	—	—	77	25	15	23	0	60	1	3	1	5	0	1.00	1	.217	.288	.328
1996 Edmonton	AAA	98	350	105	27	3	10	—	—	168	61	60	43	3	83	4	3	4	5	3	.63	8	.300	.379	.480
1997 Edmonton	AAA	118	422	133	39	6	19	—	—	241	89	77	59	4	104	6	3	3	5	2	.71	11	.315	.404	.571
1998 Oklahoma	AAA	131	493	126	31	4	29	—	—	252	74	96	62	3	143	3	0	6	2	2	.50	7	.256	.339	.511
1997 Oakland	AL	13	24	6	0	0	1	(1	0)	9	2	2	1	0	6	1	1	0	0	0	.00	0	.250	.308	.375
1998 Texas	AL	7	16	2	0	0	0	(0	0)	2	0	1	1	0	6	0	0	0	0	0	.00	1	.125	.176	.125
2 ML YEARS		20	40	8	0	0	1	(1	0)	11	2	3	2	0	12	1	1	0	0	0	.00	1	.200	.256	.275

Craig Shipley

B: R **T:** R **Pos:** 3B-48; PH/PR-15; 2B-11; 1B-8; SS-5; DH-1; LF-1; RF-1   **Ht:** 6'1" **Wt:** 190 **Born:** 1/7/63 **Age:** 36

Year Team	Lg	G	AB	H	2B	3B	HR	(Hm	Rd)	TB	R	RBI	TBB	IBB	SO	HBP	SH	SF	SB	CS	SB%	GDP	Avg	OBP	SLG
1986 Los Angeles	NL	12	27	3	1	0	0	(0	0)	4	3	4	2	1	5	1	1	0	0	0	.00	1	.111	.200	.148
1987 Los Angeles	NL	26	35	9	1	0	0	(0	0)	10	3	2	0	0	6	0	0	0	0	0	.00	0	.257	.257	.286
1989 New York	NL	4	7	1	0	0	0	(0	0)	1	3	0	0	0	1	0	0	0	0	0	.00	0	.143	.143	.143
1991 San Diego	NL	37	91	25	3	0	1	(0	1)	31	6	6	2	0	14	1	1	0	1	1	.50	0	.275	.298	.341
1992 San Diego	NL	52	105	26	6	0	0	(0	0)	32	7	7	2	1	21	0	1	1	1	1	.50	2	.248	.262	.305
1993 San Diego	NL	105	230	54	9	0	4	(2	2)	75	25	22	10	0	31	3	1	1	12	3	.80	3	.235	.275	.326
1994 San Diego	NL	81	240	80	14	4	4	(2	2)	114	32	30	9	1	28	3	4	2	6	6	.50	3	.333	.362	.475
1995 Houston	NL	92	232	61	8	1	3	(1	2)	80	23	24	8	3	28	2	1	2	6	1	.86	13	.263	.291	.345
1996 San Diego	NL	33	92	29	5	0	1	(0	1)	37	13	7	2	1	15	2	1	2	7	0	1.00	0	.315	.337	.402
1997 San Diego	NL	63	139	38	9	0	5	(3	2)	62	22	19	7	0	20	0	1	1	1	1	.50	1	.273	.306	.446
1998 Anaheim	AL	77	147	38	7	1	2	(0	2)	53	18	17	5	0	22	5	4	1	0	4	.00	3	.259	.304	.361
11 ML YEARS		582	1345	364	63	6	20	(8	12)	499	155	138	47	7	191	17	15	9	33	17	.66	29	.271	.302	.371

Brian Shouse

Pitches: Left **Bats:** Left **Pos:** RP-7   **Ht:** 5'11" **Wt:** 175 **Born:** 9/26/68 **Age:** 30

Year Team	Lg	G	GS	CG	GF	IP	BFP	H	R	ER	HR	SH	SF	HB	TBB	IBB	SO	WP	Bk	W	L	Pct.	ShO	Sv-Op	Hld	ERA
1990 Welland	A-	17	1	0	7	39.2	177	50	27	23	2	4	1	3	7	0	39	1	2	4	3	.571	0	2- —	—	5.22
1991 Augusta	A	26	0	0	25	31	124	22	13	11	1	1	1	3	9	1	32	5	0	2	3	.400	0	8- —	—	3.19
Salem	A+	17	0	0	9	33.2	147	35	12	11	2	2	0	0	15	2	25	1	0	2	1	.667	0	3- —	—	2.94
1992 Carolina	AA	59	0	0	33	77.1	323	71	31	21	3	8	2	2	28	4	79	4	1	5	6	.455	0	4- —	—	2.44
1993 Buffalo	AAA	48	0	0	14	51.2	218	54	24	22	7	0	3	2	17	2	25	1	0	1	0	1.000	0	0- —	—	3.83
1994 Buffalo	AAA	43	0	0	20	52	212	44	22	21	6	4	2	1	15	4	31	0	0	3	4	.429	0	0- —	—	3.63
1995 Calgary	AAA	8	8	1	0	39.1	185	62	35	27	2	1	1	1	7	0	17	3	0	4	4	.500	0	0- —	—	6.18
Carolina	AA	21	20	0	0	114.2	480	126	64	57	14	5	3	4	19	2	76	1	1	7	6	.538	0	0- —	—	4.47
1996 Calgary	AAA	12	1	0	0	12.2	65	22	15	15	4	0	1	0	4	1	12	1	0	1	0	1.000	0	0- —	—	10.66
Rochester	AAA	32	0	0	10	50	217	53	27	25	6	2	2	1	16	1	45	5	0	1	2	.333	0	2- —	—	4.50
1997 Rochester	AAA	54	0	0	29	71.1	282	48	21	18	6	5	1	3	21	4	81	2	0	6	2	.750	0	9- —	—	2.27
1998 Pawtucket	AAA	22	1	0	15	31	121	21	11	10	7	1	1	0	7	0	25	0	0	2	0	1.000	0	6- —	—	2.90
1993 Pittsburgh	NL	6	0	0	1	4	22	7	4	4	1	0	1	0	2	0	3	1	0	0	0	.000	0	0-0	—	9.00
1998 Boston	AL	7	0	0	4	8	36	9	5	5	2	0	0	0	4	0	5	0	0	0	1	.000	0	0-0	1	5.63
2 ML YEARS		13	0	0	5	12	58	16	9	9	3	0	1	0	6	0	8	1	0	0	1	.000	0	0-0	1	6.75

Paul Shuey

Pitches: Right **Bats:** Right **Pos:** RP-43   **Ht:** 6'3" **Wt:** 215 **Born:** 9/16/70 **Age:** 28

Year Team	Lg	G	GS	CG	GF	IP	BFP	H	R	ER	HR	SH	SF	HB	TBB	IBB	SO	WP	Bk	W	L	Pct.	ShO	Sv-Op	Hld	ERA
1998 Akron *	AA	1	0	0	0	0.1	5	3	2	2	0	0	0	0	1	0	0	0	0	0	0	.000	0	0- —	—	54.00
Buffalo *	AAA	11	0	0	4	14.1	61	11	4	4	0	0	1	0	6	0	22	1	0	0	0	.000	0	2- —	—	2.51
1994 Cleveland	AL	14	0	0	11	11.2	62	14	11	11	0	0	0	0	12	1	16	4	0	0	1	.000	0	5-5	1	8.49
1995 Cleveland	AL	7	0	0	3	6.1	28	5	4	3	0	2	0	0	5	0	5	1	0	0	0	.000	0	0-0	0	4.26
1996 Cleveland	AL	42	0	0	18	53.2	225	45	19	17	6	1	3	0	26	3	44	3	1	5	2	.714	0	4-7	7	2.85
1997 Cleveland	AL	40	0	0	16	45	212	52	31	31	5	4	2	1	28	3	46	2	0	4	2	.667	0	2-3	4	6.20
1998 Cleveland	AL	43	0	0	16	51	222	44	19	17	6	2	0	3	25	5	58	3	0	5	4	.556	0	2-5	12	3.00
5 ML YEARS		146	0	0	64	167.2	749	160	84	79	18	9	5	4	96	12	169	13	1	14	11	.560	0	13-20	24	4.24

Terry Shumpert

Bats: Right **Throws:** Right **Pos:** PH/PR-19; 2B-6   **Ht:** 6'0" **Wt:** 195 **Born:** 8/16/66 **Age:** 32

Year Team	Lg	G	AB	H	2B	3B	HR	(Hm	Rd)	TB	R	RBI	TBB	IBB	SO	HBP	SH	SF	SB	CS	SB%	GDP	Avg	OBP	SLG
1998 Colo Sprngs *	AAA	97	376	115	29	8	12	—	—	196	66	50	35	4	59	4	4	1	11	11	.50	11	.306	.370	.521
1990 Kansas City	AL	32	91	25	6	1	0	(0	0)	33	7	8	2	0	17	1	0	2	3	3	.50	4	.275	.292	.363
1991 Kansas City	AL	144	369	80	16	4	5	(1	4)	119	45	34	30	0	75	5	10	3	17	11	.61	10	.217	.283	.322

205

Year Team	Lg	G	AB	H	2B	3B	HR	(Hm	Rd)	TB	R	RBI	TBB	IBB	SO	HBP	SH	SF	SB	CS	SB%	GDP	Avg	OBP	SLG
1992 Kansas City	AL	36	94	14	5	1	1	(0	1)	24	6	11	3	0	17	0	2	0	2	2	.50	2	.149	.175	.255
1993 Kansas City	AL	8	10	1	0	0	0	(0	0)	1	0	0	2	0	2	0	0	0	1	0	1.00	0	.100	.250	.100
1994 Kansas City	AL	64	183	44	6	2	8	(2	6)	78	28	24	13	0	39	0	5	1	18	3	.86	0	.240	.289	.426
1995 Boston	AL	21	47	11	3	0	0	(0	0)	14	6	3	4	0	13	0	0	0	3	1	.75	0	.234	.294	.298
1996 Chicago	NL	27	31	7	1	0	2	(2	0)	14	5	6	2	0	11	1	0	1	0	1	.00	0	.226	.286	.452
1997 San Diego	NL	13	33	9	3	0	1	(0	1)	15	4	6	3	0	4	0	0	1	0	0	.00	1	.273	.324	.455
1998 Colorado	NL	23	26	6	1	0	1	(0	1)	10	3	2	2	0	8	0	0	0	0	0	.00	0	.231	.286	.385
9 ML YEARS		368	884	197	41	8	18	(5	13)	308	104	94	61	0	186	7	17	8	44	21	.68	17	.223	.276	.348

Joe Siddall

Bats: Left **Throws:** Right **Pos:** C-27; PH/PR-2; RF-1   **Ht:** 6'1" **Wt:** 200 **Born:** 10/25/67 **Age:** 31

Year Team	Lg	G	AB	H	2B	3B	HR	(Hm	Rd)	TB	R	RBI	TBB	IBB	SO	HBP	SH	SF	SB	CS	SB%	GDP	Avg	OBP	SLG
1998 Toledo *	AAA	43	129	31	5	0	4	(Hm	Rd)	48	16	16	11	0	42	2	2	0	2	1	.67	2	.240	.310	.372
1993 Montreal	NL	19	20	2	1	0	0	(0	0)	3	0	1	1	1	5	0	0	0	0	0	.00	0	.100	.143	.150
1995 Montreal	NL	7	10	3	0	0	0	(0	0)	3	4	1	3	0	3	1	0	0	0	0	.00	0	.300	.500	.300
1996 Florida	NL	18	47	7	1	0	0	(0	0)	8	0	3	2	0	8	0	0	0	0	0	.00	0	.149	.184	.170
1998 Detroit	AL	29	65	12	3	0	1	(1	0)	18	3	6	7	0	25	0	2	0	0	0	.00	1	.185	.264	.277
4 ML YEARS		73	142	24	5	0	1	(1	0)	32	7	11	13	1	41	1	2	0	0	0	.00	1	.169	.244	.225

Ruben Sierra

Bats: B **Throws:** R **Pos:** RF-12; PH/PR-10; DH-5; LF-2   **Ht:** 6'1" **Wt:** 200 **Born:** 10/6/65 **Age:** 33

Year Team	Lg	G	AB	H	2B	3B	HR	(Hm	Rd)	TB	R	RBI	TBB	IBB	SO	HBP	SH	SF	SB	CS	SB%	GDP	Avg	OBP	SLG
1998 Norfolk *	AAA	28	108	28	5	0	3	—	—	42	16	19	13	2	18	0	0	3	3	0	1.00	4	.259	.331	.389
1986 Texas	AL	113	382	101	13	10	16	(8	8)	182	50	55	22	3	65	1	1	5	7	8	.47	8	.264	.302	.476
1987 Texas	AL	158	643	169	35	4	30	(15	15)	302	97	109	39	4	114	2	0	12	16	11	.59	18	.263	.302	.470
1988 Texas	AL	156	615	156	32	2	23	(15	8)	261	77	91	44	10	91	1	0	8	18	4	.82	15	.254	.301	.424
1989 Texas	AL	162	634	194	35	14	29	(21	8)	344	101	119	43	2	82	2	0	10	8	2	.80	7	.306	.347	.543
1990 Texas	AL	159	608	170	37	2	16	(10	6)	259	70	96	49	13	86	1	0	4	9	0	1.00	15	.280	.330	.426
1991 Texas	AL	161	661	203	44	5	25	(12	13)	332	110	116	56	7	91	0	0	9	16	4	.80	17	.307	.357	.502
1992 Tex-Oak	AL	151	601	167	34	7	17	(10	7)	266	83	87	45	12	68	0	0	10	14	4	.78	11	.278	.323	.443
1993 Oakland	AL	158	630	147	23	5	22	(9	13)	246	77	101	52	16	97	0	0	9	25	5	.83	15	.233	.288	.390
1994 Oakland	AL	110	426	114	21	1	23	(11	12)	206	71	92	23	4	64	0	0	11	8	5	.62	15	.268	.298	.484
1995 Oak-NYA	AL	126	479	126	32	0	19	(8	11)	215	73	86	46	4	76	0	0	8	5	4	.56	8	.263	.323	.449
1996 NYA-Det	AL	142	518	128	26	2	12	(4	8)	194	61	72	60	12	83	0	0	9	4	4	.50	12	.247	.320	.375
1997 Cin-Tor	NL	39	138	32	5	3	3	(3	0)	52	10	12	9	2	34	0	0	1	0	0	.00	1	.232	.277	.377
1998 Chicago	AL	27	74	16	4	1	4	(0	4)	34	7	11	3	0	11	0	0	2	2	0	1.00	2	.216	.247	.459
1992 Texas	AL	124	500	139	30	6	14	(8	6)	223	66	70	31	6	59	0	0	8	12	4	.75	9	.278	.315	.446
Oakland	AL	27	101	28	4	1	3	(2	1)	43	17	17	14	6	9	0	0	2	2	0	1.00	2	.277	.359	.426
1995 Oakland	AL	70	264	70	17	0	12	(3	9)	123	40	42	24	2	42	0	0	3	4	4	.50	2	.265	.323	.428
New York	AL	56	215	56	15	0	7	(5	2)	92	33	44	22	2	34	0	0	5	1	0	1.00	6	.260	.322	.428
1996 New York	AL	96	360	93	17	1	11	(4	7)	145	39	52	40	11	58	0	0	7	1	3	.25	10	.258	.327	.403
Detroit	AL	46	158	35	9	1	1	(0	1)	49	22	20	20	1	25	0	0	2	3	1	.75	2	.222	.306	.310
1997 Cincinnati	NL	25	90	22	5	1	2	(2	0)	35	6	7	6	1	21	0	0	0	0	0	.00	1	.244	.292	.389
Toronto	AL	14	48	10	0	2	1	(1	0)	17	4	5	3	1	13	0	0	1	0	0	.00	0	.208	.250	.354
13 ML YEARS		1662	6409	1723	341	56	239	(126	113)	2893	887	1047	491	89	962	7	1	101	132	51	.72	146	.269	.317	.451

Jose Silva

Pitches: Right **Bats:** Right **Pos:** SP-18   **Ht:** 6'5" **Wt:** 230 **Born:** 12/19/73 **Age:** 25

Year Team	Lg	G	GS	CG	GF	IP	BFP	H	R	ER	HR	SH	SF	HB	TBB	IBB	SO	WP	Bk	W	L	Pct.	ShO	Sv-Op	Hld	ERA
1992 Blue Jays	R	12	12	0	0	59.1	231	42	23	15	1	0	1	2	18	0	78	1	2	6	4	.600	0	0- -		2.28
1993 Hagerstown	A	24	24	0	0	142.2	581	103	50	40	6	0	4	4	62	0	161	9	1	12	5	.706	0	0- -		2.52
1994 Dunedin	A+	8	7	0	0	43	188	41	32	18	4	2	6	4	24	0	41	5	0	0	2	.000	0	0- -		3.77
Knoxville	AA	16	16	1	0	91.1	381	89	47	42	9	2	3	2	31	0	71	4	0	4	8	.333	1	0- -		4.14
1995 Knoxville	AA	3	0	0	0	2	15	3	2	2	0	1	1	0	6	0	2	0	0	0	0	.000	0	0- -		9.00
1996 Knoxville	AA	22	6	0	4	44	196	45	27	24	3	3	1	3	22	2	26	4	0	2	3	.400	0	0- -		4.91
1997 Calgary	AAA	17	11	0	1	66	288	74	27	25	3	3	1	3	22	0	54	2	1	5	1	.833	0	0- -		3.41
1998 Nashville	AAA	3	3	0	0	9.1	40	10	5	5	2	0	0	0	4	0	6	0	2	0	0	.000	0	0- -		4.82
1996 Toronto	AL	2	0	0	0	2	11	5	3	3	1	0	0	0	0	0	4	0	0	0	0	.000	0	0-0	0	13.50
1997 Pittsburgh	NL	11	4	0	0	36.1	174	52	26	24	4	4	3	1	16	3	30	0	1	2	1	.667	0	0-0	0	5.94
1998 Pittsburgh	NL	18	18	1	0	100.1	425	104	55	49	7	5	1	1	30	2	64	2	2	6	7	.462	0	0-0	0	4.40
3 ML YEARS		31	22	1	0	138.2	610	161	84	76	12	9	4	2	46	5	94	2	3	8	8	.500	0	0-0	0	4.93

Dave Silvestri

Bats: R **Throws:** R **Pos:** PH/PR-4; 3B-3; DH-2; 2B-2; SS-1   **Ht:** 6'0" **Wt:** 196 **Born:** 9/29/67 **Age:** 31

Year Team	Lg	G	AB	H	2B	3B	HR	(Hm	Rd)	TB	R	RBI	TBB	IBB	SO	HBP	SH	SF	SB	CS	SB%	GDP	Avg	OBP	SLG
1998 Durham *	AAA	129	480	133	31	2	8	—	—	192	74	56	61	1	73	4	6	6	12	9	.57	7	.277	.359	.400
1992 New York	AL	7	13	4	0	2	0	(0	0)	8	3	1	0	0	3	0	0	0	0	0	.00	1	.308	.308	.615
1993 New York	AL	7	21	6	1	0	1	(0	1)	10	4	4	5	0	3	0	0	0	0	0	.00	0	.286	.423	.476
1994 New York	AL	12	18	2	0	1	1	(1	0)	7	3	2	4	0	9	0	0	1	0	1	.00	0	.111	.261	.476
1995 NYA-Mon	AL	56	93	21	6	0	3	(0	3)	36	16	11	13	0	36	1	1	2	2	0	1.00	3	.226	.321	.387

Year Team	Lg	G	AB	H	2B	3B	HR	(Hm	Rd)	TB	R	RBI	TBB	IBB	SO	HBP	SH	SF	SB	CS	SB%	GDP	Avg	OBP	SLG
1996 Montreal	NL	86	162	33	4	0	1	(0	1)	40	16	17	34	6	41	0	3	1	2	1	.67	5	.204	.340	.247
1997 Texas	AL	2	4	0	0	0	0	(0	0)	0	0	0	0	0	0	1	0	0	0	0	.00	0	.000	.000	.000
1998 Tampa Bay	AL	8	14	1	0	0	0	(0	0)	1	0	0	0	0	2	0	0	0	0	0	.00	0	.071	.071	.071
1995 New York	AL	17	21	2	0	0	0	(0	1)	5	4	4	4	0	9	1	0	1	0	0	.00	1	.095	.259	.238
Montreal	NL	39	72	19	6	0	2	(0	2)	31	12	7	9	0	27	0	1	1	2	0	1.00	2	.264	.341	.431
7 ML YEARS		178	325	67	11	3	6	(1	5)	102	42	35	56	6	95	1	4	4	4	2	.67	11	.206	.321	.314

Bill Simas

Pitches: **Right** Bats: **Left** Pos: **RP-60**   Ht: **6'3"** Wt: **220** Born: **11/28/71** Age: **27**

Year Team	Lg	G	GS	CG	GF	IP	BFP	H	R	ER	HR	SH	SF	HB	TBB	IBB	SO	WP	Bk	W	L	Pct.	ShO	Sv-Op	Hld	ERA
1998 Calgary *	AAA	5	0	0	4	9	33	3	1	0	0	0	0	0	2	1	11	0	0	1	0	1.000	0	1--	—	0.00
1995 Chicago	AL	14	0	0	4	14	66	15	5	4	1	0	0	1	10	2	16	1	0	1	1	.500	0	0-0	3	2.57
1996 Chicago	AL	64	0	0	16	72.2	328	75	39	37	5	1	2	3	39	6	65	0	0	2	8	.200	0	2-8	15	4.58
1997 Chicago	AL	40	0	0	11	41.1	193	46	23	19	6	1	1	2	24	3	38	2	0	3	1	.750	0	1-2	3	4.14
1998 Chicago	AL	60	0	0	41	70.2	287	54	29	28	12	2	0	1	22	4	56	1	0	4	3	.571	0	18-24	6	3.57
4 ML YEARS		178	0	0	72	198.2	874	190	96	88	24	4	3	7	95	15	175	4	0	10	13	.435	0	21-34	27	3.99

Brian Simmons

Bats: **Both** Throws: **Right** Pos: **CF-4; LF-2**   Ht: **6'2"** Wt: **190** Born: **9/4/73** Age: **25**

Year Team	Lg	G	AB	H	2B	3B	HR	(Hm	Rd)	TB	R	RBI	TBB	IBB	SO	HBP	SH	SF	SB	CS	SB%	GDP	Avg	OBP	SLG
1995 White Sox	R	5	17	3	1	0	1	—	—	7	5	5	6	0	1	0	0	0	0	0	.00	1	.176	.391	.412
Hickory	A	41	163	31	6	1	2	—	—	45	13	11	19	0	44	2	0	0	4	4	.50	2	.190	.283	.276
1996 South Bend	A	92	356	106	29	6	17	—	—	198	73	58	48	2	69	2	1	4	14	9	.61	3	.298	.380	.556
Pr William	A+	33	131	26	4	3	4	—	—	48	17	14	9	1	39	0	1	0	2	0	1.00	3	.198	.250	.366
1997 Birmingham	AA	138	546	143	28	12	15	—	—	240	108	72	88	5	124	2	2	3	15	12	.56	10	.262	.365	.440
1998 White Sox	R	5	12	2	0	0	0	—	—	2	0	1	0	0	1	0	0	0	0	0	.00	0	.167	.231	.167
Calgary	AAA	94	355	103	21	4	13	—	—	171	72	51	41	1	82	1	3	3	10	6	.63	6	.290	.363	.482
1998 Chicago	AL	5	19	7	0	0	2	(0	2)	13	4	6	0	0	2	0	0	0	1	0	1.00	0	.368	.368	.684

Mike Simms

Bats: **R** Throws: **R** Pos: **RF-40; DH-24; PH/PR-20; 1B-16; LF-3**   Ht: **6'4"** Wt: **230** Born: **1/12/67** Age: **32**

Year Team	Lg	G	AB	H	2B	3B	HR	(Hm	Rd)	TB	R	RBI	TBB	IBB	SO	HBP	SH	SF	SB	CS	SB%	GDP	Avg	OBP	SLG
1990 Houston	NL	12	13	4	1	0	1	(0	1)	8	3	2	0	0	4	0	0	0	0	0	.00	1	.308	.308	.615
1991 Houston	NL	49	123	25	5	0	3	(1	2)	39	18	16	18	0	38	0	0	2	1	0	1.00	2	.203	.301	.317
1992 Houston	NL	15	24	6	1	0	1	(0	1)	10	1	3	2	0	9	1	0	0	1	0	1.00	0	.250	.333	.417
1994 Houston	NL	6	12	1	1	0	0	(0	0)	2	1	0	0	0	5	0	0	0	1	0	1.00	0	.083	.083	.167
1995 Houston	NL	50	121	31	4	0	9	(5	4)	62	14	24	13	0	28	3	0	1	1	2	.33	3	.256	.341	.512
1996 Houston	NL	49	68	12	2	1	1	(1	0)	19	6	8	4	0	16	1	0	0	1	0	1.00	1	.176	.233	.279
1997 Texas	AL	59	111	28	8	0	5	(3	2)	51	13	22	8	1	27	0	0	3	0	1	.00	3	.252	.298	.459
1998 Texas	AL	86	186	55	11	0	16	(9	7)	114	36	46	24	0	47	3	0	2	0	1	.00	4	.296	.381	.613
8 ML YEARS		326	658	162	33	1	36	(19	17)	305	92	121	69	1	174	8	0	7	4	4	.50	15	.246	.322	.464

Randall Simon

Bats: **Left** Throws: **Left** Pos: **1B-4; PH/PR-3**   Ht: **6'0"** Wt: **180** Born: **5/26/75** Age: **24**

Year Team	Lg	G	AB	H	2B	3B	HR	(Hm	Rd)	TB	R	RBI	TBB	IBB	SO	HBP	SH	SF	SB	CS	SB%	GDP	Avg	OBP	SLG
1993 Danville	R+	61	232	59	17	1	3	—	—	87	28	31	10	2	34	2	0	2	1	1	.50	4	.254	.289	.375
1994 Macon	A	106	358	105	23	1	10	—	—	160	45	54	6	2	56	1	1	2	7	6	.54	7	.293	.305	.447
1995 Durham	A+	122	420	111	18	1	18	—	—	185	56	79	36	14	63	5	0	5	6	5	.55	15	.264	.326	.440
1996 Greenville	A+	134	498	139	26	2	18	—	—	223	74	77	37	7	61	4	0	4	9	31	.13	13	.279	.331	.448
1997 Richmond	AAA	133	519	160	45	1	14	—	—	249	62	102	17	2	76	4	1	1	1	6	.14	18	.308	.335	.480
1998 Richmond	AAA	126	484	124	20	1	13	—	—	185	52	70	24	3	62	2	0	4	4	4	.50	22	.256	.292	.382
1997 Atlanta	NL	13	14	6	1	0	0	(0	0)	7	2	1	1	0	2	0	0	0	0	0	.00	1	.429	.467	.500
1998 Atlanta	NL	7	16	3	0	0	0	(0	0)	3	2	4	0	0	1	0	0	1	0	0	.00	0	.188	.176	.188
2 ML YEARS		20	30	9	1	0	0	(0	0)	10	4	5	1	0	3	0	0	1	0	0	.00	1	.300	.313	.333

Steve Sinclair

Pitches: **Left** Bats: **Left** Pos: **RP-24**   Ht: **6'2"** Wt: **190** Born: **8/2/71** Age: **27**

Year Team	Lg	G	GS	CG	GF	IP	BFP	H	R	ER	HR	SH	SF	HB	TBB	IBB	SO	WP	Bk	W	L	Pct.	ShO	Sv-Op	Hld	ERA
1991 Medicine Ha	R+	12	0	0	8	14.2	76	17	15	11	1	1	0	3	11	0	14	0	0	1	0	1.000	0	0--	—	6.75
1992 Blue Jays	R	5	4	0	0	23	92	23	10	7	2	0	0	0	5	0	18	1	0	1	2	.333	0	0--	—	2.74
Medicine Ha	R+	9	7	0	0	43	189	54	25	22	2	2	3	1	12	0	28	3	0	2	3	.400	0	0--	—	4.60
1993 Medicine Ha	R+	15	12	0	0	78.1	335	87	41	29	5	2	2	1	16	0	45	5	1	5	2	.714	0	0--	—	3.33
1994 Hagerstown	A	38	1	0	16	105	458	127	53	44	9	4	5	2	25	0	75	3	0	9	2	.818	0	3--	—	3.77
1995 Dunedin	A+	46	0	0	18	73	297	69	26	21	4	1	1	3	17	1	52	2	3	5	3	.625	0	2--	—	2.59
1996 Dunedin	A+	3	0	0	1	2.2	12	4	2	1	1	0	0	1	0	0	1	0	0	1	.000	0	0--	—	3.38
1997 Dunedin	A+	43	0	0	20	68.1	296	63	36	22	4	4	1	2	26	3	66	4	1	2	5	.286	0	3--	—	2.90
Syracuse	AAA	6	0	0	1	9	40	11	6	6	0	0	0	0	3	0	9	0	0	0	0	.000	0	0--	—	6.00

		HOW MUCH HE PITCHED					WHAT HE GAVE UP										THE RESULTS					
Year Team	Lg	G	GS	CG	GF	IP	BFP	H	R	ER	HR	SH	SF	HB	TBB	IBB	SO	WP	Bk	W	L	Pct.	ShO	Sv-Op	Hld	ERA
1998 Syracuse	AAA	43	1	0	16	49.2	204	37	15	12	2	1	2	1	23	2	45	0	0	3	1	.750	0	3--	—	2.17
1998 Toronto	AL	24	0	0	3	15	61	13	7	6	0	0	0	0	5	0	8	0	0	0	2	.000	0	0-2	3	3.60

Mike Sirotka

Pitches: Left **Bats:** Left **Pos:** SP-33   **Ht:** 6'1" **Wt:** 200 **Born:** 5/13/71 **Age:** 28

		HOW MUCH HE PITCHED						WHAT HE GAVE UP											THE RESULTS					
Year Team	Lg	G	GS	CG	GF	IP	BFP	H	R	ER	HR	SH	SF	HB	TBB	IBB	SO	WP	Bk	W	L	Pct.	ShO	Sv-Op	Hld	ERA
1995 Chicago	AL	6	6	0	0	34.1	152	39	16	16	2	1	3	0	17	0	19	2	0	1	2	.333	0	0-0	0	4.19
1996 Chicago	AL	15	4	0	2	26.1	122	34	27	21	3	0	2	0	12	0	11	1	0	1	2	.333	0	0-0	0	7.18
1997 Chicago	AL	7	4	0	1	32	130	36	9	8	4	0	0	1	5	1	24	0	0	3	0	1.000	0	0-0	1	2.25
1998 Chicago	AL	33	33	5	0	211.2	911	255	137	119	30	5	7	2	47	0	128	3	1	14	15	.483	0	0-0	0	5.06
4 ML YEARS		61	47	5	3	304.1	1315	364	189	164	39	6	12	3	81	1	182	6	1	19	19	.500	0	0-0	1	4.85

Heathcliff Slocumb

Pitches: Right **Bats:** Right **Pos:** RP-57   **Ht:** 6'3" **Wt:** 220 **Born:** 6/7/66 **Age:** 33

		HOW MUCH HE PITCHED						WHAT HE GAVE UP											THE RESULTS					
Year Team	Lg	G	GS	CG	GF	IP	BFP	H	R	ER	HR	SH	SF	HB	TBB	IBB	SO	WP	Bk	W	L	Pct.	ShO	Sv-Op	Hld	ERA
1991 Chicago	NL	52	0	0	21	62.2	274	53	29	24	3	6	6	3	30	6	34	9	0	2	1	.667	0	1-3	6	3.45
1992 Chicago	NL	30	0	0	11	36	174	52	27	26	3	2	2	1	21	3	27	1	0	0	3	.000	0	1-1	1	6.50
1993 ChN-Cle		30	0	0	9	38	164	35	19	17	3	1	3	0	20	2	22	0	0	4	1	.800	0	0-2	3	4.03
1994 Philadelphia	NL	52	0	0	16	72.1	322	75	32	23	0	2	4	2	28	4	58	9	0	5	1	.833	0	0-5	18	2.86
1995 Philadelphia	NL	61	0	0	54	65.1	289	64	26	21	2	4	0	1	35	3	63	3	0	5	6	.455	0	32-38	3	2.89
1996 Boston	AL	75	0	0	60	83.1	368	68	31	28	2	1	3	3	55	5	88	10	0	5	5	.500	0	31-39	2	3.02
1997 Bos-Sea	AL	76	0	0	61	75	353	84	45	43	6	4	2	4	49	5	64	10	0	0	9	.000	0	27-33	3	5.16
1998 Seattle	AL	57	0	0	29	67.2	313	72	40	40	5	4	2	1	44	1	51	10	0	2	5	.286	0	3-4	2	5.32
1993 Chicago	NL	10	0	0	4	10.2	42	7	5	4	0	0	1	0	4	0	4	0	0	1	0	1.000	0	0-0	2	3.38
Cleveland	AL	20	0	0	5	27.1	122	28	14	13	3	1	2	0	16	2	18	0	0	3	1	.750	0	0-2	1	4.28
1997 Boston	AL	49	0	0	37	46.2	227	58	32	30	4	2	2	3	34	4	36	6	0	0	5	.000	0	17-22	1	5.79
Seattle	AL	27	0	0	24	28.1	126	26	13	13	2	2	0	1	15	1	28	4	0	0	4	.000	0	10-11	2	4.13
8 ML YEARS		433	0	0	261	500.1	2257	503	249	222	24	24	22	15	282	29	407	52	0	23	31	.426	0	95-125	38	3.99

Aaron Small

Pitches: Right **Bats:** Right **Pos:** RP-47   **Ht:** 6'5" **Wt:** 226 **Born:** 11/23/71 **Age:** 27

		HOW MUCH HE PITCHED						WHAT HE GAVE UP											THE RESULTS					
Year Team	Lg	G	GS	CG	GF	IP	BFP	H	R	ER	HR	SH	SF	HB	TBB	IBB	SO	WP	Bk	W	L	Pct.	ShO	Sv-Op	Hld	ERA
1994 Toronto	AL	1	0	0	1	2	13	5	2	2	1	0	1	0	2	0	0	0	0	0	0	.000	0	0-0	0	9.00
1995 Florida	NL	7	0	0	1	6.1	32	7	2	1	1	0	0	0	6	0	5	0	0	1	0	1.000	0	0-0	0	1.42
1996 Oakland	AL	12	3	0	4	28.2	144	37	28	26	3	0	1	1	22	1	17	2	0	1	3	.250	0	0-0	0	8.16
1997 Oakland	AL	71	0	0	22	96.2	425	109	50	46	6	5	6	3	40	6	57	4	0	9	5	.643	0	4-6	4	4.28
1998 Oak-Ari		47	0	0	13	67.2	304	83	48	42	8	5	1	4	22	4	33	4	0	4	2	.667	0	0-2	4	5.59
1998 Oakland	AL	24	0	0	4	36	174	51	34	29	3	3	1	3	14	3	19	4	0	1	1	.500	0	0-0	3	7.25
Arizona	NL	23	0	0	9	31.2	130	32	14	13	5	2	0	1	8	1	14	0	0	3	1	.750	0	0-2	1	3.69
5 ML YEARS		138	3	0	41	201.1	918	241	130	117	19	10	9	8	92	11	112	10	0	15	10	.600	0	4-8	12	5.23

John Smiley

Pitches: Left **Bats:** Left **Pos:** SP   **Ht:** 6'4" **Wt:** 210 **Born:** 3/17/65 **Age:** 34

		HOW MUCH HE PITCHED						WHAT HE GAVE UP											THE RESULTS					
Year Team	Lg	G	GS	CG	GF	IP	BFP	H	R	ER	HR	SH	SF	HB	TBB	IBB	SO	WP	Bk	W	L	Pct.	ShO	Sv-Op	Hld	ERA
1986 Pittsburgh	NL	12	0	0	2	11.2	42	4	6	5	2	0	0	0	4	0	9	0	0	1	0	1.000	0	0--	—	3.86
1987 Pittsburgh	NL	63	0	0	19	75	336	69	49	48	7	0	3	0	50	8	58	5	1	5	5	.500	0	4-6	12	5.76
1988 Pittsburgh	NL	34	32	5	0	205	835	185	81	74	15	11	8	3	46	4	129	6	6	13	11	.542	1	0-0	1	3.25
1989 Pittsburgh	NL	28	28	8	0	205.1	835	174	78	64	22	5	7	4	49	5	123	5	2	12	8	.600	1	0-0	0	2.81
1990 Pittsburgh	NL	26	25	2	0	149.1	632	161	83	77	15	5	4	2	36	1	86	2	2	9	10	.474	0	0-0	0	4.64
1991 Pittsburgh	NL	33	32	2	0	207.2	836	194	78	71	17	11	4	3	44	0	129	3	1	20	8	.714	2	0-0	0	3.08
1992 Minnesota	AL	34	34	5	0	241	970	205	93	86	17	4	9	6	65	0	163	4	0	16	9	.640	2	0-0	0	3.21
1993 Cincinnati	NL	18	18	2	0	105.2	455	117	69	66	15	5	5	5	31	0	60	2	1	3	9	.250	0	0-0	0	5.62
1994 Cincinnati	NL	24	24	1	0	158.2	672	169	80	68	18	16	0	4	37	3	112	4	2	11	10	.524	1	0-0	0	3.86
1995 Cincinnati	NL	28	27	1	0	176.2	724	173	72	68	11	17	5	4	39	3	124	5	1	12	5	.706	0	0-0	0	3.46
1996 Cincinnati	NL	35	34	2	0	217.1	889	207	100	88	20	16	7	4	54	5	171	7	1	13	14	.481	0	0-1	0	3.64
1997 Cin-Cle		26	26	0	0	154.1	674	184	99	91	26	6	2	7	41	3	120	5	0	11	14	.440	0	0-0	0	5.31
1997 Cincinnati	NL	20	20	0	0	117	514	139	76	68	17	6	1	6	31	3	94	2	0	9	10	.474	0	0-0	0	5.23
Cleveland	AL	6	6	0	0	37.1	160	45	23	23	9	0	1	1	10	0	26	3	0	2	4	.333	0	0-0	0	5.54
12 ML YEARS		361	280	28	21	1907.2	7900	1842	888	806	185	101	52	39	496	32	1284	48	17	126	103	.550	8	4--	—	3.80

Bobby Smith

Bats: R **Throws:** R **Pos:** 3B-97; PH/PR-22; DH-7; SS-7; 2B-6   **Ht:** 6'3" **Wt:** 190 **Born:** 5/10/74 **Age:** 25

		BATTING																	BASERUNNING				PERCENTAGES		
Year Team	Lg	G	AB	H	2B	3B	HR	(Hm	Rd)	TB	R	RBI	TBB	IBB	SO	HBP	SH	SF	SB	CS	SB%	GDP	Avg	OBP	SLG
1992 Braves	R	57	217	51	9	1	3	—	—	71	31	28	17	1	55	3	0	2	5	6	.45	5	.235	.297	.327
1993 Macon	A	108	384	94	16	7	4	—	—	136	53	38	23	1	81	5	8	0	12	8	.60	1	.245	.296	.354
1994 Durham	A+	127	478	127	27	2	12	—	—	194	49	71	41	1	112	4	1	0	18	7	.72	19	.266	.329	.406
1995 Greenville	AA	127	444	116	27	3	14	—	—	191	75	58	40	2	109	7	4	1	12	6	.67	12	.261	.331	.430

Year Team	Lg	G	AB	H	2B	3B	HR	(Hm	Rd)	TB	R	RBI	TBB	IBB	SO	HBP	SH	SF	SB	CS	SB%	GDP	Avg	OBP	SLG
							BATTING												BASERUNNING				PERCENTAGES		
1996 Richmond	AAA	124	445	114	27	0	8	—	—	165	49	58	32	0	114	4	2	3	15	9	.63	12	.256	.310	.371
1997 Richmond	AAA	100	357	88	10	2	12	—	—	138	47	47	44	2	109	7	2	1	6	5	.55	4	.246	.340	.387
1998 Tampa Bay	AL	117	370	102	15	3	11	(4	7)	156	44	55	34	0	110	6	2	4	5	3	.63	9	.276	.343	.422

Mark Smith

Bats: R **Throws:** R **Pos:** PH/PR-27; LF-16; RF-9; 1B-6; DH-3 **Ht:** 6'3" **Wt:** 235 **Born:** 5/7/70 **Age:** 29

Year Team	Lg	G	AB	H	2B	3B	HR	(Hm	Rd)	TB	R	RBI	TBB	IBB	SO	HBP	SH	SF	SB	CS	SB%	GDP	Avg	OBP	SLG
							BATTING												BASERUNNING				PERCENTAGES		
1998 Nashville *	AAA	24	93	33	10	1	8	—	—	69	18	30	11	1	20	3	0	1	3	1	.75	1	.355	.435	.742
1994 Baltimore	AL	3	7	1	0	0	0	(0	0)	1	0	2	0	0	2	0	0	0	0	0	.00	0	.143	.143	.143
1995 Baltimore	AL	37	104	24	5	0	3	(1	2)	38	11	15	12	2	22	1	2	1	3	0	1.00	4	.231	.314	.365
1996 Baltimore	AL	27	78	19	2	0	4	(3	1)	33	9	10	3	0	20	3	0	0	2	0	.00	4	.244	.298	.423
1997 Pittsburgh	NL	71	193	55	13	1	9	(6	3)	97	29	35	28	1	36	0	0	1	3	1	.75	3	.285	.374	.503
1998 Pittsburgh	NL	59	128	25	6	0	2	(1	1)	37	18	13	10	0	26	3	0	3	7	0	1.00	1	.195	.264	.289
5 ML YEARS		197	510	124	26	1	18	(11	7)	206	67	75	53	3	106	7	2	5	13	3	.81	8	.243	.320	.404

Pete Smith

Pitches: Right **Bats:** Right **Pos:** RP-25; SP-12 **Ht:** 6'2" **Wt:** 200 **Born:** 2/27/66 **Age:** 33

Year Team	Lg	G	GS	CG	GF	IP	BFP	H	R	ER	HR	SH	SF	HB	TBB	IBB	SO	WP	Bk	W	L	Pct.	ShO	Sv-Op	Hld	ERA
			HOW MUCH HE PITCHED					WHAT HE GAVE UP												THE RESULTS						
1987 Atlanta	NL	6	6	0	0	31.2	143	39	21	17	3	0	2	0	14	0	11	3	1	1	2	.333	0	0-0	0	4.83
1988 Atlanta	NL	32	32	5	0	195.1	837	183	89	80	15	12	4	1	88	3	124	5	7	7	15	.318	3	0-0	0	3.69
1989 Atlanta	NL	28	27	1	0	142	613	144	83	75	13	4	5	0	57	2	115	3	7	5	14	.263	0	0-0	0	4.75
1990 Atlanta	NL	13	13	0	0	77	327	77	45	41	11	4	3	0	24	2	56	2	1	5	6	.455	0	0-0	0	4.79
1991 Atlanta	NL	14	10	0	2	48	211	48	33	27	5	2	4	0	22	3	29	1	4	1	3	.250	0	0-0	0	5.06
1992 Atlanta	NL	12	11	2	0	79	323	63	19	18	3	4	1	0	28	2	43	2	1	7	0	1.000	1	0-0	0	2.05
1993 Atlanta	NL	20	14	0	2	90.2	390	92	45	44	15	6	5	2	36	3	53	1	1	4	8	.333	0	0-0	1	4.37
1994 New York	NL	21	21	1	0	131.1	565	145	83	81	25	5	7	2	42	4	62	3	1	4	10	.286	0	0-0	0	5.55
1995 Cincinnati	NL	11	2	0	3	24.1	106	30	19	18	8	1	3	1	7	1	14	1	0	1	2	.333	0	0-0	1	6.66
1997 San Diego	NL	37	15	0	7	118	511	120	66	63	16	7	2	1	52	2	68	0	3	7	6	.538	0	1-1	2	4.81
1998 SD-Bal	AL	37	12	0	5	88.1	397	102	54	54	12	4	4	3	34	2	65	8	1	5	5	.500	0	0-1	2	5.50
1998 San Diego	NL	10	8	0	2	43.1	193	45	23	23	5	1	2	3	18	1	36	2	0	3	2	.600	0	0-0	0	4.78
Baltimore	AL	27	4	0	3	45	204	57	31	31	7	3	2	0	16	1	29	6	1	2	3	.400	0	0-1	2	6.20
11 ML YEARS		231	163	12	19	1025.2	4423	1043	557	518	126	49	40	10	404	24	640	29	27	47	71	.398	4	1-2	5	4.55

Travis Smith

Pitches: Right **Bats:** Right **Pos:** RP-1 **Ht:** 5'10" **Wt:** 165 **Born:** 11/7/72 **Age:** 26

Year Team	Lg	G	GS	CG	GF	IP	BFP	H	R	ER	HR	SH	SF	HB	TBB	IBB	SO	WP	Bk	W	L	Pct.	ShO	Sv-Op	Hld	ERA
			HOW MUCH HE PITCHED					WHAT HE GAVE UP												THE RESULTS						
1995 Helena	R+	20	7	0	11	56	224	41	16	15	4	0	0	7	19	0	63	4	2	4	2	.667	0	5- -	—	2.41
1996 Stockton	A+	14	6	0	3	58.2	241	56	17	12	4	1	0	4	21	0	48	2	4	6	1	.857	0	1- -	—	1.84
El Paso	AA	17	17	3	0	107.2	478	119	56	50	6	4	5	6	39	0	68	2	0	7	4	.636	1	0- -	—	4.18
1997 El Paso	AA	28	28	5	0	184.1	805	210	106	85	12	7	5	7	58	2	107	7	3	16	3	.842	1	0- -	—	4.15
1998 Louisville	AAA	12	11	0	0	67.2	296	77	44	40	9	3	4	2	25	1	36	3	0	4	6	.400	0	0- -	—	5.32
1998 Milwaukee	NL	1	0	0	0	2	7	1	0	0	0	0	0	0	0	0	1	0	0	0	0	.000	0	0-0	0	0.00

John Smoltz

Pitches: Right **Bats:** Right **Pos:** SP-26 **Ht:** 6'3" **Wt:** 205 **Born:** 5/15/67 **Age:** 32

Year Team	Lg	G	GS	CG	GF	IP	BFP	H	R	ER	HR	SH	SF	HB	TBB	IBB	SO	WP	Bk	W	L	Pct.	ShO	Sv-Op	Hld	ERA
			HOW MUCH HE PITCHED					WHAT HE GAVE UP												THE RESULTS						
1998 Greenville *	AA	3	3	0	0	14	54	11	4	4	2	0	0	0	3	0	16	2	0	0	0	.000	0	0- -	—	2.57
Macon *	A	2	2	0	0	10	40	7	4	4	1	0	0	0	1	0	14	1	0	0	0	.000	0	0- -	—	3.60
1988 Atlanta	NL	12	12	0	0	64	297	74	40	39	10	2	0	2	33	4	37	2	1	2	7	.222	0	0-0	0	5.48
1989 Atlanta	NL	29	29	5	0	208	847	160	79	68	15	10	7	2	72	2	168	8	3	12	11	.522	0	0-0	0	2.94
1990 Atlanta	NL	34	34	6	0	231.1	966	206	109	99	20	9	8	1	90	3	170	14	3	14	11	.560	2	0-0	0	3.85
1991 Atlanta	NL	36	36	5	0	229.2	947	206	101	97	16	9	9	3	77	1	148	20	1	14	13	.519	2	0-0	0	3.80
1992 Atlanta	NL	35	35	9	0	246.2	1021	206	90	78	17	7	8	5	80	5	215	17	1	15	12	.556	3	0-0	0	2.85
1993 Atlanta	NL	35	35	3	0	243.2	1028	208	104	98	23	13	4	6	100	12	208	13	1	15	11	.577	1	0-0	0	3.62
1994 Atlanta	NL	21	21	1	0	134.2	568	120	69	62	15	7	6	4	48	4	113	7	0	6	10	.375	0	0-0	0	4.14
1995 Atlanta	NL	29	29	2	0	192.2	808	166	76	68	15	13	5	4	72	8	193	13	0	12	7	.632	1	0-0	0	3.18
1996 Atlanta	NL	35	35	6	0	253.2	995	199	93	83	19	12	4	2	55	3	276	10	1	24	8	.750	2	0-0	0	2.94
1997 Atlanta	NL	35	35	7	0	256	1043	234	97	86	21	10	3	1	63	9	241	10	1	15	12	.556	2	0-0	0	3.02
1998 Atlanta	NL	26	26	2	0	167.2	681	145	58	54	10	4	2	4	44	2	173	3	1	17	3	.850	2	0-0	0	2.90
11 ML YEARS		327	327	46	0	2228	9201	1924	916	832	181	96	56	34	734	53	1942	117	14	146	105	.582	13	0-0	0	3.36

Chris Snopek

Bats: R **Throws:** R **Pos:** SS-33; 2B-15; PH/PR-13; 3B-6; DH-3; 1B-1; RF-1 **Ht:** 6'1" **Wt:** 185 **Born:** 9/20/70 **Age:** 28

Year Team	Lg	G	AB	H	2B	3B	HR	(Hm	Rd)	TB	R	RBI	TBB	IBB	SO	HBP	SH	SF	SB	CS	SB%	GDP	Avg	OBP	SLG
							BATTING												BASERUNNING				PERCENTAGES		
1995 Chicago	AL	22	68	22	4	1	1	(1	0)	29	12	7	9	0	12	0	0	0	1	0	1.00	2	.324	.403	.426
1996 Chicago	AL	46	104	27	6	1	6	(3	3)	53	18	18	6	0	16	1	1	1	0	1	.00	5	.260	.304	.510
1997 Chicago	AL	86	298	65	15	0	5	(3	2)	95	27	35	18	0	51	1	4	2	3	2	.60	4	.218	.263	.319

Year Team	Lg	G	AB	H	2B	3B	HR	(Hm Rd)	TB	R	RBI	TBB	IBB	SO	HBP	SH	SF	SB	CS	SB%	GDP	Avg	OBP	SLG
1998 ChA-Bos	AL	61	137	28	2	0	1	(0 1)	33	19	6	16	0	29	1	0	1	3	0	1.00	4	.204	.290	.241
1998 Chicago	AL	53	125	26	2	0	1	(0 1)	31	17	4	14	0	24	1	0	1	3	0	1.00	4	.208	.291	.248
Boston	AL	8	12	2	0	0	0	(0 0)	2	2	2	2	0	5	0	0	0	0	0	.00	0	.167	.286	.167
4 ML YEARS		215	607	142	27	1	13	(7 6)	210	76	66	49	0	108	3	5	4	7	3	.70	15	.234	.293	.346

J.T. Snow

Bats: Both **Throws:** Left **Pos:** 1B-136; PH/PR-9 **Ht:** 6'2" **Wt:** 202 **Born:** 2/26/68 **Age:** 31

Year Team	Lg	G	AB	H	2B	3B	HR	(Hm Rd)	TB	R	RBI	TBB	IBB	SO	HBP	SH	SF	SB	CS	SB%	GDP	Avg	OBP	SLG
1992 New York	AL	7	14	2	1	0	0	(0 0)	3	1	2	5	1	5	0	0	0	0	0	.00	0	.143	.368	.214
1993 California	AL	129	419	101	18	2	16	(10 6)	171	60	57	55	4	88	2	7	6	3	0	1.00	10	.241	.328	.408
1994 California	AL	61	223	49	4	0	8	(7 1)	77	22	30	19	1	48	3	2	1	0	1	.00	2	.220	.289	.345
1995 California	AL	143	544	157	22	1	24	(14 10)	253	80	102	52	4	91	3	5	2	2	1	.67	16	.289	.353	.465
1996 California	AL	155	575	148	20	1	17	(8 9)	221	69	67	56	5	96	5	2	3	1	6	.14	19	.257	.327	.384
1997 San Francisco	NL	157	531	149	36	1	28	(14 14)	271	81	104	96	13	124	1	2	7	6	4	.60	8	.281	.387	.510
1998 San Francisco	NL	138	435	108	29	1	15	(9 6)	184	65	79	58	3	84	0	0	7	1	2	.33	12	.248	.332	.423
7 ML YEARS		790	2741	714	130	6	108	(62 46)	1180	378	441	341	32	536	14	18	26	13	14	.48	67	.260	.342	.430

John Snyder

Pitches: Right **Bats:** Right **Pos:** SP-14; RP-1 **Ht:** 6'3" **Wt:** 185 **Born:** 8/16/74 **Age:** 24

Year Team	Lg	G	GS	CG	GF	IP	BFP	H	R	ER	HR	SH	SF	HB	TBB	IBB	SO	WP	Bk	W	L	Pct.	ShO	Sv-Op	Hld	ERA
1992 Angels	R	15	0	0	7	44	195	40	27	16	0	2	5	3	16	1	38	1	4	2	4	.333	0	3- -	—	3.27
1993 Cedar Rapds	A	21	16	1	0	99	467	126	88	65	13	7	5	8	39	1	79	6	4	5	6	.455	1	0- -	—	5.91
1994 Lk Elsinore	A+	26	26	2	0	159	698	181	101	79	16	5	5	6	56	0	108	11	2	10	11	.476	0	0- -	—	4.47
1995 Midland	AA	21	21	4	0	133.1	591	158	93	85	12	3	6	10	48	1	81	7	3	8	9	.471	0	0- -	—	5.74
Birmingham	AA	5	4	0	0	20.1	87	24	16	15	6	0	1	2	6	0	13	1	0	1	0	1.000	0	0- -	—	6.64
1996 White Sox	R	4	4	0	0	16.1	58	5	3	3	1	1	0	0	4	0	23	0	0	1	0	1.000	0	0- -	—	1.65
Birmingham	AA	9	9	0	0	54	236	59	35	29	10	2	2	1	16	1	58	4	3	3	5	.375	0	0- -	—	4.83
1997 Birmingham	AA	20	20	2	0	114.1	510	130	76	59	9	1	3	6	43	0	90	6	2	7	8	.467	1	0- -	—	4.64
1998 Calgary	AAA	15	15	1	0	97	429	112	49	47	11	5	2	5	34	1	63	2	2	7	3	.700	0	0- -	—	4.36
1998 Chicago	AL	15	14	1	0	86.1	367	96	49	46	14	2	4	2	23	1	52	2	0	7	2	.778	0	0-0	0	4.80

Clint Sodowsky

Pitches: Right **Bats:** Left **Pos:** RP-39; SP-6 **Ht:** 6'4" **Wt:** 200 **Born:** 7/13/72 **Age:** 26

Year Team	Lg	G	GS	CG	GF	IP	BFP	H	R	ER	HR	SH	SF	HB	TBB	IBB	SO	WP	Bk	W	L	Pct.	ShO	Sv-Op	Hld	ERA
1998 Tucson *	AAA	2	2	0	0	9.1	42	11	4	4	0	0	0	0	3	0	7	0	1	0	1	.000	0	0- -	—	3.86
1995 Detroit	AL	6	6	0	0	23.1	112	24	15	13	4	1	0	0	18	0	14	1	1	2	2	.500	0	0-0	0	5.01
1996 Detroit	AL	7	7	0	0	24.1	132	40	34	32	5	1	0	3	20	0	9	3	0	1	3	.250	0	0-0	0	11.84
1997 Pittsburgh	NL	45	0	0	8	52	236	49	22	21	6	1	2	2	34	7	51	6	0	2	2	.500	0	0-2	5	3.63
1998 Arizona	NL	45	6	0	10	77.2	357	86	56	49	5	2	7	7	39	5	42	4	2	3	6	.333	0	0-3	2	5.68
4 ML YEARS		103	19	0	18	177.1	837	199	127	115	20	4	12	11	111	12	116	14	3	8	13	.381	0	0-5	7	5.84

Luis Sojo

Bats: R **Throws:** R **Pos:** SS-20; 1B-19; 2B-8; PH/PR-8; 3B-6; DH-2 **Ht:** 5'11" **Wt:** 175 **Born:** 1/3/66 **Age:** 33

Year Team	Lg	G	AB	H	2B	3B	HR	(Hm Rd)	TB	R	RBI	TBB	IBB	SO	HBP	SH	SF	SB	CS	SB%	GDP	Avg	OBP	SLG
1998 Tampa *	A+	3	9	2	0	0	0	— —	2	1	0	2	0	0	0	0	0	0	0	.00	0	.222	.364	.222
Columbus *	AAA	6	23	5	2	0	0	— —	7	1	2	1	0	1	0	0	0	1	0	1.00	1	.217	.250	.304
1990 Toronto	AL	33	80	18	3	0	1	(0 1)	24	14	9	5	0	5	0	0	0	1	1	.50	1	.225	.271	.300
1991 California	AL	113	364	94	14	1	3	(1 2)	119	38	20	14	0	26	5	19	0	4	2	.67	12	.258	.295	.327
1992 California	AL	106	368	100	12	3	7	(2 5)	139	37	43	14	0	24	1	7	1	7	11	.39	14	.272	.299	.378
1993 Toronto	AL	19	47	8	2	0	0	(0 0)	10	5	6	4	0	2	0	2	1	0	0	.00	3	.170	.231	.213
1994 Seattle	AL	63	213	59	9	2	6	(4 2)	90	32	22	8	0	25	2	3	1	2	1	.67	9	.277	.308	.416
1995 Seattle	AL	102	339	98	18	2	7	(4 3)	141	50	39	23	0	19	1	6	1	4	2	.67	9	.289	.335	.416
1996 Sea-NYA	AL	95	287	63	10	1	1	(1 0)	78	23	21	11	0	17	1	8	1	2	2	.50	10	.220	.250	.272
1997 New York	AL	77	215	66	6	1	2	(2 0)	80	27	25	16	0	14	1	5	2	3	1	.75	5	.307	.355	.372
1998 New York	AL	54	147	34	3	1	0	(0 0)	39	16	14	4	0	15	0	1	1	0	0	1.00	5	.231	.250	.265
1996 Seattle	AL	77	247	52	8	1	1	(1 0)	65	20	16	10	0	13	1	6	0	2	2	.50	8	.211	.244	.263
New York	AL	18	40	11	2	0	0	(0 0)	13	3	5	1	0	4	0	2	1	0	0	.00	2	.275	.286	.325
9 ML YEARS		662	2060	540	77	11	27	(14 13)	720	242	199	99	0	147	11	51	8	24	20	.55	61	.262	.298	.350

Paul Sorrento

Bats: L **Throws:** R **Pos:** DH-86; 1B-27; RF-14; PH/PR-12; LF-4 **Ht:** 6'2" **Wt:** 220 **Born:** 11/17/65 **Age:** 33

Year Team	Lg	G	AB	H	2B	3B	HR	(Hm Rd)	TB	R	RBI	TBB	IBB	SO	HBP	SH	SF	SB	CS	SB%	GDP	Avg	OBP	SLG
1989 Minnesota	AL	14	21	5	0	0	0	(0 0)	5	2	1	5	1	4	0	0	0	0	0	.00	0	.238	.370	.238
1990 Minnesota	AL	41	121	25	4	1	5	(2 3)	46	11	13	12	0	31	1	0	1	1	1	.50	3	.207	.281	.380
1991 Minnesota	AL	26	47	12	2	0	4	(2 2)	26	6	13	4	2	11	0	0	0	0	0	.00	0	.255	.314	.553
1992 Cleveland	AL	140	458	123	24	1	18	(11 7)	203	52	60	51	7	89	1	1	3	0	3	.00	13	.269	.341	.443
1993 Cleveland	AL	148	463	119	26	1	18	(8 10)	201	75	65	58	11	121	2	0	4	3	1	.75	10	.257	.340	.434

Year Team	Lg	G	AB	H	2B	3B	HR	(Hm Rd)	TB	R	RBI	TBB	IBB	SO	HBP	SH	SF	SB	CS	SB%	GDP	Avg	OBP	SLG
1994 Cleveland	AL	95	322	90	14	0	14	(8 6)	146	43	62	34	6	68	0	1	3	0	1	.00	7	.280	.345	.453
1995 Cleveland	AL	104	323	76	14	0	25	(12 13)	165	50	79	51	6	71	0	0	4	1	1	.50	10	.235	.336	.511
1996 Seattle	AL	143	471	136	32	1	23	(13 10)	239	67	93	57	10	103	7	2	5	0	2	.00	10	.289	.370	.507
1997 Seattle	AL	146	457	123	19	0	31	(18 13)	235	68	80	51	9	112	3	0	2	0	2	.00	13	.269	.345	.514
1998 Tampa Bay	AL	137	435	98	27	0	17	(10 7)	176	40	57	54	1	133	3	0	3	2	3	.40	8	.225	.313	.405
10 ML YEARS		994	3118	807	162	4	155	(84 71)	1442	414	523	377	53	743	17	4	26	7	14	.33	77	.259	.339	.462

Sammy Sosa

Bats: Right **Throws:** Right **Pos:** RF-156; CF-7   **Ht:** 6'0" **Wt:** 200 **Born:** 11/12/68 **Age:** 30

Year Team	Lg	G	AB	H	2B	3B	HR	(Hm Rd)	TB	R	RBI	TBB	IBB	SO	HBP	SH	SF	SB	CS	SB%	GDP	Avg	OBP	SLG
1989 Tex-ChA	AL	58	183	47	8	0	4	(1 3)	67	27	13	11	2	47	2	5	2	7	5	.58	6	.257	.303	.366
1990 Chicago	AL	153	532	124	26	10	15	(10 5)	215	72	70	33	4	150	6	2	6	32	16	.67	10	.233	.282	.404
1991 Chicago	AL	116	316	64	10	1	10	(3 7)	106	39	33	14	2	98	2	5	1	13	6	.68	5	.203	.240	.335
1992 Chicago	NL	67	262	68	7	2	8	(4 4)	103	41	25	19	1	63	4	4	2	15	7	.68	4	.260	.317	.393
1993 Chicago	NL	159	598	156	25	5	33	(23 10)	290	92	93	38	6	135	4	0	1	36	11	.77	14	.261	.309	.485
1994 Chicago	NL	105	426	128	17	6	25	(11 14)	232	59	70	25	1	92	2	1	4	22	13	.63	7	.300	.339	.545
1995 Chicago	NL	**144**	564	151	17	3	36	(19 17)	282	89	119	58	11	134	5	0	2	34	7	.83	8	.268	.340	.500
1996 Chicago	NL	124	498	136	21	2	40	(26 14)	281	84	100	34	6	134	5	0	4	18	5	.78	14	.273	.323	.564
1997 Chicago	NL	**162**	642	161	31	4	36	(25 11)	308	90	119	45	9	**174**	2	0	5	22	12	.65	16	.251	.300	.480
1998 Chicago	NL	159	643	198	20	0	66	(35 31)	416	**134**	**158**	73	14	171	1	0	5	18	9	.67	20	.308	.377	.647
1989 Texas	AL	25	84	20	3	0	1	(0 1)	26	8	3	0	0	20	0	4	0	0	2	.00	3	.238	.238	.310
Chicago	AL	33	99	27	5	0	3	(1 2)	41	19	10	11	2	27	2	1	2	7	3	.70	3	.273	.351	.414
10 ML YEARS		1247	4664	1233	182	33	273	(157 116)	2300	727	800	350	56	1198	33	17	32	217	91	.70	104	.264	.318	.493

Steve Sparks

Pitches: Right **Bats:** Right **Pos:** SP-20; RP-2   **Ht:** 6'0" **Wt:** 180 **Born:** 7/2/65 **Age:** 33

Year Team	Lg	G	GS	CG	GF	IP	BFP	H	R	ER	HR	SH	SF	HB	TBB	IBB	SO	WP	Bk	W	L	Pct.	ShO	Sv-Op	Hld	ERA
1998 Midland *	AA	7	7	0	0	40.2	184	49	38	32	3	2	1	0	15	0	34	3	1	0	4	.000	0	0- -	—	7.08
Vancouver *	AAA	4	4	2	0	28	114	23	11	9	2	1	3	1	6	0	19	2	0	0	4	.000	0	0- -	—	2.89
1995 Milwaukee	AL	33	27	3	2	202	875	210	114	104	17	5	**12**	5	86	1	96	5	1	9	11	.450	0	0-0	0	4.63
1996 Milwaukee	AL	20	13	1	2	88.2	406	103	66	65	19	3	1	3	52	0	21	6	0	4	7	.364	0	0-0	0	6.60
1998 Anaheim	AL	22	20	0	1	128.2	562	130	66	62	14	2	3	5	58	0	90	6	0	9	4	.692	0	0-0	0	4.34
3 ML YEARS		75	60	4	5	419.1	1843	443	243	231	50	10	16	13	196	1	207	17	1	22	22	.500	0	0-0	0	4.96

Tim Spehr

Bats: Right **Throws:** Right **Pos:** C-32; 1B-1   **Ht:** 6'2" **Wt:** 200 **Born:** 7/2/66 **Age:** 32

Year Team	Lg	G	AB	H	2B	3B	HR	(Hm Rd)	TB	R	RBI	TBB	IBB	SO	HBP	SH	SF	SB	CS	SB%	GDP	Avg	OBP	SLG
1998 St. Lucie *	A+	14	38	7	2	0	1	— —	12	7	6	9	0	16	3	0	1	0	0	.00	0	.184	.373	.316
Norfolk *	AAA	1	1	1	0	0	0	— —	1	0	0	0	0	0	0	0	0	0	0	.00	0	1.000	1.000	1.000
1991 Kansas City	AL	37	74	14	5	0	3	(1 2)	28	7	14	9	0	18	1	3	1	1	0	1.00	2	.189	.282	.378
1993 Montreal	NL	53	87	20	6	0	2	(0 2)	32	14	10	6	1	20	1	3	2	2	0	1.00	0	.230	.281	.368
1994 Montreal	NL	52	36	9	3	1	0	(0 0)	14	8	5	4	0	11	0	1	0	2	0	1.00	0	.250	.325	.389
1995 Montreal	NL	41	35	9	5	0	1	(0 1)	17	4	3	6	0	7	0	3	0	1	0	1.00	0	.257	.366	.486
1996 Montreal	NL	63	44	4	1	0	1	(1 0)	8	4	3	3	0	15	1	1	0	1	0	1.00	1	.091	.167	.182
1997 KC-Atl		25	49	9	1	0	2	(1 1)	16	5	6	2	0	16	1	0	0	1	0	1.00	0	.184	.231	.327
1998 NYN-KC		32	76	13	3	0	1	(1 0)	19	8	5	15	1	19	4	1	0	1	0	1.00	1	.171	.337	.250
1997 Kansas City	AL	17	35	6	0	0	1	(0 1)	9	3	2	2	0	12	1	0	0	0	0	.00	0	.171	.237	.257
Atlanta	NL	8	14	3	1	0	1	(1 0)	7	2	4	0	0	4	0	0	0	1	0	1.00	0	.214	.214	.500
1998 New York	NL	21	51	7	1	0	0	(0 0)	8	3	3	7	1	16	2	0	0	1	0	1.00	0	.137	.267	.157
Kansas City	AL	11	25	6	2	0	1	(1 0)	11	5	2	8	0	3	2	1	0	0	0	.00	1	.240	.457	.440
7 ML YEARS		303	401	78	24	1	10	(4 6)	134	50	46	45	2	106	8	12	3	8	0	1.00	4	.195	.287	.334

Justin Speier

Pitches: Right **Bats:** Right **Pos:** RP-19   **Ht:** 6'4" **Wt:** 205 **Born:** 11/6/73 **Age:** 25

Year Team	Lg	G	GS	CG	GF	IP	BFP	H	R	ER	HR	SH	SF	HB	TBB	IBB	SO	WP	Bk	W	L	Pct.	ShO	Sv-Op	Hld	ERA
1995 Williamsprt	A-	30	0	0	22	36.1	142	27	6	6	1	2	2	1	4	0	39	0	0	2	1	.667	0	12- -	—	1.49
1996 Daytona	A+	33	0	0	29	38.1	168	32	19	16	3	3	2	2	19	3	34	5	0	2	4	.333	0	13- -	—	3.76
Orlando	AA	24	0	0	19	26.1	110	23	7	6	2	1	1	2	5	1	14	0	0	4	1	.800	0	6- -	—	2.05
1997 Orlando	AA	50	0	0	20	78.1	328	77	46	39	8	4	2	3	23	0	63	2	2	6	5	.545	0	6- -	—	4.48
Iowa	AAA	8	0	0	4	12.1	41	5	0	0	0	1	0	0	1	0	9	0	0	2	0	1.000	0	1- -	—	0.00
1998 Iowa	AAA	45	0	0	33	51.2	226	52	31	29	10	3	0	5	19	1	49	6	0	3	3	.500	0	12- -	—	5.05
1998 ChN-Fla	NL	19	0	0	10	20.2	99	27	20	20	7	2	1	0	13	1	17	3	0	0	3	.000	0	0-1	1	8.71
1998 Chicago	NL	1	0	0	0	1.1	7	2	2	2	0	0	0	0	1	0	2	1	0	0	0	.000	0	0-0	0	13.50
Florida	NL	18	0	0	10	19.1	92	25	18	18	7	2	1	0	12	1	15	2	0	0	3	.000	0	0-1	1	8.38

Shane Spencer

Bats: R **Throws:** R **Pos:** RF-15; LF-9; PH/PR-9; DH-4; 1B-1   **Ht:** 5'11" **Wt:** 210 **Born:** 2/20/72 **Age:** 27

				BATTING																BASERUNNING				PERCENTAGES		
Year Team	Lg	G	AB	H	2B	3B	HR	(Hm	Rd)	TB	R	RBI	TBB	IBB	SO	HBP	SH	SF		SB	CS	SB%	GDP		Avg	OBP	SLG
1990 Yankees	R	42	147	27	4	0	0	—	—	31	20	7	20	0	23	1	0	1		11	2	.85	3		.184	.284	.211
1991 Yankees	R	41	160	49	7	0	0	—	—	56	25	30	14	0	19	2	0	4		8	2	.80	6		.306	.361	.350
Oneonta	A-	18	53	13	2	1	0	—	—	17	10	3	10	0	9	1	3	0		2	2	.50	1		.245	.375	.321
1992 Greensboro	A	83	258	74	10	2	3	—	—	97	43	27	33	0	37	3	1	2		8	2	.80	12		.287	.372	.376
1993 Greensboro	A	122	431	116	35	2	12	—	—	191	89	80	52	0	62	3	0	8		14	2	.88	8		.269	.346	.443
1994 Tampa	A+	90	334	97	22	3	8	—	—	149	44	53	30	0	53	1	1	1		5	3	.63	8		.290	.350	.446
1995 Tampa	A+	134	500	150	31	3	16	—	—	235	87	88	61	2	60	7	2	3		14	8	.64	7		.300	.382	.470
1996 Norwich	AA	126	450	114	19	0	29	—	—	220	70	89	68	2	99	4	1	5		4	2	.67	6		.253	.353	.489
Columbus	AAA	9	31	11	4	0	3	—	—	24	7	6	5	0	5	1	0	0		0	1	.00	0		.355	.459	.774
1997 Columbus	AAA	125	452	109	34	4	30	—	—	241	78	86	71	1	105	4	1	5		0	2	.00	8		.241	.346	.533
1998 Columbus	AAA	87	342	110	29	1	18	—	—	195	66	67	41	0	59	3	0	2		1	3	.25	8		.322	.397	.570
1998 New York	AL	27	67	25	6	0	10	(8	2)	61	18	27	5	0	12	0	0	1		0	1	.00	0		.373	.411	.910

Stan Spencer

Pitches: Right **Bats:** Right **Pos:** SP-5; RP-1   **Ht:** 6'4" **Wt:** 205 **Born:** 8/7/69 **Age:** 29

		HOW MUCH HE PITCHED						WHAT HE GAVE UP												THE RESULTS						
Year Team	Lg	G	GS	CG	GF	IP	BFP	H	R	ER	HR	SH	SF	HB	TBB	IBB	SO	WP	Bk		W	L	Pct.	ShO	Sv-Op	Hld	ERA
1991 Harrisburg	AA	17	17	1	0	92	389	90	52	45	6	4	2	4	30	0	66	2	3		6	1	.857	0	0- -	—	4.40
1993 High Desert	A+	13	13	0	0	61.2	265	67	33	28	4	0	2	3	18	0	38	1	0		4	4	.500	0	0- -	—	4.09
1994 Brevard Cty	A+	6	5	0	1	20	84	20	9	7	0	0	1	1	6	0	22	1	0		1	0	1.000	0	0- -	—	3.15
Portland	AA	20	20	1	0	124	505	113	52	48	12	4	6	2	30	2	96	3	1		9	4	.692	0	0- -	—	3.48
1995 Charlotte	AAA	9	9	0	0	41.1	198	61	37	36	9	0	0	3	24	1	19	0	0		1	4	.200	0	0- -	—	7.84
Portland	AA	8	8	0	0	39	193	57	39	32	9	0	4	2	19	0	32	0	0		1	4	.200	0	0- -	—	7.38
1997 Rancho Cuca	A+	7	7	0	0	40.1	164	37	18	15	6	0	1	2	5	0	46	1	0		3	1	.750	0	0- -	—	3.35
Las Vegas	AAA	8	8	0	0	48	208	48	23	20	5	1	0	1	18	2	47	1	0		3	2	.600	0	0- -	—	3.75
1998 Las Vegas	AAA	22	22	0	0	137.1	570	120	67	60	17	3	3	5	42	2	136	6	1		12	6	.667	0	0- -	—	3.93
1998 San Diego	NL	6	5	0	0	30.2	124	29	16	16	5	0	0	1	4	0	31	0	0		1	0	1.000	0	0-0	0	4.70

Bill Spiers

Bats: L **Throws:** R **Pos:** 3B-99; PH/PR-25; 2B-9; 1B-7; SS-2   **Ht:** 6'2" **Wt:** 190 **Born:** 6/5/66 **Age:** 33

				BATTING																BASERUNNING				PERCENTAGES		
Year Team	Lg	G	AB	H	2B	3B	HR	(Hm	Rd)	TB	R	RBI	TBB	IBB	SO	HBP	SH	SF		SB	CS	SB%	GDP		Avg	OBP	SLG
1989 Milwaukee	AL	114	345	88	9	3	4	(1	3)	115	44	33	21	1	63	1	4	2		10	2	.83	2		.255	.298	.333
1990 Milwaukee	AL	112	363	88	15	3	2	(2	0)	115	44	36	16	0	45	1	6	3		11	6	.65	12		.242	.274	.317
1991 Milwaukee	AL	133	414	117	13	6	8	(1	7)	166	71	54	34	0	55	2	10	4		14	8	.64	9		.283	.337	.401
1992 Milwaukee	AL	12	16	5	2	0	0	(0	0)	7	2	2	1	0	4	0	1	0		1	1	.50	0		.313	.353	.438
1993 Milwaukee	AL	113	340	81	8	4	2	(2	0)	103	43	36	29	2	51	4	9	4		9	8	.53	11		.238	.302	.303
1994 Milwaukee	AL	73	214	54	10	1	0	(0	0)	66	27	17	19	1	42	1	3	0		7	1	.88	5		.252	.316	.308
1995 New York	NL	63	72	15	2	1	0	(0	0)	19	5	11	12	1	15	0	1	2		0	1	.00	0		.208	.314	.264
1996 Houston	NL	122	218	55	10	1	6	(3	3)	85	27	26	20	4	34	2	1	1		7	0	1.00	3		.252	.320	.390
1997 Houston	NL	132	291	93	27	4	4	(0	4)	140	51	48	61	6	42	1	1	1		10	5	.67	4		.320	.438	.481
1998 Houston	NL	123	384	105	27	4	4	(1	3)	152	66	43	45	0	62	5	1	2		11	2	.85	9		.273	.356	.396
10 ML YEARS		997	2657	701	123	27	30	(10	20)	968	380	306	258	15	413	17	37	19		80	34	.70	55		.264	.331	.364

Scott Spiezio

Bats: Both **Throws:** Right **Pos:** 2B-112; PH/PR-3; DH-1   **Ht:** 6'2" **Wt:** 226 **Born:** 9/21/72 **Age:** 26

				BATTING																BASERUNNING				PERCENTAGES		
Year Team	Lg	G	AB	H	2B	3B	HR	(Hm	Rd)	TB	R	RBI	TBB	IBB	SO	HBP	SH	SF		SB	CS	SB%	GDP		Avg	OBP	SLG
1998 Edmonton *	AAA	5	13	3	1	0	1	—	—	7	3	4	3	0	2	0	0	0		0	0	.00	0		.231	.375	.538
1996 Oakland	AL	9	29	9	2	0	2	(1	1)	17	6	8	4	1	4	0	2	0		0	1	.00	0		.310	.394	.586
1997 Oakland	AL	147	538	131	28	4	14	(6	8)	209	58	65	44	2	75	1	3	4		9	3	.75	13		.243	.300	.388
1998 Oakland	AL	114	406	105	19	1	9	(6	3)	153	54	50	44	3	56	2	7	2		1	3	.25	10		.259	.333	.377
3 ML YEARS		270	973	245	49	5	25	(13	12)	379	118	123	92	6	135	3	12	6		10	7	.59	23		.252	.317	.390

Paul Spoljaric

Pitches: Left **Bats:** Right **Pos:** RP-47; SP-6   **Ht:** 6'3" **Wt:** 210 **Born:** 9/24/70 **Age:** 28

		HOW MUCH HE PITCHED						WHAT HE GAVE UP												THE RESULTS						
Year Team	Lg	G	GS	CG	GF	IP	BFP	H	R	ER	HR	SH	SF	HB	TBB	IBB	SO	WP	Bk		W	L	Pct.	ShO	Sv-Op	Hld	ERA
1994 Toronto	AL	2	1	0	0	2.1	21	5	10	10	3	0	0	0	9	1	2	0	0		0	1	.000	0	0-0	0	38.57
1996 Toronto	AL	28	0	0	12	38	163	30	17	13	6	1	1	2	19	1	38	0	0		2	2	.500	0	1-1	5	3.08
1997 Tor-Sea	AL	57	0	0	10	70.2	302	61	30	29	4	2	2	3	36	6	70	6	3		0	3	.000	0	3-5	10	3.69
1998 Seattle	AL	53	6	0	10	83.1	387	85	67	60	14	5	3	1	55	3	89	10	0		4	6	.400	0	0-2	9	6.48
1997 Toronto	AL	37	0	0	10	48	198	37	17	17	3	1	2	2	21	4	43	5	1		0	3	.000	0	3-3	8	3.19
Seattle	AL	20	0	0	0	22.2	104	24	13	12	1	1	0	1	15	2	27	1	2		0	0	.000	0	0-2	2	4.76
4 ML YEARS		140	7	0	32	194.1	873	181	124	112	27	8	6	6	119	11	199	16	3		6	12	.333	0	4-8	24	5.19

Jerry Spradlin

Pitches: Right **Bats:** Both **Pos:** RP-69   **Ht:** 6'7" **Wt:** 246 **Born:** 6/14/67 **Age:** 32

Year Team	Lg	G	GS	CG	GF	IP	BFP	H	R	ER	HR	SH	SF	HB	TBB	IBB	SO	WP	Bk	W	L	Pct.	ShO	Sv-Op	Hld	ERA
1993 Cincinnati	NL	37	0	0	16	49	193	44	20	19	4	3	4	0	9	0	24	3	1	2	1	.667	0	2-3	0	3.49
1994 Cincinnati	NL	6	0	0	2	8	38	12	11	9	2	0	2	0	2	0	4	0	0	0	0	.000	0	0-0	0	10.13
1996 Cincinnati	NL	1	0	0	1	0.1	1	0	0	0	0	0	0	0	0	0	0	1	0	0	0	.000	0	0-0	0	0.00
1997 Philadelphia	NL	76	0	0	23	81.2	345	86	45	43	9	1	2	1	27	3	67	5	2	4	8	.333	0	1-5	18	4.74
1998 Philadelphia	NL	69	0	0	20	81.2	319	63	34	32	9	4	2	2	20	1	76	6	1	4	4	.500	0	1-4	5	3.53
5 ML YEARS		189	0	0	62	220.2	896	205	110	103	24	8	10	3	58	4	171	15	4	10	13	.435	0	4-12	23	4.20

Ed Sprague

Bats: Right **Throws:** Right **Pos:** 3B-128; PH/PR-3; 1B-1   **Ht:** 6'2" **Wt:** 205 **Born:** 7/25/67 **Age:** 31

Year Team	Lg	G	AB	H	2B	3B	HR	(Hm	Rd)	TB	R	RBI	TBB	IBB	SO	HBP	SH	SF	SB	CS	SB%	GDP	Avg	OBP	SLG
1991 Toronto	AL	61	160	44	7	0	4	(3	1)	63	17	20	19	2	43	3	0	1	0	3	.00	2	.275	.361	.394
1992 Toronto	AL	22	47	11	2	0	1	(1	0)	16	6	7	3	0	7	0	0	0	0	0	.00	0	.234	.280	.340
1993 Toronto	AL	150	546	142	31	1	12	(8	4)	211	50	73	32	1	85	10	2	6	1	0	1.00	23	.260	.310	.386
1994 Toronto	AL	109	405	97	19	1	11	(6	5)	151	38	44	23	1	95	11	2	4	1	0	1.00	11	.240	.296	.373
1995 Toronto	AL	144	521	127	27	2	18	(12	6)	212	77	74	58	3	96	15	1	7	0	0	.00	19	.244	.333	.407
1996 Toronto	AL	159	591	146	35	2	36	(17	19)	293	88	101	60	1	146	12	0	7	0	0	.00	7	.247	.325	.496
1997 Toronto	AL	138	504	115	29	4	14	(5	9)	194	63	48	51	0	102	6	0	1	0	1	.00	10	.228	.306	.385
1998 Tor-Oak	AL	132	469	104	25	0	20	(9	11)	189	57	58	26	2	90	13	0	2	1	2	.33	16	.222	.280	.403
1998 Toronto	AL	105	382	91	20	0	17	(6	11)	162	49	51	24	1	73	11	0	2	0	2	.00	15	.238	.301	.424
Oakland	AL	27	87	13	5	0	3	(3	0)	27	8	7	2	1	17	2	0	0	1	0	1.00	1	.149	.187	.310
8 ML YEARS		915	3243	786	175	10	116	(61	55)	1329	396	425	272	12	664	70	5	28	3	6	.33	88	.242	.312	.410

Dennis Springer

Pitches: Right **Bats:** Right **Pos:** SP-17; RP-12   **Ht:** 5'10" **Wt:** 185 **Born:** 2/12/65 **Age:** 34

Year Team	Lg	G	GS	CG	GF	IP	BFP	H	R	ER	HR	SH	SF	HB	TBB	IBB	SO	WP	Bk	W	L	Pct.	ShO	Sv-Op	Hld	ERA
1998 Durham *	AAA	5	5	0	0	37.2	157	34	13	12	1	1	1	1	15	0	23	1	0	2	3	.400	0	0- -	—	2.87
1995 Philadelphia	NL	4	4	0	0	22.1	94	21	15	12	3	2	0	1	9	1	15	1	0	0	3	.000	0	0-0	0	4.84
1996 California	AL	20	15	2	3	94.2	413	91	65	58	24	0	1	6	43	0	64	1	0	5	6	.455	1	0-0	1	5.51
1997 Anaheim	AL	32	28	3	0	194.2	846	199	118	112	32	4	13	10	73	0	75	7	0	9	9	.500	1	0-0	0	5.18
1998 Tampa Bay	AL	29	17	1	8	115.2	517	120	77	70	21	1	2	12	60	1	46	6	0	3	11	.214	0	0-0	0	5.45
4 ML YEARS		85	64	6	11	427.1	1870	431	275	252	80	7	16	29	185	2	200	15	0	17	29	.370	2	0-0	1	5.31

Russ Springer

Pitches: Right **Bats:** Right **Pos:** RP-48   **Ht:** 6'4" **Wt:** 205 **Born:** 11/7/68 **Age:** 30

Year Team	Lg	G	GS	CG	GF	IP	BFP	H	R	ER	HR	SH	SF	HB	TBB	IBB	SO	WP	Bk	W	L	Pct.	ShO	Sv-Op	Hld	ERA
1992 New York	AL	14	0	0	5	16	75	18	11	11	0	0	0	1	10	0	12	0	0	0	0	.000	0	0-0	2	6.19
1993 California	AL	14	9	1	3	60	278	73	48	48	11	1	1	3	32	1	31	6	0	1	6	.143	0	0-0	0	7.20
1994 California	AL	18	5	0	6	45.2	198	53	28	28	9	1	1	0	14	0	28	2	0	2	2	.500	0	2-3	1	5.52
1995 Cal-Phi		33	6	0	6	78.1	350	82	48	46	16	2	2	7	35	4	70	2	0	1	2	.333	0	1-2	0	5.29
1996 Philadelphia	NL	51	7	0	12	96.2	437	106	60	50	12	5	3	1	38	6	94	5	0	3	10	.231	0	0-3	6	4.66
1997 Houston	NL	54	0	0	13	55.1	241	48	28	26	4	2	4	2	27	2	74	4	0	3	3	.500	0	3-7	9	4.23
1998 Ari-Atl	NL	48	0	0	14	52.2	232	51	26	24	4	2	1	1	30	4	56	5	0	5	4	.556	0	0-4	7	4.10
1995 California	AL	19	6	0	3	51.2	238	60	37	35	11	1	0	5	25	1	38	1	0	1	2	.333	0	1-2	0	6.10
Philadelphia	NL	14	0	0	3	26.2	112	22	11	11	5	1	2	2	10	3	32	1	0	0	0	.000	0	0-0	0	3.71
1998 Arizona	NL	26	0	0	13	32.2	140	29	16	15	4	0	0	1	14	1	37	3	0	4	3	.571	0	0-3	1	4.13
Atlanta	NL	22	0	0	1	20	92	22	10	9	0	2	1	0	16	3	19	2	0	1	1	.500	0	0-1	6	4.05
7 ML YEARS		232	27	1	59	404.2	1811	431	249	233	56	12	10	17	186	17	365	24	0	15	27	.357	0	6-19	25	5.18

Scott Stahoviak

Bats: Left **Throws:** Right **Pos:** 1B-4; PH/PR-4; RF-1   **Ht:** 6'5" **Wt:** 222 **Born:** 3/6/70 **Age:** 29

Year Team	Lg	G	AB	H	2B	3B	HR	(Hm	Rd)	TB	R	RBI	TBB	IBB	SO	HBP	SH	SF	SB	CS	SB%	GDP	Avg	OBP	SLG
1998 Salt Lake *	AAA	111	399	126	33	6	18	—	—	225	71	82	45	4	94	1	0	7	5	2	.71	9	.316	.381	.564
1993 Minnesota	AL	20	57	11	4	0	0	(0	0)	15	1	1	3	0	22	0	0	0	0	2	.00	2	.193	.233	.263
1995 Minnesota	AL	94	263	70	19	0	3	(1	2)	98	28	23	30	1	61	1	0	2	5	1	.83	3	.266	.341	.373
1996 Minnesota	AL	130	405	115	30	3	13	(8	5)	190	72	61	59	7	114	2	1	2	3	3	.50	9	.284	.376	.469
1997 Minnesota	AL	91	275	63	17	0	10	(4	6)	110	33	33	24	1	73	6	0	4	5	2	.71	7	.229	.301	.400
1998 Minnesota	AL	9	19	2	0	0	1	(1	0)	5	1	1	0	0	7	0	0	0	0	0	.00	0	.105	.105	.263
5 ML YEARS		344	1019	261	70	3	27	(14	13)	418	135	119	116	9	277	9	1	8	13	8	.62	21	.256	.335	.410

Matt Stairs

Bats: L **Throws:** R **Pos:** DH-120; PH/PR-14; LF-11; 1B-6; RF-2   **Ht:** 5'9" **Wt:** 206 **Born:** 2/27/68 **Age:** 31

Year Team	Lg	G	AB	H	2B	3B	HR	Hm	Rd	TB	R	RBI	TBB	IBB	SO	HBP	SH	SF	SB	CS	SB%	GDP	Avg	OBP	SLG
1992 Montreal	NL	13	30	5	2	0	0	(0	0)	7	2	5	7	0	7	0	0	1	0	0	.00	0	.167	.316	.233
1993 Montreal	NL	6	8	3	1	0	0	(0	0)	4	1	2	0	0	1	0	0	0	0	0	.00	1	.375	.375	.500
1995 Boston	AL	39	88	23	7	1	1	(0	1)	35	8	17	4	0	14	1	1	1	0	1	.00	4	.261	.298	.398
1996 Oakland	AL	61	137	38	5	1	10	(5	5)	75	21	23	19	2	23	1	0	1	1	1	.50	2	.277	.367	.547
1997 Oakland	AL	133	352	105	19	0	27	(20	7)	205	62	73	50	1	60	3	1	4	3	2	.60	6	.298	.386	.582
1998 Oakland	AL	149	523	154	33	1	26	(16	10)	267	88	106	59	4	93	6	1	4	8	3	.73	13	.294	.370	.511
6 ML YEARS		401	1138	328	67	3	64	(41	23)	593	182	226	139	7	198	11	3	11	12	7	.63	26	.288	.368	.521

Robby Stanifer

Pitches: Right **Bats:** Right **Pos:** RP-38   **Ht:** 6'3" **Wt:** 205 **Born:** 3/10/72 **Age:** 27

Year Team	Lg	G	GS	CG	GF	IP	BFP	H	R	ER	HR	SH	SF	HB	TBB	IBB	SO	WP	Bk	W	L	Pct.	ShO	Sv-Op	Hld	ERA
1994 Elmira	A-	9	8	1	0	49	211	54	17	14	2	0	1	2	12	1	38	2	3	2	1	.667	0	0- -	—	2.57
Brevard Cty	A+	5	5	0	0	24.1	115	32	20	17	2	1	1	3	10	0	12	2	1	1	2	.333	0	0- -	—	6.29
1995 Brevard Cty	A+	18	13	0	0	82.2	360	97	47	38	4	4	5	7	15	0	45	2	0	3	6	.333	0	0- -	—	4.14
1996 Brevard Cty	A+	22	0	0	4	49	206	54	17	13	3	0	1	1	9	0	32	1	0	4	2	.667	0	0- -	—	2.39
Portland	AA	18	0	0	10	34.1	137	27	15	6	3	1	2	1	9	0	33	2	0	3	1	.750	0	2- -	—	1.57
1997 Charlotte	AAA	22	0	0	16	27.2	123	34	16	15	3	1	1	1	7	0	25	2	0	4	0	1.000	0	5- -	—	4.88
1998 Charlotte	AAA	21	1	0	10	39.2	166	39	20	19	1	1	5	1	13	2	29	1	0	4	2	.667	0	4- -	—	4.31
1997 Florida	NL	36	0	0	10	45	188	43	23	23	9	4	0	3	16	0	28	1	0	1	2	.333	0	1-2	4	4.60
1998 Florida	NL	38	0	0	11	48	222	54	33	30	5	2	3	0	22	3	30	1	0	2	4	.333	0	1-3	3	5.63
2 ML YEARS		74	0	0	21	93	410	97	56	53	14	6	3	3	38	3	58	2	0	3	6	.333	0	2-5	7	5.13

Andy Stankiewicz

Bats: Right **Throws:** Right **Pos:** 2B-61; PH/PR-30   **Ht:** 5'9" **Wt:** 165 **Born:** 8/10/64 **Age:** 34

Year Team	Lg	G	AB	H	2B	3B	HR	Hm	Rd	TB	R	RBI	TBB	IBB	SO	HBP	SH	SF	SB	CS	SB%	GDP	Avg	OBP	SLG
1998 Diamondbcks *	R	3	10	3	0	0	0	—	—	3	2	3	0	0	0	0	0	0	0	0	.00	0	.300	.300	.300
Tucson *	AAA	5	20	6	0	0	0	—	—	6	1	2	0	0	0	1	0	0	0	0	.00	1	.300	.333	.300
1992 New York	AL	116	400	107	22	2	2	(2	0)	139	52	25	38	0	42	5	7	1	9	5	.64	13	.268	.338	.348
1993 New York	AL	16	9	0	0	0	0	(0	0)	0	5	0	1	0	1	0	0	0	0	0	.00	0	.000	.100	.000
1994 Houston	NL	37	54	14	3	0	1	(1	0)	20	7	6	12	0	12	1	1	0	1	1	.50	2	.259	.403	.370
1995 Houston	NL	43	52	6	1	0	0	(0	0)	7	6	7	12	2	19	0	1	0	4	2	.67	1	.115	.281	.135
1996 Montreal	NL	64	77	22	5	1	0	(0	0)	29	12	9	6	1	12	3	1	1	1	0	1.00	1	.286	.356	.377
1997 Montreal	NL	76	107	24	9	0	1	(0	1)	36	11	5	4	0	22	0	7	1	1	1	.50	1	.224	.250	.336
1998 Arizona	NL	77	145	30	5	0	0	(0	0)	35	9	8	7	0	33	2	0	1	1	0	1.00	3	.207	.252	.241
7 ML YEARS		429	844	203	45	3	4	(3	1)	266	105	59	80	3	141	11	18	4	17	9	.65	21	.241	.313	.315

Mike Stanley

Bats: R **Throws:** R **Pos:** DH-107; 1B-35; PH/PR-3; LF-1   **Ht:** 6'0" **Wt:** 190 **Born:** 6/25/63 **Age:** 36

Year Team	Lg	G	AB	H	2B	3B	HR	Hm	Rd	TB	R	RBI	TBB	IBB	SO	HBP	SH	SF	SB	CS	SB%	GDP	Avg	OBP	SLG
1986 Texas	AL	15	30	10	3	0	1	(0	1)	16	4	1	3	0	7	0	0	0	1	0	1.00	0	.333	.394	.533
1987 Texas	AL	78	216	59	8	1	6	(3	3)	87	34	37	31	0	48	1	1	4	3	0	1.00	0	.273	.361	.403
1988 Texas	AL	94	249	57	8	0	3	(1	2)	74	21	27	37	0	62	0	1	5	0	0	.00	6	.229	.323	.297
1989 Texas	AL	67	122	30	3	1	1	(1	0)	38	9	11	12	1	29	2	1	0	1	0	1.00	5	.246	.324	.311
1990 Texas	AL	103	189	47	8	1	2	(1	1)	63	21	19	30	2	25	0	6	1	1	0	1.00	5	.249	.350	.333
1991 Texas	AL	95	181	45	13	1	3	(1	2)	69	25	25	34	0	44	2	5	1	0	0	.00	2	.249	.372	.381
1992 New York	AL	68	173	43	7	0	8	(5	3)	74	24	27	33	0	45	1	0	0	0	0	.00	2	.249	.372	.428
1993 New York	AL	130	423	129	17	1	26	(17	9)	226	70	84	57	4	85	5	0	6	1	1	.50	10	.305	.389	.534
1994 New York	AL	82	290	87	20	0	17	(8	9)	158	54	57	39	2	56	2	0	2	0	0	.00	6	.300	.384	.545
1995 New York	AL	118	399	107	29	1	18	(13	5)	192	63	83	57	1	106	5	0	9	1	1	.50	14	.268	.360	.481
1996 Boston	AL	121	397	107	20	1	24	(10	14)	201	73	69	69	3	62	5	0	2	2	1	1.00	4	.270	.383	.506
1997 Bos-NYA	AL	125	347	103	25	0	16	(6	10)	176	61	65	54	4	72	6	0	8	0	1	.00	13	.297	.393	.507
1998 Tor-Bos	AL	145	497	127	25	0	29	(12	17)	239	74	79	82	5	129	7	0	7	3	1	.75	12	.256	.364	.481
1997 Boston	AL	97	260	78	17	0	13	(5	8)	134	45	53	39	0	50	6	0	7	0	1	.00	9	.300	.394	.515
New York	AL	28	87	25	8	0	3	(1	2)	42	16	12	15	4	22	0	0	1	0	0	.00	4	.287	.388	.483
1998 Toronto	AL	98	341	82	13	0	22	(11	11)	161	49	47	56	3	86	5	0	3	2	1	.67	6	.240	.353	.472
Boston	AL	47	156	45	12	0	7	(1	6)	78	25	32	26	2	43	2	0	4	1	0	1.00	6	.288	.388	.500
13 ML YEARS		1241	3513	951	186	7	154	(78	76)	1613	533	584	538	22	770	36	14	45	13	4	.76	96	.271	.369	.459

Mike Stanton

Pitches: Left **Bats:** Left **Pos:** RP-67   **Ht:** 6'1" **Wt:** 215 **Born:** 6/2/67 **Age:** 32

Year Team	Lg	G	GS	CG	GF	IP	BFP	H	R	ER	HR	SH	SF	HB	TBB	IBB	SO	WP	Bk	W	L	Pct.	ShO	Sv-Op	Hld	ERA
1989 Atlanta	NL	20	0	0	10	24	94	17	4	4	0	4	0	0	8	1	27	1	0	0	1	.000	0	7-8	2	1.50
1990 Atlanta	NL	7	0	0	4	7	42	16	14	14	1	1	0	1	4	2	7	1	0	0	3	.000	0	2-3	0	18.00
1991 Atlanta	NL	74	0	0	20	78	314	62	27	25	6	6	0	1	21	6	54	0	0	5	5	.500	0	7-10	15	2.88
1992 Atlanta	NL	65	0	0	23	63.2	264	59	32	29	6	1	2	2	20	2	44	3	0	5	4	.556	0	8-11	15	4.10
1993 Atlanta	NL	63	0	0	41	52	236	51	35	27	4	5	2	0	29	7	43	2	0	4	6	.400	0	27-33	5	4.67

		HOW MUCH HE PITCHED			WHAT HE GAVE UP								THE RESULTS			
Year Team	Lg	G GS CG GF	IP	BFP	H R ER HR SH SF HB	TBB IBB	SO WP Bk	W L Pct.	ShO Sv-Op Hld	ERA
1994 Atlanta	NL	49 0 0 15	45.2	197	41 18 18 2 2 1 3	26 3	35 1 0	3 1 .750	0 3-4 10	3.55
1995 Atl-Bos		48 0 0 22	40.1	178	48 23 19 6 2 1 1	14 2	23 2 1	2 1 .667	0 1-3 8	4.24
1996 Bos-Tex	AL	81 0 0 28	78.2	327	78 32 32 11 4 2 0	27 5	60 3 2	4 4 .500	0 1-6 22	3.66
1997 New York	AL	64 0 0 15	66.2	283	50 19 19 3 2 0 3	34 2	70 3 2	6 1 .857	0 3-5 26	2.57
1998 New York	AL	67 0 0 26	79	330	71 51 48 13 1 4 2	26 1	69 0 0	4 1 .800	0 6-10 18	5.47
1995 Atlanta	NL	26 0 0 10	19.1	94	31 14 12 3 2 1 1	6 2	13 1 1	1 1 .500	0 1-2 4	5.59
Boston	AL	22 0 0 12	21	87	17 9 7 3 0 0 0	8 0	10 1 0	1 0 1.000	0 0-1 4	3.00
1996 Boston	AL	59 0 0 19	56.1	239	58 24 24 9 3 2 0	23 4	46 3 2	4 3 .571	0 1-5 15	3.83
Texas	AL	22 0 0 9	22.1	88	20 8 8 2 1 0 0	4 1	14 0 0	0 1 .000	0 0-1 7	3.22
10 ML YEARS		538 0 0 204	535	2265	493 257 235 52 28 10 15	209 31	432 15 5	33 27 .550	0 65-93 121	3.95

Kennie Steenstra

Pitches: Right **Bats:** Right **Pos:** RP-4   **Ht:** 6'5" **Wt:** 215 **Born:** 10/13/70 **Age:** 28

		HOW MUCH HE PITCHED			WHAT HE GAVE UP								THE RESULTS			
Year Team	Lg	G GS CG GF	IP	BFP	H R ER HR SH SF HB	TBB IBB	SO WP Bk	W L Pct.	ShO Sv-Op Hld	ERA
1992 Geneva	A-	3 3 1 0	20	76	11 4 2 0 0 0 0	3 0	12 0 1	1 0 1.000	0 0- —	0.90
Peoria	A	12 12 4 0	89.2	364	79 29 21 5 2 1 3	21 1	68 4 3	6 3 .667	2 0- —	2.11
1993 Daytona	A+	13 13 1 0	81.1	317	64 26 23 2 3 2 8	12 1	57 2 1	5 3 .625	1 0- —	2.55
Iowa	AAA	1 1 0 0	6.2	32	9 5 5 2 0 0 0	4 0	6 0 0	1 0 1.000	0 0- —	6.75
Orlando	AA	14 14 2 0	100.1	427	103 47 40 4 4 2 9	25 0	60 5 2	8 3 .727	2 0- —	3.59
1994 Iowa	AAA	3 3 0 0	13	68	24 21 19 2 0 2 2	4 0	10 0 0	1 2 .333	0 0- —	13.15
Orlando	AA	23 23 2 0	158.1	654	146 55 46 12 9 3 9	39 4	83 4 1	9 7 .563	1 0- —	2.61
1995 Iowa	AAA	29 26 6 1	171.1	722	174 85 74 15 6 6 8	48 3	96 6 0	9 12 .429	2 0- —	3.89
1996 Iowa	AAA	26 26 3 0	158	686	170 96 88 24 5 9 9	47 4	101 2 0	8 12 .400	0 0- —	5.01
1997 Iowa	AAA	25 25 4 0	160.2	663	161 85 70 15 4 9 0	41 4	111 7 0	5 10 .333	0 0- —	3.92
1998 Iowa	AAA	25 24 1 0	148	639	171 84 72 16 6 3 1	36 1	104 0 0	11 5 .688	1 0- —	4.38
1998 Chicago	NL	4 0 0 1	3.1	18	7 4 4 2 0 0 0	1 0	4 0 0	0 0 .000	0 0-0 0	10.80

Blake Stein

Pitches: Right **Bats:** Right **Pos:** SP-20; RP-4   **Ht:** 6'7" **Wt:** 210 **Born:** 8/3/73 **Age:** 25

		HOW MUCH HE PITCHED			WHAT HE GAVE UP								THE RESULTS			
Year Team	Lg	G GS CG GF	IP	BFP	H R ER HR SH SF HB	TBB IBB	SO WP Bk	W L Pct.	ShO Sv-Op Hld	ERA
1994 Johnson Cty	R+	13 13 1 0	59.2	242	44 21 19 4 4 2 1	24 0	69 3 0	4 1 .800	0 0- —	2.87
1995 Peoria	A	27 27 1 0	139.2	596	122 69 59 12 1 4 5	61 0	133 2 1	10 6 .625	0 0- —	3.80
1996 St. Pete	A+	28 27 2 1	172	667	122 48 41 4 3 4 5	54 0	159 4 0	16 5 .762	1 1- —	2.15
1997 Arkansas	AA	22 22 1 0	133.2	557	128 67 63 17 5 1 1	49 2	114 5 0	8 7 .533	0 0- —	4.24
Huntsville	AA	7 7 0 0	34.2	157	36 24 22 3 0 1 0	20 1	25 6 0	3 2 .600	0 0- —	5.71
1998 Edmonton	AAA	5 4 0 0	23.1	104	22 13 9 1 1 0 0	11 0	31 1 0	3 1 .750	0 0- —	3.47
1998 Oakland	AL	24 20 1 0	117.1	538	117 92 83 22 1 2 5	71 3	89 15 0	5 9 .357	1 0-0 0	6.37

Terry Steinbach

Bats: Right **Throws:** Right **Pos:** C-119; PH/PR-5; DH-3   **Ht:** 6'1" **Wt:** 212 **Born:** 3/2/62 **Age:** 37

						BATTING										BASERUNNING				PERCENTAGES		
Year Team	Lg	G	AB	H	2B 3B HR	(Hm Rd)	TB	R	RBI	TBB	IBB	SO	HBP	SH	SF	SB CS SB% GDP	Avg	OBP	SLG
1986 Oakland	AL	6	15	5	0 0 2	(0 2)	11	3	4	1	0	0	0	0	0	0 0 .00 0	.333	.375	.733
1987 Oakland	AL	122	391	111	16 3 16	(6 10)	181	66	56	32	2	66	9	3	3	1 2 .33 10	.284	.349	.463
1988 Oakland	AL	104	351	93	19 1 9	(6 3)	141	42	51	33	2	47	6	3	5	3 0 1.00 13	.265	.334	.402
1989 Oakland	AL	130	454	124	13 1 7	(5 2)	160	37	42	30	2	66	2	2	3	1 2 .33 10	.273	.319	.352
1990 Oakland	AL	114	379	95	15 2 9	(3 6)	141	32	57	19	1	66	4	5	3	0 1 .00 11	.251	.291	.372
1991 Oakland	AL	129	456	125	31 1 6	(1 5)	176	50	67	22	4	70	7	0	9	2 2 .50 15	.274	.312	.386
1992 Oakland	AL	128	438	122	20 1 12	(3 9)	180	48	53	45	3	58	1	0	3	2 3 .40 20	.279	.345	.411
1993 Oakland	AL	104	389	111	19 1 10	(5 5)	162	47	43	25	1	65	3	0	1	3 3 .50 13	.285	.333	.416
1994 Oakland	AL	103	369	105	21 2 11	(5 6)	163	51	57	26	4	62	0	1	6	2 1 .67 10	.285	.327	.442
1995 Oakland	AL	114	406	113	26 1 15	(9 6)	186	43	65	25	4	74	3	1	4	1 3 .25 15	.278	.322	.458
1996 Oakland	AL	145	514	140	25 1 35	(16 19)	272	79	100	49	5	115	6	0	2	0 1 .00 16	.272	.342	.529
1997 Minnesota	AL	122	447	111	27 1 12	(6 6)	176	60	54	35	2	106	1	0	4	6 1 .86 14	.248	.302	.394
1998 Minnesota	AL	124	422	102	25 2 14	(6 8)	173	45	54	38	0	89	4	0	1	0 1 .00 16	.242	.310	.410
13 ML YEARS		1445	5031	1357	257 17 158	(71 87)	2122	603	703	380	30	884	46	15	44	21 20 .51 167	.270	.324	.422

Garrett Stephenson

Pitches: Right **Bats:** Right **Pos:** SP-6   **Ht:** 6'5" **Wt:** 208 **Born:** 1/2/72 **Age:** 27

		HOW MUCH HE PITCHED			WHAT HE GAVE UP								THE RESULTS			
Year Team	Lg	G GS CG GF	IP	BFP	H R ER HR SH SF HB	TBB IBB	SO WP Bk	W L Pct.	ShO Sv-Op Hld	ERA
1998 Scranton-WB *	AAA	13 11 2 1	73.2	314	81 49 43 15 0 5 2	16 0	48 1 0	1 8 .111	0 0- —	5.25
1996 Baltimore	AL	3 0 0 2	6.1	35	13 9 9 1 1 0 1	3 1	3 0 0	0 1 .000	0 0-0 0	12.79
1997 Philadelphia	NL	20 18 2 0	117	474	104 45 41 11 2 5 3	38 0	81 1 0	8 6 .571	0 0-0 0	3.15
1998 Philadelphia	NL	6 6 0 0	23	118	31 24 23 3 1 0 0	19 0	17 0 1	0 2 .000	0 0-0 0	9.00
3 ML YEARS		29 24 2 2	146.1	627	148 78 73 15 4 5 4	60 1	101 1 1	8 9 .471	0 0-0 0	4.49

215

Dave Stevens

Pitches: Right **Bats:** Right **Pos:** RP-31   **Ht:** 6'3" **Wt:** 210 **Born:** 3/4/70 **Age:** 29

Year Team	Lg	HOW MUCH HE PITCHED						WHAT HE GAVE UP										THE RESULTS						
		G	GS	CG	GF	IP	BFP	H	R	ER	HR	SH	SF	HB	TBB	IBB	SO	WP	Bk	W	L	Pct.	ShO	Sv-Op	Hld	ERA
1998 Iowa *	AAA	26	0	0	10	49.2	198	41	19	17	2	0	0	0	16	1	39	1	0	4	1	.800	0	2- -	—	3.08
1994 Minnesota	AL	24	0	0	6	45	208	55	35	34	6	2	0	1	23	2	24	3	0	5	2	.714	0	0-0	1	6.80
1995 Minnesota	AL	56	0	0	34	65.2	302	74	40	37	14	4	5	1	32	1	47	2	0	5	4	.556	0	10-12	5	5.07
1996 Minnesota	AL	49	0	0	38	58	251	58	31	30	12	3	3	0	25	2	29	1	0	3	3	.500	0	11-16	0	4.66
1997 Min-ChN		16	6	0	0	32.1	174	54	34	33	8	0	1	1	26	0	29	1	3	1	5	.167	0	0-0	0	9.19
1998 Chicago	NL	31	0	0	13	38	169	42	20	20	6	4	1	1	17	5	31	1	1	1	2	.333	0	0-0	0	4.74
1997 Minnesota	AL	6	6	0	0	23	124	41	23	23	8	0	0	0	17	0	16	1	2	1	3	.250	0	0-0	0	9.00
Chicago	NL	10	0	0	0	9.1	50	13	11	10	0	0	1	1	9	0	13	0	1	0	2	.000	0	0-0	0	9.64
5 ML YEARS		176	6	0	91	239	1104	283	160	154	46	13	10	4	123	10	160	8	4	15	16	.484	0	21-28	6	5.80

Lee Stevens

Bats: L **Throws:** L **Pos:** DH-72; 1B-37; PH/PR-22; RF-7   **Ht:** 6'4" **Wt:** 235 **Born:** 7/10/67 **Age:** 31

Year Team	Lg	BATTING															BASERUNNING				PERCENTAGES		
		G	AB	H	2B	3B	HR	(Hm	Rd)	TB	R	RBI	TBB	IBB	SO	HBP	SH	SF	SB	CS	SB%	GDP	Avg	OBP	SLG
1998 Oklahoma *	AAA	3	12	4	0	0	1	—	—	7	2	1	0	0	2	0	0	0	0	0	.00	0	.333	.333	.583
1990 California	AL	67	248	53	10	0	7	(4	3)	84	28	32	23	3	75	0	2	3	1	1	.50	8	.214	.275	.339
1991 California	AL	18	58	17	7	0	0	(0	0)	24	8	9	6	2	12	0	1	1	1	2	.33	0	.293	.354	.414
1992 California	AL	106	312	69	19	0	7	(2	5)	109	25	37	29	6	64	1	1	2	1	4	.20	4	.221	.288	.349
1996 Texas	AL	27	78	18	2	3	3	(2	1)	35	6	12	6	0	22	1	0	1	0	0	.00	2	.231	.291	.449
1997 Texas	AL	137	426	128	24	2	21	(12	9)	219	58	74	23	2	83	1	1	3	1	3	.25	18	.300	.336	.514
1998 Texas	AL	120	344	91	17	4	20	(13	7)	176	52	59	31	4	93	0	0	1	0	2	.00	6	.265	.324	.512
6 ML YEARS		475	1466	376	79	9	58	(33	25)	647	177	223	117	17	349	3	5	11	4	12	.25	38	.256	.311	.441

Shannon Stewart

Bats: Right **Throws:** Right **Pos:** LF-110; CF-44; PH/PR-4   **Ht:** 6'1" **Wt:** 194 **Born:** 2/25/74 **Age:** 25

Year Team	Lg	BATTING															BASERUNNING				PERCENTAGES		
		G	AB	H	2B	3B	HR	(Hm | Rd)	TB	R	RBI	TBB	IBB	SO	HBP	SH	SF	SB	CS	SB%	GDP	Avg	OBP	SLG
1995 Toronto	AL	12	38	8	0	0	0	(0 | 0)	8	2	1	5	0	5	1	0	0	1	0	1.00	0	.211	.318	.211
1996 Toronto	AL	7	17	3	1	0	0	(0 | 0)	4	2	2	1	0	4	0	0	0	1	0	1.00	1	.176	.222	.235
1997 Toronto	AL	44	168	48	13	7	0	(0 | 0)	75	25	22	19	1	24	4	0	2	10	3	.77	3	.286	.368	.446
1998 Toronto	AL	144	516	144	29	3	12	(6 | 6)	215	90	55	67	1	77	15	6	1	51	18	.74	5	.279	.377	.417
4 ML YEARS		207	739	203	43	10	12	(6 | 6)	302	119	80	92	2	110	20	6	3	64	21	.75	9	.275	.369	.409

Dave Stieb

Pitches: Right **Bats:** Right **Pos:** RP-16; SP-3   **Ht:** 6'1" **Wt:** 195 **Born:** 7/22/57 **Age:** 41

Year Team	Lg	HOW MUCH HE PITCHED						WHAT HE GAVE UP										THE RESULTS						
		G	GS	CG	GF	IP	BFP	H	R	ER	HR	SH	SF	HB	TBB	IBB	SO	WP	Bk	W	L	Pct.	ShO	Sv-Op	Hld	ERA
1998 Dunedin *	A+	3	3	0	0	15	65	17	8	5	2	0	0	0	5	0	19	1	0	2	0	1.000	0	0- -	—	3.00
Syracuse *	AAA	9	9	2	0	66	252	44	23	20	5	4	4	2	17	1	47	2	0	5	4	.556	0	0- -	—	2.73
1979 Toronto	AL	18	18	7	0	129.1	563	139	70	62	11	4	4	4	48	3	52	3	1	8	8	.500	1	0-0	0	4.31
1980 Toronto	AL	34	32	14	0	242.2	1004	232	108	100	12	12	9	6	83	6	108	6	2	12	15	.444	4	0- -	—	3.71
1981 Toronto	AL	25	25	11	0	183.2	748	148	70	65	10	5	7	11	61	2	89	1	2	11	10	.524	2	0-0	0	3.19
1982 Toronto	AL	38	38	19	0	288.1	1187	271	116	104	27	10	9	5	75	4	141	3	1	17	14	.548	5	0-0	0	3.25
1983 Toronto	AL	36	36	14	0	278	1141	223	105	94	21	6	9	14	93	6	187	5	1	17	12	.586	4	0-0	0	3.04
1984 Toronto	AL	35	35	11	0	267	1085	215	87	84	19	8	6	11	88	1	198	2	0	16	8	.667	2	0-0	0	2.83
1985 Toronto	AL	36	36	8	0	265	1087	206	89	73	22	14	2	9	96	3	167	4	1	14	13	.519	2	0-0	0	2.48
1986 Toronto	AL	37	34	1	2	205	919	239	128	108	29	6	6	15	87	1	127	7	0	7	12	.368	1	1-1	0	4.74
1987 Toronto	AL	33	31	3	1	185	789	164	92	84	16	5	5	7	87	4	115	4	0	13	9	.591	1	0-0	0	4.09
1988 Toronto	AL	32	31	8	1	207.1	844	157	76	70	15	10	4	13	79	0	147	4	5	16	8	.667	4	0-0	0	3.04
1989 Toronto	AL	33	33	3	0	206.2	850	164	83	77	12	10	3	13	76	2	101	3	1	17	8	.680	2	0-0	0	3.35
1990 Toronto	AL	33	33	2	0	208.2	861	179	73	68	11	6	3	10	64	0	125	5	0	18	6	.750	2	0-0	0	2.93
1991 Toronto	AL	9	9	1	0	59.2	244	52	22	21	4	4	1	2	23	0	29	0	0	4	3	.571	0	0-0	0	3.17
1992 Toronto	AL	21	14	1	3	96.1	415	98	58	54	9	6	5	4	43	3	45	4	0	4	6	.400	0	0-0	0	5.04
1993 Chicago	AL	4	4	0	0	22.1	107	27	17	15	1	2	1	0	14	0	11	0	0	1	3	.250	0	0-0	0	6.04
1998 Toronto	AL	19	3	0	7	50.1	228	58	31	27	6	0	2	5	17	1	27	0	0	1	2	.333	0	2-2	1	4.83
16 ML YEARS		443	412	103	14	2895.1	12072	2572	1225	1106	225	98	70	129	1034	36	1669	51	14	176	137	.562	30	3- -	—	3.44

Kelly Stinnett

Bats: Right **Throws:** Right **Pos:** C-86; PH/PR-8; DH-1   **Ht:** 5'11" **Wt:** 195 **Born:** 2/14/70 **Age:** 29

Year Team	Lg	BATTING															BASERUNNING				PERCENTAGES		
		G	AB	H	2B	3B	HR	(Hm | Rd)	TB	R	RBI	TBB	IBB	SO	HBP	SH	SF	SB	CS	SB%	GDP	Avg	OBP	SLG
1994 New York	NL	47	150	38	6	2	2	(0 | 2)	54	20	14	11	1	28	5	0	1	2	0	1.00	3	.253	.323	.360
1995 New York	NL	77	196	43	8	1	4	(1 | 3)	65	23	18	29	3	65	6	0	0	2	0	1.00	3	.219	.338	.332
1996 Milwaukee	AL	14	26	2	0	0	0	(0 | 0)	2	1	0	2	0	11	1	0	0	0	0	.00	0	.077	.172	.077
1997 Milwaukee	AL	30	36	9	4	0	0	(0 | 0)	13	2	3	3	0	9	0	0	0	0	1	.00	0	.250	.308	.361
1998 Arizona	NL	92	274	71	14	1	11	(5 | 6)	120	35	34	35	3	74	6	1	2	0	0	.00	9	.259	.353	.438
5 ML YEARS		260	682	163	32	4	17	(6 | 11)	254	81	69	80	7	187	18	1	3	4	1	.80	15	.239	.333	.372

Kevin Stocker

Bats: Both **Throws:** Right **Pos:** SS-110; PH/PR-2 **Ht:** 6'1" **Wt:** 175 **Born:** 2/13/70 **Age:** 29

							BATTING											BASERUNNING				PERCENTAGES		
Year Team	Lg	G	AB	H	2B	3B	HR	(Hm | Rd)	TB	R	RBI	TBB	IBB	SO	HBP	SH	SF	SB	CS	SB%	GDP	Avg	OBP	SLG
1993 Philadelphia	NL	70	259	84	12	3	2	(1 | 1)	108	46	31	30	11	43	8	4	1	5	0	1.00	8	.324	.409	.417
1994 Philadelphia	NL	82	271	74	11	2	2	(2 | 0)	95	38	28	44	8	41	7	4	4	2	2	.50	3	.273	.383	.351
1995 Philadelphia	NL	125	412	90	14	3	1	(1 | 0)	113	42	32	43	9	75	9	10	3	6	1	.86	7	.218	.304	.274
1996 Philadelphia	NL	119	394	100	22	6	5	(0 | 5)	149	46	41	43	9	89	8	3	4	6	4	.60	6	.254	.336	.378
1997 Philadelphia	NL	149	504	134	23	5	4	(2 | 2)	179	51	40	51	7	91	2	2	1	11	6	.65	14	.266	.335	.355
1998 Tampa Bay	AL	112	336	70	11	3	6	(4 | 2)	105	37	25	27	1	80	8	8	2	5	3	.63	7	.208	.282	.313
6 ML YEARS		657	2176	552	93	22	20	(10 | 10)	749	260	197	238	45	419	42	31	15	35	16	.69	45	.254	.337	.344

Jim Stoops

Pitches: Right **Bats:** Right **Pos:** RP-3 **Ht:** 6'3" **Wt:** 180 **Born:** 6/30/72 **Age:** 27

		HOW MUCH HE PITCHED						WHAT HE GAVE UP											THE RESULTS						
Year Team	Lg	G	GS	CG	GF	IP	BFP	H	R	ER	HR	SH	SF	HB	TBB	IBB	SO	WP	Bk	W	L	Pct.	ShO	Sv-Op	Hld	ERA
1995 Bellingham	A-	24	0	0	14	42	178	32	23	16	1	2	1	5	17	0	58	2	0	6	5	.545	0	4- -	—	3.43
1996 Burlington	A	46	0	0	18	60.2	262	43	24	17	2	4	1	6	40	4	69	6	1	3	3	.500	0	5- -	—	2.52
1997 San Jose	A+	50	0	0	16	91.2	401	92	56	53	3	2	3	7	45	2	114	7	1	2	5	.286	0	4- -	—	5.20
1998 San Jose	A+	45	0	0	43	55.1	222	28	7	6	0	0	0	3	25	0	96	1	0	2	1	.667	0	31- -	—	0.98
Salem	A+	3	0	0	1	4.1	16	2	0	0	0	1	0	0	1	0	8	0	0	0	0	.000	0	0- -	—	0.00
Colo Sprngs	AAA	11	0	0	6	14.2	58	6	6	2	0	0	2	1	8	0	17	0	0	1	0	1.000	0	1- -	—	1.23
1998 Colorado	NL	3	0	0	0	4	17	5	1	1	0	0	1	0	3	0	0	0	0	1	0	1.000	0	0-0	0	2.25

Todd Stottlemyre

Pitches: Right **Bats:** Left **Pos:** SP-33 **Ht:** 6'3" **Wt:** 200 **Born:** 5/20/65 **Age:** 34

		HOW MUCH HE PITCHED						WHAT HE GAVE UP											THE RESULTS						
Year Team	Lg	G	GS	CG	GF	IP	BFP	H	R	ER	HR	SH	SF	HB	TBB	IBB	SO	WP	Bk	W	L	Pct.	ShO	Sv-Op	Hld	ERA
1988 Toronto	AL	28	16	0	4	98	443	109	70	62	15	5	3	4	46	5	67	2	3	4	8	.333	0	0-1	0	5.69
1989 Toronto	AL	27	18	0	4	127.2	545	137	56	55	11	3	7	5	44	4	63	4	1	7	7	.500	0	0-0	0	3.88
1990 Toronto	AL	33	33	4	0	203	866	214	101	98	18	3	5	8	69	4	115	6	1	13	17	.433	0	0-0	0	4.34
1991 Toronto	AL	34	34	1	0	219	921	194	97	92	21	0	8	12	75	3	116	4	0	15	8	.652	0	0-0	0	3.78
1992 Toronto	AL	28	27	6	0	174	755	175	99	87	20	2	11	10	63	4	98	7	0	12	11	.522	2	0-0	0	4.50
1993 Toronto	AL	30	28	1	0	176.2	786	204	107	95	11	5	11	3	69	5	98	7	1	11	12	.478	1	0-0	0	4.84
1994 Toronto	AL	26	19	3	5	140.2	605	149	67	66	19	4	5	7	48	2	105	0	0	7	7	.500	1	1-3	0	4.22
1995 Oakland	AL	31	31	2	0	209.2	920	228	117	106	26	4	4	6	80	7	205	11	0	14	7	.667	0	0-0	0	4.55
1996 St. Louis	NL	34	33	5	0	223.1	944	191	100	96	30	12	9	4	93	8	194	8	1	14	11	.560	2	0-0	0	3.87
1997 St. Louis	NL	28	28	0	0	181	761	155	86	78	16	8	5	12	65	3	160	6	0	12	9	.571	0	0-0	0	3.88
1998 StL-Tex		33	33	3	0	221.2	949	214	107	92	25	8	6	4	81	1	204	5	2	14	13	.519	0	0-0	0	3.74
1998 St. Louis	NL	23	23	3	0	161.1	674	146	74	63	20	7	3	4	51	0	147	4	2	9	9	.500	0	0-0	0	3.51
Texas	AL	10	10	0	0	60.1	275	68	33	29	5	1	3	0	30	1	57	1	0	5	4	.556	0	0-0	0	4.33
11 ML YEARS		332	300	25	11	1974.2	8495	1970	1007	927	212	54	74	75	733	46	1425	60	9	123	110	.528	6	1-4	0	4.23

DaRond Stovall

Bats: B **Throws:** L **Pos:** LF-27; PH/PR-22; CF-14; RF-7 **Ht:** 6'1" **Wt:** 185 **Born:** 1/3/73 **Age:** 26

							BATTING											BASERUNNING				PERCENTAGES		
Year Team	Lg	G	AB	H	2B	3B	HR	(Hm	Rd)	TB	R	RBI	TBB	IBB	SO	HBP	SH	SF	SB	CS	SB%	GDP	Avg	OBP	SLG
1991 Johnson Cty	R+	48	134	19	2	2	0	—	—	25	16	5	23	1	63	0	0	0	8	3	.73	1	.142	.268	.187
1992 Savannah	A	135	450	92	13	7	7	—	—	140	51	40	63	0	138	0	1	1	20	14	.59	13	.204	.302	.311
1993 Springfield	A	135	460	118	19	4	20	—	—	205	73	81	53	2	143	0	2	3	18	12	.60	5	.257	.333	.446
1994 St. Pete	A+	134	507	113	20	6	15	—	—	190	68	69	62	4	154	0	2	5	24	8	.75	10	.223	.305	.375
1995 Wst Plm Bch	A+	121	461	107	22	2	4	—	—	145	52	51	44	2	117	0	2	3	18	12	.60	4	.232	.297	.315
1996 Expos	R	9	34	15	3	2	0	—	—	22	5	7	3	0	6	0	0	0	3	0	1.00	0	.441	.486	.647
Wst Plm Bch	A+	8	31	14	4	0	1	—	—	21	8	8	6	0	7	0	0	0	2	2	.50	1	.452	.541	.677
Harrisburg	AA	74	272	60	7	1	10	—	—	99	38	36	32	1	86	2	4	0	15	5	.67	5	.221	.307	.364
1997 Harrisburg	AA	45	169	48	4	1	9	—	—	81	29	39	23	1	30	0	0	3	4	0	1.00	3	.284	.364	.479
Ottawa	AAA	98	342	83	23	2	4	—	—	122	40	48	31	3	114	2	3	4	10	13	.43	6	.243	.306	.357
1998 Ottawa	AAA	44	150	34	7	1	8	—	—	67	15	22	21	1	51	0	1	1	6	2	.75	6	.227	.320	.447
1998 Montreal	NL	62	78	16	2	1	2	(0	2)	26	11	6	6	0	29	0	0	0	1	0	1.00	1	.205	.262	.333

Doug Strange

Bats: B **Throws:** R **Pos:** 3B-42; PH/PR-39; 2B-9; 1B-3 **Ht:** 6'1" **Wt:** 185 **Born:** 4/13/64 **Age:** 35

							BATTING											BASERUNNING				PERCENTAGES		
Year Team	Lg	G	AB	H	2B	3B	HR	(Hm	Rd)	TB	R	RBI	TBB	IBB	SO	HBP	SH	SF	SB	CS	SB%	GDP	Avg	OBP	SLG
1998 Carolina *	AA	4	14	5	0	0	0	—	—	5	4	0	2	0	1	0	0	0	0	0	.00	0	.357	.438	.357
1989 Detroit	AL	64	196	42	4	1	1	(1	0)	51	16	14	17	0	36	1	3	0	3	3	.50	6	.214	.280	.260
1991 Chicago	NL	3	9	4	1	0	0	(0	0)	5	0	1	0	0	1	1	0	1	1	0	1.00	0	.444	.455	.556
1992 Chicago	NL	52	94	15	1	0	1	(0	1)	19	7	5	10	2	15	0	2	0	1	0	1.00	1	.160	.240	.202
1993 Texas	AL	145	484	124	29	6	7	(4	3)	174	58	60	43	3	69	3	8	4	6	4	.60	12	.256	.318	.360
1994 Texas	AL	73	226	48	12	1	5	(3	2)	77	26	26	15	0	38	3	4	2	1	3	.25	6	.212	.268	.341
1995 Seattle	AL	74	155	42	9	2	2	(1	1)	61	19	21	10	0	25	2	1	0	0	3	.00	4	.271	.323	.394
1996 Seattle	AL	88	183	43	7	1	3	(2	1)	61	19	23	14	0	31	1	0	2	1	0	1.00	3	.235	.290	.333
1997 Montreal	NL	118	327	84	16	2	12	(6	6)	140	40	47	36	9	76	2	5	2	0	2	.00	4	.257	.332	.428
1998 Pittsburgh	NL	90	185	32	8	0	0	(0	0)	40	9	14	10	1	39	1	3	2	1	0	1.00	5	.173	.217	.216

Year Team	Lg	G	AB	H	2B	3B	HR	(Hm	Rd)	TB	R	RBI	TBB	IBB	SO	HBP	SH	SF	SB	CS	SB%	GDP	Avg	OBP	SLG
9 ML YEARS		707	1859	434	87	7	31	(17	14)	628	194	211	155	15	330	14	26	13	14	15	.48	41	.233	.295	.338

Darryl Strawberry

Bats: Left **Throws:** Left **Pos:** DH-81; LF-16; PH/PR-7 **Ht:** 6'6" **Wt:** 215 **Born:** 3/12/62 **Age:** 37

					BATTING														BASERUNNING				PERCENTAGES		
Year Team	Lg	G	AB	H	2B	3B	HR	(Hm	Rd)	TB	R	RBI	TBB	IBB	SO	HBP	SH	SF	SB	CS	SB%	GDP	Avg	OBP	SLG
1983 New York	NL	122	420	108	15	7	26	(10	16)	215	63	74	47	9	128	4	0	2	19	6	.76	5	.257	.336	.512
1984 New York	NL	147	522	131	27	4	26	(8	18)	244	75	97	75	15	131	0	1	4	27	8	.77	8	.251	.343	.467
1985 New York	NL	111	393	109	15	4	29	(14	15)	219	78	79	73	13	96	1	0	3	26	11	.70	9	.277	.389	.557
1986 New York	NL	136	475	123	27	5	27	(11	16)	241	76	93	72	9	141	6	0	9	28	12	.70	4	.259	.358	.507
1987 New York	NL	154	532	151	32	5	39	(20	19)	310	108	104	97	13	122	7	0	4	36	12	.75	4	.284	.398	.583
1988 New York	NL	153	543	146	27	3	39	(21	18)	296	101	101	85	21	127	3	0	9	29	14	.67	6	.269	.366	.545
1989 New York	NL	134	476	107	26	1	29	(15	14)	222	69	77	61	13	105	1	0	3	11	4	.73	4	.225	.312	.466
1990 New York	NL	152	542	150	18	1	37	(24	13)	281	92	108	70	15	110	4	0	5	15	8	.65	5	.277	.361	.518
1991 Los Angeles	NL	139	505	134	22	4	28	(14	14)	248	86	99	75	4	125	3	0	5	10	8	.56	8	.265	.361	.491
1992 Los Angeles	NL	43	156	37	8	0	5	(3	2)	60	20	25	19	4	34	1	0	1	3	1	.75	2	.237	.322	.385
1993 Los Angeles	NL	32	100	14	2	0	5	(3	2)	31	12	12	16	1	19	2	0	2	1	0	1.00	1	.140	.267	.310
1994 San Francisco	NL	29	92	22	3	1	4	(2	2)	39	13	17	19	4	22	0	0	2	0	3	.00	2	.239	.363	.424
1995 New York	AL	32	87	24	4	1	3	(3	0)	39	15	13	10	1	22	2	0	0	0	0	.00	0	.276	.364	.448
1996 New York	AL	63	202	53	13	0	11	(8	3)	99	35	36	31	5	55	1	0	3	6	5	.55	3	.262	.359	.490
1997 New York	AL	11	29	3	1	0	0	(0	0)	4	1	2	3	0	9	0	0	0	0	0	.00	0	.103	.188	.138
1998 New York	AL	101	295	73	11	2	24	(14	10)	160	44	57	46	4	90	3	0	1	8	7	.53	1	.247	.354	.542
16 ML YEARS		1559	5369	1385	251	38	332	(170	162)	2708	888	994	799	131	1336	38	1	53	219	99	.69	64	.258	.355	.504

Mark Strittmatter

Bats: Right **Throws:** Right **Pos:** C-3; PH/PR-1 **Ht:** 6'1" **Wt:** 210 **Born:** 4/4/69 **Age:** 30

					BATTING														BASERUNNING				PERCENTAGES		
Year Team	Lg	G	AB	H	2B	3B	HR	(Hm	Rd)	TB	R	RBI	TBB	IBB	SO	HBP	SH	SF	SB	CS	SB%	GDP	Avg	OBP	SLG
1992 Bend	A-	35	101	26	6	0	2	—	—	38	17	13	12	0	28	3	0	0	0	4	.00	2	.257	.353	.376
1993 Central Val	A+	59	179	47	8	0	2	—	—	61	21	15	31	0	29	2	2	3	0	0	1.00	8	.263	.372	.341
Colo Sprngs	AAA	5	10	2	1	0	0	—	—	3	1	2	0	0	2	1	0	0	0	0	.00	2	.200	.273	.300
1994 New Haven	AA	73	215	49	8	0	2	—	—	63	20	26	33	1	39	9	3	4	1	2	.33	7	.228	.349	.293
1995 Colo Sprngs	AAA	5	17	5	2	0	0	—	—	7	1	3	0	0	3	0	0	0	0	0	.00	0	.294	.294	.412
New Haven	AA	90	288	70	12	1	7	—	—	105	44	42	47	1	51	6	1	2	1	0	1.00	5	.243	.359	.365
1996 Colo Sprngs	AAA	58	159	37	8	1	2	—	—	53	21	18	17	3	30	7	1	0	2	1	.67	5	.233	.333	.333
1997 Colo Sprngs	AAA	45	114	28	8	0	2	—	—	42	16	12	11	3	21	5	4	1	0	1	.00	4	.246	.336	.368
1998 Colo Sprngs	AAA	87	255	71	15	3	6	—	—	110	32	38	30	1	48	12	2	2	0	0	.00	6	.278	.378	.431
1998 Colorado	NL	4	4	0	0	0	0	(0	0)	0	0	0	0	0	3	0	0	0	0	0	.00	0	.000	.000	.000

Chris Stynes

B: R **T:** R **Pos:** LF-64; PH/PR-23; 3B-22; RF-20; 2B-11; SS-2; CF-2 **Ht:** 5'10" **Wt:** 185 **Born:** 1/19/73 **Age:** 26

					BATTING														BASERUNNING				PERCENTAGES		
Year Team	Lg	G	AB	H	2B	3B	HR	(Hm	Rd)	TB	R	RBI	TBB	IBB	SO	HBP	SH	SF	SB	CS	SB%	GDP	Avg	OBP	SLG
1995 Kansas City	AL	22	35	6	1	0	0	(0	0)	7	7	2	4	0	3	0	0	0	0	0	.00	3	.171	.256	.200
1996 Kansas City	AL	36	92	27	6	0	0	(0	0)	33	8	6	2	0	5	0	1	0	5	2	.71	1	.293	.309	.359
1997 Cincinnati	NL	49	198	69	7	1	6	(2	4)	96	31	28	11	1	13	4	2	0	11	2	.85	5	.348	.394	.485
1998 Cincinnati	NL	123	347	88	10	1	6	(3	3)	118	52	27	32	1	36	4	4	1	15	1	.94	5	.254	.323	.340
4 ML YEARS		230	672	190	24	2	12	(5	7)	254	98	63	49	2	57	8	7	1	31	5	.86	14	.283	.338	.378

Scott Sullivan

Pitches: Right **Bats:** Right **Pos:** RP-67 **Ht:** 6'5" **Wt:** 210 **Born:** 3/13/71 **Age:** 28

		HOW MUCH HE PITCHED					WHAT HE GAVE UP											THE RESULTS					
Year Team	Lg	G	GS	CG	GF	IP	BFP	H	R	ER	HR	SH	SF	HB	TBB	IBB	SO	WP	Bk	W	L	Pct.	ShO	Sv-Op	Hld	ERA
1995 Cincinnati	NL	3	0	0	1	3.2	17	4	2	2	0	1	0	0	2	0	2	0	0	0	0	.000	0	0-0	0	4.91
1996 Cincinnati	NL	7	0	0	4	8	35	7	2	2	0	1	0	1	5	0	3	1	0	0	0	.000	0	0-0	0	2.25
1997 Cincinnati	NL	59	0	0	15	97.1	402	79	36	35	12	3	3	7	30	8	96	7	1	5	3	.625	0	1-2	13	3.24
1998 Cincinnati	NL	67	0	0	13	102	440	98	62	59	14	3	4	9	36	4	86	4	0	5	5	.500	0	1-4	5	5.21
4 ML YEARS		136	0	0	33	211	894	188	102	98	26	8	7	17	73	12	187	12	1	10	8	.556	0	2-6	18	4.18

Jeff Suppan

Pitches: Right **Bats:** Right **Pos:** SP-14; RP-3 **Ht:** 6'2" **Wt:** 210 **Born:** 1/2/75 **Age:** 24

		HOW MUCH HE PITCHED					WHAT HE GAVE UP											THE RESULTS					
Year Team	Lg	G	GS	CG	GF	IP	BFP	H	R	ER	HR	SH	SF	HB	TBB	IBB	SO	WP	Bk	W	L	Pct.	ShO	Sv-Op	Hld	ERA
1998 Tucson *	AAA	13	12	0	0	67	292	75	29	27	4	1	0	3	17	1	62	4	0	4	3	.571	0	0- -	—	3.63
1995 Boston	AL	8	3	0	1	22.2	100	29	15	15	4	1	1	0	5	1	19	0	0	1	2	.333	0	0-0	1	5.96
1996 Boston	AL	8	4	0	2	22.2	107	29	19	19	3	1	4	1	13	0	13	3	0	1	1	.500	0	0-0	0	7.54
1997 Boston	AL	23	22	0	0	112.1	503	140	75	71	12	0	4	4	36	1	67	5	0	7	3	.700	0	0-0	0	5.69
1998 Ari-KC	AL	17	14	1	2	78.2	345	91	56	50	13	3	2	1	22	1	51	2	0	1	7	.125	0	0-0	0	5.72
1998 Arizona	NL	13	13	1	0	66	299	82	55	49	12	3	2	1	21	1	39	2	0	1	7	.125	0	0-0	0	6.68
Kansas City	AL	4	1	0	2	12.2	46	9	1	1	1	0	0	0	1	0	12	0	0	0	0	.000	0	0-0	0	0.71
4 ML YEARS		56	43	1	6	236.1	1055	289	165	155	32	5	11	6	76	3	150	10	0	10	13	.435	0	0-0	1	5.90

B.J. Surhoff

Bats: Left **Throws:** Right **Pos:** LF-157; PH/PR-9; 1B-1 **Ht:** 6'1" **Wt:** 200 **Born:** 8/4/64 **Age:** 34

Year Team	Lg	G	AB	H	2B	3B	HR	(Hm	Rd)	TB	R	RBI	TBB	IBB	SO	HBP	SH	SF	SB	CS	SB%	GDP	Avg	OBP	SLG
1987 Milwaukee	AL	115	395	118	22	3	7	(5	2)	167	50	68	36	1	30	0	5	9	11	10	.52	13	.299	.350	.423
1988 Milwaukee	AL	139	493	121	21	0	5	(2	3)	157	47	38	31	9	49	3	11	3	21	6	.78	12	.245	.292	.318
1989 Milwaukee	AL	126	436	108	17	4	5	(3	2)	148	42	55	25	1	29	3	3	10	14	12	.54	8	.248	.287	.339
1990 Milwaukee	AL	135	474	131	21	4	6	(4	2)	178	55	59	41	5	37	1	7	7	18	7	.72	8	.276	.331	.376
1991 Milwaukee	AL	143	505	146	19	4	5	(3	2)	188	57	68	26	2	33	0	13	9	5	8	.38	21	.289	.319	.372
1992 Milwaukee	AL	139	480	121	19	1	4	(3	1)	154	63	62	46	8	41	2	5	10	14	8	.64	9	.252	.314	.321
1993 Milwaukee	AL	148	552	151	38	3	7	(4	3)	216	66	79	36	5	47	2	4	5	12	9	.57	9	.274	.318	.391
1994 Milwaukee	AL	40	134	35	11	2	5	(2	3)	65	20	22	16	0	14	0	2	2	0	1	.00	5	.261	.336	.485
1995 Milwaukee	AL	117	415	133	26	3	13	(7	6)	204	72	73	37	4	43	4	2	4	7	3	.70	7	.320	.378	.492
1996 Baltimore	AL	143	537	157	27	6	21	(12	9)	259	74	82	47	8	79	3	2	1	0	1	.00	7	.292	.352	.482
1997 Baltimore	AL	147	528	150	30	4	18	(10	8)	242	80	88	49	14	60	5	3	10	1	1	.50	7	.284	.345	.458
1998 Baltimore	AL	162	573	160	34	1	22	(9	13)	262	79	92	49	9	81	1	1	10	9	7	.56	13	.279	.332	.457
12 ML YEARS		1554	5522	1531	285	35	118	(64	54)	2240	705	786	439	66	543	24	58	80	112	73	.61	119	.277	.329	.406

Larry Sutton

Bats: L **Throws:** L **Pos:** RF-47; LF-39; PH/PR-29; 1B-6; DH-3 **Ht:** 6'0" **Wt:** 185 **Born:** 5/14/70 **Age:** 29

Year Team	Lg	G	AB	H	2B	3B	HR	(Hm	Rd)	TB	R	RBI	TBB	IBB	SO	HBP	SH	SF	SB	CS	SB%	GDP	Avg	OBP	SLG
1992 Eugene	A-	70	238	74	17	3	15	—	—	142	45	58	48	5	33	5	0	2	3	6	.33	3	.311	.433	.597
Appleton	A	1	2	0	0	0	0	—	—	0	1	0	2	0	1	0	0	0	0	1	.00	0	.000	.500	.000
1993 Rockford	A	113	361	97	24	1	7	—	—	144	67	50	95	5	65	8	0	8	3	5	.38	3	.269	.424	.399
1994 Wilmington	A+	129	480	147	33	1	26	—	—	260	91	94	81	10	71	6	1	9	2	1	.67	7	.306	.406	.542
1995 Wichita	AA	53	197	53	11	1	5	—	—	81	31	32	26	0	33	2	0	2	1	1	.50	3	.269	.357	.411
1996 Wichita	AA	125	463	137	22	2	22	—	—	229	84	84	77	3	66	8	0	6	4	1	.80	11	.296	.401	.495
1997 Omaha	AAA	106	380	114	27	1	19	—	—	200	61	72	61	4	57	0	0	2	0	0	.00	6	.300	.395	.526
1997 Kansas City	AL	27	69	20	2	0	2	(1	1)	28	9	8	5	0	12	0	1	0	0	0	.00	0	.290	.338	.406
1998 Kansas City	AL	111	310	76	14	2	5	(3	2)	109	29	42	29	3	46	3	4	5	3	3	.50	5	.245	.311	.352
2 ML YEARS		138	379	96	16	2	7	(4	3)	137	38	50	34	3	58	3	5	5	3	3	.50	5	.253	.316	.361

Makoto Suzuki

Pitches: Right **Bats:** Right **Pos:** SP-5; RP-1 **Ht:** 6'3" **Wt:** 195 **Born:** 5/31/75 **Age:** 24

		HOW MUCH HE PITCHED						WHAT HE GAVE UP											THE RESULTS						
Year Team	Lg	G	GS	CG	GF	IP	BFP	H	R	ER	HR	SH	SF	HB	TBB	IBB	SO	WP	Bk	W	L	Pct.	ShO	Sv-Op	Hld	ERA
1992 Salinas	A	1	0	0	0	1	3	0	0	0	0	0	0	0	1	0	1	0	0	0	0	—	0	0--	—	0.00
1993 San Berndno	A+	48	1	0	35	80.2	351	59	37	33	5	3	2	2	56	4	87	12	2	4	4	.500	0	12--	—	3.68
1994 Jacksnville	AA	8	0	0	1	12.2	58	15	4	4	1	0	1	0	6	0	10	0	0	1	0	1.000	0	1--	—	2.84
1995 Mariners	R	4	3	0	0	4	19	5	4	3	1	0	0	1	0	0	3	0	0	1	0	1.000	0	0--	—	6.75
Riverside	A+	6	0	0	1	7.2	39	10	4	4	0	0	1	0	6	0	6	2	0	1	0	1.000	0	0--	—	4.70
1996 Port City	AA	16	16	0	0	74.1	320	69	44	39	10	2	1	2	32	0	66	0	0	3	6	.333	0	0--	—	4.72
Tacoma	AAA	13	2	0	6	22.1	110	31	19	18	3	2	0	0	12	2	14	3	0	0	3	.000	0	0--	—	7.25
1997 Tacoma	AAA	32	10	0	7	83.1	384	79	60	55	13	2	1	0	64	1	63	6	1	4	9	.308	0	0--	—	5.94
1998 Tacoma	AAA	28	21	2	1	131.2	578	130	70	64	19	2	3	5	70	0	117	8	0	9	10	.474	1	0--	—	4.37
1996 Seattle	AL	1	0	0	0	1.1	8	2	3	3	0	0	0	0	2	1	1	0	0	0	0	.000	0	0-0	0	20.25
1998 Seattle	AL	6	5	0	0	26.1	127	34	23	21	3	0	0	0	15	0	19	0	0	1	2	.333	0	0-0	0	7.18
2 ML YEARS		7	5	0	0	27.2	135	36	26	24	3	0	0	0	17	1	20	0	0	1	2	.333	0	0-0	0	7.81

Dale Sveum

Bats: B **Throws:** R **Pos:** 1B-21; 3B-6; PH/PR-6; DH-3 **Ht:** 6'2" **Wt:** 212 **Born:** 11/23/63 **Age:** 35

Year Team	Lg	G	AB	H	2B	3B	HR	(Hm	Rd)	TB	R	RBI	TBB	IBB	SO	HBP	SH	SF	SB	CS	SB%	GDP	Avg	OBP	SLG
1986 Milwaukee	AL	91	317	78	13	2	7	(4	3)	116	35	35	32	0	63	1	5	1	4	3	.57	7	.246	.316	.366
1987 Milwaukee	AL	153	535	135	27	3	25	(9	16)	243	86	95	40	4	133	1	5	5	2	6	.25	11	.252	.303	.454
1988 Milwaukee	AL	129	467	113	14	4	9	(2	7)	162	41	51	21	0	122	1	3	3	1	0	1.00	6	.242	.274	.347
1990 Milwaukee	AL	48	117	23	7	0	1	(1	0)	33	15	12	12	0	30	2	0	2	1	0	.00	2	.197	.278	.282
1991 Milwaukee	AL	90	266	64	19	1	4	(3	1)	97	33	43	32	0	78	1	5	4	2	4	.33	8	.241	.320	.365
1992 Phi-ChA		94	249	49	13	0	4	(1	3)	74	28	28	28	4	68	0	2	5	1	1	.50	6	.197	.273	.297
1993 Oakland	AL	30	79	14	2	1	2	(0	2)	24	12	6	16	1	21	0	0	0	0	0	.00	2	.177	.316	.304
1994 Seattle	AL	10	27	5	0	0	1	(0	1)	8	3	2	2	0	10	0	0	0	0	0	.00	1	.185	.241	.296
1996 Pittsburgh	NL	12	34	12	5	0	1	(0	1)	20	9	5	6	0	6	0	0	0	0	0	.00	0	.353	.450	.588
1997 Pittsburgh	NL	126	306	80	20	1	12	(5	7)	138	30	47	27	2	81	0	4	2	0	3	.00	8	.261	.319	.451
1998 New York	NL	30	58	9	0	0	0	(0	0)	9	6	3	4	0	16	0	0	0	0	0	.00	2	.155	.203	.155
1992 Philadelphia	NL	54	135	24	4	0	2	(0	2)	34	13	16	16	4	39	0	2	0	0	0	.00	5	.178	.261	.252
Chicago	AL	40	114	25	9	0	2	(1	1)	40	15	12	12	0	29	0	2	3	1	1	.50	1	.219	.287	.351
11 ML YEARS		813	2455	582	120	12	66	(25	41)	924	298	327	220	11	628	6	25	24	10	18	.36	53	.237	.299	.376

Mark Sweeney

Bats: L **Throws:** L **Pos:** PH/PR-76; RF-29; 1B-21; LF-5; DH-1 **Ht:** 6'1" **Wt:** 195 **Born:** 10/26/69 **Age:** 29

Year Team	Lg	G	AB	H	2B	3B	HR	(Hm	Rd)	TB	R	RBI	TBB	IBB	SO	HBP	SH	SF	SB	CS	SB%	GDP	Avg	OBP	SLG
1995 St. Louis	NL	37	77	21	2	0	2	(0	2)	29	5	13	10	0	15	0	1	2	1	1	.50	3	.273	.348	.377

Year Team	Lg	G	AB	H	2B	3B	HR	(Hm	Rd)	TB	R	RBI	TBB	IBB	SO	HBP	SH	SF	SB	CS	SB%	GDP	Avg	OBP	SLG
1996 St. Louis	NL	98	170	45	9	0	3	(0	3)	63	32	22	33	2	29	1	5	0	3	0	1.00	4	.265	.387	.371
1997 StL-SD	NL	115	164	46	7	0	2	(2	0)	59	16	23	20	1	32	1	1	2	2	3	.40	3	.280	.358	.360
1998 San Diego	NL	122	192	45	8	3	2	(1	1)	65	17	15	26	0	37	1	0	3	1	2	.33	5	.234	.324	.339
1997 St. Louis	NL	44	61	13	3	0	0	(0	0)	16	5	4	9	1	14	1	1	1	0	1	.00	2	.213	.319	.262
San Diego	NL	71	103	33	4	0	2	(2	0)	43	11	19	11	0	18	0	0	1	2	2	.50	1	.320	.383	.417
4 ML YEARS		372	603	157	26	3	9	(3	6)	216	70	73	89	3	113	3	7	7	7	6	.54	15	.260	.355	.358

Mike Sweeney

Bats: Right **Throws:** Right **Pos:** C-91; PH/PR-9   **Ht:** 6'2" **Wt:** 215 **Born:** 7/22/73 **Age:** 25

Year Team	Lg	G	AB	H	2B	3B	HR	(Hm	Rd)	TB	R	RBI	TBB	IBB	SO	HBP	SH	SF	SB	CS	SB%	GDP	Avg	OBP	SLG
1995 Kansas City	AL	4	4	1	0	0	0	(0	0)	1	1	0	0	0	0	0	0	0	0	0	.00	0	.250	.250	.250
1996 Kansas City	AL	50	165	46	10	0	4	(1	3)	68	23	24	18	0	21	4	0	3	1	2	.33	7	.279	.358	.412
1997 Kansas City	AL	84	240	58	8	0	7	(5	2)	87	30	31	17	0	33	6	1	2	3	2	.60	8	.242	.306	.363
1998 Kansas City	AL	92	282	73	18	0	8	(6	2)	115	32	35	24	1	38	2	2	1	2	3	.40	7	.259	.320	.408
4 ML YEARS		230	691	178	36	0	19	(12	7)	271	86	90	59	1	92	12	3	6	6	7	.46	22	.258	.324	.392

Bill Swift

Pitches: Right **Bats:** Right **Pos:** SP-26; RP-3   **Ht:** 6'0" **Wt:** 191 **Born:** 10/27/61 **Age:** 37

Year Team	Lg	G	GS	CG	GF	IP	BFP	H	R	ER	HR	SH	SF	HB	TBB	IBB	SO	WP	Bk	W	L	Pct.	ShO	Sv-Op	Hld	ERA
1985 Seattle	AL	23	21	0	0	120.2	532	131	71	64	7	6	5	5	48	5	55	5	3	6	10	.375	0	0--	—	4.77
1986 Seattle	AL	29	17	1	3	115.1	534	148	85	70	5	5	3	7	55	2	55	2	1	2	9	.182	0	0--	—	5.46
1988 Seattle	AL	38	24	6	4	174.2	757	199	99	89	10	5	3	8	65	3	47	6	2	8	12	.400	1	0-1	1	4.59
1989 Seattle	AL	37	16	0	7	130	551	140	72	64	7	4	3	2	38	4	45	4	1	7	3	.700	0	1-1	2	4.43
1990 Seattle	AL	55	8	0	18	128	533	135	46	34	4	5	4	7	21	6	42	8	3	6	4	.600	0	6-7	7	2.39
1991 Seattle	AL	71	0	0	30	90.1	359	74	22	20	3	2	0	1	26	4	48	2	1	1	2	.333	0	17-18	13	1.99
1992 San Francisco	NL	30	22	3	2	164.2	655	144	41	38	6	5	2	3	43	3	77	0	1	10	4	.714	2	1-1	3	**2.08**
1993 San Francisco	NL	34	34	1	0	232.2	922	195	82	73	18	4	2	6	55	5	157	4	0	21	8	.724	1	0-0	0	2.82
1994 San Francisco	NL	17	17	0	0	109.1	457	109	49	41	10	7	2	1	31	6	62	2	0	8	7	.533	0	0-0	0	3.38
1995 Colorado	NL	19	19	0	0	105.2	463	122	62	58	12	6	1	1	43	2	68	2	0	9	3	.750	0	0-0	0	4.94
1996 Colorado	NL	7	3	0	2	18.1	78	23	12	11	1	0	1	0	5	0	5	0	0	1	1	.500	0	2-2	1	5.40
1997 Colorado	NL	14	13	0	1	65.1	304	85	57	46	11	4	4	2	26	0	29	2	2	4	6	.400	0	0-0	0	6.34
1998 Seattle	AL	29	26	0	0	144.2	663	183	103	94	21	2	2	10	51	2	77	1	2	11	9	.550	0	0-0	—	5.85
13 ML YEARS		403	220	11	67	1599.2	6817	1688	801	702	116	55	30	53	507	42	767	38	16	94	78	.547	4	27--	—	3.95

Greg Swindell

Pitches: Left **Bats:** Right **Pos:** RP-81   **Ht:** 6'3" **Wt:** 230 **Born:** 1/2/65 **Age:** 34

Year Team	Lg	G	GS	CG	GF	IP	BFP	H	R	ER	HR	SH	SF	HB	TBB	IBB	SO	WP	Bk	W	L	Pct.	ShO	Sv-Op	Hld	ERA
1986 Cleveland	AL	9	9	1	0	61.2	255	57	35	29	9	3	1	1	15	0	46	3	2	5	2	.714	0	0-0	0	4.23
1987 Cleveland	AL	16	15	4	0	102.1	441	112	62	58	18	4	3	1	37	1	97	0	1	3	8	.273	1	0-0	1	5.10
1988 Cleveland	AL	33	33	12	0	242	988	234	97	86	18	9	5	1	45	3	180	5	0	18	14	.563	4	0-0	0	3.20
1989 Cleveland	AL	28	28	5	0	184.1	749	170	71	69	16	4	4	0	51	3	129	3	1	13	6	.684	2	0-0	0	3.37
1990 Cleveland	AL	34	34	3	0	214.2	912	245	110	105	27	8	6	1	47	2	135	3	2	12	9	.571	0	0-0	0	4.40
1991 Cleveland	AL	33	33	7	0	238	971	241	112	92	21	**13**	8	1	31	1	169	3	1	9	16	.360	0	0-0	0	3.48
1992 Cincinnati	NL	31	30	5	0	213.2	867	210	72	64	14	9	7	2	41	4	138	3	2	12	8	.600	3	0-0	0	2.70
1993 Houston	NL	31	30	1	0	190.1	818	215	98	88	24	13	3	1	40	3	124	2	2	12	13	.480	1	0-0	0	4.16
1994 Houston	NL	24	24	1	0	148.1	623	175	80	72	20	9	7	1	26	2	74	1	1	8	9	.471	0	0-0	0	4.37
1995 Houston	NL	33	26	1	3	153	659	180	86	76	21	4	8	2	39	2	96	3	0	10	9	.526	1	0-2	0	4.47
1996 Hou-Cle		21	6	0	0	51.2	237	66	46	41	13	1	2	1	19	0	36	0	0	1	4	.200	0	0-2	1	7.14
1997 Minnesota	AL	65	1	0	12	115.2	460	102	46	46	12	2	3	2	25	3	75	0	0	7	4	.636	0	1-7	12	3.58
1998 Min-Bos	AL	81	0	0	15	90.1	385	92	40	36	13	4	2	3	31	3	63	3	0	5	6	.455	0	2-5	24	3.59
1996 Houston	NL	8	4	0	0	23	116	35	25	20	5	0	1	1	11	0	15	0	0	0	3	.000	0	0-2	0	7.83
Cleveland	AL	13	2	0	1	28.2	121	31	21	21	8	1	1	0	8	0	21	0	0	1	1	.500	0	0-0	1	6.59
1998 Minnesota	AL	52	0	0	12	66.1	281	67	27	27	10	3	2	3	18	2	45	3	0	3	3	.500	0	2-4	18	3.66
Boston	AL	29	0	0	3	24	104	25	13	9	3	1	0	0	13	1	18	0	0	2	3	.400	0	0-1	6	3.38
13 ML YEARS		439	269	40	34	2006	8365	2099	955	862	226	83	59	19	447	25	1362	29	12	115	108	.516	12	3-16	38	3.87

Jeff Tabaka

Pitches: Left **Bats:** Right **Pos:** RP-37   **Ht:** 6'2" **Wt:** 200 **Born:** 1/17/64 **Age:** 35

Year Team	Lg	G	GS	CG	GF	IP	BFP	H	R	ER	HR	SH	SF	HB	TBB	IBB	SO	WP	Bk	W	L	Pct.	ShO	Sv-Op	Hld	ERA
1998 Nashville *	AAA	4	0	0	2	4.2	24	9	4	4	0	0	2	1	0	0	4	0	0	1	0	1.000	0	0--	—	7.71
1994 Pit-SD	NL	39	0	0	10	41	181	32	29	24	1	3	1	0	27	3	32	1	0	3	1	.750	0	1-1	1	5.27
1995 SD-Hou	NL	34	0	0	6	30.2	128	27	11	11	2	0	0	0	17	1	25	1	0	1	0	1.000	0	0-1	5	3.23
1996 Houston	NL	18	0	0	5	20.1	105	28	18	15	5	1	0	0	14	0	18	3	0	0	2	.000	0	0-1	1	6.64
1997 Cincinnati	NL	3	0	0	1	2	10	1	1	1	1	0	0	2	1	0	1	0	0	0	0	.000	0	0-0	0	4.50
1998 Pittsburgh	NL	37	0	0	9	50.2	212	37	19	17	6	2	2	5	22	4	40	1	0	2	2	.500	0	0-0	2	3.02
1994 Pittsburgh	NL	5	0	0	2	4	24	4	8	8	1	0	0	0	8	0	2	0	0	0	0	.000	0	0-0	0	18.00
San Diego	NL	34	0	0	8	37	157	28	21	16	0	3	1	0	19	3	30	1	0	3	1	.750	0	1-1	1	3.89
1995 San Diego	NL	10	0	0	3	6.1	32	10	5	5	1	0	0	0	5	1	6	1	0	0	0	.000	0	0-1	0	7.11
Houston	NL	24	0	0	3	24.1	96	17	6	6	1	0	0	0	12	0	19	0	0	1	0	1.000	0	0-0	5	2.22
5 ML YEARS		131	0	0	31	144.2	636	125	78	68	15	6	3	10	81	8	116	6	0	6	5	.545	0	2-3	8	4.23

Jeff Tam

Pitches: Right **Bats:** Right **Pos:** RP-15 — **Ht:** 6'1" **Wt:** 202 **Born:** 8/19/70 **Age:** 28

			HOW MUCH HE PITCHED						WHAT HE GAVE UP											THE RESULTS					
Year Team	Lg	G	GS	CG	GF	IP	BFP	H	R	ER	HR	SH	SF	HB	TBB	IBB	SO	WP	Bk	W	L	Pct.	ShO	Sv-Op	Hld	ERA
1993 Pittsfield	A-	21	1	0	13	40.1	180	50	21	15	0	0	1	1	7	0	31	1	3	3	3	.500	0	0- -	—	3.35
1994 Capital City	A	26	0	0	26	28	115	23	14	4	0	1	0	2	6	0	22	0	2	1	1	.500	0	18- -	—	1.29
St. Lucie	A+	24	0	0	22	26.2	99	13	0	0	0	0	0	3	6	1	15	1	2	0	0	.000	0	16- -	—	0.00
Binghamton	AA	4	0	0	1	6.2	35	9	6	6	0	1	0	1	5	0	7	0	0	0	0	.000	0	0- -	—	8.10
1995 Mets	R	2	1	0	0	3	13	2	1	1	0	1	0	1	1	0	2	1	0	0	0	.000	0	0- -	—	3.00
Binghamton	AA	14	0	0	7	18	83	20	11	9	1	1	4	1	4	2	9	3	0	0	2	.000	0	3- -	—	4.50
1996 Binghamton	AA	49	0	0	18	62.2	241	51	19	17	6	2	1	2	16	3	48	2	4	6	2	.750	0	2- -	—	2.44
1997 Norfolk	AAA	40	11	0	15	111.2	480	137	72	58	9	6	4	7	14	4	67	5	0	7	5	.583	0	6- -	—	4.67
1998 Norfolk	AAA	45	0	0	24	64	239	42	14	13	3	3	2	3	6	0	54	0	0	3	3	.500	0	11- -	—	1.83
1998 New York	NL	15	0	0	5	14.1	60	13	10	10	2	0	0	2	4	1	8	0	0	1	1	.500	0	0-1	1	6.28

Kevin Tapani

Pitches: Right **Bats:** Right **Pos:** SP-34; RP-1 — **Ht:** 6'1" **Wt:** 190 **Born:** 2/18/64 **Age:** 35

			HOW MUCH HE PITCHED						WHAT HE GAVE UP											THE RESULTS					
Year Team	Lg	G	GS	CG	GF	IP	BFP	H	R	ER	HR	SH	SF	HB	TBB	IBB	SO	WP	Bk	W	L	Pct.	ShO	Sv-Op	Hld	ERA
1989 NYN-Min		8	5	0	1	40	169	39	18	17	3	1	2	0	12	1	23	0	1	2	2	.500	0	0-0	0	3.83
1990 Minnesota	AL	28	28	1	0	159.1	659	164	75	72	12	3	4	2	29	2	101	1	0	12	8	.600	1	0-0	0	4.07
1991 Minnesota	AL	34	34	4	0	244	974	225	84	81	23	9	6	2	40	2	135	3	3	16	9	.640	1	0-0	0	2.99
1992 Minnesota	AL	34	34	4	0	220	911	226	103	97	17	8	11	5	48	2	138	4	0	16	11	.593	1	0-0	0	3.97
1993 Minnesota	AL	36	35	3	0	225.2	964	243	123	111	21	3	5	6	57	1	150	4	0	12	15	.444	1	0-0	0	4.43
1994 Minnesota	AL	24	24	4	0	156	672	181	86	80	13	2	5	4	39	0	91	1	0	11	7	.611	0	0-0	0	4.62
1995 Min-LA		33	31	3	0	190.2	834	227	116	105	29	6	5	5	48	4	131	4	0	10	13	.435	1	0-0	0	4.96
1996 Chicago	AL	34	34	1	0	225.1	971	236	123	115	34	6	6	3	76	5	150	13	0	13	10	.565	1	0-0	0	4.59
1997 Chicago	NL	13	13	1	0	85	352	77	33	32	7	7	2	2	23	2	55	0	2	9	3	.750	1	0-0	0	3.39
1998 Chicago	NL	35	34	2	0	219	945	244	120	118	30	11	9	5	62	4	136	7	0	19	9	.679	2	0-0	0	4.85
1989 New York	NL	3	0	0	1	7.1	31	5	3	3	1	0	1	0	4	0	2	0	1	0	0	.000	0	0-0	0	3.68
1995 Minnesota	AL	5	5	0	0	32.2	138	34	15	14	2	1	1	0	8	1	21	0	0	2	2	.500	0	0-0	0	3.86
1995 Minnesota	AL	20	20	3	0	133.2	579	155	79	73	21	3	3	4	34	2	88	3	0	6	11	.353	1	0-0	0	4.92
Los Angeles	NL	13	11	0	0	57	255	72	37	32	8	3	2	1	14	2	43	1	0	4	2	.667	0	0-0	0	5.05
10 ML YEARS		279	272	23	1	1765	7451	1862	881	828	189	56	55	34	434	21	1110	37	6	120	87	.580	9	0-0	0	4.22

Tony Tarasco

Bats: L **Throws:** R **Pos:** PH/PR-10; LF-4; RF-2; CF-1 — **Ht:** 6'1" **Wt:** 205 **Born:** 12/9/70 **Age:** 28

					BATTING														BASERUNNING				PERCENTAGES		
Year Team	Lg	G	AB	H	2B	3B	HR	(Hm	Rd)	TB	R	RBI	TBB	IBB	SO	HBP	SH	SF	SB	CS	SB%	GDP	Avg	OBP	SLG
1998 Indianapols *	AAA	90	319	100	19	1	16	—	—	169	53	45	43	1	46	1	2	2	3	2	.60	4	.313	.395	.530
1993 Atlanta	NL	24	35	8	2	0	0	(0	0)	10	6	2	0	0	5	1	0	1	0	1	.00	1	.229	.243	.286
1994 Atlanta	NL	87	132	36	6	0	5	(2	3)	57	16	19	9	1	17	0	0	3	5	0	1.00	5	.273	.313	.432
1995 Montreal	NL	126	438	109	18	4	14	(7	7)	177	64	40	51	12	78	2	3	1	24	3	.89	5	.249	.329	.404
1996 Baltimore	AL	31	84	20	3	0	1	(1	0)	26	14	9	7	0	15	0	1	0	5	3	.63	1	.238	.297	.310
1997 Baltimore	AL	100	166	34	8	1	7	(4	3)	65	26	26	25	1	33	1	1	0	2	2	.50	3	.205	.313	.392
1998 Cincinnati	NL	15	24	5	2	0	1	(1	0)	10	5	4	3	0	5	0	0	0	0	0	.00	0	.208	.296	.417
6 ML YEARS		383	879	212	39	5	28	(15	13)	345	131	100	95	14	153	4	6	5	36	9	.80	12	.241	.316	.392

Fernando Tatis

Bats: Right **Throws:** Right **Pos:** 3B-149; SS-3; PH/PR-1 — **Ht:** 5'10" **Wt:** 170 **Born:** 1/1/75 **Age:** 24

					BATTING														BASERUNNING				PERCENTAGES		
Year Team	Lg	G	AB	H	2B	3B	HR	(Hm	Rd)	TB	R	RBI	TBB	IBB	SO	HBP	SH	SF	SB	CS	SB%	GDP	Avg	OBP	SLG
1994 Rangers	R	60	212	70	10	2	6	—	—	102	34	32	25	4	33	3	0	2	20	4	.83	4	.330	.405	.481
1995 Chston-SC	A	131	499	151	43	4	15	—	—	247	74	84	45	4	94	7	1	4	22	19	.54	5	.303	.366	.495
1996 Charlotte	A+	85	325	93	25	0	12	—	—	154	46	53	30	4	48	6	1	4	9	3	.75	9	.286	.353	.474
Okla City	AAA	2	4	2	1	0	0	—	—	3	0	0	0	0	1	0	0	0	0	0	.00	0	.500	.500	.750
1997 Tulsa	AA	102	382	120	26	1	24	—	—	220	73	61	46	4	72	3	0	2	17	8	.68	15	.314	.390	.576
1997 Texas	AL	60	223	57	9	0	8	(6	2)	90	29	29	14	0	42	0	2	2	3	0	1.00	6	.256	.297	.404
1998 Tex-StL		150	532	147	33	4	11	(6	5)	221	69	58	36	3	123	6	4	1	13	5	.72	16	.276	.329	.415
1998 Texas	AL	95	330	89	17	2	3	(1	2)	119	41	32	12	2	66	4	4	0	6	2	.75	10	.270	.303	.361
St. Louis	NL	55	202	58	16	2	8	(5	3)	102	28	26	24	1	57	2	0	1	7	3	.70	6	.287	.367	.505
2 ML YEARS		210	755	204	42	4	19	(12	7)	311	98	87	50	3	165	6	6	3	16	5	.76	22	.270	.319	.412

Ramon Tatis

Pitches: Left **Bats:** Left **Pos:** RP-22 — **Ht:** 6'3" **Wt:** 195 **Born:** 5/2/73 **Age:** 26

			HOW MUCH HE PITCHED						WHAT HE GAVE UP											THE RESULTS					
Year Team	Lg	G	GS	CG	GF	IP	BFP	H	R	ER	HR	SH	SF	HB	TBB	IBB	SO	WP	Bk	W	L	Pct.	ShO	Sv-Op	Hld	ERA
1992 Mets	R	11	5	0	0	36	184	56	40	34	2	0	1	4	15	0	25	7	1	1	3	.250	0	0- -	—	8.50
1993 Kingsport	R+	13	3	0	5	42.2	204	51	42	29	1	3	1	5	23	0	25	4	0	0	2	.000	0	1- -	—	6.12
1994 Kingsport	R+	13	4	0	8	40.2	187	35	25	15	2	2	1	2	31	0	36	5	2	1	3	.250	0	0- -	—	3.32
1995 Pittsfield	A-	13	13	1	0	79.1	341	88	40	32	2	1	1	3	27	0	69	8	3	4	5	.444	1	0- -	—	3.63
Capital City	A	18	2	0	9	32	141	34	27	20	1	2	1	1	14	0	27	5	0	2	3	.400	0	0- -	—	5.63
1996 St. Lucie	A+	46	1	0	20	74.1	325	71	35	28	4	7	2	2	38	8	46	14	1	4	2	.667	0	6- -	—	3.39
1998 Durham	AAA	19	9	0	4	61.1	267	66	29	25	5	1	2	3	24	2	44	4	1	1	3	.250	0	2- -	—	3.67

		HOW MUCH HE PITCHED						WHAT HE GAVE UP											THE RESULTS					
Year Team	Lg	G	GS	CG	GF	IP	BFP	H	R	ER	HR	SH	SF	HB	TBB	IBB	SO	WP	Bk	W	L	Pct.	ShO	Sv-Op Hld	ERA
1997 Chicago	NL	56	0	0	12	55.2	255	66	36	33	13	6	3	3	29	6	33	4	2	1	1	.500	0	0-1 8	5.34
1998 Tampa Bay	AL	22	0	0	7	11.2	72	23	19	18	2	0	0	1	16	1	5	1	1	0	0	.000	0	0-0 1	13.89
2 ML YEARS		78	0	0	19	67.1	327	89	55	51	15	6	3	4	45	7	38	5	3	1	1	.500	0	0-1 9	6.82

Jimmy Tatum

Bats: R **Throws:** R **Pos:** PH/PR-20; 1B-9; C-4; LF-4; 3B-3; DH-1 **Ht:** 6'2" **Wt:** 200 **Born:** 10/9/67 **Age:** 31

		BATTING																	BASERUNNING				PERCENTAGES		
Year Team	Lg	G	AB	H	2B	3B	HR	(Hm	Rd)	TB	R	RBI	TBB	IBB	SO	HBP	SH	SF	SB	CS	SB%	GDP	Avg	OBP	SLG
1992 Milwaukee	AL	5	8	1	0	0	0	(0	0)	1	0	0	1	0	2	0	0	0	0	0	.00	0	.125	.222	.125
1993 Colorado	NL	92	98	20	5	0	1	(0	1)	28	7	12	5	0	27	1	0	2	0	0	.00	0	.204	.245	.286
1995 Colorado	NL	34	34	8	1	1	0	(0	0)	11	4	4	1	0	7	0	0	0	0	0	.00	1	.235	.257	.324
1996 Bos-SD		7	11	1	0	0	0	(0	0)	1	1	0	0	0	3	0	0	0	0	0	.00	0	.091	.091	.091
1998 New York	NL	35	50	9	1	2	2	(2	0)	20	4	13	3	0	19	0	0	4	0	0	.00	0	.180	.211	.400
1996 Boston	AL	2	8	1	0	0	0	(0	0)	1	1	0	0	0	2	0	0	0	0	0	.00	0	.125	.125	.125
San Diego	NL	5	3	0	0	0	0	(0	0)	0	0	0	0	0	1	0	0	0	0	0	.00	0	.000	.000	.000
5 ML YEARS		173	201	39	7	3	3	(2	1)	61	16	29	10	0	58	1	0	6	0	0	.00	1	.194	.229	.303

Eddie Taubensee

Bats: Left **Throws:** Right **Pos:** C-126; PH/PR-15 **Ht:** 6'4" **Wt:** 225 **Born:** 10/31/68 **Age:** 30

		BATTING																	BASERUNNING				PERCENTAGES		
Year Team	Lg	G	AB	H	2B	3B	HR	(Hm	Rd)	TB	R	RBI	TBB	IBB	SO	HBP	SH	SF	SB	CS	SB%	GDP	Avg	OBP	SLG
1991 Cleveland	AL	26	66	16	2	1	0	(0	0)	20	5	8	5	1	16	0	0	2	0	0	.00	1	.242	.288	.303
1992 Houston	NL	104	297	66	15	0	5	(2	3)	96	23	28	31	3	78	2	0	1	2	1	.67	4	.222	.299	.323
1993 Houston	NL	94	288	72	11	1	9	(4	5)	112	26	42	21	5	44	0	1	2	1	0	1.00	8	.250	.299	.389
1994 Hou-Cin	NL	66	187	53	8	2	8	(2	6)	89	29	21	15	2	31	0	1	2	2	0	1.00	2	.283	.333	.476
1995 Cincinnati	NL	80	218	62	14	2	9	(4	5)	107	32	44	22	2	52	1	1	1	2	2	.50	2	.284	.354	.491
1996 Cincinnati	NL	108	327	95	20	0	12	(6	6)	151	46	48	26	5	64	0	1	5	3	4	.43	4	.291	.338	.462
1997 Cincinnati	NL	108	254	68	18	0	10	(7	3)	116	26	34	22	2	66	1	1	5	0	1	.00	2	.268	.323	.457
1998 Cincinnati	NL	130	431	120	27	0	11	(8	3)	180	61	72	52	6	93	0	2	6	1	0	1.00	4	.278	.352	.418
1994 Houston	NL	5	10	1	0	0	0	(0	0)	1	0	0	0	0	3	0	0	0	0	0	.00	1	.100	.100	.100
Cincinnati	NL	61	177	52	8	2	8	(2	6)	88	29	21	15	2	28	0	1	2	2	0	1.00	1	.294	.345	.497
8 ML YEARS		716	2068	552	115	6	64	(33	31)	871	248	297	194	26	444	5	7	24	11	8	.58	27	.267	.328	.421

Jesus Tavarez

Bats: Both **Throws:** Right **Pos:** CF-5; RF-4; PH/PR-2 **Ht:** 6'0" **Wt:** 170 **Born:** 3/26/71 **Age:** 28

		BATTING																	BASERUNNING				PERCENTAGES		
Year Team	Lg	G	AB	H	2B	3B	HR	(Hm	Rd)	TB	R	RBI	TBB	IBB	SO	HBP	SH	SF	SB	CS	SB%	GDP	Avg	OBP	SLG
1998 Rochester *	AAA	102	364	102	17	6	1	—	—	134	62	30	27	0	59	2	5	3	22	3	.88	4	.280	.331	.368
1994 Florida	NL	17	39	7	0	0	0	(0	0)	7	4	4	1	0	5	0	1	0	1	1	.50	0	.179	.200	.179
1995 Florida	NL	63	190	55	6	2	2	(1	1)	71	31	13	16	1	27	1	3	1	7	5	.58	1	.289	.346	.374
1996 Florida	NL	98	114	25	3	0	0	(0	0)	28	14	6	7	0	18	0	3	0	5	1	.83	2	.219	.264	.246
1997 Boston	AL	42	69	12	3	1	0	(0	1)	17	12	9	4	0	9	0	0	1	0	0	.00	2	.174	.216	.246
1998 Baltimore	AL	8	11	2	0	0	1	(0	1)	5	2	1	2	0	3	0	0	0	0	1	.00	0	.182	.308	.455
5 ML YEARS		228	423	101	12	3	3	(1	2)	128	63	33	30	1	62	1	7	2	13	8	.62	5	.239	.289	.303

Julian Tavarez

Pitches: Right **Bats:** Left **Pos:** RP-60 **Ht:** 6'2" **Wt:** 190 **Born:** 5/22/73 **Age:** 26

		HOW MUCH HE PITCHED						WHAT HE GAVE UP											THE RESULTS					
Year Team	Lg	G	GS	CG	GF	IP	BFP	H	R	ER	HR	SH	SF	HB	TBB	IBB	SO	WP	Bk	W	L	Pct.	ShO	Sv-Op Hld	ERA
1998 Fresno *	AAA	1	0	0	0	2.1	13	6	5	5	0	0	0	1	0	0	1	0	0	0	0	.000	0	0- —	19.29
1993 Cleveland	AL	8	7	0	0	37	172	53	29	27	7	0	1	2	13	2	19	3	1	2	2	.500	0	0-0	6.57
1994 Cleveland	AL	1	1	0	0	1.2	14	8	4	4	1	0	1	0	1	1	0	0	0	0	1	.000	0	0-0	21.60
1995 Cleveland	AL	57	0	0	15	85	350	76	36	23	7	0	2	3	21	0	68	3	2	10	2	.833	0	0-4 19	2.44
1996 Cleveland	AL	51	4	0	13	80.2	353	101	49	48	9	5	4	1	22	5	46	1	0	4	7	.364	0	0-0 13	5.36
1997 San Francisco	NL	89	0	0	13	88.1	378	91	43	38	6	3	8	4	34	5	38	4	0	6	4	.600	0	0-3 26	3.87
1998 San Francisco	NL	60	0	0	12	85.1	374	96	41	36	5	5	3	8	36	11	52	1	1	5	3	.625	0	1-6 10	3.80
6 ML YEARS		266	12	0	53	378	1641	423	206	176	35	13	19	18	127	24	223	12	4	27	19	.587	0	1-13 68	4.19

Billy Taylor

Pitches: Right **Bats:** Right **Pos:** RP-70 **Ht:** 6'8" **Wt:** 230 **Born:** 10/16/61 **Age:** 37

		HOW MUCH HE PITCHED						WHAT HE GAVE UP											THE RESULTS					
Year Team	Lg	G	GS	CG	GF	IP	BFP	H	R	ER	HR	SH	SF	HB	TBB	IBB	SO	WP	Bk	W	L	Pct.	ShO	Sv-Op Hld	ERA
1994 Oakland	AL	41	0	0	11	46.1	195	38	24	18	4	1	1	2	18	5	48	0	0	1	3	.250	0	1-3 2	3.50
1996 Oakland	AL	55	0	0	30	60.1	261	52	30	29	5	4	3	4	25	4	67	1	0	6	3	.667	0	17-19 4	4.33
1997 Oakland	AL	72	0	0	45	73	320	70	32	31	3	1	2	5	36	9	66	0	0	3	4	.429	0	23-30 7	3.82
1998 Oakland	AL	70	0	0	58	73	311	71	37	29	7	3	5	3	22	4	58	0	1	4	9	.308	0	33-37 0	3.58
4 ML YEARS		238	0	0	144	252.2	1087	231	123	107	19	9	11	14	101	22	239	1	1	14	19	.424	0	74-89 13	3.81

Miguel Tejada

Bats: Right **Throws:** Right **Pos:** SS-104; PH/PR-1 **Ht:** 5'9" **Wt:** 192 **Born:** 5/25/76 **Age:** 23

		BATTING																	BASERUNNING				PERCENTAGES		
Year Team	Lg	G	AB	H	2B	3B	HR	(Hm	Rd)	TB	R	RBI	TBB	IBB	SO	HBP	SH	SF	SB	CS	SB%	GDP	Avg	OBP	SLG
1995 Sou. Oregon	A-	74	269	66	15	5	8	—	—	115	45	44	41	2	54	2	0	3	19	2	.90	3	.245	.346	.428
1996 Modesto	A+	114	458	128	12	5	20	—	—	210	97	72	51	3	93	4	1	7	27	16	.63	9	.279	.352	.459
1997 Huntsville	AA	128	502	138	20	3	22	—	—	230	85	97	50	0	99	7	1	8	15	11	.58	9	.275	.344	.458
1998 Edmonton	AAA	1	3	0	0	0	0	—	—	0	0	0	1	0	1	0	0	0	0	0	.00	1	.000	.250	.000
Huntsville	AA	15	52	17	6	0	2	—	—	29	9	7	4	0	8	0	1	2	1	0	1.00	2	.327	.362	.558
1997 Oakland	AL	26	99	20	3	2	2	(1	1)	33	10	10	2	0	22	3	0	0	2	0	1.00	3	.202	.240	.333
1998 Oakland	AL	105	365	85	20	1	11	(5	6)	140	53	45	28	0	86	7	4	3	5	6	.45	8	.233	.298	.384
2 ML YEARS		131	464	105	23	3	13	(6	7)	173	63	55	30	0	108	10	4	3	7	6	.54	11	.226	.286	.373

Amaury Telemaco

Pitches: Right **Bats:** Right **Pos:** RP-23; SP-18 **Ht:** 6'3" **Wt:** 210 **Born:** 1/19/74 **Age:** 25

		HOW MUCH HE PITCHED						WHAT HE GAVE UP											THE RESULTS					
Year Team	Lg	G	GS	CG	GF	IP	BFP	H	R	ER	HR	SH	SF	HB	TBB	IBB	SO	WP	Bk	W	L	Pct.	ShO	Sv-Op	Hld	ERA
1996 Chicago	NL	25	17	0	2	97.1	427	108	67	59	20	5	3	3	31	2	64	3	0	5	7	.417	0	0-0	0	5.46
1997 Chicago	NL	10	5	0	2	38	169	47	26	26	4	2	1	0	11	0	29	1	0	0	3	.000	0	0-0	0	6.16
1998 ChN-Ari	NL	41	18	0	5	148.2	637	150	75	65	18	8	6	4	46	2	78	7	0	7	10	.412	0	0-0	1	3.93
1998 Chicago	NL	14	0	0	4	27.2	118	23	12	12	5	0	0	0	13	0	18	3	0	1	1	.500	0	0-0	1	3.90
Arizona	NL	27	18	0	1	121	519	127	63	53	13	8	6	4	33	2	60	4	0	6	9	.400	0	0-0	0	3.94
3 ML YEARS		76	40	0	9	284	1233	305	168	150	42	15	10	7	88	4	171	11	0	12	20	.375	0	0-0	1	4.75

Anthony Telford

Pitches: Right **Bats:** Right **Pos:** RP-77 **Ht:** 6'0" **Wt:** 195 **Born:** 3/6/66 **Age:** 33

		HOW MUCH HE PITCHED						WHAT HE GAVE UP											THE RESULTS					
Year Team	Lg	G	GS	CG	GF	IP	BFP	H	R	ER	HR	SH	SF	HB	TBB	IBB	SO	WP	Bk	W	L	Pct.	ShO	Sv-Op	Hld	ERA
1990 Baltimore	AL	8	8	0	0	36.1	168	43	22	20	4	0	2	1	19	0	20	1	0	3	3	.500	0	0-0	0	4.95
1991 Baltimore	AL	9	1	0	4	26.2	109	27	12	12	3	0	1	0	6	1	24	1	0	0	0	.000	0	0-0	0	4.05
1993 Baltimore	AL	3	0	0	2	7.1	34	11	8	8	3	0	0	1	1	0	6	1	0	0	0	.000	0	0-0	0	9.82
1997 Montreal	NL	65	0	0	17	89	369	77	34	32	11	4	1	5	33	4	61	6	0	4	6	.400	0	1-5	11	3.24
1998 Montreal	NL	77	0	0	24	91	398	85	45	39	9	10	4	4	36	1	59	8	1	3	6	.333	0	1-5	8	3.86
5 ML YEARS		162	9	0	47	250.1	1078	243	121	111	30	14	8	11	95	6	170	17	1	10	15	.400	0	2-10	19	3.99

Dave Telgheder

Pitches: Right **Bats:** Right **Pos:** RP-6; SP-2 **Ht:** 6'2" **Wt:** 223 **Born:** 11/11/66 **Age:** 32

		HOW MUCH HE PITCHED						WHAT HE GAVE UP											THE RESULTS					
Year Team	Lg	G	GS	CG	GF	IP	BFP	H	R	ER	HR	SH	SF	HB	TBB	IBB	SO	WP	Bk	W	L	Pct.	ShO	Sv-Op	Hld	ERA
1998 Edmonton *	AAA	3	3	0	0	16	74	26	14	13	2	0	1	0	3	0	9	0	1	1	2	.333	0	0- -	—	7.31
1993 New York	NL	24	7	0	7	75.2	325	82	40	40	10	2	1	4	21	2	35	1	0	6	2	.750	0	0-0	1	4.76
1994 New York	NL	6	0	0	0	10	48	11	8	8	2	1	0	0	8	2	4	0	0	0	1	.000	0	0-0	0	7.20
1995 New York	NL	7	4	0	0	25.2	118	34	18	16	4	3	1	0	7	3	16	0	1	1	2	.333	0	0-0	0	5.61
1996 Oakland	AL	16	14	1	1	79.1	348	92	42	41	12	3	3	1	26	1	43	2	0	4	7	.364	1	0-0	0	4.65
1997 Oakland	AL	20	19	0	0	101	458	134	71	68	15	0	7	2	35	1	55	4	0	4	6	.400	0	0-0	0	6.06
1998 Oakland	AL	8	2	0	4	20	91	19	12	8	4	2	0	2	6	0	5	2	1	0	1	.000	0	0-0	0	3.60
6 ML YEARS		81	46	1	14	311.2	1388	372	191	181	47	11	12	9	103	9	158	9	2	15	19	.441	1	0-0	1	5.23

Jay Tessmer

Pitches: Right **Bats:** Right **Pos:** RP-7 **Ht:** 6'3" **Wt:** 190 **Born:** 12/26/71 **Age:** 27

		HOW MUCH HE PITCHED						WHAT HE GAVE UP											THE RESULTS					
Year Team	Lg	G	GS	CG	GF	IP	BFP	H	R	ER	HR	SH	SF	HB	TBB	IBB	SO	WP	Bk	W	L	Pct.	ShO	Sv-Op	Hld	ERA
1995 Oneonta	A-	34	0	0	33	38	156	27	8	4	0	0	0	3	12	2	52	3	2	2	0	1.000	0	20- -	—	0.95
1996 Tampa	A+	68	0	0	63	97.1	381	68	18	16	2	6	0	6	19	3	104	1	0	12	4	.750	0	35- -	—	1.48
1997 Norwich	AA	55	0	0	49	62.2	289	78	41	37	7	3	2	2	24	2	51	4	0	3	6	.333	0	17- -	—	5.31
1998 Norwich	AA	45	0	0	44	49.2	208	50	8	6	0	3	0	0	13	5	57	0	1	3	4	.429	0	29- -	—	1.09
Columbus	AAA	12	0	0	11	18.1	64	8	2	1	1	0	1	0	1	0	14	0	0	1	1	.500	0	5- -	—	0.49
1998 New York	AL	7	0	0	3	8.2	33	4	3	3	1	0	1	0	4	0	6	1	0	1	0	1.000	0	0-0	1	3.12

Bob Tewksbury

Pitches: Right **Bats:** Right **Pos:** SP-25; RP-1 **Ht:** 6'4" **Wt:** 206 **Born:** 11/30/60 **Age:** 38

		HOW MUCH HE PITCHED						WHAT HE GAVE UP											THE RESULTS					
Year Team	Lg	G	GS	CG	GF	IP	BFP	H	R	ER	HR	SH	SF	HB	TBB	IBB	SO	WP	Bk	W	L	Pct.	ShO	Sv-Op	Hld	ERA
1986 New York	AL	23	20	2	0	130.1	558	144	58	48	8	4	7	5	31	0	49	3	2	9	5	.643	0	0-0	0	3.31
1987 NYA-ChN		15	9	0	4	51.1	242	79	41	38	6	5	1	1	20	3	22	1	2	1	8	.111	0	0-1	0	6.66
1988 Chicago	NL	1	1	0	0	3.1	18	6	5	3	1	0	1	0	2	0	1	0	0	0	0	.000	0	0-0	0	8.10
1989 St. Louis	NL	7	4	1	2	30	125	25	12	11	2	1	1	2	10	3	17	0	0	1	0	1.000	1	0-0	0	3.30
1990 St. Louis	NL	28	20	3	1	145.1	595	151	67	56	7	5	7	3	15	3	50	2	0	10	9	.526	2	1-1	2	3.47
1991 St. Louis	NL	30	30	3	0	191	798	206	86	69	13	12	10	5	38	2	75	0	0	11	12	.478	0	0-0	0	3.25
1992 St. Louis	NL	33	33	5	1	233	915	217	63	56	15	9	7	3	20	0	91	2	0	16	5	.762	0	0-0	0	2.16
1993 St. Louis	NL	32	32	2	0	213.2	907	258	99	91	15	15	9	6	20	1	97	2	0	17	10	.630	0	0-0	0	3.83
1994 St. Louis	NL	24	24	4	0	155.2	667	190	97	92	19	4	3	3	22	1	79	1	0	12	10	.545	1	0-0	0	5.32

Year Team	Lg	G	GS	CG	GF	IP	BFP	H	R	ER	HR	SH	SF	HB	TBB	IBB	SO	WP	Bk	W	L	Pct.	ShO	Sv-Op	Hld	ERA
1995 Texas	AL	21	21	4	0	129.2	561	169	75	66	8	6	3	3	20	4	53	4	0	8	7	.533	1	0-0	0	4.58
1996 San Diego	NL	36	33	1	0	206.2	881	224	116	99	17	10	11	3	43	3	126	2	3	10	10	.500	0	0-0	0	4.31
1997 Minnesota	AL	26	26	5	0	168.2	721	200	83	79	12	8	7	1	31	1	92	2	0	8	13	.381	2	0-0	0	4.22
1998 Minnesota	AL	26	25	1	0	148.1	635	174	82	79	19	7	6	6	20	1	60	5	0	7	13	.350	0	0-0	0	4.79
1987 New York	AL	8	6	0	1	33.1	149	47	26	25	5	2	0	1	7	0	12	0	0	1	4	.200	0	0-0	0	6.75
Chicago	NL	7	3	0	3	18	93	32	15	13	1	3	1	0	13	3	10	1	2	0	4	.000	0	0-1	0	6.50
13 ML YEARS		302	277	31	8	1807	7623	2043	884	787	142	94	74	41	292	22	812	24	7	110	102	.519	7	1-2	2	3.92

Frank Thomas

Bats: Right **Throws:** Right **Pos:** DH-146; 1B-14 **Ht:** 6'5" **Wt:** 270 **Born:** 5/27/68 **Age:** 31

Year Team	Lg	G	AB	H	2B	3B	HR	(Hm	Rd)	TB	R	RBI	TBB	IBB	SO	HBP	SH	SF	SB	CS	SB%	GDP	Avg	OBP	SLG
1990 Chicago	AL	60	191	63	11	3	7	(2	5)	101	39	31	44	0	54	2	0	3	0	1	.00	5	.330	.454	.529
1991 Chicago	AL	158	559	178	31	2	32	(24	8)	309	104	109	**138**	13	112	1	0	2	1	2	.33	20	.318	**.453**	.553
1992 Chicago	AL	160	573	185	**46**	2	24	(10	14)	307	108	115	**122**	6	88	5	0	11	6	3	.67	19	.323	**.439**	.536
1993 Chicago	AL	153	549	174	36	0	41	(**26**	15)	333	106	128	112	23	54	2	0	13	4	2	.67	10	.317	.426	.607
1994 Chicago	AL	113	399	141	34	1	38	(**22**	16)	291	106	101	**109**	12	61	2	0	7	2	4	.40	15	.353	**.487**	**.729**
1995 Chicago	AL	**145**	493	152	27	0	40	(15	**25**)	299	102	111	**136**	**29**	74	6	0	**12**	3	2	.60	14	.308	.454	.606
1996 Chicago	AL	141	527	184	26	0	40	(16	24)	330	110	134	109	**26**	70	5	0	8	1	1	.50	25	.349	.459	.626
1997 Chicago	AL	146	530	184	35	0	35	(16	19)	324	110	125	109	9	69	3	0	7	1	1	.50	15	**.347**	**.456**	.611
1998 Chicago	AL	160	585	155	35	2	29	(15	14)	281	109	109	110	2	93	6	0	11	7	0	1.00	14	.265	.381	.480
9 ML YEARS		1236	4406	1416	281	10	286	(146	140)	2575	894	963	989	120	675	32	0	74	25	15	.63	137	.321	.443	.584

Jim Thome

Bats: Left **Throws:** Right **Pos:** 1B-117; DH-6; PH/PR-3 **Ht:** 6'4" **Wt:** 225 **Born:** 8/27/70 **Age:** 28

Year Team	Lg	G	AB	H	2B	3B	HR	(Hm	Rd)	TB	R	RBI	TBB	IBB	SO	HBP	SH	SF	SB	CS	SB%	GDP	Avg	OBP	SLG
1991 Cleveland	AL	27	98	25	4	2	1	(0	1)	36	7	9	5	1	16	1	0	0	1	1	.50	4	.255	.298	.367
1992 Cleveland	AL	40	117	24	3	1	2	(1	1)	35	8	12	10	2	34	2	0	2	2	0	1.00	3	.205	.275	.299
1993 Cleveland	AL	47	154	41	11	0	7	(5	2)	73	28	22	29	1	36	4	0	5	2	1	.67	3	.266	.385	.474
1994 Cleveland	AL	98	321	86	20	1	20	(10	10)	168	58	52	46	5	84	0	1	1	3	3	.50	11	.268	.359	.523
1995 Cleveland	AL	137	452	142	29	3	25	(13	12)	252	92	73	97	3	113	5	0	3	4	3	.57	8	.314	.438	.558
1996 Cleveland	AL	151	505	157	28	5	38	(18	20)	309	122	116	123	8	141	6	0	2	2	2	.50	13	.311	.450	.612
1997 Cleveland	AL	147	496	142	25	0	40	(17	23)	287	104	102	**120**	9	146	3	0	8	1	1	.50	9	.286	.423	.579
1998 Cleveland	AL	123	440	129	34	2	30	(18	12)	257	89	85	90	8	141	3	0	4	1	0	1.00	7	.293	.413	.584
8 ML YEARS		770	2583	746	154	14	163	(82	81)	1417	508	471	520	37	711	24	1	25	16	11	.59	58	.289	.409	.549

Justin Thompson

Pitches: Left **Bats:** Left **Pos:** SP-34 **Ht:** 6'4" **Wt:** 215 **Born:** 3/8/73 **Age:** 26

Year Team	Lg	G	GS	CG	GF	IP	BFP	H	R	ER	HR	SH	SF	HB	TBB	IBB	SO	WP	Bk	W	L	Pct.	ShO	Sv-Op	Hld	ERA
1996 Detroit	AL	11	11	0	0	59	267	62	35	30	7	0	2	2	31	2	44	1	0	1	6	.143	0	0-0	0	4.58
1997 Detroit	AL	32	32	4	0	223.1	891	188	82	75	20	5	10	2	66	1	151	4	0	15	11	.577	0	0-0	0	3.02
1998 Detroit	AL	34	34	5	0	222	946	227	114	100	20	10	6	2	79	4	149	4	0	11	15	.423	0	0-0	0	4.05
3 ML YEARS		77	77	9	0	504.1	2104	477	231	205	47	15	18	6	176	7	344	9	0	27	32	.458	0	0-0	0	3.66

Mark Thompson

Pitches: Right **Bats:** Right **Pos:** SP-6 **Ht:** 6'2" **Wt:** 213 **Born:** 4/7/71 **Age:** 28

Year Team	Lg	G	GS	CG	GF	IP	BFP	H	R	ER	HR	SH	SF	HB	TBB	IBB	SO	WP	Bk	W	L	Pct.	ShO	Sv-Op	Hld	ERA
1998 Rockies *	R	1	1	0	0	3	9	1	0	0	0	0	0	0	0	0	2	0	0	0	0	.000	0	0- -	—	0.00
Salem *	A+	3	3	0	0	13.2	61	17	7	6	2	0	0	1	3	0	10	0	0	0	1	.000	0	0- -	—	3.95
Colo Sprngs *	AAA	1	1	0	0	3.1	19	10	7	7	3	0	0	1	1	0	1	0	0	0	1	.000	0	0- -	—	18.90
1994 Colorado	NL	2	2	0	0	9	49	16	9	9	2	0	0	1	8	0	5	0	0	1	1	.500	0	0-0	0	9.00
1995 Colorado	NL	21	5	0	3	51	240	73	42	37	7	4	4	1	22	2	30	2	0	2	3	.400	0	0-0	2	6.53
1996 Colorado	NL	34	28	3	2	169.2	763	189	109	100	25	10	3	13	74	1	99	1	1	9	11	.450	1	0-1	0	5.30
1997 Colorado	NL	6	6	0	0	29.2	146	40	27	26	8	3	2	4	13	0	9	0	1	3	3	.500	0	0-0	0	7.89
1998 Colorado	NL	6	6	0	0	23.1	116	36	22	20	8	2	2	5	12	0	14	1	0	1	2	.333	0	0-0	0	7.71
5 ML YEARS		69	47	3	5	282.2	1314	354	209	192	50	19	11	24	129	3	157	4	2	16	20	.444	1	0-1	2	6.11

John Thomson

Pitches: Right **Bats:** Right **Pos:** SP-26 **Ht:** 6'3" **Wt:** 185 **Born:** 10/1/73 **Age:** 25

Year Team	Lg	G	GS	CG	GF	IP	BFP	H	R	ER	HR	SH	SF	HB	TBB	IBB	SO	WP	Bk	W	L	Pct.	ShO	Sv-Op	Hld	ERA
1993 Rockies	R	11	11	0	0	50.2	228	43	40	26	0	0	2	3	31	0	36	14	1	3	5	.375	0	0- -	—	4.62
1994 Asheville	A	19	15	1	1	88.1	361	70	34	28	3	2	1	5	33	1	79	1	0	6	6	.500	1	0- -	—	2.85
Central Val	A+	9	8	0	0	49.1	201	43	20	18	0	0	2	1	18	1	41	3	1	3	1	.750	0	0- -	—	3.28
1995 New Haven	AA	26	24	0	0	131.1	572	132	69	61	8	2	7	2	56	0	82	3	2	7	8	.467	0	0- -	—	4.18
1996 New Haven	AA	16	16	1	0	97.2	389	82	35	31	8	2	2	2	27	1	86	2	1	9	4	.692	0	0- -	—	2.86
Colo Sprngs	AAA	11	11	0	0	69.2	305	76	45	39	6	3	1	4	26	2	62	4	1	4	7	.364	0	0- -	—	5.04
1997 Colo Sprngs	AAA	7	7	0	0	42	169	36	18	16	4	1	0	0	14	1	49	2	0	4	2	.667	0	0- -	—	3.43
1998 Asheville	A	2	2	0	0	9	32	5	1	0	0	0	0	0	1	0	12	1	0	1	0	1.000	0	0- -	—	0.00

Year Team	Lg	G	GS	CG	GF	IP	BFP	H	R	ER	HR	SH	SF	HB	TBB	IBB	SO	WP	Bk	W	L	Pct.	ShO	Sv-Op	Hld	ERA
1997 Colorado	NL	27	27	2	0	166.1	721	193	94	87	15	10	3	5	51	0	106	2	0	7	9	.438	1	0-0	0	4.71
1998 Colorado	NL	26	26	2	0	161	680	174	86	86	21	8	5	2	49	0	106	4	2	8	11	.421	0	0-0	0	4.81
2 ML YEARS		53	53	4	0	327.1	1401	367	180	173	36	18	8	7	100	0	212	6	2	15	20	.429	1	0-0	0	4.76

Mike Thurman

Pitches: Right Bats: Right Pos: SP-13; RP-1   Ht: 6'4" Wt: 210 Born: 7/22/73 Age: 25

Year Team	Lg	G	GS	CG	GF	IP	BFP	H	R	ER	HR	SH	SF	HB	TBB	IBB	SO	WP	Bk	W	L	Pct.	ShO	Sv-Op	Hld	ERA
1994 Vermont	A-	2	2	0	0	6.2	28	6	4	4	1	0	0	0	2	0	3	0	0	0	1	.000	0	0- -	—	5.40
1995 Albany	A	22	22	2	0	110.1	482	133	79	67	4	3	7	4	32	0	77	7	0	3	8	.273	0	0- -	—	5.47
1996 Wst Plm Bch	A+	19	19	0	0	113.2	479	122	53	43	3	2	2	5	23	0	68	7	1	6	8	.429	0	0- -	—	3.40
Harrisburg	AA	4	4	1	0	24.2	101	25	14	14	6	1	1	3	5	0	14	0	0	3	1	.750	0	0- -	—	5.11
1997 Harrisburg	AA	20	20	1	0	115.2	474	102	54	49	16	3	7	5	30	0	85	3	0	9	6	.600	0	0- -	—	3.81
Ottawa	AAA	4	4	0	0	19.2	85	17	13	12	1	0	0	1	9	0	15	2	1	1	3	.250	0	0- -	—	5.49
1998 Ottawa	AAA	19	19	0	0	105.2	464	107	50	40	13	2	2	2	49	0	76	5	2	7	7	.500	0	0- -	—	3.41
1997 Montreal	NL	5	2	0	1	11.2	48	8	9	7	3	0	0	1	4	0	8	0	0	1	0	1.000	0	0-0	0	5.40
1998 Montreal	NL	14	13	0	1	67	287	60	38	35	7	2	4	3	26	2	32	3	0	4	5	.444	0	0-0	0	4.70
2 ML YEARS		19	15	0	2	78.2	335	68	47	42	10	2	4	4	30	2	40	3	0	5	5	.500	0	0-0	0	4.81

Mike Timlin

Pitches: Right Bats: Right Pos: RP-70   Ht: 6'4" Wt: 210 Born: 3/10/66 Age: 33

Year Team	Lg	G	GS	CG	GF	IP	BFP	H	R	ER	HR	SH	SF	HB	TBB	IBB	SO	WP	Bk	W	L	Pct.	ShO	Sv-Op	Hld	ERA
1991 Toronto	AL	63	3	0	17	108.1	463	94	43	38	6	6	2	1	50	11	85	5	0	11	6	.647	0	3-8	9	3.16
1992 Toronto	AL	26	0	0	14	43.2	190	45	23	20	0	2	1	1	20	5	35	0	0	0	2	.000	0	1-1	1	4.12
1993 Toronto	AL	54	0	0	27	55.2	254	63	32	29	7	1	3	1	27	3	49	1	0	4	2	.667	0	1-4	5	4.69
1994 Toronto	AL	34	0	0	16	40	179	41	25	23	5	0	0	2	20	0	38	3	0	0	1	.000	0	2-4	5	5.18
1995 Toronto	AL	31	0	0	19	42	179	38	13	10	1	3	0	2	17	5	36	3	1	4	3	.571	0	5-9	4	2.14
1996 Toronto	AL	59	0	0	56	56.2	230	47	25	23	4	2	3	2	18	4	52	3	0	1	6	.143	0	31-38	2	3.65
1997 Tor-Sea	AL	64	0	0	31	72.2	297	69	30	26	8	6	1	1	20	5	45	1	1	6	4	.600	0	10-18	9	3.22
1998 Seattle	AL	70	0	0	40	79.1	321	78	26	26	5	4	2	3	16	2	60	0	0	3	3	.500	0	19-24	6	2.95
1997 Toronto	AL	38	0	0	26	47	190	41	17	15	6	4	1	1	15	4	36	1	1	3	2	.600	0	9-13	2	2.87
Seattle	AL	26	0	0	5	25.2	107	28	13	11	2	2	0	0	5	1	9	0	0	3	2	.600	0	1-5	7	3.86
8 ML YEARS		401	3	0	220	498.1	2113	475	217	195	36	24	12	13	188	35	400	16	2	29	27	.518	0	72-106	45	3.52

Andy Tomberlin

Bats: L Throws: L Pos: DH-21; PH/PR-13; LF-4; RF-1   Ht: 5'11" Wt: 185 Born: 11/7/66 Age: 32

Year Team	Lg	G	AB	H	2B	3B	HR	(Hm	Rd)	TB	R	RBI	TBB	IBB	SO	HBP	SH	SF	SB	CS	SB%	GDP	Avg	OBP	SLG
1998 Toledo *	AAA	14	47	16	2	1	2	—	—	26	13	4	8	0	15	4	0	0	1	1	.50	0	.340	.475	.553
Richmond *	AAA	39	104	27	3	0	4	—	—	42	12	15	15	1	29	7	0	1	1	1	.50	3	.260	.386	.404
1993 Pittsburgh	NL	27	42	12	0	1	1	(0	1)	17	4	5	2	0	14	1	0	0	0	0	.00	0	.286	.333	.405
1994 Boston	AL	18	36	7	0	1	1	(1	0)	12	1	1	6	0	12	0	0	0	1	0	1.00	0	.194	.310	.333
1995 Oakland	AL	46	85	18	0	0	4	(3	1)	30	15	10	5	0	22	0	2	0	4	1	.80	2	.212	.256	.353
1996 New York	NL	63	66	17	4	0	3	(2	1)	30	12	10	9	0	27	1	0	0	0	0	.00	0	.258	.355	.455
1997 New York	NL	6	7	2	0	0	0	(0	0)	2	0	0	1	0	3	0	0	0	0	0	.00	0	.286	.375	.286
1998 Detroit	AL	32	69	15	2	0	2	(1	1)	23	8	12	3	1	25	3	0	0	1	0	1.00	3	.217	.280	.333
6 ML YEARS		192	305	71	6	2	11	(7	4)	114	40	38	26	1	103	5	2	0	6	1	.86	5	.233	.304	.374

Brett Tomko

Pitches: Right Bats: Right Pos: SP-34   Ht: 6'4" Wt: 215 Born: 4/7/73 Age: 26

Year Team	Lg	G	GS	CG	GF	IP	BFP	H	R	ER	HR	SH	SF	HB	TBB	IBB	SO	WP	Bk	W	L	Pct.	ShO	Sv-Op	Hld	ERA
1995 Chston-WV	A	9	7	0	0	49	192	41	12	10	1	1	1	1	9	1	46	4	2	4	2	.667	0	0- -	—	1.84
1996 Chattanooga	AA	27	27	0	0	157.2	647	131	73	68	20	3	4	5	54	4	164	6	5	11	7	.611	0	0- -	—	3.88
1997 Indianapols	AAA	10	10	0	0	61	239	53	21	20	7	0	1	1	9	0	60	0	0	6	3	.667	0	0- -	—	2.95
1997 Cincinnati	NL	22	19	0	1	126	519	106	50	48	14	5	9	4	47	4	95	5	0	11	7	.611	0	0-0	0	3.43
1998 Cincinnati	NL	34	34	1	0	210.2	887	198	111	104	22	12	2	7	64	3	162	9	1	13	12	.520	0	0-0	0	4.44
2 ML YEARS		56	53	1	1	336.2	1406	304	161	152	36	17	11	11	111	7	257	14	1	24	19	.558	0	0-0	0	4.06

Steve Trachsel

Pitches: Right Bats: Right Pos: SP-33   Ht: 6'4" Wt: 205 Born: 10/31/70 Age: 28

Year Team	Lg	G	GS	CG	GF	IP	BFP	H	R	ER	HR	SH	SF	HB	TBB	IBB	SO	WP	Bk	W	L	Pct.	ShO	Sv-Op	Hld	ERA
1993 Chicago	NL	3	3	0	0	19.2	78	16	10	10	4	1	1	0	3	0	14	1	0	0	2	.000	0	0-0	0	4.58
1994 Chicago	NL	22	22	1	0	146	612	133	57	52	19	3	3	3	54	4	108	6	0	9	7	.563	0	0-0	0	3.21
1995 Chicago	NL	30	29	2	0	160.2	722	174	104	92	25	12	5	0	76	8	117	2	1	7	13	.350	0	0-0	0	5.15
1996 Chicago	NL	31	31	3	0	205	845	181	82	69	30	3	3	8	62	3	132	5	2	13	9	.591	2	0-0	0	3.03
1997 Chicago	NL	34	34	0	0	201.1	878	225	110	101	32	8	11	5	69	6	160	4	1	8	12	.400	0	0-0	0	4.51
1998 Chicago	NL	33	33	1	0	208	894	204	107	103	27	9	7	8	84	5	149	3	2	15	8	.652	0	0-0	0	4.46
6 ML YEARS		153	152	7	0	940.2	4029	933	470	427	137	36	30	24	348	26	680	21	6	52	51	.505	2	0-0	0	4.09

Bubba Trammell

Bats: R **Throws:** R **Pos:** LF-23; DH-19; RF-16; PH/PR-7   **Ht:** 6'2" **Wt:** 220 **Born:** 11/6/71 **Age:** 27

Year Team	Lg	G	AB	H	2B	3B	HR	(Hm	Rd)	TB	R	RBI	TBB	IBB	SO	HBP	SH	SF	SB	CS	SB%	GDP	Avg	OBP	SLG
1994 Jamestown	A-	65	235	70	18	6	5	—	—	115	37	41	23	0	32	4	0	4	9	7	.56	1	.298	.365	.489
1995 Lakeland	A+	122	454	129	32	3	16	—	—	215	61	72	48	2	80	4	0	4	13	3	.81	9	.284	.355	.474
1996 Jacksnville	AA	83	311	102	23	2	27	—	—	210	63	75	32	6	61	8	0	1	3	2	.60	11	.328	.403	.675
Toledo	AAA	51	180	53	14	1	6	—	—	87	32	24	22	1	44	0	0	1	5	1	.83	1	.294	.369	.483
1997 Toledo	AAA	90	319	80	15	1	28	—	—	181	56	75	38	1	91	5	0	4	2	2	.50	1	.251	.336	.567
1998 Durham	AAA	57	217	63	12	0	16	—	—	123	46	48	38	1	42	0	0	1	6	1	.86	2	.290	.395	.567
1997 Detroit	AL	44	123	28	5	0	4	(2	2)	45	14	13	15	0	35	0	0	2	3	1	.75	2	.228	.307	.366
1998 Tampa Bay	AL	59	199	57	18	1	12	(6	6)	113	28	35	16	0	45	0	0	1	0	2	.00	4	.286	.338	.568
2 ML YEARS		103	322	85	23	1	16	(8	8)	158	42	48	31	0	80	0	0	3	3	3	.50	6	.264	.326	.491

Chris Tremie

Bats: Right **Throws:** Right **Pos:** DH-2; PH/PR-2   **Ht:** 6'0" **Wt:** 200 **Born:** 10/17/69 **Age:** 29

Year Team	Lg	G	AB	H	2B	3B	HR	(Hm	Rd)	TB	R	RBI	TBB	IBB	SO	HBP	SH	SF	SB	CS	SB%	GDP	Avg	OBP	SLG
1992 Utica	A	6	16	1	0	0	0	—	—	1	1	0	0	0	5	0	0	0	0	0	.00	0	.063	.063	.063
1993 White Sox	R	2	4	0	0	0	0	—	—	0	0	0	0	0	0	0	0	0	0	0	.00	0	.000	.000	.000
Sarasota	A+	14	37	6	1	0	0	—	—	7	2	5	2	0	4	3	0	0	0	0	.00	1	.162	.262	.189
Hickory	A	49	155	29	6	1	1	—	—	40	7	17	9	0	26	4	1	0	0	0	.00	5	.187	.250	.258
1994 Birmingham	AA	92	302	68	13	0	2	—	—	87	32	29	17	0	44	6	3	2	4	1	.80	3	.225	.278	.288
1995 Nashville	AAA	67	190	38	4	0	2	—	—	48	13	16	13	0	37	2	4	0	0	0	.00	6	.200	.259	.253
1996 Nashville	AAA	70	215	47	10	1	0	—	—	59	17	26	18	0	48	2	6	3	2	0	1.00	2	.219	.282	.274
1997 Reading	AA	97	295	60	11	1	2	—	—	79	20	31	36	0	61	5	5	5	0	5	.00	7	.203	.296	.268
1998 Oklahoma	AAA	78	247	55	10	0	0	—	—	65	35	12	24	0	47	5	4	1	1	1	.50	12	.223	.303	.263
1995 Chicago	AL	10	24	4	0	0	0	(0	0)	4	0	0	1	0	2	1	0	0	0	0	.00	0	.167	.200	.167
1998 Texas	AL	2	3	1	1	0	0	(0	0)	2	2	0	1	0	1	0	0	0	0	0	.00	0	.333	.500	.667
2 ML YEARS		12	27	5	1	0	0	(0	0)	6	2	0	2	0	3	1	0	0	0	0	.00	0	.185	.241	.222

Mike Trombley

Pitches: Right **Bats:** Right **Pos:** RP-76; SP-1   **Ht:** 6'2" **Wt:** 203 **Born:** 4/14/67 **Age:** 32

Year Team	Lg	G	GS	CG	GF	IP	BFP	H	R	ER	HR	SH	SF	HB	TBB	IBB	SO	WP	Bk	W	L	Pct.	ShO	Sv-Op	Hld	ERA
1992 Minnesota	AL	10	7	0	0	46.1	194	43	20	17	5	2	0	1	17	0	38	0	0	3	2	.600	0	0-0	0	3.30
1993 Minnesota	AL	44	10	0	8	114.1	506	131	72	62	15	3	7	3	41	4	85	5	0	6	6	.500	0	2-5	8	4.88
1994 Minnesota	AL	24	0	0	8	48.1	219	56	36	34	10	1	2	3	18	2	32	3	0	2	0	1.000	0	0-1	1	6.33
1995 Minnesota	AL	20	18	0	0	97.2	442	107	68	61	18	3	2	3	42	1	68	4	0	4	8	.333	0	0-0	0	5.62
1996 Minnesota	AL	43	0	0	19	68.2	292	61	24	23	2	0	3	5	25	8	57	4	0	5	1	.833	0	6-9	4	3.01
1997 Minnesota	AL	67	0	0	21	82.1	349	77	43	40	7	2	3	2	31	4	74	5	0	2	3	.400	0	1-1	11	4.37
1998 Minnesota	AL	77	1	0	17	96.2	413	90	41	39	16	2	1	5	41	3	89	6	1	6	5	.545	0	1-4	23	3.63
7 ML YEARS		285	36	0	73	554.1	2415	565	304	276	73	13	18	22	215	22	443	27	1	28	25	.528	0	10-20	47	4.48

Michael Tucker

Bats: Left **Throws:** Right **Pos:** RF-118; PH/PR-17   **Ht:** 6'2" **Wt:** 185 **Born:** 6/25/71 **Age:** 28

Year Team	Lg	G	AB	H	2B	3B	HR	(Hm	Rd)	TB	R	RBI	TBB	IBB	SO	HBP	SH	SF	SB	CS	SB%	GDP	Avg	OBP	SLG
1995 Kansas City	AL	62	177	46	10	0	4	(1	3)	68	23	17	18	2	51	1	2	0	2	1	.67	7	.260	.332	.384
1996 Kansas City	AL	108	339	88	18	4	12	(2	10)	150	55	53	40	1	69	7	3	4	10	4	.71	7	.260	.346	.442
1997 Atlanta	NL	138	499	141	25	7	14	(5	9)	222	80	56	44	0	116	6	4	7	12	7	.63	7	.283	.347	.445
1998 Atlanta	NL	130	414	101	27	3	13	(10	3)	173	54	46	49	10	112	3	1	2	8	3	.73	4	.244	.327	.418
4 ML YEARS		438	1429	376	80	14	43	(18	25)	613	212	172	151	13	348	17	10	7	32	17	.65	21	.263	.339	.429

Chris Turner

Bats: Right **Throws:** Right **Pos:** C-4   **Ht:** 6'1" **Wt:** 190 **Born:** 3/23/69 **Age:** 30

Year Team	Lg	G	AB	H	2B	3B	HR	(Hm	Rd)	TB	R	RBI	TBB	IBB	SO	HBP	SH	SF	SB	CS	SB%	GDP	Avg	OBP	SLG
1998 Omaha *	AAA	66	196	60	14	1	1	—	—	79	31	16	38	2	36	3	1	1	6	3	.67	3	.306	.424	.403
1993 California	AL	25	75	21	5	0	1	(0	1)	29	9	13	9	0	16	1	0	1	1	1	.50	1	.280	.360	.387
1994 California	AL	58	149	36	7	1	1	(1	0)	48	23	12	10	0	29	1	1	2	3	0	1.00	2	.242	.290	.322
1995 California	AL	5	10	1	0	0	0	(0	0)	1	0	1	0	0	3	0	0	0	0	0	.00	0	.100	.100	.100
1996 California	AL	4	3	1	0	0	0	(0	0)	1	1	1	1	0	0	0	0	0	0	0	.00	0	.333	.400	.333
1997 Anaheim	AL	13	23	6	1	1	1	(0	1)	12	4	2	5	0	8	0	1	0	0	0	.00	0	.261	.393	.522
1998 Kansas City	AL	4	9	0	0	0	0	(0	0)	0	0	0	0	0	4	1	0	0	0	0	.00	1	.000	.100	.000
6 ML YEARS		109	269	65	13	2	3	(1	2)	91	37	29	25	0	60	3	2	4	4	1	.80	4	.242	.309	.338

Ugueth Urbina

Pitches: Right **Bats:** Right **Pos:** RP-64   **Ht:** 6'2" **Wt:** 165 **Born:** 2/15/74 **Age:** 25

		HOW MUCH HE PITCHED						WHAT HE GAVE UP										THE RESULTS					
Year Team	Lg	G	GS	CG	GF	IP	BFP	H	R	ER	HR	SH	SF	HB	TBB	IBB	SO	WP	Bk	W	L	Pct.	ShO	Sv-Op	Hld	ERA
1995 Montreal	NL	7	4	0	0	23.1	109	26	17	16	6	2	0	0	14	1	15	2	0	2	2	.500	0	0-0	0	6.17
1996 Montreal	NL	33	17	0	2	114	484	102	54	47	18	1	3	1	44	4	108	3	1	10	5	.667	0	0-1	6	3.71
1997 Montreal	NL	63	0	0	50	64.1	276	52	29	27	9	3	0	1	29	2	84	2	0	5	8	.385	0	27-32	1	3.78
1998 Montreal	NL	64	0	0	59	69.1	272	37	11	10	2	2	1	0	33	2	94	3	2	6	3	.667	0	34-38	0	1.30
4 ML YEARS		167	21	0	111	271	1141	217	111	100	35	8	4	2	120	9	301	10	3	23	18	.561	0	61-71	7	3.32

Ismael Valdes

Pitches: Right **Bats:** Right **Pos:** SP-27   **Ht:** 6'3" **Wt:** 215 **Born:** 8/21/73 **Age:** 25

		HOW MUCH HE PITCHED						WHAT HE GAVE UP										THE RESULTS					
Year Team	Lg	G	GS	CG	GF	IP	BFP	H	R	ER	HR	SH	SF	HB	TBB	IBB	SO	WP	Bk	W	L	Pct.	ShO	Sv-Op	Hld	ERA
1998 Vero Beach *	A+	1	1	0	0	3	11	2	0	0	0	0	0	0	1	0	3	0	0	0	0	.000	0	0- —	—	0.00
San Berndno *	A+	1	1	0	0	6.1	27	7	2	2	0	1	0	0	1	0	4	0	0	1	0	1.000	0	0- —	—	2.84
1994 Los Angeles	NL	21	1	0	7	28.1	115	21	10	10	2	3	0	0	10	2	28	1	2	3	1	.750	0	0-0	4	3.18
1995 Los Angeles	NL	33	27	6	1	197.2	804	168	76	67	17	10	5	1	51	5	150	1	3	13	11	.542	2	1-1	2	3.05
1996 Los Angeles	NL	33	33	0	0	225	945	219	94	83	20	7	7	3	54	10	173	1	5	15	7	.682	0	0-0	0	3.32
1997 Los Angeles	NL	30	30	0	0	196.2	795	171	68	58	16	11	3	3	47	1	140	3	2	10	11	.476	0	0-0	0	2.65
1998 Los Angeles	NL	27	27	2	0	174	745	171	82	77	17	5	3	2	66	4	122	4	2	11	10	.524	2	0-0	0	3.98
5 ML YEARS		144	118	8	8	821.2	3404	750	330	295	72	36	18	9	228	22	613	10	14	52	40	.565	4	1-1	6	3.23

Marc Valdes

Pitches: Right **Bats:** Right **Pos:** RP-16; SP-4   **Ht:** 6'0" **Wt:** 185 **Born:** 12/20/71 **Age:** 27

		HOW MUCH HE PITCHED						WHAT HE GAVE UP										THE RESULTS					
Year Team	Lg	G	GS	CG	GF	IP	BFP	H	R	ER	HR	SH	SF	HB	TBB	IBB	SO	WP	Bk	W	L	Pct.	ShO	Sv-Op	Hld	ERA
1995 Florida	NL	3	3	0	0	7	49	17	13	11	1	1	1	1	9	0	2	1	0	0	0	.000	0	0-0	0	14.14
1996 Florida	NL	11	8	0	0	48.2	228	63	32	26	5	1	3	1	23	0	13	3	2	1	3	.250	0	0-1	0	4.81
1997 Montreal	NL	48	7	0	9	95	407	84	36	33	2	5	5	8	39	5	54	2	0	4	4	.500	0	2-2	1	3.13
1998 Montreal	NL	20	4	0	3	36.1	169	41	34	30	6	1	2	1	21	2	28	4	0	1	3	.250	0	0-0	1	7.43
4 ML YEARS		82	22	0	12	187	853	205	115	100	14	8	11	11	92	7	97	10	2	6	10	.375	0	2-3	2	4.81

Pedro Valdes

Bats: Left **Throws:** Left **Pos:** PH/PR-8; LF-6; RF-1   **Ht:** 6'1" **Wt:** 180 **Born:** 6/29/73 **Age:** 26

		BATTING																		BASERUNNING				PERCENTAGES		
Year Team	Lg	G	AB	H	2B	3B	HR	(Hm	Rd)	TB	R	RBI	TBB	IBB	SO	HBP	SH	SF	SB	CS	SB%	GDP	Avg	OBP	SLG
1991 Huntington	R+	50	157	45	11	1	0	—	—	58	18	16	17	3	31	2	1	5	5	1	.83	7	.287	.354	.369
1992 Peoria	A	33	112	26	7	0	0	—	—	33	8	20	7	3	32	0	0	4	0	0	.00	1	.232	.268	.295
Geneva	A-	66	254	69	10	0	5	—	—	94	27	24	3	1	33	3	2	2	4	5	.44	2	.272	.286	.370
1993 Peoria	A	65	234	74	11	1	7	—	—	108	33	36	10	4	40	0	5	4	2	2	.50	3	.316	.339	.462
Daytona	A+	60	230	66	16	1	8	—	—	108	27	49	9	1	30	2	0	5	3	4	.43	8	.287	.313	.470
1994 Orlando	AA	116	365	103	14	4	1	—	—	128	39	37	20	3	45	2	2	1	2	6	.25	10	.282	.322	.351
1995 Orlando	AA	114	426	128	28	3	7	—	—	183	57	68	37	3	77	5	0	6	3	6	.33	7	.300	.359	.430
1996 Iowa	AAA	103	397	117	23	0	15	—	—	185	61	60	31	1	57	1	1	5	2	0	1.00	12	.295	.343	.466
1997 Iowa	AAA	125	464	132	30	1	14	—	—	206	65	60	48	5	67	2	1	6	9	2	.82	13	.284	.350	.444
1998 Iowa	AAA	65	229	72	12	0	17	—	—	135	49	40	27	3	38	0	0	2	2	1	.67	6	.314	.384	.590
1996 Chicago	NL	9	8	1	1	0	0	(0	0)	2	2	1	1	0	5	0	0	0	0	0	.00	0	.125	.222	.250
1998 Chicago	NL	14	23	5	1	1	0	(0	0)	8	1	2	1	0	3	0	0	0	0	1	.00	1	.217	.250	.348
2 ML YEARS		23	31	6	2	1	0	(0	0)	10	3	3	2	0	8	0	0	0	0	1	.00	1	.194	.242	.323

Carlos Valdez

Pitches: Right **Bats:** Right **Pos:** RP-4   **Ht:** 5'11" **Wt:** 175 **Born:** 12/26/71 **Age:** 27

		HOW MUCH HE PITCHED						WHAT HE GAVE UP										THE RESULTS					
Year Team	Lg	G	GS	CG	GF	IP	BFP	H	R	ER	HR	SH	SF	HB	TBB	IBB	SO	WP	Bk	W	L	Pct.	ShO	Sv-Op	Hld	ERA
1991 Giants	R	13	10	0	1	63.1	288	75	48	40	3	1	4	0	32	0	48	6	1	2	3	.400	0	0- —	—	5.68
1992 Everett	A-	3	0	0	2	6.1	29	4	2	1	0	0	1	2	7	0	6	1	0	0	1	.000	0	0- —	—	1.42
Giants	R	6	0	0	3	14.2	56	7	2	0	0	1	0	0	5	0	14	1	0	3	1	.750	0	0- —	—	0.00
1993 Clinton	A	35	2	0	14	90.1	389	74	47	40	6	7	3	2	44	1	85	8	0	4	7	.364	0	3- —	—	3.99
1994 San Jose	A+	36	17	0	10	123.2	536	109	70	62	7	3	6	12	61	0	116	6	0	8	6	.571	0	0- —	—	4.51
1995 Shreveport	AA	22	3	0	8	64	240	40	11	9	0	1	0	3	14	2	51	1	0	3	2	.600	0	5- —	—	1.27
Phoenix	AAA	18	0	0	12	29.1	131	29	10	9	2	2	0	1	13	2	30	3	0	1	0	1.000	0	2- —	—	2.76
1996 Phoenix	AAA	44	0	0	17	59.2	276	63	38	33	4	4	2	4	34	5	38	6	1	4	3	.571	0	5- —	—	4.98
1997 Pawtucket	AAA	35	8	0	6	78.2	346	73	49	41	7	3	4	0	46	4	64	5	0	0	4	.000	0	1- —	—	4.69
1998 Pawtucket	AAA	37	5	0	8	74.2	321	74	38	34	12	2	2	4	22	2	75	6	0	4	3	.571	0	0- —	—	4.10
1995 San Francisco	NL	11	0	0	3	14.2	69	19	10	10	1	0	1	1	8	1	7	1	1	0	1	.000	0	0-0	0	6.14
1998 Boston	AL	4	0	0	1	3.1	16	1	0	0	0	0	1	0	5	0	4	0	0	1	0	1.000	0	0-0	0	0.00
2 ML YEARS		15	0	0	4	18	85	20	10	10	1	0	2	1	13	1	11	1	1	1	1	.500	0	0-0	0	5.00

227

Efrain Valdez

Pitches: Left   Bats: Left   Pos: RP-6   Ht: 5'11" Wt: 170 Born: 6/11/66 Age: 33

Year Team	Lg	G	GS	CG	GF	IP	BFP	H	R	ER	HR	SH	SF	HB	TBB	IBB	SO	WP	Bk	W	L	Pct.	ShO	Sv-Op	Hld	ERA
1998 Norfolk *	AAA	18	0	0	10	20.2	92	23	9	9	0	1	0	3	10	0	15	1	0	1	0	1.000	0	1--	—	3.92
Tucson *	AAA	28	2	0	10	57.2	247	59	31	28	5	5	2	3	18	1	41	7	1	1	4	.200	0	0--	—	4.37
1990 Cleveland	AL	13	0	0	4	23.2	104	20	10	8	2	1	3	0	14	3	13	1	0	1	1	.500	0	0-0	0	3.04
1991 Cleveland	AL	7	0	0	0	6	27	5	1	1	0	1	1	1	3	1	1	0	0	0	0	.000	0	0-0	1	1.50
1998 Arizona	NL	6	0	0	2	4.1	20	7	2	2	2	0	0	0	1	0	2	0	0	0	0	.000	0	0-0	0	4.15
3 ML YEARS		26	0	0	6	34	151	32	13	11	4	2	4	1	18	4	16	1	0	1	1	.500	0	0-0	1	2.91

Javier Valentin

Bats: Both   Throws: Right   Pos: C-53; DH-1; PH/PR-1   Ht: 5'10" Wt: 185 Born: 9/19/75 Age: 23

Year Team	Lg	G	AB	H	2B	3B	HR	(Hm	Rd)	TB	R	RBI	TBB	IBB	SO	HBP	SH	SF	SB	CS	SB%	GDP	Avg	OBP	SLG
1993 Twins	R	32	103	27	6	1	1	—	—	38	18	19	14	0	19	1	0	4	0	2	.00	1	.262	.344	.369
Elizabethtn	R+	9	24	5	1	0	0	—	—	6	3	3	4	0	2	1	0	0	0	0	.00	0	.208	.345	.250
1994 Elizabethtn	R+	54	210	44	5	0	9	—	—	76	23	27	15	0	44	2	0	5	0	1	.00	9	.210	.263	.362
1995 Fort Wayne	A	112	383	123	26	5	19	—	—	216	59	65	47	7	75	2	1	0	5	5	.00	7	.321	.398	.564
1996 Fort Myers	A+	87	338	89	26	1	7	—	—	138	34	54	32	4	65	4	0	5	1	0	1.00	5	.263	.330	.408
Hardware City	AA	48	165	39	8	0	3	—	—	56	22	14	16	1	35	1	3	0	0	3	.00	2	.236	.308	.339
1997 New Britain	AA	102	370	90	17	0	8	—	—	131	41	50	30	1	61	1	2	6	2	3	.40	5	.243	.297	.354
1997 Minnesota	AL	4	7	2	0	0	0	(0	0)	2	1	0	0	0	3	0	0	0	0	0	.00	0	.286	.286	.286
1998 Minnesota	AL	55	162	32	7	1	3	(1	2)	50	11	18	11	0	30	0	3	1	0	0	.00	7	.198	.247	.309
2 ML YEARS		59	169	34	7	1	3	(1	2)	52	12	18	11	0	33	0	3	1	0	0	.00	7	.201	.249	.308

John Valentin

Bats: Right   Throws: Right   Pos: 3B-153; 2B-1   Ht: 6'0" Wt: 180 Born: 2/18/67 Age: 32

Year Team	Lg	G	AB	H	2B	3B	HR	(Hm	Rd)	TB	R	RBI	TBB	IBB	SO	HBP	SH	SF	SB	CS	SB%	GDP	Avg	OBP	SLG
1992 Boston	AL	58	185	51	13	0	5	(1	4)	79	21	25	20	0	17	2	4	1	1	0	1.00	9	.276	.351	.427
1993 Boston	AL	144	468	130	40	3	11	(7	4)	209	50	66	49	2	77	2	16	4	3	4	.43	9	.278	.346	.447
1994 Boston	AL	84	301	95	26	2	9	(6	3)	152	53	49	42	1	38	5	3	1	3	1	.75	4	.316	.400	.505
1995 Boston	AL	135	520	155	37	2	27	(11	16)	277	108	102	81	2	67	10	4	6	20	5	.80	7	.298	.399	.533
1996 Boston	AL	131	527	156	29	3	13	(9	4)	230	84	59	63	0	59	7	2	7	9	10	.47	15	.296	.374	.436
1997 Boston	AL	143	575	176	47	5	18	(11	7)	287	95	77	58	5	66	5	1	5	7	4	.64	21	.306	.372	.499
1998 Boston	AL	153	588	145	44	1	23	(11	12)	260	113	73	77	3	82	9	2	5	4	5	.44	9	.247	.340	.442
7 ML YEARS		848	3164	908	236	16	106	(56	50)	1494	524	451	390	13	406	38	34	32	47	29	.62	69	.287	.369	.472

Jose Valentin

Bats: Both   Throws: Right   Pos: SS-139; PH/PR-22; DH-1   Ht: 5'10" Wt: 173 Born: 10/12/69 Age: 29

Year Team	Lg	G	AB	H	2B	3B	HR	(Hm	Rd)	TB	R	RBI	TBB	IBB	SO	HBP	SH	SF	SB	CS	SB%	GDP	Avg	OBP	SLG
1992 Milwaukee	AL	4	3	0	0	0	0	(0	0)	0	1	1	0	0	0	0	0	1	0	0	.00	0	.000	.000	.000
1993 Milwaukee	AL	19	53	13	1	2	1	(1	0)	21	10	7	7	1	16	1	2	0	1	0	1.00	1	.245	.344	.396
1994 Milwaukee	AL	97	285	68	19	0	11	(8	3)	120	47	46	38	1	75	2	4	2	12	3	.80	1	.239	.330	.421
1995 Milwaukee	AL	112	338	74	23	3	11	(3	8)	136	62	49	37	0	83	0	7	4	16	8	.67	0	.219	.293	.402
1996 Milwaukee	AL	154	552	143	33	7	24	(10	14)	262	90	95	66	9	145	0	6	4	17	4	.81	4	.259	.336	.475
1997 Milwaukee	AL	136	494	125	23	1	17	(4	13)	201	58	58	39	4	109	4	4	5	9	8	.70	5	.253	.310	.407
1998 Milwaukee	NL	151	428	96	24	0	16	(7	9)	168	65	49	63	4	105	1	2	3	10	7	.59	2	.224	.323	.393
7 ML YEARS		673	2153	519	123	13	80	(33	47)	908	333	305	250	23	533	8	25	19	75	30	.71	13	.241	.320	.422

John Vander Wal

Bats: L   Throws: L   Pos: PH/PR-82; RF-25; 1B-5; LF-5; DH-3   Ht: 6'2" Wt: 197 Born: 4/29/66 Age: 33

Year Team	Lg	G	AB	H	2B	3B	HR	(Hm	Rd)	TB	R	RBI	TBB	IBB	SO	HBP	SH	SF	SB	CS	SB%	GDP	Avg	OBP	SLG
1991 Montreal	NL	21	61	13	4	1	1	(0	1)	22	4	8	1	0	18	0	0	0	0	0	.00	2	.213	.222	.361
1992 Montreal	NL	105	213	51	8	2	4	(2	2)	75	21	20	24	2	36	0	0	0	3	0	1.00	2	.239	.316	.352
1993 Montreal	NL	106	215	50	7	4	5	(1	4)	80	34	30	27	2	30	1	0	1	6	3	.67	4	.233	.320	.372
1994 Colorado	NL	91	110	27	3	1	5	(1	4)	47	12	15	16	0	31	0	0	1	2	1	.67	4	.245	.339	.427
1995 Colorado	NL	105	101	35	8	1	5	(2	3)	60	15	21	16	5	23	0	0	1	1	1	.50	2	.347	.432	.594
1996 Colorado	NL	104	151	38	6	2	5	(5	0)	63	20	31	19	2	38	1	0	2	2	2	.50	1	.252	.335	.417
1997 Colorado	NL	76	92	16	2	0	1	(0	1)	21	7	11	10	0	33	0	0	1	1	1	.50	2	.174	.255	.228
1998 Col-SD	NL	109	129	36	13	1	5	(3	2)	66	21	20	22	0	34	0	0	1	0	0	.00	2	.279	.382	.512
1998 Colorado	NL	89	104	30	10	1	5	(3	2)	57	18	20	16	0	29	0	0	1	0	0	.00	1	.288	.380	.548
San Diego	NL	20	25	6	3	0	0	(0	0)	9	3	0	6	0	5	0	0	0	0	0	.00	1	.240	.387	.360
8 ML YEARS		717	1072	266	51	12	31	(14	17)	434	134	156	135	11	243	2	0	7	15	8	.65	19	.248	.331	.405

Todd Van Poppel

Pitches: Right **Bats:** Right **Pos:** SP-11; RP-11   **Ht:** 6'5" **Wt:** 210 **Born:** 12/9/71 **Age:** 27

		HOW MUCH HE PITCHED						WHAT HE GAVE UP										THE RESULTS						
Year Team	Lg	G	GS	CG	GF	IP	BFP	H	R	ER	HR	SH	SF	HB	TBB	IBB	SO	WP	Bk	W	L	Pct.	ShO	Sv-Op	Hld	ERA
1998 Tulsa *	AA	1	1	0	0	4	17	2	2	2	1	0	0	0	4	0	2	0	0	0	0	.000	0	0- --	—	4.50
Oklahoma *	AAA	15	13	2	0	87	370	88	44	36	11	0	2	1	25	0	69	3	1	5	5	.500	0	0- --	—	3.72
1991 Oakland	AL	1	1	0	0	4.2	21	7	5	5	1	0	0	0	2	0	6	0	0	0	0	.000	0	0-0	0	9.64
1993 Oakland	AL	16	16	0	0	84	380	76	50	47	10	1	2	2	62	0	47	3	0	6	6	.500	0	0-0	0	5.04
1994 Oakland	AL	23	23	0	0	116.2	532	108	80	79	20	4	4	3	89	2	83	3	1	7	10	.412	0	0-0	0	6.09
1995 Oakland	AL	36	14	1	10	138.1	582	125	77	75	16	3	6	4	56	1	122	4	0	4	8	.333	0	0-0	1	4.88
1996 Oak-Det	AL	37	15	1	8	99.1	491	139	107	100	24	4	7	3	62	3	53	7	0	3	9	.250	1	1-2	0	9.06
1998 Tex-Pit		22	11	0	3	66.1	303	79	52	47	9	3	3	2	28	3	42	7	3	2	4	.333	0	0-0	0	6.38
1996 Oakland	AL	28	6	0	8	63	301	86	56	54	13	3	5	2	33	3	37	4	0	1	5	.167	0	1-2	0	7.71
Detroit	AL	9	9	1	0	36.1	190	53	51	46	11	1	2	1	29	0	16	3	0	2	4	.333	1	0-0	0	11.39
1998 Texas	AL	4	4	0	0	19.1	95	26	20	19	5	0	1	1	10	0	10	2	0	1	2	.333	0	0-0	0	8.84
Pittsburgh	NL	18	7	0	3	47	208	53	32	28	4	3	2	0	18	3	32	5	3	1	2	.333	0	0-0	0	5.36
6 ML YEARS		135	80	2	21	509.1	2309	534	371	353	80	15	22	13	299	9	353	24	4	22	37	.373	1	1-2	1	6.24

Ben VanRyn

Pitches: Left **Bats:** Left **Pos:** RP-25   **Ht:** 6'5" **Wt:** 195 **Born:** 8/9/71 **Age:** 27

		HOW MUCH HE PITCHED						WHAT HE GAVE UP										THE RESULTS						
Year Team	Lg	G	GS	CG	GF	IP	BFP	H	R	ER	HR	SH	SF	HB	TBB	IBB	SO	WP	Bk	W	L	Pct.	ShO	Sv-Op	Hld	ERA
1990 Expos	R	10	9	0	0	51.2	205	44	13	10	0	0	2	1	15	0	56	0	0	5	3	.625	0	0- --	—	1.74
1991 Sumter	A	20	20	0	0	109.1	506	122	96	79	14	3	7	6	61	0	77	10	4	2	13	.133	0	0- --	—	6.50
Jamestown	A-	6	6	1	0	32.1	143	37	19	18	1	0	0	2	12	0	23	4	0	3	3	.500	0	0- --	—	5.01
1992 Vero Beach	A+	26	25	1	0	137.2	583	125	58	49	4	5	8	2	54	1	108	4	5	10	7	.588	1	0- --	—	3.20
1993 San Antonio	AA	21	21	1	0	134.1	557	118	43	33	5	4	1	3	38	1	144	2	4	14	4	.778	0	0- --	—	2.21
Albuquerque	AAA	6	6	0	0	24.1	120	35	30	29	1	1	2	0	17	0	9	0	0	1	4	.200	0	0- --	—	10.73
1994 Albuquerque	AAA	12	9	0	1	50.2	251	75	42	36	6	3	1	0	24	1	44	0	1	4	1	.800	0	0- --	—	6.39
San Antonio	AA	17	17	0	0	102.1	418	93	42	34	5	3	1	0	35	0	72	2	0	8	3	.727	0	0- --	—	2.99
1995 Chattanooga	AA	5	3	0	0	12.2	69	22	18	13	2	0	2	1	6	0	6	0	0	1	0	1.000	0	0- --	—	9.24
Vancouver	AAA	11	5	0	2	29.1	123	29	10	10	1	2	2	0	9	1	20	2	0	2	0	1.000	0	0- --	—	3.07
Midland	AA	19	0	0	8	32.1	133	33	10	10	4	0	0	2	12	0	24	2	0	1	1	.500	0	1- --	—	2.78
1996 Vancouver	AAA	18	1	0	0	34.2	154	35	17	15	2	3	1	1	13	1	28	3	0	3	3	.500	0	0- --	—	3.89
Louisville	AAA	19	10	0	4	66.1	288	69	43	36	9	2	3	0	27	0	42	2	0	4	6	.400	0	1- --	—	4.88
1997 Iowa	AAA	51	5	0	12	80.1	343	88	43	41	10	5	3	1	25	2	64	5	0	2	2	.500	0	3- --	—	4.59
1998 Syracuse	AAA	30	0	0	7	41	164	34	16	16	3	1	3	0	13	1	30	0	0	2	1	.667	0	2- --	—	3.51
1996 California	AL	1	0	0	1	1	5	1	0	0	0	0	0	0	1	0	0	0	0	0	0	.000	0	0-0	0	0.00
1998 ChN-SD-Tor		25	0	0	6	14.2	72	18	10	10	1	1	1	0	12	0	10	1	0	0	2	.000	0	0-1	3	6.14
1998 Chicago	NL	9	0	0	2	8	39	9	3	3	0	0	1	0	6	0	6	0	0	0	0	.000	0	0-0	2	3.38
San Diego	NL	6	0	0	1	2.2	16	3	3	3	0	0	0	0	4	0	1	1	0	0	1	.000	0	0-1	0	10.13
Toronto	AL	10	0	0	3	4	17	6	4	4	0	0	0	0	2	0	3	0	0	0	1	.000	0	0-0	1	9.00
2 ML YEARS		26	0	0	7	15.2	77	19	10	10	1	1	1	0	13	0	10	1	0	0	2	.000	0	0-1	3	5.74

Jason Varitek

Bats: Both **Throws:** Right **Pos:** C-75; PH/PR-24; DH-3   **Ht:** 6'2" **Wt:** 210 **Born:** 4/11/72 **Age:** 27

		BATTING																	BASERUNNING				PERCENTAGES		
Year Team	Lg	G	AB	H	2B	3B	HR	(Hm	Rd)	TB	R	RBI	TBB	IBB	SO	HBP	SH	SF	SB	CS	SB%	GDP	Avg	OBP	SLG
1995 Port City	AA	104	352	79	14	2	10	—	—	127	42	44	61	4	126	2	3	3	0	1	.00	8	.224	.340	.361
1996 Port City	AA	134	503	132	34	1	12	—	—	204	63	67	66	7	93	4	0	4	7	6	.54	14	.262	.350	.406
1997 Tacoma	AAA	87	307	78	13	0	15	—	—	136	54	48	34	2	71	2	4	4	0	1	.00	13	.254	.329	.443
Pawtucket	AAA	20	66	13	5	0	1	—	—	21	6	5	8	0	12	0	0	0	0	0	.00	4	.197	.284	.318
1997 Boston	AL	1	1	1	0	0	0	(0	0)	1	0	0	0	0	0	0	0	0	0	0	.00	0	1.000	1.000	1.000
1998 Boston	AL	86	221	56	13	0	7	(1	6)	90	31	33	17	1	45	2	4	3	2	2	.50	8	.253	.309	.407
2 ML YEARS		87	222	57	13	0	7	(1	6)	91	31	33	17	1	45	2	4	3	2	2	.50	8	.257	.311	.410

Greg Vaughn

Bats: Right **Throws:** Right **Pos:** LF-151; DH-4; PH/PR-3   **Ht:** 6'0" **Wt:** 202 **Born:** 7/3/65 **Age:** 33

		BATTING																	BASERUNNING				PERCENTAGES		
Year Team	Lg	G	AB	H	2B	3B	HR	(Hm	Rd)	TB	R	RBI	TBB	IBB	SO	HBP	SH	SF	SB	CS	SB%	GDP	Avg	OBP	SLG
1989 Milwaukee	AL	38	113	30	3	0	5	(1	4)	48	18	23	13	0	23	0	0	2	4	1	.80	0	.265	.336	.425
1990 Milwaukee	AL	120	382	84	26	2	17	(9	8)	165	51	61	33	1	91	1	7	6	7	4	.64	11	.220	.280	.432
1991 Milwaukee	AL	145	542	132	24	5	27	(16	11)	247	81	98	62	2	125	1	2	7	2	2	.50	5	.244	.319	.456
1992 Milwaukee	AL	141	501	114	18	2	23	(11	12)	205	77	78	60	1	123	5	2	5	15	15	.50	8	.228	.313	.409
1993 Milwaukee	AL	154	569	152	28	2	30	(12	18)	274	97	97	89	14	118	5	0	4	10	7	.59	6	.267	.369	.482
1994 Milwaukee	AL	95	370	94	24	1	19	(9	10)	177	59	55	51	6	93	1	0	1	9	5	.64	6	.254	.345	.478
1995 Milwaukee	AL	108	392	88	19	1	17	(8	9)	160	67	59	55	3	89	0	0	4	10	4	.71	10	.224	.317	.408
1996 Mil-SD		145	516	134	19	1	41	(22	19)	278	98	117	82	6	130	6	0	5	9	3	.75	7	.260	.365	.539
1997 San Diego	NL	120	361	78	10	0	18	(11	7)	142	60	57	56	1	110	2	0	3	7	4	.64	7	.216	.322	.393
1998 San Diego	NL	158	573	156	28	4	50	(23	27)	342	112	119	79	6	121	5	0	4	11	4	.73	7	.272	.363	.597
1996 Milwaukee	AL	102	375	105	16	0	31	(16	15)	214	78	95	58	4	99	4	0	5	5	2	.71	6	.280	.378	.571
San Diego	NL	43	141	29	3	1	10	(6	4)	64	20	22	24	2	31	2	0	0	4	1	.80	1	.206	.329	.454
10 ML YEARS		1224	4319	1062	199	18	247	(122	125)	2038	720	764	580	40	1023	26	11	41	84	49	.63	67	.246	.336	.472

Mo Vaughn

Bats: Left   **Throws:** Right   **Pos:** 1B-142; DH-12   **Ht:** 6'1"   **Wt:** 240   **Born:** 12/15/67   **Age:** 31

							BATTING												BASERUNNING				PERCENTAGES		
Year Team	Lg	G	AB	H	2B	3B	HR	(Hm	Rd)	TB	R	RBI	TBB	IBB	SO	HBP	SH	SF	SB	CS	SB%	GDP	Avg	OBP	SLG
1991 Boston	AL	74	219	57	12	0	4	(1	3)	81	21	32	26	2	43	2	0	4	2	1	.67	7	.260	.339	.370
1992 Boston	AL	113	355	83	16	2	13	(8	5)	142	42	57	47	7	67	3	0	3	3	3	.50	8	.234	.326	.400
1993 Boston	AL	152	539	160	34	1	29	(13	16)	283	86	101	79	23	130	8	0	7	4	3	.57	14	.297	.390	.525
1994 Boston	AL	111	394	122	25	1	26	(15	11)	227	65	82	57	20	112	10	0	2	4	4	.50	7	.310	.408	.576
1995 Boston	AL	140	550	165	28	3	39	(15	24)	316	98	126	68	17	150	14	0	4	11	4	.73	17	.300	.388	.575
1996 Boston	AL	161	635	207	29	1	44	(27	17)	370	118	143	95	19	154	14	0	8	2	0	1.00	17	.326	.420	.583
1997 Boston	AL	141	527	166	24	0	35	(20	15)	295	91	96	86	17	154	12	0	3	2	2	.50	10	.315	.420	.560
1998 Boston	AL	154	609	205	31	2	40	(19	21)	360	107	115	61	13	144	8	0	3	0	0	.00	13	.337	.402	.591
8 ML YEARS		1046	3828	1165	199	10	230	(118	112)	2074	628	752	519	118	954	71	0	34	28	17	.62	93	.304	.394	.542

Javier Vazquez

Pitches: Right   **Bats:** Right   **Pos:** SP-32; RP-1   **Ht:** 6'2"   **Wt:** 180   **Born:** 7/25/76   **Age:** 22

		HOW MUCH HE PITCHED						WHAT HE GAVE UP											THE RESULTS						
Year Team	Lg	G	GS	CG	GF	IP	BFP	H	R	ER	HR	SH	SF	HB	TBB	IBB	SO	WP	Bk	W	L	Pct.	ShO	Sv-Op Hld	ERA
1994 Expos	R	15	11	1	0	67.2	260	37	25	19	0	1	2	3	15	0	56	9	2	5	2	.714	1	0- —	2.53
1995 Albany	A	21	21	1	0	102.2	459	109	67	58	8	1	2	9	47	0	87	2	2	6	6	.500	0	0- — —	5.08
1996 Delmarva	A	27	27	1	0	164.1	668	138	64	49	12	1	1	7	57	0	173	12	2	14	3	.824	0	0- — —	2.68
1997 Wst Plm Bch	A+	19	19	1	0	112.2	461	98	40	27	8	1	2	6	28	0	100	2	2	6	3	.667	0	0- — —	2.16
Harrisburg	AA	6	6	1	0	42	155	15	5	5	2	0	1	2	12	0	47	2	0	4	0	1.000	1	0- — —	1.07
1998 Montreal	NL	33	32	0	1	172.1	764	196	121	116	31	9	4	11	68	2	139	2	0	5	15	.250	0	0-0 0	6.06

Jorge Velandia

Bats: Right   **Throws:** Right   **Pos:** SS-7; 2B-1; PH/PR-1   **Ht:** 5'9"   **Wt:** 160   **Born:** 1/12/75   **Age:** 24

							BATTING												BASERUNNING				PERCENTAGES		
Year Team	Lg	G	AB	H	2B	3B	HR	(Hm	Rd)	TB	R	RBI	TBB	IBB	SO	HBP	SH	SF	SB	CS	SB%	GDP	Avg	OBP	SLG
1992 Bristol	R+	45	119	24	6	1	0	—	—	32	20	9	15	0	16	0	3	0	3	2	.60	1	.202	.291	.269
1993 Fayetteville	A	37	106	17	4	0	0	—	—	21	15	11	13	0	21	3	0	2	5	0	1.00	3	.160	.266	.198
Niagara Fal	A-	72	212	41	11	0	1	—	—	55	30	22	19	0	48	0	3	2	22	4	.85	2	.193	.258	.259
1994 Lakeland	A+	22	60	14	4	0	0	—	—	18	8	3	6	0	14	0	3	1	0	2	.00	0	.233	.299	.300
Springfield	A	98	290	71	14	0	4	—	—	97	42	36	21	0	46	4	6	3	5	6	.45	8	.245	.302	.334
1995 Memphis	AA	63	186	38	10	2	4	—	—	64	23	17	14	2	37	1	1	1	2	2	.00	4	.204	.262	.344
Las Vegas	AAA	66	206	54	12	3	0	—	—	72	25	25	13	1	37	2	7	2	0	0	.00	5	.262	.309	.350
1996 Memphis	AA	122	392	94	19	0	9	—	—	140	42	48	31	3	65	3	5	8	3	7	.30	10	.240	.295	.357
1997 Las Vegas	AAA	114	405	110	15	2	3	—	—	138	46	35	29	3	62	4	8	1	13	3	.81	5	.272	.326	.341
1998 Edmonton	AAA	128	488	140	35	1	6	—	—	195	64	57	37	0	52	6	5	5	8	6	.57	19	.287	.341	.400
1997 San Diego	NL	14	29	3	2	0	0	(0	0)	5	0	1	0	1	7	0	0	0	0	0	.00	0	.103	.133	.172
1998 Oakland	AL	8	4	1	0	0	0	(0	0)	1	0	0	0	0	1	0	0	0	0	0	.00	0	.250	.250	.250
2 ML YEARS		22	33	4	2	0	0	(0	0)	6	0	1	0	1	8	0	0	0	0	0	.00	0	.121	.147	.182

Randy Velarde

Bats: Right   **Throws:** Right   **Pos:** 2B-51; PH/PR-1   **Ht:** 6'0"   **Wt:** 200   **Born:** 11/24/62   **Age:** 36

							BATTING												BASERUNNING				PERCENTAGES		
Year Team	Lg	G	AB	H	2B	3B	HR	(Hm	Rd)	TB	R	RBI	TBB	IBB	SO	HBP	SH	SF	SB	CS	SB%	GDP	Avg	OBP	SLG
1998 Lk Elsinore *	A+	5	20	11	2	1	1	—	—	18	6	7	2	0	0	1	0	0	1	1	.50	0	.550	.609	.900
Vancouver *	AAA	4	16	4	2	0	0	—	—	6	0	2	1	0	4	1	0	0	1	1	.50	0	.250	.333	.375
1987 New York	AL	8	22	4	0	0	0	(0	0)	4	1	1	0	0	6	0	0	0	0	0	.00	1	.182	.182	.182
1988 New York	AL	48	115	20	6	0	5	(2	3)	41	18	12	8	0	24	2	0	0	1	1	.50	3	.174	.240	.357
1989 New York	AL	33	100	34	4	2	2	(1	1)	48	12	11	7	0	14	1	3	0	0	3	.00	0	.340	.389	.480
1990 New York	AL	95	229	48	6	2	5	(1	4)	73	21	19	20	0	53	1	2	1	0	3	.00	6	.210	.275	.319
1991 New York	AL	80	184	45	11	1	1	(0	1)	61	19	15	18	0	43	3	5	0	3	1	.75	6	.245	.322	.332
1992 New York	AL	121	412	112	24	1	7	(2	5)	159	57	46	38	1	78	2	4	5	7	2	.78	13	.272	.333	.386
1993 New York	AL	85	226	68	13	2	7	(4	3)	106	28	24	18	2	39	4	3	2	2	2	.50	12	.301	.360	.469
1994 New York	AL	77	280	78	16	1	9	(3	6)	123	47	34	22	0	61	4	2	2	4	2	.67	7	.279	.338	.439
1995 New York	AL	111	367	102	19	1	7	(2	5)	144	60	46	55	0	64	4	3	3	5	1	.83	9	.278	.375	.392
1996 California	AL	136	530	151	27	3	14	(8	6)	226	82	54	70	0	118	5	4	2	7	7	.50	7	.285	.372	.426
1997 Anaheim	AL	1	0	0	0	0	0	(0	0)	0	0	0	0	0	0	0	0	0	0	0	.00	0	.000	.000	.000
1998 Anaheim	AL	51	188	49	13	1	4	(1	3)	76	29	26	34	0	42	1	0	1	7	2	.78	8	.261	.375	.404
12 ML YEARS		846	2653	711	139	14	61	(24	37)	1061	374	288	290	3	542	27	26	16	36	24	.60	72	.268	.344	.400

Robin Ventura

Bats: Left   **Throws:** Right   **Pos:** 3B-161   **Ht:** 6'1"   **Wt:** 198   **Born:** 7/14/67   **Age:** 31

							BATTING												BASERUNNING				PERCENTAGES		
Year Team	Lg	G	AB	H	2B	3B	HR	(Hm	Rd)	TB	R	RBI	TBB	IBB	SO	HBP	SH	SF	SB	CS	SB%	GDP	Avg	OBP	SLG
1989 Chicago	AL	16	45	8	3	0	0	(0	0)	11	5	7	8	0	6	1	1	3	0	0	.00	1	.178	.298	.244
1990 Chicago	AL	150	493	123	17	1	5	(2	3)	157	48	54	55	2	53	1	13	3	1	4	.20	5	.249	.324	.318
1991 Chicago	AL	157	606	172	25	1	23	(16	7)	268	92	100	80	3	67	4	8	7	2	4	.33	22	.284	.367	.442
1992 Chicago	AL	157	592	167	38	1	16	(7	9)	255	85	93	93	9	71	0	1	8	2	4	.33	14	.282	.375	.431
1993 Chicago	AL	157	554	145	27	1	22	(12	10)	240	85	94	105	16	82	3	1	6	1	6	.14	18	.262	.379	.433
1994 Chicago	AL	109	401	113	15	1	18	(8	10)	184	57	78	61	15	69	2	2	8	3	1	.75	8	.282	.373	.459
1995 Chicago	AL	135	492	145	22	0	26	(8	18)	245	79	93	75	11	98	1	1	8	4	3	.57	8	.295	.384	.498

230

	BATTING																			BASERUNNING				PERCENTAGES		
Year Team	Lg	G	AB	H	2B	3B	HR	(Hm	Rd)	TB	R	RBI	TBB	IBB	SO	HBP	SH	SF		SB	CS	SB%	GDP	Avg	OBP	SLG
1996 Chicago	AL	158	586	168	31	2	34	(13	21)	305	96	105	78	10	81	2	0	8		1	3	.25	18	.287	.368	.520
1997 Chicago	AL	54	183	48	10	1	6	(2	4)	78	27	26	34	5	21	0	0	3		0	0	.00	3	.262	.373	.426
1998 Chicago	AL	161	590	155	31	4	21	(15	6)	257	84	91	79	15	111	1	1	3		1	1	.50	10	.263	.349	.436
10 ML YEARS		1254	4542	1244	219	12	171	(83	88)	2000	658	741	668	86	659	15	28	57		15	26	.37	107	.274	.365	.440

Dario Veras

Pitches: Right **Bats:** Right **Pos:** RP-7   **Ht:** 6'1" **Wt:** 155 **Born:** 3/13/73 **Age:** 26

	HOW MUCH HE PITCHED						WHAT HE GAVE UP												THE RESULTS						
Year Team	Lg	G	GS	CG	GF	IP	BFP	H	R	ER	HR	SH	SF	HB	TBB	IBB	SO	WP	Bk	W	L	Pct.	ShO	Sv-Op	Hld	ERA
1998 Las Vegas *	AAA	31	0	0	27	35.2	153	36	15	15	5	0	0	2	11	0	29	4	0	2	1	.667	0	9--	—	3.79
Pawtucket *	AAA	23	0	0	21	29	124	30	12	12	4	1	1	0	11	3	27	0	0	2	0	1.000	0	7--	—	3.72
1996 San Diego	NL	23	0	0	6	29	117	24	10	9	3	1	1	0	10	4	23	1	0	3	1	.750	0	0-0	1	2.79
1997 San Diego	NL	23	0	0	7	24.2	114	28	18	14	5	0	0	2	12	3	21	0	0	2	1	.667	0	0-1	2	5.11
1998 Boston	AL	7	0	0	4	8	43	12	9	9	0	0	0	1	7	0	2	2	0	0	1	.000	0	0-0	0	10.13
3 ML YEARS		53	0	0	17	61.2	274	64	37	32	8	1	1	4	29	7	46	3	0	5	3	.625	0	0-1	3	4.67

Quilvio Veras

Bats: Both **Throws:** Right **Pos:** 2B-131; PH/PR-7   **Ht:** 5'9" **Wt:** 166 **Born:** 4/3/71 **Age:** 28

	BATTING																			BASERUNNING				PERCENTAGES		
Year Team	Lg	G	AB	H	2B	3B	HR	(Hm	Rd)	TB	R	RBI	TBB	IBB	SO	HBP	SH	SF		SB	CS	SB%	GDP	Avg	OBP	SLG
1995 Florida	NL	124	440	115	20	7	5	(2	3)	164	86	32	80	0	68	9	7	2		56	21	.73	7	.261	.384	.373
1996 Florida	NL	73	253	64	8	1	4	(1	3)	86	40	14	51	1	42	2	1	1		8	8	.50	3	.253	.381	.340
1997 San Diego	NL	145	539	143	23	1	3	(3	0)	177	74	45	72	0	84	7	9	4		33	12	.73	9	.265	.357	.328
1998 San Diego	NL	138	517	138	24	2	6	(5	1)	184	79	45	84	2	78	6	1	4		24	9	.73	6	.267	.373	.356
4 ML YEARS		480	1749	460	75	11	18	(11	7)	611	279	136	287	3	272	24	18	11		121	50	.71	25	.263	.372	.349

Dave Veres

Pitches: Right **Bats:** Right **Pos:** RP-63   **Ht:** 6'2" **Wt:** 195 **Born:** 10/19/66 **Age:** 32

	HOW MUCH HE PITCHED						WHAT HE GAVE UP												THE RESULTS						
Year Team	Lg	G	GS	CG	GF	IP	BFP	H	R	ER	HR	SH	SF	HB	TBB	IBB	SO	WP	Bk	W	L	Pct.	ShO	Sv-Op	Hld	ERA
1994 Houston	NL	32	0	0	7	41	168	39	13	11	4	0	2	1	7	3	28	2	0	3	3	.500	0	1-1	3	2.41
1995 Houston	NL	72	0	0	15	103.1	418	89	29	26	5	6	8	4	30	6	94	4	0	5	1	.833	0	1-3	19	2.26
1996 Montreal	NL	68	0	0	22	77.2	351	85	39	36	10	3	3	6	32	2	81	3	2	6	3	.667	0	4-6	15	4.17
1997 Montreal	NL	53	0	0	11	62	281	68	28	24	5	6	1	2	27	3	47	7	0	2	3	.400	0	1-4	10	3.48
1998 Colorado	NL	63	0	0	26	76.1	319	67	26	24	6	0	2	2	27	2	74	2	2	3	1	.750	0	8-13	8	2.83
5 ML YEARS		288	0	0	81	360.1	1537	348	135	121	30	15	16	15	123	16	324	18	4	19	11	.633	0	15-27	55	3.02

Jose Vidro

Bats: Both **Throws:** Right **Pos:** 2B-56; PH/PR-27; 3B-7   **Ht:** 6'0" **Wt:** 185 **Born:** 8/27/74 **Age:** 24

	BATTING																			BASERUNNING				PERCENTAGES		
Year Team	Lg	G	AB	H	2B	3B	HR	(Hm	Rd)	TB	R	RBI	TBB	IBB	SO	HBP	SH	SF		SB	CS	SB%	GDP	Avg	OBP	SLG
1992 Expos	R	54	200	66	6	2	4	—	—	88	29	31	16	1	31	0	1	2		10	1	.91	5	.330	.376	.440
1993 Burlington	A	76	287	69	19	0	2	—	—	94	39	34	28	3	54	5	4	2		3	2	.60	7	.240	.317	.328
1994 Wst Plm Bch	A+	125	465	124	30	2	4	—	—	170	57	49	51	4	56	5	3	3		8	2	.80	5	.267	.344	.366
1995 Harrisburg	AA	64	246	64	16	2	4	—	—	96	33	38	20	2	37	1	4	3		3	7	.30	5	.260	.315	.390
Wst Plm Bch	A+	44	163	53	15	2	3	—	—	81	20	24	8	0	21	2	2	2		0	1	.00	5	.325	.360	.497
1996 Harrisburg	AA	126	452	117	25	3	18	—	—	202	57	82	29	3	71	2	9	10		3	1	.75	4	.259	.300	.447
1997 Ottawa	AAA	73	279	90	17	0	13	—	—	146	40	47	22	5	40	1	0	3		2	0	1.00	6	.323	.370	.523
1998 Ottawa	AAA	63	235	68	14	2	2	—	—	92	35	32	24	1	25	4	1	3		5	2	.71	4	.289	.361	.391
1997 Montreal	NL	67	169	42	12	1	2	(0	2)	62	19	17	11	0	20	2	0	3		1	0	1.00	5	.249	.297	.367
1998 Montreal	NL	83	205	45	12	0	0	(0	0)	57	24	18	27	0	33	4	6	3		2	2	.50	5	.220	.318	.278
2 ML YEARS		150	374	87	24	1	2	(0	2)	119	43	35	38	0	53	6	6	6		3	2	.60	6	.233	.309	.318

Ron Villone

Pitches: Left **Bats:** Left **Pos:** RP-25   **Ht:** 6'3" **Wt:** 237 **Born:** 1/16/70 **Age:** 29

	HOW MUCH HE PITCHED						WHAT HE GAVE UP												THE RESULTS						
Year Team	Lg	G	GS	CG	GF	IP	BFP	H	R	ER	HR	SH	SF	HB	TBB	IBB	SO	WP	Bk	W	L	Pct.	ShO	Sv-Op	Hld	ERA
1998 Buffalo *	AAA	23	0	0	20	22.1	98	20	11	5	2	1	1	0	11	0	28	0	0	2	2	.500	0	7--	—	2.01
1995 Sea-SD		38	0	0	15	45	212	44	31	29	11	3	1	1	34	0	63	3	0	2	3	.400	0	1-5	6	5.80
1996 SD-Mil		44	0	0	19	43	182	31	15	15	6	0	2	5	25	0	38	2	0	2	3	.500	0	2-3	9	3.14
1997 Milwaukee	AL	50	0	0	15	52.2	238	54	23	20	4	2	0	1	36	2	40	3	0	1	0	1.000	0	0-2	8	3.42
1998 Cleveland	AL	25	0	0	6	27	129	30	18	18	3	2	2	2	22	0	15	0	0	0	0	.000	0	0-0	1	6.00
1995 Seattle	AL	19	0	0	7	19.1	101	20	19	17	6	3	0	1	23	0	26	1	0	0	2	.000	0	0-3	5	7.91
San Diego	NL	19	0	0	8	25.2	111	24	12	12	5	0	1	0	11	0	37	2	0	2	1	.667	0	1-2	3	4.21
1996 San Diego	NL	21	0	0	9	18.1	78	17	6	6	2	0	0	1	7	0	19	0	0	1	1	.500	0	0-1	4	2.95
Milwaukee	AL	23	0	0	10	24.2	104	14	9	9	4	0	2	4	18	0	19	2	0	0	0	.000	0	2-2	5	3.28
4 ML YEARS		157	0	0	55	167.2	761	159	87	82	24	7	5	9	117	2	156	8	0	4	4	.500	0	3-10	24	4.40

Fernando Vina

Bats: Left **Throws:** Right **Pos:** 2B-158; PH/PR-1 **Ht:** 5'9" **Wt:** 170 **Born:** 4/16/69 **Age:** 30

Year Team	Lg	G	AB	H	2B	3B	HR	(Hm	Rd)	TB	R	RBI	TBB	IBB	SO	HBP	SH	SF	SB	CS	SB%	GDP	Avg	OBP	SLG
1993 Seattle	AL	24	45	10	2	0	0	(0	0)	12	5	2	4	0	3	3	1	0	6	0	1.00	0	.222	.327	.267
1994 New York	NL	79	124	31	6	0	0	(0	0)	37	20	6	12	0	11	12	2	0	3	1	.75	4	.250	.372	.298
1995 Milwaukee	AL	113	288	74	7	7	3	(3	4)	104	46	29	22	0	28	9	4	2	6	3	.67	6	.257	.337	.361
1996 Milwaukee	AL	140	554	157	19	10	7	(3	4)	217	94	46	38	3	35	13	6	4	16	7	.70	15	.283	.342	.392
1997 Milwaukee	AL	79	324	89	12	2	4	(1	3)	117	37	28	12	1	23	7	2	3	8	7	.53	4	.275	.312	.361
1998 Milwaukee	NL	159	637	198	39	7	7	(2	5)	272	101	45	54	2	46	25	5	1	22	16	.58	7	.311	.386	.427
6 ML YEARS		594	1972	559	85	26	21	(7	14)	759	303	156	142	6	146	69	20	10	61	34	.64	36	.283	.351	.385

Joe Vitiello

Bats: Right **Throws:** Right **Pos:** DH-2; PH/PR-1 **Ht:** 6'3" **Wt:** 230 **Born:** 4/11/70 **Age:** 29

Year Team	Lg	G	AB	H	2B	3B	HR	(Hm	Rd)	TB	R	RBI	TBB	IBB	SO	HBP	SH	SF	SB	CS	SB%	GDP	Avg	OBP	SLG
1998 Omaha *	AAA	103	376	107	20	2	18	—	—	185	44	71	39	2	68	6	0	7	0	0	.00	19	.285	.355	.492
1995 Kansas City	AL	53	130	33	4	0	7	(3	4)	58	13	21	8	0	25	4	0	0	0	0	.00	4	.254	.317	.446
1996 Kansas City	AL	85	257	62	15	1	8	(3	5)	103	29	40	38	2	69	3	0	3	2	0	1.00	12	.241	.342	.401
1997 Kansas City	AL	51	130	31	6	0	5	(4	1)	52	11	18	14	1	37	2	0	0	0	0	.00	2	.238	.322	.400
1998 Kansas City	AL	3	7	1	0	0	0	(0	0)	1	0	0	1	0	2	0	0	0	0	0	.00	0	.143	.250	.143
4 ML YEARS		192	524	127	25	1	20	(10	10)	214	53	79	61	3	133	9	0	3	2	0	1.00	18	.242	.330	.408

Jose Vizcaino

Bats: Both **Throws:** Right **Pos:** SS-66; PH/PR-2 **Ht:** 6'1" **Wt:** 180 **Born:** 3/26/68 **Age:** 31

Year Team	Lg	G	AB	H	2B	3B	HR	(Hm	Rd)	TB	R	RBI	TBB	IBB	SO	HBP	SH	SF	SB	CS	SB%	GDP	Avg	OBP	SLG
1989 Los Angeles	NL	7	10	2	0	0	0	(0	0)	2	2	0	0	0	1	0	1	0	0	0	.00	0	.200	.200	.200
1990 Los Angeles	NL	37	51	14	1	1	0	(0	0)	17	3	2	4	1	8	0	0	1	1	1	.50	1	.275	.327	.333
1991 Chicago	NL	93	145	38	5	0	0	(0	0)	43	7	10	5	0	18	0	2	2	2	1	.67	1	.262	.283	.297
1992 Chicago	NL	86	285	64	10	4	1	(0	1)	85	25	17	14	2	35	0	5	1	3	0	1.00	4	.225	.260	.298
1993 Chicago	NL	151	551	158	19	4	4	(1	3)	197	74	54	46	2	71	3	8	9	12	9	.57	9	.287	.340	.358
1994 New York	NL	103	410	105	13	3	3	(1	2)	133	47	33	33	3	62	2	5	6	1	11	.08	5	.256	.310	.324
1995 New York	NL	135	509	146	21	5	3	(2	1)	186	66	56	35	4	76	1	13	3	8	3	.73	14	.287	.332	.365
1996 NYN-Cle		144	542	161	17	8	1	(1	0)	197	70	45	35	0	82	3	10	3	15	7	.68	3	.297	.341	.363
1997 San Francisco	NL	151	568	151	19	7	5	(1	4)	199	77	50	48	1	87	0	13	1	8	8	.50	13	.266	.323	.350
1998 Los Angeles	NL	67	237	62	9	0	3	(0	3)	80	30	29	17	0	35	1	10	2	7	3	.70	4	.262	.311	.338
1996 New York	NL	96	363	110	12	6	1	(1	0)	137	47	32	28	0	58	3	6	2	9	5	.64	6	.303	.356	.377
Cleveland	AL	48	179	51	5	2	0	(0	0)	60	23	13	7	0	24	0	4	1	6	2	.75	2	.285	.310	.335
10 ML YEARS		974	3308	901	114	32	20	(6	14)	1139	401	296	237	13	475	10	67	27	57	43	.57	59	.272	.320	.344

Omar Vizquel

Bats: Both **Throws:** Right **Pos:** SS-151 **Ht:** 5'9" **Wt:** 170 **Born:** 4/24/67 **Age:** 32

Year Team	Lg	G	AB	H	2B	3B	HR	(Hm	Rd)	TB	R	RBI	TBB	IBB	SO	HBP	SH	SF	SB	CS	SB%	GDP	Avg	OBP	SLG
1989 Seattle	AL	143	387	85	7	3	1	(1	0)	101	45	20	28	0	40	1	13	2	1	4	.20	6	.220	.273	.261
1990 Seattle	AL	81	255	63	3	2	2	(0	2)	76	19	18	18	0	22	0	10	2	4	1	.80	7	.247	.295	.298
1991 Seattle	AL	142	426	98	16	4	1	(1	0)	125	42	41	45	0	37	0	8	3	7	2	.78	8	.230	.302	.293
1992 Seattle	AL	136	483	142	20	4	0	(0	0)	170	49	21	32	0	38	2	9	1	15	13	.54	14	.294	.340	.352
1993 Seattle	AL	158	560	143	14	2	2	(1	1)	167	68	31	50	2	71	4	13	3	12	14	.46	7	.255	.319	.298
1994 Cleveland	AL	69	286	78	10	1	1	(0	1)	93	39	33	23	0	23	0	11	2	13	4	.76	4	.273	.325	.325
1995 Cleveland	AL	136	542	144	28	0	6	(3	3)	190	87	56	59	0	59	1	10	10	29	11	.73	4	.266	.333	.351
1996 Cleveland	AL	151	542	161	36	1	9	(2	7)	226	98	64	56	0	42	4	12	9	35	9	.80	10	.297	.362	.417
1997 Cleveland	AL	153	565	158	23	6	5	(3	2)	208	89	49	57	1	58	2	16	2	43	12	.78	16	.280	.347	.368
1998 Cleveland	AL	151	576	166	30	6	2	(0	2)	214	86	50	62	1	64	4	12	6	37	12	.76	10	.288	.358	.372
10 ML YEARS		1320	4622	1238	187	29	29	(11	18)	1570	622	383	430	4	454	18	114	40	196	82	.71	86	.268	.330	.340

Jack Voigt

Bats: R **Throws:** R **Pos:** 1B-27; PH/PR-26; CF-10; LF-9; DH-3; 3B-2; RF-2 **Ht:** 6'1" **Wt:** 178 **Born:** 5/17/66 **Age:** 33

Year Team	Lg	G	AB	H	2B	3B	HR	(Hm	Rd)	TB	R	RBI	TBB	IBB	SO	HBP	SH	SF	SB	CS	SB%	GDP	Avg	OBP	SLG
1998 Edmonton *	AAA	18	68	22	6	0	4	—	—	40	10	11	8	0	15	0	0	0	1	2	.33	0	.324	.395	.588
Oklahoma *	AAA	20	70	24	6	0	2	—	—	36	10	11	14	0	19	1	0	1	0	1	.00	1	.343	.453	.514
1992 Baltimore	AL	1	0	0	0	0	0	(0	0)	0	0	0	0	0	0	0	0	0	0	0	.00	0	.000	.000	.000
1993 Baltimore	AL	64	152	45	11	1	6	(5	1)	76	32	23	25	0	33	0	0	0	1	0	1.00	3	.296	.395	.500
1994 Baltimore	AL	59	141	34	5	0	3	(1	2)	48	15	20	18	1	25	1	1	2	0	0	.00	0	.241	.327	.340
1995 Bal-Tex	AL	36	63	11	3	0	2	(2	0)	20	9	8	10	0	14	0	0	1	0	0	.00	2	.175	.284	.317
1996 Texas	AL	5	9	1	0	0	0	(0	0)	1	1	0	0	0	2	0	0	0	0	0	.00	0	.111	.111	.111
1997 Milwaukee	AL	72	151	37	9	2	8	(5	3)	74	20	22	19	2	36	1	2	1	1	2	.33	5	.245	.331	.490
1998 Oakland	AL	57	72	10	4	0	1	(1	0)	17	7	10	6	0	19	0	1	0	5	1	.83	1	.139	.205	.236
1995 Baltimore	AL	3	1	1	0	0	0	(0	0)	1	1	0	0	0	0	0	0	0	0	0	.00	0	1.000	1.000	1.000
Texas	AL	33	62	10	3	0	2	(2	0)	19	8	8	10	0	14	0	0	1	0	0	.00	2	.161	.274	.306
7 ML YEARS		294	588	138	32	3	20	(14	6)	236	84	83	78	3	129	2	4	4	7	3	.70	11	.235	.324	.401

Terrell Wade

Pitches: Left **Bats:** Left **Pos:** SP-2 **Ht:** 6'3" **Wt:** 205 **Born:** 1/25/73 **Age:** 26

Year Team	Lg	G	GS	CG	GF	IP	BFP	H	R	ER	HR	SH	SF	HB	TBB	IBB	SO	WP	Bk	W	L	Pct.	ShO	Sv-Op	Hld	ERA
1998 St. Pete *	A+	3	3	0	0	15	66	12	8	6	2	0	1	1	7	0	16	1	0	0	1	.000	0	0--	—	3.60
Durham *	AAA	4	4	0	0	19.2	92	21	12	10	1	0	0	1	12	1	14	0	0	1	1	.500	0	0--	—	4.58
1995 Atlanta	NL	3	0	0	0	4	18	3	2	2	1	0	0	0	4	0	3	1	0	0	1	.000	0	0-0	0	4.50
1996 Atlanta	NL	44	8	0	13	69.2	305	57	28	23	9	5	1	1	47	6	79	2	0	5	0	1.000	0	1-2	4	2.97
1997 Atlanta	NL	12	9	0	1	42	197	60	31	25	6	2	5	2	16	1	35	1	0	2	3	.400	0	0-0	0	5.36
1998 Tampa Bay	AL	2	2	0	0	10.2	46	14	6	6	3	0	0	0	2	0	8	1	0	1	1	.500	0	0-0	0	5.06
4 ML YEARS		61	19	0	14	126.1	566	134	67	56	19	7	6	3	69	7	125	5	0	8	5	.615	0	1-2	4	3.99

Billy Wagner

Pitches: Left **Bats:** Left **Pos:** RP-58 **Ht:** 5'11" **Wt:** 180 **Born:** 7/25/71 **Age:** 27

Year Team	Lg	G	GS	CG	GF	IP	BFP	H	R	ER	HR	SH	SF	HB	TBB	IBB	SO	WP	Bk	W	L	Pct.	ShO	Sv-Op	Hld	ERA
1998 Jackson *	AA	3	1	0	1	3	10	1	0	0	0	0	0	0	0	0	7	0	0	0	0	.000	0	0--	—	0.00
1995 Houston	NL	1	0	0	0	0.1	1	0	0	0	0	0	0	0	0	0	0	0	0	0	0	.000	0	0-0	0	0.00
1996 Houston	NL	37	0	0	20	51.2	212	28	16	14	6	7	2	3	30	2	67	1	0	2	2	.500	0	9-13	3	2.44
1997 Houston	NL	62	0	0	49	66.1	277	49	23	21	5	3	1	3	30	1	106	3	0	7	8	.467	0	23-29	1	2.85
1998 Houston	NL	58	0	0	50	60	247	46	19	18	6	4	0	0	25	1	97	2	0	4	3	.571	0	30-35	1	2.70
4 ML YEARS		158	0	0	119	178.1	737	123	58	53	17	14	3	6	85	4	270	6	0	13	13	.500	0	62-77	5	2.67

Paul Wagner

Pitches: Right **Bats:** Right **Pos:** SP-9; RP-4 **Ht:** 6'1" **Wt:** 211 **Born:** 11/14/67 **Age:** 31

Year Team	Lg	G	GS	CG	GF	IP	BFP	H	R	ER	HR	SH	SF	HB	TBB	IBB	SO	WP	Bk	W	L	Pct.	ShO	Sv-Op	Hld	ERA
1998 Beloit *	A	1	1	0	0	5	21	7	4	4	0	1	1	0	0	3	3	1	0	0	1	.000	0	0--	—	7.20
Louisville *	AAA	3	3	0	0	12.1	58	17	12	12	3	0	0	0	5	0	6	1	0	1	0	1.000	0	0--	—	8.76
Richmond *	AAA	8	0	0	1	13.2	54	11	4	3	0	1	0	0	3	0	9	0	0	1	0	1.000	0	0--	—	1.98
1992 Pittsburgh	NL	6	1	0	1	13	52	9	1	1	0	0	0	0	5	0	5	1	0	2	0	1.000	0	0-0	0	0.69
1993 Pittsburgh	NL	44	17	1	9	141.1	599	143	72	67	15	6	7	1	42	2	114	12	0	8	8	.500	1	2-5	4	4.27
1994 Pittsburgh	NL	29	17	1	4	119.2	534	136	69	61	7	8	4	8	50	4	86	4	0	7	8	.467	0	0-0	2	4.59
1995 Pittsburgh	NL	33	25	3	1	165	725	174	96	88	18	7	2	7	72	7	120	8	0	5	16	.238	1	1-1	1	4.80
1996 Pittsburgh	NL	16	15	1	0	81.2	361	86	49	49	10	5	1	3	39	2	81	7	0	4	8	.333	0	0-0	0	5.40
1997 Pit-Mil		16	0	0	3	18	87	20	9	9	3	1	0	0	13	3	9	3	2	1	0	1.000	0	0-1	0	4.50
1998 Milwaukee	NL	13	9	0	0	55.2	261	67	49	44	10	5	2	1	31	1	37	3	0	1	5	.167	0	0-0	0	7.11
1997 Pittsburgh	NL	14	0	0	2	16	79	17	7	7	3	1	0	0	13	3	9	3	0	1	0	.000	0	0-1	0	3.94
Milwaukee	AL	2	0	0	1	2	8	3	2	2	0	0	0	0	0	0	0	0	0	1	0	1.000	0	0-0	0	9.00
7 ML YEARS		157	84	6	19	594.1	2619	635	345	319	64	34	17	20	252	19	452	38	2	28	45	.384	2	3-7	7	4.83

David Wainhouse

Pitches: Right **Bats:** Left **Pos:** RP-10 **Ht:** 6'2" **Wt:** 190 **Born:** 11/7/67 **Age:** 31

Year Team	Lg	G	GS	CG	GF	IP	BFP	H	R	ER	HR	SH	SF	HB	TBB	IBB	SO	WP	Bk	W	L	Pct.	ShO	Sv-Op	Hld	ERA
1998 Colo Sprngs *	AAA	38	0	0	30	50	214	47	25	20	4	3	2	3	23	0	44	1	1	2	3	.400	0	4--	—	3.60
1991 Montreal	NL	2	0	0	1	2.2	14	2	2	2	0	1	0	0	4	0	1	2	0	0	1	.000	0	0-0	0	6.75
1993 Seattle	AL	3	0	0	0	2.1	20	7	7	7	1	0	0	1	5	0	2	0	0	0	0	.000	0	0-0	0	27.00
1996 Pittsburgh	NL	17	0	0	6	23.2	101	22	16	15	3	1	2	0	10	1	16	2	0	1	0	1.000	0	0-0	1	5.70
1997 Pittsburgh	NL	25	0	0	6	28	137	34	28	25	2	3	1	3	17	0	21	1	1	0	1	.000	0	0-0	0	8.04
1998 Colorado	NL	10	0	0	3	11	51	15	6	6	1	0	0	2	5	0	3	0	0	1	0	1.000	0	0-1	0	4.91
5 ML YEARS		57	0	0	16	67.2	323	80	59	55	7	4	4	6	41	1	43	5	1	2	2	.500	0	0-1	2	7.32

Tim Wakefield

Pitches: Right **Bats:** Right **Pos:** SP-33; RP-3 **Ht:** 6'2" **Wt:** 206 **Born:** 8/2/66 **Age:** 32

Year Team	Lg	G	GS	CG	GF	IP	BFP	H	R	ER	HR	SH	SF	HB	TBB	IBB	SO	WP	Bk	W	L	Pct.	ShO	Sv-Op	Hld	ERA
1992 Pittsburgh	NL	13	13	4	0	92	373	76	26	22	3	6	4	1	35	1	51	3	1	8	1	.889	1	0-0	0	2.15
1993 Pittsburgh	NL	24	20	3	1	128.1	595	145	83	80	14	7	5	9	75	2	59	6	0	6	11	.353	2	0-0	0	5.61
1995 Boston	AL	27	27	6	0	195.1	804	163	76	64	22	3	7	9	68	0	119	11	0	16	8	.667	1	0-0	0	2.95
1996 Boston	AL	32	32	6	0	211.2	963	238	151	121	38	1	9	12	90	0	140	4	1	14	13	.519	0	0-0	0	5.14
1997 Boston	AL	35	29	4	2	201.1	866	193	109	95	24	3	7	16	87	5	151	6	0	12	15	.444	2	0-0	1	4.25
1998 Boston	AL	36	33	2	1	216	939	211	123	110	30	1	8	14	79	1	146	6	1	17	8	.680	0	0-0	0	4.58
6 ML YEARS		167	154	25	4	1044.2	4540	1026	568	492	131	21	40	61	434	9	666	36	3	73	56	.566	6	0-0	1	4.24

Matt Walbeck

Bats: Both **Throws:** Right **Pos:** C-104; PH/PR-9; DH-2 **Ht:** 5'11" **Wt:** 206 **Born:** 10/2/69 **Age:** 29

Year Team	Lg	G	AB	H	2B	3B	HR	(Hm	Rd)	TB	R	RBI	TBB	IBB	SO	HBP	SH	SF	SB	CS	SB%	GDP	Avg	OBP	SLG
1993 Chicago	NL	11	30	6	2	0	1	(1	0)	11	2	6	1	0	6	0	0	0	0	0	.00	0	.200	.226	.367
1994 Minnesota	AL	97	338	69	12	0	5	(0	5)	96	31	35	17	1	37	2	1	1	1	1	.50	7	.204	.246	.284
1995 Minnesota	AL	115	393	101	18	1	1	(1	0)	124	40	44	25	2	71	1	1	2	3	1	.75	11	.257	.302	.316

Year Team	Lg	G	AB	H	2B	3B	HR	(Hm	Rd)	TB	R	RBI	TBB	IBB	SO	HBP	SH	SF	SB	CS	SB%	GDP	Avg	OBP	SLG
								BATTING											BASERUNNING				PERCENTAGES		
1996 Minnesota	AL	63	215	48	10	0	2	(1	1)	64	25	24	9	0	34	0	1	2	3	1	.75	6	.223	.252	.298
1997 Detroit	AL	47	137	38	3	0	3	(1	2)	50	18	10	12	0	19	0	0	2	3	3	.50	4	.277	.331	.365
1998 Anaheim	AL	108	338	87	15	2	6	(3	3)	124	41	46	30	0	68	2	5	5	1	1	.50	9	.257	.317	.367
6 ML YEARS		441	1451	349	60	3	18	(7	11)	469	157	165	94	3	235	5	8	12	11	7	.61	37	.241	.287	.323

Jamie Walker

Pitches: Left   **Bats:** Left   **Pos:** RP-4; SP-2   **Ht:** 6'2"   **Wt:** 190   **Born:** 7/1/71   **Age:** 28

Year Team	Lg	G	GS	CG	GF	IP	BFP	H	R	ER	HR	SH	SF	HB	TBB	IBB	SO	WP	Bk	W	L	Pct.	ShO	Sv-Op	Hld	ERA
		HOW MUCH HE PITCHED						WHAT HE GAVE UP												THE RESULTS						
1992 Auburn	A-	15	14	0	0	83.1	341	75	35	29	4	4	1	6	21	0	67	4	1	4	6	.400	0	0--	—	3.13
1993 Quad City	A	25	24	1	1	131.2	585	140	92	75	12	10	5	6	48	1	121	12	0	3	11	.214	1	0--	—	5.13
1994 Quad City	A	32	18	0	4	125	569	133	80	58	10	14	3	16	42	2	104	5	1	8	10	.444	0	1--	—	4.18
1995 Jackson	AA	50	0	0	19	58	250	59	29	29	6	3	2	2	24	5	38	4	1	4	2	.667	0	2--	—	4.50
1996 Jackson	AA	45	7	0	13	101	424	94	34	28	7	1	8	8	35	2	79	2	0	5	1	.833	0	2--	—	2.50
1997 Wichita	AA	5	0	0	1	6.2	32	6	8	7	1	1	1	2	5	0	6	0	0	0	1	.000	0	0--	—	9.45
1998 Omaha	AAA	7	7	0	0	46.2	198	57	15	14	3	2	1	2	11	1	21	1	0	5	1	.833	0	0--	—	2.70
1997 Kansas City	AL	50	0	0	15	43	197	46	28	26	6	2	2	3	20	3	24	2	0	3	3	.500	0	0-1	3	5.44
1998 Kansas City	AL	6	2	0	2	17.1	86	30	20	19	5	1	1	2	3	0	15	0	0	0	1	.000	0	0-0	1	9.87
2 ML YEARS		56	2	0	17	60.1	283	76	48	45	11	3	3	5	23	3	39	2	0	3	4	.429	0	0-1	4	6.71

Larry Walker

Bats: L   **Throws:** R   **Pos:** RF-123; PH/PR-8; CF-3; DH-1; 2B-1; 3B-1   **Ht:** 6'3"   **Wt:** 235   **Born:** 12/1/66   **Age:** 32

Year Team	Lg	G	AB	H	2B	3B	HR	(Hm	Rd)	TB	R	RBI	TBB	IBB	SO	HBP	SH	SF	SB	CS	SB%	GDP	Avg	OBP	SLG
								BATTING											BASERUNNING				PERCENTAGES		
1989 Montreal	NL	20	47	8	0	0	0	(0	0)	8	4	4	5	0	13	1	3	0	1	1	.50	0	.170	.264	.170
1990 Montreal	NL	133	419	101	18	3	19	(9	10)	182	59	51	49	5	112	5	3	2	21	7	.75	8	.241	.326	.434
1991 Montreal	NL	137	487	141	30	2	16	(5	11)	223	59	64	42	2	102	5	1	4	14	9	.61	7	.290	.349	.458
1992 Montreal	NL	143	528	159	31	4	23	(13	10)	267	85	93	41	10	97	6	0	8	18	6	.75	9	.301	.353	.506
1993 Montreal	NL	138	490	130	24	5	22	(13	9)	230	85	86	80	20	76	6	0	6	29	7	.81	8	.265	.371	.469
1994 Montreal	NL	103	395	127	44	2	19	(7	12)	232	76	86	47	5	74	4	0	6	15	5	.75	8	.322	.394	.587
1995 Colorado	NL	131	494	151	31	5	36	(24	12)	300	96	101	49	13	72	14	0	5	16	3	.84	13	.306	.381	.607
1996 Colorado	NL	83	272	75	18	4	18	(12	6)	155	58	58	20	2	58	9	0	3	18	2	.90	7	.276	.342	.570
1997 Colorado	NL	153	568	208	46	4	49	(20	29)	409	143	130	78	14	90	14	0	4	33	8	.80	15	.366	.452	.720
1998 Colorado	NL	130	454	165	46	3	23	(17	6)	286	113	67	64	2	61	4	0	2	14	4	.78	11	.363	.445	.630
10 ML YEARS		1171	4154	1265	288	32	225	(120	105)	2292	778	740	475	73	755	68	7	40	179	52	.77	86	.305	.382	.552

Todd Walker

Bats: Left   **Throws:** Right   **Pos:** 2B-140; PH/PR-2; DH-1   **Ht:** 6'0"   **Wt:** 181   **Born:** 5/25/73   **Age:** 26

Year Team	Lg	G	AB	H	2B	3B	HR	(Hm	Rd)	TB	R	RBI	TBB	IBB	SO	HBP	SH	SF	SB	CS	SB%	GDP	Avg	OBP	SLG
								BATTING											BASERUNNING				PERCENTAGES		
1996 Minnesota	AL	25	82	21	6	0	0	(0	0)	27	8	6	4	0	13	0	0	3	2	0	1.00	4	.256	.281	.329
1997 Minnesota	AL	52	156	37	7	1	3	(1	2)	55	15	16	11	1	30	1	1	2	7	0	1.00	5	.237	.288	.353
1998 Minnesota	AL	143	528	167	41	3	12	(7	5)	250	85	62	47	9	65	2	0	4	19	7	.73	13	.316	.372	.473
3 ML YEARS		220	766	225	54	4	15	(8	7)	332	108	84	62	10	108	3	1	9	28	7	.80	22	.294	.345	.433

Donne Wall

Pitches: Right   **Bats:** Right   **Pos:** RP-45; SP-1   **Ht:** 6'1"   **Wt:** 180   **Born:** 7/11/67   **Age:** 31

Year Team	Lg	G	GS	CG	GF	IP	BFP	H	R	ER	HR	SH	SF	HB	TBB	IBB	SO	WP	Bk	W	L	Pct.	ShO	Sv-Op	Hld	ERA
		HOW MUCH HE PITCHED						WHAT HE GAVE UP												THE RESULTS						
1998 Las Vegas *	AAA	3	3	0	0	15	62	11	8	8	2	0	1	0	8	0	12	0	0	2	0	1.000	0	0--	—	4.80
1995 Houston	NL	6	5	0	0	24.1	110	33	19	15	5	0	2	0	5	0	16	1	0	3	1	.750	0	0-0	1	5.55
1996 Houston	NL	26	23	2	1	150	643	170	84	76	17	4	5	6	34	3	99	3	2	9	8	.529	1	0-0	0	4.56
1997 Houston	NL	8	8	0	0	41.2	186	53	31	29	8	0	0	2	16	0	25	2	1	2	5	.286	0	0-0	0	6.26
1998 San Diego	NL	46	1	0	14	70.1	287	50	20	19	6	4	2	1	32	2	56	3	1	5	4	.556	0	1-4	16	2.43
4 ML YEARS		86	37	2	15	286.1	1226	306	154	139	36	8	9	9	87	5	196	9	4	19	18	.514	1	1-4	17	4.37

Jerome Walton

Bats: Right   **Throws:** Right   **Pos:** PH/PR-5; LF-4; RF-4; DH-3   **Ht:** 6'1"   **Wt:** 200   **Born:** 7/8/65   **Age:** 33

Year Team	Lg	G	AB	H	2B	3B	HR	(Hm	Rd)	TB	R	RBI	TBB	IBB	SO	HBP	SH	SF	SB	CS	SB%	GDP	Avg	OBP	SLG
								BATTING											BASERUNNING				PERCENTAGES		
1989 Chicago	NL	116	475	139	23	3	5	(3	2)	183	64	46	27	1	77	6	2	5	24	7	.77	6	.293	.335	.385
1990 Chicago	NL	101	392	103	16	2	2	(2	0)	129	63	21	50	1	70	4	1	2	14	7	.67	4	.263	.350	.329
1991 Chicago	NL	123	270	59	13	1	5	(3	2)	89	42	17	19	0	55	3	3	3	7	3	.70	7	.219	.275	.330
1992 Chicago	NL	30	55	7	0	1	0	(0	0)	9	7	1	9	0	13	2	3	0	1	2	.33	1	.127	.273	.164
1993 California	NL	5	2	0	0	0	0	(0	0)	0	1	0	2	0	0	0	0	0	0	1	1.00	0	.000	.333	.000
1994 Cincinnati	NL	46	68	21	4	0	1	(1	0)	28	10	9	4	0	12	0	1	0	1	3	.25	1	.309	.347	.412
1995 Cincinnati	NL	102	162	47	12	1	8	(4	4)	85	32	22	17	0	25	4	3	2	10	7	.59	0	.290	.368	.525
1996 Atlanta	NL	37	47	16	5	0	1	(1	0)	24	9	4	5	0	10	0	1	2	0	0	.00	1	.340	.389	.511
1997 Baltimore	AL	26	68	20	1	0	3	(1	2)	30	8	9	4	0	10	1	0	0	0	0	.00	3	.294	.333	.441
1998 Tampa Bay	AL	12	34	11	3	0	0	(0	0)	14	4	3	2	0	6	0	0	0	0	0	.00	1	.324	.361	.412
10 ML YEARS		598	1573	423	77	8	25	(15	10)	591	241	132	138	2	280	19	16	14	58	29	.67	25	.269	.333	.376

Bryan Ward

Pitches: Left **Bats:** Left **Pos:** RP-28 **Ht:** 6'2" **Wt:** 210 **Born:** 1/25/72 **Age:** 27

		HOW MUCH HE PITCHED				WHAT HE GAVE UP				THE RESULTS					
Year Team	Lg	G GS CG GF	IP	BFP	H R ER	HR SH SF HB	TBB IBB	SO	WP Bk	W L	Pct.	ShO	Sv-Op	Hld	ERA
1993 Elmira	A-	14 11 0 2	61.1	291	82 41 34	6 3 4 4	26 2	63	5 5	2 5	.286	0	0--	—	4.99
1994 Kane County	A	47 0 0 40	55.2	235	46 27 21	4 3 4 2	21 2	62	2 0	3 4	.429	0	11--	—	3.40
1995 Portland	AA	20 11 1 5	72	321	70 42 36	9 1 1 2	31 3	71	7 3	7 3	.700	1	2--	—	4.50
Brevard Cty	A+	11 11 0 0	72	296	68 27 23	5 4 0 2	17 0	65	1 1	5 1	.833	0	0--	—	2.88
1996 Portland	AA	28 25 2 0	146.2	633	170 97 80	23 9 6 7	32 3	124	0 2	9 9	.500	0	0--	—	4.91
1997 Portland	AA	12 12 0 0	76	316	71 39 33	17 2 2 2	19 1	69	6 0	6 3	.667	0	0--	—	3.91
Charlotte	AAA	15 14 2 0	75.1	349	102 62 58	17 5 4 4	30 4	48	5 1	2 9	.182	0	0--	—	6.93
1998 Birmingham	AA	29 0 0 24	42	187	33 19 11	0 2 3 1	25 3	40	5 0	2 3	.400	0	12--	—	2.36
1998 Chicago	AL	28 0 0 9	27	116	30 13 10	4 0 1 0	7 0	17	0 0	1 2	.333	0	1-4	3	3.33

Daryle Ward

Bats: Left **Throws:** Left **Pos:** PH/PR-4 **Ht:** 6'2" **Wt:** 230 **Born:** 6/27/75 **Age:** 24

		BATTING											BASERUNNING	PERCENTAGES		
Year Team	Lg	G AB H	2B 3B HR	(Hm Rd)	TB	R RBI	TBB	IBB	SO	HBP SH SF		SB CS SB% GDP	Avg	OBP	SLG
1994 Bristol	R+	48 161 43	6 0 5	— —	64	17 30	19	4	33	0 1 1		5 1 .83 3	.267	.343	.398
1995 Fayetteville	A	137 524 149	32 4 14	— —	223	75 106	46	11	111	5 0 7		1 2 .33 13	.284	.344	.426
1996 Toledo	AAA	6 23 4	0 0 0	— —	4	1 1	0	0	3	0 0 0		0 0 .00 2	.174	.174	.174
Lakeland	A+	128 464 135	29 4 10	— —	202	65 68	57	6	77	6 0 4		1 1 .50 9	.291	.373	.435
1997 Jackson	AA	114 422 139	25 0 19	— —	221	72 90	46	4	68	3 0 1		4 2 .67 11	.329	.398	.524
New Orleans	AAA	14 48 18	1 0 2	— —	25	4 8	7	1	7	0 0 0		0 0 .00 0	.375	.455	.521
1998 New Orleans	AAA	116 463 141	31 1 23	— —	243	78 96	41	7	78	2 0 4		2 0 1.00 17	.305	.361	.525
1998 Houston	NL	4 3 1	0 0 0	(0 0)	1	1 0	1	0	2	0 0 0		0 0 .00 0	.333	.500	.333

Turner Ward

Bats: B **Throws:** R **Pos:** CF-48; LF-41; PH/PR-37; RF-22; DH-1 **Ht:** 6'2" **Wt:** 200 **Born:** 4/11/65 **Age:** 34

		BATTING											BASERUNNING	PERCENTAGES		
Year Team	Lg	G AB H	2B 3B HR	(Hm Rd)	TB	R RBI	TBB	IBB	SO	HBP SH SF		SB CS SB% GDP	Avg	OBP	SLG
1990 Cleveland	AL	14 46 16	2 1 1	(0 1)	23	10 10	3	0	8	0 1 0		3 0 1.00 1	.348	.388	.500
1991 Cle-Tor	AL	48 113 27	7 0 0	(0 0)	34	12 7	11	0	18	0 4 0		0 0 .00 2	.239	.306	.301
1992 Toronto	AL	18 29 10	3 0 1	(0 1)	16	7 3	4	0	4	0 0 0		0 1 .00 1	.345	.424	.552
1993 Toronto	AL	72 167 32	4 2 4	(2 2)	52	20 28	23	2	26	1 3 4		3 3 .50 7	.192	.287	.311
1994 Milwaukee	AL	102 367 85	15 2 9	(3 6)	131	55 45	52	4	68	3 0 5		6 2 .75 9	.232	.328	.357
1995 Milwaukee	AL	44 129 34	3 1 4	(3 1)	51	19 16	14	1	21	1 1 1		6 1 .86 2	.264	.338	.395
1996 Milwaukee	AL	43 67 12	2 1 2	(2 0)	22	7 10	13	0	17	1 0 1		3 0 1.00 3	.179	.309	.328
1997 Pittsburgh	NL	71 167 59	16 1 7	(5 2)	98	33 33	18	2	17	2 3 1		4 1 .80 1	.353	.420	.587
1998 Pittsburgh	NL	123 282 74	13 3 9	(6 3)	120	33 46	27	1	40	4 4 7		5 4 .56 4	.262	.328	.426
1991 Cleveland	AL	40 100 23	7 0 0	(0 0)	30	11 5	10	0	16	0 4 0		0 0 .00 1	.230	.300	.300
Toronto		8 13 4	0 0 0	(0 0)	4	1 2	1	0	2	0 0 0		0 0 .00 1	.308	.357	.308
9 ML YEARS		535 1367 349	65 11 37	(21 16)	547	196 198	165	10	219	11 16 19		30 12 .71 30	.255	.336	.400

John Wasdin

Pitches: Right **Bats:** Right **Pos:** RP-39; SP-8 **Ht:** 6'2" **Wt:** 193 **Born:** 8/5/72 **Age:** 26

		HOW MUCH HE PITCHED				WHAT HE GAVE UP				THE RESULTS					
Year Team	Lg	G GS CG GF	IP	BFP	H R ER	HR SH SF HB	TBB IBB	SO	WP Bk	W L	Pct.	ShO	Sv-Op	Hld	ERA
1998 Pawtucket *	AAA	4 2 0 2	12	52	11 6 4	0 1 0	5 0	10	1 0	1 0	1.000	0	0--	—	3.00
1995 Oakland	AL	5 2 0 3	17.1	69	14 9 9	4 0 0 1	3 0	6	0 0	1 1	.500	0	0-0	0	4.67
1996 Oakland	AL	25 21 1 2	131.1	575	145 96 87	24 3 6 4	50 5	75	2 2	8 7	.533	0	0-1	0	5.96
1997 Boston	AL	53 7 0 10	124.2	534	121 68 61	18 4 7 3	38 4	84	4 0	4 6	.400	0	0-2	11	4.40
1998 Boston	AL	47 8 0 13	96	424	111 57 56	14 3 6 2	27 8	59	1 0	6 4	.600	0	0-1	4	5.25
4 ML YEARS		130 38 1 28	369.1	1602	391 230 213	60 10 19 10	118 17	224	7 2	19 18	.514	0	0-4	15	5.19

Jarrod Washburn

Pitches: Left **Bats:** Left **Pos:** SP-11; RP-4 **Ht:** 6'1" **Wt:** 200 **Born:** 8/13/74 **Age:** 24

		HOW MUCH HE PITCHED				WHAT HE GAVE UP				THE RESULTS					
Year Team	Lg	G GS CG GF	IP	BFP	H R ER	HR SH SF HB	TBB IBB	SO	WP Bk	W L	Pct.	ShO	Sv-Op	Hld	ERA
1995 Boise	A-	8 8 0 0	46	185	35 17 17	1 0 1 2	14 0	54	1 0	3 2	.600	0	0--	—	3.33
Cedar Rapds	A	3 3 0 0	18.1	79	17 7 7	1 2 1 3	7 0	20	1 0	1 0	1.000	0	0--	—	3.44
1996 Lk Elsinore	A+	14 14 3 0	92.2	384	79 38 34	5 2 2 2	33 0	93	8 0	6 3	.667	0	0--	—	3.30
Vancouver	AAA	2 2 0 0	8.1	48	12 16 10	1 0 0 0	12 0	5	1 0	0 2	.000	0	0--	—	10.80
Midland	AA	13 13 1 0	88	361	77 44 43	11 1 2 5	25 0	58	1 1	5 6	.455	0	0--	—	4.40
1997 Midland	AA	29 29 5 0	189.1	818	211 115 101	23 7 4 9	65 0	146	9 1	15 12	.556	1	0--	—	4.80
Vancouver	AAA	1 1 0 0	5	21	4 2 2	0 0 0 0	2 0	6	2 0	0 0	.000	0	0--	—	3.60
1998 Midland	AA	1 1 0 0	8.2	40	13 8 6	2 1 0 0	2 0	8	0 0	0 1	.000	0	0--	—	6.23
Vancouver	AAA	14 14 2 0	91.2	402	91 44 44	7 5 1 5	43 0	66	5 0	4 5	.444	0	0--	—	4.32
1998 Anaheim	AL	15 11 0 0	74	317	70 40 38	11 2 3 3	27 1	48	0 0	6 3	.667	0	0-0	1	4.62

Pat Watkins

Bats: R **Throws:** R **Pos:** CF-39; RF-28; PH/PR-18; LF-13   **Ht:** 6'2"   **Wt:** 195   **Born:** 9/2/72   **Age:** 26

Year Team	Lg	G	AB	H	2B	3B	HR	(Hm	Rd)	TB	R	RBI	TBB	IBB	SO	HBP	SH	SF	SB	CS	SB%	GDP	Avg	OBP	SLG
1993 Billings	R+	66	235	63	10	3	6	—	—	97	46	30	22	0	44	2	1	1	15	4	.79	4	.268	.335	.413
1994 Winston-Sal	A+	132	524	152	24	5	27	—	—	267	107	83	62	3	84	7	1	6	31	13	.70	8	.290	.369	.510
1995 Winston-Sal	A+	27	107	22	3	1	4	—	—	39	14	13	10	0	24	0	1	2	1	0	1.00	5	.206	.269	.364
Chattanooga	AA	105	358	104	26	2	12	—	—	170	57	57	33	4	53	3	0	4	5	5	.50	7	.291	.352	.475
1996 Chattanooga	AA	127	492	136	31	2	8	—	—	195	63	59	30	0	64	7	2	4	15	11	.58	17	.276	.325	.396
1997 Chattanooga	AA	46	177	62	15	1	7	—	—	100	35	30	15	1	16	2	0	1	9	3	.75	3	.350	.405	.565
Indianapols	AAA	84	325	91	14	7	9	—	—	146	46	35	24	2	55	1	3	1	13	9	.59	10	.280	.330	.449
1998 Indianapols	AAA	44	188	71	12	1	3	—	—	94	37	24	15	0	26	1	1	1	8	3	.73	5	.378	.424	.500
1997 Cincinnati	NL	17	29	6	2	0	0	(0	0)	8	2	0	0	0	5	0	1	0	1	0	1.00	1	.207	.207	.276
1998 Cincinnati	NL	83	147	39	8	1	2	(1	1)	55	11	15	8	0	26	1	2	4	1	3	.25	3	.265	.300	.374
2 ML YEARS		100	176	45	10	1	2	(1	1)	63	13	15	8	0	31	1	3	4	2	3	.40	4	.256	.286	.358

Allen Watson

Pitches: Left   **Bats:** Left   **Pos:** SP-14; RP-14   **Ht:** 6'3"   **Wt:** 212   **Born:** 11/18/70   **Age:** 28

Year Team	Lg	G	GS	CG	GF	IP	BFP	H	R	ER	HR	SH	SF	HB	TBB	IBB	SO	WP	Bk	W	L	Pct.	ShO	Sv-Op	Hld	ERA
1998 Midland *	AA	1	1	0	0	4	19	6	2	1	0	0	1	1	1	0	3	1	0	0	0	.000	0	0--	—	2.25
Lk Elsinore *	A+	1	1	0	0	5	17	3	0	0	0	0	0	0	1	0	6	0	0	1	0	1.000	0	0--	—	0.00
Vancouver *	AAA	1	1	0	0	6	26	6	3	3	1	0	0	0	2	0	8	1	0	0	0	.000	0	0--	—	4.50
1993 St. Louis	NL	16	15	0	1	86	373	90	53	44	11	6	4	3	28	2	49	2	1	6	7	.462	0	0-1	0	4.60
1994 St. Louis	NL	22	22	0	0	115.2	523	130	73	71	15	7	0	8	53	0	74	2	2	6	5	.545	0	0-0	0	5.52
1995 St. Louis	NL	21	19	0	1	114.1	491	126	68	63	17	2	1	5	41	0	49	2	2	7	9	.438	0	0-0	0	4.96
1996 San Francisco	NL	29	29	2	0	185.2	793	189	105	95	28	18	9	5	69	2	128	9	2	8	12	.400	0	0-0	0	4.61
1997 Anaheim	AL	35	34	0	0	199	880	220	121	109	37	5	6	8	73	0	141	8	2	12	12	.500	0	0-0	0	4.93
1998 Anaheim	AL	28	14	1	4	92.1	421	122	67	62	12	0	6	3	34	0	64	6	1	6	7	.462	0	0-0	0	6.04
6 ML YEARS		151	133	3	6	793	3481	877	487	444	120	38	26	32	298	4	505	29	10	45	52	.464	0	0-1	0	5.04

Dave Weathers

Pitches: Right   **Bats:** Right   **Pos:** RP-35; SP-9   **Ht:** 6'3"   **Wt:** 220   **Born:** 9/25/69   **Age:** 29

Year Team	Lg	G	GS	CG	GF	IP	BFP	H	R	ER	HR	SH	SF	HB	TBB	IBB	SO	WP	Bk	W	L	Pct.	ShO	Sv-Op	Hld	ERA
1991 Toronto	AL	15	0	0	4	14.2	79	15	9	8	1	2	1	2	17	3	13	0	0	1	0	1.000	0	0-0	1	4.91
1992 Toronto	AL	2	0	0	0	3.1	15	5	3	3	1	0	0	0	2	0	3	0	0	0	0	.000	0	0-0	0	8.10
1993 Florida	NL	14	6	0	2	45.2	202	57	26	26	3	2	0	1	13	1	34	0	4	2	3	.400	0	0-0	0	5.12
1994 Florida	NL	24	24	0	0	135	621	166	87	79	13	12	4	4	59	9	72	7	1	8	12	.400	0	0-0	0	5.27
1995 Florida	NL	28	15	0	0	90.1	419	104	68	60	8	7	3	5	52	3	60	3	0	4	5	.444	0	0-0	1	5.98
1996 Fla-NYA		42	12	0	9	88.2	409	108	60	54	8	5	2	6	42	5	53	3	0	2	4	.333	0	0-0	3	5.48
1997 NYA-Cle	AL	19	1	0	5	25.2	126	38	24	24	3	2	1	1	15	0	18	3	0	1	3	.250	0	0-1	0	8.42
1998 Cin-Mil	NL	44	9	0	9	110	492	130	69	60	6	6	2	3	41	3	94	7	2	6	5	.545	0	0-1	3	4.91
1996 Florida		31	8	0	8	71.1	319	85	41	36	7	5	1	4	28	4	40	2	0	2	2	.500	0	0-0	3	4.54
New York	AL	11	4	0	1	17.1	90	23	19	18	1	0	1	2	14	1	13	1	0	0	2	.000	0	0-0	0	9.35
1997 New York	AL	10	0	0	3	9	47	15	10	10	1	0	0	0	7	0	4	2	0	0	1	.000	0	0-1	0	10.00
Cleveland	AL	9	1	0	2	16.2	79	23	14	14	2	2	1	1	8	0	14	1	0	1	2	.333	0	0-0	0	7.56
1998 Cincinnati	NL	16	9	0	0	62.1	294	86	47	43	3	4	1	1	27	2	51	5	1	2	4	.333	0	0-0	0	6.21
Milwaukee	NL	28	0	0	9	47.2	198	44	22	17	3	2	1	2	14	1	43	2	1	4	1	.800	0	0-1	3	3.21
8 ML YEARS		188	67	0	29	513.1	2363	623	346	314	43	36	13	22	241	24	347	29	3	24	32	.429	0	0-2	8	5.51

Eric Weaver

Pitches: Right   **Bats:** Right   **Pos:** RP-7   **Ht:** 6'5"   **Wt:** 230   **Born:** 8/4/73   **Age:** 25

Year Team	Lg	G	GS	CG	GF	IP	BFP	H	R	ER	HR	SH	SF	HB	TBB	IBB	SO	WP	Bk	W	L	Pct.	ShO	Sv-Op	Hld	ERA
1992 Vero Beach	A+	19	18	1	0	89.2	394	73	52	41	7	5	6	1	57	0	73	17	2	4	11	.267	0	0--	—	4.12
1993 Bakersfield	A+	28	27	0	0	157.2	703	135	89	75	10	2	9	2	118	2	110	16	0	6	11	.353	0	0--	—	4.28
1994 Vero Beach	A+	7	7	0	0	24	109	28	20	18	3	0	0	1	9	1	22	1	0	1	3	.250	0	0--	—	6.75
1995 San Antonio	AA	27	26	1	1	141.2	635	147	83	64	10	9	7	7	72	1	105	8	2	8	11	.421	0	0--	—	4.07
1996 San Antonio	AA	18	18	1	0	122.2	509	106	51	45	6	7	2	3	44	0	69	2	1	10	5	.667	1	0--	—	3.30
Albuquerque	AAA	13	8	0	0	46.2	225	63	39	28	5	2	1	3	22	0	38	3	0	1	4	.200	0	0--	—	5.40
1997 San Antonio	AA	13	13	2	0	84.2	363	80	43	34	4	1	4	5	38	0	60	2	0	7	2	.778	1	0--	—	3.61
Albuquerque	AAA	21	8	0	5	68.2	335	101	53	49	6	3	4	2	38	1	54	4	0	3	3	.000	0	0--	—	6.42
1998 Albuquerque	AAA	46	0	0	26	61.2	277	65	41	38	7	2	2	3	32	2	63	2	0	2	5	.286	0	3--	—	5.55
1998 Los Angeles	NL	7	0	0	4	9.2	35	5	1	1	1	1	0	0	6	0	5	0	0	2	0	1.000	0	0-0	0	0.93

Neil Weber

Pitches: Left   **Bats:** Left   **Pos:** RP-4   **Ht:** 6'5"   **Wt:** 215   **Born:** 12/6/72   **Age:** 26

Year Team	Lg	G	GS	CG	GF	IP	BFP	H	R	ER	HR	SH	SF	HB	TBB	IBB	SO	WP	Bk	W	L	Pct.	ShO	Sv-Op	Hld	ERA
1993 Jamestown	A-	16	16	2	0	94.1	398	84	46	29	3	0	4	4	36	0	80	3	3	6	5	.545	1	0--	—	2.77
1994 Wst Plm Bch	A+	25	24	1	0	135	566	113	58	48	8	4	4	4	62	0	134	7	3	9	7	.563	0	0--	—	3.20
1995 Harrisburg	AA	28	28	0	0	152.2	696	157	98	85	16	11	7	8	90	1	119	7	1	6	11	.353	0	0--	—	5.01
1996 Harrisburg	AA	18	18	0	0	107	440	90	37	36	8	3	3	5	44	0	74	5	0	7	4	.636	0	0--	—	3.03

236

Year Team	Lg	G GS CG GF	IP	BFP	H	R	ER	HR	SH	SF	HB	TBB	IBB	SO	WP	Bk	W	L	Pct.	ShO	Sv-Op	Hld	ERA
1997 Ottawa	AAA	9 9 0 0	39.2	204	46	46	35	7	2	1	2	40	0	27	2	0	2	5	.286	0	0- -	—	7.94
Harrisburg	AA	18 18 1 0	112.2	477	93	56	48	17	6	1	8	51	1	121	6	0	7	6	.538	1	0- -	—	3.83
1998 Tucson	AAA	46 11 1 6	112.2	508	116	82	64	17	5	3	4	55	0	79	12	1	5	9	.357	0	1- -	—	5.11
1998 Arizona	NL	4 0 0 0	2.1	15	5	3	3	0	0	0	0	3	0	4	0	0	0	0	.000	0	0-0	0	11.57

Lenny Webster

Bats: Right **Throws:** Right **Pos:** C-102; PH/PR-12; DH-4   **Ht:** 5'9" **Wt:** 200 **Born:** 2/10/65 **Age:** 34

Year Team	Lg	G	AB	H	2B	3B	HR	(Hm	Rd)	TB	R	RBI	TBB	IBB	SO	HBP	SH	SF	SB	CS	SB%	GDP	Avg	OBP	SLG
1989 Minnesota	AL	14	20	6	2	0	0	(0	0)	8	3	1	3	0	2	0	0	0	0	0	.00	0	.300	.391	.400
1990 Minnesota	AL	2	6	2	1	0	0	(0	0)	3	1	0	1	0	1	0	0	0	0	0	.00	0	.333	.429	.500
1991 Minnesota	AL	18	34	10	1	0	3	(1	2)	20	7	8	6	0	10	0	0	1	0	0	.00	2	.294	.390	.588
1992 Minnesota	AL	53	118	33	10	1	1	(1	0)	48	10	13	9	0	11	0	2	0	0	2	.00	3	.280	.331	.407
1993 Minnesota	AL	49	106	21	2	0	1	(1	0)	26	14	8	11	1	8	0	0	0	1	0	1.00	6	.198	.274	.245
1994 Montreal	NL	57	143	39	10	0	5	(2	3)	64	13	23	16	1	24	6	1	0	0	0	.00	7	.273	.370	.448
1995 Philadelphia	NL	49	150	40	9	0	4	(1	3)	61	18	14	16	0	27	0	1	0	0	0	.00	6	.267	.337	.407
1996 Montreal	NL	78	174	40	10	0	2	(1	1)	56	18	17	25	2	21	2	1	1	0	0	.00	10	.230	.332	.322
1997 Baltimore	AL	59	259	66	8	1	7	(3	4)	97	29	37	22	0	46	2	3	1	0	1	.00	10	.255	.317	.375
1998 Baltimore	AL	108	309	88	16	0	10	(6	4)	134	37	46	15	0	38	0	3	1	0	0	.00	10	.285	.317	.434
10 ML YEARS		526	1319	345	69	2	33	(16	17)	517	150	167	124	4	188	10	11	4	1	3	.25	47	.262	.329	.392

John Wehner

Bats: R **Throws:** R **Pos:** PH/PR-27; LF-12; RF-11; 3B-8; CF-2   **Ht:** 6'3" **Wt:** 206 **Born:** 6/29/67 **Age:** 32

Year Team	Lg	G	AB	H	2B	3B	HR	(Hm	Rd)	TB	R	RBI	TBB	IBB	SO	HBP	SH	SF	SB	CS	SB%	GDP	Avg	OBP	SLG
1998 Charlotte *	AAA	30	83	27	1	0	3	—	—	37	12	15	4	0	16	2	1	0	5	1	.83	5	.325	.371	.446
1991 Pittsburgh	NL	37	106	36	7	0	0	(0	0)	43	15	7	7	0	17	0	0	0	3	0	1.00	4	.340	.381	.406
1992 Pittsburgh	NL	55	123	22	6	0	0	(0	0)	28	11	4	12	2	22	0	2	0	3	0	1.00	4	.179	.252	.228
1993 Pittsburgh	NL	29	35	5	0	0	0	(0	0)	5	3	0	6	1	10	0	2	0	0	0	.00	0	.143	.268	.143
1994 Pittsburgh	NL	2	4	1	1	0	0	(0	0)	2	1	3	0	0	1	0	0	0	0	0	.00	0	.250	.250	.500
1995 Pittsburgh	NL	52	107	33	0	3	0	(0	0)	39	13	5	10	1	17	0	4	2	3	1	.75	2	.308	.361	.364
1996 Pittsburgh	NL	86	139	36	9	1	2	(1	1)	53	19	13	8	1	22	0	2	0	1	5	.17	3	.259	.299	.381
1997 Florida	NL	44	36	10	2	0	0	(0	0)	12	8	2	2	0	5	1	1	0	1	0	1.00	1	.278	.333	.333
1998 Florida	NL	53	88	20	2	0	0	(0	0)	22	10	5	7	0	12	0	0	1	1	0	1.00	3	.227	.281	.250
8 ML YEARS		358	638	163	27	4	2	(1	1)	204	80	39	52	5	106	1	11	3	12	6	.67	14	.255	.311	.320

Walt Weiss

Bats: Both **Throws:** Right **Pos:** SS-96   **Ht:** 6'0" **Wt:** 175 **Born:** 11/28/63 **Age:** 35

Year Team	Lg	G	AB	H	2B	3B	HR	(Hm	Rd)	TB	R	RBI	TBB	IBB	SO	HBP	SH	SF	SB	CS	SB%	GDP	Avg	OBP	SLG
1987 Oakland	AL	16	26	12	4	0	0	(0	0)	16	3	1	2	0	2	0	1	0	1	2	.33	0	.462	.500	.615
1988 Oakland	AL	147	452	113	17	3	3	(0	3)	145	44	39	35	1	56	9	8	7	4	4	.50	9	.250	.312	.321
1989 Oakland	AL	84	236	55	11	0	3	(2	1)	75	30	21	21	0	39	1	5	0	6	1	.86	5	.233	.298	.318
1990 Oakland	AL	138	445	118	17	1	2	(1	1)	143	50	35	46	5	53	4	6	4	9	3	.75	7	.265	.337	.321
1991 Oakland	AL	40	133	30	6	1	0	(0	0)	38	15	13	12	0	14	0	1	2	6	0	1.00	3	.226	.286	.286
1992 Oakland	AL	103	316	67	5	2	0	(0	0)	76	36	21	43	1	39	1	11	4	6	3	.67	10	.212	.305	.241
1993 Florida	NL	158	500	133	14	2	1	(0	1)	154	50	39	79	13	73	3	5	4	7	3	.70	5	.266	.367	.308
1994 Colorado	NL	110	423	106	11	4	1	(1	0)	128	58	32	56	0	58	0	4	3	12	7	.63	6	.251	.336	.303
1995 Colorado	NL	137	427	111	17	3	1	(0	1)	137	65	25	98	8	57	5	6	1	15	3	.83	5	.260	.403	.321
1996 Colorado	NL	155	517	146	20	2	8	(5	3)	194	89	48	80	5	78	6	14	6	10	2	.83	9	.282	.381	.375
1997 Colorado	NL	121	393	106	23	5	4	(2	2)	151	52	38	66	3	56	2	7	1	5	2	.71	7	.270	.377	.384
1998 Atlanta	NL	96	347	97	18	2	0	(0	0)	119	64	27	59	0	53	3	12	3	7	1	.88	4	.280	.386	.343
12 ML YEARS		1305	4215	1094	163	25	23	(11	12)	1376	556	339	597	36	578	34	80	35	88	31	.74	72	.260	.353	.326

Mike Welch

Pitches: Right **Bats:** Left **Pos:** RP-8; SP-2   **Ht:** 6'2" **Wt:** 210 **Born:** 8/25/72 **Age:** 26

Year Team	Lg	G GS CG GF	IP	BFP	H	R	ER	HR	SH	SF	HB	TBB	IBB	SO	WP	Bk	W	L	Pct.	ShO	Sv-Op	Hld	ERA
1993 Pittsfield	A-	17 0 0 14	31	126	23	9	5	0	2	4	0	6	1	34	3	1	3	1	.750	0	9- -	—	1.45
1994 Capital City	A	24 24 5 0	159.2	667	151	81	64	14	7	5	11	33	0	127	5	0	7	11	.389	2	0- -	—	3.61
1995 St. Lucie	A+	44 6 0 33	70	322	96	50	42	7	4	3	6	18	4	51	4	0	4	4	.500	0	15- -	—	5.40
Binghamton	AA	1 0 0 1	1	3	0	0	0	0	0	0	0	0	0	2	0	0	0	0	.000	0	0- -	—	0.00
1996 Binghamton	AA	46 0 0 37	51	216	55	29	26	4	3	1	3	10	0	53	0	0	4	2	.667	0	27- -	—	4.59
Norfolk	AAA	10 0 0 5	8.2	36	8	4	4	0	0	0	0	2	0	6	0	0	1	0	1.000	0	2- -	—	4.15
1997 Norfolk	AAA	46 0 0 38	51.2	216	53	21	21	6	2	2	1	16	2	35	0	0	2	2	.500	0	20- -	—	3.66
1998 Scranton-WB	AAA	31 6 0 9	75.1	342	98	56	50	5	8	3	6	17	6	32	1	0	3	4	.429	0	2- -	—	5.97
1998 Philadelphia	NL	10 2 0 0	20.2	94	26	19	19	7	1	0	2	7	0	15	0	0	0	2	.000	0	0-0	0	8.27

Bob Wells

Pitches: Right **Bats:** Right **Pos:** RP-30   **Ht:** 6'0" **Wt:** 190 **Born:** 11/1/66 **Age:** 32

Year Team	Lg	G	GS	CG	GF	IP	BFP	H	R	ER	HR	SH	SF	HB	TBB	IBB	SO	WP	Bk	W	L	Pct.	ShO	Sv-Op	Hld	ERA
1998 Wisconsin *	A	1	1	0	0	3	13	4	2	1	1	0	0	0	0	0	2	1	0	0	1	.000	0	0- --	---	3.00
1994 Phi-Sea		7	0	0	2	9	38	8	2	2	0	0	0	1	4	0	6	0	0	2	0	1.000	0	0-0	0	2.00
1995 Seattle	AL	30	4	0	3	76.2	358	88	51	49	11	1	5	3	39	3	38	1	0	4	3	.571	0	0-1	0	5.75
1996 Seattle	AL	36	16	1	6	130.2	574	141	78	77	25	3	4	6	46	5	94	0	0	12	7	.632	1	0-0	1	5.30
1997 Seattle	AL	46	1	0	19	67.1	304	88	49	43	11	1	2	3	18	1	51	1	0	2	0	1.000	0	2-4	5	5.75
1998 Seattle	AL	30	0	0	4	51.2	228	54	38	35	12	2	1	2	16	1	29	1	0	2	2	.500	0	0-1	1	6.10
1994 Philadelphia	NL	6	0	0	2	5	21	4	1	1	0	0	0	1	3	0	3	0	0	1	0	1.000	0	0-0	0	1.80
Seattle	AL	1	0	0	0	4	17	4	1	1	0	0	0	0	1	0	3	0	0	1	0	1.000	0	0-0	0	2.25
5 ML YEARS		149	21	1	34	335.1	1502	379	218	206	59	7	12	15	123	10	218	3	0	22	12	.647	1	2-6	7	5.53

David Wells

Pitches: Left **Bats:** Left **Pos:** SP-30   **Ht:** 6'4" **Wt:** 225 **Born:** 5/20/63 **Age:** 36

Year Team	Lg	G	GS	CG	GF	IP	BFP	H	R	ER	HR	SH	SF	HB	TBB	IBB	SO	WP	Bk	W	L	Pct.	ShO	Sv-Op	Hld	ERA
1987 Toronto	AL	18	2	0	6	29.1	132	37	14	13	0	1	0	0	12	0	32	4	0	4	3	.571	0	1-2	3	3.99
1988 Toronto	AL	41	0	0	19	64.1	279	65	36	33	12	2	2	2	31	9	56	6	2	3	5	.375	0	4-6	9	4.62
1989 Toronto	AL	54	0	0	19	86.1	352	66	25	23	5	3	2	0	28	7	78	6	3	7	4	.636	0	2-9	8	2.40
1990 Toronto	AL	43	25	0	8	189	759	165	72	66	14	9	2	2	45	3	115	7	1	11	6	.647	0	3-3	3	3.14
1991 Toronto	AL	40	28	2	3	198.1	811	188	88	82	24	6	6	2	49	1	106	10	3	15	10	.600	0	1-2	3	3.72
1992 Toronto	AL	41	14	0	14	120	529	138	84	72	16	3	4	8	36	6	62	3	1	7	9	.438	0	2-4	3	5.40
1993 Detroit	AL	32	30	0	0	187	776	183	93	87	26	3	3	7	42	6	139	13	0	11	9	.550	0	0-0	1	4.19
1994 Detroit	AL	16	16	5	0	111.1	464	113	54	49	13	3	1	2	24	0	71	5	0	5	7	.417	1	0-0	0	3.96
1995 Det-Cin		29	29	6	0	203	839	194	88	73	23	7	3	2	53	9	133	7	2	16	8	.667	0	0-0	0	3.24
1996 Baltimore	AL	34	34	3	0	224.1	946	247	132	128	32	8	14	7	51	7	130	4	2	11	14	.440	0	0-0	0	5.14
1997 New York	AL	32	32	5	0	218	922	239	109	102	24	7	3	6	45	0	156	8	0	16	10	.615	2	0-0	0	4.21
1998 New York	AL	30	30	8	0	214.1	851	195	86	83	29	2	2	1	29	0	163	2	0	18	4	.818	5	0-0	0	3.49
1995 Detroit	AL	18	18	3	0	130.1	539	120	54	44	17	3	2	2	37	5	83	6	1	10	3	.769	0	0-0	0	3.04
Cincinnati	NL	11	11	3	0	72.2	300	74	34	29	6	4	1	0	16	4	50	1	1	6	5	.545	0	0-0	0	3.59
12 ML YEARS		410	240	29	65	1845.1	7660	1830	881	811	218	54	42	39	445	54	1241	75	14	124	89	.582	8	13-26	30	3.96

Turk Wendell

Pitches: Right **Bats:** Left **Pos:** RP-66   **Ht:** 6'2" **Wt:** 205 **Born:** 5/19/67 **Age:** 32

Year Team	Lg	G	GS	CG	GF	IP	BFP	H	R	ER	HR	SH	SF	HB	TBB	IBB	SO	WP	Bk	W	L	Pct.	ShO	Sv-Op	Hld	ERA
1993 Chicago	NL	7	4	0	1	22.2	98	24	13	11	0	2	0	0	8	1	15	1	1	1	2	.333	0	0-0	4	4.37
1994 Chicago	NL	6	2	0	1	14.1	76	22	20	19	3	2	1	0	10	1	9	1	0	0	1	.000	0	0-0	0	11.93
1995 Chicago	NL	43	0	0	17	60.1	270	71	35	33	11	3	3	2	24	4	50	1	0	3	1	.750	0	0-0	3	4.92
1996 Chicago	NL	70	0	0	49	79.1	339	58	26	25	8	3	1	3	44	4	75	3	2	4	5	.444	0	18-21	6	2.84
1997 ChN-NYN	NL	65	0	0	21	76.1	345	68	42	37	7	4	3	2	53	6	64	4	0	3	5	.375	0	5-7	2	4.36
1998 New York	NL	66	0	0	17	76.2	319	62	25	25	4	2	1	2	33	9	58	1	0	5	1	.833	0	4-8	11	2.93
1997 Chicago	NL	52	0	0	18	60	269	53	32	28	4	3	3	1	39	5	54	4	0	3	5	.375	0	4-5	2	4.20
New York	NL	13	0	0	3	16.1	76	15	10	9	3	1	0	1	14	1	10	0	0	0	0	.000	0	1-2	0	4.96
6 ML YEARS		257	6	0	106	329.2	1447	305	161	150	33	16	9	9	172	25	271	11	3	16	15	.516	0	27-36	22	4.10

Don Wengert

Pitches: Right **Bats:** Right **Pos:** RP-25; SP-6   **Ht:** 6'2" **Wt:** 212 **Born:** 11/6/69 **Age:** 29

Year Team	Lg	G	GS	CG	GF	IP	BFP	H	R	ER	HR	SH	SF	HB	TBB	IBB	SO	WP	Bk	W	L	Pct.	ShO	Sv-Op	Hld	ERA
1998 Iowa *	AAA	9	9	1	0	53	227	58	30	27	2	3	1	1	14	0	48	1	1	3	1	.750	0	0- --	---	4.58
1995 Oakland	AL	19	0	0	10	29.2	129	30	14	11	3	1	1	1	12	2	16	1	0	1	1	.500	0	0-0	1	3.34
1996 Oakland	AL	36	25	1	2	161.1	725	200	102	100	29	3	5	6	60	5	75	4	0	7	11	.389	1	0-0	2	5.58
1997 Oakland	AL	49	12	1	16	134	612	177	96	90	21	5	7	6	41	4	68	2	0	5	11	.313	0	2-3	0	6.04
1998 SD-ChN	NL	31	6	0	9	63.1	288	76	38	37	10	1	0	3	28	0	46	1	0	1	5	.167	0	1-1	0	5.26
1998 San Diego	NL	10	0	0	3	13.2	64	21	9	9	2	0	0	0	5	0	5	0	0	0	0	.000	0	1-1	0	5.93
Chicago	NL	21	6	0	6	49.2	224	55	29	28	8	1	0	3	23	0	41	1	0	1	5	.167	0	0-0	0	5.07
4 ML YEARS		135	43	2	37	388.1	1754	483	250	238	63	10	13	18	141	11	205	8	0	14	28	.333	1	3-4	3	5.52

David West

Pitches: Left **Bats:** Left **Pos:** RP-6   **Ht:** 6'6" **Wt:** 247 **Born:** 9/1/64 **Age:** 34

Year Team	Lg	G	GS	CG	GF	IP	BFP	H	R	ER	HR	SH	SF	HB	TBB	IBB	SO	WP	Bk	W	L	Pct.	ShO	Sv-Op	Hld	ERA
1998 New Orleans *	AAA	19	2	0	3	31.2	136	26	11	9	2	0	0	1	22	0	33	3	0	1	1	.500	0	0- --	---	2.56
Pawtucket *	AAA	17	0	0	11	24	106	19	4	3	1	0	0	0	12	1	23	1	0	5	0	1.000	0	3- --	---	1.13
1988 New York	NL	2	1	0	0	6	25	6	2	2	0	0	0	0	3	0	3	0	2	1	0	1.000	0	0-0	0	3.00
1989 NYN-Min		21	7	0	4	63.2	294	73	49	48	9	2	3	3	33	3	50	2	0	3	4	.429	0	0-1	2	6.79
1990 Minnesota	AL	29	27	2	0	146.1	646	142	88	83	21	6	4	4	78	1	92	4	1	7	9	.438	0	0-0	0	5.10
1991 Minnesota	AL	15	12	0	0	71.1	305	66	37	36	13	2	3	1	28	0	52	3	0	4	4	.500	0	0-0	0	4.54
1992 Minnesota	AL	9	3	0	1	28.1	139	32	24	22	3	0	2	1	20	0	19	2	0	1	3	.250	0	0-0	0	6.99
1993 Philadelphia	NL	76	0	0	27	86.1	375	60	37	28	6	8	2	5	51	4	87	3	0	6	4	.600	0	3-9	21	2.92
1994 Philadelphia	NL	31	14	0	7	99	429	74	44	39	7	4	2	1	61	2	83	9	0	4	10	.286	0	0-2	3	3.55

Year Team	Lg	G	GS	CG	GF	IP	BFP	H	R	ER	HR	SH	SF	HB	TBB	IBB	SO	WP	Bk	W	L	Pct.	ShO	Sv-Op	Hld	ERA
1995 Philadelphia	NL	8	8	0	0	38	163	34	17	16	5	2	0	1	19	0	25	1	0	3	2	.600	0	0-0	0	3.79
1996 Philadelphia	NL	7	6	0	0	28.1	126	31	17	15	0	1	0	0	11	0	22	1	1	2	2	.500	0	0-0	0	4.76
1998 Boston	AL	6	0	0	0	2	20	7	6	6	1	0	0	0	7	0	4	1	0	0	0	.000	0	0-0	1	27.00
1989 New York	NL	11	2	0	0	24.1	112	25	20	20	4	0	1	1	14	2	19	1	0	0	2	.000	0	0-0	2	7.40
Minnesota	AL	10	5	0	4	39.1	182	48	29	28	5	2	2	2	19	1	31	1	0	3	2	.600	0	0-1	0	6.41
10 ML YEARS		204	78	2	39	569.1	2522	525	321	295	65	25	16	16	311	10	437	26	4	31	38	.449	0	3-12	27	4.66

John Wetteland

Pitches: Right **Bats:** Right **Pos:** RP-63 **Ht:** 6'2" **Wt:** 215 **Born:** 8/21/66 **Age:** 32

Year Team	Lg	G	GS	CG	GF	IP	BFP	H	R	ER	HR	SH	SF	HB	TBB	IBB	SO	WP	Bk	W	L	Pct.	ShO	Sv-Op	Hld	ERA
1989 Los Angeles	NL	31	12	0	7	102.2	411	81	46	43	8	4	2	0	34	4	96	16	1	5	8	.385	0	1-1	1	3.77
1990 Los Angeles	NL	22	5	0	7	43	190	44	28	23	6	1	1	4	17	3	36	8	0	2	4	.333	0	0-1	0	4.81
1991 Los Angeles	NL	6	0	0	3	9	36	5	2	0	0	0	1	1	3	0	9	1	0	1	0	1.000	0	0-0	0	0.00
1992 Montreal	NL	67	0	0	58	83.1	347	64	27	27	6	5	1	4	36	3	99	4	0	4	4	.500	0	37-46	1	2.92
1993 Montreal	NL	70	0	0	58	85.1	344	58	17	13	3	5	1	2	28	3	113	7	0	9	3	.750	0	43-49	0	1.37
1994 Montreal	NL	52	0	0	43	63.2	261	46	22	20	5	5	4	3	21	4	68	0	0	4	6	.400	0	25-35	0	2.83
1995 New York	AL	60	0	0	56	61.1	233	40	22	20	6	1	2	0	14	2	66	1	0	1	5	.167	0	31-37	0	2.93
1996 New York	AL	62	0	0	58	63.2	265	54	23	20	9	1	2	0	21	4	69	1	0	2	3	.400	0	**43-47**	0	2.83
1997 Texas	AL	61	0	0	58	65	259	43	18	14	5	1	1	0	21	3	63	1	0	7	2	.778	0	31-37	0	1.94
1998 Texas	AL	63	0	0	59	62	249	47	17	14	6	2	2	0	14	1	72	1	0	3	1	.750	0	42-47	0	2.03
10 ML YEARS		494	17	0	407	639	2595	482	222	194	54	25	17	14	209	27	691	40	1	38	36	.514	0	253-300	1	2.73

Matt Whisenant

Pitches: Left **Bats:** Right **Pos:** RP-70 **Ht:** 6'3" **Wt:** 215 **Born:** 6/8/71 **Age:** 28

Year Team	Lg	G	GS	CG	GF	IP	BFP	H	R	ER	HR	SH	SF	HB	TBB	IBB	SO	WP	Bk	W	L	Pct.	ShO	Sv-Op	Hld	ERA
1990 Princeton	R+	9	2	0	2	15	85	16	27	19	3	0	1	3	20	0	25	7	0	0	0	.000	0	0- -	—	11.40
1991 Batavia	A-	11	10	0	1	47.2	208	31	19	13	2	1	1	0	42	0	55	4	2	2	1	.667	0	0- -	—	2.45
1992 Spartanburg	A	27	27	2	0	150.2	652	117	69	54	9	5	6	10	85	0	151	10	6	11	7	.611	0	0- -	—	3.23
1993 Kane County	A	15	15	0	0	71	331	68	45	37	3	8	2	3	56	0	74	8	3	2	6	.250	0	0- -	—	4.69
1994 Brevard Cty	A+	28	26	5	0	160	679	125	71	60	7	6	7	9	82	2	103	18	1	6	9	.400	1	0- -	—	3.38
1995 Portland	AA	23	22	2	0	128.2	544	106	57	50	8	7	4	9	65	3	107	8	0	10	6	.625	0	0- -	—	3.50
1996 Charlotte	AAA	28	22	1	1	121	590	149	107	93	15	8	2	3	101	3	97	30	0	8	10	.444	0	0- -	—	6.92
1997 Brevard Cty	A+	2	1	0	0	3.1	15	3	3	3	0	0	0	0	3	0	4	1	0	0	0	.000	0	0- -	—	8.10
Charlotte	AAA	16	0	0	4	15	73	16	12	12	0	1	0	3	12	0	19	4	0	2	1	.667	0	0- -	—	7.20
1997 Fla-KC		28	0	0	5	21.2	105	19	13	11	0	1	0	3	18	0	20	3	0	1	0	1.000	0	0-0	4	4.57
1998 Kansas City	AL	70	0	0	23	60.2	267	61	37	33	3	1	5	3	33	2	45	9	0	2	1	.667	0	2-5	16	4.90
1997 Florida	NL	4	0	0	2	2.2	19	4	6	5	0	1	0	0	6	0	4	0	0	0	0	.000	0	0-0	0	16.88
Kansas City	AL	24	0	0	3	19	86	15	7	6	0	0	0	3	12	0	16	3	0	1	0	1.000	0	0-0	5	2.84
2 ML YEARS		98	0	0	28	82.1	372	80	50	44	3	2	5	6	51	2	65	12	0	3	1	.750	0	2-5	21	4.81

Derrick White

Bats: Right **Throws:** Right **Pos:** PH/PR-18; LF-3; DH-1 **Ht:** 6'1" **Wt:** 225 **Born:** 10/12/69 **Age:** 29

Year Team	Lg	G	AB	H	2B	3B	HR	(Hm	Rd)	TB	R	RBI	TBB	IBB	SO	HBP	SH	SF	SB	CS	SB%	GDP	Avg	OBP	SLG
1998 Iowa *	AAA	66	251	91	17	2	18	(—	—)	166	57	76	38	3	48	4	0	2	4	5	.44	4	.363	.451	.661
Colo Sprngs *	AAA	22	81	23	5	0	2	(—	—)	34	15	10	10	0	14	2	0	2	2	1	.67	3	.284	.368	.420
1993 Montreal	NL	17	49	11	3	0	2	(1	1)	20	6	4	2	1	12	1	0	0	2	0	1.00	1	.224	.269	.408
1996 Detroit	AL	30	18	0	2	0	0	(0	0)	11	3	2	0	0	7	0	0	0	1	0	1.00	0	.199	.199	.220
1998 ChN-Col	NL	20	19	1	0	0	1	(1	0)	4	1	2	0	0	9	0	0	0	0	0	.00	0	.053	.053	.211
1998 Chicago	NL	11	10	1	0	0	1	(1	0)	4	1	2	0	0	5	0	0	0	0	0	.00	0	.100	.100	.400
Colorado	NL	9	9	0	0	0	0	(0	0)	0	0	0	0	0	4	0	0	0	0	0	.00	0	.000	.000	.000
3 ML YEARS		76	116	21	5	0	3	(2	1)	35	10	8	2	1	28	1	0	0	3	0	1.00	2	.181	.202	.302

Devon White

Bats: Both **Throws:** Right **Pos:** CF-144; PH/PR-3 **Ht:** 6'2" **Wt:** 190 **Born:** 12/29/62 **Age:** 36

Year Team	Lg	G	AB	H	2B	3B	HR	(Hm	Rd)	TB	R	RBI	TBB	IBB	SO	HBP	SH	SF	SB	CS	SB%	GDP	Avg	OBP	SLG
1985 California	AL	21	7	1	0	0	0	(0	0)	1	7	0	1	0	3	1	0	0	3	1	.75	0	.143	.333	.143
1986 California	AL	29	51	12	1	1	1	(0	1)	18	8	3	6	0	8	0	0	0	6	0	1.00	0	.235	.316	.353
1987 California	AL	159	639	168	33	5	24	(11	13)	283	103	87	39	2	135	2	14	2	32	11	.74	8	.263	.306	.443
1988 California	AL	122	455	118	22	2	11	(3	8)	177	76	51	23	1	84	2	5	1	17	8	.68	5	.259	.297	.389
1989 California	AL	156	636	156	18	13	12	(9	3)	236	86	56	31	3	129	2	7	2	44	16	.73	12	.245	.282	.371
1990 California	AL	125	443	96	17	3	11	(5	6)	152	57	44	44	5	116	3	10	3	21	6	.78	6	.217	.290	.343
1991 Toronto	AL	156	642	181	40	10	17	(9	8)	292	110	60	55	1	135	7	5	6	33	10	.77	7	.282	.342	.455
1992 Toronto	AL	153	641	159	26	7	17	(7	10)	250	98	60	47	0	133	5	0	3	37	4	.90	9	.248	.303	.390
1993 Toronto	AL	146	598	163	42	6	15	(10	5)	262	116	52	57	1	127	7	3	3	34	4	**.89**	3	.273	.341	.438
1994 Toronto	AL	100	403	109	24	6	13	(5	8)	184	67	49	21	3	80	5	4	2	11	3	.79	4	.270	.313	.457
1995 Toronto	AL	101	427	121	23	5	10	(4	6)	184	61	53	29	1	97	5	1	3	11	2	.85	5	.283	.334	.431
1996 Florida	NL	146	552	151	37	6	17	(5	12)	251	77	84	38	6	99	8	4	9	22	6	.79	5	.274	.325	.455
1997 Florida	NL	74	265	65	13	1	6	(4	2)	98	37	34	32	2	65	7	0	4	13	5	.72	3	.245	.338	.370
1998 Arizona	NL	146	563	157	32	1	22	(11	11)	257	84	85	42	4	102	9	7	6	22	8	.73	6	.279	.335	.456
14 ML YEARS		1634	6322	1657	328	66	176	(83	93)	2645	987	718	465	29	1313	63	60	44	306	84	.78	79	.262	.317	.418

Gabe White

Pitches: Left **Bats:** Left **Pos:** RP-66; SP-3   **Ht:** 6'2" **Wt:** 200 **Born:** 11/20/71 **Age:** 27

Year Team	Lg	G	GS	CG	GF	IP	BFP	H	R	ER	HR	SH	SF	HB	TBB	IBB	SO	WP	Bk	W	L	Pct.	ShO	Sv-Op	Hld	ERA
1994 Montreal	NL	7	5	0	2	23.2	106	24	16	16	4	1	1	1	11	0	17	0	0	1	1	.500	0	1-1	0	6.08
1995 Montreal	NL	19	1	0	8	25.2	115	26	21	20	7	2	3	1	9	0	25	0	0	1	2	.333	0	0-0	1	7.01
1997 Cincinnati	NL	12	6	0	2	41	168	39	20	20	6	3	2	0	8	1	25	0	0	2	2	.500	0	1-1	3	4.39
1998 Cincinnati	NL	69	3	0	29	98.2	404	86	46	44	17	2	2	1	27	6	83	3	0	5	5	.500	0	9-13	6	4.01
4 ML YEARS		107	15	0	41	189	793	175	103	100	34	8	8	4	55	7	150	3	0	9	10	.474	0	11-15	9	4.76

Rick White

Pitches: Right **Bats:** Right **Pos:** RP-35; SP-3   **Ht:** 6'4" **Wt:** 215 **Born:** 12/23/68 **Age:** 30

Year Team	Lg	G	GS	CG	GF	IP	BFP	H	R	ER	HR	SH	SF	HB	TBB	IBB	SO	WP	Bk	W	L	Pct.	ShO	Sv-Op	Hld	ERA
1998 Durham *	AAA	9	9	1	0	53.1	230	63	29	25	3	1	1	3	11	0	31	3	0	4	2	.667	0	0--	—	4.22
1994 Pittsburgh	NL	43	5	0	23	75.1	317	79	35	32	9	7	5	3	17	3	38	2	2	4	5	.444	0	6-9	3	3.82
1995 Pittsburgh	NL	15	9	0	2	55	247	66	33	29	3	3	3	2	18	0	29	0	0	2	3	.400	0	0-0	0	4.75
1998 Tampa Bay	AL	38	3	0	12	68.2	289	66	32	29	8	0	2	2	23	2	39	3	0	2	6	.250	0	0-0	2	3.80
3 ML YEARS		96	17	0	37	199	853	211	100	90	20	10	11	10	58	5	106	7	2	8	14	.364	0	6-9	5	4.07

Rondell White

Bats: Right **Throws:** Right **Pos:** CF-82; LF-15; DH-1   **Ht:** 6'1" **Wt:** 210 **Born:** 2/23/72 **Age:** 27

Year Team	Lg	G	AB	H	2B	3B	HR	(Hm	Rd)	TB	R	RBI	TBB	IBB	SO	HBP	SH	SF	SB	CS	SB%	GDP	Avg	OBP	SLG
1993 Montreal	NL	23	73	19	3	1	2	(1	1)	30	9	15	7	0	16	0	2	1	1	2	.33	2	.260	.321	.411
1994 Montreal	NL	40	97	27	10	1	2	(1	1)	45	16	13	9	0	18	3	0	0	1	1	.50	1	.278	.358	.464
1995 Montreal	NL	130	474	140	33	4	13	(6	7)	220	87	57	41	1	87	6	0	4	25	5	.83	11	.295	.356	.464
1996 Montreal	NL	88	334	98	19	4	6	(2	4)	143	35	41	22	0	53	2	0	1	14	6	.70	11	.293	.340	.428
1997 Montreal	NL	151	562	160	29	5	28	(9	19)	283	84	82	31	3	111	10	1	4	16	8	.67	18	.270	.316	.478
1998 Montreal	NL	97	357	107	21	2	17	(9	8)	183	54	58	30	2	57	7	0	3	16	7	.70	7	.300	.363	.513
6 ML YEARS		529	1927	551	115	17	68	(28	40)	904	285	266	140	6	342	28	3	13	73	29	.72	50	.286	.341	.469

Mark Whiten

Bats: B **Throws:** R **Pos:** LF-43; CF-22; PH/PR-16; RF-13; DH-5; P-1   **Ht:** 6'3" **Wt:** 235 **Born:** 11/25/66 **Age:** 32

Year Team	Lg	G	AB	H	2B	3B	HR	(Hm	Rd)	TB	R	RBI	TBB	IBB	SO	HBP	SH	SF	SB	CS	SB%	GDP	Avg	OBP	SLG
1990 Toronto	AL	33	88	24	1	1	2	(1	1)	33	12	7	7	0	14	0	0	1	2	0	1.00	2	.273	.323	.375
1991 Tor-Cle	AL	116	407	99	18	7	9	(4	5)	158	46	45	30	2	85	2	3	0	4	3	.57	12	.243	.297	.388
1992 Cleveland	AL	148	508	129	19	4	9	(6	3)	183	73	43	72	10	102	2	3	3	16	12	.57	12	.254	.347	.360
1993 St. Louis	NL	152	562	142	13	4	25	(12	13)	238	81	99	58	9	110	2	0	4	15	8	.65	11	.253	.323	.423
1994 St. Louis	NL	92	334	98	18	2	14	(6	8)	162	57	53	37	9	75	1	0	1	10	5	.67	8	.293	.364	.485
1995 Bos-Phi	NL	92	320	77	13	1	12	(5	7)	128	51	47	39	1	86	1	0	1	8	0	1.00	9	.241	.324	.400
1996 Phi-Atl-Sea	AL	136	412	108	20	1	22	(9	13)	196	76	71	70	6	127	3	0	1	17	9	.65	12	.262	.372	.476
1997 New York	AL	69	215	57	11	0	5	(4	1)	83	34	24	30	5	47	2	1	0	4	2	.67	6	.265	.360	.386
1998 Cleveland	AL	87	226	64	14	0	6	(3	3)	96	31	29	29	0	60	3	1	0	2	1	.67	7	.283	.372	.425
1991 Toronto	AL	46	149	33	4	3	2	(2	0)	49	12	19	11	1	35	1	0	3	0	1	.00	5	.221	.274	.329
Cleveland	AL	70	258	66	14	4	7	(2	5)	109	34	26	19	1	50	1	3	0	4	2	.67	8	.256	.310	.422
1995 Boston	AL	32	108	20	3	0	1	(0	1)	26	13	10	8	0	23	0	0	1	1	0	1.00	5	.185	.239	.241
Philadelphia	NL	60	212	57	10	1	11	(5	6)	102	38	37	31	1	63	1	0	0	7	0	1.00	4	.269	.365	.481
1996 Philadelphia	NL	60	182	43	8	0	7	(4	3)	72	33	21	33	2	62	1	0	1	13	3	.81	9	.236	.356	.396
Atlanta	NL	36	90	23	5	1	3	(1	2)	39	12	17	16	0	25	0	0	1	2	5	.29	2	.256	.364	.433
Seattle	AL	40	140	42	7	0	12	(4	8)	85	31	33	21	4	40	2	0	0	2	1	.67	1	.300	.399	.607
9 ML YEARS		925	3072	798	127	20	104	(50	54)	1277	461	418	372	42	706	17	5	17	78	40	.66	80	.260	.341	.416

Matt Whiteside

Pitches: Right **Bats:** Right **Pos:** RP-10   **Ht:** 6'0" **Wt:** 205 **Born:** 8/8/67 **Age:** 31

Year Team	Lg	G	GS	CG	GF	IP	BFP	H	R	ER	HR	SH	SF	HB	TBB	IBB	SO	WP	Bk	W	L	Pct.	ShO	Sv-Op	Hld	ERA
1998 Scranton-WB *	AAA	30	1	0	20	33.1	151	47	24	24	4	1	0	0	7	0	21	0	1	1	4	.200	0	5--	—	6.48
1992 Texas	AL	20	0	0	8	28	118	26	8	6	1	0	1	0	11	2	13	2	0	1	1	.500	0	4-4	0	1.93
1993 Texas	AL	60	0	0	10	73	305	78	37	35	7	2	1	0	23	6	39	0	2	2	1	.667	0	1-5	14	4.32
1994 Texas	AL	47	0	0	16	61	272	68	40	34	6	3	2	1	28	3	37	1	0	2	2	.500	0	1-3	7	5.02
1995 Texas	AL	40	0	0	18	53	223	48	24	24	5	2	3	1	19	2	46	4	0	5	4	.556	0	3-4	7	4.08
1996 Texas	AL	14	0	0	7	32.1	148	43	24	24	8	1	2	0	11	1	15	1	0	0	1	.000	0	0-0	1	6.68
1997 Texas	AL	42	1	0	8	72.2	323	85	45	41	4	2	5	3	26	3	44	3	2	4	1	.800	0	0-4	2	5.08
1998 Philadelphia	NL	10	0	0	1	18	85	27	18	17	6	0	0	0	5	0	14	0	1	1	1	.500	0	0-0	0	8.50
7 ML YEARS		233	1	0	68	338	1474	375	196	181	37	10	14	6	123	17	208	11	5	15	11	.577	0	9-20	31	4.82

Bob Wickman

Pitches: Right **Bats:** Right **Pos:** RP-72   **Ht:** 6'1" **Wt:** 227 **Born:** 2/6/69 **Age:** 30

Year Team	Lg	G	GS	CG	GF	IP	BFP	H	R	ER	HR	SH	SF	HB	TBB	IBB	SO	WP	Bk	W	L	Pct.	ShO	Sv-Op	Hld	ERA
1992 New York	AL	8	8	0	0	50.1	213	51	25	23	2	1	3	2	20	0	21	3	0	6	1	.857	0	0-0	0	4.11
1993 New York	AL	41	19	1	9	140	629	156	82	72	13	4	1	5	69	7	70	2	0	14	4	.778	1	4-8	2	4.63
1994 New York	AL	53	0	0	19	70	286	54	26	24	3	0	5	1	27	3	56	2	0	5	4	.556	0	6-10	11	3.09
1995 New York	AL	63	1	0	14	80	347	77	38	36	6	4	1	5	33	3	51	2	0	2	4	.333	0	1-10	21	4.05
1996 NYA-Mil	AL	70	0	0	18	95.2	429	106	50	47	10	2	4	5	44	5	75	4	0	7	1	.875	0	0-4	10	4.42
1997 Milwaukee	AL	74	0	0	20	95.2	405	89	32	29	8	6	2	3	41	7	78	8	0	7	6	.538	0	1-5	28	2.73
1998 Milwaukee	NL	72	0	0	51	82.1	357	79	38	34	5	10	3	4	39	2	71	1	0	6	9	.400	0	25-32	5	3.72
1996 New York	AL	58	0	0	14	79	358	94	41	41	7	1	4	5	34	1	61	3	0	4	1	.800	0	0-3	6	4.67
Milwaukee	AL	12	0	0	4	16.2	71	12	9	6	3	1	0	0	10	2	14	1	0	3	0	1.000	0	0-1	4	3.24
7 ML YEARS		381	28	1	131	614	2666	612	291	265	47	27	19	25	273	25	422	22	0	47	29	.618	1	37-69	81	3.88

Chris Widger

Bats: Right **Throws:** Right **Pos:** C-123; PH/PR-2   **Ht:** 6'3" **Wt:** 210 **Born:** 5/21/71 **Age:** 28

						BATTING													BASERUNNING				PERCENTAGES		
Year Team	Lg	G	AB	H	2B	3B	HR	(Hm	Rd)	TB	R	RBI	TBB	IBB	SO	HBP	SH	SF	SB	CS	SB%	GDP	Avg	OBP	SLG
1995 Seattle	AL	23	45	9	0	0	1	(1	0)	12	2	2	3	0	11	0	0	1	0	0	.00	0	.200	.245	.267
1996 Seattle	AL	8	11	2	0	0	0	(0	0)	2	1	0	0	0	5	1	0	0	0	0	.00	0	.182	.250	.182
1997 Montreal	NL	91	278	65	20	3	7	(4	3)	112	30	37	22	1	59	1	2	2	2	0	1.00	7	.234	.290	.403
1998 Montreal	NL	125	417	97	18	1	15	(6	9)	162	36	53	29	2	85	0	0	2	6	1	.86	5	.233	.281	.388
4 ML YEARS		247	751	173	38	4	23	(11	12)	288	69	92	54	3	160	2	2	5	8	1	.89	12	.230	.282	.383

Marc Wilkins

Pitches: Right **Bats:** Right **Pos:** RP-16   **Ht:** 5'11" **Wt:** 207 **Born:** 10/21/70 **Age:** 28

Year Team	Lg	G	GS	CG	GF	IP	BFP	H	R	ER	HR	SH	SF	HB	TBB	IBB	SO	WP	Bk	W	L	Pct.	ShO	Sv-Op	Hld	ERA
1998 Carolina *	AA	2	0	0	1	2	7	1	1	1	1	0	0	0	0	0	4	0	0	0	0	.000	0	0- -	—	4.50
Nashville *	AAA	5	0	0	1	4.1	21	3	5	5	1	0	0	1	3	0	4	1	0	1	0	1.000	0	0- -	—	10.38
1996 Pittsburgh	NL	47	0	0	11	75	331	75	36	32	6	3	4	6	36	6	62	5	0	4	3	.571	0	1-5	4	3.84
1997 Pittsburgh	NL	70	0	0	21	75.2	310	65	33	31	7	4	0	4	33	2	47	5	1	9	5	.643	0	2-4	15	3.69
1998 Pittsburgh	NL	16	0	0	6	15.1	67	13	6	6	1	0	1	2	9	2	17	1	1	0	0	.000	0	0-1	4	3.52
3 ML YEARS		133	2	0	38	166	708	153	75	69	14	7	5	12	78	10	126	11	1	13	8	.619	0	3-10	23	3.74

Rick Wilkins

Bats: Left **Throws:** Right **Pos:** C-10; PH/PR-9; 1B-6; DH-1   **Ht:** 6'2" **Wt:** 215 **Born:** 6/4/67 **Age:** 32

						BATTING													BASERUNNING				PERCENTAGES		
Year Team	Lg	G	AB	H	2B	3B	HR	(Hm	Rd)	TB	R	RBI	TBB	IBB	SO	HBP	SH	SF	SB	CS	SB%	GDP	Avg	OBP	SLG
1998 Norfolk *	AAA	45	158	41	13	1	1	—	—	59	17	20	14	1	37	0	0	4	1	0	1.00	3	.259	.313	.373
1991 Chicago	NL	86	203	45	9	0	6	(3	3)	72	21	22	19	2	56	6	7	0	3	3	.50	3	.222	.307	.355
1992 Chicago	NL	83	244	66	9	1	8	(3	5)	101	20	22	28	7	53	0	1	1	2	0	.00	6	.270	.344	.414
1993 Chicago	NL	136	446	135	23	1	30	(10	20)	250	78	73	50	13	99	3	0	1	2	1	.67	6	.303	.376	.561
1994 Chicago	NL	100	313	71	25	2	7	(4	3)	121	44	39	40	5	86	2	1	2	4	3	.57	3	.227	.317	.387
1995 ChN-Hou	NL	65	202	41	3	0	7	(3	4)	65	30	19	46	2	61	1	0	2	0	0	.00	9	.203	.351	.322
1996 Hou-SF	NL	136	411	100	18	2	14	(6	8)	164	53	59	67	13	121	1	0	10	0	3	.00	5	.243	.344	.399
1997 SF-Sea	NL	71	202	40	6	0	7	(3	4)	67	20	27	18	0	67	0	0	0	0	0	.00	0	.198	.259	.332
1998 Sea-NYN	NL	24	56	10	1	1	1	(1	0)	16	8	5	6	0	16	0	0	1	0	0	.00	0	.179	.254	.286
1995 Chicago	NL	50	162	31	2	0	6	(3	3)	51	24	14	36	1	51	1	0	1	0	0	.00	8	.191	.340	.315
Houston	NL	15	40	10	1	0	1	(0	1)	14	6	5	10	1	10	0	0	1	0	0	.00	1	.250	.392	.350
1996 Houston	NL	84	254	54	8	2	6	(3	3)	84	34	23	46	10	81	1	0	5	0	1	.00	1	.213	.330	.331
San Francisco	NL	52	157	46	10	0	8	(3	5)	80	19	36	21	3	40	0	0	5	0	2	.00	4	.293	.366	.510
1997 San Francisco	NL	66	190	37	5	0	5	(1	5)	60	18	23	17	0	65	0	0	3	0	0	.00	0	.195	.257	.316
Seattle	AL	5	12	3	1	0	1	(1	0)	7	2	4	1	0	2	0	0	1	0	0	.00	0	.250	.286	.583
1998 Seattle	AL	19	41	8	1	1	1	(1	0)	14	5	4	4	0	14	0	0	1	0	0	.00	1	.195	.261	.341
New York	NL	5	15	2	0	0	0	(0	0)	2	3	1	2	0	2	0	0	0	0	0	.00	0	.133	.235	.133
8 ML YEARS		701	2077	508	94	7	80	(31	49)	856	274	266	274	42	559	13	9	21	9	12	.43	33	.245	.333	.412

Bernie Williams

Bats: Both **Throws:** Right **Pos:** CF-123; DH-5   **Ht:** 6'2" **Wt:** 205 **Born:** 9/13/68 **Age:** 30

						BATTING													BASERUNNING			PERCENTAGES		
Year Team	Lg	G	AB	H	2B	3B	HR	(Hm	Rd)	TB	R	RBI	TBB	IBB	SO	HBP	SH	SF	SB	CS	SB%	GDP	Avg	OBP	SLG
1998 Tampa *	A+	1	2	1	0	0	0	—	—	2	0	0	1	0	0	0	0	0	0	0	.00	0	.500	.667	1.000
Norwich *	AA	3	11	6	2	0	2	—	—	14	6	5	2	0	1	0	0	1	0	0	.00	1	.545	.571	1.273
1991 New York	AL	85	320	76	19	4	3	(1	2)	112	43	34	48	0	57	1	2	3	10	5	.67	4	.238	.336	.350
1992 New York	AL	62	261	73	14	2	5	(3	2)	106	39	26	29	1	36	1	2	0	7	6	.54	5	.280	.354	.406
1993 New York	AL	139	567	152	31	4	12	(5	7)	227	67	68	53	4	106	4	1	3	9	9	.50	17	.268	.333	.400
1994 New York	AL	108	408	118	29	1	12	(4	8)	185	80	57	61	2	54	3	1	2	16	9	.64	11	.289	.384	.453
1995 New York	AL	144	563	173	29	9	18	(7	11)	274	93	82	75	1	98	5	2	3	8	6	.57	12	.307	.392	.487
1996 New York	AL	143	551	168	26	7	29	(12	17)	295	108	102	82	8	72	0	1	7	17	4	.81	15	.305	.391	.535
1997 New York	AL	129	509	167	35	6	21	(13	8)	277	107	100	73	7	80	1	0	8	15	8	.65	10	.328	.408	.544
1998 New York	AL	128	499	169	30	5	26	(14	12)	287	101	97	74	9	81	1	0	4	15	9	.63	19	.339	.422	.575
8 ML YEARS		938	3678	1096	213	38	126	(59	67)	1763	638	566	495	32	584	16	9	30	97	56	.63	93	.298	.381	.479

Eddie Williams

Bats: Right **Throws:** Right **Pos:** PH/PR-10; 1B-7   **Ht:** 6'0" **Wt:** 210 **Born:** 11/1/64 **Age:** 34

Year Team	Lg	G	AB	H	2B	3B	HR	(Hm	Rd)	TB	R	RBI	TBB	IBB	SO	HBP	SH	SF	SB	CS	SB%	GDP	Avg	OBP	SLG
1998 Las Vegas *	AAA	90	307	103	24	0	20	—	—	187	69	77	33	7	66	6	0	7	1	1	.50	6	.336	.402	.609
1986 Cleveland	AL	5	7	1	0	0	0	(0	0)	1	2	1	0	0	3	0	0	0	0	0	.00	0	.143	.143	.143
1987 Cleveland	AL	22	64	11	4	0	1	(0	1)	18	9	4	9	0	19	1	0	1	0	0	.00	2	.172	.280	.281
1988 Cleveland	AL	10	21	4	0	0	0	(0	0)	4	3	1	0	0	3	1	1	0	0	0	.00	1	.190	.227	.190
1989 Chicago	AL	66	201	55	8	0	3	(2	1)	72	25	10	18	3	31	4	3	3	1	2	.33	4	.274	.341	.358
1990 San Diego	NL	14	42	12	3	0	3	(1	2)	24	5	4	5	2	6	0	0	0	0	1	.00	1	.286	.362	.571
1994 San Diego	NL	49	175	58	11	1	11	(5	6)	104	32	42	15	1	26	3	2	1	0	1	.00	10	.331	.392	.594
1995 San Diego	NL	97	296	77	11	1	12	(4	8)	126	35	47	23	0	47	4	0	2	0	0	.00	21	.260	.320	.426
1996 Detroit	AL	77	215	43	5	0	6	(3	3)	66	22	26	18	0	50	2	0	1	0	0	.00	8	.200	.267	.307
1997 LA-Pit	NL	38	96	23	5	0	3	(1	2)	37	12	12	11	2	25	2	1	1	1	0	1.00	2	.240	.327	.385
1998 San Diego	NL	17	28	4	0	0	0	(0	0)	4	1	3	2	0	6	0	0	1	0	0	.00	1	.143	.194	.143
1997 Los Angeles	NL	8	7	1	0	0	0	(0	0)	1	0	1	1	1	1	0	0	0	0	0	.00	0	.143	.250	.143
Pittsburgh	NL	30	89	22	5	0	3	(1	2)	36	12	11	10	1	24	2	1	1	1	0	1.00	2	.247	.333	.404
10 ML YEARS		395	1145	288	47	2	39	(16	23)	456	146	150	101	8	216	17	7	10	2	6	.25	50	.252	.319	.398

Gerald Williams

Bats: R **Throws:** R **Pos:** RF-61; LF-56; PH/PR-39; CF-11   **Ht:** 6'2" **Wt:** 187 **Born:** 8/10/66 **Age:** 32

Year Team	Lg	G	AB	H	2B	3B	HR	(Hm	Rd)	TB	R	RBI	TBB	IBB	SO	HBP	SH	SF	SB	CS	SB%	GDP	Avg	OBP	SLG
1992 New York	AL	15	27	8	2	0	3	(2	1)	19	7	6	0	0	3	0	0	0	2	0	1.00	0	.296	.296	.704
1993 New York	AL	42	67	10	2	3	0	(0	0)	18	11	6	1	0	14	2	0	1	2	0	1.00	2	.149	.183	.269
1994 New York	AL	57	86	25	8	0	4	(2	2)	45	19	13	4	0	17	0	0	1	1	3	.25	6	.291	.319	.523
1995 New York	AL	100	182	45	18	2	6	(4	2)	85	33	28	22	1	34	1	0	3	4	2	.67	4	.247	.327	.467
1996 NYA-Mil		125	325	82	19	4	5	(3	2)	124	43	34	19	3	57	5	3	5	10	9	.53	8	.252	.299	.382
1997 Milwaukee	AL	155	566	143	32	2	10	(3	7)	209	73	41	19	1	90	6	5	5	23	9	.72	9	.253	.282	.369
1998 Atlanta	NL	129	266	81	19	2	10	(5	5)	134	46	44	17	1	48	3	2	1	11	5	.69	5	.305	.352	.504
1996 Milwaukee	NL	99	233	63	15	4	5	(3	2)	101	37	30	15	2	39	4	1	5	7	8	.47	7	.270	.319	.433
Milwaukee	AL	26	92	19	4	0	0	(0	0)	23	6	4	4	1	18	1	2	0	3	1	.75	1	.207	.247	.250
7 ML YEARS		623	1519	394	100	13	38	(19	19)	634	232	172	82	6	263	17	10	16	53	28	.65	34	.259	.302	.417

Matt Williams

Bats: Right **Throws:** Right **Pos:** 3B-134; PH/PR-5   **Ht:** 6'2" **Wt:** 210 **Born:** 11/28/65 **Age:** 33

Year Team	Lg	G	AB	H	2B	3B	HR	(Hm	Rd)	TB	R	RBI	TBB	IBB	SO	HBP	SH	SF	SB	CS	SB%	GDP	Avg	OBP	SLG
1998 Tucson *	AAA	2	5	1	0	0	0	—	—	1	0	0	0	0	0	0	0	0	0	0	.00	0	.200	.200	.200
1987 San Francisco	NL	84	245	46	9	2	8	(5	3)	83	28	21	16	4	68	1	3	1	4	3	.57	5	.188	.240	.339
1988 San Francisco	NL	52	156	32	6	1	8	(7	1)	64	17	19	8	0	41	2	3	1	0	1	.00	7	.205	.251	.410
1989 San Francisco	NL	84	292	59	18	1	18	(10	8)	133	31	50	14	1	72	2	1	2	1	2	.33	5	.202	.242	.455
1990 San Francisco	NL	159	617	171	27	2	33	(20	13)	301	87	**122**	33	9	138	7	2	5	7	4	.64	13	.277	.319	.488
1991 San Francisco	NL	157	589	158	24	5	34	(17	17)	294	72	98	33	6	128	6	0	7	5	5	.50	11	.268	.310	.499
1992 San Francisco	NL	146	529	120	13	5	20	(9	11)	203	58	66	39	11	109	6	1	0	7	7	.50	15	.227	.286	.384
1993 San Francisco	NL	145	579	170	33	4	38	(19	19)	325	105	110	27	4	80	4	0	9	1	3	.25	12	.294	.325	.561
1994 San Francisco	NL	112	445	119	16	3	**43**	(20	**23**)	270	74	96	33	7	87	2	0	3	1	0	1.00	11	.267	.319	.607
1995 San Francisco	NL	76	283	95	17	1	23	(9	14)	183	53	65	30	8	58	2	0	3	2	0	1.00	8	.336	.399	.647
1996 San Francisco	NL	105	404	122	16	1	22	(13	9)	206	69	85	39	9	91	6	0	6	1	2	.33	10	.302	.367	.510
1997 Cleveland	AL	151	596	157	32	3	32	(7	25)	291	86	105	34	4	108	4	0	2	12	4	.75	14	.263	.307	.488
1998 Arizona	NL	135	510	136	26	1	20	(11	9)	224	72	71	43	8	102	3	0	1	5	1	.83	19	.267	.327	.439
12 ML YEARS		1406	5245	1385	237	29	299	(147	152)	2577	752	908	349	71	1082	45	9	42	46	32	.59	130	.264	.313	.491

Mike Williams

Pitches: Right **Bats:** Right **Pos:** RP-36; SP-1   **Ht:** 6'3" **Wt:** 195 **Born:** 7/29/68 **Age:** 30

		HOW MUCH HE PITCHED						WHAT HE GAVE UP										THE RESULTS					
Year Team	Lg	G	GS	CG	GF	IP	BFP	H	R	ER	HR	SH	SF	HB	TBB	IBB	SO	WP	Bk	W	L	Pct.	ShO	Sv-Op	Hld	ERA
1998 Nashville *	AAA	16	4	0	6	37	163	36	25	23	11	3	1	1	14	2	34	3	0	0	2	.000	0	1- -	—	5.59
1992 Philadelphia	NL	5	5	1	0	28.2	121	29	20	17	3	1	1	0	7	0	5	0	0	1	1	.500	0	0-0	0	5.34
1993 Philadelphia	NL	17	4	0	2	51	221	50	32	30	5	1	0	0	22	2	33	2	0	1	3	.250	0	0-0	0	5.29
1994 Philadelphia	NL	12	8	0	2	50.1	222	61	31	28	7	2	3	0	20	3	29	0	0	2	4	.333	0	0-0	0	5.01
1995 Philadelphia	NL	33	8	0	7	87.2	367	78	37	32	10	5	3	3	29	2	57	7	0	3	3	.500	0	0-0	1	3.29
1996 Philadelphia	NL	32	29	0	1	167	732	188	107	101	25	6	5	6	67	6	103	**16**	1	6	14	.300	0	0-0	0	5.44
1997 Kansas City	AL	10	0	0	4	14	70	20	11	10	1	0	1	0	8	1	10	0	0	0	2	.000	0	1-1	0	6.43
1998 Pittsburgh	NL	37	1	0	9	51	204	39	12	11	1	1	2	0	16	4	59	3	0	4	2	.667	0	0-1	7	1.94
7 ML YEARS		146	55	1	25	449.2	1937	465	250	229	52	16	15	10	169	18	296	28	1	17	29	.370	0	1-2	9	4.58

Reggie Williams

Bats: B **Throws:** R **Pos:** LF-19; PH/PR-12; CF-5; DH-2; RF-2   **Ht:** 6'1" **Wt:** 189 **Born:** 5/5/66 **Age:** 33

Year Team	Lg	G	AB	H	2B	3B	HR	(Hm	Rd)	TB	R	RBI	TBB	IBB	SO	HBP	SH	SF	SB	CS	SB%	GDP	Avg	OBP	SLG
1988 Everett	A-	60	223	56	8	1	3	—	—	75	52	29	47	1	43	1	0	2	36	10	.78	5	.251	.385	.336
1989 Clinton	A	68	236	46	9	2	3	—	—	68	38	18	29	0	66	3	5	1	14	9	.61	1	.195	.290	.288
Boise	A-	42	153	41	5	1	3	—	—	57	33	14	24	0	29	2	0	1	18	5	.78	2	.268	.372	.373

					BATTING															BASERUNNING				PERCENTAGES		
Year Team	Lg	G	AB	H	2B	3B	HR	(Hm	Rd)	TB	R	RBI	TBB	IBB	SO	HBP	SH	SF	SB	CS	SB%	GDP	Avg	OBP	SLG
1990 Quad City	A	58	189	46	11	2	3	—	—	70	50	12	39	0	60	4	2	1	24	6	.80	2	.243	.382	.370
1991 Palm Spring	A+	14	44	13	1	0	1	—	—	17	10	2	21	0	15	1	1	0	6	5	.55	0	.295	.530	.386
Midland	AA	83	319	99	12	3	1	—	—	120	77	30	62	2	67	0	5	3	21	9	.70	3	.310	.419	.376
1992 Edmonton	AAA	139	519	141	26	9	3	—	—	194	96	64	88	1	110	3	7	8	44	14	.76	9	.272	.375	.374
1993 Vancouver	AAA	130	481	132	17	6	2	—	—	167	92	53	88	2	99	5	9	6	50	17	.75	7	.274	.388	.347
1994 Albuquerque	AAA	104	288	90	15	8	4	—	—	133	55	42	33	1	62	0	1	2	21	10	.68	6	.313	.381	.462
1995 Albuquerque	AAA	66	234	73	15	5	6	—	—	116	44	29	30	0	46	1	1	3	6	4	.60	3	.312	.388	.496
1996 Albuquerque	AAA	92	352	101	25	2	6	—	—	148	60	42	37	5	72	1	5	1	17	7	.71	6	.287	.355	.420
1997 Vancouver	AAA	12	40	10	3	0	2	—	—	19	10	5	6	0	13	0	0	0	3	2	.60	0	.250	.348	.475
1998 Vancouver	AAA	100	373	105	25	5	5	—	—	155	58	39	53	2	98	6	1	2	13	12	.52	2	.282	.378	.416
1992 California	AL	14	26	6	1	1	0	(0	0)	9	5	2	1	0	10	0	0	0	1	0	.00	0	.231	.259	.346
1995 Los Angeles	NL	15	11	1	0	0	0	(0	0)	1	2	1	2	0	3	0	0	0	0	0	.00	0	.091	.231	.091
1998 Anaheim	AL	29	36	13	1	0	1	(0	1)	17	7	5	7	0	11	1	1	0	2	3	.50	0	.361	.477	.472
3 ML YEARS		58	73	20	2	1	1	(0	1)	27	14	8	10	0	24	1	1	0	3	3	.38	0	.274	.369	.370

Todd Williams

Pitches: Right **Bats:** Right **Pos:** RP-6   **Ht:** 6'4" **Wt:** 190 **Born:** 3/13/71 **Age:** 28

			HOW MUCH HE PITCHED						WHAT HE GAVE UP												THE RESULTS					
Year Team	Lg	G	GS	CG	GF	IP	BFP	H	R	ER	HR	SH	SF	HB	TBB	IBB	SO	WP	Bk	W	L	Pct.	ShO	Sv-Op	Hld	ERA
1991 Great Falls	R+	28	0	0	14	53	232	50	26	16	1	0	0	1	24	1	59	4	1	5	2	.714	0	8- -	—	2.72
1992 Bakersfield	A+	13	0	0	13	15.2	64	11	4	4	1	1	0	0	7	1	11	0	0	0	0	.000	0	9- -	—	2.30
San Antonio	AA	39	0	0	34	44	196	47	17	16	0	4	1	1	23	6	35	3	0	7	4	.636	0	13- -	—	3.27
1993 Albuquerque	AAA	65	0	0	50	70.1	321	87	44	39	2	0	1	1	31	6	56	6	0	5	5	.500	0	21- -	—	4.99
1994 Albuquerque	AAA	59	0	0	36	72.1	299	78	29	25	1	1	3	6	17	3	30	6	1	4	2	.667	0	13- -	—	3.11
1995 Albuquerque	AAA	25	0	0	9	45.1	203	59	21	17	4	1	1	1	15	4	23	1	2	4	1	.800	0	0- -	—	3.38
1996 Edmonton	AAA	35	10	0	7	91.2	427	125	71	56	4	2	5	3	37	3	33	3	0	5	3	.625	0	0- -	—	5.50
1997 Chattanooga	AAA	48	0	0	44	55.2	231	38	16	13	1	0	0	2	25	2	45	6	0	3	3	.500	0	31- -	—	2.10
Indianapolis	AAA	12	0	0	5	12.2	54	11	4	3	0	1	0	1	6	1	11	2	0	2	0	1.000	0	2- -	—	2.13
1998 Indianapolis	AAA	53	0	0	45	58.1	243	54	19	15	0	2	2	3	24	2	35	5	1	0	3	.000	0	26- -	—	2.31
1995 Los Angeles	NL	16	0	0	5	19.1	83	19	11	11	3	3	1	0	7	2	8	0	0	2	2	.500	0	0-1	0	5.12
1998 Cincinnati	NL	6	0	0	2	9.1	50	15	8	8	1	0	0	0	6	0	4	0	0	0	1	.000	0	0-0	0	7.71
2 ML YEARS		22	0	0	7	28.2	133	34	19	19	4	3	1	0	13	2	12	0	0	2	3	.400	0	0-1	0	5.97

Woody Williams

Pitches: Right **Bats:** Right **Pos:** SP-32   **Ht:** 6'0" **Wt:** 190 **Born:** 8/19/66 **Age:** 32

			HOW MUCH HE PITCHED						WHAT HE GAVE UP												THE RESULTS					
Year Team	Lg	G	GS	CG	GF	IP	BFP	H	R	ER	HR	SH	SF	HB	TBB	IBB	SO	WP	Bk	W	L	Pct.	ShO	Sv-Op	Hld	ERA
1993 Toronto	AL	30	0	0	0	37	172	40	18	18	2	2	1	2	22	3	24	2	1	3	1	.750	0	0-2	4	4.38
1994 Toronto	AL	38	0	0	14	59.1	253	44	24	24	5	1	2	2	33	1	56	4	0	1	3	.250	0	0-0	5	3.64
1995 Toronto	AL	23	3	0	10	53.2	232	44	23	22	6	2	0	2	28	1	41	0	0	1	2	.333	0	0-1	1	3.69
1996 Toronto	AL	12	10	1	0	59	255	64	33	31	8	2	1	1	21	1	43	2	0	4	5	.444	0	0-0	0	4.73
1997 Toronto	AL	31	31	0	0	194.2	833	201	98	94	31	4	8	5	66	3	124	7	0	9	14	.391	0	0-0	0	4.35
1998 Toronto	AL	32	32	1	0	209.2	894	196	112	104	36	5	6	2	81	3	151	2	1	10	9	.526	1	0-0	0	4.46
6 ML YEARS		166	76	2	33	613.1	2639	589	308	293	88	18	18	13	251	12	439	17	2	28	34	.452	1	0-3	10	4.30

Craig Wilson

Bats: Right **Throws:** Right **Pos:** SS-8; 2B-4; 3B-2   **Ht:** 6'0" **Wt:** 185 **Born:** 9/3/70 **Age:** 28

					BATTING															BASERUNNING				PERCENTAGES		
Year Team	Lg	G	AB	H	2B	3B	HR	(Hm	Rd)	TB	R	RBI	TBB	IBB	SO	HBP	SH	SF	SB	CS	SB%	GDP	Avg	OBP	SLG
1993 South Bend	A	132	455	118	27	?	5	—	—	164	56	59	49	2	60	9	7	6	4	1	.80	16	.259	.000	.000
1994 Pr William	A+	131	496	131	36	4	4	—	—	187	70	66	58	2	44	6	5	6	1	2	.33	16	.264	.345	.377
1995 Birmingham	AA	132	471	136	19	1	4	—	—	169	56	46	43	0	44	5	10	2	2	2	.50	21	.289	.353	.359
1996 Nashville	AAA	44	123	22	4	1	1	—	—	31	13	6	10	0	15	0	5	1	0	0	.00	6	.179	.239	.252
Birmingham	AA	58	202	57	9	0	3	—	—	75	36	26	40	1	28	1	6	4	1	1	.50	7	.282	.397	.371
1997 Nashville	AAA	137	453	123	20	2	6	—	—	165	71	42	48	1	31	1	12	0	4	4	.50	19	.272	.343	.364
1998 Calgary	AAA	120	432	132	21	1	14	—	—	197	67	69	37	1	41	3	9	5	4	2	.67	13	.306	.361	.456
1998 Chicago	AL	13	47	22	5	0	3	(1	2)	36	14	10	3	0	6	0	2	1	1	0	1.00	0	.468	.490	.766

Dan Wilson

Bats: Right **Throws:** Right **Pos:** C-94; PH/PR-4   **Ht:** 6'3" **Wt:** 202 **Born:** 3/25/69 **Age:** 30

					BATTING															BASERUNNING				PERCENTAGES		
Year Team	Lg	G	AB	H	2B	3B	HR	(Hm	Rd)	TB	R	RBI	TBB	IBB	SO	HBP	SH	SF	SB	CS	SB%	GDP	Avg	OBP	SLG
1992 Cincinnati	NL	12	25	9	1	0	0	(0	0)	10	2	3	3	0	8	0	0	0	0	0	.00	2	.360	.429	.400
1993 Cincinnati	NL	36	76	17	3	0	0	(0	0)	20	6	8	9	4	16	0	2	1	0	0	.00	2	.224	.302	.263
1994 Seattle	AL	91	282	61	14	2	3	(1	2)	88	24	27	10	0	57	1	8	2	1	2	.33	11	.216	.244	.312
1995 Seattle	AL	119	399	111	22	3	9	(5	4)	166	40	51	33	1	63	2	5	1	2	1	.67	12	.278	.336	.416
1996 Seattle	AL	138	491	140	24	0	18	(7	11)	218	51	83	32	2	88	3	9	5	1	2	.33	15	.285	.330	.444
1997 Seattle	AL	146	508	137	31	1	15	(9	6)	215	66	74	39	1	72	5	8	3	7	2	.78	12	.270	.326	.423
1998 Seattle	AL	96	325	82	17	1	9	(6	3)	128	39	44	24	0	56	5	8	6	2	1	.67	6	.252	.308	.394
7 ML YEARS		638	2106	557	112	7	54	(28	26)	845	228	290	150	8	360	16	40	18	13	8	.62	60	.264	.316	.401

Enrique Wilson

Bats: B **Throws:** R **Pos:** 2B-22; SS-10; PH/PR-3; 3B-2   **Ht:** 5'11" **Wt:** 160 **Born:** 7/27/75 **Age:** 23

Year Team	Lg	G	AB	H	2B	3B	HR	(Hm	Rd)	TB	R	RBI	TBB	IBB	SO	HBP	SH	SF	SB	CS	SB%	GDP	Avg	OBP	SLG
1992 Twins	R	13	44	15	1	0	0	—	—	16	12	8	4	0	4	4	0	1	3	0	1.00	0	.341	.434	.364
1993 Elizabethtn	R+	58	197	57	8	4	13	—	—	112	42	50	14	1	18	6	0	2	5	4	.56	1	.289	.352	.569
1994 Columbus	A	133	512	143	28	12	10	—	—	225	82	72	44	5	34	6	0	4	21	13	.62	7	.279	.341	.439
1995 Kinston	A+	117	464	124	24	7	6	—	—	180	55	52	25	2	38	2	4	10	18	19	.49	10	.267	.301	.388
1996 Canton-Akrn	AA	117	484	147	17	5	5	—	—	189	70	50	31	2	46	4	0	7	23	16	.59	9	.304	.346	.390
Buffalo	AAA	3	8	4	1	0	0	—	—	5	1	0	1	0	1	0	0	0	0	2	.00	1	.500	.556	.625
1997 Buffalo	AAA	118	451	138	20	3	11	—	—	197	78	39	42	2	41	5	4	4	9	8	.53	7	.306	.369	.437
1998 Buffalo	AAA	56	221	62	13	0	4	—	—	87	40	23	19	0	21	0	3	2	8	3	.73	6	.281	.335	.394
1997 Cleveland	AL	5	15	5	0	0	0	(0	0)	5	2	1	0	0	2	0	0	0	0	0	.00	0	.333	.333	.333
1998 Cleveland	AL	32	90	29	6	0	2	(1	1)	41	13	12	4	0	8	1	1	1	2	4	.33	1	.322	.354	.456
2 ML YEARS		37	105	34	6	0	2	(1	1)	46	15	13	4	0	10	1	1	1	2	4	.33	1	.324	.351	.438

Preston Wilson

Bats: Right **Throws:** Right **Pos:** CF-9; PH/PR-9; LF-7; RF-2   **Ht:** 6'2" **Wt:** 193 **Born:** 7/19/74 **Age:** 24

Year Team	Lg	G	AB	H	2B	3B	HR	(Hm	Rd)	TB	R	RBI	TBB	IBB	SO	HBP	SH	SF	SB	CS	SB%	GDP	Avg	OBP	SLG
1993 Kingsport	R+	66	259	60	9	3	16	—	—	117	44	48	24	0	75	3	1	1	6	2	.75	6	.232	.303	.452
Pittsfield	A-	8	29	16	5	1	1	—	—	26	6	12	2	0	7	1	0	1	1	0	1.00	0	.552	.576	.897
1994 Capital City	A	131	474	108	17	4	14	—	—	175	55	58	20	0	135	3	0	3	10	5	.57	4	.228	.262	.369
1995 Capital City	A	111	442	119	26	5	20	—	—	215	70	61	19	2	114	9	1	3	20	6	.77	4	.269	.311	.486
1996 St. Lucie	A+	23	85	15	3	0	1	—	—	21	6	7	8	0	21	2	0	0	1	1	.50	3	.176	.263	.247
1997 St. Lucie	A+	63	245	60	12	1	11	—	—	107	32	48	8	0	66	1	0	4	3	4	.43	4	.245	.267	.437
Binghamton	AA	70	259	74	12	1	19	—	—	145	37	47	21	0	71	2	0	3	7	1	.88	5	.286	.340	.560
1998 Norfolk	AAA	18	73	18	5	1	1	—	—	28	9	9	2	0	22	1	0	1	1	1	.50	2	.247	.273	.384
Charlotte	AAA	94	356	99	25	3	25	—	—	205	71	77	34	0	121	2	0	4	14	6	.70	6	.278	.341	.576
1998 NYN-Fla	NL	22	51	8	2	0	1	(1	0)	13	7	3	6	0	21	1	2	0	1	1	.50	1	.157	.259	.255
1998 New York	NL	8	20	6	2	0	0	(0	0)	8	3	2	2	0	8	0	0	0	1	1	.50	0	.300	.364	.400
Florida	NL	14	31	2	0	0	1	(1	0)	5	4	1	4	0	13	1	2	0	0	0	.00	0	.065	.194	.161

Trevor Wilson

Pitches: Left **Bats:** Left **Pos:** RP-15   **Ht:** 6'0" **Wt:** 204 **Born:** 6/7/66 **Age:** 33

Year Team	Lg	G	GS	CG	GF	IP	BFP	H	R	ER	HR	SH	SF	HB	TBB	IBB	SO	WP	Bk	W	L	Pct.	ShO	Sv-Op	Hld	ERA
1998 Vancouver *	AAA	21	21	4	0	141.2	604	130	67	57	14	1	2	11	59	0	94	6	4	5	9	.357	1	0--	—	3.62
1988 San Francisco	NL	4	4	0	0	22	96	25	14	10	1	3	1	0	8	0	15	0	1	0	2	.000	0	0-0	0	4.09
1989 San Francisco	NL	14	4	0	2	39.1	167	28	20	19	2	3	1	4	24	0	22	0	1	2	3	.400	0	0-0	0	4.35
1990 San Francisco	NL	27	17	3	3	110.1	457	87	52	49	11	6	2	1	49	3	66	5	2	8	7	.533	2	0-0	2	4.00
1991 San Francisco	NL	44	29	2	6	202	841	173	87	80	13	14	5	5	77	4	139	5	3	13	11	.542	1	0-1	3	3.56
1992 San Francisco	NL	26	26	1	0	154	661	152	82	72	11	8	6	6	64	5	88	2	7	8	14	.364	1	0-0	0	4.21
1993 San Francisco	NL	22	18	1	1	110	455	110	45	44	8	6	3	6	40	3	57	0	0	7	5	.583	0	0-0	0	3.60
1995 San Francisco	NL	17	17	0	0	82.2	354	82	42	36	8	5	2	4	38	1	38	0	0	3	4	.429	0	0-0	0	3.92
1998 Anaheim	AL	15	0	0	2	7.2	37	8	4	3	0	0	1	1	5	2	6	0	0	0	0	.000	0	0-2	2	3.52
8 ML YEARS		169	115	7	14	728	3068	665	346	313	61	48	21	27	305	18	431	12	15	41	46	.471	4	0-3	7	3.87

Scott Winchester

Pitches: Right **Bats:** Right **Pos:** SP-16   **Ht:** 6'2" **Wt:** 210 **Born:** 4/20/73 **Age:** 26

Year Team	Lg	G	GS	CG	GF	IP	BFP	H	R	ER	HR	SH	SF	HB	TBB	IBB	SO	WP	Bk	W	L	Pct.	ShO	Sv-Op	Hld	ERA
1995 Watertown	A-	23	0	0	22	28.2	116	24	10	9	0	1	2	2	6	2	27	2	2	3	1	.750	0	11--	—	2.83
1996 Columbus	A	52	0	0	47	61.1	254	50	27	22	8	5	2	5	16	4	60	4	0	7	3	.700	0	26--	—	3.23
1997 Kinston	A+	34	0	0	34	36.2	146	21	6	6	2	0	1	1	11	0	45	3	0	2	1	.667	0	29--	—	1.47
Akron	AA	6	0	0	6	7	32	8	3	3	1	0	0	1	2	1	8	1	0	0	0	.000	0	1--	—	3.86
Chattanooga	AA	9	0	0	7	10.2	45	9	4	2	0	2	2	0	3	1	3	1	0	2	1	.667	0	3--	—	1.69
Indianapols	AAA	4	0	0	4	5.2	21	2	0	0	0	0	1	0	2	0	2	0	0	0	0	.000	0	0--	—	0.00
1998 Indianapols	AAA	6	5	0	0	29.2	134	39	23	22	7	0	0	1	8	0	12	2	0	3	2	.600	0	0--	—	6.67
1997 Cincinnati	NL	5	0	0	4	6	30	9	5	4	1	2	1	0	3	0	3	0	0	0	0	.000	0	0-0	0	6.00
1998 Cincinnati	NL	16	16	1	0	79	359	101	56	51	12	2	2	4	27	2	40	3	0	3	6	.333	0	0-0	0	5.81
2 ML YEARS		21	16	1	4	85	389	110	61	55	13	4	2	5	29	2	43	3	0	3	6	.333	0	0-0	0	5.82

Randy Winn

Bats: B **Throws:** R **Pos:** CF-70; PH/PR-24; LF-16; RF-12; DH-4   **Ht:** 6'2" **Wt:** 175 **Born:** 6/9/74 **Age:** 25

Year Team	Lg	G	AB	H	2B	3B	HR	(Hm	Rd)	TB	R	RBI	TBB	IBB	SO	HBP	SH	SF	SB	CS	SB%	GDP	Avg	OBP	SLG
1995 Elmira	A-	51	213	67	7	4	0	—	—	82	38	22	15	0	31	3	0	2	19	7	.73	1	.315	.365	.385
1996 Kane County	A	130	514	139	16	3	0	—	—	161	90	35	47	0	115	8	11	3	30	18	.63	3	.270	.340	.313
1997 Brevard Cty	A+	36	143	45	8	2	0	—	—	57	26	15	16	1	28	5	2	1	16	8	.67	3	.315	.400	.399
Portland	AA	96	384	112	15	6	8	—	—	163	66	36	42	2	92	7	6	1	35	20	.64	4	.292	.371	.424
1998 Durham	AAA	29	123	35	5	2	1	—	—	47	25	16	15	0	24	0	4	0	10	4	.71	1	.285	.362	.382
1998 Tampa Bay	AL	109	338	94	9	9	1	(0	1)	124	51	17	29	0	69	1	11	0	26	12	.68	2	.278	.337	.367

Darrin Winston

Pitches: Left **Bats:** Right **Pos:** RP-27 **Ht:** 6'0" **Wt:** 195 **Born:** 7/6/66 **Age:** 32

Year Team	Lg	G	GS	CG	GF	IP	BFP	H	R	ER	HR	SH	SF	HB	TBB	IBB	SO	WP	Bk	W	L	Pct.	ShO	Sv-Op	Hld	ERA
1988 Jamestown	A-	14	7	0	5	44	194	47	28	24	3	3	2	0	19	0	29	2	4	2	4	.333	0	2-–	—	4.91
1989 Rockford	A	47	0	0	30	65	256	52	16	11	0	3	3	0	11	0	70	7	1	7	1	.875	0	16-–	—	1.52
1990 Jacksnville	AA	47	0	0	20	63	246	38	16	15	3	5	2	0	28	2	45	4	0	6	2	.750	0	7-–	—	2.14
1991 Indianapols	AAA	27	0	0	4	31	143	26	10	5	3	6	2	1	21	5	23	2	0	1	0	1.000	0	0-–	—	1.45
1993 Harrisburg	AA	24	0	0	9	44.2	206	53	30	23	4	4	4	2	19	2	36	3	0	1	0	1.000	0	1-–	—	4.63
Wst Plm Bch	A+	8	2	1	3	24.2	88	18	6	4	0	0	0	0	3	0	21	0	0	2	0	1.000	0	0-–	—	1.46
1994 Harrisburg	AA	25	0	0	11	35.1	144	32	12	6	3	3	0	2	9	3	27	0	0	4	2	.667	0	0-–	—	1.53
Ottawa	AAA	23	0	0	9	28.1	116	27	15	12	6	1	0	0	10	1	17	0	0	2	0	1.000	0	0-–	—	3.81
1995 Calgary	AAA	53	0	0	20	50.2	226	59	33	27	8	0	2	0	17	2	40	2	0	4	6	.400	0	2-–	—	4.80
1997 Scranton-WB	AAA	39	9	1	9	89.1	371	74	38	34	9	2	3	5	36	4	66	6	1	7	4	.636	0	0-–	—	3.43
1998 Scranton-WB	AAA	16	2	0	4	23.2	119	40	27	25	6	0	2	1	10	0	18	2	0	0	2	.000	0	0-–	—	9.51
1997 Philadelphia	NL	7	1	0	1	12	50	8	8	7	4	0	0	2	3	1	8	0	0	2	0	1.000	0	0-0	—	5.25
1998 Philadelphia	NL	27	0	0	5	25	114	31	18	17	7	2	0	2	6	0	11	1	0	2	2	.500	0	1-2	5	6.12
2 ML YEARS		34	1	0	6	37	164	39	26	24	11	2	0	4	9	1	19	1	0	4	2	.667	0	1-2	6	5.84

Jay Witasick

Pitches: Right **Bats:** Right **Pos:** RP-4; SP-3 **Ht:** 6'4" **Wt:** 210 **Born:** 8/28/72 **Age:** 26

Year Team	Lg	G	GS	CG	GF	IP	BFP	H	R	ER	HR	SH	SF	HB	TBB	IBB	SO	WP	Bk	W	L	Pct.	ShO	Sv-Op	Hld	ERA
1993 Johnson Cty	R+	12	12	0	0	67.2	288	65	42	31	8	4	1	0	19	0	74	5	1	4	3	.571	0	0-–	—	4.12
Savannah	A	1	1	0	0	6	27	7	3	3	0	0	0	2	0	8	0	0	1	0	1.000	0	0-–	—	4.50
1994 Madison	A	18	18	2	0	112.1	443	74	36	29	5	5	3	2	42	0	141	5	0	10	4	.714	0	0-–	—	2.32
1995 St. Pete	A+	18	18	1	0	105	425	80	39	32	4	1	4	0	36	1	109	5	1	7	7	.500	1	0-–	—	2.74
Arkansas	AA	7	7	0	0	34	161	46	29	26	4	0	0	0	16	1	26	2	0	2	4	.333	0	0-–	—	6.88
1996 Huntsville	AA	25	6	0	12	66.2	274	47	21	17	3	3	1	3	26	2	63	2	2	0	3	.000	0	4-–	—	2.30
Edmonton	AAA	6	0	0	5	8.2	39	9	4	4	1	1	1	1	6	0	9	2	0	0	0	.000	0	0-–	—	4.15
1997 Modesto	A+	9	2	0	1	17.1	75	16	9	8	1	0	0	1	5	0	29	1	0	0	1	.000	0	1-–	—	4.15
Edmonton	AAA	13	1	0	4	27.1	121	25	13	13	3	1	2	0	15	3	17	2	0	3	2	.600	0	0-–	—	4.28
1998 Edmonton	AAA	27	26	2	1	149	621	126	74	64	19	2	6	7	49	0	155	5	1	11	7	.611	1	0-–	—	3.87
1996 Oakland	AL	12	0	0	6	13	55	12	9	9	5	0	1	0	5	0	12	2	0	1	1	.500	0	0-1	0	6.23
1997 Oakland	AL	8	0	0	1	11	53	14	7	7	2	1	0	0	6	0	8	0	0	0	0	.000	0	0-0	1	5.73
1998 Oakland	AL	7	3	0	1	27	131	36	24	19	9	0	0	0	15	1	29	2	0	1	3	.250	0	0-0	0	6.33
3 ML YEARS		27	3	0	8	51	239	62	40	35	16	1	1	0	26	1	49	4	0	2	4	.333	0	0-1	1	6.18

Shannon Withem

Pitches: Right **Bats:** Right **Pos:** RP-1 **Ht:** 6'3" **Wt:** 185 **Born:** 9/21/72 **Age:** 26

Year Team	Lg	G	GS	CG	GF	IP	BFP	H	R	ER	HR	SH	SF	HB	TBB	IBB	SO	WP	Bk	W	L	Pct.	ShO	Sv-Op	Hld	ERA
1990 Bristol	R+	14	13	0	1	62	288	70	46	37	4	0	0	5	35	1	48	12	3	3	9	.250	0	0-–	—	5.37
1991 Fayettevlle	A	11	11	0	0	47.2	241	71	53	45	2	2	0	0	30	0	19	8	0	2	6	.250	0	0-–	—	8.50
Niagara Fal	A-	8	3	0	2	27	115	26	12	10	0	0	2	2	11	0	17	2	0	1	2	.333	0	0-–	—	3.33
1992 Fayettevlle	A	22	2	0	8	38	173	40	23	20	3	2	2	4	20	0	34	9	2	1	3	.250	0	2-–	—	4.74
1993 Lakeland	A+	16	16	2	0	113	462	108	47	43	5	1	5	5	24	0	62	3	0	10	2	.833	1	0-–	—	3.42
1994 Trenton	AA	25	25	5	0	178	735	190	80	68	10	4	4	4	37	0	135	5	2	7	12	.368	1	0-–	—	3.44
1995 Jacksnville	AA	19	18	0	1	108	481	142	77	69	17	5	1	5	24	1	80	4	0	5	8	.385	0	0-–	—	5.75
1996 St. Lucie	A+	2	2	0	0	14	53	8	2	2	0	0	0	1	1	0	13	1	0	1	0	1.000	0	0-–	—	1.29
Binghamton	AA	12	12	1	0	86	355	86	32	31	8	3	0	3	17	0	59	2	0	6	3	.667	1	0-–	—	3.24
Norfolk	AAA	8	8	0	0	42.2	188	56	25	22	6	2	1	0	6	0	30	2	0	3	3	.500	0	0-–	—	4.64
1997 Norfolk	AAA	29	27	1	2	155.2	668	167	85	75	21	2	4	4	48	1	109	5	0	9	10	.474	0	0-–	—	4.34
1998 Syracuse	AAA	28	27	4	1	189.2	781	176	72	69	14	4	5	10	58	2	113	2	0	17	5	.773	2	0-–	—	3.27
1998 Toronto	AL	1	0	0	0	3	14	3	1	1	0	0	0	0	2	0	2	0	0	0	0	.000	0	0-0	0	3.00

Bobby Witt

Pitches: Right **Bats:** Right **Pos:** SP-18; RP-13 **Ht:** 6'2" **Wt:** 205 **Born:** 5/11/64 **Age:** 35

Year Team	Lg	G	GS	CG	GF	IP	BFP	H	R	ER	HR	SH	SF	HB	TBB	IBB	SO	WP	Bk	W	L	Pct.	ShO	Sv-Op	Hld	ERA
1986 Texas	AL	31	31	0	0	157.2	741	130	104	96	18	3	9	3	143	2	174	22	3	11	9	.550	0	0-0	0	5.48
1987 Texas	AL	26	25	1	0	143	673	114	82	78	10	5	5	3	140	1	160	7	2	8	10	.444	0	0-0	0	4.91
1988 Texas	AL	22	22	13	0	174.1	736	134	83	76	13	7	6	1	101	2	148	16	8	8	10	.444	2	0-0	0	3.92
1989 Texas	AL	31	31	5	0	194.1	869	182	123	111	14	11	8	2	114	3	166	7	4	12	13	.480	1	0-0	0	5.14
1990 Texas	AL	33	32	7	1	222	954	197	98	83	12	5	6	4	110	3	221	11	2	17	10	.630	1	0-0	0	3.36
1991 Texas	AL	17	16	1	0	88.2	413	84	66	60	4	3	4	1	74	1	82	8	0	3	7	.300	1	0-0	0	6.09
1992 Tex-Oak	AL	31	31	0	0	193	848	183	99	92	16	7	10	2	114	2	125	9	1	10	14	.417	0	0-0	0	4.29
1993 Oakland	AL	35	33	5	0	220	950	226	112	103	16	9	8	3	91	5	131	8	1	14	13	.519	1	0-0	0	4.21
1994 Oakland	AL	24	24	5	0	135.2	618	151	88	76	22	2	7	5	70	4	111	6	1	8	10	.444	3	0-0	0	5.04
1995 Fla-Tex	AL	29	29	2	0	172	748	185	87	79	12	7	5	3	68	2	141	7	0	5	11	.313	0	0-0	0	4.13
1996 Texas	AL	33	32	2	1	199.2	903	235	129	120	28	2	7	2	96	3	157	4	0	16	12	.571	0	0-0	0	5.41
1997 Texas	AL	34	32	3	1	209	919	245	118	112	33	3	7	2	74	4	121	7	0	12	12	.500	0	0-0	0	4.82
1998 Tex-StL	AL	31	18	0	8	116.2	546	150	94	85	21	6	5	2	53	2	58	3	2	7	9	.438	0	0-0	0	6.56
1992 Texas	AL	25	25	0	0	161.1	708	152	87	80	14	5	8	2	95	1	100	6	1	9	13	.409	0	0-0	0	4.46
Oakland	AL	6	6	0	0	31.2	140	31	12	12	2	2	2	0	19	1	25	3	0	1	1	.500	0	0-0	0	3.41
1995 Florida	NL	19	19	1	0	110.2	472	104	52	48	8	5	3	2	47	1	95	2	0	2	7	.222	0	0-0	0	3.90

Year Team	Lg	G	GS	CG	GF	IP	BFP	H	R	ER	HR	SH	SF	HB	TBB	IBB	SO	WP	Bk	W	L	Pct.	ShO	Sv-Op	Hld	ERA
Texas	AL	10	10	1	0	61.1	276	81	35	31	4	2	2	1	21	1	46	5	0	3	4	.429	0	0-0	0	4.55
1998 Texas	AL	14	13	0	0	69.1	329	95	62	59	14	2	4	0	33	1	30	2	1	5	4	.556	0	0-0	0	7.66
St. Louis	NL	17	5	0	8	47.1	217	55	32	26	7	4	1	2	20	1	28	1	1	2	5	.286	0	0-0	0	4.94
13 ML YEARS		377	356	44	11	2226	9918	2216	1283	1171	219	70	87	33	1248	34	1795	115	25	131	140	.483	9	0-0	0	4.73

Kevin Witt

Bats: Left   **Throws:** Right   **Pos:** PH/PR-4; 1B-1   **Ht:** 6'4"   **Wt:** 195   **Born:** 1/5/76   **Age:** 23

Year Team	Lg	G	AB	H	2B	3B	HR	(Hm	Rd)	TB	R	RBI	TBB	IBB	SO	HBP	SH	SF	SB	CS	SB%	GDP	Avg	OBP	SLG
1994 Medicine Ha	R+	60	243	62	10	4	7	—	—	101	37	36	15	0	52	1	1	1	4	1	.80	3	.255	.300	.416
1995 Hagerstown	A	119	479	111	35	1	14	—	—	190	58	50	28	2	148	4	3	0	1	5	.17	5	.232	.280	.397
1996 Dunedin	A+	124	446	121	18	6	13	—	—	190	63	70	39	3	96	6	2	5	9	4	.69	9	.271	.335	.426
1997 Knoxville	AA	127	501	145	27	4	30	—	—	270	76	91	44	7	109	3	1	2	1	0	1.00	13	.289	.349	.539
1998 Syracuse	AAA	126	455	124	20	3	23	—	—	219	71	67	53	6	124	7	1	5	3	3	.50	5	.273	.354	.481
1998 Toronto	AL	5	7	1	0	0	0	(0	0)	1	0	0	0	0	3	0	0	0	0	0	.00	0	.143	.143	.143

Mark Wohlers

Pitches: Right   **Bats:** Right   **Pos:** RP-27   **Ht:** 6'4"   **Wt:** 207   **Born:** 1/23/70   **Age:** 29

Year Team	Lg	G	GS	CG	GF	IP	BFP	H	R	ER	HR	SH	SF	HB	TBB	IBB	SO	WP	Bk	W	L	Pct.	ShO	Sv-Op	Hld	ERA
1998 Greenville *	AA	1	1	0	0	1	5	1	1	0	0	0	1	0	1	0	1	0	0	0	0	.000	0	0- -	—	0.00
Richmond *	AAA	16	0	0	1	12.1	91	21	28	28	5	0	0	0	36	0	16	17	0	0	3	.000	0	0- -	—	20.43
1991 Atlanta	NL	17	0	0	4	19.2	89	17	7	7	1	2	1	2	13	3	13	0	0	3	1	.750	0	2-4	2	3.20
1992 Atlanta	NL	32	0	0	16	35.1	140	28	11	10	0	5	1	1	14	4	17	1	0	1	2	.333	0	4-6	2	2.55
1993 Atlanta	NL	46	0	0	13	48	199	37	25	24	2	5	1	1	22	3	45	0	0	6	2	.750	0	0-0	12	4.50
1994 Atlanta	NL	51	0	0	15	51	236	51	35	26	1	4	6	0	33	9	58	2	0	7	2	.778	0	1-2	7	4.59
1995 Atlanta	NL	65	0	0	49	64.2	269	51	16	15	2	2	0	1	24	3	90	4	0	7	3	.700	0	25-29	2	2.09
1996 Atlanta	NL	77	0	0	64	77.1	323	71	30	26	8	2	2	2	21	3	100	10	0	2	4	.333	0	39-44	0	3.03
1997 Atlanta	NL	71	0	0	55	69.1	300	57	29	27	4	4	4	0	38	0	92	6	0	5	7	.417	0	33-40	1	3.50
1998 Atlanta	NL	27	0	0	17	20.1	113	18	23	23	2	1	0	1	33	0	22	7	0	0	1	.000	0	8-8	0	10.18
8 ML YEARS		386	0	0	233	385.2	1669	330	176	158	20	25	15	8	198	25	437	30	0	31	22	.585	0	112-133	26	3.69

Bob Wolcott

Pitches: Right   **Bats:** Right   **Pos:** SP-6   **Ht:** 6'0"   **Wt:** 190   **Born:** 9/8/73   **Age:** 25

Year Team	Lg	G	GS	CG	GF	IP	BFP	H	R	ER	HR	SH	SF	HB	TBB	IBB	SO	WP	Bk	W	L	Pct.	ShO	Sv-Op	Hld	ERA
1998 Tucson *	AAA	23	21	2	0	128.2	551	156	79	74	13	4	3	4	26	1	100	0	1	8	6	.571	1	0- -	—	5.18
1995 Seattle	AL	7	6	0	0	36.2	164	43	18	18	6	0	3	2	14	0	19	0	0	3	2	.600	0	0-0	0	4.42
1996 Seattle	AL	30	28	1	0	149.1	672	179	101	95	26	5	3	7	54	5	78	3	1	7	10	.412	0	0-0	0	5.73
1997 Seattle	AL	19	18	0	0	100	451	129	71	67	22	4	2	5	29	2	58	0	0	6	6	.455	0	0-0	0	6.03
1998 Arizona	NL	6	6	0	0	33	141	32	27	26	7	1	0	0	13	1	21	1	0	1	3	.250	0	0-0	0	7.09
4 ML YEARS		62	58	1	0	319	1428	383	217	206	61	10	8	14	110	8	176	4	1	16	21	.432	0	0-0	0	5.81

Tony Womack

Bats: L **Throws:** R **Pos:** 2B-152; CF-5; SS-2; PH/PR-2   **Ht:** 5'9"   **Wt:** 155   **Born:** 9/25/69   **Age:** 29

Year Team	Lg	G	AB	H	2B	3B	HR	(Hm	Rd)	TB	R	RBI	TBB	IBB	SO	HBP	SH	SF	SB	CS	SB%	GDP	Avg	OBP	SLG
1993 Pittsburgh	NL	15	24	2	0	0	0	(0	0)	2	5	0	3	0	3	0	1	0	2	0	1.00	0	.083	.185	.083
1994 Pittsburgh	NL	5	12	4	0	0	0	(0	0)	4	4	1	2	0	3	0	0	0	1	0	.00	0	.333	.429	.333
1996 Pittsburgh	NL	17	30	10	3	1	0	(0	0)	15	11	7	6	0	1	1	3	0	2	0	1.00	0	.333	.459	.500
1997 Pittsburgh	NL	155	641	178	26	9	6	(5	1)	240	85	50	43	2	109	3	2	0	60	7	.90	6	.278	.326	.374
1998 Pittsburgh	NL	159	655	185	26	7	3	(2	1)	234	85	45	38	1	94	0	6	6	58	8	.88	4	.282	.319	.357
5 ML YEARS		351	1362	379	55	17	9	(7	2)	495	190	103	92	3	210	4	12	5	122	15	.89	10	.278	.325	.363

Jason Wood

Bats: R **Throws:** R **Pos:** 1B-6; DH-3; SS-3; PH/PR-2; 3B-1   **Ht:** 6'1"   **Wt:** 170   **Born:** 12/16/69   **Age:** 29

Year Team	Lg	G	AB	H	2B	3B	HR	(Hm	Rd)	TB	R	RBI	TBB	IBB	SO	HBP	SH	SF	SB	CS	SB%	GDP	Avg	OBP	SLG
1991 Sou. Oregon	A-	44	142	44	3	4	3	—	—	64	30	23	28	0	30	2	2	5	5	2	.71	0	.310	.423	.451
1992 Modesto	A+	128	454	105	28	3	6	—	—	157	66	49	40	1	106	4	3	5	5	4	.56	15	.231	.296	.346
1993 Huntsville	AA	103	370	85	21	2	3	—	—	119	44	36	33	0	97	2	9	3	2	4	.33	7	.230	.294	.322
1994 Huntsville	AA	134	468	128	29	2	6	—	—	179	54	84	46	1	83	6	5	15	3	6	.33	9	.274	.336	.382
1995 Edmonton	AAA	127	421	99	20	5	2	—	—	135	49	50	29	3	72	5	3	6	1	4	.20	13	.235	.282	.321
1996 Huntsville	AA	133	491	128	21	1	20	—	—	211	77	84	72	2	87	5	2	11	2	5	.29	14	.261	.354	.430
Edmonton	AAA	3	12	0	0	0	0	—	—	0	0	0	5	0	6	0	0	0	0	1	.00	0	.000	.294	.000
1997 Edmonton	AAA	130	505	162	35	7	19	—	—	268	83	87	45	0	74	8	2	4	2	4	.33	21	.321	.383	.531
1998 Edmonton	AAA	80	307	86	20	0	18	—	—	160	52	73	37	1	71	2	0	6	1	1	.50	5	.280	.355	.521
Toledo	AAA	46	169	47	9	0	7	—	—	77	24	29	16	1	30	1	0	1	0	0	.00	5	.278	.342	.456
1998 Oak-Det	AL	13	24	8	2	0	1	(0	1)	13	6	1	3	0	5	0	0	0	0	1	.00	0	.333	.407	.542
1998 Oakland	AL	3	1	0	0	0	0	(0	0)	0	1	0	0	0	1	0	0	0	0	0	.00	0	.000	.000	.000
Detroit	AL	10	23	8	2	0	1	(0	1)	13	5	1	3	0	4	0	0	0	0	1	.00	0	.348	.423	.565

Kerry Wood

Pitches: Right **Bats:** Right **Pos:** SP-26 | **Ht:** 6'5" **Wt:** 225 **Born:** 6/16/77 **Age:** 22

| | | HOW MUCH HE PITCHED | | | | | | WHAT HE GAVE UP | | | | | | | | | | | | THE RESULTS | | | | | | |
Year Team	Lg	G	GS	CG	GF	IP	BFP	H	R	ER	HR	SH	SF	HB	TBB	IBB	SO	WP	Bk	W	L	Pct.	ShO	Sv-Op	Hld	ERA
1995 Cubs	R	1	1	0	0	3	9	0	0	0	0	0	0	0	1	0	2	0	0	0	0	.000	0	0- -	—	0.00
Williamsprt	A-	2	2	0	0	4.1	23	5	8	5	0	0	0	0	5	0	5	1	0	0	0	.000	0	0- -	—	10.38
1996 Daytona	A+	22	22	0	0	114.1	495	72	51	37	6	5	4	14	70	0	136	10	7	10	2	.833	0	0- -	—	2.91
1997 Orlando	AA	19	19	0	0	94	416	58	49	47	2	0	6	10	79	2	106	10	4	6	7	.462	0	0- -	—	4.50
Iowa	AAA	10	10	0	0	57.2	254	35	35	30	2	3	0	6	52	0	80	8	2	4	2	.667	0	0- -	—	4.68
1998 Iowa	AAA	1	1	0	0	5	17	1	0	0	0	0	0	0	2	0	11	0	0	1	0	1.000	0	0- -	—	0.00
1998 Chicago	NL	26	26	1	0	166.2	699	117	69	63	14	2	4	11	85	1	233	6	3	13	6	.684	1	0-0	0	3.40

Brad Woodall

Pitches: Left **Bats:** Both **Pos:** SP-20; RP-11 | **Ht:** 6'0" **Wt:** 175 **Born:** 6/25/69 **Age:** 30

| | | HOW MUCH HE PITCHED | | | | | | WHAT HE GAVE UP | | | | | | | | | | | | THE RESULTS | | | | | | |
Year Team	Lg	G	GS	CG	GF	IP	BFP	H	R	ER	HR	SH	SF	HB	TBB	IBB	SO	WP	Bk	W	L	Pct.	ShO	Sv-Op	Hld	ERA
1998 Louisville *	AAA	5	5	0	0	30	135	32	19	13	3	0	0		15	0	27	4	0	1	1	.500	0	0- -	—	3.90
1994 Atlanta	NL	1	1	0	0	6	24	5	3	3	2	0	0		2	0	2	0	0	0	1	.000	0	0-0	0	4.50
1995 Atlanta	NL	9	0	0	3	10.1	52	13	10	7	1	1	1	0	8	1	5	1	0	1	1	.500	0	0-0	0	6.10
1996 Atlanta	NL	8	3	0	2	19.2	91	28	19	16	4	1	2	0	4	0	20	1	0	2	2	.500	0	0-0	0	7.32
1998 Milwaukee	NL	31	20	0	4	138	594	145	81	76	25	7	2	6	47	4	85	3	0	7	9	.438	0	0-0	1	4.96
4 ML YEARS		49	24	0	9	174	761	191	113	102	32	9	5	6	61	5	112	5	0	10	13	.435	0	0-0	1	5.28

Steve Woodard

Pitches: Right **Bats:** Left **Pos:** SP-26; RP-8 | **Ht:** 6'4" **Wt:** 236 **Born:** 5/15/75 **Age:** 24

| | | HOW MUCH HE PITCHED | | | | | | WHAT HE GAVE UP | | | | | | | | | | | | THE RESULTS | | | | | | |
Year Team	Lg	G	GS	CG	GF	IP	BFP	H	R	ER	HR	SH	SF	HB	TBB	IBB	SO	WP	Bk	W	L	Pct.	ShO	Sv-Op	Hld	ERA
1994 Brewers	R	15	12	2	1	82.2	336	68	29	22	3	2	3	4	13	1	85	8	1	8	0	1.000	0	0- -	—	2.40
1995 Beloit	A	21	21	1	0	115	490	113	68	58	12	6	2	5	31	0	94	6	5	7	4	.636	0	0- -	—	4.54
1996 Stockton	A+	28	28	3	0	181.1	762	201	89	81	14	4	6	3	33	1	142	7	2	12	9	.571	0	0- -	—	4.02
1997 El Paso	AA	19	19	6	0	136.1	561	136	56	48	8	8	0	2	25	2	97	9	0	14	3	.824	1	0- -	—	3.17
Tucson	AAA	1	1	0	0	7	26	3	0	0	0	0	0	1	1	0	6	1	0	1	0	1.000	0	0- -	—	0.00
1997 Milwaukee	AL	7	7	0	0	36.2	153	39	25	21	5	0	0	2	6	0	32	0	0	3	3	.500	0	0-0	0	5.15
1998 Milwaukee	NL	34	26	0	2	165.2	692	170	83	77	19	2	4	9	33	4	135	3	2	10	12	.455	0	0-0	0	4.18
2 ML YEARS		41	33	0	2	202.1	845	209	108	98	24	2	4	11	39	4	167	3	2	13	15	.464	0	0-0	0	4.36

Tim Worrell

Pitches: Right **Bats:** Right **Pos:** RP-34; SP-9 | **Ht:** 6'4" **Wt:** 215 **Born:** 7/5/67 **Age:** 31

| | | HOW MUCH HE PITCHED | | | | | | WHAT HE GAVE UP | | | | | | | | | | | | THE RESULTS | | | | | | |
Year Team	Lg	G	GS	CG	GF	IP	BFP	H	R	ER	HR	SH	SF	HB	TBB	IBB	SO	WP	Bk	W	L	Pct.	ShO	Sv-Op	Hld	ERA
1993 San Diego	NL	21	21	0	1	100.2	443	104	63	55	11	8	5	0	43	5	52	3	0	2	7	.222	0	0-0	1	4.92
1994 San Diego	NL	3	3	0	1	14.2	59	9	7	6	0	0	1	0	5	0	14	0	0	0	1	.000	0	0-0	0	3.68
1995 San Diego	NL	9	0	0	4	13.1	63	16	7	7	2	1	0	1	6	0	13	1	0	1	0	1.000	0	0-0	0	4.73
1996 San Diego	NL	50	11	0	8	121	510	109	45	41	9	3	1	6	39	1	99	0	0	9	7	.563	0	1-2	10	3.05
1997 San Diego	NL	60	10	0	14	106.1	483	116	67	61	14	6	6	7	50	2	81	2	1	4	8	.333	0	3-7	16	5.16
1998 Det-Cle-Oak	AL	43	9	0	5	103	440	106	62	60	16	2	3	1	29	3	82	2	0	2	7	.222	0	0-3	6	5.24
1998 Detroit	AL	15	9	0	1	61.2	265	66	42	41	11	0	1	1	19	2	47	0	0	2	6	.250	0	0-1	0	5.98
Cleveland	AL	3	0	0	1	5.1	24	6	3	3	0	0	2	0	2	0	2	0	0	0	0	.000	0	0-0	0	5.06
Oakland	AL	25	0	0	4	36	151	34	17	16	5	2	0	0	8	1	33	2	0	0	1	.000	0	0-2	6	4.00
6 ML YEARS		186	49	0	32	459	1998	460	251	230	52	20	16	15	172	11	341	8	1	18	30	.375	0	4-12	33	4.51

Jamey Wright

Pitches: Right **Bats:** Right **Pos:** SP-34 | **Ht:** 6'5" **Wt:** 214 **Born:** 12/24/74 **Age:** 24

| | | HOW MUCH HE PITCHED | | | | | | WHAT HE GAVE UP | | | | | | | | | | | | THE RESULTS | | | | | | |
Year Team	Lg	G	GS	CG	GF	IP	BFP	H	R	ER	HR	SH	SF	HB	TBB	IBB	SO	WP	Bk	W	L	Pct.	ShO	Sv-Op	Hld	ERA
1996 Colorado	NL	16	15	0	0	91.1	406	105	60	50	8	4	2	7	41	1	45	1	2	4	4	.500	0	0-0	1	4.93
1997 Colorado	NL	26	26	1	0	149.2	698	198	113	104	19	8	3	11	71	3	59	6	2	8	12	.400	0	0-0	0	6.25
1998 Colorado	NL	34	34	1	0	206.1	919	235	143	130	24	8	6	11	95	3	86	6	3	9	14	.391	0	0-0	0	5.67
3 ML YEARS		76	75	2	0	447.1	2023	538	316	284	51	20	11	29	207	7	190	13	7	21	30	.412	0	0-0	1	5.71

Jaret Wright

Pitches: Right **Bats:** Right **Pos:** SP-32 | **Ht:** 6'2" **Wt:** 230 **Born:** 12/29/75 **Age:** 23

| | | HOW MUCH HE PITCHED | | | | | | WHAT HE GAVE UP | | | | | | | | | | | | THE RESULTS | | | | | | |
Year Team	Lg	G	GS	CG	GF	IP	BFP	H	R	ER	HR	SH	SF	HB	TBB	IBB	SO	WP	Bk	W	L	Pct.	ShO	Sv-Op	Hld	ERA
1994 Burlington	R+	4	4	0	0	13.1	62	13	10	8	1	1	2	2	9	0	16	0	0	0	1	.000	0	0- -	—	5.40
1995 Columbus	A	24	24	0	0	129	554	93	55	43	9	3	6	13	79	0	113	11	3	5	6	.455	0	0- -	—	3.00
1996 Kinston	A+	19	19	0	0	101	413	65	36	28	1	6	3	7	55	0	109	7	1	7	4	.636	0	0- -	—	2.50
1997 Akron	AA	8	8	1	0	54	221	43	26	22	4	5	0	2	23	2	59	2	1	3	3	.500	0	0- -	—	3.67
Buffalo	AAA	7	7	1	0	45	183	30	16	9	4	0	1	1	19	0	47	2	0	4	1	.800	1	0- -	—	1.80
1997 Cleveland	AL	16	16	0	0	90.1	388	81	45	44	9	3	4	5	35	0	63	1	0	8	3	.727	0	0-0	0	4.38
1998 Cleveland	AL	32	32	1	0	192.2	855	207	109	101	22	4	6	11	87	4	140	6	0	12	10	.545	1	0-0	0	4.72
2 ML YEARS		48	48	1	0	283	1243	288	154	145	31	7	10	16	122	4	203	7	0	20	13	.606	1	0-0	0	4.61

Esteban Yan

Pitches: Right **Bats:** Right **Pos:** RP-64 **Ht:** 6'4" **Wt:** 230 **Born:** 6/22/74 **Age:** 25

		HOW MUCH HE PITCHED						WHAT HE GAVE UP											THE RESULTS					
Year Team	Lg	G	GS	CG	GF	IP	BFP	H	R	ER	HR	SH	SF	HB	TBB	IBB	SO	WP	Bk	W	L	Pct.	ShO	Sv-Op	Hld	ERA
1993 Danville	R+	14	14	0	0	71.1	324	73	46	24	4	3	3	5	24	1	50	3	0	4	7	.364	0	0- -	—	3.03
1994 Macon	A	28	28	4	0	170.2	696	155	85	62	15	4	3	13	34	1	121	4	1	11	12	.478	3	0- -	—	3.27
1995 Wst Plm Bch	A+	24	21	1	1	137.2	580	139	63	47	3	7	5	10	33	0	89	8	3	6	8	.429	0	1- -	—	3.07
1996 Bowie	AA	9	1	0	3	16	75	18	12	10	2	1	1	0	8	0	16	1	1	0	2	.000	0	0- -	—	5.63
Rochester	AAA	22	10	0	3	71.2	306	75	37	34	6	3	4	2	18	0	61	4	1	5	4	.556	0	1- -	—	4.27
1997 Rochester	AAA	34	12	0	8	119	490	107	54	41	13	1	6	5	37	0	131	5	0	11	5	.688	0	2- -	—	3.10
1996 Baltimore	AL	4	0	0	2	9.1	42	13	7	6	3	0	0	0	3	1	7	0	0	0	0	.000	0	0-0	0	5.79
1997 Baltimore	AL	3	2	0	0	9.2	58	20	18	17	3	0	1	2	7	0	4	1	0	0	1	.000	0	0-0	0	15.83
1998 Tampa Bay	AL	64	0	0	18	88.2	381	78	41	38	11	1	3	5	41	2	77	6	0	5	4	.556	0	1-5	8	3.86
3 ML YEARS		71	2	0	20	107.2	481	111	66	61	17	1	4	7	51	3	88	7	0	5	5	.500	0	1-5	8	5.10

Masato Yoshii

Pitches: Right **Bats:** Right **Pos:** SP-29 **Ht:** 6'2" **Wt:** 210 **Born:** 4/20/65 **Age:** 34

		HOW MUCH HE PITCHED						WHAT HE GAVE UP											THE RESULTS					
Year Team	Lg	G	GS	CG	GF	IP	BFP	H	R	ER	HR	SH	SF	HB	TBB	IBB	SO	WP	Bk	W	L	Pct.	ShO	Sv-Op	Hld	ERA
1998 New York	NL	29	29	1	0	171.2	724	166	79	75	22	9	4	6	53	5	117	5	1	6	8	.429	0	0-0	0	3.93

Dmitri Young

Bats: B **Throws:** R **Pos:** LF-91; 1B-44; RF-14; PH/PR-8 **Ht:** 6'2" **Wt:** 235 **Born:** 10/11/73 **Age:** 25

		BATTING															BASERUNNING				PERCENTAGES		
Year Team	Lg	G	AB	H	2B	3B	HR	(Hm | Rd)	TB	R	RBI	TBB	IBB	SO	HBP	SH	SF	SB	CS	SB%	GDP	Avg	OBP	SLG
1996 St. Louis	NL	16	29	7	0	0	0	(0 | 0)	7	3	2	4	0	5	1	0	0	0	1	.00	1	.241	.353	.241
1997 St. Louis	NL	110	333	86	14	3	5	(2 | 3)	121	38	34	38	3	63	2	1	3	6	5	.55	8	.258	.335	.363
1998 Cincinnati	NL	144	536	166	48	1	14	(3 | 11)	258	81	83	47	4	94	2	0	5	2	4	.33	16	.310	.364	.481
3 ML YEARS		270	898	259	62	4	19	(5 | 14)	386	122	119	89	7	162	5	1	8	8	10	.44	25	.288	.353	.430

Eric Young

Bats: Right **Throws:** Right **Pos:** 2B-114; PH/PR-3; DH-1 **Ht:** 5'9" **Wt:** 170 **Born:** 5/18/67 **Age:** 32

		BATTING															BASERUNNING				PERCENTAGES		
Year Team	Lg	G	AB	H	2B	3B	HR	(Hm | Rd)	TB	R	RBI	TBB	IBB	SO	HBP	SH	SF	SB	CS	SB%	GDP	Avg	OBP	SLG
1992 Los Angeles	NL	49	132	34	1	0	1	(0 | 1)	38	9	11	8	0	9	0	4	0	6	1	.86	3	.258	.300	.288
1993 Colorado	NL	144	490	132	16	8	3	(3 | 0)	173	82	42	63	3	41	4	4	4	42	19	.69	9	.269	.355	.353
1994 Colorado	NL	90	228	62	13	1	7	(6 | 1)	98	37	30	38	1	17	2	5	2	18	7	.72	5	.272	.378	.430
1995 Colorado	NL	120	366	116	21	9	6	(5 | 1)	173	68	36	49	3	29	5	3	1	35	12	.74	4	.317	.404	.473
1996 Colorado	NL	141	568	184	23	4	8	(7 | 1)	239	113	74	47	1	31	21	2	5	53	19	.74	9	.324	.393	.421
1997 Col-LA	NL	155	622	174	33	8	8	(2 | 6)	247	106	61	71	1	54	9	10	6	45	14	.76	18	.280	.359	.397
1998 Los Angeles	NL	117	452	129	24	1	8	(7 | 1)	179	78	43	45	0	32	5	9	2	42	13	.76	4	.285	.355	.396
1997 Colorado	NL	118	468	132	29	6	6	(2 | 4)	191	78	45	57	0	37	5	8	5	32	12	.73	16	.282	.363	.408
Los Angeles	NL	37	154	42	4	2	2	(0 | 2)	56	28	16	14	1	17	4	2	1	13	2	.87	2	.273	.347	.364
7 ML YEARS		816	2858	831	131	31	41	(30 | 11)	1147	493	297	321	9	213	46	37	20	241	85	.74	50	.291	.369	.401

Ernie Young

Bats: R **Throws:** R **Pos:** RF-19; PH/PR-7; CF-5; LF-1 **Ht:** 6'1" **Wt:** 190 **Born:** 7/8/69 **Age:** 29

		BATTING															BASERUNNING				PERCENTAGES		
Year Team	Lg	G	AB	H	2B	3B	HR	(Hm | Rd)	TB	R	RBI	TBB	IBB	SO	HBP	SH	SF	SB	CS	SB%	GDP	Avg	OBP	SLG
1998 Omaha *	AAA	79	297	97	13	1	22	—	—	178	58	55	29	2	68	5	0	1	6	4	.60	8	.327	.395	.599
1994 Oakland	AL	11	30	2	1	0	0	(0 | 0)	3	2	3	1	0	8	0	0	0	0	0	.00	1	.067	.097	.100
1995 Oakland	AL	26	50	10	3	0	2	(2 | 0)	19	9	5	8	0	12	0	0	0	0	0	.00	1	.200	.310	.380
1996 Oakland	AL	141	462	112	19	4	19	(10 | 9)	196	72	64	52	1	118	7	3	4	7	5	.58	13	.242	.326	.424
1997 Oakland	AL	71	175	39	7	0	5	(3 | 2)	61	22	15	19	0	57	2	2	2	1	3	.25	6	.223	.303	.349
1998 Kansas City	AL	25	53	10	3	0	1	(0 | 1)	16	2	3	2	0	9	1	0	0	2	1	.67	3	.189	.232	.302
5 ML YEARS		274	770	173	33	4	27	(15 | 12)	295	107	90	82	1	204	10	5	6	10	9	.53	24	.225	.305	.383

Kevin Young

Bats: Right **Throws:** Right **Pos:** 1B-157; PH/PR-2 **Ht:** 6'3" **Wt:** 220 **Born:** 6/16/69 **Age:** 30

		BATTING															BASERUNNING				PERCENTAGES		
Year Team	Lg	G	AB	H	2B	3B	HR	(Hm | Rd)	TB	R	RBI	TBB	IBB	SO	HBP	SH	SF	SB	CS	SB%	GDP	Avg	OBP	SLG
1992 Pittsburgh	NL	10	7	4	0	0	0	(0 | 0)	4	2	4	2	0	0	0	0	0	1	0	1.00	0	.571	.667	.571
1993 Pittsburgh	NL	141	449	106	24	3	6	(6 | 0)	154	38	47	36	3	82	9	5	9	2	2	.50	10	.236	.300	.343
1994 Pittsburgh	NL	59	122	25	7	2	1	(1 | 0)	39	15	11	8	2	34	1	2	1	0	2	.00	3	.205	.258	.320
1995 Pittsburgh	NL	56	181	42	9	0	6	(5 | 1)	69	13	22	8	0	53	2	1	3	1	3	.25	5	.232	.268	.381
1996 Kansas City	AL	55	132	32	6	0	8	(4 | 4)	62	20	23	11	0	32	0	0	0	3	3	.50	2	.242	.301	.470
1997 Pittsburgh	NL	97	333	100	18	3	18	(11 | 7)	178	59	74	16	1	89	4	1	8	11	2	.85	6	.300	.332	.535
1998 Pittsburgh	NL	159	592	160	40	2	27	(15 | 12)	285	88	108	44	1	127	11	0	9	15	7	.68	20	.270	.328	.481
7 ML YEARS		577	1816	469	104	10	66	(42 | 24)	791	235	289	125	7	417	27	9	30	33	19	.63	46	.258	.311	.436

Tim Young

Pitches: Left **Bats:** Left **Pos:** RP-10 **Ht:** 5'9" **Wt:** 170 **Born:** 10/15/73 **Age:** 25

Year Team	Lg	G	GS	CG	GF	IP	BFP	H	R	ER	HR	SH	SF	HB	TBB	IBB	SO	WP	Bk	W	L	Pct.	ShO	Sv-Op	Hld	ERA
1996 Vermont	A-	27	0	0	26	29.1	106	14	1	1	1	2	1	2	4	0	46	0	1	1	0	1.000	0	18-	—	0.31
1997 Cape Fear	A	45	0	0	41	54	214	33	12	9	0	1	2	2	15	0	66	8	0	1	1	.500	0	18-	—	1.50
Wst Plm Bch	A+	11	0	0	8	15.2	56	8	1	1	0	2	0	1	4	0	13	0	0	0	0	.000	0	5-	—	0.57
Harrisburg	AA	1	0	0	0	2	7	1	0	0	0	0	0	0	0	0	3	0	0	0	0	.000	0	--	—	0.00
1998 Harrisburg	AA	26	0	0	19	35.2	146	28	17	15	3	5	0	1	10	0	52	1	0	3	3	.500	0	3-	—	3.79
Ottawa	AAA	20	0	0	10	26.2	119	26	14	6	1	0	0	1	12	2	34	0	0	1	1	.500	0	2-	—	2.03
1998 Montreal	NL	10	0	0	0	6	29	6	4	4	0	1	0	0	4	0	7	0	0	0	0	.000	0	0-0	3	6.00

Gregg Zaun

Bats: Both **Throws:** Right **Pos:** C-88; PH/PR-25; 2B-1 **Ht:** 5'10" **Wt:** 180 **Born:** 4/14/71 **Age:** 28

Year Team	Lg	G	AB	H	2B	3B	HR	(Hm	Rd)	TB	R	RBI	TBB	IBB	SO	HBP	SH	SF	SB	CS	SB%	GDP	Avg	OBP	SLG
1995 Baltimore	AL	40	104	27	5	0	3	(1	2)	41	18	14	16	0	14	0	2	0	1	1	.50	2	.260	.358	.394
1996 Bal-Fla		60	139	34	9	1	2	(1	1)	51	20	15	14	3	20	2	1	2	1	0	1.00	5	.245	.318	.367
1997 Florida	NL	58	143	43	10	2	2	(0	2)	63	21	20	26	4	18	2	1	0	1	0	1.00	3	.301	.415	.441
1998 Florida	NL	106	298	56	12	2	5	(2	3)	87	19	29	35	2	52	1	2	2	5	2	.71	7	.188	.274	.292
1996 Baltimore	AL	50	108	25	8	1	1	(1	0)	38	16	13	11	2	15	2	0	2	0	0	.00	3	.231	.309	.352
Florida	NL	10	31	9	1	0	1	(0	1)	13	4	2	3	1	5	0	1	0	1	0	1.00	2	.290	.353	.419
4 ML YEARS		264	684	160	36	5	12	(4	8)	242	78	78	91	9	104	5	6	4	8	3	.73	17	.234	.327	.354

Todd Zeile

Bats: Right **Throws:** Right **Pos:** 3B-157; PH/PR-2; 1B-1 **Ht:** 6'1" **Wt:** 200 **Born:** 9/9/65 **Age:** 33

Year Team	Lg	G	AB	H	2B	3B	HR	(Hm	Rd)	TB	R	RBI	TBB	IBB	SO	HBP	SH	SF	SB	CS	SB%	GDP	Avg	OBP	SLG
1989 St. Louis	NL	28	84	21	3	1	1	(0	1)	29	7	8	9	1	14	0	1	1	0	0	.00	1	.256	.326	.354
1990 St. Louis	NL	144	495	121	25	3	15	(8	7)	197	62	57	67	3	77	2	0	6	2	4	.33	11	.244	.333	.398
1991 St. Louis	NL	155	565	158	36	3	11	(7	4)	233	76	81	62	3	94	5	0	6	17	11	.61	15	.280	.353	.412
1992 St. Louis	NL	126	439	113	18	4	7	(4	3)	160	51	48	68	4	70	0	0	7	7	10	.41	11	.257	.352	.364
1993 St. Louis	NL	157	571	158	36	4	17	(8	9)	247	82	103	70	5	76	0	0	6	5	4	.56	15	.277	.352	.433
1994 St. Louis	NL	113	415	111	25	1	19	(9	10)	195	62	75	52	3	56	3	0	7	1	3	.25	13	.267	.348	.470
1995 StL-ChN	NL	113	426	105	22	0	14	(8	6)	169	50	52	34	1	76	4	4	5	1	0	1.00	13	.246	.305	.397
1996 Phi-Bal		163	617	162	32	0	25	(10	15)	269	78	99	82	4	104	1	0	4	1	1	.50	18	.263	.348	.436
1997 Los Angeles	NL	160	575	154	17	0	31	(17	14)	264	89	90	85	7	112	6	0	6	8	7	.53	18	.268	.365	.459
1998 LA-Fla-Tex		158	572	155	32	3	19	(7	12)	250	85	94	69	2	90	4	1	7	4	4	.50	12	.271	.350	.437
1995 St. Louis	NL	34	127	37	6	0	5	(2	3)	58	16	22	18	1	23	1	0	2	1	0	1.00	2	.291	.378	.457
Chicago	NL	79	299	68	16	0	9	(6	3)	111	34	30	16	0	53	3	4	3	0	0	.00	11	.227	.271	.371
1996 Philadelphia	NL	134	500	134	24	0	20	(9	11)	218	61	80	67	4	88	1	0	4	1	1	.50	16	.268	.353	.436
Baltimore	AL	29	117	28	8	0	5	(1	4)	51	17	19	15	0	16	0	0	0	0	0	.00	2	.239	.326	.436
1998 Los Angeles	NL	40	158	40	6	1	7	(1	6)	69	22	27	10	0	24	1	0	1	1	1	.50	5	.253	.300	.437
Florida	NL	66	234	68	12	1	6	(2	4)	100	37	39	31	2	34	2	0	3	2	3	.40	4	.291	.374	.427
Texas	AL	52	180	47	14	1	6	(4	2)	81	26	28	28	0	32	1	1	3	1	0	1.00	3	.261	.358	.450
10 ML YEARS		1317	4757	1258	246	16	159	(78	81)	2013	642	707	598	33	769	25	6	55	46	44	.51	127	.264	.346	.423

Jon Zuber

Bats: Left **Throws:** Left **Pos:** PH/PR-29; LF-5; 1B-4 **Ht:** 6'0" **Wt:** 190 **Born:** 12/10/69 **Age:** 29

Year Team	Lg	G	AB	H	2B	3B	HR	(Hm	Rd)	TB	R	RBI	TBB	IBB	SO	HBP	SH	SF	SB	CS	SB%	GDP	Avg	OBP	SLG
1992 Batavia	A	22	86	30	6	0	1	—	—	45	14	21	9	1	11	1	0		1	1	.50	1	.341	.404	.511
Spartanburg	A	54	206	59	13	1	3	—	—	83	24	36	33	1	31	1	0		1	1	.75	6	.286	.386	.403
1993 Clearwater	A+	129	494	152	37	5	5	—	—	214	70	69	49	5	47	0	3	4	6	6	.50	15	.308	.367	.433
1994 Reading	AA	138	498	146	29	5	9	—	—	212	81	70	71	4	71	1	1	5	2	4	.33	11	.293	.379	.426
1995 Scranton-WB	AAA	119	418	120	19	5	3	—	—	158	53	50	49	2	68	0	1	2	1	2	.33	11	.287	.360	.378
1996 Scranton-WB	AAA	118	412	128	22	5	4	—	—	172	62	59	58	3	50	1	2	4	4	2	.67	15	.311	.394	.417
1997 Scranton-WB	AAA	126	435	137	37	2	6	—	—	196	85	64	79	0	53	3	1	3	3	4	.43	11	.315	.421	.451
1998 Scranton-WB	AAA	80	280	91	23	4	4	—	—	134	47	56	45	1	34	2	1	6	0	0	.00	8	.325	.414	.479
1996 Philadelphia	NL	30	91	23	4	0	1	(1	0)	30	7	10	6	1	11	0	1	1	1	0	1.00	3	.253	.296	.330
1998 Philadelphia	NL	38	45	11	3	1	2	(0	2)	22	6	6	6	0	9	1	0	0	0	0	.00	1	.244	.346	.489
2 ML YEARS		68	136	34	7	1	3	(1	2)	52	13	16	12	1	20	1	1	1	1	0	1.00	4	.250	.313	.382

1998 Team Statistics

All the statistics you need about your favorite team are here. Final standings, record breakdowns, team batting, pitching and fielding can be found here. Also included in this section are team's records against the other league. American League teams have a split vs. NL teams and National League teams have a split vs. AL teams.

1998 American League Final Standings

Overall

EAST

Team	W-L	Pct	GB	Clinch	1st	Lead
New York Yankees	114-48	.704	—	9/9	153	22
Boston Red Sox*	92-70	.568	22	—	6	0.5
Toronto Blue Jays	88-74	.543	26	—	2	0
Baltimore Orioles	79-83	.488	35	—	16	2.5
Tampa Bay Devil Rays	63-99	.389	51	—	—	—

CENTRAL

Team	W-L	Pct	GB	Clinch	1st	Lead
Cleveland Indians	89-73	.549	—	9/16	182	14
Chicago White Sox	80-82	.494	9	—	1	0
Kansas City Royals	72-89	.447	16.5	—	1	0
Minnesota Twins	70-92	.432	19	—	1	0
Detroit Tigers	65-97	.401	24	—	1	0

WEST

Team	W-L	Pct	GB	Clinch	1st	Lead
Texas Rangers	88-74	.543	—	9/25	104	6
Anaheim Angels	85-77	.525	3	—	84	3.5
Seattle Mariners	76-85	.472	11.5	—	2	0
Oakland Athletics	74-88	.457	14	—	1	0

* represents playoff wild-card berth

East Division

Team	AT Home	Road	VERSUS East	Cent	West	NL	LHS	RHS	CONDITIONS Grass	Turf	Day	Night	XInn	RUNS 1-R	5+R	MONTHLY Apr	May	June	July	Aug	Sep/Oct	ALL-STAR Pre	Post
New York	62-19	52-29	33-15	39-15	29-15	13-3	33-11	81-37	97-39	17-9	36-14	78-34	9-2	21-10	42-13	17-6	20-7	19-7	20-7	22-10	16-11	61-20	53-28
Boston	51-30	41-40	25-23	31-23	27-17	9-7	31-15	61-55	81-57	11-13	27-26	65-44	7-4	24-25	30-11	18-8	13-14	17-10	15-12	17-11	12-15	52-33	40-37
Toronto	51-30	37-44	27-21	28-26	24-20	9-7	23-19	65-55	27-34	61-40	35-15	53-59	8-8	28-17	27-22	10-16	18-11	14-14	12-15	17-10	17-8	46-42	42-32
Baltimore	42-39	37-44	19-29	29-25	26-18	5-11	22-27	57-56	66-67	13-16	26-22	53-61	5-2	18-24	27-18	14-12	11-17	12-16	18-8	14-14	10-15	38-50	41-33
Tampa Bay	33-48	30-51	16-32	22-32	20-24	5-11	13-27	50-72	23-38	40-61	18-25	45-74	5-10	15-20	20-32	12-13	12-16	10-17	9-16	10-20	10-16	34-52	29-47

Central Division

Team	AT Home	Road	VERSUS East	Cent	West	NL	LHS	RHS	CONDITIONS Grass	Turf	Day	Night	XInn	RUNS 1-R	5+R	MONTHLY Apr	May	June	July	Aug	Sep/Oct	ALL-STAR Pre	Post
Cleveland	46-35	43-38	27-27	29-19	23-21	10-6	25-20	64-53	74-63	15-10	21-29	68-44	5-10	23-23	27-23	13-12	18-10	14-12	16-12	13-15	14-12	50-35	39-38
Chicago	44-37	36-45	28-26	26-22	19-25	7-9	17-25	63-57	70-64	10-18	20-29	60-53	4-6	20-22	23-33	9-15	12-16	11-17	14-12	15-15	18-7	35-51	45-31
Kansas City	29-51	43-38	23-31	21-27	19-24	9-7	19-30	53-59	53-80	19-9	19-24	53-65	7-5	17-16	15-41	11-15	9-17	15-13	12-15	16-13	8-16	38-48	34-41
Minnesota	35-46	35-46	24-30	21-27	18-26	7-9	16-19	54-73	26-32	44-60	24-26	46-66	5-12	25-29	19-26	11-16	13-13	14-14	13-13	9-20	10-16	40-46	30-46
Detroit	32-49	33-48	19-35	23-25	16-28	7-9	17-25	48-72	53-84	12-13	21-29	44-68	7-8	20-21	19-28	5-18	15-12	10-18	13-15	8-22	13-12	34-50	31-47

West Division

Team	AT Home	Road	VERSUS East	Cent	West	NL	LHS	RHS	CONDITIONS Grass	Turf	Day	Night	XInn	RUNS 1-R	5+R	MONTHLY Apr	May	June	July	Aug	Sep/Oct	ALL-STAR Pre	Post
Texas	48-33	40-41	27-28	33-22	20-16	8-8	26-22	62-52	79-61	9-13	16-23	72-51	3-3	19-17	30-28	18-7	15-13	13-15	11-15	18-12	15-10	48-39	40-35
Anaheim	42-39	43-38	27-28	29-26	19-17	10-6	23-18	62-59	71-68	14-9	18-24	67-53	6-6	24-19	26-26	15-11	12-15	22-6	9-18	18-12	9-15	49-37	36-40
Seattle	42-39	34-46	22-33	32-22	15-21	7-9	14-18	62-67	22-41	54-44	26-24	50-61	3-5	10-20	30-26	12-14	14-14	8-20	14-11	14-14	14-11	37-51	39-34
Oakland	39-42	35-46	18-37	30-25	18-18	8-8	23-29	51-59	64-76	10-12	33-37	41-51	7-5	16-19	23-29	12-14	10-17	15-13	11-16	15-15	11-13	41-45	33-43

Team vs. Team Breakdown

	Ana	Bal	Bos	ChA	Cle	Det	KC	Min	NYA	Oak	Sea	TB	Tex	Tor
Anaheim Angels	—	5	6	5	4	8	6	6	6	5	9	6	5	4
Baltimore Orioles	6	—	6	2	5	10	5	7	3	8	6	5	6	5
Boston Red Sox	5	6	—	5	8	5	8	5	5	9	7	9	6	5
Chicago White Sox	6	9	6	—	6	6	8	6	4	4	4	5	5	4
Cleveland Indians	7	6	3	6	—	9	8	6	4	3	9	7	4	7
Detroit Tigers	3	1	5	6	3	—	6	8	3	7	3	5	3	5
Kansas City Royals	5	6	3	4	4	6	—	7	0	7	4	8	3	6
Minnesota Twins	5	3	6	6	6	4	5	—	4	4	2	7	7	4
New York Yankees	5	9	7	7	7	8	10	7	—	8	8	11	8	6
Oakland Athletics	7	3	2	7	8	4	4	7	3	—	5	5	6	5
Seattle Mariners	3	5	4	7	2	8	6	9	3	7	—	6	5	4
Tampa Bay Devil Rays	5	7	3	6	3	6	3	4	1	6	5	—	4	5
Texas Rangers	7	5	5	6	7	8	8	4	3	6	7	7	—	7
Toronto Blue Jays	7	7	7	6	4	6	5	7	6	6	7	7	4	—

(read wins across and losses down)

1998 National League Final Standings

Overall

EAST

Team	W-L	Pct	GB	Clinch	1st	Lead
Atlanta Braves	106-56	.654	—	9/14	169	18
New York Mets	88-74	.543	18	—	19	1.5
Philadelphia Phillies	75-87	.463	31	—	4	0.5
Montreal Expos	65-97	.401	41	—	1	0
Florida Marlins	54-108	.333	52	—	1	0

CENTRAL

Team	W-L	Pct	GB	Clinch	1st	Lead
Houston Astros	102-60	.630	—	9/14	150	13
Chicago Cubs*	90-73	.552	12.5	—	13	0.5
St. Louis Cardinals	83-79	.512	19	—	4	0.5
Cincinnati Reds	77-85	.475	25	—	—	—
Milwaukee Brewers	74-88	.457	28	—	20	2.5
Pittsburgh Pirates	69-93	.426	33	—	2	0

WEST

Team	W-L	Pct	GB	Clinch	1st	Lead
San Diego Padres	98-64	.605	—	9/12	176	16
San Francisco Giants	89-74	.546	9.5	—	13	1
Los Angeles Dodgers	83-79	.512	15	—	—	—
Colorado Rockies	77-85	.475	21	—	6	1
Arizona Diamondbacks	65-97	.401	33	—	—	—

* represents playoff wild-card berth

East Division

Team	AT Home	Road	VERSUS East	Cent	West	AL	LHS	RHS	CONDITIONS Grass	Turf	Day	Night	XInn	RUNS 1-R	5+R	MONTHLY Apr	May	June	July	Aug	Sep	ALL-STAR Pre	Post
Atlanta	56-25	50-31	30-18	34-20	33-11	9-7	25-13	81-43	86-43	20-13	33-12	73-44	2-4	23-21	35-8	17-9	21-9	15-11	18-9	18-10	16-8	59-29	47-27
New York	47-34	41-40	22-26	33-21	24-20	9-7	25-19	63-55	75-60	13-14	33-25	55-49	7-9	25-26	21-14	12-18	12-15	13-15	20-12	12-12		44-39	44-35
Philadelphia	40-41	35-46	21-27	29-25	18-26	7-9	15-25	60-62	23-37	52-50	22-26	53-61	13-9	29-28	10-23	12-12	13-15	15-12	15-12	11-20	9-15	43-42	32-45
Montreal	39-42	26-55	26-22	13-41	20-24	6-10	14-22	51-75	19-42	46-55	14-32	51-65	4-4	21-27	14-23	7-18	13-17	13-13	9-19	11-19	12-11	34-52	31-45
Florida	31-50	23-58	21-27	12-42	13-31	8-8	11-25	43-83	47-83	7-25	20-30	34-78	7-14	31-29	8-29	8-18	8-20	12-15	10-18	8-20	7-17	32-55	22-53

Central Division

Team	AT Home	Road	VERSUS East	Cent	West	AL	LHS	RHS	CONDITIONS Grass	Turf	Day	Night	XInn	RUNS 1-R	5+R	MONTHLY Apr	May	June	July	Aug	Sep	ALL-STAR Pre	Post
Houston	55-26	47-34	30-15	38-18	24-23	10-4	24-17	78-43	30-27	72-33	31-18	71-42	10-12	30-18	35-9	17-9	16-12	17-10	15-12	22-7	15-9	53-34	49-26
Chicago	51-31	39-42	27-18	28-28	30-19	5-8	23-22	67-51	78-59	12-14	52-41	38-32	11-11	30-27	20-17	14-12	17-11	12-15	19-9	14-14	14-11	48-39	42-34
St. Louis	48-34	35-45	23-22	30-26	26-22	4-9	26-22	57-57	74-61	9-18	25-26	58-53	9-7	28-30	22-20	15-11	12-15	11-16	12-15	14-15	18-7	40-46	43-33
Cincinnati	39-42	38-43	26-19	27-29	17-31	7-6	14-23	63-62	30-31	47-54	28-28	49-57	7-7	16-26	18-21	12-13	15-16	8-19	13-13	17-11	12-12	39-50	38-35
Milwaukee	38-43	36-45	22-23	22-34	22-25	8-6	20-27	54-61	64-73	10-15	24-30	50-58	10-4	26-26	10-23	16-8	12-16	15-12	12-17	9-19	10-15	43-42	31-46
Pittsburgh	40-40	29-53	21-24	23-33	19-29	6-7	19-24	50-69	19-40	50-53	15-30	54-63	4-9	19-30	20-25	11-16	15-14	13-14	11-15	14-12	5-22	40-48	29-45

West Division

Team	AT Home	Road	VERSUS East	Cent	West	AL	LHS	RHS	CONDITIONS Grass	Turf	Day	Night	XInn	RUNS 1-R	5+R	MONTHLY Apr	May	June	July	Aug	Sep	ALL-STAR Pre	Post
San Diego	54-27	44-37	26-18	35-22	31-17	6-7	28-24	70-40	83-55	15-9	29-20	69-44	9-5	31-23	18-13	18-7	16-14	18-9	18-8	18-11	9-15	57-31	41-33
San Francisco	49-32	40-42	28-16	31-27	22-26	8-5	23-17	66-57	79-65	10-9	42-29	47-45	12-8	25-29	24-15	13-13	19-11	15-12	10-15	16-13	15-10	52-37	37-37
Los Angeles	48-33	35-46	19-25	31-26	25-23	8-5	19-19	64-60	73-68	10-11	21-23	62-56	9-8	30-24	15-15	14-11	13-13	13-13	17-10	11-18	15-9	43-44	40-35
Colorado	42-39	35-46	24-20	25-33	24-24	4-8	18-32	59-53	61-71	16-14	25-28	52-57	6-5	23-24	19-19	11-16	12-16	13-15	11-14	15-14	14-10	37-52	40-33
Arizona	34-47	31-50	15-29	27-30	18-30	5-8	18-22	47-75	55-83	10-14	16-25	49-72	6-5	16-23	16-33	7-19	10-19	12-15	11-15	13-16	12-12	30-58	35-39

Team vs. Team Breakdown

	Ari	Atl	ChN	Cin	Col	Fla	Hou	LA	Mil	Mon	NYN	Phi	Pit	SD	SF	StL
Arizona Diamondbacks	—	1	5	4	6	6	4	4	6	2	4	2	6	3	5	2
Atlanta Braves	8	—	3	7	5	7	4	8	7	6	9	8	7	5	7	6
Chicago Cubs	7	6	—	6	7	7	4	4	6	7	4	3	8	5	7	4
Cincinnati Reds	5	2	5	—	4	9	3	5	6	8	3	4	5	1	2	8
Colorado Rockies	6	3	2	5	—	6	6	6	4	7	3	5	5	5	7	3
Florida Marlins	2	5	2	0	3	—	3	4	0	5	5	6	3	4	0	4
Houston Astros	5	5	7	8	5	6	—	3	9	7	5	7	9	5	6	5
Los Angeles Dodgers	8	1	5	4	6	5	6	—	5	5	3	5	7	5	6	4
Milwaukee Brewers	3	2	6	5	7	9	2	4	—	6	1	4	6	3	5	3
Montreal Expos	7	6	2	1	2	7	2	4	3	—	8	5	2	4	3	3
New York Mets	5	3	5	6	6	7	4	5	8	4	—	8	4	4	4	6
Philadelphia Phillies	7	4	6	5	4	6	2	4	5	7	4	—	8	1	2	3
Pittsburgh Pirates	3	2	3	7	4	6	2	5	5	7	5	1	—	5	2	6
San Diego Padres	9	4	4	11	7	5	4	7	6	4	5	8	4	—	8	6
San Francisco Giants	7	2	3	7	5	9	3	6	4	6	5	6	7	4	—	7
St. Louis Cardinals	7	3	7	3	6	5	7	5	8	6	3	6	5	3	5	—

(read wins across and losses down)

American League Batting

Tm	G	AB	H	2B	3B	HR	(Hm	Rd)	TB	R	RBI	TBB	IBB	SO	HBP	SH	SF	ShO	SB	CS	SB%	GDP	LOB	Avg	OBP	SLG
NYA	162	5643	1625	290	31	207	(97	110)	2598	965	907	653	34	1025	57	32	59	5	153	63	.71	145	1203	.288	.364	.460
Tex	162	5672	1637	314	32	201	(101	100)	2618	940	894	595	27	1045	39	41	54	6	82	47	.64	137	1184	.289	.357	.462
Bos	162	5601	1568	338	35	205	(93	112)	2591	876	827	541	32	1049	70	35	52	4	72	39	.65	144	1150	.280	.348	.463
ChA	163	5585	1516	291	38	198	(106	92)	2477	861	806	551	34	916	47	38	59	9	127	46	.73	119	1104	.271	.339	.444
Sea	161	5628	1553	321	28	234	(117	117)	2632	859	822	558	26	1081	57	36	48	6	115	39	.75	107	1189	.276	.345	.468
Cle	162	5616	1530	334	30	198	(104	94)	2518	850	811	631	35	1061	40	30	59	6	143	60	.70	123	1169	.272	.347	.448
Bal	162	5565	1520	303	11	214	(109	105)	2487	817	783	593	30	903	58	44	44	3	86	48	.64	136	1187	.273	.347	.447
Tor	163	5580	1482	316	19	221	(112	109)	2499	816	776	564	43	1132	87	43	49	4	184	81	.69	108	1133	.266	.340	.448
Oak	162	5490	1413	295	13	149	(71	78)	2181	804	755	633	22	1122	55	58	46	9	131	47	.74	120	1159	.257	.338	.397
Ana	162	5630	1530	314	27	147	(53	94)	2339	787	739	510	31	1028	48	49	41	6	93	45	.67	122	1180	.272	.335	.415
Min	162	5641	1499	285	32	115	(51	64)	2193	734	691	506	33	915	45	18	52	10	112	54	.67	155	1151	.266	.328	.389
Det	162	5664	1494	306	29	165	(92	73)	2353	722	691	455	25	1070	62	16	45	8	122	62	.66	111	1131	.264	.323	.415
KC	162	5546	1459	274	40	134	(76	58)	2215	714	686	475	24	984	60	45	65	10	135	50	.73	118	1140	.263	.324	.399
TB	162	5555	1450	267	43	111	(67	44)	2136	620	579	473	24	1107	37	53	38	17	120	73	.62	127	1155	.261	.321	.385
AL	1134	78416	21276	4248	408	2499	(1249	1250)	33837	11365	10767	7738	420	14438	762	538	711	103	1675	754	.69	1772	16235	.271	.340	.432

American League Pitching

Tm	G	CG	Rel	IP	BFP	H	R	ER	HR	SH	SF	HB	TBB	IBB	SO	WP	Bk	W	L	Pct.	ShO	Sv-Op	Hld	OAvg	OOBP	OSLG	ERA
NYA	162	22	334	1456.2	6100	1357	656	619	156	34	47	68	466	25	1080	37	5	114	48	.704	16	48-66	46	.247	.312	.387	3.82
Bos	162	5	432	1436	6141	1406	729	667	168	26	47	53	504	33	1025	62	2	92	70	.568	8	53-71	68	.255	.321	.402	4.18
TB	162	7	410	1443	6269	1425	751	698	171	34	45	81	643	27	1008	43	3	69	93	.389	7	28-48	38	.261	.345	.412	4.35
Tor	163	10	384	1465	6352	1443	768	697	169	42	44	45	587	26	1154	34	4	88	74	.543	11	47-68	69	.256	.329	.417	4.28
Cle	162	9	423	1460	6393	1552	779	721	171	43	49	67	563	48	1037	35	5	89	73	.549	4	47-70	83	.274	.344	.428	4.44
Ana	162	3	415	1444	6326	1481	783	720	164	44	57	47	630	23	1091	70	4	85	77	.525	5	52-69	63	.267	.344	.423	4.49
Bal	162	16	402	1431.1	6213	1505	785	754	169	46	50	46	535	33	1065	51	6	79	83	.488	10	37-55	52	.272	.338	.424	4.74
Min	162	7	432	1447.2	6322	1622	818	764	180	37	68	43	458	21	952	55	5	70	92	.432	8	42-64	70	.284	.338	.448	4.75
Sea	161	17	368	1424.1	6271	1530	855	781	196	49	37	60	528	23	1156	61	6	76	85	.472	7	31-52	36	.273	.340	.451	4.93
Det	162	9	446	1446.1	6327	1551	863	792	185	46	49	40	595	53	947	60	0	65	97	.401	4	32-47	37	.277	.348	.440	4.93
Oak	162	12	408	1434	6310	1555	866	766	179	44	53	56	529	29	922	68	5	74	88	.457	4	39-59	64	.276	.342	.441	4.81
Tex	162	10	402	1431.1	6357	1624	871	794	164	35	63	45	519	32	994	62	2	88	74	.543	8	46-59	52	.285	.346	.446	4.99
KC	161	6	388	1436.1	6369	1590	899	822	196	30	58	60	568	28	999	72	5	72	89	.447	5	46-62	49	.281	.350	.445	5.15
ChA	163	8	405	1438.2	6368	1569	931	835	211	32	51	54	580	20	911	58	10	80	82	.494	4	42-63	55	.278	.348	.453	5.22
AL	1134	141	5649	20194.2	88118	21210	11354	10430	2479	542	718	765	7705	421	14341	768	62	1135	1131	.501	101	590-853	782	.271	.339	.430	4.65

American League Fielding

Team	G	PO	Ast	OFAst	E	(Throw	Field)	TC	DP	GDP Opp	GDP	GDP%	PB	OSB	OCS	OSB%	CPkof	PPkof	AVG
Baltimore	162	4294	1758	26	81	(39	42)	6133	144	213	121	.568	12	182	53	.77	0	4	.987
Tampa Bay	162	4329	1763	48	94	(39	55)	6186	178	253	147	.581	19	97	61	.61	3	2	.985
New York	162	4370	1639	32	98	(41	57)	6107	146	210	117	.557	12	102	51	.67	1	6	.984
Boston	162	4308	1624	26	105	(54	51)	6037	128	191	106	.555	35	132	58	.69	1	2	.983
Anaheim	162	4332	1646	27	106	(57	49)	6084	146	225	119	.529	28	156	65	.71	0	8	.983
Cleveland	162	4380	1727	44	110	(47	63)	6217	146	254	125	.492	8	110	47	.70	0	2	.982
Minnesota	162	4343	1585	33	108	(38	70)	6036	135	203	115	.567	11	101	45	.69	2	4	.982
Detroit	162	4339	1812	44	115	(45	70)	6266	164	224	147	.656	14	120	69	.63	2	4	.982
Texas	162	4294	1580	25	121	(42	79)	5995	140	215	112	.521	10	64	55	.54	7	0	.980
Kansas City	161	4309	1689	27	125	(60	65)	6123	172	240	143	.596	11	80	43	.65	1	7	.980
Toronto	163	4395	1531	29	125	(52	73)	6051	131	204	106	.520	9	149	47	.76	0	3	.979
Seattle	161	4273	1571	33	125	(62	63)	5969	139	207	120	.580	11	127	49	.72	0	3	.979
Chicago	163	4316	1706	27	140	(65	75)	6162	161	240	141	.588	9	122	59	.67	4	4	.977
Oakland	162	4302	1654	32	141	(61	80)	6097	155	238	130	.546	13	103	48	.68	0	11	.977
American League	1134	60584	23285	453	1594	(702	892)	85463	2085	3117	1749	.561	202	1645	750	.69	21	60	.981

National League Batting

Tm	G	AB	H	2B	3B	HR	(Hm	Rd)	TB	R	RBI	TBB	IBB	SO	HBP	SH	SF	ShO	SB	CS	SB%	GDP	LOB	Avg	OBP	SLG
Hou	162	5641	1578	326	28	166	(82	84)	2458	874	818	621	52	1122	72	58	49	6	155	51	.75	146	1217	.280	.356	.436
SF	163	5628	1540	292	26	161	(84	77)	2367	845	800	678	53	1040	44	81	53	8	102	51	.67	123	1235	.274	.353	.421
ChN	163	5649	1494	250	34	212	(111	101)	2448	831	788	601	52	1223	39	67	37	7	65	44	.60	123	1162	.264	.337	.433
Atl	162	5484	1489	297	26	215	(104	111)	2483	826	794	548	37	1062	61	76	46	6	98	43	.70	104	1148	.272	.342	.453
Col	162	5632	1640	333	36	183	(111	72)	2594	826	791	469	29	949	37	98	41	6	67	47	.59	148	1138	.291	.347	.461
StL	163	5593	1444	292	30	223	(113	110)	2465	810	781	676	65	1179	42	68	34	2	133	41	.76	117	1200	.258	.341	.441
Cin	162	5496	1441	298	28	138	(66	72)	2209	750	723	608	39	1107	37	78	49	10	95	42	.69	134	1183	.262	.337	.402
SD	162	5490	1390	292	30	167	(79	88)	2243	749	715	604	40	1072	48	56	45	7	79	37	.68	112	1179	.253	.330	.409
Phi	162	5617	1482	286	36	126	(68	58)	2218	713	672	508	44	1080	45	65	65	11	97	45	.68	110	1179	.264	.326	.395
Mil	162	5541	1439	266	17	152	(68	84)	2195	707	673	532	36	1039	66	61	32	11	81	59	.58	135	1148	.260	.330	.396
NYN	162	5510	1425	289	24	136	(66	70)	2170	706	671	572	55	1049	37	88	48	9	62	46	.57	126	1193	.259	.330	.394
LA	162	5459	1374	209	27	159	(78	81)	2114	669	630	447	31	1056	36	91	43	9	137	53	.72	98	1069	.252	.310	.387
Fla	162	5558	1381	277	36	114	(52	62)	2072	667	621	525	30	1120	45	70	29	6	115	57	.67	121	1132	.248	.317	.373
Ari	162	5491	1353	235	46	159	(82	77)	2157	665	621	489	32	1239	64	45	27	16	73	38	.66	125	1104	.246	.314	.393
Pit	163	5493	1395	271	35	107	(58	49)	2057	650	613	393	22	1060	91	78	56	14	159	51	.76	102	1089	.254	.311	.374
Mon	162	5418	1348	280	32	147	(65	82)	2133	644	602	439	31	1058	60	87	37	13	91	46	.66	109	1068	.249	.310	.394
NL	1298	88700	23213	4493	491	2565	(1287	1278)	36383	11932	11313	8710	648	17455	824	1167	691	141	1609	751	.68	1933	18444	.262	.331	.410

National League Pitching

Tm	G	CG	Rel	IP	BFP	H	R	ER	HR	SH	SF	HB	TBB	IBB	SO	WP	Bk	W	L	Pct.	ShO	Sv-Op	Hld	OAvg	OOBP	OSLG	ERA
Atl	162	24	354	1438.2	5967	1291	581	520	117	59	27	35	467	37	1232	51	3	106	56	.654	23	45-62	68	.240	.303	.353	3.25
Hou	162	12	340	1471.1	6214	1435	620	572	147	52	41	42	465	25	1187	50	5	102	60	.630	11	44-59	33	.256	.315	.394	3.50
SD	162	14	369	1454.2	6151	1384	635	587	139	75	29	49	501	45	1217	63	6	98	64	.605	11	59-75	66	.252	.318	.381	3.63
NYN	162	9	399	1458	6161	1381	645	609	152	64	42	68	532	59	1129	40	11	88	74	.543	16	46-72	51	.253	.325	.401	3.76
LA	162	16	342	1447.1	6168	1332	678	612	135	72	38	56	587	26	1178	46	9	83	79	.512	10	47-74	39	.246	.324	.376	3.81
Pit	163	7	395	1449	6217	1433	718	629	147	64	50	31	530	53	1112	45	14	69	93	.426	10	41-60	50	.259	.324	.400	3.91
SF	163	6	433	1477	6362	1457	739	686	171	80	46	52	562	68	1089	58	3	89	74	.546	6	44-67	70	.259	.330	.412	4.18
Cin	162	6	366	1441.1	6206	1400	760	711	170	74	44	52	573	42	1098	60	7	77	85	.475	8	42-57	28	.256	.330	.417	4.44
StL	163	6	428	1469.2	6392	1513	782	703	151	92	45	54	558	38	972	42	14	83	79	.512	10	44-75	70	.268	.338	.407	4.31
Mon	162	4	443	1427	6207	1448	783	695	156	77	50	57	533	39	1017	50	12	65	97	.401	5	39-52	45	.264	.333	.408	4.38
ChN	163	7	449	1477.1	6472	1528	792	733	187	80	62	46	575	48	1207	48	14	90	73	.552	7	56-78	66	.266	.336	.424	4.47
Phi	162	21	385	1463	6339	1476	808	754	188	73	43	54	544	27	1176	73	5	75	87	.463	10	32-56	41	.262	.331	.432	4.64
Ari	162	7	368	1432.1	6151	1463	812	737	188	80	40	41	489	32	908	52	14	65	97	.401	6	37-55	23	.266	.328	.428	4.63
Mil	162	2	416	1451	6325	1538	812	746	188	82	44	61	550	29	1063	48	7	74	88	.457	2	39-62	72	.275	.344	.444	4.63
Col	162	9	406	1432.2	6277	1583	855	794	174	62	43	63	562	17	951	47	9	77	85	.475	5	36-55	59	.285	.355	.448	4.99
Fla	162	11	420	1449.2	6553	1617	923	834	182	95	56	58	715	62	1016	62	10	54	108	.333	3	24-46	45	.287	.370	.454	5.18
NL	1298	161	6313	23240	100162	23279	11943	10922	2585	1163	684	821	8743	647	17552	835	143	1295	1299	.499	143	675-1005	826	.262	.332	.411	4.23

National League Fielding

Team	G	PO	Ast	OFAst	E	(Throw	Field)	TC	DP	GDP Opp	GDP	GDP%	PB	OSB	OCS	OSB%	CPkof	PPkof	AVG
Atlanta	162	4316	1681	36	91	(27	64)	6088	139	200	119	.595	13	85	40	.68	2	5	.985
San Francisco	163	4431	1806	11	101	(51	50)	6338	157	233	133	.571	13	97	39	.71	0	1	.984
Arizona	162	4297	1718	25	100	(38	62)	6115	125	196	105	.536	7	93	63	.60	1	7	.984
Chicago	163	4432	1622	34	101	(39	62)	6155	107	192	77	.422	7	100	10	.71	0	0	.984
New York	162	4374	1672	39	101	(49	52)	6147	151	211	118	.559	11	117	64	.65	0	10	.984
Colorado	162	4298	1795	36	102	(44	58)	6195	193	271	158	.583	9	108	52	.68	0	10	.984
San Diego	162	4364	1727	26	104	(50	54)	6195	155	234	126	.538	17	94	40	.70	4	3	.983
Houston	162	4414	1782	35	108	(49	59)	6304	144	240	111	.463	9	75	43	.64	0	1	.983
Philadelphia	162	4389	1747	43	110	(48	62)	6246	131	205	108	.527	15	87	33	.73	1	4	.982
Milwaukee	162	4353	1761	35	110	(44	66)	6224	192	241	156	.647	14	125	34	.79	4	5	.982
Cincinnati	162	4324	1563	25	122	(49	73)	6009	142	198	117	.591	10	117	46	.72	1	11	.980
Florida	162	4349	1738	45	129	(67	62)	6216	177	241	144	.598	18	109	54	.67	0	8	.979
Los Angeles	162	4342	1731	31	134	(54	80)	6207	154	216	127	.588	8	93	57	.62	0	5	.978
St. Louis	163	4409	1781	39	142	(56	86)	6332	160	216	123	.569	6	92	44	.68	1	5	.978
Pittsburgh	163	4347	1698	38	140	(58	82)	6185	161	252	135	.536	14	95	39	.71	0	6	.977
Montreal	162	4281	1686	36	155	(63	92)	6122	127	189	96	.508	18	132	64	.67	0	5	.975
National League	1298	69720	27508	534	1850	(786	1064)	99078	2415	3525	1953	.554	189	1639	755	.68	14	95	.981

255

1998 Fielding Stats

Ah, fielding—that murky realm that even the great Branch Rickey dismissed as "hopeless." Thanks to STATS, Inc., fielding statistics have come a long way since the days when all we had were games, putouts, assists, errors, fielding percentage and double plays. On the following pages, you'll see that we've added games started and defensive innings, as well as range factor. In the STATS *All-Time Major League Handbook*, range factor is calculated as (putouts plus assists) per game. On the following pages, we've used the formula (putouts plus assists) *per nine innings,* which is a bit more precise. The catchers have an additional section of "special" stats, where you'll find opponents' stolen base/caught stealing data and team ERA with a particular catcher behind the plate. Although these stats are unofficial, we don't expect that the "official" ones will be substantially different when they arrive in a few months.

One last note: make it a point to take a look at Andruw Jones' stats. He replaced Kenny Lofton as the Braves' center fielder last year, and they say he played even better defense than Lofton had. It sure shows up in the numbers—Jones led all major league center fielders in assists, putouts and double plays, and only one regular center fielder committed fewer errors.

First Basemen - Regulars

Player	Tm	G	GS	Inn	PO	A	E	DP	Pct.	Rng
Segui,David	Sea	134	133	1143.1	1044	115	1	106	.999	—
Snow,J.T.	SF	136	113	1037.0	1039	93	1	99	.999	—
Lee,Travis	Ari	146	145	1268.1	1270	98	3	104	.998	—
Brogna,Rico	Phi	151	143	1272.2	1239	140	5	103	.996	—
Olerud,John	NYN	157	149	1337.0	1257	116	5	119	.996	—
McGriff,Fred	TB	135	134	1186.1	1151	78	6	140	.995	—
King,Jeff	KC	112	110	944.1	932	85	5	103	.995	—
Fielder,Cecil	TOT	75	74	633.1	563	41	3	61	.995	—
Bagwell,Jeff	Hou	147	146	1311.1	1239	129	7	114	.995	—
Helton,Todd	Col	146	134	1208.0	1163	146	7	156	.995	—
Young,Kevin	Pit	157	153	1359.0	1335	80	8	138	.994	—
Grace,Mark	ChN	156	154	1390.1	1281	118	8	82	.994	—
Palmeiro,Rafael	Bal	159	158	1378.1	1433	125	9	127	.994	—
Casey,Sean	Cin	86	79	683.1	643	36	4	65	.994	—
Norton,Greg	ChA	79	67	630.1	643	30	4	57	.994	—
Joyner,Wally	SD	127	113	1013.2	988	78	7	99	.993	—
Lee,Derrek	Fla	132	114	1046.2	951	114	8	116	.993	—
Martinez,Tino	NYA	142	139	1215.0	1182	93	10	109	.992	—
Cordero,Wil	ChA	83	81	687.1	698	67	6	78	.992	—
Delgado,Carlos	Tor	141	141	1256.2	1165	86	10	110	.992	—
McGwire,Mark	StL	152	152	1326.1	1326	96	12	128	.992	—
Galarraga,Andres	Atl	149	149	1278.2	1219	81	11	114	.992	—
Thome,Jim	Cle	117	114	1015.2	998	85	10	97	.991	—
Vaughn,Mo	Bos	142	142	1238.1	1176	87	12	91	.991	—
Karros,Eric	LA	136	136	1168.2	1151	108	12	122	.991	—
Clark,Tony	Det	142	142	1234.0	1265	96	13	134	.991	—
Giambi,Jason	Oak	146	146	1236.2	1258	71	14	120	.990	—
Clark,Will	Tex	134	133	1147.1	1077	75	13	112	.989	—
Fullmer,Brad	Mon	137	135	1082.2	1070	78	17	81	.985	—
Average	—	132	128	1128.1	1095	91	7	106	.993	

First Basemen - The Rest

Player	Tm	G	GS	Inn	PO	A	E	DP	Pct.	Rng
Amaral,Rich	Sea	7	1	22.0	16	2	0	1	1.000	—
Arias,George	SD	1	1	5.0	4	0	0	1	1.000	—
Ashley,Billy	Bos	2	0	6.0	6	0	1	2	.857	—
Ball,Jeff	SF	1	1	7.0	10	0	0	1	1.000	—
Banks,Brian	Mil	2	1	9.0	8	0	0	0	1.000	—
Bell,David	Cle	1	0	7.0	4	0	0	0	1.000	—
Bell,David	Sea	5	3	29.0	35	2	0	3	1.000	—
Benjamin,Mike	Bos	10	4	42.2	41	9	0	3	1.000	—
Blowers,Mike	Oak	8	5	47.1	47	0	0	3	1.000	—
Bolick,Frank	Ana	0	0	2.0	2	0	0	1	1.000	—
Branson,Jeff	Cle	3	1	10.0	9	2	0	1	1.000	—
Brede,Brent	Ari	12	5	60.0	58	5	1	4	.984	—
Brosius,Scott	NYA	3	1	13.0	7	2	0	1	1.000	—
Brown,Brant	ChN	7	4	35.0	32	2	0	2	1.000	—
Carter,Joe	Bal	1	0	2.0	3	1	0	0	1.000	—
Carter,Joe	SF	16	10	97.0	87	8	1	5	.990	—
Catalanotto,Frank	Det	18	12	116.0	124	10	0	9	1.000	—
Cianfrocco,Archi	SD	19	9	92.2	91	11	0	11	1.000	—
Cirillo,Jeff	Mil	6	6	51.0	50	13	0	8	1.000	—
Colbrunn,Greg	Col	27	24	193.2	216	21	2	18	.992	—
Colbrunn,Greg	Atl	9	5	61.0	55	4	0	2	1.000	—
Conine,Jeff	KC	12	9	85.1	101	3	0	15	1.000	—
Coomer,Ron	Min	54	39	388.2	371	34	1	32	.998	—

First Basemen - The Rest

Player	Tm	G	GS	Inn	PO	A	E	DP	Pct.	Rng
Crespo,Felipe	Tor	1	0	2.0	4	0	1	0	.800	—
Dalesandro,Mark	Tor	2	0	2.0	5	0	0	0	1.000	—
Daubach,Brian	Fla	4	3	24.0	22	1	0	4	1.000	—
DeShields,Delino	StL	1	0	1.0	0	0	0	0	.000	—
Echevarria,Angel	Col	4	3	26.0	20	2	0	3	1.000	—
Eisenreich,Jim	Fla	10	8	64.0	53	2	2	7	.965	—
Eisenreich,Jim	LA	9	2	30.0	20	2	0	5	1.000	—
Erstad,Darin	Ana	72	57	503.2	463	38	2	46	.996	—
Fasano,Sal	KC	5	0	12.0	16	0	0	2	1.000	—
Fick,Robert	Det	1	1	9.0	9	0	0	1	1.000	—
Fielder,Cecil	Ana	72	72	613.1	551	39	2	60	.997	—
Fielder,Cecil	Cle	3	2	20.0	12	2	1	1	.933	—
Fox,Andy	Ari	12	12	103.0	104	6	0	7	1.000	—
Franco,Matt	NYN	11	6	72.1	68	3	0	3	1.000	—
Gaetti,Gary	StL	3	1	9.0	15	0	0	2	1.000	—
Garcia,Freddy	Pit	4	2	20.0	25	2	1	2	.964	—
Gates,Brent	Min	1	0	1.0	2	0	0	1	1.000	—
Greene,Todd	Ana	3	2	15.0	16	1	0	2	1.000	—
GriffeyJr.,Ken	Sea	1	0	1.0	0	0	0	0	.000	—
Guillen,Ozzie	Atl	1	0	2.0	2	0	0	0	1.000	—
Halter,Shane	KC	1	0	1.0	2	0	0	0	1.000	—
Hamelin,Bob	Mil	51	21	248.1	230	7	2	22	.992	—
Harris,Lenny	NYN	1	0	1.0	1	0	0	0	1.000	—
Hayes,Charlie	SF	45	39	335.2	347	34	2	37	.995	—
Hernandez,Carlos	SD	1	0	1.0	1	0	0	0	1.000	—
Hernandez,Jose	ChN	3	2	16.0	19	1	0	2	1.000	—
Hocking,Denny	Min	2	0	2.0	3	0	0	0	1.000	—
Hoiles,Chris	Bal	6	0	12.0	13	0	0	3	1.000	—
Hollins,Dave	Ana	7	6	48.0	44	5	1	4	.980	—
Houston,Tyler	ChN	7	3	34.0	32	2	0	1	1.000	—
Howell,Jack	Hou	10	5	53.0	63	6	0	3	1.000	—
Hudler,Rex	Phi	1	0	7.0	8	1	0	1	1.000	—
Hunter,Brian	StL	10	2	35.0	23	1	0	2	1.000	—
Huson,Jeff	Sea	7	2	25.0	22	1	0	1	1.000	—
Ibanez,Raul	Sea	16	12	119.0	93	5	1	12	.990	—
Jackson,Ryan	Fla	44	37	310.2	300	20	9	30	.973	—
Jaha,John	Mil	57	55	445.2	442	24	3	57	.994	—
Jefferies,Gregg	Ana	3	3	24.0	23	2	0	2	1.000	—
Jefferson,Reggie	Bos	7	4	40.0	37	4	2	2	.953	—
Johnson,Mark	Ana	5	1	17.1	13	1	0	1	1.000	—
Jordan,Kevin	Phi	24	18	169.1	158	15	0	15	1.000	—
Kent,Jeff	SF	1	0	0.1	1	0	0	0	1.000	—
Klesko,Ryan	Atl	7	5	50.0	48	4	1	4	.981	—
Konerko,Paul	LA	23	18	165.0	170	14	1	8	.995	—
Konerko,Paul	Cin	7	5	44.0	38	5	0	1	1.000	—
Kotsay,Mark	Fla	3	0	3.1	3	1	0	0	1.000	—
Laker,Tim	Pit	4	4	28.0	33	1	0	4	1.000	—
Lampkin,Tom	StL	2	0	4.0	5	0	0	1	1.000	—
Larkin,Stephen	Cin	1	1	6.0	6	0	0	1	1.000	—
Ledesma,Aaron	TB	2	1	4.0	4	0	0	1	1.000	—
Lesher,Brian	Oak	1	0	1.0	0	0	1	0	.000	—
Leyritz,Jim	Bos	1	0	3.0	3	0	0	1	1.000	—
Leyritz,Jim	SD	20	17	139.2	134	8	1	12	.993	—
Livingstone,Scott	Mon	3	1	12.0	10	1	1	4	.917	—
Loretta,Mark	Mil	70	32	360.0	353	23	3	41	.992	—
Luke,Matt	LA	18	6	82.0	64	13	0	5	1.000	—
Mabry,John	StL	16	8	90.1	93	11	0	8	1.000	—
Magadan,Dave	Oak	7	2	29.0	33	3	0	3	1.000	—

258

First Basemen - The Rest

Player	Tm	G	GS	Inn	PO	A	E	DP	Pct.	Rng
Manto,Jeff	Cle	7	5	44.0	49	3	1	4	.981	—
Manto,Jeff	Det	10	4	45.0	43	0	1	3	.977	—
Marrero,Eli	StL	2	0	2.0	1	1	0	0	1.000	—
Martinez,Dave	TB	1	0	0.2	0	0	0	0	.000	—
Martinez,Edgar	Sea	4	4	31.0	22	6	0	3	1.000	—
McCarty,Dave	Sea	2	2	17.0	14	0	0	1	1.000	—
McClain,Scott	TB	5	2	27.0	24	4	1	1	.966	—
McGee,Willie	StL	1	0	2.0	2	2	0	0	1.000	—
McGuire,Ryan	Mon	78	21	291.0	275	25	6	18	.980	—
Merced,Orlando	Min	38	34	294.1	299	20	6	32	.982	—
Mientkiewicz,D.	Min	8	7	64.0	61	3	0	3	1.000	—
Miller,Damian	Ari	1	0	1.0	0	1	0	0	1.000	—
Minor,Ryan	Bal	3	1	8.0	5	1	0	2	1.000	—
Mitchell,Kevin	Oak	2	1	7.1	5	0	0	1	1.000	—
Molitor,Paul	Min	9	9	74.0	79	7	0	4	1.000	—
Mordecai,Mike	Mon	1	0	1.0	2	0	0	0	1.000	—
Morris,Hal	KC	46	40	357.2	349	34	4	35	.990	—
Nevin,Phil	Ana	2	0	4.0	3	0	0	2	1.000	—
Nilsson,Dave	Mil	49	47	337.0	354	22	6	43	.984	—
Oliver,Joe	Det	2	0	3.0	2	1	0	0	1.000	—
Ortiz,David	Min	71	69	586.2	503	46	6	51	.989	—
Ortiz,Hector	KC	1	0	1.0	0	0	0	0	.000	—
Paquette,Craig	NYN	2	0	2.2	3	0	0	0	1.000	—
Perez,Eddie	Atl	8	0	17.0	15	0	1	1	.938	—
Perez,Eduardo	Cin	51	36	340.0	290	45	5	35	.985	—
Petagine,Roberto	Cin	15	2	43.1	46	4	0	4	1.000	—
Phillips,J.R.	Hou	12	8	76.1	70	6	3	7	.962	—
Pickering,Calvin	Bal	5	3	28.0	31	0	1	3	.969	—
Posada,Jorge	NYA	1	1	5.2	7	1	0	2	1.000	—
Pratt,Todd	NYN	3	3	10.0	11	0	0	1	1.000	—
Pritchett,Chris	Ana	29	19	189.2	190	20	1	12	.995	—
Radmanovich,R.	Sea	1	0	1.0	1	0	0	0	1.000	—
Randa,Joe	Det	1	0	3.0	3	1	0	1	1.000	—
Ripken,Billy	Det	2	0	2.0	5	0	0	0	1.000	—
Roskos,John	Fla	1	0	1.0	1	0	0	0	1.000	—
Samuel,Juan	Tor	3	0	3.0	2	0	0	0	1.000	—
Seguignol,F.	Mon	7	5	40.1	44	5	0	3	1.000	—
Servais,Scott	ChN	1	0	2.0	2	1	0	0	1.000	—
Sexson,Richie	Cle	45	40	363.1	321	38	6	36	.984	—
Shave,Jon	Min	1	0	1.0	1	0	0	0	1.000	—
Choate,Andy	CD	2	1	10.0	0	0	0	2	1.000	
Sheldon,Scott	Tex	1	0	1.0	0	0	0	0	.000	—
Shipley,Craig	Ana	8	2	27.0	27	3	1	3	.968	—
Simms,Mike	Tex	16	10	84.0	72	7	2	8	.975	—
Simon,Randall	Atl	4	3	30.0	36	1	0	3	1.000	—
Smith,Mark	Pit	6	4	37.0	30	4	0	3	1.000	—
Snopek,Chris	ChA	1	1	7.0	9	0	0	1	1.000	—
Sojo,Luis	NYA	19	12	120.0	107	8	1	8	.991	—
Sorrento,Paul	TB	27	25	225.0	220	23	0	22	1.000	—
Spehr,Tim	NYN	1	0	1.0	2	0	0	0	1.000	—
Spencer,Shane	NYA	1	1	6.0	3	1	0	0	1.000	—
Spiers,Bill	Hou	7	3	30.2	34	1	0	1	1.000	—
Sprague,Ed	Oak	1	0	2.0	1	0	0	0	1.000	—
Stahoviak,Scott	Min	4	4	36.0	35	4	1	4	.975	—
Stairs,Matt	Oak	6	5	46.2	45	8	0	6	1.000	—
Stanley,Mike	Tor	22	22	193.2	171	12	1	14	.995	—
Stanley,Mike	Bos	13	12	106.0	107	6	0	14	1.000	—
Stevens,Lee	Tex	37	19	199.0	207	15	1	11	.996	—

First Basemen - The Rest

Player	Tm	G	GS	Inn	PO	A	E	DP	Pct.	Rng
Strange,Doug	Pit	3	0	5.0	2	1	0	0	1.000	
Surhoff,B.J.	Bal	1	0	3.0	2	0	0	0	1.000	
Sutton,Larry	KC	6	2	35.0	32	3	0	5	1.000	
Sveum,Dale	NYA	21	8	97.0	108	9	3	9	.975	
Sweeney,Mark	SD	21	13	131.2	127	5	1	11	.992	
Tatum,Jimmy	NYN	9	4	34.0	32	1	0	1	1.000	
Thomas,Frank	ChA	14	14	114.0	116	6	2	12	.984	
VanderWal,John	Col	2	1	5.0	8	1	0	0	1.000	
VanderWal,John	SD	3	2	18.0	14	2	0	1	1.000	
Voigt,Jack	Oak	27	3	64.0	73	2	1	8	.987	
Wilkins,Rick	Sea	6	4	36.0	43	2	0	2	1.000	
Williams,Eddie	SD	7	6	43.0	47	3	0	3	1.000	
Witt,Kevin	Tor	1	0	7.2	5	1	0	0	1.000	
Wood,Jason	Det	6	3	34.1	36	2	0	4	1.000	
Young,Dmitri	Cin	44	39	324.2	304	22	2	25	.994	
Zeile,Todd	LA	1	0	1.2	2	0	0	0	1.000	
Zuber,Jon	Phi	4	1	14.0	15	1	0	1	1.000	

Second Basemen - Regulars

Player	Tm	G	GS	Inn	PO	A	E	DP	Pct.	Rng
Vina,Fernando	Mil	158	158	1382.2	404	468	12	135	.986	5.68
Easley,Damion	Det	140	136	1179.1	285	439	11	102	.985	5.53
Lansing,Mike	Col	153	148	1275.0	346	425	10	118	.987	5.44
Counsell,Craig	Fla	104	101	892.2	237	297	5	72	.991	5.38
Bell,David	TOT	116	105	928.2	215	335	10	70	.982	5.33
Veras,Quilvio	SD	132	130	1126.0	255	406	9	88	.987	5.28
Kent,Jeff	SF	134	134	1166.0	277	403	20	87	.971	5.25
DeShields,Delino	StL	111	102	896.1	248	274	9	66	.983	5.24
Lewis,Mark	Phi	140	137	1228.2	276	437	16	73	.978	5.22
Graffanino,Tony	Atl	93	67	632.2	139	227	11	41	.971	5.21
Cairo,Miguel	TB	148	139	1233.0	279	429	16	110	.978	5.17
Womack,Tony	Pit	152	149	1316.0	304	450	17	104	.978	5.16
Alomar,Roberto	Bal	144	141	1236.1	250	449	11	86	.985	5.09
McLemore,Mark	Tex	122	122	1055.2	249	331	15	71	.975	4.94
Young,Eric	LA	114	113	968.0	226	305	13	67	.976	4.94
Boone,Bret	Cin	156	155	1358.0	329	415	9	100	.988	4.93
Biggio,Craig	Hou	159	154	1368.0	318	430	15	91	.980	4.92
Benjamin,Mike	Bos	87	73	636.2	159	189	2	40	.994	4.92
Grebeck,Craig	Tor	91	77	723.0	144	249	10	38	.975	4.89
Offerman,Jose	KC	152	152	1325.1	278	440	19	112	.974	4.88
Baerga,Carlos	NYN	144	135	1164.0	289	341	9	97	.986	4.87
Spiezio,Scott	Oak	112	110	955.2	195	316	13	71	.975	4.81
Durham,Ray	ChA	158	156	1357.1	282	438	18	129	.976	4.77
Knoblauch,Chuck	NYA	149	149	1292.2	274	408	13	85	.981	4.75
Lockhart,Keith	Atl	97	86	730.1	130	250	6	56	.984	4.68
Morandini,Mickey	ChN	152	146	1304.0	265	404	5	70	.993	4.62
Guerrero,Wilton	TOT	84	80	694.2	155	198	10	41	.972	4.57
Fernandez,Tony	Tor	82	81	692.2	129	222	9	43	.975	4.56
Walker,Todd	Min	140	139	1171.2	219	363	13	72	.978	4.47
Cora,Joey	TOT	151	147	1268.0	241	308	20	75	.965	3.90
Average	—	129	124	1085.0	246	354	11	80	.981	4.99

Second Basemen - The Rest

Player	Tm	G	GS	Inn	PO	A	E	DP	Pct.	Rng
Abbott,Kurt	Col	7	5	43.0	13	17	0	3	1.000	6.28
Alexander,Manny	ChN	27	16	163.1	43	51	2	11	.979	5.18
Alicea,Luis	Tex	45	37	342.0	81	111	6	26	.970	5.05
Amaral,Rich	Sea	11	6	61.2	17	10	0	1	1.000	3.94
Anderson,Marlon	Phi	9	9	79.2	14	30	1	6	.978	4.97
Arias,Alex	Phi	1	0	1.0	0	1	0	0	1.000	9.00
Bates,Jason	Col	17	7	80.2	14	24	1	4	.974	4.24
Batista,Tony	Ari	41	31	280.2	72	83	1	23	.994	4.97
Baughman,Justin	Ana	59	53	472.2	104	153	6	22	.977	4.89
Bell,David	StL	1	1	5.1	0	2	0	1	1.000	3.38
Bell,David	Cle	101	91	807.1	192	293	9	58	.982	5.41
Bell,David	Sea	14	13	116.0	23	40	1	11	.984	4.89
Bell,Jay	Ari	15	15	131.1	28	38	1	7	.985	4.52
Bellhorn,Mark	Oak	1	0	1.0	0	0	0	0	.000	.00
Belliard,Ron	Mil	1	0	1.0	0	0	0	0	.000	.00
Berg,Dave	Fla	27	18	176.2	57	47	0	13	1.000	5.30
Bogar,Tim	Hou	11	2	46.1	10	14	0	4	1.000	4.66
Boone,Aaron	Cin	1	0	3.0	0	0	1	0	.000	.00
Bournigal,Rafael	Oak	48	26	269.2	55	81	0	20	1.000	4.54
Branson,Jeff	Cle	31	11	125.1	35	37	3	14	.960	5.17
Buford,Damon	Bos	1	0	0.1	0	0	0	0	.000	.00
Bush,Homer	NYA	24	10	126.0	36	29	2	4	.970	4.64
Cabrera,Orlando	Mon	28	24	210.0	59	72	4	16	.970	5.61
Castillo,Luis	Fla	44	43	378.1	118	113	6	34	.975	5.50
Castro,Juan	LA	38	20	220.0	47	73	2	22	.984	4.91
Catalanotto,Frank	Det	31	12	126.0	38	36	2	10	.974	5.29
Cedeno,Domingo	Tex	7	3	33.2	4	12	2	1	.889	4.28
Cianfrocco,Archi	SD	3	0	3.0	3	1	0	1	1.000	12.00
Cora,Alex	LA	4	1	14.0	4	8	0	3	1.000	7.71
Cora,Joey	Sea	130	126	1086.1	211	268	19	67	.962	3.97
Cora,Joey	Cle	21	21	181.2	30	40	1	8	.986	3.47
Crespo,Felipe	Tor	8	4	37.1	6	14	3	2	.870	4.82
Diaz,Edwin	Ari	3	2	20.0	6	8	1	2	.933	6.30
Dunston,Shawon	Cle	24	19	161.1	31	56	2	9	.978	4.85
Dunston,Shawon	SF	1	0	2.0	0	1	0	1	1.000	4.50
Febles,Carlos	KC	11	6	64.0	16	18	0	2	1.000	4.78
Forbes,P.J.	Bal	1	1	21.0	6	9	0	2	1.000	6.43
Fox,Andy	Ari	60	55	443.1	103	119	4	23	.982	4.51
Frias,Hanley	Ari	3	2	18.2	5	5	0	2	1.000	4.82
Gaetti,Gary	StL	1	0	2.0	0	0	0	0	.000	.00
Garcia,Carlos	Ana	11	8	72.0	19	25	1	7	.978	5.50
Gates,Brent	Min	21	13	131.0	23	43	2	8	.971	4.53
Gilbert,Shawn	StL	2	0	3.0	1	0	0	0	1.000	3.00
Giovanola,Ed	SD	36	17	188.2	46	79	1	13	.992	5.96
Guerrero,Wilton	LA	32	28	244.1	53	67	4	16	.968	4.42
Guerrero,Wilton	Mon	52	52	450.1	102	131	6	25	.975	4.66
Guevara,Giomar	Sea	5	2	24.1	6	9	0	2	1.000	5.55
Guillen,Carlos	Sea	10	10	81.0	15	29	0	5	1.000	4.89
Guillen,Ozzie	Atl	2	1	10.0	1	5	0	1	1.000	5.40
HairstonJr,Jerry	Bal	4	2	16.0	4	2	2	1	.750	3.38
Halter,Shane	KC	6	1	16.0	2	8	1	0	.909	5.63
Haney,Todd	NYN	1	0	2.0	0	0	0	0	.000	.00
Hansen,Jed	KC	2	0	5.0	1	0	0	0	1.000	1.80
Harris,Lenny	NYN	2	0	3.0	1	0	0	0	1.000	3.00
Hernandez,Jose	ChN	2	1	9.0	2	4	0	1	1.000	6.00
Hocking,Denny	Min	47	10	145.0	38	46	0	9	1.000	5.21
Holbert,Ray	Mon	1	1	9.0	2	3	0	0	1.000	5.00
Howard,David	StL	19	12	125.1	37	49	0	5	1.000	6.18
Hubbard,Mike	Mon	1	0	3.0	0	0	0	0	.000	.00
Huson,Jeff	Sea	8	3	35.0	7	6	0	2	1.000	3.34
Johns,Keith	Bos	1	0	2.0	1	1	0	1	1.000	9.00
Johnson,Russ	Hou	1	1	8.0	2	2	0	0	1.000	4.50
Jordan,Kevin	Phi	22	16	152.2	32	54	3	12	.966	5.07
Kelly,Pat	StL	41	36	306.1	79	108	7	18	.964	5.49
Klassen,Danny	Ari	29	28	238.0	60	73	5	16	.964	5.03
Ledesma,Aaron	TB	19	16	149.0	39	54	2	10	.979	5.62
Lemke,Mark	Bos	31	29	248.2	38	71	0	15	1.000	3.95
Liriano,Nelson	Col	3	1	14.0	5	2	0	1	1.000	4.50
Lopez,Luis	NYN	50	27	281.1	73	86	4	16	.975	5.09
Loretta,Mark	Mil	13	4	57.1	12	15	0	5	1.000	4.24
Lovullo,Torey	Cle	5	5	37.0	4	14	1	3	.947	4.38
Malloy,Marty	Atl	10	8	65.2	16	22	0	4	1.000	5.21
Manto,Jeff	Cle	1	0	4.1	0	1	0	1	1.000	2.08
Martin,Norberto	Ana	54	43	394.0	88	138	4	31	.983	5.16
Martinez,Felix	KC	2	0	2.0	0	0	0	0	.000	.00
Martinez,R.	SF	14	4	56.1	15	20	0	7	1.000	5.59
Maxwell,Jason	ChN	1	0	1.0	0	1	0	0	1.000	9.00
McEwing,Joe	StL	6	4	37.0	9	10	0	3	1.000	4.62
Merloni,Lou	Bos	32	22	210.0	47	66	3	10	.974	4.84
Metcalfe,Mike	LA	1	0	1.0	0	0	0	0	.000	.00
Milliard,Ralph	NYN	5	0	7.2	3	2	1	0	.833	5.87
Mordecai,Mike	Mon	21	10	113.0	18	32	1	7	.980	3.98
Mueller,Bill	SF	10	6	58.0	16	14	1	4	.968	4.66
Norton,Greg	ChA	1	0	1.0	0	2	0	0	1.000	18.00
Ordaz,Luis	StL	1	1	6.0	2	3	0	1	1.000	7.50
Owens,Eric	Mil	4	0	10.0	1	0	1	0	.500	0.90
Perez,Tomas	Tor	1	0	1.0	0	1	0	0	1.000	9.00
Polanco,Placido	StL	14	8	88.1	34	21	1	10	.982	5.60
Polcovich,Kevin	Pit	15	7	71.2	15	37	0	9	1.000	6.53
Randa,Joe	Det	20	11	117.0	24	40	0	9	1.000	4.92
Reboulet,Jeff	Bal	28	18	158.0	27	49	2	13	.974	4.33
Reese,Pokey	Cin	3	1	13.2	6	9	0	3	1.000	9.88
Ripken,Billy	Det	2	2	17.0	2	2	0	1	1.000	2.12
Rivera,Luis	KC	6	2	24.0	5	6	0	0	1.000	4.13
Roberts,Bip	Det	1	1	7.0	2	3	0	3	1.000	6.43
Roberts,Bip	Oak	30	25	199.2	38	58	3	18	.970	4.33
Rossy,Rico	Sea	6	1	20.0	1	12	0	1	1.000	5.85
Sadler,Donnie	Bos	50	38	333.0	77	96	5	17	.972	4.68
Samuel,Juan	Tor	2	1	11.0	2	4	0	0	1.000	4.91
Sanchez,Rey	SF	36	19	194.2	36	76	1	18	.991	5.18
Sanford,Chance	Pit	1	0	2.0	1	0	1	0	.500	4.50
Santangelo,F.P.	Mon	35	29	237.0	47	71	2	7	.983	4.48
Sefcik,Kevin	Phi	1	0	1.0	1	0	0	0	1.000	9.00
Sheets,Andy	SD	22	15	137.0	38	39	2	7	.975	5.06
Shipley,Craig	Ana	11	8	69.0	20	31	0	11	1.000	6.65
Shumpert,Terry	Col	1	1	20.0	2	14	0	3	1.000	7.20
Silvestri,Dave	TB	2	2	16.0	4	5	0	1	1.000	5.06
Smith,Bobby	TB	6	5	45.0	11	19	1	3	.968	6.00
Snopek,Chris	ChA	12	4	54.1	6	19	1	3	.962	4.14
Snopek,Chris	Bos	3	0	4.2	1	2	1	0	.750	5.79
Sojo,Luis	NYA	3	3	38.0	7	14	0	4	1.000	4.97
Spiers,Bill	Hou	9	5	49.0	10	13	1	2	.958	4.22
Stankiewicz,Andy	Ari	61	29	300.1	61	94	1	17	.994	4.64
Strange,Doug	Pit	9	7	59.1	17	18	0	6	1.000	5.31
Stynes,Chris	Cin	11	6	66.2	15	22	0	4	1.000	5.00
Valentin,John	Bos	1	0	0.2	0	0	0	0	.000	.00

Second Basemen - The Rest

Player	Tm	G	GS	Inn	PO	A	E	DP	Pct.	Rng
Velandia,Jorge	Oak	1	1	8.0	1	3	0	0	1.000	4.50
Velarde,Randy	Ana	51	50	436.1	88	132	4	25	.982	4.54
Vidro,Jose	Mon	56	46	404.2	78	121	5	25	.975	4.43
Walker,Larry	Col	1	0	0.0	0	0	0	0	.000	.00
Wilson,Craig	ChA	4	3	26.0	7	9	0	4	1.000	5.54
Wilson,Enrique	Cle	22	15	143.0	35	52	1	6	.989	5.48
Zaun,Gregg	Fla	1	0	2.0	0	1	0	0	1.000	4.50

Third Basemen - Regulars

Player	Tm	G	GS	Inn	PO	A	E	DP	Pct.	Rng
Andrews,Shane	Mon	147	143	1232.0	95	322	20	28	.954	3.05
Williams,Matt	Ari	134	129	1126.2	99	281	11	18	.972	3.04
Cirillo,Jeff	Mil	149	147	1307.2	99	339	11	45	.976	3.01
Orie,Kevin	TOT	105	100	888.1	88	207	15	12	.952	2.99
Tatis,Fernando	TOT	149	145	1281.2	109	306	27	22	.939	2.91
Rolen,Scott	Phi	159	159	1419.0	135	318	14	27	.970	2.87
Smith,Bobby	TB	97	81	739.2	70	165	9	11	.963	2.86
Berry,Sean	Hou	87	75	654.1	55	150	10	13	.953	2.82
Mueller,Bill	SF	137	126	1137.1	83	273	18	32	.952	2.82
Ventura,Robin	ChA	161	158	1380.2	101	328	15	38	.966	2.80
Valentin,John	Bos	153	153	1325.2	121	289	15	26	.965	2.78
Spiers,Bill	Hou	99	81	742.1	57	169	8	9	.966	2.74
Brosius,Scott	NYA	150	147	1312.2	107	292	22	29	.948	2.74
Gaetti,Gary	TOT	119	112	971.1	71	220	5	17	.983	2.70
Randa,Joe	Det	118	105	950.1	72	212	7	18	.976	2.69
Castilla,Vinny	Col	162	162	1422.2	110	315	13	39	.970	2.69
Alfonzo,Edgardo	NYN	144	136	1232.2	117	245	9	20	.976	2.64
Greene,Willie	Cin	76	69	618.0	48	128	12	20	.936	2.56
Boggs,Wade	TB	78	75	639.1	52	130	5	12	.973	2.56
Jones,Chipper	Atl	159	159	1399.2	105	291	12	28	.971	2.55
Gates,Brent	Min	77	66	608.1	59	113	7	5	.961	2.54
Hollins,Dave	Ana	91	91	746.1	63	145	16	13	.929	2.51
Sprague,Ed	TOT	128	126	1111.1	110	196	26	10	.922	2.48
Coomer,Ron	Min	76	75	627.2	56	116	5	9	.972	2.47
Caminiti,Ken	SD	127	126	1049.0	77	208	21	14	.931	2.45
Zeile,Todd	TOT	157	155	1364.2	104	265	23	19	.941	2.43
Ripken,Cal	Bal	161	161	1365.1	101	266	8	23	.979	2.42
Blowers,Mike	Oak	120	99	895.1	66	174	19	14	.927	2.41
Davis,Russ	Sea	127	122	1144.0	66	250	22	26	.935	2.41
Bonilla,Bobby	TOT	85	82	687.0	59	124	17	14	.915	2.40
Fryman,Travis	Cle	144	142	1266.0	100	236	13	21	.963	2.39
Ramirez,Aramis	Pit	71	71	605.1	29	114	9	12	.941	2.13
Palmer,Dean	KC	129	127	1102.1	69	185	22	16	.920	2.07
Average	—	123	118	1041.0	83	223	14	20	.955	2.65

Third Basemen - The Rest

Player	Tm	G	GS	Inn	PO	A	E	DP	Pct.	Rng
Abbott,Kurt	Oak	1	0	1.0	0	0	0	0	.000	.00
Abbott,Kurt	Col	3	0	6.0	2	1	0	0	1.000	4.50
Alexander,Manny	ChN	19	13	121.1	8	18	1	1	.963	1.93
Alicea,Luis	Tex	26	16	157.1	15	32	3	1	.940	2.69
Alvarez,Gabe	Det	55	52	460.0	37	93	19	6	.872	2.54
Amaral,Rich	Sea	1	0	1.0	0	0	0	0	.000	.00
Arias,Alex	Phi	5	0	7.2	0	1	0	0	1.000	1.17

Third Basemen - The Rest

Player	Tm	G	GS	Inn	PO	A	E	DP	Pct.	Rng
Arias,George	SD	14	8	86.0	4	23	2	2	.931	2.83
Banks,Brian	Mil	1	0	2.0	0	0	0	0	.000	.00
Barrett,Michael	Mon	3	3	25.0	0	5	2	0	.714	1.80
Bates,Jason	Col	3	0	4.0	0	0	0	0	.000	.00
Batista,Tony	Ari	15	12	111.0	9	28	1	1	.974	3.00
Bell,David	StL	4	1	16.2	1	2	0	0	1.000	1.62
Bell,David	Cle	6	5	46.0	4	12	0	1	1.000	3.13
Bell,David	Sea	5	2	21.0	2	5	0	0	1.000	3.00
Bellhorn,Mark	Oak	5	2	24.0	3	7	0	0	1.000	3.75
Beltre,Adrian	LA	74	54	516.2	31	130	13	13	.925	2.80
Benjamin,Mike	Bos	11	5	60.0	6	19	0	0	1.000	3.75
Berg,Dave	Fla	25	16	163.1	19	41	3	2	.952	3.31
Bogar,Tim	Hou	11	3	41.2	4	6	1	1	.909	2.16
Bolick,Frank	Ana	7	5	47.0	6	7	0	0	1.000	2.49
Bonilla,Bobby	Fla	26	25	216.1	18	41	5	6	.922	2.45
Bonilla,Bobby	LA	59	57	470.2	41	83	12	8	.912	2.37
Boone,Aaron	Cin	52	49	426.0	37	98	7	7	.951	2.85
Booty,Josh	Fla	7	6	51.0	4	10	3	1	.824	2.47
Borders,Pat	Cle	1	0	3.0	0	1	0	0	1.000	3.00
Branson,Jeff	Cle	20	7	77.2	5	16	2	1	.913	2.43
Branyan,Russ	Cle	1	1	7.0	0	1	0	0	1.000	1.29
Buford,Damon	Bos	1	0	0.2	0	0	0	0	.000	.00
Bush,Homer	NYA	3	2	19.0	1	6	0	0	1.000	3.32
Castro,Juan	LA	12	3	45.0	6	7	1	2	.929	2.60
Catalanotto,Frank	Det	3	3	21.0	0	5	1	1	.833	2.14
Chavez,Eric	Oak	13	11	95.0	11	21	0	2	1.000	3.03
Cianfrocco,Archi	SD	13	7	73.0	7	14	3	0	.875	2.59
Crespo,Felipe	Tor	2	1	10.0	1	2	0	0	1.000	2.70
Dalesandro,Mark	Tor	8	2	28.0	3	5	1	0	.889	2.57
Evans,Tom	Tor	7	3	32.2	5	3	1	0	.889	2.20
Fasano,Sal	KC	1	0	1.0	0	0	0	0	.000	.00
Fernandez,Tony	Tor	54	52	452.2	32	73	4	3	.963	2.09
Forbes,P.J.	Bal	1	0	1.0	0	0	0	0	.000	.00
Fox,Andy	Ari	26	21	191.0	23	48	2	4	.973	3.35
Franco,Matt	NYN	13	11	84.0	5	18	0	2	1.000	2.46
Frias,Hanley	Ari	2	0	3.2	0	1	0	0	1.000	2.45
Gaetti,Gary	StL	83	78	676.0	47	152	3	15	.985	2.65
Gaetti,Gary	ChN	36	34	295.1	24	68	2	2	.979	2.80
Garcia,Freddy	Pit	47	46	397.1	28	102	7	9	.949	2.94
Gilbert,Shawn	NYN	1	0	2.0	0	0	0	0	.000	.00
Giovanola,Ed	SD	38	14	157.2	11	43	2	2	.964	3.08
Gipson,Charles	Sea	4	3	24.0	6	3	1	0	.900	3.38
Glaus,Troy	Ana	48	45	402.0	27	85	7	7	.941	2.51
Graffanino,Tony	Atl	1	0	1.0	0	0	0	0	.000	.00
Grebeck,Craig	Tor	4	2	23.0	2	4	1	0	.857	2.35
Guillen,Ozzie	Bal	1	0	1.0	0	0	0	0	.000	.00
Guillen,Ozzie	Atl	1	0	9.0	1	1	0	0	1.000	2.00
Halter,Shane	KC	8	1	28.0	1	3	0	0	1.000	1.29
Hardtke,Jason	ChN	7	0	14.1	0	3	0	0	1.000	1.88
Harris,Lenny	NYN	10	7	48.0	2	11	1	1	.929	2.44
Hayes,Charlie	SF	46	37	339.2	22	67	1	6	.989	2.36
Helms,Wes	Atl	4	2	21.0	1	2	1	0	.750	1.29
Hernandez,Jose	ChN	72	54	507.2	45	115	7	4	.958	2.84
Hocking,Denny	Min	11	4	46.2	1	11	0	1	1.000	2.31
Houston,Tyler	ChN	12	9	64.1	1	13	2	1	.875	1.96
Howard,David	StL	14	1	27.2	3	2	0	0	1.000	1.63
Howell,Jack	Hou	2	2	16.0	1	5	0	0	1.000	3.38
Hubbard,Trenidad	LA	1	0	1.0	0	0	0	0	.000	.00

Third Basemen - The Rest

Player	Tm	G	GS	Inn	PO	A	E	DP	Pct.	Rng
Huson,Jeff	Sea	8	6	53.0	1	7	2	0	.800	1.36
Johnson,Russ	Hou	5	1	17.0	1	7	0	0	1.000	4.24
Jordan,Brian	StL	1	0	3.0	0	1	0	0	1.000	3.00
Jordan,Kevin	Phi	6	3	32.1	5	8	1	1	.929	3.62
King,Jeff	KC	4	3	34.0	3	6	0	2	1.000	2.38
Kinkade,Mike	NYN	1	0	3.0	0	0	0	0	.000	.00
Konerko,Paul	LA	11	8	61.0	5	16	1	1	.955	3.10
Konerko,Paul	Cin	9	9	74.0	2	18	0	0	1.000	2.43
Koskie,Corey	Min	10	7	71.0	6	10	1	1	.941	2.03
Lansing,Mike	Col	1	0	0.0	0	0	0	0	.000	.00
Ledesma,Aaron	TB	7	3	32.2	5	6	2	0	.846	3.03
Leius,Scott	KC	15	11	94.0	8	18	4	2	.867	2.49
Leyritz,Jim	SD	1	1	6.0	3	0	0	0	1.000	4.50
Livingstone,Scott	Mon	17	11	96.0	6	24	2	0	.938	2.81
Lockhart,Keith	Atl	1	1	8.0	0	0	0	0	.000	.00
Lopez,Luis	NYN	11	3	45.1	1	12	0	2	1.000	2.58
Lopez,Mendy	KC	2	1	10.0	1	4	0	0	1.000	4.50
Loretta,Mark	Mil	22	15	141.1	18	33	0	9	1.000	3.25
Lovullo,Torey	Cle	1	0	1.1	0	1	0	0	1.000	6.75
Lowell,Mike	NYA	7	3	36.0	2	6	0	2	1.000	2.00
Mabry,John	StL	38	31	272.1	18	46	6	1	.914	2.12
Magadan,Dave	Oak	30	26	203.2	15	52	6	7	.918	2.96
Manto,Jeff	Cle	8	5	44.0	0	5	0	2	1.000	1.02
Martin,Norberto	Ana	5	3	26.1	2	4	0	1	1.000	2.05
McClain,Scott	TB	3	3	23.0	2	2	0	0	1.000	1.57
Merloni,Lou	Bos	5	3	36.2	5	7	2	0	.857	2.95
Millar,Kevin	Fla	2	1	6.0	2	3	1	1	.833	7.50
Minor,Ryan	Bal	6	1	23.0	1	4	1	0	.833	1.96
Mordecai,Mike	Mon	11	2	40.2	3	5	1	0	.889	1.77
Norton,Greg	ChA	11	5	46.0	12	10	2	0	.917	4.30
Ordaz,Luis	StL	2	0	2.0	0	0	0	0	.000	.00
Orie,Kevin	ChN	57	53	474.1	39	101	5	7	.966	2.66
Orie,Kevin	Fla	48	47	414.0	49	106	10	5	.939	3.37
Osik,Keith	Pit	7	7	64.2	9	18	1	4	.964	3.76
Paquette,Craig	NYN	4	3	26.0	2	2	0	1	1.000	1.38
Pendleton,Terry	KC	23	18	150.0	12	32	2	1	.957	2.64
Perez,Eduardo	Cin	1	0	3.0	0	2	0	0	1.000	6.00
Polcovich,Kevin	Pit	8	4	43.1	2	17	0	1	1.000	3.95
Reboulet,Jeff	Bal	23	0	41.0	1	8	1	2	.900	1.98
Reese,Pokey	Cin	32	24	210.2	20	45	1	7	.985	2.78
Ripken,Billy	Det	2	2	15.0	2	5	0	1	1.000	4.20
Rivera,Luis	KC	6	0	17.0	1	3	0	0	1.000	2.12
Roberts,Bip	Oak	3	2	18.1	3	3	0	0	1.000	2.95
Rossy,Rico	Sea	25	17	181.1	11	44	0	5	1.000	2.73
Sanford,Chance	Pit	5	5	46.0	4	5	1	2	.900	1.76
Santangelo,F.P.	Mon	1	0	0.2	0	0	0	0	.000	.00
Sefcik,Kevin	Phi	2	0	4.0	1	0	1	0	.500	2.25
Shave,Jon	Min	15	10	94.0	6	20	0	2	1.000	2.49
Sheets,Andy	SD	22	6	83.0	8	12	2	2	.909	2.17
Sheldon,Scott	Tex	3	1	13.0	1	4	0	0	1.000	3.46
Shipley,Craig	Ana	48	18	222.1	15	37	2	1	.963	2.10
Silvestri,Dave	TB	3	0	8.1	1	1	0	0	1.000	2.16
Snopek,Chris	ChA	3	0	6.0	0	0	0	0	.000	.00
Snopek,Chris	Bos	3	1	13.0	0	2	0	0	1.000	1.38
Sojo,Luis	NYA	6	5	44.0	4	8	0	1	1.000	2.45
Sprague,Ed	Tor	105	104	918.2	87	157	20	8	.924	2.39
Sprague,Ed	Oak	23	22	192.2	23	39	6	2	.912	2.90
Strange,Doug	Pit	42	30	292.1	25	54	5	3	.940	2.43

Third Basemen - The Rest

Player	Tm	G	GS	Inn	PO	A	E	DP	Pct.	Rng
Stynes,Chris	Cin	22	11	109.2	9	26	2	3	.946	2.87
Sveum,Dale	NYA	6	5	45.0	4	6	1	0	.909	2.00
Tatis,Fernando	Tex	94	93	809.2	74	187	15	15	.946	2.90
Tatis,Fernando	StL	55	52	472.0	35	119	12	7	.928	2.94
Tatum,Jimmy	NYN	3	2	17.0	2	2	0	0	1.000	2.12
Vidro,Jose	Mon	7	3	32.2	4	5	1	2	.900	2.48
Voigt,Jack	Oak	2	0	3.0	0	1	0	0	1.000	3.00
Walker,Larry	Col	1	0	0.0	0	0	0	0	.000	.00
Wehner,John	Fla	8	4	38.2	2	10	0	0	1.000	2.79
Wilson,Craig	ChA	2	0	6.0	0	1	0	0	1.000	1.50
Wilson,Enrique	Cle	2	2	15.0	1	0	0	0	1.000	0.60
Wood,Jason	Oak	1	0	1.0	0	1	0	0	1.000	9.00
Zeile,Todd	LA	40	40	353.0	25	53	6	2	.929	1.99
Zeile,Todd	Fla	65	63	560.1	41	121	5	11	.970	2.60
Zeile,Todd	Tex	52	52	451.1	38	91	12	6	.915	2.57

Shortstops - Regulars

Player	Tm	G	GS	Inn	PO	A	E	DP	Pct.	Rng
Perez,Neifi	Col	162	156	1385.2	271	517	20	127	.975	5.12
Stocker,Kevin	TB	110	108	940.0	185	335	11	80	.979	4.98
Cruz,Deivi	Det	135	132	1163.1	196	445	11	100	.983	4.96
Bordick,Mike	Bal	150	144	1238.1	236	445	7	90	.990	4.95
Clayton,Royce	TOT	141	138	1225.2	230	438	20	79	.971	4.91
Tejada,Miguel	Oak	104	104	915.0	173	325	26	74	.950	4.90
Vizquel,Omar	Cle	151	149	1316.0	271	442	5	94	.993	4.88
Gutierrez,Ricky	Hou	141	129	1147.2	215	403	15	81	.976	4.85
Meares,Pat	Min	149	145	1270.0	263	411	24	92	.966	4.78
Caruso,Mike	ChA	131	129	1121.0	217	377	35	91	.944	4.77
Rodriguez,Alex	Sea	160	160	1389.1	271	447	18	89	.976	4.65
Ordonez,Rey	NYN	151	147	1289.0	265	398	17	82	.975	4.63
Grudzielanek,M.	TOT	156	156	1336.2	230	456	33	90	.954	4.62
Valentin,Jose	Mil	139	112	1060.2	173	370	21	69	.963	4.61
Aurilia,Rich	SF	120	107	917.2	154	311	10	71	.979	4.56
Bell,Jay	Ari	138	135	1175.2	197	397	18	77	.971	4.55
Collier,Lou	Pit	107	98	862.1	148	287	18	56	.960	4.54
DiSarcina,Gary	Ana	157	155	1370.2	253	438	14	103	.980	4.54
Renteria,Edgar	Fla	130	129	1129.0	194	374	20	93	.966	4.53
Garciaparra,N.	Bos	143	143	1255.1	228	401	25	67	.962	4.51
Elster,Kevin	Tex	84	84	734.2	107	255	9	49	.976	4.43
Gonzalez,Alex	Tor	158	157	1398.1	260	426	17	98	.976	4.42
Gomez,Chris	SD	143	136	1191.1	181	395	12	92	.980	4.35
Relaford,Desi	Phi	137	135	1190.0	189	380	24	72	.960	4.30
Jeter,Derek	NYA	148	148	1304.2	225	391	9	81	.986	4.25
Larkin,Barry	Cin	145	142	1236.0	207	358	12	79	.979	4.11
Weiss,Walt	Atl	96	95	789.1	96	255	12	63	.967	4.00
Blauser,Jeff	ChN	106	100	892.1	129	255	14	36	.965	3.87
Average	—	135	131	1151.1	205	383	17	81	.972	4.60

Shortstops - The Rest

Player	Tm	G	GS	Inn	PO	A	E	DP	Pct.	Rng
Abbott,Kurt	Oak	28	28	232.0	41	70	11	16	.910	4.31
Abbott,Kurt	Col	7	3	25.0	4	6	0	2	1.000	3.60
Alexander,Manny	ChN	50	26	267.1	37	71	4	15	.964	3.64
Alfonzo,Edgardo	NYN	1	0	1.0	0	0	0	0	.000	.00
Arias,Alex	Phi	38	27	273.0	43	87	2	10	.985	4.29
Bates,Jason	Col	3	2	15.0	2	3	1	2	.833	3.00
Batista,Tony	Ari	34	26	246.2	43	93	4	13	.971	4.96
Baughman,Justin	Ana	3	1	10.2	2	2	2	0	.667	3.38
Bell,David	Cle	1	0	1.0	1	0	0	0	1.000	9.00
Bellhorn,Mark	Oak	2	0	6.1	0	0	0	0	.000	.00
Belliard,Rafael	Atl	7	6	51.0	7	13	1	4	.952	3.53
Beltre,Adrian	LA	2	0	2.0	1	1	0	1	1.000	9.00
Benjamin,Mike	Bos	20	18	162.2	26	59	1	11	.988	4.70
Berg,Dave	Fla	17	10	111.1	16	40	4	8	.933	4.53
Bogar,Tim	Hou	55	33	320.2	49	126	2	16	.989	4.91
Boone,Aaron	Cin	1	0	3.0	0	0	0	0	.000	.00
Bournigal,Rafael	Oak	38	29	265.2	54	89	0	18	1.000	4.84
Branson,Jeff	Cle	2	0	3.0	0	0	0	0	.000	.00
Bush,Homer	NYA	2	0	11.0	0	3	0	0	1.000	2.45
Cabrera,Jolbert	Cle	1	0	5.0	2	2	0	0	1.000	7.20
Cabrera,Orlando	Mon	52	48	411.1	64	123	3	20	.984	4.09
Castilla,Vinny	Col	1	0	0.0	0	0	0	0	.000	.00
Castro,Juan	LA	47	35	301.0	43	102	7	29	.954	4.34
Cedeno,Domingo	Tex	35	25	231.2	37	67	4	14	.963	4.04
Clayton,Royce	StL	89	86	777.1	141	286	13	53	.970	4.94
Clayton,Royce	Tex	52	52	448.1	89	152	7	26	.972	4.84
Cora,Alex	LA	21	4	76.1	22	21	2	6	.956	5.07
Delgado,Wilson	SF	6	1	17.1	3	6	0	2	1.000	4.67
DeRosa,Mark	Atl	4	0	8.0	1	1	0	1	1.000	2.25
Dunston,Shawon	Cle	14	6	65.1	13	21	2	3	.944	4.68
Dunston,Shawon	SF	9	3	37.0	11	4	1	0	.938	3.65
Easley,Damion	Det	30	10	121.0	29	41	1	10	.986	5.21
Forbes,P.J.	Bal	1	0	2.0	0	0	0	0	.000	.00
Frias,Hanley	Ari	2	1	10.0	3	4	0	1	1.000	6.30
Fryman,Travis	Cle	3	1	9.2	1	5	0	2	1.000	5.59
Garcia,Carlos	Ana	5	2	23.2	5	8	0	2	1.000	4.94
Gates,Brent	Min	1	0	3.0	1	1	0	0	1.000	6.00
Giovanola,Ed	SD	1	0	1.0	0	0	0	0	.000	.00
Gonzalez,Alex	Fla	25	23	209.1	29	57	3	17	.966	3.70
Graffanino,Tony	Atl	2	0	3.0	0	1	0	0	1.000	3.00
Grebeck,Craig	Tor	6	4	40.0	4	15	0	3	1.000	4.28
Greene,Willie	Cin	2	0	4.0	1	3	1	1	.800	9.00
Grudzielanek,M.	Mon	105	105	891.0	151	284	23	56	.950	4.39
Grudzielanek,M.	LA	51	51	445.2	79	172	10	34	.962	5.07
Guerrero,Wilton	LA	14	7	66.2	12	24	2	6	.947	4.86
Guevara,Giomar	Sea	5	1	20.0	2	4	0	1	1.000	2.70
Guillen,Ozzie	Bal	6	3	29.0	3	11	1	1	.933	4.34
Guillen,Ozzie	Atl	71	58	550.0	93	159	6	25	.977	4.12
Halter,Shane	KC	66	45	420.0	73	166	9	28	.964	5.12
Hernandez,Jose	ChN	45	37	315.2	53	103	6	19	.963	4.45
Hocking,Denny	Min	28	17	174.0	29	43	3	7	.960	3.72
Holbert,Ray	Atl	7	3	37.1	6	14	1	3	.952	4.82
Howard,David	StL	16	10	92.0	12	29	2	4	.953	4.01
Huson,Jeff	Sea	1	0	2.0	0	0	0	0	.000	.00
Jackson,Damian	Cin	10	7	73.0	14	21	1	3	.972	4.32
Kelly,Pat	StL	2	0	2.0	0	1	0	0	1.000	4.50
Ledesma,Aaron	TB	58	49	448.1	104	165	8	51	.971	5.40
Leius,Scott	KC	2	0	2.0	0	1	0	0	1.000	4.50

Shortstops - The Rest

Player	Tm	G	GS	Inn	PO	A	E	DP	Pct.	Rng
Liriano,Nelson	Col	1	1	7.0	0	2	0	1	1.000	2.57
Lopez,Luis	NYN	39	15	167.0	36	47	6	17	.933	4.47
Lopez,Mendy	KC	72	66	562.2	101	221	15	53	.955	5.15
Loretta,Mark	Mil	56	50	390.1	67	147	3	39	.986	4.93
Martin,Norberto	Ana	2	2	15.0	1	2	0	1	1.000	1.80
Martinez,Felix	KC	32	28	244.2	49	80	6	23	.956	4.75
Merloni,Lou	Bos	1	0	2.0	0	0	0	0	.000	.00
Milliard,Ralph	NYN	1	0	1.0	0	0	0	0	.000	.00
Mordecai,Mike	Mon	30	9	124.2	16	45	3	6	.953	4.40
Nieves,Jose	ChN	1	0	2.0	0	0	0	0	.000	.00
Nunez,Abraham	Pit	23	20	163.2	32	61	7	12	.930	5.11
Ordaz,Luis	StL	54	46	394.1	68	154	13	34	.945	5.07
Perez,Tomas	Tor	4	2	26.2	6	5	0	1	1.000	3.71
Polanco,Placido	StL	28	21	196.0	38	82	6	18	.952	5.51
Polcovich,Kevin	Pit	54	45	415.2	60	159	20	32	.916	4.74
Reboulet,Jeff	Bal	28	15	162.0	25	63	3	8	.967	4.89
Reese,Pokey	Cin	18	13	120.1	24	24	7	7	.873	3.59
Ripken,Billy	Det	21	19	155.0	23	51	6	11	.925	4.30
Rivera,Luis	KC	30	22	207.0	41	81	5	20	.961	5.30
Rossy,Rico	Sea	4	0	13.0	3	5	0	1	1.000	5.54
Sadler,Donnie	Bos	4	1	16.0	5	6	0	2	1.000	6.19
Sanchez,Rey	SF	76	52	505.0	106	185	7	33	.977	5.19
Sanford,Chance	Pit	1	0	5.0	0	1	0	0	1.000	1.80
Shave,Jon	Min	1	0	0.2	0	0	0	0	.000	.00
Sheets,Andy	SD	39	26	262.1	41	93	5	18	.964	4.60
Sheldon,Scott	Tex	2	1	16.2	7	7	1	3	.933	7.56
Shipley,Craig	Ana	5	2	24.0	6	5	0	4	1.000	4.13
Silvestri,Dave	TB	1	0	5.0	0	3	1	0	.750	5.40
Smith,Bobby	TB	7	5	49.2	7	20	3	4	.900	4.89
Snopek,Chris	ChA	33	26	243.2	47	93	4	16	.972	5.17
Sojo,Luis	NYA	20	14	141.0	29	44	2	11	.973	4.66
Spiers,Bill	Hou	2	0	3.0	0	0	0	0	.000	.00
Stynes,Chris	Cin	2	0	5.0	1	2	0	1	1.000	5.40
Tatis,Fernando	StL	3	0	8.0	1	3	0	1	1.000	4.50
Velandia,Jorge	Oak	7	1	12.0	4	7	1	1	.917	8.25
Vizcaino,Jose	LA	66	65	555.2	89	169	4	32	.985	4.18
Wilson,Craig	ChA	8	8	74.0	13	17	0	4	1.000	3.65
Wilson,Enrique	Cle	10	6	60.0	9	23	1	4	.970	4.80
Womack,Tony	Pit	2	0	2.1	1	1	0	0	1.000	7.71
Wood,Jason	Oak	2	0	3.0	1	2	0	1	1.000	9.00
Wood,Jason	Det	1	1	7.0	2	0	0	0	1.000	2.57

Left Fielders - Regulars

Player	Tm	G	GS	Inn	PO	A	E	DP	Pct.	Rng
Cordova,Marty	Min	115	113	982.0	257	5	6	1	.978	2.40
Henderson,Rickey	Oak	142	128	1104.0	290	2	4	1	.986	2.38
Curtis,Chad	NYA	100	76	759.0	195	5	3	3	.985	2.37
Giles,Brian	Cle	95	85	792.0	199	7	5	1	.976	2.34
Rodriguez,Henry	ChN	114	112	876.1	215	7	1	1	.996	2.28
Stewart,Shannon	Tor	110	89	843.0	204	1	5	0	.976	2.19
Belle,Albert	ChA	159	159	1365.0	315	11	8	3	.976	2.15
Greer,Rusty	Tex	154	151	1324.1	304	6	3	0	.990	2.11
Dellucci,David	Ari	95	80	714.1	164	3	2	3	.988	2.10
O'Leary,Troy	Bos	155	154	1342.0	302	9	3	1	.990	2.09
Bichette,Dante	Col	134	131	1103.2	237	14	9	6	.965	2.05
Bonds,Barry	SF	155	154	1337.1	301	2	5	0	.984	2.04

Left Fielders - Regulars

Player	Tm	G	GS	Inn	PO	A	E	DP	Pct.	Rng
Gilkey,Bernard	TOT	103	88	795.2	163	12	2	1	.989	1.98
Hill,Glenallen	TOT	99	95	723.1	153	4	5	1	.969	1.95
Martin,Al	Pit	114	110	922.1	192	6	3	1	.985	1.93
Vaughn,Greg	SD	151	150	1307.1	270	5	2	0	.993	1.89
Gonzalez,Luis	Det	132	131	1144.0	232	8	3	0	.988	1.89
Floyd,Cliff	Fla	146	145	1267.0	251	10	7	1	.974	1.85
Gant,Ron	StL	104	101	819.0	162	4	5	0	.971	1.82
Surhoff,B.J.	Bal	157	147	1311.1	253	12	3	2	.989	1.82
Young,Dmitri	Cin	91	85	725.1	142	3	9	0	.942	1.80
Jefferies,Gregg	TOT	136	134	1055.0	193	7	1	0	.995	1.71
Alou,Moises	Hou	152	148	1330.0	227	11	4	2	.983	1.61
Klesko,Ryan	Atl	120	119	917.0	146	9	1	1	.994	1.52
Average	—	126	120	1035.2	223	6	4	1	.982	2.00

Left Fielders - The Rest

Player	Tm	G	GS	Inn	PO	A	E	DP	Pct.	Rng
Abbott,Jeff	ChA	20	0	31.0	10	0	0	0	1.000	2.90
Abbott,Kurt	Oak	5	0	14.0	6	0	0	0	1.000	3.86
Abbott,Kurt	Col	4	2	17.0	7	0	0	0	1.000	3.71
Agbayani,Benny	NYN	1	0	2.0	0	0	0	0	.000	.00
Alexander,Manny	ChN	1	0	0.1	1	0	0	0	1.000	27.00
Alicea,Luis	Tex	2	1	6.0	2	0	0	0	1.000	3.00
Allensworth,J.	KC	1	0	2.0	0	0	0	0	.000	.00
Allensworth,J.	NYN	4	0	7.0	2	0	0	0	1.000	2.57
Amaral,Rich	Sea	43	17	195.1	49	2	0	0	1.000	2.35
Amaro,Ruben	Phi	43	3	119.0	18	1	0	0	1.000	1.44
Anderson,Garret	Ana	39	32	303.0	64	0	0	1	1.000	1.96
Ashley,Billy	Bos	2	0	5.0	0	1	0	0	1.000	1.80
Banks,Brian	Mil	1	0	1.0	0	1	1	0	.500	9.00
Barry,Jeff	Col	1	0	3.0	0	0	0	0	.000	.00
Bartee,Kimera	Det	11	3	42.0	12	1	0	0	1.000	2.79
Bautista,Danny	Atl	53	27	292.1	45	0	2	0	.957	1.39
Beamon,Trey	Det	2	1	10.0	7	0	0	0	1.000	6.30
Becker,Rich	NYN	17	7	81.1	19	2	1	0	.955	2.32
Becker,Rich	Bal	5	1	14.0	5	0	0	0	1.000	3.21
Bell,David	Sea	1	0	3.0	0	0	0	0	.000	.00
Benard,Marvin	SF	12	3	46.2	6	0	0	0	1.000	1.16
Benitez,Yamil	Ari	49	35	296.1	83	4	2	1	.978	2.64
Berroa,Geronimo	Cle	14	14	111.0	26	1	0	0	1.000	2.19
Berroa,Geronimo	Det	2	1	11.0	1	0	0	0	1.000	0.82
Bieser,Steve	Pit	1	0	2.2	0	0	0	0	.000	.00
Bonilla,Bobby	LA	12	12	85.2	16	0	1	0	.941	1.68
Bragg,Darren	Bos	7	4	41.0	10	0	0	0	1.000	2.20
Brede,Brent	Ari	26	15	136.2	23	0	0	0	1.000	1.51
Brown,Adrian	Pit	3	3	23.0	7	0	1	0	.875	2.74
Brown,Brant	ChN	48	11	165.0	31	0	3	0	.912	1.69
Brown,Emil	Pit	9	9	69.2	17	2	0	0	1.000	2.45
Burks,Ellis	Col	45	17	193.0	45	0	3	0	.938	2.10
Butler,Rich	TB	39	37	327.0	70	2	0	0	1.000	1.98
Cangelosi,John	Fla	9	1	22.2	7	0	1	0	.875	2.78
Canseco,Jose	Tor	50	47	360.1	81	3	4	2	.955	2.10
Carter,Joe	Bal	3	1	9.2	2	1	0	0	1.000	2.79
Carter,Joe	SF	4	1	18.0	3	0	0	0	1.000	1.50
Cedeno,Roger	LA	45	21	215.2	42	1	1	0	.977	1.79
Christenson,Ryan	Oak	1	0	1.0	0	0	0	0	.000	.00
Clark,Dave	Hou	9	7	57.1	9	0	2	0	.818	1.41

Left Fielders - The Rest

Player	Tm	G	GS	Inn	PO	A	E	DP	Pct.	Rng
Clyburn,Danny	Bal	5	3	25.0	6	0	0	0	1.000	2.16
Conine,Jeff	KC	50	46	407.0	88	4	0	0	1.000	2.03
Cordero,Wil	ChA	4	3	29.0	5	0	0	0	1.000	1.55
Cradle,Rickey	Sea	1	0	2.0	0	0	0	0	.000	.00
Crespo,Felipe	Tor	19	7	99.0	30	0	0	0	1.000	2.73
Cruz Jr.,Jose	Tor	6	1	19.0	4	0	0	0	1.000	1.89
Damon,Johnny	KC	14	2	43.0	13	0	0	0	1.000	2.72
Davis,Russ	Sea	3	3	19.0	1	0	2	0	.333	0.47
Devereaux,Mike	LA	1	1	9.0	2	0	0	0	1.000	2.00
Diaz,Alex	SF	4	0	6.2	1	0	0	0	1.000	1.35
Drew,J.D.	StL	6	4	35.0	11	1	0	1	1.000	3.09
Ducey,Rob	Sea	23	9	102.1	28	1	1	0	.967	2.55
Dunston,Shawon	Cle	11	9	76.0	16	0	0	0	1.000	1.89
Echevarria,Angel	Col	3	3	26.0	3	0	0	0	1.000	1.04
Eisenreich,Jim	Fla	5	2	21.2	5	0	0	0	1.000	2.08
Eisenreich,Jim	LA	22	16	136.1	31	1	1	0	.970	2.11
Encarnacion,Juan	Det	8	7	65.1	14	1	0	0	1.000	2.07
Erstad,Darin	Ana	70	67	573.1	109	4	1	2	.991	1.77
Fox,Andy	Ari	10	6	55.0	12	1	0	0	1.000	2.13
Franco,Matt	NYN	12	8	75.0	11	1	1	0	.923	1.44
Frank,Mike	Cin	1	0	1.0	1	0	0	0	1.000	9.00
Giambi,Jeremy	KC	9	9	76.0	14	1	0	0	1.000	1.78
Gibson,Derrick	Col	7	6	49.2	11	2	1	0	.929	2.36
Gilkey,Bernard	NYN	76	62	566.2	114	9	1	1	.992	1.95
Gilkey,Bernard	Ari	27	26	229.0	49	3	1	0	.981	2.04
Gipson,Charles	Sea	14	1	34.1	10	0	0	0	1.000	2.62
Goodwin,Curtis	Col	14	0	20.1	7	0	0	0	1.000	3.10
Greene,Todd	Ana	12	11	80.0	12	0	0	0	1.000	1.54
Greene,Willie	Cin	9	6	58.1	9	1	0	0	1.000	1.54
Greene,Willie	Bal	1	1	3.1	0	0	0	0	.000	.00
GriffeyJr.,Ken	Sea	1	0	3.0	0	0	0	0	.000	.00
Guerrero,Wilton	LA	3	3	26.1	5	0	1	0	.833	1.71
Halter,Shane	KC	6	4	44.2	9	0	0	0	1.000	1.81
Hammonds,J.	Bal	7	5	40.0	6	1	0	0	1.000	1.58
Haney,Todd	NYN	1	0	2.0	0	0	0	0	.000	.00
Harris,Lenny	Cin	13	7	64.2	14	2	3	0	.842	2.23
Harris,Lenny	NYN	21	2	49.1	7	2	0	0	1.000	1.64
Hatcher,Chris	KC	5	4	38.0	7	0	0	0	1.000	1.66
Hernandez,Jose	ChN	31	0	45.2	9	0	0	0	1.000	1.77
Hidalgo,Richard	Hou	9	3	41.0	10	0	1	0	.909	2.20
Higginson,Bob	Det	17	17	151.0	26	2	1	0	.966	1.67
Hill,Glenallen	Sea	71	70	526.0	106	2	4	1	.964	1.85
Hill,Glenallen	ChN	28	25	197.1	47	2	1	0	.980	2.23
Hocking,Denny	Min	17	13	125.2	34	2	1	1	.973	2.58
Hollandsworth,T.	LA	48	35	327.0	64	1	4	0	.942	1.79
Hollins,Damon	Atl	2	2	14.0	2	0	0	0	1.000	1.29
Hollins,Damon	LA	1	0	3.0	1	0	0	0	1.000	3.00
Howard,Thomas	LA	11	3	40.2	12	0	0	0	1.000	2.66
Hubbard,Trenidad	LA	34	21	185.2	44	1	0	0	1.000	2.18
Hudler,Rex	Phi	3	2	18.0	5	0	0	0	1.000	2.50
Hundley,Todd	NYN	34	34	215.0	42	2	5	0	.898	1.84
Hunter,Brian	StL	16	11	98.1	23	2	2	1	.926	2.29
Ibanez,Raul	Sea	6	4	35.0	5	1	0	0	1.000	1.54
Incaviglia,Pete	Det	1	0	1.0	0	0	0	0	.000	.00
Incaviglia,Pete	Hou	3	2	16.0	3	0	0	0	1.000	1.69
Jackson,Darrin	Mil	55	10	190.1	38	1	2	0	.951	1.84
Jackson,Ryan	Fla	10	6	49.1	8	0	0	0	1.000	1.46
Javier,Stan	SF	6	3	37.0	12	0	0	0	1.000	2.92

Left Fielders - The Rest

Left Fielders - The Rest

Player	Tm	G	GS	Inn	PO	A	E	DP	Pct.	Rng
Jefferies,Gregg	Phi	121	119	954.2	168	7	1	0	.994	1.65
Jefferies,Gregg	Ana	15	15	100.1	25	0	0	0	1.000	2.24
Jenkins,Geoff	Mil	81	67	592.2	115	6	4	2	.968	1.84
Johnson,Brian	SF	1	0	2.0	1	0	0	0	1.000	4.50
Jones,Chris	Ari	1	0	1.0	0	0	0	0	.000	.00
Jones,Chris	SF	5	2	22.1	2	0	1	0	.667	0.81
Justice,David	Cle	19	18	149.0	32	0	0	0	1.000	1.93
Kelly,Mike	TB	43	37	333.1	78	2	0	1	1.000	2.16
Kelly,Pat	StL	3	0	4.0	0	0	0	0	.000	.00
Kelly,Roberto	Tex	14	8	70.0	14	2	0	0	1.000	2.06
Kirby,Wayne	NYN	3	0	6.0	0	0	0	0	.000	.00
Konerko,Paul	LA	11	9	70.2	12	0	0	0	1.000	1.53
Konerko,Paul	Cin	7	4	36.0	8	0	0	0	1.000	2.00
Lampkin,Tom	StL	4	0	4.0	1	0	0	0	1.000	2.25
Latham,Chris	Min	13	10	95.0	22	0	1	0	.957	2.08
Lawton,Matt	Min	12	11	100.0	22	0	0	0	1.000	1.98
Ledee,Ricky	NYA	36	18	190.1	43	4	1	0	.979	2.22
Lesher,Brian	Oak	4	2	16.0	4	2	0	1	1.000	3.38
Lewis,Darren	Bos	4	1	15.0	5	0	0	0	1.000	3.00
Leyritz,Jim	SD	1	0	1.0	0	0	0	0	.000	.00
Little,Mark	StL	3	1	12.1	2	0	0	0	1.000	1.46
Lopez,Luis	NYN	8	5	48.1	8	0	0	0	1.000	1.49
Loretta,Mark	Mil	1	0	1.0	0	0	0	0	.000	.00
Lowery,Terrell	ChN	2	0	2.0	0	0	0	0	.000	.00
Luke,Matt	LA	50	41	347.1	76	4	1	0	.988	2.07
Mabry,John	StL	46	28	260.2	42	6	0	2	1.000	1.66
Mack,Shane	KC	30	30	252.0	52	1	1	0	.981	1.89
Magee,Wendell	Phi	19	19	170.1	31	1	2	0	.941	1.69
Manto,Jeff	Det	1	0	2.0	0	0	0	0	.000	.00
Martin,Norberto	Ana	5	2	20.1	2	0	0	0	1.000	0.89
Martinez,Greg	Mil	6	0	11.2	0	0	0	0	.000	.00
Martinez,Manny	Pit	26	16	153.2	30	0	0	0	1.000	1.76
Mashore,Damon	Ana	1	1	3.0	1	0	0	0	1.000	3.00
May,Derrick	Mon	48	38	306.2	57	3	1	1	.984	1.76
McCracken,Q.	TB	58	47	434.1	106	6	1	1	.991	2.32
McDonald,Jason	Oak	11	7	70.0	15	0	0	0	1.000	1.93
McEwing,Joe	StL	1	0	1.0	0	0	0	0	.000	.00
McGee,Willie	StL	56	18	235.1	43	3	3	0	.939	1.76
McGuire,Ryan	Mon	33	22	199.1	35	0	1	0	.972	1.58
Merced,Orlando	ChN	4	0	7.0	3	0	0	0	1.000	3.86
Mieske,Matt	ChN	50	11	150.2	22	0	1	0	.957	1.31
Mitchell,Keith	Bos	4	2	24.0	2	0	0	0	1.000	0.75
Mitchell,Kevin	Oak	10	6	49.0	10	0	0	0	1.000	1.84
Monahan,Shane	Sea	61	56	492.1	113	3	1	1	.991	2.12
Montgomery,Ray	Hou	1	0	1.0	0	0	0	0	.000	.00
Morris,Hal	KC	39	37	288.0	47	1	0	0	1.000	1.50
Mouton,James	SD	16	1	38.2	10	0	1	0	.909	2.33
Mouton,Lyle	Bal	6	4	28.0	3	0	0	0	1.000	0.96
Neill,Mike	Oak	4	1	15.0	7	0	0	0	1.000	4.20
Newfield,Marc	Mil	55	49	369.0	73	3	3	0	.962	1.85
Newson,Warren	Tex	6	1	22.0	6	0	0	0	1.000	2.45
Nieves,Melvin	Cin	3	2	21.0	3	0	0	0	1.000	1.29
Nilsson,Dave	Mil	37	34	260.0	49	2	2	0	.962	1.77
Nixon,Trot	Bos	1	1	9.0	4	0	0	0	1.000	4.00
Nunnally,Jon	Cin	3	2	28.0	6	1	0	0	1.000	2.25
Ochoa,Alex	Min	21	15	145.0	28	4	1	0	.970	1.99
Owens,Eric	Mil	10	2	25.1	5	0	0	0	1.000	1.78
Palmeiro,Orlando	Ana	46	31	303.2	81	0	0	0	1.000	2.40
Paquette,Craig	NYN	1	1	7.0	0	0	0	0	.000	.00
Payton,Jay	NYN	8	3	36.0	6	1	0	0	1.000	1.75
Perez,Eduardo	Cin	1	0	2.0	1	0	0	0	1.000	4.50
Perez,Robert	Sea	2	0	4.0	1	0	0	0	1.000	2.25
Perez,Robert	Mon	29	20	169.1	20	3	4	0	.852	1.22
Petagine,Roberto	Cin	1	0	2.0	2	0	0	0	1.000	9.00
Phillips,J.R.	Hou	6	2	26.0	2	0	0	0	1.000	0.69
Phillips,Tony	Tor	11	10	81.2	20	0	1	0	.952	2.20
Phillips,Tony	NYN	43	34	315.1	61	2	2	0	.969	1.80
Pride,Curtis	Atl	8	6	49.0	14	0	0	0	1.000	2.57
Raines,Tim	NYA	47	46	353.0	60	3	1	2	.984	1.61
Ramirez,Alex	Cle	2	1	9.0	4	0	0	0	1.000	4.00
Rios,Armando	SF	2	0	7.0	2	0	0	0	1.000	2.57
Rivera,Ruben	SD	13	7	69.2	13	0	0	0	1.000	1.68
Roberts,Bip	Det	2	2	13.0	1	0	0	0	1.000	0.69
Roberts,Bip	Oak	8	2	25.0	9	0	1	0	.900	3.24
Robinson,Kerry	TB	2	0	6.0	4	0	0	0	1.000	6.00
Samuel,Juan	Tor	8	8	54.0	14	0	2	0	.875	2.33
Santangelo,F.P.	Mon	72	53	470.2	103	5	3	0	.973	2.07
Sefcik,Kevin	Phi	35	14	162.0	24	0	0	0	1.000	1.33
Segui,David	Sea	1	1	8.0	0	0	0	0	.000	.00
Seguignol,F.	Mon	8	6	51.1	20	0	0	0	1.000	3.51
Sexson,Richie	Cle	3	2	19.0	4	0	0	0	1.000	1.89
Shipley,Craig	Ana	1	1	7.0	2	0	0	0	1.000	2.57
Sierra,Ruben	ChA	2	1	9.0	2	0	0	0	1.000	2.00
Simmons,Brian	ChA	2	0	4.2	0	0	0	0	.000	.00
Simms,Mike	Tex	3	1	9.0	2	0	0	0	1.000	2.00
Smith,Mark	Pit	16	11	108.1	24	0	0	0	1.000	1.99
Sorrento,Paul	TB	4	4	31.0	3	0	0	0	1.000	0.87
Spencer,Shane	NYA	9	7	57.0	10	1	0	0	1.000	1.74
Stairs,Matt	Oak	11	10	81.0	20	3	0	0	1.000	2.56
Stanley,Mike	Tor	1	1	8.0	1	0	0	0	1.000	1.13
Stovall,DaRond	Mon	27	8	97.2	19	1	2	0	.909	1.84
Strawberry,Darryl	NYA	16	15	97.1	19	0	2	0	.905	1.76
Stynes,Chris	Cin	64	48	425.1	105	3	0	1	1.000	2.29
Sutton,Larry	KC	39	29	280.2	56	2	0	0	1.000	1.86
Sweeney,Mark	SD	5	2	21.0	3	0	0	0	1.000	1.29
Tarasco,Tony	Cin	4	3	28.2	9	0	0	0	1.000	2.83
Tatum,Jimmy	NYN	4	3	22.0	6	0	0	0	1.000	2.45
Tomberlin,Andy	Det	4	0	7.0	4	0	0	0	1.000	5.14
Trammell,Bubba	TB	23	21	174.0	33	2	0	0	1.000	1.81
Valdes,Pedro	ChN	6	4	32.0	9	0	0	0	1.000	2.53
VanderWal,John	Col	3	3	16.0	2	0	0	0	1.000	1.13
VanderWal,John	SD	2	2	17.0	7	0	0	0	1.000	3.71
Voigt,Jack	Oak	9	6	59.0	17	1	0	0	1.000	2.75
Walton,Jerome	TB	4	3	27.0	10	2	0	0	1.000	4.00
Ward,Turner	Pit	41	14	169.1	32	1	2	0	.943	1.75
Watkins,Pat	Cin	13	4	49.0	16	0	1	0	.941	2.94
Wehner,John	Fla	12	6	63.0	11	1	0	0	1.000	1.71
White,Derrick	ChN	1	0	1.0	0	0	0	0	.000	.00
White,Derrick	Col	2	0	4.0	1	0	0	0	1.000	2.25
White,Rondell	Mon	15	15	132.0	26	3	0	1	1.000	1.98
Whiten,Mark	Cle	43	33	304.0	80	6	3	0	.966	2.55
Williams,Gerald	Atl	56	8	166.1	34	0	1	0	.971	1.84
Williams,Reggie	Ana	19	2	53.1	16	0	0	0	1.000	2.70
Wilson,Preston	NYN	4	3	25.0	5	0	0	0	1.000	1.80
Wilson,Preston	Fla	3	2	26.0	6	0	0	0	1.000	2.08
Winn,Randy	TB	16	13	110.1	18	3	0	0	1.000	1.71

265

Left Fielders - The Rest

Player	Tm	G	GS	Inn	PO	A	E	DP	Pct.	Rng
Young,Ernie	KC	1	0	5.0	0	0	0	0	.000	.00
Zuber,Jon	Phi	5	5	39.0	7	0	0	0	1.000	1.62

Center Fielders - Regulars

Player	Tm	G	GS	Inn	PO	A	E	DP	Pct.	Rng
White,Rondell	Mon	82	81	699.1	234	4	1	2	.996	3.06
Lewis,Darren	Bos	109	104	888.2	288	5	0	0	1.000	2.97
Hunter,Brian L.	Det	139	137	1212.1	386	11	5	0	.988	2.95
Goodwin,Tom	Tex	150	129	1149.1	370	5	3	1	.992	2.94
Cameron,Mike	ChA	136	104	972.1	310	5	4	0	.987	2.92
Dunwoody,Todd	Fla	111	96	874.2	272	9	3	4	.989	2.89
Jones,Andruw	Atl	159	156	1372.2	413	20	2	6	.995	2.84
Christenson,Ryan	Oak	113	100	891.0	275	6	5	2	.983	2.84
Griffey Jr.,Ken	Sea	158	158	1344.2	407	11	5	2	.988	2.80
White,Devon	Ari	144	141	1219.1	371	3	5	0	.987	2.76
Nixon,Otis	Min	108	106	922.2	278	4	3	0	.989	2.75
Edmonds,Jim	Ana	153	150	1312.1	389	10	5	1	.988	2.74
Everett,Carl	Hou	121	111	1028.0	290	12	4	3	.987	2.64
Damon,Johnny	KC	130	127	1123.1	315	9	2	1	.994	2.60
Cruz Jr.,Jose	Tor	103	95	871.2	243	7	4	1	.984	2.58
McCracken,Q.	TB	103	101	880.2	238	12	2	2	.992	2.55
Lankford,Ray	StL	145	137	1216.1	337	7	5	2	.986	2.55
Allensworth,J.	TOT	94	82	747.0	204	4	4	2	.981	2.51
Grissom,Marquis	Mil	137	133	1168.2	317	8	3	3	.991	2.50
Williams,Bernie	NYA	123	123	1095.0	299	4	3	0	.990	2.49
Finley,Steve	SD	157	146	1335.1	350	12	7	5	.981	2.44
Lofton,Kenny	Cle	154	150	1321.2	340	18	8	4	.978	2.44
Glanville,Doug	Phi	158	155	1398.0	360	14	2	1	.995	2.41
Sanders,Reggie	Cin	88	79	658.1	169	3	5	0	.972	2.35
Anderson,Brady	Bal	130	121	1076.0	269	1	4	0	.985	2.26
Johnson,Lance	ChN	78	68	636.0	154	5	4	2	.975	2.25
Burks,Ellis	TOT	114	109	891.2	213	8	3	0	.987	2.23
Hamilton,Darryl	TOT	144	136	1221.1	297	5	1	1	.997	2.23
McRae,Brian	NYN	154	144	1306.1	301	8	4	3	.987	2.13
Mondesi,Raul	LA	94	94	803.1	178	5	4	1	.979	2.05
Average	—	126	119	1054.1	295	7	3	1	.988	2.59

Center Fielders - The Rest

Player	Tm	G	GS	Inn	PO	A	E	DP	Pct.	Rng
Abbott,Jeff	ChA	38	34	264.1	71	0	3	0	.959	2.42
Agbayani,Benny	NYN	2	2	11.0	1	0	0	0	1.000	0.82
Allensworth,J.	Pit	66	61	554.0	144	4	3	2	.980	2.40
Allensworth,J.	KC	24	18	169.0	53	0	1	0	.981	2.82
Allensworth,J.	NYN	3	2	24.0	7	0	0	0	1.000	2.63
Alou,Moises	Hou	6	4	33.1	5	0	1	0	.833	1.35
Amaral,Rich	Sea	4	0	6.0	2	0	0	0	1.000	3.00
Amaro,Ruben	Phi	3	1	13.0	5	0	0	0	1.000	3.46
Barry,Jeff	Col	8	6	53.0	14	1	0	0	1.000	2.55
Bartee,Kimera	Det	18	13	123.0	37	2	2	0	.951	2.85
Bautista,Danny	Atl	1	0	2.1	2	0	0	0	1.000	7.71
Becker,Rich	NYN	14	8	75.1	12	0	0	0	1.000	1.43
Becker,Rich	Bal	13	8	76.2	16	0	0	0	1.000	1.88
Beltran,Carlos	KC	14	13	117.0	44	0	1	0	.978	3.38
Benard,Marvin	SF	9	6	49.0	11	0	0	0	1.000	2.02

Center Fielders - The Rest

Player	Tm	G	GS	Inn	PO	A	E	DP	Pct.	Rng
Bragg,Darren	Bos	12	6	60.1	21	1	0	0	1.000	3.28
Brown,Adrian	Pit	34	32	277.1	72	3	1	2	.987	2.43
Brown,Brant	ChN	69	62	537.1	149	1	4	0	.974	2.51
Brown,Emil	Pit	1	1	8.0	4	0	0	0	1.000	4.50
Buford,Damon	Bos	67	52	487.0	133	4	0	1	1.000	2.53
Burks,Ellis	Col	78	76	605.2	142	7	2	0	.987	2.21
Burks,Ellis	SF	36	33	286.0	71	1	1	0	.986	2.27
Burnitz,Jeromy	Mil	1	0	1.0	0	0	0	0	.000	.00
Cangelosi,John	Fla	33	26	196.2	49	1	1	0	.980	2.29
Cedeno,Roger	LA	29	24	220.0	37	3	1	1	.976	1.64
Clemente,Edgard	Col	1	1	8.0	1	0	0	0	1.000	1.13
Cradle,Rickey	Sea	2	0	4.0	1	0	0	0	1.000	2.25
Curtis,Chad	NYA	45	38	348.2	98	4	2	0	.981	2.63
Cuyler,Milt	Tex	3	1	16.0	5	0	0	0	1.000	2.81
Davis,Eric	Bal	11	10	77.0	14	0	0	0	1.000	1.64
Dellucci,David	Ari	19	14	129.0	45	0	1	0	.978	3.14
Devereaux,Mike	LA	3	2	18.2	7	0	0	0	1.000	3.38
Diaz,Alex	SF	15	9	82.0	26	2	0	0	1.000	3.07
Drew,J.D.	StL	2	0	3.0	0	0	0	0	.000	.00
Ducey,Rob	Sea	6	2	26.2	8	0	0	0	1.000	2.70
Dunston,Shawon	Cle	1	0	4.1	2	0	0	0	1.000	4.15
Dunston,Shawon	SF	6	4	36.0	9	0	1	0	.900	2.25
Encarnacion,Juan	Det	13	12	107.0	11	2	0	0	1.000	1.09
Erstad,Darin	Ana	3	3	26.0	7	0	0	0	1.000	2.42
Floyd,Cliff	Fla	2	0	3.2	1	0	0	0	1.000	2.45
Fox,Andy	Ari	8	6	57.0	24	0	0	0	1.000	3.79
Frank,Mike	Cin	25	20	197.2	59	1	0	0	1.000	2.73
Frazier,Lou	ChA	3	1	14.2	5	0	0	0	1.000	3.07
Garcia,Karim	Ari	8	1	27.0	7	0	1	0	.875	2.33
Giles,Brian	Cle	3	0	11.0	2	0	0	0	1.000	1.64
Gilkey,Bernard	NYN	1	1	9.0	4	0	0	0	1.000	4.00
Gipson,Charles	Sea	11	0	32.0	8	0	0	0	1.000	2.25
Gonzalez,Luis	Det	3	0	4.0	1	0	0	0	1.000	2.25
Goodwin,Curtis	Col	74	33	354.2	111	1	2	0	.982	2.84
Green,Shawn	Tor	33	32	276.1	77	1	1	0	.987	2.54
Greer,Rusty	Tex	2	0	2.0	0	0	0	0	.000	.00
Guerrero,Wilton	LA	1	0	2.0	1	0	0	0	1.000	4.50
Guillen,Jose	Pit	2	2	18.0	5	0	0	0	1.000	2.50
Hamilton,Darryl	SF	96	90	814.0	194	4	0	1	1.000	2.19
Hamilton,Darryl	Col	48	46	407.1	103	1	1	0	.990	2.30
Hammonds,J.	Bal	24	20	167.2	47	1	1	1	.980	2.58
Hammonds,J.	Cin	25	24	205.0	64	3	1	1	.985	2.94
Harris,Lenny	NYN	1	0	2.0	2	0	0	0	1.000	9.00
Henderson,Rickey	Oak	24	16	135.0	36	1	0	0	1.000	2.47
Hernandez,Jose	ChN	31	25	209.2	65	3	0	0	1.000	2.92
Hidalgo,Richard	Hou	57	47	410.0	116	3	1	1	.992	2.61
Hocking,Denny	Min	1	0	3.0	3	0	0	0	1.000	9.00
Hollandsworth,T.	LA	10	7	51.2	22	0	0	0	1.000	3.83
Howard,David	StL	2	0	2.0	0	0	0	0	.000	.00
Howard,Thomas	LA	13	8	74.0	19	2	0	0	1.000	2.55
Hubbard,Trenidad	LA	46	27	277.2	63	2	1	0	.985	2.11
Hudler,Rex	Phi	1	0	2.0	2	0	0	0	1.000	9.00
Hunter,Torii	Min	6	5	45.0	8	0	0	0	1.000	1.60
Jackson,Damian	Cin	3	2	19.0	6	0	0	0	1.000	2.84
Jackson,Darrin	Mil	43	24	245.2	65	2	0	0	1.000	2.45
Javier,Stan	SF	29	21	193.0	49	0	1	0	.980	2.28
Jones,Terry	Mon	60	57	492.2	162	4	2	3	.988	3.03
Jordan,Brian	StL	33	24	222.1	61	2	1	2	.984	2.55

266

Center Fielders - The Rest

Player	Tm	G	GS	Inn	PO	A	E	DP	Pct.	Rng
Kelly,Roberto	Tex	41	32	264.0	87	2	4	1	.957	3.03
Kingsale,Gene	Bal	4	0	7.0	2	0	0	0	1.000	2.57
Kirby,Wayne	NYN	4	2	17.1	4	0	0	0	1.000	2.08
Kotsay,Mark	Fla	46	37	339.0	132	5	2	1	.986	3.64
Latham,Chris	Min	15	10	101.0	33	0	1	0	.971	2.94
Lawton,Matt	Min	47	40	365.0	113	2	1	2	.991	2.84
Ledee,Ricky	NYA	3	1	13.0	2	0	0	0	1.000	1.38
Lowery,Terrell	ChN	20	2	47.0	13	0	1	0	.929	2.49
Martinez,Dave	TB	2	1	8.0	3	0	0	0	1.000	3.38
Martinez,Manny	Pit	37	24	237.1	58	0	1	0	.983	2.20
Mashore,Damon	Ana	7	4	49.1	11	0	0	0	1.000	2.01
McDonald,Jason	Oak	33	29	247.2	83	5	4	1	.957	3.20
McEwing,Joe	StL	1	0	2.0	1	0	0	0	1.000	4.50
McGee,Willie	StL	7	2	24.0	8	0	2	0	.800	3.00
McGuire,Ryan	Mon	7	1	19.0	8	0	0	0	1.000	3.79
Mieske,Matt	ChN	3	0	4.0	0	0	0	0	.000	.00
Monahan,Shane	Sea	3	1	11.0	2	0	0	0	1.000	1.64
Mouton,James	SD	4	4	31.0	3	1	0	0	1.000	1.16
Neill,Mike	Oak	2	2	18.0	7	0	0	0	1.000	3.50
Nunnally,Jon	Cin	24	18	138.2	46	1	0	0	1.000	3.05
Ochoa,Alex	Min	4	1	11.0	1	0	0	0	1.000	0.82
Ordonez,Magglio	ChA	22	20	152.1	47	3	0	1	1.000	2.95
Owens,Eric	Mil	5	5	35.2	7	2	0	0	1.000	2.27
Palmeiro,Orlando	Ana	6	2	26.0	7	0	0	0	1.000	2.42
Powell,Dante	SF	8	0	14.1	2	0	0	0	1.000	1.26
Rios,Armando	SF	1	0	2.2	3	0	0	0	1.000	10.13
Rivera,Ruben	SD	13	12	88.1	23	2	1	0	.962	2.55
Roberts,Bip	Oak	12	12	100.0	30	0	1	0	.968	2.70
Santangelo,F.P.	Mon	23	22	181.0	61	1	0	0	1.000	3.08
Sefcik,Kevin	Phi	8	6	50.0	15	0	0	0	1.000	2.70
Simmons,Brian	ChA	4	4	35.0	13	0	0	0	1.000	3.34
Sosa,Sammy	ChN	7	6	43.1	15	0	0	0	1.000	3.12
Stewart,Shannon	Tor	44	36	317.0	91	2	1	1	.989	2.64
Stovall,DaRond	Mon	14	1	35.0	7	0	1	0	.875	1.80
Stynes,Chris	Cin	2	0	3.0	0	0	0	0	.000	.00
Tarasco,Tony	Cin	1	0	2.0	0	0	0	0	.000	.00
Tavarez,Jesus	Bal	5	3	27.0	6	0	0	0	1.000	2.00
Voigt,Jack	Oak	10	3	42.1	10	1	0	0	1.000	2.34
Walker,Larry	Col	3	0	4.0	0	0	0	0	.000	.00
Ward,Turner	Pit	48	38	314.1	95	5	1	0	.990	2.86
Watkins,Pat	Cin	39	19	217.2	60	0	1	0	.984	2.48
Wehner,John	Fla	2	0	3.1	0	1	0	0	1.000	2.70
Whiten,Mark	Cle	22	12	123.0	38	2	1	1	.976	2.93
Williams,Gerald	Atl	11	6	63.2	24	0	1	0	.960	3.39
Williams,Reggie	Ana	5	3	30.0	8	0	0	0	1.000	2.40
Wilson,Preston	NYN	2	2	13.0	3	0	1	0	.750	2.08
Wilson,Preston	Fla	7	3	32.1	7	0	0	0	1.000	1.95
Winn,Randy	TB	70	60	554.1	165	3	3	0	.982	2.73
Womack,Tony	Pit	5	5	40.0	4	0	0	0	1.000	0.90
Young,Ernie	KC	5	3	27.0	9	1	0	0	1.000	3.33

Right Fielders - Regulars

Player	Tm	G	GS	Inn	PO	A	E	DP	Pct.	Rng
Lawton,Matt	Min	100	96	855.0	263	9	3	3	.989	2.86
Ordonez,Magglio	ChA	136	118	1074.2	276	7	5	1	.983	2.37
Garcia,Karim	Ari	100	83	735.2	185	6	4	1	.979	2.34
Anderson,Garret	Ana	122	119	1050.1	262	9	6	2	.978	2.32
Kotsay,Mark	Fla	107	99	888.2	213	15	4	1	.983	2.31
Higginson,Bob	Det	136	136	1196.1	277	16	5	3	.983	2.20
Guerrero,Vladimir	Mon	157	157	1360.0	321	10	17	3	.951	2.19
Jordan,Brian	StL	124	110	945.2	221	9	8	4	.966	2.19
Sosa,Sammy	ChN	156	153	1379.0	319	14	9	2	.974	2.17
Walker,Larry	Col	123	118	1010.2	236	8	4	2	.984	2.17
Martinez,Dave	TB	85	80	699.2	158	9	1	1	.994	2.15
Guillen,Jose	Pit	149	144	1254.1	279	16	10	4	.967	2.12
O'Neill,Paul	NYA	150	148	1298.2	292	11	4	5	.987	2.10
Green,Shawn	Tor	127	115	1071.0	234	13	6	4	.976	2.08
Ramirez,Manny	Cle	148	147	1318.2	292	10	7	1	.977	2.06
Abreu,Bob	Phi	146	139	1260.1	271	17	8	0	.973	2.06
Burnitz,Jeromy	Mil	161	144	1403.1	306	10	9	3	.972	2.03
Huskey,Butch	NYN	103	94	795.1	167	8	4	1	.978	1.98
Bragg,Darren	Bos	112	102	881.1	188	5	1	2	.995	1.97
Gonzalez,Juan	Tex	116	115	1007.0	212	8	4	2	.982	1.97
Bell,Derek	Hou	154	149	1337.2	282	8	8	2	.973	1.95
Javier,Stan	SF	95	78	719.2	156	0	2	1	.987	1.95
Grieve,Ben	Oak	151	150	1280.2	262	8	2	0	.993	1.90
Tucker,Michael	Atl	118	112	953.2	194	5	1	1	.995	1.88
Sheffield,Gary	TOT	126	126	1098.2	216	9	2	4	.991	1.84
Gwynn,Tony	SD	116	115	901.2	143	5	1	0	.993	1.48
Average	—	127	121	1068.1	239	9	5	2	.980	2.10

Right Fielders - The Rest

Player	Tm	G	GS	Inn	PO	A	E	DP	Pct.	Rng
Abbott,Jeff	ChA	27	27	214.0	51	0	1	0	.981	2.14
Abbott,Kurt	Oak	1	1	7.0	0	0	0	0	.000	.00
Abbott,Kurt	Col	5	4	31.0	6	0	1	0	.857	1.74
Agbayani,Benny	NYN	6	1	19.0	5	0	0	0	1.000	2.37
Allensworth,J.	KC	2	0	3.0	1	0	0	0	1.000	3.00
Allensworth,J.	NYN	25	9	102.1	13	0	0	0	1.000	1.14
Amaral,Rich	Sea	9	8	59.0	7	0	0	0	1.000	1.07
Amaro,Ruben	Phi	6	2	26.2	4	2	0	0	1.000	2.03
Barry,Jeff	Col	5	0	0.0	0	0	0	0	1.000	0.00
Bartee,Kimera	Det	1	0	6.0	2	0	0	0	1.000	3.00
Bautista,Danny	Atl	4	0	5.2	0	0	0	0	.000	.00
Beamon,Trey	Det	2	0	5.0	0	0	0	0	.000	.00
Becker,Rich	NYN	13	8	71.0	25	2	0	0	1.000	3.42
Becker,Rich	Bal	43	17	189.0	38	1	1	0	.975	1.86
Benard,Marvin	SF	64	48	444.1	92	1	2	1	.979	1.88
Benitez,Yamil	Ari	13	13	103.0	18	0	1	0	.947	1.57
Berroa,Geronimo	Det	2	0	6.0	3	0	0	0	1.000	4.50
Bichette,Dante	Col	29	25	213.0	51	0	2	0	.962	2.15
Bolick,Frank	Ana	1	1	8.0	2	0	0	0	1.000	2.25
Brede,Brent	Ari	39	26	239.0	55	2	3	1	.950	2.15
Brosius,Scott	NYA	1	0	2.0	0	0	0	0	.000	.00
Brown,Adrian	Pit	1	1	8.0	4	0	0	0	1.000	4.50
Brown,Dermal	KC	2	0	3.0	1	0	0	0	1.000	3.00
Brown,Emil	Pit	1	0	4.0	0	0	0	0	.000	.00
Buhner,Jay	Sea	70	70	571.2	127	5	2	2	.985	2.08
Burks,Ellis	SF	10	8	64.0	18	0	0	0	1.000	2.53

Right Fielders - The Rest

Player	Tm	G	GS	Inn	PO	A	E	DP	Pct.	Rng
Butler,Rich	TB	22	19	171.1	43	3	0	1	1.000	2.42
Cameron,Mike	ChA	2	1	11.0	3	0	0	0	1.000	2.45
Cangelosi,John	Fla	8	1	22.0	6	0	0	0	1.000	2.45
Canseco,Jose	Tor	26	26	190.1	35	1	1	0	.973	1.70
Carter,Joe	Bal	47	43	365.0	94	3	4	1	.960	2.39
Carter,Joe	SF	14	12	91.1	12	0	0	0	1.000	1.18
Cedeno,Roger	LA	10	4	45.0	7	1	0	0	1.000	1.60
Christenson,Ryan	Oak	4	1	17.0	9	1	0	0	1.000	5.29
Cianfrocco,Archi	SD	3	0	4.0	2	0	0	0	1.000	4.50
Clark,Dave	Hou	13	9	72.2	13	1	1	0	.933	1.73
Clemente,Edgard	Col	6	3	38.0	5	0	1	0	.833	1.18
Clyburn,Danny	Bal	5	3	21.0	5	0	0	0	1.000	2.14
Colbrunn,Greg	Col	5	3	25.0	6	0	0	0	1.000	2.16
Colbrunn,Greg	Atl	1	1	5.0	2	0	0	0	1.000	3.60
Conine,Jeff	KC	31	27	233.1	46	0	1	0	.979	1.77
Coomer,Ron	Min	3	1	10.0	1	0	0	0	1.000	0.90
Cordero,Wil	ChA	8	6	49.0	10	0	1	0	.909	1.84
Cradle,Rickey	Sea	1	1	9.0	1	0	0	0	1.000	1.00
Crespo,Felipe	Tor	25	15	148.0	26	1	0	1	1.000	1.64
Cummings,Midre	Bos	17	8	84.1	16	0	1	0	.941	1.71
Curtis,Chad	NYA	9	7	58.0	13	0	0	0	1.000	2.02
Dalesandro,Mark	Tor	1	1	7.0	0	0	0	0	.000	.00
Damon,Johnny	KC	24	22	188.0	43	1	2	0	.957	2.11
Davis,Eric	Bal	64	59	494.2	105	4	1	0	.991	1.98
Dellucci,David	Ari	15	9	84.2	21	0	0	0	1.000	2.23
Devereaux,Mike	LA	1	0	1.0	0	1	0	0	1.000	9.00
Diaz,Alex	SF	3	1	12.0	1	0	0	0	1.000	0.75
Drew,J.D.	StL	5	4	37.0	8	0	0	0	1.000	1.95
Ducey,Rob	Sea	61	41	390.1	90	3	3	1	.969	2.14
Dye,Jermaine	KC	59	56	513.1	153	4	2	3	.987	2.75
Echevarria,Angel	Col	1	0	3.0	0	0	0	0	.000	.00
Eisenreich,Jim	Fla	3	2	19.0	4	0	0	0	1.000	1.89
Eisenreich,Jim	LA	2	2	17.0	2	0	0	0	1.000	1.06
Encarnacion,Juan	Det	21	20	177.0	35	1	1	1	.973	1.83
Everett,Carl	Hou	5	2	19.0	5	0	0	0	1.000	2.37
Fox,Andy	Ari	33	22	198.0	40	2	2	0	.955	1.91
Franco,Matt	NYN	1	0	1.0	0	0	0	0	.000	.00
Frank,Mike	Cin	2	0	3.0	0	0	0	0	.000	.00
Gaetti,Gary	StL	1	0	2.0	0	0	0	0	.000	.00
Giles,Brian	Cle	6	5	41.0	11	0	0	0	1.000	2.41
Gilkey,Bernard	NYN	4	4	27.0	3	0	0	0	1.000	1.00
Gipson,Charles	Sea	13	4	55.0	16	2	1	1	.947	2.95
Goodwin,Curtis	Col	7	0	12.0	1	0	0	0	1.000	0.75
Greene,Willie	Cin	22	17	137.0	34	0	0	0	1.000	2.23
Greene,Willie	Bal	13	10	90.2	15	1	1	0	.941	1.59
GriffeyJr.,Ken	Sea	1	0	2.0	1	0	0	0	1.000	4.50
Halter,Shane	KC	3	2	15.0	4	0	0	0	1.000	2.40
Hammonds,J.	Bal	29	21	189.0	41	0	1	0	.976	1.95
Hardtke,Jason	ChN	1	0	1.0	0	0	0	0	.000	.00
Harris,Lenny	Cin	20	12	108.1	23	0	0	0	1.000	1.91
Harris,Lenny	NYN	53	27	279.2	71	1	1	0	.986	2.32
Hernandez,Jose	ChN	2	0	2.0	0	0	0	0	.000	.00
Hidalgo,Richard	Hou	13	2	40.0	5	0	1	0	.833	1.13
Hill,Glenallen	ChN	6	6	43.0	12	1	0	0	1.000	2.72
Hocking,Denny	Min	7	5	40.0	10	0	0	0	1.000	2.25
Hollandsworth,T.	LA	1	1	6.2	1	0	0	0	1.000	1.35
Hollins,Damon	Atl	1	0	1.0	0	0	0	0	.000	.00
Hollins,Damon	LA	3	2	20.0	4	0	0	0	1.000	1.80
Howard,David	StL	1	0	1.0	1	1	0	1	1.000	18.00
Howard,Thomas	LA	6	1	21.0	2	0	0	0	1.000	0.86
Hubbard,Trenidad	LA	4	0	9.0	2	0	0	0	1.000	2.00
Hudler,Rex	Phi	5	5	41.0	12	0	0	0	1.000	2.63
Hughes,Bobby	Mil	3	0	4.0	1	0	0	0	1.000	2.25
Hunter,Brian	StL	12	9	67.1	20	0	1	0	.952	2.67
Huson,Jeff	Sea	1	0	1.0	1	0	0	0	1.000	9.00
Ibanez,Raul	Sea	12	7	53.0	7	0	0	0	1.000	1.19
Jackson,Darrin	Mil	5	3	25.2	3	0	0	0	1.000	1.05
Jackson,Ryan	Fla	23	14	133.1	33	0	1	0	.971	2.23
Jenkins,Geoff	Mil	1	0	1.0	0	0	0	0	.000	.00
Jones,Chris	Ari	7	5	43.2	11	0	0	0	1.000	2.27
Jones,Chris	SF	24	16	143.2	29	1	1	0	.968	1.88
Justice,David	Cle	2	2	18.0	5	0	0	0	1.000	2.50
Kapler,Gabe	Det	6	6	53.0	9	0	0	0	1.000	1.53
Kelly,Mike	TB	51	30	294.2	58	2	0	0	1.000	1.83
Kelly,Roberto	Tex	31	17	167.0	54	1	0	0	1.000	2.96
Kirby,Wayne	NYN	12	2	33.1	11	1	0	1	1.000	3.24
Lampkin,Tom	StL	1	0	0.1	0	0	0	0	.000	.00
Latham,Chris	Min	5	5	45.0	14	1	0	0	1.000	3.00
Ledee,Ricky	NYA	4	1	17.0	2	0	0	0	1.000	1.06
Lennon,Patrick	Tor	2	1	7.2	3	0	0	0	1.000	3.52
Lewis,Darren	Bos	55	46	408.1	89	1	3	0	.968	1.98
Little,Mark	StL	4	3	26.0	9	0	0	0	1.000	3.12
Lombard,George	Atl	2	1	11.0	2	0	0	0	1.000	1.64
Lopez,Luis	NYN	1	1	5.1	4	0	1	0	.800	6.75
Luke,Matt	LA	14	10	94.1	21	2	0	0	1.000	2.19
Mabry,John	StL	37	18	170.2	53	1	3	1	.947	2.85
Mack,Shane	KC	3	1	13.0	2	0	0	0	1.000	1.38
Martinez,Manny	Pit	3	0	8.0	4	0	0	0	1.000	4.50
Mashore,Damon	Ana	28	19	183.1	42	1	0	0	1.000	2.11
McCarty,Dave	Sea	5	4	31.0	7	0	0	0	1.000	2.03
McDonald,Jason	Oak	25	8	102.1	24	2	2	0	.929	2.29
McEwing,Joe	StL	1	0	1.0	0	0	0	0	.000	.00
McGee,Willie	StL	38	19	218.2	50	3	2	1	.964	2.18
McGuire,Ryan	Mon	8	2	26.0	8	1	0	0	1.000	3.12
Merced,Orlando	Min	13	12	101.0	25	2	0	1	1.000	2.41
Merced,Orlando	Bos	1	0	3.0	2	0	0	0	1.000	6.00
Meulens,Hensley	Ari	4	4	25.1	6	1	0	0	1.000	2.49
Mieske,Matt	ChN	12	3	49.1	14	1	0	0	1.000	2.74
Miller,Damian	Ari	2	0	3.0	0	0	0	0	.000	.00
Mitchell,Keith	Bos	6	2	20.0	4	0	0	0	1.000	1.80
Monahan,Shane	Sea	2	0	4.0	2	0	0	0	1.000	4.50
Mondesi,Raul	LA	54	53	457.1	106	1	2	0	.982	2.11
Montgomery,Ray	Hou	1	0	2.0	1	0	0	0	1.000	4.50
Mouton,James	SD	14	4	71.1	17	0	0	0	1.000	2.14
Mouton,Lyle	Bal	12	7	68.0	16	1	0	0	1.000	2.25
Nieves,Melvin	Cin	22	16	140.0	28	1	0	0	1.000	1.86
Nilsson,Dave	Mil	3	0	5.0	1	0	0	0	1.000	1.80
Nixon,Trot	Bos	6	4	39.0	12	0	0	0	1.000	2.77
Nunnally,Jon	Cin	53	30	279.0	74	3	6	0	.928	2.48
Ochoa,Alex	Min	52	43	393.2	88	4	3	0	.968	2.10
Otanez,Willis	Bal	2	2	8.0	1	0	0	0	1.000	1.13
Owens,Eric	Mil	2	1	12.0	1	0	0	0	1.000	0.75
Palmeiro,Orlando	Ana	4	1	17.2	4	0	0	0	1.000	2.04
Payton,Jay	NYN	1	0	2.0	0	0	0	0	.000	.00
Perez,Robert	Sea	15	8	77.1	19	1	0	0	1.000	2.33
Petagine,Roberto	Cin	15	11	83.0	26	0	0	0	1.000	2.82

Right Fielders - The Rest

Player	Tm	G	GS	Inn	PO	A	E	DP	Pct.	Rng
Phillips,Tony	Tor	4	3	27.0	4	0	0	0	1.000	1.33
Phillips,Tony	NYN	15	15	113.0	25	0	1	0	.962	1.99
Pride,Curtis	Atl	14	11	94.0	27	0	0	0	1.000	2.59
Radmanovich,R.	Sea	24	18	171.0	33	2	0	0	1.000	1.84
Ramirez,Alex	Cle	1	1	8.0	1	0	1	0	.500	1.13
Rios,Armando	SF	2	0	2.0	0	0	0	0	.000	.00
Rivera,Ruben	SD	73	24	317.0	68	1	2	0	.972	1.96
Roberts,Bip	Oak	3	0	5.0	1	0	0	0	1.000	1.80
Salmon,Tim	Ana	19	19	162.2	45	1	2	0	.958	2.55
Samuel,Juan	Tor	2	2	14.0	1	0	0	0	1.000	0.64
Sanders,Reggie	Cin	57	43	383.2	94	1	1	0	.990	2.23
Santangelo,F.P.	Mon	1	0	1.0	0	0	0	0	.000	.00
Sefcik,Kevin	Phi	20	16	135.0	48	1	1	0	.980	3.27
Seguignol,F.	Mon	1	0	2.0	1	0	0	0	1.000	4.50
Sheffield,Gary	Fla	37	37	322.2	68	3	1	2	.986	1.98
Sheffield,Gary	LA	89	89	776.0	148	6	1	2	.994	1.79
Shipley,Craig	Ana	1	1	6.0	2	0	0	0	1.000	3.00
Siddall,Joe	Det	1	0	1.0	0	0	0	0	.000	.00
Sierra,Ruben	ChA	12	11	89.0	17	1	0	0	1.000	1.82
Simms,Mike	Tex	40	26	224.1	43	1	0	0	1.000	1.77
Smith,Mark	Pit	9	9	72.1	18	0	1	0	.947	2.24
Snopek,Chris	ChA	1	0	1.0	0	0	0	0	.000	.00
Sorrento,Paul	TB	14	13	87.0	27	0	0	0	1.000	2.79
Spencer,Shane	NYA	15	6	81.0	15	0	0	0	1.000	1.67
Stahoviak,Scott	Min	1	0	3.0	0	0	0	0	.000	.00
Stairs,Matt	Oak	2	1	12.0	3	0	0	0	1.000	2.25
Stevens,Lee	Tex	7	4	33.0	12	0	0	0	1.000	3.27
Stovall,DaRond	Mon	7	3	38.0	10	1	0	0	1.000	2.61
Stynes,Chris	Cin	20	12	108.2	18	1	0	1	1.000	1.57
Sutton,Larry	KC	47	43	365.0	91	2	2	1	.979	2.29
Sweeney,Mark	SD	29	19	157.1	34	0	0	0	1.000	1.94
Tarasco,Tony	Cin	2	1	10.0	1	0	0	0	1.000	0.90
Tavarez,Jesus	Bal	4	0	6.0	1	0	0	0	1.000	1.50
Tomberlin,Andy	Det	1	0	2.0	1	0	0	0	1.000	4.50
Trammell,Bubba	TB	16	13	113.0	17	1	0	0	1.000	1.43
Valdes,Pedro	ChN	1	1	3.0	1	0	0	0	1.000	3.00
VanderWal,John	Col	22	9	91.0	18	2	0	1	1.000	1.98
VanderWal,John	SD	3	0	3.1	0	0	0	0	.000	.00
Voigt,Jack	Oak	2	1	10.0	2	0	0	0	1.000	1.80
Walton,Jerome	TB	4	2	19.0	3	0	0	0	1.000	1.42
Ward,Turner	Pit	22	0	102.1	35	1	0	1	1.000	3.17
Watkins,Pat	Cin	28	8	94.1	22	1	1	0	.958	2.19
Wehner,John	Fla	11	8	55.0	14	0	0	0	1.000	2.29
Whiten,Mark	Cle	13	7	74.1	6	0	0	0	1.000	0.73
Williams,Gerald	Atl	61	37	368.1	101	2	3	0	.972	2.52
Williams,Reggie	Ana	2	2	16.0	1	0	0	0	1.000	0.56
Wilson,Preston	NYN	1	1	9.0	2	0	0	0	1.000	2.00
Wilson,Preston	Fla	1	1	9.0	0	0	0	0	.000	.00
Winn,Randy	TB	12	5	58.1	9	1	1	1	.909	1.54
Young,Dmitri	Cin	14	12	94.1	12	0	1	0	.923	1.14
Young,Ernie	KC	19	10	102.2	34	1	0	0	1.000	3.07

Catchers - Regulars

Player	Tm	G	GS	Inn	PO	A	E	DP	PB	Pct.
Lopez,Javy	Atl	128	123	1092.1	978	68	5	6	11	.995
Girardi,Joe	NYA	78	76	655.2	541	38	3	5	5	.995
Hoiles,Chris	Bal	83	78	645.0	516	39	3	6	2	.995
Wilson,Dan	Sea	94	92	797.1	677	34	4	6	5	.994
Servais,Scott	ChN	110	87	811.2	652	47	4	6	3	.994
Posada,Jorge	NYA	99	85	792.0	586	46	4	3	7	.994
Rodriguez,Ivan	Tex	139	137	1197.1	864	71	6	6	10	.994
Johnson,Brian	SF	95	86	764.0	590	33	4	4	7	.994
Flaherty,John	TB	91	86	763.0	541	45	4	2	5	.993
Hatteberg,Scott	Bos	108	105	904.0	665	60	5	7	17	.993
Webster,Lenny	Bal	102	78	726.2	529	38	4	5	9	.993
DiFelice,Mike	TB	84	75	671.0	483	51	4	8	13	.993
Ausmus,Brad	Hou	124	117	1054.1	850	58	7	8	4	.992
Alomar,Sandy	Cle	111	106	930.0	713	42	6	7	4	.992
Hernandez,Carlos	SD	122	102	907.2	793	54	7	6	13	.992
Johnson,Charles	TOT	131	129	1143.2	908	59	8	10	6	.992
Kendall,Jason	Pit	144	143	1253.1	1015	58	9	10	9	.992
Marrero,Eli	StL	73	67	613.0	426	30	4	3	1	.991
Fletcher,Darrin	Tor	121	114	971.1	832	49	8	1	3	.991
Mayne,Brent	SF	88	72	664.0	492	39	5	5	6	.991
Walbeck,Matt	Ana	104	91	831.1	682	46	7	3	8	.990
Steinbach,Terry	Min	119	116	1007.0	665	52	7	3	4	.990
Piazza,Mike	TOT	141	140	1190.0	984	85	11	7	5	.990
Bako,Paul	Det	94	83	755.0	493	45	6	5	9	.989
Manwaring,Kirt	Col	108	95	796.0	527	49	7	6	8	.988
Taubensee,Eddie	Cin	126	109	991.2	776	44	10	5	8	.988
Lieberthal,Mike	Phi	83	78	706.0	607	41	8	5	5	.988
Matheny,Mike	Mil	107	91	795.0	570	45	8	9	6	.987
Zaun,Gregg	Fla	88	77	711.1	531	47	8	12	10	.986
Hinch,A.J.	Oak	118	109	940.1	602	47	9	8	8	.986
Reed,Jeff	Col	99	66	625.2	452	26	7	4	1	.986
Stinnett,Kelly	Ari	86	78	710.0	458	38	8	3	1	.984
Sweeney,Mike	KC	91	75	705.1	517	33	9	7	9	.984
Widger,Chris	Mon	123	118	1014.0	752	62	14	12	14	.983
Kreuter,Chad	TOT	94	74	670.0	438	35	9	4	5	.981
Average	—	105	95	851.1	648	47	6	5	6	.991

Catchers - The Rest

Player	Tm	G	GS	Inn	PO	A	E	DP	PB	Pct.
Banks,Brian	Mil	5	1	11.0	4	0	0	0	0	1.000
Barrett,Michael	Mon	3	3	23.0	22	4	1	1	0	.963
Bennett,Gary	Phi	9	8	78.2	50	2	0	0	0	1.000
Borders,Pat	Cle	53	42	399.1	283	19	8	1	4	.974
Brown,Kevin L.	Tor	52	32	313.1	261	19	2	2	5	.993
Casanova,Raul	Det	14	13	105.0	81	6	3	0	0	.967
Castillo,Alberto	NYN	35	28	245.2	193	15	2	3	1	.990
Chavez,Raul	Sea	1	0	4.0	3	1	0	0	0	1.000
Colbrunn,Greg	Col	1	0	1.0	0	0	0	0	0	.000
Dalesandro,Mark	Tor	18	11	112.1	68	4	1	0	0	.986
Davis,Ben	SD	1	0	2.1	2	0	0	0	0	1.000
Diaz,Einar	Cle	17	14	130.2	101	9	3	0	0	.973
Estalella,Bobby	Phi	47	44	393.2	321	12	4	0	5	.988
Eusebio,Tony	Hou	54	45	409.0	352	19	3	2	4	.992
Fabregas,Jorge	Ari	41	41	334.0	228	30	1	2	0	.996
Fabregas,Jorge	NYN	12	5	63.1	62	6	2	2	2	.971
Fasano,Sal	KC	70	68	579.1	421	25	2	5	2	.996

Catchers - The Rest

Player	Tm	G	GS	Inn	PO	A	E	DP	PB	Pct.
Fick,Robert	Det	3	3	22.0	18	1	1	0	0	.950
Figga,Mike	NYA	1	1	9.0	3	0	0	0	0	1.000
Fordyce,Brook	Cin	54	44	367.0	288	20	7	3	0	.978
Garcia,Guillermo	Cin	11	9	82.2	74	5	1	1	2	.988
Greene,Charlie	Bal	13	6	59.2	57	5	0	0	1	1.000
Haselman,Bill	Tex	36	25	234.0	177	7	1	0	0	.995
Henley,Bob	Mon	35	30	270.2	189	14	1	1	3	.995
Houston,Tyler	ChN	63	56	473.2	418	21	3	4	3	.993
Hubbard,Mike	Mon	24	11	119.1	83	5	0	1	1	1.000
Hughes,Bobby	Mil	72	56	510.2	397	29	2	5	6	.995
Hundley,Todd	NYN	2	2	18.0	18	2	0	0	0	1.000
Jensen,Marcus	Mil	1	0	1.0	1	0	0	0	0	1.000
Johnson,Charles	Fla	31	31	273.0	193	9	2	2	1	.990
Johnson,Charles	LA	100	98	870.2	715	50	6	8	5	.992
Johnson,Mark L.	ChA	7	5	53.2	36	2	0	1	0	1.000
Knorr,Randy	Fla	15	15	119.0	82	7	1	2	4	.989
Kreuter,Chad	ChA	91	71	647.0	424	34	7	4	5	.985
Kreuter,Chad	Ana	3	3	23.0	14	1	2	0	0	.882
Laker,Tim	TB	2	1	9.0	5	0	0	0	1	1.000
Laker,Tim	Pit	1	0	3.0	2	0	0	0	1	1.000
Lampkin,Tom	StL	62	54	482.1	331	19	5	5	4	.986
Levis,Jesse	Mil	14	8	87.1	83	2	0	0	1	1.000
Leyritz,Jim	Bos	1	1	8.0	10	0	0	0	0	1.000
Leyritz,Jim	SD	24	20	163.1	139	11	2	1	1	.987
LoDuca,Paul	LA	4	2	24.0	18	2	0	1	0	1.000
Macfarlane,Mike	KC	3	3	24.2	13	3	0	1	0	1.000
Macfarlane,Mike	Oak	70	53	485.1	355	20	4	6	5	.989
Machado,Robert	ChA	34	33	283.0	189	17	4	1	3	.981
Martinez,Sandy	ChN	33	20	192.0	185	7	3	1	1	.985
Marzano,John	Sea	48	40	362.1	317	24	1	2	5	.997
Meluskey,Mitch	Hou	3	0	8.0	9	0	0	0	1	1.000
Miller,Damian	Ari	46	43	388.1	255	26	4	2	6	.986
Mirabelli,Doug	SF	10	5	49.0	34	4	1	0	0	.974
Molina,Ben	Ana	2	0	3.0	1	0	0	0	0	1.000
Molina,Izzy	Oak	5	0	8.1	8	1	0	0	0	1.000
Myers,Greg	SD	52	38	357.2	276	29	4	4	2	.987
Nevin,Phil	Ana	69	64	555.2	399	32	5	3	20	.989
Nilsson,Dave	Mil	7	6	46.0	31	1	1	0	1	.970
O'Brien,Charlie	ChA	57	54	455.0	305	22	4	3	1	.988
O'Brien,Charlie	Ana	5	4	31.0	20	2	0	0	0	1.000
Oliver,Joe	Det	48	44	379.0	259	16	5	2	0	.982
Oliver,Joe	Sea	29	24	218.2	174	9	3	0	1	.984
Ortiz,Hector	KC	3	1	12.0	4	0	0	0	0	1.000
Osik,Keith	Pit	26	20	192.2	143	12	0	1	4	1.000
Pagnozzi,Tom	StL	44	42	374.1	259	17	5	5	1	.982
Parent,Mark	Phi	34	32	284.2	211	15	3	4	5	.987
Pena,Angel	LA	4	3	29.0	26	2	0	0	1	1.000
Perez,Eddie	Atl	45	39	346.1	275	28	1	2	2	.997
Perez,Neifi	Col	1	0	0.0	0	0	0	0	0	.000
Piazza,Mike	LA	37	37	309.2	276	26	2	1	0	.993
Piazza,Mike	Fla	4	4	35.0	27	3	1	1	0	.968
Piazza,Mike	NYN	100	99	845.1	681	56	8	5	5	.989
Pierzynski,A.J.	Min	6	4	37.0	33	2	0	1	0	1.000
Pratt,Todd	NYN	16	8	90.2	67	4	2	1	2	.973
Prince,Tom	LA	32	22	214.0	175	14	0	2	1	1.000
Redmond,Mike	Fla	37	35	311.1	216	25	2	3	3	.992
Romero,Mandy	SD	6	2	23.2	24	2	1	0	1	.963
Romero,Mandy	Bos	4	0	8.0	11	0	0	0	0	1.000

270

Catchers - The Rest

Player	Tm	G	GS	Inn	PO	A	E	DP	PB	Pct.
Santiago,Benito	Tor	15	6	68.0	45	2	0	0	1	1.000
Siddall,Joe	Det	27	19	185.1	142	15	1	3	3	.994
Spehr,Tim	NYN	21	15	147.0	119	10	0	1	1	1.000
Spehr,Tim	KC	11	11	93.0	62	2	0	0	0	1.000
Strittmatter,Mark	Col	3	1	10.0	10	1	0	1	0	1.000
Tatum,Jimmy	NYN	4	1	14.0	11	3	0	0	0	1.000
Turner,Chris	KC	4	3	22.0	16	0	0	0	0	1.000
Valentin,Javier	Min	53	42	403.2	281	16	5	0	7	.983
Varitek,Jason	Bos	75	56	516.0	367	32	5	3	18	.988
Wilkins,Rick	Sea	6	5	42.0	28	2	0	0	0	1.000
Wilkins,Rick	NYN	4	4	34.0	21	1	1	0	0	.957

Catchers - Regulars - Special

Player	Tm	G	GS	Inn	SBA	CS	PCS	CS%	ER	CERA
Lopez,Javy	Atl	128	123	1092.1	80	27	0	.34	420	3.46
Hernandez,C.	SD	122	102	907.2	82	24	5	.29	355	3.52
Ausmus,Brad	Hou	124	117	1054.1	88	32	13	.36	414	3.53
Marrero,Eli	StL	73	67	613.0	51	19	7	.37	256	3.76
Girardi,Joe	NYA	78	76	655.2	73	19	5	.26	277	3.80
Posada,Jorge	NYA	99	85	792.0	80	32	3	.40	338	3.84
Kendall,Jason	Pit	144	143	1253.1	115	32	4	.28	537	3.86
Fletcher,Darrin	Tor	121	114	971.1	133	32	1	.24	425	3.94
Piazza,Mike	TOT	141	140	1190.0	156	41	6	.26	532	4.02
Johnson,Brian	SF	95	86	764.0	61	20	4	.33	345	4.06
Johnson,Charles	TOT	131	129	1143.2	93	37	11	.40	520	4.09
Hatteberg,Scott	Bos	108	105	904.0	120	39	8	.33	412	4.10
DiFelice,Mike	TB	84	75	671.0	81	32	3	.40	314	4.21
Widger,Chris	Mon	123	118	1014.0	129	47	13	.36	486	4.31
Mayne,Brent	SF	88	72	664.0	68	15	1	.22	319	4.32
Walbeck,Matt	Ana	104	91	831.1	137	41	11	.30	404	4.37
Webster,Lenny	Bal	102	78	726.2	107	25	5	.23	354	4.38
Alomar,Sandy	Cle	111	106	930.0	95	28	4	.29	454	4.39
Flaherty,John	TB	91	86	763.0	77	29	3	.38	373	4.40
Servais,Scott	ChN	110	87	811.2	89	25	6	.28	406	4.50
Hinch,A.J.	Oak	118	109	940.1	103	35	13	.34	471	4.51
Taubensee,E.	Cin	126	109	991.2	102	23	5	.23	498	4.52
Stinnett,Kelly	Ari	86	78	710.0	78	29	10	.37	359	4.55
Lieberthal,Mike	Phi	83	78	706.0	51	18	2	.35	362	4.61
Matheny,Mike	Mil	107	91	795.0	88	21	3	.24	411	4.65
Steinbach,Terry	Min	119	116	1007.0	97	34	3	.35	534	4.77
Bako,Paul	Det	94	83	755.0	106	36	7	.34	408	4.86
Manwaring,Kirt	Col	108	95	796.0	94	30	3	.32	433	4.90
Rodriguez,Ivan	Tex	139	137	1197.1	87	49	7	.56	655	4.92
Wilson,Dan	Sea	94	92	797.1	100	28	11	.28	443	5.00
Hoiles,Chris	Bal	83	78	645.0	126	27	6	.21	361	5.04
Reed,Jeff	Col	99	66	625.2	65	22	3	.34	353	5.08
Zaun,Gregg	Fla	88	77	711.1	78	26	7	.33	407	5.15
Sweeney,Mike	KC	91	75	705.1	71	21	4	.30	404	5.16
Kreuter,Chad	TOT	94	74	670.0	79	26	4	.33	399	5.36
Average	—	105	95	851.1	92	29	5	.32	412	4.36

Catchers - The Rest - Special

Player	Tm	G	GS	Inn	SBA	CS	PCS	CS%	ER	CERA
Banks,Brian	Mil	5	1	11.0	2	0	0	0	4	3.27
Barrett,Michael	Mon	3	3	23.0	6	2	0	.33	18	7.04
Bennett,Gary	Phi	9	8	78.2	1	0	0	0	39	4.46
Borders,Pat	Cle	53	42	399.1	46	13	1	.28	207	4.67
Brown,Kevin L.	Tor	52	32	313.1	41	12	0	.29	167	4.80
Casanova,Raul	Det	14	13	105.0	18	7	3	.39	63	5.40
Castillo,Alberto	NYN	35	28	245.2	28	15	5	.54	84	3.08
Chavez,Raul	Sea	1	0	4.0	0	0	0	0	0	0.00
Colbrunn,Greg	Col	1	0	1.0	0	0	0	0	0	0.00
Dalesandro,Mark	Tor	18	11	112.1	12	3	0	.25	67	5.37
Davis,Ben	SD	1	0	2.1	0	0	0	0	4	15.43
Diaz,Einar	Cle	17	14	130.2	16	6	0	.38	60	4.13
Estalella,Bobby	Phi	47	44	393.2	43	7	2	.16	202	4.62
Eusebio,Tony	Hou	54	45	409.0	30	11	1	.37	154	3.39
Fabregas,Jorge	Ari	41	41	334.0	43	22	4	.51	196	5.28
Fabregas,Jorge	NYN	12	5	63.1	11	3	1	.27	41	5.83
Fasano,Sal	KC	70	68	579.1	41	18	3	.44	327	5.08

Catchers - The Rest - Special

Player	Tm	G	GS	Inn	SBA	CS	PCS	CS%	ER	CERA
Fick,Robert	Det	3	3	22.0	3	1	1	.33	11	4.50
Figga,Mike	NYA	1	1	9.0	0	0	0	0	4	4.00
Fordyce,Brook	Cin	54	44	367.0	45	16	3	.36	154	3.78
Garcia,Guillermo	Cin	11	9	82.2	16	7	0	.44	59	6.42
Greene,Charlie	Bal	13	6	59.2	2	1	0	.50	39	5.88
Haselman,Bill	Tex	36	25	234.0	32	6	1	.19	139	5.35
Henley,Bob	Mon	35	30	270.2	30	10	1	.33	130	4.32
Houston,Tyler	ChN	63	56	473.2	58	14	3	.24	229	4.35
Hubbard,Mike	Mon	24	11	119.1	31	5	2	.16	61	4.60
Hughes,Bobby	Mil	72	56	510.2	57	12	2	.21	269	4.74
Hundley,Todd	NYN	2	2	18.0	3	2	0	.67	4	2.00
Jensen,Marcus	Mil	1	0	1.0	0	0	0	0	1	9.00
Johnson,Charles	Fla	31	31	273.0	24	7	2	.29	165	5.44
Johnson,Charles	LA	100	98	870.2	69	30	9	.43	355	3.67
Johnson,Mark L.	ChA	7	5	53.2	4	2	1	.50	21	3.52
Knorr,Randy	Fla	15	15	119.0	17	3	1	.18	87	6.58
Kreuter,Chad	ChA	91	71	647.0	74	25	4	.34	385	5.36
Kreuter,Chad	Ana	3	3	23.0	5	1	0	.20	14	5.48
Laker,Tim	TB	2	1	9.0	0	0	0	0	11	11.00
Laker,Tim	Pit	1	0	3.0	0	0	0	0	3	9.00
Lampkin,Tom	StL	62	54	482.1	43	13	0	.30	258	4.81
Levis,Jesse	Mil	14	8	87.1	9	1	0	.11	36	3.71
Leyritz,Jim	Bos	1	1	8.0	2	0	0	0	6	6.75
Leyritz,Jim	SD	24	20	163.1	12	2	1	.17	67	3.69
LoDuca,Paul	LA	4	2	24.0	4	2	0	.50	7	2.63
Macfarlane,Mike	KC	3	3	24.2	3	2	0	.67	21	7.66
Macfarlane,Mike	Oak	70	53	485.1	46	13	4	.28	290	5.38
Machado,Robert	ChA	34	33	283.0	35	11	7	.31	150	4.77
Martinez,Sandy	ChN	33	20	192.0	16	4	0	.25	98	4.59
Marzano,John	Sea	48	40	362.1	45	13	2	.29	191	4.74
Meluskey,Mitch	Hou	3	0	8.0	0	0	0	0	4	4.50
Miller,Damian	Ari	46	43	388.1	35	12	1	.34	182	4.22
Mirabelli,Doug	SF	10	5	49.0	7	4	0	.57	22	4.04
Molina,Ben	Ana	2	0	3.0	0	0	0	0	0	0.00
Molina,Izzy	Oak	5	0	8.1	2	0	0	0	5	5.40
Myers,Greg	SD	52	38	357.2	37	13	1	.35	151	3.80
Nevin,Phil	Ana	69	64	555.2	75	21	3	.28	279	4.52
Nilsson,Dave	Mil	7	6	46.0	3	0	0	0	25	4.89
O'Brien,Charlie	ChA	57	54	455.0	68	21	5	.31	279	5.52
O'Brien,Charlie	Ana	5	4	31.0	4	2	0	.50	23	6.68
Oliver,Joe	Det	48	44	379.0	38	14	3	.37	223	5.30
Oliver,Joe	Sea	29	24	218.2	28	7	3	.25	125	5.14
Ortiz,Hector	KC	3	1	12.0	0	0	0	0	17	12.75
Osik,Keith	Pit	26	20	192.2	19	7	2	.37	89	4.16
Pagnozzi,Tom	StL	44	42	374.1	42	12	2	.29	189	4.54
Parent,Mark	Phi	34	32	284.2	25	8	0	.32	151	4.77
Pena,Angel	LA	4	3	29.0	2	1	0	.50	9	2.79
Perez,Eddie	Atl	45	39	346.1	45	13	1	.29	100	2.60
Piazza,Mike	LA	37	37	309.2	50	12	2	.24	142	4.13
Piazza,Mike	Fla	4	4	35.0	4	1	0	.25	23	5.91
Piazza,Mike	NYN	100	99	845.1	102	28	4	.27	367	3.91
Pierzynski,A.J.	Min	6	4	37.0	5	1	0	.20	10	2.43
Pratt,Todd	NYN	16	8	90.2	9	4	0	.44	38	3.77
Prince,Tom	LA	32	22	214.0	25	12	1	.48	99	4.16
Redmond,Mike	Fla	37	35	311.1	40	17	4	.43	152	4.39
Romero,Mandy	SD	6	2	23.2	3	1	0	.33	10	3.80
Romero,Mandy	Bos	4	0	8.0	0	0	0	0	3	3.38

Catchers - The Rest - Special

Player	Tm	G	GS	Inn	SBA	CS	PCS	CS%	ER	CERA
Santiago,Benito	Tor	15	6	68.0	10	0	0	0	38	5.03
Siddall,Joe	Det	27	19	185.1	24	11	3	.46	87	4.22
Spehr,Tim	NYN	21	15	147.0	19	7	0	.37	51	3.12
Spehr,Tim	KC	11	11	93.0	7	2	0	.29	42	4.06
Strittmatter,Mark	Col	3	1	10.0	1	0	0	0	7	6.30
Tatum,Jimmy	NYN	4	1	14.0	5	4	1	.80	9	5.79
Turner,Chris	KC	4	3	22.0	1	0	0	0	11	4.50
Valentin,Javier	Min	53	42	403.2	44	10	2	.23	220	4.91
Varitek,Jason	Bos	75	56	516.0	68	19	3	.28	246	4.29
Wilkins,Rick	Sea	6	5	42.0	3	1	0	.33	22	4.71
Wilkins,Rick	NYN	4	4	34.0	4	1	1	.25	15	3.97

Pitchers Hitting & Fielding, and Hitters Pitchings

The 1998 baseball season contained dozens of remarkable performances, even beyond those accomplished by Mark McGwire and Sammy Sosa. In the following section, you'll find complete 1998 hitting, fielding, and opponent basestealing data for each major league pitcher. Take a look at Mike Morgan, who never had batted above .125 and carried a lowly .089 career batting average into the season. Last year, he broke out with a double and four singles in eight at-bats. Then there's Omar Daal, who completely neutralized the running game. He picked off one baserunner, threw out three more stealing, and helped his catchers throw out nine of 12 potential thieves. Randy Johnson showed that he's still got that old wildness on throws to first base: he committed nine errors, almost twice as many as any other pitcher. Then there's Kerry Ligtenberg, who threw 73 innings and handled only five chances all year. He barely managed to record more clean chances (three) than errors (two). In the final section, "hitters pitching," you'll find the unique pitching line of Mark Whiten, who became the first non-pitcher in history to work a full inning and strike out the side.

Pitchers Hitting

	1998 Hitting														Career Hitting													
Pitcher,Team	Avg	OBP	SLG	AB	H	2B	3B	HR	R	RBI	BB	SO	SH	SB-CS	Avg	OBP	SLG	AB	H	2B	3B	HR	R	RBI	BB	SO	SH	SB-CS
Acevedo,Juan,StL	.176	.222	.235	17	3	1	0	0	2	0	1	5	2	0-0	.098	.140	.122	41	4	1	0	0	2	0	2	16	3	0-0
Adams,Terry,ChN	.000	.000	.000	1	0	0	0	0	0	0	0	1	0	0-0	.000	.100	.000	9	0	0	0	0	0	0	1	5	0	0-0
Adamson,Joel,Ari	.429	.429	.571	7	3	1	0	0	0	1	0	0	1	0-0	.300	.300	.400	10	3	1	0	0	0	1	0	0	1	0-0
Aguilera,Rick,Min	.000	.000	.000	0	0	0	0	0	0	0	0	0	0	0-0	.203	.236	.290	138	28	3	0	3	12	11	6	37	16	0-0
Aldred,Scott,TB	.000	.000	.000	0	0	0	0	0	0	0	0	0	0	0-0	.000	.000	.000	0	0	0	0	0	0	0	0	0	0	0-0
Alfonseca,Antonio,Fla	.000	.000	.000	4	0	0	0	0	0	0	0	2	0	0-0	.000	.000	.000	7	0	0	0	0	0	0	0	5	0	0-0
Anderson,Brian,Ari	.106	.145	.106	66	7	0	0	0	6	0	3	19	6	1-0	.106	.145	.106	66	7	0	0	0	6	0	3	19	6	1-0
Anderson,Matt,Det	.000	.000	.000	0	0	0	0	0	0	0	0	0	0	0-0	.000	.000	.000	0	0	0	0	0	0	0	0	0	0	0-0
Andujar,Luis,Tor	.000	.000	.000	0	0	0	0	0	0	0	0	0	0	0-0	.000	.000	.000	0	0	0	0	0	0	0	0	0	0	0-0
Arrojo,Rolando,TB	.000	.000	.000	3	0	0	0	0	0	0	0	2	0	0-0	.000	.000	.000	3	0	0	0	0	0	0	0	2	0	0-0
Ashby,Andy,SD	.111	.135	.139	72	8	2	0	0	1	2	2	35	9	0-0	.138	.157	.171	334	46	11	0	0	15	13	8	140	56	1-0
Assenmacher,P.,Cle	.000	.000	.000	0	0	0	0	0	0	0	0	0	0	0-0	.083	.195	.111	36	3	1	0	0	3	0	5	12	7	0-0
Astacio,Pedro,Col	.129	.156	.161	62	8	2	0	0	4	3	0	21	11	0-0	.117	.128	.129	341	40	4	0	0	15	10	2	144	48	0-1
Avery,Steve,Bos	.000	.000	.000	1	0	0	0	0	2	0	0	0	0	0-0	.178	.199	.261	410	73	14	4	4	33	31	12	124	39	1-1
Ayala,Bobby,Sea	.000	.000	.000	0	0	0	0	0	0	0	0	0	0	0-0	.067	.067	.100	30	2	1	0	0	2	1	0	13	3	0-1
Aybar,Manny,StL	.222	.222	.333	27	6	0	0	1	4	3	0	9	1	0-0	.188	.188	.250	48	9	0	0	1	4	4	0	18	1	0-0
Bailes,Scott,Tex	.000	.000	.000	0	0	0	0	0	0	0	0	0	0	0-0	.000	.000	.000	0	0	0	0	0	0	0	0	0	0	0-0
Bailey,Cory,SF	.000	.000	.000	0	0	0	0	0	0	0	0	0	0	0-0	.500	.750	.500	2	1	0	0	0	2	0	2	0	1	0-0
Baldwin,James,ChA	.000	.000	.000	2	0	0	0	0	0	0	0	1	0	0-0	.000	.000	.000	5	0	0	0	0	0	0	0	3	1	0-0
Banks,Willie,NYA-Ari	.000	.000	.000	1	0	0	0	0	0	0	0	1	0	0-0	.176	.222	.206	68	12	2	0	0	5	1	2	23	8	0-1
Barrios,Manuel,Fla-LA	.000	.000	.000	0	0	0	0	0	0	0	0	0	0	0-0	.000	.000	.000	0	0	0	0	0	0	0	0	0	0	0-0
Batista,Miguel,Mon	.000	.000	.000	32	0	0	0	0	0	0	0	21	2	0-0	.000	.000	.000	40	0	0	0	0	0	0	0	26	2	0-0
Beck,Rod,ChN	.000	.000	.000	1	0	0	0	0	0	0	0	0	0	0-0	.222	.222	.222	18	4	0	0	0	0	1	0	9	1	0-0
Beech,Matt,Phi	.152	.152	.152	33	5	0	0	0	2	2	0	10	6	0-0	.143	.143	.156	77	11	1	0	0	4	4	0	28	17	0-0
Belcher,Tim,KC	.200	.200	.200	5	1	0	0	0	1	0	0	2	1	0-0	.123	.136	.159	383	47	8	0	2	19	25	2	145	42	0-1
Belinda,Stan,Cin	.000	.000	.000	1	0	0	0	0	0	0	0	1	0	0-0	.150	.227	.200	20	3	1	0	0	1	3	2	11	3	0-0
Beltran,Rigo,NYN	.000	.000	.000	1	0	0	0	0	0	0	0	0	0	0-0	.125	.125	.250	8	1	1	0	0	1	0	0	1	0	0-0
Benes,Andy,Ari	.169	.250	.262	65	11	3	0	1	8	3	6	28	10	0-0	.143	.183	.199	567	81	17	0	5	37	38	24	247	75	0-0
Benitez,Armando,Bal	.000	.000	.000	0	0	0	0	0	0	0	0	0	0	0-0	.000	.000	.000	0	0	0	0	0	0	0	0	0	0	0-0
Bennett,Shayne,Mon	.000	.143	.000	6	0	0	0	0	0	0	1	1	1	0-0	.000	.222	.000	7	0	0	0	0	0	0	2	1	1	0-0
Bere,Jason,ChA-Cin	.000	.067	.000	14	0	0	0	0	0	0	1	5	0	0-0	.000	.067	.000	14	0	0	0	0	0	0	1	5	0	0-0
Bergman,Sean,Hou	.083	.083	.117	60	5	2	0	0	3	4	0	30	8	0-0	.107	.107	.165	103	11	3	0	1	6	9	0	46	11	0-0
Bevil,Brian,KC	.000	.000	.000	0	0	0	0	0	0	0	0	0	0	0-0	.000	.000	.000	0	0	0	0	0	0	0	0	0	0	0-0
Blair,Willie,Ari-NYN	.096	.145	.096	52	5	0	0	0	3	0	3	27	4	0-0	.070	.108	.077	142	10	1	0	0	6	5	6	86	12	0-0
Bochtler,Doug,Det	.000	.000	.000	0	0	0	0	0	0	0	0	0	0	0-0	.000	.000	.000	2	0	0	0	0	0	0	0	0	0	0-0
Boehringer,Brian,SD	.000	.125	.000	7	0	0	0	0	0	0	1	4	0	0-0	.000	.125	.000	7	0	0	0	0	0	0	1	4	0	0-0
Bohanon,B.,NYN-LA	.279	.311	.372	43	12	2	1	0	1	5	2	13	4	0-0	.237	.253	.289	76	18	2	1	0	1	9	2	28	5	0-0
Bones,Ricky,KC	.000	.000	.000	1	0	0	0	0	0	0	0	0	0	0-0	.063	.167	.063	16	1	0	0	0	1	1	2	5	4	0-0
Borland,Toby,Phi	.000	.000	.000	0	0	0	0	0	0	0	0	0	0	0-0	.083	.077	.083	12	1	0	0	0	1	2	0	3	1	0-0
Borowski,Joe,NYA	.000	.000	.000	0	0	0	0	0	0	0	0	0	0	0-0	.000	.000	.000	2	0	0	0	0	0	0	0	2	1	0-0
Boskie,Shawn,Mon	.000	.200	.000	4	0	0	0	0	1	0	1	3	0	0-0	.179	.227	.262	145	26	5	2	1	10	8	9	45	9	0-0
Bottalico,Ricky,Phi	.000	.000	.000	0	0	0	0	0	0	0	0	0	0	0-0	.111	.111	.222	9	1	1	0	0	0	0	0	7	1	0-0
Bottenfield,Kent,StL	.088	.088	.088	34	3	0	0	0	3	2	0	9	5	0-0	.182	.198	.182	99	18	0	0	0	6	5	1	31	14	1-0
Brantley,Jeff,StL	.000	.000	.000	0	0	0	0	0	0	0	0	0	1	0-0	.118	.143	.132	68	8	1	0	0	5	5	2	23	11	0-0
Brewer,Billy,Phi	.000	.000	.000	0	0	0	0	0	0	0	0	0	0	0-0	.000	.000	.000	1	0	0	0	0	0	0	0	1	0	0-0
Brocail,Doug,Det	.000	.000	.000	0	0	0	0	0	0	0	0	0	0	0-0	.164	.164	.194	67	11	0	1	0	9	1	0	18	15	2-0
Brock,Chris,SF	.250	.250	.250	4	1	0	0	0	0	0	0	0	0	0-0	.143	.143	.143	14	2	0	0	0	0	1	0	2	0	0-0
Brow,Scott,Ari	.000	.000	.000	1	0	0	0	0	0	0	0	1	0	0-0	.000	.000	.000	1	0	0	0	0	0	0	0	1	0	0-0
Brown,Kevin,SD	.207	.244	.244	82	17	3	0	0	4	10	4	29	7	0-0	.152	.204	.174	230	35	5	0	0	9	17	15	82	17	0-0
Brownson,Mark,Col	.000	.000	.000	5	0	0	0	0	0	0	0	0	0	0-0	.000	.000	.000	5	0	0	0	0	0	0	0	0	0	0-0
Brunson,Will,LA-Det	.000	.000	.000	0	0	0	0	0	0	0	0	0	0	0-0	.000	.000	.000	0	0	0	0	0	0	0	0	0	0	0-0
Bruske,J.,LA-SD-NYA	.000	.000	.000	3	0	0	0	0	0	0	0	1	0	0-0	.111	.111	.222	9	1	1	0	0	0	0	0	2	0	0-0
Buddie,Mike,NYA	.000	.000	.000	0	0	0	0	0	0	0	0	0	0	0-0	.000	.000	.000	0	0	0	0	0	0	0	0	0	0	0-0
Bullinger,Kirk,Mon	.000	.000	.000	1	0	0	0	0	0	0	0	0	0	0-0	.000	.000	.000	1	0	0	0	0	0	0	0	0	0	0-0
Burba,Dave,Cle	.167	.167	.667	6	1	0	0	1	1	2	0	1	0	0-0	.142	.194	.201	169	24	1	0	3	9	12	9	71	17	0-0
Burkett,John,Tex	.000	.000	.000	3	0	0	0	0	1	0	0	0	0	0-0	.089	.132	.101	427	38	5	0	0	18	14	20	179	47	0-0
Busby,Mike,StL	.000	.250	.000	3	0	0	0	0	0	1	1	1	0	0-0	.333	.400	.333	9	3	0	0	0	0	1	1	4	0	0-0
Butler,Adam,Atl	.000	.000	.000	0	0	0	0	0	0	0	0	0	0	0-0	.000	.000	.000	0	0	0	0	0	0	0	0	0	0	0-0
Byrd,Paul,Atl-Phi	.167	.250	.167	18	3	0	0	0	1	1	1	7	0	0-0	.179	.233	.179	28	5	0	0	0	1	2	1	9	2	0-0
Cabrera,Jose,Hou	.000	.000	.000	0	0	0	0	0	0	0	0	0	0	0-0	.000	.000	.000	2	0	0	0	0	0	0	0	0	0	0-0
Cadaret,G.,Ana-Tex	.000	.000	.000	0	0	0	0	0	0	0	0	0	0	0-0	.000	.000	.000	2	0	0	0	0	0	0	0	1	0	0-0
Candiotti,Tom,Oak	1.000	1.000	2.000	1	1	1	0	0	0	0	0	0	1	0-0	.117	.140	.134	299	35	5	0	0	11	12	7	71	52	0-0
Carpenter,Chris,Tor	.000	.000	.000	1	0	0	0	0	0	0	0	0	0	0-0	.000	.000	.000	1	0	0	0	0	0	0	0	0	0	0-0
Carrasco,Hector,Min	.000	.000	.000	0	0	0	0	0	0	0	0	0	0	0-0	.056	.056	.056	18	1	0	0	0	0	0	0	12	0	0-0
Castillo,Carlos,ChA	.000	.000	.000	1	0	0	0	0	0	0	0	0	0	0-0	.500	.500	.500	2	1	0	0	0	0	0	0	0	0	0-0
Castillo,Frank,Det	.000	.000	.000	1	0	0	0	0	0	0	0	0	0	0-0	.110	.144	.110	327	36	0	0	0	7	13	13	106	40	0-1
Castillo,Tony,ChA	.000	.000	.000	0	0	0	0	0	0	0	0	0	0	0-0	.077	.143	.077	13	1	0	0	0	1	0	1	6	4	0-0
Cather,Mike,Atl	.000	.000	.000	0	0	0	0	0	0	0	0	0	0	0-0	.000	.000	.000	1	0	0	0	0	0	0	0	0	0	0-0
Charlton,Norm,Bal-Atl	.000	.000	.000	1	0	0	0	0	0	0	0	0	0	0-0	.092	.151	.115	87	8	2	0	0	6	1	3	50	10	0-0
Chen,Bruce,Atl	.143	.143	.143	7	1	0	0	0	0	1	0	4	2	0-0	.143	.143	.143	7	1	0	0	0	0	1	0	4	2	0-0
Chouinard,B.,Mil-Ari	.000	.000	.000	2	0	0	0	0	0	0	0	1	0	0-0	.000	.000	.000	2	0	0	0	0	0	0	0	1	0	0-0
Christiansen,Jason,Pit	.250	.250	.250	4	1	0	0	0	0	1	0	1	0	0-0	.111	.111	.111	9	1	0	0	0	0	1	0	6	1	0-0
Clark,Mark,ChN	.065	.108	.097	62	4	2	0	0	1	3	3	27	8	0-0	.058	.088	.083	240	14	3	0	1	7	9	8	104	29	0-0
Clemens,Roger,Tor	.000	.200	.000	4	0	0	0	0	0	0	1	0	1	0-0	.286	.444	.429	7	2	1	0	0	1	0	2	0	1	0-0
Clement,Matt,SD	.000	.000	.000	2	0	0	0	0	0	0	0	2	2	0-0	.000	.000	.000	2	0	0	0	0	0	0	0	2	2	0-0
Clontz,Brad,LA-NYN	.000	.000	.000	2	0	0	0	0	0	0	0	1	0	0-0	.000	.222	.000	7	0	0	0	0	1	0	2	4	1	0-0
Cloude,Ken,Sea	.000	.000	.000	3	0	0	0	0	0	0	0	0	0	0-0	.000	.000	.000	5	0	0	0	0	0	0	0	0	0	0-0
Colon,Bartolo,Cle	.500	.500	.500	2	1	0	0	0	0	1	0	1	0	0-0	.333	.333	.333	3	1	0	0	0	0	1	0	2	0	0-0
Cone,David,NYA	.000	.000	.000	3	0	0	0	0	1	1	0	0	1	0-0	.152	.190	.172	401	61	8	0	0	27	21	16	88	37	0-1
Connelly,Steve,Oak	.000	.000	.000	0	0	0	0	0	0	0	0	0	0	0-0	.000	.000	.000	0	0	0	0	0	0	0	0	0	0	0-0
Cook,Dennis,NYN	.000	.000	.000	3	0	0	0	0	0	0	0	0	0	0-0	.269	.288	.361	108	29	2	1	2	15	9	3	12	8	0-0
Cooke,Steve,Cin	.500	.500	.500	2	1	0	0	0	0	0	0	0	0	0-0	.140	.145	.164	171	24	4	0	0	8	7	0	47	20	0-0
Cordova,Francisco,Pit	.120	.143	.160	75	9	1	1	0	3	1	2	29	2	0-0	.109	.144	.129	147	16	1	1	0	6	3	6	62	12	0-0

	1998 Hitting														Career Hitting													
Pitcher,Team	Avg	OBP	SLG	AB	H	2B	3B	HR	R	RBI	BB	SO	SH	SB-CS	Avg	OBP	SLG	AB	H	2B	3B	HR	R	RBI	BB	SO	SH	SB-CS
Corey,Bryan,Ari	.000	.000	.000	0	0	0	0	0	0	0	0	0	0	0-0	.000	.000	.000	0	0	0	0	0	0	0	0	0	0	0-0
Corsi,Jim,Bos	.000	.000	.000	1	0	0	0	0	0	0	0	0	0	0-0	.000	.000	.000	2	0	0	0	0	0	0	0	1	0	0-0
Crabtree,Tim,Tex	.000	.000	.000	1	0	0	0	0	0	0	0	0	0	0-0	.000	.000	.000	1	0	0	0	0	0	0	0	0	0	0-0
Croushore,Rich,StL	.000	.000	.000	0	0	0	0	0	0	0	0	0	2	0-0	.000	.000	.000	0	0	0	0	0	0	0	0	0	2	0-0
Crow,Dean,Det	.000	.000	.000	0	0	0	0	0	0	0	0	0	0	0-0	.000	.000	.000	0	0	0	0	0	0	0	0	0	0	0-0
Cunnane,Will,SD	.000	.000	.000	0	0	0	0	0	0	0	0	0	0	0-0	.357	.438	.500	14	5	0	1	0	4	4	2	4	1	0-0
Daal,Omar,Ari	.109	.196	.109	46	5	0	0	0	3	1	5	17	5	0-0	.097	.176	.097	62	6	0	0	0	3	2	6	22	5	0-0
Darensbourg,Vic,Fla	.000	.111	.000	8	0	0	0	0	0	0	1	3	0	0-0	.000	.111	.000	8	0	0	0	0	0	0	1	3	0	0-0
Darwin,Danny,SF	.089	.128	.111	45	4	1	0	0	2	1	1	30	4	0-0	.128	.146	.197	305	39	11	2	2	15	22	6	171	20	2-0
DeLosSantos,V.,Mil	.000	.000	.000	0	0	0	0	0	0	0	0	0	0	0-0	.000	.000	.000	0	0	0	0	0	0	0	0	0	0	0-0
DeHart,Rick,Mon	.000	.000	.000	0	0	0	0	0	0	0	0	0	0	0-0	.000	.000	.000	2	0	0	0	0	0	0	0	2	0	0-0
DeJean,Mike,Col	.000	.000	.000	5	0	0	0	0	0	0	0	4	0	0-0	.125	.125	.250	8	1	1	0	0	0	0	0	5	1	0-0
DeLucia,Rich,Ana	.000	.000	.000	0	0	0	0	0	0	0	0	0	0	0-0	.214	.313	.214	14	3	0	0	0	2	0	2	3	1	0-0
Dempster,Ryan,Fla	.000	.000	.000	13	0	0	0	0	0	0	0	8	1	0-0	.000	.000	.000	13	0	0	0	0	0	0	0	8	1	0-0
Dessens,Elmer,Pit	.000	.111	.000	8	0	0	0	0	0	1	1	4	3	0-0	.154	.214	.154	13	2	0	0	0	1	3	1	4	3	0-0
Dickson,Jason,Ana	.000	.200	.000	4	0	0	0	0	1	0	1	3	0	0-0	.000	.143	.000	6	0	0	0	0	1	0	1	3	0	0-0
Dipoto,Jerry,Col	.000	.500	.000	1	0	0	0	0	0	0	1	0	0	0-0	.063	.118	.063	16	1	0	0	0	0	0	1	9	1	0-0
Dodd,Robert,Phi	.000	.000	.000	0	0	0	0	0	0	0	0	0	0	0-0	.000	.000	.000	0	0	0	0	0	0	0	0	0	0	0-0
Dougherty,Jim,Oak	.000	.000	.000	0	0	0	0	0	0	0	0	0	0	0-0	.125	.125	.125	8	1	0	0	0	1	0	0	2	1	0-0
Drabek,Doug,Bal	.000	.000	.000	1	0	0	0	0	0	0	0	1	0	0-0	.166	.193	.207	716	119	17	3	2	42	46	17	207	66	0-1
Dreifort,Darren,LA	.224	.255	.286	49	11	0	0	1	10	2	2	22	5	0-0	.217	.242	.267	60	13	0	0	1	10	3	2	29	6	0-0
EdmondsonB.Atl-Fla	.000	.000	.000	12	0	0	0	0	0	0	0	5	1	0-0	.000	.000	.000	12	0	0	0	0	0	0	0	5	1	0-0
Elarton,Scott,Hou	.000	.000	.000	7	0	0	0	0	0	0	0	4	3	0-0	.000	.000	.000	7	0	0	0	0	0	0	0	4	3	0-0
Eldred,Cal,Mil	.125	.176	.156	32	4	1	0	0	1	2	2	19	5	0-1	.114	.162	.143	35	4	1	0	0	1	2	2	19	6	0-1
Embree,Alan,Atl-Ari	.000	.500	.000	1	0	0	0	0	0	0	1	1	0	0-0	.000	.500	.000	1	0	0	0	0	0	0	1	1	0	0-0
Erickson,Scott,Bal	.000	.600	.000	2	0	0	0	0	2	0	3	2	1	0-0	.000	.500	.000	4	0	0	0	0	2	0	4	4	3	0-0
Estes,Shawn,SF	.190	.209	.214	42	8	1	0	0	4	0	1	17	8	0-0	.157	.187	.187	134	21	1	0	1	15	4	3	51	21	0-0
Eversgerd,Bryan,StL	.000	.000	.000	0	0	0	0	0	0	0	0	0	0	0-0	.000	.000	.000	7	0	0	0	0	0	0	0	3	2	0-0
Eyre,Scott,ChA	.000	.000	.000	3	0	0	0	0	0	0	0	3	0	0-0	.200	.200	.200	5	1	0	0	0	0	0	0	3	0	0-0
Fassero,Jeff,Sea	.000	.000	.000	3	0	0	0	0	0	0	0	2	0	0-0	.079	.146	.098	215	17	2	1	0	15	5	17	120	39	1-0
Fetters,Mike,Oak-Ana	.000	.000	.000	0	0	0	0	0	0	0	0	0	0	0-0	.000	.000	.000	0	0	0	0	0	0	0	0	0	0	0-0
Finley,Chuck,Ana	.000	.000	.000	4	0	0	0	0	0	0	0	3	0	0-0	.000	.000	.000	10	0	0	0	0	1	0	0	5	0	0-0
Florie,Bryce,Det	.333	.600	.333	3	1	0	0	0	0	0	2	1	1	0-0	.125	.300	.125	8	1	0	0	0	0	0	2	4	1	0-0
Fontenot,Joe,Fla	.000	.000	.000	10	0	0	0	0	1	0	0	6	1	0-0	.000	.000	.000	10	0	0	0	0	1	0	0	6	1	0-0
Ford,Ben,Ari	.000	.000	.000	0	0	0	0	0	0	0	0	0	0	0-0	.000	.000	.000	0	0	0	0	0	0	0	0	0	0	0-0
Fordham,Tom,ChA	.000	.000	.000	1	0	0	0	0	0	0	0	1	0	0-0	.000	.000	.000	1	0	0	0	0	0	0	0	1	0	0-0
FossasSea-ChN-Tex	.000	.000	.000	0	0	0	0	0	0	0	0	0	0	0-0	.000	.000	.000	1	0	0	0	0	0	0	0	0	0	0-0
Foster,Kevin,ChN	.000	.000	.000	0	0	0	0	0	0	0	0	0	0	0-0	.190	.237	.270	163	31	6	2	1	15	19	9	59	22	2-0
Foulke,Keith,ChA	.000	.000	.000	0	0	0	0	0	0	0	0	0	0	0-0	.154	.154	.154	13	2	0	0	0	0	0	0	4	2	0-0
Fox,Chad,Mil	.000	.000	.000	3	0	0	0	0	0	0	0	2	1	0-0	.000	.000	.000	3	0	0	0	0	0	0	0	2	1	0-0
Franco,John,NYN	.000	.000	.000	2	0	0	0	0	0	0	0	1	0	0-0	.091	.091	.091	33	3	0	0	0	2	1	0	13	3	0-0
Frascatore,John,StL	.167	.167	.167	6	1	0	0	0	0	0	0	3	0	0-0	.059	.111	.059	17	1	0	0	0	0	0	1	12	1	0-0
Garces,Rich,Bos	.000	.000	.000	0	0	0	0	0	0	0	0	0	0	0-0	.000	.000	.000	1	0	0	0	0	0	0	0	0	0	0-0
Gardner,Mark,SF	.164	.228	.178	73	12	1	0	0	4	4	5	26	4	0-0	.132	.164	.149	403	53	3	2	0	18	18	12	161	44	0-0
Glauber,Keith,Cin	.000	.000	.000	2	0	0	0	0	0	0	0	0	0	0-0	.000	.000	.000	2	0	0	0	0	0	0	0	0	0	0-0
Glavine,Tom,Atl	.239	.250	.282	71	17	3	0	0	3	7	1	15	14	0-0	.205	.255	.234	766	157	15	2	1	59	58	50	194	117	1-0
Gomes,Wayne,Phi	.000	.000	.000	2	0	0	0	0	0	0	0	2	0	0-0	.000	.200	.000	4	0	0	0	0	0	0	1	3	0	0-0
Gonzalez,Gabe,Fla	.000	.000	.000	0	0	0	0	0	0	0	0	0	0	0-0	.000	.000	.000	0	0	0	0	0	0	0	0	0	0	0-0
Gonzalez,Jeremi,ChN	.188	.188	.219	32	6	1	0	0	0	2	0	11	8	0-0	.139	.173	.153	72	10	1	0	0	1	3	3	23	16	0-0
Gonzalez,Lariel,Col	.000	.000	.000	0	0	0	0	0	0	0	0	0	0	0-0	.000	.000	.000	0	0	0	0	0	0	0	0	0	0	0-0
Gooden,Dwight,Cle	.000	.000	.000	2	0	0	0	0	0	0	0	1	0	0-0	.196	.211	.258	736	144	15	5	7	59	65	13	133	85	1-1
Gordon,Tom,Bos	.000	.000	.000	0	0	0	0	0	0	0	0	0	0	0-0	.000	.000	.000	0	0	0	0	0	0	0	0	0	0	0-0
Grace,Mike,Phi	.087	.160	.087	23	2	0	0	0	1	1	2	11	3	0-0	.106	.169	.106	66	7	0	0	0	2	1	4	33	6	0-0
Graves,Danny,Cin	.000	.000	.000	4	0	0	0	0	0	0	0	3	0	0-0	.000	.000	.000	5	0	0	0	0	0	0	0	4	0	0-0
Green,Tyler,Phi	.146	.178	.171	41	6	1	0	0	2	3	2	21	6	0-0	.195	.205	.301	113	22	9	0	1	6	10	2	44	16	0-1
Greisinger,Seth,Det	.250	.250	.250	4	1	0	0	0	0	1	0	0	0	0-0	.250	.250	.250	4	1	0	0	0	0	1	0	0	0	0-0
Groom,Buddy,Oak	.000	.000	.000	0	0	0	0	0	0	0	0	0	0	0-0	.000	.000	.000	0	0	0	0	0	0	0	0	0	0	0-0
Grzanich,Mike,Hou	.000	.000	.000	0	0	0	0	0	0	0	0	0	0	0-0	.000	.000	.000	0	0	0	0	0	0	0	0	0	0	0-0
Guardado,Eddie,Min	.000	.000	.000	0	0	0	0	0	0	0	0	0	0	0-0	.000	.000	.000	0	0	0	0	0	0	0	0	0	0	0-0
Gunderson,Eric,Tex	.000	.000	.000	0	0	0	0	0	0	0	0	0	0	0-0	.000	.143	.000	6	0	0	0	0	1	0	0	4	0	0-0
Guthrie,Mark,LA	.000	.000	.000	1	0	0	0	0	0	0	0	0	0	0-0	.111	.111	.111	9	1	0	0	0	0	0	0	0	1	0-0
Guzman,Juan,Tor-Bal	.000	.000	.000	2	0	0	0	0	0	0	0	0	0	0-0	.000	.000	.000	2	0	0	0	0	0	0	0	0	0	0-0
Halama,John,Hou	.000	.167	.000	10	0	0	0	0	1	0	2	7	1	0-0	.000	.167	.000	10	0	0	0	0	1	0	2	7	1	0-0
Hall,Darren,LA	.000	.000	.000	0	0	0	0	0	0	0	0	0	0	0-0	.000	.000	.000	0	0	0	0	0	0	0	0	0	0	0-0
Hamilton,Joey,SD	.141	.153	.211	71	10	0	1	1	1	6	1	31	2	0-0	.117	.139	.178	298	35	4	1	4	16	20	8	151	32	0-0
Hammond,Chris,Fla	.200	.200	.200	5	1	0	0	0	0	0	0	2	0	0-0	.205	.286	.295	234	48	7	1	4	30	14	27	94	19	0-0
Hampton,Mike,Hou	.262	.348	.328	61	16	4	0	0	3	2	7	12	7	2-0	.191	.265	.227	225	43	6	1	0	25	13	20	59	28	2-1
Haney,Chris,KC-ChN	.000	.000	.000	0	0	0	0	0	0	0	0	0	0	0-0	.111	.111	.111	36	4	0	0	0	2	4	0	4	4	0-0
Hanson,Erik,Tor	.000	.000	.000	0	0	0	0	0	0	0	0	0	0	0-0	.154	.154	.179	39	6	1	0	0	5	3	0	17	2	0-0
Harnisch,Pete,Cin	.106	.119	.106	66	7	0	0	0	3	1	1	22	9	0-0	.115	.140	.145	393	45	12	0	0	28	16	11	111	47	0-2
Harris,Pep,Ana	.000	.000	.000	0	0	0	0	0	0	0	0	0	0	0-0	.000	.000	.000	0	0	0	0	0	0	0	0	0	0	0-0
Harris,Reggie,Hou	.000	.000	.000	0	0	0	0	0	0	0	0	0	0	0-0	.000	.000	.000	0	0	0	0	0	0	0	0	0	0	0-0
Hartgraves,Dean,SF	.000	.000	.000	0	0	0	0	0	0	0	0	0	0	0-0	.000	.000	.000	3	0	0	0	0	0	0	0	1	2	0-0
Hasegawa,S.,Ana	.000	.000	.000	0	0	0	0	0	0	0	0	0	0	0-0	.000	.000	.000	0	0	0	0	0	0	0	0	0	0	0-0
Hawkins,LaTroy,Min	.000	.000	.000	1	0	0	0	0	0	0	0	1	0	0-0	.000	.000	.000	2	0	0	0	0	0	0	0	2	0	0-0
Haynes,Jimmy,Oak	.000	.250	.000	3	0	0	0	0	1	0	1	3	0	0-0	.000	.167	.000	5	0	0	0	0	1	0	1	4	0	0-0
Helling,Rick,Tex	.200	.200	.200	5	1	0	0	0	0	0	0	2	1	0-0	.107	.107	.107	28	3	0	0	0	1	0	0	10	2	0-0
Henderson,Ro.,Mil	.000	.000	.000	0	0	0	0	0	0	0	0	0	0	0-0	.000	.000	.000	1	0	0	0	0	0	0	0	1	0	0-0
Henriquez,Oscar,Fla	.000	.000	.000	1	0	0	0	0	0	0	0	0	0	0-0	.000	.000	.000	1	0	0	0	0	0	0	0	0	0	0-0
Henry,Doug,Hou	.000	.000	.000	4	0	0	0	0	0	0	0	2	1	0-0	.067	.067	.067	15	1	0	0	0	1	0	0	5	2	0-0
Hentgen,Pat,Tor	.000	.000	.000	5	0	0	0	0	0	0	0	2	1	0-0	.000	.000	.000	12	0	0	0	0	0	0	0	4	1	0-0
Heredia,Felix,Fla-ChN	.000	.000	.000	3	0	0	0	0	0	0	0	1	0	0-0	.200	.200	.200	5	1	0	0	0	0	0	0	2	1	0-0
Hermanson,D.,Mon	.115	.270	.192	52	6	1	0	1	7	2	10	29	5	0-0	.110	.212	.190	100	11	2	0	2	8	3	12	53	10	0-0
Hernandez,Livan,Fla	.195	.205	.232	82	16	3	0	0	3	6	0	20	1	0-0	.196	.211	.241	112	22	5	0	0	6	8	1	26	4	0-0
Hernandez,O.,NYA	.000	.000	.000	7	0	0	0	0	0	0	0	5	1	0-0	.000	.000	.000	7	0	0	0	0	0	0	0	5	1	0-0
Hernandez,R.,TB	.000	.000	.000	0	0	0	0	0	0	0	0	0	0	0-0	.500	.500	.500	2	1	0	0	0	0	0	0	1	0	0-0

Pitcher,Team	1998 Hitting														Career Hitting													
	Avg	OBP	SLG	AB	H	2B	3B	HR	R	RBI	BB	SO	SH	SB-CS	Avg	OBP	SLG	AB	H	2B	3B	HR	R	RBI	BB	SO	SH	SB-CS
Hernandez,Xavier,Tex	.000	.000	.000	0	0	0	0	0	0	0	0	0	0	0-0	.027	.077	.027	37	1	0	0	0	2	0	2	20	4	0-0
Hershiser,Orel,SF	.152	.200	.182	66	10	2	0	0	7	1	3	16	8	1-0	.208	.238	.251	741	154	28	2	0	62	47	26	162	98	7-3
Hill,Ken,Ana	.000	.000	.000	1	0	0	0	0	0	0	0	0	0	0-0	.150	.210	.187	327	49	7	1	1	22	21	24	94	66	0-0
Hitchcock,Sterling,SD	.140	.157	.140	50	7	0	0	0	5	2	1	21	5	0-0	.120	.154	.120	100	12	0	0	0	9	3	4	51	13	0-1
Hoffman,Trevor,SD	.000	.000	.000	3	0	0	0	0	0	0	0	2	0	0-0	.115	.115	.154	26	3	1	0	0	1	3	0	9	2	0-0
Holmes,Darren,NYA	.000	.000	.000	0	0	0	0	0	0	0	0	0	0	0-0	.130	.160	.261	23	3	0	0	1	2	2	1	11	6	0-0
Holtz,Mike,Ana	.000	.000	.000	0	0	0	0	0	0	0	0	0	0	0-0	.000	.000	.000	1	0	0	0	0	0	0	0	1	0	0-0
Howry,Bob,ChA	.000	.000	.000	0	0	0	0	0	0	0	0	0	0	0-0	.000	.000	.000	0	0	0	0	0	0	0	0	0	0	0-0
Hudek,John,NYN-Cin	.000	.000	.000	3	0	0	0	0	0	0	0	3	1	0-0	.250	.250	.250	4	1	0	0	0	0	2	0	3	1	0-0
Hudson,Joe,Mil	.000	.000	.000	0	0	0	0	0	0	0	0	0	0	0-0	.000	.000	.000	0	0	0	0	0	0	0	0	0	0	0-0
Hutton,Mark,Cin	1.000	1.000	1.000	1	1	0	0	0	0	1	0	0	0	0-0	.304	.304	.435	23	7	0	0	1	2	2	0	6	1	0-0
Irabu,Hideki,NYA	.250	.250	.250	4	1	0	0	0	0	0	0	3	1	0-0	.200	.200	.200	5	1	0	0	0	0	0	0	3	1	0-0
Jackson,Mike,Cle	.000	.000	.000	0	0	0	0	0	0	0	0	0	0	0-0	.185	.214	.259	27	5	2	0	0	3	1	1	4	4	0-0
Jimenez,Jose,StL	.000	.000	.000	6	0	0	0	0	0	1	0	4	2	0-0	.000	.000	.000	6	0	0	0	0	0	1	0	4	2	0-0
Johns,Doug,Bal	1.000	1.000	1.000	2	2	0	0	0	1	0	0	0	0	0-0	1.000	1.000	1.000	2	2	0	0	0	2	0	0	0	0	0-0
Johnson,Jason,TB	.000	.000	.000	2	0	0	0	0	0	0	0	2	0	0-0	.000	.000	.000	3	0	0	0	0	0	0	0	3	0	0-0
Johnson,Mike,Mon	.333	.333	.333	3	1	0	0	0	0	1	0	1	0	0-0	.125	.125	.125	16	2	0	0	0	1	2	0	6	2	0-0
Johnson,R.,Sea-Hou	.077	.077	.103	39	3	1	0	0	2	2	0	19	3	0-0	.091	.091	.109	55	5	1	0	0	3	2	0	28	5	0-0
Johnstone,John,SF	.000	.000	.000	2	0	0	0	0	0	0	0	0	1	0-0	.000	.000	.000	4	0	0	0	0	0	0	0	1	2	0-0
Jones,Bobby,NYN	.188	.220	.208	48	9	1	0	0	1	4	2	21	12	0-0	.134	.159	.154	292	39	6	0	0	17	13	9	110	53	0-0
Jones,BobbyM.,Col	.178	.178	.200	45	8	1	0	0	3	4	0	14	5	0-0	.180	.196	.200	50	9	1	0	0	4	4	1	14	6	0-0
Jones,Doug,Mil-Cle	.000	.000	.000	2	0	0	0	0	0	0	0	2	0	0-0	.143	.250	.143	7	1	0	0	0	0	0	1	4	0	0-0
Jones,Todd,Det	.000	.000	.000	0	0	0	0	0	0	0	0	0	0	0-0	.273	.273	.364	11	3	1	0	0	1	0	0	1	0	0-0
Jordan,Ricardo,Cin	.000	.000	.000	0	0	0	0	0	0	0	0	0	0	0-0	.000	.000	.000	2	0	0	0	0	0	0	0	1	0	0-0
Judd,Mike,LA	.000	.000	.000	1	0	0	0	0	0	0	0	0	0	0-0	.000	.000	.000	2	0	0	0	0	0	0	0	1	0	0-0
Juden,Jeff,Mil-Ana	.122	.122	.146	41	5	1	0	0	3	4	0	12	3	0-0	.109	.124	.160	119	13	3	0	1	5	13	1	60	11	0-0
KarchnerM.,ChA-ChN	.000	.000	.000	0	0	0	0	0	0	0	0	0	0	0-0	.000	.000	.000	0	0	0	0	0	0	0	0	0	0	0-0
Karl,Scott,Mil	.071	.133	.107	56	4	0	1	0	3	0	4	17	9	0-0	.067	.125	.100	60	4	0	1	0	3	0	4	20	9	0-0
Kile,Darryl,Col	.254	.293	.324	71	18	5	0	0	5	5	4	22	9	0-0	.137	.186	.185	439	60	18	0	1	25	29	23	200	57	0-0
King,Curtis,StL	.000	.000	.000	5	0	0	0	0	0	0	0	1	0	0-0	.000	.000	.000	6	0	0	0	0	0	0	0	2	0	0-0
Kline,Steve,Mon	.000	.000	.000	4	0	0	0	0	0	0	0	1	1	0-0	.000	.000	.000	5	0	0	0	0	0	0	0	2	1	0-0
Klingenbeck,Scott,Cin	.000	.000	.000	6	0	0	0	0	0	0	0	4	0	0-0	.000	.000	.000	6	0	0	0	0	0	0	0	4	0	0-0
Krivda,Rick,Cle-Cin	.000	.000	.000	4	0	0	0	0	0	0	0	3	0	0-0	.000	.000	.000	4	0	0	0	0	0	0	0	3	0	0-0
Kroon,Marc,SD-Cin	.000	.000	.000	0	0	0	0	0	0	0	0	0	0	0-0	.000	.000	.000	0	0	0	0	0	0	0	0	0	0	0-0
Kubenka,Jeff,LA	.000	.000	.000	0	0	0	0	0	0	0	0	0	0	0-0	.000	.000	.000	0	0	0	0	0	0	0	0	0	0	0-0
Langston,Mark,SD	.083	.154	.125	24	2	1	0	0	0	2	2	9	4	0-0	.144	.161	.178	90	13	3	0	0	5	5	2	37	5	0-0
Lankford,Frank,LA	.000	.000	.000	2	0	0	0	0	0	0	0	1	0	0-0	.000	.000	.000	2	0	0	0	0	0	0	0	1	0	0-0
Larkin,Andy,Fla	.138	.167	.138	29	4	0	0	0	1	0	1	19	2	0-0	.129	.156	.129	31	4	0	0	0	1	0	1	20	2	0-0
Lawrence,Sean,Pit	.000	.000	.000	6	0	0	0	0	0	0	0	4	0	0-0	.000	.000	.000	6	0	0	0	0	0	0	0	4	0	0-0
Leiter,Al,NYN	.105	.203	.158	57	6	3	0	0	1	4	7	32	5	0-0	.103	.169	.120	175	18	3	0	0	6	6	14	102	14	0-0
Leiter,Mark,Phi	.000	.000	.000	2	0	0	0	0	0	0	0	2	0	0-0	.110	.153	.116	181	20	1	0	0	8	14	9	98	28	0-0
Leskanic,Curt,Col	.000	.000	.000	2	0	0	0	0	1	0	0	1	1	0-0	.156	.182	.250	32	5	3	0	0	3	4	1	13	5	0-0
Levine,Al,Tex	.000	.000	.000	0	0	0	0	0	0	0	0	0	0	0-0	.000	.000	.000	0	0	0	0	0	0	0	0	0	0	0-0
Lieber,Jon,Pit	.167	.216	.188	48	8	1	0	0	3	1	3	20	7	0-0	.134	.178	.168	202	27	7	0	0	11	12	11	82	14	0-0
Ligtenberg,Kerry,Atl	.000	.000	.000	0	0	0	0	0	0	0	0	0	0	0-0	.000	.000	.000	0	0	0	0	0	0	0	0	0	0	0-0
Lima,Jose,Hou	.139	.159	.165	79	11	2	0	0	6	4	2	27	9	0-0	.134	.153	.159	82	11	2	0	0	6	4	2	30	11	0-0
Lloyd,Graeme,NYA	.000	.000	.000	0	0	0	0	0	0	0	0	0	0	0-0	.000	.000	.000	0	0	0	0	0	0	0	0	0	0	0-0
Loaiza,E.,Pit-Tex	.241	.267	.241	29	7	0	0	0	2	3	1	5	3	0-0	.184	.198	.209	158	29	2	1	0	11	11	3	35	23	0-0
Loewer,Carlton,Phi	.086	.158	.086	35	3	0	0	0	4	1	3	10	5	0-0	.086	.158	.086	35	3	0	0	0	4	1	3	10	5	0-0
Loiselle,Rich,Pit	.000	.000	.000	0	0	0	0	0	0	0	0	0	1	0-0	.222	.222	.333	9	2	1	0	0	0	2	0	4	1	0-0
Looper,Braden,StL	.000	.000	.000	0	0	0	0	0	0	0	0	0	0	0-0	.000	.000	.000	0	0	0	0	0	0	0	0	0	0	0-0
Lopez,Albie,TB	.000	.000	.000	1	0	0	0	0	0	0	0	0	0	0-0	.000	.000	.000	2	0	0	0	0	0	0	0	1	0	0-0
Lowe,Derek,Bos	.000	.200	.000	4	0	0	0	0	0	0	1	3	0	0-0	.000	.125	.000	7	0	0	0	0	0	0	1	5	0	0-0
Lowe,Sean,StL	.000	.000	.000	2	0	0	0	0	0	0	0	0	0	0-0	.200	.200	.200	5	1	0	0	0	0	0	0	1	0	0-0
Ludwick,Eric,Fla	.000	.000	.000	7	0	0	0	0	0	0	0	3	0	0-0	.000	.000	.000	11	0	0	0	0	0	0	0	5	0	0-0
Maddux,Greg,Atl	.240	.278	.280	75	18	3	0	0	4	4	4	18	6	0-1	.178	.199	.208	926	165	22	0	2	68	45	23	251	93	4-2
Maddux,Mike,Mon	.000	.000	.000	2	0	0	0	0	0	0	0	1	0	0-0	.067	.125	.078	90	6	1	0	0	4	4	6	32	14	0-0
Magnante,Mike,Hou	1.000	1.000	1.000	2	2	0	0	0	0	1	0	0	0	0-0	.400	.400	.400	5	2	0	0	0	0	1	0	2	0	0-0
Mahay,Ron,Bos	.000	.000	.000	0	0	0	0	0	0	0	0	0	0	0-0	.200	.273	.450	20	4	2	0	1	3	3	1	6	0	0-0
Maloney,Sean,LA	.000	.000	.000	1	0	0	0	0	0	0	0	1	0	0-0	.000	.000	.000	1	0	0	0	0	0	0	0	1	0	0-0
Mantei,Matt,Fla	.333	.333	.333	3	1	0	0	0	0	0	0	0	0	0-0	.250	.250	.250	4	1	0	0	0	0	0	0	1	0	0-0
Manuel,Barry,Ari	.000	.000	.000	0	0	0	0	0	0	0	0	0	0	0-0	.000	.100	.000	9	0	0	0	0	0	0	1	4	1	0-0
Martinez,Dennis,Atl	.091	.167	.182	11	1	1	0	0	0	3	1	7	1	0-0	.142	.169	.165	520	74	12	0	0	25	33	15	168	65	1-0
Martinez,Javier,Pit	.000	.000	.000	1	0	0	0	0	0	0	0	1	0	0-0	.000	.000	.000	1	0	0	0	0	0	0	0	1	0	0-0
Martinez,Pedro,Bos	.000	.000	.000	7	0	0	0	0	0	0	0	5	0	0-0	.099	.141	.126	253	25	3	2	0	13	11	10	116	37	0-0
Martinez,Ramon,LA	.176	.176	.265	34	6	1	1	0	3	1	0	16	5	0-0	.154	.164	.183	586	90	12	1	1	32	33	7	197	68	0-2
Mathews,T.J.,Oak	.000	.000	.000	0	0	0	0	0	0	0	0	0	0	0-0	.000	.000	.000	7	0	0	0	0	0	0	0	4	0	0-0
Mathews,Terry,Bal	.000	.000	.000	0	0	0	0	0	0	0	0	0	0	0-0	.391	.391	.522	23	9	3	0	0	3	3	0	8	0	0-0
McCarthy,Greg,Sea	.000	.000	.000	0	0	0	0	0	0	0	0	0	0	0-0	.000	.000	.000	0	0	0	0	0	0	0	0	0	0	0-0
McCurry,Jeff,Pit	.000	.000	.000	0	0	0	0	0	0	0	0	0	0	0-0	.000	.000	.000	4	0	0	0	0	0	0	0	2	0	0-0
McElroy,Chuck,Col	.200	.200	.200	5	1	0	0	0	0	0	0	3	1	0-0	.237	.237	.368	38	9	3	1	0	4	4	0	12	1	0-1
McMichael,G.,NYN-LA	.000	.000	.000	1	0	0	0	0	0	0	0	0	0	0-0	.133	.188	.133	15	2	0	0	0	0	0	1	7	0	0-0
Meadows,Brian,Fla	.130	.186	.130	54	7	0	0	0	4	3	4	19	2	0-0	.130	.186	.130	54	7	0	0	0	4	3	4	19	2	0-0
Mecir,Jim,TB	.000	.000	.000	1	0	0	0	0	0	0	0	0	0	0-0	.000	.000	.000	1	0	0	0	0	0	0	0	0	0	0-0
Medina,Rafael,Fla	.053	.053	.053	19	1	0	0	0	1	0	0	6	6	0-0	.053	.053	.053	19	1	0	0	0	1	0	0	6	6	0-0
Mendoza,Ramiro,NYA	.000	.000	.000	0	0	0	0	0	0	0	0	0	1	0-0	.000	.000	.000	0	0	0	0	0	0	0	0	0	1	0-0
Mercedes,Jose,Mil	.091	.167	.091	11	1	0	0	0	0	0	0	6	0	0-0	.077	.143	.077	13	1	0	0	0	0	0	0	8	0	0-0
Mercker,Kent,StL	.148	.179	.241	54	8	0	1	1	3	6	2	25	5	0-0	.106	.142	.157	216	23	4	2	1	7	16	9	104	18	0-0
Mesa,Jose,Cle-SF	.000	1.000	.000	0	0	0	0	0	1	0	1	0	0	0-0	.000	1.000	.000	0	0	0	0	0	1	0	1	0	0	0-0
Miceli,Dan,SD	1.000	1.000	1.000	1	1	0	0	0	0	0	0	0	0	0-0	.056	.056	.056	18	1	0	0	0	0	0	0	7	0	0-0
Michalak,Chris,Ari	.000	.000	.000	0	0	0	0	0	0	0	0	0	0	0-0	.000	.000	.000	0	0	0	0	0	0	0	0	0	0	0-0
Miller,Kurt,ChN	.000	.000	.000	0	0	0	0	0	0	0	0	0	0	0-0	.286	.286	.286	14	4	0	0	0	1	2	0	2	2	0-0
Miller,Trever,Hou	.333	.333	.667	3	1	1	0	0	1	0	0	0	0	0-0	.333	.333	.667	3	1	1	0	0	1	0	0	0	0	0-0
Mills,Alan,Bal	.000	.000	.000	0	0	0	0	0	0	0	0	0	0	0-0	.000	.000	.000	0	0	0	0	0	0	0	0	0	0	0-0
Millwood,Kevin,Atl	.080	.179	.100	50	4	1	0	0	1	1	6	22	6	0-0	.065	.159	.081	62	4	1	0	0	1	1	7	30	7	0-0
Milton,Eric,Min	.444	.444	.444	9	4	0	0	0	0	1	0	4	0	0-0	.444	.444	.444	9	4	0	0	0	0	1	0	4	0	0-0

	1998 Hitting													Career Hitting												
Pitcher,Team	Avg	OBP	SLG	AB	H	2B	3B	HR	R	RBI	BB	SO	SH	SB-CS	Avg	OBP	SLG	AB	H	2B	3B	HR	R	RBI	BB	SO	SH	SB-CS
Mlicki,Dave,NYN-LA	.100	.167	.120	50	5	1	0	0	4	0	4	15	10	0-0	.116	.201	.143	147	17	4	0	0	9	5	16	52	25	0-0
Moehler,Brian,Det	.000	.000	.000	4	0	0	0	0	1	0	0	2	0	0-0	.000	.000	.000	7	0	0	0	0	1	0	0	4	0	0-0
Mohler,Mike,Oak	.000	.000	.000	0	0	0	0	0	0	0	0	0	0	0-0	.000	.000	.000	0	0	0	0	0	0	0	0	0	0	0-0
Montgomery,Jeff,KC	.000	.000	.000	0	0	0	0	0	0	0	0	0	0	0-0	.000	.000	.000	2	0	0	0	0	0	0	0	1	0	0-0
Moore,Trey,Mon	.235	.278	.294	17	4	1	0	0	1	0	1	3	1	0-0	.235	.278	.294	17	4	1	0	0	1	0	1	3	1	0-0
Morgan,Mike,Min-ChN	.625	.625	.750	8	5	1	0	0	1	0	0	3	1	0-0	.096	.120	.107	477	46	3	1	0	13	14	12	144	58	0-0
Morman,Alvin,Cle-SF	.000	.000	.000	0	0	0	0	0	0	0	0	0	0	0-0	.000	.000	.000	1	0	0	0	0	0	0	0	0	0	0-0
Morris,Matt,StL	.069	.206	.103	29	2	1	0	0	1	3	5	16	7	0-0	.167	.241	.196	102	17	3	0	0	5	9	10	52	9	0-1
Moyer,Jamie,Sea	.000	.000	.000	2	0	0	0	0	0	0	0	0	0	0-0	.141	.211	.154	156	22	2	0	0	10	4	14	51	19	0-0
Mulholland,Terry,ChN	.294	.368	.412	17	5	2	0	0	3	3	2	10	1	0-0	.105	.125	.140	522	55	10	1	2	21	16	11	237	39	1-1
Mullins,Greg,Mil	.000	.000	.000	0	0	0	0	0	0	0	0	0	0	0-0	.000	.000	.000	0	0	0	0	0	0	0	0	0	0	0-0
Munoz,Mike,Col	.000	.000	.000	2	0	0	0	0	1	0	0	2	1	0-0	.143	.400	.286	7	1	1	0	0	2	1	3	6	1	0-0
Mussina,Mike,Bal	.000	.000	.000	2	0	0	0	0	0	0	0	1	0	0-0	.167	.167	.167	6	1	0	0	0	0	0	0	2	0	0-0
Myers,Mike,Mil	.000	.000	.000	0	0	0	0	0	0	0	0	0	0	0-0	.000	.000	.000	0	0	0	0	0	0	0	0	0	0	0-0
Myers,Randy,Tor-SD	.000	.000	.000	1	0	0	0	0	0	0	0	1	0	0-0	.183	.222	.233	60	11	3	0	0	5	7	3	33	5	0-0
Myers,Rodney,ChN	.000	.000	.000	1	0	0	0	0	0	0	0	1	0	0-0	.000	.000	.000	6	0	0	0	0	0	0	0	5	0	0-0
Nagy,Charles,Cle	.000	.000	.000	5	0	0	0	0	0	0	0	4	0	0-0	.100	.100	.100	10	1	0	0	0	1	0	0	5	0	0-0
Naulty,Dan,Min	.000	.000	.000	0	0	0	0	0	0	0	0	0	0	0-0	.000	.000	.000	0	0	0	0	0	0	0	0	0	0	0-0
Navarro,Jaime,ChA	.000	.000	.000	1	0	0	0	0	0	0	0	0	0	0-0	.153	.164	.194	144	22	6	0	0	1	10	1	51	17	0-0
Neagle,Denny,Atl	.175	.224	.190	63	11	1	0	0	2	3	4	12	9	0-0	.148	.181	.191	345	51	6	0	3	18	29	14	110	48	0-1
Nelson,Jeff,NYA	.000	.000	.000	1	0	0	0	0	0	0	0	0	1	0-0	.000	.000	.000	1	0	0	0	0	0	0	0	0	1	0-0
Nen,Robb,SF	.000	.000	.000	3	0	0	0	0	0	0	0	2	0	0-0	.000	.000	.000	12	0	0	0	0	0	0	0	3	0	0-0
Nitkowski,C.J.,Hou	.000	.000	.000	4	0	0	0	0	0	0	0	3	1	0-0	.143	.143	.143	14	2	0	0	0	1	1	0	9	1	0-0
Nomo,Hideo,LA-NYN	.180	.196	.240	50	9	0	0	1	4	5	1	17	4	0-0	.138	.151	.185	260	36	9	0	1	10	14	4	120	24	0-0
Nunez,Vladimir,Ari	.000	.000	.000	0	0	0	0	0	0	0	0	0	0	0-0	.000	.000	.000	0	0	0	0	0	0	0	0	0	0	0-0
Nye,Ryan,Phi	.000	.000	.000	0	0	0	0	0	0	0	0	0	0	0-0	.000	.000	.000	2	0	0	0	0	0	0	0	1	1	0-0
Ojala,Kirt,Fla	.154	.241	.192	26	4	1	0	0	2	3	3	10	2	0-0	.121	.194	.152	33	4	1	0	0	2	3	3	12	3	0-0
Olivares,Omar,Ana	.000	.333	.000	2	0	0	0	0	1	0	1	1	0	0-0	.236	.256	.337	208	49	7	1	4	22	23	6	60	13	0-0
Oliver,Darren,Tex-StL	.103	.133	.172	29	3	2	0	0	1	1	1	14	0	0-0	.129	.182	.194	31	4	2	0	0	2	3	1	15	0	0-0
Olson,Gregg,Ari	.500	.500	2.000	2	1	0	0	1	1	2	0	1	0	0-0	.250	.250	1.000	4	1	0	0	1	1	2	0	3	0	0-0
Oquist,Mike,Oak	.000	.000	.000	1	0	0	0	0	0	0	0	0	1	0-0	.200	.200	.200	5	1	0	0	0	0	0	0	0	2	0-0
Orosco,Jesse,Bal	.000	.000	.000	0	0	0	0	0	0	0	0	0	0	0-0	.169	.250	.169	59	10	0	0	0	2	4	7	25	7	0-0
Ortiz,Russ,SF	.280	.333	.400	25	7	0	0	1	3	2	2	9	5	0-0	.280	.333	.400	25	7	0	0	1	3	2	2	9	5	0-0
Osborne,Donovan,StL	.040	.143	.040	25	1	0	0	0	0	0	3	5	4	0-0	.167	.208	.224	246	41	9	1	1	17	19	12	84	27	1-1
Osuna,Antonio,LA	.000	.000	.000	2	0	0	0	0	0	0	0	0	0	0-0	.143	.222	.143	7	1	0	0	0	0	1	1	0	0	0-0
Painter,Lance,StL	1.000	1.000	1.000	1	1	0	0	0	0	0	0	0	1	0-0	.175	.197	.246	57	10	2	1	0	6	5	2	28	8	0-0
Pall,Donn,Fla	.000	.000	.000	2	0	0	0	0	0	0	0	1	0	0-0	.000	.167	.000	5	0	0	0	0	0	0	1	2	0	0-0
Park,ChanHo,LA	.194	.216	.250	72	14	2	1	0	2	3	2	30	6	0-0	.168	.207	.224	143	24	6	1	0	7	7	7	61	20	0-0
Parque,Jim,ChA	.000	.000	.000	1	0	0	0	0	0	0	0	0	2	0-0	.000	.000	.000	1	0	0	0	0	0	0	0	0	2	0-0
Parris,Steve,Cin	.138	.138	.138	29	4	0	0	0	0	3	0	9	3	0-0	.190	.203	.222	63	12	2	0	0	3	7	1	20	6	0-0
Patrick,Bronswell,Mil	.200	.294	.400	15	3	0	0	1	1	1	2	3	1	0-0	.200	.294	.400	15	3	0	0	1	1	1	2	3	1	0-0
Patterson,Bob,ChN	.000	.000	.000	0	0	0	0	0	0	0	0	0	1	0-0	.125	.155	.143	56	7	1	0	0	3	4	2	24	7	0-0
Patterson,Danny,Tex	.000	.000	.000	0	0	0	0	0	0	0	0	0	0	0-0	.000	.000	.000	0	0	0	0	0	0	0	0	0	0	0-0
Pavano,Carl,Mon	.158	.158	.184	38	6	1	0	0	1	3	0	14	6	0-0	.158	.158	.184	38	6	1	0	0	1	3	0	14	6	0-0
Percival,Troy,Ana	.000	.000	.000	0	0	0	0	0	0	0	0	0	0	0-0	.000	.000	.000	1	0	0	0	0	0	0	0	1	0	0-0
Perez,Carlos,Mon-LA	.155	.200	.225	71	11	2	0	1	5	3	4	32	14	0-0	.156	.200	.244	180	28	5	1	3	9	10	10	84	23	0-0
Perez,Odalis,Atl	.000	.000	.000	0	0	0	0	0	0	0	0	0	0	0-0	.000	.000	.000	0	0	0	0	0	0	0	0	0	0	0-0
Perez,Yorkis,Phi	.000	.000	.000	2	0	0	0	0	0	0	0	1	0	0-0	.000	.000	.000	8	0	0	0	0	0	0	0	5	0	0-0
Person,Robert,Tor	.000	.000	.000	0	0	0	0	0	0	0	0	0	0	0-0	.179	.207	.214	28	5	1	0	0	2	0	1	13	5	0-0
Peters,Chris,Pit	.231	.250	.231	39	9	0	0	0	2	2	1	9	4	1-0	.226	.238	.242	62	14	1	0	0	4	5	1	19	5	1-0
Petkovsek,Mark,StL	.318	.348	.364	22	7	1	0	0	5	1	1	2	2	0-0	.163	.232	.174	86	14	1	0	0	10	3	7	18	6	0-0
Pettitte,Andy,NYA	.000	.000	.000	4	0	0	0	0	0	0	0	3	2	0-0	.000	.000	.000	4	0	0	0	0	0	0	0	3	2	0-0
Pichardo,Hipolito,KC	.000	.000	.000	2	0	0	0	0	0	0	0	2	0	0-0	.000	.000	.000	4	0	0	0	0	0	0	0	2	0	0-0
Pickett,Ricky,Ari	.000	.000	.000	0	0	0	0	0	0	0	0	0	0	0-0	.000	.000	.000	0	0	0	0	0	0	0	0	0	0	0-0
Pisciotta,Marc,ChN	.333	.333	.333	3	1	0	0	0	0	0	0	1	0	0-0	.250	.250	.250	4	1	0	0	0	0	0	0	2	0	0-0
Pittsley,Jim,KC	.000	.000	.000	2	0	0	0	0	0	0	0	2	1	0-0	.250	.250	.500	4	1	1	0	0	0	0	0	3	1	0-0
Plesac,Dan,Tor	.000	.000	.000	0	0	0	0	0	0	0	0	0	0	0-0	.071	.071	.071	14	1	0	0	0	0	0	0	9	0	0-0
Plunk,Eric,Cle-Mil	.000	.500	.000	1	0	0	0	0	1	0	1	1	0	0-0	.000	.333	.000	2	0	0	0	0	1	0	1	2	0	0-0
Rolitto,Cliff,StL	.071	.133	.071	14	1	0	0	0	0	0	1	8	1	0-0	.071	.133	.071	14	1	0	0	0	0	0	1	8	1	0-0
Ponson,Sidney,Bal	.500	.500	.500	4	2	0	0	0	1	0	0	2	0	0-0	.500	.500	.500	4	2	0	0	0	1	0	0	2	0	0-0
Poole,Jim,SF-Cle	.250	.250	.500	4	1	1	0	0	1	0	0	0	2	0-0	.167	.167	.333	6	1	1	0	0	1	0	0	1	3	0-0
Portugal,Mark,Phi	.260	.315	.360	50	13	5	0	0	6	4	4	10	4	0-0	.199	.233	.262	447	89	20	1	2	33	36	20	87	53	0-0
Powell,Brian,Det	.000	.000	.000	1	0	0	0	0	0	0	0	1	0	0-0	.000	.000	.000	1	0	0	0	0	0	0	0	1	0	0-0
Powell,Jay,Fla-Hou	.000	.000	.000	1	0	0	0	0	0	0	0	1	0	0-0	.200	.200	.200	10	2	0	0	0	0	1	0	6	1	0-0
Powell,Jeremy,Mon	.000	.000	.000	6	0	0	0	0	0	0	0	3	0	0-0	.000	.000	.000	6	0	0	0	0	0	0	0	3	0	0-0
Priest,Eddie,Cin	.000	.000	.000	2	0	0	0	0	0	0	0	2	0	0-0	.000	.000	.000	2	0	0	0	0	0	0	0	2	0	0-0
Pulsipher,Bill,NYN-Mil	.150	.150	.150	20	3	0	0	0	2	0	0	6	1	0-0	.121	.185	.155	58	7	2	0	0	6	4	5	25	5	0-0
Quantrill,Paul,Tor	.000	.000	.000	0	0	0	0	0	0	0	0	0	0	0-0	.098	.141	.098	61	6	0	0	0	5	0	3	26	7	0-0
Radinsky,Scott,LA	.000	.000	.000	0	0	0	0	0	0	0	0	0	0	0-0	.000	.000	.000	5	0	0	0	0	0	0	0	4	0	0-0
Radke,Brad,Min	.000	.000	.000	2	0	0	0	0	0	0	0	1	0	0-0	.000	.000	.000	5	0	0	0	0	0	0	0	1	1	0-0
Raggio,Brady,StL	.000	.000	.000	1	0	0	0	0	0	0	0	0	1	0-0	.000	.000	.000	4	0	0	0	0	0	1	0	0	1	0-0
Ramirez,Roberto,SD	.000	.000	.000	0	0	0	0	0	0	0	0	0	0	0-0	.000	.000	.000	0	0	0	0	0	0	0	0	0	0	0-0
Rapp,Pat,KC	.000	.000	.000	2	0	0	0	0	0	0	0	1	1	0-0	.122	.126	.152	237	29	4	0	1	10	13	1	89	21	0-0
Rath,Fred,Col	.000	.000	.000	2	0	0	0	0	0	0	0	1	0	0-0	.000	.000	.000	2	0	0	0	0	0	0	0	1	0	0-0
Rath,Gary,LA	.000	.000	.000	0	0	0	0	0	0	0	0	0	0	0-0	.000	.000	.000	0	0	0	0	0	0	0	0	0	0	0-0
Reed,Rick,NYN	.125	.164	.172	64	8	0	0	1	6	5	3	21	12	0-0	.151	.195	.226	159	24	6	0	2	13	13	9	51	20	0-0
Reed,Steve,SF-Cle	.333	.333	.333	3	1	0	0	0	0	0	0	0	0	0-0	.143	.143	.143	21	3	0	0	0	0	0	0	6	2	0-0
Remlinger,Mike,Cin	.106	.143	.128	47	5	1	0	0	1	1	2	7	7	0-1	.081	.142	.111	99	8	3	0	0	4	8	7	29	17	0-1
Reyes,Al,Mil	.200	.200	.200	5	1	0	0	0	1	0	0	4	0	0-0	.200	.200	.200	5	1	0	0	0	1	0	0	4	0	0-0
Reyes,Carlos,SD-Bos	.000	.000	.000	0	0	0	0	0	0	0	0	0	1	0-0	.000	.000	.000	0	0	0	0	0	0	0	0	0	1	0-0
Reyes,Dennis,LA-Cin	.059	.059	.118	17	1	1	0	0	1	0	0	5	1	0-0	.038	.074	.077	26	1	1	0	0	2	0	1	10	2	1-0
Reynolds,Shane,Hou	.159	.188	.207	82	13	4	0	0	10	9	2	39	7	0-0	.150	.176	.204	313	47	11	0	2	24	17	9	143	47	0-0
Reynoso,A.,NYN	.167	.167	.233	30	5	2	0	0	2	0	0	15	1	0-0	.157	.201	.209	230	36	3	0	3	14	9	13	96	20	0-0
Rhodes,Arthur,Bal	.500	.500	.500	2	1	0	0	0	0	0	0	1	0	0-0	.333	.333	.333	3	1	0	0	0	0	0	0	2	0	0-0
Rincon,Ricardo,Pit	.000	.000	.000	2	0	0	0	0	0	0	0	0	0	0-0	.000	.000	.000	3	0	0	0	0	0	0	0	1	1	0-0
Risley,Bill,Tor	.000	.000	.000	0	0	0	0	0	0	0	0	0	0	0-0	.000	.000	.000	2	0	0	0	0	0	0	0	0	0	0-0

	1998 Hitting														Career Hitting													
Pitcher,Team	Avg	OBP	SLG	AB	H	2B	3B	HR	R	RBI	BB	SO	SH	SB-CS	Avg	OBP	SLG	AB	H	2B	3B	HR	R	RBI	BB	SO	SH	SB-CS
Ritz,Kevin,Col	.333	.333	.333	3	1	0	0	0	0	0	0	1	0	0-0	.158	.226	.193	171	27	3	0	1	14	7	13	77	29	2-1
Rivera,Mariano,NYA	.000	.000	.000	0	0	0	0	0	0	0	0	0	0	0-0	.000	.000	.000	0	0	0	0	0	0	0	0	0	0	0-0
Rocker,John,Atl	.000	.000	.000	0	0	0	0	0	0	0	0	0	0	0-0	.000	.000	.000	0	0	0	0	0	0	0	0	0	0	0-0
Rodriguez,Felix,Ari	.000	.000	.000	0	0	0	0	0	0	0	0	0	0	0-0	.000	.000	.000	3	0	0	0	0	0	0	0	1	0	0-0
Rodriguez,Rich,SF	.167	.167	.167	6	1	0	0	0	0	0	0	4	1	0-0	.077	.172	.077	26	2	0	0	0	2	0	3	8	3	0-0
Rogers,Kenny,Oak	.000	.000	.000	4	0	0	0	0	1	0	0	2	0	0-0	.000	.000	.000	7	0	0	0	0	1	0	0	2	0	0-0
Rojas,Mel,NYN	.000	.000	.000	0	0	0	0	0	0	0	0	0	0	0-0	.119	.119	.136	59	7	1	0	0	1	3	0	32	6	0-0
Roque,Rafael,Mil	.077	.077	.077	13	1	0	0	0	0	1	0	6	4	0-0	.077	.077	.077	13	1	0	0	0	0	1	0	6	4	0-0
Rosado,Jose,KC	.500	.500	.500	2	1	0	0	0	0	0	0	0	0	0-0	.250	.250	.250	4	1	0	0	0	0	0	0	1	0	0-0
Rueter,Kirk,SF	.209	.209	.224	67	14	1	0	0	7	3	0	12	9	0-1	.138	.171	.142	240	33	1	0	0	15	16	10	55	30	0-1
Runyan,Sean,Det	.000	.000	.000	0	0	0	0	0	0	0	0	0	0	0-0	.000	.000	.000	0	0	0	0	0	0	0	0	0	0	0-0
Rusch,Glendon,KC	.000	.000	.000	3	0	0	0	0	0	0	0	0	0	0-0	.000	.000	.000	6	0	0	0	0	0	0	0	2	0	0-0
Ryan,Ken,Phi	.000	.000	.000	1	0	0	0	0	0	0	0	0	0	0-0	.125	.125	.125	8	1	0	0	0	0	0	0	4	1	0-0
Saberhagen,Bret,Bos	.000	.000	.000	5	0	0	0	0	0	0	0	2	0	0-0	.124	.177	.145	186	23	4	0	0	13	1	12	47	24	0-0
Sager,A.J.,Det	.000	.000	.000	1	0	0	0	0	0	0	0	0	0	0-0	.071	.071	.214	14	1	0	1	0	0	2	0	6	1	0-0
Saipe,Mike,Col	.000	.500	.000	1	0	0	0	0	0	0	1	0	0	0-0	.000	.500	.000	1	0	0	0	0	0	0	1	0	0	0-0
Sanchez,Jesus,Fla	.135	.151	.173	52	7	0	1	0	2	1	1	15	4	0-0	.135	.151	.173	52	7	0	1	0	2	1	1	15	4	0-0
Sanders,Scott,Det-SD	.000	.000	.000	0	0	0	0	0	0	0	0	0	1	0-0	.180	.216	.216	111	20	4	0	0	4	7	5	36	18	1-0
Santana,Julio,Tex-TB	.000	.000	.000	4	0	0	0	0	0	0	0	3	0	0-0	.167	.167	.167	6	1	0	0	0	0	0	0	3	0	0-0
Saunders,Tony,TB	1.000	1.000	1.000	2	2	0	0	0	0	0	0	0	0	0-0	.128	.171	.205	39	5	0	0	1	2	1	2	19	1	0-0
Scanlan,Bob,Hou	.000	.000	.000	0	0	0	0	0	0	0	0	0	0	0-0	.067	.094	.067	30	2	0	0	0	1	3	1	12	3	0-0
Schilling,Curt,Phi	.132	.165	.158	76	10	2	0	0	3	3	3	26	12	0-0	.156	.173	.174	430	67	8	0	0	17	18	9	148	58	1-0
Schmidt,Jason,Pit	.097	.123	.129	62	6	2	0	0	1	2	2	25	12	0-0	.091	.130	.117	154	14	4	0	0	4	7	7	68	24	0-0
Schourek,P.,Hou-Bos	.211	.211	.263	19	4	1	0	0	2	2	0	6	5	1-0	.175	.197	.217	240	42	4	0	2	14	19	7	67	34	2-0
Seanez,Rudy,Atl	.000	.000	.000	1	0	0	0	0	0	0	0	1	0	0-0	.000	.000	.000	3	0	0	0	0	0	0	0	3	0	0-0
Sele,Aaron,Tex	.250	.250	.500	4	1	1	0	0	0	0	0	0	0	0-0	.167	.167	.333	6	1	1	0	0	0	0	0	1	0	0-0
Serafini,Dan,Min	.000	.000	.000	1	0	0	0	0	0	0	0	1	0	0-0	.000	.000	.000	1	0	0	0	0	0	0	0	1	0	0-0
Service,Scott,KC	.000	.000	.000	1	0	0	0	0	0	0	0	1	0	0-0	.063	.063	.063	16	1	0	0	0	0	1	0	9	0	0-0
Shaw,Jeff,Cin-LA	.000	.000	.000	2	0	0	0	0	0	0	0	2	1	0-0	.079	.167	.079	38	3	0	0	0	4	0	4	20	3	0-0
Shuey,Paul,Cle	.000	.000	.000	1	0	0	0	0	0	0	0	0	0	0-0	.000	.000	.000	2	0	0	0	0	0	0	0	1	0	0-0
Silva,Jose,Pit	.037	.133	.074	27	1	1	0	0	0	0	2	10	5	0-0	.059	.135	.088	34	2	1	0	0	1	0	2	14	8	0-0
Simas,Bill,ChA	.000	.000	.000	0	0	0	0	0	0	0	0	0	0	0-0	.000	.000	.000	0	0	0	0	0	0	0	0	0	0	0-0
Sirotka,Mike,ChA	.000	.200	.000	4	0	0	0	0	0	0	1	0	0	0-0	.000	.167	.000	5	0	0	0	0	0	0	1	1	0	0-0
Slocumb,H.,Sea	.000	.000	.000	0	0	0	0	0	0	0	0	0	0	0-0	.091	.091	.091	11	1	0	0	0	0	2	0	6	1	0-0
Small,Aaron,Oak-Ari	.000	.000	.000	0	0	0	0	0	0	0	0	0	0	0-0	.000	.000	.000	1	0	0	0	0	0	0	0	0	0	0-0
Smith,Pete,SD-Bal	.063	.167	.063	16	1	0	0	0	1	1	2	7	1	0-0	.118	.174	.147	279	33	4	2	0	15	15	19	83	38	0-0
Smith,Travis,Mil	.000	.000	.000	1	0	0	0	0	0	0	0	0	0	0-0	.000	.000	.000	1	0	0	0	0	0	0	0	0	0	0-0
Smoltz,John,Atl	.196	.317	.216	51	10	1	0	0	4	5	8	16	8	0-0	.165	.240	.211	665	110	16	1	4	58	44	64	250	86	3-2
Snyder,John,ChA	.000	.000	.000	0	0	0	0	0	0	0	0	0	0	0-0	.000	.000	.000	0	0	0	0	0	0	0	0	0	0	0-0
Sodowsky,Clint,Ari	.300	.300	.400	10	3	1	0	0	2	0	0	2	1	0-0	.333	.333	.417	12	4	1	0	0	2	0	0	2	1	0-0
Sparks,Steve,Ana	.000	.500	.000	1	0	0	0	0	1	0	1	0	1	0-0	.000	.500	.000	1	0	0	0	0	1	0	1	0	1	0-0
Speier,Justin,ChN-Fla	.000	.000	.000	0	0	0	0	0	0	0	0	0	0	0-0	.000	.000	.000	0	0	0	0	0	0	0	0	0	0	0-0
Spencer,Stan,SD	.111	.111	.222	9	1	1	0	0	0	0	0	4	3	0-0	.111	.111	.222	9	1	1	0	0	0	0	0	4	3	0-0
Spoljaric,Paul,Sea	.000	.000	.000	0	0	0	0	0	0	0	0	0	0	0-0	.000	.000	.000	1	0	0	0	0	0	0	0	0	0	0-0
Spradlin,Jerry,Phi	1.000	1.000	2.000	1	1	1	0	0	0	0	0	0	0	0-0	.250	.250	.500	4	1	1	0	0	0	0	0	2	0	0-0
Springer,Dennis,TB	.000	.000	.000	1	0	0	0	0	0	0	0	1	0	0-0	.083	.083	.083	12	1	0	0	0	0	0	0	7	0	0-0
Springer,Russ,Ari-Atl	.000	.000	.000	1	0	0	0	0	0	0	0	1	0	0-0	.050	.050	.050	20	1	0	0	0	1	0	0	14	3	0-0
Stanifer,Robby,Fla	.000	.000	.000	5	0	0	0	0	0	0	0	3	0	0-0	.250	.333	.375	8	2	1	0	0	1	1	0	3	0	0-0
Stanton,Mike,NYA	.000	.000	.000	1	0	0	0	0	0	0	0	0	0	0-0	.500	.538	.583	12	6	1	0	0	1	2	1	1	1	0-0
Steenstra,Kennie,ChN	.000	.000	.000	0	0	0	0	0	0	0	0	0	0	0-0	.000	.000	.000	0	0	0	0	0	0	0	0	0	0	0-0
Stein,Blake,Oak	.000	.000	.000	5	0	0	0	0	0	0	0	4	1	0-0	.000	.000	.000	5	0	0	0	0	0	0	0	4	1	0-0
Stephenson,G.,Phi	.167	.286	.167	6	1	0	0	0	0	0	1	1	1	0-0	.105	.150	.132	38	4	1	0	0	0	1	1	17	6	0-0
Stevens,Dave,ChN	.250	.250	.250	4	1	0	0	0	0	0	0	2	0	0-0	.200	.200	.200	5	1	0	0	0	0	0	0	2	0	0-0
Stieb,Dave,Tor	.000	.000	.000	1	0	0	0	0	0	0	0	0	0	0-0	.000	.000	.000	2	0	0	0	0	2	0	0	0	0	0-0
Stoops,Jim,Col	.000	.000	.000	0	0	0	0	0	0	0	0	0	0	0-0	.000	.000	.000	0	0	0	0	0	0	0	0	0	0	0-0
Stottlemyre,T.,StL-Tex	.226	.281	.226	53	12	0	0	0	3	1	4	24	5	0-0	.229	.304	.263	175	40	4	1	0	17	7	19	65	19	1-1
Sullivan,Scott,Cin	.091	.091	.091	11	1	0	0	0	0	0	0	6	1	0-0	.050	.050	.050	20	1	0	0	0	0	1	0	11	3	0-0
Suppan,Jeff,Ari-KC	.273	.304	.273	22	6	0	0	0	1	1	0	6	1	1-0	.250	.280	.250	24	6	0	0	0	1	1	0	7	1	1-0
Swift,Bill,Sea	.000	.000	.000	5	0	0	0	0	0	0	0	2	0	0-0	.210	.260	.262	229	48	9	0	1	27	15	15	54	29	1-0
Swindell,G.,Min-Bos	.000	.000	.000	0	0	0	0	0	0	0	0	0	0	0-0	.192	.204	.233	240	46	10	0	0	10	13	4	55	33	0-0
Tabaka,Jeff,Pit	.000	.000	.000	1	0	0	0	0	0	0	0	1	0	0-0	.250	.400	.500	4	1	1	0	0	1	0	1	2	1	0-0
Tam,Jeff,NYN	.000	.000	.000	1	0	0	0	0	0	0	0	0	0	0-0	.000	.000	.000	1	0	0	0	0	0	0	0	0	0	0-0
Tapani,Kevin,ChN	.133	.205	.200	75	10	2	0	1	7	11	7	30	5	0-0	.138	.198	.190	116	16	3	0	1	9	13	9	50	12	1-0
Tavarez,Julian,SF	.111	.111	.111	9	1	0	0	0	0	0	0	4	1	0-0	.100	.100	.100	10	1	0	0	0	0	0	0	5	1	0-0
Taylor,Billy,Oak	.000	.000	.000	0	0	0	0	0	0	0	0	0	0	0-0	.000	.000	.000	0	0	0	0	0	0	0	0	0	0	0-0
Telemaco,A.,ChN-Ari	.086	.108	.171	35	3	1	1	0	2	2	1	16	1	0-0	.110	.143	.151	73	8	1	1	0	3	3	3	37	5	0-0
Telford,Anthony,Mon	.250	.250	.250	4	1	0	0	0	0	1	0	0	0	0-0	.211	.211	.263	19	4	1	0	0	0	2	0	3	1	0-0
Tewksbury,Bob,Min	.000	.000	.000	1	0	0	0	0	0	0	0	1	0	0-0	.132	.177	.150	380	50	7	0	0	20	19	21	148	41	0-0
Thompson,Justin,Det	.143	.143	.143	7	1	0	0	0	1	0	0	3	0	0-0	.111	.111	.111	9	1	0	0	0	1	0	0	4	0	0-0
Thompson,Mark,Col	.143	.143	.143	7	1	0	0	0	1	0	0	3	0	0-0	.172	.181	.247	93	16	4	0	1	7	3	1	40	9	0-0
Thomson,John,Col	.120	.148	.120	50	6	0	0	0	4	2	2	23	9	0-1	.165	.194	.165	97	16	0	0	0	6	7	4	46	15	0-1
Thurman,Mike,Mon	.000	.080	.000	23	0	0	0	0	1	0	2	17	2	0-0	.040	.111	.040	25	1	0	0	0	2	0	2	18	3	0-0
Timlin,Mike,Sea	.000	.000	.000	0	0	0	0	0	0	0	0	0	0	0-0	.000	.000	.000	0	0	0	0	0	0	0	0	0	0	0-0
Tomko,Brett,Cin	.108	.157	.123	65	7	1	0	0	4	3	4	29	9	0-0	.119	.159	.139	101	12	2	0	0	6	6	5	43	12	0-0
Trachsel,Steve,ChN	.266	.338	.359	64	17	3	0	1	11	8	7	18	9	0-0	.184	.229	.243	288	53	11	0	2	26	23	16	85	40	0-1
Trombley,Mike,Min	.000	.000	.000	0	0	0	0	0	0	0	0	0	0	0-0	.000	.000	.000	1	0	0	0	0	0	0	0	1	0	0-0
Urbina,Ugueth,Mon	.000	.000	.000	6	0	0	0	0	0	0	0	3	0	0-0	.109	.146	.109	46	5	0	0	0	3	1	2	28	3	0-0
Valdes,Ismael,LA	.167	.216	.188	48	8	1	0	0	3	2	3	6	8	0-0	.121	.150	.134	239	29	3	0	0	11	6	8	75	35	2-0
Valdes,Marc,Mon	.400	.500	.400	5	2	0	0	0	1	0	0	2	0	0-0	.100	.163	.100	40	4	0	0	0	1	1	2	13	0	0-0
Valdez,Efrain,Ari	.000	.000	.000	0	0	0	0	0	0	0	0	0	0	0-0	.000	.000	.000	0	0	0	0	0	0	0	0	0	0	0-0
VanPoppel,T.,Tex-Pit	.214	.267	.286	14	3	1	0	0	3	1	1	4	3	0-0	.214	.267	.286	14	3	1	0	0	3	1	1	4	3	0-0
VanRyn,ChN-SD-Tor	.000	.000	.000	1	0	0	0	0	0	0	0	0	0	0-0	.000	.000	.000	1	0	0	0	0	0	0	0	0	0	0-0
Vazquez,Javier,Mon	.173	.200	.250	52	9	2	1	0	3	5	2	7	6	0-0	.173	.200	.250	52	9	2	1	0	3	5	2	7	6	0-0
Veres,Dave,Col	.333	.333	.333	3	1	0	0	0	0	0	0	1	0	0-0	.316	.350	.368	19	6	1	0	0	1	1	1	10	2	0-0
Wagner,Billy,Hou	.333	.333	.333	3	1	0	0	0	0	0	0	2	0	0-0	.111	.111	.111	9	1	0	0	0	0	0	0	4	0	0-0
Wagner,Paul,Mil	.158	.158	.158	19	3	0	0	0	1	0	0	2	1	0-0	.166	.199	.178	169	28	2	0	0	10	9	7	47	16	0-1

Pitcher,Team	1998 Hitting														Career Hitting													
	Avg	OBP	SLG	AB	H	2B	3B	HR	R	RBI	BB	SO	SH	SB-CS	Avg	OBP	SLG	AB	H	2B	3B	HR	R	RBI	BB	SO	SH	SB-CS
Wainhouse,David,Col	.000	.000	.000	1	0	0	0	0	0	0	0	0	0	0-0	.000	.000	.000	4	0	0	0	0	0	0	0	0	0	0-0
Wakefield,Tim,Bos	.000	.333	.000	2	0	0	0	0	0	0	1	2	2	0-0	.122	.145	.189	74	9	2	0	1	3	3	2	22	10	0-0
Wall,Donne,SD	.286	.286	.286	7	2	0	0	0	0	0	0	3	0	0-0	.182	.217	.197	66	12	1	0	0	5	1	3	20	12	0-0
Wasdin,John,Bos	.000	1.000	.000	0	0	0	0	0	1	0	1	0	0	0-0	.000	1.000	.000	0	0	0	0	0	1	0	1	0	0	0-0
Washburn,Jarrod,Ana	.000	.000	.000	1	0	0	0	0	0	0	0	1	2	0-0	.000	.000	.000	1	0	0	0	0	0	0	0	1	2	0-0
Weathers,D.,Cin-Mil	.087	.160	.217	23	2	0	0	1	2	1	2	14	4	0-0	.107	.148	.156	122	13	0	0	2	6	4	5	76	16	0-0
Weaver,Eric,LA	.000	.000	.000	1	0	0	0	0	0	0	0	1	0	0-0	.000	.000	.000	1	0	0	0	0	0	0	0	1	0	0-0
Weber,Neil,Ari	.000	.000	.000	0	0	0	0	0	0	0	0	0	0	0-0	.000	.000	.000	0	0	0	0	0	0	0	0	0	0	0-0
Welch,Mike,Phi	.000	.000	.000	3	0	0	0	0	0	0	0	2	0	0-0	.000	.000	.000	3	0	0	0	0	0	0	0	2	0	0-0
Wells,Bob,Sea	.000	.000	.000	0	0	0	0	0	0	0	0	0	0	0-0	.000	1.000	.000	0	0	0	0	0	1	0	1	0	0	0-0
Wells,David,NYA	.250	.250	.250	4	1	0	0	0	0	0	0	1	0	0-0	.156	.156	.156	32	5	0	0	0	2	0	0	6	1	0-0
Wendell,Turk,NYN	.000	.000	.000	4	0	0	0	0	0	0	0	2	0	0-0	.074	.194	.074	27	2	0	0	0	1	0	4	13	1	0-0
Wengert,Don,SD-ChN	.000	.059	.000	16	0	0	0	0	0	0	1	3	1	0-0	.000	.059	.000	16	0	0	0	0	0	0	1	3	1	0-0
Wetteland,John,Tex	.000	.000	.000	0	0	0	0	0	0	0	0	0	0	0-0	.167	.167	.286	42	7	2	0	1	4	8	0	19	9	0-0
Whisenant,Matt,KC	.000	.000	.000	0	0	0	0	0	0	0	0	0	0	0-0	.000	.000	.000	0	0	0	0	0	0	0	0	0	0	0-0
White,Gabe,Cin	.167	.167	.167	6	1	0	0	0	0	0	0	3	4	0-0	.091	.130	.091	22	2	0	0	0	0	1	1	14	8	0-0
White,Rick,TB	.333	.333	.333	3	1	0	0	0	0	0	0	1	0	0-0	.097	.125	.129	31	3	1	0	0	1	1	0	8	2	0-0
Whiteside,Matt,Phi	.000	.000	.000	2	0	0	0	0	0	0	0	2	0	0-0	.000	.000	.000	2	0	0	0	0	0	0	0	2	0	0-0
Wickman,Bob,Mil	.000	.000	.000	1	0	0	0	0	0	0	0	0	0	0-0	.000	.000	.000	1	0	0	0	0	0	0	0	0	0	0-0
Wilkins,Marc,Pit	.000	.000	.000	0	0	0	0	0	0	0	0	0	0	0-0	.154	.267	.154	13	2	0	0	0	1	2	2	9	1	0-0
Williams,Mike,Pit	.000	.000	.000	3	0	0	0	0	0	0	0	2	2	0-0	.163	.187	.183	104	17	2	0	0	7	7	3	32	24	1-0
Williams,Todd,Cin	.000	.000	.000	2	0	0	0	0	0	0	0	2	0	0-0	.250	.250	.250	4	1	0	0	0	0	0	0	2	0	0-0
Williams,Woody,Tor	.333	.333	.333	6	2	0	0	0	0	0	0	1	0	0-0	.375	.375	.375	8	3	0	0	0	0	0	0	2	0	0-0
Winchester,Scott,Cin	.130	.167	.130	23	3	0	0	0	0	1	0	9	2	0-0	.130	.167	.130	23	3	0	0	0	0	1	0	9	2	0-0
Winston,Darrin,Phi	.000	.000	.000	1	0	0	0	0	0	0	0	1	0	0-0	.333	.500	.333	3	1	0	0	0	0	1	1	1	0	0-0
Witt,Bobby,Tex-StL	.182	.250	.273	11	2	1	0	0	1	1	1	5	1	0-0	.120	.151	.240	50	6	3	0	1	2	5	2	17	5	0-0
Wohlers,Mark,Atl	.000	.000	.000	0	0	0	0	0	0	0	0	1	0	0-0	.083	.083	.083	12	1	0	0	0	1	0	0	11	1	0-0
Wolcott,Bob,Ari	.222	.222	.222	9	2	0	0	0	1	0	0	1	0	0-0	.200	.200	.200	10	2	0	0	0	1	0	0	1	0	0-0
Wood,Kerry,ChN	.130	.145	.241	54	7	0	0	2	3	8	1	16	8	0-0	.130	.145	.241	54	7	0	0	2	3	8	1	16	8	0-0
Woodall,Brad,Mil	.237	.310	.342	38	9	1	0	1	7	2	4	10	5	0-0	.261	.333	.348	46	12	1	0	1	7	3	5	12	5	0-0
Woodard,Steve,Mil	.140	.140	.180	50	7	2	0	0	1	4	0	12	2	0-0	.140	.140	.180	50	7	2	0	0	1	4	0	12	2	0-0
Worrell,T,Det-Cle-Oak	.000	.000	.000	0	0	0	0	0	0	0	0	0	0	0-0	.116	.164	.130	69	8	1	0	0	6	4	4	34	9	0-0
Wright,Jamey,Col	.175	.217	.298	57	10	2	1	1	5	4	3	29	8	0-0	.137	.187	.214	131	18	5	1	1	12	7	8	64	16	0-0
Wright,Jaret,Cle	.429	.429	.429	7	3	0	0	0	2	1	0	2	0	0-0	.300	.300	.300	10	3	0	0	0	2	1	0	3	2	0-0
Yan,Esteban,TB	.000	.000	.000	0	0	0	0	0	0	0	0	0	0	0-0	.000	.000	.000	0	0	0	0	0	0	0	0	0	0	0-0
Yoshii,Masato,NYN	.063	.118	.083	48	3	1	0	0	3	3	3	27	8	0-0	.063	.118	.083	48	3	1	0	0	3	3	3	27	8	0-0
Young,Tim,Mon	.000	.000	.000	0	0	0	0	0	0	0	0	0	0	0-0	.000	.000	.000	0	0	0	0	0	0	0	0	0	0	0-0

Pitchers Fielding and Holding Runners

1998 Fielding and Holding Runners

Pitcher,Team	G	Inn	PO	A	E	DP	Pct.	SBA	CS	PCS	PPO	CS%
Abbott,Jim,ChA	5	31.2	2	10	0	1	1.000	10	0	2	0	.20
Abbott,Paul,Sea	4	24.2	1	3	0	0	1.000	5	0	1	0	.20
Acevedo,Juan,StL	50	98.1	6	18	1	0	.960	7	5	0	2	.71
Adams,Terry,ChN	63	72.2	4	13	3	0	.850	14	2	0	0	.14
Adamson,Joel,Ari	5	23.0	0	4	1	0	.800	3	0	2	0	.67
Aguilera,Rick,Min	68	74.1	3	9	0	2	1.000	6	0	0	0	.00
Aldred,Scott,TB	48	31.1	3	7	0	2	1.000	3	0	1	0	.33
Alfonseca,Antonio,Fla	58	70.2	5	6	1	1	.917	4	1	0	0	.25
Almanzar,Carlos,Tor	25	28.2	2	3	1	0	.833	3	0	0	0	.00
Alvarez,Wilson,TB	25	142.2	5	6	0	1	1.000	8	4	1	0	.63
Anderson,Brian,Ari	32	208.0	11	46	2	4	.966	13	1	8	4	.69
Anderson,Matt,Det	42	44.0	0	8	1	0	.889	3	2	0	0	.67
Andujar,Luis,Tor	5	5.2	0	1	0	0	1.000	0	0	0	0	.00
Appier,Kevin,KC	3	15.0	0	1	0	0	1.000	1	1	0	0	1.00
Arrojo,Rolando,TB	32	202.0	17	42	4	5	.937	27	9	1	1	.37
Ashby,Andy,SD	33	226.2	14	35	1	4	.980	31	11	2	0	.42
Assenmacher,P.,Cle	69	47.0	2	4	0	0	1.000	8	0	0	0	.00
Astacio,Pedro,Col	35	209.1	22	31	0	3	1.000	22	6	1	0	.32
Avery,Steve,Bos	34	123.2	7	39	1	5	.979	19	3	6	0	.47
Ayala,Bobby,Sea	62	75.1	8	8	5	1	.762	7	1	0	0	.14
Aybar,Manny,StL	20	81.1	8	8	0	0	1.000	14	2	0	0	.14
Bailes,Scott,Tex	46	40.1	2	3	1	0	.833	3	2	0	0	.67
Bailey,Cory,SF	5	3.1	0	0	0	0	.000	0	0	0	0	.00
Baldwin,James,ChA	37	159.0	7	15	5	0	.815	18	5	0	0	.28
Banks,Willie,NYA-Ari	42	58.0	10	10	1	1	.952	8	4	0	0	.50
Baptist,Travis,Min	13	27.0	6	2	0	0	1.000	1	0	1	0	1.00
Barber,Brian,KC	8	42.0	0	3	0	0	1.000	2	0	0	0	.00
Barkley,Brian,Bos	6	11.0	1	0	0	0	1.000	5	0	0	0	.00
Barrios,Manuel,Fla-LA	3	3.2	0	0	0	0	.000	0	0	0	0	.00
Batista,Miguel,Mon	56	135.0	10	21	1	1	.969	17	6	1	0	.41
Beck,Rod,ChN	81	80.1	8	11	0	1	1.000	9	1	0	0	.11
Beech,Matt,Phi	21	117.0	0	13	0	2	1.000	7	3	1	0	.57
Belcher,Tim,KC	34	234.0	18	17	2	2	.946	17	10	0	0	.59
Belinda,Stan,Cin	40	61.1	2	10	2	1	.857	10	2	1	0	.30
Beltran,Rigo,NYN	7	8.0	0	1	0	0	1.000	0	0	0	0	.00
Benes,Andy,Ari	34	231.1	23	25	0	2	1.000	35	11	0	0	.31
Benitez,Armando,Bal	71	68.1	3	5	0	0	1.000	9	1	0	0	.11
Bennett,Joel,Bal	2	2.0	0	0	0	0	.000	0	0	0	0	.00
Bennett,Shayne,Mon	62	91.2	4	14	0	1	1.000	13	3	0	1	.23
Bere,Jason,ChA-Cin	27	127.1	8	11	1	0	.950	18	6	1	2	.39
Bergman,Sean,Hou	31	172.0	16	14	1	0	.968	10	2	0	0	.20
Bevil,Brian,KC	39	40.0	1	1	0	0	1.000	1	0	0	0	.00
Blair,Willie,Ari-NYN	34	175.1	10	34	1	3	.978	27	10	1	1	.41
Bochtler,Doug,Det	51	67.1	6	4	2	0	.833	10	3	0	0	.30
Boehringer,Brian,SD	56	76.1	7	8	0	0	1.000	7	2	0	0	.29
Bohanon,B.,NYN-LA	39	151.2	10	37	2	3	.959	8	1	2	0	.38
Bones,Ricky,KC	32	53.1	8	15	1	1	.958	5	0	1	0	.20
Borland,Toby,Phi	6	9.0	0	1	0	0	1.000	2	1	0	0	.50
Borowski,Joe,NYA	8	9.2	0	2	0	0	1.000	0	0	0	0	.00
Boskie,Shawn,Mon	5	17.2	0	4	1	0	.800	3	0	0	0	.00
Bottalico,Ricky,Phi	39	43.1	5	6	0	1	1.000	1	0	0	0	.00
Bottenfield,Kent,StL	44	133.2	3	27	0	0	1.000	9	3	0	2	.33
Bradford,Chad,ChA	29	30.2	1	9	1	0	.909	1	0	0	0	.00
Bradley,Ryan,NYA	5	12.2	2	0	0	0	1.000	2	0	0	0	.00
Brantley,Jeff,StL	48	50.2	4	0	0	0	1.000	3	0	0	0	.00
Brewer,Billy,Phi	2	0.1	0	0	0	0	.000	0	0	0	0	.00
Brocail,Doug,Det	60	62.2	8	7	0	1	1.000	7	2	1	0	.43
Brock,Chris,SF	13	27.2	1	2	1	0	.750	2	0	0	0	.00
Brow,Scott,Ari	17	21.1	5	1	1	0	.857	3	1	0	0	.33
Brown,Kevin,SD	36	257.0	32	41	2	2	.973	12	6	1	3	.58
Brownson,Mark,Col	2	13.1	1	0	0	0	1.000	4	0	0	0	.00
Brunson,Will,LA-Det	10	5.1	0	1	0	0	1.000	1	0	0	0	.00
Bruske,J.,LA-SD-NYA	42	60.0	4	4	0	0	1.000	8	1	0	0	.13
Buddie,Mike,NYA	24	41.2	4	3	0	0	1.000	7	3	0	0	.43
Bullinger,Jim,Sea	2	5.2	1	0	0	0	1.000	1	0	0	0	.00
Bullinger,Kirk,Mon	8	7.0	0	3	0	0	1.000	1	0	0	1	.00
Burba,Dave,Cle	32	203.2	15	26	2	4	.953	17	5	0	0	.29
Burkett,John,Tex	32	195.0	11	19	1	0	.968	16	6	1	0	.44
Busby,Mike,StL	26	46.0	3	4	0	1	1.000	3	0	0	0	.00
Butler,Adam,Atl	8	5.0	0	0	1	0	.000	3	0	0	0	.00
Byrd,Paul,Atl-Phi	9	57.0	3	7	1	1	.909	4	1	0	0	.25
Byrdak,Tim,KC	3	1.2	0	0	0	0	.000	0	0	0	0	.00
Cabrera,Jose,Hou	3	4.1	0	1	0	0	1.000	0	0	0	0	.00
Cadaret,G.,Ana-Tex	50	44.2	1	4	0	1	1.000	1	0	0	0	.00
Candiotti,Tom,Oak	33	201.0	16	39	1	2	.982	29	6	1	1	.24
Carlson,Dan,TB	10	17.2	1	2	0	0	1.000	2	2	0	0	1.00
Carpenter,Chris,Tor	33	175.0	20	13	1	2	.971	20	11	0	0	.55
Carrasco,Hector,Min	63	61.2	9	6	0	0	1.000	5	1	0	0	.20
Casian,Larry,ChA	4	4.0	1	1	0	0	1.000	0	0	0	0	.00
Castillo,Carlos,ChA	54	100.1	5	15	1	2	.952	11	1	1	1	.18
Castillo,Frank,Det	27	116.0	8	14	0	1	1.000	17	7	0	0	.41
Castillo,Tony,ChA	25	27.0	1	9	0	1	1.000	4	1	0	0	.50
Cather,Mike,Atl	36	41.1	0	7	1	0	.875	2	2	0	0	1.00

1998 Fielding and Holding Runners

Pitcher,Team	G	Inn	PO	A	E	DP	Pct.	SBA	CS	PCS	PPO	CS%
Charlton,Norm,Bal-Atl	49	48.0	6	9	1	0	.938	7	0	1	0	.14
Checo,Robinson,Bos	2	7.2	0	0	0	0	.000	4	4	0	0	1.00
Chen,Bruce,Atl	4	20.1	0	1	0	0	1.000	1	1	0	0	1.00
Cho,Jin Ho,Bos	4	18.2	3	0	0	0	1.000	2	0	0	0	.00
Chouinard,B.,Mil-Ari	27	41.1	3	4	0	0	1.000	5	1	0	0	.20
Christiansen,Jason,Pit	60	64.2	2	5	1	0	.875	4	2	0	0	.50
Clark,Mark,ChN	33	213.2	11	24	0	0	1.000	36	6	2	0	.22
Clemens,Roger,Tor	33	234.2	7	27	1	1	.971	37	8	1	0	.24
Clement,Matt,SD	4	13.2	0	0	0	0	.000	0	0	0	0	.00
Clontz,Brad,LA-NYN	20	23.2	1	1	1	0	.667	4	1	0	0	.25
Cloude,Ken,Sea	30	155.1	11	15	2	2	.929	12	7	0	1	.58
Colon,Bartolo,Cle	31	204.0	14	34	1	1	.980	8	1	0	0	.13
Cone,David,NYA	31	207.2	12	24	1	3	.973	27	6	0	0	.22
Connelly,Steve,Oak	3	4.2	1	1	0	0	1.000	1	0	0	0	.00
Cook,Dennis,NYN	73	68.0	2	9	1	1	.917	7	0	4	0	.57
Cooke,Steve,Cin	1	6.0	0	1	0	0	1.000	1	0	0	0	.00
Coppinger,Rocky,Bal	6	15.2	1	0	0	0	1.000	2	0	0	0	.00
Cordova,Francisco,Pit	33	220.1	12	30	1	1	.977	16	3	0	3	.19
Corey,Bryan,Ari	3	4.0	0	1	0	0	1.000	0	0	0	0	.00
Corsi,Jim,Bos	59	66.0	3	16	2	2	.905	9	5	0	0	.56
Crabtree,Tim,Tex	64	85.1	4	8	1	2	.923	11	5	0	0	.45
Croushore,Rich,StL	41	54.1	2	13	0	0	1.000	10	0	0	0	.00
Crow,Dean,Det	32	45.2	2	6	0	0	1.000	10	3	1	0	.40
Cunnane,Will,SD	3	3.0	0	1	0	0	1.000	0	0	0	0	.00
Daal,Omar,Ari	33	162.2	6	33	1	2	.975	15	9	3	1	.80
Darensbourg,Vic,Fla	59	71.0	1	5	0	0	1.000	11	2	1	0	.27
Darwin,Danny,SF	33	148.2	11	23	2	1	.944	17	7	0	0	.41
DeLosSantos,V.,Mil	13	21.2	0	2	0	0	1.000	0	0	0	0	.00
DeHart,Rick,Mon	26	28.0	7	6	0	0	1.000	1	0	0	0	.00
DeJean,Mike,Col	59	74.1	6	6	0	3	1.000	11	6	0	0	.55
DeLucia,Rich,Ana	61	71.2	0	6	0	0	1.000	12	4	0	1	.33
Dempster,Ryan,Fla	14	54.2	2	12	0	2	1.000	7	1	0	0	.14
Dessens,Elmer,Pit	43	74.2	4	9	1	0	.929	5	1	0	0	.20
Dickson,Jason,Ana	27	122.0	9	10	1	0	.950	12	5	0	0	.42
Dipoto,Jerry,Col	68	71.1	3	7	0	2	1.000	6	1	0	0	.17
Dodd,Robert,Phi	4	5.0	0	0	0	0	.000	0	0	0	0	.00
Dougherty,Jim,Oak	9	12.0	1	5	0	2	1.000	3	1	1	0	.67
Drabek,Doug,Bal	23	108.2	8	15	1	1	.958	19	3	0	1	.16
Dreifort,Darren,LA	32	180.0	18	41	4	4	.937	20	6	2	0	.40
Duran,Roberto,Det	18	15.1	1	2	0	0	1.000	0	0	0	0	.00
Duvall,Mike,TB	3	4.0	2	1	0	0	1.000	0	0	0	0	.00
Dykhoff,R.,Bal	1	1.0	0	0	0	0	.000	0	0	0	0	.00
Eckersley,Dennis,Bos	50	39.2	2	4	1	0	.857	13	1	0	0	.08
Edmondson,B.,Atl-Fla	53	76.0	7	9	2	0	.889	8	5	0	0	.63
Eiland,Dave,TB	1	2.2	0	0	0	0	.000	1	0	0	0	.00
Elarton,Scott,Hou	28	57.0	4	4	0	1	1.000	1	0	0	0	.00
Eldred,Cal,Mil	23	133.0	9	12	2	4	.913	15	6	0	1	.40
Embree,Alan,Atl-Ari	55	53.2	3	5	0	1	1.000	4	2	1	0	.75
Erdos,Todd,NYA	2	2.0	0	0	0	0	.000	0	0	0	0	.00
Erickson,Scott,Bal	36	251.1	24	50	3	5	.961	35	7	0	1	.20
Escobar,Kelvim,Tor	22	79.2	2	4	0	0	1.000	13	0	0	0	.00
Estes,Shawn,SF	25	149.1	6	28	2	0	.944	10	3	0	0	.30
Evans,Bart,KC	8	9.0	1	1	0	0	1.000	0	0	0	0	.00
Eversgerd,Bryan,StL	8	6.0	2	1	0	0	1.000	0	0	0	0	.00
Eyre,Scott,ChA	33	107.0	1	17	1	3	.947	16	4	3	0	.44
Fassero,Jeff,Sea	32	224.2	11	31	2	0	.955	35	3	8	0	.31
Fetters,Mike,Oak-Ana	60	58.2	2	15	2	1	.895	8	1	1	2	.25
Finley,Chuck,Ana	34	223.1	13	24	3	4	.925	42	9	6	0	.36
Florie,Bryce,Det	42	133.0	14	22	3	5	.923	14	6	0	0	.43
Fontenot,Joe,Fla	8	42.2	4	9	0	1	1.000	4	0	0	0	.00
Ford,Ben,Ari	8	10.0	0	1	1	0	.500	2	0	0	0	.00
Fordham,Tom,ChA	29	48.0	3	11	0	0	1.000	5	3	1	0	.80
Fossas,Sea-ChN-Tex	41	22.2	3	3	0	0	1.000	5	2	0	0	.40
Foster,Kevin,ChN	3	3.1	0	0	0	0	.000	1	0	0	0	.00
Foulke,Keith,ChA	54	65.1	1	8	2	0	.818	4	1	0	0	.25
Fox,Chad,Mil	49	57.0	3	5	0	0	1.000	6	3	0	0	.50
Franco,John,NYN	61	64.2	4	16	0	2	1.000	3	0	1	1	.33
Frascatore,John,StL	69	95.2	11	11	2	1	.917	16	2	0	0	.13
Fussell,Chris,Bal	3	9.2	1	2	0	1	1.000	0	0	0	0	.00
Gaillard,Eddie,TB	6	7.2	0	1	0	0	1.000	0	0	0	0	.00
Gajkowski,Steve,Sea	9	8.2	0	0	0	0	.000	0	0	0	0	.00
Garces,Rich,Bos	30	46.0	2	5	0	0	1.000	6	1	0	0	.17
Gardner,Mark,SF	33	212.0	14	33	0	2	1.000	20	7	0	1	.35
Glauber,Keith,Cin	3	7.2	0	0	0	0	.000	1	0	0	0	.00
Glavine,Tom,Atl	33	229.1	11	50	1	3	.984	13	7	0	0	.54
Gomes,Wayne,Phi	71	93.1	13	6	1	0	.950	11	1	0	0	.09
Gonzalez,Gabe,Fla	3	1.0	0	1	0	0	1.000	0	0	0	0	.00
Gonzalez,Jeremi,ChN	20	110.0	6	13	1	0	.950	10	2	2	2	.40
Gonzalez,Lariel,Col	1	1.0	0	0	0	0	.000	0	0	0	0	.00
Gooden,Dwight,Cle	23	134.0	6	18	0	1	1.000	20	4	0	0	.20
Gordon,Tom,Bos	73	79.1	7	1	0	0	1.000	7	0	0	0	.00
Gorecki,Rick,TB	3	16.2	0	2	0	0	1.000	3	1	0	0	.33
Grace,Mike,Phi	21	90.1	1	10	0	0	1.000	6	1	0	1	.17

1998 Fielding and Holding Runners

Pitcher,Team	G	Inn	PO	A	E	DP	Pct.	SBA	CS	PCS	PPO	CS%
Graves,Danny,Cin	62	81.1	7	15	2	0	.917	8	2	0	0	.25
Green,Tyler,Phi	27	159.1	12	16	4	1	.875	19	8	0	2	.42
Greisinger,Seth,Det	21	130.0	4	15	2	0	.905	24	5	3	0	.33
Groom,Buddy,Oak	75	57.1	1	7	0	0	1.000	10	0	2	0	.20
Grzanich,Mike,Hou	1	1.0	0	0	0	0	.000	0	0	0	0	.00
Guardado,Eddie,Min	79	65.2	6	5	0	0	1.000	3	0	0	0	.00
Gunderson,Eric,Tex	68	67.2	6	10	0	0	1.000	1	0	1	0	1.00
Guthrie,Mark,LA	53	54.0	3	9	1	0	.923	9	0	3	0	.33
Guzman,Juan,Tor-Bal	33	211.0	11	19	4	2	.882	40	8	1	0	.23
Halama,John,Hou	6	32.1	2	5	0	0	1.000	0	0	0	0	.00
Hall,Darren,LA	11	11.1	3	0	0	0	1.000	4	0	0	0	.00
Halladay,Roy,Tor	2	14.0	1	2	0	0	1.000	2	0	0	0	.00
Hamilton,Joey,SD	34	217.1	15	31	3	3	.939	20	7	1	0	.40
Hammond,Chris,Fla	3	13.2	0	0	0	0	.000	0	0	0	0	.00
Hampton,Mike,Hou	32	211.2	11	48	4	7	.937	16	3	4	0	.44
Haney,Chris,KC-ChN	38	102.1	3	22	0	3	1.000	11	0	2	0	.18
Hanson,Erik,Tor	11	49.0	8	7	0	1	1.000	6	0	0	0	.00
Harnisch,Pete,Cin	32	209.0	20	18	0	4	1.000	15	6	0	1	.40
Harriger,Denny,Det	4	12.0	1	1	0	0	1.000	1	0	0	0	.00
Harris,Pep,Ana	49	60.0	4	13	2	1	.895	4	0	1	0	.25
Harris,Reggie,Hou	6	6.0	1	0	0	0	1.000	1	0	0	0	.00
Hartgraves,Dean,SF	5	5.2	0	0	0	0	.000	1	0	0	0	.00
Hasegawa,S.,Ana	61	97.1	3	16	0	2	1.000	4	1	0	0	.25
Hawkins,LaTroy,Min	33	190.1	17	29	0	5	1.000	29	7	1	1	.28
Haynes,Jimmy,Oak	33	194.1	11	19	1	1	.968	18	6	0	4	.33
Heathcott,Mike,ChA	1	3.0	0	0	0	0	.000	0	0	0	0	.00
Helling,Rick,Tex	33	216.1	8	12	1	0	.952	23	12	0	0	.52
Henderson,Ro.,Mil	2	3.2	0	0	0	0	.000	0	0	0	0	.00
Henriquez,Oscar,Fla	15	20.0	0	1	0	0	1.000	1	0	0	0	.00
Henry,Butch,Bos	2	9.0	1	3	0	0	1.000	2	0	1	0	.50
Henry,Doug,Hou	59	71.0	4	4	0	1	1.000	9	0	0	0	.00
Hentgen,Pat,Tor	29	177.2	15	22	2	1	.949	16	4	0	0	.25
Heredia,Felix,Fla-ChN	71	58.2	4	3	1	0	.875	7	3	0	0	.43
Heredia,Gil,Oak	8	42.2	1	9	0	0	1.000	2	1	1	1	1.00
Hermanson,D.,Mon	32	187.0	18	24	4	3	.913	18	6	3	1	.50
Hernandez,Livan,Fla	33	234.1	15	35	0	3	1.000	20	10	1	3	.55
Hernandez,O.,NYA	21	141.0	10	23	0	0	1.000	23	9	0	0	.39
Hernandez,R.,TB	67	71.1	4	9	1	0	.929	7	2	0	0	.29
Hernandez,Xavier,Tex	46	58.0	3	3	0	0	1.000	2	1	0	0	.50
Hershiser,Orel,SF	34	202.0	21	36	1	3	.983	12	3	0	0	.25
Hill,Ken,Ana	19	103.0	14	20	0	3	1.000	29	8	1	0	.31
Hitchcock,Sterling,SD	39	176.1	6	17	0	2	1.000	18	0	2	0	.11
Hoffman,Trevor,SD	66	73.0	3	4	0	1	1.000	7	0	0	0	.00
Holdridge,David,Sea	7	6.2	0	0	0	0	.000	0	0	0	0	.00
Holmes,Darren,NYA	34	51.1	4	5	1	2	.900	6	1	0	0	.17
Holtz,Mike,Ana	53	30.1	0	2	0	0	1.000	4	3	0	0	.75
Holzemer,Mark,Oak	13	9.2	2	0	0	0	1.000	1	0	0	0	.00
Howry,Bob,ChA	44	54.1	2	7	1	0	.900	5	2	0	0	.40
Hudek,John,NYN-Cin	58	64.0	3	7	0	0	1.000	9	3	1	0	.44
Hudson,Joe,Mil	1	0.1	0	0	0	0	.000	0	0	0	0	.00
Hutton,Mark,Cin	10	17.0	3	4	0	1	1.000	3	0	0	0	.00
Irabu,Hideki,NYA	29	173.0	6	18	2	1	.923	25	9	0	2	.36
Jackson,Mike,Cle	69	64.0	6	11	1	2	.944	5	4	0	1	.80
Jacome,Jason,Cle	1	5.0	0	0	0	0	.000	1	1	0	0	1.00
James,Mike,Ana	11	14.0	0	1	0	0	1.000	2	2	0	0	1.00
Jerzembeck,M.,NYA	3	6.1	0	1	0	0	1.000	1	0	0	0	.00
Jimenez,Jose,StL	4	21.1	0	5	0	0	1.000	0	0	0	0	.00
Johns,Doug,Bal	31	86.2	6	24	1	2	.968	18	3	7	0	.56
Johnson,Jason,TB	13	60.0	2	4	0	0	1.000	8	4	0	0	.50
Johnson,J.,Tex	1	4.1	1	1	0	0	1.000	1	0	0	0	.00
Johnson,Mike,Mon	2	7.1	0	1	0	0	1.000	2	0	0	0	.00
Johnson,R.,Sea-Hou	34	244.1	6	30	9	3	.800	50	13	6	0	.38
Johnstone,John,SF	70	88.0	8	5	0	0	1.000	15	3	0	0	.20
Jones,Bobby,NYN	30	195.1	14	33	2	3	.959	31	11	0	1	.35
Jones,BobbyM.,Col	35	141.1	8	18	3	0	.897	22	5	2	0	.32
Jones,Doug,Mil-Cle	69	85.1	4	14	1	2	.947	3	1	0	0	.33
Jones,Todd,Det	65	63.1	7	7	0	2	1.000	4	0	0	0	.00
Jordan,Ricardo,Cin	6	3.1	1	0	0	0	1.000	0	0	0	0	.00
Judd,Mike,LA	7	11.1	0	4	0	0	1.000	2	0	0	0	.00
Juden,Jeff,Mil-Ana	32	178.1	9	19	3	2	.903	53	6	0	0	.11
Kamieniecki,Scott,Bal	12	54.2	12	10	0	0	1.000	10	2	0	2	.20
Karchner,M.,ChA-ChN	61	64.2	3	11	0	0	1.000	11	1	0	0	.09
Karl,Scott,Mil	33	192.1	12	38	0	3	1.000	15	3	1	1	.27
Karsay,Steve,Cle	11	24.1	3	2	0	0	1.000	2	2	0	0	1.00
Keagle,Greg,Det	9	38.2	3	5	0	0	1.000	6	1	0	0	.17
Key,Jimmy,Bal	25	79.1	4	11	0	3	1.000	9	6	0	0	.67
Kile,Darryl,Col	36	230.1	22	32	3	1	.947	20	5	0	0	.25
King,Curtis,StL	36	51.0	9	9	0	1	1.000	2	0	0	0	.00
Kline,Steve,Mon	78	71.2	3	10	1	0	.929	9	3	0	0	.33
Klingenbeck,Scott,Cin	4	22.2	4	3	0	0	1.000	1	0	0	0	.00
Krivda,Rick,Cle-Cin	27	51.1	3	5	0	0	1.000	5	1	1	0	.40
Kroon,Marc,SD-Cin	6	7.2	0	3	0	0	1.000	2	0	1	0	.50
Kubenka,Jeff,LA	6	9.1	0	3	1	0	.750	3	2	0	0	.67
Langston,Mark,SD	22	81.1	2	17	1	1	.950	10	1	1	0	.20
Lankford,Frank,LA	12	19.2	6	8	0	0	1.000	4	1	0	0	.25
Larkin,Andy,Fla	17	74.2	4	11	0	1	1.000	15	2	0	0	.13

1998 Fielding and Holding Runners

Pitcher,Team	G	Inn	PO	A	E	DP	Pct.	SBA	CS	PCS	PPO	CS%
Lawrence,Sean,Pit	7	19.2	0	2	0	0	1.000	0	0	0	0	.00
Leiter,Al,NYN	28	193.0	4	18	0	0	1.000	15	4	0	0	.27
Leiter,Mark,Phi	69	88.2	12	8	1	2	.952	4	2	0	0	.50
Leskanic,Curt,Col	66	75.2	5	9	0	0	1.000	4	3	0	0	.75
Levine,Al,Tex	30	58.0	4	7	0	1	1.000	2	0	0	0	.00
Lewis,Richie,Bal	2	4.2	1	0	0	0	1.000	1	1	0	0	1.00
Lieber,Jon,Pit	29	171.0	12	16	0	1	1.000	13	6	0	0	.46
Ligtenberg,Kerry,Atl	75	73.0	1	2	2	0	.600	7	1	0	0	.14
Lima,Jose,Hou	33	233.1	24	32	3	3	.949	17	3	1	0	.24
Lira,Felipe,Sea	7	15.2	2	2	0	1	1.000	1	0	0	0	.00
Lloyd,Graeme,NYA	50	37.2	3	5	1	1	.889	2	0	0	0	.00
Loaiza,E.,Pit-Tex	35	171.0	22	23	0	3	1.000	20	6	0	0	.30
Loewer,Carlton,Phi	21	122.2	6	15	1	0	.955	17	3	1	0	.24
Loiselle,Rich,Pit	54	55.0	2	10	0	0	1.000	5	2	0	0	.40
Looper,Braden,StL	4	3.1	0	0	0	0	.000	0	0	0	0	.00
Lopez,Albie,TB	54	79.2	3	15	0	0	1.000	8	4	0	0	.50
Lorraine,Andrew,Sea	4	3.2	0	0	0	0	.000	0	0	0	0	.00
Lowe,Derek,Bos	63	123.0	12	24	4	4	.900	22	5	0	0	.23
Lowe,Sean,StL	4	5.1	1	1	0	0	1.000	0	0	0	0	.00
Ludwick,Eric,Fla	13	32.2	2	4	1	1	.857	6	1	0	0	.17
Maddux,Greg,Atl	34	251.0	31	64	4	5	.960	39	10	1	0	.28
Maddux,Mike,Mon	51	55.2	3	10	0	0	1.000	6	0	0	0	.00
Magnante,Mike,Hou	48	51.2	6	17	0	0	1.000	4	0	1	0	.25
Mahay,Ron,Bos	29	26.0	1	2	1	0	.750	6	0	0	0	.00
Maloney,Sean,LA	11	12.2	2	2	0	1	1.000	1	0	0	0	.00
Mantei,Matt,Fla	42	54.2	4	5	0	1	1.000	3	2	0	1	.67
Manuel,Barry,Ari	13	15.2	1	0	0	0	1.000	1	0	0	0	.00
Martin,Tom,Cle	14	14.2	1	2	0	0	1.000	1	0	0	0	.00
Martinez,Dennis,Atl	53	91.0	6	16	1	2	.957	9	2	0	1	.22
Martinez,Javier,Pit	37	41.0	2	0	1	0	.667	8	1	0	0	.13
Martinez,Pedro,Bos	33	233.2	11	19	4	3	.882	20	5	1	1	.30
Martinez,Ramon,LA	15	101.2	10	17	0	1	1.000	8	4	0	0	.50
Mathews,T.J.,Oak	66	72.2	4	7	1	1	.917	8	1	0	0	.13
Mathews,Terry,Bal	17	20.1	3	6	0	0	1.000	3	0	0	0	.00
McCarthy,Greg,Sea	29	23.1	1	6	0	0	1.000	6	0	1	0	.17
McCurry,Jeff,Pit	16	19.1	1	3	0	0	1.000	2	0	0	1	.00
McDill,Allen,KC	7	6.0	0	1	0	0	1.000	0	0	0	0	.00
McDowell,Jack,Ana	14	76.0	3	12	0	1	1.000	12	3	2	1	.42
McElroy,Chuck,Col	78	68.1	0	6	0	2	1.000	6	2	1	0	.50
McMichael,G.,NYN-LA	64	68.0	5	16	0	1	1.000	12	2	2	0	.33
Meadows,Brian,Fla	31	174.1	18	21	1	2	.975	17	4	0	0	.24
Mecir,Jim,TB	68	84.0	9	16	0	2	1.000	8	3	0	0	.38
Medina,Rafael,Fla	12	67.1	5	4	0	2	1.000	11	0	0	0	.00
Mendoza,Ramiro,NYA	41	130.1	11	25	1	3	.973	6	4	0	0	.67
Mercedes,Jose,Mil	7	32.0	0	3	0	0	1.000	5	1	0	0	.20
Mercker,Kent,StL	31	161.2	3	26	2	0	.935	18	7	3	0	.56
Mesa,Jose,Cle-SF	76	84.2	5	11	2	1	.889	4	2	0	0	.50
Miceli,Dan,SD	67	72.2	4	3	0	1	1.000	3	1	0	0	.33
Michalak,Chris,Ari	5	5.1	0	0	0	0	.000	1	0	0	0	.00
Miller,Kurt,ChN	3	4.0	0	0	0	0	.000	0	0	0	0	.00
Miller,Travis,Min	14	23.1	1	2	1	0	.750	0	0	0	0	.00
Miller,Trever,Hou	37	53.1	4	6	0	0	1.000	5	1	1	0	.40
Mills,Alan,Bal	72	77.0	8	9	0	2	1.000	13	2	0	0	.15
Millwood,Kevin,Atl	31	174.1	9	16	1	1	.962	12	5	0	0	.42
Milton,Eric,Min	32	172.1	8	20	0	1	1.000	16	4	2	0	.38
Mlicki,Dave,NYN-LA	30	181.1	21	22	1	1	.977	18	8	0	1	.44
Moehler,Brian,Det	33	221.1	10	35	1	1	.978	21	8	1	1	.43
Mohler,Mike,Oak	57	61.0	1	7	1	1	.889	6	2	0	0	.33
Montgomery,Jeff,KC	56	56.0	5	4	0	1	1.000	2	0	0	0	.00
Moore,Trey,Mon	13	61.0	6	10	0	0	1.000	13	0	3	0	.23
Morgan,Mike,Min-ChN	23	120.2	15	21	1	3	.973	11	4	0	2	.36
Morman,Alvin,Cle-SF	40	29.0	2	5	0	0	1.000	6	1	1	0	.33
Morris,Matt,StL	17	113.2	4	17	1	5	.955	10	3	0	1	.30
Moyer,Jamie,Sea	34	234.1	16	31	1	1	.979	25	3	1	0	.16
Mulholland,Terry,ChN	70	112.0	7	10	4	1	.810	0	0	0	1	.00
Mullins,Greg,Mil	2	1.0	0	0	0	0	.000	0	0	0	0	.00
Munoz,Bobby,Bal	9	12.0	1	2	0	0	1.000	3	0	0	0	.00
Munoz,Mike,Col	40	41.1	3	6	0	1	1.000	5	1	1	0	.40
Mussina,Mike,Bal	29	206.1	12	38	0	1	1.000	27	7	0	0	.26
Myers,Mike,Mil	70	50.0	3	10	2	4	.867	8	1	1	0	.25
Myers,Randy,Tor-SD	62	56.2	0	4	0	0	1.000	4	2	0	0	.50
Myers,Rodney,ChN	12	18.0	0	2	0	0	1.000	0	0	0	1	.00
Nagy,Charles,Cle	33	210.1	17	46	2	4	.969	30	9	0	1	.30
Naulty,Dan,Min	19	23.2	1	0	0	0	1.000	3	1	0	0	.33
Navarro,Jaime,ChA	37	172.2	8	20	1	1	.966	32	6	0	0	.19
Neagle,Denny,Atl	32	210.1	4	20	0	0	1.000	12	4	0	4	.33
Nelson,Jeff,NYA	45	40.1	3	9	0	0	1.000	6	1	0	0	.17
Nen,Robb,SF	78	88.2	4	8	1	1	.923	10	0	0	0	.00
Nitkowski,C.J.,Hou	43	59.2	1	10	0	2	1.000	7	2	2	0	.57
Nomo,Hideo,LA-NYN	29	157.1	10	14	0	0	1.000	33	8	0	0	.24
Nunez,Vladimir,Ari	4	5.1	0	0	0	0	.000	0	0	0	0	.00
Nye,Ryan,Phi	1	1.0	0	0	0	0	.000	0	0	0	0	.00
Ogea,Chad,Cle	19	69.0	2	9	0	1	1.000	7	1	0	0	.14
Ojala,Kirt,Fla	41	125.0	9	24	3	4	.917	16	2	4	0	.38
Olivares,Omar,Ana	37	183.0	21	39	5	3	.923	18	7	0	0	.39
Oliver,Darren,Tex-StL	29	160.1	5	26	1	1	.969	26	5	8	0	.50

1998 Fielding and Holding Runners

Pitcher,Team	G	Inn	PO	A	E	DP	Pct.	SBA	CS	PCS	PPO	CS%
Olson,Gregg,Ari	64	68.2	4	7	0	0	1.000	9	2	0	0	.22
Oquist,Mike,Oak	31	175.0	7	15	0	3	1.000	15	6	0	0	.40
Orosco,Jesse,Bal	69	56.2	1	6	0	1	1.000	10	1	0	0	.10
Ortiz,Russ,SF	22	88.1	9	13	1	2	.957	15	4	0	0	.27
Osborne,Donovan,StL	14	83.2	6	8	3	2	.824	4	2	0	0	.50
Osuna,Antonio,LA	54	64.2	3	8	1	1	.917	4	3	0	2	.75
Painter,Lance,StL	65	47.1	6	12	0	1	1.000	1	0	1	0	1.00
Pall,Donn,Fla	23	33.1	3	5	0	0	1.000	5	2	0	0	.40
Paniagua,Jose,Sea	18	22.0	2	5	0	1	1.000	1	1	0	0	1.00
Park,ChanHo,LA	34	220.2	19	28	4	5	.922	18	7	1	1	.44
Parque,Jim,ChA	21	113.0	7	16	0	1	1.000	14	2	6	2	.57
Parris,Steve,Cin	18	99.0	5	21	0	0	1.000	10	3	0	0	.30
Patrick,Bronswell,Mil	32	78.2	2	7	0	0	1.000	4	1	0	1	.25
Patterson,Bob,ChN	33	20.1	0	2	0	0	1.000	5	0	1	0	.20
Patterson,Danny,Tex	56	60.2	3	7	0	0	1.000	4	1	2	0	.75
Pavano,Carl,Mon	24	134.2	15	13	2	1	.933	23	6	0	0	.26
Pavlik,Roger,Tex	5	14.0	0	2	0	0	1.000	0	0	0	0	.00
Pennington,Brad,TB	1	0.0	0	0	0	0	.000	0	0	0	0	.00
Percival,Troy,Ana	67	66.2	2	4	1	1	.857	18	2	0	0	.11
Perez,Carlos,Mon-LA	34	241.0	11	44	0	3	1.000	38	7	8	1	.39
Perez,Odalis,Atl	10	10.2	0	1	0	0	1.000	0	0	0	0	.00
Perez,Yorkis,Phi	57	52.0	3	7	1	0	.909	6	0	0	0	.00
Perisho,Matt,Tex	2	5.0	0	0	0	0	.000	2	0	0	0	.00
Person,Robert,Tor	27	38.1	2	2	1	0	.800	4	1	0	0	.25
Peters,Chris,Pit	39	148.0	3	16	3	2	.864	12	1	1	0	.17
Petkovsek,Mark,StL	48	105.2	8	11	1	1	.950	7	4	0	0	.57
Pettitte,Andy,NYA	33	216.1	11	36	1	5	.979	23	1	5	3	.26
Pichardo,Hipolito,KC	27	112.1	11	18	0	5	1.000	11	0	0	0	.00
Pickett,Ricky,Ari	2	0.2	0	0	0	0	.000	0	0	0	0	.00
Pisciotta,Marc,ChN	43	44.0	2	5	0	1	1.000	4	0	0	0	.00
Pittsley,Jim,KC	39	68.1	5	11	2	1	.889	8	2	0	0	.25
Plesac,Dan,Tor	78	50.0	0	1	0	0	1.000	9	2	0	0	.22
Plunk,Eric,Cle-Mil	63	72.2	0	5	1	0	.833	16	3	2	0	.31
Politte,Cliff,StL	8	37.0	3	4	1	0	.875	4	2	0	0	.50
Ponson,Sidney,Bal	31	135.0	10	11	1	1	.955	23	4	0	0	.17
Poole,Jim,SF-Cle	38	39.1	4	6	0	0	1.000	5	0	1	0	.20
Portugal,Mark,Phi	26	166.1	24	17	3	2	.932	9	2	0	1	.22
Powell,Brian,Det	18	83.2	6	8	1	0	.933	6	4	0	0	.67
Powell,Jay,Fla-Hou	62	70.1	8	5	0	0	1.000	4	2	0	0	.50
Powell,Jeremy,Mon	7	25.0	2	3	0	0	1.000	9	4	0	0	.44
Priest,Eddie,Cin	2	6.0	0	0	0	0	.000	0	0	0	0	.00
Prieto,Ariel,Oak	2	8.1	0	1	0	0	1.000	3	1	0	0	.33
Pulsipher,Bill,NYN-Mil	26	72.1	1	12	0	0	1.000	2	0	1	0	.50
Quantrill,Paul,Tor	82	80.0	4	14	0	2	1.000	5	0	0	0	.00
Radinsky,Scott,LA	62	61.2	2	9	1	0	.917	5	4	0	1	.80
Radke,Brad,Min	32	213.2	12	34	1	1	.979	35	12	0	0	.34
Raggio,Brady,StL	4	7.0	1	1	0	1	1.000	0	0	0	0	.00
Rakers,Jason,Cle	1	1.0	0	0	0	0	.000	0	0	0	0	.00
Ramirez,Roberto,SD	21	14.2	0	1	0	0	1.000	0	0	0	0	.00
Rapp,Pat,KC	32	188.1	20	23	1	0	.977	19	10	0	1	.53
Rath,Fred,Col	2	5.1	0	0	0	0	.000	0	0	0	0	.00
Rath,Gary,LA	3	3.1	0	0	0	0	.000	0	0	0	0	.00
Reed,Rick,NYN	31	212.1	12	37	1	2	.980	21	14	0	2	.67
Reed,Steve,SF-Cle	70	80.1	4	9	1	1	.929	7	3	0	0	.43
Rekar,Bryan,TB	16	86.2	12	7	2	0	.905	5	1	0	0	.20
Remlinger,Mike,Cin	35	164.1	7	16	2	1	.920	22	6	1	2	.32
Reyes,Al,Mil	50	57.0	2	6	2	1	.800	6	3	0	0	.50
Reyes,Carlos,SD-Bos	46	66.0	5	10	0	0	1.000	8	4	1	0	.63
Reyes,Dennis,LA-Cin	19	67.1	1	12	3	0	.813	10	2	2	4	.40
Reynolds,Shane,Hou	35	233.1	24	40	2	9	.970	17	11	0	1	.65
Reynoso,A.,NYN	11	68.1	5	24	1	2	.967	5	2	0	2	.40
Rhodes,Arthur,Bal	45	77.0	2	5	2	0	.778	16	2	1	0	.19
Rincon,Ricardo,Pit	60	65.0	3	9	2	2	.857	3	1	0	0	.33
Rios,Danny,KC	5	7.1	1	0	0	0	1.000	1	0	0	0	.00
Risley,Bill,Tor	44	54.2	2	3	0	1	1.000	13	3	0	0	.23
Ritchie,Todd,Min	15	24.0	0	0	0	0	.000	0	0	0	0	.00
Ritz,Kevin,Col	2	9.0	2	3	0	0	1.000	5	1	0	0	.20
Rivera,Mariano,NYA	54	61.1	3	14	0	1	1.000	2	0	0	1	.00
Rizzo,Todd,ChA	9	6.2	0	0	1	0	.000	0	0	0	0	.00
Robertson,Rich,Ana	5	5.2	1	3	0	0	1.000	0	0	0	0	.00
Rocker,John,Atl	47	38.0	1	6	0	0	1.000	2	0	0	0	.00
Rodriguez,Felix,Ari	43	44.0	1	11	0	0	1.000	4	0	0	0	.00
Rodriguez,Frank,Min	20	70.0	8	9	2	0	.895	7	3	0	0	.43
Rodriguez,N.,Bal-Tor	13	27.1	0	1	0	0	1.000	6	2	0	0	.33
Rodriguez,Rich,SF	68	65.2	10	11	1	0	.955	4	0	1	0	.25
Rogers,Kenny,Oak	34	238.2	18	67	2	4	.977	15	2	7	3	.60
Rojas,Mel,NYN	50	58.0	6	11	1	1	.944	17	3	1	0	.24
Roque,Rafael,Mil	9	48.0	3	10	0	1	1.000	2	0	0	0	.00
Rosado,Jose,KC	38	174.2	8	28	2	1	.947	11	2	0	2	.18
Rose,Brian,Bos	8	37.2	4	4	0	1	1.000	6	0	0	0	.00
Ruebel,Matt,TB	7	8.2	1	0	0	0	1.000	2	1	0	0	.50
Rueter,Kirk,SF	33	187.2	12	39	2	2	.962	9	2	2	0	.44
Runyan,Sean,Det	88	50.1	2	1	0	0	1.000	8	1	1	0	.25
Rusch,Glendon,KC	29	154.2	9	22	1	4	.969	15	5	1	0	.40
Ryan,Ken,Phi	17	22.2	1	4	0	0	1.000	1	0	0	0	.00
Saberhagen,Bret,Bos	31	175.0	13	20	1	1	.971	11	7	0	1	.64

1998 Fielding and Holding Runners

Pitcher,Team	G	Inn	PO	A	E	DP	Pct.	SBA	CS	PCS	PPO	CS%
Sager,A.J.,Det	31	59.1	3	14	0	2	1.000	14	3	0	0	.21
Saipe,Mike,Col	2	10.0	2	2	0	0	1.000	2	0	0	0	.00
Sampson,Benj,Min	5	17.1	0	1	0	0	1.000	2	0	0	0	.00
Sanchez,Jesus,Fla	35	173.0	6	33	2	4	.951	19	3	8	4	.58
Sanders,Scott,Det-SD	26	40.1	5	5	1	0	.909	7	0	1	0	.14
Santana,Julio,Tex-TB	35	145.2	6	11	2	0	.895	13	5	0	0	.38
Santana,Marino,Det	7	7.1	0	1	0	0	1.000	0	0	0	0	.00
Santiago,Jose,KC	2	2.0	0	1	0	0	1.000	0	0	0	0	.00
Saunders,Tony,TB	31	192.1	12	18	1	4	.968	23	7	3	0	.43
Scanlan,Bob,Hou	27	26.1	4	1	1	0	.833	2	2	0	0	1.00
Schilling,Curt,Phi	35	268.2	17	33	2	3	.962	15	4	1	0	.33
Schmidt,Jason,Pit	33	214.1	7	16	2	2	.920	20	5	2	0	.35
Schourek,P.,Hou-Bos	25	124.0	1	9	0	0	1.000	16	4	3	0	.44
Seanez,Rudy,Atl	34	36.0	3	1	0	0	1.000	4	1	0	0	.25
Sele,Aaron,Tex	33	212.2	18	20	2	3	.950	12	8	0	0	.67
Serafini,Dan,Min	28	75.0	1	8	0	1	1.000	7	1	0	1	.14
Service,Scott,KC	73	82.2	4	15	1	0	.950	11	4	1	3	.45
Shaw,Jeff,Cin-LA	73	85.0	8	18	3	0	.897	7	0	0	1	.00
Shouse,Brian,Bos	7	8.0	0	2	0	0	1.000	0	0	0	0	.00
Shuey,Paul,Cle	43	51.0	3	5	1	0	.889	11	3	0	0	.27
Silva,Jose,Pit	18	100.1	3	18	0	1	1.000	10	3	0	0	.30
Simas,Bill,ChA	60	70.2	9	5	0	1	1.000	6	0	0	0	.00
Sinclair,Steve,Tor	24	15.0	0	4	0	1	1.000	2	1	0	0	.50
Sirotka,Mike,ChA	33	211.2	9	33	1	1	.977	24	7	3	0	.42
Slocumb,H.,Sea	57	67.2	6	8	1	0	.933	11	4	0	0	.36
Small,Aaron,Oak-Ari	47	67.2	3	4	0	0	1.000	4	1	1	0	.50
Smith,Pete,SD-Bal	37	88.1	5	17	1	3	.957	23	0	1	0	.04
Smith,Travis,Mil	1	2.0	0	0	0	0	.000	1	0	0	0	.00
Smoltz,John,Atl	26	167.2	12	20	0	2	1.000	10	2	0	0	.20
Snyder,John,ChA	15	86.1	8	14	1	0	.957	8	6	0	1	.75
Sodowsky,Clint,Ari	45	77.2	4	12	1	1	.941	8	1	0	1	.13
Sparks,Steve,Ana	22	128.2	12	30	0	2	1.000	14	3	1	4	.29
Speier,Justin,ChN-Fla	19	20.2	0	2	0	0	1.000	4	1	0	0	.25
Spencer,Stan,SD	6	30.2	1	1	0	0	1.000	3	0	0	0	.00
Spoljaric,Paul,Sea	53	83.1	3	9	0	0	1.000	11	0	1	1	.09
Spradlin,Jerry,Phi	69	81.2	8	8	0	1	1.000	10	2	1	0	.30
Springer,Dennis,TB	29	115.2	7	11	0	2	1.000	19	4	0	0	.21
Springer,Russ,Ari-Atl	48	52.2	2	2	1	0	.800	9	2	0	0	.22
Stanifer,Robby,Fla	38	48.0	5	4	1	0	.900	6	1	0	0	.17
Stanton,Mike,NYA	67	79.0	7	6	1	0	.929	2	1	1	0	1.00
Steenstra,Kennie,ChN	4	3.1	0	0	0	0	.000	2	0	0	0	.00
Stein,Blake,Oak	24	117.1	0	15	1	1	.938	15	2	3	1	.33
Stephenson,G.,Phi	6	23.0	3	1	0	0	1.000	2	1	0	0	.50
Stevens,Dave,ChN	31	38.0	1	1	0	0	1.000	12	4	0	0	.33
Stieb,Dave,Tor	19	50.1	5	5	0	0	1.000	8	3	0	0	.38
Stoops,Jim,Col	3	4.0	1	1	0	1	1.000	3	3	0	0	1.00
Stottlemyre,T.,StL-Tex	33	221.2	20	27	1	2	.979	18	4	1	0	.28
Sullivan,Scott,Cin	67	102.0	9	11	1	1	.952	13	2	1	0	.23
Suppan,Jeff,Ari-KC	17	78.2	7	18	0	2	1.000	9	4	0	0	.44
Suzuki,Makoto,Sea	6	26.1	0	2	0	0	1.000	3	0	0	0	.00
Swift,Bill,Sea	29	144.2	16	28	4	3	.917	19	3	0	1	.16
Swindell,G.,Min-Bos	81	90.1	10	9	0	1	1.000	6	0	3	0	.50
Tabaka,Jeff,Pit	37	50.2	1	10	1	1	.917	2	0	1	0	.50
Tam,Jeff,NYN	15	14.1	3	1	0	0	1.000	1	0	0	0	.00
Tapani,Kevin,ChN	35	219.0	11	31	0	1	1.000	16	3	0	0	.19
Tatis,Ramon,TB	22	11.2	1	4	0	1	1.000	1	1	0	0	1.00
Tavarez,Julian,SF	60	85.1	4	10	1	1	.933	9	1	1	0	.22
Taylor,Billy,Oak	70	73.0	4	8	0	2	1.000	7	0	0	0	.00
Telemaco,A.,ChN-Ari	41	148.2	13	20	2	0	.943	9	2	0	1	.22
Telford,Anthony,Mon	77	91.0	5	18	1	1	.958	4	2	1	0	.75
Telgheder,Dave,Oak	8	20.0	0	2	0	0	1.000	1	0	0	0	.00
Tessmer,Jay,NYA	7	8.2	0	0	0	0	.000	1	1	0	0	1.00
Tewksbury,Bob,Min	26	148.1	12	31	2	3	.956	14	3	0	0	.21
Thompson,Justin,Det	34	222.0	6	35	0	2	1.000	37	7	9	3	.43
Thompson,Mark,Col	6	23.1	3	2	0	0	1.000	1	1	0	0	1.00
Thomson,John,Col	26	161.0	15	15	0	3	1.000	13	3	0	1	.23
Thurman,Mike,Mon	14	67.0	1	12	0	0	1.000	13	5	1	0	.46
Timlin,Mike,Sea	70	79.1	10	13	0	1	1.000	1	0	0	0	.00
Tomko,Brett,Cin	34	210.2	14	25	1	1	.975	22	6	0	1	.27
Trachsel,Steve,ChN	33	208.0	23	34	2	1	.966	16	6	2	4	.50
Trombley,Mike,Min	77	96.2	4	9	0	0	1.000	6	4	0	0	.67
Urbina,Ugueth,Mon	64	69.1	2	3	0	0	1.000	6	0	0	1	.00
Valdes,Ismael,LA	27	174.0	12	25	1	1	.974	16	5	0	0	.31
Valdes,Marc,Mon	20	36.1	3	6	0	0	1.000	10	0	0	0	.00
Valdez,Carlos,Bos	4	3.1	0	0	0	0	.000	0	0	0	0	.00
Valdez,Efrain,Ari	6	4.1	1	1	0	0	1.000	0	0	0	0	.00
VanPoppel,T.,Tex-Pit	22	66.1	1	3	0	0	1.000	14	2	0	0	.14
VanRyn,ChN-SD-Tor	25	14.2	1	0	0	0	1.000	3	1	0	0	.33
Vazquez,Javier,Mon	33	172.1	12	24	0	3	1.000	18	7	2	0	.50
Veras,Dario,Bos	7	8.0	1	0	0	0	1.000	0	0	0	0	.00
Veres,Dave,Col	63	76.1	7	11	0	0	1.000	8	2	1	1	.38
Villone,Ron,Cle	25	27.0	2	4	0	0	1.000	4	1	1	0	.50
Wade,Terrell,TB	2	10.2	0	0	0	0	.000	0	0	0	0	.00
Wagner,Billy,Hou	58	60.0	2	2	1	0	.800	2	0	0	0	.00
Wagner,Paul,Mil	13	55.2	3	7	0	1	1.000	8	1	0	0	.13
Wainhouse,David,Col	10	11.0	2	4	0	2	1.000	0	0	0	0	.00

1998 Fielding and Holding Runners

Pitcher,Team	G	Inn	PO	A	E	DP	Pct.	SBA	CS	PCS	PPO	CS%
Wakefield,Tim,Bos	36	216.0	16	22	3	1	.927	32	8	0	0	.25
Walker,Jamie,KC	6	17.1	2	4	0	1	1.000	5	1	2	0	.60
Wall,Donne,SD	46	70.1	4	10	0	2	1.000	5	2	0	0	.40
Ward,Bryan,ChA	28	27.0	2	0	0	0	1.000	3	0	0	0	.00
Wasdin,John,Bos	47	96.0	6	14	1	1	.952	13	2	0	0	.15
Washburn,Jarrod,Ana	15	74.0	4	8	0	0	1.000	12	1	1	0	.17
Watson,Allen,Ana	28	92.1	4	15	0	0	1.000	22	2	2	1	.18
Weathers,D.,Cin-Mil	44	110.0	5	14	0	1	1.000	14	2	1	1	.21
Weaver,Eric,LA	7	9.2	0	1	0	1	1.000	3	3	0	0	1.00
Weber,Neil,Ari	4	2.1	0	0	0	0	.000	0	0	0	0	.00
Welch,Mike,Phi	10	20.2	2	2	0	1	1.000	2	0	0	0	.00
Wells,Bob,Sea	30	51.2	5	4	0	0	1.000	0	0	0	0	.00
Wells,David,NYA	30	214.1	8	27	3	1	.921	16	5	2	0	.44
Wendell,Turk,NYN	66	76.2	5	12	1	0	.944	10	0	1	2	.10
Wengert,Don,SD-ChN	31	63.1	2	8	0	1	1.000	4	0	0	0	.00
West,David,Bos	6	2.0	0	0	0	0	.000	0	0	0	0	.00
Wetteland,John,Tex	63	62.0	2	7	1	0	.900	1	0	0	0	.00
Whisenant,Matt,KC	70	60.2	3	10	0	1	1.000	3	1	0	1	.33
White,Gabe,Cin	69	98.2	4	12	0	0	1.000	9	2	3	0	.56
White,Rick,TB	38	68.2	5	11	2	1	.889	6	4	0	0	.67
Whiteside,Matt,Phi	10	18.0	2	2	0	0	1.000	3	0	0	0	.00
Wickman,Bob,Mil	72	82.1	10	13	2	1	.920	9	1	0	0	.11
Wilkins,Marc,Pit	16	15.1	0	1	0	0	1.000	1	0	0	1	.00
Williams,Mike,Pit	37	51.0	0	13	1	0	.929	9	3	2	1	.56
Williams,Todd,Cin	6	9.1	0	1	0	0	1.000	0	0	0	0	.00
Williams,Woody,Tor	32	209.2	12	18	3	4	.909	22	5	0	3	.23
Wilson,Trevor,Ana	15	7.2	1	1	0	1	1.000	0	0	0	0	.00
Winchester,Scott,Cin	16	79.0	6	8	0	1	1.000	14	2	0	0	.14
Winston,Darrin,Phi	27	25.0	2	3	0	0	1.000	1	0	0	0	.00
Witasick,Jay,Oak	7	27.0	1	2	0	1	1.000	2	1	0	0	.50
Withem,Shannon,Tor	1	3.0	0	1	0	0	1.000	0	0	0	0	.00
Witt,Bobby,Tex-StL	31	116.2	5	12	2	2	.895	13	5	0	0	.38
Wohlers,Mark,Atl	27	20.1	3	1	0	0	1.000	3	0	0	0	.00
Wolcott,Bob,Ari	6	33.0	3	2	1	1	.833	4	3	0	0	.75
Wood,Kerry,ChN	26	166.2	4	9	0	1	1.000	22	8	2	1	.45
Woodall,Brad,Mil	32	138.0	5	26	2	4	.939	8	1	1	1	.25
Woodard,Steve,Mil	34	165.2	9	15	1	0	.960	21	3	1	1	.19
Worrell,T,Det-Cle-Oak	43	103.0	8	15	0	1	1.000	9	0	0	0	.00
Wright,Jamey,Col	34	206.1	18	36	2	5	.964	28	7	0	8	.25
Wright,Jaret,Cle	32	192.2	16	26	1	0	.977	20	5	0	0	.25
Yan,Esteban,TB	64	88.2	9	11	1	1	.952	15	3	0	1	.20
Yoshii,Masato,NYN	29	171.2	14	20	3	2	.919	18	3	0	0	.17
Young,Tim,Mon	10	6.0	0	2	0	0	1.000	0	0	0	0	.00

Hitters Pitching

Player	1998 Pitching											Career Pitching										
	G	W	L	Sv	IP	H	R	ER	BB	SO	ERA	G	W	L	Sv	IP	H	R	ER	BB	SO	ERA
Alexander, Manny	0	0	0	0	0.0	0	0	0	0	0	0.00	1	0	0	0	0.2	1	5	5	4	0	67.50
Benjamin, Mike	0	0	0	0	0.0	0	0	0	0	0	0.00	1	0	0	0	1.0	0	0	0	0	0	0.00
Boggs, Wade	0	0	0	0	0.0	0	0	0	0	0	0.00	1	0	0	0	1.0	0	0	0	1	1	0.00
Cangelosi, John	0	0	0	0	0.0	0	0	0	0	0	0.00	3	0	0	0	4.0	1	0	0	2	0	0.00
Canseco, Jose	0	0	0	0	0.0	0	0	0	0	0	0.00	1	0	0	0	1.0	2	3	3	3	0	27.00
Davis, Chili	0	0	0	0	0.0	0	0	0	0	0	0.00	1	0	0	0	2.0	0	0	0	0	0	0.00
Gaetti, Gary	1	0	0	0	1.0	2	0	0	0	0	0.00	2	0	0	0	1.1	3	0	0	0	0	0.00
Halter, Shane	1	0	0	0	1.0	1	0	0	0	0	0.00	1	0	0	0	1.0	1	0	0	0	0	0.00
Harris, Lenny	1	0	0	0	1.0	0	0	0	0	1	0.00	1	0	0	0	1.0	0	0	0	0	1	0.00
Howard, David	0	0	0	0	0.0	0	0	0	0	0	0.00	1	0	0	0	2.0	2	1	1	5	0	4.50
Jackson, Darrin	0	0	0	0	0.0	0	0	0	0	0	0.00	1	0	0	0	2.0	3	2	2	2	0	9.00
Martinez, Dave	0	0	0	0	0.0	0	0	0	0	0	0.00	2	0	0	0	1.1	2	2	2	4	0	13.50
O'Neill, Paul	0	0	0	0	0.0	0	0	0	0	0	0.00	1	0	0	0	2.0	2	3	3	4	2	13.50
Tomberlin, Andy	0	0	0	0	0.0	0	0	0	0	0	0.00	1	0	0	0	2.0	1	0	0	1	1	0.00
Whiten, Mark	1	0	0	0	1.0	1	1	1	2	3	9.00	1	0	0	0	1.0	1	1	1	2	3	9.00

Park Data

Is the remodeled Edison International Field of Anaheim less hitter-friendly than the old Big A? How much did Tropicana Field and Bank One Ballpark contribute to their respective teams' pitching woes? You'll find the answers on the following pages.

For each park, we show how the home team and its opponents performed, both at home and on the road with the exception being that we do *not* include data from interleague games. By comparing the overall totals at the home park and on the road, we can evaluate the park's impact. We simply divide the home total by the road total and multiply the result by 100, generating a "park index." If the home and road totals are equal, the index equals 100, and we can conclude that the park had no impact. An index above 100 means that the park favors that particular statistic.

The indexes for at-bats, runs, hits, errors, and infield errors are determined on a per-game basis; all other stats are calculated on a per-at-bat basis. "E-infield" denotes infield *fielding* errors. "Alt" is the approximate elevation of the ballpark.

For most parks, data is presented both for 1998 and for the last three years overall. If the park's dimensions have changed over that time, however, we do not combine the data from its "old" and "new" configurations. At the end, you'll find a rankings section that shows which parks inflate runs, homers and batting average the most.

Anaheim Angels—Edison Int'l Field of Anaheim

Alt: 160 feet **Surface:** Grass

	1998 Season							1996-1997						
	Home Games			Away Games				Home Games			Away Games			
	Angels	Opp	Total	Angels	Opp	Total	Index	Angels	Opp	Total	Angels	Opp	Total	Index
G	73	73	146	73	73	146	—	155	155	310	152	152	304	98
Avg	.264	.258	.261	.280	.273	.276	94	.277	.264	.270	.273	.278	.276	98
AB	2445	2522	4967	2631	2449	5080	98	5336	5525	10861	5412	5118	10530	101
R	327	362	689	379	345	724	95	803	820	1623	726	823	1549	103
H	645	650	1295	736	668	1404	92	1476	1461	2937	1478	1425	2903	99
2B	125	146	271	164	155	319	87	260	261	521	244	274	518	98
3B	17	10	27	8	11	19	145	17	12	29	29	29	58	48
HR	48	82	130	81	64	145	92	184	232	416	155	162	317	127
BB	223	292	515	235	286	521	101	542	570	1112	535	642	1177	92
SO	447	527	974	474	456	930	107	921	1099	2020	903	902	1805	109
E	48	57	105	47	54	101	104	137	136	273	118	110	228	117
E-Infield	40	50	90	44	44	88	102	100	98	198	93	84	177	110
LHB-Avg	.282	.259	.271	.287	.278	.283	96	.280	.263	.273	.280	.264	.274	100
LHB-HR	25	31	56	44	28	72	76	87	87	174	78	54	132	126
RHB-Avg	.246	.257	.252	.274	.269	.271	93	.274	.265	.269	.266	.286	.277	97
RHB-HR	23	51	74	37	36	73	107	97	145	242	77	108	185	128

ANAHEIM

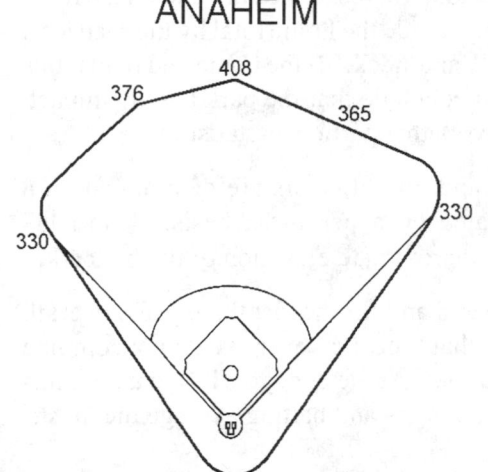

ARIZONA

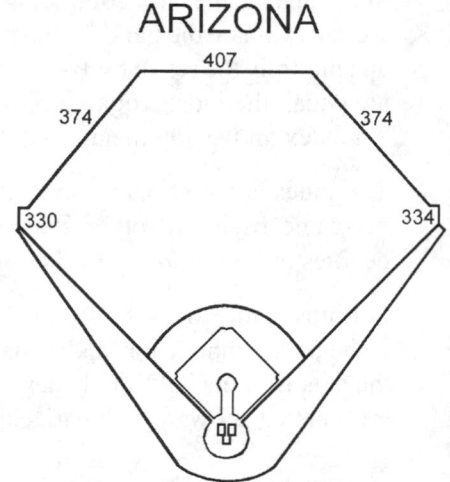

Arizona Diamondbacks—Bank One Ballpark

Alt: 1090 feet **Surface:** Grass

	1998 Season							1998 Season						
	Home Games			Away Games				Home Games			Away Games			
	D-backs	Opp	Total	D-backs	Opp	Total	Index	D-backs	Opp	Total	D-backs	Opp	Total	Index
G	73	73	146	76	76	152	—	73	73	146	76	76	152	—
Avg	.256	.263	.260	.231	.264	.247	105	.256	.263	.260	.231	.264	.247	105
AB	2443	2565	5008	2576	2473	5049	103	2443	2565	5008	2576	2473	5049	103
R	301	351	652	286	379	665	102	301	351	652	286	379	665	102
H	626	675	1301	595	654	1249	108	626	675	1301	595	654	1249	108
2B	99	123	222	116	118	234	96	99	123	222	116	118	234	96
3B	23	19	42	19	10	29	146	23	19	42	19	10	29	146
HR	66	81	147	73	89	162	91	66	81	147	73	89	162	91
BB	218	188	406	236	267	503	81	218	188	406	236	267	503	81
SO	511	392	903	634	440	1074	85	511	392	903	634	440	1074	85
E	42	47	89	43	58	101	92	42	47	89	43	58	101	92
E-Infield	34	39	73	31	43	74	103	34	39	73	31	43	74	103
LHB-Avg	.252	.264	.258	.238	.271	.252	102	.252	.264	.258	.238	.271	.252	102
LHB-HR	25	27	52	30	27	57	92	25	27	52	30	27	57	92
RHB-Avg	.260	.262	.261	.224	.261	.244	107	.260	.262	.261	.224	.261	.244	107
RHB-HR	41	54	95	43	62	105	91	41	54	95	43	62	105	91

Atlanta Braves—Turner Field

Alt: 1050 feet **Surface:** Grass

| | 1998 Season | | | | | | | 1997-1998 | | | | | | |
| | Home Games | | | Away Games | | | | Home Games | | | Away Games | | | |
	Braves	Opp	Total	Braves	Opp	Total	Index	Braves	Opp	Total	Braves	Opp	Total	Index
G	73	73	146	73	73	146	—	148	148	296	145	145	290	—
Avg	.280	.243	.261	.263	.234	.249	105	.278	.240	.258	.263	.241	.252	102
AB	2385	2473	4858	2542	2366	4908	99	4876	5053	9929	5043	4740	9783	99
R	365	252	617	372	256	628	98	722	523	1245	735	515	1250	98
H	667	602	1269	669	553	1222	104	1354	1212	2566	1328	1142	2470	102
2B	135	98	233	133	89	222	106	242	214	456	268	193	461	97
3B	13	14	27	10	10	20	136	33	24	57	24	19	43	131
HR	93	47	140	98	53	151	94	161	97	258	185	101	286	89
BB	248	217	465	254	207	461	102	540	440	980	513	401	914	106
SO	476	559	1035	478	560	1038	101	993	1117	2110	1008	1083	2091	99
E	41	54	95	38	59	97	98	105	119	224	80	119	199	110
E-Infield	37	42	79	34	48	82	96	88	95	183	66	100	166	108
LHB-Avg	.277	.236	.258	.253	.245	.250	103	.284	.236	.263	.263	.252	.259	101
LHB-HR	35	14	49	32	21	53	91	70	30	100	78	35	113	84
RHB-Avg	.282	.248	.264	.271	.227	.249	106	.271	.242	.255	.263	.234	.248	103
RHB-HR	58	33	91	66	32	98	96	91	67	158	107	66	173	92

ATLANTA

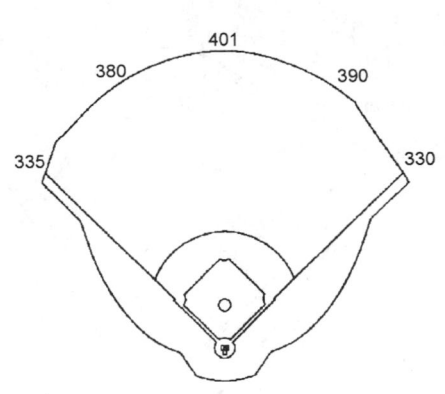

BALTIMORE

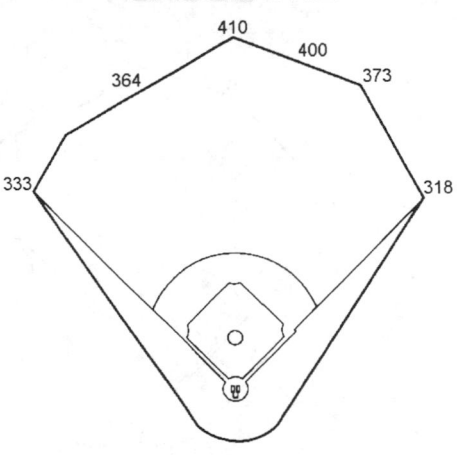

Baltimore Orioles—Oriole Park at Camden Yards

Alt: 20 feet **Surface:** Grass

| | 1998 Season | | | | | | | 1996-1998 | | | | | | |
| | Home Games | | | Away Games | | | | Home Games | | | Away Games | | | |
	Orioles	Opp	Total	Orioles	Opp	Total	Index	Orioles	Opp	Total	Orioles	Opp	Total	Index
G	73	73	146	73	73	146	—	227	227	454	229	229	458	—
Avg	.274	.257	.265	.275	.282	.278	95	.268	.262	.265	.277	.273	.275	96
AB	2459	2518	4977	2568	2465	5033	99	7609	7947	15556	8164	7764	15928	99
R	353	328	681	400	372	772	88	1138	1081	2219	1307	1134	2441	92
H	674	646	1320	705	696	1401	94	2038	2086	4124	2260	2123	4383	95
2B	115	121	236	156	122	278	86	343	361	704	478	406	884	82
3B	6	9	15	4	15	19	80	24	30	54	35	46	81	68
HR	99	73	172	97	81	178	98	313	258	571	316	249	565	103
BB	256	221	477	294	258	552	87	821	751	1572	898	832	1730	93
SO	380	498	878	426	461	887	100	1268	1564	2832	1302	1475	2777	104
E	30	37	67	47	41	88	76	142	133	275	139	148	287	97
E-Infield	24	35	59	37	31	68	87	110	118	228	103	112	215	107
LHB-Avg	.268	.245	.257	.271	.290	.280	92	.280	.254	.268	.285	.281	.283	95
LHB-HR	47	26	73	48	31	79	92	167	94	261	170	97	267	99
RHB-Avg	.279	.266	.273	.278	.276	.277	99	.256	.269	.263	.269	.268	.269	98
RHB-HR	52	47	99	49	50	99	102	146	164	310	146	152	298	107

Boston Red Sox—Fenway Park

Alt: 21 feet **Surface:** Grass

	1998 Season							1996-1998						
	Home Games			Away Games				Home Games			Away Games			
	Red Sox	Opp	Total	Red Sox	Opp	Total	Index	Red Sox	Opp	Total	Red Sox	Opp	Total	Index
G	73	73	146	73	73	146	—	226	226	452	229	229	458	—
Avg	.292	.265	.278	.264	.249	.257	108	.299	.273	.286	.272	.270	.271	105
AB	2456	2573	5029	2581	2400	4981	101	7861	8140	16001	8217	7746	15963	102
R	394	337	731	381	323	704	104	1296	1166	2462	1188	1195	2383	105
H	717	681	1398	681	597	1278	109	2347	2223	4570	2238	2089	4327	107
2B	166	133	299	131	108	239	124	521	458	979	422	374	796	123
3B	18	7	25	15	7	22	113	51	36	87	44	36	80	108
HR	86	75	161	104	78	182	88	289	221	510	280	246	526	97
BB	247	227	474	242	235	477	98	825	826	1651	762	918	1680	98
SO	477	499	976	462	444	906	107	1421	1567	2988	1484	1440	2924	102
E	46	48	94	48	39	87	108	203	145	348	171	163	334	106
E-Infield	42	42	84	44	32	76	111	162	113	275	144	125	269	104
LHB-Avg	.302	.271	.286	.268	.271	.270	106	.312	.282	.297	.271	.280	.276	108
LHB-HR	40	28	68	54	39	93	74	133	93	226	133	101	234	94
RHB-Avg	.284	.260	.272	.260	.229	.245	111	.288	.265	.276	.273	.261	.268	103
RHB-HR	46	47	93	50	39	89	101	156	128	284	147	145	292	99

BOSTON

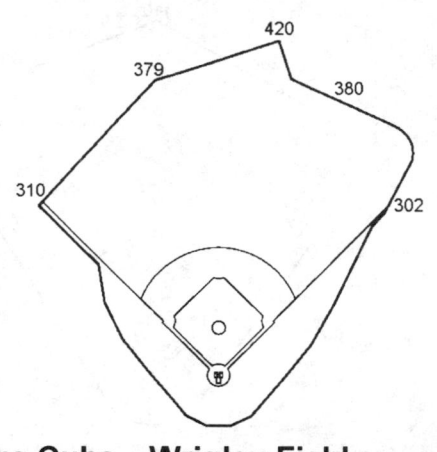

CHICAGO CUBS

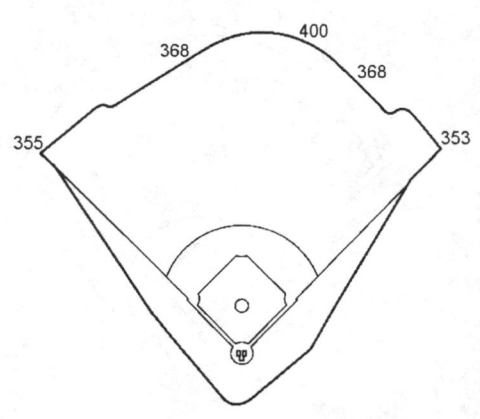

Chicago Cubs—Wrigley Field

Alt: 595 feet **Surface:** Grass

	1998 Season							1996-1998						
	Home Games			Away Games				Home Games			Away Games			
	Cubs	Opp	Total	Cubs	Opp	Total	Index	Cubs	Opp	Total	Cubs	Opp	Total	Index
G	77	77	154	73	73	146	—	229	229	458	230	230	460	—
Avg	.275	.262	.269	.256	.266	.261	103	.268	.257	.262	.247	.270	.258	102
AB	2589	2744	5333	2614	2520	5134	98	7706	8062	15768	8004	7717	15721	101
R	390	372	762	379	354	733	99	1148	1065	2213	992	1122	2114	105
H	713	720	1433	670	671	1341	101	2069	2070	4139	1978	2082	4060	102
2B	115	145	260	111	128	239	105	352	400	752	383	432	815	92
3B	17	15	32	15	16	31	99	45	42	87	40	54	94	92
HR	102	84	186	91	82	173	104	269	273	542	214	249	463	117
BB	284	270	554	263	256	519	103	771	794	1565	707	816	1523	102
SO	534	607	1141	593	512	1105	99	1513	1652	3165	1626	1470	3096	102
E	49	51	100	46	57	103	92	160	201	361	162	173	335	108
E-Infield	38	38	76	35	49	84	86	123	161	284	117	149	266	107
LHB-Avg	.295	.273	.284	.272	.280	.275	103	.297	.263	.279	.264	.274	.269	104
LHB-HR	40	34	74	34	29	63	111	80	91	171	81	97	178	98
RHB-Avg	.258	.254	.256	.243	.256	.250	103	.251	.252	.251	.236	.267	.251	100
RHB-HR	62	50	112	57	53	110	99	189	182	371	133	152	285	127

Chicago White Sox—Comiskey Park

Alt: 595 feet **Surface:** Grass

| | 1998 Season | | | | | | | 1996-1998 | | | | | | |
| | Home Games | | | Away Games | | | Index | Home Games | | | Away Games | | | Index |
	White Sox	Opp	Total	White Sox	Opp	Total		White Sox	Opp	Total	White Sox	Opp	Total	
G	74	74	148	73	73	146	—	230	230	460	225	225	450	98
Avg	.282	.272	.277	.261	.281	.271	102	.277	.265	.271	.275	.280	.277	98
AB	2417	2580	4997	2589	2508	5097	97	7595	8069	15664	8061	7751	15812	97
R	395	409	804	381	410	791	100	1154	1154	2308	1243	1239	2482	91
H	682	702	1384	677	704	1381	99	2105	2140	4245	2217	2169	4386	95
2B	139	138	277	125	135	260	109	385	402	787	401	440	841	94
3B	16	14	30	18	11	29	106	48	41	89	46	39	85	106
HR	95	86	181	87	101	188	98	236	250	486	284	274	558	88
BB	262	256	518	242	253	495	107	875	820	1695	864	842	1706	100
SO	360	407	767	450	412	862	91	1153	1401	2554	1387	1341	2728	95
E	59	54	113	73	61	134	83	173	148	321	207	168	375	84
E-Infield	49	47	96	64	52	116	82	136	110	246	160	124	284	85
LHB-Avg	.276	.297	.287	.266	.291	.279	103	.278	.271	.275	.279	.291	.285	96
LHB-HR	28	40	68	22	42	64	114	75	103	178	108	125	233	79
RHB-Avg	.286	.256	.271	.259	.273	.265	102	.276	.261	.268	.271	.271	.271	99
RHB-HR	67	46	113	65	59	124	90	161	147	308	176	149	325	94

CHICAGO WHITE SOX

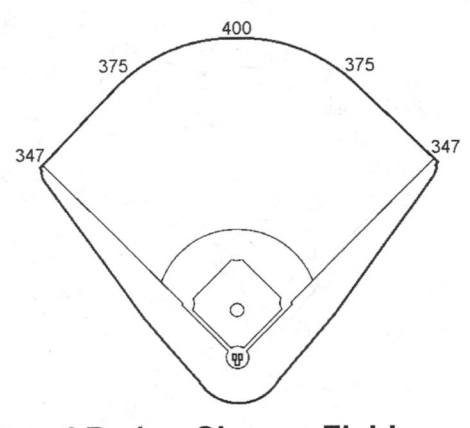

CINCINNATI

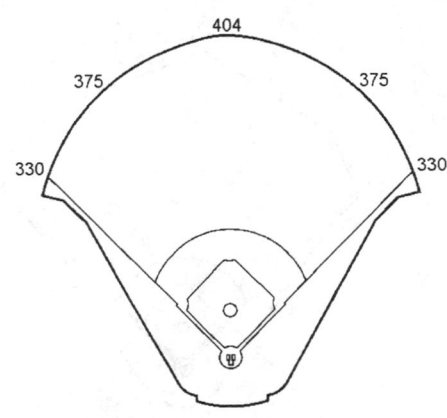

Cincinnati Reds—Cinergy Field

Alt: 550 feet **Surface:** Turf

| | 1998 Season | | | | | | | 1996-1998 | | | | | | |
| | Home Games | | | Away Games | | | Index | Home Games | | | Away Games | | | Index |
	Reds	Opp	Total	Reds	Opp	Total		Reds	Opp	Total	Reds	Opp	Total	
G	73	73	146	76	76	152	—	226	226	452	232	232	464	—
Avg	.257	.241	.249	.266	.267	.266	93	.261	.247	.254	.252	.269	.260	98
AB	2386	2468	4854	2655	2522	5177	98	7401	7756	15157	8082	7752	15834	98
R	356	344	700	347	359	706	103	1066	1059	2125	998	1122	2120	103
H	614	594	1208	705	674	1379	91	1935	1918	3853	2033	2087	4120	96
2B	144	140	284	136	138	274	111	416	416	832	360	420	780	111
3B	11	14	25	13	17	30	89	42	53	95	44	49	93	107
HR	63	72	135	67	81	148	97	217	239	456	233	239	472	101
BB	303	285	588	262	251	513	122	895	816	1711	750	823	1573	114
SO	491	511	1002	544	496	1040	103	1490	1604	3094	1710	1535	3245	100
E	57	43	100	58	58	116	90	168	157	325	189	198	387	86
E-Infield	47	35	82	40	47	87	98	136	112	248	137	152	289	88
LHB-Avg	.256	.255	.256	.287	.264	.276	93	.267	.263	.265	.262	.268	.265	100
LHB-HR	25	20	45	28	23	51	103	90	88	178	94	73	167	115
RHB-Avg	.258	.231	.245	.251	.270	.260	94	.257	.238	.247	.243	.270	.257	96
RHB-HR	38	52	90	39	58	97	93	127	151	278	139	166	305	93

Cleveland Indians—Jacobs Field

Alt: 660 feet **Surface:** Grass

	1998 Season							1996-1998						
	Home Games			Away Games			Index	Home Games			Away Games			Index
	Indians	Opp	Total	Indians	Opp	Total		Indians	Opp	Total	Indians	Opp	Total	
G	73	73	146	73	73	146	—	228	228	456	225	225	450	—
Avg	.286	.287	.286	.253	.263	.258	111	.290	.277	.283	.277	.270	.274	103
AB	2476	2641	5117	2561	2472	5033	102	7726	8133	15859	8030	7654	15684	100
R	410	380	790	350	342	692	114	1295	1146	2441	1204	1090	2294	105
H	709	757	1466	648	649	1297	113	2240	2253	4493	2224	2070	4294	103
2B	145	157	302	150	126	276	108	448	474	922	454	381	835	109
3B	15	13	28	13	16	29	95	41	29	70	30	47	77	90
HR	92	74	166	85	83	168	97	286	233	519	313	268	581	88
BB	287	273	560	276	242	518	106	933	792	1725	868	737	1605	106
SO	426	501	927	536	451	987	92	1266	1546	2812	1393	1387	2780	100
E	61	53	114	43	43	86	133	179	204	383	171	172	343	110
E-Infield	48	44	92	34	35	69	133	126	154	280	126	136	262	105
LHB-Avg	.297	.294	.295	.257	.261	.259	114	.300	.285	.292	.277	.280	.278	105
LHB-HR	39	40	79	40	40	80	100	131	108	239	137	121	258	92
RHB-Avg	.277	.280	.278	.249	.264	.257	109	.282	.270	.276	.277	.261	.270	102
RHB-HR	53	34	87	45	43	88	94	155	125	280	176	147	323	86

CLEVELAND

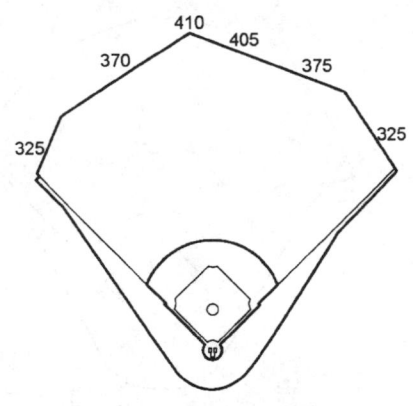

COLORADO

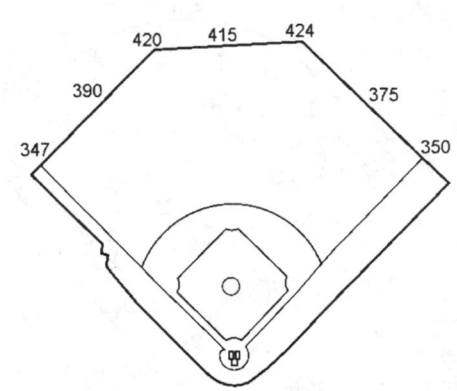

Colorado Rockies—Coors Field

Alt: 5280 feet **Surface:** Grass

	1998 Season							1996-1998						
	Home Games			Away Games			Index	Home Games			Away Games			Index
	Rockies	Opp	Total	Rockies	Opp	Total		Rockies	Opp	Total	Rockies	Opp	Total	
G	75	75	150	75	75	150	—	229	229	458	229	229	458	—
Avg	.326	.302	.314	.256	.263	.259	121	.330	.307	.318	.245	.270	.257	124
AB	2653	2715	5368	2561	2403	4964	108	8104	8356	16460	7731	7452	15183	108
R	485	465	950	280	314	594	160	1629	1478	3107	925	1082	2007	155
H	864	819	1683	656	632	1288	131	2674	2565	5239	1895	2013	3908	134
2B	168	142	310	140	126	266	108	492	473	965	348	408	756	118
3B	18	25	43	14	15	29	137	66	69	135	40	57	97	128
HR	102	94	196	68	63	131	138	361	328	689	245	209	454	140
BB	242	249	491	195	269	464	98	807	800	1607	673	851	1524	97
SO	389	421	810	478	452	930	81	1292	1275	2567	1635	1306	2941	81
E	50	60	110	43	49	92	120	182	223	405	183	176	359	113
E-Infield	32	46	78	36	42	78	100	131	170	301	152	128	280	108
LHB-Avg	.329	.310	.319	.278	.267	.272	117	.332	.315	.322	.253	.286	.271	119
LHB-HR	38	39	77	26	29	55	125	101	129	230	83	92	175	119
RHB-Avg	.323	.295	.309	.242	.260	.250	124	.329	.301	.316	.241	.258	.249	127
RHB-HR	64	55	119	42	34	76	149	260	199	459	162	117	279	154

Detroit Tigers—Tiger Stadium

Alt: 585 feet **Surface:** Grass

	1998 Season							1997-1998						
	Home Games			Away Games			Index	Home Games			Away Games			Index
	Tigers	Opp	Total	Tigers	Opp	Total		Tigers	Opp	Total	Tigers	Opp	Total	
G	73	73	146	73	73	146	—	145	145	290	148	148	296	—
Avg	.260	.271	.266	.268	.287	.278	96	.256	.263	.260	.266	.283	.274	95
AB	2466	2582	5048	2627	2468	5095	99	4819	5107	9926	5263	4999	10262	99
R	326	396	722	323	396	719	100	688	746	1434	673	780	1453	101
H	641	700	1341	705	709	1414	95	1236	1342	2578	1400	1415	2815	93
2B	109	130	239	169	129	298	81	216	241	457	306	258	564	84
3B	11	13	24	15	21	36	67	27	28	55	26	39	65	87
HR	83	100	183	64	70	134	138	166	189	355	139	150	289	127
BB	205	277	482	200	263	463	105	505	524	1029	429	533	962	111
SO	468	442	910	486	408	894	103	987	891	1878	1011	853	1864	104
E	61	61	122	48	43	91	134	103	123	226	90	85	175	132
E-Infield	51	51	102	41	37	78	131	86	102	188	73	74	147	131
LHB-Avg	.256	.264	.260	.278	.292	.285	91	.267	.263	.265	.272	.290	.281	94
LHB-HR	45	36	81	34	37	71	116	88	77	165	73	72	145	122
RHB-Avg	.263	.276	.270	.261	.283	.271	99	.249	.263	.256	.262	.277	.269	95
RHB-HR	38	64	102	30	33	63	162	78	112	190	66	78	144	133

DETROIT

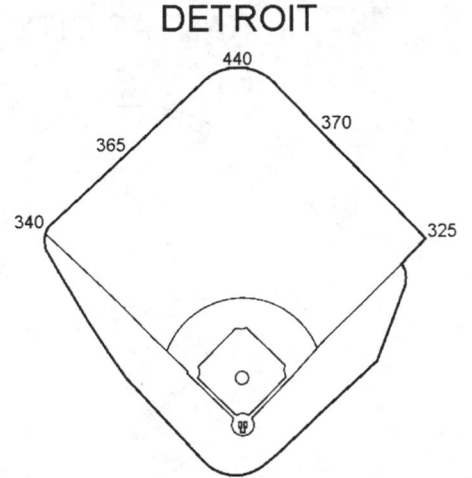

440 · 370 · 365 · 340 · 325

FLORIDA

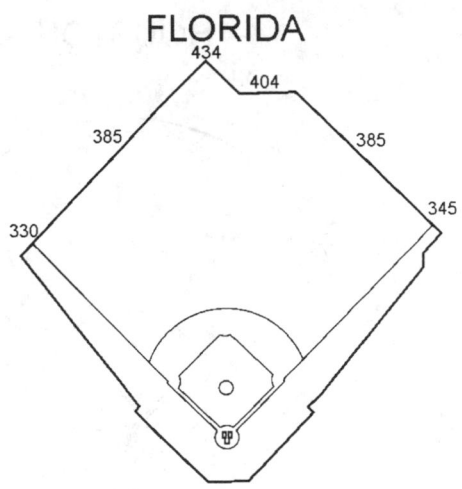

434 · 404 · 385 · 385 · 330 · 345

Florida Marlins—Pro Player Stadium

Alt: 10 feet **Surface:** Grass

	1998 Season							1996-1998						
	Home Games			Away Games			Index	Home Games			Away Games			Index
	Marlins	Opp	Total	Marlins	Opp	Total		Marlins	Opp	Total	Marlins	Opp	Total	
G	73	73	146	73	73	146	—	229	229	458	226	226	452	—
Avg	.246	.270	.258	.253	.308	.280	92	.258	.246	.252	.253	.285	.269	94
AB	2462	2575	5037	2544	2480	5024	100	7509	7776	15285	7928	7613	15541	97
R	297	395	692	309	462	771	90	991	970	1961	965	1202	2167	89
H	605	695	1300	643	763	1406	92	1937	1912	3849	2005	2170	4175	91
2B	121	135	256	130	148	278	92	340	342	682	394	403	797	87
3B	17	20	37	17	19	36	103	54	52	106	36	62	98	110
HR	46	84	130	58	82	140	93	176	190	366	204	212	416	89
BB	252	314	566	220	341	561	101	872	894	1766	773	917	1690	106
SO	500	480	980	521	421	942	104	1504	1583	3087	1620	1438	3058	103
E	58	62	120	65	46	111	108	174	180	354	191	173	364	96
E-Infield	49	55	104	55	38	93	112	137	140	277	154	126	280	98
LHB-Avg	.249	.283	.264	.261	.323	.287	92	.253	.260	.256	.252	.298	.274	94
LHB-HR	22	29	51	26	26	52	95	43	64	107	59	70	129	82
RHB-Avg	.242	.262	.254	.244	.299	.274	93	.261	.237	.249	.254	.277	.265	94
RHB-HR	24	55	79	32	56	88	92	133	126	259	145	142	287	93

Houston Astros—The Astrodome   Alt: 40 feet   Surface: Turf

	1998 Season							1996-1998						
	Home Games			Away Games			Index	Home Games			Away Games			Index
	Astros	Opp	Total	Astros	Opp	Total		Astros	Opp	Total	Astros	Opp	Total	
G	73	73	146	75	75	150	—	226	226	452	231	231	462	—
Avg	.285	.251	.267	.270	.264	.267	100	.270	.248	.259	.263	.274	.268	96
AB	2487	2585	5072	2666	2552	5218	100	7558	7926	15484	8127	7813	15940	99
R	387	275	662	385	303	688	99	1095	880	1975	1157	1081	2238	90
H	708	648	1356	721	674	1395	100	2043	1966	4009	2141	2138	4279	96
2B	157	145	302	141	108	249	125	454	415	869	435	369	804	111
3B	14	8	22	12	18	30	75	45	36	81	46	38	84	99
HR	70	68	138	75	71	146	97	186	179	365	213	234	447	84
BB	307	199	506	262	232	494	105	847	646	1493	862	787	1649	93
SO	501	591	1092	530	505	1035	109	1500	1851	3351	1594	1465	3059	113
E	45	52	97	55	63	118	84	178	176	354	216	199	415	87
E-Infield	34	45	79	46	53	99	82	136	145	281	158	153	311	92
LHB-Avg	.264	.243	.249	.272	.262	.265	94	.259	.254	.256	.262	.276	.271	94
LHB-HR	7	23	30	10	21	31	89	26	70	96	33	80	113	84
RHB-Avg	.289	.256	.275	.270	.265	.268	102	.274	.244	.260	.264	.272	.268	97
RHB-HR	63	45	108	65	50	115	101	160	109	269	180	154	334	84

HOUSTON

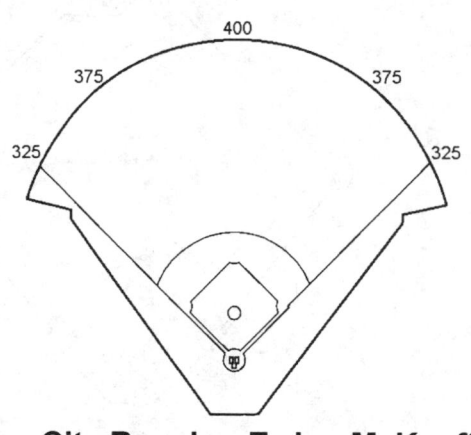

KANSAS CITY

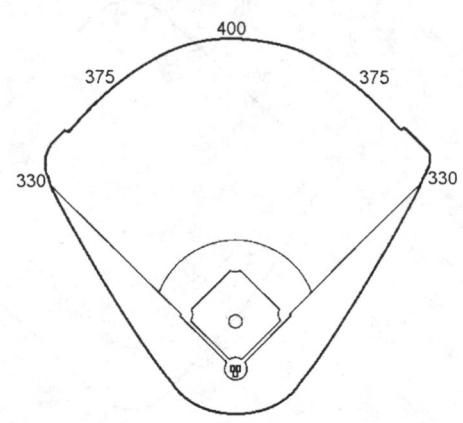

Kansas City Royals—Ewing M. Kauffman Stadium   Alt: 750 feet   Surface: Grass

	1998 Season							1996-1998						
	Home Games			Away Games			Index	Home Games			Away Games			Index
	Royals	Opp	Total	Royals	Opp	Total		Royals	Opp	Total	Royals	Opp	Total	
G	72	72	144	73	73	146	—	226	226	452	226	226	452	—
Avg	.255	.289	.273	.267	.278	.272	100	.264	.279	.272	.263	.277	.270	101
AB	2405	2622	5027	2576	2461	5037	101	7697	8139	15836	7917	7672	15589	102
R	314	447	761	336	382	718	107	1033	1217	2250	1031	1145	2176	103
H	614	758	1372	687	684	1371	101	2034	2267	4301	2084	2128	4212	102
2B	103	133	236	146	133	279	85	366	378	744	392	414	806	91
3B	23	13	36	11	8	19	190	67	54	121	39	30	69	173
HR	64	101	165	53	81	134	123	191	282	473	189	248	437	107
BB	234	242	476	199	276	475	100	754	689	1443	705	781	1486	96
SO	416	445	861	462	439	901	96	1287	1297	2584	1488	1396	2884	88
E	59	51	110	52	56	108	103	162	168	330	158	182	340	97
E-Infield	54	40	94	46	48	94	101	129	138	267	121	141	262	102
LHB-Avg	.269	.274	.271	.278	.263	.271	100	.268	.283	.275	.275	.273	.274	100
LHB-HR	15	31	46	13	27	40	119	56	110	166	55	101	156	106
RHB-Avg	.247	.299	.274	.259	.289	.273	100	.261	.275	.269	.253	.281	.267	101
RHB-HR	49	70	119	40	54	94	124	135	172	307	134	147	281	107

Los Angeles Dodgers—Dodger Stadium

Alt: 340 feet **Surface:** Grass

| | 1998 Season | | | | | | | 1996-1998 | | | | | | |
| | Home Games | | | Away Games | | | Index | Home Games | | | Away Games | | | Index |
	Dodgers	Opp	Total	Dodgers	Opp	Total		Dodgers	Opp	Total	Dodgers	Opp	Total	
G	76	76	152	73	73	146	—	230	230	460	227	227	454	—
Avg	.255	.233	.244	.247	.261	.254	96	.254	.228	.241	.258	.263	.261	93
AB	2466	2566	5032	2536	2414	4950	98	7537	7812	15349	7987	7647	15634	97
R	310	265	575	301	364	665	83	927	804	1731	1039	1048	2087	82
H	630	599	1229	627	631	1258	94	1918	1785	3703	2064	2011	4075	90
2B	88	111	199	100	116	216	91	277	299	576	341	388	729	80
3B	10	3	13	15	20	35	37	35	15	50	53	55	108	47
HR	74	61	135	73	67	140	95	206	176	382	243	217	460	85
BB	201	262	463	211	285	496	92	661	743	1404	722	819	1541	93
SO	473	558	1031	491	532	1023	99	1472	1757	3229	1664	1656	3320	99
E	56	57	113	64	59	123	88	197	193	390	182	192	374	103
E-Infield	49	48	97	55	43	98	95	148	152	300	144	135	279	106
LHB-Avg	.231	.247	.241	.234	.270	.255	94	.238	.244	.242	.252	.267	.260	93
LHB-HR	13	24	37	11	27	38	100	21	78	99	31	92	123	80
RHB-Avg	.264	.224	.246	.252	.255	.253	97	.262	.216	.241	.261	.260	.261	92
RHB-HR	61	37	98	62	40	102	93	185	98	283	212	125	337	87

LOS ANGELES

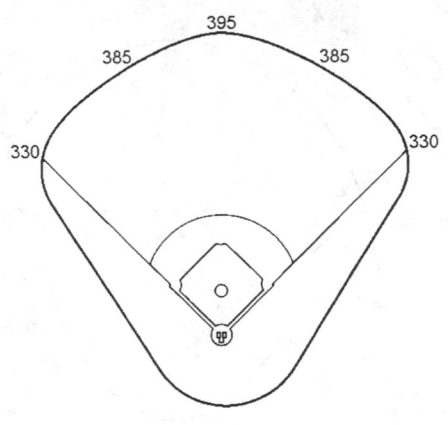

395
385 385
330 330

MILWAUKEE

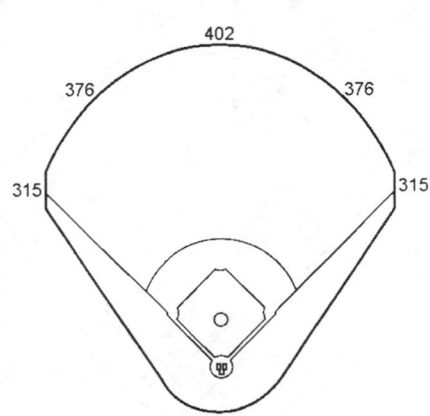

402
376 376
315 315

Milwaukee Brewers—County Stadium

Alt: 635 feet **Surface:** Grass

| | 1998 Season | | | | | | | 1996-1998 | | | | | | |
| | Home Games | | | Away Games | | | Index | Home Games | | | Away Games | | | Index |
	Brewers	Opp	Total	Brewers	Opp	Total		Brewers	Opp	Total	Brewers	Opp	Total	
G	75	75	150	73	73	146	—	230	230	460	226	226	452	—
Avg	.262	.281	.272	.254	.268	.261	104	.271	.273	.272	.262	.271	.266	102
AB	2508	2660	5168	2531	2418	4949	102	7733	8141	15874	7939	7532	15471	101
R	325	395	720	308	349	657	107	1109	1193	2302	1051	1136	2187	103
H	656	748	1404	643	648	1291	106	2097	2225	4322	2083	2039	4122	103
2B	130	135	265	109	140	249	102	409	434	843	401	400	801	103
3B	7	13	20	9	18	27	71	46	39	85	36	49	85	97
HR	65	84	149	76	88	164	87	200	278	478	245	277	522	89
BB	256	239	495	226	254	480	99	848	820	1668	712	807	1519	107
SO	425	473	898	529	492	1021	84	1302	1398	2700	1513	1340	2853	92
E	52	53	105	48	48	96	106	184	171	355	173	157	330	106
E-Infield	37	41	78	40	39	79	96	141	130	271	140	127	267	100
LHB-Avg	.254	.283	.268	.253	.251	.252	106	.270	.265	.267	.258	.283	.270	99
LHB-HR	39	22	61	43	26	69	86	86	100	186	111	123	234	77
RHB-Avg	.268	.280	.274	.255	.277	.267	103	.272	.279	.276	.266	.262	.264	105
RHB-HR	26	62	88	33	62	95	88	114	178	292	134	154	288	99

Minnesota Twins—Hubert H. Humphrey Metrodome   Alt: 815 feet   Surface: Turf

| | 1998 Season | | | | | | | 1996-1998 | | | | | | |
| | Home Games | | | Away Games | | | | Home Games | | | Away Games | | | |
	Twins	Opp	Total	Twins	Opp	Total	Index	Twins	Opp	Total	Twins	Opp	Total	Index
G	73	73	146	73	73	146	—	230	230	460	225	225	450	—
Avg	.277	.283	.280	.257	.288	.272	103	.283	.280	.281	.268	.283	.276	102
AB	2519	2667	5186	2570	2504	5074	102	7928	8291	16219	7947	7660	15607	102
R	345	372	717	338	376	714	100	1149	1270	2419	1107	1180	2287	103
H	697	756	1453	660	720	1380	105	2240	2322	4562	2129	2171	4300	104
2B	137	150	287	120	140	260	108	464	490	954	402	450	852	108
3B	19	20	39	13	15	28	136	60	54	114	54	43	97	113
HR	47	86	133	60	83	143	91	160	294	454	182	283	465	94
BB	245	223	468	221	185	406	113	754	757	1511	749	683	1432	102
SO	413	447	860	388	412	800	105	1408	1409	2817	1363	1244	2607	104
E	44	62	106	56	63	119	89	151	185	336	145	179	324	101
E-Infield	39	53	92	43	58	101	91	123	143	266	109	141	250	104
LHB-Avg	.295	.283	.289	.263	.303	.283	102	.281	.280	.280	.251	.296	.274	102
LHB-HR	26	49	75	27	33	60	119	70	144	214	70	120	190	108
RHB-Avg	.261	.284	.273	.252	.274	.263	104	.283	.280	.282	.279	.274	.277	102
RHB-HR	21	37	58	33	50	83	70	90	150	240	112	163	275	84

MINNESOTA   MONTREAL

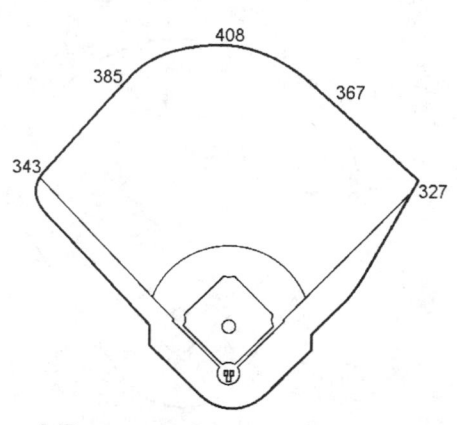 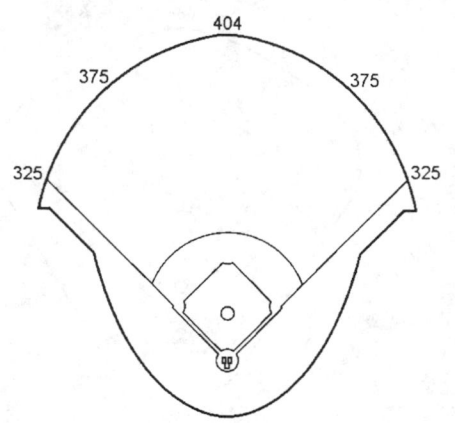

Montreal Expos—Olympic Stadium   Alt: 90 feet   Surface: Turf

| | 1998 Season | | | | | | | 1996-1998 | | | | | | |
| | Home Games | | | Away Games | | | | Home Games | | | Away Games | | | |
	Expos	Opp	Total	Expos	Opp	Total	Index	Expos	Opp	Total	Expos	Opp	Total	Index
G	73	73	146	73	73	146	—	229	229	458	226	226	452	—
Avg	.239	.250	.244	.260	.270	.265	92	.261	.247	.254	.252	.261	.257	99
AB	2381	2550	4931	2506	2370	4876	101	7612	7931	15543	7803	7413	15216	101
R	269	294	563	315	394	709	79	1011	986	1997	945	1072	2017	98
H	568	637	1205	652	640	1292	93	1989	1962	3951	1970	1936	3906	100
2B	108	117	225	140	120	260	86	449	358	807	405	354	759	104
3B	14	11	25	15	13	28	88	52	44	96	36	39	75	125
HR	61	55	116	75	82	157	73	214	197	411	222	230	452	89
BB	207	229	436	197	262	459	94	683	729	1412	591	765	1356	102
SO	487	462	949	477	452	929	101	1476	1605	3081	1550	1537	3087	98
E	69	60	129	64	53	117	110	200	178	378	202	175	377	99
E-Infield	55	48	103	48	46	94	110	153	129	282	152	132	284	98
LHB-Avg	.225	.254	.241	.249	.259	.254	95	.259	.257	.258	.245	.258	.251	103
LHB-HR	7	23	30	18	34	52	57	82	70	152	84	74	158	93
RHB-Avg	.246	.247	.247	.267	.277	.272	91	.262	.241	.252	.257	.263	.260	97
RHB-HR	54	32	86	57	48	105	81	132	127	259	138	156	294	87

New York Mets—Shea Stadium

Alt: 20 feet **Surface:** Grass

	1998 Season							1996-1998						
	Home Games			Away Games				Home Games			Away Games			
	Mets	Opp	Total	Mets	Opp	Total	Index	Mets	Opp	Total	Mets	Opp	Total	Index
G	73	73	146	73	73	146	—	229	229	458	226	226	452	—
Avg	.259	.247	.253	.265	.260	.262	96	.265	.254	.259	.264	.272	.268	97
AB	2419	2513	4932	2563	2421	4984	99	7661	7999	15660	7943	7560	15503	100
R	323	277	600	316	301	617	97	1031	939	1970	1062	1049	2111	92
H	627	620	1247	678	629	1307	95	2030	2033	4063	2095	2055	4150	97
2B	131	132	263	142	134	276	96	378	371	749	400	396	796	93
3B	9	15	24	9	8	17	143	44	44	88	49	43	92	95
HR	60	63	123	58	71	129	96	190	198	388	215	226	441	87
BB	268	225	493	252	256	508	98	760	710	1470	710	749	1459	100
SO	450	516	966	488	499	987	99	1389	1551	2940	1557	1347	2904	100
E	45	48	93	49	40	89	104	198	178	376	200	179	379	98
E-Infield	35	39	74	38	31	69	107	141	137	278	139	141	280	98
LHB-Avg	.288	.253	.271	.255	.253	.254	107	.285	.263	.274	.274	.280	.277	99
LHB-HR	31	23	54	24	28	52	104	101	80	181	96	85	181	101
RHB-Avg	.236	.243	.240	.272	.264	.268	90	.251	.248	.249	.256	.266	.261	96
RHB-HR	29	40	69	34	43	77	91	89	118	207	119	141	260	78

NEW YORK METS

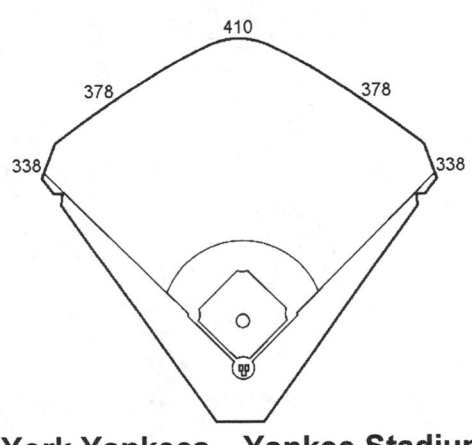

410

378   378

338   338

NEW YORK YANKEES

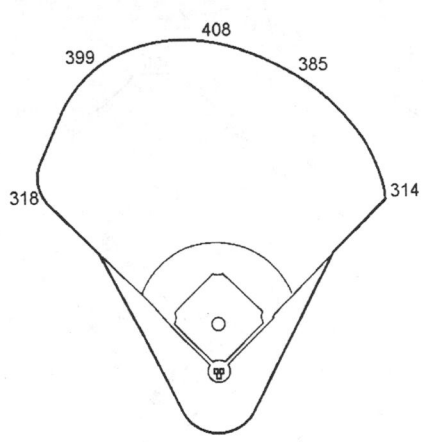

408

399   385

318   314

New York Yankees—Yankee Stadium

Alt: 55 feet **Surface:** Grass

	1998 Season							1996-1998						
	Home Games			Away Games				Home Games			Away Games			
	Yankees	Opp	Total	Yankees	Opp	Total	Index	Yankees	Opp	Total	Yankees	Opp	Total	Index
G	72	72	144	74	74	148	—	223	223	446	232	232	464	—
Avg	.298	.239	.269	.282	.265	.274	98	.297	.255	.276	.284	.265	.275	100
AB	2440	2498	4938	2664	2472	5136	99	7561	7765	15326	8390	7857	16247	98
R	422	284	706	445	321	766	95	1250	962	2212	1341	1061	2402	96
H	728	598	1326	750	656	1406	97	2243	1980	4223	2382	2080	4462	98
2B	141	120	261	129	120	249	109	407	379	786	457	399	856	97
3B	11	6	17	17	11	28	63	37	25	62	41	40	81	81
HR	83	64	147	101	80	181	84	231	205	436	272	216	488	95
BB	287	186	473	297	239	536	92	885	713	1598	952	806	1758	96
SO	425	516	941	496	443	939	104	1189	1585	2774	1488	1564	3052	96
E	42	53	95	42	68	110	89	120	168	288	160	219	379	79
E-Infield	36	47	83	35	59	94	91	102	126	228	127	161	288	82
LHB-Avg	.292	.259	.275	.271	.275	.273	101	.294	.259	.278	.281	.278	.279	100
LHB-HR	41	38	79	55	36	91	92	130	89	219	151	91	242	98
RHB-Avg	.303	.225	.264	.290	.258	.275	96	.299	.253	.274	.287	.256	.271	101
RHB-HR	42	26	68	46	44	90	78	101	116	217	121	125	246	92

295

Oakland Athletics—Oakland-Alameda County Coliseum Alt: 25 feet Surface: Grass

	1998 Season							1996-1998						
	Home Games			Away Games			Index	Home Games			Away Games			Index
	Athletics	Opp	Total	Athletics	Opp	Total		Athletics	Opp	Total	Athletics	Opp	Total	
G	73	73	146	73	73	146	—	221	221	442	233	233	466	—
Avg	.248	.265	.257	.265	.288	.276	93	.264	.283	.274	.257	.293	.275	100
AB	2377	2567	4944	2569	2504	5073	97	7417	7944	15361	8202	8028	16230	100
R	324	342	666	387	424	811	82	1071	1197	2268	1177	1319	2496	96
H	590	680	1270	680	720	1400	91	1959	2251	4210	2109	2351	4460	100
2B	116	135	251	152	148	300	86	374	450	824	427	463	890	98
3B	8	13	21	4	20	24	90	27	41	68	24	65	89	81
HR	63	72	135	72	86	158	88	266	248	514	289	294	583	93
BB	271	220	491	299	265	564	89	857	766	1623	927	947	1874	92
SO	465	430	895	540	392	932	99	1445	1269	2714	1744	1282	3026	95
E	57	58	115	72	58	130	88	168	162	330	183	154	337	103
E-Infield	49	52	101	61	48	109	93	128	122	250	146	116	262	101
LHB-Avg	.278	.273	.275	.287	.286	.286	96	.281	.286	.284	.270	.294	.283	100
LHB-HR	36	35	71	38	36	74	94	96	119	215	96	128	224	98
RHB-Avg	.224	.258	.241	.248	.289	.268	90	.253	.281	.267	.250	.292	.269	99
RHB-HR	27	37	64	34	50	84	81	170	129	299	193	166	359	90

OAKLAND

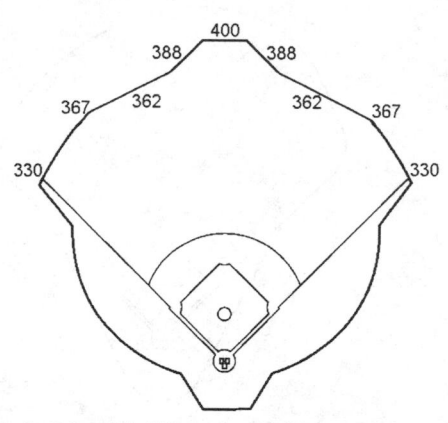

PHILADELPHIA

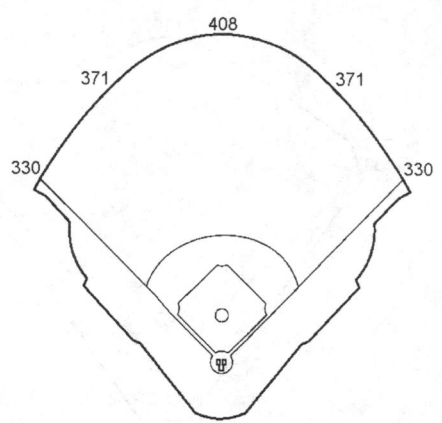

Philadelphia Phillies—Veterans Stadium Alt: 20 feet Surface: Turf

	1998 Season							1996-1998						
	Home Games			Away Games			Index	Home Games			Away Games			Index
	Phillies	Opp	Total	Phillies	Opp	Total		Phillies	Opp	Total	Phillies	Opp	Total	
G	73	73	146	73	73	146	—	229	229	458	226	226	452	—
Avg	.272	.268	.270	.248	.254	.251	108	.266	.260	.263	.248	.268	.258	102
AB	2441	2586	5027	2592	2478	5070	99	7673	8017	15690	7797	7466	15263	101
R	349	376	725	281	339	620	117	993	1127	2120	908	1144	2052	102
H	665	693	1358	643	630	1273	107	2044	2087	4131	1936	1999	3935	104
2B	128	156	284	121	140	261	110	407	493	900	357	410	767	114
3B	19	18	37	12	9	21	178	60	50	110	41	53	94	114
HR	66	84	150	46	84	130	116	179	243	422	172	244	416	99
BB	244	241	485	218	243	461	106	770	751	1521	708	798	1506	98
SO	472	570	1042	511	486	997	105	1464	1722	3186	1548	1477	3025	102
E	47	55	102	52	58	110	93	151	182	333	189	174	363	91
E-Infield	42	39	81	45	45	90	90	115	133	248	146	126	272	90
LHB-Avg	.292	.281	.286	.260	.263	.262	109	.275	.262	.269	.261	.280	.270	100
LHB-HR	28	31	59	17	32	49	121	67	74	141	56	95	151	92
RHB-Avg	.262	.258	.260	.242	.248	.244	106	.259	.259	.259	.238	.259	.249	104
RHB-HR	38	53	91	29	52	81	114	112	169	281	116	149	265	102

Pittsburgh Pirates—Three Rivers Stadium

Alt: 730 feet **Surface:** Turf

	1998 Season							1996-1998						
	Home Games			Away Games				Home Games			Away Games			
	Pirates	Opp	Total	Pirates	Opp	Total	Index	Pirates	Opp	Total	Pirates	Opp	Total	Index
G	73	73	146	77	77	154	—	225	225	450	234	234	468	—
Avg	.265	.251	.258	.241	.265	.253	102	.267	.268	.268	.255	.274	.264	101
AB	2411	2508	4919	2625	2565	5190	100	7516	7893	15409	8197	7913	16110	99
R	328	305	633	274	358	632	106	1045	1090	2135	1009	1092	2101	106
H	640	629	1269	633	681	1314	102	2010	2112	4122	2088	2166	4254	101
2B	137	141	278	110	132	242	121	429	440	869	405	391	796	114
3B	21	8	29	12	14	26	118	70	43	113	43	50	93	127
HR	56	64	120	45	75	120	106	190	212	402	167	238	405	104
BB	189	231	420	173	265	438	101	678	728	1406	649	768	1417	104
SO	487	520	1007	506	494	1000	106	1480	1574	3054	1593	1459	3052	105
E	59	60	119	68	58	126	100	200	201	401	201	198	399	105
E-Infield	51	53	104	58	51	109	101	157	165	322	160	158	318	105
LHB-Avg	.267	.246	.255	.236	.305	.272	94	.270	.274	.272	.257	.295	.276	99
LHB-HR	12	22	34	12	34	46	78	72	76	148	57	94	151	106
RHB-Avg	.265	.254	.260	.244	.240	.242	107	.266	.264	.265	.253	.260	.257	103
RHB-HR	44	42	86	33	41	74	122	118	136	254	110	144	254	102

PITTSBURGH

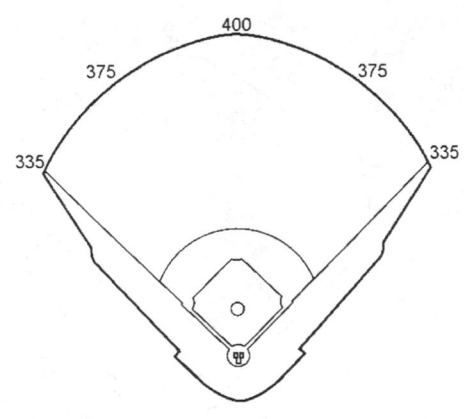

SAN DIEGO

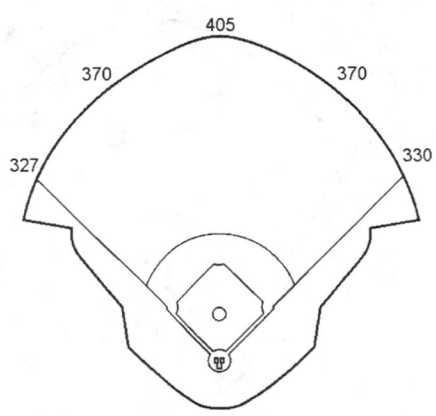

San Diego Padres—Qualcomm Stadium

Alt: 20 feet **Surface:** Grass

	1998 Season							1996-1998						
	Home Games			Away Games				Home Games			Away Games			
	Padres	Opp	Total	Padres	Opp	Total	Index	Padres	Opp	Total	Padres	Opp	Total	Index
G	76	76	152	73	73	146	—	224	224	448	233	233	466	—
Avg	.238	.226	.232	.262	.277	.269	86	.255	.248	.251	.266	.270	.268	94
AB	2464	2581	5045	2564	2483	5047	96	7451	7833	15284	8262	7953	16215	98
R	311	236	547	365	332	697	75	950	926	1876	1188	1114	2302	85
H	586	583	1169	671	688	1359	83	1903	1939	3842	2199	2150	4349	92
2B	112	88	200	148	135	283	71	342	316	658	440	418	858	81
3B	9	8	17	20	15	35	49	26	33	59	41	49	90	70
HR	75	58	133	82	67	149	89	209	211	420	227	200	427	104
BB	290	197	487	274	244	518	94	810	656	1466	897	807	1704	91
SO	523	633	1156	466	482	948	122	1478	1715	3193	1559	1561	3120	109
E	45	53	98	49	52	101	93	176	153	329	172	191	363	94
E-Infield	39	43	82	42	44	86	92	135	121	256	141	143	284	94
LHB-Avg	.244	.237	.241	.279	.278	.279	86	.272	.250	.262	.291	.274	.284	92
LHB-HR	32	19	51	38	24	62	86	97	76	173	122	68	190	98
RHB-Avg	.232	.218	.224	.243	.276	.261	86	.241	.246	.243	.244	.267	.256	95
RHB-HR	43	39	82	44	43	87	91	112	135	247	105	132	237	110

San Francisco Giants—3Com Park

Alt: 65 feet   **Surface:** Grass

| | 1998 Season | | | | | | | 1996-1998 | | | | | | |
| | Home Games | | | Away Games | | | | Home Games | | | Away Games | | | |
	Giants	Opp	Total	Giants	Opp	Total	Index	Giants	Opp	Total	Giants	Opp	Total	Index
G	73	73	146	77	77	154	—	228	228	456	230	230	460	—
Avg	.283	.247	.264	.268	.267	.268	99	.263	.259	.261	.259	.274	.266	98
AB	2395	2486	4881	2782	2673	5455	94	7530	7947	15477	8108	7750	15858	98
R	387	290	677	390	391	781	91	1114	1066	2180	1117	1180	2297	96
H	677	614	1291	746	715	1461	93	1983	2059	4042	2099	2126	4225	97
2B	128	111	239	144	146	290	92	356	372	728	394	397	791	94
3B	11	14	25	13	18	31	90	37	40	77	44	49	93	85
HR	79	77	156	70	78	148	118	230	242	472	216	245	461	105
BB	313	233	546	318	282	600	102	942	776	1718	887	821	1708	103
SO	450	522	972	496	484	980	111	1551	1578	3129	1602	1367	2969	108
E	49	44	93	43	40	83	118	192	210	402	173	163	336	121
E-Infield	42	38	80	37	32	69	122	144	159	303	141	130	271	113
LHB-Avg	.300	.253	.278	.275	.260	.268	104	.279	.271	.275	.273	.272	.272	101
LHB-HR	32	27	59	30	23	53	127	110	95	205	104	78	182	117
RHB-Avg	.267	.243	.254	.262	.273	.267	95	.250	.252	.251	.246	.276	.262	96
RHB-HR	47	50	97	40	55	95	112	120	147	267	112	167	279	97

SAN FRANCISCO

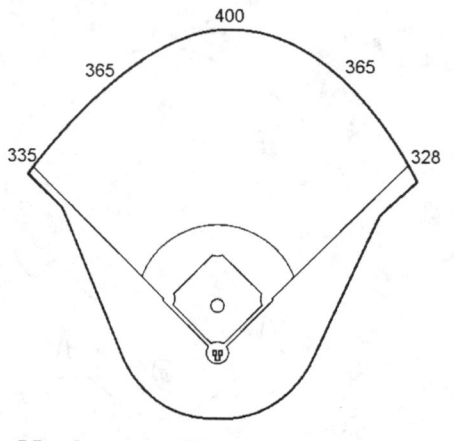

SEATTLE

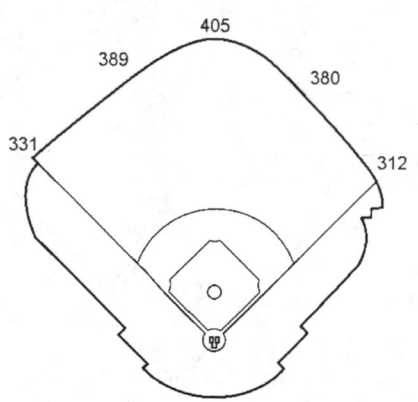

Seattle Mariners—The Kingdome

Alt: 16 feet   **Surface:** Turf

| | 1998 Season | | | | | | | 1996-1998 | | | | | | |
| | Home Games | | | Away Games | | | | Home Games | | | Away Games | | | |
	Mariners	Opp	Total	Mariners	Opp	Total	Index	Mariners	Opp	Total	Mariners	Opp	Total	Index
G	73	73	146	72	72	144	—	227	227	454	225	225	450	—
Avg	.279	.266	.272	.272	.282	.277	98	.281	.267	.274	.282	.279	.280	98
AB	2495	2599	5094	2568	2440	5008	100	7739	8033	15772	8061	7670	15731	99
R	389	388	777	394	389	783	98	1257	1213	2470	1341	1193	2534	97
H	696	692	1388	699	687	1386	99	2176	2141	4317	2270	2140	4410	97
2B	144	171	315	146	158	304	102	479	467	946	434	450	884	107
3B	8	10	18	15	12	27	66	27	28	55	35	38	73	75
HR	105	94	199	107	85	192	102	339	297	636	349	259	608	104
BB	281	269	550	221	224	445	122	888	864	1752	832	776	1608	109
SO	485	569	1054	496	460	956	108	1526	1718	3244	1508	1409	2917	111
E	47	43	90	63	48	111	80	165	141	306	183	152	335	91
E-Infield	36	38	74	57	42	99	74	135	125	260	155	120	275	94
LHB-Avg	.282	.292	.287	.263	.304	.282	102	.285	.286	.286	.275	.309	.291	98
LHB-HR	38	46	84	40	39	79	103	137	126	263	143	117	260	101
RHB-Avg	.277	.251	.263	.278	.269	.274	96	.279	.255	.267	.285	.262	.274	96
RHB-HR	67	48	115	67	46	113	101	202	171	373	206	142	348	107

St. Louis Cardinals—Busch Stadium

Alt: 455 feet   **Surface:** Grass

| | 1998 Season | | | | | | | 1996-1998 | | | | | | |
| | Home Games | | | Away Games | | | | Home Games | | | Away Games | | | |
	Cards	Opp	Total	Cards	Opp	Total	Index	Cards	Opp	Total	Cards	Opp	Total	Index
G	77	77	154	73	73	146	—	230	230	460	229	229	458	—
Avg	.268	.254	.261	.252	.280	.266	98	.269	.247	.258	.253	.270	.261	99
AB	2657	2787	5444	2505	2409	4914	105	7734	8036	15770	7956	7653	15609	101
R	419	360	779	344	347	691	107	1125	982	2107	1030	1070	2100	100
H	712	707	1419	631	675	1306	103	2080	1983	4063	2011	2070	4081	99
2B	151	130	281	128	134	262	97	435	337	772	367	378	745	103
3B	18	11	29	11	11	22	119	49	27	76	45	48	93	81
HR	110	79	189	100	55	155	110	240	214	454	245	201	446	101
BB	351	263	614	281	259	540	103	856	770	1626	763	789	1552	104
SO	555	480	1035	553	417	970	96	1586	1548	3134	1709	1419	3128	99
E	74	44	118	58	40	98	114	201	135	336	181	176	357	94
E-Infield	62	33	95	42	32	74	122	154	104	258	150	139	289	89
LHB-Avg	.284	.239	.259	.252	.274	.264	98	.282	.254	.267	.270	.277	.273	98
LHB-HR	34	26	60	24	16	40	136	77	88	165	88	70	158	104
RHB-Avg	.260	.264	.262	.252	.285	.267	98	.261	.242	.251	.242	.266	.253	99
RHB-HR	76	53	129	76	39	115	101	163	126	289	157	131	288	99

ST. LOUIS

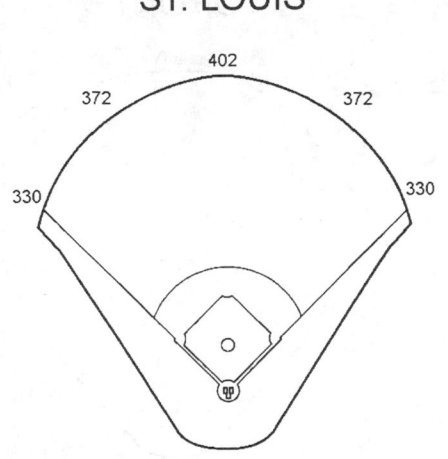

402

372   372

330   330

TAMPA BAY

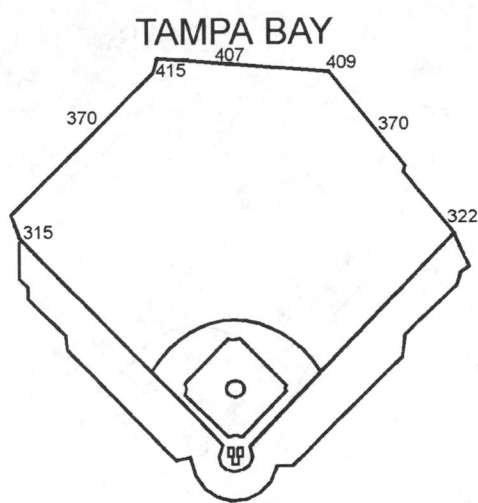

407

415   409

370   370

315   322

Tampa Bay Devil Rays—Tropicana Field

Alt: 15 feet   **Surface:** Turf

| | 1998 Season | | | | | | | 1998 Season | | | | | | |
| | Home Games | | | Away Games | | | | Home Games | | | Away Games | | | |
	Devil Rays	Opp	Total	Devil Rays	Opp	Total	Index	Devil Rays	Opp	Total	Devil Rays	Opp	Total	Index
G	73	73	146	73	73	146	—	73	73	146	73	73	146	—
Avg	.256	.266	.261	.268	.256	.262	100	.256	.266	.261	.268	.256	.262	100
AB	2461	2574	5035	2533	2338	4871	103	2461	2574	5035	2533	2338	4871	103
R	292	356	648	280	319	599	108	292	356	648	280	319	599	108
H	630	685	1315	678	599	1277	103	630	685	1315	678	599	1277	103
2B	120	131	251	125	104	229	106	120	131	251	125	104	229	106
3B	16	10	26	23	14	37	68	16	10	26	23	14	37	68
HR	63	83	146	41	70	111	127	63	83	146	41	70	111	127
BB	211	280	491	216	304	520	91	211	280	491	216	304	520	91
SO	469	454	923	504	455	959	93	469	454	923	504	455	959	93
E	45	55	100	39	45	84	119	45	55	100	39	45	84	119
E-Infield	40	49	89	38	40	78	114	40	49	89	38	40	78	114
LHB-Avg	.258	.271	.264	.266	.266	.266	99	.258	.271	.264	.266	.266	.266	99
LHB-HR	43	31	74	15	30	45	152	43	31	74	15	30	45	152
RHB-Avg	.253	.263	.259	.269	.249	.259	100	.253	.263	.259	.269	.249	.259	100
RHB-HR	20	52	72	26	40	66	110	20	52	72	26	40	66	110

Texas Rangers—The Ballpark in Arlington

Alt: 551 feet   **Surface:** Grass

| | 1998 Season | | | | | | | 1996-1998 | | | | | | |
| | Home Games | | | Away Games | | | | Home Games | | | Away Games | | | |
	Rangers	Opp	Total	Rangers	Opp	Total	Index	Rangers	Opp	Total	Rangers	Opp	Total	Index
G	73	73	146	73	73	146	—	227	227	454	228	228	456	—
Avg	.306	.292	.299	.273	.282	.278	108	.295	.286	.290	.268	.280	.273	106
AB	2523	2647	5170	2591	2479	5070	102	7801	8159	15960	8091	7685	15776	102
R	460	418	878	398	369	767	114	1319	1212	2531	1171	1115	2286	111
H	771	774	1545	707	700	1407	110	2302	2332	4634	2166	2148	4314	108
2B	146	165	311	138	137	275	111	435	438	873	450	411	861	100
3B	18	27	45	10	14	24	184	56	64	120	27	47	74	160
HR	94	78	172	89	75	164	103	291	250	541	284	222	506	106
BB	271	215	486	270	246	516	92	865	752	1617	781	791	1572	102
SO	446	442	888	496	442	938	93	1430	1362	2792	1582	1338	2920	95
E	63	50	113	40	55	95	119	162	164	326	139	168	307	107
E-Infield	58	39	97	35	49	84	115	138	123	261	113	142	255	103
LHB-Avg	.302	.294	.298	.270	.270	.270	110	.302	.284	.293	.269	.278	.274	107
LHB-HR	37	40	77	30	37	67	115	115	120	235	98	93	191	123
RHB-Avg	.309	.291	.300	.275	.293	.284	106	.289	.287	.288	.266	.280	.273	105
RHB-HR	57	38	95	59	38	97	94	176	130	306	186	129	315	95

TEXAS

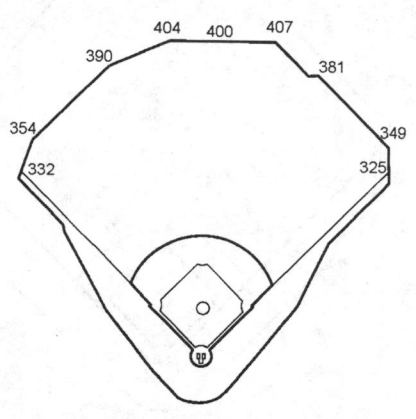

TORONTO

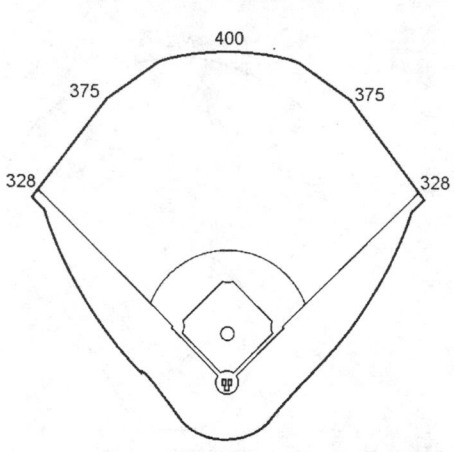

Toronto Blue Jays—SkyDome

Alt: 300 feet   **Surface:** Turf

| | 1998 Season | | | | | | | 1996-1998 | | | | | | |
| | Home Games | | | Away Games | | | | Home Games | | | Away Games | | | |
	Blue Jays	Opp	Total	Blue Jays	Opp	Total	Index	Blue Jays	Opp	Total	Blue Jays	Opp	Total	Index
G	73	73	146	74	74	148	—	226	226	452	230	230	460	—
Avg	.265	.236	.250	.266	.269	.267	94	.257	.256	.256	.257	.266	.262	98
AB	2438	2557	4995	2583	2481	5064	100	7560	7943	15503	8033	7662	15695	101
R	381	316	697	352	373	725	97	1046	1030	2076	1058	1096	2154	98
H	645	603	1248	686	667	1353	94	1944	2030	3974	2067	2041	4108	98
2B	153	150	303	133	148	281	109	436	438	874	403	403	806	110
3B	9	9	18	9	21	30	61	49	34	83	43	38	81	104
HR	97	66	163	97	86	183	90	242	232	474	260	262	522	92
BB	285	261	546	233	292	525	105	776	786	1562	713	826	1539	103
SO	496	543	1039	516	510	1026	103	1559	1595	3154	1567	1547	3114	103
E	61	42	103	54	49	103	101	173	146	319	151	195	346	94
E-Infield	50	35	85	43	41	84	103	138	111	249	116	147	263	96
LHB-Avg	.271	.233	.250	.281	.282	.281	89	.274	.252	.262	.270	.267	.268	98
LHB-HR	41	30	71	43	48	91	79	98	105	203	102	126	228	91
RHB-Avg	.260	.239	.250	.255	.255	.255	98	.246	.259	.252	.249	.265	.256	98
RHB-HR	56	36	92	54	38	92	101	144	127	271	158	136	294	93

1996-98 Ballpark Index Rankings—Runs per Game

	AMERICAN LEAGUE									NATIONAL LEAGUE								
	Home Games				Away Games						Home Games				Away Games				
	Gm	Team	Opp	Total	Gm	Team	Opp	Total	Index		Gm	Team	Opp	Total	Gm	Team	Opp	Total	Index
Tex	227	1319	1212	2531	228	1171	1115	2286	111	Col	229	1629	1478	3107	229	925	1082	2007	155
TB**	73	292	356	648	73	280	319	599	108	Pit	225	1045	1090	2135	234	1009	1092	2101	106
Bos	226	1296	1166	2462	229	1188	1195	2383	105	ChN	229	1148	1065	2213	230	992	1122	2114	105
Cle	228	1295	1146	2441	225	1204	1090	2294	105	Mil	230	1109	1193	2302	226	1051	1136	2187	103
KC	226	1033	1217	2250	226	1031	1145	2176	103	Cin	226	1066	1059	2125	232	998	1122	2120	103
Min	230	1149	1270	2419	225	1107	1180	2287	103	Phi	229	993	1127	2120	226	908	1144	2052	102
Det*	145	688	746	1434	148	673	780	1453	101	Ari**	73	301	351	652	76	286	379	665	102
Tor	226	1046	1030	2076	230	1058	1096	2154	98	StL	230	1125	982	2107	229	1030	1070	2100	100
Sea	227	1257	1213	2470	225	1341	1193	2534	97	Atl*	148	722	523	1245	145	735	515	1250	98
NYA	223	1250	962	2212	232	1341	1061	2402	96	Mon	229	1011	986	1997	226	945	1072	2017	98
Oak	221	1071	1197	2268	233	1177	1319	2496	96	SF	228	1114	1066	2180	230	1117	1180	2297	96
Ana**	73	327	362	689	73	379	345	724	95	NYN	229	1031	939	1970	226	1062	1049	2111	92
Bal	227	1138	1081	2219	229	1307	1134	2441	92	Hou	226	1095	880	1975	231	1157	1081	2238	90
ChA	230	1154	1154	2308	225	1243	1239	2482	91	Fla	229	991	970	1961	226	965	1202	2167	89
										SD	224	950	926	1876	233	1188	1114	2302	85
										LA	230	927	804	1731	227	1039	1048	2087	82

*—Current dimensions began 1997; **—Current dimensions began 1998

1996-98 Ballpark Index Rankings—Home Runs per At Bat

	AMERICAN LEAGUE									NATIONAL LEAGUE								
	Home Games				Away Games						Home Games				Away Games				
	Gm	Team	Opp	Total	Gm	Team	Opp	Total	Index		Gm	Team	Opp	Total	Gm	Team	Opp	Total	Index
Det*	145	166	189	355	148	139	150	289	127	Col	229	361	328	689	229	245	209	454	140
TB**	73	63	83	146	73	41	70	111	127	ChN	229	269	273	542	230	214	249	463	117
KC	226	191	282	473	226	189	248	437	107	SF	228	230	242	472	230	216	245	461	105
Tex	227	291	250	541	228	284	222	506	106	Pit	225	190	212	402	234	167	238	405	104
Sea	227	339	297	636	225	349	259	608	104	SD	224	209	211	420	233	227	200	427	104
Bal	227	313	258	571	229	316	249	565	103	Cin	226	217	239	456	232	233	239	472	101
Bos	226	289	221	510	229	280	246	526	97	StL	230	240	214	454	229	245	201	446	101
NYA	223	231	205	436	232	272	216	488	95	Phi	229	179	243	422	226	172	244	416	99
Min	230	160	294	454	225	182	283	465	94	Ari**	73	66	81	147	76	73	89	162	91
Oak	221	266	248	514	233	289	294	583	93	Mil	230	200	278	478	226	245	277	522	89
Ana**	73	48	82	130	73	81	64	145	92	Atl*	148	161	97	258	145	185	101	286	89
Tor	226	242	232	474	230	260	262	522	92	Mon	229	214	197	411	226	222	230	452	89
ChA	230	236	250	486	225	284	274	558	88	Fla	229	176	190	366	226	204	212	416	89
Cle	228	286	233	519	225	313	268	581	88	NYN	229	190	198	388	226	215	226	441	87
										LA	230	206	176	382	227	243	217	460	85
										Hou	226	186	179	365	231	213	234	447	84

*—Current dimensions began 1997; **—Current dimensions began 1998

1996-98 Ballpark Index Rankings—Batting Average

	AMERICAN LEAGUE									NATIONAL LEAGUE								
	Home Games				Away Games						Home Games				Away Games				
	Gm	Team	Opp	Avg	Gm	Team	Opp	Avg	Index		Gm	Team	Opp	Avg	Gm	Team	Opp	Avg	Index
Tex	227	.295	.286	.290	228	.268	.280	.273	106	Col	229	.330	.307	.318	229	.245	.270	.257	124
Bos	226	.299	.273	.286	229	.272	.270	.271	105	Ari**	73	.256	.263	.260	76	.231	.264	.247	105
Cle	228	.290	.277	.283	225	.277	.270	.274	103	Mil	230	.271	.273	.272	226	.262	.271	.266	102
Min	230	.283	.280	.281	225	.268	.283	.276	102	Atl*	148	.278	.240	.258	145	.263	.241	.252	102
KC	226	.264	.279	.272	226	.263	.277	.270	101	ChN	229	.268	.257	.262	230	.247	.270	.258	102
NYA	223	.297	.255	.276	232	.284	.265	.275	100	Phi	229	.266	.260	.263	226	.248	.268	.258	102
Oak	221	.264	.283	.274	233	.257	.293	.275	100	Pit	225	.267	.268	.268	234	.255	.274	.264	101
TB**	73	.256	.266	.261	73	.268	.256	.262	100	Mon	229	.261	.247	.254	226	.252	.261	.257	99
ChA	230	.277	.265	.271	225	.275	.280	.277	98	StL	230	.269	.247	.258	229	.253	.270	.261	99
Sea	227	.281	.267	.274	225	.282	.279	.280	98	Cin	226	.261	.247	.254	232	.252	.269	.260	98
Tor	226	.257	.256	.256	230	.257	.266	.262	98	SF	228	.263	.259	.261	230	.259	.274	.266	98
Bal	227	.268	.262	.265	229	.277	.273	.275	96	NYN	229	.265	.254	.259	226	.264	.272	.268	97
Det*	145	.256	.263	.260	148	.266	.283	.274	95	Hou	226	.270	.248	.259	231	.263	.274	.268	96
Ana**	73	.264	.258	.261	73	.280	.273	.276	94	SD	224	.255	.248	.251	233	.266	.270	.268	94
										Fla	229	.258	.246	.252	226	.253	.285	.269	94
										LA	230	.254	.228	.241	227	.258	.263	.261	93

*—Current dimensions began 1997; **—Current dimensions began 1998

301

1998 Lefty-Righty Stats

In the 163rd game of the 1998 season, Giants manager Dusty Baker was confronted with one of his most important choices of the year. The Giants trailed the Cubs 2-0 in the bottom of the sixth, and the Cubs had the bases loaded. Cubs manager Jim Riggleman sent up pinch-hitter Matt Mieske to face lefthander Rich Rodriguez, and Baker had to decide whether or not to change pitchers.

If Baker had had the following section of this book in front of him, his decision might have been a little easier. Mieske, you see, batted .389 against lefties last year. What's more, Rodriguez was hammered by righthanded hitters to the tune of a .336 average. If Baker had known this, he might have brought in righthander John Johnstone, who held righties to a .226 average. Even if Riggleman had responded by sending up a lefthanded hitter, the Giants would have been covered—lefties had hit only .220 off Johnstone.

But Baker elected to leave Rodriguez in, and Mieske touched him for a big two-run single to give the Cubs a four-run lead. Baker sent for Johnstone, but it was a batter too late. The Cubs ultimately prevailed, 5-3, ending the Giants' season.

Would Baker have played it any differently if he'd had the numbers in front of him? Perhaps not, but at least he would have known what he was getting into.

Batters vs. Lefthanded and Righthanded Pitchers

Batter	vs	Avg	AB	H	2B	3B	HR	BI	BB	SO	OBP	SLG
Abbott,Jeff	L	.313	67	21	3	0	4	12	4	7	.347	.537
Bats Right	R	.266	177	47	11	1	8	29	5	21	.280	.475
Abbott,Kurt	L	.236	72	17	8	0	1	8	3	25	.260	.389
Bats Right	R	.279	122	34	5	1	4	16	9	28	.336	.434
Abreu,Bob	L	.320	103	33	5	2	0	12	11	30	.379	.408
Bats Left	R	.310	394	122	24	4	17	62	73	103	.416	.520
Agbayani,B	L	.167	6	1	0	0	0	0	0	1	.167	.167
Bats Right	R	.111	9	1	0	0	0	0	1	4	.200	.111
Alexander,M	L	.230	100	23	3	0	2	9	9	25	.300	.320
Bats Right	R	.226	164	37	7	1	3	16	9	41	.264	.335
Alfonzo,E	L	.234	141	33	6	0	4	14	18	22	.321	.362
Bats Right	R	.293	416	122	22	2	13	64	47	55	.367	.450
Alicea,Luis	L	.302	43	13	3	0	2	7	7	8	.423	.512
Bats Both	R	.269	216	58	12	3	4	26	30	32	.361	.407
Allensworth,J	L	.288	139	40	9	0	2	9	15	31	.373	.396
Bats Right	R	.262	221	58	11	3	3	22	13	45	.325	.380
Alomar,R	L	.311	167	52	12	0	7	20	17	27	.376	.509
Bats Both	R	.271	421	114	24	1	7	36	42	43	.335	.382
Alomar,Sandy	L	.250	104	26	10	0	2	15	4	9	.275	.404
Bats Right	R	.230	305	70	16	2	4	29	14	36	.269	.334
Alou,Moises	L	.288	125	36	9	0	6	20	26	14	.405	.504
Bats Right	R	.318	459	146	25	5	32	104	58	73	.397	.603
Alvarez,Gabe	L	.262	42	11	4	0	1	8	6	7	.354	.429
Bats Right	R	.223	157	35	7	0	4	21	12	58	.283	.344
Amaral,Rich	L	.257	74	19	4	0	1	3	5	9	.304	.351
Bats Right	R	.300	60	18	2	0	0	1	8	15	.386	.333
Amaro,Ruben	L	.184	38	7	1	0	1	3	1	6	.200	.289
Bats Both	R	.188	69	13	4	0	0	7	5	9	.237	.246
Anderson,B	L	.179	134	24	6	2	3	12	15	32	.270	.321
Bats Left	R	.258	345	89	22	1	15	39	60	46	.388	.458
Anderson,G	L	.292	168	49	11	1	4	29	5	26	.312	.440
Bats Left	R	.295	454	134	30	6	11	50	24	54	.330	.460
Anderson,M	L	.000	3	0	0	0	0	0	0	1	.000	.000
Bats Left	R	.350	40	14	3	0	1	4	1	5	.357	.500
Andrews,S.	L	.241	108	26	8	1	5	18	12	24	.311	.472
Bats Right	R	.237	384	91	22	0	20	51	46	113	.315	.451
Arias,Alex	L	.207	29	6	1	0	1	2	5	3	.343	.345
Bats Right	R	.317	104	33	7	0	0	14	8	15	.363	.385
Arias,George	L	.333	12	4	0	1	0	2	0	4	.333	.500
Bats Right	R	.125	24	3	1	0	1	2	3	12	.276	.292
Ashley,Billy	L	.263	19	5	2	0	2	2	1	9	.300	.684
Bats Right	R	.400	5	2	1	0	1	5	1	2	.500	1.200
Aurilia,Rich	L	.275	109	30	10	0	4	12	9	12	.331	.477
Bats Right	R	.263	304	80	17	2	5	37	22	50	.315	.382
Ausmus,Brad	L	.267	86	23	3	0	1	8	18	14	.396	.337
Bats Right	R	.270	326	88	7	4	5	37	35	46	.344	.362
Baerga,Carlos	L	.204	103	21	2	0	2	17	9	16	.267	.282
Bats Both	R	.282	408	115	25	1	5	36	15	39	.313	.385
Bagwell,Jeff	L	.402	107	43	10	0	7	24	33	16	.538	.692
Bats Right	R	.279	433	121	23	1	27	87	76	74	.391	.524
Baines,Harold	L	.204	49	10	1	0	1	6	5	9	.291	.286
Bats Left	R	.320	244	78	16	0	8	51	27	31	.385	.484
Bako,Paul	L	.174	46	8	1	0	1	5	5	16	.255	.261
Bats Left	R	.290	259	75	11	1	2	25	18	66	.331	.363
Ball,Jeff	L	.333	3	1	0	0	0	0	0	0	.333	.333
Bats Right	R	.000	1	0	0	0	0	0	0	0	.000	.000
Banks,Brian	L	.143	7	1	0	0	1	2	2	3	.333	.571
Bats Both	R	.353	17	6	2	0	0	3	2	4	.421	.471
Barrett,M	L	.000	5	0	0	0	0	0	1	0	.167	.000
Bats Right	R	.389	18	7	2	0	1	2	2	6	.476	.667
Barry,Jeff	L	.091	11	1	0	0	0	0	1	5	.167	.091
Bats Both	R	.217	23	5	1	0	0	2	1	6	.240	.261
Bartee,Kimera	L	.229	35	8	2	0	2	7	0	10	.222	.457
Bats Both	R	.175	63	11	3	1	1	8	6	25	.246	.302
Bates,Jason	L	.176	17	3	2	0	0	0	2	8	.263	.294
Bats Both	R	.193	57	11	1	0	0	3	6	13	.270	.211
Batista,Tony	L	.320	103	33	6	1	6	13	9	16	.381	.573
Bats Right	R	.247	190	47	10	0	12	28	9	36	.283	.489
Baughman,J	L	.339	62	21	3	1	1	7	2	11	.359	.468
Bats Right	R	.216	134	29	6	0	0	13	4	25	.239	.261
Bautista,D	L	.259	85	22	8	0	2	12	6	12	.301	.424
Bats Right	R	.237	59	14	3	0	1	5	1	9	.250	.339
Beamon,Trey	L	.333	3	1	1	0	0	0	0	0	.333	.667
Bats Left	R	.256	39	10	3	0	0	2	5	13	.341	.333
Becker,Rich	L	.129	31	4	0	0	1	3	7	12	.308	.226
Bats Left	R	.209	182	38	5	2	5	18	36	64	.342	.341
Bell,David	L	.254	114	29	5	1	3	6	9	19	.312	.395
Bats Right	R	.279	315	88	25	1	7	43	18	46	.317	.432
Bell,Derek	L	.347	147	51	13	1	6	34	13	25	.400	.571
Bats Right	R	.304	483	147	28	1	16	74	38	101	.353	.466
Bell,Jay	L	.255	145	37	6	0	4	17	25	32	.370	.379
Bats Right	R	.250	404	101	23	5	16	50	56	97	.347	.450
Belle,Albert	L	.313	134	42	11	1	12	28	15	23	.380	.679
Bats Right	R	.333	475	158	37	1	37	124	66	61	.405	.648
Bellhorn,Mark	L	.111	9	1	1	0	0	1	1	3	.200	.222
Bats Both	R	.000	3	0	0	0	0	0	2	1	.500	.000
Belliard,R	L	.000	3	0	0	0	0	0	0	0	.000	.000
Bats Right	R	.294	17	5	0	0	0	1	0	1	.294	.294
Belliard,Ron	L	.200	5	1	0	0	0	0	0	0	.200	.200
Bats Right	R	.000	0	0	0	0	0	0	0	0	.000	.000
Beltran,C	L	.333	21	7	0	0	0	2	2	2	.391	.429
Bats Both	R	.243	37	9	3	3	0	5	1	10	.275	.486
Beltre,Adrian	L	.175	40	7	2	0	0	3	5	8	.267	.225
Bats Right	R	.226	155	35	7	0	7	19	9	29	.281	.406
Benard,Marvin	L	.237	38	9	1	0	0	4	6	8	.348	.263
Bats Left	R	.335	248	83	20	1	3	32	28	31	.404	.460
Benitez,Yamil	L	.204	103	21	3	1	5	17	6	17	.265	.398
Bats Right	R	.194	103	20	4	0	4	13	8	29	.259	.350
Benjamin,Mike	L	.284	95	27	7	0	1	11	4	16	.317	.389
Bats Right	R	.268	254	68	16	0	3	28	11	57	.310	.366

Batters vs. Lefthanded and Righthanded Pitchers

Batter	vs	Avg	AB	H	2B	3B	HR	BI	BB	SO	OBP	SLG
Bennett,Gary	L	.125	8	1	0	0	0	0	1	2	.222	.125
Bats Right	R	.348	23	8	0	0	0	3	4	3	.429	.348
Berg,Dave	L	.290	69	20	5	0	2	12	10	19	.375	.449
Bats Right	R	.327	113	37	6	0	0	9	16	27	.405	.381
Berroa,G	L	.288	73	21	4	2	0	4	13	14	.395	.397
Bats Right	R	.186	118	22	3	0	1	9	11	30	.267	.237
Berry,Sean	L	.383	107	41	6	1	5	24	9	20	.429	.598
Bats Right	R	.276	192	53	11	0	8	28	22	30	.365	.458
Bichette,D	L	.292	185	54	8	0	4	31	9	19	.320	.400
Bats Right	R	.346	477	165	40	2	18	91	19	57	.371	.551
Bieser,Steve	L	.000	0	0	0	0	0	0	0	0	.000	.000
Bats Left	R	.273	11	3	1	0	0	1	2	2	.385	.364
Biggio,Craig	L	.343	137	47	12	0	4	19	13	21	.438	.518
Bats Right	R	.320	509	163	39	2	16	69	51	92	.393	.499
Blauser,Jeff	L	.270	100	27	3	1	2	8	17	21	.387	.380
Bats Right	R	.199	261	52	8	2	2	18	43	72	.323	.268
Blowers,Mike	L	.292	171	50	11	2	5	30	18	48	.360	.468
Bats Right	R	.197	238	47	13	0	6	41	21	68	.261	.328
Bogar,Tim	L	.182	44	8	2	0	0	2	2	9	.229	.227
Bats Right	R	.143	112	16	2	1	1	6	7	27	.200	.205
Boggs,Wade	L	.254	118	30	3	1	3	13	7	23	.294	.373
Bats Left	R	.290	317	92	20	3	4	39	39	31	.367	.410
Bolick,Frank	L	.200	5	1	1	0	0	0	2	1	.429	.400
Bats Both	R	.150	40	6	1	0	1	2	9	7	.306	.250
Bonds,Barry	L	.280	168	47	9	0	9	37	39	25	.418	.494
Bats Left	R	.313	384	120	35	7	28	85	91	67	.447	.659
Bonilla,Bobby	L	.276	58	16	0	0	4	10	6	8	.338	.483
Bats Both	R	.244	275	67	11	1	7	35	35	51	.324	.367
Boone,Aaron	L	.208	53	11	3	0	0	4	2	10	.250	.264
Bats Right	R	.313	128	40	10	2	2	24	13	26	.388	.469
Boone,Bret	L	.230	135	31	7	0	4	15	12	31	.291	.370
Bats Right	R	.277	448	124	31	1	20	80	36	73	.334	.484
Booty,Josh	L	.000	2	0	0	0	0	0	0	0	.000	.000
Bats Right	R	.176	17	3	1	0	0	3	3	8	.300	.235
Borders,Pat	L	.237	38	9	2	0	0	0	3	12	.293	.289
Bats Right	R	.238	122	29	4	0	0	6	7	28	.288	.270
Bordick,Mike	L	.184	114	21	6	1	4	13	11	11	.256	.360
Bats Right	R	.285	351	100	23	0	9	38	28	54	.352	.427
Bournigal,R	L	.233	60	14	2	0	1	7	2	2	.270	.317
Bats Right	R	.221	149	33	9	0	0	12	8	9	.263	.282
Bragg,Darren	L	.246	61	15	6	0	1	11	9	15	.352	.393
Bats Left	R	.284	348	99	23	3	7	46	33	84	.351	.428
Branson,Jeff	L	.083	12	1	0	0	0	0	0	4	.083	.083
Bats Left	R	.216	88	19	4	1	1	9	3	17	.239	.318
Branyan,Russ	L	.000	1	0	0	0	0	0	0	1	.000	.000
Bats Left	R	.000	3	0	0	0	0	0	0	1	.000	.000
Brede,Brent	L	.121	33	4	1	0	0	1	4	12	.256	.152
Bats Left	R	.246	179	44	8	3	2	16	20	31	.322	.358
Brogna,Rico	L	.231	143	33	7	1	3	24	8	33	.270	.357
Bats Left	R	.277	422	117	29	2	17	80	41	92	.335	.476
Brosius,Scott	L	.370	119	44	16	0	7	30	12	20	.436	.681
Bats Right	R	.280	411	115	18	0	12	68	40	77	.353	.411
Brown,Adrian	L	.395	43	17	2	0	0	4	2	6	.422	.442
Bats Both	R	.239	109	26	2	1	0	1	7	12	.284	.275
Brown,Brant	L	.234	64	15	3	1	3	10	3	27	.275	.453
Bats Left	R	.304	283	86	14	6	11	38	27	68	.365	.512
Brown,Dermal	L	.000	1	0	0	0	0	0	0	0	.000	.000
Bats Left	R	.000	2	0	0	0	0	0	0	1	.000	.000
Brown,Emil	L	.167	12	2	0	0	0	0	1	6	.231	.167
Bats Right	R	.296	27	8	1	0	0	3	0	5	.321	.333
Brown,K	L	.273	55	15	4	0	0	5	4	16	.323	.345
Bats Right	R	.255	55	14	3	1	2	10	5	15	.317	.455
Buford,Damon	L	.333	132	44	12	1	8	29	13	25	.390	.621
Bats Right	R	.202	84	17	3	0	2	13	9	18	.284	.369
Buhner,Jay	L	.173	52	9	1	0	4	7	5	18	.241	.423
Bats Right	R	.260	192	50	6	1	11	38	33	53	.370	.474
Burks,Ellis	L	.324	139	45	6	2	7	19	23	31	.415	.547
Bats Right	R	.279	365	102	22	4	14	57	35	80	.345	.477
Burnitz,J	L	.271	199	54	9	1	8	32	13	56	.321	.447
Bats Left	R	.259	410	106	19	0	30	93	57	102	.347	.524
Bush,Homer	L	.294	17	5	1	0	0	0	2	6	.368	.353
Bats Right	R	.407	54	22	2	0	1	5	3	13	.439	.500
Butler,Rich	L	.214	28	6	0	1	1	2	3	3	.313	.393
Bats Left	R	.228	189	43	3	2	6	18	12	34	.273	.360
Cabrera,J	L	.000	2	0	0	0	0	0	0	1	.000	.000
Bats Right	R	.000	0	0	0	0	0	0	0	0	.000	.000
Cabrera,O	L	.308	52	16	1	0	0	5	4	4	.357	.327
Bats Right	R	.273	209	57	15	5	3	17	14	23	.317	.435
Cairo,Miguel	L	.328	125	41	8	1	2	19	9	9	.375	.456
Bats Right	R	.249	390	97	18	4	3	27	15	35	.285	.338
Cameron,Mike	L	.218	87	19	4	0	2	11	14	17	.324	.333
Bats Right	R	.207	309	64	12	5	6	32	23	84	.273	.337
Caminiti,Ken	L	.230	161	37	9	0	9	30	20	43	.317	.453
Bats Both	R	.265	291	77	20	0	20	52	51	65	.372	.540
Cangelosi,J	L	.230	87	20	6	0	1	5	13	10	.327	.333
Bats Both	R	.274	84	23	2	0	0	5	17	13	.402	.298
Canseco,Jose	L	.213	141	30	3	0	15	34	25	41	.327	.553
Bats Right	R	.244	442	108	23	0	31	73	40	118	.314	.507
Carter,Joe	L	.297	148	44	9	0	10	25	9	21	.340	.561
Bats Right	R	.238	240	57	1	0	8	38	15	40	.282	.400
Caruso,Mike	L	.314	102	32	6	0	1	10	2	13	.327	.402
Bats Left	R	.304	421	128	11	6	4	45	12	25	.332	.387
Casanova,Raul	L	.200	5	1	1	0	0	0	2	0	.429	.400
Bats Both	R	.135	37	5	1	0	1	3	3	10	.220	.243
Casey,Sean	L	.222	45	10	2	0	1	8	5	11	.308	.333
Bats Left	R	.280	257	72	19	1	6	44	38	34	.375	.432
Castilla,V	L	.320	172	55	7	2	11	34	11	25	.362	.576
Bats Right	R	.319	473	151	21	2	35	110	29	64	.361	.594
Castillo,A	L	.222	18	4	0	0	1	1	4	1	.364	.389
Bats Right	R	.200	65	13	4	0	1	6	5	16	.268	.308

Batters vs. Lefthanded and Righthanded Pitchers

Batter	vs	Avg	AB	H	2B	3B	HR	BI	BB	SO	OBP	SLG
Castillo,Luis	L	.200	45	9	1	1	1	3	12	7	.368	.333
Bats Right	R	.204	108	22	2	1	0	7	10	26	.277	.241
Castro,Juan	L	.217	60	13	1	0	1	5	6	8	.284	.283
Bats Both	R	.188	160	30	6	0	1	9	9	29	.229	.244
Catalanotto,F	L	.364	11	4	1	0	0	5	1	1	.467	.455
Bats Left	R	.277	202	56	12	2	6	20	11	38	.315	.446
Cedeno,D	L	.327	49	16	4	0	1	6	1	11	.340	.469
Bats Both	R	.228	92	21	5	1	1	15	9	21	.294	.337
Cedeno,Roger	L	.186	70	13	2	1	1	3	9	24	.278	.286
Bats Both	R	.265	170	45	9	0	1	14	18	33	.333	.335
Chavez,Eric	L	.333	3	1	0	1	0	0	0	1	.333	1.000
Bats Left	R	.310	42	13	4	0	0	6	3	4	.356	.405
Chavez,Raul	L	.000	0	0	0	0	0	0	0	0	.000	.000
Bats Right	R	.000	1	0	0	0	0	0	0	0	.000	.000
Christenson,R	L	.241	108	26	6	0	1	6	18	29	.349	.324
Bats Right	R	.263	262	69	16	2	4	34	18	77	.309	.385
Cianfrocco,A	L	.171	41	7	2	0	1	2	4	9	.261	.293
Bats Right	R	.065	31	2	1	0	0	3	1	13	.094	.097
Cirillo,Jeff	L	.299	167	50	6	0	3	21	28	26	.400	.389
Bats Right	R	.330	437	144	25	1	11	47	51	62	.403	.467
Clark,Dave	L	.000	4	0	0	0	0	0	2	2	.333	.000
Bats Left	R	.213	127	27	7	0	0	4	12	43	.286	.268
Clark,Tony	L	.331	172	57	11	0	10	30	19	34	.394	.570
Bats Both	R	.274	430	118	26	0	24	73	44	94	.344	.502
Clark,Will	L	.327	147	48	13	0	5	25	14	34	.386	.517
Bats Left	R	.297	407	121	28	1	18	77	58	63	.383	.504
Clayton,Royce	L	.303	142	43	11	1	5	20	22	20	.392	.500
Bats Right	R	.233	399	93	20	1	4	33	31	63	.291	.318
Clemente,E	L	.333	6	2	0	1	0	1	0	3	.333	.667
Bats Right	R	.364	11	4	0	0	0	1	2	5	.462	.364
Clyburn,Danny	L	.333	12	4	0	0	0	2	1	7	.385	.333
Bats Right	R	.231	13	3	0	0	1	1	0	3	.231	.462
Colbrunn,Greg	L	.291	110	32	4	2	2	9	5	25	.328	.418
Bats Right	R	.339	56	19	7	0	1	14	5	9	.422	.518
Collier,Lou	L	.266	79	21	5	1	0	9	14	21	.379	.354
Bats Right	R	.239	255	61	8	5	2	25	17	49	.295	.333
Conine,Jeff	L	.241	79	19	5	0	0	8	9	16	.311	.304
Bats Right	R	.261	230	60	21	0	8	35	17	52	.312	.457
Coomer,Ron	L	.281	135	38	7	1	5	21	3	16	.285	.459
Bats Right	R	.274	394	108	15	0	10	51	15	56	.299	.388
Cora,Alex	L	.000	3	0	0	0	0	0	0	1	.000	.000
Bats Left	R	.133	30	4	0	1	0	0	2	7	.212	.200
Cora,Joey	L	.239	113	27	7	0	0	8	18	14	.346	.301
Bats Both	R	.284	489	139	20	6	6	24	55	45	.360	.387
Cordero,Wil	L	.265	102	27	4	0	6	12	8	21	.324	.480
Bats Right	R	.268	239	64	14	2	7	37	14	45	.309	.431
Cordova,Marty	L	.330	91	30	5	1	3	16	18	21	.436	.505
Bats Right	R	.233	347	81	15	1	7	53	32	82	.303	.343
Counsell,C	L	.235	68	16	2	1	0	6	2	10	.268	.294
Bats Left	R	.255	267	68	17	4	4	34	49	37	.375	.393
Cradle,Rickey	L	.000	3	0	0	0	0	0	1	3	.250	.000
Bats Right	R	.250	4	1	0	0	0	2	0	2	.250	.250
Crespo,Felipe	L	.261	23	6	0	0	1	6	5	6	.379	.391
Bats Both	R	.262	107	28	8	1	0	9	10	21	.333	.355
Cromer,Tripp	L	.000	2	0	0	0	0	0	0	1	.000	.000
Bats Right	R	.250	4	1	0	0	1	1	0	1	.250	1.000
Cruz,Deivi	L	.340	103	35	9	1	2	15	4	12	.370	.505
Bats Right	R	.236	351	83	13	2	3	30	9	43	.258	.311
Cruz,Jacob	L	.000	1	0	0	0	0	0	0	0	.000	.000
Bats Left	R	.000	3	0	0	0	0	0	0	2	.000	.000
Cruz Jr.,Jose	L	.289	90	26	6	0	2	6	21	22	.420	.422
Bats Both	R	.240	262	63	8	3	9	36	36	77	.329	.397
Cummings,M	L	.111	9	1	0	0	1	3	0	2	.111	.444
Bats Left ,	R	.297	111	33	8	0	4	12	17	17	.400	.477
Curtis,Chad	L	.241	137	33	7	1	8	25	23	19	.358	.482
Bats Right	R	.245	319	78	14	0	2	31	52	61	.354	.307
Cuyler,Milt	L	.500	4	2	2	0	0	0	0	0	.500	1.000
Bats Both	R	.500	2	1	0	0	1	3	1	0	.667	2.000
Dalesandro,M	L	.333	33	11	2	0	1	7	0	4	.333	.485
Bats Right	R	.265	34	9	3	0	1	7	1	2	.278	.441
Damon,Johnny	L	.245	192	47	9	1	3	12	14	29	.301	.349
Bats Left	R	.291	450	131	21	9	15	54	44	55	.355	.478
Daubach,Brian	L	.000	1	0	0	0	0	0	0	1	.000	.000
Bats Left	R	.214	14	3	1	0	0	3	1	4	.313	.286
Davis,Ben	L	.000	0	0	0	0	0	0	0	0	.000	.000
Bats Both	R	.000	1	0	0	0	0	0	0	0	.000	.000
Davis,Chili	L	.357	42	15	5	0	3	7	5	7	.426	.690
Bats Both	R	.246	61	15	2	0	0	2	9	11	.338	.279
Davis,Eric	L	.296	162	48	12	0	10	30	18	38	.368	.556
Bats Right	R	.345	290	100	17	1	18	59	26	70	.399	.597
Davis,Russ	L	.278	97	27	9	0	2	15	7	22	.321	.433
Bats Right	R	.254	405	103	21	1	18	67	27	112	.301	.444
Delgado,C	L	.303	155	47	13	0	5	39	18	42	.387	.484
Bats Left	R	.288	375	108	30	1	33	76	55	97	.385	.637
Delgado,W	L	.000	4	0	0	0	0	1	0	1	.000	.000
Bats Both	R	.250	8	2	1	0	0	0	1	2	.333	.375
Dellucci,D	L	.273	99	27	8	2	1	12	6	26	.321	.424
Bats Left	R	.256	317	81	11	10	4	39	27	77	.317	.391
DeRosa,Mark	L	.000	1	0	0	0	0	0	0	1	.000	.000
Bats Right	R	.500	2	1	0	0	0	0	0	0	.500	.500
DeShields,D	L	.267	101	27	4	4	0	12	10	13	.333	.386
Bats Left	R	.298	319	95	17	4	7	32	46	48	.382	.442
Devereaux,M	L	.333	9	3	1	0	0	1	3	0	.500	.444
Bats Right	R	.250	4	1	0	0	0	0	0	2	.250	.250
Diaz,Alex	L	.185	27	5	1	0	0	2	0	5	.185	.222
Bats Both	R	.086	35	3	1	0	0	3	0	10	.086	.114
Diaz,Edwin	L	.000	1	0	0	0	0	0	0	0	.000	.000
Bats Right	R	.000	6	0	0	0	0	0	0	2	.000	.000
Diaz,Einar	L	.188	16	3	0	0	0	2	0	0	.250	.188
Bats Right	R	.250	32	8	1	0	2	7	3	2	.306	.469

Batters vs. Lefthanded and Righthanded Pitchers

Batter	vs	Avg	AB	H	2B	3B	HR	BI	BB	SO	OBP	SLG
DiFelice,Mike	L	.279	61	17	2	1	1	8	3	13	.308	.393
Bats Right	R	.214	187	40	10	2	2	15	12	43	.264	.321
DiSarcina,G	L	.311	135	42	11	0	1	15	6	11	.345	.415
Bats Right	R	.279	416	116	28	3	2	41	15	40	.313	.375
Drew,J.D.	L	.400	10	4	0	0	2	3	0	3	.400	1.000
Bats Left	R	.423	26	11	3	1	3	10	4	7	.484	.962
Ducey,Rob	L	.118	17	2	1	0	0	1	1	7	.167	.176
Bats Left	R	.250	200	50	17	2	5	22	22	54	.349	.430
Dunston,S	L	.209	86	18	4	1	3	4	3	7	.250	.384
Bats Right	R	.231	121	28	9	2	3	16	3	21	.258	.413
Dunwoody,T.	L	.221	68	15	1	0	2	6	4	24	.284	.324
Bats Left	R	.257	366	94	26	7	3	22	17	89	.294	.391
Durham,Ray	L	.281	171	48	8	1	6	19	10	32	.322	.444
Bats Both	R	.287	464	133	27	7	13	48	63	73	.376	.459
Dye,Jermaine	L	.256	43	11	2	0	1	5	3	11	.304	.372
Bats Right	R	.228	171	39	3	1	4	18	8	35	.261	.327
Easley,Damion	L	.290	138	40	9	0	4	13	10	23	.355	.442
Bats Right	R	.265	456	121	29	2	23	87	29	89	.325	.489
Echevarria,A	L	.267	15	4	1	0	0	5	1	2	.353	.333
Bats Right	R	.500	14	7	2	0	1	4	1	1	.563	.857
Edmonds,Jim	L	.272	195	53	10	0	4	22	15	52	.324	.385
Bats Left	R	.324	404	131	32	1	21	69	42	62	.388	.564
Eisenreich,J	L	.200	15	3	0	0	0	0	0	6	.200	.200
Bats Left	R	.216	176	38	3	2	1	13	16	30	.281	.273
Elster,Kevin	L	.240	75	18	5	1	2	12	7	13	.313	.413
Bats Right	R	.230	222	51	5	0	6	25	26	53	.311	.333
Encarnacion,J	L	.250	28	7	0	1	0	2	4	7	.344	.321
Bats Right	R	.346	136	47	9	3	7	19	3	24	.357	.610
Erstad,Darin	L	.263	167	44	11	1	7	29	14	25	.335	.467
Bats Left	R	.311	370	115	28	2	12	53	29	52	.361	.495
Estalella,B	L	.130	46	6	2	1	0	2	5	14	.212	.217
Bats Right	R	.210	119	25	4	0	8	18	8	35	.262	.445
Eusebio,Tony	L	.262	42	11	2	0	0	7	4	10	.326	.310
Bats Right	R	.250	140	35	4	1	1	29	14	21	.318	.314
Evans,Tom	L	.000	4	0	0	0	0	0	0	1	.000	.000
Bats Right	R	.000	6	0	0	0	0	0	1	1	.143	.000
Everett,Carl	L	.268	82	22	4	0	3	15	2	17	.294	.427
Bats Both	R	.301	385	116	30	4	12	61	42	85	.371	.494
Fabregas,J	L	.217	23	5	1	0	0	2	2	4	.280	.261
Bats Left	R	.194	160	31	3	0	2	18	12	28	.251	.250
Fasano,Sal	L	.157	51	8	3	0	1	8	2	14	.211	.275
Bats Right	R	.248	165	41	7	0	7	23	8	42	.337	.418
Febles,Carlos	L	.333	6	2	1	0	0	0	0	2	.333	.500
Bats Right	R	.421	19	8	0	2	0	2	4	5	.522	.632
Fernandez,T	L	.361	122	44	15	1	2	21	6	8	.389	.549
Bats Both	R	.308	364	112	21	1	7	51	39	45	.386	.429
Fick,Robert	L	.000	2	0	0	0	0	0	0	1	.000	.000
Bats Left	R	.400	20	8	1	0	3	7	2	6	.455	.900
Fielder,Cecil	L	.254	130	33	4	0	7	19	19	41	.358	.446
Bats Right	R	.224	286	64	13	1	10	49	34	70	.308	.381
Figga,Mike	L	.500	2	1	0	0	0	0	0	1	.500	.500
Bats Right	R	.000	2	0	0	0	0	0	0	0	.000	.000
Finley,Steve	L	.188	197	37	12	1	2	12	12	40	.244	.289
Bats Left	R	.277	422	117	28	5	12	55	33	63	.328	.453
Flaherty,John	L	.234	64	15	4	0	1	4	5	9	.282	.344
Bats Right	R	.200	240	48	7	0	2	20	17	37	.255	.254
Fletcher,D	L	.203	59	12	2	0	1	7	4	8	.279	.288
Bats Left	R	.296	348	103	21	1	8	45	21	31	.337	.431
Floyd,Cliff	L	.329	155	51	13	2	3	27	5	36	.352	.497
Bats Left	R	.266	433	115	32	1	19	63	42	76	.332	.476
Forbes,P.J.	L	.000	4	0	0	0	0	0	0	0	.000	.000
Bats Right	R	.167	6	1	0	0	0	2	0	0	.167	.167
Fordyce,Brook	L	.302	63	19	6	0	2	9	7	12	.371	.492
Bats Right	R	.217	83	18	3	0	1	5	4	16	.253	.289
Fox,Andy	L	.333	96	32	7	1	0	15	9	17	.413	.427
Bats Left	R	.264	406	107	14	5	9	29	34	80	.341	.389
Franco,Matt	L	.333	12	4	0	0	0	0	1	2	.385	.333
Bats Left	R	.268	149	40	7	2	1	13	22	24	.364	.362
Frank,Mike	L	.154	13	2	1	0	0	2	0	0	.154	.231
Bats Left	R	.237	76	18	5	0	0	5	7	12	.298	.303
Frazier,Lou	L	.000	0	0	0	0	0	0	0	0	.000	.000
Bats Both	R	.000	7	0	0	0	0	0	2	6	.222	.000
Frias,Hanley	L	.333	3	1	0	1	0	0	0	0	.333	1.000
Bats Both	R	.100	20	2	0	0	1	2	0	5	.100	.250
Fryman,Travis	L	.309	136	42	10	0	4	17	14	24	.375	.471
Bats Right	R	.280	421	118	23	2	24	79	30	101	.329	.515
Fullmer,Brad	L	.244	90	22	8	0	2	10	8	14	.320	.400
Bats Left	R	.280	415	116	36	2	11	63	31	56	.329	.455
Gaetti,Gary	L	.291	141	41	12	0	10	29	19	23	.377	.589
Bats Right	R	.276	293	81	22	1	9	41	24	39	.347	.451
Galarraga,A	L	.328	134	44	6	0	12	32	19	24	.414	.642
Bats Right	R	.297	421	125	21	1	32	89	44	122	.391	.580
Gant,Ron	L	.286	105	30	4	1	8	24	18	23	.392	.571
Bats Right	R	.223	278	62	13	0	18	43	33	69	.307	.464
Garcia,Carlos	L	.333	3	1	0	0	0	0	1	0	.500	.333
Bats Right	R	.125	32	4	1	0	0	0	2	11	.200	.156
Garcia,Freddy	L	.233	60	14	2	0	3	8	4	20	.292	.417
Bats Right	R	.268	112	30	9	1	6	18	14	25	.352	.527
Garcia,G	L	.160	25	4	1	0	1	2	1	10	.192	.320
Bats Right	R	.273	11	3	1	0	1	2	1	3	.333	.636
Garcia,Karim	L	.302	43	13	4	3	0	10	3	9	.348	.535
Bats Left	R	.210	290	61	6	5	9	33	15	69	.247	.359
Garciaparra,N	L	.320	153	49	9	3	7	29	14	20	.374	.556
Bats Right	R	.324	451	146	28	5	28	93	19	42	.358	.594
Gates,Brent	L	.239	92	22	3	0	0	8	12	11	.321	.272
Bats Both	R	.253	241	61	12	0	3	34	24	35	.325	.340
Giambi,Jason	L	.257	206	53	8	0	8	33	26	47	.351	.413
Bats Left	R	.317	356	113	20	0	19	77	55	55	.402	.534
Giambi,Jeremy	L	.143	7	1	0	0	0	3	3	1	.364	.143
Bats Left	R	.235	51	12	4	0	2	5	8	8	.339	.431

Batters vs. Lefthanded and Righthanded Pitchers

Batter	vs	Avg	AB	H	2B	3B	HR	BI	BB	SO	OBP	SLG	Batter	vs	Avg	AB	H	2B	3B	HR	BI	BB	SO	OBP	SLG
Gibson,D	L	.462	13	6	1	0	0	2	0	3	.462	.538	Griffey Jr.,K	L	.299	177	53	6	1	21	47	16	33	.360	.701
Bats Right	R	.375	8	3	0	0	0	0	1	1	.500	.375	Bats Left	R	.279	456	127	27	2	35	99	60	88	.367	.577
Gilbert,Shawn	L	.333	3	1	0	0	0	0	0	2	.333	.333	Grissom,M	L	.253	150	38	8	0	3	18	8	18	.289	.367
Bats Right	R	.000	2	0	0	0	0	0	0	0	.000	.000	Bats Right	R	.278	392	109	20	1	7	42	16	60	.309	.388
Giles,B	L	.229	48	11	1	0	0	6	12	13	.383	.250	Grudzielanek,M	L	.264	129	34	5	0	3	15	8	16	.302	.372
Bats Left	R	.275	302	83	18	0	16	60	61	62	.398	.493	Bats Right	R	.274	460	126	16	1	7	47	18	57	.314	.359
Gilkey,B	L	.208	101	21	4	0	1	7	11	20	.298	.277	Guerrero,V	L	.339	127	43	9	0	5	17	10	21	.391	.528
Bats Right	R	.242	264	64	11	0	4	26	32	60	.328	.330	Bats Right	R	.321	496	159	28	7	33	92	32	74	.365	.605
Giovanola,Ed	L	.231	13	3	0	0	0	0	3	4	.375	.231	Guerrero,W	L	.325	83	27	3	2	1	5	0	14	.325	.446
Bats Left	R	.230	126	29	3	3	1	9	19	18	.331	.325	Bats Both	R	.273	319	87	11	7	1	22	14	49	.303	.361
Gipson,C	L	.318	22	7	0	0	0	1	1	1	.348	.318	Guevara,G	L	.500	2	1	1	0	0	0	2	0	.750	1.000
Bats Right	R	.172	29	5	1	0	0	1	4	8	.294	.207	Bats Both	R	.182	11	2	1	0	0	0	2	4	.357	.273
Girardi,Joe	L	.239	46	11	2	0	0	6	5	4	.321	.283	Guillen,C	L	.286	7	2	1	0	0	1	1	0	.375	.429
Bats Right	R	.284	208	59	9	4	3	25	9	34	.317	.409	Bats Both	R	.344	32	11	0	1	0	4	2	9	.382	.406
Glanville,D	L	.259	162	42	6	1	2	17	9	21	.298	.346	Guillen,Jose	L	.275	131	36	9	0	7	22	6	26	.304	.504
Bats Right	R	.285	516	147	22	6	6	32	33	68	.333	.386	Bats Right	R	.265	442	117	29	2	7	62	15	74	.296	.387
Glaus,Troy	L	.281	32	9	4	0	0	4	5	7	.378	.406	Guillen,Ozzie	L	.258	66	17	2	1	0	7	5	5	.306	.318
Bats Right	R	.203	133	27	5	0	1	19	10	44	.255	.263	Bats Left	R	.266	214	57	13	0	1	15	20	22	.331	.341
Gomez,Chris	L	.283	120	34	8	0	1	12	16	24	.377	.375	Gutierrez,R	L	.287	122	35	7	1	0	15	16	16	.366	.361
Bats Right	R	.261	329	86	24	3	3	27	35	63	.335	.380	Bats Right	R	.252	369	93	17	2	2	31	38	68	.327	.325
Gonzalez,Alex	L	.272	136	37	12	0	4	17	5	20	.296	.449	Gwynn,Tony	L	.323	161	52	10	0	8	22	10	6	.358	.534
Bats Right	R	.229	432	99	16	1	9	34	23	101	.276	.333	Bats Left	R	.320	300	96	25	0	8	47	25	12	.367	.483
Gonzalez,Alex	L	.043	23	1	0	0	1	1	5	11	.214	.174	Hairston Jr,J	L	.000	3	0	0	0	0	0	0	0	.000	.000
Bats Right	R	.190	63	12	2	0	2	6	4	19	.250	.317	Bats Right	R	.000	4	0	0	0	0	0	0	1	.000	.000
Gonzalez,Juan	L	.355	155	55	13	0	11	42	19	25	.429	.652	Halter,Shane	L	.320	75	24	7	0	2	9	3	16	.346	.493
Bats Right	R	.306	451	138	37	2	34	115	27	101	.344	.623	Bats Right	R	.163	129	21	5	0	0	4	9	22	.220	.202
Gonzalez,Luis	L	.278	151	42	8	2	1	13	13	24	.359	.377	Hamelin,Bob	L	.143	14	2	0	0	0	1	2	5	.235	.143
Bats Left	R	.263	396	104	27	3	22	58	44	38	.333	.513	Bats Left	R	.227	132	30	6	0	7	21	14	25	.302	.432
Goodwin,C	L	.219	32	7	1	0	0	1	3	8	.278	.250	Hamilton,D	L	.317	164	52	9	1	2	16	17	26	.385	.421
Bats Left	R	.252	127	32	6	0	1	5	13	32	.321	.323	Bats Left	R	.305	397	121	19	2	4	35	65	47	.403	.393
Goodwin,Tom	L	.300	80	24	0	1	0	1	8	17	.364	.325	Hammonds,J	L	.271	96	26	7	1	3	17	10	26	.343	.458
Bats Left	R	.289	440	127	13	2	2	32	65	73	.380	.341	Bats Right	R	.286	161	46	9	1	3	22	29	30	.395	.410
Grace,Mark	L	.271	203	55	9	0	4	21	23	23	.351	.374	Haney,Todd	L	.000	2	0	0	0	0	0	1	0	.333	.000
Bats Left	R	.329	392	129	30	3	13	68	70	33	.426	.520	Bats Right	R	.000	1	0	0	0	0	0	0	0	.000	.000
Graffanino,T	L	.199	136	27	7	1	2	8	13	34	.272	.309	Hansen,Jed	L	.000	0	0	0	0	0	0	0	0	.000	.000
Bats Right	R	.222	153	34	7	0	3	14	11	34	.279	.327	Bats Right	R	.000	3	0	0	0	0	0	0	3	.000	.000
Grebeck,Craig	L	.244	78	19	4	0	1	7	6	9	.294	.333	Hardtke,Jason	L	1.000	1	1	0	0	0	1	1	0	1.000	1.000
Bats Right	R	.260	223	58	13	2	1	20	23	33	.339	.350	Bats Both	R	.200	20	4	0	0	0	1	1	6	.238	.200
Green,Shawn	L	.221	172	38	9	0	8	31	10	50	.265	.413	Harris,Lenny	L	.263	19	5	0	0	0	1	1	1	.333	.263
Bats Left	R	.299	458	137	24	4	27	69	40	92	.360	.546	Bats Left	R	.258	271	70	15	0	6	26	16	20	.298	.380
Greene,C	L	.000	1	0	0	0	0	0	0	0	.000	.000	Haselman,Bill	L	.405	37	15	2	0	3	11	1	6	.400	.703
Bats Right	R	.200	20	4	1	0	0	0	0	8	.200	.250	Bats Right	R	.265	68	18	4	0	3	6	2	11	.286	.456
Greene,Todd	L	.133	30	4	2	0	0	2	1	8	.161	.200	Hatcher,Chris	L	.077	13	1	0	0	0	1	1	6	.143	.077
Bats Right	R	.341	41	14	2	0	1	5	1	12	.357	.463	Bats Right	R	.000	2	0	0	0	0	0	0	1	.000	.000
Greene,Willie	L	.250	80	20	2	0	3	12	12	15	.362	.388	Hatteberg,S	L	.234	47	11	1	0	1	8	7	9	.339	.319
Bats Left	R	.259	316	82	17	1	12	42	57	75	.372	.434	Bats Left	R	.282	312	88	22	1	11	35	36	49	.362	.465
Greer,Rusty	L	.337	175	59	4	2	4	33	19	28	.401	.451	Hayes,Charlie	L	.338	130	44	5	0	5	26	15	23	.407	.492
Bats Left	R	.293	423	124	27	3	12	75	61	65	.380	.456	Bats Right	R	.251	199	50	3	0	7	36	19	38	.314	.372
Grieve,Ben	L	.253	217	55	15	0	8	38	30	57	.345	.433	Helms,Wes	L	.200	5	1	1	0	0	0	0	2	.200	.400
Bats Left	R	.309	366	113	26	2	10	51	55	66	.410	.473	Bats Right	R	.375	8	3	0	0	1	2	0	2	.375	.750

Batters vs. Lefthanded and Righthanded Pitchers

Batter	vs	Avg	AB	H	2B	3B	HR	BI	BB	SO	OBP	SLG	Batter	vs	Avg	AB	H	2B	3B	HR	BI	BB	SO	OBP	SLG
Helton,Todd	L	.304	112	34	5	0	5	21	13	12	.394	.482	Hunter,B	L	.264	148	39	8	0	1	6	9	17	.306	.338
Bats Left	R	.318	418	133	32	1	20	76	40	42	.377	.543	Bats Right	R	.251	447	112	21	3	3	30	27	77	.296	.331
Henderson,R	L	.256	156	40	9	0	5	18	36	35	.396	.410	Hunter,Torii	L	.400	5	2	0	0	0	1	1	1	.500	.400
Bats Right	R	.228	386	88	7	1	9	39	82	79	.368	.321	Bats Right	R	.167	12	2	1	0	0	1	1	5	.231	.250
Henley,Bob	L	.333	21	7	1	0	1	5	2	3	.375	.524	Huskey,Butch	L	.299	117	35	5	0	5	19	13	12	.363	.470
Bats Right	R	.298	94	28	7	1	2	13	9	23	.377	.457	Bats Right	R	.230	252	58	13	0	8	40	13	54	.268	.377
Hernandez,C	L	.288	132	38	6	0	3	12	9	13	.343	.402	Huson,Jeff	L	.333	3	1	1	0	0	1	0	0	.333	.667
Bats Right	R	.248	258	64	9	0	6	40	7	41	.285	.353	Bats Left	R	.152	46	7	0	0	1	3	5	6	.235	.217
Hernandez,J	L	.255	157	40	7	4	9	25	14	37	.314	.522	Ibanez,Raul	L	.182	11	2	1	0	0	1	0	3	.182	.273
Bats Right	R	.254	331	84	16	3	14	50	26	103	.309	.447	Bats Left	R	.264	87	23	6	1	2	11	5	19	.304	.425
Hidalgo,R	L	.313	80	25	7	0	1	8	8	13	.378	.438	Incaviglia,P	L	.067	15	1	0	0	0	0	2	4	.176	.067
Bats Right	R	.298	131	39	8	0	6	27	9	24	.340	.496	Bats Right	R	.133	15	2	1	0	0	2	0	6	.133	.200
Higginson,Bob	L	.277	188	52	8	2	6	33	18	40	.343	.436	Jackson,D	L	.273	11	3	1	0	0	0	1	1	.333	.364
Bats Left	R	.288	424	122	29	2	19	52	45	61	.360	.500	Bats Right	R	.333	27	9	4	0	0	7	5	3	.424	.481
Hill,G	L	.315	130	41	4	0	6	16	12	25	.373	.485	Jackson,D	L	.250	72	18	4	0	2	6	6	12	.308	.389
Bats Right	R	.308	260	80	21	2	14	40	16	54	.354	.565	Bats Right	R	.235	132	31	9	1	2	14	3	25	.257	.364
Hinch,A.J.	L	.220	91	20	5	0	3	8	5	19	.253	.374	Jackson,Ryan	L	.308	39	12	2	0	0	2	4	9	.386	.359
Bats Right	R	.236	246	58	5	0	6	27	25	70	.312	.329	Bats Left	R	.240	221	53	13	1	5	29	16	64	.290	.376
Hocking,Denny	L	.158	57	9	0	0	0	6	8	18	.254	.158	Jaha,John	L	.197	66	13	2	0	2	12	21	19	.391	.318
Bats Both	R	.220	141	31	6	1	3	9	8	26	.262	.340	Bats Right	R	.213	150	32	4	1	5	26	28	47	.355	.353
Hoiles,Chris	L	.257	70	18	2	0	3	15	19	14	.413	.414	Javier,Stan	L	.291	103	30	2	0	0	9	8	17	.342	.311
Bats Right	R	.264	197	52	10	0	12	41	19	36	.335	.497	Bats Both	R	.290	314	91	11	5	4	40	57	46	.397	.395
Holbert,Ray	L	.000	4	0	0	0	0	0	0	0	.000	.000	Jefferies,G	L	.286	119	34	5	1	2	14	5	4	.313	.395
Bats Right	R	.125	16	2	0	0	0	1	2	5	.211	.125	Bats Both	R	.305	436	133	23	2	7	44	24	28	.339	.415
Hollandsworth	L	.286	35	10	2	0	1	5	0	10	.286	.429	Jefferson,R	L	.333	18	6	2	0	0	2	2	3	.409	.444
Bats Left	R	.264	140	37	4	4	2	15	9	32	.313	.393	Bats Left	R	.303	178	54	14	1	8	29	19	37	.371	.528
Hollins,Damon	L	.111	9	1	0	0	0	0	0	2	.111	.111	Jenkins,Geoff	L	.200	45	9	2	1	0	5	1	15	.229	.289
Bats Right	R	.333	6	2	0	0	0	2	0	1	.333	.333	Bats Left	R	.235	217	51	10	0	9	23	19	46	.300	.406
Hollins,Dave	L	.252	115	29	3	0	3	8	16	23	.351	.357	Jensen,Marcus	L	.000	0	0	0	0	0	0	0	0	.000	.000
Bats Both	R	.238	248	59	13	2	8	31	28	46	.326	.403	Bats Both	R	.000	2	0	0	0	0	0	0	2	.000	.000
Houston,Tyler	L	.263	19	5	0	0	0	0	4	5	.391	.263	Jeter,Derek	L	.345	148	51	6	5	6	26	16	14	.409	.574
Bats Left	R	.254	236	60	7	1	9	33	9	48	.280	.407	Bats Right	R	.318	478	152	19	3	13	58	41	105	.376	.452
Howard,David	L	.324	34	11	0	1	1	8	5	7	.410	.471	Johns,Keith	L	.000	0	0	0	0	0	0	0	0	.000	.000
Bats Both	R	.206	68	14	1	0	1	4	7	15	.276	.265	Bats Right	R	.000	0	0	0	0	0	0	1	0	1.000	.000
Howard,T.	L	.000	7	0	0	0	0	0	1	3	.125	.000	Johnson,Brian	L	.227	97	22	3	1	6	12	16	23	.336	.464
Bats Left	R	.203	69	14	4	0	2	4	2	12	.225	.348	Bats Right	R	.242	211	51	5	0	7	22	12	44	.297	.365
Howell,Jack	L	.250	8	2	1	0	0	1	1	2	.333	.375	Johnson,C	L	.265	83	22	3	0	3	10	10	23	.344	.410
Bats Left	R	.300	30	9	4	0	1	6	3	10	.364	.533	Bats Right	R	.207	376	78	15	0	16	48	35	106	.276	.375
Hubbard,Mike	L	.143	14	2	1	0	0	0	0	8	.143	.214	Johnson,Lance	L	.257	109	28	4	0	2	9	12	8	.331	.349
Bats Right	R	.146	41	6	0	0	1	3	0	9	.167	.220	Bats Left	R	.292	195	57	4	4	0	12	14	14	.338	.354
Hubbard,T	L	.366	82	30	4	0	4	8	7	19	.407	.561	Johnson,Mark	L	.000	1	0	0	0	0	0	0	1	.000	.000
Bats Right	R	.254	126	32	5	1	3	10	11	27	.326	.381	Bats Left	R	.077	13	1	0	0	0	0	0	5	.077	.077
Hudler,Rex	L	.133	30	4	1	0	0	1	3	7	.212	.167	Johnson,M	L	.000	2	0	0	0	0	0	0	0	.000	.000
Bats Right	R	.091	11	1	0	0	0	1	1	5	.167	.091	Bats Left	R	.095	21	2	0	2	0	1	1	8	.136	.286
Hughes,Bobby	L	.240	50	12	2	0	2	4	2	12	.269	.400	Johnson,Russ	L	.500	4	2	1	0	0	0	1	1	.600	.750
Bats Right	R	.226	168	38	5	2	7	25	14	42	.288	.405	Bats Right	R	.111	9	1	0	0	0	0	0	4	.200	.111
Hundley,Todd	L	.059	17	1	0	0	0	0	3	14	.200	.059	Jones,Andruw	L	.312	141	44	10	3	12	22	12	28	.370	.681
Bats Both	R	.178	107	19	4	0	3	12	13	41	.270	.299	Bats Right	R	.259	441	114	23	5	19	68	28	101	.305	.463
Hunter,Brian	L	.208	53	11	5	0	2	7	4	8	.276	.415	Jones,Chipper	L	.298	181	54	11	1	2	18	24	42	.380	.403
Bats Right	R	.203	59	12	4	1	2	6	3	15	.242	.407	Bats Both	R	.319	420	134	18	4	32	89	72	51	.413	.610

Batters vs. Lefthanded and Righthanded Pitchers

Batter	vs	Avg	AB	H	2B	3B	HR	BI	BB	SO	OBP	SLG	Batter	vs	Avg	AB	H	2B	3B	HR	BI	BB	SO	OBP	SLG
Jones,Chris	L	.236	72	17	1	0	2	9	5	20	.286	.333	Laker,Tim	L	.375	8	3	0	0	0	0	2	3	.500	.375
Bats Right	R	.122	49	6	2	1	0	4	6	17	.211	.204	Bats Right	R	.333	21	7	1	0	1	2	0	1	.318	.524
Jones,Terry	L	.167	42	7	1	0	1	2	6	7	.271	.262	Lampkin,Tom	L	.079	38	3	1	0	0	1	8	6	.271	.105
Bats Both	R	.229	170	39	6	2	0	13	15	39	.292	.288	Bats Left	R	.264	178	47	11	1	6	27	16	26	.342	.438
Jordan,Brian	L	.351	151	53	15	3	6	26	11	16	.393	.609	Lankford,Ray	L	.264	140	37	9	0	6	27	24	45	.376	.457
Bats Right	R	.303	413	125	19	4	19	65	29	50	.359	.506	Bats Left	R	.303	393	119	28	1	25	78	62	106	.397	.570
Jordan,Kevin	L	.210	81	17	5	0	0	6	2	10	.229	.272	Lansing,Mike	L	.248	161	40	9	0	5	13	13	25	.309	.398
Bats Right	R	.308	169	52	8	0	2	21	6	20	.337	.391	Bats Right	R	.286	423	121	30	2	7	53	26	63	.331	.416
Joyner,Wally	L	.307	114	35	7	0	3	18	11	11	.365	.447	Larkin,Barry	L	.285	123	35	12	1	4	18	27	15	.411	.496
Bats Left	R	.295	325	96	23	1	9	62	40	33	.372	.455	Bats Right	R	.316	415	131	22	9	13	54	52	54	.393	.506
Justice,David	L	.232	155	36	14	0	3	21	10	35	.275	.381	Larkin,S	L	.000	0	0	0	0	0	0	0	0	.000	.000
Bats Left	R	.299	385	115	25	2	18	67	66	63	.395	.514	Bats Left	R	.333	3	1	0	0	0	0	0	1	.333	.333
Kapler,Gabe	L	.286	7	2	0	0	0	0	0	0	.286	.286	Latham,Chris	L	.077	13	1	0	0	0	1	1	6	.143	.077
Bats Right	R	.167	18	3	0	1	0	0	1	4	.211	.278	Bats Both	R	.173	81	14	1	0	1	4	12	30	.280	.222
Karros,Eric	L	.297	101	30	4	0	4	14	13	23	.377	.455	Lawton,Matt	L	.275	131	36	10	1	6	23	21	15	.392	.504
Bats Right	R	.296	406	120	16	1	19	73	34	70	.349	.480	Bats Left	R	.279	426	119	26	5	15	54	65	49	.385	.469
Kelly,Mike	L	.244	119	29	2	1	6	15	10	32	.300	.429	Ledee,Ricky	L	.167	12	2	0	0	0	0	1	5	.231	.167
Bats Right	R	.238	160	38	9	1	4	18	12	48	.291	.381	Bats Left	R	.254	67	17	5	2	1	12	6	24	.311	.433
Kelly,Pat	L	.200	60	12	1	0	3	6	3	22	.234	.367	Ledesma,A.	L	.393	84	33	8	1	0	9	3	9	.409	.512
Bats Right	R	.226	93	21	4	0	1	8	10	26	.314	.301	Bats Right	R	.298	215	64	8	2	0	20	6	42	.318	.353
Kelly,Roberto	L	.349	146	51	4	2	9	26	4	26	.367	.589	Lee,Derrek	L	.215	130	28	10	0	5	23	16	39	.309	.408
Bats Right	R	.288	111	32	3	1	7	20	4	20	.328	.523	Bats Right	R	.241	324	78	19	1	12	51	31	81	.321	.417
Kendall,Jason	L	.372	129	48	16	0	5	20	14	15	.443	.612	Lee,Travis	L	.239	180	43	6	1	4	20	12	38	.286	.350
Bats Right	R	.313	406	127	20	3	7	55	37	36	.401	.429	Bats Left	R	.283	382	108	14	1	18	52	55	85	.372	.466
Kent,Jeff	L	.254	126	32	9	2	4	28	17	24	.342	.452	Leius,Scott	L	.167	30	5	0	0	0	4	0	3	.167	.167
Bats Right	R	.310	400	124	28	1	27	100	31	86	.365	.588	Bats Right	R	.188	16	3	0	0	0	0	1	3	.235	.188
King,Jeff	L	.308	133	41	8	0	6	26	14	16	.376	.504	Lemke,Mark	L	.063	32	2	0	0	0	1	2	7	.118	.063
Bats Right	R	.246	353	87	9	1	18	67	28	57	.297	.431	Bats Both	R	.254	59	15	4	0	0	6	4	8	.292	.322
Kingsale,Gene	L	.000	0	0	0	0	0	0	0	0	.000	.000	Lennon,P	L	.667	3	2	2	0	0	0	0	0	.667	1.333
Bats Both	R	.000	2	0	0	0	0	0	0	1	.000	.000	Bats Right	R	.000	1	0	0	0	0	0	0	1	.000	.000
Kinkade,Mike	L	.000	1	0	0	0	0	0	0	0	.000	.000	Lesher,Brian	L	.143	7	1	1	0	0	1	0	3	.143	.286
Bats Right	R	.000	1	0	0	0	0	0	0	0	.000	.000	Bats Right	R	.000	0	0	0	0	0	0	0	0	.000	.000
Kirby,Wayne	L	.333	3	1	0	0	0	0	0	1	.333	.333	Levis,Jesse	L	.455	11	5	0	0	0	1	2	2	.500	.455
Bats Left	R	.179	28	5	0	1	0	0	1	8	.207	.250	Bats Left	R	.308	26	8	0	0	0	3	5	4	.455	.308
Klassen,Danny	L	.231	26	6	0	0	1	2	3	6	.310	.346	Lewis,Darren	L	.313	163	51	9	0	3	15	25	20	.414	.423
Bats Right	R	.183	82	15	2	1	2	6	6	27	.247	.305	Bats Right	R	.251	422	106	16	3	5	48	45	74	.327	.339
Klesko,Ryan	L	.213	61	13	3	0	0	4	11	11	.342	.262	Lewis,Mark	L	.254	134	34	6	1	0	10	17	24	.333	.313
Bats Left	R	.284	366	104	26	1	18	66	45	55	.362	.508	Bats Right	R	.247	384	95	15	1	9	44	31	87	.304	.362
Knoblauch,C	L	.252	139	35	8	1	3	14	24	17	.369	.388	Leyritz,Jim	L	.265	155	41	11	0	8	25	23	34	.378	.490
Bats Right	R	.269	464	125	17	3	14	50	52	53	.358	.409	Bats Right	R	.291	117	34	5	0	4	17	19	40	.393	.436
Knorr,Randy	L	.136	22	3	1	0	1	6	1	4	.167	.318	Lieberthal,M	L	.308	65	20	4	0	2	8	6	7	.392	.462
Bats Right	R	.259	27	7	3	1	1	5	0	6	.259	.556	Bats Right	R	.242	248	60	11	3	6	37	11	37	.280	.383
Konerko,Paul	L	.288	66	19	4	0	2	17	4	10	.315	.439	Liriano,N	L	.000	6	0	0	0	0	0	0	3	.000	.000
Bats Right	R	.185	151	28	0	0	5	12	12	30	.259	.285	Bats Both	R	.000	11	0	0	0	0	0	0	4	.000	.000
Koskie,Corey	L	.400	5	2	0	0	1	2	0	1	.400	1.000	Little,Mark	L	.000	9	0	0	0	0	0	1	4	.100	.000
Bats Left	R	.083	24	2	0	0	0	0	2	9	.154	.083	Bats Right	R	.333	3	1	0	0	0	0	1	1	.500	.333
Kotsay,Mark	L	.266	139	37	2	5	3	15	3	18	.282	.417	Livingstone,S	L	.000	3	0	0	0	0	0	0	1	.000	.000
Bats Left	R	.282	439	124	23	2	8	53	31	43	.329	.399	Bats Left	R	.215	107	23	6	0	0	12	5	14	.243	.271
Kreuter,Chad	L	.261	46	12	3	0	0	3	7	9	.370	.326	Lockhart,K	L	.189	37	7	2	0	0	1	3	3	.250	.243
Bats Both	R	.248	206	51	7	1	2	30	26	40	.336	.320	Bats Left	R	.264	329	87	19	0	9	36	26	34	.318	.404

Batters vs. Lefthanded and Righthanded Pitchers

Batter	vs	Avg	AB	H	2B	3B	HR	BI	BB	SO	OBP	SLG
LoDuca,Paul	L	.500	6	3	0	0	0	1	0	0	.500	.500
Bats Right	R	.125	8	1	1	0	0	0	0	1	.125	.250
Lofton,Kenny	L	.293	188	55	7	1	4	22	25	30	.377	.404
Bats Left	R	.277	412	114	24	5	8	42	62	50	.369	.417
Lombard,G	L	.000	1	0	0	0	0	0	0	0	.000	.000
Bats Left	R	.400	5	2	0	0	1	1	0	1	.400	1.000
Lopez,Javy	L	.275	109	30	5	1	7	19	7	20	.316	.532
Bats Right	R	.287	380	109	16	0	27	87	23	65	.332	.542
Lopez,Luis	L	.241	87	21	4	1	1	7	2	15	.275	.345
Bats Both	R	.257	179	46	9	1	1	15	18	45	.328	.335
Lopez,Mendy	L	.255	51	13	4	0	1	4	8	9	.356	.392
Bats Right	R	.239	155	37	6	2	0	11	4	31	.261	.303
Loretta,Mark	L	.347	144	50	13	0	1	16	18	11	.423	.458
Bats Right	R	.300	290	87	16	0	5	38	24	36	.361	.407
Lovullo,Torey	L	.000	3	0	0	0	0	0	0	1	.000	.000
Bats Both	R	.250	16	4	1	0	0	1	1	1	.294	.313
Lowell,Mike	L	.333	6	2	0	0	0	0	0	0	.333	.333
Bats Right	R	.222	9	2	0	0	0	0	0	1	.222	.222
Lowery,T	L	.143	7	1	0	0	0	0	2	4	.333	.143
Bats Right	R	.250	8	2	1	0	0	1	1	3	.333	.375
Luke,Matt	L	.200	20	4	2	0	0	1	2	6	.273	.300
Bats Left	R	.237	219	52	10	1	12	33	15	54	.288	.457
Mabry,John	L	.218	78	17	3	0	0	9	4	18	.259	.256
Bats Left	R	.258	299	77	19	0	9	37	26	58	.317	.411
Macfarlane,M	L	.266	64	17	1	0	6	16	4	8	.304	.563
Bats Right	R	.234	154	36	11	0	1	18	8	28	.286	.325
Machado,R	L	.175	40	7	2	0	1	6	2	7	.214	.300
Bats Right	R	.225	71	16	4	0	2	9	5	15	.276	.366
Mack,Shane	L	.228	79	18	5	0	2	12	11	14	.319	.367
Bats Right	R	.308	130	40	10	1	4	17	4	22	.357	.492
Magadan,Dave	L	.125	16	2	1	0	0	1	2	2	.222	.188
Bats Left	R	.355	93	33	7	0	1	12	11	10	.419	.462
Magee,Wendell	L	.258	31	8	1	1	0	5	2	4	.303	.355
Bats Right	R	.318	44	14	5	0	1	6	5	7	.388	.500
Malloy,Marty	L	.000	0	0	0	0	0	0	0	0	.000	.000
Bats Left	R	.179	28	5	1	0	1	1	2	2	.233	.321
Manto,Jeff	L	.256	43	11	2	0	1	6	4	16	.319	.372
Bats Right	R	.208	24	5	1	0	2	3	1	5	.269	.500
Manwaring,K	L	.233	129	30	4	2	1	12	19	20	.336	.318
Bats Right	R	.259	162	42	8	1	1	14	19	29	.342	.340
Marrero,Eli	L	.293	92	27	9	1	1	10	9	16	.353	.446
Bats Right	R	.216	162	35	9	0	3	10	19	26	.298	.327
Martin,Al	L	.216	88	19	4	0	1	9	3	22	.258	.295
Bats Left	R	.244	352	86	11	2	11	38	29	69	.306	.381
Martin,N	L	.217	46	10	2	0	0	2	1	8	.229	.261
Bats Right	R	.215	149	32	0	0	1	11	5	21	.239	.235
Martinez,Dave	L	.250	84	21	2	0	0	5	7	20	.319	.274
Bats Left	R	.258	225	58	9	0	3	15	28	32	.340	.338
Martinez,E	L	.311	106	33	12	0	2	11	32	22	.468	.481
Bats Right	R	.324	450	146	34	1	27	91	74	74	.418	.584
Martinez,F	L	.190	21	4	0	0	0	1	1	6	.261	.190
Bats Both	R	.109	64	7	1	1	0	4	4	15	.162	.156
Martinez,Greg	L	.000	1	0	0	0	0	0	0	1	.000	.000
Bats Both	R	.000	2	0	0	0	0	0	1	1	.333	.000
Martinez,M	L	.274	95	26	7	2	5	16	5	22	.317	.547
Bats Right	R	.224	85	19	4	0	1	8	4	22	.261	.306
Martinez,R	L	.500	6	3	0	0	0	0	2	1	.625	.500
Bats Right	R	.231	13	3	1	0	0	0	2	1	.333	.308
Martinez,S	L	.364	11	4	1	0	0	1	0	2	.364	.455
Bats Left	R	.250	76	19	8	1	0	6	13	19	.363	.382
Martinez,Tino	L	.268	168	45	10	0	9	38	13	37	.330	.488
Bats Left	R	.287	363	104	23	1	19	85	48	46	.366	.512
Marzano,John	L	.185	27	5	2	0	1	1	4	5	.313	.370
Bats Right	R	.245	106	26	5	1	3	11	5	19	.328	.396
Mashore,D.	L	.250	48	12	4	0	2	7	4	13	.308	.458
Bats Right	R	.220	50	11	2	0	0	4	5	9	.328	.260
Matheny,Mike	L	.252	103	26	1	0	4	13	5	15	.287	.379
Bats Right	R	.230	217	50	12	0	2	14	6	48	.274	.313
Maxwell,Jason	L	.500	2	1	0	0	1	2	0	1	.500	2.000
Bats Right	R	.000	1	0	0	0	0	0	0	1	.000	.000
May,Derrick	L	.154	13	2	1	0	0	0	2	3	.267	.231
Bats Left	R	.246	167	41	7	0	5	15	9	21	.282	.377
Mayne,Brent	L	.306	36	11	4	0	0	2	1	7	.324	.417
Bats Left	R	.268	239	64	11	0	3	30	36	40	.363	.351
McCarty,Dave	L	.429	7	3	0	0	1	2	3	4	.600	.857
Bats Right	R	.182	11	2	0	0	0	0	2	0	.308	.182
McClain,Scott	L	.111	9	1	0	0	0	0	2	2	.273	.111
Bats Right	R	.091	11	1	0	0	0	0	0	4	.167	.091
McCracken,Q	L	.282	156	44	9	0	0	18	7	26	.313	.340
Bats Both	R	.295	458	135	29	7	7	41	34	81	.342	.434
McDonald,J	L	.233	43	10	2	0	0	5	2	13	.267	.279
Bats Both	R	.258	132	34	7	0	1	11	25	20	.385	.333
McEwing,Joe	L	.111	9	1	0	0	0	1	1	3	.200	.111
Bats Right	R	.273	11	3	1	0	0	0	0	0	.333	.364
McGee,Willie	L	.224	76	17	1	0	0	8	2	17	.241	.237
Bats Both	R	.264	193	51	9	1	3	26	12	32	.304	.368
McGriff,Fred	L	.274	179	49	8	0	3	19	26	41	.365	.369
Bats Left	R	.288	385	111	25	0	16	62	53	77	.374	.478
McGuire,Ryan	L	.182	44	8	1	0	0	1	10	14	.333	.205
Bats Right	R	.187	166	31	8	0	1	9	22	41	.280	.253
McGwire,Mark	L	.254	130	33	4	0	15	27	49	38	.459	.631
Bats Right	R	.314	379	119	17	0	55	120	113	117	.474	.794
McLemore,M.	L	.259	135	35	8	0	0	12	30	15	.394	.319
Bats Both	R	.242	326	79	7	1	5	41	59	49	.359	.316
McRae,Brian	L	.252	151	38	9	1	2	13	20	27	.341	.364
Bats Both	R	.269	401	108	27	4	19	66	60	63	.367	.499
Meares,Pat	L	.248	133	33	2	1	3	15	5	25	.284	.346
Bats Right	R	.263	410	108	24	2	6	55	19	61	.300	.376
Meluskey,M	L	.333	3	1	0	0	0	0	0	1	.333	.333
Bats Both	R	.200	5	1	1	0	0	0	1	3	.333	.400

Batters vs. Lefthanded and Righthanded Pitchers

Batter	vs	Avg	AB	H	2B	3B	HR	BI	BB	SO	OBP	SLG
Merced,O	L	.133	15	2	0	0	1	2	1	7	.235	.333
Bats Left	R	.288	208	60	12	0	5	38	19	27	.343	.418
Merloni,Lou	L	.265	34	9	2	0	1	5	5	8	.359	.412
Bats Right	R	.290	62	18	4	0	0	10	2	12	.333	.355
Metcalfe,Mike	L	.000	0	0	0	0	0	0	0	0	.000	.000
Bats Right	R	.000	1	0	0	0	0	0	0	1	.000	.000
Meulens,H	L	.083	12	1	0	0	1	1	0	4	.083	.333
Bats Right	R	.000	3	0	0	0	0	0	0	2	.000	.000
Mientkiewicz,D	L	.500	2	1	0	0	0	0	1	0	.667	.500
Bats Left	R	.174	23	4	1	0	0	2	3	3	.269	.217
Mieske,Matt	L	.389	54	21	5	0	0	8	8	9	.460	.481
Bats Right	R	.186	43	8	2	0	1	4	3	8	.255	.302
Millar,Kevin	L	.000	0	0	0	0	0	0	0	0	.000	.000
Bats Right	R	.500	2	1	0	0	0	0	0	1	.667	.500
Miller,Damian	L	.299	67	20	6	1	2	6	5	15	.347	.507
Bats Right	R	.277	101	28	8	1	1	8	6	28	.330	.406
Milliard,R	L	.000	0	0	0	0	0	0	0	0	.000	.000
Bats Right	R	.000	1	0	0	0	0	0	0	1	.000	.000
Minor,Ryan	L	.500	6	3	0	0	0	0	0	2	.500	.500
Bats Right	R	.375	8	3	1	0	0	1	0	1	.375	.500
Mirabelli,D	L	.600	5	3	1	0	1	2	1	1	.667	1.400
Bats Right	R	.083	12	1	1	0	0	2	1	5	.154	.167
Mitchell,K	L	.222	18	4	1	0	0	3	6	2	.417	.278
Bats Right	R	.333	15	5	1	0	0	3	1	3	.375	.400
Mitchell,K	L	.218	78	17	4	1	2	12	5	17	.265	.372
Bats Right	R	.245	49	12	3	0	0	9	4	9	.302	.306
Molina,Ben	L	.000	1	0	0	0	0	0	0	0	.000	.000
Bats Right	R	.000	0	0	0	0	0	0	0	0	.000	.000
Molina,Izzy	L	.000	1	0	0	0	0	0	0	0	.000	.000
Bats Right	R	1.000	1	1	0	0	0	0	0	0	1.000	1.000
Molitor,Paul	L	.264	121	32	9	1	1	13	12	12	.328	.380
Bats Right	R	.286	381	109	20	4	3	56	33	29	.337	.383
Monahan,S.	L	.379	29	11	3	0	1	8	1	4	.400	.586
Bats Left	R	.220	182	40	5	1	3	20	7	49	.249	.308
Mondesi,Raul	L	.241	116	28	3	0	6	14	6	24	.285	.422
Bats Right	R	.289	464	134	23	5	24	76	24	88	.324	.515
Montgomery,R	L	.000	1	0	0	0	0	0	0	0	.000	.000
Bats Right	R	.500	4	2	0	0	0	0	0	0	.500	.500
Morandini,M	L	.224	156	35	4	0	0	11	26	24	.337	.250
Bats Left	R	.322	426	137	16	4	8	42	46	60	.397	.434
Mordecai,Mike	L	.167	42	7	0	0	2	5	3	9	.222	.310
Bats Right	R	.221	77	17	4	2	1	5	6	11	.277	.364
Morris,Hal	L	.294	102	30	4	0	0	7	11	17	.363	.333
Bats Left	R	.314	370	116	23	2	1	33	21	35	.346	.395
Mouton,James	L	.152	33	5	0	0	0	1	4	5	.243	.152
Bats Right	R	.233	30	7	2	1	0	6	3	6	.294	.367
Mouton,Lyle	L	.333	27	9	1	0	2	5	2	5	.379	.593
Bats Right	R	.250	12	3	1	0	0	2	2	3	.357	.333
Mueller,Bill	L	.298	121	36	9	0	3	22	23	21	.407	.446
Bats Both	R	.293	413	121	18	0	6	37	56	62	.376	.380

Batter	vs	Avg	AB	H	2B	3B	HR	BI	BB	SO	OBP	SLG
Myers,Greg	L	.105	19	2	0	0	0	0	1	9	.150	.105
Bats Left	R	.263	152	40	10	0	4	20	16	27	.331	.408
Neill,Mike	L	.000	1	0	0	0	0	0	0	0	.000	.000
Bats Left	R	.286	14	4	1	0	0	0	2	4	.375	.357
Nevin,Phil	L	.242	91	22	5	0	4	11	8	21	.310	.429
Bats Right	R	.219	146	32	3	1	4	16	9	46	.280	.336
Newfield,Marc	L	.258	97	25	3	0	2	13	9	16	.327	.351
Bats Right	R	.213	89	19	4	0	1	12	10	13	.284	.292
Newson,W.	L	.000	0	0	0	0	0	0	0	0	.000	.000
Bats Left	R	.190	21	4	1	0	0	2	1	5	.227	.238
Nieves,Jose	L	.000	0	0	0	0	0	0	0	0	.000	.000
Bats Right	R	.000	1	0	0	0	0	0	0	0	.000	.000
Nieves,Melvin	L	.270	37	10	3	0	1	6	8	13	.400	.432
Bats Both	R	.244	82	20	1	0	1	11	18	29	.373	.293
Nilsson,Dave	L	.127	55	7	2	0	0	7	7	9	.222	.164
Bats Left	R	.299	254	76	12	1	12	49	26	39	.365	.496
Nixon,Otis	L	.216	102	22	2	0	1	6	10	14	.283	.265
Bats Both	R	.321	346	111	4	6	0	14	34	42	.384	.367
Nixon,Trot	L	.000	1	0	0	0	0	0	0	0	.000	.000
Bats Left	R	.269	26	7	1	0	0	1	1	3	.296	.308
Norton,Greg	L	.231	39	9	3	1	2	8	1	16	.250	.513
Bats Both	R	.238	260	62	14	1	7	28	25	61	.308	.381
Nunez,A.	L	.000	9	0	0	0	0	0	1	4	.100	.000
Bats Both	R	.233	43	10	2	0	1	2	11	10	.389	.349
Nunnally,Jon	L	.300	20	6	2	0	1	3	0	2	.333	.550
Bats Left	R	.195	154	30	7	0	6	17	34	36	.335	.357
O'Brien,C	L	.234	47	11	0	0	3	5	5	6	.302	.426
Bats Right	R	.266	128	34	9	0	1	13	5	27	.299	.359
O'Leary,Troy	L	.284	197	56	11	3	4	29	12	38	.329	.431
Bats Left	R	.263	414	109	25	5	19	54	24	70	.306	.486
O'Neill,Paul	L	.286	182	52	8	1	6	39	11	46	.320	.440
Bats Left	R	.331	420	139	32	1	18	77	46	57	.394	.540
Ochoa,Alex	L	.245	106	26	2	1	1	13	6	14	.286	.311
Bats Right	R	.266	143	38	12	1	1	12	4	21	.291	.385
Offerman,Jose	L	.338	195	66	8	4	1	18	27	26	.422	.436
Bats Both	R	.303	412	125	20	9	6	48	62	70	.394	.439
Olerud,John	L	.375	152	57	6	0	5	22	25	22	.467	.513
Bats Left	R	.346	405	140	30	4	17	71	71	51	.440	.565
Oliver,Joe	L	.218	87	19	5	0	1	13	9	16	.289	.310
Bats Right	R	.229	153	35	6	0	5	19	8	32	.262	.366
Ordaz,Luis	L	.115	52	6	2	0	0	1	5	6	.193	.154
Bats Right	R	.248	101	25	3	0	0	7	7	12	.296	.277
Ordonez,M	L	.267	120	32	5	0	5	15	5	9	.302	.433
Bats Right	R	.287	415	119	20	2	9	50	23	44	.333	.410
Ordonez,Rey	L	.255	137	35	5	1	0	14	8	14	.297	.307
Bats Right	R	.242	368	89	15	1	1	28	15	46	.270	.296
Orie,Kevin	L	.286	112	32	7	0	3	15	10	14	.352	.429
Bats Right	R	.191	267	51	15	1	5	23	22	45	.264	.311
Ortiz,David	L	.245	53	13	5	0	1	11	10	12	.388	.396
Bats Left	R	.284	225	64	15	0	8	35	29	60	.367	.458

Batters vs. Lefthanded and Righthanded Pitchers

Batter	vs	Avg	AB	H	2B	3B	HR	BI	BB	SO	OBP	SLG
Ortiz,Hector	L	.000	2	0	0	0	0	0	0	0	.000	.000
Bats Right	R	.000	2	0	0	0	0	0	0	0	.000	.000
Osik,Keith	L	.273	22	6	1	0	0	1	3	1	.385	.318
Bats Right	R	.197	76	15	3	0	0	6	10	15	.295	.237
Otanez,Willis	L	.333	3	1	0	0	0	0	0	1	.333	.333
Bats Right	R	.000	2	0	0	0	0	0	0	1	.000	.000
Owens,Eric	L	.158	19	3	2	0	0	1	1	2	.200	.263
Bats Right	R	.095	21	2	0	0	1	3	1	4	.136	.238
Pagnozzi,Tom	L	.255	51	13	5	0	1	4	6	12	.328	.412
Bats Right	R	.202	109	22	4	0	0	6	8	25	.256	.239
Palmeiro,O	L	.231	13	3	0	0	0	2	2	1	.333	.231
Bats Left	R	.329	152	50	7	2	0	19	18	10	.400	.401
Palmeiro,R	L	.317	230	73	16	1	15	39	23	34	.387	.591
Bats Left	R	.283	389	110	20	0	28	82	56	57	.375	.550
Palmer,Dean	L	.317	139	44	9	0	6	32	11	26	.357	.511
Bats Right	R	.266	433	115	18	2	28	87	37	108	.326	.510
Paquette,C	L	.429	7	3	2	0	0	0	0	1	.429	.714
Bats Right	R	.167	12	2	0	0	0	0	0	5	.167	.167
Parent,Mark	L	.267	30	8	0	0	1	6	2	6	.313	.367
Bats Right	R	.205	83	17	4	0	0	7	8	24	.266	.253
Payton,Jay	L	.267	15	4	1	0	0	0	1	3	.313	.333
Bats Right	R	.429	7	3	0	0	0	0	0	1	.429	.429
Pena,Angel	L	.250	4	1	0	0	0	0	0	2	.250	.250
Bats Right	R	.222	9	2	0	0	0	0	0	4	.222	.222
Pendleton,T	L	.314	51	16	1	0	1	10	4	7	.357	.392
Bats Both	R	.242	186	45	9	0	2	19	11	42	.283	.323
Perez,Eddie	L	.306	49	15	2	0	1	7	6	7	.404	.408
Bats Right	R	.350	100	35	10	0	5	25	9	21	.404	.600
Perez,Eduardo	L	.205	78	16	2	0	2	10	17	20	.354	.308
Bats Right	R	.266	94	25	2	0	2	20	4	25	.297	.351
Perez,Neifi	L	.302	215	65	8	2	6	21	10	20	.333	.442
Bats Both	R	.259	432	112	17	7	3	38	28	50	.303	.352
Perez,Robert	L	.253	91	23	1	0	3	13	2	16	.266	.363
Bats Right	R	.160	50	8	1	0	0	1	0	12	.176	.180
Perez,Tomas	L	.143	7	1	0	0	0	0	0	3	.143	.143
Bats Right	R	.000	2	0	0	0	0	0	1	0	.333	.000
Petagine,R	L	.000	7	0	0	0	0	1	3	3	.273	.000
Bats Left	R	.291	55	16	2	1	3	6	13	8	.426	.527
Phillips,J.R.	L	.300	10	3	0	0	1	4	1	3	.364	.600
Bats Left	R	.167	48	8	0	0	1	5	6	19	.259	.229
Phillips,Tony	L	.271	59	16	6	0	2	6	22	13	.469	.475
Bats Both	R	.243	177	43	10	0	2	15	25	37	.338	.333
Piazza,Mike	L	.323	130	42	9	0	8	28	17	22	.396	.577
Bats Right	R	.329	431	142	29	1	24	83	41	58	.388	.568
Pickering,C	L	.000	1	0	0	0	0	0	0	0	.000	.000
Bats Left	R	.250	20	5	0	0	2	3	3	4	.348	.550
Pierzynski,A	L	1.000	1	1	0	0	0	0	0	0	1.000	1.000
Bats Left	R	.222	9	2	0	0	0	1	1	2	.273	.222
Polanco,P	L	.188	32	6	2	1	0	3	1	5	.212	.313
Bats Right	R	.280	82	23	1	1	1	8	4	4	.322	.354

Batter	vs	Avg	AB	H	2B	3B	HR	BI	BB	SO	OBP	SLG
Polcovich,K	L	.181	72	13	5	0	0	6	7	10	.256	.250
Bats Right	R	.193	140	27	7	0	0	8	8	23	.255	.243
Posada,Jorge	L	.357	112	40	10	0	5	23	9	26	.402	.580
Bats Both	R	.228	246	56	13	0	12	40	38	66	.328	.427
Powell,Dante	L	.500	2	1	0	0	0	0	2	0	.750	.500
Bats Right	R	.500	2	1	0	0	1	1	1	0	.667	2.000
Pratt,Todd	L	.267	30	8	4	0	0	9	2	9	.313	.400
Bats Right	R	.282	39	11	5	1	2	9	0	11	.282	.615
Pride,Curtis	L	.000	5	0	0	0	0	0	1	4	.167	.000
Bats Left	R	.265	102	27	6	1	3	9	8	25	.333	.431
Prince,Tom	L	.316	19	6	3	0	0	1	4	5	.458	.474
Bats Right	R	.145	62	9	2	1	0	4	3	19	.197	.210
Pritchett,C	L	.500	10	5	1	0	0	4	0	2	.500	.600
Bats Left	R	.257	70	18	1	1	2	4	4	14	.297	.386
Radmanovich	L	.556	9	5	0	0	1	3	0	2	.556	.889
Bats Left	R	.167	60	10	4	0	1	7	4	23	.219	.283
Raines,Tim	L	.307	127	39	3	0		18	28	13	.428	.331
Bats Both	R	.278	194	54	10	1	5	29	27	36	.372	.418
Ramirez,Alex	L	.167	6	1	0	0	0	0	0	1	.167	.167
Bats Right	R	.000	2	0	0	0	0	0	0	2	.000	.000
Ramirez,A	L	.255	51	13	1	1	2	4	5	16	.345	.431
Bats Right	R	.230	200	46	8	0	4	20	13	56	.282	.330
Ramirez,Manny	L	.340	150	51	8	1	18	53	17	26	.402	.767
Bats Right	R	.278	421	117	27	1	27	92	59	95	.368	.539
Randa,Joe	L	.254	130	33	6	2	2	15	16	18	.345	.377
Bats Right	R	.255	330	84	15	0	7	35	25	52	.314	.364
Reboulet,Jeff	L	.275	51	14	3	0	0	2	7	9	.362	.333
Bats Right	R	.227	75	17	3	0	1	6	12	25	.344	.307
Redmond,Mike	L	.413	63	26	5	0	2	8	2	7	.439	.587
Bats Right	R	.236	55	13	4	0	0	4	3	9	.288	.309
Reed,Jeff	L	.333	18	6	1	0	1	1	1	6	.368	.556
Bats Left	R	.286	241	69	16	1	8	38	36	51	.377	.461
Reese,Pokey	L	.133	30	4	1	0	0	1	3	5	.212	.167
Bats Right	R	.291	103	30	1	2	1	15	11	23	.353	.369
Relaford,Desi	L	.242	128	31	5	1	1	7	9	28	.290	.320
Bats Both	R	.246	366	90	20	2	4	34	24	59	.294	.344
Renteria,E	L	.234	111	26	4	1	1	7	13	14	.317	.315
Bats Right	R	.296	406	120	14	1	2	24	35	64	.355	.350
Rios,Armando	L	.667	3	2	0	0	0	0	0	0	.667	.667
Bats Right	R	.500	4	2	0	0	2	3	3	2	.714	2.000
Ripken,Billy	L	.192	26	5	0	0	0	2	3	3	.267	.192
Bats Right	R	.313	48	15	3	0	0	3	2	7	.353	.375
Ripken,Cal	L	.258	163	42	8	0	5	20	16	16	.331	.399
Bats Right	R	.276	438	121	19	1	9	41	35	52	.331	.386
Rivera,Luis	L	.182	22	4	1	0	0	0	1	4	.217	.227
Bats Right	R	.269	67	18	3	0	0	7	6	13	.329	.313
Rivera,Ruben	L	.268	97	26	6	1	5	20	11	26	.343	.505
Bats Right	R	.133	75	10	1	1	1	9	17	26	.305	.213
Roberts,Bip	L	.203	79	16	5	0	0	3	7	11	.276	.266
Bats Both	R	.292	216	63	12	0	1	21	24	27	.369	.361

Batters vs. Lefthanded and Righthanded Pitchers

Batter	vs	Avg	AB	H	2B	3B	HR	BI	BB	SO	OBP	SLG
Robertson,M	L	.000	0	0	0	0	0	0	0	0	.000	.000
Bats Left	R	.154	13	2	0	0	0	0	0	2	.154	.154
Robinson,K	L	.000	1	0	0	0	0	0	0	0	.000	.000
Bats Left	R	.000	2	0	0	0	0	0	0	1	.000	.000
Rodriguez,A	L	.313	144	45	8	0	12	32	9	21	.353	.618
Bats Right	R	.310	542	168	27	5	30	92	36	100	.362	.544
Rodriguez,H	L	.250	96	24	5	0	3	17	10	35	.321	.396
Bats Left	R	.251	319	80	16	1	28	68	44	78	.338	.571
Rodriguez,I	L	.317	139	44	8	0	5	22	11	19	.368	.482
Bats Right	R	.323	440	142	32	4	16	69	21	69	.355	.523
Rolen,Scott	L	.280	132	37	8	1	11	26	33	30	.422	.606
Bats Right	R	.292	469	137	37	3	20	84	60	111	.382	.512
Romero,Mandy	L	.250	4	1	0	0	0	0	0	1	.250	.250
Bats Both	R	.111	18	2	1	0	0	1	4	5	.273	.167
Roskos,John	L	.167	6	1	0	0	0	0	0	2	.167	.167
Bats Right	R	.000	4	0	0	0	0	0	0	3	.000	.000
Rossy,Rico	L	.182	22	4	0	0	0	1	1	5	.217	.182
Bats Right	R	.203	59	12	6	0	1	3	5	8	.266	.356
Sadler,Donnie	L	.310	29	9	0	1	0	5	1	4	.323	.379
Bats Right	R	.200	95	19	4	3	3	10	5	24	.262	.400
Salmon,Tim	L	.273	128	35	6	0	4	13	26	22	.395	.414
Bats Right	R	.310	335	104	22	1	22	75	64	78	.416	.579
Samuel,Juan	L	.217	23	5	2	0	1	2	3	7	.333	.435
Bats Right	R	.148	27	4	0	0	0	0	4	6	.258	.148
Sanchez,Rey	L	.377	69	26	5	0	2	10	6	13	.429	.536
Bats Right	R	.259	247	64	9	2	0	20	10	34	.295	.312
Sanders,R	L	.248	113	28	4	1	4	14	12	25	.325	.407
Bats Right	R	.274	368	101	14	5	10	45	39	112	.352	.421
Sanford,C	L	.000	2	0	0	0	0	0	0	1	.000	.000
Bats Left	R	.154	26	4	1	1	0	3	1	5	.185	.269
Santangelo,F	L	.289	83	24	5	0	1	8	10	12	.398	.386
Bats Both	R	.193	300	58	13	0	3	15	34	60	.312	.267
Santiago,B	L	.429	14	6	4	0	0	1	0	1	.429	.714
Bats Right	R	.200	15	3	1	0	0	3	1	5	.250	.267
Sasser,Rob	L	.000	1	0	0	0	0	0	0	0	.000	.000
Bats Right	R	.000	0	0	0	0	0	0	0	0	.000	.000
Sefcik,Kevin	L	.321	56	18	5	0	1	5	10	13	.426	.464
Bats Right	R	.310	113	35	2	2	2	15	15	19	.418	.416
Segui,David	L	.297	118	35	4	0	6	19	12	11	.356	.483
Bats Both	R	.307	404	124	32	1	13	65	37	69	.359	.488
Seguignol,F	L	.250	12	3	2	0	0	0	0	3	.250	.417
Bats Both	R	.267	30	8	2	0	2	3	3	12	.324	.533
Servais,Scott	L	.286	133	38	8	0	5	22	13	13	.351	.459
Bats Right	R	.177	192	34	7	1	2	14	13	39	.244	.255
Sexson,Richie	L	.241	58	14	4	0	3	7	1	13	.254	.466
Bats Right	R	.345	116	40	10	1	8	29	5	29	.387	.655
Shave,Jon	L	.263	19	5	1	0	1	5	2	7	.333	.474
Bats Right	R	.238	21	5	2	0	0	0	1	3	.273	.333
Sheets,Andy	L	.237	93	22	2	2	0	10	9	26	.304	.301
Bats Right	R	.248	101	25	3	1	7	19	12	36	.330	.505

Batter	vs	Avg	AB	H	2B	3B	HR	BI	BB	SO	OBP	SLG
Sheffield,G	L	.312	77	24	1	0	6	19	15	8	.417	.558
Bats Right	R	.300	360	108	26	2	16	66	80	38	.430	.517
Sheldon,Scott	L	.125	8	1	0	0	0	1	0	1	.125	.125
Bats Right	R	.125	8	1	0	0	0	0	1	5	.222	.125
Shipley,Craig	L	.182	44	8	4	0	0	2	2	8	.234	.273
Bats Right	R	.291	103	30	3	1	2	15	3	14	.333	.398
Shumpert,T	L	.364	11	4	0	0	1	2	2	3	.462	.636
Bats Right	R	.133	15	2	1	0	0	0	0	5	.133	.200
Siddall,Joe	L	.263	19	5	0	0	1	3	2	9	.333	.421
Bats Left	R	.152	46	7	3	0	0	3	5	16	.235	.217
Sierra,Ruben	L	.333	12	4	0	0	0	0	1	2	.385	.333
Bats Both	R	.194	62	12	4	1	4	11	2	9	.219	.484
Silvestri,D	L	.000	2	0	0	0	0	0	0	1	.000	.000
Bats Right	R	.083	12	1	0	0	0	0	0	1	.083	.083
Simmons,Brian	L	.333	3	1	0	0	1	2	0	1	.333	1.333
Bats Both	R	.375	16	6	0	0	1	4	0	1	.375	.563
Simms,Mike	L	.306	121	37	10	0	11	32	14	28	.381	.661
Bats Right	R	.277	65	18	1	0	5	14	10	19	.382	.523
Simon,Randall	L	.000	1	0	0	0	0	0	0	0	.000	.000
Bats Left	R	.200	15	3	0	0	0	4	0	1	.188	.200
Smith,Bobby	L	.269	130	35	8	1	5	19	11	33	.329	.462
Bats Right	R	.279	240	67	7	2	6	36	23	77	.351	.400
Smith,Mark	L	.159	44	7	1	0	1	4	3	12	.224	.250
Bats Right	R	.214	84	18	5	0	1	9	7	14	.284	.310
Snopek,Chris	L	.194	62	12	0	0	1	3	6	8	.261	.242
Bats Right	R	.213	75	16	2	0	0	3	10	21	.314	.240
Snow,J.T.	L	.164	73	12	3	0	1	6	10	21	.259	.247
Bats Both	R	.265	362	96	26	1	14	73	48	63	.347	.459
Sojo,Luis	L	.327	49	16	2	0	0	7	0	3	.327	.367
Bats Right	R	.184	98	18	1	0	0	7	4	12	.214	.214
Sorrento,Paul	L	.203	74	15	7	0	1	6	14	27	.322	.338
Bats Left	R	.230	361	83	20	0	16	51	40	106	.311	.418
Sosa,Sammy	L	.287	164	47	5	0	12	35	37	54	.418	.537
Bats Right	R	.315	479	151	15	0	54	123	36	117	.361	.685
Spehr,Tim	L	.103	29	3	1	0	0	0	6	4	.278	.138
Bats Right	R	.213	47	10	2	0	1	5	9	15	.373	.319
Spencer,Shane	L	.465	43	20	6	0	7	19	3	6	.500	1.093
Bats Right	R	.208	24	5	0	0	3	8	2	6	.259	.583
Spiers,Bill	L	.143	35	5	0	1	0	5	4	9	.220	.200
Bats Left	R	.287	349	100	27	3	4	38	41	53	.370	.415
Spiezio,Scott	L	.264	121	32	6	0	1	16	15	22	.343	.339
Bats Both	R	.256	285	73	13	1	8	34	29	34	.328	.393
Sprague,Ed	L	.189	106	20	6	0	3	7	6	29	.237	.330
Bats Right	R	.231	363	84	19	0	17	51	20	61	.293	.424
Stahoviak,S	L	.000	2	0	0	0	0	0	0	1	.000	.000
Bats Left	R	.118	17	2	0	0	1	1	0	6	.118	.294
Stairs,Matt	L	.280	164	46	10	0	8	23	14	30	.352	.488
Bats Left	R	.301	359	108	23	1	18	83	45	63	.378	.521
Stankiewicz,A	L	.208	53	11	2	0	0	3	1	9	.218	.245
Bats Right	R	.207	92	19	3	0	0	5	6	24	.270	.239

Batters vs. Lefthanded and Righthanded Pitchers

Batter	vs	Avg	AB	H	2B	3B	HR	BI	BB	SO	OBP	SLG	Batter	vs	Avg	AB	H	2B	3B	HR	BI	BB	SO	OBP	SLG
Stanley,Mike	L	.299	117	35	6	0	10	22	26	25	.428	.607	Trammell,B	L	.324	74	24	10	0	3	13	5	15	.367	.581
Bats Right	R	.242	380	92	19	0	19	57	56	104	.344	.442	Bats Right	R	.264	125	33	8	1	9	22	11	30	.321	.560
Steinbach,T	L	.222	99	22	9	1	1	6	11	16	.300	.364	Tremie,Chris	L	.000	0	0	0	0	0	0	1	0	1.000	.000
Bats Right	R	.248	323	80	16	1	13	48	27	73	.313	.424	Bats Right	R	.333	3	1	1	0	0	0	0	1	.333	.667
Stevens,Lee	L	.167	30	5	0	0	1	4	0	10	.161	.267	Tucker,M	L	.263	38	10	4	1	1	7	4	12	.364	.500
Bats Left	R	.274	314	86	17	4	19	55	31	83	.339	.535	Bats Left	R	.242	376	91	23	2	12	39	45	100	.323	.410
Stewart,S	L	.296	135	40	7	0	2	16	24	17	.418	.393	Turner,Chris	L	.000	0	0	0	0	0	0	0	0	.000	.000
Bats Right	R	.273	381	104	22	3	10	39	43	60	.362	.425	Bats Right	R	.000	9	0	0	0	0	0	0	4	.100	.000
Stinnett,K	L	.253	79	20	4	0	2	7	10	18	.341	.380	Valdes,Pedro	L	.000	1	0	0	0	0	0	0	1	.000	.000
Bats Right	R	.262	195	51	10	1	9	27	25	56	.358	.462	Bats Left	R	.227	22	5	1	1	0	2	1	2	.261	.364
Stocker,Kevin	L	.253	83	21	3	1	2	9	6	17	.340	.386	Valentin,J	L	.207	29	6	2	0	0	3	1	10	.226	.276
Bats Both	R	.194	253	49	8	2	4	16	21	63	.262	.289	Bats Both	R	.195	133	26	5	1	3	15	10	20	.252	.316
Stovall,D	L	.167	18	3	0	0	0	0	2	7	.250	.167	Valentin,John	L	.250	160	40	12	0	9	28	27	20	.354	.494
Bats Both	R	.217	60	13	2	1	2	6	4	22	.266	.383	Bats Right	R	.245	428	105	32	1	14	45	50	62	.335	.423
Strange,Doug	L	.077	13	1	0	0	0	3	0	1	.077	.077	Valentin,Jose	L	.229	105	24	5	0	0	6	13	25	.308	.276
Bats Both	R	.180	172	31	8	0	0	11	10	38	.227	.227	Bats Both	R	.223	323	72	19	0	16	43	50	80	.328	.430
Strawberry,D	L	.250	36	9	1	0	2	4	6	14	.357	.444	Vander Wal,J	L	.167	6	1	0	0	0	0	2	1	.375	.167
Bats Left	R	.247	259	64	10	2	22	53	40	76	.353	.556	Bats Left	R	.285	123	35	13	1	5	20	20	33	.382	.528
Strittmatter,M	L	.000	3	0	0	0	0	0	0	3	.000	.000	Varitek,Jason	L	.278	133	37	10	0	3	15	13	30	.345	.421
Bats Right	R	.000	1	0	0	0	0	0	0	0	.000	.000	Bats Both	R	.216	88	19	3		4	18	4	15	.253	.386
Stynes,Chris	L	.277	119	33	5	1	0	6	7	12	.323	.336	Vaughn,Greg	L	.267	191	51	11	0	14	38	31	35	.371	.545
Bats Right	R	.241	228	55	5	0	6	21	25	24	.323	.342	Bats Right	R	.275	382	105	17	4	36	81	48	86	.359	.623
Surhoff,B.J.	L	.254	177	45	8	0	7	27	12	26	.302	.418	Vaughn,Mo	L	.333	198	66	8	0	14	45	17	61	.400	.586
Bats Left	R	.290	396	115	26	1	15	65	37	55	.345	.475	Bats Left	R	.338	411	139	23	2	26	70	44	83	.403	.594
Sutton,Larry	L	.200	20	4	1	0	0	2	1	1	.238	.250	Velandia,J	L	.250	4	1	0	0	0	0	0	1	.250	.250
Bats Left	R	.248	290	72	13	2	5	40	28	45	.316	.359	Bats Right	R	.000	0	0	0	0	0	0	0	0	.000	.000
Sveum,Dale	L	.083	12	1	0	0	0	1	2	5	.200	.083	Velarde,Randy	L	.303	33	10	2	0	1	5	13	6	.500	.455
Bats Both	R	.174	46	8	0	0	0	2	2	11	.204	.174	Bats Right	R	.252	155	39	11	1	3	21	21	36	.343	.394
Sweeney,Mark	L	.000	10	0	0	0	0	0	2	4	.167	.000	Ventura,Robin	L	.277	155	43	8	1	7	30	20	31	.360	.477
Bats Left	R	.247	182	45	8	3	2	15	24	33	.333	.357	Bats Left	R	.257	435	112	23	3	14	61	59	80	.345	.421
Sweeney,Mike	L	.302	63	19	6	0	3	13	10	4	.397	.540	Veras,Quilvio	L	.279	154	43	9	1	2	18	17	22	.352	.390
Bats Right	R	.247	219	54	12	0	5	22	14	34	.297	.370	Bats Both	R	.262	363	95	15	1	4	27	67	56	.382	.342
Tarasco,Tony	L	.000	0	0	0	0	0	0	0	0	.000	.000	Vidro,Jose	L	.125	32	4	2	0	0	2	4	7	.237	.188
Bats Left	R	.208	24	5	2	0	1	4	3	5	.296	.417	Bats Both	R	.237	173	41	10	0	0	16	23	26	.333	.295
Tatis,F	L	.287	150	43	10	0	0	15	9	30	.325	.353	Vina,Fernando	L	.324	185	60	9	3	0	15	12	15	.399	.405
Bats Right	R	.272	382	104	23	4	11	43	27	93	.330	.440	Bats Left	R	.305	452	138	30	4	7	30	42	31	.381	.436
Tatum,Jimmy	L	.094	32	3	0	1	1	6	3	13	.154	.250	Vitiello,Joe	L	.250	4	1	0	0	0	0	1	1	.400	.250
Bats Right	R	.333	18	6	1	1	1	7	0	6	.333	.667	Bats Right	R	.000	3	0	0	0	0	0	0	1	.000	.000
Taubensee,E	L	.240	75	18	5	0	2	13	3	18	.269	.387	Vizcaino,Jose	L	.380	50	19	2	0	1	7	4	8	.418	.480
Bats Left	R	.287	356	102	22	0	9	59	49	75	.367	.424	Bats Both	R	.230	187	43	7	0	2	22	13	27	.282	.299
Tavarez,Jesus	L	.000	2	0	0	0	0	0	1	1	.333	.000	Vizquel,Omar	L	.274	168	46	10	2	1	13	23	21	.363	.375
Bats Both	R	.222	9	2	0	0	1	1	1	2	.300	.556	Bats Both	R	.294	408	120	20	4	1	37	39	43	.356	.370
Tejada,Miguel	L	.210	100	21	4	0	5	11	9	28	.282	.400	Voigt,Jack	L	.114	35	4	1	0	0	3	3	9	.184	.143
Bats Right	R	.242	265	64	16	1	6	34	19	58	.304	.377	Bats Right	R	.162	37	6	3	0	1	7	3	10	.225	.324
Thomas,Frank	L	.226	137	31	4	0	5	18	21	24	.327	.365	Walbeck,Matt	L	.354	48	17	3	0	0	9	7	5	.436	.458
Bats Right	R	.277	448	124	31	2	24	91	89	69	.396	.516	Bats Both	R	.241	290	70	12	1	6	37	23	63	.297	.352
Thome,Jim	L	.289	142	41	9	0	7	24	21	49	.386	.500	Walker,Larry	L	.321	131	42	16	0	3	16	20	21	.412	.511
Bats Left	R	.295	298	88	25	2	23	61	69	92	.426	.624	Bats Left	R	.381	323	123	30	3	20	51	44	40	.458	.678
Tomberlin,A	L	.000	11	0	0	0	0	1	0	4	.000	.000	Walker,Todd	L	.271	96	26	3	0	0	4	4	14	.307	.302
Bats Left	R	.259	58	15	2	0	2	11	3	21	.328	.397	Bats Left	R	.326	432	141	38	3	12	58	43	51	.385	.512

Batters vs. Lefthanded and Righthanded Pitchers

Batter	vs	Avg	AB	H	2B	3B	HR	BI	BB	SO	OBP	SLG
Walton,Jerome	L	.391	23	9	2	0	0	2	1	2	.417	.478
Bats Right	R	.182	11	2	1	0	0	1	1	4	.250	.273
Ward,Daryle	L	.000	0	0	0	0	0	0	1	0	1.000	.000
Bats Left	R	.333	3	1	0	0	0	0	0	2	.333	.333
Ward,Turner	L	.333	33	11	2	0	0	3	4	6	.405	.394
Bats Both	R	.253	249	63	11	3	9	43	23	34	.318	.430
Watkins,Pat	L	.269	52	14	2	1	1	5	4	4	.310	.404
Bats Right	R	.263	95	25	6	0	1	10	4	22	.294	.358
Webster,Lenny	L	.333	93	31	3	0	4	9	6	13	.374	.495
Bats Right	R	.264	216	57	13	0	6	37	9	25	.292	.407
Wehner,John	L	.296	54	16	2	0	0	4	6	5	.361	.333
Bats Right	R	.118	34	4	0	0	0	1	1	7	.143	.118
Weiss,Walt	L	.250	96	24	7	0	0	2	14	20	.348	.323
Bats Both	R	.291	251	73	11	2	0	25	45	33	.400	.351
White,Derrick	L	.083	12	1	0	0	1	2	0	8	.083	.333
Bats Right	R	.000	7	0	0	0	0	0	0	1	.000	.000
White,Devon	L	.291	165	48	6	1	5	22	10	23	.337	.430
Bats Both	R	.274	398	109	26	0	17	63	32	79	.335	.466
White,Rondell	L	.346	78	27	6	1	6	16	7	8	.395	.679
Bats Right	R	.287	279	80	15	1	11	42	23	49	.354	.466
Whiten,Mark	L	.278	90	25	6	0	0	9	7	16	.337	.344
Bats Both	R	.287	136	39	8	0	6	20	22	44	.394	.478
Widger,Chris	L	.250	88	22	5	1	3	10	9	21	.320	.432
Bats Right	R	.228	329	75	13	0	12	43	20	64	.271	.377
Wilkins,Rick	L	.000	3	0	0	0	0	0	1	2	.250	.000
Bats Left	R	.189	53	10	1	1	1	5	5	14	.254	.302
Williams,B	L	.350	163	57	7	2	9	33	29	24	.443	.583
Bats Both	R	.333	336	112	23	3	17	64	45	57	.411	.571
Williams,E	L	.050	20	1	0	0	0	2	2	4	.130	.050
Bats Right	R	.375	8	3	0	0	0	1	0	2	.375	.375
Williams,G	L	.363	146	53	16	0	7	28	10	22	.408	.616
Bats Right	R	.233	120	28	3	2	3	16	7	26	.285	.367
Williams,Matt	L	.300	130	39	5	0	5	19	15	22	.372	.454
Bats Right	R	.255	380	97	21	1	15	52	28	80	.311	.434
Williams,R	L	.333	18	6	1	0	0	1	2	2	.400	.389
Bats Both	R	.389	18	7	0	0	1	4	5	9	.542	.556
Wilson,Craig	L	.611	18	11	4	0	1	4	0	2	.611	1.000
Bats Right	R	.379	29	11	1	0	2	6	3	4	.424	.621
Wilson,Dan	L	.317	63	20	5	1	1	6	8	10	.378	.476
Bats Right	R	.237	262	62	12	0	8	38	16	46	.290	.374
Wilson,E	L	.388	49	19	5	0	2	10	1	0	.400	.612
Bats Both	R	.244	41	10	1	0	0	2	3	8	.304	.268
Wilson,P	L	.080	25	2	0	0	0	1	1	11	.148	.080
Bats Right	R	.231	26	6	2	0	1	2	5	10	.355	.423
Winn,Randy	L	.289	90	26	3	5	1	6	6	13	.333	.467
Bats Both	R	.274	248	68	6	4	0	11	23	56	.338	.331
Witt,Kevin	L	.500	2	1	0	0	0	0	0	1	.500	.500
Bats Left	R	.000	5	0	0	0	0	0	0	2	.000	.000
Womack,Tony	L	.244	164	40	2	1	0	16	14	25	.302	.268
Bats Left	R	.295	491	145	24	6	3	29	24	69	.326	.387

Batter	vs	Avg	AB	H	2B	3B	HR	BI	BB	SO	OBP	SLG
Wood,Jason	L	.438	16	7	1	0	1	1	2	1	.500	.688
Bats Right	R	.125	8	1	1	0	0	0	1	4	.222	.250
Young,Dmitri	L	.320	147	47	12	0	1	19	16	19	.387	.422
Bats Both	R	.306	389	119	36	1	13	64	31	75	.356	.504
Young,Eric	L	.258	93	24	5	0	2	7	11	6	.349	.376
Bats Right	R	.292	359	105	19	1	6	36	34	26	.357	.401
Young,Ernie	L	.250	36	9	3	0	1	3	0	6	.270	.417
Bats Right	R	.059	17	1	0	0	0	0	2	3	.158	.059
Young,Kevin	L	.248	137	34	11	2	5	22	11	31	.302	.467
Bats Right	R	.277	455	126	29	0	22	86	33	96	.335	.486
Zaun,Gregg	L	.085	47	4	0	0	0	4	4	12	.154	.085
Bats Both	R	.207	251	52	12	2	5	25	31	40	.296	.331
Zeile,Todd	L	.279	129	36	10	2	6	21	16	17	.359	.527
Bats Right	R	.269	443	119	22	1	13	73	53	73	.347	.411
Zuber,Jon	L	.667	3	2	1	0	0	0	1	1	.800	1.000
Bats Left	R	.214	42	9	2	1	2	6	5	8	.298	.452
AL	L	.276	—	—	—	—	—	—	—	—	.345	.438
	R	.270	—	—	—	—	—	—	—	—	.338	.429
NL	L	.259	—	—	—	—	—	—	—	—	.331	.398
	R	.263	—	—	—	—	—	—	—	—	.331	.414
MLB	L	.267	—	—	—	—	—	—	—	—	.338	.417
	R	.266	—	—	—	—	—	—	—	—	.334	.421

Pitchers vs. Lefthanded and Righthanded Batters

Pitcher	vs	Avg	AB	H	2B	3B	HR	BI	BB	SO	OBP	SLG
Abbott,Jim	L	.393	28	11	2	0	1	4	2	0	.452	.571
Throws Left	R	.261	92	24	4	0	1	10	10	14	.330	.337
Abbott,Paul	L	.228	57	13	1	0	2	5	7	15	.313	.351
Throws Right	R	.297	37	11	1	0	0	6	3	7	.341	.324
Acevedo,Juan	L	.269	175	47	6	0	4	15	14	29	.325	.371
Throws Right	R	.203	177	36	3	0	3	12	15	27	.277	.271
Adams,Terry	L	.223	121	27	4	0	2	16	16	32	.312	.306
Throws Right	R	.280	161	45	5	1	5	33	25	41	.376	.416
Adamson,Joel	L	.357	14	5	0	0	0	2	2	1	.444	.357
Throws Left	R	.270	74	20	3	0	5	18	9	13	.365	.514
Aguilera,Rick	L	.239	138	33	7	1	3	18	9	30	.282	.370
Throws Right	R	.284	148	42	9	1	5	18	6	27	.316	.459
Aldred,Scott	L	.207	58	12	3	0	0	6	4	11	.270	.259
Throws Left	R	.350	60	21	4	0	1	10	8	10	.435	.467
Alfonseca,A	L	.330	100	33	5	0	4	20	22	13	.444	.500
Throws Right	R	.251	167	42	9	0	6	30	11	33	.303	.413
Almanzar,C	L	.277	47	13	3	0	1	4	7	4	.370	.404
Throws Right	R	.292	72	21	6	1	3	14	1	16	.311	.528
Alvarez,W	L	.250	116	29	5	0	3	10	19	18	.371	.371
Throws Left	R	.236	428	101	24	0	15	61	49	89	.321	.397
Anderson,B	L	.295	139	41	10	0	7	21	2	15	.305	.518
Throws Left	R	.270	667	180	27	3	32	76	22	80	.296	.463
Anderson,Matt	L	.304	56	17	1	2	0	14	22	15	.500	.393
Throws Right	R	.219	96	21	6	0	3	13	9	29	.287	.375
Andujar,Luis	L	.308	13	4	1	0	0	4	1	1	.357	.385
Throws Right	R	.533	15	8	2	0	0	3	1	0	.563	.667
Appier,Kevin	L	.333	39	13	3	0	1	9	3	5	.381	.487
Throws Right	R	.348	23	8	1	0	2	4	2	4	.407	.652
Arrojo,R	L	.300	413	124	29	4	12	44	43	68	.378	.477
Throws Right	R	.204	348	71	4	2	9	31	22	84	.270	.305
Ashby,Andy	L	.251	458	115	27	4	10	49	33	75	.300	.393
Throws Right	R	.268	403	108	15	2	13	32	25	76	.320	.412
Assenmacher,P	L	.313	99	31	5	1	3	15	7	22	.358	.475
Throws Left	R	.256	90	23	3	0	2	7	12	21	.343	.356
Astacio,Pedro	L	.257	416	107	16	2	20	61	50	82	.342	.450
Throws Right	R	.332	416	138	19	6	19	81	24	88	.384	.543
Avery,Steve	L	.294	109	32	12	1	1	17	15	19	.384	.450
Throws Left	R	.262	366	96	15	2	13	46	49	38	.354	.421
Ayala,Bobby	L	.322	143	46	10	2	6	30	13	30	.373	.545
Throws Right	R	.323	167	54	9	0	3	27	13	38	.368	.431
Aybar,Manny	L	.244	164	40	11	1	2	22	27	25	.349	.444
Throws Right	R	.321	156	50	14	1	4	19	15	32	.387	.500
Bailes,Scott	L	.298	84	25	6	2	1	17	6	18	.341	.452
Throws Left	R	.400	90	36	12	1	4	25	5	12	.427	.689
Bailey,Cory	L	.000	4	0	0	0	0	0	0	1	.000	.000
Throws Right	R	.250	8	2	0	0	1	1	1	1	.333	.625
Baldwin,James	L	.291	344	100	23	3	8	49	33	66	.358	.445
Throws Right	R	.262	290	76	21	1	10	46	27	42	.334	.445
Banks,Willie	L	.248	101	25	3	1	2	14	18	19	.358	.356
Throws Right	R	.246	118	29	6	1	4	25	19	21	.360	.415

Pitcher	vs	Avg	AB	H	2B	3B	HR	BI	BB	SO	OBP	SLG
Baptist,T	L	.281	32	9	2	0	2	6	3	5	.324	.531
Throws Left	R	.338	74	25	9	0	3	15	8	6	.384	.581
Barber,Brian	L	.286	84	24	5	1	4	14	9	11	.347	.512
Throws Right	R	.266	79	21	5	0	1	11	4	13	.306	.367
Barkley,Brian	L	.308	13	4	0	0	0	3	6	0	.476	.308
Throws Left	R	.353	34	12	0	0	2	7	3	2	.421	.529
Barrios,M	L	.143	7	1	0	0	0	0	1	1	.250	.143
Throws Right	R	.500	6	3	0	0	1	4	3	0	.667	1.000
Batista,M	L	.310	226	70	12	0	7	29	42	35	.415	.456
Throws Right	R	.246	289	71	13	0	5	36	23	57	.312	.343
Beck,Rod	L	.270	148	40	5	2	6	17	10	35	.323	.453
Throws Right	R	.267	172	46	9	1	5	21	10	46	.301	.419
Beech,Matt	L	.274	62	17	3	1	1	9	7	12	.352	.403
Throws Left	R	.275	396	109	18	2	18	54	56	101	.368	.467
Belcher,Tim	L	.256	449	115	17	1	22	71	50	63	.331	.445
Throws Right	R	.287	460	132	23	4	15	52	23	67	.324	.452
Belinda,Stan	L	.222	90	20	1	2	2	11	18	24	.349	.344
Throws Right	R	.205	127	26	6	0	5	11	10	33	.268	.370
Beltran,Rigo	L	.000	5	0	0	0	0	1	3	2	.333	.000
Throws Left	R	.261	23	6	2	0	1	1	1	3	.292	.478
Benes,Andy	L	.258	458	118	30	5	11	47	34	76	.311	.417
Throws Right	R	.244	422	103	19	3	14	55	40	88	.311	.403
Benitez,A	L	.181	94	17	1	1	4	19	28	39	.371	.340
Throws Right	R	.211	147	31	6	0	6	20	11	48	.278	.374
Bennett,Joel	L	.333	3	1	0	1	0	0	3	0	.667	1.000
Throws Right	R	.200	5	1	1	0	0	1	0	0	.200	.400
Bennett,S	L	.258	151	39	12	2	3	29	26	23	.367	.424
Throws Right	R	.290	200	58	7	0	5	34	19	36	.360	.400
Bere,Jason	L	.315	248	78	18	3	7	39	48	42	.419	.496
Throws Right	R	.238	248	59	10	1	10	43	30	42	.325	.407
Bergman,Sean	L	.275	349	96	23	1	12	39	25	42	.325	.450
Throws Right	R	.261	333	87	17	2	8	35	17	58	.304	.396
Bevil,Brian	L	.314	70	22	2	0	2	10	8	16	.388	.429
Throws Right	R	.260	96	25	6	3	2	15	14	31	.363	.448
Blair,Willie	L	.275	316	87	19	3	10	35	38	28	.356	.449
Throws Right	R	.288	351	101	14	3	21	60	23	64	.332	.524
Bochtler,Doug	L	.243	115	28	3	2	8	26	21	20	.367	.513
Throws Right	R	.306	147	45	6	4	9	30	21	25	.392	.585
Boehringer,B	L	.263	118	31	5	0	1	17	24	21	.392	.331
Throws Right	R	.253	174	44	12	0	9	29	21	46	.342	.477
Bohanon,Brian	L	.267	135	36	9	3	3	13	10	22	.324	.444
Throws Left	R	.205	414	85	18	2	10	41	47	89	.299	.331
Bones,Ricky	L	.195	77	15	3	0	1	6	12	12	.303	.273
Throws Right	R	.274	124	34	7	1	3	19	12	26	.343	.419
Borland,Toby	L	.182	11	2	0	0	0	1	0	2	.182	.182
Throws Right	R	.273	22	6	2	0	1	8	5	7	.407	.500
Borowski,Joe	L	.350	20	7	2	0	0	2	2	4	.409	.450
Throws Right	R	.222	18	4	1	0	0	4	2	3	.300	.278
Boskie,Shawn	L	.432	44	19	3	0	3	12	2	7	.458	.705
Throws Right	R	.395	38	15	2	0	2	8	2	3	.439	.605

Pitchers vs. Lefthanded and Righthanded Batters

Pitcher	vs	Avg	AB	H	2B	3B	HR	BI	BB	SO	OBP	SLG
Bottalico,R	L	.375	72	27	4	0	3	17	12	6	.460	.556
Throws Right	R	.257	105	27	8	1	4	17	13	21	.339	.467
Bottenfield,K	L	.235	247	58	7	0	3	29	31	41	.323	.300
Throws Right	R	.273	256	70	16	0	10	37	26	57	.344	.453
Bradford,Chad	L	.288	52	15	6	0	0	10	3	3	.327	.404
Throws Right	R	.182	66	12	0	0	0	2	4	8	.229	.182
Bradley,Ryan	L	.333	27	9	1	0	2	7	6	2	.471	.593
Throws Right	R	.143	21	3	2	0	0	3	3	11	.240	.238
Brantley,Jeff	L	.236	72	17	2	0	6	15	10	19	.325	.514
Throws Right	R	.209	110	23	3	0	6	12	8	29	.264	.400
Brewer,Billy	L	1.000	2	2	0	0	0	0	0	0	1.000	1.000
Throws Left	R	.500	2	1	0	0	0	1	2	0	.750	.500
Brocail,Doug	L	.221	86	19	6	0	1	12	12	22	.310	.326
Throws Right	R	.204	137	28	5	1	1	10	6	33	.241	.277
Brock,Chris	L	.277	47	13	3	0	1	8	4	7	.333	.404
Throws Right	R	.281	64	18	5	2	2	7	3	12	.313	.516
Brow,Scott	L	.333	36	12	3	1	1	13	8	6	.444	.556
Throws Right	R	.222	45	10	2	0	1	12	6	7	.314	.333
Brown,Kevin	L	.245	490	120	16	0	3	34	30	111	.292	.296
Throws Right	R	.225	467	105	16	0	5	35	19	146	.265	.291
Brownson,Mark	L	.294	17	5	0	1	1	4	0	4	.294	.588
Throws Right	R	.297	37	11	2	0	1	3	2	4	.350	.432
Brunson,Will	L	.100	10	1	1	0	0	1	2	1	.250	.200
Throws Left	R	.444	9	4	0	0	0	0	1	1	.500	.444
Bruske,Jim	L	.319	94	30	9	0	2	11	11	18	.390	.479
Throws Right	R	.250	144	36	10	1	3	24	13	20	.325	.396
Buddie,Mike	L	.333	72	24	5	0	3	13	7	8	.415	.528
Throws Right	R	.247	89	22	5	0	2	17	6	12	.292	.371
Bullinger,Jim	L	.563	16	9	4	0	2	8	1	1	.556	1.188
Throws Right	R	.286	14	4	1	0	1	1	1	3	.333	.571
Bullinger,K	L	.438	16	7	0	0	0	2	0	1	.438	.438
Throws Right	R	.368	19	7	2	0	1	6	0	1	.368	.632
Burba,Dave	L	.253	411	104	23	2	13	47	38	68	.320	.414
Throws Right	R	.286	370	106	15	1	17	46	31	64	.341	.470
Burkett,John	L	.276	395	109	16	6	11	48	28	75	.328	.430
Throws Right	R	.308	393	121	29	1	8	56	18	56	.343	.448
Busby,Mike	L	.224	85	19	5	0	0	10	10	21	.309	.282
Throws Right	R	.286	91	26	6	1	3	19	5	12	.347	.473
Butler,Adam	L	.300	10	3	0	0	1	3	1	2	.417	.600
Throws Left	R	.250	8	2	1	0	0	1	5	5	.500	.375
Byrd,Paul	L	.214	84	18	3	2	2	6	11	10	.305	.369
Throws Right	R	.213	127	27	7	0	4	13	7	29	.252	.362
Byrdak,Tim	L	.667	3	2	1	0	0	2	0	0	.667	1.000
Throws Left	R	.500	6	3	0	0	1	1	0	1	.500	1.000
Cabrera,Jose	L	.714	7	5	2	0	0	4	1	0	.750	1.000
Throws Right	R	.182	11	2	2	0	0	2	0	1	.182	.364
Cadaret,Greg	L	.227	75	17	2	0	2	8	8	16	.310	.333
Throws Right	R	.308	104	32	5	0	5	19	10	26	.376	.500
Candiotti,Tom	L	.290	427	124	18	3	15	57	34	55	.339	.452
Throws Right	R	.269	364	98	24	2	15	54	29	43	.336	.470
Carlson,Dan	L	.290	31	9	3	0	2	7	4	7	.389	.581
Throws Right	R	.390	41	16	3	0	1	9	4	9	.458	.537
Carpenter,C	L	.267	345	92	18	1	8	46	38	61	.341	.394
Throws Right	R	.264	322	85	24	1	10	45	24	75	.316	.438
Carrasco,H	L	.309	94	29	1	0	2	14	12	17	.382	.383
Throws Right	R	.301	153	46	8	0	2	29	19	29	.367	.392
Casian,Larry	L	.600	5	3	1	0	0	0	0	2	.667	.800
Throws Left	R	.333	15	5	1	1	0	4	1	4	.412	.533
Castillo,C	L	.247	154	38	8	1	4	18	16	28	.318	.390
Throws Right	R	.246	228	56	11	1	13	51	19	36	.309	.474
Castillo,F	L	.276	225	62	15	1	5	30	36	41	.371	.418
Throws Right	R	.353	249	88	16	4	12	47	8	40	.381	.594
Castillo,Tony	L	.365	52	19	5	0	4	15	2	8	.411	.692
Throws Left	R	.297	64	19	4	0	3	12	9	6	.384	.500
Cather,Mike	L	.246	65	16	4	1	1	10	7	10	.311	.385
Throws Right	R	.261	88	23	3	0	6	18	5	23	.316	.500
Charlton,Norm	L	.279	61	17	4	0	2	13	11	10	.384	.443
Throws Left	R	.273	132	36	7	0	3	13	22	37	.378	.394
Checo,R	L	.375	16	6	2	0	1	1	3	4	.474	.688
Throws Right	R	.385	13	5	0	0	2	5	2	1	.467	.923
Chen,Bruce	L	.364	11	4	2	1	0	1	2	2	.500	.727
Throws Left	R	.275	69	19	2	0	3	8	7	15	.342	.435
Cho,Jin Ho	L	.375	40	15	6	1	0	3	2	5	.405	.575
Throws Right	R	.310	42	13	1	0	4	12	1	10	.333	.619
Chouinard,B	L	.365	74	27	6	1	3	14	4	16	.397	.595
Throws Right	R	.211	90	19	3	1	2	16	7	11	.263	.333
Christiansen,J	L	.195	82	16	5	0	0	9	10	24	.283	.256
Throws Left	R	.227	154	35	8	0	2	21	17	47	.302	.318
Clark,Mark	L	.299	364	109	22	2	9	40	25	59	.343	.445
Throws Right	R	.262	484	127	27	1	14	57	23	102	.299	.409
Clemens,Roger	L	.197	456	90	21	2	9	41	58	147	.290	.311
Throws Right	R	.198	399	79	24	1	2	30	30	124	.263	.278
Clement,Matt	L	.294	17	5	0	0	0	1	4	4	.429	.294
Throws Right	R	.278	36	10	2	0	0	4	3	9	.333	.333
Clontz,Brad	L	.296	27	8	1	0	2	7	10	4	.486	.556
Throws Right	R	.183	60	11	3	0	2	12	2	12	.234	.333
Cloude,Ken	L	.319	345	110	32	3	21	54	49	69	.404	.612
Throws Right	R	.270	285	77	20	2	8	44	31	45	.343	.439
Colon,Bartolo	L	.271	410	111	29	2	10	50	46	83	.346	.424
Throws Right	R	.248	379	94	14	1	5	30	33	75	.310	.330
Cone,David	L	.252	429	108	25	2	12	46	37	103	.329	.403
Throws Right	R	.220	355	78	16	0	8	30	22	106	.267	.332
Connelly,S	L	.600	10	6	0	0	0	3	2	0	.692	.600
Throws Right	R	.308	13	4	0	0	0	1	2	1	.400	.308
Cook,Dennis	L	.299	97	29	5	0	2	15	4	22	.320	.412
Throws Left	R	.203	153	31	7	0	3	16	23	57	.317	.307
Cooke,Steve	L	.000	6	0	0	0	0	0	0	1	.000	.000
Throws Left	R	.250	16	4	0	0	0	1	0	2	.294	.250
Coppinger,R	L	.286	28	8	3	0	2	5	6	6	.412	.607
Throws Right	R	.216	37	8	0	0	1	3	1	7	.237	.324

Pitchers vs. Lefthanded and Righthanded Batters

Pitcher	vs	Avg	AB	H	2B	3B	HR	BI	BB	SO	OBP	SLG
Cordova,F	L	.270	408	110	17	3	13	42	26	55	.317	.422
Throws Right	R	.221	426	94	20	2	9	38	43	102	.289	.340
Corey,Bryan	L	.429	7	3	0	0	1	4	0	1	.429	.857
Throws Right	R	.333	9	3	0	0	0	0	2	0	.500	.333
Corsi,Jim	L	.211	114	24	3	0	3	7	16	24	.305	.316
Throws Right	R	.256	133	34	4	1	3	15	7	25	.298	.368
Crabtree,Tim	L	.228	114	26	5	1	2	19	14	21	.303	.342
Throws Right	R	.283	212	60	9	1	1	28	21	39	.353	.349
Croushore,R	L	.149	87	13	2	0	0	3	17	22	.288	.172
Throws Right	R	.258	120	31	9	1	6	26	12	25	.343	.500
Crow,Dean	L	.274	73	20	0	0	2	4	9	11	.361	.356
Throws Right	R	.340	103	35	8	0	4	18	7	7	.384	.534
Cunnane,Will	L	.250	4	1	0	0	0	0	1	0	.400	.250
Throws Right	R	.333	9	3	0	0	1	2	0	1	.333	.667
Daal,Omar	L	.283	113	32	4	1	1	13	10	26	.341	.363
Throws Left	R	.237	482	114	19	0	11	42	41	106	.297	.344
Darensbourg,V	L	.168	107	18	2	1	0	4	14	35	.264	.206
Throws Left	R	.236	144	34	7	0	5	18	16	39	.307	.389
Darwin,Danny	L	.287	303	87	16	3	10	37	21	37	.331	.459
Throws Right	R	.307	290	89	17	1	13	44	28	44	.373	.507
De Los Santos,V	L	.167	18	3	2	0	0	0	1	4	.211	.278
Throws Left	R	.145	55	8	1	0	4	9	1	14	.161	.382
DeHart,Rick	L	.316	38	12	3	0	0	10	5	4	.395	.395
Throws Left	R	.278	79	22	7	0	3	17	8	10	.341	.481
DeJean,Mike	L	.286	112	32	6	1	1	20	6	10	.317	.384
Throws Right	R	.284	162	46	8	1	3	17	18	17	.355	.401
DeLucia,Rich	L	.250	96	24	5	0	3	14	22	25	.385	.396
Throws Right	R	.204	157	32	8	1	7	20	24	48	.310	.401
Dempster,Ryan	L	.394	99	39	8	0	4	21	24	11	.504	.596
Throws Right	R	.287	115	33	6	1	2	21	14	24	.391	.409
Dessens,Elmer	L	.298	114	34	10	1	5	19	9	13	.347	.535
Throws Right	R	.301	186	56	8	0	5	27	16	30	.353	.425
Dickson,Jason	L	.308	240	74	13	1	11	40	30	26	.383	.508
Throws Right	R	.298	245	73	14	1	6	43	11	35	.333	.437
Dipoto,Jerry	L	.297	128	38	9	0	5	20	12	16	.362	.484
Throws Right	R	.170	135	23	5	1	3	10	13	33	.250	.289
Dodd,Robert	L	.167	6	1	0	1	0	2	1	2	.286	.500
Throws Left	R	.400	15	6	2	0	1	4	0	2	.389	.733
Dougherty,Jim	L	.364	22	8	1	0	2	9	3	3	.462	.682
Throws Right	R	.321	28	9	2	0	0	4	4	0	.406	.393
Drabek,Doug	L	.318	242	77	13	2	5	36	13	27	.355	.450
Throws Right	R	.303	201	61	9	0	15	39	16	28	.356	.572
Dreifort,D	L	.284	356	101	24	4	5	36	38	94	.357	.416
Throws Right	R	.224	312	70	13	0	7	34	19	74	.279	.333
Duran,Roberto	L	.182	22	4	1	0	0	0	9	3	.455	.227
Throws Left	R	.161	31	5	2	0	0	5	8	9	.333	.226
Duvall,Mike	L	.200	5	1	0	0	0	1	1	1	.333	.200
Throws Left	R	.300	10	3	2	1	0	2	1	0	.364	.700
Dykhoff,R	L	.000	1	0	0	0	0	0	0	1	.000	.000
Throws Left	R	.500	4	2	1	0	0	2	1	0	.600	.750
Eckersley,D	L	.311	45	14	3	0	4	11	8	4	.415	.644
Throws Right	R	.283	113	32	6	0	2	14	0	18	.293	.389
Edmondson,B	L	.248	125	31	7	2	2	15	7	21	.288	.384
Throws Right	R	.280	161	45	9	1	8	33	30	19	.396	.497
Eiland,Dave	L	.444	9	4	1	0	0	4	3	0	.583	.556
Throws Right	R	.400	5	2	1	0	0	0	0	1	.400	.600
Elarton,Scott	L	.174	92	16	5	0	3	11	12	26	.269	.326
Throws Right	R	.214	112	24	8	0	2	11	8	30	.270	.339
Eldred,Cal	L	.280	257	72	22	2	4	30	28	46	.356	.428
Throws Right	R	.313	272	85	14	1	10	41	33	40	.386	.482
Embree,Alan	L	.260	77	20	3	0	3	11	5	19	.305	.416
Throws Left	R	.275	131	36	9	0	4	19	18	24	.364	.435
Erdos,Todd	L	.500	4	2	1	0	0	0	1	0	.600	.750
Throws Right	R	.500	6	3	1	0	0	2	0	0	.500	.667
Erickson,S	L	.309	570	176	32	4	12	65	47	82	.368	.442
Throws Right	R	.245	441	108	12	0	11	52	22	104	.290	.347
Escobar,K	L	.238	151	36	4	1	3	17	18	41	.316	.338
Throws Right	R	.237	152	36	7	3	2	17	17	31	.312	.362
Estes,Shawn	L	.247	93	23	5	0	2	12	15	27	.369	.366
Throws Left	R	.274	464	127	22	1	12	64	65	109	.363	.403
Evans,Bart	L	.188	16	3	1	0	1	2	0	3	.188	.438
Throws Right	R	.222	18	4	0	0	0	1	0	4	.222	.222
Eversgerd,B	L	.429	7	3	0	0	0	2	0	0	.429	.429
Throws Left	R	.316	19	6	1	0	1	6	2	4	.375	.526
Eyre,Scott	L	.290	107	31	7	0	6	22	16	9	.387	.523
Throws Left	R	.265	313	83	11	2	18	48	48	64	.362	.486
Fassero,Jeff	L	.288	170	49	10	1	2	13	11	33	.351	.394
Throws Left	R	.251	692	174	40	1	31	95	55	143	.307	.447
Fetters,Mike	L	.292	106	31	7	2	2	20	7	15	.336	.453
Throws Right	R	.246	126	31	5	3	3	24	18	28	.340	.405
Finley,Chuck	L	.263	179	47	5	1	6	17	30	48	.371	.402
Throws Left	R	.242	674	163	40	1	14	66	79	164	.324	.366
Florie,Bryce	L	.289	249	72	9	0	9	28	39	36	.386	.434
Throws Right	R	.262	263	69	16	4	7	42	20	61	.321	.433
Fontenot,Joe	L	.326	89	29	7	0	4	17	11	11	.400	.539
Throws Right	R	.314	86	27	8	1	1	11	9	13	.406	.465
Ford,Ben	L	.250	12	3	0	0	2	4	1	3	.308	.750
Throws Right	R	.313	32	10	1	0	0	7	2	2	.389	.344
Fordham,Tom	L	.257	70	18	3	0	1	7	17	12	.409	.343
Throws Left	R	.292	113	33	2	2	6	20	25	11	.417	.504
Fossas,Tony	L	.278	54	15	3	1	1	15	9	17	.375	.426
Throws Left	R	.405	37	15	1	0	0	8	7	6	.500	.432
Foster,Kevin	L	.556	9	5	2	0	1	3	1	0	.600	1.111
Throws Right	R	.429	7	3	1	0	0	2	1	3	.400	.571
Foulke,Keith	L	.267	101	27	5	1	4	14	13	30	.348	.455
Throws Right	R	.174	138	24	6	1	5	22	7	27	.233	.341
Fox,Chad	L	.241	83	20	5	1	3	10	8	31	.308	.434
Throws Right	R	.273	132	36	5	0	1	15	12	33	.338	.333
Franco,John	L	.340	53	18	1	0	0	4	3	10	.386	.358
Throws Left	R	.247	194	48	7	2	4	25	26	49	.338	.366

Pitchers vs. Lefthanded and Righthanded Batters

Pitcher	vs	Avg	AB	H	2B	3B	HR	BI	BB	SO	OBP	SLG	Pitcher	vs	Avg	AB	H	2B	3B	HR	BI	BB	SO	OBP	SLG
Frascatore,J	L	.245	163	40	12	1	3	19	19	16	.328	.387	Halama,John	L	.261	23	6	3	0	0	2	2	9	.346	.391
Throws Right	R	.264	208	55	10	1	8	29	17	33	.325	.438	Throws Left	R	.304	102	31	10	2	0	14	11	12	.364	.441
Fussell,Chris	L	.353	17	6	0	0	1	3	5	3	.500	.529	Hall,Darren	L	.381	21	8	2	0	1	6	3	3	.480	.619
Throws Right	R	.263	19	5	0	1	0	4	4	5	.375	.368	Throws Right	R	.321	28	9	2	0	1	8	2	5	.355	.500
Gaillard,E	L	.250	12	3	0	0	3	5	0	3	.250	1.000	Halladay,Roy	L	.226	31	7	1	0	2	4	2	9	.273	.452
Throws Right	R	.067	15	1	1	0	0	0	3	2	.222	.133	Throws Right	R	.100	20	2	0	0	0	0	0	4	.100	.100
Gajkowski,S	L	.286	14	4	0	0	1	2	1	3	.333	.500	Hamilton,Joey	L	.282	387	109	25	7	8	46	49	72	.368	.444
Throws Right	R	.455	22	10	2	0	2	12	3	0	.556	.818	Throws Right	R	.253	438	111	19	2	7	52	57	75	.341	.354
Garces,Rich	L	.205	73	15	5	0	2	8	12	11	.322	.356	Hammond,Chris	L	.400	5	2	0	0	0	0	0	1	.400	.400
Throws Right	R	.219	96	21	4	0	4	12	15	23	.330	.385	Throws Left	R	.353	51	18	2	0	3	8	8	7	.450	.569
Gardner,Mark	L	.276	373	103	22	5	9	35	35	72	.338	.434	Hampton,Mike	L	.277	166	46	11	0	2	13	20	26	.358	.380
Throws Right	R	.233	429	100	18	5	20	60	30	79	.288	.438	Throws Left	R	.278	651	181	27	3	16	66	61	111	.340	.402
Glauber,Keith	L	.250	12	3	1	0	0	1	0	2	.231	.333	Haney,Chris	L	.241	108	26	6	0	3	15	7	24	.292	.380
Throws Right	R	.188	16	3	1	0	0	2	1	2	.222	.250	Throws Left	R	.333	306	102	20	0	17	56	30	31	.389	.565
Glavine,Tom	L	.245	212	52	5	0	6	20	15	34	.294	.354	Hanson,Erik	L	.381	118	45	10	1	4	24	13	8	.443	.585
Throws Left	R	.235	638	150	28	1	7	43	59	123	.301	.315	Throws Right	R	.304	92	28	4	0	6	11	16	13	.413	.543
Gomes,Wayne	L	.293	150	44	6	1	3	19	17	29	.371	.407	Harnisch,Pete	L	.216	380	82	20	2	13	36	34	71	.278	.382
Throws Right	R	.234	214	50	7	0	6	21	18	57	.296	.350	Throws Right	R	.240	391	94	23	2	11	33	30	86	.304	.394
Gonzalez,Gabe	L	1.000	1	1	0	0	0	3	0	0	1.000	1.000	Harriger,D	L	.286	21	6	0	0	1	5	6	3	.444	.429
Throws Left	R	.000	2	0	0	0	0	0	1	0	.333	.000	Throws Right	R	.355	31	11	1	0	0	4	2	0	.394	.387
Gonzalez,J	L	.298	208	62	18	2	3	32	19	41	.358	.447	Harris,Pep	L	.239	92	22	5	0	5	12	14	13	.336	.457
Throws Right	R	.265	234	62	10	1	10	28	22	29	.332	.444	Throws Right	R	.239	138	33	2	1	2	14	9	21	.286	.312
Gonzalez,L	L	.000	2	0	0	0	0	0	0	0	.000	.000	Harris,Reggie	L	.333	9	3	1	0	1	2	1	1	.400	.778
Throws Right	R	.000	1	0	0	0	0	0	0	0	.000	.000	Throws Right	R	.214	14	3	1	0	0	2	1	1	.250	.286
Gooden,Dwight	L	.275	273	75	14	1	10	31	25	40	.340	.443	Hartgraves,D	L	.400	5	2	0	0	0	3	1	2	.375	.400
Throws Right	R	.248	242	60	11	1	3	18	26	43	.333	.339	Throws Left	R	.381	21	8	2	0	1	5	3	2	.458	.619
Gordon,Tom	L	.189	169	32	2	0	0	12	12	42	.242	.201	Hasegawa,S	L	.212	146	31	10	1	4	17	10	35	.259	.377
Throws Right	R	.193	119	23	6	1	2	16	13	36	.271	.311	Throws Right	R	.261	211	55	14	0	10	31	22	38	.331	.469
Gorecki,Rick	L	.258	31	8	1	1	0	3	5	3	.361	.355	Hawkins,L	L	.296	419	124	26	4	15	60	37	62	.348	.484
Throws Right	R	.259	27	7	1	1	1	5	5	4	.353	.481	Throws Right	R	.302	341	103	17	1	12	47	24	43	.354	.463
Grace,Mike	L	.370	173	64	17	3	5	31	14	12	.423	.590	Haynes,Jimmy	L	.308	390	120	29	2	8	41	60	67	.400	.454
Throws Right	R	.261	199	52	14	0	5	29	16	34	.333	.407	Throws Right	R	.288	378	109	24	3	17	63	28	67	.337	.503
Graves,Danny	L	.254	130	33	5	0	4	18	13	15	.317	.385	Heathcott,M	L	.333	3	1	1	0	0	0	0	0	.333	.667
Throws Right	R	.250	172	43	6	1	2	21	15	29	.313	.331	Throws Right	R	.125	8	1	0	0	0	1	1	3	.222	.125
Green,Tyler	L	.231	286	66	17	1	7	35	35	55	.319	.371	Helling,Rick	L	.253	419	106	25	3	16	52	52	90	.332	.442
Throws Right	R	.247	308	76	15	0	16	55	50	58	.359	.451	Throws Right	R	.252	408	103	19	2	11	46	26	74	.295	.390
Greisinger,S	L	.313	259	81	15	2	8	40	23	34	.368	.479	Henderson,R	L	.000	2	0	0	0	0	0	0	0	.000	.000
Throws Right	R	.250	244	61	10	1	9	31	25	32	.324	.410	Throws Right	R	.357	14	5	1	0	2	4	0	1	.400	.857
Groom,Buddy	L	.243	111	27	7	0	2	14	10	19	.309	.360	Henriquez,O	L	.289	38	11	4	0	0	4	6	13	.391	.395
Throws Left	R	.304	115	35	6	0	2	21	10	17	.354	.409	Throws Right	R	.319	47	15	3	1	4	15	6	6	.389	.681
Grzanich,Mike	L	.000	0	0	0	0	0	0	0	0	.000	.000	Henry,Butch	L	.250	8	2	1	0	0	0	3	1	.455	.375
Throws Right	R	.333	3	1	0	0	0	2	2	1	.500	.333	Throws Left	R	.231	26	6	1	0	2	4	0	5	.259	.500
Guardado,E	L	.206	126	26	6	0	5	23	13	30	.273	.373	Henry,Doug	L	.157	108	17	2	0	2	11	21	31	.292	.231
Throws Left	R	.325	123	40	6	3	5	32	15	23	.393	.545	Throws Right	R	.259	147	38	6	0	7	22	14	28	.319	.442
Gunderson,E	L	.297	145	43	8	0	8	31	7	26	.331	.517	Hentgen,Pat	L	.288	364	105	23	1	13	50	39	49	.361	.464
Throws Left	R	.336	134	45	9	2	5	20	12	15	.385	.545	Throws Right	R	.299	345	103	24	0	15	53	30	45	.352	.499
Guthrie,Mark	L	.256	86	22	5	0	1	7	4	16	.289	.349	Heredia,Felix	L	.204	108	22	7	1	0	15	10	32	.269	.287
Throws Left	R	.274	124	34	5	1	2	17	20	29	.384	.379	Throws Left	R	.297	118	35	7	2	2	24	28	22	.432	.441
Guzman,Juan	L	.257	432	111	23	5	13	52	59	64	.346	.424	Heredia,Gil	L	.229	83	19	5	1	3	7	3	13	.256	.422
Throws Right	R	.220	373	82	28	3	10	50	39	104	.303	.391	Throws Right	R	.282	85	24	8	0	1	4	0	14	.307	.412

Pitcher	vs	Avg	AB	H	2B	3B	HR	BI	BB	SO	OBP	SLG
Hermanson,D	L	.234	346	81	11	2	10	32	36	66	.308	.364
Throws Right	R	.234	351	82	14	0	11	39	20	88	.276	.368
Hernandez,L	L	.276	421	116	23	2	18	59	48	74	.351	.468
Throws Right	R	.300	496	149	26	2	19	63	56	88	.374	.476
Hernandez,O	L	.271	280	76	15	2	8	33	33	47	.354	.425
Throws Right	R	.162	228	37	8	0	3	18	19	84	.231	.237
Hernandez,R	L	.184	136	25	1	1	2	12	25	32	.311	.250
Throws Right	R	.242	124	30	4	0	3	21	16	23	.352	.347
Hernandez,X	L	.213	80	17	1	0	3	13	17	15	.354	.338
Throws Right	R	.203	128	26	8	0	2	19	13	26	.275	.313
Hershiser,O	L	.247	377	93	15	1	6	35	49	47	.335	.340
Throws Right	R	.271	395	107	20	3	16	58	36	79	.346	.458
Hill,Ken	L	.319	216	69	22	1	3	31	28	27	.395	.472
Throws Right	R	.300	180	54	7	1	3	21	19	30	.369	.400
Hitchcock,S	L	.256	156	40	8	2	4	16	11	29	.331	.410
Throws Left	R	.249	518	129	20	1	25	61	37	129	.301	.436
Hoffman,T	L	.171	123	21	3	1	0	9	11	41	.244	.211
Throws Right	R	.159	126	20	3	1	2	7	10	45	.221	.246
Holdridge,D	L	.182	11	2	1	0	0	2	2	2	.308	.273
Throws Right	R	.267	15	4	2	0	0	1	2	4	.333	.400
Holmes,Darren	L	.245	94	23	3	0	3	14	5	16	.294	.372
Throws Right	R	.294	102	30	5	2	1	12	9	15	.345	.412
Holtz,Mike	L	.308	78	24	6	0	0	18	9	23	.371	.385
Throws Left	R	.350	40	14	4	0	0	5	6	6	.447	.450
Holzemer,Mark	L	.071	14	1	0	0	0	2	1	1	.176	.071
Throws Left	R	.480	25	12	2	1	1	10	2	2	.519	.760
Howry,Bob	L	.149	87	13	3	0	4	10	14	25	.260	.322
Throws Right	R	.231	104	24	5	1	3	10	5	26	.279	.385
Hudek,John	L	.200	85	17	3	2	2	6	24	21	.381	.353
Throws Right	R	.231	143	33	8	1	6	28	23	47	.339	.427
Hudson,Joe	L	1.000	1	1	1	0	0	3	2	0	1.000	2.000
Throws Right	R	1.000	1	1	1	0	0	3	2	0	.750	2.000
Hutton,Mark	L	.333	24	8	3	0	1	4	9	1	.515	.583
Throws Right	R	.356	45	16	2	1	1	10	8	2	.463	.511
Irabu,Hideki	L	.218	331	72	10	3	18	41	48	72	.322	.429
Throws Right	R	.250	304	76	12	0	9	30	28	54	.320	.378
Jackson,Mike	L	.210	100	21	8	0	1	5	8	15	.288	.320
Throws Right	R	.182	121	22	1	0	3	7	5	40	.220	.264
Jacome,Jason	L	.200	5	1	0	0	0	0	1	0	.333	.200
Throws Left	R	.500	18	9	1	1	2	8	2	2	.550	1.000
James,Mike	L	.250	24	6	3	0	0	3	1	7	.280	.375
Throws Right	R	.167	24	4	0	0	0	1	6	5	.333	.167
Jerzembeck,M	L	.375	16	6	2	0	2	6	2	0	.444	.875
Throws Right	R	.300	10	3	0	0	0	2	2	1	.385	.300
Jimenez,Jose	L	.316	38	12	1	0	0	4	5	4	.386	.342
Throws Right	R	.217	46	10	3	0	0	4	3	8	.265	.283
Johns,Doug	L	.242	95	23	4	1	1	15	6	13	.296	.337
Throws Left	R	.353	241	85	17	1	8	31	26	21	.415	.531
Johnson,Jason	L	.292	137	40	10	1	3	15	15	22	.370	.445
Throws Right	R	.324	105	34	8	0	6	16	12	14	.395	.571

Pitcher	vs	Avg	AB	H	2B	3B	HR	BI	BB	SO	OBP	SLG
Johnson,J	L	.429	7	3	2	0	0	3	2	1	.500	.714
Throws Right	R	.222	9	2	0	0	0	1	3	2	.417	.222
Johnson,Mike	L	.316	19	6	2	0	0	2	1	2	.350	.421
Throws Right	R	.556	18	10	1	0	4	9	1	2	.600	1.278
Johnson,Randy	L	.181	83	15	2	0	0	5	10	40	.284	.205
Throws Left	R	.228	824	188	36	1	23	91	76	289	.302	.358
Johnstone,J	L	.220	132	29	9	1	5	19	19	37	.312	.417
Throws Right	R	.226	190	43	10	2	5	19	19	49	.297	.379
Jones,Bobby	L	.232	353	82	19	1	9	38	25	58	.284	.368
Throws Right	R	.290	379	110	21	2	14	49	28	57	.346	.467
Jones,B	L	.291	103	30	8	0	1	15	12	20	.378	.398
Throws Left	R	.280	439	123	26	4	11	55	54	89	.359	.433
Jones,Doug	L	.271	140	38	7	0	7	19	12	27	.325	.471
Throws Right	R	.307	199	61	9	0	10	28	5	44	.330	.503
Jones,Todd	L	.240	121	29	3	0	4	22	19	26	.340	.364
Throws Right	R	.259	112	29	7	0	3	15	17	31	.353	.402
Jordan,R	L	.286	7	2	1	0	1	3	3	1	.455	.857
Throws Left	R	.333	6	2	0	0	1	5	4	0	.600	.833
Judd,Mike	L	.290	31	9	1	0	3	12	6	11	.405	.613
Throws Right	R	.500	20	10	2	0	1	8	3	3	.583	.750
Juden,Jeff	L	.279	333	93	17	5	14	54	49	72	.373	.486
Throws Right	R	.250	356	89	19	2	13	51	35	76	.330	.424
Kamieniecki,S	L	.255	106	27	9	0	3	19	19	10	.375	.425
Throws Right	R	.370	108	40	6	0	4	16	7	15	.415	.537
Karchner,Matt	L	.268	112	30	3	0	6	24	14	19	.352	.455
Throws Right	R	.241	137	33	7	0	2	16	19	33	.352	.336
Karl,Scott	L	.250	148	37	9	0	2	9	7	29	.297	.351
Throws Left	R	.299	608	182	39	3	19	86	59	73	.361	.467
Karsay,Steve	L	.288	52	15	3	0	1	10	3	5	.345	.404
Throws Right	R	.333	48	16	5	0	2	11	3	8	.365	.563
Keagle,Greg	L	.355	93	33	5	1	5	17	12	14	.434	.591
Throws Right	R	.206	63	13	2	0	0	8	8	11	.324	.238
Key,Jimmy	L	.233	73	17	5	0	2	14	3	13	.282	.384
Throws Left	R	.265	226	60	10	6	3	23	20	40	.327	.403
Kile,Darryl	L	.312	477	149	30	4	8	54	53	69	.381	.442
Throws Right	R	.259	417	108	17	3	20	70	43	89	.333	.458
King,Curtis	L	.244	90	22	2	1	4	15	9	15	.310	.422
Throws Right	R	.277	101	28	5	0	1	14	11	13	.362	.356
Kline,Steve	L	.178	90	16	1	2	1	11	13	33	.292	.267
Throws Left	R	.253	182	46	12	0	3	19	28	43	.354	.368
Klingenbeck,S	L	.261	46	12	1	1	2	9	2	8	.300	.457
Throws Right	R	.311	45	14	4	0	4	7	5	5	.380	.667
Krivda,Rick	L	.269	67	18	3	2	4	11	9	10	.355	.552
Throws Left	R	.333	141	47	11	2	5	27	26	19	.444	.546
Kroon,Marc	L	.250	12	3	0	0	0	2	6	2	.526	.250
Throws Right	R	.250	16	4	1	1	0	4	3	4	.368	.438
Kubenka,Jeff	L	.125	8	1	0	0	0	0	4	4	.417	.125
Throws Left	R	.143	21	3	0	0	0	2	4	6	.269	.143
Langston,Mark	L	.360	50	18	2	1	2	11	6	5	.421	.560
Throws Left	R	.319	279	89	19	2	9	38	35	51	.393	.498

Pitchers vs. Lefthanded and Righthanded Batters

Pitcher	vs	Avg	AB	H	2B	3B	HR	BI	BB	SO	OBP	SLG	Pitcher	vs	Avg	AB	H	2B	3B	HR	BI	BB	SO	OBP	SLG
Lankford,F	L	.282	39	11	1	0	0	2	6	4	.391	.308	Mahay,Ron	L	.243	37	9	2	0	1	8	6	8	.333	.378
Throws Right	R	.293	41	12	2	0	2	11	1	3	.326	.488	Throws Left	R	.274	62	17	1	0	1	16	9	6	.373	.339
Larkin,Andy	L	.364	143	52	9	2	6	43	31	19	.474	.580	Maloney,Sean	L	.200	20	4	0	1	0	2	1	4	.238	.300
Throws Right	R	.299	164	49	11	1	6	30	24	24	.399	.488	Throws Right	R	.310	29	9	1	0	2	7	4	7	.429	.552
Lawrence,Sean	L	.348	23	8	2	0	1	5	4	5	.444	.565	Mantei,Matt	L	.200	75	15	4	0	1	11	12	25	.303	.293
Throws Left	R	.298	57	17	6	1	3	11	6	7	.354	.596	Throws Right	R	.205	112	23	5	2	0	12	11	38	.311	.286
Leiter,Al	L	.263	133	35	11	0	2	13	8	31	.315	.391	Manuel,Barry	L	.333	21	7	1	0	3	8	8	3	.533	.810
Throws Left	R	.205	566	116	26	1	6	33	63	143	.294	.286	Throws Right	R	.233	43	10	4	1	2	10	6	9	.327	.512
Leiter,Mark	L	.240	150	36	9	1	8	24	22	35	.341	.473	Martin,Tom	L	.444	27	12	3	0	1	6	3	4	.500	.667
Throws Right	R	.194	160	31	7	0	0	16	25	49	.321	.238	Throws Left	R	.386	44	17	5	1	2	15	9	5	.481	.682
Leskanic,Curt	L	.325	123	40	8	1	5	22	19	14	.415	.528	Martinez,D	L	.299	154	46	4	1	3	17	11	23	.351	.396
Throws Right	R	.210	167	35	6	1	4	19	21	41	.302	.329	Throws Right	R	.293	215	63	11	2	5	32	8	39	.319	.433
Levine,Al	L	.266	94	25	6	0	2	16	8	3	.320	.394	Martinez,J	L	.271	70	19	4	1	1	12	15	18	.398	.400
Throws Right	R	.314	137	43	8	2	4	22	8	16	.347	.489	Throws Right	R	.230	87	20	3	0	4	19	19	24	.382	.402
Lewis,Richie	L	.556	9	5	2	0	1	6	2	1	.583	1.111	Martinez,P	L	.225	472	106	18	1	12	36	40	125	.289	.343
Throws Right	R	.300	10	3	0	0	1	3	3	3	.462	.600	Throws Right	R	.209	393	82	12	1	14	40	27	126	.264	.351
Lieber,Jon	L	.311	315	98	24	3	17	51	21	49	.354	.568	Martinez,R	L	.211	161	34	8	0	6	15	23	28	.316	.373
Throws Right	R	.232	362	84	18	1	6	34	19	89	.273	.337	Throws Right	R	.202	208	42	10	0	2	21	18	63	.266	.279
Ligtenberg,K	L	.176	119	21	6	0	1	9	10	35	.238	.252	Mathews,T.J.	L	.324	108	35	6	2	2	22	20	16	.421	.472
Throws Right	R	.207	145	30	3	0	5	16	14	44	.277	.331	Throws Right	R	.216	167	36	7	2	4	22	9	37	.261	.353
Lima,Jose	L	.267	449	120	21	4	11	44	21	78	.299	.405	Mathews,Terry	L	.259	27	7	1	0	0	4	4	3	.355	.296
Throws Right	R	.244	446	109	17	1	23	50	11	91	.271	.442	Throws Right	R	.388	49	19	2	1	6	19	4	7	.426	.837
Lira,Felipe	L	.314	35	11	2	0	3	7	0	8	.314	.629	McCarthy,Greg	L	.200	35	7	1	0	4	12	9	12	.404	.571
Throws Right	R	.324	34	11	2	1	2	4	5	8	.400	.618	Throws Left	R	.224	49	11	3	0	2	4	8	13	.333	.408
Lloyd,Graeme	L	.198	81	16	2	0	3	13	3	13	.235	.333	McCurry,Jeff	L	.407	27	11	5	0	1	4	2	3	.448	.704
Throws Left	R	.182	55	10	3	0	0	5	3	7	.233	.236	Throws Right	R	.277	47	13	2	0	3	10	7	8	.375	.511
Loaiza,E	L	.290	341	99	15	3	13	40	35	53	.354	.466	McDill,Allen	L	.300	10	3	1	0	0	4	1	1	.364	.400
Throws Right	R	.299	334	100	12	3	15	58	17	55	.333	.488	Throws Left	R	.353	17	6	1	0	3	5	1	2	.389	.941
Loewer,C	L	.327	223	73	21	2	5	32	14	22	.362	.507	McDowell,Jack	L	.279	172	48	12	1	4	24	13	30	.330	.430
Throws Right	R	.299	271	81	18	1	13	46	25	36	.359	.517	Throws Right	R	.350	137	48	12	1	7	18	6	15	.377	.606
Loiselle,Rich	L	.269	78	21	6	0	0	9	16	19	.394	.346	McElroy,Chuck	L	.292	113	33	9	1	3	22	8	23	.333	.469
Throws Right	R	.257	136	35	3	0	2	20	20	29	.358	.324	Throws Left	R	.248	141	35	6	1	0	12	16	38	.323	.305
Looper,Braden	L	.667	6	4	0	0	1	4	0	1	.667	1.167	McMichael,G	L	.275	102	28	4	0	1	7	12	18	.356	.343
Throws Right	R	.125	8	1	0	0	0	1	1	3	.200	.125	Throws Right	R	.317	167	53	7	0	8	36	23	37	.404	.503
Lopez,Albie	L	.227	110	25	6	0	4	15	18	27	.343	.391	Meadows,Brian	L	.350	346	121	27	0	12	46	27	42	.395	.532
Throws Right	R	.262	183	48	6	1	3	22	14	35	.315	.355	Throws Right	R	.281	359	101	13	3	8	50	19	46	.320	.401
Lorraine,A	L	.000	2	0	0	0	0	0	3	0	.600	.000	Mecir,Jim	L	.227	150	34	4	1	5	22	21	37	.328	.367
Throws Left	R	.300	10	3	1	0	0	1	1	0	.364	.400	Throws Right	R	.224	152	34	5	1	1	12	12	40	.283	.289
Lowe,Derek	L	.292	219	64	12	1	2	26	25	23	.360	.384	Medina,Rafael	L	.283	113	32	6	3	2	18	24	19	.409	.442
Throws Right	R	.245	253	62	9	1	3	35	17	54	.301	.324	Throws Right	R	.293	150	44	10	2	6	26	28	30	.405	.507
Lowe,Sean	L	.500	14	7	3	0	1	8	4	0	.611	.929	Mendoza,R	L	.289	263	76	15	1	5	32	23	23	.344	.411
Throws Right	R	.364	11	4	1	0	0	1	1	2	.417	.455	Throws Right	R	.236	233	55	13	0	4	18	7	33	.278	.343
Ludwick,Eric	L	.491	55	27	3	0	3	12	10	8	.561	.709	Mercedes,Jose	L	.339	59	20	1	0	2	12	6	4	.397	.458
Throws Right	R	.229	83	19	8	1	4	12	7	19	.286	.494	Throws Right	R	.297	74	22	4	0	3	9	3	7	.325	.473
Maddux,Greg	L	.218	417	91	15	1	5	34	25	94	.269	.295	Mercker,Kent	L	.324	111	36	8	0	1	13	7	9	.367	.423
Throws Right	R	.221	498	110	17	0	8	35	20	110	.253	.303	Throws Left	R	.308	530	163	34	1	10	73	46	63	.360	.432
Maddux,Mike	L	.293	82	24	4	0	1	13	7	11	.344	.378	Mesa,Jose	L	.338	142	48	5	0	4	24	13	19	.399	.458
Throws Right	R	.210	124	26	8	0	2	12	8	22	.259	.323	Throws Right	R	.225	191	43	8	1	4	29	25	44	.320	.340
Magnante,Mike	L	.235	68	16	0	0	1	6	7	9	.316	.279	Miceli,Dan	L	.321	112	36	5	0	2	11	11	22	.379	.420
Throws Left	R	.296	135	40	9	2	1	21	19	30	.392	.415	Throws Right	R	.178	157	28	6	0	4	17	16	48	.257	.293

Pitchers vs. Lefthanded and Righthanded Batters

Pitcher	vs	Avg	AB	H	2B	3B	HR	BI	BB	SO	OBP	SLG	Pitcher	vs	Avg	AB	H	2B	3B	HR	BI	BB	SO	OBP	SLG
Michalak,C	L	.800	5	4	0	0	0	3	1	1	.714	.800	Naulty,Dan	L	.289	38	11	3	2	2	9	5	6	.372	.632
Throws Left	R	.263	19	5	1	0	1	7	3	4	.364	.474	Throws Right	R	.255	55	14	2	1	1	4	5	9	.311	.382
Miller,Kurt	L	.200	5	1	0	0	0	0	0	2	.200	.200	Navarro,Jaime	L	.327	376	123	25	1	15	62	39	37	.392	.519
Throws Right	R	.200	10	2	0	0	0	0	0	4	.200	.200	Throws Right	R	.301	332	100	13	0	15	62	38	34	.375	.476
Miller,Travis	L	.147	34	5	3	0	0	3	3	9	.211	.235	Neagle,Denny	L	.257	148	38	5	3	3	10	12	27	.317	.392
Throws Left	R	.345	58	20	4	0	0	8	8	14	.424	.414	Throws Left	R	.248	637	158	28	2	22	76	48	138	.304	.402
Miller,Trever	L	.217	60	13	2	1	0	5	5	10	.277	.283	Nelson,Jeff	L	.295	61	18	6	1	0	8	8	14	.411	.426
Throws Left	R	.286	154	44	12	0	4	19	15	20	.353	.442	Throws Right	R	.268	97	26	3	2	1	8	14	21	.373	.371
Mills,Alan	L	.207	92	19	1	1	2	5	22	12	.360	.304	Nen,Robb	L	.234	167	39	5	1	1	11	12	49	.285	.293
Throws Right	R	.201	179	36	5	0	6	24	28	45	.308	.330	Throws Right	R	.125	160	20	4	0	3	11	13	61	.193	.206
Millwood,K	L	.277	303	84	14	3	8	34	37	59	.358	.422	Nitkowski,C	L	.186	59	11	4	0	0	5	7	14	.310	.254
Throws Right	R	.243	375	91	15	3	10	41	19	104	.281	.379	Throws Left	R	.244	156	38	6	1	4	18	16	30	.320	.372
Milton,Eric	L	.361	155	56	9	1	9	29	14	25	.412	.606	Nomo,Hideo	L	.210	271	57	8	2	11	36	45	77	.324	.376
Throws Left	R	.259	537	139	39	3	16	67	56	82	.328	.432	Throws Right	R	.239	305	73	13	1	8	36	49	90	.346	.367
Mlicki,Dave	L	.297	344	102	22	2	13	43	46	47	.377	.485	Nunez,V	L	.200	5	1	0	0	0	0	1	0	.333	.200
Throws Right	R	.239	360	86	21	1	10	43	17	70	.282	.386	Throws Right	R	.353	17	6	1	0	0	4	1	2	.368	.412
Moehler,Brian	L	.267	431	115	22	5	16	53	37	65	.323	.452	Nye,Ryan	L	.500	2	1	1	0	0	0	0	1	.500	1.000
Throws Right	R	.252	416	105	16	2	14	38	19	58	.288	.401	Throws Right	R	.500	4	2	0	0	1	3	0	2	.500	1.250
Mohler,Mike	L	.333	99	33	3	1	3	20	16	21	.436	.475	Ogea,Chad	L	.280	132	37	8	3	5	26	12	22	.340	.500
Throws Left	R	.259	143	37	5	1	3	22	10	21	.312	.371	Throws Right	R	.266	139	37	4	1	4	16	13	21	.352	.396
Montgomery,J	L	.293	116	34	4	0	5	12	11	23	.352	.457	Ojala,Kirt	L	.303	109	33	3	0	3	13	12	22	.382	.413
Throws Right	R	.231	104	24	6	0	3	22	11	31	.316	.375	Throws Left	R	.257	370	95	26	5	11	55	47	53	.342	.443
Moore,Trey	L	.302	53	16	4	0	1	6	6	9	.373	.434	Olivares,Omar	L	.281	345	97	16	1	10	42	58	66	.384	.420
Throws Left	R	.307	202	62	15	0	4	32	11	26	.341	.441	Throws Right	R	.260	354	92	16	3	9	37	33	46	.328	.398
Morgan,Mike	L	.286	245	70	17	3	9	26	24	26	.352	.490	Oliver,Darren	L	.274	135	37	7	0	5	15	17	21	.355	.437
Throws Right	R	.301	226	68	11	1	12	29	15	34	.359	.518	Throws Left	R	.320	522	167	46	1	13	81	49	66	.384	.487
Morman,Alvin	L	.250	52	13	3	0	2	13	6	11	.328	.423	Olson,Gregg	L	.163	135	22	5	1	0	7	17	37	.257	.215
Throws Left	R	.328	61	20	2	1	3	10	8	12	.400	.541	Throws Left	R	.293	116	34	5	2	4	17	8	18	.341	.474
Morris,Matt	L	.234	197	46	10	1	4	12	23	43	.312	.355	Oquist,Mike	L	.291	375	109	17	2	13	58	34	67	.351	.451
Throws Right	R	.251	219	55	10	1	4	21	19	36	.320	.361	Throws Right	R	.307	329	101	23	2	14	51	23	45	.354	.517
Moyer,Jamie	L	.258	271	70	17	2	10	31	10	47	.301	.446	Orosco,Jesse	L	.205	83	17	2	0	2	8	9	25	.280	.301
Throws Left	R	.255	644	164	47	1	13	56	32	111	.292	.391	Throws Left	R	.232	125	29	5	0	4	18	19	25	.336	.368
Mulholland,T	L	.256	125	32	6	0	3	15	8	18	.299	.376	Ortiz,Russ	L	.283	180	51	13	0	8	23	20	33	.355	.489
Throws Left	R	.227	300	68	12	0	4	29	31	54	.305	.307	Throws Right	R	.252	155	39	13	0	3	20	26	42	.366	.394
Mullins,Greg	L	.000	2	0	0	0	0	0	0	1	.333	.000	Osborne,D	L	.150	60	9	2	0	0	1	4	12	.203	.183
Throws Left	R	.500	2	1	0	0	0	0	0	0	.500	.500	Throws Left	R	.280	268	75	15	2	11	41	18	48	.323	.474
Munoz,Bobby	L	.250	24	6	3	0	1	6	5	4	.387	.500	Osuna,Antonio	L	.173	98	17	3	0	1	5	20	35	.314	.235
Throws Right	R	.522	23	12	2	0	3	9	1	2	.500	1.000	Throws Right	R	.243	136	33	6	1	7	20	12	37	.309	.456
Munoz,Mike	L	.359	64	23	5	1	1	18	4	8	.406	.516	Painter,Lance	L	.205	73	15	3	0	2	7	13	16	.330	.329
Throws Left	R	.283	106	30	8	2	1	15	12	16	.353	.425	Throws Left	R	.281	96	27	4	0	3	13	15	23	.391	.406
Mussina,Mike	L	.246	399	98	23	2	9	42	24	107	.287	.381	Pall,Donn	L	.293	58	17	2	0	3	8	4	8	.333	.483
Throws Right	R	.239	381	91	17	0	13	37	17	68	.278	.386	Throws Right	R	.352	71	25	6	0	2	7	3	18	.387	.521
Myers,Mike	L	.162	68	11	0	0	2	11	14	24	.305	.250	Paniagua,Jose	L	.211	38	8	1	0	2	5	2	10	.250	.395
Throws Left	R	.303	109	33	4	2	3	19	8	16	.376	.459	Throws Right	R	.189	37	7	1	0.	1	3	3	6	.302	.297
Myers,Randy	L	.282	71	20	5	0	2	9	5	14	.338	.437	Park,Chan Ho	L	.252	409	103	27	2	9	47	49	90	.329	.394
Throws Left	R	.260	150	39	9	0	4	20	21	27	.353	.400	Throws Right	R	.235	408	96	16	1	7	33	48	101	.328	.331
Myers,Rodney	L	.455	22	10	4	0	0	3	2	2	.500	.636	Parque,Jim	L	.300	100	30	8	0	3	14	8	19	.364	.470
Throws Right	R	.296	54	16	0	0	3	10	4	13	.345	.463	Throws Left	R	.299	351	105	25	2	11	52	41	58	.379	.476
Nagy,Charles	L	.271	399	108	24	3	17	53	34	58	.336	.474	Parris,Steve	L	.291	175	51	14	0	2	20	20	24	.369	.406
Throws Right	R	.322	441	142	28	2	17	68	32	62	.368	.510	Throws Right	R	.188	202	38	4	2	7	21	12	53	.241	.332

Pitchers vs. Lefthanded and Righthanded Batters

Pitcher	vs	Avg	AB	H	2B	3B	HR	BI	BB	SO	OBP	SLG	Pitcher	vs	Avg	AB	H	2B	3B	HR	BI	BB	SO	OBP	SLG
Patrick,B	L	.283	127	36	13	2	3	20	11	12	.341	.488	Powell,Brian	L	.232	181	42	7	2	5	23	20	29	.307	.376
Throws Right	R	.275	171	47	9	2	6	28	18	37	.339	.456	Throws Right	R	.364	162	59	15	0	12	38	16	17	.428	.679
Patterson,Bob	L	.354	48	17	3	2	0	11	6	9	.411	.500	Powell,Jay	L	.221	113	25	4	2	3	19	15	39	.328	.372
Throws Left	R	.432	44	19	4	0	2	8	6	8	.500	.659	Throws Right	R	.228	145	33	5	2	3	20	22	23	.327	.352
Patterson,D	L	.330	91	30	4	2	4	11	8	15	.390	.549	Powell,Jeremy	L	.237	38	9	1	1	1	8	3	5	.286	.395
Throws Right	R	.238	143	34	8	1	7	22	11	18	.295	.455	Throws Right	R	.327	55	18	1	0	4	16	8	9	.441	.564
Pavano,Carl	L	.260	231	60	12	2	7	26	27	33	.340	.420	Priest,Eddie	L	.375	8	3	0	0	1	2	0	1	.375	.750
Throws Right	R	.244	287	70	15	2	11	36	16	50	.294	.425	Throws Left	R	.474	19	9	2	0	1	5	1	0	.476	.737
Pavlik,Roger	L	.263	19	5	0	0	0	3	4	3	.375	.263	Prieto,Ariel	L	.409	22	9	1	0	2	5	4	5	.500	.727
Throws Right	R	.297	37	11	4	1	2	6	1	5	.333	.622	Throws Right	R	.421	19	8	1	2	0	6	1	3	.476	.684
Pennington,B	L	1.000	1	1	0	0	0	1	2	0	1.000	1.000	Pulsipher,B	L	.320	50	16	4	1	2	10	6	9	.386	.560
Throws Left	R	.000	0	0	0	0	0	1	1	0	1.000	.000	Throws Left	R	.304	230	70	11	3	6	34	25	42	.371	.457
Percival,Troy	L	.206	126	26	9	0	2	18	22	42	.336	.325	Quantrill,P	L	.258	132	34	7	0	2	15	13	27	.327	.356
Throws Right	R	.164	116	19	5	1	3	16	15	45	.258	.302	Throws Right	R	.305	177	54	9	1	3	30	9	32	.340	.418
Perez,Carlos	L	.301	186	56	9	4	1	22	6	19	.330	.409	Radinsky,S	L	.281	64	18	3	0	2	13	3	17	.324	.422
Throws Left	R	.254	739	188	31	5	20	72	57	109	.308	.391	Throws Left	R	.268	168	45	4	1	3	23	17	28	.342	.357
Perez,Odalis	L	.500	8	4	0	0	0	0	1	3	.556	.500	Radke,Brad	L	.322	457	147	26	3	15	64	24	68	.359	.490
Throws Left	R	.182	33	6	1	0	1	4	3	2	.250	.303	Throws Right	R	.238	383	91	16	2	8	37	19	78	.283	.352
Perez,Yorkis	L	.202	84	17	3	1	2	12	8	23	.269	.333	Raggio,Brady	L	.565	23	13	1	0	1	9	2	1	.577	.739
Throws Left	R	.215	107	23	11	0	1	14	17	19	.317	.346	Throws Right	R	.600	15	9	2	0	0	5	1	2	.647	.733
Perisho,Matt	L	.556	9	5	1	0	2	9	2	1	.667	1.333	Rakers,Jason	L	.000	2	0	0	0	0	0	0	0	.000	.000
Throws Right	R	.476	21	10	3	0	0	6	6	1	.607	.619	Throws Right	R	.000	0	0	0	0	0	1	3	0	.750	.000
Person,Robert	L	.311	74	23	3	0	5	16	12	17	.400	.554	Ramirez,R	L	.321	28	9	1	0	4	10	5	6	.424	.786
Throws Right	R	.278	79	22	4	1	4	13	10	14	.359	.506	Throws Right	R	.103	29	3	1	0	0	2	7	11	.278	.138
Peters,Chris	L	.263	133	35	2	0	4	12	6	24	.305	.368	Rapp,Pat	L	.289	405	117	22	0	8	48	73	79	.397	.402
Throws Left	R	.249	430	107	19	1	9	42	49	79	.324	.360	Throws Right	R	.281	324	91	15	3	16	52	34	53	.362	.494
Petkovsek,M	L	.311	206	64	13	2	0	21	17	18	.368	.393	Rath,Fred	L	.429	7	3	0	0	0	1	0	0	.429	.429
Throws Right	R	.313	214	67	8	2	9	42	19	37	.381	.495	Throws Right	R	.231	13	3	2	0	0	1	2	2	.313	.385
Pettitte,Andy	L	.283	184	52	7	0	8	27	14	43	.347	.451	Rath,Gary	L	.000	3	0	0	0	0	0	0	2	.000	.000
Throws Left	R	.271	642	174	31	1	12	70	73	103	.344	.379	Throws Left	R	.333	9	3	0	0	1	2	2	2	.455	.667
Pichardo,H	L	.300	233	70	15	1	4	32	22	21	.364	.425	Reed,Rick	L	.249	358	89	17	1	14	35	15	68	.280	.419
Throws Right	R	.258	217	56	11	0	7	25	21	34	.326	.406	Throws Right	R	.271	439	119	21	4	16	42	14	85	.299	.446
Pickett,Ricky	L	.500	2	1	1	0	0	0	1	1	.667	1.000	Reed,Steve	L	.231	104	24	4	0	6	20	17	23	.344	.442
Throws Left	R	.667	3	2	0	0	0	1	3	1	.833	.667	Throws Right	R	.174	184	32	7	0	2	15	10	50	.232	.245
Pisciotta,M	L	.161	56	9	2	0	2	6	22	11	.400	.304	Rekar,Bryan	L	.290	176	51	7	2	5	23	17	28	.343	.438
Throws Right	R	.307	114	35	6	0	2	15	10	20	.368	.412	Throws Right	R	.273	161	44	9	0	11	29	4	27	.294	.534
Pittsley,Jim	L	.304	102	31	11	1	1	16	18	20	.398	.461	Remlinger,M	L	.267	120	32	7	0	1	9	14	20	.355	.350
Throws Right	R	.333	171	57	8	2	12	40	19	24	.402	.614	Throws Left	R	.266	496	132	31	0	22	68	73	124	.359	.462
Plesac,Dan	L	.198	111	22	8	0	2	11	7	38	.244	.324	Reyes,Al	L	.233	86	20	4	2	5	17	23	21	.400	.500
Throws Left	R	.264	72	19	5	1	2	14	9	17	.345	.444	Throws Right	R	.269	130	35	6	1	4	21	8	37	.314	.423
Plunk,Eric	L	.280	93	26	5	1	2	9	7	20	.333	.419	Reyes,Carlos	L	.220	100	22	3	0	4	17	4	17	.255	.370
Throws Right	R	.276	185	51	4	2	7	35	23	54	.363	.432	Throws Right	R	.257	140	36	7	0	2	13	16	30	.340	.350
Politte,Cliff	L	.315	73	23	4	1	2	15	8	9	.378	.479	Reyes,Dennis	L	.236	72	17	5	1	0	6	9	23	.321	.333
Throws Right	R	.293	75	22	4	1	4	9	10	13	.384	.533	Throws Left	R	.263	171	45	11	1	3	25	38	54	.396	.392
Ponson,Sidney	L	.263	270	71	11	3	8	31	23	41	.321	.415	Reynolds,S	L	.256	464	119	27	3	11	50	31	113	.299	.399
Throws Right	R	.323	266	86	12	1	11	44	19	44	.370	.500	Throws Right	R	.303	455	138	26	3	14	43	22	96	.338	.466
Poole,Jim	L	.258	66	17	4	1	1	13	5	12	.315	.394	Reynoso,A	L	.230	122	28	5	1	2	13	13	10	.312	.336
Throws Left	R	.333	90	30	7	1	4	15	7	15	.381	.567	Throws Right	R	.281	128	36	9	0	2	13	19	30	.387	.398
Portugal,Mark	L	.267	341	91	16	1	16	38	16	55	.299	.460	Rhodes,Arthur	L	.172	93	16	1	0	2	8	7	33	.230	.247
Throws Right	R	.300	317	86	24	2	10	47	16	49	.340	.483	Throws Left	R	.263	186	49	11	1	6	25	27	50	.352	.430

Pitchers vs. Lefthanded and Righthanded Batters

Pitcher	vs	Avg	AB	H	2B	3B	HR	BI	BB	SO	OBP	SLG
Rincon,R	L	.131	84	11	3	1	0	4	8	28	.207	.190
Throws Left	R	.250	156	39	11	0	6	26	21	36	.335	.436
Rios,Danny	L	.154	13	2	0	0	0	1	3	4	.353	.154
Throws Right	R	.412	17	7	3	0	1	7	3	2	.476	.765
Risley,Bill	L	.244	78	19	5	1	3	13	17	13	.381	.449
Throws Right	R	.268	123	33	6	1	4	19	17	29	.366	.431
Ritchie,Todd	L	.255	47	12	4	0	0	7	3	12	.300	.340
Throws Right	R	.316	57	18	3	2	1	9	6	9	.381	.491
Ritz,Kevin	L	.368	19	7	3	0	1	6	2	2	.455	.684
Throws Right	R	.417	24	10	4	0	0	5	0	1	.417	.583
Rivera,M	L	.235	115	27	6	0	0	9	9	9	.294	.287
Throws Right	R	.194	108	21	6	0	3	8	8	27	.246	.333
Rizzo,Todd	L	.533	15	8	1	0	0	5	1	2	.529	.600
Throws Left	R	.250	16	4	1	0	0	4	5	1	.429	.313
Robertson,R	L	.154	13	2	0	0	0	2	0	2	.143	.154
Throws Left	R	.600	15	9	1	0	3	6	2	1	.647	1.267
Rocker,John	L	.164	55	9	0	0	2	7	4	19	.258	.273
Throws Left	R	.178	73	13	2	1	2	7	18	23	.341	.315
Rodriguez,F	L	.268	71	19	5	1	4	23	15	20	.391	.535
Throws Right	R	.253	99	25	2	0	1	14	14	16	.345	.303
Rodriguez,F	L	.356	149	53	10	2	3	30	22	28	.434	.510
Throws Right	R	.248	141	35	10	0	3	20	8	34	.294	.383
Rodriguez,N	L	.321	56	18	5	0	0	10	8	4	.409	.411
Throws Right	R	.298	57	17	9	2	1	15	9	7	.388	.579
Rodriguez,R	L	.185	108	20	2	0	2	13	9	24	.246	.259
Throws Left	R	.336	146	49	8	0	5	30	11	20	.380	.493
Rogers,Kenny	L	.226	199	45	8	0	4	12	26	51	.325	.327
Throws Left	R	.247	688	170	37	4	15	68	41	87	.291	.378
Rojas,Mel	L	.220	100	22	8	0	2	17	18	19	.342	.360
Throws Right	R	.374	123	46	10	0	7	25	12	22	.435	.626
Roque,Rafael	L	.311	45	14	4	0	0	4	2	7	.354	.400
Throws Left	R	.212	132	28	0	0	9	20	22	27	.325	.417
Rosado,Jose	L	.217	166	36	3	0	3	16	13	50	.286	.289
Throws Left	R	.274	525	144	25	4	22	81	44	85	.331	.463
Rose,Brian	L	.289	76	22	4	0	5	14	12	8	.393	.539
Throws Right	R	.280	75	21	5	0	4	16	2	10	.304	.507
Ruebel,Matt	L	.357	14	5	0	0	1	4	1	2	.400	.571
Throws Left	R	.286	21	6	0	0	2	3	3	4	.375	.571
Rueter,Kirk	L	.238	143	34	3	0	5	14	6	33	.273	.364
Throws Left	R	.271	586	159	28	5	22	73	51	69	.332	.449
Runyan,Sean	L	.271	107	29	5	0	4	21	16	25	.367	.430
Throws Left	R	.234	77	18	3	0	3	12	12	14	.323	.390
Rusch,Glendon	L	.237	135	32	3	0	1	16	9	36	.295	.281
Throws Left	R	.322	494	159	31	1	21	79	41	58	.375	.516
Ryan,Ken	L	.258	31	8	1	0	0	2	9	4	.425	.290
Throws Right	R	.250	52	13	5	1	1	12	11	12	.379	.442
Saberhagen,B	L	.300	367	110	22	2	12	42	19	45	.337	.469
Throws Right	R	.223	318	71	12	2	10	34	10	55	.254	.368
Sager,A.J.	L	.306	121	37	5	1	3	16	10	10	.359	.438
Throws Right	R	.344	122	42	8	0	4	35	13	13	.406	.508
Saipe,Mike	L	.444	18	8	2	0	3	5	0	0	.444	1.056
Throws Right	R	.424	33	14	3	0	2	7	0	2	.457	.697
Sampson,Benj	L	.182	11	2	1	0	0	0	2	5	.308	.273
Throws Left	R	.170	47	8	1	0	0	3	5	11	.241	.191
Sanchez,Jesus	L	.269	78	21	2	0	1	10	18	11	.408	.333
Throws Left	R	.273	576	157	25	3	17	74	73	126	.356	.415
Sanders,Scott	L	.329	79	26	4	0	3	16	7	12	.384	.494
Throws Right	R	.330	94	31	7	0	3	23	4	20	.357	.500
Santana,Julio	L	.296	270	80	15	2	8	35	34	34	.372	.456
Throws Right	R	.248	286	71	13	1	10	30	28	27	.323	.406
Santana,M	L	.333	12	4	0	0	0	0	5	3	.529	.333
Throws Right	R	.294	17	5	2	0	1	5	3	7	.429	.588
Santiago,Jose	L	.500	4	2	0	0	0	0	0	1	.500	.500
Throws Right	R	.400	5	2	1	0	0	2	0	1	.400	.600
Saunders,Tony	L	.256	172	44	9	4	1	16	14	45	.325	.372
Throws Left	R	.268	549	147	26	3	14	66	97	127	.376	.403
Scanlan,Bob	L	.152	33	5	1	1	0	3	6	6	.268	.242
Throws Right	R	.292	65	19	1	1	4	10	7	3	.365	.523
Schilling,C	L	.249	497	124	33	3	12	51	39	153	.304	.400
Throws Right	R	.223	503	112	23	3	11	45	22	147	.260	.346
Schmidt,Jason	L	.279	365	102	17	1	10	40	34	67	.340	.414
Throws Right	R	.272	463	126	24	2	14	53	37	91	.330	.423
Schourek,Pete	L	.258	97	25	6	1	4	14	9	22	.336	.464
Throws Left	R	.273	373	102	18	2	13	46	41	73	.344	.437
Seanez,Rudy	L	.286	56	16	3	0	2	7	6	14	.365	.446
Throws Right	R	.125	72	9	0	0	0	4	10	36	.226	.125
Sele,Aaron	L	.295	434	128	25	5	8	44	50	89	.373	.431
Throws Right	R	.270	411	111	22	1	6	57	34	78	.333	.372
Serafini,Dan	L	.330	91	30	6	1	2	16	6	13	.366	.484
Throws Left	R	.302	215	65	14	1	8	33	23	33	.365	.488
Service,Scott	L	.222	117	26	6	2	2	17	15	29	.314	.359
Throws Right	R	.237	186	44	9	0	5	29	19	66	.327	.366
Shaw,Jeff	L	.228	149	34	5	0	3	13	14	27	.299	.322
Throws Right	R	.252	163	41	3	0	5	19	5	28	.271	.362
Shouse,Brian	L	.273	11	3	0	0	0	1	2	2	.385	.273
Throws Left	R	.286	21	6	1	0	2	4	2	3	.348	.619
Shuey,Paul	L	.230	87	20	5	0	2	8	11	18	.330	.356
Throws Right	R	.229	105	24	4	0	4	12	14	40	.325	.381
Silva,Jose	L	.310	184	57	12	2	3	22	19	34	.369	.446
Throws Right	R	.235	200	47	11	0	4	24	11	30	.276	.350
Simas,Bill	L	.224	125	28	5	1	8	21	17	26	.317	.472
Throws Right	R	.190	137	26	3	1	4	12	5	30	.224	.314
Sinclair,S	L	.184	38	7	2	0	0	1	2	5	.225	.237
Throws Left	R	.333	18	6	1	0	0	4	3	3	.429	.389
Sirotka,Mike	L	.330	188	62	12	2	7	30	9	34	.360	.527
Throws Left	R	.292	662	193	36	1	23	95	38	94	.329	.453
Slocumb,H	L	.328	125	41	9	1	3	25	27	21	.444	.488
Throws Right	R	.226	137	31	7	0	2	20	17	30	.314	.321
Small,Aaron	L	.260	104	27	6	0	2	14	14	16	.350	.375
Throws Right	R	.333	168	56	9	0	6	33	8	17	.374	.494

Pitchers vs. Lefthanded and Righthanded Batters

Pitcher	vs	Avg	AB	H	2B	3B	HR	BI	BB	SO	OBP	SLG
Smith,Pete	L	.288	163	47	6	0	4	18	21	25	.376	.399
Throws Right	R	.291	189	55	12	1	8	38	13	40	.333	.492
Smith,Travis	L	.000	2	0	0	0	0	1	0	0	.000	.000
Throws Right	R	.200	5	1	0	0	0	0	0	1	.200	.200
Smoltz,John	L	.248	335	83	11	4	7	29	28	76	.308	.367
Throws Right	R	.212	292	62	11	3	3	25	16	97	.259	.301
Snyder,John	L	.271	192	52	10	1	9	25	11	24	.312	.474
Throws Right	R	.306	144	44	9	1	5	21	12	28	.356	.486
Sodowsky,C	L	.248	129	32	6	1	2	16	20	20	.358	.357
Throws Right	R	.309	175	54	10	0	3	31	19	22	.388	.417
Sparks,Steve	L	.289	246	71	15	1	7	26	33	45	.370	.443
Throws Right	R	.238	248	59	13	0	7	31	25	45	.319	.375
Speier,Justin	L	.240	25	6	1	0	1	7	5	6	.367	.400
Throws Right	R	.362	58	21	3	1	6	17	8	11	.433	.759
Spencer,Stan	L	.281	57	16	4	1	2	9	2	9	.305	.491
Throws Right	R	.210	62	13	0	0	3	6	2	22	.246	.355
Spoljaric,P	L	.262	107	28	5	1	6	19	18	35	.365	.495
Throws Left	R	.264	216	57	19	0	8	35	37	54	.371	.463
Spradlin,J	L	.231	104	24	2	1	2	11	7	34	.289	.327
Throws Right	R	.209	187	39	4	1	7	18	13	42	.259	.353
Springer,D	L	.311	209	65	10	1	12	38	35	21	.411	.541
Throws Right	R	.236	233	55	10	0	9	30	25	25	.337	.395
Springer,Russ	L	.267	86	23	4	0	1	13	17	23	.390	.349
Throws Right	R	.250	112	28	2	0	3	18	13	33	.328	.348
Stanifer,R	L	.321	56	18	4	0	2	15	6	8	.375	.500
Throws Right	R	.259	139	36	7	0	3	24	16	22	.333	.374
Stanton,Mike	L	.253	99	25	5	0	6	22	4	27	.295	.485
Throws Left	R	.232	198	46	8	0	7	22	22	42	.313	.379
Steenstra,K	L	.125	8	1	0	0	0	1	0	2	.125	.125
Throws Right	R	.667	9	6	0	1	2	4	1	2	.700	1.556
Stein,Blake	L	.229	223	51	13	1	10	35	43	40	.359	.430
Throws Right	R	.280	236	66	15	1	12	43	28	49	.360	.504
Stephenson,G	L	.404	47	19	7	0	2	8	8	6	.491	.681
Throws Right	R	.235	51	12	3	0	1	14	11	11	.371	.353
Stevens,Dave	L	.352	54	19	5	0	2	11	4	5	.397	.556
Throws Right	R	.250	92	23	4	0	4	12	13	26	.346	.424
Stieb,Dave	L	.304	102	31	5	0	3	12	9	11	.365	.441
Throws Right	R	.265	102	27	5	0	3	15	8	16	.336	.402
Stoops,Jim	L	.500	6	3	1	0	1	1	2	0	.625	1.167
Throws Right	R	.286	7	2	1	0	0	0	1	0	.444	.429
Stottlemyre,T	L	.277	441	122	29	6	14	52	55	87	.359	.465
Throws Right	R	.226	407	92	12	2	11	47	26	117	.272	.346
Sullivan,S	L	.288	156	45	13	0	2	21	19	24	.362	.410
Throws Right	R	.228	232	53	10	0	12	38	17	62	.304	.427
Suppan,Jeff	L	.236	157	37	8	2	3	20	11	28	.282	.369
Throws Right	R	.338	160	54	8	1	10	29	11	23	.384	.588
Suzuki,Makoto	L	.355	62	22	5	3	3	15	8	7	.429	.677
Throws Right	R	.240	50	12	5	0	0	5	7	12	.333	.340
Swift,Bill	L	.309	314	97	24	0	16	65	29	35	.378	.538
Throws Right	R	.303	284	86	25	1	5	28	22	42	.359	.451

Pitcher	vs	Avg	AB	H	2B	3B	HR	BI	BB	SO	OBP	SLG
Swindell,Greg	L	.265	155	41	6	0	7	20	10	25	.313	.439
Throws Left	R	.268	190	51	15	1	6	17	21	38	.344	.453
Tabaka,Jeff	L	.175	57	10	3	0	1	8	5	12	.258	.281
Throws Left	R	.218	124	27	4	1	5	14	17	28	.326	.387
Tam,Jeff	L	.286	14	4	2	0	0	2	0	1	.286	.429
Throws Right	R	.225	40	9	3	0	2	6	4	7	.326	.450
Tapani,Kevin	L	.303	399	121	29	5	13	46	34	61	.358	.499
Throws Right	R	.268	459	123	21	2	17	64	28	75	.310	.434
Tatis,Ramon	L	.333	27	9	0	0	0	5	8	4	.486	.333
Throws Left	R	.500	28	14	4	0	2	11	8	1	.622	.857
Tavarez,J	L	.329	140	46	7	1	2	11	22	15	.415	.436
Throws Right	R	.275	182	50	12	0	3	30	14	37	.351	.390
Taylor,Billy	L	.278	144	40	10	2	4	22	10	21	.329	.458
Throws Right	R	.231	134	31	2	0	3	19	12	37	.294	.313
Telemaco,A	L	.306	281	86	20	1	10	40	23	34	.360	.491
Throws Right	R	.219	292	64	11	2	8	33	23	44	.277	.353
Telford,A	L	.236	140	33	5	0	3	13	20	28	.337	.336
Throws Right	R	.255	204	52	10	1	6	34	16	31	.311	.402
Telgheder,D	L	.275	40	11	2	0	4	9	3	4	.341	.625
Throws Right	R	.195	41	8	3	0	0	4	3	1	.267	.268
Tessmer,Jay	L	.111	9	1	1	0	0	2	2	1	.250	.222
Throws Right	R	.158	19	3	1	0	1	1	2	5	.238	.368
Tewksbury,Bob	L	.261	314	82	12	3	7	29	12	38	.293	.385
Throws Right	R	.326	282	92	14	4	12	44	8	22	.347	.532
Thompson,J	L	.317	183	58	7	1	8	33	14	30	.362	.497
Throws Left	R	.254	666	169	33	2	12	66	65	119	.320	.363
Thompson,Mark	L	.395	38	15	3	0	4	13	1	7	.390	.789
Throws Right	R	.368	57	21	2	0	4	6	11	7	.507	.614
Thomson,John	L	.303	317	96	10	3	10	40	27	44	.354	.448
Throws Right	R	.261	299	78	11	4	11	40	22	62	.314	.435
Thurman,Mike	L	.214	103	22	2	1	2	11	10	5	.278	.311
Throws Right	R	.255	149	38	5	1	5	20	16	27	.335	.403
Timlin,Mike	L	.263	137	36	1	0	4	18	4	29	.285	.358
Throws Right	R	.264	159	42	8	2	1	23	12	31	.324	.358
Tomko,Brett	L	.253	371	94	24	2	5	26	34	75	.322	.369
Throws Right	R	.241	431	104	25	3	17	73	30	87	.295	.432
Trachsel,S	L	.240	371	89	15	1	9	41	43	64	.321	.358
Throws Right	R	.277	415	115	26	3	18	58	41	85	.346	.484
Trombley,Mike	L	.257	148	38	5	1	9	18	12	36	.313	.486
Throws Right	R	.242	215	52	10	1	7	26	29	53	.344	.395
Urbina,Ugueth	L	.159	113	18	7	0	1	6	21	39	.289	.248
Throws Right	R	.154	123	19	4	0	1	6	12	55	.230	.211
Valdes,Ismael	L	.250	308	77	14	4	7	29	39	56	.335	.390
Throws Right	R	.260	361	94	15	2	10	42	27	66	.312	.396
Valdes,Marc	L	.327	49	16	2	0	3	8	9	9	.433	.551
Throws Right	R	.263	95	25	3	0	3	20	12	19	.343	.389
Valdez,Carlos	L	.000	4	0	0	0	0	0	2	1	.333	.000
Throws Right	R	.167	6	1	0	0	0	1	3	3	.400	.167
Valdez,Efrain	L	.286	7	2	0	0	0	1	1	2	.375	.286
Throws Left	R	.417	12	5	1	0	2	2	0	0	.417	1.000

Pitchers vs. Lefthanded and Righthanded Batters

Pitcher	vs	Avg	AB	H	2B	3B	HR	BI	BB	SO	OBP	SLG
Van Poppel,T	L	.376	101	38	13	2	3	17	16	12	.466	.634
Throws Right	R	.246	167	41	7	1	6	25	12	30	.291	.407
VanRyn,Ben	L	.393	28	11	4	0	0	6	7	4	.528	.536
Throws Left	R	.241	29	7	2	0	0	2	5	6	.361	.310
Vazquez,J	L	.276	352	97	14	1	22	63	33	68	.338	.509
Throws Right	R	.309	320	99	20	3	9	42	35	71	.393	.475
Veras,Dario	L	.429	14	6	2	0	0	3	2	1	.500	.571
Throws Right	R	.286	21	6	1	0	0	3	5	1	.444	.333
Veres,Dave	L	.239	117	28	8	0	3	15	14	26	.326	.385
Throws Right	R	.228	171	39	4	0	3	21	13	48	.283	.304
Villone,Ron	L	.229	35	8	1	0	0	1	11	5	.426	.257
Throws Left	R	.333	66	22	5	0	3	21	11	10	.425	.545
Wade,Terrell	L	.231	13	3	1	0	2	3	0	6	.231	.769
Throws Left	R	.355	31	11	6	0	1	3	2	2	.394	.645
Wagner,Billy	L	.302	43	13	2	0	0	1	7	17	.400	.349
Throws Left	R	.189	175	33	2	0	6	17	18	80	.264	.303
Wagner,Paul	L	.306	108	33	7	1	3	16	17	17	.402	.472
Throws Right	R	.298	114	34	4	2	7	30	14	20	.372	.553
Wainhouse,D	L	.304	23	7	0	1	1	4	2	2	.407	.522
Throws Right	R	.381	21	8	2	0	0	3	3	1	.458	.476
Wakefield,Tim	L	.285	389	111	24	3	16	56	34	64	.345	.486
Throws Right	R	.223	448	100	26	0	14	48	45	82	.306	.375
Walker,Jamie	L	.318	22	7	0	0	3	6	1	9	.348	.727
Throws Left	R	.404	57	23	6	0	2	15	2	6	.435	.614
Wall,Donne	L	.204	108	22	5	0	3	8	15	26	.296	.333
Throws Right	R	.200	140	28	6	0	3	11	17	30	.291	.307
Ward,Bryan	L	.325	40	13	1	0	3	13	3	6	.372	.575
Throws Left	R	.250	68	17	7	0	1	7	4	11	.288	.397
Wasdin,John	L	.297	192	57	12	1	10	29	24	23	.372	.526
Throws Right	R	.278	194	54	16	1	4	32	3	36	.291	.433
Washburn,J	L	.276	58	16	4	0	4	13	3	12	.317	.552
Throws Left	R	.241	224	54	17	1	7	25	24	36	.317	.420
Watson,Allen	L	.255	106	27	10	2	1	14	9	24	.322	.415
Throws Left	R	.349	272	95	24	1	11	46	25	40	.399	.566
Weathers,Dave	L	.328	177	58	11	3	4	29	23	39	.404	.492
Throws Right	R	.274	263	72	11	2	2	30	18	55	.325	.354
Weaver,Eric	L	.286	14	4	0	0	1	1	4	4	.444	.500
Throws Right	R	.071	14	1	0	0	0	2	2	1	.188	.071
Weber,Neil	L	.600	5	3	0	0	0	1	2	1	.714	.600
Throws Left	R	.286	7	2	0	0	0	0	1	3	.375	.286
Welch,Mike	L	.394	33	13	5	1	3	3	3	7	.444	.879
Throws Right	R	.255	51	13	3	0	4	14	4	8	.333	.549
Wells,Bob	L	.357	84	30	6	0	6	23	7	7	.407	.643
Throws Right	R	.195	123	24	6	1	6	18	9	22	.259	.407
Wells,David	L	.245	184	45	8	0	7	15	6	29	.272	.402
Throws Left	R	.237	633	150	27	4	22	61	23	134	.263	.397
Wendell,Turk	L	.229	96	22	5	1	4	15	19	17	.357	.427
Throws Right	R	.216	185	40	15	1	0	18	14	41	.277	.308
Wengert,Don	L	.333	108	36	6	2	4	20	15	18	.419	.537
Throws Right	R	.270	148	40	6	1	6	21	13	28	.337	.446
West,David	L	.667	6	4	0	0	0	2	4	2	.800	.667
Throws Left	R	.429	7	3	0	0	1	2	3	2	.600	.857
Wetteland,J	L	.197	132	26	1	2	1	8	5	33	.223	.258
Throws Right	R	.212	99	21	2	1	5	16	9	39	.278	.404
Whisenant,M	L	.194	93	18	0	0	1	10	12	20	.296	.226
Throws Left	R	.326	132	43	8	0	2	29	21	25	.411	.432
White,Gabe	L	.231	121	28	4	0	5	19	9	34	.282	.388
Throws Left	R	.231	251	58	11	1	12	30	18	49	.284	.426
White,Rick	L	.246	126	31	7	0	4	16	13	19	.312	.397
Throws Right	R	.259	135	35	6	0	4	22	10	20	.318	.393
Whiteside,M	L	.231	26	6	0	0	1	3	1	3	.259	.346
Throws Right	R	.389	54	21	3	0	5	18	4	11	.431	.722
Wickman,Bob	L	.270	137	37	4	0	1	15	21	34	.365	.321
Throws Right	R	.256	164	42	6	0	4	22	18	37	.340	.366
Wilkins,Marc	L	.300	20	6	1	0	0	0	6	9	.462	.350
Throws Right	R	.200	35	7	2	0	1	5	3	8	.293	.343
Williams,Mike	L	.182	55	10	0	1	0	3	8	20	.286	.218
Throws Right	R	.223	130	29	10	0	1	13	8	39	.264	.323
Williams,Todd	L	.333	18	6	2	0	0	3	5	3	.478	.444
Throws Right	R	.346	26	9	0	0	1	7	1	1	.370	.462
Williams,W	L	.268	422	113	29	7	19	49	49	77	.342	.505
Throws Right	R	.220	378	83	19	1	17	55	32	74	.281	.410
Wilson,Trevor	L	.235	17	4	0	0	0	3	2	4	.333	.235
Throws Left	R	.308	13	4	4	0	0	3	3	2	.438	.615
Winchester,S	L	.373	153	57	11	3	3	21	16	10	.435	.542
Throws Right	R	.257	171	44	12	1	9	29	11	30	.310	.497
Winston,D	L	.341	44	15	3	0	4	9	2	5	.383	.682
Throws Left	R	.267	60	16	3	0	3	11	4	6	.323	.467
Witasick,Jay	L	.254	59	15	2	0	6	12	10	18	.362	.593
Throws Right	R	.368	57	21	5	1	3	10	5	11	.419	.649
Withem,S	L	.200	5	1	1	0	0	0	2	1	.429	.400
Throws Right	R	.286	7	2	0	1	0	1	0	1	.286	.571
Witt,Bobby	L	.333	252	84	16	3	9	34	37	33	.421	.528
Throws Right	R	.289	228	66	15	2	12	51	16	25	.332	.531
Wohlers,Mark	L	.171	41	7	2	0	1	8	16	16	.414	.293
Throws Right	R	.297	37	11	5	0	1	6	17	6	.519	.514
Wolcott,Bob	L	.323	65	21	0	1	5	11	7	9	.389	.585
Throws Right	R	.177	62	11	5	0	2	13	6	12	.250	.355
Wood,Kerry	L	.228	272	62	12	3	5	32	57	95	.371	.349
Throws Right	R	.169	325	55	12	1	9	28	28	138	.244	.295
Woodall,Brad	L	.287	108	31	6	0	5	14	12	15	.364	.481
Throws Left	R	.269	424	114	27	1	20	55	35	70	.330	.479
Woodard,Steve	L	.240	275	66	18	1	7	31	16	44	.281	.389
Throws Right	R	.282	369	104	26	1	12	38	17	91	.327	.455
Worrell,Tim	L	.241	187	45	9	2	4	18	14	25	.292	.374
Throws Right	R	.280	218	61	16	0	12	45	15	57	.326	.518
Wright,Jamey	L	.275	378	104	23	3	9	57	51	38	.361	.423
Throws Right	R	.311	421	131	28	2	15	63	44	48	.386	.494
Wright,Jaret	L	.303	402	122	34	2	12	57	43	70	.378	.488
Throws Right	R	.246	345	85	9	1	10	42	44	70	.336	.365

Pitchers vs. Lefthanded and Righthanded Batters

Pitcher	vs	Avg	AB	H	2B	3B	HR	BI	BB	SO	OBP	SLG
Yan, Esteban	L	.222	135	30	7	0	3	25	23	31	.340	.341
Throws Right	R	.245	196	48	6	0	8	24	18	46	.317	.398
Yoshii, Masato	L	.274	288	79	14	0	12	26	31	49	.350	.448
Throws Right	R	.240	362	87	26	2	10	37	22	68	.287	.406
Young, Tim	L	.333	15	5	0	1	0	3	1	5	.375	.467
Throws Left	R	.111	9	1	0	0	0	0	3	2	.333	.111
AL	L	.275	—	—	—	—	—	—	—	—	.349	.436
	R	.267	—	—	—	—	—	—	—	—	.331	.425
NL	L	.267	—	—	—	—	—	—	—	—	.340	.413
	R	.259	—	—	—	—	—	—	—	—	.326	.410
MLB	L	.271	—	—	—	—	—	—	—	—	.345	.425
	R	.263	—	—	—	—	—	—	—	—	.328	.417

Runs Created/
Component Earned Run Average

In the past year, STATS has produced two books which we feel set the standard for encyclopedic information. Ask any question about baseball, and the chances are good you'll find the answer in either our *All-Time Major League Handbook* or *All-Time Baseball Sourcebook*.

Among the mountain of statistics available in each book, it's likely that two of them—Runs Created per 27 Outs (RC/27) and Component ERA (ERC)—are the ones we find most compelling. For a definition of each stat, please consult the glossary. But since the two historical volumes are complete through the 1997 season, the following section provides a complementary update for active players through the year just completed. If you need any more evidence confirming the greatness of Mark McGwire or Roger Clemens, this is the section to consult.

Runs Created

Player, Team	1998 RC	1998 RC/27	1998 LRC/27	Career RC	Career RC/27	Career LRC27
Abbott, Jeff, ChA	39	5.57	5.01	40	4.91	5.00
Abbott, Kurt, Oak/Col	22	3.87	4.86	195	4.21	4.67
Abreu, Bob, Phi	109	8.03	4.60	138	7.06	4.60
Acevedo, Juan, StL	1	1.69	4.60	1	0.64	4.61
Adams, Terry, ChN	0	0.00	4.60	0	0.00	4.66
Adamson, Joel, Ari	0	0.00	4.60	0	0.00	4.71
Agbayani, Benny, NYN	0	0.00	4.60	0	0.00	4.60
Aguilera, Rick, Min	0	—	—	10	2.14	4.23
Alexander, Manny, ChN	23	2.86	4.60	76	3.02	4.81
Alfonseca, Antonio, Fla	0	0.00	4.60	0	0.00	4.60
Alfonzo, Edgardo, NYN	91	5.83	4.60	274	5.47	4.62
Alicea, Luis, Tex	47	6.34	5.01	367	4.68	4.59
Allensworth, J, Pit/KC/NYN	51	4.95	4.69	129	4.57	4.65
Alomar, Roberto, Bal	85	5.12	5.01	1001	5.87	4.61
Alomar Jr., Sandy, Cle	30	2.38	5.01	351	4.12	4.84
Alou, Moises, Hou	130	8.25	4.60	602	6.62	4.52
Alvarez, Gabe, Det	24	4.03	5.01	24	4.03	5.01
Amaral, Rich, Sea	14	3.76	5.01	200	4.31	4.99
Amaro, Ruben, Phi	6	1.76	4.60	96	3.41	4.35
Anderson, Brady, Bal	73	5.09	5.01	810	5.63	4.79
Anderson, Brian, Ari	0	0.00	4.60	0	0.00	4.60
Anderson, Garret, Ana	91	5.30	5.01	298	4.78	5.10
Anderson, Marlon, Phi	9	8.09	4.60	9	8.09	4.60
Andrews, Shane, Mon	58	3.91	4.60	135	3.93	4.63
Arias, Alex, Phi	17	4.73	4.60	124	3.82	4.54
Arias, George, SD	4	3.72	4.60	26	2.74	5.23
Arrojo, Rolando, TB	0	0.00	5.01	0	0.00	5.01
Ashby, Andy, SD	0	0.00	4.60	5	0.39	4.57
Ashley, Billy, Bos	4	6.32	5.01	66	3.62	4.52
Assenmacher, Paul, Cle	0	—	—	2	1.32	4.14
Astacio, Pedro, Col	1	0.41	4.60	0	0.00	4.55
Aurilia, Rich, SF	53	4.52	4.60	101	4.12	4.63
Ausmus, Brad, Hou	55	4.54	4.60	231	3.86	4.70
Avery, Steve, Bos	0	0.00	5.01	16	1.12	4.34
Ayala, Bobby, Sea	0	—	—	0	0.00	4.30
Aybar, Manny, StL	2	2.45	4.60	2	1.35	4.60
Baerga, Carlos, NYN	50	3.31	4.60	638	4.86	4.73
Bagwell, Jeff, Hou	124	8.32	4.60	902	7.75	4.43
Bailey, Cory, SF	0	—	—	2	13.52	4.68
Baines, Harold, Bal	50	6.00	5.01	1445	5.66	4.61
Bako, Paul, Det	27	3.14	5.01	27	3.14	5.01
Baldwin, James, ChA	0	0.00	5.01	0	0.00	4.96
Ball, Jeff, SF	0	0.00	4.60	0	0.00	4.60
Banks, Brian, Mil	6	9.52	4.60	16	5.60	4.87
Banks, Willie, Ari	0	0.00	4.60	2	0.83	4.62
Barrett, Michael, Mon	4	6.74	4.60	4	6.74	4.60
Barry, Jeff, Col	0	0.00	4.60	0	0.00	4.61
Bartee, Kimera, Det	11	3.44	5.01	31	3.01	5.26
Bates, Jason, Col	3	1.26	4.60	86	4.27	4.64
Batista, Miguel, Mon	-1	-0.79	4.60	-1	-0.64	4.60
Batista, Tony, Ari	48	5.75	4.60	103	4.94	4.94
Baughman, Justin, Ana	18	2.98	5.01	18	2.98	5.01
Bautista, Danny, Atl	15	3.46	4.60	67	2.87	4.92
Beamon, Trey, Det	4	3.07	5.01	18	3.82	4.74
Beck, Rod, ChN	0	0.00	4.60	1	1.80	4.50
Becker, Rich, NYN/Bal	27	4.01	4.82	229	4.64	5.10
Beech, Matt, Phi	0	0.00	4.60	2	0.64	4.61
Belcher, Tim, KC	0	0.00	5.01	3	0.21	4.09
Belinda, Stan, Cin	0	0.00	4.60	2	2.47	4.23
Bell, David, StL/Cle/Sea	47	3.79	5.00	79	3.12	4.82
Bell, Derek, Hou	107	6.29	4.60	471	4.97	4.59
Bell, Jay, Ari	93	5.73	4.60	785	4.70	4.42
Belle, Albert, ChA	151	9.11	5.01	932	7.05	4.85
Bellhorn, Mark, Oak	2	4.88	5.01	29	4.08	4.94
Belliard, Rafael, Atl	0	0.00	4.60	149	2.10	4.22
Belliard, Ron, Mil	0	0.00	4.60	0	0.00	4.60
Beltran, Carlos, KC	11	6.57	5.01	11	6.57	5.01
Beltran, Rigo, NYN	0	0.00	4.60	0	0.00	4.60
Beltre, Adrian, LA	23	3.88	4.60	23	3.88	4.60
Benard, Marvin, SF	48	6.29	4.60	121	4.58	4.65
Benes, Andy, Ari	6	2.53	4.60	19	0.89	4.39
Benitez, Yamil, Ari	14	2.17	4.60	45	3.40	4.74
Benjamin, Mike, Bos	38	3.65	5.01	107	2.86	4.63
Bennett, Gary, Phi	3	3.37	4.60	3	2.19	4.63
Bennett, Shayne, Mon	0	0.00	4.60	0	0.00	4.60
Bere, Jason, ChA/Cin	0	0.00	4.60	0	0.00	4.60
Berg, Dave, Fla	36	7.30	4.60	36	7.30	4.60
Bergman, Sean, Hou	0	0.00	4.60	1	0.26	4.62
Berroa, Geronimo, Cle/Det	18	3.14	5.01	375	5.47	5.04
Berry, Sean, Hou	53	6.53	4.60	324	5.41	4.58
Bichette, Dante, Col	112	6.39	4.60	772	5.75	4.54
Bieser, Steve, Pit	2	5.99	4.60	9	3.73	4.60
Biggio, Craig, Hou	141	8.29	4.60	1017	6.36	4.37
Blair, Willie, Ari/NYN	0	0.00	4.60	0	0.00	4.50
Blauser, Jeff, ChN	39	3.57	4.60	648	5.18	4.38
Blowers, Mike, Oak	57	4.63	5.01	321	4.82	4.85
Bochtler, Doug, Det	0			0	0.00	4.63
Boehringer, Brian, SD	0	0.00	4.60	0	0.00	4.60
Bogar, Tim, Hou	1	0.19	4.60	87	3.23	4.59
Boggs, Wade, TB	52	4.23	5.01	1610	6.83	4.64
Bohanon, Brian, NYN/LA	6	4.37	4.60	7	2.86	4.60
Bolick, Frank, Ana	3	2.07	5.01	22	2.79	4.58
Bonds, Barry, SF	140	9.01	4.60	1544	8.33	4.33
Bones, Ricky, KC	0	0.00	5.01	0	0.00	4.20
Bonilla, Bobby, Fla/LA	37	3.64	4.60	1124	5.96	4.41
Boone, Aaron, Cin	27	5.24	4.60	29	4.39	4.60
Boone, Bret, Cin	79	4.55	4.60	340	4.03	4.62
Booty, Josh, Fla	1	1.69	4.60	3	4.04	4.61
Borders, Pat, Cle	3	0.62	5.01	274	3.09	4.65
Bordick, Mike, Bal	54	3.79	5.01	385	3.54	4.91
Borland, Toby, Phi	0			0	0.00	4.60
Borowski, Joe, NYA	0	—		0	0.00	4.68
Boskie, Shawn, Mon	0	0.00	4.60	7	1.48	4.22
Bottalico, Ricky, Phi	0	—		1	3.01	4.64
Bottenfield, Kent, StL	0	0.00	4.60	3	0.85	4.51
Bournigal, Rafael, Oak	16	2.43	5.01	74	2.89	5.01
Bragg, Darren, Bos	61	5.09	5.01	206	4.63	5.10
Branson, Jeff, Cle	3	0.97	5.01	148	3.27	4.59
Brantley, Jeff, StL	0	0.00	4.60	1	0.37	4.26
Branyan, Russ, Cle	0	0.00	5.01	0	0.00	5.01
Brede, Brent, Ari	20	3.17	4.60	47	3.86	4.78
Brewer, Billy, Phi	0	—		0	0.00	4.60
Brocail, Doug, Det	0	—		3	1.14	4.52
Brock, Chris, SF	0	0.00	4.60	0	0.00	4.60
Brogna, Rico, Phi	77	4.68	4.60	281	5.08	4.61
Brow, Scott, Ari	0	0.00	4.60	0	0.00	4.60
Brown, Adrian, Pit	14	3.26	4.60	23	2.53	4.60
Brown, Brant, ChN	58	6.16	4.60	79	5.12	4.61
Brown, Dermal, KC	0			0	0.00	5.01
Brown, Emil, Pit	2	1.86	4.60	7	1.73	4.60
Brown, Kevin, SD	6	2.25	4.60	8	1.01	4.63
Brown, Kevin L., Tor	14	4.22	5.01	15	4.15	5.03
Brownson, Mark, Col	0	0.00	4.60	0	0.00	4.60
Bruske, Jim, LA/SD	0	0.00	4.60	0	0.00	4.60
Buford, Damon, Bos	39	6.27	5.01	125	4.19	4.96
Buhner, Jay, Sea	42	5.94	5.01	765	6.03	4.79
Bullinger, Kirk, Mon	0	0.00	4.60	0	0.00	4.60
Burba, Dave, Cle	2	10.74	5.01	8	1.30	4.57
Burkett, John, Tex	0	0.00	5.01	-4	-0.24	4.37
Burks, Ellis, Col/SF	84	5.78	4.60	877	5.92	4.55
Burnitz, Jeromy, Mil	95	5.45	4.60	278	5.63	4.77
Busby, Mike, StL	0	0.00	4.60	1	4.49	4.61
Bush, Homer, NYA	11	5.91	4.60	14	6.60	5.00
Butler, Rich, TB	21	3.19	5.01	24	3.43	5.01
Byrd, Paul, Atl/Phi	2	3.60	4.60	3	2.16	4.61
Cabrera, Jolbert, Cle	0	0.00	5.01	0	0.00	5.01
Cabrera, Jose, Hou	0	—		0	0.00	4.60
Cabrera, Orlando, Mon	29	3.87	4.60	30	3.68	4.60
Cadaret, Greg, Ana	0	—		0	0.00	4.49
Cairo, Miguel, TB	57	3.76	5.01	59	3.51	5.01
Cameron, Mike, ChA	39	3.14	5.01	108	4.29	4.98
Caminiti, Ken, SD	82	6.25	4.60	825	5.31	4.35
Candiotti, Tom, Oak	1	26.86	5.01	0	-0.00	4.45
Cangelosi, John, Fla	18	3.42	4.60	281	4.67	4.48
Canseco, Jose, Tor	92	5.22	5.01	1094	6.21	4.73
Carpenter, Chris, Tor	0	0.00	5.01	0	0.00	5.01
Carrasco, Hector, Min	0	—		0	0.00	4.64
Carter, Joe, Bal/SF	51	4.56	4.90	1235	5.08	4.68
Caruso, Mike, ChA	69	4.78	5.01	69	4.78	5.01
Casanova, Raul, Det	4	2.98	5.01	35	2.67	5.04
Casey, Sean, Cin	51	5.85	4.60	52	5.77	4.61
Castilla, Vinny, Col	125	7.05	4.60	488	6.06	4.61
Castillo, Alberto, NYN	8	2.88	4.60	13	2.16	4.61
Castillo, Carlos, ChA	0	0.00	5.01	1	0.00	5.01
Castillo, Frank, Det	0	0.00	5.01	0	-0.00	4.41
Castillo, Luis, Fla	16	3.48	4.60	52	3.00	4.62
Castillo, Tony, ChA	0	—		0	0.00	4.19
Castro, Juan, LA	17	2.38	4.60	25	1.79	4.62
Catalanotto, Frank, Det	29	4.75	5.01	35	5.17	5.00

Player, Team	1998 RC	RC/27	LRC/27	Career RC	RC/27	LRC27
Cather, Mike, Atl	0	—		0	0.00	4.60
Cedeno, Domingo, Tex	16	3.87	5.01	117	3.56	5.10
Cedeno, Roger, LA	22	3.14	4.60	88	4.46	4.63
Charlton, Norm, Bal/Atl	0	0.00	5.01	2	0.30	4.07
Chavez, Eric, Oak	9	7.33	5.01	9	7.33	5.01
Chavez, Raul, Sea	0	0.00	5.01	2	2.07	4.63
Chen, Bruce, Atl	0	0.00	4.60	0	0.00	4.60
Chouinard, Bobby, Mil/Ari	0	0.00	4.60	0	0.00	4.60
Christenson, Ryan, Oak	47	4.26	5.01	47	4.26	5.01
Christiansen, Jason, Pit	1	8.99	4.60	1	3.00	4.65
Cianfrocco, Archi, SD	1	0.40	4.60	149	3.93	4.46
Cirillo, Jeff, Mil	99	5.97	4.60	371	6.04	4.99
Clark, Dave, Hou	6	1.51	4.60	262	4.60	4.51
Clark, Mark, ChN	0	0.00	4.60	-3	-0.31	4.51
Clark, Tony, Det	94	5.60	5.01	278	5.91	5.07
Clark, Will, Tex	106	7.00	5.01	1249	7.08	4.47
Clayton, Royce, StL/Tex	58	3.53	4.74	343	3.38	4.55
Clemens, Roger, Tor	0	0.00	5.01	1	0.00	5.00
Clement, Matt, SD	0	0.00	4.60	0	0.00	4.60
Clemente, Edgard, Col	3	7.36	4.60	3	7.36	4.60
Clontz, Brad, LA/NYN	0	0.00	4.60	0	0.00	4.64
Cloude, Ken, Sea	0	0.00	5.01	0	0.00	4.98
Clyburn, Danny, Bal	1	1.49	5.01	1	1.28	5.00
Colbrunn, Greg, Col/Atl	26	5.89	4.60	255	4.61	4.60
Collier, Lou, Pit	37	3.70	4.60	37	3.29	4.60
Colon, Bartolo, Cle	0	0.00	5.01	0	0.00	4.97
Cone, David, NYA	0	0.00	5.01	9	0.63	4.06
Conine, Jeff, KC	41	4.51	5.01	449	5.45	4.64
Cook, Dennis, NYN	0	0.00	4.60	11	3.31	4.11
Cooke, Steve, Cin	0	0.00	4.60	-1	-0.15	4.54
Coomer, Ron, Min	55	3.56	5.01	182	4.60	5.05
Cora, Alex, LA	1	0.87	4.60	1	0.87	4.60
Cora, Joey, Sea/Cle	73	4.24	5.01	488	4.47	4.91
Cordero, Wil, ChA	46	4.70	5.01	357	4.79	4.74
Cordova, Francisco, Pit	0	0.00	4.60	0	0.00	4.61
Cordova, Marty, Min	57	4.34	5.01	287	5.24	5.12
Corsi, Jim, Bos	0	0.00	5.01	0	0.00	4.56
Counsell, Craig, Fla	54	5.50	4.60	80	5.52	4.60
Crabtree, Tim, Tex	0	0.00	5.01	0	0.00	5.01
Cradle, Rickey, Sea	1	4.48	5.01	1	4.48	5.01
Crespo, Felipe, Tor	20	5.07	5.01	32	5.12	5.09
Cromer, Tripp, LA	1	5.40	4.60	35	2.49	4.62
Croushore, Rich, StL	0	0.00	4.60	0	0.00	4.60
Cruz, Deivi, Det	41	3.08	5.01	78	2.91	4.97
Cruz, Jacob, SF/Cle	0	0.00	4.70	9	2.65	4.66
Cruz Jr., Jose, Tor	54	5.35	5.01	116	5.37	4.97
Cummings, Midre, Bos	18	5.25	5.01	93	4.06	4.67
Cunnane, Will, SD	0	—		4	10.77	4.60
Curtis, Chad, NYA	64	4.67	5.01	465	4.59	4.93
Cuyler, Milt, Tex	4	35.81	5.01	144	3.40	4.66
Daal, Omar, Ari	0	0.00	4.60	1	0.43	4.61
Dalesandro, Mark, Tor	10	5.27	5.01	13	4.26	5.07
Damon, Johnny, KC	94	5.19	5.01	252	4.87	5.10
Darensbourg, Vic, Fla	0	0.00	4.60	0	0.00	4.60
Darwin, Danny, SF	0	0.00	4.60	6	0.56	4.35
Daubach, Brian, Fla	2	4.50	4.60	2	4.50	4.60
Davis, Ben, SD	0	0.00	4.60	0	0.00	4.60
Davis, Chili, NYA	14	4.64	5.01	1335	5.65	4.49
Davis, Eric, Bal	90	7.33	5.01	877	6.49	4.34
Davis, Russ, Sea	67	4.54	5.01	161	4.62	5.04
DeHart, Rick, Mon	0	—		0	0.00	4.60
DeJean, Mike, Col	0	0.00	4.60	1	2.99	4.60
Delgado, Carlos, Tor	112	7.73	5.01	316	6.29	5.11
Delgado, Wilson, SF	0	0.00	4.60	4	3.49	4.64
Dellucci, David, Ari	57	4.81	4.60	59	4.64	4.62
DeLucia, Rich, Ana	0	—		1	2.08	4.64
Dempster, Ryan, Fla	0	0.00	4.60	0	0.00	4.60
DeRosa, Mark, Atl	0	0.00	4.60	0	0.00	4.60
DeShields, Delino, StL	67	5.61	4.60	622	4.84	4.41
Dessens, Elmer, Pit	0	0.00	4.60	2	3.86	4.62
Devereaux, Mike, LA	1	2.25	4.60	447	4.03	4.64
Diaz, Alex, SF	0	0.00	4.60	61	2.56	5.04
Diaz, Edwin, Ari	0	0.00	4.60	0	0.00	4.60
Diaz, Einar, Cle	7	4.48	5.01	7	3.84	5.01
Dickson, Jason, Ana	0	0.00	4.60	0	0.00	4.98
DiFelice, Mike, TB	18	2.32	5.01	46	2.88	4.80
Dipoto, Jerry, Col	0	0.00	4.60	0	0.00	4.62
DiSarcina, Gary, Ana	66	4.16	5.01	321	3.12	4.92
Dougherty, Jim, Oak	0	—		0	0.00	4.63
Drabek, Doug, Bal	0	0.00	5.01	22	0.89	4.26
Dreifort, Darren, LA	3	1.88	4.60	4	2.04	4.60
Drew, J.D., StL	12	12.45	4.60	12	12.45	4.60

Player, Team	1998 RC	RC/27	LRC/27	Career RC	RC/27	LRC27
Ducey, Rob, Sea	28	4.35	5.01	96	3.76	4.71
Dunston, Shawon, Cle/SF	20	3.13	4.90	605	4.10	4.30
Dunwoody, Todd, Fla	43	3.46	4.60	52	3.76	4.60
Durham, Ray, ChA	111	6.25	5.01	328	4.96	5.09
Dye, Jermaine, KC	14	2.11	5.01	69	3.02	4.86
Easley, Damion, Det	102	6.12	5.01	311	4.57	4.98
Echevarria, Angel, Col	7	8.58	4.60	11	5.50	4.63
Edmonds, Jim, Ana	101	6.19	5.01	411	6.12	5.09
Edmondson, Brian, Atl/Fla	0	0.00	4.60	0	0.00	4.60
Eisenreich, Jim, Fla/LA	7	1.23	4.60	530	4.75	4.48
Elarton, Scott, Hou	0	0.00	4.60	0	0.00	4.60
Eldred, Cal, Mil	0	0.00	4.60	0	0.00	4.63
Elster, Kevin, Tex	37	4.12	5.01	304	3.82	4.46
Embree, Alan, Atl/Ari	0	0.00	4.60	0	0.00	4.60
Encarnacion, Juan, Det	25	5.64	5.01	30	5.48	5.00
Erickson, Scott, Bal	1	8.95	5.01	1	3.84	4.97
Erstad, Darin, Ana	99	6.82	5.01	221	6.25	5.04
Estalella, Bobby, Phi	9	1.72	4.60	22	3.43	4.60
Estes, Shawn, SF	1	0.64	4.60	2	0.40	4.62
Eusebio, Tony, Hou	21	3.88	4.60	141	4.71	4.62
Evans, Tom, Tor	0	0.00	5.01	4	2.76	4.95
Everett, Carl, Hou	71	5.37	4.60	199	4.68	4.62
Eversgerd, Bryan, StL	0	—		0	0.00	4.62
Eyre, Scott, ChA	0	0.00	5.01	0	0.00	4.99
Fabregas, Jorge, Ari/NYN	9	1.58	4.60	105	3.04	5.03
Fasano, Sal, KC	28	4.27	5.01	47	3.88	5.14
Fassero, Jeff, Sea	0	0.00	5.01	0	0.00	4.60
Febles, Carlos, KC	7	11.75	5.01	7	11.75	5.01
Fernandez, Tony, Tor	82	6.15	5.01	1007	4.82	4.51
Fick, Robert, Det	7	12.53	5.01	7	12.53	5.01
Fielder, Cecil, Ana/Cle	53	4.17	5.01	862	5.71	4.78
Figga, Mike, NYA	0	0.00	5.01	0	0.00	4.97
Finley, Chuck, Ana	0	0.00	5.01	0	0.00	4.96
Finley, Steve, SD	71	3.96	4.60	711	4.75	4.42
Flaherty, John, TB	14	1.44	5.01	156	3.17	4.88
Fletcher, Darrin, Tor	49	4.13	5.01	304	4.14	4.57
Florie, Bryce, Det	0	0.00	5.01	0	0.00	4.79
Floyd, Cliff, Fla	91	5.47	4.60	206	5.16	4.62
Fontenot, Joe, Fla	0	0.00	4.60	0	0.00	4.60
Forbes, P.J., Bal	1	2.98	5.01	1	2.98	5.01
Fordham, Tom, ChA	0	0.00	5.01	0	0.00	5.01
Fordyce, Brook, Cin	14	3.34	4.60	25	3.44	4.60
Fossas, Tony, ChN	0	—		0	0.00	4.68
Foster, Kevin, ChN	0	0.00	4.60	16	2.81	4.63
Foulke, Keith, ChA	0	—		0	0.00	4.60
Fox, Andy, Ari	78	5.64	4.60	96	4.57	4.84
Fox, Chad, Mil	0	0.00	4.60	0	0.00	4.60
Franco, John, NYN	0	0.00	4.60	1	0.82	4.22
Franco, Matt, NYN	20	4.22	4.60	44	4.10	4.61
Frank, Mike, Cin	10	3.65	4.60	10	3.65	4.60
Frascatore, John, StL	0	0.00	4.60	0	0.00	4.61
Frazier, Lou, ChA	1	3.36	5.01	65	3.97	4.74
Frias, Hanley, Ari	1	1.28	4.60	2	1.25	4.77
Fryman, Travis, Cle	94	6.00	5.01	742	5.35	4.85
Fullmer, Brad, Mon	81	5.66	4.60	90	5.86	4.60
Gaetti, Gary, StL/ChN	71	5.80	4.60	1139	4.47	4.57
Galarraga, Andres, Atl	119	7.93	4.60	1102	6.01	4.34
Gant, Ron, StL	59	5.32	4.60	771	5.41	4.29
Garces, Rich, Bos	0	—		0	0.00	4.63
Garcia, Carlos, Ana	0	0.00	5.01	233	3.71	4.64
Garcia, Freddy, Pit	25	5.03	4.60	27	3.33	4.61
Garcia, Guillermo, Cin	3	2.61	4.60	3	2.61	4.60
Garcia, Karim, Ari	32	3.17	4.60	36	3.00	4.60
Garciaparra, Nomar, Bos	121	7.35	5.01	249	6.61	5.00
Gardner, Mark, SF	3	1.19	4.60	3	0.20	4.40
Gates, Brent, Min	44	4.46	5.01	237	3.95	5.01
Giambi, Jason, Oak	111	7.05	5.01	322	6.41	5.11
Giambi, Jeremy, KC	5	2.69	5.01	5	2.69	5.01
Gibson, Derrick, Col	5	11.24	4.60	5	11.24	4.60
Gilbert, Shawn, NYN/StL	1	6.74	4.60	1	1.17	4.60
Giles, Brian S., Cle	68	6.71	5.01	165	6.70	5.02
Gilkey, Bernard, NYN/Ari	33	2.97	4.60	562	5.42	4.48
Giovanola, Ed, SD	16	3.72	4.60	22	2.87	4.63
Gipson, Charles, Sea	5	3.28	5.01	5	3.28	5.01
Girardi, Joe, NYA	25	3.24	5.01	344	3.81	4.62
Glanville, Doug, Phi	82	4.33	4.60	150	4.30	4.61
Glauber, Keith, Cin	0	0.00	4.60	0	0.00	4.60
Glaus, Troy, Ana	20	4.01	5.01	20	4.01	5.01
Glavine, Tom, Atl	5	1.98	4.60	49	1.81	4.34
Gomes, Wayne, Phi	0	0.00	4.60	0	0.00	4.60
Gomez, Chris, SD	48	3.67	4.60	254	3.73	4.83
Gonzalez, Alex, Tor	47	2.70	5.01	195	3.28	5.11

Player, Team	1998 RC	RC/27	LRC/27	Career RC	RC/27	LRC27
Gonzalez, Alex, Fla	3	1.05	4.60	3	1.05	4.60
Gonzalez, Jeremi, ChN	0	0.00	4.60	0	0.00	4.60
Gonzalez, Juan, Tex	129	7.79	5.01	792	6.64	4.84
Gonzalez, Luis, Det	80	5.06	5.01	562	5.01	4.52
Gooden, Dwight, Cle	0	0.00	5.01	38	1.48	4.15
Goodwin, Curtis, Col	15	3.00	4.60	79	3.02	4.77
Goodwin, Tom, Tex	76	5.05	5.01	271	4.16	5.05
Grace, Mark, ChN	113	6.90	4.60	1029	6.25	4.32
Grace, Mike, Phi	0	0.00	4.60	0	0.00	4.63
Graffanino, Tony, Atl	23	2.57	4.60	49	3.05	4.61
Graves, Danny, Cin	0	0.00	4.60	0	0.00	4.60
Grebeck, Craig, Tor	33	3.63	5.01	194	4.03	4.71
Green, Shawn, Tor	101	5.69	5.01	286	5.39	5.09
Green, Tyler, Phi	0	0.00	4.60	7	1.72	4.61
Greene, Charlie, Bal	0	0.00	5.01	0	0.00	4.99
Greene, Todd, Ana	5	2.53	5.01	31	3.97	5.10
Greene, Willie, Cin/Bal	62	5.43	4.64	207	5.16	4.58
Greer, Rusty, Tex	107	6.44	5.01	459	6.96	5.11
Greisinger, Seth, Det	1	8.95	5.01	1	8.95	5.01
Grieve, Ben, Oak	107	6.59	5.01	126	6.74	5.00
Griffey Jr., Ken, Sea	135	7.62	5.01	1063	7.39	4.75
Grissom, Marquis, Mil	61	3.93	4.60	685	4.81	4.46
Grudzielanek, M., Mon/LA	65	3.75	4.60	239	3.89	4.63
Guerrero, Vladimir, Mon	125	7.49	4.60	173	6.50	4.60
Guerrero, Wilton, LA/Mon	42	3.74	4.60	83	3.82	4.60
Guevara, Giomar, Sea	1	2.44	5.01	1	1.79	4.99
Guillen, Carlos, Sea	10	10.33	5.01	10	10.33	5.01
Guillen, Jose, Pit	68	4.20	4.60	121	3.96	4.60
Guillen, Ozzie, Bal/Atl	34	4.15	4.63	632	3.35	4.70
Gunderson, Eric, Tex	0	—	—	0	0.00	4.20
Guthrie, Mark, LA	0	0.00	4.60	0	0.00	4.63
Gutierrez, Ricky, Hou	48	3.24	4.60	189	3.41	4.59
Guzman, Juan, Tor	0	0.00	5.01	0	0.00	5.01
Gwynn, Tony, SD	78	6.26	4.60	1496	6.53	4.26
Hairston Jr, Jerry, Bal	0	0.00	5.01	0	0.00	5.01
Halama, John, Hou	0	0.00	4.60	0	0.00	4.60
Halter, Shane, KC	12	1.83	5.01	22	2.17	4.98
Hamelin, Bob, Mil	14	3.00	4.60	198	5.24	5.06
Hamilton, Darryl, SF/Col	96	6.20	4.60	567	5.20	4.75
Hamilton, Joey, SD	2	0.86	4.60	3	0.27	4.63
Hammond, Chris, Fla	0	0.00	4.60	22	2.86	4.38
Hammonds, J., Bal/Cin	44	6.01	4.87	206	4.98	5.06
Hampton, Mike, Hou	7	3.50	4.60	16	2.01	4.62
Haney, Chris, KC/ChN	0	—	—	1	0.73	4.05
Haney, Todd, NYN	0	0.00	4.60	21	3.44	4.61
Hansen, Jed, KC	0	0.00	5.01	17	6.09	4.93
Hanson, Erik, Tor	0	—	—	0	0.00	4.62
Hardtke, Jason, ChN	3	5.06	4.60	12	2.97	4.64
Harnisch, Pete, Cin	-1	-0.39	4.60	2	0.13	4.40
Harris, Lenny, Cin/NYN	25	2.80	4.60	319	3.78	4.30
Hartgraves, Dean, SF	0	—	—	0	0.00	4.65
Haselman, Bill, Tex	19	6.71	5.01	113	3.95	5.04
Hatcher, Chris, KC	0	0.00	5.01	0	0.00	5.01
Hatteberg, Scott, Bos	47	4.61	5.01	93	4.50	4.98
Hawkins, LaTroy, Min	0	0.00	5.01	0	0.00	4.97
Hayes, Charlie, SF	50	5.55	4.60	546	4.13	4.46
Haynes, Jimmy, Oak	0	0.00	5.01	0	0.00	4.98
Helling, Rick, Tex	0	0.00	5.01	0	0.00	4.74
Helms, Wes, Atl	1	3.00	4.60	1	3.00	4.60
Helton, Todd, Col	102	7.09	4.60	115	6.79	4.60
Henderson, Rickey, Oak	99	6.08	5.01	1898	6.98	4.57
Henderson, Rodney, Mil	0	—	—	0	0.00	4.62
Henley, Bob, Mon	18	5.58	4.60	18	5.58	4.60
Henriquez, Oscar, Fla	0	0.00	4.60	0	0.00	4.60
Henry, Doug, Hou	0	0.00	4.60	1	1.59	4.66
Hentgen, Pat, Tor	0	0.00	5.01	0	0.00	4.97
Heredia, Felix, Fla/ChN	0	0.00	4.60	0	0.00	4.60
Hermanson, Dustin, Mon	2	1.06	4.60	2	0.54	4.60
Hernandez, Carlos, SD	42	3.64	4.60	93	3.14	4.45
Hernandez, Jose, ChN	71	4.96	4.60	171	3.83	4.62
Hernandez, Livan, Fla	2	0.76	4.60	3	0.55	4.60
Hernandez, Orlando, NYA	0	0.00	5.01	0	0.00	5.01
Hernandez, Roberto, TB	0	—	—	0	0.00	4.60
Hernandez, Xavier, Tex	0	—	—	0	0.00	4.27
Hershiser, Orel, SF	1	0.42	4.60	40	1.56	4.20
Hidalgo, Richard, Hou	30	5.09	4.60	39	5.21	4.60
Higginson, Bob, Det	94	5.48	5.01	364	6.44	5.08
Hill, Glenallen, Sea/ChN	60	5.63	4.88	444	5.00	4.58
Hill, Ken, Ana	0	0.00	5.01	11	0.86	4.25
Hinch, A.J., Oak	34	3.20	5.01	34	3.20	5.01
Hitchcock, Sterling, SD	0	0.00	4.60	0	0.00	4.60
Hocking, Denny, Min	14	2.27	5.01	54	2.61	5.05

Player, Team	1998 RC	RC/27	LRC/27	Career RC	RC/27	LRC27
Hoffman, Trevor, SD	0	0.00	4.60	2	2.16	4.61
Hoiles, Chris, Bal	51	6.46	5.01	476	5.84	4.89
Holbert, Ray, Atl/Mon	0	0.00	4.60	5	1.52	4.62
Hollandsworth, Todd, LA	26	5.20	4.60	149	4.97	4.64
Hollins, Damon, Atl/LA	1	2.08	4.60	1	2.08	4.60
Hollins, Dave, Ana	50	4.68	5.01	515	5.55	4.65
Holmes, Darren, NYA	0	—	—	0	0.00	4.61
Holtz, Mike, Ana	0	—	—	0	0.00	4.93
Houston, Tyler, ChN	30	4.05	4.60	80	4.74	4.62
Howard, David, StL	11	3.62	4.60	138	2.95	4.91
Howard, Thomas, LA	3	1.26	4.60	247	3.94	4.50
Howell, Jack, Hou	5	4.82	4.60	354	4.61	4.53
Hubbard, Mike, Mon	0	0.00	4.60	1	0.17	4.62
Hubbard, Trenidad, LA	27	4.50	4.60	55	4.84	4.63
Hudek, John, NYN/Cin	0	0.00	4.60	1	0.00	4.60
Hudler, Rex, Phi	1	0.73	4.60	211	4.05	4.53
Hughes, Bobby, Mil	21	3.24	4.60	21	3.24	4.60
Hundley, Todd, NYN	7	1.78	4.60	363	4.83	4.47
Hunter, Brian, StL	8	2.22	4.60	147	3.96	4.47
Hunter, Brian L., Det	64	3.68	5.01	250	4.07	4.85
Hunter, Torii, Min	2	3.58	5.01	2	3.58	5.01
Huskey, Butch, NYN	41	3.67	4.60	162	3.97	4.62
Huson, Jeff, Sea	3	1.92	5.01	139	2.94	4.50
Hutton, Mark, Cin	1	—	—	1	0.00	4.67
Ibanez, Raul, Sea	9	3.14	5.01	11	2.84	5.01
Incaviglia, Pete, Det/Hou	0	0.00	4.79	562	4.53	4.49
Irabu, Hideki, NYA	0	0.00	5.01	0	0.00	5.00
Jackson, Damian, Cin	8	7.71	4.60	14	5.72	4.72
Jackson, Darrin, Mil	22	3.69	4.60	278	3.84	4.35
Jackson, Mike, Cle	0	—	—	2	2.08	4.49
Jackson, Ryan, Fla	29	3.87	4.60	29	3.87	4.60
Jaha, John, Mil	31	4.62	4.60	370	5.90	4.97
Javier, Stan, SF	61	5.13	4.60	522	4.45	4.58
Jefferies, Gregg, Phi/Ana	73	4.72	4.65	741	5.12	4.40
Jefferson, Reggie, Bos	34	6.34	5.01	295	5.62	4.96
Jenkins, Geoff, Mil	16	2.03	4.60	16	2.03	4.60
Jensen, Marcus, Mil	0	0.00	4.60	9	2.64	4.65
Jeter, Derek, NYA	113	6.77	5.01	288	5.46	5.10
Jimenez, Jose, StL	0	0.00	4.60	0	0.00	4.60
Johns, Doug, Bal	1	—	—	1	—	—
Johns, Keith, Bos	0	—	—	0	—	—
Johnson, Brian, SF	32	3.41	4.60	114	3.28	4.66
Johnson, Charles, Fla/LA	52	3.75	4.60	184	3.83	4.63
Johnson, Jason, TB	0	0.00	5.01	0	0.00	4.88
Johnson, Lance, ChN	36	4.19	4.60	676	4.79	4.63
Johnson, Mark, Ana	0	0.00	5.01	112	4.78	4.65
Johnson, Mark L., ChA	0	0.00	5.01	0	0.00	5.01
Johnson, Mike, Mon	1	13.49	4.60	1	1.69	4.60
Johnson, Randy, Sea/Hou	0	0.00	4.66	0	0.00	4.45
Johnson, Russ, Hou	1	2.45	4.60	10	4.72	4.60
Johnstone, John, SF	0	0.00	4.60	0	0.00	4.60
Jones, Andruw, Atl	91	5.54	4.60	156	4.87	4.61
Jones, Bobby, NYN	4	2.08	4.60	4	0.35	4.62
Jones, Bobby M., Col	1	0.63	4.60	1	0.56	4.60
Jones, Chipper, Atl	119	7.21	4.60	437	6.79	4.63
Jones, Chris, Ari/SF	9	2.36	4.60	133	4.49	4.50
Jones, Doug, Mil	0	0.00	4.60	1	0.00	4.12
Jones, Terry, Mon	17	2.45	4.60	18	2.49	4.60
Jones, Todd, Det	0	—	—	1	3.37	4.63
Jordan, Brian, StL	96	6.27	4.60	367	5.70	4.55
Jordan, Kevin, Phi	23	3.32	4.60	58	3.31	4.62
Jordan, Ricardo, Cin	0	—	—	0	0.00	4.64
Joyner, Wally, SD	83	6.91	4.60	1072	5.95	4.60
Judd, Mike, LA	0	0.00	4.60	0	0.00	4.60
Juden, Jeff, Mil	-1	-0.64	4.60	3	0.68	4.59
Justice, David, Cle	89	5.83	5.01	760	7.00	4.49
Kapler, Gabe, Det	1	1.34	5.01	1	1.34	5.01
Karl, Scott, Mil	0	0.00	4.60	0	0.00	4.62
Karros, Eric, LA	89	6.44	4.60	539	4.85	4.50
Kelly, Mike, TB	29	3.42	5.01	77	3.76	4.79
Kelly, Pat, StL	12	2.57	4.60	187	3.26	4.75
Kelly, Roberto, Tex	45	6.64	5.01	630	4.95	4.58
Kendall, Jason, Pit	110	7.79	4.60	251	6.43	4.62
Kent, Jeff, SF	103	6.93	4.60	499	5.40	4.58
Kile, Darryl, Col	6	2.57	4.60	10	0.61	4.50
King, Curtis, StL	0	0.00	4.60	0	0.00	4.60
King, Jeff, KC	70	4.95	5.01	578	4.68	4.52
Kingsale, Gene, Bal	0	0.00	5.01	0	0.00	5.01
Kinkade, Mike, NYN	0	0.00	4.60	0	0.00	4.60
Kirby, Wayne, NYN	0	0.00	4.60	131	3.67	4.82
Klassen, Danny, Ari	4	1.16	4.60	4	1.16	4.60
Klesko, Ryan, Atl	63	5.21	4.60	360	6.30	4.62

	1998			Career		
Player, Team	RC	RC/27	LRC/27	RC	RC/27	LRC27
Kline, Steve, Mon	0	0.00	4.60	0	0.00	4.60
Klingenbeck, Scott, Cin	0	0.00	4.60	0	0.00	4.60
Knoblauch, Chuck, NYA	93	5.24	5.01	799	6.29	4.87
Knorr, Randy, Fla	7	4.72	4.60	55	3.48	4.89
Konerko, Paul, LA/Cin	15	2.20	4.60	15	2.12	4.60
Koskie, Corey, Min	2	2.15	5.01	2	2.15	5.01
Kotsay, Mark, Fla	72	4.33	4.60	75	4.10	4.60
Kreuter, Chad, ChA/Ana	32	4.23	5.01	191	3.80	4.80
Krivda, Rick, Cle/Cin	0	0.00	4.60	0	0.00	4.60
Laker, Tim, TB/Pit	4	4.90	4.69	24	2.43	4.51
Lampkin, Tom, StL	27	4.19	4.60	117	3.84	4.57
Langston, Mark, SD	1	1.04	4.60	2	0.65	4.16
Lankford, Frank, LA	0	0.00	4.60	0	0.00	4.60
Lankford, Ray, StL	113	7.82	4.60	738	6.24	4.42
Lansing, Mike, Col	72	4.28	4.60	423	4.66	4.61
Larkin, Andy, Fla	0	0.00	4.60	0	0.00	4.60
Larkin, Barry, Cin	102	6.98	4.60	1000	6.34	4.33
Larkin, Stephen, Cin	0	0.00	4.60	0	0.00	4.60
Latham, Chris, Min	6	1.97	5.01	6	1.61	5.00
Lawrence, Sean, Pit	0	0.00	4.60	0	0.00	4.60
Lawton, Matt, Min	103	6.52	5.01	231	6.06	5.06
Ledee, Ricky, NYA	11	4.69	5.01	11	4.69	5.01
Ledesma, Aaron, TB	36	4.34	5.01	57	4.94	4.96
Lee, Derrek, Fla	59	4.37	4.60	67	4.46	4.60
Lee, Travis, Ari	77	4.88	4.60	77	4.88	4.60
Leiter, Al, NYN	2	0.96	4.60	0	-0.00	4.63
Leiter, Mark, Phi	0	0.00	4.60	3	0.42	4.64
Leius, Scott, KC	2	1.34	5.01	155	3.53	4.81
Lemke, Mark, Bos	3	1.03	5.01	318	3.26	4.42
Lennon, Patrick, Tor	2	26.86	5.01	23	5.16	4.98
Lesher, Brian, Oak	0	0.00	5.01	22	3.27	5.10
Leskanic, Curt, Col	0	0.00	4.60	3	2.45	4.58
Levis, Jesse, Mil	7	6.51	4.60	69	3.89	5.03
Lewis, Darren, Bos	84	4.92	5.01	376	3.99	4.65
Lewis, Mark, Phi	49	3.15	4.60	277	3.93	4.73
Leyritz, Jim, Bos/SD	44	5.69	4.80	341	5.33	4.85
Lieber, Jon, Pit	2	1.15	4.60	5	0.68	4.62
Lieberthal, Mike, Phi	41	4.55	4.60	131	4.20	4.62
Lima, Jose, Hou	0	0.00	4.60	0	0.00	4.60
Liriano, Nelson, Col	0	0.00	4.60	283	4.33	4.49
Little, Mark, StL	1	2.25	4.60	1	2.25	4.60
Livingstone, Scott, Mon	6	1.74	4.60	167	3.86	4.57
Loaiza, Esteban, Pit	2	2.08	4.60	4	0.69	4.62
Lockhart, Keith, Atl	44	4.22	4.60	172	4.79	4.97
LoDuca, Paul, LA	1	2.70	4.60	1	2.70	4.60
Loewer, Carlton, Phi	0	0.00	4.60	0	0.00	4.60
Lofton, Kenny, Cle	105	6.17	5.01	694	6.43	4.89
Loiselle, Rich, Pit	0	0.00	4.60	1	3.01	4.67
Lombard, George, Atl	2	13.49	4.60	2	13.49	4.60
Lopez, Albie, TB	0	0.00	5.01	0	0.00	4.97
Lopez, Javy, Atl	88	6.18	4.60	307	5.30	4.62
Lopez, Luis, NYN	27	3.37	4.60	79	3.05	4.61
Lopez, Mendy, KC	20	3.16	5.01	20	3.16	5.01
Loretta, Mark, Mil	66	5.48	4.60	143	4.70	4.87
Lovullo, Torey, Cle	1	1.58	5.01	66	3.05	4.76
Lowe, Derek, Bos	0	0.00	5.01	0	0.00	4.98
Lowe, Sean, StL	0	0.00	4.60	0	0.00	4.60
Lowell, Mike, NYA	0	0.00	5.01	0	0.00	5.01
Lowery, Terrell, ChN	2	4.50	4.60	4	4.90	4.60
Ludwick, Eric, Fla	0	0.00	4.60	0	0.00	4.67
Luke, Matt, LA/Cle	25	3.55	4.60	25	3.55	4.60
Mabry, John, StL	38	3.46	4.60	215	4.46	4.63
Macfarlane, Mike, KC/Oak	25	3.90	5.01	449	4.55	4.75
Machado, Robert, ChA	8	2.29	5.01	12	2.93	5.01
Mack, Shane, Oak/KC	33	5.54	5.01	475	5.89	4.58
Maddux, Greg, Atl	4	1.69	4.60	20	0.63	4.31
Maddux, Mike, Mon	0	0.00	4.60	0	0.00	4.09
Magadan, Dave, Oak	21	6.96	5.01	591	5.82	4.34
Magee, Wendell, Phi	10	4.73	4.60	26	2.52	4.64
Magnante, Mike, Hou	1	—	—	1	0.00	4.60
Mahay, Ron, Bos	0	—	—	1	1.68	5.06
Malloy, Marty, Atl	1	1.17	4.60	1	1.17	4.60
Maloney, Sean, LA	0	0.00	4.60	0	0.00	4.60
Mantei, Matt, Fla	0	0.00	4.60	0	0.00	4.63
Manto, Jeff, Cle/Det	5	2.36	5.01	88	4.33	4.89
Manuel, Barry, Ari	0	—	—	0	0.00	4.67
Manwaring, Kirt, Col	24	2.72	4.60	256	3.00	4.40
Marrero, Eli, StL	25	3.36	4.60	31	3.53	4.60
Martin, Al, Pit	44	3.36	4.60	399	5.24	4.60
Martin, Norberto, Ana	5	0.80	5.01	92	3.72	5.09
Martinez, Dave, TB	30	3.32	5.01	599	4.58	4.48
Martinez, Dennis, Atl	0	0.00	4.60	3	0.16	4.14

	1998			Career		
Player, Team	RC	RC/27	LRC/27	RC	RC/27	LRC27
Martinez, Edgar, Sea	123	8.30	5.01	905	7.66	4.79
Martinez, Felix, KC	1	0.34	5.01	6	1.52	4.99
Martinez, Greg, Mil	0	0.00	4.60	0	0.00	4.60
Martinez, Javier, Pit	0	0.00	4.60	0	0.00	4.60
Martinez, Manny, Pit	22	4.06	4.60	25	3.53	4.67
Martinez, Pedro, Bos	0	0.00	5.01	-1	-0.10	4.64
Martinez, Ramon, LA	0	0.00	4.60	11	0.52	4.37
Martinez, Ramon E., SF	2	3.85	4.60	2	3.85	4.60
Martinez, Sandy, ChN	10	3.97	4.60	48	3.23	5.13
Martinez, Tino, NYA	101	6.60	5.01	601	5.79	4.93
Marzano, John, Sea	14	3.51	5.01	75	3.14	4.79
Mashore, Damon, Ana	11	3.74	5.01	62	4.31	5.04
Matheny, Mike, Mil	28	2.99	4.60	110	3.08	5.00
Mathews, T.J., Oak	0	—	—	0	0.00	4.66
Mathews, Terry, Bal	0	—	—	4	7.21	4.64
Maxwell, Jason, ChN	1	8.99	4.60	1	8.99	4.60
May, Derrick, Mon	14	2.64	4.60	270	4.41	4.48
Mayne, Brent, SF	38	4.81	4.60	193	3.72	4.74
McCarty, Dave, Sea	5	10.33	5.01	61	2.67	4.82
McClain, Scott, TB	0	0.00	5.01	0	0.00	5.01
McCracken, Quinton, TB	79	4.48	5.01	175	4.94	4.82
McCurry, Jeff, Pit	0	—	—	0	0.00	4.62
McDonald, Jason, Oak	22	4.10	5.01	57	4.66	4.97
McElroy, Chuck, Col	0	0.00	4.60	5	4.37	4.41
McEwing, Joe, StL	1	1.50	4.60	1	1.50	4.60
McGee, Willie, StL	25	3.18	4.60	973	4.76	4.24
McGriff, Fred, TB	91	5.76	5.01	1149	6.56	4.48
McGuire, Ryan, Mon	13	1.93	4.60	35	2.77	4.60
McGwire, Mark, StL	165	12.06	4.60	1165	7.89	4.63
McLemore, Mark, Tex	71	5.01	5.01	478	4.11	4.89
McMichael, Greg, NYN/LA	0	0.00	4.60	1	1.92	4.58
McRae, Brian, NYN	88	5.52	4.60	628	4.58	4.63
Meadows, Brian, Fla	0	0.00	4.60	0	0.00	4.60
Meares, Pat, Min	61	3.85	5.01	276	3.78	5.06
Mecir, Jim, TB	0	0.00	5.01	0	0.00	5.01
Medina, Rafael, Fla	0	0.00	4.60	0	0.00	4.60
Meluskey, Mitch, Hou	1	3.85	4.60	1	3.85	4.60
Mendoza, Ramiro, NYA	0	0.00	5.01	0	0.00	5.01
Merced, O., Min/Bos/ChN	28	4.32	4.99	507	5.65	4.51
Mercedes, Jose, Mil	0	0.00	4.60	0	0.00	4.65
Mercker, Kent, StL	2	1.04	4.60	3	0.38	4.56
Merloni, Lou, Bos	18	6.81	5.01	18	6.81	5.01
Mesa, Jose, Cle/SF	0	—	—	0	—	—
Metcalfe, Mike, LA	0	0.00	4.60	0	0.00	4.60
Meulens, Hensley, Ari	0	0.00	4.60	47	3.10	4.48
Miceli, Dan, SD	1	—	—	1	0.00	4.67
Mientkiewicz, Doug, Min	2	2.56	5.01	2	2.56	5.01
Mieske, Matt, ChN	17	6.55	4.60	170	4.41	5.11
Millar, Kevin, Fla	1	26.98	4.60	1	26.98	4.60
Miller, Damian, Ari	24	5.22	4.60	32	4.87	4.70
Miller, Kurt, ChN	0	—	—	0	0.00	4.65
Miller, Trever, Hou	1	13.49	4.60	1	13.49	4.60
Milliard, Ralph, NYN	0	0.00	4.60	4	1.30	4.66
Millwood, Kevin, Atl	0	0.00	4.60	0	0.00	4.60
Milton, Eric, Min	3	16.12	5.01	3	16.12	5.01
Minor, Ryan, Bal	3	10.07	5.01	3	10.07	5.01
Mirabelli, Doug, SF	5	10.38	4.60	8	6.55	4.63
Mitchell, Keith, Bos	6	6.71	5.01	32	4.66	4.88
Mitchell, Kevin, Oak	16	4.21	5.01	724	6.27	4.29
Mlicki, Dave, NYN/LA	1	0.49	4.60	4	0.69	4.61
Moehler, Brian, Det	0	0.00	5.01	0	0.00	4.98
Molina, Ben, Ana	0	0.00	5.01	0	0.00	5.01
Molina, Izzy, Oak	0	0.00	5.01	8	1.92	5.01
Molitor, Paul, Min	74	5.06	5.01	1876	6.28	4.63
Monahan, Shane, Sea	19	3.07	5.01	19	3.07	5.01
Mondesi, Raul, LA	84	5.15	4.60	459	5.79	4.62
Montgomery, Jeff, KC	0	—	—	0	0.00	4.52
Montgomery, Ray, Hou	1	8.99	4.60	8	3.04	4.62
Moore, Trey, Mon	2	3.85	4.60	2	3.85	4.60
Morandini, Mickey, ChN	97	6.07	4.60	484	4.57	4.47
Mordecai, Mike, Mon	9	2.45	4.60	36	3.03	4.63
Morgan, Mike, Min/ChN	2	13.49	4.70	-3	-0.16	4.30
Morman, Alvin, Cle/SF	0	—	—	0	0.00	4.93
Morris, Hal, KC	50	3.82	5.01	520	5.07	4.48
Morris, Matt, StL	1	0.79	4.60	6	1.70	4.60
Mouton, James, SD	4	1.86	4.60	120	3.44	4.64
Mouton, Lyle, Bal	9	8.95	5.01	94	4.96	5.11
Moyer, Jamie, Sea	0	0.00	5.01	5	0.86	4.19
Mueller, Bill, SF	78	5.26	4.60	174	5.59	4.61
Mulholland, Terry, ChN	3	6.23	4.60	-4	-0.21	4.27
Munoz, Mike, Col	0	0.00	4.60	1	3.87	4.56
Mussina, Mike, Bal	0	0.00	5.01	0	0.00	4.96

Player, Team	1998			Career		
	RC	RC/27	LRC/27	RC	RC/27	LRC27
Myers, Greg, SD	18	3.54	4.60	208	3.41	4.79
Myers, Randy, Tor/SD	0	0.00	5.01	4	1.93	4.13
Myers, Rodney, ChN	0	0.00	4.60	0	0.00	4.67
Nagy, Charles, Cle	0	0.00	5.01	0	0.00	4.98
Navarro, Jaime, ChA	0	0.00	5.01	3	0.58	4.67
Neagle, Denny, Atl	1	0.44	4.60	13	1.01	4.59
Neill, Mike, Oak	1	2.44	5.01	1	2.44	5.01
Nelson, Jeff, NYA	0	0.00	5.01	0	0.00	5.01
Nen, Robb, SF	0	0.00	4.60	0	0.00	4.58
Nevin, Phil, Ana	21	2.95	5.01	92	4.05	5.01
Newfield, Marc, Mil	23	4.06	4.60	109	3.84	4.88
Newson, Warren, Tex	1	1.49	5.01	142	4.93	4.94
Nieves, Jose, ChN	0	0.00	4.60	0	0.00	4.60
Nieves, Melvin, Cin	15	4.30	4.60	166	4.51	4.96
Nilsson, Dave, Mil	51	5.64	4.60	376	5.45	4.95
Nitkowski, C.J., Hou	0	0.00	4.60	1	2.08	4.62
Nixon, Otis, Min	55	4.32	5.01	613	4.18	4.63
Nixon, Trot, Bos	2	2.69	5.01	2	2.44	5.05
Nomo, Hideo, LA/NYN	2	1.20	4.60	3	0.32	4.63
Norton, Greg, ChA	31	3.40	5.01	37	3.43	5.03
Nunez, Abraham, Pit	6	3.37	4.60	11	3.66	4.60
Nunnally, Jon, Cin	21	3.78	4.60	136	5.81	4.88
Nye, Ryan, Phi	0		—	0	0.00	4.60
O'Brien, Charlie, ChA/Ana	18	3.48	5.01	239	3.59	4.61
O'Leary, Troy, Bos	82	4.69	5.01	311	5.22	5.09
O'Neill, Paul, NYA	114	6.88	5.01	973	6.12	4.57
Ochoa, Alex, Min	25	3.44	5.01	87	3.76	4.76
Offerman, Jose, KC	120	7.28	5.01	495	4.81	4.67
Ojala, Kirt, Fla	2	2.16	4.60	2	1.63	4.60
Olerud, John, NYN	126	8.83	4.60	784	6.80	4.73
Olivares, Omar, Ana	0	0.00	5.01	20	3.11	4.21
Oliver, Darren, Tex/StL	1	1.03	4.68	2	1.99	4.69
Oliver, Joe, Det/Sea	19	2.54	5.01	341	3.84	4.43
Olson, Gregg, Ari	1	26.98	4.60	1	8.99	4.64
Oquist, Mike, Oak	0	0.00	5.01	0	0.00	4.96
Ordaz, Luis, StL	11	2.30	4.60	13	2.42	4.60
Ordonez, Magglio, ChA	71	4.58	5.01	82	4.72	5.00
Ordonez, Rey, NYN	38	2.46	4.60	100	2.41	4.63
Orie, Kevin, ChN/Fla	34	2.95	4.60	89	4.02	4.60
Orosco, Jesse, Bal	0		—	4	1.84	4.17
Ortiz, David, Min	50	6.30	5.01	59	6.42	5.00
Ortiz, Hector, KC	0	0.00	5.01	0	0.00	5.01
Ortiz, Russ, SF	3	3.52	4.60	3	3.52	4.60
Osborne, Donovan, StL	0	0.00	4.60	12	1.39	4.44
Osik, Keith, Pit	7	2.20	4.60	42	4.18	4.63
Osuna, Antonio, LA	0	0.00	4.60	0	0.00	4.63
Otanez, Willis, Bal	0	0.00	5.01	0	0.00	5.01
Owens, Eric, Mil	2	1.38	4.60	22	2.31	4.66
Pagnozzi, Tom, StL	11	2.23	4.60	275	3.23	4.30
Painter, Lance, StL	1	26.98	4.60	5	2.33	4.61
Pall, Donn, Fla	0	0.00	4.60	0	0.00	4.63
Palmeiro, Orlando, Ana	25	5.37	5.01	49	4.14	5.06
Palmeiro, Rafael, Bal	117	6.82	5.01	1172	6.30	4.67
Palmer, Dean, KC	81	4.88	5.01	511	5.00	4.88
Paquette, Craig, NYN	0	0.00	4.60	139	3.21	5.04
Parent, Mark, Phi	10	2.90	4.60	122	3.05	4.48
Park, Chan Ho, LA	2	0.84	4.60	4	0.78	4.61
Parque, Jim, ChA	0	0.00	5.01	0	0.00	5.01
Parris, Steve, Cin	2	1.93	4.60	5	2.37	4.62
Patrick, Bronswell, Mil	2	4.15	4.60	2	4.15	4.60
Patterson, Bob, ChN	0	0.00	4.60	3	1.45	4.25
Pavano, Carl, Mon	2	1.42	4.60	2	1.42	4.60
Payton, Jay, NYN	1	1.80	4.60	1	1.80	4.60
Pena, Angel, LA	0	0.00	4.60	0	0.00	4.60
Pendleton, Terry, KC	26	3.88	5.01	866	4.28	4.28
Percival, Troy, Ana	0		—	0	0.00	5.39
Perez, Carlos, Mon/LA	2	0.73	4.60	6	0.93	4.61
Perez, Eddie, Atl	32	8.30	4.60	60	4.06	4.63
Perez, Eduardo, Cin	25	4.92	4.60	111	4.17	4.76
Perez, Neifi, Col	68	3.60	4.60	111	3.79	4.60
Perez, Robert, Sea/Mon	8	1.86	4.70	44	3.15	5.06
Perez, Tomas, Tor	1	2.69	5.01	39	2.40	5.21
Perez, Yorkis, Phi	0	0.00	4.60	0	0.00	4.62
Person, Robert, Tor	0		—	1	0.97	4.72
Petagine, Roberto, Cin	9	4.95	4.60	38	4.06	4.64
Peters, Chris, Pit	1	0.79	4.60	3	1.53	4.62
Petkovsek, Mark, StL	3	4.76	4.60	5	1.69	4.63
Pettitte, Andy, NYA	0	0.00	5.01	0	0.00	5.01
Phillips, J.R., Hou	6	3.37	4.60	40	2.79	4.63
Phillips, Tony, Tor/NYN	37	5.39	4.67	1138	5.42	4.68
Piazza, Mike, LA/Fla/NYN	112	7.61	4.60	647	7.94	4.58
Pichardo, Hipolito, KC	0	0.00	5.01	0	0.00	5.04

Player, Team	1998			Career		
	RC	RC/27	LRC/27	RC	RC/27	LRC27
Pickering, Calvin, Bal	2	2.98	5.01	2	2.98	5.01
Pierzynski, A.J., Min	3	10.07	5.01	3	10.07	5.01
Pisciotta, Marc, ChN	0	0.00	4.60	0	0.00	4.60
Pittsley, Jim, KC	0	0.00	5.01	1	6.72	4.99
Plesac, Dan, Tor	0		—	0	0.00	4.64
Plunk, Eric, Cle/Mil	0	0.00	4.60	0	0.00	4.76
Polanco, Placido, StL	11	3.37	4.60	11	3.37	4.60
Polcovich, Kevin, Pit	13	1.87	4.60	40	2.81	4.60
Polite, Cliff, StL	0	0.00	4.60	0	0.00	4.60
Ponson, Sidney, Bal	1	13.43	5.01	1	13.43	5.01
Poole, Jim, SF	1	5.40	4.60	3	3.37	4.62
Portugal, Mark, Phi	5	3.14	4.60	25	1.59	4.39
Posada, Jorge, NYA	57	5.45	5.01	88	5.34	5.00
Powell, Brian, Det	0	0.00	5.01	0	0.00	5.01
Powell, Dante, SF	3	40.46	4.60	9	7.82	4.60
Powell, Jay, Fla/Hou	0	0.00	4.60	1	2.69	4.65
Powell, Jeremy, Mon	0	0.00	4.60	0	0.00	4.60
Pratt, Todd, NYN	11	5.93	4.60	62	4.53	4.52
Pride, Curtis, Atl	12	3.85	4.60	88	4.90	5.02
Priest, Eddie, Cin	0	0.00	4.60	0	0.00	4.60
Prince, Tom, LA	7	2.78	4.60	66	2.97	4.36
Pritchett, Chris, Ana	7	3.13	5.01	7	2.65	5.07
Pulsipher, Bill, NYN/Mil	0	0.00	4.60	2	0.93	4.62
Quantrill, Paul, Tor	0		—	-1	-0.43	4.64
Radinsky, Scott, StL	0		—	0	0.00	4.62
Radke, Brad, Min	0	0.00	5.01	0	0.00	4.96
Radmanovich, Ryan, Sea	6	2.83	5.01	6	2.83	5.01
Raggio, Brady, StL	0	0.00	4.60	0	0.00	4.60
Raines, Tim, NYA	57	6.41	5.01	1556	6.57	4.37
Ramirez, Alex, Cle	0	0.00	5.01	0		5.01
Ramirez, Aramis, Pit	22	3.00	4.60	22	3.00	4.60
Ramirez, Manny, Cle	124	7.67	5.01	502	7.17	5.10
Randa, Joe, Det	55	4.05	5.01	183	4.87	4.98
Rapp, Pat, KC	0	0.00	5.01	0	0.00	4.61
Rath, Fred, Col	0	0.00	4.60	0	0.00	4.60
Reboulet, Jeff, Bal	11	2.76	5.01	159	3.82	4.97
Redmond, Mike, Fla	15	4.55	4.60	15	4.55	4.60
Reed, Jeff, Col	42	5.78	4.60	302	3.92	4.37
Reed, Rick, NYN	2	0.79	4.60	10	1.73	4.60
Reed, Steve, SF	0	0.00	4.60	1	1.35	4.55
Reese, Pokey, Cin	17	4.25	4.60	48	3.01	4.60
Relaford, Desi, Phi	42	2.81	4.60	49	2.81	4.60
Remlinger, Mike, Cin	-2	-1.04	4.60	-1	-0.24	4.56
Renteria, Edgar, Fla	59	3.82	4.60	185	4.04	4.62
Reyes, Al, Mil	0	0.00	4.60	0	0.00	4.60
Reyes, Carlos, SD/Bos	0	0.00	4.60	0	0.00	4.60
Reyes, Dennis, LA/Cin	0	0.00	4.60	0	0.00	4.60
Reynolds, Shane, Hou	4	1.42	4.60	4	0.34	4.62
Reynoso, Armando, NYN	0	0.00	4.60	5	0.62	4.57
Rhodes, Arthur, Bal	0	0.00	5.01	0	0.00	4.60
Rincon, Ricardo, Pit	0	0.00	4.60	0	0.00	4.60
Rios, Armando, SF	5	44.96	4.60	5	44.96	4.60
Ripken, Billy, Det	5	2.28	5.01	245	2.94	4.55
Ripken Jr., Cal, Bal	74	4.40	5.01	1555	5.22	4.66
Risley, Bill, Tor	0		—	0	0.00	3.88
Ritz, Kevin, Col	0	0.00	4.60	8	1.22	4.64
Rivera, Luis, KC	10	3.78	5.01	192	2.85	4.32
Rivera, Ruben, SD	25	4.82	4.60	43	5.13	4.84
Roberts, Bip, Det/Oak	40	4.67	5.01	610	5.25	4.45
Robertson, Mike, Ari	0	0.00	4.60	6	3.44	4.70
Robinson, Kerry, TB	0	0.00	5.01	0	0.00	5.01
Rodriguez, Alex, Sea	131	6.97	5.01	394	6.99	5.10
Rodriguez, Felix, Ari	0		—	0	0.00	4.60
Rodriguez, Henry, ChN	71	5.91	4.60	324	5.14	4.57
Rodriguez, Ivan, Tex	97	6.29	5.01	538	5.02	4.93
Rodriguez, Rich, SF	1	4.50	4.60	2	1.80	4.24
Rogers, Kenny, Oak	0	0.00	5.01	0	0.00	4.98
Rojas, Mel, NYN	0		—	1	0.47	4.34
Rolen, Scott, Phi	121	7.25	4.60	246	6.79	4.61
Romero, Mandy, SD/Bos	1	1.34	4.82	4	1.82	4.68
Roque, Rafael, Mil	0	0.00	4.60	0	0.00	4.60
Rosado, Jose, KC	0	0.00	5.01	0	0.00	4.97
Roskos, John, Fla	0	0.00	4.60	0	0.00	4.60
Rossy, Rico, Sea	5	2.00	5.01	27	2.69	4.59
Rueter, Kirk, SF	2	0.84	4.60	5	0.56	4.60
Rusch, Glendon, KC	0	0.00	5.01	0	0.00	4.97
Ryan, Ken, Phi	0	0.00	4.60	0	0.00	4.67
Saberhagen, Bret, Bos	0	0.00	5.01	1	0.14	4.49
Sadler, Donnie, Bos	16	4.17	5.01	16	4.17	5.01
Sager, A.J., Det	0	0.00	5.01	1	1.93	4.65
Saipe, Mike, Col	0	0.00	4.60	0	0.00	4.60
Salmon, Tim, Ana	101	8.00	5.01	646	7.49	5.03

Player, Team	1998 RC	RC/27	LRC/27	Career RC	RC/27	LRC27
Samuel, Juan, Tor	3	1.61	5.01	822	4.64	4.25
Sanchez, Jesus, Fla	0	0.00	4.60	0	0.00	4.60
Sanchez, Rey, SF	33	3.71	4.60	220	3.29	4.54
Sanders, Reggie, Cin	70	5.01	4.60	474	5.69	4.50
Sanders, Scott, SD	0	0.00	4.60	4	0.99	4.62
Sanford, Chance, Pit	0	0.00	4.60	0	0.00	4.60
Santana, Julio, TB	0	0.00	5.01	0	0.00	5.00
Santangelo, F.P., Mon	42	3.53	4.60	173	4.76	4.63
Santiago, Benito, Tor	3	3.84	5.01	554	3.96	4.32
Sasser, Rob, Tex	0	0.00	5.01	0	0.00	5.01
Saunders, Tony, TB	1	—	—	1	0.00	4.60
Scanlan, Bob, Hou	0	—	—	1	0.77	4.11
Schilling, Curt, Phi	1	0.35	4.60	1	0.06	4.49
Schmidt, Jason, Pit	0	0.00	4.60	0	0.00	4.62
Schourek, Pete, Hou	1	1.35	4.60	10	1.14	4.43
Seanez, Rudy, Atl	0	0.00	4.60	0	0.00	4.62
Sefcik, Kevin, Phi	30	6.47	4.60	50	4.23	4.62
Segui, David, Sea	79	5.51	5.01	442	4.93	4.66
Seguignol, Fernando, Mon	3	2.45	4.60	3	2.45	4.60
Sele, Aaron, Tex	1	8.95	5.01	1	5.37	4.98
Serafini, Dan, Min	0	0.00	5.01	0	0.00	5.01
Servais, Scott, ChN	25	2.51	4.60	233	3.57	4.53
Service, Scott, KC	0	0.00	5.01	1	1.80	4.52
Sexson, Richie, Cle	30	6.50	5.01	30	6.01	5.01
Shave, Jon, Min	4	3.36	5.01	9	3.36	4.84
Shaw, Jeff, Cin/LA	0	0.00	4.60	0	0.00	4.58
Sheets, Andy, SD	31	5.36	4.60	47	3.91	4.90
Sheffield, Gary, Fla/LA	108	8.88	4.60	800	6.87	4.43
Sheldon, Scott, Tex	0	0.00	4.60	5	3.95	4.97
Shipley, Craig, Ana	17	3.77	5.01	148	3.80	4.54
Shuey, Paul, Cle	0	0.00	5.01	0	0.00	4.97
Shumpert, Terry, Col	2	2.70	4.60	86	3.09	4.64
Siddall, Joe, Det	5	2.40	5.01	8	1.78	4.80
Sierra, Ruben, ChA	7	3.13	5.01	955	5.16	4.68
Silva, Jose, Pit	0	0.00	4.60	0	0.00	4.60
Silvestri, Dave, TB	0	0.00	5.01	38	3.68	4.74
Simmons, Brian, ChA	7	14.46	5.01	7	14.46	5.01
Simms, Mike, Tex	42	8.17	5.01	100	5.16	4.65
Simon, Randall, Atl	2	3.85	4.60	5	5.86	4.60
Sirotka, Mike, ChA	0	0.00	5.01	0	0.00	5.00
Slocumb, Heathcliff, Sea	0	—	—	1	2.45	4.29
Small, Aaron, Oak/Ari	0	—	—	0	0.00	4.93
Smith, Bobby, TB	49	4.60	5.01	49	4.60	5.01
Smith, Mark, Pit	9	2.27	4.60	75	5.00	4.83
Smith, Pete, SD/Bal	1	1.69	4.65	5	0.47	4.23
Smith, Travis, Mil	0	0.00	4.60	0	0.00	4.60
Smoltz, John, Atl	5	2.70	4.60	35	1.45	4.34
Snopek, Chris, ChA/Bos	8	1.88	5.01	57	3.11	5.04
Snow, J.T., SF	62	4.81	4.60	403	5.04	4.92
Sodowsky, Clint, Ari	0	0.00	4.60	0	0.00	4.60
Sojo, Luis, NYA	8	1.79	5.01	207	3.36	4.83
Sorrento, Paul, TB	50	3.83	5.01	453	5.01	4.89
Sosa, Sammy, ChN	141	7.94	4.60	718	5.27	4.50
Sparks, Steve, Ana	0	0.00	5.01	0	0.00	5.01
Spehr, Tim, NYN/KC	8	3.31	4.73	42	3.31	4.62
Spencer, Shane, NYA	24	14.65	5.01	24	14.65	5.01
Spencer, Stan, SD	0	0.00	4.60	0	0.00	4.60
Spiers, Bill, Hou	61	5.62	4.60	358	4.59	4.57
Spiezio, Scott, Oak	50	4.16	5.01	119	4.12	4.98
Spoljaric, Paul, Sea	0	—	—	0	0.00	4.93
Spradlin, Jerry, Phi	1	—	—	1	0.00	4.53
Sprague, Ed, Tor/Oak	44	3.07	5.01	369	3.84	5.02
Springer, Dennis, TB	0	0.00	4.60	0	0.00	4.75
Springer, Russ, Ari/Atl	0	0.00	4.60	0	0.00	4.67
Stahoviak, Scott, Min	0	0.00	5.01	137	4.63	5.13
Stairs, Matt, Oak	101	6.96	5.01	215	6.74	5.00
Stanifer, Robby, Fla	0	0.00	4.60	2	8.97	4.60
Stankiewicz, Andy, Ari	7	1.59	4.60	86	3.35	4.48
Stanley, Mike, Tor/Bos	89	6.13	5.01	609	6.02	4.85
Stanton, Mike, NYA	0	0.00	5.01	3	11.58	4.35
Stein, Blake, Oak	0	0.00	5.01	0	0.00	5.01
Steinbach, Terry, Min	48	3.81	5.01	663	4.55	4.75
Stephenson, Garrett, Phi	0	0.00	4.60	0	0.00	4.60
Stevens, Dave, ChN	0	0.00	4.60	0	0.00	4.60
Stevens, Lee, Tex	56	5.74	5.01	202	4.70	4.71
Stewart, Shannon, Tor	88	5.88	5.01	124	5.79	5.01
Stieb, Dave, Tor	0	0.00	5.01	0	0.00	4.76
Stinnett, Kelly, Ari	41	5.12	4.60	87	4.36	4.66
Stocker, Kevin, TB	26	2.44	5.01	234	3.65	4.68
Stottlemyre, Todd, StL	4	2.30	4.60	14	2.42	4.64
Stovall, DaRond, Mon	6	2.57	4.60	6	2.57	4.60
Strange, Doug, Pit	2	0.33	4.60	185	3.27	4.74

Player, Team	1998 RC	RC/27	LRC/27	Career RC	RC/27	LRC27
Strawberry, Darryl, NYA	59	6.86	5.01	991	6.39	4.25
Strittmatter, Mark, Col	0	0.00	4.60	0	0.00	4.60
Stynes, Chris, Cin	34	3.40	4.60	81	4.29	4.73
Sullivan, Scott, Cin	0	0.00	4.60	0	0.00	4.60
Suppan, Jeff, Ari	2	3.17	4.60	2	2.84	4.63
Surhoff, B.J., Bal	81	4.90	5.01	764	4.76	4.71
Sutton, Larry, KC	41	4.39	5.01	54	4.82	5.00
Sveum, Dale, NYA	0	0.00	5.01	274	3.70	4.56
Sweeney, Mark, SD	19	3.26	4.60	83	4.66	4.63
Sweeney, Mike, KC	37	4.48	5.01	83	4.05	5.07
Swift, Bill, Sea	0	0.00	5.01	11	1.38	4.42
Swindell, Greg, Min/Bos	0	—	—	8	0.94	4.34
Tabaka, Jeff, Pit	0	0.00	4.60	1	0.00	4.64
Tam, Jeff, NYN	0	0.00	4.60	0	0.00	4.60
Tapani, Kevin, ChN	6	2.22	4.60	6	1.40	4.59
Tarasco, Tony, Cin	3	4.05	4.60	117	4.52	4.76
Tatis, Fernando, Tex/StL	59	3.86	4.86	82	3.76	4.88
Tatum, Jimmy, NYN	7	4.20	4.60	17	2.72	4.57
Taubensee, Eddie, Cin	74	6.18	4.60	296	5.05	4.49
Tavarez, Jesus, Bal	0	0.00	5.01	45	3.54	4.71
Tavarez, Julian, SF	0	0.00	4.60	0	0.00	4.60
Tejada, Miguel, Oak	39	3.48	5.01	49	3.44	4.99
Telemaco, A., ChN/Ari	0	0.00	4.60	1	0.37	4.63
Telford, Anthony, Mon	0	0.00	4.60	1	1.68	4.60
Tewksbury, Bob, Min	0	0.00	5.01	3	0.21	4.33
Thomas, Frank, ChA	119	7.02	5.01	1097	9.18	4.85
Thome, Jim, Cle	100	8.34	5.01	533	7.42	5.03
Thompson, Justin, Det	0	0.00	5.01	0	0.00	4.99
Thompson, Mark, Col	0	0.00	4.60	2	0.62	4.66
Thomson, John, Col	0	0.00	4.60	2	0.54	4.60
Thurman, Mike, Mon	0	0.00	4.60	0	0.00	4.60
Tomberlin, Andy, Det	9	4.24	5.01	28	3.12	4.91
Tomko, Brett, Cin	0	0.00	4.60	1	0.26	4.60
Trachsel, Steve, ChN	9	4.26	4.60	14	1.34	4.63
Trammell, Bubba, TB	31	5.59	5.01	45	4.86	4.98
Tremie, Chris, Tex	1	13.43	5.01	1	1.17	5.06
Trombley, Mike, Min	0	—	—	0	0.00	4.93
Tucker, Michael, Atl	55	4.59	4.60	203	4.93	4.85
Turner, Chris, KC	0	0.00	5.01	36	4.50	5.05
Urbina, Ugueth, Mon	0	0.00	4.60	1	0.61	4.66
Valdes, Ismael, LA	2	1.12	4.60	1	0.11	4.63
Valdes, Marc, Mon	1	8.99	4.60	1	0.75	4.64
Valdes, Pedro, ChN	0	0.00	4.60	0	0.00	4.62
Valentin, Javier, Min	7	1.33	5.01	7	1.29	5.01
Valentin, John, Bos	89	5.15	5.01	538	5.98	5.00
Valentin, Jose, Mil	56	4.37	4.60	310	4.85	5.03
Van Poppel, Todd, Tex/Pit	1	1.93	4.71	1	1.93	4.71
Vander Wal, John, Col/SD	25	7.03	4.60	156	5.02	4.42
VanRyn, Ben, ChN/SD	0	0.00	4.60	0	0.00	4.60
Varitek, Jason, Bos	27	3.98	5.01	28	3.98	5.01
Vaughn, Greg, SD	114	7.12	4.60	709	5.58	4.69
Vaughn, Mo, Bos	125	7.99	5.01	775	7.43	4.94
Vazquez, Javier, Mon	3	1.59	4.60	3	1.59	4.60
Velandia, Jorge, Oak	0	0.00	5.01	0	0.00	4.65
Velarde, Randy, Ana	33	5.91	4.60	367	4.75	4.82
Ventura, Robin, ChA	89	5.31	5.01	737	5.64	4.79
Veras, Quilvio, SD	73	4.94	4.60	242	4.69	4.62
Veres, Dave, Col	0	0.00	4.60	2	1.80	4.64
Vidro, Jose, Mon	18	2.76	4.60	37	3.25	4.60
Vina, Fernando, Mil	108	6.23	4.60	277	4.93	4.95
Vitiello, Joe, KC	0	0.00	5.01	66	4.25	5.19
Vizcaino, Jose, LA	31	4.31	4.60	379	3.93	4.55
Vizquel, Omar, Cle	83	4.95	5.01	529	3.84	4.80
Voigt, Jack, Oak	6	2.48	5.01	82	4.61	4.98
Wagner, Billy, Hou	0	0.00	4.60	0	0.00	4.65
Wagner, Paul, Mil	0	0.00	4.60	5	0.84	4.59
Wainhouse, David, Col	0	0.00	4.60	0	0.00	4.62
Wakefield, Tim, Bos	0	0.00	5.01	2	0.72	4.28
Walbeck, Matt, Ana	42	4.16	5.01	145	3.34	5.11
Walker, Larry, Col	94	8.29	4.60	799	7.02	4.39
Walker, Todd, Min	90	6.28	5.01	110	5.10	5.04
Wall, Donne, SD	0	0.00	4.60	1	0.41	4.66
Walton, Jerome, TB	3	3.36	5.01	193	4.24	4.22
Ward, Daryle, Hou	1	13.49	4.60	1	13.49	4.60
Ward, Turner, Pit	46	5.47	4.60	196	4.82	4.85
Wasdin, John, Bos	0	—	—	0	—	—
Washburn, Jarrod, Ana	0	0.00	5.01	0	0.00	5.01
Watkins, Pat, Cin	15	3.37	4.60	15	2.79	4.60
Weathers, Dave, Cin/Mil	1	1.08	4.60	1	0.22	4.61
Weaver, Eric, LA	0	0.00	4.60	0	0.00	4.60
Webster, Lenny, Bal	36	4.11	5.01	146	3.79	4.75
Wehner, John, Fla	4	1.50	4.60	49	2.60	4.40

Player, Team	1998			Career		
	RC	RC/27	LRC/27	RC	RC/27	LRC27
Weiss, Walt, Atl	52	5.20	4.60	505	4.08	4.50
Welch, Mike, Phi	0	0.00	4.60	0	0.00	4.60
Wells, Bob, Sea	0	—	—	0	—	—
Wells, David, NYA	0	0.00	5.01	0	0.00	4.67
Wendell, Turk, NYN	0	0.00	4.60	1	1.04	4.59
Wengert, Don, SD/ChN	0	0.00	4.60	0	0.00	4.60
Wetteland, John, Tex	0	—	—	3	1.23	4.10
White, Derrick, ChN/Col	1	1.50	4.60	5	1.39	4.75
White, Devon, Ari	88	5.44	4.60	860	4.70	4.60
White, Gabe, Cin	0	0.00	4.60	1	0.96	4.61
White, Rick, TB	0	0.00	5.01	0	0.00	4.66
White, Rondell, Mon	61	6.16	4.60	273	5.01	4.62
Whiten, Mark, Cle	33	5.18	5.01	422	4.71	4.62
Whiteside, Matt, Phi	0	0.00	4.60	0	0.00	4.60
Wickman, Bob, Mil	0	0.00	4.60	0	0.00	4.60
Widger, Chris, Mon	46	3.78	4.60	84	3.79	4.64
Wilkins, Marc, Pit	0	—	—	1	2.25	4.65
Wilkins, Rick, Sea/NYN	2	1.12	4.90	265	4.36	4.48
Williams, Bernie, NYA	110	8.16	5.01	654	6.35	4.94
Williams, Eddie, SD	1	1.04	4.60	127	3.68	4.71
Williams, Gerald, Atl	49	6.68	4.60	176	3.90	4.99
Williams, Matt, Ari	63	4.30	4.60	772	5.12	4.39
Williams, Mike, Pit	0	0.00	4.60	5	1.21	4.59
Williams, Reggie, Ana	8	7.96	5.01	11	5.02	4.69
Williams, Todd, Cin	0	0.00	4.60	0	0.00	4.61
Williams, Woody, Tor	1	6.71	5.01	1	5.37	5.00
Wilson, Craig, ChA	16	15.35	5.01	16	15.35	5.01
Wilson, Dan, Sea	39	3.97	5.01	272	4.37	5.09
Wilson, Enrique, Cle	12	4.74	5.01	15	5.17	5.01
Wilson, Preston, NYN/Fla	3	1.76	4.60	3	1.76	4.60
Winchester, Scott, Cin	0	0.00	4.60	0	0.00	4.60
Winn, Randy, TB	36	3.59	5.01	36	3.59	5.01
Winston, Darrin, Phi	0	0.00	4.60	1	13.46	4.60
Witt, Bobby, Tex/StL	2	5.40	4.64	4	2.15	4.66
Witt, Kevin, Tor	0	0.00	5.01	0	0.00	5.01
Wohlers, Mark, Atl	0	—	—	1	2.25	4.47
Wolcott, Bob, Ari	0	0.00	4.60	0	0.00	4.64
Womack, Tony, Pit	86	4.71	4.60	186	4.89	4.60
Wood, Jason, Oak/Det	3	4.74	5.01	3	4.74	5.01
Wood, Kerry, ChN	4	1.96	4.60	4	1.96	4.60
Woodall, Brad, Mil	3	2.38	4.60	4	2.08	4.61
Woodard, Steve, Mil	0	0.00	4.60	0	0.00	4.60
Worrell, Tim, Det	0	—	—	4	1.54	4.58
Wright, Jamey, Col	5	2.41	4.60	5	1.03	4.62
Wright, Jaret, Cle	2	13.43	5.01	2	5.97	4.97
Yoshii, Masato, NYN	0	0.00	4.60	0	0.00	4.60
Young, Dmitri, Cin	87	5.94	4.60	127	5.01	4.60
Young, Eric, LA	69	5.30	4.60	444	5.40	4.57
Young, Ernie, KC	0	0.00	5.01	79	3.32	5.23
Young, Kevin, Pit	85	4.90	4.60	229	4.26	4.63
Zaun, Gregg, Fla	24	2.54	4.60	82	3.99	4.80
Zeile, Todd, LA/Fla/Tex	99	6.05	4.73	668	4.84	4.45
Zuber, Jon, Phi	8	6.17	4.60	15	3.75	4.66

Component Earned Run Average

	1998				Career			
Pitcher, Team	OAvg	OOB	ERC	LERA	OAvg	OOB	ERC	LERA
Abbott, Jim, ChA	.292	.358	4.66	4.65	.274	.337	4.22	4.29
Abbott, Paul, Sea	.255	.324	3.85	4.65	.257	.368	4.91	4.16
Acevedo, Juan, StL	.236	.301	2.87	4.23	.274	.341	4.51	4.21
Adams, Terry, ChN	.255	.349	4.55	4.23	.264	.352	4.30	4.21
Adamson, Joel, Ari	.284	.379	6.48	4.23	.283	.350	5.28	4.46
Aguilera, Rick, Min	.262	.299	3.45	4.65	.252	.305	3.44	4.13
Aldred, Scott, TB	.280	.356	3.99	4.65	.298	.373	6.04	4.54
Alfonseca, Antonio, Fla	.281	.359	4.96	4.23	.294	.367	5.34	4.22
Almanzar, Carlos, Tor	.286	.336	4.85	4.65	.269	.321	4.45	4.64
Alvarez, Wilson, TB	.239	.332	4.30	4.65	.245	.335	4.09	4.57
Anderson, Brian, Ari	.274	.297	3.99	4.23	.285	.322	4.60	4.54
Anderson, Matt, Det	.250	.378	4.38	4.65	.250	.378	4.38	4.65
Andujar, Luis, Tor	.429	.467	10.20	4.65	.317	.379	6.55	4.73
Appier, Kevin, KC	.339	.391	7.33	4.65	.238	.303	3.12	4.41
Arrojo, Rolando, TB	.256	.329	4.03	4.65	.256	.329	4.03	4.65
Ashby, Andy, SD	.259	.309	3.55	4.23	.265	.322	3.91	4.15
Assenmacher, Paul, Cle	.286	.351	4.79	4.65	.248	.316	3.37	3.98
Astacio, Pedro, Col	.294	.363	5.91	4.23	.262	.324	3.98	4.13
Avery, Steve, Bos	.269	.361	5.06	4.65	.261	.322	3.80	4.02
Ayala, Bobby, Sea	.323	.370	5.78	4.65	.269	.343	4.59	4.52
Aybar, Manny, StL	.281	.367	5.04	4.23	.273	.357	4.75	4.22
Bailes, Scott, Tex	.351	.385	6.87	4.65	.283	.345	4.90	4.14
Bailey, Cory, SF	.167	.231	2.70	4.23	.276	.367	4.59	4.26
Baldwin, James, ChA	.278	.347	4.89	4.65	.271	.339	4.69	4.73
Banks, Willie, NYA/Ari	.247	.359	4.59	4.33	.273	.358	4.95	4.22
Baptist, Travis, Min	.321	.366	6.24	4.65	.321	.366	6.24	4.65
Barber, Brian, KC	.276	.328	4.34	4.65	.281	.355	5.09	4.45
Barkley, Brian, Bos	.340	.441	9.46	4.65	.340	.441	9.46	4.65
Barrios, Manuel, Fla/LA	.308	.471	10.01	4.23	.357	.486	10.94	4.22
Batista, Miguel, Mon	.274	.359	4.70	4.23	.272	.364	4.79	4.22
Beck, Rod, ChN	.269	.311	4.05	4.23	.240	.282	2.94	4.01
Beech, Matt, Phi	.275	.366	5.69	4.23	.281	.357	5.49	4.21
Belcher, Tim, KC	.272	.328	4.59	4.65	.255	.319	3.81	4.16
Belinda, Stan, Cin	.212	.304	2.97	4.23	.226	.309	3.28	4.14
Beltran, Rigo, NYN	.214	.303	3.32	4.23	.235	.295	2.80	4.20
Benes, Andy, Ari	.251	.311	3.64	4.23	.244	.307	3.40	4.00
Benitez, Armando, Bal	.199	.318	3.63	4.65	.197	.318	3.51	4.66
Bennett, Joel, Bal	.250	.455	7.45	4.65	.250	.455	7.45	4.65
Bennett, Shayne, Mon	.276	.363	4.83	4.23	.271	.352	4.51	4.22
Bere, Jason, ChA/Cin	.276	.373	5.73	4.50	.250	.359	4.99	4.60
Bergman, Sean, Hou	.268	.315	4.00	4.23	.290	.351	5.05	4.36
Bevil, Brian, KC	.283	.373	5.76	4.65	.273	.362	5.15	4.68
Blair, Willie, Ari/NYN	.282	.344	5.00	4.23	.279	.339	4.59	4.16
Bochtler, Doug, Det	.279	.381	6.77	4.65	.237	.348	4.42	4.33
Boehringer, Brian, SD	.257	.363	5.06	4.23	.257	.365	5.12	4.55
Bohanon, B., NYN/LA	.220	.305	3.09	4.23	.272	.347	4.69	4.33
Bones, Ricky, KC	.244	.327	3.53	4.65	.279	.341	4.82	4.50
Borland, Toby, Phi	.242	.342	4.17	4.23	.255	.355	4.41	4.21
Borowski, Joe, NYA	.289	.357	4.27	4.65	.291	.387	5.40	4.33
Boskie, Shawn, Mon	.415	.449	11.44	4.23	.286	.346	5.09	4.27
Bottalico, Ricky, Phi	.305	.390	6.63	4.23	.221	.316	3.38	4.20
Bottenfield, Kent, StL	.254	.333	4.00	4.23	.269	.343	4.41	4.11
Bradford, Chad, ChA	.229	.272	2.16	4.65	.229	.272	2.16	4.65
Bradley, Ryan, NYA	.250	.373	5.77	4.65	.250	.373	5.77	4.65
Brantley, Jeff, StL	.220	.289	3.60	4.23	.232	.313	3.44	3.88
Brewer, Billy, Phi	.750	.833	100.03	4.23	.248	.340	4.52	4.57
Brocail, Doug, Det	.211	.269	1.99	4.65	.270	.334	4.27	4.26
Brock, Chris, SF	.279	.322	4.11	4.23	.284	.351	4.64	4.21
Brow, Scott, Ari	.272	.375	5.05	4.23	.285	.382	5.86	4.67
Brown, Kevin, SD	.235	.279	2.35	4.23	.254	.312	3.33	4.21
Brownson, Mark, Col	.296	.333	4.94	4.23	.296	.333	4.94	4.23
Brunson, Will, LA/Det	.263	.364	3.90	4.47	.263	.364	3.90	4.47
Bruske, J., LA/SD/NYA	.277	.351	4.67	4.29	.267	.347	4.48	4.24
Buddie, Mike, NYA	.286	.348	4.80	4.65	.286	.348	4.80	4.65
Bullinger, Jim, Sea	.433	.455	16.02	4.65	.265	.351	4.60	4.11
Bullinger, Kirk, Mon	.400	.400	8.74	4.23	.400	.400	8.74	4.23
Burba, Dave, Cle	.269	.330	4.50	4.65	.253	.333	4.18	4.22
Burkett, John, Tex	.292	.335	4.55	4.65	.276	.322	3.95	4.12
Busby, Mike, StL	.256	.328	3.77	4.23	.301	.368	5.76	4.22
Butler, Adam, Atl	.278	.462	8.22	4.23	.278	.462	8.22	4.23
Byrd, Paul, Atl/Phi	.213	.274	2.62	4.23	.235	.313	3.56	4.21
Byrdak, Tim, KC	.556	.556	23.52	4.65	.556	.556	23.52	4.65
Cabrera, Jose, Hou	.389	.421	6.28	4.23	.197	.263	1.89	4.21
Cadaret, Greg, Ana/Tex	.274	.348	5.25	4.65	.262	.358	4.52	4.10
Candiotti, Tom, Oak	.281	.338	4.84	4.65	.255	.315	3.63	4.10
Carlson, Dan, TB	.347	.429	8.27	4.65	.328	.391	7.58	4.39
Carpenter, Chris, Tor	.265	.329	4.12	4.65	.285	.351	4.81	4.62
Carrasco, Hector, Min	.304	.373	5.47	4.65	.246	.340	3.90	4.31
Casian, Larry, ChA	.400	.478	10.86	4.65	.301	.354	5.07	4.35
Castillo, Carlos, ChA	.246	.312	4.14	4.65	.254	.326	4.42	4.61

	1998				Career			
Pitcher, Team	OAvg	OOB	ERC	LERA	OAvg	OOB	ERC	LERA
Castillo, Frank, Det	.316	.376	6.32	4.65	.274	.330	4.34	4.05
Castillo, Tony, ChA	.328	.395	8.25	4.65	.274	.333	4.16	4.45
Cather, Mike, Atl	.255	.314	3.97	4.23	.218	.301	3.00	4.22
Charlton, Norm, Bal/Atl	.275	.380	5.83	4.53	.239	.325	3.55	4.00
Checo, Robinson, Bos	.379	.471	11.82	4.65	.288	.352	5.10	4.59
Chen, Bruce, Atl	.288	.367	5.55	4.23	.288	.367	5.55	4.23
Cho, Jin Ho, Bos	.341	.368	7.12	4.65	.341	.368	7.12	4.65
Chouinard, B., Mil/Ari	.280	.322	4.15	4.23	.302	.369	5.80	4.68
Christiansen, Jason, Pit	.216	.295	2.39	4.23	.254	.340	4.00	4.21
Clark, Mark, ChN	.278	.318	4.02	4.23	.272	.321	4.05	4.26
Clemens, Roger, Tor	.198	.277	2.27	4.65	.225	.289	2.74	4.30
Clement, Matt, SD	.283	.367	4.14	4.23	.283	.367	4.14	4.23
Clontz, Brad, LA/NYN	.218	.327	3.99	4.23	.262	.334	4.07	4.20
Cloude, Ken, Sea	.297	.377	6.46	4.65	.279	.364	5.83	4.63
Colon, Bartolo, Cle	.260	.329	3.87	4.65	.268	.341	4.37	4.62
Cone, David, NYA	.237	.302	3.31	4.65	.224	.299	3.02	4.11
Connelly, Steve, Oak	.435	.536	13.87	4.65	.435	.536	13.87	4.65
Cook, Dennis, NYN	.240	.318	3.35	4.23	.251	.321	3.87	4.08
Cooke, Steve, Cin	.182	.217	1.23	4.23	.276	.339	4.39	4.11
Coppinger, Rocky, Bal	.246	.319	4.68	4.65	.262	.349	5.33	4.90
Cordova, Francisco, Pit	.245	.303	3.35	4.23	.254	.307	3.46	4.22
Corey, Bryan, Ari	.375	.474	10.40	4.23	.375	.474	10.40	4.23
Corsi, Jim, Bos	.235	.301	3.18	4.65	.251	.323	3.37	4.34
Crabtree, Tim, Tex	.264	.335	3.80	4.65	.273	.341	4.23	4.74
Croushore, Rich, StL	.213	.320	3.70	4.23	.213	.320	3.70	4.23
Crow, Dean, Det	.313	.374	5.49	4.65	.313	.374	5.49	4.65
Cunnane, Will, SD	.308	.357	6.84	4.23	.305	.391	6.49	4.20
Daal, Omar, Ari	.245	.305	3.12	4.23	.267	.338	4.14	4.23
Darensbourg, Vic, Fla	.207	.289	2.47	4.23	.207	.289	2.47	4.23
Darwin, Danny, SF	.297	.352	5.29	4.23	.256	.310	3.62	4.06
De Los Santos, V., Mil	.151	.173	1.25	4.23	.151	.173	1.25	4.23
DeHart, Rick, Mon	.291	.359	5.31	4.23	.291	.362	5.68	4.21
DeJean, Mike, Col	.285	.340	3.92	4.23	.283	.343	4.10	4.22
DeLucia, Rich, Ana	.221	.340	4.13	4.65	.250	.335	4.37	4.20
Dempster, Ryan, Fla	.336	.446	8.14	4.23	.336	.446	8.14	4.23
Dessens, Elmer, Pit	.300	.351	5.19	4.23	.317	.360	5.40	4.22
Dickson, Jason, Ana	.303	.359	5.52	4.65	.296	.349	5.28	4.64
Dipoto, Jerry, Col	.232	.304	3.31	4.23	.279	.354	4.31	4.25
Dodd, Robert, Phi	.333	.360	6.82	4.23	.333	.360	6.82	4.23
Dougherty, Jim, Oak	.340	.431	8.45	4.65	.297	.376	5.65	4.25
Drabek, Doug, Bal	.312	.355	5.94	4.65	.255	.308	3.47	3.93
Dreifort, Darren, LA	.256	.321	3.50	4.23	.257	.334	3.71	4.22
Duran, Roberto, Det	.170	.389	4.04	4.65	.178	.414	4.89	4.61
Duvall, Mike, TB	.267	.353	3.88	4.65	.267	.353	3.88	4.65
Dykhoff, Radhames, Bal	.400	.500	12.01	4.65	.400	.500	12.01	4.65
Eckersley, Dennis, Bos	.291	.331	4.64	4.65	.246	.290	3.13	3.95
Edmondson, B., Atl/Fla	.266	.353	4.74	4.23	.266	.353	4.74	4.23
Eiland, Dave, TB	.429	.529	14.42	4.65	.301	.353	5.29	3.99
Elarton, Scott, Hou	.196	.270	2.35	4.23	.196	.270	2.35	4.23
Eldred, Cal, Mil	.297	.372	5.54	4.23	.252	.327	4.13	4.47
Embree, Alan, Atl/Ari	.269	.343	4.71	4.23	.253	.342	4.48	4.40
Erdos, Todd, NYA	.500	.545	13.15	4.65	.324	.387	6.19	4.26
Erickson, Scott, Bal	.281	.334	4.40	4.65	.276	.338	4.29	4.46
Escobar, Kelvim, Tor	.238	.314	3.41	4.65	.238	.322	3.49	4.62
Estes, Shawn, SF	.269	.364	4.71	4.23	.243	.340	3.84	4.21
Evans, Bart, KC	.206	.206	1.58	4.65	.206	.206	1.58	4.65
Eversgerd, Bryan, StL	.346	.387	7.67	4.23	.299	.359	5.10	4.21
Eyre, Scott, ChA	.271	.368	6.31	4.65	.270	.363	5.97	4.62
Fassero, Jeff, Sea	.259	.316	4.10	4.65	.247	.307	3.36	4.26
Fetters, Mike, Oak/Ana	.267	.338	4.29	4.65	.263	.344	4.09	4.42
Finley, Chuck, Ana	.246	.334	4.10	4.65	.254	.330	3.97	4.35
Florie, Bryce, Det	.275	.354	4.88	4.65	.253	.348	4.33	4.49
Fontenot, Joe, Fla	.320	.403	6.83	4.23	.320	.403	6.83	4.23
Ford, Ben, Ari	.295	.367	6.78	4.23	.295	.367	6.78	4.23
Fordham, Tom, ChA	.279	.414	7.03	4.65	.275	.401	6.42	4.63
Fossas, Sea/ChN/Tex	.330	.426	6.90	4.57	.266	.342	4.24	4.18
Foster, Kevin, ChN	.500	.500	16.31	4.23	.257	.333	4.64	4.20
Foulke, Keith, ChA	.213	.283	2.95	4.65	.260	.323	4.32	4.49
Fox, Chad, Mil	.260	.326	3.66	4.23	.251	.329	3.91	4.22
Franco, John, NYN	.267	.347	4.11	4.23	.247	.317	3.23	3.83
Frascatore, John, StL	.256	.326	4.09	4.23	.263	.339	4.31	4.21
Fussell, Chris, Bal	.306	.435	7.05	4.65	.306	.435	7.05	4.65
Gaetti, Gary, StL	.400	.400	7.48	4.23	.429	.500	12.64	4.22
Gaillard, Eddie, TB	.148	.233	3.13	4.65	.194	.280	3.10	4.59
Gajkowski, Steve, Sea	.389	.476	12.46	4.65	.389	.476	12.46	4.65
Garces, Rich, Bos	.213	.327	3.83	4.65	.239	.346	4.34	4.63
Gardner, Mark, SF	.253	.311	3.83	4.23	.260	.327	4.15	4.00
Glauber, Keith, Cin	.214	.226	1.44	4.23	.214	.226	1.44	4.23
Glavine, Tom, Atl	.238	.300	2.93	4.23	.249	.311	3.27	3.92
Gomes, Wayne, Phi	.258	.328	4.00	4.23	.263	.341	4.35	4.22

	1998				Career			
Pitcher, Team	OAvg	OOB	ERC	LERA	OAvg	OOB	ERC	LERA
Gonzalez, Gabe, Fla	.333	.600	11.52	4.23	.333	.600	11.52	4.23
Gonzalez, Jeremi, ChN	.281	.344	4.80	4.23	.256	.333	4.22	4.21
Gonzalez, Lariel, Col	.000	.000	0.00	4.23	.000	.000	0.00	4.23
Gooden, Dwight, Cle	.262	.337	4.32	4.65	.240	.304	3.11	3.87
Gordon, Tom, Bos	.191	.254	1.72	4.65	.244	.331	3.87	4.40
Gorecki, Rick, TB	.259	.357	4.22	4.65	.286	.392	6.44	4.53
Grace, Mike, Phi	.312	.375	5.85	4.23	.269	.324	3.98	4.22
Graves, Danny, Cin	.252	.315	3.38	4.23	.276	.345	4.34	4.42
Green, Tyler, Phi	.239	.340	4.53	4.23	.265	.356	4.93	4.20
Greisinger, Seth, Det	.282	.346	4.89	4.65	.282	.346	4.89	4.65
Groom, Buddy, Oak	.274	.332	4.12	4.65	.298	.368	5.46	4.60
Grzanich, Mike, Hou	.333	.500	9.51	4.23	.333	.500	9.51	4.23
Guardado, Eddie, Min	.265	.332	4.42	4.65	.279	.347	4.98	4.65
Gunderson, Eric, Tex	.315	.358	6.03	4.65	.286	.350	4.97	4.46
Guthrie, Mark, LA	.267	.347	4.20	4.23	.273	.336	4.18	4.15
Guzman, Juan, Tor/Bal	.240	.326	4.02	4.65	.240	.323	3.78	4.50
Halama, John, Hou	.296	.361	4.34	4.23	.296	.361	4.34	4.23
Hall, Darren, LA	.347	.411	8.32	4.23	.278	.358	4.78	4.42
Halladay, Roy, Tor	.176	.208	1.61	4.65	.176	.208	1.61	4.65
Halter, Shane, KC	.333	.333	2.79	4.65	.333	.333	2.79	4.65
Hamilton, Joey, SD	.267	.353	4.36	4.23	.258	.329	3.89	4.21
Hammond, Chris, Fla	.357	.446	9.33	4.23	.277	.342	4.43	4.00
Hampton, Mike, Hou	.278	.344	4.45	4.23	.269	.333	4.07	4.21
Haney, Chris, KC/ChN	.309	.364	6.31	4.63	.286	.344	4.82	4.50
Hanson, Erik, Tor	.348	.429	8.95	4.65	.267	.325	3.95	4.29
Harnisch, Pete, Cin	.228	.291	3.06	4.23	.241	.312	3.56	3.97
Harriger, Denny, Det	.327	.417	7.06	4.65	.327	.417	7.06	4.65
Harris, Lenny, Cin	.000	.000	0.00	4.23	.000	.000	0.00	4.23
Harris, Pep, Ana	.239	.307	3.50	4.65	.258	.338	4.20	4.67
Harris, Reggie, Hou	.261	.308	4.18	4.23	.243	.365	4.69	4.12
Hartgraves, Dean, SF	.385	.438	10.46	4.23	.249	.343	4.15	4.20
Hasegawa, S., Ana	.241	.302	3.54	4.65	.257	.323	3.99	4.60
Hawkins, LaTroy, Min	.299	.350	5.31	4.65	.313	.371	6.24	4.65
Haynes, Jimmy, Oak	.298	.370	5.69	4.65	.291	.373	5.72	4.72
Heathcott, Mike, ChA	.182	.250	1.57	4.65	.182	.250	1.57	4.65
Helling, Rick, Tex	.253	.314	3.86	4.65	.250	.324	4.22	4.57
Henderson, Rodney, Mil	.313	.353	9.00	4.23	.326	.431	9.18	4.22
Henriquez, Oscar, Fla	.306	.390	7.53	4.23	.289	.388	6.73	4.22
Henry, Butch, Bos	.235	.316	4.51	4.65	.279	.319	3.92	4.03
Henry, Doug, Hou	.216	.307	3.30	4.23	.244	.328	3.86	4.21
Hentgen, Pat, Tor	.293	.357	5.58	4.65	.261	.327	4.17	4.65
Heredia, Felix, Fla/ChN	.252	.360	4.31	4.23	.256	.358	4.41	4.22
Heredia, Gil, Oak	.256	.282	3.05	4.65	.282	.321	3.97	4.24
Hermanson, D., Mon	.234	.292	3.12	4.23	.242	.312	3.60	4.21
Hernandez, Livan, Fla	.289	.363	5.58	4.23	.272	.347	4.76	4.22
Hernandez, O., NYA	.222	.299	2.96	4.65	.222	.299	2.96	4.65
Hernandez, R., TB	.212	.330	3.43	4.65	.223	.304	3.09	4.52
Hernandez, Xavier, Tex	.207	.307	3.08	4.65	.244	.318	3.65	4.06
Hershiser, Orel, SF	.259	.341	4.35	4.23	.246	.308	3.26	3.96
Hill, Ken, Ana	.311	.384	5.38	4.65	.255	.329	3.78	4.14
Hitchcock, Sterling, SD	.251	.308	3.95	4.23	.274	.339	4.72	4.55
Hoffman, Trevor, SD	.165	.232	1.32	4.23	.198	.266	2.25	4.17
Holdridge, David, Sea	.231	.323	3.33	4.65	.231	.323	3.33	4.65
Holmes, Darren, NYA	.270	.321	3.73	4.65	.268	.335	4.13	4.17
Holtz, Mike, Ana	.322	.397	5.39	4.65	.250	.339	4.00	4.71
Holzemer, Mark, Oak	.333	.386	6.35	4.65	.321	.406	7.48	4.66
Howry, Bob, ChA	.194	.270	2.50	4.65	.194	.270	2.50	4.65
Hudek, John, NYN/Cin	.219	.356	4.44	4.23	.219	.334	4.11	4.21
Hudson, Joe, Mil	1.000	.857	90.02	4.23	.307	.400	5.78	4.77
Hutton, Mark, Cin	.348	.483	10.12	4.23	.279	.368	5.34	4.36
Irabu, Hideki, NYA	.233	.321	4.05	4.65	.253	.333	4.74	4.63
Jackson, Mike, Cle	.195	.252	1.82	4.65	.216	.301	2.97	4.13
Jacome, Jason, Cle	.435	.500	15.40	4.65	.308	.368	5.78	4.59
James, Mike, Ana	.208	.309	2.44	4.65	.241	.340	3.84	4.77
Jerzembeck, Mike, NYA	.346	.419	9.68	4.65	.346	.419	9.68	4.65
Jimenez, Jose, StL	.262	.323	3.35	4.23	.262	.323	3.35	4.23
Johns, Doug, Bal	.321	.381	5.77	4.65	.292	.366	5.34	4.84
Johnson, Jason, TB	.306	.381	6.35	4.65	.315	.383	6.63	4.61
Johnson, Jonathan, Tex	.313	.455	7.36	4.65	.313	.455	7.36	4.65
Johnson, Mike, Mon	.432	.475	16.53	4.23	.308	.370	6.80	4.35
Johnson, R., Sea/Hou	.224	.300	3.16	4.50	.212	.310	3.21	4.31
Johnstone, John, SF	.224	.303	3.19	4.23	.254	.342	4.37	4.22
Jones, Bobby, NYN	.262	.316	3.84	4.23	.265	.320	3.87	4.20
Jones, Bobby M., Col	.282	.363	4.91	4.23	.295	.374	5.32	4.23
Jones, Doug, Mil/Cle	.292	.328	4.94	4.38	.262	.304	3.29	4.15
Jones, Todd, Det	.249	.347	4.37	4.65	.235	.328	3.54	4.32
Jordan, Ricardo, Cin	.308	.524	18.21	4.23	.270	.381	5.28	4.32
Judd, Mike, LA	.373	.475	12.61	4.23	.371	.458	11.05	4.22
Juden, Jeff, Mil/Ana	.264	.351	5.10	4.32	.254	.341	4.57	4.24
Kamieniecki, Scott, Bal	.313	.394	6.41	4.65	.270	.347	4.61	4.42
Karchner, M., ChA/ChN	.253	.352	4.61	4.47	.262	.355	4.67	4.68
Karl, Scott, Mil	.290	.349	4.78	4.23	.281	.344	4.73	4.62

	1998				Career			
Pitcher, Team	OAvg	OOB	ERC	LERA	OAvg	OOB	ERC	LERA
Karsay, Steve, Cle	.310	.355	5.40	4.65	.290	.349	5.06	4.55
Keagle, Greg, Det	.295	.389	6.41	4.65	.300	.402	7.10	4.80
Key, Jimmy, Bal	.258	.316	3.47	4.65	.255	.303	3.42	4.28
Kile, Darryl, Col	.287	.358	5.11	4.23	.257	.343	4.19	4.07
King, Curtis, StL	.262	.338	4.09	4.23	.286	.353	4.42	4.22
Kline, Steve, Mon	.228	.333	3.60	4.23	.277	.364	5.10	4.29
Klingenbeck, Scott, Cin	.286	.340	5.82	4.23	.311	.385	7.32	4.70
Krivda, Rick, Cle/Cin	.313	.417	7.73	4.43	.293	.368	5.73	4.72
Kroon, Marc, SD/Cin	.250	.447	6.49	4.23	.265	.396	6.26	4.21
Kubenka, Jeff, LA	.138	.316	2.03	4.23	.138	.316	2.03	4.23
Langston, Mark, SD	.325	.397	6.79	4.23	.245	.325	3.86	4.19
Lankford, Frank, LA	.288	.360	5.30	4.23	.288	.360	5.30	4.23
Larkin, Andy, Fla	.329	.435	8.41	4.23	.321	.431	8.07	4.23
Lawrence, Sean, Pit	.313	.380	6.98	4.23	.313	.380	6.98	4.23
Leiter, Al, NYN	.216	.298	2.65	4.23	.233	.338	3.82	4.35
Leiter, Mark, Phi	.216	.331	3.45	4.23	.266	.336	4.45	4.22
Leskanic, Curt, Col	.259	.350	4.74	4.23	.262	.338	4.42	4.18
Levine, Al, Tex	.294	.336	4.58	4.65	.298	.358	5.26	4.69
Lewis, Richie, Bal	.421	.520	16.11	4.65	.258	.366	5.25	4.43
Lieber, Jon, Pit	.269	.311	4.00	4.23	.278	.319	4.13	4.21
Ligtenberg, Kerry, Atl	.193	.260	2.13	4.23	.196	.260	2.32	4.22
Lima, Jose, Hou	.256	.285	3.36	4.23	.272	.312	4.08	4.43
Lira, Felipe, Sea	.319	.360	7.63	4.65	.278	.347	5.07	4.79
Lloyd, Graeme, NYA	.191	.234	1.67	4.65	.259	.314	3.54	4.66
Loaiza, E., Pit/Tex	.295	.344	5.19	4.42	.293	.346	4.92	4.26
Loewer, Carlton, Phi	.312	.360	5.70	4.23	.312	.360	5.70	4.23
Loiselle, Rich, Pit	.262	.372	4.43	4.23	.266	.345	4.28	4.21
Looper, Braden, StL	.357	.375	8.14	4.23	.357	.375	8.14	4.23
Lopez, Albie, TB	.249	.326	3.66	4.65	.283	.360	5.38	4.66
Lorraine, Andrew, Sea	.250	.438	5.44	4.65	.327	.402	7.32	4.66
Lowe, Derek, Bos	.267	.329	3.64	4.65	.271	.334	4.08	4.62
Lowe, Sean, StL	.440	.533	14.71	4.23	.384	.462	9.93	4.21
Ludwick, Eric, Fla	.333	.401	7.89	4.23	.331	.412	8.58	4.33
Maddux, Greg, Atl	.220	.260	2.01	4.23	.236	.284	2.53	3.90
Maddux, Mike, Mon	.243	.293	2.79	4.23	.263	.323	3.66	3.99
Magnante, Mike, Hou	.276	.368	4.62	4.23	.281	.346	4.37	4.37
Mahay, Ron, Bos	.263	.358	4.76	4.65	.234	.326	3.88	4.61
Maloney, Sean, LA	.265	.357	5.26	4.23	.278	.365	5.35	4.35
Mantei, Matt, Fla	.203	.308	2.44	4.23	.209	.344	3.49	4.22
Manuel, Barry, Ari	.266	.405	8.26	4.23	.240	.322	4.08	4.19
Martin, Tom, Cle	.408	.488	13.19	4.65	.293	.373	5.09	4.29
Martinez, Dennis, Atl	.295	.332	4.37	4.23	.256	.312	3.58	3.99
Martinez, Javier, Pit	.248	.389	5.94	4.23	.248	.389	5.94	4.23
Martinez, Pedro, Bos	.217	.278	2.78	4.65	.214	.284	2.67	4.27
Martinez, Ramon, LA	.206	.288	2.71	4.23	.235	.314	3.41	3.94
Mathews, T.J., Oak	.258	.328	3.91	4.65	.235	.310	3.32	4.37
Mathews, Terry, Bal	.342	.400	7.22	4.65	.267	.341	4.37	4.28
McCarthy, Greg, Sea	.214	.365	5.64	4.65	.224	.349	4.72	4.66
McCurry, Jeff, Pit	.324	.400	7.11	4.23	.322	.402	7.11	4.22
McDill, Allen, KC	.333	.379	9.97	4.65	.293	.442	10.90	4.61
McDowell, Jack, Ana	.311	.350	5.39	4.65	.256	.316	3.66	4.34
McElroy, Chuck, Col	.268	.327	3.61	4.23	.253	.332	3.71	4.07
McMichael, G., NYN/LA	.301	.386	5.89	4.23	.245	.311	3.18	4.17
Meadows, Brian, Fla	.315	.358	5.29	4.23	.315	.358	5.29	4.23
Mecir, Jim, TB	.225	.306	2.95	4.65	.250	.328	3.84	4.72
Medina, Rafael, Fla	.289	.407	6.59	4.23	.289	.407	6.59	4.23
Mendoza, Ramiro, NYA	.264	.314	3.44	4.65	.291	.333	4.36	4.67
Mercedes, Jose, Mil	.316	.359	5.87	4.23	.262	.331	4.52	4.58
Mercker, Kent, StL	.310	.361	4.96	4.23	.254	.333	4.07	4.13
Mesa, Jose, Cle/SF	.273	.353	4.68	4.50	.271	.341	4.30	4.36
Miceli, Dan, SD	.238	.308	3.20	4.23	.263	.343	4.66	4.30
Michalak, Chris, Ari	.375	.448	10.59	4.23	.375	.448	10.59	4.23
Miller, Kurt, ChN	.200	.200	1.13	4.23	.314	.410	6.89	4.21
Miller, Travis, Min	.272	.346	3.92	4.65	.328	.391	6.93	4.70
Miller, Trever, Hou	.266	.332	4.18	4.23	.296	.364	5.47	4.41
Mills, Alan, Bal	.203	.326	3.42	4.65	.236	.346	4.25	4.40
Millwood, Kevin, Atl	.258	.316	3.81	4.23	.263	.324	3.87	4.22
Milton, Eric, Min	.282	.347	5.21	4.65	.282	.347	5.21	4.65
Mlicki, Dave, NYN/LA	.267	.330	4.35	4.23	.263	.332	4.31	4.20
Moehler, Brian, Det	.260	.306	3.79	4.65	.271	.325	4.31	4.62
Mohler, Mike, Oak	.289	.365	5.19	4.65	.270	.366	4.97	4.65
Montgomery, Jeff, KC	.264	.335	4.60	4.65	.234	.301	3.12	4.28
Moore, Trey, Mon	.306	.348	4.95	4.23	.306	.348	4.95	4.23
Morgan, Mike, Min/ChN	.293	.355	5.51	4.57	.271	.332	4.08	4.01
Morman, Alvin, Cle/SF	.292	.367	5.86	4.55	.272	.366	5.57	4.39
Morris, Matt, StL	.243	.316	3.25	4.23	.253	.318	3.35	4.21
Moyer, Jamie, Sea	.256	.295	3.34	4.65	.271	.327	4.22	4.31
Mulholland, Terry, ChN	.235	.304	3.04	4.23	.270	.317	3.84	3.98
Mullins, Greg, Mil	.250	.400	5.48	4.23	.250	.400	5.48	4.23
Munoz, Bobby, Bal	.383	.439	10.37	4.65	.290	.357	5.05	4.25
Munoz, Mike, Col	.312	.372	5.29	4.23	.287	.365	5.05	4.14
Mussina, Mike, Bal	.242	.283	2.96	4.65	.246	.290	3.14	4.54

	1998				Career			
Pitcher, Team	OAvg	OOB	ERC	LERA	OAvg	OOB	ERC	LERA
Myers, Mike, Mil	.249	.348	4.14	4.23	.270	.362	5.16	4.63
Myers, Randy, Tor/SD	.267	.348	4.52	4.54	.233	.316	3.30	3.96
Myers, Rodney, ChN	.342	.390	7.19	4.23	.273	.364	5.11	4.22
Nagy, Charles, Cle	.298	.353	5.39	4.65	.276	.330	4.23	4.49
Naulty, Dan, Min	.269	.337	4.60	4.65	.234	.320	3.97	4.80
Navarro, Jaime, ChA	.315	.384	6.80	4.65	.281	.336	4.39	4.23
Neagle, Denny, Atl	.250	.307	3.55	4.23	.257	.310	3.61	4.14
Nelson, Jeff, NYA	.278	.387	5.13	4.65	.236	.337	3.64	4.55
Nen, Robb, SF	.180	.239	1.58	4.23	.231	.305	3.12	4.20
Nitkowski, C.J., Hou	.228	.317	3.19	4.23	.295	.391	6.21	4.52
Nomo, Hideo, LA/NYN	.226	.336	4.10	4.23	.218	.305	3.22	4.21
Nunez, Vladimir, Ari	.318	.360	4.87	4.23	.318	.360	4.87	4.23
Nye, Ryan, Phi	.500	.500	25.51	4.23	.404	.486	12.43	4.20
Ogea, Chad, Cle	.273	.346	4.93	4.65	.266	.327	4.27	4.75
Ojala, Kirt, Fla	.267	.351	4.66	4.23	.264	.352	4.74	4.22
Olivares, Omar, Ana	.270	.357	4.85	4.65	.271	.349	4.57	4.21
Oliver, Darren, Tex/StL	.311	.378	6.01	4.50	.278	.360	5.17	4.69
Olson, Gregg, Ari	.223	.295	2.74	4.23	.236	.325	3.34	4.20
Oquist, Mike, Oak	.298	.352	5.47	4.65	.284	.358	5.29	4.64
Orosco, Jesse, Bal	.221	.314	3.45	4.65	.219	.304	2.98	3.98
Ortiz, Russ, SF	.269	.360	5.05	4.23	.269	.360	5.05	4.23
Osborne, Donovan, StL	.256	.301	3.70	4.23	.262	.312	3.76	4.02
Osuna, Antonio, LA	.214	.311	3.50	4.23	.219	.300	2.95	4.21
Painter, Lance, StL	.249	.365	4.56	4.23	.288	.354	5.28	4.18
Pall, Donn, Fla	.326	.362	5.42	4.23	.268	.322	3.85	4.09
Paniagua, Jose, Sea	.200	.277	2.68	4.65	.284	.379	5.76	4.32
Park, Chan Ho, LA	.244	.328	3.69	4.23	.225	.317	3.46	4.22
Parque, Jim, ChA	.299	.375	5.88	4.65	.299	.375	5.88	4.65
Parris, Steve, Cin	.236	.302	3.22	4.23	.266	.337	4.44	4.21
Patrick, Bronswell, Mil	.279	.339	4.44	4.23	.279	.339	4.44	4.23
Patterson, Bob, ChN	.391	.453	9.40	4.23	.264	.315	3.74	4.04
Patterson, Danny, Tex	.274	.332	4.79	4.65	.269	.326	3.95	4.63
Pavano, Carl, Mon	.251	.315	3.97	4.23	.251	.315	3.97	4.23
Pavlik, Roger, Tex	.286	.349	5.18	4.65	.262	.346	4.60	4.63
Pennington, Brad, TB	1.000	1.000	inf	inf	.239	.423	7.15	4.56
Percival, Troy, Ana	.186	.299	2.74	4.65	.169	.266	2.14	4.74
Perez, Carlos, Mon/LA	.264	.312	3.55	4.23	.261	.306	3.54	4.21
Perez, Odalis, Atl	.244	.311	3.60	4.23	.244	.311	3.60	4.23
Perez, Yorkis, Phi	.209	.297	2.80	4.23	.234	.327	3.71	4.20
Perisho, Matt, Tex	.500	.625	30.09	4.65	.349	.451	9.52	4.57
Person, Robert, Tor	.294	.379	6.94	4.65	.252	.331	4.62	4.44
Peters, Chris, Pit	.252	.319	3.70	4.23	.265	.337	4.32	4.22
Petkovsek, Mark, StL	.312	.375	5.43	4.23	.287	.347	4.75	4.19
Pettitte, Andy, NYA	.274	.344	4.46	4.65	.268	.328	3.90	4.73
Pichardo, Hipolito, KC	.280	.346	4.75	4.65	.279	.345	4.39	4.47
Pickett, Ricky, Ari	.600	.778	58.14	4.23	.600	.778	58.14	4.23
Pisciotta, Marc, ChN	.259	.380	5.35	4.23	.237	.356	4.31	4.22
Pittsley, Jim, KC	.322	.401	7.35	4.65	.298	.378	6.27	4.60
Plesac, Dan, Tor	.224	.286	2.76	4.65	.245	.309	3.39	4.16
Plunk, Eric, Cle/Mil	.277	.353	4.91	4.47	.235	.337	4.03	4.30
Politte, Cliff, StL	.304	.381	6.28	4.23	.304	.381	6.28	4.23
Ponson, Sidney, Bal	.293	.345	5.07	4.65	.293	.345	5.07	4.65
Poole, Jim, SF/Cle	.301	.353	4.86	4.30	.257	.332	3.96	4.39
Portugal, Mark, Phi	.283	.319	4.39	4.23	.257	.320	3.83	3.99
Powell, Brian, Det	.294	.364	6.25	4.65	.294	.364	6.25	4.65
Powell, Jay, Fla/Hou	.225	.328	3.46	4.23	.241	.334	3.65	4.21
Powell, Jeremy, Mon	.290	.382	6.29	4.23	.290	.382	6.29	4.23
Priest, Eddie, Cin	.444	.448	12.11	4.23	.444	.448	12.11	4.23
Prieto, Ariel, Oak	.415	.489	13.54	4.65	.290	.376	5.52	4.76
Pulsipher, Bill, NYN/Mil	.307	.373	5.46	4.23	.274	.342	4.39	4.20
Quantrill, Paul, Tor	.285	.334	3.90	4.65	.296	.345	4.70	4.46
Radinsky, Scott, LA	.272	.337	4.03	4.23	.252	.326	3.59	4.18
Radke, Brad, Min	.283	.324	4.18	4.65	.267	.309	3.99	4.73
Raggio, Brady, StL	.579	.605	22.18	4.23	.391	.451	8.95	4.21
Rakers, Jason, Cle	.000	.500	7.00	4.65	.000	.500	7.00	4.65
Ramirez, Roberto, SD	.211	.348	5.61	4.23	.211	.348	5.61	4.23
Rapp, Pat, KC	.285	.381	5.84	4.65	.279	.368	4.99	4.27
Rath, Fred, Col	.300	.348	4.03	4.23	.300	.348	4.03	4.23
Rath, Gary, LA	.250	.357	5.66	4.23	.250	.357	5.66	4.23
Reed, Rick, NYN	.261	.290	3.39	4.23	.262	.298	3.44	4.08
Reed, Steve, SF/Cle	.194	.275	2.42	4.36	.236	.306	3.50	4.18
Rekar, Bryan, TB	.282	.321	4.69	4.65	.298	.351	5.57	4.36
Remlinger, Mike, Cin	.266	.358	5.04	4.23	.253	.352	4.67	4.17
Reyes, Al, Mil	.255	.352	5.01	4.23	.242	.335	4.31	4.47
Reyes, Carlos, SD/Bos	.242	.306	3.21	4.47	.272	.347	4.89	4.75
Reyes, Dennis, LA/Cin	.255	.375	4.37	4.23	.266	.364	4.37	4.22
Reynolds, Shane, Hou	.280	.318	4.05	4.23	.268	.308	3.58	4.19
Reynoso, A., NYN	.256	.351	4.01	4.23	.286	.352	4.91	4.14
Rhodes, Arthur, Bal	.233	.313	3.47	4.65	.249	.334	4.22	4.49
Rincon, Ricardo, Pit	.208	.292	2.88	4.23	.219	.300	2.98	4.22
Rios, Danny, KC	.300	.421	7.92	4.65	.391	.491	15.67	4.63
Risley, Bill, Tor	.259	.372	5.14	4.65	.225	.313	3.62	4.73

	1998				Career			
Pitcher, Team	OAvg	OOB	ERC	LERA	OAvg	OOB	ERC	LERA
Ritchie, Todd, Min	.288	.345	4.75	4.65	.290	.351	5.27	4.58
Ritz, Kevin, Col	.395	.435	9.49	4.23	.287	.371	5.28	4.14
Rivera, Mariano, NYA	.215	.270	2.21	4.65	.223	.287	2.69	4.76
Rizzo, Todd, ChA	.387	.474	10.16	4.65	.387	.474	10.16	4.65
Robertson, Rich, Ana	.393	.419	13.25	4.65	.284	.375	5.64	4.75
Rocker, John, Atl	.172	.307	2.73	4.23	.172	.307	2.73	4.23
Rodriguez, Felix, Ari	.259	.365	5.11	4.23	.266	.374	5.21	4.21
Rodriguez, Frank, Min	.303	.369	5.65	4.65	.277	.351	4.82	4.77
Rodriguez, N., Bal/Tor	.310	.398	6.21	4.65	.279	.355	4.96	4.71
Rodriguez, Rich, SF	.272	.322	3.94	4.23	.254	.325	3.67	3.93
Rogers, Kenny, Oak	.242	.299	3.13	4.65	.257	.328	4.00	4.50
Rojas, Mel, NYN	.305	.391	6.24	4.23	.234	.310	3.33	4.01
Roque, Rafael, Mil	.237	.332	4.50	4.23	.237	.332	4.50	4.23
Rosado, Jose, KC	.260	.320	4.31	4.65	.260	.318	4.02	4.69
Rose, Brian, Bos	.285	.351	6.07	4.65	.291	.359	6.24	4.64
Ruebel, Matt, TB	.314	.385	8.17	4.65	.292	.367	5.75	4.24
Rueter, Kirk, SF	.265	.321	4.27	4.23	.267	.315	3.80	4.19
Runyan, Sean, Det	.255	.348	4.67	4.65	.255	.348	4.67	4.65
Rusch, Glendon, KC	.304	.358	5.62	4.65	.302	.355	5.59	4.60
Ryan, Ken, Phi	.253	.396	5.17	4.23	.249	.350	4.07	4.39
Saberhagen, Bret, Bos	.264	.299	3.65	4.65	.251	.289	2.99	4.12
Sager, A.J., Det	.325	.383	6.09	4.65	.297	.353	4.93	4.62
Saipe, Mike, Col	.431	.453	14.60	4.23	.431	.453	14.60	4.23
Sampson, Benj, Min	.172	.254	1.49	4.65	.172	.254	1.49	4.65
Sanchez, Jesus, Fla	.272	.363	4.91	4.23	.272	.363	4.91	4.23
Sanders, Scott, Det/SD	.329	.370	6.12	4.33	.253	.322	4.05	4.29
Santana, Julio, Tex/TB	.272	.347	4.75	4.65	.294	.367	5.69	4.61
Santana, Marino, Det	.310	.474	8.74	4.65	.310	.474	8.74	4.65
Santiago, Jose, KC	.444	.444	8.38	4.65	.367	.424	7.12	4.59
Saunders, Tony, TB	.265	.364	4.78	4.65	.258	.358	4.60	4.48
Scanlan, Bob, Hou	.245	.330	4.33	4.23	.276	.344	4.33	4.19
Schilling, Curt, Phi	.236	.282	2.75	4.23	.235	.288	2.86	4.04
Schmidt, Jason, Pit	.275	.334	4.35	4.23	.274	.347	4.60	4.21
Schourek, P., Hou/Bos	.270	.342	4.69	4.38	.266	.330	4.19	4.04
Seanez, Rudy, Atl	.195	.286	2.44	4.23	.253	.355	4.64	4.13
Sele, Aaron, Tex	.283	.354	4.69	4.65	.275	.353	4.74	4.68
Serafini, Dan, Min	.310	.365	5.82	4.65	.304	.364	5.51	4.64
Service, Scott, KC	.231	.322	3.52	4.65	.258	.340	4.27	4.31
Shaw, Jeff, Cin/LA	.240	.284	2.75	4.23	.258	.313	3.61	4.15
Shouse, Brian, Bos	.281	.361	6.42	4.65	.314	.379	7.56	4.45
Shuey, Paul, Cle	.229	.327	3.83	4.65	.252	.351	4.51	4.75
Silva, Jose, Pit	.271	.321	3.70	4.23	.295	.348	4.63	4.23
Simas, Bill, ChA	.206	.270	2.87	4.65	.248	.336	4.28	4.76
Sinclair, Steve, Tor	.232	.295	2.51	4.65	.232	.295	2.51	4.65
Sirotka, Mike, ChA	.300	.336	4.91	4.65	.300	.342	4.96	4.68
Slocumb, H., Sea	.275	.379	5.27	4.65	.263	.358	4.35	4.33
Small, Aaron, Oak/Ari	.305	.365	5.38	4.45	.302	.376	5.51	4.58
Smith, Pete, SD/Bal	.290	.354	5.25	4.44	.266	.333	4.33	3.85
Smith, Travis, Mil	.143	.143	0.54	4.23	.143	.143	0.54	4.23
Smoltz, John, Atl	.231	.285	2.67	4.23	.232	.296	2.98	3.93
Snyder, John, ChA	.286	.332	4.76	4.65	.286	.332	4.76	4.65
Sodowsky, Clint, Ari	.283	.375	5.06	4.23	.283	.388	5.95	4.39
Sparks, Steve, Ana	.263	.345	4.60	4.65	.275	.356	5.01	4.75
Speier, Justin, ChN/Fla	.325	.412	8.94	4.23	.325	.412	8.94	4.23
Spencer, Stan, SD	.244	.274	3.25	4.23	.244	.274	3.25	4.23
Spoljaric, Paul, Sea	.263	.369	5.69	4.65	.247	.354	4.83	4.69
Spradlin, Jerry, Phi	.216	.270	2.50	4.23	.251	.300	3.31	4.18
Springer, Dennis, TB	.271	.372	5.94	4.65	.264	.346	5.22	4.66
Springer, Russ, Ari/Atl	.258	.357	4.38	4.23	.272	.352	5.06	4.35
Stanifer, Robby, Fla	.277	.345	4.78	4.23	.269	.342	4.78	4.22
Stanton, Mike, NYA	.239	.307	3.88	4.65	.246	.321	3.62	4.24
Steenstra, Kennie, ChN	.412	.444	15.36	4.23	.412	.444	15.36	4.23
Stein, Blake, Oak	.255	.359	5.64	4.65	.255	.359	5.64	4.65
Stephenson, G., Phi	.316	.427	8.16	4.23	.267	.340	4.37	4.24
Stevens, Dave, ChN	.288	.364	5.23	4.23	.297	.376	6.35	4.69
Stieb, Dave, Tor	.284	.351	5.16	4.65	.239	.312	3.34	4.05
Stoops, Jim, Col	.385	.529	11.67	4.23	.385	.529	11.67	4.23
Stottlemyre, T., StL/Tex	.252	.318	3.88	4.34	.261	.329	4.13	4.23
Sullivan, Scott, Cin	.253	.327	4.22	4.23	.238	.314	3.65	4.21
Suppan, Jeff, Ari/KC	.287	.333	4.95	4.30	.302	.353	5.40	4.53
Suzuki, Makoto, Sea	.304	.386	6.52	4.65	.305	.393	6.66	4.66
Swift, Bill, Sea	.306	.369	6.05	4.65	.274	.333	4.00	4.06
Swindell, Greg, Min/Bos	.267	.331	4.39	4.65	.271	.310	3.76	4.07
Tabaka, Jeff, Pit	.204	.305	3.13	4.23	.233	.343	4.15	4.21
Tam, Jeff, NYN	.241	.317	3.86	4.23	.241	.317	3.86	4.23
Tapani, Kevin, ChN	.284	.333	4.59	4.23	.271	.315	3.89	4.33
Tatis, Ramon, TB	.418	.556	16.38	4.65	.331	.430	8.44	4.28
Tavarez, Julian, SF	.298	.379	4.89	4.23	.289	.349	4.60	4.51
Taylor, Billy, Oak	.255	.312	3.56	4.65	.243	.321	3.48	4.73
Telemaco, A., ChN/Ari	.262	.318	3.97	4.23	.274	.328	4.52	4.22
Telford, Anthony, Mon	.247	.322	3.75	4.23	.256	.328	4.10	4.16
Telgheder, Dave, Oak	.235	.303	4.18	4.65	.297	.351	5.36	4.51

Pitcher, Team	1998				Career			
	OAvg	OOB	ERC	LERA	OAvg	OOB	ERC	LERA
Tessmer, Jay, NYA	.143	.242	1.74	4.65	.143	.242	1.74	4.65
Tewksbury, Bob, Min	.292	.318	4.31	4.65	.287	.316	3.79	4.10
Thompson, Justin, Det	.267	.329	4.00	4.65	.253	.316	3.61	4.65
Thompson, Mark, Col	.379	.465	11.65	4.23	.313	.392	6.83	4.21
Thomson, John, Col	.282	.335	4.51	4.23	.290	.343	4.63	4.21
Thurman, Mike, Mon	.238	.312	3.57	4.23	.231	.306	3.56	4.23
Timlin, Mike, Sea	.264	.306	3.17	4.65	.253	.324	3.55	4.47
Tomko, Brett, Cin	.247	.307	3.50	4.23	.242	.307	3.42	4.22
Trachsel, Steve, ChN	.260	.334	4.35	4.23	.260	.327	4.31	4.20
Trombley, Mike, Min	.248	.332	4.46	4.65	.263	.334	4.45	4.58
Urbina, Ugueth, Mon	.157	.259	1.59	4.23	.216	.299	3.30	4.21
Valdes, Ismael, LA	.256	.323	3.89	4.23	.241	.293	3.04	4.21
Valdes, Marc, Mon	.285	.375	6.06	4.23	.280	.364	4.95	4.21
Valdez, Carlos, Bos	.100	.375	3.41	4.65	.290	.400	5.85	4.27
Valdez, Efrain, Ari	.368	.400	10.46	4.23	.254	.342	4.26	3.98
Van Poppel, T., Tex/Pit	.295	.360	5.47	4.35	.272	.369	5.67	4.67
VanRyn, B, ChN/SD/Tor	.316	.444	7.06	4.34	.311	.442	6.95	4.39
Vazquez, Javier, Mon	.292	.364	5.79	4.23	.292	.364	5.79	4.23
Veras, Dario, Bos	.343	.465	8.80	4.65	.268	.355	4.90	4.26
Veres, Dave, Col	.233	.301	3.15	4.23	.254	.319	3.63	4.20
Villone, Ron, Cle	.297	.425	7.01	4.65	.255	.378	5.58	4.56
Wade, Terrell, TB	.318	.348	6.51	4.65	.279	.369	5.47	4.25
Wagner, Billy, Hou	.211	.292	2.87	4.23	.196	.296	2.78	4.21
Wagner, Paul, Mil	.302	.387	6.59	4.23	.277	.351	4.72	4.15
Wainhouse, David, Col	.341	.431	7.60	4.23	.299	.398	6.35	4.19
Wakefield, Tim, Bos	.252	.324	4.30	4.65	.258	.337	4.46	4.54
Walker, Jamie, KC	.380	.412	9.69	4.65	.305	.371	6.33	4.59
Wall, Donne, SD	.202	.293	2.69	4.23	.275	.330	4.39	4.21
Ward, Bryan, ChA	.278	.319	4.46	4.65	.278	.319	4.46	4.65
Wasdin, John, Bos	.288	.333	4.70	4.65	.271	.326	4.54	4.74
Washburn, Jarrod, Ana	.248	.317	4.09	4.65	.248	.317	4.09	4.65
Watson, Allen, Ana	.323	.378	6.30	4.65	.284	.351	5.17	4.33
Weathers, Dave, Cin/Mil	.295	.358	4.73	4.23	.304	.381	5.58	4.23
Weaver, Eric, LA	.179	.324	2.77	4.23	.179	.324	2.77	4.23
Weber, Neil, Ari	.417	.533	14.38	4.23	.417	.533	14.38	4.23
Welch, Mike, Phi	.310	.376	7.74	4.23	.310	.376	7.74	4.23
Wells, Bob, Sea	.261	.319	4.89	4.65	.282	.346	5.34	4.77
Wells, David, NYA	.239	.265	2.83	4.65	.259	.304	3.59	4.40
Wendell, Turk, NYN	.221	.306	2.78	4.23	.246	.340	4.10	4.20
Wengert, Don, SD/ChN	.297	.373	6.13	4.23	.307	.368	6.03	4.70
West, David, Bos	.538	.700	44.11	4.65	.244	.341	4.37	4.02
Wetteland, John, Tex	.203	.247	2.09	4.65	.207	.274	2.42	4.15
Whisenant, Matt, KC	.271	.365	4.53	4.65	.260	.370	4.57	4.61
White, Gabe, Cin	.231	.284	3.30	4.23	.244	.298	3.76	4.21
White, Rick, TB	.253	.315	3.82	4.65	.276	.331	4.17	4.35
Whiten, Mark, Cle	.250	.571	13.82	4.65	.250	.571	13.82	4.65
Whiteside, Matt, Phi	.338	.376	8.40	4.23	.284	.344	4.65	4.55
Wickman, Bob, Mil	.262	.352	4.05	4.23	.264	.345	4.20	4.53
Wilkins, Marc, Pit	.236	.358	4.07	4.23	.252	.347	4.09	4.21
Williams, Mike, Pit	.211	.271	1.95	4.23	.269	.335	4.34	4.15
Williams, Todd, Cin	.341	.420	8.58	4.23	.293	.362	5.42	4.20
Williams, Woody, Tor	.245	.314	4.15	4.65	.252	.325	4.25	4.65
Wilson, Trevor, Ana	.267	.378	4.40	4.65	.249	.330	3.73	3.76
Winchester, Scott, Cin	.312	.370	6.07	4.23	.315	.374	6.20	4.23
Winston, Darrin, Phi	.298	.348	6.36	4.23	.262	.321	5.39	4.22
Witasick, Jay, Oak	.310	.389	8.53	4.65	.294	.370	7.39	4.72
Withem, Shannon, Tor	.250	.357	4.23	4.65	.250	.357	4.23	4.65
Witt, Bobby, Tex/StL	.313	.380	6.64	4.48	.261	.355	4.73	4.29
Wohlers, Mark, Atl	.231	.464	8.41	4.23	.232	.326	3.33	4.09
Wolcott, Bob, Ari	.252	.321	4.62	4.23	.298	.358	5.87	4.75
Wood, Kerry, ChN	.196	.306	3.03	4.23	.196	.306	3.03	4.23
Woodall, Brad, Mil	.273	.337	4.89	4.23	.281	.343	5.16	4.22
Woodard, Steve, Mil	.264	.307	3.73	4.23	.265	.307	3.77	4.29
Worrell, T, Det/Cle/Oak	.262	.311	4.10	4.65	.259	.327	4.13	4.27
Wright, Jamey, Col	.294	.374	5.57	4.23	.306	.386	6.01	4.22
Wright, Jaret, Cle	.277	.358	5.07	4.65	.265	.345	4.59	4.62
Yan, Esteban, TB	.236	.326	4.02	4.65	.266	.352	5.21	4.67
Yoshii, Masato, NYN	.255	.316	3.83	4.23	.255	.316	3.83	4.23
Young, Tim, Mon	.250	.357	4.07	4.23	.250	.357	4.07	4.23

Leader Boards

The Leader Boards section always provides some of the best nuggets. Here's a sampling from this year's lists: Barry Bonds and Mark McGwire were the two most pitched-around sluggers in baseball last year, and no one else was even close. Bonds led the majors with 29 intentional walks; McGwire received 28 free passes, twice as many as anyone else, save for Bonds. It's easy to see a young Roger Clemens in Kerry Wood. In fact, the way Clemens is throwing, it's easy to see a young Roger Clemens in the old Rocket, too. Only two starting pitchers held opponents to a sub-.200 batting average last year: Wood (.196) and Clemens (.198). Who says youngsters crack under pressure? The leading hitter with runners in scoring position last year was sophomore outfielder Bob Abreu, who notched 44 hits in 103 at-bats for a cool .427 average. The "Big Cat" comes up biggest when the game's on the line. In the late innings of close games, Andres Galarraga hit .446 in 56 at-bats. No one else in the majors batted over .400 in those situations. Jose Cruz Jr. may have had a disappointing season, but he didn't ground into a single double play in 105 games. Willie Blair's ERA rose by 0.81 runs, and his record dropped from 16-8 to 5-16. Kirk Rueter's ERA rose by 0.91, and his record went from 13-6 to 16-9. What's the difference? Run support. Blair's clubs scored only 3.29 runs per nine innings for him, the worst mark in baseball. Meanwhile, Rueter enjoyed the best support in the bigs, 7.91 runs per nine innings.

There's plenty more where that came from. Read on.

1998 American League Batting Leaders

Batting Average
minimum 3.1 PA per game

Player, Team	AB	H	AVG
B Williams, NYA	**499**	**169**	**.339**
M Vaughn, Bos	609	205	.337
A Belle, ChA	609	200	.328
E Davis, Bal	452	148	.327
D Jeter, NYA	626	203	.324
N Garciaparra, Bos	604	195	.323
E Martinez, Sea	556	179	.322
I Rodriguez, Tex	579	186	.321
T Fernandez, Tor	486	156	.321
J Gonzalez, Tex	606	193	.318

On-Base Percentage
minimum 3.1 PA per game

Player, Team	PA*	OB	OBP
E Martinez, Sea	**672**	**288**	**.429**
B Williams, NYA	578	244	.422
J Thome, Cle	537	222	.413
T Salmon, Ana	566	232	.410
J Offerman, KC	707	285	.403
M Vaughn, Bos	681	274	.402
A Belle, ChA	706	282	.399
E Davis, Bal	508	197	.388
T Fernandez, Tor	548	212	.387
M Lawton, Min	662	256	.387

* AB, BB, HBP, SF

Slugging Percentage
minimum 3.1 PA per game

Player, Team	AB	TB	SLG
A Belle, ChA	**609**	**399**	**.655**
J Gonzalez, Tex	606	382	.630
K Griffey Jr., Sea	633	387	.611
M Ramirez, Cle	571	342	.599
C Delgado, Tor	530	314	.592
M Vaughn, Bos	609	360	.591
N Garciaparra, Bos	604	353	.584
J Thome, Cle	440	257	.584
E Davis, Bal	452	263	.582
B Williams, NYA	499	287	.575

Games

A Belle, ChA	**163**
B Surhoff, Bal	162
R Palmeiro, Bal	162
5 players tied with	161

Plate Appearances

A Rodriguez, Sea	**748**
R Durham, ChA	723
K Griffey Jr., Sea	720
F Thomas, ChA	712
J Damon, KC	710

At-Bats

A Rodriguez, Sea	**686**
J Damon, KC	642
R Durham, ChA	635
K Griffey Jr., Sea	633
S Green, Tor	630

Hits

A Rodriguez, Sea	**213**
M Vaughn, Bos	205
D Jeter, NYA	203
A Belle, ChA	200
N Garciaparra, Bos	195

Singles

D Jeter, NYA	**151**
J Offerman, KC	143
T Goodwin, Tex	133
M Vaughn, Bos	132
M Caruso, ChA	132

Doubles

J Gonzalez, Tex	**50**
A Belle, ChA	48
E Martinez, Sea	46
J Valentin, Bos	44
C Delgado, Tor	43

Triples

J Offerman, KC	**13**
J Damon, KC	10
R Winn, TB	9
4 players tied with	8

Home Runs

K Griffey Jr., Sea	**56**
A Belle, ChA	49
J Canseco, Tor	46
J Gonzalez, Tex	45
M Ramirez, Cle	45

Total Bases

A Belle, ChA	**399**
K Griffey Jr., Sea	387
A Rodriguez, Sea	384
J Gonzalez, Tex	382
M Vaughn, Bos	360

Runs Scored

D Jeter, NYA	**127**
R Durham, ChA	126
A Rodriguez, Sea	123
K Griffey Jr., Sea	120
C Knoblauch, NYA	117

Runs Batted In

J Gonzalez, Tex	**157**
A Belle, ChA	152
K Griffey Jr., Sea	146
M Ramirez, Cle	145
A Rodriguez, Sea	124

Ground Double Play

R Coomer, Min	**22**
P O'Neill, NYA	**22**
N Garciaparra, Bos	20
J Gonzalez, Tex	20
4 players tied with	19

Sacrifice Hits

M Bordick, Bal	**15**
A Gonzalez, Tor	13
A Hinch, Oak	13
M Benjamin, Bos	13
4 players tied with	12

Sacrifice Flies

A Belle, ChA	**15**
D Palmer, KC	13
J Gonzalez, Tex	11
F Thomas, ChA	11
P O'Neill, NYA	11

Stolen Bases

R Henderson, Oak	**66**
K Lofton, Cle	54
S Stewart, Tor	51
A Rodriguez, Sea	46
J Offerman, KC	45

Caught Stealing

T Goodwin, Tex	**20**
S Stewart, Tor	18
J Canseco, Tor	17
R Henderson, Oak	13
A Rodriguez, Sea	13

Walks

R Henderson, Oak	**118**
F Thomas, ChA	110
E Martinez, Sea	106
T Salmon, Ana	90
J Thome, Cle	90

Intentional Walks

R Ventura, ChA	**15**
C Delgado, Tor	13
M Vaughn, Bos	13
K Griffey Jr., Sea	11
A Belle, ChA	10

Hit by Pitch

C Knoblauch, NYA	**18**
D Easley, Det	16
S Fasano, KC	16
3 players tied with	15

Strikeouts

J Canseco, Tor	**159**
M Vaughn, Bos	144
S Green, Tor	142
J Thome, Cle	141
C Delgado, Tor	139

1998 National League Batting Leaders

Batting Average
minimum 3.1 PA per game

Player, Team	AB	H	AVG
L Walker, Col	454	165	.363
J Olerud, NYN	557	197	.354
D Bichette, Col	662	219	.331
M Piazza, LA-Fla-NYN	561	184	.328
J Kendall, Pit	535	175	.327
C Biggio, Hou	646	210	.325
V Guerrero, Mon	623	202	.324
J Cirillo, Mil	604	194	.321
T Gwynn, SD	461	148	.321
V Castilla, Col	645	206	.319

On-Base Percentage
minimum 3.1 PA per game

Player, Team	PA*	OB	OBP
M McGwire, StL	681	320	.470
J Olerud, NYN	664	297	.447
L Walker, Col	524	233	.445
B Bonds, SF	696	305	.438
G Sheffield, Fla-LA	549	235	.428
J Bagwell, Hou	661	280	.424
J Kendall, Pit	625	257	.411
B Abreu, Phi	585	239	.409
C Jones, Atl	706	285	.404
C Biggio, Hou	737	297	.403

* AB, BB, HBP, SF

Slugging Percentage
minimum 3.1 PA per game

Player, Team	AB	TB	SLG
M McGwire, StL	509	383	.752
S Sosa, ChN	643	416	.647
L Walker, Col	454	286	.630
B Bonds, SF	552	336	.609
G Vaughn, SD	573	342	.597
A Galarraga, Atl	555	330	.595
V Castilla, Col	645	380	.589
V Guerrero, Mon	623	367	.589
M Alou, Hou	584	340	.582
M Piazza, LA-Fla-NYN	561	320	.570

Games

N Perez, Col	162
V Castilla, Col	162
J Burnitz, Mil	161
D Bichette, Col	161
4 players tied with	160

Plate Appearances

C Biggio, Hou	738
D Glanville, Phi	735
S Sosa, ChN	722
F Vina, Mil	722
N Perez, Col	712

At-Bats

D Glanville, Phi	678
D Bichette, Col	662
T Womack, Pit	655
N Perez, Col	647
C Biggio, Hou	646

Hits

D Bichette, Col	219
C Biggio, Hou	210
V Castilla, Col	206
V Guerrero, Mon	202
3 players tied with	198

Singles

T Womack, Pit	149
J Cirillo, Mil	148
D Bichette, Col	147
D Glanville, Phi	146
F Vina, Mil	145

Doubles

C Biggio, Hou	51
D Young, Cin	48
D Bichette, Col	48
L Walker, Col	46
2 players tied with	45

Triples

D Dellucci, Ari	12
B Larkin, Cin	10
W Guerrero, LA-Mon	9
N Perez, Col	9
3 players tied with	8

Home Runs

M McGwire, StL	70
S Sosa, ChN	66
G Vaughn, SD	50
V Castilla, Col	46
A Galarraga, Atl	44

Total Bases

S Sosa, ChN	416
M McGwire, StL	383
V Castilla, Col	380
V Guerrero, Mon	367
G Vaughn, SD	342

Runs Scored

S Sosa, ChN	134
M McGwire, StL	130
J Bagwell, Hou	124
C Biggio, Hou	123
C Jones, Atl	123

Runs Batted In

S Sosa, ChN	158
M McGwire, StL	147
V Castilla, Col	144
J Kent, SF	128
J Burnitz, Mil	125

Ground Double Play

J Cirillo, Mil	26
V Castilla, Col	24
B Boone, Cin	23
J Lopez, Atl	22
D Bichette, Col	22

Sacrifice Hits

N Perez, Col	22
T Jones, Mon	15
R Ordonez, NYN	15
T Glavine, Atl	14
C Perez, Mon-LA	14

Sacrifice Flies

J Kent, SF	10
R Brogna, Phi	10
D Bell, Hou	10
3 players tied with	9

Stolen Bases

T Womack, Pit	58
C Biggio, Hou	50
E Young, LA	42
E Renteria, Fla	41
B Bonds, SF	28

Caught Stealing

E Renteria, Fla	22
F Vina, Mil	16
C Floyd, Fla	14
E Young, LA	13
2 players tied with	12

Walks

M McGwire, StL	162
B Bonds, SF	130
J Bagwell, Hou	109
C Jones, Atl	96
J Olerud, NYN	96

Intentional Walks

B Bonds, SF	29
M McGwire, StL	28
B Abreu, Phi	14
M Piazza, LA-Fla-NYN	14
S Sosa, ChN	14

Hit by Pitch

J Kendall, Pit	31
F Vina, Mil	25
A Galarraga, Atl	25
F Santangelo, Mon	23
C Biggio, Hou	23

Strikeouts

S Sosa, ChN	171
J Burnitz, Mil	158
M McGwire, StL	155
R Lankford, StL	151
A Galarraga, Atl	146

1998 American League Pitching Leaders

Earned Run Average
minimum 162 innings pitched

Pitcher, Team	IP	ER	ERA
R Clemens, Tor	**234.2**	**69**	**2.65**
P Martinez, Bos	233.2	75	2.89
K Rogers, Oak	238.2	84	3.17
C Finley, Ana	223.1	84	3.39
D Wells, NYA	214.1	83	3.49
M Mussina, Bal	206.1	80	3.49
J Moyer, Sea	234.1	92	3.53
D Cone, NYA	207.2	82	3.55
R Arrojo, TB	202.0	80	3.56
B Colon, Cle	204.0	84	3.71

Won-Lost Percentage
minimum 13 decisions

Pitcher, Team	W	L	WL%
D Wells, NYA	**18**	**4**	**.818**
R Clemens, Tor	20	6	.769
O Hernandez, NYA	12	4	.750
D Cone, NYA	20	7	.741
R Helling, Tex	20	7	.741
P Martinez, Bos	19	7	.731
J Baldwin, ChA	13	6	.684
T Wakefield, Bos	17	8	.680
K Rogers, Oak	16	8	.667
B Saberhagen, Bos	15	8	.652

Opposition Average
minimum 600 batters faced

Pitcher, Team	AB	H	AVG
R Clemens, Tor	**855**	**169**	**.198**
P Martinez, Bos	865	188	.217
H Irabu, NYA	635	148	.233
D Cone, NYA	784	186	.237
D Wells, NYA	817	195	.239
J Guzman, Tor-Bal	805	193	.240
M Mussina, Bal	780	189	.242
K Rogers, Oak	887	215	.242
W Williams, Tor	800	196	.245
C Finley, Ana	853	210	.246

Games
S Runyan, Det	**88**
P Quantrill, Tor	82
G Swindell, Min-Bos	81
E Guardado, Min	79
D Plesac, Tor	78

Games Started
S Erickson, Bal	**36**
5 pitchers tied with	34

Complete Games
S Erickson, Bal	**11**
D Wells, NYA	8
J Fassero, Sea	7
K Rogers, Oak	7
2 pitchers tied with	6

Games Finished
T Gordon, Bos	**69**
R Aguilera, Min	64
T Percival, Ana	60
J Wetteland, Tex	59
2 pitchers tied with	58

Wins
R Helling, Tex	**20**
R Clemens, Tor	**20**
D Cone, NYA	**20**
P Martinez, Bos	19
A Sele, Tex	19

Losses
T Candiotti, Oak	**16**
J Guzman, Tor-Bal	**16**
J Navarro, ChA	**16**
4 pitchers tied with	15

Saves
T Gordon, Bos	**46**
T Percival, Ana	42
J Wetteland, Tex	42
M Jackson, Cle	40
R Aguilera, Min	38

Shutouts
D Wells, NYA	**5**
J Moyer, Sea	3
R Clemens, Tor	3
B Moehler, Det	3
8 pitchers tied with	2

Hits Allowed
S Erickson, Bal	**284**
M Sirotka, ChA	255
C Nagy, Cle	250
T Belcher, KC	247
A Sele, Tex	239

Doubles Allowed
J Moyer, Sea	**64**
J Haynes, Oak	53
K Cloude, Sea	52
C Nagy, Cle	52
J Guzman, Tor-Bal	51

Triples Allowed
J Guzman, Tor-Bal	**8**
W Williams, Tor	**8**
4 pitchers tied with	7

Home Runs Allowed
T Belcher, KC	**37**
W Williams, Tor	36
C Nagy, Cle	34
J Fassero, Sea	33
6 pitchers tied with	30

Batters Faced
S Erickson, Bal	**1102**
T Belcher, KC	1003
C Finley, Ana	976
J Moyer, Sea	974
K Rogers, Oak	970

Innings Pitched
S Erickson, Bal	**251.1**
K Rogers, Oak	238.2
R Clemens, Tor	234.2
J Moyer, Sea	234.1
T Belcher, KC	234.0

Runs Allowed
C Nagy, Cle	**139**
M Sirotka, ChA	137
J Navarro, ChA	135
J Burkett, Tex	131
T Belcher, KC	127

Strikeouts
R Clemens, Tor	**271**
P Martinez, Bos	251
R Johnson, Sea	213
C Finley, Ana	212
D Cone, NYA	209

Walks Allowed
T Saunders, TB	**111**
C Finley, Ana	109
P Rapp, KC	107
J Guzman, Tor-Bal	98
O Olivares, Ana	91

Hit Batters
R Arrojo, TB	**19**
D Cone, NYA	15
T Wakefield, Bos	14
S Erickson, Bal	13
A Sele, Tex	13

Wild Pitches
J Navarro, ChA	**18**
B Stein, Oak	15
P Rapp, KC	14
T Candiotti, Oak	14
J Fassero, Sea	12

Balks
J Parque, ChA	**3**
M Jackson, Cle	**3**
C Castillo, ChA	**3**
6 pitchers tied with	2

1998 National League Pitching Leaders

Earned Run Average
minimum 162 innings pitched

Pitcher, Team	IP	ER	ERA
G Maddux, Atl	**251.0**	**62**	**2.22**
K Brown, SD	257.0	68	2.38
A Leiter, NYN	193.0	53	2.47
T Glavine, Atl	229.1	63	2.47
O Daal, Ari	162.2	52	2.88
J Smoltz, Atl	167.2	54	2.90
D Hermanson, Mon	187.0	65	3.13
P Harnisch, Cin	209.0	73	3.14
C Schilling, Phi	268.2	97	3.25
F Cordova, Pit	220.1	81	3.31

Won-Lost Percentage
minimum 13 decisions

Pitcher, Team	W	L	WL%
J Smoltz, Atl	**17**	**3**	**.850**
T Glavine, Atl	20	6	.769
A Leiter, NYN	17	6	.739
K Brown, SD	18	7	.720
S Reynolds, Hou	19	8	.704
M Gardner, SF	13	6	.684
K Wood, ChN	13	6	.684
K Millwood, Atl	17	8	.680
K Tapani, ChN	19	9	.679
G Maddux, Atl	18	9	.667

Opposition Average
minimum 600 batters faced

Pitcher, Team	AB	H	AVG
K Wood, ChN	**597**	**117**	**.196**
A Leiter, NYN	699	151	.216
G Maddux, Atl	915	201	.220
P Harnisch, Cin	771	176	.228
J Smoltz, Atl	627	145	.231
D Hermanson, Mon	697	163	.234
K Brown, SD	957	225	.235
C Schilling, Phi	1000	236	.236
T Glavine, Atl	850	202	.238
C Park, LA	817	199	.244

Games

R Beck, ChN	**81**
C McElroy, Col	78
S Kline, Mon	78
R Nen, SF	78
A Telford, Mon	77

Games Started

D Kile, Col	**35**
S Reynolds, Hou	**35**
K Brown, SD	**35**
C Schilling, Phi	**35**
10 pitchers tied with	34

Complete Games

C Schilling, Phi	**15**
G Maddux, Atl	9
L Hernandez, Fla	9
K Brown, SD	7
C Perez, Mon-LA	7

Games Finished

R Beck, ChN	**70**
J Shaw, Cin-LA	69
R Nen, SF	67
T Hoffman, SD	61
U Urbina, Mon	59

Wins

T Glavine, Atl	**20**
K Tapani, ChN	19
S Reynolds, Hou	19
G Maddux, Atl	18
K Brown, SD	18

Losses

D Kile, Col	**17**
W Blair, Ari-NYN	16
J Vazquez, Mon	15
M Remlinger, Cin	15
8 pitchers tied with	14

Saves

T Hoffman, SD	**53**
R Beck, ChN	51
J Shaw, Cin-LA	48
R Nen, SF	40
J Franco, NYN	38

Shutouts

G Maddux, Atl	**5**
R Johnson, Hou	4
T Glavine, Atl	3
K Brown, SD	3
9 pitchers tied with	2

Hits Allowed

L Hernandez, Fla	**265**
D Kile, Col	257
S Reynolds, Hou	257
P Astacio, Col	245
2 pitchers tied with	244

Doubles Allowed

C Schilling, Phi	**56**
S Reynolds, Hou	53
J Wright, Col	51
K Tapani, ChN	50
4 pitchers tied with	49

Triples Allowed

M Gardner, SF	**10**
J Hamilton, SD	9
C Perez, Mon-LA	9
A Benes, Ari	8
P Astacio, Col	8

Home Runs Allowed

B Anderson, Ari	**39**
P Astacio, Col	**39**
L Hernandez, Fla	37
J Lima, Hou	34
2 pitchers tied with	31

Batters Faced

C Schilling, Phi	**1089**
L Hernandez, Fla	1040
K Brown, SD	1032
D Kile, Col	1020
C Perez, Mon-LA	1009

Innings Pitched

C Schilling, Phi	**268.2**
K Brown, SD	257.0
G Maddux, Atl	251.0
C Perez, Mon-LA	241.0
L Hernandez, Fla	234.1

Runs Allowed

P Astacio, Col	**160**
J Wright, Col	143
D Kile, Col	141
L Hernandez, Fla	133
J Vazquez, Mon	121

Strikeouts

C Schilling, Phi	**300**
K Brown, SD	257
K Wood, ChN	233
S Reynolds, Hou	209
G Maddux, Atl	204

Walks Allowed

J Hamilton, SD	**106**
L Hernandez, Fla	104
C Park, LA	97
D Kile, Col	96
J Wright, Col	95

Hit Batters

P Astacio, Col	**17**
O Hershiser, SF	13
6 pitchers tied with	11

Wild Pitches

J Schmidt, Pit	**15**
H Nomo, LA-NYN	13
O Hershiser, SF	12
D Kile, Col	12
C Schilling, Phi	12

Balks

B Anderson, Ari	**6**
J Sanchez, Fla	5
K Mercker, StL	4
H Nomo, LA-NYN	4
10 pitchers tied with	3

1998 American League Special Batting Leaders

Scoring Position
minimum 100 PA

Player, Team	AB	H	AVG
S Brosius, NYA	155	58	.374
T Fernandez, Tor	131	46	.351
J Offerman, KC	143	50	.350
P Molitor, Min	137	47	.343
A Rodriguez, Sea	167	57	.341
D Erstad, Ana	124	42	.339
T Martinez, NYA	160	54	.338
B Williams, NYA	155	52	.335
P O'Neill, NYA	164	55	.335
M McLemore, Tex	111	37	.333

Leadoff Hitters OBP
minimum 150 PA

Player, Team	PA	OB	OBP
T Goodwin, Tex	564	216	.383
S Stewart, Tor	552	209	.379
R Henderson, Oak	663	249	.376
J Cora, Sea-Cle	560	209	.373
K Lofton, Cle	692	255	.368
D Erstad, Ana	446	162	.363
R Durham, ChA	684	247	.361
C Knoblauch, NYA	704	254	.361
O Nixon, Min	494	178	.360
N Garciaparra, Bos	154	54	.351

Cleanup Hitters SLG
minimum 150 PA

Player, Team	AB	TB	SLG
A Belle, ChA	592	391	.660
J Gonzalez, Tex	605	382	.631
N Garciaparra, Bos	249	154	.618
J Thome, Cle	314	188	.599
C Delgado, Tor	517	306	.592
M Ramirez, Cle	272	160	.588
M Vaughn, Bos	206	120	.583
R Palmeiro, Bal	464	260	.560
B Williams, NYA	388	215	.554
E Martinez, Sea	382	210	.550

Vs LHP

S Brosius, NYA	**.370**
T Fernandez, Tor	.361
J Gonzalez, Tex	.355
B Williams, NYA	.350
R Kelly, Tex	.349

Vs RHP

M Vaughn, Bos	**.338**
B Williams, NYA	.333
A Belle, ChA	.333
P O'Neill, NYA	.331
T Walker, Min	.326

BA at Home

B Williams, NYA	**.355**
A Belle, ChA	.348
M Vaughn, Bos	.345
J Gonzalez, Tex	.345
T Walker, Min	.344

BA on the Road

A Rodriguez, Sea	**.335**
M Vaughn, Bos	.329
B Grieve, Oak	.323
E Martinez, Sea	.322
N Garciaparra, Bos	.322

OBP vs LHP

E Martinez, Sea	**.468**
B Williams, NYA	.443
S Brosius, NYA	.436
J Gonzalez, Tex	.429
T Raines, NYA	.428

OBP vs RHP

E Martinez, Sea	**.418**
T Salmon, Ana	.416
B Williams, NYA	.411
B Grieve, Oak	.410
A Belle, ChA	.405

Late & Close

I Rodriguez, Tex	**.387**
A Ledesma, TB	.380
N Garciaparra, Bos	.375
E Davis, Bal	.371
M Vaughn, Bos	.365

Bases Loaded

R Durham, ChA	**.667**
M Ramirez, Cle	.500
J Giambi, Oak	.500
M Cordova, Min	.500
C Kreuter, ChA-Ana	.500

SLG vs LHP

M Ramirez, Cle	**.767**
K Griffey Jr., Sea	.701
S Brosius, NYA	.681
A Belle, ChA	.679
M Simms, Tex	.661

SLG vs RHP

A Belle, ChA	**.648**
C Delgado, Tor	.637
J Gonzalez, Tex	.623
N Garciaparra, Bos	.594
M Vaughn, Bos	.594

AB per HR

K Griffey Jr., Sea	**11.3**
A Belle, ChA	12.4
J Canseco, Tor	12.7
M Ramirez, Cle	12.7
J Gonzalez, Tex	13.5

Times on Base

E Martinez, Sea	**288**
J Offerman, KC	285
A Belle, ChA	282
M Vaughn, Bos	274
F Thomas, ChA	271

Pitches Seen

R Henderson, Oak	**2903**
F Thomas, ChA	2896
C Knoblauch, NYA	2885
J Offerman, KC	2882
R Durham, ChA	2842

Pitches per PA

R Henderson, Oak	**4.33**
C Delgado, Tor	4.14
J Thome, Cle	4.12
C Knoblauch, NYA	4.09
E Martinez, Sea	4.08

% Pitches Taken

R Henderson, Oak	**67.9**
M McLemore, Tex	67.1
E Martinez, Sea	67.1
W Boggs, TB	65.2
B Grieve, Oak	65.0

Ground/Fly Ratio

T Goodwin, Tex	**2.73**
H Morris, KC	2.72
D Lewis, Bos	2.48
D Jeter, NYA	2.46
B Hunter, Det	2.08

GDP/GDP Opp

J Cruz Jr., Tor	**0.00**
R Christenson, Oak	0.01
L Alicea, Tex	0.02
D Strawberry, NYA	0.02
D Erstad, Ana	0.02

SB Success %

K Lofton, Cle	**84.4**
O Nixon, Min	84.1
R Henderson, Oak	83.5
D Jeter, NYA	83.3
C Curtis, NYA	80.8

Steals of Third

K Lofton, Cle	**16**
R Henderson, Oak	15
A Rodriguez, Sea	14
3 players tied with	10

% CS by Catchers

I Rodriguez, Tex	**56.3**
J Posada, NYA	40.0
M DiFelice, TB	39.5
J Flaherty, TB	37.7
T Steinbach, Min	35.1

1998 National League Special Batting Leaders

Scoring Position
minimum 100 PA

Player, Team	AB	H	AVG
B Abreu, Phi	**103**	**44**	**.427**
W Joyner, SD	119	49	.412
F Vina, Mil	108	42	.389
T Helton, Col	132	51	.386
D Bichette, Col	193	72	.373
D Nilsson, Mil	94	34	.362
V Castilla, Col	180	65	.361
D Hamilton, Col	100	36	.360
C Biggio, Hou	139	50	.360
E Taubensee, Cin	112	40	.357

Leadoff Hitters OBP
minimum 150 PA

Player, Team	PA	OB	OBP
M Benard, SF	**226**	**100**	**.442**
C Biggio, Hou	734	296	.403
D Hamilton, SF-Col	636	252	.396
F Vina, Mil	716	277	.387
W Weiss, Atl	407	157	.386
Q Veras, SD	602	227	.377
C Floyd, Fla	163	59	.362
A Fox, Ari	481	174	.362
N Perez, Col	316	113	.358
R Sanders, Cin	390	139	.356

Cleanup Hitters SLG
minimum 150 PA

Player, Team	AB	TB	SLG
S Sosa, ChN	**156**	**113**	**.724**
V Guerrero, Mon	238	157	.660
M Piazza, LA-Fla-NYN	270	178	.659
G Vaughn, SD	214	138	.645
L Walker, Col	146	87	.596
A Galarraga, Atl	553	329	.595
J Bagwell, Hou	367	214	.583
J Kent, SF	480	274	.571
D Bichette, Col	312	166	.532
G Sheffield, Fla-LA	280	148	.529

Vs LHP

J Bagwell, Hou	**.402**
J Olerud, NYN	.375
J Kendall, Pit	.372
G Williams, Atl	.363
B Jordan, StL	.351

Vs RHP

D Bichette, Col	**.346**
J Olerud, NYN	.346
J Cirillo, Mil	.330
M Piazza, LA-Fla-NYN	.329
M Grace, ChN	.329

BA at Home

L Walker, Col	**.418**
D Bichette, Col	.381
V Castilla, Col	.368
T Helton, Col	.354
J Bagwell, Hou	.347

BA on the Road

J Olerud, NYN	**.373**
F Vina, Mil	.350
J Kendall, Pit	.348
M Piazza, LA-Fla-NYN	.346
D Young, Cin	.338

OBP vs LHP

J Bagwell, Hou	**.538**
J Olerud, NYN	.467
M McGwire, StL	.459
J Kendall, Pit	.443
C Biggio, Hou	.438

OBP vs RHP

M McGwire, StL	**.474**
B Bonds, SF	.447
J Olerud, NYN	.440
G Sheffield, Fla-LA	.430
M Grace, ChN	.426

Late & Close

A Galarraga, Atl	**.446**
M Grace, ChN	.385
F Vina, Mil	.368
D Bichette, Col	.364
L Walker, Col	.361

BA Bases Loaded

C Widger, Mon	**.636**
A Boone, Cin	.625
M Grace, ChN	.571
B Abreu, Phi	.571
J Snow, SF	.538

SLG vs LHP

J Bagwell, Hou	**.692**
A Jones, Atl	.681
A Galarraga, Atl	.642
M McGwire, StL	.631
G Williams, Atl	.616

SLG vs RHP

M McGwire, StL	**.794**
S Sosa, ChN	.685
B Bonds, SF	.659
G Vaughn, SD	.623
C Jones, Atl	.610

AB per HR

M McGwire, StL	**7.3**
S Sosa, ChN	9.7
G Vaughn, SD	11.5
A Galarraga, Atl	12.6
V Castilla, Col	14.0

Times on Base

M McGwire, StL	**320**
B Bonds, SF	305
C Biggio, Hou	297
J Olerud, NYN	297
C Jones, Atl	285

Pitches Seen

S Rolen, Phi	**2899**
S Sosa, ChN	2872
J Burnitz, Mil	2766
M McGwire, StL	2692
2 players tied with	2677

Pitches per PA

R Lankford, StL	**4.23**
J Bell, Ari	4.15
E Alfonzo, NYN	4.11
S Rolen, Phi	4.08
B Abreu, Phi	4.04

% Pitches Taken

W Weiss, Atl	**66.8**
J Olerud, NYN	63.3
Q Veras, SD	62.5
M Grace, ChN	62.2
B Bonds, SF	61.6

Ground/Fly Ratio

R Gutierrez, Hou	**2.85**
D Hamilton, SF-Col	2.28
E Renteria, Fla	2.17
Q Veras, SD	2.13
R Sanders, Cin	2.03

GDP/GDP Opp

R Rivera, SD	**0.02**
K Lockhart, Atl	0.02
J Valentin, Mil	0.02
A Fox, Ari	0.03
R Lankford, StL	0.03

SB Success %

B Larkin, Cin	**89.7**
T Womack, Pit	87.9
A Jones, Atl	87.1
A Martin, Pit	87.0
C Biggio, Hou	86.2

Steals of Third

C Biggio, Hou	**11**
B McRae, NYN	9
T Womack, Pit	9
E Renteria, Fla	8
E Young, LA	8

% CS by Catchers

C Johnson, Fla-LA	**39.8**
K Stinnett, Ari	37.2
C Widger, Mon	36.4
B Ausmus, Hou	36.4
J Lopez, Atl	33.8

1998 American League Special Pitching Leaders

Baserunners Per 9 IP
minimum 162 IP

Player, Team	IP	BR	BR/9
D Wells, NYA	**214.1**	**225**	**9.45**
R Clemens, Tor	234.2	264	10.13
P Martinez, Bos	233.2	263	10.13
M Mussina, Bal	206.1	234	10.21
K Rogers, Oak	238.2	289	10.90
J Moyer, Sea	234.1	286	10.98
B Saberhagen, Bos	175.0	216	11.11
D Cone, NYA	207.2	260	11.27
B Moehler, Det	221.1	278	11.30
W Williams, Tor	209.2	279	11.98

Strikeouts Per 9 IP
minimum 162 IP

Player, Team	IP	SO	SO/9
R Clemens, Tor	**234.2**	**271**	**10.39**
P Martinez, Bos	233.2	251	9.67
D Cone, NYA	207.2	209	9.06
C Finley, Ana	223.1	212	8.54
T Saunders, TB	192.1	172	8.05
M Mussina, Bal	206.1	175	7.63
J Guzman, Tor-Bal	211.0	168	7.17
A Sele, Tex	212.2	167	7.07
J Fassero, Sea	224.2	176	7.05
C Carpenter, Tor	175.0	136	6.99

Run Support Per 9 IP
minimum 162 IP

Player, Team	IP	R	R/9
T Wakefield, Bos	**216.0**	**175**	**7.29**
D Cone, NYA	207.2	159	6.89
D Wells, NYA	214.1	163	6.84
A Sele, Tex	212.2	158	6.69
R Helling, Tex	216.1	159	6.61
J Wright, Cle	192.2	135	6.31
J Haynes, Oak	194.1	133	6.16
M Sirotka, ChA	211.2	143	6.08
P Hentgen, Tor	177.2	120	6.08
C Carpenter, Tor	175.0	117	6.02

OBP Allowed
D Wells, NYA	**.265**
R Clemens, Tor	.277
P Martinez, Bos	.278
M Mussina, Bal	.283
J Moyer, Sea	.295

SLG Allowed
R Clemens, Tor	**.296**
P Martinez, Bos	.347
K Rogers, Oak	.366
D Cone, NYA	.371
C Finley, Ana	.374

Hits per 9 IP
R Clemens, Tor	**6.48**
P Martinez, Bos	7.24
H Irabu, NYA	7.70
D Cone, NYA	8.06
K Rogers, Oak	8.11

Home Runs per 9 IP
R Clemens, Tor	**0.42**
A Sele, Tex	0.59
B Colon, Cle	0.66
T Saunders, TB	0.70
K Rogers, Oak	0.72

Vs LHB
R Clemens, Tor	**.197**
H Irabu, NYA	.218
P Martinez, Bos	.225
K Rogers, Oak	.226
B Stein, Oak	.229

Vs RHB
R Clemens, Tor	**.198**
R Arrojo, TB	.204
P Martinez, Bos	.209
W Williams, Tor	.220
D Cone, NYA	.220

BA Allowed ScPos
R Clemens, Tor	**.176**
P Martinez, Bos	.192
W Williams, Tor	.203
C Finley, Ana	.217
K Rogers, Oak	.224

OBP Leadoff Inning
P Martinez, Bos	**.249**
D Wells, NYA	.252
M Mussina, Bal	.266
D Cone, NYA	.271
R Johnson, Sea	.284

K/BB Ratio
D Wells, NYA	**5.62**
M Mussina, Bal	4.27
J Moyer, Sea	3.76
P Martinez, Bos	3.75
D Cone, NYA	3.54

Grd/Fly Ratio Off
S Erickson, Bal	**2.85**
O Olivares, Ana	2.33
A Pettitte, NYA	2.22
C Nagy, Cle	1.91
R Clemens, Tor	1.86

Pitches per Start
R Clemens, Tor	**115.4**
P Martinez, Bos	114.1
C Finley, Ana	111.7
W Williams, Tor	110.7
J Fassero, Sea	110.5

Pitches per Batter
T Wakefield, Bos	**3.43**
J Burkett, Tex	3.51
C Nagy, Cle	3.53
S Erickson, Bal	3.54
T Belcher, KC	3.59

Steals Allowed
J Guzman, Tor-Bal	**31**
S Erickson, Bal	28
R Clemens, Tor	28
C Finley, Ana	27
J Navarro, ChA	26

Caught Stealing Off
J Thompson, Det	**16**
C Finley, Ana	15
R Johnson, Sea	13
R Helling, Tex	12
B Radke, Min	12

SB% Allowed
A Sele, Tex	**33.3**
B Saberhagen, Bos	36.4
K Rogers, Oak	40.0
T Belcher, KC	41.2
C Carpenter, Tor	45.0

Pickoffs
J Thompson, Det	**12**
K Rogers, Oak	10
J Fassero, Sea	8
J Parque, ChA	8
A Pettitte, NYA	8

PkOf Throw/Runner
K Rogers, Oak	**1.67**
C Finley, Ana	1.42
J Guzman, Tor-Bal	1.35
J Haynes, Oak	1.31
R Arrojo, TB	1.29

GDPs Induced
K Rogers, Oak	**34**
A Pettitte, NYA	29
M Sirotka, ChA	28
B Moehler, Det	28
P Rapp, KC	27

GDP per 9 IP
P Rapp, KC	**1.3**
K Rogers, Oak	1.3
O Olivares, Ana	1.3
A Pettitte, NYA	1.2
M Sirotka, ChA	1.2

Quality Starts
P Martinez, Bos	**25**
R Clemens, Tor	24
S Erickson, Bal	21
J Moyer, Sea	21
K Rogers, Oak	21

1998 National League Special Pitching Leaders

Baserunners Per 9 IP
minimum 162 IP

Player, Team	IP	BR	BR/9
G Maddux, Atl	251.0	253	9.07
K Brown, SD	257.0	284	9.95
C Schilling, Phi	268.2	303	10.15
R Reed, NYN	212.1	243	10.30
J Lima, Hou	233.1	268	10.34
J Smoltz, Atl	167.2	193	10.36
P Harnisch, Cin	209.0	246	10.59
D Hermanson, Mon	187.0	222	10.68
B Anderson, Ari	208.0	249	10.77
A Leiter, NYN	193.0	233	10.87

Strikeouts Per 9 IP
minimum 162 IP

Player, Team	IP	SO	SO/9
K Wood, ChN	166.2	233	12.58
C Schilling, Phi	268.2	300	10.05
J Smoltz, Atl	167.2	173	9.29
K Brown, SD	257.0	257	9.00
K Millwood, Atl	174.1	163	8.41
D Dreifort, LA	180.0	168	8.40
A Leiter, NYN	193.0	174	8.11
S Hitchcock, SD	176.1	158	8.06
S Reynolds, Hou	233.1	209	8.06
M Remlinger, Cin	164.1	144	7.89

Run Support Per 9 IP
minimum 162 IP

Player, Team	IP	R	R/9
K Rueter, SF	187.2	165	7.91
S Reynolds, Hou	233.1	175	6.75
S Bergman, Hou	172.0	121	6.33
K Tapani, ChN	219.0	152	6.25
J Smoltz, Atl	167.2	116	6.23
S Trachsel, ChN	208.0	143	6.19
D Neagle, Atl	210.1	143	6.12
M Gardner, SF	212.0	144	6.11
J Lima, Hou	233.1	158	6.09
C Park, LA	220.2	141	5.75

OBP Allowed

G Maddux, Atl	.260
K Brown, SD	.279
C Schilling, Phi	.282
J Smoltz, Atl	.285
J Lima, Hou	.285

SLG Allowed

K Brown, SD	.294
G Maddux, Atl	.299
A Leiter, NYN	.306
K Wood, ChN	.320
T Glavine, Atl	.325

Hits per 9 IP

K Wood, ChN	6.32
A Leiter, NYN	7.04
G Maddux, Atl	7.21
P Harnisch, Cin	7.58
J Smoltz, Atl	7.78

Home Runs per 9 IP

K Brown, SD	0.28
A Leiter, NYN	0.37
G Maddux, Atl	0.47
T Glavine, Atl	0.51
J Smoltz, Atl	0.54

Vs LHB

H Nomo, LA-NYN	.210
P Harnisch, Cin	.216
G Maddux, Atl	.218
K Wood, ChN	.228
T Green, Phi	.231

Vs RHB

K Wood, ChN	.169
R Johnson, Hou	.189
A Leiter, NYN	.205
B Bohanon, NYN-LA	.205
J Smoltz, Atl	.212

BA Allowed ScPos

K Wood, ChN	.153
P Harnisch, Cin	.174
M Yoshii, NYN	.199
F Cordova, Pit	.199
J Lima, Hou	.203

OBP Leadoff Inning

B Bohanon, NYN-LA	.244
G Maddux, Atl	.244
K Brown, SD	.250
C Schilling, Phi	.262
R Reed, NYN	.262

K/BB Ratio

J Lima, Hou	5.28
R Reed, NYN	5.28
K Brown, SD	5.24
C Schilling, Phi	4.92
G Maddux, Atl	4.53

Grd/Fly Ratio Off

G Maddux, Atl	3.25
K Brown, SD	3.02
M Hampton, Hou	2.70
A Ashby, SD	2.18
O Hershiser, SF	2.07

Pitches per Start

C Schilling, Phi	120.4
L Hernandez, Fla	119.0
T Glavine, Atl	108.8
A Benes, Ari	108.4
J Schmidt, Pit	105.5

Pitches per Batter

M Portugal, Phi	3.29
B Meadows, Fla	3.30
S Bergman, Hou	3.31
G Maddux, Atl	3.33
B Anderson, Ari	3.34

Steals Allowed

J Juden, Mil	34
G Maddux, Atl	28
M Clark, ChN	28
H Nomo, LA-NYN	25
A Benes, Ari	24

Caught Stealing Off

C Perez, Mon-LA	15
R Reed, NYN	14
A Ashby, SD	13
O Daal, Ari	12
7 pitchers tied with	11

SB% Allowed

O Daal, Ari	20.0
B Anderson, Ari	30.8
R Reed, NYN	33.3
S Reynolds, Hou	35.3
K Brown, SD	41.7

Pickoffs

J Sanchez, Fla	12
B Anderson, Ari	12
C Perez, Mon-LA	9
J Wright, Col	8
2 pitchers tied with	6

PkOf Throw/Runner

B Tomko, Cin	1.55
M Remlinger, Cin	1.47
I Valdes, LA	1.27
F Cordova, Pit	1.14
A Benes, Ari	1.13

GDPs Induced

M Hampton, Hou	31
J Wright, Col	29
C Park, LA	25
L Hernandez, Fla	25
A Ashby, SD	25

GDP per 9 IP

M Hampton, Hou	1.3
J Wright, Col	1.3
A Leiter, NYN	1.1
D Dreifort, LA	1.0
S Karl, Mil	1.0

Quality Starts

K Brown, SD	29
G Maddux, Atl	27
T Glavine, Atl	26
S Reynolds, Hou	26
2 pitchers tied with	25

1998 Active Career Batting Leaders

Batting Average

Player	AB	H	AVG
1 Tony Gwynn	8648	2928	.339
2 Mike Piazza	3119	1038	.333
3 Wade Boggs	8888	2922	.329
4 Frank Thomas	4406	1416	.321
5 Edgar Martinez	4374	1389	.318
6 Alex Rodriguez	2070	648	.313
7 Kenny Lofton	3914	1216	.311
8 Rusty Greer	2435	756	.310
9 Mark Grace	6053	1875	.310
10 Nomar Garciaparra	1375	425	.309
11 Jason Kendall	1435	442	.308
12 Derek Jeter	1910	588	.308
13 Paul Molitor	10835	3319	.306
14 Hal Morris	3727	1140	.306
15 Larry Walker	4154	1265	.305
16 Mo Vaughn	3828	1165	.304
17 Jeff Bagwell	4197	1276	.304
18 Vinny Castilla	2901	880	.303
19 Reggie Jefferson	1917	580	.303
20 Will Clark	6495	1964	.302
21 Jeff Cirillo	2204	666	.302
22 Manny Ramirez	2509	758	.302
23 Roberto Alomar	6048	1825	.302
24 John Olerud	4184	1261	.301
25 Dante Bichette	4822	1448	.300

On-Base Percentage

Player	PA	OB	OBP
1 Frank Thomas	5501	2437	.443
2 Edgar Martinez	5249	2223	.424
3 Wade Boggs	10377	4319	.416
4 Jeff Bagwell	5068	2083	.411
5 Barry Bonds	8096	3324	.411
6 Jim Thome	3152	1290	.409
7 Rickey Henderson	11504	4652	.404
8 John Olerud	4978	2005	.403
9 Mike Piazza	3482	1380	.396
10 Tim Salmon	3717	1468	.395
11 Mo Vaughn	4452	1755	.394
12 Jason Kendall	1664	654	.393
13 Dave Magadan	4331	1701	.393
14 Mark McGwire	6311	2468	.391
15 Rusty Greer	2802	1095	.391
16 Gary Sheffield	4876	1904	.390
17 Manny Ramirez	2921	1138	.390
18 Tony Gwynn	9489	3691	.389
19 Chuck Knoblauch	5268	2038	.387
20 Tim Raines	9934	3837	.386
21 Mark Grace	6912	2664	.385
22 Chipper Jones	2682	1024	.382
23 Kenny Lofton	4411	1684	.382
24 Larry Walker	4737	1808	.382
25 Bill Mueller	1293	493	.381

Slugging Percentage

Player	AB	TB	SLG
1 Frank Thomas	4406	2575	.584
2 Albert Belle	4684	2705	.577
3 Mark McGwire	5131	2953	.576
4 Mike Piazza	3119	1794	.575
5 Ken Griffey Jr.	5226	2967	.568
6 Juan Gonzalez	4269	2423	.568
7 Manny Ramirez	2509	1401	.558
8 Barry Bonds	6621	3679	.556
9 Nomar Garciaparra	1375	759	.552
10 Larry Walker	4154	2292	.552
11 Jim Thome	2583	1417	.549
12 Alex Rodriguez	2070	1123	.543
13 Mo Vaughn	3828	2074	.542
14 Vinny Castilla	2901	1564	.539
15 Jeff Bagwell	4197	2260	.538
16 Tim Salmon	3130	1653	.528
17 Ryan Klesko	2027	1062	.524
18 Matt Stairs	1138	593	.521
19 Edgar Martinez	4374	2274	.520
20 Kevin Mitchell	4134	2149	.520
21 Carlos Delgado	1759	911	.518
22 Jose Canseco	6042	3121	.517
23 Fred McGriff	6257	3218	.514
24 Raul Mondesi	2886	1467	.508
25 David Justice	3893	1977	.508

Hits

Paul Molitor	3319
Tony Gwynn	2928
Wade Boggs	2922
Cal Ripken	2878
Rickey Henderson	2678
Harold Baines	2649
Tim Raines	2532
Chili Davis	2252
Gary Gaetti	2223
Willie McGee	2186
Joe Carter	2184
Tony Fernandez	2081
Rafael Palmeiro	1975
Will Clark	1964
Tony Phillips	1924
Andres Galarraga	1921
Barry Bonds	1917
Terry Pendleton	1897
Bobby Bonilla	1893
Wally Joyner	1881

Home Runs

Mark McGwire	457
Barry Bonds	411
Jose Canseco	397
Joe Carter	396
Cal Ripken	384
Fred McGriff	358
Gary Gaetti	351
Ken Griffey Jr.	350
Harold Baines	348
Darryl Strawberry	332
Andres Galarraga	332
Chili Davis	331
Albert Belle	321
Cecil Fielder	319
Rafael Palmeiro	314
Juan Gonzalez	301
Matt Williams	299
Frank Thomas	286
Bobby Bonilla	273
Sammy Sosa	273

Runs Batted In

Cal Ripken	1514
Harold Baines	1480
Joe Carter	1445
Paul Molitor	1307
Gary Gaetti	1294
Chili Davis	1294
Barry Bonds	1216
Jose Canseco	1214
Andres Galarraga	1172
Mark McGwire	1130
Bobby Bonilla	1106
Will Clark	1106
Fred McGriff	1088
Rafael Palmeiro	1079
Ruben Sierra	1047
Tony Gwynn	1042
Albert Belle	1019
Ken Griffey Jr.	1018
Wally Joyner	1017
Cecil Fielder	1008

Stolen Bases

Rickey Henderson	1297
Tim Raines	803
Otis Nixon	594
Paul Molitor	504
Barry Bonds	445
Kenny Lofton	408
Juan Samuel	396
Delino DeShields	382
Marquis Grissom	358
Willie McGee	345
Eric Davis	342
Roberto Alomar	340
Craig Biggio	318
Barry Larkin	315
Lance Johnson	312
Tony Gwynn	311
Chuck Knoblauch	307
Devon White	306
Bip Roberts	264
Brady Anderson	247

Seasons Played	
Paul Molitor	21
Rickey Henderson	20
Tim Raines	20
Harold Baines	19
Gary Gaetti	18
Cal Ripken	18
Chili Davis	18
5 players tied with	17

Games	
Cal Ripken	2704
Paul Molitor	2683
Rickey Henderson	2612
Harold Baines	2567
Gary Gaetti	2389
Wade Boggs	2350
Tim Raines	2295
Chili Davis	2290
Tony Gwynn	2222
Joe Carter	2189

At-Bats	
Paul Molitor	10835
Cal Ripken	10433
Rickey Henderson	9473
Harold Baines	9111
Wade Boggs	8888
Gary Gaetti	8661
Tony Gwynn	8648
Tim Raines	8559
Joe Carter	8422
Chili Davis	8197

Runs Scored	
Rickey Henderson	2014
Paul Molitor	1782
Tim Raines	1528
Cal Ripken	1510
Wade Boggs	1473
Barry Bonds	1364
Tony Gwynn	1302
Tony Phillips	1224
Harold Baines	1208
Chili Davis	1181

Doubles	
Paul Molitor	605
Wade Boggs	564
Cal Ripken	544
Tony Gwynn	495
Harold Baines	456
Rickey Henderson	442
Gary Gaetti	434
Joe Carter	432
Tim Raines	414
Barry Bonds	403

Triples	
Paul Molitor	114
Tim Raines	112
Lance Johnson	111
Juan Samuel	102
Willie McGee	94
Tony Fernandez	92
Tony Gwynn	84
Steve Finley	75
Ozzie Guillen	69
Devon White	66

AB per HR	
Mark McGwire	11.2
Juan Gonzalez	14.2
Albert Belle	14.6
Ken Griffey Jr.	14.9
Jose Canseco	15.2
Frank Thomas	15.4
Mike Piazza	15.6
Jim Thome	15.8
Barry Bonds	16.1
Cecil Fielder	16.2

AB per RBI	
Juan Gonzalez	4.5
Mark McGwire	4.5
Frank Thomas	4.6
Albert Belle	4.6
Mike Piazza	4.8
Manny Ramirez	4.9
Jose Canseco	5.0
Jeff Bagwell	5.0
Matt Stairs	5.0
Mo Vaughn	5.1

Total Bases	
Paul Molitor	4854
Cal Ripken	4662
Harold Baines	4245
Rickey Henderson	4038
Tony Gwynn	3960
Wade Boggs	3954
Joe Carter	3910
Gary Gaetti	3786
Chili Davis	3702
Barry Bonds	3679

Walks	
Rickey Henderson	1890
Wade Boggs	1374
Barry Bonds	1357
Tim Raines	1264
Tony Phillips	1248
Chili Davis	1121
Paul Molitor	1094
Cal Ripken	1067
Mark McGwire	1052
Frank Thomas	989

Intentional Walks	
Barry Bonds	289
Tony Gwynn	195
Chili Davis	181
Wade Boggs	178
Harold Baines	177
Ken Griffey Jr.	153
Will Clark	150
Tim Raines	143
Darryl Strawberry	131
Fred McGriff	125

Hit by Pitch	
Craig Biggio	142
Andres Galarraga	137
Brady Anderson	112
Mike Macfarlane	96
Gary Gaetti	94
Chuck Knoblauch	92
Joe Carter	90
Rickey Henderson	84
Jeff Blauser	83
Jason Kendall	77

Strikeouts	
Jose Canseco	1630
Andres Galarraga	1615
Chili Davis	1598
Gary Gaetti	1548
Juan Samuel	1442
Tony Phillips	1405
Rickey Henderson	1390
Joe Carter	1387
Fred McGriff	1365
Darryl Strawberry	1336

K/BB Ratio	
Wade Boggs	.525
Tony Gwynn	.549
Mark Grace	.637
Eric Young	.664
Frank Thomas	.683
Tim Raines	.729
Rickey Henderson	.735
Gregg Jefferies	.738
Gary Sheffield	.741
Dave Magadan	.742

Sacrifice Hits	
Jay Bell	140
Ozzie Guillen	135
Omar Vizquel	114
Roberto Alomar	95
Joey Cora	84
Walt Weiss	80
Mike Bordick	77
Mark McLemore	76
Paul Molitor	75
2 tied with	72

Sacrifice Flies	
Cal Ripken	111
Paul Molitor	109
Joe Carter	105
Ruben Sierra	101
Gary Gaetti	98
Harold Baines	94
Bobby Bonilla	94
Will Clark	94
Wade Boggs	92
Chili Davis	91

SB Success %	
Tony Womack	89.1
Eric Davis	85.1
Tim Raines	84.7
Barry Larkin	84.7
Stan Javier	84.3
Rickey Henderson	81.2
Kenny Lofton	80.2
Marquis Grissom	80.1
Alex Rodriguez	79.5
Paul Molitor	79.4

Caught Stealing	
Rickey Henderson	301
Otis Nixon	179
Tim Raines	145
Juan Samuel	143
Paul Molitor	131
Barry Bonds	130
Tony Fernandez	128
Delino Deshields	126
Tony Gwynn	122
Willie McGee	117

GDP	
Cal Ripken	311
Harold Baines	274
Tony Gwynn	240
Gary Gaetti	231
Wade Boggs	222
Chili Davis	220
Paul Molitor	209
Terry Pendleton	178
Cecil Fielder	169
Terry Steinbach	167

AB per GDP	
Jose Valentin	165.6
Johnny Damon	139.9
Tony Womack	136.2
Darin Erstad	128.4
Tom Goodwin	109.8
Brady Anderson	104.7
F.P. Santangelo	102.0
Milt Cuyler	92.4
Craig Biggio	85.8
Darryl Strawberry	83.9

1998 Active Career Pitching Leaders

Wins			Losses			Winning Percentage			ERA	
Dennis Martinez	245		**Dennis Martinez**	193		**Mike Mussina**	.667		**John Franco**	2.64
Roger Clemens	233		Danny Darwin	182		Andy Pettitte	.657		Greg Maddux	2.75
Greg Maddux	202		Dennis Eckersley	171		Roger Clemens	.653		Roger Clemens	2.95
Dennis Eckersley	197		Mike Morgan	170		Pedro Martinez	.646		Jesse Orosco	2.96
Orel Hershiser	190		Tom Candiotti	158		Randy Johnson	.644		Pedro Martinez	2.98
Jimmy Key	186		Mark Langston	156		David Cone	.644		Jeff Montgomery	3.05
Dwight Gooden	185		Bobby Witt	140		Dwight Gooden	.642		Jeff Brantley	3.15
Mark Langston	178		Dave Stieb	137		Greg Maddux	.633		David Cone	3.17
Dave Stieb	176		Doug Drabek	134		Tom Glavine	.622		Randy Myers	3.19
Tom Glavine	173		Orel Hershiser	133		Ramon Martinez	.615		Mike Jackson	3.21

Games			Games Started			Innings Pitched			Batters Faced	
Dennis Eckersley	1071		**Dennis Martinez**	562		**Dennis Martinez**	3999.2		**Dennis Martinez**	16754
Jesse Orosco	1025		Roger Clemens	449		Dennis Eckersley	3285.2		Dennis Eckersley	13534
John Franco	832		Orel Hershiser	428		Roger Clemens	3274.2		Roger Clemens	13389
Paul Assenmacher	829		Mark Langston	423		Danny Darwin	3016.2		Danny Darwin	12716
Mike Jackson	763		Dave Stieb	412		Orel Hershiser	2926.2		Mark Langston	12288
Dan Plesac	758		Greg Maddux	399		Mark Langston	2901.0		Orel Hershiser	12238
Randy Myers	728		Tom Candiotti	397		Dave Stieb	2895.1		Dave Stieb	12072
Doug Jones	722		Jimmy Key	389		Greg Maddux	2849.1		Greg Maddux	11517
Danny Darwin	716		Doug Drabek	387		Tom Candiotti	2653.2		Tom Candiotti	11242
Dennis Martinez	692		Mike Morgan	381		Jimmy Key	2591.2		Jimmy Key	10719

Complete Games			CG Freq			Shutouts			Quality Start %*	
Dennis Martinez	122		**Dennis Eckersley**	0.28		**Roger Clemens**	44		**Greg Maddux**	71.1
Roger Clemens	114		Curt Schilling	0.26		Dennis Martinez	30		Roger Clemens	68.8
Dave Stieb	103		Roger Clemens	0.25		Dave Stieb	30		Curt Schilling	68.6
Dennis Eckersley	100		Dave Stieb	0.25		Greg Maddux	28		Kevin Brown	66.9
Greg Maddux	89		Jack McDowell	0.23		Orel Hershiser	25		David Cone	66.7
Mark Langston	81		Greg Maddux	0.22		Dwight Gooden	24		Ismael Valdes	66.1
Bret Saberhagen	76		Bret Saberhagen	0.22		Randy Johnson	23		Pedro Martinez	65.4
Tom Candiotti	68		Dennis Martinez	0.22		Doug Drabek	21		Randy Johnson	65.2
Orel Hershiser	68		Kevin Brown	0.20		David Cone	21		Tom Glavine	65.1
Dwight Gooden	68		Randy Johnson	0.20		2 pitchers tied with	20		Mike Mussina	65.0
									* since 1987	

Strikeouts			Walks Allowed			Strikeouts/9 IP			Walks/9 IP	
Roger Clemens	3153		**Mark Langston**	1260		**Randy Johnson**	10.60		**Bob Tewksbury**	1.45
Mark Langston	2421		Bobby Witt	1248		Hideo Nomo	9.98		Bret Saberhagen	1.70
Dennis Eckersley	2401		Dennis Martinez	1165		Pedro Martinez	9.59		Shane Reynolds	1.92
Randy Johnson	2329		Dave Stieb	1034		Randy Myers	8.99		Doug Jones	1.94
David Cone	2243		Chuck Finley	1024		Roger Clemens	8.67		Greg Swindell	2.01
Dwight Gooden	2150		Roger Clemens	1012		Eric Plunk	8.52		Dennis Eckersley	2.02
Dennis Martinez	2149		Randy Johnson	943		Paul Assenmacher	8.51		Brad Radke	2.03
Greg Maddux	2024		Orel Hershiser	916		Curt Schilling	8.45		Greg Maddux	2.07
Chuck Finley	1951		David Cone	895		David Cone	8.42		Mike Mussina	2.12
2 pitchers tied with	1942		Danny Darwin	874		Dan Plesac	8.22		David Wells	2.17

K/BB Ratio

Shane Reynolds	**4.07**
Doug Jones	3.86
Bret Saberhagen	3.53
Curt Schilling	3.46
Pedro Martinez	3.27
Dennis Eckersley	3.25
Mike Mussina	3.12
Roger Clemens	3.12
Greg Maddux	3.09
Greg Swindell	3.05

Hits/9 IP

Randy Johnson	**6.93**
Pedro Martinez	6.99
Mike Jackson	7.03
Jesse Orosco	7.16
Hideo Nomo	7.19
David Cone	7.44
Roger Clemens	7.51
Jeff Brantley	7.66
Randy Myers	7.71
Al Leiter	7.71

Baserunners/9 IP

Greg Maddux	**10.21**
Pedro Martinez	10.28
Bret Saberhagen	10.48
Curt Schilling	10.48
Mike Mussina	10.55
Roger Clemens	10.58
Dennis Eckersley	10.65
Ismael Valdes	10.81
John Smoltz	10.87
David Cone	11.08

Home Runs/9 IP

Greg Maddux	**0.45**
John Franco	0.49
Kevin Brown	0.50
Roger Clemens	0.59
Dwight Gooden	0.59
Tom Glavine	0.59
Kevin Appier	0.62
Al Leiter	0.62
Mike Maddux	0.64
Bill Swift	0.65

Opposition Avg*

Randy Johnson	**.212**
Pedro Martinez	.214
Mike Jackson	.216
Hideo Nomo	.218
Jesse Orosco	.219
David Cone	.224
Roger Clemens	.225
Jeff Brantley	.232
John Smoltz	.232
Randy Myers	.233
*since 1987	

Opposition OBP*

Greg Maddux	**.283**
Pedro Martinez	.284
Curt Schilling	.288
Bret Saberhagen	.290
Mike Mussina	.290
Roger Clemens	.291
Ismael Valdes	.293
John Smoltz	.296
David Cone	.298
Dennis Martinez	.299
*since 1987	

Opposition SLG*

Mariano Rivera	**.320**
Roberto Hernandez	.320
Greg Maddux	.322
John Wetteland	.323
Gregg Olson	.323
Mark Wohlers	.325
Trevor Hoffman	.329
Roger Clemens	.329
Randy Johnson	.332
John Franco	.333
*since 1987	

Home Runs Allowed

Dennis Martinez	**372**
Dennis Eckersley	347
Danny Darwin	321
Mark Langston	302
Jimmy Key	254
Doug Drabek	246
Tom Candiotti	236
Chuck Finley	231
Tim Belcher	229
2 pitchers tied with	226

Hit Batsmen

Dave Stieb	**129**
Dennis Martinez	122
Roger Clemens	105
Kevin Brown	101
Orel Hershiser	95
Randy Johnson	92
Tom Candiotti	82
Danny Darwin	81
Darryl Kile	79
2 pitchers tied with	76

Wild Pitches

David Cone	**122**
John Smoltz	117
Bobby Witt	115
Orel Hershiser	113
Tom Candiotti	107
Chuck Finley	102
Mike Morgan	97
Juan Guzman	93
Tom Gordon	91
Dennis Martinez	89

GDPs Induced*

Greg Maddux	**247**
Kevin Brown	235
Chuck Finley	232
Orel Hershiser	231
Tom Glavine	227
Scott Erickson	224
Mike Morgan	216
Bill Swift	206
Mark Langston	192
Jim Abbott	190
*since 1987	

GDP/9 IP

Bill Swift	**1.36**
Bob Wickman	1.25
Trevor Wilson	1.16
Scott Erickson	1.13
Hipolito Pichardo	1.13
Donn Pall	1.10
Andy Pettitte	1.10
Mike Fetters	1.08
Bob Scanlan	1.08
Jim Abbott	1.07

Saves

John Franco	**397**
Dennis Eckersley	390
Randy Myers	347
Jeff Montgomery	292
Doug Jones	291
Rick Aguilera	275
John Wetteland	253
Rod Beck	250
Gregg Olson	203
Roberto Hernandez	191

Save %

Troy Percival	**87.1**
Trevor Hoffman	87.0
Ugueth Urbina	85.9
Rod Beck	85.6
Robb Nen	85.5
Randy Myers	85.3
Dennis Eckersley	84.6
Jose Mesa	84.6
John Wetteland	84.3
Mark Wohlers	84.2

Games Finished

John Franco	**677**
Doug Jones	583
Dennis Eckersley	577
Randy Myers	548
Jeff Montgomery	513
Rick Aguilera	472
Jesse Orosco	461
Rod Beck	416
John Wetteland	407
Gregg Olson	392

SB% Allowed*

Terry Mulholland	**38.6**
Kirk Rueter	40.0
Kenny Rogers	40.4
Trevor Wilson	41.7
Rich DeLucia	43.4
Pat Rapp	44.6
Randy Myers	46.4
Chan Ho Park	46.5
Brian Anderson	48.1
Bob Patterson	50.9
*since 1987	

1998 American League Bill James Leaders

Top Game Scores of the Year

Pitcher, Team	Date	Opp	IP	H	R	ER	BB	K	SC
R Clemens, Tor	8/25	KC	9.0	3	0	0	0	18	99
D Wells, NYA	5/17	Min	9.0	0	0	0	0	11	98
D Wells, NYA	9/1	Oak	9.0	2	0	0	0	13	96
P Martinez, Bos	4/11	Sea	9.0	2	0	0	2	12	93
R Johnson, Sea	7/16	Min	9.0	1	0	0	3	11	93
D Cone, NYA	6/7	Fla	9.0	2	1	1	2	14	91
M Mussina, Bal	8/4	Det	9.0	2	0	0	0	8	91
R Johnson, Sea	7/11	Ana	9.0	5	0	0	2	15	90
O Hernandez, NYA	9/14	Bos	9.0	3	0	0	0	9	90
R Halladay, Tor	9/27	Det	9.0	1	1	1	0	8	89

Worst Game Scores of the Year

Pitcher, Team	Date	Opp	IP	H	R	ER	BB	K	SC
M Oquist, Oak	8/3	NYA	5.0	16	14	14	3	3	−21
S Sanders, Det	4/14	Tex	4.0	16	11	11	3	2	−15
M Perisho, Tex	6/21	Ana	2.2	10	10	9	5	1	−4
O Hernandez, NYA	7/29	Ana	3.1	13	10	10	0	3	−3
J Bullinger, Sea	4/7	NYA	3.1	12	10	10	0	2	−2
C Nagy, Cle	8/14	Bal	5.0	12	11	10	4	2	−1
A Sele, Tex	6/3	Oak	4.0	12	10	8	3	2	1
K Cloude, Sea	8/29	NYA	3.1	12	9	8	3	2	1
J Burkett, Tex	4/24	KC	4.2	11	11	11	2	6	2
B Swift, Sea	5/1	Det	4.0	10	10	10	1	1	2

Runs Created

A Belle, ChA	158
M Vaughn, Bos	144
K Griffey Jr., Sea	142
E Martinez, Sea	141
A Rodriguez, Sea	138
J Gonzalez, Tex	134
R Palmeiro, Bal	132
M Ramirez, Cle	128
C Delgado, Tor	126
N Garciaparra, Bos	120

Runs Created per 27 Outs

A Belle, ChA	9.1
J Thome, Cle	8.3
E Martinez, Sea	8.3
B Williams, NYA	8.2
T Salmon, Ana	8.0
M Vaughn, Bos	8.0
J Gonzalez, Tex	7.8
C Delgado, Tor	7.7
M Ramirez, Cle	7.7
K Griffey Jr., Sea	7.6

Offensive Win Pct

A Belle, ChA	.786
E Martinez, Sea	.785
J Thome, Cle	.781
M Vaughn, Bos	.774
T Salmon, Ana	.755
B Williams, NYA	.753
C Delgado, Tor	.752
J Gonzalez, Tex	.724
E Davis, Bal	.724
K Griffey Jr., Sea	.720

Secondary Average

J Thome, Cle	.495
K Griffey Jr., Sea	.471
A Belle, ChA	.463
C Delgado, Tor	.443
M Ramirez, Cle	.441
E Martinez, Sea	.435
R Henderson, Oak	.426
T Salmon, Ana	.425
F Thomas, ChA	.415
J Canseco, Tor	.413

Isolated Power (Power Pct)

K Griffey Jr., Sea	.327
A Belle, ChA	.327
J Gonzalez, Tex	.312
M Ramirez, Cle	.305
C Delgado, Tor	.300
J Thome, Cle	.291
J Canseco, Tor	.281
R Palmeiro, Bal	.270
N Garciaparra, Bos	.262
M Vaughn, Bos	.255

Power/Speed Number

A Rodriguez, Sea	43.9
J Canseco, Tor	35.6
S Green, Tor	35.0
K Griffey Jr., Sea	29.5
R Durham, ChA	24.9
D Jeter, NYA	23.3
R Henderson, Oak	23.1
C Knoblauch, NYA	22.0
J Damon, KC	21.3
K Lofton, Cle	19.6

Speed Scores

T Goodwin, KC	8.15
B Hunter, Det	8.04
J Damon, KC	7.90
C Knoblauch, NYA	7.25
J Offerman, KC	7.08
O Vizquel, Cle	7.02
R Durham, ChA	6.99
S Green, Tor	6.97
D Erstad, Ana	6.93
D Jeter, NYA	6.88

Cheap Wins

P Rapp, KC	7
T Wakefield, Bos	7
C Nagy, Cle	6
R Helling, Tex	5
7 pitchers tied with	4

Tough Losses

J Thompson, Det	7
J Guzman, Tor-Bal	5
P Martinez, Bos	5
T Candiotti, Oak	4
T Belcher, KC	4
S Erickson, Bal	4
D Burba, Cle	4
J Fassero, Sea	4
B Radke, Min	4
9 pitchers tied with	3

1998 National League Bill James Leaders

Top Game Scores of the Year

Pitcher, Team	Date	Opp	IP	H	R	ER	BB	K	SC
K Wood, ChN	5/6	Hou	9.0	1	0	0	0	20	105
K Millwood, Atl	4/14	Pit	9.0	1	0	0	0	13	98
K Brown, SD	8/16	Mil	9.0	1	0	0	2	11	94
J Smoltz, Atl	9/6	NYN	9.0	3	0	0	0	12	93
C Schilling, Phi	4/10	Atl	9.0	2	0	0	1	10	92
I Valdes, LA	6/27	Pit	9.0	1	0	0	0	7	92
T Stottlemyre, StL	5/11	Mil	8.0	2	0	0	0	13	91
I Valdes, LA	6/10	Oak	9.0	2	0	0	1	9	91
J Smoltz, Atl	7/24	Pit	9.0	3	0	0	0	10	91
D Kile, Col	9/20	SD	10.0	3	0	0	2	7	91

Worst Game Scores of the Year

Pitcher, Team	Date	Opp	IP	H	R	ER	BB	K	SC
J Mercedes, Mil	5/4	SD	3.1	12	11	11	2	1	−9
D Kile, Col	7/2	Sea	2.0	10	10	10	1	2	−3
S Winchester, Cin	7/24	SF	3.1	11	10	10	2	2	−2
L Hernandez, Fla	9/7	Col	4.1	14	9	9	3	2	−2
J Thomson, Col	4/11	Cin	2.0	11	9	9	1	2	−1
M Saipe, Col	7/1	Sea	4.0	13	9	9	0	1	1
M Gardner, SF	5/13	Mon	2.1	11	8	8	0	0	3
B Raggio, StL	5/15	Fla	0.2	9	7	7	2	0	4
A Larkin, Fla	7/29	Hou	2.1	10	8	8	3	2	4
D Kile, Col	7/29	Pit	4.0	11	9	9	0	1	5

Runs Created

M McGwire, StL	193
B Bonds, SF	153
S Sosa, ChN	149
C Biggio, Hou	142
J Olerud, NYN	141
M Alou, Hou	138
C Jones, Atl	136
J Bagwell, Hou	134
A Galarraga, Atl	134
S Rolen, Phi	131

Runs Created per 27 Outs

M McGwire, StL	12.1
B Bonds, SF	9.0
G Sheffield, Fla-LA	8.9
J Olerud, NYN	8.8
J Bagwell, Hou	8.3
L Walker, Col	8.3
C Biggio, Hou	8.3
M Alou, Hou	8.3
B Abreu, Phi	8.0
S Sosa, ChN	7.9

Offensive Win Pct

M McGwire, StL	.905
L Walker, Col	.861
J Olerud, NYN	.823
B Bonds, SF	.821
J Bagwell, Hou	.793
A Galarraga, Atl	.790
G Sheffield, Fla-LA	.790
M Alou, Hou	.785
R Lankford, StL	.774
S Sosa, ChN	.770

Secondary Average

M McGwire, StL	.774
B Bonds, SF	.571
J Bagwell, Hou	.478
G Vaughn, SD	.475
G Sheffield, Fla-LA	.474
S Sosa, ChN	.467
R Lankford, StL	.448
L Walker, Col	.430
M Alou, Hou	.428
K Caminiti, SD	.423

Isolated Power (Power Pct)

M McGwire, StL	.454
S Sosa, ChN	.339
G Vaughn, SD	.325
B Bonds, SF	.306
A Galarraga, Atl	.290
H Rodriguez, ChN	.280
M Alou, Hou	.271
V Castilla, Col	.270
L Walker, Col	.267
V Guerrero, Mon	.265

Power/Speed Number

B Bonds, SF	31.9
A Jones, Atl	28.9
C Biggio, Hou	28.6
S Sosa, ChN	28.3
R Lankford, StL	28.3
J Bagwell, Hou	24.4
C Floyd, Fla	24.2
G Sheffield, Fla-LA	22.0
D White, Ari	22.0
C Jones, Atl	21.8

Speed Scores

D DeShields, StL	8.20
T Womack, Pit	8.14
C Biggio, Hou	7.78
D Glanville, Phi	7.29
S Finley, SD	7.29
N Perez, Col	7.28
E Young, LA	7.20
A Jones, Atl	6.87
S Javier, SF	6.83
D White, Ari	6.77

Cheap Wins

K Tapani, ChN	7
P Astacio, Col	6
D Oliver, StL	5
D Darwin, SF	4
J Gonzalez, ChN	4
10 pitchers tied with	3

Tough Losses

C Schilling, Phi	11
K Brown, SD	6
J Schmidt, Pit	6
C Perez, Mon-LA	6
A Ashby, SD	5
M Remlinger, Cin	5
D Neagle, Atl	5
J Lima, Hou	5
8 pitchers tied with	4

1998 American League Relief Pitching Leaders

Saves

Player, Team	Saves
T Gordon, Bos	**46**
T Percival, Ana	42
J Wetteland, Tex	42
M Jackson, Cle	40
R Aguilera, Min	38
J Montgomery, KC	36
M Rivera, NYA	36
B Taylor, Oak	33
T Jones, Det	28
R Myers, Tor	28

Save Percentage
minimum 10 save opportunities

Player, Team	Sv	Op	Pct
T Gordon, Bos	**46**	**47**	**97.9**
J Wetteland, Tex	42	47	89.4
B Taylor, Oak	33	37	89.2
M Jackson, Cle	40	45	88.9
J Montgomery, KC	36	41	87.8
M Rivera, NYA	36	41	87.8
T Jones, Det	28	32	87.5
T Percival, Ana	42	48	87.5
R Myers, Tor	28	33	84.8
A Benitez, Bal	22	26	84.6

Relief ERA
minimum 50 relief innings

Player, Team	IP	ER	ERA
M Jackson, Cle	**64.0**	**11**	**1.55**
M Rivera, NYA	61.1	13	1.91
J Wetteland, Tex	62.0	14	2.03
P Quantrill, Tor	80.0	23	2.59
J Corsi, Bos	66.0	19	2.59
A Lopez, TB	79.2	23	2.60
T Gordon, Bos	79.1	24	2.72
D Brocail, Det	62.2	19	2.73
D Lowe, Bos	75.0	24	2.88
M Timlin, Sea	79.1	26	2.95

Relief Wins

S Hasegawa, Ana	**8**
T Gordon, Bos	7
A Lopez, TB	7
T Mathews, Oak	7
J Mecir, TB	7

Relief Losses

B Ayala, Sea	**10**
R Aguilera, Min	9
B Taylor, Oak	9
M Fetters, Oak-Ana	8
T Percival, Ana	7

Holds

D Plesac, Tor	**27**
P Quantrill, Tor	**27**
P Assenmacher, Cle	25
G Swindell, Min-Bos	24
M Trombley, Min	23

Blown Saves

R Aguilera, Min	**11**
R Hernandez, TB	9
B Ayala, Sea	9
P Quantrill, Tor	7
3 pitchers tied with	6

Games

S Runyan, Det	**88**
P Quantrill, Tor	82
G Swindell, Min-Bos	81
E Guardado, Min	79
D Plesac, Tor	78

Games Finished

T Gordon, Bos	**69**
R Aguilera, Min	64
T Percival, Ana	60
J Wetteland, Tex	59
2 pitchers tied with	58

Relief Innings

S Hasegawa, Ana	**97.1**
M Trombley, Min	92.0
C Castillo, ChA	90.2
G Swindell, Min-Bos	90.1
E Yan, TB	88.2

K/BB Ratio

J Wetteland, Tex	**5.14**
M Jackson, Cle	4.23
T Worrell, Det-Cle-Oak	3.92
R Aguilera, Min	3.80
M Timlin, Sea	3.75

Opposition Avg

T Percival, Ana	**.186**
T Gordon, Bos	.191
B Howry, ChA	.194
M Jackson, Cle	.195
A Benitez, Bal	.199

Opposition OBP

J Wetteland, Tex	**.247**
M Jackson, Cle	.252
T Gordon, Bos	.254
D Brocail, Det	.269
B Howry, ChA	.270

Opposition SLG

T Gordon, Bos	**.247**
M Jackson, Cle	.290
D Brocail, Det	.296
R Hernandez, TB	.296
D Lowe, Bos	.301

1st Batter Avg

T Jones, Det	**.117**
T Gordon, Bos	.119
R DeLucia, Ana	.137
X Hernandez, Tex	.150
M Jackson, Cle	.152

Vs LHB

B Howry, ChA	**.149**
A Rhodes, Bal	.172
A Benitez, Bal	.181
R Hernandez, TB	.184
T Gordon, Bos	.189

Vs RHB

T Percival, Ana	**.164**
K Foulke, ChA	.174
M Jackson, Cle	.182
B Simas, ChA	.190
T Gordon, Bos	.193

BA Runners On

T Percival, Ana	**.164**
P Shuey, Cle	.175
A Mills, Bal	.178
X Hernandez, Tex	.188
B Howry, ChA	.189

BA Allowed ScPos

P Shuey, Cle	**.132**
P Harris, Ana	.143
M Jackson, Cle	.143
R Person, Tor	.159
G Lloyd, NYA	.159

% Inherited Scored

G Swindell, Min-Bos	**10.4**
D Plesac, Tor	18.8
A Mills, Bal	19.0
R DeLucia, Ana	19.6
P Assenmacher, Cle	20.5

Grd/Fly Ratio Off

D Lowe, Bos	**4.58**
P Quantrill, Tor	2.45
M Timlin, Sea	2.22
J Mecir, TB	2.03
T Jones, Det	2.02

Pitches per Batter

D Patterson, Tex	**3.36**
E Gunderson, Tex	3.43
A Levine, Tex	3.44
B Ayala, Sea	3.45
P Harris, Ana	3.46

Strike:Ball Ratio

M Timlin, Tor	**2.11**
M Rivera, NYA	2.08
J Wetteland, Tex	2.01
R Aguilera, Min	1.98
J Wasdin, Bos	1.97

1998 National League Relief Pitching Leaders

Saves

Player, Team	Saves
T Hoffman, SD	**53**
R Beck, ChN	51
J Shaw, Cin-LA	48
R Nen, SF	40
J Franco, NYN	38
U Urbina, Mon	34
G Olson , Ari	30
B Wagner, Hou	30
K Ligtenberg, Atl	30
B Wickman, Mil	25

Save Percentage
minimum 10 save opportunities

Player, Team	Sv	Op	Pct
T Hoffman, SD	**53**	**54**	**98.1**
J Acevedo, StL	15	16	93.8
U Urbina, Mon	34	38	89.5
R Nen, SF	40	45	88.9
G Olson, Ari	30	34	88.2
K Ligtenberg, Atl	30	34	88.2
R Beck, ChN	51	58	87.9
B Wagner, Hou	30	35	85.7
J Shaw, Cin-LA	48	57	84.2
2 pitchers tied with			82.6

Relief ERA
minimum 50 relief innings

Player, Team	IP	ER	ERA
U Urbina, Mon	**69.1**	**10**	**1.30**
T Hoffman, SD	73.0	12	1.48
S Reed, SF	54.2	9	1.48
R Nen, SF	88.2	15	1.52
J Shaw, Cin-LA	85.0	20	2.12
D Cook, NYN	68.0	18	2.38
D Wall, SD	65.1	18	2.48
J Christiansen, Pit	64.2	18	2.51
S Radinsky, LA	61.2	18	2.63
2 pitchers tied with			2.70

Relief Wins

D Miceli, SD	**10**
W Gomes, Phi	9
D Cook, NYN	8
D Henry, Hou	8
5 pitchers tied with	7

Relief Losses

B Wickman, Mil	**9**
J Franco, NYN	8
S Belinda, Cin	8
J Shaw, Cin-LA	8
6 pitchers tied with	7

Holds

M Myers, Mil	**23**
R Rodriguez, SF	22
D Cook, NYN	21
L Painter, StL	21
2 pitchers tied with	20

Blown Saves

M Leiter, Phi	**12**
S Radinsky, LA	11
J Shaw, Cin-LA	9
4 pitchers tied with	8

Games

R Beck, ChN	**81**
C McElroy, Col	78
R Nen, SF	78
S Kline, Mon	78
A Telford, Mon	77

Games Finished

R Beck, ChN	**70**
J Shaw, Cin-LA	69
R Nen, SF	67
T Hoffman, SD	61
U Urbina, Mon	59

Relief Innings

S Sullivan, Cin	**102.0**
J Frascatore, StL	95.2
W Gomes, Phi	93.1
S Bennett, Mon	91.2
A Telford, Mon	91.0

K/BB Ratio

R Nen, SF	**4.40**
T Hoffman, SD	4.10
R Beck, ChN	4.05
D Jones, Mil	3.91
B Wagner, Hou	3.88

Opposition Avg

U Urbina, Mon	**.157**
S Reed, SF	.160
T Hoffman, SD	.165
R Nen, SF	.180
K Ligtenberg, Atl	.193

Opposition OBP

T Hoffman, SD	**.232**
R Nen, SF	.239
S Reed, SF	.251
U Urbina, Mon	.259
K Ligtenberg, Atl	.260

Opposition SLG

U Urbina, Mon	**.229**
T Hoffman, SD	.229
R Nen, SF	.251
S Reed, SF	.261
M Mantei, Fla	.289

1st Batter Avg

S Reed, SF	**.111**
R Croushore, StL	.114
T Hoffman, SD	.129
U Urbina, Mon	.138
Y Perez, Phi	.140

Vs LHB

R Rincon, Pit	**.131**
R Croushore, StL	.149
D Henry, Hou	.157
U Urbina, Mon	.159
M Myers, Mil	.162

Vs RHB

R Nen, SF	**.125**
S Reed, SF	.132
U Urbina, Mon	.154
T Hoffman, SD	.159
J DiPoto, Col	.170

BA Runners On

S Reed, SF	**.111**
U Urbina, Mon	.126
V Darensbourg, Fla	.149
T Hoffman, SD	.158
D Wall, SD	.163

BA Allowed ScPos

U Urbina, Mon	**.123**
M Wohlers, Atl	.143
S Reed, SF	.143
V Darensbourg, Fla	.148
J Rocker, Atl	.149

% Inherited Scored

V Darensbourg, Fla	**12.1**
B Wickman, Mil	16.1
J Rocker, Atl	18.2
L Painter, StL	18.6
A Osuna, LA	18.9

Grd/Fly Ratio Off

T Adams, ChN	**2.82**
J Tavarez, SF	2.56
M Petkovsek, StL	2.56
D Graves, Cin	2.55
C King, StL	2.51

Pitches per Batter

D Graves, Cin	**3.29**
A Alfonseca, Fla	3.35
D Jones, Mil	3.39
M Maddux, Mon	3.46
J Powell, Fla-Hou	3.47

Strike:Ball Ratio

D Jones, Mil	**2.47**
J Shaw, Cin-LA	2.20
R Nen, SF	2.19
G White, Cin	2.15
R Beck, ChN	2.04

Player Profiles

Kevin Brown, Tom Gordon, Trevor Hoffman, Greg Vaughn, Kerry Wood, Vlad Guerrero. . . many players put together seasons in 1998 that deserve a closer look. Unfortunately, we've only got room for three: Mark McGwire, Sammy Sosa and Roger Clemens. But we're sure you'll find their breakdowns intriguing. Take a look at McGwire, for example. When you hit close to .300 with 70 home runs, is it possible to take your game to another level? Somehow, McGwire found a way to do it: in 85 at-bats during the late innings of close games, he hit .306 with 16 home runs and an ungodly .894 slugging percentage. And please note that Sosa, who has a well-earned reputation as a free-swinger, actually saw *more* pitches per plate appearance than McGwire last year. That's no fluke; Sosa topped McGwire in '97, also. And if you think Clemens has lost even an inch off his fastball, take a look at his 11-0 record and 1.71 ERA in the second half. Do you know how many home runs he allowed to righthanded hitters last year? Exactly two.

The *Major League Handbook's* companion volume, the STATS *Player Profiles 1999,* contains breakdowns like these for *every* major league player.

Roger Clemens — Blue Jays

Age 36 – Pitches Right (groundball pitcher)

	ERA	W	L	Sv	G	GS	IP	BB	SO	Avg	H	2B	3B	HR	RBI	OBP	SLG	CG	ShO	Sup	QS	#P/S	SB	CS	GB	FB	G/F
1998 Season	2.65	20	6	0	33	33	234.2	88	271	.198	169	45	3	11	71	.277	.296	5	3	4.99	24	115	28	9	307	165	1.86
Last Five Years	2.96	70	38	0	148	148	1052.0	393	1120	.220	854	174	17	69	339	.298	.327	23	9	4.78	101	118	90	51	1369	790	1.73

1998 Season

	ERA	W	L	Sv	G	GS	IP	H	HR	BB	SO		Avg	AB	H	2B	3B	HR	RBI	BB	SO	OBP	SLG
Home	2.77	12	4	0	20	20	149.2	104	5	53	173	vs. Left	.197	456	90	21	2	9	41	58	147	.290	.311
Away	2.44	8	2	0	13	13	85.0	65	6	35	98	vs. Right	.198	399	79	24	1	2	30	30	124	.263	.278
Day	2.72	6	1	0	11	11	82.2	53	5	28	104	Inning 1-6	.195	683	133	36	2	8	54	73	210	.278	.288
Night	2.61	14	5	0	22	22	152.0	116	6	60	167	Inning 7+	.209	172	36	9	1	3	17	15	61	.273	.326
Grass	2.50	4	1	0	8	8	54.0	37	5	26	68	None on	.205	497	102	26	2	7	7	53	156	.288	.308
Turf	2.69	16	5	0	25	25	180.2	132	6	62	203	Runners on	.187	358	67	19	1	4	64	35	115	.262	.279
March/April	3.62	2	3	0	5	5	27.1	17	0	17	24	Scoring Posn	.176	233	41	11	1	2	58	24	73	.251	.258
May	3.43	3	3	0	6	6	42.0	32	3	21	45	Close & Late	.185	81	15	3	0	1	7	11	36	.283	.259
June	4.04	4	0	0	6	6	42.1	42	4	14	44	None on/out	.224	223	50	11	2	5	5	22	61	.302	.359
July	1.73	4	0	0	5	5	36.1	25	1	13	35	vs. 1st Batter (relief)	.000	0	0	0	0	0	0	0	0	.000	.000
August	0.90	4	0	0	6	6	50.0	25	0	10	68	1st Inning Pitched	.123	106	13	2	0	2	7	14	41	.231	.198
Sept/Oct	2.70	3	0	0	5	5	36.2	28	3	13	55	First 75 Pitches	.184	522	96	26	2	6	32	56	164	.267	.276
Starter	2.65	20	6	0	33	33	234.2	169	11	88	271	Pitch 76-90	.284	116	33	6	1	3	15	8	26	.346	.431
Reliever	0.00	0	0	0	0	0	0.0	0	0	0	0	Pitch 91-105	.224	98	22	6	0	2	11	12	41	.309	.347
0-3 Days Rest (Start)	0.00	0	0	0	0	0	0.0	0	0	0	0	Pitch 106+	.151	119	18	7	0	0	13	12	40	.229	.210
4 Days Rest	2.35	13	3	0	20	20	149.2	106	8	52	174	First Pitch	.257	109	28	6	0	0	12	0	0	.261	.312
5+ Days Rest	3.18	7	3	0	13	13	85.0	63	3	36	97	Ahead in Count	.119	395	47	13	2	1	16	0	224	.130	.170
vs. AL	2.47	18	6	0	30	30	211.2	144	9	83	248	Behind in Count	.295	166	49	14	0	5	21	48	0	.453	.470
vs. NL	4.30	2	0	0	3	3	23.0	25	2	5	23	Two Strikes	.113	462	52	19	2	2	22	40	271	.188	.175
Pre-All Star	3.55	9	6	0	18	18	119.0	96	7	56	120	Pre-All Star	.215	446	96	27	2	7	49	56	120	.308	.332
Post-All Star	1.71	11	0	0	15	15	115.2	73	4	32	151	Post-All Star	.178	409	73	18	1	4	22	32	151	.243	.257

Last Five Years

	ERA	W	L	Sv	G	GS	IP	H	HR	BB	SO		Avg	AB	H	2B	3B	HR	RBI	BB	SO	OBP	SLG
Home	2.79	38	18	0	75	75	554.0	434	25	186	599	vs. Left	.221	2089	461	92	13	36	187	244	615	.307	.329
Away	3.14	32	20	0	73	73	498.0	420	44	207	521	vs. Right	.220	1787	393	82	4	33	152	149	505	.286	.326
Day	3.06	21	13	0	51	51	356.1	301	22	139	378	Inning 1-6	.217	3160	686	141	12	55	278	328	910	.297	.322
Night	2.91	49	25	0	97	97	695.2	553	47	254	742	Inning 7+	.235	716	168	33	5	14	61	65	210	.300	.353
Grass	3.20	42	25	0	93	93	640.1	523	49	265	687	None on	.221	2280	505	98	10	48	48	233	678	.301	.336
Turf	2.58	28	13	0	55	55	411.2	331	20	128	433	Runners on	.219	1596	349	76	7	21	291	160	442	.292	.315
March/April	3.14	9	8	0	22	22	143.1	106	9	61	129	Scoring Posn	.196	892	175	36	5	8	246	112	264	.285	.275
May	2.90	14	5	0	23	23	167.2	127	11	65	189	Close & Late	.212	378	80	14	2	11	39	41	113	.290	.347
June	3.47	9	6	0	28	28	194.2	175	17	69	197	None on/out	.226	1005	227	33	6	24	24	95	286	.299	.342
July	3.03	13	10	0	27	27	190.1	155	16	76	189	vs. 1st Batr (relief)	.000	0	0	0	0	0	0	0	0	.000	.000
August	1.97	15	3	0	25	25	192.1	150	7	60	212	1st Inning Pitched	.181	515	93	15	2	3	35	62	164	.277	.235
Sept/Oct	3.35	10	6	0	23	23	163.2	141	9	62	204	First 75 Pitches	.224	2330	523	103	12	38	197	245	676	.304	.328
Starter	2.96	70	38	0	148	148	1052.0	854	69	393	1120	Pitch 76-90	.204	491	100	21	1	9	41	44	131	.277	.305
Reliever	0.00	0	0	0	0	0	0.0	0	0	0	0	Pitch 91-105	.202	471	95	20	0	13	43	45	143	.275	.327
0-3 Days Rest (Start)	0.00	0	0	0	0	0	0.0	0	0	0	0	Pitch 106+	.233	584	136	30	4	9	58	59	170	.306	.344
4 Days Rest	2.92	48	29	0	102	102	738.2	605	48	266	800	First Pitch	.316	469	148	28	1	8	52	3	0	.328	.431
5+ Days Rest	3.04	22	9	0	46	46	313.1	249	21	127	320	Ahead in Count	.142	1844	261	50	6	18	100	0	913	.152	.204
vs. AL	2.97	63	32	0	132	132	936.1	748	62	357	999	Behind in Count	.331	771	255	51	8	21	94	180	0	.457	.499
vs. NL	2.88	7	6	0	16	16	115.2	106	7	36	121	Two Strikes	.133	2068	276	59	6	22	119	209	1120	.218	.200
Pre-All Star	3.12	34	22	0	81	81	563.1	455	41	218	568	Pre-All Star	.219	2078	455	104	8	41	188	218	568	.299	.336
Post-All Star	2.78	36	16	0	67	67	488.2	399	28	175	552	Post-All Star	.221	1798	399	70	9	28	151	175	552	.296	.318

Pitcher vs. Batter (career)

Pitches Best Vs.	Avg	AB	H	2B	3B	HR	RBI	BB	SO	OBP	SLG	Pitches Worst Vs.	Avg	AB	H	2B	3B	HR	RBI	BB	SO	OBP	SLG
Cecil Fielder	.043	46	2	0	0	0	2	4	21	.120	.043	Gary Sheffield	.533	15	8	1	0	0	2	1	1	.563	.600
Darren Bragg	.050	20	1	0	0	0	2	1	5	.130	.050	Jim Leyritz	.385	13	5	1	0	1	4	0	4	.385	.692
Jeff Cirillo	.067	15	1	1	0	0	0	0	8	.067	.133	Ken Griffey Jr	.382	68	26	7	0	6	15	10	10	.462	.750
Dave Magadan	.083	12	1	0	0	0	0	0	1	.083	.083	Will Clark	.353	17	6	3	0	1	4	4	4	.476	.706
Kimera Bartee	.083	12	1	0	0	0	0	0	10	.083	.083	Jim Thome	.324	34	11	2	0	5	11	7	9	.442	.824

Mark McGwire — Cardinals
Age 35 – Bats Right (flyball hitter)

	Avg	G	AB	R	H	2B	3B	HR	RBI	BB	SO	HBP	GDP	SB	CS	OBP	SLG	IBB	SH	SF	#Pit	#P/PA	GB	FB	G/F
1998 Season	.299	155	509	130	152	21	0	70	147	162	155	6	8	1	0	.470	.752	28	0	4	2692	3.95	92	177	0.52
Last Five Years	.287	592	1924	421	553	85	0	228	498	504	543	34	43	5	1	.440	.687	68	0	18	9602	3.87	357	744	0.48

1998 Season

	Avg	AB	H	2B	3B	HR	RBI	BB	SO	OBP	SLG		Avg	AB	H	2B	3B	HR	RBI	BB	SO	OBP	SLG
vs. Left	.254	130	33	4	0	15	27	49	38	.459	.631	First Pitch	.425	73	31	6	0	11	23	20	0	.558	.959
vs. Right	.314	379	119	17	0	55	120	113	117	.474	.794	Ahead in Count	.396	111	44	5	0	24	51	73	0	.633	1.090
Groundball	.283	159	45	6	0	18	43	50	43	.458	.660	Behind in Count	.239	222	53	6	0	24	55	0	114	.241	.590
Flyball	.345	87	30	4	0	13	23	25	24	.500	.839	Two Strikes	.163	258	42	2	0	21	48	69	155	.340	.415
Home	.316	263	83	10	0	38	80	94	83	.497	.787	Batting #1	1.000	2	2	1	0	1	2	0	0	1.000	3.000
Away	.280	246	69	11	0	32	67	68	72	.438	.715	Batting #3	.296	506	150	20	0	69	145	162	155	.469	.745
Day	.296	159	47	8	0	21	45	63	56	.496	.742	Other	.000	1	0	0	0	0	0	0	0	.000	.000
Night	.300	350	105	13	0	49	102	99	99	.457	.757	March/April	.318	88	28	7	0	11	36	27	30	.470	.773
Grass	.305	426	130	17	0	60	129	139	136	.477	.768	May	.326	86	28	2	0	16	32	33	27	.513	.907
Turf	.265	83	22	4	0	10	18	23	19	.430	.675	June	.313	83	26	3	0	10	19	19	17	.457	.711
Pre-All Star	.310	268	83	12	0	37	87	88	78	.483	.769	July	.213	80	17	0	0	8	13	33	18	.443	.513
Post-All Star	.286	241	69	9	0	33	60	74	77	.455	.734	August	.289	90	26	7	0	10	19	31	39	.472	.700
Scoring Posn	.278	115	32	5	0	20	79	61	36	.517	.843	Sept/Oct	.329	82	27	2	0	15	28	19	24	.461	.902
Close & Late	.306	85	26	2	0	16	32	27	32	.473	.894	vs. AL	.298	47	14	1	0	6	10	7	9	.389	.702
None on/out	.287	101	29	5	0	10	10	28	30	.442	.634	vs. NL	.299	462	138	20	0	64	137	155	146	.477	.758

1998 By Position

Position	Avg	AB	H	2B	3B	HR	RBI	BB	SO	OBP	SLG	G	GS	Innings	PO	A	E	DP	Fld Pct	Rng Fctr	In Zone	Zone Outs	Zone Rtg	MLB Zone
As 1b	.296	506	150	20	0	69	145	162	155	.469	.745	152	152	1326.1	1326	96	12	128	.992	---	263	230	.875	.876

Last Five Years

	Avg	AB	H	2B	3B	HR	RBI	BB	SO	OBP	SLG		Avg	AB	H	2B	3B	HR	RBI	BB	SO	OBP	SLG
vs. Left	.282	490	138	21	0	57	121	161	135	.461	.673	First Pitch	.381	312	119	23	0	45	106	50	0	.476	.888
vs. Right	.289	1434	415	64	0	171	377	343	408	.432	.692	Ahead in Count	.412	381	157	21	0	78	163	232	0	.634	1.081
Groundball	.310	471	146	23	0	54	121	131	125	.467	.703	Behind in Count	.207	828	171	23	0	64	140	0	405	.216	.466
Flyball	.259	351	91	13	0	41	86	85	94	.416	.647	Two Strikes	.156	925	144	15	0	60	132	222	543	.322	.366
Home	.296	931	276	45	0	113	249	261	261	.456	.709	Batting #3	.292	636	186	23	0	89	179	199	202	.464	.748
Away	.279	993	277	40	0	115	249	243	282	.424	.667	Batting #4	.286	1187	339	60	0	130	297	279	317	.427	.665
Day	.298	711	212	39	0	86	183	201	198	.460	.716	Other	.277	101	28	2	0	9	22	26	24	.426	.564
Night	.281	1213	341	46	0	142	315	303	345	.428	.670	March/April	.300	270	81	19	0	29	82	83	79	.462	.693
Grass	.291	1670	486	75	0	197	435	447	478	.445	.690	May	.308	357	110	17	0	43	99	84	80	.442	.717
Turf	.264	254	67	10	0	31	63	57	65	.404	.669	June	.291	364	106	17	0	46	90	91	96	.441	.717
Pre-All Star	.299	1096	328	57	0	127	296	290	283	.449	.699	July	.258	333	86	11	0	32	67	83	88	.411	.700
Post-All Star	.272	828	225	28	0	101	202	214	260	.427	.671	August	.276	275	76	11	0	30	65	80	98	.442	.644
Scoring Posn	.284	469	133	28	0	58	266	194	137	.488	.714	Sept/Oct	.289	325	94	10	0	48	95	83	102	.444	.763
Close & Late	.275	291	80	7	0	33	75	98	97	.462	.639	vs. AL	.283	1189	336	51	0	133	296	290	315	.428	.661
None on/out	.289	467	135	21	0	58	58	96	130	.417	.707	vs. NL	.295	735	217	34	0	95	202	214	228	.458	.729

Batter vs. Pitcher (career)

Hits Best Against	Avg	AB	H	2B	3B	HR	RBI	BB	SO	OBP	SLG	Hits Worst Against	Avg	AB	H	2B	3B	HR	RBI	BB	SO	OBP	SLG
Rich Robertson	.600	10	6	1	0	3	7	3	1	.692	1.600	Juan Guzman	.000	11	0	0	0	0	0	2	5	.214	.000
Orel Hershiser	.529	17	9	1	0	4	9	1	5	.556	1.294	Roger Clemens	.085	47	4	1	0	2	2	6	14	.189	.234
Scott Kamieniecki	.444	18	8	2	0	4	8	2	3	.500	1.222	Troy Percival	.091	11	1	0	0	0	0	4	5	.333	.091
Scott Erickson	.429	28	12	3	0	5	11	3	5	.484	1.071	Rich DeLucia	.105	19	2	1	0	0	0	1	4	.150	.158
Rick Reed	.400	10	4	1	0	2	3	2	1	.500	1.100	Eric Plunk	.125	16	2	0	0	0	3	3	8	.263	.125

	Avg	G	AB	R	H	2B	3B	HR	RBI	BB	SO	HBP	GDP	SB	CS	OBP	SLG	IBB	SH	SF	#Pit	#P/PA	GB	FB	G/F
1998 Season	.308	159	643	134	198	20	0	66	158	73	171	1	20	18	9	.377	.647	14	0	5	2872	3.98	189	185	1.02
Last Five Years	.279	694	2773	456	774	106	15	203	566	235	705	15	65	114	46	.337	.548	41	1	20	11771	3.87	848	802	1.06

1998 Season

	Avg	AB	H	2B	3B	HR	RBI	BB	SO	OBP	SLG		Avg	AB	H	2B	3B	HR	RBI	BB	SO	OBP	SLG
vs. Left	.287	164	47	5	0	12	35	37	54	.418	.537	First Pitch	.340	47	16	1	0	3	11	12	0	.475	.553
vs. Right	.315	479	151	15	0	54	123	36	117	.361	.685	Ahead in Count	.426	169	72	11	0	26	69	32	0	.515	.953
Groundball	.354	212	75	9	0	17	49	17	44	.403	.637	Behind in Count	.259	286	74	7	0	26	55	0	125	.257	.556
Flyball	.284	141	40	4	0	17	41	11	50	.333	.674	Two Strikes	.203	325	66	1	0	25	45	29	171	.267	.437
Home	.300	310	93	11	0	35	77	34	79	.366	.674	Batting #3	.292	487	142	14	0	49	114	48	123	.353	.622
Away	.315	333	105	9	0	31	81	39	92	.387	.622	Batting #4	.359	156	56	6	0	17	44	25	48	.448	.724
Day	.294	360	106	11	0	33	77	45	88	.370	.600	Other	.000	0	0	0	0	0	0	0	0	.000	.000
Night	.325	283	92	9	0	33	81	28	83	.386	.707	March/April	.343	108	37	5	0	6	17	11	25	.403	.556
Grass	.305	531	162	17	0	57	133	61	134	.381	.659	May	.344	96	33	5	0	7	22	16	24	.426	.615
Turf	.321	112	36	3	0	9	25	6	37	.353	.589	June	.298	114	34	2	0	20	40	6	27	.331	.842
Pre-All Star	.324	333	108	15	0	33	81	35	80	.384	.667	July	.262	107	28	5	0	9	29	12	25	.336	.561
Post-All Star	.290	310	90	5	0	33	77	38	91	.369	.626	August	.322	115	37	2	0	13	28	16	35	.406	.678
Scoring Posn	.313	150	47	6	0	13	81	29	32	.413	.613	Sept/Oct	.282	103	29	1	0	11	22	12	35	.357	.612
Close & Late	.311	106	33	2	0	11	27	14	30	.388	.642	vs. AL	.255	55	14	2	0	6	14	4	13	.305	.618
None on/out	.276	127	35	0	0	10	10	14	34	.352	.512	vs. NL	.313	588	184	18	0	60	144	69	158	.383	.650

1998 By Position

Position	Avg	AB	H	2B	3B	HR	RBI	BB	SO	OBP	SLG	G	GS	Innings	PO	A	E	DP	Fld Pct	Rng Fctr	In Zone	Zone Outs	Zone Rtg	MLB Zone
As rf	.311	624	194	20	0	65	155	68	167	.377	.655	156	153	1379.0	319	14	9	2	.974	2.17	376	308	.819	.813

Last Five Years

	Avg	AB	H	2B	3B	HR	RBI	BB	SO	OBP	SLG		Avg	AB	H	2B	3B	HR	RBI	BB	SO	OBP	SLG
vs. Left	.278	679	189	26	3	50	132	94	172	.366	.546	First Pitch	.349	341	119	14	4	25	82	33	0	.407	.633
vs. Right	.279	2094	585	80	12	153	434	141	533	.327	.548	Ahead in Count	.405	551	223	36	4	73	196	77	0	.472	.882
Groundball	.304	773	235	34	3	49	149	60	166	.357	.546	Behind in Count	.212	1313	278	36	5	65	181	0	562	.216	.395
Flyball	.268	473	127	13	2	37	98	32	156	.314	.539	Two Strikes	.182	1405	256	29	4	58	157	124	705	.250	.332
Home	.282	1392	392	45	11	116	318	126	330	.341	.580	Batting #3	.285	847	241	25	1	67	178	70	215	.339	.554
Away	.277	1381	382	61	4	87	248	109	375	.332	.516	Batting #4	.277	1680	466	71	9	121	353	150	432	.338	.546
Day	.282	1563	440	59	12	120	326	151	380	.345	.565	Other	.272	246	67	10	5	15	35	15	58	.318	.537
Night	.276	1210	334	47	3	83	240	84	325	.325	.526	March/April	.262	416	109	14	3	19	61	35	102	.322	.447
Grass	.287	2223	638	89	15	178	489	203	549	.347	.581	May	.308	519	160	25	6	46	116	45	139	.364	.645
Turf	.247	550	136	17	0	25	77	32	156	.291	.415	June	.274	541	148	22	1	40	110	29	130	.307	.540
Pre-All Star	.279	1623	453	70	10	111	310	123	407	.330	.540	July	.284	542	154	25	0	36	113	50	121	.349	.530
Post-All Star	.279	1150	321	36	5	92	256	112	298	.345	.559	August	.273	450	123	13	4	39	104	41	127	.334	.580
Scoring Posn	.288	754	217	27	6	55	347	96	198	.363	.558	Sept/Oct	.262	305	80	7	1	23	62	35	86	.339	.518
Close & Late	.269	450	121	17	2	32	95	42	118	.329	.529	vs. AL	.330	103	34	8	0	9	24	9	25	.384	.670
None on/out	.268	597	160	22	1	43	43	44	137	.320	.524	vs. NL	.277	2670	740	98	15	194	542	226	680	.335	.543

Batter vs. Pitcher (career)

Hits Best Against	Avg	AB	H	2B	3B	HR	RBI	BB	SO	OBP	SLG	Hits Worst Against	Avg	AB	H	2B	3B	HR	RBI	BB	SO	OBP	SLG
Orel Hershiser	.520	25	13	1	0	4	9	2	3	.571	1.040	Dwight Gooden	.000	12	0	0	0	0	0	1	8	.077	.000
Ken Hill	.500	12	6	1	0	2	2	3	1	.600	1.083	Mike Jackson	.000	10	0	0	0	0	0	2	6	.167	.000
Mark Petkovsek	.462	13	6	1	0	3	8	1	1	.500	1.231	Mike Hampton	.100	30	3	0	0	0	2	1	9	.129	.100
Bryan Rekar	.455	11	5	0	1	2	4	0	0	.455	1.182	John Franco	.100	10	1	0	0	0	1	1	3	.182	.100
Robb Nen	.429	14	6	0	1	3	5	0	3	.429	1.214	Steve Cooke	.111	18	2	0	0	0	2	1	4	.158	.111

Manager Tendencies

One of the things about baseball which appeals to many of us is the game's endless opportunity for analysis. . . and few things are analyzed more than managerial decisions. Major League skippers may not have batting averages and slugging percentages to point to at the end of the season, but when it comes time to judge their performance and production, there's no reason we can't take a look at their statistics.

Which manager posted the best stolen-base success rate?

Which skippers were constantly tinkering with their lineups?

Which managers wore out a path to the pitching mound?

It's questions like these that get our second-guessing juices going, and it's questions like these that inspired the following pages, which look at managerial tendencies in a number of situations. Once again, the skippers are compared based on offense, defense, lineups, and pitching use. We don't rank the managers; there is plenty of room for argument on whether certain moves are good or bad. We are simply providing fodder for the discussion.

Offensively, managers have control over bunting, stealing and the timing of hit-and-runs. The *Handbook* looks at the quantity, timing and success of these moves.

Defensively, the *Handbook* looks at the success of pitchouts, the frequency of intentional walks, and the pattern of defensive substitutions.

Most managers spend large amounts of their time devising lineups. The *Handbook* shows the number of lineups used, as well as the platoon percentage. The use of pinch hitters and pinch runners is also explored.

Finally, how does the manager use pitchers? For starters, the *Handbook* shows slow and quick hooks, along with the number of times a starter was allowed to throw more than 120 and 140 pitches. For relievers, we look at the number of relief appearances, mid-inning changes and how often a pitcher gets a save going more than one inning (a rare occurrence these days). The categories include:

Stolen Base Success Percentage: SB/Attempts

Pitchout Runners Moving: The number of times the opposition is running when a

manager calls a pitchout.

Double Steals: The number of double steals attempted in 1998.

Out Percentage: The proportion of stolen bases with that number of outs.

Sacrifice Bunt Attempts: A bunt is considered a sac attempt if no runner is on third, there are no outs, or the pitcher attempts a bunt.

Sacrifice Bunt Success%: A bunt that results in a sacrifice or a hit, divided by the number of attempts.

Favorite Inning: The most common inning in which an event occurred.

Hit and Run Success: The hit-and-run results in baserunner advancement with no double play.

Intentional Walk Situation: Runners on base, first base open, and anyone but the pitcher up.

Defensive Substitutions: Straight defensive substitutions, with the team leading by four runs or less.

Number of Lineups: Based on batting order, 1-8 for National Leaguers, 1-9 for American Leaguers.

Percent LHB vs. RHSP and RHB vs. LHSP: A measure of platooning. A batter is considered to always have the platoon advantage if he is a switch-hitter.

Percent PH platoon: Frequency the manager gets his pinch hitter the platoon advantage. Switch-hitters always have the advantage.

Score Diff: The most common score differential on which an intentional walk is called for.

Slow and Quick Hooks: See the glossary for complete information. This measures how often a pitcher is left in longer than is standard practice, or pulled earlier than normal.

Mid-Inning Change: The number of times a manager changed pitchers in the middle of an inning.

1-Batter Appearance: The number of times a pitcher was brought in to face only one batter. Called the "Tony La Russa special" because of his penchant for trying to orchestrate specific match-ups for specific situations.

3 Pitchers (2 runs or less): The club gives up two runs or fewer in a game, but uses at least three pitchers.

Offense

	G	Att	SB%	Ptchout Rn Mvg	2nd SB-CS	3rd SB-CS	Home SB-CS	Double Steals	Out Percentage 0	1	2	Sac. Bunts Att	Suc. %	Fav. Inning	Sqz	Hit & Run Att	Suc. %
AL Managers																	
Bell, Buddy, Det	137	143	64.3	7	80-43	11-6	1-2	3	23.1	33.6	33.6	24	70.8	3	1	68	25.0
Collins, Terry, Ana	162	138	67.4	5	84-40	9-5	0-0	2	13.8	46.4	46.4	69	82.6	8	6	88	38.6
Hargrove, Mike, Cle	162	203	70.4	4	114-49	29-8	0-4	7	22.2	27.1	27.1	53	84.9	7	0	93	37.6
Howe, Art, Oak	162	178	73.6	5	111-39	19-4	1-4	6	18.0	37.6	37.6	75	89.3	7	1	75	37.3
Johnson, Tim, Tor	163	265	69.4	10	154-70	30-9	0-2	12	18.1	40.4	40.4	59	79.7	7	0	78	34.6
Kelly, Tom, Min	162	166	67.5	5	97-51	14-3	1-1	5	17.5	42.8	42.8	28	78.6	8	2	91	44.0
Manuel, Jerry, ChA	163	173	73.4	3	114-41	13-5	0-0	2	17.9	35.3	35.3	54	79.6	7	2	73	35.6
Miller, Ray, Bal	162	134	64.2	3	74-42	12-5	0-0	6	17.2	35.8	35.8	66	86.4	3	6	101	34.7
Muser, Tony, KC	161	185	73.0	3	112-44	21-4	2-2	6	18.9	40.5	40.5	70	75.7	8	2	111	34.2
Oates, Johnny, Tex	162	129	63.6	4	71-43	11-3	0-1	5	20.2	44.2	44.2	58	74.1	3	1	64	43.8
Parrish, Larry, Det	25	41	73.2	0	27-11	3-0	0-0	0	17.1	34.1	34.1	4	100.0	9	2	28	39.3
Piniella, Lou, Sea	161	154	74.7	4	94-32	20-7	1-0	7	16.9	43.5	43.5	58	67.2	7	4	68	36.8
Rothschild, Larry, TB	162	193	62.2	8	111-66	8-3	1-4	3	20.7	34.7	34.7	66	81.8	8	3	149	38.3
Torre, Joe, NYA	162	216	70.8	5	128-55	25-6	0-2	5	25.5	37.0	37.0	44	81.8	6	1	115	33.9
Williams, Jimy, Bos	162	111	64.9	1	70-38	2-0	0-1	1	18.0	36.0	36.0	48	83.3	7	5	89	27.0
NL Managers																	
Alou, Felipe, Mon	162	137	66.4	5	84-42	6-2	1-2	2	16.1	43.8	43.8	111	82.0	3	4	73	28.8
Baker, Dusty, SF	163	153	66.7	1	97-43	5-7	0-1	2	21.6	30.7	30.7	111	83.8	5	4	111	42.3
Baylor, Don, Col	162	114	58.8	2	52-43	14-1	1-2	4	31.6	30.7	30.7	131	80.2	3	8	79	40.5
Bochy, Bruce, SD	162	116	63.1	0	66-33	12-2	1-2	4	24.1	32.8	32.8	84	72.6	7	3	83	34.9
Cox, Bobby, Atl	162	141	69.5	3	88-33	9-9	1-1	2	18.4	38.3	38.3	97	82.5	3	8	61	42.6
Dierker, Larry, Hou	162	206	75.2	5	127-42	28-7	0-2	10	24.8	35.0	35.0	79	79.7	5	5	106	34.0
Francona, Terry, Phi	162	142	68.3	2	87-41	10-4	0-0	3	16.9	32.4	32.4	85	80.0	3	5	83	33.7
Garner, Phil, Mil	162	140	57.9	6	68-45	11-9	2-4	4	19.3	31.4	31.4	85	75.3	5	12	73	41.1
Hoffman, Glenn, LA	88	105	72.4	3	67-26	8-2	1-1	2	25.7	35.2	35.2	59	86.4	3	2	75	42.7
La Russa, Tony, StL	163	174	76.4	4	108-29	25-11	0-1	4	22.4	36.8	36.8	85	85.9	2	10	108	44.4
Lamont, Gene, Pit	163	210	75.7	6	129-43	28-8	2-0	8	19.0	35.2	35.2	116	81.0	3	8	117	35.9
Leyland, Jim, Fla	162	172	66.9	4	101-45	13-8	1-4	7	15.7	35.5	35.5	91	80.2	1	3	117	41.9
McKeon, Jack, Cin	162	137	69.3	6	87-37	7-3	1-2	3	25.5	29.2	29.2	98	79.6	8	3	64	29.7
Riggleman, Jim, ChN	163	109	59.6	2	58-40	7-1	0-3	3	19.3	33.0	33.0	89	79.8	3	8	85	41.2
Russell, Bill, LA	74	85	71.8	3	55-22	7-2	0-0	1	20.0	32.9	32.9	52	84.6	3	2	56	37.5
Showalter, Buck, Ari	162	111	65.8	2	68-32	4-4	1-2	1	15.3	35.1	35.1	68	69.1	3	0	37	27.0
Valentine, Bobby, NYN	162	108	57.4	3	49-40	13-6	0-0	2	20.4	33.3	33.3	113	84.1	2	8	92	34.8

Defense

	G	Pitchout Total	Runners Moving	CS%	Non-PO CS%	IBB	Pct. of Situations	Favorite Score Diff.	Defensive Subs Total	Favorite Inning	Pos. 1	Pos. 2	Pos. 3
AL Managers													
Bell, Buddy, Det	137	38	8	62.5	35.9	29	5.4	0	7	9	3b-3	ss-3	1b-1
Collins, Terry, Ana	162	38	10	30.0	29.4	16	2.1	1	33	9	3b-13	lf-7	cf-5
Hargrove, Mike, Cle	162	47	17	47.1	27.9	39	5.3	-1	32	8	2b-12	lf-8	cf-5
Howe, Art, Oak	162	26	5	40.0	31.5	19	2.7	0	40	8	2b-9	1b-8	cf-7
Johnson, Tim, Tor	163	22	8	50.0	22.9	22	2.8	0	34	8	lf-10	cf-9	rf-6
Kelly, Tom, Min	162	37	12	33.3	30.6	16	2.3	-2	32	9	2b-19	3b-4	cf-4
Manuel, Jerry, ChA	163	26	4	25.0	32.8	13	1.9	0	31	8	cf-20	rf-4	3b-3
Miller, Ray, Bal	162	51	14	28.6	22.2	22	3.0	-1	32	9	rf-15	c-9	1b-2
Muser, Tony, KC	161	21	2	100.0	33.9	22	3.7	-2	21	8	rf-7	lf-6	cf-4
Oates, Johnny, Tex	162	18	9	88.9	42.7	23	4.1	-1	18	8	cf-8	1b-5	2b-3
Parrish, Larry, Det	25	7	1	0.0	34.3	7	6.0	-2	6	7	lf-2	c-1	2b-1
Piniella, Lou, Sea	161	20	7	85.7	25.4	18	2.6	-2	43	8	lf-20	rf-10	3b-6
Rothschild, Larry, TB	162	23	5	80.0	37.3	21	3.4	-1	14	9	rf-4	cf-3	1b-2
Torre, Joe, NYA	162	9	3	33.3	33.3	18	3.0	0	28	7	lf-20	1b-3	rf-2
Williams, Jimy, Bos	162	75	21	33.3	30.2	23	3.4	-1	14	8	2b-4	rf-3	3b-2
NL Managers													
Alou, Felipe, Mon	162	18	2	50.0	32.5	30	4.4	-1	37	9	1b-16	lf-9	2b-2
Baker, Dusty, SF	163	41	6	50.0	27.7	51	7.6	0	12	7	1b-4	cf-4	ss-2
Baylor, Don, Col	162	99	22	45.5	30.4	12	2.0	-1	26	8	cf-12	lf-7	rf-5
Bochy, Bruce, SD	162	27	6	66.7	28.1	30	4.6	-2	44	8	rf-16	3b-8	c-6
Cox, Bobby, Atl	162	40	10	70.0	28.7	26	4.9	0	25	8	lf-16	ss-4	rf-4
Dierker, Larry, Hou	162	12	1	100.0	35.9	21	3.2	0	12	8	rf-4	cf-3	2b-2
Francona, Terry, Phi	162	16	4	25.0	27.6	23	3.3	-1	19	8	lf-13	1b-4	ss-1
Garner, Phil, Mil	162	59	6	33.3	20.9	21	2.9	-2	46	8	lf-21	1b-13	c-5
Hoffman, Glenn, LA	88	2	0	—	42.0	10	3.1	-2	25	8	lf-16	cf-8	c-5
La Russa, Tony, StL	163	34	7	42.9	31.8	32	4.5	1	18	8	ss-7	3b-6	lf-5
Lamont, Gene, Pit	163	61	11	45.5	27.6	38	6.0	-1	14	8	cf-6	1b-3	lf-3
Leyland, Jim, Fla	162	31	4	50.0	32.7	45	6.4	-1	15	7	1b-6	cf-5	rf-5
McKeon, Jack, Cin	162	7	2	50.0	28.0	31	4.6	-2	25	8	cf-8	3b-6	rf-5
Riggleman, Jim, ChN	163	26	5	20.0	26.6	36	5.0	-2	35	8	lf-16	cf-8	c-5
Russell, Bill, LA	74	21	7	42.9	33.8	9	3.2	-2	13	8	2b-3	ss-3	lf-2
Showalter, Buck, Ari	162	13	3	33.3	40.5	18	2.9	-2	15	9	rf-6	2b-4	cf-3
Valentine, Bobby, NYN	162	54	15	40.0	34.9	41	5.7	-1	34	8	rf-12	lf-9	3b-5

Lineups

	G	Starting Lineup				Substitutes				
		Lineups Used	% LHB Vs. RHSP	%RHB vs. LHSP	#PH	Percent PH Platoon	PH BA	PH HR	#PR	PR SB-CS
AL Managers										
Bell, Buddy, Det	137	88	51.4	76.5	102	84.3	.227	3	25	4-3
Collins, Terry, Ana	162	119	52.4	72.4	100	79.0	.195	0	64	1-2
Hargrove, Mike, Cle	162	108	56.4	75.3	88	83.0	.250	1	21	2-0
Howe, Art, Oak	162	129	51.5	74.6	136	61.0	.299	1	47	7-1
Johnson, Tim, Tor	163	91	49.3	80.2	61	73.8	.204	1	35	10-5
Kelly, Tom, Min	162	140	54.3	81.9	101	83.2	.301	0	22	1-0
Manuel, Jerry, ChA	163	110	45.7	84.4	65	75.4	.186	1	19	1-1
Miller, Ray, Bal	162	132	52.5	72.3	162	79.0	.209	1	45	0-2
Muser, Tony, KC	161	133	47.5	86.2	127	69.3	.186	1	25	2-1
Oates, Johnny, Tex	162	81	56.6	78.0	133	88.0	.233	2	22	1-0
Parrish, Larry, Det	25	20	52.6	79.6	32	84.4	.071	1	9	3-0
Piniella, Lou, Sea	161	111	44.6	86.8	99	79.8	.187	0	38	5-1
Rothschild, Larry, TB	162	139	62.8	78.9	126	70.6	.272	3	45	7-2
Torre, Joe, NYA	162	96	53.5	83.3	94	83.0	.203	2	36	3-2
Williams, Jimy, Bos	162	95	52.7	76.8	165	81.8	.220	2	53	4-0
NL Managers										
Alou, Felipe, Mon	162	133	40.0	86.7	235	83.0	.245	2	27	2-0
Baker, Dusty, SF	163	130	56.7	80.0	224	70.5	.223	10	20	0-1
Baylor, Don, Col	162	96	45.9	83.3	316	77.5	.224	9	31	4-1
Bochy, Bruce, SD	162	110	59.1	78.0	280	79.3	.177	2	62	5-5
Cox, Bobby, Atl	162	80	56.6	88.0	245	70.6	.243	5	28	2-1
Dierker, Larry, Hou	162	81	21.2	96.7	233	75.1	.188	2	12	0-0
Francona, Terry, Phi	162	84	42.3	86.1	256	55.9	.232	5	20	1-0
Garner, Phil, Mil	162	125	54.5	69.7	265	71.7	.226	7	54	3-1
Hoffman, Glenn, LA	88	66	24.7	96.0	126	76.2	.216	2	16	4-1
La Russa, Tony, StL	163	146	40.5	80.8	259	71.0	.235	10	7	0-0
Lamont, Gene, Pit	163	106	36.5	84.0	197	73.1	.202	4	16	0-0
Leyland, Jim, Fla	162	96	54.1	72.5	277	80.1	.209	3	13	0-0
McKeon, Jack, Cin	162	132	44.9	90.4	288	80.9	.205	2	30	0-1
Riggleman, Jim, ChN	163	104	51.2	72.3	273	71.1	.254	10	26	0-0
Russell, Bill, LA	74	49	35.6	95.8	108	84.3	.222	1	17	0-0
Showalter, Buck, Ari	162	124	56.6	76.7	252	65.9	.173	3	17	0-0
Valentine, Bobby, NYN	162	124	51.4	88.1	305	81.0	.223	4	42	1-2

Pitching

	G	Starters					Relievers					
		Slow Hooks	Quick Hooks	>120 Pitches	>140 Pitches	3 Days Rest	Relief App	Mid-Inning Change	Save >1 IP	1st Batter Platoon Pct	1-Batter App	3 Pitchers (<=2 runs)
AL Managers												
Bell, Buddy, Det	137	15	15	10	0	1	362	176	4	63.5	35	16
Collins, Terry, Ana	162	11	15	28	3	8	415	236	11	67.7	62	20
Hargrove, Mike, Cle	162	13	15	19	0	0	423	194	9	64.7	48	26
Howe, Art, Oak	162	20	15	12	1	2	408	239	15	65.7	54	19
Johnson, Tim, Tor	163	21	7	36	2	0	384	203	6	64.3	52	21
Kelly, Tom, Min	162	8	14	9	0	1	432	233	7	68.5	48	28
Manuel, Jerry, ChA	163	18	18	6	0	0	405	184	14	59.5	24	17
Miller, Ray, Bal	162	17	19	19	1	5	402	206	13	64.2	31	22
Muser, Tony, KC	161	23	11	10	0	0	388	156	9	65.5	17	15
Oates, Johnny, Tex	162	20	10	18	0	3	402	228	7	67.1	39	15
Parrish, Larry, Det	25	1	2	0	0	0	84	45	1	57.1	15	5
Piniella, Lou, Sea	161	24	19	32	4	1	368	173	4	63.3	28	16
Rothschild, Larry, TB	162	7	26	14	0	2	410	182	6	60.2	33	26
Torre, Joe, NYA	162	14	10	27	2	2	334	162	17	57.2	31	25
Williams, Jimy, Bos	162	11	26	14	1	1	432	188	18	62.7	36	25
NL Managers												
Alou, Felipe, Mon	162	8	27	2	0	0	443	174	15	60.4	33	27
Baker, Dusty, SF	163	12	15	8	0	2	433	175	5	59.7	31	28
Baylor, Don, Col	162	35	11	18	0	4	406	126	4	63.5	34	16
Bochy, Bruce, SD	162	7	18	9	0	1	369	136	12	66.1	25	31
Cox, Bobby, Atl	162	12	14	14	0	1	354	92	1	56.2	28	36
Dierker, Larry, Hou	162	7	12	15	0	1	340	113	11	47.8	22	22
Francona, Terry, Phi	162	23	15	20	1	1	385	119	7	59.0	20	17
Garner, Phil, Mil	162	18	23	6	0	1	416	172	9	60.7	33	33
Hoffman, Glenn, LA	88	7	7	13	0	0	169	57	3	46.7	6	13
La Russa, Tony, StL	163	14	22	13	0	3	429	166	14	60.0	22	22
Lamont, Gene, Pit	163	10	17	10	0	0	395	149	12	65.1	29	26
Leyland, Jim, Fla	162	24	18	25	6	5	420	182	8	68.3	26	17
McKeon, Jack, Cin	162	8	21	10	0	3	366	138	20	59.7	20	15
Riggleman, Jim, ChN	163	14	16	20	0	0	449	216	6	66.4	43	17
Russell, Bill, LA	74	5	8	10	0	0	173	70	5	54.3	14	8
Showalter, Buck, Ari	162	11	14	7	0	1	368	122	6	59.2	17	15
Valentine, Bobby, NYN	162	9	15	21	0	1	399	120	7	56.8	22	27

Player Projections

Over the course of a season, a .290 hitter will tend to hit about .290, and a .240 hitter will tend to hit about .240. This is basically all that we know, which enables us to predict what baseball players will do next season. Well, that's not all that we know. We also know that ballplayers tend to slow down as they get older, that baseball teams only play 162 games a season, and that players who hit in the minor leagues are going to tend to hit in the majors, only not quite as much. OK, that's it; that's all we know. This is not an adventurous process, is what I'm saying. We don't know who is going to work hard this winter and come back to have a career year, and we don't know who is going to eat too many chocolate bon-bons, and miss 40 games next season with tooth decay. Because we don't know these things, we don't make any radical guesses about players getting much better next year or much worse. We play everything straight down the middle. Of course, sometimes players do have career years. When this happens, we wind up with a bad projection. That happened last year to Bob Abreu, Cliff Floyd, and Carlos Hernandez:

Bob Abreu

	G	AB	R	H	2B	3B	HR	RBI	BB	SO	SB	CS	Avg
Actual 1998	151	497	68	155	29	6	17	74	84	133	19	10	.312
Projected 1998	127	383	49	98	17	7	6	47	44	101	12	9	.256

Cliff Floyd

	G	AB	R	H	2B	3B	HR	RBI	BB	SO	SB	CS	Avg
Actual 1998	153	588	85	166	45	3	22	90	47	112	27	14	.282
Projected 1998	100	228	32	59	14	2	7	31	27	56	6	2	.259

Carlos Hernandez

	G	AB	R	H	2B	3B	HR	RBI	BB	SO	SB	CS	Avg
Actual 1998	129	390	34	102	15	0	9	52	16	54	2	2	.262
Projected 1998	57	124	8	27	4	0	2	11	5	26	1	1	.218

Actually, our projection for Floyd isn't really off by all that much, except for the playing time. We had projected him as a regular for several years, but gave up on him when he didn't come through. Of course, we hadn't projected that Mark McGwire would hit 70 homers, Sammy Sosa 66, or Greg Vaughn 50:

Mark McGwire

	G	AB	R	H	2B	3B	HR	RBI	BB	SO	SB	CS	Avg
Actual 1998	155	509	130	152	21	0	70	147	162	155	1	0	.299
Projected 1998	154	539	100	143	23	0	52	116	132	152	1	1	.265

Sammy Sosa

	G	AB	R	H	2B	3B	HR	RBI	BB	SO	SB	CS	Avg
Actual 1998	159	643	134	198	20	0	66	158	73	171	18	9	.308
Projected 1998	153	603	89	155	23	4	37	108	51	156	28	11	.257

Greg Vaughn

	G	AB	R	H	2B	3B	HR	RBI	BB	SO	SB	CS	Avg
Actual 1998	158	573	112	156	28	4	50	119	79	121	11	4	.272
Projected 1998	116	387	65	89	19	1	22	69	60	100	8	4	.230

Vladimir Guerrero, we were almost exactly right on except that he hit twice as many home runs as we had expected:

Vladimir Guerrero

	G	AB	R	H	2B	3B	HR	RBI	BB	SO	SB	CS	Avg
Actual 1998	159	623	108	202	37	7	38	109	42	95	11	9	.324
Projected 1998	149	569	87	181	41	6	19	82	43	59	13	10	.318

Details, details. Scott Rolen was about the same as Vladimir: we hit his batting average on the nose, .290, but failed to anticipate his power surge. Shawn Green was in that class; we had projected him about right, except that we had 17 homers instead of 35. Other players who played far better than we had expected them to include but are not limited to Moises Alou, Derek Bell, Bret Boone, Scott Brosius, Eric Davis, Carl Everett and Tony Fernandez. About the same number of players hit far less than we had expected them to hit. Rich Becker, for one:

Rich Becker

	G	AB	R	H	2B	3B	HR	RBI	BB	SO	SB	CS	Avg
Actual 1998	128	213	37	42	5	2	6	21	43	76	5	1	.197
Projected 1998	144	501	76	142	25	3	11	57	64	121	16	7	.283

Geronimo Berroa and John Jaha, for two more:

Geronimo Berroa

	G	AB	R	H	2B	3B	HR	RBI	BB	SO	SB	CS	Avg
Actual 1998	72	191	23	43	7	2	1	13	24	44	1	1	.225
Projected 1998	151	568	86	155	24	1	27	93	64	118	6	4	.273

John Jaha

	G	AB	R	H	2B	3B	HR	RBI	BB	SO	SB	CS	Avg
Actual 1998	73	216	29	45	6	1	7	38	49	66	1	3	.208
Projected 1998	143	513	88	141	24	1	30	93	74	112	3	2	.275

Mike Cameron, Chris Stynes and Ernie Young, for three more:

Mike Cameron

	G	AB	R	H	2B	3B	HR	RBI	BB	SO	SB	CS	Avg
Actual 1998	141	396	53	83	16	5	8	43	37	101	27	11	.210
Projected 1998	148	523	96	137	28	7	21	74	65	139	28	10	.262

Chris Stynes

	G	AB	R	H	2B	3B	HR	RBI	BB	SO	SB	CS	Avg
Actual 1998	123	347	52	88	10	1	6	27	32	36	15	1	.254
Projected 1998	156	557	76	165	29	3	10	65	31	37	15	7	.296

Ernie Young

	G	AB	R	H	2B	3B	HR	RBI	BB	SO	SB	CS	Avg
Actual 1998	25	53	2	10	3	0	1	3	2	9	2	1	.189
Projected 1998	111	340	52	83	16	2	12	48	44	87	4	5	.244

They say that confession is good for the soul, and, just on that theory, we'll throw out the names Bobby Bonilla, Bernard Gilkey, Marc Newfield, Jon Nunnally and Kevin Orie. We projected that they would hit 91 homers as a group. They hit 34, and each of them was at least 25 points under his projected average. Nunnally and Orie were 60 points under. Sometimes we project that a young player will play, and he doesn't. That happened last year to Brian Lesher and Jacob Cruz:

Brian Lesher

	G	AB	R	H	2B	3B	HR	RBI	BB	SO	SB	CS	Avg
Actual 1998	7	7	0	1	1	0	0	1	0	3	0	0	.143
Projected 1998	70	234	33	61	12	1	9	34	22	53	4	3	.261

Jacob Cruz

	G	AB	R	H	2B	3B	HR	RBI	BB	SO	SB	CS	Avg
Actual 1998	4	4	0	0	0	0	0	0	0	3	0	0	.000
Projected 1998	136	421	63	120	28	1	8	61	47	68	7	6	.285

Sometimes players who are projected to play get hurt, like Benito Santiago and Todd Greene. Occasionally players who we don't expect to play much do play, like David Bell and Dmitri Young. But I will say this for our system: if a player doesn't hit less than we expect him to, and he doesn't hit more than we expect him to, and he plays about as much as we expect him to, then we usually wind up with a pretty accurate projection. No, seriously, the last thing I would want is to make any exaggerated claims about the accuracy of our projections, but it is amazing how many players in any season deliver no surprises. There is a system of "similarity scores", which has been explained in several of my books. We do a study every year, comparing the similarity of each player's projected record to his actual record. If the similarity is 980 to 1000, we score that an "A+" projection. 960 to 979 is an "A", etc. We had 396 projections of players who actually played in the majors last year.

This is a summary of our self-scored accuracy:

Grade	Range	#	Grade	Range	#
A+	(980 and up)	8	C	(840 to 859)	17
A	(960 to 979)	52	C−	(820 to 839)	16
A−	(940 to 959)	71	D+	(800 to 819)	13
B+	(920 to 939)	83	D	(780 to 799)	7
B	(900 to 919)	45	D−	(760 to 779)	8
B−	(880 to 899)	41	F	(Up to 759)	14
C+	(860 to 879)	21			

It was actually the best year we had ever had, with an average score of 905. The 14 players for whom we had "F" projections were Mark Bellhorn, Geronimo Berroa, Jacob Cruz, Eric Davis, Carlos Garcia, Todd Greene, John Jaha, Mark Johnson, Paul Konerko, Jon Nunnally, Dante Powell, Benito Santiago, Dale Sveum, and Greg Vaughn; I discussed most of those earlier, and the others were just guys that we had projected to play who didn't play for one reason or another. The 8 players for whom we had "A+" projections were, alphabetically, John Cangelosi, Mike DiFelice, Shane Halter, Mike Lansing, Mike Matheny, Greg Myers, Craig Shipley, and Matt Stairs. These are their projected and actual records:

John Cangelosi

	G	AB	R	H	2B	3B	HR	RBI	BB	SO	SB	CS	Avg
Actual 1998	104	171	19	43	8	0	1	10	30	23	2	3	.251
Projected 1998	99	136	22	33	5	1	1	8	23	24	8	3	.243

Mike DiFelice

	G	AB	R	H	2B	3B	HR	RBI	BB	SO	SB	CS	Avg
Actual 1998	84	248	17	57	12	3	3	23	15	56	0	0	.230
Projected 1998	84	230	18	57	11	0	4	24	18	42	1	1	.248

Shane Halter

	G	AB	R	H	2B	3B	HR	RBI	BB	SO	SB	CS	Avg
Actual 1998	86	204	17	45	12	0	2	13	12	38	2	5	.221
Projected 1998	78	202	22	45	10	0	2	16	17	43	3	3	.223

Mike Lansing

	G	AB	R	H	2B	3B	HR	RBI	BB	SO	SB	CS	Avg
Actual 1998	153	584	73	161	39	2	12	66	39	88	10	3	.276
Projected 1998	152	592	77	158	37	2	14	63	43	85	22	8	.267

Mike Matheny

	G	AB	R	H	2B	3B	HR	RBI	BB	SO	SB	CS	Avg
Actual 1998	108	320	24	76	13	0	6	27	11	63	1	0	.237
Projected 1998	128	330	29	75	18	1	5	37	18	74	2	1	.227

Greg Myers

	G	AB	R	H	2B	3B	HR	RBI	BB	SO	SB	CS	Avg
Actual 1998	69	171	19	42	10	0	4	20	17	36	0	1	.246
Projected 1998	77	180	19	45	9	0	4	22	12	31	0	0	.250

Craig Shipley

	G	AB	R	H	2B	3B	HR	RBI	BB	SO	SB	CS	Avg
Actual 1998	77	147	18	38	7	1	2	17	5	22	0	4	.259
Projected 1998	65	137	15	35	7	0	2	13	5	20	3	2	.255

Matt Stairs

	G	AB	R	H	2B	3B	HR	RBI	BB	SO	SB	CS	Avg
Actual 1998	149	523	88	154	33	1	26	106	59	93	8	3	.294
Projected 1998	157	543	78	153	34	1	29	101	64	94	6	5	.282

I always thought it would be fun to nail somebody's triple crown stats on the nose, but I don't think we've ever done that. Last year we hit the batting average dead on for nine players: Domingo Cedeno, Darin Erstad, Marquis Grissom, Ricky Gutierrez, Luis Lopez, Orlando Merced, Edgar Renteria, Scott Rolen and Terry Steinbach. We had a straight "A" projection for Lopez:

Luis Lopez

	G	AB	R	H	2B	3B	HR	RBI	BB	SO	SB	CS	Avg
Actual 1998	117	266	37	67	13	2	2	22	20	60	2	2	.252
Projected 1998	95	258	29	65	16	1	3	26	14	50	3	3	.252

I'll show you the projections for the regulars in that group:

Darin Erstad

	G	AB	R	H	2B	3B	HR	RBI	BB	SO	SB	CS	Avg
Actual 1998	133	537	84	159	39	3	19	82	43	77	20	6	.296
Projected 1998	147	567	100	168	32	4	14	72	57	81	18	10	.296

Marquis Grissom

	G	AB	R	H	2B	3B	HR	RBI	BB	SO	SB	CS	Avg
Actual 1998	142	542	57	147	28	1	10	60	24	78	13	8	.271
Projected 1998	152	612	92	166	28	4	15	58	46	76	32	12	.271

Edgar Renteria

	G	AB	R	H	2B	3B	HR	RBI	BB	SO	SB	CS	Avg
Actual 1998	133	517	79	146	18	2	3	31	48	78	41	22	.282
Projected 1998	153	586	79	165	21	4	5	53	38	92	27	11	.282

Scott Rolen

	G	AB	R	H	2B	3B	HR	RBI	BB	SO	SB	CS	Avg
Actual 1998	160	601	120	174	45	4	31	110	93	141	14	7	.290
Projected 1998	152	555	82	161	40	2	18	83	69	107	12	8	.290

Terry Steinbach

	G	AB	R	H	2B	3B	HR	RBI	BB	SO	SB	CS	Avg
Actual 1998	124	422	45	102	25	2	14	54	38	89	0	1	.242
Projected 1998	130	459	52	111	22	1	18	65	37	107	2	2	.242

The projections for Renteria and Steinbach we scored as "A", for Grissom and Erstad as A–. The projection for Rolen, because we missed on his power by a significant amount, is scored a "B". To give you a clearer idea of what these groupings or "grades" mean, I'll show you examples of borderline cases, players who straddle the fence between groups. Edgar Renteria, for example, is right on the border between an "A" and an "A–", as is Ken Griffey Jr.:

Ken Griffey Jr.

	G	AB	R	H	2B	3B	HR	RBI	BB	SO	SB	CS	Avg
Actual 1998	161	633	120	180	33	3	56	146	76	121	20	5	.284
Projected 1998	154	588	127	178	34	3	50	128	91	116	14	4	.303

Brad Fullmer sits right on the line between an "A–" and a "B+":

Brad Fullmer

	G	AB	R	H	2B	3B	HR	RBI	BB	SO	SB	CS	Avg
Actual 1998	140	505	58	138	44	2	13	73	39	70	6	6	.273
Projected 1998	146	558	69	157	34	1	22	80	27	46	4	3	.281

While Neifi Perez is right between a "B+" and a straight "B":

Neifi Perez

	G	AB	R	H	2B	3B	HR	RBI	BB	SO	SB	CS	Avg
Actual 1998	162	647	80	177	25	9	9	59	38	70	5	6	.274
Projected 1998	156	602	84	187	40	11	11	66	26	57	10	8	.311

Carlos Delgado is on the fence between a "B" and a "B–":

Carlos Delgado

	G	AB	R	H	2B	3B	HR	RBI	BB	SO	SB	CS	Avg
Actual 1998	142	530	94	155	43	1	38	115	73	139	3	0	.292
Projected 1998	152	560	78	150	28	2	31	94	67	146	1	1	.268

While Bret Boone is just between a "B-" and a "C+":

Bret Boone

	G	AB	R	H	2B	3B	HR	RBI	BB	SO	SB	CS	Avg
Actual 1998	157	583	76	155	38	1	24	95	48	104	6	4	.266
Projected 1998	136	476	55	120	27	2	11	63	40	92	4	3	.252

That scores at 880. Exactly three-fourths of our projections from last year score better than 880, better than that one. David Bell is on the line between the lowest "C–" and the highest "D+":

David Bell

	G	AB	R	H	2B	3B	HR	RBI	BB	SO	SB	CS	Avg
Actual 1998	132	429	48	117	30	2	10	49	27	65	0	4	.273
Projected 1998	55	153	15	37	6	1	2	17	9	23	1	1	.242

While Scott Stahoviak represents the lowest "D–" and Benito Santiago the highest "F":

Scott Stahoviak

	G	AB	R	H	2B	3B	HR	RBI	BB	SO	SB	CS	Avg
Actual 1998	9	19	1	2	0	0	1	1	0	7	0	0	.105
Projected 1998	94	274	40	71	20	1	8	37	34	71	4	3	.259

Benito Santiago

	G	AB	R	H	2B	3B	HR	RBI	BB	SO	SB	CS	Avg
Actual 1998	15	29	3	9	5	0	0	4	1	6	0	0	.310
Projected 1998	117	395	46	95	17	1	17	54	33	87	1	1	.241

Why isn't Stahoviak an "F"? It has to do with the DISTANCE by which we missed. If we had projected him to play a couple more games, hit one more homer, etc., our projection would have been thrown into the "F" range. That's what most of the "F" grades are: they're guys who we projected to play, but who didn't play for one reason or another. We had projected that Lee Stevens would hit 20 home runs:

Lee Stevens

	G	AB	R	H	2B	3B	HR	RBI	BB	SO	SB	CS	Avg
Actual 1998	120	344	52	91	17	4	20	59	31	93	0	2	.265
Projected 1998	116	377	54	102	24	1	20	62	35	80	1	1	.271

We projected that Jose Guillen would hit 14 home runs, which he did:

Jose Guillen

	G	AB	R	H	2B	3B	HR	RBI	BB	SO	SB	CS	Avg
Actual 1998	153	573	60	153	38	2	14	84	21	100	3	5	.267
Projected 1998	144	500	60	137	21	5	14	70	18	80	2	1	.274

Those are both straight "A"s. We had the home run totals projected right for Sean Berry (B+), Barry Bonds (B+), Wilfredo Cordero (B+) and Alex Gonzalez (A–):

Sean Berry

	G	AB	R	H	2B	3B	HR	RBI	BB	SO	SB	CS	Avg
Actual 1998	102	299	48	94	17	1	13	52	31	50	3	1	.314
Projected 1998	122	378	44	105	24	1	13	61	27	60	8	5	.278

Barry Bonds

	G	AB	R	H	2B	3B	HR	RBI	BB	SO	SB	CS	Avg
Actual 1998	156	552	120	167	44	7	37	122	130	92	28	12	.303
Projected 1998	154	519	117	143	31	3	37	103	141	85	35	10	.276

Wil Cordero

	G	AB	R	H	2B	3B	HR	RBI	BB	SO	SB	CS	Avg
Actual 1998	96	341	58	91	18	2	13	49	22	66	2	1	.267
Projected 1998	125	480	68	138	30	2	13	63	31	88	9	4	.288

Alex Gonzalez

	G	AB	R	H	2B	3B	HR	RBI	BB	SO	SB	CS	Avg
Actual 1998	158	568	70	136	28	1	13	51	28	121	21	6	.239
Projected 1998	140	479	62	117	26	4	13	52	47	119	16	7	.244

We are proud of our projections for Edgar Martinez (B+) and Tino Martinez (A):

Edgar Martinez

	G	AB	R	H	2B	3B	HR	RBI	BB	SO	SB	CS	Avg
Actual 1998	154	556	86	179	46	1	29	102	106	96	1	1	.322
Projected 1998	145	512	101	156	38	1	25	101	121	88	4	3	.305

Tino Martinez

	G	AB	R	H	2B	3B	HR	RBI	BB	SO	SB	CS	Avg
Actual 1998	142	531	92	149	33	1	28	123	61	83	2	1	.281
Projected 1998	158	594	89	165	31	1	33	116	75	88	2	1	.278

We did well on our projections for the veterans David Justice (A−) and Jay Bell (A):

David Justice

	G	AB	R	H	2B	3B	HR	RBI	BB	SO	SB	CS	Avg
Actual 1998	146	540	94	151	39	2	21	88	76	98	9	3	.280
Projected 1998	139	506	82	143	24	2	28	90	86	82	4	4	.283

Jay Bell

	G	AB	R	H	2B	3B	HR	RBI	BB	SO	SB	CS	Avg
Actual 1998	155	549	79	138	29	5	20	67	81	129	3	5	.251
Projected 1998	151	555	78	143	30	4	15	67	62	109	6	5	.258

We are most proud, however, of our projections for young players, first-time regulars. In addition to the good projections shown above for Brad Fullmer and Neifi Perez, we had a "B+" projection for Jeff Abbott:

Jeff Abbott

	G	AB	R	H	2B	3B	HR	RBI	BB	SO	SB	CS	Avg
Actual 1998	89	244	33	68	14	1	12	41	9	28	3	3	.279
Projected 1998	110	260	40	81	16	0	6	33	19	28	5	3	.312

We had an "A" projection for rookie Danny Bautista:

Danny Bautista

	G	AB	R	H	2B	3B	HR	RBI	BB	SO	SB	CS	Avg
Actual 1998	82	144	17	36	11	0	3	17	7	21	1	0	.250
Projected 1998	67	165	20	40	7	1	4	20	11	34	2	2	.242

An "A−" projection for Aaron Boone:

Aaron Boone

	G	AB	R	H	2B	3B	HR	RBI	BB	SO	SB	CS	Avg
Actual 1998	58	181	24	51	13	2	2	28	15	36	6	1	.282
Projected 1998	92	252	33	66	16	2	7	33	15	37	6	2	.262

And an "A" for Adrian Brown:

Adrian Brown

	G	AB	R	H	2B	3B	HR	RBI	BB	SO	SB	CS	Avg
Actual 1998	41	152	20	43	4	1	0	5	9	18	4	0	.283
Projected 1998	53	182	25	48	6	1	1	13	13	22	10	5	.264

We evaluate our Todd Dunwoody projection at "B+":

Todd Dunwoody

	G	AB	R	H	2B	3B	HR	RBI	BB	SO	SB	CS	Avg
Actual 1998	116	434	53	109	27	7	5	28	21	113	5	1	.251
Projected 1998	121	361	47	87	15	4	12	45	24	109	13	6	.241

And chalk up an "A" for Karim Garcia:

Karim Garcia

	G	AB	R	H	2B	3B	HR	RBI	BB	SO	SB	CS	Avg
Actual 1998	113	333	39	74	10	8	9	43	18	78	5	4	.222
Projected 1998	91	282	36	69	11	3	9	39	16	69	5	4	.245

Garcia, who had only 9 major league hits before last season, hit 23 points less than we said he would, a discrepance of 8 hits, but we nailed his power, his strikeout/walk ratio, his stolen

bases and his playing time. We claim an "A–" projection for the American League's apparent Rookie of the Year, Ben Grieve:

Ben Grieve

	G	AB	R	H	2B	3B	HR	RBI	BB	SO	SB	CS	Avg
Actual 1998	155	583	94	168	41	2	18	89	85	123	2	2	.288
Projected 1998	149	556	100	162	35	1	23	105	71	116	3	3	.291

And the same grade—in fact, the same similarity score (956)—for his National League counterpart:

Todd Helton

	G	AB	R	H	2B	3B	HR	RBI	BB	SO	SB	CS	Avg
Actual 1998	152	530	78	167	37	1	25	97	53	54	3	3	.315
Projected 1998	148	551	91	180	40	4	19	93	72	72	3	3	.327

We had a "B+" projection for Mark Kotsay of Florida:

Mark Kotsay

	G	AB	R	H	2B	3B	HR	RBI	BB	SO	SB	CS	Avg
Actual 1998	154	578	72	161	25	7	11	68	34	61	10	5	.279
Projected 1998	140	479	79	121	23	2	12	59	50	79	13	4	.253

We didn't do quite as well for Eli Marrero of St. Louis:

Eli Marrero

	G	AB	R	H	2B	3B	HR	RBI	BB	SO	SB	CS	Avg
Actual 1998	83	254	28	62	18	1	4	20	28	42	6	2	.244
Projected 1998	123	381	52	96	18	3	15	55	22	56	7	5	.252

That's a "C+". We're not in the excuse business, but you all probably know why that was. Phil Nevin batted 100 times in a season for the first time:

Phil Nevin

	G	AB	R	H	2B	3B	HR	RBI	BB	SO	SB	CS	Avg
Actual 1998	75	237	27	54	8	1	8	27	17	67	0	0	.228
Projected 1998	81	248	32	59	12	0	9	35	26	65	1	1	.238

That's an "A", and Greg Norton is another one:

Greg Norton

	G	AB	R	H	2B	3B	HR	RBI	BB	SO	SB	CS	Avg
Actual 1998	105	299	38	71	17	2	9	36	26	77	3	3	.237
Projected 1998	101	313	46	80	16	1	10	43	33	67	5	6	.256

We got an "A–" for his teammate, Magglio Ordonez:

Magglio Ordonez

	G	AB	R	H	2B	3B	HR	RBI	BB	SO	SB	CS	Avg
Actual 1998	145	535	70	151	25	2	14	65	28	53	9	7	.282
Projected 1998	138	451	55	129	30	1	13	64	25	59	9	9	.286

And also an "A–" for David Ortiz:

David Ortiz

	G	AB	R	H	2B	3B	HR	RBI	BB	SO	SB	CS	Avg
Actual 1998	86	278	47	77	20	0	9	46	39	72	1	0	.277
Projected 1998	90	221	32	60	16	1	11	41	12	65	1	5	.271

We got a straight "B" for Kevin Sefcik:

Kevin Sefcik

	G	AB	R	H	2B	3B	HR	RBI	BB	SO	SB	CS	Avg
Actual 1998	104	169	27	53	7	2	3	20	25	32	4	2	.314
Projected 1998	61	140	16	37	6	1	1	11	8	14	3	2	.264

Larry Sutton earned us a "B+":

Larry Sutton

	G	AB	R	H	2B	3B	HR	RBI	BB	SO	SB	CS	Avg
Actual 1998	111	310	29	76	14	2	5	42	29	46	3	3	.245
Projected 1998	110	241	33	67	12	0	8	34	28	35	1	0	.278

And a solid "A" for Miguel Tejada:

Miguel Tejada

	G	AB	R	H	2B	3B	HR	RBI	BB	SO	SB	CS	Avg
Actual 1998	105	365	53	85	20	1	11	45	28	86	5	6	.233
Projected 1998	129	413	52	97	14	3	12	58	24	90	9	8	.235

We claim another "A" for Todd Walker, who opened the season on the bench, but had a breakthrough season:

Todd Walker

	G	AB	R	H	2B	3B	HR	RBI	BB	SO	SB	CS	Avg
Actual 1998	143	528	85	167	41	3	12	62	47	65	19	7	.316
Projected 1998	146	513	73	151	30	3	16	72	47	91	13	7	.294

We expected Bubba Trammell to earn more playing time earlier in the year—but we were exactly right about what kind of a hitter he was:

Bubba Trammell

	G	AB	R	H	2B	3B	HR	RBI	BB	SO	SB	CS	Avg
Actual 1998	59	199	28	57	18	1	12	35	16	45	0	2	.286
Projected 1998	131	442	73	122	25	0	31	81	46	106	4	2	.276

That scores at a straight "C", because we missed the playing time. We do not claim to be mystics or sooth-sayers; we're just a bunch of lousy statisticians. But we were pretty much right about all of these rookies and first-year players because a) we were able to correctly interpret their minor league statistics, and b) they all had seasons which fairly reflected their ability. We were wrong about Paul Konerko, Jacob Cruz and Mark Bellhorn, we believe, because a) we're not omniscient, and b) they didn't have seasons that reflected their ability.

But we'll get 'em next year. Thanks for reading, thanks for buying the book, and thanks to Mark McGwire and Sammy Sosa for a great season. It was never more fun to be wrong by 47 home runs on two players.

— *Bill James*

Pitcher Projections

Trying to project the statistics for major league pitchers is such a difficult task that even Bill James hasn't tried to do it. So much can change in a pitcher from year to year—his velocity, the sharpness of his curve, his command, his health, his role—that it's nearly impossible to predict what a pitcher will do with any accuracy.

But it's not *totally* impossible. Thanks to STATS president and CEO John Dewan and systems manager Mike Canter, we have a formula that projects 1999 pitching performances. All pitchers who have 150 games or 500 innings in their major league careers are covered.

How accurate are John and Mike? Just ask Bobby Jones and Scott Karl:

Bobby Jones

	W	L	ERA	G	IP	H	BB	SO	BR/9
Actual 1998	9	9	4.05	30	195.1	192	53	115	11.7
Projected 1998	11	12	4.13	30	194.0	198	63	120	12.1

Scott Karl

	W	L	ERA	G	IP	H	BB	SO	BR/9
Actual 1998	10	11	4.40	33	192.1	219	66	102	13.5
Projected 1998	11	13	4.68	32	198.0	217	69	119	13.0

Are the projections perfect? Of course not. If we were that good, we'd all be working as general managers for big league clubs. Our projections vastly underestimated Trevor Hoffman and Kenny Rogers:

Trevor Hoffman

	W	L	ERA	Sv	G	IP	H	BB	SO	BR/9
Actual 1998	4	2	1.48	53	66	73.0	41	21	86	7.8
Projected 1998	3	3	2.68	40	70	84.0	61	26	103	9.3

Kenny Rogers

	W	L	ERA	G	IP	H	BB	SO	BR/9
Actual 1998	16	8	3.17	34	238.2	215	67	138	10.9
Projected 1998	9	9	4.38	31	156.0	153	67	82	12.7

While the projections may not be infallible, we do think they're the best ones available on the market. So enjoy them.

— *Jim Callis*

Projections for 1999 Batters

Batter	Age	Avg	G	AB	R	H	2B	3B	HR	RBI	BB	SO	SB	CS	OBP	SLG
Abbott,Jeff, ChA	26	.301	125	422	61	127	25	1	13	56	27	46	7	6	.343	.457
Abbott,Kurt, Col	30	.254	103	280	37	71	17	3	8	34	20	81	3	2	.303	.421
Abreu,Bob, Phi	25	.270	154	560	71	151	27	9	15	80	75	146	20	13	.356	.430
Alexander,Manny, ChN	28	.223	113	260	35	58	12	2	4	24	18	60	9	4	.273	.331
Alfonzo,Edgardo, NYN	25	.288	150	517	73	149	26	3	16	79	58	66	7	3	.360	.443
Alicea,Luis, Tex	33	.245	125	351	52	86	17	3	5	35	55	65	12	6	.347	.353
Allensworth,J., NYN	27	.256	122	281	41	72	15	2	3	25	27	59	12	6	.321	.356
Alomar,Roberto, Bal	31	.297	141	539	87	160	30	4	15	67	65	60	20	5	.373	.451
Alomar Jr.,Sandy, Cle	33	.267	119	404	49	108	22	1	12	53	18	44	1	1	.299	.416
Alou,Moises, Hou	32	.288	149	546	89	157	33	3	27	107	68	84	9	4	.366	.507
Alvarez,Gabe, Det	25	.253	121	379	47	96	20	0	14	55	38	83	2	2	.321	.417
Amaral,Rich, Sea	37	.263	62	118	22	31	7	0	1	10	13	23	8	2	.336	.347
Anderson,Brady, Bal	35	.251	140	529	88	133	26	4	22	63	77	97	20	9	.347	.440
Anderson,Garret, Ana	27	.302	157	632	77	191	38	3	13	89	31	80	9	5	.335	.434
Anderson,Marlon, Phi	25	.265	112	317	41	84	14	3	5	32	15	44	12	6	.298	.375
Andrews,Shane, Mon	27	.229	152	555	63	127	24	1	27	81	59	163	3	3	.303	.422
Arias,Alex, Phi	31	.262	75	126	14	33	6	0	1	14	12	16	1	0	.326	.333
Arias,George, SD	27	.261	131	402	53	105	21	3	16	63	29	83	2	1	.311	.448
Aurilia,Rich, SF	27	.254	123	417	49	106	21	2	8	49	33	64	5	4	.309	.372
Ausmus,Brad, Hou	30	.253	137	431	55	109	18	2	5	43	48	75	13	7	.328	.339
Baerga,Carlos, NYN	30	.285	147	537	65	153	30	2	10	69	25	49	4	3	.317	.404
Bagwell,Jeff, Hou	31	.291	155	550	110	160	37	2	34	116	124	107	22	9	.421	.551
Baines,Harold, Bal	40	.270	121	326	40	88	14	1	11	49	43	47	1	1	.355	.420
Bako,Paul, Det	27	.258	89	267	25	69	14	0	4	29	23	67	1	1	.317	.356
Batista,Tony, Ari	25	.273	147	528	76	144	29	2	20	71	40	84	7	7	.324	.449
Bautista,Danny, Atl	27	.250	81	160	22	40	9	1	3	18	12	28	2	1	.302	.375
Becker,Rich, Bal	27	.260	120	342	54	89	17	2	8	39	53	94	11	5	.359	.392
Bell,David, Sea	26	.255	147	474	46	121	22	2	8	48	29	70	3	4	.298	.361
Bell,Derek, Hou	30	.279	151	592	83	165	29	2	17	94	46	115	23	7	.331	.421
Bell,Jay, Ari	33	.251	149	534	75	134	29	4	17	68	68	114	5	5	.336	.416
Belle,Albert, ChA	32	.300	156	597	106	179	41	2	41	128	77	89	6	3	.380	.581
Belliard,Ron, Mil	24	.262	128	381	56	100	23	3	5	39	38	54	14	6	.329	.378
Beltran,Carlos, KC	22	.298	139	500	101	149	33	13	20	81	35	90	15	0	.344	.536
Beltre,Adrian, LA	21	.243	97	309	38	75	18	1	11	45	26	56	11	4	.301	.414
Benard,Marvin, SF	29	.269	122	320	52	86	17	2	3	28	40	54	12	8	.350	.363
Benitez,Yamil, Ari	27	.246	63	187	21	46	8	1	8	26	11	50	3	2	.288	.428
Benjamin,Mike, Bos	33	.225	89	231	24	52	10	1	3	20	13	50	5	2	.266	.316
Berg,Dave, Fla	28	.274	81	248	31	68	14	2	3	28	24	43	6	4	.338	.383
Berroa,Geronimo, Det	34	.264	78	254	38	67	11	1	10	37	28	56	2	2	.337	.433
Berry,Sean, Hou	33	.275	118	360	43	99	22	1	13	60	29	59	5	5	.329	.450
Bichette,Dante, Col	35	.309	149	585	86	181	34	2	24	109	33	89	15	7	.346	.497
Biggio,Craig, Hou	33	.281	159	629	120	177	36	3	18	76	77	102	37	9	.360	.434
Blauser,Jeff, ChN	33	.249	118	374	58	93	19	2	9	37	57	84	5	2	.348	.382
Blowers,Mike, Oak	34	.248	98	282	34	70	15	1	8	45	32	76	1	0	.325	.394
Boggs,Wade, TB	41	.298	107	373	52	111	23	2	4	39	48	39	1	1	.378	.402
Bonds,Barry, SF	34	.293	151	509	109	149	31	3	34	101	138	84	32	10	.444	.566
Bonilla,Bobby, LA	36	.267	127	454	64	121	26	2	16	70	59	79	2	3	.351	.438
Boone,Aaron, Cin	26	.258	134	411	55	106	26	2	9	52	29	67	12	4	.307	.397
Boone,Bret, Cin	30	.246	154	540	62	133	31	2	16	73	46	107	5	3	.305	.400
Borders,Pat, Cle	36	.231	45	104	8	24	6	0	1	7	6	23	0	0	.273	.317

379

Projections for 1999 Batters

Batter	Age	Avg	G	AB	R	H	2B	3B	HR	RBI	BB	SO	SB	CS	OBP	SLG
Bordick,Mike, Bal	33	.241	149	485	50	117	18	1	9	48	41	64	6	4	.300	.338
Bournigal,Rafael, Oak	33	.240	71	171	19	41	7	0	1	13	11	11	2	1	.286	.298
Bragg,Darren, Bos	29	.266	130	403	57	107	26	2	8	47	55	83	11	5	.354	.400
Brede,Brent, Ari	27	.261	90	268	40	70	17	2	4	31	34	56	5	3	.344	.384
Brogna,Rico, Phi	29	.257	154	560	72	144	34	3	20	86	46	126	6	3	.314	.436
Brosius,Scott, NYA	32	.263	135	486	72	128	23	1	16	62	50	96	8	4	.332	.414
Brown,Adrian, Pit	25	.261	68	234	30	61	8	2	1	15	16	28	12	5	.308	.325
Brown,Brant, ChN	28	.271	114	347	46	94	20	3	12	42	24	79	5	6	.318	.450
Brown,Emil, Pit	24	.274	102	270	38	74	14	1	5	28	19	51	9	4	.322	.389
Brown,Kevin L., Tor	26	.255	68	204	29	52	10	0	8	28	21	59	0	0	.324	.422
Buford,Damon, Bos	29	.243	114	272	45	66	15	1	8	33	26	60	13	8	.309	.393
Buhner,Jay, Sea	34	.236	128	450	79	106	20	1	31	95	82	141	0	0	.353	.491
Burks,Ellis, SF	34	.277	138	505	87	140	27	3	26	83	55	102	14	5	.348	.497
Burnitz,Jeromy, Mil	30	.258	159	559	90	144	30	5	30	109	80	136	14	8	.351	.490
Bush,Homer, NYA	26	.264	54	125	16	33	4	1	1	9	7	29	6	4	.303	.336
Butler,Rich, TB	26	.246	61	199	26	49	7	2	6	24	19	39	5	3	.312	.392
Cabrera,Orlando, Mon	24	.249	129	401	58	100	21	5	3	38	29	43	15	8	.300	.349
Cairo,Miguel, TB	25	.256	153	555	63	142	24	3	4	45	25	54	27	11	.288	.332
Cameron,Mike, ChA	26	.250	123	392	67	98	20	5	13	51	47	102	23	9	.330	.426
Caminiti,Ken, SD	36	.265	134	476	74	126	27	1	25	81	75	114	8	4	.365	.483
Cangelosi,John, Fla	36	.240	84	150	21	36	6	1	1	9	23	25	7	3	.341	.313
Canseco,Jose, Tor	34	.245	141	526	83	129	25	1	37	100	72	150	13	6	.336	.508
Caruso,Mike, ChA	22	.295	140	549	87	162	19	6	5	62	15	36	22	9	.314	.379
Casanova,Raul, Det	26	.238	53	160	16	38	6	0	6	18	15	26	1	1	.303	.388
Casey,Sean, Cin	24	.316	126	456	65	144	34	1	12	82	53	61	1	1	.387	.474
Castilla,Vinny, Col	31	.303	158	617	93	187	29	2	40	114	40	93	5	6	.346	.551
Castillo,Luis, Fla	23	.265	73	253	37	67	7	2	0	14	31	47	18	8	.345	.308
Castro,Juan, LA	27	.215	74	163	18	35	7	1	1	13	11	29	1	1	.264	.288
Catalanotto,Frank, Det	25	.262	88	279	38	73	15	2	7	32	25	47	5	6	.322	.405
Cedeno,Domingo, Tex	30	.269	99	301	39	81	13	3	3	28	20	59	4	3	.315	.362
Cedeno,Roger, LA	24	.249	92	229	31	57	10	2	2	19	27	48	8	4	.328	.336
Chavez,Eric, Oak	21	.289	148	533	78	154	40	1	22	94	35	100	9	8	.333	.492
Christenson,Ryan, Oak	25	.274	98	317	56	87	18	3	4	34	37	78	7	6	.350	.388
Cirillo,Jeff, Mil	29	.297	157	586	91	174	38	3	13	74	69	77	8	5	.371	.439
Clark,Tony, Det	27	.272	159	588	90	160	27	1	33	102	75	155	2	2	.354	.490
Clark,Will, Tex	35	.286	146	538	85	154	32	2	18	88	73	91	1	1	.372	.454
Clayton,Royce, Tex	29	.256	157	566	74	145	27	4	8	55	44	99	31	13	.310	.360
Colbrunn,Greg, Atl	29	.280	91	175	20	49	9	0	5	24	9	29	3	2	.315	.417
Collier,Lou, Pit	25	.258	111	333	37	86	16	3	1	30	25	54	8	5	.310	.333
Conine,Jeff, KC	33	.270	121	389	48	105	22	1	15	64	44	86	2	1	.344	.447
Coomer,Ron, Min	32	.277	129	441	50	122	22	1	13	67	20	64	3	2	.308	.420
Cora,Joey, Cle	34	.273	145	550	86	150	22	3	7	40	53	47	12	7	.337	.362
Cordero,Wil, ChA	27	.287	136	499	72	143	32	2	15	67	31	98	4	3	.328	.449
Cordova,Marty, Min	29	.275	115	429	62	118	25	2	13	68	43	90	9	5	.341	.434
Counsell,Craig, Fla	28	.281	107	352	48	99	22	4	4	39	46	37	6	3	.364	.401
Crespo,Felipe, Tor	26	.259	71	201	28	52	12	1	4	22	28	27	5	5	.349	.388
Cruz,Deivi, Det	24	.254	145	456	46	116	26	2	4	46	15	52	4	4	.278	.346
Cruz Jr.,Jose, Tor	25	.263	144	521	86	137	28	3	22	78	79	127	12	5	.360	.455
Cummings,Midre, Bos	27	.259	69	139	16	36	7	1	3	14	10	25	1	1	.309	.388
Curtis,Chad, NYA	30	.255	126	322	54	82	15	1	9	37	48	56	14	7	.351	.391

Projections for 1999 Batters

Batter	Age	Avg	G	AB	R	H	2B	3B	HR	RBI	BB	SO	SB	CS	OBP	SLG
Damon,Johnny, KC	25	.282	158	568	84	160	23	9	12	60	48	74	23	9	.338	.417
Davis,Chili, NYA	39	.255	119	384	50	98	16	1	17	61	65	80	3	2	.363	.435
Davis,Eric, Bal	37	.272	118	386	58	105	17	1	21	60	49	113	12	6	.354	.484
Davis,Russ, Sea	29	.261	141	490	67	128	30	1	20	73	37	116	4	2	.313	.449
Delgado,Carlos, Tor	27	.274	155	551	85	151	35	2	33	103	73	147	1	1	.359	.525
Dellucci,David, Ari	25	.280	138	436	54	122	23	6	9	53	39	89	6	6	.339	.422
DeShields,Delino, StL	30	.269	137	506	76	136	19	6	8	47	55	84	44	14	.340	.377
Diaz,Einar, Cle	26	.266	54	158	18	42	8	1	2	16	6	12	1	1	.293	.367
DiFelice,Mike, TB	30	.241	101	286	20	69	13	1	4	30	19	56	1	1	.289	.336
DiSarcina,Gary, Ana	31	.255	153	541	60	138	27	2	4	46	20	38	8	6	.282	.335
Drew,J.D., StL	23	.305	152	561	109	171	34	3	29	103	96	141	3	13	.406	.531
Ducey,Rob, Sea	34	.240	89	179	23	43	14	2	4	16	15	46	3	2	.299	.408
Dunston,Shawon, SF	36	.254	84	248	28	63	14	2	6	26	7	39	8	3	.275	.399
Dunwoody,Todd, Fla	24	.252	149	527	70	133	26	7	14	60	34	147	15	6	.298	.408
Durham,Ray, ChA	27	.276	158	616	106	170	33	7	18	76	68	100	34	11	.348	.440
Dye,Jermaine, KC	25	.258	82	271	31	70	13	1	10	35	14	50	3	3	.295	.424
Easley,Damion, Det	29	.253	155	582	84	147	29	2	22	80	59	110	19	9	.321	.423
Edmonds,Jim, Ana	29	.292	151	575	107	168	33	2	28	91	64	111	5	5	.363	.503
Eisenreich,Jim, LA	40	.278	62	126	14	35	8	1	1	14	12	16	2	0	.341	.381
Encarnacion,Juan, Det	23	.290	155	572	85	166	29	5	20	75	36	116	23	10	.332	.463
Erstad,Darin, Ana	25	.299	148	578	99	173	35	4	17	79	55	80	20	9	.360	.462
Estalella,Bobby, Phi	24	.234	67	205	27	48	11	0	10	30	27	53	1	1	.323	.434
Eusebio,Tony, Hou	32	.281	77	192	19	54	10	1	2	29	20	27	1	1	.349	.375
Evans,Tom, Tor	24	.261	136	402	57	105	24	0	13	51	55	100	4	3	.350	.418
Everett,Carl, Hou	28	.263	123	361	53	95	20	2	10	49	33	84	11	8	.325	.413
Fabregas,Jorge, NYN	29	.242	83	227	19	55	7	0	3	25	14	29	0	0	.286	.313
Fasano,Sal, KC	27	.226	80	230	27	52	9	0	9	28	15	54	1	1	.273	.383
Febles,Carlos, KC	23	.293	128	417	78	122	22	10	9	37	48	75	31	13	.366	.458
Fernandez,Tony, Tor	37	.278	128	439	55	122	24	4	8	52	34	54	8	6	.330	.405
Fick,Robert, Det	25	.279	125	401	62	112	30	3	13	70	36	75	5	3	.339	.466
Finley,Steve, SD	34	.258	145	574	91	148	25	5	19	65	46	93	20	7	.313	.418
Flaherty,John, TB	31	.243	98	321	27	78	15	0	6	34	20	47	2	2	.287	.346
Fletcher,Darrin, Tor	32	.260	123	388	38	101	21	1	12	51	25	41	0	0	.305	.412
Floyd,Cliff, Fla	26	.276	151	576	80	159	29	3	21	82	59	121	26	12	.343	.446
Fordyce,Brook, Cin	29	.239	81	226	22	54	13	1	5	25	17	33	1	0	.292	.372
Fox,Andy, Ari	28	.245	116	241	36	59	8	2	4	20	27	47	11	5	.321	.344
Franco,Matt, NYN	29	.269	110	193	21	52	11	1	2	21	15	25	1	1	.322	.368
Frye,Jeff, Bos	32	.278	86	273	37	76	18	1	2	27	27	35	9	3	.343	.374
Fryman,Travis, Cle	30	.274	152	587	85	161	33	3	23	97	51	118	8	4	.332	.458
Fullmer,Brad, Mon	24	.280	147	521	62	146	39	1	17	75	33	54	6	4	.323	.457
Gaetti,Gary, ChN	40	.240	115	354	41	85	16	1	14	49	28	65	2	1	.296	.410
Galarraga,Andres, Atl	38	.270	143	544	88	147	26	1	35	108	49	148	11	5	.331	.515
Gant,Ron, StL	34	.225	129	435	66	98	21	2	23	71	62	122	13	5	.322	.441
Garcia,Freddy, Pit	26	.243	148	503	64	122	28	4	24	70	30	119	1	1	.285	.457
Garcia,Karim, Ari	23	.239	87	276	35	66	10	4	9	39	18	67	5	4	.286	.402
Garciaparra,N., Bos	25	.308	150	637	110	196	37	9	31	117	36	71	21	9	.345	.540
Gates,Brent, Min	29	.262	99	302	35	79	18	1	3	37	30	41	2	2	.328	.358
Giambi,Jason, Oak	28	.283	153	566	83	160	39	1	23	92	69	100	1	1	.361	.477
Giambi,Jeremy, KC	24	.310	138	422	65	131	24	1	17	66	57	74	6	5	.392	.493
Gibson,Derrick, Col	24	.316	73	206	30	65	10	1	8	28	12	42	4	4	.353	.490

381

Projections for 1999 Batters

Batter	Age	Avg	G	AB	R	H	2B	3B	HR	RBI	BB	SO	SB	CS	OBP	SLG
Giles,Brian S., Cle	28	.277	144	494	83	137	24	3	22	81	84	72	10	4	.382	.472
Gilkey,Bernard, Ari	32	.255	105	361	54	92	22	2	11	50	47	78	9	6	.341	.418
Giovanola,Ed, SD	30	.251	74	171	20	43	8	1	1	14	24	28	2	2	.344	.327
Girardi,Joe, NYA	34	.264	111	345	40	91	14	2	3	38	23	49	4	3	.310	.342
Glanville,Doug, Phi	28	.270	151	612	84	165	27	4	6	47	32	70	21	11	.306	.356
Glaus,Troy, Ana	22	.253	146	538	77	136	29	1	25	88	52	150	5	4	.319	.450
Gomez,Chris, SD	28	.253	151	558	67	141	26	2	6	55	66	111	5	5	.332	.339
Gonzalez,Alex, Tor	26	.249	151	559	69	139	29	4	15	60	41	122	17	8	.300	.395
Gonzalez,Juan, Tex	29	.295	151	600	98	177	34	3	45	141	47	113	1	1	.346	.587
Gonzalez,Luis, Det	31	.267	150	524	75	140	32	4	16	73	64	59	10	7	.347	.435
Goodwin,Curtis, Col	26	.249	113	297	44	74	12	2	1	20	37	63	26	11	.332	.313
Goodwin,Tom, Tex	30	.271	155	560	91	152	16	4	2	37	57	89	57	22	.339	.325
Grace,Mark, ChN	35	.297	153	572	86	170	35	2	13	78	84	50	4	4	.387	.434
Graffanino,Tony, Atl	27	.230	102	261	35	60	15	1	6	23	25	61	4	4	.297	.364
Grebeck,Craig, Tor	34	.246	84	187	19	46	11	1	1	16	19	25	1	1	.316	.332
Green,Shawn, Tor	26	.287	153	617	90	177	33	4	32	95	52	128	20	8	.342	.509
Greene,Todd, Ana	28	.278	121	403	57	112	22	0	21	66	26	63	3	3	.322	.489
Greene,Willie, Bal	27	.252	134	385	60	97	16	2	19	61	63	94	4	2	.357	.452
Greer,Rusty, Tex	30	.309	157	606	104	187	37	3	20	107	82	93	6	3	.391	.479
Grieve,Ben, Oak	23	.291	148	571	96	166	36	1	20	97	77	115	3	3	.375	.462
Griffey Jr.,Ken, Sea	29	.291	160	625	130	182	35	3	55	146	84	121	16	5	.375	.621
Grissom,Marquis, Mil	32	.268	143	570	73	153	27	3	13	56	35	77	22	10	.311	.395
Grudzielanek,Mark, LA	29	.279	158	641	78	179	36	2	7	57	27	79	25	8	.308	.374
Guerrero,Vladimir, Mon	23	.324	153	611	101	198	41	7	31	109	44	73	12	10	.369	.566
Guerrero,Wilton, Mon	24	.290	126	438	52	127	13	7	2	32	15	56	14	7	.313	.365
Guillen,Carlos, Sea	23	.246	113	342	42	84	13	1	5	32	23	68	4	4	.293	.333
Guillen,Jose, Pit	23	.275	148	535	61	147	30	3	14	78	20	86	3	3	.301	.421
Guillen,Ozzie, Atl	35	.252	102	309	36	78	12	2	2	28	14	20	4	4	.285	.324
Gutierrez,Ricky, Hou	29	.258	137	415	50	107	16	3	2	37	42	72	11	6	.326	.325
Gwynn,Tony, SD	39	.321	134	499	66	160	26	3	12	74	40	23	9	4	.371	.457
Halter,Shane, KC	29	.227	93	233	24	53	13	1	2	20	17	43	3	2	.280	.318
Hamelin,Bob, Mil	31	.245	55	106	15	26	8	0	5	18	19	25	1	1	.360	.462
Hamilton,Darryl, Col	34	.286	138	539	79	154	22	3	5	46	65	68	14	7	.363	.365
Hammonds,Jeffrey, Cin	28	.261	115	368	64	96	21	3	13	52	41	73	10	4	.335	.440
Harris,Lenny, NYN	34	.260	103	215	26	56	9	1	4	21	15	19	7	4	.309	.367
Haselman,Bill, Tex	33	.257	55	140	17	36	8	0	5	20	9	25	1	1	.302	.421
Hatteberg,Scott, Bos	29	.261	125	380	52	99	24	0	11	45	54	75	0	0	.353	.411
Hayes,Charlie, SF	34	.252	106	313	33	79	15	1	8	48	29	58	2	1	.316	.383
Helton,Todd, Col	25	.332	149	546	82	181	37	2	22	91	62	63	3	3	.400	.527
Henderson,Rickey, Oak	40	.237	130	418	79	99	17	2	9	38	103	93	38	11	.388	.352
Henley,Bob, Mon	26	.250	61	172	18	43	9	0	4	21	20	37	1	1	.328	.372
Hernandez,Carlos, SD	32	.255	137	384	27	98	13	0	7	42	14	69	3	3	.281	.344
Hernandez,Jose, ChN	29	.243	152	555	83	135	15	5	23	73	45	154	6	5	.300	.413
Hidalgo,Richard, Hou	23	.261	125	379	42	99	24	2	8	45	20	51	5	6	.298	.398
Higginson,Bob, Det	28	.290	156	573	93	166	32	3	26	87	75	90	8	5	.372	.492
Hill,Glenallen, ChN	34	.259	121	398	51	103	21	2	16	59	27	92	9	4	.306	.442
Hinch,A.J., Oak	25	.267	122	341	40	91	12	0	9	41	35	70	2	1	.335	.381
Hocking,Denny, Min	29	.224	70	161	18	36	7	1	2	16	12	31	3	3	.277	.317
Hoiles,Chris, Bal	34	.250	115	344	48	86	15	0	17	59	52	84	1	0	.348	.442
Hollandsworth,Todd, LA	26	.273	86	256	35	70	13	2	5	30	19	50	8	5	.324	.398

Projections for 1999 Batters

Batter	Age	Avg	G	AB	R	H	2B	3B	HR	RBI	BB	SO	SB	CS	OBP	SLG
Hollins,Dave, Ana	33	.249	102	349	57	87	17	1	10	45	47	78	6	3	.338	.390
Houston,Tyler, ChN	28	.250	106	252	26	63	11	1	6	32	13	44	2	2	.287	.373
Howard,David, StL	32	.225	51	102	12	23	4	1	1	9	9	19	1	1	.288	.314
Hubbard,Trenidad, LA	33	.288	76	191	30	55	12	2	6	20	22	33	8	4	.362	.466
Hughes,Bobby, Mil	28	.238	83	239	24	57	14	1	7	28	15	45	1	1	.283	.393
Hundley,Todd, NYN	30	.243	137	441	65	107	20	1	25	74	79	130	2	2	.358	.463
Hunter,Brian L., Det	28	.268	145	590	85	158	27	4	4	43	41	102	49	14	.315	.347
Huskey,Butch, NYN	27	.260	124	412	48	107	18	1	17	65	27	75	6	5	.305	.432
Jackson,Darrin, Mil	35	.245	70	143	16	35	8	1	3	18	5	26	2	1	.270	.378
Jackson,Ryan, Fla	27	.275	61	153	19	42	8	1	4	21	11	32	1	1	.323	.418
Jaha,John, Mil	33	.252	102	309	52	78	14	0	16	55	54	78	2	1	.364	.453
Javier,Stan, SF	35	.273	120	381	57	104	14	2	4	38	50	65	22	5	.357	.352
Jefferies,Gregg, Ana	31	.283	132	498	68	141	27	2	9	54	41	28	14	6	.338	.400
Jefferson,Reggie, Bos	30	.301	106	346	50	104	21	1	12	52	24	72	0	0	.346	.471
Jenkins,Geoff, Mil	24	.244	123	385	46	94	19	3	9	49	26	85	2	2	.292	.379
Jeter,Derek, NYA	25	.310	155	619	115	192	28	7	17	85	62	112	22	9	.373	.460
Johnson,Brian, SF	31	.253	109	324	31	82	13	1	12	44	19	50	1	1	.294	.410
Johnson,Charles, LA	27	.229	138	459	47	105	22	1	18	57	55	120	1	1	.311	.399
Johnson,Lance, ChN	35	.283	116	448	66	127	14	6	5	36	33	31	26	8	.333	.375
Johnson,Mark L., ChA	23	.241	101	278	39	67	10	3	4	34	51	60	0	1	.359	.342
Jones,Andruw, Atl	22	.272	158	570	89	155	29	4	32	94	53	126	28	9	.334	.505
Jones,Chipper, Atl	27	.302	160	605	114	183	33	4	29	109	92	91	16	5	.395	.514
Jones,Terry, Mon	28	.260	45	146	19	38	3	1	0	9	10	22	10	4	.308	.295
Jordan,Brian, StL	32	.291	151	532	84	155	28	4	19	85	35	74	21	8	.335	.466
Jordan,Kevin, Phi	29	.264	91	208	23	55	15	1	3	25	6	26	1	0	.285	.389
Joyner,Wally, SD	37	.272	126	426	51	116	26	1	10	67	56	58	3	2	.357	.408
Justice,David, Cle	33	.278	140	514	82	143	25	2	24	88	79	91	6	4	.374	.475
Kapler,Gabe, Det	23	.277	136	459	72	127	31	4	19	90	35	87	4	3	.328	.486
Karros,Eric, LA	31	.260	151	578	73	150	27	1	27	95	54	109	8	4	.323	.450
Kelly,Mike, TB	29	.239	95	251	41	60	13	1	8	31	26	68	11	4	.310	.394
Kelly,Pat, StL	31	.234	48	107	16	25	7	0	3	12	11	28	4	1	.305	.383
Kelly,Roberto, Tex	34	.282	105	344	46	97	18	2	11	49	20	63	8	5	.321	.442
Kendall,Jason, Pit	25	.307	151	551	85	169	33	3	9	71	54	50	18	7	.369	.426
Kent,Jeff, SF	31	.266	143	522	77	139	30	2	24	93	44	108	7	4	.323	.469
King,Jeff, KC	34	.241	139	507	73	122	26	1	23	93	64	86	11	4	.326	.432
Klassen,Danny, Ari	23	.267	51	172	23	46	10	1	4	19	10	36	3	2	.308	.407
Klesko,Ryan, Atl	28	.271	141	468	70	127	25	3	24	80	59	107	6	4	.353	.491
Knoblauch,Chuck, NYA	30	.287	155	602	120	173	31	6	13	64	91	77	48	15	.381	.424
Konerko,Paul, Cin	23	.262	110	355	45	93	15	0	15	57	34	55	1	2	.326	.431
Koskie,Corey, Min	26	.272	119	331	52	90	18	3	14	51	39	76	6	5	.349	.471
Kotsay,Mark, Fla	23	.275	154	585	87	161	28	5	13	73	50	70	13	6	.332	.407
Kreuter,Chad, Ana	34	.229	93	236	26	54	11	1	3	27	29	57	1	1	.313	.322
Lampkin,Tom, StL	35	.230	101	222	27	51	11	1	6	27	26	31	3	2	.310	.369
Lankford,Ray, StL	32	.290	145	511	89	148	33	4	26	88	88	135	27	9	.394	.523
Lansing,Mike, Col	31	.272	151	595	76	162	37	1	14	64	43	88	19	6	.321	.408
Larkin,Barry, Cin	35	.282	146	531	95	150	28	4	18	64	94	63	39	8	.390	.452
Lawton,Matt, Min	27	.280	152	546	88	153	35	4	19	74	81	78	15	9	.373	.463
Ledee,Ricky, NYA	25	.279	95	240	43	67	14	1	11	36	26	64	3	2	.350	.483
Ledesma,Aaron, TB	28	.282	99	326	38	92	17	1	1	33	23	50	6	4	.330	.350
Lee,Derrek, Fla	23	.268	143	471	71	126	29	1	19	69	48	135	8	4	.335	.454

Projections for 1999 Batters

Batter	Age	Avg	G	AB	R	H	2B	3B	HR	RBI	BB	SO	SB	CS	OBP	SLG
Lee,Travis, Ari	24	.290	153	576	76	167	25	2	27	90	68	115	6	2	.365	.481
Lewis,Darren, Bos	31	.240	138	367	57	88	14	3	4	36	46	56	23	11	.324	.327
Lewis,Mark, Phi	29	.255	141	486	58	124	24	2	10	53	41	98	4	3	.313	.374
Leyritz,Jim, SD	35	.258	114	314	39	81	15	0	10	48	46	78	1	1	.353	.401
Lieberthal,Mike, Phi	27	.251	117	399	46	100	22	1	13	55	32	64	2	2	.306	.409
Lockhart,Keith, Atl	34	.272	120	323	41	88	18	2	8	39	25	33	5	3	.325	.415
Lofton,Kenny, Cle	32	.300	144	584	106	175	27	6	10	58	72	81	57	18	.377	.418
Lopez,Javy, Atl	28	.283	138	484	61	137	22	2	28	81	36	87	2	3	.333	.510
Lopez,Luis, NYN	28	.249	117	297	34	74	17	1	2	28	18	59	3	3	.292	.333
Lopez,Mendy, KC	24	.234	143	461	46	108	20	3	4	37	30	92	8	5	.281	.317
Loretta,Mark, Mil	27	.279	144	484	59	135	22	2	5	56	52	59	8	7	.349	.364
Luke,Matt, LA	28	.239	65	138	17	33	6	1	5	19	9	27	1	1	.286	.406
Mabry,John, StL	28	.269	127	401	42	108	23	0	8	45	34	73	1	1	.326	.387
Macfarlane,Mike, Oak	35	.247	87	259	34	64	14	1	10	36	21	44	1	1	.304	.425
Machado,Robert, ChA	26	.234	55	171	19	40	9	0	3	16	9	30	1	1	.272	.339
Mack,Shane, KC	35	.283	85	205	26	58	13	2	5	28	15	38	5	2	.332	.439
Magadan,Dave, Oak	36	.268	66	127	15	34	9	0	1	15	21	19	0	0	.372	.362
Magee,Wendell, Phi	26	.255	110	357	41	91	20	2	10	41	28	66	5	6	.309	.406
Malloy,Marty, Atl	26	.258	68	163	21	42	7	1	1	13	13	21	4	3	.313	.331
Manwaring,Kirt, Col	33	.230	111	304	20	70	11	1	2	24	32	61	1	2	.304	.293
Marrero,Eli, StL	25	.245	122	444	57	109	22	3	15	56	32	67	9	7	.296	.410
Martin,Al, Pit	31	.276	112	416	60	115	21	3	12	46	37	80	22	8	.336	.428
Martin,Norberto, Ana	32	.268	48	97	12	26	4	0	1	10	3	13	2	1	.290	.340
Martinez,Dave, TB	34	.270	100	315	45	85	12	3	5	30	36	45	8	4	.345	.375
Martinez,Edgar, Sea	36	.298	142	503	91	150	38	1	24	90	112	91	3	2	.426	.521
Martinez,Manny, Pit	28	.250	67	212	27	53	11	1	4	20	13	47	6	5	.293	.368
Martinez,Tino, NYA	31	.277	151	570	87	158	30	1	31	119	69	81	2	1	.355	.496
Matheny,Mike, Mil	28	.224	121	340	28	76	16	1	5	36	15	76	2	1	.256	.321
May,Derrick, Mon	30	.258	61	159	17	41	7	1	4	20	15	22	2	1	.322	.390
Mayne,Brent, SF	31	.253	101	241	21	61	12	0	3	21	26	39	1	1	.326	.340
McCracken,Q., TB	29	.289	155	602	91	174	28	6	6	60	59	114	35	16	.352	.385
McDonald,Jason, Oak	27	.239	95	289	50	69	10	2	3	24	46	53	19	8	.343	.318
McGee,Willie, StL	40	.260	81	177	22	46	11	2	2	20	11	37	3	1	.303	.379
McGriff,Fred, TB	35	.275	147	552	73	152	27	1	21	87	69	114	5	3	.356	.442
McGuire,Ryan, Mon	27	.242	86	211	24	51	14	0	3	20	27	42	3	2	.328	.351
McGwire,Mark, StL	35	.264	147	526	103	139	22	0	54	117	138	158	1	1	.417	.614
McLemore,Mark, Tex	34	.249	124	449	67	112	16	2	4	38	74	66	17	8	.356	.321
McRae,Brian, NYN	31	.259	155	572	89	148	31	5	16	56	73	85	26	11	.343	.414
Meares,Pat, Min	30	.261	149	510	64	133	24	4	10	63	21	89	9	6	.290	.382
Meluskey,Mitch, Hou	25	.297	66	172	25	51	13	0	4	23	22	32	0	0	.376	.442
Merced,Orlando, ChN	32	.273	101	337	45	92	19	2	10	51	39	55	5	3	.348	.430
Merloni,Lou, Bos	28	.279	85	240	32	67	14	1	5	30	21	38	2	2	.337	.408
Miller,Damian, Ari	29	.269	75	238	25	64	13	1	4	29	14	44	2	2	.310	.382
Monahan,Shane, Sea	24	.272	35	114	13	31	5	1	2	16	7	26	3	2	.314	.386
Mondesi,Raul, LA	28	.293	154	607	95	178	33	6	29	92	37	113	24	10	.334	.511
Morandini,Mickey, ChN	33	.267	145	546	72	146	25	4	4	41	61	89	16	7	.341	.350
Morris,Hal, KC	34	.296	119	426	55	126	25	2	5	48	34	57	3	2	.348	.399
Mueller,Bill, SF	28	.290	148	542	80	157	27	3	7	54	68	79	4	4	.369	.389
Myers,Greg, SD	33	.243	80	210	23	51	11	1	5	26	17	38	0	0	.300	.376
Nevin,Phil, Ana	28	.230	101	305	37	70	14	0	11	39	30	87	2	1	.299	.384

384

Projections for 1999 Batters

Batter	Age	Avg	G	AB	R	H	2B	3B	HR	RBI	BB	SO	SB	CS	OBP	SLG
Newfield,Marc, Mil	26	.271	72	177	21	48	13	0	4	25	15	30	0	0	.328	.412
Nieves,Melvin, Cin	27	.246	93	167	24	41	7	1	8	26	21	64	1	2	.330	.443
Nilsson,Dave, Mil	29	.280	131	446	65	125	26	2	16	74	55	68	2	2	.359	.455
Nixon,Otis, Min	40	.279	117	459	63	128	9	1	1	26	55	67	39	11	.356	.309
Nixon,Trot, Bos	25	.260	138	492	70	128	20	3	15	58	55	78	11	7	.335	.404
Norton,Greg, ChA	26	.245	86	269	38	66	14	1	9	35	28	65	4	5	.316	.405
Nunez,Abraham, Pit	23	.242	118	351	37	85	12	2	2	26	31	66	13	8	.304	.305
Nunnally,Jon, Cin	27	.249	96	285	47	71	15	2	14	42	41	77	6	5	.344	.463
O'Brien,Charlie, Ana	38	.204	73	201	15	41	10	0	5	21	17	44	0	0	.266	.328
O'Leary,Troy, Bos	29	.278	155	551	78	153	33	6	18	78	44	89	3	3	.331	.457
O'Neill,Paul, NYA	36	.308	143	535	76	165	30	1	21	101	75	93	6	3	.393	.486
Ochoa,Alex, Min	27	.274	96	259	35	71	15	2	3	29	19	31	6	6	.324	.382
Offerman,Jose, KC	30	.290	146	558	81	162	21	7	5	47	75	90	22	11	.374	.380
Olerud,John, NYN	30	.303	159	535	86	162	36	1	20	84	92	64	1	1	.405	.486
Oliver,Joe, Sea	33	.235	82	243	23	57	12	0	8	32	20	46	1	1	.293	.383
Ordaz,Luis, StL	23	.254	89	283	26	72	12	2	3	31	16	28	6	5	.294	.343
Ordonez,Magglio, ChA	25	.282	153	556	68	157	33	1	15	73	31	65	11	11	.320	.426
Ordonez,Rey, NYN	26	.238	138	442	44	105	15	3	1	38	21	47	6	7	.272	.292
Orie,Kevin, Fla	26	.268	125	414	53	111	26	2	12	55	43	64	2	1	.337	.428
Ortiz,David, Min	23	.294	135	435	68	128	32	1	17	74	41	119	3	4	.355	.490
Palmeiro,Orlando, Ana	30	.280	97	232	34	65	14	2	0	26	26	20	5	4	.353	.358
Palmeiro,Rafael, Bal	34	.268	153	589	91	158	33	2	36	110	78	98	6	3	.354	.514
Palmer,Dean, KC	30	.260	152	574	84	149	27	1	30	97	53	140	4	2	.322	.467
Payton,Jay, NYN	26	.234	78	201	23	47	7	2	3	14	13	34	5	4	.280	.333
Perez,Eddie, Atl	31	.251	89	203	21	51	12	0	6	26	14	30	1	1	.300	.399
Perez,Eduardo, Cin	29	.249	77	209	31	52	12	1	8	32	23	44	3	1	.323	.431
Perez,Neifi, Col	24	.295	153	614	79	181	35	10	9	61	30	61	9	8	.328	.428
Phillips,Tony, NYN	40	.239	99	355	61	85	14	1	7	32	75	87	7	5	.372	.344
Piazza,Mike, NYN	30	.332	154	567	97	188	28	1	35	111	74	85	2	1	.409	.570
Pickering,Calvin, Bal	22	.278	138	417	67	116	20	1	23	80	58	113	3	5	.366	.496
Polanco,Placido, StL	23	.261	96	291	33	76	12	1	1	25	13	25	7	3	.293	.320
Polcovich,Kevin, Pit	29	.230	77	213	23	49	10	0	1	17	13	34	4	3	.274	.291
Posada,Jorge, NYA	27	.255	113	377	61	96	22	1	13	55	61	83	2	3	.358	.422
Pride,Curtis, Atl	30	.253	85	186	31	47	9	2	4	20	25	43	9	4	.341	.387
Raines,Tim, NYA	39	.260	91	281	46	73	14	3	5	35	47	44	7	2	.366	.384
Ramirez,Aramis, Pit	21	.238	68	231	20	55	10	1	5	20	20	57	0	1	.299	.355
Ramirez,Manny, Cle	27	.310	153	568	102	176	37	1	40	118	85	115	6	5	.400	.590
Randa,Joe, Det	29	.268	137	451	53	121	24	3	8	53	41	66	8	5	.329	.388
Reboulet,Jeff, Bal	35	.230	60	100	12	23	5	0	1	10	12	20	1	1	.313	.310
Redmond,Mike, Fla	28	.245	87	212	18	52	10	0	2	19	8	24	1	1	.273	.321
Reed,Jeff, Col	36	.283	112	290	33	82	12	1	9	33	40	65	1	1	.370	.424
Reese,Pokey, Cin	26	.227	94	282	34	64	13	1	3	26	24	53	9	4	.288	.312
Relaford,Desi, Phi	25	.232	138	482	50	112	23	2	5	39	34	86	18	7	.283	.320
Renteria,Edgar, Fla	23	.286	146	573	83	164	20	3	4	49	47	89	34	15	.340	.353
Rios,Armando, SF	27	.268	83	194	31	52	10	1	7	30	21	32	5	4	.340	.438
Ripken Jr.,Cal, Bal	38	.253	155	584	67	148	27	2	16	75	53	75	1	1	.316	.389
Rivera,Ruben, SD	25	.242	112	264	40	64	12	2	8	33	29	77	10	6	.317	.394
Roberts,Bip, Oak	35	.275	108	364	47	100	17	2	2	37	29	51	17	5	.328	.349
Rodriguez,Alex, Sea	23	.327	156	651	123	213	39	4	36	115	53	109	31	10	.378	.565
Rodriguez,Henry, ChN	31	.239	139	485	59	116	25	1	29	83	46	144	2	2	.305	.474

Projections for 1999 Batters

Batter	Age	Avg	G	AB	R	H	2B	3B	HR	RBI	BB	SO	SB	CS	OBP	SLG
Rodriguez,Ivan, Tex	27	.304	151	608	93	185	35	2	20	82	38	78	5	2	.345	.467
Rolen,Scott, Phi	24	.296	160	582	100	172	43	3	25	102	82	117	13	9	.383	.509
Sadler,Donnie, Bos	24	.231	68	225	32	52	9	2	4	19	21	45	9	3	.297	.342
Salmon,Tim, Ana	30	.291	154	561	98	163	30	2	31	103	101	127	5	5	.399	.517
Sanchez,Rey, SF	31	.249	123	337	39	84	17	1	2	22	19	48	4	3	.289	.323
Sanders,Reggie, Cin	31	.256	114	395	62	101	21	3	16	55	49	116	23	10	.338	.446
Santangelo,F.P., Mon	31	.236	99	263	35	62	15	1	3	24	34	48	4	3	.323	.335
Santiago,Benito, Tor	34	.236	68	203	23	48	8	1	8	28	16	47	1	0	.292	.404
Sefcik,Kevin, Phi	28	.280	108	257	33	72	13	3	2	23	21	30	6	4	.335	.377
Segui,David, Sea	32	.291	139	506	74	147	28	1	17	70	61	72	3	3	.367	.451
Servais,Scott, ChN	32	.240	122	379	37	91	20	0	8	47	27	60	1	1	.291	.356
Sexson,Richie, Cle	24	.269	125	387	54	104	22	1	19	64	27	81	2	1	.316	.478
Sheets,Andy, SD	27	.248	75	161	23	40	9	1	4	18	17	48	3	1	.320	.391
Sheffield,Gary, LA	30	.279	139	455	90	127	26	2	25	84	122	62	20	9	.432	.510
Simmons,Brian, ChA	25	.251	73	203	34	51	9	3	5	24	21	45	5	4	.321	.399
Simms,Mike, Tex	32	.246	86	207	27	51	12	1	11	37	21	52	2	2	.316	.473
Smith,Bobby, TB	25	.245	99	323	37	79	14	1	8	37	27	89	6	5	.303	.368
Smith,Mark, Pit	29	.260	82	227	32	59	16	0	9	37	22	44	5	2	.325	.449
Snopek,Chris, Bos	28	.256	78	223	26	57	12	1	6	29	19	35	2	2	.314	.399
Snow,J.T., SF	31	.254	145	496	68	126	24	1	19	79	69	98	3	3	.345	.421
Sojo,Luis, NYA	33	.248	47	109	12	27	5	0	1	10	5	8	1	1	.281	.321
Sorrento,Paul, TB	33	.243	109	337	42	82	17	0	17	58	41	90	1	1	.325	.445
Sosa,Sammy, ChN	30	.266	161	643	105	171	24	4	48	130	58	173	25	9	.327	.540
Spencer,Shane, NYA	27	.253	126	340	52	86	21	0	18	58	39	69	1	2	.330	.474
Spiers,Bill, Hou	33	.256	129	301	41	77	16	2	4	35	43	48	8	3	.349	.362
Spiezio,Scott, Oak	26	.249	134	478	60	119	25	3	12	62	46	64	5	4	.315	.389
Sprague,Ed, Oak	31	.232	119	367	48	85	20	1	15	48	33	79	0	0	.295	.414
Stairs,Matt, Oak	31	.285	154	544	85	155	36	1	29	106	67	97	5	3	.363	.515
Stanley,Mike, Bos	36	.256	129	402	61	103	19	0	21	68	68	93	1	1	.364	.460
Steinbach,Terry, Min	37	.234	127	444	49	104	22	1	16	60	40	108	2	1	.298	.396
Stevens,Lee, Tex	31	.262	109	336	47	88	20	1	18	56	30	77	1	1	.322	.488
Stewart,Shannon, Tor	25	.279	154	537	85	150	30	6	8	55	69	78	39	15	.361	.402
Stinnett,Kelly, Ari	29	.255	94	263	36	67	14	1	10	35	30	64	1	1	.331	.430
Stocker,Kevin, TB	29	.242	123	396	43	96	18	3	5	35	39	82	7	4	.310	.341
Strawberry,Darryl, NYA	37	.247	78	215	31	53	11	1	13	40	33	69	4	3	.347	.488
Stynes,Chris, Cin	26	.282	83	241	34	68	11	1	5	26	14	18	6	2	.322	.398
Surhoff,B.J., Bal	34	.277	146	527	69	146	26	2	17	75	48	74	4	3	.337	.431
Sutton,Larry, KC	29	.259	85	263	33	68	13	1	7	36	29	37	1	1	.332	.395
Sweeney,Mark, SD	29	.259	112	170	23	44	11	1	2	24	27	32	2	1	.360	.371
Sweeney,Mike, KC	25	.260	108	338	43	88	19	0	11	47	29	41	3	2	.319	.414
Tatis,Fernando, StL	24	.286	150	549	80	157	33	2	18	70	42	107	14	7	.337	.452
Taubensee,Eddie, Cin	30	.263	133	384	49	101	21	1	12	56	40	85	2	2	.333	.417
Tejada,Miguel, Oak	23	.240	151	529	70	127	24	3	15	68	34	107	10	9	.286	.382
Thomas,Frank, ChA	31	.313	158	576	111	180	36	1	36	127	117	81	3	1	.429	.566
Thome,Jim, Cle	28	.284	139	472	101	134	28	2	33	89	115	140	2	2	.424	.561
Trammell,Bubba, TB	27	.266	141	477	72	127	27	1	29	81	48	110	5	3	.333	.509
Tucker,Michael, Atl	28	.259	140	463	66	120	24	5	13	53	52	110	11	6	.334	.417
Valentin,Javier, Min	23	.227	56	172	17	39	8	0	3	18	12	31	1	1	.277	.326
Valentin,John, Bos	32	.279	143	563	97	157	39	2	20	77	67	69	10	6	.356	.462
Valentin,Jose, Mil	29	.241	131	353	55	85	21	2	13	49	42	86	13	6	.322	.422

Projections for 1999 Batters

Batter	Age	Avg	G	AB	R	H	2B	3B	HR	RBI	BB	SO	SB	CS	OBP	SLG
Vander Wal,John, SD	33	.235	78	98	12	23	6	1	2	14	12	28	1	1	.318	.378
Varitek,Jason, Bos	27	.249	84	265	33	66	14	0	8	33	26	54	2	1	.316	.392
Vaughn,Greg, SD	33	.234	151	538	95	126	25	1	36	100	82	139	10	5	.335	.485
Vaughn,Mo, Bos	31	.300	151	587	99	176	28	1	36	113	82	150	4	2	.386	.535
Velarde,Randy, Ana	36	.248	113	351	48	87	18	1	7	36	51	86	5	3	.343	.365
Ventura,Robin, ChA	31	.262	157	583	84	153	28	1	24	91	82	90	2	2	.353	.437
Veras,Quilvio, SD	28	.256	146	532	84	136	23	3	5	41	86	82	38	16	.359	.338
Vidro,Jose, Mon	24	.253	94	288	33	73	18	1	4	35	22	40	2	2	.306	.365
Vina,Fernando, Mil	30	.283	140	555	82	157	20	5	6	46	40	38	17	11	.331	.369
Vizcaino,Jose, LA	31	.265	128	472	58	125	16	3	3	43	36	71	10	5	.317	.331
Vizquel,Omar, Cle	32	.263	150	552	81	145	21	2	4	48	59	54	36	12	.334	.330
Walbeck,Matt, Ana	29	.236	106	331	36	78	13	1	4	35	24	59	3	2	.287	.317
Walker,Larry, Col	32	.333	134	480	100	160	33	2	29	86	61	78	22	6	.409	.592
Walker,Todd, Min	26	.301	149	549	79	165	35	3	15	72	49	86	16	8	.358	.457
Ward,Turner, Pit	34	.263	95	213	28	56	13	1	6	30	23	32	5	2	.335	.418
Watkins,Pat, Cin	26	.272	86	272	32	74	16	1	4	28	15	39	7	5	.310	.382
Webster,Lenny, Bal	34	.253	106	265	29	67	14	0	7	33	23	39	0	0	.313	.385
Weiss,Walt, Atl	35	.261	125	417	59	109	15	2	3	30	69	65	8	2	.366	.329
White,Devon, Ari	36	.262	143	539	69	141	27	4	16	70	45	113	18	6	.318	.416
White,Rondell, Mon	27	.285	135	501	74	143	29	4	20	69	34	85	20	8	.331	.479
Whiten,Mark, Cle	32	.244	55	164	25	40	6	1	5	21	25	45	4	2	.344	.384
Widger,Chris, Mon	28	.243	126	407	41	99	20	2	13	48	31	84	4	1	.297	.398
Williams,Bernie, NYA	30	.301	137	529	100	159	31	5	23	89	81	79	14	7	.393	.509
Williams,Gerald, Atl	32	.259	127	270	37	70	17	2	6	29	13	46	9	5	.293	.404
Williams,Matt, Ari	33	.254	133	507	69	129	22	2	23	81	40	105	5	2	.309	.442
Wilson,Craig, ChA	28	.257	96	241	31	62	9	0	4	24	22	25	1	1	.319	.344
Wilson,Dan, Sea	30	.262	125	431	47	113	21	2	12	60	32	70	3	2	.313	.404
Wilson,Enrique, Cle	23	.287	143	513	72	147	22	2	7	48	33	47	13	10	.330	.378
Wilson,Preston, Fla	24	.244	65	217	30	53	11	1	10	32	14	69	5	3	.290	.442
Winn,Randy, TB	25	.272	95	324	47	88	10	6	2	25	27	69	23	11	.328	.358
Womack,Tony, Pit	29	.257	159	618	74	159	20	6	3	42	38	98	48	11	.300	.324
Young,Dmitri, Cin	25	.284	149	546	76	155	36	3	12	70	51	92	7	6	.345	.427
Young,Eric, LA	32	.283	139	551	90	156	22	4	8	53	56	39	47	17	.349	.381
Young,Kevin, Pit	30	.257	154	567	76	146	34	3	25	95	39	132	12	7	.305	.460
Zaun,Gregg, Fla	28	.237	96	245	31	58	13	1	4	26	34	34	3	2	.330	.347
Zeile,Todd, Tex	33	.251	154	565	77	142	28	1	22	83	77	102	4	3	.341	.421

Projections for 1999 Pitchers

Pitcher	Age	ERA	W	L	Sv	G	GS	IP	H	HR	BB	SO	BR/9
Abbott,Jim, ChA	31	4.78	9	9	0	25	25	160	179	17	61	71	13.5
Adams,Terry, ChN	26	4.19	4	5	0	67	0	73	74	4	38	63	13.8
Aguilera,Rick, Min	37	3.75	2	4	36	66	0	72	71	9	19	63	11.3
Alvarez,Wilson, TB	29	4.26	10	13	0	32	32	190	177	20	91	153	12.7
Anderson,Brian, Ari	27	4.48	11	14	0	32	32	207	226	40	24	95	10.9
Appier,Kevin, KC	31	3.39	13	8	0	29	29	178	158	16	59	146	11.0
Ashby,Andy, SD	31	3.63	13	12	0	32	32	218	214	21	56	150	11.1
Assenmacher,Paul, Cle	38	3.94	4	3	2	71	0	48	49	5	17	48	12.4
Astacio,Pedro, Col	29	5.61	12	12	0	34	33	207	238	36	73	169	13.5
Avery,Steve, Bos	29	5.17	6	8	0	30	21	115	123	13	59	56	14.2
Ayala,Bobby, Sea	29	4.61	5	4	0	65	0	82	87	11	32	76	13.1
Bailes,Scott, Tex	36	5.29	2	3	0	39	0	34	43	4	12	24	14.6
Baldwin,James, ChA	27	4.75	11	11	0	32	32	180	193	22	68	124	13.1
Banks,Willie, Ari	30	5.02	2	3	0	30	0	43	45	5	26	29	14.9
Beck,Rod, ChN	30	3.62	3	5	40	78	0	77	77	10	14	66	10.6
Belcher,Tim, KC	37	4.84	12	14	0	33	33	227	248	35	71	123	12.6
Belinda,Stan, Cin	32	3.88	3	2	2	37	0	51	42	5	22	51	11.3
Benes,Andy, Ari	31	3.73	14	13	0	34	34	234	223	23	75	194	11.5
Benitez,Armando, Bal	26	3.47	3	3	27	71	0	70	49	9	39	96	11.3
Bere,Jason, Cin	28	5.74	4	8	0	20	17	94	102	14	58	64	15.3
Bergman,Sean, Hou	29	4.62	8	9	0	35	21	148	170	18	36	95	12.5
Blair,Willie, NYN	33	4.47	9	11	0	32	26	175	179	23	61	91	12.3
Bochtler,Doug, LA	28	4.43	4	4	0	52	0	65	56	9	44	53	13.8
Bohanon,Brian, LA	30	3.93	10	10	0	32	32	183	179	17	75	132	12.5
Bones,Ricky, KC	30	5.16	3	3	0	31	4	68	78	10	29	33	14.2
Bottalico,Ricky, Phi	29	3.63	2	3	23	55	0	57	49	7	31	59	12.6
Bottenfield,Kent, StL	30	3.92	5	4	0	51	11	117	113	12	47	86	12.3
Brantley,Jeff, StL	35	3.57	2	3	22	56	0	53	41	8	21	56	10.5
Brocail,Doug, Det	32	4.10	4	4	0	60	0	68	67	7	27	52	12.4
Brown,Kevin, SD	34	2.41	20	8	0	35	35	250	217	10	48	234	9.5
Burba,Dave, Cle	32	4.00	13	9	0	31	30	189	181	23	64	137	11.7
Burkett,John, Tex	34	4.38	12	11	0	31	31	193	220	20	46	136	12.4
Cadaret,Greg, Tex	37	4.50	2	2	0	38	0	34	35	5	15	31	13.2
Candiotti,Tom, Oak	41	4.59	11	13	0	33	33	196	204	30	61	109	12.2
Carrasco,Hector, Min	29	3.86	4	4	0	64	0	70	68	4	37	57	13.5
Castillo,Frank, Det	30	5.12	7	10	0	29	24	139	156	19	53	96	13.5
Castillo,Tony, ChA	36	4.62	2	2	0	38	0	39	44	5	12	24	12.9
Christiansen,Jason, Pit	29	3.00	3	4	3	53	0	54	52	4	24	55	12.7
Clark,Mark, ChN	31	4.05	12	13	0	33	32	211	226	22	47	143	11.6
Clemens,Roger, Tor	36	2.84	19	8	0	33	33	244	194	13	92	276	10.5
Clontz,Brad, NYN	28	4.22	2	2	0	30	0	32	32	3	13	22	12.7
Cone,David, NYA	36	3.41	17	7	0	30	30	203	168	17	58	218	10.0
Cook,Dennis, NYN	36	3.27	5	3	0	68	0	66	58	4	30	68	12.0
Cooke,Steve, Cin	29	3.15	5	3	0	11	11	60	65	5	0	39	9.8
Corsi,Jim, Bos	37	3.29	5	3	0	57	0	63	58	4	22	45	11.4
Crabtree,Tim, Tex	29	3.99	4	4	0	55	0	70	75	5	27	52	13.1
Daal,Omar, Ari	27	3.98	11	11	0	31	31	183	186	17	57	146	12.0
DeLucia,Rich, Ana	34	3.92	4	3	4	53	0	62	51	8	36	60	12.6
Dipoto,Jerry, Col	31	3.99	5	4	17	70	0	79	82	5	33	57	13.1
Drabek,Doug, Bal	36	5.44	8	9	0	26	24	129	157	25	34	65	13.3

Projections for 1999 Pitchers

Pitcher	Age	ERA	W	L	Sv	G	GS	IP	H	HR	BB	SO	BR/9
Eckersley,Dennis, Bos	44	4.70	3	3	0	52	0	44	45	7	8	32	10.8
Eldred,Cal, Mil	31	5.02	8	11	0	27	27	156	165	20	72	97	13.7
Embree,Alan, Ari	29	4.24	3	4	0	59	0	51	48	6	25	47	12.9
Erickson,Scott, Bal	31	4.18	15	13	0	35	35	241	265	21	66	162	12.4
Fassero,Jeff, Sea	36	3.79	16	10	0	33	33	228	220	24	67	181	11.3
Fetters,Mike, Ana	34	4.00	4	4	5	57	0	63	64	4	28	52	13.1
Finley,Chuck, Ana	36	3.88	11	12	0	31	31	204	196	22	99	193	13.0
Florie,Bryce, Det	29	4.11	5	4	0	39	13	114	108	11	58	88	13.1
Fossas,Tony, Tex	41	5.63	2	3	0	51	0	32	40	3	18	28	16.3
Franco,John, NYN	38	3.29	2	3	36	60	0	63	58	4	25	57	11.9
Frascatore,John, StL	29	4.00	5	4	0	66	0	90	91	8	36	55	12.7
Gardner,Mark, SF	37	4.30	11	13	0	32	32	201	201	29	62	147	11.8
Glavine,Tom, Atl	33	3.17	16	10	0	33	33	233	207	14	75	153	10.9
Gooden,Dwight, Cle	34	4.39	8	7	0	22	22	125	128	14	47	77	12.6
Gordon,Tom, Bos	31	3.00	3	4	45	71	0	75	57	3	33	73	10.8
Groom,Buddy, Oak	33	5.10	4	5	0	76	0	60	71	7	23	41	14.1
Guardado,Eddie, Min	28	4.42	4	4	0	76	0	59	58	9	25	58	12.7
Gunderson,Eric, Tex	33	4.65	4	4	0	65	1	62	69	9	19	36	12.8
Guthrie,Mark, LA	33	3.97	4	4	0	56	0	59	59	6	23	43	12.5
Guzman,Juan, Bal	32	4.31	12	11	0	30	30	186	173	22	86	151	12.5
Hamilton,Joey, SD	28	4.44	11	14	0	33	33	209	206	18	102	138	13.3
Hampton,Mike, Hou	26	4.14	13	12	0	33	33	215	219	17	82	137	12.6
Haney,Chris, ChN	30	4.62	3	3	0	28	9	76	88	10	20	40	12.8
Harnisch,Pete, Cin	32	3.43	12	12	0	32	32	207	199	27	63	149	11.4
Henry,Butch, Bos	30	4.24	2	2	0	13	3	34	36	3	11	21	12.4
Henry,Doug, Hou	35	4.18	4	4	0	64	0	71	68	7	37	61	13.3
Hentgen,Pat, Tor	30	4.50	12	12	0	31	31	206	214	23	80	119	12.8
Heredia,Gil, Oak	33	3.77	3	2	0	8	6	43	49	4	3	27	10.9
Hernandez,Roberto, TB	34	3.53	2	4	25	69	0	74	63	6	37	69	12.2
Hernandez,Xavier, Tex	33	4.09	3	3	0	45	0	55	53	7	24	47	12.6
Hershiser,Orel, SF	40	4.55	11	13	0	33	33	200	201	24	84	117	12.8
Hill,Ken, Ana	33	4.66	9	11	0	28	28	166	176	15	76	92	13.7
Hitchcock,Sterling, SD	28	4.10	12	12	0	33	33	188	190	22	51	147	11.5
Hoffman,Trevor, SD	31	2.25	3	2	48	67	0	76	51	7	24	97	8.9
Holmes,Darren, NYA	33	4.08	4	3	2	43	0	64	68	6	23	51	12.8
Hudek,John, Cin	32	4.50	3	4	0	52	0	56	47	8	40	55	14.0
Jackson,Mike, Cle	34	2.78	3	2	41	70	0	68	53	6	21	64	9.8
James,Mike, Ana	31	3.60	2	2	0	27	0	30	27	2	15	26	12.6
Johnson,Randy, Hou	35	3.00	17	9	0	33	33	234	180	23	82	317	10.1
Jones,Bobby, NYN	29	4.11	11	12	0	30	30	195	199	23	53	120	11.6
Jones,Doug, Cle	42	3.96	6	3	0	71	0	84	81	11	13	77	10.1
Jones,Todd, Det	31	3.95	2	4	27	66	0	66	60	5	35	59	13.0
Juden,Jeff, Ana	28	5.57	10	11	0	31	29	173	164	23	81	144	12.7
Kamieniecki,Scott, Bal	35	5.25	5	7	0	18	17	96	106	12	46	55	14.3
Karchner,Matt, ChN	32	4.57	3	4	3	58	0	61	61	7	35	44	14.2
Karl,Scott, Mil	27	4.71	10	13	0	33	33	193	213	22	66	110	13.0
Key,Jimmy, Bal	38	3.85	5	4	0	28	19	124	122	12	45	82	12.1
Kile,Darryl, Col	30	4.97	15	12	0	35	35	239	258	26	100	168	13.5
Leiter,Al, NYN	33	3.02	13	8	0	28	28	179	145	12	66	159	10.6
Leiter,Mark, Phi	36	3.77	3	5	7	65	0	74	70	9	34	62	12.6

Projections for 1999 Pitchers

Pitcher	Age	ERA	W	L	Sv	G	GS	IP	H	HR	BB	SO	BR/9
Leskanic,Curt, Col	31	4.37	4	4	2	62	0	70	68	8	34	62	13.1
Lieber,Jon, Pit	29	4.17	8	13	0	30	29	177	196	22	41	147	12.1
Lloyd,Graeme, NYA	32	3.73	3	2	0	49	0	41	40	4	14	22	11.9
Loaiza,Esteban, Tex	27	4.93	10	12	0	34	29	179	207	23	55	112	13.2
Maddux,Greg, Atl	33	2.17	21	6	0	34	34	245	201	11	44	193	9.0
Maddux,Mike, Mon	37	3.73	2	2	0	36	0	41	43	2	14	25	12.5
Magnante,Mike, Hou	34	3.96	3	3	0	45	0	50	50	4	20	37	12.6
Martinez,Dennis, Atl	44	5.14	3	4	0	38	6	77	96	9	26	43	14.3
Martinez,Pedro, Bos	27	2.78	19	8	0	32	32	236	185	22	68	277	9.6
Martinez,Ramon, LA	31	3.54	7	6	0	17	17	112	97	10	45	101	11.4
Mathews,T.J., Oak	29	3.45	5	3	0	65	0	73	64	7	29	64	11.5
Mathews,Terry, Bal	34	4.63	2	2	0	30	0	35	34	5	17	24	13.1
McElroy,Chuck, Col	31	3.80	5	4	2	72	0	71	71	5	25	62	12.2
McMichael,Greg, NYN	32	3.60	5	4	0	67	0	75	69	7	27	66	11.5
Mercker,Kent, StL	31	4.44	10	10	0	29	28	156	167	17	51	75	12.6
Mesa,Jose, SF	33	3.64	5	4	0	73	0	84	80	6	33	69	12.1
Miceli,Dan, SD	28	3.79	4	5	0	68	0	76	77	10	35	68	13.3
Mills,Alan, Bal	32	4.64	4	4	3	61	0	64	55	9	44	52	13.9
Mlicki,Dave, LA	31	4.38	10	12	0	31	31	185	189	23	64	135	12.3
Mohler,Mike, Oak	30	4.56	4	4	0	59	0	75	79	7	37	53	13.9
Montgomery,Jeff, KC	37	4.11	2	3	35	56	0	57	55	8	20	51	11.8
Morgan,Mike, ChN	39	4.50	7	10	0	26	25	134	144	16	43	78	12.6
Moyer,Jamie, Sea	36	3.74	16	9	0	33	33	219	224	25	39	140	10.8
Mulholland,Terry, ChN	36	3.94	6	6	0	60	13	137	143	14	38	70	11.9
Munoz,Mike, Col	33	5.02	3	3	2	48	0	43	53	5	15	31	14.2
Mussina,Mike, Bal	30	3.38	17	10	0	34	34	240	223	28	48	219	10.2
Myers,Mike, Mil	30	4.76	3	4	2	76	0	51	53	7	25	48	13.8
Myers,Randy, SD	36	3.88	4	4	13	62	0	58	55	5	26	57	12.6
Nagy,Charles, Cle	32	4.58	13	12	0	33	33	216	236	26	68	133	12.7
Navarro,Jaime, ChA	31	5.17	8	9	0	36	22	148	167	17	66	82	14.2
Neagle,Denny, Atl	30	3.76	14	11	0	33	32	218	212	22	62	166	11.3
Nelson,Jeff, NYA	32	3.40	4	2	2	56	0	53	45	4	26	57	12.1
Nen,Robb, SF	29	2.89	3	3	42	76	0	84	70	5	29	97	10.6
Nomo,Hideo, NYN	30	4.03	10	11	0	30	30	174	138	17	104	191	12.5
Ogea,Chad, Cle	28	4.13	9	8	0	30	22	144	147	17	48	94	12.2
Olivares,Omar, Ana	31	5.02	9	12	0	35	28	181	195	19	90	108	14.2
Oliver,Darren, StL	28	5.02	9	12	0	30	30	174	195	21	72	92	13.8
Olson,Gregg, Ari	32	3.77	2	4	33	58	0	62	60	5	32	46	13.4
Orosco,Jesse, Bal	42	3.27	5	3	4	70	0	55	39	6	30	49	11.3
Osborne,Donovan, StL	30	3.98	11	9	0	28	28	172	170	22	45	116	11.3
Osuna,Antonio, LA	26	3.09	4	3	2	52	0	64	50	6	25	68	10.5
Painter,Lance, StL	31	5.11	2	3	0	48	0	37	39	6	20	32	14.4
Park,Chan Ho, LA	26	3.50	14	11	0	33	33	211	174	19	93	183	11.4
Patterson,Bob, ChN	40	4.09	2	3	0	47	0	33	35	5	9	31	12.0
Percival,Troy, Ana	29	2.32	3	2	43	63	0	62	37	6	29	83	9.6
Perez,Carlos, LA	28	3.83	13	13	0	34	33	230	231	23	60	122	11.4
Perez,Yorkis, Phi	31	4.03	2	3	0	41	0	38	34	3	21	33	13.0
Petkovsek,Mark, StL	33	4.24	5	4	0	50	7	102	110	10	36	53	12.9
Pettitte,Andy, NYA	27	3.70	14	11	0	34	33	224	229	17	90	153	12.8
Pichardo,Hipolito, KC	29	4.55	5	5	0	34	12	91	98	8	35	50	13.2

Projections for 1999 Pitchers

Pitcher	Age	ERA	W	L	Sv	G	GS	IP	H	HR	BB	SO	BR/9
Plesac,Dan, Tor	37	3.60	5	3	4	76	0	50	44	6	17	58	11.0
Plunk,Eric, Mil	35	3.99	4	4	2	61	0	70	63	9	32	73	12.2
Poole,Jim, Cle	33	4.81	3	3	0	46	0	43	46	5	20	28	13.8
Portugal,Mark, Phi	36	3.99	6	7	0	18	18	115	120	16	22	68	11.1
Powell,Jay, Hou	27	3.45	5	4	2	66	0	73	66	4	34	59	12.3
Quantrill,Paul, Tor	30	3.14	5	5	7	80	0	83	99	10	25	55	13.4
Radinsky,Scott, LA	31	3.77	4	4	2	66	0	62	63	5	20	48	12.0
Radke,Brad, Min	26	4.14	13	13	0	33	33	222	232	32	45	157	11.2
Rapp,Pat, KC	31	5.15	9	12	0	30	30	173	185	16	98	117	14.7
Reed,Rick, NYN	33	3.28	14	10	0	32	32	211	199	26	29	133	9.7
Reed,Steve, Cle	33	3.04	6	3	0	68	0	74	57	9	25	57	10.0
Remlinger,Mike, Cin	33	4.53	8	10	0	46	23	151	139	18	80	151	13.1
Reyes,Carlos, SD	30	4.76	3	4	0	43	2	70	76	10	28	44	13.4
Reynolds,Shane, Hou	31	3.75	14	11	0	33	33	216	223	20	49	188	11.3
Reynoso,A., NYN	33	3.98	7	13	0	28	28	165	185	20	77	90	14.3
Rhodes,Arthur, Bal	29	3.47	5	3	8	48	0	83	71	10	31	91	11.1
Risley,Bill, Tor	32	4.50	2	2	0	30	0	38	34	5	23	27	13.5
Rivera,Mariano, NYA	29	2.77	3	2	39	58	0	65	55	4	19	63	10.2
Rodriguez,Frank, Min	26	4.84	8	11	0	28	25	160	173	17	69	96	13.6
Rodriguez,Rich, SF	36	3.95	4	4	0	69	0	66	67	7	21	38	12.0
Rogers,Kenny, Oak	34	3.73	15	11	0	33	33	227	220	23	64	128	11.3
Rojas,Mel, NYN	32	3.76	4	4	0	59	0	67	63	7	28	68	12.2
Rueter,Kirk, SF	28	4.05	11	12	0	33	33	189	191	21	57	108	11.8
Saberhagen,Bret, Bos	35	3.95	11	9	0	28	28	171	180	23	28	97	10.9
Sanders,Scott, SD	30	4.19	3	3	0	33	8	73	72	11	27	70	12.2
Schilling,Curt, Phi	32	2.83	18	11	0	35	35	264	221	25	60	312	9.6
Schmidt,Jason, Pit	26	4.30	10	15	0	33	33	205	218	20	68	150	12.6
Schourek,Pete, Bos	30	4.23	10	9	0	27	27	164	155	20	66	121	12.1
Sele,Aaron, Tex	29	4.88	11	13	0	33	33	201	228	19	79	149	13.7
Service,Scott, KC	32	3.57	4	3	7	54	0	63	56	7	24	67	11.4
Shaw,Jeff, LA	32	2.97	3	4	44	75	0	88	80	7	19	61	10.1
Shuey,Paul, Cle	28	4.22	3	2	2	42	0	49	46	5	26	48	13.2
Simas,Bill, ChA	27	4.13	4	3	8	53	0	61	58	7	28	53	12.7
Slocumb,Heathcliff, Sea	33	4.24	5	4	0	63	0	70	69	4	46	63	14.8
Smith,Pete, Bal	33	4.96	4	4	0	37	13	98	108	16	41	63	13.7
Smoltz,John, Atl	32	2.90	16	8	0	31	31	211	181	16	55	206	10.1
Spradlin,Jerry, Phi	32	3.40	5	4	0	71	0	82	74	9	23	71	10.6
Springer,Russ, Atl	30	4.50	3	3	0	50	0	54	55	7	25	59	13.3
Stanton,Mike, NYA	32	3.96	5	4	0	66	0	75	70	9	29	66	11.9
Stevens,Dave, ChN	29	6.00	1	3	0	26	2	36	42	7	19	25	15.3
Stieb,Dave, Tor	41	4.83	2	2	0	18	2	41	47	5	14	22	13.4
Stottlemyre,Todd, Tex	34	4.02	13	11	0	31	31	208	197	24	76	188	11.8
Swift,Bill, Sea	37	5.87	6	8	0	24	22	118	151	18	42	60	14.7
Swindell,Greg, Bos	34	3.73	6	5	5	76	0	99	107	14	29	67	12.4
Tapani,Kevin, ChN	35	4.37	11	14	0	33	33	206	217	28	58	129	12.0
Tavarez,Julian, SF	26	4.08	5	5	0	70	0	86	92	7	31	46	12.9
Taylor,Billy, Oak	37	3.70	3	4	31	71	0	73	71	5	29	62	12.3
Telford,Anthony, Mon	33	3.60	5	5	6	73	0	90	81	10	35	60	11.6
Tewksbury,Bob, Min	38	4.18	9	9	0	26	25	155	183	15	21	74	11.8
Thompson,Justin, Det	26	3.81	14	11	0	33	33	222	210	21	79	150	11.7

Projections for 1999 Pitchers

Pitcher	Age	ERA	W	L	Sv	G	GS	IP	H	HR	BB	SO	BR/9
Timlin,Mike, Sea	33	3.04	3	3	24	68	0	77	71	5	20	58	10.6
Trachsel,Steve, ChN	28	4.24	10	15	0	33	33	206	209	30	83	155	12.8
Trombley,Mike, Min	32	4.11	5	5	9	74	1	92	89	12	36	82	12.2
Urbina,Ugueth, Mon	25	2.65	2	4	34	64	0	68	54	9	29	78	11.0
Valdes,Ismael, LA	25	3.71	11	10	0	28	28	182	166	16	69	128	11.6
Van Poppel,Todd, Pit	27	6.00	1	3	0	21	5	51	57	8	28	29	15.0
Veres,Dave, Col	32	3.75	5	3	11	60	0	72	69	6	29	67	12.3
Villone,Ron, Cle	29	5.00	2	2	0	33	0	36	34	5	24	27	14.5
Wagner,Billy, Hou	27	2.86	3	3	34	63	0	66	46	6	32	100	10.6
Wakefield,Tim, Bos	32	4.35	13	12	0	36	32	211	205	29	77	150	12.0
Watson,Allen, Ana	28	4.92	4	5	0	30	21	128	142	20	47	89	13.3
Weathers,Dave, Mil	29	4.94	3	4	0	36	6	82	99	7	36	60	14.8
Wells,Bob, Sea	32	5.05	3	3	0	35	0	57	65	10	18	40	13.1
Wells,David, NYA	36	3.75	15	9	0	31	31	216	224	28	29	159	10.5
Wendell,Turk, NYN	32	3.62	4	4	9	66	0	77	68	8	43	65	13.0
Wetteland,John, Tex	32	2.57	3	2	45	62	0	63	46	7	19	67	9.3
Whiteside,Matt, Phi	31	4.75	1	2	0	21	0	36	41	5	12	21	13.3
Wickman,Bob, Mil	30	3.62	3	5	29	73	0	87	86	7	39	71	12.9
Williams,Mike, Pit	30	4.15	2	2	0	28	1	39	39	4	15	29	12.5
Williams,Woody, Tor	32	4.57	12	12	0	32	32	205	200	32	79	139	12.2
Witt,Bobby, StL	35	5.87	5	8	0	32	16	112	134	17	51	62	14.9
Worrell,Tim, LA	31	4.15	5	4	0	49	9	104	105	12	37	83	12.3

These Guys Can Play Too And Might Get A Shot

It's difficult to predict which players will end up getting significant playing time in the major leagues next year. That said, we can say with confidence that if the following players land major league jobs, their final numbers should be consistent with the stats listed below. What you'll find below are the players' Major League Equivalencies (or MLEs) for their 1998 seasons. An MLE is not a projection for what a player will do in the future; it is an interpretation of what he did in the minors last year. The MLE method adjusts the player's minor league stats and re-expresses them in major league terms. In short, an MLE shows you what a player would have hit if he'd been playing in the majors. It has just as much predictive value as a major leaguer's 1998 stats, but no more. Look for the following players to succeed in 1999 if given the chance.

Batter	Age	Avg	G	AB	R	H	2B	3B	HR	RBI	BB	SO	SB	CS	OBP	SLG
Banks, Brian	28	.261	85	287	45	75	16	0	14	51	41	74	10	2	.354	.463
Barrett, Michael	22	.289	120	433	60	125	29	1	13	67	18	46	5	5	.317	.450
Berkman, Lance	23	.260	139	457	70	119	32	0	17	75	57	113	3	4	.342	.442
Buxbaum, Danny	26	.282	103	372	46	105	17	1	13	48	16	54	0	2	.312	.438
Clemente, Edgard	23	.247	135	490	56	121	19	6	22	58	28	116	3	5	.288	.445
Cline, Pat	24	.251	122	407	39	102	18	1	10	45	28	61	1	2	.299	.373
Conti, Jason	24	.277	130	502	90	139	26	8	10	48	38	102	12	13	.328	.420
Darr, Mike	23	.269	132	494	77	133	33	2	4	66	38	83	17	7	.321	.368
Daubach, Brian	27	.270	140	466	73	126	36	3	22	88	57	119	6	2	.350	.502
Davis, Ben	22	.252	116	413	48	104	22	1	11	55	25	63	2	1	.295	.390
Figga, Mike	28	.251	123	443	45	111	26	2	20	75	27	112	1	2	.294	.454
Gonzalez, Raul	25	.281	118	427	58	120	25	0	11	59	33	53	7	8	.333	.417
Hermansen, Chad	21	.224	126	438	57	98	23	3	19	55	35	159	14	5	.281	.420
Horne, Tyrone	28	.276	126	431	70	119	11	2	27	104	44	107	11	7	.343	.499
Jones, Jacque	24	.281	134	505	67	142	36	2	18	73	27	147	13	11	.318	.467
Kirgan, Chris	26	.298	140	527	68	157	40	0	32	85	37	121	1	1	.344	.556
Krause, Scott	25	.264	117	375	55	99	22	1	19	63	36	107	8	3	.328	.480
LaRue, Jason	25	.306	120	409	53	125	36	5	9	60	27	70	2	2	.349	.484
Lee, Carlos	23	.272	138	526	60	143	28	1	16	83	25	58	7	5	.305	.420
Lennon, Patrick	31	.267	126	424	71	113	20	3	22	78	71	127	9	3	.372	.483
Liefer, Jeff	24	.253	135	478	67	121	30	4	14	76	40	145	0	2	.311	.421
Lombard, George	23	.263	122	396	57	104	20	2	14	44	41	149	21	8	.332	.429
Mateo, Ruben	21	.286	107	419	66	120	28	2	14	63	21	59	12	7	.320	.463
McClain, Scott	27	.255	126	444	60	113	28	0	22	72	44	118	3	2	.322	.466
Mientkiewicz, Doug	25	.303	139	488	82	148	42	0	14	76	71	63	8	4	.392	.475
Morgan, Scott	25	.265	119	438	75	116	27	2	19	70	37	132	2	5	.322	.466
Morris, Warren	25	.303	139	519	67	157	25	6	15	80	44	102	11	7	.357	.461
Pena, Angel	24	.280	126	446	56	125	23	1	14	73	28	85	6	5	.323	.430
Perez, Santiago	23	.252	143	551	58	139	19	11	8	48	18	105	18	6	.276	.370
Quinn, Mark	25	.305	100	348	57	106	21	5	10	58	25	54	2	1	.351	.480
Ramirez, Alex	24	.276	121	504	78	139	19	6	27	86	13	106	4	4	.294	.498
Stenson, Dernell	21	.241	138	494	73	119	21	0	18	58	58	144	3	2	.321	.393
Taylor, Jamie	28	.332	113	377	51	125	29	0	13	57	33	60	0	2	.385	.512
Valdes, Pedro	26	.283	65	219	37	62	10	0	12	30	20	39	1	1	.343	.493
Valdez, Mario	24	.289	123	422	65	122	27	0	13	61	45	107	0	2	.358	.445
Veras, Wilton	21	.273	126	458	57	125	27	3	12	55	10	70	3	3	.288	.424
Ward, Daryle	24	.268	116	440	61	118	27	0	15	75	30	85	1	0	.315	.432
Witt, Kevin	23	.248	126	440	58	109	18	2	18	55	43	130	2	2	.315	.420

Career Projections

Can Ken Griffey Jr. break Hank Aaron's career home run record? Can Alex Rodriguez make it to 4,000 hits, or even top Pete Rose's record total of 4,256? To answer questions like this this, Bill James came up with a formula he called "The Favorite Toy" back in the days he was still doing the *Baseball Abstract*. For several years, we've run projections based on Bill's formula in the *STATS Baseball Scoreboard*, and last year we began doing so in the *Major League Handbook* as well. We continue the tradition this year; the only difference is that from now on, we'll just call them "Career Projections."

Rather than run the formula, which is fairly complex, we'll just say that the Career Projections use a player's age and recent performance to estimate his chances of reaching the goal. So is it better than 50-50 that Ken Griffey Jr. will make it to 3,000 hits? Will Griffey drive in 2,000 runs before his career is through? Here's what the formula says. (Age here is the player's age as of July 1, 1998).

— Don Zminda

Player	Age	H	HR	RBI	500	600	700	756	800	3000	4000	4257	2000	2298
		Current			Home Runs					Hits			RBI	
Mark McGwire	34	1353	457	1130	98%	93%	54%	34%	23%	—	—	—	11%	—
Barry Bonds	33	1917	411	1216	93%	42%	10%	1%	—	17%	—	—	17%	—
Ken Griffey Jr.	28	1569	350	1018	92%	87%	60%	45%	35%	38%	2%	—	54%	29%
Jose Canseco	33	1608	397	1214	92%	32%	5%	—	—	—	—	—	3%	—
Sammy Sosa	29	1233	273	800	88%	55%	30%	21%	15%	14%	—	—	23%	9%
Juan Gonzalez	28	1238	301	947	87%	54%	28%	18%	12%	21%	—	—	47%	26%
Albert Belle	31	1388	321	1019	81%	34%	12%	4%	—	15%	—	—	28%	10%
Rafael Palmeiro	33	1975	314	1079	48%	14%	—	—	—	26%	—	—	9%	—
Frank Thomas	30	1416	286	963	42%	13%	—	—	—	14%	—	—	19%	3%
Alex Rodriguez	22	648	106	352	38%	20%	8%	3%	—	35%	10%	6%	17%	7%
Mo Vaughn	30	1165	230	752	37%	13%	—	—	—	13%	—	—	4%	—
Manny Ramirez	26	758	154	517	35%	16%	4%	—	—	12%	—	—	15%	4%
Greg Vaughn	32	1062	247	764	29%	7%	—	—	—	—	—	—	—	—
Vinny Castilla	30	880	170	509	28%	10%	—	—	—	6%	—	—	2%	—
Jeff Bagwell	30	1276	221	835	28%	8%	—	—	—	8%	—	—	12%	—
Jim Thome	27	746	163	471	27%	9%	—	—	—	—	—	—	—	—
Vladimir Guerrero	22	305	50	150	18%	5%	—	—	—	10%	—	—	—	—
Carlos Delgado	26	466	105	333	17%	4%	—	—	—	—	—	—	—	—
Dean Palmer	29	888	197	601	17%	—	—	—	—	—	—	—	—	—
Andres Galarraga	37	1921	332	1172	15%	—	—	—	—	—	—	—	—	—
Tony Clark	26	453	96	303	14%	1%	—	—	—	—	—	—	—	—
Tino Martinez	30	1001	185	693	13%	—	—	—	—	—	—	—	9%	—
Larry Walker	31	1265	225	740	12%	—	—	—	—	2%	—	—	—	—
Fred McGriff	34	1782	358	1088	11%	—	—	—	—	3%	—	—	—	—
Matt Williams	32	1385	299	908	11%	—	—	—	—	—	—	—	—	—
Chipper Jones	26	690	108	414	9%	—	—	—	—	14%	—	—	5%	—
Raul Mondesi	27	852	130	419	9%	—	—	—	—	11%	—	—	—	—
Nomar Garciaparra	24	425	69	236	9%	—	—	—	—	10%	—	—	—	—
Tim Salmon	29	921	179	591	9%	—	—	—	—	—	—	—	—	—
Andruw Jones	21	273	54	173	8%	—	—	—	—	—	—	—	—	—
Shawn Green	25	528	77	253	6%	—	—	—	—	1%	—	—	—	—
Jay Buhner	33	1112	268	840	5%	—	—	—	—	—	—	—	—	—
Gary Sheffield	29	1180	202	706	5%	—	—	—	—	—	—	—	—	—
Mike Piazza	29	1038	200	644	4%	—	—	—	—	—	—	—	—	—
Scott Rolen	23	366	56	220	3%	—	—	—	—	2%	—	—	—	—
Eric Karros	30	1041	177	622	1%	—	—	—	—	—	—	—	—	—
Tony Gwynn	38	2928	123	1042	—	—	—	—	—	99%	—	—	—	—
Cal Ripken	37	2878	384	1514	—	—	—	—	—	98%	—	—	—	—
Wade Boggs	40	2922	116	985	—	—	—	—	—	98%	—	—	—	—
Roberto Alomar	30	1825	127	709	—	—	—	—	—	32%	—	—	—	—
Craig Biggio	32	1680	136	633	—	—	—	—	—	25%	—	—	—	—
Derek Jeter	24	588	39	239	—	—	—	—	—	23%	2%	—	—	—
Chuck Knoblauch	29	1357	60	455	—	—	—	—	—	18%	—	—	—	—
Mark Grace	34	1875	121	831	—	—	—	—	—	14%	—	—	—	—
Travis Fryman	29	1336	177	775	—	—	—	—	—	13%	—	—	2%	—
John Olerud	29	1261	153	666	—	—	—	—	—	13%	—	—	—	—
Garret Anderson	26	670	51	313	—	—	—	—	—	13%	—	—	—	—
Edgar Renteria	22	450	12	114	—	—	—	—	—	10%	—	—	—	—
Gregg Jefferies	30	1513	118	631	—	—	—	—	—	8%	—	—	—	—
Ray Durham	26	627	47	236	—	—	—	—	—	8%	—	—	—	—
Will Clark	34	1964	253	1106	—	—	—	—	—	7%	—	—	—	—
Bernie Williams	29	1096	126	566	—	—	—	—	—	7%	—	—	—	—
Ivan Rodriguez	26	1134	109	508	—	—	—	—	—	6%	—	—	—	—
Johnny Damon	24	501	35	187	—	—	—	—	—	6%	—	—	—	—
Derek Bell	29	970	99	520	—	—	—	—	—	5%	—	—	—	—
Jeff Cirillo	28	666	51	284	—	—	—	—	—	5%	—	—	—	—
Rickey Henderson	39	2678	266	978	—	—	—	—	—	4%	—	—	—	—
Jose Offerman	29	990	22	312	—	—	—	—	—	4%	—	—	—	—
Kenny Lofton	31	1216	56	373	—	—	—	—	—	4%	—	—	—	—
Rusty Greer	29	756	83	402	—	—	—	—	—	4%	—	—	—	—
Marquis Grissom	31	1389	111	518	—	—	—	—	—	3%	—	—	—	—
Carlos Baerga	29	1367	121	676	—	—	—	—	—	3%	—	—	—	—
Edgardo Alfonzo	24	507	35	231	—	—	—	—	—	3%	—	—	—	—
Dante Bichette	34	1448	205	869	—	—	—	—	—	2%	—	—	—	—
Omar Vizquel	31	1238	29	383	—	—	—	—	—	1%	—	—	—	—
Bob Higginson	27	570	92	310	—	—	—	—	—	1%	—	—	—	—

Glossary

% Inherited Scored

A Relief Pitching statistic indicating the percentage of runners on base at the time a relief pitcher enters a game that he allows to score.

% Pitches Taken

The number of pitches a batter does not swing at divided by the total number of pitches he sees.

1st Batter OBP

The On-Base Percentage allowed by a relief pitcher to the first batter he faces in a game.

Active Career Batting Leaders

Minimum of 1,000 At-Bats required for Batting Average, On-Base Percentage, Slugging Percentage, At-Bats Per HR, At-Bats Per GDP, At-Bats Per RBI, and Strikeout-to-Walk Ratio. One hundred (100) Stolen Base Attempts required for Stolen Base Success %. Any player who appeared in 1998 is eligible for inclusion provided he meets the category's minimum requirements.

Active Career Pitching Leaders

Minimum of 750 Innings Pitched required for Earned Run Average, Opponent Batting Average, all of the "Per 9 Innings" categories, and Strikeout-to-Walk Ratio. Two hundred fifty (250) Games Started required for Complete Game Frequency. One hundred (100) decisions required for Win-Loss Percentage. Any player who appeared in 1998 is eligible for inclusion provided he meets the category's minimum requirements.

Bases Loaded

Batting Average with the Bases Loaded.

BA ScPos Allowed

Batting Average Allowed with Runners in Scoring Position.

Batting Average

Hits divided by At-Bats.

Blown Save

Entering a game in a Save Situation (see Save Situation in Glossary) and allowing the tying or go-ahead run to score.

Catcher's ERA

The Earned Run Average of a club's pitchers with a particular catcher behind the plate. To figure this for a catcher, multiply the Earned Runs Allowed by the pitchers while he was catching times nine and divide that by his number of Innings Caught.

Cheap Wins/Tough Losses/Top Game Scores

First determine the starting pitcher's Game Score as follows: (1) Start with 50. (2) Add 1 point for each out recorded by the starting pitcher. (3) Add 2 points for each inning the pitcher completes after the fourth inning. (4) Add 1 point for each strikeout. (5) Subtract 2 points for each hit allowed. (6) Subtract 4 points for each earned run allowed. (7) Subtract 2 points for an unearned run. (8) Subtract 1 point for each walk.

If the starting pitcher scores over 50 and loses, it's a Tough Loss. If he wins with a game score under 50, it's a Cheap Win. The top Game Scores of 1998 are listed.

Cleanup Slugging%

The Slugging Percentage of a player when batting fourth in the batting order.

Complete Game Frequency

Complete Games divided by Games Started.

Component ERA (ERC)

The steps in producing a pitcher's Component ERA are as follows:

1) Subtract the pitcher's Home Runs Allowed from his Hits Allowed,

2) Multiply that by 1.255,

3) Multiply his Home Runs allowed by four, and

4) Add those two [(2) + (3)] together.

5) Multiply all of that by .89.

6) Add his Walks and Hit Batsmen, and

7) Multiply that by .475, then

8) Add those two [(5) + (7)] together.

That makes:

$$((((H - HR) * 1.255) + (HR * 4)) * .89) + ((BB + HB) * .475)$$

For those pitchers for whom there is intentional walk data, use this formula instead:

$$((((H - HR) * 1.255) + (HR * 4)) * .89) + ((BB + HB - IBB) * .56)$$

9) Call that "PTB" for "Pitcher's Total Base Estimate."

10) Figure his baserunners allowed (Hits + Walks + Hit Batsmen).

11) Multiply that by his PTB.

12) Divide by his Batters Facing Pitcher.

13) Multiply by 9.

14) Divide by Innings Pitched, and

15) Subtract 0.56.

The result will be the pitcher's ERC.

NOTE: If the result after step 14 is less than 2.24, modify step 15 by multiplying by 0.75 rather than subtracting 0.56.

When BFP is not known, use this formula to estimate it:

$$(IP * 2.9) + H + BB + HBP \text{ (when known)}$$

Earned Run Average
(Earned Runs * 9) divided by Innings Pitched.

Fielding Percentage
(Putouts plus Assists) divided by (Putouts plus Assists plus Errors).

Games Finished
The last relief pitcher for either team in any given game is credited with a Game Finished.

GDP
Ground into Double Play.

GDP Opportunity
Any situation with a runner on first and less than two out.

Ground/Fly Ratio (Grd/Fly)
For batters, groundballs hit divided by flyballs hit. For pitchers, groundballs allowed divided by flyballs allowed. All batted balls except line drives and bunts are included.

Hold
A Hold is credited any time a relief pitcher enters a game in a Save Situation (see definition), records at least one out, and leaves the game never having relinquished the lead. Note: a pitcher cannot finish the game and receive credit for a Hold, nor can he earn a hold and a save.

Isolated Power
Slugging Percentage minus Batting Average.

K/BB Ratio

Strikeouts divided by Walks.

Late & Close

A Late & Close situation meets the following requirements: (1) the game is in the seventh inning or later, and (2) the batting team is either leading by one run, tied, or has the potential tying run on base, at bat, or on deck. Note: this situation is very similar to the characteristics of a Save Situation.

Leadoff On Base%

The On-Base Percentage of a player when batting first in the batting order.

LHS

Lefthanded Starter.

Offensive Winning Percentage

The Winning Percentage a team of nine Sammy Sosas (or anybody) would compile against average pitching and defense. The formula: (Runs Created per 27 outs) divided by the League average of runs scored per game. Square the result and divide it by (1+itself).

On-Base Percentage

(Hits plus Walks plus Hit by Pitcher) divided by (At-Bats plus Walks plus Hit by Pitcher plus Sacrifice Flies).

Opponent Batting Average

Hits Allowed divided by (Batters Faced minus Walks minus Hit Batsmen minus Sacrifice Hits minus Sacrifice Flies minus Catcher's Interference).

PA*

The divisor for On-Base Percentage: At-Bats plus Walks plus Hit By Pitcher plus Sacrifice Flies; or Plate Appearances minus Sacrifice Hits and Times Reached Base on Defensive Interference.

PCS (Pitchers' Caught Stealing)

The number of runners officially counted as Caught Stealing where the initiator of the fielding play was the pitcher, not the catcher. Note: such plays are often referred to as "pickoffs," but appear in official records as Caught Stealings. The most common "pitcher caught stealing scenario" is a 1-3-6 fielding play, where the runner is officially charged a Caught Stealing because he broke for second base. "Pickoff" (fielding play 1-3 being the most common) is not an official statistic.

Pitches per PA

For a hitter, the total number of pitches seen divided by total number of At-Bats.

PkOf Throw/Runner

The number of Pickoff Throws made by a pitcher divided by the number of runners on first base.

Plate Appearances

At-Bats plus Total Walks plus Hit By Pitcher plus Sacrifice Hits plus Sacrifice Flies plus Times Reached on Defensive Interference.

Power/Speed Number

A way to look at power and speed in one number. A player must score high in both areas to earn a high Power/Speed Number. The formula: (HR x SB x 2) divided by (HR + SB).

Quick Hooks and Slow Hooks

A Quick Hook is the removal of a pitcher who has pitched less than six innings and given up three runs or less. A Slow Hook occurs when a pitcher pitches more than nine innings, or allows seven or more runs, or whose combined innings pitched and runs allowed totals 13 or more.

Range Factor

The number of Successful Chances (Putouts plus Assists) times nine divided by the number of Defensive Innings Played. The average for a player at each position in 1998:

Second Base: 4.97	Left Field: 1.99
Third Base: 2.63	Center Field: 2.60
Shortstop: 4.62	Right Field: 2.10

RHS

Righthanded Starter.

Run Support Per 9 IP

The number of runs scored by a pitcher's team while he was still in the game times nine divided by his Innings Pitched.

Runs Created

A way to combine a batter's total offensive contributions into one number. The formula:

(H + BB + HBP - CS - GIDP) times (Total Bases + .26(TBB - IBB + HBP) + .52(SH + SF + SB)) divided by (AB + TBB + HBP + SH + SF).

Runs Created per 27 Outs (RC/27)

The name of this statistic is actually a misnomer. Bill James has revised the formula to use the actual league average of outs per game, rather than 27 outs. The new formula is:

Runs Created * (3 * League Outs/League Team Games)/Outs Made

The results estimates how many runs per game a team of nine Mickey Mantles would have produced in 1956, to use one example.

Save Percentage

Saves (SV) divided by Save Opportunities (OP).

Save Situation

Credit a pitcher with a save when he meets all three of the following conditions:

(1) he is the finishing pitcher in a game won by his club; and

(2) he is not the winning pitcher; and

(3) he qualifies under one of the following conditions:

(a) he enters the game with a lead of no more than three runs and pitches for at least one inning; or

(b) he enters the game, regardless of the count, with the potential tying run either on base, or at-bat, or on deck (that is, the potential tying run is either already on base or is one of the first two batsmen he faces); or

(c) he pitches effectively for at least three innings.

No more than one save may be credited in each game.

SB Success%

Stolen Bases divided by (Stolen Bases plus Caught Stealing).

Secondary Average

A way to look at a player's extra bases gained, independent of Batting Average. The formula:

(Total Bases - Hits + TBB + SB) divided by At-Bats.

Slugging Percentage

Total Bases divided by At-Bats.

Total Bases

Hits plus Doubles plus (2 * Triples) plus (3 * Home Runs).

Win-Loss Percentage or Winning Percentage

Wins divided by (Wins plus Losses).

About STATS, Inc.

STATS, Inc. is the nation's leading independent sports information and statistical analysis company, providing detailed sports services for a wide array of commercial clients.

As one of the fastest growing companies in sports, STATS provides the most up-to-the-minute sports information to professional teams, print and broadcast media, software developers and interactive service providers around the country. STATS was recently recognized as "One of Chicago's 100 most influential technology players" by *Crain's Chicago Business* and was one of 16 finalists for KPMG/Peat Marwick's Illinois High Tech Award. Some of our major clients are ESPN, the Associated Press, AOL, *The Sporting News*, Fox Sports, Electronic Arts, MSNBC, SONY and Topps. Much of the information we provide is available to the public via STATS On-Line. With a computer and a modem, you can follow action in the four major professional sports, as well as NCAA football and basketball. . . as it happens!

STATS Publishing, a division of STATS, Inc., produces 12 annual books, including the *Major League Handbook*, *The Scouting Notebook*, the *Pro Football Handbook*, the *Pro Basketball Handbook* and the *Hockey Handbook,* as well as the *STATS Fantasy Insider* magazine. This year we introduced two all-inclusive baseball encyclopedias, *The All-Time Baseball Sourcebook* and *The All-Time Major League Handbook*. Together they combine for over 5,000 pages of baseball history. These publications deliver STATS' expertise to fans, scouts, general managers and media around the country.

In addition, STATS offers the most innovative—and fun—fantasy sports games around, from *Bill James Fantasy Baseball* and *Bill James Classic Baseball* to *STATS Fantasy Football* and *STATS Fantasy Hoops*. Check out our immensely popular Fantasy Portfolios, and our great new web-based product, STATS Fantasy Advantage.

Information technology has grown by leaps and bounds in the last decade, and STATS will continue to be at the forefront as both a vendor and supplier of the most up-to-date, in-depth sports information available. For those of you on the information superhighway, you can always catch STATS in our area on America Online or at our Internet site.

For more information on our products, or on joining our reporter network, contact us on:

America Online — (Keyword: STATS)
Internet — www.stats.com
Toll Free in the USA at 1-800-63-STATS (1-800-637-8287)
Outside the USA at 1-847-676-3383

Or write to:

STATS, Inc.
8131 Monticello Ave.
Skokie, IL 60076-3300

There is NO Offseason!

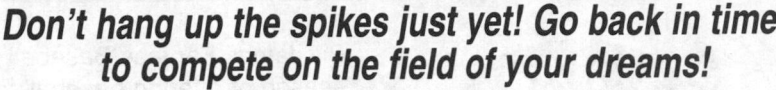

Don't hang up the spikes just yet! Go back in time to compete on the field of your dreams!

If you're not ready to give up baseball in the fall, or if you're looking to relive its glorious past, then Bill James Classic Baseball is the game for you! The Classic Game features players from all eras of Major League Baseball at all performance levels—not just the stars. You could see Honus Wagner, Josh Gibson, Carl Yastrzemski, Bob Uecker, Billy Grabarkewitz, and Pete Rose...on the SAME team!

As owner, GM and manager all in one, you'll be able to...

- "Buy" your team of up to 25 players from our catalog of over 2,000 historical players (You'll receive $1 million to buy your favorite players)
- Choose the park your team will call home—current or historical, 63 in all!
- Rotate batting lineups for a right or lefthanded starting pitcher
- Change your pitching rotation for each series. Determine your set-up man, closer, and long reliever
- Alter in-game strategies, including stealing frequency, holding runners on base, hit-and-run, and much more!
- Select your best pinch hitter and late-inning defensive replacements (For example, Curt Flood will get to more balls than Hack Wilson!)

How to Play The Classic Game:

1. Sign up to be a team owner TODAY! Leagues forming year-round
2. STATS, Inc. will supply you with a catalog of eligible players and a rule book
3. You'll receive $1 million to buy your favorite major leaguers
4. Take part in a player and ballpark draft with 11 other owners
5. Set your pitching rotation, batting lineup, and managerial strategies
6. STATS runs the game simulation...a 154-game schedule, 14 weeks!
7. You'll receive customized in-depth weekly reports, featuring game summaries, stats, and boxscores

Order from  today!

Order form in Back of This Book

1-800-63-STATS   847-676-3383   www.stats.com

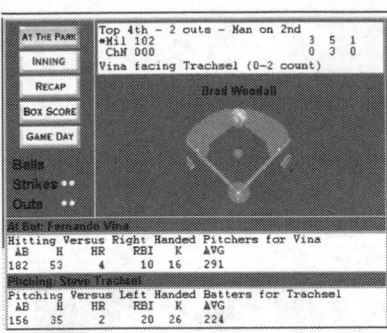

STATS, Inc. Order Form

Name _____

Address _____

City _____ State _____ Zip _____

Phone _____ Fax _____ E-mail Address _____

Method of Payment (U.S. Funds Only):
☐ Check   ☐ Money Order   ☐ Visa   ☐ MasterCard   ☐ Discover   ☐ AMEX

Credit Card Information:

Cardholder Name _____

Credit Card Number _____ Exp. Date _____

Signature _____

BOOKS (STATS Publications include free first class shipping)

Qty.	Product Name	Item Number	Price	Total
	STATS Major League Handbook 1999	HB99	$19.95	
	STATS Major League Handbook 1999 (Comb-bound)	HC99	$24.95	
	*STATS Projections Update 1999	PJUP	$9.95	
	STATS ALL-TIME Major League Handbook	ATHA	$79.95	
	STATS ALL-TIME Baseball Sourcebook	ATSA	$79.95	
	STATS ALL-TIME Combo (BOTH ALL-TIMERS)	ATCA	$149.95	
	The Scouting Notebook 1999	SN99	$19.95	
	The Scouting Notebook 1999 (Comb-bound)	SC99	$24.95	
	STATS Minor League Scouting Notebook 1999	MN99	$19.95	
	STATS Minor League Handbook 1999	MH99	$19.95	
	STATS Minor League Handbook 1999 (Comb-bound)	MC99	$24.95	
	STATS Player Profiles 1999	PP99	$19.95	
	STATS Player Profiles 1999 (Comb-bound)	PC99	$24.95	
	STATS 1999 Batter Vs. Pitcher Match-Ups!	BP99	$24.95	
	Ballpark Sourcebook Diamond Diagrams	BSDD	$24.95	
	STATS Diamond Chronicles	CH99	$19.95	
	STATS Baseball Scoreboard 1999	SB99	$19.95	
	Pro Football Revealed: The 100 Yard War (1998 Edition)	PF98	$19.95	
	Pro Football Handbook 1998	FH98	$19.95	
	Pro Football Handbook 1998 (Comb-bound)	FC98	$21.95	
	STATS Pro Basketball Handbook 1998-1999	BH99	$19.95	
	STATS Hockey Handbook 1998-1999	HH99	$19.95	
	*STATS Fantasy Insider: 1998 Pro Football Edition	IF98	$5.95	
	Prior Editions (Please circle appropriate year)			
	STATS Major League Handbook '91 '92 '93 '94 '95 '96 '97 '98		$9.95	
	The Scouting Notebook/Report '94 '95 '96 '97 '98		$9.95	
	STATS Player Profiles '93 '94 '95 '96 '97 '98		$9.95	
	STATS Minor League Handbook '92 '93 '94 '95 '96 '97 '98		$9.95	
	STATS Minor League Scouting Notebook '95 '96 '97 '98		$9.95	
	STATS Batter Vs. Pitcher Match-Ups! '94 '95 '96 '97 '98		$9.95	
	STATS Diamond Chronicles '97 '98		$9.95	
	STATS Baseball Scoreboard '92 '93 '94 '95 '96 '97 '98		$9.95	
	Pro Football Revealed: The 100 Yard War '94 '95 '96 '97		$9.95	
	STATS Pro Football Handbook '95 '96 '97		$9.95	
	STATS Pro Basketball Handbook '93-94 '94-95 '95-96 '96-97 '97-98		$9.95	
	STATS Hockey Handbook '96-'97 '97-'98		$9.95	

Denotes Magazine

FANTASY GAMES

Qty.	Product Name	Item Number	Price	Total
	Bill James Classic Baseball	BJCB	$129.00	
	STATS Fantasy Football	SFF	$49.00	
	Bill James Fantasy Baseball	BJFB	$89.00	

1st Fantasy Team Name (ex. Colt 45's): _____

      What Fantasy Game is this team for? _____

2nd Fantasy Team Name (ex. Colt 45's): _____

      What Fantasy Game is this team for? _____

Note: $1.00/player is charged for all roster moves and transactions.

For Bill James Fantasy Baseball:

Would you like to play in a league drafted by Bill James?   ☐ Yes   ☐ No

STATSfax and e-STATS Services (*be SURE to include fax or e-mail address on form)

Game	Format (circle one)	Price/Service (circle one)	Total
Bill James Classic Baseball	Fax / e-mail	$5/week $20/month $60/season *all Classic Game services: 5 days/week*	
Bill James Fantasy Baseball	Fax / e-mail	$5/5 days a week $7/7 days a week $20/month (5 days) $25/month (7 days) $100/season (5 days) $125/season (7 days)	
STATS Fantasy Hoops	Fax / e-mail	$5/5 days a week $7/7 days a week $20/month (5 days) $25/month (7 days) $100/season (5 days) $125/season (7 days)	
STATS Fantasy Football	Fax / e-mail	$15/month $60/season *both: 3 days/week*	

For faster service, call:

**1-800-63-STATS or
847-676-3383**

or fax this form to STATS:

847-676-0821

STATS, Inc.
8131 Monticello Avenue
Skokie, IL 60076-3300

FANTASY GAMES	Price	Total
Product Total (excl. Fantasy Games)		
Canada—all orders—add:	$3.50/book	
Magazines—add: $2.00 S&H	$2.00/book	
Order 2 or more books—subtract:	$1.00/book	
IL residents add 8.5% sales tax		
Subtotal		
Fantasy Games Total		
STATSfax and 2-STATS Service Total		
(NO other discounts apply) **GRAND TOTAL**		

* orders subject to availability

All books include free 1st class shipping!
Thanks for ordering from STATS, Inc.

We want to know what you think about our books

Name_____
Address_____
City_____State_____Zip_____
Day Phone_____Evening Phone_____
Fax_____
E-mail Address_____

1) Where did you purchase this book?_____
_____

2) What other STATS publications do you buy?_____
_____

3) What do you like most about this book?_____
_____

4) What would you change about this book?_____
_____

5) What new information or book would you like to see STATS publish next?_____
_____

6) Would you be interested in a STATS Publication about baseball's most outrageous and funny nicknames?_____
_____

7) Would you be interested in a STATS Publication about baseball's all-time greatest players?
_____

8) Do you purchase books on the Internet? If yes, where?_____

Two Great Reasons to mail a copy of this questionnaire back to STATS:

1) You'll be entered in a drawing for a FREE STATS All-Time Major League Handbook and All-Time Baseball Sourcebook - valued at *$159.90*.

2) Attach your order for the *1999 Player Projections Update* to this questionnaire and save 10% - just $8.95.

STATS Inc.
Attn: Publishing/Marketing
8131 Monticello Avenue
Skokie, IL 60076-3300